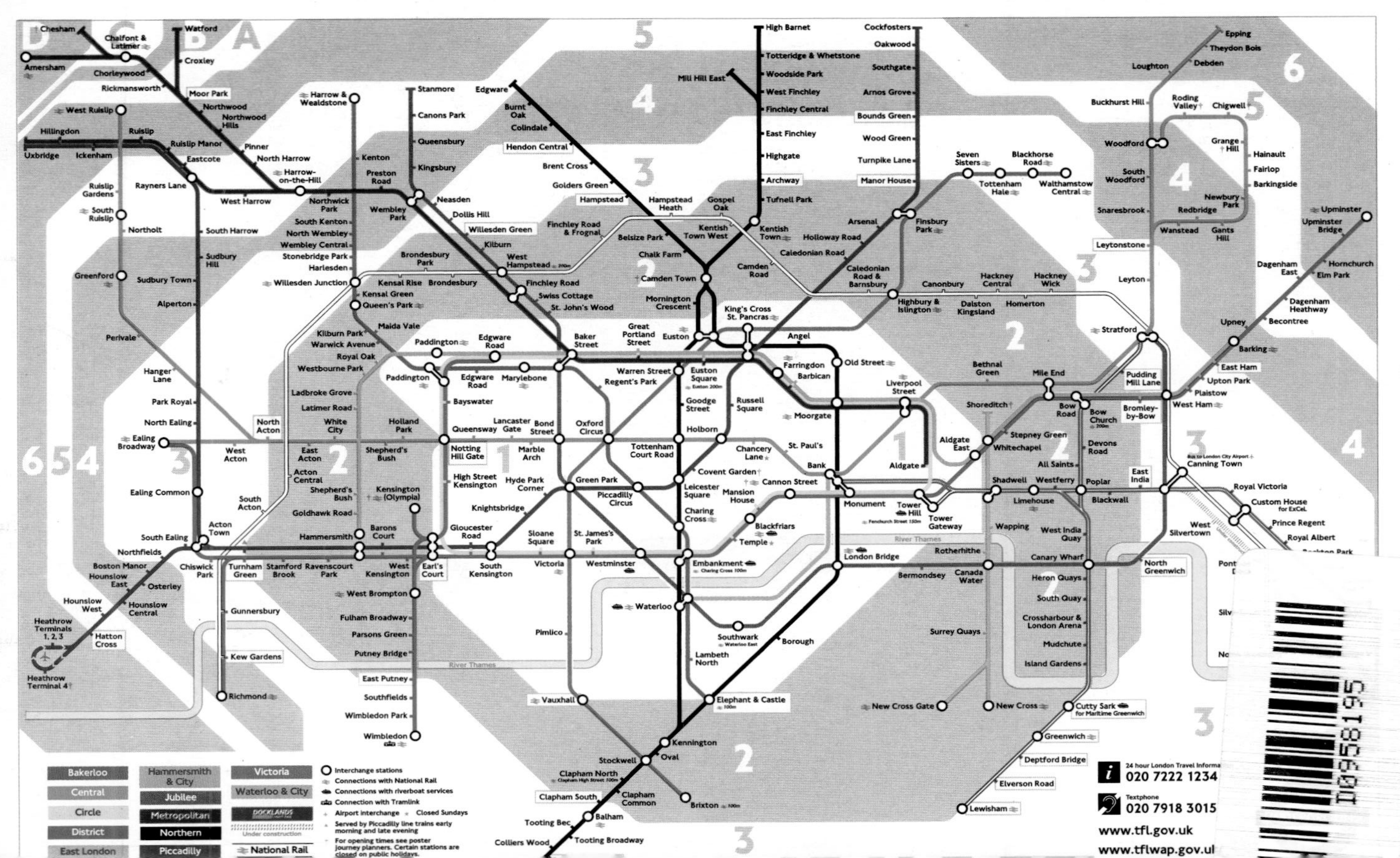

Chesham
Chalfont & Latimer
Amersham
Chorleywood
Rickmansworth
Watford
Croxley
Moor Park
Northwood
Northwood Hills
Pinner
North Harrow
Harrow-on-the-Hill
West Ruislip
Hillingdon
Ruislip
Ruislip Manor
Uxbridge
Ickenham
Eastcote
Rayners Lane
West Harrow
Ruislip Gardens
South Ruislip
Northolt
South Harrow
Sudbury Hill
Sudbury Town
Alperton
Greenford
Perivale
Hanger Lane
Park Royal
North Ealing
Ealing Broadway
West Acton
North Acton
Ealing Common
South Ealing
Northfields
Boston Manor
Hounslow East
Osterley
Hounslow West
Hounslow Central
Heathrow Terminals 1, 2, 3
Hatton Cross
Heathrow Terminal 4
Acton Town
Chiswick Park
Turnham Green
Stamford Brook
Ravenscourt Park
Gunnersbury
Kew Gardens
Richmond
Harrow & Wealdstone
Kenton
Preston Road
Northwick Park
Wembley Park
South Kenton
North Wembley
Wembley Central
Stonebridge Park
Harlesden
Willesden Junction
Kensal Green
Kensal Rise
Brondesbury
Brondesbury Park
Queen's Park
Stanmore
Canons Park
Queensbury
Kingsbury
Neasden
Dollis Hill
Willesden Green
Kilburn
West Hampstead
Finchley Road
Swiss Cottage
St. John's Wood
Edgware
Burnt Oak
Colindale
Hendon Central
Brent Cross
Golders Green
Hampstead
Finchley Road & Frognal
Belsize Park
Chalk Farm
Hampstead Heath
Gospel Oak
Kentish Town West
Kentish Town
Camden Road
Camden Town
Mornington Crescent
High Barnet
Totteridge & Whetstone
Woodside Park
West Finchley
Mill Hill East
Finchley Central
East Finchley
Highgate
Archway
Tufnell Park
Holloway Road
Caledonian Road
Caledonian Road & Barnsbury
Cockfosters
Oakwood
Southgate
Arnos Grove
Bounds Green
Wood Green
Turnpike Lane
Manor House
Arsenal
Finsbury Park
Seven Sisters
Tottenham Hale
Blackhorse Road
Walthamstow Central
Highbury & Islington
Canonbury
Dalston Kingsland
Hackney Central
Homerton
Hackney Wick
Epping
Theydon Bois
Debden
Loughton
Buckhurst Hill
Roding Valley
Chigwell
Grange Hill
Hainault
Fairlop
Barkingside
Woodford
South Woodford
Snaresbrook
Newbury Park
Redbridge
Wanstead
Gants Hill
Leytonstone
Leyton
Upminster
Upminster Bridge
Hornchurch
Elm Park
Dagenham East
Dagenham Heathway
Becontree
Upney
Barking
East Ham
Upton Park
Plaistow
West Ham
Stratford
Pudding Mill Lane
Bromley-by-Bow
Bow Church
Bow Road
Mile End
Bethnal Green
Maida Vale
Kilburn Park
Warwick Avenue
Royal Oak
Westbourne Park
Ladbroke Grove
Latimer Road
White City
Shepherd's Bush
East Acton
Acton Central
South Acton
Goldhawk Road
Hammersmith
Barons Court
Kensington (Olympia)
Holland Park
West Kensington
Earl's Court
West Brompton
Fulham Broadway
Parsons Green
Putney Bridge
East Putney
Southfields
Wimbledon Park
Wimbledon
Paddington
Edgware Road
Marylebone
Baker Street
Great Portland Street
Euston
King's Cross St. Pancras
Bayswater
Queensway
Notting Hill Gate
Lancaster Gate
Marble Arch
Bond Street
Oxford Circus
Warren Street
Regent's Park
Euston Square
Euston 200m
Goodge Street
Russell Square
Angel
Farringdon
Barbican
Old Street
Moorgate
Liverpool Street
Aldgate
Aldgate East
High Street Kensington
Gloucester Road
South Kensington
Knightsbridge
Hyde Park Corner
Green Park
Piccadilly Circus
Tottenham Court Road
Holborn
Chancery Lane
St. Paul's
Bank
Covent Garden
Leicester Square
Mansion House
Cannon Street
Monument
Tower Hill
Fenchurch Street 150m
Tower Gateway
Sloane Square
Victoria
St. James's Park
Westminster
Charing Cross
Embankment
Charing Cross 100m
Temple
Blackfriars
London Bridge
River Thames
Waterloo
Southwark
Waterloo East
Lambeth North
Borough
Elephant & Castle
100m
Pimlico
Vauxhall
Kennington
Oval
Stockwell
Brixton
Clapham North
Clapham High Street 100m
Clapham Common
Clapham South
Balham
Tooting Bec
Tooting Broadway
Colliers Wood
Shoreditch
Whitechapel
Stepney Green
Shadwell
Limehouse
Westferry
All Saints
Devons Road
Poplar
East India
Blackwall
Canning Town
Bus to London City Airport
Royal Victoria
Custom House for ExCeL
Prince Regent
Royal Albert
West Silvertown
Wapping
Rotherhithe
Canada Water
Bermondsey
Surrey Quays
West India Quay
Canary Wharf
Heron Quays
South Quay
Crossharbour & London Arena
Mudchute
Island Gardens
North Greenwich
Cutty Sark for Maritime Greenwich
Greenwich
Deptford Bridge
Elverson Road
Lewisham
New Cross Gate
New Cross
Bakerloo
Central
Circle
District
East London
Hammersmith & City
Jubilee
Metropolitan
Northern
Piccadilly
Victoria
Waterloo & City
DOCKLANDS
Under construction
National Rail
Interchange stations
Connections with National Rail
Connections with riverboat services
Connection with Tramlink
Airport interchange
Closed Sundays
Served by Piccadilly line trains early morning and late evening
For opening times see poster journey planners. Certain stations are closed on public holidays.
24 hour London Travel Informa
020 7222 1234
Textphone
020 7918 3015
www.tfl.gov.uk
www.tflwap.gov.ul
D0958195

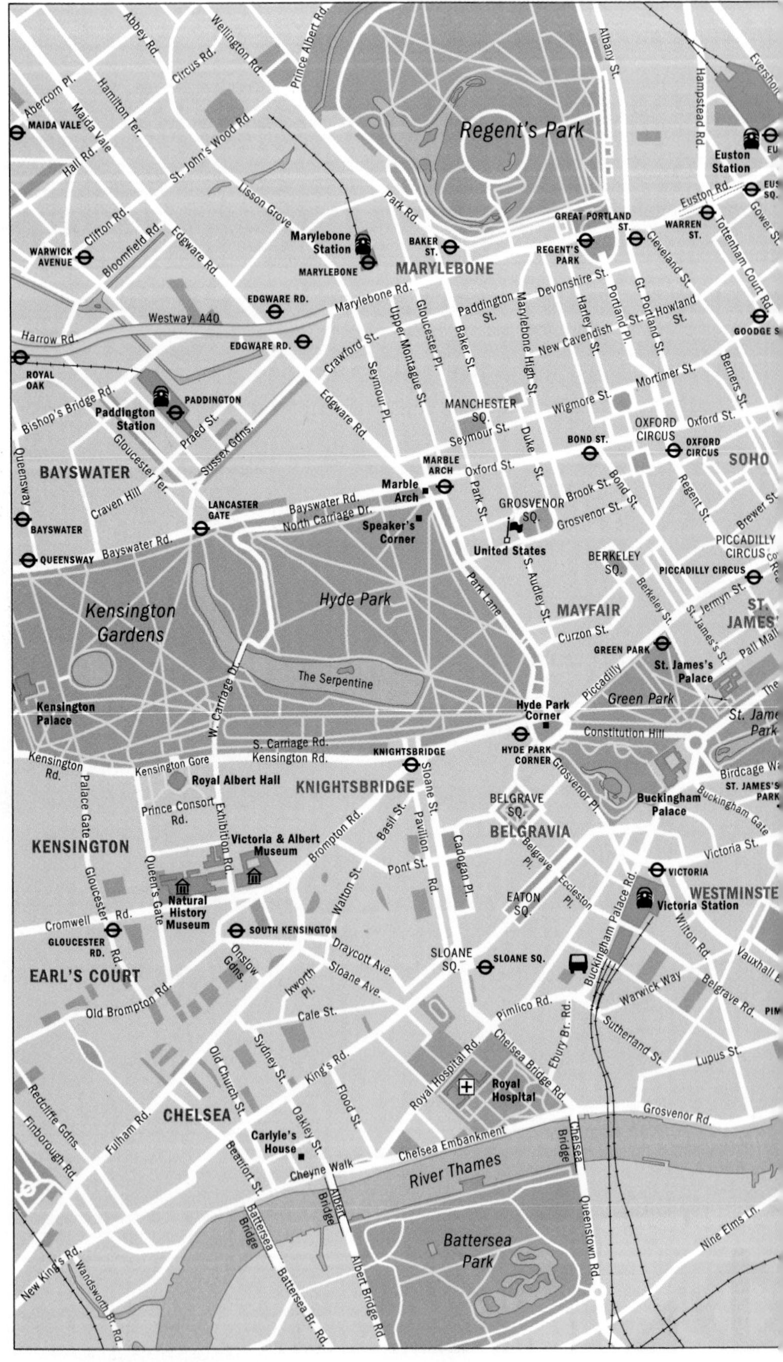

Regent's Park
Abbey Rd.
Wellington Rd.
Prince Albert Rd.
Circus Rd.
Albany St.
Hampstead Rd.
Eversholt
Euston Station
Abercorn Pl.
Hamilton Ter.
Maida Vale
MAIDA VALE
Hall Rd.
St. John's Wood Rd.
Lisson Grove
Park Rd.
Euston Rd.
EUS SQ.
Gower St.
Clifton Rd.
Bloomfield Rd.
Edgware Rd.
WARWICK AVENUE
Marylebone Station
MARYLEBONE
BAKER ST.
MARYLEBONE
GREAT PORTLAND ST.
WARREN ST.
REGENT'S PARK
Cleveland St.
Tottenham Court Rd.
Devonshire St.
EDGWARE RD.
Marylebone Rd.
Westway A40
Harrow Rd.
Paddington St.
Gloucester Pl.
Upper Montague St.
Baker St.
Marylebone High St.
Harley St.
Portland Pl.
Gt. Portland St.
Howland St.
New Cavendish St.
GOODGE S
Crawford St.
Seymour Pl.
ROYAL OAK
PADDINGTON
Paddington Station
Bishop's Bridge Rd.
Praed St.
Sussex Gdns.
Gloucester Ter.
MANCHESTER SQ.
Wigmore St.
Mortimer St.
Berners St.
Seymour St.
Duke St.
BOND ST.
OXFORD CIRCUS
Oxford St.
OXFORD CIRCUS
SOHO
Queensway
BAYSWATER
Craven Hill
MARBLE ARCH
Marble Arch
Oxford St.
Park St.
Brook St.
Bond St.
Regent St.
LANCASTER GATE
Bayswater Rd.
North Carriage Dr.
Speaker's Corner
GROSVENOR SQ.
Grosvenor St.
Brewer St.
BAYSWATER
QUEENSWAY
Bayswater Rd.
United States
BERKELEY SQ.
PICCADILLY CIRCUS
PICCADILLY CIRCUS
Park Lane
S. Audley St.
Berkeley St.
Jermyn St.
ST. JAMES'
Kensington Gardens
Hyde Park
MAYFAIR
St. James's St.
Curzon St.
GREEN PARK
Pall Mall
St. James's Palace
The Serpentine
Piccadilly
Green Park
Kensington Palace
W. Carriage Dr.
Hyde Park Corner
St. James Park
Constitution Hill
S. Carriage Rd.
Kensington Rd.
KNIGHTSBRIDGE
HYDE PARK CORNER
Kensington Rd.
Kensington Gore
Royal Albert Hall
KNIGHTSBRIDGE
Sloane St.
Grosvenor Pl.
Birdcage Wa
ST. JAMES'S PARK
Palace Gate
Prince Consort Rd.
Exhibition Rd.
Brompton Rd.
Basil St.
Pavilion Rd.
BELGRAVE SQ.
BELGRAVIA
Buckingham Palace
Buckingham Gate
KENSINGTON
Victoria & Albert Museum
Cadogan Pl.
Belgrave Pl.
Victoria St.
Gloucester Rd.
Queen's Gate
Natural History Museum
Walton St.
Pont St.
Eccleston Pl.
EATON SQ.
VICTORIA
WESTMINSTE
Victoria Station
Cromwell Rd.
GLOUCESTER RD.
SOUTH KENSINGTON
Buckingham Palace Rd.
Wilton Rd.
Onslow Gdns.
Draycott Ave.
SLOANE SQ.
SLOANE SQ.
Vauxhall B
EARL'S COURT
Ixworth Pl.
Sloane Ave.
Warwick Way
Belgrave Rd.
PIM
Old Brompton Rd.
Cale St.
Pimlico Rd.
Ebury Br. Rd.
Sutherland St.
Lupus St.
Old Church St.
Sydney St.
King's Rd.
Flood St.
Royal Hospital Rd.
Chelsea Bridge Rd.
Royal Hospital
Redcliffe Gdns.
Finborough Rd.
Fulham Rd.
CHELSEA
Oakley St.
Carlyle's House
Beaufort St.
Cheyne Walk
Chelsea Embankment
Chelsea Bridge
Grosvenor Rd.
River Thames
Albert Bridge
Battersea Bridge
Battersea Park
Queenstown Rd.
Nine Elms Ln.
New King's Rd.
Wandsworth Br. Rd.
Battersea Br. Rd.
Albert Bridge Rd.

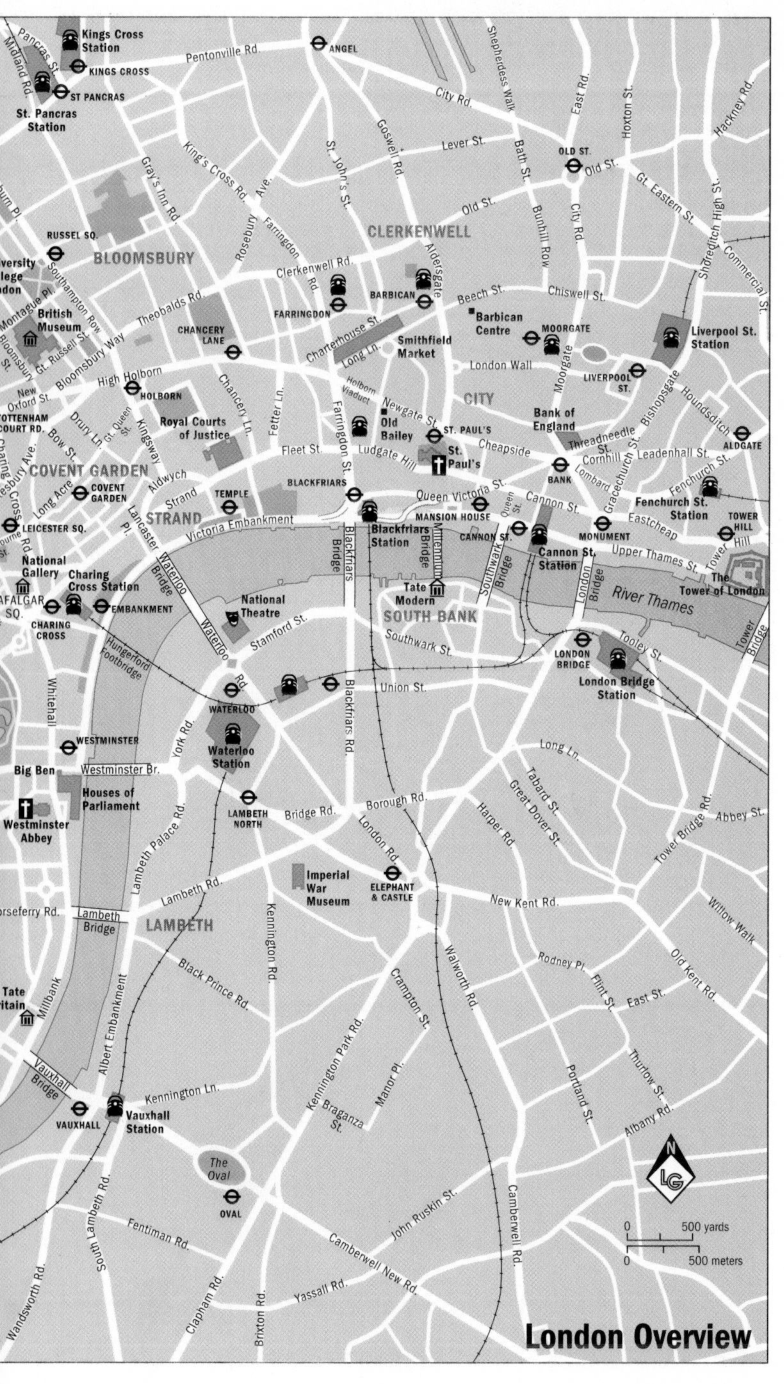

London Overview
Kings Cross Station
KINGS CROSS
ST PANCRAS
St. Pancras Station
ANGEL
Pentonville Rd.
City Rd.
Lever St.
OLD ST.
Old St.
CLERKENWELL
BLOOMSBURY
RUSSEL SQ.
University College London
British Museum
CHANCERY LANE
HOLBORN
Royal Courts of Justice
TOTTENHAM COURT RD.
COVENT GARDEN
LEICESTER SQ.
STRAND
TEMPLE
BLACKFRIARS
Blackfriars Station
FARRINGDON
BARBICAN
Barbican Centre
MOORGATE
Liverpool St. Station
LIVERPOOL ST.
Smithfield Market
CITY
Bank of England
Old Bailey
ST. PAUL'S
St. Paul's
BANK
ALDGATE
Fenchurch St. Station
TOWER HILL
MANSION HOUSE
CANNON ST.
Cannon St. Station
MONUMENT
The Tower of London
River Thames
National Gallery
Charing Cross Station
EMBANKMENT
TRAFALGAR SQ.
CHARING CROSS
National Theatre
Tate Modern
SOUTH BANK
LONDON BRIDGE
London Bridge Station
WATERLOO
Waterloo Station
WESTMINSTER
Big Ben
Houses of Parliament
Westminster Abbey
LAMBETH NORTH
Imperial War Museum
ELEPHANT & CASTLE
LAMBETH
Tate Britain
VAUXHALL
Vauxhall Station
The Oval
OVAL
Blackfriars Bridge
Millennium Bridge
Southwark Bridge
London Bridge
Tower Bridge
Waterloo Bridge
Hungerford Footbridge
Westminster Br.
Lambeth Bridge
Vauxhall Bridge
Victoria Embankment
Albert Embankment
Union St.
Southwark St.
Borough Rd.
New Kent Rd.
Old Kent Rd.
Kennington Rd.
Walworth Rd.
Camberwell Rd.
Camberwell New Rd.
500 yards
500 meters

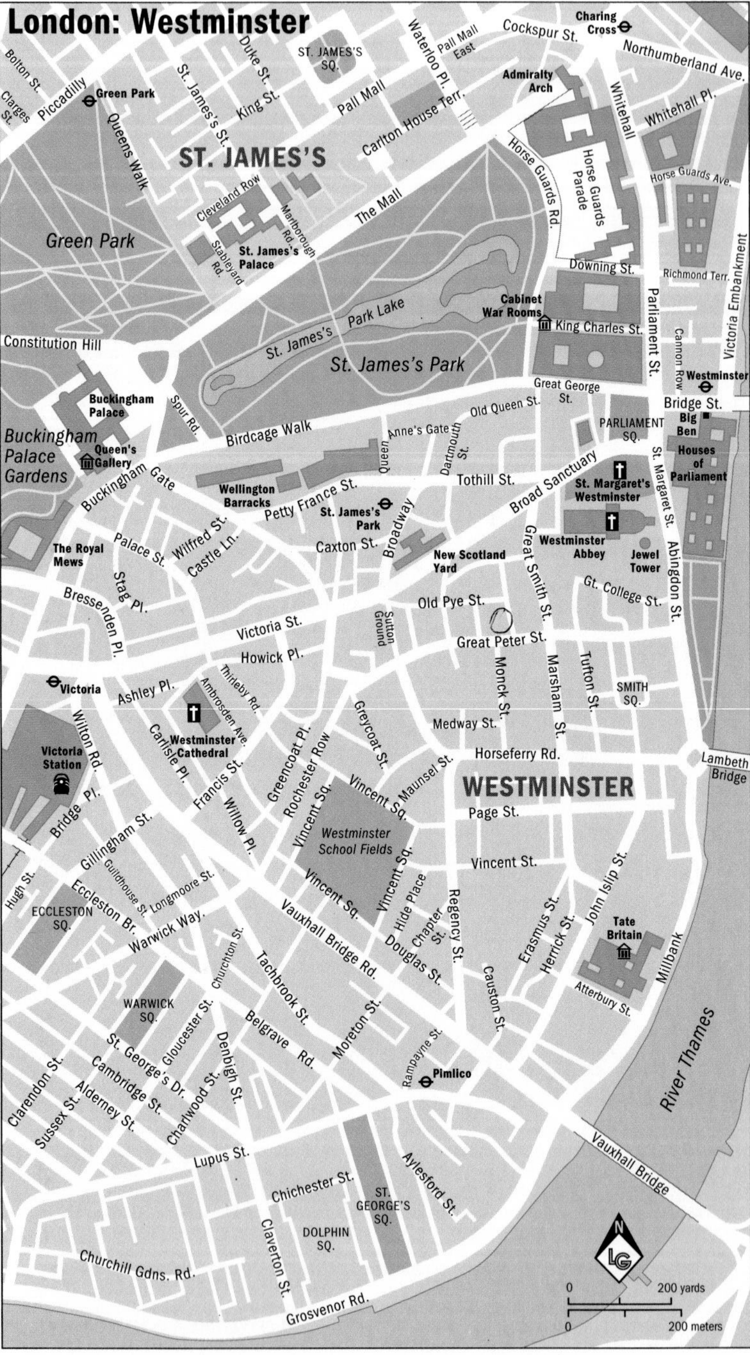
London: Westminster
ST. JAMES'S
WESTMINSTER
Green Park
St. James's Park
Buckingham Palace Gardens
Charing Cross
Green Park
St. James's Park
Westminster
Victoria
Pimlico
Admiralty Arch
Horse Guards Parade
St. James's Palace
Cabinet War Rooms
Buckingham Palace
Queen's Gallery
The Royal Mews
Wellington Barracks
New Scotland Yard
Westminster Abbey
St. Margaret's Westminster
Jewel Tower
Big Ben
Houses of Parliament
Westminster Cathedral
Victoria Station
Westminster School Fields
Tate Britain
River Thames
Lambeth Bridge
Vauxhall Bridge
ST. JAMES'S SQ.
PARLIAMENT SQ.
SMITH SQ.
ECCLESTON SQ.
WARWICK SQ.
ST. GEORGE'S SQ.
DOLPHIN SQ.
Piccadilly
Pall Mall
The Mall
Whitehall
Birdcage Walk
Victoria St.
Horseferry Rd.
Vauxhall Bridge Rd.
Grosvenor Rd.
Millbank
Victoria Embankment
0
200 yards
0
200 meters

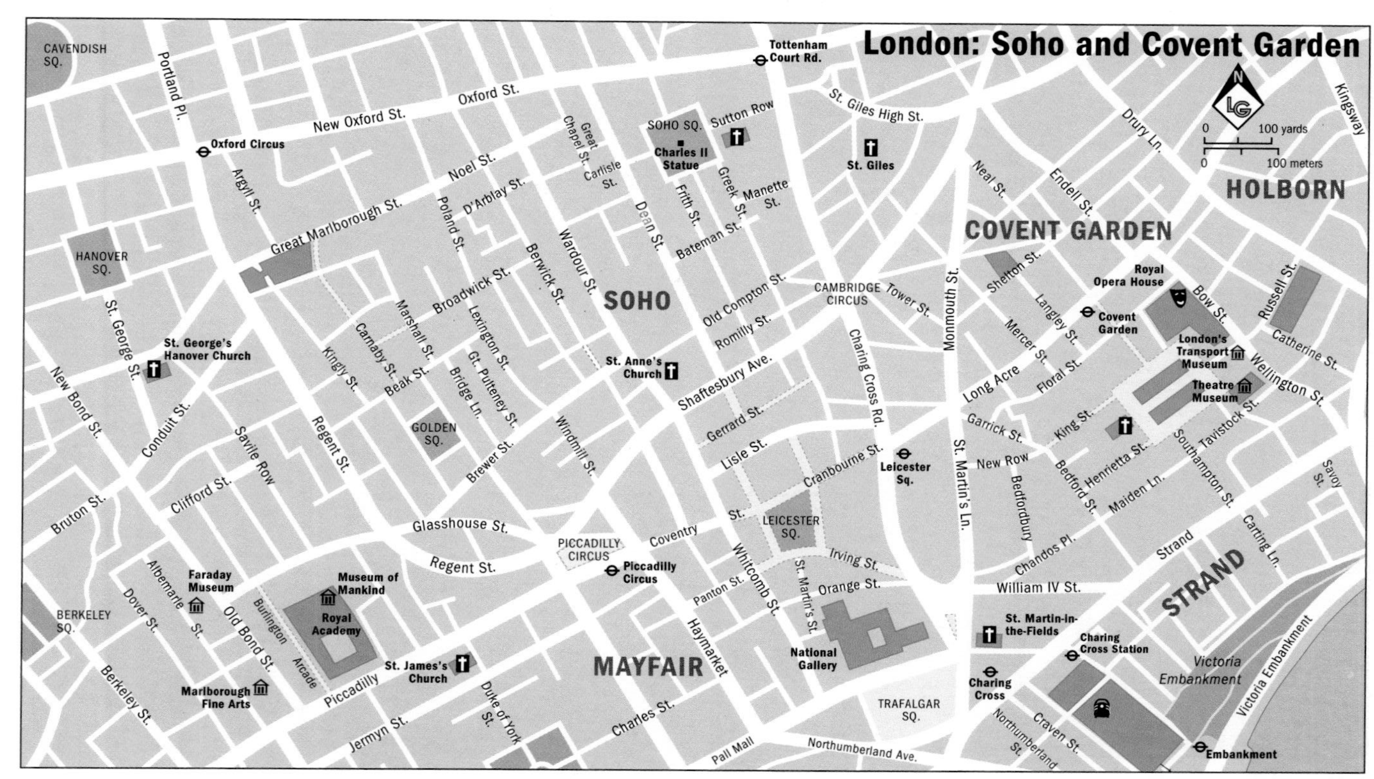
London: Soho and Covent Garden
N
LG
0
100 yards
0
100 meters
HOLBORN
COVENT GARDEN
SOHO
MAYFAIR
STRAND
CAVENDISH SQ.
Portland Pl.
Oxford Circus
Oxford St.
New Oxford St.
Tottenham Court Rd.
St. Giles High St.
St. Giles
Drury Ln.
Kingsway
Argyll St.
Great Marlborough St.
Noel St.
D'Arblay St.
Poland St.
Great Chapel St.
Carlisle St.
SOHO SQ.
Charles II Statue
Sutton Row
Frith St.
Greek St.
Manette St.
Bateman St.
Dean St.
Wardour St.
Berwick St.
Neal St.
Endell St.
HANOVER SQ.
St. George St.
St. George's Hanover Church
New Bond St.
Conduit St.
Savile Row
Clifford St.
Bruton St.
Regent St.
Kingly St.
Carnaby St.
Marshall St.
Broadwick St.
Lexington St.
Beak St.
Bridge Ln.
Gt. Pulteney St.
GOLDEN SQ.
Brewer St.
Windmill St.
St. Anne's Church
Shaftesbury Ave.
Old Compton St.
Romilly St.
CAMBRIDGE CIRCUS
Tower St.
Charing Cross Rd.
Monmouth St.
Shelton St.
Langley St.
Mercer St.
Royal Opera House
Covent Garden
Bow St.
Russell St.
Catherine St.
London's Transport Museum
Theatre Museum
Wellington St.
Long Acre
Floral St.
Garrick St.
King St.
Tavistock St.
Southampton St.
Henrietta St.
Bedford St.
Maiden Ln.
New Row
Bedfordbury
St. Martin's Ln.
Savoy St.
Carting Ln.
Strand
Chandos Pl.
William IV St.
Gerrard St.
Lisle St.
Cranbourne St.
Leicester Sq.
LEICESTER SQ.
Coventry St.
Irving St.
Glasshouse St.
PICCADILLY CIRCUS
Piccadilly Circus
Regent St.
Whitcomb St.
St. Martin's St.
Orange St.
Panton St.
Haymarket
National Gallery
TRAFALGAR SQ.
St. Martin-in-the-Fields
Charing Cross Station
Charing Cross
Victoria Embankment
Victoria Embankment
Embankment
Craven St.
Northumberland St.
Northumberland Ave.
Pall Mall
Charles St.
Duke of York St.
Jermyn St.
St. James's Church
Piccadilly
Museum of Mankind
Royal Academy
Burlington Arcade
Old Bond St.
Albemarle St.
Faraday Museum
Dover St.
BERKELEY SQ.
Berkeley St.
Marlborough Fine Arts

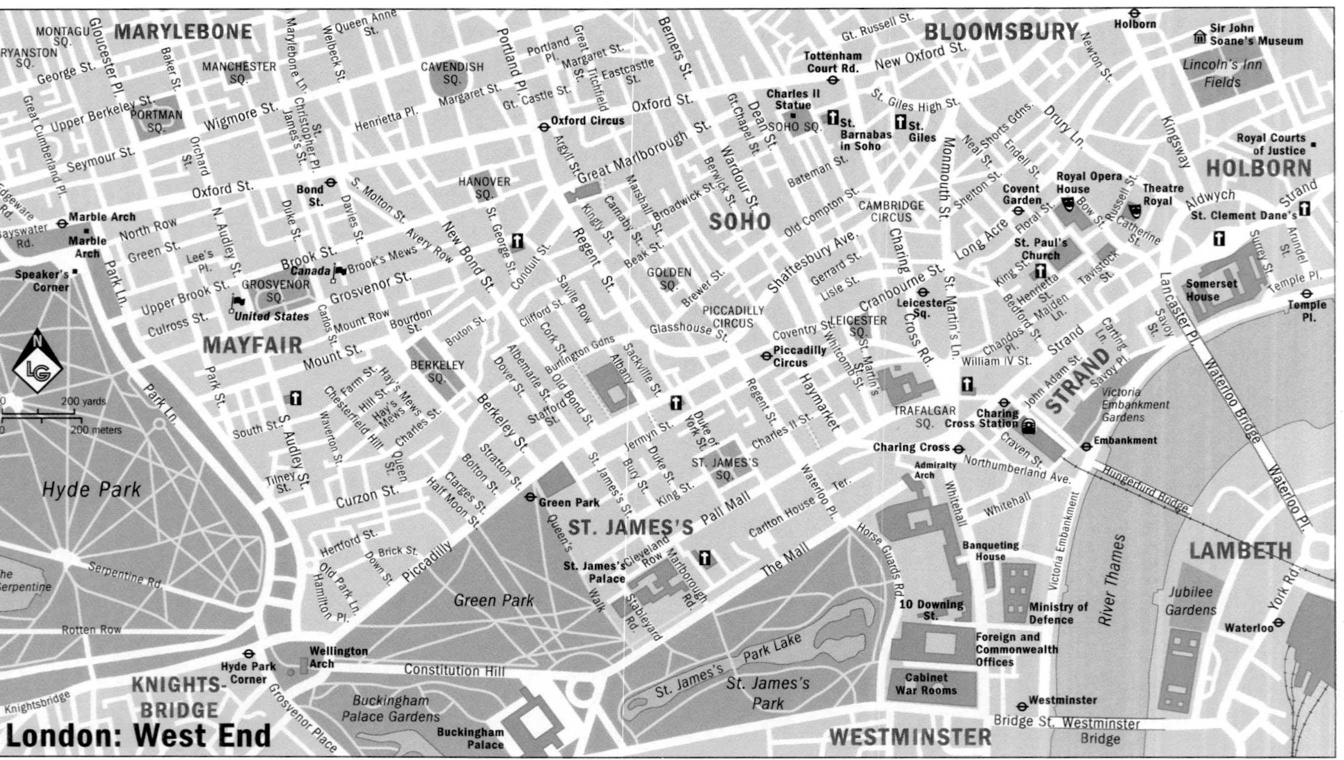

London: West End
MARYLEBONE
BLOOMSBURY
HOLBORN
SOHO
MAYFAIR
ST. JAMES'S
STRAND
LAMBETH
WESTMINSTER
KNIGHTS-BRIDGE
Hyde Park
Green Park
St. James's Park
Buckingham Palace Gardens
River Thames
Lincoln's Inn Fields
Jubilee Gardens
Victoria Embankment Gardens
The Serpentine
Park Lake
Sir John Soane's Museum
Royal Courts of Justice
Holborn
Tottenham Court Rd.
Charles II Statue
St. Barnabas in Soho
St. Giles
Royal Opera House
Theatre Royal
Covent Garden
St. Paul's Church
St. Clement Dane's
Somerset House
Temple Pl.
Oxford Circus
Bond St.
Marble Arch
Speaker's Corner
Canada
United States
Leicester Sq.
Piccadilly Circus
Charing Cross
Charing Cross Station
Embankment
Admiralty Arch
Banqueting House
Ministry of Defence
10 Downing St.
Foreign and Commonwealth Offices
Cabinet War Rooms
Westminster
Waterloo
Green Park
St. James's Palace
Wellington Arch
Hyde Park Corner
Buckingham Palace
MONTAGU SQ.
BRYANSTON SQ.
MANCHESTER SQ.
PORTMAN SQ.
CAVENDISH SQ.
HANOVER SQ.
SOHO SQ.
GOLDEN SQ.
GROSVENOR SQ.
BERKELEY SQ.
ST. JAMES'S SQ.
LEICESTER SQ.
TRAFALGAR SQ.
CAMBRIDGE CIRCUS
PICCADILLY CIRCUS
200 yards
200 meters

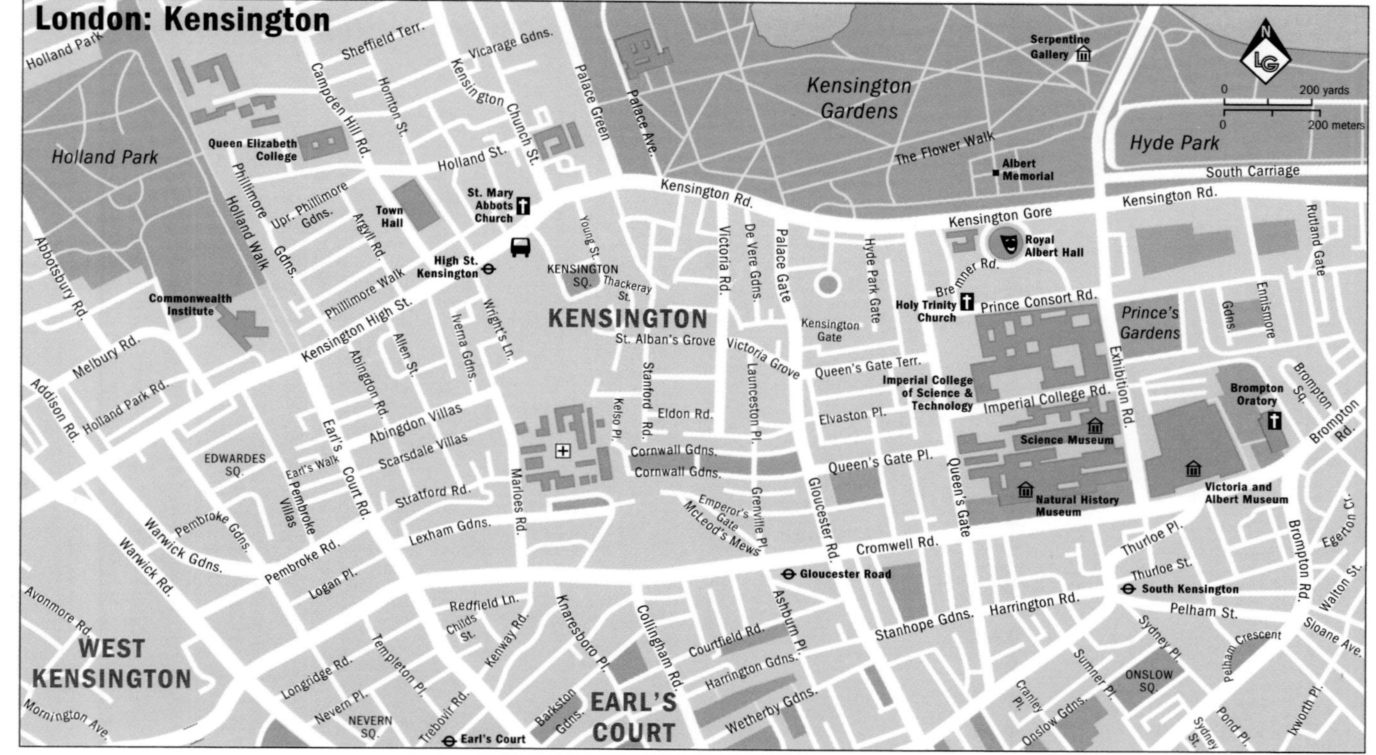
London: Kensington
Holland Park
Holland Park
Queen Elizabeth College
Phillimore Gdns.
Holland Walk
Upr. Phillimore Gdns.
Campden Hill Rd.
Sheffield Terr.
Hornton St.
Argyll Rd.
Town Hall
Holland St.
Vicarage Gdns.
Kensington Church St.
St. Mary Abbots Church
Palace Green
Palace Ave.
Kensington Gardens
Serpentine Gallery
The Flower Walk
Albert Memorial
Hyde Park
South Carriage
Kensington Rd.
Kensington Rd.
Kensington Gore
Royal Albert Hall
Rutland Gate
Abbotsbury Rd.
Commonwealth Institute
Phillimore Walk
High St. Kensington
Kensington High St.
Young St.
KENSINGTON SQ.
Thackeray St.
KENSINGTON
Victoria Rd.
De Vere Gdns.
Palace Gate
Kensington Gate
Hyde Park Gate
Bremner Rd.
Holy Trinity Church
Prince Consort Rd.
Prince's Gardens
Gdns.
Ennismore
Melbury Rd.
Allen St.
Iverna Gdns.
Wright's Ln.
St. Alban's Grove
Victoria Grove
Queen's Gate Terr.
Imperial College of Science & Technology
Exhibition Rd.
Brompton Sq.
Brompton Oratory
Addison Rd.
Holland Park Rd.
Abingdon Rd.
Abingdon Villas
Stanford Rd.
Eldon Rd.
Kelso Pl.
Launceston Pl.
Elvaston Pl.
Imperial College Rd.
Science Museum
Brompton Rd.
EDWARDES SQ.
Earl's Walk
Earl's Court Rd.
Scarsdale Villas
Marloes Rd.
Cornwall Gdns.
Cornwall Gdns.
Gloucester Rd.
Queen's Gate Pl.
Queen's Gate
Natural History Museum
Victoria and Albert Museum
Pembroke Villas
Pembroke Gdns.
Stratford Rd.
Emperor's Gate
McLeod's Mews
Grenville Pl.
Egerton Cr.
Warwick Gdns.
Warwick Rd.
Pembroke Rd.
Lexham Gdns.
Cromwell Rd.
Thurloe Pl.
Logan Pl.
Gloucester Road
Thurloe St.
Walton St.
Brompton Rd.
Avonmore Rd.
Redfield Ln.
Childs St.
Kenway Rd.
Knaresboro Pl.
Collingham Rd.
Ashburn Pl.
South Kensington
Harrington Rd.
Pelham St.
Stanhope Gdns.
Sloane Ave.
WEST KENSINGTON
Templeton Pl.
Longridge Rd.
Courtfield Rd.
Harrington Gdns.
Sydney Pl.
Sumner Pl.
Pelham Crescent
Nevern Pl.
NEVERN SQ.
Trebovir Rd.
Barkston Gdns.
EARL'S COURT
Wetherby Gdns.
Cranley Pl.
ONSLOW SQ.
Onslow Gdns.
Sydney St.
Pond Pl.
Ixworth Pl.
Mornington Ave.
Earl's Court
0 200 yards
0 200 meters
N
LG

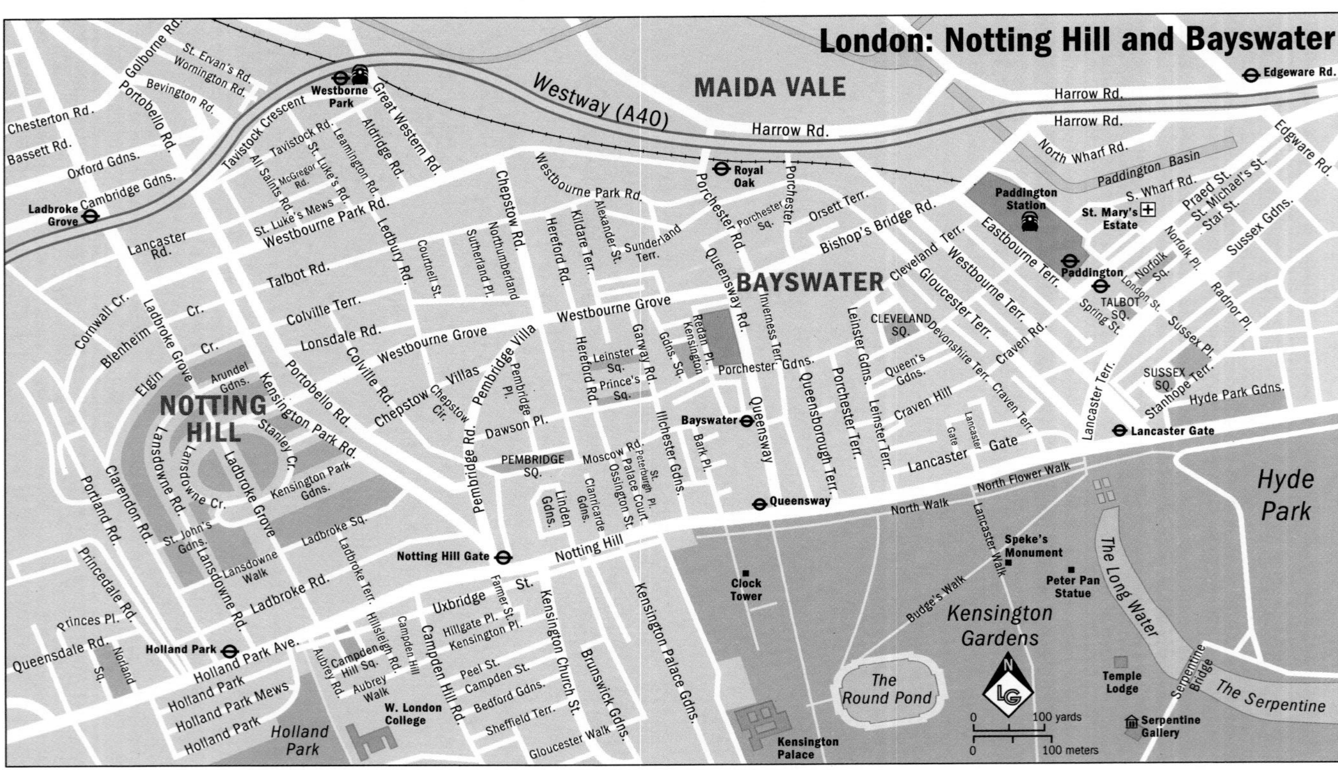
London: Notting Hill and Bayswater
MAIDA VALE
BAYSWATER
NOTTING HILL
Westway (A40)
Harrow Rd.
Edgeware Rd.
Paddington Station
Paddington
Paddington Basin
North Wharf Rd.
S. Wharf Rd.
St. Mary's Estate
Praed St.
St. Michael's St.
Star St.
Sussex Gdns.
Norfolk Pl.
Norfolk Sq.
London St.
TALBOT SQ.
Spring St.
Radnor Pl.
Sussex Pl.
SUSSEX SQ.
Stanhope Terr.
Hyde Park Gdns.
Lancaster Terr.
Lancaster Gate
Eastbourne Terr.
Westbourne Terr.
Gloucester Terr.
Cleveland Terr.
Bishop's Bridge Rd.
Orsett Terr.
Porchester
Porchester Sq.
Porchester Rd.
Royal Oak
Craven Rd.
Devonshire Terr.
Craven Terr.
CLEVELAND SQ.
Queen's Gdns.
Craven Hill
Leinster Gdns.
Leinster Terr.
Porchester Terr.
Queensborough Terr.
Inverness Terr.
Porchester Gdns.
Queensway Rd.
Queensway
Bayswater
Redan Pl.
Kensington Gdns. Sq.
Garway Rd.
Leinster Sq.
Prince's Sq.
Hereford Rd.
Bark Pl.
Ilchester Gdns.
Moscow Rd.
St. Peterburgh Pl.
Palace Court
Ossington St.
Clanricarde Gdns.
Linden Gdns.
PEMBRIDGE SQ.
Dawson Pl.
Pembridge Pl.
Pembridge Villa
Pembridge Rd.
Westbourne Grove
Westbourne Park Rd.
Alexander St.
Sunderland Terr.
Kildare Terr.
Chepstow Rd.
Northumberland
Sutherland Pl.
Courtnell St.
Ledbury Rd.
Talbot Rd.
Colville Terr.
Lonsdale Rd.
Colville Rd.
Chepstow Villas
Chepstow Cir.
Portobello Rd.
Kensington Park Rd.
Stanley Cr.
Kensington Park Gdns.
Ladbroke Sq.
Ladbroke Terr.
Ladbroke Grove
Lansdowne Cr.
Lansdowne Rd.
Lansdowne Walk
St. John's Gdns.
Ladbroke Rd.
Arundel Gdns.
Elgin Cr.
Blenheim Cr.
Cornwall Cr.
Clarendon Rd.
Portland Rd.
Princedale Rd.
Princes Pl.
Queensdale Rd.
Norland Sq.
Holland Park
Holland Park Ave.
Holland Park Mews
Lancaster Rd.
Westbourne Park
Great Western Rd.
Aldridge Rd.
Leamington Rd.
St. Luke's Rd.
Tavistock Rd.
Tavistock Crescent
McGregor Rd.
All Saints Rd.
St. Luke's Mews
Westbourne Park Rd.
Golborne Rd.
St. Ervan's Rd.
Wornington Rd.
Bevington Rd.
Chesterton Rd.
Bassett Rd.
Oxford Gdns.
Cambridge Gdns.
Ladbroke Grove
Notting Hill Gate
Notting Hill
Uxbridge St.
Farmer St.
Hillgate Pl.
Kensington Pl.
Campden Hill
Hillsleigh Rd.
Campden Hill Sq.
Aubrey Walk
Aubrey Rd.
Campden Hill Rd.
Peel St.
Campden St.
Bedford Gdns.
Sheffield Terr.
W. London College
Kensington Church St.
Gloucester Walk
Brunswick Gdns.
Kensington Palace Gdns.
Kensington Palace
Clock Tower
The Round Pond
Kensington Gardens
Budge's Walk
Lancaster Walk
North Walk
North Flower Walk
Speke's Monument
Peter Pan Statue
The Long Water
Temple Lodge
Serpentine Bridge
The Serpentine
Serpentine Gallery
Hyde Park
Queensway
0
100 yards
100 meters

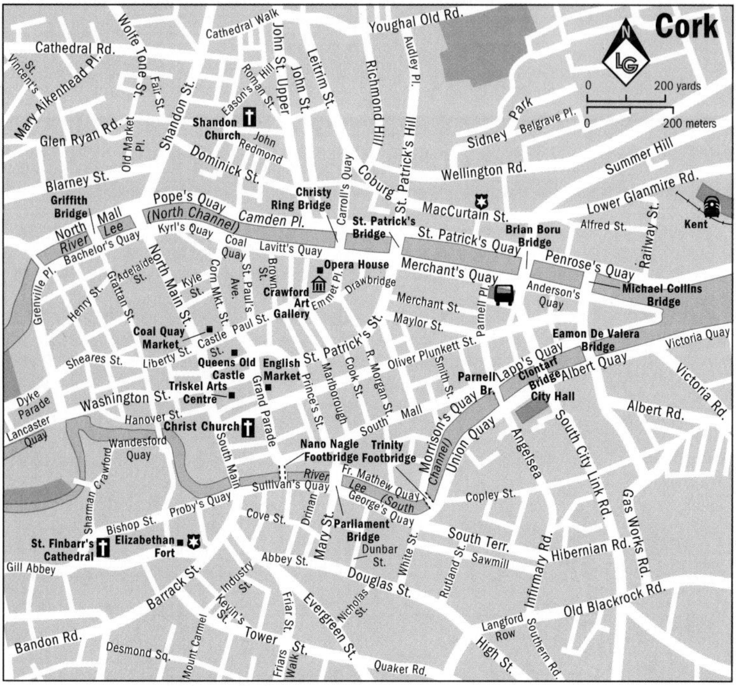

Cork

0 200 yards
0 200 meters

Youghal Old Rd.
Cathedral Walk
Cathedral Rd.
St. Vincent's
Mary Aikenhead Pl.
Wolfe Tone St.
Fair St.
Shandon St.
Eason's Hill
Roman St.
John St. Upper
John St.
Leitrim St.
Richmond Hill
Audley Pl.
St. Patrick's Hill
Shandon Church
John Redmond
Glen Ryan Rd.
Old Market Pl.
Dominick St.
Sidney Park
Belgrave Pl.
Blarney St.
Carroll's Quay
Coburg
Wellington Rd.
Summer Hill
Lower Glanmire Rd.
Griffith Bridge
North Mall
Pope's Quay
(North Channel)
Camden Pl.
Christy Ring Bridge
MacCurtain St.
Kent
North River Lee
Bachelor's Quay
Kyrl's Quay
Coal Quay
Lavitt's Quay
St. Patrick's Bridge
St. Patrick's Quay
Brian Boru Bridge
Alfred St.
Railway St.
Grenville Pl.
Adelaide St.
Kyle St.
Grattan St.
North Main St.
Corn Mkt. St.
St. Paul's Ave.
Brown St.
Opera House
Crawford Art Gallery
Emmet Pl.
Drawbridge
Merchant's Quay
Penrose's Quay
Anderson's Quay
Michael Collins Bridge
Henry St.
Merchant St.
Parnell Pl.
Coal Quay Market
Castle St.
Paul St.
Maylor St.
Eamon De Valera Bridge
Victoria Quay
Sheares St.
Liberty St.
Queens Old Castle
English Market
St. Patrick's St.
Oliver Plunkett St.
Lapp's Quay
Clontarf Bridge
Albert Quay
Dyke Parade
Washington St.
Triskel Arts Centre
Grand Parade
Prince's St.
Marlborough
Cook St.
R. Morgan St.
Smith St.
Parnell Br.
City Hall
Victoria Rd.
Albert Rd.
Lancaster Quay
Hanover St.
Christ Church
South Mall
Morrison's Quay
Union Quay
Angelsea
South City Link Rd.
Wandesford Quay
Crawford
South Main
Nano Nagle Footbridge
Trinity Footbridge
River Lee (South Channel)
Fr. Mathew Quay
Sharman Crawford
Sullivan's Quay
Proby's Quay
George's Quay
Copley St.
Gas Works Rd.
Bishop St.
Cove St.
Drinan
Mary St.
Parliament Bridge
South Terr.
Hibernian Rd.
St. Finbarr's Cathedral
Elizabethan Fort
Dunbar St.
White St.
Rutland St.
Sawmill
Infirmary Rd.
Gill Abbey
Abbey St.
Douglas St.
Barrack St.
Industry St.
Old Blackrock Rd.
Kevin's St.
Friar St.
Evergreen St.
Nicholas St.
Langford Row
Southern Rd.
Bandon Rd.
Tower St.
High St.
Desmond Sq.
Mount Carmel
Friars Walk
Quaker Rd.

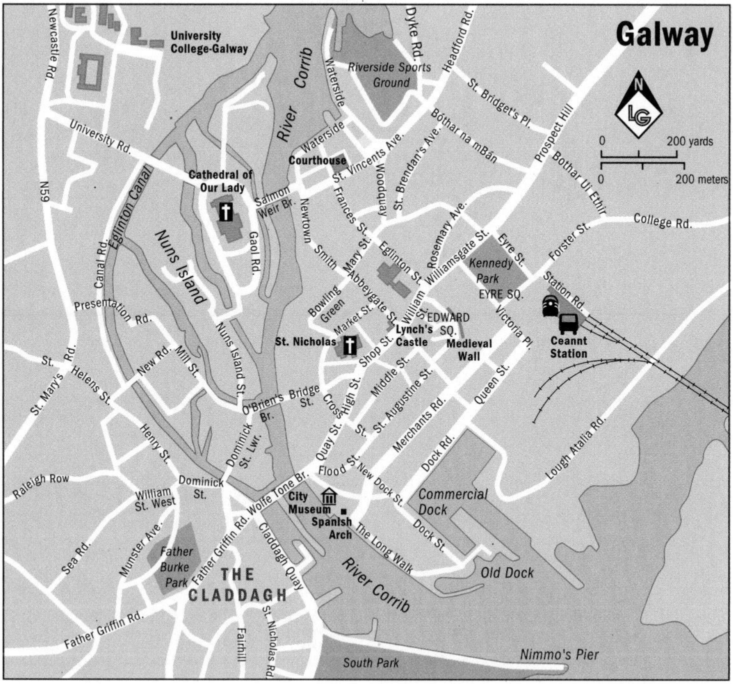

Galway

0 200 yards
0 200 meters

Newcastle Rd.
University College-Galway
Dyke Rd.
Headford Rd.
River Corrib
Waterside
Riverside Sports Ground
St. Bridget's Pl.
Bóthar na mBan
Prospect Hill
University Rd.
St. Vincents Ave.
Woodquay
St. Brendan's Ave.
Bothar Ui Ethir
Courthouse
Cathedral of Our Lady
Salmon Weir Br.
Newtown Smith
St. Frances St.
N59
Eglinton Canal
Nuns Island
Gaol Rd.
Rosemary Ave.
College Rd.
Forster St.
Eyre St.
Canal Rd.
Mary St.
Eglinton St.
Williamsgate St.
Kennedy Park
EYRE SQ.
Station Rd.
Presentation Rd.
Bowling Green
Abbeygate St.
William St.
EDWARD SQ.
Victoria Pl.
Market St.
Lynch's Castle
Medieval Wall
Ceannt Station
St. Nicholas
Shop St.
Nuns Island St.
St. Mary's Rd.
New Rd.
Mill St.
Middle St.
St. Helens St.
Queen St.
O'Brien's Bridge St.
O'Brien's Br.
Cross St.
High St.
St. Augustine St.
Merchants Rd.
Henry St.
Dominick St. Lwr.
Quay St.
Dock Rd.
Lough Atalia Rd.
Flood St.
New Dock St.
Raleigh Row
Dominick St.
William St. West
Wolfe Tone Br.
City Museum
Commercial Dock
Father Griffin Rd.
Spanish Arch
Claddagh Quay
Dock St.
The Long Walk
Sea Rd.
Munster Ave.
Father Burke Park
THE CLADDAGH
River Corrib
Old Dock
Father Griffin Rd.
Fairhill
St. Nicholas Rd.
South Park
Nimmo's Pier

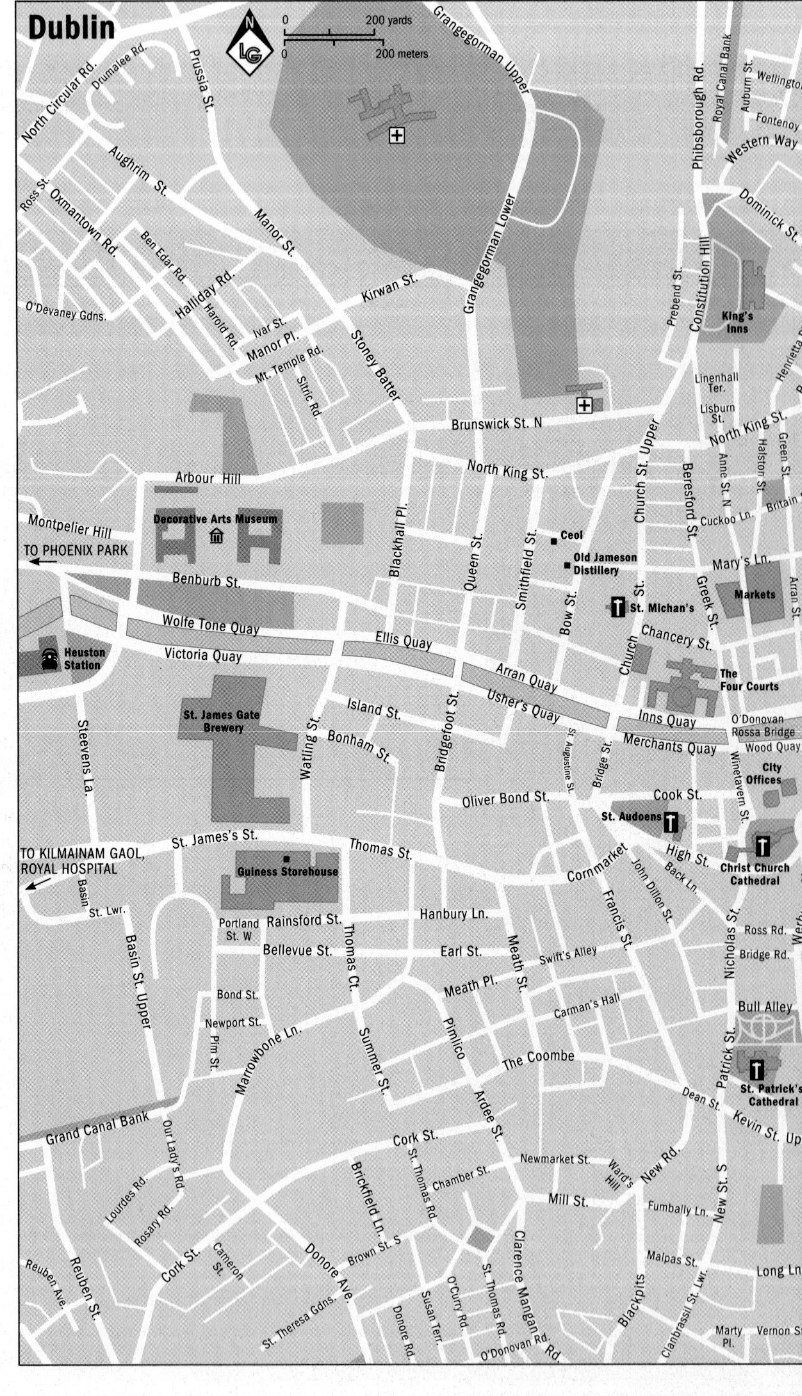
Dublin
0
200 yards
200 meters
Grangegorman Upper
North Circular Rd.
Drumalee Rd.
Prussia St.
Aughrim St.
Ross St.
Oxmantown Rd.
Manor St.
Ben Edar Rd.
Halliday Rd.
Harold Rd.
O'Devaney Gdns.
Kirwan St.
Ivar St.
Manor Pl.
Mt. Temple Rd.
Sitric Rd.
Stoney Batter
Grangegorman Lower
Brunswick St. N
Phibsborough Rd.
Royal Canal Bank
Auburn St.
Wellington
Fontenoy St.
Western Way
Dominick St.
Prebend St.
Constitution Hill
King's Inns
Henrietta Pl.
Linenhall Ter.
Lisburn St.
North King St.
Arbour Hill
North King St.
Church St. Upper
Beresford St.
Anne St. N
Halston St.
Green St.
Britain St.
Cuckoo Ln.
Montpelier Hill
Decorative Arts Museum
TO PHOENIX PARK
Blackhall Pl.
Queen St.
Smithfield St.
Ceol
Old Jameson Distillery
Mary's Ln.
Benburb St.
Bow St.
Church St.
St. Michan's
Greek St.
Markets
Arran St.
Wolfe Tone Quay
Ellis Quay
Chancery St.
Heuston Station
Victoria Quay
Arran Quay
Church St.
The Four Courts
Usher's Quay
Island St.
Inns Quay
O'Donovan Rossa Bridge
St. James Gate Brewery
Steevens La.
Watling St.
Bonham St.
Bridgefoot St.
St. Augustine St.
Bridge St.
Merchants Quay
Wood Quay
Winetavern St.
City Offices
Oliver Bond St.
Cook St.
St. Audoens
St. James's St.
Thomas St.
High St.
Christ Church Cathedral
TO KILMAINAM GAOL, ROYAL HOSPITAL
Basin St. Lwr.
Gulness Storehouse
Cornmarket
John Dillon St.
Back Ln.
Francis St.
Hanbury Ln.
Portland St. W
Rainsford St.
Thomas Ct.
Nicholas St.
Ross Rd.
Werburgh St.
Basin St. Upper
Bellevue St.
Earl St.
Meath St.
Swift's Alley
Bridge Rd.
Bond St.
Meath Pl.
Newport St.
Carman's Hall
Bull Alley
Pim St.
Marrowbone Ln.
Summer St.
Pimlico
Patrick St.
The Coombe
St. Patrick's Cathedral
Dean St.
Grand Canal Bank
Ardee St.
Kevin St. Upr
Our Lady's Rd.
Cork St.
St. Thomas Rd.
Newmarket St.
Ward's Hill
New Rd.
Lourdes Rd.
Brickfield Ln.
Chamber St.
Mill St.
New St. S
Rosary Rd.
Fumbally Ln.
Cork St.
Cameron St.
Brown St. S
Donore Ave.
Clarence Mangan Rd.
Malpas St.
Long Ln.
Reuben Ave.
Reuben St.
St. Thomas Rd.
O'Curry Rd.
Susan Terr.
Donore Rd.
St. Theresa Gdns.
O'Donovan Rd.
Blackpits
Clanbrassil St. Lwr.
Marty Pl.
Vernon St

TO
St. George's
Berkeley St.
Temple St. N
N. Circular Rd.
William St. N
Mountjoy Sq.
North
East
West
South
Charles St. Great
Rutland St. Upr.
Summer St. N
Dunne St.
Portland Row
Blessington St.
Wellington St. Lwr.
Dorset St. Upper
Mountjoy
Paradise Pl.
Gardiner Pl.
Hill St.
Middle Gardiner St.
Gardiner Ln.
Empress Pl.
Upr. Buckingham St.
Rutland St. Lwr.
Summerhill Rd.
Dublin Writers Museum
Hugh Lane Gallery
Abbey Presbyterian
Denmark St.
N. Great George's
Nat'l Wax Museum
Parnell Sq. N
Garden of Remembrance
Parnell Sq. E
James Joyce Center
Killarney St.
Amiens St.
Parnell Sq.
Sean Mac Dermott St.
Lwr Buckingham St.
Dominick Pl.
Parnell Sq. W
Gate Theatre
Lower Gardiner St.
Railway St.
Connolly Station
Marlborough St.
DART Trains
Dominick St. Lower
Rotunda Hospital
Parnell Sq. S
Corporation St.
Foley St.
Main Entrance
Sheriff St. Lwr.
O'Connell St. Upper
Moore Ln.
Moore St.
Tyrone House
Talbot Ln.
Parnell St.
Talbot St.
Inner Dock
Moore St. Market
Earl St. N
Store St.
Commons St.
Central Library
Busarus
Memorial Rd.
Financial Services Center
Wolf Tone St.
Jervis St.
Jervis Ln.
Henry St.
Mary St.
Beresford Pl.
Prince's St. N
O'Connell St. Lower
Liffey St. Upr.
Lower Abbey St.
Custom House
George's Dock
St. Mary's Church
Liberty Hall
Middle Abbey St.
Custom House Quay
Eden Quay
North Wall
Upper Abbey St.
Liffey St. Lwr.
Lotts Row
River Liffey
O'Connell Bridge
Burgh Quay
George's Quay
City Quay
Strand St. Great
Bachelors Walk
Tara St.
Tara St. Station
Princes St.
Sir Rogerson's Quay
Poolbeg
Luke St.
Ormond Quay
Ha'Penny Footbridge
Aston Quay
Westmoreland St.
D'Olier St.
Moss St.
Gloucester St.
Lombard St.
Millennium Bridge
Grattan Bridge
Wellington Quay
Fleet St.
Garda
Townsend St.
Creighton St.
Temple Bar
Stock Exchange
Pearse St.
Lombard St. E
Parliament St.
Sycamore St.
Eustace St.
Temple Ln. S
Anglesea St.
Bank of Ireland
Cope St.
College Green
Sandwith St. Lwr.
City Hall
Irish Film Centre
Dame St.
Pearse Station
Trinity College
Dublin Castle
Suffolk St.
Westland Row
Chester Beatty Library
Wicklow St.
American Express
Nassau St.
Sandwith St. Upr.
Boyne St.
S. Great Georges St.
Drury St.
William St. S.
Clarendon St.
Grafton St.
Duke St.
Frederick St. S
Lincoln Pl.
Ship St. Great
Stephen St. Upr.
Dublin Civic Museum
Frederick Ln.
National Library
National Gallery
Fenian St.
Stephen St. Lwr.
Chatham St.
Anne St. S
Molesworth St.
National History
Denzille Ln.
Longford St. Gt.
Mansion House
National Museums
Leinster House
North
Holles St.
Adelaide Hospital
Mercer St. Lwr.
St. Steven's Green Shopping Centre
Dawson St.
Kildare St.
West
Merrion Sq.
Peter Row
Aungier St.
Archaeology and History Museum
Mount St. Lwr.
St. Stephen's Green N
Merrion St. Upper
York St.
St. Stephen's Green W
South
East
Mercer St. Upr.
Merrion Row
Fitzwilliam La.
Wexford St.
St. Stephen's Green
Hume St.
Ely Pl.
Baggot St. Lower
Mount St. Upr.
St. Stephen's Green E
Number 29
Fitzwilliam St. Lwr.
James's St. E
St. Stephen's Green S
Camden Row
Pembroke St. Lwr.
Bank of Ireland
Harcourt St.
University College Dublin
Quinn's Ln.
Fitzwilliam St. Upr.
Leeson St. Lwr.
Earlsfort Ter.
Lad Ln.
Pleasants St.
Camden St.
National Concert Hall
Pembroke St. Upr.
Fitzwilliam Sq.

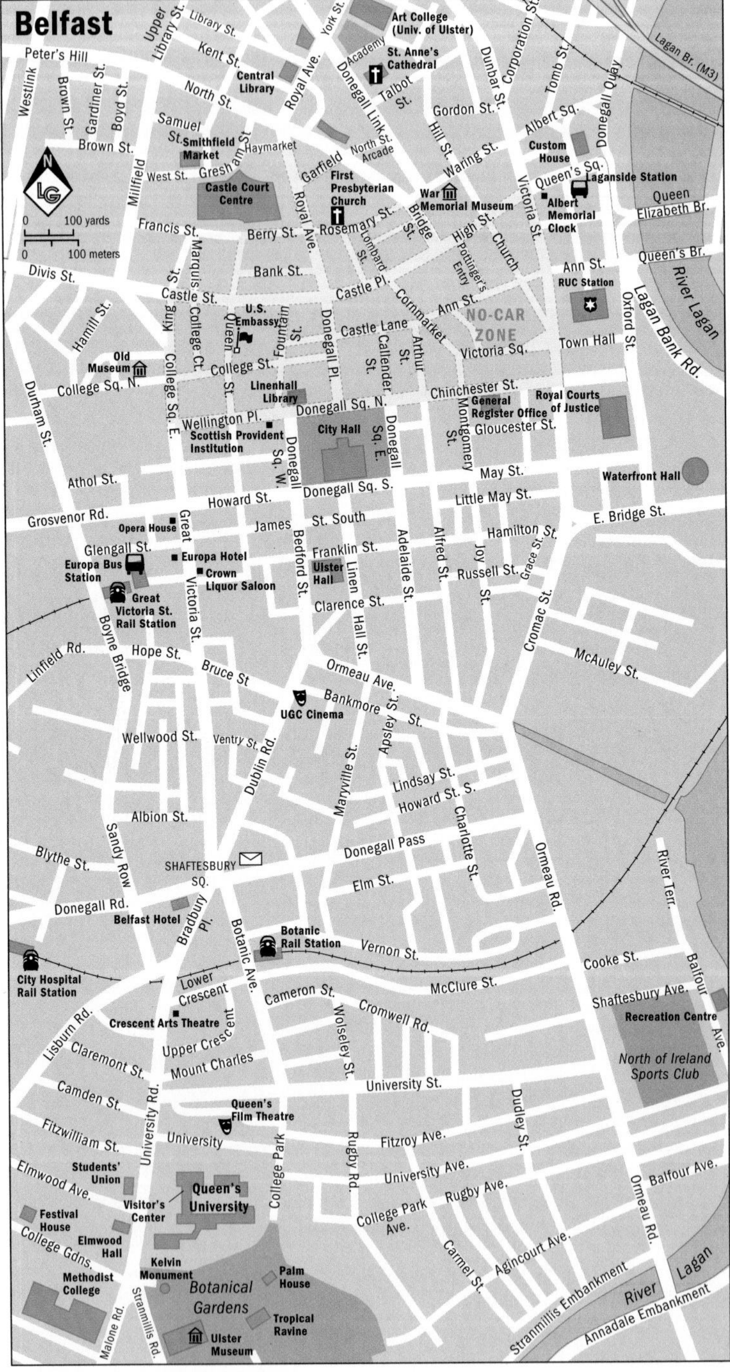
Belfast
100 yards
100 meters
Art College (Univ. of Ulster)
St. Anne's Cathedral
Central Library
Smithfield Market
Castle Court Centre
First Presbyterian Church
War Memorial Museum
Custom House
Laganside Station
Albert Memorial Clock
RUC Station
NO-CAR ZONE
U.S. Embassy
Old Museum
Linenhall Library
Royal Courts of Justice
General Register Office
City Hall
Scottish Provident Institution
Waterfront Hall
Opera House
Europa Hotel
Europa Bus Station
Crown Liquor Saloon
Ulster Hall
Great Victoria St. Rail Station
UGC Cinema
Shaftesbury Sq.
Belfast Hotel
Botanic Rail Station
City Hospital Rail Station
Crescent Arts Theatre
Recreation Centre
North of Ireland Sports Club
Queen's Film Theatre
Students' Union
Queen's University
Visitor's Center
Festival House
Elmwood Hall
Kelvin Monument
Methodist College
Botanical Gardens
Palm House
Tropical Ravine
Ulster Museum
River Lagan
Queen Elizabeth Br.
Queen's Br.
Lagan Br. (M3)
Donegall Quay
Lagan Bank Rd.
Oxford St.
Ormeau Rd.
Ormeau Ave.
Donegall Pass
Donegall Rd.
Botanic Ave.
University Rd.
Lisburn Rd.
Malone Rd.
Stranmillis Rd.
Stranmillis Embankment
Annadale Embankment
Grosvenor Rd.
Divis St.
Great Victoria St.
Dublin Rd.
Sandy Row
Boyne Bridge
Cromac St.
Victoria St.
Royal Ave.
Donegall Pl.
Bedford St.
Linen Hall St.
Adelaide St.
Alfred St.
University St.
Fitzroy Ave.
University Ave.
College Park
Rugby Rd.
Dudley St.
Balfour Ave.
McAuley St.
E. Bridge St.
Chichester St.
May St.
Howard St.
Castle St.
Castle Pl.
High St.
North St.
Peter's Hill
Westlink
Millfield
Durham St.

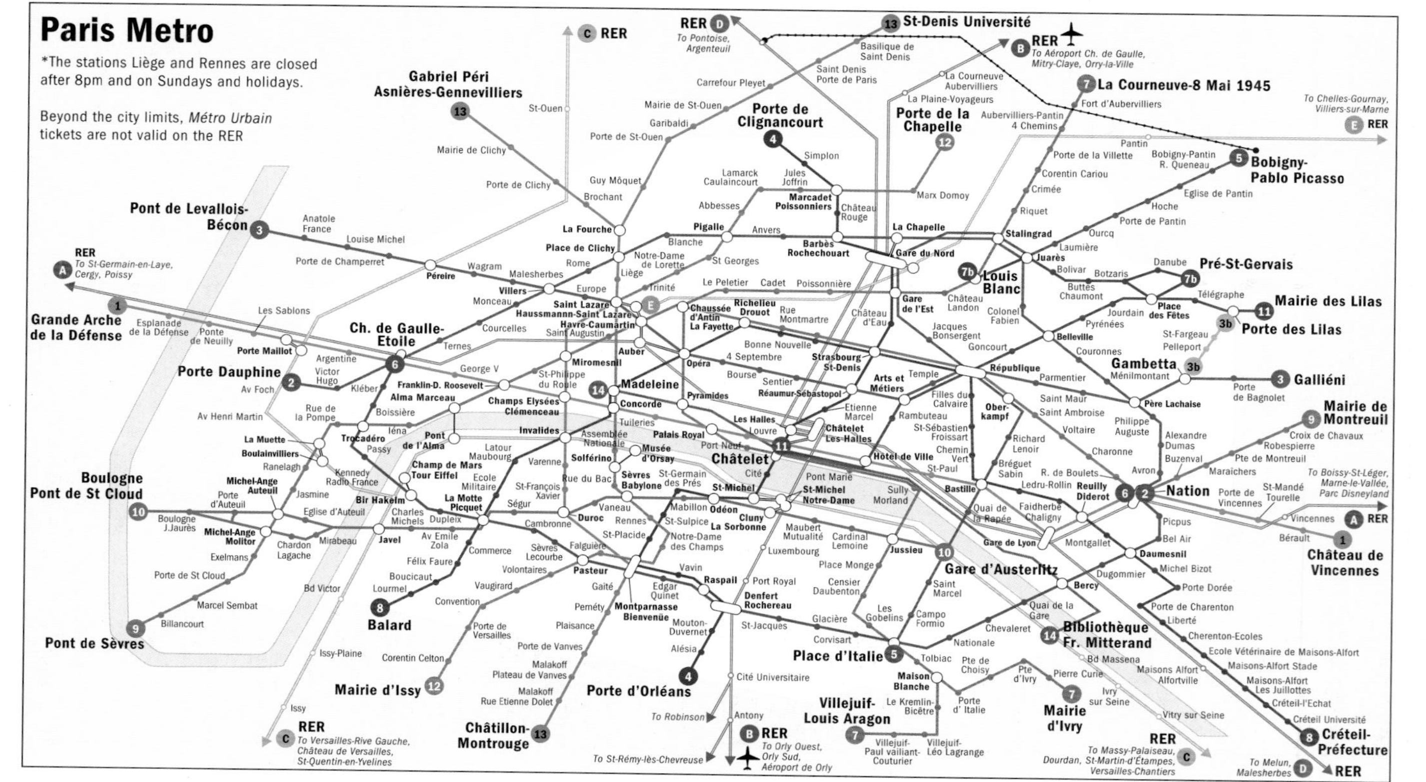

Paris Metro
*The stations Liège and Rennes are closed after 8pm and on Sundays and holidays.
Beyond the city limits, Métro Urbain tickets are not valid on the RER
RER A To St-Germain-en-Laye, Cergy, Poissy
RER C
RER D To Pontoise, Argenteuil
St-Denis Université
RER B To Aéroport Ch. de Gaulle, Mitry-Claye, Orry-la-Ville
La Courneuve-8 Mai 1945
To Chelles-Gournay, Villiers-sur-Marne
RER E
Gabriel Péri Asnières-Gennevilliers
Porte de Clignancourt
Porte de la Chapelle
Bobigny-Pablo Picasso
Pont de Levallois-Bécon
Grande Arche de la Défense
Pré-St-Gervais
Mairie des Lilas
Porte des Lilas
Ch. de Gaulle-Etoile
Porte Dauphine
Gambetta
Gallièni
Mairie de Montreuil
To Boissy-St-Léger, Marne-le-Vallée, Parc Disneyland
RER A
Château de Vincennes
Boulogne Pont de St Cloud
Nation
Châtelet
Gare d'Austerlitz
Pont de Sèvres
Balard
Bibliothèque Fr. Mitterand
Place d'Italie
Mairie d'Issy
Porte d'Orléans
Villejuif-Louis Aragon
Mairie d'Ivry
Créteil-Préfecture
Châtillon-Montrouge
RER C To Versailles-Rive Gauche, Château de Versailles, St-Quentin-en-Yvelines
To Robinson
To St-Rémy-lès-Chevreuse
RER B To Orly Ouest, Orly Sud, Aéroport de Orly
RER C To Massy-Palaiseau, Dourdan, St-Martin-d'Étampes, Versailles-Chantiers
To Melun, Malesherbes
RER D
Basilique de Saint Denis
Saint Denis Porte de Paris
Carrefour Pleyel
Mairie de St-Ouen
Garibaldi
Porte de St-Ouen
Guy Môquet
Brochant
La Fourche
Place de Clichy
St-Ouen
Mairie de Clichy
Porte de Clichy
Anatole France
Louise Michel
Porte de Champerret
Péreire
Wagram
Malesherbes
Villiers
Monceau
Courcelles
Ternes
Rome
Europe
Liège
Notre-Dame de Lorette
Blanche
Pigalle
Anvers
Abbesses
Lamarck Caulaincourt
Jules Joffrin
Simplon
Marcadet Poissonniers
Château Rouge
Marx Domoy
Barbès Rochechouart
La Chapelle
Gare du Nord
Stalingrad
Jaurès
Riquet
Crimée
Corentin Cariou
Porte de la Villette
Fort d'Aubervilliers
Aubervilliers-Pantin 4 Chemins
La Courneuve Aubervilliers
La Plaine-Voyageurs
Pantin
Bobigny-Pantin R. Queneau
Eglise de Pantin
Hoche
Porte de Pantin
Ourcq
Laumière
Bolivar
Buttes Chaumont
Botzaris
Danube
Place des Fêtes
Télégraphe
St-Fargeau
Pelleport
Jourdain
Pyrénées
Belleville
Couronnes
Ménilmontant
Porte de Bagnolet
Père Lachaise
Philippe Auguste
Alexandre Dumas
Buzenval
Maraichers
Pte de Montreuil
Robespierre
Croix de Chavaux
Louis Blanc
Château Landon
Colonel Fabien
Gare de l'Est
Château d'Eau
Jacques Bonsergent
Goncourt
République
Parmentier
Saint Maur
Saint Ambroise
Voltaire
Charonne
Avron
St Georges
Trinité
Le Peletier
Cadet
Poissonnière
Saint Lazare
Haussmann-Saint Lazare
Havre-Caumartin
Saint Augustin
Chaussée d'Antin La Fayette
Richelieu Drouot
Rue Montmartre
Bonne Nouvelle
Strasbourg St-Denis
4 Septembre
Opéra
Auber
Miromesnil
St-Philippe du Roule
Franklin-D. Roosevelt
George V
Argentine
Victor Hugo
Kléber
Les Sablons
Esplanade de la Défense
Pont de Neuilly
Porte Maillot
Av Foch
Rue de la Pompe
Boissière
Alma Marceau
Champs Elysées Clémenceau
Madeleine
Concorde
Pyramides
Bourse
Sentier
Réaumur-Sébastopol
Arts et Métiers
Temple
Filles du Calvaire
Oberkampf
Rambuteau
Etienne Marcel
Les Halles
Châtelet Les-Halles
Louvre
Palais Royal
Tuileries
Assemblée Nationale
Invalides
Iéna
Trocadéro
Passy
Pont de l'Alma
Av Henri Martin
La Muette
Boulainvilliers
Ranelagh
Kennedy Radio France
Jasmine
Michel-Ange Auteuil
Porte d'Auteuil
Boulogne J.Jaurès
Michel-Ange Molitor
Eglise d'Auteuil
Chardon Lagache
Mirabeau
Exelmans
Porte de St Cloud
Marcel Sembat
Billancourt
Bir Hakeim
Champ de Mars Tour Eiffel
Charles Michels
Dupleix
La Motte Picquet
Ecole Militaire
Latour Maubourg
Varenne
Musée d'Orsay
Solférino
Sèvres Babylone
St-François Xavier
Ségur
Rue du Bac
Vaneau
Duroc
Rennes
St-Placide
Cambronne
Javel
Av Emile Zola
Félix Faure
Commerce
Boucicault
Lourmel
Bd Victor
Issy-Plaine
Issy
Convention
Vaugirard
Volontaires
Sèvres Lecourbe
Falguière
Pasteur
Gaité
Pernety
Plaisance
Porte de Vanves
Porte de Versailles
Corentin Celton
Malakoff Plateau de Vanves
Malakoff Rue Etienne Dolet
Montparnasse Bienvenüe
Edgar Quinet
Vavin
Raspail
Denfert Rochereau
Mouton-Duvernet
Alésia
Notre-Dame des Champs
St-Sulpice
Mabillon
Odéon
St-Germain des Prés
St-Michel
Cluny La Sorbonne
St-Michel Notre-Dame
Cité
Pont Neuf
Pont Marie
Hôtel de Ville
St-Paul
Chemin Vert
St-Sébastien Froissart
Richard Lenoir
Bréguet Sabin
Bastille
Sully Morland
Maubert Mutualité
Cardinal Lemoine
Jussieu
Luxembourg
Port Royal
Place Monge
Censier Daubenton
Les Gobelins
Campo Formio
Saint Marcel
St-Jacques
Glacière
Corvisart
Cité Universitaire
Antony
Quai de la Rapée
Gare de Lyon
Faidherbe Chaligny
Ledru-Rollin
R. de Boulets
Reuilly Diderot
Montgallet
Dugommier
Daumesnil
Bercy
Quai de la Gare
Chevaleret
Nationale
Tolbiac
Maison Blanche
Le Kremlin-Bicêtre
Villejuif-Paul vaillant-Couturier
Villejuif-Léo Lagrange
Porte d'Italie
Pte de Choisy
Pte d'Ivry
Pierre Curie
Bd Massena
Ivry sur Seine
Vitry sur Seine
Maisons Alfort Alfortville
Picpus
Bel Air
Michel Bizot
Porte Dorée
Porte de Charenton
Liberté
Cherenton-Ecoles
Ecole Vétérinaire de Maisons-Alfort
Maisons-Alfort Stade
Maisons-Alfort Les Juillottes
Créteil-l'Echat
Créteil Université
Porte de Vincennes
St-Mandé Tourelle
Vincennes
Bérault

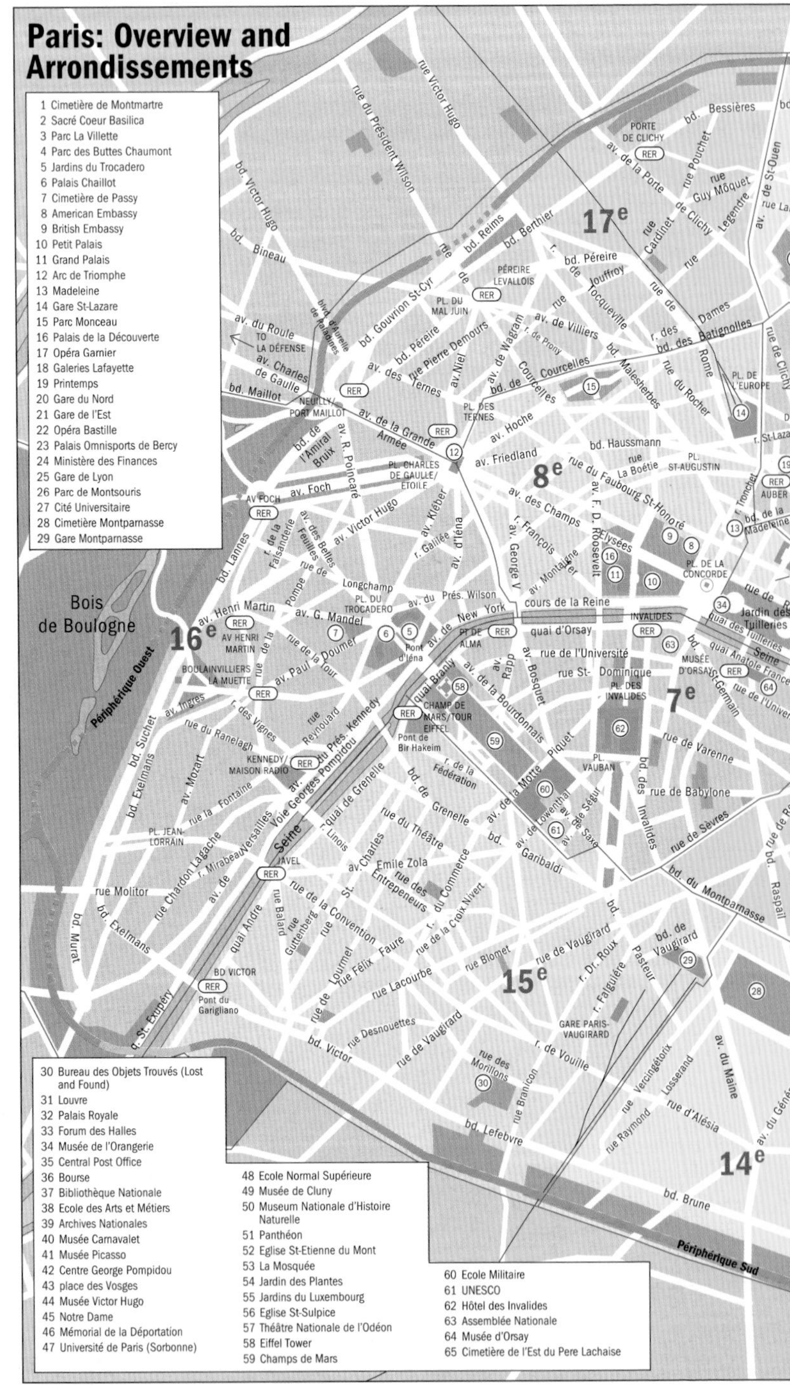
Paris: Overview and Arrondissements
1 Cimetière de Montmartre
2 Sacré Coeur Basilica
3 Parc La Villette
4 Parc des Buttes Chaumont
5 Jardins du Trocadero
6 Palais Chaillot
7 Cimetière de Passy
8 American Embassy
9 British Embassy
10 Petit Palais
11 Grand Palais
12 Arc de Triomphe
13 Madeleine
14 Gare St-Lazare
15 Parc Monceau
16 Palais de la Découverte
17 Opéra Garnier
18 Galeries Lafayette
19 Printemps
20 Gare du Nord
21 Gare de l'Est
22 Opéra Bastille
23 Palais Omnisports de Bercy
24 Ministère des Finances
25 Gare de Lyon
26 Parc de Montsouris
27 Cité Universitaire
28 Cimetière Montparnasse
29 Gare Montparnasse
30 Bureau des Objets Trouvés (Lost and Found)
31 Louvre
32 Palais Royale
33 Forum des Halles
34 Musée de l'Orangerie
35 Central Post Office
36 Bourse
37 Bibliothèque Nationale
38 Ecole des Arts et Métiers
39 Archives Nationales
40 Musée Carnavalet
41 Musée Picasso
42 Centre George Pompidou
43 place des Vosges
44 Musée Victor Hugo
45 Notre Dame
46 Mémorial de la Déportation
47 Université de Paris (Sorbonne)
48 Ecole Normal Supérieure
49 Musée de Cluny
50 Museum Nationale d'Histoire Naturelle
51 Panthéon
52 Eglise St-Etienne du Mont
53 La Mosquée
54 Jardin des Plantes
55 Jardins du Luxembourg
56 Eglise St-Sulpice
57 Théâtre Nationale de l'Odéon
58 Eiffel Tower
59 Champs de Mars
60 Ecole Militaire
61 UNESCO
62 Hôtel des Invalides
63 Assemblée Nationale
64 Musée d'Orsay
65 Cimetière de l'Est du Pere Lachaise
17e
8e
16e
7e
15e
14e
Bois de Boulogne
Périphérique Ouest
Périphérique Sud
Seine
TO LA DÉFENSE
PORTE DE CLICHY
PÉREIRE LEVALLOIS
PL. DU MAL JUIN
NEUILLY/ PORT MAILLOT
PL. DES TERNES
PL. CHARLES DE GAULLE/ ETOILE
AV FOCH
PL. DU TROCADERO
AV HENRI MARTIN
BOULAINVILLIERS LA MUETTE
KENNEDY/ MAISON RADIO
CHAMP DE MARS/TOUR EIFFEL
PT DE ALMA
Pont d'Iéna
Pont de Bir Hakeim
INVALIDES
MUSÉE D'ORSAY
PL. DES INVALIDES
PL. VAUBAN
PL. DE LA CONCORDE
PL. ST-AUGUSTIN
AUBER
PL. DE L'EUROPE
PL. JEAN-LORRAIN
JAVEL
BD VICTOR
Pont du Garigliano
GARE PARIS-VAUGIRARD
Jardin des Tuileries
RER
bd. Bessières
rue Victor Hugo
rue du Président Wilson
bd. Victor Hugo
bd. Bineau
bd. Berthier
bd. Reims
bd. Péreire
av. de la Porte de Clichy
rue Guy Môquet
av. de St-Ouen
rue Cardinet
rue Legendre
rue Pouchet
rue Lamarck
rue de Tocqueville
rue Jouffroy
bd. des Batignolles
rue des Dames
rue de Rome
rue du Rocher
rue de Clichy
av. du Roule
av. Charles de Gaulle
bd. Maillot
bd. Gouvrion St-Cyr
av. de Villiers
r. de Prony
av. de Wagram
rue Pierre Demours
av. des Ternes
av. Niel
rue de Courcelles
bd. de Courcelles
bd. Malesherbes
av. de la Grande Armée
bd. de l'Amiral Bruix
av. R. Poincaré
av. Hoche
av. Friedland
bd. Haussmann
rue La Boétie
rue du Faubourg St-Honoré
r. St-Lazare
bd. de la Madeleine
av. Foch
av. Victor Hugo
av. Kléber
av. d'Iéna
r. Galilée
av. des Champs Elysées
av. F. D. Roosevelt
r. François 1er
av. George V
av. Montaigne
cours de la Reine
av. du Prés. Wilson
rue de Longchamp
av. Henri Martin
av. G. Mandel
av. Paul Doumer
rue de la Pompe
rue de la Tour
av. de New York
quai d'Orsay
rue de l'Université
rue St-Dominique
av. Rapp
av. Bosquet
av. de la Bourdonnais
quai Branly
rue de Rivoli
quai Anatole France
bd. St-Germain
rue de Varenne
rue de Babylone
rue de Sèvres
bd. des Invalides
bd. du Montparnasse
bd. Raspail
rue de Rennes
av. de la Motte Piquet
av. de Lowenthal
av. de Saxe
av. de Ségur
bd. Garibaldi
bd. de Grenelle
r. de la Fédération
rue du Théâtre
av. Emile Zola
rue des Entrepeneurs
rue du Commerce
rue de la Croix Nivert
quai de Grenelle
av. du Prés. Kennedy
Voie Georges Pompidou
r. Linois
rue St. Charles
rue de la Convention
rue Balard
rue Guttenberg
rue de Lourmel
rue Félix Faure
rue Lacourbe
rue Blomet
rue de Vaugirard
r. Dr. Roux
r. Falguière
bd. Pasteur
bd. de Vaugirard
av. du Maine
rue Vercingétorix
rue Losserand
rue d'Alésia
rue Raymond
av. du Général Leclerc
r. de Vouille
rue des Morillons
rue Brancion
bd. Lefebvre
bd. Brune
bd. Victor
rue Desnouettes
quai André
av. de Versailles
r. Mirabeau
rue Chardon Lagache
rue Molitor
bd. Exelmans
bd. Murat
q. St. Exupéry
bd. Suchet
av. Mozart
rue la Fontaine
rue du Ranelagh
av. Ingres
r. des Vignes
rue Reynouard
bd. Lannes
r. de la Faisanderie
av. des Belles Feuilles

Périphérique Nord
Périphérique Est
bd. Ney
bd. Macdonald
Canal de l'Ourcq
18e
19e
20e
9e
10e
11e
12e
13e
1er
2e
3e
4e
5e
6e
rue Championnet
bd. Ornano
rue Ordener
rue Duhesme
Marcadet
Caulaincourt
rue Custine
rue de Clignancourt
bd. Barbès
rue des Poissonniers
rue de la Chapelle
rue Marx Dormoy
r. l'Evangile
rue Riquet
rue d'Aubervilliers
rue Archereau
rue de l'Ourcq
av. Corentin Cariou
bd. Sérurier
av. Jean Lolive
rue de Flandre
rue de Crimée
Bassin de la Villette
av. Jean Jaurès
bd. Indochine
bd. d'Algérie
rue Manin
r. David d'Angiers
r. Armand Carel
av. Secrétan
bd. de Rochechouart
bd. de la Chapelle
bd. de Clichy
PL. PIGALLE
av. Trudaine
PL. DE STALINGRAD
PL. DU COLONEL FABIEN
Canal St-Martin
RER
rue La Fayette
rue Poissonnière
r. Paradis
rue de Châteaudun
rue du Fg. Poissonnière
r. d'Hauteville
r. de Fg. St-Denis
bd. de Strasbourg
bd. de Magenta
r. Château d'Eau
bd. de la Villette
bd. Mortier
bd. Montmartre
bd. des Italiens
bd. Poissonnière
bd. St-Denis
blvd. St-Martin
rue du Faubourg du Temple
rue des Pyrénées
PL. GAMBETTA
av. Gambetta
av. Parmentier
rue St-Maur
bd. de Belleville
4 Sept.
rue Montmartre
rue Réaumur
bd. Petit Champs
PL. DE LA RÉPUBLIQUE
rue de Turbigo
r. Etienne Marcel
rue du Louvre
rue St-Honoré
rue de Rivoli
rue des Halles
bd. de Sébastopol
rue St-Denis
rue St-Martin
rue Beaubourg
rue du Temple
rue des Archives
rue Vieille du Temple
av. de la République
rue Oberkampf
bd. Beaumarchais
bd. R. Lenoir
bd. Voltaire
rue du Chemin Vert
rue de la Roquette
Ménilmontant
bd. de Ménilmontant
av. Philippe Auguste
bd. de Charonne
rue de Charonne
bd. Davout
quai du Louvre
Pont Neuf
Ile de la Cité
quai St-Michel
r. de Seine
St-Germain
ST-MICHEL
quai de la Tournelle
PL. MAUBERT
rue St-Antoine
Ile St-Louis
bd. Henri IV
Pont de Sully
rue du Faubourg St-Antoine
rue de Lyon
av. Ledru Rollin
rue de Montreuil
NATION
PL. DE LA NATION
Cours de Vincennes
bd. Diderot
bd. Picpus
rue de Picpus
av. du Dr. Arnold Netter
r. des Écoles
LUXEMBOURG
bd. St-Michel
rue Monge
quai St-Bernard
Seine
Pont d'Austerlitz
PL. DE LA CONTRE-SCARPE
rue d'Ulm
rue Guy Lussac
rue Mouffetard
r. G. St-Hilaire
rue Censier
rue Buffon
av. Daumesnil
PL. FÉLIX ÉBOUÉ
bd. de Bercy
rue de Bercy
GARE D'AUSTERLITZ
Pont de Bercy
quai de Bercy
rue de Charenton
bd. Mt. Bizot
bd. Soult
PORT ROYAL
r. C. Bernard
bd. St-Marcel
bd. de Port Royal
rue St-Jacques
av. des Gobelins
bd. de l'Hôpital
bd. Arago
Pont de Tolbiac
av. du Gén. Bizot
bd. Poniatowski
Parc Zoologique
Bois de Vincennes
bd. St-Jacques
DENFERT ROCHEREAU
PL. D'ALESIA
bd. A. Blanqui
bd. de la Gare
rue Jeanne d'Arc
rue du Chevaleret
rue de Tolbiac
Pont National
rue d'Alésia
rue de Tolbiac
av. de Choisy
rue Nationale
av. d'Ivry
av. d'Italie
rue Regnault
bd. de Masséna
BD. MASSÉNA
rue de Paris
bd. Kellerman
CITÉ UNIVERSITAIRE
Jourdan
l'Observatoire
0
1 mile
1 km

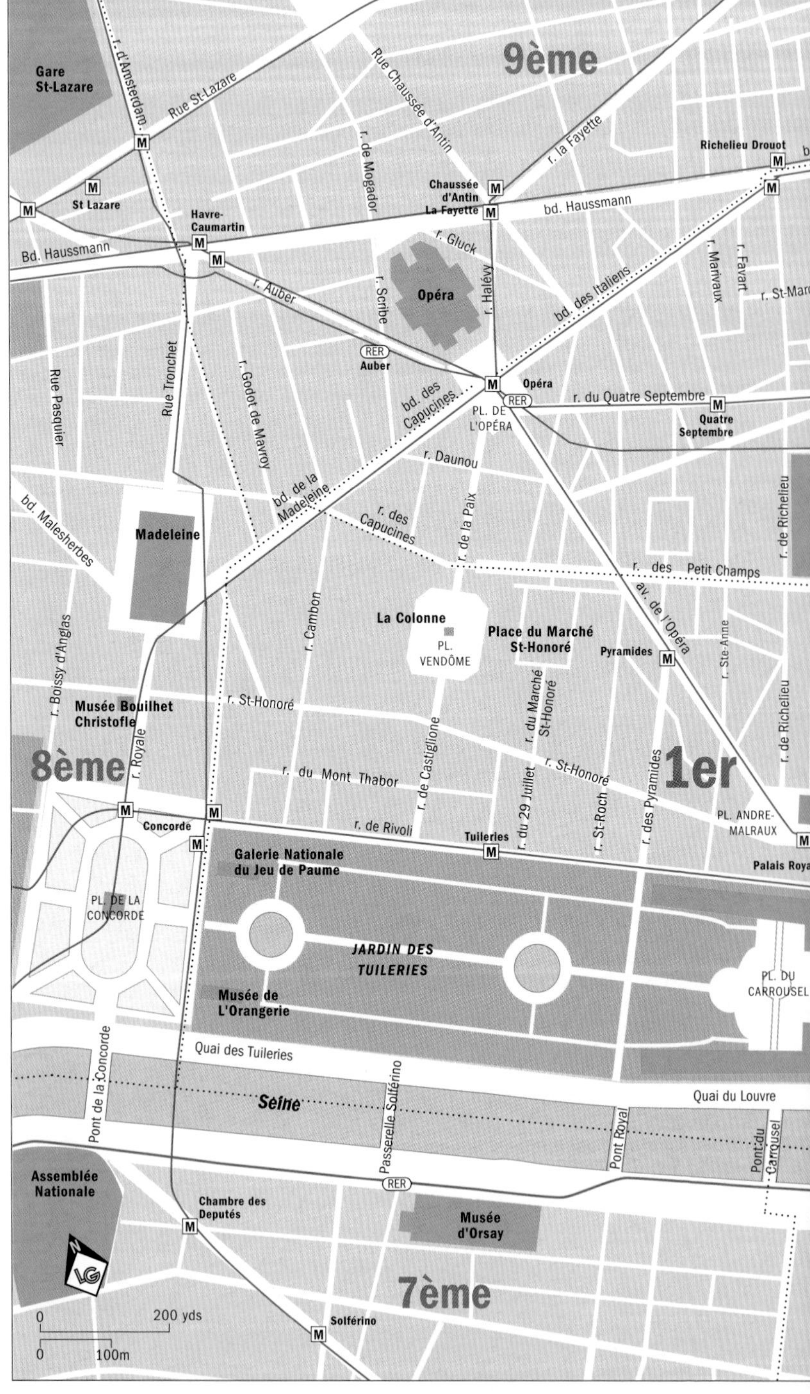

9ème
8ème
1er
7ème
Gare St-Lazare
r. d'Amsterdam
Rue St-Lazare
Rue Chaussée d'Antin
r. de Mogador
r. la Fayette
Richelieu Drouot
St Lazare
Havre-Caumartin
Chaussée d'Antin La Fayette
bd. Haussmann
Bd. Haussmann
r. Gluck
r. Auber
Opéra
r. Scribe
r. Halévy
bd. des Italiens
r. Marivaux
r. Favart
r. St-Marc
RER
Auber
Rue Pasquier
Rue Tronchet
r. Godot de Mavroy
bd. des Capucines
Opéra
PL. DE L'OPÉRA
r. du Quatre Septembre
Quatre Septembre
r. Daunou
bd. Malesherbes
bd. de la Madeleine
r. des Capucines
r. de la Paix
r. de Richelieu
Madeleine
r. des Petit Champs
av. de l'Opéra
La Colonne
PL. VENDÔME
Place du Marché St-Honoré
Pyramides
r. Cambon
r. Boissy d'Anglas
r. Ste-Anne
Musée Bouilhet Christofle
r. St-Honoré
r. du Marché St-Honoré
r. de Castiglione
r. Royale
r. du Mont Thabor
r. St-Honoré
r. des Pyramides
r. St-Roch
r. du 29 Juillet
PL. ANDRE-MALRAUX
Concorde
r. de Rivoli
Tuileries
Palais Royal
Galerie Nationale du Jeu de Paume
PL. DE LA CONCORDE
JARDIN DES TUILERIES
PL. DU CARROUSEL
Musée de L'Orangerie
Quai des Tuileries
Pont de la Concorde
Seine
Passerelle Solférino
Quai du Louvre
Pont Royal
Pont du Carrousel
Assemblée Nationale
Chambre des Deputés
Musée d'Orsay
LG
0
200 yds
0
100m
Solférino

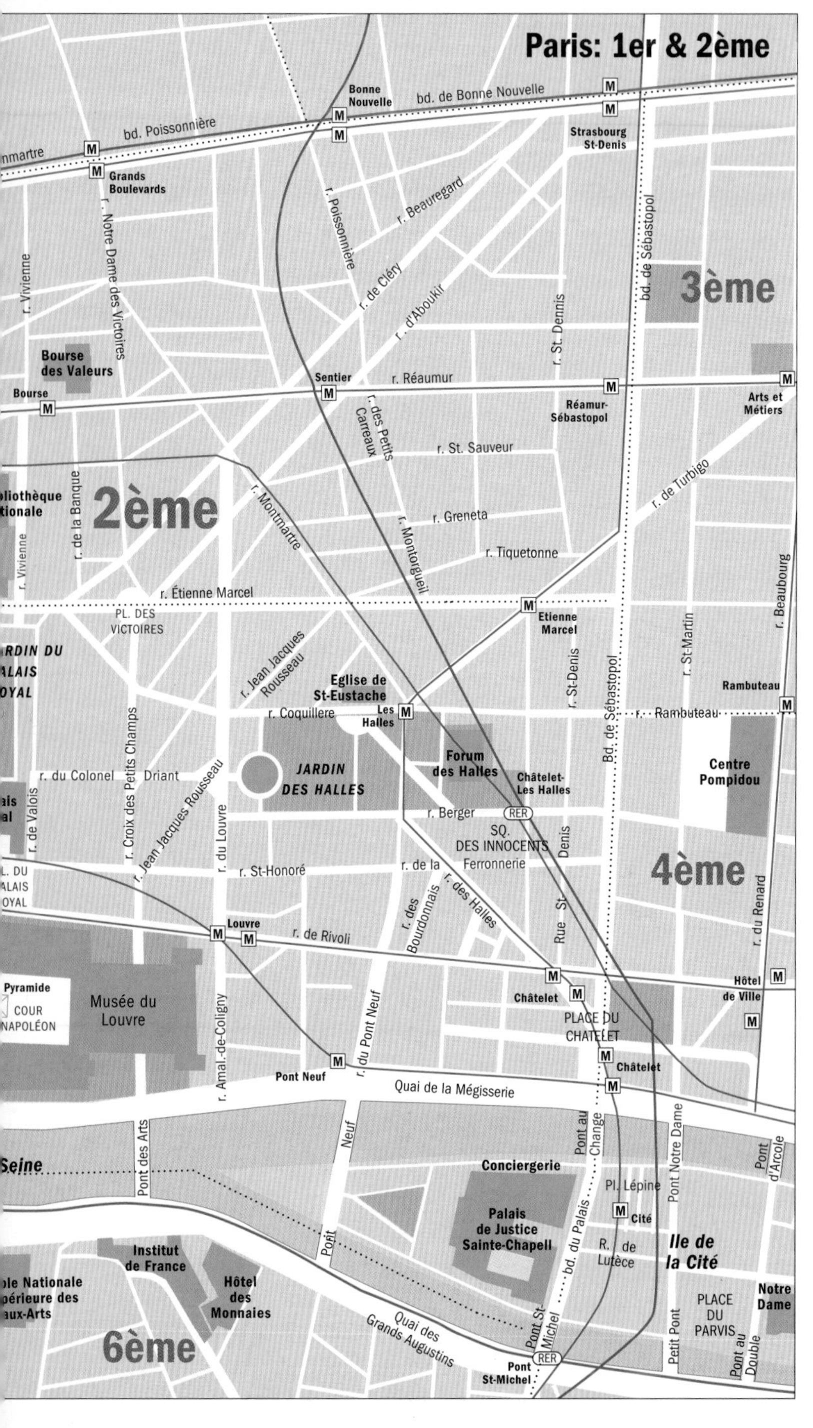

Paris: 1er & 2ème
bd. Poissonnière
bd. de Bonne Nouvelle
Bonne Nouvelle
Grands Boulevards
Strasbourg St-Denis
r. Notre Dame des Victoires
r. Poissonnière
r. Beauregard
r. de Cléry
r. d'Aboukir
bd. de Sébastopol
3ème
r. Vivienne
Bourse des Valeurs
Bourse
Sentier
r. Réaumur
Réaumur-Sébastopol
Arts et Métiers
r. des Petits Carreaux
r. St. Sauveur
r. St. Dennis
r. de la Banque
2ème
r. Montmartre
r. Greneta
r. de Turbigo
r. Montorgueil
r. Tiquetonne
r. Étienne Marcel
PL. DES VICTOIRES
Etienne Marcel
r. Beaubourg
r. Jean Jacques Rousseau
Eglise de St-Eustache
r. St-Denis
r. St-Martin
Rambuteau
r. Coquillere
Les Halles
r. Rambuteau
r. Croix des Petits Champs
r. du Colonel Driant
JARDIN DES HALLES
Forum des Halles
Châtelet-Les Halles
Bd. de Sébastopol
Centre Pompidou
r. de Valois
r. du Louvre
r. Berger
RER
SQ. DES INNOCENTS
r. St-Honoré
r. de la Ferronnerie
4ème
r. des Bourdonnais
r. des Halles
Rue St Denis
r. du Renard
Louvre
r. de Rivoli
Châtelet
Hôtel de Ville
Pyramide
COUR NAPOLÉON
Musée du Louvre
r. Amal.-de-Coligny
r. du Pont Neuf
PLACE DU CHATELET
Pont Neuf
Quai de la Mégisserie
Pont des Arts
Pont Neuf
Pont au Change
Pont Notre Dame
Pont d'Arcole
Seine
Conciergerie
Pl. Lépine
Palais de Justice Sainte-Chapell
Cité
bd. du Palais
R. de Lutèce
Ile de la Cité
Institut de France
Hôtel des Monnaies
Notre Dame
PLACE DU PARVIS
Quai des Grands Augustins
Pont St Michel
Petit Pont
Pont au Double
6ème
Pont St-Michel

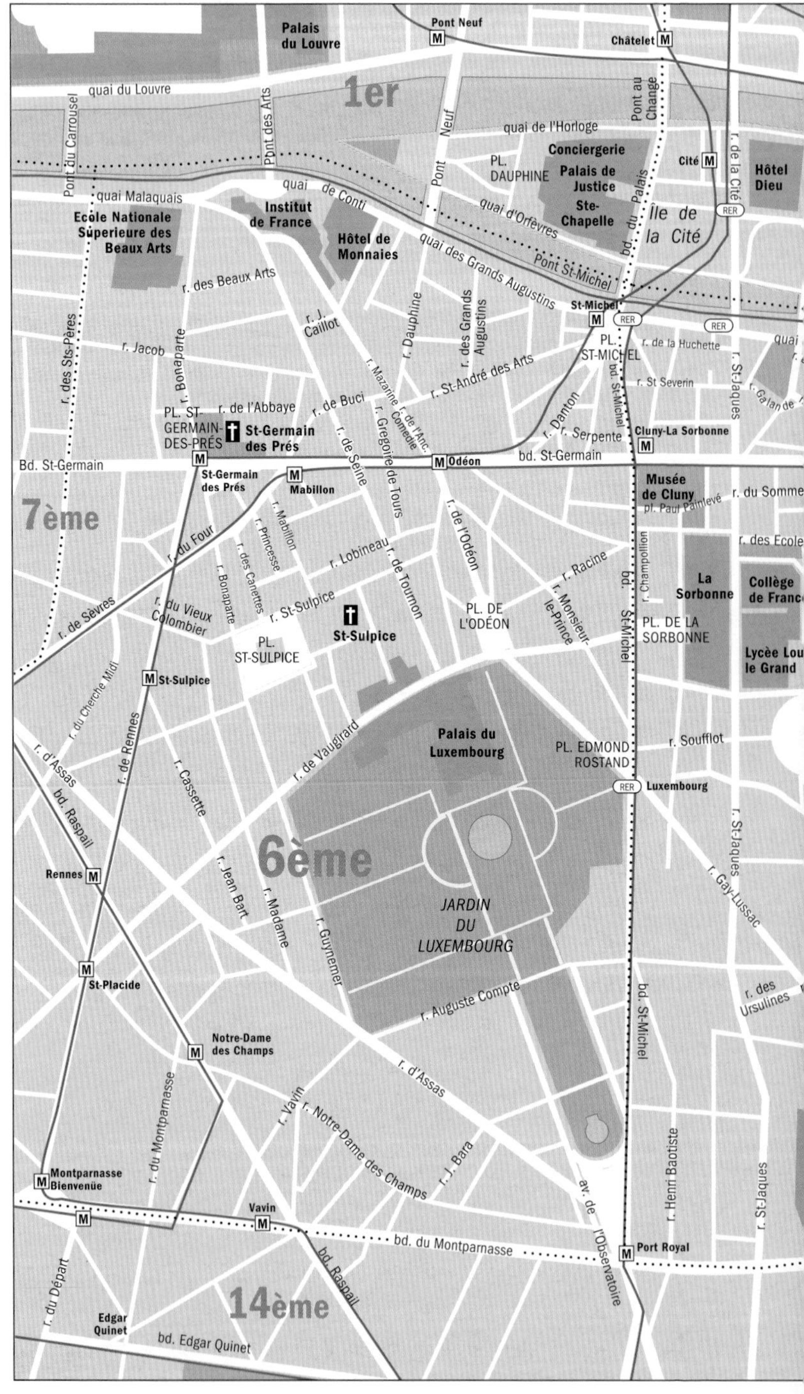

Palais du Louvre
Pont Neuf
Châtelet
1er
quai du Louvre
Pont du Carrousel
Pont des Arts
Pont Neuf
Pont au Change
quai de l'Horloge
PL. DAUPHINE
Conciergerie
Palais de Justice
Ste-Chapelle
Cité
r. de la Cité
Hôtel Dieu
Île de la Cité
quai Malaquais
quai de Conti
Institut de France
Hôtel de Monnaies
Ecole Nationale Supérieure des Beaux Arts
quai d'Orfèvres
quai des Grands Augustins
Pont St-Michel
bd. du Palais
r. des Beaux Arts
r. J. Caillot
r. Dauphine
r. des Grands Augustins
St-Michel
RER
r. des Sts-Pères
r. Jacob
r. Bonaparte
r. Mazarine
r. St-André des Arts
PL. ST-MICHEL
r. de la Huchette
r. St Severin
quai
r. Galande
r. St-Jaques
PL. ST-GERMAIN-DES-PRÉS
r. de l'Abbaye
St-Germain des Prés
r. de Buci
r. de Seine
r. Gregoire de Tours
r. de l'Anc. Comédie
r. Danton
r. Serpente
bd. St-Michel
Cluny-La Sorbonne
Bd. St-Germain
Odéon
bd. St-Germain
St-Germain des Prés
Mabillon
Musée de Cluny
pl. Paul Painlevé
r. du Somme
7ème
r. Mabillon
r. Princesse
r. des Canettes
r. du Four
r. Lobineau
r. de Tournon
r. de l'Odéon
r. Racine
r. des Ecole
r. Bonaparte
r. St-Sulpice
r. du Vieux Colombier
r. de Sèvres
St-Sulpice
PL. DE L'ODÉON
r. Monsieur-le-Prince
bd. St-Michel
r. Champollion
La Sorbonne
Collège de Franc
PL. DE LA SORBONNE
PL. ST-SULPICE
Lycèe Lou le Grand
St-Sulpice
r. du Cherche Midi
r. de Rennes
r. Cassette
r. de Vaugirard
Palais du Luxembourg
PL. EDMOND ROSTAND
r. Soufflot
Luxembourg
r. d'Assas
bd. Raspail
6ème
r. Jean Bart
r. Madame
r. Guynemer
JARDIN DU LUXEMBOURG
r. St-Jaques
r. Gay-Lussac
Rennes
St-Placide
r. Auguste Compte
r. des Ursulines
Notre-Dame des Champs
r. d'Assas
r. du Montparnasse
r. Vavin
r. Notre-Dame des Champs
r. J. Bara
av. de l'Observatoire
bd. St-Michel
r. Henri Baotiste
r. St-Jaques
Montparnasse Bienvenüe
Vavin
bd. du Montparnasse
Port Royal
bd. Raspail
r. du Départ
14ème
Edgar Quinet
bd. Edgar Quinet

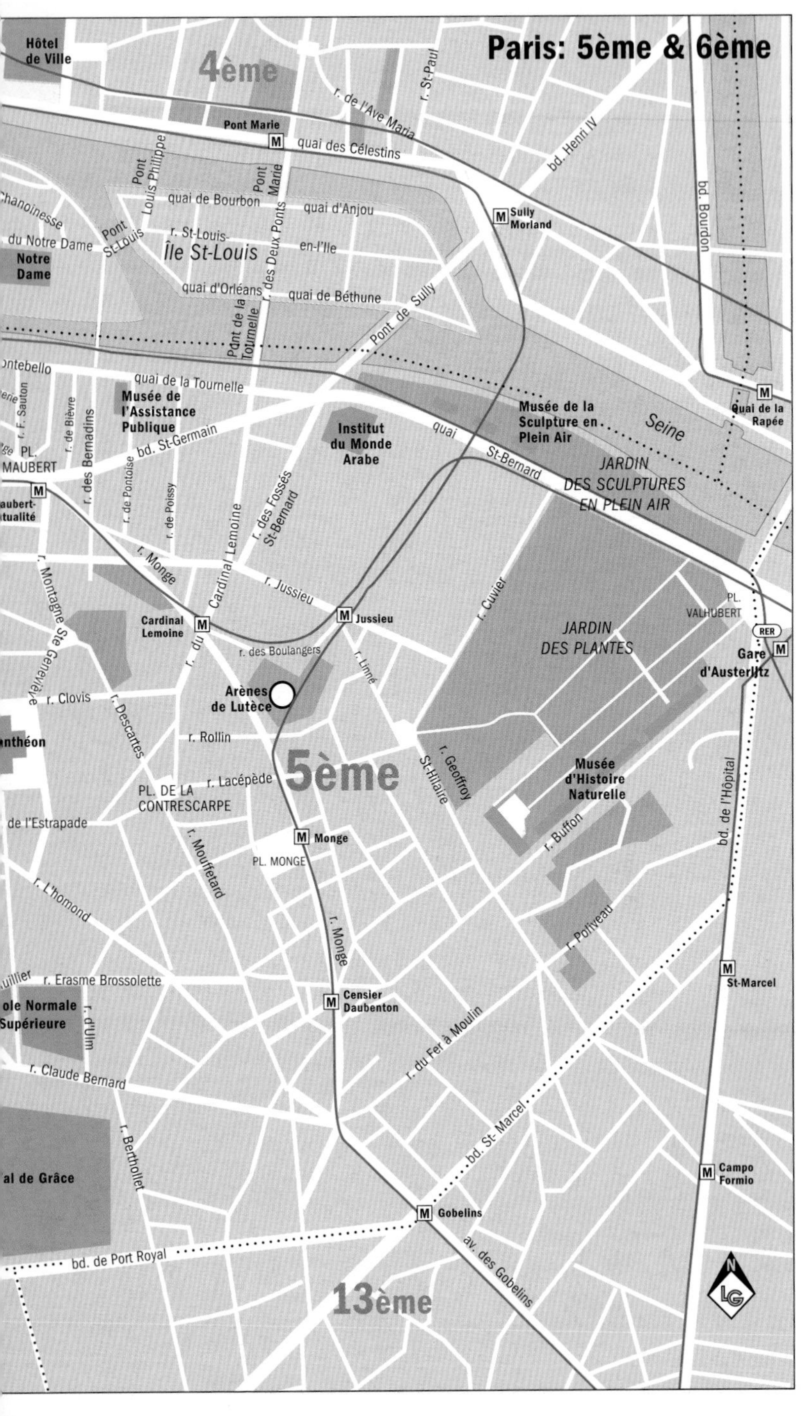
Paris: 5ème & 6ème
4ème
5ème
13ème
Hôtel de Ville
Pont Marie
quai des Célestins
r. de l'Ave Maria
r. St-Paul
bd. Henri IV
bd. Bourdon
Sully Morland
Pont Louis Philippe
Pont Marie
quai de Bourbon
quai d'Anjou
Pont St-Louis
r. St-Louis-en-l'Île
Île St-Louis
du Notre Dame
Notre Dame
quai d'Orléans
quai de Béthune
r. des Deux Ponts
Pont de la Tournelle
Pont de Sully
quai de la Tournelle
Musée de l'Assistance Publique
Institut du Monde Arabe
Musée de la Sculpture en Plein Air
Seine
Quai de la Rapée
quai St-Bernard
JARDIN DES SCULPTURES EN PLEIN AIR
bd. St-Germain
PL. MAUBERT
r. F. Sauton
r. de Bièvre
r. des Bernadins
r. de Pontoise
r. de Poissy
r. Cardinal Lemoine
r. des Fossés St-Bernard
r. Monge
r. Jussieu
Jussieu
r. Cuvier
PL. VALHUBERT
RER
Gare d'Austerlitz
JARDIN DES PLANTES
r. Montagne Ste Geneviève
Cardinal Lemoine
r. du Cardinal Lemoine
r. des Boulangers
r. Linné
Arènes de Lutèce
r. Clovis
r. Descartes
r. Rollin
r. Lacépède
PL. DE LA CONTRESCARPE
r. Geoffroy St-Hilaire
Musée d'Histoire Naturelle
r. Buffon
bd. de l'Hôpital
de l'Estrapade
r. Mouffetard
Monge
PL. MONGE
r. L'homond
r. Monge
r. Poliveau
r. Erasme Brossolette
Censier Daubenton
St-Marcel
r. d'Ulm
r. du Fer à Moulin
r. Claude Bernard
bd. St-Marcel
r. Berthollet
Campo Formio
Gobelins
bd. de Port Royal
av. des Gobelins
N
LG

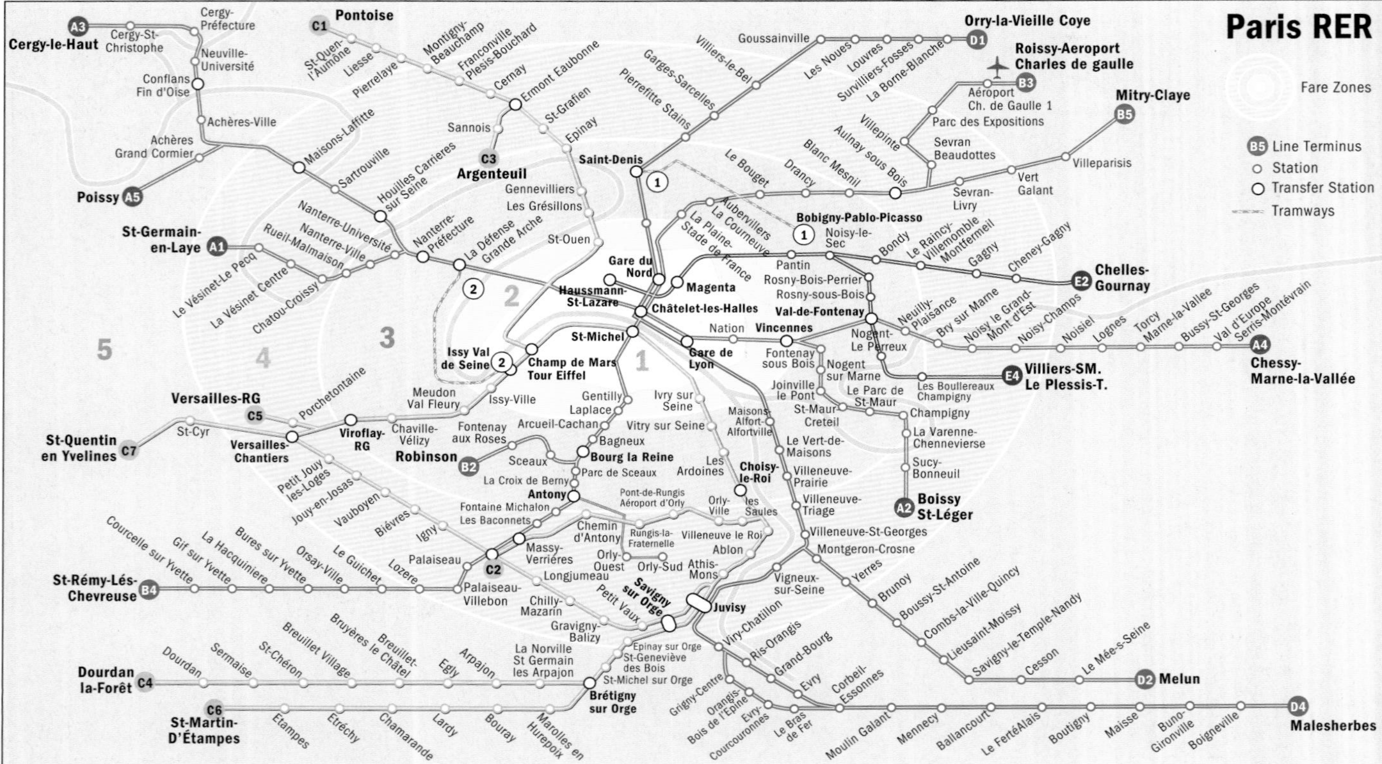

Paris RER
Fare Zones
Line Terminus
Station
Transfer Station
Tramways
Cergy-le-Haut
Cergy-St-Christophe
Cergy-Préfecture
Neuville-Université
Conflans Fin d'Oise
Achères-Ville
Achères Grand Cormier
Poissy
St-Germain-en-Laye
Pontoise
St-Quen-l'Aumône
Liesse
Pierrelaye
Montigny-Beauchamp
Franconville Plessis-Bouchard
Cernay
Ermont Eaubonne
Sannois
Argenteuil
St-Grafien
Epinay
Maisons-Laffitte
Sartrouville
Houilles Carrieres sur Seine
Nanterre-Université
Nanterre-Ville
Rueil-Malmaison
Le Vésinet-Le Pecq
La Vésinet Centre
Chatou-Croissy
Nanterre-Préfecture
La Défense Grande Arche
Gennevilliers
Les Grésillons
St-Ouen
Saint-Denis
Pierrefitte Stains
Garges-Sarcelles
Villiers-le-Bel
Goussainville
Les Noues
Louvres
Survilliers-Fosses
La Borne-Blanche
Orry-la-Vieille Coye
Roissy-Aeroport Charles de gaulle
Aéroport Ch. de Gaulle 1
Parc des Expositions
Villepinte
Sevran Beaudottes
Mitry-Claye
Villeparisis
Vert Galant
Sevran-Livry
Aulnay sous Bois
Blanc Mesnil
Drancy
Le Bouget
Aubervillers La Courneuve
La Plaine-Stade de France
Bobigny-Pablo-Picasso
Noisy-le-Sec
Bondy
Le Raincy-Villemomble Montfermeil
Gagny
Cheney-Gagny
Chelles-Gournay
Gare du Nord
Magenta
Haussmann-St-Lazare
Châtelet-les-Halles
Pantin
Rosny-Bois-Perrier
Rosny-sous-Bois
Val-de-Fontenay
Neuilly-Plaisance
Bry sur Marne
Noisy le Grand-Mont d'Est
Noisy-Champs
Noisiel
Lognes
Torcy
Marne-la-Vallee
Bussy-St-Georges
Val d'Europe
Serris-Montévrain
Chessy-Marne-la-Vallée
Nation
Vincennes
Nogent-Le Perreux
Les Boullereaux Champigny
Villiers-SM. Le Plessis-T.
St-Michel
Gare de Lyon
Fontenay sous Bois
Nogent sur Marne
Joinville le Pont
Le Parc de St-Maur
St-Maur Creteil
Champigny
La Varenne-Chennevierse
Sucy-Bonneuil
Boissy St-Léger
Issy Val de Seine
Champ de Mars Tour Eiffel
Issy-Ville
Meudon Val Fleury
Versailles-RG
Porchefontaine
St-Quentin en Yvelines
St-Cyr
Versailles-Chantiers
Viroflay-RG
Chaville-Vélizy
Fontenay aux Roses
Robinson
Sceaux
Gentilly
Laplace
Arcueil-Cachan
Bagneux
Bourg la Reine
Parc de Sceaux
La Croix de Berny
Antony
Ivry sur Seine
Vitry sur Seine
Les Ardoines
Choisy-le-Roi
Maisons-Alfort-Alfortville
Le Vert-de-Maisons
Villeneuve-Prairie
Villeneuve-Triage
Villeneuve-St-Georges
Montgeron-Crosne
Yerres
Brunoy
Boussy-St-Antoine
Combs-la-Ville-Quincy
Lieusaint-Moissy
Savigny-le-Temple-Nandy
Cesson
Le Mée-s-Seine
Melun
Petit Jouy les-Loges
Jouy-en-Josas
Vauboyen
Bièvres
Igny
Fontaine Michalon
Les Baconnets
Massy-Verrières
Chemin d'Antony
Pont-de-Rungis Aéroport d'Orly
Rungis-la-Fraternelle
Orly-Ville
les Saules
Villeneuve le Roi
Ablon
Orly-Ouest
Orly-Sud
Athis-Mons
Palaiseau
Longjumeau
Savigny sur Orge
Juvisy
Vigneux-sur-Seine
St-Rémy-Lés-Chevreuse
Courcelle sur Yvette
Gif sur Yvette
La Hacquiniere
Bures sur Yvette
Orsay-Ville
Le Guichet
Lozere
Palaiseau-Villebon
Chilly-Mazarin
Petit Vaux
Gravigny-Balizy
Dourdan la-Forêt
Dourdan
Sermaise
St-Chéron
Breuillet Village
Bruyères le Châtel
Breuillet-
Egly
Arpajon
La Norville St Germain les Arpajon
Epinay sur Orge
St-Geneviève des Bois
St-Michel sur Orge
Brétigny sur Orge
Viry-Chatillon
Ris-Orangis
Grand-Bourg
Evry
Corbeil-Essonnes
Grigny-Centre
Orangis Bois de l'Epine
Evry-Courcouronnes
Le Bras de Fer
St-Martin-D'Étampes
Etampes
Etréchy
Chamarande
Lardy
Bouray
Marolles en Hurepoix
Moulin Galant
Mennecy
Ballancourt
Le FertéAlais
Boutigny
Maisse
Buno-Gironville
Boigneville
Malesherbes

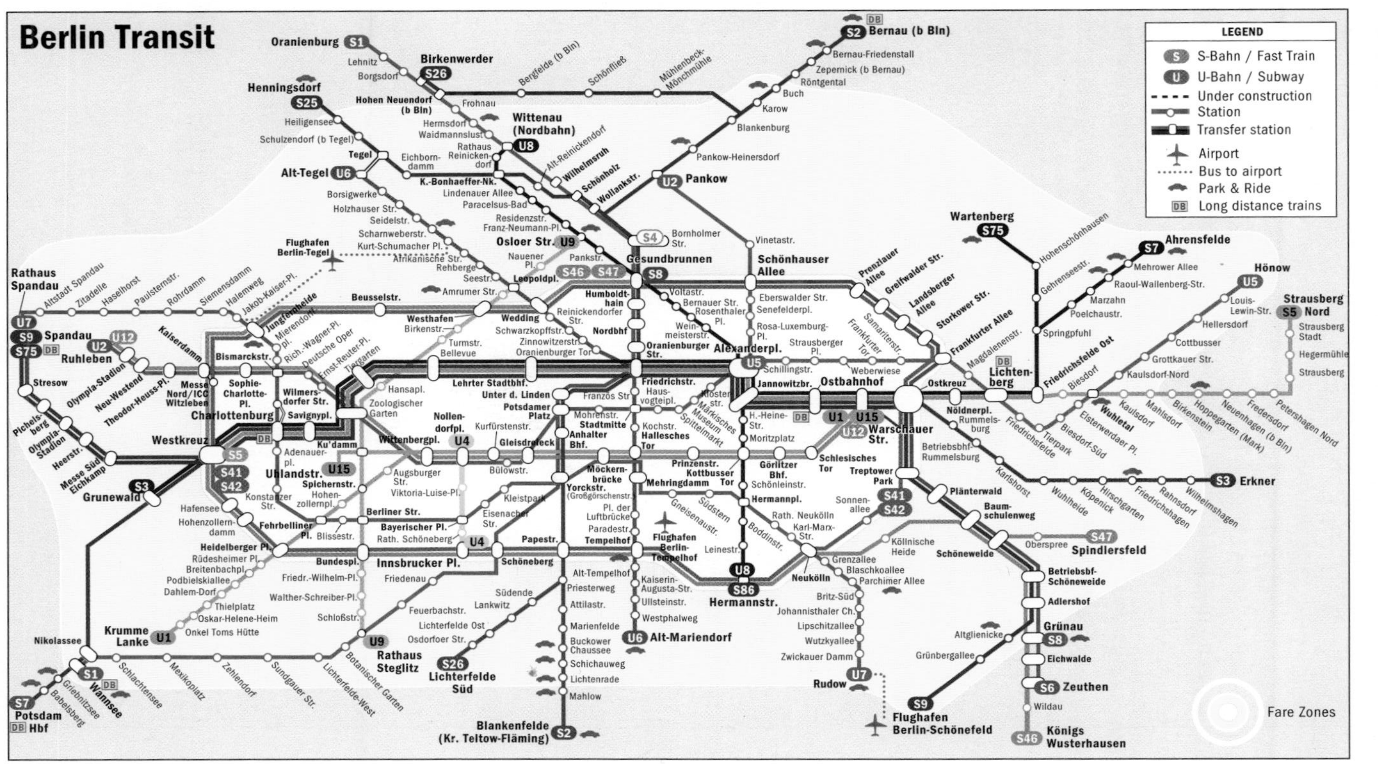

Berlin Transit
LEGEND
S-Bahn / Fast Train
U-Bahn / Subway
Under construction
Station
Transfer station
Airport
Bus to airport
Park & Ride
Long distance trains
Fare Zones
Oranienburg S1
Lehnitz
Borgsdorf
Birkenwerder S26
Hohen Neuendorf (b Bln)
Frohnau
Hermsdorf
Waidmannslust
Bergfelde (b Bln)
Schönfließ
Mühlenbeck-Mönchmühle
Bernau (b Bln) S2
Bernau-Friedenstall
Zepernick (b Bernau)
Röntgental
Buch
Karow
Blankenburg
Pankow-Heinersdorf
U2 Pankow
Henningsdorf S25
Heiligensee
Schulzendorf (b Tegel)
Tegel
Alt-Tegel U6
Eichborn-damm
Wittenau (Nordbahn) U8
Rathaus Reinicken-dorf
Alt-Reinickendorf
Wilhelmsruh
Schönholz
Wollankstr.
K.-Bonhaeffer-Nk.
Lindenauer Allee
Paracelsus-Bad
Residenzstr.
Franz-Neumann-Pl.
Borsigwerke
Holzhauser Str.
Seidelstr.
Scharnweberstr.
Kurt-Schumacher Pl.
Afrikanische Str.
Rehberge
Seestr.
Amrumer Str.
Flughafen Berlin-Tegel
Osloer Str. U9
Nauener Pl.
Pankstr.
Leopoldpl.
S46 S47
S4
Bornholmer Str.
Gesundbrunnen S8
Vinetastr.
Schönhauser Allee
Wartenberg S75
Hohenschönhausen
Gehrenseestr.
Ahrensfelde S7
Mehrower Allee
Raoul-Wallenberg-Str.
Marzahn
Poelchaustr.
Springpfuhl
Hönow U5
Louis-Lewin-Str.
Hellersdorf
Cottbusser
Grottkauer Str.
Kaulsdorf-Nord
Strausberg S5 Nord
Strausberg Stadt
Hegermühle
Strausberg
Rathaus Spandau
U7
Altstadt Spandau
Zitadelle
Haselhorst
Paulsternstr.
Rohrdamm
Siemensdamm
Halemweg
Jakob-Kaiser-Pl.
Jungfernheide
Mierendorff pl.
S9 Spandau
S75
U2 U12
Ruhleben
Stresow
Olympia-Stadion
Neu-Westend
Theodor-Heuss-Pl.
Kaiserdamm
Messe Nord/ICC Witzleben
Pichelsberg
Olympia-Stadion
Heerstr.
Messe Süd Eichkamp
Westkreuz
Charlottenburg
Bismarckstr.
Sophie-Charlotte-Pl.
Rich.-Wagner-Pl.
Deutsche Oper
Ernst-Reuter-Pl.
Tiergarten
Wilmersdorfer Str.
Savignypl.
Beusselstr.
Westhafen
Birkenstr.
Turmstr.
Bellevue
Wedding
Reinickendorfer Str.
Schwarzkopffstr.
Zinnowitzerstr.
Oranienburger Tor
Humboldthain
Nordbhf
Voltastr.
Bernauer Str.
Rosenthaler Pl.
Weinmeisterstr.
Oranienburger Str.
Eberswalder Str.
Senefelderpl.
Rosa-Luxemburg-Pl.
Alexanderpl.
U5
Strausberger Pl.
Prenzlauer Allee
Greifswalder Str.
Landsberger Allee
Storkower Str.
Frankfurter Allee
Samariterstr.
Frankfurter Tor
Magdalenenstr.
Lichtenberg
Friedrichsfelde Ost
Biesdorf
Wuhletal
Kaulsdorf
Mahlsdorf
Birkenstein
Hoppegarten (Mark)
Neuenhagen (b Bln)
Fredersdorf
Petershagen Nord
Schillingstr.
Weberwiese
Lehrter Stadtbhf.
Hansapl.
Zoologischer Garten
Unter d. Linden
Friedrichstr.
Hausvogteipl.
Französ Str
Klosterstr.
Märkisches Museum
Spittelmarkt
Jannowitzbr.
Ostbahnhof
Ostkreuz
Nöldnerpl.
Rummelsburg
Friedrichsfelde
Tierpark
Biesdorf-Süd
Elsterwerdaer Pl.
Potsdamer Platz
Mohrenstr.
Stadtmitte
Kochstr.
Anhalter Bhf.
Hallesches Tor
H.-Heine-Str.
Moritzplatz
U1 U15
U12
Warschauer Str.
Betriebsbhf-Rummelsburg
Karlshorst
Wuhlheide
Köpenick
Hirschgarten
Friedrichshagen
Rahnsdorf
Wilhelmshagen
S3 Erkner
Nollendorfpl.
Kurfürstenstr.
Wittenbergpl.
U4
Gleisdreieck
Ku'damm
Adenauerpl.
Uhlandstr.
U15
Spichernstr.
Augsburger Str.
Viktoria-Luise-Pl.
Bülowstr.
Möckernbrücke
Mehringdamm
Prinzenstr.
Kottbusser Tor
Görlitzer Bhf.
Schönleinstr.
Schlesisches Tor
Treptower Park
S41 S42
S5 S41 S42
Grunewald S3
Hafensee
Hohenzollerndamm
Konstanzer Str.
Hohenzollernpl.
Fehrbelliner Pl.
Blissestr.
Berliner Str.
Bayerischer Pl.
Rath. Schöneberg
U4
Kleistpark
Eisenacher Str.
Yorckstr. (Großgörschenstr.)
Pl. der Luftbrücke
Paradestr.
Tempelhof
Flughafen Berlin-Tempelhof
Gneisenaustr.
Südstern
Hermannpl.
Boddinstr.
Rath. Neukölln
Karl-Marx-Str.
Sonnenallee
Plänterwald
Baumschulenweg
Schöneweide
Köllnische Heide
Oberspree
S47 Spindlersfeld
Heidelberger Pl.
Rüdesheimer Pl.
Breitenbachpl.
Podbielskiallee
Dahlem-Dorf
Thielplatz
Oskar-Helene-Heim
Onkel Toms Hütte
Krumme Lanke U1
Bundespl.
Innsbrucker Pl.
Schöneberg
Papestr.
Friedr.-Wilhelm-Pl.
Walther-Schreiber-Pl.
Schloßstr.
U9 Rathaus Steglitz
Friedenau
Südende
Lankwitz
Feuerbachstr.
Lichterfelde Ost
Osdorfoer Str.
S26 Lichterfelde Süd
Alt-Tempelhof
Priesterweg
Attilastr.
Marienfelde
Buckower Chaussee
Schichauweg
Lichtenrade
Mahlow
Blankenfelde (Kr. Teltow-Fläming) S2
Kaiserin-Augusta-Str.
Ullsteinstr.
Westphalweg
U6 Alt-Mariendorf
Leinestr.
U8
S86
Hermannstr.
Neukölln
Grenzallee
Blaschkoallee
Parchimer Allee
Britz-Süd
Johannisthaler Ch.
Lipschitzallee
Wutzkyallee
Zwickauer Damm
Rudow U7
Flughafen Berlin-Schönefeld
S9
Altglienicke
Grünbergallee
Betriebsbf. Schöneweide
Adlershof
Grünau S8
Eichwalde
S6 Zeuthen
Wildau
S46 Königs Wusterhausen
Nikolassee
S1 Wannsee
Schlachtensee
Mexikoplatz
Zehlendorf
Sundgauer Str.
Lichterfelde-West
Botanischer Garten
Griebnitzsee
Babelsberg
S7 Potsdam Hbf
DB

Berlin Overview

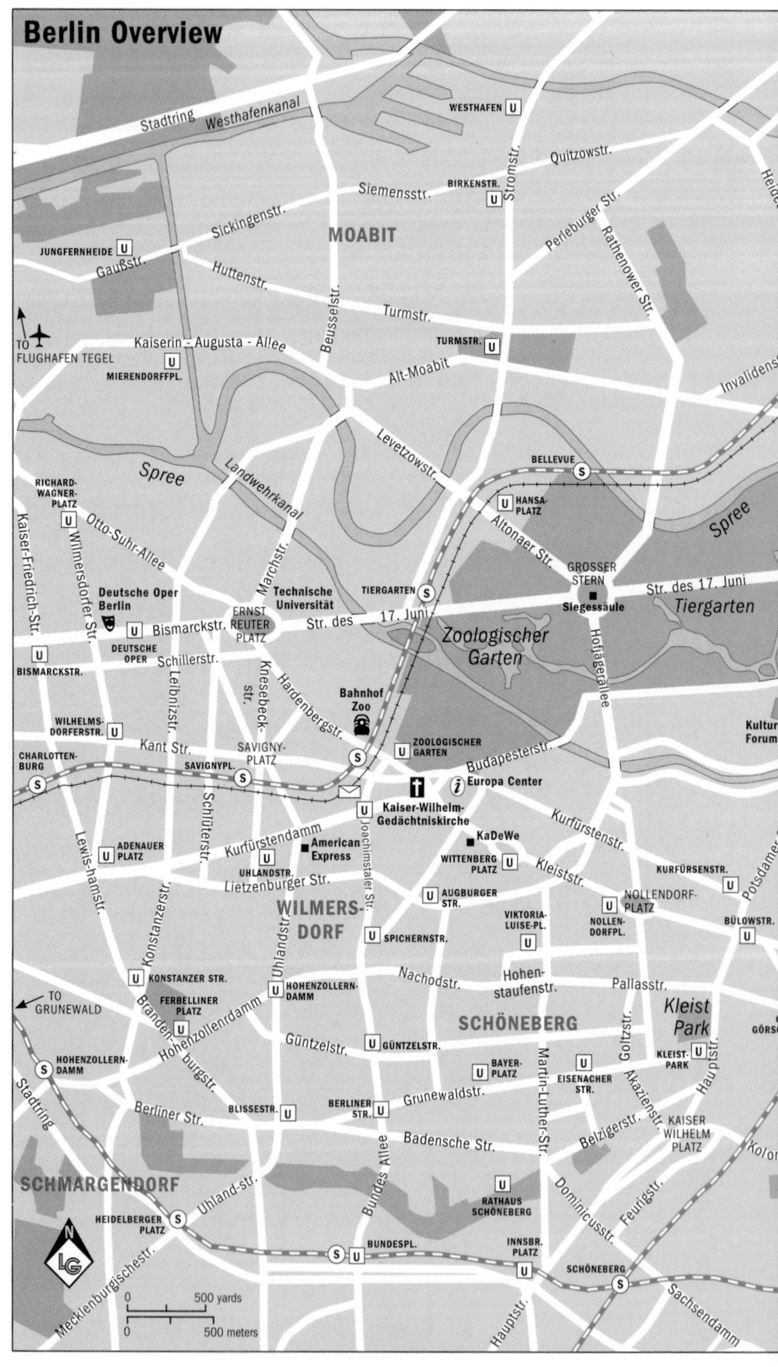

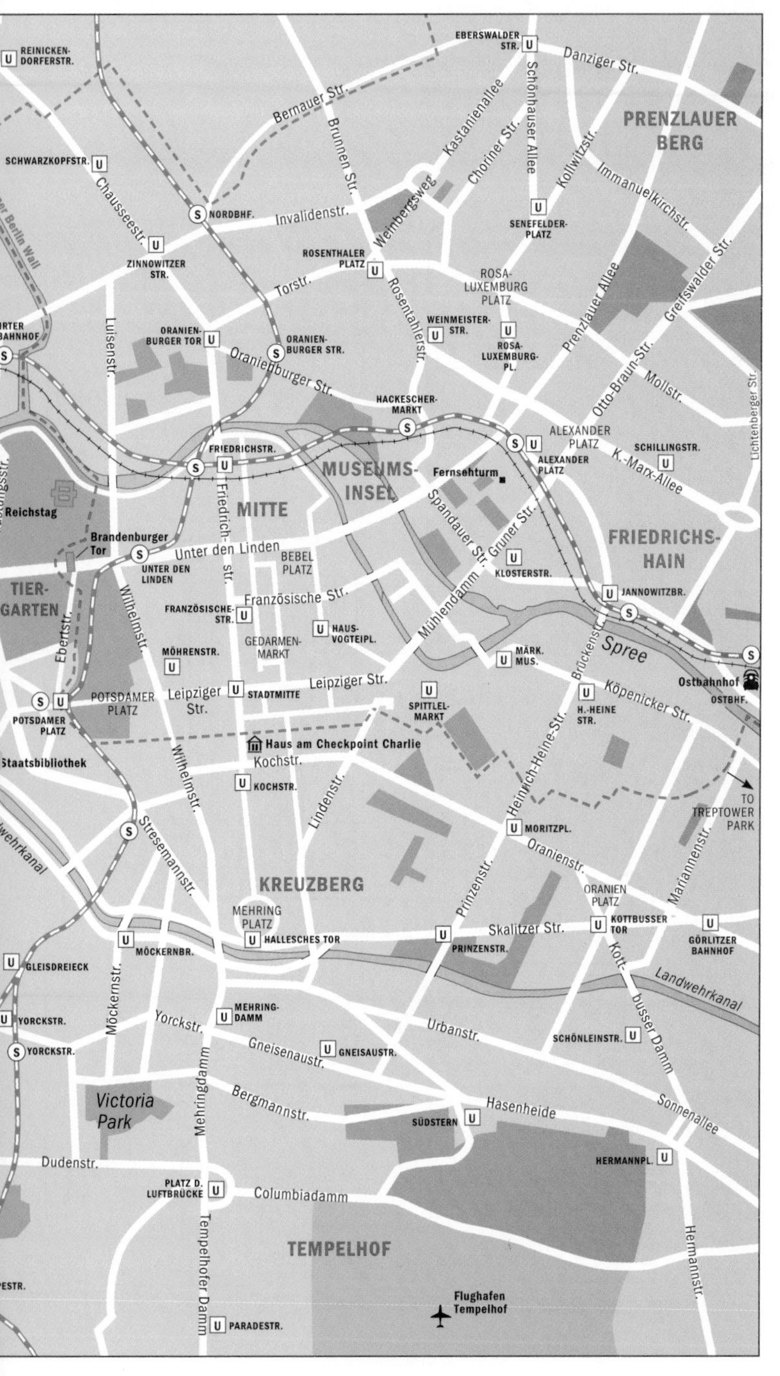

PRENZLAUER BERG
MITTE
MUSEUMS-INSEL
TIER-GARTEN
FRIEDRICHS-HAIN
KREUZBERG
TEMPELHOF
Reichstag
Brandenburger Tor
Fernsehturm
Haus am Checkpoint Charlie
Staatsbibliothek
Ostbahnhof
Flughafen Tempelhof
Victoria Park
Spree
Landwehrkanal
TO TREPTOWER PARK
Bernauer Str.
Brunnen Str.
Kastanienallee
Schönhauser Allee
Danziger Str.
Choriner Str.
Kollwitzstr.
Immanuelkirchstr.
Greifswalder Str.
Prenzlauer Allee
Otto-Braun-Str.
Mollstr.
Lichtenberger Str.
K.-Marx-Allee
Invalidenstr.
Chausseestr.
Weinbergsweg
Torstr.
Rosenthaler Str.
Oranienburger Str.
Luisenstr.
Friedrich-str.
Unter den Linden
Französische Str.
Spandauer Str.
Gruner Str.
Mühlendamm
Wilhelmstr.
Ebertstr.
Leipziger Str.
Kochstr.
Lindenstr.
Heinrich-Heine-Str.
Brückenstr.
Köpenicker Str.
Stresemannstr.
Oranienstr.
Prinzenstr.
Skalitzer Str.
Mariannenstr.
Kottbusser Damm
Möckernstr.
Yorckstr.
Gneisenaustr.
Urbanstr.
Mehringdamm
Bergmannstr.
Hasenheide
Sonnenallee
Dudenstr.
Columbiadamm
Tempelhofer Damm
Hermannstr.
Berlin Wall
ROSA-LUXEMBURG PLATZ
ALEXANDER PLATZ
BEBEL PLATZ
GEDARMEN-MARKT
POTSDAMER PLATZ
MEHRING PLATZ
ORANIEN PLATZ
REINICKEN-DORFERSTR.
EBERSWALDER STR.
SCHWARZKOPFSTR.
NORDBHF.
SENEFELDER-PLATZ
ZINNOWITZER STR.
ROSENTHALER PLATZ
WEINMEISTER-STR.
ROSA-LUXEMBURG-PL.
ORANIEN-BURGER TOR
ORANIEN-BURGER STR.
HACKESCHER-MARKT
FRIEDRICHSTR.
SCHILLINGSTR.
UNTER DEN LINDEN
KLOSTERSTR.
JANNOWITZBR.
FRANZÖSISCHE-STR.
HAUS-VOGTEIPL.
MÖHRENSTR.
MÄRK. MUS.
STADTMITTE
SPITTEL-MARKT
H.-HEINE STR.
OSTBHF.
KOCHSTR.
MORITZPL.
HALLESCHES TOR
MÖCKERNBR.
PRINZENSTR.
KOTTBUSSER TOR
GÖRLITZER BAHNHOF
GLEISDREIECK
MEHRING-DAMM
YORCKSTR.
GNEISAUSTR.
SCHÖNLEINSTR.
SÜDSTERN
HERMANNPL.
PLATZ D. LUFTBRÜCKE
PARADESTR.

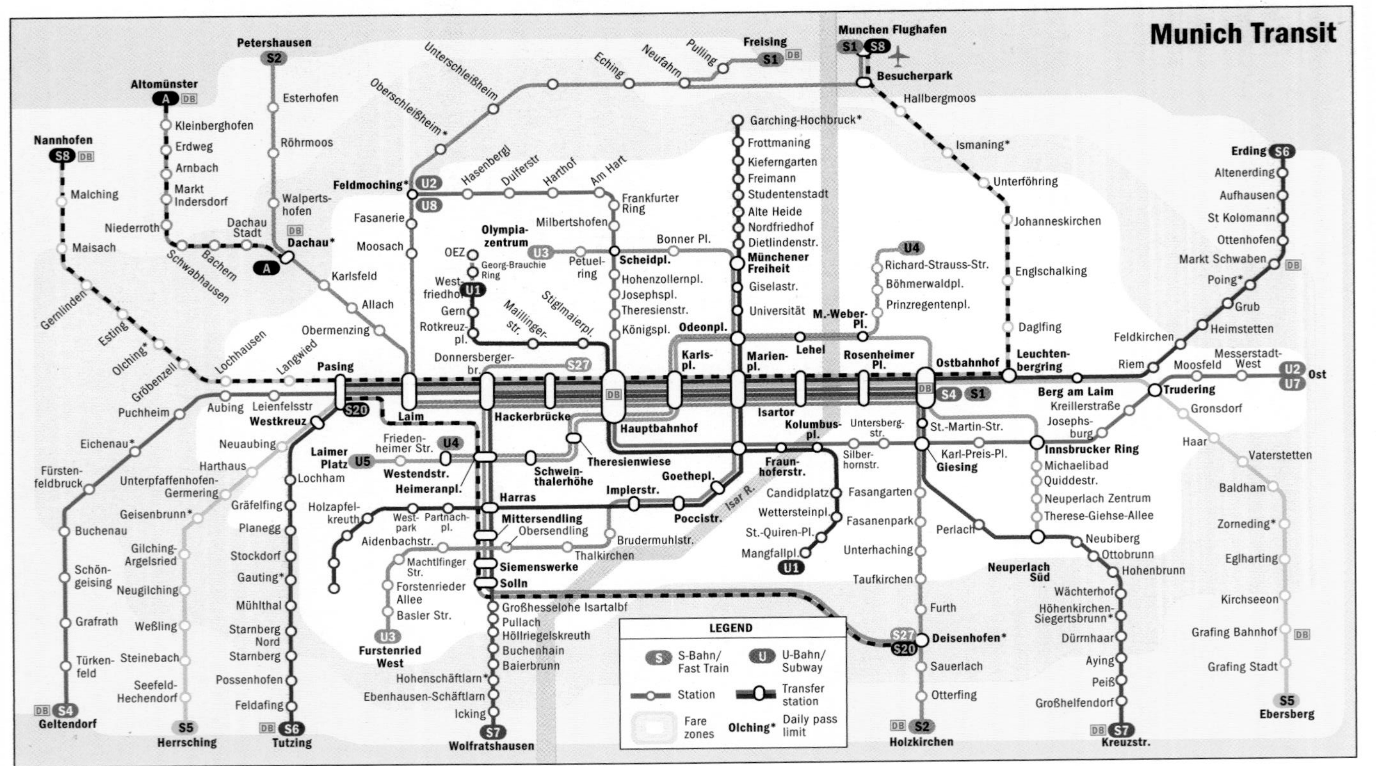
Munich Transit
Petershausen
S2
Esterhofen
Röhrmoos
Walperts-hofen
Dachau*
Dachau Stadt
Altomünster
A
Kleinberghofen
Erdweg
Arnbach
Markt Indersdorf
Niederroth
Bachern
Schwabhausen
Nannhofen
S8
Malching
Maisach
Gernlinden
Esting
Olching*
Gröbenzell
Lochhausen
Langwied
Pasing
Karlsfeld
Allach
Obermenzing
Unterschleißheim
Oberschleißheim*
Feldmoching*
U2
U8
Hasenbergl
Dulferstr
Harthof
Am Hart
Frankfurter Ring
Milbertshofen
Fasanerie
Moosach
Olympia-zentrum
OEZ
Georg-Brauchle Ring
West-friedhof
U1
Gern
Rotkreuz-pl.
Maillinger-str.
Stiglmaierpl.
U3
Petuel-ring
Scheidpl.
Bonner Pl.
Hohenzollernpl.
Josephspl.
Theresienstr.
Königspl.
Eching
Neufahrn
Pulling
Freising
S1
Munchen Flughafen
S1
S8
Besucherpark
Hallbergmoos
Ismaning*
Unterföhring
Johanneskirchen
Englschalking
Daglfing
Leuchten-bergring
Garching-Hochbruck*
Frottmaning
Kieferngarten
Freimann
Studentenstadt
Alte Heide
Nordfriedhof
Dietlindenstr.
Münchener Freiheit
Giselastr.
Universität
Odeonpl.
U4
Richard-Strauss-Str.
Böhmerwaldpl.
Prinzregentenpl.
M.-Weber-Pl.
Lehel
Rosenheimer Pl.
Ostbahnhof
Erding
S6
Altenerding
Aufhausen
St Kolomann
Ottenhofen
Markt Schwaben
Poing*
Grub
Heimstetten
Feldkirchen
Riem
Messerstadt-West
Moosfeld
U2
U7
Ost
Trudering
Berg am Laim
S4
S1
Donnersberger-br.
S27
Laim
Hackerbrücke
Hauptbahnhof
Karls-pl.
Marien-pl.
Isartor
Puchheim
Aubing
Leienfelsstr
Westkreuz
S20
Eichenau*
Fürsten-feldbruck
Neuaubing
Harthaus
Unterpfaffenhofen-Germering
Geisenbrunn*
Gilching-Argelsried
Neugilching
Weßling
Steinebach
Seefeld-Hechendorf
S5
Herrsching
Buchenau
Schön-geising
Grafrath
Türken-feld
S4
Geltendorf
Lochham
Gräfelfing
Planegg
Stockdorf
Gauting*
Mühlthal
Starnberg Nord
Starnberg
Possenhofen
Feldafing
S6
Tutzing
Laimer Platz
U5
Frieden-heimer Str.
U4
Westendstr.
Heimeranpl.
Schwein-thalerhöhe
Theresienwiese
Holzapfel-kreuth
West-park
Partnach-pl.
Aidenbachstr.
Harras
Mittersendling
Obersendling
Machtlfinger Str.
Forstenrieder Allee
Basler Str.
U3
Furstenried West
Thalkirchen
Brudermuhlstr.
Implerstr.
Poccistr.
Goethepl.
Siemenswerke
Solln
Großhesselohe Isartalbf
Pullach
Höllriegelskreuth
Buchenhain
Baierbrunn
Hohenschäftlarn*
Ebenhausen-Schäftlarn
Icking
S7
Wolfratshausen
Kolumbus-pl.
Fraun-hoferstr.
Isar R.
Candidplatz
Wettersteinpl.
St.-Quiren-Pl.
Mangfallpl.
U1
Untersberg-str.
Silber-hornstr.
St.-Martin-Str.
Karl-Preis-Pl.
Giesing
Fasangarten
Fasanenpark
Unterhaching
Taufkirchen
Furth
S27
S20
Deisenhofen*
Sauerlach
Otterfing
S2
Holzkirchen
Kreillerstraße
Josephs-burg
Innsbrucker Ring
Michaelibad
Quiddestr.
Neuperlach Zentrum
Therese-Giehse-Allee
Perlach
Neuperlach Süd
Neubiberg
Ottobrunn
Hohenbrunn
Wächterhof
Höhenkirchen-Siegertsbrunn*
Dürrnhaar
Aying
Peiß
Großhelfendorf
S7
Kreuzstr.
Gronsdorf
Haar
Vaterstetten
Baldham
Zorneding*
Eglharting
Kirchseeon
Grafing Bahnhof
Grafing Stadt
S5
Ebersberg
DB
LEGEND
S S-Bahn/ Fast Train
U U-Bahn/ Subway
Station
Transfer station
Fare zones
Olching* Daily pass limit

Florence
Accademia, 23
American Church, 19
American Express, 1
Badia, 5
Bargello, 4
Basilica di San Lorenzo, 15
Bus Station, 17
Casa Buonarroti, 25
Casa di Dante, 6
Chiesa di S. Maria Novella, 16
Chiesa di San Marco, 22
Chiesa di Santa Croce, 26
Chiesa di Santa Maria del Carmine, 30
Chiesa di Santa Trinità, 9
Chiesa di Santo Spirito, 29
Duomo, 14
Museo Archeologico, 24
Museo di Storia della Scienza, 27
Orsanmichele, 7
Palazzo Davanzati, 8
Palazzo Medici-Riccardi, 13
Palazzo Pitti, 28
Palazzo Pucci, 21
Palazzo Rucellai, 11
Palazzo Strozzi, 12
Palazzo Vecchio, 3
S. Maria Novella Station, 20
Uffizi Gallery, 2
U.K. Embassy, 10
U.S. Embassy, 18
0 300 yards
0 300 meters
N
LG
Giardino Della Gherardesca
PIAZZA STAZIONE
PIAZZA DEL MERCATO CENTRALE
PIAZZA DELL' UNITA ITALIANA
PIAZZA SANTA MARIA NOVELLA
PIAZZA SAN LORENZO
PIAZZA S.S. ANNUNZIATA
PIAZZA S. GIOVANNI
PIAZZA DEL DUOMO
PIAZZA S.M. NUOVA
SYNAGOGUE OF FLORENCE
PIAZZA DELLA REPUBBLICA
PIAZZA S. PIER MAGGIORE
MERCATO NUOVO
PIAZZA S. FIRENZE
PIAZZA SIGNORIA
PIAZZA SANTA CROCE
S. CROCE
PIAZZA DEL CAVALLEGGERI
PIAZZA DEL CARMINE
S. M. DEL CARMINE
S. SPIRITO
PIAZZA SAN SPIRITO
PALAZZO PITTI
Giardino Di Boboli
Ponte A. Vespucci
Ponte Alla Carraia
Ponte S. Trinita
Ponte Vecchio
Ponte Alle Grazie
Fiume Arno
Fiume Arno
Via Luigi Almanni
Via Valfonda
Via Fiume
Via Faenza
Via Guelfa
Via XXVII Aprile
Via Guelfa
Via Giorgio La Pira
Gino Capponi
Via Giuseppe Giusti
Borgo Pinti
Viale Antonio Gramsci
Via Montebello
Il Prato
Via Della Scala
Via Rucellai
Via Solferino
Via Magenta
Via Garibaldi
Via Palestro
Via S. Lucia
Via Palazzuolo
Via S.C. da Siena
Via Finiguerra dell'Albero
Via Nazionale
Via Dell' Ariento
V. S. Antonino
Via De' Ginori
Via Cavour
Via Ricasoli
Via dei Servi
Via Laura
Via Della Colonna
Via Degli Alfani
Via L. C. Farini
Via G. Carducci
Via Della Mattonaia
Via De' Panzan
Via De' Conti
Borgo S. Lorenzo
V. De' Martelli
Via De' Pucci
Via Bufalini
Via Della Pergola
Via Nuova dei Caccini
Borgo Pinti
Via Fiesolana
Via dei Pilastri
Via Di Mezzo
Borgo Ognissant
Via Montebello
Via Della Scala
Via Del Porcellana
V. De' Cerretani
V. De' Pecori
V.D. Belle Donne
Via Del Sole
Via Della Spada
Via De' Fossi
Lungarno Amerigo Vespucci
Via Tournabuoni
Via Strozzi
Via Roma
Via del Medici
Via Dei Calzaiuoli
Via Del Proconsolo
Via Dell' Oriuolo
Via S. Edigo
Borgo Degli Albizi
Via Pietrapiana
Borgo La Croce
V. D. Vigna Nuova
Via Del Parione
Lungarno Corsini
Via Pellicceria
Via Calimala
Via Del Corso
Via dei Tavolini
Via Alighieri
Via dell'Agnolo
Via Ghibellina
Via G. Verdi
Via De' Pepi
V.M. Buonarroti
Borgo Allegri
Via F. Paolieri
Via dell'Agnolo
Via Ghibellina
Via de Macci
Via Porta Rossa
Via Delle Terme
Via Dell' Anguillara
Borgo dei Greci
Via Magliabechi
Via S. Giuseppe
Viale Gramsci
Lungarno Soderini
Borgo S. Frediano
Lungarno Guicciardini
Via Di S. Spirito
Lungarno Acciaiuoli
Via dei Neri
Via Benci
Corso dei Tintori
Via De' Malcontenti
Via S. Monaca
Via dei Serragli
Via Maffia
Via S. Agostino
Borgo Tegolaio
Via Maggio
Via Toscanella
Via De' Guicciardini
Borgo S. Jacopo
Lungarno Gen. Diaz
Lungarno D. Grazie
Via Tripoli
Lungarno Della Zecca Vecchia
Lungarno Torrigiani
Via D. Bardi
Via Della Chiesa
TO PIAZZLE MICHELANGELO AND SAN MINIATO AL. MONTE

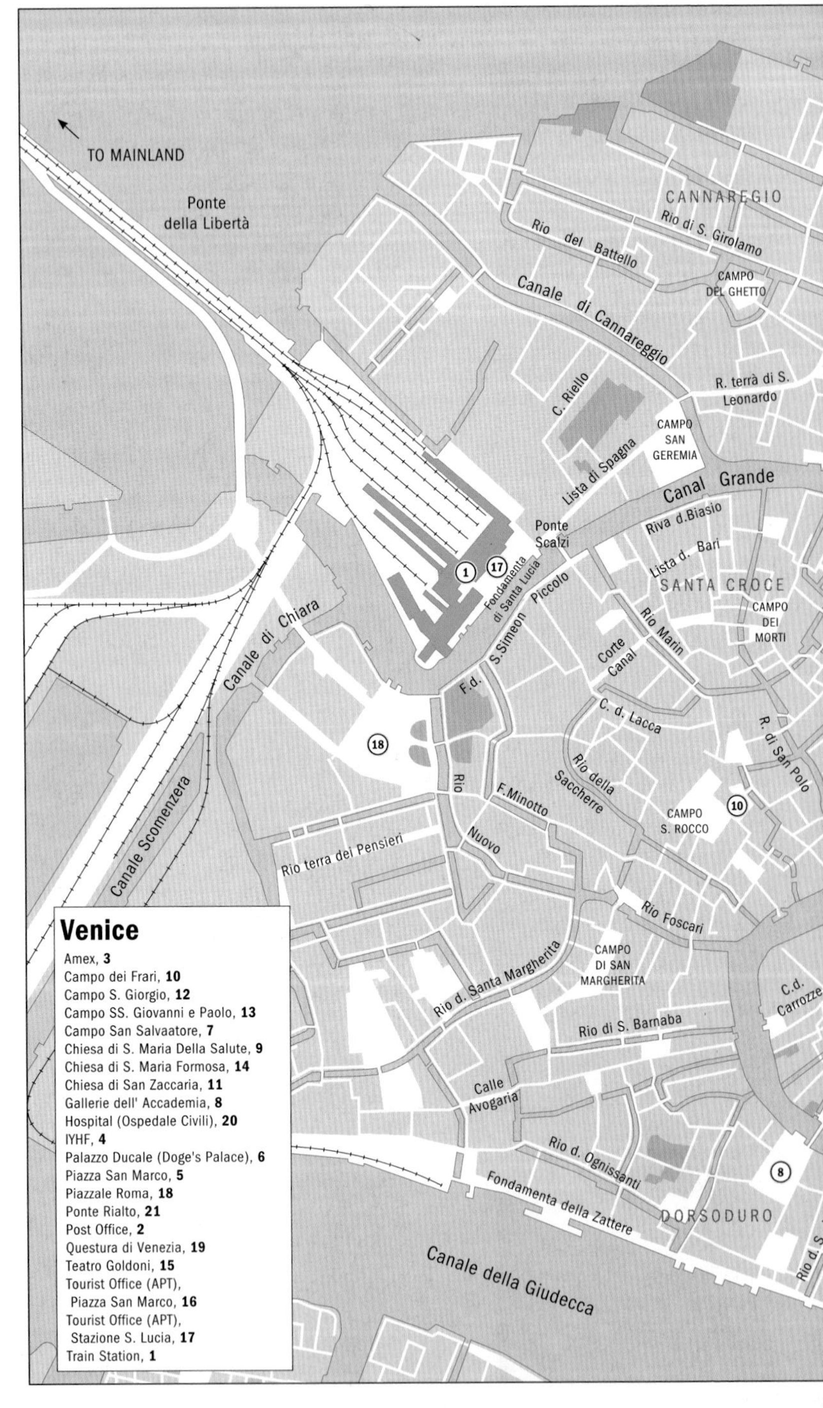

Venice

Amex, **3**
Campo dei Frari, **10**
Campo S. Giorgio, **12**
Campo SS. Giovanni e Paolo, **13**
Campo San Salvaatore, **7**
Chiesa di S. Maria Della Salute, **9**
Chiesa di S. Maria Formosa, **14**
Chiesa di San Zaccaria, **11**
Gallerie dell' Accademia, **8**
Hospital (Ospedale Civili), **20**
IYHF, **4**
Palazzo Ducale (Doge's Palace), **6**
Piazza San Marco, **5**
Piazzale Roma, **18**
Ponte Rialto, **21**
Post Office, **2**
Questura di Venezia, **19**
Teatro Goldoni, **15**
Tourist Office (APT), Piazza San Marco, **16**
Tourist Office (APT), Stazione S. Lucia, **17**
Train Station, **1**

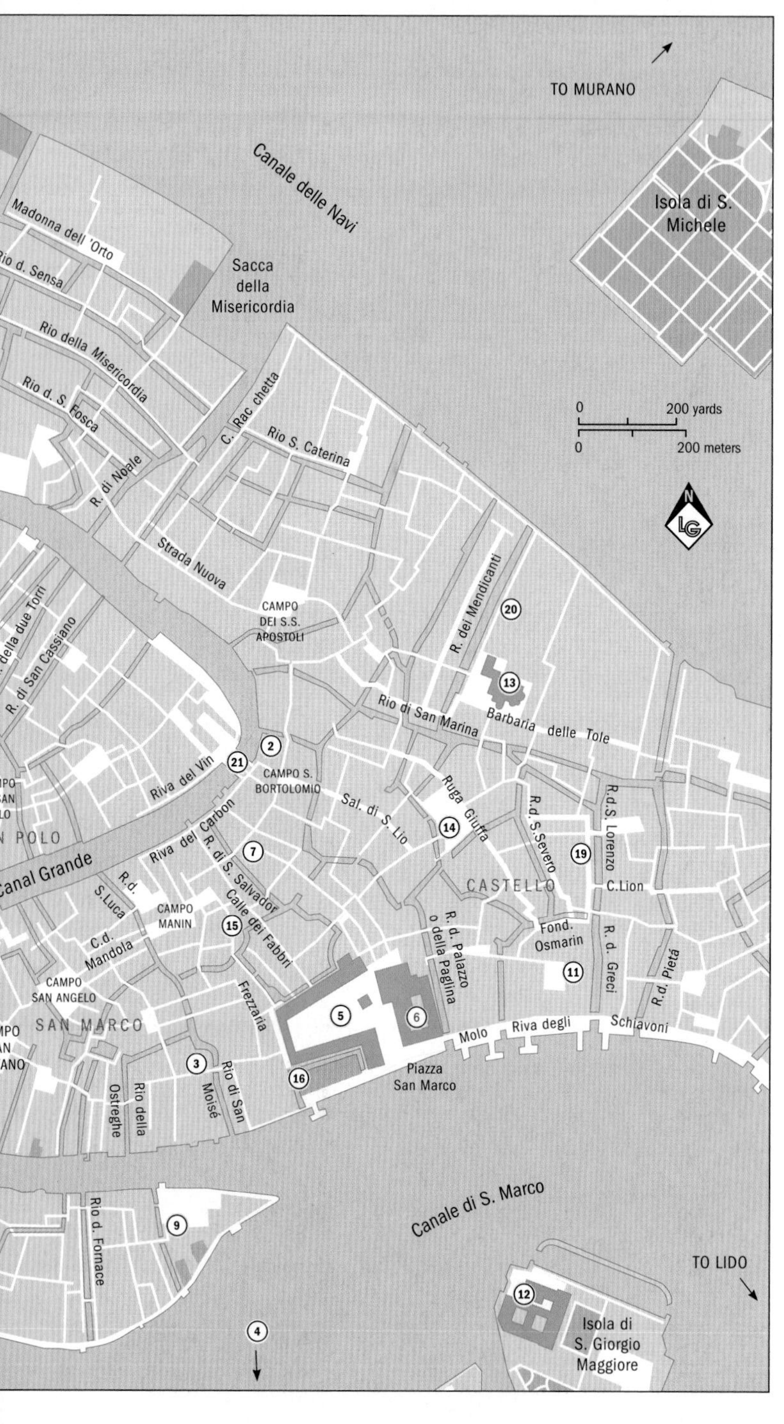

TO MURANO
Canale delle Navi
Isola di S. Michele
Madonna dell 'Orto
Rio d. Sensa
Sacca della Misericordia
Rio della Misericordia
Rio d. S. Fosca
C. Rac chetta
Rio S. Caterina
R. di Noale
0
200 yards
0
200 meters
Strada Nuova
R. dei Mendicanti
CAMPO DEI S.S. APOSTOLI
R. della due Torri
R. di San Cassiano
Rio di San Marina
Barbaria delle Tole
Riva del Vin
CAMPO S. BORTOLOMIO
Sal. di S. Lio
Ruga Giuffa
R.d. S.Severo
R.d.S. Lorenzo
Riva del Carbon
R. di S. Salvador
Canal Grande
R.d. S.Luca
CASTELLO
C.Lion
Calle dei Fabbri
CAMPO MANIN
C.d. Mandola
R. d. Palazzo o della Paglina
Fond. Osmarin
R. d. Greci
R.d. Pietá
CAMPO SAN ANGELO
SAN MARCO
Frezzaria
Molo
Riva degli Schiavoni
Piazza San Marco
Rio della Ostreghe
Rio di San Moisé
Canale di S. Marco
Rio d. Fornace
TO LIDO
Isola di S. Giorgio Maggiore

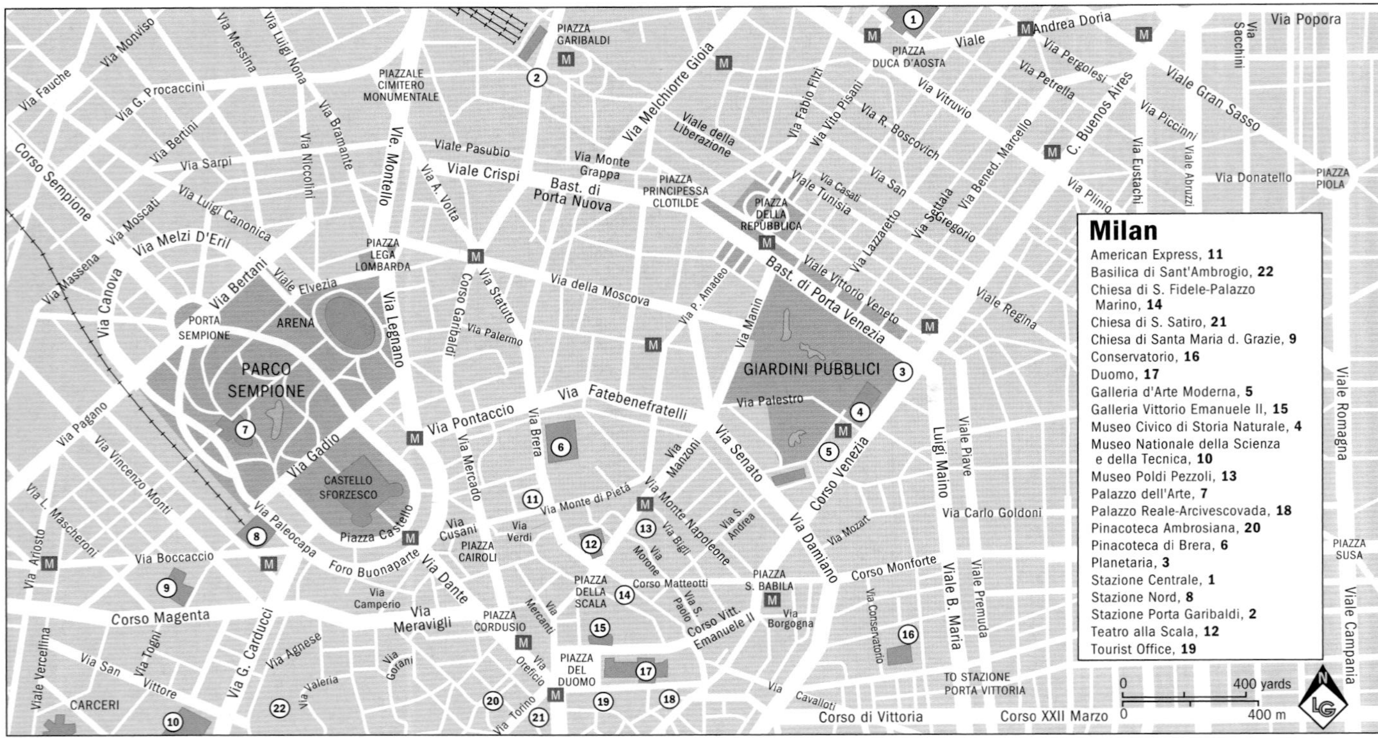

Milan
American Express, 11
Basilica di Sant'Ambrogio, 22
Chiesa di S. Fidele-Palazzo Marino, 14
Chiesa di S. Satiro, 21
Chiesa di Santa Maria d. Grazie, 9
Conservatorio, 16
Duomo, 17
Galleria d'Arte Moderna, 5
Galleria Vittorio Emanuele II, 15
Museo Civico di Storia Naturale, 4
Museo Nationale della Scienza e della Tecnica, 10
Museo Poldi Pezzoli, 13
Palazzo dell'Arte, 7
Palazzo Reale-Arcivescovada, 18
Pinacoteca Ambrosiana, 20
Pinacoteca di Brera, 6
Planetaria, 3
Stazione Centrale, 1
Stazione Nord, 8
Stazione Porta Garibaldi, 2
Teatro alla Scala, 12
Tourist Office, 19
0 400 yards
0 400 m
N
LG
PARCO SEMPIONE
ARENA
PORTA SEMPIONE
CASTELLO SFORZESCO
GIARDINI PUBBLICI
PIAZZA GARIBALDI
PIAZZALE CIMITERO MONUMENTALE
PIAZZA LEGA LOMBARDA
PIAZZA PRINCIPESSA CLOTILDE
PIAZZA DELLA REPUBBLICA
PIAZZA DUCA D'AOSTA
PIAZZA PIOLA
PIAZZA SUSA
PIAZZA CAIROLI
PIAZZA CORDUSIO
PIAZZA DELLA SCALA
PIAZZA DEL DUOMO
PIAZZA S. BABILA
CARCERI
TO STAZIONE PORTA VITTORIA
Via Popora
Via Sacchini
Viale Gran Sasso
Via Donatello
Viale Abruzzi
Via Eustachi
Via Piccinni
Via Plinio
C. Buenos Aires
Via Pergolesi
Via Petrella
Andrea Doria
Viale
Via Vitruvio
Via Bened. Marcello
Via R. Boscovich
Via San Gregorio
Via Settala
Via Lazzaretto
Viale Regina
Viale Vittorio Veneto
Bast. di Porta Venezia
Via Casati
Viale Tunisia
Via Vito Pisani
Via Fabio Filzi
Viale della Liberazione
Via Melchiorre Gioia
Via Monte Grappa
Bast. di Porta Nuova
Viale Crispi
Viale Pasubio
Via A. Volta
Vle. Montello
Via Bramante
Via Niccolini
Via Luigi Nona
Via Messina
Via Monviso
Via Fauche
Via G. Procaccini
Via Bertini
Via Sarpi
Via Luigi Canonica
Via Moscati
Corso Sempione
Via Melzi D'Eril
Via Massena
Via Canova
Via Bertani
Viale Elvezia
Via Legnano
Via della Moscova
Via P. Amadeo
Via Manin
Corso Garibaldi
Via Statuto
Via Palermo
Via Pontaccio
Via Fatebenefratelli
Via Palestro
Via Senato
Corso Venezia
Luigi Maino
Viale Piave
Viale Romagna
Viale Campania
Via Carlo Goldoni
Via Brera
Via Mercado
Via Monte di Pietá
Via Manzoni
Via Monte Napoleone
Via S. Andrea
Via Mozart
Via Damiano
Corso Monforte
Viale B. Maria
Viale Premuda
Via Conservatorio
Via Borgogna
Corso Vitt. Emanuele II
Via S. Paolo
Corso Matteotti
Via Bigli
Via Morone
Via Verdi
Via Cusani
Via Gadio
Piazza Castello
Via Paleocapa
Foro Buonaparte
Via Dante
Via Camperio
Via Meravigli
Via Mercanti
Via Orefici
Via Torino
Via Gorani
Via Valeria
Via Agnese
Via G. Carducci
Corso Magenta
Via Boccaccio
Via Ariosto
Via L. Mascheroni
Via Vincenzo Monti
Via Pagano
Via Togni
Via San Vittore
Viale Vercellina
Via Cavallotti
Corso di Vittoria
Corso XXII Marzo

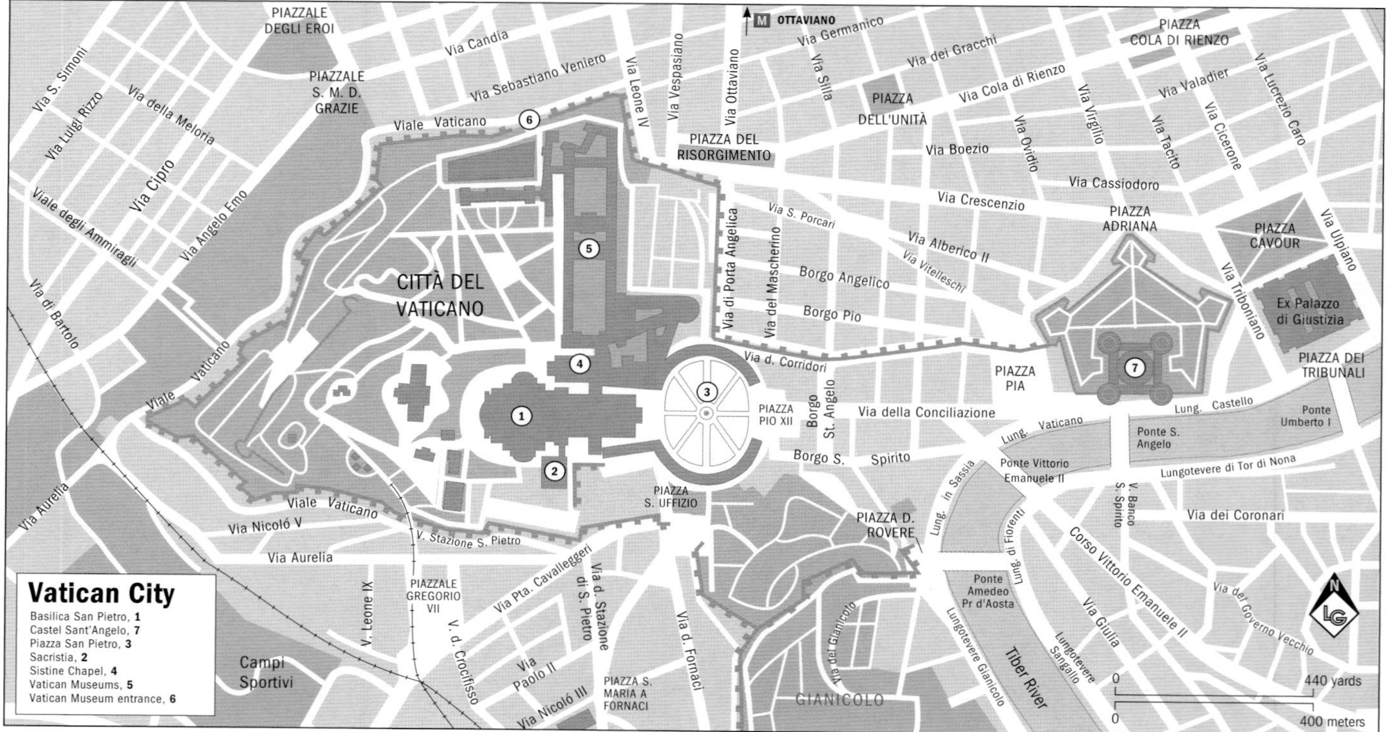
Vatican City
Basilica San Pietro, 1
Castel Sant'Angelo, 7
Piazza San Pietro, 3
Sacristia, 2
Sistine Chapel, 4
Vatican Museums, 5
Vatican Museum entrance, 6
CITTÀ DEL VATICANO
OTTAVIANO
PIAZZALE DEGLI EROI
PIAZZALE S. M. D. GRAZIE
PIAZZA DEL RISORGIMENTO
PIAZZA DELL'UNITÀ
PIAZZA COLA DI RIENZO
PIAZZA ADRIANA
PIAZZA CAVOUR
Ex Palazzo di Giustizia
PIAZZA DEI TRIBUNALI
PIAZZA PIA
PIAZZA PIO XII
PIAZZA S. UFFIZIO
PIAZZA D. ROVERE
PIAZZALE GREGORIO VII
PIAZZA S. MARIA A FORNACI
GIANICOLO
Campi Sportivi
Tiber River
Via S. Simoni
Via Luigi Rizzo
Via della Meloria
Via Cipro
Viale degli Ammiragli
Via Angelo Emo
Via di Bartolo
Via Aurelia
Viale Vaticano
Via Candia
Via Sebastiano Veniero
Via Leone IV
Via Vespasiano
Via Ottaviano
Via Silla
Via Germanico
Via dei Gracchi
Via Cola di Rienzo
Via Boezio
Via Ovidio
Via Virgilio
Via Tacito
Via Cicerone
Via Valadier
Via Lucrezio Caro
Via Ulpiano
Via Cassiodoro
Via Crescenzio
Via S. Porcari
Via Alberico II
Via Vitelleschi
Via di Porta Angelica
Via del Mascherino
Borgo Angelico
Borgo Pio
Via Tribonano
Via d. Corridori
Borgo St. Angelo
Via della Conciliazione
Borgo S. Spirito
Lung. Castello
Ponte Umberto I
Ponte S. Angelo
Lung. Vaticano
Ponte Vittorio Emanuele II
Lungotevere di Tor di Nona
V. Banco S. Spirito
Via dei Coronari
Lung. in Sassia
Lung. di Fiorenti
Corso Vittorio Emanuele II
Via del Governo Vecchio
Via Giulia
Ponte Amedeo Pr d'Aosta
Lungotevere Gianicolo
Lungotevere Sangallo
Via del Gianicolo
Via d. Fornaci
Via d. Stazione di S. Pietro
Via Pta. Cavalleggeri
V. Stazione S. Pietro
Via Nicoló V
Via Aurelia
V. Leone IX
V. d. Crocifisso
Via Paolo II
Via Nicoló III
0
440 yards
0
400 meters

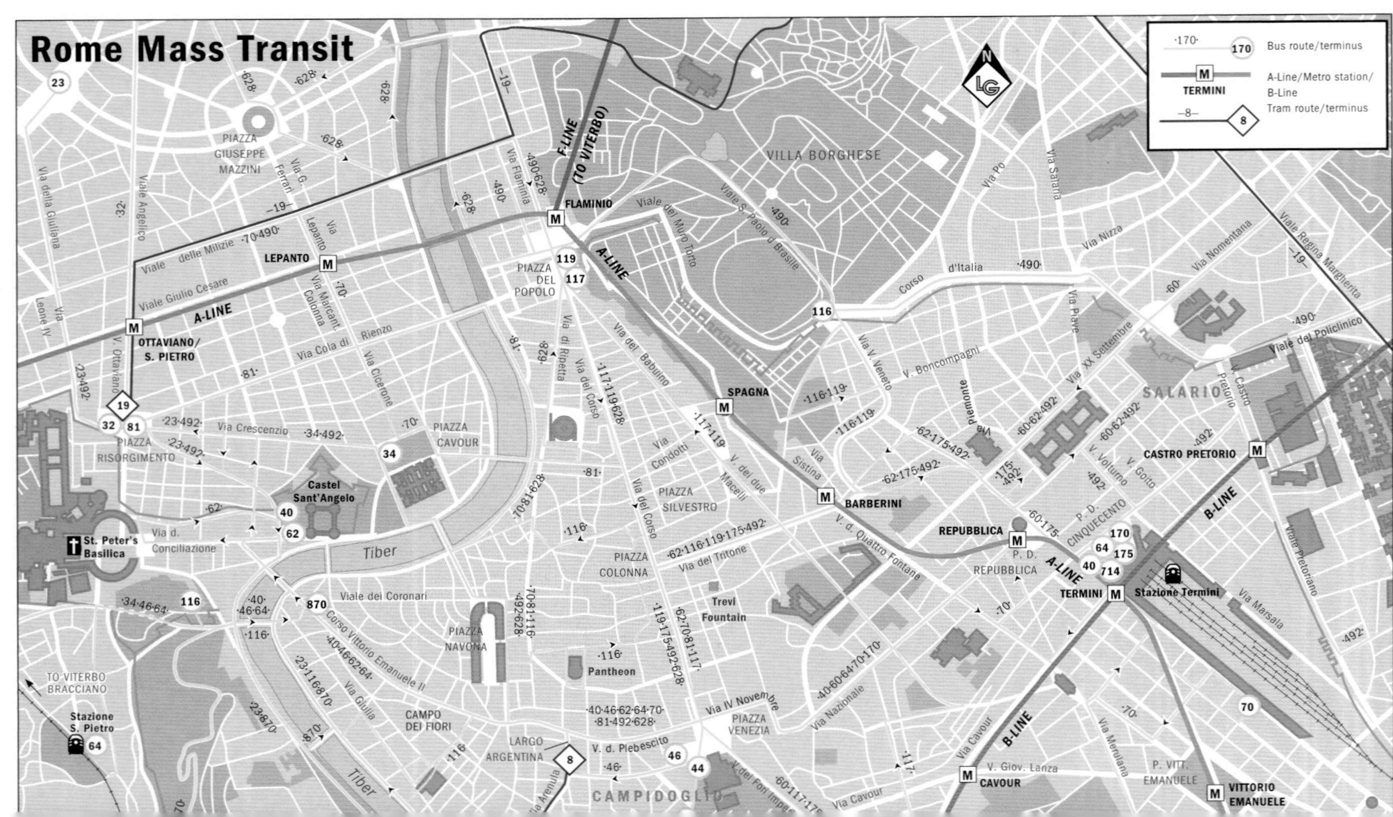

Rome Mass Transit
Bus route/terminus
A-Line/Metro station/
B-Line
TERMINI
Tram route/terminus
VILLA BORGHESE
F-LINE
(TO VITERBO)
FLAMINIO
A-LINE
B-LINE
LEPANTO
OTTAVIANO/
S. PIETRO
SPAGNA
BARBERINI
REPUBBLICA
TERMINI
CASTRO PRETORIO
CAVOUR
VITTORIO
EMANUELE
Stazione Termini
Stazione
S. Pietro
TO VITERBO
BRACCIANO
PIAZZA
GIUSEPPE
MAZZINI
PIAZZA
DEL
POPOLO
PIAZZA
CAVOUR
PIAZZA
RISORGIMENTO
Castel
Sant'Angelo
St. Peter's
Basilica
Tiber
PIAZZA
COLONNA
PIAZZA
SILVESTRO
Trevi
Fountain
Pantheon
PIAZZA
NAVONA
CAMPO
DEI FIORI
LARGO
ARGENTINA
PIAZZA
VENEZIA
CAMPIDOGLIO
SALARIO
P. D.
REPUBBLICA
P. D.
CINQUECENTO
P. VITT.
EMANUELE
Viale Angelico
Via della Giuliana
Via
Leone IV
V. Ottaviano
Viale delle Milizie
Viale Giulio Cesare
Via G.
Ferrari
Via
Lepanto
Via Marcant.
Colonna
Via Cola di Rienzo
Via Cicerone
Via Crescenzio
Via d.
Conciliazione
Viale dei Coronari
Corso Vittorio Emanuele II
Via Giulia
Via Flaminia
Via di Ripetta
Via del Corso
Via del Babuino
Via
Condotti
V. dei due
Macelli
Via
Sistina
Via del Tritone
Via IV Novembre
V. d. Plebescito
Via Arenula
V. dei Fori Imperiali
Via Cavour
Via Nazionale
V. d. Quattro Fontane
Viale del Muro Torto
Viale S. Paolo d. Brasile
Via V. Veneto
V. Boncompagni
Via Piemonte
Corso d'Italia
Via Po
Via Salaria
Via Piave
Via Nizza
Via Nomentana
Via XX Settembre
V. Volturno
V. Goito
V. Castro
Pretorio
Viale del Policlinico
Viale Regina Margherita
Viale Pretoriano
Via Marsala
V. Giov. Lanza
Via Merulana
23
32
81
19
34
40
62
116
870
119
117
46
44
8
64
170
175
40
714
70
·628·
–19–
·32·
·490·628·
·490·
·70·490·
·70·
·81·
·23·492·
·34·492·
·62·
·34·46·64·
·40·
·46·64·
·116·
·23·116·870·
·40·46·62·64·
·23·870·
·870·
·628·
·117·119·628·
·70·81·628·
·70·81·116·
·492·628·
·117·119·
·62·116·119·175·492·
·119·175·492·628·
·62·70·81·117·
·40·46·62·64·70·
·81·492·628·
·46·
·116·119·
·62·175·492·
·175·
·492·
·60·62·492·
·60·175·
·40·60·64·70·170·
·60·117·175·
·117·
·490·
·60·
·492·

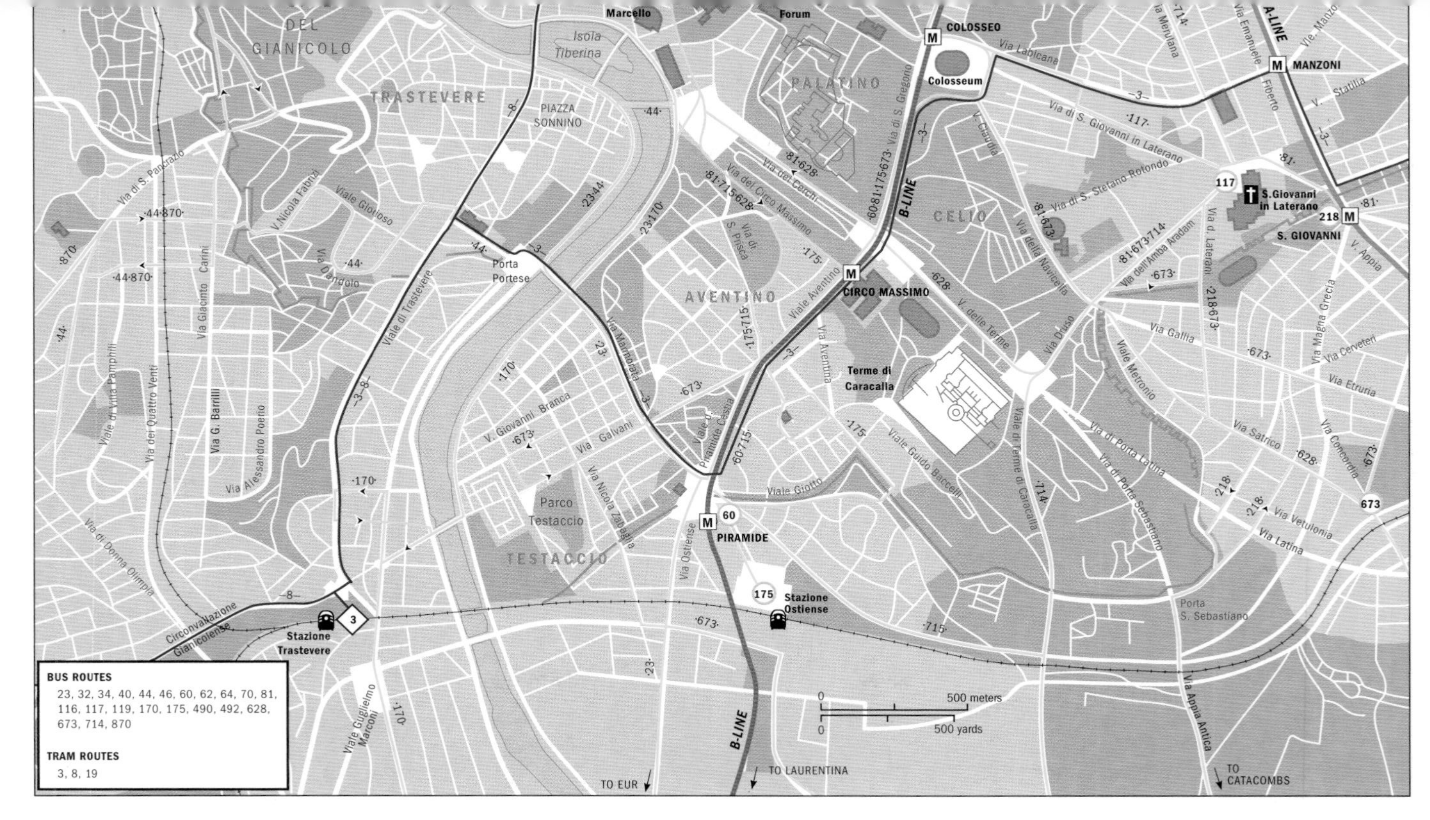

BUS ROUTES
23, 32, 34, 40, 44, 46, 60, 62, 64, 70, 81, 116, 117, 119, 170, 175, 490, 492, 628, 673, 714, 870
TRAM ROUTES
3, 8, 19
COLOSSEO
Colosseum
MANZONI
A-LINE
B-LINE
CIRCO MASSIMO
PIRAMIDE
S. GIOVANNI
S.Giovanni in Laterano
Terme di Caracalla
Stazione Ostiense
Stazione Trastevere
Marcello
Forum
PALATINO
CELIO
AVENTINO
TESTACCIO
TRASTEVERE
DEL GIANICOLO
Isola Tiberina
PIAZZA SONNINO
Porta Portese
Parco Testaccio
Porta S. Sebastiano
Via Labicana
Via Merulana
Via Emanuele Fiberto
Via di S. Gregorio
Via di S. Giovanni in Laterano
Via di S. Stefano Rotondo
Via d. Laterani
Via dell'Amba Aradam
Via della Navicella
V. Claudia
V. delle Terme
Via del Circo Massimo
Via dei Cerchi
Viale Aventino
Via Aventina
Via di S. Prisca
Via Marmorata
Via Galvani
V. Giovanni Branca
Via Nicola Zabaglia
Viale d. Piramide Cestia
Via Ostiense
Viale Giotto
Viale Guido Baccelli
Viale di Terme di Caracalla
Via di Porta Latina
Via di Porta Sebastiano
Viale Metronio
Via Druso
Via Gallia
Via Magna Grecia
Via Cerveteri
Via Etruria
Via Satrico
Via Concordia
Via Vetulonia
Via Latina
Via Appia Antica
V. Appia
V. Statilia
Vle. Manzoni
Viale di Trastevere
Viale Glorioso
V. Nicola Fabrizi
Via Dandolo
Via di S. Pancrazio
Via Giacinto Carini
Via G. Barrili
Via Alessandro Poerio
Via dei Quattro Venti
Viale di Villa Pamphili
Via di Donna Olimpia
Circonvallazione Gianicolense
Viale Guglielmo Marconi
TO EUR
TO LAURENTINA
TO CATACOMBS
500 meters
500 yards

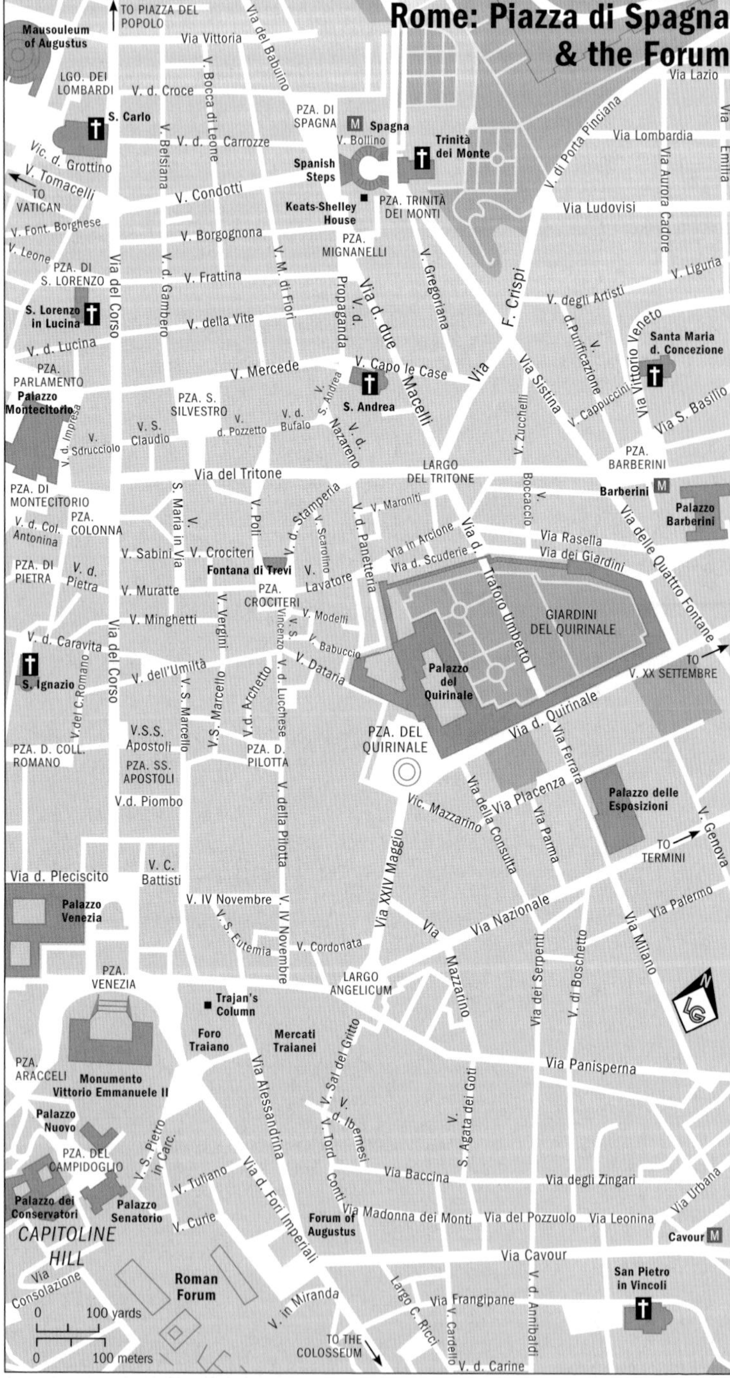
Rome: Piazza di Spagna & the Forum
TO PIAZZA DEL POPOLO
Mausoleum of Augustus
Via Vittoria
Via del Babuino
LGO. DEI LOMBARDI
V. d. Croce
V. Bocca di Leone
S. Carlo
V. d. Carrozze
V. Belsiana
PZA. DI SPAGNA
Spagna
V. Bollino
Trinità dei Monte
Spanish Steps
Vic. d. Grottino
V. Tomacelli
TO VATICAN
V. Condotti
Keats-Shelley House
PZA. TRINITÀ DEI MONTI
V. Font. Borghese
V. Borgognona
PZA. MIGNANELLI
V. Leone
PZA. DI S. LORENZO
V. Frattina
V. d. Gambero
V. M. di Fiori
V. d. Propaganda
Via d. due Macelli
V. Gregoriana
S. Lorenzo in Lucina
V. della Vite
Via del Corso
V. d. Lucina
PZA. PARLAMENTO
V. Mercede
V. Capo le Case
Palazzo Montecitorio
V. d. Impresa
PZA. S. SILVESTRO
V. S. Andrea
S. Andrea
V. S. Claudio
V. d. Pozzetto
V. d. Bufalo
V. d. Nazareno
V. Sdrucciolo
Via del Tritone
LARGO DEL TRITONE
PZA. DI MONTECITORIO
V. S. Maria in Via
V. Poli
V. d. Stamperia
V. Scarolino
V. d. Panetteria
V. Maroniti
V. d. Col. Antonina
PZA. COLONNA
V. Sabini
V. Crociteri
Fontana di Trevi
V. Lavatore
Via in Arcione
Via d. Scuderie
PZA. DI PIETRA
V. d. Pietra
V. Muratte
PZA. CROCITERI
V. Minghetti
V. Vergini
V. S. Vincenzo
V. Modelli
V. Babuccio
V. d. Caravita
V. Dataria
S. Ignazio
V. dell'Umiltà
V. S. Marcello
V. d. Archetto
V. d. Lucchese
V. del C. Romano
V.S.S. Apostoli
PZA. D. COLL. ROMANO
PZA. D. PILOTTA
PZA. SS. APOSTOLI
V.d. Piombo
V. della Pilotta
Via F. Crispi
V. di Porta Pinciana
Via Lazio
Via Emilia
Via Lombardia
Via Aurora
Via Ludovisi
Cadore
V. Liguria
V. degli Artisti
V. d. Purificazione
Via Vittorio Veneto
Santa Maria d. Concezione
Via Sistina
V. Zucchelli
V. Cappuccini
Via S. Basilio
PZA. BARBERINI
Barberini
Palazzo Barberini
V. Boccaccio
Via Rasella
Via dei Giardini
Via d. Traforo Umberto I
Via delle Quattro Fontane
GIARDINI DEL QUIRINALE
Palazzo del Quirinale
TO V. XX SETTEMBRE
Via d. Quirinale
PZA. DEL QUIRINALE
Via Ferrara
Via della Consulta
Via Placenza
Palazzo delle Esposizioni
Vic. Mazzarino
Via Parma
TO TERMINI
V. Genova
Via XXIV Maggio
Via d. Plebiscito
V. C. Battisti
Palazzo Venezia
V. IV Novembre
V. S. Eutemia
V. Cordonata
Via Mazzarino
Via Nazionale
Via Palermo
Via dei Serpenti
V. di Boschetto
Via Milano
PZA. VENEZIA
LARGO ANGELICUM
Trajan's Column
Foro Traiano
Mercati Traianei
PZA. ARACCELI
Monumento Vittorio Emmanuele II
Via Panisperna
Via Alessandrina
V. Sal del Gritto
V. d. Ibernesi
V. Tord Conti
V. S. Agata dei Goti
Palazzo Nuovo
V. S. Pietro in Carc.
PZA. DEL CAMPIDOGLIO
V. Tuliano
Via d. Fori Imperiali
Via Baccina
Via degli Zingari
Palazzo dei Conservatori
Palazzo Senatorio
V. Curie
Forum of Augustus
Via Madonna dei Monti
Via del Pozzuolo
Via Leonina
Via Urbana
Cavour
CAPITOLINE HILL
Via Cavour
Via Consolazione
Roman Forum
Largo C. Ricci
Via Frangipane
V. d. Annibaldi
San Pietro in Vincoli
V. in Miranda
V. Cardello
0 100 yards
0 100 meters
TO THE COLOSSEUM
V. d. Carine
N

Ancient City

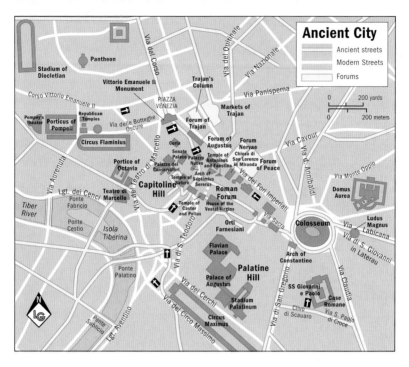

Ancient streets
Modern Streets
Forums

0 200 yards
0 200 meters

Stadium of Diocletian
Pantheon
Vittorio Emanuele II Monument
Via del Corso
Via del Quirinale
Via Nazionale
Trajan's Column
Via Panisperna
Corso Vittorio Emanuele II
PIAZZA VENEZIA
Markets of Trajan
Pompey's Theater
Porticus of Pompeii
Republican Temples
Via delle Botteghe Oscure
Forum of Trajan
Circus Flaminius
Curia
Forum of Augustus
Forum Nervae
Via Cavour
Senate Palace
Palazzo Nuovo
Temple of Antoninus and Faustina
Chiesa di San Lorenzo in Miranda
Forum of Peace
Via d. Annibaldi
Portico of Octavia
Palazzo dei Conservatori
Arch of Septimius Sererus
Via Monte Oppio
Via del Teatro di Marcello
Temple of Saturn
Via dei Fori Imperiali
Via Aurenula
Capitoline Hill
Roman Forum
Domus Aurea
Lgt. dei Cenci
Teatro di Marcello
Ponte Fabricio
Tiber River
Temple of Castor and Pollux
House of the Vestal Virgins
Via Sacra
Ponte Cestio
Isola Tiberina
Orti Farnesiani
Colosseum
Via Labicana
Ludus Magnus
Via di S. Teodoro
Via di S. Giovanni in Laterau
Flavian Palace
Arch of Constantine
Ponte Palatino
Palatine Hill
Palace of Augustus
Via di San Gregorio
Via Claudia
SS Giovanni e Paolo
Via dei Cerchi
Stadium Palatinum
Case Romane
Clivo di Scauaro
Via S. Paolo di Croce
Via del Circo Massimo
Circus Maximus
Ponte Sublicio
Lgt. Aventino
N
LG

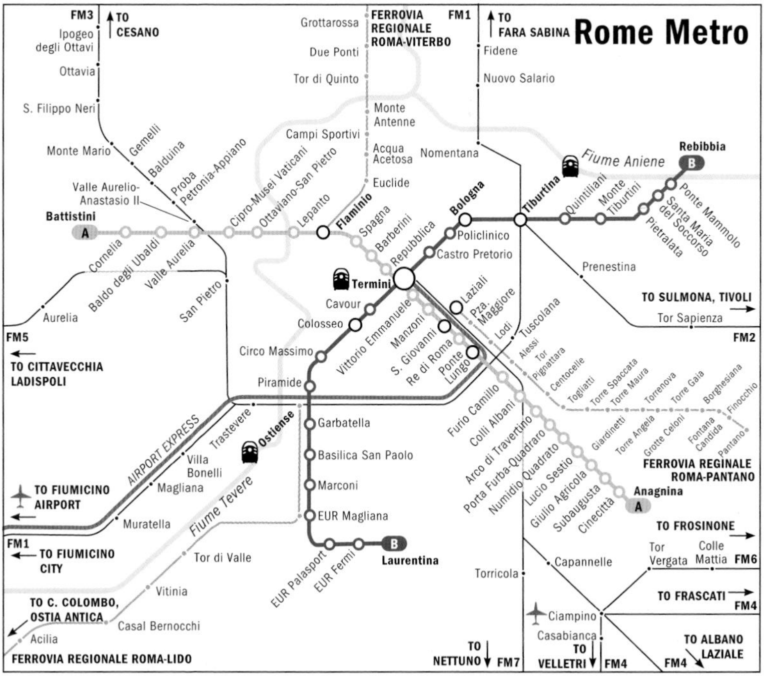

Rome Metro

FM3 TO CESANO
Ipogeo degli Ottavi
Ottavia
S. Filippo Neri
Monte Mario
Gemelli
Balduina
Proba Petronia-Appiano
Valle Aurelio-Anastasio II
Battistini
A
Cornelia
Baldo degli Ubaldi
Valle Aurelia
Cipro-Musei Vaticani
Ottaviano-San Pietro
Lepanto
Flaminio
Spagna
Barberini
Repubblica
San Pietro
Aurelia
FM5 TO CITTAVECCHIA LADISPOLI
Grottarossa
Due Ponti
Tor di Quinto
Campi Sportivi
FERROVIA REGIONALE ROMA-VITERBO
Monte Antenne
Acqua Acetosa
Euclide
FM1 TO FARA SABINA
Fidene
Nuovo Salario
Nomentana
Fiume Aniene
Rebibbia
B
Bologna
Policlinico
Castro Pretorio
Tiburtina
Quintiliani
Monte Tiburtini
Pietralata
Santa Maria del Soccorso
Ponte Mammolo
Prenestina
TO SULMONA, TIVOLI
Tor Sapienza
FM2
Termini
Cavour
Colosseo
Circo Massimo
Piramide
Vittorio Emanuele
Manzoni
S. Giovanni
Re di Roma
Ponte Lungo
Laziali
Pza. Maggiore
Lodi
Tuscolana
Alessi
Tor Pignattara
Centocelle
Togliatti
Torre Spaccata
Torre Maura
Torrenova
Torre Gaia
Borghesiana
Finocchio
Pantano
Fontana Candida
Grotte Celoni
Torre Angela
Giardinetti
FERROVIA REGIONALE ROMA-PANTANO
Furio Camillo
Colli Albani
Arco di Travertino
Porta Furba-Quadraro
Numidio Quadrato
Lucio Sestio
Giulio Agricola
Subaugusta
Cinecittà
Anagnina
A
AIRPORT EXPRESS
Trastevere
Ostiense
Villa Bonelli
Magliana
Muratella
TO FIUMICINO AIRPORT
Fiume Tevere
Garbatella
Basilica San Paolo
Marconi
EUR Magliana
EUR Palasport
EUR Fermi
B
Laurentina
FM1 TO FIUMICINO CITY
Tor di Valle
Vitinia
TO C. COLOMBO, OSTIA ANTICA
Casal Bernocchi
Acilia
FERROVIA REGIONALE ROMA-LIDO
Torricola
TO NETTUNO FM7
TO FROSINONE
Capannelle
Tor Vergata
Colle Mattia
FM6
TO FRASCATI
FM4
Ciampino
Casabianca
TO VELLETRI
FM4
TO ALBANO LAZIALE
FM4

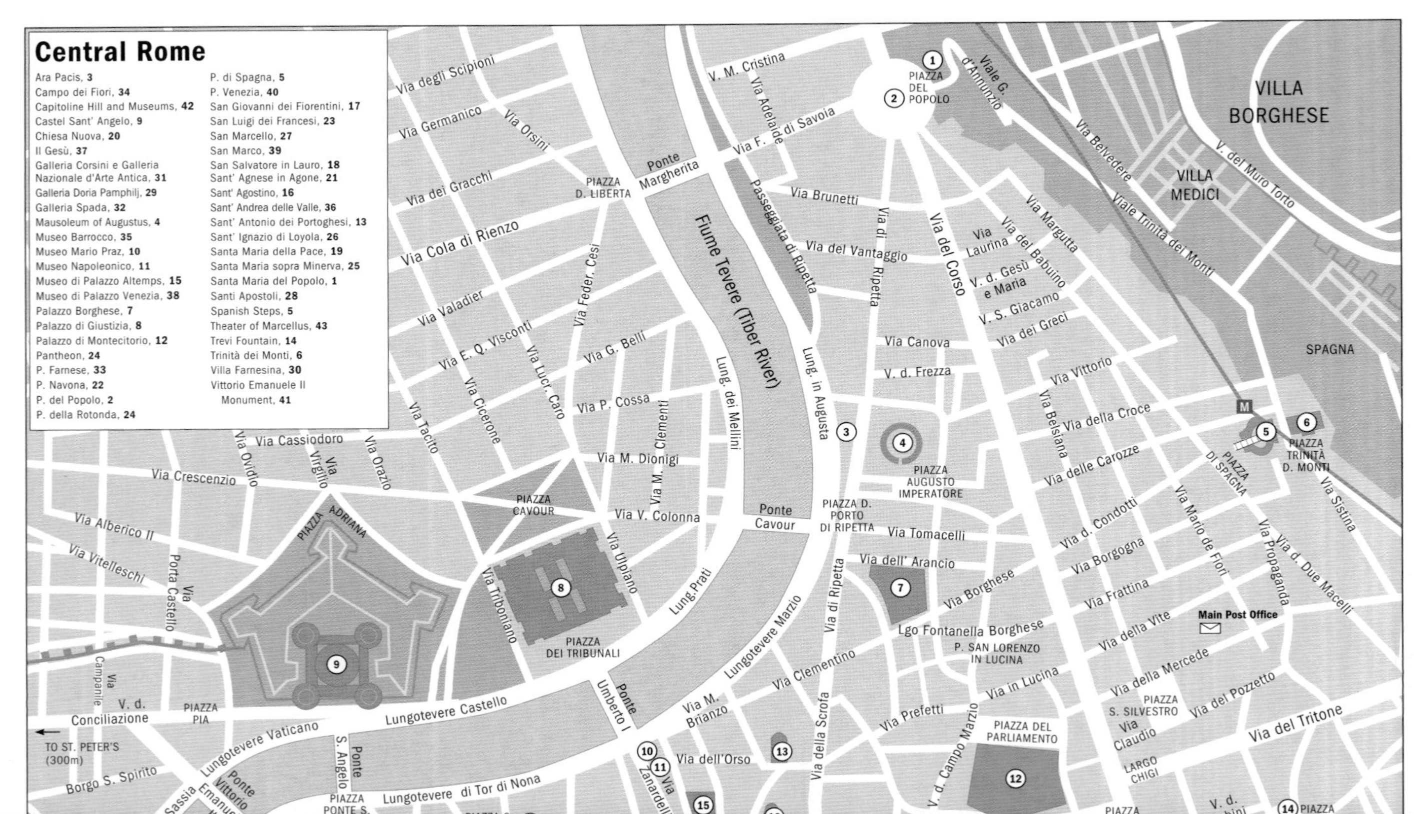

Central Rome
Ara Pacis, 3
Campo dei Fiori, 34
Capitoline Hill and Museums, 42
Castel Sant' Angelo, 9
Chiesa Nuova, 20
Il Gesù, 37
Galleria Corsini e Galleria Nazionale d'Arte Antica, 31
Galleria Doria Pamphilj, 29
Galleria Spada, 32
Mausoleum of Augustus, 4
Museo Barrocco, 35
Museo Mario Praz, 10
Museo Napoleonico, 11
Museo di Palazzo Altemps, 15
Museo di Palazzo Venezia, 38
Palazzo Borghese, 7
Palazzo di Giustizia, 8
Palazzo di Montecitorio, 12
Pantheon, 24
P. Farnese, 33
P. Navona, 22
P. del Popolo, 2
P. della Rotonda, 24
P. di Spagna, 5
P. Venezia, 40
San Giovanni dei Fiorentini, 17
San Luigi dei Francesi, 23
San Marcello, 27
San Marco, 39
San Salvatore in Lauro, 18
Sant' Agnese in Agone, 21
Sant' Agostino, 16
Sant' Andrea delle Valle, 36
Sant' Antonio dei Portoghesi, 13
Sant' Ignazio di Loyola, 26
Santa Maria della Pace, 19
Santa Maria sopra Minerva, 25
Santa Maria del Popolo, 1
Santi Apostoli, 28
Spanish Steps, 5
Theater of Marcellus, 43
Trevi Fountain, 14
Trinità dei Monti, 6
Villa Farnesina, 30
Vittorio Emanuele II Monument, 41
VILLA BORGHESE
VILLA MEDICI
SPAGNA
PIAZZA DEL POPOLO
PIAZZA TRINITÀ D. MONTI
PIAZZA DI SPAGNA
PIAZZA AUGUSTO IMPERATORE
PIAZZA D. PORTO DI RIPETTA
PIAZZA D. LIBERTA
PIAZZA CAVOUR
PIAZZA ADRIANA
PIAZZA DEI TRIBUNALI
PIAZZA PIA
PIAZZA PONTE S.
P. SAN LORENZO IN LUCINA
PIAZZA DEL PARLIAMENTO
PIAZZA S. SILVESTRO
LARGO CHIGI
Main Post Office
Fiume Tevere (Tiber River)
Ponte Margherita
Ponte Cavour
Ponte Umberto I
Ponte S. Angelo
Ponte Vittorio Emanuele II
TO ST. PETER'S (300m)
Via del Corso
Via di Ripetta
Via Cola di Rienzo
Via Crescenzio
Via Cassiodoro
Via del Tritone
Via Sistina
Via d. Due Macelli
Via Propaganda
Via Mario de Fiori
Via d. Condotti
Via Borgogna
Via Frattina
Via della Vite
Via della Mercede
Via del Pozzetto
Via delle Carozze
Via della Croce
Via Belsiana
Via Vittorio
Via dei Greci
V. S. Giacamo
V. d. Gesù e Maria
Via Laurina
Via del Babuino
Via Margutta
Via Canova
V. d. Frezza
Via Tomacelli
Via dell' Arancio
Via Borghese
Lgo Fontanella Borghese
Via in Lucina
Via Prefetti
V. d. Campo Marzio
Via della Scrofa
Via Clementino
Lungotevere Marzio
Via M. Brianzo
Via dell'Orso
Via Zanardelli
Lung. in Augusta
Passeggiata di Ripetta
Via del Vantaggio
Via Brunetti
Via F. di Savoia
Via Adelaide
V. M. Cristina
Viale G. d'Annunzio
Via Belvedere
Viale Trinità dei Monti
V. del Muro Torto
Lung. dei Mellini
Lung. Prati
Via M. Clementi
Via M. Dionigi
Via V. Colonna
Via Ulpiano
Via P. Cossa
Via G. Belli
Via Feder. Cesi
Via Lucr. Caro
Via Cicerone
Via Tacito
Via Orazio
Via Virgilio
Via Ovidio
Via Tribroniano
Via Valadier
Via E. Q. Visconti
Via dei Gracchi
Via Germanico
Via Orsini
Via degli Scipioni
Via Alberico II
Via Vitelleschi
Via Porta Castello
Via Campanile
V. d. Conciliazione
Borgo S. Spirito
Lungotevere Vaticano
Lungotevere Castello
Lungotevere di Tor di Nona
Via Claudio

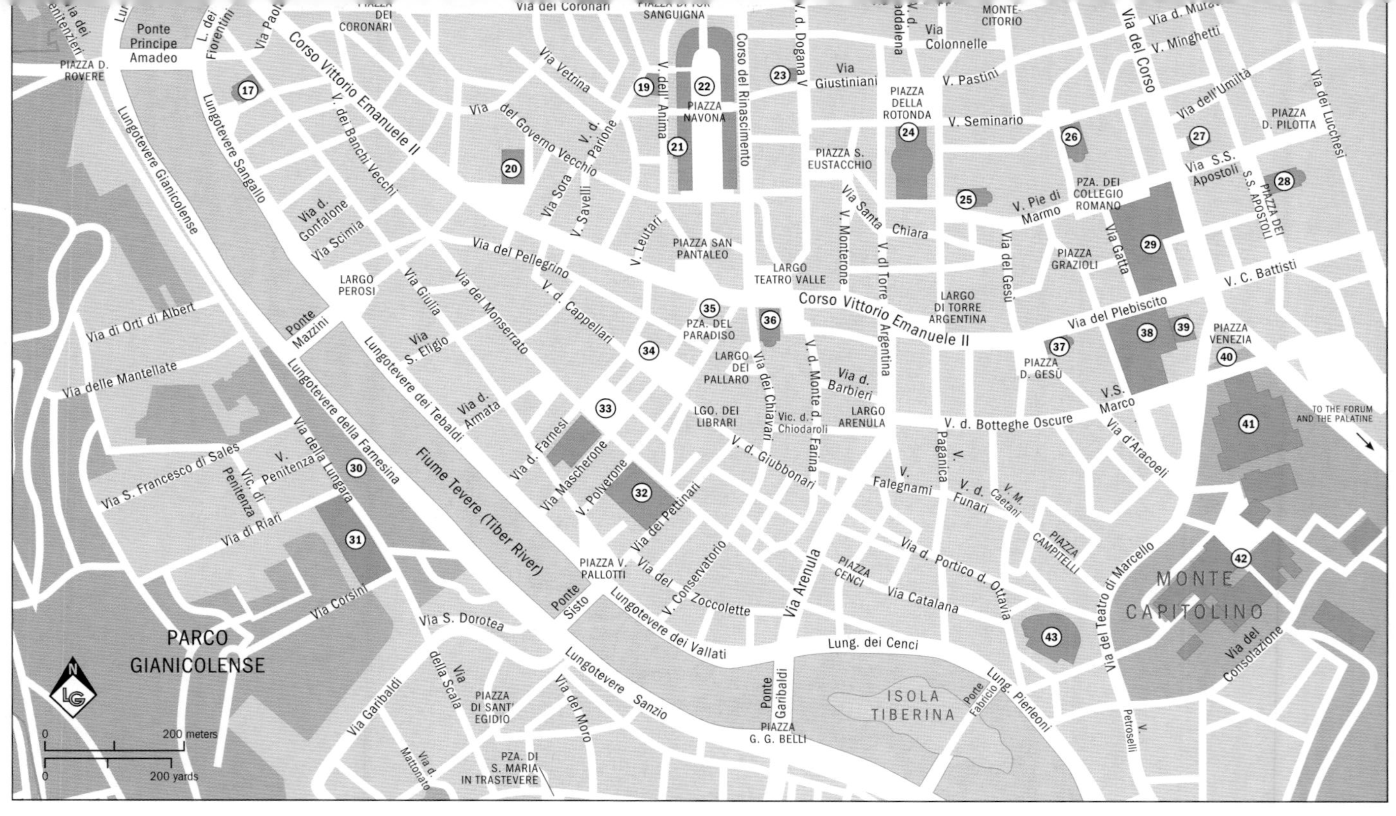

Ponte Principe Amadeo
PIAZZA D. ROVERE
L. dei Fiorentini
Via Paola
Corso Vittorio Emanuele II
DEI CORONARI
Via dei Coronari
SANGUIGNA
Corso del Rinascimento
V. d. Dogana V
Via Giustiniani
Via Colonnelle
MONTE-CITORIO
Via del Corso
Via d. Muratte
V. Minghetti
Via dei Lucchesi
PIAZZA D. PILOTTA
Via dell'Umiltà
Via S.S. Apostoli
PIAZZA DEI S.S. APOSTOLI
V. Pastini
V. Seminario
PIAZZA DELLA ROTONDA
PIAZZA S. EUSTACCHIO
Via Vetrina
V. dell' Anima
PIAZZA NAVONA
Via del Governo Vecchio
V. d. Parione
Via Sora
V. Savelli
V. Leutari
PIAZZA SAN PANTALEO
Via Santa Chiara
V. Monterone
V. di Torre Argentina
LARGO TEATRO VALLE
LARGO DI TORRE ARGENTINA
V. Pie di Marmo
PZA. DEI COLLEGIO ROMANO
Via Gatta
PIAZZA GRAZIOLI
Via del Gesù
V. C. Battisti
Via del Plebiscito
PIAZZA VENEZIA
PIAZZA D. GESÙ
V.S. Marco
TO THE FORUM AND THE PALATINE
Lungotevere Gianicolense
Lungotevere Sangallo
V. dei Banchi Vecchi
Via d. Gonfalone
Via Scimia
LARGO PEROSI
Via del Pellegrino
Via Giulia
Via del Monserrato
V. d. Cappellari
PZA. DEL PARADISO
LARGO DEI PALLARO
Via dei Chiavari
V. d. Monte d. Farina
Via d. Barbieri
Ponte Mazzini
Via di Orti di Albert
Via delle Mantellate
Via S. Eligio
Lungotevere dei Tebaldi
Via d. Armata
LGO. DEI LIBRARI
Vic. d. Chiodaroli
LARGO ARENULA
V. d. Botteghe Oscure
Via d'Aracoeli
Lungotevere della Farnesina
Fiume Tevere (Tiber River)
Via d. Farnesi
Via Mascherone
V. Polverone
V. d. Giubbonari
V. Paganica
V. Falegnami
V. d. Funari
V. M. Caetani
Via S. Francesco di Sales
Vic. di Penitenza
V. Penitenza
Via della Lungara
Via dei Pettinari
Via di Riari
PIAZZA CAMPITELLI
PIAZZA V. PALLOTTI
Via del Zoccolette
V. Conservatorio
Via Arenula
PIAZZA CENCI
Via d. Portico d. Ottavia
Via Catalana
Via del Teatro di Marcello
MONTE CAPITOLINO
Via Corsini
Via S. Dorotea
Ponte Sisto
Lungotevere dei Vallati
Lung. dei Cenci
Via del Consolazione
PARCO GIANICOLENSE
Via Garibaldi
Via della Scala
PIAZZA DI SANT' EGIDIO
Via del Moro
Lungotevere Sanzio
Ponte Garibaldi
PIAZZA G. G. BELLI
ISOLA TIBERINA
Ponte Fabricio
Lung. Pierleoni
V. Petroselli
PZA. DI S. MARIA IN TRASTEVERE
Via d. Mattonato
N
LG
0
200 meters
0
200 yards
17
19
20
21
22
23
24
25
26
27
28
29
30
31
32
33
34
35
36
37
38
39
40
41
42
43

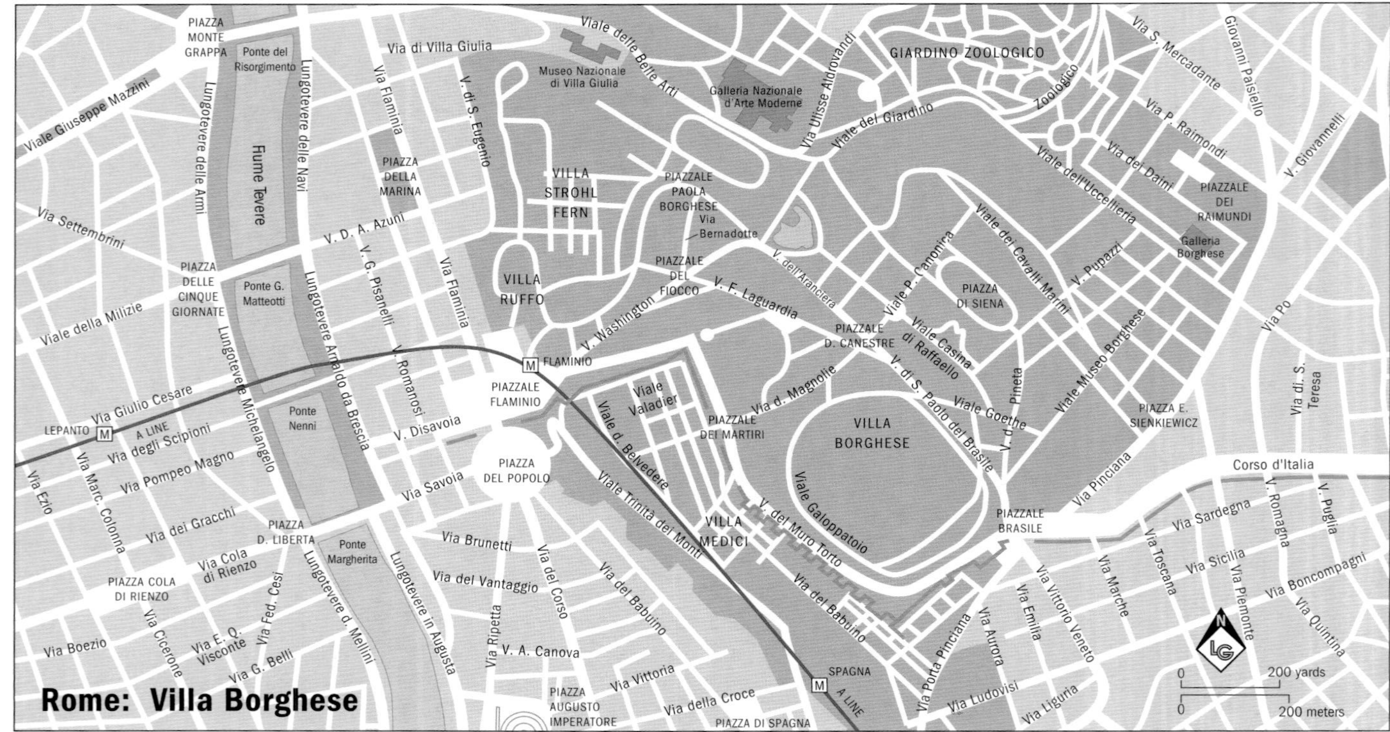

Rome: Villa Borghese
GIARDINO ZOOLOGICO
Zoologico
VILLA BORGHESE
VILLA STROHL FERN
VILLA RUFFO
VILLA MEDICI
Museo Nazionale di Villa Giulia
Galleria Nazionale d'Arte Moderne
Galleria Borghese
PIAZZALE DEI RAIMUNDI
PIAZZA DI SIENA
PIAZZALE D. CANESTRE
PIAZZALE PAOLA BORGHESE
PIAZZALE DEL FIOCCO
PIAZZALE DEI MARTIRI
PIAZZALE FLAMINIO
PIAZZA DEL POPOLO
PIAZZALE BRASILE
PIAZZA E. SIENKIEWICZ
PIAZZA MONTE GRAPPA
PIAZZA DELLA MARINA
PIAZZA DELLE CINQUE GIORNATE
PIAZZA D. LIBERTA
PIAZZA COLA DI RIENZO
PIAZZA AUGUSTO IMPERATORE
PIAZZA DI SPAGNA
Ponte del Risorgimento
Ponte G. Matteotti
Ponte Nenni
Ponte Margherita
Fiume Tevere
FLAMINIO
LEPANTO
SPAGNA
A LINE
Viale delle Belle Arti
Via di Villa Giulia
V. di S. Eugenio
Via Flaminia
V. D. A. Azuni
V. G. Pisanelli
V. Romanosi
V. Disavoia
Via Savoia
Viale Giuseppe Mazzini
Via Settembrini
Viale della Milizie
Via Giulio Cesare
Via degli Scipioni
Via Pompeo Magno
Via Marc. Colonna
Via Ezio
Via dei Gracchi
Via Cola di Rienzo
Via Cicerone
Via Boezio
Via E. Q. Visconte
Via Fed. Cesi
Via G. Belli
Lungotevere delle Armi
Lungotevere delle Navi
Lungotevere Michelangelo
Lungotevere Arnaldo da Brescia
Lungotevere d. Mellini
Lungotevere in Augusta
Via Brunetti
Via del Vantaggio
Via Ripetta
V. A. Canova
Via del Corso
Via del Babuino
Via Vittoria
Via della Croce
Viale Trinità dei Monti
Viale d. Belvedere
Viale Valadier
V. Washington
V. F. Laguardia
Via Bernadotte
V. dell'Aranciera
Via Ulisse Aldrovandi
Viale del Giardino
Via S. Mercadante
Giovanni Paisiello
Via P. Raimondi
Via dei Daini
Viale dell'Uccelliera
V. Giovannelli
Viale dei Cavalli Marini
V. Pupazzi
Viale P. Canonica
Viale Casina di Raffaello
V. di S. Paolo del Brasile
Via d. Magnolie
Viale Goethe
V. d. Pineta
Viale Museo Borghese
Via Po
Via di S. Teresa
Viale Galoppatoio
V. del Muro Torto
Via Pinciana
Corso d'Italia
V. Romagna
V. Puglia
Via Sardegna
Via Toscana
Via Sicilia
Via Boncompagni
Via Piemonte
Via Quintina
Via Marche
Via Vittorio Veneto
Via Emilia
Via Aurora
Via Porta Pinciana
Via Ludovisi
Via Liguria
N
LG
0
200 yards
200 meters

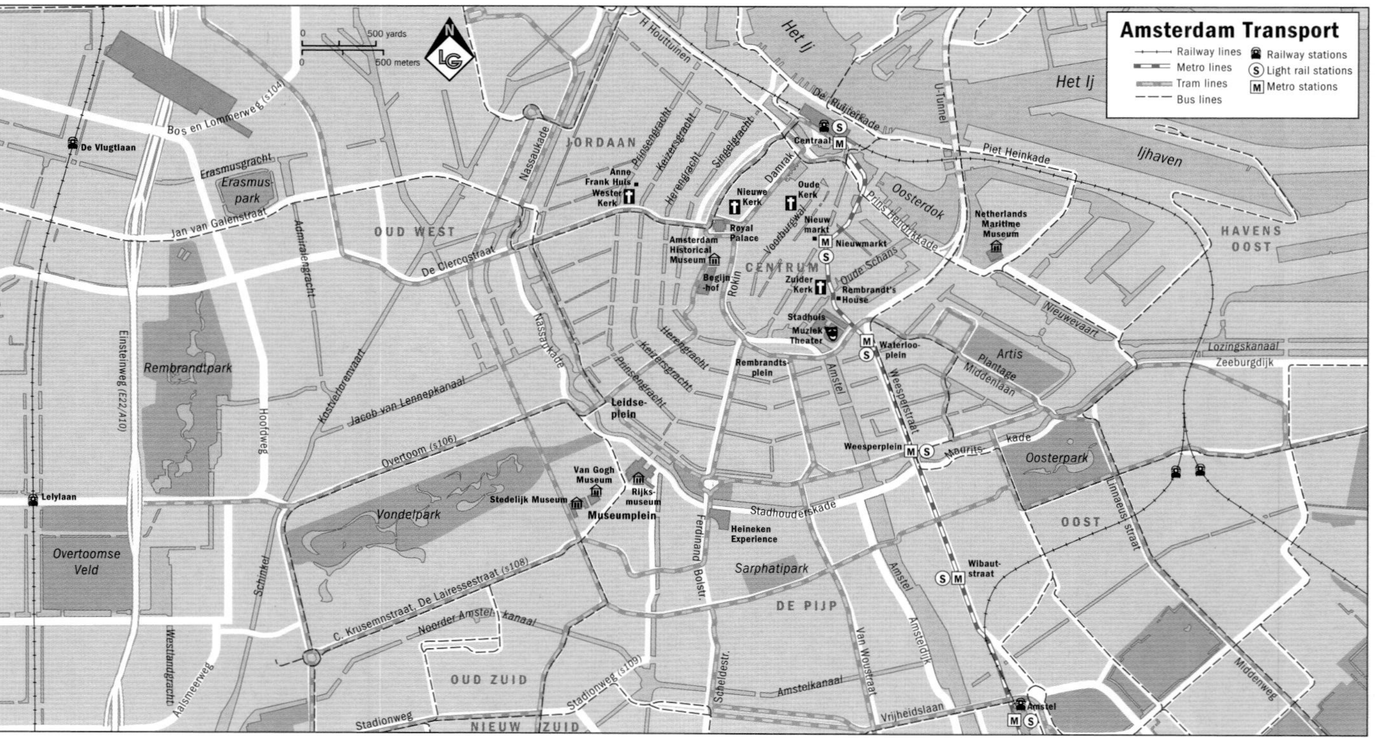
Amsterdam Transport
Railway lines
Metro lines
Tram lines
Bus lines
Railway stations
Light rail stations
Metro stations
0 500 yards
0 500 meters
N
LG
Het Ij
Het Ij
Ijhaven
U-Tunnel
De Ruijterkade
Piet Heinkade
H Houttuinen
Centraal
Oosterdok
Prins Hendrikkade
Netherlands Maritime Museum
HAVENS OOST
JORDAAN
Nassaukade
Prinsengracht
Keizersgracht
Herengracht
Singelgracht
Damrak
Anne Frank Huis
Wester Kerk
Nieuwe Kerk
Oude Kerk
Royal Palace
Voorburgwal
Nieuw markt
Nieuwmarkt
Amsterdam Historical Museum
Begijn -hof
CENTRUM
Rokin
Oude Schans
Zuider Kerk
Rembrandt's House
Stadhuis Muziek Theater
Waterloo-plein
Nieuwevaart
Artis Plantage
Middenlaan
Lozingskanaal
Zeeburgdijk
OUD WEST
Jan van Galenstraat
De Clercqstraat
Bos en Lommerweg (s104)
De Vlugtlaan
Erasmusgracht
Erasmus-park
Admiralengracht
Kostverlorenvaart
Jacob van Lennepkanaal
Rembrandtpark
Einsteinweg (E22/A10)
Hoofdweg
Leidse-plein
Rembrandts-plein
Amstel
Weesperstraat
Weesperplein
Mauritskade
Oosterpark
Overtoom (s106)
Van Gogh Museum
Rijks-museum
Stedelijk Museum
Museumplein
Vondelpark
Lelylaan
Overtoomse Veld
Schinkel
Stadhouderskade
Ferdinand Bolstr.
Heineken Experience
Sarphatipark
DE PIJP
OOST
Linnaeusstraat
Wibaut-straat
Amstel
Amsteldijk
Van Woustraat
C. Krusemnstraat. De Lairessestraat (s108)
Noorder Amstelkanaal
OUD ZUID
Westlandgracht
Aalsmeerweg
Stadionweg (s109)
Scheldestr.
Amstelkanaal
Stadionweg
NIEUW ZUID
Vrijheidslaan
Amstel
Middenweg

Centraal Station
Frederik Hendrik Plantsoen
VAN OLDENBARNEVELDTPLEIN
Anne Frank Huis
Westerkerk
Nieuwe Kerk
Koninklijk Paleis
DAM SQ.
Oude Kerk
BEURSPLEIN
Amsterdams Historisch Museum
Begijnhof
KONINGSPLEIN
MUNTPLEIN
REMBRANDTPLEIN
DA COSTAPLEIN
LEIDSEPLEIN
Rijksmuseum
Van Gogh Museum
Stedelijk Museum
Museumplein
Vondelpark
Weteringplantsoen
Heineken Experience
Sarphatipark
Singelgracht
Herengracht
Keizersgracht
Prinsengracht
Damrak
Rokin
Vijzelstr.
Raadhuisstr.
Leidsestr.
Nassaukade
Marnixstr.
Stadhouderskade
Weteringschans
Overtoom
Albert Cuypstr.

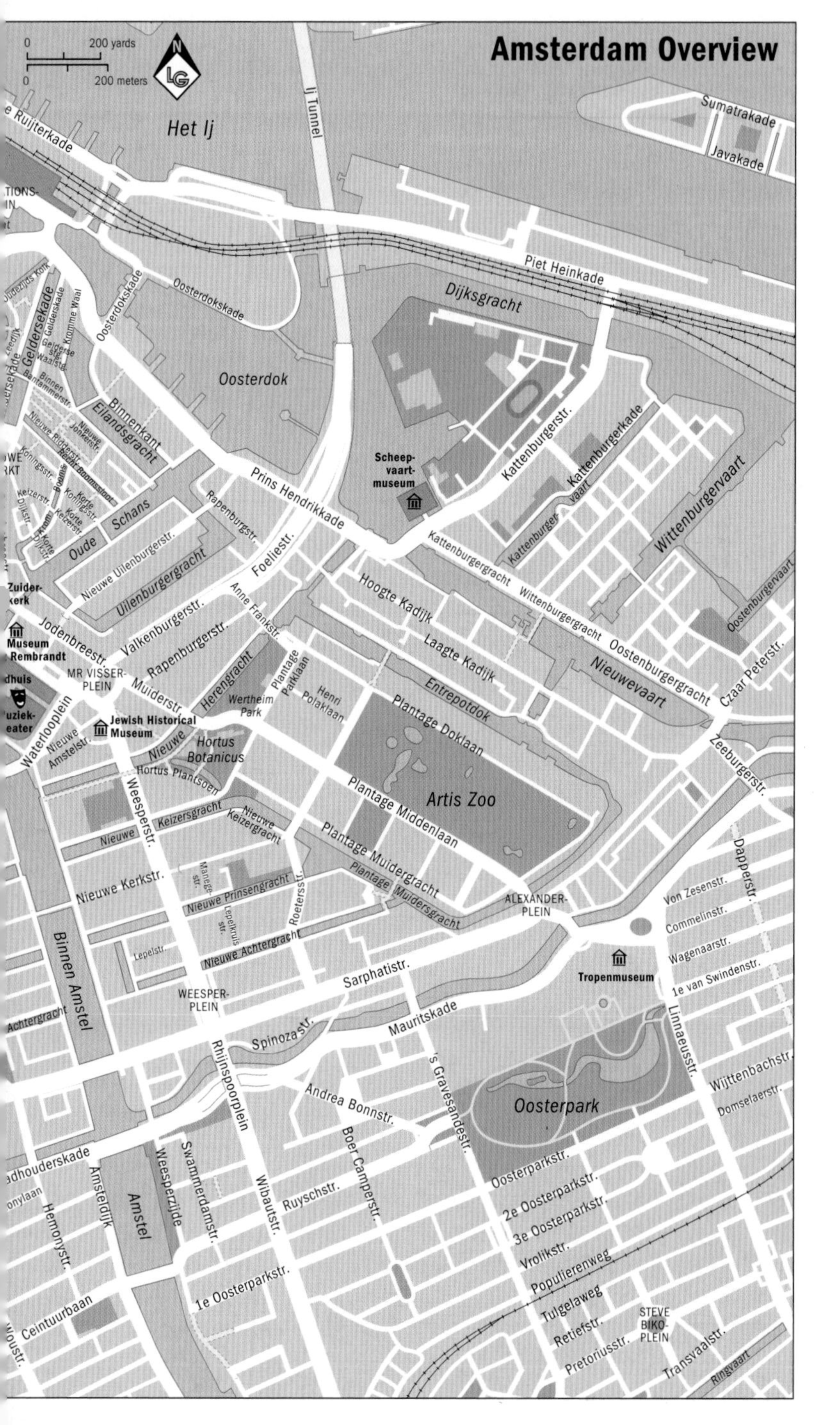

Amsterdam Overview
0 200 yards
0 200 meters
Het IJ
IJ Tunnel
Sumatrakade
Javakade
Piet Heinkade
Dijksgracht
Oosterdokskade
Oosterdok
Scheepvaartmuseum
Kattenburgerstr.
Kattenburgerkade
Wittenburgervaart
Kattenburgergracht
Wittenburgergracht
Oostenburgergracht
Nieuwevaart
Czaar Peterstr.
Prins Hendrikkade
Rapenburgstr.
Foeliestr.
Schans
Oude
Nieuwe Uilenburgerstr.
Uilenburgergracht
Binnenkant
Eilandsgracht
Geldersekade
Zuiderkerk
Museum Rembrandt
Jodenbreestr.
Valkenburgerstr.
Rapenburgerstr.
Anne Frankstr.
MR VISSER-PLEIN
Muiderstr.
Herengracht
Wertheim Park
Plantage Parklaan
Henri Polaklaan
Hoogte Kadijk
Laagte Kadijk
Entrepotdok
Plantage Doklaan
Artis Zoo
Plantage Middenlaan
Plantage Muidergracht
Jewish Historical Museum
Waterlooplein
Nieuwe Amstelstr.
Hortus Botanicus
Hortus Plantsoen
Weesperstr.
Nieuwe Keizersgracht
Nieuwe Kerkstr.
Nieuwe Prinsengracht
Nieuwe Achtergracht
Roetersstr.
Binnen Amstel
WEESPERPLEIN
Sarphatistr.
Spinozastr.
Mauritskade
ALEXANDERPLEIN
Tropenmuseum
Zeeburgerstr.
Dapperstr.
Von Zesenstr.
Commelinstr.
Wagenaarstr.
1e van Swindenstr.
Linnaeusstr.
Wijttenbachstr.
Domselaerstr.
Oosterpark
's Gravesandestr.
Andrea Bonnstr.
Boer Camperstr.
Rhijnspoorplein
Wibautstr.
Ruyschstr.
Swammerdamstr.
Weesperzijde
Amstel
Amsteldijk
Hemonystr.
Oosterparkstr.
2e Oosterparkstr.
3e Oosterparkstr.
Vrolikstr.
Populierenweg
Tulgelaweg
Retiefstr.
Pretoriusstr.
STEVE BIKO-PLEIN
Transvaalstr.
Ringvaart
1e Oosterparkstr.
Ceintuurbaan
Stadhouderskade
Achtergracht

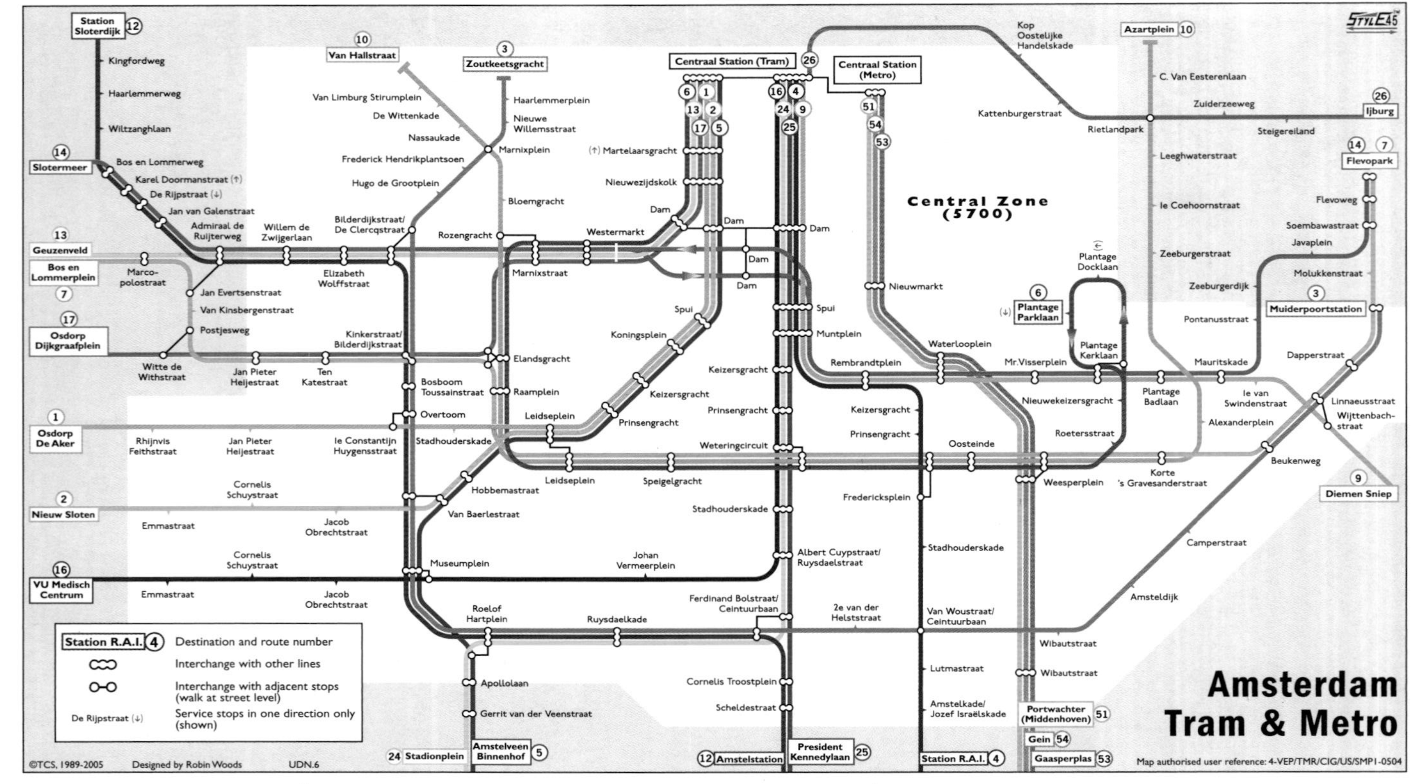

Amsterdam
Tram & Metro
Central Zone
(5700)
Station Sloterdijk 12
Kingfordweg
Haarlemmerweg
Wiltzanghlaan
14 Slotermeer
Bos en Lommerweg
Karel Doormanstraat (↑)
De Rijpstraat (↓)
Jan van Galenstraat
Admiraal de Ruijterweg
Willem de Zwijgerlaan
Elizabeth Wolffstraat
Bilderdijkstraat/ De Clercqstraat
13 Geuzenveld
Bos en Lommerplein 7
Marco-polostraat
Jan Evertsenstraat
Van Kinsbergenstraat
Postjesweg
17 Osdorp Dijkgraafplein
Witte de Withstraat
Jan Pieter Heijestraat
Ten Katestraat
Kinkerstraat/ Bilderdijkstraat
10 Van Hallstraat
Van Limburg Stirumplein
De Wittenkade
Nassaukade
Frederick Hendrikplantsoen
Hugo de Grootplein
3 Zoutkeetsgracht
Haarlemmerplein
Nieuwe Willemsstraat
Marnixplein
Bloemgracht
Rozengracht
Marnixstraat
Westermarkt
Elandsgracht
Bosboom Toussainstraat
Raamplein
Overtoom
Stadhouderskade
1 Osdorp De Aker
Rhijnvis Feithstraat
Jan Pieter Heijestraat
Ie Constantijn Huygensstraat
2 Nieuw Sloten
Cornelis Schuystraat
Emmastraat
Jacob Obrechtstraat
Hobbemastraat
Van Baerlestraat
Leidseplein
Prinsengracht
Keizersgracht
Koningsplein
Spui
Dam
Centraal Station (Tram)
6 1 13 2 17 5
(↑) Martelaarsgracht
Nieuwezijdskolk
26
16 4 24 9 25
Centraal Station (Metro)
51 54 53
Nieuwmarkt
Muntplein
Rembrandtplein
Keizersgracht
Prinsengracht
Weteringcircuit
Speigelgracht
Stadhouderskade
Albert Cuypstraat/ Ruysdaelstraat
16 VU Medisch Centrum
Emmastraat
Cornelis Schuystraat
Jacob Obrechtstraat
Museumplein
Johan Vermeerplein
Roelof Hartplein
Ruysdaelkade
Ferdinand Bolstraat/ Ceintuurbaan
2e van der Helststraat
Van Woustraat/ Ceintuurbaan
Apollolaan
Gerrit van der Veenstraat
24 Stadionplein
Amstelveen Binnenhof 5
12 Amstelstation
Cornelis Troostplein
Scheldestraat
President Kennedylaan 25
Stadhouderskade
Lutmastraat
Amstelkade/ Jozef Israëlskade
Station R.A.I. 4
Frederiksplein
Oosteinde
Weesperplein
Waterlooplein
Mr. Visserplein
Nieuwekeizersgracht
Roetersstraat
6 Plantage Parklaan (↓)
Plantage Docklaan (←)
Plantage Kerklaan
Plantage Badlaan
Korte 's Gravesanderstraat
Ie van Swindenstraat
Alexanderplein
Mauritskade
Dapperstraat
Linnaeusstraat
Wijttenbach-straat
Beukenweg
9 Diemen Sniep
Camperstraat
Amsteldijk
Wibautstraat
Wibautstraat
Portwachter (Middenhoven) 51
Gein 54
Gaasperplas 53
Kop Oostelijke Handelskade
Kattenburgerstraat
Rietlandpark
Azartplein 10
C. Van Eesterenlaan
Zuiderzeeweg
Steigereiland
26 Ijburg
Leeghwaterstraat
Ie Coehoornstraat
Zeeburgerstraat
Zeeburgerdijk
Pontanusstraat
14 7 Flevopark
Flevoweg
Soembawastraat
Javaplein
Molukkenstraat
3 Muiderpoortstation
STYLE45
Station R.A.I. 4 Destination and route number
Interchange with other lines
Interchange with adjacent stops (walk at street level)
De Rijpstraat (↓) Service stops in one direction only (shown)
©TCS, 1989-2005
Designed by Robin Woods
UDN.6
Map authorised user reference: 4-VEP/TMR/CIG/US/SMP1-0504

Central Barcelona

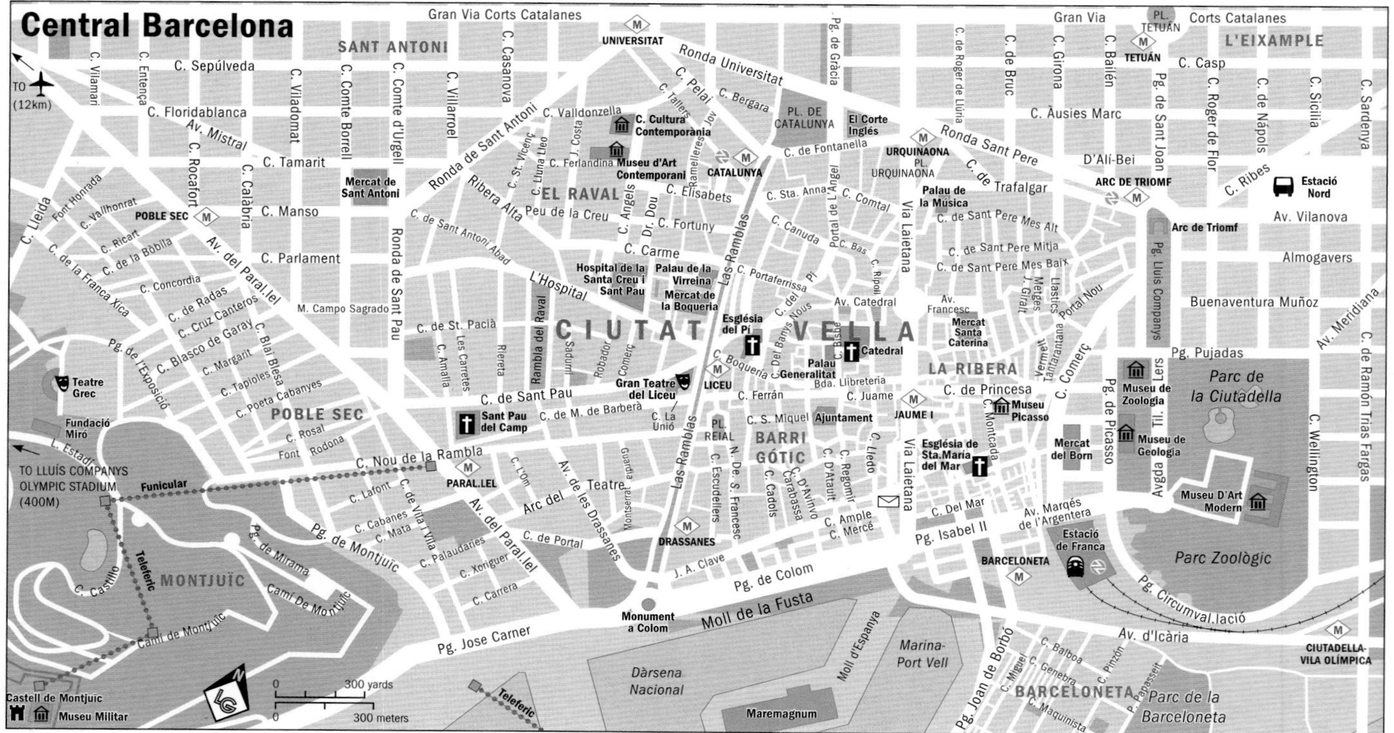

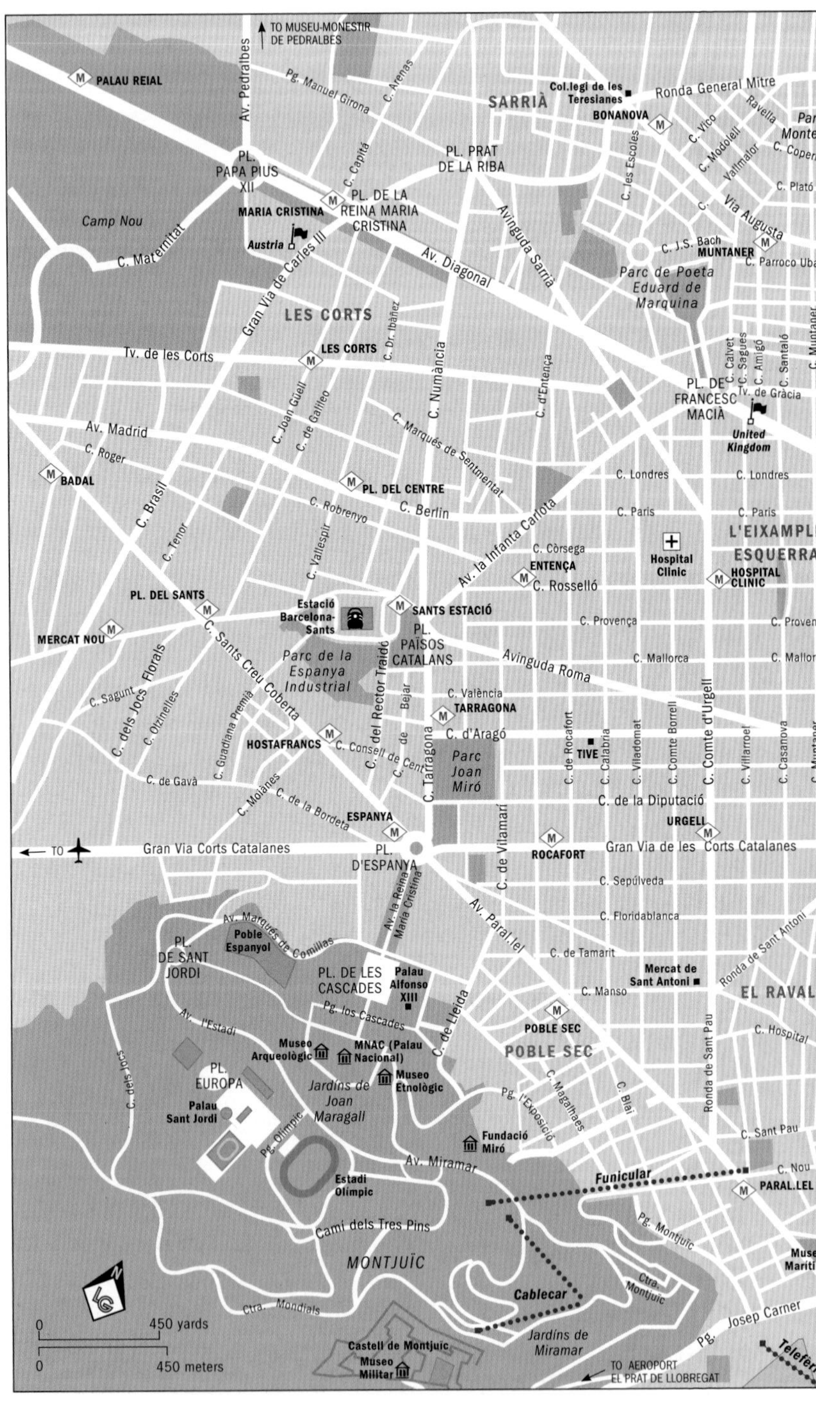

TO MUSEU-MONESTIR DE PEDRALBES
PALAU REIAL
Av. Pedralbes
Pg. Manuel Girona
C. Arenas
SARRIÀ
Col.legi de les Teresianes
Ronda General Mitre
BONANOVA
Parc Monter
C. Vico
Ravella
C. Modolell
C. Copern
Vallmajor
C. Plató
Via Augusta
C. Les Escoles
PL. PAPA PIUS XII
PL. PRAT DE LA RIBA
C. Capità
PL. DE LA REINA MARIA CRISTINA
MARIA CRISTINA
Camp Nou
Austria
Avinguda Sarrià
C. J.S. Bach
MUNTANER
C. Parroco Ubac
C. Maternitat
Gran Via de Carles III
Av. Diagonal
Parc de Poeta Eduard de Marquina
LES CORTS
C. Dr. Ibáñez
Tv. de les Corts
LES CORTS
C. Numància
C. d'Entença
C. Calvet
C. Sagues
C. Amigó
C. Santaló
C. Muntaner
PL. DE FRANCESC MACIÀ
Tv. de Gràcia
United Kingdom
C. Joan Güell
C. de Galileo
C. Marquès de Sentmenat
Av. Madrid
C. Roger
BADAL
PL. DEL CENTRE
C. Londres
C. Robrenyo
C. Berlin
C. Paris
L'EIXAMPLE ESQUERRA
C. Brasil
C. Tenor
Av. la Infanta Carlota
C. Vallespir
C. Còrsega
Hospital Clinic
ENTENÇA
C. Rosselló
HOSPITAL CLINIC
PL. DEL SANTS
Estació Barcelona-Sants
SANTS ESTACIÓ
MERCAT NOU
C. Provença
PL. PAÏSOS CATALANS
C. Sants Creu Coberta
C. dels Jocs Florals
Parc de la Espanya Industrial
C. del Rector Triadó
Avinguda Roma
C. Mallorca
C. Sagunt
C. Olzinelles
C. Guadiana Premià
Bejar
C. València
TARRAGONA
C. Comte d'Urgell
C. d'Aragó
HOSTAFRANCS
C. Consell de Cent
C. Tarragona
Parc Joan Miró
C. de Rocafort
TIVE
C. Calabria
C. Viladomat
C. Comte Borrell
C. Villarroel
C. Casanova
C. Muntaner
C. de Gavà
C. Moianès
C. de la Bordeta
C. de la Diputació
ESPANYA
URGELL
TO
Gran Via Corts Catalanes
PL. D'ESPANYA
ROCAFORT
Gran Via de les Corts Catalanes
C. de Vilamarí
C. Sepúlveda
Av. la Reina Maria Cristina
Av. Paral.lel
C. Floridablanca
Av. Marquès de Comillas
Poble Espanyol
PL. DE SANT JORDI
C. de Tamarit
Ronda de Sant Antoni
PL. DE LES CASCADES
Palau Alfonso XIII
Mercat de Sant Antoni
C. Manso
EL RAVAL
Av. l'Estadi
Pg. los Cascades
C. de Lleida
POBLE SEC
C. Hospital
Museo Arqueològic
MNAC (Palau Nacional)
POBLE SEC
PL. EUROPA
Museo Etnològic
C. Magalhaes
C. dels Jocs
Jardíns de Joan Maragall
Pg. l'Exposició
C. Blai
Ronda de Sant Pau
Palau Sant Jordi
Pg. Olímpic
Fundació Miró
C. Sant Pau
Av. Miramar
C. Nou
Funicular
Estadi Olímpic
PARAL.LEL
Camí dels Tres Pins
Pg. Montjuïc
MONTJUÏC
Museu Marítim
Ctra. Montjuïc
Cablecar
Ctra. Mondials
0
450 yards
0
450 meters
Pg. Josep Carner
Jardíns de Miramar
Castell de Montjuïc
Museo Militar
TO AEROPORT EL PRAT DE LLOBREGAT
Telefèric

Barcelona
PARK GÜELL
Parc Carmel
C. de Marianao
C. Balmes
Av. la República Argentina
C. Verdi
C. Muntanya
C. de Molist
C. Pàdua
PÀDUA
C. Zaragoza
C. Vallirana
LESSEPS
PL. DE LESSEPS
Travessera de Dalt
C. Sanjoanistes
C. Sant Salvador
C. Camèlies
Av. de Montserrat
C. de Castillejos
C. Guillem Tell
PL. MOLINA
Canada
C. Gran de Gràcia
C. Verdi
C. de Martí
C. Sors
C. Torrent de les Flors
C. Alegre de Dalt
PL. ALFONS EL SAVI
Tenerife
Parc de les Aigües
C. Alfons XII
C. Lincoln
Casa Vicens
C. Providència
C. Robí
FONTANA
C. d'Astúries
C. Torren de l'Olla
C. l'Escorial
C. Coloma
ALFONS X
Ronda Guinardó
GRÀCIA
Montseny
C. Sant Marc
C. de l'Or
C. Sant Lluís
Ros de Olano
C. Terol Bruniguer
C. Ramón y Cajal
C. Pi. i Margall
JOANIC
C. de Cartagena
Via Agusta
Tusset
Tv. de Gràcia
C. Martínez
C. Siracusa
C. Sant Antoni Maria Claret
HOSPITAL DE SANT PAU
Av. Diagonal
C. Bonavista
PL. JOAN CARLES I
C. Indústria
L'EIXAMPLE DRETA
C. Còrsega
DIAGONAL
C. de Bailen
Pg. de Sant Joan
C. Roger de Flor
C. Nàpols
C. Sicília
C. Sardenya
C. Marina
Av. de Gaudí
C. Rosselló
C. Granados
PROVENÇA
La Pedrera
LA SAGRADA FAMILIA
C. Provença
CARTAGENA
C. de Balmes
Rambla de Catalunya
Pg. de Gràcia
C. Pau Claris
C. Roger Llúria
VERDAGUER
La Sagrada Familia
PL. JACINT VERDAGUER
C. València
Fundació Tàpies
PG. DE GRÀCIA
C. d'Aragó
PL. PABLO NERUDA
Manzana de la Discòrdia
C. Consell de Cent
GIRONA
C. Bruc
C. de la Diputació
(Pg. Carles I)
PL. DE LES GLÒRIES CATALANES
Plaza de Toros Monumentales
UNIVERSITAT
PG. DE GRÀCIA
TETUÁN
PL. TETUÁN
Gran Via de les Corts Catalanes
Teatre Nacional de Catalunya
Ronda Universitat
C. Pelai
C. Casp
MONUMENTAL
GLÒRIES
Auditori Municipal
C. Girona
C. Bailen
CATALUNYA
PL. DE CATALUNYA
C. d'Ausiàs Marc
Aero-bus
URQUINAONA
Ronda de Sant Pere
Fontanella
ARC DE TRIOMF
Estació Nord
C. Tànger
CIUTAT VELLA
Portal de l'Àngel
Palau de la Música Catalana
S. Pere Més Alt
C. de Marina
Av. Meridiana
MARINA
Carme
Las Ramblas
S. Pere Més Baix
C. dels Almogàvers
Mercat
PL. DE PI
Palau de la Generalitat
Sta. Maria del Pi
LA RIBERA
C. Pamplona
C. d'Alaba
C. d'Àvila
LICEU
United States
C. Comerç
Pg. Pujades
BOGATELL
PL. DE ST. JAUME
C. Princesa
Ajuntament
Museu Picasso
JAUME I
Pg. Picasso
Museu d'Art Modern
C. Llull
POBLE NOU
C. Ramón Turró
PL. REIAL
C. Ciutat
Via Laietana
Pg. Born
Santa Maria del Mar
PARC DE LA CIUTADELLA
C. Wellington
BARRI GÒTIC
Av. Marquès de l'Argentera
Av. Bogatell
DRASSANES
Estació França
Parc Zoologic
Pg. Colom
Monument a Colom
Av. d'Icària
Pg. Circumval.lació
Av. d'Icària
Vila Olímpica
Moll de la Fusta
CIUTADELLA-VILA OLIMPICA
Moll d'Espanya
BARCELONETA
The Towers
PORT OLÍMPIC

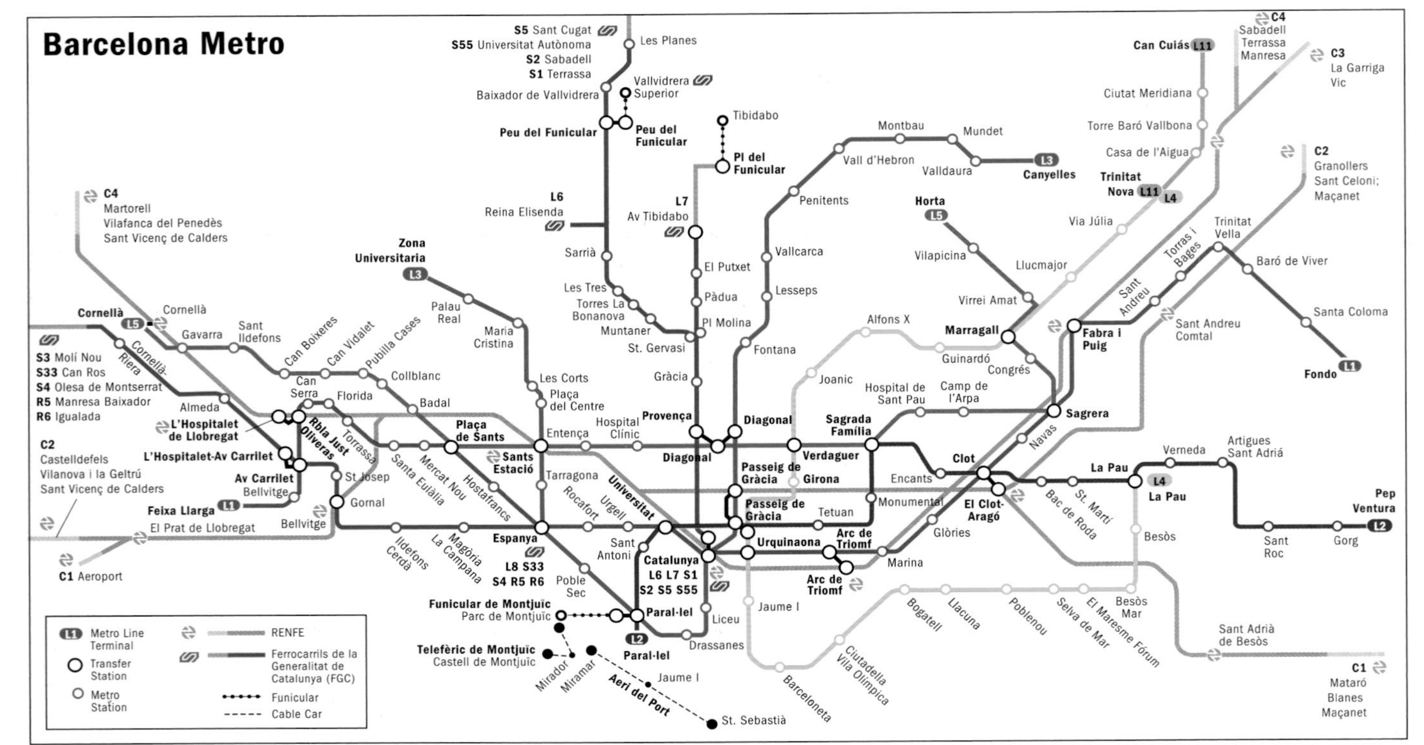

Barcelona Metro
S5 Sant Cugat
S55 Universitat Autònoma
S2 Sabadell
S1 Terrassa
Les Planes
Baixador de Vallvidrera
Vallvidrera Superior
Peu del Funicular
Peu del Funicular
Tibidabo
Pl del Funicular
L6
Reina Elisenda
L7
Av Tibidabo
Sarrià
El Putxet
Pàdua
Les Tres Torres
La Bonanova
Muntaner
St. Gervasi
Pl Molina
Gràcia
Montbau
Mundet
Vall d'Hebron
Valldaura
Canyelles
Penitents
Vallcarca
Lesseps
Fontana
Can Cuiás
Ciutat Meridiana
Torre Baró Vallbona
Casa de l'Aigua
Trinitat Nova
C4
Sabadell
Terrassa
Manresa
C3
La Garriga
Vic
C2
Granollers
Sant Celoni;
Maçanet
Horta
Vilapicina
Llucmajor
Via Júlia
Virrei Amat
Trinitat Vella
Torras i Bages
Baró de Viver
Sant Andreu
Santa Coloma
Fondo
Sant Andreu Comtal
Marragall
Fabra i Puig
Alfons X
Guinardó
Congrés
Joanic
Hospital de Sant Pau
Camp de l'Arpa
Sagrera
Sagrada Família
Navas
Verdaguer
Clot
Verneda
Artigues Sant Adriá
La Pau
La Pau
Encants
El Clot-Aragó
St. Martí
Bac de Roda
Sant Roc
Gorg
Pep Ventura
Besòs
Monumental
Glòries
Tetuan
Marina
Arc de Triomf
Arc de Triomf
Urquinaona
Jaume I
Besòs Mar
El Maresme Fórum
Selva de Mar
Poblenou
Llacuna
Bogatell
Ciutadella Vila Olímpica
Barceloneta
Sant Adrià de Besòs
C1
Mataró
Blanes
Maçanet
C4
Martorell
Vilafanca del Penedès
Sant Vicenç de Calders
Zona Universitaria
Palau Real
Maria Cristina
Les Corts
Plaça del Centre
Cornellà
Cornellà
Gavarra
Sant Ildefons
Can Boixeres
Can Vidalet
Pubilla Cases
Collblanc
Badal
Can Serra
Florida
Cornellà-Riera
S3 Molí Nou
S33 Can Ros
S4 Olesa de Montserrat
R5 Manresa Baixador
R6 Igualada
Almeda
L'Hospitalet de Llobregat
Rbla Just Oliveras
Torrassa
L'Hospitalet-Av Carrilet
Av Carrilet
Bellvitge
St Josep
Gornal
Bellvitge
Santa Eulàlia
Mercat Nou
Plaça de Sants
Sants Estació
Hostafrancs
Entença
Hospital Clínic
Provença
Diagonal
Diagonal
Tarragona
Rocafort
Urgell
Universitat
Passeig de Gràcia
Girona
Passeig de Gràcia
C2
Castelldefels
Vilanova i la Geltrú
Sant Vicenç de Calders
Feixa Llarga
El Prat de Llobregat
C1 Aeroport
Ildefons Cerdà
La Campana
Magòria
Espanya
L8 S33
S4 R5 R6
Sant Antoni
Poble Sec
Catalunya
L6 L7 S1
S2 S5 S55
Liceu
Paral·lel
Drassanes
Paral·lel
Funicular de Montjuïc
Parc de Montjuïc
Telefèric de Montjuïc
Castell de Montjuïc
Mirador
Miramar
Aeri del Port
Jaume I
St. Sebastià
Metro Line Terminal
Transfer Station
Metro Station
RENFE
Ferrocarrils de la Generalitat de Catalunya (FGC)
Funicular
Cable Car

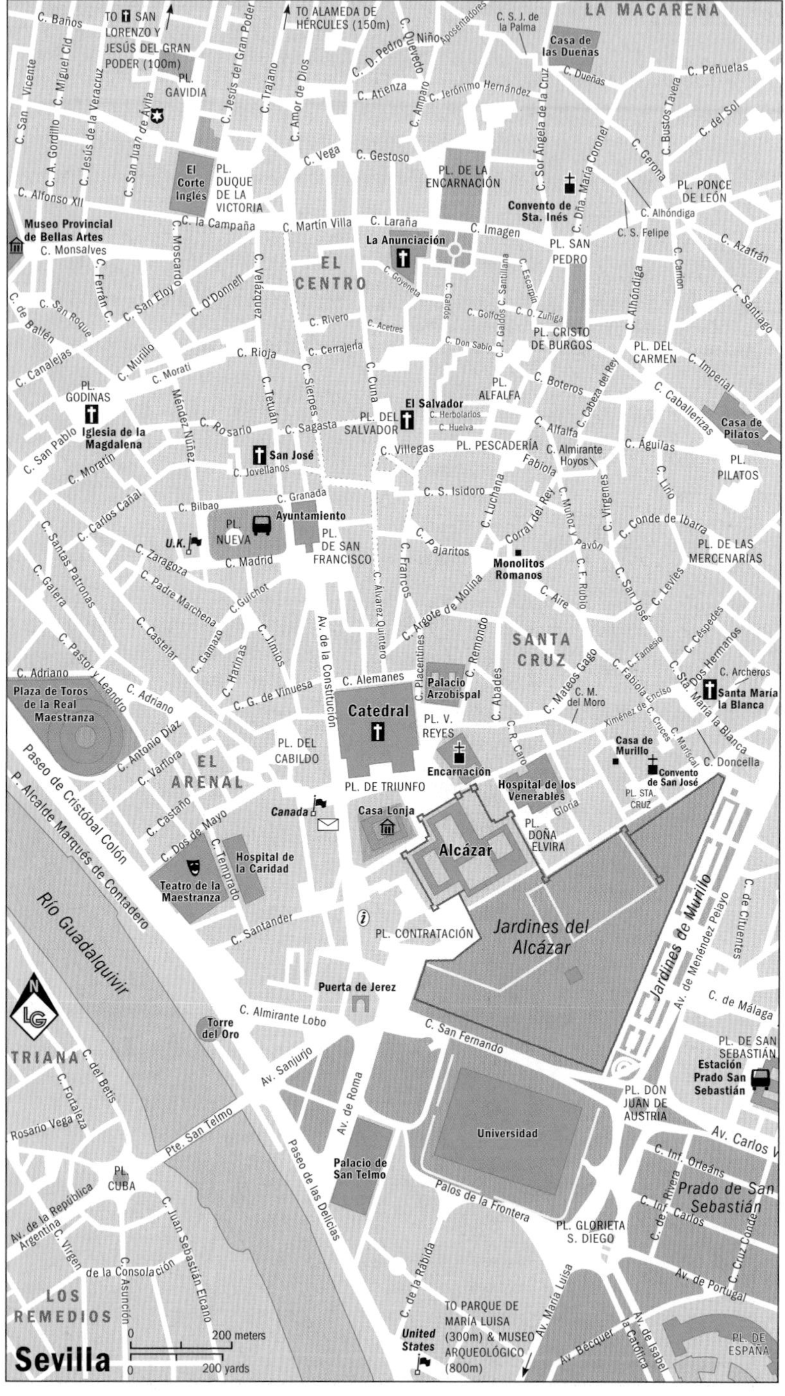
Sevilla
LA MACARENA
EL CENTRO
SANTA CRUZ
EL ARENAL
TRIANA
LOS REMEDIOS
TO SAN LORENZO Y JESÚS DEL GRAN PODER (100m)
TO ALAMEDA DE HÉRCULES (150m)
TO PARQUE DE MARÍA LUISA (300m) & MUSEO ARQUEOLÓGICO (800m)
Casa de las Dueñas
El Corte Inglés
PL. GAVIDIA
PL. DUQUE DE LA VICTORIA
PL. DE LA ENCARNACIÓN
Convento de Sta. Inés
PL. PONCE DE LEÓN
Museo Provincial de Bellas Artes
La Anunciación
PL. SAN PEDRO
PL. CRISTO DE BURGOS
PL. DEL CARMEN
PL. GODINAS
Iglesia de la Magdalena
PL. ALFALFA
El Salvador
PL. DEL SALVADOR
Casa de Pilatos
PL. PILATOS
San José
PL. PESCADERÍA
Ayuntamiento
PL. NUEVA
U.K.
PL. DE SAN FRANCISCO
Monolitos Romanos
PL. DE LAS MERCENARÍAS
Palacio Arzobispal
Catedral
PL. V. REYES
PL. DEL CABILDO
Santa María la Blanca
Casa de Murillo
Convento de San José
Encarnación
Hospital de los Venerables
PL. DE TRIUNFO
PL. STA. CRUZ
Plaza de Toros de la Real Maestranza
Canada
Casa Lonja
PL. DOÑA ELVIRA
Alcázar
Hospital de la Caridad
Teatro de la Maestranza
PL. CONTRATACIÓN
Jardines del Alcázar
Jardines de Murillo
Puerta de Jerez
Torre del Oro
Río Guadalquivir
PL. DE SAN SEBASTIÁN
Estación Prado San Sebastián
PL. DON JUAN DE AUSTRIA
Universidad
Palacio de San Telmo
Prado de San Sebastián
PL. GLORIETA S. DIEGO
PL. CUBA
United States
PL. DE ESPAÑA
0 200 meters
0 200 yards
C. Baños
C. San Vicente
C. Miguel Cid
C. Jesús de la Veracruz
C. San Juan de Ávila
C. Jesús del Gran Poder
C. Trajano
C. Amor de Dios
C. D. Pedro Niño
C. Quevedo
C. Aposentadores
C. S. J. de la Palma
C. Dueñas
C. Peñuelas
C. Atienza
C. Jerónimo Hernández
C. Amparo
C. Sor Ángela de la Cruz
C. Dña. María Coronel
C. Bustos Tavera
C. del Sol
C. Gerona
C. A. Gordillo
C. Vega
C. Gestoso
C. Alfonso XII
C. la Campaña
C. Martín Villa
C. Laraña
C. Imagen
C. Alhóndiga
C. S. Felipe
C. Azafrán
C. Monsalves
C. Moscardo
C. Ferrán
C. Velázquez
C. Goyeneta
C. Gallos
C. Santillana
C. Escarpín
C. Carrión
C. Santiago
C. de Ballén
C. San Roque
C. San Eloy
C. O'Donnell
C. Rivero
C. Acetres
C. Golfo
C. O. Zuñiga
C. Don Sabio
C. P. Galdós
C. Cerrajería
C. Rioja
C. Canalejas
C. Murillo
C. Morati
C. Méndez Núñez
C. Tetuán
C. Sierpes
C. Cuna
C. Boteros
C. Cabeza del Rey
C. Imperial
C. Caballerizas
C. Herbolarios
C. Huelva
C. Rosario
C. Sagasta
C. Alfalfa
C. San Pablo
C. Moratín
C. Villegas
C. Almirante Hoyos
C. Águilas
C. Jovellanos
Fabiola
C. Lirio
C. Carlos Cañal
C. Bilbao
C. Granada
C. S. Isidoro
C. Luchana
Corral del Rey
C. Muñoz y Pavón
C. Virgenes
C. Conde de Ibarra
C. Santas Patronas
C. Zaragoza
C. Madrid
C. Pajaritos
C. Francos
C. Galera
C. Padre Marchena
C. Guichot
C. Álvarez Quintero
C. Argote de Molina
C. F. Rubio
C. Aire
C. San José
C. Levíes
C. Castelar
C. Gamazo
C. Harinas
C. Jimios
Av. de la Constitución
C. Placentines
C. Remondo
C. Abades
C. Mateos Gago
C. Farnesio
C. Céspedes
C. Dos Hermanos
C. Pastor y Leandro
C. Adriano
C. G. de Vinuesa
C. Alemanes
C. M. del Moro
C. Fabiola
Ximénez de Enciso
C. Sta. María la Blanca
C. Archeros
C. Antonio Díaz
C. Varflora
C. R. Caro
C. Cruces
C. Mariscal
C. Doncella
Paseo de Cristóbal Colón
P. Alcalde Marqués de Contadero
C. Castaño
C. Dos de Mayo
C. Temprado
Gloria
C. Santander
C. de Cifuentes
Av. de Menéndez Pelayo
C. de Málaga
C. Almirante Lobo
C. San Fernando
C. del Betis
C. Fortaleza
Av. Sanjurjo
Av. de Roma
Rosario Vega
Pte. San Telmo
Paseo de las Delicias
Av. Carlos V
C. Inf. Orleáns
C. de Rivera
C. Inf. Carlos
Palos de la Frontera
Av. de la República Argentina
C. Virgen de la Consolación
C. Juan Sebastián Elcano
C. Asunción
C. de la Rábida
Av. María Luisa
Av. Bécquer
Av. de Isabel la Católica
Av. de Portugal
C. Cruz Conde

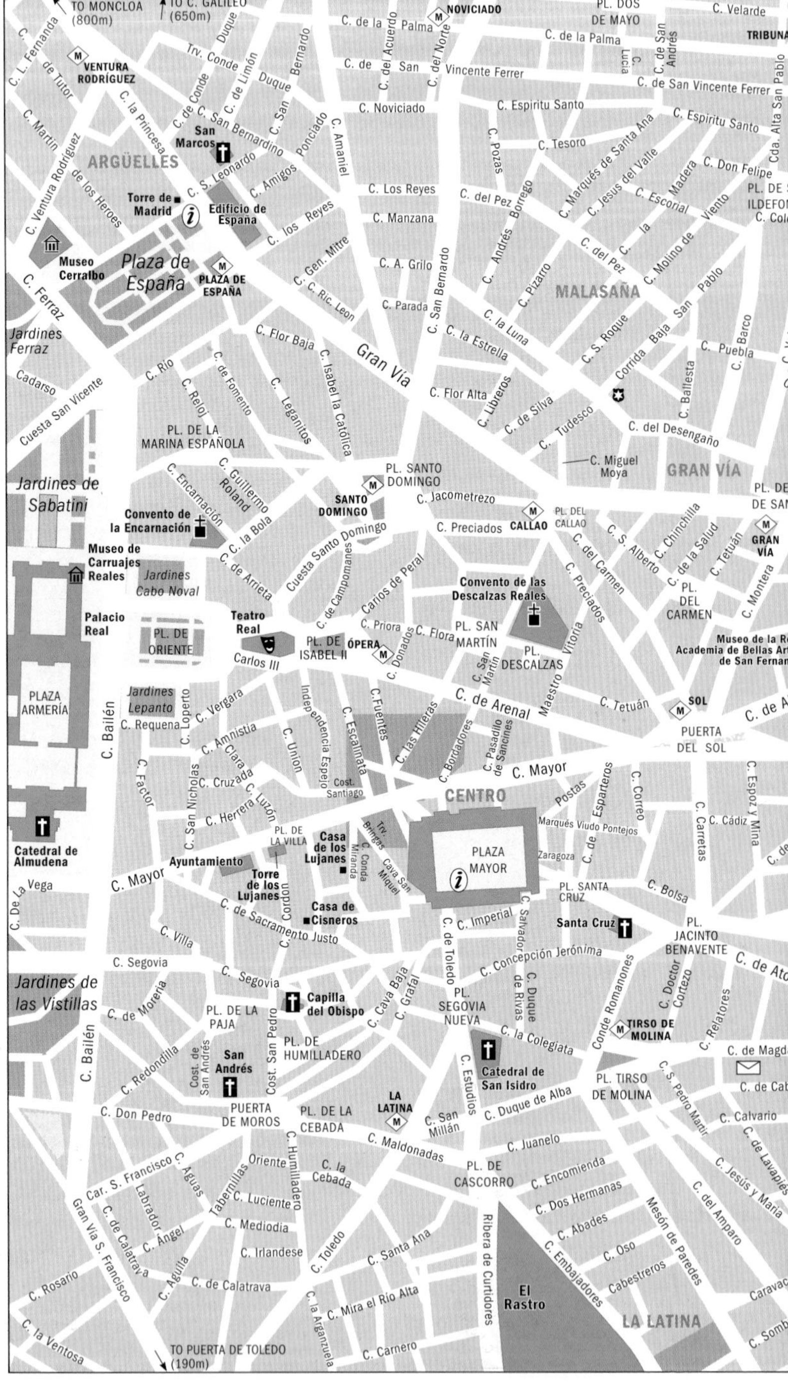

TO MONCLOA (800m)
TO C. GALILEO (650m)
VENTURA RODRÍGUEZ
NOVICIADO
PL. DOS DE MAYO
TRIBUNAL
ARGÜELLES
San Marcos
Torre de Madrid
Edificio de España
Museo Cerralbo
Plaza de España
PLAZA DE ESPAÑA
MALASAÑA
Gran Vía
Jardines Ferraz
PL. DE LA MARINA ESPAÑOLA
Jardines de Sabatini
Convento de la Encarnación
Museo de Carruajes Reales
Jardines Cabo Noval
Palacio Real
PL. DE ORIENTE
Teatro Real
PL. DE ISABEL II
ÓPERA
PLAZA ARMERÍA
Jardines Lepanto
PL. SANTO DOMINGO
SANTO DOMINGO
CALLAO
PL. DEL CALLAO
GRAN VÍA
Convento de las Descalzas Reales
PL. SAN MARTÍN
PL. DESCALZAS
PL. DEL CARMEN
Museo de la Real Academia de Bellas Artes de San Fernando
SOL
PUERTA DEL SOL
CENTRO
Catedral de Almudena
Ayuntamiento
PL. DE LA VILLA
Torre de los Lujanes
Casa de los Lujanes
Casa de Cisneros
PLAZA MAYOR
PL. SANTA CRUZ
Santa Cruz
PL. JACINTO BENAVENTE
Jardines de las Vistillas
Capilla del Obispo
PL. DE LA PAJA
PL. DE HUMILLADERO
San Andrés
PL. SEGOVIA NUEVA
Catedral de San Isidro
TIRSO DE MOLINA
PL. TIRSO DE MOLINA
PUERTA DE MOROS
PL. DE LA CEBADA
LA LATINA
PL. DE CASCORRO
El Rastro
LA LATINA
TO PUERTA DE TOLEDO (190m)
C. Mayor
C. de Arenal
C. de Toledo
C. Bailén
C. Segovia
Cuesta San Vicente
C. San Bernardo
C. de la Princesa
C. Preciados
C. de Atocha

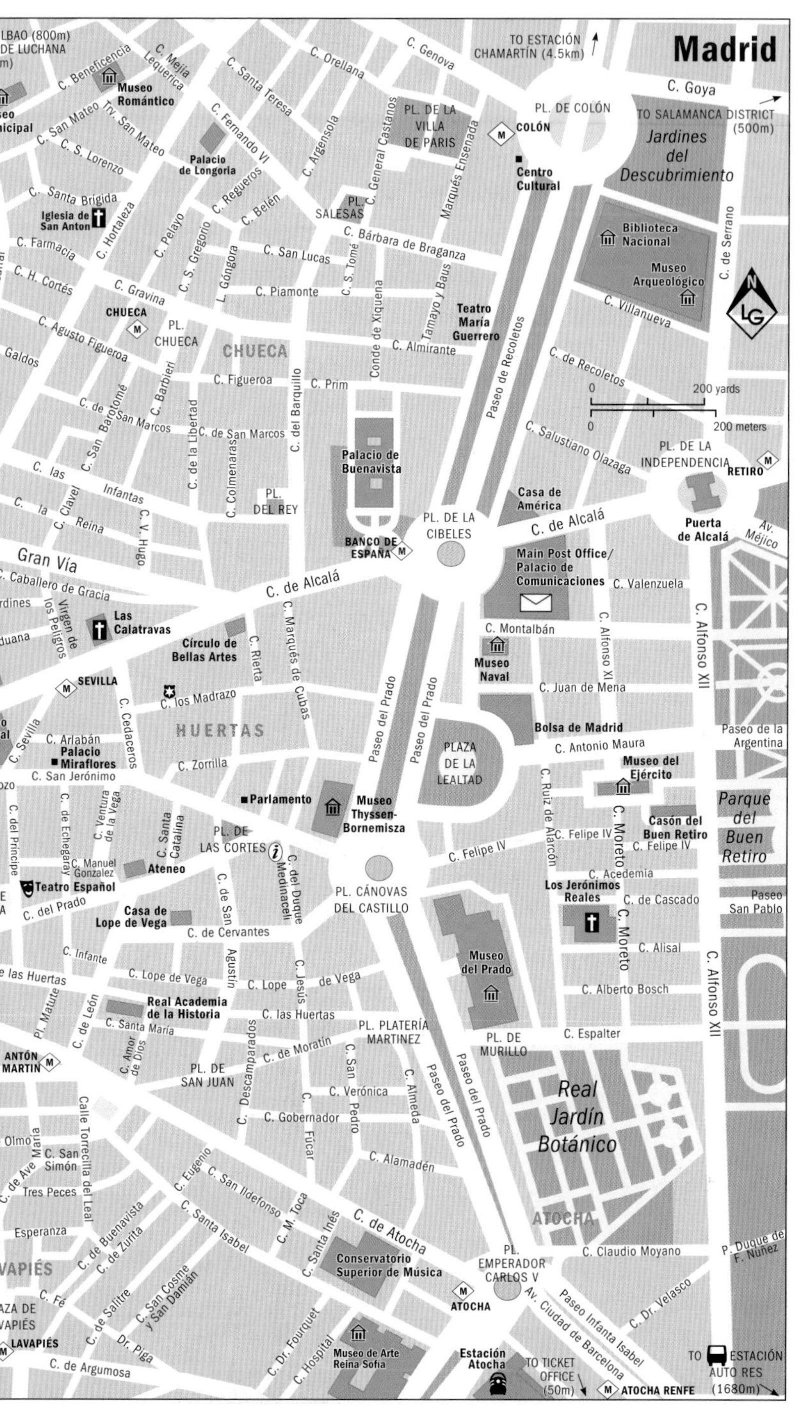
Madrid
TO ESTACIÓN CHAMARTÍN (4.5km)
TO SALAMANCA DISTRICT (500m)
PL. DE COLÓN
COLÓN
Centro Cultural
Jardines del Descubrimiento
Biblioteca Nacional
Museo Arqueológico
Museo Romántico
Palacio de Longoria
Iglesia de San Anton
PL. DE LA VILLA DE PARIS
PL. SALESAS
CHUECA
PL. CHUECA
Teatro María Guerrero
Palacio de Buenavista
PL. DEL REY
PL. DE LA CIBELES
BANCO DE ESPAÑA
PL. DE LA INDEPENDENCIA
RETIRO
Puerta de Alcalá
Casa de América
Main Post Office/ Palacio de Comunicaciones
Museo Naval
Bolsa de Madrid
Museo del Ejército
Casón del Buen Retiro
Parque del Buen Retiro
Las Calatravas
Círculo de Bellas Artes
SEVILLA
HUERTAS
Palacio Miraflores
Parlamento
Museo Thyssen-Bornemisza
PLAZA DE LA LEALTAD
PL. DE LAS CORTES
Ateneo
Teatro Español
Casa de Lope de Vega
PL. CÁNOVAS DEL CASTILLO
Los Jerónimos Reales
Museo del Prado
Real Academia de la Historia
PL. PLATERÍA MARTINEZ
PL. DE MURILLO
Real Jardín Botánico
ANTÓN MARTIN
PL. DE SAN JUAN
ATOCHA
LAVAPIÉS
PLAZA DE LAVAPIÉS
Conservatorio Superior de Música
PL. EMPERADOR CARLOS V
Museo de Arte Reina Sofia
Estación Atocha
TO TICKET OFFICE (50m)
ATOCHA RENFE
TO ESTACIÓN AUTO RES (1680m)
0 200 yards
0 200 meters
Gran Vía
C. de Alcalá
Paseo de Recoletos
Paseo del Prado
C. de Atocha
C. Alfonso XII
C. de Serrano
C. Goya
C. Genova

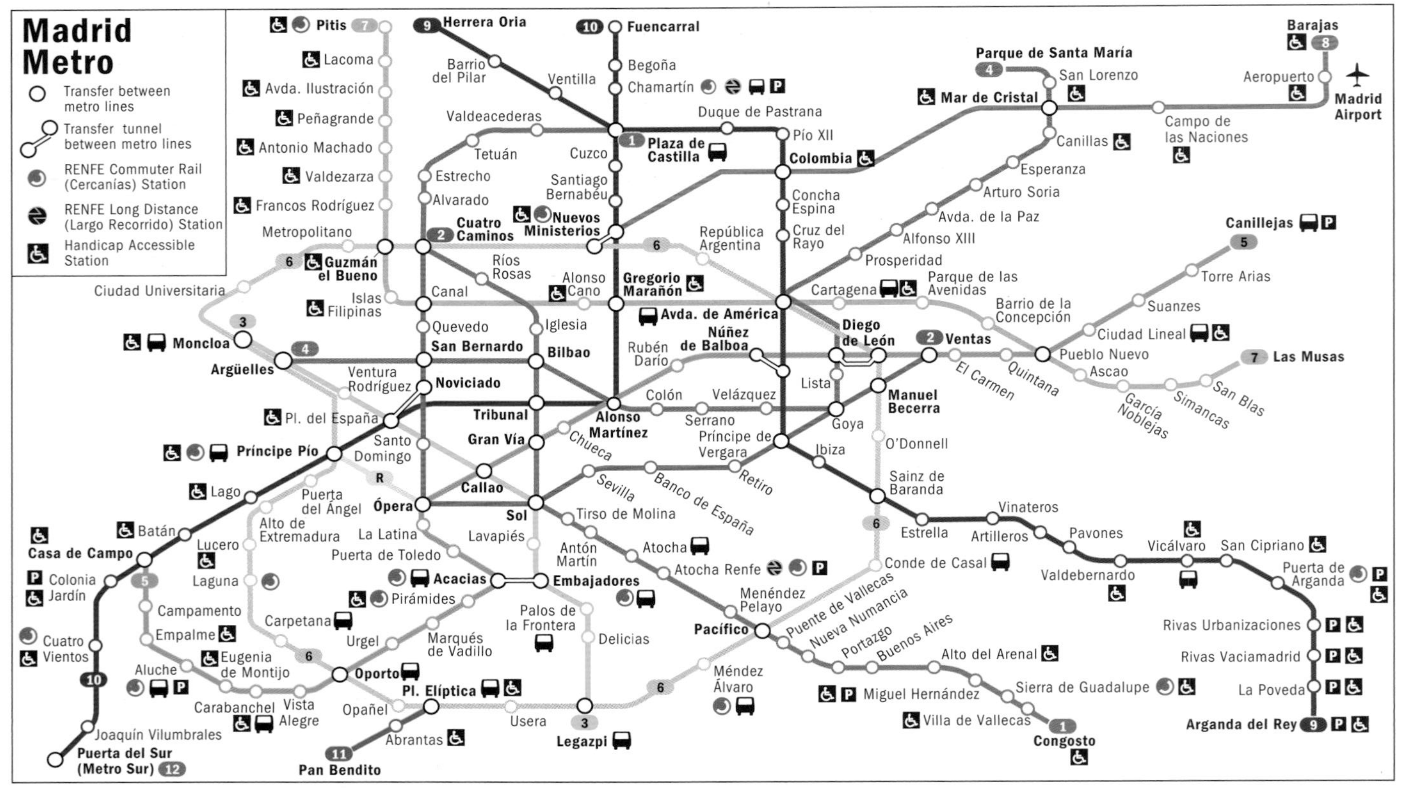

Madrid Metro
Transfer between metro lines
Transfer tunnel between metro lines
RENFE Commuter Rail (Cercanías) Station
RENFE Long Distance (Largo Recorrido) Station
Handicap Accessible Station
Pitis
Lacoma
Avda. Ilustración
Peñagrande
Antonio Machado
Valdezarza
Francos Rodríguez
Metropolitano
Guzmán el Bueno
Ciudad Universitaria
Islas Filipinas
Moncloa
Argüelles
Ventura Rodríguez
Pl. del España
Príncipe Pío
Santo Domingo
Lago
Batán
Casa de Campo
Colonia Jardín
Cuatro Vientos
Joaquín Vilumbrales
Puerta del Sur (Metro Sur)
Lucero
Laguna
Campamento
Empalme
Aluche
Eugenia de Montijo
Carabanchel
Vista Alegre
Puerta del Ángel
Alto de Extremadura
Carpetana
Urgel
Oporto
Opañel
Pl. Elíptica
Abrantas
Pan Bendito
Usera
Legazpi
Herrera Oria
Barrio del Pilar
Ventilla
Valdeacederas
Tetuán
Estrecho
Alvarado
Cuatro Caminos
Canal
Quevedo
San Bernardo
Noviciado
Ríos Rosas
Iglesia
Bilbao
Tribunal
Gran Vía
Callao
Ópera
La Latina
Puerta de Toledo
Acacias
Pirámides
Marqués de Vadillo
Lavapiés
Sol
Embajadores
Palos de la Frontera
Delicias
Fuencarral
Begoña
Chamartín
Plaza de Castilla
Cuzco
Santiago Bernabéu
Nuevos Ministerios
Alonso Cano
Gregorio Marañón
Avda. de América
Rubén Darío
Alonso Martínez
Chueca
Núñez de Balboa
Colón
Serrano
Velázquez
Sevilla
Banco de España
Retiro
Tirso de Molina
Antón Martín
Atocha
Atocha Renfe
Menéndez Pelayo
Pacífico
Méndez Álvaro
Duque de Pastrana
Pío XII
Colombia
Concha Espina
Cruz del Rayo
República Argentina
Prosperidad
Cartagena
Parque de las Avenidas
Barrio de la Concepción
Diego de León
Lista
Goya
Príncipe de Vergara
Ibiza
Manuel Becerra
O'Donnell
Sainz de Baranda
Conde de Casal
Puente de Vallecas
Nueva Numancia
Portazgo
Buenos Aires
Alto del Arenal
Miguel Hernández
Sierra de Guadalupe
Villa de Vallecas
Congosto
Ventas
El Carmen
Quintana
Pueblo Nuevo
Ascao
García Noblejas
Simancas
San Blas
Las Musas
Ciudad Lineal
Suanzes
Torre Arias
Canillejas
Estrella
Vinateros
Artilleros
Pavones
Valdebernardo
Vicálvaro
San Cipriano
Puerta de Arganda
Rivas Urbanizaciones
Rivas Vaciamadrid
La Poveda
Arganda del Rey
Parque de Santa María
San Lorenzo
Mar de Cristal
Canillas
Esperanza
Arturo Soria
Avda. de la Paz
Alfonso XIII
Campo de las Naciones
Aeropuerto
Barajas
Madrid Airport

St. Petersburg

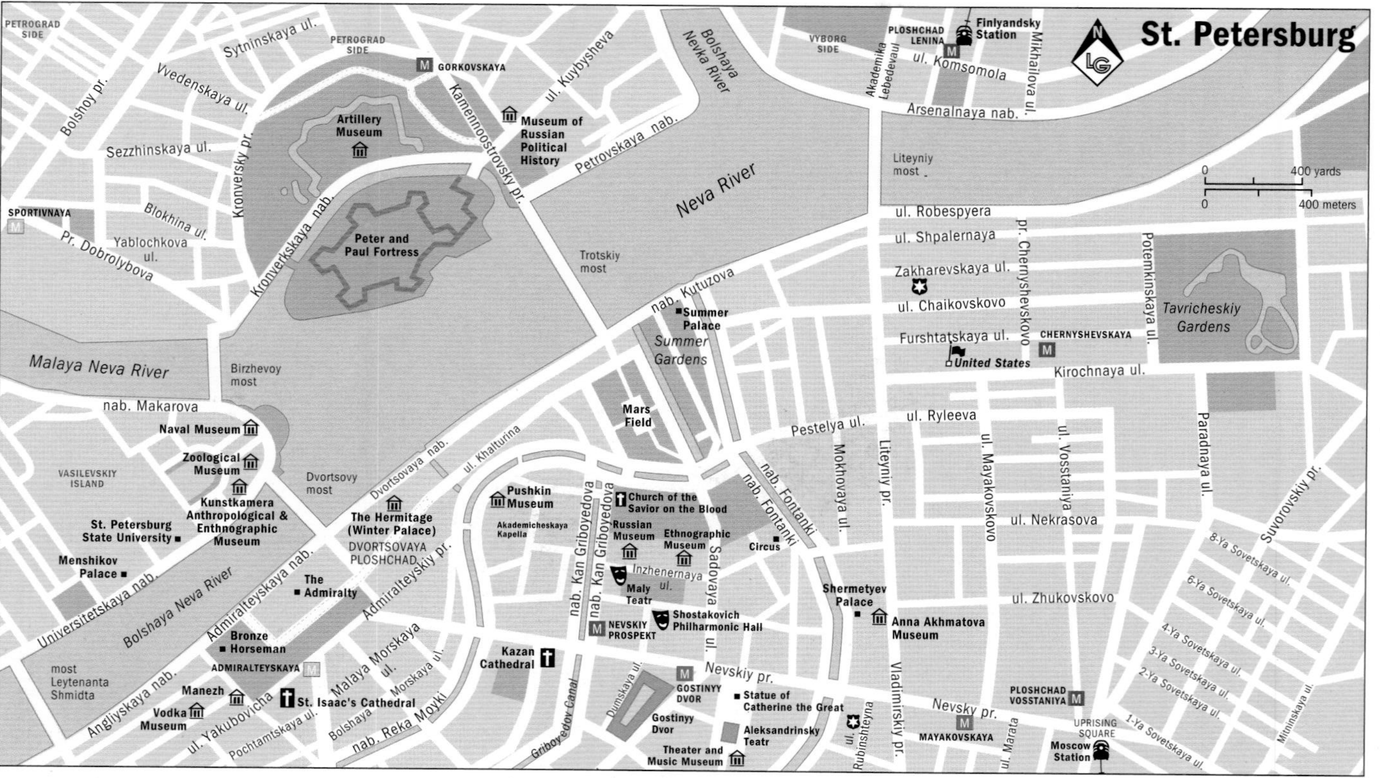

St. Petersburg
N
LG
0
400 yards
400 meters
PETROGRAD SIDE
Sytninskaya ul.
Vvedenskaya ul.
Bolshoy pr.
Sezzhinskaya ul.
Kronversky pr.
Blokhina ul.
Yablochkova ul.
Pr. Dobrolybova
SPORTIVNAYA
GORKOVSKAYA
Artillery Museum
Peter and Paul Fortress
Kronverkskaya nab.
Kamennoostrovsky pr.
ul. Kuybysheva
Museum of Russian Political History
Petrovskaya nab.
Bolshaya Nevka River
Neva River
Trotskiy most
VYBORG SIDE
PLOSHCHAD LENINA
Finlyandsky Station
Akademika Lebedeva ul.
ul. Komsomola
Mikhailova ul.
Arsenalnaya nab.
Liteyniy most
ul. Robespyera
ul. Shpalernaya
Zakharevskaya ul.
ul. Chaikovskovo
Furshtatskaya ul.
United States
pr. Chernyshevskovo
CHERNYSHEVSKAYA
Potemkinskaya ul.
Tavricheskiy Gardens
Kirochnaya ul.
Paradnaya ul.
Malaya Neva River
Birzhevoy most
nab. Makarova
Naval Museum
Zoological Museum
VASILEVSKIY ISLAND
Kunstkamera Anthropological & Enthnographic Museum
St. Petersburg State University
Menshikov Palace
Universitetskaya nab.
Bolshaya Neva River
most Leytenanta Shmidta
Angliyskaya nab.
Manezh
Vodka Museum
Dvortsovy most
Dvortsovaya nab.
nab. Kutuzova
Summer Palace
Summer Gardens
Mars Field
ul. Khalturina
The Hermitage (Winter Palace)
DVORTSOVAYA PLOSHCHAD
Admiralteyskaya nab.
The Admiralty
Admiralteyskiy pr.
Bronze Horseman
ADMIRALTEYSKAYA
ul. Yakubovicha
St. Isaac's Cathedral
Pochtamtskaya ul.
Malaya Morskaya ul.
Bolshaya Morskaya ul.
nab. Reka Moyki
Pushkin Museum
Akademicheskaya Kapella
nab. Kan Griboyedova
Church of the Savior on the Blood
Russian Museum
Ethnographic Museum
Inzhenernaya ul.
Maly Teatr
Sadovaya ul.
Shostakovich Philharmonic Hall
NEVSKIY PROSPEKT
Kazan Cathedral
Griboyedov Canal
Dumskaya ul.
GOSTINYY DVOR
Gostinyy Dvor
Nevskiy pr.
Statue of Catherine the Great
Aleksandrinsky Teatr
Theater and Music Museum
nab. Fontanki
Circus
Pestelya ul.
ul. Ryleeva
Mokhovaya ul.
Liteyniy pr.
Shermetyev Palace
Anna Akhmatova Museum
ul. Rubinshteyna
Vladimirskiy pr.
ul. Mayakovskovo
ul. Vosstaniya
ul. Nekrasova
ul. Zhukovskovo
MAYAKOVSKAYA
ul. Marata
PLOSHCHAD VOSSTANIYA
Nevsky pr.
UPRISING SQUARE
Moscow Station
Suvorovskiy pr.
8-Ya Sovetskaya ul.
6-Ya Sovetskaya ul.
4-Ya Sovetskaya ul.
3-Ya Sovetskaya ul.
2-Ya Sovetskaya ul.
1-Ya Sovetskaya ul.
Mitninskaya ul.

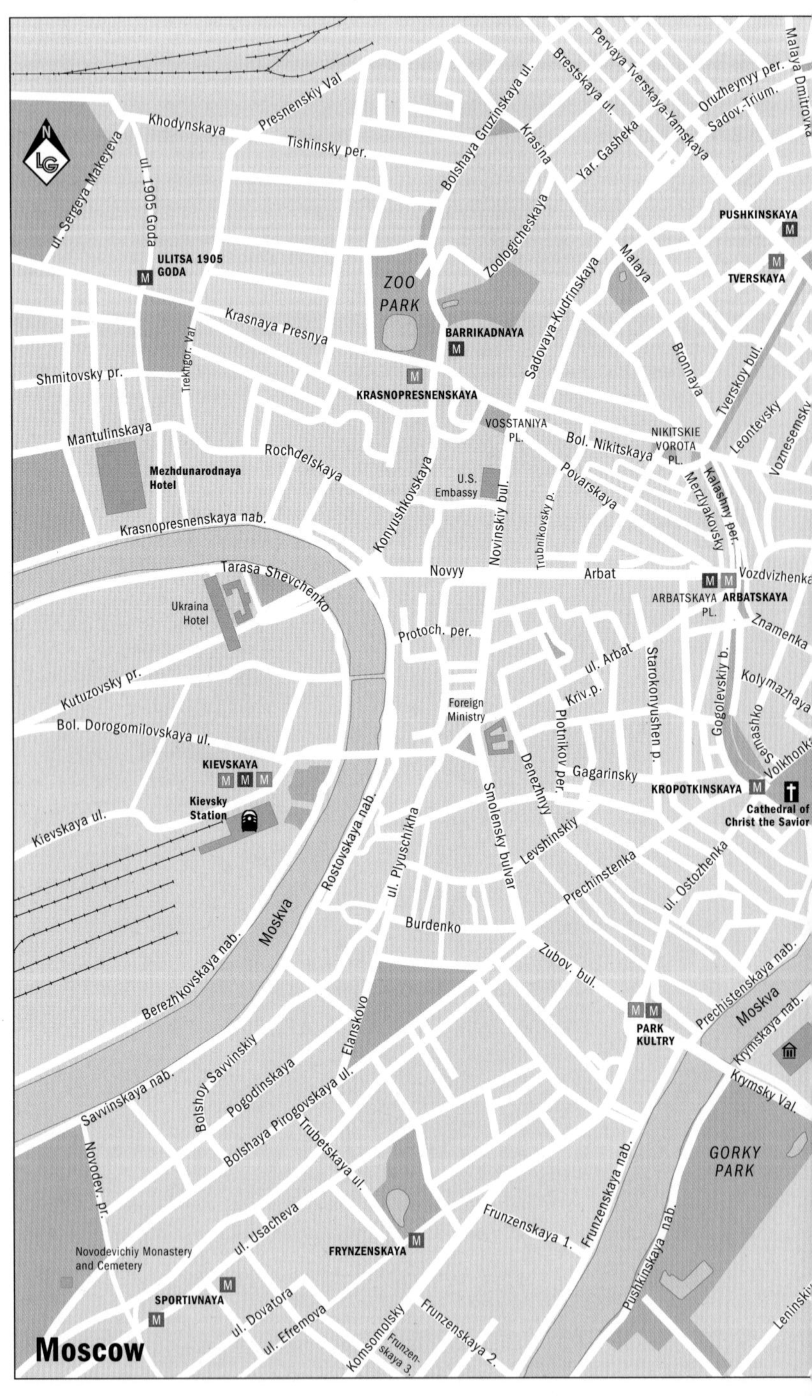
Moscow
Ulitsa 1905 Goda
Zoo Park
Barrikadnaya
Krasnopresnenskaya
Vosstaniya Pl.
Nikitskie Vorota Pl.
Pushkinskaya
Tverskaya
Mezhdunarodnaya Hotel
U.S. Embassy
Ukraina Hotel
Arbatskaya Pl.
Arbatskaya
Foreign Ministry
Kievskaya
Kievsky Station
Kropotkinskaya
Cathedral of Christ the Savior
Park Kultry
Gorky Park
Frynzenskaya
Novodevichiy Monastery and Cemetery
Sportivnaya
Moskva
Khodynskaya
Presnenskiy Val
Tishinsky per.
ul. Sergeya Makeyeva
ul. 1905 Goda
Bolshaya Gruzinskaya ul.
Brestskaya ul.
Pervaya Tverskaya-Yamskaya
Krasina
Yar. Gasheka
Oruzheynyy per.
Sadov.-Trium.
Malaya Dmitrovka
Zoologicheskaya
Sadovaya-Kudrinskaya
Malaya
Bronnaya
Tverskoy bul.
Leontevsky
Voznesemsky
Krasnaya Presnya
Trekhgor. Val
Shmitovsky pr.
Mantulinskaya
Rochdelskaya
Konyushkovskaya
Novinskiy bul.
Trubnikovsky p.
Bol. Nikitskaya
Povarskaya
Merzlyakovsky
Kalashny per.
Krasnopresnenskaya nab.
Tarasa Shevchenko
Novyy
Arbat
Vozdvizhenka
Znamenka
Protoch. per.
ul. Arbat
Kriv. p.
Starokonyushen p.
Gogolevskiy b.
Kolymazhaya
Semashko
Volkhonka
Kutuzovsky pr.
Bol. Dorogomilovskaya ul.
Plotnikov per.
Gagarinsky
Denezhny
Smolensky bulvar
Levshinskiy
Kievskaya ul.
Rostovskaya nab.
ul. Plyuschikha
Prechinstenka
ul. Ostozhenka
Burdenko
Zubov. bul.
Berezhkovskaya nab.
Elanskovo
Prechistenskaya nab.
Krymskaya nab.
Krymsky Val.
Bolshoy Savvinskiy
Pogodinskaya
Bolshaya Pirogovskaya ul.
Savvinskaya nab.
Trubetskaya ul.
Novodev. pr.
Frunzenskaya nab.
Frunzenskaya 1.
Pushkinskaya nab.
ul. Usacheva
ul. Dovatora
ul. Efremova
Komsomolsky
Frunzenskaya 3
Frunzenskaya 2.
Leninsk

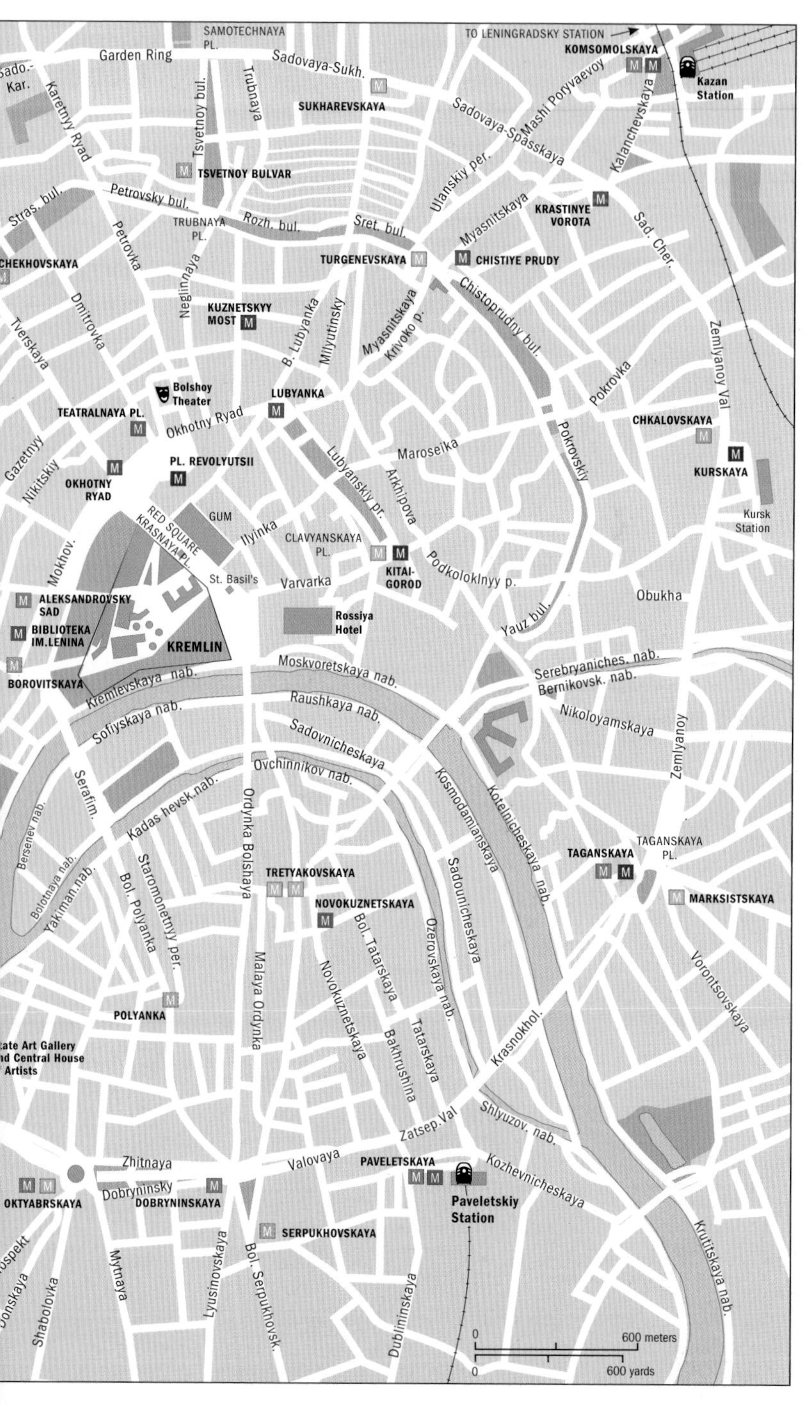

SAMOTECHNAYA PL.
TO LENINGRADSKY STATION
KOMSOMOLSKAYA
Kazan Station
Garden Ring
Sado.-Kar.
Sadovaya-Sukh.
SUKHAREVSKAYA
Sadovaya-Spasskaya
Mashi Poryvaevoy
Kalanchevskaya
Karetnyy Ryad
Tsvetnoy bul.
Trubnaya
TSVETNOY BULVAR
Ulanskiy per.
KRASTINYE VOROTA
Stras. bul.
Petrovsky bul.
TRUBNAYA PL.
Rozh. bul.
Sret. bul.
Myasnitskaya
Sad. Cher.
TURGENEVSKAYA
CHISTIYE PRUDY
CHEKHOVSKAYA
Petrovka
Neglinnaya
Chistoprudny bul.
KUZNETSKYY MOST
Dmitrovka
Tverskaya
B. Lubyanka
Milyutinsky
Myasnitskaya
Krivoko p.
Zemlyanoy Val
Pokrovka
Bolshoy Theater
LUBYANKA
TEATRALNAYA PL.
Okhotny Ryad
CHKALOVSKAYA
Pokrovskiy
Maroseika
KURSKAYA
Gazetnyy
Nikitskiy
OKHOTNY RYAD
PL. REVOLYUTSII
Lubyanskiy pr.
Arkhipova
Kursk Station
RED SQUARE KRASNAYA PL.
GUM
Ilyinka
CLAVYANSKAYA PL.
Mokhov.
KITAI-GOROD
Podkoloklnyy p.
St. Basil's
Varvarka
Obukha
ALEKSANDROVSKY SAD
BIBLIOTEKA IM.LENINA
Rossiya Hotel
Yauz bul.
KREMLIN
BOROVITSKAYA
Moskvoretskaya nab.
Serebryaniches. nab.
Bernikovsk. nab.
Kremlevskaya nab.
Raushkaya nab.
Sofiyskaya nab.
Sadovnicheskaya
Nikoloyamskaya
Zemlyanoy
Ovchinnikov nab.
Serafim.
Kadas hevsk.nab.
Kosmodamianskaya
Kotelnicheskaya nab.
Bersenev nab.
Bolotnaya nab.
Yakiman.nab.
Staromonetnyy per.
Bol. Polyanka
Ordynka Bolshaya
TRETYAKOVSKAYA
Sadovnicheskaya
TAGANSKAYA
TAGANSKAYA PL.
MARKSISTSKAYA
NOVOKUZNETSKAYA
Bol. Tatarskaya
Ozerovskaya nab.
Novokuznetskaya
Malaya Ordynka
Vorontsovskaya
POLYANKA
Tatarskaya
Bakhrushina
Krasnokhol.
Shlyuzov. nab.
Zatsep.Val
Zhitnaya
Valovaya
PAVELETSKAYA
Kozhevnicheskaya
Dobryninsky
OKTYABRSKAYA
DOBRYNINSKAYA
Paveletskiy Station
SERPUKHOVSKAYA
Krutitskaya nab.
Shabolovka
Mytnaya
Lysinovskaya
Bol. Serpukhovsk.
Dubininskaya
0
600 meters
600 yards

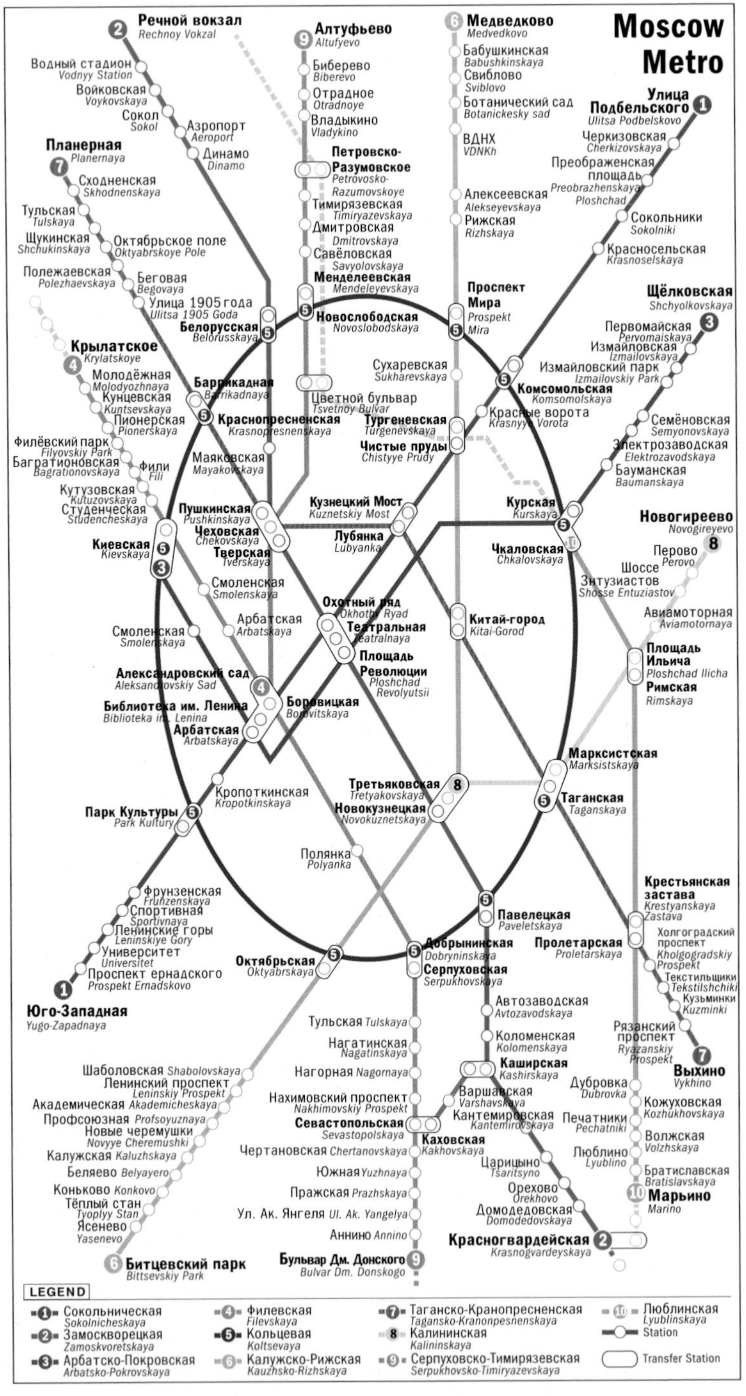

Moscow Metro
Речной вокзал
Rechnoy Vokzal
Водный стадион
Vodnyy Station
Войковская
Voykovskaya
Сокол
Sokol
Аэропорт
Aeroport
Динамо
Dinamo
Алтуфьево
Altufyevo
Бибирево
Biberevo
Отрадное
Otradnoye
Владыкино
Vladykino
Петровско-Разумовское
Petrovosko-Razumovskoye
Тимирязевская
Timiryazevskaya
Дмитровская
Dmitrovskaya
Савёловская
Savyolovskaya
Менделеевская
Mendeleyevskaya
Новослободская
Novoslobodskaya
Медведково
Medvedkovo
Бабушкинская
Babushkinskaya
Свиблово
Sviblovo
Ботанический сад
Botanickesky sad
ВДНХ
VDNKh
Алексеевская
Alekseyevskaya
Рижская
Rizhskaya
Проспект Мира
Prospekt Mira
Улица Подбельского
Ulitsa Podbelskovo
Черкизовская
Cherkizovskaya
Преображенская площадь
Preobrazhenskaya Ploshchad
Сокольники
Sokolniki
Красносельская
Krasnoselskaya
Щёлковская
Shchyolkovskaya
Первомайская
Pervomaiskaya
Измайловская
Izmailovskaya
Измайловский парк
Izmailovskiy Park
Комсомольская
Komsomolskaya
Красные ворота
Krasnyye Vorota
Семёновская
Semyonovskaya
Электрозаводская
Elektrozavodskaya
Бауманская
Baumanskaya
Планерная
Planernaya
Сходненская
Skhodnenskaya
Тульская
Tulskaya
Щукинская
Shchukinskaya
Октябрьское поле
Oktyabrskoye Pole
Полежаевская
Polezhaevskaya
Беговая
Begovaya
Улица 1905 года
Ulitsa 1905 Goda
Белорусская
Belorusskaya
Крылатское
Krylatskoye
Молодёжная
Molodyozhnaya
Кунцевская
Kuntsevskaya
Пионерская
Pionerskaya
Филёвский парк
Filyovskiy Park
Багратионовская
Bagrationovskaya
Фили
Fili
Кутузовская
Kutuzovskaya
Студенческая
Studencheskaya
Баррикадная
Barrikadnaya
Краснопресненская
Krasnopresnenskaya
Цветной бульвар
Tsvetnoy Bulvar
Сухаревская
Sukharevskaya
Тургеневская
Turgenevskaya
Чистые пруды
Chistyye Prudy
Маяковская
Mayakovskaya
Пушкинская
Pushkinskaya
Чеховская
Chekovskaya
Тверская
Tverskaya
Кузнецкий Мост
Kuznetskiy Most
Лубянка
Lubyanka
Курская
Kurskaya
Чкаловская
Chkalovskaya
Новогиреево
Novogireyevo
Перово
Perovo
Шоссе Энтузиастов
Shosse Entuziastov
Авиамоторная
Aviamotornaya
Киевская
Kievskaya
Смоленская
Smolenskaya
Арбатская
Arbatskaya
Смоленская
Smolenskaya
Охотный ряд
Okhotny Ryad
Театральная
Teatralnaya
Площадь Революции
Ploshchad Revolyutsii
Китай-город
Kitai-Gorod
Площадь Ильича
Ploshchad Ilicha
Римская
Rimskaya
Александровский сад
Aleksandrovskiy Sad
Библиотека им. Ленина
Biblioteka im. Lenina
Арбатская
Arbatskaya
Боровицкая
Borovitskaya
Марксистская
Marksistskaya
Таганская
Taganskaya
Кропоткинская
Kropotkinskaya
Парк Культуры
Park Kultury
Третьяковская
Tretyakovskaya
Новокузнецкая
Novokuznetskaya
Полянка
Polyanka
Крестьянская застава
Krestyanskaya Zastava
Пролетарская
Proletarskaya
Холгоградский проспект
Kholgogradskiy Prospekt
Текстильщики
Tekstilshchiki
Кузьминки
Kuzminki
Рязанский проспект
Ryazanskiy Prospekt
Выхино
Vykhino
Павелецкая
Paveletskaya
Фрунзенская
Frunzenskaya
Спортивная
Sportivnaya
Ленинские горы
Leninskiye Gory
Университет
Universitet
Проспект ернадского
Prospekt Ernadskovo
Юго-Западная
Yugo-Zapadnaya
Октябрьская
Oktyabrskaya
Добрынинская
Dobryninskaya
Серпуховская
Serpukhovskaya
Автозаводская
Avtozavodskaya
Коломенская
Kolomenskaya
Каширская
Kashirskaya
Варшавская
Varshavskaya
Кантемировская
Kantemirovskaya
Царицыно
Tsaritsyno
Орехово
Orekhovo
Домодедовская
Domodedovskaya
Красногвардейская
Krasnogvardeyskaya
Тульская Tulskaya
Нагатинская
Nagatinskaya
Нагорная Nagornaya
Нахимовский проспект
Nakhimovskiy Prospekt
Севастопольская
Sevastopolskaya
Каховская
Kakhovskaya
Чертановская Chertanovskaya
Южная Yuzhnaya
Пражская Prazhskaya
Ул. Ак. Янгеля Ul. Ak. Yangelya
Аннино Annino
Бульвар Дм. Донского
Bulvar Dm. Donskogo
Шаболовская Shabolovskaya
Ленинский проспект
Leninskiy Prospekt
Академическая Akademicheskaya
Профсоюзная Profsoyuznaya
Новые черемушки
Novyye Cheremushki
Калужская Kaluzhskaya
Беляево Belyayero
Коньково Konkovo
Тёплый стан
Tyoplyy Stan
Ясенево
Yasenevo
Битцевский парк
Bittsevskiy Park
Дубровка
Dubrovka
Кожуховская
Kozhukhovskaya
Печатники
Pechatniki
Волжская
Volzhskaya
Люблино
Lyublino
Братиславская
Bratislavskaya
Марьино
Marino
LEGEND
Сокольническая
Sokolnicheskaya
Замоскворецкая
Zamoskvoretskaya
Арбатско-Покровская
Arbatsko-Pokrovskaya
Филевская
Filevskaya
Кольцевая
Koltsevaya
Калужско-Рижская
Kauzhsko-Rizhskaya
Таганско-Кранопресненская
Tagansko-Kranopresnenskaya
Калининская
Kalininskaya
Серпуховско-Тимирязевская
Serpukhovsko-Timiryazevskaya
Люблинская
Lyublinskaya
Station
Transfer Station

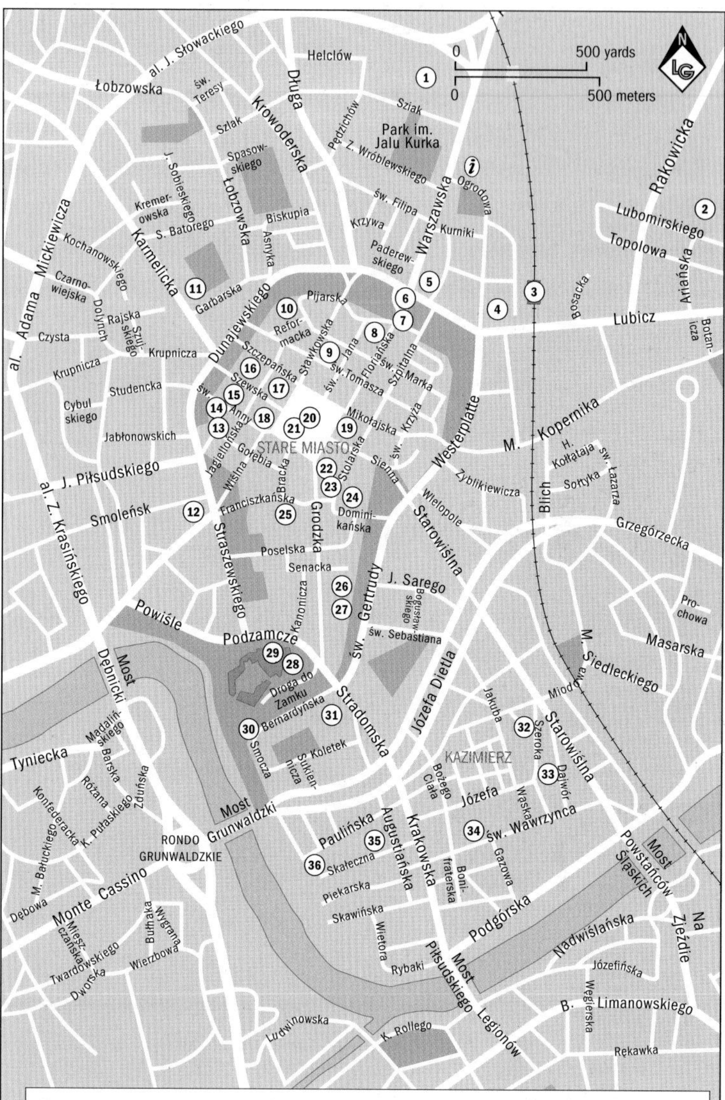

Central Kraków

Akademia Ekonomiczna, **2**
Almatur Office, **22**
Barbican, **6**
Bernardine Church, **31**
Bus Station, **4**
Carmelite Church, **11**
Cartoon Gallery, **9**
Collegium Maius, **14**
Corpus Christi Church, **34**
Czartoryski Art Museum, **8**
Dominican Church, **24**
Dragon Statue, **30**
Filharmonia, **12**
Franciscan Church, **25**
Grunwald Memorial, **5**
History Museum of Kraków, **17**
Jewish Cemetery, **32**
Jewish Museum, **33**
Kraków Glowny Station, **3**
Monastery of the Reformed Franciscans, **10**
Pauline Church, **36**
Police Station, **18**
Politechnika Krakowska, **1**
St. Andrew's Church, **27**
St. Anne's Church, **15**
St. Catherine's Church, **35**
St. Florian's Gate, **7**
St. Mary's Church, **19**
St. Peter and Paul Church, **26**
Stary Teatr (Old Theater), **16**
Sukiennice (Cloth Hall), **20**
Town Hall, **21**
United States Embassy, **23**
University Museum, **13**
Wawel Castle, **28**
Wawel Cathedral, **29**

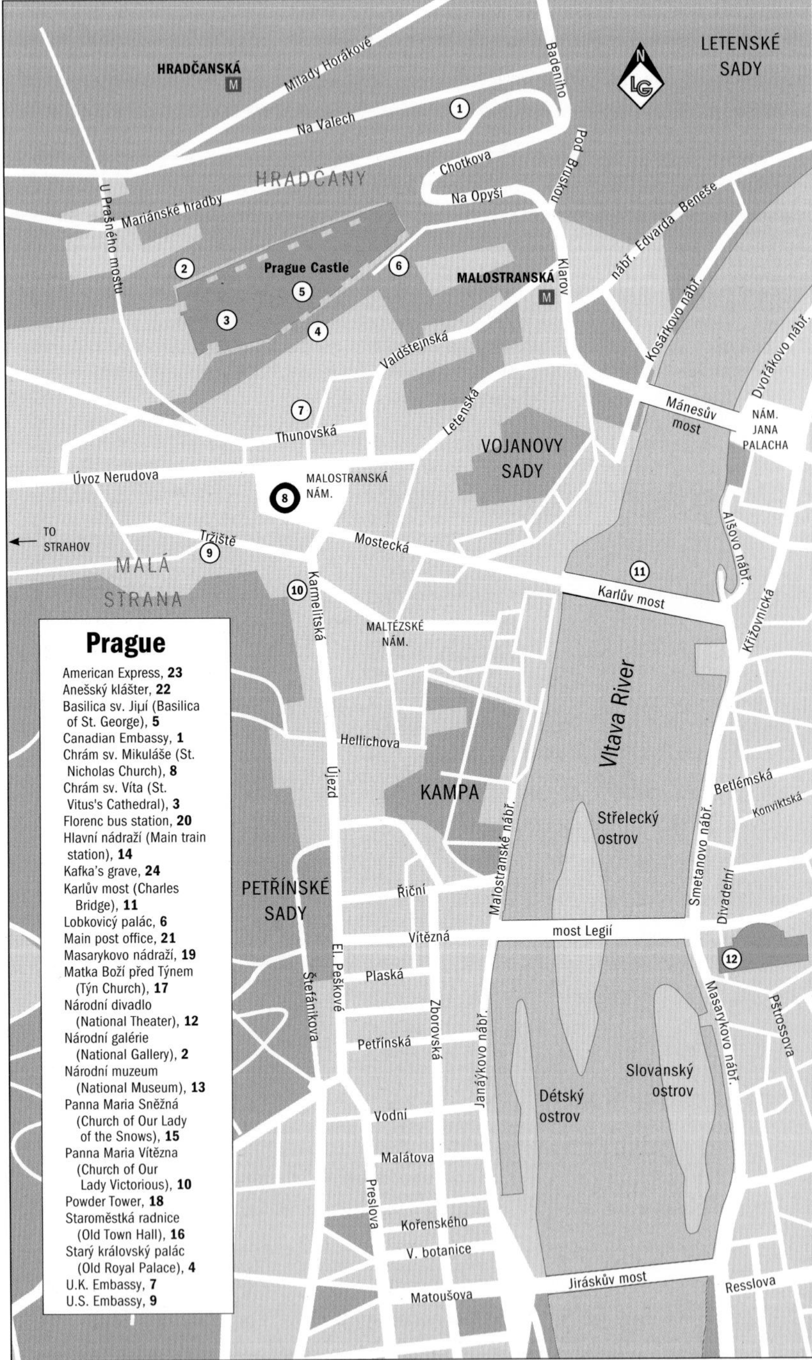

Prague
American Express, 23
Anešský klášter, 22
Basilica sv. Jiµí (Basilica of St. George), 5
Canadian Embassy, 1
Chrám sv. Mikuláše (St. Nicholas Church), 8
Chrám sv. Víta (St. Vitus's Cathedral), 3
Florenc bus station, 20
Hlavní nádraží (Main train station), 14
Kafka's grave, 24
Karlův most (Charles Bridge), 11
Lobkovicý palác, 6
Main post office, 21
Masarykovo nádraží, 19
Matka Boží před Týnem (Týn Church), 17
Národní divadlo (National Theater), 12
Národní galérie (National Gallery), 2
Národní muzeum (National Museum), 13
Panna Maria Sněžná (Church of Our Lady of the Snows), 15
Panna Maria Vítězna (Church of Our Lady Victorious), 10
Powder Tower, 18
Staroměstká radnice (Old Town Hall), 16
Starý královský palác (Old Royal Palace), 4
U.K. Embassy, 7
U.S. Embassy, 9
HRADČANSKÁ
M
LETENSKÉ SADY
Milady Horákové
Badeniho
Na Valech
Pod Bruskou
Chotkova
HRADČANY
Na Opyši
U Prašného mostu
Mariánské hradby
nábř. Edvarda Beneše
Prague Castle
MALOSTRANSKÁ
Klárov
Kosárkovo nábř.
Dvořákovo nábř.
Valdštejnská
Letenská
Mánesův most
NÁM. JANA PALACHA
Thunovská
VOJANOVY SADY
Úvoz Nerudova
MALOSTRANSKÁ NÁM.
TO STRAHOV
Tržiště
Mostecká
Alšovo nábř.
MALÁ STRANA
Karmelitská
Karlův most
Křižovnická
MALTÉZSKÉ NÁM.
Vltava River
Hellichova
Újezd
Betlémská
KAMPA
Konviktská
Malostranské nábř.
Střelecký ostrov
Smetanovo nábř.
PETŘÍNSKÉ SADY
Říční
Divadelní
Vítězná
most Legií
El. Peškové
Plaská
Štefánikova
Zborovská
Masarykovo nábř.
Pštrossova
Petřínská
Janáýkovo nábř.
Slovanský ostrov
Dětský ostrov
Vodní
Malátova
Preslova
Kořenského
V. botanice
Jiráskův most
Resslova
Matoušova

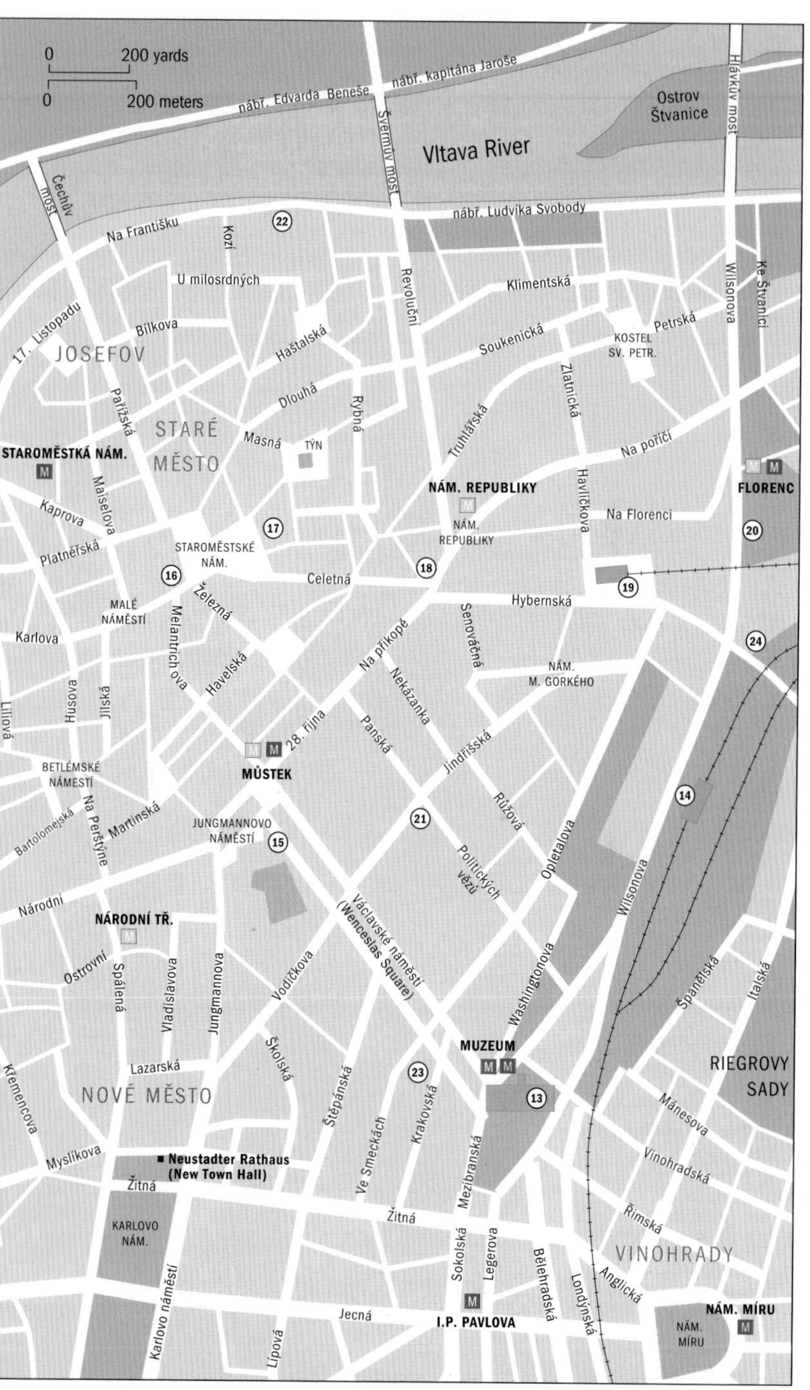

0 200 yards
0 200 meters
Vltava River
Ostrov Štvanice
nábř. Edvarda Beneše
nábř. kapitána Jaroše
nábř. Ludvíka Svobody
Čechův most
Švermův most
Hlávkův most
Na Františku
Kozí
U milosrdných
Revoluční
Klimentská
Wilsonova
Ke Štvanici
17. Listopadu
Bílkova
Haštalská
Soukenická
Petrská
KOSTEL SV. PETR.
JOSEFOV
Pařížská
Dlouhá
Rybná
Zlatnická
Truhlářská
STARÉ MĚSTO
Masná
TÝN
Na poříčí
STAROMĚSTSKÁ NÁM.
Maiselova
NÁM. REPUBLIKY
Havlíčkova
FLORENC
Kaprova
Na Florenci
Platnéřská
STAROMĚSTSKÉ NÁM.
Celetná
Železná
MALÉ NÁMĚSTÍ
Melantrichova
Hybernská
Senovážná
Karlova
Na příkopě
Havelská
Nekázanka
NÁM. M. GORKÉHO
Liliová
Husova
Jilská
28. října
Panská
Jindřišská
MŮSTEK
BETLÉMSKÉ NÁMĚSTÍ
Bartolomějská
Na Perštýně
Martinská
JUNGMANNOVO NÁMĚSTÍ
Růžová
Opletalova
Politických vězňů
Wilsonova
Národní
NÁRODNÍ TŘ.
Václavské náměstí (Wencesias Square)
Ostrovní
Spálená
Vladislavova
Jungmannova
Vodičkova
Washingtonova
Španělská
Italská
Školská
MUZEUM
Lazarská
Štěpánská
RIEGROVY SADY
NOVÉ MĚSTO
Křemencova
Ve Smečkách
Krakovská
Mezibranská
Mánesova
Myslíkova
Neustadter Rathaus (New Town Hall)
Vinohradská
Žitná
Žitná
KARLOVO NÁM.
Římská
Sokolská
Legerova
Bělehradská
VINOHRADY
Karlovo náměstí
Londýnská
Anglická
Jecná
I.P. PAVLOVA
NÁM. MÍRU
NÁM. MÍRU
Lípová
13
14
15
16
17
18
19
20
21
22
23
24

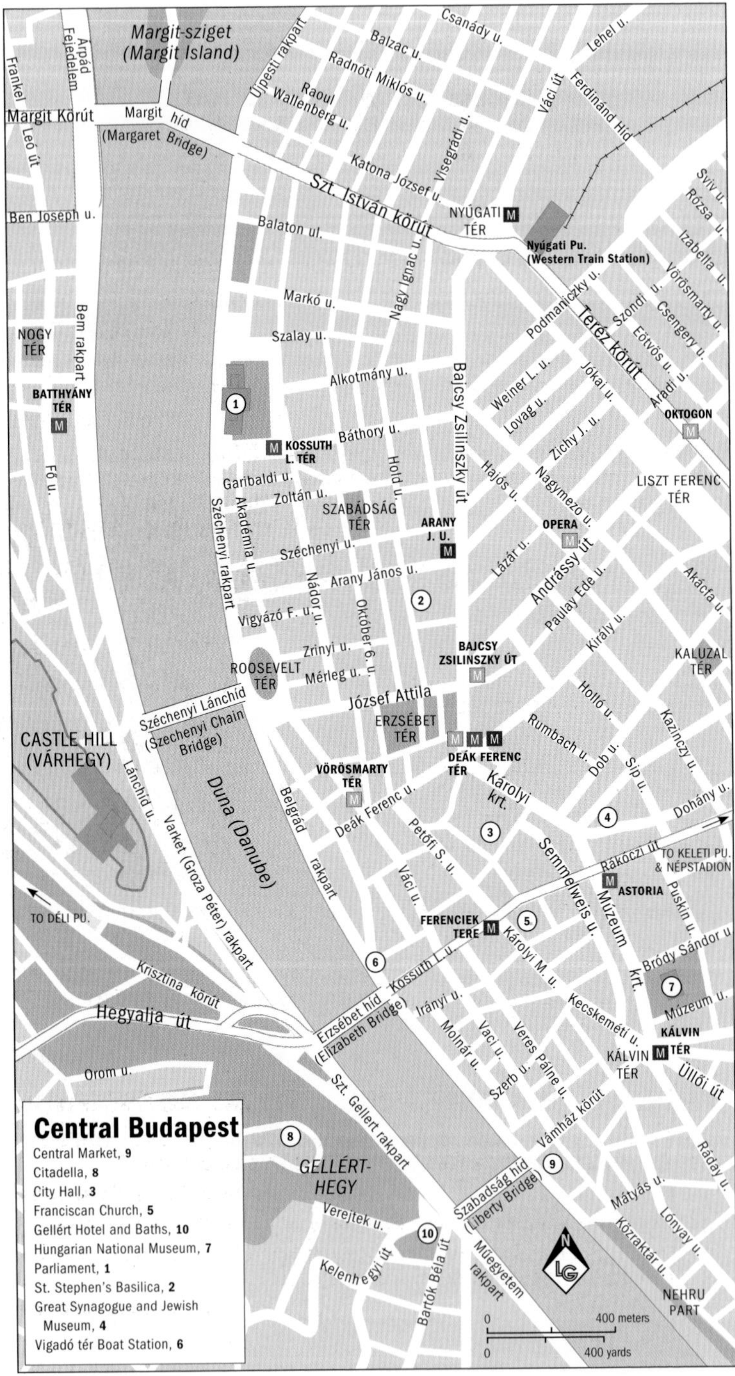
Central Budapest
Central Market, 9
Citadella, 8
City Hall, 3
Franciscan Church, 5
Gellért Hotel and Baths, 10
Hungarian National Museum, 7
Parliament, 1
St. Stephen's Basilica, 2
Great Synagogue and Jewish Museum, 4
Vigadó tér Boat Station, 6
Margit-sziget
(Margit Island)
Margit híd
(Margaret Bridge)
Margit Körút
Szt. István körút
NYÚGATI TÉR
Nyúgati Pu.
(Western Train Station)
Teréz körút
OKTOGON
LISZT FERENC TÉR
OPERA
Andrássy út
KOSSUTH L. TÉR
SZABÁDSÁG TÉR
ARANY J. U.
BATTHYÁNY TÉR
NOGY TÉR
ROOSEVELT TÉR
BAJCSY ZSILINSZKY ÚT
Bajcsy Zsilinszky út
József Attila
ERZSÉBET TÉR
DEÁK FERENC TÉR
VÖRÖSMARTY TÉR
KALUZAL TÉR
Széchenyi Lánchíd
(Szechenyi Chain Bridge)
CASTLE HILL
(VÁRHEGY)
Duna (Danube)
Károlyi krt.
Rákóczi út
TO KELETI PU. & NÉPSTADION
ASTORIA
FERENCIEK TERE
Múzeum krt.
KÁLVIN TÉR
Üllői út
TO DÉLI PU.
Krisztina körút
Hegyalja út
Erzsébet híd
(Elizabeth Bridge)
Szt. Gellert rakpart
GELLÉRT-HEGY
Szabadság híd
(Liberty Bridge)
Vámház körút
NEHRU PART
Műegyetem rakpart
Bartók Béla út
0 400 meters
0 400 yards

LET'S GO

■ PAGES PACKED WITH ESSENTIAL INFORMATION

"Value-packed, unbeatable, accurate, and comprehensive."

—The Los Angeles Times

"The guides are aimed not only at young budget travelers but at the independent traveler; a sort of streetwise cookbook for traveling alone."

—The New York Times

"Unbeatable; good sight-seeing advice; up-to-date info on restaurants, hotels, and inns; a commitment to money-saving travel; and a wry style that brightens nearly every page."

—The Washington Post

■ THE BEST TRAVEL BARGAINS IN YOUR BUDGET

"All the dirt, dirt cheap."

—People

"Let's Go follows the creed that you don't have to toss your life's savings to the wind to travel—unless you want to."

—The Salt Lake Tribune

■ REAL ADVICE FOR REAL EXPERIENCES

"The writers seem to have experienced every rooster-packed bus and lunar-surfaced mattress about which they write."

—The New York Times

"[Let's Go's] devoted updaters really walk the walk (and thumb the ride, and trek the trail). Learn how to fish, haggle, find work—anywhere."

—Food & Wine

"A world-wise traveling companion—always ready with friendly advice and helpful hints, all sprinkled with a bit of wit."

—The Philadelphia Inquirer

■ A GUIDE WITH A SPIRIT AND A SOCIAL CONSCIENCE

"Lighthearted and sophisticated, informative and fun to read. [Let's Go] helps the novice traveler navigate like a knowledgeable old hand."

—Atlanta Journal-Constitution

"The serious mission at the book's core reveals itself in exhortations to respect the culture and the environment—and, if possible, to visit as a volunteer, a student, or a teacher rather than a tourist."

—San Francisco Chronicle

LET'S GO PUBLICATIONS

TRAVEL GUIDES

Australia 8th edition
Austria & Switzerland 12th edition
Brazil 1st edition
Britain 2006
California 10th edition
Central America 9th edition
Chile 2nd edition
China 5th edition
Costa Rica 2nd edition
Eastern Europe 12th edition
Ecuador 1st edition
Egypt 2nd edition
Europe 2006
France 2006
Germany 12th edition
Greece 8th edition
Hawaii 3rd edition
India & Nepal 8th edition
Ireland 12th edition
Israel 4th edition
Italy 2006
Japan 1st edition
Mexico 21st edition
Middle East 4th edition
New Zealand 7th edition
Peru 1st edition
Puerto Rico 2nd edition
South Africa 5th edition
Southeast Asia 9th edition
Spain & Portugal 2006
Thailand 2nd edition
Turkey 5th edition
USA 23rd edition
Vietnam 1st edition
Western Europe 2006

ROADTRIP GUIDE

Roadtripping USA

ADVENTURE GUIDES

Alaska 1st edition
Pacific Northwest 1st edition
Southwest USA 3rd edition

CITY GUIDES

Amsterdam 4th edition
Barcelona 3rd edition
Boston 4th edition
London 15th edition
New York City 15th edition
Paris 13th edition
Rome 12th edition
San Francisco 4th edition
Washington, D.C. 13th edition

POCKET CITY GUIDES

Amsterdam
Berlin
Boston
Chicago
London
New York City
Paris
San Francisco
Venice
Washington, D.C.

LET'S GO EUROPE 2006

Jeremy Todd Editor
Virginia Fisher Associate Editor
Jody M. Kelman Associate Editor
Sarah Inez Levy Associate Editor
Meghan Sherlock Associate Editor
Stefan Zebrowski-Rubin Associate Editor

Kelly Whelan Heuer Map Editor
Laura E. Martin Managing Editor

St. Martin's Press New York

HELPING LET'S GO. If you want to share your discoveries, suggestions, or corrections, please drop us a line. We read every piece of correspondence, whether a postcard, a 10-page email, or a coconut. **Address mail to:**

Let's Go: Europe
67 Mount Auburn St.
Cambridge, MA 02138
USA

Visit Let's Go at **http://www.letsgo.com,** or send email to:

feedback@letsgo.com
Subject: "Let's Go: Europe"

In addition to the invaluable travel advice our readers share with us, many are kind enough to offer their services as researchers or editors. Unfortunately, our charter enables us to employ only currently enrolled Harvard students.

Distributed outside the USA and Canada by Macmillan.

ISBN: 0-312-34894-0
EAN: 978-0-312-34894-6
First edition
10 9 8 7 6 5 4 3 2 1

Let's Go: Europe is written by Let's Go Publications, 67 Mount Auburn St., Cambridge, MA 02138, USA.

HOW TO USE THIS BOOK

Hello, friend. This book was written with one goal in mind: providing the most accurate and useful information possible to travelers who are preparing to tackle the infinitely rewarding adventure that is travel in Europe. This effort has—we hope you'll find—paid off handsomely; we're extremely proud of the tips our researchers have come up with on topics as varied as the best way to get from Bruges to Budapest and how to tell the good gelato from the bad. More to the point, we hope you'll find that the investment you've made in this book will be returned many times over, and not only through budget travel hints. This guide will not only keep you from busting your wallet; it will help you better navigate all facets of your Europe adventure, regardless of your budget, interests, or itinerary.

Things are changing in Europe: You can now travel between half the countries on the continent without so much as pulling out a passport, and you're more likely to come across an Internet terminal than a coin-operated pay phone. Whether you're a long-time expat or an first-time backpacker, the freshly reformatted and always updated *Let's Go: Europe 2006* will keep you in good company.

ORGANIZATION. *Let's Go: Europe 2006* is arranged to make the information you need easy to find. The **Discover** chapter offers Europe-wide highlights, tips on when to travel (including a calendar of festivals), and suggested itineraries. The **Essentials** chapter details the nitty-gritty of money, communications, passports, dirty laundry, and more—everything you'll need to plan your trip and stay safe on the road. The **Transportation** section will get you to and around Europe, while the ensuing **Beyond Tourism** chapter gives advice on how to work or volunteer your way across the continent. Next come 32 jam-packed **country chapters,** from Austria to Ukraine; each begins with essential information on traveling in that specific country. Don't overlook the **language phrasebook** (p. 1056), offering a crash course in the local tongues you're sure to encounter.

PRICE RANGES AND RANKINGS. Our 50 indefatigable researchers list establishments in order of value from best to worst; absolute favorites are denoted by the *Let's Go* thumbs-up (☒). Since the best value does not always mean the cheapest price, we have incorporated a system of **price ranges (❶❷❸❹❺)** into our coverage of accommodations and restaurants. At a glance, you can compare the cost of a night's stay in towns a mile apart or halfway across the country. The price ranges for each country can be found in the introductory sections of each chapter, and for more information on what to expect from each ranking, see p. xix.

NEW FEATURES. Long-time readers will notice a number of other changes in our series, most notably the sidebars that accompany much of our coverage. At the end of the Discover chapter, you'll also find a series of longer **Scholarly Articles** focused on issues affecting Europe as a whole. Whether read on a long train ride or in a quiet hostel, we hope these articles will inform as well as entertain.

A NOTE TO OUR READERS. The information for this book was gathered by *Let's Go* researchers from May through August of 2005. Each listing is based on one researcher's opinion, formed during his or her visit at a particular time. Those traveling at other times may have different experiences since prices, dates, hours, and conditions are always subject to change. You are urged to check the facts presented in this book beforehand to avoid inconvenience and surprises.

CONTENTS

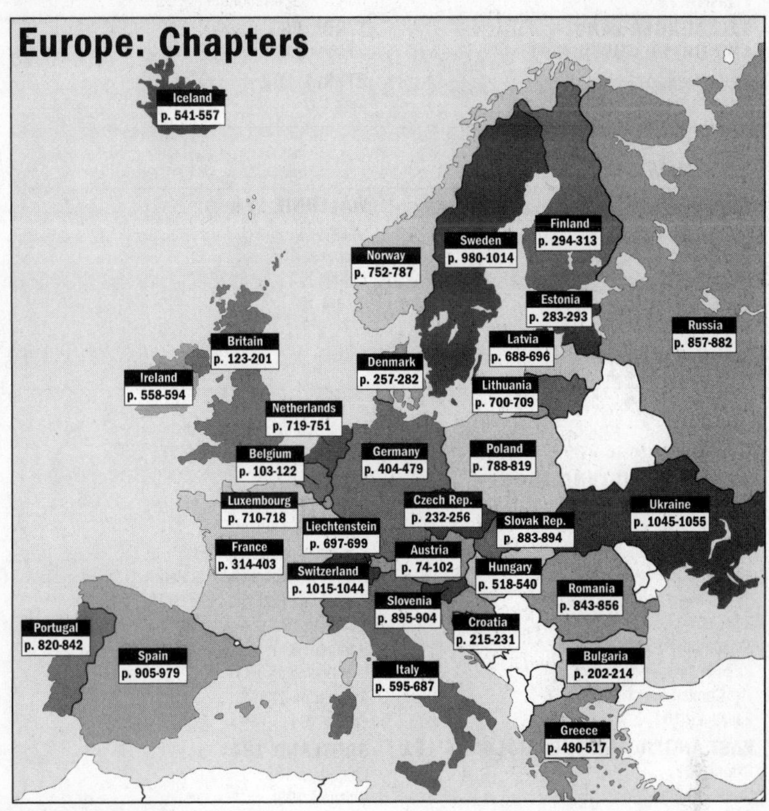

Europe: Chapters
Iceland
p. 541-557
Finland
p. 294-313
Sweden
p. 980-1014
Norway
p. 752-787
Estonia
p. 283-293
Russia
p. 857-882
Latvia
p. 688-696
Britain
p. 123-201
Denmark
p. 257-282
Ireland
p. 558-594
Lithuania
p. 700-709
Netherlands
p. 719-751
Belgium
p. 103-122
Germany
p. 404-479
Poland
p. 788-819
Luxembourg
p. 710-718
Czech Rep.
p. 232-256
Ukraine
p. 1045-1055
Slovak Rep.
p. 883-894
Liechtenstein
p. 697-699
France
p. 314-403
Austria
p. 74-102
Switzerland
p. 1015-1044
Hungary
p. 518-540
Romania
p. 843-856
Slovenia
p. 895-904
Croatia
p. 215-231
Portugal
p. 820-842
Spain
p. 905-979
Bulgaria
p. 202-214
Italy
p. 595-687
Greece
p. 480-517

RESEARCHER-WRITERS

Candace Bertotti *Berlin, Northern Germany, Luxembourg*

Candace, a yoga fanatic and dedicated vegan, navigated her way through the urban landscape of Berlin before stopping to savor the marzipan in the beautiful cities of northern Germany and to climb through the casemates of Luxembourg City. With a keen eye for detail and an instinct for bargain-hunting, Candace unearthed offbeat attractions that even her editors hadn't heard about, chatting up locals as she went.

Ieva Chaleckyte *Reykjavík, Finland, Sweden*

This tenacious, take-no-prisoners Lithuanian fought off drunken Finns during midsummer and all-too-friendly hostelers in Sweden, even as she did battle with her ornery stone-age laptop. Bronzed and lean from biking back-road Scandinavia, Ieva kept her editors exceedingly happy, churning out tight, detailed prose, color-coded map edits, and laugh-out-loud travelogues in between soaks in Reykjavík's thermal baths and early morning Swedish ferry hops.

Shelley Jiang *Austria, Bavaria*

A caffeine connoisseur and dazzling writer, Shelley whirled through elegant Vienna and boisterous Munich, castle-hopped along the Romantic Road, and followed Mozart's footsteps in Salzburg before tromping through the Austrian Alps and braving the summer snow. Snapping gorgeous photographs wherever she went, this editorial goddess sent back reams of beautiful, beautiful prose, ensuring that even the European wilderness was punctuated by philosophy.

Laura Maludzinski *Switzerland, Liechtenstein, Germany*

This cheerful runner and veteran researcher ripped through her fast-paced itinerary with style, partying in Vaduz with Liechtenstein's professional soccer team before paragliding around the Matterhorn and scaling the walls of a glacier in Interlaken. Laura impressed on all fronts, digging up deal after deal as she traipsed through the Rhine Valley and sending Swiss chocolate back to her all-too-grateful editors along with every batch of amazing copy.

Allen Pope *Belgium, Denmark*

This boy-wonder from Newton, MA channeled his well-honed eye for detail into precise prose as he traipsed through Belgium and Denmark. Bound (for eternity) to his editor in (pretend) matrimony, Allen ensured marital bliss through his prompt delivery of crisp copy and obsessively detailed maps—even if his rapturous descriptions of Brussels's ornate Grand-Place and Denmark's surreal Skagen did make her jealous at times.

Lauri Tähitinen *Rural Iceland, Norway*

Lauri, an intrepid globetrotter from Finland, charmed (or perhaps muscled) his way across rural Iceland and through the fjords of Norway. Obsessed with outing the overtouristed, Lauri used his easy wit to strike up friendships that took him to the farthest reaches of every place he stopped—from the private bars of Trondheim to the polar-bear-filled wilds of Svalbard. In his precious downtime, this ambitious polyglot relaxed by learning Norwegian.

REGIONAL EDITORS AND RESEARCHER-WRITERS

LET'S GO: AMSTERDAM

Dustin A. Lewis *Editor*
Eric Philip Lesser *Researcher-Writer*
Haven Thompson *Researcher-Writer*

LET'S GO: BRITAIN

Annie M. Lowrey *Editor*
Eoghan O'Donnell *Associate Editor*
Madeleine Bäverstam *Researcher-Writer*
Mary Kate Burke *Researcher-Writer*
Lindsay Crouse *Researcher-Writer*
John Arthur Epley *Researcher-Writer*
Terrence Costello *Researcher-Writer*

LET'S GO: EASTERN EUROPE

Jane Yager *Editor*
Alexander Pasternack *Associate Editor*
Alexander Rothman *Associate Editor*
Amelia "Molly" Atlas *Researcher-Writer*
Piotr Brzezinski *Researcher-Writer*
Jason Campbell *Researcher-Writer*
Neasa Coll *Researcher-Writer*
Alexie Harper *Researcher-Writer*
Jordan Hylden *Researcher-Writer*
Justin Jennings *Researcher-Writer*
Jennifer Kan *Researcher-Writer*
Stephanie O'Rourke *Researcher-Writer*

LET'S GO: FRANCE

Claire Pasternack *Editor*
Carl Hughes *Associate Editor*
Samantha Gelfand *Associate Editor*
Amanda Gann *Researcher-Writer*
Geoffrey S. Johnston *Researcher-Writer*
Malgorzata Maria Kurjanska *Researcher-Writer*
Brandon Presser *Researcher-Writer*
Cindy Obst *Researcher-Writer*
Julia Reischel *Researcher-Writer*
Ashley Shuyler *Researcher-Writer*

LET'S GO: GREECE

Julia Bonnheim *Editor*
Simon William Vozick-Levinson *Associate Editor*
B. Britt Caputo *Researcher-Writer*
Alex Economou *Researcher-Writer*
Mishy Harman *Researcher-Writer*
Kevin Paik *Researcher-Writer*
Laurie Schnidman *Researcher-Writer*
Jenny Wong *Researcher-Writer*

LET'S GO: IRELAND

Rachel Nolan *Editor*
Kevin Joseph Feeney *Associate Editor*
Emma Beavers *Researcher-Writer*
Kate Cosgrove *Researcher-Writer*
Margo Hoppin *Researcher-Writer*
Christopher Schonberger *Researcher-Writer*

LET'S GO: ITALY

Inna Livitz *Editor*
Anna A. Mattson-DiCecca *Associate Editor*
Samantha Gelfand *Associate Editor*
Lauren Holmes *Researcher-Writer*
Morgan Kruger *Researcher-Writer*
Diana Limbach *Researcher-Writer*
Stephanie Plant *Researcher-Writer*
Jennifer Rugani *Researcher-Writer*
Chris Starr *Researcher-Writer*

LET'S GO: LONDON

David Blazar *Editor*
Amber Johnson *Researcher-Writer*
Yaran Noti *Researcher-Writer*

LET'S GO: SPAIN AND PORTUGAL

Diana Garvin *Editor*
Silvia Killingsworth *Associate Editor*
Lucy Lindsey *Associate Editor*
Emily Chau *Researcher-Writer*
Peter Ekman *Researcher-Writer*
Steve Fiascone *Researcher-Writer*
Anthony Johnson *Researcher-Writer*
Zhenzhen Lu *Researcher-Writer*
Ines Pacheco *Researcher-Writer*
Emma Sevitt *Researcher-Writer*

CONTRIBUTING WRITERS

Patrice M. Dabrowski *Celebrating the New Europe (p. 6)*

Dr. Patrice M. Dabrowski is a postdoctoral fellow at Brown University's Watson Institute for International Studies.

Derek Glanz *Maintaining Borders in an Expanding EU (p. 7)*

Derek Glanz was the editor of Let's Go: Spain & Portugal 1998. He is a doctoral candidate in political science at the University of North Carolina at Chapel Hill.

Barbara Richter *Test Tubes and Teutons (p. 73)*

Barbara Richter was a Researcher-Writer for *Let's Go: Austria and Switzerland 2005.*

Editor
Jeremy Todd
Associate Editors
Virginia Fisher, Jody M. Kelman, Sarah Inez Levy, Meghan Sherlock, Stefan Zebrowski-Rubin
Managing Editor
Laura E. Martin
Map Editor
Kelly Whelan Heuer
Typesetter
Christine Yokoyama

LET'S GO

Publishing Director
Seth Robinson
Editor-in-Chief
Stuart J. Robinson
Production Manager
Alexandra Hoffer
Cartography Manager
Katherine J. Thompson
Editorial Managers
Rachel M. Burke, Ashley Eva Isaacson, Laura E. Martin
Financial Manager
Adrienne Taylor Gerken
Publicity Manager
Alexandra C. Stanek
Personnel Manager
Ella M. Steim
Production Associate
Ansel S. Witthaus
IT Director
Jeffrey Hoffman Yip
Director of E-Commerce
Michael Reckhow
Office Coordinator
Matthew Gibson

Director of Advertising Sales
Jillian N. London
Senior Advertising Associates
Jessica C.L. Chiu, Katya M. Golovchenko, Mohammed J. Herzallah
Advertising Graphic Designer
Emily E. Maston

President
Caleb J. Merkl
General Manager
Robert B. Rombauer
Assistant General Manager
Anne E. Chisholm

ACKNOWLEDGMENTS

TEAM EUROPE THANKS: Our researchers, who left no laundromat unturned, Kelly, for leaving no laundromat unplotted, and Laura, who is in many ways like a laundromat for books stained with bad format and lousy writing. Also, in—never you fret—a definite and particular order: Adrienne, Alexandra, Alex, Also Alex, Ashley, Ella, google, Jane, Joanna, Laura, Seth, and Stuart.

JEREMY THANKS: Laura, who is the best; Virginia, for braving the borderland, Jody, for conjuring polar bears and cutting mercilessly, Sarah, who will undoubtedly make San Francisco even more pleasant, Meghan, who almost made me appreciate Germany, and Stefan, last in the AE alphabet race but otherwise first-rate in every regard; to my parents, whose support is more valuable than they can possibly know; and Katherine, who is always worth coming back to.

VIRGINIA THANKS: Dan, for bringing us all together; Jeremy, for stepping in with *schnell* and style; Laura, for caffeine and primal screams; Meghan, Jody, Stefan, and Sarah, my unstoppable teammates; Julia and Simon, the Helladic Heroes; Sonja, Matu, and Ensio, the Hipster Bloc; Dashenka, for stopping in Cambridge on your world tour; Silas, for hosting the Californian getaway; Noah, the inimitable Africa correspondent; and Mama, Papa, Buggi, and Dot, for holdin' down the fort.

JODY THANKS: First and foremost, thanks to the incredible RWs, Allen, Ieva, and Lauri, who pushed themselves to the limit for this book. Next, in no particular order, thanks to my AE partners-in-crime, for our days downing sour candy by the handful; Jeremy, for squirrels, clowns, *schnell*, and unending patience; Dan, for envelope-licking parties; Laura, for un-italicizing commas with love; and of course, Team Eastern Europe, for the whisperings across the wall. Finally, thanks to Barb, goddess of sushi, and to Otis, nester extraordinaire.

SARAH THANKS: Laura, who is a superwoman; Jeremy, who would be our desert island editor, too; Jody, Meghan, Stefan, and Virginia, who are simply vibrant and who kept me smiling; Wales, for not believing in vowels; Mom, Dad, and Becca, because it's easy to go on adventures with so much love to come back to; and Oren, because it's easy to leave home when home is sitting next to you all the way.

MEGHAN THANKS: Jeremy, for witty titles and caffeine enablement; Laura, for her extreme generosity with thin mints and sharp eye for detail; Dan, for getting everything started; my wonderful teammates, Jody, Stefan, Sarah, and Virginia, for jumping parties and never letting me settle for a mere "vibrant"; Shelley, Laura, and Candace, who wrote beautiful things about beautiful places and me feel as if I were travelling, too; the Eastern Europe bookteam, for the liberation of Fruit by the People; and especially Mom, Dad, and Will, who are always there for me.

STEFAN THANKS: Henderson and my family, for constant support; hugs go a long way. The AEs for their dedication and comradery: Starbucks Jody, the nutter neighbour/cutter queen, Sarah, with a spirit that could melt rock, Meghan, Fruit-by-the-Foot addict and marzipan supplier, and Virginia, agile redhead and jumper extraordinaire. Jeremy, the LG vet who came to the rescue and became our hero. Laura for positive reinforcement and fine-toothed edits. EEUR, for playing the accent thick. LG for giving me a thirst for travel and a fresh agility with words.

KELLY THANKS: Katherine, for knowing absolutely everything; Jess and David for their amazing maps and friendship; Jeremy for keeping me sane and up-to-date; Jody, Meghan, Stefan, Virginia, and Sarah for surviving the avalanche of maps I gave them; our amazing RWs, especially Ieva, for their incredible sense of place; Kevin, for walking me home; and Bean, just because.

1 2 3 4 5

PRICE RANGES>>EUROPE

Our researchers list establishments in order of value from best to worst; our favorites are denoted by the Let's Go thumbs-up (☒). Since the best value is not always the cheapest price, however, we have also incorporated a system of price ranges, based on a rough expectation of what you will spend. For **accommodations,** we base our range on the cheapest price for which a single traveler can stay for one night. For **restaurants** and other dining establishments, we estimate the average amount a traveler will spend. The table below tells you what you will *typically* find in Europe at the corresponding price range; keep in mind that no system can allow for every individual establishment's quirks.

ACCOMMODATIONS	WHAT YOU'RE *LIKELY* TO FIND
❶	Camping; most dorm rooms, such as HI or other hostels or university dorm rooms. Expect bunk beds and a communal bath; you may have to provide or rent towels and sheets.
❷	Upper-end hostels or small hotels. You may have a private bathroom, or there may be a sink in your room and communal shower in the hall.
❸	A small room with a private bath. Should have decent amenities, such as a phone and TV. Breakfast may be included in the price of the room.
❹	Similar to 3, but may have more amenities or may be located in a more touristed area.
❺	Large hotels or upscale chains. If it's a 5 and it doesn't have the perks you want, you've paid too much.
FOOD	**WHAT YOU'RE *LIKELY* TO FIND**
❶	Mostly street-corner stands, falafel and Shawarma huts, or fast-food joints. Soups and simple noodle dishes in minimalist (or downright tacky) surroundings. You may have the option of sitting down or takeaway.
❷	Sandwiches, appetizers at a bar, or low-priced entrees and tapas. Ethnic eateries and pan-Asian noodle houses. Takeaway is less frequent; generally a sit-down meal, sometimes with servers, but only slightly more upscale decor.
❸	Mid-priced entrees, seafood and exotic pasta dishes. More upscale ethnic eateries. Tip'll bump you up a couple dollars, since you will have a waiter.
❹	A somewhat fancy restaurant or a steakhouse. Either way, you'll have a special knife. Few restaurants in this range have a dress code, but some may look down on t-shirt and jeans.
❺	Food with foreign names and a decent wine list. Slacks and dress shirts may be expected. Don't order PB&J.

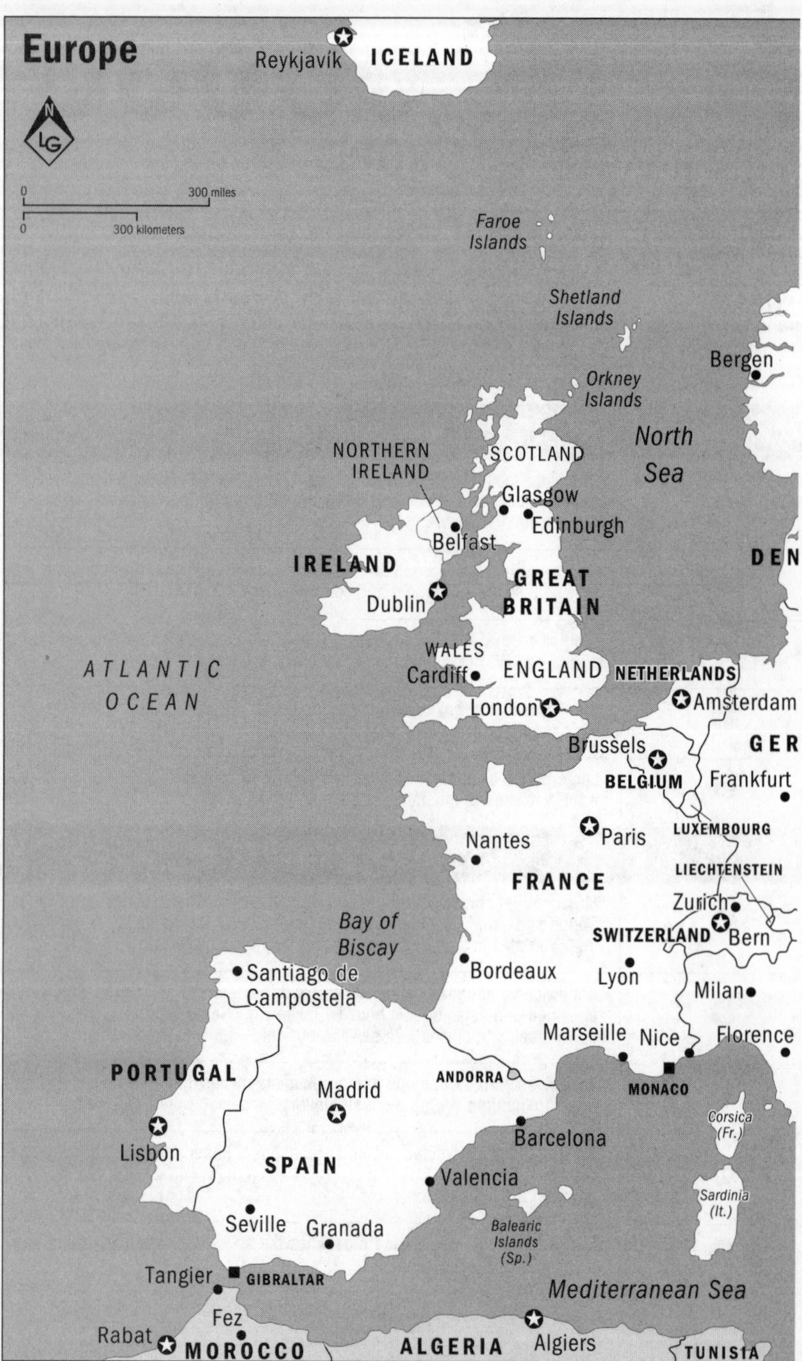
Europe
N
LG
0
300 miles
0
300 kilometers
Reykjavík
ICELAND
Faroe Islands
Shetland Islands
Orkney Islands
Bergen
North Sea
NORTHERN IRELAND
SCOTLAND
Glasgow
Edinburgh
Belfast
DEN
IRELAND
GREAT BRITAIN
Dublin
WALES
ATLANTIC OCEAN
Cardiff
ENGLAND
NETHERLANDS
London
Amsterdam
Brussels
GER
BELGIUM
Frankfurt
Paris
LUXEMBOURG
Nantes
FRANCE
LIECHTENSTEIN
Zurich
Bay of Biscay
SWITZERLAND
Bern
Bordeaux
Lyon
Santiago de Campostela
Milan
Marseille
Nice
Florence
PORTUGAL
ANDORRA
MONACO
Madrid
Corsica (Fr.)
Lisbon
Barcelona
SPAIN
Valencia
Sardinia (It.)
Seville
Granada
Balearic Islands (Sp.)
Tangier
GIBRALTAR
Mediterranean Sea
Fez
Rabat
MOROCCO
ALGERIA
Algiers
TUNISIA

Rovaniemi
Trondheim
Gulf of Bothnia
FINLAND
NORWAY
Oslo
SWEDEN
Helsinki
Tallinn
St. Petersburg
Stockholm
ESTONIA
Gothenburg
Rīga
Moscow
LATVIA
MARK
Baltic Sea
LITHUANIA
Copenhagen
Vilnius
RUSSIA
RUSSIA
Hamburg
Gdańsk
Minsk
Berlin
Warsaw
BELARUS
MANY
POLAND
Kiev
Prague
Kraków
Lviv
CZECH REPUBLIC
UKRAINE
SLOVAK REPUBLIC
Munich
Bratislava
Vienna
MOLDOVA
Budapest
Sea of Azov
AUSTRIA
Chişinău
Odessa
Ljubljana
HUNGARY
Venice
SLOVENIA
ROMANIA
Yalta
Zagreb
Bucharest
CROATIA
BOSNIA AND HERZEGOVINA
Belgrade
Black Sea
Sarajevo
SERBIA AND MONTENEGRO
BULGARIA
SAN MARINO
Dubrovnik
Adriatic Sea
Sofia
Rome
Istanbul
ITALY
F.Y.R. MACEDONIA
Ankara
Tiranë
Thessaloniki
Naples
ALBANIA
Tyrrhenian Sea
GREECE
Aegean Sea
TURKEY
Izmir
Ionian Sea
Sicily
Athens

ABOUT LET'S GO

NOT YOUR PARENTS' TRAVEL GUIDE

At Let's Go, we see every trip as the chance of a lifetime. If your dream is to grab a machete and forge through the jungles of Brazil, we can take you there. If you'd rather bask in the Riviera sun at a beachside cafe, we'll set you a table. We write for readers who know that there's more to travel than sharing double deckers with tourists and who believe that travel can change both themselves and the world—whether they plan to spend six days in London or six months in Latin America. We'll show you just how far your money can go, and prove that the greatest limitation on your adventures is not your wallet, but your imagination.

BEYOND THE TOURIST EXPERIENCE

To help you gain a deeper connection with the places you travel, our fearless researchers scour the globe to give you the heads-up on both world-renowned and off-the-beaten-track attractions, sights, and destinations. They engage with the local culture, only to emerge with the freshest insights on everything from local festivals to regional cuisine. We've also opened our pages to respected writers and scholars to hear their takes on the countries and regions we cover, and asked travelers who have worked, studied, or volunteered abroad to contribute first-person accounts of their experiences. In addition, we increased our coverage of responsible travel and expanded each guide's Beyond Tourism chapter to share more ideas about how to give back while on the road.

FORTY-SIX YEARS OF WISDOM

Let's Go got its start in 1960, when a group of creative and well-traveled students compiled their experience and advice into a 20-page mimeographed pamphlet, which they gave to travelers on charter flights to Europe. Four and a half decades later, we've expanded to cover six continents and all kinds of travel—while retaining our founders' adventurous attitude toward the world. Laced with witty prose and total candor, our guides are still researched and written entirely by students on shoestring budgets, experienced travelers who know that train strikes, stolen luggage, food poisoning, and marriage proposals are all part of a day's work.

THE LET'S GO COMMUNITY

More than just a travel guide company, Let's Go is a community. Our small staff comes together because of our shared passion for travel and our desire to help other travelers see the world the way it was meant to be seen. We love it when our readers become part of the Let's Go community as well—when you travel, drop us a postcard (67 Mt. Auburn St., Cambridge, MA 02138, USA), send us an e-mail (feedback@letsgo.com), or post on our forum (http://www.letsgo.com/connect/forum) to tell us about your adventures and discoveries.

For more information, visit us online: www.letsgo.com.

DISCOVER EUROPE

Europe offers as many unique pathways as it has travelers to take them. For many, the continent's draw comes from familiar imagery. Aspiring writers still spin impassioned romances in Parisian alleyways; a glass of sangria at twilight on the Plaza Mayor tastes as sweet as ever; and iconic treasures, from the onion domes of St. Basil's cathedral to the behemoth slabs of Stonehenge, inspire no small amount of awe. Yet against this ancient backdrop, a freshly costumed continent takes the stage. As the European Union has grown from a small clique of nations trading coal and steel to a 25-member commonwealth with a parliament and a central bank, Eastern and Western Europe find themselves more closely connected than ever before. Those lucky enough to be traveling in a continent that seems simultaneously to be shrinking and expanding can take advantage of increased ease of travel to venture off the beaten path and determine on their own the must-see destinations of 21st century Europe.

While Prague and Budapest may have been the hot spots a few years ago, emerging cities like Kraków and Stockholm are poised to inherit the lucrative tourist money train. Newly minted cultural meccas like Bilbao's Guggenheim and London's Tate Modern have breezily joined the ranks of timeless galleries like the Louvre and the Hermitage, while a constant influx of students and DJs keep Europe's nightlife dependably hot. Whether it's the pubs of Dublin, the upscale bistros of Lyon, the frozen north country of Sweden, or the dazzling beaches of Croatia's Dalmatian Coast that call to you, *Let's Go: Europe 2006* will help keep you informed, alive, and on-budget.

TACKLING EUROPE

Anyone who tells you that there exists any one "best way" to see Europe should be politely ignored. This book is designed to facilitate a variety of travel through Europe, from a few days in Prague to a continent-wide summer sprint. This chapter is made up of tools to help you make your own itinerary: **themed categories** let you know where to find your museums, your mountains, and your madhouses; **suggested itineraries** outline common paths across Europe. After getting a general impression of the continent, make sure to turn to the country-specific **Discover** section at the beginning of each chapter for more detailed information.

WHEN TO GO

While summer sees the most tourist traffic in Euorpe, the best mix of value and accessibility comes in early fall and late spring. To the delight of skiing and ice-climbing enthusiasts, traveling during the low season (mid-Sept. to June) brings cheaper airfares and accommodations, in addition to freeing you from the hordes of fanny-pack-toting tourists. On the flip side, many attractions, hostels, and tourist offices close in the winter, and in some rural areas local transportation dwindles or shuts down altogether. Most of Europe's best **festivals** (see below) also take place during the summer months. For more info on the best time to make your excursion, see each country's **Essentials** section and the **Weather Chart** on p. 1068.

MUSEUMS

It is something of a truism to say that Europe has bred all the masterworks of Western art from ancient Greece through the Renaissance to Impressionism and beyond, but what a breathtaking truism it is. Most of these have been kept close to home in cultural strongholds like the Louvre, the Prado, and the Vatican Museums. Imperial conquest helped Britain add to the marvels that outfit the British Museum and Russia to amass the wealth so picturesquely on display in the galleries of the Hermitage. European museums do not merely house art, however. They also shelter torture instruments, marijuana, puppets, erotica, marzipan, leprosy, secret police, and spirits both undead and delicious—in short, whatever can be classified and captioned. A trip across Europe qualifies as little more than a stopover without an afternoon spent among some of the paintings and artifacts below—whether they include pinnacles of Western culture or more risqué fare.

THE PICTURESQUE	AND THE OFTEN GROTESQUE
FRANCE: THE LOUVRE (p. 337). Along with troves of work by nearly every other master, Da Vinci's *Mona Lisa* smiles out from behind her glass case and her crowds of beady-eyed tourists.	**SWITZERLAND: COLLECTION DE L'ART BRUT** (p. 1041). Inspiration and madness have never been harder to separate than in these artworks by institutionalized schizophrenics and criminals.
RUSSIA: THE HERMITAGE (p. 879). In the palatial St. Petersburg home of the Tsars resides the world's largest art collection. Only 5% of its 3 million pieces is on display at any one time.	**CZECH REPUBLIC: MUSEUM OF MEDIEVAL TORTURE INSTRUMENTS** (p. 247). Save lunch for after visiting these exhibits and the accompanying explanations, all in meticulous detail.
SPAIN: MUSEO DEL PRADO (p. 919). It's an art-lover's heaven to harrow the hell painted by Hieronymus Bosch. Also here are works by El Greco, Goya, Rubens, Titian, and Velázquez.	**GERMANY: MUSEUM FÜR PUPPENTHEATER** (p. 446). Thousands of hand, string, shadow, and stick puppets from around the globe make up the largest private puppet collection in the world.
BRITAIN: THE BRITISH MUSEUM (p. 145). Gathering world artifacts like Egypt's Rosetta Stone or Iran's Oxus Treasure, the British Museum ironically contains almost nothing British at all.	**THE NETHERLANDS: CANNABIS COLLEGE** (p. 736). Cannabis College is just like college, except there are no libraries, no lectures, no studying, no liquor, no dorms, and no full-time students.
ITALY: VATICAN MUSEUMS (p. 620). Look for the *School of Athens* here, in Rome; the painting crowns a mindblowing amount of Renaissance and other art, including the incredible Raphael Rooms.	**FRANCE: MUSÉE DU VIN** (p. 396). See the vats and winepresses housed in the 15th-century Hôtel des Ducs de Bourgogne for free before splurging on the age-ripened vintages themselves.
AUSTRIA: KUNSTHISTORISCHES MUSEUM (p. 88). Venetian paintings, an Egyptian burial chamber, and medieval arms in the world's 4th-largest art collection impress the history geek in all of us.	**LITHUANIA: DEVIL MUSEUM** (p. 707). Devil-worshippers can practice idolatry in 2000 different ways in this museum, which has amassed that many depictions of devils in various media.
GREECE: NATIONAL ARCHAEOLOGICAL MUSEUM (p. 492). Athens itself may be museum enough for some, but this building collects what's too small to be seen with a placard on the street.	**GERMANY: EROTIC ART MUSEUM** (p. 445). Picasso's visual imagination is harnessed to add class to an otherwise naughty assortment of *Kama Sutra* poses and Victorian pornography.
BRITAIN: TATE GALLERIES (p. 146). While the Tate Modern collects Picassos, Duchamps, and others, the Tate Britain assembles the works of Blake, Hockney, Rosetti, and Turner.	**RUSSIA: KGB MUSEUM** (p. 872). Quiz a current FSB agent and learn everything about Russia's secret police from Ivan the Terrible to the present. Everything, that is, except for its secrets.
ITALY: GALLERIA BORGHESE (p. 620). Vivid paintings and graceful sculpture by Bernini, Caravaggio, Rubens, and Titian are a sight for sore eyes after staring at miles of Renaissance canvas.	**NORWAY: LEPROSY MUSEUM** (p. 771). Ancient treatments of this fabled disease are exhibited here in cells that housed as many as three patients at once into the 1940s.
THE NETHERLANDS: RIJKSMUSEUM (p. 737). Renovations should not deter anyone from seeing the pinnacles of the Dutch Golden Age, including Rembrandts and Vermeers, line up along the walls.	**HUNGARY: SZABÓ MARZIPAN MUSEUM** (p. 534). Only one statuette on display at this museum is not composed of marzipan: an 80kg white chocolate effigy of Michael Jackson.

ARCHITECTURE

European history is legible not only in textbooks, but also in the architecture left behind by millennia of secular and religious tradition. Royal lines from the early Welsh dynasties and Polish kings to the Bourbons, Hapsburgs, and Romanovs have all been outlasted by the emblems of their magnificence—castles, palaces, and chateaux. Monarchs were careless of expense, and prodigiously jealous: Louis XIV's palace at Versailles, which has become a byword for opulence, whet the ambition of rival monarchs and spurred the construction of rival domiciles, among them Peter the Great's Peterhof, Charles III's Reggia, and Ludwig II's Herreninsel. No expense was spared for God, either, as attest the many splendid cathedrals, monasteries, synagogues, temples, and mosques that rise skyward from their low cityscapes. Córdoba's Mezquita mosque and Budapest's Great Synagogue are among the finest of their kind, while Chartres's Cathédrale de Notre Dame and Cologne's Dom are high points—pun intended—of the Gothic style.

ROYAL REAL ESTATE	SACRED SITES
GERMANY: NEUSCHWANSTEIN (p. 478). A waterfall, an artificial grotto, a byzantine throne room, and a Wagnerian opera hall deck out the inspiration for Disney's Cinderella Castle.	**ITALY: SISTINE CHAPEL** (p. 618). Since the 16th century, white smoke has risen from the chapel after the election of a new pope. Michelangelo's ceiling frescoes are also worth a glance.
FRANCE: VERSAILLES PALACE (p. 345). Little can compare to Versailles, testimony to the extravagance of pre-Revolutionary France and the prototype for regal self-indulgence down the ages.	**SPAIN: MEZQUITA** (p. 931). Córdoba's Mezquita, one of the most important Islamic monuments in the West, is supported by 850 pink-and-blue marble and alabaster columns.
BRITAIN: BUCKINGHAM PALACE (p. 138). Queen Elizabeth still resides here, among the Throne Room, the Music Room, the opulent White Room, the gardens, and the galleries.	**FRANCE: CHARTRES CATHEDRAL** (p. 345). Arguably the world's finest example of early Gothic architecture has intact stained-glass windows from the 12th century and a crypt from the 9th.
RUSSIA: PETERHOF (p. 882). Nothing was too good for the tsars, or too holy to have been built by more than serf labor. Peter the Great's project stretches magnificently along the Gulf of Finland.	**HUNGARY: THE GREAT SYNAGOGUE** (p. 531). Europe's largest synagogue can hold 3000 faithful. Inscribed leaves of a metal tree in the courtyard commemorate the victims of the Holocaust.
ITALY: PALAZZO PITTI (p. 668). The Medici family left this 15th-century *palazzo* slathered in artistic treasures and its adjacent Boboli gardens exquisitely landscaped.	**BRITAIN: WESTMINSTER ABBEY** (p. 139). Royal weddings and coronations take place in the sanctuary; nearby, poets and politicians from the earliest kings to Winston Churchill rest in peace.
SPAIN: THE ALHAMBRA (p. 944). At an impressionistic distance, the Alhambra looks like a worn-out toy; zoom in, and its wood, stucco, and ceramics reveal exquisite beauty.	**ITALY: THE DUOMO** (p. 664). It is hard to know which to be more impressed by, the massive nave built by Arnolfo di Cambrio, or the dome built by Filippo Brunelleschi that crowns it.
POLAND: WAWEL CASTLE (p. 805). Kraków's hillside masterpiece includes a castle begun in the 900s, as well as a cathedral that was once the seat of the archbishopric of Pope John Paul II.	**GERMANY: KÖLNER DOM** (p. 452). With a ceiling 44m high and 1350 sq. m of stained glass illuminating the interior with particolored sunlight, Cologne's cathedral is Germany's greatest.
AUSTRIA: SCHLOß SCHÖNBRUNN (p. 88). It's hard to tell which is more impressive, the palace or the classical gardens that stretch a full four times the length of the structure.	**RUSSIA: SERGIYEV POSAD** (p. 873). Under the trademark Orthodox onion domes, Russia's most celebrated pilgrimage site now thrives again after seven decades of state-propagated atheism.
BRITAIN: CAERNARFON CASTLE (p. 183). Edward I began this architectural feat in 1283 in order to maintain control over northern Wales, but left it unfinished when he ran out of money.	**GREECE: THE PARTHENON** (p. 491). Keeping vigil over Athens from the Acropolis, the Parthenon is a needful pilgrimage for any culture-worshipper; the Greek mythology has become common to all.
FRANCE: CHENONCEAU (p. 355). A series of noblewomen crafted one of the most graceful chateaux in France, which arches elegantly over the Cher River.	**AUSTRIA: STEPHANSDOM** (p. 86). Work on the north tower of Vienna's cathedral stopped, according to legend, after a pact with the devil went awry and the builder plunged to his death.

OUTDOORS

Granted, it may not be what you came for. Europe, as the seat of modern civilization, tends to draw people to its museums and ruins more than its mountains and rivers. But for any traveler, budget or poor, solo or companioned, expert or neophyte, an excursion to the outdoors can round off (or salvage, as the case may be) any journey. Fjords, volcanoes, vales, gorges, plateaus, and upthrusts pock the spots where the Earth's plates wreck and unwreck at their edges. Waters of innumerable shades of blue wash up on uninhabited shores of black-, white-, and red-sand beaches. Mountains, whether sprawling with trees or culminating in ice, continue to challenge mankind and dwarf the man-made—just as they, and the rest of the European landscape, did when civilization began.

LANDSCAPES	SEAVIEWS
GERMANY: THE SCHWARZWALD (p. 465). The eerie darkness pervading this tangled expanse of evergreen, once the inspiration of the Brothers Grimm, continues to lure hikers and skiers alike.	**ITALY: THE AMALFI COAST** (p. 681). The azure waters that make up the coastline south of Naples are second only to the jagged, gravity-defying rocks which overlook them.
SWITZERLAND: INTERLAKEN (p. 1022). Thanks to its mild climate and pristine landscape, Interlaken quenches the thirst for anything outdoors, whether it be hiking, bungee jumping, or skydiving.	**NORWAY: SOGNEFJORD** (p. 775). Thundering waterfalls give way to halcyon lakes, sweeping green meadows, and regal glaciers at the longest fjord in the world.
GREECE: MOUNT OLYMPUS (p. 502). Erupting out of the Thermaic Gulf, the 3000m height and formidable slopes of Olympus so awed the ancients that they believed it to be the divine dwelling of their immortal pantheon.	**FRANCE: D-DAY BEACHES** (p. 347). The heroism of the Allied forces is tastefully preserved on the beaches near Bayeux, where thousands of soldiers were killed in battle over 60 years ago.
BRITAIN: LAKE DISTRICT NATIONAL PARK (p. 177). Four million sheep have cast their votes for the loveliest park in England–an equal number of summertime tourists seem to agree.	**DENMARK: ÆRØSKØBING** (p. 278). Economic stagnation and recent conservation efforts have successfully fossilized the 19th-century lifestyle and charm of this tiny island town.
THE NETHERLANDS: HOGE VELUWE NATIONAL PARK (p. 747). Wild boars and red deer inhabit the 13,500 acres of forestry, while the park's museum houses works by Van Gogh and Picasso.	**BRITAIN: NEWQUAY** (p. 160). Believe it or not, the best surfing in Europe may just be at this little city on the Cornish coast.
ICELAND: ÞINGVELLIR NATIONAL PARK (p. 553). Few sights in the world allow visitors to straddle separating tectonic plates amid lava fields.	**FRANCE: CANNES** (p. 375). Never mind the annual film festival; the essence of Cannes is on its stunning beaches and palm-lined boardwalks.
SLOVAKIA: SLOVENSKÝ RAJ NATIONAL PARK (p. 893). Hikers who tire of the views overlooking the Tatras can rest in the frozen columns, gigantic walls, and hardened waterfalls of the Dobăinksá Ice Caves, which date back to the last Ice Age.	**SWEDEN: SKÄRGÅRD ARCHIPELAGO** (p. 996). A popular daytrip from the capital city, this archipelago has become a favorite of sailing enthusiasts, hikers and picnickers.
ITALY: MT. VESUVIUS (p. 680). The only active volcano on the continent is overdue for another eruption. Scientists claim that the next tantrum the ancient mountain throws will be more violent than the one which buried Pompeii in AD 79.	**SPAIN: SITGES** (p. 964). One of the many destinations vying for the title "Jewel of the Mediterranean," Sitges's maintains its credibility as a must-see beach town with prime tanning grounds and a nightlife almost as hot as the beaches.
AUSTRIA: THE HOHE TAUERN NATIONAL PARK (p. 97). Saturated with glaciers, mountains, lakes, and endangered species, the largest park in Europe offers ice-free mountain paths once trod by Celts and Romans.	**BRITAIN: LOCH LOMOND** (p. 197). While tales of monsters are generally reserved for another Loch, Lomond still manages to attract travelers with the largest lake in Britain, along with the 38 islands which dot it.
POLAND: WIELICZKA SALT MINES (p. 808). Discovered by monks digging a well, miners and artists transformed the salt deposits into a maze of chambers full of sculptures and carvings.	**CROATIA: HVAR ISLAND** (p. 227). Hordes of sun-soaked and salt-licked revelers descend upon Hvar, internationally regarded as one of the 10 most beautiful beaches in the world.

FESTIVALS

COUNTRIES	APR. – JUNE	JULY – AUG.	SEPT. – MAR.
AUSTRIA AND SWITZERLAND	**Vienna Festwochen** (early May to mid-June)	**Salzburger Festspiele** (July 24-Aug. 31)	**Escalade** (Geneva; early Dec.) **Fasnacht** (Basel; late Feb.)
BELGIUM	**Festival of Fairground Arts** (Wallonie; late May)	**Gentse Feesten** (Ghent; July 16-25)	**International French Language Film Festival** (Namur; late Sept.)
BRITAIN AND IRELAND	**Bloomsday** (Dublin; June 16) **Wimbledon** (London; June 26-July 9)	**Fringe Festival** (Edinburgh; Aug. 6-28) **Edinburgh Int'l Festival** (Aug.13-Sept. 3)	**Matchmaking Festival** (Lisdoonvarna; Sept.) **St. Patrick's Day** (Mar. 17)
CROATIA	**World Festival of Animated Film** (Zagreb; May)	**Int'l Folklore Festival** (July) **Dubrovnik Summer Fest.** (July and Aug.)	**Int'l Puppet Festival** (Sept.) **Zagreb Fest** (Nov.)
CZECH REPUBLIC	**Prague Spring Festival** (May)	**Český Krumlov Int'l Music Fest** (Aug.)	**Int'l Organ Fest** (Olomouc; Sept.)
FRANCE	**Cannes Film Festival** (May)	**Tour de France** (July) **Festival d'Avignon** (July-Aug.)	**Carnevale** (Nice, Nantes; Feb.)
GERMANY	**May Day** (Berlin; May 1) **Christopher St. Day** (late June)	**Rhine in Flames Festival** (Rhine Valley; Sep. 16)	**Oktoberfest** (Munich; Sept. 16-Oct. 1) **Fasching** (Munich; Feb. 24-28)
HUNGARY	**Golden Shell Folklore** (Siófok; June)	**Sziget Rock Fest** (Budapest; July) **Baroque Festival** (Eger; July)	**Eger Vintage Days** (Sept.) **Festival of Wine Songs** (Pécs; Sept.)
ITALY	**Maggio Musicale** (Florence; Apr. 30-June 14) **Festa di San Gennaro** (Naples; May 6, Sept. 19)	**Il Palio** (Siena; July 2 and Aug. 16) **Umbria Jazz Festival** (July)	**Carnevale** (late Feb.) **Scoppio del Carro** (Florence; Easter Su)
THE NETHERLANDS	**Queen's Day** (Apr. 30) **Holland Festival** (June)	**Gay Pride Parade** (Aug.)	**Flower Parade** (Aalsmeer; Sept. 2) **Cannabis Cup** (Nov.)
POLAND	**Int'l Short Film** (Kraków; May) **Festival of Jewish Culture** (Kraków; June)	**Street Theater** (Kraków; July) **Highlander Folklore** (Zakopane; Aug.)	**Kraków Jazz Fest** (Oct.) **Nat'l Blues Music** (Torún; Nov.)
PORTUGAL	**Burning of the Ribbons** (Coimbra; early May)	**Lisbon Beer Festival** (July)	**Carnival** (Mar. 4) **Semana Santa** (Mar. 20-27)
SCANDINAVIA	**Midsummer** (June 21-23) **Festspillene** (Bergen; May 31-June 1)	**Savonlinna Opera Festival** (July) **Quart Music Festival** (Kristiansand; early July)	**Helsinki Festival** (late Aug.-early Sept.) **Tromsø International Film Festival** (Jan. 17-22)
SPAIN	**Feria de Abril** (Seville; Apr. 12-17)	**San Fermines** (Pamplona; July 6-14)	**Las Fallas** (Valencia; Mar.) **Carnaval** (Mar.) **Semana Santa** (Mar. 20-27)

Manufacturing Continental Unity

As midnight approached on April 30th, 2004, corks could be heard popping across much of what used to be known as Eastern Europe. May 1st marked the beginning of a new era: Ten new countries—Cyprus, the Czech Republic, Estonia, Hungary, Latvia, Lithuania, Malta, Poland, the Slovak Republic, and Slovenia—were admitted into the European Union. The union, now 25 strong, set about commemorating its expansion across what had long been a divided continent. Concerts were held in Berlin and Warsaw, and all of Europe was able to watch televised broadcasts of the fireworks in Malta. All of this testified to the transformation of a Europe no longer divided into East and West.

Celebrations such as these can be enlightening. What and how we commemorate often tells more about who we are and what we claim to value than about the event or person being commemorated. May 1 had traditionally been a day to celebrate the working class (in the East) or labor more generally (in the West). This time, these themes were overshadowed by a different kind of internationalism: a sense on the part of the 10 inductees that they had finally become full-fledged members of "Europe." Examining this new Europe's celebrations tells us a good deal about just what the reinvented continent aspires to be.

What Europeans choose to remember or forget, how they recast their past and imagine the future can all be gleaned from commemorations choreographed and spontaneous, solemn and joyous, permanent and ephemeral. Take, for example, the 60th anniversary of D-Day, celebrated in 2004. Those festivities brought not only aging war veterans and their families, but numerous international dignitaries to the coasts of Normandy for a week's worth of events. American president George W. Bush underscored the contributions the United States had made to the security of Europe and the world as a whole, doubtless hoping that the luster of Normandy would rub off on his country's latest attempts at ridding the world of tyranny. Indeed, the American invasion of Normandy has long been a symbol of the larger Pax Americana that followed World War II, and although this vision has come under siege in recent years, it continues to be trumpeted in the public realm.

The festivities of 2004 brought changes to the D-Day anniversary, which had been celebrated regularly in previous decades. For the first time, the heads of Germany and Russia were present. The participation of both tells us much more about current alliances than about those that prevailed during the war. Recall that 20 years earlier, Ronald Reagan had been criticized for his visit to the Bitburg cemetery, where Nazi fighters lay buried. This time, the presence of Chancellor Gerhard Schroeder at the festivities reflected the fact that a united Germany lies at the center of the new Europe. Russian participation in the D-Day festivities is even more interesting, since it signified recognition of one of the Allied Powers not often given its due. In the Cold War decades, after the Axis Powers were vanquished, Soviet efforts in World War II were conveniently "forgotten" in the West. Given the improved relations between post-Communist Russia and the West, it had become acceptable to recall the Soviet Union's wartime sacrifices as well as those of Britain, France, and America.

Of course, not only battles are commemorated. A newly-minted tradition, initiated by the European Union, is the designation of European Capitals of Culture. Each year, the designated city organizes festivities, exhibits, and events to showcase its cultural heritage. Genoa, Italy and Lille, France split the honor in 2004, while Cork, Ireland enjoyed top billing in 2005. Such celebrations say much about the identity of these particular urban centers, and to some extent about how they situate themselves within European culture as a whole. The same is true of the European Heritage Days set aside each autumn, again celebrated in different ways in cities and towns across the continent. That the European Union promotes such local expressions of cultural inheritance suggests that it values the rich cultural mosaic that comprises Europe.

Thus, the second half of the European Union's slogan "unity in diversity" continues to receive attention. However, the first half of the slogan—unity—still lacks its own celebration. Is not European Unity Day—"E-Day"—equally worth celebrating in the aftermath of May 1, 2004? Perhaps Europeans will take it upon themselves to transform May Day into E-Day on a permanent basis. This might make up for the fact that the revolutions of 1989, which helped to initiate the reunification of Europe's two halves, received so little notice on their 15th anniversary. With the tearing down of the Berlin Wall, Europe lost one site for spontaneous celebrations such as those that took place on November 9, 1989. One fitting tribute to both 1989 and to the European reunification of 2004 might be fireworks over Budapest's Statue Park, with its collection of monuments to Karl Marx and V.I. Lenin. Here, perhaps, one could best appreciate the irony of Europe's slogan for the 21st century: "Europeans of the world, unite!"

Patrice M. Dabrowski is a postdoctoral fellow at Brown University's Watson Institute for International Studies. She is the author of Commemorations and the Shaping of Modern Poland, *published by Indiana University Press in 2004 and hailed by fellow scholars for its "tremendous erudition."*

The Struggle for a European Immigration Policy

n June of 2003, 200 would-be European immi-;rants believed to have embarked from Libya lrowned in the rough waters south of Sicily; hat same month, 2666 migrants from Africa sur-ived the journey, landing on the isolated Italian sland, Lampedusa, and creating a study in con-rasts in the ongoing EU immigration debate. In he annals of European immigration, tragedies f this caliber are far from rare: The Sicily rowning occurred four years to the month after 8 Chinese refugees were asphyxiated in a con-ainer lorry at the English port of Dover. Even he illegal immigrants who beat the odds and the order control do not always escape tragic cir-umstances. Many are forced into black-market abor, such as prostitution, to pay back smug-,lers for their passage. While it is fairly clear hat current EU immigration policies are harm-ul to refugees, opening the floodgates on legal mmigration is not only in the best interests of hose seeking entrance—it now appears that the U needs immigrants as desperately as immi-rants need the EU.

Western European birth-rates have crashed to n all-time low, averaging only 1.5 children per voman, and dipping as low as Spain's scant 1.1. t the other end of things, Europe's aging popula-on has become a major strain on its pension sys-ems. French Parliamentarian Elisabeth Guigou eports that, if present demographic trends con-nue, without relaxing immigration constraints, ne mighty new 25-nation European Union will xperience a net decline in population of 50 mil-on people by 2050. Even now Europe is facing hortages in both its skilled and unskilled labor ools, making even more apparent its need for nmigrants for economic prosperity to continue.

With so much at stake, the recent Europe-wide wing to the politcal right on immigration policy ay be difficult to comprehend. Some of the ost developed, prosperous nations, such as ermany and France, worry that an influx of nmigrants will destabilize their economies and opardize publicly funded medical and social rograms. Tensions have been primarily focused n African and Arab ghettos, commonly seen as rags on the welfare state and feared to be security threats in the wake of September 11. This explosive combination of fear and uncertainty has fueled the popularity of far-right populist political candidates running on anti-immigration platforms, spawning legislation severely restricting legal immigration.

Between June and July of 2003 at the Thessaloniki Summit, Germany, Britain, and Italy were the most vocal and influential players in the debate over how to manage illegal immigration while integrating legal immigrants. Some leaders, such as German Interior Minister Otto Schily, think agreements with countries of origin are the best way to curbing illegal immigration. Supporters of such efforts point to Italy's bilateral agreements with Lybia, a hub for human trafficking from Africa to Europe, and Albania as models. In the former scenario, Italy will provide technical assistance to Libya, and the two countries will cooperate on offshore patrols. The 1997 Italian-Albanian cooperation deal contains a simplified repatriation scheme, quotas for seasonal workers, and joint patrols in Albanian waters of the Adriatic Sea that separate Italy and the former Stalinist state.

The stage is set for what promises to be an ongoing debate, as Germany leads the fight to retain autonomous control of its border policies while nations like Britain and Italy attempt to institute centralized, EU-wide control of immigration policy and enforcement. For the moment, a stopgap EU program intended to "promote a tolerant and inclusive society by raising awareness of fundamental European values" and to project accurate information about immigrants' culture, traditions, and religion underscores the complexity of the situation. By educating immigrants in the cultural, social, and political characteristics of their adoptive state—and providing EU citizens with accurate information about immigrants' cultures—there is hope that some of the elements of mistrust and misunderstanding that have plagued the discussion thus far can be mitigated, and that the frustrated desperation that has cost the lives of so many refugees will give way to a peaceful, legal, and mutually beneficial solution.

Derek Glanz is a doctoral candidate in political science at the University of North Carolina at Chapel Hill. He was the Editor of Let's Go: Spain & Portugal 1998.

SUGGESTED ITINERARIES

THE GRAND TOUR - EUROPE IN SIX (OR

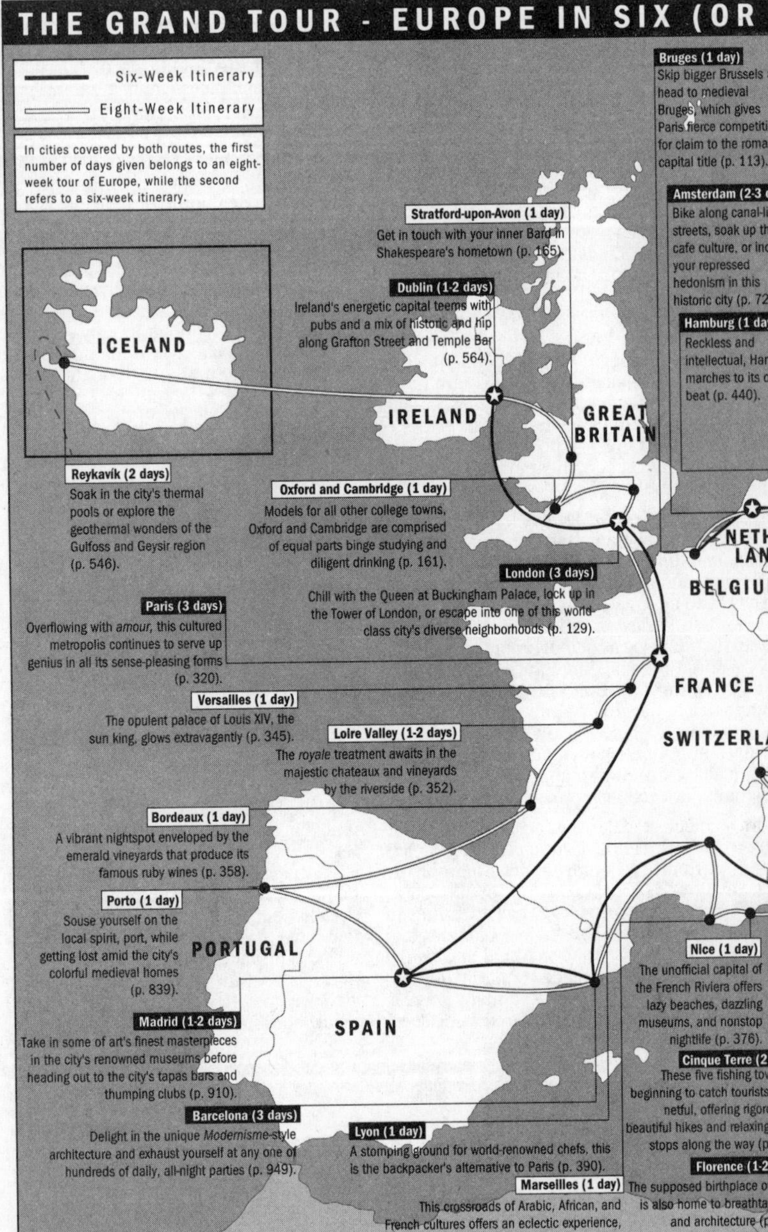

Six-Week Itinerary
Eight-Week Itinerary
In cities covered by both routes, the first number of days given belongs to an eight-week tour of Europe, while the second refers to a six-week itinerary.
ICELAND
IRELAND
GREAT BRITAIN
NETHERLAND
BELGIUM
FRANCE
SWITZERLAN
PORTUGAL
SPAIN
Reykavík (2 days)
Soak in the city's thermal pools or explore the geothermal wonders of the Gulfoss and Geysir region (p. 546).
Stratford-upon-Avon (1 day)
Get in touch with your inner Bard in Shakespeare's hometown (p. 165).
Dublin (1-2 days)
Ireland's energetic capital teems with pubs and a mix of historic and hip along Grafton Street and Temple Bar (p. 564).
Oxford and Cambridge (1 day)
Models for all other college towns, Oxford and Cambridge are comprised of equal parts binge studying and diligent drinking (p. 161).
London (3 days)
Chill with the Queen at Buckingham Palace, lock up in the Tower of London, or escape into one of this world-class city's diverse neighborhoods (p. 129).
Paris (3 days)
Overflowing with amour, this cultured metropolis continues to serve up genius in all its sense-pleasing forms (p. 320).
Versailles (1 day)
The opulent palace of Louis XIV, the sun king, glows extravagantly (p. 345).
Loire Valley (1-2 days)
The royale treatment awaits in the majestic chateaux and vineyards by the riverside (p. 352).
Bordeaux (1 day)
A vibrant nightspot enveloped by the emerald vineyards that produce its famous ruby wines (p. 358).
Porto (1 day)
Souse yourself on the local spirit, port, while getting lost amid the city's colorful medieval homes (p. 839).
Madrid (1-2 days)
Take in some of art's finest masterpieces in the city's renowned museums before heading out to the city's tapas bars and thumping clubs (p. 910).
Barcelona (3 days)
Delight in the unique Modernisme-style architecture and exhaust yourself at any one of hundreds of daily, all-night parties (p. 949).
Lyon (1 day)
A stomping ground for world-renowned chefs, this is the backpacker's alternative to Paris (p. 390).
Marseilles (1 day)
This crossroads of Arabic, African, and French cultures offers an eclectic experience, especially in Cours Julien (p. 367).
Bruges (1 day)
Skip bigger Brussels and head to medieval Bruges, which gives Paris fierce competition for claim to the romance capital title (p. 113).
Amsterdam (2-3 day
Bike along canal-lined streets, soak up the cafe culture, or indulg your repressed hedonism in this historic city (p. 723).
Hamburg (1 day)
Reckless and intellectual, Hambu marches to its own beat (p. 440).
Nice (1 day)
The unofficial capital of the French Riviera offers lazy beaches, dazzling museums, and nonstop nightlife (p. 376).
Cinque Terre (2 da
These five fishing towns beginning to catch tourists by netful, offering rigorous beautiful hikes and relaxing be stops along the way (p. 6
Florence (1-2 da
The supposed birthplace of ge is also home to breathtaking and architecture (p. 6
Siena (1
A medieval treasure often overshadowed, never replaced, by Florence and Rome (p. 66

EIGHT) WEEKS

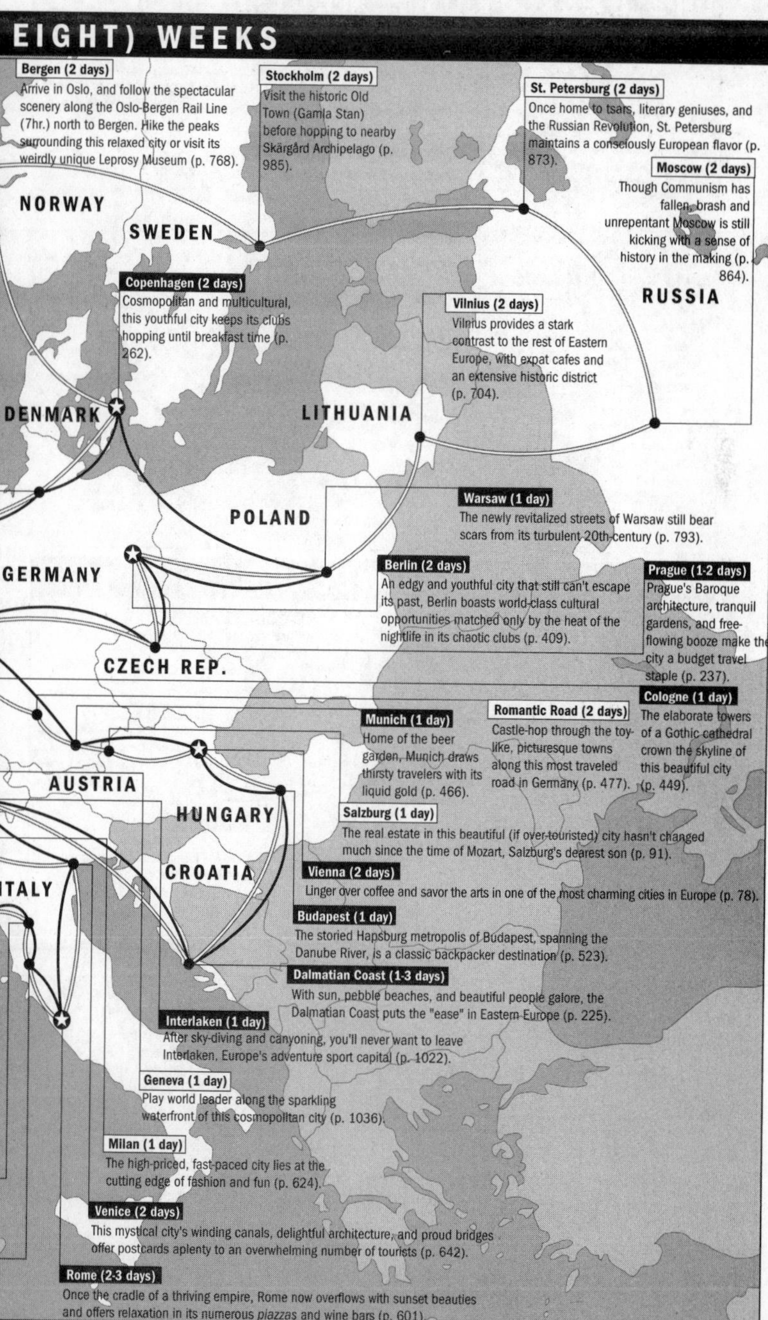

Bergen (2 days)
Arrive in Oslo, and follow the spectacular scenery along the Oslo-Bergen Rail Line (7hr.) north to Bergen. Hike the peaks surrounding this relaxed city or visit its weirdly unique Leprosy Museum (p. 768).

Stockholm (2 days)
Visit the historic Old Town (Gamla Stan) before hopping to nearby Skärgård Archipelago (p. 985).

St. Petersburg (2 days)
Once home to tsars, literary geniuses, and the Russian Revolution, St. Petersburg maintains a consciously European flavor (p. 873).

Moscow (2 days)
Though Communism has fallen, brash and unrepentant Moscow is still kicking with a sense of history in the making (p. 864).

Copenhagen (2 days)
Cosmopolitan and multicultural, this youthful city keeps its clubs hopping until breakfast time (p. 262).

Vilnius (2 days)
Vilnius provides a stark contrast to the rest of Eastern Europe, with expat cafes and an extensive historic district (p. 704).

Warsaw (1 day)
The newly revitalized streets of Warsaw still bear scars from its turbulent 20th-century (p. 793).

Berlin (2 days)
An edgy and youthful city that still can't escape its past, Berlin boasts world-class cultural opportunities matched only by the heat of the nightlife in its chaotic clubs (p. 409).

Prague (1-2 days)
Prague's Baroque architecture, tranquil gardens, and free-flowing booze make the city a budget travel staple (p. 237).

Cologne (1 day)
The elaborate towers of a Gothic cathedral crown the skyline of this beautiful city (p. 449).

Romantic Road (2 days)
Castle-hop through the toy-like, picturesque towns along this most traveled road in Germany (p. 477).

Munich (1 day)
Home of the beer garden, Munich draws thirsty travelers with its liquid gold (p. 466).

Salzburg (1 day)
The real estate in this beautiful (if over-touristed) city hasn't changed much since the time of Mozart, Salzburg's dearest son (p. 91).

Vienna (2 days)
Linger over coffee and savor the arts in one of the most charming cities in Europe (p. 78).

Budapest (1 day)
The storied Hapsburg metropolis of Budapest, spanning the Danube River, is a classic backpacker destination (p. 523).

Dalmatian Coast (1-3 days)
With sun, pebble beaches, and beautiful people galore, the Dalmatian Coast puts the "ease" in Eastern Europe (p. 225).

Interlaken (1 day)
After sky-diving and canyoning, you'll never want to leave Interlaken, Europe's adventure sport capital (p. 1022).

Geneva (1 day)
Play world leader along the sparkling waterfront of this cosmopolitan city (p. 1036).

Milan (1 day)
The high-priced, fast-paced city lies at the cutting edge of fashion and fun (p. 624).

Venice (2 days)
This mystical city's winding canals, delightful architecture, and proud bridges offer postcards aplenty to an overwhelming number of tourists (p. 642).

Rome (2-3 days)
Once the cradle of a thriving empire, Rome now overflows with sunset beauties and offers relaxation in its numerous *piazzas* and wine bars (p. 601).

THE BEST OF THE MEDITERRANEAN

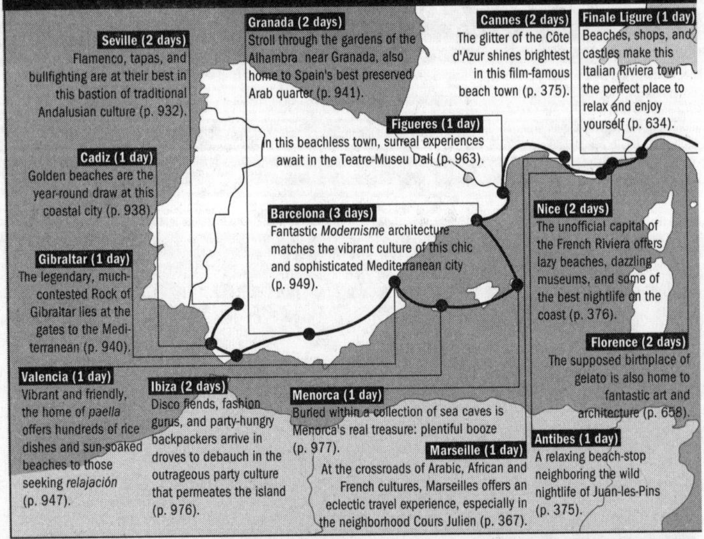

Seville (2 days) Flamenco, tapas, and bullfighting are at their best in this bastion of traditional Andalusian culture (p. 932).

Granada (2 days) Stroll through the gardens of the Alhambra near Granada, also home to Spain's best preserved Arab quarter (p. 941).

Cannes (2 days) The glitter of the Côte d'Azur shines brightest in this film-famous beach town (p. 375).

Finale Ligure (1 day) Beaches, shops, and castles make this Italian Riviera town the perfect place to relax and enjoy yourself (p. 634).

Figueres (1 day) In this beachless town, surreal experiences await in the Teatre-Museu Dalí (p. 963).

Cadiz (1 day) Golden beaches are the year-round draw at this coastal city (p. 938).

Barcelona (3 days) Fantastic *Modernisme* architecture matches the vibrant culture of this chic and sophisticated Mediterranean city (p. 949).

Nice (2 days) The unofficial capital of the French Riviera offers lazy beaches, dazzling museums, and some of the best nightlife on the coast (p. 376).

Gibraltar (1 day) The legendary, much-contested Rock of Gibraltar lies at the gates to the Mediterranean (p. 940).

Florence (2 days) The supposed birthplace of gelato is also home to fantastic art and architecture (p. 658).

Valencia (1 day) Vibrant and friendly, the home of *paella* offers hundreds of rice dishes and sun-soaked beaches to those seeking *relajación* (p. 947).

Ibiza (2 days) Disco fiends, fashion gurus, and party-hungry backpackers arrive in droves to debauch in the outrageous party culture that permeates the island (p. 976).

Menorca (1 day) Buried within a collection of sea caves is Menorca's real treasure: plentiful booze (p. 977).

Marseille (1 day) At the crossroads of Arabic, African and French cultures, Marseilles offers an eclectic travel experience, especially in the neighborhood Cours Julien (p. 367).

Antibes (1 day) A relaxing beach-stop neighboring the wild nightlife of Juan-les-Pins (p. 375).

HEADING EAST (6 WEEKS)

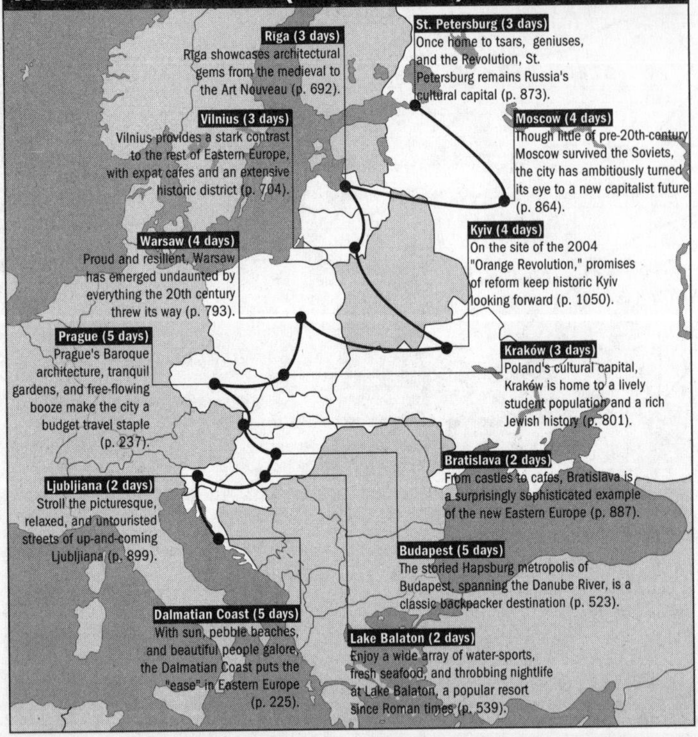

Riga (3 days) Riga showcases architectural gems from the medieval to the Art Nouveau (p. 692).

St. Petersburg (3 days) Once home to tsars, geniuses, and the Revolution, St. Petersburg remains Russia's cultural capital (p. 873).

Vilnius (3 days) Vilnius provides a stark contrast to the rest of Eastern Europe, with expat cafes and an extensive historic district (p. 704).

Moscow (4 days) Though little of pre-20th-century Moscow survived the Soviets, the city has ambitiously turned its eye to a new capitalist future (p. 864).

Warsaw (4 days) Proud and resilient, Warsaw has emerged undaunted by everything the 20th century threw its way (p. 793).

Kyiv (4 days) On the site of the 2004 "Orange Revolution," promises of reform keep historic Kyiv looking forward (p. 1050).

Prague (5 days) Prague's Baroque architecture, tranquil gardens, and free-flowing booze make the city a budget travel staple (p. 237).

Kraków (3 days) Poland's cultural capital, Kraków is home to a lively student population and a rich Jewish history (p. 801).

Bratislava (2 days) From castles to cafes, Bratislava is a surprisingly sophisticated example of the new Eastern Europe (p. 887).

Ljubljiana (2 days) Stroll the picturesque, relaxed, and untouristed streets of up-and-coming Ljubljiana (p. 899).

Budapest (5 days) The storied Hapsburg metropolis of Budapest, spanning the Danube River, is a classic backpacker destination (p. 523).

Dalmatian Coast (5 days) With sun, pebble beaches, and beautiful people galore, the Dalmatian Coast puts the "ease" in Eastern Europe (p. 225).

Lake Balaton (2 days) Enjoy a wide array of water-sports, fresh seafood, and throbbing nightlife at Lake Balaton, a popular resort since Roman times (p. 539).

(6 WEEKS)

Piran (2 days)
At the foot of the Alps, on Slovenia's sliver of coastline, Piran offers scuba diving and Venetian architecture (p. 903).
Pula (1 day)
On the Istrian Peninsula, Pula's Roman ruins are as stunning as its cool, clear waters (p. 223).
Dubrovnik (2 days)
Watch the sun set over the Adriatic from atop Dubrovnik's limestone city walls (p. 228).
Split (1 day)
Wedged between mountains and sea, Split's cultural attractions are as much of a draw as the palm-lined waterfront (p. 226).
Mykonos (1 day)
The chic playground of Mykonos is home to hedonistic nighttime revelry (p. 508).
Delos (1 day)
The archaeological site of the Sanctuary of Apollo takes up the entire island of Delos, sacred center of the Cyclades (p. 509).
Corfu (1 day)
Lush beauty attracts hordes of admirers, but the island is big enough to find unspoiled beaches and traditional towns not far from the beaten path (p. 505).
Siena (1 day)
A medieval gem often unfairly overshadowed by Florence and Rome (p. 669).
Bay of Naples Islands (1 day)
Capri's pristine waters and pricey shops appeal to the rich, while Ischia's hot springs and ruins have a more earthy beauty (p. 682).
Nafplion (2 days)
Cross the Peleponnese to Nafplion, with its historic architecture and majestic harbor (p. 496).
Iraklion (2 days)
From Iraklion, visit the Minoan palaces at Knossos, famous as the home of the Minotaur, then return for the glitzy nightlife (p. 512).
Naples (2 days)
The chaotic home of pizza offers treats for gourmands and history buffs alike (p. 676).
Olympia (1 day)
Visit the ancient arena at Olympia, site of the original pan-Hellenic games (p. 495).
Hania (1 day)
Relax in Hania's cafes or take a bus to hike through the spectacular Samaria Gorge (p. 513).

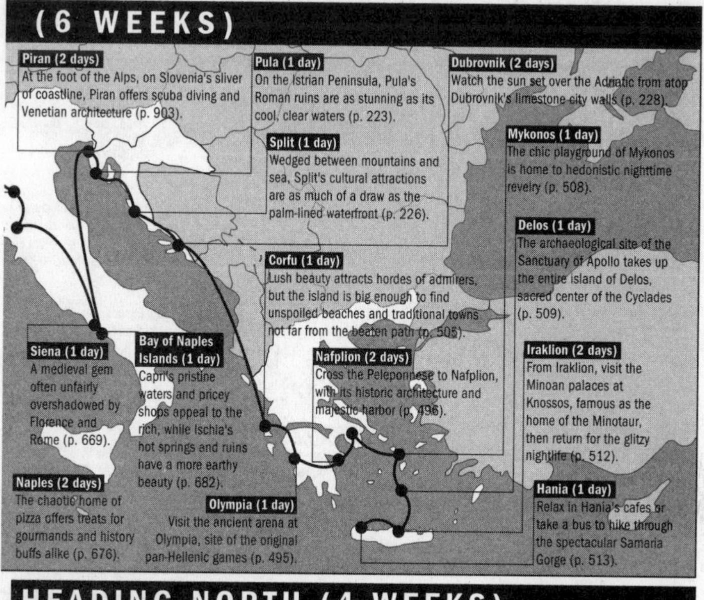

HEADING NORTH (4 WEEKS)

Reykjavík (1 day)
Start your trip in this stark, striking city; any trip to Europe via IcelandAir includes a free stopover in Iceland (p. 546).
Þingvellir National Park (1 day)
Make your way through jagged lava fields to Lake Þingvallavatn, Iceland's largest lake, and see why Iceland is celebrated for its spectacular natural wonders (p. 554).
Stockholm (3 days)
Built upon a delicate latticework of bridges, islands, and peninsulas, Stockholm's unique architecture speaks to its understanding of harmony (p. 985).
Gulfoss and Geysir (1 day)
Escape the city to watch the Strokkur geyser spew sulfurous water 35m into the air (p. 552).
Turku (1 day)
Drink up in the unusual pubs of Finland's oldest city (p. 307).
Geirangerfjord (1 day)
Soak in the splendor of the region's narrow cliffs and waterfalls (p. 778).
Bergen (2 days)
Hike the peaks surrounding this relaxed city or visit its unique Leprosy Museum (p. 768).
Sognefjord (1 day)
Admire Norway's natural beauty along the country's deepest fjord (p. 775).
Helsinki (2 days)
Tour Alvar Aalto's Modernist buildings in the midst of this neoclassical city (p. 298).
Uppsala (1 day)
Take in the academic vibe of this university town (p. 996).
Oslo (2 days)
Experience Oslo's world-class museums and ethnic eateries, or return to traditional Norway with a trip to the Viking Ship Museum and a whale burger (p. 758).
Gothenburg (2 days)
Enjoy the youthful atmosphere of this up-and-coming city in southwestern Sweden (p. 1003).
Hillerød (1 day)
Daytrip from Copenhagen to play in hedge mazes on the well-kept grounds at Fredericksborg Slot, a 16th-century castle (p. 272).
Malmo (1 day)
Visit the bustling open-air markets and packed cafes of Sweden's most diverse city (p. 1000).
Copenhagen (3 days)
Party until breakfast time in this multicultural, cosmopolitan city (p. 262).
Århus (1 day)
Stroll through the pedestrian walkways of this laidback city en route to the modern art in the Århus Kunstmuseum (p. 278).
Odense (1 day)
Come for Hans Christian Andersen, but stay for the nightlife and music scene (p. 276).

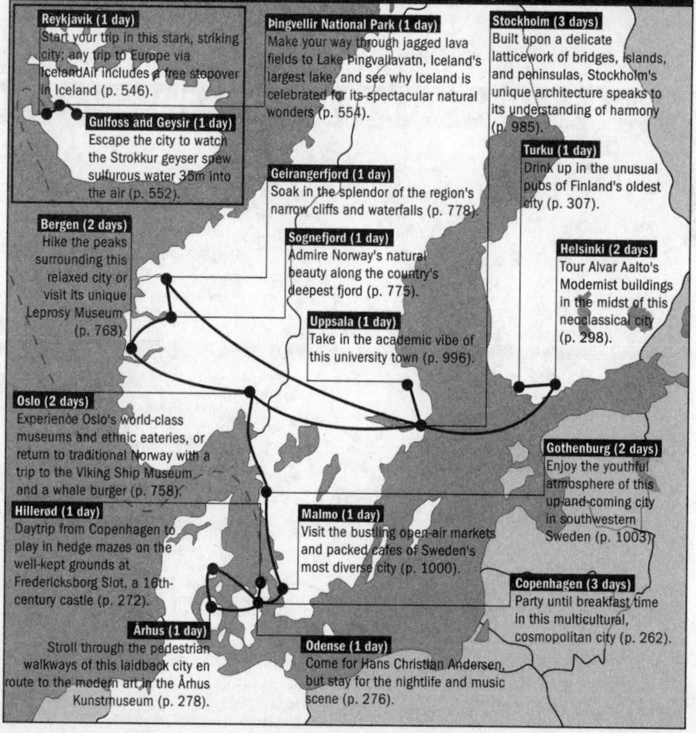

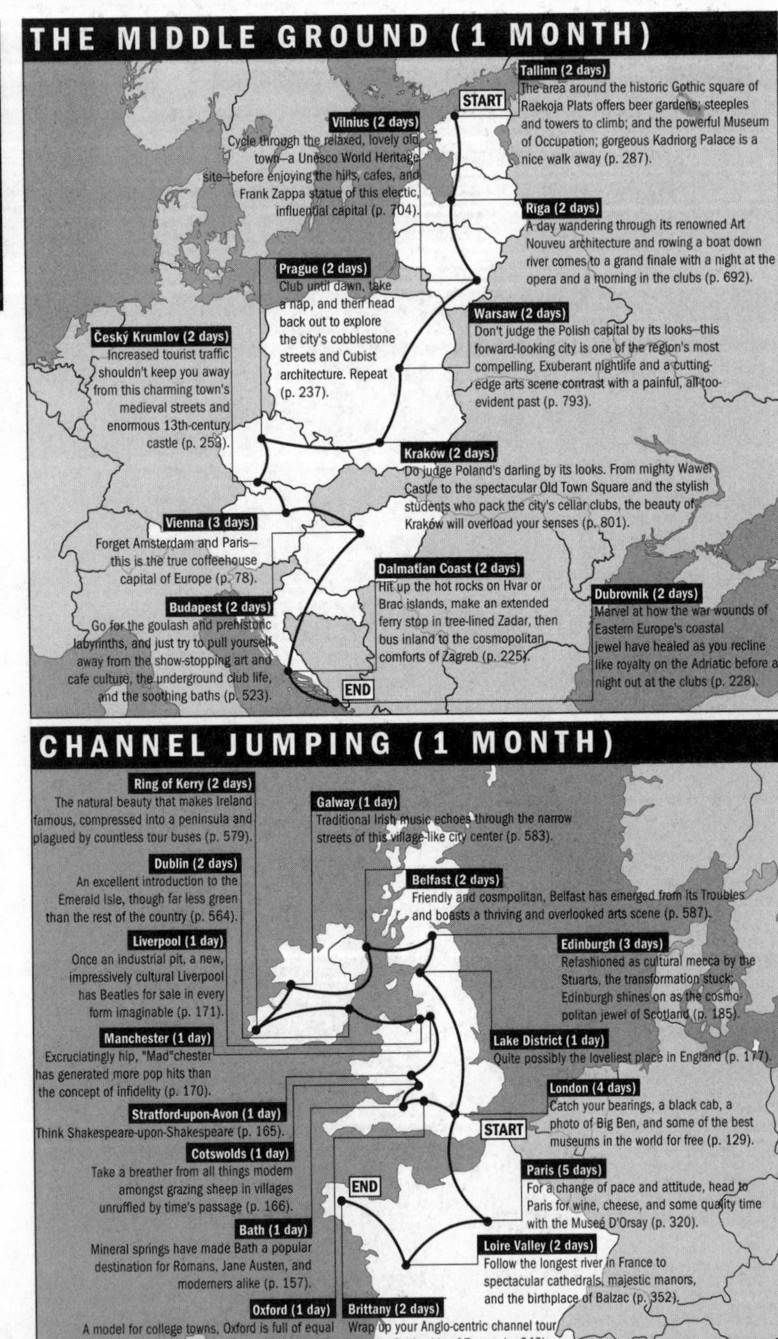
THE MIDDLE GROUND (1 MONTH)
START
Tallinn (2 days)
The area around the historic Gothic square of Raekoja Plats offers beer gardens; steeples and towers to climb; and the powerful Museum of Occupation; gorgeous Kadriorg Palace is a nice walk away (p. 287).
Vilnius (2 days)
Cycle through the relaxed, lovely old town—a Unesco World Heritage site—before enjoying the hills, cafes, and Frank Zappa statue of this electic, influential capital (p. 704).
Rīga (2 days)
A day wandering through its renowned Art Nouveu architecture and rowing a boat down river comes to a grand finale with a night at the opera and a morning in the clubs (p. 692).
Prague (2 days)
Club until dawn, take a nap, and then head back out to explore the city's cobblestone streets and Cubist architecture. Repeat (p. 237).
Warsaw (2 days)
Don't judge the Polish capital by its looks—this forward-looking city is one of the region's most compelling. Exuberant nightlife and a cutting-edge arts scene contrast with a painful, all-too-evident past (p. 793).
Český Krumlov (2 days)
Increased tourist traffic shouldn't keep you away from this charming town's medieval streets and enormous 13th-century castle (p. 253).
Kraków (2 days)
Do judge Poland's darling by its looks. From mighty Wawel Castle to the spectacular Old Town Square and the stylish students who pack the city's cellar clubs, the beauty of Kraków will overload your senses (p. 801).
Vienna (3 days)
Forget Amsterdam and Paris—this is the true coffeehouse capital of Europe (p. 78).
Dalmatian Coast (2 days)
Hit up the hot rocks on Hvar or Brac islands, make an extended ferry stop in tree-lined Zadar, then bus inland to the cosmopolitan comforts of Zagreb (p. 225).
Dubrovnik (2 days)
Marvel at how the war wounds of Eastern Europe's coastal jewel have healed as you recline like royalty on the Adriatic before a night out at the clubs (p. 228).
Budapest (2 days)
Go for the goulash and prehistoric labyrinths, and just try to pull yourself away from the show-stopping art and cafe culture, the underground club life, and the soothing baths (p. 523).
END
CHANNEL JUMPING (1 MONTH)
Ring of Kerry (2 days)
The natural beauty that makes Ireland famous, compressed into a peninsula and plagued by countless tour buses (p. 579).
Galway (1 day)
Traditional Irish music echoes through the narrow streets of this village-like city center (p. 583).
Dublin (2 days)
An excellent introduction to the Emerald Isle, though far less green than the rest of the country (p. 564).
Belfast (2 days)
Friendly and cosmpolitan, Belfast has emerged from its Troubles and boasts a thriving and overlooked arts scene (p. 587).
Liverpool (1 day)
Once an industrial pit, a new, impressively cultural Liverpool has Beatles for sale in every form imaginable (p. 171).
Edinburgh (3 days)
Refashioned as cultural mecca by the Stuarts, the transformation stuck; Edinburgh shines on as the cosmopolitan jewel of Scotland (p. 185).
Manchester (1 day)
Excruciatingly hip, "Mad"chester has generated more pop hits than the concept of infidelity (p. 170).
Lake District (1 day)
Quite possibly the loveliest place in England (p. 177).
London (4 days)
Catch your bearings, a black cab, a photo of Big Ben, and some of the best museums in the world for free (p. 129).
Stratford-upon-Avon (1 day)
Think Shakespeare-upon-Shakespeare (p. 165).
START
Cotswolds (1 day)
Take a breather from all things modern amongst grazing sheep in villages unruffled by time's passage (p. 166).
Paris (5 days)
For a change of pace and attitude, head to Paris for wine, cheese, and some quality time with the Museé D'Orsay (p. 320).
END
Bath (1 day)
Mineral springs have made Bath a popular destination for Romans, Jane Austen, and moderners alike (p. 157).
Loire Valley (2 days)
Follow the longest river in France to spectacular cathedrals, majestic manors, and the birthplace of Balzac (p. 352).
Oxford (1 day)
A model for college towns, Oxford is full of equal parts binge studying and diligent drinking (p. 161).
Brittany (2 days)
Wrap up your Anglo-centric channel tour with the Celtic side of France (p. 348).

THE ULTIMATE PUB CRAWL

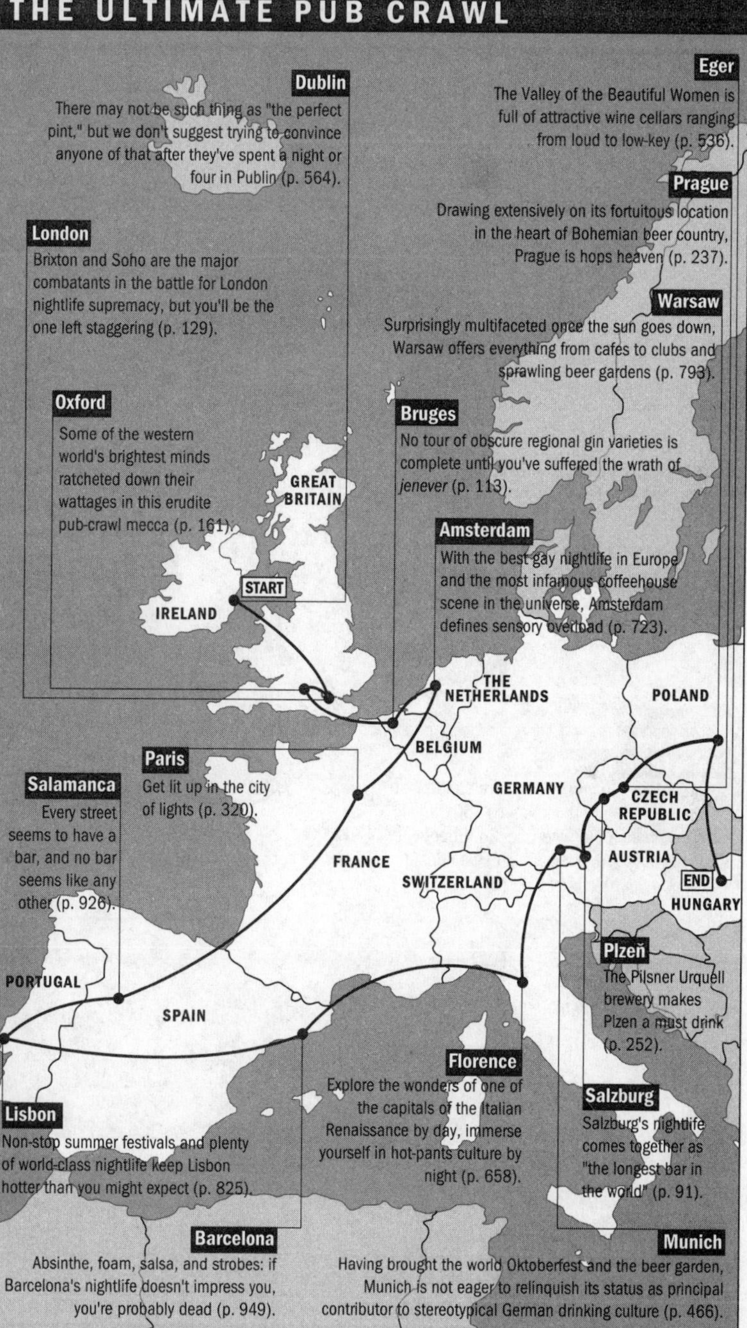
Dublin
There may not be such thing as "the perfect pint," but we don't suggest trying to convince anyone of that after they've spent a night or four in Publin (p. 564).
London
Brixton and Soho are the major combatants in the battle for London nightlife supremacy, but you'll be the one left staggering (p. 129).
Oxford
Some of the western world's brightest minds ratcheted down their wattages in this erudite pub-crawl mecca (p. 161).
Eger
The Valley of the Beautiful Women is full of attractive wine cellars ranging from loud to low-key (p. 536).
Prague
Drawing extensively on its fortuitous location in the heart of Bohemian beer country, Prague is hops heaven (p. 237).
Warsaw
Surprisingly multifaceted once the sun goes down, Warsaw offers everything from cafes to clubs and sprawling beer gardens (p. 793).
Bruges
No tour of obscure regional gin varieties is complete until you've suffered the wrath of jenever (p. 113).
Amsterdam
With the best gay nightlife in Europe and the most infamous coffeehouse scene in the universe, Amsterdam defines sensory overload (p. 723).
GREAT BRITAIN
START
IRELAND
THE NETHERLANDS
POLAND
BELGIUM
Paris
Get lit up in the city of lights (p. 320).
Salamanca
Every street seems to have a bar, and no bar seems like any other (p. 926).
GERMANY
CZECH REPUBLIC
FRANCE
AUSTRIA
SWITZERLAND
END
HUNGARY
Plzeň
The Pilsner Urquell brewery makes Plzen a must drink (p. 252).
PORTUGAL
SPAIN
Florence
Explore the wonders of one of the capitals of the Italian Renaissance by day, immerse yourself in hot-pants culture by night (p. 658).
Salzburg
Salzburg's nightlife comes together as "the longest bar in the world" (p. 91).
Lisbon
Non-stop summer festivals and plenty of world-class nightlife keep Lisbon hotter than you might expect (p. 825).
Barcelona
Absinthe, foam, salsa, and strobes: if Barcelona's nightlife doesn't impress you, you're probably dead (p. 949).
Munich
Having brought the world Oktoberfest and the beer garden, Munich is not eager to relinquish its status as principal contributor to stereotypical German drinking culture (p. 466).

FESTIVALS

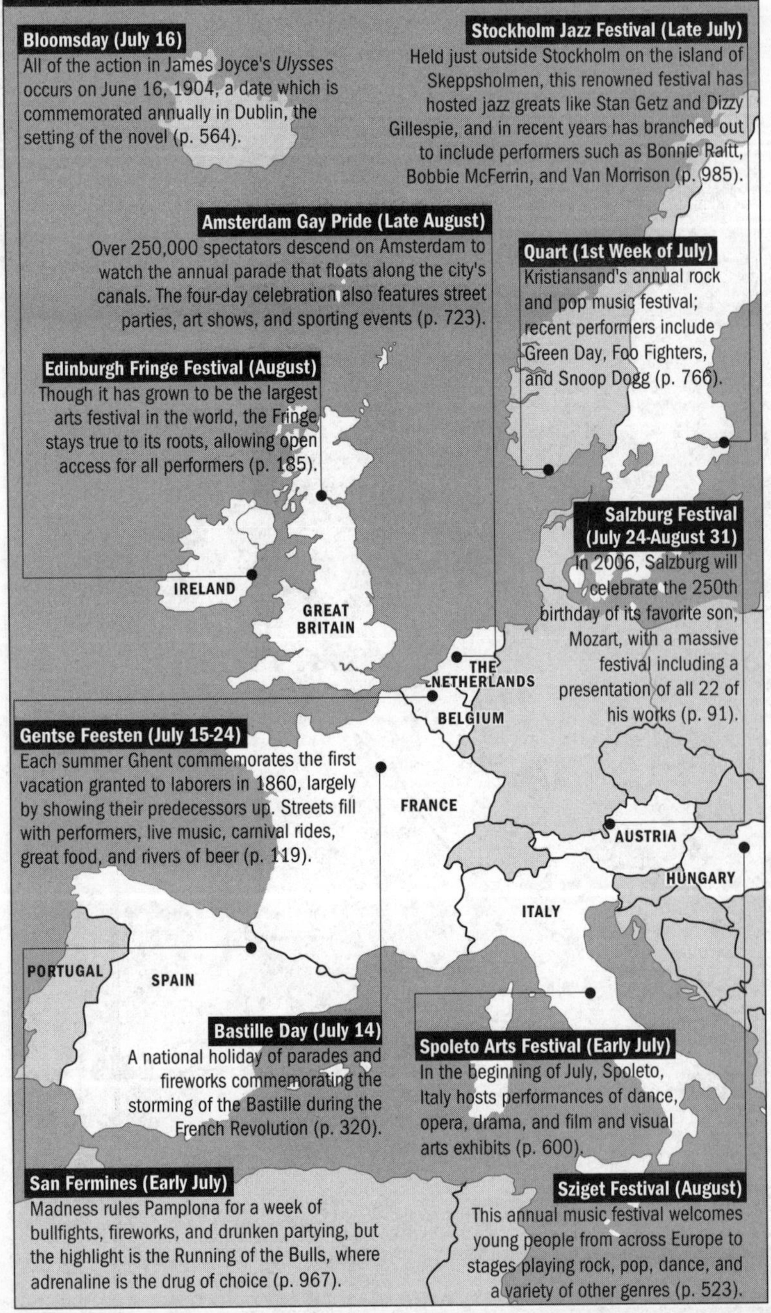

Bloomsday (July 16)
All of the action in James Joyce's *Ulysses* occurs on June 16, 1904, a date which is commemorated annually in Dublin, the setting of the novel (p. 564).

Stockholm Jazz Festival (Late July)
Held just outside Stockholm on the island of Skeppsholmen, this renowned festival has hosted jazz greats like Stan Getz and Dizzy Gillespie, and in recent years has branched out to include performers such as Bonnie Raitt, Bobbie McFerrin, and Van Morrison (p. 985).

Amsterdam Gay Pride (Late August)
Over 250,000 spectators descend on Amsterdam to watch the annual parade that floats along the city's canals. The four-day celebration also features street parties, art shows, and sporting events (p. 723).

Quart (1st Week of July)
Kristiansand's annual rock and pop music festival; recent performers include Green Day, Foo Fighters, and Snoop Dogg (p. 766).

Edinburgh Fringe Festival (August)
Though it has grown to be the largest arts festival in the world, the Fringe stays true to its roots, allowing open access for all performers (p. 185).

Salzburg Festival (July 24-August 31)
In 2006, Salzburg will celebrate the 250th birthday of its favorite son, Mozart, with a massive festival including a presentation of all 22 of his works (p. 91).

IRELAND
GREAT BRITAIN
THE NETHERLANDS
BELGIUM

Gentse Feesten (July 15-24)
Each summer Ghent commemorates the first vacation granted to laborers in 1860, largely by showing their predecessors up. Streets fill with performers, live music, carnival rides, great food, and rivers of beer (p. 119).

FRANCE
AUSTRIA
HUNGARY
ITALY
PORTUGAL
SPAIN

Bastille Day (July 14)
A national holiday of parades and fireworks commemorating the storming of the Bastille during the French Revolution (p. 320).

Spoleto Arts Festival (Early July)
In the beginning of July, Spoleto, Italy hosts performances of dance, opera, drama, and film and visual arts exhibits (p. 600).

San Fermines (Early July)
Madness rules Pamplona for a week of bullfights, fireworks, and drunken partying, but the highlight is the Running of the Bulls, where adrenaline is the drug of choice (p. 967).

Sziget Festival (August)
This annual music festival welcomes young people from across Europe to stages playing rock, pop, dance, and a variety of other genres (p. 523).

ESSENTIALS

PLANNING YOUR TRIP

BEFORE YOU GO

Passport (p. 15). Required for all non-EU citizens traveling in Europe.

Visa (p. 16). Not required for citizens of Australia, Canada, Ireland, New Zealand, the UK, and the US for stays shorter than 90 days in a 6-month period in most European countries.

Work Permit (p. 16). Required for all foreigners planning to work in any European country.

Recommended Vaccinations (p. 27). All visitors should be up to date on vaccines, especially for diphtheria, hepatitis A, hepatitis B, and mumps. Visitors to Eastern Europe should also have measles, rabies, and typhoid vaccines.

EMBASSIES AND CONSULATES

CONSULAR SERVICES

Information about European consular services abroad and foreign consular services in Europe is located in individual country chapters; it can also be found at www.embassiesabroad.com and www.embassyworld.com.

TOURIST OFFICES

Information about national tourist boards in Europe is located in individual country chapters; it can also be found at www.towd.com.

DOCUMENTS AND FORMALITIES

PASSPORTS

REQUIREMENTS

Citizens of Australia, Canada, Ireland, New Zealand, the UK, and the US need valid passports to enter European countries and to re-enter their home countries. Most countries do not allow entrance if the holder's passport expires within six months; returning home with an expired passport is illegal, and may result in a fine.

NEW PASSPORTS

Citizens of Australia, Canada, Ireland, New Zealand, the UK, and the US can apply for a passport at any passport office, most post offices, and courts of law. New passport or renewal applications must be filed at least two months in advance of departure, though most passport offices offer rush services for a steep fee. Even "rushed" passports take up to two weeks to arrive. Citizens living abroad who need a new passport should contact the passport office of their home country.

PASSPORT MAINTENANCE

If you lose your passport, immediately notify local police and the nearest embassy or consulate of your home government. To expedite its replacement, you must know all personal information on record, and show ID and proof of citizenship. A

ESSENTIALS

ONE EUROPE. European unity has come a long way since 1958, when the European Economic Community (EEC) was created to promote European solidarity and cooperation. Since then, the EEC has become the European Union (EU), a mighty political, legal, and economic institution. On May 1, 2004, 10 South, Central, and Eastern European countries—Cyprus, the Czech Republic, Estonia, Hungary, Latvia, Lithuania, Malta, Poland, the Slovak Republic, and Slovenia—were admitted to the EU, joining 15 other member states: Austria, Belgium, Denmark, Finland, France, Germany, Greece, Ireland, Italy, Luxembourg, the Netherlands, Portugal, Spain, Sweden, and the UK.

What does this mean for travelers to the EU? The EU's policy of **freedom of movement** means that border controls between the 1st 15 member states (minus Ireland and the UK, but plus Norway and Iceland) have been abolished, and visa policies harmonized. Under this treaty, formally known as the **Schengen Agreement,** you're still required to carry a passport (a government-issued ID card for EU citizens) when crossing an internal border, but once you've been admitted to one country, you're free to travel to other participating states. On June 5, 2005, Switzerland signed on, and will be a full participant by 2007. The 10 newest member states will implement the policy after 2006. Britain and Ireland have also formed a **common travel area,** abolishing passport controls between the UK and the Republic of Ireland. For more important consequences of the EU for travelers, see **The Euro** (p. 21) and **Customs in the EU** (p. 19).

replacement may take weeks to process, and may be valid for a limited time. Any visas stamped in your old passport will be lost. In an emergency, ask for immediate temporary traveling papers that will permit you to re-enter your home country.

VISAS AND WORK PERMITS

VISAS

As of August 2005, citizens of Australia, Canada, Ireland, New Zealand, the UK, or the US do not need a visa to visit the following countries for less than 90 days: Austria, Belgium, Croatia, Czech Republic, Denmark, Estonia, Finland, France, Germany, Greece, Hungary, Iceland, Italy, Latvia, Liechtenstein, Lithuania, Luxembourg, the Netherlands, Norway, Poland, Portugal, Slovak Republic, Slovenia, Spain, Sweden, and Switzerland. Furthermore, citizens of Australia, Canada, New Zealand, and the US do not need visas to enter Ireland or the UK for less than 90 days. Canadian citizens do not need a visa to visit Romania for less than 90 days; citizens of Ireland, the UK, and the US do not need a visa for stays under 30 days; citizens of Australia and New Zealand need a visa to enter Romania.

For travelers planning to spend more than three months in any European country, visas cost US$35-200 and typically allow you to spend six months in that country. Visas can usually be purchased at a consulate or at www.itseasypassport.com/services/visas/visas.htm. All travelers to Russia and the Ukraine must have a visa. For details on Russian visas see p. 857, on Ukrainian visas see p. 1045.

Double-check entrance requirements at the nearest embassy or consulate of your destination for up-to-date info before departure. US citizens can also consult http://travel.state.gov/foreignentryreqs.html.

WORK PERMITS

Admission as a visitor does not include the right to work, which is authorized only by a work permit. Entering a country in Europe to study often requires a special study visa, though many study-abroad programs subsidize it. For more information, see p. 66.

BETTER SAFE THAN STRANDED. Europe is a nice place to visit, but a bad place to be stuck without money or identification. Before you go, make copies of the photo page of your passport, your visa, travelers' checks' serial numbers, as well as any other important documents you will have with you on your trip. Carry one set of copies in a safe place, apart from the originals, and leave another set at home. In case you lose your passport, you will have the necessary information to obtain a temporary one to return home. Consulates also recommend that you carry an expired passport or an official copy of your birth certificate in a part of your baggage separate from other documents.

IDENTIFICATION

When you travel, always carry at least two forms of identification on your person, including a photo ID; a passport and a driver's license or birth certificate is usually adequate. Never carry all of your IDs together; split them up in case of theft or loss, and keep photocopies of all of them in your luggage and at home.

STUDENT, TEACHER, AND YOUTH IDENTIFICATION

SAVING AROUND THE WORLD. Those in possession of the ISIC, ITIC or IYTC pay less to sightsee, eat, shop, and travel. The US$22 card will gain access to over 17,000 discounts in Europe alone, and can often secure cheaper airfares when booking through travel agents. ISIC works as a phone card that can be activated online with a credit card or can be used to call collect. Consult www.isic.org for more discount information. Like all discount cards, ISIC only works if you ask about student discounts when making purchases; don't be shy to seek out these deals.

The **International Student Identity Card (ISIC),** the most widely accepted form of student ID, provides discounts on some sights, accommodations, food, and transport; access to a 24hr. emergency helpline; and insurance benefits for US cardholders (see **Insurance,** p. 27). Applicants must be full-time secondary or post-secondary school students at least 12 years of age. Because of the proliferation of fake ISICs, some services (particularly airlines) require additional proof of student status.

The **International Teacher Identity Card (ITIC)** offers teachers the same insurance coverage as the ISIC and similar but more limited discounts. For travelers who are under 26 years old but are not students, the **International Youth Travel Card (IYTC)** also offers many of the same benefits as the ISIC.

Each of these identity cards costs US$22. ISICs and ITICs are valid until the new year; if purchased between September and December, they are valid for the rest of that year and the next calendar year; IYTCs are valid for one year from the date of issue. Many student travel agencies issue the cards; for a list of agencies, see the **International Student Travel Confederation (ISTC)** website (www.istc.org).

CUSTOMS

When you enter a European country, you have to declare certain foreign items and pay a duty on the value of those items if they exceed a set allowance. Goods purchased at **duty-free** shops aren't exempt from duty or sales tax; "duty-free" only means that you don't need to pay a tax in the country of purchase. When you go home, you must again declare all articles bought abroad and pay a duty on the value of articles in excess of your home country's allowance.

Every country in the European Union has a **Value Added Tax (VAT)** which can be claimed upon departure. Policies granting such refunds to travelers are set by individual countries (see **Taxes,** p. 23).

CUSTOMS IN THE EU. In addition to the freedom of movement of people within the EU (p. 16), travelers in the 15 original EU member countries (Austria, Belgium, Denmark, Finland, France, Germany, Greece, Ireland, Italy, Luxembourg, the Netherlands, Portugal, Spain, Sweden, and the UK) can also take advantage of the freedom of movement of goods. This means that there are no customs controls at internal EU borders (i.e., you can take the blue customs channel at the airport), and travelers are free to transport whatever legal substances they like as long as it is for their own personal (non-commercial) use—up to 800 cigarettes, 10L of spirits, 90L of wine (including up to 60L of sparkling wine), and 110L of beer. Duty-free allowances have been abolished for travel between the original 15 EU member states; this now also applies to Cyprus and Malta. However, travelers between the EU and the rest of the world still get a duty-free allowance when passing through customs.

MONEY

CURRENCY AND EXCHANGE

EUROS (€)	
AUS$1 = EUR€0.61	EUR€1 = AUS$1.62
CDN$1 = EUR€0.68	EUR€1 = CDN$1.46
NZ$1 = EUR€0.56	EUR€1 = NZ$1.74
UK£1 = EUR€1.46	EUR€1 = UK£0.68
US$1 = EUR€0.81	EUR€1 = US$1.23

The currency chart above is based on August 2005 exchange rates between European Union euros (EUR€) and Australian dollars (AUS$), Canadian dollars (CDN$), New Zealand dollars (NZ$), British pounds (UK£), and US dollars (US$). Check the currency converter on websites like www.xe.com/ucc or a large newspaper for the latest exchange rates. As a general rule, it's cheaper to convert money in Europe than at home. However, you should bring enough foreign currency for the first few days of a trip to avoid being penniless if you arrive after bank hours or on a holiday. When changing money abroad, try to go only to banks or change bureaus that have at most a 5% margin between their buy and sell prices.

MONEY, MONEY, MONEY. Since you lose money with every transaction, convert large sums (unless the currency is depreciating rapidly), but no more than you'll need.

If you use traveler's checks or bills, carry some in small denominations (the equivalent of US$50 or less) for times when you are forced to exchange money at disadvantageous rates, but bring a range of denominations since charges may be levied per check cashed. Store your money in a variety of forms; ideally, at any given time you will be carrying some cash, some traveler's checks, and an ATM and/or credit card. All travelers should also consider carrying some US dollars (about US$50 worth), which are often preferred by local tellers.

For more info on currency and exchange rates, see individual country chapters.

TRAVELER'S CHECKS

Traveler's checks are one of the safest and least troublesome means of carrying funds. American Express and Visa are the most recognized brands. Many banks and agencies sell traveler's checks for a small fee. Check issuers provide refunds if the checks are lost or stolen; many provide additional services, like toll-free

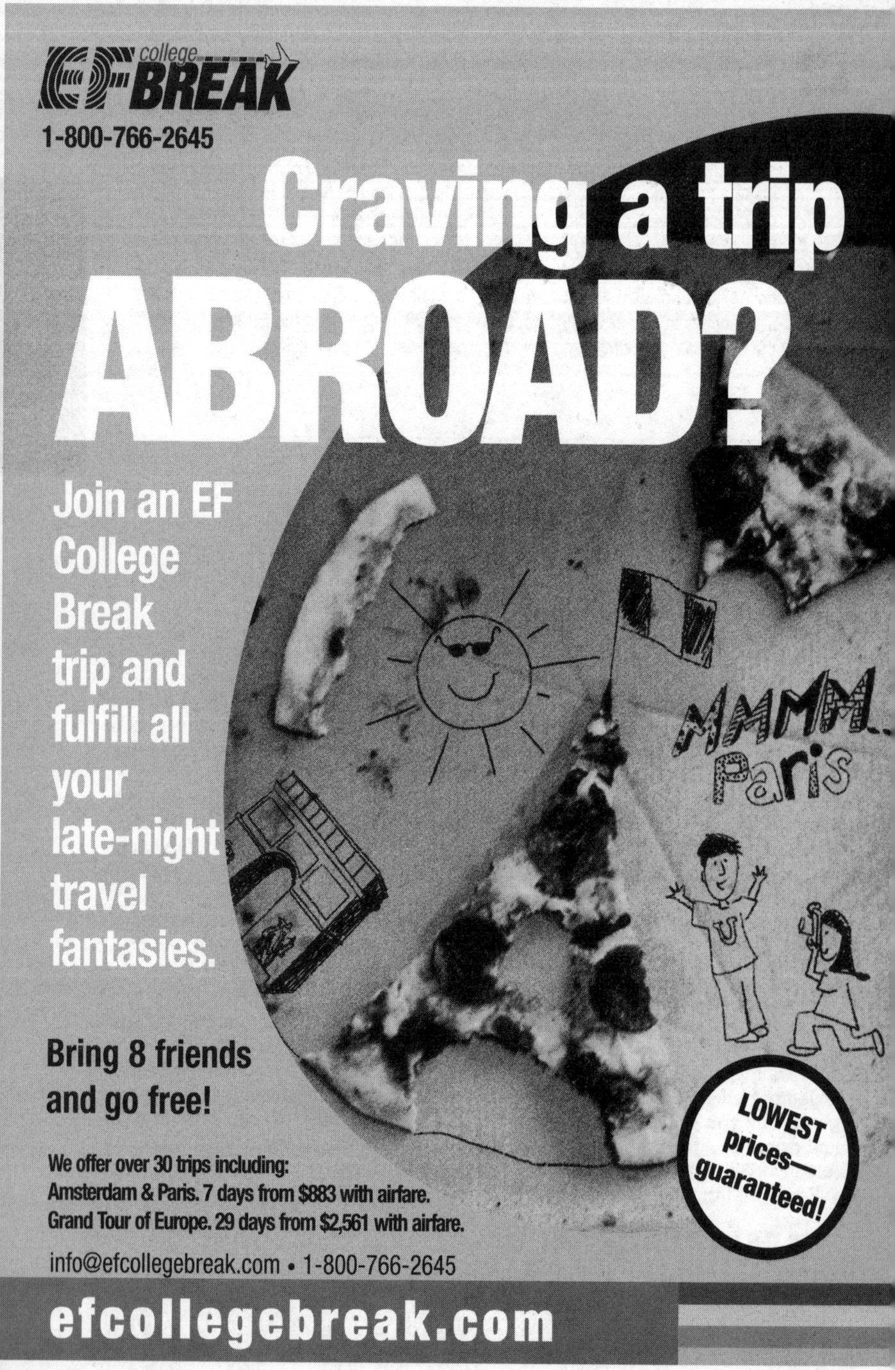

EF college BREAK
1-800-766-2645
Craving a trip ABROAD?
Join an EF College Break trip and fulfill all your late-night travel fantasies.
MMMM... Paris
U
Bring 8 friends and go free!
We offer over 30 trips including:
Amsterdam & Paris. 7 days from $883 with airfare.
Grand Tour of Europe. 29 days from $2,561 with airfare.
info@efcollegebreak.com • 1-800-766-2645
efcollegebreak.com
LOWEST prices— guaranteed!

THE EURO. The official currency of 12 members of the European Union–Austria, Belgium, Finland, France, Germany, Greece, Ireland, Italy, Luxembourg, the Netherlands, Portugal, and Spain–is now the euro.

The currency has some important–and positive–consequences for travelers hitting more than one euro-zone country. For one thing, money-changers across the euro-zone are obliged to exchange money at the official, fixed rate, and at no commission (though they may still charge a small service fee). Second, traveler's checks in euros allow you to pay for goods and services across the euro-zone, again at the official rate and commission-free.

refund hotlines, emergency message services, and stolen credit card assistance. Traveler's checks are accepted throughout Europe, though you may have trouble using them in less touristed areas and small towns, especially in Eastern Europe. Ask about toll-free refund hotlines and the location of refund centers when purchasing checks, and always carry emergency cash. If you pay for traveler's checks with a credit card, it may count as a cash advance, carrying hefty fees and interest.

American Express: Cheques available with commission at select banks, AmEx offices, and online (www.americanexpress.com; US residents only). AmEx cardholders can also purchase checks by phone (☎800-721-9768). Available in Australian, British, Canadian, European, Japanese, and US currencies, among others. American Express also offers the Travelers Cheque Card, a prepaid reloadable card. Cheques for Two can be signed by either of 2 people traveling together. For more information, contact AmEx's service centers: Australia ☎800 688 022, New Zealand 423 74 409, the UK 0800 587 6023, the US and Canada 800-221-7282; elsewhere, call the US collect at 801-964-6665.

Travelex: Thomas Cook MasterCard and Interpayment Visa traveler's checks are other options. For information about Thomas Cook MasterCard call: Canada and the US ☎800-223-7373, the UK 0800 622 101; elsewhere call the UK collect at +44 1733 318 950. For information about Interpayment Visa in the US and Canada call ☎800-732-1322, in the UK 0800 515 884; elsewhere call the UK collect at +44 1733 318 949. For more information, visit www.travelex.com.

Visa: Checks available (generally with commission) at banks worldwide. For the location of the nearest office, call the Visa Travelers Cheque Global Refund and Assistance Center: the UK ☎0800 515 884, the US 800-227-6811, elsewhere, call the UK collect at +44 2079 378 091. Checks available in British, Canadian, European, Japanese, and US currencies, among others. Visa also offers TravelMoney, a prepaid debit card that can be reloaded online or by phone. For more information on Visa travel services, see http://usa.visa.com/personal/using_visa/travel_with_visa.html.

CREDIT, ATM, AND DEBIT CARDS

Where they are accepted, credit cards often offer superior exchange rates—up to 5% better than the retail rate used by banks and other currency exchange establishments. Credit cards may also offer services such as insurance or emergency help, and are sometimes required to reserve hotel rooms or rental cars. **Mastercard** (a.k.a. **EuroCard** or **Access** in Europe) and **Visa** (a.k.a. **Carte Bleue** or **Barclaycard**) are the most widely accepted; **American Express** cards work at some ATMs and at AmEx offices and most major airports. A **debit card** can be used wherever its associated credit card company (usually Mastercard or Visa) is accepted. Debit cards often function as ATM cards and can be used to withdraw cash from associated banks and ATMs throughout Europe. Ask your local bank about obtaining one.

ATM machines are common in Europe and usually have instructions in several languages. You can most likely access your personal bank account from abroad. ATMs get the same wholesale exchange rate as credit cards, but there is often a limit on the amount of money you can withdraw per day (usually around US$500). There is typically a surcharge of US$1-5 per withdrawal.

Some banks add conversion fees (1-4%) on international purchases. Read your card agreement carefully to avoid hidden fines. Be sure to have backup finances if you'll be traveling extensively in Eastern Europe or rural areas of Western Europe; many places don't accept credit cards, and functional ATMs may be hard to find.

PINS AND ATMS. To use a cash or credit card to withdraw money from an ATM in Europe, you must have a 4-digit **Personal Identification Number (PIN).** If your PIN is longer than 4 digits, ask your bank whether you can just use the first 4, or whether you'll need a new one. **Credit cards** don't usually come with PINs, so if you intend to hit up ATMs in Europe with a credit card to get cash advances, call your credit card company before leaving to request one.
Travelers with alphabetic, rather than numerical PINs may also be thrown off by the lack of letters on European cash machines. The following are the corresponding numbers to use: 1=QZ; 2=ABC; 3=DEF; 4=GHI; 5=JKL; 6=MNO; 7=PRS; 8=TUV; and 9=WXY. Note that if you mistakenly punch the wrong code into the machine 3 times, it will swallow your card for good.

ESSENTIALS

GETTING MONEY FROM HOME

If you run out of money while traveling, the easiest and cheapest solution is to have someone at home deposit to the bank account linked to your card. Failing that, consider the options below. The **International Money Transfer Consumer Guide** (http://international-money-transfer-consumer-guide.info) may also be of help.

WIRING MONEY

It is possible to arrange a **bank money transfer,** which means asking a bank back home to wire money to a bank in Europe. This is the cheapest and slowest way to transfer cash, usually taking several days or more. Note that some banks may only release your funds in local currency, potentially sticking you with a poor exchange rate; ask about this in advance. Money transfer services like **Western Union** are faster and more convenient than bank transfers—but also much pricier. Western Union has many locations worldwide. To find one, visit www.westernunion.com, or call ☎800-325-6000. To wire money using a major credit card, call in Canada and the US ☎800-225-5227, in the UK 0800 833 833. Money transfer services are available to **American Express** cardholders and at selected **Thomas Cook** offices.

US STATE DEPARTMENT (US CITIZENS ONLY)

In serious emergencies only, the US State Department will forward money within hours to the nearest consular office, which will then disburse it according to instructions for a US$30 fee. If you wish to use this service, you must contact the Overseas Citizens Service division (☎202-647-5225, toll-free 888-407-4747).

COSTS

The cost of your trip will vary considerably, depending on where you go, how you travel, and where you stay. The most significant expenses will probably be your round-trip (return) **airfare** to Europe (see **Getting to Europe: By Plane,** p. 48) and a **railpass** or **bus pass** (see **Getting around Europe,** p. 53).

STAYING ON A BUDGET

Your daily budget will vary greatly from country to country. A bare-bones day in Europe would include camping or sleeping in hostels and buying food at supermarkets. A slightly more comfortable day would include sleeping in hostels or guesthouses and the occasional budget hotel, eating one meal per day at a restaurant, and going out at night. For a luxurious day, the sky's the limit. In any case, be sure to factor in emergency reserve funds (at least US$200) when planning how much money you'll need.

TIPS FOR SAVING MONEY

Simple ways to save include searching out free entertainment, splitting accommodation and food costs with trustworthy fellow travelers, and buying food in grocery stores or markets rather than eating out. Full- or multi-day local transportation passes can also save you pocket change. Bring a **sleepsack** (p. 24) to save at hostels that charge for linen, and do your **laundry** in the sink (unless you're prohibited from doing so). Museums often have certain days once a month or once a week when admission is free. If eligible, consider getting an ISIC or an IYTC; many sights and museums offer reduced admission to students and youths. For getting around quickly, bikes are the most economical option. Renting a bike is cheaper than a moped or scooter. Purchasing drinks at bars and clubs becomes expensive. It's cheaper to buy alcohol at a supermarket and drink before going out.

TIPPING AND BARGAINING

HOW TO HAGGLE. If you're not sure whether bargaining is appropriate, let the seller make the first move. Show some interest in an item and then lament that it's too expensive. If he makes a lower offer, you're safe to begin bargaining. Decide what you're willing to pay, don't let on that you just *have* to have that bag/necklace/Pope John Paul II statuette, and stay tough. Walking away is often an effective strategy for getting a lower price.

In most European countries, a 5-10% gratuity is included in the food service bill. An additional tip is not expected, but an extra 5-10% for good service is not unusual. If the gratuity is not included, 10-15% tips are standard and rounding up is common. Tipping in bars and pubs is unnecessary; money left on the bar may not make it into the bartender's hands. For other services like taxis or hairdressers, a 10-15% tip is recommended. Watch other customers to gauge what is appropriate. Bargaining is useful in Greece and outdoor markets across Europe. See individual country chapters for more specific information.

TAXES

The EU imposes a **Value Added Tax (VAT)** on goods and services, usually included in the sticker price. Non-EU citizens visiting Europe may obtain a refund for taxes

TOP TEN LIST

EUROPE ON THE CHEAP

1. Ask about discounts. If under 26, for example, you shouldn't go a day without being rewarded for your youth and inexperience.
2. Be aware that room prices tend to shoot up and transportation hassles abound on festival dates and local holidays.
3. Consider purchasing the combination transportation and sights discount passes offered by many city tourist offices; they often pay for themselves many times over.
4. Get out of the city. A day hiking or beach-lounging provides relief for both you and your wallet.
5. Travel early; trains, buses, and ferries leaving early in the day or on weekdays (as opposed to weekends) are generally cheaper than those leaving at other times.
6. If you live off ramen noodles at home, don't expect to eat out every meal in Europe. Street markets are excellent places to find cheap fruits and vegetables, and most hostels have kitchens.
7. In major cities, make your base on the outskirts of the town, where food and beds tend to be both cheaper and less touristed.
8. Bring a sleepsack to avoid the occasional linen rental charge.
9. In Eastern Europe, be wary of any establishment with English words in its name. Many of these will turn out to be tourist traps.
10. Be your own tour guide; the best pictures, and often the best memories, are acheived at no cost by simply walking through the cities you're visiting.

paid on unused retail goods, but not for taxes paid on services. The VAT is 15-25%; it may be worthwhile to file for a refund. To do so, you must obtain Tax-Free Shopping Cheques, available from shops with the Europe Tax-Free Shopping logo, and save your receipts. Upon leaving the EU, present your goods, invoices, and passport to customs and have your checks stamped. Go to an on site ETS cash refund office or file for a refund once back home. Keep in mind that goods must be taken out of the country within three months of the month of purchase, and most countries require minimum purchase amounts per store to become eligible for a refund. See www.globalrefund.org for more information and downloads of relevant forms.

PACKING

Let's Go advocates the golden rule of packing light: lay out only what you absolutely need, then take half the clothes and twice the money. The Travelite FAQ (www.travelite.org) is a good resource for packing tips. The online **Universal Packing List** (http://upl.codeq.info) will generate a customized list of suggested items based on your trip length, the expected climate, your planned activities, and other factors. If you plan to do a lot of hiking, also consult **The Great Outdoors**, p. 39.

Luggage: If you plan to cover most of your itinerary by foot, a sturdy **frame backpack** is unbeatable. (For the basics on buying a pack, see p. 41.) Toting a **suitcase** or **trunk** is fine if you plan to live in 1 or 2 cities and explore from there, but not a great idea if you plan to move around frequently. In addition to your main piece of luggage, a **daypack** (a small backpack or courier bag) is useful.

Clothing: No matter when you're traveling, it's a good idea to bring a warm jacket or wool sweater, a rain jacket (Gore-Tex® is both waterproof and breathable), sturdy shoes or hiking boots, and thick socks. Waterproof sandals are must-haves for grubby hostel showers. You may also want one outfit for going out, and maybe a nicer pair of shoes. If you plan to visit religious or cultural sites, remember that you will need modest and respectful dress. Our mothers always told us that cotton underwear is best. It's breathable, and keeps away that nasty bacteria that you don't want as your traveling buddies.

Sleepsack: Some hostels require that you either provide your own linen or rent sheets from them. Save cash by making your own sleepsack: fold a full-size sheet in half the long way, then sew it closed along the long side and one of the short sides.

Converters and Adapters: In Europe, electricity is 230V AC, enough to fry any 120V North American appliance. 220/240V electrical appliances won't work with a 120V current, either. Americans and Canadians should buy an adapter (changes the shape of the plug; US$15) and a converter (changes the voltage; US$10-30). Don't make the mistake of using only an adapter unless appliance instructions explicitly state otherwise. Australians and New Zealanders, who use 230V at home, won't need a converter, but will need a set of adapters. Check out http://kropla.com/electric.htm.

Toiletries: Toothbrushes, towels, cold-water soap, talcum powder (to keep feet dry), deodorant, razors, tampons, and condoms are generally available, but it may be difficult to find your preferred brand. If you insist on bringing your own shampoo and conditioner, pour it into travel-sized plastic bottles. Contact lenses are likely to be expensive and difficult to find, so bring extras and solution for your entire trip. Also bring your glasses and a copy of your prescription in case you need emergency replacements.

First-Aid: For a basic first-aid kit, pack bandages, a pain reliever, antibiotic cream, a thermometer, tweezers, moleskin, decongestant, motion-sickness remedy, diarrhea or upset-stomach medication (Pepto Bismol® or Imodium®), an antihistamine, insect repellent, and burn ointment. If you will be in regions of less-developed Eastern European countries, consider packing a syringe for emergencies (get an explanatory letter from your doctor). When flying, leave all sharp objects in your checked luggage.

Photography: Always pack film in your carry-on luggage since airport security uses high-intensity X-rays that can fog film in checked luggage. Some claim that carry-on X-rays can also fog film. If you are concerned, buy a lead-lined camera pouch or ask security to hand-inspect it. Consider using a digital camera. Although it requires a steep initial investment, a digital camera means you never have to buy film again. For more info on digital cameras, visit www.shortcourses.com/choosing/contents.htm.

Other Useful Items: For safety, you should bring a **money belt** and a small **padlock.** Basic **outdoors equipment** (plastic water bottle, compass, waterproof matches, pocketknife, sunglasses, sunscreen, hat) may also prove useful. You can make **quick repairs** of torn garments on the road with a needle and thread; also consider bringing electrical tape for patching tears. To do laundry by hand, bring detergent, a small rubber ball to stop up the sink, and string for a makeshift clothes line. Extra **plastic bags** are crucial for storing food, dirty shoes, and wet clothes, and for keeping sunscreen and other liquids from exploding all over your clothes. Other things you might forget include: an umbrella, a battery-powered **alarm clock,** safety pins, rubber bands, a flashlight, earplugs, garbage bags, and a small calculator. A **mobile phone** can be a lifesaver (literally) on the road; see p. 33for information on acquiring one that will work at your destination.

Important Documents: Don't forget your passport, traveler's checks, ATM and/or credit cards, adequate ID, and photocopies of all of the aforementioned in case these documents are lost or stolen (p. 17). Also check that you have any of the following that might apply to you: a hostelling membership card (p. 35); driver's license (p. 17); travel insurance forms (p. 27); ISIC (p. 17), and rail or bus pass (p. 53).

SAFETY AND HEALTH

GENERAL ADVICE

In any type of crisis situation, the most important thing to do is **stay calm.** Your country's embassy abroad (p. 15) is usually your best resource when things go wrong; registering with that embassy upon arrival in the country is often a good idea. The government offices listed in the **Travel Advisories** box (p. 26) provide information on the services they offer their citizens in case of emergencies abroad.

DRUGS AND ALCOHOL

Drug and alcohol laws vary widely throughout Europe. In the Netherlands "soft" drugs are available on the open market while in much of Eastern Europe drug possession may lead to a heavy prison sentence. If you carry **prescription drugs,** you must carry both a copy of the prescriptions themselves and a note from a doctor, especially at border crossings. **Public drunkenness** is culturally unacceptable and against the law in many countries; it can also jeopardize your safety.

TERRORISM AND CIVIL UNREST

In the wake of September 11 and the war in Iraq, exercise increased vigilance near embassies and be wary of big crowds and demonstrations. Keep an eye on the news, heed travel warnings, and comply with security measures. Overall, risks of civil unrest tend to be localized and rarely directed toward tourists. Though the peace process in Northern Ireland is progressing, tension tends to surround the July "marching season." Notoriously violent separatist movements include ETA, a Basque group that operates in southern France and Spain, and FLNC, a Corsican separatist group in France. The November 17 group in Greece is known for anti-Western acts, though they do not target tourists. The **Travel Advisories** box lists offices to contact and websites to visit to get the most updated list of your home country's government travel advisories.

TRAVEL ADVISORIES. The following government offices provide travel information and advisories by telephone, by fax, or via the web:

Australian Department of Foreign Affairs and Trade: ☎1300 555 135; www.dfat.gov.au.

Canadian Department of Foreign Affairs and International Trade (DFAIT): ☎800-267-8376; www.dfait-maeci.gc.ca. Free booklet, *Bon Voyage...But.*

New Zealand Ministry of Foreign Affairs: ☎044 398 000; www.mft.govt.nz/travel/index.html.

United Kingdom Foreign and Commonwealth Office: ☎020 7008 1500; www.fco.gov.uk.

US Department of State: ☎202-647-5225; http://travel.state.gov. Visit the website for the booklet *A Safe Trip Abroad.*

PERSONAL SAFETY

EXPLORING AND TRAVELING

To avoid unwanted attention, try to blend in as much as possible. Respecting local customs (in many cases, dressing more conservatively than you would at home) may placate would-be hecklers. Take extra care in your dress and demeanor upon visits to churches an other culturally sensitive areas. Familiarize yourself with your surroundings before setting out, and carry yourself with confidence. Check maps in shops and restaurants rather than on the street. If you are traveling alone, be sure someone at home knows your itinerary, and never admit that you're by yourself. When walking at night, stick to busy, well-lit streets. If you ever feel uncomfortable, leave the area as quickly and as directly as you can.

There is no sure-fire way to avoid all the threatening situations you might encounter while traveling, but a **self-defense course** will teach you ways to react to unwanted advances. **Impact, Prepare,** and **Model Mugging** can refer you to local self-defense courses in the US. Visit www.modelmugging.org for a list of nearby chapters. Workshops (2-4hr.) start at US$50; full courses (20hr.) run US$350-500.

POSSESSIONS AND VALUABLES

Never leave your belongings unattended; crime occurs even in hostels and hotels that feel safe. Bring a **padlock** for hostel lockers, and keep valuables on your person. Be particularly careful on **buses** and **trains,** especially in Eastern Europe; thieves wait for travelers to fall asleep. Carry your backpack in front of you where you can see it and don't keep your wallet in back pockets. When traveling with others, sleep in shifts. When alone, use good judgment in selecting a train compartment: never stay in an empty one, and lock your pack to the luggage rack. Try to sleep on top bunks with your luggage above you (if not in bed with you), and keep important documents and other valuables on your person.

To minimize the risk of theft, **bring as little with you as possible.** Also, **carry as little cash as possible.** Keep your traveler's checks and ATM/credit cards in a **money belt**—not a "fanny pack"—along with your passport and ID cards, and **keep a small cash reserve separate from your primary stash.** This should be about US$50 (US$ or euros are best) sewn into or stored in the depths of your pack, along with your traveler's check serial numbers and important photocopies.

In large cities **con artists** often work in groups and may employ children. Beware of certain classics: sob stories that require money, rolls of bills "found" on the street, mustard spilled (or saliva spit) onto your shoulder to distract you while they snatch your bag. Be wary while using ATMs; stand in front of the display and never turn your back on the machine when your card is inside. **Never let your pass-**

port and bags out of your sight. Beware of **pickpockets** in crowds and on public transportation. Be alert in phone booths: if you must say your calling card number, do so quietly; if you punch it in, make sure no one can look over your shoulder.

If you will be traveling with electronic devices, such as a laptop or a PDA, check if your homeowner's insurance covers loss, theft, or damage when you travel. If not, you might consider purchasing a low-cost property insurance policy. **Safeware** (☎800-800-1492; www.safeware.com) specializes in covering computers and charges US$90 for 90-day comprehensive travel coverage up to US$4000.

PRE-DEPARTURE HEALTH

In your **passport,** write the names of any people you wish to be contacted in case of a medical emergency, and list any allergies or medical conditions you have. Matching a prescription to a foreign equivalent is not always easy, safe, or possible, so if you take prescription drugs, consider carrying prescriptions or a statement from your doctor stating the medication's trade name, manufacturer, chemical name, and dosage. While traveling, keep all medication with you in your carry-on luggage. For tips on packing a basic **first-aid kit** and other health essentials, see p. 24.

IMMUNIZATIONS AND PRECAUTIONS

Travelers should make sure that they are up to date on the following vaccines: MMR (for measles, mumps, and rubella); DTaP or Td (for diphtheria, tetanus, and pertussis); IPV (for polio); Hib (for *haemophilus* influenza B); and HepB (for Hepatitis B). For travelers going to Eastern Europe, a Hepatitis A and/or immune globulin (IG) vaccine is also recommended, as well as typhoid and rabies vaccines. Some countries may deny access to travelers arriving from parts of South America and sub-Saharan Africa without a certificate of vaccination for yellow fever. For recommendations on immunizations, consult the CDC (p. 27) in the US or the equivalent in your home country, and check with a doctor for guidance.

INSURANCE

Travel insurance covers four basic areas: medical/health problems, property loss, trip cancellation/interruption, and emergency evacuation. Regular insurance policies may extend to travel-related accidents, but you may consider purchasing travel insurance if the cost of trip cancellation, interruption, or emergency medical evacuation is greater than you can absorb. Prices for independent travel insurance run about US$50 per week for full coverage, while trip cancellation/interruption may be purchased separately at a rate of US$3-5 per day depending on length of stay. **Medical insurance** often covers costs incurred abroad; check with your provider. **Australians** traveling in Finland, Ireland, Italy, the Netherlands, Sweden, or the UK are entitled to many services that they would receive at home as part of the Reciprocal Health Care Agreement. **Homeowners' insurance** often covers theft and loss of travel documents (passport, plane ticket, railpass, etc.) up to US$500.

ISIC and **ITIC** (p. 17) provide basic insurance benefits to US cardholders, including US$100 per day of in-hospital sickness for up to 100 days and US$10,000 of accident-related medical reimbursement (see www.isicus.com for details). Cardholders have access to a toll-free 24hr. helpline for medical, legal, and financial emergencies. **American Express** (☎800-338-1670) grants most cardholders automatic collision and theft insurance on car rentals made with the card.

USEFUL ORGANIZATIONS AND PUBLICATIONS

The US **Centers for Disease Control and Prevention** (CDC; ☎877-FYI-TRIP; www.cdc.gov/travel) maintains an international travelers' hotline and an informative website. The CDC's comprehensive booklet *Health Information for International Travel* (The Yellow Book), a biannual rundown of disease, immunization, and general health advice, is free online (☎877-252-1200; http://bookstore.phfg.org/cat24.htm). Consult the appropriate government agency of your home country for consular information sheets on health, entry requirements, and other issues for various countries (see the listings in the box on **Travel Advisories,** p. 26). For quick information on health and other travel warnings, call the **Overseas Citizens Services** (M-F 8am-8pm ☎888-407-4747, from overseas 202-501-4444), or contact a passport agency, embassy, or consulate abroad. For information on medical evacuation services and travel insurance firms, see the US government's website at http://travel.state.gov/travel/abroad_health.html or the **British Foreign and Commonwealth Office** (www.fco.gov.uk). For general health info, contact the **American Red Cross** (☎800-564-1234; www.redcross.org).

STAYING HEALTHY

Common sense is the simplest prescription for good health while you travel. Drink lots of fluids, and wear sturdy, broken-in shoes and clean socks.

ONCE IN EUROPE

ENVIRONMENTAL HAZARDS

Heat exhaustion and dehydration: Heat exhaustion leads to nausea, excessive thirst, headache, and dizziness. Avoid it by drinking plenty of fluids, eating salty foods (e.g., crackers), abstaining from dehydrating beverages (e.g., alcohol and caffeinated beverages), and always wearing sunscreen. Continuous heat stress can eventually lead to heatstroke, characterized by a rising temperature, severe headache, delirium and cessation of sweating. Victims should be cooled off with wet towels and taken to a doctor.

Sunburn: Always wear sunscreen (SPF 30) when spending excessive amounts of time outdoors. If you get sunburned, drink more fluids than usual and apply an aloe-based lotion. Severe sunburns can lead to sun poisoning, a condition that causes fever, chills, nausea, and vomiting. Sun poisoning should always be treated by a doctor.

Hypothermia and frostbite: A rapid drop in body temperature is the clearest sign of overexposure to cold. Victims may also shiver, feel exhausted, have poor coordination or slurred speech, hallucinate, or suffer amnesia. *Do not let hypothermia victims fall asleep*. To avoid hypothermia, keep dry, wear layers, and stay out of the wind. When the temperature is below freezing, watch out for frostbite. If skin turns white or blue, waxy, and cold, do not rub the area. Drink warm beverages, stay dry, and slowly warm the area with dry fabric or steady body contact until a doctor can be found.

High altitude: Allow your body a couple of days to adjust to less oxygen before exerting yourself. Note that alcohol is more potent and UV rays are stronger at high elevations.

INSECT-BORNE DISEASES

Many diseases are transmitted by insects—mainly mosquitoes, fleas, ticks, and lice. Be aware of insects in wet or forested areas. Especially while hiking and camping, wear long pants and long sleeves, tuck your pants into your socks, and use a mosquito net. **Ticks**—which can carry Lyme and other diseases—can be particularly dangerous in rural and forested regions.

Tick-borne encephalitis: A viral infection of the central nervous system transmitted during the summer by tick bites (primarily in wooded areas) or by consumption of unpasteurized dairy products. The risk of contracting the disease is relatively low, especially if precautions are taken against tick bites. Tick-borne encephalitis has been known to occur in Austria, the Czech Republic, Germany, Hungary, Poland, the former Soviet Union, Switzerland and less frequently in Bulgaria, Romania, and Scandinavia.

Leishmaniasis: A parasite transmitted by sand flies; can occasionally occur in Southern Europe and the eastern Mediterranean, usually in rural areas. Common symptoms are fever, weakness, and swelling of the spleen, as well as skin sores weeks to months after the bite. There is a treatment but no vaccine. Regardless of infection, sand fly bites are annoying enough; carry plenty of bug spray in these areas.

Lyme disease: A bacterial infection carried by ticks and marked by a circular bull's-eye rash 2 in. or more in diameter. Lyme disease is most common in central and northern Europe, including Scandinavia. Later symptoms include fever, headache, fatigue, and aches and pains. Antibiotics are effective if administered early. Left untreated, Lyme can cause problems in joints, the heart, and the nervous system. If you find a tick attached to your skin, grasp the head with tweezers as close to your skin as possible and apply slow, steady traction. Removing a tick within 24hr. greatly reduces the risk of infection. Do not try to remove ticks with petroleum jelly, nail polish remover, or a hot match. It is bad form to taunt the tick. Tick bites usually occur in moist and heavily wooded areas. If hiking in these areas, wear long clothes and insect repellent with DEET.

FOOD- AND WATER-BORNE DISEASES

COMING IN HANDY. A small bottle of liquid hand cleanser, a stash of cleansing towelettes, or even a package of baby wipes can keep your hands and face germ-free and refreshed on the road.

Prevention is the best cure: be sure that your food is properly cooked and the water you drink is clean. Unpeeled fruits and vegetables and tap water should be safe throughout most of Europe, particularly in Western Europe. In some parts of Southern and Eastern Europe (in particular Moscow and St. Petersburg), you'll need to peel fruits and vegetables and avoid tap water (including ice cubes and anything washed in tap water, like salad). Watch out for food from markets or street vendors that may have been cooked in unhygienic conditions. Other culprits are raw shellfish, unpasteurized milk, and sauces containing raw eggs. Buy bottled water, or purify your own water by bringing it to a rolling boil or treating it with **iodine tablets;** note, however, that some parasites such as *giardia* have iodine-resistant exteriors, so boiling is more reliable as well as more palatable. Always wash your hands before eating or bring a quick-drying liquid hand cleaner.

Cholera: An intestinal disease caused by a bacteria in contaminated food. Symptoms include severe diarrhea, dehydration, vomiting, and muscle cramps. See a doctor immediately; if left untreated, it may be deadly within hours. Antibiotics are available, but the most important treatment is rehydration. Cholera is a serious problem in parts the former Soviet Union and Ukraine.

Giardiasis: Occurs worldwide. Transmitted through parasites (microbes, tapeworms, etc. in contaminated water and food) and acquired by drinking untreated water from streams or lakes. Symptoms include diarrhea, abdominal cramps, bloating, fatigue, weight loss, and nausea. If untreated it can lead to severe dehydration.

Hepatitis A: A viral infection of the liver acquired primarily through contaminated water, including through shellfish from contaminated water. Symptoms include fatigue, fever, loss of appetite, nausea, dark urine, jaundice, vomiting, aches and pains, and light stools. There is a moderate risk in Eastern Europe, mainly in rural areas, the countryside, and the former Soviet Union. Ask your doctor about the hepatitis A vaccine (Havrix or Vaqta) or an injection of immune globulin (IG; formerly called gamma globulin).

Traveler's diarrhea: Results from drinking fecally contaminated water or eating uncooked and contaminated foods. Symptoms include nausea, bloating, and urgency. Try quick-energy, non-sugary foods with protein and carbohydrates to keep your strength up. Over-the-counter anti-diarrheals (e.g., Imodium) may counteract the problems. The most dangerous side effect is dehydration; drink 8 oz. of water with ½ tsp. of sugar or honey and a pinch of salt, try uncaffeinated soft drinks, or eat salted crackers. If you develop a fever or your symptoms don't go away after 4-5 days, consult a doctor. Consult a doctor immediately for treatment of diarrhea in children.

Typhoid fever: Caused by the salmonella bacteria; travelers to villages and rural areas in Eastern Europe may be at risk. Mostly transmitted through contaminated food and water, it may also be acquired by direct contact with another person. Early symptoms include persistent high fever, headache, fatigue, loss of appetite, constipation, and sometimes a rash on the abdomen or chest. Antibiotics can treat typhoid, but a vaccination (70-90% effective) is recommended.

OTHER INFECTIOUS DISEASES

AIDS and HIV: For detailed information on Acquired Immune Deficiency Syndrome (AIDS) in the regions you will be visiting, call the US Centers for Disease Control 24hr. hotline at ☎800-342-2437, or contact the Joint United Nations Programme on HIV/AIDS (UNAIDS), 20 ave. Appia, CH-1211 Geneva 27, Switzerland (☎+41 22 791 3666; fax 22 791 4187). Note that Belarus, Bulgaria, Hungary, Russia, the Slovak Republic, and Ukraine screen incoming travelers for AIDS, primarily those planning extended visits for work or study, and deny entrance to those who test HIV-positive. Contact the country's consulate for information.

Hepatitis B: A viral infection of the liver transmitted via blood or other bodily fluids. Symptoms, which may not surface until years after infection, include jaundice, loss of appetite, fever, and joint pain. It is transmitted through activities like unprotected sex, illegal drug injections, and unprotected health work. A 3-shot vaccination sequence is recommended for health-care workers, sexually active travelers, and anyone planning to seek medical treatment abroad; begin the course of vaccine 6 months before traveling.

Hepatitis C: Like hepatitis B, but mode of transmission differs. IV drug users, those with occupational exposure to blood, hemodialysis patients, and recipients of blood transfusions are at the highest risk, but the disease can also spread through sexual contact or sharing items like razors and toothbrushes that may have traces of blood on them. No symptoms are usually exhibited; if there are any, they include loss of appetite, abdominal pain, fatigue, nausea, and jaundice. Untreated, hepatitis C can lead to liver failure.

Rabies: Transmitted through the saliva of infected animals; fatal if untreated. By the time symptoms (thirst and muscle spasms) appear, the disease is in its terminal stage. If bitten, wash the wound thoroughly, seek immediate medical care, and have the animal located. A rabies vaccine consists of 3 shots over a 21-day period, is recommended for developing world travel, but is only semi-effective. Rabies is found all over the world, with high incidences in Eastern Europe, and is often transmitted through dogs.

Sexually transmitted diseases (STDs): Chlamydia, genital warts, gonorrhea, herpes, syphilis, and other STDs are more common than HIV and can be just as deadly. **Hepatitis** B and C can also be transmitted sexually. Though condoms may protect you from some STDs, oral or even tactile contact can lead to transmission. If you think you may have contracted an STD, see a doctor immediately.

OTHER HEALTH CONCERNS

MEDICAL CARE ON THE ROAD

While health-care systems in Western Europe tend to be quite accessible and of high quality, medical care varies greatly across Eastern and Southern Europe. Major cities such as Prague and Budapest have English-speaking medical centers or hospitals for foreigners, whereas English-speaking facilities are nearly nonexistent in countries like Bulgaria or Latvia. In general, medical service in these regions is not up to Western standards; though basic supplies are always there, specialized treatment is not. Private hospitals tend to have better facilities than state-operated ones. Tourist offices may have names of local doctors who speak English. In the event of a medical emergency, contact your embassy for aid and recommendations. All EU citizens can receive free or reduced-cost first aid and emergency services by presenting a **European Health Insurance Card.**

If you are concerned about obtaining medical assistance while traveling, you may wish to employ special support services. The *MedPass* from **GlobalCare, Inc.**, 6875 Shiloh Rd. East, Alpharetta, GA 30005, USA (☎800-860-1111; www.globalcare.net), provides 24hr. international medical assistance, support, and medical evacuation resources. The **International Association for Medical Assistance to Travelers** (**IAMAT;** Canada ☎519-836-0102, US 716-754-4883; www.iamat.org) has free membership, lists English-speaking doctors worldwide, and offers detailed info on immunization requirements and sanitation. If your regular **insurance** policy does not cover travel abroad, you may wish to purchase additional coverage (p. 27).

Those with medical conditions (such as diabetes, allergies to antibiotics, epilepsy, or heart conditions) may want to obtain a **MedicAlert** membership (first year US$35, annually thereafter US$20), which includes a stainless steel ID tag, among other benefits. Contact the MedicAlert Foundation, 2323 Colorado Ave., Turlock, CA 95382, USA (☎888-633-4298, outside US 209-668-3333; www.medicalert.org).

WOMEN'S HEALTH

Women traveling in unsanitary conditions are vulnerable to **infections of the urinary tract** (including bladder and kidneys). Over-the-counter medicines can sometimes alleviate symptoms, but if they persist, see a doctor. **Vaginal yeast infections** may flare up in hot and humid climates. Wearing loosely fitting trousers or a skirt and cotton underwear will help, as will over-the-counter remedies like Monostat or Gynelotrimin. Bring supplies from home if you are prone to infection, as it may be difficult to find the brands you prefer on the road. **Tampons, pads,** and **contraceptive devices** are widely available in most of Western Europe, but they can be hard to find in areas of Eastern Europe—bring supplies with you. **Abortion** laws also vary from country to country. In most of Western Europe, abortion is legal during at least the first 10-12 weeks of pregnancy, but it remains illegal in Ireland, Liechtenstein, Monaco, Poland, and Portugal, except in extreme circumstances.

KEEPING IN TOUCH

BY EMAIL AND INTERNET

Email is popular and accessible in most of Europe. In some places it's possible to forge a remote link with your home server, but this is a slower (and more expensive) option than taking advantage of free **web-based email** (e.g., www.gmail.com or www.hotmail.com). **Internet cafes** and the occasional free Internet terminal at a public library or university are listed in the **Practical Information** sections, and hostels frequently offer Internet access. For lists of additional cybercafes in Europe, check www.cybercaptive.com or www.world66.com/netcafeguide.

Increasingly, travelers find that taking their **laptops** on the road can be a convenient option for staying connected. Laptop users can call an Internet service provider via a modem using long-distance phone cards intended for such calls. Internet cafes may also allow them to connect their laptops to the Internet. Travelers with wireless-enabled computers may take advantage of an increasing number of Internet "hot spots," where they can get online for free or for a small fee. Newer computers detect these hot spots automatically; websites like www.jiwire.com, www.wi-fihotspotlist.com and www.locfinder.net can help you find them.

BY TELEPHONE

CALLING HOME

You can usually make direct international calls from pay phones, but if you aren't using a phone card, you may wind up spending more on your call than you will on a bed for the night. Prepaid phone cards are a common and relatively inexpensive means of calling abroad. Each one comes with a Personal Identification Number (PIN) and a toll-free access number. You call the access number and then follow the directions for dialing your PIN. To purchase prepaid phone cards, check online for the best rates; www.callingcards.com is a good place to start. Online providers generally send your access number and PIN via email, with no actual "card" involved. Keep in mind that phone cards can be problematic in Russia, Ukraine, and Slovenia, so buying an international phone card once you arrive will probably save you headaches. You can also call home with prepaid phone cards purchased in Europe (see **Calling Within Europe,** below).

PLACING INTERNATIONAL CALLS. All international dialing prefixes and country codes for Europe are shown in a chart inside the back cover of this book. To place international calls, dial:

1. The **international dialing prefix.** To call from **Australia,** dial 0011; **Canada** or the **US,** 011; **Ireland, New Zealand,** or the **UK,** 00.
2. The **country code** of the country you want to call. To call **Australia,** dial 61; **Canada** or the **US,** 1; **Ireland,** 353; **New Zealand,** 64; the **UK,** 44.
3. The **city/area code.** *Let's Go* lists the city/area codes for cities and towns in Europe opposite the city or town name, next to a ☎. If the 1st digit is a zero (e.g., 020 for London), omit the zero when calling from abroad (e.g., dial 20 from Canada to reach London).
4. The **local number.**

Another option is a **calling card,** linked to a major national telecommunications service in your home country. Calls are billed collect or to your account. Companies in the US that offer calling cards include: **AT&T** (☎800-364-9292; www.att.com); **MCI** (☎800-777-5000; consumer.mci.com); **Canada Direct** (☎800-561-8868; www.infocanadadirect.com); **Telecom New Zealand Direct** (www.telecom.co.nz); **Telstra Australia** (☎13 22 00; www.telstra.com). Where available, there are often advantages to purchasing calling cards online, including better rates and immediate account access. To call home with a calling card, contact the local operator for your service provider by dialing the appropriate toll-free access number. Placing a **collect call** through an international operator can be expensive, but may be necessary in an emergency. You can call collect without even possessing a calling card just by calling an access number and following the instructions.

CALLING WITHIN EUROPE

Many travelers are opting to buy mobile phones for placing calls within Europe. (For more info, see **Mobile Phones,** p. 33.) Beyond that, perhaps the simplest way to call within a country is to use a public pay phone. However, much of Europe has switched to a **prepaid phone card** system, and in some countries you may have a hard time finding any coin-operated phones at all. Prepaid phone cards, available at newspaper kiosks and tobacco stores, carry a certain amount of phone time depending on the card's denomination and usually save time and money in the long run. The computerized phone will tell you how much time, in units, you have left on your card. Another kind of prepaid telephone card comes with a PIN and a toll-free access number. Instead of inserting the card into the phone, you call the access number and follow the directions on the card. These cards can be used to make international as well as domestic calls. Phone rates tend to be highest in the morning, lower in the evening, and lowest on Sunday and late at night.

MOBILE PHONES

Mobile phones are a popular option for travelers calling within Europe. In addition to greater convenience, mobile phones provide an economical alternative to expensive landline calls. Unlike North America, virtually all areas of Western Europe receive excellent coverage, and the widespread use of the **Global System for Mobiles (GSM)** allows one phone to function in multiple countries. To make and receive calls in Europe, you will need a GSM-compatible phone and a **SIM (subscriber identity module) card,** a thumbnail-sized chip that gives you a local phone number and plugs you into the local network. SIM cards can be purchased from any European country for any GSM phone, but some companies lock their phones to prevent switches to competitor carriers, so inquire about using the phone in other countries before buying. Phones in Europe cost around US$100; instead of requiring a service contract, they often run on prepaid minutes that are easily purchased. Incoming calls are often free. When you use up the prepaid time, you can buy additional cards or vouchers (usually available at convenience stores) to get more. For more information on GSM phones, check out www.telestial.com, www.vodafone.com, www.orange.co.uk, www.roadpost.com, www.t-mobile.com, or www.planetomni.com. Companies like **Cellular Abroad** (www.cellularabroad.com) and **Telestial** rent phones that work in destinations around the world, providing a simpler option than picking up a phone in-country.

GSM PHONES. Just having a GSM phone doesn't mean you're necessarily good to go when you travel abroad. The majority of GSM phones sold in the United States operate on a different **frequency** (1900) than international phones (900/1800) and will not work abroad. Tri-band phones work on all 3 frequencies (900/1800/1900) and will operate through most of the world. Some GSM phones are **SIM-locked** and will only accept SIM cards from a single carrier. You'll need a **SIM-unlocked** phone to use a SIM card from a local carrier when you travel.

TIME DIFFERENCES

All of Europe falls within 3hr. of **Greenwich Mean Time (GMT).** For more info, consult the **time zone chart** on the inside back cover. GMT is 5hr. ahead of New York time, 8hr. ahead of Vancouver and San Francisco time, 10hr. behind Sydney time, and 12hr. behind Auckland time. Iceland is the only country in Europe to ignore **Daylight Saving Time;** fall and spring switchover times vary in countries that observe Daylight Saving. A good source of information is www.worldtimeserver.com.

BY MAIL

SENDING MAIL HOME

Airmail is the best way to send mail from Europe. From Western Europe to North America, it averages seven days; from Central or Eastern Europe, allow anywhere from seven days to three weeks. **Aerogrammes,** printed sheets that fold into envelopes and travel via airmail, are available at post offices. Write "par avion" (or *por avion, mit Luftpost, via aerea,* etc.) on the front. Most post offices will charge exorbitant fees or simply refuse to send aerogrammes with enclosures. **Surface mail** is by far the cheapest and slowest way to send mail. It takes one to two months to cross the Atlantic and one to three to cross the Pacific—good for heavy items you won't need for a while, or articles you've acquired along the way. Check the beginning of each chapter for country-specific postal information.

RECEIVING MAIL IN EUROPE

To send mail abroad, mark envelopes "airmail" in your country's language; otherwise, your letter may never arrive. In addition to the standard postage systems, **Federal Express** (Australia ☎ 13 26 10, Canada and US 800-463-3339, Ireland 1800 535 800, New Zealand 0800 733 339, UK 0800 123 800; www.fedex.com) handles express mail services from most countries to Europe.

There are several ways to arrange pickup of letters sent to you while you are abroad. Mail can be sent via **Poste Restante** (General Delivery; *Lista de Correos, Fermo Posta, Postlagernde Briefe*, etc.) to almost any city or town in Europe with a post office. See individual country chapters to find out how to address *Poste Restante* letters. The mail goes to the central post office, unless you specify a post office by street address or postal code. It's best to use the largest post office, since mail may be sent there regardless. It is usually safer and quicker, though more expensive, to send mail express or registered. Bring your passport (or other photo ID) for pickup; there may be a fee. If the clerks insist that there is nothing for you, have them check under your first name as well. *Let's Go* lists post offices in the **Practical Information** section for each city and most towns.

American Express's travel offices throughout the world offer a free **Client Letter Service** (mail held up to 30 days and forwarded upon request) for cardholders who contact them in advance. Some offices provide these services to non-cardholders (especially AmEx Travelers Cheque holders), but call ahead to make sure. *Let's Go* lists AmEx locations for most large cities in **Practical Information** sections; for a complete list, call ☎ 800-528-4800 or visit www.americanexpress.com/travel.

ACCOMMODATIONS

HOSTELS

A HOSTELER'S BILL OF RIGHTS. There are certain standard features that we do not include in our hostel listings. Unless we state otherwise, you can expect that every hostel has no lockout, no curfew, a kitchen, free hot showers, some system of secure luggage storage, and no key deposit.

In the summer Europe is overrun by young budget travelers drawn to hostels' low prices and common spaces. Many are laid out dorm-style with bunk beds in large single-sex rooms, although private rooms sleeping two to four are becoming more common. They sometimes have kitchens and utensils for your use, bike or moped rentals, storage areas, airport transportation, breakfast, laundry facilities, and Internet access. However, there can be drawbacks: some hostels close during certain daytime "lockout" hours, have a curfew, don't accept reservations, impose a maximum stay, or, less often, require that you do chores. In Western and Eastern Europe a hostel bed will average US$15-25 and US$5-20, and a private room around US$30 and US$20, respectively. Comprehensive hosteling websites include www.hostels.com, www.hostelplanet.com, and www.hostelseurope.com.

HOSTELLING INTERNATIONAL

Joining the youth hostel association in your country automatically grants you membership privileges in **Hostelling International (HI),** a federation of national hosteling associations. HI hostels are extremely common throughout Western Europe and in most major Eastern European cities; in general HI hostels are cheaper than private hostels. Non-HI members are often allowed to stay in HI hostels, but pay extra to do so. When determining whether or not to purchase an HI membership, it is important to take into account how many nights you plan on staying in HI hostels, then factor in the 10-15% HI discount. Travelers planning to spend several weeks in Europe often find the membership investment pays off. HI's website (www.hihostels.com), which lists the websites and phone numbers of national associations, can be a great place to begin researching hosteling in a specific region. All prices listed below are valid for individual **one-year memberships** unless otherwise noted.

Australian Youth Hostels Association (AYHA), 422 Kent St., Sydney, NSW 200 (☎02 9261 1111; www.yha.com.au). AUS$52, under 18 AUS$19.

Hostelling International-Canada (HI-C), 205 Catherine St. #400, Ottawa, ON K2P 1C3 (☎613-237-7884; www.hihostels.ca). CDN$35, under 18 free.

An Óige (Irish Youth Hostel Association), 61 Mountjoy St., Dublin 7 (☎830 4555; www.irelandyha.org). EUR€20, under 18 EUR€10.

Hostelling International Northern Ireland (HINI), 22-32 Donegall Rd., Belfast BT12 5JN (☎02890 32 47 33; www.hini.org.uk). UK£13, under 18 UK£6.

Youth Hostels Association of New Zealand (YHANZ), Level 1, Moorhouse City, 166 Moorhouse Ave., P.O. Box 436, Christchurch (☎0800 278 299 (NZ only) or 03 379 9970; www.yha.org.nz). NZ$40, under 18 free.

Scottish Youth Hostels Association (SYHA), 7 Glebe Cres., Stirling FK8 2JA (☎01786 89 14 00; www.syha.org.uk). UK£6, under 17 £2.50.

Youth Hostels Association (England and Wales), Trevelyan House, Dimple Rd., Matlock, Derbyshire DE4 3YH (☎08707 708 868; www.yha.org.uk). UK£15.50, under 26 UK£10.

Hostelling International-USA, 8401 Colesville Rd., Ste. 600, Silver Spring, MD 20910 (☎301-495-1240; www.hiayh.org). US$28, under 18 free.

BOOKING HOSTELS ONLINE. One of the easiest ways to ensure you've got a bed for the night is by reserving online. Click to the **Hostelworld** booking engine through **www.letsgo.com,** and you'll have access to bargain accommodations from Argentina to Zimbabwe with no added commission.

OTHER TYPES OF ACCOMMODATIONS

YMCAS

Young Men's Christian Association (YMCA) lodgings are usually cheaper than hotels but more expensive than hostels. Not all YMCA locations offer lodging. Many YMCAs accept women and families; some will not lodge those under 18 without parental permission. **World Alliance of YMCAs** (☎+41 22 849 5100; www.ymca.int) has more info and a register of Western European YMCAs with housing options.

HOTELS, GUESTHOUSES, AND PENSIONS

In Western Europe, **hotels** generally start at US$30 per person. Elsewhere or for couples and larger groups, however, hotels can be a more reasonable option. You'll typically share a hall bathroom; private bathrooms cost extra, as may hot showers. Some hotels offer "full pension" (all meals) and "half pension" (no lunch). Smaller **guesthouses** and **pensions** are often cheaper than hotels. If you make **reservations** in writing, indicate your day of arrival and the length of your stay. The hotel will send you a confirmation and may request payment for the first night. Often it is easiest to make reservations over the phone with a credit card.

BED AND BREAKFASTS (B&BS)

For a cozy alternative to impersonal hotel rooms, B&Bs (private homes with rooms available to travelers) range from the acceptable to the sublime. B&Bs are particularly popular in Britain and Ireland, where rooms average UK£20/€30 per person. For more information, check out **InnFinder** (www.inncrawler.com), **InnSite** (www.innsite.com), or **BedandBreakfast.com** (www.bedandbreakfast.com).

PRIVATE ROOMS

In much of Eastern Europe, due to a lack of budget travel infrastructure, the only budget accommodations are often rooms in private houses. Owners seek out tourists at the train or bus stations; tourist offices are often more reliable. In larger towns and cities, agencies book private rooms, often for a fee. If renting from the owner, feel free to negotiate, and don't agree to anything before you see the room.

UNIVERSITY DORMS

Many **universities** open their residence halls to travelers when school is not in session; some do so during term-time. Getting a room may take a couple of phone calls in advance, but rates tend to be low and many offer free local calls and Internet. When available, university dorms are listed in the **Accommodations** section.

HOME EXCHANGES AND HOSPITALITY CLUBS

Home exchange offers the traveler various types of homes (houses, apartments, condominiums, villas, and even castles in some cases), plus the opportunity to live like a native and save money. For more information, contact Intervac International Home Exchange (http://intervac-online.com; see site for phone listings by country) or HomeExchange.Com, P.O. Box 787, Hermosa Beach, CA 90254, USA (☎800-877-8723; fax 310-798-3865; www.homeexchange.com).

Hospitality clubs link their members with individuals or families abroad who are willing to host travelers for free or for a small fee to promote cultural exchange and general good karma. In exchange, members usually must be willing to host travelers in their own homes; a small membership fee may also be required. **The Hospitality Club** (www.hospitalityclub.org) and **GlobalFreeloaders.com** (www.globalfreeloaders.com) are good places to start. An Internet search will find many similar organizations, some of which cater to special interests (e.g., women, gay and lesbian travelers, members of certain professions). As always, use common sense when planning to stay with or host someone you do not know.

LONG-TERM ACCOMMODATIONS

Travelers planning to stay in Europe for extended periods of time may find it cost-effective to rent an **apartment.** Rents vary widely. Generally, for stays shorter than three months, it is more feasible to **sublet,** than lease your own apartment. Sublets are also more likely to be furnished. Out of session, it may be possible to arrange to sublet rooms from departed university students. It is far easier to find an apartment once you have arrived at your destination than attempting to use the Internet or phone from home. By staying in a hostel for your first week or so, you can make local contacts and, more importantly, check out your new digs before you commit.

THE GREAT OUTDOORS

Camping can be a thrilling way to see Europe on the cheap. **Organized campgrounds** exist just outside most European cities. Showers, bathrooms, and a small restaurant or store are common; some have more elaborate facilities. Prices are usually US$5-15 per person plus charges for tents and/or cars. While camping is cheaper than hosteling, the cost of transportation to and from campsites can add up. Certain parks allow **free camping,** but check local regulations before you pitch your tent. The **Great Outdoor Recreation Pages** (www.gorp.com) provides information for travelers planning on spending time outdoors.

LEAVE NO TRACE. *Let's Go* encourages travelers to embrace the "Leave No Trace" ethic, minimizing their impact on natural environments and protecting them for future generations. Trekkers and wilderness enthusiasts should set up camp on durable surfaces, use cookstoves instead of campfires, bury human waste away from water supplies, bag trash and carry it out with them, and respect wildlife and natural objects. For more detailed information, contact the **Leave No Trace Center for Outdoor Ethics,** P.O. Box 997, Boulder, CO 80306 (☎800-332-4100 or 303-442-8222; www.lnt.org).

USEFUL RESOURCES

A variety of publishing companies offer hiking guidebooks to meet the educational needs of novice or expert. For information about camping, hiking, and biking, write or call the publishers listed below to receive a free catalog. Campers heading to Europe should consider buying an **International Camping Carnet.** Similar to a hostel membership card, it's required at a few campgrounds and provides discounts at others. It is available in North America from the **Family Campers and RVers Association** (www.fcrv.org) and in the UK from **The Caravan Club** (see p. 40).

Automobile Association, Contact Centre, Carr Ellison House, William Armstrong Dr., Newcastle-upon-Tyne NE4 7YA, UK (☎08706 000 371; www.theAA.com). Publishes *Caravan and Camping Europe* and *Britain & Ireland* (UK£10) as well as road atlases for Europe as a whole and for Britain, France, Germany, Ireland, Italy, and Spain.

The Caravan Club, East Grinstead House, East Grinstead, West Sussex, RH19 1UA, UK (☎01342 326 944; www.caravanclub.co.uk). For UK£32, members receive access to campsites, insurance services, equipment discounts, maps, and a monthly magazine.

The Mountaineers Books, 1001 SW Klickitat Way, Ste. 201, Seattle, WA 98134, USA (☎206-223-6303; www.mountaineersbooks.org). Over 600 titles on hiking, biking, mountaineering, natural history, and conservation.

WILDERNESS SAFETY

Staying **warm, dry,** and **well hydrated** is the key to a happy and safe experience. Before any hike, prepare yourself for an emergency by packing a first-aid kit, a reflector, a whistle, high-energy food, extra water, raingear, a hat, mittens, and several **extra pairs of socks.** Wear wool or insulating synthetic materials designed for the outdoors. Cotton is a bad choice as it takes a long time to dry. Check **weather forecasts** often and pay attention to the skies; weather patterns can change suddenly, especially in mountainous areas. Let someone—your hostel, a park ranger, or a local hiking organization—know when and where you are going. Know your physical limits and do not attempt a hike beyond your ability.

CAMPING AND HIKING EQUIPMENT

WHAT TO BUY

Good camping equipment is both sturdy and light. North American suppliers tend to offer the most competitive prices.

Sleeping Bags: Most sleeping bags are rated by season; "summer" means 30-40°F (around 0°C) at night; "four-season" or "winter" often means below 0°F (-17°C). Bags are made of **down** (warm and light, but expensive, and miserable when wet) or of **synthetic** material (heavy, durable, and warm when wet). Prices range US$50-250 for a summer synthetic to US$200-300 for a good down winter bag. **Sleeping bag pads** include foam pads (US$10-30), air mattresses (US$15-50), and self-inflating mats (US$30-120). Line your **stuff sack** with a garbage bag to keep your bag dry.

Tents: The best tents are free-standing, quick to set up, and only require staking in high winds. Low-profile dome tents are the best. 2-person tents start at US$100, 4-person at US$160. Make sure your tent has a rain fly and waterproof its seams. Other useful accessories include a **battery-operated lantern,** plastic **groundcloth,** and a nylon **tarp.**

Backpacks: Internal-frame packs mold well to your back, keep a lower center of gravity, and flex adequately to allow you to hike difficult trails, while **external-frame packs** are more comfortable for long hikes over even terrain, as they carry weight higher and distribute it more evenly. Make sure your pack has a strong, padded hip-belt to transfer weight to your legs. There are models designed specifically for women. Any serious backpacking requires a pack of at least 4000cubic in. (16,000cc), plus 500 cubic in. for sleeping bags in internal-frame packs. Sturdy backpacks can cost as much as US$425, but your pack is an area where it doesn't pay to economize. On your hunt for the perfect pack, fill up prospective models with something heavy, strap it on correctly, and walk around the store to get a sense of how the pack distributes weight. Either buy a **rain cover** (US$10-20) or store all of your belongings in plastic bags inside your pack.

Boots: Be sure to wear hiking boots with good **ankle support.** They should fit snugly and comfortably over 1-2 pairs of **wool socks** and a pair of thin **liner socks.** Break in boots over several weeks before you go to spare yourself blisters.

Other Necessities: Synthetic layers, like those made of polypropylene or polyester, and a pile jacket will keep you warm even when wet. A **space blanket** (US$5-15) will help you to retain body heat and doubles as a groundcloth. Plastic **water bottles** are vital; look for shatter- and leak-resistant models. Carry **water-purification tablets** for when you can't boil water. Virtually every organized campground in Europe forbids fires or the gathering of firewood, so you'll need a **camp stove** (the classic Coleman starts at US$50) and a propane-filled **fuel bottle** to operate it. Also bring a **first-aid kit, pocketknife, insect repellent,** and **waterproof matches** or a **lighter.**

WHERE TO BUY IT

The online/mail-order companies listed below offer lower prices than many retail stores. However, a visit to a local camping or outdoors store will give you a good sense of the look and weight of certain items before you buy.

Campmor, 28 Parkway, P.O. Box 700, Upper Saddle River, NJ 07458, USA (☎800-525-4784; www.campmor.com).

Discount Camping, 880 Main North Rd., Pooraka, South Australia 5095, Australia (☎08 8262 3399; www.discountcamping.com.au).

Eastern Mountain Sports (EMS), 1 Vose Farm Rd., Peterborough, NH 03458, USA (☎888-463-6367; www.ems.com).

Gear-Zone, 8 Burnet Rd., Sweetbriar Road Industrial Estate, Norwich, NR3 2BS, UK (☎1603 410 108; www.gear-zone.co.uk).

L.L. Bean, Freeport, ME 04033, USA (US and Canada ☎800-441-5713, UK 0800 891 297; www.llbean.com).

Recreational Equipment, Inc. (REI), Sumner, WA 98352, USA (US and Canada ☎800-426-4840, elsewhere 253-891-2500; www.rei.com).

ORGANIZED ADVENTURE TRIPS. Another way of exploring the wild, activities include hiking, biking, skiing, canoeing, kayaking, rafting, climbing, photo safaris, and archaeological digs. Organizations that specialize in camping and outdoor equipment like REI and EMS are often a good source for info. **Specialty Travel Index** lists organized tour opportunities throughout Europe. (US ☎888-624-4030, elsewhere ☎415-455-1643; www.specialtytravel.com.)

SPECIFIC CONCERNS

SUSTAINABLE TRAVEL

As the number of travelers on the road continues to rise, the detrimental effect they can have on natural environments becomes an increasing concern. With this in mind, *Let's Go* promotes **sustainable travel.** Through a sensitivity to issues of ecology and sustainability, travelers can be a powerful force in preserving and restoring the places they visit. **Ecotourism,** a growing trend in sustainable travel, focuses on conserving natural habitats and using them to build up the economy without exploitation or overdevelopment. Travelers can make a difference by doing advance research and by supporting organizations and establishments that pay attention to their impact on their natural surroundings and strive to be environmentally friendly. Delicate ecosystems like coastal and marine areas, riverbanks, islands, mountain ranges and watersheds receive the most attention from conservationists, and travelers should approach these areas with particular care. **International Friends of Nature** (www.nfi.at) has info about sustainable travel options in Europe. For more information, see **Beyond Tourism,** p. 67.

ECOTOURISM RESOURCES. For more information on environmentally responsible tourism, contact one of the organizations below:

Green Globe 21 (☎61 2 6257 9102; www.greenglobe21.com/Travellers.aspx).

International Ecotourism Society, 733 15th St. NW, Washington, D.C. 20005, USA (☎202-347-9203; www.ecotourism.org).

United Nations Environment Program (**UNEP;** ☎+33 1 44 37 14 41; www.uneptie.org/pc/tourism).

RESPONSIBLE TRAVEL

The impact of tourist money on the destinations you visit should not be underestimated. The choices you make during your trip can have potent effects on local communities—for better or for worse. Travelers who care about the destinations and environments they explore should become aware of the social, cultural, and political implications of the choices they make when they travel. Simple decisions such as buying local products instead of global brands, paying a fair price for the product or service, and attempting to say a few words in the local language can have a strong, positive effect on the community. **Community-based tourism** aims to channel tourist money into the local economy by emphasizing tours and cultural programs run by members of the host community and that often benefit disadvantaged groups. These tours often take travelers beyond the traditional attractions of the region, benefitting the visitors as well as the locals. An excellent resource for community-based travel is *The Good Alternative Travel Guide* (UK£10), a project of **Tourism Concern** (☎+44 020 7133 3330; www.tourismconcern.org.uk).

TRAVELING ALONE

There are many benefits to traveling alone, including independence and greater interaction with locals. On the other hand, any solo traveler is a more vulnerable target of harassment and street theft. As a lone traveler, try not to stand out as a tourist, look confident, and be especially careful in deserted or very crowded areas. Stay away from areas that are not well lit. If questioned, never admit that you are traveling alone. Maintain regular contact with someone at home who knows your itinerary and research your destination before traveling. For more tips, pick up *Traveling Solo* by Eleanor Berman (Globe Pequot Press; US$18).

WOMEN TRAVELERS

Women exploring on their own inevitably face some additional safety concerns, but it's easy to be adventurous without taking undue risks. If you are concerned, consider staying in hostels which offer single rooms that lock from the inside or rooms for women only. Stick to centrally located accommodations and avoid solitary late-night treks or metro rides. Always carry extra money for a phone call, bus, or taxi. **Hitchhiking** is never safe for lone women, or even for two women traveling together. Look as if you know where you're going and approach older women or couples for directions if you're lost or uncomfortable. Dress conservatively, especially in rural areas, and try not to look like a tourist.

Your best answer to verbal harassment is no answer at all; walking away or pretending not to hear the speaker, sitting motionless, and staring straight ahead at nothing in particular will often defuse situations that more pointed reactions may only exacerbate. The extremely persistent can sometimes be dissuaded by a firm, loud, and very public "Go away!" in the appropriate language. Don't hesitate to seek out a police officer or a passerby if you are being harassed. Memorize the emergency numbers in places you visit, and consider carrying a whistle on your keychain. A self-defense course will both prepare you for a potential attack and raise your level of awareness of your surroundings (p. 26). Also be sure you are aware of the health concerns that women face when traveling (p. 31).

GLBT TRAVELERS

Attitudes toward gay, lesbian, bisexual, and transgendered (GLBT) travelers are particular to each region in Europe. Countries in Northern and Western Europe (especially the Netherlands) tend to be queer-friendly; Central and Eastern Europe harbors enclaves of tolerance in major cities amid stretches of cultural conservatism. Countries like Romania that outlawed homosexuality as recently as 2002 are becoming more liberal today, and can be considered viable destinations for the GLBT traveler. **Out and About** (www.planetout.com) offers a bi-weekly newsletter and comprehensive website addressing gay travel concerns. The online newspaper **365gay.com** (www.365gay.com/travel/travelchannel.htm) has a solid travel section, while the French-language site **netgai.com** (netgai.com/international/Europe) includes links to country-specific resources, including many in English.

To avoid hassles at airports and border crossings, transgendered travelers should make sure that all of their travel documents report the same gender. Many countries will amend the passports and other documents of post-operative transsexuals to reflect their true gender. Some helpful resources include:

Gay's the Word, 66 Marchmont St., London WC1N 1AB, UK (☎+44 020 7278 7654; www.gaystheword.co.uk). The largest gay and lesbian bookshop in the UK, with both fiction and non-fiction titles. Mail-order service available.

Giovanni's Room, 1145 Pine St., Philadelphia, PA 19107, USA (☎215-923-2960; www.queerbooks.com). An international lesbian/feminist and gay bookstore with mail-order service.

International Lesbian and Gay Association (ILGA; ☎+32 2 502 2471; www.ilga.org). Provides political information, such as homosexuality laws of individual countries.

ADDITIONAL RESOURCES.

Spartacus 2004-2005: International Gay Guide. Bruno Gmunder Verlag (US$33).

Ferrari Guides' Gay Travel A to Z, Ferrari Guides' Men's Travel in Your Pocket, Ferrari Guides' Women's Travel in Your Pocket, and *Ferrari Guides' Inn Places.* Ferrari Publications (US$16-20).

The Gay Vacation Guide: The Best Trips and How to Plan Them. Mark Chesnut, Kensington Books (US$15).

TRAVELERS WITH DISABILITIES

European countries vary in accessibility to travelers with disabilities. Some national and regional tourist boards, particularly in Western and Northern Europe, provide directories on accommodation and transportation accessibility. If these services are not available, contact establishments directly. Be sure to inform airlines and hostels of any pertinent disabilities when making reservations; some time may be needed to prepare special accommodations. Call ahead to restaurants, museums, etc., to find out if they are wheelchair accessible. **Guide dog owners** should inquire as to the quarantine policies of each destination country. At the very least, you will need to provide a certificate of immunization against rabies.

Rail is probably the most convenient form of travel for disabled travelers: many stations have ramps; some trains have wheelchair lifts, special seating, and specially equipped toilets. All Eurostar, some InterCity (IC) and some EuroCity (EC) trains are wheelchair accessible. CityNightLine trains, French TGV (high speed) and Conrail trains feature special compartments. The countries with the most **wheelchair-accessible rail networks** are: Denmark (IC and Lyn trains), France (TGVs and other long-distance trains), Germany (ICE, EC, IC, and IR trains), Italy (EC and IC trains), the Netherlands (most trains), the Republic of Ireland (most major trains), Sweden (X2000s, most IC and IR trains), and Switzerland (all IC, most EC, and some regional trains). Austria, Poland, and Great Britain offer accessibility on select routes. Bulgaria, the Czech Republic, Greece, Hungary, the Slovak Republic, and Spain's rail systems have limited resources for wheelchair accessibility.

USEFUL ORGANIZATIONS

Access Abroad, www.umabroad.umn.edu/access. A website devoted to making study abroad available to students with disabilities. The site is maintained by Disability Services and the Learning Abroad Center, University of Minnesota, University Gateway, Ste. 180, 200 Oak St. SE, Minneapolis, MN 55455, USA (☎612-626-7379).

Accessible Journeys, 35 West Sellers Ave., Ridley Park, PA 19078, USA (☎800-846-4537; www.disabilitytravel.com). Designs tours for wheelchair users and slow walkers. The site has tips and forums for all travelers.

Flying Wheels, 143 W. Bridge St., P.O. Box 382, Owatonna, MN 55060, USA (☎507-451-5005; www.flyingwheelstravel.com). Specializes in escorted trips to Europe and the Middle East for people with physical disabilities; plans custom trips worldwide.

The Guided Tour Inc., 7900 Old York Rd., Ste. 114B, Elkins Park, PA 19027, USA (☎800-783-5841; www.guidedtour.com). Organizes travel programs for persons with developmental and physical challenges in France, Iceland, Ireland, Spain, and the UK.

Mobility International USA (MIUSA), P.O. Box 10767, Eugene, OR 97440, USA (☎541-343-1284; www.miusa.org). Provides a variety of books and other publications containing information for travelers with disabilities.

Society for Accessible Travel and Hospitality (SATH), 347 Fifth Ave., Ste. 610, New York, NY 10016, USA (☎212-447-7284; www.sath.org). An advocacy group that publishes free online travel info and the travel magazine *OPEN WORLD* (annual subscription US$13, free for members). Annual membership US$45, students and seniors US$30.

MINORITY TRAVELERS

In general, minority travelers will find a high level of tolerance in large cities; small towns and the countryside are more unpredictable. The increasingly mainstream reality of anti-immigrant sentiments means that travelers of African or Arab descent (regardless of their citizenship) may be the object of unwarranted assumptions and even hostility. The September 11 terrorist attacks on the United States corresponded to an upsurge in anti-Muslim sentiments in Europe, while anti-Semitism also remains a very real problem in many countries, most visibly in France and Germany. Jews, Muslims, and other minority travelers should keep an eye out for skinheads, who have been linked to racist violence in Central and Eastern Europe, and elsewhere. **The European Monitoring Centre on Racism and Xenophobia** (☎+43 15 80 30; http://eumc.eu.int) publishes a wealth of country-specific statistics and reports. Travelers can also consult **United for Intercultural Action** (☎31

20 6834778; www.unitedagainstracism.org) for a list of over 500 country-specific organizations that work against racism and discrimination. Or contact **Youth United Against Racism in Europe** (☎+44 020 8558 7947) for educational resources.

DIETARY CONCERNS

Vegetarians will find no shortage of meat-free dining options throughout most of Northern and Western Europe, although **vegans** may have a trickier time away from urban centers, where eggs and dairy can dominate traditional cuisine. The cuisine of Eastern Europe still tends to be heavy on meat and gravy, although major cities often boast surprisingly inventive vegetarian and ethnic fare.

The travel section of The Vegetarian Resource Group website, www.vrg.org/travel, has a list of organizations that are geared toward helping vegetarians and vegans traveling abroad. The website for the **European Vegetarian Union (EVU)**, www.europeanvegetarian.org, links to organizations in 26 European countries. For more information, try *The Vegetarian Traveler: Where to Stay if You're Vegetarian, Vegan, Environmentally Sensitive*, by Jed and Susan Civic (Larson Publications; US$16), *Vegan Passport* (The Vegan Society; US$5), www.vegdining.com, www.happycow.net, and www.vegetariansabroad.com.

Those looking to keep **kosher** will find abundant dining options across Europe; contact synagogues in larger cities for information, or consult www.kashrut.com/travel/Europe for country-specific resources. Hebrew College Online also offers a searchable database of kosher restaurants at www.shamash.org/kosher. Another good resource is the *Jewish Travel Guide*, edited by Michael Zaidner (Vallentine Mitchell; US$18). Travelers looking for **halal** groceries and restaurants will have the most success in France and Eastern European nations with substantial Muslim populations; consult www.zabihah.com for establishment reviews. If you are strict in your observance, you may have to prepare your own food on the road.

OTHER RESOURCES

Let's Go tries to cover all aspects of budget travel, but we can't put *everything* in our guides. Listed below are books and websites that can serve as jumping-off points for your own research.

TRAVEL PUBLISHERS AND BOOKSTORES

Globe Corner Bookstore (☎617-492-6277; www.globecorner.com), sponsors an Adventure Travel Lecture Series and carries a vast selection of guidebooks and maps. Online catalog includes atlases and monthly staff picks of outstanding travel writing.

Hippocrene Books, 171 Madison Ave., New York, NY 10016 (☎212-454-2366; www.hippocrenebooks.com), publishes foreign-language dictionaries and learning guides, along with ethnic cookbooks and a smattering of guidebooks.

Rand McNally, 8255 N. Central Park, Skokie, IL 60076 (☎800-275-7263, outside the US 847-329-6656; www.randmcnally.com), sells its own maps (US$10) and maps from European companies including Michelin, Hallwag, and Freytag & Berndt.

WORLD WIDE WEB

Info on almost every aspect of budget travel is accessible via the web. In 10 minutes online, you can make a hostel reservation, get advice on travel hot spots from other travelers, or find out how much a train from Geneva to Nice costs.

Listed here are some regional and travel-related sites to start your surfing; other relevant websites are listed throughout the book. Because website turnover is high, use search engines (www.google.com) to strike out on your own.

WWW.LETSGO.COM. Let's Go's website features a wealth of information and valuable advice at your fingertips. It offers excerpts from all our guides as well as monthly features on new hot spots in the most popular destinations. In addition to our online bookstore, we have great deals on everything from airfares to mobile phones. Our resources section is full of information you'll need before you hit the road, and our forums are buzzing with advice from other travelers. Check back often to see constant updates, exciting new tips, and prize giveaways.

THE ART OF TRAVEL

Backpacker's Ultimate Guide: www.bugeurope.com. Tips on packing, transportation, and where to go, as well as tons of country-specific travel information.

BootsnAll.com: www.bootsnall.com. Numerous resources for independent travelers, from planning your trip to reporting on it when you get back.

How to See the World: www.artoftravel.com. A compendium of great travel tips, from cheap flights to self defense to interacting with local culture.

Travel Intelligence: www.travelintelligence.net. An extensive collection of travel writing by distinguished travel writers.

World Hum: www.worldhum.com. An independently produced collection of "travel dispatches from a shrinking planet."

INFORMATION ON EUROPE

BBC News: news.bbc.co.uk/europe. The latest coverage, free, from one of Europe's most reputable sources for English-language news.

EUROPA: europa.eu.int/index_en.htm. English-language gateway to the European Union, featuring recent news articles and a citizen's guide to EU institutions.

European Visits: www.eurodata.com. An online magazine of European travel, including feature articles, an advice column, and the odd book review.

TRANSPORTATION

GETTING TO EUROPE

BY PLANE

When it comes to airfare, a little effort can save you a bundle. If your plans are flexible enough to deal with the restrictions, courier fares are the cheapest. Tickets bought from consolidators and standby seating are also good deals, but last-minute specials, airfare wars, and charter flights often beat these fares. The key is to hunt around, to be flexible, and to ask persistently about discounts. Students, seniors, and those under 26 should never pay full price for a ticket.

AIRFARES

Airfares to Europe peak between mid-June and early September; holidays are also expensive. The cheapest times to travel are November to mid-December and early January to March. Midweek (M-Th morning) round-trip flights run US$40-50 cheaper than weekend flights, but they are generally more crowded and less likely to permit frequent-flier upgrades. Not fixing a return date ("open return") or arriving in and departing from different cities ("open-jaw") can be pricier than round-trip flights. Patching one-way flights together is the most expensive way to travel. Flights between Europe's capitals or regional hubs (Amsterdam, Frankfurt, London, Paris, Prague, and Warsaw) will tend to be cheaper.

If your European destinations are part of a more extensive globe-hop, consider a round-the-world (RTW) ticket. Tickets usually include at least five stops and are valid for about a year; prices range US$1200-5000. Try **Northwest Airlines/KLM** (☎800-225-2525; www.nwa.com) or **Star Alliance,** a consortium of 16 airlines including United Airlines (www.staralliance.com).

Fares for round-trip flights to European hubs from the US or Canadian east coast cost US$600-1000 in the high season and US$250-400 in the low season; from the west coast US$800-1000/400-500; from the UK to the continent, UK£50-100; from Australia AUS$1700-2300/2100-2400; from New Zealand NZ$1800-2200/1500-1800.

BUDGET AND STUDENT TRAVEL AGENCIES

While agents specializing in flights to Europe can make your life easy, they may not spend the time to find you the lowest possible fare—they get paid on commission. Travelers holding **ISICs** and **IYTCs** (p. 17) qualify for big discounts from student travel agencies. Most flights from budget agencies are on major airlines, but in peak season some may sell seats on less reliable chartered aircraft.

STA Travel, 5900 Wilshire Blvd., Ste. 900, Los Angeles, CA 90036, USA (24hr. reservations and info ☎800-781-4040; www.sta-travel.com). A student and youth travel organization with over 150 offices worldwide (check their website for a listing of all their offices), including US offices in Boston, Chicago, L.A., New York, San Francisco, Seattle, and Washington, D.C. Ticket booking, travel insurance, railpasses, and more. Walk-in offices are located throughout Australia (☎03 9349 4344), New Zealand (☎09 309 9723), and the UK (☎08701 600 599).

Travel CUTS (Canadian Universities Travel Services Limited), 187 College St., Toronto, ON M5T 1P7, Canada (☎800-592-2887; www.travelcuts.com). Offices across Canada and the US including Los Angeles, New York, San Francisco, and Seattle.

USIT, 19-21 Aston Quay, Dublin 2, Ireland (☎01 602 1904; www.usit.ie), Ireland's leading student/budget travel agency has 20 offices throughout Northern Ireland and the Republic of Ireland. Offers programs to work, study, and volunteer worldwide.

Wasteels, Skoubogade 6, 1158 Copenhagen K., Denmark (☎3314 4633; www.wasteels.com). A huge chain with 180 locations across Europe. Sells Wasteels BIJ tickets discounted 30-45% off regular fare, 2nd-class international point-to-point train tickets with unlimited stopovers for those under 26 (sold only in Europe).

FLIGHT PLANNING ON THE INTERNET. The Internet may be the budget traveler's dream when it comes to finding and booking bargain fares, but the array of options can be overwhelming. Many airline sites offer special last-minute deals on the web, although some may require membership logins or email subscriptions. Try www.icelandair.com, www.airfrance.com, www.lufthansa.de, and www.britishairways.com. (For a great set of links to practically every airline in every country, see www.travelpage.com.) **STA** (www.sta-travel.com) and **StudentUniverse** (www.studentuniverse.com) provide quotes on student tickets, while **Expedia** (www.expedia.com), **Orbitz** (www.orbitz.com), **Opodo** (www.opodo.com), and **Travelocity** (www.travelocity.com) offer full travel services. **Priceline** (www.priceline.com) lets you specify a price, and obligates you to buy any ticket that meets or beats it; **Hotwire** (www.hotwire.com) offers bargain fares but won't reveal the airline or flight times until you buy. Other sites that compile deals for you include www.bestfares.com, www.flights.com, www.lowestfare.com, www.onetravel.com, and www.travelzoo.com. Increasingly, there are online tools available to help sift through multiple offers; **Booking Buddy** (www.bookingbuddy.com) and **SideStep** (www.sidestep.com; download required) let you enter your trip information once and search multiple sites. An indispensable resource on the Internet is the **Air Traveler's Handbook** (www.faqs.org/faqs/travel/air/handbook), a comprehensive listing of links to everything you need to know before you board a plane.

MAJOR AIRLINES

The major airlines' lowest regular offer is the **APEX** (Advance Purchase Excursion) fare, which provides confirmed reservations and allows "open-jaw" tickets. Generally, reservations must be made seven to 21 days ahead of departure, with seven- to 14-day minimum stay and 90-day maximum stay restrictions. These fares carry hefty cancellation and change penalties. Book peak-season APEX fares early. Use **Expedia** (www.expedia.com) or **Travelocity** (www.travelocity.com) to get an idea of the lowest published fares, then use the resources below to try to beat those fares.

TRAVELING FROM NORTH AMERICA

Round-trip fares to Europe range from roughly US$200-750: to Frankfurt, US$350-750; London, US$250-550; Paris, US$300-700; Warsaw $300-700. Standard commercial carriers like **American** (☎800-433-7300; www.aa.com), **United** (☎800-538-2929; www.ual.com), and **Northwest** (☎800-447-4747; www.nwa.com) will probably offer the most convenient flights, but they may not be the cheapest. Check **Lufthansa** (☎800-399-5838; www.lufthansa.com), **British Airways** (☎800-247-9297; www.britishairways.com), **Air France** (☎800-237-2747; www.airfrance.us), and **Alitalia** (☎800-223-5730; www.alitaliausa.com) for cheap tickets from destinations throughout the US to all over Europe. You might find an even better deal on one of the following airlines, if any of their limited departure points is convenient for you.

Icelandair: ☎800-223-5500; www.icelandair.com. Stopovers in Iceland for no extra cost on most flights. New York to Frankfurt Apr.-Sept. US$700; Sept.-Oct. US$400; Dec.-Mar. US$300. For last-minute offers, subscribe to their Lucky Fares email list.

Finnair: ☎800-950-5000; www.us.finnair.com. Cheap round-trips from San Francisco, New York, and Toronto to Helsinki; connections throughout Europe. New York to Helsinki June-Sept. US$850-1130; Sept.-Mar. US$550-750; Apr.-May US$650-800.

Martinair: ☎800-627-8462; www.martinair.com. Fly from Florida to Amsterdam mid-June to mid-Aug. US$880; mid-Aug. to mid-June US$730.

TRAVELING FROM THE UK AND IRELAND

Because of the many carriers flying from the British Isles to the continent, we only include discount airlines or those with cheap specials here. The **Air Travel Advisory Bureau** in London (☎870 737 0021; www.atab.co.uk) provides referrals to travel agencies and consolidators that offer discounted airfares out of the UK. **Cheapflights** (www.cheapflights.co.uk) publishes airfare bargains.

Aer Lingus: Ireland ☎0818 365 000; www.aerlingus.com. Round-trip tickets from Dublin, Cork, and Shannon to destinations across Europe (€4-244).

bmibaby: UK ☎08702 642 229; www.bmibaby.com. Departures from throughout the UK to destinations across Europe. London to Amsterdam (UK£60); Venice (UK£70).

easyJet: UK ☎08712 442 366; www.easyjet.com. London to Athens, Barcelona, Madrid, Nice, Palma, and Zurich, among others. Average fare UK£42.

KLM: UK ☎08705 074 074; www.klmuk.com. Cheap round-trip tickets from London and Amsterdam to cities across Europe.

Ryanair: Ireland ☎0818 303 030, UK 08712 460 000; www.ryanair.com. Rock bottom fares (starting around €20, including taxes and fees) from Dublin, Glasgow, Liverpool, London, and Shannon to destinations throughout Western Europe.

TRAVELING FROM AUSTRALIA AND NEW ZEALAND

Air New Zealand: New Zealand ☎0800 73 70 00; www.airnz.co.nz. Auckland to London.

Qantas Air: Australia ☎13 13 13, New Zealand 0800 808 767; www.qantas.com.au. Flights from Australia and New Zealand to London for around AUS$2000.

Singapore Air: Australia ☎13 10 11, New Zealand 0800 808 909; www.singaporeair.com. Flies from Auckland, Christchurch, Melbourne, Perth, and Sydney to Western Europe.

Thai Airways: Australia ☎1300 65 19 60, New Zealand 09 377 38 86; www.thaiair.com. Auckland, Melbourne, Perth, and Sydney to cities throughout Europe.

AIR COURIER FLIGHTS

Light packers should consider courier flights. Couriers transport cargo on international flights by using their checked luggage space for freight. Generally, couriers must travel with carry-ons only and deal with complex flight restrictions. Most flights are round-trip only, with short, fixed-length stays (usually one week) and a limit of a one ticket per issue. Most of these flights also operate only from major gateway cities, mostly in North America. Generally, you must be over 18 (in some cases 21). In summer, the most popular destinations usually require an advance reservation of about two weeks; otherwise, book up to two months ahead. Super-discounted fares are common for "last-minute" flights (three to 14 days ahead).

FROM NORTH AMERICA

Round-trip courier fares from the US to Western Europe run about US$200-500. Most flights leave from New York, Los Angeles, San Francisco, or Miami in the US; and from Montreal, Toronto, or Vancouver in Canada. The organizations below provide members with lists of opportunities and courier brokers for an annual fee. Prices quoted below are round-trip.

Air Courier Association, 1767 A Denver West Blvd., Golden, CO 80401 (☎800-211-5119; www.aircourier.org). 10 departure cities throughout the US and Canada to London, Madrid, Paris, Rome, and throughout Western Europe (high-season US$110-640). 1-year membership US$49.

International Association of Air Travel Couriers (IAATC; www.courier.org). From 7 North American cities to Western European cities, including London, Madrid, Paris, and Rome. 1-year membership US$45.

Courier Travel (www.couriertravel.org). Searchable online database. Multiple departure points in the US to various European destinations.

FROM THE UK, AUSTRALIA, AND NEW ZEALAND

The minimum age for couriers from the UK is usually 18. The **International Association of Air Travel Couriers** (www.courier.org; see above) often offers courier flights from London to Tokyo, Sydney, and Bangkok and from Auckland to Frankfurt and London. **Courier Travel** (see above) also offers flights from London and Sydney.

STANDBY FLIGHTS

Traveling standby requires considerable flexibility in arrival and departure dates and cities. Companies dealing in standby flights sell vouchers rather than tickets, along with the promise to get you to your destination (or near your destination) within a certain window of time (typically 1-5 days). You call in before your specific window of time to hear your flight options and the probability that you will be able to board each flight. You can then decide which flights you want to try to make, show up at the appropriate airport at the appropriate time, present your voucher, and board if space is available. Vouchers can usually be bought for both one-way and round-trip travel. You may receive a refund only if every available flight within your date range is full; if you opt not to take an available (but less convenient) flight, you can only get credit toward future travel. Carefully read agreements with any company offering standby flights as tricky fine print abounds. It is difficult to receive refunds, and clients' vouchers will not be honored when an airline fails to receive payment in time. To check on a company's service record in the US, contact the Better Business Bureau (☎703-276-0100; www.bbb.org).

TICKET CONSOLIDATORS

Ticket consolidators, or **"bucket shops,"** buy unsold tickets in bulk from commercial airlines and sell them at discounted rates. Look is in the Sunday travel section of any major newspaper, where many shops place tiny ads, and call quickly, as availability is extremely limited. Not all bucket shops are reliable, so insist on a receipt that gives full details of restrictions, refunds, and tickets, and pay by credit card (in spite of the 2-5% fee) so you can stop payment if you don't receive your tickets. For more info, see www.travel-library.com/air-travel/consolidators.html.

TRAVELING FROM THE US AND CANADA

NOW Voyager, 315 W. 49th St. Plaza Arcade, New York, NY 10019, USA (☎212-459-1616; www.nowvoyagertravel.com) arranges discounted flights, mostly from New York, to cities in Western Europe. Other consolidators worth trying are **Rebel** (☎800-732-3588; www.rebeltours.com) and **Cheap Tickets** (www.cheaptickets.com). Additional options include **Flights.com** (www.flights.com) and **TravelHUB** (www.travelhub.com), but keep in mind that these are only suggestions; *Let's Go* does not endorse any of these agencies. As always, be cautious, and research companies before you hand over your credit card number.

CHARTER FLIGHTS

Charters are flights a tour operator contracts with an airline to fly extra loads of passengers during peak season. Charter flights fly less frequently than major airlines, make refunds particularly difficult, and are almost always fully booked. Schedules and itineraries may also change or be cancelled at the last moment (as late as 48hr. before the trip, and without a full refund), and check-in, boarding, and

baggage claim are often much slower. However, they can also be cheaper. Discount clubs and fare brokers offer members savings on last-minute charter and tour deals. Study contracts closely; you don't want to end up with an unwanted overnight layover. **Travelers Advantage** (☎877-259-2691; www.travelersadvantage.com; US$90 annual fee includes discounts and cheap flight directories) specializes in European travel and tour packages.

GETTING AROUND EUROPE

GOING MY WAY, SAILOR? In Europe, fares are listed as either **single** (one-way) or **return** (round-trip). "Period returns" require you to return within a specific number of days; "day return" means you must return on the same day. Round-trip fares on trains and buses in Europe are simply twice the one-way fare. Unless stated otherwise, *Let's Go* always lists single fares.

BY PLANE

The recent emergence of no-frills airlines has made hopscotching around Europe by air increasingly affordable. Though these flights often feature inconvenient hours and serve less-popular regional airports, with one-way flights averaging about US$80, it's never been cheaper to jet set across the continent. **Ryanair** is often the least expensive option, with fares starting around US$25, including taxes and fees. Ryanair serves 95 destinations in Austria, Belgium, the Czech Republic, France, Germany, Ireland, Italy, Latvia, the Netherlands, Poland, Portugal, Scandinavia, Spain, and the UK. (Ireland ☎0818 303 030, UK 0871 246 00 00; www.ryanair.com.) With an average fare of US$70, **easyJet** serves 62 destinations in Belgium, the Czech Republic, Denmark, Estonia, France, Germany, Greece, Hungary, Italy, Latvia, the Netherlands, Poland, Portugal, the Slovak Republic, Slovenia, Spain, Switzerland, and the UK. (UK ☎0871 244 2366; www.easyjet.com.)

The **Star Alliance European Airpass** offers economy-class fares as low as US$65 for travel within Europe to more than 200 destinations in 41 countries. The pass is available to non-European passengers on Star Alliance carriers, including Air Canada, Air New Zealand, Austrian Airlines, BMI British Midland, LOT Polish Airlines, Lufthansa, SAS (Scandinavian Airlines), Singapore Airlines, SpanAir, Thai International, United Airlines, USAirways, and Varig, as well as on certain partner airlines. See www.staralliance.com for more information. In addition, a number of European airlines offer discount coupon packets. Most are only available as tack-ons for transatlantic passengers, but some are stand-alone offers. Most must be purchased before departure, so research in advance. **Europe by Air's** *FlightPass* allows you to country-hop to over 150 European cities for US$99 per flight. (☎888-321-4737; www.europebyair.com.) **Iberia's** *Europass* allows Iberia passengers flying from the US to Spain to tack on a minimum of two additional destinations in Europe for US$133 each. (☎800-772-4642; www.iberia.com.)

BY TRAIN

Trains in Europe are generally comfortable, convenient, and reasonably fast, although quality varies by country. Second-class compartments, which seat two to six, are great places to meet fellow travelers. However, trains can be unsafe; for safety tips, see p. 23. For long trips, make sure you are on the correct car, as trains sometimes split at crossroads. Towns listed in parentheses on European train schedules require a switch at the town listed immediately before the parentheses.

Rail prices and times are subject to wide variation, and student or other discounts may be available. This map gives only a general picture of train travel in Europe. Consult *Thomas Cook's European Timetable* for accurate schedule info.
0 300 miles
0 300 kilometers
Shetland Islands
Orkney Islands
North Sea
ATLANTIC OCEAN
SCOTLAND
NORTHERN IRELAND
IRELAND
GREAT BRITAIN
ENGLAND
WALES
DENMARK
NETHERLANDS
GERMANY
BELGIUM
LUXEMBOURG
SWITZERLAND
FRANCE
PORTUGAL
SPAIN
ANDORRA
MONACO
GIBRALTAR
Bay of Biscay
Mediterranean Sea
Corsica (Fr.)
Sardinia (It.)
Balearic Islands (Sp.)
Bergen
$105 6-8hr.
Glasgow
$14-16 1hr.
Edinburgh
Belfast
$58 2hr.
Dublin
$69 3hr.
Cork
$145-156 4¾hr.
$159 5-6hr.
Cardiff
London
Hamburg
$90 5hr.
Amsterdam
$126 6¼hr.
$59 2¾hr.
$95-270 2¾hr.
$35-57 3½hr.
Brussels
Cologne
$11-13 20min.
Bonn
$32-46 2hr.
Frankfurt
$195-255 3hr.
$87 1½hr.
$105-145 4hr.
Paris
$106 3¾hr.
$150 8-10hr.
Nantes
$89 6hr.
$76-89 3¼-6¼hr.
$104 2hr.
$87 3½hr.
Zurich
$87 4½hr.
$35 1¼hr.
Bern
$35 2hr.
Geneva
$49 2hr.
$116-137 12hr.
Lyon
$72 4hr.
$33-37 1½hr.
$119 5½hr.
Milan
Verona
Bordeaux
Santiago de Campostela
$38-42 1½hr.
Turin
$52 2¾hr.
$38-42 2¼-3hr
San Sebastián
$77 2hr.
Montpellier
$42 2hr.
Nice
$47 8hr.
$44 3hr.
$51 2¾hr.
Florence
$59 4½hr.
Marseille
$52 1½hr.
Lisbon
$65 10hr.
Madrid
$42-113 4½-9hr.
Barcelona
$46-54 3½hr.
$24-47 3½hr.
$55-60 1¾hr.
$37-41 6-7hr.
Valencia
Palma
Seville
$9-30 45min.
Córdoba
$20 2hr.
Málaga
Granada

Rail Planner

You can either buy a **railpass,** which allows you unlimited travel within a particular region for a given period of time, or rely on buying individual **point-to-point** tickets as you go. Almost all countries give students or youths (usually defined as anyone under 26) direct discounts on regular domestic rail tickets, and many also sell a student or youth card that provides 20-50% off all fares for up to a year.

RESERVATIONS

While seat reservations are required only for select trains (usually on major lines), you are not guaranteed a seat without one (usually US$5-30). You should strongly consider reserving in advance during peak holiday and tourist seasons (at the very latest, a few hours ahead). You will also have to purchase a **supplement** (US$10-50) or special fare for high-speed or high quality trains such as Spain's AVE, Switzerland's Cisalpino, Finland's Pendolino, Italy's ETR500 and Pendolino, Germany's ICE, and certain French TGVs. InterRail holders must also purchase supplements (US$3-20) for trains like EuroCity, InterCity, Sweden's X2000, and many French TGVs; supplements are often unnecessary for Eurailpass and Europass holders.

OVERNIGHT TRAINS

On night trains, you won't waste valuable daylight hours traveling and you can avoid the expense of staying at a hotel. However, the main drawbacks include discomfort, sleepless nights, and the lack of scenery. **Sleeping accommodations** on trains differ from country to country, but typically cost more than day fares; you can either sleep upright in your seat (supplement about $2-10) or pay for a separate space. **Couchettes** (berths) typically have four to six seats per compartment (supplement about US$10-50 per person); **sleepers** (beds) in private sleeping cars offer more privacy and comfort, but are considerably more expensive (supplement US$40-150). If you are using a railpass valid only for a restricted number of days, inspect train schedules to maximize the use of your pass: an overnight train or boat journey often uses up only one of your travel days if it departs after 7pm.

SHOULD YOU BUY A RAILPASS? Railpasses were conceived to allow you to jump on any train in Europe, go wherever you want whenever you want, and change your plans at will. In practice, it's not so simple. You still must stand in line to validate your pass, pay for supplements, and fork over cash for seat and couchette reservations. More importantly, railpasses don't always pay off. Consult our **railplanner** (at the front of this book) to estimate the point-to-point cost of each leg of your journey; add them up and compare the total with the cost of a railpass. If you are planning to spend extensive time on trains, hopping between big cities, a railpass will probably be worth it. But in many cases, especially if you are under 26, point-to-point tickets may prove a cheaper option.

In Scandinavia, where distances are long and rail prices high, a railpass is often your best bet. You may find it tough to make your railpass pay for itself in the Balkans, Belgium, Eastern Europe, Greece, Iceland, Ireland, Italy, Luxembourg, the Netherlands, Portugal, or Spain, where train fares are reasonable, distances short, or buses preferable. If, however, the total cost of your trips nears the price of the pass, the convenience of avoiding ticket lines may be worth the difference.

MULTINATIONAL RAILPASSES

EURAILPASSES. Eurail is **valid** in most of Western Europe: Austria, Belgium, Denmark, Finland, France, Germany, Greece, Hungary, Italy, Luxembourg, the Netherlands, Norway, Portugal, the Republic of Ireland, Spain, Sweden, and Switzerland. It is **not valid** in the UK. Standard **Eurailpasses,** valid for a consecutive given number of days, are best for those planning on spending extensive time on trains every few days. **Eurailpass Flexi,** valid for any 10 or 15 (not necessarily consecutive) days within a two-month period, is more cost-effective for those traveling longer distances less frequently. **Eurailpass Saver** provides first-class travel for travelers in groups of two to five (prices are per person). **Eurailpass Youth** and **Eurailpass Youth Flexi** provide parallel second-class perks for those under 26. Passholders receive a

EURAILPASSES	15 DAYS	21 DAYS	1 MONTH	2 MONTHS	3 MONTHS
1st class Eurailpass	US$588	US$762	US$946	US$1338	US$1654
Eurailpass Saver	US$498	US$648	US$804	US$1138	US$1408
Eurailpass Youth	US$382	US4934	US$615	US$870	US$1075

EURAILPASS FLEXI	10 DAYS IN 2 MONTHS	15 DAYS IN 2 MONTHS
1st class Eurailpass Flexi	US$694	US$914
Eurailpass Saver Flexi	US$592	US$778
Eurailpass Youth Flexi	US$451	US$594

timetable for major routes and a map with details on possible bike rental, car rental, hotel, and museum discounts. Often they receive reduced fares or free passage on many boat, bus, and private railroad lines.

The **Eurail Selectpass** is a slimmed-down version of the Eurailpass: it allows five to 15 days of unlimited travel in any two-month period within three, four, or five bordering countries of 22 European countries; 15-day routes automatically include five countries. **Eurail Selectpasses** cost US$370-456 per person for a five-day pass and US$826 for 15 days. **Eurail Selectpass Savers,** for people traveling in groups of two to five, cost US$316-388 per person for a five-day pass and US$702 for 15 days. The **Eurail Selectpass Youth** (2nd-class), for those aged 12-25, costs US$241-296 per person for a five-day pass and US$537 for 15 days. You are entitled to the same **freebies** afforded by the Eurailpass, but only when they are within or between countries that you have purchased.

SHOPPING AROUND FOR A EURAIL. Eurailpasses can be bought only by non-Europeans, generally from non-European distributors. These passes must be sold at uniform prices determined by the EU. However, some travel agents tack on a US$10 handling fee, and others offer certain bonuses with purchase, so shop around. Also, keep in mind that pass prices usually go up each year, so if you're planning to travel early in the year, you can save cash by purchasing before January 1 (you have 3 months from the purchase date to validate your pass in Europe).

It is best to buy your Eurail before leaving; only a few places in major European cities sell them, and at a marked-up price. You can get a replacement for a lost pass only if you have purchased insurance on it under the Pass Security Plan (US$10-17). Eurailpasses are available through travel agents, student travel agencies like STA (p. 48), and **Rail Europe** (Canada ☎800-361-7245, US 877-257-2887; www.raileurope.com) or **Flight Centre** (1-866-967-5351; www.flightcentre.com). It is also possible to buy directly from Eurail's website, www.eurail.com. Book well in advance of your trip, however, as the company does not ship to Europe.

OTHER MULTINATIONAL PASSES. If your travels will be limited to one area, regional passes are often good values. Options available through Rail Europe include the **Balkan Flexipass,** which is valid for travel in Bulgaria, Greece, the Former Yugoslav Republic of Macedonia, Montenegro, Romania, Serbia, and Turkey (1st-class travel 5 days in 1 month US$189, under 26 US$112; 10 days in 1 month US$330/196; 15 days in 1 month US$397/238); the **Benelux Tourrail Pass** for Belgium, the Netherlands, and Luxembourg (2nd-class travel 5 days in 1 month US$163, under 26 US$109; 25% discount for companion traveler); the **European East Pass** for Austria, the Czech Republic, Hungary, Poland, and Slovakia (1st-class travel 5 days in 1 month US$230, 2nd-class US$162); and the **Scanrail Pass** for Denmark, Finland, Norway, and Sweden (standard/under 26 passes for 2nd-class travel 5 days in 2 months US$291/203; 10 days in 2 months US$390/273; 21 consecutive days US$453/316). Check www.raileurope.com and www.eurail.com for the regional passes most applicable to your country.

If you have lived for at least six months in one of the European countries where **InterRail Passes** are valid, they prove an economical option. The InterRail Pass allows travel within 30 European countries (excluding the passholder's country of residence), which are divided into eight **zones.** Passes may be purchased for one, two, or all eight zones. The one-zone pass (€286, under 26 €195) is good for 16 days of travel, the two-zone pass (€396, under 26 €275) is good for 22 days of travel, and the global pass (8 zones; €546, under 26 €385). Passholders receive free admission to many museums, as well as **discounts** on accommodations, food, and many ferries to Ireland, Scandinavia, and the rest of Europe. Passes are available at www.interrailnet.com, as well as from travel agents, at major train stations throughout Europe, and through online vendors (www.railpassdirect.co.uk).

DOMESTIC RAILPASSES

If you are planning to spend a significant amount of time within one country, a national pass—valid on all rail lines of a country's rail company—may be more cost-effective than a multinational pass. But many national passes are limited and don't provide the free or discounted travel on private railways and ferries that Eurail does. Some of these passes can be bought only in Europe, some only outside of Europe; check with a railpass agent or with national tourist offices.

NATIONAL RAILPASSES. The domestic analogs of the Eurailpass, national railpasses are valid either for a given number of consecutive days or for a specific number of days within a given time period. Usually, they must be purchased before you leave. Though they will usually save travelers some money, in some cases you may find that they are actually a more expensive alternative to point-to-point tickets, particularly in Eastern Europe. For more information, check out www.raileurope.com/us/rail/passes/single_country_index.htm.

EURODOMINO. Like the InterRail Pass, the EuroDomino Pass is available to anyone who has lived in Europe for at least six months; however, it is only valid in one country, which you designate when buying the pass. It is available for 28 European countries. Reservations must still be paid for separately. **Supplements** are included for many high-speed trains (e.g., TGV, ICE). The pass must be bought within your country of residence; each country has its own price. For more information, check www.raileurope.co.uk/railpasses/eurodomino.htm.

RAIL-AND-DRIVE PASSES. In addition to railpasses, many countries (as well as Eurail) offer rail-and-drive passes, which combine car rental with rail travel—a good option for travelers who wish both to visit cities accessible by rail and to travel in the surrounding areas. Prices range US$235-660, depending on the type of pass, type of car, and number of people included. Children under the age of 11 cost US$95-150, and adding more days costs US$39-215 per day (see **By Car**, p. 60).

BY BUS

In some cases buses prove a better option than train travel. In Britain and Hungary, the bus and train systems are on par; in the Baltics, Greece, Ireland, and Portugal, bus networks are more extensive, efficient, and often more comfortable; in Iceland and parts of northern Scandinavia, bus service is the only ground transportation available. In the rest of Europe, bus travel is more of a gamble; scattered

RESOURCES ON TRAIN TRAVEL

Info on rail travel and railpasses: www.raileurope.com.

Point-to-point fares and schedules: www.raileurope.com/us/rail/fares_schedules/index.htm. Allows you to calculate whether buying a railpass would save you money. For a more portable resource, see our **railplanner** at the front of this book.

Railsaver: www.railpass.com/new. Uses your itinerary to calculate the best railpass for your trip.

European Railway Server: www.railfaneurope.net. Links to rail servers throughout Europe.

offerings from private companies are often cheap, but sometimes unreliable. Amsterdam, Athens, London, Munich, and Oslo are centers for lines that offer long-distance rides across Europe. **International bus passes** allow unlimited travel on a hop-on, hop-off basis between major European cities, often at cheaper prices than railpasses. The prices below are based on high-season travel.

Eurolines, 4 Vicarage Rd., Edgbaston, Birmingham B15 3ES, UK (☎08705 143 219; www.eurolines.co.uk or www.eurolines.com). The largest operator of Europe-wide coach services. Unlimited 15-day (high season UK£195, under 26 and over 60 UK£165; low season UK£149/129); 30-day (high season UK£290/235; low season UK£209/169); or 60-day (high season UK£333/259; low season UK£265/211) travel passes that offer unlimited transit between 35 major European cities.

Busabout, 258 Vauxhall Bridge Rd., London SW1V 1BS, UK (☎0207 950 1661; www.busabout.com). Offers 5 interconnecting bus circuits covering 60 cities and towns in Europe. Unlimited (consecutive-day) Passes, Flexipasses, and Add On Passes are available. Unlimited standard/student passes are valid for 2 weeks (US$469/419), 4 weeks (US$739/659), 6 weeks (US$919/819), 8 weeks (US$1049/939), 12 weeks (US$1319/1179), or for the season (US$1649/1469).

ADDITIONAL READING

Thomas Cook European Timetable, updated monthly, covers all major and most minor train routes in Europe. Buy directly from Thomas Cook (www.thomascooktimetables.com).

Independent Travellers Europe by Rail 2005: The Inter-railer's and Eurailer's Guide. Thomas Cook Publishing (US$19.95).

BY CAR

Cars offer speed, freedom, access to the countryside, and an escape from the town-to-town mentality of trains. Although a single traveler won't save by renting a car, four usually will. If you can't decide between train and car travel, you may benefit from a combination of the two; RailEurope and other railpass vendors offer rail-and-drive packages. Fly-and-drive packages are also often available from travel agents and airline/rental agency partnerships.

Before setting off, know the laws of the countries in which you'll be driving (e.g., both seat belts and headlights must be on at all times in Scandinavia, and remember to keep left in Ireland and the UK). For an informal primer on European road signs and conventions, check out www.travlang.com/signs. The **Association for Safe International Road Travel (ASIRT),** 11769 Gainsborough Rd., Potomac, MD 20854, USA (☎301-983-5252; www.asirt.org), can provide more specific information about road conditions. ASIRT considers road travel (by car or bus) to be relatively **safe** in Denmark, Ireland, the Netherlands, Norway, Sweden, Switzerland, and the UK, and less safe in France, Greece, Italy, and Portugal.

RENTING A CAR

You can rent a car from a US-based firm (Alamo, Avis, Budget, or Hertz) with European offices, from a European-based company with local representatives (Europcar), or from a tour operator (Auto Europe, Europe By Car, and Kemwel Holiday Autos) that will arrange a rental for you from a European company. Multinationals offer greater flexibility, but tour operators often strike better deals. Ask airlines about special fly-and-drive packages; you may get up to a week of free or discounted rental. See **Costs and Insurance** section, p. 61, for more info. Minimum age requirements vary but tend to fall in the range of 21-25, with some as low as 18; there may be an additional insurance fee for drivers under 25. At most agencies, all that's needed to rent a car is a license from home and proof that you've had it for a year. Car rental in Europe is available through the following agencies:

Auto Europe (US and Canada ☎888-223-5555; www.autoeurope.com).

Avis (Australia ☎136 333, Canada 800-272-5871, New Zealand 0800 65 51 11, UK 0870 606 0100, US 800-230-4898; www.avis.com).

Budget (Canada ☎800-268-8900; UK 8701 565 656; US 800-527-0700; www.budgetrentacar.com).

Europcar International, 3 Av. du Centre, 78 881 Saint Quentin en Yvelines Cedex, France (UK ☎870 607 5000, US 877-940-6900; www.europcar.com).

Europe by Car (US ☎800-223-1516 or 212-581-3040; www.europebycar.com).

Hertz (Australia ☎9698 2555, Canada 800-263-0600, UK 08708 44 88 44, US 800-654-3030; www.hertz.com).

Kemwel (US ☎877-820-0668; www.kemwel.com).

COSTS AND INSURANCE

Expect to pay US$100-500 per week, plus tax (5-25%), for a tiny car with a manual transmission; automatics can double or triple the price. Larger vehicles and 4WD will also raise prices. Reserve ahead and pay in advance if at all possible. It is less expensive to reserve a car from the US than from Europe. Rates are generally lowest in Belgium, Germany, Holland, and the UK, higher in Ireland, and Italy, and highest in Scandinavia and Eastern Europe. Some companies charge fees for traveling into Eastern Europe. National chains often allow one-way rentals: pick-up in one city and drop-off in another. There is usually a minimum hire period and sometimes an extra drop-off charge of several hundred dollars.

Many rental packages offer unlimited kilometers, while others offer a fixed distance per day with a per-kilometer surcharge after that. Be sure to ask whether the price includes **insurance** against theft and collision. Remember that if you are driving a conventional vehicle on an **unpaved road** in a rental car, you are almost never covered by insurance; ask about this before leaving the rental agency. Always check if prices quoted include tax and collision insurance; some credit card companies provide insurance, allowing their customers to decline the collision damage waiver. Ask about discounts and check the terms of insurance, particularly the size of the deductible. Beware that cars rented on an **American Express** or **Visa/Mastercard Gold or Platinum** credit cards in Europe might *not* carry the automatic insurance that they would in some other countries; check with your credit card company. Insurance plans almost always come with an **excess** (or deductible) for conventional vehicles; excess is usually higher for younger drivers and for 4WD. This provision means you pay for all damages up to the specified sum, unless they are the fault of another vehicle. The excess you will be quoted applies to collisions with other vehicles; collisions with non-vehicles like trees ("single-vehicle collisions") will cost you even more. The excess can often be reduced or waived for an additional charge. Remember to return the car with a full tank of **gasoline** to

TRANSPORTATION

avoid high fuel charges in the end. Gas prices vary by country, and are generally highest in Scandinavia. Throughout Europe, fuel tends to be cheaper in cities than in outlying areas. Western Europeans and Scandinavians use unleaded gas almost exclusively, but it's not available in many gas stations in Eastern Europe.

LEASING A CAR

For longer than 17 days, leasing can be cheaper than renting; it is often the only option for those ages 18 to 21. The cheapest leases are agreements to buy the car and then sell it back to the manufacturer at a prearranged price. Leases generally include insurance coverage and are not taxed. The most affordable ones usually originate in Belgium, France, or Germany. Expect to pay around US$1100-1800 (depending on size of car) for 60 days. Contact **Auto Europe, Europe by Car,** or **Kemwel** (p. 61) before you go.

BUYING A CAR

If you're brave and know what you're doing, buying a used car or van in Europe and selling it just before you leave can provide the cheapest wheels for longer trips. Check with consulates for import-export laws concerning used vehicles, registration, and safety and emission standards.

ON THE ROAD

Road conditions and **regional hazards** are variable throughout Europe. Roads in mountainous areas are often steep and curvy and may be closed in the winter. Road conditions in Eastern Europe are often poor as a result of maintenance issues and inadequately enforced traffic laws; many travelers prefer public transportation. Western European roads are generally excellent, but keep in mind that each area has its own dangers. In Scandinavia, for example, drivers should be on the lookout for moose and elk, while on the Autobahn the threat will come from cars speeding at 150kph. In this book, region-specific hazards are listed in country introductions. The Association for Safe International Road Travel (p. 60) can provide more extended info on road safety. Carry emergency equipment with you (see box on **Driving Precautions,** below) and know what to do in case of a breakdown. Car rental companies will often have phone numbers for emergency service.

DRIVING PRECAUTIONS. When traveling in the summer or in the desert, bring substantial amounts of water (a suggested 5L of water per person per day) for drinking and for the radiator. For long drives to unpopulated areas, register with police before beginning the trek, and again upon arrival at the destination. Check with the local automobile club for details. When traveling for long distances, make sure tires are in good repair and have enough air, and get good maps. A compass and a car manual can also be very useful. Always carry a spare tire and jack, jumper cables, extra oil, flares, a flashlight (torch), and heavy blankets (in case your car breaks down at night or in the winter). If you don't know how to change a tire, learn before heading out, especially if you are planning on traveling in deserted areas. Blowouts on dirt roads are exceedingly common. If you do have a breakdown, stay with your car; if you wander off, there's less likelihood trackers will find you.

DRIVING PERMITS AND CAR INSURANCE

INTERNATIONAL DRIVING PERMIT (IDP)

If you plan to drive a car while in Europe, you must be over 18 and have an International Driving Permit (IDP), though certain countries (such as the UK) allow travelers to drive with a valid American or Canadian license for a limited number of months. It may be a good idea to get one anyway, in case you're in a situation (e.g., an accident or stranded in a small town) where the police do not know English; information on the IDP is printed in 11 languages, including French, German, Italian, Portuguese, Russian, Spanish, and Swedish.

Your IDP, valid for one year, must be issued in your own country before you depart. An application for an IDP usually requires one or two photos, a current local license, an additional form of identification, and a fee. To apply, contact your home country's automobile association. Be careful when purchasing an IDP online or anywhere other than your home automobile association. Many vendors sell permits of questionable legitimacy for higher prices.

CAR INSURANCE

Most credit cards cover standard insurance. If you rent, lease, or borrow a car, you will need a Green Card, or International Insurance Certificate, to certify that you have liability insurance and that it applies abroad. Green cards can be obtained at car rental agencies, car dealers (for those leasing cars), some travel agents, and some border crossings. Rental agencies may require you to purchase theft insurance in countries that they consider to have a high risk of auto theft.

BY CHUNNEL FROM THE UK

Traversing 43km under the sea, the Chunnel is undoubtedly the fastest, most convenient, and least scenic route from England to France.

BY TRAIN. Eurostar, Eurostar House, Waterloo Station, London SE1 8SE (UK ☎08705 186 186; www.eurostar.com) runs frequent trains between London and the continent. Trains run to 100 destinations, including Paris (4hr., US$75-400, 2nd class). Book online, at major rail stations in the UK, or at the office above.

BY BUS. Eurolines (p. 60) provides bus/ferry combinations.

BY CAR. Eurotunnel, Customer relations, P.O. Box 2000, Folkestone, Kent CT18 8XY (UK ☎08705 353 535; www.eurotunnel.co.uk) shuttles cars and passengers between Kent and Nord-Pas-de-Calais. Round-trip fares for vehicle and all passengers range from UK£223-253 with car. Same-day round-trip costs UK£19-34, two- to five-day round-trip for a car UK£123-183. Book online or via phone. Travelers with cars can also look into sea crossings by ferry (see below).

BY BOAT

Most European ferries are quite comfortable; the cheapest ticket typically includes a reclining chair or couchette. Fares jump sharply in July and August. Ask for discounts; ISIC holders can often get student fares, and Eurailpass holders get many reductions and free trips. You'll occasionally have to pay a port tax (under US$10). The fares below are **one-way** for **adult foot passengers** unless otherwise noted. Though standard round-trip fares are usually twice the one-way fare, **fixed-period returns** (usually within 5 days) are generally cheaper. Ferries run **year-round** unless otherwise noted. **Bikes** cost up to US$15 in high season.

ENGLISH CHANNEL AND IRISH SEA FERRIES

Ferries are frequent and dependable. The main route across the English Channel, from England to France, is Dover-Calais. The main ferry port on the southern coast of England is Portsmouth, with connections to France and Spain. Ferries also cross the Irish Sea, connecting Northern Ireland with Scotland and England, and the Republic of Ireland with Wales. A directory of ferries in this region can be found at www.seaview.co.uk/ferries.html.

Brittany Ferries: UK ☎08703 665 333, France 08 25 82 88 28; www.brittany-ferries.com. Plymouth, England to **Roscoff, France** (6hr., in summer 1-3 per day, UK£20-58) and **Santander, Spain** (18hr., 2 per week, round-trip UK£80-145). Portsmouth, England to **St-Malo, France** (11hr., 1 per day, €23-49) and **Caen, France** (5¾hr., 2-4 per day, €21-44). Poole, England to **Cherbourg, France** (4¼hr., 2-3 per day, €21-44). Cork, Ireland to **Roscoff, France** (14hr., mid-Mar. to early Nov. 1 per week, €52-99).

DFDS Seaways: UK ☎08705 444 333; www.dfdsse aways.co.uk. Harwich, England to **Cuxhaven, Germany** (19½hr., UK£29-49) and **Esbjerg, Denmark** (18hr., UK£29-49). Newcastle, England to **Amsterdam, the Netherlands** (16hr., UK£19-39); **Kristiansand, Norway** (18¼hr., UK£19-59); **Gothenburg, Sweden** (26hr., UK£19-59).

Fjord Line: UK ☎08701 439 669; www.fjordline.no. Newcastle, England to **Stavanger, Norway** (19½hr., UK£30-40) and **Bergen, Norway** (26hr., UK£30-40).

Hoverspeed: UK ☎08702 408 070; www.hoverspeed.co.uk. Dover, England to Calais, France (2hr., every 1-2hr., UK£15).

Irish Ferries: Ireland ☎353 818 300 400; www.irishferries.ie. Rosslare Harbour, Ireland to **Cherbourg** and **Roscoff, France** (18hr., €49-99), and **Pembroke, Wales** (3¾hr., €26-54). Holyhead, Wales to **Dublin, Ireland** (2-3hr., €24-40).

P&O Ferries: UK ☎08705 980 333; www.posl.com. Dover, England to **Calais, France** (1¼hr., every hr. 50 per day; from UK£10). Daily ferries from Hull, England to **Rotterdam, the Netherlands** (10hr.) and **Zeebrugge, Belgium** (12½hr.). Both from UK£100.

SeaFrance: UK ☎08705 711 711; France ☎08 03 04 40 45; www.seafrance.com. Dover, England to **Calais, France** (1½hr., 15 per day, UK£7-11).

Stena Line: UK ☎08705 707 070; www.stenaline.co.uk. Harwich, England to **Hook of Holland** (3½hr., €31). Fishguard, Wales to **Rosslare Harbour, Ireland** (1¾hr., €32). Holyhead, Wales to **Dublin** or **Dún Laoghaire, Ireland** (1¾hr., €32).

NORTH AND BALTIC SEA FERRIES

Ferries run to many North Sea destinations. Those content with deck passage rarely need to book ahead. Baltic Sea ferries sail between Poland and Scandinavia.

Color Line: Norway ☎0810 00 811; www.colorline.com. Ferries run between Norway and Denmark, Sweden, and Germany.

Silja Line: US sales ☎800-533-3755, ext. 114, Finland ☎09 18 041, Stockholm 086 66 33 30; www.silja.com. Helsinki to **Stockholm** (16hr.; June-Dec.); **Tallinn, Estonia** (3hr.; June to mid-Sept.); **Rostock, Germany** (23-25hr.; June to mid-Sept.).

Viking Line: US Sales ☎800-843-0602, Sweden ☎0452 40 00; www.vikingline.fi. Ferries run between Helsinki and Turku in Finland to destinations in Sweden and Estonia. One-way €11-44. M-Th, Su min. age 20; F-Sa 23. Eurail discounts available.

MEDITERRANEAN AND AEGEAN FERRIES

Mediterranean ferries may be the most glamorous, but they can also be the most rocky; bring toilet paper. Ferries run from Spain to Morocco, from Italy to Tunisia, and from France to Morocco and Tunisia. Reservations are recommended, especially in July and August. Schedules are erratic, with varying prices for similar routes. Shop around, and beware of small companies that don't take reservations.

Ferries float across the Adriatic from Ancona and Bari, Italy to Split and Dubrovnik, respectively, in Croatia. Ferries also run across the Aegean, from Ancona, Italy to Patras, Greece (19hr.), and from Bari, Italy to Igoumenitsa (9hr.) and Patras (15hr.), Greece. **Eurail** is valid on certain ferries between Brindisi, Italy and Corfu (8hr.), Igoumenitsa, and Patras, Greece. Countless ferry companies operate on these routes; see specific country chapters for more information.

BY MOPED AND MOTORCYCLE

Motorized bikes and mopeds don't use much gas, can be put on trains and ferries, and are a good compromise between costly car travel and the limited range of bicycles. However, they're uncomfortable for long distances, dangerous in the rain, and unpredictable on rough roads. Always wear a helmet, and never ride with a backpack. If you've never ridden a moped before, a twisting Alpine road is not the place to start. Expect to pay about US$20-35 per day; try auto repair shops, and remember to bargain. Motorcycles are more expensive and normally require a license, but are better for long distances. Before renting, ask if the price includes tax and insurance, or you may be hit with an unexpected fee. Avoid handing your passport over as a deposit; if you have an accident or mechanical failure you may not get it back until you cover all repairs. Pay ahead of time instead.

BY THUMB

Let's Go strongly urges you to consider the risks before you choose to hitch. We do not recommend hitchhiking, and none of the information presented here is intended to do so.

No one should hitch without careful consideration of the risks involved. Hitching means entrusting your life to a unknown person and risking theft, assault, sexual harassment, and unsafe driving. Some travelers report that hitchhiking allows them to meet local people and travel in areas where public transportation is sketchy. The choice, however, remains yours.

Britain and **Ireland** are probably the easiest places in Western Europe to get a lift. Hitching in **Scandinavia** is slow but steady. Long-distance hitching in the developed countries of **northwestern Europe** demands close attention to expressway junctions, rest stop locations, and often a destination sign. Hitching in **southern Europe** is generally mediocre; **France** is the worst. In some **Central** and **Eastern European** countries, the line between hitching and taking a taxi is virtually nonexistent.

Hitchhiking at night can be particularly dangerous; experienced hitchers stand in well-lit places. For women traveling alone, hitching is just too dangerous. A man and a woman are a safer combination, two men will have a harder time, and three will go nowhere. Experienced hitchers pick a spot outside of built-up areas, where drivers can stop, return to the road without causing an accident, and have time to look over potential passengers as they approach. Hitching (or even standing) on super-highways is usually illegal: one may only thumb at rest stops or at the entrance ramps to highways. Finally, success often depends on appearance.

Most Western European countries offer a ride service, which pairs drivers with riders; the fee varies according to destination. **Eurostop** (www.taxistop.be/index_ils.htm), Taxistop's ride service, is one of the largest in Europe. Also try **Allostop** (French-language website www.allostop.net) in France and **Verband der Deutschen Mitfahrzentralen** in Germany (German-language website www.mitfahrzentrale.de). Not all organizations screen drivers and riders; ask in advance.

BEYOND TOURISM

A PHILOSOPHY FOR TRAVELERS

BEYOND TOURISM HIGHLIGHTS

NURTURE endangered griffons on the island Cres in Croatia (p. 220).

RESTORE castles in France (p. 67) and Germany (p. 409).

POLITICK as an intern at NATO in Belgium (p. 107).

Let's Go believes that the connection between travelers and their destinations is an important one. We know that many travelers care passionately about the communities and environments they explore, but we also know that even conscientious tourists can inadvertently damage natural wonders and harm cultural environments. With this Beyond Tourism chapter, *Let's Go* hopes to provide a valuable alternative to the typical itinerary through Europe. You'll also find Beyond Tourism information throughout the book in the form of new "Giving Back" sidebar features that highlight regional Beyond Tourism opportunities.

There are several options for those who seek to contribute to or take part in the communities they visit. Opportunities for **volunteerism** abound, both with local and international organizations. **Studying** can also be instructive, whether through direct enrollment in a local university or in an independent research project. **Working** is a way to both immerse yourself in the local culture and finance your travels.

As a volunteer in Europe, you can participate in projects—from castle-cleaning in France to protecting the endangered Loggerhead turtles in Greece—either on a short-term basis or as the main component of your trip. Later in this chapter, we recommend organizations that can help you find the opportunities that best suit your interests, whether you're looking to pitch in for a day or a year.

Studying is another option. Those who choose to study abroad in Europe often find the immersion in the region's educational environment to be much more rewarding and genuine than the backpacker trail alone. With hundreds of programs to choose from, students can select from a full spectrum of fields that cater to their individual interests. Many travelers also structure their trips by the work that they can do along the way—either odd jobs as they go, or full-time stints in cities where they plan to stay for some time. The availability and legality of temporary work vary widely across Europe. If you are interested in working your way across the continent, we recommend picking up *Let's Go* city and country guides.

Start your search at **www.beyondtourism.com,** Let's Go's searchable database of alternatives to tourism to find exciting articles and helpful program listings divided by country, continent, and program type. For a sampling of country-specific offerings, check the Essentials chapter of each chapter in this book.

VOLUNTEERING

Volunteering can be challenging in direct proportion to the extent to which it is unpaid. It can also be phenomenally rewarding, especially when combined with the thrill of travel. Whether your passion is for ecological, political, or social work, Europe can make use of your energies.

Most people who volunteer in Europe do so on a short-term basis, at organizations that make use of drop-in or once-a-week volunteers. The best way to find opportunities that match up with your interests and schedule may be to check with local or national volunteer centers. Opportunities for volunteer work are more abundant in Eastern Europe than in other areas of the continent. Habitat for Humanity and Peace Corps placements, for example, are not usually available in Western Europe. Those looking for longer, more intensive volunteer experiences usually choose to go through a parent organization that takes care of logistical details and often provides a group environment and support system—for a fee. There are two main types of organizations—religious and non-sectarian—although there are rarely restrictions on participation for either.

WHY PAY MONEY TO VOLUNTEER? Many volunteers are surprised to learn that some organizations require large fees or "donations." Such fees often keep the organization afloat, in addition to covering airfare, room, board, and administrative expenses. (Other organizations must rely on private donations and government subsidies.) If you're concerned about how a program spends its fees, request an annual report or finance account. A reputable organization won't refuse to inform you of how volunteer money is spent.

Pay-to-volunteer programs may be good for travelers are looking for support and structure (e.g., pre-arranged transportation and housing), or who would rather not deal with the uncertainty in creating a volunteer experience from scratch.

PROGRAMS

COMMUNITY DEVELOPMENT

Cross-Cultural Solutions, 2 Clinton Pl., New Rochelle, NY 10801, USA (☎800-380-4777; http://crossculturalsolutions.org). 2- to 12-week education and social service placements in Russia and many other countries. 18+. From US$2279.

Global Volunteers, 375 E. Little Canada Rd., St. Paul, MN 55117, USA (☎800-487-1074; www.globalvolunteers.org). A variety of 1- to 3-week volunteer programs throughout Europe. Fees range US$1370-2750, including room and board but not airfare.

Service Civil International Voluntary Service (SCI-IVS), SCI USA main office, 5505 Walnut Level Rd., Crozet, VA 22932, USA (☎206-350-6585; www.sci-ivs.org). Arranges placement in outdoor "workcamps" throughout Europe. 18+. Registration fee US$175.

CONSERVATION

Club du Vieux Manoir, Ancienne Abbaye du Moncel, 60700 Pontpoint, France (☎+33 03 44 72 33 98; http://cvmclubduvieuxmanoir.free.fr). Offers year-long and summer programs restoring castles and churches throughout France. €14 annual membership and insurance fee. €12.5 per day, including food and tent. Website in French.

Earthwatch Institute, 3 Clocktower Pl., Ste. 100, P.O. Box 75, Maynard, MA 01754, USA (☎800-776-0188; www.earthwatch.org). Arranges 1- to 3-week programs to promote conservation of natural resources. Fees vary based on program location and duration. Costs range US$700-4000 plus airfare.

The National Trust, Community Learning and Volunteering, Rowan, Swindon, Wilts, SN2 8YL, UK (☎+44 0870 609 5383; www.nationaltrust.org.uk/volunteers). Arranges numerous volunteer opportunities, including Working Holidays.

World Wide Opportunities on Organic Farms (WWOOF), Main Office, P.O. Box 2675, Lewes, East Sussex, BN7 1RB, UK (www.wwoof.org). Arranges volunteer work with organic and eco-conscious farms around the world.

HUMANITARIAN AND SOCIAL SERVICES

Coalition for Work with Psychotrauma and Peace, Gunduliceva 18, 32000 Vukovar, Croatia (☎+385 32 444 662; www.cwwpp.org). Work for 1½-2 years in education and health care related to long-term conflict stress in Bosnia, Croatia, and Serbia.

Simon Wiesenthal Center, 1399 South Roxbury Dr., Los Angeles, CA 90035, USA (☎800-900-9036; www.wiesenthal.org). Fights anti-Semitism and Holocaust denial throughout Europe. Small, variable donation required for membership.

Volunteers for Peace, 1034 Tiffany Rd., Belmont, VT 05730, USA (☎802-259-2759; www.vfp.org). Arranges placement in camps throughout Europe. US$20 Membership required for registration. Programs average US$200-400 for 2-3 weeks.

STUDYING

Study abroad programs range from basic language and culture courses to college-level classes. In order to choose a program that best fits your needs, research before making your decision—determine costs, duration, what kind of students participate, and what accommodations are provided. In programs that have large groups of students who speak the same language you may feel more comfortable, but you will not have the same opportunity to practice a foreign language or to befriend other international students. Dorm life provides a better opportunity to mingle with students, but there is less of a chance to experience the local scene. If you live with a family, there is a potential to build friendships with natives and to experience day-to-day life, but conditions vary greatly from family to family.

VISA INFORMATION. Different countries have different requirements for study-abroad students. Ask the local consulate for information about acquiring the proper visa. Generally speaking, applicants must be able to provide a passport and proof of enrollment, medical insurance, and financial support before their visa can be issued. Since the process may take months to complete, it is advisable to apply for a visa well in advance of your departure date.

UNIVERSITIES

Most university-level programs are meant as language and culture enrichment opportunities, and are conducted in the local language. Still, many programs offer classes in English and lower-level language courses. Those relatively fluent in a foreign language may find it cheaper to enroll directly in a university abroad, although getting college credit may be more difficult. Websites like www.studyabroad.com, www.petersons.com/stdyabrd/sasector.html, and www.westudyabroad.com/europe.htm are good resources for finding programs that cater to your particular interests. Each has links to various study-abroad programs broken down by a variety of criteria, including desired location and focus of study.

AMERICAN PROGRAMS

The following is a list of organizations that can help place students in university programs abroad, or that have their own branch in Europe.

American Institute for Foreign Study (AIFS), College Division, River Plaza, 9 West Broad St., Stamford, CT 06902 (☎800-727-2437; www.aifsabroad.com). Organizes programs for high school and college study at universities in Austria, Britain, the Czech Republic, France, Ireland, Italy, Russia, and Spain. Scholarships available.

American Field Service (AFS), 71 W. 23rd St., 17th fl., New York, NY 10010 (☎212-807-8686; www.afs.org), has branches in over 50 countries. Summer-, semester-, and year-long homestay exchange programs for high school students and graduating seniors in locations including the Czech Republic, Hungary, Latvia, Russia, and the Slovak Republic. Community service programs are also offered to young adults, 18+. Teaching programs available for current and retired teachers. Financial aid available.

American School of Classical Studies (ASCSA), 54 Souidias St., GR-106 76 Athens, Greece (☎+30 210 72 36 313; www.ascsa.edu.gr). Offers a variety of archaeological and classical studies programs to undergraduates, graduate students, and doctoral candidates. Visit the website to find a list of publications and links to other archaeological programs. Costs vary from summer to academic year. US$2950-16,000.

Council on International Educational Exchange (CIEE), 7 Custom House St., 3rd fl., Portland, ME 04101 (☎800-407-8839; www.ciee.org). Sponsors academic programs in Belgium, Britain, the Czech Republic, France, Hungary, Ireland, Italy, the Netherlands, Poland, Russia, and Spain for around US$10,000 per semester, as well as volunteer opportunities across Europe. US$30 application fee. Scholarships available.

Cultural Experiences Abroad (CEA), 1400 East Southern Ave. Ste. B-108, Tempe, AZ 85282 (☎800-266-4441; www.gowithcea.com). Operates programs in Britain, France, Ireland, Italy, and Spain for undergraduates studying in the US and Canada. Financial aid available. Costs depend on program and range from US$3295 for a summer course to US$17,395 for the academic year. Financial aid available.

Institute for the International Education of Students (IES), 33 N. LaSalle St., 15th fl., Chicago, IL 60602 (☎800-995-2300; www.IESabroad.org). Offers year-, semester-, and summer-long study abroad programs in Austria, England, France, Germany, Ireland, Italy, the Netherlands, and Spain for college students. US$10,000-15,000 per semester. Internship opportunities available. US$50 application fee. Scholarships available.

School for International Training (SIT), College Semester Abroad, Kipling Rd., P.O. Box 676, Brattleboro, VT 05302 (☎800-257-7751; www.sit.edu). Each semester-long study abroad program is planned around a theme, with a focus on social responsibility and intercultural understanding. Courses in Europe cost around US$15,000. Also runs the **Experiment in International Living** (☎800-345-2929; www.usexperiment.org), 3- to 5-week summer programs that offer high school students cross-cultural homestays in Britain, France, Germany, Italy, Poland, Spain, and Switzerland for around US$5000.

Youth for Understanding International Exchange (YFU), 6400 Goldsboro Rd., Ste. 100, Bethesda, MD 20817 (☎800-833-6243; www.yfu-usa.org). Places US high school students with host families throughout Europe. Semester or year about US$7000. Summer approx. US$5000. US$75 application fee plus US$500 deposit.

LANGUAGE SCHOOLS

Language schools can be independently run international or local organizations or divisions of foreign universities. They rarely offer college credit. They are a good alternative to university study if you desire a deeper focus on the language or a less rigorous courseload. These programs are also good for high school students who might not feel comfortable with older students in a university program.

Eurocentres, 101 N. Union St. Ste. 300, Alexandria, VA 22314, USA (☎703-684-1494; www.eurocentres.com). Language programs for beginning to advanced students with optional homestays in France, Germany, Italy, Russia, Spain, and Switzerland.

Language Immersion Institute, JFT 214, SUNY New Paltz, 75 South Manheim Blvd., New Paltz, NY 12561, USA (☎845-257-3500; www.newpaltz.edu/lii). 2-week summer overseas courses in France, Italy, and Spain in addition to a wide variety of stateside offerings. US$950 plus US$360-600 for accommodations.

Sprachcaffe Languages Plus, 413 Ontario St., Toronto, Ontario M5A 2V9, Canada (☎888-526-4758; www.sprachcaffe.com). Language classes in France, Germany, Italy, and Spain for US$200-600 per week. Price depends on course and accommodations. Homestays available. Also offers a French language and travel program for teenagers.

WORKING

VISA INFORMATION. EU Citizens: The 2004 enlargement of the EU inspired fear in the 15 current member states (EU-15) that waves of Central and Eastern European immigrants would flood their labor markets. This fear forced the union to institute a transition period of up to seven years during which citizens of the new EU countries may still need a visa or permit to work in the EU-15 countries. EU-15 citizens generally have the right to work in the pre-enlargement countries for up to three months without a visa; longer-term employment usually requires a residency or work permit. By law, all EU-15 citizens are given equal consideration when applying to jobs not directly related to national security.

Everyone else: For non-EU citizens, getting a work visa in Western Europe is extremely difficult. Different countries have different laws for employment of non-EU foreigners; inquire at the local embassy or consulate for specific information. Even when possible, the process is invariably time-consuming and frustrating. Non-EU citizens planning to work in Europe must carefully research country-specific requirements and limitations before their departure. Having a job lined-up *before* braving the bureaucratic gauntlet can generally speed up the application process, as employers can perform much of the administrative leg-work.

As with volunteering, work opportunities tend to fall into two categories: long- and short-term. Some travelers want long-term jobs that allow them to get to know another part of the world as a member of the community, while other travelers seek out short-term jobs to finance the next leg of their travels. In Europe, people who want to work long-term might find success where their language skills are in demand, such as in teaching or working with tourists. Employment opportunities for those who want short-term work may be more limited and are generally contingent upon the economic needs of the city or region. In addition to local papers, international English-language newspapers, such as the *International Herald Tribune* (www.iht.com), often list job opportunities in their classified sections. If applicable, travelers should also consult federally run employment offices.

LONG-TERM WORK

If you're planning on spending more than three months working in Europe, search for a job in advance. International placement agencies are often the easiest way to find employment abroad. **Internships** are a good way to segue from traveling into working abroad, although they often offer no or low wages (many say the experience, however, is worth it). Be wary of companies that claim the ability to get you a job abroad for a fee—often the same listings are available online or in newspapers, or are even out-of-date. Some reputable organizations include:

Escapeartist.com (http://jobs.escapeartist.com). International employers post directly to this website; various European jobs advertised.

International Cooperative Education, 15 Spiros Way, Menlo Park, CA 94025, USA (☎650-323-4944; www.icemenlo.com). Finds summer jobs and internships for students in Belgium, Britain, Germany, and Switzerland. Participants must be aged 18-30. Costs include a US$250 application fee and a US$700 placement fee.

ResortJobs.com (www.resortjobs.com). Searchable database of service and entertainment jobs at resorts in Greece and Switzerland.

StepStone (www.stepstone.com, branches across Europe listed at www.stepstone.com/offices.htm). Database covering international employment openings for most of Europe. Several search options and a constantly updated list of openings.

TEACHING ENGLISH

Teaching jobs abroad are rarely well paid, although some elite private American schools can pay more competitive salaries. Volunteering as a teacher in lieu of getting paid is also a popular option; even in those cases, teachers often get some sort of a daily stipend to help with living expenses. In almost all cases, you must have at least a bachelor's degree to be a full-fledged teacher, although college undergraduates can often get summer positions teaching or tutoring.

Many schools require teachers to have a **Teaching English as a Foreign Language (TEFL)** certificate. Not having this certification does not exclude you from finding a teaching job, but certified teachers often find higher-paying positions. Native English speakers working in private schools are often hired for English-immersion classrooms where not a word of the local language is spoken. Those teaching in poorer, public schools are more likely to work in both English and the native tongue. Placement agencies and university fellowship programs are the best resources for finding teaching jobs. The alternative is to make contact directly with schools or just to try your luck once you get there. If you are going to try the latter, the best time to look is several weeks before the start of the school year. The following organizations are extremely helpful in placing teachers in Europe:

Central European Teaching Program (CETP), 3800 NE 72nd Ave., Portland, OR 97213 (☎503-287-4977; www.ticon.net/~cetp). Provides college graduates with job placement as English teachers in Hungary and Romania. Placement fees vary; summer US$500, semester US$1500, academic year US$2000.

International Schools Services (ISS), 15 Roszel Rd., P.O. Box 5910, Princeton, NJ 08543, USA (☎609-452-0990; www.iss.edu). Hires teachers for more than 200 international and American schools around the world; candidates should have 2 years teaching experience and/or teacher certification. 2-year commitment expected.

Teaching English as a Foreign Language (TEFL), TEFL Professional Network Ltd., 72 Pentyla Baglan Rd., Port Talbot, SA12 8AD, UK (www.tefl.com). Maintains the most extensive database of openings throughout Europe. Offers job training and certification.

AU PAIR WORK

Au pairs are typically women (although sometimes men) aged 18-27, who work as live-in nannies, caring for children and doing light housework in foreign countries in exchange for room, board, and a small stipend. Most former au pairs speak favorably of their experience. The job allows you to get to know the country without the high expenses of traveling. Drawbacks, however, often include long hours of constantly being on duty and mediocre pay. Au pairs in Europe typically work 25-40hr. per week and receive US$300-450 per month. Much of the au pair experience really does depend on the family with whom you're placed. The agencies below are a good starting point for looking for employment as an au pair.

Childcare International, Ltd., Trafalgar House, Grenville Pl., London NW7 3SA, UK (☎020 8906 3116; www.childint.co.uk). Offers au pair and nanny placement in Britain, France, Germany, the Netherlands, Italy, and Spain.

InterExchange, 161 6th Ave., New York, NY 10013, USA (☎212-924-0446; www.interexchange.org). Au pair, internship, and short-term work placement in Belgium, Britain, France, Germany, the Netherlands, Norway, and Spain. US$400-600 placement fee.

Sunny AuPairs (☎+44 (0)1722 415864; www.sunnyaupairs.com). Online, worldwide database connecting au pairs with families. Free registration. No placement fee.

SHORT-TERM WORK

Traveling for long periods of time can get expensive; therefore, many travelers try their hand at odd jobs for a few weeks at a time to help finance another month or two abroad. Another popular option is to work several hours a day at a hostel in exchange for free or discounted room and/or board. Most often, these short-term jobs are found by word of mouth or simply by talking to the owner of a hostel or restaurant. Due to the high turnover in the tourism industry, many places are eager for help, even if it is only temporary.

FURTHER READING ON BEYOND TOURISM

Alternatives to the Peace Corps: A Directory of Third World and U.S. Volunteer Opportunities, by Jennifer S. Willsea. Food First Books, 2003 (US$10).

Back Door Guide to Short-Term Job Adventures: Internships, Extraordinary Experiences, Seasonal Jobs, Volunteering, Working Abroad, by Michael Landes. Ten Speed Press, 2002 (US$22).

Green Volunteers: The World Guide to Voluntary Work in Nature, by Ausenda and McCloskey. Universe, 2003 (US$15).

How to Get a Job in Europe, by Sanborn and Matherly. Planning Communications, 2003 (US$22).

How to Live Your Dream of Volunteering Overseas, by Collins, DeZerega, and Heckscher. Penguin Books, 2002 (US$17).

International Directory of Voluntary Work, by Whetter and Pybus. Peterson's Guides and Vacation Work, 2000 (US$16).

International Job Finder: Where the Jobs Are Worldwide, by Daniel Lauber. Planning Communications, 2002 (US$20).

Invest Yourself: The Catalogue of Volunteer Opportunities, published by the Commission on Voluntary Service and Action (☎646-486-2446).

Live and Work Abroad: A Guide for Modern Nomads, by Francis and Callan. Vacation-Work Publications, 2001 (US$16).

Overseas Summer Jobs 2002, by Collier and Woodworth. Peterson's Guides and Vacation Work, 2002 (US$18).

Volunteer Vacations: Short-term Adventures That Will Benefit You and Others, by Cutchins and Geissinger. Chicago Review Press, 2003 (US$18).

Work Abroad: The Complete Guide to Finding a Job Overseas, by Hubbs, Griffith, and Nolting. Transitions Abroad Publishing, 2002 (US$16).

Work Your Way Around the World, by Susan Griffith. Vacation Work Publications, 2003 (US$18).

TEST TUBES AND TEUTONS

Research in Germany

During my time as a college student in the United States, I took an unforgettable semester off to work at the University of Ulm doing chemistry research. I was interested not only in learning about polypeptides and phenolphthalein, but also in discovering how Germans differ in their approaches to research, academics, and life. I wanted to get to know Germany (and Europe) more intimately than the average tourist, using the city of Ulm as the stronghold from which I would sally forth to other nations.

For centuries, Germany has been known for its rigorous intellectual tradition, especially in the physical sciences. After sitting in on a mind-blowing statistical mechanics lecture in Ulm, I learned that the professor was also deeply interested in history. In particular, he emphasized Einstein's variegate contributions to the field and the fact that Ulm was his birthplace. Germany may have lost some of its academic luster since the times of Boltzmann, Leibniz, and Hegel, but its academic research is still as vital as the flow of the mighty Rhine.

I began my search for a position in a German lab by talking to my academic advisor in the States about potential contacts in Germany. Finding professors who wanted an American protégé ended up being much easier than finding a reliable, sufficient, and legal method of financing my trip. I eventually was lucky enough to come upon a professor whose university could fund my studies, which meant I could stop trying to arrange my own funding through the **German Academic Exchange Program** (www.daad.de).

Undertaking academic research in Germany had several advantages over participating in a mere study abroad program, the biggest being the financial backing. I also appreciated the interaction afforded by eating with students in their dining hall. During my time in Germany, I lived in university housing with visiting scholars from many different countries, all of whom had very different academic and personal backgrounds, and fascinating stories. The true highlight of my research experience, however, was the opportunity to get involved in intense, focused scholarship, which can be far more intellectually rewarding than the academic dabbling of broad overview classes.

To pursue academic research in Germany, you usually have to be a university student or graduate with a strong interest in pursuing a narrow research topic in a rigorous academic setting. In most fields, especially scientific ones, you do not need to speak any German at all, let alone know how to decline an unpreceded adjective in front of a feminine noun in the dative case. Everyone in my lab spoke some heartfelt variant of English, and I was actually required to give my presentations in English.

My six-month stay in Germany was one of the most rewarding experiences I've had abroad. Academically, my project succeeded beyond our wildest dreams. I worked hard, but received unending support from my labmates. I survived the student dining hall, sat in on classes, and went to a few raging university parties. But even as we climbed scientific mountains together, I saw firsthand the ways in which German students differed from Americans. One day I arrived at work to find that the students had gone on strike (by refusing to attend classes, a tough move for the industrious Germans) to protest an administrative fee that the university was planning to establish.

While based in Ulm, I also had the opportunities to explore Munich and Stuttgart and spend a strenuous but rewarding weekend biking at the glorious Chiemsee in Bavaria. Since I was a wage-earning chemist instead of a starving backpacker, my quick trips to Austria, France, and England had a more generous budget than they otherwise would have, and the superb European train system and new discount airlines helped make them relatively hassle-free. Academic research was a phenomenal way for me to get to know Germany, change the shape of my life for a while, see much of Europe, and even learn a little bit of science.

Barbara Richter was a Researcher-Writer for Let's Go: Austria & Switzerland. *A native Austrian, then New Jersian, she'll be continuing her studies in chemistry and physics as a graduate student.*

AUSTRIA (ÖSTERREICH)

With high culture in Vienna and high mountains in the Alps, Austria veers between very different extremes of beauty. Travelers delight in the high, clear voices of the Vienna Boys' Choir, the jagged peaks that define the horizon, and the fresh-fallen snow. Austria's capital city, Vienna, dazzles the senses with cosmopolitan flair, but follow any road away from the city and you'll find golden onion-domed churches gracing small villages, vines curling over half-timbered houses, and friendly people who take the time for a smile and a *"Grüß Gott"* (hello) to passing strangers.

DISCOVER AUSTRIA: SUGGESTED ITINERARIES

THREE DAYS Spend all three days in **Vienna,** the Imperial headquarters of romance. From the stately **Staatsoper** to the majestic **Hofburg,** Vienna's attractions will leave you with enough sensory stimulation to last until your next trip.

ONE WEEK Begin in **Zell am See** (1 day; p. 97) to take advantage of its outdoor offerings. Stop in **Salzburg** (2 days; p. 91) to see the home of Mozart and the Festung Hohensalzburg (p. 94). Move on to the Salzkammergut for the **Dachstein Ice Caves** (1 day; p. 96). End by basking in the glory of **Vienna** (3 days).

TWO WEEKS Start in **Innsbruck,** where museums and mountains meet (2 days; p. 98), then swing by **Zell am See** (1 day). Spend another two days wandering **Hohe Tauern National Park** (p. 97), visiting the Pasterze Glacier and the Großglockner Hochalpenstraße. Next, tour **Hallstatt** and its nearby ice caves (2 days; p. 96). Follow your ears to **Salzburg** (2 days) before heading to the throbbing nightlife of **Graz** (1 day; p. 102). Finally, make your way to **Vienna** for a grand finale of romance, waltzes, and high coffeehouse culture (4 days).

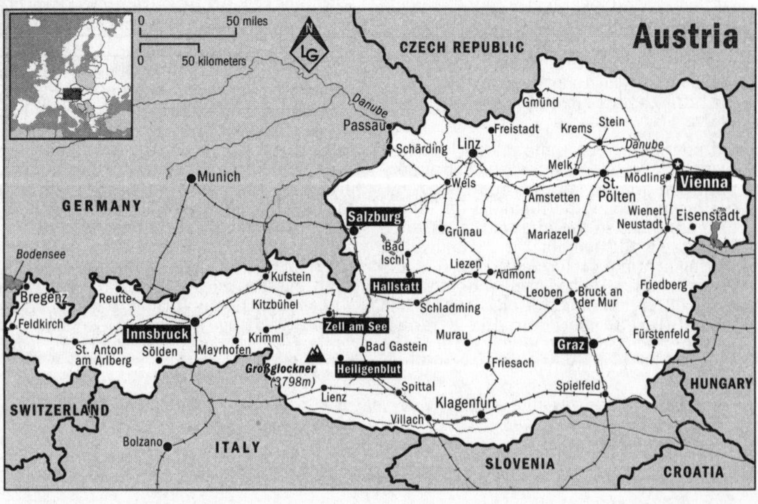

ESSENTIALS

FACTS AND FIGURES

Official Name: Republic of Austria.
Capital: Vienna.
Major Cities: Graz, Innsbruck, Salzburg.
Population: 8,185,000.
Time Zone: GMT +1.
Language: German.
Religions: Roman Catholic (74%), Protestant (5%), Muslim (4%), other (17%).

WHEN TO GO

Ski season reaches its peak between November and March, when prices in western Austria double and travelers need reservations months in advance. The situation reverses in the summer, when the eastern half fills with tourists. Accommodations are cheaper and less crowded in the shoulder season (May-June and Sept.-Oct.). However, some Alpine resorts close in May and June—call ahead. Cultural opportunities also vary with the seasons: the Vienna State Opera, the Vienna Boys' Choir, and many major theaters don't perform during the summer.

DOCUMENTS AND FORMALITIES

EMBASSIES. All foreign embassies in Austria are in Vienna (p. 78). Austrian embassies abroad include: **Australia,** 12 Talbot St., Forrest, Canberra ACT 2603 (☎02 6295 1533; www.austriaemb.org.au); **Canada,** 445 Wilbrod St., Ottawa, ON K1N 6M7 (☎613-789-1444; www.austro.org); **Ireland,** 15 Ailesbury Court, 93 Ailesbury Rd., Dublin 4 (☎01 269 14 51); **New Zealand,** Level 2, Willbank House, 57 Willis St., Wellington 6001 (☎04 499 63 93); **UK,** 18 Belgrave Mews West, London SW1X 8HU (☎020 7235 3731; www.bmaa.gv.at/london); **US,** 3524 International Ct. NW, Washington, D.C. 20008 (☎202-895-6700; austrianembassy@washington.nu).

VISA AND ENTRY INFORMATION. EU citizens do not need a visa. Citizens of Australia, Canada, New Zealand, the UK, and the US do not need a visa for stays of up to 90 days, although this three-month period begins upon entry into any of the countries that belong to the EU's freedom of movement zone.

TOURIST SERVICES AND MONEY

EMERGENCY	Ambulance: ☎144. Fire: ☎122. Police: ☎133.

TOURIST OFFICES. Tourist offices are marked by signs with a green "i"; most brochures are available in English. Visit www.austria-tourism.at for more info.

MONEY. The unit of currency in Austria in the **euro (€).** As a general rule, it's cheaper to exchange money in Austria than at home. Railroad stations, airports, hotels, and most travel agencies offer exchange services, as do banks. If you stay in hostels and prepare most of your own food, expect to spend anywhere from €30-60 per person per day. Accommodations start at about €12 and a basic sit-down meal usually costs around €8. Menus will say whether service is included (*preise inclusive* or *bedienung inclusiv*); if it is, a tip is not expected. If not, 10% will do. Austrian restaurants expect you to seat yourself, and servers will not bring the bill until you ask them to do so. Say "*Zahlen bitte*" (TSAHL-en BIT-uh) to settle your accounts, and don't leave tips on the table. Except at street markets, don't expect to bargain. Austria has a 10-20% **Value Added Tax (VAT),** which is applied to purchased goods. You can get refunds for one-time purchases of over €75 if you carry the goods out of Austria within three months of their purchase. Remember to keep your receipt or ask the customs office to endorse an invoice before you leave Austria. Contact the customs office to apply for your refund.

TRANSPORTATION

BY PLANE. The only major international airport is Vienna's Schwechat Flughafen (VIE). Others are in Innsbruck, Graz, Klagenfurt, Linz, and Salzburg. From London-Stansted, **Ryanair** (☎3531 303 030; www.ryanair.com) flies to the latter four. For more information on flying to Austria from other locations, see p. 48.

BY TRAIN. The **Österreichische Bundesbahn (ÖBB),** Austria's state railroad, operates an efficient system with fast, comfortable trains. **Eurail, InterRail,** and **Europe East** are valid in Austria, but they do not guarantee a seat. The **Austrian Railpass** allows three days of travel within any 15-day period. It also entitles holders to 40% off bike rentals at train stations (2nd-class US$107, each additional day US$16).

BY BUS. The Austrian bus system consists mainly of **PostBuses,** which cover areas inaccessible by train for comparably high prices. Buy tickets at the station or from the driver. For info, call ☎0222 711 01 between 7am-8pm.

BY CAR. Driving is a good way to see more isolated parts of Austria, but gas is costly, an international license is required, and some small towns prohibit cars. The roads are well maintained and marked, and Austrian drivers are quite careful. **Mitfahrzentrale** (ride-sharing services) in larger cities pair drivers with riders for a small fee. Riders negotiate fares with the drivers. Not all organizations screen their drivers or riders; ask in advance.

BY BIKE. Bikes are a great way to get around Austria, where roads are generally smooth and safe. Many train stations rent bikes and allow you to return them to any participating station. Consult local tourist offices for bike routes and maps.

KEEPING IN TOUCH

PHONE CODES	**Country code:** 43. **International dialing prefix:** 00 (from Vienna, 900). For more information on how to place international calls, see inside back cover.

EMAIL AND THE INTERNET. It's not hard to find Internet cafes, especially in larger cities. It costs €2-6 per hour and rates sometimes fall during slow times of the day or night.

TELEPHONE. Wherever possible, use a calling card for international phone calls, as long-distance rates for national phone services are often exorbitant. Prepaid phone cards and major credit cards can be used for direct international calls, but they are still less cost-efficient. For information on mobile phones, see p. 33. Direct dial access numbers for calling out of Austria include **AT&T** (☎0800 200 288), **British Telecom** (☎0800 200 209), **Canada Direct** (☎0800 200 217), **MCI WorldPhone** (☎0800 999 762), **Sprint** (☎0800 200 236), **Telecom New Zealand** (☎0800 200 222), and **Telstra Australia** (☎0800 200 202).

MAIL. Letters take one or two days within Austria. Airmail to North America takes four to seven days, up to nine days to Australia and New Zealand. Mark all letters and packages *"mit Flugpost"* (airmail). Aerogrammes are the cheapest option. *Let's Go* lists the addresses for mail to be held *(Postlagernde Briefe)* in the **Practical Information** section of big cities.

LANGUAGE. German is the official language. English is the most common second language, but it's less common outside of cities and among older residents. For basic German words and phrases, see p. 1060.

ACCOMMODATIONS AND CAMPING

AUSTRIA	❶	❷	❸	❹	❺
ACCOMMODATIONS	under €16	€16-26	€26-34	€34-55	over €55

Lodgings may provide a **guest card** *(Gästekarte)*, which grants discounts on activities, museums, and public transportation. The **Österreichischer Jugendherbergsverband-Hauptverband (ÖJH)** runs over 80 HI **hostels** in Austria. Because of rigorous national standards, these tend to be clean. Most charge €18-30 per night for dorms, with a €3-5 HI discount. **Independent hostels** vary in quality, but often have a lively backpacking culture. Slightly more expensive, **Pensionen** are similar to B&Bs. In small to mid-sized towns, singles will cost €20-30; expect to pay twice as much in cities. **Hotels** are expensive (singles over €35; doubles over €48). The cheapest ones generally have "*Gasthof*," "*Gästehaus*," or "*Pension-Garni*" in the name. Renting a **Privatzimmer** (room in a family home) is an inexpensive option. Rooms range €16-30 per person; contact the local tourist office. **Camping** in Austria is less about communing with nature than having a cheap place to sleep; most sites are plots glutted with RVs and are open in summer only. Tent sites run €10-12 and €5-7 per extra person. In the high Alps, hikers and mountaineers can retire to the well-maintained system of **mountain huts** *(Hütten)*, where traditional Austrian fare and a good night's rest await them—provided they book ahead.

HIKING AND SKIING. Nearly every town has hiking trails; consult the local tourist office. Trails are usually marked with either a red-white-red marker (only sturdy boots and hiking poles necessary) or a blue-white-blue marker (mountaineering equipment needed). Because of snow in the higher passes, most mountain hiking trails and huts are open only from late June to early September. Western Austria is one of the world's best skiing regions; the areas around Innsbruck and Kitzbühel are saturated with lifts and runs. High season usually runs December through March. Local tourist offices provide information on skiing and can suggest budget travel agencies that offer ski packages.

FOOD AND DRINK

AUSTRIA	❶	❷	❸	❹	❺
FOOD	under €5	€5-10	€10-16	€16-25	over €25

Loaded with fat, salt, and cholesterol, traditional Austrian cuisine is bad for your skin, your heart, and your figure; enjoy! Austria's best known dish, *wienerschnitzel*, is a breaded meat cutlet (usually veal or pork) fried in butter. Natives nurse their sweet tooth with *kaffee und kuchen* (coffee and cake), *sacher torte* (rich chocolate cake layered with marmalade), and *linzer torte* (light yellow cake with currant jam). Austrian beers are outstanding—try Stiegl, a Salzburg brew; Zipfer, from Upper Austria; and Styrian Gösser.

EAT YOUR VEGGIES. Vegetarians should look on the menu for *spätzle* (noodles), *eierschwammerl* (mushrooms), or anything with the word "*vegi*" in it.

HOLIDAYS AND FESTIVALS

Holidays: Just about everything closes on public holidays, so plan accordingly. New Year's Day (Jan. 1); Epiphany (Jan. 6); Good Friday (Mar. 25); Easter Monday (Apr. 17); Labor Day (May 1); Ascension (May 25); Corpus Christi (June 15); Assumption Day (Aug. 15); Austrian National Day (Oct. 26); All Saints' Day (Nov. 1); Immaculate Conception (Dec. 8); Christmas (Dec. 25); Boxing Day (Dec. 26).

Festivals: Vienna celebrates *Fasching* (Carnival) during the last 2 weeks of Feb. Austria's most famous summer music festivals are the *Vienna Festwochen* (early May to mid-June) and the *Salzburger Festspiele* (July 24-Aug. 31).

BEYOND TOURISM

Austria caters more to tourism than volunteerism; there are only limited opportunities to give back, so your best bet is to find them through a placement service. Opportunities for short-term work abound at hotels, ski resorts, and farms.

Concordia, Heversham House, 2nd fl. 20-22 Boundary Rd., Hove, BN3 4ET (☎01273 422218; www.concordia-iye.co.uk). UK organization has many projects in Austria: renovate historic buildings and parks, direct a youth drama project, and create hiking paths.

Actilingua Academy, Glorietteg. 8, A-1130 Vienna, Austria (☎431 877 67 01; www.actilingua.com). Study German in Vienna.

VIENNA (WIEN) ☎01

AUSTRIA

Vienna (pop. 1,500,000) was transformed by war, marriage, and Hapsburg maneuvering from a Roman camp along the Danube into the political linchpin of the continent. Beethoven and Schönberg have made Vienna an arbiter of high culture—yet Vienna, as always, keeps to the beat of the younger generation. On any given afternoon, cafes turn the sidewalks into a sea of umbrellas, and on warm summer nights, bars and clubs pulse with experimental techno and indie rock until dawn.

INTERCITY TRANSPORTATION

Flights: The **Wien-Schwechat Flughafen** (VIE; ☎700 70), 18km from the city center, is home to **Austrian Airlines** (☎517 89; www.aua.com). The cheapest way to reach the city is S7 Flughafen/Wolfsthal, which stops at **Wien Mitte** (30min., every 20-30min. 5am-10pm, €3). The Vienna Airport Lines **shuttle** (☎65 17 17; english.viennaairport.com/bus.html) takes 25min. to reach Südbahnhof and 40min. to Westbahnhof (every 30min. 6:05am-12:05am; €6, round-trip €11). The **City Airport Train** (CAT; ☎25 250; www.cityairporttrain.com) takes only 16min. to reach **Wien Mitte** (every 30min. 6:05am-11:35pm) but is expensive (€9, round-trip €16; €1 discount when bought from ticket machine, further discounts when bought online; Eurail not valid).

Trains: Vienna has 2 main train stations with international connections. Call ☎05 17 17 (24hr.) or check www.oebb.at for general train information.

Westbahnhof, XV, Mariahilferstr. 132. To: **Amsterdam** (12hr., 10 per day, €111); **Berlin** (11hr., every 2hr., €80); **Budapest** (3hr., 10 per day, €36); **Hamburg** (9hr., every 2hr., €80); **Innsbruck** (5-6hr., every 1½hr., €49); **Munich** (5hr., 1 per hr., €68); **Paris** (14hr., 1 per hr. 7am-4pm, €110); **Salzburg** (3hr., 1 per hr., €37); **Zurich** (9hr., 8 per day, €165). Info counter open daily 7:30am-9pm.

Südbahnhof, X, Wiener Gürtel 1a. Trains generally go south and east. To: **Graz** (2½hr., every 2hr., €32); **Kraków** (7-11hr., 5 per day, €48); **Prague** (4hr., 9-10 per day, €43); **Rome** (14hr., every 2hr., €100); **Venice** (9-10hr., 4 per day, €70). Info counter open daily 7am-8pm.

Buses: Buses in Austria are rarely cheaper than trains; compare prices before buying. **City bus terminals** at Wien Mitte/Landstr., Hütteldorf, Heiligenstadt, Floridsdorf, Kagran, Erdberg, and Reumannpl. Tickets are sold onboard. Many international bus lines also have agencies in the stations. For info, call ☎711 01 between 7am-8pm.

ORIENTATION

Vienna is divided into 23 **districts** *(bezirke)*. The first is **Innenstadt** (city center), defined by the **Ringstraße** (ring road) on three sides and the Danube Canal on the fourth. At the center of Innenstadt lies **Stephansplatz** and much of the pedestrian district. To reach Innenstadt, take the U-bahn to Stephanspl. (U1, U3) or **Karlsplatz** (U1, U2, U4); other options include **Herrengasse** and **Stubentor** (both U3) and **Schwedenplatz** (U1, U4), close to the city's nightlife.

The Ringstraße consists of many different segments, each with its own name, like Opernring or Kärntner Ring. Many of Vienna's major attractions are in District I and immediately around the Ringstr. Districts II-IX spread out from the city center following the clockwise traffic of the Ring. The remaining districts expand from another ring road, the **Gürtel** (Belt). Like the Ring, this major thoroughfare has many segments, including Margaretengürtel, Währinger Gürtel, and Neubaugürtel. Street signs indicate the district number in Roman or Arabic numerals before the street and number, as does *Let's Go.*

LOCAL TRANSPORTATION

Public Transportation: (general info ☎790 91 00.) The **subway** (U-Bahn), **tram** (Straßenbahn), **elevated train** (S-Bahn), and **bus** lines operate on a 1-ticket system, so you can transfer between types of transportation without buying a new ticket. Buy tickets onboard or at a machine, counter, or tobacco shop. A **single fare** (€2 onboard, €1.50 in advance) lets you travel anywhere in the city and switch from bus to U-Bahn to tram to S-Bahn, as long as your travel is uninterrupted. Other ticket options include a **1-day pass** (€5), **3-day rover ticket** (€12), **7-day pass** (€12.50; valid M 9am to the next M 9am), and an **8-day pass** (€24; valid any 8 days, not necessarily consecutive; valid also for several people traveling together). The **Vienna Card** (€16.90) offers free travel for 72hr. as well as discounts at sights and events. To **validate a ticket,** punch it in the machine before entering the 1st vehicle; don't stamp it again when you switch trains or plainclothes inspectors may fine you €60. Regular trams and subway cars stop running midnight-5am. **Night buses** run every 30min. along most routes; designated by "N" signs. Schedule available in U-Bahn stations. Single-fare €1.50; day passes not valid.

AUSTRIA

Taxis: ☎313 00, 401 00, 601 60, or 814 00. Stands are at Westbahnhof, Südbahnhof, Karlspl. in the city center, and by the Bermuda Dreieck for late-night revelers. Accredited taxis have yellow-and-black signs on the roof. Base rate €2.50, €0.20 per additional 0.2km; slightly more expensive holidays and 11pm-6am.

Car Rental: Avis, I, Opernring 3-5 (☎587 6241 or 700 327 00). Open M-F 7am-6pm, Sa 8am-2pm, Su 8am-1pm. **Hertz** (☎70 07 32 661), at the airport. Open M-F 8am-11pm, Sa 8am-8pm, Su 7am-11pm.

Bike Rental: Pick up *Vienna By Bike* at the tourist office. **Pedal Power,** II, Ausstellungsstr. 3 (☎729 7234). Bike rental by hr. (€5, students €4), 4hr. (€17/14), or day (€27/24). They run bike tours (€19-23) daily May-Sept. Vienna Card discounts. Open daily Apr.-Oct. 8am-7pm. Hostels (p. 82) are also a cheap and convenient option.

PRACTICAL INFORMATION

TOURIST AND FINANCIAL SERVICES

Main Tourist Office: I, Albertinapl. (☎211 140). Follow Operng. up 1 block from the Opera House. The staff books rooms for a €2 fee and gives out free city maps, the pamphlet *Youth Scene,* and brochures on events and festivals. Open daily 9am-7pm.

Vienna
U3 U-Bahn
S-Bahn
ACCOMMODATIONS
Believe It Or Not, 1 B4
Camping Neue Donau, 2 F2
Hostel Ruthensteiner, 4 B5
Myrtheng./Neustiftg. (HI), 5 B4
Panda Hostel, 6 A4
Pension Hargita, 7 A5
Pension Kraml, 8 B5
Porzellaneum der Wiener Universität, 9 C3
Studentenwohnheim der Hochschule für Musik, 10 D4
Wien Süd, 3 A6
Westend City Hostel, 11 A5
Wombats City Hostel, 12 A5
FOOD
Amerlingbeisl, 13 B4
Bizi Pizza, 14 D4
Bodega El Gusto, 15 D4
Centimeter, 16 C3
Fischerbräu, 17 B1
Inigo, 18 D4
Levante, 19 D4
OH Pot, OH Pot, 20 C3
Sato Café-Restaurant, 21 A5
Smutny, 22 D4
Trzesniewski, 23 C4
Vegetasia, 24 B4

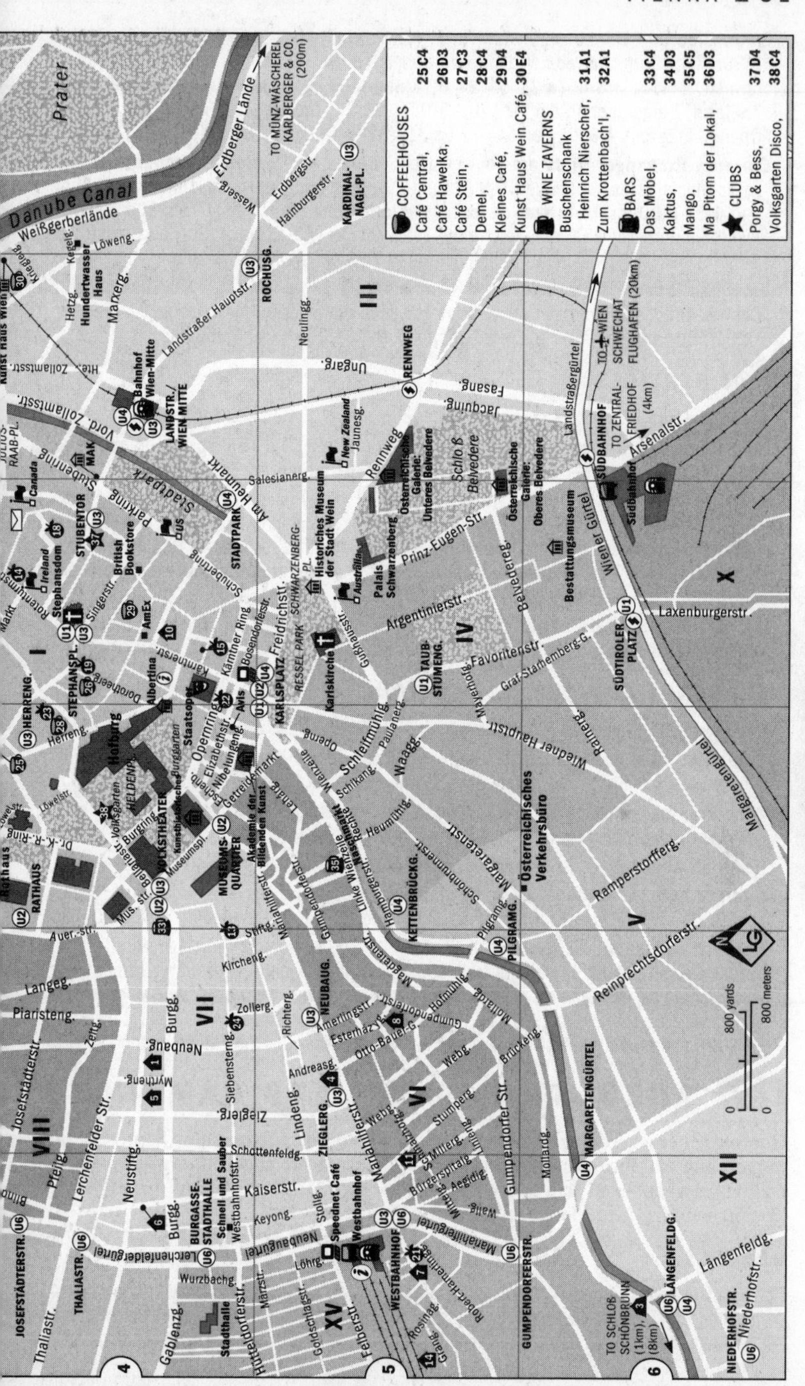
COFFEEHOUSES
Café Central, 25 C4
Café Hawelka, 26 D3
Café Stein, 27 C3
Demel, 28 C4
Kleines Café, 29 D4
Kunst Haus Wein Café, 30 E4
WINE TAVERNS
Buschenschank Heinrich Nierscher, 31 A1
Zum Krottenbach'l, 32 A1
BARS
Das Möbel, 33 C4
Kaktus, 34 D3
Mango, 35 C5
Ma Pitom der Lokal, 36 D3
CLUBS
Porgy & Bess, 37 D4
Volksgarten Disco, 38 C4
Danube Canal
Prater
Stadtpark
Hofburg
Staatsoper
Karlskirche
Schloß Belvedere
Südbahnhof
Westbahnhof
0 800 yards
0 800 meters

Embassies and Consulates: Australia, IV, Mattiellistr. 2-3 (☎506 74). Open M-F 8:30am-4:30pm. **Canada,** I, Laurenzerberg 2 (☎531 38 30 00). **Ireland,** I, Rotenturmstr. 16-18, 3rd fl. (☎71 54 24 6). Open M-F 9:30-11am and 1:30-4pm. **New Zealand,** Salesianerstr. 15 (☎318 85 05). **UK,** III, Jauresg. 10 (☎716 13 51 51). Open M-F 2-4pm. **US,** IX, Parkring 12 (☎313 390). Open M-F 8-11:30am.

Currency Exchange: ATMs are your best bet. **Banks** and **airport exchanges** use the same official rates. Most open M-W, F 8am-12:30pm and 1:30-3pm, Th 8am-12:30pm and 1:30-5:30pm. **Train station** exchanges offer long hours (daily 7am-10pm at the Westbahnhof) and a €6 min. fee for the 1st 3 checks (€300 max.). Stay away from the 24hr. bill-exchange machines in Innenstadt, as they generally charge outrageous prices.

American Express Travel Agency: I, Kärntnerstr. 21-23 (☎515 40), near Stephanspl. Cashes AmEx and Thomas Cook checks (€7 min. commission for up to €250, €12 for €251-500) and sells event tickets. Open M-F 9am-5:30pm, Sa 9am-noon.

LOCAL SERVICES

Luggage Storage: Lockers available at all trains stations. €2 per 24hr.

Bookstores: The **British Bookshop,** I, Weihburgg. 24 (☎512 19 45), has an extensive travel section. Open M-F 9:30am-6:30pm, Sa 9:30am-5pm. AmEx/DC/MC/V.

GLBT Resources: Pick up the *Vienna Gay Guide* (www.gayguide.at), *Extra Connect, Bussi,* or the *Queer Guide* from any tourist office or gay bar, cafe, or club. **Rosa Lila Tip,** VI, Linke Wienzeile 102 (lesbians ☎586 5150, gays 585 4343; lesbenberatung@villa.at), is a knowledgeable resource and social center for homosexual Viennese and visitors. U4 to Pilgrimg.; look for the pink house. Open M, W, F 5-8pm.

Laundromat: Schnell und Sauber, VII, Westbahnhofstr. 60. U6: Burgg./Stadthalle. Wash €4.50, dry €1 per 20min. Soap included. Open 24hr.

AUSTRIA

EMERGENCY AND COMMUNICATION

Emergency: Police: ☎133. **Ambulance:** ☎144. **Fire:** ☎122. **Emergency care:** ☎141.

Crisis Hotlines: All have English speakers. **Rape Crisis Hotline:** ☎523 22 22. Line staffed M, Th 1-6pm, Tu, F 10am-3pm. **24hr. immediate help for women:** ☎717 19.

24hr. Pharmacy Hotline: ☎15 50. Consulates have lists of English-speaking doctors, or call **Wolfgang Molnar** ☎330 34 68.

Hospital: Allgemeines Krankenhaus, IX, Währinger Gürtel 18-20 (☎404 00 19 64).

Internet Access: Speednet Cafe, Europapl. 1 (☎892 56 66), in Westbahnhof. €3.30 per 30min., €5.80 per hr. Open M-Sa 7am-midnight, Su 8am-midnight. AmEx/MC/V.

Post Office: Hauptpostamt (☎0577 677 1010), I, Fleischmarkt 19. Open 24hr. Branches throughout city and at train stations; look for yellow signs with trumpet logo. Address *Poste Restante* as follows: SURNAME, Firstname, *Postlagernde Briefe;* Hauptpostamt; Fleischmarkt 19, A-1010 Wien AUSTRIA. **Postal Codes:** A-1010 (1st district); A-1020 (2nd district); A-1030 (3rd district); continues to A-1230 (23rd district).

ACCOMMODATIONS AND CAMPING

Hunting for cheap rooms in Vienna during peak tourist season (June-Sept.) can be unpleasant; call for reservations at least five days in advance. Otherwise, plan on calling between 6 and 9am to put your name down for a reservation. For information on camping near Vienna, visit www.campingwien.at.

HOSTELS

Hostel Ruthensteiner, XV, Robert-Hamerlingg. 24 (☎893 4202; www.hostelruthensteiner.com). Exit Westbahnhof, turn right on Mariahilferstr., and continue until Haidmannsg. Turn left, then right on Robert-Hamerlingg. Spotless rooms and kitchenettes. Bike rental €12 per day, half-day €8. Breakfast €2.50. Linen €2; included with private rooms. Internet €2 per 25min. 4-night max. stay. Reception 24hr. 32-bed summer dorm €12; 4- to 10-bed dorms €13-15; singles €26; doubles €44; quads €60. AmEx/MC/V; €0.40 per day surcharge. ❶

Wombats City Hostel, XV, Grang. 6 (☎897 2336). Exit Westbahnhof, turn right on Mariahilferstr., right on Rosinag., and left on Grang. Wildly colorful hostel compensates for its proximity to train tracks with an in-house pub, English-language movie nights, and guided tours. Bike rental €12 per day, €3 per hr. Breakfast €3.50. Internet €3 per hr. All rooms with bath. Dorms €18; singles €24; doubles €48. Cash only. ❷

Westend City Hostel, VI, Fügerg. 3 (☎597 67 29), near Westbahnhof. Exit on Äussere Mariahilferstr., cross the intersection, go right on Mullerg. and left on Fügerg. Plain dorms with bath. Breakfast included. Internet €2 per 20min. Reception 24hr. Check-out 10am. Lockout 10am-2pm. Dorms €17-20; singles €43-58; doubles €52-68. Cash only. ❷

Myrthengasse (HI), VII, Myrtheng. 7. U6 to Burgg./Stadthalle, then bus #48A (dir.: Ring) to Neubaug. Backtrack on Burgg. 1 block; take 1st right on Myrtheng. Or take U3 to Neubaug. Also runs the nearby **Neustiftgasse (HI),** VII, Neustiftg. 85 (☎523 63 16). 20min. walk from Innenstadt. Breakfast included. Locks €4. Internet €2.60 per 18min. Reception for both at Myrthengasse 24hr. 5-night max. stay. Dorms €19.50-21.50. €3.50 HI discount. AmEx/MC/V. ❷

Panda Hostel, VII, Kaiserstr. 77 (☎522 25 55). Sea-gray walls, paper lanterns, and modernist furniture. Dorms lack usual hostel amenities like laundry and Internet. Reception 8am-2pm. Check-in 2pm. Lockout 10am-2pm. Dorms €13.50. Cash only. ❶

Believe It Or Not, VII, Myrtheng. 10, Apt. #14 (☎526 46 58). A converted apartment with kitchen. 2-night min. stay. Reception 8:15am-12:30pm. Lockout 10am-noon. Tightly packed 12-bed dorm €13.50; roomier 4-bed dorm €15.50. Ages 18-30. ❶

HOTELS AND PENSIONS

Pension Hargita, VII, Andreasg. 1 (☎526 19 28). U3: Zieglerg. Exit on Andreasg. Sunflowers and hardwood floors accompany blue-and-white furniture and bedding. Breakfast €3. Reception 8am-8pm. Singles €35, with shower €40, with shower and toilet €52; doubles €48, with shower €55; triples €63, with shower and toilet €70. MC/V. ❹

Pension Kraml, VI, Brauerg. 5 (☎587 85 88). U3: Zierierg. Exit on Otto-Bauerg., take 1st left, then 1st right. Near the Naschmarkt. Plush rooms. Lounge and cable TV. Breakfast included. Reception 24hr. Singles €28; doubles €48, with shower €58; triples €68/75. 2- to 5-person apartment with bath €68-120. Cash only. ❸

UNIVERSITY DORMITORIES

July through September, many university dorms become hotels and alleviate the budget crunch. Their cleanliness and low cost make them suited to longer stays.

Porzellaneum der Wiener Universität, IX, Porzellang. 30 (☎317 7282; www.porzellaneum.sth.ac.at). U4: Roßauer Lände. From Südbahnhof, take tram D (dir.: Nußdorf) to Bauernfeldpl. Reception Tu 3-5pm, Th 10am-1pm. Reserve by mail or in person 1 week in advance. Singles daily €20, monthly €500; doubles €36/440 per person; quads €72. ❷

Studentenwohnheim der Hochschule für Musik, I, Johannesg. 8 (M-F 10am-2pm ☎514 84 7701). Walk 3 blocks down Kärntnerstr. from Stephansdom and turn left on Johannesg. 23 practice rooms with grand pianos (€5 per hr.). Breakfast included. Reception 24hr. Reserve in advance. Singles €35; doubles €33; triples €66; quads €80; quints €100; 4-person apartment €120. ❹

CAMPING

Camping Neue Donau, XXII, Am Kleehäufel 119 (☎202 40 10). U1: Kaisermühlen. From Schüttaustr. exit, cross the street and take bus #91a (every 30min.) to Kleehäufel. 4km from the city center and adjacent to Neue Donau beaches. Boat and bike rental. Reception 8am-12:30pm and 3-6:15pm. Open Easter-Sept. Tent sites €10.20-12.20, extra person €5.70-6.70. DC/MC/V. ❶

Wien Süd, XXIII, Breitenfurterstr. 269 (☎867 36 49). U6: Philadelphiabrücke, and bus #62A to Wien Süd. This former imperial park features a cafe, playground, supermarket, and kitchen. Laundry €4.50. Reception 7:45am-8pm. Open May-Sept. Tent sites €10.20-12.20, extra person €5.70-6.70. AmEx/DC/MC/V. ❶

FOOD

Restaurants that call themselves *stüberl* or advertise *schmankerl* all serve Viennese fare. Innenstadt restaurants are expensive, but north of the university, where Universitätsstr. and Währingerstr. meet (U2: Schottentor), is a more budget-friendly area. Affordable cafes and restaurants line **Burggasse** in District VI and the area surrounding the Rechte and Linke Wienzeile near Naschmarkt (U4: Kettenbrückeg). Supermarket chains include **Zielpunkt, Billa,** and **Spar.** The **kosher** supermarket is at District II, Hollandstr. 10. (☎216 96 75. Open M-Th 8:30am-6:30pm, F 8am-3pm, Su 10am-noon.)

INSIDE THE RING

Trzesniewski, I, Dorotheerg. 1 (☎512 32 91), 3 blocks down the Graben from Stephansdom. Once Kafka's favorite place to eat, this stand-up establishment has been serving open-faced mini-sandwiches (€0.80) for over 100 years. Toppings include salmon, onion, paprika, and egg. Open M-F 8:30am-7:30pm, Sa 9am-5pm. Cash only. ❶

Bizi Pizza, I, Rotenturmstr. 4 (☎513 37 05), 1 block up Rotenturmstr. from Stephanspl. One of the best deals in the city, this self-serve restaurant grills up meats with 2 sides for €5-6. Pizza slice €2.50. Pastas €5-6. Open daily 10:30am-11:30pm. Cash only. ❷

Smutny, I, Elisabethstr. 8 (☎587 13 56), off Karlspl. A traditional Austrian restaurant that serves tasty *schnitzel* and *gulasch* (€8.50). M-F lunchtime *menü* €7.80, Sa-Su €8.20. Open daily 10am-11:30pm. AmEx/MC/V. ❷

Inigo, I, Bäckerstr. 18 (☎512 74 51). Founded by a Jesuit priest, Inigo hires the long-term unemployed as cooks, and serves international dishes (€5-10) like *schnitzel* and marinated tofu. Salads €5-6. Open July-Aug. M-F 10:30am-midnight; Sept.-June also Sa 10:30am-midnight, Su 10am-4pm. AmEx/DC/MC/V. ❷

Levante, I, Wallnerstr. 2 (☎533 23 26). Walk down Graben away from Stephansdom, turn left on Kohlmarkt and right onto Wallnerstr. Easily a meal for 2, Greek pizza (€5-7.50) comes on a doughy golden crust. Other Greek and Turkish dishes, including vegetarian options, €7-13. Open daily 11am-11pm. MC/V. ❷

Bodega El Gusto, I, Mahlerstr. 7 (☎512 06 73). Walk in the direction of Stephansdom on Kärntnerstr. and turn right on Mahlerstr. This cozy restaurant serves a wide variety of tapas (€2-7; vegetarian options available) and meat and seafood Spanish dishes (€4-20). Open M-Sa 5pm-1am. MC/V. ❸

OUTSIDE THE RING

OH Pot, OH Pot, IX, Währingerstr. 22 (☎513 42 59). U2: Schottentor. Serves filling "pots," stew-like veggie or meat concoctions with influences from Ethiopia to Bolivia (€8.20). Lunch special: any pot, soup or salad, and dessert for €6.20. Open daily 11am-midnight. AmEx/DC/MC/V. ❷

Centimeter, IX, Liechtensteinstr. 42 (☎319 84 04). Tram D to Bauernfeldpl. This chain offers huge portions of greasy Austrian fare (€4.50-6.50) and an unbelievable selection of beers (€3-4 per L). Cold and warm sandwiches for €0.15 per centimeter. Open M-F 10am-midnight, Sa-Su 11am-midnight. AmEx/MC/V. ❶

Amerlingbeisl, VII, Stiftg. 8 (☎526 1660). U3: Neubaug. Soft lighting and a grapevine-covered courtyard are a perfect backdrop for Mediterranean-influenced entrees (€6-9). Vegetarian options. Open daily 9am-2am. Kitchen open until 1am. AmEx/MC/V. ❷

Sato Café-Restaurant, XV, Mariahilferstr. 151 (☎897 54 97). U3 or U6: Westbahnhof. Near the Ruthensteiner and Wombats hostels. Free baskets of fluffy, sesame-studded Turkish bread accompany the scrumptious Turkish food. Vegetarian options. Entrees €5-9. Delicious breakfast omelettes €3-4. Open daily 8am-midnight. Cash only. ❶

Fischerbräu, XIX, Billrothstr. 17 (☎369 59 49). U6: Nußdorfer Str. Exit on Währinger Gürtel, continue until Döblinger Hauptpl., take a left, and left again onto Billrothstr. Try the home-brewed beer (0.3L, €2.30) and breads with delicious toppings (€3-5). Austrian dishes €5-11. Piano trio Sa 8pm, jazz brunch Su 11am. Open July-Aug. daily 4pm-1am; Sept.-June M-Sa 4pm-1am, Su 11am-1am. Cash only. ❷

Vegetasia, III, Ungarg. 57 (☎713 8332). Tram O to Neulingg. A Taiwanese vegetarian nirvana. Lunch buffet M-Sa €6.80. Entrees €6-11. Meat dishes available. Another branch at VII, Kaiserstr. 45 (☎523 10 91). Both open Tu-Su 11:30am-3pm and 5:30-11pm. Branch in III closed Tu dinner Tu, branch in VII closed M dinner. AmEx/MC/V. ❷

COFFEEHOUSES

Using Viennese coffeehouses for a midafternoon pick-me-up is akin to using the Magna Carta to clean up after a spill. These establishments have been havens for artists, writers, and thinkers. The most important dictate of coffeehouse etiquette is that you linger; the waiter *(Herr Ober)* will serve you, then will leave you to sip, read, and cogitate. When you're ready to leave, just ask to pay *("Zahlen bitte")*.

Kleines Café, I, Franziskanerpl. 3. Turn off Kärntnerstr. onto Weihburg.; follow it to the Franziskanerkirche. Escape from the busy pedestrian streets with a *mélange* (espresso with hot milk; €2.90). Sandwiches €2.80-4. Open daily 10am-2am. Cash only.

Café Central, I, Herreng. 14 (☎533 37 6246), at Strauchg. inside Palais Ferstel. With green-gold arches and live music, this luxurious coffeehouse deserves its status as mecca of the cafe world. Open M-Sa 8am-10pm, Su 10am-6pm. AmEx/DC/MC/V.

Café Hawelka, I, Dorotheerg. 6 (☎512 82 30), off Graben. Josephine and Leopold Hawelka put this legendary cafe on the map in 1939. Today, customers enjoy a mean *buchteln* (cake with plum marmalade; €3) amid sofas scattered along the walls and old-fashioned lamps. Open M, W-Sa 8am-2am, Su 4pm-2am. Cash only.

Kunst Haus Wien Café, III, Untere Weißgerberstr. 13 (☎712 04 97). Tram N from Schwedenpl. to Radetzkypl. Serves creative vegetarian fare (€4-15) in a vine-covered courtyard of the Kunst Haus Wien museum (p. 89). Open daily 10am-11pm. MC.

COFFEE CULTURE

Far more than that extra kick to get you out the door in the mornings, Viennese coffee has attained the status of high art and acquired a language of its own along the way. Here's our quick guide to ordering in a cafe:

A **Mokka** or a **Schwarzer** is the pure black stuff, strong espresso and nothing more. The **Braune** lightens the espresso with milk or cream, and the **Verlängerter** lowers the stakes still more with weaker coffee. The quintessential Viennese cafe drink, the **Wiener mélange,** melds black espresso with hot milk. Somewhat similar, the **Kapuziner** consists of espresso with gently foamed milk and is more commonly known by its Italian name, "cappuccino." **Eiskaffee,** or hot coffee with vanilla ice cream, has a refreshing jolt on hot summer days.

Vienna's specialty coffee drinks combine espresso with a variety of liqueurs for caffeine with a punch. Café Central (p. 85) has a special liqueur named after the cafe itself; it also serves the **Maria-Theresia,** with orange liqueur, and the **Pharisär,** with rum and sugar. Other liqueurs include **Marillen** (apricot) and **Kirsche** (cherry). Be prepared to shell out €6-7 for one of these indulgent delights.

Viennese coffee typically comes on a silver platter with a chocolate or a cookie. If you must pass up the hefty dollop of fresh cream that tops most cups, say *"Ohne Schlag, bitte."*

Demel, I, Kohlmarkt 14 (☎535 17 17). 5min. from the Stephansdom, down Graben. Demel once served its creations to the imperial court. The chocolate is made fresh every morning. *Mélange* €3.80. Tortes €4. Open daily 10am-7pm. AmEx/MC/V.

Café Stein, IX, Währingerstr. 6 (☎319 72 41), near Schottentor. This lively, trendy cafe transforms into Stein's Diner at night and hosts poetry slams. Breakfast until 8pm. Open M-Sa 7am-1am, Su 9am-1am. Stein's Diner open M-Sa 7pm-1am. Cash only.

WINE TAVERNS (HEURIGEN)

Marked by a hanging branch of evergreen, *heurigen* serve wine and savory Austrian delicacies, often outdoors. The wine, *heuriger*, is from the most recent harvest. Tourist buses head to the most famous region, **Grinzing,** in District XIX; you'll find better atmosphere in the hills of **Sievering, Neustift am Walde** (both in District XIX), and **Neuwaldegg** (in XVII). Authentic *heurigen* also abound on Hochstr. in **Perchtoldsdorf,** southwest of the city. To reach Perchtoldsdorf, take U4 to Hietzing and tram #6 to Rodaun. Walk down Ketzerg. until Hochstr. True *heuriger* devotees make the trip to **Gumpoldskirchen.** Take the S-Bahn from the Südbahnhof.

Buschenschank Heinrich Nierscher, XIX, Strehlg. 21 (☎440 21 46). U6: Währingerstr. Tram #41 to Plötzleinsdorf (the last stop); then take bus #41A to Plötzleinsfriedhof or walk up Pötzleing. which becomes Khevenhuller Str.; go right on Strehlg. Enjoy a white wine spritzer (€1.60) in the serene backyard. Open M, Th-Su 3pm-midnight. Cash only.

Zum Krottenbach'l, XIX, Krottenbachstr. 148 (☎440 12 40). U6: Nußdorfer Str., then bus #35A (dir.: Salmannsdorf) to Kleingartenverein. Ask bus driver to stop. Larger but more touristy than Heinrich Nierscher, with tables under vine-covered terraces. 0.25L of wine €1.80. Open daily 3pm-midnight. Cash only.

AUSTRIA

SIGHTS

Expect contrasts around every corner of Vienna's streets: the expanse of the Ringstraße and the confines of a cobblestone courtyard, the flourishes of a Baroque palace and the spare lines of public housing. To wander on your own, grab the brochure *Vienna from A to Z* (€4 with Vienna Card) from the tourist office. The range of **tours** is overwhelming—there are 50 themed walking tours in the brochure *Walks in Vienna.* Contact **Pedal Power,** II, Ausstellungsstr. 3 (☎729 7234; www.pedalpower.at.), for **bike rental** (€5) or **cycling tours** (€20). **Bus tours** (€34) are given by **Vienna Sightseeing Tours,** IV, Graf Starhemberg (☎712 46 83).

INSIDE THE RING

A stroll in District I, the social and geographical center, is a feast for the senses. Cafe tables spill into the streets and musicians attract onlookers as Romanesque arches, *Jugendstil* apartments, and the modern **Haas Haus** overlook the action.

STEPHANSDOM, GRABEN, AND PETERSPLATZ. In the heart of the city, the massive **Stephansdom** is one of Vienna's most treasured symbols. For a view of the old city, take the elevator up the North Tower or climb the 343 steps of the South Tower. *(☎515 52 3526. North Tower open daily July-Aug. 9am-5pm; Apr.-June and Sept.-Oct. 8:30am-5:30pm; Nov.-Mar. 8:30am-5pm. South Tower open daily 9am-5:30pm. South Tower €3. North Tower €4.)* Downstairs, skeletons of plague victims fill the **catacombs.** *(Tours M-Sa every 30min. 10-11:30am and 1:30-4:30pm, Su and holidays 1:30-4:30pm. €4.)* From Stephanspl., follow Graben for *Jugendstil* architecture, including the **Ankerhaus** (#10), the red-marble **Grabenhof,** and the underground public toilet complex designed by Adolf Loos. Graben leads to Peterspl. and the 1663 **Pestsaüle** (Plague Column), built to celebrate the passing of the Black Death *(U1 or 3: Stephanspl.).*

HOHER MARKT AND STADTTEMPEL. The biggest draw in Hoher Market is the 1914 *Jugendstil* **Ankeruhr** (clock), whose 3m figures—from Marcus Aurelius to Maria Theresia—rotate past the Viennese coat of arms. *(1 figure per hr. At noon all figures appear.)* Hidden on Ruprechtspl., the **Stadttempel** is the only synagogue in Vienna to escape *Kristallnacht*. *(Seitenstetteng. 4. Judeng. from Hoher Markt to Ruprechtspl. Required guided tours M and Th 11:30am, 2pm. Bring passport. €2, students €1.)*

AM HOF AND FREYUNG. Once a medieval jousting square, Am Hof now houses the **Kirche am Hof** and **Collalto Palace,** where Mozart gave his first public performance. *(From Stephanspl., walk down Graben to the end, go right and continue on Bognerg.)* Just west of Am Hof is Freyung, the square with the **Austriabrunnen** in the center. Medieval fugitives took asylum in the **Schottenstift** (Monastery of the Scots), thus the name Freyung, or "sanctuary." Today, the annual **Christkindl market** fills the plaza with baked goods and holiday cheer.

HOFBURG. The sprawling Hofburg was the Hapsburg winter residence. Construction began in 1275, and additions continued until the end of the family's reign in 1918. Coming from Michaelerpl., the **Silberkammer** (Silver Treasury) is immediately to your right under the dome. The Silberkammer displays the 100 ft. gilded candelabra that once adorned the imperial table and other riches. Also included in the same ticket are the **Kaiserappartements** and the **Sisi Museum.** *(☎533 75 70. Open daily July-Aug. 9am-5:30pm; Sept.-June 9am-5pm. €8.90, students €7.)*

The Michaelerkuppel opens onto the **In der Berg** courtyard. On the left, the red-and-black **Schweizertor** (Swiss Gate) leads to the **Schweizerhof,** the inner courtyard of the **Alte Burg** (Old Fortress), which stands on the same site as the original 13th-century palace. The **Vienna Boys' Choir** *(Wiener Sängerknaben)* sing every Sunday in the Gothic **Hofburgkapelle,** at the top of the stairs. *(Open to visitors M-Th 11am-3pm, F 11am-1pm. €1.50.)* Beneath the stairs is the entrance to the **Weltliche und Geistliche Schatzkammer,** which contains the Hapsburg jewels and Napoleon's cradle. *(☎525 24 448. Open M, W-Su 10am-6pm. €8, students €6. Free English-language audio tour available.)*

Enter from Josefs Pl. or from opposite the Silberkammer for the Lipizzaner stallions and the **Spanische Reitschule** (Spanish Riding School). The cheapest way to see the snow-white horses is to watch them train. *(Morning exercises mid-Feb. to June and late Aug. to early Nov. Tu-F 10am-noon. Check ahead for exact dates and times. Open for tours Jan. to mid.-Feb. Tu and F 9am-5pm; mid-Feb. to Dec. Tu-Sa 9am-5pm. Morning exercise tickets sold at the door at Josefspl., Gate 2, €12, students €6. Tours €15/12.)*

Built between 1881 and 1913, the **Neue Burg** is the youngest wing of the palace. The double-headed golden eagle on the roof symbolizes the empire of Austria-Hungary. Today it houses Austria's largest library, the **Österreichische Nationalbibliothek.** *(Open July-Sept. M-F 9am-4pm, Sa 9am-12:45pm; Oct.-June M-F 9am-9pm, Sa 9am-12:45pm; closed Sept. 1-7.)* High Mass is still held in 14th-century **Augustinerkirche** (St. Augustine's Church) on Josefspl. The hearts of the Hapsburgs are stored in the **Herzgrüftel.** *(Augustinerstr. 3. Through the Michaelertor in Michaelerpl. Mass 11am. Open M-Sa 8am-5pm, Su 11am-6pm. Free.)*

OUTSIDE THE RING

Some of Vienna's most famous modern architecture is outside the Ring, where 20th-century designers found more space to build. This area is also home to a number of Baroque palaces and parks that were once beyond the city limits.

KARLSPLATZ. Karlsplatz is home to Vienna's most beautiful Baroque church, the **Karlskirche,** an eclectic masterpiece combining a Neoclassical portico with a Baroque dome and towers on either side. Under renovation until the end of 2006, the church may be best viewed from the outside; save your money unless you want to take an elevator to the top of the dome. *(Kreuzherreng. 1. U1, 2, or 4 to Karlspl. ☎504 61 87. Open M-F 7:30am-7pm, Sa 8:30am-7pm, Su 9am-7pm. €6, students €4.)*

SCHLOß BELVEDERE. The Schloß Belvedere was the summer residence of Prince Eugène of Savoy, one of Austria's greatest military heroes. The grounds, stretching from Schwarzenberg Palace to the Südbahnhof, contain three excellent museums (p. 88) and an equal number of gardens. *(Take tram D or #71 one stop past Schwarzenbergpl. Gardens open daily dawn to dusk. Free.)*

SCHLOß SCHÖNBRUNN. Schönbrunn began as a humble hunting lodge, but Maria Theresia transformed it into the palace it is today. The **Imperial Tour** passes through the **Great Gallery,** where the Congress of Vienna met, and the dazzling **Hall of Mirrors,** where six-year-old Mozart played. The **Grand Tour** also visits the rooms of Maria Theresia's time, including the ornate Millions Room. *(Schönbrunnerstr. 47. U4: Schönbrunn. Apartments open daily July-Aug. 8:30am-6pm; Apr.-June and Sept.-Oct. 8:30am-5pm; Nov.-Mar. 8:30am-4:30pm. Imperial Tour €8.90, students €7.90. Grand Tour €11.50/10.20. English-language audio tours included.)* As impressive as Schönbrunn, the **gardens** behind the palace contain a **labyrinth,** manicured greenery, flowers, and statuettes. *(Park open daily 6am-dusk. Labyrinth open daily July-Aug. 9am-7pm; Apr.-June and Sept. 9am-6pm; Oct. 9am-5pm; also Nov. 9am-3:30pm. Park free. Labyrinth €2.60, students €2.20.)*

MUSEUMS

The tourist office's free *Museums* brochure lists all opening hours and admission prices. All museums run by the city are free Friday before noon (except on public holidays), and private collections often have their own special discounted or free days as well. If you're going to be in town for a while, invest in the **Museum Card,** which is available at any museum ticket window.

AUSTRIA

INSIDE THE RING

HAUS DER MUSIK. Science meets music in this über-interactive museum. Experience the physics of sound, learn about famous Viennese composers, and entertain yourself with a fascinating invention called the Brain Opera. *(I, Seilerstatte 30, near the opera house. ☎516 480. Open daily 10am-10pm. €10, students €8.50.)*

ALBERTINA. First an Augustinian monastery and then the largest of the Hapsburg residences, the Albertina now houses the Collection of Graphic Arts. Past exhibits have featured Rembrandt and various Pop artists. The Prunkräume, or state rooms, exhibit some of Albrecht Dürer's finest prints, including the famous praying hands. *(Open M-Tu and Th-Su 10am-6pm, W 10am-9pm. €9, students €6.50.)*

JÜDISCHES MUSEUM (JEWISH MUSEUM). Jewish culture and history told through holograms and more traditional displays. Temporary exhibits focus on prominent Jewish figures and contemporary Jewish art. *(I, Dorotheerg. 11, near Stephanspl. ☎535 04 31. Open M-W, F, Su 10am-6pm, Th 10am-8pm. €5, students €2.90.)*

OUTSIDE THE RING

ÖSTERREICHISCHE GALERIE (AUSTRIAN GALLERY). The Österreichische Galerie's two museums are housed in the grounds of Schloß Belvedere. Home to *The Kiss* and other works by Klimt, the **Oberes Belvedere** supplements its permanent collection of 19th- and 20th-century art with rotating exhibits. The **Unteres Belvedere** contains the Austrian Museum of Baroque Art and of Medieval Art. *(Oberes Belvedere, III, Prinz-Eugen-Str. 27, in Schloß Belvedere behind Schwarzenbergpl. Walk up from the Südbahnhof, or take tram D to Schloß Belvedere. Unteres Belvedere, III, Rennweg 6. Tram #71 to Unteres Belvedere. ☎795 570. Both open Tu-Su 10am-6pm. €7.50, students €5.)*

KUNST HAUS WIEN. Artist-environmentalist Friedenreich Hundertwasser built this museum without straight lines—even the floor bends. Besides the comprehensive Hundertwasser exhibit, Kunst Haus also hosts contemporary art. *(III, Untere Weißgerberstr. 13. U1 or 4 to Schwedenpl., then tram N to Hetzg. ☎712 04 91; www.kunsthauswien.com. Open daily 10am-7pm. Each exhibit €9, students €7. M €4.50, except holidays.)*

ÖSTERREICHISCHES MUSEUM FÜR ANGEWANDTE KUNST (MAK). This intimate and eclectic museum is dedicated to design, from the smooth curves of Thonet bentwood chairs to the intricacies of Venetian glass to the steel heights of modern architecture. *(I, Stubenring 5. U3: Stubentor. ☎711 360; www.mak.at. Open Tu 10am-midnight, W-Su 10am-6pm. €7.90, students €4. Sa free.)*

KUNSTHISTORISCHES MUSEUM (MUSEUM OF FINE ARTS). One of the world's largest art collections features Venetian and Flemish paintings, Classical art, and an Egyptian burial chamber. The **Ephesos Museum** exhibits findings from excavations in Turkey, the **Hofjagd- und Rustkammer** is the second-largest collection of arms in the world, and the **Sammlung alter Musikinstrumente** includes Beethoven's harpsichord and Mozart's piano. *(U2: Museumsquartier. Across from the Burgring and Heldenpl. on Maria Theresia's right. ☎525 2441. Open Tu-W and F-Su 10am-6pm, Th 10am-9pm. €10, students €7.50. English-language audio tour €2.)*

MUSEUMSQUARTIER. At 60 sq. km, it's one of the 10 biggest art districts in the world. Central Europe's largest collection of modern art, the **Museum Moderner Kunst (MUMOK),** highlights Classical Modernism, Pop Art, Photo Realism, Fluxus, and Viennese Actionism in a building made from basalt lava. Twentieth-century masters include Kandinsky, Klee, Magritte, Miró, Picasso, Pollock, and Warhol. *(Open Tu-Su 10am-6pm, Th 10am-9pm. €8, students €6.50.)* The **Leopold Museum** has the world's largest Schiele collection, plus works by Egger-Lienz, Gerstl, Klimt, and Kokoschka. *(Open M, W, F-Su 10am-7pm, Th 10am-9pm. €9, students €5.50.)* Themed exhibits of contemporary artists fill **Kunsthalle Wien.** *(U2: Museumsquartier. Open M-W and F-Su 10am-7pm, Th 10am-10pm. Exhibition Hall 1 €7.50, students €6. Exhibition Hall 2 €6/4.50; both €10.50/8.50. Students €2 on M. "Art" combination ticket admits visitors to all three museums; €21.50. "Duo" ticket admits to Leopold and MUMOK; €16, students €11.)*

HISTORISCHES MUSEUM DER STADT WIEN. The Historical Museum of Vienna documents the city's evolution from a Roman encampment to the center of 640 years of Hapsburg rule. *(IV, Karlspl., to the left of Karlskirche. Open Tu-Su 9am-6pm. €4 per exhibit, students €2; combination ticket €5/2.50. All exhibits F morning and the permanent exhibit Su free.)*

AKADEMIE DER BILDENDEN KUNST (ACADEMY OF FINE ARTS). This building houses the art academy famous for having rejected Hitler's application. The excellent collection includes several works by Peter Paul Rubens and Hieronymus Bosch's *The Last Judgment*. *(I, Schillerpl. 3. From Karlspl. turn left onto Friedrichstr., right onto Operng., and left on Nibelungeng. ☎588 16 225. Open Tu-Su and holidays 10am-6pm. €5, students €3. Call ahead for English-language guided tours. Audio tours €2.)*

FREUD MUSEUM. Freud's former home has bric-a-brac that includes his report cards and circumcision certificate. *(IX, Bergg. 19. U2: Schottentor; walk up Währingerstr. to Bergg. ☎319 15 96. Open daily July-Sept. 9am-6pm; Oct.-June 9am-5pm. €5, students €3.)*

ENTERTAINMENT

All but a few of classical music's marquee names lived, composed, and performed in Vienna. Vienna hosts many performances accessible to the budget traveler throughout the year, although none of the venues listed below has performances

AUSTRIA

in July or August. The **Bundestheaterkasse,** I, Hanuschg. 3, sells tickets for the Staatsoper, the Volksoper, and the Burgtheater. (☎514 44 78 80. Open M-F 8am-6pm, Sa-Su 9am-noon; Sa during Advent 9am-5pm.)

Staatsoper, I, Opernring 2 (☎514 442 250; www.wiener-staatsoper.at). Vienna's premier opera performs nearly every night Sept.-June. No shorts. Seats €5-254. 500 standing-room tickets sold 80min. before every show (1 per person; €2-3.50); arrive 2hr. before curtain. Foyer box office open 9am until 1hr. before curtain, Sa 9am-noon; 1st Sa of each month and during Advent 9am-5pm.

Vienna Philharmonic Orchestra (Wiener Philharmoniker; www.wienerphilharmoniker.at) plays in the **Musikverein,** Austria's premiere concert hall. Even if you only want standing-room tickets, visit the box office (Bösendorferstr. 12) well in advance.

Vienna Boys' Choir (Wiener Sängerknaben; reservations ☎533 99 27) sings during mass every Su at 9:15am (mid-Sept. to late June) in the Hofburgkapelle (U3: Herreng.). Despite rumors to the contrary, standing room is free; arrive before 8am.

NIGHTLIFE

With one of the highest bar-to-cobblestone ratios in the world, Vienna is the place to party. Take U1 or 4 to Schwedenpl., which will drop you within blocks of the **Bermuda Dreieck** (Bermuda Triangle), an area packed with crowded clubs. If you make it out, head down **Rotenturmstraße** toward Stephansdom or walk around the areas bounded by the synagogue and Ruprechtskirche. Slightly outside the Ring, the streets off **Burggasse** and **Stiftgasse** in District VII and the **university quarter** in Districts XIII and IX have outdoor courtyards and hip bars. Viennese nightlife starts late, often after 11pm. For listings, pick up the indispensable *Falter* (€2).

Das Möbel (☎524 9497; www.das-moebel.net), VII, Burgg. 10. U2 or 3: Volkstheater. An artsy crowd chats and reads amid metal couches and Swiss-army tables, all created by designers and available for sale. Don't leave without seeing the bathroom. Internet free for first 15min. Open daily 10am-1am. Cash only. MC/V accepted for furniture.

Ma Pitom der Lokal, I, Seitenstetteng. 5 (☎535 43 13). A cavernous, arched space draws together a diverse crowd to chat over cheap drinks and price-skewing pub grub. Beers €1.60 during daily 5-7pm happy hour. Open M-Th, Su 5pm-3am, F-Sa 5pm-4am.

Kaktus, I, Seitenstetteng. 1 (☎0676 67 04 496; www.kaktus.at), in the heart of the Bermuda Triangle. Packed with 20-somethings and dripping with alcohol, this bar plays mostly mainstream music. 0.5L beer €3.40. All drinks half-price during happy hour M-Th 7-10pm. Dress to impress. Open M-Th, Su 7pm-3am, F-Sa 7pm-4am.

Volksgarten Disco, I, Volksgarten (☎532 42 41; www.volksgarten.at). U2: Volkstheater. One of the trendiest clubs in Vienna. M tango with all levels welcome. Th alternative and house; F hip-hop; Sa house. Cover €5-10. Open M 8pm-2am, Th 8pm-4am, F 11pm-6am, Sa June-Aug. 9pm-6am; Sept.-May 11pm-6am. MC/V; €70 minimum charge.

Porgy & Bess, I, Riemerg. 11 (☎512 8811; www.porgy.at). U1: Stubentor. The best jazz club in Vienna. Prices vary €15-20. Open M-Th and Su 8pm-2am, F-Sa 8pm-4am. Box office open M-Sa 3-8pm, Su 5-8pm. MC/V.

Mango, VI, Laimgrubeng. 3 (☎587 44 48). U2: Museumsquartier. Down Getreidemarkt toward city center, right on Gumpendorferstr. and left on Laimgrubeng. Mango draws gay men with pop music and casual atmosphere. Open daily 9pm-4am. AmEx/MC/V.

FESTIVALS

Vienna hosts an array of annual festivals. The **Vienna Festwochen** (early May to mid-June) has a program of exhibitions, plays, and concerts. (☎58 92 20; www.festwochen.or.at.) The Staatsoper and Volkstheater host the **Jazzfest Wien** (☎503 5647; www.viennajazz.org) during the first weeks of July. The Social Democrats host the late-June **Danube Island Festival,** drawing millions of revelers for fireworks and concerts (☎535 35 35; www.donauinselfest.at). Mid-July through mid-August, the **ImPulsTanz Festival** (☎523 55 58; www.impulstanz.com) attracts some of the world's greatest dance troupes and offers seminars to enthusiasts. The city-wide film festival, the **Viennale** (www.viennale.at), kicks off in mid-October.

SALZBURGER LAND AND UPPER AUSTRIA

Salzburger Land's precious white gold, salt *(salz)*, drew the first settlers over 3000 ago. Modern travelers prefer to seek instead the lakes and hills of the Salzkammergut, where Salzburg and Hallstatt are among the more enticing destinations.

SALZBURG ☎0662

Graced with Baroque wonders, Salzburg was the ecclesiastical center of Austria in the 17th and 18th centuries. Its rich musical culture lives on today, in everything from high concert halls to impromptu folk performances in the public squares.

AUSTRIA

TRANSPORTATION

Trains: Hauptbahnhof, in Südtirolerpl. (24hr. reservations ☎05 17 17). To: **Graz** (4hr., every hr. 8am-6:30pm, €40); **Innsbruck** (2hr., 11 per day, €32); **Munich** (2hr., 30 per day, €26); **Vienna** (3½hr., 26 per day, €40); **Zurich** (6hr., 7 per day, €70).

Public Transportation: Buses depart from the depot in front of the train station. The information desk (☎44 80 61 66) at the bus depot can answer questions about local transportation. Open M-F 6am-6:45pm, Sa 7:30am-2:45pm. Single tickets (€1.60) available at automatic machines or from the drivers. 5-ticket books (€8), day passes (€4.20), and week passes (€11) are available at machines, the ticket office, or *Tabak* (newsstand/tobacco) shops. Punch your ticket when you board or risk a €36 fine. Buses usually make their last run 10:30-11:30pm.

ORIENTATION AND PRACTICAL INFORMATION

Three hills and the **Salzach River** define Salzburg, just a few kilometers from the German border. The **Neustadt** (new town) is north of the river, and the beautiful **Altstadt** (old town) squeezes between the southern bank and the **Mönchsberg** hill. The Hauptbahnhof is on the northern side of town beyond the *Neustadt;* buses #1, 3, 5, 6, 51, and 55 connect it to **Hanuschplatz,** the main public transportation hub in the *Altstadt,* by the river near Griesg. and the Staatsbrücke. Hubs in the *Neustadt* include **Mirabellplatz** and the **Mozartsteg,** the pedestrian bridge that leads across the Salzach to Mozartpl. To reach the *Altstadt* on foot, turn left out of the station onto Rainerstr. and follow it straight under the tunnel and on to Mirabellpl.

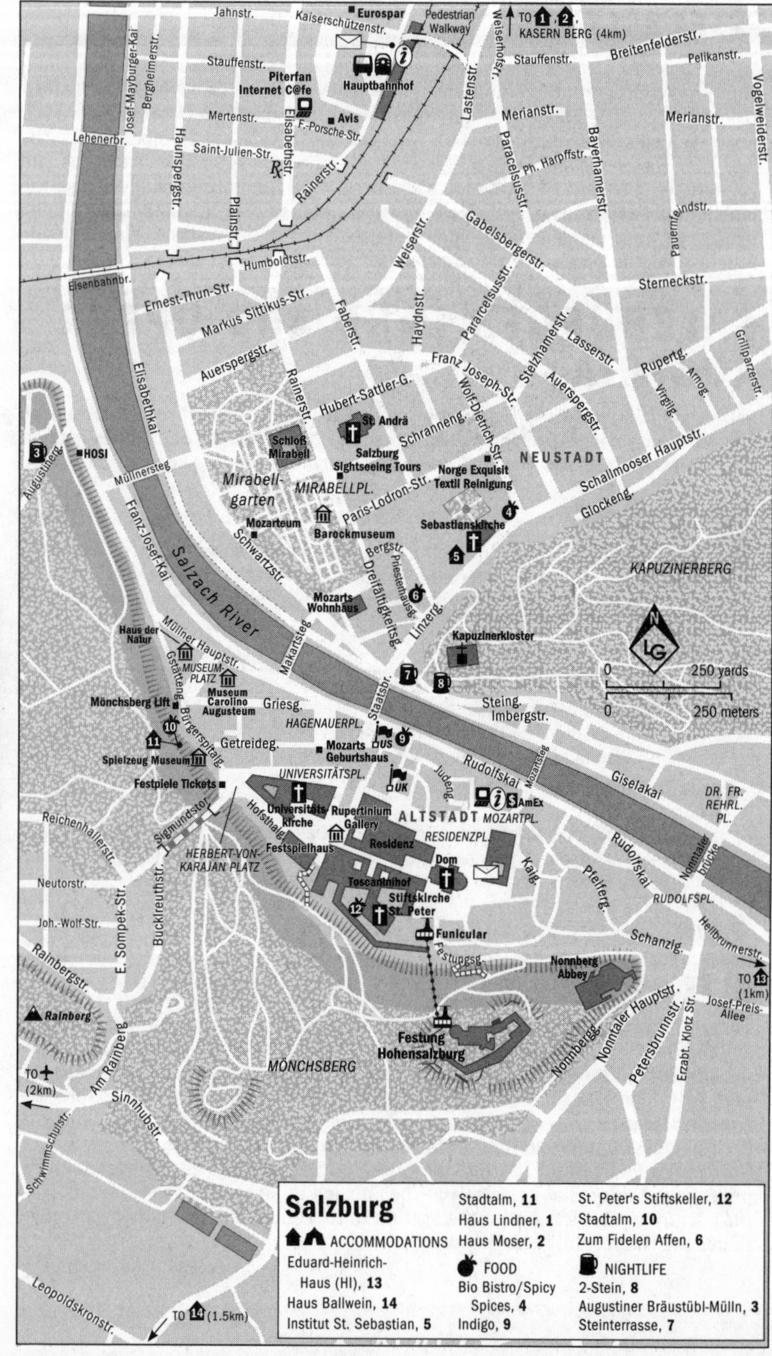
Salzburg
ACCOMMODATIONS
Eduard-Heinrich-Haus (HI), 13
Haus Ballwein, 14
Institut St. Sebastian, 5
Stadtalm, 11
Haus Lindner, 1
Haus Moser, 2
FOOD
Bio Bistro/Spicy Spices, 4
Indigo, 9
St. Peter's Stiftskeller, 12
Stadtalm, 10
Zum Fidelen Affen, 6
NIGHTLIFE
2-Stein, 8
Augustiner Bräustübl-Mülln, 3
Steinterrasse, 7
Hauptbahnhof
Piterfan Internet C@fe
Eurospar
Avis
Pedestrian Walkway
TO 1, 2, KASERN BERG (4km)
Salzach River
Schloß Mirabell
Mirabellgarten
MIRABELLPL.
Mozarteum
Barockmuseum
St. Andrä
Salzburg Sightseeing Tours
Norge Exquisit Textil Reinigung
Sebastianskirche
NEUSTADT
KAPUZINERBERG
Kapuzinerkloster
Mozarts Wohnhaus
Haus der Natur
MUSEUMPLATZ
Museum Carolino Augusteum
Mönchsberg Lift
HAGENAUERPL.
Mozarts Geburtshaus
Spielzeug Museum
Festpiele Tickets
UNIVERSITÄTSPL.
Universitäts-kirche
Rupertinium Gallery
ALTSTADT
MOZARTPL.
AmEx
Festspielhaus
Residenz
RESIDENZPL.
HERBERT-VON-KARAJAN PLATZ
Dom
Toscaninihof
Stiftskirche St. Peter
Funicular
Nonnberg Abbey
Festung Hohensalzburg
MÖNCHSBERG
Rainberg
HOSI
DR. FR. REHRL. PL.
RUDOLFSPL.
TO 13 (1km)
TO 14 (1.5km)
TO (2km)
0 250 yards
0 250 meters

Tourist Office: Mozartpl. 5 (☎88 98 73 30), in the *Altstadt.* The office books rooms (€2.20 fee and 10% deposit), offers guided tours of the city (daily 12:15pm, €8), and gives out free hotel maps. It also sells a city map (€0.70) and the **Salzburg Card,** which grants admission to all museums and sights as well as unlimited public transportation (1-day card €22, 2-day €29, 3-day €34). Open daily 9am-6pm.

Currency Exchange: Banks offer better rates for cash than AmEx but often charge higher commissions. Banking hours M-F 8am-12:30pm and 2-4:30pm. Train station exchange open M-F 7am-9pm.

American Express: Mozartpl. 5 (☎80 80). Cashes AmEx cheques without commission and books tours. Open M-F 9am-5:30pm, Sa 9am-noon.

Luggage Storage: At the train station. 24hr. lockers €2-3.50.

GLBT Resources: Homosexual Initiative of Salzburg (HOSI), Müllner Hauptstr. 11 (☎43 59 27; www.hosi.or.at), hosts regular workshops and meetings and offers a free guide to Salzburg. Open M from 7pm, F-Sa from 8pm. Phone staffed F 7-9pm.

Emergency: Police: ☎133. **Ambulance:** ☎144. **Fire:** ☎122.

Pharmacies: Elisabeth-Apotheke, Elisabethstr. 1a (☎87 14 84). Pharmacies in the city center open M-F 8am-6pm, Sa 8am-noon. 3 pharmacies are open 24hr.; ask for an after-hours calendar at any pharmacy or check the list on the door if they're closed.

Internet Access: Internet Café, Mozartpl. 5 (☎84 48 22), near the tourist office. €0.15 per min. Open daily Sept.-June 10am-11pm; July-Aug. 9am-midnight.

Post Office: ☎88 30 30. At the train station. Address *Poste Restante* mail with Postal Code 5021 and it will be held at the post office for 3 weeks. Open M-F 7am-8:30pm, counter closes 6pm; Sa 8am-2pm; Su 1-6pm. **Postal Code:** A-5020.

ACCOMMODATIONS

IN SALZBURG

Stadtalm, Mönchsberg 19c (☎84 17 29; www.diestadtalm.com). Bus #1 (dir.: Maxglan) to Mönchsbergaufzug; down the street and through the stone arch to the Mönchsberg lift (☎4480 6285; M-Tu, Th-Su 8am-7pm, W 8am-10pm; €2.90). Follow signs at the top. Turreted hostel proves you don't have to have own mutual funds to enjoy one of the best views in Salzburg. Breakfast included. Reception 9am-10pm. Curfew 1am. Open Apr.-Sept. Dorms €15. Cash only. ❶

Eduard-Heinrich-Haus (HI), Eduard-Heinrich-Str. 2 (☎62 59 76; www.hostel-ehh.at). Bus #3 (dir.: Salzburg-Süd) or 8 (dir.: Alpensiedlung) to Polizeidirektion. Cross Alpenstr., turn right on Billrothstr., left on Robert-Stolz-Promenade; walk 200m, and take 1st right; the pink building on the left. Spacious rooms look out into the garden. Common areas with TV, table tennis, and chess. Breakfast included. Internet €2.60 per 20min. Laundry €6. Key deposit of ID or €20. Reception 7-10am and 5pm-midnight. All rooms with bath except 4 dorms (€15-18). Other dorms €18-21; singles €27. MC/V. ❶

Institut St. Sebastian, Linzerg. 41 (☎87 13 86). Bus #1, 3, 5, or 6 to Mirabellpl. Cross the street, walk same direction as bus, turn left onto Bergstr., left again onto Linzerg.; hostel is through the arch. Clean rooms. Breakfast included. Dorms linen €2. Wash €3, dry €3. Reception 8am-noon and 4-9pm. Dorms €16; singles €30, with shower €37; doubles €48/60; triples €68/73; quads €78/88. MC/V; €18 minimum charge. ❷

OUTSIDE SALZBURG

Most *Privatzimmer* (rooms in a family home) are officially outside of Salzburg, but welcoming hosts and bargain prices make them the best deal in the city. To get to the rooms on **Kasern Berg,** north of the city, take the S2 train to Kasern Berg (4min.; every 30min.; €1.60, Eurail valid). Get off at Salzburg-Maria Plain and walk up Bergstr., the only uphill road. To get to southern *Privatzimmer* from the train station, take a bus to Hanuschpl., for south-bound bus #16. Get off at the Gserngeweg stop. Reservations recommended, especially in summer.

Haus Ballwein, Moosstr. 69a (☎82 40 29; www.haus-ballwein.at), south of the city. Colorful curtains, natural wood paneling, and braided rugs will rejuvenate any traveler. Bike rental €5 per day. Breakfast included. Singles €23, with shower €33-35; doubles €44/48-52; triples with bath €65-70; apartment for 4 with kitchenette €80. Cash only. ❷

Haus Lindner, Panoramaweg 5 (☎45 66 81; www.haus-lindner.at), north of the city. Some of the tastefully furnished rooms have balconies. Breakfast included. Call for pickup from the station. Doubles, triples, and quads €16-18 per person. Cash only. ❷

Haus Moser, Turnerbühel (☎45 66 76), north of the city. Walk up the driveway near the start of Bergstr. near Kasern Berg. Comfortable rooms in a dark-timbered home. Breakfast and laundry included. Doubles, triples, and quads €16 per person. Cash only. ❷

FOOD

Local specialties include the world-famous *Mozartkugeln* (hazelnuts coated in pistachio marzipan, nougat, and chocolate). **Supermarkets** cluster to the north of the river. Another market, **Billa,** Griesg. 19, is next to Hanuschpl. (Open M-W 8am-7pm, Th 7:30am-7pm, F 7:30am-7:30pm, Sa 7:30am-6pm.) **Open-air markets** sell fruits, meats, and cheeses in Universitätpl. (Open M-F 6am-7pm, Sa 6am-1pm.)

Indigo, Rudolfskai 8 (☎84 34 80), to the left of Staatsbrücke when facing the *Altstadt*. Draws a daily local crowd with Asian noodles, sushi, and meals (€4.50-4.90). Noodles €4.90. Sushi roll €2.20, 8 pieces €5.90. Open M-Sa 10am-10pm. Cash only. ❶

Zum Fidelen Affen, Priesterhausg. 8 (☎87 73 61), off Linzerg. Hearty Austrian food keeps everyone coming back "To the Faithful Ape." Try the Monkey Steak, a roasted pork dish, for €10. Vegetarian options. Open M-Sa 5pm-midnight. DC/MC/V. ❷

Stadtalm, Mönchsberg 19c (☎84 17 29). Enjoy chicken cordon bleu (€10) or a Greek salad (€6) while soaking up a view of the *Altstadt* at the Stadtalm hostel's delightful cafe. Entrees €4-11. Open daily Mar.-Oct. 10am-10pm. Cash only. ❷

Bio Bistro/Spicy Spices, Wolf-Dietrich-Str. 1 (☎87 07 12), at Linzerg. Everything is vegetarian and organic, with many vegan options. Dish of the day, *chapati* bread, and lentils €4.50. Other entrees with 2 *naan* €6.50. Open daily 10am-10pm. Cash only. ❶

St. Peter's Stiftskeller, St.-Peter-Bezirk 1/4 (☎84 12 680). At the foot of the cliffs next to St. Peter's Monastery, this is the oldest restaurant in Central Europe. Entrees €10-23. Open M-F 11am-midnight, during the *Festspiele* until 1am. AmEx/DC/MC/V. ❸

SIGHTS

FESTUNG HOHENSALZBURG. Built between 1077 and 1681 atop Mönchsberg, Hohensalzburg Fortress is the largest completely preserved castle in Europe. The castle contains formidable Gothic state rooms and a watchtower that provides visitors with an unmatched panorama of the city. The **Burgmuseum** inside the fortress displays medieval instruments of torture and has side-by-side histories of Salzburg and the fortress. *(Take the trail or the Festungsbahn funicular up to the fortress from Festungsg. Funicular every 10min. 9am-10pm. Open daily Jun.-Aug. 9am-7:30pm; Sept. and May 9am-7pm; Oct.-Apr. 9am-5:30pm. Funicular round-trip €9.60; includes fortress admission. If you walk, ticket including fortress and museums €8.40.)*

MOZARTS GEBURTSHAUS. Mozart's birthplace features the child genius's belongings, including his first violin and a pair of keyboard instruments. Several rooms recreate his young years. Come before 11am to avoid the crowd. *(Getreideg. 9. Open daily July-Aug. 9am-6pm. Last entrance 30min. before closing. €6, students €5.)*

AUSTRIA

UNIVERSITÄTSKIRCHE. In Mozart's backyard stands the **University Church,** one of the largest Baroque chapels on the continent and designer Fischer von Erlach's masterpiece. Sculpted clouds coat the nave, while pudgy cherubim frolic all over the church's immense apse. *(Hours vary, generally open daily 9am-5pm. Free.)*

TOSCANINIHOF, CATACOMBS, AND THE DOM. Steps lead from Toscaninihof, the courtyard of **St. Peter's Monastery,** up the Mönchsberg cliffs. **Stiftskirche St. Peter,** a church within the monastery, features a marble portal from 1244. In the 18th century, the building was remodeled in Rococo style. *(☎844 5760. Open daily 9am-12:15pm and 2:30-6:30pm.)* The entrance to the Catacombs is near the far end of the cemetery, against the Mönchsberg. In the lower room (St. Gertrude's Chapel), a fresco commemorates the martyrdom of Thomas à Becket. *(Open May-Sept. Tu-Su 10:30am-5pm; Oct.-Apr. W-Th 10:30am-3:30pm. €1, students €0.60.)* The exit at the other end of the cemetery leads to the immense Baroque *Dom* (cathedral), where Mozart was christened in 1756 and later worked as concertmaster and court organist. The square leading out of the cathedral, **Domplatz,** features a statue of the Virgin Mary and figures representing Wisdom, Faith, the Church, and the Devil.

RESIDENZ. The archbishops of Salzburg have resided in the magnificent Residenz since 1595. Stunning Baroque **State Rooms** have ceiling frescoes, gilded furniture, Flemish tapestries, and ornate stucco work. A **gallery** exhibits 16th- to 19th-century art. *(Open daily 10am-5pm, closed some M. €8, students €6. Audio tour included.)*

MIRABELL PALACE AND GARDENS. Mirabellpl. holds the marvelous **Mirabell Schloß,** which the supposedly celibate Archbishop Wolf Dietrich built for his mistress and their 10 children in 1606. *(Open daily 7am-9pm. Free.)* Behind the palace, the **Mirabellgarten** is a maze of flower beds. The garden contains the moss-covered **Zauberflötenhäuschen,** where Mozart purportedly composed *The Magic Flute.*

ENTERTAINMENT

During the **Salzburger Festspiele** (July 24-Aug. 31, 2006), everyone from the Vienna Philharmonic to rising stars arrives for a month of performances. Room prices rise accordingly; plan ahead. In 2006, the festival celebrates the 250th anniversary of Mozart's birth with performances of all 22 of his stage works. Info and tickets for *Festspiele* are available through the ticket office *(Festspiele Kartenbüro)* and daily box office *(Direkt Verkauf)* at Karajanpl. 11, next to the tunnel. (☎804 5500; www.salzburg-festival.at. Tickets €15-360. Ticket offices open mid-Mar. to June M-F 9:30am-3pm; July 1-24 M-Sa 9:30am-5pm, July 25-Aug. 31 daily 9:30am-6pm.)

BARS AND BEER GARDENS

Munich may be known as the world's beer capital, but much of that liquid gold flows south to Austria's pubs and *Biergärten* (beer gardens). These lager oases cluster in the city center along the **Salzach River.** The boisterous stick to **Rudolfskai,** between the Staatsbrücke and Mozartsteg. Along **Chiemseegasse** and around **Anton-Neumayr-Platz,** you can throw back a few drinks in a pub.

Augustiner Bräustübl-Mülln, Augustinerg. 4 (☎43 12 46). Even though the monks are no more, the *Bräukloster* they founded in 1621 continues to turn out home-brewed beer (€2.50-2.80). Open M-F 3-11pm, Sa-Su 2:30-11pm; last drink 10:30pm. Cash only.

2-Stein, Giselakai 9 (☎87 71 79). The place to come for Salzburg's gay and lesbian scene. Mixed drinks from €5. Open M-W 6pm-4am, Th-Su 6pm-5am. AmEx/DC/MC/V.

Steinterrasse, Giselakai 3-5 (☎88 20 70), on the 7th fl. of the Stein Hotel. This hip cafe-bar knows that a lofty rooftop panorama doesn't have to mean equally lofty prices. Beer €2-4. Mixed drinks €5-10. Open daily 9am-1am. AmEx/DC/MC/V.

HALLSTATT ☎06134

On the banks of the Hallstättersee, tiny Hallstatt (pop. 960) clings to the mountainside and to the blue-green waters of the lake. Easily the most striking lakeside village in the Salzkammergut, Hallstatt also boasts salt-rich earth that has helped to preserve its archaeological treasures—so extensive that one era in Celtic studies (800-400 BC) is dubbed "the Hallstatt era."

TRANSPORTATION AND PRACTICAL INFORMATION. **Buses** are the cheapest way (€18) to get to Hallstatt from Salzburg but require two layovers. The bus station is in the neighboring town of Lahn; face away from the lake and head right for 10min. to reach the Hallstatt tourist office. The **train** station, across the lake, is not staffed. All trains come from Attnang-Puchheim in the north or Stainach-Irdning in the south. **Trains** run every hour 7am-6pm to Bad Ischl (30min., €3.50) and Salzburg (2½hr., €19.50) via Attnang-Puchheim. The **tourist office,** Seestr. 169, finds rooms and helps with the confusing system of street addresses. (☎82 08. Open July-Aug. M-F 9am-noon and 2-5pm; Nov.-May M-F 9am-noon.) There is an **ATM** at Volksbank, 114 Seestr. (☎48 13. Open M-Tu and Th-F 8am-noon and 2-5pm, W 8am-noon.) **Postal Code:** A-4830.

ACCOMMODATIONS AND FOOD. To reach **Gästehaus Zur Mühle ❶,** Kirchenweg 36, from the tourist office, walk uphill to the tunnel at the upper right corner of the square; it's at the end of the tunnel by the waterfall. (☎48 13. €15 locker deposit. Linen €3. Reception 11am-2pm and 4-10pm. Closed Nov. Dorms €12. DC/MC/V.) Enjoy a glorious view of the lake from **Frühstückspension Sarstein ❷,** Gosamühlstr. 83. From the ferry, turn right on Seestr. and walk 10min. (☎82 17; pension.sarstein@aon.at. Breakfast included. Showers €1 per 10min. Singles €18-20, with bath €25-27; doubles €37-40, with shower €50-53, with bath €56-59; triples €58-62, with bath €76-78. 2- to 5-person apartment with 4-night min. stay €50-90. Cash only.) The cheapest eats are at **Konsum** supermarket, Kernmagazinpl. 8, across from the bus stop; the butcher prepares sandwiches on request. (☎8226. Open M-F 7:30am-noon and 3-6pm, Sa 7:30am-noon. Cash only.) The meat shop **Karl Forstinger ❶,** 139 Seestr., grills up fresh *wurst.* (☎0676 788 7299. *Wurst* and roll €2-3. Open M-F 10am-5pm, Sa 10am-4pm, Su 11am-4pm. Cash only.)

SIGHTS AND HIKING. Back when Rome was still a village, the salt mines earned Hallstatt international renown. The 2500-year-old **Salzbergwerk** is the oldest salt mine in the world. Take the 1hr. guided tour and zip down a wooden mining slide to a lake deep inside the mountain. (☎200 2400. Open daily Apr. 24-Sept. 18 9:30am-4:30pm; Sept. 19-Oct. 26 9:30am-3pm. English-language tours every 15min. €15.50, students €9.30.) In the 19th century, Hallstatt was the site of an Iron Age archaeological find. The **Charnel House** next to St. Michael's Chapel is filled with the remains of over 610 villagers from as early as the 16th century. From the ferry dock, follow the signs marked "*Katholische Kirche.*" (☎82 79. Open daily June-Sept. 10am-6pm; May and Oct. 10am-4pm; Nov.-Apr. call for an appointment. €1.)

Hallstatt offers some of the most spectacular day hikes in the Salzkammergut. The tourist office has bike maps (€7) and an excellent English-language hiking guide (€6), which details 38 hikes in the area. The easy **Waldbachstrub Waterfall hike** (1¾-2hr. round-trip) follows a glacial stream up to a waterfall. From the bus station, follow the brown Malerweg signs near the supermarket until you reach the Waldbachstrub sign (about 40min.). The waterfall is in the **Echental,** a valley blazed with trails leading deep into the valley. The **Gangsteig,** a slippery stairway carved into the side of a cliff, requires sturdy shoes and a strong will to climb.

DAYTRIP FROM HALLSTATT: DACHSTEIN ICE CAVES. Across the lake from Hallstatt, frozen waterfalls and curtains of ice in the Rieseneishöhle (Giant Ice Cave) transport visitors to a chilly wonderland. The Rieseneishöhle and the

Mammuthöhle (Mammoth Cave) are on the mountain near the Schönbergalm cable car station, while the Koppenbrüllerhöhle, a giant spring, is in the valley. English-language tours are required; you'll be assigned to a group at Schönbergalm. The cave temperatures are near freezing, so bring warm clothes. (☎84 00; www.dachsteinhoehlen.at. Buses to Dachstein leave every hr. 8:48am-4:52pm from the Lahn station; 10min., €1.60. Koppenbrüller cave is a 15min. walk from the Dachstein bus stop in Obertraun. Cable car runs every 15min. 8:40am-5:40pm from Obertraun to the ice caves at Schönbergalm, round-trip €13.70. Open May to mid-Oct. daily 9am-5pm. Each cave €8.50, Rieseneishöhle and Mammuthöhle €13.10.)

ZELL AM SEE ☎06542

Surrounded by a ring of snow-capped mountains cradling a turquoise lake, Zell am See (pop. 9700) lures visitors craving the outdoors. The **Schmittenhöhebahn** cable car leads to many hikes. (Runs daily every 30min. Round-trip €19.60, up €15.50, down €11.50. Guest card discounts available.) PostBus #661 (every 30min., €1.80) goes to the lift. The moderate **Pinzgauer Spaziergang,** marked "Alpenvereinsweg" #19 or 719, begins at the top of the lift and levels off high in the Alps. Most devote an entire day to this trail, taking a side path to a town west of Zell am See and returning by bus. For those desiring a faster-paced experience, **Adventure Service,** Steinerg. 9 (☎0664 132 8552 or 735 25), leads a variety of trips.

Ask at your hostel for a free **guest card,** which provides discounts on activities throughout the city. **Haus der Jugend (HI) ❷,** Seespitzstr. 13, redefines "budget" with a terrace on the lake and spacious rooms with bath. From the station, take the exit facing the lake and turn right on the lakeside footpath; at the end, turn left on Seespitzstr. (☎571 85; www.jungehotels.at/seespitzstrasse. Breakfast included. Reception 7-9am and 4-10pm. Dorms €17-19; doubles €21. AmEx/DC/MC/V.) **Ristorante Pizzeria Giuseppe ❷,** Kircheng. 1, has an Italian ambience. From the station, walk up Bahnhofstr. past the church. (☎723 73. Pizza €5.90-9.80. Open Tu-Su 11:30am-11pm. DC/MC/V; €40 min. charge.) The **SPAR** is at Brucker-Bundesstr. 4. (☎700 19. Open M-Th 7:30am-6:30pm, F 7:30am-7pm, Sa 7:30am-5pm.)

The **train** station (☎7321 4357) is at the intersection of Bahnhofstr. and Salzmannstr. Trains run to Innsbruck (1½-2hr., every 2hr., €21.90); Vienna (5hr., €43.50) via Salzburg (1½hr., 1-2 per hr., €12.40). The **bus station** is at Gartenstr. and Schulstr. Buy tickets onboard or at the kiosk. (☎54 44. Kiosk open M-F 7:45am-1:45pm.) Buses service: Franz-Josefs-Höhe (mid-June to mid-Sept.; 9:20am, 12:20pm; €10.40) and Salzburg (2hr., every 2hr. 6:40am-4:50pm, €10.20). The **tourist office** is at Brucker-Bundesstr. 1a. (☎770; www.europasportregion.info. Open July to mid-Sept. and mid-Dec. to Mar. M-F 9am-6pm, Sa 9am-noon and 2-6pm, Su 10am-noon; Apr.-June and Sept. to mid-Dec. closed Su.) The **post office** is at Postpl. 4. (☎73 79 10. Open M-F 7:30am-6pm, Sa 7-10am; July to mid-Sept. and Christmas-Easter Sa 7-11am.) **Postal Code:** A-5700.

HOHE TAUERN NATIONAL PARK

The enormous Hohe Tauern range, the largest national park in Europe, encompasses 246 glaciers and 304 mountains. The best way to explore this preserve is to hike through it. *An Experience in Nature*, available at park centers and most area tourist offices, plots 84 different hikes. The center of the park is Franz-Josefs-Höhe and the Pasterze Glacier, which hovers above the town of Heiligenblut.

TRANSPORTATION. Hohe Tauern National Park sits at the meeting point of the three provinces of Salzburger Land, Tyrol, and Kärnten. **Zell am See** (above) is the most convenient base to access the park. **PostBus** provides a scenic ride from Zell am See to Franz-Josefs-Höhe (2hr.; departs 9:20am, 12:20pm, returns 3pm; €10.40, round-trip €20.70). The park itself is criss-crossed by **bus** lines that operate on a complicated timetable.

HIKING. Make sure to pick up a hiking map from the National Park Office or tourist office. From the Franz-Josefs-Höhe parking lot, the moderately difficult **Gletscherweg** (3hr.) passes through the varied terrain created by the retreating Pasterze Glacier before taking hikers onto the glacier itself. **Heiligenblut** hikes depart from the Retschitzbrücke parking area outside of town via Gemeindestr.

FRANZ-JOSEFS-HÖHE. This tourist center, stationed above the Pasterze Glacier, has a great view of the Großglockner (3797m) on clear days. The Höhe has its own **park office** in the parking area. (☎04824 27 27. Open mid-May to mid-Oct. daily 10am-4pm.) The elevator next to the info center leads to a path across the ridge to the **Swarovski Observation Center.** (Open daily 10am-4pm. Free.)

HEILIGENBLUT. Close to the highest mountain in Austria, Heiligenblut is a great starting point for hikes. Reach the town by **bus** from Franz-Josefs-Höhe (30min., €3.60) and Lienz (1hr., 2-6 per day, €6). The **tourist office,** Hof 4, up the street from the bus stop, dispenses info on rooms, hikes, and transport. (☎20 01 21. Open July-Aug. M-F 9am-6pm, Sa 9am-noon and 4-6pm; Sept.-June M-F 9am-noon and 2-6pm, Sa 9am-noon and 4-6pm.) To reach the **Jugendgästehaus (HI)** ❷, Hof 36, take the path down from the wall behind the bus stop parking lot. (☎22 59. HI members only. Breakfast included. Reception July-Aug. 7-11am and 5-10pm; Sept.-June 7-10am and 5-9pm. Lockout 10am-4pm. Curfew 10pm. Dorms €16.50.)

TYROL (TIROL)

Tyrol's soaring peaks challenge hikers with their celestial scale. Craggy summits in the northeast and south cradle the pristine Ötzal and Zillertal valleys while the mighty Hohe Tauern mountain range marches across eastern Tyrol.

AUSTRIA

INNSBRUCK ☎0512

The 1964 and 1976 winter Olympics were held in Innsbruck (pop. 128,000), bringing international recognition to this beautiful mountain city. The nearby Tyrolean Alps await skiers and hikers, and the tiny cobblestone streets of the *Altstadt* (old town) are peppered with fancy architecture and relics of the Hapsburg Empire.

TRANSPORTATION AND PRACTICAL INFORMATION

Trains: Hauptbahnhof, Südtirolerpl. (☎517 17). To: **Munich** (2hr., 9 per day, €31.80); **Vienna** (5½-7hr., €49.80) via **Salzburg** (2½hr., 5am-5:30pm 1-2 per hr., €31.80); **Zurich** (4hr.; 8:39am, 12:39pm; €45.40).

Public Transportation: The **IVB** Office, Stainerstr. 2 (☎530 799), off Marktgraben, has bus schedules and route maps. Open M-F 7:30am-6pm. The main bus station is in front of the train station. Single fare €1.60, 24hr. pass €3.50, week €11. Most buses stop running at around 11:30pm, but 4 **Nachtbus** lines run every hr. midnight-5am; almost every one passes through Maria-Theresien-Str., the train station, and Museumstr.

Bike Rental: Neuner Radsport, Maximilianstr. 23 (☎56 15 01). Mountain bikes and helmets €16 per half-day, €20 per day. Open M-F 9am-6pm, Sa 9am-noon.

Tourist Office: Innsbruck Tourist Office, Burggraben 3 (☎598 50), off the end of Museumstr. Sells maps (€1) and the **Innsbruck Card,** which provides unlimited access to public transportation and free admission to most sights. 1-day card €23, 2-day €28, 3-day €33. Open daily 9am-6pm.

Police: ☎133. **Ambulance:** ☎144 or 142. **Fire:** ☎122. **Mountain Rescue:** ☎140.

Internet Access: International Telephone Discount, Südtirolerpl. 1 (☎282 3690). Turn right from the Hauptbahnhof. €0.07 per min. Open daily 9am-11pm.

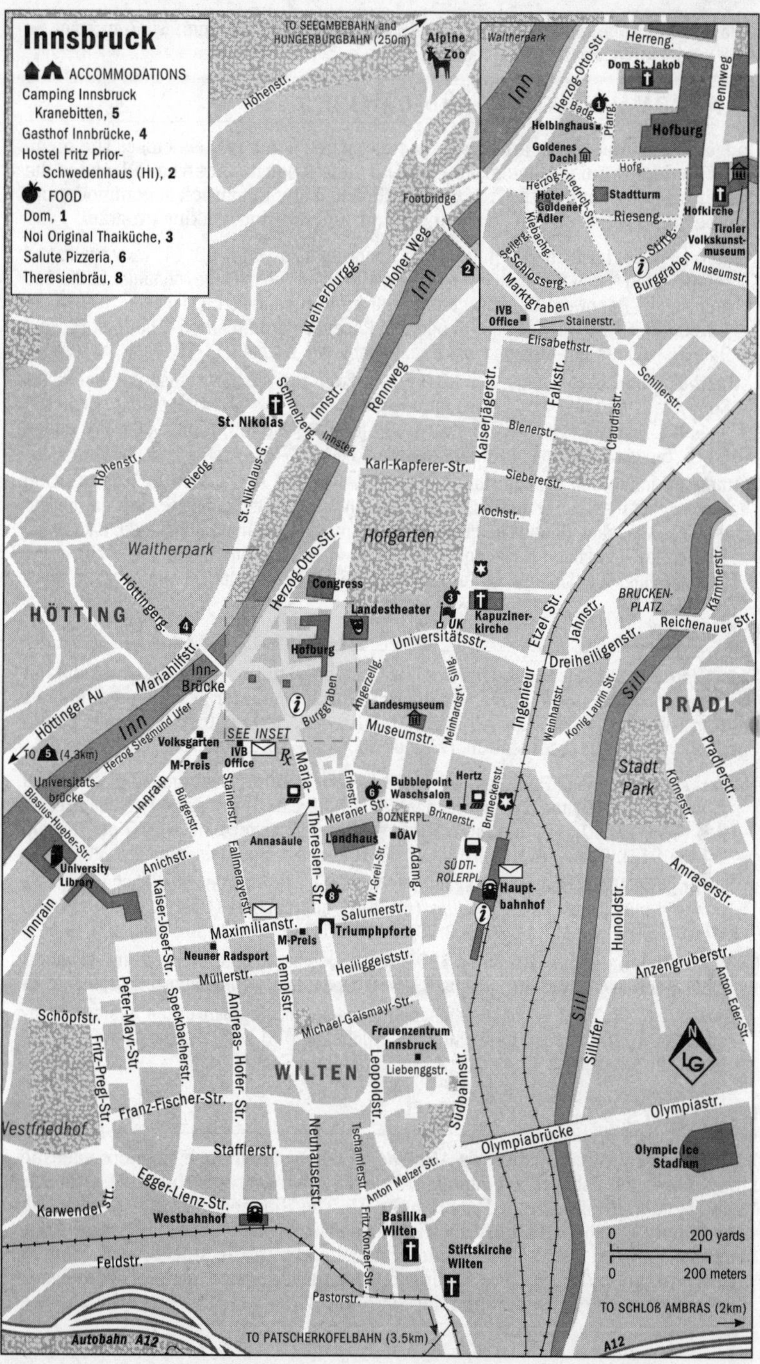
Innsbruck
ACCOMMODATIONS
Camping Innsbruck Kranebitten, 5
Gasthof Innbrücke, 4
Hostel Fritz Prior-Schwedenhaus (HI), 2
FOOD
Dom, 1
Noi Original Thaiküche, 3
Salute Pizzeria, 6
Theresienbräu, 8
TO SEEGMBEBAHN and HUNGERBURGBAHN (250m)
Alpine Zoo
Höhenstr.
Footbridge
Hoher Weg
Inn
Weiherburgg.
Rennweg
Schmelzerg.
Innstr.
St. Nikolas
Innsteg
Karl-Kapferer-Str.
Riedg.
Höhenstr.
St.-Nikolaus-G.
Hofgarten
Waltherpark
Herzog-Otto-Str.
Congress
Landestheater
Kapuziner-kirche
UK
HÖTTING
Höttingerg.
Mariahilfstr.
Inn-Brücke
Hofburg
Universitätsstr.
Höttinger Au
Burggraben
Angerzellg.
Landesmuseum
SEE INSET
Museumstr.
Herzog Siegmund Ufer
Volksgarten
IVB Office
M-Preis
TO 5 (4.3km)
Universitäts-brücke
Blasius-Hueber-Str.
Innrain
Bürgerstr.
Stainerstr.
Maria-Theresien-Str.
Erlerstr.
Bubblepoint Waschsalon
Hertz
Meraner Str.
BOZNERPL.
Brixnerstr.
Bruneckerstr.
Annasäule
Landhaus
ÖAV
W.-Greil-Str.
Adamg.
SÜDTIROLERPL.
Hauptbahnhof
University Library
Anichstr.
Kaiser-Josef-Str.
Fallmerayerstr.
Salurnerstr.
Maximilianstr.
Triumphpforte
M-Preis
Neuner Radsport
Heiliggeiststr.
Müllerstr.
Templstr.
Schöpfstr.
Peter-Mayr-Str.
Speckbacherstr.
Andreas-Hofer-Str.
Michael-Gaismayr-Str.
Frauenzentrum Innsbruck
Liebenggstr.
WILTEN
Leopoldstr.
Südbahnstr.
Fritz-Pregl-Str.
Franz-Fischer-Str.
Westfriedhof
Neuhauserstr.
Tschamlerstr.
Stafflerstr.
Olympiabrücke
Olympiastr.
Olympic Ice Stadium
Anton Melzer Str.
Egger-Lienz-Str.
Karwendelstr.
Westbahnhof
Basilika Wilten
Fritz Konzert-Str.
Stiftskirche Wilten
Feldstr.
Pastorstr.
Autobahn A12
TO PATSCHERKOFELBAHN (3.5km)
TO SCHLOß AMBRAS (2km)
A12
0 200 yards
0 200 meters
Elisabethstr.
Kaiserjägerstr.
Falkstr.
Schillerstr.
Bienerstr.
Claudiastr.
Sieberer str.
Kochstr.
Ingenieur Etzel Str.
BRUCKEN-PLATZ
Jahnstr.
Kärntnerstr.
Reichenauer Str.
Dreiheiligenstr.
Weinhartstr.
Konig Laurin Str.
Meinhardstr.
Sillg.
Sill
PRADL
Stadt Park
Pradlerstr.
Körnerstr.
Amraserstr.
Hunoldstr.
Anzengruberstr.
Anton Eder-Str.
Sillufer
Waltherpark
Herreng.
Dom St. Jakob
Herzog-Otto-Str.
Rennweg
Badg.
Pfarrg.
Helbinghaus
Hofburg
Goldenes Dachl
Hofg.
Herzog-Friedrich-Str.
Hotel Goldener Adler
Stadtturm
Riesengg.
Hofkirche
Tiroler Volkskunst-museum
Kiebachg.
Seilerg.
Schlosserg.
Stiftg.
Burggraben
Museumstr.
Marktgraben
IVB Office
Stainerstr.

Post Office: Maximilianstr. 2 (☎500 7900). Open M-F 7am-9pm, Sa 7am-3pm, Su 10am-7:30pm. **Postal Code:** A-6010.

ACCOMMODATIONS AND CAMPING

Budget accommodations are scarce in June, when some hostels close. The opening of student dorms to backpackers in July and August somewhat alleviates the crunch. Visitors can join the free **Club Innsbruck** at any Innsbruck accommodation; membership gives discounts on skiing, tours, and the club's hiking program.

Hostel Fritz Prior-Schwedenhaus (HI), Rennweg 17b (☎58 58 14; www.tirol.com/youth-hostel). From the station, take bus #4 to Handelsakademie, continue to the end and across Rennweg. Cheerful rooms with bath. Breakfast €5. Linen €1.50. Wash €3.60, dry €1.80. Internet €0.05 per min. Reception 7-9am and 5-10:30pm. Lockout 9am-5pm. Open July-Aug. and late Dec. to early Jan. Dorms €11-16. Cash only. ❶

Gasthof Innbrücke, Innstr. 1 (☎28 19 34). From the *Altstadt,* cross the Innbrücke. Comfy beds and fat pillows make for a restful night at this 581-year-old inn. Breakfast included. Singles €30, with shower €38; doubles €50/65; triples €63/93; quads €115; 5-person apartment €135; 6-person €160. DC/MC/V. ❸

Camping Innsbruck Kranebitten, Kranebitter Allee 214 (☎28 41 80). Take bus O to Technik and then bus LK (every 30min., last run 8:30pm) to Klammstr. Walk downhill to the right. Pleasant grounds in the shadow of a mountain. Showers included. Bike rental €5 per day. Reception 8am-noon and 2-9pm; after 9pm, find a site and check in the next morning. Tent sites €8.55, extra person €5.55. Tent rental €8. AmEx/MC/V. ❶

FOOD

The *Altstadt* cafes on Maria-Theresien-Str. are good but overpriced. Cross the Inn River to **Innstraße,** in the university district, for cheap pizzerias. There are **M-Preis** supermarkets at Maximilianstr. 3 (☎580 5110; open M-F 7:30am-7pm, Sa 7:30am-5pm) and inside the train station. (☎58 07 30. Open daily 6am-9pm. MC/V.)

Theresienbräu, Maria-Theresien-Str. 51-53 (☎58 75 80), is built around giant copper brewing kettles. Try the dark house lager (*Pfiff;* 0.4L €2.70) alongside Tyrolean specialties (€5.90-6.60). Fondue for 2 or more after 6pm (chocolate €6.70 per person; cheese €12). Open M-W 10am-1am, Th-Sa 10am-2am, Su 10am-midnight. MC/V. ❷

Noi Original Thaiküche, Kaiserjägerstr. 1 (☎58 97 77). This tiny Thai kitchen packs a powerful punch with its spicy soups (€4.20-9) and noodles (€7-10). Lunch specials €7.70-8.90. Open M-F 11:30am-2:30pm and 6-11pm, Sa 6-11pm. Cash only. ❷

Salute Pizzeria, Innrainstr. 35 (☎585 818). Students flock to the best and cheapest pizza in town (€3.20-6.60). Salads €3-4.50. Open daily 11am-midnight. Cash only. ❶

Dom, Pfarrg. 3 (☎23 85 51). Atmospheric cafe-bar in the heart of the *Altstadt.* Enjoy soups (€3.30), salads (€4-8), and sandwiches (€4-6) with a glass of wine (€3-4) under vaulted ceilings. Open daily 11am-2am. AmEx/DC/MC/V. ❶

SIGHTS

The stony facades of Innsbruck's *Altstadt* repose beneath the even more majestic stony faces of Innsbruck's mountains. The old town centers around the **Goldenes Dachl** (Golden Roof), Herzog-Friedrich-Str. 15. The 16th-century gold-shingled balcony honors Maximilian I, Innsbruck's favorite Hapsburg emperor. The nearby **Helbinghaus** is graced with pale-green floral detail and intricate stucco work. Church domes and shopping boutiques line Innsbruck's most distinctive street, **Maria-Theresien-Straße,** which runs south from the edge of the *Altstadt.* At its far end stands the

Triumphpforte (Triumphal Arch), built in 1765 after the betrothal of Emperor Leopold II. Up the street, the **Annasäule** (Anna Column) commemorates the Tyroleans' 1703 victory over the Bavarians. At **Dom St. Jakob,** *1 block behind the Goldenes Dachl,* the unassuming gray facade conceals a riot of pink-and-white High Baroque ornamentation within. The cathedral's prized possession is the small altar painting of *Our Lady of Succor* by Lukas Cranach the Elder. (Open Apr.-Sept. M-Sa 8am-7:30pm, Su 12:30-7:30pm; Oct.-Mar. M-Sa 10am-6:30pm, Su 12:30-6:30pm. Mass M-Sa 9:30am, Su 10, 11:30am. Free.) Behind the Dom, **Hofburg,** the imperial palace, was built in 1460 but completely remodeled under Maria Theresia. Don't miss the gilded tableau in the Audience Room, depicting the whole Hapsburg gang in gold medallions. (☎58 71 86. Open daily 9am-5pm. Last admission 4:30pm. €5.45, students €3.63. English-language guidebook €1.80.) Twenty-eight bronze statues of the ancestors and heroes of Maximilian I line the nave at **Hofkirche,** in the Volkskunstmuseum building at Universitätsstr. 8, appropriately surrounding the massive tomb of the *kaiser* himself. (☎58 43 02. Open July-Aug. M-Sa 9am-5:30pm, Su 12:30-5pm; Sept.-June M-Sa 9am-5pm, Su 12:30-5pm. €3, students €2.)

HIKING AND SKIING

A **Club Innsbruck** membership (free; see **Accommodations,** p. 100) lets you in on one of the best deals in Austria. The club's popular **hiking** program provides free guides, transportation, and equipment, including boots. To hike on your own, take the J bus to **Patscherkofel Seilbahnen** (20min.). The lift provides access to moderate 1½-5hr. hikes near the summit of the Patscherkofel. (Open daily 9am-4:30pm, July-Aug. 9am-5pm. Round-trip €16, students €13.) For more challenging climbs, head to the lifts that ferry passengers up to the **Nordkette** mountains. For those more interested in flying, Innsbruck-Information has a €95 **paragliding** package, including transport and equipment (bookings ☎37 84 88).

For Club-led **ski excursions,** take the complimentary ski shuttle (schedules at the tourist office) to any cable car. The **Innsbruck Gletscher Ski Pass** (available at all cable cars) is valid for all 60 lifts in the region (with Club Innsbruck membership: 3-day €90, 6-day €155). Individual lift passes might be a better option for the budget-conscious: skiers can buy day passes for Nordpark-Seegrube (€23.50), Patscherkofel (€25.50), and Glungezer (€21). The tourist office also rents **ski equipment** (€9-18 per day). One day of winter glacier skiing costs €32; summer ski packages (bus, lift, and rental) cost €49.

FROM THE ROA

SNOW IN JULY

I blinked in the sunlight. "Yo must be joking...snow?" The bu driver nodded. "*Ja,* snow. Tomorrow it will most likely snow."

Looking at the clear blue sky, couldn't believe what I had jus heard. But sure enough, the nex day the clouds sat low and dark and rain splattered moodily. O the mountain slopes, a dusting o new snow could be glimpse whenever the clouds broke apart.

My plans to go hiking wer seemingly ruined, but I refused t surrender to a day spent inside. put on all the shirts I had (3, to b exact) and my denim jacket, an headed up the mountain. The goin started easy. By the time I reache about 1800m, it was getting cold but I dug my hands into my pocket and ploughed on through the thic mists that huddled close to the ground. Then I noticed that the falling rain had suddenly become a lo more solid. Crystalline. Flecks o white were appearing all over m jacket. It was, indeed, snow in July.

I kicked myself for what nov seemed like a stupid decision The higher I went, the colder i became, and the snow began t fall steadily, white gusts smearin the sky into near-invisibility. But had to keep going: the next cluster of houses was closer tha Sölden below. Everyone seeme to be hibernating when I reache the town, with the exception o one cafe. I was never so glad t see a hot cappuccino.

-Shelly Jiang

STYRIA (STEIERMARK)

Many of southern Austria's folk traditions live on in the emerald hills and sloping pastures of Styria, where even the largest city, Graz, remains calm and relatively untouristed. The Styrian vineyards are also essential to any wine tour of Europe.

GRAZ ☎0316

Graz may be Austria's second-largest city (pop. 226,000), but that seems to be a well-kept secret. The *Altstadt* (old town) has an unhurried Mediterranean feel, picturesque red-tiled roofs, and Baroque domes. To the right of the tourist office, **Landeszeughaus** (Provincial Arsenal), Herreng. 16, has enough spears, muskets, and armor to outfit 28,000 mercenaries. (☎8017 9660; www.museum-joanneum.at. Open Apr.-Oct. daily 10am-6pm, Th 2hr. later; Nov.-Mar. Tu-Su 10am-3pm. English-language tours daily 10:30am, 3:30pm. €4.50, with tour €6, students €1.50/3.) North of Hauptpl., the **Schloßberg** (Castle Mountain) rises above Graz. Climb the steps of the **Schloßbergstiege,** built by Russian prisoners during WWI, for views of the Styrian plain. The newest addition to the riverscape, the shell-shaped **Murinsel,** houses a cafe, open-air theater, and playground. The **Opernhaus,** Franz-Josef-Pl. 10, at the corner of Opernring and Burgg., stages high-quality performances.

Most accommodations in Graz are pricey and far from the city center, but local transportation provides an easy commute. To reach **Jugendgästehaus Graz (HI) ❷,** Idlhofg. 74, from the station, cross the street, head right on Eggenberger Gürtel, left on Josef-Huber-G., then take the first right; the complex is through the parking lot on the right. Buses #31, 32, and 33 run from Jakominipl. (☎71 48 76. All rooms with bath. Breakfast included. Wash €2, dry €2. Internet €1.50 per 20min. Reception 7am-11pm. Dorms €20; singles €30, with bath €45; doubles €50. MC/V.) Concession stands sell sandwiches, *wurst* (€2-3), and other fast-food on **Hauptplatz.** Student hangouts line **Zinzendorfgasse** near the university. **Continuum ❶,** Spörg. 29, dishes up pizza (€3.30-7.50) in a space filled with flowers. At night it transforms into a bar. (☎81 57 78. Weekend brunch buffet 10am-2pm €5. Open M-F 3pm-2am, Sa-Su 10am-2am. MC/V.) **SPAR** supermarket is in the train station. (Open daily 6am-9pm.) The hub of after-hours activity is the so-called **Bermuda Triangle,** the area behind Hauptpl., bordered by Mehlpl., Färberg., and Prokopig. At **Kulturhauskeller,** Elisabethstr. 30, music throbs all night. (19+. Cover €2. Open Tu-Sa 9pm-late.)

Trains run from the Hauptbahnhof to: Innsbruck (5-6hr., 7 per day, €45); Munich (6¼hr., 4 per day, €68); Salzburg (4¼hr., every 2hr., €40); Vienna Südbahnhof (2½hr., every hr., €28); Zurich (10hr.; daily 5:40, 9:40am; €79). From the train station, go down Annenstr. and cross the main bridge to reach **Hauptplatz,** the city center. The **tourist office,** Herreng. 16, has free maps and books rooms for no fee. (☎807 50. Open June-Sept. M-F 9am-7pm, Sa 9am-6pm, Su 10am-6pm; Oct.-May M-Sa 9am-6pm, Su 10am-6pm.) **Postal Code:** A-8010.

BELGIUM (BELGIQUE, BELGIË)

Chocoholics, Europhiles, and art-lovers come together to worship in Belgium. Sweet-toothed foreigners flock to capital city Brussels to down Godiva chocolates on their way to comb the hallways of the European Union and NATO. In Flanders, Gothic towers crane their necks above the cobblestone squares of Flanders, while visitors below souse themselves on the canvases of Old Masters by day and the perfumed ales of hop-slinging monks by night. French-speaking Wallonie may not have a polished tourist schtick down pat yet, but the caves of the Lesse Valley and the forested trails of the Ardennes speak for themselves.

DISCOVER BELGIUM: SUGGESTED ITINERARIES

Plan for at least two days in **Brussels** (p. 107), the capital whose **Grand-Place** Victor Hugo called "the most beautiful square in the world." Head north to the elegant boulevards of **Antwerp** (p. 117) and the historic districts of **Ghent** (p. 119), then angle west to the winding streets and canals of romantic **Bruges** (p. 113). Connect to eastbound trains in the gritty university town of **Liège** (p. 121), or else take your time exploring the leafy Ardennes, using **Namur** (p. 122) as a base for hikes or bike rides into Belgium's rural south country.

ESSENTIALS

FACTS AND FIGURES

Official Name: Kingdom of Belgium.

Capital: Brussels.

Major Cities: Antwerp, Ghent, Liège.

Population: 10,350,000.

Time Zone: GMT +1.

Language: Flemish and French; pockets of German in the east.

Religions: Roman Catholic (75%).

WHEN TO GO

May, June, and September are the best times to visit, with temperatures around 18-22°C (64-72°F) in Brussels and Antwerp, and about 10° higher in Liège and Ghent. July and August tend to be humid and rainy. Winters are cloudy and cool, with temperatures averaging 2-7°C (36-45°F), and a bit colder in the eastern Ardennes. Bring a sweater and rain gear whenever you go and a heavy jacket in the winter.

DOCUMENTS AND FORMALITIES

EMBASSIES AND CONSULATES. All foreign embassies are in Brussels. For Belgian embassies in your home country: **Australia,** 19 Arkana St., Yarralumla, ACT 2600 (☎02 62 73 25 02; www.diplomatie.be/canberra); **Canada,** 360 Albert St., Ste. 820, Ottawa, ON K1R 7X7 (☎613-236-7267; www.diplomatie.be/

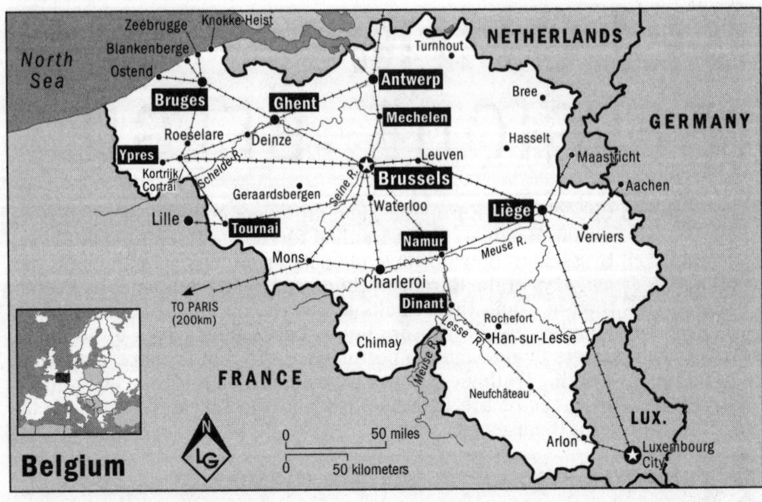

ottawa); **Ireland,** 2 Shrewsbury Rd., Ballsbridge, Dublin 4 (☎01 205 71 00; www.diplomatie.be/dublin); **UK,** 103-105 Eaton Sq., London SW1W 9AB (☎020 7470 3700; www.diplobel.org/uk/uk.htm); **US,** 3330 Garfield St. NW, Washington, D.C. 20008 (☎202-333-6900; www.diplobel.us). **New Zealanders** should contact the Belgian Honorary Consul for Auckland (ismackenzie@extra.co.nz), or the Australian embassy.

VISA AND ENTRY INFORMATION. EU citizens do not need a visa. Citizens of Australia, Canada, New Zealand, and the US do not need a visa for stays of up to 90 days, beginning upon entry into any of the countries within EU's freedom of movement zone. For more information, see p. 16.

TOURIST SERVICES AND MONEY

EMERGENCY	**Ambulance:** ☎100. **Fire:** ☎100. **Police:** ☎101.

TOURIST OFFICES. Bureaux de Tourisme, marked by green-and-white or blue signs labeled "i," are supplemented by **Infor Jeunes/Info-Jeugd,** information centers that help young people find work and secure accommodations in Wallonie and Flanders, respectively. The **Belgian Tourist Information Center (BBB),** Grasmarkt 63, Brussels (☎025 04 03 90), has national tourist info. The weekly English-language *Bulletin* (€2.35 at newsstands) includes movie listings, cultural events, and news.

MONEY. The **euro (€)** has replaced the Belgian Franc as the unit of currency in Belgium. For exchange rates and more information on the euro, see p. 21. ATMs generally offer the best exchange rates, but checking accounts are often required in order to withdraw money. A bare-bones day in Belgium might cost €35; a more comfortable day €50-65. Restaurant bills usually include a service charge, although outstanding service warrants an extra 5-10% tip. EU member countries impose a **Value Added Tax (VAT)** on goods and services purchased within the EU. Prices in Belgium already include the country's stiff 21% VAT rate, although partial refunds are available for visitors who are not EU citizens (p. 23).

TRANSPORTATION

BY PLANE. Several major airlines fly into **Brussels International Airport (BRU)** from Europe, North America, and Australia. **SN Brussels Airlines** (Belgium ☎070 35 11 11, UK 0870 735 2345; www.flysn.com) flies into Brussels from most major European cities, while budget airline **Ryanair** (☎353 1249 7700; www.ryanair.com) flies into **Brussels South Charleroi Airport (CRL)** from across Europe. Ryanair's rock-bottom fares, which start as low as €0.99 excluding taxes and fees (generally €15-20), are by far the best deal for those willing to trade-off convenience for price.

BY TRAIN AND BUS. The extensive, reliable **Belgian Rail** (www.b-rail.be) network traverses the country. **Eurail** is valid in Belgium. A **Benelux Tourrail Pass** (€126) allows five days of unlimited train travel in a one-month period in Belgium, the Netherlands, and Luxembourg, and is discounted to €95 for travelers under 26. Travelers who have time to explore small town Belgium might consider the **Rail Pass** (€65), which allows 10 single trips within the country over a six-month period, though it is invalid in July, August, and on weekends. For travelers under 26, the similar **Go Pass** (€43) carries the same restrictions. Both passes may be used by more than one person. **Buses** are used primarily for local transport (€1-2).

BY FERRY. P&O Ferries (UK ☎087 05 980 333, Belgium 070 70 77 71; www.poferries.com) cross the Channel from **Hull, England** to **Zeebrugge,** north of Bruges (12½hr., departure at 7pm, from €150).

BY CAR, BIKE, AND THUMB. Belgium honors most foreign drivers' licenses, including those from Australia, Canada, the EU, and the US. **New Zealanders** must contact the New Zealand Automobile Association (☎0800 822 422; www.aa.co.nz) for an International Driving Permit. **Speed limits** are 120kph on motorways, 90kph on main roads, and 50kph elsewhere. **Biking** is popular, and many roads in Flanders have bike lanes, while Wallonie has started to convert old railroad beds into paths for pedestrians and cyclists. **Hitchhiking** is illegal and uncommon, and *Let's Go* does not recommend it as a safe means of transport.

KEEPING IN TOUCH

PHONE CODES	**Country code:** 32. **International dialing prefix:** 00. For more information on how to place international calls, see inside back cover.

EMAIL AND THE INTERNET. There are cybercafes in all of the larger towns and cities in Belgium. Expect to pay €2-3 per 30min. In smaller towns, Internet is generally available in hostels for €0.08-0.10 per minute.

TELEPHONE. Most pay phones require a phone card (from €5), available at post offices, supermarkets, and newsstands. Calls are cheapest 6:30pm-8am and on weekends. Mobile phones are increasingly popular and economical (p. 33). For operator assistance, dial ☎12 07; international assistance ☎12 04 (€0.25). International direct dial numbers include: **AT&T** (☎0800 100 10); **British Telecom** (☎0800 89 0032); **Canada Direct** (☎0800 100 19); **MCI** (☎0800 100 12); **Sprint** (☎0800 100 14); **Telecom New Zealand** (☎0800 100 64); and **Telstra Australia** (☎0800 100 61).

MAIL. A postcard or letter (up to 50g) sent within Belgium costs €0.44/0.50, within the EU €0.60/0.70, and to the rest of the world €0.65/0.80. Additional info is available at www.post.be.

LANGUAGE. Belgium's three official languages are each associated with particular regions and fierce regional sentiment. Flemish, a variant of Dutch, is spoken in Flanders, the northern half of the country; French is spoken in Wallonie, the southern region; German is spoken in a few districts east of Liège. Both Flemish and French are spoken in Brussels. In Flanders, most people speak English; some knowledge of French is very helpful in Wallonie. For basic French words and phrases, see p. 1059; for German, see p. 1060.

ACCOMMODATIONS AND CAMPING

BELGIUM	❶	❷	❸	❹	❺
ACCOMMODATIONS	under €10	€10-20	€20-30	€30-40	over €40

Hotels in Belgium are fairly expensive, with rock-bottom singles from €30 and doubles from €40-45. Belgium's 31 **HI youth hostels** are run by the Flemish Youth Hostel Federation (☎03 232 72 18; www.vjh.be) in Flanders, and Les Auberges de Jeunesses (☎02 219 56 76; www.laj.be), in Wallonie. Expect to pay around €18 per night including linen with a €3 HI discount for modern, basic hostels. **Private hostels** often cost about the same but are much nicer, although they may charge separately for linen. Most receptionists speak some English. Reservations are a good idea, particularly in the summer and on weekends. **Campgrounds** charge about €4 per night, and are common in Wallonie but not in Flanders. An **International Camping Card** is not required in Belgium.

FOOD AND DRINK

BELGIUM	❶	❷	❸	❹	❺
FOOD	under €5	€5-8	€8-12	€12-18	over €18

Belgian cuisine, a combination of French and German traditions, is praised throughout Western Europe, but an authentic evening meal may cost as much as that night's accommodations. Seafood, fresh from the coast, is served in a variety of dishes. **Moules** or **mosselen** (steamed mussels), regarded as the national dish, are tasty and reasonably affordable (€14 is the cheapest, usually €17-20). Often paired with mussels are **frites** (french fries), a Belgian invention, which locals dip in mayonnaise. Belgian **beer** is a source of national pride and a national pastime; more varieties—over 300, ranging from ordinary **pilsners** (€1) to religiously brewed **Trappist ales** (€3)—are produced here than in any other country. Leave room for chocolate **pralines** from Leonidas, and Belgian **waffles** *(gaufres)*—soft, warm, glazed ones on the street (€1.50) and thin, crispier ones piled high with toppings at cafes (€2-5). See p. 111 for a guide to the best waffle stops in Brussels.

HOLIDAYS AND FESTIVALS

Holidays: Easter Sunday and Monday (Apr. 16-17); Labor Day (May 1); Feast of the Ascension (May 25); Whit Sunday and Monday (June 4-5); Flemish Community Day (July 11); National Day (July 21); Feast of the Assumption (Aug. 15); French Community Day (Sept. 27); All Saints' Day (Nov. 1); Armistice Day (Nov. 11).

Festivals: Ghent hosts Gentse Feesten (mid-July; www.gentsefeesten.be) cultural festival, with dance festival 10 Days Off (www.10daysoff.be). Music events like Bruges's Cactus Festival (mid-July; www.cactusfestival.be), draw alt-pop and hip-hop acts; eastern Belgium's Pukkelpop (late Aug.; www.pukkelpop.be) draws an alternative set.

BEYOND TOURISM

Volunteer and work opportunities in Belgium center around its strong international offerings, especially in Brussels, which is home to both NATO and the EU. Private sector short- and long-term employment are listed at www.jobs-in-europe.net. A limited selection of public sector job and volunteer opportunities are listed below. See p. 66 for Beyond Tourism opportunities throughout Europe.

The International School of Brussels, Kattenberg-Botisfort 19, Brussels (☎02 661 42 11; www.isb.be). The ISB hires teachers to positions lasting a year or more. Must have permission to work in Belgium.

North American Treaty Organization (NATO), Blvd. Leopold III, Brussels (www.nato.int). People under 30 who are fluent in at least 2 NATO languages can apply for internships. Requirements and application details available at www.nato.int/structur/interns/index.html. Be advised that application deadlines are far ahead of start dates.

BRUSSELS (BRUXELLES, BRUSSEL) ☎02

The headquarters of both NATO and the EU, Brussels (pop. 1,200,000) is often identified by its population of terminally bland functionaries. Yet these civil servants aren't the only ones who speak for Belgium's capital; beneath the drone of parliamentary procedure bustles the witty clamor of local life. These voices echo throughout the city's intricate architecture, alternately Gothic and Art Nouveau, and jabber in both French and Flemish into the waning hours of Brussels nightlife.

TRANSPORTATION

Flights: Brussels Airport (BRU; ☎753 77 53 or 09007 00000, €0.45 per min.; www.brusselsairport.be) is 14km from the city. See www.flysn.be for info on **SN Brussels Airline,** the Belgian national carrier. Trains run to the airport from Gare du Midi (25min., every 25min., €2.60) stopping at Gare Centrale and Gare du Nord. Bus #12 traces the same route (every 30min.; Sept.-June 5am-midnight, July-Aug. 5am-11pm; €3). **Brussels South Charleroi** (CRL; ☎71 25 12 11; www.charleroi-airport.com) is 46km outside the city, between Brussels and Charleroi, and services a number of European airlines, including Ryanair. The TEC Bus A runs to the airport from r. de France just outside the Gare du Midi in Brussels (2½hr. before each Ryanair flight, €10).

Trains: (☎555 25 55). All international trains stop at **Gare du Midi;** most also stop at **Gare Centrale** (near Grand-Place) or **Gare du Nord** (near the Botanical Gardens). To: **Amsterdam** (3hr.; €32, under 26 €24); **Antwerp** (45min., €5.80); **Bruges** (45min., €11.30); **Cologne** (2¾hr.; €38.50, under 26 €19.50); **Luxembourg City** (1¾hr.; €27.40, under 26 €17.80); **Paris** (1½hr.; €71.50, under 26 €36). **Eurostar** goes to **London** (2¾hr.; €79-224, under 26 from €60, with Eurail or Benelux pass from €75).

Public Transportation: The **Métro (M), buses,** and **trams** run daily 5:30am-12:30am. 1hr. ticket €1.50, day pass €3.80, 5 trips €6.50, 10 trips €10. All 3 are run by the **Société des Transports Intercommunaux Bruxellois** (STIB; ☎0900 10 310, €0.45 per min.; www.stib.irisnet.be). STIB also offers the **Carte 3/5** (€9), providing 3 24hr. periods of unlimited intracity transport within 5 days' time.

HOLD THAT STUB. Always hold on to your receipt or ticket stub to avoid steep fines on public transportation; authorities conduct spot checks.

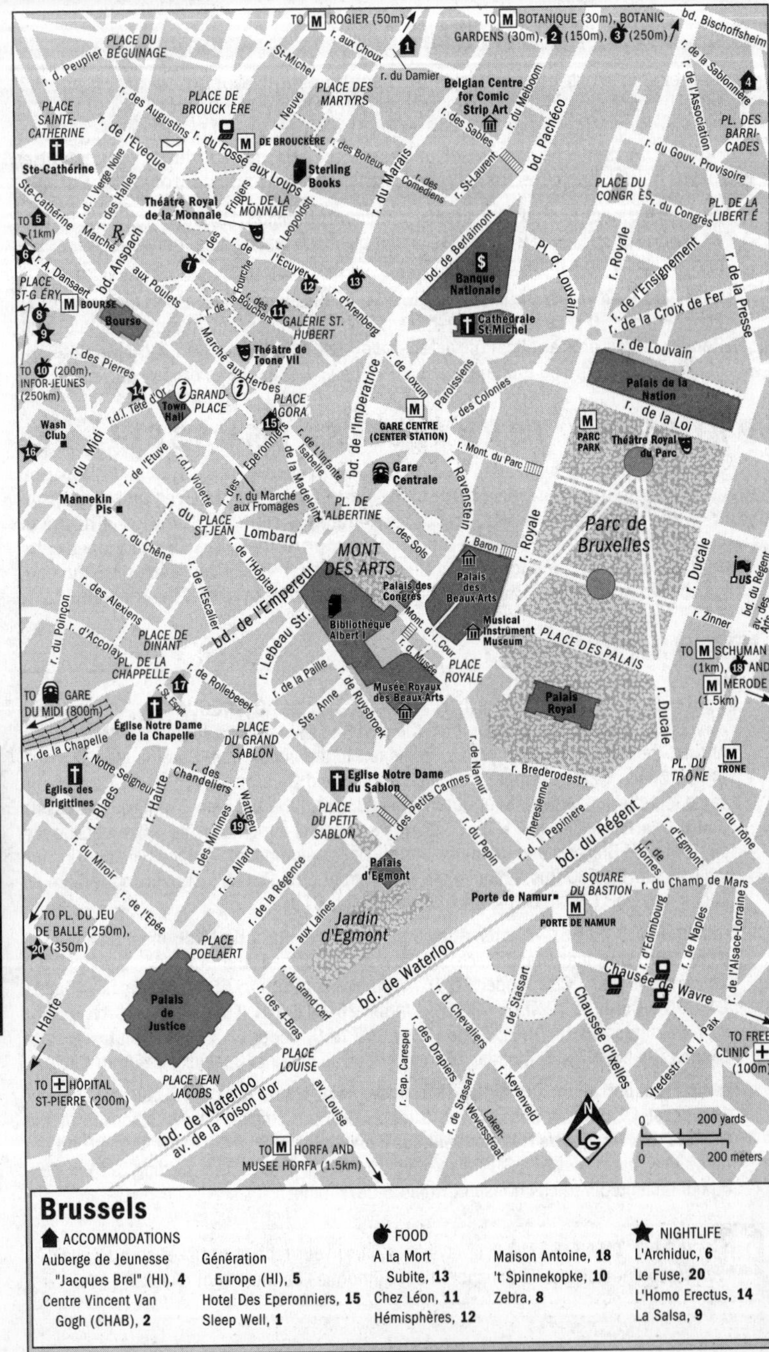
TO M ROGIER (50m)
TO M BOTANIQUE (30m), BOTANIC GARDENS (30m), 2 (150m), 3 (250m)
bd. Bischoffsheim
PLACE DU BÉGUINAGE
r. d. Peuplier
r. aux Choux
r. St-Michel
r. du Damier
Belgian Centre for Comic Strip Art
PLACE DES MARTYRS
PLACE DE BROUCK ÈRE
PLACE SAINTE-CATHERINE
r. des Augustins
r. de l'Eveque
r. du Fossé aux Loups
M DE BROUCKÈRE
r. Neuve
r. des Sables
r. du Meiboom
bd. Pachéco
r. de la Sablonnière
r. de l'Association
PL. DES BARRICADES
Ste-Cathérine
Sterling Books
r. des Boiteux
r. des Comediens
r. St-Laurent
r. du Marais
r. du Gouv. Provisoire
PLACE DU CONGR ÈS
r. du Congrès
PL. DE LA LIBERT É
r. d. l. Vierge Noire
r. des Halles
Ste-Catherine
Théatre Royal de la Monnaie
PL. DE LA MONNAIE
Fripiers
r. Leopoldstr.
TO 5 (1km)
Marché
bd. Anspach
r. des
r. de l'Ecuyer
r. d'Arenberg
bd. de Berlaimont
Banque Nationale
Pl. d. Louvain
r. Royale
r. de l'Enseignement
r. de la Croix de Fer
r. de la Presse
r. A. Dansaert
PLACE ST-G ÉRY
aux Poulets
M BOURSE
Bourse
r. de la Fourche
r. des Bouchers
GALÉRIE ST. HUBERT
Cathédrale St-Michel
r. de Louvain
Palais de la Nation
r. des Pierres
Théatre de Toone VII
Marché aux Herbes
TO 10 (200m), INFOR-JEUNES (250km)
r.d.l. Tête d'Or
Town Hall
GRAND-PLACE
PLACE AGORA
bd. de l'Imperatrice
r. de Loxum
Paroissiens
r. des Colonies
M GARE CENTRE (CENTER STATION)
r. de la Loi
M PARC PARK
Théâtre Royal du Parc
Wash Club
r. du Midi
r. de l'Etuve
r.d.l. Violette
r. des Eperonniers
r. de l'Infante Isabelle
r. de la Madeleine
r. du Marché aux Fromages
r. Mont. du Parc
Gare Centrale
r. Ravenstein
Mannekin Pis
r. du Lombard
PLACE ST-JEAN
PL. DE L'ALBERTINE
r. des Sols
r. Baron
r. Royale
Parc de Bruxelles
r. du Chêne
r. de l'Hôpital
MONT DES ARTS
r. de l'Escalier
bd. de l'Empereur
Palais des Congrès
Palais des Beaux-Arts
r. Ducale
US
bd. du Régent
av. des Arts
r. des Alexiens
r. du Poinçon
r. d'Accolay
PLACE DE DINANT
PL. DE LA CHAPPELLE
r. Lebeau Str.
Bibliothèque Albert I
Mont. d. l. Cour
r. d. Musée
Musical Instrument Museum
PLACE DES PALAIS
r. Zinner
TO M SCHUMAN (1km), 18 AND M MERODE (1.5km)
TO GARE DU MIDI (800m)
r. de Rollebeeek
r. St. Esprit
r. de la Paille
r. de Ruysbroek
PLACE ROYALE
Musée Royaux des Beaux-Arts
Palais Royal
Église Notre Dame de la Chapelle
r. de la Chapelle
r. Ste. Anne
PLACE DU GRAND SABLON
r. de Namur
r. Ducale
M TRONE
PL. DU TRÔNE
r. Notre Seigneur
r. des Chandeliers
Eglise Notre Dame du Sablon
r. Brederodestr.
Église des Brigittines
r. Blaes
r. Haute
r. Watteeu
r. des Minimes
PLACE DU PETIT SABLON
r. des Petits Carmes
r. Theresienne
r. d. l. Pepiniere
r. du Trône
r. du Pepin
r. d'Egmont
r. de Hornes
r. du Miroir
r. E. Allard
Palais d'Egmont
SQUARE DU BASTION
r. du Champ de Mars
Porte de Namur
M PORTE DE NAMUR
TO PL. DU JEU DE BALLE (250m), 20 (350m)
r. de l'Epée
r. de la Régence
r. aux Laines
Jardin d'Egmont
r. d'Edimbourg
r. de Naples
r. de l'Alsace-Lorraine
PLACE POELAERT
bd. de Waterloo
Chaussée de Wavre
Palais de Justice
r. du Grand Cerf
r. des 4-Bras
r. d. Chevaliers
r. de Stassart
Chaussée d'Ixelles
r. Haute
PLACE LOUISE
r. Cap. Carespel
r. des Drapiers
r. Keyenveld
Vredestr. r. d. l. Paix
TO FREE CLINIC (100m)
TO HÔPITAL ST-PIERRE (200m)
PLACE JEAN JACOBS
bd. de Waterloo
av. de la Toison d'or
av. Louise
r. de Stassart
Wevesrsstraat
Laken.
N
LG
0 200 yards
0 200 meters
TO M HORFA AND MUSEE HORFA (1.5km)
Brussels
ACCOMMODATIONS
Auberge de Jeunesse "Jacques Brel" (HI), 4
Centre Vincent Van Gogh (CHAB), 2
Génération Europe (HI), 5
Hotel Des Eperonniers, 15
Sleep Well, 1
FOOD
A La Mort Subite, 13
Chez Léon, 11
Hémisphères, 12
Maison Antoine, 18
't Spinnekopke, 10
Zebra, 8
NIGHTLIFE
L'Archiduc, 6
Le Fuse, 20
L'Homo Erectus, 14
La Salsa, 9

BELGIUM

ORIENTATION AND PRACTICAL INFORMATION

Most major attractions are clustered around **Grand-Place,** between the **Bourse** (Stock Market) to the west and the **Parc de Bruxelles** to the east. One **Métro** line circles the city and another bisects it, while efficient **trams** run north-south. Signs list street names in both French and Flemish; *Let's Go* lists all addresses in French.

Tourist Offices: Brussels International Tourism and Congress (BITC; ☎513 89 40; www.brusselsinternational.be). M: Bourse. On Grand-Place in the Town Hall; the official tourist office of the city. Books rooms within the city for no fee, and sells the **Brussels Card** (€30), which provides free public transportation and access to 30 museums for 3 days. Open daily 9am-6pm; Jan.-Easter closed Su. **Belgian Tourist Office,** 63 r. des Marché aux Herbes (☎504 30 90; www.visitbelgium.com). M: Bourse. 1 block from Grand-Place. Books rooms all over Belgium and offers free copies of *What's On,* published in *The Bulletin*. Open July-Aug. M-F 9am-7pm, Sa-Su 9am-1pm and 2-7pm; Sept.-June M-F 9am-6pm, Sa-Su 9am-1pm and 2-6pm; Nov.-Apr. closed Su 2-6pm.

Budget Travel: Infor-Jeunes Bruxelles, 155 r. Van Arteveld (☎514 41 11; www.inforjeunes-bxl.be). M: Bourse. Offers budget travel info for students and helps to find jobs and apartments. Free Internet for students. Open M-F noon-5:30pm.

Embassies and Consulates: Australia, 6-8 r. Guimard (☎286 05 00). **Canada,** 2 av. Tervuren (☎741 06 11). **Ireland,** 50 r. Wiertz (☎235 66 76). **New Zealand,** 1 sq. de Meeus (☎512 10 40). **UK,** 85 r. d'Arlon (☎287 62 11; www.british-embassy.be). **US,** 27 bd. du Régent (☎508 21 11; www.usembassy.be).

Currency Exchange: Many exchange booths near Grand-Place stay open until 11pm. Most banks and booths charge a commission (€2.50-3.75) to cash checks. **CBC-Automatic Change,** 7 Grand-Place. (☎547 16 16). Open M-F 8:45am-4:10 pm.

GLBT Resources: The tourist office offers the *Safer Guide* to gay nightlife.

English-Language Bookstore: Sterling Books, 38 r. du Fossé aux Loups (☎223 62 23). M: De Brouckère. Open M-Sa 10am-7pm, Su noon-6:30pm. AmEx/MC/V.

Laundromat: Wash Club, 68 r. du Marché au Charbon. M: Bourse. Wash €3.50 per 8 kg. €7 per 18 kg. Open daily 7am-10pm.

Emergencies: Ambulance and **Fire:** ☎100. **Police:** ☎101.

Pharmacy: Neos-Bourse Pharmacie, bd. Anspach at r. du Marché aux Poulets (☎218 06 40). M: Bourse. Open M-Sa 8:30am-6:30pm. Neon crosses light all pharmacies.

Medical Services: Free Clinic, 154a ch. de Wavre (☎512 13 14). M: Porte de Namur. Ignore the name—you'll have to pay. Open M-F 9am-7pm, Sa 10am-noon. **Centre Hospitalier Universitaire St. Pierre,** 322 r. Haute (☎535 31 11). M: Porte de Namur. You can also call ☎479 18 18 to reach an on-call doctor 24hr. a day.

Internet Access: A bevy of Internet cafes can be found on ch. de Wavre (M: Porte de Namur), charging €1-1.50 per hr. **Call Center,** in the De Brouckère Métro station, charges €1.50 per hr. Open M-F 8am-11pm, Sa-Su 10am-10pm.

Post Office: Corner of bd. Anspach and r. des Augustes (☎078 155 15 16; www.laposte.be). M: De Brouckère. Open M-F 8am-6pm, Sa 10:30am-4:30pm. Address mail to be held in the following format: First name SURNAME, *Poste Restante,* pl. de la Monnaie, 1000 Bruxelles, BELGIUM.

Solo women navigating Brussels are often the target of unwanted advances from male admirers, ranging from playful requests for a kiss to cruder overtures. Sexual harassment is illegal in Belgium but isolated incidents are rarely prosecuted. Consider venturing out with a companion, and see p. 43 for further tips.

ACCOMMODATIONS

Accommodations can be difficult to find, especially on weekends in the summer. Overall, accommodations are well-kept and centrally located. The BITC (see **Practical Information,** p. 109) books rooms for free, sometimes at discounts up to 50%.

Centre Vincent Van Gogh (CHAB), 8 r. Traversière (☎217 01 58). M: Botanique. Take a right out of the station onto r. Royale and turn right again onto Ch. d'Haecht, which becomes r. Traversière. Spartan rooms are made up for by the hotel-like reception, candlelit bar, and sunroom, all with a laidback vibe. Under 35 only. Breakfast included. Locker deposit €6. Linen €3.80. Laundry €4.50. Internet €1 per 15min. Reception 24hr. Lockout 10am-2pm. Dorms €12-16; singles €27; doubles €40. AmEx/MC/V. ❷

Sleep Well, 23 r. du Damier (☎218 50 50). M: Rogier. Common spaces create lively atmosphere. "Star" service includes TV and private bath. Breakfast included. Lockout for non-Star, 11am-4pm. Dorms €16-20; singles €27; doubles €48; triples €64. €2.75 discount after 1st night. Star singles €37-50; doubles €55-77.50. MC/V. ❷

Auberge de Jeunesse "Jacques Brel" (HI), 30 r. de la Sablonnière (☎218 01 87), on pl. des Barricades. M: Botanique. Relaxed courtyard with a picturesque fountain and spacious rooms, although it can get noisy at night. Breakfast included. Reception 8am-1am. Lockout noon-3pm. Laundry €8. Free Internet 7pm-1am. Dorms €18.30-20.30; singles €29; doubles €47; triples €61. €3 HI discount. MC/V. ❷

Génération Europe (HI), 4 r. de L'Eléphant (☎410 38 58). M: Compte de Flandres. Turn left onto r. de compte de Flandres, right on ch. de Gand, and your 2nd left on r. Borre. Bear left onto r. de L'Eléphant. A short trip from the city center, in a lively neighborhood. Breakfast included. Laundry €3.50. Internet €1 per 30min. Reception 8am-11pm. Dorms €18.30; singles €29; doubles €52; quads €81.20. €3 HI discount. MC/V. ❷

Hotel Des Eperonniers, 1 r. des Eperonniers (☎513 53 66). M: Gare Centrale. Choose between basic singles and spacious studios for up to 5 people, just around the corner from Grand-Place. Prices vary depending on amenities such as private bath. Reception 7am-midnight. Singles €25-55; doubles €42-70. AmEx/MC/V. ❹

FOOD

Brussels has earned its reputation as one of the culinary capitals of Europe, although the city's restaurants are often more suited to the five-star port-wine-reduction set than to the budget traveler. Inexpensive restaurants cluster outside the **Grand-Place.** Vendors along the **Rue du Marché aux Fromages** to the south hawk cheap Middle Eastern food, while restaurants along the narrow **Rue des Bouchers** offer shellfish and paella. Seafood is also available at the small restaurants on **Quai aux Briques,** in the Ste-Catherine area behind pl. St-Géry. An **AD Delhaize** supermarket is on the corner of bd. Anspach and r. du Marché aux Poulets. (M: Bourse. Open M-Th and Sa 9am-8pm, F 9am-9pm, Su 9am-6pm. AmEx/DC/MC/V.)

't Spinnekopke, 1 pl. du Jardin aux Fleurs (☎511 86 95). M: Bourse. Locals "inside the spider's head" savor the authentically Belgian, game-heavy menu in this cottage-like setting. Entrees €15-25. Open M-F 11am-11pm, Sa 6-11pm. AmEx/MC/V. ❺

Zebra, 33 pl. St-Géry. M: Bourse. Known for its cocktails, this chic, centrally located cafe and bar also serves light sandwiches and generous portions of pasta (€2-6). Kitchen closes at 11pm. Open M-Th and Su 11:45am-1am, F-Sa 11:45am-2am. MC/V. ❶

Hémisphères, 65 r. de l'Ecuyer (☎513 93 70; www.hemispheres-resto.be). With a citizen-of-the world atmosphere, this restaurant, art gallery, and "intercultural space" serves Middle Eastern and Asian cuisine amid cozy furnishings. Entrees €9-13. Open M-F noon-3pm and 6:30-10:30pm, Sa 6:30pm-midnight. MC/V. ❸

Maison Antoine, 1 pl. Jourdan. M: Schuman. Walk down r. Froissart from the roundabout; it's the brown kiosk. After 56 years, the Maison makes the best *frites* (€1.60-1.80) in town. Open M-Th and Su 11:30am-1am, F-Sa 11:30am-2am. Cash only. ❶

A La Mort Subite, 7 r. Montagne-aux-Herbes-Potagères (☎513 13 18; www.alamortsubite.com). M: Gare Centrale or De Brouckère. Tuck into a sandwich (€4-8) and enjoy the mirrored walls and gilded detail. Open M-Sa 11am-1am, Su 1-11pm. AmEx/MC/V. ❷

Chez Léon, 18 r. des Bouchers (☎511 14 15). Though it's surrounded by competitors, locals swear allegiance to Chez Léon's generous plate of *moules frites* (fried mussels; €13-22). Open daily noon-11pm. AmEx/DC/MC/V. ❹

SIGHTS

GRAND-PLACE AND ENVIRONS. Victor Hugo once called the densely statued and ornately gilded Grand-Place "the most beautiful square in the world." The buildings around the squares were built to house the market's guilds that became the source of much of the city's wealth. By night, the town hall and its soaring towers takes center stage in a swirling light show, illuminated by 800 colored floodlights. *(Light show daily late June to Aug. and Dec. around 10:30pm. Town hall tours €3, students €2.50.)* You'll find an introduction to Brussels's famed beers at the **Belgian Brewer's Museum,** left of the town hall. *(10 Grand-Place. ☎511 49 87; www.beerparadise.be. Open daily 10am-5pm. €4.)* Nearby, the **Museum of Cocoa and Chocolate** tells the story of Belgium's other renowned food export. *(11 r. de la Tête d'Or. ☎514 20 48; www.mucc.be. Open July-Aug. daily 10am-4:30pm; low season closed M. €5, students €4.)* Three blocks behind the town hall, on the corner of r. de l'Etuve and r. du Chêne, is Brussels's most giggled-at sight, the **Mannekin Pis,** a tiny statue of a boy with an apparently gargantuan bladder peeing continuously. Local legend has it that the statue commemorates a boy who defused a bomb destined for the Grand-Place. In reality, the fountain was installed to supply the neighborhood with drinking water during the reign of Archduke Albert and Archduchess Isabelle. Locals have created hundreds of outfits for him, with strategically placed holes for his you-know-what. In the lavish **Galeries St-Hubert** arcade, one block behind Grand-Place, you can window-shop for everything from haute couture to marzipan frogs. Just north of Gare Centrale, the **Cathédrale St-Michel et Ste-Gudule** hosts royal affairs under its ribbed vaults. If you are lucky enough to be there at the right time, a pipe organ or carillon might serenade your visit. *(Pl. St-Gudule. Open M-F 7am-6pm, Sa-Su 8:30am-6pm. Free. Open M-F 10am-12:30pm and 2-5pm, Sa 10am-12:30pm and 2-3:45pm, Su 2-5pm.)*

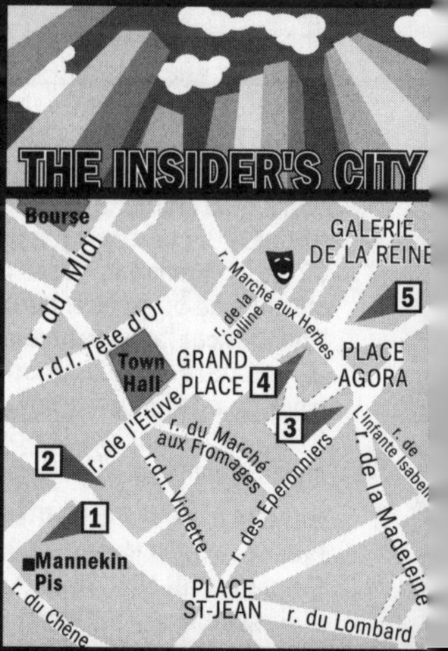

WAFFLE WALK

Instead of breakfasting on their waffles *(gaufres)*, Belgians nab the golden-brown confections from street carts as an afternoon snack. The vendors around Grand-Place serve these sweet squares day and night.

1. Start off with a *gaufre natur* sprinkled with sugar at **Funambule,** 42 r. de l'Etuve.
2. Move on to **J. Dandoy,** 18 r. Charles Buls, for a light waffle dripping with Belgian *stracciatella* (chocolate chip) or raspberry ice cream.
3. **Les Gaufres d'Augustin,** 2 r. des Harengs, serves up its delicious waffles in scrumptious chocolate sauce.
4. The dense, glazed Liège waffles at **Papillon,** 87 r. Marché aux Herbes, are even better with fresh strawberries.
5. Finish with a fluffy Brussels waffle at **Gaufre de Bruxelles,** 113 r. du Marché aux Herbes. A dollop of freshly whipped *crème de Chantilly* is a must.

MONT DES ARTS. The **Musées Royaux des Beaux-Arts** encompass the **Musée d'Art Ancien,** the **Musée d'Art Moderne,** a **sculpture gallery,** and temporary exhibits. Together, the museums steward a huge collection of Belgian art, including Bruegel the Elder's *Landscape with the Fall of Icarus*, and pieces by Rubens and Brussels native René Magritte. Other masterpiecesinclude David's *Death of Marat* and paintings by Delacroix, Ingres, Gauguin, van Gogh, and Seurat. The great hall itself is a work of architectural beauty; the view of Brussels's cityscape from the fourth floor of the 19th-century wing justifies the admission fee. *(3 r. de la Régence. M: Parc. ☎508 32 11; www.fine-arts-museum.be. Open Tu-Su 10am-5pm. Some wings close noon-2pm. €5, students €3.50, special exhibits extra. 1st W of each month 1-5pm free. Audio tours €2.50.)* The **Musical Instrument Museum (MIM),** houses over 1500 instruments; stand in front of one and your headphones play a sample of its music. *(2 r. Montagne de la Cour. One block from the Musées Royaux des Beaux-Arts. ☎545 01 30; www.mim.fgov.be. Open Tu-F 9:30am-5pm, Sa-Su 10am-5pm. €5, students €3.50; headphones included. 1st W of each month 1-5pm free.)* The nearby **Palais de la Justice** boasts a glorious view of the city.

BELGIAN CENTER FOR COMIC STRIP ART. Comic strips *(les BD)* are serious business in Belgium. This restored Art Nouveau warehouse pays tribute to what Belgians call the Ninth Art. Amusing displays document comic strip history, the museum library makes thousands of books available to scholarly researchers, and the store hawks merchandise festooned with Tintin, the Smurfs, among a cast of lesser characters. *(☎219 19 80. 20 r. des Sables. M: Rogier. From the station, take a right onto bd. du Jardin Botanique, a right onto r. du Marais, and turn left onto r. des Sables. Open Tu-Su 10am-6pm. Library open Tu-Th noon-5pm, Sa noon-6pm, Su 10am-6pm. Museum €6.20, students with ISIC €5. €0.50 to enter the reading room and €1.20 for the study library.)*

OTHER SIGHTS. The eerily illuminated Treasure Room and the Greco-Roman collection are the main attractions at the **Musées Royaux d'Art et d'Histoire;** the Gothic Room and the Chinese draw-loom exhibits are quirkily enjoyable. *(10 Parc du Cinquantenaire. ☎741 72 11. M: Mérode. From the station, next to the big arch. Open Tu-F 9:30am-5pm, Sa-Su 10am-5pm. €4, students €3.)* The **Musée Horta,** home of 20th-century architect Victor Horta, applies his Art Nouveau style to a domestic setting. *(25 r. Américaine. M: Horta. Right out of the stop, walk 7min. uphill on ch. de Waterloo, left onto ch. de Charleroi and right onto r. Américaine. ☎543 04 90; www.hortamuseum.be. Open Tu-Su 2-5:30pm. €5, students €3.70.)*

BELGIUM

ENTERTAINMENT AND NIGHTLIFE

The weekly *What's On*, part of the *Bulletin* newspaper and free at the tourist office, contains information on cultural events. The **Théâtre Royal de la Monnaie,** on pl. de la Monnaie, is renowned worldwide for its opera and ballet. (M: de Brouckère. ☎229 12 00, tickets 70 233 939; www.lamonnaie.be. Tickets from €8.) The **Théâtre Royal de Toone VII,** 21 Petite r. des Bouchers, stages marionette performances, a distinctly Belgian art form. (☎513 54 86. Shows in French; English available for groups upon request. F-Sa 8:30pm, occasionally Tu-Th. €10, students €7.) The rebellious **Nova,** 3 r. d'Arenberg, screens foreign, independent, and experimental films. A free "Open Screen" the last Thursday of every month at 8:30pm, allows filmmakers to project a 15min. piece. (☎511 24 77; www.nova-cinema.com. €5, students €3.50.)

On summer nights, **Grand-Place** and the **Bourse** spark to life with street performances and live concerts. *All the Fun*, available at the tourist office, lists the newest clubs and bars. On **Place St-Géry,** patios are jammed with a laidback crowd of students and backpackers. **Zebra** (p. 110) and a host of other bars are lively until late. **L'Archiduc,** 6 r. Antoine Dansaert, unites occasional live jazz, mixed drinks (€7-8), and a horseshoe-shaped Art Deco balcony for a cool vibe. (☎512 06 52. Open daily 4pm-late.) For throbbing techno amid a sea of people, all roads lead to **Le Fuse,** 208 r. Blaes. (☎511 97 89; www.fuse.be. Cover €4 before midnight, €8 after. Open daily 10pm-late.) Take it down a notch at **La Salsa,** 9 r. Borgval, with daily salsa lessons. (Lessons 8-10pm. Prices vary, F free. Open daily 8pm-late.) **Gay nightlife** centers around r. des Pierres and r. du Marché au Charbon, next to Grand-Place. **L'Homo Erectus,** 57 r. des Pierres, is popular, even on Monday nights. (☎514 74 93; www.lhomoerectus.com. Open M-F noon-5am, Sa-Su 3pm-late.)

DAYTRIP FROM BRUSSELS: MECHELEN (MALINES)

The residents of Mechelen (pop. 78,000) are nicknamed the Moon Exinguishers *(Maneblussers)* for once mistaking fog and a red moon for a fire in the tower of **St-Rombouts Tower and Cathedral.** Today, the cathedral's tower holds two 49-bell carillons and is home to the world's foremost bell-ringing school. (**Carillon recitals** June-Sept. daily 8:30pm.) To reach St-Rombouts, walk down Consciencestr. from Centraal Station to the Grote Markt. (Cathedral open daily 9:30am-5:30pm; low season until 4:30pm. Tower climb and tour July-Aug. daily 7pm, Sa-Su also 2:15pm; June and Sept. M 7pm, Sa-Su 2:15pm. €5.) Nearby, the 15th-century **Church of St. John boasts** Rubens's magnificent triptych *The Adoration of the Magi* as well as a host of lesser works. From the Grote Markt, walk down Fr. de Merodestr. and turn left onto St-Janstr. (Open Tu-Su 1:30-5:30pm; low season until 4:30pm.) To reach the **Jewish Museum of Deportation and Resistance,** 153 Goswin de Stassartstr., follow Wollemarkt from behind St. Rumbouts until it becomes Goswin de Stassartstr. The museum is housed in 18th-century barracks that were used as a holding pen for Jews en route to Auschwitz-Birkenau. It can be difficult to find; look for the sign on the right side of the apartment complex that shares the converted barracks. (Open M-Th and Su 10am-5pm, F 10am-1pm. Free.) Sample *mechelse koekoek* (spiced chicken braised in beer), or mild white asparagus grown locally during the springtime at cafes around the **Grote Markt. Trains** arrive from Antwerp (20min., 5 per hr., €3.10) and Brussels (20min., 5 per hr., €3.60). The **tourist office** is in the corner of the Grote Markt. (☎015 29 76 55; www.mechelen.be. Open April to mid-Dec. M 9:30am-7pm, Tu-F 9:30am-5:30pm, Sa-Su 10am-4:30pm; mid-Dec. to Mar. M-F 9:30am-4:30pm, Sa-Su 10:30am-3:30pm.)

THE REAL DEAL. Skip the boring trip to Waterloo, the location of the famous battle. Hordes of tourists bear down on the site's unimaginatively displayed artifacts, ensuring that your trip to this historic battlefield will lack even a semblance of meaning. If you really must see Waterloo, take Bus W from the Gare du Midi (1hr., 2 per hr., €2.40-3). The tourist office is at 218 ch. de Bruxelles. (☎354 99 10; www.waterloo-tourisme.be. Open daily Apr.-Sept. 9:30am-6:30pm; Oct.-Mar. 10:30am-5pm.)

BELGIUM

FLANDERS (VLAANDEREN)

Flanders, the moneyed, Flemish-speaking half of Belgium, spans quaint cities and a coastline firmly in the grip of the leisure industry. Ports created great prosperity through trade in linen, wool, and diamonds. Over time, rivers have silted in, closing off former sources of wealth. Tourism buoys the region's economy, although its workforce continues to innovate in fields from biotechnology to graphic design.

BRUGES (BRUGGE) ☎50

Famed for its relationship with painter Jan van Eyck, Bruges (pop. 116,000) is Belgium's most touristed city, and arguably its most romantic. Canals carve through rows of stone houses and streets en route to the breathtaking Gothic Markt. The city remains one of the best examples of Northern Renaissance architecture, although rows of sleek wind turbines are visible behind traditional windmills.

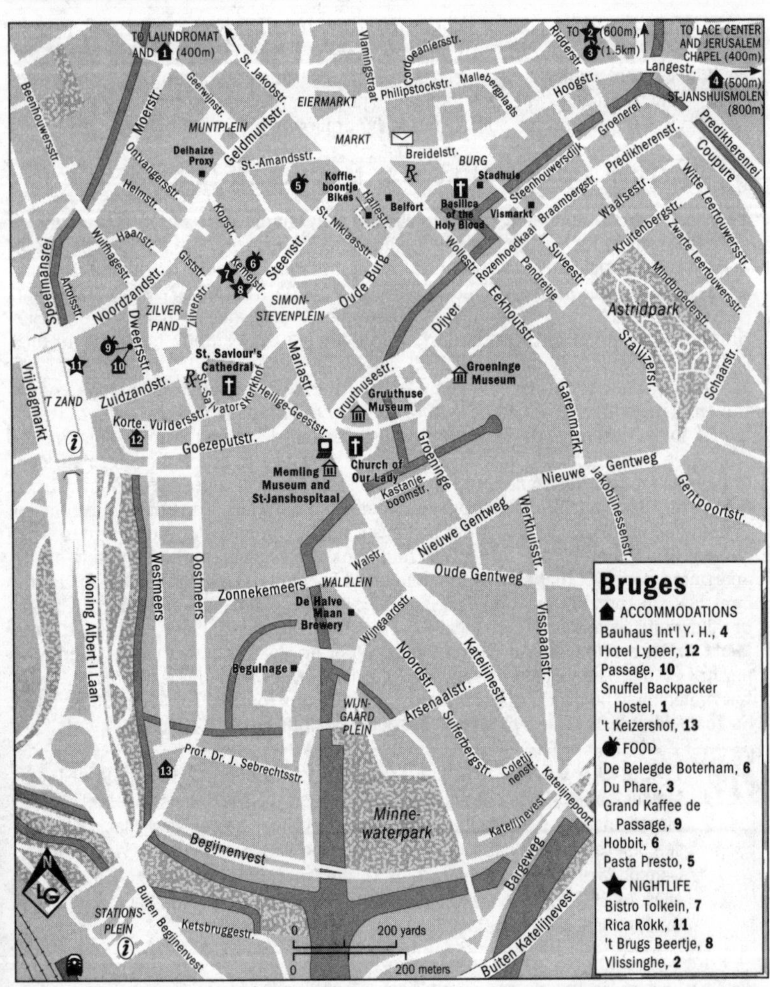

TRANSPORTATION

Trains leave from the Stationsplein, a 15min. walk south of the city. (☎38 23 82. Open daily 4:30am-11pm.) Trains head to: Antwerp (1½hr., 2 per hr., €11.90); Brussels (1hr., 1-3 per hr., €11.30); Ghent (40min., 1-2 per hr., €5.10); Knokke (20min., every hr., €2.90); Ostend (13min., 3 per hr., €3.20).

ORIENTATION AND PRACTICAL INFORMATION

Bruges is enclosed by a circular canal. The main train station, **Stationsplein,** is south of the canal. The historic district is walkable; bikes are popular for the countryside. The **Belfort** (belfry) presides over the **Markt.** Locals consider the windmill-lined **Kruisvestraat** and **Minnewater Park** two of the most beautiful spots in Bruges.

Tourist Office: In and Uit, 't Zand 34 (☎44 86 86; www.brugge.be). From train station, go left to 't Zand; walk 10min.; office is in red concert hall. Books rooms for €2.50 service fee and €20 deposit, and sells **maps** (€0.20) and **info guides** (€1). Free **Internet.** Open daily 10am-6pm, Th until 8pm. Branch office at the **train station.** Open Apr.-Sept. Tu-Sa 10am-1pm and 2-6pm; Oct.-Mar. Tu-Sa 9:30am-12:30pm and 1-5pm.

Tours: Tourist office provides maps for self-guided walking tours. 5 companies offer **boat tours** of Bruges's canals, otherwise inaccessible corners of the city (Mar.-Nov., every 30min. 10am-6pm, €5.70); ask for info at tourist office. **QuasiMundo Tours** offers 3 **bike tours** which depart daily from the Burg, all of which include a drink in a pub. (☎33 07 75; www.quasimundo.com. Tours Mar.-Oct. €20, under 26 €18.) **Pink Bear Bicycle Company** leads a tour of Bruges and countryside; departs 10:30am from underneath belfry in Markt. (☎61 66 86; www.pinkbear.freeservers.com. €18, under 26 €16.)

Luggage Storage: At the train station. €2.50-3.50.

Laundromat: Belfort, Ezelstr. 51. Wash €3-6, dry €1. Open daily 7am-10pm.

Bike Rental: Train station (☎30 23 28). €6.50 per half-day, €9.50 per day. €20 deposit. **Koffieboontje,** Hallestr. 4 (☎33 80 27), right of the belfry. €7 per 4hr.; €10 per day, students €7. Open daily 9am-10pm. Some hostels rent bikes. €5-9 per day.

Emergency: ☎100.

Police: Hauwerstr. 7 (☎44 89 30). In emergency, dial ☎101.

Pharmacies: Apotheek Dryepondt, Wollestr. 7. Open M-F 9am-12:30pm and 2-6:30pm, Sa until 6pm. **Apotheek K. Dewolf/Fevery-Dewitte,** Zuidzandstr. 1. Open M-F 9am-12:30pm and 2-6:30pm, Sa until 6pm.

Hospitals: A. Z. St-Jan (☎45 21 11; not to be confused with Oud St-Janshospitaal, a museum). St-Lucas (☎36 91 11). St-Franciscus Xaveriuskliniek (☎47 04 70). Call tourist office for doctors on call.

Internet Access: Coffee Link, Mariastr. 38 (☎34 99 73), in the Oud St-Janshospitaal. €1.25 for 1st 15min., €0.07 per min. thereafter. Open M noon-6pm, Tu-Sa 10am-6pm.

Post Office: Markt 5. Open M-F 9am-6pm, Sa 9:30am-12:30pm. Address mail to be held: First name SURNAME, *Poste Restante,* Markt 5, 8000 Brugge, BELGIUM.

WATCH THAT BIKE! In Bruges, as in many Flemish cities, bike lanes are marked in red. To escape cyclists' ire, pedestrians should avoid these areas.

BELGIUM

ACCOMMODATIONS

Despite Bruges's popularity, reasonably priced accommodations are available just blocks from the city center. Reserve in advance for weekend stays.

Passage, Dweersstr. 26 (☎34 02 32; www.passagebruges.com). Ideal location, friendly service, great rooms, and popular cafe. No locks on doors, but safes are available. Free beer with dinner. Breakfast €3. Internet €1 per 15min. Reception 9am-midnight. Dorms €12; singles €25-40; doubles €40-60; triples and quads €60. AmEx/DC/MC/V. ❷

Snuffel Backpacker Hostel, Ezelstr. 47-49 (☎33 31 33; www.snuffel.be). Bus #3 or 13 to after Markt, then 1st left. Free tours. Serves own beer (€2) in on-site bar. Bike rental €6 per day. Breakfast €3. Linen €2. €5 key deposit. Internet €1 per 30min. Reception 8am-midnight. Dorms €13; doubles €34; quads €60. AmEx/MC/V. ❷

Hotel Lybeer, Korte Vuldersstr. 31 (☎33 43 55; hotellybeer@hotmail.com). Old-fashioned charm in a great location. Breakfast included. Free Internet. Reception 7:30am-11pm. Singles €25-38; doubles €45-55; triples €56-75; quads €90. AmEx/MC/V. ❸

Bauhaus International Youth Hostel and Hotel, Langestr. 133-137 (☎34 10 93; www.bauhaus.be). Bus #6 or 16; ask to stop at hostel. Colorful rooms. Bike rental €9 per day. Breakfast €3. Lockers €1.50. Reception 8am-midnight. Dorms €13-14; singles with bath €26; doubles €34/40; triples €48/57; quads €60/72. AmEx/MC/V. ❷

't Keizershof, Oostmeers 126 (☎33 87 28; www.hotelkeizershof.be). Pretty, sunlit rooms on a quiet street. Breakfast included. Reception 8am-6pm; call ahead for arrivals after 6pm. Singles €25; doubles €40; triples €62; quads €72. Cash only. ❸

FOOD

Inexpensive restaurants can be hard to find in Bruges, but seafood lovers should splurge at least once on its famous mussels (*mosselen;* usually €15-22) or buy fresh raw seafood at the **Vismarkt,** near the Burg. (Open Tu-Sa 8am-1pm.) Grab groceries at **Delhaize Proxy,** Noordzandstr. 4, near the Markt. (Open M-Sa 9am-7pm.)

Grand Kaffee de Passage, Dweersstr. 26-28 (☎34 02 32). Next to the Passage hostel. Traditional Belgian cuisine in a candlelit setting. The excellent Flemish stew comes with Belgian fries *(frites)* and a salad for €9.50. Open daily 6am-midnight. AmEx/MC/V. ❷

Du Phare, Sasplein 2 (☎34 35 90; www.duphare.be). From the Burg, walk down Hoogstr.; turn left at the canal onto Verversdijk. Follow the canal 15min. to Sasplein. Bus #4 stops right outside. Jazz and blues bistro serves international fare (€10-17). Open M-W 11:30am-2:30pm and 7pm-midnight, F-Sa 11:30am-2:30pm and 6:30pm-midnight, Su 11:30am-3pm and 6pm-midnight. AmEx/DC/MC/V. ❸

Hobbit, Kemelstr. 8-10 (☎33 55 20; www.hobbitgrill.be). Order filling meats and pastas from clever newsprint menus. Entrees €7.50-15. Open daily 6pm-1am. AmEx/MC/V. ❷

Pasta Presto, St-Amandsstr. 17 (☎34 55 36). Bargain-priced Italian fare, just off the Markt. Opt for the pasta with choice of 9 sauces (€5-7), or snack on sandwiches and salads. Open M, W-Th, Su 11:30am-8pm, F-Sa 11:30am-9pm. Cash only. ❷

De Belegde Boterham, Kleine St-Amandsstr. 5 (☎34 91 31). Health-conscious spot serves sandwiches (€7) and innovative salads (€10) in chic interior or on lovingly mismatched tables outside. Open M-Sa noon-5pm. Cash only. ❷

SIGHTS

Filled with Gothic and neo-Gothic buildings and criss-crossed by canals, Bruges is best experienced on foot. Avoid visiting on Mondays, when museums are closed; if you plan to visit many museums, buy a combination ticket (€15, admission to 5).

BELGIUM

MARKT AND BURG. Medieval **Belfort** looms over the Markt; climb its dizzying 366 steps for a great view. *(Open Tu-Su 9:30am-5pm. Tickets sold until 4:15pm. €5. Bell concerts Oct. to mid-June W and Sa-Su 2:15pm; mid-June to Sept. M, W, Sa 9pm, Su 2:15pm.)* Behind the Markt, the Burg is dominated by the detailed facade of the **Stadhuis.** Inside, wander through the gilded **Gothic Hall,** where residents of Bruges still get married. *(☎44 81 10. Open Tu-Su 9:30am-5pm. €2.50, students €1.50. Audio tour included.)* Tucked away in a corner of the Burg, the **Basilica of the Holy Blood** supposedly holds the blood of Christ in an ornate sanctuary, and hosts a museum that contains a disappointing collection of paintings and clerical garments. *(Open daily Apr.-Sept. 9:30-noon and 2-6pm; Oct.-Mar. 10am-noon and 2-4pm; closed W afternoon. Free. Museum €1.50.)*

MUSEUMS. From the Burg, follow Wollestr. left and head right on Dijver to the **Groeninge Museum;** highlights include works by Jan van Eyck and Bruges-born Hans Memling. *(Dijver 12. ☎44 87 41. Open Tu-Su 9:30am-5pm. €8, students €5. Audio tour €3.)* A former palace, the **Gruuthuse Museum** houses a collection of 16th- and 17th-century tapestries. *(Dijver 17. ☎44 87 62. Open Tu-Su 9:30am-5pm. €6, students €4. Audio tour included.)* Continue on Dijver as it becomes Gruuthusestr. and walk under the archway to the **Memling Museum,** in **Oud St-Janshospitaal,** one of the oldest surviving medieval hospitals in Europe. The museum reconstructs everyday life in the hospital and has several paintings by its namesake, Hans Memling. *(Mariastr. 38. ☎44 87 71. Open Tu-Su 9:30am-5pm. €8, students €5. Audio tour included.)* To get to the **Lace Center,** Peperstr. 3A, walk down Hoogstr. from the Burg. Turn left onto Molenmeers after the canal and right onto Peperstr.; the center is through the same gate as the **Jerusalem Chapel.** Afternoon lace-making demonstrations by a brood of wrinkled octogenarians are surprisingly fun to watch. *(☎33 00 72; www.kantcentrum.com. Open M-F 10am-noon and 2-6pm, Sa-Su 10am-noon and 2-5pm. €2.50, students €1.50.)*

OTHER SIGHTS. The 14th-century **Church of Our Lady,** at Mariastr. and Gruuthusestr., contains Michelangelo's *Madonna and Child. (Open M-F 9:30am-12:30pm and 1:30-5pm, Sa 9:30am-12:30pm and 1:30-4pm, Su 1:30-5pm. Church free. Tomb viewing €2.50, students €1.50. Ticket for the tomb included in Gruuthuse Museum ticket.)* Beer aficionados will enjoy the free samples at **De Halve Maan,** a beer museum and brewery renowned for its *Straffe Hendrik* beer. *(Welplein 26. From the Church of Our Lady, turn left, follow Mariastr., turn right onto Wijngaardstr., and turn right onto Welplein. ☎33 26 97; www.halvemaan.be. Tours Apr.-Sept. every hr. 11am-4pm, Sa-Su until 5pm; Oct.-Mar. 11am, 3pm, Sa-Su every hr. 11am-4pm. €4.)* For God-sanctioned fun, wander the grounds of the **Beguinage,** home to Benedictine nuns. The Beguine's House displays furnishings typical of medieval Flemish households for a small fee. *(From Simon Stevinplein, follow Mariastr., turn right on Wijngaardstr.; at the canal, turn right and cross the footbridge. ☎33 00 11.Open daily Mar.-Nov. 10am-noon and 1:45-5pm; gate open 6:30am-6:30pm. Admission to house €2, students €1.)* The 235-year-old windmill **St-Janshuismolen** still gives occasional flour grinding demonstrations during the summer. *(☎33 00 44. From the Burg, follow Hoogstr., which becomes Langestr.; turn left at the end on Kruisvestr. From bus #6 or 16, get off right before the bus crosses the canal, and continue along the water to the 2nd windmill. Open May-Sept. daily 9:30am-12:30pm and 1:30-5pm. €2, students €1.)*

ENTERTAINMENT AND NIGHTLIFE

Bruges hosts the **Cactusfestival** (☎33 20 14; www.cactusfestival.be), a series of alt-pop and hip-hop concerts in July. The city also sponsors **Klinkers,** a free open-air music and film series during July and August. (☎33 20 14; www.klinkers-brugge.be.) Bruges has over 420 historic pubs. At **'t Brugs Beertje,** Kemelstr. 5, off Steenstr, sample one of the 250 beers. (Open M-Tu, Th, Su 4pm-12:30am, F-Sa 4pm-1:30am.) Next door, the candlelit **Bistro Tolkien** dishes out fruity *jenever* (€2), a flavored Dutch gin that packs a wallop at upward of 70 proof. (☎34 24 21. Open M, Th-Su noon-2pm, 6pm-midnight.) For a quieter night, try Bruges's oldest pub, **Vlissinghe,** Blekersstr. 2, established in 1515. From the Burg, take Hoogstr. and turn left onto Verversdijk before the canal. Cross the second bridge onto Blekersstr. (Open W-Th 11am-midnight, F-Sa 11am-late, Su 11am-7pm.) Steer clear of the tourist clubs behind the Markt. Belgian students prefer the dance floor of **Rica Rokk,** 't Zand 6, where shots are €3 and a meter of beer starts at €20. (☎33 24 34. Open daily 9:30pm-late.) The tourist office has a list of GLBT establishments.

THE LONG ARM OF THE LAW. If you're wobbling back to your hostel with a bellyful of beer, think twice before yielding to nature's call en route. Police will fine you up to €152 if they catch you urinating in public. Keep €0.30 handy for public toilets, although many of these stalls close at 8pm.

ANTWERP (ANTWERPEN, ANVERS) ☎03

Once home to master painter Peter Paul Rubens, Antwerp (pop. 455,000) has become distinctly cosmopolitan. Formerly known for its avant-garde fashions and jet-setting party hoppers, the scene has calmed down, making way for young professionals. Window-shopping in the city's gritty diamond quarter or along the Meir shows that Antwerp holds an attraction for the backpacker and the fashionista. Try to visit Antwerp on Friday; admission is free at many of the smaller museums.

TRANSPORTATION AND PRACTICAL INFORMATION. Antwerp has two train stations: **Berchem** handles international traffic and **Centraal** is the domestic station. Centraal's arches make it a tourist destination in its own right. **Trains** go from Berchem to: Amsterdam (2hr., every hr., €27.40); Brussels (1hr., 5 per hr., €6.20); Rotterdam (1hr., every hr., €16.60). For the **tourist office,** Grote Markt 15, take tram #8 (all trams/buses €1) to Groenpl. From Centraal take tram #2 or the pedestrian thoroughfare to Groenpl. The office books rooms for a small fee and provides €1 maps or information guides. (☎232 01 03; www.visitantwerpen.be. Open M-Sa 9am-6pm, Su 9am-5pm.) **Postal Code:** 2000.

ACCOMMODATIONS AND FOOD. The cozy, worn **New International Youth Hotel ❷,** Provinciestr. 256, is a 15min. walk from Centraal Station, on the corner of De Boeystr. and Provinciestr. Turn left from the station on Pelikaanstr., which becomes Simonsstr.; turn left on Plantin en Moretus, walk under the bridge, turn right on Provinciestr. Or take tram #2 or 15 to Plantin. (☎230 05 22; www.youthhotel.be. Breakfast included. Linen €4. Dorms €18.50-19.50, under 26 €14.50; singles €30; doubles €46-58; quads €78-90. MC/V.) For **Guesthouse 26 ❺,** Pelgrimsstr. 26, take Reyndersstr. from Groenpl.; turn right on Pelgrimsstr. Decor keeps guests coming back, even as prices skyrocket. (☎289 39 95. M: Groenpl. Breakfast included. Reserve in advance. Reception 8am-10pm. Singles €45, with bath €65; doubles €55/75. AmEx/MC/V.) To reach **Camping Vogelzang ❶** from Groenplaats, take tram #2 (dir.: Hoboken) to Bouwcentrum; walk away from the fountain; take the first left. (☎238 57 17. Open Apr.-Sept. Reception July-Aug. 8am-9pm; Apr.-June, Sept. 9am-8pm. Tent sites €3.75. 4-bed huts €32. €15 deposit. Cash only.)

Grote Markt and **Groenplaats** are surrounded by restaurants. **Suikerrui,** off Grote Markt, is the street for seafood lovers. At **Da Giovanni ❷,** Jan Blomstr. 8, Groenpl., a flirtatious waitstaff serves pizzas (€4.50-12) and faux marriage proposals. (Open daily 11am-midnight. 20% student discount. AmEx/MC/V.) More than 400 religious figurines accompany a meal at **'t Elfde Gebod ❹,** Torfburg 10, off Kaasrui. (☎289 34 65. Entrees €11-19. Open daily noon-2am. Kitchen closes 11:30pm. MC/V.) The **Super GB** supermarket is in the Grand Shopping Bazar; enter on the corner of Beddenstr. and Schoenmarkt. (Open M-Th, Sa 8:30am-8pm, F 8:30am-9pm. MC/V.)

SIGHTS AND NIGHTLIFE. Antwerp's main promenades, **De Keyserlei** and the **Meir,** draw a trendy crowd to their department stores and boutiques. On the western edge of the buying spree, the **Cathedral of Our Lady,** Groenpl. 21, holds Rubens's *Descent from the Cross.* (☎213 99 51; www.dekathedraal.be. Open M-F 10am-5pm, Sa 10am-3pm, Su 1-4pm. Included guided tours 11am, 2:15pm; mid-July to Aug. also 3:45pm. €2.) Take in the busy exterior of the **Stadhuis,** then hop tram #11 toward Eksterlaar to see the mansions that line **Cogels Osylei.** A stroll by the Schelde River leads to **Steen Castle,** Steenplein 1, which holds the collections of the **National Maritime Museum.** (☎201 93 40. Open Tu-Su 10am-5pm. Last entry at 4:30pm. €4, students €3.) The **Royal Museum of Fine Arts,** Leopold De Waelpl. 1-9, has one of the world's finest collections of Old Flemish Master paintings. (☎238 78 09; http://museum.antwerpen.be/kmska. Open Tu-Sa 10am-5pm, Su 10am-6pm. €5, under 25 €4. €3 supplement for rotating exhibits. Audio tours €1.50.) The **Mayer van den Bergh Museum,** Lange Gasthuisstr. 19, showcases Bruegel's *Mad Meg,* and other 14th- to 16th-century works. (☎232 01 03. Open Tu-Su 10am-5pm. €4, students €2.) The **Rubens Huis,** Wapper 9, off Meir, was built by Antwerp's favorite son and is filled with his works, including *The Assumption.* (☎201 15 55; www.antwerpen.be/cultuur/rubenshuis. Open Tu-Su 10am-5pm. €6, students €4. Audio tour included.) The **Diamant Museum,** Kon. Astridplein 19-23, a self-described "sight-sound" museum, chronicles Antwerp's role as the world's diamond center through weird audiovisual displays. (☎202 48 90. Open M-Tu, Th-Su 10am-5:30pm. €6, students €4.)

The palatial club **Café d'Anvers,** Verversrui 15, is north of Grote Markt in the red-light district. (☎226 38 70; www.cafe-d-anvers.com. Open F-Sa 11pm-late.) Otherwise, **bars** are the place to be, behind the cathedral, and around the Museum of Fine Arts. For live jazz, hole up in **De Muze,** Melkmarkt 15, or sip your beer outside. (Open daily 11am-4am.) The basement at **Pelgrom,** Pelgrimstr. 15, has the local *elixir d'Anvers* (strong, sweet herbal liqueur) doled out by bartenders in traditional dress. (Open daily noon-late.) Gay nightlife clusters around **Van Schoonhovenstraat,** north of Centraal Station.

GHENT (GENT) ☎09

Once the heart of Flanders's textile industry, Ghent (pop. 228,000) still celebrates its medieval greatness and its more recent industrial past. Buildings in the main square are a testament to its former grandeur, and each summer the Gentse Feesten brings performers, carnival rides, and rivers of *jenever* to the city. (July 15-24, 2006. ☎269 46 00; www.gentsefeesten.be.) Steer clear on Mondays, when museums close, and the two weeks after the festival, when most of the city shuts down.

TRANSPORTATION AND PRACTICAL INFORMATION. **Trains** run from St-Pietersstation (accessible by tram #1) to: Antwerp (50min., 2 per hr., €7.50); Brussels (35min., 5 per hr., €7.10); and Bruges (25min., 4 per hr., €5.10). The **tourist office,** Botermarkt 17A, in the belfry crypt, books rooms. (☎266 52 32; www.visitgent.be. Open daily Apr.-Oct. 9:30am-6:30pm; Nov.-Mar. 9:30am-4:30pm.) **Use-It,** St-Pietersnieuwstr. 21, is a great resource for budget-conscious backpackers, with maps and information on walking tours as well as free **Internet.** Check their website for a database of rooms in the city, including university dorms (€25) during the summer. (☎324 39 06; www.use-it.be. Open M-F 1-6pm.) **Postal Code:** 9000.

ACCOMMODATIONS AND FOOD. To reach **De Draecke (HI) ❷**, St-Widostr. 11, from the station, take tram #1 to Gravensteen (15min.). Facing the castle, go over the canal, right on Gewad and right on St-Widostr. (☎233 70 50; www.ghent-hostels.com. Breakfast included. Internet €2 per 30min. Reception 7am-11pm. Dorms €19.30; singles €29; doubles €50. €3 HI discount. AmEx/MC/V.) For **Camping Blaarmeersen ❶**, Zuiderlaan 12, take bus #9 from St-Pietersstation toward Mariakerke. Get off at Europabrug; cross the street and hop on bus #38 or 39 to Blaarmeersen. Take the first street on the left to the end. (☎266 81 60. Open Mar. to mid-Oct. Tent sites €8; low season €6.50.) **Oudburg,** near Patershol, and **St-Pietersnieuwstraat,** by the university, have inexpensive kebab and pita joints. **Magazijn ❷**, Penitentenstr. 24, has hearty fare, including vegetarian options. (☎234 07 08. Open M-Th and Sa-Su 6-11pm. Bar open until late. AmEx/DC/MC/V.) To self-cater, stop by **Contact GB** at Hoogpoort 42. (☎225 05 92. Open M-Sa 8:30am-6pm. MC/V.)

SIGHTS AND NIGHTLIFE. The **Leie canal** runs through the city and wraps around the **Gravensteen,** St-Veerlepl. 11, a partially restored medieval fortress. The torture museum inside will make even the strong-willed shudder. (☎225 93 06; www.gent.be. Open daily Apr.-Sept. 9am-5pm; Oct.-Mar. 9am-4:15pm. Last tickets 1hr. before closing. €6, students €1.20.) Nearby is the **Partershol** quarter, a network of well-preserved 16th- to 18th-century houses. Walk across **St-Michielshelling** (St. Michael's Bridge) for the best view of Ghent's skyline. The **Graslei** is a medieval street lined with guild houses. Nearby on Limburgstr., the elaborate **St-Baafskathedraal** holds Hubert and Jan van Eyck's many-paneled *Adoration of the Mystic Lamb* and Rubens's *St. Bavo's Entrance into the Monastery of Ghent,* as well as a temporary display from the Museum of Fine Arts. (Cathedral and crypt open daily Apr.-Oct. 8:30am-6pm; Nov.-Mar. 8:30am-5pm. *Mystic Lamb* exhibit open Apr.-Oct. M-Sa 9:30am-5pm, Su 1-4:30pm; Nov.-Mar. M-Sa 10:30am-4pm, Su 1-3:30pm.

Cathedral and crypt free. *Mystic Lamb* exhibit €3. Audio tour included.) The **St-Niklaaskerk,** where rich merchants once worshipped, was built with limestone drawn from quarries along the Schelde River. (☎225 37 00. Open M 2:30-5pm, Tu-Su 10am-5pm. Free.) The **Design Museum,** on Jan Breydelstr., has a large collection of Rococo and Art Nouveau designs. (☎267 99 99; www.design.museum.gent.be. Open Tu-Su 10am-6pm. €2.50, students €1.20.) **Stedelijk Museum voor Actuele Kunst (SMAK),** in Citadel Park, regularly rotates its collection of cutting-edge modern art. (☎240 76 01; www.smak.be. Open Tu-Su 10am-6pm. €5, students €3.80.)

Korenmarkt and **Vrijdagmarkt** are filled with restaurants and pubs. Use-It's guide to nightlife can direct you to live music almost every night of the week. One popular haunt is the dimly lit **Charlatan,** Vlasmarkt 6, which features live bands every Thursday and Sunday, and a nightly DJ. (www.charlatan.be. Open Tu-Su 7pm-7am.) For GLBT nightlife options, consult Use-It's *Ghent Gay Map* or head to the **Foyer Casa Rosa,** Kammerstr. 22/Belfortstr. 39, a combination infocenter and bar. (☎269 28 16; www.casarosa.be. Open M-F 3pm-1am, Sa-Su until 2am.)

YPRES (IEPER) ☎57

Famous for its poppy-filled, cross-lined fields, Ypres and the surrounding area continue to bear witness to their role in WWI. What the Germans believed would be a quick victory became a bitter stalemate punctuated by the first use of chemical warfare in Western history. Ypres (pop. 35,000) was destroyed by four years of combat, but was impressively—and defiantly—rebuilt as a near-perfect replica of its former self. Today, the town is surrounded by over 150 **British cemeteries** and filled with memorials. In the **Cloth Hall,** one of the guild halls that preside over **Grote Markt,** the **In Flanders Field Museum,** Grote Markt 34, documents the history of the war with an emphasis on the individuals who lived through the destruction. (☎239 220; www.inflandersfields.be. Open Tu-Su Apr.-Sept. 10am-6pm; Oct.-Mar. 10am-5pm. Last admission 1hr. before closing. €7.50.) Next door stands **St. Martin's Cathedral,** rebuilt from pre-war plans. It features a collection of stained glass, including a rose window given to Belgium by the British Army and the Royal Air Force. (☎208 004. Free.) Across the Markt, the names of 54,896 British soldiers lost in the trenches are inscribed on the **Menin Gate.** At 8pm each evening, the **Last Post** bugle ceremony honors those who defended Ypres. From Menin Gate, take the **Rose Coombs Walk** along the moat to the nearby **Ramparts Cemetery,** where crosses line the river. The battlefields are an easy 3-4km **bike** ride from town.

BELGIUM

B&B Nooit Gedacht ❸, Ligywijk 129, provides modern luxuries. From Grote Markt, walk through Menin Gate and continue 7min. Turn right on Ligywijk, take the first left, and the first right. (☎20 84 00. Free Internet. Singles €27; doubles €45; triples €65. Cash only.) Spend a more rustic night at **Camping Jeugdstadion ❶,** 16 Leopold III laan. (☎21 72 82; www.jeugdstadion.be. Bike rental €6 per day. Tent sites €4.50. 4-bed huts with kitchenette €32. Open Mar.-Oct.) Restaurants line the Grote Markt. Locals single out **Old Tom ❹,** Grote Markt 8, for its menu and large portions. (☎20 15 41. Entrees €9-20. Open M-Tu and Th-Su noon-2:30pm and 6-9:30pm. AmEx/DC/MC/V.) Free chocolate is available in the square; try **Vandaele,** Grote Markt 9. (☎20 03 87. Open Tu-Su 9:30am-7pm. AmEx/DC/MC/V.) **Super GB,** Vandepeereboompl. 15, has groceries. (☎20 29 35. Open M-Sa 9am-7pm.) **Trains** run to: Bruges (2hr., every hr., €9.70); Brussels (1½hr., every hr., €14); Ghent (1¼hr., every hr., €9.20). The **tourist office** is in the Cloth Hall. Head down Stationsstr.; turn left on Tempelstr., then right on Boterstr. (☎239 220; www.ieper.be. Open Apr.-Sept. M-Sa 9am-6pm, Su 10am-6pm; Oct.-Mar. M-Sa 9am-5pm, Su 10am-5pm.)

WALLONIE

Wallonie, the French-speaking region of Belgium, is less wealthy than its Flemish neighbor, but its small towns and stunning grottoes reveal a more relaxed side of the country. In the province of Namur, visitors sample local brews or head out to hiking trails and river expeditions in the nearby Ardennes. Nature-lovers will want to spend at least a night here, but those pressed for time can enjoy the scenery from trains heading to Brussels, Luxembourg City, or Paris.

LIÈGE (LUIK) ☎041

Industrial Liège (pop. 200,000), the largest city in Wallonie, is often dismissed as a mere transportation hub, but its cutting edge art scene and night-owl student hangouts temper the city's nondescript reputation. The **Coeur Historique** (Historic Heart) is a knot of alleyways and medieval architecture at the center of the city. There you'll find the **Musée de L'Art Wallon,** 86 Féronstrée, a collection of Belgian art dating back to the Renaissance, including several works by Magritte. (☎221 92 31. Open Tu-Sa 1-6pm, Su 11am-4:30pm. €3.80, students €2.50.) Turn right on Féronstrée and left at the Pl. du Nord to reach the **Montagne de Bueren.** Scale the steep steps for a view of the city. From Féronstrée, turn left on r. Léopold and right on r. de la Cathédrale (15min.) to reach the Gothic naves of the **Cathédrale de St-Paul.** (☎232 61 32. Cathedral open daily 8am-noon and 2-5pm. Treasure room open Tu-Su 2-5pm. Tour 3pm. Cathedral free. Treasure room €4, students €2.50.) Across the Meuse River, a large island makes up the working-class neighborhood of **Outremeuse.** The island is home to the **Musée d'Art Moderne et d'Art Contemporain (MAMAC),** 3 Parc de la Boverie, which showcases works by Gauguin and Chagall and will host an exhibit of Lambert Lombard's work in spring 2006. To reach the museum and the remains of the 1905 World's Fair, cross any bridge, turn right, and follow the river until you reach the Parc de la Boverie. (☎343 04 03; www.mamac.org. Open Tu-Sa 1-6pm, Su 11am-4:30pm. €3.80, students €2.50.) **Flea markets** are big on weekends. **La Batte** is the oldest and largest in Belgium, with stalls stretching 4km around Quai Roosevelt and Quai de Maastricht. (Open Su 8am-2pm.) At night, students from the University of Liège pack the streets, in **Le Carré**—a pedestrian area with narrow, bar-lined streets bisected by r. du Pot-d'Or.

The modern **Auberge Georges Simenon de Jeunesse de Liège (HI) ❷,** 2 r. Georges Simenon, is across the Pont des Arches from the Coeur Historique. Take bus #4 from the station and get off at Auberge Simenon. (☎344 56 89. Breakfast included. Laundry €6. Reception 7:30am-1am. Dorms €19.30; singles €28; doubles €45. €3 HI discount. MC/V.) Steer clear of the expensive fare on r. Roture in favor of hole-in-the wall pita joints. **Newave à la Passerelle ❷,** 13 bvd. Saucy, serves vegetarian couscous for €6. (☎341 15 66. Open M-F noon-9pm, Su noon-5pm. Cash only.) Pick up **groceries** at Colruyt, r. Gaston Grégoire. (Open M-F 9am-8pm, Sa 9am-7pm.) **Trains** run to: Brussels (1½hr., 2-5 per hr., €11.40); Maastricht (30min.; every hr.; €7.20). For the **tourist office,** 92 Féronstrée, take bus #1 or 4. (☎221 92 21; www.liege.be. Open M-F 9am-5pm.) On summer weekends, there is a branch on Pl. St. Lambert. (☎237 92 92. Open daily June-Sept. 9:30am-5:30pm.) Cyberman, 48 r. Léopold, has **Internet.** (☎222 12 48. Open daily 10am-12:30am. €0.30 per 15min.)

TOURNAI (DOORNIK) ☎069

The first city liberated from the Nazis by Allied forces, Tournai (pop. 68,000) has bounced between various empires—once a Roman trading post and later the capital of Gaul. The most spectacular sight is the 800-year-old **Cathédrale Notre-Dame,** the only cathedral in the world with five steeples. A 1999 tornado left the landmark in need of renovations and half of the building is inaccessible, but visitors are welcome as the repairs continue. (Open daily Apr.-Oct. 9:30am-noon and 2-5:30pm; Nov.-Mar. 10am-noon and 2-4pm. Free.) Climb the 257 steps of the **belfry,** the oldest in Belgium, for a stunning view. (Open Mar.-Oct. Tu-Sa 10am-1pm and 2-5:30pm, Su 11am-1pm and 2-6:30pm; Nov.-Feb. Tu-Sa 10am-noon and 2-5pm, Su 2-5pm. Last entrance 45min. before tower closes. €2, under 20 €1.) Two blocks away, Victor Horta's **Musée des Beaux-Arts** (Museum of Fine Arts), Enclos St-Martin, holds a collection of Belgian and Dutch paintings including Louis Gallait's *Peste de Tournai* and the works of Roger de la Pasture. (Open Apr.-Sept. daily 9:30am-12:30pm and 2-5:30pm; Oct.-Mar. Tu-Sa 10am-noon and 2-5pm, Su 2-5pm. €3, students €1.)

The **Auberge de Jeunesse (HI)** ❷ is at 64 r. St-Martin, up the hill from the tourist office. Take bus #4, W, or R (€1.20) from the station. (☎21 61 36. Breakfast included. Reception 8am-noon and 5-10pm. Closed Dec.-Jan. Dorms €17.30; singles €28; doubles €48. €3 HI discount. MC/V.) Avoid getting mauled by tourists by searching for food at **Quai du Marché Poisson.** Shimmy into the wee hours at medieval-chic **Hangar,** 6 r. de l'Arbalète, off r. de l'Hôpital de Notre-Dame. (Open Tu-Su 9pm-late.) **Trains** arrive at pl. Crombez from Brussels (1hr., every hr., €10.20). The **tourist office,** 14 Vieux Marché aux Poteries, is at the base of the belfry; from the station, take r. Royale. (☎22 20 45; www.tournai.be. Open Apr.-Sept. M-F 8:30am-6pm, Sa 9:30am-noon and 2-5pm, Su 10am-noon and 2:30-6pm; Oct.-Mar. M-F 8:30am-5:30pm, Sa 10am-noon and 2-5pm, Su 2:30-6pm.) Free **Internet** is available for students at **Infor Jeunes,** 6 r. St-Martin, between the Grand-Place and the youth hostel. (☎070 233 444; www.inforjeunes.be. Open M-F noon-5pm, Sa 10am-5pm.)

NAMUR ☎081

Friendly Namur (pop. 110,000) is the last sizable outpost before the wilderness of the Ardennes, and a gateway for **hiking, biking, caving,** and **kayaking.** In September, Namur hosts a multicultural crowd at the **International French Language Film Festival** (☎24 12 36; www.fiff.be). The foreboding **citadel** remained an active Belgian military base until 1978. Pick up a free copy of *Storming the Citadel of Namur* at the tourist office before taking bus #3 up the hill. (☎25 02 83; www.citadelle.namur.be. Bus runs 5min. after every hr.; €1. Open daily 10am-6pm.) Bike paths thread through the surrounding Parc de Champeau. Flocks of geese dally next to **Auberge Félicien Rops (HI)** ❷, 8 av. Félicien Rops. Take bus #3 (dir.: La Plante) from the train station. (☎22 36 88. Breakfast included. Free Internet. Reception 7:30am-11:30pm. Lockout 11am-4pm. Dorms €17.30-19.30. €3 HI discount.) Take bus #6 to **camp** at **Les Trieux** ❶, 99 r. des Tris. (☎44 55 83. Open Apr.-Oct. Tent sites €6.) To reach the **tourist office,** Sq. Léopold, turn left out of the train station on r. de la Gare. (☎24 64 49; www.ville.namur.be. Open daily 9:30am-6pm.) Rent bikes at nearby **Maison des Cyclistes.** (☎81 38 48. Open Tu-F 10am-noon and 1:30-4pm, Sa 10am-12:30pm and 1-5pm. €2 per hr., €8 per day.) **Trains** link Namur to: Brussels (1hr., 2 per hr., €7.10); Dinant (30min., every hr., €3.70); Luxembourg City (2hr., every hr., €24.20).

DINANT ☎082

Razed by the German army in 1914, Dinant (pop. 13,000) has reinvented itself as a tourist destination. The **citadel** towers over the Meuse River behind an onion-domed cathedral. For a spectacular view, climb the stairs or take the gondola. (☎22 36 70. Open Mar.-Sept. M-F 10am-5pm, Sa-Su 10am-6pm; Oct.-Feb. M-Th and Sa-Su 10am-5pm. Required 1hr. tour in French or Dutch. €6.50.) Descend into the beautiful **Grotte Merveilleuse,** 142 rte. de Phillipeville, 600m from the train station, for a witty tour of the hidden limestone formations. Bring a jacket. (☎22 22 10; www.dinantourism.com. Open daily July-Aug. 10am-6pm; Apr.-June and Sept.-Oct. 11am-5pm; Oct.-Mar. Sa-Su 1-4pm. Tours every hr. in English. €6, students €4.) Get information about **kayaking** on the Meuse at the **tourist office,** 8 Quai Cadoux. From the train station, turn right, then left, then left again. (☎22 28 70; www.dinant-tourisme.be. Open M-F 8:30am-6pm, Sa 9:30am-5pm, Su 10am-4:30pm; low season reduced hours.) Trains run from Brussels (1½hr., every hr., €10.20) and Namur (30min., every hr., €3.70). On summer Sundays, a one-way **river cruise** from Namur is also available (3½hr., €14).

HOW NOT TO BE A CAVE MAN. Small tips (€0.50-1) are considered courteous on cave tours, even though it is not customary to tip in restaurants.

BRITAIN

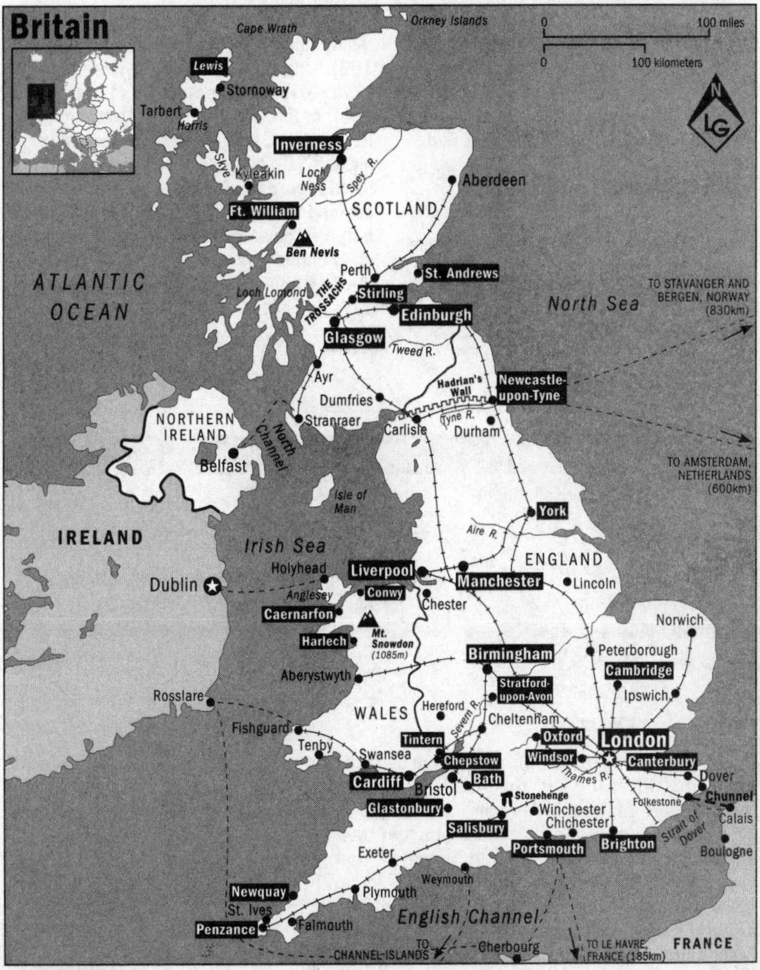

Having colonized two-fifths of the globe, spearheaded the Industrial Revolution, and won every foreign war in its history but two, Britain seems intent on making the world forget its tiny size. It's hard to believe that the rolling farms of the south and the rugged cliffs of the north are only a day's train ride apart, or that people as diverse as London clubbers, Cornish miners, Welsh students, and Gaelic monks all occupy a land area half the size of Spain. Beyond the stereotypical fairy-tale cottages and quaint sheep farms of "Merry Olde England," today's Britain is a cosmopolitan destination driven by international energy. Though the sun may have set on the British Empire, a colonial legacy survives in multicultural urban centers and a dynamic arts and theater scene. Brits now eat kebabs and curry as often as they do scones, and five-story dance clubs in post-industrial settings draw as much attention as picturesque country inns.

Travelers should be aware that names hold political force. "Great Britain" refers to England, Scotland, and Wales; "United Kingdom" encompasses Northern Ireland as well. *Let's Go* uses "Britain" to refer to England, Scotland, and Wales.

DISCOVER BRITAIN: SUGGESTED ITINERARIES

THREE DAYS Spend it all in **London** (p. 129), the city of tea, royalty, and James Bond. After a stroll through **Hyde Park,** head to **Buckingham Palace** for the changing of the guard. Check out the renowned collections of the **British Museum** and the **Tate Modern.** Stop at storied **Westminster Abbey** and catch a play at **Shakespeare's Globe Theatre** before sipping a drink in the **East End.**

ONE WEEK Begin in **London** (3 days), then immerse yourself in academia at the colleges in **Oxford** (1 day; p. 161). Travel north to Scotland for a day in the museums and galleries of **Glasgow** (p. 193) and finish off with pubs and parties in lively **Edinburgh** (2 days; p. 185).

THREE WEEKS Start in **London** (4 days), where you'll explore the museums, theaters, and clubs. Tour the college greens in **Cambridge** (2 days; p. 167) and **Oxford** (2 days), then amble through the rolling hills of the **Cotswolds** (1 day; p. 166). Don't miss Shakespeare's hometown, **Stratford-upon-Avon** (1 day; p. 165), or that of the Beatles, **Liverpool** (1 day; p. 171). Head to **Manchester** for its nightlife (1 day; p. 170) before moving on to **Glasgow** (1 day) and nearby **Loch Lomond** (1 day; p. 197). Exuberant **Edinburgh** (4 days) will keep you busy, especially during festival season. Finally, enjoy the beautiful **Lake District** (2 days; p. 177) and historic **York** (1 day; p. 174).

ESSENTIALS

FACTS AND FIGURES

Official Name: United Kingdom of Great Britain and Northern Ireland.

Capital: London.

Major Cities: Cardiff, Edinburgh, Glasgow, Liverpool, Manchester.

Population: 60,441,457.

Land Area: 242,500 sq. km.

Time Zone: GMT.

Language: English; also Welsh and Scottish Gaelic.

Religions: Anglican and Roman Catholic (72%), Muslim (3%), other (25%).

Total No. *Harry Potter* Books Sold: More than the populations of Britain, France, Germany, and Italy combined.

WHEN TO GO

It may be wise to plan around the high season (June-Aug.). Spring or fall are more appealing times to visit; the weather is still reasonable and flights are cheaper, though there may be fewer services in rural areas. If you intend to visit the large cities and linger indoors at museums and theaters, the low season (Nov.-Mar.) is most economical. Keep in mind, however, that sights and accommodations often close or have reduced hours, especially in rural regions. Another factor to consider is hours of daylight. In Scotland, summer light lasts almost to midnight, but in winter the sun may set as early as 3:45pm. Regardless of when you go, it will rain—have warm, waterproof clothing on hand.

DOCUMENTS AND FORMALITIES

EMBASSIES AND CONSULATES. All foreign embassies in Britain are in London (p. 129). British embassies at home include: **Australia,** Commonwealth Ave., Yarralumla, ACT 2600 (☎02 6270 6666; http://bhc.britaus.net); **Canada,** 80 Elgin St., Ottawa, ON K1P 5K7 (☎613-237-1530; www.britainincanada.org); **Ireland,** 29 Merrion Rd., Ballsbridge, Dublin 4 (☎01 205 3700; www.britishembassy.ie); **New Zealand,** 44 Hill St., Thorndon, Wellington 1 (☎04 924 2888; www.britain.org.nz); **US,** 3100 Massachusetts Ave. NW, Washington, D.C. 20008 (☎900-255-6685; www.britainusa.com).

VISA AND ENTRY INFORMATION. EU citizens, and citizens of Iceland, Liechtenstein, Norway, and Switzerland, do not need a visa to enter Britain. Citizens of Australia, Canada, New Zealand, and the US do not need a visa for stays up to six months. Students planning to study in the UK for six months or more must obtain a student visa. For more information, call your local British embassy or complete an inquiry at www.ukvisas.gov.uk.

TOURIST SERVICES AND MONEY

EMERGENCY	**Police, ambulance, fire:** ☎999.

TOURIST OFFICES. Formerly the British Tourist Authority, **Visit Britain** (☎020 8563 3000; www.visitbritain.com) is an umbrella organization for the separate UK tourist boards. Tourist offices within Britain, listed under **Practical Information** for each city and town, go by the name Tourist Information Centres.

MONEY. The **pound sterling (£)** is the unit of currency in the United Kingdom. It is divided into 100 pence, with standard denominations of 1p, 2p, 5p, 10p, 20p, 50p, £1, and £2 in coins, and £5, £10, £20, and £50 in notes. The term *quid* is slang for pounds. Scotland has its own bank notes, which can be used interchangeably with English currency, though you may have difficulty using Scottish £1 notes outside Scotland. As a general rule, it's cheaper to exchange money in Britain than at home. ATMs offer the best exchange rates. Expect to spend anywhere from £25-50 per day when traveling in Britain. London in particular is a budget-buster, with the bare minimum for accommodations, food, and transport costing £30-40. **Tips** in restaurants are often included in the bill, sometimes as a "service charge." If gratuity is not included, you should tip your server 12.5%. Taxi drivers should receive a 10% tip, and bellhops and chambermaids usually expect £1-3. Tipping is not expected at pubs and bars in Britain. Aside from open-air markets, don't expect to bargain.

The UK has a 17.5% **Value Added Tax (VAT),** a sales tax applied to everything but food, books, medicine, and children's clothing. The tax is **included** in the amount indicated on the price tag. The prices stated in *Let's Go* include VAT. In the airport, upon exiting the EU, non-EU citizens can claim a refund on the tax paid for purchases at participating stores. You can obtain refunds only for goods you take out of the country (i.e., not accommodations or meals). Participating shops display a "Tax Free Shopping" sign. They may have a purchase minimum of £50-100 before they offer refunds, and the complex procedure is probably only worthwhile for large purchases. To apply for a refund, fill out the form you are given in the shop and present it with the goods and receipts at customs upon departure—look for the Tax Free Refund desk at the airport. At peak times, this process can take up to an hour. You must leave the country within three months of your purchase in order to claim a refund, and you must apply before leaving the UK.

BRITISH POUNDS (£)		
	AUS$1 = UK£0.42	UK£1 = AUS$2.38
	CDN$1 = UK£0.46	UK£1 = CDN$2.16
	EUR€1 = UK£0.68	UK£1 = EUR€1.47
	NZ$1 = UK£0.39	UK£1 = NZ$2.59
	US$1 = UK£0.55	UK£1 = US$1.80

TRANSPORTATION

BY PLANE. For info on flying to Britain from continental Europe, see p. 48. Most flights into Britain that originate outside Europe land at London's Heathrow (LHR; ☎0870 000 0123) or Gatwick (LGW; ☎0870 000 2468) airports, but some fly directly to regional airports such as Manchester (MAN; ☎0161 489 3000) and Edinburgh (EDI; ☎0870 040 0007).

BY TRAIN. Trains run to Britain from the Continent through the **Chunnel** (p. 63). Britain's train network is extensive, criss-crossing the length and breadth of the island. Prices and schedules often change; find up-to-date information from **National Rail Enquiries** (☎08457 484 950; www.nationalrail.co.uk/planmyjourney) or **Network Rail** (www.networkrail.co.uk; schedules only). The **BritRail Pass,** only sold outside Britain, allows unlimited travel in England, Wales, and Scotland (www.britrail.net). In Canada and the US, contact **Rail Europe** (Canada ☎800-361-7245, US 800-257-2887; www.raileurope.com). **Eurail passes are not valid in Britain.** Rail discount cards (£20), available at rail stations and through travel agents, grant 33% off most point-to-point fares and are available to those ages 16-25, full-time students, seniors over 60, and families. In general, traveling by train costs more than by bus.

BY BUS. The British distinguish between **buses,** which cover short local routes, and **coaches,** which cover long distances; *Let's Go* refers to both as "buses." **National Express** (☎08705 808 080; www.nationalexpress.com) is the principal operator of long-distance bus service in Britain, although **Scottish Citylink** (☎08705 505 050; www.citylink.co.uk) has the most extensive coverage in Scotland. The **Brit Xplorer Pass** offers unlimited travel on National Express buses. (7-day £79, 14-day £139, 28-day £219.) **NX2** cards (£10), available online for those ages 16-26, reduce fares by up to 30%. For those who plan far ahead, the cheapest rides are National Express's **Fun Fares,** available only online, which offer a limited number of seats on buses out of London from £1.

BY CAR. To drive, you must be 18 and have a valid license from your home country; to rent, you must be over 21. Britain is covered by a high-speed system of **motorways** (M-roads) that connect London with other major cities. Visitors may not be accustomed to **driving on the left,** and automatic transmission is rare in rental cars. Roads are generally well maintained, but gasoline (petrol) gasoline prices are high. In London, driving is restricted during weekday working hours, with charges imposed in certain congestion zones; parking can be similarly nightmarish.

BY FERRY. Several ferry lines provide service between Britain and the Continent. Ask for discounts; ISIC holders can sometimes get student fares, and Eurail passholders are eligible for reductions and free trips. Seaview Ferries (www.seaview.co.uk/ferries.html) has a directory of UK ferries. Book ahead in summer. For more information on boats to Ireland and the Continent, see p. 63.

BY BIKE AND FOOT. Much of the British countryside is well suited for **biking.** Many cities and villages have bike rental shops and maps of local cycle routes. Large-scale Ordnance Survey maps, often available at tourist offices, detail the extensive system of long-distance **hiking** paths. Tourist offices and National Park Information Centres can provide extra information about routes.

BY THUMB. *Let's Go* does not recommend hitchhiking and strongly urges you to consider the risks before you choose to do it. Hitchhiking is fairly common in Britain, especially in rural parts of Scotland and Wales (England is tougher) where public transportation is unreliable. Hitchhiking (M-roads) in is illegal in Britain.

KEEPING IN TOUCH

PHONE CODES	**Country code:** 44. **International dialing prefix:** 00. Within Britain, dial city code + local number, even when dialing inside the city. For more information on how to place international calls, see inside back cover.

EMAIL AND THE INTERNET. Internet access is ubiquitous in big cities, common in towns, and sparse in rural areas. **Cybercafes** or public terminals can be found almost everywhere; they usually cost £4-6 per hour, but you often pay only for the time used. Refer to www.cybercafes.com for an online guide to cybercafes in Britain. Public **libraries** usually have free or inexpensive Internet access, but you might have to wait or make an advance reservation. Many coffee shops, particularly chains such as Caffe Nero and Starbucks, also have wireless Internet

TELEPHONE. For information on buying a **mobile phone,** see p. 33. Most public pay phones in Britain are run by **British Telecom (BT).** Public phones charge a minimum of 30p and don't accept 1, 2, or 5p coins. A BT **Chargecard** will bill phone calls to your credit card, but most pay phones now allow you to swipe credit cards directly, generally AmEx/MC/V. The number for the **operator** in Britain is ☎100, and the number for the **international operator** is ☎155. International direct dial numbers include: **AT&T** ☎0800 013 0011; **British Telecom** ☎0800 14 41 44; **Canada Direct** ☎0800 096 0634 or 0800 559 3141; **MCI** ☎0800 279 5088; and **Sprint** ☎0800 890 877.

MAIL. Royal Mail has taken great care to standardize their rates around the world. To check how much a shipment will cost, use the Royal Mail Postal Calculator at www.royalmail.com. From Britain, it costs £0.21 to send a postcard domestically, within Europe £0.42, and to the rest of the world £0.47. Airmail letters up to 20g cost £0.21 domestically, within Europe £0.42, and elsewhere £0.68. Write "Par Avion—By Airmail" on the top left corner of your envelope or swing by any post office to get a free airmail label. Address mail to be held as follows: First name SURNAME, *Poste Restante*, Letter St. Post Office, City A12 3BC, UK.

ACCOMMODATIONS AND CAMPING

BRITAIN	❶	❷	❸	❹	❺
ACCOMMODATIONS	under £15	£15-20	£20-30	£30-40	over £40

Hostelling International (HI) hostels are prevalent throughout Britain. They are run by the **Youth Hostels Association of England and Wales** (**YHA;** ☎0870 770 8868; www.yha.org.uk) and the **Scottish Youth Hostels Association** (**SYHA;** ☎01786 89 14 00; www.syha.org.uk). Hostel dorms will cost around £11 in rural areas, £14 in larger cities, and £15-25 in London. You can book **B&Bs** by calling directly, or by asking the local tourist office to help you find accommodations. Tourist offices usually charge a flat fee of £1-3 plus a 10% deposit, deductible from the amount you pay the B&B proprietor. **Campsites** tend to be privately owned and cost £3-10 per person per night. Camping in national parks is illegal.

FOOD AND DRINK

BRITAIN	❶	❷	❸	❹	❺
FOOD	under £6	£6-10	£10-15	£15-20	over £20

A pillar of traditional British fare, the famous, cholesterol-filled, meat-anchored **English breakfast** is still served in most B&Bs across the country. **Beans on toast** or toast smothered in **Marmite** (the most acquired of tastes—a salty, brown spread made from yeast) are breakfast staples. The best native dishes for lunch or dinner are **roasts**—beef, lamb, and Wiltshire hams—and **Yorkshire pudding,** a type of popover drizzled with meat juices. Despite their intriguing names, **bangers and mash** and **bubble and squeak** are just sausages and potatoes and cabbage and potatoes, respectively. Pubs often serve savory meat pies like **Cornish pasties** (PASS-tees) or **ploughman's lunches** of bread, cheese, and pickles. **Fish and chips** (french fries) are traditionally drowned in malt vinegar and salt. **Crisps,** or potato chips, come in astonishing variety, with flavors like prawn cocktail. Britons make their **desserts** (often called "puddings" or "afters") sweet and gloopy. Sponges, trifles, tarts, and the ill-named spotted dick (spongy currant cake) will satiate the sweetest tooth. British "tea" refers to both a drink and a social ritual. **High tea** might include cooked meats, salad, sandwiches, and pastries, while the oft-stereotyped **afternoon tea** comes with finger sandwiches, scones with jam and clotted cream (a sinful cross between whipped cream and butter), and small cakes. **Cream tea,** a specialty of Cornwall and Devon, includes scones or crumpets, jam, and clotted cream.

HOLIDAYS AND FESTIVALS

Holidays: New Year's Day (Jan. 1); Good Friday (Apr. 14); Easter Sunday and Monday (Apr. 16 and 17); May Day (May 1); Bank Holidays (May 29 and Aug. 28); Boxing Day (Dec. 26).

Festivals: Scotland's New Year's Eve celebration, Hogmanay, takes over the streets in Edinburgh and Glasgow. The National Eisteddfod of Wales (Aug. 5-12) has brought Welsh writers, musicians, and artists together since 1176. One of the largest music and theater festivals in the world is the Edinburgh International Festival (Aug. 13-Sept. 3); also highly recommended is the Fringe Festival (Aug. 6-28). Manchester's Gay Village hosts Manchester Pride in August (www.manchesterpride.com), and London throws a huge street party at the Notting Hill Carnival (Aug. 28-29). Bonfires and fireworks abound at England's Guy Fawkes Day (Nov. 5) in celebration of a conspirator's failed attempt to destroy the Houses of Parliament in 1605.

BEYOND TOURISM

As a volunteer, you can participate in projects from archaeological digs to political activism. Explore academic passions at prestigious institutions or pursue an independent research project. If you'd like to take an internship in Parliament or try your hand at teaching, Britain has plenty opportunities for paid work.

The Teacher Recruitment Company, Ste. G5, MLS Business Centre, 1-3 The Queensway, Redhill RH1 1NG (☎0870 922 0316; www.teachers.eu.com). International recruitment agency lists positions and provides information on jobs in the UK.

University of Oxford, College Admissions Office, Wellington Sq., Oxford OX1 2JD (☎0186 528 8000; www.ox.ac.uk). Large range of summer programs (£880-3780) and year-long courses (£8170-£10,890).

ENGLAND

A land where the stately once prevailed, England is now a youthful, hip, and forward-looking nation at the cutting edge of art, music, and film. But traditionalists can rest easy; for all the moving and shaking in large cities, around the corner there are still scores of ancient towns, opulent castles, and comforting cups of tea.

LONDON ☎020

London offers visitors a bewildering array of choices: Leonardo at the National or Hirst at the Tate Modern; Rossini at the Royal Opera or *Les Mis* at the Queen's; Bond Street couture or Camden cutting-edge—you could spend your entire stay just deciding what to do. London is often described not as a unified city but rather a conglomeration of villages, whose heritage and traditions are still alive and evolving. Thanks to the feisty independence and diversity of each area, the London "buzz" is continually on the move.

INTERCITY TRANSPORTATION

Flights: Heathrow (LON; ☎08700 000 123) is London's main airport. The **Piccadilly Line** heads from the airport to central London (50min.-1hr., every 4-5min., from £5). **Heathrow Connect** runs to Paddington (20min., every 30min., £9.50), as does the more expensive **Heathrow Express** (15min.; every 15min.; £14, round-trip £26). From **Gatwick Airport** (LGW; ☎08700 002 468), the **Gatwick Express** heads to Victoria (30min.; every 15min.; £13, round-trip £24).

Trains: London has 8 major stations: **Charing Cross** (serves south England); **Euston** (the northwest); **King's Cross** (the northeast); **Liverpool Street** (East Anglia); **Paddington** (the west and south Wales); **St. Pancras** (the Midlands and the northwest); **Victoria** (the south); and **Waterloo** (the south, the southwest, and the Continent). All stations are linked by the Underground (Tube; ⊖). Itineraries involving a change of stations in London usually include a cross-town transfer by Tube. Get info at the station ticket office or from the **National Rail Enquiries Line** (☎08457 484 950; www.britrail.com).

Buses: Long-distance buses (a.k.a **coaches**) arrive in London at **Victoria Coach Station,** 164 Buckingham Palace Rd. ⊖Victoria. National Express (☎08705 808 080; www.nationalexpress.com) is the largest operator of intercity services.

ORIENTATION

The **West End,** stretching east from Park Lane to Kingsway and south from Oxford St. to the River Thames, is the heart of London. In this area you'll find aristocratic **Mayfair,** the shopping streets near **Oxford Circus,** the clubs of **Soho,** and the boutiques of **Covent Garden.** Heading east of the West End, you'll pass legalistic **Holborn** before hitting the ancient **City of London** ("the City"), the site of the original Roman settlement and home to St. Paul's Cathedral and the Tower of London. The City's eastern border jostles the ethnically diverse, working-class **East End.**

Westminster encompasses the grandeur of **Trafalgar Square** and extends south along the Thames; this is royal and political London, with the Houses of Parliament, Buckingham Palace, and Westminster Abbey. Across the river from Westminster and the West End, the **South Bank** has an incredible variety of entertainment and museums. The huge expanse of **Hyde Park** lies west of the West End; along its southern border are chic **Knightsbridge** and posh **Kensington.** North of Hyde Park is the media-infested **Not-**

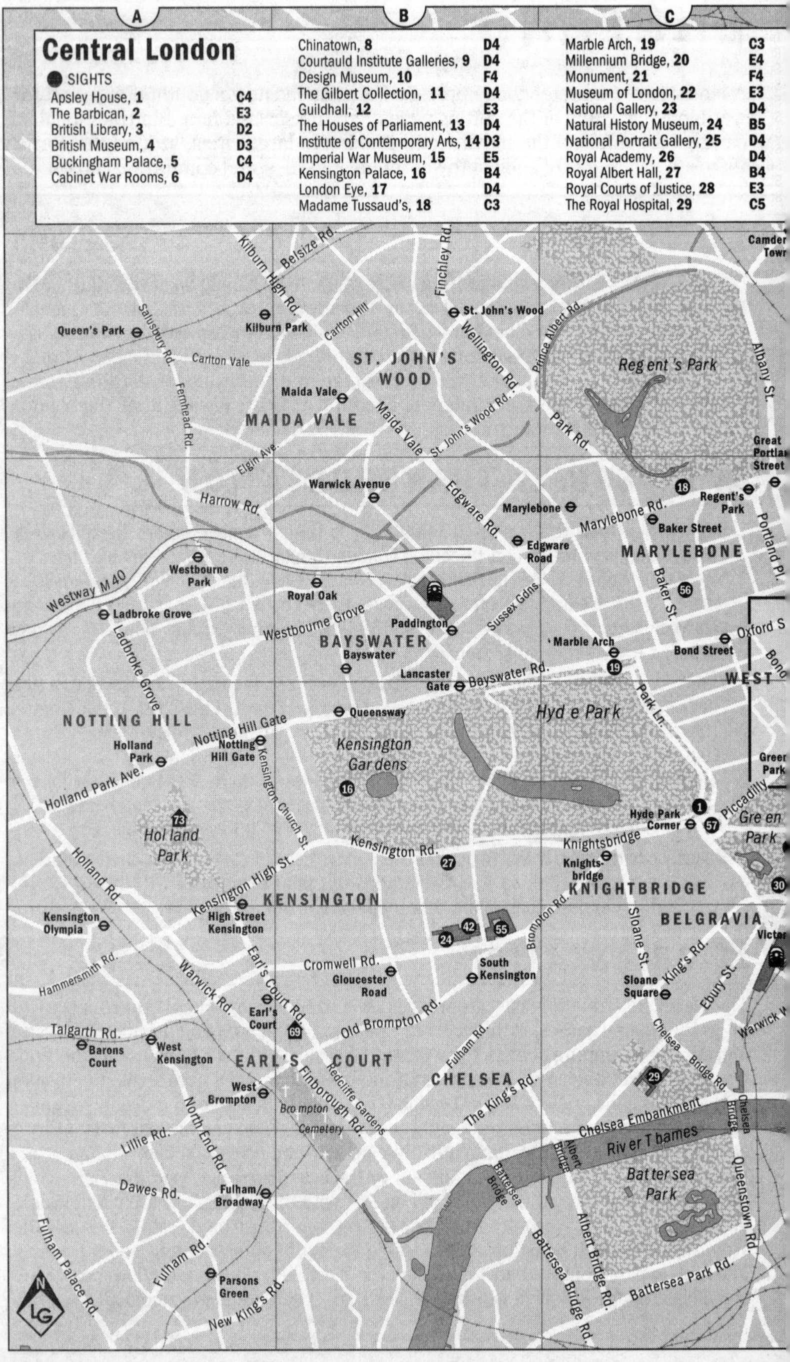

Central London

● SIGHTS

Sight	Grid
Apsley House, **1**	**C4**
The Barbican, **2**	**E3**
British Library, **3**	**D2**
British Museum, **4**	**D3**
Buckingham Palace, **5**	**C4**
Cabinet War Rooms, **6**	**D4**
Chinatown, **8**	**D4**
Courtauld Institute Galleries, **9**	**D4**
Design Museum, **10**	**F4**
The Gilbert Collection, **11**	**D4**
Guildhall, **12**	**E3**
The Houses of Parliament, **13**	**D4**
Institute of Contemporary Arts, **14**	**D3**
Imperial War Museum, **15**	**E5**
Kensington Palace, **16**	**B4**
London Eye, **17**	**D4**
Madame Tussaud's, **18**	**C3**
Marble Arch, **19**	**C3**
Millennium Bridge, **20**	**E4**
Monument, **21**	**F4**
Museum of London, **22**	**E3**
National Gallery, **23**	**D4**
Natural History Museum, **24**	**B5**
National Portrait Gallery, **25**	**D4**
Royal Academy, **26**	**D4**
Royal Albert Hall, **27**	**B4**
Royal Courts of Justice, **28**	**E3**
The Royal Hospital, **29**	**C5**

A
B
C

ST. JOHN'S WOOD
MAIDA VALE
MARYLEBONE
BAYSWATER
NOTTING HILL
KENSINGTON
KNIGHTBRIDGE
BELGRAVIA
EARL'S COURT
CHELSEA
Regent's Park
Hyde Park
Kensington Gardens
Holland Park
Battersea Park
Brompton Cemetery
River Thames
Queen's Park
Kilburn Park
St. John's Wood
Maida Vale
Warwick Avenue
Marylebone
Baker Street
Regent's Park
Great Portland Street
Edgware Road
Westbourne Park
Royal Oak
Ladbroke Grove
Paddington
Bayswater
Marble Arch
Bond Street
Lancaster Gate
Queensway
Notting Hill Gate
Holland Park
Hyde Park Corner
Knightsbridge
Kensington Olympia
High Street Kensington
Gloucester Road
South Kensington
Sloane Square
Earl's Court
Barons Court
West Kensington
West Brompton
Fulham/Broadway
Parsons Green
Kilburn High Rd.
Belsize Rd.
Finchley Rd.
Salusbury Rd.
Carlton Hill
Carlton Vale
Fernhead Rd.
Wellington Rd.
Prince Albert Rd.
Albany St.
St. John's Wood Rd.
Park Rd.
Elgin Ave.
Harrow Rd.
Edgware Rd.
Marylebone Rd.
Portland Pl.
Baker St.
Westway M 40
Westbourne Grove
Sussex Gdns.
Oxford St.
Bayswater Rd.
Park Ln.
Ladbroke Grove
Notting Hill Gate
Holland Park Ave.
Kensington Church St.
Piccadilly
Kensington Rd.
Knightsbridge
Holland Rd.
Kensington High St.
Brompton Rd.
Sloane St.
King's Rd.
Ebury St.
Hammersmith Rd.
Cromwell Rd.
Warwick Rd.
Earl's Court Rd.
Old Brompton Rd.
Talgarth Rd.
Fulham Rd.
Chelsea Bridge Rd.
Finborough Rd.
Redcliffe Gardens
The King's Rd.
Chelsea Embankment
Chelsea Bridge
Albert Bridge
Battersea Bridge
North End Rd.
Lillie Rd.
Dawes Rd.
Queenstown Rd.
Albert Bridge Rd.
Battersea Bridge Rd.
Battersea Park Rd.
Fulham Rd.
Fulham Palace Rd.
New King's Rd.

BRITAIN

The Royal Mews, **30**	**C4**
Royal Opera House, **31**	**D3**
St. Bride's, **32**	**E3**
St. Etheldreda's, **33**	**E3**
St. James's Palace, **34**	**D4**
St. John's Square, **35**	**E3**
St. Margaret's Westminster, **36**	**D4**
St. Martin-in-the-Fields, **37**	**D4**
St. Mary-le-Bow, **38**	**E3**
St. Pancras Station, **39**	**D2**
St. Paul's Cathedral, **40**	**E3**
St. Paul's Church, **41**	**D3**
Science Museum, **42**	**B5**
Shakespeare's Globe Theatre, **43**	**E4**
Sir John Soane's Museum, **44**	**E3**
Smithfield Market, **45**	**E3**
Southwark Cathedral, **46**	**E4**
Tate Britain, **47**	**D5**
Tate Modern, **48**	**E4**
The Temple, **49**	**E3**
Theatre Royal, Drury Lane, **50**	**D3**
Tower Bridge, **51**	**F4**
The Tower of London, **52**	**F4**
Trafalgar Square, **53**	**D4**
University College London, **54**	**D3**
Victoria and Albert Museum, **55**	**B5**
The Wallace Collection, **56**	**C3**
The Wellington Arch, **57**	**C4**
Westminster Abbey, **58**	**D4**
Westminster Cathedral, **59**	**D5**
Whitehall, **60**	**D4**

SEE "WEST END NIGHTLIFE," p. 151

BRITAIN

ting Hill and the B&B-filled **Bayswater.** Bayswater, Mayfair, and **Marylebone** meet at Marble Arch, on Hyde Park's northeast corner; from there, Marylebone stretches west to meet academic **Bloomsbury,** north of Soho and Holborn. **Camden Town, Islington,** and **Hampstead** lie north of Bloomsbury and the City. A good street atlas is essential; **London A to Z** (£5) is available at newsstands and bookstores.

LOCAL TRANSPORTATION

Public Transportation: Run by **Transport for London** (TfL; 24hr. info ☎7222 1234; www.tfl.gov.uk). The **Underground** (a.k.a. the **Tube**) network is divided into 6 concentric zones; fares depend on the number of zones crossed. Buy your ticket before you board and pass it through automatic gates at both ends of your journey. 1-way trip in Zone 1 £2. The Tube runs approximately 5:30am-12:30am, depending on the line. See the color maps section of this book. **Buses** are divided into 4 zones. Zones 1-3 are identical to the Tube zones. Buses run 5:30am-midnight, after which a limited network of **Night Buses,** prefixed by an "N," take over. Fares £0.70-1. The **Travelcard** is valid for travel on all TfL services. Daily, weekend, weekly, monthly, and annual cards. 1-day Travelcard from £6 (Zones 1-2).

Licensed Taxicabs: An illuminated "taxi" sign on the roof of a black cab signals availability. Very expensive, but drivers know their stuff. Tip 10%. For pickup (min. £2 extra charge), call **Taxi One-Number** (☎08718 718 710).

Minicabs: Private cars. Cheaper than black cabs, but less reliable–stick to a reputable company. **London Radio Cars** (☎8905 0000) offers 24hr. pickup.

PRACTICAL INFORMATION

TOURIST, FINANCIAL, AND LOCAL SERVICES

Tourist Offices: Britain Visitor Centre, 1 Regent St. (www.visitbritain.com). ⊖Oxford Circus. Open M 9:30am-6:30pm, Tu-F 9am-6:30pm, Sa-Su 10am-4pm. **London Information Centre,** 1 Leicester Pl. (☎7930 6769; www.londoninformation.org). ⊖Leicester Sq. Open M-F 8am-midnight, Sa-Su 9am-6pm.

Tours: The **Big Bus Company** is the biggest bus service, with multiple routes and buses every 5-15min. 1hr. walking tours and mini Thames cruise included. 48 Buckingham Palace Rd. ⊖Victoria. (☎7233 9533; www.bigbus.co.uk.) £20. £2 discount when purchased online. AmEx/MC/V. **Original London Walks** runs themed walks, from "Haunted London" to "Slice of India." Most 2hr. (☎7624 3978; recorded info 7624 9255; www.walks.com.) £6, students £4, children under 16 free.

Embassies: Australia, Australia House, Strand (☎7379 4334). ⊖Temple. Open M-F 9am-5pm. **Canada,** MacDonald House, 1 Grosvenor Sq. (☎7258 6600). ⊖Bond St. Open M-F 9am-5pm. **Ireland,** 17 Grosvenor Pl. (☎7235 2171). ⊖Hyde Park Corner. Open M-F 9:30am-1pm and 2:15-5pm. **New Zealand,** New Zealand House, 80 Haymarket (☎7930 8422). ⊖Piccadilly Circus. Open M-F 9am-5pm. **US,** 24 Grosvenor Sq. (☎7499 9000). ⊖Bond St. Open M-F 8:30am-5:30pm.

Currency Exchange: Banks, such as **Barclays, HSBC, Lloyd's,** and **National Westminster** (NatWest) have the best rates. **Branches** open M-F 9:30am-4:30pm. Call ☎0800 521 313 for the nearest **American Express** location.

GLBT Resources: London Lesbian and Gay Switchboard (☎7837 7324; www.queery.org.uk). 24hr. helpline and information service.

EMERGENCY AND COMMUNICATIONS

Emergency: ☎999 from any land phone, or 122 from a mobile phone. Free.

Police: London is covered by 2 police forces: the **City of London Police** (☎7601 2222) for the City and the **Metropolitan Police** (☎7230 1212) for the rest. At least 1 station in each borough is open 24hr. Call ☎7230 1212 to find the nearest station.

Pharmacies: Usually open M-Sa 9:30am-5:30pm; a "duty" chemist in each neighborhood opens Su, but hours may be limited. Late-night and 24hr. chemists are rare; one 24hr. option is **Zafash Pharmacy,** 233 Old Brompton Rd. (☎7373 2798). ⊖Earl's Ct.

Hospitals: Charing Cross, Fulham Palace Rd. (☎8846 1234), entrance on St. Dunstan's Rd., ⊖Hammersmith. **Royal Free,** Pond St. (☎7794 0500). ⊖Belsize Park. **St. Thomas's,** Lambeth Palace Rd. (☎7188 7982). ⊖Waterloo. **University College London Hospital,** Grafton Way (☎7387 9300). ⊖Warren St.

Internet Access: Don't pay more than £2 per hr. Try the ubiquitous **easyEverything** (☎7241 9000; www.easyeverything.com). Locations include 9-16 Tottenham Ct. Rd. (⊖Tottenham Ct. Rd.); 456-459 Strand (⊖Charing Cross); 358 Oxford St. (⊖Bond St.); 160-166 Kensington High St. (⊖High St. Kensington). Generally open until 11pm.

Post Office: Post offices everywhere. When sending mail to London, be sure to include the full post code. The largest office is **Trafalgar Square Post Office.** (24-28 William IV St. ⊖Charing Cross. ☎7484 9304. Open M-F 8:30am-6:30pm, Sa 9am-5:30pm.)

ACCOMMODATIONS

Sheets are included at all YHAs, but towels are not; buy one from reception (£3.50). YHAs also sell discount tickets to theaters and major attractions. The best deals in town are student residence halls, which rent out rooms over the summer and sometimes over Easter vacation. "B&B" encompasses accommodations of wildly varying quality, personality, and price. Be aware that in-room showers are often prefabricated units jammed into a corner.

BAYSWATER

Quest Hostel, 45 Queensborough Terr. (☎7229 7782; www.astorhostels.com). ⊖Bayswater. Night Bus #N15, 94, 148. Simple hostel with friendly staff. Continental breakfast included. Internet £2 per hr. Dorms £14-18; twins £25. MC/V. ❶

Hyde Park Hostel, 2-6 Inverness Terr. (☎7229 5101; www.astorhostels.com). ⊖Bayswater. Night Bus #N15, 94, 148. Jungle-themed basement bar and dance space hosts DJs and parties (open W-Sa 8pm-3am). Ages 16-35 only. Laundry, TV lounge, secure luggage room. Breakfast included. Reception 24hr. Book 2 weeks ahead in summer. Dorms £11-18; twins £25. MC/V. ❶

Leinster Inn, 7-12 Leinster Sq. (☎7729 9641; www.astorhostels.com). ⊖Bayswater. Night Bus #N15, 94, 148. Some decent rooms have bath. TV/pool room and small bar (open W-Sa until 3am). Safe deposit boxes, kitchen, luggage room, and laundry. Continental breakfast included. Internet £1-1.60 per hr. £10 key deposit. Reception 24hr. Dorms £14.50-17.50; singles £27.50-33; twins £44-55; triples £57. MC/V. ❷

BLOOMSBURY

Many B&Bs are on busy roads, so be wary of noise levels. The area becomes seedier closer to King's Cross.

The Generator, Compton Pl. (☎7388 7666; www.generatorhostels.com), off 37 Tavistock Pl. ⊖Russell Sq. or King's Cross St. Pancras. Night Bus #N19, 35, 38, 41, 55, 91, 243. The ultimate party hostel. 18+. Bar and well-equipped common rooms. Continental breakfast included. Internet £0.50 per 7min. Reception 24hr. Book 1 week in ahead for Sa-Su. Credit card required for reservation. Dorms £12.50-17.50; singles £35/56; twin beds £50/56; triples £60/69; quads £68/80. MC/V. ❶

Ashlee House, 261-265 Gray's Inn Rd. (☎7833 9400; www.ashleehouse.co.uk). ⊖King's Cross. Night Bus #N10, 63, 73, 91, 390. Dorms are small but bright at this laidback "designer" hostel. Private rooms include table, sink, and kettle. Continental breakfast included. Linen included; towels £1. Internet £1 per hr. 2-week max. stay. Reception 24hr. Apr.-Oct. dorms £16-20; singles £37; doubles £50. MC/V. ❷

George Hotel, 58-60 Cartwright Gardens (☎7387 8777; www.georgehotel.com). ⊖Russell Sq. Night Bus #N10, 73, 91, 390. Meticulously kept blue and yellow rooms with satellite TV, kettle, phone, and sink. Breakfast included. Free Internet. Book 3 weeks ahead in summer. Singles £47.50, with shower £60; doubles £66.50, with shower £74, with bath £89; triples £79/89/99; quads £89. MC/V. ❺

Astor's Museum Hostel, 27 Montague St. (☎7580 5360). ⊖Tottenham Ct. Rd., Russell Sq., or Goodge St. Night Bus #N19, 35, 38. Bare-bones but friendly. Under-35 only. Free DVD rental. English breakfast and linen included. Towel purchase £5. Reservations recommended. Dorms £16-£20; double £50. AmEx/MC/V. ❷

KENSINGTON AND EARL'S COURT

YHA Holland House (HI), Holland Walk (☎7937 0748; www.hihostels.com). ⊖High St. Kensington or Holland Park. Night Bus #N27, 94, 148. If location is everything, this 17th-century mansion smack-dab in gorgeous Holland Park has it made. Internet £0.50 for 7min. Breakfast included. Reception 24hr. Dorms £21.60, under 18 £19.30; singles £30; doubles £50; triples £70; quads £90. £3 student discount. AmEx/MC/V. ❷

YHA Earl's Court (HI), 38 Bolton Gardens (☎7373 7083; www.hihostels.com). ⊖Earl's Ct. Night Bus #N31, 74, 97. Bright, tidy, dorms with wooden bunks. Breakfast included for private rooms; otherwise £3.80. Laundry. Internet £3 per hr. Book private rooms at least 24hr. in advance. Dorms £22.50, under 18 £20.20; doubles £56.60; quads £81. £3 HI discount. MC/V. ❷

Oxford Hotel, 24 Penywern Rd. (☎7370 1161; www.the-oxford-hotel.com). ⊖Earl's Ct. Night Bus #N31, 74, 97. Impress your geek friends: the physicist who discovered helium once lived here. Bright rooms with minimal but high-quality furnishings. Continental breakfast included. Reception 24hr. Reserve 2-3 weeks in advance for June. Singles with shower £40, with bath £55; doubles £60/70; triples with bath £82; quads £89/96; quints £110/120. MC/V. ❹

OTHER NEIGHBORHOODS

YHA Oxford Street (HI), 14 Noel St. (☎0870 770 5984; www.yhalondon.org.uk), in the West End. ⊖Oxford Circus. Night Bus #N7, 74, 159, among others. Unbeatable location for Soho nightlife, though triple-decker bunk beds may feel cramped. Towels £3.50. Book 1 month ahead. Dorms £22.60, under 18 £18.20; twins £49.20. ❷

City University Finsbury Residences, 15 Bastwick St. (☎7040 8811; www.city.ac.uk/ems/accomm/fins.html), in Clerkenwell. ⊖Barbican. Newly renovated rooms hide behind a grim facade. Evening meals available at the City University cafeteria (£4.70). Open June 12-Sept. 10, 2006. Singles £21. MC/V. ❸

Luna Simone Hotel, 47-49 Belgrave Rd. (☎7834 5897; www.lunasimonehotel.com), in Westminster. ⊖Victoria or Pimlico. Night Bus #N2, 24, 36. Overachieving staff and attractive yellow rooms. Full English breakfast included. Free Internet. Book at least 2 weeks ahead. Singles £40, with bath £60; doubles with bath £80; triples with bath £100; quads with bath £120. 10-20% low-season discount. MC/V. ❺

IES Chelsea Pointe, corner of Manresa Rd. and King's Rd. (☎7808 9200; www.iesreshall.com). Entrance on Manresa Rd. in Chelsea. ⊖Sloane Sq., then bus #11, 19, 22, 319. Or, ⊖South Kensington, then us #49. Unheard of prices in posh Soho; don't expect this brand-new residence hall to start a trend. All rooms have bath, data ports, phone, kitchen, and laundry. Reservations highly recommended. Singles £40; doubles £100. AmEx/MC/V. ❺

International Student House, 229 Great Portland St. (☎7631 8310; www.ish.org.uk), in Marylebone and Regent's Park. ⊖Great Portland St. If the institutional vibe starts getting you down, take another look at the price. Most rooms have sink and fridge; some have private bath. Facilities include a bar, cafeteria, and fitness center (£5 per day). Continental breakfast included with private rooms (dorms £2); English breakfast £3. Internet £2 per hr. £10 key deposit. Dorms £12; singles £33.50; doubles £51; triples £61.50; quads £74. 10% ISIC discount on private rooms. MC/V. ❶

St. Christopher's Inn, 48-50 Camden High St. (☎7407 1856; www.st-christophers.co.uk), in North London. ⊖Mornington Crescent. Night Bus #N5, 20, 253. The reception in Belushi's Bar downstairs serves as a fitting entrance to this party-friendly backpacker hostel. Most rooms have private bath. Continental breakfast included. Reception 24hr. Dorms £15-23. Discount with online booking. ❶

FOOD

Forget stale stereotypes about British food, it *is* possible to eat cheaply—and well—in London. For the best and cheapest **ethnic restaurants,** head to the source: **Whitechapel** for Bengali *baltis,* **Chinatown** for dim sum, **South Kensington** for French pastries, and **Edgware Road** for Lebanese Shawarma. The cheapest places to get your own ingredients are local **street markets** (see **Shopping,** p. 150). To find all your food under one roof, head to supermarket chains **Tesco, Safeway, Sainsbury's,** or **Marks & Spencer.**

BAYSWATER

Mr. Jerk, 19 Westbourne Grove (☎7221 4678; www.mrjerk.co.uk). ⊖Bayswater or Royal Oak. 2nd location at 189 Wardour St. (☎7287 2878), in the West End. No-frills cafe with mouth-wateringly inexpensive food. Specialty jerk chicken £6.50. Takeaway available. Open M-Sa 10am-11pm, Su noon-8pm. AmEx/MC/V. ❷

Levantine, 26 London St. (☎7262 1111). ⊖Paddington. Seductive Lebanese restaurant with loads of vegetarian options and featured nights of belly-dancing and *shisha* (water pipe). Set lunch menu £5. Open daily noon-midnight. MC/V. ❷

BLOOMSBURY

ICCo (Italiano Coffee Company), 46 Goodge St. (☎7580 9688). ⊖Goodge St. Delicious 11in. pizzas for an eye-popping £3. Pasta from £2. Sandwiches and baguettes half-price after 4pm. Takeaway available. Pizzas available from noon. Open daily 7am-11pm. AmEx/MC/V. ❶

Navarro's Tapas Bar, 67 Charlotte St. (☎7637 7713; www.navarros.co.uk). ⊖Goodge St. Colorful, bustling, and reasonably authentic–try the spicy and deliciously thick lentil stew. Tapas £3-6; 2-3 per person is plenty (£7.50 min.). Open M-F noon-3pm and 6-10pm, Sa 6-10pm. AmEx/MC/V. ❸

Newman Arms, 23 Rathbone St., entrance to pie room on Newman Passage. (☎7636 1127). ⊖Tottenham Ct Rd. or Russell Sq. Dig into homemade meat pies (£8.50). Pints start at £3. Book ahead. Pub open M-F 11am-11pm. Restaurant open M-F noon-3pm and M-Th 6-9pm. MC/V. ❷

CHELSEA

Buona sera, at the Jam, 289a King's Rd. (☎7352 8827). ⊖Sloane Sq., then bus #19 or 319. "Bunk" tables stacked high into the air. Meat and pasta entrees £7-12. Open Tu-F noon-3pm and 6pm-midnight, Sa-Su noon-midnight. Reservations recommended F-Sa. AmEx/MC/V. ❸

Chelsea Bun, 9a Limerston St. (☎7352 3635). ⊖Sloane Sq., then bus #11 or 22. Relaxed diner serves heaping portions of everything from roast lamb (£11) to Tijuana Benedict (eggs with chorizo; £8). Extensive vegetarian and vegan options. Breakfast (from £4) served until 6pm. Lunch £3.50 min. per person, dinner £5.50. Open M-Sa 7am-11:30pm, Su 9am-7pm. MC/V. ❷

THE CITY OF LONDON

Café Spice Namaste, 16 Prescot St. (☎7488 9242). ⊖Tower Hill or DLR: Tower Gateway. Worth the trek. Carnivalesque decorations in a converted Victorian warehouse. Meat entrees are on the pricey side (from £10). Vegetarian meals (from £7) are affordable. Open M-F noon-3pm and 6:15-10:30pm, Sa 6:30-10:30pm. AmEx/MC/V. ❸

Futures, 8 Botolph Alley (☎7623 4529), between Botolph and Lovat Ln. ⊖Monument. Suits and their lackeys besiege this tiny takeaway joint during the lunch hour. Vegetarian soups, salads, and entrees (from £2-4) change weekly. Open M-F 7:30-10am and 11:30am-3pm. ❶

CLERKENWELL AND HOLBORN

Anexo, 61 Turnmill St. (☎7250 3401; www.anexo.co.uk). ⊖Farringdon. Funky and laid-back. Iberian lunch specials are hard to beat (£6 for 2 courses, £8 for 3 courses). M 2-for-1 tapas. Happy hour M-Sa 5-7pm. Open M-F 10am-10pm, Sa 6-11pm, Su 4:30-10pm. Bar open 11am-2am. AmEx/MC/V. ❷

Bleeding Heart Tavern, corner of Greville St. and Bleeding Heart Yard (☎7404 0333). ⊖Farringdon. Highlights include the roast suckling pig with delicately spiced apple (£12). Entrees £8-13. Open M-F 7-10:30am, noon-2:30pm, and 6-10:30pm. Upstairs pub open M-F 11:30am-11pm. AmEx/MC/V. ❸

KENSINGTON AND EARL'S COURT

Utsav, 17 Kensington High St. (☎7368 0022; www.utsav-restaurant.co.uk). ⊖High St. Kensington. Artistically presented Indian specialties with a creative twist. 2-course lunch £5-6. Open M-Sa 11am-11pm, Su 11am-10pm. AmEx/MC/V. ❷

Raison d'Être, 18 Bute St. (☎7584 5008). ⊖South Kensington. Offers a bewildering range of filled baguettes and focaccia (£2.50-5.50). Open M-F 8am-6pm, Sa 9:30am-4pm. Cash only. ❶

The Orangery, Kensington Palace (☎7938 1406). ⊖High St. Kensington. Built for Queen Anne's dinner parties and full of white, high-ceilinged stateliness. Light gourmet lunches £8-11. Afternoon tea from £7. Open daily 10am-noon for breakfast, noon-3pm for lunch, and 3-6pm for tea. MC/V. ❷

MARYLEBONE AND REGENT'S PARK

Mandalay, 444 Edgware Rd. (☎7258 3696). ⊖Edgware Rd. Burmese entrees, including a sizable vegetarian selection, £4-7.50. Lunch specials offer great value (curry and rice £3.90; 4 courses £6). Open M-Sa noon-2:30pm and 6-10:30pm. Dinner reservations recommended. AmEx/MC/V. ❶

Patogh, 8 Crawford Pl. (☎7262 4015). ⊖Edgware Rd. This tiny Persian restaurant gives new meaning to "hole in the wall." Generous portions of sesame-seed flatbread (£2) and freshly prepared starters (£2.50-5). Entrees (£6-11) could feed you for days. Open daily noon-midnight. ❷

The Golden Hind, 73 Marylebone Ln. (☎7486 3644). ⊖Baker St. or Bond St. No-nonsense "chippie" serves up fried cod and haddock (£3.40-£5.70) to a local clientele and a growing number of travelers in on the secret. Open M-F noon-3pm and 6-10pm, Sa 6-10pm. Reservations recommended after 7pm. AmEx/MC/V. ❷

THE WEST END

Masala Zone, 9 Marshall St. (☎7287 9966; www.realindianfood.com). ⊖Oxford Circus. South Indian favorites (£6-8), in addition to small bowls of "street food" (£3.40-5.50), and large *thali* (sampler platters; £7.50-11.50). Open M-F noon-2:45pm and 5:30-11pm, Sa 12:30-11pm, Su 12:30-3:30pm and 6-10:30pm. MC/V. ❷

Rock and Sole Plaice, 47 Endell St. (☎7836 3785; www.rockandsoleplaice.com). ⊖Covent Garden. A self-proclaimed "master fryer" (qualifications unclear) turns out tasty fillets (all with chips) for £8-11. Meat pies £4.50-7. Vegetarians samosas £4.50. Open M-Sa 11:30am-11:30pm, Su 11:30am-10pm. MC/V. ❷

Cafe in the Crypt, Duncannon St. (☎7839 4342). ⊖Embankment or Charing Cross. In the basement of St. Martin-in-the-Fields Church. An excellent salad bar (£6.75), freshly made sandwiches (£3.95), and warm puddings (£3) served cafeteria-style. Jazz some W nights. Open M-W 10am-7:30pm, Th-Sa 8am-10:30pm, Su noon-7:30pm. AmEx/MC/V; £5 min. charge. ❶

NORTH LONDON

Gallipoli, 102 Upper St. (☎7359 0630), **Gallipoli Again,** 120 Upper St. (☎7359 1578), and **Gallipoli Bazaar,** 107 Upper St. ⊖Angel. Spectacular Lebanese, North African, and Turkish delights. 2-course lunch £6. Open M-Th 10:30am-11pm, F-Sa 10:30am-midnight, Su 10:30am-11pm. Reservations recommended F-Sa. MC/V. ❷

Mango Room, 10-12 Kentish Town Rd. (☎7482 5065). ⊖Camden Town. The small Caribbean menu features plenty of mango, avocado, and coconut sauces. Lunch from £5.50. Entrees from £9.50. Open daily noon-11pm. MC/V. ❷

New Culture Revolution, 43 Parkway (☎017 1267 2700). ⊖Camden Town. Huge portions of noodles and steaming soups for £5. Open daily noon-11pm. AmEx/MC/V. ❶

EAST LONDON

Café 1001, Dray Walk (☎7247 9679). ⊖Aldgate East. In an alley just off Brick Ln. Dreadlocked 20-somethings lounge around the spacious, smoke-filled upstairs, while staff dole out homemade food straight from casserole dishes downstairs. Pre-made salads and sandwiches £2.50. Weather-permitting outdoor barbecue. Nightly DJs or live bands 7pm-close. Open M-W and Su 7am-11pm, Th-Sa 7pm-midnight. ❶

Aladin, 132 Brick Ln. (☎7247 8210). ⊖Shoreditch. Serving up Pakistani, Bangladeshi, and Indian food, Aladin stands out among Brick Ln.'s overwhelming *balti* options. Plenty of vegetarian dishes. Entrees £3-8.50. 3-course lunch £6. Daily special noon-4:30pm. Open M-Th and Su noon-11:30pm, F-Sa noon-midnight. ❷

OTHER NEIGHBORHOODS

Jenny Lo's Teahouse, 14 Eccleston St. (☎7259 0399), in Knightsbridge and Belgravia. ⊖Victoria. The small modern interior bustles on weekdays, but the broad selection of Asian noodles (£5.75-8) make it worth the wait. Takeaway and delivery available. £5 min. per person. Open M-F noon-3pm and 6-10pm. Cash only. ❷

George's Portobello Fish Bar, 329 Portobello Rd. (☎8969 7895), in Notting Hill. ⊖Ladbroke Grove. Fish come with a huge helping of chunky chips (from £4.50). Burgers, kebabs, and falafel also available. Open M-F 11am-midnight, Sa 11am-9pm, Su noon-9:30pm. ❶

Lazy Daisy Café, 59a Portobello Rd. (☎7221 8417), in Notting Hill. ⊖Notting Hill Gate. Tucked into an alley. A range of periodicals and a bin of toys keep customers of all ages happily occupied. All-day breakfast £4-6. Open M-F 9:30am-5:30pm, Sa 9am-5pm, Su noon-2:30pm. ❶

SIGHTS

WESTMINSTER

The City of Westminster, now a borough of London, has been the seat of British power for over a thousand years. William the Conqueror was crowned in Westminster Abbey on Christmas Day, 1066, and his successors built the Palace of Westminster that today houses Parliament.

WESTMINSTER ABBEY. Originally founded as a Benedictine monastery, Westminster Abbey has evolved to become a house of kings and queens both living and dead. Almost nothing remains of St. Edward's Abbey: Henry III's 13th-century Gothic reworking created most of the grand structure you see today. A door off the east cloister leads to the octagonal **Chapter House,** the original meeting place of the House of Commons. Next door to the Abbey (through the cloisters), the lackluster **Abbey Museum** is housed in the Norman undercroft. Just north of the Abbey, **St. Margaret's Church** enjoys a strange status: as a part of the Royal Peculiar, it is

THE LOCAL STORY

QUEEN'S GUARD

Let's Go got the scoop on a London icon, interviewing Corporal of Horse Simon Knowles, an 18-year veteran of the Queen's Guard.

LG: What sort of training did you undergo?

A: In addition to a year of basic military camp, which involves mainly training on tanks and armored cars, I was also trained as a gunner and radio operator. Then I joined the service regiment at 18 years of age.

LG: So it's not all glamor?

A: Not at all, that's a common misconception. After armored training, we go through mounted training on horseback in Windsor for six months where we learn the tools of horseback riding, beginning with bareback training. The final month is spent in London training in full state uniform.

LG: Do the horses ever act up?

A: Yes, but it's natural. During the Queen's Jubilee Parade, with three million people lining the Mall, to expect any animal to be fully relaxed is absurd. The horses rely on the rider to give them confidence. If the guard is riding the horses confidently and strongly, the horse will settle down.

LG: Your uniforms look pretty heavy. Are they comfortable?

not under the jurisdiction of the diocese of England or even the archbishop of Canterbury. Since 1614, it's been the official worshipping place of the House of Commons. *(Parliament Sq., in Westminster. Access Old Monastery, Cloister, and Garden from Dean's Yard, behind the Abbey. ⊖Westminster. No photography. Abbey Open M-Tu and Th-F 9:30am-3:45pm, W 9:30am-7pm, Sa 9:30am-1:45pm, Su open for services only. Museum open daily 10:30am-4pm. Chapter House open daily 10:30am-4pm. Cloisters open daily 8am-6pm. Garden open Tu-Th Apr.-Sept. 10am-6pm; Oct.-Mar. daily 10am-4pm. St. Margaret's open M-F 9:30am-3:45pm, Sa 9:30am-1:45pm, Su 2-5pm. Hours subject to change, call ahead. 90min. tours M-F 10, 11am, 2, 3pm; Sa 10, 11am; Apr.-Oct. also M-F 10:30am and 2:30pm. Audio tours M-F 9:30am-3pm, Sa 9:30am-1pm. Abbey and museum £8, students 11-17 £6. Tours £4. Audio tours £3. Services free. Chapter House, Gardens, and St. Margaret's free. AmEx/MC/V.)*

BUCKINGHAM PALACE. Originally built for the Dukes of Buckingham, Buckingham House was acquired by George III in 1762 and converted into a full-scale palace by George IV. During the summer opening of the **State Rooms,** visitors have access to the **Throne Room,** the **Galleries** (with works by Rubens and Rembrandt), and the **Music Room,** where Mendelssohn played for Queen Victoria. In the opulent **White Room,** the large mirrored fireplace hides a door used by the Royal Family at formal dinners. Since 2001, Queen Elizabeth has also allowed visitors into the **gardens.** *(At the end of the Mall, between Westminster, Belgravia, and Mayfair. ⊖St. James's Park, Victoria, Green Park, or Hyde Park Corner. State room tickets available at ☎7766 7300. Book ahead.)* "God Save the Queen" is the rallying cry at the **Queens Gallery,** dedicated to changing exhibitions of jaw-droppingly valuable items from the Royal Collection. *(☎7766 7301. Open daily 10am-5:30pm, last admission 4:30pm. £7.50, students £6.)* Detached from the palace and tour, the **Royal Mews's** main attraction is the Queen's collection of coaches, including the four-ton Gold State Coach, which can occasionally be seen tooling around the streets in the early morning on practice runs for major events. *(☎7766 7302. Open daily late July to late Sept. 10am-5pm, last admission 4:15pm; Mar.-July and late Sept. to late Oct. M-Th and Sa-Su 11am–4pm, last admission 3:15pm. £6, under 17 £3.50. AmEx/MC/V.)* To witness the spectacle of the Palace without the cost, attend a session of **Changing of the Guard.** Show up well before 11:30am and stand in front of the Palace in view of the morning guards, or use the steps of the Victoria Memorial as a vantage point. *(☎7766 7324. Daily Apr. to late July, every other day Aug.-Mar., provided the Queen is in residence, it's not raining hard, and there are no pressing state functions. Free.)*

THE HOUSES OF PARLIAMENT. The Palace of Westminster has been home to both the House of Lords and the House of Commons (together known as Parliament) since the 11th century, when Edward the Confessor established his court here. Standing guard on the northern side of the building is the Clock Tower, **Big Ben,** whose name actually refers to the 14-ton bell that hangs inside. **Victoria Tower,** at the south end of the Palace building, was erected in 1834 to celebrate the emancipation of slaves in the British Empire. The tower contains copies of every Act of Parliament since 1497. A flag flown from the top indicates that Parliament is in session. When the Queen is in the building a special Royal banner is flown instead of the Union flag. Visitors with enough patience or luck to make it inside the chambers can hear the raucous debates between members of both the House of Lords and the House of Commons. *(Parliament Sq. ⊖Westminster. ☎08709 063 773, commons info office 7219 4272. "Line of Route" Tour includes both houses. Tours Aug.-Oct. Book online, by phone, or in person at Abingdon Green ticket office (open mid-July) across from Palace of Westminster. Open Aug. M-Tu and F-Sa 9:15am-4pm, W-Th 1:15-4:30pm; Sept.-Oct. M and F-Sa 9:15am-4:30pm, Tu-Th 1:15-4:30pm. Tours depart every few min. and last 75min. £7. MC/V. House of Lords open during session M-Th 9am-6pm, F 9am-4:30pm; during recess M-F 10am-5pm. Chamber open Oct.-July M-W 2:30-10pm, Th 11am-7:30pm, and occasionally F from 11am. House of Commons open during session M-Th 9am-6pm, F 9am-4:30pm; during recess M-F 10am-5pm. Chamber open Oct.-July M-Tu 2:30-10:30pm, W 11:30am-7:30pm, Th 10:30am-6:30pm, occasionally F 9:30am-3pm. Hours subject to change.)*

ST. JAMES'S PARK AND GREEN PARK. The streets leading up to Buckingham Palace are flanked by two sprawling expanses of greenery: St. James's Park and Green Park. In the middle of St. James's Park is the placid **St. James's Park Lake**—the lake and the grassy area surrounding it is an official waterfowl preserve. Across the Mall, the lush Green Park is the creation of Charles II, connecting Westminster and St. James. *(The Mall. ⊖St. James's Park or Green Park. Open daily 5am-midnight. Lawn chairs available Mar.-Oct. 10am-6pm, weather permitting; June-Aug. 10am-10pm. £2 per 2hr. Last rental 2hr. before close. ☎7930 1793.)*

WESTMINSTER CATHEDRAL. Westminster, London's first Catholic cathedral after Henry VIII espoused Protestantism, was started in 1887. In 1903, money ran out, leaving the interior only partially completed. The blackened brick domes contrast dramatically with the swirling marble of the lower walls and the magnificence of the side chapels. An elevator carries visitors up the striped 90m **bell tower.** *(Cathe-*

A: They're not comfortable at all. They were designed way back in Queen Victoria's time, and the leather trousers and boots are very solid. The uniform weighs about 3 stone [about 45 lb.].

LG: How do you overcome the itches, sneezes, and bees?

A: Discipline is instilled in every British soldier during training. We know not to move a muscle while on parade no matter what the provocation or distraction—unless, of course, it is a security matter. But our helmets are akin to wearing a boiling kettle on your head; to relieve the pressure, sometimes we use the back of our sword blade to ease the back of the helmet forward.

LG: How do you make the time pass while on duty?

A: The days are long. At Whitehall the shift system is derived upon inspection in Barracks. Smarter men work on horseback in the boxes in shifts from 10am-4pm; less smart men work on foot from 7am-8pm. Some guys count the number of buses that drive past. Unofficially, there are lots of pretty girls around here, and we *are* allowed to move our eyeballs.

LG: What has been your funniest distraction attempt?

A: One day a taxi pulled up, and out hopped four Playboy bunnies, who then posed for a photo shoot right in front of us. You could call that a distraction if you like.

dral Piazza, off Victoria St. ⊖Victoria. Open daily 8am-7pm. Bell tower open daily Mar.-Nov. 9am-12:30pm and 1pm-5pm; Dec.-Feb. Tu-Sa 9am-12:30pm. Organ recitals Su 4:45pm. Cathedral uggested donation £2. Bell tower £3, students £1.50.)

WHITEHALL. The stretch of road connecting Trafalgar Sq. with **Parliament Square** and is synonymous with the British civil service. Toward the north end of Whitehall, **Great Scotland Yard** marks the former headquarters of the Metropolitan Police. Nearer Parliament Sq., heavily guarded steel gates mark the entrance to **Downing Street.** The prime minister traditionally lives at #10, but Tony Blair's family is so big that he's had to swap with the Chancellor, Gordon Brown at #11. The street is closed to visitors, but if you wait long enough you might see the PM going to or coming from work. *(Between Trafalgar Sq. and Parliament Sq. ⊖Westminster, Embankment, or Charing Cross.)*

THE CITY OF LONDON

ST. PAUL'S CATHEDRAL. Christopher Wren's masterpiece is the 5th cathedral to occupy the site; the original was built in AD 604. After three designs were rejected by the bishops, Wren, with Charles II's support, started building—sneakily, he had persuaded the king to let him make "necessary alterations" as work progressed, and the building that emerged from the scaffolding in 1708 bore little resemblance to what Charles II had approved. The **Nave** has space to seat 2500 worshippers. The tombs, including those of Nelson, Wellington, and Florence Nightingale, are all downstairs in the **crypt.** Christopher Wren lies beneath the epitaph "*Lector, si monumentum requiris circumspice*" ("Reader, if you seek his monument, look around"). To see the inside of the second-tallest freestanding **dome** in Europe (after St. Peter's in the Vatican), climb the 259 steps to the **Whispering Gallery.** From here, 119 more steps lead to the **Stone Gallery,** on the outer base of the dome, and it's another 152 to the summit's **Golden Gallery.** *(⊖St. Paul's. ☎7246 8348; www.stpauls.co.uk. Open M-Sa 8:30am-4:30pm; last admission 4pm. Dome and galleries open M-Sa 9:30am-4pm. Open for worship daily 7:15am-6pm. "Supertour" M-F 11, 11:30am, 1:30, 2pm. "Triforium" tour M-F 11:30am, 2:30pm. Audio tour available 10am-3:30pm. Admission £8, students £7. Worshippers free. 90min. Supertour £2.50, students £2. Triforium tour £5, book in advance. Audio tour £3.50, students £3.)*

ST. PAUL'S FOR POCKET CHANGE. To gain access to the cathedral's nave for free, attend an Evensong service (45min., M-Sa 5pm). Arrive at 4:50pm to be admitted to seats in the quire.

THE TOWER OF LONDON. The Tower of London, palace and prison of English monarchs for over 900 years, is steeped in blood and history. Conceived by William the Conqueror in 1067 to provide protection *from* rather than *for* his new subjects, the original wooden palisade was replaced by a stone structure that over the next 20 years would grow into the **White Tower.** From the western entrance near the **Middle Tower,** you pass over the old moat, now a garden. Beyond **Byward Tower** is a massive **bell tower;** the curfew bell has been rung nightly for over 500 years. **Traitor's Gate** was built by Edward I for his personal use, but is now associated with the prisoners who passed through it on their way to execution at **Tower Green.** Some victims are buried in the **Chapel Royal of St. Peter and Vincula,** including Henry VIII's wives Catherine Howard and Anne Boleyn. Across the green is the **Bloody Tower,** so named because Richard III allegedly imprisoned and murdered his nephews here before usurping the throne in 1483.

The most famous sights in the Tower are the **crown jewels;** moving walkways ensure that no awestruck gazers hold up the queue. While eyes are naturally drawn to the **Imperial State Crown,** featuring the Stuart Sapphire and 2876 diamonds, don't miss the **Sceptre with the Cross,** topped with the First Star of Africa, the largest quality-cut diamond in the world. Other famous gems include the **Koh-**

i-Noor, set into the **Queen Mother's Crown;** legend claims the stone will bring luck only to women. *(⊖Tower Hill. ☎08707 566 060, ticket sales 0870 756 7070. Open Mar.-Oct. M 10am-6pm, Tu-Sa 9am-6pm, Su 10am-6pm; Nov.-Feb. closes 1hr. earlier. Tickets also sold at Tube stations; buy ahead to avoid queues. 1hr.* ***"Yeoman Warder Tours"*** *meet near the entrance every 90min., M 10am-3:30pm, Tu-Sa 9:30am-3:30pm, Su 10am-3:30pm. £13.50, students £10.50. Audio tours £3.)*

ALL HALLOWS-BY-THE-TOWER. Nearly hidden by redevelopment projects and nearby office buildings, All Hallows bears its longevity proudly, incorporating a Saxon arch from AD 675. The undercroft is home to an array of archaeological finds, including Roman pavement and some stunning Celtic carvings. *(Byward St. ⊖Tower Hill. ☎7481 2928; www.allhallowsbythetower.org.uk. Church open M-F 9am-5:45pm, Sa-Su 10am-5pm. Crypt and museum open daily 10:30am-4pm. Free.)*

TOWER BRIDGE. Not to be mistaken for its plainer sibling, **London Bridge,** Tower Bridge is the one you know from all the London-based movies. Historians and technophiles will appreciate the **Tower Bridge Exhibition,** which combines scenic 140 ft. glass-enclosed walkways with videos presenting a bell-and-whistle history of the bridge. *(Entrance to the Exhibition through the west side, upriver, of the North Tower. ⊖Tower Hill or London Bridge. ☎7940 3985, lifting schedule 7940 3984; www.towerbridge.org.uk. Open daily 10am-6pm. £5.50, students £4.25.)*

THE SOUTH BANK

SHAKESPEARE'S GLOBE THEATRE. This incarnation of the Globe is faithful to the original, thatch roof and all. The first Globe burned down in 1613 after a 14-year run as the Bard's preferred playhouse. Today's reconstruction had its first full season in 1997 and now stands as the cornerstone of the International Shakespeare Globe Centre. For info on performances, see p. 148. *(Close to Bankside pier. ⊖Southwark or London Bridge. Open daily May-Sept. 9am-noon; Oct.-Apr. 10am-5pm. Tours every 30min. No tours on days when there's a matinee. £9, students £7.50.)*

SOUTHWARK CATHEDRAL. A site of worship since AD 606, the cathedral has undergone numerous transformations in the last 1400 years. Shakespeare's brother Edmund is buried here. In the rear of the nave, there are four smaller chapels; the northernmost Chapel of St. Andrew is specifically dedicated to those living with and dying from HIV and AIDS. Near the center, the **archaeological gallery** is actually a small excavation of a first-century Roman road. *(Montague Close. ⊖London Bridge. Open daily 8am-6pm. Suggested donation £3.50. Audio tour £5, students £4.)*

LONDON EYE. Also known as the Millennium Wheel, at 135m (430 ft.) the British Airways London Eye is the biggest observational wheel in the world. The ellipsoidal glass "pods" give uninterrupted views throughout each 30min. revolution. *(Jubilee Gardens, between County Hall and the Festival Hall. ⊖Waterloo. Open daily late May to June and Sept. 9:30am-9pm; July-Aug. 9:30am-10pm; Feb.-Apr. and Oct.-Dec. 9:30am-8pm. Buy tickets from box office at the corner of County Hall before joining the queue at the Eye; advance booking recommended; check the weather in advance. £12.50, students £10.)*

THE REAL DEAL. While the **London Eye** does offer magnificent views, the queues are long and it's overpriced. For equally impressive sights in a quieter atmosphere, head to the **Monument**, **Primrose Hill,** or **Hampstead Heath.**

BLOOMSBURY AND MARYLEBONE

Marylebone's most famous resident (and address) never existed. 221b Baker St. was the fictional home of Sherlock Holmes, but 221 Baker St. is actually the headquarters of the Abbey National Bank. Bloomsbury's intellectual reputation was bolstered in the early 20th century when Gordon Sq., east of Marylebone, resounded with the philosophizing and womanizing of the **Bloomsbury Group,** a set of intellectuals including John Maynard Keynes, Bertrand Russell, Lytton Strachey, and Virginia Woolf.

REGENT'S PARK. This is perhaps London's most attractive and most popular park, with landscapes ranging from football-scarred fields to Italian-style formal plantings. It's all very different from John Nash's vision of wealthy villas hidden among exclusive gardens; fortunately for us common folk, Parliament intervened in 1811 and guaranteed the space would remain open to all. *(⊖Baker St. 500 acres of gardens stretching north from Marylebone Rd. to Camden Town. Open daily 7am-dusk. Free.)*

BRITISH LIBRARY. Criticized during its long construction by traditionalists for being too modern and by modernists for being too traditional, the completed British Library building is unequivocally impressive. The bulk of the library is underground, with 12 million books on 200 mi. of shelving. The brick building aboveground is home to cavernous reading rooms and an engrossing **Museum.** *(96 Euston Rd. ⊖Euston Sq. or King's Cross. ☎7412 7332; www.bl.uk. All public spaces open M 9:30am-6pm, Tu 9:30am-8pm, W-F 9:30am-6pm, Sa 9:30am-5pm, Su 11am-5pm. Admission free. To use reading rooms, bring 2 forms of ID, one with a signature and one with a home address. Tours of public areas M, W, and F 3pm, Sa also 10:30am. Tours including one of the reading rooms Su and Bank Holidays 11:30am and 3pm. Reservations recommended for all tours. Tours £6, students £4.50; including reading room £7/£5.50. Audio tours £3.50/£2.50.)*

OTHER BLOOMSBURY SIGHTS. Established in 1828, **University College London** was the first in Britain to admit Catholics, Jews, and women. The embalmed body of founder Jeremy Bentham has been on display in the South Cloister since 1850. *(Main entrance on Gower St. South Cloister entrance through the courtyard. ⊖Euston. www.ucl.ac.uk. Quadrangle gates close at midnight; access to Bentham until 6pm. Free.)* Next to the British Library soar the Gothic spires of **St. Pancras Station.** Formerly the the Midland Grand Hotel, Sir George Gilbert Scott's facade is a hollow shell awaiting rebirth as a Marriott. *(Euston Rd. ⊖King's Cross or St. Pancras.)*

HOLBORN AND CLERKENWELL

Although most are inaccessible to tourists, Clerkenwell is full of beautiful buildings. The **Clerkenwell Historic Trail** is a nice walk past many of them. Maps are available at the 3 Things Coffee Room. (53 Clerkenwell Close. ⊖Farringdon. ☎7251 6311. Open M-Sa 11am-6pm.)

THE TEMPLE. South of Fleet St., the land upon which this labyrinthine compound rests belonged to the crusading Knights Templar in the 13th century. The only remnant of that time is the round **Temple Church,** adjoined by a Gothic nave with an altar screen by Wren. *(☎7353 3470. Hours vary and are posted outside the door of the church. Organ recitals W 1:15-1:45pm. No services Aug.-Sept. Free.)* According to Shakespeare's *Henry VI*, the red and white flowers that served as emblems in the Wars of the Roses were plucked in **Middle Temple Garden,** south of the hall. *(Open May-Sept. M-F noon-3pm. Free.)*

ROYAL COURTS OF JUSTICE. Straddling the official division between the City of Westminster and the City of London, this sprawling neo-Gothic structure encloses courtrooms and the Great Hall (home to Europe's largest mosaic floor) amid confusing passageways. All courtrooms are open to the public during trials. *(Where the Strand becomes Fleet St.; rear entrance on Carey St. ⊖Temple or Chancery Ln. ☎7947 6000. Open M-F 9am-4:30pm; cases are heard 10am-1pm and 2-3:30pm. Be prepared to go through a metal-detector security checkpoint when you enter. Cameras not permitted; 50p to check them at the door. Free.)*

KENSINGTON AND EARL'S COURT

Nobody took much notice of Kensington before 1689, when the newly crowned William III and Mary II moved into Kensington Palace. In 1851, the Great Exhibition brought in enough money to finance museums and colleges. Now that the neighborhood is home to expensive stores like Harrods and Harvey Nichols, it's hard to imagine the days when the area was known for taverns and highwaymen.

HYDE PARK AND KENSINGTON GARDENS. Surrounded by London's wealthiest neighborhoods, Hyde Park has served as the model for city parks around the world. **Kensington Gardens,** adjacent to Hyde Park and originally part of it, was created in the late 17th century when William and Mary set up house in Kensington Palace. In the middle of the park is **The Serpentine,** filled with dog-paddling tourists, rowers, and pedal boaters. Nowhere near the water, the **Serpentine Gallery** holds contemporary art. At the northeast corner of the park, near **Marble Arch,** you can see free speech in action as proselytizers, politicos, and flat-out crazies dispense the fruits of their knowledge to bemused tourists at **Speaker's Corner** on Sundays, the only place in London where demonstrators can assemble without a permit. *(Framed by Kensington Rd., Knightsbridge, Park Ln., and Bayswater Rd. ⊖Queensway, or High St. Kensington. Park open daily 5am-midnight. Gardens open daily dawn-dusk. Both free.)*

KENSINGTON PALACE. Remodeled by Christopher Wren for William and Mary, parts of the palace are still in use today as a royal residence. Princess Diana lived here until her death. The **Royal Ceremonial Dress Collection** features 19th-century court costumes along with the Queen's demure evening gowns and some of Diana's sexier numbers. *(West edge of Kensington Gardens; enter through the park. ⊖High St. Kensington. Open daily Mar.-Oct. 10am-6pm; Nov.-Feb. 10am-5pm. £11, students £8.30.)*

KNIGHTSBRIDGE AND BELGRAVIA

APSLEY HOUSE AND WELLINGTON ARCH. Apsley House, with the convenient address of "No. 1, London," was bought in 1817 by the Duke of Wellington. On display is his outstanding art collection, much of it given by grateful European royalty following the Battle of Waterloo. The majority of the paintings hang in the **Waterloo Gallery.** *(Hyde Park Corner. ⊖Hyde Park Corner. Open Apr.-Oct. Tu-Su 10am-5pm; Nov.-Mar. 10am-4pm. £4.50, students £3.)* Across from Apsley House, the Wellington Arch dedicated to the Duke of Wellington in 1838. Later, to the horror of its architect, Decimus Burton, an enormous statue of the Duke was placed on top. *(⊖Hyde Park Corner. Open Apr.-Oct. W-Su 10am-5pm; Nov.-Mar. W-Su 10am-4pm. £3, students £2.30.)*

THE WEST END

TRAFALGAR SQUARE. John Nash first suggested laying out this square in 1820, but it took almost 50 years for London's largest roundabout to take on its current appearance. The square is named in commemoration of the defeat of Napoleon's navy at Trafalgar, considered England's greatest naval victory. It has traditionally been a site for public rallies and protest movements. Towering over the square is the 51m granite **Nelson's Column,** which until recently was one of the world's tallest displays of decades-old pigeon droppings. Now, thanks to a deep-clean sponsored by the mayor, this monument to naval hero Lord Nelson sparkles once again. *(⊖Charing Cross or Leicester Sq.)*

ST. MARTIN-IN-THE-FIELDS. The 4th church to stand here, James Gibbs's 1726 creation is instantly recognizable: the rectangular portico building supporting a soaring steeple made it the model for countless Georgian churches in Ireland and America. Handel and Mozart both performed here, and the church hosts frequent concerts. In order to support the cost of keeping the church open, there is a tourist-oriented **daily market** outside as well as a surprisingly extensive and delicious **cafe**, bookshop, and art gallery in the crypt. *(St. Martin's Ln., northeast corner of Trafalgar Sq.; crypt entrance on Duncannon St. ⊖Leicester Sq. or Charing Cross. ☎7766 1100; www.stmartin-in-the-fields.org. Market open daily 11am-7pm. Church open M-Sa 10am-7pm, Su noon-6pm. Tours Th 11:30am. Free. Brass rubbing £3-15.)*

SOHO. Soho is one of the most diverse areas in central London. **Old Compton Street** is the center of London's GLBT culture. In the 1950s, immigrants from Hong Kong started moving en masse the few blocks just north of Leicester Sq., around **Gerrard Street** and grittier **Lisle Street,** which now form **Chinatown.** Gaudy, brash, and world-famous, **Piccadilly Circus** is made up of four of the West End's major arteries (Piccadilly, Regent St., Shaftesbury Ave., and the Haymarket). In the middle of all the glitz and neon stands Gilbert's famous **Statue of Eros,** dedicated to the Victorian philanthropist, Lord Shaftesbury. Eros originally pointed down Shaftesbury Ave., but recent restoration work has put his aim significantly off. *(⊖Piccadilly Circus.)* Lined with tour buses, overpriced clubs, fast-food restaurants, and generic cafes, **Leicester Square** is one destination that Londoners go out of their way to avoid. *(⊖Piccadilly Circus or Leicester Sq.)* A calm in the midst of the storm, **Soho Square** is a rather scruffy patch of green-space popular with picnickers. Its removed location makes the square more hospitable and less trafficked than its big brother, Leicester. *(⊖Tottenham Ct. Rd. Park open daily 10am-dusk.)*

MUSEUMS AND GALLERIES

Centuries spent as the capital of an empire, together with a decidedly English penchant for collecting, have given London a spectacular set of museums. Art lovers, history buffs, and amateur ethnologists won't know which way to turn when they arrive. And there's even better news for museum lovers: in celebration of the Queen's Golden Jubilee, all major museums are free indefinitely.

MAJOR COLLECTIONS

TATE MODERN. Since opening in May 2000, Tate Modern has been credited with single-handedly reversing the long-term decline in museum attendance in Britain. One of the largest modern art museums in the world, its most striking aspect is the building itself, formerly Bankside Power Station. The conversion to a gallery added a 7th floor with wraparound views, and turned the old **Turbine Hall** into an immense atrium that often overpowers the installations commissioned for it. The Tate groups works according to theme rather than period or artist—the four overarching divisions are **Still Life/Object/Real Life** and **Landscape/Matter/Environment** on Level 3, and **Nude/Action/Body** and **History/Memory/Society** on Level 5—even skeptics admit that this arrangement throws up some interesting contrasts and forces visitors into contact with an exceptionally wide range of art. It's now impossible to see the Tate's more famous pieces, which include Picasso's *Nude Woman with Necklace*, without also confronting challenging and invigorating works by less well-known contemporary artists. *(Bankside, on the South Bank. ØSouthwark or Blackfriars. From Southwark Tube, turn left up Union then left on Great Suffolk, then left on Holland. ☎7887 8000. Open M-Th and Su 10am-6pm, F-Sa 10am-10pm. Free tours meet on the gallery concourses. Audio tours £2.)*

BRITAIN

NATIONAL GALLERY. The National Gallery was founded by an Act of Parliament in 1824, with 38 pictures displayed in a townhouse; it grew so rapidly in size and popularity that a new gallery was constructed in 1838. If you're pressed for time, head to **Art Start** in the Sainsbury Wing, where you can design and print out a personalized tour. Climate-controlled rooms house the oldest, most fragile paintings, including Botticelli's *Venus and Mars*, and the *Leonardo Cartoon*, a detailed preparatory drawing by da Vinci for a never-executed painting. With paintings that date from

1510 to 1600, the **West Wing** is dominated by the Italian High Renaissance, German, and Flemish art. The **North Wing** spans the 17th century, with an exceptional display of Flemish and Spanish Renaissance works. The **East Wing,** home to paintings from 1700 to 1900, is the most crowded, with the most famous works and the Impressionist galleries. The focus is primarily on Room #45, which features one of Van Gogh's *Sunflowers. (Main entrance on north side of Trafalgar Sq. ⊖Charing Cross or Leicester Sq. Open M-Tu and Th-Su 10am-6pm, W 10am-9pm. Special exhibitions in the Sainsbury Wing occasionally open until 10pm. Free 1hr. tours start at Sainsbury Wing information desk daily 11:30am, 12:30, 2:30, 3:30pm; W also 6, 6:30pm. Free; some temporary exhibits £5-9, students £2-3. Audio tours £4 suggested donation. AmEx/MC/V for ticketed events.)*

NATIONAL PORTRAIT GALLERY. This artistic Who's Who in Britain began in 1856 and has grown to be the place to see Britain's freshest new artwork as well as centuries-old portraiture. New facilities include an IT Gallery, with computers allowing you to search for pictures and print out a personalized tour, and a 3rd-floor restaurant offering an aerial view of London. To see the paintings in historical order, take the escalator from the reception hall in the Ondaatje Wing to the top floor. *(St. Martin's Pl., at the start of Charing Cross Rd., Trafalgar Sq.; in the West End. ⊖Leicester Sq. or Charing Cross. ☎7312 2463; www.npg.org.uk. Open M-W and Sa-Su 10am-6pm, Th-F 10am-8:50pm. Lectures Tu, Th, and Sa-Su 1:10 and 3pm; free, but popular events require tickets, available from the information desk. Evening Events: Talks Th 7pm; free-£3. Admission free; special exhibits up to £6. Audio tours £2.)*

BRITISH MUSEUM. With 50,000 items, this magnificent collection is somewhat undermined by a chaotic layout and poor labeling, while staff shortages mean that even famous galleries are randomly closed. That said, the building itself is magnificent, especially the Great Court and the Reading Room, and a leisurely stroll through the less-frequented galleries is worth an afternoon visit. Most people don't even make it past the main floor, but they should—the galleries upstairs and downstairs are some of the best, if not the most famous. *(Great Russell St., in Bloomsbury. ⊖Tottenham Ct. Rd., Russell Sq., or Holborn. ☎7323 8299; www.thebritishmuseum.ac.uk. Great Court open M-W and Su 9am-6pm, Th-Sa 9am-11pm, until 9pm in winter. Galleries open daily 10am-5:30pm, selected galleries open Th-F until 8pm. Free tours daily 12:30pm from the Enlightenment Desk. 90min. "Highlights Tour" daily 10:30am, 1, 3pm; advance booking recommended. Various other themed tours run throughout the week; check website or info desk for details. Admission free; £3 suggested donation. Temporary exhibits around £5, students £3.50. Highlights Tour £8, students £5. Audio tour £3.50. MC/V.)*

VICTORIA AND ALBERT MUSEUM. The V&A is dedicated to displaying "the fine and applied arts of all countries, all styles, and all periods." The subject of a £31 million refit, the vast **British Galleries** hold a series of recreated rooms from every period between 1500 and 1900, mirrored by the vast **Dress Collection,** a dazzling array of the finest *haute couture* through the ages. The ground-floor **European** collections range from 4th-century Byzantine tapestries to Alfonse Mucha posters; if you only see one thing, make it the **Raphael Gallery,** hung with six massive paintings commissioned by Pope Leo X in 1515. The **Sculpture Gallery** and its fine works are not to be confused with the **Cast Courts,** a plaster-replica collection of the world's greatest sculptural hits, from Trajan's Column to Michelangelo's *David.* The V&A's **Asian** collections are particularly formidable. In contrast to the geographically laid-out ground floor, the **upper levels** are mostly arranged by material; here you'll find specialist galleries devoted to everything from jewelry to musical instruments to stained glass. The six-level **Henry Cole wing** is home to British paintings, a display of Rodin bronzes, donated by the artist in 1914, and the "world's greatest collection" of miniature portraits. *(Main entrance on Cromwell Rd.; in Kensington and Earl's Court. ⊖South Kensington.*

☎7942 2000; www.vam.ac.uk. Open daily 10am-5:45pm, plus W and last F of month until 10pm. Tours meet at rear of main entrance. Call ahead for times. Talks and tours W from 6:30pm; last F of month also draws a young artistic crowd with live performances, guest DJs, late-night exhibition openings, bar, and food. Free.)

TATE BRITAIN. The original Tate opened in 1897 as a showcase for modern British art. Before long, it had expanded to include contemporary art from all over the world, as well as British art from the Middle Ages on. Despite many expansions, it was clear that the dual role was too much for one building; the problem was resolved with the relocation of almost all the contemporary art to the Tate Modern at Bankside (p. 144). At the same time, the original Tate was rededicated to British art. The **Clore Gallery** continues to display the Turner Bequest of 282 oils and 19,000 watercolors; other painters featured heavily are William Blake, John Constable, Lucien Freud, David Hockney, and Dante Gabriel Rossetti. Despite the Tate Modern's popular explosion, the annual **Turner Prize** for contemporary art is still held here. *(Millbank, near Vauxhall Bridge. ⊖Pimlico. Open daily 10am-5:50pm; last admission 5pm. Free. Special exhibits £3-9.50. Audio tour free.)*

OTHER MUSEUMS AND GALLERIES

Courtauld Institute, Somerset House, The Strand, Westminster (☎7420 9400; www.courtauld.ac). ⊖Charing Cross. Small, outstanding collection. 14th- to 20th-century abstractions, focusing on Impressionism. Cézanne's *The Card Players*, Manet's *A Bar at the Follies Bergères*, and Van Gogh's *Self Portrait with Bandaged Ear.* Open daily 10am-6pm. £5, students £4. Tours £1.50, students £2. Free M 10am-2pm.

Cabinet War Rooms, Clive Steps, Westminster (☎7766 0130). ⊖Westminster. The rooms where Churchill and his ministers, generals, and support staff lived and worked underground from 1939 to 1945. Highlights include the small room containing the top-secret transatlantic hotline—the official story was that it was Churchill's personal toilet. Open daily 9:30am-6pm. Last admission 5pm. £10, students £8, under 16 free. MC/V.

British Library Galleries, 96 Euston Rd. (☎7412 7332). ⊖King's Cross. A stunning display of texts, from the 2nd-century *Unknown Gospel* to the Beatles' hand-scrawled lyrics. Other highlights include a Gutenberg Bible, Joyce's handwritten *Finnegan's Wake*, and pages from da Vinci's notebooks. Open M and W-F 9:30am-6pm, Tu 9:30am-8pm, Sa 9:30am-5pm, Su 11am-5pm. Free.

Science Museum, Exhibition Rd., Kensington (☎0870 870 4868). ⊖South Kensington. A mix of state-of-the-art interactive displays and priceless historical artifacts, encompassing all forms of technology. Open daily 10am-6pm. Free.

Natural History Museum, on Cromwell Rd., Kensington (☎7942 5000). ⊖South Kensington. Cathedral-like building home to an array of minerals and stuffed animals. Highlights include a frighteningly realistic T-Rex and the engrossing, interactive Human Biology gallery. Open M-Sa 10am-5:50pm, Su 11am-5:50pm. Free.

Museum of London, London Wall, The City of London (☎7600 3699). ⊖Barbican. Enter through the Barbican. The engrossing collection traces the history of London from its foundations—literally—to the present day, cleverly incorporating adjacent ruins. Open M-Sa 10am-6pm, Su noon-6pm. Last admission 5:30pm. Free.

Whitechapel Art Gallery, Whitechapel High St. (☎7522 7888). ⊖Aldgate East. At the forefront of the East End's art scene, Whitechapel hosts excellent, often controversial, shows of contemporary art. Closes between exhibits; call ahead. Open Tu-W and F-Su 11am-6pm, Th 11am-9pm. Free.

Wallace Collection, Manchester Sq., Marylebone (☎7563 9500). ⊖Bond St. Palatial Hertford House holds a stunning array of porcelain, medieval armor, and weaponry. Open M-Sa 10am-5pm, Su noon-5pm. Suggested donation £2.

ENTERTAINMENT

Although West End ticket prices are through the roof and the quality of some shows highly questionable, the city that brought the world Shakespeare, the Sex Pistols, and Andrew Lloyd Webber still retains its originality and theatrical edge. London is a city of immense talent, full of student up-and-comers, experimental writers, and humble undergrounders.

CINEMA

The heart of the celluloid monster is **Leicester Square,** where the latest releases premier a day before hitting the city's chains. The dominant cinema chain is **Odeon** (☎0870 5050 007; www.odeon.co.uk). Tickets to West End cinemas cost £8-10+; weekday matinees are cheaper. For less mainstream offerings, try the **Electric Cinema,** 191 Portobello Rd. For an extra special experience, choose a luxury armchair or loveseat. (⊖Ladbroke Grove. ☎7908 9696; www.the-electric.co.uk. Tickets £5-12.50; loveseat £20-30. MC/V.) **Riverside Studios,** Crips Rd., shows a wide range of foreign and classic films. (⊖Hammersmith. ☎8237 1111; www.riversidestudios.co.uk. £6.50, students £5.50.) The **National Film Theatre (NFT)** screens a mind-boggling array of films every evening starting around 6pm. (South Bank, underneath Waterloo Bridge. ⊖Waterloo, Embankment, or Temple. ☎7928 3232; www.bfi.org.uk/nft. £7.50, concessions £5.70.)

COMEDY

Summertime visitors should note that London empties of comedians in **August,** when most head to Edinburgh to take part in the annual festivals (p. 192). That means, however, that **July** provides plenty of comedians trying out material; check listings in *Time Out* or a newspaper **Comedy Store,** 1a Oxendon St., is the UK's top comedy club and sower of the seeds that gave rise to *Ab Fab*, *Whose Line is it Anyway?*, and *Blackadder*. (⊖Piccadilly Circus. ☎7839 6642, tickets 08700 602 340; www.thecomedystore.biz. Shows Tu-Su 8pm, F-Sa also midnight. 18+. Tu-W, F late show, and Su £13; students £8. Th-F early show and Sa £15. Box office open Tu-Su 6:30-9:30pm, F-Sa 6:30pm-1:30am. 100 seats always available at the door. AmEx/MC/V.) North London's **Canal Cafe Theatre,** Delamere Terr., above the Bridge House pub, is one of the few comedy venues to specialize in sketch, as opposed to stand-up. (⊖Warwick Ave. ☎7289 6054. Shows W-Sa 7:30, 9:30pm; £5, students £4. Newsrevue £8, students £6. £1 membership included in price.)

MUSIC

CLASSICAL

Barbican Hall, Silk St. (☎0845 120 7500; www.barbican.org.uk), in City of London. ⊖Barbican or Moorgate. The resident **London Symphony Orchestra** plays here frequently; the hall also hosts concerts by international orchestras, jazz artists, and world musicians. Call in advance for tickets. Online and phone box offices often have good last-minute options. Tickets £5-35.

Royal Albert Hall, Kensington Gore (☎7589 8212; www.royalalberthall.com), in Kensington and Earl's Court. ⊖High St. Kensington. Best known for the **Proms,** the summer season of classical music (mid-July to mid-Sept.). Box office open daily 9am-9pm.MC/V.

Royal Opera, Bow St. (☎7304 4000; www.royaloperahouse.org), in Covent Garden. ⊖Covent Garden. Lavish, traditional productions with recent contemporary ventures. Prices for the best seats (orchestra stalls) top £75, but standing room and restricted-view seating in the upper balconies run as low as £5. For some performances, 100 seats are available for £10; apply at least 2 weeks in advance at www.travelex.royaloperahouse.org.uk. 67 seats available from 10am on day of performance, limit 1 per person. Box office open M-Sa 10am-8pm. AmEx/MC/V.

JAZZ

Jazz Café, 5 Parkway (☎7344 0044; www.jazzcafe.co.uk), in North London. ⊖Camden Town. Shows can be pricey (£10-30), but an impressive roster of jazz, hip hop, funk, and Latin performers explains Jazz Café's popularity. Jazzy DJs spin F-Sa following the shows until 2am. Cover F-Sa £8-9, with flyer £5; Su £3, with musical instrument £1. Open M-Th 7pm-1am, F-Sa 7pm-2am, Su 7pm-midnight. MC/V.

Spitz, 109 Commercial St. (☎7392 9032; www.spitz.co.uk), in East London. ⊖Liverpool St. Fresh range of live music, from klezmer, jazz, and world music to indie, pop, and rap. All profits to charity. Cover free-£15. Open M-W 7pm-midnight, Th-Sa 7pm-1am, Su 4-10:30pm. MC/V.

606 Club, 90 Lots Rd. (☎7352 5953; www.606club.co.uk), in Chelsea. ⊖Sloane Sq., then bus #11 or 22. Look for the brick arch labeled 606 opposite the "Fire Access" garage across the street; ring the doorbell. Brilliant British and European jazz in a smoky, candlelit basement venue. Reservations highly recommended. Cover added to the food bill, M-Th £7-8, F-Sa £9, Su £8. M-W doors open 7:30pm, music from 8pm; Th-Sa doors open 8pm, music from 9:30pm; Su (vocalists) doors open 8pm, music from 9pm. Music continues until the musicians don't want to play anymore. MC/V.

ROCK AND POP

The Water Rats, 328 Grays Inn Rd., in Bloomsbury (☎7837 7269). ⊖King's Cross. Pub-cafe by day, stomping ground for top new talent by night (from 8pm). Oasis was signed here after their first London gig. Cover £5-6, with band flyer £4-5. Music M-Sa 8pm to late (headliner 9:45pm). MC/V; £7 min. charge.

Carling Academy, Brixton, 211 Stockwell Rd. (☎7771 3000; www.brixton-academy.co.uk), in South London. ⊖Brixton. Art Deco ex-cinema with a pitched floor for universal good views. Buy tickets online, by telephone, or at the Carling Academy box office (16 Parkfield Street, Islington; open M-Sa noon-4pm). Tickets generally £20-30.

London Astoria (LA1), 157 Charing Cross Rd. (info ☎8963 0940, 24hr. ticket line 08701 500 044; www.londonastoria.com), in Soho. ⊖Tottenham Ct. Rd. Formerly a pickle factory, strip club, and music hall before becoming a full-time rock venue. The 2000-person venue occasionally hosts big names, but is more popular for G-A-Y club night (p. 153). Box office open M-Sa 10am-6pm. AmEx/MC/V.

THEATER

London's West End is dominated by musicals and plays that run for years, if not decades. For a list of shows and discount tickets, head to the **tkts** booth in Leicester Sq. (⊖Leicester Sq. www.tkts.co.uk. Most shows £20-22; up to £2.50 booking fee per ticket. Open M-Sa 10am-7pm, Su noon-3pm. MC/V.)

REPERTORY

Shakespeare's Globe Theatre, 21 New Globe Walk (☎7401 9919; www.shakespearesglobe.org), in the South Bank. ⊖Southwark or London Bridge. Stages plays by Shakespeare and his contemporaries. Sit in one of three covered tiers of backless wooden benches or stand in the open as a "groundling"; arrive 30min. before the show to get as close as you can. Performances mid-May to late Sept. Tu-Sa 7:30pm, Su 6:30pm; June-Sept. also Tu-Sa 2pm, Su 1pm. Box office open M-Sa 10am-6pm, 8pm on performance days. Seats from £12, students from £10, groundlings £5. Raingear £2.50.

National Theatre, South Bank (info ☎7452 3400, box office 7452 3000; www.nationaltheatre.org.uk), in the South Bank. ⊖Waterloo or Embankment. Laurence Olivier founded the National Theatre in 1976, and it has been at the forefront of British theater ever since. Box office open M-Sa 10am-8pm. Complicated pricing scheme. Contact box office for details. Tickets typically start at £10. MC/V.

Royal Court Theatre, Sloane Sq. (☎7565 5000; www.royalcourttheatre.com), in Chelsea. ⊖Sloane Sq. Recognized by *The New York Times* as a standout theater in Europe. Main auditorium £7.50-27.50, students £9. M all seats £7.50. Box office open M-Sa 10am-7:45pm, closes 6pm non-performance weeks. AmEx/MC/V.

"OFF-WEST END"

The Almeida, Almeida St. (☎7359 4404; www.almeida.co.uk), in North London. ⊖Angel or Highbury and Islington. The top fringe theater in London, if not the world. Shows M-Sa 7:30pm, Sa matinees 3pm. Tickets from £10. MC/V.

Donmar Warehouse, 41 Earlham St. (☎08700 606 624; www.donmarwarehouse.com), in Covent Garden. ⊖Covent Garden. In the mid-90s, artistic director Sam Mendes transformed this gritty space into one of the best theaters in the country. Tickets £13-29; students and under-18 standby 30min. before curtain £12 (call in advance for availability); £5 standing-room tickets available once performance sells out. Box office open M-Sa 10am-7:30pm. AmEx/MC/V.

Royal Academy of Dramatic Arts (RADA), 62-64 Gower St. (☎7908 4800; www.rada.org), entrance on Malet St.; in Bloomsbury. ⊖Goodge St. A cheaper alternative to the West End, Britain's most famous drama school has 3 on-site theaters. Tickets £3-10, students £2-7.50. Regular Foyer events during the academic year including plays, music, and readings M-Th at 7 or 7:30pm (free-£4). Box office open M-F 10am-6pm, until 7:30pm performance nights. AmEx/MC/V.

SHOPPING

London has long been considered one of the fashion capitals of the world. The truly budget-conscious should forget buying altogether and stick to window-shopping in **Knightsbridge** and on **Regent Street.** Vintage shopping in **Notting Hill** is also a viable alternative. As with any large city, London retail is dominated by chains, as on **Oxford St.** Fortunately, local shoppers are picky enough that buying from a chain doesn't mean abandoning the flair for which Londoners are famed. Stores are usually open 10am-7pm weekdays, and noon-5pm on weekends.

DEPARTMENT STORES

Harrods, 87-135 Brompton Rd. (☎7730 1234; www.harrods.com), in Knightsbridge and Belgravia. ⊖Knightsbridge. The only thing bigger than the bewildering store is the mark-up on the goods. Still, the over-the-top food halls are a sight to behold. Open M-Sa 10am-7pm, Su noon-6pm. AmEx/MC/V.

Harvey Nichols, 109-125 Knightsbridge (☎7235 5000; www.harveynichols.com), in Knightsbridge and Belgravia. ⊖Knightsbridge. Fifth Avenue meets London on 5 floors of fashion. Open M-F 10am-8pm, Sa 10am-7pm, Su noon-6pm. AmEx/MC/V.

Selfridges, 400 Oxford St. (☎0870 837 7377; www.selfridges.com), in the West End. ⊖Bond St. The total department store covers everything from traditional tweeds to space-age clubwear. Massive Jan. and July sales. Open M-F 10am-8pm, Sa 9:30am-8pm, Su noon-6pm. AmEx/MC/V.

Liberty, 210-220 Regent St. (☎7734 1234; www.liberty.co.uk), main entrance on Gt. Marlborough St.; in the West End. ⊖Oxford Circus. The focus on top-quality design and handcrafts makes it more like a giant boutique than a full-blown department store, famous for custom fabric prints. Open M-W and F-Sa 10am-7pm, Th 10am-8pm, Su noon-6pm. AmEx/MC/V.

Fortnum & Mason, 181 Piccadilly (☎7734 8040; www.fortnumandmason.co.uk), in the West End. ⊖Green Park or Piccadilly Circus. Gourmet department store provides foodstuffs fit for a queen. Open M-Sa 10am-6:30pm, Su noon-6pm (food hall and patio restaurant only). AmEx/MC/V.

STREET MARKETS

Better for people-watching than hardcore shopping, street markets may not bring you the big goods, but they are a much better alternative to a day on Oxford St. **Portobello Road Markets** include food, antiques, and second-hand clothing. Come Friday or Saturday when everything is sure to be open. (⊖Notting Hill Gate; also Westbourne Park and Ladroke Grove. Stalls set their own times. General hours M-W and F-Sa 8am-6:30pm, Th 8am-1pm.) **Camden Passage Market** is more for looking than for buying—London's premier antique shops line these quaint alleyways. (Islington High St., in North London. ⊖Angel. Stalls open W and Sa 8:30am-6pm; some stores open daily, but W is by far the best day to go.) **Brixton Market** has London's best selection of Afro-Caribbean fruits, vegetables, spices, and fish. (Along Electric Ave., Pope's Rd., and Brixton Station Rd., and inside markets in Granville Arcade and Market Row; in South London. ⊖Brixton. Open daily 8am-6pm; closes W at 3pm.) Formerly a wholesale vegetable markets, **Spitalfields** has matured to be the best of the East End markets. On Sunday, the food shares space with rows of clothing by local independent designers. (Commercial St., in East London. ⊖Shoreditch, Liverpool St., or Aldgate East. Crafts market open M-F 11am-3:30pm, Su 10am-5pm. Antiques market open Th 9am-5pm. Organic market open F and Su 10am-5pm.)

NIGHTLIFE

First-time visitors may initially head directly to the **West End,** drawn by the flashy lights and pumping music of Leicester Sq. Be warned, though, that like much of the West End, nightlife here is not the definitive voice of Londoners who like to get jiggy; for a more authentic experience, head to the **East End** or **Brixton.** Soho's **Old Compton Street,** though, is still the center of GLBT nightlife. Before heading out for the evening, make sure to plan **Night Bus** travel. Listings open past 11pm include local Night Bus routes. Night Buses in the West End are ubiquitous—head to Trafalgar Sq., Oxford St., or Piccadilly Circus.

PUBS

Ye Olde Cheshire Cheese, Wine Office Ct. (☎7353 6170; www.yeoldecheshirecheese.com), in Holborn. By 145 Fleet St., not to be confused with The Cheshire Cheese on the other side of Fleet St. ⊖Blackfriars or St. Paul's. Once a haunt of Dickens, Mark Twain, and Theodore Roosevelt. Front open M-Sa 11am-11pm, Su noon-3pm. Cellar Bar open M-F noon-2:30pm, M-Th and Sa also 5:30-11pm. Chop Room open M-F noon-9:30pm, Sa noon-2:30pm and 6-9:30pm, Su noon-2:30pm. Johnson Room open M-F noon-2:30pm and 7-9:30pm. AmEx/MC/V.

Fitzroy Tavern, 16 Charlotte St. (☎7580 3714), in Bloomsbury. ⊖Goodge St. Once popular with artists and writers, this pub now oozes with good-looking students. W comedy 8:30pm (£5). Open M-Sa 11am-11pm, Su noon-10:30pm. MC/V.

The Jerusalem Tavern, 55 Britton St. (☎7490 4281; www.stpetersbrewery.co.uk), in Clerkenwell. ⊖Farringdon. Ideal for an evening of intense conversation. A broad selection of specialty ales (£2.40), including grapefruit, cinnamon, and apple, rewards the adventuresome. Open M-F 11am-11pm, Sa 5-11pm, Su 11am-5pm. MC/V.

The Troubadour, 265 Old Brompton Rd. (☎7370 1434; www.troubadour.co.uk), in Kensington and Earl's Court. ⊖Earl's Court. A combination pub/cafe/deli. Once upon a time, Bob Dylan, Joni Mitchell, and Paul Simon played in the intimate basement club, and the place retains a bohemian appeal. Entrees £5.50-10. 2-for-1 mixed drinks in the cafe weekdays 4:30-7:30pm. Open daily 9am-midnight. MC/V.

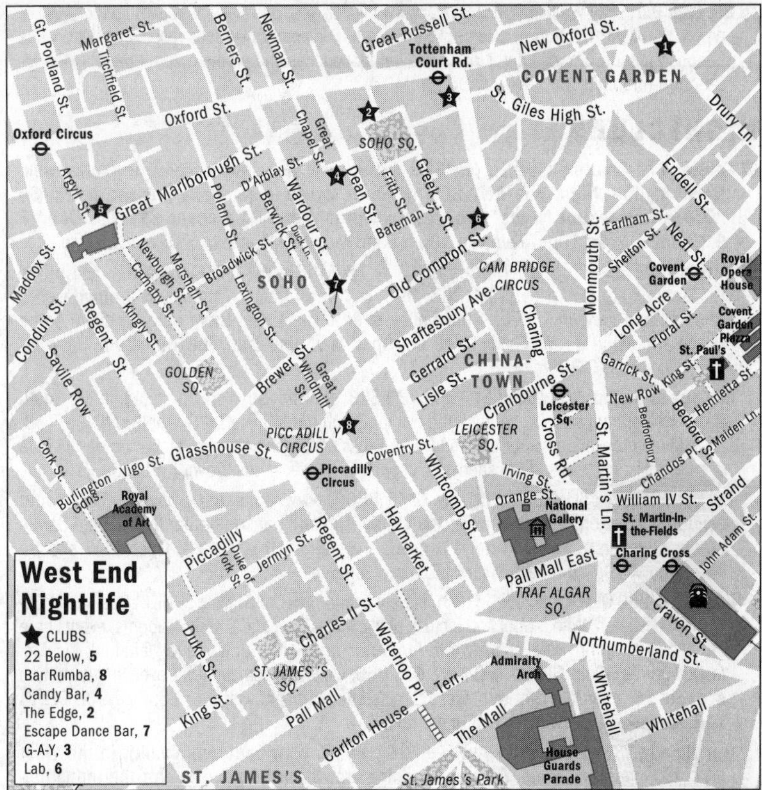

BARS

Vibe Bar, 91-95 Brick Ln. (☎7377 2899; www.vibe-bar.co.uk), in East London. ⊖Aldgate East or Liverpool St. Night Bus hub at Liverpool St. Station. Plop down on a sofa, or get there early for an outside table. Free Internet. A young crowd grooves to hip hop, soul, acoustic, and jazz. DJs spin M-Sa from 7:30pm, Su from 7pm. Cover F-Sa after 8pm £3.50. Open M-Th and Su 11am-11:30pm, F-Sa 11am-1am.

Lab, 12 Old Compton St. (☎7437 7820), in the West End. ⊖Leicester Sq. or Tottenham Ct. Rd. With restrooms for "bitches" and "bastards," the only thing this funky cocktail bar takes seriously is its stellar drink menu. DJs spin house and funk from 8pm nightly. Open M-Sa 4pm-midnight, Su 4-10:30pm. AmEx/MC/V.

Filthy MacNasty's Whiskey Café, 68 Amwell St. (☎7837 6067), in North London. ⊖Angel or King's Cross. Night Bus #N10, 63, 73, 91, 390. Shane MacGowan, U2, and the Libertines have all played in this laidback Irish pub. Live music and occasional literary readings add to the bad-boy-cum-intellectual atmosphere. Open M-Sa noon-11pm, Su noon-10:30pm.

22 Below, 22 Great Marlborough St. (☎0871 223 5531), in the West End. ⊖Oxford St. In a basement next to Cafe Libre and opposite Carnaby St. Entertaining Old Rope comedy nights, over-sized fresh fruit martinis (£6-7), and a friendly, casual crowd will make it hard to pull yourself off the comfy leather couches. M comedy (£3). Open M-F 5pm-midnight, Sa 7:30pm-midnight. MC/V.

Big Chill Bar, Dray Walk (☎7392 9180; www.bigchill.net), off Brick Ln. in East London. ⊖Liverpool St. Night Bus hub at Liverpool St. Station. DJs spin an eclectic mix every night, while famously friendly crowds chat it up on big leather couches and on the outdoor patio. Open M-Sa noon-midnight, Su noon-10:30pm. MC/V.

NIGHTCLUBS

Fabric, 77a Charterhouse St. (☎7336 8898; www.fabriclondon.com), in Clerkenwell. ⊖Farringdon. Night Bus #N242. The young crowd is generally dressed down. Su **"DTPM Polysexual Night"** (house; www.dtpm.net). F-Sa cover £11-15. Open F 9:30pm-5am, Sa 10pm-7am, Su 10pm-5am. MC/V; only at bar, £15 min. charge.

Notting Hill Arts Club, 21 Notting Hill Gate (☎7460 4459), in Notting Hill. ⊖Notting Hill Gate. Night Bus #94, 148, 207, 390. Not at all touristy, thanks to a non-descript exterior, and very chill. 1-in, 1-out policy later at night. Get there early to claim some space and avoid a wait. Cover up to £6. Open M-W 6pm-1am, Th-F 6pm-2am, Sa 4pm-2am, Su 4pm-12:30am. MC/V.

Ministry of Sound, 103 Gaunt St. (☎7378 6528; www.ministryofsound.co.uk), in the South Bank. ⊖Elephant and Castle; take the exit for South Bank University. Night Bus #N35, 133, 343. Mecca for serious clubbers worldwide. Dress code generally casual, but err on the side of smartness: no tracksuits or sneakers, especially on weekends. Cover F £12, Sa £15.

Tongue&Groove, 50 Atlantic Rd. (☎7274 8600; www.tongueandgroove.org), in South London. ⊖Brixton. Un-self-consciously trendy club and bar so popular that people dance on the speakers. Cover Th after 11pm £2, F-Sa after 10:30pm £3. Open M-W and Su 7pm-3am, Th-Sa 7pm-5am. MC/V; £10 min. charge.

Aquarium, 256 Old St. (☎7251 6136), in East London. ⊖Old St.; Exit 3. Night Bus hub at Liverpool St. Station. With a pool and jacuzzi, along with 4 bars and 2 chillout rooms, events here are hilarious, campy affairs. Sa world-famous "Carwash" (funky/retro-glam-funk fashion-fest). 10pm-3:30am (Tickets ☎08702 461 966; www.carwash.co.uk.). Cover Th guys before midnight £5, after midnight with flyer £8, girls after midnight with flyer £5; F guys £15, girls £10; Sa £12.50 in advance, £15 at the door.

Bar Rumba, 36 Shaftesbury Ave. (☎7287 6933; www.barrumba.co.uk), in the West End. ⊖Piccadilly Circus. A young dancing crowd makes good use of the industrial-strength interior. Cover £3-8. Open M-Tu varied hours, W 9pm-3am, Th 8:30pm-3am, F 10pm-4am, Sa 9pm-4am, Su 8pm-1am. MC/V; £10 min. charge.

GLBT NIGHTLIFE

Many venues have Gay and Lesbian nights on a rotating basis. Check *TimeOut* and look for flyers/magazines floating around Soho: *The Pink Paper* (free from newsagents) and *Boyz* (www.boyz.co.uk; free from gay bars and clubs), the main gay listings magazine for London.

The Edge, 11 Soho Sq. (☎7439 1313; www.edge.uk.com), in the West End. ⊖Oxford Circus or Tottenham Ct. Rd. A chill, friendly gay and lesbian drinking spot. Tu-Sa DJ. Tu-F piano bar. F-Sa dancing. Cover F-Sa after 11pm £2. Open M-Sa noon-1am, Su noon-10:30pm. MC/V.

The Black Cap, 171 Camden High St. (☎7428 2721; www.theblackcap.com), in North London. ⊖Camden Town. North London's most popular gay bar and cabaret is always buzzing with a male and female crowd. Cover M-Th and Su downstairs £3, before 11pm £2; F-Sa before 11pm £3, after 11pm £4. Food served daily noon-6pm. Open M-Th noon-2am, F-Sa noon-3am, Su noon-12:30am.

Escape Dance Bar, 10a Brewer St. (☎7731 2626; www.kudosgroup.com), in the West End. ⊖Leicester Sq. Dance to the latest pop hits in an enjoyably cramped space. Cover Tu-Th after 11pm £3; F-Sa £4. Open M-Sa 5pm-3am, Su 5-10:30pm. AmEx/MC/V.

Candy Bar, 4 Carlisle St. (☎7494 4041; www.thecandybar.co.uk), in the West End. ⊖Tottenham Ct. Rd or Oxford Circus. This estrogen-packed, pink-hued drinking spot is a one-stop shop for lesbian entertainment. W karaoke. F-Sa cover £5 after 9pm. Open M-Th and Su 5-11:30pm, F-Sa 5pm-2am. MC/V.

G-A-Y, 157 Charing Cross Rd. (☎7434 9592; www.g-a-y.co.uk), in the West End. ⊖Tottenham Ct. Rd. London's biggest gay/lesbian venue. Sa night rocks a capacity crowd with DJs and live pop. Cover £0.50-15. Open M and Th-F 11pm-4am, Sa 10:30pm-5am. Cash only.

DAYTRIP FROM LONDON

WINDSOR AND ETON

Windsor has 2 train stations, both within walking distance of the castle. Trains (☎08457 484 950) to Windsor and Eton Central arrive from Paddington station (40min., 2 per hr., round-trip £7) via Slough, while those to Windsor and Eton Riverside come from Waterloo (50min., 2 per hr., round-trip £7). Green Line bus #702 arrives at Central from Victoria station (1¼hr., every hr., round-trip £5-10.)

Built by William the Conqueror in the 11th century to be a fortress, **Windsor Castle** is the largest and oldest continuously inhabited castle in the world. The queen is officially in residence for the month of April and one week in June. The **Upper Ward** houses the **state apartments,** which are filled with works by Rembrandt, Rubens, and Queen Victoria herself. A stroll to the **Lower Ward** brings you to **St. George's Chapel,** which boasts delicate vaulting and exquisite stained glass. Ten sovereigns lie here, including George V, Edward IV, Charles I, and Henrys VI and VIII. (☎01753 831 118. As a "working castle," large areas may be closed on short notice. Open daily Mar.-Oct. 9:45am-5:30pm; Nov.-Feb. 9:45am-4pm. Last admission 1¼hr. before closing. £12.50, under 17 £6.50. Audio tours £3.50. Guides £5.) **Eton College,** Across Windsor Bridge and along Eton High St., was founded by Henry VI in 1440 as a school for paupers, and has ironically evolved into England's pre-eminent "public" (i.e., private) school. Pupils still wear tailcoats to every class and raise one finger in greeting to any teacher they pass. For all its air of privilege, Eton has shaped some notable dissidents, including Aldous Huxley and George Orwell. (☎01753 671 177. Open daily late Mar. to mid-Apr. and July-Aug. 10:30am-4:30pm; mid.-Apr. to June and Sept. to late Mar. 2-4:30pm. Schedule varies due to academic calendar. Daily tours 2:15 and 3:15pm. £3.80, under 16 £3. Tours £4.90, under 16 £4.)

TOP TEN LIST

ETON-SPEAK

The elite prep school Eton College has educated philosophers, princes, and Prime Ministers for over 500 years and has a vernacular to describe the school's many ranks, quirks, and rituals. Common words (with example sentences) include:

1. **Stick-ups:** collars worn with the school's black morning suit. "With a stiff upper lip and bruised neck, Ansel regretted over-starching his stick-ups."
2. **Colleger:** one of 70 student scholars selected by examination. "Truant Kevin was no colleger."
3. **Wet bob:** a boy who rows crew in summer. "David, a wet bob, suffered from tan lines."
4. **Dry bob:** a boy who plays cricket in summer. "Dustin, a dry bob, suffered from shin splints."
5. **Half:** a school term. "Studious Seth hated the end of half."
6. **Division:** a form, class, or grade. "Silly Stuart failed sixth division."
7. **Tutor:** a faculty member responsible for supervising studies. "The tutor advised that Jeremy repeat maths."
8. **The Block:** a stool-shaped bench where students were flogged. "Michael, and his buttocks, shivered as he passed the Block."
9. **Pop, popper:** one of 25 self-elected student prefects. "Owen abused his power as a popper."
10. **Montem:** A procession made by the students from the school to Salt Hill in Slough, stopped due to rowdy behavior. "The sixth division rioted gleefully during Montem."

SOUTHERN ENGLAND

History and myth cloak Southern England as densely as the Atlantic fog. Cornwall, the alleged birthplace of King Arthur, was the last stronghold of the Celts in England, but traces of even older Neolithic communities linger in the massive stone circles they left behind. During WWII, German bombings uncovered long-buried evidence of an invasion by Caesar, whose Romans dotted the countryside with settlements that included the elaborate spas at Bath. William the Conqueror left his mark in the form of awe-inspiring castles and cathedrals. The voices of such British literati as Jane Austen, Geoffrey Chaucer, Charles Dickens, and E. M. Forster also seem to echo above the sprawling pastures and seaside cliffs.

CANTERBURY ☎01227

Archbishop Thomas Becket met his demise at **Canterbury Cathedral** in 1170 after an irate Henry II asked, "Will no one rid me of this troublesome priest?" Later, in his famed *Canterbury Tales*, Chaucer caricatured the pilgrims who traveled the road from London to England's most famous execution site. (☎762 862; www.canterbury-cathedral.org. Open Easter-Oct. M-Sa 9am-6pm; Oct.-Easter M-Sa 9am-5pm, Su 12:30-2:30pm and 4:30-5:30pm. M-Sa 3 1¼hr. tours per day. Cathedral £5, students £4. Tour £3.50, students £2.50. 40min. audio tour £3, students £2.) The skeletons of soaring arches and crumbling walls are all that remain of **Saint Augustine's Abbey,** outside the city wall near the cathedral. St. Augustine himself is buried under a pile of rocks. (☎767 345. Open Apr.-Sept. daily 10am-6pm; Oct.-Mar. W-Su 10am-4pm. £3.70, students £2.80.) **The Canterbury Tales,** on St. Margaret's St., plays abbreviated portions of Chaucer's masterpiece through headphones to herds of tourists browsing recreated scenes. (☎479 227; www.canterburytales.org.uk. Open daily July-Aug. 9:30am-5pm; Sept.-June reduced hours. £7, students £6.)

B&Bs cluster around **High Street,** and on **New Dover Road.** For a laidback social atmosphere, try **Kipps Independent Hostel ❶,** 40 Nunnery Fields, home to a friendly management and a great movie selection. (☎786 121. Laundry £3. Internet £2 per hr. Key deposit £10. Dorms £14; singles £19; doubles £33. £0.50 surcharge for MC/V.) There's a **Safeway** supermarket on St. George's Pl. (☎769 335. Open M-F 8am-9pm, Sa 8am-8pm, Su 11am-5pm.) **Trains** from London Victoria arrive at Canterbury's East Station (1¾hr., 2 per hr., £18), while trains from London Charing Cross and Waterloo arrive at West Station (1½hr., every hr., £15). National Express **buses** (☎08705 808 080) arrive at St. George's Ln. from London (2hr., 2 per hr., £11.40). The **tourist office,** 12-13 Sun St., in the Buttermarket, books rooms for a £2.50 fee plus a 10% deposit. (☎378 100. Open Easter-Christmas M-Sa 9:30am-5pm, Su 10am-4pm; Christmas-Easter M-Sa 10am-4pm.) **Postal Code:** CT1 2BA.

BRIGHTON ☎01273

According to legend, the future King George IV sidled into Brighton (pop. 180,000) for some decidedly common hanky-panky around 1784. Today, Brighton is still the unrivaled home of the "dirty weekend"—it sparkles with a tawdry luster all its own. Check out England's long-time obsession with the Far East at the excessive **Royal Pavilion,** on Pavilion Parade, next to Old Steine. Rumor has it that King George IV wept tears of joy upon entering it, proving that wealth does not give you taste. (☎292 880. Open daily Apr.-Sept. 9:30am-5:45pm; Oct.-Mar. 10am-5:15pm. Tours daily 11:30am and 2:30pm. Pavilion £6, students £4.30. Tours £1.55.) Around the corner on Church St. stands the **Brighton Museum and Art Gallery,** showcasing Art Nouveau and Art Deco pieces, English pottery, and a Brighton historical exhibit that thoroughly explains the phrase "dirty weekend." (☎292 882. Open Tu 10am-7pm, W-Sa 10am-5pm, Su 2-5pm. Free.) Before heading to the rocky **beach,** stroll the novelty shops and colorful cafes of the **North Laines,** off Trafalgar St.

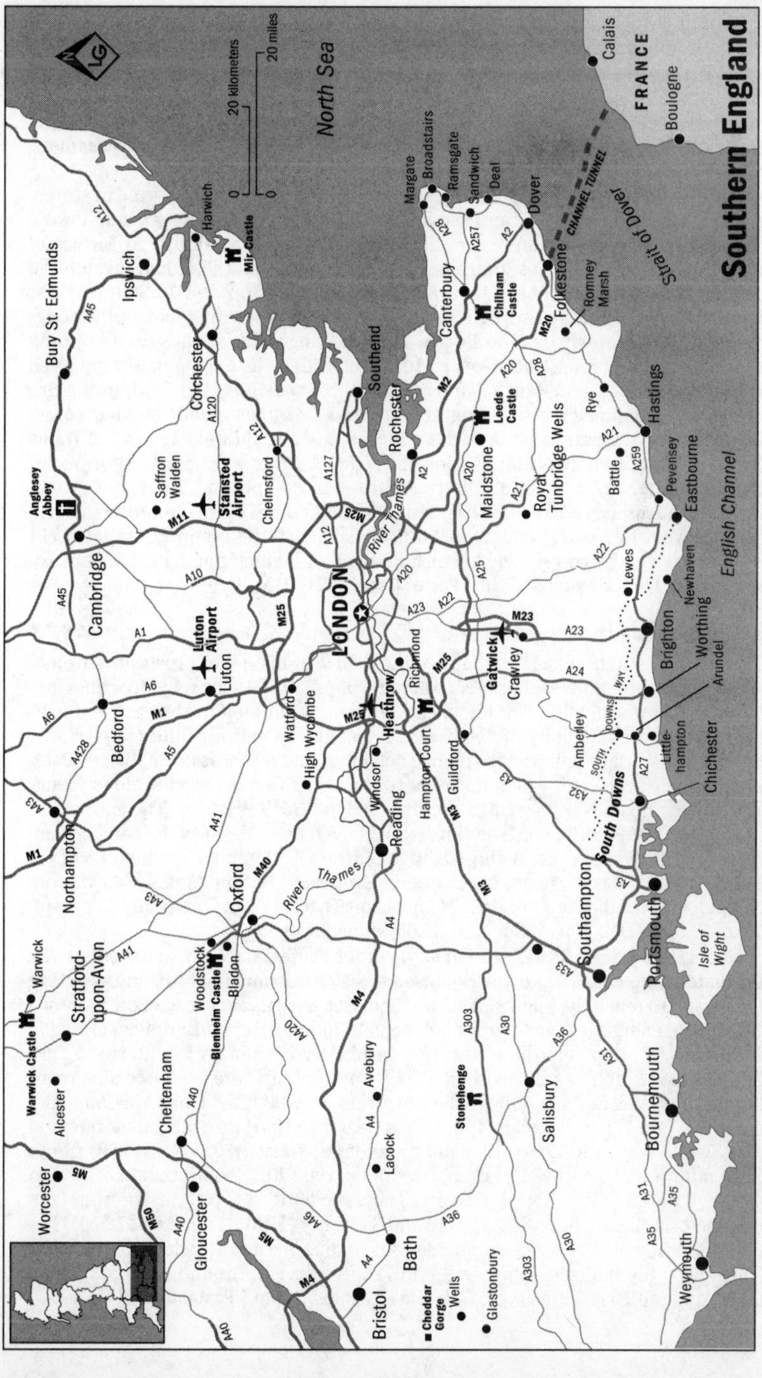
Southern England
North Sea
English Channel
Strait of Dover
FRANCE
Calais
Boulogne
CHANNEL TUNNEL
0
20 kilometers
0
20 miles
LONDON
River Thames
River Thames
Worcester
Gloucester
Cheltenham
Bristol
Bath
Cheddar Gorge
Wells
Glastonbury
Lacock
Avebury
Stonehenge
Salisbury
Bournemouth
Weymouth
Alcester
Warwick Castle
Warwick
Stratford-upon-Avon
Woodstock
Blenheim Castle
Bladon
Oxford
Northampton
Bedford
Luton
Luton Airport
Cambridge
Anglesey Abbey
Bury St. Edmunds
Ipswich
Harwich
Mir Castle
Colchester
Saffron Walden
Stansted Airport
Chelmsford
Southend
Rochester
Canterbury
Margate
Broadstairs
Ramsgate
Sandwich
Deal
Dover
Folkestone
Romney Marsh
Chilham Castle
Leeds Castle
Maidstone
Royal Tunbridge Wells
Rye
Hastings
Battle
Pevensey
Eastbourne
Newhaven
Lewes
Brighton
Worthing
Arundel
Littlehampton
Amberley
Chichester
South Downs
SOUTH DOWNS WAY
Portsmouth
Isle of Wight
Southampton
Guildford
Hampton Court
Richmond
Heathrow
Windsor
Reading
High Wycombe
Watford
Gatwick
Crawley
M1
M4
M5
M11
M20
M23
M25
M3
M40
M50
M2
A1
A2
A3
A4
A5
A6
A10
A12
A20
A21
A22
A23
A24
A25
A27
A28
A30
A31
A32
A33
A35
A36
A40
A41
A43
A45
A46
A120
A127
A257
A259
A303
A420
A428

BRITAIN

West of West Pier along King's Rd. Arches, **Baggies Backpackers ❶,** 33 Oriental Pl., is a mellow hostel with frequent live music and spontaneous parties, though co-ed bathrooms are cramped and rooms can get smoky. (☎733 740. Dorms £13; doubles £35. Cash only.) At **Bombay Aloo ❶,** 39 Ship St., loyal patrons return for blissfully cheap Indian vegetarian food and an unbeatable £5 all-you-can-eat special. (Entrees £3-7. Open daily noon-midnight. MC/V.) Buy groceries at **Somerfield,** 6 St. James's St. (☎570 363. Open M-Sa 8am-10pm, Su 11am-5pm.)

For nightlife tips, pick up *The Source* or *What's On* for free at music stores, newsstands, and pubs. Gay and lesbian venues are listed in *G Scene* and *3Sixty* (both free from newsstands); the tourist office also has a full list. At **Fortune of War,** 157 King's Rd. Arches, patrons can relax with a pint (£3.10) and watch the sun set over the Channel. (Open M-Sa noon-11pm, Su noon-10:30pm.) Most **clubs** are open Monday through Saturday 9pm-2am; after they close, the party moves to the waterfront. **The Beach,** 171-181 King's Rd. Arches, is a hopping shore-side club. (☎722 272. Cover £10, with student ID £8. Open M and W-Th 10pm-2am, F-Sa 10pm-3am.) The lesbian club **Candy Bar,** 129 St. James's St., draws an all-female crowd for nightly fun. (☎662 414; www.thecandybar.co.uk. Cover F-Sa £5. Open M-Th 9pm-2am, F-Sa 9pm-3am, Su 9pm-12:30am.) **Trains** (☎08457 484 950) leave from the northern end of Queen's Rd. for London Victoria (1hr., 2 per hr., £16.70) and Portsmouth (1½hr., 2 per hr., £13.40). National Express **buses** (☎08705 808 080) run to Pool Valley from London Victoria (2½hr., every hr., £9.30). The **tourist office** is at 10 Bartholomew Sq. (☎0906 711 2255; www.visitbrighton.com. Open June-Sept. M-F 9am-5pm, Sa 10am-5pm, Su 10am-4pm; Oct.-May closed Su.) **Postal Code:** BN1 1BA.

PORTSMOUTH ☎023

Though its reputation has been tainted by a 900-year history of prostitutes, drunkards, and foul-mouthed sailors, Portsmouth (pop. 190,500) has recently come into its own as a respectable seaside vacation town. Stretching to the east, the half-hearted resort community of **Southsea** can feel like an entirely different city. War buffs and historians will want to plunge head-first into the **Portsmouth Historic Dockyard,** in the Naval Yard, which houses a trio of Britain's most storied ships: Henry VIII's *Mary Rose*, Nelson's *HMS Victory*, and the *HMS Warrior*. The entrance is next to the tourist office on The Hard. (Ships open daily Mar.-Oct. 9:45am-5:30pm; Nov.-Feb. 10am-5pm. Each ship £9.70, children £8. Combination ticket £15.50/£12.50.) The **D-Day Museum,** on Clarence Esplanade in Southsea, leads visitors through life-size dioramas of the 1944 invasion. (☎9282 7261. Open daily Apr.-Sept. 10am-5:30pm; Oct.-Mar. 10am-5pm. £5.50, students £3.30.)

Moderately priced **B&Bs** (around £25) clutter **Southsea,** 2.5km southeast of The Hard along the coast. Take any Southsea bus from Commercial Rd. and get off at the Strand to reach the **Portsmouth and Southsea Backpackers Lodge ❶,** 4 Florence Rd., where energetic owners offer immaculate rooms to a pan-European crowd in a fabulous location near the waterfront. (☎9283 2495. Laundry £2. Internet £2 per hr. Dorms £12; doubles £26, with bath £29. Cash only.) There is a **Tesco** supermarket on Crasswell St., just outside the town center. (☎839 222. Open M-F 7am-midnight, Sa 7am-10pm, Su 10am-4pm.) **Pubs** near The Hard provide galley fare and grog, while those on Albert Rd. cater to students. **Trains** (☎08457 484 950) run to Portsmouth and Southsea Station, on Commercial Rd., from London Waterloo (1¾hr., 4 per hr., £22). National Express **buses** (☎08705 808 080) arrive from London Victoria (2½hr., every hr., £18.50) and Salisbury (1½hr., 1 per day, £12.50). The **tourist office,** which books accommodations for a £2 fee and 10% deposit, is on The Hard, near the historic ships. (☎9282 6722; www.visitportsmouth.co.uk. Open daily Apr.-Sept. 9:30am-5:45pm; Oct.-Mar. 9:30am-5:15pm.) **Postal Code:** PO1 1AA.

SALISBURY ☎01722

Salisbury (pop. 37,000) centers around the mammoth **Salisbury Cathedral,** built between 1220 and 1258. Its astounding 123m spire was the tallest of medieval England, and the bases of its marble pillars actually bend inward under 6400 tons of limestone. The cathedral also houses the world's oldest functioning mechanical clock. (☎555 120. Open June-Aug. M-Sa 7:15am-8:15pm, Su 7:15am-6:15pm; Sept.-May daily 7:15am-6:15pm. Cathedral tours free. Roof and tower tours £3, students £2. Call ahead. Suggested donation £4, students £3.50.) The best surviving copy of the **Magna Carta** rests in the nearby **Chapter House.** (Open June-Aug. M-Sa 9:30am-6:45pm, Su noon-5:30pm; Sept.-May daily 9:30am-5:30pm. Free.)

From the tourist office, head left on Fish Row, turn right on Queen St., go left on Milford St. and then under the overpass to find the **YHA Salisbury ❶,** Milford Hill House, on Milford Hill, which offers a TV lounge and a cafeteria. (☎327 572. Reservations recommended. Breakfast included. Laundry £3. Internet £4.20 per hr. Dorms £16, under 18 £12.50. MC/V.) At **Harper's "Upstairs Restaurant" ❷,** 6-7 Ox Rd., Market Sq., inventive international and English dishes (£6-10) make hearty meals. (☎333 118. Open M-F noon-2pm and 6-9:30pm, Sa noon-2pm and 6-10pm, Su 6-9pm. Oct.-May closed Su. AmEx/MC/V.) **Trains** arrive at South Western Rd., west of town across the River Avon, from London Waterloo (1½hr., 2 per hr., £24.20) and Portsmouth (1½hr., 2 per hr., £12). **Buses** pull into 8 Endless St. from Bath (#X4; every hr., £4.20) and London (3hr., 3 per day, £13.50). The **tourist office** is on Fish Row, in back of the Guildhall in Market Sq. (☎334 956; www.visitsalisbury.com. Open June-Sept. M-Sa 9:30am-6pm, Su 10:30am-4:30pm; Oct.-May M-Sa 9:30am-5pm.) **Postal Code:** SP1 1AB.

STONEHENGE AND AVEBURY

A sunken colossus amid swaying grass and indifferent sheep, Stonehenge has been battered for millennia by winds whipping at 80km per hour and visited by legions of people for over 5000 years. The monument, which has retained its present shape since about 1500 BC, was once a complete circle of 6.5m tall stones weighing up to 45 tons. Though the construction of Stonehenge has been attributed to builders from Merlin to extraterrestrials, the more plausible explanation—Neolithic builders using still unknown methods—is perhaps the most astonishing of all. You may admire Stonehenge for free from nearby Amesbury Hill, 2.5km up A303, or pay admission at the site, which includes a 30min. audio tour; the effect may be more haunting than the rocks themselves—a bizarre march of tourists who all appear engaged in phone calls between photo breaks. Ropes confine the throngs to a path around the outside of the monument. (☎01980 624 715. Open daily June-Aug. 9am-7pm; mid-Mar. to May and Sept. to mid-Oct. 9:30am-6pm; mid-Oct. to mid-Mar. 9:30am-4pm. £5.50, students £4.) The neighboring megaliths at **Avebury** are a good and less crowded alternative. Dating from 2500 BC, Avebury's stones are older and larger than their favored cousins at Stonehenge. Wilts & Dorset **buses** (☎336 855) run from Salisbury's center and train station, to both sites (#3, 5, and 6; 40-120min., round-trip £4-7). An **Explorer** ticket (£6.50) allows travel all day on any bus. The closest accommodations are in **Salisbury** (above).

BATH ☎01225

Bath (pop. 83,000) has been a must-see for travelers since AD 43, when the Romans built an elaborate complex to house the town's curative waters. Roman Bath flourished for 400 years, its hot (47°C) springs making the city a pilgrimage site for religious miracles, physical healing, and, later, social climbing. The **Roman Baths Museum,** Stall St., showcases the complexity of Roman engineering, which included central heating and internal plumbing. (☎447 785; www.romanbaths.co.uk. Open daily July-Aug. 9am-10pm; Sept.-Oct. and Mar.-June 9am-6pm; Jan.-Feb. and Nov.-Dec.

9:30am-5:30pm. Last admission 1hr. before closing. Audio tour included. £9.50. Joint ticket with Museum of Costume £12.50.) Next to the baths, the towering **Bath Abbey** fulfills masons George and William Vertue's promise to build "the goodliest vault in all England and France." (☎422 462; www.bathabbey.org. Open Apr.-Oct. M-Sa 9am-6pm, Su 1-2:30pm and 4:30-5:30pm; Nov.-Mar. M-Sa 9am-4pm, Su between services. Requested donation £2.50.) Walk up Gay St. to **The Circus,** a classic Georgian block where Thomas Gainsborough lived. Left of The Circus, the **Museum of Costume,** on Bennet St., hosts a dazzling parade of 400 years of catwalk fashions, from 17th-century silver tissue garments to a racy Versace ensemble worn by Jennifer Lopez. (☎477 785; www.museumofcostume.co.uk. Open daily Mar.-Oct. 11am-5pm; Nov.-Feb. 11am-4pm. £6.25, students £5.25.) From The Circus, proceed up Brock St. to the **Royal Crescent,** a half-moon of stately 18th-century townhouses bordering **Royal Victoria Park.**

Extremely convenient **St. Christopher's Inn ❷,** 16 Green St., has clean beds, and the downstairs pub is an ideal hangout. (☎481 444; www.st-christophers.co.uk. Internet £3 per hr. Dorms £16-19.50. Discount for online booking. MC/V.) The **International Backpackers Hostel ❶,** 13 Pierrepont St., three blocks from the baths, is a laidback backpacker's lair with music-themed rooms. (☎446 787. Luggage storage £1 per bag. Laundry £2.50. Internet £2 per hr. Reception 8am-midnight. Check-out 10:30am. Dorms M-Th and Su £13, F-Sa £14; doubles £35; triples £52.50. £5 deposit. MC/V.) **The Pump Room ❹,** Abbey Churchyard, exercises its monopoly over Bath Spa drinking water (£0.50 per glass) in a palatial Victorian ballroom. (☎444 477; www.searcys.co.uk. Breakfast, brunch, and lunch £6.25-16.25. Dinner July-Aug. £17.50-19.50. Open daily July-Aug. 8am-9pm; Sept.-June 9:30am-6pm. AmEx/MC/V.) Prepare a picnic with the fresh breads, fruits and vegetables available at **Waitrose** supermarket, in the Podium Shopping Centre on Northgate St., across from the post office. (☎442 550. Open M-Sa 8:30am-8pm, Su 11am-5pm.)

Trains leave from Dorchester St. for: Birmingham (2hr., every hr., £30); Bristol (15min., 3 per hr., £5); London Paddington (1½hr., 2 per hr., £36); London Waterloo (2-2½hr., 2 per day, £34). National Express **buses** (☎08705 808 080) run from Manvers St. to London (3½hr., every 1½hr., £15) and Oxford (2¼hr., 1 per day, £8.40). The train and bus stations are near the south end of Manvers St.; walk toward the town center and turn left on York St. to reach the **tourist office,** in Abbey Chambers. (☎08704 446 442; http://visitbath.co.uk. Open May-Sept. M-Sa 9:30am-6pm, Su 10am-4pm; Oct.-Apr. M-Sa 9:30am-5pm, Su 10am-4pm.) **Postal Code:** BA1 1AJ.

GLASTONBURY ☎01458

The reputed birthplace of Christianity in England, an Arthurian hot spot, and home to England's biggest summer music festival, Glastonbury (pop. 6900) is a quirky intersection of mysticism and pop culture. Legend has it that Joseph of Arimathea founded the massive **Glastonbury Abbey,** on Magdalene St., in AD 63. Though the abbey was destroyed during the English Reformation, the colossal pile of ruins and its accompanyting museum evoke the abbey's original grandeur. (☎832 267; www.glastonburyabbey.com. Open daily June-Aug. 9am-6pm; Sept.-May 10am-dusk. €4, students €3.50.) The 160m **Glastonbury Tor** is reputedly the site where King Arthur sleeps until his country needs him. To reach the Tor turn right at the top of High St. onto Lambrook, which becomes Chilkwell St.; turn left onto Wellhouse Ln. and follow the path up the hill, looking out for cow dung. (Open year-round. Free.) The annual **Glastonbury Festival** is the biggest and best of Britain's summer music festivals. The week-long at the end of June has featured some of the world's biggest bands. (Tickets ☎834 596; www.glastonburyfestivals.co.uk.)

At **Glastonbury Backpackers ❷,** 4 Market Pl., in the dead center of town at the corner of Magdalene St. and High St., a friendly staff and a lively cafe-bar complement the superb location. (☎833 353; www.glastonburybackpackers.com. Internet £5 per hr. Check-in 4:30-11pm. Dorms £12; doubles £30, with bath £35. MC/V.) **Heri-**

tage Fine Foods, 32-34 High St., has groceries. (☎831 003. Open M-W 7am-9pm, Th-Sa 9am-10pm, Su 8am-9pm.) No trains serve Glastonbury, but First **buses** (☎08706 082 608) run from town hall to London (3½hr., 7pm, £17) via Wells. From the bus stop, turn right on High St. to reach the **tourist office,** the Tribunal, 9 High St., which books rooms for a £3 fee plus a 10% deposit. (☎832 954; www.glastonburytic.co.uk. Open Apr.-Sept. M-Th and Su 10am-5pm, F-Sa 10am-5:30pm; Oct.-Mar. M-Th and Su 10am-4pm, F-Sa 10am-5:30pm.) **Postal Code:** BA6 9HG.

CHANNEL ISLANDS

Jersey, Guernsey, and seven smaller islands comprise the 194 sq. km known as the Channel Islands. Situated 128km south of England and 64km west of France, the islands tempt visitors with cultural fusion and a touch of (expensive) elegance.

FERRIES TO THE CHANNEL ISLANDS

Condor Ferries (☎01202 207 216) runs one early and one late ferry per day from Portsmouth, docking at St. Peter Port, Guernsey and the Elizabeth Harbor at St. Helier, Jersey. Times, frequencies, and ticket prices are affected by the season and the tides. Call ☎0845 124 2003 or check www.condorferries.com for up-to-date scheduling. ISIC holders are eligible for a 20% discount; ask before purchasing a ticket.

THE REAL DEAL. Though part of the UK, Jersey and Guernsey are essentially self-governing nations. The British pound is the official currency, but ATMs dish out Jersey or Guernsey pounds. These local pounds are on par with their British counterparts, but are not accepted outside the Channel Islands; you will have to exchange them upon returning to the mainland. Toward the end of your stay in the islands, make sure to ask local merchants to give you change in British pounds. Another quirk to keep in mind is that your mobile phone carrier may think you are in France (or not recognize you at all) and charge accordingly.

JERSEY. The largest of the Channel Islands, Jersey offers the bustling city center of St. Helier, gorgeous countryside, and rocky coastlines with extreme tides. Perhaps the most memorable of Jersey's sights is the gigantic **Mont Orgueil** castle on Gorey Pier. Climb to the top for a spectacular panorama. (☎01534 853 292. Open daily Apr.-Oct. 10am-6pm; Nov.-Mar. 10am-dusk. £5.25, students £4.40.) Across from Liberation Sq. by St. Helier Marina, the **Maritime Museum** features hands-on exhibits about the seas surrounding the island. (☎01534 811 043. Open daily Apr.-Oct. 10am-5pm; Nov.-Mar. 10am-4pm. £6, students £5.) In the fall, Jersey plays host to **Tennerfest,** challenging local restaurants to come up with the best £10 menu. Check out www.jersey.com for more on festivals throughout the year.

The only hostel on the island is the spanking-new **YHA Jersey (HI) ❷,** Haut de la Garenne, La Rue de la Pouclée des Quatre Chemis, St. Martin. To get there, take bus #3a from St. Helier (20min., every hr.) or after 5:45pm take #1 to Gorey and walk 0.8km up the nearly vertical hill, then cross the road and turn left up the larger hill. (☎840 100. Fabulous breakfast included. Open Jan.-Nov. daily 7-10am and 5-11pm; Dec.-Jan. F-Sa only. Dorms £18, under 18 £13. MC/V.) Peer at mosaics and a fountain (and that's just the bathroom) at the **Beach House ❷,** on Gorey Pier. (☎01534 859 902. Wraps £6. Salmon £9. Open M 11am-6pm, Tu-Su 12:30-3:30pm and 6:30pm-9:30pm. MC/V.) An efficient **bus** system makes travel around Jersey painless. From Weighbridge Terminal in St. Helier, Connex buses travel around the island. (☎01534 877 772; www.mybus.je. £0.90-1.60.) Easylink also offers a hop-on/hop-off tour service from the Terminal. (☎01534 876 418. M-F and Su. 1-day Explorer ticket

CLUBBING WITH CAUTION

urther steps in a region-wide ttempt to curb drink-spiking and ate rape have been taken by one lewquay nightclub. **Sailors** ecame the first club in Cornwall o install a drink-dispensing nachine—similar to a soda or andy dispenser—in July 2004. he machine allows clubbers ooking for bottled drinks to avoid ong lines at the bar, and allevi-ites stress on busy bartenders, is Newquay's beachgoers gener-illy pack clubs to capacity.

The machine also promotes lrink safety: patrons open drinks hemselves, preventing any possi-oility of tampering. This coincides vith the Spike Campaign, inaugu-ated by Cornish authorities in pril 2004. The campaign is eing carried by clubs like Sail-rs, who now use drink mats eminding customers to mind heir drinks. Bartenders have also mployed the help of "Spike," a reen monster atop a drink stirrer ontaining contact information—if hey pass an unattended drink wice, they will drop in the stirrer o remind patrons how easily omeone could compromise their lrinks.

Bars UK-wide have also begun elling "alcotops," brightly col-red reusable bottle tops www.alcotop.co.uk). Clubbers an put the top on when they put lown their drinks, dissuading otential spikers whose actions vould take much longer and vould be more conspicuous.

£7, 3-day £16.50, 5-day £21.) Exit the harbor, head left, follow signs to the Esplanade, and turn right for the **tourist office,** Liberation Sq., St. Helier. (☎01534 500 700; www.jersey.com. Open M-Sa 8:30am-7pm, Su 8:30am-2:15pm.)

GUERNSEY. Smaller in size but not in charm, Guernsey flaunts its French roots more than neighboring Jersey—cultural fusion is evident in the architecture, cuisine, and speech of the locals. **Hauteville House,** St. Peter Port, was Victor Hugo's home during his exile from France. It remains virtually unaltered from the days when he wrote *Les Misérables* here. The house is full of secret passages, inverted decorations (e.g., doors for tables and table legs for pillars), and hidden inscriptions. (☎01481 721 911. Open Apr.-Oct. M-Sa 10am-4pm. £4, students £2.)

For lodgings near town with views of nearby Sark and Herm, try **St. George's Hotel ❹**, St. George's Esplanade, St. Peter Port. (☎721 027. Breakfast included. £33 per person; Aug. £35. MC/V.) Farther down the road, **Christies ❸**, Le Pollet, is an airy French bistro serving local seafood salads and sandwiches. (☎726 624. Entrees £4.50-14.95. Open daily noon-2:30pm and 6-10:30pm. MC/V.) Island Coachways (☎01481 720 210; www.buses.gg) **buses** operate throughout the island and offer tours from May through September; call the office for fares and information. Routes #7 and 7a circle the coast every hour for £0.50. A **tourist office** is right near the ferry at St. Peter Port; its larger office is located across the harbor on North Esplanade. The staff books rooms for a £2 fee plus a 10% deposit, and distributes maps. *Naturally Guernsey* is a helpful guide to the island. (☎01481 723 552; www.guernseytouristboard.com. Open in summer M-Sa 9am-6pm, Su 9am-1pm; in winter M-F 9am-5pm, Sa 9am-4pm.)

THE CORNISH COAST

With lush cliffsides stretching out into the Atlantic, Cornwall's terrain doesn't feel quite like England. Years ago, the Celts fled westward in the face of Saxon conquest; today, the migration to Cornwall continues in the form of artists, vacationers, and surfers. Though the Cornish language is no longer spoken, the area remains protective of its distinctive past and its ubiquitous pasties.

NEWQUAY. Known as "the new California," Newquay (NEW-key; pop. 20,000) is an incongruous slice of surfer culture in the middle of Cornwall. Atlantic winds descend with a vengeance on **Fistral Beach,** creating arguably the best surfing conditions in Europe. **Sunset Surf Shop,** 106 Fore St., rents equipment and books lessons. (☎877 624. Board rental £5-

10 per day, £12-25 per 3 days, £25-40 per week. Wetsuits or bodyboards £4-5/10-12/20. Open Apr.-Oct. daily 9am-6pm.) For tamer waters, head to **Lusty Glaze** and **Tolcarne Beaches.** Enjoy sea views at **Original Backpackers ❷,** 16 Beachfield Ave. (☎874 668. Laundry £3. Dorms £11-17; low season £10. MC/V.) Restaurants in Newquay tend to be bland and costly. For a cheap alternative, head to pubs or the **Somerfield** supermarket at the end of Fore St. (☎876 006. Open M-Th and Sa 8am-8pm, F 8am-9pm, Su 11am-4pm; July-Aug. closes 1hr. later.) At night, watch out for the ubiquitous stag and hen parties, and head to the shore for more relaxed venues. Surfers and locals alike enjoy **The Koola,** 8-10 Beach Rd., one of Newquay's newest and classiest clubs. (☎873 415; www.thekoola.com. Open daily.)

Trains (☎08457 484 950) from Newquay go to Penzance (1½hr., 12 per day, £11) and Plymouth (50min., 15 per day, £8.60) via Par (50min., summer 5-8 per day, £4.50). National Express **buses** (☎08705 808 080) leave Manor Rd. for London (7hr., 2-4 per day, £33). The **tourist office** is on Marcus Hill, a few blocks toward the city center from the train station. It has free maps and books accommodations for £3.50 plus a 20% deposit. (☎854 020; www.newquay.co.uk. Open June-Sept. M-Sa 9:30am-5:30pm, Su 9:30am-12:30pm; Oct.-May reduced hours.)

PENZANCE ☎01736

Penzance is the very model of an ancient English pirate town. A Benedictine monastery, **St. Michael's Mount,** marks the spot where the archangel St. Michael is said to have appeared in AD 495. The interior is modest, but the grounds are lovely and the views are well worth the 30-story climb. (☎710 507. Open Apr.-Oct. M-F and Su 10:30am-5:30pm; Nov.-Mar. M, W, F by appointment only. £5.50, children £2.75.) During low tide, visitors can walk to the Mount; during high tide, take the ferry (£1). Penzance boasts an impressive number of art galleries; pick up the *Cornwall Galleries Guide* (£1) at the tourist office. Walk 30min. from the bus station, or take Sunset Coach #5 or 6 to the Pirate Pub and walk 10min. up Castle Horneck Rd. to reach the **YHA Penzance (HI) ❶,** Castle Horneck. Housed in an 18th-century mansion, the hostel has a friendly staff and clean rooms. (☎362 666. Internet £4.20 per hr. Lockout 10am-noon. Dorms £14, under 18 £10; twins £28. Tent sites £5.50. MC/V.) **Admiral Benbow,** 46 Chapel St., is a pub decorated with paraphernalia from local shipwrecks. (☎363 448. Pints £2.80. Open M-Sa 11am-11pm, Su noon-10:30pm.) **Trains** leave Wharf Rd., at the head of Albert Pier, for: London (5½hr., 7 per day, £67.50) and Newquay (3hr., 8 per day, €10.70). **Buses** also leave Wharf Rd. for London (8½hr., 7 per day, £34). The **tourist office** is between the train and bus stations on Station Rd. (☎362 207; www.go-cornwall.com. Open May-Sept. M-Sa 9am-5:30pm, Su 9am-1pm; Oct.-Apr. M-F 9am-5pm, Sa 10am-1pm.)

EAST ANGLIA AND THE MIDLANDS

The rich farmland and watery flats of East Anglia stretch northeast from London, cloaking the counties of Cambridgeshire, Norfolk, Suffolk, and parts of Essex. Mention of The Midlands inevitably evokes grim urban images, but there is a unique heritage and quiet grandeur to this smokestacked landscape. Even Birmingham, the region's much-maligned center, has its saving graces, among them lively nightlife and the Cadbury chocolate empire.

OXFORD ☎01865

Sprawling college grounds and 12th-century spires mark this Holy Grail of British academia. Nearly a millenium of scholarship at Oxford (pop. 120,000) has seen the education of 25 British prime ministers and countless other world leaders. Despite

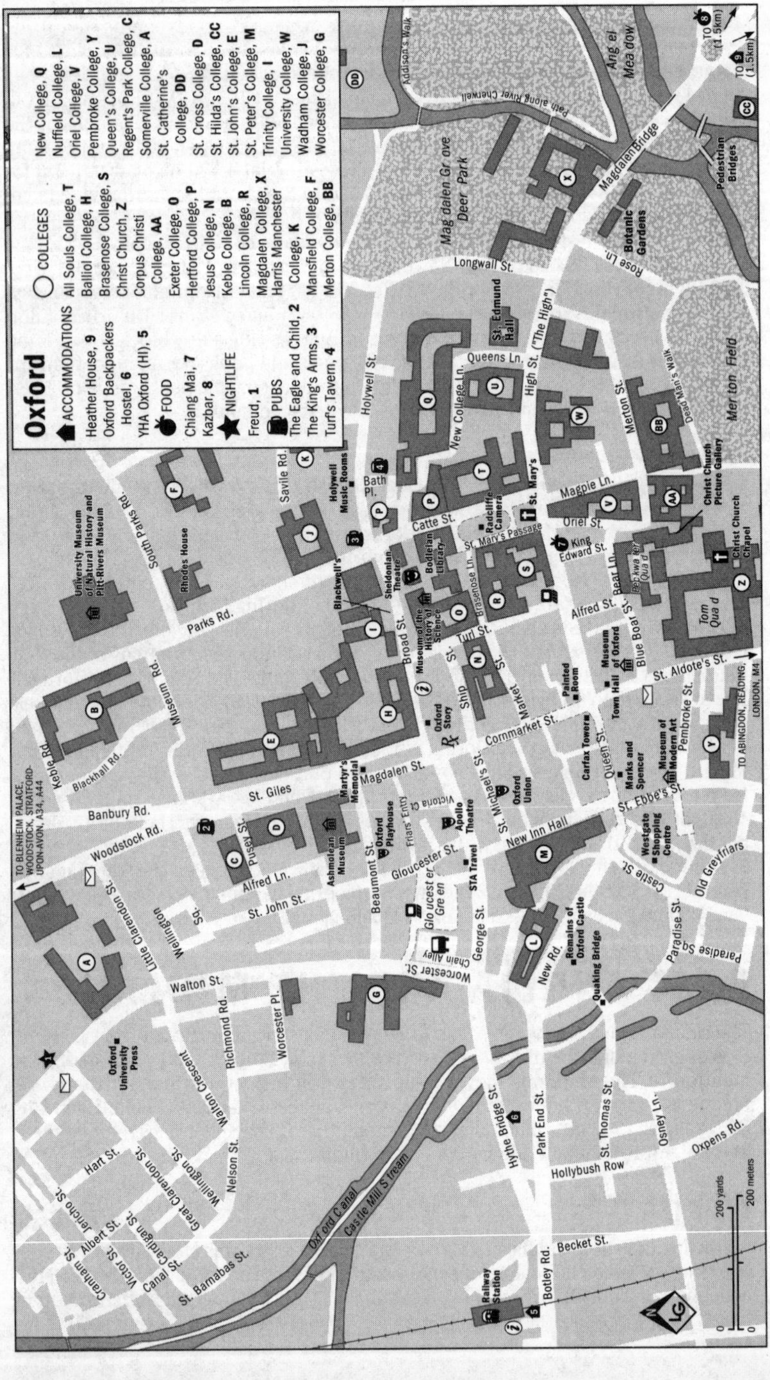

Oxford

ACCOMMODATIONS
Heather House, **9**
Oxford Backpackers Hostel, **6**
YHA Oxford (HI), **5**

FOOD
Chiang Mai, **7**
Kazbar, **8**

NIGHTLIFE
Freud, **1**

PUBS
The Eagle and Child, **2**
The King's Arms, **3**
Turf's Tavern, **4**

COLLEGES
All Souls College, **T**
Balliol College, **H**
Brasenose College, **S**
Christ Church, **Z**
Corpus Christi College, **AA**
Exeter College, **O**
Hertford College, **P**
Jesus College, **N**
Keble College, **B**
Lincoln College, **R**
Magdalen College, **X**
Harris Manchester College, **K**
Mansfield College, **F**
Merton College, **BB**
New College, **Q**
Nuffield College, **L**
Oriel College, **V**
Pembroke College, **Y**
Queen's College, **U**
Regent's Park College, **C**
Somerville College, **A**
St. Catherine's College, **DD**
St. Cross College, **D**
St. Hilda's College, **CC**
St. John's College, **E**
St. Peter's College, **M**
Trinity College, **I**
University College, **W**
Wadham College, **J**
Worcester College, **G**

all the tourists, Oxford has an irrepressible grandeur and pockets of tranquility that lift the spirits: the basement of Blackwell's Bookshop, the galleries of the Ashmolean, and the perfectly maintained quadrangles of the university's 39 colleges.

TRANSPORTATION AND PRACTICAL INFORMATION. **Trains** (☎08457 484 950) run from Botley Rd., down Park End, to: Birmingham (1¼hr., 2 per hr., £18); Glasgow (7hr., every hr., £70); London Paddington (1hr., 2-4 per hr., £15); Manchester (3¼hr., 1-2 per hr., £38.50). Stagecoach **buses** (☎772 250; www.stagecoachbus.com) run to Cambridge (3hr., 2 per hr., £6) and London (1¾hr.; 3-5 per hr.; £10, students £8). Oxford Bus Company (☎785 400; www.oxfordbus.co.uk) sends **buses** from Gloucester Green to: London Gatwick (2hr.; every hr.; £20, students £10); Heathrow (1¼hr.; 3 per hr.; £15, students £7.50); Victoria (1¾hr.; 3-5 per hr.; £10, students £8). The **tourist office,** 15-16 Broad St., books rooms for a £4 fee and offers 2hr. walking tours for £6.50. (☎726 871; www.visitoxford.org. Open Easter-Oct. M-Sa 9:30am-5:30pm, Su 10am-3:30pm; Nov.-Easter closed Su.) You can access the **Internet** for free at the **Oxford Central Library,** on Queen St. near the Westgate Shopping Center. (☎815 549. Open M-Th 9:15am-7pm, F-Sa 9:15am-5pm.) **Postal Code:** OX1 1ZZ.

ACCOMMODATIONS AND FOOD. Book at least a week ahead in summer. If it's late and you're homeless, call the **Oxford Association of Hotels and Guest Houses** (East Oxford ☎721 561, West Oxford 862 138, North Oxford 244 691, South Oxford 244 268). Make an right from the train station to reach the superbly located **YHA Oxford (HI) ❷,** 2a Botley Rd., with comfortable, clean rooms. (☎727 275. Breakfast included. Laundry £3. Internet £4.20 per hr. Dorms £20.50, under 18 £15.40; doubles £46. £3 HI discount. MC/V.) The **Oxford Backpackers Hostel ❶,** 9a Hythe Bridge St., between the bus and train stations, fosters a social atmosphere with an inexpensive bar, a pool table, and constant music. (☎721 761. Passport required. Laundry £2.50. Internet £2 per hr. Dorms £13-14; quads £64. MC/V.) Chatty proprietress Vivian offers sparkling, modern rooms at **Heather House ❹,** 192 Iffley Rd. Walk 10-15min. from Magdalen Bridge, or take the "Rose Hill" bus from the bus or train stations or Carfax Tower. (☎/fax 249 757. Singles £40; doubles £60-75. MC/V.)

Students fed up with bland college food and tourists on the go are easily seduced by a bevy of budget options in Oxford. If you're cooking for yourself, try **Gloucester Green Market,** behind the bus station, for cheap treats. (Open W 8am-3:30pm.) The **Covered Market** between Market St. and Carfax has fresh produce and bread. (Open M-Sa 8am-5pm.) Watch out for after-hours **kebab vans,** usually at Broad, High, Queen, and St. Aldate's St. **Kazbar ❶,** 25-27 Cowley Rd., is a Mediterranean tapas bar with Spanish-style decor and a posh atmosphere. (☎202 920. Tapas £2.20-4.75. Open daily noon-11pm. AmEx/MC/V.) **Chiang Mai ❷,** 130a High St., serves Thai dishes in a quaint 14th-century home. (☎202 233. Entrees £7-10. Open daily noon-2pm; also M-Th 6-10:15pm, F-Sa 6-10:30pm, Su 6-10pm. Reservations highly recommended. AmEx/MC/V.)

SIGHTS. The tourist office sells a map (£1.25) and the *Welcome to Oxford* guide (£1), which lists the visiting hours of Oxford's **colleges.** Don't bother trying to sneak in outside opening hours; even after hiding your pack and copy of *Let's Go*, bouncers, affectionately known as "bulldogs," will squint their eyes and kick you out. Just down St. Aldate's St. from Carfax, **Christ Church College** has Oxford's grandest quad and most distinguished alumni, including 13 former prime ministers. The dining hall and Tom Quad are also shooting locations for the *Harry Potter* movies. The **Christ Church Chapel** functions as the university's cathedral. It was here that the Rev. Charles Dodgson (better known as Lewis Carroll) first met Alice Liddell, the dean's daughter; the White Rabbit is immortalized in the hall's stained glass. **Tom Quad** takes its name from Great Tom, the seven-ton bell in Tom Tower that has faithfully rung 101 strokes (the original number of students) at 9:05pm (the original undergraduate curfew) every evening since 1682. (☎286 573; www.chch.ox.ac.uk. Open M-Sa 9am-

5pm, Su 1-5pm. Chapel services weekdays 6pm; Su 8, 10, 11:15am, and 6pm. £4, students £3.) J. R. R. Tolkien lectured at **Merton College,** Merton St., whose library houses the first printed Welsh Bible. Nearby **St. Alban's Quad** has some of the university's best gargoyles. (☎276 310; www.merton.ox.ac.uk. Open M-F 2-4pm, Sa-Su 10am-4pm. Free.) Soot-blackened **University College,** High St., was built in 1249 and vies with Merton for the title of oldest, claiming Alfred the Great as its founder. (☎276 602; www.univ.ox.ac.uk. Open to tours only.) **Oriel College,** wedged between High and Merton St., was once the turf of Sir Walter Raleigh. (☎276 555; www.oriel.ox.ac.uk. Open to tours only.) South of Oriel, **Corpus Christi College** surrounds a sundialed quad. The garden gate here was built for visits between Charles I and his queen, who lived nearby during the Civil Wars. (☎276 700; www.ccc.ox.ac.uk. Open daily 2-5pm.) The prestigious **All Souls College,** at the corner of High and Cattle St., admits only the best—and stores only the best in its wine cellar. (☎279 379; www.allsouls.ox.ac.uk. Open M-F 2-4:30pm.) At **The Queen's College,** High St., a boar's head graces the table at Christmas to commemorate a student who, attacked by a boar on the outskirts of town, choked the animal to death with a volume of Aristotle. (☎279 120; www.queens.ox.ac.uk. Open to tours only.) With extensive grounds, flower-edged quads, and a deer park, **Magdalen College** (MAUD-lin), on High St. near the Cherwell, is considered Oxford's handsomest. Seamus Heaney, C.S. Lewis, and Oscar Wilde are among the college's alumni. (☎276 000; www.magd.ox.ac.uk. Open daily July-Sept. noon-6pm; Oct.-June 1-6pm. £3, students £2.)

The grand **Ashmolean Museum,** on Beaumont St., houses works by van Gogh, Matisse, Monet, Michelangelo, Rodin, and da Vinci. Opened in 1683, the Ashmolean was Britain's first public museum. (☎278 000. Open Tu-Sa 10am-5pm, Su noon-5pm; in summer Th until 7pm. Free. Tours £2.) **Bodleian Library,** on Broad St., is Oxford's principal reading and research library with over five million books and 50,000 manuscripts. It receives a copy of every book printed in Great Britian but no one has ever been permitted to check one out. (☎277 000; www.bodley.ox.ac.uk. Guided tours leave from the Divinity School, in the main quad, M-Sa 2-4 per day in the afternoon. Open M-F 9am-10pm, Sa 9am-1pm; fall through spring M-F 9am-7pm, Sa 9am-1pm. Tours £4, audio tours £2.) Next door on Broad St. is the **Sheldonian Theatre,** a Romanesque auditorium designed by a teenage Christopher Wren. Graduation ceremonies, conducted in Latin, take place in the Sheldonian, as do world-class opera performances. The cupola affords a picturesque view of Oxford's scattered quads. (☎277 299. Open M-Sa 10am-12:30pm and 2-4:30pm; in winter until 3:30pm. £1.50, under 15 £1.) You could browse the 10km of bookshelves for days at **Blackwell's Bookstore,** 53 Broad St., a local favorite. (☎792 792. Open M and W-Sa 9am-6pm, Tu 9:30am-6pm, Su 11am-5pm.) **Carfax Tower,** at the corner of Queen and Cornmarket St., marks the center of the original city, and all roads seem to lead here. Hike up its 99 narrow steps for a great view. (☎792 653. Open daily Apr.-Oct. 10am-5pm; Nov.-Mar. 10am-3:30pm. £1, under 16 £0.80.)

ENTERTAINMENT AND NIGHTLIFE. Punting on the River Thames or on the River Cherwell (CHAR-wul) is a traditional Oxford pastime. **Magdalen Bridge Boat Company,** just under Magdalen Bridge, rents boats. (☎202 643. £10-12 per hr.; deposit £30 and ID. Open daily Mar.-Oct. 7:30am-9pm. Cash and checks only.) Bring along your own wine or bottle of champagne for a floating toast.

Music and drama at Oxford are cherished arts. *This Month in Oxford* and *Daily Information* (www.dailyinfo.co.uk), both available at the tourist office for free, list upcoming events. **Pubs** far outnumber colleges in Oxford. Many are so small that a single band of students will squeeze out other patrons—luckily, there's usually another place just around the corner, so be ready to crawl. Known to students as "the Turf," **Turf's Tavern,** 4 Bath Pl., off Holywell St., is a wildly popular 13th-century pub tucked in the alley of an alley, against the ruins of the city wall. (☎243 235. Open M-Sa 11am-11pm, Su noon-10:30pm. Food served noon-7:30pm. AmEx/MC/V.) **The Eagle and Child,** 49 St. Giles (a.k.a. "the Bird and Baby") soothed the parched throats of C. S. Lewis and J. R. R. Tolkien for 25 years. *The Chronicles of Narnia* and *The Hobbit* were first read aloud here. (☎302 925. Open M-Sa 11am-11pm, Su noon-10:30pm. Food served M-F noon-10pm, Sa-Su noon-9pm. AmEx/MC/V.) Merry masses gravitate to back rooms at **The King's Arms,** 40 Holywell St., Oxford's unofficial student union. (☎242 369. Open M-Sa 10:30am-11pm, Su 10:30am-10:30pm. MC/V.) After happy hour at the pubs, head to the clubs at **Walton Street** or **Cowley Road.** In a former church, **Freud,** 119 Walton St., is a cafe by day and chic cocktail bar by night. (☎311 171. Open M and Su 11am-midnight, Tu 11am-1am, W 11am-1:30am, Th-Sa 11am-2am. MC/V.)

STRATFORD-UPON-AVON ☎01789

Local son William Shakespeare is the area's industry, and proprietors tout a dozen-odd properties linked, however remotely, to the Bard. Stratford's Will-centered sights are best seen before the daytrippers arrive at 11am, or after 4pm when the crowds disperse. Diehard fans can buy the **All Five Houses** ticket for admission to the official Shakespeare properties: Anne Hathaway's Cottage, Mary Arden's House and Countryside Museum, Hall's Croft, New Place and Nash's House, and Shakespeare's Birthplace. (Tickets available from any house. £13, students £12.) The **Three In-Town Houses** pass covers only the latter three. (£10, students £8.) **Shakespeare's Birthplace,** on Henley St., is part period re-creation and part exhibit of Shakespeare's life and works. (☎201 823. Open June-Aug. M-Sa 9am-5pm, Su 9:30am-5pm; Apr.-May and Sept.-Oct. daily 10am-5pm; Nov.-Mar. M-Sa 10am-4pm, Su 10:30am-4pm. £6.70, students £5.50.) **New Place,** on High St., was Stratford's finest home when Shakespeare bought it in 1597—now only the foundation remains. View it from **Nash's House,** on Chapel St., which belonged to the first husband of Shakespeare's granddaughter. Pay homage to the Bard's **grave** in the **Holy Trinity Church,** on Trinity St. (☎266 316. Open Apr.-Sept. M-Sa 8:30am-6pm, Su noon-5pm; low season reduced hours. Requested donation £1.) The world-famous **Royal Shakespeare Company** sells over one million tickets each year. Tickets for the **Royal Shakespeare Theatre,** the **Swan Theatre,** and **The Other Place** are sold through the box office in the Royal Shakespeare Theatre, on the Waterside. Five student standing-room-only tickets offer spectacular views. (Information ☎403 444, ticket hotline 0870 609 1110; www.rsc.org.uk. Open M-Sa 9:30am-8pm. Tickets £5-40. Students and under 30 eligible for half-price tickets available in advance M-W performances, available same day for Th-Su. Standbys £12-15. Tours £5, students £4.)

B&Bs line **Evesham Place, Evesham Road, Grove Road,** and **Shipston Road,** but reservations are a must. **Carlton Guest House ❸,** 22 Evesham Pl., has spacious rooms and friendly service. (☎293 548. £20-26 per person. Cash only.) Classy yet cozy, **The Oppo ❸,** 13 Sheep St., gets rave reviews for its varied cuisine. (☎269 980. Transcendent lasagna £9. Open daily noon-2pm, also M-Th 5:30-9:30pm, F-Sa 5-11pm, Su 6-9:30pm. MC/V.) A **Somerfield** supermarket is in Town Sq. (☎292 604. Open M-W 8am-7pm, Th-Sa 8am-8pm, Su 10am-4pm.) RSC actors make almost nightly appearances at **Dirty Duck Pub,** 66 Waterside. (☎297 312. Open M-Sa 11am-11pm, Su noon-10:30pm.) **Trains** (☎08457 484 950) arrive at Station Rd., off Alcester Rd., from Birmingham (50min., 1 per hr., £5) and London Paddington (2¼hr., 5 per day, £34.20). National Express (☎08705 808 080) runs **buses** to London (3hr., 3 per day, £14). Local Stratford Blue bus #X20 stops at Wood and Bridge St., and goes to Birmingham (1¼hr., every hr., £3.50). The **tourist office,** Bridgefoot, across Warwick Rd., books rooms for a £3 charge and a 10% deposit. (☎08701 607 930. Open Apr.-Sept. M-Sa 9am-5:30pm, Su 10:30am-4:30pm; Oct.-Mar. M-Sa 9am-5pm.) Surf the **Internet** at **Cyber Junction,** 28 Greenhill St. (£2.50 per 30min., £4 per hr.; students £2/3.50. Open M-F 10am-6pm, Sa 10:30am-5:30pm, Su 11am-5pm.) **Postal Code:** CV37 6PU.

THE COTSWOLDS

"Cotswolds" means "sheep enclosure in rolling hillsides," and that pretty much covers it. Grazing sheep and cattle roam 2000 sq. km of postcard-ready hillsides linking heavily touristed towns.

TRANSPORTATION AND PRACTICAL INFORMATION. Public transportation to and in the Cotswolds is scarce; planning ahead is a must as some locations may be impossible to reach by public transportation. Useful gateway cities are Bath, Cheltenham, and Oxford. **Moreton-in-Marsh,** one of the bigger villages, has **trains** to London (1½hr., every 1-2hr., £21.20) via Oxford (30min., £8.20). It's far easier to reach the Cotswolds by **bus.** The Cheltenham tourist office's free *Getting There* pamphlet has detailed bus information. *Explore the Cotswolds by Public Transport*, available for free at village tourist offices, has timetables. Pulham's Coaches (☎01451 820 369) run from Cheltenham to Moreton-in-Marsh (1hr., M-Sa 7 per day, £1.75) via Stow-on-the-Wold (50min., £1.70).

Local roads are perfect for **biking. The Toy Shop,** on High St. in Moreton-in-Marsh, rents bikes. (☎01608 650 756. £12 per half-day, £14 per day. Open M and W-Sa 9am-1pm and 2-5pm.) Visitors can also experience the Cotswolds as the English have for centuries, by treading the well-worn footpaths from village to village. The **Cotswold Way,** spanning over 160km from Bath to Chipping Camden, offers lovely vistas of hills and dales. Contact the **National Trails Office** (☎01865 810 224) for details on this and other trails. The free *Cotswold Events* booklet lists everything from music festivals and antique markets to cheese-rolling and wool-sack races. The **Cotswold Discovery Tour** is a full-day bus tour that starts in Bath and visits five of the most scenic and touristed villages. (☎09067 112 000; www.madmax.abel.co.uk. Apr.-Oct. Tu, Th, Su 9am-5:15pm. £25.)

WINCHCOMBE, MORETON-IN-MARSH, AND STOW-ON-THE-WOLD. Ten kilometers north of Cheltenham on A46, **Sudeley Castle,** once the manor of King Ethelred the Unready, crowns the town of **Winchcombe.** (☎01242 602 308; www.sudeleycastle.co.uk. Open Mar.-Oct. daily 11am-5pm. £7.20, students £6.20.) The Winchcombe **tourist office** is on High St., next to Town Hall. (☎01242 602 925. Open Apr.-Oct. M-Sa 10am-1pm and 2-5pm, Su 10am-1pm and 2-4pm; Nov.-Mar. Sa-Su 10am-1pm and 2-4pm.) With a train station, relatively frequent bus service, and bike shop, **Moreton-in-Marsh** is a convenient base for exploring the Cotswolds. Its **tourist office** is in the District Council Building on High St. (☎01608 650 881. Open M 8:45am-4pm, Tu-Th 8:45am-5:15pm, F 8:45am-4:45pm, Sa 10am-1pm.) **Warwick House B&B ❸**, on London Rd., offers amazing value with a pleasant garden and free access to a nearby leisure center. (☎01608 650 733; www.snoozeandsizzle.com. Free pickup from train station. £21-25 per person. Cash only.) **Stow-on-the-Wold,** the self-proclaimed "Heart of the Cotswolds," sits atop a hill, offering visitors fine views and a sense of the Cotswold pace of life. The **tourist office** is in Hollis House on The Square. (☎01451 831 082. Open M-Sa Easter-Oct. 9:30am-5:30pm; Nov.-Easter 9:30am-4:30pm.) The **YHA (HI) ❷,** beside the tourist office, has bright rooms in a beautiful building. (☎01451 830 497. Laundry £3. Reception 8-10am and 5-10pm. Lockout 10am-5pm. Curfew 11pm. Book 1 month ahead. Open mid-Feb. to Oct. daily; Nov.-Dec. F-Sa. Dorms £14, under 18 £10. AmEx/MC/V.) A **Tesco** supermarket is on Fosse Way. (Open M-F 6am-midnight, Sa 6am-10pm, Su 10am-4pm.)

BIRMINGHAM ☎0121

Industrial Birmingham (pop. 1,000,000) may seem at first to have nothing to suit the suitless. However, a walk through "Brum" reveals the fruits of focused efforts to overcome an ugly reputation. At night, the city truly comes alive, fueled by world-class entertainers and a university crowd. The most popular attractions are regenerated **shopping** districts. The sprawling **Bullring,** recognizable by the wavy, scaled Selfridges, is Europe's largest retail project. (☎632 1500; www.bullring.co.uk. Open M-F 9:30am-8pm, Sa 9am-8pm, Su 11am-5pm.) Twelve minutes south of town by rail or bus lies **Cadbury World,** an unabashed, cavity-inducing celebration of the famed chocolate empire. Take a train from New St. to Bournville, or bus #84 from the city center. (☎451 4159. Open Mar.-Oct. daily 10am-3pm; Nov.-Feb. closed M and F. £10.50, students £8.30.) The **Birmingham International Jazz Festival** brings over 200 performers to town during the first two weeks of July. (☎454 7020; www.birminghamjazzfestival.com. Most events free.)

Despite its size, Birmingham has no hostels, and inexpensive B&Bs are rare. Busy **Hagley Road** is your best bet. Many of the rooms in the Victorian **Cook House** ❸, 425 Hagley Rd., have fireplaces and original furnishings. (☎429 1916. Singles £20-22, with bath £28; doubles £38/46. Cash only.) Get groceries from **Sainsbury's,** Martineau Pl., 17 Union St. (☎236 6496. Open M-Sa 7am-8pm, Su 11am-5pm.) **Broad Street** is teeming with trendy cafe-bars and clubs. Pick up the bimonthly *What's On* to discover the latest hot spots. **9 Bar,** 192 Broad St., is a futuristic warehouse with alluringly dark decor. (☎643 5100. Cover F £1, Sa £3-5. Open W-Sa 8pm-2am, Su 8pm-1am.) A thriving gay-friendly scene centers around **Essex Street.**

Trains arrive at New St. Station (☎08457 484 950) from: Liverpool Lime St. (1½hr., every hr., £19.80); London Euston (2hr., 2 per hr., £27.40); Manchester Piccadilly (2hr., every hr., £21); Oxford (1¼hr., 2 per hr., £19). National Express **buses** (☎08705 808 080) arrive at Digbeth Station from: Cardiff (2½hr., 3 per day, £19.40); Liverpool (3hr., 4 per day, £13); London (3hr., every hr., £14); Manchester (2½hr., every 2hr., £10.50). The **tourist office,** in The Rotunda, 150 New St., books rooms for a 10% deposit. (☎202 5099; www.beinbirmingham.com. Open M-Sa 9:30am-5:30pm, Su 10:30am-4:30pm.) **Postal Code:** B2 4TU.

CAMBRIDGE ☎01223

In contrast to museum-oriented, metropolitan Oxford, Cambridge is determined to retain its pastoral academic robes; the city manages, rather than encourages, visitors. Once the exclusive preserve of sons of privilege, the university now welcomes women and state-school pupils. During May Week (cleverly named to disguise the fact that the party occurs over two weeks in June), which marks term's end, Cambridge shakes off its reserve with Pimms-soaked glee.

TRANSPORTATION AND PRACTICAL INFORMATION. **Trains** (☎08457 484 950) run from Station Rd. to London King's Cross (45min., 3 per hr., £16.40) and London Liverpool St. (1¼hr., 5 per hr., £16.40). From Drummer St., National Express **buses** (☎08705 808 080) go to London Victoria (2hr., 2 per hr., £9.30); Stagecoach Express buses (☎01604 676 060) go to Oxford (3hr., every hr., from £6). Bicycles are the primary mode of transportation in Cambridge. Try **Mike's Bikes,** 28 Mill Rd., for **bicycle rentals.** (☎312 591. £10 per day plus £35 deposit. Open M-Sa 9am-6pm, Su 10am-4pm. MC/V.) The **tourist office,** is south of Market Sq. on Wheeler St. (☎09065 862 526; www.visitcambridge.org. Open M-F 10am-5:30pm, Sa 10am-5pm, Su 11am-4pm.) **Postal Code:** CB2 3AA.

BRITAIN

ACCOMMODATIONS AND FOOD. Rooms are scarce in Cambridge, which makes prices high and quality low. Most **B&Bs** aren't in the town center, but those around **Portugal Street** and **Tenison Road** are close to the train station. Check the guide to accommodations (£0.50) at the tourist office. Two blocks from the train station, **Tenison Towers Guest House** ❸, 148 Tenison Rd., has impeccably clean, airy rooms with fresh flowers as well as free breakfast. (☎363 924; www.cambridgecitytenisontowers.com. Singles £28-30; doubles £55. Cash only.) **YHA Cambridge (HI)** ❷, 97

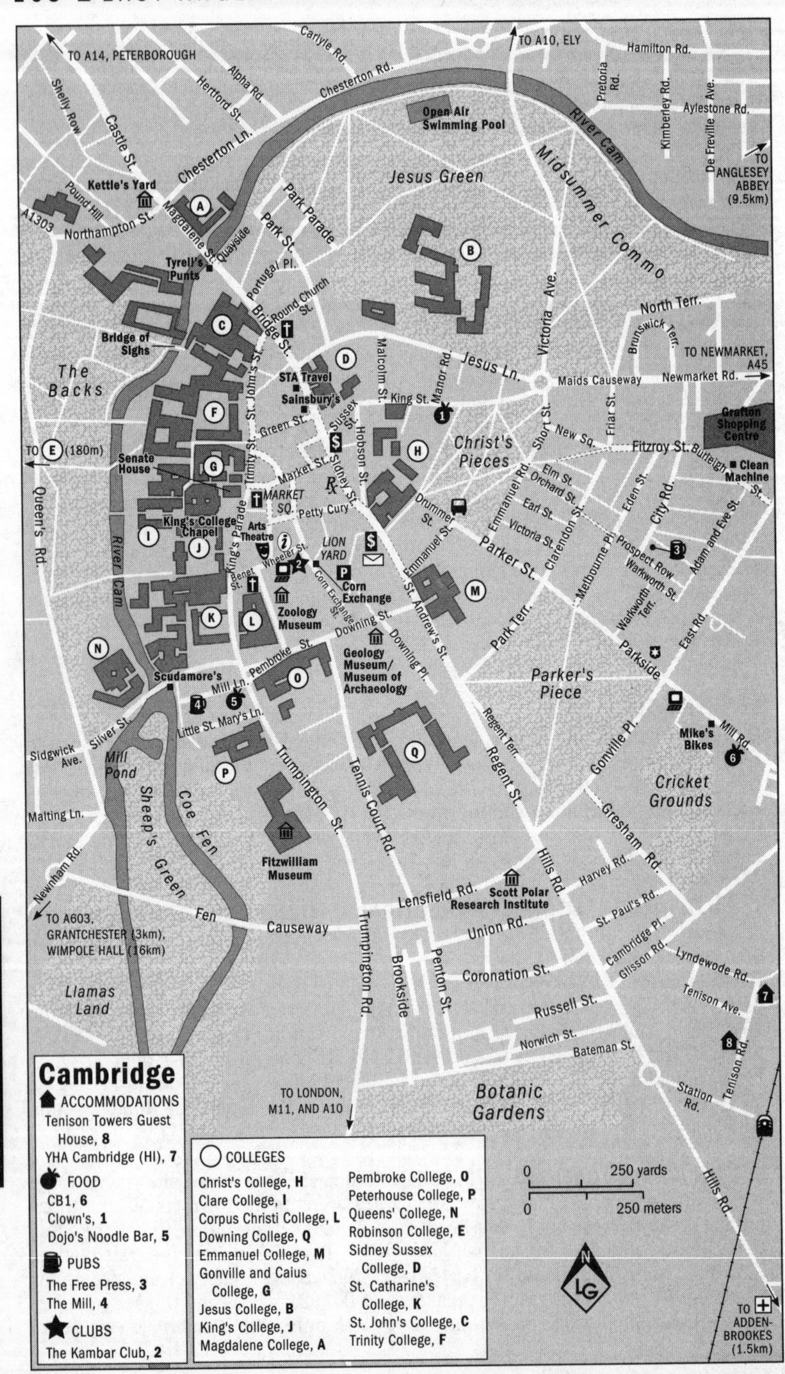
Cambridge
ACCOMMODATIONS
Tenison Towers Guest House, 8
YHA Cambridge (HI), 7
FOOD
CB1, 6
Clown's, 1
Dojo's Noodle Bar, 5
PUBS
The Free Press, 3
The Mill, 4
CLUBS
The Kambar Club, 2
COLLEGES
Christ's College, H
Clare College, I
Corpus Christi College, L
Downing College, Q
Emmanuel College, M
Gonville and Caius College, G
Jesus College, B
King's College, J
Magdalene College, A
Pembroke College, O
Peterhouse College, P
Queens' College, N
Robinson College, E
Sidney Sussex College, D
St. Catharine's College, K
St. John's College, C
Trinity College, F
TO A14, PETERBOROUGH
TO A10, ELY
TO NEWMARKET, A45
TO ANGLESEY ABBEY (9.5km)
TO A603, GRANTCHESTER (3km), WIMPOLE HALL (16km)
TO LONDON, M11, AND A10
TO ADDENBROOKES (1.5km)
TO E (180m)
Jesus Green
Midsummer Commo
Christ's Pieces
Parker's Piece
The Backs
Cricket Grounds
Botanic Gardens
Llamas Land
Sheep's Green
Coe Fen
Mill Pond
River Cam
Open Air Swimming Pool
Kettle's Yard
Tyrell's Punts
Bridge of Sighs
Senate House
King's College Chapel
Arts Theatre
STA Travel
Sainsbury's
MARKET SQ.
LION YARD
Corn Exchange
Zoology Museum
Geology Museum/ Museum of Archaeology
Fitzwilliam Museum
Scott Polar Research Institute
Scudamore's
Mike's Bikes
Grafton Shopping Centre
Clean Machine
0 250 yards
0 250 meters

Tenison Rd., has a popular TV lounge and a welcoming atmosphere close to the train station. (☎354 601. Breakfast included. Lockers £1. Laundry £3. Internet £4 per hr. Reception 24hr. Call ahead. Dorms £17, under 18 £13. MC/V.)

Market Square has pyramids of fruit and vegetables. (Open M-Sa 9:30am-4:30pm.) Students buy their Pimms and baguettes at **Sainsbury's,** 44 Sidney St. (☎366 891. Open M-F 8am-9pm, Sa 7:30am-9pm, Su 11am-5pm.) South of town, **Hills Road** and **Mill Road** have good budget options. Children's drawings plaster the orange walls at **Clown's ❶,** 54 King St., which serves a variety of homemade pastas and Italian desserts. (☎355 711. Entrees £3-7. Open M-Sa 8am-midnight, Su 8am-11pm. Cash only.) **Dojo's Noodle Bar ❶,** 1-2 Mill Rd., whips up enormous plates of asian noodles for less than £6.50. (☎363 471; www.dojonoodlebar.co.uk. Open M-Th noon-2:30pm and 5:30-11pm, F noon-4pm and 5:30-11pm, Sa-Su noon-11pm. Cash only.) Students sip coffee at the book-filled **CB1 ❶,** 32 Mill Rd. (☎576 306. Internet £2.40 per hr. Coffee £1-1.50. Open daily 10am-8pm. Cash only.)

SIGHTS. Cambridge is an architect's dream, packing some of England's most breathtaking monuments into less than three square kilometers. Soaring **King's College Chapel** and St. John's **Bridge of Sighs** are sightseeing staples, while more obscure college courts veil largely undiscovered gardens and courtyards. Many colleges at the **University of Cambridge** close to sightseers during Easter term, and virtually all are closed during exams (mid-May to mid-June); your best bet is to call ahead for hours. Porters (bowler-wearing former servicemen) guard the gates. Travelers that look like undergrads (no backpack, camera, or Cambridge sweatshirt) can often wander freely after hours. The fastest way to blow your cover is to trample the sacred grass of the courtyards, a privilege reserved for the elite.

If you only have time for a few colleges, try Trinity, King's, Saint John's, and Queens'. Sir Isaac Newton originally measured the speed of sound by timing the echo in the cloisters along the north side of the Great Court at **Trinity College,** on Trinity St. Trinity also houses the stunning **Wren Library,** with A.A. Milne's handwritten manuscript of *Winnie the Pooh* and the original copy of Newton's *Principia.* (☎338 400. Chapel and courtyard open daily 10am-5pm. Wren Library open M-F noon-2pm. Easter-Oct. £2.20, students £1.30. Nov.-Easter free.) At **King's College,** Reubens's magnificent *Adoration of the Magi* hangs behind the altar of the spectacular Gothic chapel. (☎331 100. Open M-Sa 9:30am-4:30pm, Su 10am-5pm. Tours arranged through the tourist office. £4.50, students £3.) Established in 1511 by the mother of Henry VIII, **St. John's College,** on St. John's St., is one of seven colleges founded by women. It boasts the 12th-century School of Pythagoras, thought to be the oldest complete building in Cambridge. (☎338 600. Open daily 10am-5:30pm. £2, students £1.20.) **Queens' College,** Silver St., has the only unaltered Tudor courtyard in Cambridge. Despite rumors to the contrary, its Mathematical Bridge has always been supported by screws and bolts, not just mathematical principle. (☎335 511. Open Mar.-Oct. daily 10am-4:30pm. £1.30.) A welcome break from academia, the **Fitzwilliam Museum,** on Trumpington St., displays Egyptian, Greek, and Asian treasures in addition to works by Brueghel, Monet, and Reubens. (☎332 900. Open Tu-Sa 10am-5pm, Su noon-5pm. Suggested donation £3.)

ENTERTAINMENT AND NIGHTLIFE. The best source for info on student activities is the student newspaper, *Varsity* (£0.20). **Punting** on the River Cam is a favored form of entertainment. **Scudamore's,** Silver St. Bridge, rents boats. (☎359 750; www.scudamores.com. M-F £14 per hr. plus a £70 deposit, Sa-Su £2 per extra hr. MC/V.) **Pubs** make up the core of Cambridge nightlife, but clubs and bars are also in the curriculum. **King Street** has a diverse array of pubs. **The Mill,** 14 Mill Ln., off Silver St. Bridge, sits beside a riverside park for punt- and people-watching. (Open M-Sa 11am-11pm, Su noon-10:30pm.) Locals haunt **The Free Press,** Prospect Row, named after an abolitionist newspaper. (No smoking. Open M-F noon-

2:30pm and 6-11pm, Sa noon-3pm and 6-11pm, Su noon-3pm and 7-10:30pm.) **The Kambar Club,** 1 Wheeler St., plays indie rock, garage, goth, electronica, and drum 'n' bass music, changing nightly. (Cover £5, students £3. Open M-Sa 10pm-2:30am.)

NORTHERN ENGLAND

The north's major cities grew out of the wool and coal industries, and bear the 19th-century scars to prove it, but their reinvigorated city centers have embraced post-industrial hipness with fresh youth culture. The region's innovative music and arts scenes are world-famous: Liverpool and Manchester alone have produced four of *Q Magazine's* 10 biggest rock stars of the 20th century. When you need a break from frenetic urbanity, find respite in the Peak District's green hills or the Lake District's crags and waters.

MANCHESTER ☎0161

Teeming with electronic beats and post-industrial glitz, Manchester (pop. 430,000) has risen from factory soot to become one of England's hippest spots. "Madchester" played an instrumental role in the evolution of pop and punk, especially during the New Wave of the 80s. Though still dodgy in parts, the city is increasingly accessible to the street smart seeking its vibrant arts and notorious nightclubs.

TRANSPORTATION AND PRACTICAL INFORMATION. Flights arrive at Manchester International Airport (MAN; ☎489 3000). **Trains** leave Piccadilly Station on London Rd., and Victoria Station on Victoria St., for: Birmingham (1¾hr., every hr., £21); Edinburgh (4hr., 5 per day, £49); Liverpool (50min., 2 per hr., £8); London Euston (2½-3hr., every hr., £54); York (40min., 2 per hr., £16.20). National Express **buses** (☎08705 808 080) go from Chorlton St. to Liverpool (55min., every hr., £5.50) and London (4-6hr., 7-12 per day, £19.50). Piccadilly Gardens is home to about 50 stops for local bus routes; pick up a route map at the tourist office. (All-day bus ticket £3.30.) **Manchester Visitor Centre,** in the Town Hall Extension on Lloyd St., books accommodations for £2.50 plus a 10% deposit. (☎234 3157; www.visitmanchester.com. Open M-Sa 10am-5:30pm, Su 10:30am-4:30pm.) Free **Internet** available at **Central Library,** St. Peter's Sq. (☎234 1982. Open M-Tu and Th 10am-7:45pm, W 1-7:45pm, F-Sa 10am-4:30pm.) **Postal Code:** M2 1BB.

ACCOMMODATIONS AND FOOD. Cheap stays in the city center are hard to find. The highest concentration of budget lodgings is 3-5km south in the suburbs of **Didsbury, Fallowfield,** and **Withington;** take bus #40, 42, or 157. Browse *Where to Stay* (free at tourist office) for listings. Take the metro to G-Mex Station or bus #33 (dir.: Wigan) from Piccadilly Gardens to Deansgate to reach the clean and spacious **YHA Manchester (HI) ❷,** Potato Wharf, Castlefield. (☎0870 770 5950; www.yhamanchester.org.uk. Breakfast included. Laundry £1.50. Internet £5 per hr. Reception 24hr. Dorms £20.50; doubles £45. MC/V.) In a renovated hat factory in the Northern Quarter, **The Hatters Tourist Hostel ❷,** 50 Newton St., provides clean, crowded rooms and incredibly friendly service, as well as fierce Manchester pride. (☎236 9500; www.hattersgroup.com. Breakfast included. Laundry £1.50. Reception 24hr. Dorms £14-17.50; doubles £45; triples £60. MC/V.)

Restaurants in **Chinatown** can be pricey, but most offer a reasonable, multi-course "Businessman's Lunch" (M-F noon-2pm; £4-8). Better yet, visit **Curry Mile,** a stretch of Asian restaurants on Wilmslow Rd. **Tampopo Noodle House ❷,** 16 Albert Sq., is one of Manchester's favorites, serving up noodles from Indonesia, Japan, Malaysia, Thailand, and Vietnam. (☎819 1966; www.tampopo.co.uk. Noodles £6-11. Open daily noon-11pm. AmEx/MC/V.) **Cornerhouse Cafe ❷,** 70 Oxford St., is part of the Cornerhouse Arts Centre and features a bar, three galleries, three cinemas, and trendy crowds. Create your own panini for £4.75 until 5pm. (☎200 1508. Entrees £6-8. Open M-Sa 11am-11pm, Su 11:30am-10:30pm. Food served until 10pm. Bar open M-Sa 9:30am-11pm, Su 12:30-10:30pm. MC/V.)

SIGHTS AND ENTERTAINMENT. Be sure to take a peek at the neo-Gothic **Manchester Town Hall,** at Albert St., and the **Central Library,** behind the Town Hall Extension. One of the largest municipal libraries in Europe, the domed building has a music and theater library, a language and literature library, and the UK's second-largest Judaica collection. (☎234 1900. Call for hours.) Do not miss the fantastic new **Urbis** museum, Cathedral Gardens, which explores modern urban culture and art. The awe-inspiring museum is a sculpture in itself, clad in 2200 handmade plates of glass beneath a "ski-slope" copper roof. Recent exhibits include an exploration of British punk culture. (☎605 8200; www.urbis.org.uk. Open Tu-Su 10am-6pm. Free.) The **Manchester Art Gallery,** Nicholas St., holds Rossetti's stunning *Astarte Syriaca* in its gigantic collection. (☎235 8888. Open Tu-Su and bank holidays 10am-5pm. Free.)

Loved and reviled in equal proportion, Manchester United is England's reigning football team. From the Old Trafford Metrolink stop, follow signs up Warwick Rd. to reach the **Manchester United Museum and Tour Centre,** Sir Matt Busby Way, at the Old Trafford football stadium. Memorabilia from the club's inception in 1878 to its recent trophy-hogging success may just convert you. (☎0870 442 1994. Open daily 9:30am-5pm. Tours every 10min. except on match days. Book ahead. £9.)

NIGHTLIFE. At **The Temple,** on Bridgewater St., an entrance in the middle of the street leads downstairs to a small, smoky bar, once a bathroom. Locals squeeze in for drinks before clubbing. (Open M-Sa noon-11pm, Su noon-10:30pm.) Centered around **Oldham Street,** the **Northern Quarter** is the city's youthful outlet for live music. Partiers flock to **Oxford Street** for late-night clubbing. Don't forget to collect flyers—they'll often score you a discount. **Music Box,** 65 Oxford St., is a small, underground venue that hosts live bands and enormously popular parties. (Cover £5-8. Open Th-Sa from 10pm, closes between 3am and 6am depending on the event.) GLBT clubbers flock to the **Gay Village,** northeast of Princess St. Bars line **Canal Street,** in the heart of the area, which is also lively during the day.

At night, streets in the Northern Quarter are dimly lit. If you're crossing from Piccadilly to Swan St. or Great Ancoats St., use Oldham St., where the neon-lit clubs provide reassurance. There's no shame in short taxi trips at night in this town.

LIVERPOOL ☎0151

Many Brits still scoff at once-industrial Liverpool, but Scousers—as Liverpudlians are colloquially known—have recently watched their metropolis undergo a cultural face-lift, trading in working-class grit for offbeat vitality. Several free museums, two deified football squads, and top-notch nightlife helped earn the city the title of European Capital of Culture 2008. Some fuss is also made over the Beatles.

TICKET TO RIDE. **Trains** (☎08457 484 950) leave Lime St. Station for: Birmingham (1¾hr., M-Sa every hr., £19.80); London Euston (3hr., every hr., £12, book Virgin Value Tickits at least 2 weeks in advance); and Manchester Piccadilly (1hr., 2-4 per hr., £8). National Express **buses** (☎08705 808 080) run from Norton St. Station to: Birmingham (3hr., 5 per day, £9.50); London (4½-5½hr., 5-6 per day, £20); and Manchester Piccadilly (1hr., 1-3 per hr., £5.25). The Isle of Man Steam Packet Company (☎08705 523 523; www.steam-packet.com) runs **ferries** from Princess Dock to Dublin. The **tourist office,** in Queen Sq. Centre, gives away the handy brochure *Visitor Guide to Liverpool and Merseyside* and books rooms for a 10% fee. (☎0906 680 6886; www.visitliverpool.com. Open M and W-Sa 9am-5:30pm, Tu 10am-5:30pm, Su 10:30am-4:30pm.) Expert guide Phil Hughes runs personalized 3-4hr. Beatles tours leaving from Strawberry Fields and Eleanor Rigby's grave (☎228 4565; £12). Surf the **Internet** for free at the Central **Library** on William Brown St. (☎233 5835. Open M-F 9am-6pm, Sa 9am-5pm, Su noon-4pm.) **Postal Code:** L1 1AA.

A HARD DAY'S NIGHT. Most budget hotels are located around **Lord Nelson Street,** next to the train station, and **Mount Pleasant,** one block from Brownlow Hill. Housed in a former Victorian warehouse, **International Inn ❷,** 4 South Hunter St., is clean and fun, with a lounge and adjoining Internet cafe. (☎709 8135; www.internationalinn.co.uk. Free coffee, tea, and toast. Linen included. All rooms with bathroom. Internet £2 per hr. Dorms £15-16; doubles £36. AmEx/MC/V.) **Embassie Backpackers ❷,** 1 Falkner Sq., is a bit louder. Tireless guests socialize at the pool table, in one of three lounges, in the kitchen, or over 24hr. free tea and toast. (☎707 1089; www.embassie.com. Linen included. Laundry facilities. Dorms £14.50, £13.50 after first night. Cash only.) Trendy cafes and budget-friendly kebab stands line **Bold** and **Hardman Streets.** There is a **Tesco Metro** supermarket in Clayton Sq., across from St. John's Shopping Centre. (Open M-F 6am-midnight, Sa 6am-10pm, Su 11am-5pm.) At **Tabac ❶,** 126 Bold St., sleek, minimalist decor belies surprisingly affordable food. Sandwiches (from £3.50) on fresh focaccia are served all day. (☎709 9502. Breakfast from £2. Dinner specials £6.50-9.50. Open M-F 8:30am-11pm, Sa 9am-midnight, Su 10am-11pm. MC/V.) The Mediterranean and North African cuisine at **Kimos ❶,** 46 Mt. Pleasant, satisfies for vegetarians and carnivores alike. (☎709 2355. Entrees £4-7. Open daily 10am-11pm. Cash only.)

MAGICAL MYSTERY TOUR. The tourist office's **Beatles Map** (£3) leads visitors through Beatles-themed sights including **Strawberry Fields** and **Penny Lane.** At Albert Dock, **The Beatles Story** traces the rise and fall of the band through Hamburg, the Cavern Club, and a pseudo-shrine to John's legacy of love. (☎709 1963; www.beatlesstory.com. Open daily 10am-6pm. £9, students £6.) The Liverpool branch of the **Tate Gallery,** also on Albert Dock, contains a select collection of 20th-century artwork. (☎702 7400; www.tate.org.uk/liverpool. Open Tu-Su 10am-6pm. Free. Special exhibits £5, students £4.) Completed in 1978, the Anglican **Liverpool Cathedral,** on Upper Duke St., boasts the highest Gothic arches and the heaviest bells in the world. Climb the tower for a view that extends to Wales. (☎709 6271; www.liverpoolcathedral.org.uk. Cathedral open daily 8am-6pm. Tower open daily Mar.-Sept. 11am-5pm; Oct.-Feb. 11am-4pm. Suggested donation for Cathedral £2.50. Tower £3.25.) The **Liverpool** and **Everton football clubs**—intense rivals—offer tours of their grounds. Bus #26 runs from the city center to the Liverpool stadium. Bus #19 runs to the Everton stadium. (Everton ☎330 2277; tour £9, students £5. Liverpool ☎260 6677; tour £8.50, students £5.50. Book in advance.)

HIPPY HIPPY SHAKE. Consult the *Liverpool Echo* (£0.35), sold daily by street vendors, for up-to-date information on nightlife. **Slater Street** brims with £1 pints, while the downtown **Ropewalks** area—especially **Matthew Street, Church Street,** and **Bold Street**—overflows with clubbers on weekend nights. John Lennon once said that the worst thing about fame was "not being able to get a quiet pint at the Phil." Fortunately, the rest of us can sip in peace with the old-boy crowd at elegant **The Philharmonic,** 36 Hope St. (☎707 2837. Open M-Sa noon-11pm, Su noon-10:30pm.) **The Cavern Club,** 10 Matthew St., where the Fab Four gained prominence, draws live bands hoping that history will repeat itself. (☎236 9091. Cover £2-4 after 9pm. Club open M-W 6pm-midnight, Th-Sa 6pm-2:30am. Pub open M-Sa from 11am, Su noon-11:30pm.) Fabulous **Society,** 47 Fleet St., draws decadent crowds and posh VIPs to its steamy dance floor. (☎707 3575. Cover F £7, Sa £10, Su £5. Open F 10:30pm-2am, Sa 10:30pm-4am, Su 10:30pm-1am.)

PEAK DISTRICT NATIONAL PARK

Though the Peak District can't lay claim to any true mountains, its 1400 sq. km offer a bit of almost everything else: deep gullies, green pastures, rocky hillsides, and soft peat moorland. The natural beauty of the area may come as a surprise because of its location between industrial giants Manchester, Nottingham, and Sheffield. Transportation is easiest in the south and near outlying cities, but hikers should head north for a more isolated escape.

TRANSPORTATION AND PRACTICAL INFORMATION. The invaluable *Peak District Timetables* (£0.60), available at tourist offices, has accommodation and bike rental information, transport routes, and map. Two **train** lines (☎08457 484 950) originate in Manchester and enter the park at New Mills. One stops at Buxton, near the park's edge (1hr., every hr., £5.70). The other crosses the park (11-16 per day) via Edale (55min., £6.90), Hope, and Hathersage (both 1hr., £7.20), terminating in Sheffield (1½hr., £11.20). **Buses** make a noble effort to connect the scattered Peak towns, and **Traveline** (☎0870 608 2608) is a vital resource. "Transpeak" makes the 3hr. journey between Buxton, Bakewell, Matlock, stopping at towns in between (6 per day). Bus #173 runs from Bakewell to Castleton (50min., 3-5 per day). Bus #200 runs from Castleton to Edale (20min., M-F 3-7 per day). The **Derbyshire Wayfarer** ticket, available at Manchester train stations and NPICs, allows one day of train and bus travel through the Peak District as far north as Sheffield and as far south as Derby. (£7.50, students £3.75.)

The **National Park Information Centres (NPICs)** at Bakewell, Castleton, and Edale carry walking guides. Information is also available at the Buxton **tourist office** (☎01298 25 106). **YHA** operates 20 **hostels** ❶ in the park (reservations highly recommended; dorms £9-16). For Bakewell, Castleton, and Edale, see p. 173. For the park's 11 **YHA Camping Barns (HI)** ❷ (£5 per person), book at the **Camping Barns Reservation Office,** 6 King St., Clitheroe, Lancashire BB7 2EP (☎0870 770 8868). The park has seven **Cycle Hire Centres** (£13 per day); the free brochure *Cycle Derbyshire*, available at NPICs, includes phone numbers, hours, locations, and a map with on- and off-road tracks.

CASTLETON. For such a small town, Castleton (pop. 705) has an incredible amount of natural beauty. Its main attraction is the **Treak Cliff Cavern,** which hides purple seams of Blue John, a semi-precious mineral found only in these hills. (☎620 571; www.bluejohnstone.com. Open daily Mar.-Oct. 10am-4:20pm; Nov.-Feb. 10am-3:20pm. 40min. tours every 15-30min. £6, students and YHA members £5.) Castleton's **NPIC** is on Buxton Rd. (☎0870 444 7275. Open daily Apr.-Oct. 9:30am-5:30pm; Nov.-Mar. 10am-5pm.) **YHA Castleton (HI)** ❷ is in Castleton Hall in the heart of town. (☎620 235. Kitchen. Internet £5 per hr. Book 2-3 weeks in advance. Open Feb.-Dec. Dorms £12.50, under 18 £9. Members only. Cash only.)

BAKEWELL AND EDALE. The town of **Bakewell,** 50km southeast of Manchester, is the best base from which to explore the region. Several scenic walks through the **White Peaks** begin nearby. Bakewell's **NPIC** is in Old Market Hall, on Bridge St. (☎0870 444 7275. Open daily Mar.-Oct. 9:30am-5:30pm; Nov.-Feb. 10am-5pm.) The cozy **YHA Bakewell (HI)** ❶, on Fly Hill, is 5min. from the town center. (☎01629 812 313. Dorms £11, under 18 £8. Cash only.) A **Midlands Co-op** sells groceries at the corner of Granby Rd. and Market St. (Open M-Sa 8am-10pm, Su 10am-4pm.)

The northern Dark Peak area contains some of the wildest and most rugged hill country in England, including spectacular peat marshes around **Edale.** For details on shorter **trails** nearby, check out the National Park Authority's *8 Walks Around Edale* (£1.40). The town of Edale itself offers little more than a church, cafe, pub, school, and the nearby **YHA Edale (HI)** ❶, Rowland Cote. (☎01433 670 302. Dorms £12, under 18 £8.50. Cash only.)

YORK ☎01904

Once impenetrable to outsiders, the crumbling medieval walls of York (pop. 105,000) are now defenseless against hordes of tourists. Brandishing cameras in place of swords, the invaders come to ogle Britain's largest Gothic cathedral and roam through the tiny medieval alleyways of "the most haunted city in the world."

TRANSPORTATION AND PRACTICAL INFORMATION. Trains (☎08457 484 950) leave Station Rd. for: Edinburgh (2½hr., 2 per hr., £22-83); London King's Cross (2hr., 2 per hr., £19-144); Manchester Piccadilly (1½hr., 3 per hr., £17.10-21.10); and Newcastle (1hr., 4 per hr., £19-28). National Express **buses** (☎08705 808 080) leave 20 Rougier St., Exhibition Sq., the train station and The Stonebow for: Edinburgh (5½hr., daily 10:55am, £29); London (5hr., 4 per day, £23); Manchester (2¾hr., daily 5pm, £7.90). Follow Station Rd. as it becomes

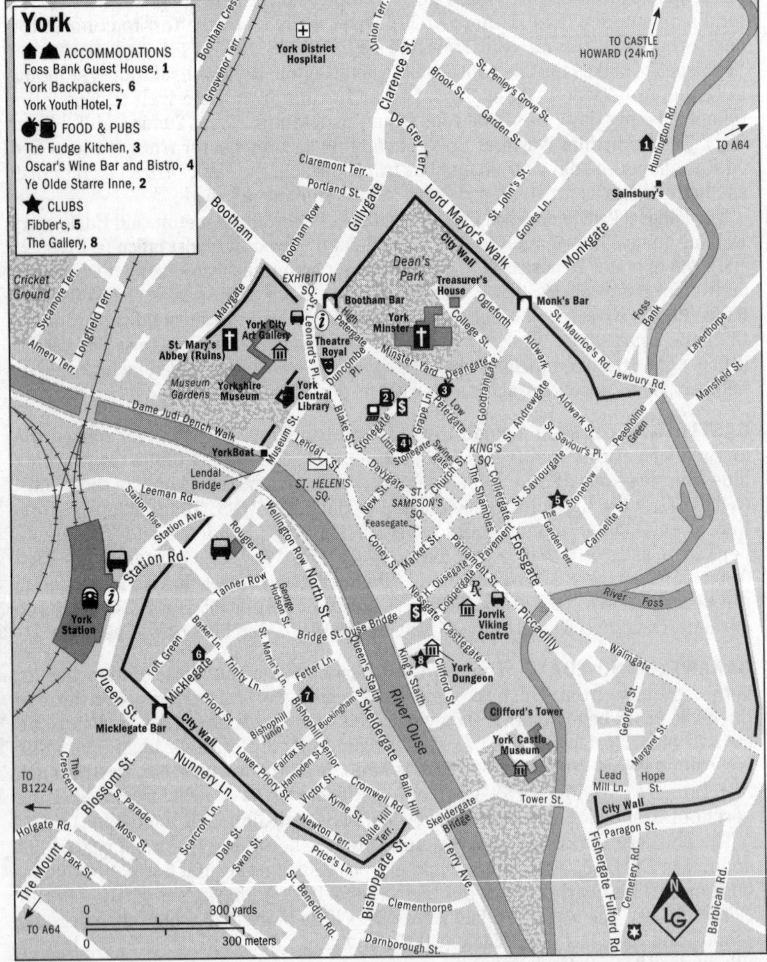

Museum St., cross the bridge, and go left on St. Leonard's Pl. for the **tourist office,** Exhibition Sq. (☎621 756; www.visityork.org. Open June-Oct. M-Sa 9am-6pm, Su 10am-5pm; Nov.-May M-Sa 9am-5pm, Su 10am-4pm.) **Cafe of the Evil Eye,** 42 Stonegate, has **Internet.** (☎640 002. £2 per hr.) **Postal Code:** YO1 8DA.

ACCOMMODATIONS AND FOOD. **B&Bs** (from £18) are concentrated on the side streets along **Bootham** and **Clifton,** in the Mount area down **Blossom Street,** and on **Bishopthorpe Road,** south of town. Book weeks ahead in the summer, when competition for inexpensive beds is fierce; the tourist office can help book rooms. **York Backpackers ❷,** 88-90 Micklegate, is a Georgian mansion with a kitchen, laundry (£3), TV lounge, and "dungeon bar" with 24hr. liquor license. (☎627 720; www.yorkbackpackers.co.uk. Continental breakfast included. Large dorms £13-14; doubles £35. Ask about working in exchange for accommodation. MC/V.) At **Foss Bank Guest House ❸,** 16 Huntington Rd., friendly owner Kevin offers elegant rooms and an inviting guest lounge. (☎635 548. Singles £27; doubles £48, with bath £56. Discount for *Let's Go* users. Cash only.) The **York Youth Hotel ❷,** 11-13 Bishophill Senior, is a conveniently located, no-frills hostel catering primarily to groups. (☎625 904; www.yorkyouthhotel.com. Laundry and Internet. Key deposit £3. Reception 24hr. Dorms £12; singles £25; twins £38. AmEx/MC/V.)

Greengrocers peddle at **Newgate Market** between Parliament St. and the Shambles. (Open M-Sa 9am-5pm; Apr.-Dec. also Su 9am-4:30pm.) Buy groceries at **Sainsbury's,** at the intersection of Foss Bank and Heworth Green. (☎643 801. Open M-Sa 8am-8pm, Su 11am-5pm.) **Oscar's Wine Bar and Bistro ❷,** 8 Little Stonegate, dishes up huge portions of hearty grub in an ivy-covered courtyard. (☎652 002. Entrees £6-8. Happy hour M 4-11pm, Tu-F 5-7pm, Su 4-10:30pm. Open M-Sa 11:30am-11pm, Su noon-10:30pm. MC/V.) At **The Fudge Kitchen ❶,** 58 Low Petergate, over 20 flavors of gooey fudge are made right before your eyes. (☎645 596. Free samples. Slices £3.50-4. Open M-Sa 10am-6pm, Su 10am-5:30pm. MC/V.) The city's oldest pub, **Ye Olde Starre Inne ❶,** 40 Stonegate, makes award-winning sausages and meat pies. (☎623 063. Meals £5-7. Open M-Sa 11am-11pm, Su noon-10:30pm. AmEx/MC/V.)

SIGHTS AND ENTERTAINMENT. The best introduction to York is the 4km walk along its **medieval walls.** The **Association of Voluntary Guides** (☎630 284) offers free 2hr. **walking tours,** which leave at 10:15am, 2:15pm, and 6:45pm in summer and 10:15am in winter from the York City Art Gallery, across from the tourist office. It's estimated that half of all the medieval stained glass in England lines the walls of **York Minster,** the largest Gothic cathedral in Britain. The Great East Window depicts the beginning and end of the world in over 100 scenes. (☎557 216; www.yorkminster.org. Open daily 7:30am-6:30pm. Evensong M-Sa 5pm, Su 4pm. Free 1hr. tours leave from the entrance every 30min. 9:30am-3:30pm. £5, students £3.50. Combined ticket with Undercroft, Treasury, and Crypt £7/4.50.) Climb the 275 steps of **Central Tower** for a view of York. (Open daily 9:30am-5pm. £2.50.)

The **York Castle Museum,** between Tower St. and Piccadilly, is arguably Britain's premier museum of everyday life. Rooms include Kirkgate, a reconstructed Victorian shopping street, and Half Moon Court, its Edwardian counterpart. (☎650 335; www.yorkcastlemuseum.org.uk. Open mid-July to Aug. daily 9:30am-5pm; Sept. to mid-July M-Th and Sa-Su 9:30am-5pm, F 10am-5pm. £6, students £4.50.) **Clifford's Tower,** Tower St., is one of the last remaining pieces of **York Castle** and a chilling reminder of the worst anti-Jewish violence in English history. In 1190, Christian merchants tried to erase their debts to Jewish bankers by destroying York's Jewish community. Faced with starvation or butchery, 150 Jews took refuge in the tower, where they committed mass suicide. (☎646 940. Open daily Apr.-Sept. 10am-6pm; Oct. 10am-5pm; Nov.-Mar. 10am-4pm. £2.80, students £2.10.) The **Jorvik Viking Centre,** on Coppergate, is one of the busiest of York's attractions; go early or late, or book at least a day ahead. Visitors float in "time cars" through the

York of AD 948, past authentic artifacts, life-like mannequins, and painfully accurate smells. (☎643 211; www.jorvik-viking-centre.co.uk, advance booking 543 403. Open daily Apr.-Oct. 9am-6pm; Nov.-Mar. 10am-5pm. £7.45, students £6.30.)

The *What's On* and *Artscene* guides, available at the tourist office, publish info on performances and exhibitions. In the evenings, barbershop quartets share the pavement of **King's Square** and **Stonegate** with magicians, and soapboxers. York's dressy club, **The Gallery,** 12 Clifford St., has two hot dance floors and six bars. (☎647 947. No sneakers or sportswear on weekends. Cover £3.50-8. Open M-Th and Su 10pm-2am, F-Sa 10pm-3am.) **Fibber's,** Stonebow House, the Stonebow, hosts high-quality live music nightly at 8pm and dancing after 10:30pm. (☎651 250; www.fibbers.co.uk. Check website or *What's On* for events. Cover varies.)

NEWCASTLE-UPON-TYNE ☎0191

The largest city in the northeast, Newcastle (pop. 278,000) all but shed its image as a faded capital of industry. Ambitious building efforts have jumpstarted the city's daytime energy, and its nightlife is hotter than ever as students, tourists, and proud locals swarm to its pubs and clubs. The **BALTIC Centre for Contemporary Art,** in a renovated grain warehouse, is Britain's largest center for contemporary art outside of London. (☎478 1810; www.balticmill.com. Open M-W and F-Sa 10am-7pm, Th 10am-10pm, Su 10am-5pm. Free.) The Centre is part of a trio of new structures on the river, also including the steel and glass **Sage Gateshead,** a complex of concert halls, and the **Gateshead Millenium Bridge,** the only rotating bridge in the world, which opens like a giant eyelid to allow ships to pass. The largely intact **Castle Garth Keep,** at the foot of St. Nicholas St., is all that remains of the 12th-century New Castle complex, though the city actually derives its name from a castle that existed over 100 years earlier. (☎232 7938. Open daily Apr.-Sept. 9:30am-5:30pm; Oct.-Mar. 9:30am-4:30pm. £1.50, students £0.50.) Theater buffs can treat themselves to an evening at the gilt-and-velvet **Theatre Royal,** 100 Grey St., undoubtedly northern England's premier stage. (☎0870 905 5060; www.theatreroyal.co.uk.)

To get to the small but friendly **YHA Newcastle (HI) ❷,** 107 Jesmond Rd., take the metro to Jesmond, turn left onto Jesmond Rd., and walk past the traffic lights. Book in advance. (☎0870 770 5972. Internet £5 per hr. Reception 7-11pm. Curfew 11pm. Closed mid-Dec. to mid-Jan. Dorms £16-19, under 18 £12.50-15.50. AmEx/V.) **Blake's Coffee House ❶,** 53 Grey St., is a popular, central hangout with a range of lunch fare (£4-5) and tasty sandwiches for £2-3. (☎261 5463. Open M-F 7am-5:30pm, Sa-Su 7am-4pm. Cash only.) **Safeway** is on Clayton St., in the city center. (☎261 2805. Open M-Sa 8am-7pm, Su 11am-5pm.)

Home of the nectar known as brown ale, Newcastle's party scene is legendary. *The Crack* (free at record stores) has the best nightlife listings in Newcastle. Rowdy **Bigg Market** features the highest concentration of pubs in England, while neighboring **Quayside** attracts herds of 20-somethings to its packed clubs. **The Head of Steam,** 2 Neville St., near the train station, features live soul, funk, jazz, and reggae with packed shows most nights and occasional local DJs. (☎230 4236. Open daily noon-1:30am.) Lined with bars, **Ikon,** 49 New Bridge St., consistently produces a surging sea of dancing bodies. (☎261 2526. Cover £3-7. Open Th-Sa 10pm-2am.) For a happening GLBT scene, head to **Times Square.** No matter what your plans, finish the night Newcastle-style with a kebab and extra chili sauce.

Trains leave from Central Station, Neville St., for Edinburgh (1½hr., approx. every hr., £36) and London King's Cross (3½hr., every hr., £83). National Express **buses** (☎08705 808 080) leave St. James Blvd. for Edinburgh (3hr., 4 per day, £13.50) and London (7hr., 4 per day, £24). The **tourist office** is at 132 Grainger St., in the Central Arcade. (☎277 8000. Open June-Sept. M-F 9:30am-5:30pm, Sa 9am-5:30pm, Su 10am-4pm; Oct.-May closed Su.) **Postal Code:** NE1 7AB.

LAKE DISTRICT NATIONAL PARK

With some of the most stunning scenery in England, the Lake District owes its jagged peaks, windswept fells, and serene mountain lakes to a thorough glacier-gouging during the last Ice Age. Though summertime hikers, bikers, and boaters almost equal sheep in number—and with four million sheep, that's quite a feat—there is always some lonely hill or quiet cove where your footprints will seem the first for generations. Use Windermere, Ambleside, Grasmere, and Keswick as bases from which to ascend into the hills—the farther west you go from the A591, which connects these towns, the more countryside you'll have to yourself.

TRANSPORTATION AND PRACTICAL INFORMATION. Trains (☎08457 484 950) run to Oxenholme, the primary gateway to the lakes, from: Birmingham (2hr., every 2hr., £40); Edinburgh (2hr., 6 per day, £29); London Euston (3½hr., 11-16 per day, £62); Manchester Piccadilly (1½hr., 9-10 per day, £13). Trains also run from Oxenholme to Windermere (20min., every hr., £3.25), and from Manchester Piccadilly to Windermere (1¾hr., every hr., £13). National Express **buses** (☎08705 808 080) arrive in Windermere from Birmingham (4½hr., 1 per day, £29) and London (7½hr., 1 per day, £27), continuing north through Ambleside and Grasmere to Keswick. **Stagecoach in Cumbria** (☎0870 608 2608) is the primary bus service in the region; a complete timetable, *The Lakeland Explorer*, is available for free at tourist offices. An **Explorer ticket** offers unlimited travel on all area Stagecoach buses (1-day £8; 4-day £18). YHA Ambleside offers a convenient **minibus** service (☎01539 432 304) between hostels (2 per day, £3) as well as free service from the Windermere train station to the hostels in Windermere and Ambleside.

The **National Park Visitor Centre** is in **Brockhole,** halfway between Windermere and Ambleside. (☎01539 446 601; www.lake-district.gov.uk. Open Apr.-Oct. daily 10am-5pm.) **National Park Information Centres (NPICs)** book accommodations and dispense free information and maps. Though B&Bs line every street in every town and there's a hostel around every bend, lodgings fill up in summer; book ahead.

WINDERMERE AND BOWNESS. Windermere and its sidekick **Bowness-on-Windermere** fill to the gills with vacationers in summer, when sailboats and waterskiers swarm the lake. The short, steep climb to **Orrest Head** (2.5km round-trip) is moderately difficult, but affords one of the best views in the Lake District. It begins opposite the TIC on the other side of A591. To get to the spacious **YHA Windermere (HI) ❶,** Bridge Ln., 3.2km north of Windermere off A591, catch the YHA shuttle from the train station. (☎01539 443 543. Internet £5 per hr. Open Feb.-Nov. daily; early Dec. F-Sa only. Breakfast, packed lunch, and dinner £3.40-5.50. Dorms £12.50-15.50, under 18 £9-10.50.) To camp at **Park Cliffe ❷,** Birks Rd., 7km south of Bowness, take bus #618 from Windermere. (☎01539 531 344. Tent sites £11-12. AmEx/MC/V.) **Windermere Lake Cruises** (☎01539 443 360), at the northern end of Bowness Pier, sends boats north to Waterhead Pier in Ambleside (30min., round-trip £6.65) and south to Lakeside (40min., round-trip £6.85). The Lakeland Experience **bus** #599 (3 per hr., £1) leaves for Bowness pier from the train station in Windermere. The **tourist office** is near the train station. (☎01539 446 499. Open daily July-Aug. 9am-6:30pm; Easter-June and Sept.-Oct. 9am-6pm; Nov.-Easter 9am-5pm.) The local **NPIC,** on Glebe Rd., is beside Bowness Pier. (☎01539 442 895. Open daily mid-July to Aug. 9:30am-6pm; Sept. to mid-July reduced hours.)

AMBLESIDE. Set in a valley 1.5km north of Lake Windermere, Ambleside is an attractive village with convenient access to the southern lakes. **Hiking** trails extend in all directions. Splendid views of high fells can be had from the top of **Loughrigg,** a moderately difficult climb (11km round-trip). The lovely **Stockghyll Force** waterfall is an easy 1.5km from town. The tourist office has guides to these and other walks. Bus #555 stops in front of **YHA Ambleside (HI)** ❶, 1.5km south of Ambleside and 5km north of Windermere, a magnificent former hotel with refurbished rooms, great food, and swimming off the pier. (☎01539 432 304. Bike rental £1.50 per hr. Internet £5 per hr. Dorms £15, under 18 £11.) Pick up organic fruits and veggies at **Granny Smith's,** Market Pl. (☎01539 433 145. Open M-F 8am-5pm, Sa 8am-6pm, Su 9am-4pm. Cash only.) Lakeslink **bus** #555 (☎01539 432 231) leaves from Kelsick Rd. for Grasmere, Keswick, and Windermere (1 per hr., £2-6.50). The **tourist office** is in the Central Building on Market Cross. (☎01539 432 582; www.amblesideonline.co.uk. Open daily 9am-5pm.) To reach the **NPIC,** walk south on Lake Rd. or Borrans Rd. to the pier. (☎01539 4342 895. Open Easter-Oct. daily 9:30am-5:30pm.)

GRASMERE. The peace that William Wordsworth enjoyed in the village of Grasmere is still palpable on quiet mornings. Guides provide 30min. tours of the early 17th-century Dove Cottage, where the poet lived from 1799 to 1808; the cottage is almost exactly as he left it. Next door is the outstanding Wordsworth Museum. (☎01539 435 544. Both open daily mid-Feb. to mid-Jan. 9:30am-5pm. Cottage and museum £6, students and HI members £4.60. Museum only £4.) The 10km Wordsworth Walk circles the two lakes of the Rothay River, passing the cottage, the poet's grave in St. Oswald's churchyard, and Rydal Mount, where he died in 1850. (Rydal ☎01539 433 002. Open Mar.-Oct. daily 9:30am-5pm; Nov.-Dec. and Feb. M and W-Su 10am-4pm. £4.50, students £3.50.) A steep, strenuous scramble leads to the top of Helm Cragg (6km round-trip). **YHA Butharlyp Howe (HI)** ❷, on Easedale Rd., is a large Victorian house with Internet. (☎01539 435 316. Dorms £11-14, under 18 £8-9.50. MC/V.) A staple since 1854, the famous gingerbread at **Sarah Nelson's Grasmere Gingerbread Shop** ❶, in Church Cottage, outside St. Oswald's Church, is a bargain at £0.30 a piece. (☎01593 435 428; www.grasmeregingerbread.co.uk. Open M-Sa 9:15am-5:30pm, Su 12:30-5:30pm; Dec.-Easter closes earlier.) **Bus** #555 stops in Grasmere every hour on its way south to Ambleside or north to Keswick. The combined **tourist office** and **NPIC** is on Redbank Rd. (☎01539 435 245. Open Easter-Oct. daily 9:30am-5:30pm; Nov.-Easter F-Su 10am-4pm.)

KESWICK. Between towering Skiddaw peak and the northern edge of Lake Derwentwater, Keswick (KEZ-ick) rivals Windermere as the Lake District's tourist capital. A standout 6km dayhike from Keswick culminates with the eerily striking **Castlerigg Stone Circle,** a 5000-year-old neolithic henge. Another short walk leads to the beautiful **Friar's Crag,** on the shore of Derwentwater, and **Castlehead,** a viewpoint encompassing the town, the lakes, and the peaks beyond. Both of these walks are fairly easy, with only a few strenuous moments. **YHA Derwentwater (HI)** ❶, Barrow House, Borrowdale, is a 200-year-old house with its own waterfall. Take bus #79 (every hr.) 3km south out of Keswick. (☎01768 777 246. Open Mar.-Oct. daily; Nov.-Feb. F-Sa only. Dorms £12.50-15.50, under 18 £9-10.50. MC/V.) Maps and information on area walks are available at the **NPIC,** in Moot Hall, Market Sq. (☎01768 772 645. Open Apr.-Oct. daily 9:30am-5:30pm.)

WALES (CYMRU)

If many of the nearly three million Welsh people had their druthers, they would be floating miles away from the English. Ever since England solidified its control over Wales with the murder of Prince Llywelyn ap Gruffydd in 1282, relations between the two countries have been marked by a powerful unease. Wales clings steadfastly to its Celtic heritage, and the Welsh language endures in conversation, commerce, and literature. As mines faltered in the mid-20th century, Wales turned its economic eye from heavy industry to tourism. Travelers today come for the dramatic beaches, cliffs, mountains, and brooding castles—remnants of the long battle with England.

CARDIFF (CAERDYDD) ☎029

The "Come on, Cardiff!" signs that flutter all around the city speak to the vigor with which Cardiff (pop. 306,000) is reinventing itself. Formerly the main port of call for Welsh coal, Cardiff is now the port of arrival for a colorful international population. "Europe's youngest capital" stakes its reputation on its progressive attitudes, yet tradition, evidenced by the red dragons emblazoned on every flag and store window, remains as strong as ever.

TRANSPORTATION AND PRACTICAL INFORMATION. Trains (☎08457 484 950) leave Central Station, Central Sq., for: Bath (1-1½hr., 1-3 per hr., £12.40); Birmingham (2hr., 2 per hr., £22); Edinburgh (7-7½hr., 3 per day, £91); London Paddington (2hr., 2 per hr., £59). National Express **buses** (☎08705 808 080) leave from Wood St. for: Birmingham (2¼hr., 8 per day, £20.40); London (3½hr., 9 per day, £19); Manchester (6hr., 8 per day, £31). Pick up a free *Wales Bus, Rail, and Tourist Map and Guide* at the tourist office. Cardiff Bus (Bws Caerdydd), St. David's House, Wood St. (☎2066 6444), runs green and orange city buses in Cardiff and surrounding areas. (Service ends M-Sa 11:20pm, Su 11pm. £0.65-1.55, week-long pass £12.) The **tourist office,** the Old Library, The Hayes, books rooms for a £2 fee and a 10% deposit. (☎2022 7281; www.visitcardiff.info. Open M-Sa 10am-6pm, Su 10am-4pm.) The public **library,** at Frederick St. and Bridge St., offers free **Internet** in 30min. slots. (☎2038 2116. Open M-W and F 9am-6pm, Th 9am-7pm, Sa 9am-5:30pm.) **Postal Code:** CF10 2SJ.

ACCOMMODATIONS AND FOOD. Budget accommodations are hard to come by in Cardiff; the cheapest **B&Bs** (from £20) are on the outskirts of the city. **Cardiff International Backpacker ❷**, 98 Neville St., is a backpacker's dream, with a happy hour (M-Th and Su 7-9pm) and a rooftop patio complete with hammocks. (☎2034 5577. Light breakfast included. Internet £2 per hr. M-Th and Su curfew 2:30am. Dorms £16.50; doubles £38; triples £48; quads £60. Credit card required for advance booking. MC/V.) **Jollies Lodge ❷**, 109 Cathedral Rd., has the best price in town for a private room. (☎2022 1495. £20 per person. Cash only.)

Downtown Cardiff is full of corner stalls, pubs, and coffee shops. **Europa Cafe ❶**, 25 Castle St., across from Cardiff Castle, is a trendy but comfortable coffee house, with plush couches and live music. (☎2066 7776. Drinks £1-3. Open daily

WELSH RABBIT

Switzerland has gooey fondue Italy has hot pizza, and Mexic has steaming quesadillas, bu none of these are quite as deli cious as Wales's contribution t the culinary pantheon of carbohy drates and cheese. Take a piec of bread, smear it with a thic concoction of beer, mustard spices, and, of course, cheese and then melt it all under hig heat until brown and bubbly- you've just made traditiona Welsh rabbit.

Erroneously spelled and pro nounced "rarebit" by some, rabbi has a contested etymology. Som claim it was coined by patronizin Englishmen, who considered th Welsh so hopeless that the couldn't even catch a hare fo supper–and instead were force to eat bread and cheese. Anothe story contends that St. Peter lure the Welsh people out of heave using a "rabbit" of sorts–a bait o roasted cheese (*caws pobi*) to ge them outside the pearly gates.

The Welsh don't have an Isl wide monopoly on the tasty dis older cookbooks contain Scottis and English rabbit recipes. Th instructions for these often call fo a "salamander," a large iron sla on a stick (it looks much like pizza wheel) that was heated an then rested just inches above th bread as a rudimentary broile Now toaster ovens do the tric and rabbit is common througho Wales in local cafes and vegeta ian hangouts.

10:30am-5:30pm; later in summer. Cash only.) **Celtic Cauldron Wholefoods ❶,** 47-49 Castle Arcade, is the place to gorge on traditional Glamorganshire sausage, seaweed-based laverbread, Welsh rarebit, and local desserts. (☎2238 7185. Entrees £5. Open M-Sa 8:30am-5pm, Su 11am-4pm. MC/V.) **Caroline Street** is a surefire post-club hot spot with curried or fried goodies at shops that stay open until 3 or 4am.

SIGHTS AND ENTERTAINMENT. After 2000 years, the peacocks that strut around the green of **Cardiff Castle** still wear crowns (of sorts) suited for the royalty that inspired the castle's extravagant buildings, including a Norman keep and a Victorian mansion. Watch out for owls Billy and Floyd during falconry shows. (☎2087 8100. Open daily Mar.-Oct. 9:30am-6pm; Nov.-Feb. 9:30am-5pm. £6.50, students £5.) The **Civic Centre,** in Cathays Park, includes Alexandra Gardens, City Hall, and the **National Museum and Gallery.** The museum's diverse local exhibits range from a room full of carved Celtic crosses to a walk-through display of Wales's indigenous flora and fauna. (☎2039 7951. Open Tu-Su 10am-5pm. Free.)

After 11pm the majority of Cardiff's popular downtown pubs stop serving alcohol, and the action migrates to an array of nearby clubs, most located on or around **St. Mary Street.** For up-to-date nightlife info, check the free *Buzz* guide or the *Itchy Cardiff Guide* (£3.50), available at the tourist office. Locals love **The Toucan,** 95-97 St. Mary St., for its musical diversity and inviting atmosphere. (☎2037 2212; www.toucanclub.co.uk. Open Tu 7pm-12:30am, W 7pm-1am, Th-Sa 7pm-2am, Su 8pm-12:30am. Food served until 11pm.) Trendy clubbers of every persuasion girate at **Club X,** 35 Charles St., on weekends after other clubs close. (Cover €3-7. Open W 9pm-2am, F-Sa 10pm-6am.)

DAYTRIP FROM CARDIFF: CAERPHILLY CASTLE. Visitors to **Caerphilly Castle,** 13km north of Cardiff, may find the 30-acre castle easy to navigate today, but 13th-century invaders had to contend with pivoting drawbridges, trebuchets, crossbows, and catapults when attacking this menacing stronghold, the most technologically advanced fortification of its time. Take the train (20min., M-Sa 2 per hr., £3) or bus #26 from Central Station. (☎2088 3143. Open June-Sept. daily 9:30am-6pm; Apr.-May daily 9:30am-5pm; Oct.-Mar. M-Sa 9:30am-4pm, Su 11am-4pm. Last admission 30min. before closing. £3, students £2.50. Audio tour £1.)

WYE VALLEY

It's no wonder that Wordsworth mused on the tranquility and pastoral majesty that suffuse this once-troubled Welsh-English border territory. As the Wye River (Afon Gwy) meanders through the tranquil valley riddled with sheep farms, trails, abbeys, and castles, much of the landscape still seems completely untouched.

TRANSPORTATION

Chepstow provides the easiest entrance to the valley. **Trains** (☎08457 484 950) run to Chepstow from Cardiff (45min., 1-2 per hr., £5.40). National Express **buses** (☎08705 808 080) arrive from Cardiff (50min., 13 per day, £4.30) and London (2½hr., 7 per day, £17). For information on walking trails acessible by local bus, pick up *Discover the Wye Valley on Foot and by Bus* (£0.50) in tourist offices. Those who wander the hills near the Wye are rewarded with quiet wooded trails, open meadows, and lovely vistas of the valley. **Hiking** is a great way to explore. The 220km **Wye Valley Walk** (www.wyevalleywalk.com) treks north from Chepstow, through Hay-on-Wye, and on to Prestatyn along wooded cliffs and farmland. **Offa's Dyke Path** consists of 285km of hiking and biking paths along the Welsh-English border. For info, consult the **Offa's Dyke Association** (☎01547 528 753).

CHEPSTOW AND TINTERN ☎01291

Chepstow's position at the mouth of the river and the base of the English border made it an important fortification in Norman times. Flowers spring from the cliff-side ruins of **Castell Casgwent,** Britain's oldest datable stone castle (c. 1070), which offers stunning views from its tower walls. (☎624 065. Open daily 9:30am-6pm. £3, students £2.50.) The **First Hurdle Guest House ❸**, 9-10 Upper Church St., offers leather couches and comfortable rooms. (☎622 189. Singles £35; doubles £50. AmEx/MC/V.) Find groceries at **Tesco** on Station Rd. (Open M 8am-midnight, Tu-F 24hr., Sa midnight-10pm, Su 10am-4pm.) **Trains** arrive on Station Rd.; **buses** stop in front of Somerfield supermarket. Buy tickets at **The Travel House,** 9 Moor St. (☎623 031. Open M-Sa 9am-5:30pm.) The **tourist office** is on Bridge St. (☎623 772; www.chepstow.co.uk. Open daily Apr.-Oct. 10am-5:30pm; Nov.-Mar. 10am-3:30pm.)

Eight kilometers north of Chepstow on A466, the haunting Gothic arches of **Tintern Abbey** "connect the landscape with the quiet of the sky"—as described in Wordsworth's famous poem, written just a few kilometers away. The roof opens to the clouds, arches point skyward, and grass sprouts in the transepts. (☎689 251. Open June-Sept. daily 9:30am-6pm; Apr.-May and Oct. daily 9:30am-5pm; Nov.-Mar. M-Sa 9:30am-4pm, Su 11am-4pm. £3.25, students £2.75. 45min. audio tour £1, plus £5 deposit.) A 3km hike along **Monk's Trail** will get you to **Devil's Pulpit,** a huge stone from which Satan is said to have tempted the monks as they worked in the fields. **YHA St. Briavel's Castle (HI) ❶,** 6km northeast of Tintern across the English border, occupies a 13th-century fortress. While a unique experience—it was formerly King John's hunting lodge—St. Briavel's is a nearly 3km uphill hike. From A466 (bus #69 from Chepstow; ask to be let off at Bigsweir Bridge) or Offa's Dyke, follow signs from the edge of the bridge. (☎01594 530 272. Lockout 10am-5pm. Curfew 11:15pm. Dorms £12.50, under 18 £9. MC/V.) The cozy **Holmleigh B&B ❷** is near the edge of Tintern Village on A466. (☎689 521. £19 per person.) Campers can use the **field ❶** next to the old train station (£2). Try **The Moon and Sixpence ❷,** next to Holmleigh B&B on High St., for classic pub grub. (☎689 284. Food served noon-2:30pm and 6:30-9:30pm. Open daily noon-11pm.)

BRECON BEACONS NATIONAL PARK

The *Parc Cenedlaethol Bannau Brycheiniog* encompasses 1340 dramatic sq. km of red sandstone crags, shaded forests, and breathtaking views. The park is divided into four regions: Brecon Beacons, where King Arthur's fortress is thought to have stood; Fforest Fawr, home to the spectacular waterfalls of Ystradfellte; the eastern, Tolkien-esque Black Mountains; and the remote, western, and confusingly named Black Mountain. Brecon, on the park's edge, is the best touring base.

TRANSPORTATION. Trains (☎08457 484 950) run from London Paddington via Cardiff to Abergavenny, at the park's southeastern corner, and to Merthyr Tydfil, on the southern edge. National Express (☎08705 808 080) **bus** #509 runs to Brecon once per day from Cardiff (1¼hr., £3.30) and London (5hr., £21) . Stagecoach Red and White bus #21 arrives in Brecon from Abergavenny (50min., 7 per day, £4.50). The free *Brecon Beacons: A Visitor's Guide*, available at NPICs, details bus coverage and lists walks accessible by public transportation.

BRECON (ABERHONDDU). Most hikers start from Brecon, at the northern edge of the mountains. Accommodations fill up far in advance during the mid-August **Jazz Festival**—remember to book ahead. **Bikes and Hikes ❶,** 10 the Struet (the building is marked "The Elms"), near the tourist office, lives up to its name: the outdoors-enthusiast owners rent equipment and lead trips. (☎01874 610 071. Bikes £16 per day. Assorted activities £25-35 per day. Dorms £12.50.) Camp at **Brynich Caravan Park ❶,** 2.5km east on the A40, signposted from the A40-A470 roundabout. (☎01874 623 325; www.brynich.co.uk. Open Easter-Oct. £5 per person, £11 for 2 people with car. Cash only.) **Buses** arrive at the **Bulwark** in the central square from Cardiff (1¼hr., 1 per day, £3.30). The **tourist office** is in the Cattle Market parking lot with the **National Park Information Centre (NPIC);** walk through Bethel Square off Lion St. (☎01874 622 485. Open M-F 9:30am-5:30pm.)

FFOREST FAWR. Forests abound with moss and ferns and funnel water over spectacular falls near **Ystradfellte** (uh-strahd-FELTH-tuh), about 11km southwest of the Beacons. The **YHA Ystradfellte (HI)** ❶ is a perfect launching pad for those willing to make the hike. Located south of the woods and waterfall district, 4.8km from the A4059 on a paved road, 6.4km from the village of Penderyn, or a 5min. walk from the Porth-yr-Ogof cave. Hard to reach by public transport; the X5 stops 5 mi. away. (☎01639 720 301. Open Easter-late Sept. Call 48hr. in advance. Dorms £10.60, under 18 £7.60. MC/V.) From the hostel, 16km of trails pass **Fforest Fawr,** the headlands of the waterfall district, on their way to the somewhat touristy **Dan-yr-Ogof Showcaves.** (☎01639 730 284. Open daily Apr.-Oct. 10am-3pm. £9, children £6.) Stagecoach Red and White **bus** #63 (1½hr., 2-3 per day, £3-4) stops at the hostel and caves en route to Brecon.

THE BLACK MOUNTAINS. Located in the easternmost section of the park, the Black Mountains are a group of long, lofty ridges offering 200 sq. km of solitude and unsurpassed ridge-walks. Begin forays from **Crickhowell,** on the A40, or travel the eastern boundary along **Offa's Dyke Path,** which is dotted with impressive ruins. The **YHA Capel-y-ffin (HI)** ❶ (kap-EL-uh-fin), along Offa's Dyke Path, is 13km from Hay-on-Wye. Take Stagecoach Red and White **bus** #39 from Hereford to Brecon, stop before Hay-on-Wye, and walk uphill. The road to the hostel climbs up Gospel Pass past Hay Bluff. A taxi from Hay (Border Taxis ☎01497 821 266) costs £12. (☎01873 890 650. Lockout 10am-5pm. Curfew 11pm. Open mid-Apr. to Sept. Call 48hr. in advance. Dorms £10, under 18 £7. MC/V.)

THE BRECON BEACONS. These peaks at the center of the park lure hikers with idyllic farmland and pastoral slopes. The most convenient (and most overcrowded) route to the top begins at **Storey Arms** (a parking lot and bus stop on the A470) and offers views of **Llyn Cwm Llwch** (HLIN koom hlooch), a 600m deep glacial pool. Consult guides at the NPICs in Brecon or Abergavenny for recommendations on alternate trails.

SNOWDONIA NATIONAL PARK

Amid Edward I's impressive man-made battlements in Northern Wales lies the 2175 sq. km natural fortress of Snowdonia National Park. Snowdonia's craggy peaks, the highest in England and Wales, yield surprisingly diverse terrain—pristine, glittering blue lakes dot rolling grasslands and desolate slate cliffs slope into thickly wooded hills. Although these lands have largely fallen into private hands, endless public footpaths easily accommodate visitors.

TRANSPORTATION AND PRACTICAL INFORMATION. **Trains** (☎08457 484 950) stop at larger towns on the park's outskirts, including Conwy (p. 184). The Conwy Valley Line runs across the park from Llandudno through Betws-y-Coed to Blaenau Ffestiniog (1hr., 2-7 per day). There it connects with the narrow-gauge Ffestiniog Railway (p. 183), which runs through the mountains to Porthmadog, meeting the Cambrian Coaster line to Llanberis and Aberystwyth. **Buses** run to the interior of the park from Conwy and Caernarfon; consult the *Gwynedd Public Transport Maps and Timetables* and *Conwy Public Transport Information*, available for free in all regional tourist offices. The **Snowdonia National Park Information Headquar-**

ters (NPIC), Penrhyndeudraeth, Gwynedd (☎01766 770 274; www.eryri-npa.gov.uk or www.gwynedd.gov.uk), provides hiking info and can direct you to the seven quality YHA hostels in the park as well as the region's other **tourist offices.**

HIKING. The highest peak in England and Wales at 1085m, **Mount Snowdon** is the park's most popular destination. Its Welsh name is *Yr Wyddfa* (the burial place)—local lore holds that Rhita Gawr, a giant cloaked with the beards of the kings he slaughtered, is buried here. Six paths of varying difficulties wind their way up Snowdon; pick up *Ordnance Survey Landranger Map #115* (£6.50) and *Outdoor Leisure Map #17* (£7.50), as well as individual trail guides, at tourist offices and NPICs. No matter how beautiful the weather is below, it will be cold, wet, and unpredictable high up—dress accordingly. Contact **Mountaincall Snowdonia** (☎09068 500 449) for local forecasts and ground conditions or visit an NPIC.

LLANBERIS ☎01286

Llanberis owes its outdoorsy bustle to the appeal of Mt. Snowdon, whose ridges and peaks unfurl just south of town. The immensely popular and pricey **Snowdon Mountain Railway** has been helping visitors "climb" to Snowdon's summit since 1896. (☎0870 458 0033; www.snowdonrailway.co.uk. Open daily Mar. to early Nov. 9am-5pm. Mar.-May trains stop halfway to the summit. Round-trip £20.) From the bus station, walk up the hill past the railway station and the Victoria Hotel, and round the bend to the right to reach the lovely **Snowdon Cottage ❸.** A garden with a castle-view, sweet-smelling rooms, a welcoming hearth, and a gracious hostess will make you never want to go outside. (☎872 015. £22 per person. Discount for multiple nights. Cash only.) KMP (☎870 880) **bus** #88 runs from Caernarfon (25min.; 1-2 per hr.; £1.50, round-trip £2). The **tourist office** is at 41b High St. (☎870 765. Open Easter-Oct. daily 9:30am-5pm; Nov.-Easter M and F-Su 11am-4pm.)

HARLECH ☎01766

This tiny hillside town just south of the Llyn Peninsula commands panoramic views of sea, sand, and Snowdonian summits. **Harlech Castle** is one of the "iron ring" of fortresses built by Edward I to keep an eye on Welsh troublemakers, but it later served as the insurrection headquarters of Welsh rebel Owain Glyndŵr. (☎780 552. Open June-Sept. daily 9:30am-6pm; Apr.-May and Oct. daily 9:30am-5pm; Nov.-Mar. M-Sa 9:30am-4pm, Su 11am-4pm. £3, students £2.50.) Enjoy spacious rooms and breakfast served in a glassed-walled patio overlooking the ocean and castle at **Arundel ❷,** Stryd Fawr. Energetic Mrs. Stein (pronounced "Steen") will pick you up from the train station. (☎780 637. £16 per person. Cash only.) At the **Plâs Cafe ❷,** Stryd Fawr, guests linger over cream tea (£3.50) and sunset dinners (from £8) on a grassy patio. (☎780 204. Open daily Mar.-Oct. 10am-8:30pm; Nov.-Feb. 10am-5:30pm. AmEx/MC/V.) Harlech lies midway on the Cambrian Coaster line; Arriva Cymru **train** T5 arrives from Porthmadog (20min., 3-7 per day, £6.20) and connects to other towns on the Llyn Peninsula. The **Day Ranger** pass allows unlimited travel on the Coaster line for one day (£6.60, children £3.30). The **tourist office,** on Stryd Fawr, doubles as an NPIC. (☎780 658. Open daily Easter-Oct. 9:30am-12:30pm and 1:30-5:30pm.) **Postal Code:** LL46 2YA.

LLYN PENINSULA ☎01766

The seclusion and sublime tranquility of the Llyn have humbled visitors since the Middle Ages, when pilgrims traversed it on their way to Bardsey Island. Today, sun worshippers make the pilgrimage to the beaches that line the southern coast. **Porthmadog,** on the southeastern part of the peninsula, is the main gateway. The main attraction here is the **Ffestiniog Railway,** which offers a bumpy, scenic ride from Harbour Station,

High St., into the hills of Snowdonia. (☎516 000; www.festrail.co.uk. Call for timetables. 3hr. round-trip; 2-10 per day; £16, students £12.80.) Despite a less than convenient location and owners who charge for everything under the roof, **Snowdon Backpackers Hostel ❶**, is still a nice, clean place to stay. (☎515 354. Breakfast included. Laundry £2. Dorms £12.50-13.50; doubles £29-33; triples £44-50. AmEx/MC/V.) The northern end of the Cambrian Coaster **train** (☎08457 489 450) runs from Aberystwyth or Birmingham to Porthmadog (2hr., 3-7 per day) via Machynlleth. Express Motors (☎01286 881 108) **bus** #1 stops in Porthmadog on its way from Blaenau Ffestiniog to Caernarfon (1hr., every hr., £2.60). The **tourist office** is on High St. by the harbor. (☎512 981. Open daily Easter-Oct. 9:30am-5:30pm; Nov.-Easter 10am-5pm.) **Postal Code:** LL49 9AD.

CAERNARFON ☎01286

Majestic and fervently Welsh, the walled city of Caernarfon (car-NAR-von) has a world-famous castle at its prow and mountains in its wake. Edward I began building **Caernarfon Castle** in 1283 to contain and intimidate the rebellious Welsh, but it was left unfinished when he ran out of money. The castle is nonetheless an architectural feat; its walls withstood a rebel siege in 1404 with only 28 defenders. (☎677 617. Open June-Sept. daily 9:30am-6pm; Apr.-May and Oct. daily 9:30am-5pm; Nov.-Mar. M-Sa 9:30am-4pm, Su 11am-4pm. £4.75, students £3.75.) **Totter's Hostel ❶**, 2 High St., has spacious rooms, a comfortable living room, and terrific owners. (☎672 963. Dorms £13. Cash only.) Charming **Hole-in-the-Wall Street** offers a tremendous collection of bistros, cafes, and restaurants from which to choose. Arriva Cymru (☎08706 082 608) **buses** #5 and 5x leave the city center at Penllyn for Conwy (1¾hr., 1-3 per hr.). National Express (☎08705 808 080) runs to London (9hr., 1 per day, £26). The **tourist office** is on Castle St. (☎672 232. Open Apr.-Oct. daily 9:30am-5:30pm; Nov.-Mar. M-Sa 10am-4:30pm.) **Postal Code:** LL55 2ND.

CONWY ☎01492

The central attraction of this tourist mecca is the imposing, 13th-century **Conwy Castle**, another link in Edward I's chain of Welsh fortresses. Try to get on "celebrity" guide Neville Hortop's extremely entertaining tour. (☎592 358. Open June-Sept. daily 9:30am-6pm; Apr.-May and Oct. daily 9:30am-5pm; Nov.-Mar. M-Sa 9:30am-4pm, Su 11am-4pm. £4, students £3.50. Tours £1.) Cozy rooms and timber ceilings await at **Swan Cottage ❷**, 18 Berry St. (☎596 840; www.swancottage.btinternet.co.uk. Singles £19; doubles £38. Cash only.) **Edward's Butchery ❶**, 18 High St., serves huge, hearty meat pies. (☎592 443; www.edwardsofconwy.co.uk. Pies from £1.25. AmEx/MC/V.) Arriva Cymru **buses** (☎08706 082 608) #5 and 5X stop in Conwy on their way to Caernarfon from Llandudno (1-1¼hr., 1-2 per hr., £5). National Express buses (☎08705 808 080) arrive from: Liverpool (2¾hr., 1 per day, £8.40); Manchester (4½hr., 1 per day, £13.20); Newcastle (10hr., 1 per day, £45). The **tourist office**, at the castle entrance, books beds for £2 plus a 10% deposit. (☎592 248. Open daily June-Sept. 9:30am-6pm; Oct.-Nov. and May 9:30am-5pm; Dec.-Apr. 9:30am-4pm.) **Postal Code:** LL32 8H7.

SCOTLAND

A little over half the size of England but with only one-tenth of its population, Scotland possesses the open spaces and natural splendor its southern neighbor cannot hope to rival. The craggy, heathered Highlands and the luminescent mists of the Hebrides will elicit any traveler's awe, while farmlands and fishing villages harbor a gentler beauty. Scotland at its best is a world apart from the rest of the UK, and its people revel in a culture all their own. The Scots doggedly defended their independence for hundreds of years before reluctantly joining with England in 1707. While the kilts, bagpipes, and souvenir clan paraphernalia of the big cities may grow tiresome, a visit to the less touristed regions of Scotland will allow you to rub elbows with the inheritors of ancient traditions: a B&B owner speaking Gaelic to her grandchildren, a crofter cutting peat, or a fisherman setting out in his skiff at dawn.

GETTING THERE AND AROUND

Bus travel from London is generally cheaper than **train** fares. **British Airways** (☎0845 773 3377; www.ba.com) sells round-trip England-to-Scotland tickets starting at £80. **British Midland** (☎0870 607 0555; www.flybmi.com) offers saver fares from London to Glasgow (from £78 round-trip). Some of the cheapest fares available are through **easyJet** (☎0870 600 0000; www.easyjet.com), which flies to Edinburgh and Glasgow from London (fares are web-only; prices vary).

In the **Lowlands** (south of Stirling and north of the Borders), train and bus connections are frequent. In the **Highlands,** trains snake slowly on a few restricted routes, bypassing the northwest almost entirely. Many stations are unstaffed or nonexistent—buy tickets onboard. A great money-saver is the **Freedom of Scotland Travelpass,** which allows unlimited train travel, transportation on most Caledonian MacBrayne ferries, and discounts on some other ferry lines. Purchase the pass *before* traveling to Britain from any BritRail distributor (p. 126). **Buses** tend to be the best way to travel; Scottish Citylink (☎08705 505 050) provides most intercity service. **Postbuses** (Royal Mail customer service ☎08457 740 740) are a unique British phenomenon. Red mail vans pick up passengers and mail once or twice a day in the most remote parts of the country, charging 40p-£4 (and often nothing). They're a reliable way to get around the Highlands. HAGGiS (☎0131 557 9393; www.haggisadventures.com) and MacBackpackers (☎0131 558 9900; www.macbackpackers.com) cater to the young and adventurous with witty and informative pre-packaged or hop-on/hop-off tours that let you see Scotland at your own pace.

EDINBURGH ☎0131

A city of elegant stone amid rolling hills and ancient volcanoes, Edinburgh (ED-in-bur-ra; pop. 500,000) is Scotland's jewel. Since Daid I granted it burgh (town) status in 1130, the "Athens of the North" has been a hotbed for forward-thinking artists and intellectuals. In August, Edinburgh becomes a mecca for the arts, drawing talent and crowds from around the world to its International and Fringe Festivals.

TRANSPORTATION

Flights: Edinburgh International Airport (EDI; ☎333 1000), 11km west of the city. Lothian's **Airlink** (☎555 6363) shuttles between the airport and Waverley Bridge (25min.; every 10-15min. 6am-midnight, every hr. midnight-6am; £3). An **Airsaver** ticket (£4.20) scores a trip on Airlink plus 1 day of unlimited travel on Lothian buses.

Trains: Waverley Station (☎08457 484 950), between Princes St., Market St., and Waverley Bridge. Trains to: **Aberdeen** (2½hr.; M-Sa every hr., Su 8 per day; £32); **Glasgow** (1hr., 4 per hr., £8-9); **Inverness** (3½hr., every 2hr., £32); **London King's Cross** (4¾hr., every hr., £83-89); **Stirling** (50min., 2 per hr., £5.30).

Buses: Edinburgh Bus Station, on the eastern side of St. Andrew Sq. Open daily 6am-midnight. National Express (☎08705 808 080) to **London** (10hr., 4 per day, £29). Scottish Citylink (☎08705 505 050) to: **Aberdeen** (4hr., every hr., £15); **Glasgow** (1hr., 2-3 per hr., £4); **Inverness** (4½hr., 8-10 per day, £15). A combination bus-ferry route via Stranraer goes to **Belfast** (2 per day, £20) and **Dublin** (1 per day, £28).

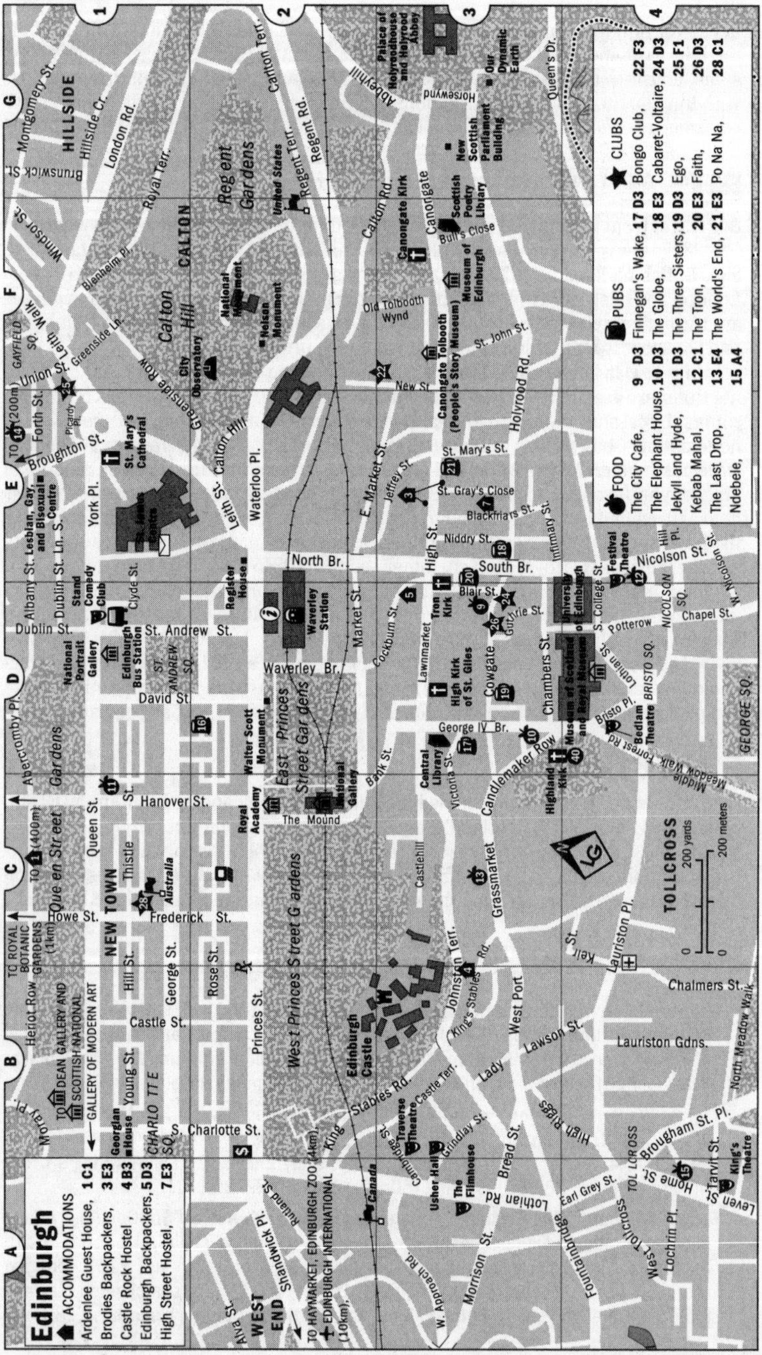
Edinburgh
ACCOMMODATIONS
Ardenlee Guest House, 1 C1
Brodies Backpackers, 3 E3
Castle Rock Hostel, 4 B3
Edinburgh Backpackers, 5 D3
High Street Hostel, 7 E3
FOOD
The City Cafe, 9 D3
The Elephant House, 10 D3
Jekyll and Hyde, 11 D3
Kebab Mahal, 12 C1
The Last Drop, 13 E4
Ndebele, 15 A4
PUBS
Finnegan's Wake, 17 D3
The Globe, 18 E3
The Three Sisters, 19 D3
The Tron, 20 E3
The World's End, 21 E3
CLUBS
Bongo Club, 22 F3
Cabaret-Voltaire, 24 D3
Ego, 25 F1
Faith, 26 D3
Po Na Na, 28 C1
NEW TOWN
CALTON
Calton Hill
Regent Gardens
HILLSIDE
WEST END
TOLLCROSS
Queen Street Gardens
West Princes Street Gardens
East Princes Street Gardens
Edinburgh Castle
Waverley Station
National Gallery
Royal Academy
Walter Scott Monument
National Monument
Nelson Monument
City Observatory
St. Mary's Cathedral
St. James Centre
Edinburgh Bus Station
National Portrait Gallery
Register House
High Kirk of St. Giles
Tron Kirk
Canongate Kirk
Canongate Tolbooth (People's Story Museum)
Museum of Edinburgh
Scottish Poetry Library
New Scottish Parliament Building
Our Dynamic Earth
Palace of Holyroodhouse and Holyrood Abbey
University of Edinburgh
Museum of Scotland and Royal Museum
Festival Theatre
Bedlam Theatre
Central Library
Highland Kirk
Traverse Theatre
Usher Hall
The Filmhouse
King's Theatre
Lesbian, Gay, and Bisexual Centre
Stand Comedy Club
Georgian House
TO ROYAL BOTANIC GARDENS (1km)
TO DEAN GALLERY AND SCOTTISH NATIONAL GALLERY OF MODERN ART
TO HAYMARKET, EDINBURGH ZOO (4km), EDINBURGH INTERNATIONAL (10km)
200 yards
200 meters

BRITAIN

Public Transportation: Lothian buses (☎555 6363; www.lothianbuses.co.uk) provide most services. Exact change required (£0.40-1). **Daysaver** ticket (£2.30) available from any driver. **Night buses** cover selected routes after midnight (£2). **First Edinburgh** (☎08708 727 271) also operates locally. **Traveline** (☎0800 232 323) has information on all area public transport.

ORIENTATION AND PRACTICAL INFORMATION

Edinburgh is a glorious city for walking. **Princes Street** is the main thoroughfare in **New Town,** the northern section of the city. From there you can view the impressive stone facade of the towering **Old Town** to the south. The **Royal Mile** (Castle Hill, Lawnmarket, High St., and Canongate) is the major road in the Old Town and connects Edinburgh Castle in the west to the Palace of Holyroodhouse in the east. **North Bridge, Waverley Bridge,** and **The Mound** connect Old and New Town. Three kilometers northeast, **Leith** is the city's seaport on the Firth of Forth.

Tourist Office: Waverley Market, 3 Princes St. (☎473 3800; www.edinburgh.org), on the north side of the Waverley Station complex. Books rooms for £3 plus a 10% deposit; sells bus, museum, tour, and theater tickets. Open July-Aug. M-Sa 9am-8pm, Su 10am-8pm; May-June and Sept. 9am-7pm; Apr. and Oct. M-Sa 9am-6pm, Su 10am-6pm; Nov.-Mar. M-Sa 9am-5pm, Su 10am-5pm. In summer, look for blue-jacketed **Guiding Stars** who wander through the city center and answer questions in several languages.

GLBT Resources: Pick up *Gay Information* at the tourist office or stop by **Edinburgh Lesbian, Gay, and Bisexual Centre,** 58a-60 Broughton St. (☎478 7069), inside Sala Cafe-Bar.

Emergency: ☎999 or 112, free from any payphone.

Police: Headquarters at Fettes Ave. (☎311 3901; www.lbp.police.uk).

Hospital: Royal Infirmary of Edinburgh, 41 Lauriston Pl. (☎536 1000, emergencies 536 6000).

Internet Access: Free at the **Central Library** (☎242 8000) on George IV Bridge. Open M-Th 10am-8pm, F 10am-5pm, Sa 9am-1pm. **easyInternet Cafe,** 58 Rose St. (☎220 3577), inside Caffe Nero. £2 per hr. Open M-Sa 7am-10pm, Su 9am-10pm.

Post Office: (☎556 9546; www.postoffice.co.uk), in the St. James Centre beside the bus station. Open M-Sa 9am-5:30pm. **Postal Code:** EH1 3SR.

ACCOMMODATIONS

Edinburgh accommodations cater to every kind of traveler. Hostels and hotels are the only city-center options, while B&Bs and guest houses begin on the periphery. It's a good idea to book ahead in summer, and absolutely essential to be well ahead of the game at New Year's and during festival season (late July-early Sept.).

High St. Hostel, 8 Blackfriars St. (☎557 3984). Good facilities, a party atmosphere, and a convenient Royal Mile location have made this a long-time Edinburgh favorite. Continental breakfast £1.90. Dorms £12.50. AmEx/MC/V. ❷

Castle Rock Hostel, 15 Johnston Terr. (☎225 9666), just steps from the castle. Regal views and top-notch common areas. Continental breakfast £1.90. Internet £1.60 per hr. Dorms £12.50, £14 during festival season. AmEx/MC/V. ❷

Ardenlee Guest House, 9 Eyre Pl. (☎556 2838). Take bus #23 or 27 from Hanover St. northbound to the corner of Dundas St. and Eyre Pl. Near the Royal Botanic Gardens, this friendly guest house has big, comfy rooms. £30-45 per person. MC/V. ❸

Brodies Backpackers 2, 93 High St. (☎556 2223; www.brodieshostels.co.uk). The best deal along the Royal Mile. Spotless kitchen, and heavenly beds. Free Internet. Dorms £11-16, festival season £17.50; doubles £34-45; quads from £55. MC/V. ❷

Edinburgh Backpackers, 65 Cockburn (CO-burn) St. (☎220 1717; www.hoppo.com). Friendly hostel with common areas, pool table, ping-pong, and TV. 15% discount at the downstairs Southern Cross cafe. Internet £2 per hr. Reception 24hr. Check-out 10am. Dorms £13-15.50, festival season £18; private rooms £44.50-72. MC/V. ❷

FOOD

Edinburgh features an exceptionally wide range of cuisines and restaurants. For a traditional taste of Scotland, the capital offers everything from haggis to creative "modern Scottish." Many pubs offer student and hosteler discounts in the early evening. Takeaway shops on **South Clerk Street, Leith Street,** and **Lothian Road** have reasonably priced Chinese and Indian food. Buy groceries at **Sainsbury's,** 9-10 St. Andrew Sq. (☎225 8400. Open M-Sa 7am-10pm, Su 10am-8pm.)

The City Cafe, 19 Blair St. (☎220 0125), off the Royal Mile behind Tron Kirk. Relaxed cafe by day, flashy pre-club spot by night. Creative wraps for £6 and incredible shakes. Happy hour daily 5-8pm. Open daily 11am-1am. Food served until 11pm. MC/V. ❷

The Elephant House, 21 George IV Bridge (☎220 5355). Harry Potter and Hogwarts were born here as hasty scribblings on napkins. A perfect place to chill, chat, or pore over the stack of newspapers. Exotic teas and coffees, delicious shortbread, and filling fare for less than £5. Th 8pm live music. Open daily 8am-11pm. MC/V. ❶

Ndebele, 57 Home St., Tolcross (☎221 1141; www.ndebele.co.uk), 0.5km south from the west end of Princes St. Serves heaping portions of South African food including smoked ostrich and mango sandwiches for £3.80. Open daily 10am-10pm. MC/V. ❶

Kebab Mahal, 7 Nicolson Sq. (☎667 5214). This casual student hot spot will stuff you with spicy Indian food. Entrees under £5. Open M-Th noon-1am, F-Sa noon-2am, Su noon-midnight. AmEx/MC/V. ❶

Jekyll and Hyde, 112 Hanover St. (☎235 2022; www.eeriepubco.com). 2 blocks from Robert Louis Stevenson's house, this themed restaurant serves "food to die for." Entrees £4.75-8. Open daily 11am-1am, until 3am during festival season. Food served until 9pm. MC/V. ❷

The Last Drop, 74-78 Grassmarket (☎225 4851). Tourist-friendly pub by the old gallows—hence the name. "Haggis, tatties, and neeps" in carnivore and herbivore versions £5. Student and hosteler discounts until 7pm. Open daily 10am-2am. AmEx/MC/V. ❶

IAGGIS AND TATTIES AND NEEPS, OH MY!

Scotland's regional cuisine usually comes beer-battered and leep-fried. But the country does offer delicacies beyond fish and chips. Here is a culinary translaion of a traditional and coronary-nducing Scottish meal.

Haggis: Perhaps the best-known Scottish dish, haggis consists of ninced and boiled offal (organ neats), which is encased in stomach lining and shaped into sauage. Don't be fooled by the ocals who tell you it's made from a three legged-bird, and don't believe weak-kneed foreigners who tell you it's disgusting.

Neeps: They're techincally rutabegas, although the nickname comes from the word turnip. Neeps are delicious stir-fried, nashed, baked, or deep-fried, especially accompanying haggis.

Tatties: Yet another name for the humble potato. Chips are served with fish. Tatties, more like steak ries, go well with heartier fare.

rn-Bru: Wash down your Scottish linner with this peculiar caffeinated orange soda. It tastes a little ike liquid bubblegum and is often nixed with liquor.

Cranachan: For dessert, try this semi-sweet fruit parfait, made with raspberries, honey, whipped cream, oatmeal, and (unsurprisngly) whisky.

SIGHTS

A boggling array of Edinburgh tour companies tout themselves as "the original," but the most worthwhile is the **Edinburgh Literary Pub Tour.** Led by professional actors, this alcohol-sodden 2hr. crash course in Scottish literature meets outside the Beehive Inn in the Grassmarket. (☎226 6665; www.edinburghliterarypub-tour.co.uk. June-Sept. daily 7:30pm; Apr.-May and Oct. Th-Su 7:30pm; Nov.-Mar. F 7:30pm. £7, students £6. £1 discount for online booking.)

THE OLD TOWN AND THE ROYAL MILE

Edinburgh's medieval center, the fascinating **Royal Mile** defines the Old Town. Once lined with narrow shopfronts and slums towering to a dozen stories, this famous strip is now a playground for hostelers and locals alike, buzzing with bars, attractions, and the inevitable cheesy souvenir shops.

EDINBURGH CASTLE. Dominating the city skyline from atop an extinct volcano, Edinburgh castle is a testament to the city's past strategic importance. The castle is the result of centuries of renovation and rebuilding; the most recent additions date to the 1920s. The **One O'Clock Gun** fires Monday through Saturday at 1pm. *(You can't miss it. ☎225 9846. Open daily Apr.-Oct. 9:30am-6pm; Nov.-Mar. 9:30am-5pm. Last admission 45min. before close. Guided tour included. £9.50. Audio tours £3.)*

CASTLE HILL AND LAWNMARKET AREA. The Scotch Whisky Experience at the **Scotch Whisky Heritage Centre** provides a Disney-style 50min. tour through the "history and mystery" of Scotland's most famous export. *(354 Castle Hill. Open daily 9:45am-5:30pm; reduced winter hours. Tours every 15min. £8.50, students £6.40.)* Staffed with knowledgeable guides, **Gladstone's Land** (c. 1617) is the oldest surviving house on the Royal Mile. *(477b Lawnmarket. ☎226 5856. Open Apr.-Oct. M-Sa 10am-5pm, Su 2-5pm. £5, students £3.75.)* Nearby, the 17th-century **Lady Stair's House** contains the **Writer's Museum,** featuring memorabilia of three of Scotland's greatest literary figures: Robert Burns, Sir Walter Scott, and Robert Louis Stevenson. *(Lawnmarket. ☎529 4901. Open M-Sa 10am-5pm; during Festival also Su 2-5pm. Free.)* For incredible views of the city, visit the **Outlook Tower** on Castle Hill. Its 150-year-old **camera obscura** captures a moving image of the streets below. *(Open daily July-Aug. 9:30am-7:30pm; Apr.-June and Sept.-Oct. 9:30am-6pm; Nov.-Mar. 10am-5pm. £6, students £4.70.)*

HIGH STREET AND CANONGATE AREA. At the beautiful **High Kirk of St. Giles** (St. Giles Cathedral), Scotland's principal church, John Knox delivered the fiery Presbyterian sermons that drove Mary, Queen of Scots, into exile. Most of the present structure was built in the 15th century, but parts date as far back as 1126. The Kirk hosts free concerts throughout the year. *(Where Lawnmarket becomes High St. ☎225 4363. Open Easter to mid-Sept. M-F 9am-7pm, Sa 9am-5pm, Su 1-5pm; mid-Sept. to Easter M-Sa 9am-5pm, Su 1-5pm. Suggested donation £1.)* The 17th-century **Canongate Kirk,** on the hill at the end of the Royal Mile, is the resting place of economist Adam Smith; royals used to worship here when in residence. *(Same hours as High Kirk. Free.)*

THE PALACE OF HOLYROODHOUSE. This Stuart palace, at the base of the Royal Mile beside Holyrood Park, remains Queen Elizabeth II's official Scottish residence. As a result, only parts of the ornate interior are open to the public. On the palace grounds stand the 12th-century ruins of **Holyrood Abbey,** built by David I in 1128 and ransacked during the Reformation. Only a single doorway remains from the original construction; most of the ruins date from the 13th century. Located in a recently renovated 17th-century schoolhouse near the palace entrance, the **Queen's Gallery** displays rotating exhibits from the royal art collection. *(☎556 5100. Open Apr.-Oct. daily*

GREYFRIARS BOBBY

Undoubtedly the most famous resident of the Greyfriars Tolbooth and Highland Kirk's ancient cemetery is a certain John Gray. The night after Gray's burial in 1858, his scruffy Skye terrier, Bobby, lay down on his master's grave. The next night Bobby returned and again held vigil, as he would every night for the next 14 years. As word spread of this extraordinary display of canine loyalty, the legend of Greyfriars Bobby became permanent part of Edinburgh lore.

After living to the age of 16, Greyfriars Bobby finally passed away, having spent all but two of his years guarding the tombstone. To honor his loyalty, the city erected a statue of the dog and buried him near his beloved master in the very same kirk.

Over the years this sweet story has found its way into numerous books and even a Disney film. The statue, which sits at the intersection of George IV Bridge and Candlemaker Row, is the most photographed statue in Scotland. Still, there are those who have their doubts about this touching saga. Some claim that the grave that Bobby so admirably watched over belonged in fact to another John Gray and not his master. Others claim that the dog's real affection was for a nearby bakery. Such spoilsports have been unsuccessful in tarnishing the legend, however, which is still alive and well.

9:30am-6pm; Nov.-Mar. M-Sa 9:30am-4:30pm. Last admission 45min. before close. Closed to visitors while royals are in residence—often late May to early July. £8, students £6.50. Queen's Gallery £5/4. Joint ticket £11/9. Audio tour free.)

OTHER SIGHTS IN THE OLD TOWN. The **Museum of Scotland** and the connected **Royal Museum,** on Chambers St., just south of the George IV Bridge, are not to be missed. The former houses a collection of Scottish artifacts in a stunning modern building. Highlights include the working **Corliss Steam Engine** and the **Maiden,** Edinburgh's pre-French Revolution guillotine. The Royal Museum has a mix of European art and ancient Roman and Egyptian artifacts. *(☎247 4422. Both open M and W-Sa 10am-5pm, Tu 10am-8pm, Su noon-5pm. Free.)* Across the street, a statue of Greyfriar's loyal pooch, Bobby, marks the entrance to **Highland Kirk,** surrounded by a beautiful, supposedly haunted churchyard. *(Off Candlemaker Row. ☎225 1900. Open Apr.-Oct. M-F 10:30am-4:30pm, Sa 10:30am-2:30pm; Nov.-Mar. Th 1:30-3:30pm. Free.)*

THE NEW TOWN

Edinburgh's new town is a masterpiece of Georgian design. James Craig, a 23-year-old architect, won the city-planning contest in 1767; his rectangular grid of three parallel streets (**Queen, George,** and **Princes**) linking two large squares (**Charlotte** and **St. Andrew**) reflects the Scottish Enlightenment's love of order.

ROYAL YACHT BRITANNIA. Northeast of the city center floats one of Edinburgh's top tourist attractions, the Royal Yacht *Britannia.* Used by the Queen and her family from 1953 to 1997, *Britannia* sailed around the world on state visits and royal holidays before settling here for permanent retirement. Visitors can follow an audio tour of the entire flagship, which remains exactly as it was when decommissioned. *(Entrance on the Ocean Terminal's 3rd fl. Take bus #22 from Princes St. or #35 from the Royal Mile to Ocean Terminal; £1. ☎555 5566; www.royalyachtbritannia.co.uk. Open daily Mar.-Oct. 9:30am-4:30pm; Oct.-Mar. 10am-3:30pm. £9, students £5.)*

THE GEORGIAN HOUSE AND THE WALTER SCOTT MONUMENT. The elegantly restored **Georgian House** gives a fair picture of how Edinburgh's elite lived 200 years ago. *(7 Charlotte Sq. ☎226 3318. Open daily Apr.-Oct. 10am-5pm; Mar. and Nov. 11am-3pm. Last admission 30min. before close. £5, students £4.)* The **Walter Scott Monument** is a Gothic "steeple without a church"; climb the 287-step staircase for views stretching out to Princes St., the castle, and the surrounding city. *(Princes St. between The Mound and Waverley Bridge. ☎529 4068. Open Apr.-Sept. M-Sa 9am-6pm, Su 10am-6pm; Oct.-Mar. 10am-3pm. £2.50.)*

THE NATIONAL GALLERIES

The National Galleries of Scotland in Edinburgh form an elite group, with excellent collections housed in stately buildings, all connected by a free shuttle that runs every 45min. The flagship is the **National Gallery of Scotland,** on The Mound, which contains a superb collection of works by Renaissance, Romantic, and Impressionist masters, including Degas, Gauguin, Monet, Raphael, and Titian. Be sure not to miss the octagonal room which displays Poussin's entire *Seven Sacraments.* The basement houses a fine spread of Scottish art. The **Scottish National Portrait Gallery,** 1 Queen St., north of St. Andrew Sq., features the faces of men and women who have shaped Scotland's history, including wordsmith Robert Louis Stevenson, renegade Bonnie Prince Charlie, and royal troublemaker Mary, Queen of Scots. The gallery also hosts excellent visiting exhibits of contemporary artists. Take the free bus #13 from George St., or walk to the **Scottish National Gallery of Modern Art,** 75 Belford Rd., west of town, to see works by Braque, Matisse, and Picasso. Part of the Gallery of Modern Art, **Dean Gallery,** 73 Belford Rd., is dedicated to Dadaist and Surrealist art. *(All open daily 10am-5pm; during festival 10am-6pm. Free.)*

GARDENS AND PARKS

Just off the eastern end of the Royal Mile, the oasis of **Holyrood Park** is a natural wilderness replete with hills, moorland, and lochs. **Arthur's Seat** is the park's highest point; the windy walk to the summit takes about 45min. Traces of forts and Bronze Age terraces dot the surrounding hillside. Located directly in the city center and affording fantastic views of the Old Town and the castle, the **Princes Street Gardens** are on the site of the now drained Nor'Loch, where Edinburghers used to drown their accused witches. The loch has been replaced with impeccably manicured lawns and stone fountains. On fine summer days all of Edinburgh eats lunch here. The lovely **Royal Botanic Gardens** are north of the city center. Guided tours wander across the lush grounds and through massive greenhouses. *(Take bus #23 or 27 from Hanover St. ☎552 7171. Open daily Apr.-Sept. 10am-7pm; Mar. and Oct. 10am-6pm; Nov.-Feb. 10am-4pm. Free. Greenhouses £3.50, students £3.)*

ENTERTAINMENT AND NIGHTLIFE

In winter, shorter days and the crush of students promote a flourishing nightlife. For the most up-to-date info on what's going on, check out *The List* (£2.20), a comprehensive bi-weekly guide to events, available from any local newsstand. The **Festival Theatre,** 13-29 Nicholson St., stages ballet and opera, while the affiliated **King's Theatre,** 2 Leven St., hosts comedy, drama, musicals, and opera. (☎529 6000. Box office open M-Sa 10am-6pm. Tickets £8-52.) **The Stand Comedy Club,** 5 York Pl., has nightly acts. (☎558 7272. Tickets £1-8.) The **Filmhouse,** 88 Lothian Rd., shows quality European, arthouse, and Hollywood cinema. (☎228 2688. Box office open daily noon-9pm. Tickets £2.50-5.80.) Edinburgh's live music scene is particularly vibrant. Enjoy live jazz at **Henry's Jazz Cellar,** 8 Morrison St. (Open daily 8pm-3am. £5.) **Whistle Binkie's,** 4-6 South Bridge, off High St., is a subterranean pub with at least two live bands per night. (M open mic; Tu open bands. Open daily until 3am.)

BRITAIN

PUBS

Students and backpackers gather each night in the Old Town. Pubs on the **Royal Mile** attract a mixed crowd. Casual pub-goers groove to live music on **Grassmarket, Candlemaker Row,** and **Victoria Street.** Historical pubs in the New Town cluster on **Rose Street,** parallel to Princes St. Wherever you are, you'll hear last call sometime between 11pm and 1am, 3am during Festival season.

The Tron, 9 Hunter Sq., behind the Tron Kirk. Wildly popular. 3 hopping floors frequently host live music. Students and hostelers get £1 drinks on W nights. A mix of alcoves and pool tables downstairs. Open M-Sa 11:30am-1am, Su 12:30pm-1am.

The Globe, 13 Niddry St. Backpackers recommend this hole-in-the-wall up and down the Royal Mile. Airs international sports, hosts DJs, and holds karaoke and quiz nights. Open M-F 4pm-1am, Sa noon-1am, Su 12:30pm-1am; during festivals until 3am.

The Three Sisters, 139 Cowgate. Loads of space for dancing, drinking, and chilling. Attracts a young crowd to its 3 bars (Irish, Gothic, and American). Close to 1000 people pass through the beer garden and barbecue on Sa nights. Open daily 9am-1am.

Finnegan's Wake, 9b Victoria St. Drink Ireland-style with several stouts on tap, road signs from Cork, and live Irish music every night. Open daily 1pm-1am.

The World's End, 2-8 High St., at the corner of St. Mary's St. Serves traditional pub grub in a historical setting. Open daily 11am-1am.

CLUBS

Club venues are constantly closing down and reopening under new management; consult *The List* for updated info. Clubs cluster around the historically disreputable **Cowgate,** just downhill from and parallel to the Royal Mile. Most close at 3am, 5am during the Festival. The Broughton St. area of the New Town (better known as the **Broughton Triangle**) is the center of Edinburgh's gay community.

Cabaret-Voltaire, 36-38 Blair St. (☎220 6176). With a wide range of live music, dance, and art, this innovative club throws a great party. Occasional cover up to £15. Open 10pm-3am.

Bongo Club, 14 New St. (☎558 7604). Students and backpackers flock to the long-running and immensely popular Messenger (reggae) and Headspin (funk and dance) nights, which run on alternate Sa. Occasional cover up to £10.

Faith, 207 Cowgate (☎225 9764). Inside an old church, this purple-hued club specializes in R&B. Very popular Su Chocolate. Occasional cover up to £6.

Po Na Na, 43b Frederick St. (☎226 2224), beneath Cafe Rouge. Moroccan-themed with parachute ceilings, red velvet couches, and an eclectic mix of music. Cover £2.50-6. Open Th 11pm-3am, F-Sa 10pm-3am.

Ego, 14 Picardy Pl. (☎478 7434). Not strictly a gay club, Ego hosts gay nights, including Vibe (Tu) and Blaze (3 F per month). Cover £2-10.

FESTIVALS

In August, Edinburgh is *the* place to be in Europe. What's commonly referred to as "the Festival" actually encompasses a number of independent events. For more info, check out www.edinburghfestivals.co.uk. The **Edinburgh International Festival** (www.eif.co.uk; Aug. 13-Sept. 3, 2006), the largest of them all, features a kaleidoscopic program of music, drama, dance, and art. Tickets (£7-58; 50% discount for students) are sold beginning in April, but you a limited number of £5 tickets are available 1hr. before every event. Bookings can be made by post, phone, fax, web, or in person at **The HUB** (☎473 2000), Edinburgh's Festival Centre, Castlehill.

A less formal **Fringe Festival** (www.edfringe.com; Aug. 6-28, 2006) has grown around the established festival. Anyone who can afford the small registration fee can perform, guaranteeing a multitude of great and not-so-good independent acts and an absolutely wild month. The **Edinburgh Jazz and Blues Festival** is in late July. (www.jazzmusic.co.uk. Tickets on sale in June.) The excellent **Edinburgh International Film Festival** occurs during the second and third weeks of August at The Filmhouse. (www.edfilmfest.org.uk. Tickets on sale starting late July.) The fun doesn't stop for winter: **Hogmanay,** the traditional New Year's Eve festival, is a serious street party with a week of associated events (www.edinburghshogmanay.org).

DAYTRIP FROM EDINBURGH: ST. ANDREWS

Golf overruns the small city of St. Andrews, where the rules of the sport were formally established. Today, a mix of golfers, college students, and royalty-spotters all converge on its three medieval streets. Mary Queen of Scots supposedly played at the **Old Course** just days after her husband was murdered. Nonmembers must present a handicap certificate or letter of introduction from a golf club. Book at least a year in advance; enter your name into a near-impossible lottery by 2pm the day before you hope to play, or get in line before dawn by the caddie master's hut as a single. (☎01334 466 666. Apr.-Oct. £80-115 per round; Nov.-Mar. £56.) The lovely budget option is the nine-hole **Balgove Course** (£10). If you need a break from the green, visit the **British Golf Museum,** next to the Old Course on Bruce Embankment, which details the ancient origins of the game. (☎01334 460 046. Open mid-Mar. to Oct. M-Sa 9:30am-5:30pm, Su 10am-5pm; Nov. to mid-Mar. daily 10am-4pm. £5, students £4.) The nearby **St. Andrews Castle** hides medieval siege tunnels and bottle-shaped dungeons. (☎01334 477 196. Open daily Apr.-Sept. 9:30am-6:30pm; Oct.-Mar. 9:30am-4:30pm. £4.) **Trains** (☎08457 484 950) stop 8km away in Leuchars, where buses #94 and 96 depart for St. Andrews (£1.60). **Buses** (☎01383 621 249) pull into City Rd. from Edinburgh (#X60; 2hr., 1-2 per hr., £6.50) and Glasgow (#X24; 2½hr., every hr., £6.50). To get from the bus station to the **tourist office,** 70 Market St., turn right on City Rd. and take the first left. Ask for the free *St. Andrews Town Map and Guide.* (☎01334 472 021. Open July-Sept. M-Sa 9:30am-7pm, Su 9:30am-5pm; Oct.-June reduced hours.)

GLASGOW ☎0141

Glasgow (pop. 700,000), Scotland's largest city, has reinvented itself many times and retains the mark of each transformation. Stately architecture recalls Queen Victoria's reign, while cranes littering the River Clyde bear witness to its sooty past as a major industrial hub. Today, world-class art museums and collections give Glasgow a thriving creative energy. The city comes alive at night, fueled by football-crazed locals and the largest student population in Scotland.

TRANSPORTATION AND PRACTICAL INFORMATION. Flights land at **Glasgow International Airport** (GLA; ☎08740 040 0008; www.baa.co.uk/glasgow), 16km west in Abbotsinch. Citylink bus #905 connects to Buchanan Station (25min., 6 per hr., £3.30). From **Glasgow Prestwick International Airport** (PIK; ☎0871 223 0700; www.gpia.co.uk), 52km away, express bus #X99 runs to Buchanan Station (50min., £3.40) and trains leave for Central Station every hour (30min.; £5.20, half price with Ryanair flight printout). **Trains** pull into Central Station, on Gordon St. (U: St. Enoch), from London King's Cross (5-6hr., every hr., £90.60) and Manchester (4hr., every hr., £40). From Queen St. Station, on George Sq. (U: Buchanan St.), trains go to: Aberdeen (2½hr., 7-11 per day, £34); Edinburgh (50min., 4 per hr., £8.20); Inverness (3¼hr., 4-7 per day, £34). Bus #88 (£0.50) connects the two stations, but it's only a 5-10min. walk. Scottish Citylink (☎08705 505 050) **buses** leave Buchanan Station, on Killermont St., for: Aberdeen (4hr., every hr., £17); Edinburgh (1¼hr., 3 per hr., £4); Inverness (3½hr., every hr., £17). National Express (☎08705 808 080) goes to London (8½hr., 3 per day, £30). Local transportation includes the circular **Underground (U)** subway line (M-Sa 6:30am-11pm, Su 11am-5:30pm; £1, all-day Discovery Ticket £1.70). The **tourist office,** 11 George Sq., south of Queen St. Station and northeast of Central Station, books rooms for a £3 fee plus 10% deposit. (☎204 4400; www.seeglasgow.com. U: Buchanan St. Open July-Aug. M-Sa 9am-8pm, Su 10am-6pm; Sept.-June M-Sa 9am-7pm,

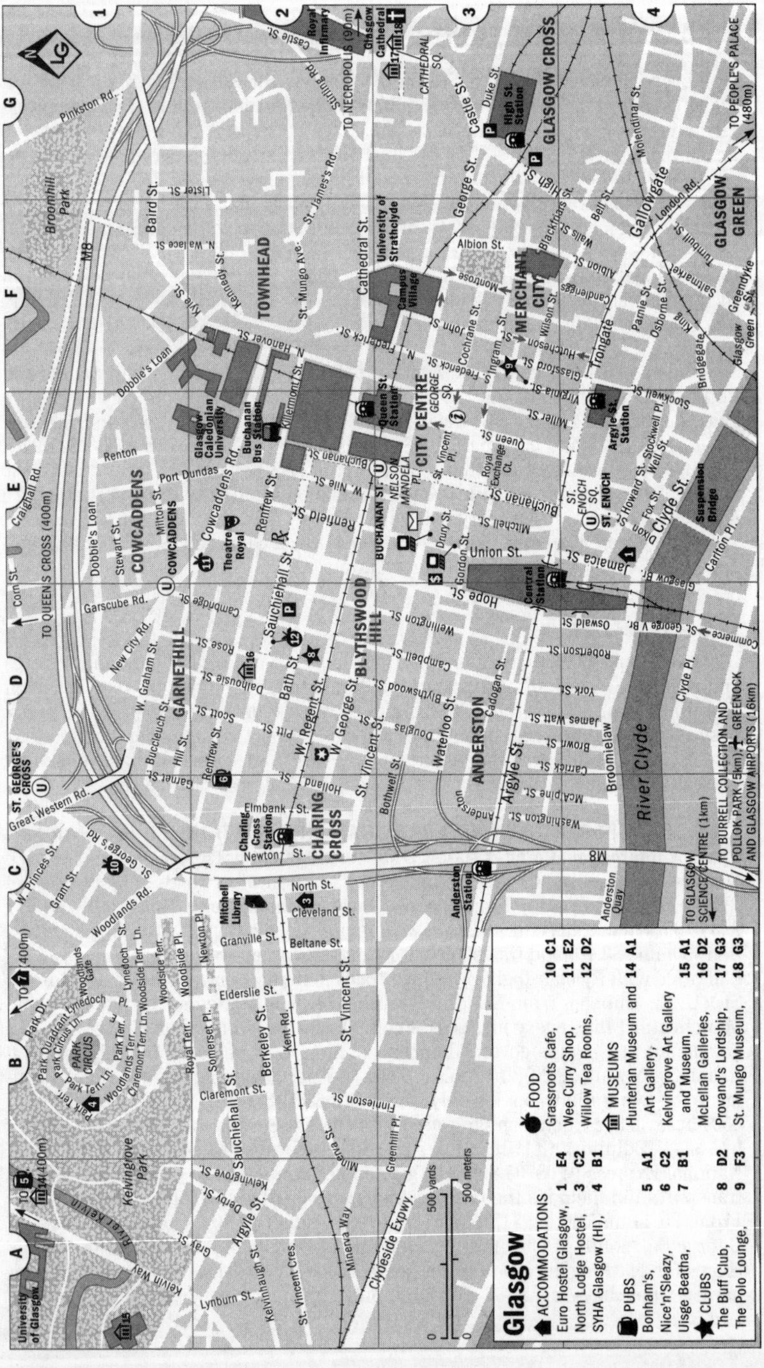

Glasgow

ACCOMMODATIONS

Euro Hostel Glasgow,	1	E4
North Lodge Hostel,	3	C2
SYHA Glasgow (HI),	4	B1

PUBS

Bonham's,	5	A1
Nice'n'Sleazy,	6	C2
Uisge Beatha,	7	B1

CLUBS

The Buff Club,	8	D2
The Polo Lounge,	9	F3

FOOD

Grassroots Cafe,	10	C1
Wee Curry Shop,	11	E2
Willow Tea Rooms,	12	D2

MUSEUMS

Hunterian Museum and Art Gallery,	14	A1
Kelvingrove Art Gallery and Museum,	15	A1
McLellan Galleries,	16	D2
Provand's Lordship,	17	G3
St. Mungo Museum,	18	G3

Su 10am-6pm.) Connect to the **Internet** at **Hub,** 8 Renfield St. (☎222 2227. £1.80 per hr.; day pass or wireless connection £3.50. Open M-Th 7:30am-10pm, F-Sa 7:30am-9pm, Su 10am-9pm.) **Postal Code:** G2 5QX.

ACCOMMODATIONS AND FOOD. Reserve rooms in advance, especially in the summer months. B&Bs are scattered on either side of **Argyle Street,** near the university and **Kelvingrove Park.** The newly renovated rooms of the **SYHA Glasgow (HI) ❶**, 7-8 Park Terr., are the best in town. (☎332 3004. U: St. George's Cross. Internet £3 per hr. June-Sept. dorms £14, under 18 £12. Low-season rates vary. MC/V.) At the **North Lodge Hostel ❶**, 163 North St., near the West End, you'll find a communal, friendly vibe as you banter with the owner and get voted in by the other guests. Free breakfast, laundry, and Internet. (☎221 3852. Dorms £10. MC/V.) The **Euro Hostel Glasgow ❶**, the gray behemoth on the corner of Clyde and Jamaica St., is most notable for its convenience to the city center. (☎222 2828; www.euro-hostels.com. Breakfast included. Internet £4 per hr. Dorms £13.95-18.95. MC/V.)

The area bordered by **Otago Street** in the west, **St. George's Road** in the east, and along **Great Western Road, Woodlands Road,** and **Eldon Street** brims with cheap kebab-and-curry joints. **Byres Road** and tiny, parallel **Ashton Lane** overflow with cheap, trendy cafes while bakeries along **High Street** serve scones for as little as £0.20. The **Willow Tea Rooms ❷**, 217 Sauchiehall St., upstairs from Henderson the Jewellers, are a cozy local landmark. (☎332 0521; www.willowtearooms.co.uk. U: Buchanan St. Tea £1.80 per pot. Afternoon tea £9.50. Open M-Sa 9am-4:30pm, Su 11am-4:15pm. MC/V.) Find Glasgow's best vegetarian food at **Grassroots Cafe ❷**, 97 St. George's Rd. (☎333 0534. U: St. George's Cross. Handmade pastas from £6.80. Open daily 10am-10pm. AmEx/MC/V.) **The Wee Curry Shop ❶**, 7 Buccleuch St., is the best deal in a town full of pakora. (☎353 0777. U: Cowcaddens. 2-course lunch £4.75. Entrees £5.50-7. Open M-Sa noon-2:30pm and 5:30-10:30pm. Cash only.)

SIGHTS. Glasgow is a budget sightseer's paradise, with splendid period architecture, grand museums, and chic galleries, many of which are free. Your first stop should be the Gothic **Glasgow Cathedral,** on Castle St., the only full-scale cathedral spared by the 16th-century Scottish Reformation. (☎552 6891. Open Apr.-Sept. M-Sa 9:30am-6pm, Su 1-5pm; Oct.-Mar. M-Sa 9:30am-4pm, Su 1-4pm. Ask for free personal tours.) Behind the cathedral is the **necropolis,** a terrifying hilltop cemetery. Be careful after dark. (Open 24hr. Free.) Down the street from the cathedral, the **St. Mungo Museum of Religious Life and Art,** 2 Castle St., surveys every religion from Islam to Yoruba, and displays Dalí's *Christ of St. John's Cross.* (☎553 2557. Open M-Th and Sa 10am-5pm, F and Su 11am-5pm. Free.) Built in 1471, **Provand's Lordship,** 3-7 Castle St., is the oldest house in Glasgow and has creaky floors to prove it. (☎552 8819. Open M-Th and Sa 10am-5pm, F and Su 11am-5pm. Free.)

In the West End, wooded **Kelvingrove Park** lies on the banks of the River Kelvin. In the park's southwestern corner, at Argyle and Sauchiehall St., the magnificent **Kelvingrove Art Gallery and Museum** shelters works by Monet, Rembrandt, and van Gogh. Due to renovations, the museum's collection will be on display at the **McLellan Galleries,** 270 Sauchiehall St., until summer 2006. (☎565 4137. Open M-Th and Sa 10am-5pm, F and Su 11am-5pm. Free.) Farther west rise the Gothic edifices of the **University of Glasgow.** The main building is on University Ave., which runs into Byres Rd. While walking through campus, stop by the **Hunterian Museum,** home to the Blackstone chair, in which all students once sat their oral examinations while timed by an hourglass. You can also see 19th-century Scottish art at the **Hunterian Art Gallery,** across the street. (U: Hillhead. Both open M-Sa 9:30am-5pm. Free.)

Take bus #45, 47, 48, or 57 from Jamaica St. (15min., £1.20) to reach the famous **Burrell Collection,** 5km south of the city in the Pollok Country Park. Once the private stash of ship magnate William Burrell, the collection includes paintings by Cézanne and Degas, needlework from European tapestries and Persian textiles, and fine china. (☎287 2550. Open M-Th and Sa 10am-5pm, F and Su 11am-5pm. Tours daily 11am, 2pm. Free.) Also in the park is the less spectacular **Pollok House,** a Victorian mansion with a small collection of paintings, some by El Greco and Goya. (☎616 6410. Open daily 10am-5pm. £5, students £3.75; Nov.-Mar. free.)

ENTERTAINMENT AND NIGHTLIFE. *The List* (£2.40 at newsstands) has detailed nightlife and entertainment listings. The infamous **Byres Road** pub crawl slithers past the University area, starting at Tennant's Bar and proceeding toward the River Clyde. With its 100 varieties, **Uisge Beatha,** 232 Woodlands Rd., reminds you that in Scotland, it's spelled "whisky." (☎564 1596. U: Kelvinbridge. Whisky from £2. Open M-Sa noon-midnight, Su 12:30pm-midnight.) **Bonham's,** 192 Byres Rd., has great food and a student-friendly atmosphere. (☎357 3424. U: Hillhead. Open daily 11am-11pm.) **Nice'n'Sleazy,** 421 Sauchiehall St., features local bands in its underground lair. (☎333 0900. Open daily 11:30am-midnight.) After hours, **The Buff Club,** 142 Bath Ln., is the place to be. (☎248 1777. Cover £3-6, free with receipt from local bar; ask at the door for details. Open M-Th and Su 11pm-3am, F-Sa 10:30pm-3am.) Labrynthine club **The Polo Lounge,** 58 Wilson St., is home to Glasgow's most popular gay scene. (☎553 1221. Open M-Th 5pm-1am, F-Sa 5pm-3am.)

STIRLING ☎01786

It was once said that "he who controls Stirling controls Scotland." The third point of a strategic triangle completed by Glasgow and Edinburgh, Stirling has historically presided over north-south travel in the region. At the 1297 Battle of Stirling Bridge, William Wallace (of *Braveheart* fame) overpowered the English army, enabling Robert the Bruce to finally overthrow the English at **Bannockburn,** 3km south of town. Take bus #51 or 52 from Murray Pl. in Stirling. (Visitors Center open daily Apr.-Oct. 10am-5:30pm; Feb.-Mar. and Nov.-Dec. 10:30am-4pm. Battlefield open year-round. £3.50.) **Stirling Castle** is decorated with prim gardens that belie its turbulent history. (☎450 000. Open daily Apr.-Oct. 9:30am-6pm; Nov.-Mar. 9:30am-5pm. 30min. guided tours leave every 30min. from inside the castle gates. £8, students £4. Tours free.) **Argyll's Lodging,** a 17th-century mansion below the castle, has been impressively restored. (Open daily Apr.-Sept. 9:30am-6pm; Oct.-Mar. 9:30am-5pm. £3.30, students £2.50, with castle admission free.)

At colorful **Willy Wallace Hostel ❶,** 77 Murray Pl., near the train station, the warm staff fosters a fun atmosphere. (☎446 773. Internet £1 per hr. Dorms £10-12. MC/V.) Hearty French fare awaits at the intimate **Cottage Cafe ❶,** 52 Spittal St. (☎446 124. Toasties £3. Lunch £4.50-5.25. Open M-Tu and Th-Su 11am-3pm, Th-Sa also 5:30-9pm. Cash only.) Tucked into an alley, **The Greengrocer Grocer,** 81 Port St., has the freshest fruits and veggies in town. (☎479 159. Open M-Sa 9am-5:30pm.) **Trains** (☎08457 484 950) run from Goosecroft Rd. to: Aberdeen (2hr., M-Sa every hr., £31); Edinburgh (50min., 2 per hr., £5.30); Glasgow (40min., 2-3 per hr., £5.40); Inverness (3hr., 3-4 per day, £31); London King's Cross (5½hr., every hr., £44-84). Scottish Citylink **buses** (☎446 474) also leave Goosecroft Rd. for: Edinburgh (1¼hr., every hr., £4); Fort William (2¾hr., 1 per day, £14.20); Glasgow (40min., 2-3 per hr., £4); Inverness (3¾hr., every hr., £13). The **tourist office** is at 41 Dumbarton Rd. (☎200 620. Open M-Sa 9am-7pm, low season reduced hours.) **Postal Code:** FK8 2BP.

THE TROSSACHS ☎01877

The most accessible tract of Scotland's wilderness, the mountains and misty lochs of the Trossachs (from Gaelic for "bristly country") are popular for their moderate hikes and unbeatable beauty. The Trossachs and Loch Lomond form Scotland's first national park, justifiably billed as the "Highlands in miniature."

TRANSPORTATION. Access to the Trossachs is easiest from Stirling. First **buses** (☎01324 613 777) connect to the region's two main towns, running from Stirling to Aberfoyle (#11; 45min., 4 per day, £2.50) and Callander (#59; 45min., 12 per day, £3). Scottish Citylink also runs a bus from Edinburgh to Callander (1¾hr., 1 per day, £8) via Stirling. In summer, the useful **Trossachs Trundler** (☎01786 442 707) ferries between Callander, Aberfoyle, and the Trossachs Pier at Loch Katrine; one daily trip begins and ends in Stirling. (June-Sept. M-Tu and Th-Su 4 per day; Day Rover £5, students £4.)

CALLANDER. Beside the quiet River Teith, the town of Callander is a good base for exploring the Trossachs. Dominating the horizon, **Ben Ledi** (880m) provides a strenuous but not overly challenging trek. A trail up the mountain (9km) begins just north of town along A84. A number of walks depart from Callander itself. **The Crags** (10km) heads up through the woods to the ridge above town, while the popular walk to **Bracklinn Falls** (8km) wanders through a picturesque glen. **Cyclists** can join a lovely stretch of the **Lowland Highland Trail,** which runs north to Strathyre along an old railway line. Callander's **Rob Roy and Trossachs Visitor Centre,** Main St., is a combination **tourist office** and exhibit on the 17th-century hero. (☎330 342. Open daily June-Aug. 10am-6pm; low season reduced hours. Exhibit £3.60, students £2.40.) Walkers should grab the *Callander Walks and Fort Trails* pamphlet; cyclists can consult *Rides around the Trossachs* (both £2). Rent bikes at **Cycle Hire Callander,** Ancaster Sq., beside the tourist office. (☎331 052. £10 per day, £7 per half day. Open daily 9am-6pm. MC/V.) The hidden gem of the region's lodgings is **Trossachs Backpackers ❷**, Invertrossachs Rd., 0.8km south of Callander. This hostel's forest-clearing location makes it an ideal base. Friendly owners Janet and Mark Shimitzu will often pick up guests from Callander. (☎331 200 for hostel, 331 100 for bike rental. Breakfast included. Laundry and Internet. Bikes £13 per day. Dorms £14; private rooms £18.50. MC/V.)

ABERFOYLE. Aberfoyle, another springboard into the wilderness, is at the heart of the **Queen Elizabeth Forest Park,** which covers territory from the shore of Loch Lomond to the Strathyre Mountains. For more information on **trails,** visit the **Trossachs Discovery Centre,** in town. (☎382 352. Open July-Aug. daily 9:30am-6pm; Apr.-June and Sept.-Oct. daily 10am-5pm; Nov.-Mar. Sa-Su 10am-5pm.) Ann and John Epps welcome visitors to **Crannaig House ❹**, Trossachs Rd., a Victorian home with spacious rooms. (☎382 276. Singles from £30; doubles £50-60. MC/V.)

LOCH KATRINE. The A821 winds through the heart of the Trossachs between Aberfoyle and Callander. Named the **Trossachs Trail,** this scenic drive passes near majestic Loch Katrine, the Trossachs' original attraction and the setting of Sir Walter Scott's "The Lady of the Lake." The popular **Steamship Sir Walter Scott** cruises from Trossachs Pier and tours the loch, stopping at Stronachlachar, on the northwestern bank. (☎376 316. Apr.-Oct. daily 11am, 1:45, 3:15pm; W no 11am sailing. £6-7.) At the pier, rent bikes from **Katrinewheelz.** (☎376 284. £12 per day.) For a good daytrip, take the ferry to Stronachlachar and then walk or ride back along the 22km wooded shore road to the pier. Above the loch hulks **Ben A'an** (460m), a reasonable 3km ascent that begins from a parking lot 1.5km along A821.

LOCH LOMOND ☎01389

Immortalized by the famous ballad, the pristine wilderness surrounding Loch Lomond continues to awe visitors. Britain's largest loch is dotted by some 38 islands, but given their proximity to Glasgow, parts of these bonnie banks can get crowded, especially during summer. Hikers adore the **West Highland Way,** which snakes along the entire eastern side of the loch and stretches north to Fort William. The *West Highland Way* official guide (£15) includes maps for each section of the route. At the southern tip of the lake is **Balloch,** the largest tourist center. Attractions and services at the **Loch Lomond Shores** visitor complex/shopping mall in Balloch include a big-screen film about the loch, a National Park Gateway Centre, a **tourist office,** and bike and canoe rentals. (☎722 406. Shores open daily June-Sept. 10am-6pm; Oct.-May 10am-5pm. £5, students £3.70.) Departing from Loch Lomond Shores and the Balloch tourist office on the River Leven, **Sweeney's Cruises** provide excellent 1hr. introductions to the area. (☎752 376; www.sweeney.uk.com. Every hr. 10:30am-5:30pm. £9.) The **SYHA Loch Lomond (HI) ❷,** 3km north of town, is a stunning 19th-century mansion. From the train station, follow the main road for 1km, turn right at the roundabout, continue 2.5km, and follow signs to the hostel. (☎0870 004 1136. Internet £3 per hr. Open Mar.-Oct. Dorms £13-14.50, under 18 £12.25. MC/V.) **Trains** (☎08457 484 950) leave Balloch Rd. for Glasgow (45min., 2 per hr., £3.40). Scottish Citylink (☎08705 505 050) **buses** also serve Glasgow (45min., 7 per day, £3.60). First (☎0141 423 6600) buses go to Stirling (1½hr., 4 per day, £3.80). The **tourist office,** Balloch Rd., is in the Old Station Building. (☎200 607. Open daily Apr.-Sept. 9:30am-6pm.)

INVERNESS AND LOCH NESS ☎01463

Inverness, the "hub of the Highlands," is a traveler's town, worth a stop before exploring the hills, lochs, and castles of the nearby Highland region. Every year, thousands of tourists descend upon **Loch Ness,** 8km south of Inverness, drawn by fantastic tales of its legendary inhabitant. In AD 565, St. Columba repelled a savage sea beast as it attacked a monk; the monster has captivated the world's imagination ever since. The loch is 700 ft. deep just 70 ft. from its shore; no one has determined how vast it really is, or what life exists at the bottom. The easiest way to see the loch is with a tour group, departing from the Inverness tourist office. **Jacobite Cruises,** Tomnahurich Bridge, Glenurquhart Rd., whisks you around on coach or boat trips. (☎233 999. £8-20, includes admission to Urquhart Castle. Student discounts available.) Five kilometers south on A82 sits **Urquhart Castle** (URK-hart), one of the largest in Scotland before it was blown up in 1692 to prevent Jacobite occupation. (☎450 551. Open June-Aug. daily 9:30am-6:30pm; Apr.-May and Sept. daily 9:30am-5:45pm; Oct.-Mar. M-Sa 9:30am-3:45pm. £6.) Highland Country bus #7 (30min., every hr., £5), leaving from the Inverness post office at 14-16 Queensgate, will take you to **Cawdor Castle,** complete with drawbridge, garden maze, and humorous placards describing the castle sights. Gorgeous hikes through the forest behind the gardens are an added bonus. (☎01667 4404 401; www.cawdorcastle.com. Open May-Oct. daily 10am-5pm. £6.80, students £5.80.)

A few blocks from Inverness Castle, **Bazpackers Backpackers Hotel ❶,** 4 Culduthel Rd., has a homey feel and great city views. (☎717 663. Reception 7:30am-midnight. Check-out 10:30am. Mid-June to Sept. dorms £12; doubles £14. Oct. to mid-June £10/12. MC/V.) Try the **Lemon Tree ❶,** 18 Inglis St., for all-day breakfast (£3.25), sweet orange lemonade (£1) and fabulous £2 soup. (☎241 114. Open M-Sa 8:30am-5:45pm.) Later, hit up **Hootananny,** 67 Church St., where you can stamp your feet to lively *ceilidh* bands on the first floor or groove to live bands upstairs. (Sa cover £3. Open M-Th noon-midnight, F noon-1am, Sa noon-12:30am. Upstairs Mad Hatter Club open W-Th 8pm-1am, F-Sa 8pm-3am. MC/V.) **Trains** (☎08457 484 950) run from Academy St. in Inverness's Station Sq., to: Edinburgh (3½hr., 8 per day, £34); Glasgow (3½hr., 8 per day, £34); Kyle of Lochalsh (2½hr., 4 per day, £15.20); London (8-11hr., 1 per day, £103.50). **Buses** go from Farraline Park, off Academy St., to: Edinburgh (4½hr., every hr., £16.70); Glasgow (4hr., every hr., £16.70); Kyle of Lochalsh (2hr., 2 per day, £12); London (13hr., 1 per day, £39). To reach the **tourist office,** Castle Wynd, from the stations, turn left on Academy St. and right on Union St. (☎234 353. Internet £3 per hr. Open mid-June to Aug. M-Sa 9am-6pm, Su 9:30am-4pm; Sept. to mid-June M-Sa 9am-5pm, Su 10am-4pm.)

FORT WILLIAM AND BEN NEVIS ☎01397

In 1654, General Monck founded the town of Fort William among Britain's highest peaks in order to keep out "savage clans and roving barbarians." His scheme backfired: today, thousands of Highlands-bound hikers invade Fort William, an ideal base for exploring some of Scotland's most impressive wilderness. Just outside of town, beautiful **Glen Nevis** runs southeast into Britain's tallest mountain. The breathtaking peak of **Ben Nevis** (1343m), the region's biggest draw, offers a challenging but manageable hike. One trail originates from the **Glen Nevis Visitor Centre,** where hikers stock up on maps and useful advice. (☎705 922. Open Apr.-Sept. daily 9am-5pm.) The ascent (13km; 6-8hr. round-trip) is difficult more for its length than for its terrain, but harsh conditions near the summit can be treacherous for the unprepared. Bring plenty of water and warm, waterproof clothes, and be sure to inform someone of your route. The **West Coast Railway's** Jacobite steam train rose to stardom as the Hogwarts Express in the *Harry Potter* films. The rail line, connecting Fort William and Mallaig, traverses some of Scotland's finest scenery. (☎0124 732 100; www.westcoastrailway.co.uk. 2hr.; June to mid-Oct. M-F departs Fort William 10:20am, departs Mallaig 2:10pm; £19.50, round-trip £26.)

Accommodations fill quickly in summer. From the train station, turn left onto Belford Rd. and right onto Alma Rd., then bear left at the fork and vault into a top bunk at **Fort William Backpackers ❶,** 6 Alma Rd., a welcoming hostel with beds named after famous Scottish characters. (☎700 711; www.scotlandstophostels.com. Breakfast £1.90. Laundry £2.50. Internet £0.80 per hr. Curfew 2am. Dorms £11-14. AmEx/MC/V.) Before heading for the hills, pick up a packed lunch (£3) or award-winning savories at the **Nevis Bakery ❶,** 49 High St., across from the tourist office. (☎704 101. Open M-Sa 8am-9pm, Su 9:30am-6pm.) **Trains** (☎08457 484 950) depart from the station beyond the north end of High St. for Glasgow Queen St. (3¾hr., 2-3 per day, £19.50). The Caledonian overnight sleeper train runs to London Euston (12hr., 1 per day, £99). **Buses** arrive next to Morrison's grocery store by the train station. Scottish Citylink (☎08705 505 050) runs to: Edinburgh (4hr., 3 per day, £21); Glasgow (3hr., 4 per day, £14); Inverness (2hr., 7-8 per day, £8.80); Kyle of Lochalsh (2hr., 3 per day, £13.30). The **tourist office,** Cameron Sq., in the center of High St., books accommodations for a £3 fee plus a 10% deposit. (☎703 781. Open July-Aug. M-Sa 9am-6pm, Su 10am-4pm; Sept.-June reduced hours.) Find free **Internet** at the **Fort William Library,** High St. (Open M and Th 10am-8pm, Tu and F 10am-6pm, W and Sa 10am-1pm.) **Postal Code:** PH33 6AR.

ISLE OF SKYE

From the serrated peaks of the Cuillin Hills to the commanding cliffs of the Trotternish Peninsula, the Isle of Skye possesses unmatched natural beauty. The island's charms well known; Skye has been fought over for centuries. Today, the tourists pour in each summer in an endless procession of vehicles crossing Skye Bridge to take part in the Isle's year-round celebration of Scottish heritage.

TRANSPORTATION. The **Skye Bridge** links the island to the mainland's Kyle of Lochalsh. **Pedestrians** can take either the bridge's 2.5km footpath or the **shuttle bus** (every hr., £0.70). **Trains** (☎08457 484 950) run to Kyle from Inverness (2½hr., 2-3 per day, £15.20). Scottish Citylink **buses** arrive daily from: Fort William (2hr., 3 per day, £13.30); Glasgow (6hr., 3 per day, £22); Inverness (2hr., 2 per day, £12). Buses on Skye are infrequent and expensive; grab the handy *Public Transport Guide to Skye* at any tourist office.

KYLE OF LOCHALSH AND KYLEAKIN. Kyle of Lochalsh ("Kyle" for short) and Kyleakin (Ky-LOCK-in) bookend the Skye Bridge. Kyle, on the mainland, wishes travelers would dally, but is most often used en route to Skye. Though Kyleakin is short on conveniences, it operates three hostels and countless tours, making it a boisterous backpacker's hub. **MacBackpackers Skye Trekker Tour,** departing from the hostel in Kyleakin, offers a one-day tour emphasizing the history and legends of the island and a two-day eco-conscious hike into the Cuillin Hills, with all necessary gear provided. (☎01599 534 510. Call ahead. Weekly departure Sa 7:30am. 1-day £18, 2-day £30.) Located between Kyle of Lochalsh and Inverness, **Eilean Donan Castle** is the restored 13th-century seat of the MacKenzie family, and the most photographed monument in Scotland. It offers one of the country's best castle tours. (☎01599 555 202; www.eileandonancastle.com. Open Apr.-Oct. daily 10am-5:30pm. £4.50, students £3.60.) The friendly owners of **Dun-Caan Hostel ❶**, in Kyleakin, have masterfully renovated a 200-year-old cottage. (☎01599 534 087; www.skyerover.co.uk. Bikes £10 per day. Dorms £11-12. MC/V. Book ahead.) The amiable staff of **Harry's ❶**, on the pier in Kyleakin, serves steaming pots of tea (£0.95) with tasty sandwiches and hot entrees (£4-7) to backpackers and seafarers alike. (☎01599 534 641. Open M-Tu and Th-Sa 9am-5:30pm, Su 10am-3pm. Cash only.)

SLIGACHAN. Renowned for their cloud and mist formations as well as their hiking trails, the **Cuillin Hills** (COO-leen), the highest peaks in the Hebrides, are visible from nearly every part of Skye. Legend says the warrior Cúchulainn was the lover of the Amazon ruler of Skye, who named the hills for him after he returned to Ireland to die. The Cuillins are great for experienced hikers, but can be risky for beginners. Tourist offices, campsites, and hostels are well stocked with maps and books for walks in the region. West of Kyleakin, the smooth, conical Red Cuillins and craggy Black Cuillin Hills meet in Sligachan (SLIG-a-chan), little more than a bunkhouse, hotel, pub, and campsite in a jaw-dropping setting. A convenient base for hiking, **Sligachan Bunkhouse ❶**, is a new mountain lodge with a classic look and feel. (☎650 204. Linen £2. Dorms £10. MC/V.) To get to **Glenbrittle Campsite ❶**, at the foot of the Black Cuillins, take bus #53 (M-Sa 2 per day) from Portree or Sligachan to Glenbrittle. (☎01478 640 404. Open Apr.-Oct. £4.50 per person. MC/V.)

PORTREE. The island's cheerful harbor capital is a festive hub for music, arts, crafts, and transportation. **Dunvegan Castle,** the seat of the MacLeod clan, holds the record for the longest-inhabited Scottish castle, with continual residence since the 13th century. Lose yourself in the expansive sculpted gardens surrounding the castle. Highland Country bus #56 (☎01478 612 622. M-Sa 3 per day) runs from Portree to the castle. (☎01478 521 206; www.dunvegancastle.com. Open daily mid-Mar. to Oct. 10am-5:30pm; Nov. to mid-Mar. 11am-4pm. £6.80, students £5.80.) The **Portree Independent Hostel ❶**, The Green, has a prime location and enthusiastic staff. (☎01478 613 737. Dorms £12-13. MC/V.) **Buses** to Portree from Kyle of Lochalsh and Kyleakin stop at Somerled Sq. (5-10 per day, £8). The **tourist office,** on Bayfield Rd., books accommodations and helps explain bus routes. (☎01478 612 137. Open July-Aug. M-Sa 9am-6pm, Su 10am-4pm; Sept.-June reduced hours.)

TROTTERNISH PENINSULA. The east side of Trotternish is a geological masterpiece of rock punctuated by thundering waterfalls, while the western side has a softer landscape of rolling hills. Northeast of Portree, the A855 snakes along the the east coast past the black stone **Old Man of Storr** and the **Quirang** rock pinnacles. Geologists may enjoy the science behind these formations, but others just stare dumbfoundedly at one of Mother Nature's most spectacular playgrounds. The Old Man of Storr is accessible by a steep **hike** (1hr. round-trip). Take Highland Country bus #57 on the Portree-Staffin route (M-Sa 4-6 per day, June-Sept. also Su 3 per day; Day Rover pass £5) and ask the driver to let you off at the parking lot.

ISLE OF LEWIS (LEODHAS) ☎01851

Fantastic hiking, biking, surfing, and archaeological sites attract adventurers and historians alike to Lewis, the most populous of the Outer Hebridean Islands. The small city of **Stornoway** is a splash of urban life in the untouched moorland and half-cut fields of peat. Second only to Stonehenge in grandeur, the **Callanish Stones,** 22km west of Stornoway on the A858, are considerably less overrun with tourists. (Always open. Free.) Most of Lewis's biggest attractions, including the Callanish Stones and other archaeological sites, line the west coast and can be reached via the W2 bus, which operates on a circuit beginning at the Stornoway bus station (M-Sa 4-6 per day in either direction). Galson Motors offers a day pass on this route (£6), or a round-trip ticket to see one, two, or three of the sights (May-Oct.; £4-5). Alternatively, travel with **Out and About Tours** (☎612 288; personalized group tours from £67 for a half day, £102 for a full day) or **Albannach Guided Tours** (☎830 433; from £10 per hr. per person), both departing from the tourist office. Lewis is also home to "the most consistent surf in Europe." Warm currents and long daylight hours draw **surfers** to spots like the popular **Dalmor Beach,** near the village of Dalbeg, which has hosted several competitions (take the W2 bus from Stornoway).

Mr. and Mrs. Hill ❷, Robertson Rd., is a better pick than the abysmal hostels in town. Head north up Church St. from the tourist office, turn left on Matheson Rd., and right onto Robertson. (☎705 553. £25 per person. Cash only.) Buy groceries at the **Co-op** on Cromwell St. (☎702 703. Open M-Sa 8am-8pm.) Stornoway's only affordable sit-down restaurant is **Thai Cafe ❷,** 27 Church St. (☎701 811. Entrees £4-6. Open M-Sa noon-2:30pm and 5-11pm. Cash only.) CalMac **ferries** sail to Stornoway from Ullapool (2¾hr.; 2-3 per day; £14.40, round-trip £24.65, with car £70/120). Western Isles **buses** depart from Stornoway's Beach St. station; pick up a free *Lewis and Harris Bus Timetable* for destinations. Be aware that the only things running on Sundays are planes and churchgoers late for services. The **tourist office** is at 26 Cromwell St. From the ferry, turn left onto South Beach, then right on Cromwell St. (☎703 088. Open Apr.-Oct. daily 9am-6pm and 8-9pm; Nov.-Mar. M-F 9am-5pm.) Rent bikes at **Alex Dan's Cycle Centre,** 67 Kenneth St. (☎704 025. £10 per day, £30 per week. Open M-Sa 9am-6pm.) **Internet** is free at **Stornoway Library.** (☎708 631. Open M-W and Sa 10am-5pm, Th-F 10am-6pm.) **Postal Code:** HS1 2AA.

BULGARIA (БЪЛГАРИЯ)

Bulgaria's history is not as serene as its landscape. Once the most powerful state in the Balkans, Bulgaria fell to the Turks in the late 14th century. In their 500 years of rule, the conquerors obliterated Bulgaria's nobility and enserfed its peasants. Underground monasteries, however, preserved Bulgarian culture, enabling the construction of much of the majestic architecture that now graces Bulgarian cities during the National Revival of the 1870s. Today, still reeling from the recent Balkan wars, the country struggles to increase its economic output and join the EU. Even as this transition continues, many travelers will be rewarded by journeys to cosmopolitan Sofia, the lush countryside, or the beautiful Black Sea Coast.

DISCOVER BULGARIA: SUGGESTED ITINERARIES

THREE DAYS Two days is probably enough to take in **Sofia's** (p. 208) museums, cathedrals, and cafes. Going to the **Rila Monastery** (1 day; p. 211) is easier said than done, but its gorgeous atmosphere and environs are worth it.

ONE WEEK If two days exploring the stunning ruins of **Veliko Târnovo** (p. 213) isn't enough, bus down to **Plovdiv** (p. 212) for even more Roman remains before heading to the **Rila Monastery** and then ending up in bustling **Sofia.**

ESSENTIALS

FACTS AND FIGURES

Official Name: Republic of Bulgaria.
Capital: Sofia.
Major Cities: Burgas, Plovdiv, Varna.
Population: 7,451,000.
Land Area: 110,550 sq. km.
Time Zone: GMT +2.
Language: Bulgarian.
Religions: Bulgarian Orthodox (83%).

WHEN TO GO

Bulgaria's temperate climate makes it easy to catch good weather. Spring (Apr.-May) is nice, and offers a bevy of festivals and cultural events. Summer (June-Sept.) isn't too hot, making it perfect for hiking and beachgoing. Beware of the crowds that gravitate toward the coast and fill up campgrounds. Skiing season runs from December until April.

DOCUMENTS AND FORMALITIES

EMBASSIES AND CONSULATES. Foreign embassies for Bulgaria are in Sofia (p. 208). For Bulgarian embassies abroad, contact: **Australia,** 14 Carlotta Rd., Double Bay, NSW 2028 (☎2 327 7592); **Canada,** 325 Stewart St., Ottawa, ON N1K 6K5 (☎613-789-3215); **Ireland,** 22 Bulington Rd., Dublin 4 (☎1 660 3293; bgemb@eircom.net); **UK,** Bulgarian Embassy, 186-188 Queensgate, London SW7 5HL (☎20 7584 9400; http://bulgaria.embassyhomepage.com); **US,** 1621 22nd St. NW, Washington, D.C. 20008 (☎202-387-0174; www.bulgaria-embassy.org).

VISA AND ENTRY INFORMATION. Citizens of Australia, Canada, Ireland, New Zealand, the UK, and the US do not need a visa for stays of up to 30 days. Citizens of other EU countries and those planning to stay more than 30 days must obtain a 90-day visa from their local embassy or consulate. Due to a reciprocal

agreement, US citizens may obtain a visa for US$60. For non-US citizens, single-entry visas are approximately US$50 for 10 business days processing; US$65 for priority processing; US$120 for multiple-entry visas. Single (US$40) and double transit visas (US$60) are valid for 24hr. Prices include a border tax of approximately US$20; those not needing visas are also required to pay the tax upon entering the country. The application requires a passport valid for more than six months after return from Bulgaria, a passport photograph, an invitation, a copy of your green card (if applicable), proof of medical insurance, payment by cash or money order, and a self-addressed, stamped envelope. There is no express service for multiple-entry visas. The easiest way to extend your visa is to temporarily leave and return.

If staying in a private residence, register your visa with police within 48hr. of entering Bulgaria; hotels and hostels will do this for you. Keep the registration with your passport, and make sure you are re-registered every time you change accommodations. A Bulgarian **border crossing** can take several hours, as there are three different checkpoints: passport control, customs, and police. Visas are very difficult to purchase at the border. Crossing the border on bus or train is often an arduous process. The border crossing into Turkey is particularly difficult. Try to enter from Romania at Ruse or Durankulak.

ENTRANCE REQUIREMENTS

Passport: Required for all travelers; must be valid for 6 months beyond stay.

Visa: Not required for citizens of Australia, Canada, New Zealand, Ireland, the UK, and US for up to 30 days.

Letter of Invitation: Not required for those who do not need a visa.

Inoculations: Not required. Recommended up-to-date on DTaP (diphtheria, tetanus, and pertussis), Hepatitis A, Hepatitis B, MMR (measles, mumps, and rubella), Polio booster, and Typhoid.

Work Permit: Required for all foreigners planning to work in Bulgaria.

International Driving Permit: Required for all those planning to drive.

TOURIST SERVICES AND MONEY

TOURIST OFFICES. Tourist offices and local travel agencies are generally knowledgeable and good at reserving private rooms; some mostly plan itineraries. Staffs are helpful and sometimes speak English, German, and/or Russian. Big hotels often have an English-speaking receptionist and maps and make good resources.

MONEY. The **lev** (lv; plural leva) is the standard monetary unit (1 lev=100 stotinki), though sometimes US dollars or euro are accepted. **Inflation** is around 6%, so expect prices to fluctuate over the next year. Private banks and exchange bureaus exchange money, but bank rates are more reliable. The four largest **banks** are Bulbank, Biochim, Hebros, and DSK. **Traveler's checks** can only be cashed at banks (with the exception of a few exchange bureaus). Many banks also give Visa **cash advances. Credit cards** are rarely accepted. **ATMs** give the best exchange rates and are common throughout Bulgaria; they usually accept MasterCard, Visa, Plus, and Cirrus. It is illegal and unwise to exchange currency on the street. Beware of officially sanctioned tourist overcharging; museums and theaters will charge foreigners double or more, a practice that many locals frown upon. **Businesses** usually open at 8 or 9am and take a 1hr. lunch break sometime between 11am and 2pm. Banks are usually open 8:30am to 4pm, but some close at 2pm. Tourist offices, post offices, and shops stay open until 6 or 8pm; in tourist areas and big cities, shops may close as late as 10pm.

LEVA (LV)		
	AUS$1 = 1.20LV	1LV = AUS$0.83
	CDN$1 = 1.32LV	1LV = CDN$0.76
	EUR€1 = 1.96LV	1LV = EUR€0.51
	NZ$1 = 1.12LV	1LV = NZ$0.90
	UK£1 = 2.88LV	1LV = UK£0.35
	US$1 = 1.61LV	1LV = US$0.62

HEALTH AND SAFETY

While basic medical supplies are available in Bulgarian hospitals, specialized treatment is not. Emergency care is better in Sofia than in the rest of the country, but it's best to avoid hospitals entirely. Travelers are required to carry proof of insurance; most doctors expect cash payment. In the case of extreme emergency, air evacuation runs about US$50,000.

The sign "Apteka" denotes a **pharmacy.** There is always a night-duty pharmacy in larger towns. *Analgin* is headache medicine; *analgin chinin* is for colds and flu; *sitoplast* are bandages. Foreign brands of condoms *(prezervatifs)* are more reliable. Prescription drugs are difficult to obtain—bring enough of your own. Public **bathrooms** ("Ж" for women, "M" for" men) are often holes in the ground; pack toilet paper and hand sanitizer and expect to pay 0.05-0.20lv. **Tampons** are widely available. Don't buy bottles of **alcohol** from street vendors, and be careful with homemade liquor—there have been cases of poisoning and contamination. Asthmatics, beware: most of Bulgaria's restaurants, taverns, and public transportation are heavily smoke-filled; buses are an exception.

Be aware of petty **street crime,** especially pickpocketing and purse snatching. Also be wary of people posing as government officials; always ask for ID. Beverages from strangers may prove to be Trojan horses to your wallet. Be sure to take only marked taxis and ensure that the meter is on for the entire ride. Nightclubs in large cities are often associated with organized crime; beware of fights.

It's generally fine for **women** to travel alone, but it's always safer to have at least one travel companion. Wear skirts and blouses to avoid unwanted attention; only young girls wear sneakers, tank tops, or shorts outside of big cities. Although access is slowly improving, visitors with physical **disabilities** will confront many challenges in Bulgaria. **Discrimination** is focused on Roma (gypsies), who are considered a nuisance at best and thieves at worst. Dark-skinned minorities are occasionally confused for Roma and discriminated against accordingly. While hate crimes are rare, persons of a foreign ethnicity may receive stares. Though the Bulgarian government has recently officially recognized **homosexuality,** acceptance is slow in coming; it is prudent to avoid public displays of affection. For more information about GLBT clubs and resources in areas you plan to visit, check out www.queer-bulgaria.org or www.bulgayria.com.

EMERGENCY **Police:** ☎166. **Ambulance:** ☎150. **Fire:** ☎160.

TRANSPORTATION

BY PLANE. All flights to Sofia (SOF) connect through London, England or Western Europe. Though tickets to the capital may run over US$2500 during the summer months, budget airline **WizzAir** offers cheap flights from London, Paris, and Frankfurt, through Budapest. Budget travelers might also consider flying into a nearby capital—Athens, Istanbul, or Bucharest—and taking a bus to Sofia. Bulgarian airports are on par with international standards.

BY TRAIN. Bulgarian trains run to Greece, Hungary, Romania, and Turkey and are the best form of transportation in the north. The train system is comprehensive but slow, crowded, and smoke-filled. Purse-slashing, pickpocketing, and theft has been reported on more crowded lines. Buy tickets at the Ticket Center *(Bileti Tsentur)* in stations. There are three types of trains: express *(ekspres)*, fast *(burz)*, and slow *(putnicheski)*. Avoid *putnicheski* at all costs—they stop at anything that looks inhabited, even if only by goats. Arrive well in advance if you want a seat. Stations are poorly marked and often only in Cyrillic; know when you're reaching your destination, bring a map, and ask for help. First class *(purva klasa)* is identical to second *(vtora klasa)*, and therefore not worth the extra money. Store luggage at the *garderob*.

BY BUS. Buses are better for travel in eastern and western Bulgaria and are often faster than trains, but less frequent and comfortable. Buses head north from Ruse, to İstanbul from anywhere on the Black Sea Coast, and to Greece from Blagoevgrad. For long distances, **Group Travel** and **Etap** have modern buses with A/C and bathrooms for 50% more than trains. Some buses have set departure times; others leave when full.

BY BOAT. Ferries from Varna and Burgas make infrequent trips to İstanbul, Turkey and Odessa, Ukraine.

BY TAXI AND BY CAR. Yellow taxis are everywhere in cities. Refuse to pay in dollars and insist on a ride *sus apparata* (with meter); ask the distance and price per kilometer. Don't try to bargain. Some taxi drivers rig the meters to charge more. Tipping taxi drivers usually means rounding up to the nearest lev or half-lev. Some Black Sea towns can only be reached by car. Renting is cheapest from a local agent, which will charge less than the €15-30 that larger companies do. While urban roads are generally in fair condition, rural roads are often in poor repair; rocks and landslides pose a threat in mountainous areas. Seat belts are mandatory in Bulgaria.

BY BIKE AND BY THUMB. Motoroads (www.motoroads.com) and travel agencies offer bike tours; when biking in urban areas, stay alert as Bulgarian drivers disregard traffic signals. Hitchhiking is rare because drivers rarely stop. While those who hitchhike say it is generally safe, *Let's Go* does not recommend it.

KEEPING IN TOUCH

PHONE CODES	**Country code:** 359. **International dialing prefix:** 00. For more information on how to place international calls, see inside back cover.

EMAIL AND THE INTERNET. Internet cafes can be found throughout urban centers, cost approximately 0.60-1lv per hr., and are often open 24hr.

TELEPHONE. Making **international phone calls** from Bulgaria can be a challenge. Pay phones are ludicrously expensive; opt for phone offices instead. If you must make an international call from a pay phone with a card, purchase the 400 unit, 22lv card. Units run out quickly on international calls, so talk fast or have multiple cards ready. There are two brands: **BulFon** (orange) and **Mobika** (blue), which work only at telephones of the same brand; BulFon is more prevalent. One minute costs 0.40lv to Australia and New Zealand, 0.20lv to Europe and the US. To **call collect,** dial ☎01 23 for an international operator. The Bulgarian phrase for collect call is "*za tyahna smetka.*" For **local calls,** pay phones seldom accept coins, so it's best to buy a phonecard (see above). You can also call from the post office, where a clerk assigns you a booth, a meter records your bill, and you pay when finished. International access codes include: **AT&T Direct** (☎00 800 0010); **BT Payphones** (☎00 800 9944); and **MCI** (☎00 800 0001).

MAIL. "Въздушна поща" on letters indicates **airmail.** Though far more reliable than ground transport mail, it is sometimes difficult to convince postal workers to let you pay extra to have your mail sent airmail. Sending a letter abroad costs 0.60lv to Europe, 0.90lv to the US, and 0.80-1lv to Australia and New Zealand; a Bulgarian return address is required. Packages must be unwrapped for inspection. Register important packages, and allow two weeks for it to arrive. Mail can be received general delivery through **Poste Restante,** though the service is unreliable. Address envelope as follows: First name, LAST NAME, POSTE RESTANTE, писма до поискване централна поща, (post office address, optional), City, Postal Code, България (Bulgaria).

LANGUAGE. Bulgarian is a South Slavic language written in the Cyrillic alphabet. A few words are borrowed from Turkish and Greek, but most vocabulary is similar to Russian and its relatives. **English** is spoken by urban youths and in tourist areas. **German** and **Russian** are often understood. Street names are in the process of changing; you may need both old and new names. The Bulgarian alphabet is much the same as Russian (see **Cyrillic Alphabet,** p. 1056) except that "щ" is pronounced "sht" and "ъ" is "ŭ" (like the "u" in bug).

YES AND NO. Bulgarians shake their heads from side to side to indicate "yes" and up and down to indicate "no," the opposite of Brits and Yanks. For the uncoordinated, it's easier to just hold your head still and say *"da"* or *"neh."*

ACCOMMODATIONS AND CAMPING

BULGARIA	❶	❷	❸	❹	❺
ACCOMMODATIONS	under 20lv	20-35lv	35-50lv	50-70lv	over 70lv

Bulgarian **hotels** are classed on a star system and licensed by the Government Committee on Tourism; rooms in one-star hotels are nearly identical to rooms in two- and three-star hotels, but have no private bathrooms. All accommodations provide linen and towels. Expect to pay US$25-35. Beware that foreigners are often charged double or more what locals pay. **Hostels** can be found in most major cities and run from US$10-18 per bed. Almost all include free breakfast and many offer Internet and laundry services. For a complete list of hostels in Bulgaria, see www.hostels.com/en/bg.html. **Private rooms** are cheap (US$6-12) and usually have all the amenities of a good hotel; with the right language skills and persistence, they can be found in any small town.

Outside major towns, most **campgrounds** provide spartan bungalows and tent space. Call ahead in the summer to reserve bungalows. Some are poorly maintained or unpredictable, so check before it is too late to stay elsewhere.

FOOD AND DRINK

BULGARIA	❶	❷	❸	❹	❺
FOOD	under 4lv	4-9lv	9-14lv	14-20lv	over 20lv

Food from **kiosks** is cheap (0.60-2.50lv); **restaurants** average 6lv per meal. Kiosks sell *kebabcheta* (sausage burgers), sandwiches, pizzas, and *banitsa sus sirene* (feta-cheese-filled pastries). Try *shopska salata*, a mix of tomatoes, peppers, and cucumbers with feta cheese. *Tarator*, a cold soup made with yogurt, cucumber, garlic, and sometimes walnuts, is also tasty. Bulgaria enjoys meat. *Kavarma*, meat with onions, spices, and egg is slightly more expensive than *skara* (grills). **Vegetarians** should request *iastia bez meso* (iahs-tea-ah bez meh-so). **Kosher** diners would also be wise to order vegetarian meals, as pork often sneaks into Bulgarian main dishes. Bulgarians are known for cheese and yogurt—the bacteria that makes yogurt from milk has the scientific name *bacilicus bulgaricus*. *Ayran* (yogurt with water and ice) and *boza* (similar to beer, but sweet and thicker) are popular drinks that complement breakfast. Breads and meats are often plain-tasting; soups and earthenware-pot dishes offer more flavor. Bulgaria exports mineral water and locals swear by its healing qualities. **Tap water** is generally safe to drink, though home-brewed beers and other alcohols produced on hand should be approached with caution. Melnik produces famous red **wine,** while the northeast is known for its excellent white wines. On the Black Sea Coast, *Albenu* is a good sparkling wine. Bulgarians begin meals with *rakiya* (grape or plum brandy). Good Bulgarian **beers** include *Kamenitza* and *Zagorka*.

HOLIDAYS AND FESTIVALS

Holidays: Baba Marta (Spring Festival; Mar. 1); Liberation Day (1878; Mar. 3); Orthodox Easter (Apr. 23); Labor Day (May 1); St. George's Day (May 6); Education and Culture Day/Day of Slavic Heritage (St. Cyril and Methodius Day; May 24); Kazaluk (Festival of the Roses; June 5); Day of Union (Sept. 6); Independence Day (Sept. 22).

Festivals: Christmas and New Year's are holidays characterized by the two related Bulgarian customs of *koledouvane* and *sourvakari*. On Christmas, groups of people go from house to house and perform *koledouvane*, or caroling, while holding beautiful oak sticks called *koledarkas*. On New Year's, a group of *sourvakari* wish their neighbors well while holding decorated cornel rods called *sourvachka*. Baba Marta (Spring Festival) celebrates the beginning of spring. Bulgarians traditionally give each other *martenitzas*, small red-and-white tassels formed to look like a boy and a girl. These fertility charms are meant to be worn around the neck or pinned on until a stork is seen. The Festival of Roses is celebrated in Kazanlŭk and Karlovo on the 1st Sunday in June.

BEYOND TOURISM

American University in Bulgaria, Blagoevgrad 2700, Bulgaria (☎359 73 888 218; www.aubg.bg). University in Bulgaria based on the American liberal arts model. Accepts international students.

MAR-Bulgarian Youth Alliance for Development, P.O. Box 201, 1000 Sofia, Bulgaria (☎359 29 80 20 37; www.mar.bg). Places volunteers in Bulgarian work camps for 2-3 weeks. Aid Roma population or foster environmental awareness.

SOFIA (СОФИЯ) ☎02

A history of assimilation has left Bulgaria unsure of its identity. In Sofia (pop. 1,100,000), spray-painted skateboarding ramps front the Soviet Army monument, while old women tote home their bread in *Harry Potter* shopping bags. Though McDonald's arches keep surfacing, the dome of St. Alexander Nevsky Cathedral remains Sofia's most visible golden landmark, and opportunities still abound to indulge in traditional cuisine, listen to folk music, and buy handmade crafts.

TRANSPORTATION

Flights: Airport Sofia (☎937 22 11). Bus #84 (tickets 0.50lv) runs to Eagle Bridge (Орлов Мост), a 10min. walk from the city center. If you take a taxi downtown, use **OK Supertrans;** your ride should cost no more than 5lv.

Trains: Tsentralna Gara (Централна Гара; Central Train Station. www.centralnaavtogara.bg), bul. Knyaginya Mariya Luiza (Мария Луиза), 1.6km north of pl. Sv. Nedelya. Information booth and ticket counter are on 1st fl. To **Burgas** (7 per day, 13.30lv) and **Plovdiv** (7 per day, 6lv). Left of the main entrance, **Rila Travel Bureau** (Рила; ☎932 33 46) sells tickets to **Thessaloniki, Greece** (3 per day, 30lv) and **Budapest, Hungary** via **Bucharest, Romania** (1 per day, 120lv). Open daily 7am-11pm.

Buses: Private buses, which leave from the parking lot across from the train station, are a bit pricier than trains but faster and more comfortable. **Group Travel** sends buses to: **Burgas** (18 per day, 18lv); **Varna** (9 per day, 22lv); **Veliko Tŭrnovo** (9 per day, 12lv). Ticket office open daily 7am-7pm.

Local Transportation: Trams, trolleybuses, and buses cost 0.50lv per ride, 2lv for 5 rides, 1-day pass 2.20lv, 5-day pass 10lv. Buy tickets at kiosks with Билети (*bileti;* tickets) signs or buy from the driver. Validate them onboard to avoid a 5lv fine. If you put your backpack on a seat, you may be fined 5lv for an "unticketed passenger." Officially, public transportation runs 5:30am-11pm, but rides are scarce after 9pm.

Taxis: While some travelers have terrible taxi tales, **OK Supertrans** (☎973 21 21) is reliable. Always make sure that the company's name and phone number are listed on the side of the car and insist that the driver turn on the meter. Drivers frequently don't speak English, so bring Bulgarian directions. Fares are 0.40-0.45lv per km, slightly more 10pm-6am.

ORIENTATION AND PRACTICAL INFORMATION

The city center, **ploshtad Sveta Nedelya** (Света Неделя), is a triangle formed by the Tsurkva (church) Sv. Nedelya, the wide Sheraton Hotel, and the department store Tsentralen Universalen Magazin. **Bulevard Knyaginya Mariya Luiza** (Княгиня Мария Луиза) connects pl. Sv. Nedelya to the train station. Bul. Vitosha, one of the main shopping and nightlife thoroughfares, links pl. Sveta Nedelya to **ploshtad Bŭlgaria** and the huge, concrete **Natsionalen Dvorets na Kulturata** (Национален Дворец Култура; NDK, National Palace of Culture). On your right as you go down bul.

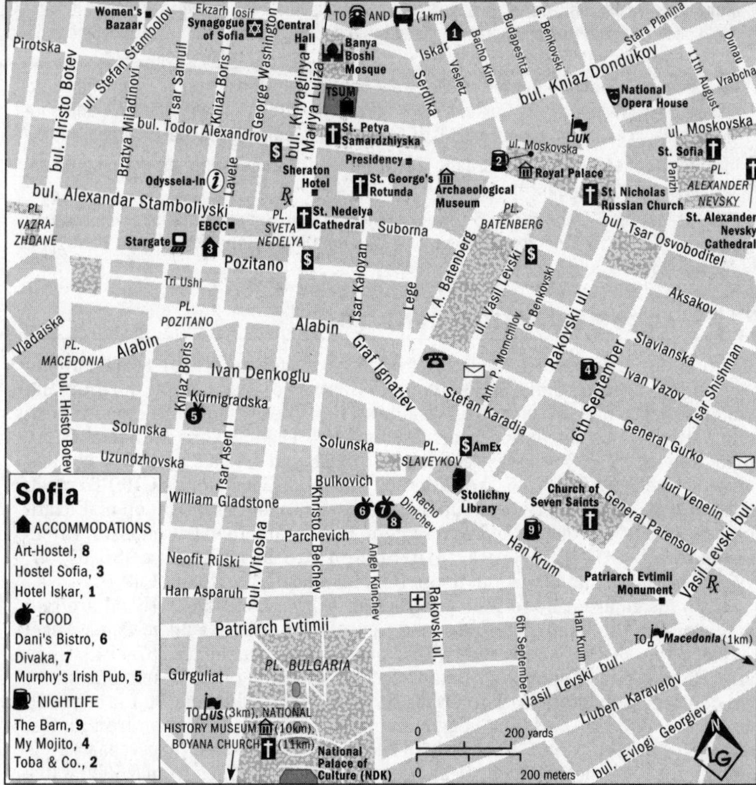

Mariya Luiza, historic **bulevard Tsar Osvoboditel** (Цар Освободител; Tsar the Liberator) leads to **Sofia University.** The *Inside & Out Guide* (free at the Sheraton Hotel and at tourist centers) has tourist info in English.

Tourist Office: **Odysseia-In/Zig Zag Holidays,** bul. Stamboliskii 20-B (Стамболийски; ☎980 51 02; www.zigzagbg.com). From pl. Sv. Nedelya, head down Stamboliskii and take the 2nd right on Lavele; Odysseia is halfway down on the left. Consultation 5lv. Open high season daily 8:30am-7:30pm; low season closed Sa-Su. MC/V.

Embassies: Australia (consulate), ul. Trakiya 37 (☎946 13 34). **Canada,** Moskovska 9 (Московска; ☎946 13 34). **Ireland, New Zealand,** and the **UK,** ul. Moskovska 9 (☎933 92 90). Open M-Th 9am-noon and 2-4pm, F 9am-noon. **US,** ul. Kozyak 16 (☎937 5100; fax 937 5122). Consulate open M-F 9am-noon, 2-4pm.

Currency Exchange: Bulbank (Булбанк), pl. Sv. Nedelya 7 (☎923 21 11), cashes **traveler's checks** and exchanges currency. Open M-F 8am-6pm.

Luggage Storage: Downstairs at the central train station. 0.80lv per piece. Claim bags 30min. before departure. Open daily 6am-midnight.

Emergency: Ambulance: ☎150. **Fire:** ☎160. **Police:** ☎166.

24hr. Pharmacies: Apteka Sv. Nedelya, pl. Sv. Nedelya 5 (☎950 50 26). **Apteka Vassil Levski,** bul. Vassil Levski 70 (☎986 17 55).

Medical Services: State-owned hospitals offer foreigners free 24hr. emergency aid; staff might not speak English. **Pirogov Emergency Hospital,** bul. Gen. Totleben 21 (Ген. Тотлебен; ☎51 531), opposite Hotel Rodina. Take trolley #5 or 19 from the city center. Open 24hr.

Telephones: Telephone Center, ul. General Gurko 4. From the post office, turn right onto Vassil Levski then left onto Gurko; it's a white building 1 block down. Offers fax and photocopy services. International calls 0.36lv per min. Internet 0.80lv per hr. Open 24hr.

Internet Access: Stargate, Pozitano 20 (Позитано), 30m on the left if facing Hostel Sofia. 1lv per hr. Open 24hr.

Post Office: ul. General Gurko 6 (Гурко; ☎949 64 46). Send international mail at windows #6-8; *Poste Restante* at window #12. Open M-Sa 7am-8:30pm, Su 8am-1pm. **Postal Code:** 1000.

ACCOMMODATIONS AND FOOD

Big hotels are rarely worth the exorbitant price; hostels or private rooms are the best option. **Hostel Sofia ❶,** Pozitano 16 (Позитано), has a great location and homey feel. From pl. Sv. Nedelya, walk down bul. Vitosha, and turn right on Pozitano. (☎989 85 82. Reception 24hr. Dorms €10.) The spacious **Art-Hostel ❶,** ul. Angel Kunchev 21A (Ангел Кънчев), is part hostel, part art gallery, with a bar and outdoor garden. (☎987 05 45. Free Internet. Reception 24hr. Dorms €10.) To reach **Hotel Iskar ❷,** ul. Iskar 11B, walk up bul. Mariya Luiza and turn right on ul. Ekzarh Iosif, then walk two blocks and turn right on Bacho Kiro, then left on Iskar. Offers well-appointed rooms in a refurbished old building. (☎986 67 50; www.hoteliskar.com. Check-out noon. Doubles €25-37; apartment €49.)

Cheap meals are easy to find. Across bul. Mariya Luiza from TSUM are two large **markets,** the Women's Bazaar and Central Hall. **Dani's Bistro ❸,** ul. Angel Kunchev 18A, is a streetside cafe with a simple, savory menu. (☎987 45 48. Open daily 10am-10pm.) Facing McDonald's in pl. Slaveikov, take the left side-street and continue right at the fork to **Divaka ❷,** ul. William Gladstone 54, for huge salads (1.70-3.50lv) and sizzling veggie and meat sacheta (6.50lv) on iron plates. (☎989 95 43. Open 24hr.) **Murphy's Irish Pub ❷,** Karnigradska 6 (Кърниградска), is a haven for homesick English-speakers. (☎980 28 70. Entrees from 6.50lv. F live music. Open daily noon-12:30am.)

SIGHTS

PLOSHTAD ALEXANDER NEVSKY. With the tsar-liberator for its patron saint, the golden-domed **St. Alexander Nevsky Cathedral** (Св. Александр Невски; Sv. Aleksandr Nevsky) was erected as a memorial to the 200,000 Russians who died in the 1877-1878 Russo-Turkish War. Through a separate entrance left of the main church, the **crypt** contains an array of painted icons and religious artifacts from the past 1500 years. *(Cathedral open daily 7am-7pm. Crypt open Tu-Su 10am-5:30pm. Cathedral free. Crypt 4lv, students 2lv. Guided tours of the crypt 25lv for 5 or more, 20lv for fewer than 5.)*

AROUND PLOSHTAD SVETA NEDELYA. The focal point of pl. Sveta Nedelya, the domed **Cathedral of St. Nedelya** (Катедрален Храм Св. Неделя; Katedralen Hram Sv. Nedelya), is a reconstruction of a 14th-century original destroyed in an attempted assassination of Tsar Boris III in 1925. The liturgy shows off the church's great acoustics. *(Open daily 7am-6:30pm. Liturgy daily 9am, Sa also 6pm.)* In the courtyard behind the Sheraton Hotel stands the 4th-century **St. George's Rotunda** (Св. Георги; Sv. Georgi), adorned with beautiful 11th- to 14th-century murals. *(Open daily 8am-6pm. Services daily 9am.)* Walk up bul. Mariya Luiza and take a left on Ekzarh Iosif to reach the recently renovated **Synagogue of Sofia** (Софийски

Синагога; Sofiiska Sinagoga), the city's only synagogue. A museum upstairs outlines the history of Jews in Bulgaria. *(Open daily 8am-4pm. Services daily 8am, Sa also 10am. Synagogue free. Museum 2lv, students 1lv.)*

ALONG BULEVARD TSAR OSVOBODITEL. Sofia's first paved street, bul. Tsar Osvoboditel stretches between the **House of Parliament** and the **Royal Palace.** Midway sits the **St. Nicholas Russian Church** (Св. Николай; Sv. Nikolai), built in 1913. Icons from the Novgorod school decorate the interior, while Russian Orthodox onion domes preside over the exterior. *(Open daily 8am-6:30pm. Liturgy W-Su 9am, W 5pm, Sa 5:30pm.)*

MUSEUMS. The Royal Palace houses the **National Museum of Ethnography** (Национален Етнографски Музей; Natsionalen Etnografski Muzey), devoted to four centuries of Bulgarian folk history. *(Open Tu-Su 10am-6pm. 3lv, students 2.50lv. Guided tours 10lv.)* In the same building, the **National Art Gallery** (Национална Художествена Галерия; Natsionalna Hudozhestvena Galeriya) displays Bulgaria's most prized traditional and contemporary art. *(Open Tu-W and F-Su 10:30am-6:30pm, Th 10am-9pm. 4lv, students 2lv. Tu free. English-language tours 20lv.)* To reach the **National History Museum,** Residence Boyana, Palace 1 (Национален Исторически Музей; Natsionalen Istoricheski Muzey), take bus #63 or 111, minibus #21, or trolley #2 to Boyana. The museum showcases archaeological finds and cultural artifacts from prehistory to the present. *(☎955 42 80. Open daily 9:30am-5:30pm. 10lv, students 5lv. Guided tour 10lv.)*

ENTERTAINMENT AND NIGHTLIFE

Half a dozen theaters lie on **Rakovski,** Bulgaria's main theater artery. From town center, a left on Rakovski leads to the columns of the National Opera House, Rakovski 59. (☎987 13 66. Performances Tu-Sa 6pm. Box office open M-Tu 9:30am-2pm and 2:30-6:30pm, W-F 8:30am-7:30pm, Sa 10:30am-6:30pm, Su 10am-6pm. Tickets 5-20lv.)

At night, smartly dressed Sofians roam the main streets, filling the outdoor bars along **bulevard Vitosha** and the cafes around the **National Palace of Culture.** For the younger set, nightlife centers around Sofia University at the intersection of Vassil Levski and Tsar Osvoboditel. At **My Mojito,** Ivan Vazov 12, students party to deafeningly loud music until morning hours. (☎088 770 94 32 Cover F-Sa 5lv for men, women free. Open daily 9:30pm-late.) Party like a tsar at **Toba & Co,** ul. Moskovska 6, behind the Royal Palace, in the courtyard and back room of the former Bulgarian monarch's residence. (☎989 46 96. Open daily 10pm-late.) Hidden away at Sixth September 22, **The Barn** is a former communist newspaper turned tavern. (Open daily 8pm-late.)

DAYTRIPS FROM SOFIA

RILA MONASTERY. Holy Ivan of Rila built the 10th-century Rila Monastery (Рилски Манастир; Rilski Manastir), the largest and most famous in Bulgaria, as a refuge from worldly temptation. The monastery sheltered the arts of icon painting and manuscript copying during the Byzantine and Ottoman occupations, and remained a bastion of Bulgarian culture during five centuries of foreign rule. Today's monastery, decorated with 1200 brilliantly colored **frescoes,** was built between 1834 and 1837, after raids and the destruction of the earlier structure, little of which now remains. The **museum** in the far right corner of the monastery displays an unbelievably detailed **wooden cross** that took 12 years to carve (with a needle) and left its creator, the monk Rafail, blind. (Open daily 8:30am-4:30pm. 5lv, students 3lv.) Signs inside and outside the monastery post maps and suggested hiking routes through nearby **Rila National Park,** or look in the **Manastirski Padarŭtsi** (Манастирски Падаръци) shop, just outside the monastery's back entry, for a Cyrillic map of the paths (6lv).

Inquire at room #170 in the monastery about staying in a spartan but heated **monastic cell ❷.** (☎70 54 22 08. Doors lock at 9pm, ring the bell after that. 25lv.) Behind the monastery is a cluster of restaurants, cafes, and a mini-market. To get to the monastery, take **tram** #5 from Pl. Sveta Nedelya to Ovcha Kŭpel Station (Овча Къпел) and take the **bus** to Rila Town (2hr., 10:20am, 5lv). From Rila Town, catch the bus to the monastery (30min., 3 per day, 1.50lv). The last bus back to Sofia leaves in mid-afternoon; confirm the exact time.

KOPRIVSHTITSA. Todor Kableshkov's 1876 "letter of blood," urging rebellion against Ottoman rule, incited the War of Liberation in this little village in the Sredna Gora mountains. Today, Koprivshtitsa (Копривщица; pop. 2600) is a charming historical village of stone cottages and winding streets, where one is just as likely to pass by a horse-drawn cart as an automobile. The well-preserved **National Revival houses** were built by the town's first settlers. Many homes have enclosed verandas and delicate woodwork, and six have been turned into **museums;** buy tickets and maps at the tourist office. (Hours differ; most open 9:30am-5:30pm, some closed M, some Tu. Combined ticket 3lv.)

Small **hotels,** often with "Kushta" (Къща) in the name, are easy to find (15-30lv). **Trains** run to Plovdiv (3½hr., 3 per day, 5lv), and Sofia (2hr., 5 per day, 5.20lv). **Private buses** also run to Plovdiv (2½hr., 1 per day, 5lv) and Sofia (2hr., 4 per day, 6lv). Backtrack along the river bisecting town to the main square, where the **tourist office** sells maps (2lv), rents mountain bikes (2lv per hr.), explains transportation options, and finds private rooms (€10-12) in the center of town. (☎21 91; tourist_center@yahoo.com. Open daily 9am-7pm.)

PLOVDIV (ПЛОВДИВ) ☎032

Though modern Plovdiv (pop. 377,000) is rather dingy and depressed, it is the logical base from which to visit the spectacular **Bachkovo Monastery.** The picturesque Old Town is filled with National Revival structures, and traces remain throughout the city from its ancient Roman days as Philippopolis. Its historical and cultural treasures are concentrated among the **Trimondium** (three hills) of **Stariya Grad** (Стария Град; Old Town). To reach the 2nd-century **Roman amphitheater** (Античен Театър; Antichen Teatŭr) from pl. Tsentralen (Централен), take a right off Knyaz Alexander (Княз Александр) onto Suborna (Съборна), then go right up the steps along Mitropolit Paisii to the steps next to the music academy. Dating from the early Roman occupation of the Balkans, this marble masterpiece now hosts concerts and shows, such as the **Opera Festival** in June and the **Festival of the Arts** in late summer and early fall. (Amphitheater open daily 9am-7pm. 3lv.) Return to Knyaz Alexander and follow it to pl. Dzhumaya (Джумая), home to the **Dzhumaya Mosque** and the remains of an ancient Roman **stadium.** (Both free.) At the end of ul. Suborna, the **Museum of Ethnography** (Етнографски Музей; Etnografski Muzey) exhibits artifacts such as *kukerski maski*, masks used to scare away evil spirits. (☎62 56 54. Open Tu-Su 9am-noon, Tu-Th and Sa-Su also 2-5pm. 4lv, students 2lv.)

Queen Mary Elizabeth Guesthouse ❶, Gustav Vaigand 7, is clean, backpacker-friendly, and cheap. From Ruski, turn left onto Gustav Vaigand; it's 100m down on the right. (☎62 93 06. Laundry €1 per kg. A/C. Reception 24hr., ring bell for entry. 15lv per person. Cash only.) **Hiker's Hostel ❶,** ul. Suborna 59, offers free Internet and big breakfasts in the Old Town. Walking north on Knyaz Alexander, turn right at Dzhumaya up onto ul. Suborna. (☎899 898 266, www.hikers-hostel.org/pd. Dorms €10. Cash only.) **Trains** run to: Burgas (5hr., 4 per day, 10lv); Sofia (2½hr., 8 per day, 6lv); Varna (5½hr., 3 per day, 12lv). Buy international tickets at **Rila,** bul. Hristo Botev 31a. (Open M-F 8am-7:30pm, Sa 8am-2pm. Cash only.) **Buses** from Sofia (2hr., every 30min., 8lv) arrive at Yug (Юг) station, bul. Hhristo Botev 47 (☎62 69 37), opposite the train station. An up-to-date map is essential; street vendors sell good ones in Cyrillic for 3lv. Check email at **Speed,** Knyaz Alexander 12, on the left before the mosque. (1lv per hr. Open 24hr.) **Postal Code:** 4000.

BACHKOVO MONASTERY

In the Rodopi mountains, 28km south of Plovdiv is Bulgaria's second-largest monastery, **Bachkovo Monastery** (Бачковски Манастир; Bachkovski Manastir; ☎03 327 277), built in 1083. The main church holds the **Icon of the Virgin Mary and Child** (Икона Света Богородица; Ikona Sveta Bogoroditsa), which is said to have miraculous healing power. (Open daily 8am-8pm. Free.) Well-maintained hiking paths lie uphill from the monastery. **Buses** (30min., every 30min., 3lv round-trip) leave from platform #1 at the Rodolpi station in Plovdiv. It's the Smolyan bus; ask to go to Bachkovo.

VELIKO TÂRNOVO (ВЕЛИКО ТЪРНОВО) ☎062

Veliko Târnovo (pop. 75,000), on the steep hills above the Yantra River, has watched over Bulgaria for more than 5000 years. The city's residents led the national uprising against Byzantine rule in 1185; its revolutionaries wrote the country's first constitution here in 1879. The ruins of the **Tsarevets** (Царевец), a fortress that once housed the royal palace and a cathedral, span a hillside outside the city and still dominate the skyline. (Open daily 8am-7pm. 4lv.) Once inside, climb uphill to the beautiful **Church of the Ascension** (Църква Възнесениегосподне; Tsŭrkva Vŭznesenieġospodne), which was restored for Bulgaria's 1300th anniversary in 1981. From the center, go down Nezavisimost, which becomes Nikola Pikolo, and turn right at ul. Ivan Vazov (Иван Вазов) to reach the **National Revival Museum** (Музей на Възраждането; Muzey na Vŭzrazhdaneto), which housed Bulgaria's first parliament and has a copy of the first constitution. (☎629 821. Open M and W-Su 9am-6pm. 4lv.) On summer evenings, there is often a **sound and light show** above Tsarevets Hill. (Begins between 9:45 and 10pm and lasts 20min.)

Hiker's Hostel ❶, Rezervoarska 91 (Резервоарска). From Stambolov, turn left on Rakovski (Раковски), left again into the small square, go straight and take the small street uphill. Hiker's serves up enormous free breakfasts in a relaxed backpacker atmosphere. (☎359 88 969 16 61; www.hikers-hostel.org/vt. Free Internet. Free pickup service. Dorms 20lv. Cash only.) **Hotel Comfort ❸,** Panayot Tipografov 5 (Панайот Типографов), has an amazing view of Tsarevets and beautiful rooms. From Stambolov, turn left on Rakovski, left again into the small square, and look for the signs. (☎628 728. Singles €25; doubles €30.) **Trains** stop at nearby Gorna Oryakhovitsa (Горна Оряховица). Bus #10 leaves from the main square in Veliko Tŭrnovo to Gorna; it's timed to meet trains (1.14lv). Destinations include: Burgas (6hr., 6 per day, 11lv); Sofia (5hr., 9 per day, 12lv); Varna (4hr., 5 per day, 11lv). Minibuses and city bus #10 go from the station to pl. Maika Bŭlgaria (Майка България), the town center. In the square is the **tourist office.** (☎622 148. Maps 3lv. Open M-F 9am-noon and 1-6pm.) Check email at **Matrix Internet Club,** Nezavisimost 32 (Независимост), along the main street. (☎605 959. Before 10pm 0.98lv per hr., after 10pm 0.68lv per hr. Open 24hr.) **Postal Code:** 5000.

BLACK SEA COAST (ЧЕРНО МОРЕ)

Bulgaria's most popular vacation spot, the Black Sea Coast is covered with secluded bays, seaside towns, and pricey resorts. The bronzed tourists and modern luxury may contrast too starkly with folk tradition, but tiny, centuries-old fishing villages are always just a step off the beaten path.

VARNA (ВАРНА) ☎052

Visitors are drawn to Varna (pop. 400,000) by its expansive beaches, Mediterranean-like climate, and frequent summer festivals. From the train station go right on bul. Primorski (Приморски) to reach **beaches** and **seaside gardens.** Despite Varna's sprawl, most sights are within a 30min. walk of one another. On San Stefano in the city's old quarter, **Grutska Makhala** (Гръцка Махала), visit the well-preserved ruins of the **Roman Thermal Baths** (Римски Терми; Rimski Termi. ☎600 059. Open Tu-Su 10am-5pm. 3lv, students 2lv.) The **Archaeological Museum** (Археологически Музей; Arkheologicheski Muzey), in the park on Mariya Luiza, has the world's oldest gold artifacts. (Open in summer Tu-Su 10am-5pm; low season Tu-Sa 10am-5pm. 5lv, students 2lv.) Varna's cultural events include the **International Jazz Festival** in late August as part of **Varna Summer,** a music, theater, and folk festival (www.varnasummerfest.org). For schedules and tickets, check the **Festival and Congress Center,** on bul. Primorski, which is also the location of **"Love is Folly,"** an international film festival in August and September.

Gregory's Backpackers Hostel ❶, 82 Fenix St., in Zvezditsa village 8km from Varna, proves itself to be one of the best in the Balkans with a swimming pool and great lounge/bar. (☎379 909. www.hostelvarna.com. Free pickup. Breakfast included. Book ahead. Dorms €10. Cash only.) **Trains** depart from near the commercial harbor for Plovdiv (7hr., 3 per day, 9-12lv) and Sofia (8hr., 6 per day, 15lv). **Buses,** at ul. Vladislav Varenchik (Владислав Варенчик), go to Burgas (2½hr., 5 per day, 8.25lv) and Sofia (6hr., 17 per day, 23lv). The **tourist office** is on bul. Knyaz Boris I, the pedestrian walkway, near the Moussala Palace Hotel. **Astra Tour,** near track #6 at the train station, finds private rooms that run for about 22lv. (☎60 58 61; astratur@yahoo.com. Open daily in summer 7am-9pm.) **Postal Code:** 9000.

CROATIA (HRVATSKA)

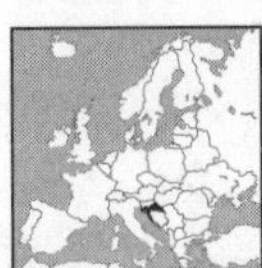

Croatia is a land of preternatural beauty, with dense forests, barren mountains, and crystal-clear waters. At the convergence of the Mediterranean, the Alps, and the Pannonian Plain, Croatia has also been situated along dangerous political boundaries—of the Frankish and Byzantine empires in the 9th century, the Catholic and Orthodox churches since the 11th century, and Christian Europe and Islamic Turkey from the 15th to 19th centuries. In the past decade, the list has extended to its own fractious ethnic groups. After the devastating 1991-1995 war, however, the country achieved full independence for the first time in 800 years, allowing natives and visitors alike to enjoy Croatia in peace.

DISCOVER CROATIA: SUGGESTED ITINERARIES

THREE DAYS Spend a day poking around the bizarre architecture of **Split** (p. 226) before ferrying down the coast to the beach paradise of either **Hvar** or **Brač** islands (1 day; p. 227) and what some consider Eastern Europe's most beautiful city–**Dubrovnik** (p. 228).

BEST OF CROATIA, ONE WEEK Enjoy the East-meets-West feel of **Zagreb** (1 day; p. 220) and make your way to **Zadar** (p. 225) on the Dalmatian Coast. Next, ferry to tree-lined **Korčula** (1 day; p. 228) before **Hvar** and **Brac** (2 days). End your journey in **Dubrovnik.**

ESSENTIALS

FACTS AND FIGURES

Official Name: Republic of Croatia.

Capital: Zagreb.

Major Cities: Dubrovnik, Ploce, Split.

Population: 4,496,000.

Land Area: 56,414 sq. km.

Time Zone: GMT +1.

Language: Croatian.

Religions: Roman Catholic (88%).

WHEN TO GO

Croatia's best weather lasts from May to September, though the crowds typically show up in July and August along the Adriatic coast. If you go in late August or September, you'll find fewer crowds, lower prices, and an abundance of figs and grapes. Come later in the fall for wine season. While April and October may be too cool for camping, the weather is usually nice along the coast and private rooms are plentiful and cheap. You can swim in the sea from mid-June to late September.

DOCUMENTS AND FORMALITIES

EMBASSIES AND CONSULATES. Embassies of other countries in Croatia are all in Zagreb (p. 220). Croatia's embassies and consulates abroad include: **Australia,** 14 Jindalee Cres., O'Malley ACT 2606, Canberra (☎2 6286 6988; croemb@dynamite.com.au); **Canada,** 229 Chapel St., Ottawa, ON K1N 7Y6 (☎613-562-7820; www.croatiaemb.net); **New Zealand** Consulate, 291 Lincoln Rd., Henderson (☎9 836 5581; cro-consulate@xtra.co.nz); **UK,** 21 Conway St., London W1P 5HL (☎20 7387 2022; amboffice@croatianembassy.co.uk); **US,** 2343 Massachusetts Ave. NW, Washington, D.C. 20008 (☎202-588-5899; www.croatiaemb.org).

VISA AND ENTRY INFORMATION. Citizens of Australia, Canada, Ireland, New Zealand, the UK, and the US do not need a visa for stays of up to 90 days. All visitors must register with the police within 48hr. of arrival—hotels, campsites, and accommodation agencies should automatically register you, but those staying with friends or in private rooms must do so themselves to avoid fines or expulsion. To register, go to room #103 on the second floor of the central police station at Petrinjska 30. Bring your passport and use form #14. (☎456 36 23, after hours 456 31 11. Open M-F 8am-4pm.) Police may check foreigners' passports anywhere and at any time. The most direct way of entering or exiting Croatia is by bus or train between Zagreb and a neighboring capital.

TOURIST SERVICES AND MONEY

TOURIST OFFICES. Even small towns have a branch of the excellent **state-run tourist board** *(turistička zajednica)*. Staff speak English, almost always Italian, and often German and French, and give out free maps and booklets. Private accommodations are handled by private agencies *(turistička/putnička agencija)*. The largest is the ubiquitous **Atlas.** Local outfits are generally cheaper.

MONEY. Croatia's monetary unit, the **kuna** (kn), which is divided into 100 lipa, is extremely difficult to exchange abroad, except in Bosnia, Hungary, and Slovenia. **Inflation** hovers around 2.5%, so prices should stay relatively constant in the near

ENTRANCE REQUIREMENTS

Passport: Required for all travelers.

Visa: Not required for stays under 90 days for citizens of Australia, Canada, Ireland, New Zealand, the UK, and the US.

Letter of Invitation: Not required for citizens of Australia, Canada, Ireland, New Zealand, the UK, and the US.

Inoculations: Not required. Recommended up-to-date on DTaP (diphtheria, tetanus, and pertussis), Hepatitis A, Hepatitis B, MMR (measles, mumps, and rubella), Polio booster, and Typhoid.

Work Permit: Required for all foreigners planning to work in Croatia.

Driving Permit: Required for all those planning to drive in Croatia.

future. Most tourist offices, hotels, and transportation stations **exchange currency** and traveler's checks, but banks generally have the best rates. Most banks give MasterCard and Visa cash advances, and credit cards are widely accepted. ATMs are everywhere. Government offices are typically open Monday through Friday 8:30am-4:30pm; banks Monday through Friday 8am-7pm, Saturday 7am-noon; grocery stores Monday through Friday 7am-8pm, Saturday 7am-3pm. Travel in Croatia is becoming more costly, with the bare minimum for accommodations, food, and transport costing 240kn. Expect to spend anywhere from to 300-470kn per day. **Tipping** is not expected, although it is appropriate to round up when paying; in some cases, the establishment will do it for you—check your change. Fancy restaurants often add a hefty service charge. **Bargaining** is reserved for only informal transactions, such as hiring a boat for a day or renting a private room directly from an owner. Posted prices should usually be followed.

KUNA (KN)		
	AUS$1 = 4.57KN	1KN = AUS$0.22
	CDN$1 = 4.98KN	1KN = CDN$0.20
	EUR€1 = 7.41KN	1KN = EUR€0.14
	NZ$1 = 4.22KN	1KN = NZ$0.24
	UK£1 = 10.87KN	1KN = UK£0.09
	US$1 = 6.06KN	1KN = US$0.17

HEALTH AND SAFETY

Travel to the former conflict area of the **Slavonia** and **Krajina regions** remains dangerous due to **unexploded landmines,** which are not expected to be cleared until at least 2010. In July 2005, a tourist was badly injured by a mine on the island of Vis, which inspectors had previously declared safe. If you choose to visit these or other regions, do not stray from areas known to be, and consult the Croatian Mine Action Center website at www.hcr.hr. **Pharmacies** are well stocked with Western products, including tampons, sanitary napkins *(sanitami ulosci)*, and condoms *(prezervativ)*. UK citizens receive free medical care with a valid passport. Tap water is normally chlorinated, and while relatively safe, may cause mild abdominal upsets. **Bottled water** is readily available. Croatians are friendly toward foreigners and sometimes a little too friendly to **females;** go out in public with a companion to ward off unwanted displays of machismo. **Disabled travelers** should contact Savez Organizacija Invalida Hrvatske (☎1 369 4502). Zagreb's cobblestones and lack of ramps make getting around difficult. Croatians are slowly beginning to accept **homosexuality;** be cautious in public.

EMERGENCY	**Police, Ambulance,** and **Fire:** ☎112.

TRANSPORTATION

BY PLANE AND TRAIN. **Croatia Airlines** flies from many cities, including Chicago, Frankfurt, London, and Paris to Zagreb, Dubrovnik, and Split. Zadar, and Pula also have tiny international airports. Trains (www.hznet.hr) run to Zagreb from Budapest, Hungary, Ljubljana, Slovenia, Venice, Italy, and Vienna, Austria, and continue to other Croatian destinations. Due to the 1991-1995 war, trains are very slow and nonexistent south of Split. *Odlazak* means departures, *dolazak* arrivals.

BY BUS. Buses (www.akz.hr) are the best option for domestic travel, running faster and farther than trains at comparable prices. Tickets are cheaper if you buy them onboard, bypassing the 2kn service charge at station kiosks. In theory, luggage must be stowed (3kn), but this is only enforced on the most crowded lines.

BY CAR AND BIKE. Anyone over 18 can rent a car in larger cities (350-400kn per day), but downtown parking and gas are expensive. Rural roads are in bad condition, and those traveling through the Krajina region and other conflict areas should be cautious of off-road **landmines.** Traveling by car can get especially expensive when island-hopping—Jadrolinija ferries charge a bundle for decking your wheels. Moped and bicycle rentals (50-80kn per day) are a good and cheap option in resort or urban areas. **Hitchhiking** is relatively uncommon and never the safest method of transportation. *Let's Go* does not recommend it.

BY FERRY. **Jadrolinija** ferries (www.jadrolinija.hr) serve the coast. Boats sail the Rijeka-Split-Dubrovnik route, stopping at islands on the way. Ferries also go to Ancona, Italy from Split and Zadar and to Bari, Italy from Split and Dubrovnik. Though slower than buses and trains, ferries are more comfortable. A basic ticket provides only a place on the deck. Cheap beds sell out fast, so buy tickets in advance. If the agency only sells basic tickets, you'll need to run to get a bed.

KEEPING IN TOUCH

PHONE CODES	**Country code:** 385. **International dialing prefix:** 00. For more information on how to place international calls, see inside back cover.

EMAIL AND THE INTERNET. Most towns, no matter how small, have at least one Internet cafe. Connections on the islands are slower and less reliable than those on the mainland.

TELEPHONE. Post offices usually have pay phones; pay after you talk. All phones on the street require a phone card (*telekarta*), sold at newsstands and post offices. Fifty "impulses" cost 23kn (1 impulse equals 3min. domestic, 36sec. international; 50% discount M-Sa 10pm-7am, Su, and holidays). Calls to the US and Europe can be expensive (20kn per min.); Voicecom and Telnet cards offer the least expensive rates. International access numbers can be found inside the back cover. For the international operator, dial ☎901. Elaborate **mobile phone** ringtones can be heard virtually everywhere in Croatia, which has two networks: T-Mobile and VIP. If you bring or buy a phone compatible with the GSM 900/1800 network, SIM cards are widely available and cost around 400kn.

MAIL. The **Croatian Post** is reliable. Mail from the US arrives within one week. Mail addressed to **Poste Restante** will be held for 30 days at the main post office. Address envelopes as follows: first name LAST NAME, POSTE RESTANTE, Pt. Republike 28 (post office street address), 20000 (postal code), Dubrovnik (city), CROATIA. *Avionski* and *zrakoplovom* both mean "airmail."

LANGUAGE. Croats speak **Croatian,** a South Slavic language written in the Latin alphabet. The language fairly recently became distinguished from Serbo-Croatian. Only a few expressions differ from Serbian, but be careful not to use the Serbian ones in Croatia—you'll make few friends. **German** and **Italian** are common second languages among adults. Most Croatians under 30 speak some **English.** For a phrasebook and glossary, see **Glossary: Croatian,** p. 1057.

ACCOMMODATIONS AND CAMPING

CROATIA	❶	❷	❸	❹	❺
ACCOMMODATIONS	under 100kn	100-150kn	150-210kn	210-360kn	over 360kn

For info on the country's seven youth **hostels** (in Zagreb, Pula, Zadar, Dubrovnik, Krk, Veli Losinj, and Punat), contact the Croatian Youth Hostel Association, Savska 5, 10000 Zagreb. (☎1 482 92 94; www.hfhs.hr.) **Hotels** in Croatia can be wildly expensive—a cheap overnight stay in a Zagreb hotel will run at least US$80. If you opt for a hotel, call a few days in advance, especially in summer along the coast. Apart from hostels, **private rooms** are the only budget accommodations. Look for *sobe* signs, especially near transportation stations. English is rarely spoken by owners. Agencies generally charge 30-50% more if you stay fewer than three nights. All accommodations are subject to a tourist tax of 5-10kn (one reason the police require foreigners to register). Croatia is one of the top **camping** destinations in Europe—33% of travelers camp. Facilities usually meet Western standards of space and utilities, and prices are among the cheapest along the Mediterranean. Camping outside of designated areas is illegal. For more info, contact the Croatian Camping Union, HR-52440 Poreč, Pionirska 1. (☎52 451 324; www.camping.hr.)

FOOD AND DRINK

CROATIA	❶	❷	❸	❹	❺
FOOD	under 40kn	40-70kn	70-110kn	110-190kn	over 190kn

Croatian cuisine is defined by the country's varied geography. In continental Croatia around and east of Zagreb, heavy meals featuring meat and creamy sauces dominate. *Purica s mlincima* (turkey with pasta) is the regional dish near Zagreb. Also popular are *burek,* a layered pie made with meat or cheese, and the spicy Slavonian *kulen,* which is considered one of the world's best **sausages** by a panel of German men who decide such things. *Pašticada* (slow-cooked meat) is another excellent option. On the coast, textures and flavors change with the presence of **seafood** and Italian influence. Don't miss out on *lignje* (squid) or *Dalmatinski pršut* (smoked ham). The **oysters** from Ston Bay have received many awards at international competitions. If your budget does not allow for such treats, *slane sardele* (salted sardines) are a tasty substitute. **Vegetarian** and **kosher** eating are difficult in Croatia, but not impossible if you're willing to live off pizza and baked goods. Croatia offers excellent **wines;** price is usually the best indicator of quality. Mix red wine with tap water to get the popular *bevanda,* and white wine with carbonated water to get *gemišt. Šljivovica* is a hard-hitting plum brandy found in many small towns. *Karlovačko* and *Ožujsko* are the two most popular beers.

HOLIDAYS AND FESTIVALS

Holidays: New Year's Day (Jan. 1); Epiphany (Jan. 6); Easter Sunday and Monday (Apr. 16 and 17); May Day (May 1); Anti-Fascist Struggle Day (June 22); National Thanksgiving Day (Aug. 5); Assumption of the Blessed Virgin Mary (Aug. 15); Independence Day (Oct. 8); All Saints' Day (Nov. 5).

Festivals: In June, Zagreb holds its own version of Woodstock, the catch-all festival Cest Is D'Best. An easygoing philosophy keeps revelers on city streets out all night. Open-air concerts and theatrical performances make the Dubrovnik Summer Festival (*Dubrovački Ljetni*; from early July to late Aug.) the event of that city's summer (p. 228). During the same period, a similar festival showcasing music and theater takes over Split. From July to August, Korčula (p. 228) unsheathes the Festival of Sword Dances *(Festival Viteških Igara)* with performances of the *Moreška, Moštra,* and *Kumpanija* sword dances swashbuckling all over the island. Zagreb's International Puppet Festival (from late Aug. to early Sept.) draws children and adults alike.

BEYOND TOURISM

Coalition for Psychotrauma and Peace, Gunduliceva 18, 32000 Vukovar, Croatia (☎385 32 444 662; www.cwwpp.org). Work for 1½-2 years in education and health care related to long-term conflict in Croatia.

Firefly UK/Bosnia, 3 Bristo Pl., Edinburgh, Midlothian, EH1 1 EY, UK (☎79 56 98 38 85; www.fireflybosnia.org). Scottish organization that arranges summer camps in Croatia for refugees from Bosnian youth centers.

Learning Enterprises, 2227 20th St. NW #304, Washington, D.C. 20009, USA (☎202-309-3453; www.learningenterprises.org). 6-week summer programs place first-time English teachers in rural Croatia, Hungary, Romania, and Slovakia, with the option to switch countries half-way. No-fee program includes orientation and room and board with a host family, but volunteers must pay for airfare and expenses.

Eco-Centre Caput Insulae-Beli, Beli 4, 51559 Beli, Cres Island, Croatia (☎385 51 840 525; www.caput-insulae.com). Volunteers protect the endangered griffons, environment, and cultural heritage of Cres Island, Croatia. 2 weeks €122-271.

ZAGREB ☎01

Zagreb (pop. 780,000) possesses the grand architecture, wide boulevards, and sprawling parks of a major European city, but the tourists are still notably absent. Those who take a chance to enjoy this laid-back, cosmopolitan capital while it still maintains its local feel, rather than rushing through en route to the Croatian coast will be richly rewarded with magnificent churches, diverse museums, lively outdoor cafes, and electric nightlife.

TRANSPORTATION AND PRACTICAL INFORMATION. Trains leave the Glavni Kolodvor (main station), Trg Kralja Tomislava 12 (☎060 333 444, international info 378 25 32; www.hznet.hr), for: Ljubljana, Slovenia (2hr.; 7 per day; 100kn, round-trip 130kn); Split (day train 6hr., 3 per day, 166kn; night train 8½hr., 2 per day, 166kn); Sarajevo, Bosnia (9hr., 1 per day, 168kn). From the station, to reach the main square, Trg bana Josipa Jelačića, cross the street, walk along the left side of the park to the end, then follow Praška. **Buses** (☎060 313 333; www.akz.hr) leave Autobusni Kolodvor (bus station), Držićeva bb, to: Dubrovnik (11hr., 8 per day, 180kn); Ljubljana, Slovenia (2½hr., 2 per day, 150kn); Split (7-9hr., 27 per day, 120kn); Vienna (8hr., 2 per day, 250kn). To reach Trg b. Josipa Jelačića, exit on Držićeva, turn left, continue past Trg Žrtava Fašizma, and turn left on Jurišićeva.

The **tourist office** is at Trg b. Josipa Jelačića 11. (☎481 40 51; www.zagreb-touristinfo.hr. Open M-F 9am-9pm, Sa 9am-5pm, Su 9am-2pm.) **Register** (p. 216) at the Department for Foreign Visitors in the central police station, Petrinjska 30, second floor, room 103. Bring your passport and use form #14. (☎456 36 23, after hours 456 31 11. Open M-F 8am-4pm.) Hotels and hostels will register guests automatically. **Internet** access is most convenient at **Charlie Net,** Gajeva 4. (☎488 02 33. Open M-Sa 8am-10pm. 16kn per hr. 20% ISIC discount.) **Postal Code:** 10000.

CROATIA

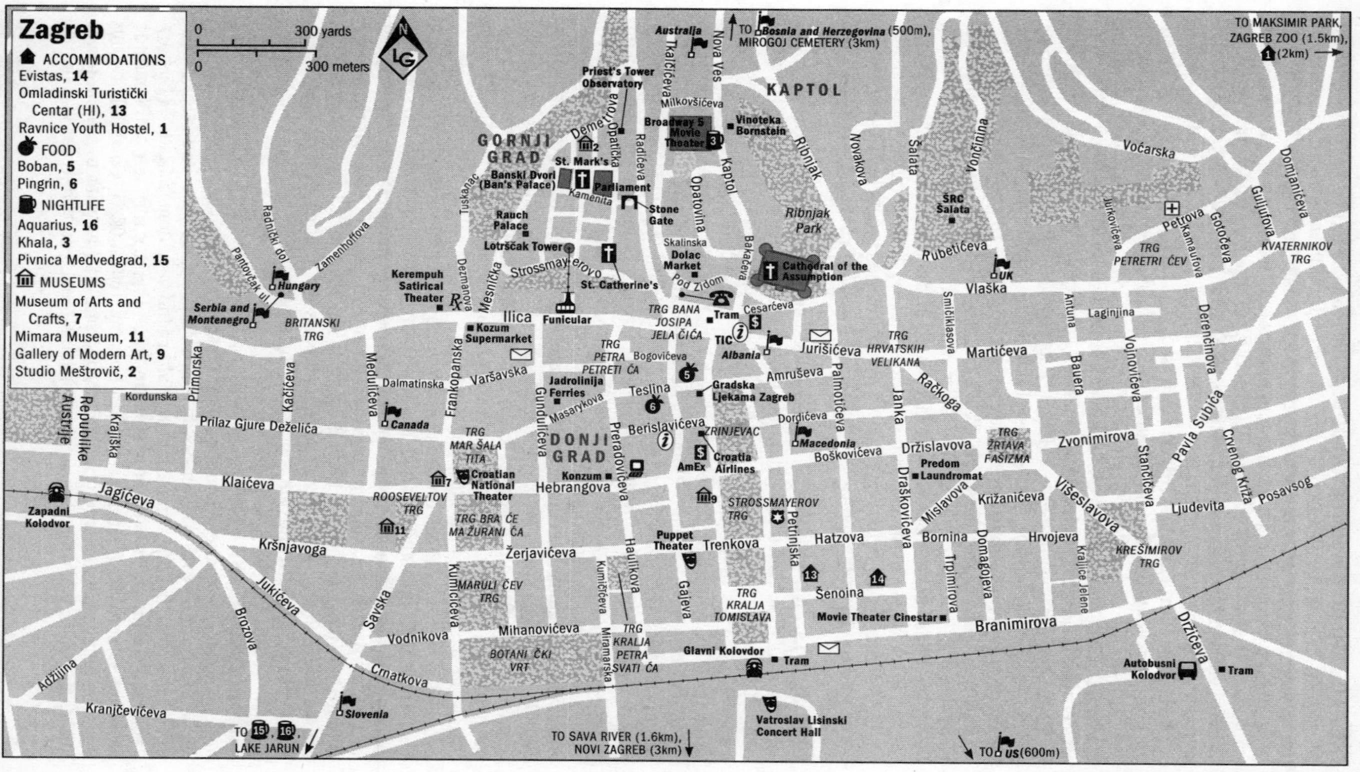
Zagreb
ACCOMMODATIONS
Evistas, 14
Omladinski Turistički Centar (HI), 13
Ravnice Youth Hostel, 1
FOOD
Boban, 5
Pingrin, 6
NIGHTLIFE
Aquarius, 16
Khala, 3
Pivnica Medvedgrad, 15
MUSEUMS
Museum of Arts and Crafts, 7
Mimara Museum, 11
Gallery of Modern Art, 9
Studio Meštrovič, 2
0
300 yards
0
300 meters
TO MAKSIMIR PARK, ZAGREB ZOO (1.5km), (2km)
TO Bosnia and Herzegovina (500m), MIROGOJ CEMETERY (3km)
TO US (600m)
TO SAVA RIVER (1.6km), NOVI ZAGREB (3km)
TO 15, 16, LAKE JARUN
KAPTOL
GORNJI GRAD
DONJI GRAD
Cathedral of the Assumption
St. Mark's
Parliament
Banski Dvori (Ban's Palace)
Lotrščak Tower
Priest's Tower Observatory
Stone Gate
Funicular
St. Catherine's
Rauch Palace
Dolac Market
Vinoteka Bornstein
Broadway 5 Movie Theater
Kerempuh Satirical Theater
Kozum Supermarket
Croatian National Theater
Puppet Theater
Movie Theater Cinestar
Vatroslav Lisinski Concert Hall
Glavni Kolovdor
Autobusni Kolodvor
Zapadni Kolodvor
Gradska Ljekama Zagreb
Jadrolinija Ferries
Croatia Airlines
AmEx
Predom Laundromat
Konzum
TIC
Tram
ŠRC Šalata
Ribnjak Park
UK
Australia
Albania
Macedonia
Canada
Hungary
Serbia and Montenegro
Slovenia
TRG BANA JOSIPA JELA ČIĆA
TRG PETRA PETRETI ĆA
TRG MAR ŠALA TITA
ROOSEVELTOV TRG
TRG BRA ĆE MA ŽURANI ĆA
MARULI ĆEV TRG
BOTANI ČKI VRT
TRG KRALJA TOMISLAVA
TRG KRALJA PETRA SVATI ĆA
STROSSMAYEROV TRG
ZRINJEVAC
TRG HRVATSKIH VELIKANA
TRG ŽRTAVA FAŠIZMA
KREŠIMIROV TRG
TRG PETRETRI ČEV
KVATERNIKOV TRG
BRITANSKI TRG
Ilica
Vlaška
Jurišićeva
Tkalčićeva
Radićeva
Opatička
Kaptol
Nova Ves
Ribnjak
Šalata
Novakova
Vončinina
Domjanićeva
Guljufova
Gotočeva
Derenčinova
Crvenog Križa
Pavla Subića
Vojnovićeva
Stančićeva
Zvonimirova
Višeslavova
Martićeva
Smičiklasova
Rubetićeva
Račkoga
Janka
Draškovićeva
Palmotićeva
Amruševa
Teslina
Bogovićeva
Berislavićeva
Preradovićeva
Gundulićeva
Hebrangova
Masarykova
Varšavska
Frankopanska
Mesnička
Tuskanac
Dezmanova
Dalmatinska
Medulićeva
Kačićeva
Prilaz Gjure Deželića
Klaićeva
Kršnjavoga
Savska
Jukićeva
Brozova
Primorska
Kordunska
Krajiška
Republike Austrije
Jagićeva
Kranjčevićeva
Adžijina
Crnatkova
Vodnikova
Mihanovićeva
Žerjavićeva
Kumičićeva
Haulikova
Miramarska
Gajeva
Trenkova
Petrinjska
Šenoina
Hatzova
Boškovićeva
Držislavova
Dordićeva
Bornina
Trpimirova
Domagojeva
Mislavova
Križanićeva
Hrvojeva
Kraljice Jelene
Branimirova
Držićeva
Ljudevita Posavsog
Bauera
Antuna
Laginjina
Jurkovićeva
Voćarska
Kamaufova
Petrova
Zamenhoffova
Radnički dol
Pantovčak ul.
Skalinska
Pod Zidom
Bakačeva
Cesarčeva
Opatovina
Milkovšićeva
Kamenita
Strossmayerovo
Demetrova

CROATIA

ACCOMMODATIONS AND FOOD. It can be hard to find a cheap room in downtown Zagreb. Impeccably clean and cheerful **Ravnice Youth Hostel ❶**, 1 Ravnice 38d, is a 20min. ride from the city center. Take tram #11 or 12 from Trg bana Jelačića, tram #4 from the train station, or tram #7 from the bus station toward Dubrava or Dubec. Get off at Ravnice, two stops past the Dinamo football stadium. Owner Vera and her daughter Lea both speak English. (☎233 23 25; fax 234 56 07. Laundry 40kn. Internet 16kn per hr. Dorms 112kn.) Although noisy and run-down, the **Omladinski Turistički Centar (HI) ❶**, Petrinjska 77, is cheap and convenient. From the train station, turn right onto Branimirova; Petrinjska is on the left. (☎484 12 61; www.hfhs.hr. Reception 24hr. Dorms 80kn; singles 158kn, with bath 218kn; doubles 211/286kn. Cash only.) **Evistas ❸**, Šenoina 28, on the street marked Augusta Šenoe off Petrinjska, past the Omladinski hostel, books private rooms downtown. (☎483 95 46; evistas@zg.hinet.hr. Open M-F 9am-1:45pm and 3-8pm, Sa 9:30am-5pm. Singles 222-240kn; doubles 317kn; triples 414kn; apartments (2-day min.) 390-750kn per night. Discount for stays longer than 1 night. Under 26 10% off. Tax 7kn.)

Near the main square, **Pingvin ❶**, Teslina 7, is a local favorite, serving grilled sandwiches of all types. (Open M-Sa 24hr., Su 5am-noon. Sandwiches 12-20kn. Cash only.) **Restaurant Boban ❷**, Gajeva 9, serves affordable pastas and salads in a vaulted brick dining room and garden patio. (Entrees 40-70kn. Open daily 10am-11pm.) **Konzum** grocery store has many locations in the city, including one on the corner of Preradoviceva and Hebrangova. (Open M-F 7am-8pm, Sa 7am-3pm.)

SIGHTS AND MUSEUMS. Zagreb is best seen on foot. From Trg b. Josipa Jelačića, take Ilica, then turn right on Tomiceva to the funicular (3kn), which gives access to many sights on the hills of Gornji Grad (upper town). **Lotrščak Tower** has a spectacular view of the city. (Open May-Sept. Tu-Su 11am-8pm. 10kn, students 5kn.) The 17th-century **St. Catherine's Church** is to the right of the tower. (Open M-F and Su 7am-11pm, Sa 7am-6:30pm. Services M-F 6pm, Su 11am. Free.) Follow ul. Cirilometodska to Markov Trg; the colorful roof tiles of Gothic **St. Mark's Church** (Crkva Sv. Marka) depict the coats of arms of Croatia, Dalmatia, and Slavonia on the left and of Zagreb on the right. (Open daily 7am-1:30pm and 5:30-7pm. Free.) Visible anywhere in Zagreb, the neo-Gothic bell towers of the 11th-century **Cathedral of the Assumption** (Katedrala Marijina Uznesenja) loom over Kaptol Hill. (Open daily 10am-5pm. Services M-Sa 7, 8, 9am, Su 7, 8, 9, 10, 11:30am. Free.) Take a bus (8min., every 15min.) from Kaptol to the beautiful **Mirogoj Cemetery,** Croatia's largest, with 12 green-and-cream-colored towers and a garden with cypress trees. (Open M-F 6am-8pm, Su 7:30am-6pm. Free.)

Zagreb's museums focus on Croatian artwork. **Studio Meštrovič,** Mletačka 8, in the former home and studio of Ivan Meštrovič, Croatia's most celebrated sculptor, displays his works in a lovely garden. The **Museum of Arts and Crafts,** Trg Maršala Tita 10, has timepieces, antique furniture, and more from the 15th century onward. (Open Tu-F 10am-7pm, Sa-Su 10am-2pm. 20kn, students 10kn.) The **Gallery of Modern Art,** Herbrangova 1, features rotating exhibits of Croatia's best artists. (Open Tu-Sa 10am-6pm, Su 10am-1pm. Prices vary by exhibit.)

NIGHTLIFE AND FESTIVALS. With a variety of clubs at **Lake Jarun** and many relaxed sidewalk cafes and bars on **Tkalčićeva,** Zagreb has a lively nightlife scene. Dance and swim at the lakeside club **Aquarius,** on Lake Jarun. Take tram #17 to Srednjaci, the third unmarked stop after Studenski dom "S. Radić" (15min.). Cross the street, and when you reach the lake (15min.), turn left and continue along the boardwalk; Aquarius is the last building. (☎364 02 31. Cover 30kn. Club open Tu-Su 10pm-4am. Cafe open daily 9am-9pm.) If you want to stay in town, **Khala,** Nova Ves 17, is a surprisingly affordable lounge and wine bar just up the street from the Cathedral in the Kaptol Center/Broadway 5 cinema complex. (☎486 06 47. Open M-Th 8am-1am, F-Su 8am-4am. Cash only.) Locals chug cheap, good quality, homemade beer at **Pivnica Medvedgrad,** Savska 56. Take tram #13, 14, or 17 from Trg bana Jelačića to the corner of Avenija Vukovar and Savska. (Beer 18kn per L. Open M-Sa 10am-midnight, Su noon-midnight.)

In late June, the city bursts with performances for the street festival **Cest is d'Best** (The Streets are the Best), and the **Eurokaz Avant-Garde Theaters Festival.** Folk culture aficionados will flock to Zagreb in mid-July for the 40th **International Folklore Festival,** the premier gathering of European folk dancers and singing groups. A huge **International Puppet Festival** greet September, and Zagreb's **International Jazz Days** say goodbye to October. Zagreb's **Christmas Fair** sets mid-December aglow. Check www.zagreb-touristinfo.hr for updated schedules.

DAYTRIP FROM ZAGREB: TRAKOŠĆAN CASTLE. The fairy-tale white walls of Trakošćan rise high above the surrounding forests and rolling hills. Inside, marvel at the impressive array of antlers and the weapons used to gather them, displayed alongside family portraits, tapestries, and suits of armor from the 15th-19th centuries in sumptuous apartments (on closer inspection, some marble is painted on). Rumor holds that the castle is also home to the ghost of Julijana Erdödy, the first female painter accepted into Croatia's Academy of Arts, whose somewhat surreal paintings are displayed throughout the castle. Julijana is reportedly fond of modern electronics; she has been spotted in the view screen of digital cameras, most recently in the northwest corner room on the second floor. To escape the crowds of schoolchildren and the absurdly overpriced restaurant at the bottom of the hill, bring a picnic and stroll the quiet grounds and lake. (☎42 79 62 81. Open daily Apr.-Oct. 9am-6pm; Nov.-Mar. 9am-4pm. 20kn, students 10kn. English-language booklet 20kn.)

Buses run from the Zagreb bus station to Varaždin (1¾hr., 20 per day, 50kn), where a local bus (1½hr., 7-11 per day, 26kn) continues to Trakošćan. From noon to 2pm, local buses are crowded with school children. Leave Zagreb early in order to make the connection and still have plenty of time at the castle before the last bus to Varaždin (M-F 9pm, Sa-Su 5pm).

NORTHERN COAST

As you approach the coast from Zagreb, you'll encounter the islands of the Gulf of Kvarner, blessed by long summers and gentle breezes; Rab in particular has some of the few sand beaches in Croatia. Roman ruins at Pula, on the Istrian Peninsula, lie farther north along the coast where the Mediterranean laps at the foot of the Alps.

PULA ☎052

Pula (pop. 62,000), the largest city on the Istrian Peninsula, typifies Adriatic charm with cool, clear water, winding medieval corridors, outdoor cafes, and breathtaking Roman ruins. Its **amphitheater** is the second largest in the world, and is often used as a concert venue. (Open daily 8am-9pm. 20kn, students 10kn.) To get there from the bus station, take a left on Istarska. Following Istarska in the opposite direction will bring you to the 29 BC stone **Arch of the Sergians** (Slavoluk obitelji Sergii). Go through the gates and down bustling ul. Sergijevaca to the **Forum,** which holds the well-preserved **Temple of Augustus** (Augustov hram), finished in AD 14. To reach the private coves of Pula's **beaches,** buy a bus ticket from any newsstand (8kn) and take bus #1 to the Stója campground.

To reach the **Omladinski Hostel (HI)** ❶, Zaljev Valsaline 4, take bus #2 (dir.: Veruda) from the bus station. Get off at the first stop on Veruda and follow the signs. Rooms are basic, but the hostel also has a zoo and campground. (☎39 11 33; www.hfhs.hr. Book ahead. Camping 50-75kn; dorms 99-120kn. 10kn registration. 10kn HI discount.) Close to the hostel, **Biska** ❶, Sisplac 15 (☎38 73 33), has superb seafood and pasta for a third of Stari Grad prices. **Corso,** Giardini 3, is a chic Old Town cafe-bar filled with trendy Pulians sipping *bijela kava* (latte; 9kn) by day and mixed drinks (40kn) by night. (☎53 51 47. Open daily 8am-midnight.)

Trains (☎54 19 82) run from Kolodvorska 5 to Ljubljana (7½hr., 2 per day, 127kn) and Zagreb (7hr., 3 per day, 112-125kn). **Buses** (☎50 29 97) run from Trg Istarske Brigade to: Dubrovnik (15hr., 1 per day, 441kn); Trieste (3hr., 5 per day, 88-112kn); Zagreb (5-6hr., 15 per day, 155kn). The **tourist office,** Forum 3, can help find private rooms. (☎21 29 87; www.pulainfo.hr. Open M-Sa 8am-midnight, Su 10am-6pm.) **Postal Code:** 52100.

ROVINJ ☎052

Purported to be one of the healthiest places in the world at the beginning of the 19th century, Rovinj (ro-VEEN; pop. 14,000) was the favorite summer resort of Austro-Hungarian emperors, and vacationers still bask in the town's unspoiled beauty. Its narrow streets lead uphill to the 18th-century Baroque **Saint Euphemia's Church** (Crkva Sv. Eufemije), which houses the sarcophagus of St. Euphemia, a 15-year-old martyr and patron saint of Rovinj. The rickety stairs up to the **bell tower** (61m) lead visitors to a majestic view of the city and sea. During the summer, there are classical music performances on the lawn. (Open M-Sa 10am-2pm and 4-6pm, Su 4-6pm. Services Su 10:30am, 7pm. Church free. Bell tower 10kn.) Rovinj's best beaches are at **Red Island,** which is actually two islands connected by a narrow bridge. The first has a huge resort and crowds, while the second is a haven for snorkelers and nude sunbathers. To get there, take the ferry to Crveni Otok (15min., 17 per day, 20kn). At night, head through the arch in the main square and follow the signs up Grisia towards the church at the top of the hill to see the artist colony display their work. Up near the church, **Valentino Bar,** via Santa Croche 28, is right on water. (☎830 683; valentinus@pu.htnet.hr.)

Across the street from the bus station, **Natale,** Carducci 4, arranges private rooms in and around the center at decent prices. (☎81 33 65; www.rovinj.com. Book ahead in summer. Singles €14-18; doubles €20-26; apartments €32-57.) The **Hotel Monte Mulini** ❸, A. Smareglia bb, offers clean but worn rooms with private baths. Facing the sea at the end of Nazora, walk to the left all the way past the marina and go up the stone steps on your left. (☎81 15 12; mulini@jadran.tdr.hr. Dinner and breakfast included. Singles €22-38; doubles €34-70.) **Camping Polari** ❶, 2.5km east of town, also has a supermarket and several bars. To get there, take one of the frequent buses (6min., 9kn) from the bus station. (☎80 15 01. July-Aug. 100kn per person; June 85kn per person.) **Stella di Mare** ❷, Santa Croche 4, with a terrace overlooking the ocean and huge pizzas, offers a great deal and filling meal in a perfect waterfront location. (Pizzas and pastas 30-45kn, seafood 45-120kn. Open daily 10am-11pm. AmEx/MC/V.) Buy **groceries** at Trg na Lokvi bb, between the bus station and the sea. (Open M-Sa 6:30am-8pm, Su 7-noon. AmEx/DC/MC/V.)

With no train station, Rovinj sends **buses** to Ljubljana, Slovenia (5hr., high season 1 per day, 146kn); Pula (1hr., 20 per day, 27kn); Zagreb (5-6hr., 9 per day, 150kn). From the bus station, turn right onto Carera to reach the main square and the **tourist office,** Pino Budičin 12. (☎81 15 66; www.tzgrovinj.hr. Open daily mid-June to Sept. 8am-9pm; Oct. to mid-June 8am-4pm.) **Postal Code:** 52210.

RAB

☎051

After centuries of Byzantine, Venetian, and Hungarian rule, Rab still has Roman ruins dating from the time of its construction during the reign of Augustus. Stroll along **Gornja Ulica** from the remains of **St. John's Church** (Crkva sv. Jvana), a Roman basilica, to **St. Justine's Church** (Crkva sv. Justine), which houses a museum of Christian art. (Open daily 10am-12:30pm and 7:30-10pm. 5kn.) Atop the bell tower of the 13th-century **St. Mary's Church** (Crkva sv. Marije), behold the sunset on the horizon or the nuns' lush garden below. (Open daily 10am-1pm and 7:30-10pm. 5kn.) **Beaches** dot the perimeter of Rab Island; the tourist office has transportation info. Most of the island's sand beaches, among the few in Croatia, are on the northern end of the island, while rocky beaches lie on the western edge and pebble beaches on the eastern.

Katurbo, M. de Dominisa, on the waterfront between the bus station and town center, arranges private rooms and rents bicycles. (☎72 44 95; www.katurbo.hr. Open daily July-Aug. 8am-9pm; Sept.-June 8am-1pm and 4-9pm. Bikes 20kn per hr. Singles €15-20; doubles €26-40. Tourist tax 7kn.) **Hotel Istra ❹,** M. de Dominisa bb, has clean, modern rooms. (☎72 41 34. Breakfast included. Doubles 190-320kn.) Walk 2km east along the bay from the bus station to reach **Camping Padova ❶** and its lovely beaches. (☎72 43 55; www.imperial.hr. Tent sites 42-64kn; 24-37kn per extra person. Tax 4.50-7kn.) **St. Maria ❸,** Dinka Dokule 6, serves Hungarian specialties in a beautiful medieval courtyard. (Entrees 60-105kn. Open daily 10am-2pm and 5pm-midnight.) A **supermarket** neighbors the post office at Dalit 88. (Open daily 6am-10pm.) **Buses** arrive from Zagreb (5½hr., M-Sa 3 per day, 157kn). The **tourist office** is behind the bus station. (☎77 11 11; www.tzg-rab.hr. Open daily 8am-10pm.) **Postal Code:** 51280.

DALMATIAN COAST

Touted as the new French Rivera, the Dalmatian Coast offers a stunning seascape of unfathomable beauty set against a backdrop of dramatic mountains. With more than 1100 islands, Dalmatia is not only Croatia's largest archipelago, but also has the cleanest and clearest waters in the Mediterranean.

ZADAR

☎023

Zadar (pop. 77,000), crushed in both WWII and the recent Balkan war, is now beautifully rejuvenated. With the extraordinary Kornati Islands just a boat ride away and a history so well preserved that Roman ruins serve as city benches, Zadar is the quintessential Dalmatian city. Rushing seawater causes pipes beneath the 70m **Sea Organ** to play notes at random. The resulting music sounds like a choir of whales. In the ancient Forum in the center of the peninsula, the circular, Byzantine **St. Donat's Church** (Crkva Sv. Donata) sits atop the ruins of an ancient Roman temple. (Open daily 9am-2pm and 4-8pm. 5kn.)

At the entrance of the Old Town, **Miatours,** Vrata Sv. Krševana, books private rooms and transportation to nearby islands. (☎254 400; www.miatours.hr. Open Jul.-Aug. 8am-8pm; Sept.-Jun. 8am-2:30pm. Singles 100-150kn; doubles 200-300kn. AmEx/DC/MC/V. **Trattoria Canzona,** Stomorica 8, is always packed with young Zadarians. (☎212 081. Entrees 30-70kn. Open daily 10am-11pm. Cash only.) **Train** run from Ante Starevića 4 for: Dubrovnik (8hr., 9 per day, 155-207kn); Ljubljana, Slovenia (8hr., 1 per day, 207kn); Split (3hr., 2 per hr., 77-91kn); Zagreb (5hr., 1 per hr., 103-107kn). From the stations, go through the pedestrian underpass and continue to Zrinsko-Frankopanska. Follow this to the water, turn left, and at the gate of Stari Grad, turn onto Široka, the main street. The **tourist office,** M. Klaića bb, in

JNTYING THE CRAVAT

While many might suspect the necktie to have originated in Italy or France, the word *cravat* (from *hrvat,* or *croat* in Serbo-Croatian) clues us into its real roots. According to legend, a Croatian woman once tied a scarf around her true love's neck as a token of her devotion; the historical record shows that the tie was first worn by Croatian soldiers fighting in the service of Austria during the Thirty Years' War.

Recently, Croatia has launched a campaign to use its *cravat* heritage to establish ties with the rest of the world. In 1990, the nonprofit organization Academia Cravatica was born, committed entirely to promoting what the group's founder Marijan Busic calls "Croatia's contribution to the global culture." In 2003, the arena in Pula served as the neck for the largest cravat in the world, an 808m long red "mega-tie." Recently, the organization opened a traveling art exhibit, The Challenge of the Tie, which addresses the neckwear's ambiguous purpose through the work of Croatian and international artists. After visiting the Baltics, the exhibit toured to acclaim in early 2005, bringing "tie art" and Croatian culture to audiences in Egypt and South Africa.

As British historian Norman Davies observes, "Of course, those who deny the influence of Europe's smaller nations should remember that Croats hold us all by our necks."

the far corner of Narodni trg, has free maps. (☎31 m61 66; tzg-zadar@zd.tel.hr. Open daily 8am-midnight; low season 8am-8pm.) **Postal Code:** 23000.

TROGIR ☎021

In Trogir (pop. 1500), made up of Trogir and Čiovo Islands, medieval buildings crowd winding streets and palmed promenades open onto lush parks. The Renaissance **North Gate** on Trogir Island frames the entrance to the **Stari Grad** (Old Town). **Trg Ivana Pavla,** the central square, contains most sights, including the **Cathedral of St. Lawrence** (Crkva sv. Lovre). Trogir's stone-carving tradition is chronicled in two buildings of the **City Museum of Trogir:** in the **lapidary,** through the arch in front of the North Gate, and in the **convent of St. Nicholas,** off Kohl-Genscher past Trg Ivana Pavla. (Lapidary open M-Sa 9am-1pm and 5-9pm. Convent open M-Sa 8am-12:30pm and 3-7:30pm. 10kn each, students 5kn.) At the tip of the island lie the remains of the **Fortress of Kamerlengo,** now an open-air cinema. (Open M-Sa 9am-11pm. 10kn, students free. Movies 20-25kn.) Trogir's best beaches lie on **Čiovo Island,** accessible from Trogir Island by the Čiovski Bridge, past Trg Ivana Pavla.

Čipiko, Gradska 41, across from the cathedral, arranges private rooms in town. (☎88 15 54. Open daily 8am-8pm. July-Aug. singles 200kn; doubles 330kn; tax 7.50kn. May-June and Sept. 150kn/250kn; tax 5.50kn.) To get to the beachside hotel **Prenocište Saldun ❶,** Sv. Andrije 1, cross Čiovski Bridge and take Put Balana up the hill, keeping right. (☎80 60 53. Call ahead. Singles 76kn; tax 6kn.) **Čiovka** supermarket is next to Atlas. (Open M-Sa 5:30am-9pm, Su 6:30am-8pm.) Lively waterfront cafes line Obala b. Berislavića. **Buses** from Zagreb stop in front of the station on the mainland on their way south to Split (30min., 22kn). Local bus #37 also runs to Split (45min., 2-3 per hr., 19kn). Across Čiovski Bridge, **Atlas,** Obala kralja Zvonimira 10, has bus schedules and ferry info. (☎88 42 79. Open in summer M-Sa 8am-9pm, Su 8am-noon.) The **tourist office,** Trg Ivana Pavla 2, gives out free maps of the city. (☎88 14 12. Open M-Sa 8am-9pm, Su 8am-noon and 5-7pm.) **Postal Code:** 21220.

SPLIT ☎021

With a welter of activities and nightlife, this city by the sea is more a cultural center than a beach resort. The **Stari Grad** (Old Town), wedged between a mountain range and palm-lined waterfront, sprawls around a luxurious **palace** where the Roman emperor Diocletian summered when not busting Christians. City **cellars** are near the palace entrance, across from the taxis on **Obala hrvatskog narodnog preporoda;** turn either way to wander the haunting labyrinth. (Open M-F 9am-9pm,

Sa-Su 10am-6pm. 10kn.) Through the cellars and up the stairs is the open-air **peristyle.** The Catholic **cathedral** to its right is the world's oldest; ironically, it was once Diocletian's mausoleum (5kn). The view from the adjoining **Bell Tower of St. Dominus** (Zvonik sv. Duje) is incredible. (Cathedral and tower open daily 8:30am-9:30pm. Cathedral 5kn. Tower 5kn.) A 25min. walk along the waterfront, the **Meštrović Gallery** (Galerija Ivana Meštrovića), Šetaliste Ivana Meštrovića 46, gathers works by Croatia's most famous modern sculptor. (Open June-Aug. Tu-Sa 9am-1pm and 5-8pm, Su 9am-2pm; Sept.-May Tu-Sa 10am-4pm, Su 10am-2pm. 15kn, students 10kn.) At night, locals skinny-dip at **Bačvice beach,** near a strip of waterfront bars.

The **Daluma Travel Agency,** Obala kneza domagoja 1, near the train station, books private rooms. (☎33 84 84; www.daluma-travel.htnet.hr. May-Oct. singles 230-255kn; doubles 340-380kn. Tourist tax 6kn. Discounts on stays longer than 4 nights. Open M-F 7am-9pm, Sa 8am-2pm.) The new **Al's Place ❷,** Kruziceva 10, is the first hostel in Split, with an enthusiastic staff and group excursions. There are only 12 beds, so book ahead. (☎098 918 29 23; www.hostelsplit.com. June-Aug. 120kn; Sept.-May. 100kn. Cash only.) For great views, at **Jugo Restoran ❷,** Uvala Baluni bb, face the water on Obala hrv. and walk right along the waterfront for 10min., following the curves onto Branimirova Obala; pass the marina, ascend the hill, and follow the signs. (Entrees 30-200kn. Open daily 11am-midnight.) A **supermarket** is at Svačićeva 4. (Open daily 7am-10pm.) **Buses** (☎33 84 83, schedule info 060 32 73 27) run to: Dubrovnik (4½hr., 19 per day, 89-122kn); Ljubljana, Slovenia (11hr., 1 per day, 260kn); Zagreb (8hr., 2 per hr., 140kn). **Ferries** (☎33 83 33) depart from the terminal across from the train and bus stations to Dubrovnik (8hr., 5 per week, 97kn) and Ancona, Italy (10hr., 4 per week, 274kn). From the bus station, follow Obala kneza domagoja (also called Riva) until Obala hrv., which runs roughly east-west. The **tourist office** is at Obala hrv. 12. (☎34 71 00. Open M-F 8am-9pm, Sa 8am-10pm.) **Postal Code:** 21000.

HVAR ISLAND ☎021

One of the most glorious isles in Europe, the thin, 88km Hvar Island grants its visitors breathtaking views of mainland mountains from its own high, rugged hills; below these lies beach enough for the many tourists that swarm here in July and August. From mid-June to early October, the **Hvar Summer Festival** brings outdoor music and drama performances (30-50kn) to the island's Franciscan monastery and elsewhere. Virtually the only place with a name is the main square, **Trg Sv. Stjepana,** directly below the bus station by the waterfront. From here, facing the sea, take a left along the waterfront to reach the tourist office and ferry terminal; a right leads to rock, pebble, and concrete beaches and the major hotels. Also to the right, stairs lead to a 13th-century **Venetian fortress** with marine archaeological relics. (Open daily 8am-midnight. 10kn.) Nearby, the **Hellish Islands** (Pakleni Otoci) include Palmižana beach, which has sparse sand and a nudist area at the far tip of the cove. (Taxi boats every 30min. 10am-6:30pm, round-trip 20-40kn.)

Pelegrini Tours, Riva bb, next to the post office, books rooms. (☎74 27 43; pelegrini@inet.hr. Open daily 7am-1pm and 5-9pm. High season singles and doubles 269-350kn.) *Sobe* (private room) signs litter the area down the waterfront from the main square. **Luna ❷,** up the steps from the square to the fortress, has a gorgeous rooftop terrace. The fettuccine with salmon (60kn) is especially tasty. (☎74 86 95. Open daily noon-3pm and 6pm-midnight.) For cheap and delicious grilled sandwiches, try **Fast Food Hello ❶,** in the main square, across from the tourist office. (Sandwiches 18-22kn. Bruschetta and mini-pizzas 20-30kn. Open daily 8am-3am. Cash only.) There is a large **Konzum** market next to the open-air market and bus station, at Dolac bb. (Open daily 7am-10pm.) At the end of Riva past the Jadrolinija office, waterfront **Carpe Diem** has a hip crowd and loud, live DJs. (Open daily 9am-2am.) **Ferries** run from Split to Stari Grad, Hvar's Old Town (1-2hr., 3-6 per day, 32kn);

from there, **buses** go to Hvar Town (25min., 7 per day, 15kn). A catamaran (1hr., 1 per day, 32kn) and a ferry (2hr., 2 per day, 32kn) run directly from Split to Hvar Town. To reach the bus station from the marina, walk through Trg Sv. Stjepana, bearing left of the church. **Jadrolinija,** Riva bb, on the left tip of the waterfront, sells ferry tickets. (☎74 11 32. Open M-Sa 5:30am-1pm and 3-8pm; Su 8-9am, noon-1pm, and 3-4pm.) The **tourist office,** Trg Sv. Stjepana 16, has island maps (20kn) and bus schedules. (☎74 10 59; www.tzhvar.hr. Open M-F 8am-8pm, Sa-Su 8am-1pm and 4-8pm; low season daily 8:30am-noon.) **Postal Code:** 21450.

BRAČ ISLAND: BOL ☎021

Central Dalmatia's largest island, Brač is an ocean-lover's paradise. Most visitors come here for **Zlatni rat,** a peninsula of white pebble beach surrounded by emerald waters, just a short walk from the town center of Bol. The 1475 **Dominican Monastery,** on the eastern tip of Bol, displays Tintoretto's altar painting *Madonna with Child.* (Open daily 10am-noon and 5-8pm. 10kn.) There are five **campsites** around Bol; the largest is **Kito ❶,** Bračka cesta bb, on the road into town. (☎63 55 51. Open May-Sept. Tent sites 44kn per person.) The **ferry** from Split docks at Supetar (1hr., 7-13 per day, 23kn). From there, take a **bus** to Bol (1hr., 7-13 per day, 15kn). The last bus back to the ferry leaves at 7pm. From the bus station, walk right, with your back to the water, for 5min. to reach the **tourist office,** Porad bolskich pomorca bb, on the far side of the small marina. (☎63 56 38; www.bol.hr. Open daily 8:30am-10pm; low season 8:30am-2pm and 5-9pm.) **Adria Tours,** Obala Vladimira Nazora 28, to the left with your back to the sea from the bus station, books rooms and rents vehicles. (☎63 59 66; www.adria-bol.hr. Rooms July-Aug. 1126-216kn. Tax 10kn. 20% discount for stays over 4 nights. Cars 400-500kn per day. Scooters 200kn per day. Open daily 8am-10pm.) **Postal Code:** 21420.

KORČULA ☎020

Within sight of the mainland, the macchia thickets and slender cypresses of Korčula mark the birthplace of Marco Polo. Sacred monuments and churches date from the time of the Apostles. The **Festival of Sword Dances** enlivens the island in July and August. (www.moreska.hr. 80kn; tickets available from tourist agencies.) **Marko Polo,** Biline 5, can arrange rooms. (☎71 54 00; www.korcula.com. Singles 150-188kn; doubles 210-263kn. Open daily 8am-9pm.) **The Korčula Backpacker ❶,** Hrvatske Bratske Zajednice 6, is the only hostel in Korčula Town. The young owner likes to party, but also provides a wealth of information on the area. (☎098 997 6353. Dorms 90kn.) **Fresh ❶,** right next to the bus station, specializes in wraps (20-25kn) and smoothies (20kn). They also have a library of English-language books and periodicals. (☎091 896 7509. Open daily 8am-2am. Cash only.) **Adio Mare ❷,** Marka Pola bb, serves authentic local specialties. (Entrees 40-80kn. Open M-Sa 5:30pm-midnight, Su 6pm-midnight.) **Buses** board ferries to the mainland and head to Dubrovnik (3½hr., 2 per day, 77kn) and Zagreb (11-13hr., 1 per day, 209kn). **Ferries** run to Dubrovnik (3½hr., 5 per week, 79kn) and Split (4½hr., 1 per day, 97kn). To reach the **tourist office,** face the water and walk left along the main street as it curves from the marina; look for the glass building just before Hotel Korčula. (Open M-Sa 8am-3pm and 4-8pm, Su 9am-1pm.) **Postal Code:** 20260.

DUBROVNIK ☎020

George Bernard Shaw once wrote: "Those who seek Paradise on earth should come to Dubrovnik." Although it would be hard for any location to live up to such praise, a stroll through the winding lanes of the Old Town *(Stari Grad)* or an evening spent watching the sun set into the sea from the city walls reveals why this Venetian city merits such praise.

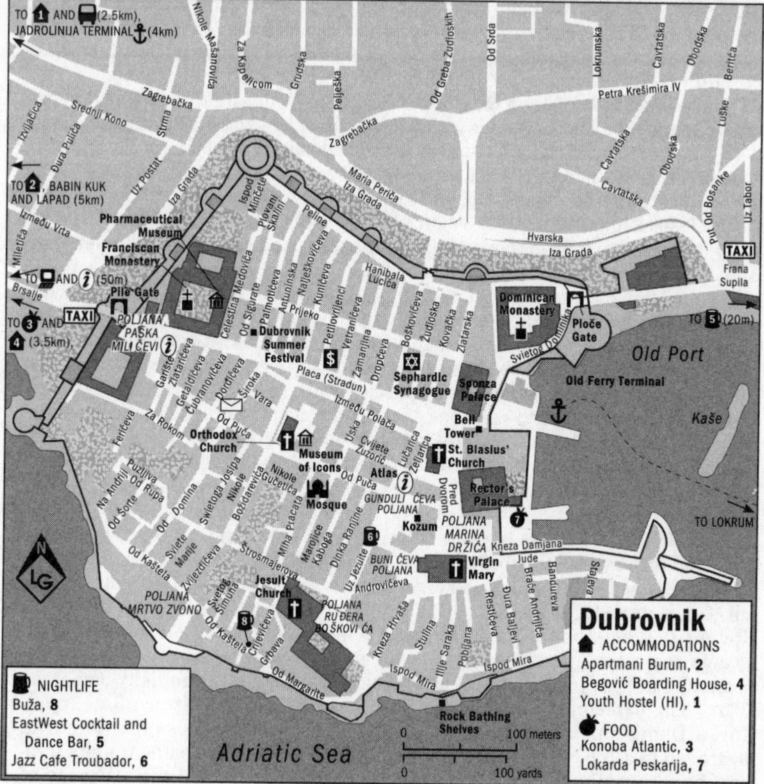

TRANSPORTATION AND PRACTICAL INFORMATION. Jadrolinija **ferries** (☎41 80 00; www.jadrolinija.hr) depart opposite Obala S. Radića 40 for: Bari, Italy (9hr., 5 per week, 329kn); Korčula (3½hr., 4 per week, 79kn); Split (8hr., 4 per day, 115kn). **Buses** (☎35 70 88) run from Pt. Republike 19 to: Ljubljana, Slovenia (14hr., 1 per day, 380kn); Split (4½hr., 16 per day, 125kn); Trieste (15hr., 1 per day, 340kn); Zagreb (11hr., 8 per day, 180kn). To reach Stari Grad, face away from the station and turn left onto Ante Starčevića; follow it uphill to the Pile Gate (25min.). To reach the ferries from the station, head left and then bear right at the fork (5min.). All local buses except #5, 7, and 8 go to the Pile Gate (8kn at kiosks, 10kn from the driver). From there, walk away from Stari Grad to reach the **tourist office,** Ante Starčevića 7, for free maps and cheap Internet. (☎42 75 91; ured.pile@tzdubrovnik.hr. Internet 20kn per hr. Open daily June-Sept. 8am-8pm; Oct.-May 8am-3pm.) **Turistička Zajednica Grada Dubrovnika,** Cvijete Zuzorić 1/2, second floor, distributes the free and invaluable *City Guide*. (☎32 38 87; www.tzdubrovnik.hr. Open June-Aug. M-F 8am-4pm, Sa 9am-3pm, Su 9am-noon; Sept.-May M-F 8am-4pm.) The **post office,** Široka 8, in Stari Grad, has a number of public telephones and offers Western Union services. (☎32 34 27. Open M-F 7:30am-9pm, Sa 10am-5pm.) **Postal Code:** 20108.

ACCOMMODATIONS AND FOOD. A private room tends to be the cheapest and most comfortable option for two; arrange one through **Atlas,** Cira Carica 3 and at kiosks throughout the city. (☎41 80 01; www.atlas-croatia.com. Open June-

Aug. M-Sa 8am-8pm, Su 8am-1pm; Sept.-May M-Sa 8am-7pm. Singles 100-150kn; doubles 120-375kn.) For even cheaper rooms, haggle with locals holding "*sobe*" signs around the ferry and bus terminals. Take bus #6 two stops past the Lapad post office, cross the street, head uphill on Mostarska, and turn left at Dubravkina to reach **Apartmani Burum ❷**, Dubravkina 16 in Babin Kuk. This social guest-house near the beach is popular with backpackers. (☎43 54 67. Pick up available. 2- to 3-bed dorms 100-125kn.) **Begović Boarding House ❷**, Primorska 17, offers 10 spacious doubles in a cozy villa with TVs and a terrace shaded by fig trees. Call ahead and Sado, the owner, will pick you up from either terminal. (☎43 51 91. Doubles 200-240kn; triples 240-300kn.) The **HI Youth Hostel ❶**, b. Josipa Jelačića 15/17, has small but clean rooms. With your back to the bus station, turn left onto Ante Starčevića, right at ul. Pera Rudenjaka, and left at the end of the street onto b. Josipa Jelačića. Look for the hidden HI sign on the left right after #17. The entrance is at the top of the stairs on the right. (☎42 32 41. Breakfast 5kn. Check-out 10am. Curfew 2am. Beds 85-120kn. 10kn HI discount.) **Lokarda Peskarija ❶**, on Na Ponti bb, has fresh, cheap seafood. From the bell tower, take a right out on Pred Dvorum and the first left out of the city walls. (☎32 47 50. Seafood 30-35kn. Open daily 8am-midnight.) Take bus #6 to the Lapad post office, follow the walk-way, then take a right up the stairs to reach **Konoba Atlantic ❷**, a tiny, family-run restaurant with delicious bread, pasta, and seafood. (☎098 185 96 25. Entrees 48-260kn. Open daily noon-11pm.)

SIGHTS. **Stari Grad** is packed with churches, museums, monasteries, palaces, and fortresses; the most popular are along **Placa.** The entrance to the 2km long limestone **city wall** (gradske zidine) lies just inside the Pile Gate, on the left. Go at dusk to be dazzled by the sunset. (Open daily May-Oct. 9am-7pm; Nov.-Apr. 10am-3pm. 30kn.) The 14th-century **Franciscan Monastery** (Franjevački samostan), next to the city wall entrance on Placa, houses the oldest pharmacy in Europe (est. 1317) and a related museum. (Open daily 9am-6pm. 10kn.) The **Cathedral of the Assumption of the Virgin Mary** (Riznica Katedrale), Kneza Damjana Jude 1, is built on the site of a Romanesque cathedral, destroyed in a 1667 earthquake and a 7th-century Byzantine cathedral. Its treasury houses relics collected by Richard the Lionheart and the "Diapers of Jesus." (Cathedral open daily 6:30am-8pm. Treasury open M-Sa 8am-5:30pm, Su 11am-5:30pm. Cathedral free. Treasury 7kn.) The 19th-century **Serbian Orthodox Church** (Pravoslavna Crkva) and its **Museum of Icons** (Muzej Ikona), Od Puča 8, stand as a symbol of Dubrovnik's tolerance. (Church open daily 8am-noon and 5-7pm. Free. Museum open M-Sa 9am-2pm. 10kn.)

As tempting as it may be to stroll through the hills above Dubrovnik or wander the unpaved paths on Lopud, both may still be laced with **landmines.** Stick to paved paths and beaches.

BEACHES. Outside the fortifications of Stari Grad are a number of **rock shelves** for sunning and swimming. To reach a pristine **pebble beach** from the bell tower, turn left onto Svetog Dominika, bear right after the footbridge, and continue on Frana Supila. Descend the stairs by the post office. For a surreal seaside swim, take a dip in the cove at the foot of the old **Hotel Libertas.** The hotel was damaged during the war and then abandoned; now it looks like a post-apocalyptic movie set. Walk 10min. along Starčevića, then take a left after the hotel. Ferries shuttle daily from the Old Port (20min., 9am and every 30min. 10am-6pm, round-trip 35kn) to the nearby island of **Lokrum,** which has a nude beach; once there, look for the FKK signs. More modest travelers can stroll through the **nature preserve.**

FESTIVALS AND NIGHTLIFE. Dubrovnik becomes a party scene and cultural mecca from mid-July to mid-August during the **Dubrovnik Summer Festival** (Dubrovački Ljetni Festival). The **festival office** on Placa has schedules and tickets. (☎42 88 64; www.dubrovnik-festival.hr. Open daily during the festival 8:30am-9pm, tickets 9am-2pm and 3-7pm. 50-300kn.)

By night Dubrovnik's crowds gravitate to bars in Stari Grad and cafes on Buničeva Poljana, where live bands and street performers turn up in summer. At **EastWest Cocktail and Dance Bar,** Frana Supila bb, dressed-to-impress clientele relax on the bar's plush white divans and recline on leather sofas directly on the beach. (Beer 12-30kn. Mixed drinks 40-100kn. Open daily 8am-3am.) Enjoy live jazz and occasional belly dancing at **Jazz Cafe Troubador,** Bunićeva 2. (Beer 18-40kn. Wine 40kn. Open daily 10am-1am, later in summer.) From the open-air market, climb the stairs toward the monastery, veer left and follow the signs marked "Cool Drinks and the Most Beautiful View" along Od Margarite to **Buža,** Crijeviceva 9. Under the city walls, this laidback watering hole perched above the Adriatic has spectacular sunsets. (Beer 17-22kn. Open daily 9am-late.)

DAYTRIP FROM DUBROVNIK: LOPUD ISLAND. Less than an hour from Dubrovnik is Lopud, an enchanting island of the Elafiti Archipelago. The tiny village's white buildings, chapels, and parks stretch along the waterfront *(obala)*. A short walk along the shore leads to an abandoned **monastery,** which can be explored—beware of crumbling floors. The island's highlight is its **beach,** Plaža Šunj. Arguably the best beach in Croatia, this cove has one thing that most of the Dalmatian Coast lacks: sand. **Ferries** run from Dubrovnik to Lopud (50min.; in summer M-Sa 4 per day, Su 1 per day; round-trip 26kn). The beach is on the opposite side of the island from the village. Facing the water, walk left and turn left onto the road between the high wall and the palm park; look for the Konoba Barbara sign and continue over the hill, keeping right when the path forks (15min.).

CZECH REPUBLIC (ČESKÁ REPUBLIKA)

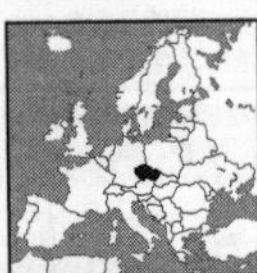

From the Holy Roman Empire through the USSR, the Czechs have long stood at a crossroads of international affairs. Unlike many of their neighbors, the citizens of this small, landlocked country have rarely resisted as armies marched across their borders, often choosing to fight with words instead of weapons. As a result, Czech towns and cities are among the best-preserved and most beautiful in Europe. Today, the path to the Czech Republic is well beaten.

DISCOVER CZECH REPUBLIC: SUGGESTED ITINERARIES

THREE DAYS You know where to go. Stroll across the **Charles Bridge** (p. 244) to see **Prague Castle** (p. 246), leave the beaten-tourist-path to explore areas like **Josefov** (p. 245), and have some beer.

ONE WEEK Keep exploring Prague (5 days; p. 237); there's plenty more to see. Relax at the **Petřín Hill Gardens** (p. 246) and visit the **Troja** chateau (p. 247). Once you need a break from the big city, head to **Český Krumlov** (2 days; p. 253) for hiking, biking, and another ancient castle.

BEST OF CZECH REPUBLIC, THREE WEEKS. Begin with 2 weeks in **Prague,** including a daytrip to the **Terezín** concentration camp (p. 249). Then spend 4 days in UNESCO-protected **Český Krumlov** getting to know the bike trails and floating down the **Vltava River** in an inner tube. Check out the weird **Revolving Theater** while you're at it. Wrap things up with 3 days in Olomouc, making sure to leave time for a daytrip to the gorgeous, Renaissance **Kroměříž** chateau (p. 255).

ESSENTIALS

FACTS AND FIGURES

Official Name: Czech Republic.

Capital: Prague.

Major Cities: Brno, České Budějovice, Český Krumlov.

Population: 10,250,000.

Time Zone: GMT +1.

Language: Czech.

Religions: Unaffiliated (68%), Roman Catholic (27%), Protestant (2%), other (3%).

WHEN TO GO

The Czech Republic is the most touristed country in Eastern Europe. It may be wise to avoid the high season (July-Aug.), though the weather is most pleasant. Book in advance for travel to any area during festivals and holidays. The best mix of good weather and minimal crowds will probably be in late spring or early fall.

DOCUMENTS AND FORMALITIES

EMBASSIES AND CONSULATES. Foreign embassies for the Czech Republic are in Prague (p. 237). Czech embassies and consulates abroad include: **Australia,** 8 Culgoa Circuit, O'Malley, Canberra, ACT 2606 (☎02 6290 1386; canberra@embassy.mzv.cz); **Canada,** 251 Cooper St., Ottawa, ON K2P OG2 (☎613-562-3875; ottawa@embassy.mzv.cz); **Ireland,** 57 Northumberland Rd., Ballsbridge, Dub-

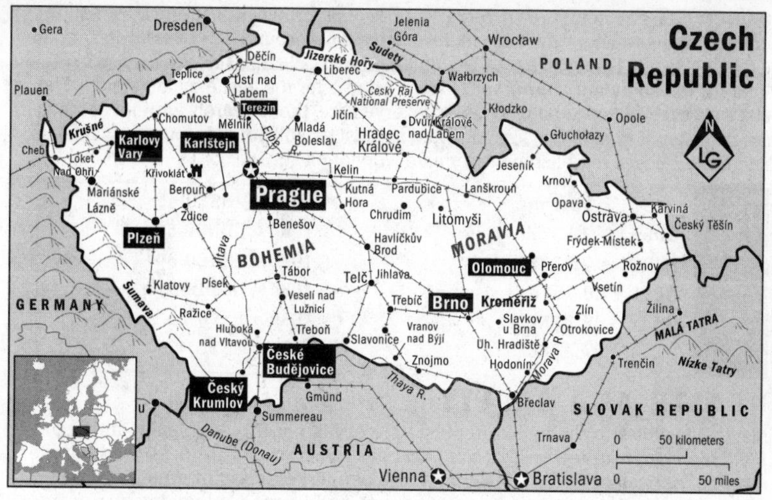

lin 4 (☎01 668 1135; dublin@embassy.mzv.cz); **New Zealand,** see Australia; **UK,** 26-30 Kensington Palace Gardens, London W8 4QY (☎20 7243 1115; www.mzv.cz/london); **US,** 3900 Spring of Freedom St. NW, Washington, D.C. 20008 (☎202-274-9100; www.mzv.cz/washington).

VISA AND ENTRY INFORMATION. Visas are available at your embassy or consulate, but **not** at the border. Processing takes seven to 10 days when submitted by mail, five days when submitted in person. With the application, you must submit your passport; one photograph (two if applying to the Czech consulate in Los Angeles) glued—not stapled—to the application; a self-addressed, stamped envelope (certified or overnight mail); and a cashier's check or money order.

ENTRANCE REQUIREMENTS

Passport: Required for all travelers.

Visa: Not required for stays under 90 days for citizens of Australia, Canada, Ireland, New Zealand, and the US. Citizens of the UK may remain in the country for up to 180 days without a visa.

Letter of Invitation: Not required for citizens of Australia, Canada, Ireland, New Zealand, the UK, and the US.

Inoculations: None required. Recommended up-to-date on DTaP (diphtheria, tetanus, and pertussis), Hepatitis A, Hepatitis B, MMR (measles, mumps, and rubella), Polio booster, and Typhoid.

TOURIST SERVICES AND MONEY

TOURIST OFFICES. Municipal tourist offices in major cities provide info on sights and events, distribute lists of hostels and hotels, and often book rooms. In Prague these offices may be crowded and staffed by disgruntled employees. **CKM,** a national student tourist agency, is helpful for young travelers, booking hostel beds and issuing ISICs and HI cards. Most bookstores sell a national hiking map, *Soubor turistických map,* with an English-language key.

MONEY. The Czech unit of currency is the **koruna** (crown; **Kč**), plural *koruny*. The country plans to adopt the euro in 2009. **Inflation** is around 3.2%. **Banks** offer good exchange rates. **Komerční banka** is a common bank chain. **ATMs** are everywhere—look for the abundant *"Bankomat"* signs—and offer the best exchange rates. **Traveler's checks** can be exchanged almost everywhere, though rarely without commission. MasterCard and Visa are accepted at most establishments, but many hostels and other budget establishments remain wary of plastic.

KORUNY (Kč)		
	AUS$1 = 18.15Kč	10Kč = AUS$0.55
	CDN$1 = 19.76Kč	10Kč = CDN$0.51
	EUR€1 = 29.33Kč	10Kč = EUR€0.34
	NZ$1 = 16.75Kč	10Kč = NZ$0.60
	UK£1 = 43.29Kč	10Kč = UK£0.23
	US$1 = 24.15Kč	10Kč = US$0.41

HEALTH AND SAFETY

Medical facilities in the Czech Republic are of high quality, especially in Prague. Major foreign insurance policies are accepted. Pharmacies are *Lékárna*, and the most common chain is Droxies; they and supermarkets carry international brands of *náplast* (bandages), *tampóny* (tampons), and *kondomy* (condoms). For prescription drugs and aspirin, look for pharmacies marked with a green cross. Petty **crime** has increased dramatically in recent years, especially on public transportation; beware of pickpockets in Prague's main squares and tourist sites.

Women traveling alone generally experience few problems in the Czech Republic. However, caution should be exercised while riding public transportation, especially after dark. **Minorities** generally do not encounter any trouble, though travelers with darker skin might be mistaken for Roma (gypsies) and discriminated against. Gay nightlife is taking off in the Czech Republic, but open displays of **homosexuality** may not be accepted; GLBT travelers may receive stares and are advised to remain cautious in public situations, especially outside Prague.

EMERGENCY	**Police:** ☎158. **Ambulance:** ☎112. **Fire:** ☎150.

TRANSPORTATION

BY PLANE. Most major European carriers, including **Air Canada, Air France, American Airlines, British Airways, ČSA, Delta, KLM, Lufthansa,** and **SAS** fly into Prague International Airport (PRG).

BY TRAIN. The easiest and cheapest way to travel between cities is by train. **Eastrail** is accepted in the Czech Republic, but **Eurail** is not. The fastest international trains are *EuroCity* and *InterCity* (*expresní;* marked in blue on schedules). *Rychlík* trains are fast domestic trains, (*zrychlený vlak;* marked in red). Avoid slow *osobní* trains, marked in white. Departures *(odjezdy)* are printed on yellow posters, arrivals *(příjezdy)* on white. Seat reservations (*místenka;* 10Kč) are recommended on express and international trains and for first-class seating.

BY BUS. Czech buses are efficient, but schedules can be confusing. For travel in the countryside, they're quicker and cheaper than trains. **ČSAD** runs national and international bus lines, and many European companies operate international service. Consult the timetables or buy your own bus schedule (25Kč) from kiosks.

BY CAR. Roads are well kept and **road-side assistance** is usually available. In addition to an International Driving Permit, US citizens must have a **US driver's license. Taxis** are safe, though many overcharge tourists, especially in Prague. Negotiate

the fare beforehand and make sure the meter is running, as exorbitant rates often result when cabbies "estimate" the fare. Calling a taxi service is often cheaper than flagging a cab. Although hitchhiking is common, *Let's Go* does not recommend it.

KEEPING IN TOUCH

PHONE CODES	**Country code:** 420. **International dialing prefix:** 00. For more information on how to place international calls, see inside back cover.

EMAIL AND THE INTERNET. Internet access is readily available throughout the Czech Republic. Internet cafes offer fast connections for about 1-2Kč per minute.

TELEPHONE. Card-operated phones (175Kč per 50 units; 320Kč per 100 units) are simpler to use than coin phones and easier to find. You can purchase **phone cards** *(telefonní karta)* at most tobacco stores *(tábaks)* and convenience stores *(trafika)*. To make domestic calls, simply dial the entire number. City codes no longer exist in the Czech Republic and dialing zero is not necessary. To make an international call to the Czech Republic, simply dial the country code followed by the phone number. Calls cost 8Kč per minute to Australia, Canada, the UK, or the US; 12Kč per minute to New Zealand. Dial ☎1181 for English-language info, ☎0800 12 34 56 for the international operator. International access codes include: **AT&T** (☎00 800 222 55288); **British Telecom** (☎00 420); **Canada Direct** (☎800 001 115); **MCI** (☎800 001 112); **Sprint** (☎00 420 87 187); and **Telstra Australia** (☎00 420 061 01).

MAIL. The postal system is reliable and efficient, though few postal employees speak English. A postcard to the US costs 12Kč, to Europe 9Kč. To send **airmail,** stress that you want your package to go on a plane *(letecky)*. Go to the customs office to send packages heavier than 2kg abroad. **Poste Restante** is generally available. Address envelopes as follows: First Name LAST NAME, POSTE RESTANTE, post office street address, postal code City, CZECH REPUBLIC.

LANGUAGE. Czech is a West Slavic language, closely related to Slovak and Polish. **English** is widely understood among young people, and **German** can be useful, especially in South Bohemia because of its proximity to the German and Austrian borders. In eastern regions, you're more likely to encounter **Polish. Russian** was taught to all school children under communism, but use it carefully, as the language is not always welcome. For a few choice expressions, see **Phrasebook: Czech,** p. 1057.

ACCOMMODATIONS AND CAMPING

CZECH REPUBLIC	❶	❷	❸	❹	❺
ACCOMMODATIONS	under 320Kč	320-500Kč	500-800Kč	800-1200Kč	over 1200Kč

University dorms are the cheapest options in July and August; two- to four-bed dorms cost 250-400Kč. **Hostels** (300-500Kč) are clean and safe, though they become scarce in areas with few students. **Pensions** are the next most affordable option at 600-800Kč, including breakfast. **Hotels** tend to be more luxurious and more expensive than hostels or pensions, from 1000Kč. From June to September reserve at least one week ahead in Prague, Český Krumlov, and Brno. Private homes are not nearly as popular (or cheap) as in the rest of Eastern Europe. Scan train stations for *"Zimmer frei"* signs. Quality varies; do not pay in advance. There are many **campgrounds** across the country; most are open only from mid-May to September.

FOOD AND DRINK

CZECH REPUBLIC	❶	❷	❸	❹	❺
FOOD	under 80Kč	80-110Kč	110-150Kč	150-200Kč	over 200Kč

Loving Czech cuisine starts with learning to pronounce *knedlíky* (KNED-lee-kee). These thick lumps of dough, feebly known in English as dumplings, are a staple. Meat lies at the heart of almost all main dishes; the **national meal** (known as *vepřo-knedlo-zelo*) is *vepřové* (roast pork), *knedlíky*, and *zelí* (sauerkraut). If you're in a hurry, grab *párky* (frankfurters) or *sýr* (cheese) at a food stand. **Vegetarian** restaurants serving meatless *(bez masa)* specialties are uncommon outside Prague; traditional restaurants serve few options beyond *smaženy sýr* (fried cheese) and *saláty* (salads), which may or may not contain meat products. Keeping **kosher** is feasible, but beware of pork, which often sneaks into Czech cuisine. Ask for *káva espresso* rather than just *káva:* the Czech brew may be unappealing to a Western palate. *Jablkový závin* (apple strudel) and *ovocné knedlíky* (fruit dumplings) are favorite sweets, but the most beloved is *koláč*—a tart filled with poppy-seed or sweet cheese. Moravian **wines** are of high quality. They're typically drunk at a *vinárna* (wine bar) that serves a variety of spirits, including *slivovice* (plum brandy) and *becherovka* (herbal bitter), the national drink. Local brews like *Plzeňský Prazdroj* (Pilsner Urquell), *Budvar*, and *Krusovice*, dominate the drinking scene.

HOLIDAYS AND FESTIVALS

Holidays: New Year's Day (Jan. 1); Easter Holiday (Apr. 16-17); May Day/Labor Day (May 1); Liberation Day (May 8); St. Cyril and Methodius Day (July 5); Jan Hus Day (July 6); Czech Statehood Day (Sept. 28); Independence Day (Oct. 28); Struggle for Freedom and Democracy Day (Nov. 17).

Festivals: The Czech Republic hosts a number of internationally renowned festivals. If you are planning to attend any of them, make sure to reserve a room and your tickets well in advance. Classical musicians and world-class orchestras descend on Prague (p. 237) for the Spring Festival held from mid-May to early June. Each June, the Five-Petaled Rose Festival, a boisterous medieval festival in Český Krumlov (p. 253) features music, dance, and a jousting tournament. Masopust, the Moravian version of Mardi Gras, is celebrated in villages across the Czech Republic from Epiphany to Ash Wednesday (Jan.-Mar.). Revelers dressed in animal masks feast, dance, and sing until Lent.

BEYOND TOURISM

INEX—Association of Voluntary Service, Senovážné nám. 24, 116 47 Praha 1, Czech Republic (☎420 234 621 527; www.inexsda.cz/en/index.php). Ecological and historical preservation efforts, as well as construction projects, in the Czech Republic.

The Prague Center for Further Education and Professional Development, Pštrossova 19, Nové Město, 110 00 Praha 1, Czech Republic (☎420 257 534 013; www.prague-center.cz/etlbar.html). Teaches courses on art, filmmaking, and design in Prague.

The Prague Post (www.praguepost.com). English-language newspaper with job ads.

University of West Bohemia, Univerzitní 8, 306 14 Plzeň, Czech Republic (☎420 377 631 111; www.zcu.cz). An international university centrally located in a student-friendly Czech brewery city.

World Wide Opportunities on Organic Farms (WWOOF), Main Office, P.O. Box 2675, Lewes BN7 1RB, England, UK (www.wwoof.org). Arranges volunteer work on organic and eco-conscious farms in the Czech Republic and around the world.

PRAGUE (PRAHA)

According to legend, Countess Libuše stood above the Vltava River and declared, "I see a grand city whose glory will touch the stars." Medieval kings, benefactors, and architects fulfilled that prophecy with cathedrals and palaces that reflected the status of Prague (pop. 1,200,000) as capital of the Holy Roman Empire. Prague's maze of alleys spawned legends of demons and occult forces, giving this "city of dreams" the dark mystique that inspired Franz Kafka's paranoid tales. Since the fall of the Iron Curtain, hordes of foreigners have flooded the city; in summer, tourists pack streets so tightly that crowd-surfing seems a viable method of transportation. Walk a few blocks away from the major sights, however, and you'll be a lone backpacker among cobblestone alleys and looming churches.

INTERCITY TRANSPORTATION

Flights: Ruzyně Airport (☎220 111 111), 20km northwest of the city. Take bus #119 to Metro A: Dejvická (daily 5am-midnight; 12Kč, luggage 6Kč per bag); buy tickets from kiosks or machines. **Airport buses** run by **Cedaz** (☎220 114 296) collect travelers from metro stops (5:30am-9:30pm 2 per hr.; nám. Republiky 90Kč, Dejvická 60Kč). **Taxis** to the airport are expensive (400-600Kč); try to settle on a price before departing.

Trains: Domestic ☎221 111 122, international 840 112 113; www.vlak.cz. Prague has 4 main terminals. **Hlavní nádraží** (☎224 615 786; Metro C: Hlavní nádraží) and **Nádraží Holešovice** (☎224 624 632; Metro C: Nádraží Holešovice) are the largest and cover most international service. Domestic trains leave **Masarykovo nádraží** (☎840 112 113; Metro B: nám. Republiky), on the corner of Hybernská and Havlíčkova, and from **Smíchovské nádraží** (☎972 226 150; Metro B: Smíchovské nádraží). International trains run to: **Berlin, Germany** (5hr., 11 per day, €52); **Budapest, Hungary** (7-9hr., 8 per day, €55); **Kraków, Poland** (9hr., 3 per day, €49); **Moscow, Russia** (35hr., 1 per day, €81); **Munich, Germany** (6hr., 2 per day, €49); **Vienna, Austria** (4½hr., 6 per day, €32); **Warsaw, Poland** (11-12hr., 3 per day, €67-77).

Buses: Schedule info ☎900 144 444; www.vlak-bus.cz. Open daily 6am-9pm. State-run **ČSAD** (Česká státní automobilová doprava; Czech National Bus Transport; ☎257 319 016) has several terminals. The biggest is **Florenc,** Křižíkova 4 (☎900 149 044). Metro B or C: Florenc. Info office open daily 6am-9pm. Buy tickets in advance. To: **Berlin, Germany** (7hr., 1 per day, 850Kč); **Budapest, Hungary** (8hr., 1 per day, 1550Kč); **Paris, France** (14hr., 3 per day, 2200Kč); **Vienna, Austria** (5hr., 1 per day, 600Kč). 10% ISIC discount. The **Tourbus** office (☎224 218 680; www.eurolines.cz), at the terminal, sells **Euroline** and airport bus tickets. Open M-F 7am-7pm, Sa 8am-7pm, Su 9am-7pm.

ORIENTATION

Spanning the **Vltava** River, greater Prague is a mess of suburbs and maze-like streets. Nearly everything of interest to the traveler lies within the compact downtown. The Vltava runs south-northeast through central Prague, separating **Staré Město** (Old Town) and **Nové Město** (New Town) from **Malá Strana** (Lesser Side). On the right bank, **Staroměstské náměstí** (Old Town Square) is the heart of Prague. From the square, the elegant **Pařížská ulice** (Paris Street) leads north to **Josefov,** the old Jewish ghetto. South of Staré Město, the Nové Město houses **Václavské náměstí** (Wenceslas Square), the commercial core of the city. West of Staroměstské nám., the **Karlův most** (Charles Bridge) spans the Vltava, connecting Staré Město with **Malostranské náměstí** (Lesser Town Square). **Pražský Hrad** (Prague Castle) looks over Malostranské nám. from **Hradčany** hill.

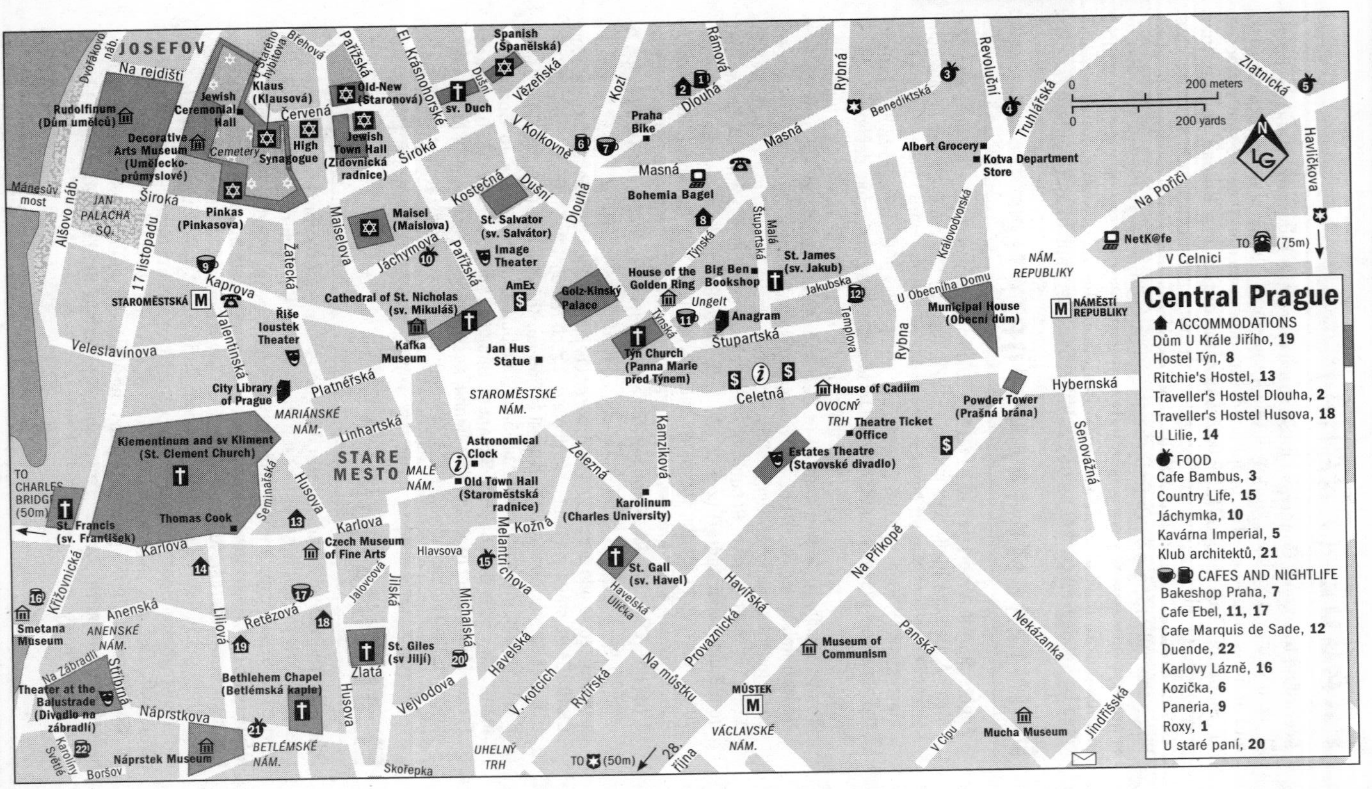
Central Prague
ACCOMMODATIONS
Dům U Krále Jiřího, 19
Hostel Týn, 8
Ritchie's Hostel, 13
Traveller's Hostel Dlouha, 2
Traveller's Hostel Husova, 18
U Lilie, 14
FOOD
Cafe Bambus, 3
Country Life, 15
Jáchymka, 10
Kavárna Imperial, 5
Klub architektů, 21
CAFES AND NIGHTLIFE
Bakeshop Praha, 7
Cafe Ebel, 11, 17
Cafe Marquis de Sade, 12
Duende, 22
Karlovy Lázně, 16
Kozička, 6
Paneria, 9
Roxy, 1
U staré paní, 20
200 meters
200 yards
Havlíčkova
Zlatnická
TO (75m)
V Celnici
Na Poříčí
NetK@fe
NÁMĚSTÍ REPUBLIKY
NÁM. REPUBLIKY
Truhlářská
Revoluční
Kotva Department Store
Albert Grocery
Králodvorská
Municipal House (Obecní dům)
U Obecního Domu
Powder Tower (Prašná brána)
Hybernská
Senovážná
Jindřišská
Nekázanka
Mucha Museum
V Cípu
Panská
Na Příkopě
Benediktská
Rybná
Rybna
Templová
Jakubská
House of Cadilm
OVOCNÝ TRH
Theatre Ticket Office
Estates Theatre (Stavovské divadlo)
Museum of Communism
MŮSTEK
VÁCLAVSKÉ NÁM.
Havířská
Provaznická
Na můstku
28. října
Rámová
Masná
Malá Štupartská
St. James (sv. Jakub)
Big Ben Bookshop
Anagram
Štupartská
Celetná
Dlouhá
Bohemia Bagel
Týnská
Ungelt
House of the Golden Ring
Týn Church (Panna Marie před Týnem)
Kamzíková
Praha Bike
Kozí
Golz-Kinský Palace
Karolinum (Charles University)
St. Gall (sv. Havel)
Havelská Ulička
Železná
TO (50m)
Rytířská
V. kotcích
Havelská
Spanish (Španělská)
Vězeňská
V Kolkovně
Dušní
St. Salvator (sv. Salvátor)
Image Theater
AmEx
Jan Hus Statue
STAROMĚSTSKÉ NÁM.
Astronomical Clock
Old Town Hall (Staroměstská radnice)
Kožná
Melantrichova
Michalská
UHELNÝ TRH
sv. Duch
El. Krásnohorské
Kostečná
Pařížská
Široká
Jáchymova
Cathedral of St. Nicholas (sv. Mikuláš)
Kafka Museum
MALÉ NÁM.
Hlavsova
Jilská
St. Giles (sv Jiljí)
Vejvodova
Skořepka
Old-New (Staronová)
Jewish Town Hall (Židovnická radnice)
Maisel (Maislova)
Maiselova
STARE MESTO
Linhartská
Platnéřská
Karlova
Czech Museum of Fine Arts
Jalovcová
Zlatá
Husova
Břehová
Červená
U Starého hřbitova
Klaus (Klausová)
High Synagogue
Žatecká
Říše Ioustek Theater
MARIÁNSKÉ NÁM.
Seminářská
Řetězová
Bethlehem Chapel (Betlémská kaple)
BETLÉMSKÉ NÁM.
Jewish Ceremonial Hall
Cemetery
Pinkas (Pinkasova)
Kaprova
Valentinská
City Library of Prague
Klementinum and sv Kliment (St. Clement Church)
Thomas Cook
Liliová
Náprstkova
JOSEFOV
Na rejdišti
Decorative Arts Museum (Uměleckoprůmyslové)
STAROMĚSTSKÁ
17 listopadu
Veleslavínova
Anenská
ANENSKÉ NÁM.
Stříbrná
Náprstek Museum
Rudolfinum (Dům umělců)
Dvořákovo nábř.
JAN PALACHA SQ.
Alšovo nábř.
Mánesův most
TO CHARLES BRIDGE (50m)
St. Francis (sv. František)
Křižovnická
Smetana Museum
Theater at the Balustrade (Divadlo na zábradlí)
Na Zábradlí
Karoliny Světlé
Boršov

Prague's **train station,** Hlavní nádraží, and Florenc **bus station** lie northeast of Václavské nám. All train and bus terminals are on or near the excellent metro. To reach Staroměstské nám., take Metro A line to Staroměstská and follow Kaprova away from the river. Bookstores sell an essential, indexed *plán města* (map).

LOCAL TRANSPORTATION

Public Transportation: Buy interchangeable tickets for the **Metro, tram,** and **bus** at newsstands, *tabák* kiosks, machines in stations, or DP (*Dopravní podnik;* transport authority) kiosks. Validate tickets in machines above escalators to avoid fines issued by plainclothes inspectors who roam transport lines. 3 **Metro** lines run daily 5am-midnight: A is green on maps, B yellow, C red. **Night trams** #51-58 and **buses** #502-514 and 601 run after the last Metro and cover same areas as day trams and buses (every 30min. 12:30-4:30am); look for dark blue signs with white letters at bus stops. The DP offices (☎222 646 350; www.dpp.cz. Open daily 7am-6pm), near the Jungmannovo nám. exit of the Můstek stop, sell **multi-day passes** (1-day 70Kč, 3-day 200Kč, 1-week 250Kč). 8Kč tickets are good for a 15min. ride or 4 stops. 12Kč ticket valid for 1hr., with transfers, for all travel in the same direction. Large bags and bikes 6Kč.

GOING THE DISTANCE. To avoid taxi scams, always ask in advance for a receipt *(Prosím, dejte mi paragon)* with distance traveled and price paid.

Taxis: Radiotaxi (☎272 731 848) or **AAA** (☎140 14). 30Kč flat rate plus 22Kč per km and 4Kč per min. waiting. These companies are particularly reliable.

PRACTICAL INFORMATION

TOURIST AND FINANCIAL SERVICES

Tourist Offices: Green "i"s mark tourist agencies, which book rooms and sell maps. **Pražská Informační Služba** (PIS; Prague Information Service; ☎12 444; www.pis.cz) is in the Old Town Hall. Open Apr.-Oct. M 11am-6pm, Tu-Su 9am-6pm; Nov.-Mar. M 11am-5pm, Tu-Su 9am-5pm. Branches at Na příkopě 20 and Hlavní nádraží (summer M-F 9am-7pm, Sa-Su 9am-5pm; low season M-F 9am-6pm, Sa 9am-3pm), and in the tower by the Malá Strana side of the Charles Bridge. (Open Apr.-Oct. daily 10am-6pm.)

Budget Travel: CKM, Mánesova 77 (☎222 721 595; www.ckm-praha.cz). Metro A: Jiřího z Poděbrad. Sells budget airfare to those under 26. Also books rooms from 250Kč. Open M-Th 10am-6pm, F 10am-4pm. **BIJ Wasteels** (☎224 641 954; www.wasteels.cz), on the 2nd fl. of Hlavní nádraží, sells discounted international train tickets to those under 26, and books couchettes and bus tickets. Open M-F 9am-7pm, Sa 9am-4pm. Wasteels tickets are also available from the **Czech Railways Travel Agency** (☎224 239 464) at Nádraží Holešovice. Open M-F 9am-5pm, Sa-Su 8am-4pm.

Passport Office: Foreigner Police Headquarters, Olšanská 2 (☎974 811 111). Metro A: Flora. From the Metro, turn right on Jičínská with the cemetery on your right and go right again on Olšanská. Or, take tram #9 from Václavské nám. toward Spojovací and get off at Olšanská. To get a **visa extension,** get a 90Kč stamp inside, line up at doors #2-12, and prepare to wait up to 2hr. Little English spoken. Open M-Tu and Th 7:30-11:30am and 12:15-3pm, W 8am-12:15pm and 1-5pm, F 7:30-11:30am.

Embassies and Consulates: Canada, Muchova 6 (☎272 101 800; www.canada.cz). Metro A: Hradčanská. Open M-F 8:30am-12:30pm and 1:30-4:30pm. **Ireland,** Tržiště 13 (☎257 530 061). Metro A: Malostranská. Open M-F 9:30am-12:30pm and 2:30-4:30pm. **UK,** Thunovská 14 (☎257 402 111). Metro A: Malostranská. Open M-Th 8:30am-5pm, F

8:30am-4pm. **US,** Tržiště 15 (☎257 530 663, after-hours emergency ☎253 12 00; www.usembassy.cz). Metro A: Malostranská. Open M-F 8am-4:30pm. **Australia,** Klimentská 10, 6th fl. (☎296 578 350; www.embassy.gov.au/cz.html) and **New Zealand,** Dykova 19 (☎222 514 672), have consulates; citizens should contact the UK embassy in an emergency. Australian consulate open M-Th 8:30am-5pm, F 8:30am-2pm.

Currency Exchange: Exchange counters are everywhere but their rates vary wildly. Never change money on the street. **Chequepoints** are convenient and open late, but usually charge a large commission or fee. **Komerční banka,** Na příkopě 33 (☎222 411 111), buys notes and checks for a 2% commission. 24hr. **ATMs** *(Bankomats)* abound and can offer the best rates, but often charge large fees.

American Express: Václavské nám. 56 (☎222 800 224). Metro A or C: Muzeum. AmEx ATM outside. Grants MC/V cash advances for a 3% commission. **Western Union** services available. Open daily 9am-7pm.

LOCAL SERVICES

Luggage Storage: Lockers in all train and bus stations take 2 5Kč coins. If these are full or if you need to store your cargo longer than 24hr., use the luggage offices to the left in the basement of **Hlavní nádraží** (15-30Kč per day; open 24hr.) or halfway up the stairs at **Florenc** (30Kč per day. Open daily 5am-11pm).

English-Language Bookstores: The Globe Bookstore, Pštrossova 6 (☎224 934 203; www.globebookstore.cz). Metro B: Národní třída. Exit Metro left on Spálená, make the 1st right on Ostrovní, then the third left on Pštrossova. Wide variety of new and used books and periodicals. Internet 1.50Kč per min. Open daily 10am-midnight.

Laundromat: Laundry Kings, Dejvická 16 (☎233 343 743). Metro A: Hradčanská. Exit metro to Dejvická, cross the street, and turn left. Wash 80Kč per 6kg, dry 90Kč. Open M-F 6am-10pm, Sa-Su 8am-10pm. Last wash 9:30pm.

EMERGENCY AND COMMUNICATION

Emergency: Police: ☎158. **Ambulance:** ☎0155. **Fire:** ☎150.

Medical Services: Na Homolce (Hospital for Foreigners), Roentgenova 2 (☎257 272 146, after hours 257 211 111; www.homolka.cz). Bus #167. Open M-F 8am-4pm. 24hr. emergency services. **Canadian Medical Center,** Velesavínská 1 (☎235 360 133, after hours 724 300 301; www.cmc.praha.cz). Open M-F 8am-6pm.

24hr. Pharmacy: U Lékárna Anděla, Štefánikova 6 (☎257 320 918, after hours 257 320 194). Metro B: Anděl. With your back to the train station, turn left and follow Nádražní until it becomes Štefánikova. For after-hours service, press the button marked "Pohotovost" to the left of the main door. Open M-F 7am-9pm, Sa-Su 8am-9pm.

Telephones: Phone cards cost 175Kč per 50 units at kiosks and post offices. Don't let kiosks rip you off. Pay phones also take coins (local calls from 4Kč per min.).

Internet Access: Prague is an Internet nirvana. **Bohemia Bagel,** Masná 2 (www.bohemiabagel.cz). Metro A: Staroměstská. 1.80Kč per min. Open M-F 7am-midnight, Sa-Su 8am-midnight. Another branch at Újezd 16. Open daily 9am-midnight.

Post Office: Jindřišská 14 (☎221 131 445). Metro A: Můstek. Airmail to the US takes 7-10 days. For **Poste Restante,** address mail: First name SURNAME, Poste Restante, Jindřišská 14, Praha 1 110 00, CZECH REPUBLIC. Open daily 2am-midnight. Tellers close 7pm. **Postal Code:** 1 110 00.

ACCOMMODATIONS AND CAMPING

Hotel prices are through the roof, but hostel rates have stabilized at around 300-600Kč per night. Hotel reservations are a must; they are also a good idea at the hostels that accept them. Most accommodations have 24hr. reception and require check-out by 10am. A growing number of Prague residents rent affordable rooms.

HOSTELS

If you tote a backpack in Hlavní nádraží or Holešovice, you will most likely be approached by hostel runners offering cheap beds. Many of these hostels are university dorms that students vacate from June to August, and often you'll be offered free transportation. These are convenient for those arriving in the middle of the night without reservations. If you prefer more than just a place to sleep, smaller establishments are a better bet. It's a good idea to call as soon as you know your plans, especially in summer. In Prague, staff at hostels typically speak English.

STARÉ MĚSTO

Hostel Týn, Týnská 19 (☎224 828 519; www.hostel-tyn.web2001.cz). Metro A: Staroměstská. From Staroměstské nám., head down Dlouhá, bear right on Masná, and again on Týnská. Clean, orderly facilities, small dorms, and a young crowd in the heart of Staré Město. English spoken. Dorms 400Kč; doubles 1100Kč. 200Kč deposit. ❷

Ritchie's Hostel, Karlova 9 (☎222 221 229; www.praguehostel.net). Metro A: Staroměstská, down Karlova from the Charles Bridge, past the small square. Surprisingly pleasant and in the thick of the tourist district. The ancient buildings are spare, but clean and functional. Dorms 450Kč; doubles 1890-2000Kč. MC/V. ❷

Travellers' Hostel, Dlouhá 33 (☎224 826 662; www.travellers.cz). Metro B: nám. Republiky. Seasonal branches at Husova 3 (☎222 220 078), Josefská (☎257 534 577), Střelecký Ostrov (☎224 932 991), U Lanové Dráhy 3 (☎257 312 403). Exit the Metro and follow Revoluční toward the river; turn left on Dlouhá. Unbeatable location and social atmosphere in the same building as the Roxy Club (p. 248). Breakfast included. Laundry 150Kč. Internet 1Kč per min. Book ahead in summer. Dorms 370-430Kč; singles 1120Kč, with bath 1300Kč; doubles 1240/1440Kč. 2- to 6-bed apartments 2100-3000Kč. 40Kč ISIC discount. ❷

NOVÉ MĚSTO AND VINOHRADY

Hostel U Melounu, Ke Karlovu 7 (☎224 918 322). Metro C: I.P. Pavlova. Follow Sokolská and go right on Na Bojišt then left onto Ke Karlovu. A historic building with great facilities. Bar and private garden. Breakfast included. Check-out 10am. Dorms 400Kč; singles 550Kč; doubles 900Kč. 30Kč ISIC discount. AmEx/MC/V. ❷

Hostel Advantage, Sokolská 11-13 (☎224 914 062; www.advantagehostel.cz). Metro C: I.P. Pavlova. From the Metro, take the stairs on the left leading to Ječná, take a left onto Sokolská. This beautifully tended hostel has simple rooms in a comfortable atmosphere. Breakfast included. Free Internet. Dorms 400Kč; doubles 1000Kč. 10% ISIC discount. MC/V. ❷

Pension Unitas Art Prison Hostel, Bartolomějská 9 (☎224 221 802; www.unitas.cz). Metro B: Národní třída. Cross Národní třída, head up Na Perštýně, and turn left on Bartolomějská. This former communist prison is now a clean and colorful hostel, though the rooms still feel like cells. Breakfast included. Reception 24hr. Book well ahead. Dorms 270Kč; singles 1100Kč; doubles 1400Kč; triples 1800Kč; quads 2100Kč. MC/V. ❶

Hostel Elf, Husitská 11 (☎222 540 963). From Metro B: Florenc, take bus #207 to U Památníku; the hostel is up the stairs through the wooden gate. Spacious rooms and a social atmosphere. Breakfast included. Free Internet. Dorms 290Kč; singles 700Kč, with bath 1000Kč; doubles 840/1200Kč. ❷

OUTSIDE THE CENTER

Hostel Boathouse, Lodnická 1 (☎241 770 051), south of the city center. Take tram #14 from Nářodni třída south toward Sídliště. Get off at Černý Kůň (20min.), go down the ramp to the left, and follow the yellow signs. Social atmosphere and caring staff generate relaxing atmosphere. Breakfast included. Dorms from 360Kč. ❶

Penzion v podzámčí, V podzámčí 27 (☎241 444 609; www.sleepinprague.com). From Metro C: Budějovická, take bus #192 and ask the driver to stop at Nad Rybníky. Homey hostel offers a personal touch. Dorms 330Kč; doubles 790Kč; triples 1080Kč. Low season reduced rates. 30Kč student discount. ❶

Hostel Sinkule, Zíkova 13 (☎224 320 202; www.bed.cz). Metro A: Dejvická. Cheap, tidy, and convenient university dorm near airport shuttle stop. Singles 400Kč; doubles 540Kč. 10% ISIC discount. Check-in 2pm. Check-out 9:30am. DC/MC/V. ❷

Welcome Hostel at Strahov Complex, Vaníčkova 7 (☎224 320 202), outside the center. Take bus #149 or 217 from Metro A: Dejvická to Koleje Strahov. Reception in Block 3. Basic rooms in high-rise dorms near the Castle. Inconveniently located, but there's always space. Open July-Sept. Singles 300Kč; doubles 440Kč. 10% ISIC discount. ❶

HOTELS AND PENSIONS

As tourists colonize Prague, hotels are upgrading their services and their prices; budget hotels are now quite scarce. Call several months ahead to book a room in summer and confirm by fax with a credit card.

Dům U Krále Jiřího (Hotel King George), Liliová 10 (☎222 220 925; www.kinggeorge.cz). Metro A: Staroměstská. Exit at nám. Jana Palacha. Walk down Křížovnická toward Charles Bridge, go left on Karlova, and take the 1st right. Gorgeous rooms with private bath worth every penny. Buffet breakfast included. Reception daily 7am-11pm. Singles 2250Kč; doubles 3100Kč; triples 4300Kč; apartments 3100Kč-6550Kč. Dec.-Feb. 300Kč discount. ❺

U Lilie, Liliová 15 (☎222 220 432; www.pensionulilie.cz). Metro A: Staroměstská. Follow the directions to Dům U Krále Jiřího. U Lilie boasts a lovely courtyard, satellite TV, phone, and minibar in every room. Breakfast included. Singles with shower 1850Kč; doubles 2150Kč, with bath 2800Kč. Cash only. ❺

CAMPING

Campsites can be found on the Vltava Islands as well as on the outskirts of Prague. Bungalows must be reserved in advance, but tent space is generally available without prior notice. Tourist offices sell a guide to sites near the city (15Kč).

Camp Sokol Troja, Trojská 171 (☎233 542 908), north of the center in the Troja district. From Metro C: Nádraží Holešovice, take bus #112 and ask for Kazanka. Similar places line the road. Clean bathrooms. July-Aug. and Dec. tent sites 220-280Kč, extra person 130Kč; singles 320Kč; doubles 640Kč. Low season reduced rates. ❶

Caravan Park, Císařská louka 599 (☎025 40 925), on the Císařská louka peninsula. Metro B: Smíchovské nádraží. Take any bus numbered in the 300s to Lihovar, or take the ferry service that leaves every hr. from the landing 1 block from Smíchovské nádraží (10Kč). On the banks of the Vltava. Tent sites 195-247Kč, extra person 100Kč. ❶

FOOD

The nearer you are to the center, the more you'll pay. Away from the center, a meal of pork, cabbage, dumplings, and .5L of beer costs about 50Kč. You will be charged for everything the waiter brings to the table; check your bill carefully. Most restaurants accept only cash. **Tesco,** Národní třída 26, right next to Metro B: Národní třída, has groceries. (Open M-F 7am-10pm, Sa 8am-8pm, Su 9am-8pm.) Look for the **daily market** in Staré Město. After a night out, grab a *párek v rohlíku* (hot dog) or a *smažený sýr* (fried cheese sandwich) from a Václavské nám. vendor.

RESTAURANTS

STARÉ MĚSTO

Klub architektů, Betlémské nám. 52A (☎224 401 214). Metro B: Národní třída. A 12th-century cellar with a 21st-century ambience. Veggie options 90-150Kč. Meat dishes 160-320Kč. Open daily 11:30am-midnight. AmEx/MC/V. ❸

Jáchymka, Jáchymova 4 (☎224 819 621). From Old Town Sq., walk up Pařížská and take a right on Jáchymova. A local favorite, Jáchymka serves gigantic, affordable cuts of meat. Salads from 30Kč. Entrees 60-260Kč. Open daily 11am-11pm. MC/V. ❸

Country Life, Melantrichova 15 (☎224 213 366; www.countrylife.cz). Metro A: Staroměstská. 3 vegetarian buffets—hot, cold, and salad—are a welcome respite from meat-heavy Czech cuisine. Buffet 22.90Kč per 100g. Soup 20Kč. Juices from 20Kč. Open M-Th 9am-10:30pm, F 9am-5pm, Su 11am-8:30pm. ❷

Cafe Bambus, Benediktská 12 (☎224 828 110; www.cafebambus.com). Metro B: nám. Republiky. Tourists and locals who look like tourists nosh on Thai and Indian dishes (pad thai and curry each 130Kč), and Czech *palančinky* (crepes; 55-75Kč). Beer from 25Kč. Open M-F 9am-2am, Sa 11am-2am, Su 11am-midnight. AmEx/MC/V. ❷

Kavárna Imperial, Na Poříčí 15 (☎222 316 012; www.hotelimperial.cz). Metro B: nám. Republiky. Kavárna Imperial is, entirely intentionally, about as close as you're going to get to life in a Fitzgerald novel. Espresso 35Kč. Vegetarian entrees 78Kč. Salads 37-88Kč. Meat entrees 108-156Kč. Open daily 9am-late. ❸

CZECH REPUBLIC

NOVÉ MĚSTO

Radost FX, Bělehradská 120. Metro C: I.P. Pavlova. A dance club and a late-night cafe with an imaginative menu and great vegetarian food. Entrees 105-195Kč. Brunch Sa-Su 95-140Kč. Open daily 11am-late. See also **Clubs and Discos,** p. 248. ❸

Velryba (The Whale), Opatovická 24. Metro B: Národní třída. Cross the tram tracks and follow Ostrovní, then go left onto Opatovická. Relaxed Italian/Czech restaurant with art gallery downstairs. Entrees 62-145Kč. Open daily 11am-midnight. ❷

Universal, V jirchářích 6 (☎224 934 416). Metro B: Národní třída. Mediterranean, French, and Asian cuisines in a bright and spacious dining room. Huge, fresh salads 119-170Kč. Entrees 149-299Kč. Su brunch buffet 135Kč. Open M-Sa 11:30am-1am, Su 11am-midnight. MC/V; 500Kč min. charge. ❸

Ultramarin Grill, Ostrovni 32 (☎224 932 249). Metro B: Národní třída. With your back to the Metro, turn left and immediately right on narrow Ostrovni. International clientele, but the portion sizes and most of the menu are purely American. Steak, duck, and lamb entrees 115-350Kč. Salads 100-180Kč. Open daily 11am-4am. AmEx/MC/V. ❸

Govinda Vegetarian Club, Soukenická 27 (☎224 816 631). Metro B: nám. Republiky. Walk down Revoluční, away from the Municipal House (Obecní Dum), and turn right on Soukenická. This tiny lunch counter serves up a set menu of stew, rice, salad, and chutney. Small portions 80Kč, large 90Kč. A la carte 21-40Kč. Open M-F 11am-5pm. ❶

MALÁ STRANA

Bar bar, Všehrdova 17 (☎257 313 246). Metro A: Malostranská. Follow the tram tracks down Letenská, through Malostranské nám., down Karmelitská, and left on Všehrdova, past the museum. Hip decor and menu at surprisingly affordable prices. Entrees 50-235Kč. Beer from 32Kč. Open M-Th and Su noon-midnight, F-Sa noon-2am. MC/V. ❶

Pivnice U Švejků, Újezd 22 (☎257 313 244). Metro A: Malostranská. Head down Klárov and turn right onto Letenská. Bear left through Malostranské nám. and follow Karmelitská until it becomes Újezd. Beer hall with 1L Pilsner Urquell, boar dishes, and live accordion from 6pm. Entrees 118-148Kč. Open daily 11am-midnight. AmEx/MC/V. ❸

CAFES AND TEAHOUSES

Cafe Ebel, Řetězová 9 (☎603 441 434). Metro A or B: Staroměstská. Ebel's espresso (40-50Kč), is blended in-house by people who clearly know what they're doing. Continental breakfast 165Kč. Quiche 60-100Kč. English spoken. Another branch at Týn 2. Both open M-F 8am-8pm, Sa-Su 8:30am-8pm. AmEx/MC/V.

Kavárna Medúza, Belgická 17. Metro A: nám. Míru. Walk down Rumunská and turn left at Belgická. Local clientele by day, hipsters by night. Well-worn antique furniture and lots of coffee (19-30Kč). Open M-F 11am-1am, Sa-Su noon-1am.

Bakeshop Praha, Kozí 1. From Old Town Sq., follow Dlouhá to the intersection with Kozí. Mouthwatering breads, pastries, salads, sandwiches, quiche, and lots of coffee and tea drinks. Another branch at Lázenska 19. 10% extra to eat in. Open daily 7am-7pm.

Paneria, Kaprova 7, on the corner of Kaprova and Valentinska. Affordable, reliable, and convenient, with 3Kč rolls, 8Kč eclairs, and espresso from 32Kč. Open daily 7am-8pm.

U zeleného čaje, Nerudova 19 (☎225 730 027). Metro A: Malostranská. Follow Letenská to Malostranské nám, stay right of the church and go down Nerudova. This adorable shop at the foot of Prague Castle takes tea to new heights. Open daily 11am-10pm.

SIGHTS

One of the only Central European cities unscathed by WWII, Prague is a blend of labyrinthine alleys and Baroque architecture. Escape crowds by venturing away from **Staroměstské náměstí, Karlův Most** (Charles Bridge), and **Václavské náměstí.** Central Prague is best explored on foot. There are plenty of opportunities for exploration in the alleys of **Josefov,** the hills of **Vyšehrad,** and **Malá Strana's** streets.

STARÉ MĚSTO (OLD TOWN)

Getting lost among the narrow roads and old-world alleys of Staré Město is probably the best way to appreciate the 1000-year-old neighborhood's charm.

CHARLES BRIDGE. Thronged with tourists and the hawkers who feed on them, the Charles Bridge (Karlův Most) is Prague's most recognizable landmark. On each side of the bridge, defense towers offer splendid views of the city and the river. Five stars and a cross mark the spot where St. Jan Nepomucký was tossed over the side of the bridge for guarding the queen's extramarital secrets from a suspicious King Wenceslas IV. *(Metro A: Malostranská or Staroměstská.)*

OLD TOWN SQUARE. Staroměstské nám. (Old Town Square) is the heart of Staré Město, surrounded by eight magnificent towers. Next to the grassy knoll stands the **Old Town Hall** (Staroměstské Radnice). The multi-facade building is missing a piece of the front facade where the Nazis partially demolished it in the final days of WWII. Crowds gather on the hour to watch the **astronomical clock** chime as the skeletal Death empties his hourglass and a procession of apostles marches by. *(Metro A: Staroměstská; Metro A or B: Můstek. Open M 10am-7pm, Tu-F 9am-7pm, Sa-Su 9am-6pm. Clock tower open daily 10am-6pm; enter through 3rd fl. Exhibition hall 20Kč, students 10Kč. Clock tower 50/40Kč.)* Opposite the Old Town Hall, the spires of **Týn Church** (Chrám Matka Boží před Týnem) rise above a mass of medieval homes. Buried inside is famous astronomer Tycho Brahe, whose overindulgence at one of Emperor Rudolf's lavish dinner parties cost him his life. Since it was deemed improper to leave the table unless the emperor himself did so, poor Tycho had to remain in his chair until his bladder burst. *(Open M-F 9am-noon, 1-2pm. Masses W-F 6pm, Sa 8am, Su 11am and 9pm. Free.)* The bronze statue of theologian **Jan Hus,** the country's most famous martyr, stands in the middle of the square. In front of the Jan Hus statue sits the flowery **Goltz-Kinský Palace,** the finest of Prague's Rococo buildings. *(Open Tu-F 10am-6pm; closes early in summer for daily concerts.)*

CATHEDRAL OF ST. NICHOLAS. While smaller and less impressive than its brother cathedral across the Vltava, this church houses a stunning crystal chandelier and beautiful ceiling frescoes. *(Metro A: Staroměstská. Next to the Kafka Museum. Open daily 10am-7pm. Mass Su 10:30am. Free.)*

NOVÉ MĚSTO (NEW TOWN)

Established in 1348 by Charles IV, Nové Město has become the commercial center of Prague, complete with American chain stores. A stroll through the Franciscan Gardens will remind you of the natural beauty that Prague has to offer.

WENCESLAS SQUARE. More a boulevard than a square, Václavské nám. (Wenceslas Square) owes its name to the equestrian statue of Czech ruler and patron St. Wenceslas (Václav) that stands in front of the National Museum. Wenceslas has presided over a century of turmoil and triumph, witnessing no fewer than five revolutions from his pedestal: the declaration of the new Czechoslovak state in 1918; the invasion by Hitler's troops in 1939; the arrival of Soviet tanks in 1968; the self-immolation of Jan Palach in protest of the Soviet invasion; and the 1989 Velvet Revolution. The square stretches from the statue past department stores, thumping discos, posh hotels, and glitzy casinos. **Radio Free Europe,** which gives global news updates and advocates peace, has been broadcasting from its glass building behind the National Museum since WWII. *(Metro A or C: Muzeum.)*

FRANCISCAN GARDEN AND VELVET REVOLUTION MEMORIAL. Monks somehow manage to preserve this serene **rose garden** in the heart of Prague's commercial district. *(Metro A or B: Můstek. Enter through the arch to the left of Jungmannova and Národní, behind the statue. Open daily mid-Apr. to mid-Sept. 7am-10pm; mid-Sept. to mid-Oct. 7am-8pm; mid-Oct. to mid-Apr. 8am-7pm. Free.)* A plaque under the arcades down Národní, across from the Black Theatre, memorializes the hundreds of citizens beaten by police on November 17, 1989. A subsequent wave of mass protests led to the collapse of communism in Czechoslovakia during the Velvet Revolution.

THE DANCING HOUSE. American architect Frank Gehry (of Guggenheim-Bilbao fame; p. 973) built the undulating "Dancing House" (Tančící dům) at the corner of Resslova and Rašínovo nábřeží. Since its 1996 unveiling, it has been called an eyesore by some and a shining example of postmodern design by others. *(Metro B: Karlovo nám. As you walk down Resslova toward the river, the building is on the left.)*

JOSEFOV

Josefov, Central Europe's oldest Jewish settlement, lies north of Staroměstské nám., along Maiselova. In 1180, Prague's citizens built a 4m wall around the area. The closed neighborhood bred exotic tales, many of which centered around Rabbi Loew ben Bezalel (1512-1609) and his legendary *golem*—a mud creature that supposedly came to life to protect Prague's Jews. The city's Jews remained clustered in Josefov until WWII when the ghetto was vacated and residents were sent to death camps. Ironically, Hitler's wish to create a "museum of an extinct race" sparked the preservation of Josefov's cemetery and synagogues. Though only a fraction of its former size, Prague still has an active Jewish community. *(Metro A: Staroměstská. Synagogues and cemetery open M-F and Su Apr.-Oct. 9am-6pm; Nov.-Mar. 9am-4:30pm. Closed Jewish holidays. Admission to all 6 synagogues except Starnová 300Kč, students 200Kč. Starnová 200/140Kč. Men must cover their heads; kippot 5Kč.)*

SYNAGOGUES. The **Maisel Synagogue** (Maiselova synagoga) displays artifacts from the Jewish Museum's collections, which were only returned to the city's Jewish community in 1994. *(On Maiselova, between Široká and Jáchymova.)* Some 80,000 names line the walls of the **Pinkas Synagogue** (Pinkasova), a sobering requiem for Czech Jews persecuted during the Holocaust. Upstairs, drawings by children interred at the Terezín camp further memorialize the inhumanity of the Holocaust. *(Turn left down Široká.)* Backtrack up Široká and go left on Maiselova to visit the oldest operating synagogue in Europe, the 700-year-old **Old-New Synagogue** (Staronová), which remains the religious center of Prague's Jewish community. Farther up Široká on Dušní is the **Spanish Synagogue** (Španělská), which has an ornate Moorish interior modeled after Granada's Alhambra.

OLD JEWISH CEMETERY. The Old Jewish Cemetery (Starý židovský hřbitov) remains Josefov's most-visited site. Between the 14th and 18th centuries, 20,000 graves were laid in 12 layers. The striking clusters of tombstones visible today were formed as older stones rose from underneath. Rabbi Loew is buried by the wall opposite the entrance. *(At the corner of Široká and Žatecká.)*

MALÁ STRANA

A seedy hangout for criminals and counter-revolutionaries for nearly a century, the cobblestone streets of Malá Strana have become prized real estate. Malá Strana is centered around **Malostranské Náměstí** and its centerpiece, the Baroque **St. Nicholas's Cathedral** (Chrám sv. Mikuláše), whose towering dome is one of Prague's most prominent landmarks. The cathedral hosts nightly concerts of classical music. *(Metro A: Malostranská; follow Letenská to Malostranské nám. Open daily 9am-4:45pm. 50Kč, students 25Kč.)* Along Letenská, a wooden gate opens into the **Wallenstein Garden** (Valdštejnská zahrada), one of Prague's best-kept secrets. *(Letenská 10. Metro A: Malostranská. Open Apr.-Oct. daily 10am-6pm. Free.)* The **Church of Our Lady Victorious** (Kostel Panna Marie Vítězné) is known for its famous wax statue of the **Infant Jesus of Prague,** said to bestow miracles on the faithful. *(Metro A: Malostranská. Follow Letecká through Malostranské nám. and continue onto Karmelitská. Church open daily 8:30am-7pm. Museum open M-Sa 9:30am-5:30pm, Su 1-6pm. Free.)* **Petřín Gardens,** on the hill beside Malá Strana, provide a tranquil retreat from Prague's urban bustle and spectacular views of the city. Climb the steep, serene, footpath, or take the funicular from just above the intersection of Vítězná and Újezd. *(Look for Lanovka Dráha signs. Funicular daily 9am-11pm, 4-6 per hr., 20Kč.)*

PRAGUE CASTLE (PRAŽSKÝ HRAD)

Prague Castle has been the seat of the Bohemian government for over 1000 years. The main castle entrance is at the end of the lush **Royal Garden** (Královská zahrada), where the Singing Fountain spouts its watery, harp-like tune in front of the newly renovated **Royal Summer Palace.** Past the main gate, the **Šternberg Palace,** houses art from the National Gallery. *(From Metro A: Malostranská, take trams #22 or 23 to Pražský Hrad and go down U Prašného Mostu. Open daily Apr.-Oct. 9am-5pm; Nov.-Mar. 9am-4pm. Royal Gardens open Apr.-Oct. Buy tickets opposite St. Vitus's Cathedral, inside the castle walls. Ticket valid for 2 days at Royal Crypt, Cathedral and Powder Tower, Old Royal Palace, and the Basilica. 350Kč, students 175Kč.)*

ST. VITUS'S CATHEDRAL. Inside the castle walls stands the colossal Gothic St. Vitus's Cathedral (Katedrála sv. Víta), which was only completed in 1929, 600 years after construction began. To the right of the high altar stands the silver **Tomb of St. Jan Nepomucký.** In the main church, the walls of **St. Wenceslas's Chapel** (Svatováclavská kaple) are lined with a painting cycle depicting the legend of Wenceslas. Climb the 287 steps of the **Great South Tower** for a great view, or descend underground to the **Royal Crypt,** which holds the tomb of Charles IV.

OLD ROYAL PALACE. The Old Royal Palace (Starý Královský Palác) is to the right of the cathedral, behind the Old Provost's House and the statue of St. George. The lengthy **Vladislav Hall** once hosted jousting competitions. Upstairs is the **Chancellery of Bohemia,** where the Second Defenestration of Prague took place.

ST. GEORGE'S BASILICA AND ENVIRONS. Across the courtyard from the Old Royal Palace stands St. George's Basilica (Bazilika sv. Jiří), where the skeleton of St. Ludmila is on display. The convent next door houses the **National Gallery of Bohemian Art,** which displays pieces ranging from Gothic to Baroque. *(Open Tu-Su 10am-6pm. 100Kč, students 50Kč.)* **Jiřská** begins to the right of the basilica. Halfway down, tiny **Golden Lane** (Zlatá ulička) heads off to the right; alchemists once worked here, attempting to create gold. Kafka later lived at #22.

OUTER PRAGUE

The city's outskirts offer green fields, churches, panoramic vistas, and peaceful respite from hordes of tourists. The beautiful neighborhood of **Troja** is the site of French architect J. B. Mathey's masterly **chateau,** overlooking the Vltava with a terraced garden, oval staircase, and magnificent collection of 19th-century Czech artwork. *(From Metro C: Nádraží Holešovice, take bus #112 to Zoologická Zahrada. Open Apr.-Oct. Tu-Su 10am-6pm; Nov.-Mar. Sa-Su 10am-5pm. 140Kč, students 70Kč.)* The oldest monastery in Bohemia, **Břevnov Monastery** was founded in AD 993 by King Boleslav II and St. Adalbert, each of whom was guided by a divine dream to build a monastery atop a bubbling stream. To the right of **St. Margaret's Church** (Bazilika sv. Markéty), the stream leads to a pond. *(From Metro A: Malostranská take tram #22 uphill to Břevnovský klášter. Church open only for mass, M-Sa 7am, 6pm, Su 7:30, 9am, 6pm. Tours Sa-Su 10am, 2, 4pm. 50Kč, students 30Kč.)* The **Prague Market** (Pražskátrznice) has acres of stalls selling all kinds of wares. *(Take tram #3 or 14 from nám. Republiky to Vozovna Kobylisy and get off at Pražskátrznice. Open M-F 8am-6pm, Sa 8am-1pm.)*

MUSEUMS

The city's museums often have striking facades but mediocre collections. Still, a few quirky exceptions are worth a visit.

MUCHA MUSEUM. The museum is devoted to the work of Alfons Mucha, the Czech Republic's most celebrated artist and pioneer of the Art Nouveau movement, who gained fame for his poster series of "la divine" Sarah Bernhardt. *(Panská 7. Metro A or B: Můstek. Walk up Václavské nám. toward the St. Wenceslas statue. Go left onto Jindřišská and left again onto Panská. Open daily 10am-6pm. 120Kč, students 60Kč.)*

MUSEUM OF COMMUNISM. This gallery is committed to exposing the flaws of the communist system that suppressed the Czech people from 1948-1989. A model factory and an interrogation office send you behind the Iron Curtain. *(Na Příkopě 10. Metro A: Můstek. Open daily 9am-9pm. 180Kč, students 140Kč.)*

MUSEUM OF MEDIEVAL TORTURE INSTRUMENTS. The collection and highly detailed explanations are sure to nauseate. In the same building, the **Exhibition of Spiders and Scorpions** shows live venomous creatures in their natural habitats. *(Mostécka 21. Metro A: Malostranská. Follow Letenská from the Metro and turn left. Open daily 10am-10pm. Torture museum 120Kč. Spiders Exhibition 100Kč, children 80Kč.)*

NATIONAL GALLERY. The collection of the National Gallery (Národní Galerie) is spread among nine locations throughout Prague; the notable Šternberský palác and Klášter sv. Jiří are in the **Prague Castle** (p. 246). The **Trade Fair Palace and the Gallery of Modern Art** (Veletržní palác a Galerie moderního umwní) exhibit an impressive collection of 20th-century Czech and European art. *(Dukelských hrdinů 47. Metro C: Nádraží Holešovice. All open Tu-Su 10am-6pm. 150Kč, students 70Kč.)*

ENTERTAINMENT

For concerts and performances, consult *Threshold, Do města-Downtown, The Pill* (all free at many cafes and restaurants), or *The Prague Post.* Most performances start at 7pm and offer standby tickets 30min. before curtain. Between mid-May and early June, the **Prague Spring Festival** draws musicians from around the world. June brings all things avant-garde with the **Prague Fringe Festival,** featuring dancers, comedians, performance artists, and—everyone's favorite—mimes. (☎224 935 183; www.praguefringe.cz). For tickets, try **Bohemia Ticket International,** Malé nám. 13, next to Čedok. (☎224 227 832; www.ticketsbti.cz. Open M-F 9am-5pm, Sa 9am-2pm.) The majority of Prague's theaters close in July and August, but the selection is extensive during the

HIGH CULTURE, LOW BUDGET. Prague's state-run theaters will often hold a group of seats in the higher balconies until the day of the performance before selling them off at reduced prices. By visiting your venue of choice the morning of a performance, you can often score tickets for as little as 50Kč.

rest of the year. Get gussied up for the **National Theater** (Národní divadlo), Národní 2/4, which stages drama, opera, and ballet. (☎224 901 487; www.narodni-divadlo.cz. Metro B: Národní třída. Box office open daily Sept.-June 10am-6pm and 45min. before performances. Tickets 30-1000Kč.) Every performance at the **Theatre Image Black Light Theatre,** Pařížská 4, is silent, conveying its message through dance, pantomime, and creative use of black light. (☎222 314 448; www.imagetheatre.cz. Performances daily 8pm. Box office open daily 9am-8pm.) The **Marionette Theater** (Říše loutek), Žatecká 1, stages a hilarious marionette version of *Don Giovanni,* now in its 14th season. (☎224 819 322. Metro A: Staroměstská. Performances June-July M-Tu and Th-Su 8pm. Box office open daily 10am-8pm. 490Kč, students 390Kč.)

NIGHTLIFE

With some of the world's best beers on tap, it's no surprise that pubs and beer halls are Prague's most popular nighttime hangouts. Tourists have overrun the city center, so authentic pub experiences are now largely restricted to the suburbs and outlying metro stops. Although dance clubs abound, Prague is not a clubbing town—locals prefer the many jazz and rock hangouts scattered about the city.

BARS

Vinárna U Sudu, Vodičkova 10. Metro A or B: Můstek. Cross Václavské nám. to Vodičkova and follow the curve left. An infinite labyrinth of cavernous cellars. Red wine 125Kč per 1L. Open M-Th 1pm-2am, F-Sa 1pm-3am, Su 3pm-1am.

Duende, Karolíny Světlé 30. A diverse crowd packs in even on those rare nights when Staroměstské nám. is dead. Beer from 19Kč. Shots 75Kč. Open daily 11am-1am.

Pivnice u Sv. Tomáše, Letenská 12 (☎257 531 835). Metro A: Malostranská. Go downhill on Letenská. These mighty dungeons are filled with boisterous revelry. Order spit-roasted meats a day in advance; 350-400Kč. Entrees 95-520Kč. Beer 40Kč. Live brass band 7-11pm. Open daily 11:30am-midnight. Kitchen closes 10pm. MC/V.

Kozička, Kozí 1 (☎224 818 308; www.kozicka.cz). Metro A: Staroměstská. Take Dlouhá from the square's northeast corner, then bear left on Kozí. An endless line of tables curves around this huge cellar bar. Beer 35Kč. Open M-F noon-4am, Sa 6pm-4am, Su 6pm-3am. MC/V.

Cafe Marquis de Sade, Melnicka 5. Metro B: nám. Republiky. Spacious microbrewery bar decorated in red velvet. Beer from 35Kč. Shots 80Kč. Open daily 2pm-2am.

U Tři Černých Ruží, Zámecká 5 (☎257 530 019). Metro A: Malostranská. At the foot of the New Castle steps. A small, quirky bar that pours endless pints at low prices (Budvar: 18Kč) for a thirsty local crowd. Open daily noon-11pm.

Jo's Bar and Garáž, Malostranské nám. 7. Metro A: Malostranská. For those desperately homesick for Anybar, USA. American bar food—nachos, burgers, burritos, and steaks 45-295Kc. Foosball, darts, card games, and a dance floor downstairs. Long Island Iced Tea 115Kč. Beer from 30Kč. Open daily 11am-2am. AmEx/MC/V.

CLUBS AND DISCOS

Radost FX, Bělehradská 120 (☎224 254 776; www.radostfx.cz). Metro C: I.P. Pavlova. Industrial metallic bar, small dance floor, and couches in this basement club. Th-F R&B, Sa house/techno. Beer from 30Kč. Cover 100-200Kč. Open Th-Sa 10pm-5am.

Roxy, Dlouhá 33. Metro B: Nám. Republiky. Same building as the Traveler's Hostel (p. 241). Artsy studio/club with experimental DJs and theme nights. Happy hour 9-11pm with 15Kč beer. Cover Tu and Th-Sa 100-350Kč. Open M-Tu and Th-Sa 9pm-late.

U staré paní (The Old Lady's Place), Michalská 9 (☎603 551 680; www.jazzlounge.cz). Metro A or B: Můstek. Classy atmosphere and quality jazz. Live music daily 9pm. Cover M-Th and Su 150Kč, F-Sa 200Kč. Beer 45Kč. Open daily 7pm-2am. AmEx/MC/V.

Palác Akropolis, Kubelíkova 27 (☎296 330 911). Metro A: Jiřího z Poděbrad. Head down Slavíkova and turn right onto Kubelíkova. Live Czech bands several times a week. Beer from 30Kč. Open daily 9pm-5am.

Deminka, Škrétova 1a (☎603 185 699). In an ancient brick cellar, Deminka provides the classic Euro techno club experience. Beer from 50Kč. Cover F-Sa 100-150Kc. No cover for women. Open Th and Su 8pm-5am, F-Sa 8pm-6am.

U Malého Glena II, Karmelitská 23 (☎257 531 717; www.malyglen.cz). Basement bar with a small stage and handful of tables. Nightly live music features blues, salsa, or jazz. Call ahead for weekend tables. Beer 35Kč. Cover 100-150Kč. Shows at 9:30pm, F-Sa 10pm. Open daily 8pm-2am. AmEx/MC/V.

Karlovy Lázně, Novotného lávka 1. 4 levels of themed dance floors under the Charles Bridge. Cover 120Kč, 50Kč before 10pm and after 4am. Open daily 9pm-5am.

Klub 007, Chaloupeckého 7 (☎257 211 439; www.klub007strahov.cz). Metro A: Dejvicka. Take bus #217 to Koleje Strahov and walk toward the high-rise dormitories. Klub 007 is in the basement of #7. Hip hop, punk, reggae, and more drinking than dancing. Beer from 20Kč. Concerts usually begin 7-9pm.

GLBT NIGHTLIFE

At any of the places below, you can pick up a copy of *Amigo* (85Kč; www.amigo.cz), the most thorough English-language guide to gay life in the Czech Republic. Check out www.praguegayguide.net or www.praguesaints.cz for a comprehensive list of attractions and resources.

The Saints, Polksá 32 (☎222 250 041; www.praguesaints.cz). Metro A: Jiřího z Poděbrad. Much more than a club, The Saints introduces GLBT visitors to Prague and organizes the local GLBT community. Small, comfy club with a mixed crowd and free wireless Internet. Beer from 22Kč. Open M-Th 1pm-2am, F-Sa 5pm-4am, Su 1pm-1am.

Friends, Bartolomejská 11 (☎224 236 272; www.friends-prague.cz). Metro B: Národní třída. From the station, turn right and head down Na Perštýně. Take a left at Bartolomejská. The only GLBT dance club in Staré Město. Rotating schedule features music videos, house, parties and theme nights. Women and straight customers welcome. Beer from 20Kč. Open daily 6pm-5am.

Tingl Tangl, Karolíny Světlé 12 (☎777 322 121; www.tingltangl.com). Metro B: Národní třída. Draws a diverse crowd for its magnificent transvestite cabarets. Women welcome. Cover 120Kč. Shows after midnight. Open W and F-Sa 9pm-5am.

DAYTRIPS FROM PRAGUE

TEREZÍN (THERESIENSTADT). In 1941, when Terezín became a concentration camp, Nazi propaganda films touted the area as a resort. In reality, over 30,000 Jews died here while another 85,000 were transported to camps farther east. The **Ghetto Museum,** left of the bus stop, places Terezín in the wider context of WWII. Across the river, the **Small Fortress,** was used as a Gestapo prison. (Museum and barracks open daily Apr.-Sept. 9am-6pm; Oct.-Mar. 9am-5:30pm. Fortress open daily Apr.-Sept. 8am-6pm; Oct.-Mar. 8am-4:30pm. Museum, barracks, and fortress 180Kč, students 140Kč.) Outside the walls lie the **cemetery** and **crematorium.** Men should cover their heads before entering. (Open M-F and Su Apr.-Sept. 10am-5pm; Nov.-Mar. 10am-

BONE-CHILLING CHAPEL

In and around Prague, you will find churches of stone, brick, iron, glass—and one of bones. Kutná Hora, a small, picturesque village 1hr. from Prague, is infamous for its ossuary, a chapel filled with artistic and religious creations made entirely from parts of human skeletons. The village was originally formed around silver mines; its morbid side only came out when the plague and a superstition about the holiness of the village's graveyard combined to leave the cemetery overflowing with corpses. The Cistercian Order built a chapel in order to house the extra remains, and in a fit of whim (or possibly insanity), one monk began designing flowers from pelvises and crania. He never finished the ossuary, but the artist František Rint eventually completed the project in 1870, decorating the chapel from floor to ceiling with the bones of over 40,000 people.

Trains run from Hlavní Nádraží (1hr., 1 per hr., round-trip 112Kč). A 1km. walk from the train station. From the train station, turn right, then left, and left again on the highway. After 500m, turn right at the church. The ossuary is at the end of the road. Open daily Apr.-Sept. 8am-6pm; Oct. 9am-noon and 1-5pm; Nov.-Mar. 9am-noon and 1-4pm. 35Kč, students 20Kč. Cameras 30Kč, video 60Kč.

4pm. Free.) Terezín has been repopulated to about half its former size. Families live in former barracks, and supermarkets occupy former Nazi offices. Take the **bus** from Prague's Florenc station to the Terezín stop (1hr., 68Kč), where the **tourist office** is located. (Open Tu-Su 9am-12:30pm and 1-4pm.)

KARLŠTEJN. A gem of the countryside, Karlštejn is a **fortress** built by Charles IV in the 14th century. (Open Tu-Su July-Aug. 9am-6pm; May-June and Sept. 9am-5pm; Apr. and Oct. 9am-4pm; Nov.-Mar. 9am-3pm. 7-8 English-language tours per day. 200Kč, students 100Kč.) The **Chapel of the Holy Cross** is inlaid with precious stones and 129 apocalyptic paintings by medieval artist Master Theodorik. (☎02 74 00 81 54; reservace@stc.npu.cz. Open July-Nov. Tu-Su 9am-5pm. Tours by reservation only. 300Kč, students 100Kč.) A **train** runs to Prague's Hlavní station (55min., 1 per hr., 46Kč). To reach the castle, turn right from the station and go left over the bridge; turn right and walk through the village (25min.; mostly uphill).

ČESKÝ RÁJ NATIONAL PRESERVE. The sandstone pillars and gorges of **Prachovské skály** (Prachovské rocks) yield climbs and hikes with stunning views. Prachovské skály boasts **Pelíšek** rock pond and the ruins of the 14th-century **Pařez** castle. (Open daily 8am-5pm. 45Kč, students 20Kč.) The 588 acres of the park are interwoven by a network of **trails;** green, blue, and yellow signs guide hikers to sights, while triangles indicate scenic vistas. Red signs mark the "Golden Trail," which connects Prachovské skály to **Hrubá Skála** (Rough Rock), a rock town surrounding a castle. From the castle, the trail leads up to what remains of **Wallenstein Castle** (Valdštejnský Hrad). The red and blue trails are open to cyclists, but only the blue trail is suited for biking. **Buses** run from Prague-Florenc station to Jičín (1½hr., 8 per day, 77Kč), from which buses go to Prachovské skály (15min., 11Kč) and other spots in Český Ráj. Buses from Jičín are unpredictable; if necessary, you can walk to the park along a 6km trail beginning at Motel Rumcajs, Koněva 331.

WEST AND SOUTH BOHEMIA

West Bohemia overflows with curative springs; over the centuries, emperors and intellectuals alike have soaked in the waters of Karlovy Vary (also known as Carlsbad). Those seeking good beer visit the *Pilsner Urquell* brewery in Plzeň or the *Budvar* brewery in České Budějovice. More rustic than West Bohemia, South Bohemia is filled with brooks, forests, and ruins.

KARLOVY VARY ☎353

The hot springs of Karlovy Vary (pop. 55,000) and the enormous spas they spawned once drew many legendary Europeans, including J. S. Bach, Sigmund Freud, Karl Marx, and Peter the Great. Older Germans and Russians seeking the therapeutic powers of the springs are the main visitors during most of the year, but film stars and fans fill the town for its International Film Festival each July.

TRANSPORTATION AND PRACTICAL INFORMATION. Buses, much more convenient than trains, run from Dolní nádraží, on Západní (☎50 45 16), to Plzeň (1¾hr., 10 per day, 80Kč) and Prague (2¼hr., 10 per day, 120Kč); buy tickets onboard. To reach the town center, turn left and take the left fork of the pedestrian underpass toward Lázně. Turn right at the next fork, follow the sign for the supermarket, and go up the stairs to reach T. G. Masaryka, which runs parallel to the main thoroughfare, Dr. Davida Bechera. **Centrum Taxi,** Zeyerova 9, offers 24hr. service (☎22 30 00). **Infocentrum,** Lázeňská 1, next to Mill Colonnade, sells maps (up to 40Kč) and theater tickets (150-600Kč), and books rooms from 450Kč. (☎22 40 97; www.karlovyvary.cz. Open Jan.-Oct. M-F 8am-6pm, Sa-Su 10am-4pm; Nov.-Dec. M-F 7am-5pm.) The **post office,** T. G. Masaryka 1, has **Western Union** and **Poste Restante.** (Open M-F 7:30am-7pm, Sa 8am-1pm, Su 8am-noon.) **Postal Code:** 36001.

ACCOMMODATIONS AND FOOD. City Info, T. G. Masaryka 9, arranges pension singles from 630Kč and hotel doubles from 950Kč. (☎22 33 51. Open daily 10am-6pm.) **Buena Vista Backpackers' Hostel ❶,** Moravská 42, offers apartments with spacious bathrooms and kitchens. Take bus #2, 8, 11, or 13 four stops to Na Vyhlídce. Continue walking, veer right at the fork past the market, go downhill, then uphill. The hostel is at the end of the street. (☎23 90 02; www.premium-hotels.com/buenavista. Internet 1Kč per min. 4- to 6-bed dorms 300Kč, low season 230Kč.) Next to the post office, **Pension Romania ❸,** Zahradní 49, has modern rooms on the Teplá. (☎22 28 22. Breakfast included. Singles 900Kč, students 715Kč; doubles 1480-1630Kč; triples 1900Kč. Oct.-Mar. reduced rates.) Karlovy Vary is known for its sweet *oplatky* (spa wafers; from 5Kč). In a town geared mainly to the old and the monied, **Bulvár ❸,** Bélehradská 9, is a haven of quality international food at reasonable prices. (☎58 51 99. Entrees 49-299Kč. Open daily 11am-2am.) **E&T Bar ❸,** Zeyerova 3, has a terrace and big portions of Czech food. (☎22 60 22. Salads and entrees 40-210Kč. Open M-Sa 9am-2am, Su 10am-2am.) Albert **supermarket,** Horova 1, is in the building marked "Městská tržnice," behind the bus station. (Open M-F 6am-7pm, Sa 7am-5pm, Su 9am-5pm. MC/V.)

SIGHTS AND ENTERTAINMENT. The **spa district,** overflowing with springs, baths, and colonnades, starts at **Elizabeth Bath 5** (Alžbětiny Lázně 5), Smetanovy Sady 1, across from the post office, which offers treatments of dubious medical value, including thermal baths (355Kč), massages (360-600Kč), and lymph drainage (380Kč). Reserve a few days in advance. (☎22 25 36; www.spa5.cz. Pool and sauna open M-F 8am-9pm, Sa 8am-6pm, Su 10am-6pm. Treatments M-F 7am-3pm. Pool 90Kč. MC/V.) Follow the Teplá River to **Bath 3,** Mlýnské nábř 5, which offers

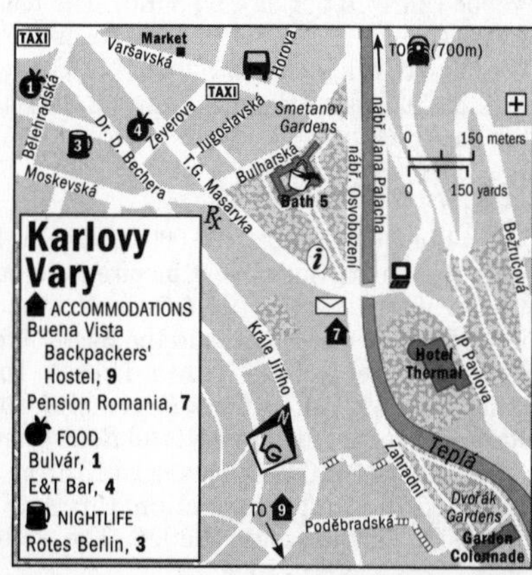

massages for 550Kč. (Treatments daily 7-11:30am and noon-3pm.) Next door, the **Mill Colonnade** (Mlýnská kolonáda) hosts free concerts in the summer. Farther down is **Zawojski House,** Tržiště 9, an ornate Art Nouveau building that now houses Živnostenská Banka. Two doors down, **Strudel Spring** (Vřídlo pramen), inside **Strudel Colonnade** (Vřídelní kolonáda), is Karlovy Vary's hottest and highest-shooting spring, spouting 30L of water each second. (Open daily 6am-7pm.)

Follow Stará Louka to find signs directing you to the **funicular,** which leads to the **Diana Observatory** and a panorama of the city. (Funicular every 15min. June-Sept. 9:15am-6:45pm; Apr.-May and Oct. 9:15am-5:45pm; Feb.-Mar. and Nov.-Dec. 9:15am-4:15pm. Tower open daily 9am-7pm. Funicular 40Kč, round-trip 60Kč. Tower 10Kč.) *Promenáda*, a monthly booklet with schedules and other info, is available at kiosks around town (15Kč). It includes info on the popular **International Film Festival,** which screens independent films in early July. **Rotes Berlin,** Jaltská 7, off Dr. Davida Bechera, attracts every young person in town with cheap beer and live music. (Beer from 15Kč. Open M-F noon-2am, Sa-Su 3pm-2am.)

DAYTRIP FROM KARLOVY VARY: PLZEŇ. Recent attempts to clean up Plzeň (pop. 175,000) have left its architecture and gardens looking fresh and new. But it's the world-famous beer, not the architecture, that lures so many to Plzeň. A beer-lover's perfect day begins at legendary **Pilsner Urquell Brewery** (Měšťanský Pivovar Plzeňský Prazdroj), where knowledgeable guides lead visitors to the cellars for samples. After the tour, take a lunch break at the on-site beerhouse **Na spilce,** which pours Pilsner for 20Kč per pint. The entrance to the complex is across the Radbuza River from Staré Město, where Pražská becomes Prazdroje u. Cross the street and take the overpass. (☎377 062 888. 70min. tours daily June-Aug. 12:30, 2pm; Sept.-May 12:30pm. Na spilce open M-Th and Sa 11am-10pm, F 11am-11pm, Su 11am-9pm. Tours 120Kč, students 60Kč.) Not just a beer mecca, Plzeň is also home to the world's third-largest **synagogue,** built in a Neo-classical style, but with onion domes. Closed from 1973 to 1988, the synagogue is now a museum; the marble halls house photography exhibits. From the southern end of Nám. Republiky, go down Prešovská to Sady Pětatřicátníků and turn left; the synagogue is on the right. Open M-F and Su Apr.-Sept. 10am-6pm; Oct. 10am-5pm; Nov. 10am-4pm. 40Kč, students 30Kč.) **Euro Café (Kavárna Europa) ❶,** Nám. Republiky 12, provides a welcome alternative to Czech fare. (Sandwiches 55Kč. Salads 50Kč. Open M-F 9am-8pm, Sa 10am-6pm.)

Buses leave from Husova 58 for Karlovy Vary (45min., 16 per day, 70-80Kč) and Prague (2hr., 16 per day, 65-80Kč). The **tourist office,** Nám. Republiky 41, books rooms (from 179Kč), sells phone cards (150-350Kč), and offers free maps. (☎378 035 330; www.icpilsen.cz. Open Apr.-Sept. daily 9am-6pm; Oct.-Mar. M-F 10am-5pm, Sa-Su 10am-3:30pm.) To reach the main square, turn left on Husova, which becomes Smetanovy Sady, then turn left on Bedřicha Smetany. **Postal Code:** 30101.

ČESKÉ BUDĚJOVICE ☎38

České Budějovice (pop. 100,000) is a great base for exploring the region's attractions. Known as Budweis, it inspired the name of the pale North American Budweiser, which bears little relation to the malty local Budvar. Rivalry lingers between Anheuser-Busch and the **Budvar Brewery,** Karoliny Světlé 4, reached from the town center by bus #2, toward Borek, Točna. (Tours M-Th and Sa-Su 9am-4pm. 92Kč, students 70Kč.) **Staré Město** (Old Town) centers on the **Náměstí Přemysla Otakara II,** surrounded by colorful Renaissance and Baroque buildings.

To reach **AT Penzion ❸,** Dukelská 15, from Nám. Otakara II, turn right on Dr. Stejskala. At the first intersection, turn left and follow Široká, veering right on Dukelská. Penzion is on the left. The rooms have private bath, TV, and fridge.

(☎7312 529. Breakfast 50Kč. Singles 500Kč; doubles 800Kč.) Eat with locals at **Restaurace Knezska ❷**, with excellent pizza. (☎777 069 002. Entrees 25-125Kč. Open M-Th 10am-11pm, F 10am-midnight, Sa 11am-midnight. Cash only.) At the **Motorcycles Legend Pub**, Radniční 9, you can join the locals, at least temporarily, in their intense love of the iron horse. (Open M-Sa 5pm-3am, Su 5pm-midnight.)

Trains (☎7854 490) leave from Nádražní 12, opposite the bus station for: Brno (4½hr., 3 per day, 274Kč); Český Krumlov (50min., 8 per day, 46Kč); Plzeň (2hr., 10 per day, 162Kč); Prague (2½hr., 12 per day, 204Kč). **Buses** run to: Brno (4½hr., 6 per day, 200Kč); Český Krumlov (50min., 25 per day, 25Kč); Prague (2½hr., 10 per day, 120-144Kč). The TIC **tourist office,** Nám. Otakara II 2, books private rooms. (☎6801 413; www.c-budejovice.cz. Open M-F 8:30am-6pm, Sa 8:30am-5pm, Su 10am-noon and 12:30-4pm.) To reach the center of town from the train station, turn right on Nádražní, take a left at the first crosswalk, and follow Lannova třída, which becomes Kanovnická. **Postal Code:** 37001.

CZECH REPUBLIC

ČESKÝ KRUMLOV

This once-hidden gem of the Czech Republic has finally been discovered—some might say besieged—by tourists escaping Prague's overcrowded streets. Yet Český Krumlov won't disappoint those who wander its medieval streets, raft down the meandering Vltava, and explore the enormous castle that looms over it all.

TRANSPORTATION AND PRACTICAL INFORMATION. **Buses** run from Kaplická 439 (☎380 715 415) to České Budějovice (30min., M-F 33 per day, Sa-Su 14 per day; 26Kč) and Prague (3hr., M-F 9 per day, Sa-Su 6 per day; 130-145Kč). To get to the main square, **Náměstí Svornosti,** take the path from the back of the terminal, to the right of stops #20-25. Go downhill at the intersection with Kaplická, then cross the highway and head to Horní, which leads to the square. The **tourist office,** Nám. Svornosti 2, books rooms (from 300Kč). (☎380 704 622; www.ckrumlov.cz/infocentrum. Open Apr.-Oct. M-Sa 9am-1pm and 2-7pm.) **Postal Code:** 38101.

ACCOMMODATIONS AND FOOD. To reach the homey **Krumlov House ❶,** Rooseveltova 68, run by an American expat couple, walk out of the square on Horní. Turn left on Rooseveltova after the lights, then follow signs. (☎380 711 935; www.krumlovhostel.com. Dorms 250Kč; doubles 600Kč; suites 750Kč.) The beds at **Hostel 99 ❷,** Věžní 99, are from a four-star hotel. From Nám. Svornosti, take Radniční, which becomes Latrán; at the red-and-yellow gate turn right on Věžní. (☎380 712 812; www.hostel99.com. Dorms 300-390Kč; doubles 700Kč.) **Hostel Merlin ❶,** Kájovská 59, on the right before the bridge, is an alternative for those weary of the backpacker scene. (☎602 432 747; www.ckrumlov.cz/nahradbach. Internet. 5-bed dorms 250Kč; doubles 500Kč; triples 750Kč.) Just off Radniční, the riverfront **U dwau Maryí ❷,** Parkán 104, specializes in medieval fare like baked millet casserole with cheese, served by an English-speaking waitstaff in period costume. (Entrees 54-120Kč. Open Apr.-Oct. daily 11am-11pm.) Right next door, **Laibon ❶,** Parkán 105, serves a meatless menu on a terrace stretching to the river. (Entrees 30-150Kč. Open daily 11am-11pm.) Get groceries at **Jidehlo Potraviny,** Latrán 55.

SIGHTS AND NIGHTLIFE. Towering above Krumlov since the 1200s, the **Zamek** (castle) has been home to a succession of Bohemian and Bavarian nobles. Follow Radniční across the river to the main entrance on Latrán. Two tours cover different parts of the interior, including a frescoed ballroom and a Baroque theater. Climb the 162 steps of the tower for a fabulous view. (☎380 704 721. Castle open June-Aug. Tu-Su 9am-noon and 1-6pm; Apr.-May and Sept.-Oct. 9am-noon and 1-5pm. Last tour 1hr. before closing. Tower open daily June-Aug. 9am-5:30pm;

Apr.-May and Sept.-Oct. 9am-4:30pm. Castle tour 160Kč, students 80Kč. Tower 35Kč, students 20Kč.) The castle gardens host the **Revolving South Bohemia Theater,** where operas and plays are performed in summer. (Gardens open daily June-Aug. 8am-7pm; May and Sept. 8am-6pm; Apr. and Oct. 8am-5pm. Free. Shows begin 8:30-9:30pm. Tickets 224-390Kč; available at the tourist office.) The painter Egon Schiele (1890-1918) lived in Český Krumlov until residents ran him out for painting burghers' daughters in the nude. The **Egon Schiele Art Center,** Široká 70-72, displays his work, and that of other 20th-century Central European artists. (☎380 704 011; www.schieleartcentrum.cz. Open daily 10am-6pm. 180Kč, students 105Kč.)

Cikánská Jizba (Gypsy Bar), Dlouhá 31, offers Roma cuisine (45-150Kč), cheap beer (18Kč), and live music. (☎380 717 585. Open M-Th 11am-10pm, F-Sa 11am-midnight.) In the bottom of an abandoned church, **Horor Bar,** Masná 129, is quite goth, with a giant metal cross above the bar, red drapes, candelabras, a broken piano, and secluded nooks. (☎728 682 724. Beer 40Kč. Open daily 6pm-late.)

OUTDOOR ACTIVITIES. Whether you'd like to float down the Vltava or bike through the countryside, stop by **VLTAVA,** Kájovská 62, for equipment rental. (☎380 711 978; www.ckvltava.cz. Bike rental 320Kč per day. Open daily 9am-5pm.) Go horseback riding at **Jezdecký klub Slupenec,** Slupenec 1. Follow Horní to the highway, take the 2nd left on Křížová, then the red trail to Slupenec. (☎380 711 052; www.jk-slupenec.cz. 250Kč per hr. Open Tu-Su 9am-6pm.)

MORAVIA

Moravia makes up the easternmost third of the Czech Republic. Home to the country's two leading universities, it's also the birthplace of Tomáš G. Masaryk, first president of the former Czechoslovakia, psychoanalyst Sigmund Freud, and chemist Johann Gregor Mendel.

BRNO

Brno (pop. 370,000) has been an international marketplace since the 13th century. Today, global corporations compete with family-owned produce stands, while ancient churches soften the glare of casinos and clubs that line the streets.

TRANSPORTATION AND PRACTICAL INFORMATION. Trains (☎541 171 111) go to: Bratislava, Slovakia (2hr., 5 per day, 250Kč); Budapest, Hungary (4hr., 3 per day, 945Kč); Prague (3-4hr., 12 per day, 130-160Kč); Vienna, Austria (1½hr., 5 per day, 536Kč). **Buses** (☎543 217 733) leave from the corner of Zvonařka and Plotní for Prague (2½hr., 36 per day, 140Kč) and Vienna, Austria (2½hr., 2 per day, 400Kč). From the exit, cross the tram lines, walk left, then right on Masarykova to reach **Náměstí Svobody** (Freedom Square), the main square. The **tourist office,** Radnická 8, is inside the town hall. From Nám. Svobody, take Masarykova and turn right on Průchodní. (☎542 211 090. Open M-F 8am-6pm, Sa-Su 9am-5pm.) **Internet Center Cafe,** Masarykova 2/24, has speedy computers in the town center. (40Kč per hr. Open M-F 8am-midnight, Sa-Su 9am-11pm.) **Postal Code:** 60100.

ACCOMMODATIONS AND FOOD. From the train station, cross the tram tracks, turn right, then take a left up the stairs. At the top, turn right to the new, centrally located **Hotel Astorka ❶,** Novobranská 3. (☎542 510 370. Open July.-Sept. Singles 520Kč; doubles 1040Kč; triples 1560Kč. 50% student discount. AmEx/MC/V.) The beautiful rooms in **Pension U Leopolda ❸,** Jeneweinova 49, have private baths. Take tram #12 or bus #A12 to Komarov, go left on Studnici, and right on

Jeneweinova. (☎545 233 036. Singles 775Kč; doubles 1250Kč; triples 1450Kč.) From Nám. Svobody, take Rašínova, and turn right to find **Caffetteria Top Shop ❶**, Jakubské nám. 4, where the coffee stands out. (Espresso from 28Kč. Open M-Th 8am-10pm, F 9am-midnight, Sa 10am-midnight, Su 10am-10pm.) Enjoy a Czech feast amid intense medieval atmosphere at **Dávně Časy ❸**, Starobrněnská 20, off Zelný trh. (Entrees 69-400Kč. Open daily 11am-11pm. AmEx/V.) Behind the train station is a **Tesco** supermarket. (Open daily 6am-10pm.)

SIGHTS AND NIGHTLIFE. From Nám. Svobody, take Zámečnická and go right on Panenská; after Husova, head uphill to **Špilberk Castle** (Hrad Špilberk), which earned a reputation as the cruelest prison in Hapsburg Europe, and is now a museum. (Open May-Sept. Tu-Su 9am-6pm; Apr. and Oct. Tu-Su 9am-5pm; Nov.-Mar. W-Su 9am-5pm. 99Kč, students 45Kč.) In the 18th century, monks at the **Capuchin Monastery Crypt** (Hrobka Kapucínského kláštera), left of Masarykova from the train station, developed a burial technique in which air ducts allowed bodies to dry naturally. One-hundred bodies of 18th-century monks and nobles attest to its effectiveness. (Open May-Sept. M-Sa 9am-noon and 2-4:30pm, Su 9am-noon. 40Kč, students 20Kč.) The newly expanded **Mendelianum**, Mendlovo nám. 1a, documents the life and work of Johann Gregor Mendel, who discovered inherited genotypes while raising peas in a Brno monastery, founding the science of genetics. (Open May-Oct. Tu-Su 10am-6pm; Nov.-Apr. W-Su 10am-4pm. 80Kč.) In summer, **raves** are announced by posters. After performances in the attached Merry Goose Theater, artsy crowds gather at **Divadelní hospoda Veselá husa**, Zelný trh. 9. (Open M-F 11am-1am, Sa-Su 3pm-1am.) Students frequent dance club **Mersey**, Minská 15. Take tram #3 or 11 from Česká to Tábor. (Beer 25Kč. Open Tu-W 8pm-2am, Th-Sa 8pm-4am.)

OLOMOUC

Today, Olomouc (pop. 103,000) is an echo of what Prague was before it was overwhelmed by tourists. Baroque architecture lines paths in the town center, locals mill about during the day, and students keep the clubs thumping until dawn.

TRANSPORTATION AND PRACTICAL INFORMATION. Trains (☎585 785 490) leave Jeremenkova 23 for Brno (1½hr., 7-8 per day, 120Kč) and Prague (3½hr., 19 per day, 294Kč). **Buses**, Rolsberská 66 (☎585 313 848), go to Brno (1½hr., 10 per day, 75-85Kč) and Prague (4½hr., 3 per day, 310Kč). From the stations, take the pedestrian way under Jeremenkova, then trams #4 or 5 to the center. The **tourist office**, Horní nám., in the town hall, has maps and books rooms. (☎685 513 385; www.olomoucko.cz. Open daily Mar.-Nov. 9am-7pm; Dec.-Feb. 9am-5pm.) **Internet u Dominika**, Slovenská 12, has plenty of terminals. (☎777 181 857. 60Kč per hr. Open M-F 9am-9pm, Sa-Su 10am-9pm.) **Postal Code:** 77127.

ACCOMMODATIONS AND FOOD. The small **Poet's Corner Hostel ❶** feels more like home than a hostel. From the train station, take trams #4-7 to Nám. Hridinů and walk two blocks. Turn left on Sokolská; the hostel is on the 4th floor. (☎777 570 730; www.hostelolomouc.com. Laundry 100Kč. 7-person dorm July-Aug. 300Kč, Sept.-June 250Kč; doubles 800Kč; triples 1000Kč.) To reach **Pension na Hradbách ❸**, Hrnčírská 3, from Horní nám., head down Školní, straight on Purkrabská, then right on Hrnčírská. This small pension is on one of the quietest streets in the center and features singles with TV and bath. (☎585 233 243; nahradback@quick.cz. Book ahead. Singles 600Kč; doubles 800Kč; triples 900Kč.) **Hanácká Hospoda ❶**, Dolní nám. 38, is packed with locals devouring excellent

Czech fare. (☎777 721 171. Entrees 56-170Kč. Open daily 10am-midnight. AmEx/MC/V.) **Supermarket Delvita,** 8 května 24, is in the basement of Prior department store at the corner of 28 října. (☎685 535 135. Open M-F 7am-8pm, Sa 7am-2pm.)

SIGHTS AND NIGHTLIFE. The massive 1378 **town hall** *(radnice)* and its clock tower dominate the town center. The tourist office arranges trips up the tower. (Daily 11am, 3pm; 15Kč.) An amusing **astronomical clock** is set in the town hall's north side. In 1955, communist clockmakers replaced the mechanical saints with archetypes of "the people"; the masses strike the hour with their hammers and sickles. The 35m black-and-gold **Trinity Column** *(Sloup Nejsvětější Trojice)*, in the middle of the square, soars higher than any other Baroque sculpture in the country. To reach **St. Wenceslas Cathedral** *(Metropolitní Kostel sv. Václava)*, follow its spires. The interior is in impeccable condition, having been reworked virtually every century since it was damaged by fire in 1265. (Open Tu and Th-Sa 9am-5pm, W 9am-4pm, Su 11am-5pm. Donations requested.) Next door to the cathedral, the walls of the **Přemyslid Palace** *(Přemyslovský palác)* are covered in beautiful frescoes. (Open Apr.-Sept. Tu-Su 10am-6pm. 15Kč, students 5Kč. W free.)

Exit Discoteque, Holická 8, is the country's largest outdoor club and Olomouc's wildest. From Horní nám., walk to Dolní nám., then follow Kateřinská 400m to 17 Listopadu. Turn left, then right on Wittgensteinova; follow it across the bridge. The club is on the right. Spotlights and techno draw clubbers like moths to a flame. Eight bars ensure that you'll never wait for a drink. (☎585 230 573. Cover 50-60Kč. Open June-Sept. F-Sa 9pm-5am.) The popular **Depo No. 9,** Nám. Republiky 1, pours *Staropramen* (20Kč) in underground rooms with comfy seats. In the wee hours, on weekends, the basement becomes Olomouc's most happening dance club, with frequent live performances. (☎585 221 273; www.depo9.cz. Occasional cover 50-100Kč. Open M-Th 10am-2am, F 10am-6am, Sa 7pm-6am, Su 7pm-midnight.)

DENMARK (DANMARK)

From Hans Christian Andersen *Hus* in rural Odense to the hopping clubs of big-city Copenhagen, fairy-tale lovers and ravers alike flock to Denmark. The nation's Viking past has given way to a vibrant multicultural society where eccentric native traditions—like downing pickled herring on New Year's Day—have merged with those of a growing immigrant population to create a dynamic modern society. With terrain that ranges from the fertile farmlands of Funen to the pristine beaches of Jutland, and Århus emerging as a nascent competitor to Copenhagen, Denmark is worth the northward trek.

DISCOVER DENMARK: SUGGESTED ITINERARIES

Start off in the cosmopolitan capital of **Copenhagen** (p. 262), soaking up some sunshine on a **bike tour** (p. 270) of the central city or waiting out showers in the medieval ruins beneath **Christianborg Slot**. Channel your inner bard at Kronborg Slot in **Helsingør** (p. 273), where the real-life Hamlet slept, then castle hop to Frederiksborg Slot in nearby **Hillerød** (p. 272). Head west to sprightly **Odense** (p. 276) for celebrations of Hans Christian Andersen's birth, and then catch a ferry to the sleepy island hamlet of **Ærø** (p. 278). Discover the museums and nightlife of little-known **Århus** (p. 278) before indulging your inner child at Legoland in **Billund** (p. 280). End up at the northern tip of Jutland, where the quaint yellow houses of **Skagen** (p. 281) look out on the tumultuous Baltic Sea.

ESSENTIALS

FACTS AND FIGURES

Official Name: Kingdom of Denmark.

Capital: Copenhagen.

Major Cities: Aalborg, Århus, Odense.

Population: 5,432,000.

Land Area: 42,394 sq. km.

Time Zone: GMT +1.

Languages: Danish. Pockets of Faroese, and Greenlandic. English is nearly universal as a second language.

Religions: Evangelical Lutheran (95%).

WHEN TO GO

Denmark is best visited between May and September, when days are usually sunny and temperatures average 10-16°C (50-61°F). Winter temperatures average 0°C (32°F). Although temperate for its northern location, Denmark can turn rainy and cool at a moment's notice; pack a sweater and an umbrella, even in summer.

DOCUMENTS AND FORMALITIES

EMBASSIES AND CONSULATES. All foreign embassies are in Copenhagen (p. 264). Danish embassies at home include: **Australia** (Consulate General), Level 14 Gold Fields House, 1 Alfred St., Circular Quay, Sydney NSW 2000 (☎02 92 47 22 24;

dtcsydney@dtcsyd.org.au); **Canada**, 47 Clarence St., Ste. 450, Ottawa, ON K1N 9K1 (☎613-562-1811; www.ambottowa.um.dk/en); **Ireland**, 121-122 St. Stephen's Green, Dublin 2 (☎01 475 64 04; www.ambdublin.um.dk/en); **New Zealand** (Consulate General), 273 Bleakhouse Rd., Howick P.O. Box 619, 1015 Auckland (☎09 537 30 99; www.danishconsulates.nz.org.nz); **UK**, 55 Sloane St., London SW1X 9SR (☎020 7333 0200; www.amblondon.um.dk/en); **US**, 3200 Whitehaven St. NW, Washington, D.C. 20008-3683 (☎202-234-4300; www.denmarkemb.org).

VISA AND ENTRY INFORMATION. EU citizens do not need a visa. Citizens of Australia, Canada, New Zealand, and the US do not need a visa for stays of up to 90 days, beginning upon entry into any of the countries belonging to the EU's freedom of movement zone. For more information, see p. 16.

TOURIST SERVICES AND MONEY

EMERGENCY	**Police, Ambulance,** and **Fire:** ☎112.

TOURIST OFFICES. The Danish Tourist Board has offices in Copenhagen at Islands Brygge 43 (☎32 88 99 00; www.visitdenmark.dt.dk).

MONEY. The Danish unit of currency is the **krona** (plural: kroner), divided into 100 *øre*. The easiest way to get cash is from **ATMs;** cash cards are widely accepted, and many machines give advances on credit cards. Expect to pay a 30kr fee to exchange money or traveler's checks. Denmark has a high cost of living, which it passes along to visitors; expect to pay 100-130kr for a hostel bed, 450-800kr for a hotel room, 80-130kr for a day's groceries, and 50-90kr for a cheap restaurant meal. A bare-bones day in Denmark might cost 250-350kr; a slightly more comfortable day might cost 400-600kr. There are no hard and fast rules for **tipping,** but it's always polite to round up to the nearest 10kr in restaurants and for taxis and to leave an additional 10-20kr for good service. In general, service at restaurants is included in the bill, although tipping up to 15% is becoming common in Copenhagen. The European Union imposes a **Value Added Tax (VAT)** on goods and services purchased within the EU, which is included in the price (p. 23). Denmark's VAT is one of the highest in Europe (25%). Non-EU citizens can get a partial VAT refund upon leaving the EU for purchases in any one store that total over 300kr.

DANISH KRONER (KR)		
	AUS$1 = 4.63KR	10KR = AUS$2.16
	CDN$1 = 5.00KR	10KR = CDN$2.00
	EUR€1 = 7.46KR	10KR = EUR€1.34
	NZ$1 = 4.24KR	10KR = NZ$2.36
	UK£1 = 10.87KR	10KR = UK£0.92
	US$1 = 5.99KR	10KR = US$1.67

DENMARK

TRANSPORTATION

BY PLANE. International flights arrive at **Kastrup Airport** in Copenhagen (CPH; ☎32 31 32 31; www.cph.dk). Flights from Europe also arrive at **Billund Airport,** outside of Århus (BLL; ☎76 50 50 50; www.billund-airport.dk). Smaller airports in Århus and Esbjerg serve as Denmark's hubs for budget airline **Ryanair** (☎353 1249 7700; www.ryanair.com), which flies from London. **SAS** (Scandinavian Airlines; Denmark ☎70 10 20 00, UK 0870 6072 7727, US 800-221-2350; www.scandinavian.net), the national airline company, offers youth discounts to some destinations.

BY TRAIN AND BY BUS. The state-run rail line in Denmark is **DSB;** visit www.rejseplanen.dk to use the helpful **journey planner. Eurail** is valid on all state-run routes. The **Scanrail pass,** purchased outside Scandinavia, is good for rail travel through Denmark, Finland, Norway, and Sweden, as well as many discounted ferry and bus rides. Passes can also be purchased within Scandinavia, but passholders can only use three travel days in the country of purchase. See p. 53 for more info. Remote towns are typically served by buses from the nearest train station. **Buses** are reliable and can be less expensive than trains. You can take buses or trains over the **Øresund bridge** from Copenhagen to Malmö, Sweden.

RAIL SAVINGS. Scanrail passes purchased outside Scandinavia are much more flexible than Scanrail passes purchased once you arrive, and may be less expensive depending on the exchange rate. Check www.scanrail.com for more information on where to purchase passes at home.

BY FERRY. Several companies operate ferries to and from Denmark. **Scandlines** (☎3315 1515; www.scandlines.dk) arrives from Germany and Sweden, as well as operates many domestic routes. **Color Line** (Norway ☎+47 810 00 811; www.color-line.com) runs ferries between Denmark and Norway. **DFDS Seaways** (UK ☎08705

444 333; www.dfdsseaways.co.uk) sails from Harwich, England to Esbjerg, Denmark. For additional info check www.aferry.to/ferry-to-denmark-ferries.htm. Tourist offices can help you sort out the dozens of smaller ferries that serve Denmark's outlying islands. For more info on connections from Bornholm to Sweden, see p. 275; for connections from Jutland to Norway and Sweden, see p. 281.

BY CAR. Denmark's only toll roads are the **Storebæltsbro** (Great Belt Bridge; 200kr) and the **Øresund bridge** (235kr). Speed limits are 50kph (30 mph) in urban areas, 80kph (50 mph) on highways, and 110-130kph (65-80 mph) on motorways. **Gas stations** *(Info-terias)*, are spaced along Danish highways. **Gas** averages 8-9kr per liter. Watch out for bikes, which have the right-of-way. High parking prices and numerous one-way streets make driving something of a nightmare in cities. For more info on driving in Denmark, contact the **Forenede Danske Motorejere (FDM),** Firskovvej 32, Box 500, 2800 Kgs. Lyngby (☎7013 3040; www.fdm.dk).

BY BIKE AND BY THUMB. Flat terrain, well-marked bike routes, and raised bike lanes on most streets in towns and cities make Denmark a cyclist's dream. You can rent bikes (50-80kr per day) from some tourist offices, rental shops, and a few train stations. The **Dansk Cyklist Forbund** (Danish Cycle Federation), Rømersg. 5, 1362 Copenhagen K (☎33 32 31 21), provides info about cycling in Denmark and investing in long-term rentals. Pick up *Bikes and Trains* at any train station for info on bringing your bike on a train (which costs 50kr or less). **Hitchhiking** on motorways is illegal and uncommon. *Let's Go* does not recommend hitchhiking.

KEEPING IN TOUCH

PHONE CODES	**Country code:** 45. **International dialing prefix:** 00. For more information on how to place international calls, see inside back cover.

EMAIL AND THE INTERNET. In Copenhagen and other cities, you can generally find at least one cybercafe; expect to pay 20-40kr per hr. DSB, the national railroad, maintains cybercafes in some of their stations as well. In smaller towns, tourist offices and libraries are your best bet. Access at public libraries is always free, although you typically have to reserve a slot in advance.

TELEPHONES. Pay phones accept both coins and phone cards, available at post offices or kiosks in 100kr denominations. Mobile phones are an increasingly popular and economical alternative (p. 33). For domestic directory info, dial ☎118; for international info, dial ☎113. International direct dial numbers include: **AT&T** (☎8001 0010); **Canada Direct** (☎8001 0011); **MCI** (☎8001 0022); **Sprint** (☎8001 0877); **Telecom New Zealand** (☎8001 0064); **Telstra Australia** (☎8001 0061).

MAIL. Mailing a postcard or letter to Australia, Canada, New Zealand, or the US costs 7.50kr, to elsewhere in Europe 6.50kr. Domestic mail costs 4.50kr.

LANGUAGES. Danish is the official language of Denmark, although natives of Greenland and the Faroe Islands still speak local dialects. The Danish add *æ* (pronounced like the "e" in egg), *ø* (pronounced "euh"), and å (sometimes written *aa;* pronounced "oh" with tightly pursed lips) to the end of the alphabet; thus Århus would follow Skagen in an alphabetical listing of cities. *Let's Go* indexes these under "ae," "o," and "a." Nearly all Danes speak flawless English.

ACCOMMODATIONS AND CAMPING

DENMARK	❶	❷	❸	❹	❺
ACCOMMODATIONS	under 100kr	100-160kr	160-220kr	220-350kr	over 350kr

Since Denmark's hotels are uniformly expensive, **youth hostels** *(vandrehjem)* tend to be mobbed by budget travelers of all ages. HI-affiliated **Danhostels** are most common, and are often the only option in smaller towns. Facilities are clean, spacious, and comfortable, but often attract vacationing families as well as backpackers. Eco-conscious tourists can choose from one of the 13 Danhostels that have earned a **Green Key** (www.green-key.org) for their environmentally friendly practices. Danhostel check-in times are usually a non-negotiable 3-4hr. window. Dorms run about 155kr per night, with a 35kr HI discount. Linen costs 40kr, and breakfast runs around 47kr. Sleeping bags are not permitted. Reserve ahead, especially during summer and near beaches. For more info, contact the Danish Youth Hostel Association (☎3331 3612; www.danhostel.dk). The country's **independent hostels,** found mostly in cities and larger towns, draw a younger backpacking crowd and tend to be more sociable, although their facilities are rarely as nice as those in Danhostels. Most tourist offices book rooms in private homes (150-250kr).

Denmark's 510 **campgrounds** (about 60kr per person) rank from one-star (toilets and drinking water) to three-star (showers and laundry) to five-star (swimming, restaurants, and stoves). You'll need either a **Camping Card Scandinavia** (1-year 80kr; available for purchase at www.camping.se; allow at least 3 weeks for delivery), valid across Scandinavia and sold at campgrounds as well as through the Danish Youth Hostel Association, or a **Camping Card International** (www.campingcardinternational.org). Camping info is available at **DK-Camp** (☎7571 2962; www.dk-camp.dk). Campsites affiliated with hostels generally do not require a card. If you only plan to camp for a night, you can buy a 24hr. pass (20kr). The **Danish Camping Council** *(Campingradet)*, Mosedalv. 15, 2500 Valby (☎3927 8844; www.campingraadet.dk) sells passes and the *Camping Denmark* handbook (95kr). Sleeping in train stations, in parks, or on public property is illegal.

DENMARK

FOOD AND DRINK

DENMARK	❶	❷	❸	❹	❺
FOOD	under 40kr	40-70kr	70-100kr	100-150kr	over 150kr

A "danish" in Denmark is a *wienerbrød* (Viennese bread), found in bakeries alongside other flaky treats. Historically, the Danes favored open-faced sandwiches called *smørrebrød* for a more substantial meal, although today they have become more of a rarefied delicacy. Herring is served in various forms, usually pickled or raw with onions or a curry mayonnaise. For cheap eats, look for lunch specials *(dagens ret)* and all-you-can-eat buffets. National beers include Carlsberg and Tuborg; bottled brew tends to be cheaper. A popular alcohol is *snaps* (or *aquavit*), a clear distilled liquor flavored with fiery spices, usually served chilled and unmixed. Many vegetarian *(vegetarret)* options are the result of Indian and Mediterranean influences, and both salads and veggies *(grønsager)* can be found on most menus. Expect to pay around 120kr for a sit down meal at a restaurant, although cheaper eats can be found in cafes and ethnic takeaways for 40-80kr.

HOLIDAYS AND FESTIVALS

Holidays: New Year's Day (Jan. 1); Easter Holidays (Mar. 13-17); Queen's Birthday (Apr. 16); Worker's Day (May 1); Whit Sunday and Monday (June 4-5); Constitution Day (June 5); Valdemar's Day (June 15); Midsummer's Eve (June 23).

Festivals: In February, Danish children assault sweet-filled barrels with birch branches on *Fastelavn* (Shrovetide), while adults take to the streets for carnivals. Yowling guitar solos ring out over Roskilde at the open-air Roskilde Festival in early July, just as Copenhagen and Århus kick off their annual jazz festivals.

BEYOND TOURISM

For short-term employment in Denmark, check www.jobs-in-europe.net. A limited number of volunteer opportunities are listed below. See p. 66 for Beyond Tourism opportunities throughout Europe.

The American-Scandinavian Foundation (AMSCAN), 725 Park Ave., New York, NY 10016, USA (☎212-879-9779; www.amscan.org/jobs/index.html). Volunteer and job opportunities throughout Scandinavia. Limited number of fellowships for study in Denmark available to Americans.

Vi Hjæper Hinanden (VHH), Asenv. 35, 9881 Bindslev, Denmark, c/o Inga Nielsen (☎45 9893 8607; www.wwoof.dk). For 50kr, Danish branch of Willing Workers on Organic Farms (WWOOF) provides a list of farmers currently accepting volunteers.

Danish Association for International Cooperation/Mellemfolkeligt Samvirke, Borgerg. 14, 1300 Copenhagen K, Denmark (☎45 7731 0000; Danish-language website: www.mstravels.dk/greenland; limited English-language website: www.ms.dk/uk). Runs summer conservation programs in Denmark and Greenland for a participation fee.

COPENHAGEN (KØBENHAVN) ☎33, 35

Copenhagen (pop. 1,800,000) embodies the laidback, progressive attitudes that have come to pervade Europe's oldest monarchy. The Strøget, the city's famed pedestrian thoroughfare, now bustles with Middle Eastern restaurants and cybercafes, as blazing neon signs conceal angels in the architecture. The up-and-coming districts of Vesterbro and Nørrebro reverberate with some of Europe's wildest nightlife, while the hippie paradise of Christiania swings to a more downbeat vibe. This is a city for every shade of maverick.

TRANSPORTATION

Flights: Kastrup Airport (CPH; ☎3231 3231; www.cph.dk). **Trains** connect the airport to København H (13min., 6 per hr., 22.50kr or 2 clips). Ryanair flies into nearby **Sturup Airport** in Malmö, Sweden (MMX; ☎40 613 1000; www.sturup.com) at low rates.

Trains: Trains stop at **København H** (Hovedbanegården or Central Station; domestic travel ☎7013 1415, international reservations 7013 1416, S-tog info 3314 1701). For travel within the country, www.dsb.dk is indispensable. Trains run to: **Berlin** (8hr., 9 per day, 800kr); **Hamburg** (5hr., 5 per day, 550kr); **Malmö** (25min., every 20min., 71kr), **Oslo** (8hr., 2 per day, 950kr); **Stockholm** (5hr., every 1-2hr., 1000kr). For international trips, fares depend on seat availability, and can drop as low as 25% of the quotes listed above; it is worth it to **book at least 14 days in advance.**

Public Transportation: Copenhagen has an extensive and efficient public transport system. **Buses** (☎3613 1415; www.hur.dk) run daily 5:30am-12:30am. Pick up a copy of the bus map on any bus. **S-togs** (subways and suburban trains; ☎3314 1701) run M-Sa 5am-12:30am, Su 6am-12:30am. Copenhagen's **metro** (☎7015 1615; www.m.dk) is small but efficient. All 3 types of public transportation operate on a zone system. To travel any distance, you must buy a minimum of a 2-zone **ticket** (17kr; additional zones 8.50kr). Most of Copenhagen is within 2 zones. For extended stays, the best deal is the **rabatkort** (rebate card; 110kr), available from supermarkets, corner stores, and kiosks, which offers 10 2-zone tickets at a discount. The **24hr. pass** (100kr), available at train stations, grants unlimited bus and train transport in the Northern Zealand region, as does the **Copenhagen Card** (see **Practical Information,** p. 264). **Night buses,** marked with an "N," run 12:30-5:30am on limited routes and charge double fare; they also accept the 24hr. pass.

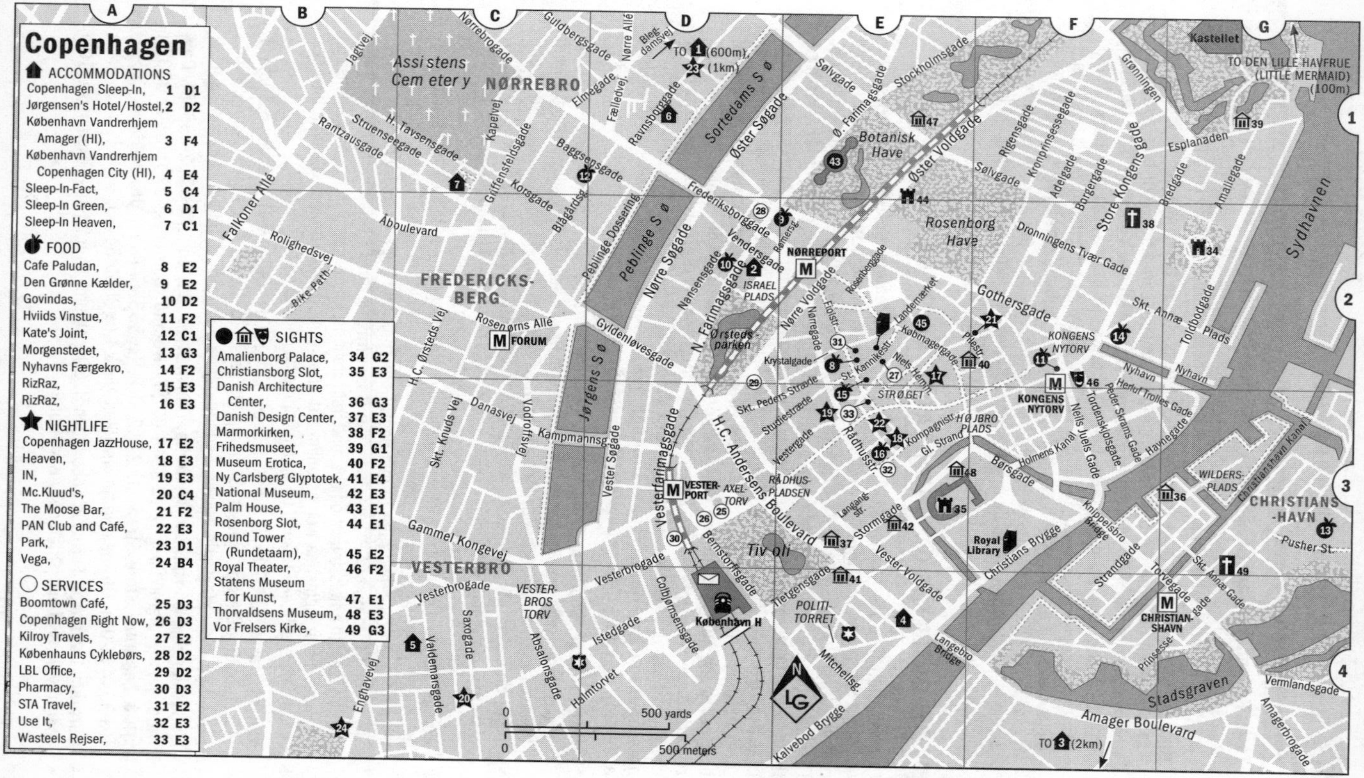

Copenhagen

ACCOMMODATIONS

Copenhagen Sleep-In,	1	D1
Jørgensen's Hotel/Hostel,	2	D2
København Vandrerhjem Amager (HI),	3	F4
København Vandrerhjem Copenhagen City (HI),	4	E4
Sleep-In-Fact,	5	C4
Sleep-In Green,	6	D1
Sleep-In Heaven,	7	C1

FOOD

Cafe Paludan,	8	E2
Den Grønne Kælder,	9	E2
Govindas,	10	D2
Hviids Vinstue,	11	F2
Kate's Joint,	12	C1
Morgenstedet,	13	G3
Nyhavns Færgekro,	14	F2
RizRaz,	15	E3
RizRaz,	16	E3

NIGHTLIFE

Copenhagen JazzHouse,	17	E2
Heaven,	18	E3
IN,	19	E3
Mc.Kluud's,	20	C4
The Moose Bar,	21	F2
PAN Club and Café,	22	E3
Park,	23	D1
Vega,	24	B4

SERVICES

Boomtown Café,	25	D3
Copenhagen Right Now,	26	D3
Kilroy Travels,	27	E2
Københauns Cyklebørs,	28	D2
LBL Office,	29	D2
Pharmacy,	30	D3
STA Travel,	31	E2
Use It,	32	E3
Wasteels Rejser,	33	E3

SIGHTS

Amalienborg Palace,	34	G2
Christiansborg Slot,	35	E3
Danish Architecture Center,	36	G3
Danish Design Center,	37	E3
Marmorkirken,	38	F2
Frihedsmuseet,	39	G1
Museum Erotica,	40	F2
Ny Carlsberg Glyptotek,	41	E4
National Museum,	42	E3
Palm House,	43	E1
Rosenborg Slot,	44	E1
Round Tower (Rundetaarn),	45	E2
Royal Theater,	46	F2
Statens Museum for Kunst,	47	E1
Thorvaldsens Museum,	48	E3
Vor Frelsers Kirke,	49	G3

DENMARK

CHEAPER THAN YOU THOUGHT. Tickets on the S-tog are covered by Eurail, Scanrail, and InterRail passes. So ride away!

Taxis: Københavns Taxa (☎3535 3535) and **Hovedstadens Taxi** (☎3877 7777) charge a base fare of 32kr for arranged pickups and 19kr otherwise, then add 10kr per km during the day and 13kr at night. København H to Kastrup Airport costs around 200kr.

Bike Rental: City Bike (www.bycyklen.dk/engelsk) lends bikes mid-Apr. to Nov. from 110 racks all over the city for a 20kr deposit. Anyone can return your bike and claim your deposit, so keep an eye on it. **Københavns Cyklebørs,** Gothersg. 157 (☎3314 0717; www.cykelborsen.dk) rents bikes for 60kr per day, 270kr per week; 200kr deposit. Open M-F 8:30am-5:30pm, Sa 10am-1:30pm; put the deposit on a credit card instead of cash to return the bike after hours. MC/V. **Københavns Cykler,** Reventlowsg. 11 (☎3333 8613; www.rentabike.dk), in København H. 75kr per day, 340kr per week; 500kr deposit. Open Sept.-June M-F 8am-5:30pm, Sa 9am-1pm; July-Aug. M-F 8am-5:30pm, Sa 9am-1pm, Su 10am-1pm. AmEx/DC/MC/V.

DENMARK

ORIENTATION AND PRACTICAL INFORMATION

Copenhagen lies on the east coast of the island of **Zealand** (Sjælland), across the Øresund Sound from Malmö, Sweden. The 28km **Øresund bridge and tunnel,** which opened July 1, 2000, established the first "fixed link" between the two countries. Copenhagen's main train station, København H, lies near the city center. North of the station, **Vesterbrogade** passes **Tivoli** and **Rådhuspladsen,** the central square, then cuts through the city center as **Strøget** (STROY-yet), the world's longest pedestrian thoroughfare. As it heads east, Strøget goes through a series of names: **Frederiksberggade, Nygade, Vimmelskaftet, Amagertorv,** and **Østergade.** The city center is ringed to the west by the five lakes, on the outside of which are the less touristed communities of **Vesterbro, Nørrebro,** and **Østerbro.** Lively Vesterbro and Nørrebro are home to many of the region's immigrants, while the wide streets of Østerbro are home to some of Copenhagen's highest income residents.

Tourist Offices: Copenhagen Right Now, Vesterbrog. 4a (☎7022 2442; www.visitcopenhagen.com). Head out the main exit of København H, turn left, and cross Vesterbrog. toward the Axelrod building. Open May-June M-Sa 9am-6pm; July-Aug. M-Sa 9am-8pm, Su 10am-6pm; Sept.-Apr. M-F 9am-4pm, Sa 9am-2pm. **Use It,** Rådhusstr. 13 (☎3373 0620; www.useit.dk). From the station, follow Vesterbrog., cross Rådhuspl. onto Strøget, and turn right on Rådhusstr. Indispensable info and free services geared toward budget travelers. Be sure to pick up a copy of *Playtime,* a comprehensive budget guide to the city. Provides daytime luggage storage, has free **Internet** (20min. max.), holds mail, and finds lodgings for no charge. Open daily mid-June to mid-Sept. 9am-7pm; mid-Sept. to mid-June M-W 11am-4pm, Th 11am-6pm, F 11am-2pm. The **Copenhagen Card** (1-day card 199kr; 3-day 429kr), sold in hotels, tourist offices, and train stations, grants free or discounted admission to most major sights, as well as unlimited travel throughout Northern Zealand; however, cardholders will need to keep up an almost manic pace to justify the cost.

Budget Travel: STA Travel, Fiolst. 18 (☎3314 1501). Open M-Th 9:30am-5:30pm, F 10am-5:30pm. **Kilroy Travels,** Skinderg. 28 (☎7015 4015). Open M-F 10am-5:30pm, Sa 10am-2pm. **Wasteels Rejser,** Skoubog. 6 (☎3314 4633). Open M-F 9am-5pm.

Embassies and Consulates: Australia, Dampfærgev. 26, 2nd fl. (☎7026 3676). **Canada,** Kristen Bernikowsg. 1 (☎3348 3200). **Ireland,** Østbaneg. 21 (☎3542 3233). **New Zealand,** Store Strandst. 21, 2nd fl. (☎3337 7702). **UK,** Kastelsv. 36-40 (☎3544 5200). **US,** Dag Hammarskjölds Allé 24 (☎3555 3144).

Currency Exchange: Forex, in København H. 20kr commission for cash exchanges, 10kr per traveler's check. Open daily 8am-9pm.

Luggage Storage: Free at **Use It** (p. 264) and most hostels. At **København H,** 30kr per bag per day; 10-day max. Lockers 25-35kr per 24hr.; 3-day max. Open M-Sa 5:30am-1am, Su 6am-1am.

Laundromats: Look for **Vascomat** and **Møntvask** chains. Locations at Borgerg. 2, Vendersg. 13, and Istedg. 45. Wash and dry each 40-50kr. Most open daily 7am-9pm. Try something different at the **Laundromat Café,** Elmeg. 15 (☎3535 2672), where you can pick up a used book, check email on the free wireless Internet, or enjoy a meal while you wait for your laundry. Bus: 3A or 80N. Salads 65kr. Entrees 95kr. Wash 32kr, dry 1kr per min. Open M-Th 8am-midnight, F-Sa 8am-2am, Su 10am-midnight. MC/V.

GLBT Resources: Landsforeningen for Bøsser and Lesbiske, Teglgårdsstr. 13 (☎3313 1948; www.lbl.dk). Open M-F 11am-5pm. The monthly *Out and About,* which lists nightlife options, is available at gay clubs and the tourist office. Other resources include www.copenhagen-gay-life.dk, www.gayguide.dk, and www.woco.dk.

Emergency: ☎112. **Police:** ☎3325 1448. Headquarters at Polititorvet, City Station at Halmtorvet 20.

24hr. Pharmacy: Steno Apotek, Vesterbrog. 6c (☎3314 8266). Ring the bell after hours. Across from the Banegårdspl. exit of København H. Cash only.

Medical Services: Doctors on Call (☎7027 5757). **Emergency rooms** at **Amager Hospital,** Italiensv. 1 (☎3234 3234), **Frederiksberg Hospital,** Nordre Fasanv. 57 (☎3816 3816), and **Bispebjerg Hospital,** Bispebjerg Bakke 23 (☎3531 3531).

Internet Access: Free at **Use It** and **Copenhagen Hovedbibliotek** (Central Library), Krystalg. 15 (☎3373 6060). Open M-F 10am-7pm, Sa 10am-2pm. **Boomtown,** Axeltorv. 1-3 (☎3332 1032), across from the Tivoli entrance (p. 267). 30kr per hr. Open 24hr.

English-Language Bookstore: Arnold Busck International Boghandel, Købmagerg. 49 (☎3373 3500; www.arnoldbusck.dk). Open M 10am-6pm, Tu-Th 9:30am-6pm, F 9:30am-7pm, Sa 10am-4pm. AmEx/DC/MC/V.

Post Office: In København H. Address mail to be held in the following format: SURNAME First name, Post Denmark, Hovedbanegårdens Posthus, Hovedbanegården, 1570 Copenhagen V, DENMARK. Open M-F 8am-9pm, Sa-Su 10am-4pm. **Use It** (p. 264) also holds mail for 2 months. Address mail to: First name SURNAME, *Poste Restante,* Use It, Rådhusstr. 13, 1466 Copenhagen K, DENMARK.

ACCOMMODATIONS AND CAMPING

Comfortable and inexpensive accommodations can be hard to find near the city center, but pedestrian-friendly streets and the great public transportation system ensure that you're never far from the action. Many hostels are also dynamic social worlds unto themselves. Reserve well in advance in summer.

Sleep-In Heaven, Struenseeg. 7 (☎3535 4648; www.sleepinheaven.com), in Nørrebro. M: Forum. From København H, take bus #250S 2 stops (dir.: Buddinge; every 10-20min.) to H.C. Ørsteds V. Take your 1st right on Kappelv., then take a left into the alley just after 44 Kappelv. Guests chat happily around the pool table, avoiding the crowded dorms. Close to nightlife. Breakfast 40kr. Linen 30kr. Free Internet. Reception 7:30am-2am. Under 35 only. Dorms 130-140kr; doubles 500kr. MC/V. ❷

Sleep-In Green, Ravnsborgg. 18, Baghuset (☎3537 7777). M: Nørreport. From there or København H, take bus #5A. Get off immediately after crossing the water, then continue in the direction of the bus and turn right. Relax in a comfortable lounge and colorful rooms at this quiet, eco-friendly hostel. Organic breakfast 30kr. Internet 20kr per 30min. Fitted sheet included; pillow and blanket 30kr. Reception 24hr. Lockout noon-4pm. Open June-Oct. 8- to 30-bed dorms 100kr. Cash only. ❷

Jørgensen's Hostel/Hotel Jørgensen, Rømersg. 11 (☎3313 8186; www.hoteljoergensen.dk), M: Nørreport. Clean, cozy rooms in a deliciously central location. Breakfast included. Linen 30kr. 5-night max. stay. Dorm lockout 11am-3pm. Dorms under 35 only. No reservations for dorms. 6- to 14-bed dorms 135kr; singles 475-575kr; doubles 575-700kr; triples 775-900kr. Cash only for dorms. DC/MC/V for private rooms. ❷

København Vandrerhjem Copenhagen City (HI), H.C. Andersens Bvd. 50 (☎3311 8585; www.danhostel.dk/copenhagencity). This 15-story "designer hostel" provides sleek accommodations. Members only. Linen 60kr. Internet 39kr per hr. Reception 24hr. Check-in 1-5pm. Dorms 120kr, private rooms 480kr. AmEx/MC/V. ❷

Sleep-In-Fact, Valdemarsg. 14 (☎3379 6779; www.sleep-in-fact.dk). Spacious, modern factory-turned-hostel. Gym available. Bike rental 50kr per day. Breakfast included. Linen 30kr. Internet 20kr per 30min. Reception 7am-noon and 3pm-3am. Lock-out noon-3pm. Curfew 3am. Open July-Aug. 10- to 30-bed dorms 100kr. Cash only. ❷

Copenhagen Sleep-In, Blegdamsv. 132 (☎3526 5059). From København H, take bus #1A (dir.: Hellerup; 15min.) to Trianglen and then walk down Blegdamsv. Popular hostel in a converted arena near Østerbro nightlife. Be prepared for the common shower divided by gender. Linen 30kr; 40kr deposit. Internet 1kr per 5min. Key deposit 20kr. Reception 24hr. Lockout noon-4pm. Open July-Aug. Dorms 110kr. Cash only. ❷

København Vandrerhjem Amager (HI), Vejlands Allé 200 (☎3252 2908). M: Bella Center. Walk across the Bella Center parking lot and turn right. This family-oriented hostel is minutes away from the city by metro. Breakfast 45kr. Lockers 25kr. Linen 35kr. Laundry 35kr. Open mid-Jan. to mid-Dec. Reception 7am-1am. Check-in 1-5pm. 6-bed dorms 135kr; private rooms 360-470kr. 35kr HI discount. AmEx/MC/V; 2% surcharge. ❷

Bellahøj Camping, Hvidkildev. 66 (☎3810 1150; www.bellahoj-camping.dk). Take bus #2A from København H (dir.: Tingbjerg; 15min., every 5-10min.) to Hulgårdsv.; backtrack and turn left onto Hulgårdsv., stay left of the church, and then make another left. Basic campsite 5km from the city center. Open June-Aug. Showers included. Electricity 25kr. Reception 24hr. Tent sites 61kr. Tent rental 100kr per person. Cash only. ❶

FOOD

Good, inexpensive food is plentiful in central Copenhagen. Strøget is lined with all-you-can-eat pizza, pasta, and Indian buffets. **Open-air markets** provide fresh fruits and veggies; try the one at **Israels Plads** near Nørreport Station. (Open M-Th 9am-5:30pm, F 9am-6:30pm, Sa 9am-3pm. Cash only.) Green grocers line the main streets in **Vesterbro** and **Nørrebro.** Around **Kongens Nytorv,** elegant cafes serve filling *smørrebrød* (open-faced sandwiches) and herring meals. **Fakta** and **Netto** supermarkets are common around Nørrebro (M: Nørreport).

Morgenstedet, Bådsmandsstr. 43 (www.morgenstedet.dk), in Christiania. Walk down Pusher St.; take a left at the end. Then take a right up the concrete ramp at the bike shop and left before the bathrooms; it will be on your right. Filling organic meals are served on the cheap in this welcoming restaurant, where complete strangers become friends. Soup 35kr. Entrees 49kr, with salad 59kr. Open Tu-Su noon-9pm. Cash only. ❷

Nyhavns Færgekro, Nyhavn 5 (☎3315 1588). M: Kongens Nytorv. Upscale fisherman's cottage atmosphere along the canal. Lunch on 10 styles of herring at the all-you-can-eat buffet (89kr) or pick just one (45kr). Sumptuous dinners from 165kr. Open daily 9am-11:30pm. Lunch served 11:30am-5pm. DC/MC/V. ❸

RizRaz, Kompagnistr. 20 (☎3315 0575) M: Kongens Nytorv. Also at Store Kannikestr. 19 (☎3332 3345). Heavily vegetarian Mediterranean buffet in a friendly environment. Lunch buffet 59kr. Dinner 69kr. Open daily 11:30am-midnight. AmEx/DC/MC/V. ❷

Govindas, Nørre Farimagsg. 82 (☎3333 7444). M: Nørreport. Hare Krishnas serve vegetarian and vegan fare in this funky cafe between Nørrebro and the city center. Buffet 69kr. Salad 15kr. Open M-F 11:30am-2pm and 4:30-9pm. Cash only. ❷

Cafe Paludan, Fiolstr. 10 (☎3315 0771). M: Nørreport. A homey, inviting eatery that doubles as a bookstore. Try a delicious bar of Scharffen Berger chocolate while you sip a warm drink. Sandwiches 48-75kr. Open M-F 10am-6pm, Sa 10am-3pm. Cash only. ❷

Kate's Joint, Blågårdsg. 12 (☎3537 4496). Bus: 5A. Diverse, rotating menu of pan-Asian cuisine with African and Middle Eastern influences. Entrees 88-98kr. Stir-fry, tofu, other appetizers 50-69kr. Open daily 5:30pm-midnight. Kitchen closes 10pm. MC/V. ❸

Den Grønne Kælder, Pilestr. 48 (☎3393 0140). M: Kongens Nytorv. Vegetarian and vegan dining in a cozy basement cafe. Sandwiches 40kr. Lunch 65kr. Dinner 85kr. Takeaway available. Open M-Sa 11am-10pm. Cash only. ❷

Hviids Vinstue, Kongens Nytorv 19 (☎3315 1064). M: Kongens Nytorv. Copenhagen's oldest pub is a delightful rabbit's warren of an establishment. 55kr lunch special includes 3 varieties of *smørrebrød* and a Danish beer. Open M-Th 10am-1am, F-Sa 10am-2am, Su 10am-10pm. MC/V. ❷

DENMARK

SIGHTS

Compact, flat Copenhagen lends itself to exploration by **bike** (p. 270). Various **walking tours** are also detailed in *Playtime* (available at **Use It,** p. 264), covering all sections of the city. Window-shop down pedestrian **Strøget** until you reach Kongens Nytorv; opposite is the picturesque **Nyhavn,** where Hans Christian Andersen penned his first fairy tale. On a clear day, take the 6.4km walk along the five **lakes** that border the western end of the city center. Wednesday is the best day to visit museums; most are free and some have extended hours.

CITY CENTER. The first sight you'll see as you exit the train station is **Tivoli,** the famous 19th-century amusement park. It features rides old-fashioned and new, shimmering fountains and colorful gardens, and a world-class **Commedia dell'arte** variety show. The **Tivoli Illuminations** is an evocative light show staged on Tivoli Lake each night 15min. before closing. *(☎3315 1001; www.tivoligardens.com. Open mid-June to mid-Aug. M-Th and Su 11am-midnight, F-Sa 11am-1am; low season reduced hours. Admission 68kr. Rides 15-60kr. Admission with unlimited rides 263kr. AmEx/DC/MC/V.)* Across the street from the back entrance of Tivoli, the **Ny Carlsberg Glyptotek** museum will be undergoing extensive renovations until July 2006; however, its Egyptian collection and most of its Impressionist works will continue to be open to the public. Tickets for free guided tours go fast; pick them up in advance. *(Dantes Pl. 7. ☎3341 8141. Open Tu-Su 10am-4pm. Tours mid-June to Aug. W at 2pm. Museum before June 28, 2006 20kr, after 40kr. Free with ISIC. W and Su free. MC/V.)* Across the street, rotating exhibits at the avant-bare **Danish Design Center** showcase trends in Danish fashion and lifestyles. *(H.C. Andersens Bvd. 27. ☎3369 3369; www.ddc.dk. Open M-F 10am-5pm, W until 9pm, Sa-Su 11am-4pm. 40kr, students 20kr. W after 5pm free. AmEx/DC/MC/V.)* To reach the **National Museum,** turn left down H.C. Andersens Bvd., another left on Stormg., a right on Vester Volg. and a left on Ny Vesterg. Its vast collections include the fabulous permanent ethnographic exhibit, "People of the Earth." *(Ny Vesterg. 10. ☎3313 4411; www.natmus.dk. Open Tu-Su 10am-5pm. 50kr, students 40kr. W free. Cash only.)* To see the vivid modernist tapestries designed by Bjørn Nørgård and given to the Queen on her 50th birthday, tour **Christiansborg Slot,** home of Parliament *(Folketing)* and the royal reception rooms. The spooky subterranean ruins underneath the Slot include plumbing from an earlier palace on the same site. *(Prins Jørgens Gård 1. ☎3392 6492. Ruins open May-Sept. daily 10am-4pm; Oct.-Apr. closed M. Call ☎3392 5259 for English-language castle tours, May-Sept. daily 11am, 1, 3pm; Oct.-Apr. Tu, Th, Sa-Su 3pm. Ruins 30kr, students 25kr. Castle tour 60kr, students 50kr.)* Nearby, the **Thorvaldsens Museum** houses works by Danish sculptor Bertel Thorvaldsen, some as original plaster models. The statues of *Jesus and the Twelve Apostles*, modeled here, are on display in the Church of Our Lady. *(Bertel Thorvaldsens Pl. 2. ☎3332 1532; www.thorvalsensmuseum.dk. Open Tu-Su 10am-5pm. 20kr. W free. V.)* For a sweeping view of the city, climb the spiral ramp of the **Round Tower,** where astronomer Tycho Brahe once observed the stars. *(Købmagerg. 52a. ☎3373 0373; www.rundetaarn.dk. Open June-Aug. M-Sa 10am-8pm, Su noon-8pm; Sept.-May M-Sa 10am-5pm, Su noon-5pm; mid-Oct. to Mar. also open Tu-W 7-10pm. 25kr. AmEx/DC/MC/V.)* Down the street, dabble in all things carnal at the **Museum Erotica,** whose Porn Room display is a far cry from high art. *(Købmagerg. 24. ☎33 12 03 11; www.museumerotica.dk. Open daily May-Sept. 10am-11pm; Oct.-Apr. M-Th and Su 11am-8pm, F-Sa 10am-10pm. 89kr, 109kr with guidebook. AmEx/MC/V.)*

CHRISTIANSHAVN. Back in 1971, the "free city" of **Christiania** was established in an abandoned Christianshavn fort by a few dozen flower children. Today, the thousand-odd residents are trying their best to continue a tradition of artistic expression and unconventionality; vendors sell clothing and jewelry out of stalls, while spots like **Woodstock Cafe** and popular **Cafe Nemoland** offer cheap beer and the most mixed crowds in town. Recent government crackdowns have driven **Pusher Street's** once-open drug trade underground; in recent years, arrests for possession have become almost commonplace (p. 268). Never take pictures on Pusher St. *(Main entrance on Prinsesseg. www.christiania.org. Take bus #66 from København H.)* The **Danish Architecture Center** hosts elegantly presented exhibits on Danish and international architecture. *(Strandg. 27b. M: Christianshavn. ☎32 57 19 30; www.dac.dk. Open daily 10am-5pm. 40kr, student 25kr. DC/MC/V.)* The steeple of **Vor Frelsers Kirke** (Our Savior's Church) will be closed for renovation until 2008. Instead, peek inside the beautiful gold-accented interior. *(Sankt Annæg. 29. M: Christianshavn or bus #66. Turn left onto Prinsesseg. ☎3257 2798; www.vorfrelserskirke.dk. Free.)*

FREDERIKSTADEN. Edvard Eriksen's **Little Mermaid** (Lille Havfrue), the tiny statue at the mouth of the harbor, honors Hans Christian Andersen's tale. *(S-tog: Østerport; turn left out of the station, left on Folke Bernadottes Allé, bear right on the path bordering the canal, left up the stairs, and then right along the street. Free.)* Head back along the canal and turn left across the moat to reach **Kastellet,** a rampart-enclosed 17th-century fortress that's now a park. *(Open daily 6am-dusk.)* Cross through Kastellet to the fascinating **Frihedsmuseet** (Museum of Danish Resistance), which documents the German occupation from 1940-1945, during which the Danes helped over 7000 Jews escape to Sweden. *(At Churchillparken.*

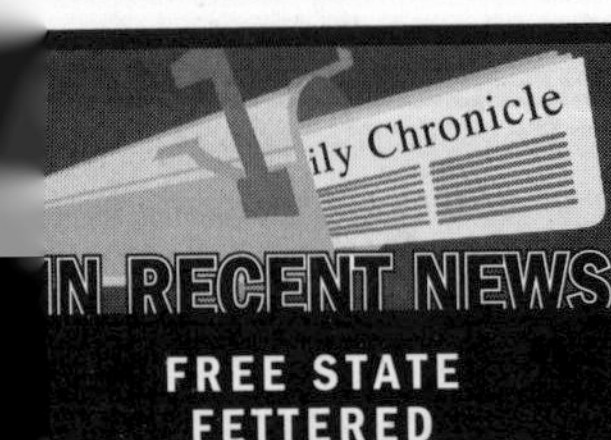

FREE STATE FETTERED

The crop of hippies who founded Christiania in 1971 shared a commitment to communal life and consensus decision-making. Many of them also shared an affection for nudism and hashish, and before long the enclave's drug culture came to outshine any mention of its New Age politics. Armed conflicts in the 1970s resulted in bans on hard drugs and weapons, but even the soft drugs that stayed attracted more stoners from abroad than the authorities liked. Once a new center-right Danish government took power in 2001, people knew that Christiania would soon have to answer for its anarchist ways.

Sure enough, police raided the area in March 2004, arresting 53 people on drug charges. Finance Minister Thor Pedersen ominously pronounced that Christiania would be "normalized," though reporters soon discovered that the government stood to gain as much as 200 million kroner by selling the land. The resulting public outcry led to a compromise solution: residents were allowed to stay if they paid for their utilities, and an independent commission was established to oversee the building of 300 new houses in compliance with government codes. The compromise has been rocky. Recent violence, including an April 2005 shooting on Pusher St. in which one man was killed, suggests a precarious future for the once free state.

☎33 13 77 14. Open May-Sept. Tu-Sa 10am-4pm, Su 10am-5pm; Oct.-Apr. Tu-Sa 10am-3pm, Su 10am-4pm. English-language tours Tu, Th, and Su at 2pm. Museum 40kr, students 30kr. W free. Cash only.) From the museum, walk south down Amalieng. to reach the lovely **Amalienborg Palace,** a complex of four enormous mansions that serve as the winter residences of Queen Margrethe II and the royal family. Several well-preserved apartments are open to the public, including the original studies of 19th-century Danish kings. The changing of the guard takes place at noon on the vast plaza; there is a smaller ceremony on even-numbered hours. *(☎3312 0808; www.rosenborgslot.dk. Open May-Oct. daily 10am-4pm; Nov.-Apr. Tu-Su 11am-4pm. 50kr, students 30kr. Combined ticket with Rosenborg Slot 80kr. MC/V.)* The imposing 19th-century **Marmorkirken** (The Marble Church), opposite the palace, features an ornate interior under Europe's third-largest dome. *(Fredriksg. 4. ☎3315 0144. Open M-Tu and Th 10am-5pm, W 10am-6pm, F-Su noon-5pm. English-language tours to the top of the dome leave mid-June to Aug. daily 1, 3pm; Oct. to mid-June Sa-Su 1, 3pm. Entrance free. Tours 25kr. Cash only.)* A few blocks north, the **Statens Museum for Kunst** (State Museum of Fine Arts) displays an eclectic collection of Danish and international art in two buildings linked by a long, glass-roof gallery nicknamed Sculpture Street. Exhibits planned for 2006 include "Rembrandt?!" (Feb. 3-May 14, 2006), which asks visitors to distinguish between works by the master himself and those of his contemporaries. *(Sølvg. 48-50. S-tog: Nørreport. Walk up Øster Voldg. ☎3374 8494; www.smk.dk. Open Tu and Th-Su 10am-5pm, W 10am-8pm. English-language tours July-Aug. Sa-Su 2pm. Museum 50kr, under 25 35kr. W free.)* Opposite the museum, the wildly Baroque **Rosenborg Slot,** built by King Christian IV as a summer residence, shows off the crown jewels as well as the opulent Unicorn Throne, which legend holds is constructed from unicorn horns. *(Øster Voldg. 4A. M: Nørreport. ☎3315 3286; www.rosenborgslot.dk. Open June-Aug. daily 10am-5pm; May and Sept. daily 10am-4pm; Oct. daily 11am-3pm; Nov.-Apr. Tu-Su 11am-2pm. 60kr, students 40kr. AmEx/DC/MC/V.)* Stroll through the 13,000 plant species in the nearby **Botanic Gardens** (Botanisk Have); tropical and subtropical plants mingle happily in the iron-and-glass **Palm House.** *(Gardens open June-Aug. daily 8:30am-6pm; Sept.-May Tu-Su 8:30am-4pm. Palm House open June-Aug. daily 10am-3pm; Sept.-May Tu-Su 10am-3pm. Free.)*

ENTERTAINMENT AND FESTIVALS

For events, consult *Copenhagen This Week* or ask at Use It. The **Royal Theater** is home to the world-famous Royal Danish Ballet. The box office at Tordenskjoldsg. 7 sells same-day half-price tickets. (☎3369 6969. Open M-Sa 10am-6pm.) For half-price tickets at the city's other theaters, head to the **Tivoli ticket office,** Vesterbrog. 3. (☎3315 1012. Open daily mid-Apr. to mid-Sept. 11am-8pm; mid-Sept. to mid-Apr. 9am-5pm.) Tickets are also available online at www.billetnet.dk. (☎3326 0954; www.vega.dk.) Relaxed **Kul-Kaféen,** Teglgårdsstr. 5, is a great place to see live performers and listen to stand-up comedy. (☎3332 1777; www.kulkafeen.dk. Cover up to 50kr. Open M 11am-midnight, Tu-Sa 11am-2am. MC/V.) In late March and early April, international and domestic releases compete for Danish distribution deals at the **NatFilm Festival** (☎3312 0005; www.natfilm.dk). During the world-class **Copenhagen Jazz Festival** (July 7-14, 2006; ☎3393 2013; http://festival.jazz.dk), the city teems with free outdoor concerts. Throughout July and August, **Zulu Sommerbio** (Summer Cinema; www.zulu.dk) holds free screenings in parks and squares all across the city. Movies are shown in their original language with Danish subtitles. October brings the well-respected **Copenhagen Gay and Lesbian Film Festival** (☎3393 0766; www.cglff.dk), followed by **cph:dox** (☎3312 0005; www.cphdox.dk), November's edgy festival of documentary cinema.

DENMARK

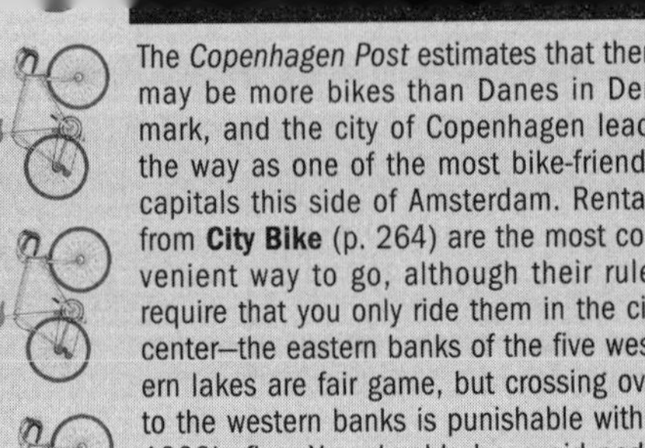

The *Copenhagen Post* estimates that there may be more bikes than Danes in Denmark, and the city of Copenhagen leads the way as one of the most bike-friendly capitals this side of Amsterdam. Rentals from **City Bike** (p. 264) are the most convenient way to go, although their rules require that you only ride them in the city center—the eastern banks of the five western lakes are fair game, but crossing over to the western banks is punishable with a 1000kr fine. You should also avoid pedestrian thoroughfares like Strøget, unless you fancy slaloming around pram-pushing newlyweds and elderly gents out taking their constitutional. If you want to ride out into the countryside, ask your hostel about rental bikes. You can take your bike onto an S-tog for 10kr. You are legally required to use lights when riding at night, and police are not shy about handing out 400kr fines. Helmets are strongly recommended, but not mandatory.

A tour of the parks, monuments, and canals just outside the central city.

TIME: 4hr. With visits to Rosenborg Slot and Christiansborg Slot, 6hr.

DISTANCE: About 6km.

SEASON: Year-round, although Rosenborg Slot has reduced hours Nov.-Apr.

This tour starts and ends at the **Rådhus.** Begin by carefully picking your way down busy Hans Christian Andersens Boulevard.

1 BOTANISK HAVE. Take a right onto Nørre Voldg. and follow it until you see the gates leading into the University of Copenhagen's lush **Botanic Gardens** (p. 268). Wander along paths lined with more than 13,000 species of plant, or hone in on the **Palm House** to view its extravagant orchids, cycads, and other tropical rarities.

2 STATENS MUSEUM FOR KUNST AND ROSENBORG SLOT. Turn left out of the gardens onto Øster Voldg. Up at the intersection with Sølvg., you'll see the gates of the **Statens Museum for Kunst** (State Museum of Fine Arts) (p. 268) to the north and the spires of **Rosenborg Slot** (p. 268) to the south. The latter served as the 16th-century summer house of King Christian IV, although the royal family took refuge here in 1801 when the British navy was shelling Copenhagen. Lock up your bike and pop inside for a look at the Sculpture Street in the museum or Denmark's crown jewels in the Slot's treasury.

3 THE ROUND TOWER. Backtrack down Øster Voldg. and turn left onto Gothersg. Make a right onto Landemærket and then hop off again to scale the heights of the **Round Tower** (p. 267), a onetime royal observatory that still affords a sweeping view of the city.

4 AMALIENBORG PALACE. Head back up to Gothersg. and turn right. Pass by **Kongens Nytorv,** the 1670 "new square" that turns into a skating rink each winter, and hang a left onto Bredg. Keep your eyes peeled for the gilded dome of the **Marmorkirken** (Marble Church; p. 268) on your left, and then turn right to enter the octagonal plaza of **Amalienborg Palace** (p. 268), a set of four Rococo mansions that the queen and her family call home.

5 NYHAVN. You've rubbed elbows with enough royalty for a bit. Continue on through the plaza, turn right on Toldbodg., and then right before the bridge onto Nyhavn. Part of the city's old waterfront, Nyhavn was known for centuries as a seedy strip for sailors to find grog, women, and a tattoo artist sober enough to wield a firm needle. Within the past 30 years, Copenhagen has embarked on a clean-up campaign, and today you're more likely to find an upscale deli serving open-faced *smørrebrod* than a tumbledown soup kitchen. Whenever a scrap of sunshine can be found, the good people of Copenhagen are soaking it up along the wharf, joined by Swedes from Malmö in search of cheap Danish beer.

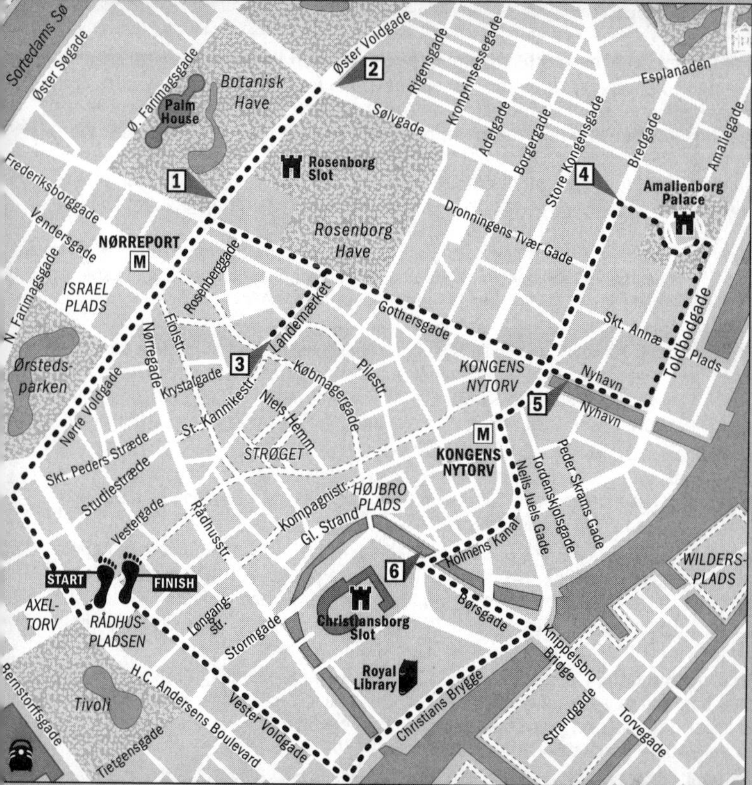

] CHRISTIANBORG SLOT. Walk your bike through Kongens Nytorv, and then thread your way etween the **Royal Theater** (p. 269) and the metro station down Neils Juels G. Turn right onto lolmens Kanal and cross the bridge to reach **Christiansborg Slot** (p. 267), seat of the Danish 'arliament. Look for the 103m tower; it's difficult to miss. If you arrive before 3:30pm, head own into the ruins of four previous castles underneath the present-day building, or try to catch tour of the Royal Reception Rooms at 11am, 1, or 3pm. The first castle was demolished to nake way for a larger one, the next two burned in spectacular fires, and the Hanseatic League 'ismantled the fourth castle stone by stone after they captured the city in 1369.

SLIDING INTO HOME. You're in the home stretch. Head east toward the Knippelsbro sridge and **Christiania** (p. 268), taking in the industrial skyline before lugging your bike 'own the steps to Christians Brygge below. Mount your trusty steed, turn right, and bike along ne canal. Keep watch for the Black Diamond annex of the **Royal Library,** built in 1996 from lack marble imported from Zimbabwe. Take a quick stop to check your email at one of the wo free terminals inside. Make a right onto Vester Voldg. and coast back up to the Rådhus. ou've earned the right to call it a day.

NIGHTLIFE

In Copenhagen, weekends often begin on Wednesday and clubs pulse with activity late enough to serve breakfast with their martinis. On Thursday, many bars and clubs have cheaper drinks and reduced covers. The streets of the city center, as well as those of **Nørrebro** and **Vesterbro,** reverberate with hip, crowded bars. Fancier options abound along Nyhavn, but laidback Danes just bring their own beer and sit on the pier; open containers are legal within the city limits. Unless otherwise noted, all bars and clubs are 18+. Copenhagen has a thriving gay and lesbian scene; check out *Playtime* or *Out and About* for listings.

> **!** The areas behind København H, the central train station, can be unsafe, especially at night. Explore with caution—and a friend.

Park, Østerbrog. 79 (☎3525 1661). Bus: 85N. A luxurious, popular club with a packed dance floor, live music hall, lavish lounges, and a rooftop patio. Dress to impress. Beer 40kr. F 20+, Sa 22+. Cover Th-Sa 50-60kr. Restaurant open Tu-Sa 11am-10pm. Club open Th-Sa 11am-5am, M-Tu and Su 11am-midnight, W 11am-2am. AmEx/DC/MC/V.

Copenhagen JazzHouse, Niels Hemmingsens G. 10 (☎3315 2600; www.jazzhouse.dk). M: Kongens Nytorv. Copenhagen's premier jazz venue becomes one of its hottest clubs after hours. Tickets from 60kr. Club cover 60kr. Concerts M-Th 8:30pm, F-Sa 9:30pm. Club open F-Sa midnight-5am. AmEx/DC/MC/V.

Vega, Enghavev. 40 (☎3326 0954; www.vega.dk). Bus: 80N, 84N. Home to Copenhagen's largest nightclub, 2 concert venues, and a popular bar, Vega is a one-stop nightlife spot. The club plays everything from 80s to trance, and the bar hosts acoustic nights and slam poetry readings. Club 20+. Club cover 60kr after 1am. Club open F-Sa 11pm-5am. Bar 18+. Bar open W 7pm-3am, Th-Sa 7pm-5am. MC/V.

PAN Club and Café, Knabrostr. 3 (☎3311 1950; www.pan-cph.dk). M: Nørreport. Gay cafe, bar, and multiple dance floors sprawl out around a seemingly endless series of staircases. Th karaoke, with cheap drinks. Cover F-Sa 50kr. Cafe open Th from 9pm, F-Sa from 10pm. Disco open from 11pm. AmEx/DC/MC/V.

Mc.Kluud's, Istedg. 126 (☎3331 6383; www.mckluud.dk). Bus: 10, 84N. Artists and students come to play sheriff and sample the cheap beer at this Wild West bar inspired by the American TV show McCloud. Beer 15-17kr. Open daily 1pm-2am. Cash only.

IN, Nørreg. 1 (☎3311 7478). M: Nørreport. Choose between **La Hacienda,** a laidback lounge, and **The Dance Floor,** a trance-driven club. Cover includes 1 free champagne. Cover for men 150kr, women 130kr. Open F 11pm-8am, Sa 11pm-11am. MC/V.

Heaven, Kompagnistr. 18 (☎3315 1900; www.heaven-copenhagen.dk). M: Kongens Nytorv. A mixed crowd gathers at this friendly, popular gay bar, a welcome break from the high-octane club scene. Open M-Th and Su noon-2am, F-Sa noon-5am. MC/V.

The Moose Bar, Sværtev. 5 (☎3391 4291). M: Kongens Nytorv. Rowdy local spirit dominates in this popular bar. Happy hour Tu, Th, Sa 9pm-late. 2 pints 30kr. 2 mixed drinks 30-35kr. Open M, Su 1pm-5am, Tu-Th 1pm-6am, F-Sa 1pm-7am. AmEx/MC/V.

DAYTRIPS FROM COPENHAGEN

When it's time for a break from the urban din of Copenhagen, the city's **S-togs** and other regional lines can whisk you all over northern Zealand. Museums, castles, countryside, and well-trodden beaches await less than an hour outside of the city.

HILLERØD. Hillerød is home to **Frederiksborg Slot,** one of Denmark's most impressive castles. Close to 90 rooms are open to the public; highlights include the Chapel, the Great Hall, and the Baroque gardens. From the train station, cross the

DENMARK

street onto Vibekev. and continue straight along the path until you can follow the signs; at the **Torvet** (main plaza), walk to the pond and follow its perimeter to reach the castle. (☎4826 0439; www.frederiksborgmuseet.dk. Gardens open May-Aug. daily 10am-9pm; low season reduced hours. Castle open daily Apr.-Oct. 10am-5pm; Nov.-Mar. 11am-3pm. Gardens free. Castle 60kr, students 50kr. AmEx/MC/V.) Hillerød is at the end of **S-tog** lines A and E. (40min., every 10min., 59.50kr or 4 clips.)

HELSINGØR. Helsingør, just 5km from the coast of Sweden, sits at a strategic entrance to the Baltic Sea. Originally built to levy taxes on ships passing through the narrows, the majestic 16th-century **Kronborg Slot** is better known as **Elsinore,** the setting for Shakespeare's *Hamlet.* Skip the underwhelming **Danish Maritime Museum** inside and head down into the dank, forbidding casemates, where a statue of Viking chief Holger Danske sleeps; legend holds that he will awake to face any threat to Denmark. Once back above ground, don't miss the Royal Apartments, where lucky fans may catch a rehearsal of *Hamlet* in progress. (☎4921 3078; www.kronborg.dk. Open May-Sept. daily 10:30am-5pm; Apr. and Oct. Tu-Su 11am-4pm; Nov.-Mar. Tu-Su 11am-3pm. Included English-language tours of the casemates daily noon, 1:30pm; castle daily at 2pm. 50kr. AmEx/MC/V.) Shakespeare buffs can head to the castle in early August, when the **Hamlet Sommer Festival** (www.hamletsommer.dk) brings Hamlet's ghost back to life in a series of avant-garde performances. To reach the lovely beach-front **Helsingør Vandrerhjem (HI) ❷,** Ndr. Strandv. 24, take bus #340 (dir.: Gilleleje; 8min., every hr.). Or, take the local train toward Hornbæk, get off at Hojstrup, and follow the path across the park; it's on the other side of the street. (☎4921 1640; www.helsingorhostel.dk. Breakfast 45kr. Linen 45kr. Reception 8am-noon and 3-9pm. Open Feb.-Nov. Dorms 115kr; private rooms 385-520kr. 35kr HI discount. AmEx/DC/MC/V; 4.75% surcharge.) The **tourist office,** Havnepl. 3, is in the Kulturhus, the large brick building across from the 19th-century train station. (☎4921 1333; www.kronborg.dk. Open mid-June to Aug. M-Th 9am-5pm, F 9am-6pm, Sa 10am-3pm; Sept. to mid-June M-F 9am-4pm, Sa 10am-1pm.) Helsingør is at the end of the northern **train** line from Malmö via Copenhagen (1hr., every 20min., 59.50kr or 4 clips).

HUMLEBÆK AND RUNGSTED. Humlebæk boasts the spectacular **Louisiana Museum of Modern Art,** 13 Gl. Strandv., named for the three wives (all named Louisa) of the estate's original owner. The museum rounds out its permanent collection—including works by Warhol, Lichtenstein, and Picasso—with six to eight major exhibits each year. Landscape architects have lavished attention on the seaside sculpture garden and the sloping lake garden, which would themselves be worth the trip. Follow signs 10min. north from the Humlebæk station or catch bus #388 across the street from the station. (☎4919 0719. Open M-Tu and Th-Su 10am-5pm, W 10am-10pm. 76kr, students 69kr. AmEx/DC/MC/V.) Near the water in Rungsted stands the house where Karen Blixen wrote her *Seven Gothic Tales* and the autobiographical novel *Out of Africa* under the pseudonym Isak Dinesen. The **Karen Blixen Museum,** Rungsted Strandv. 111, chronicles the author's life candidly and compellingly, while the grounds yield fresh flowers for the museum and are home to 40 species of birds. Follow the street leading out of the train station and turn right on Rungstedv. then right again on Rungsted Strandv.; or take bus #388 and tell the driver your destination. (☎4557 10 57. Open May-Sept. Tu-Su 10am-5pm; Oct.-Apr. W-F 1-4pm, Sa-Su 11am-4pm. 40kr. AmEx/MC/V.) Both Humlebæk (45min., every 20min., 68kr or 4 clips) and Rungsted (30min., every 20min., 59.50kr or 4 clips) are on the Copenhagen-Helsingør rail line. For Humelbæk take a Helsingør-bound **train;** for Rungsted take a train headed to Nivå. The Rungsted tourist office kiosk is on the corner of Rungstedv. and Rungsted Strandv.)

MØN. Hans Christian Andersen once called the isle of Møn, with its towering **Møns Klint** (Chalk Cliffs), the most beautiful spot in Denmark. Start your day at the "Doll Castle" **Liselund Slot,** which sits in a fairy-tale park populated by peacocks and pastel farmhouses, then work your way down the scenic 3km hike to the cliffs. (☎5581 2178. English-language castle tours daily May-Sept. 10:30, 11am, 1:30, 2pm. Tour 20kr.) Møn's unique orchids line the trail of the 143m **Aborrebjerg** (Bass Mountain), close to the youth hostel, the lakeside **Møns Klint Vandrerhjem (HI) ❷,** Langebjergv. 1. Between late June and mid-August, take bus #632 (30min., 3 per day, 13kr) from Stege, Møn's largest town, to the campground stop, then continue in the direction of the bus and take the first right. Bus #632 leaves Stege at 9:15, 11:45am, and 1:50pm. In low season, take bus #52 (every 1-2hr., 13kr) to Magleby and walk left 2.5km down the road. (☎5581 2030. Breakfast 46kr. Linen 45kr. Laundry 40kr. Reception 8-10:30am and 4-7pm. Open May to mid-Sept. Dorms 140kr; singles and doubles 335-370kr. 35kr HI discount. MC/V; 5% surcharge.) The same buses also run to the castle and the cliffs; bus #632 stops at the cliff parking lots, and bus #52 stops at Busene, a 10min. walk from the cliffs. To get to Møn, take the **train** from Copenhagen to Vordingborg (1½hr., 104kr), then bus #62 to Stege (45min., 39kr). Combination tickets (130kr), available in Copenhagen, are the cheapest option. The **Møns Turistbureau,** Storeg. 2, is next to the Stege bus stop and sells helpful maps. (☎5586 0400; www.visitmoen.com. Open mid-June to Aug. M-F 9:30am-5pm, Sa 9am-6pm; Sept. to mid-June M-F 9:30am-4:30pm, Sa 9am-noon.)

STOP THAT TRAIN! In much of Denmark, especially rural areas, trains do not stop at every station on the line. Be sure to ask at the ticket counter about exactly which train to take, and whether you need to sit in a particular car. This will prevent you from whizzing by your station unhappily.

ROSKILDE ☎46

Once the capital of the Danish Empire, Roskilde (pop. 53,000) is a comfortable daytrip from Denmark's modern-day capital. Each summer, music fans arrive in droves to hear performances by artists as diverse as Snoop Dogg and David Bowie at the **Roskilde Music Festival** (June 29-July 2, 2006; www.roskilde-festival.dk), northern Europe's largest outdoor concert. The stunning sarcophagi of the red-brick **Roskilde Domkirke,** off the Stændertorv., house the remains of generations of Danish royalty. To get there, head left out of the train station, go right on Herseg., and left onto Alg. (☎35 16 24. Open Apr.-Sept. M-F 9am-4:45pm, Sa 9am-noon, Su 12:30-4:45pm; Oct.-Mar. Tu-Sa 10am-3:45pm, Su 12:30-3:45pm. English-language tours mid-June to mid-Aug. M-F 11am, 2pm, Sa 11am, Su 2pm. Domkirke 25kr, students 15kr. Tours 20kr.) The **Vikingeskibsmuseet** (Viking Ship Museum), Vindeboder 12, houses remnants of authentic Viking ships and builds museum-quality reconstructions, some of which can be sailed out into the harbor. The tents where modern-day shipbuilders demonstrate their craft are particularly fascinating. From the Domkirke, walk downhill through the park, or take bus #216 or 607 from the train station. (☎30 02 00; www.vikingeskibsmuseet.dk. Open daily 10am-5pm. 75kr, students 55kr; low season 45/35kr. Sailing trip 50kr with museum ticket.)

The bright **Roskilde Vandrerhjem (HI) ❷,** Vindeboder 7, is next to the Viking Museum on the harbor. Book well in advance during the festival. (☎35 21 84; www.danhostel.dk/roskilde. Breakfast 45kr. Linen 45kr. Reception 7am-10pm. Dorms 155kr. 35kr HI discount. AmEx/DC/MC/V.) To reach beachside **Roskilde Camping ❶,** Baunehøjv. 7, take bus #603 (15kr) toward Veddelev to Veddelev Byg. (☎75 79 96; www.roskildecamping.dk. Open Apr. to mid-Sept. Electricity 25kr. Showers 6kr per 4min. Reception 8am-9pm. Tent sites 66kr; cabins 350-450kr. MC/V; 5% surcharge.) Restaurants and grocery stores line **Algade** and **Skomagergade.**

Trains depart for Copenhagen (25-30min., every 15min., 60kr) and Odense (1¼hr., 3 per hr., 175kr). The **tourist office,** Gullandsstr. 15, books rooms for a 25kr fee and a 10-15% deposit. Walk through the Stændertorvet with the Domkirke on your right, and turn left immediately onto Gullandsstr. (☎31 65 65. Open late June to late Aug. M-F 9am-6pm, Sa 10am-2pm; low season reduced hours.)

BORNHOLM

Bornholm natives like to say that when God was creating Scandinavia, he saved the best piece for last and then dropped it into the Baltic Sea. After a night or two on the island of Bornholm, you might be inclined to agree. The undulating farmlands of the south are ideal for bikers; nature lovers will favor the dramatic, rocky landscape of the north and the central forest, one of the largest in Denmark. The sandiest beaches are at Dueodde, on the island's southern tip. Don't miss Bornholm's four round churches, built in the 12th century and thought to be tied to the rituals of the Knights Templar. For more info, check www.bornholm.info.

TRANSPORTATION. A **train** and **ferry** combination runs from Copenhagen to Rønne, Bornholm's capital, by way of Ystad, Sweden. (Train ☎7013 1415; www.dsb.dk; 1¼hr., 5-6 per day. Ferry ☎5695 1866; www.bornholmslrafikken.dk; 80min. Combination round-trip 480kr.) A discount "red ticket" (220kr, low season 148kr) is available for the ferry with a week's advance purchase from www.bornholmslrafikken.dk, but the combo ticket above is cheaper from Copenhagen. Overnight ferries from Køge (S-tog: A+, E, Ex), south of Copenhagen, to Rønne leave at 11:30pm and arrive in Rønne at 6:30am (240kr, 315kr for a dorm bed). The cheapest way to get to Bornholm is by a **bus** and **ferry** combo. Bornhomerbussen #866 leaves from København H to Ystad, where you transfer to the ferry. (☎4468 4400. 3hr., 5 per day, 200kr.) Bornholm has an efficient local BAT **bus** service, although buses run less frequently on weekends. (☎5695 2121. 36-45kr, 24hr. pass 130kr.) Bus #7 makes a circuit of the coastline; it starts at Rønne and ends at Hammershus, stopping at most of the island's towns and attractions along the way. To go directly between Rønne and Hammershus, take bus #1 or 2. There are well-marked **bike** paths between all the major towns; pick up a guide (40kr) at Rønne's tourist office. The ride between Rønne and Sandvig or Dueodde is about 30km.

RØNNE. Busy Rønne (pop. 14,000) is Bornholm's principal port of entry. Perched on the island's southwestern coast, the town is a prime outpost for biking trips through the surrounding fields, forests, and beaches. Rent a **bike** from **Bornholms Cykeludlejning,** next door to the tourist office at Ndr. Kystv. 5. (☎5695 1359. Reserve ahead in July. 60kr per day. Open daily mid-Apr. to Sept. 7am-4pm and 8:30-9pm. AmEx/MC/V.) The **tourist office,** Ndr. Kystv. 3, books private rooms (150-215kr) for no fee. (☎5695 9500. Open mid-June to mid-Aug. daily 9am-5pm; low season reduced hours. MC/V.) To reach it, turn right out of the ferry terminal, past the BAT terminal, and cross toward the gas station; look for the green flag. The charming, family-filled **Rønne Vandrerhjem (HI) ❷,** Arsenalv. 12, is in a wooded area near the coastline. From the ferry, head toward the tourist office and then turn right on Munch Petersens V., bear left up the hill on Zahrtmannsv., follow it to the left at the top of the hill, and turn right at the roundabout onto Søndre Allé; Arsenalv. is 100m up on the right. (☎5695 1340. Breakfast 45kr. Linen 55kr. Laundry 50kr. Reception 8am-noon and 4-5pm. Open mid-June to mid-Aug. Dorms 145kr. 30kr HI discount. Cash only.) **Galløkken Camping ❶,** Strandvejen 4, is 15min. south of the city center, near the beach. Follow directions to the hostel, but continue down Søndre Allé until it becomes Strandvejen; the campground is on the right. (☎5695 2320; www.gallokken.dk. Bikes 60kr per day. Reception 8am-noon and 2-

8pm. Open May-Aug. Tent sites 58kr. MC/V; 5% surcharge.) **Sam's Corner ❷,** St. Torv 2, is a laidback burger and pizza joint with low prices (45-60kr) and large portions. (☎5695 1523. Open daily 10:30am-10pm. Cash only.) Get groceries at **Kvickly,** opposite the tourist office. (☎5695 1777. Open mid-June to Aug. daily 9am-8pm; Sept. to mid-June M-F 9am-8pm, Sa 9am-5pm, Su 10am-4pm. Cash only.)

ALLINGE AND SANDVIG. These seaside villages, 1km apart, are excellent points of entry for hikes and bike rides through the jagged heights along the northern coast. Less than 2km from Sandvig is **Hammershus,** northern Europe's largest castle ruin, situated on a breathtaking cliff overlooking the sea. Make the pleasant 20min. walk uphill from Sandvig, or catch bus #1, 2, or 7 to Hammershus. Many trails originate in Sandvig; the rocky area around **Hammeren,** northwest of the town, is a beautiful 2hr. walk that can only be covered on foot. About 20km east is the enigmatic **Østerlars Rundkirke,** the largest of the island's round churches, with a whitewashed exterior and hefty, thick-walled architecture. Take bus #3 or 9 to Østerlars Kirke. (☎5649 8264. Open Apr.-Oct. M-Sa 9am-5pm; July also Su 1-5pm. 10kr. Cash only.) The **tourist office,** Kirkeg. 4, in Allinge, offers free maps of the Hammeren area and finds rooms for free. (☎5648 0001. Open mid-June to mid-Aug. M-F 10am-5pm, Sa 10am-3pm; mid-Aug. to mid-June M-F 10am-5pm, Sa 10am-noon.) Rent **bikes** at the **Sandvig Cykeludlejning,** Strandvejen 121. (☎2145 6013. Open May-Sept. M-F 9am-3:30pm, Sa 9am-1pm, Su 10am-1pm. 60kr per day. Cash only.) Just outside Sandvig is the lakeside **Sandvig Vandrerhjem (HI) ❷,** Hammershusv. 94. Get off the bus one stop past Sandvig Gl. Station; continue up the road and follow the signs. (☎5648 0362. Breakfast 45kr. Linen 50kr. Laundry 40kr. Reception 9-10am and 4-6pm. Open May-Sept. Dorms 150kr; singles 310kr; doubles 470kr. Reservation fee 20kr. 35kr HI discount. Cash only.) **Sandvig Familie Camping ❶,** Strandlinien 5, has sites on the shore. Get off the bus at Sandvig Gl. Station and follow the signs down the hill. (☎5648 0447. Reception 8am-9pm. Open Apr.-Oct. Tent sites 69kr, extra person 54kr.) **Riccos ❷,** Strandg. 8, a pleasant cafe near the sea, has free **Internet.** (☎5648 0314. Open daily 7am-10pm. MC/V.)

FUNEN (FYN)

Nestled between Zealand to the east and the Jutland Peninsula to the west, the island of Funen has become destination spot for fairy-tale lovers and cyclists alike. Isolated in the time of golden son Hans Christian Andersen, this once remote breadbasket has since been connected to Zealand by the magnificent Storebæltsbro bridge and tunnel. Bike maps (75kr) are available at Funen tourist offices.

ODENSE ☎63, 65, 66

Most tourists are drawn to Odense (OHN-suh; pop. 200,000), the third largest city in Denmark, by the legacy of Hans Christian Andersen. While fairy tales still reign supreme, a thriving nightlife and music scene are quickly turning this city into a destination for the young and trendy.

TRANSPORTATION AND PRACTICAL INFORMATION. Trains run to Copenhagen (1½hr., 3 per hr., 210kr), Roskilde (1¼hr., 2 per hr., 175kr), and Svendborg via Kværndrup (40min., 2 per hr., 59kr). **Buses** depart from behind the train station. The **tourist office,** in the Rådhuset, offers free **Internet** and local bike maps, and will book rooms for a 35kr fee. It also sells the **Odense Adventure Pass,** good for admission to museums and unlimited public transport (1-day 120kr, 2-day 160kr). Turn left out of the train station, make a right onto Thomas B. Thriges G. at the second light, then right onto Vesterg. (☎6612 7520; www.visitodense.com. Open mid-June to Aug. M-F 9:30am-6pm, Sa-Su 10am-3pm; Sept. to mid-June M-F 9:30am-4:30pm, Sa 10am-1pm. AmEx/MC/V.) The library in the train station has free **Internet;** reserve time at the info desk. (☎6551 4421. Open Apr.-Sept. M-Th 10am-7pm, F 10am-4pm, Sa 10am-2pm; low season extended hours.) **Galaxy Netcafe,** also in the station, offers Internet and other computer services for 17kr per hr. (Open 9am-1am.) Rent **bikes** at **City Cykler.** Continue down Vesterg. from the tourist office for 10min.; it will be on your right. (99kr per day, with 750kr deposit. Open M-F 10am-5:30pm, Sa 10am-1pm.) **Postal Code:** 5000.

ACCOMMODATIONS AND FOOD. The fabulous **Danhostel Odense City (HI)** ❸ is attached to the station. (☎6311 0425; www.cityhostel.dk. Breakfast 47kr. Linen 60kr. Laundry 40kr. Internet 10kr per 15min. Reception 8am-noon and 4-8pm. Dorms 155kr; singles 435kr; doubles 550kr; triples 585kr; quads 617kr. 35kr HI discount. MC/V; 4% surcharge.) To reach **DCU-Camping Odense** ❶, Odensev. 102, 4km from town, take bus #21, 22, 23, or 24 (dir.: Højby; 14kr.) and ask the driver to drop you off. (☎6611 4702. Reception mid-June to mid-Aug. 8am-noon and 2-10pm; low season 7:30am-noon and 4-10pm. Tent sites 104kr; low season 84kr. 4-person cabin with stove 365/280kr. AmEx/MC/V.) **Vestergade,** a long pedestrian street, swarms with ethnic restaurants and cafes. Don't overlook the small alleys that wind their way off of Vesterg. **Brandts Passage,** filled with hip cafes, is the liveliest of these, while **Vintapperstræde** is slightly more low-key. Both are on the right as you walk away from the tourist office on Vesterg., just before and after Kongensg. Get groceries at **Aktiv Super,** Nørreg. 63, at the corner of Nørreg. and Skulkenborgg. (☎6612 8559. Open M-F 9am-7pm, Sa 9am-4pm. Cash only.)

DENMARK

SIGHTS AND NIGHTLIFE. At **Hans Christian Andersen's Hus,** Bangs Boder 29, where the author grew up and worked, you can learn about his eccentricities and listen to his timeless children's tales. From the tourist office, walk right on Vesterg., turn left on Thomas Thringes G. and right on Hans Jensens Str. (☎6551 4601. Open daily June-Aug. 9am-6pm; Sept.-May Tu-Su 10am-4pm. English-language performances of his works, W-Th 3pm. 50kr.) At the **Carl Nielsen Museum,** Claus Bergs G. 11, listen to the works of the famous Danish composer and musician. (☎65 51 46 01. Open Th-F 4-8pm, Su noon-4pm. 15kr.) Just down Vesterg., near the tourist office, is **St. Knud's Cathedral.** Inside, view the skeleton of St. Knud, murdered at the altar of the previous church on the same site, as well as the magnificent triptych by Claus Berg. (☎6612 0392. Open Apr.-Oct. M-Sa 10am-5pm, Su noon-5pm; low season M-Sa 10am-4pm, Su noon-5pm.)

After dinner on weekend nights, the area around Vesterg. is packed with people of all ages talking, drinking, and listening to live bands. When this crowd disperses around 11pm, the city's club and bar scene takes over. **Crazy Daisy,** Skt. Knuds Kirkestr. just past Radhuspl., has six bars on three floors. (☎6614 6788. Cover 35-40kr. Open F-Sa 11pm-late.) Farther from the center, **Boogie Dance Cafe,** on Nørreg. near Th. B. Thriges G., is packed with a young crowd pumping to Odense's best DJs. (Cover 40kr after midnight. Open Tu-Sa 10:30pm-5:30am. MC/V.) The monthly *What's On?* available at the tourist office has additional nightlife info.

DAYTRIP FROM ODENSE: KVÆRNDRUP. Just 25min. south of Odense, Kværndrup is home to **Egeskov Slot,** a magnificent castle that appears to float on the surrounding lake. Spend the afternoon exploring the grounds, which include imaginative gardens, hedge mazes, and a grab bag of small museums. On Wednesday evenings the castle hosts special activities like archery and fireworks. (☎6227 1016. Castle open July M-Tu and Th-Su 10am-7pm, W 10am-11pm; May-June and Aug.-Sept. daily 10am-5pm. Grounds open daily July 10am-8pm; June and Aug.

10am-6pm; Apr.-May and Sept. 10am-5pm. Grounds, mazes, and museums 90kr, with castle 145kr. MC/V.) Take the Svendborg-bound **train** (25min., 49kr) that leaves 38min. past the hour from Odense. Turn right out of the station and walk up to Bøjdenv., the main road, where you can catch bus #920 (every hr., 16kr), or turn right and walk 20min. to the castle. From mid-June to mid-Aug., you can also take FynBus #801 from Odense station directly to the castle (1hr., 3-8 per day, 44kr); ask at the FynBus terminal behind Odense train station for exact schedule.

ÆRØ ☎62

The wheat fields, harbors, and hamlets of Ærø (EH-ruh), a small island off the southern coast of Funen, use modern technologies to preserve an earlier era of Danish history. Almost 80% of the island is powered by renewable energy sources, leaving the countryside air pristine. The quaint town of **Ærøskøbing** (pop. 3900) serves as a gateway to the island. Hollyhocks and half-timbered houses line the town's cobblestone streets, and sleepy one-lane roads, rolling fields, and picturesque windmills lure vacationing Danes into exploring the rest of the island by bicycle. After a day of biking, relax in the summer cottage atmosphere of the **Ærøskøbing Vandrerhjem (HI) ❷,** Smedev. 15, turn left on Smedeg.; at the end, bear right onto Nørreg., which becomes Østerg. and eventually Smedev. (☎52 10 44. Bike rental 45kr per day. Breakfast 47kr. Linen 50kr. Laundry 60kr. Reception 8am-noon and 4-8pm. Check-in 4-6pm. Open Apr.-Sept. Dorms 108kr; singles 305kr; doubles 345kr. 35kr HI discount. Cash only.) Restaurants line the Vesterg. or buy groceries at **Netto,** Vestre Allé 4, across the street from the ferry landing. (Open M-F 9am-7pm, Sa 8am-5pm. Cash only.) Several **trains** run from Odense to Svendborg are timed to meet the ferry to Ærøskøbing. (☎52 40 00. 1¼hr.; 5-6 per day; 85kr, round-trip 145kr. Cash only.) On the island, bus #990 travels between the towns of Ærøskøbing, Marstal, and Søby (20kr, day-pass 60kr). Ærøskøbing's **tourist office,** Vesterg. 1, has **Internet** for 25kr per 15min. (☎52 13 00; www.arre.dk. Open M-F 9am-4pm, Sa 10am-1pm.) **Postal Code:** 5970.

JUTLAND (JYLLAND)

Jutland's sandy beaches and historic houses complement its sleek wind turbines and contemporary art. Viking trading centers used to dominate the western half of the island, but now the cultural havens of Århus and Aalborg in the east draw the region's crowds. Cyclists and canoers enjoy the vast open spaces of the central lakes region, while windsurfers head to prime waves along the western coast.

ÅRHUS ☎86-89

Pedestrian walkways thread their way through the museums, swollen nightclubs, and well-developed art scene of Århus (OR-hoos; pop. 280,000), Denmark's second-largest city. Rather than pouting in the shadow of Copenhagen, less touristy Århus takes some of the capital's urban sophistication and then tempers it with a refreshing dose of relaxed Jutland practicality.

TRANSPORTATION AND PRACTICAL INFORMATION. Trains run from Århus to: Aalborg (1½hr., 2 per hr., 147kr); Copenhagen (3hr., 2 per hr., 292kr); Fredericia (1hr., 2 per hr., 112kr); Frederikshavn (2¾hr., every hr., 192kr). **Buses** leave from outside the train station. To get to the **tourist office,** under the clock tower of the ultramodern Rådhus, go left across Banegårdspl out of the station, then take the first right on Park Allé. They book private rooms (200-500kr) for free and sell the **24hr. Tourist Ticket** (55kr), which offers unlimited use of the city's extensive bus system. The **Århus pass** includes admission to most museums and sights as well as unlimited public transit (1-day 97kr, 2-day 121kr, 1-week 171kr). (☎8731 5010; www.visitaarhus.com. Open mid-June to early Sept. M-F 9:30am-6pm, Sa 9:30am-5pm, Su 9:30am-1pm; low season reduced hours.) Between May and October, **free city bikes** are available from locations throughout the city. Check the tourist office website for additional details. **MM Cykler Værksted,** Mejlg. 41, also rents bikes for 85kr per day. (☎2835 1555 or 2072 5555. Open M-F 8am-5pm.) The main **library,** on Vesterg. 55 in Mølleparken, offers free **Internet.** (☎8940 9200. Open May-Sept. M-Th 10am-7pm, F 10am-5pm, Sa 10am-2pm; Oct.-Apr. M-Th 10am-8pm, F 10am-6pm, Sa-Su 10am-3pm.) **Postal Code:** 8000.

ACCOMMODATIONS AND FOOD. Popular and social, the **Århus City Sleep-In ❷,** Havneg. 20, is located in the heart of the city's nightlife. From the train station, follow Ryesg., which becomes Sønderg., all the way to the canal. Take the steps or elevator down to Åboulevarden, cross the canal, and turn right; at the end of the canal, turn left on Mindebrog., then left again. (☎8619 2055; www.citysleep-in.dk. Breakfast 45kr. Linen 45kr; deposit 30kr. Laundry 30kr. Internet 20kr per hr. Key deposit 50kr. Reception 24hr. Dorms 110kr; doubles 340-380kr. MC/V; 4.75% surcharge.) Just 5min. north of the city, the quieter **Århus Vandrehjem (HI) ❷,** Marienlundsv. 10, is 500m from one of Århus's nicest beaches. Take bus #1, 6, 9, or 16 to Marienlunds. (☎8616 7298; www.aarhus-danhostel.dk. Breakfast 46kr. Linen 45kr. Reception 8am-noon and 4-7pm. Dorms 143kr; doubles 502kr; triples 537kr. 35kr HI discount. MC/V; 3% surcharge.) **Blommehaven Camping ❶,** Ørneredev. 35, offers pristine facilities in the Marselisborg forest 4km south of the city. In summer, bus #19 runs directly there from the station; in low season, take bus #6 to Hørhavev., continue down the street, and turn right on Ørneredev. (☎8627 0207; blommehaven@dcu.dk. Reception 8am-noon and 2-10pm. Open mid-Mar. to late Oct. Tent sites 104kr, extra person 64kr. AmEx/DC/MC/V.) The jackpot for cheap eats is **Skolegade,** which becomes Mejlg. just behind City Sleep-In. You can see an astrologer at **Under Engle ❸,** Mejlg. 28, where delicious vegetarian fare warrants the high prices. (☎8618 2330. Veggie burgers from 75kr. Open Tu-Sa noon-10pm. Cash only.) Pick-up groceries at **Netto,** in St. Knuds Torv; from the train station go down Ryeseg. and turn right into the square across from the church. (☎8612 3112. Open M-F 9am-8pm, Sa 8am-5pm. Cash only.)

SIGHTS AND ENTERTAINMENT. The exceptional **Århus Kunstmuseum (ARoS),** Aros Allé 2, off of Vester Allé, features eight sinuous levels of gallery space, which play host to installations, multimedia exhibits, and a huge permanent collection of modern art. The view from the roof terrace is spectacular. (☎8730 6600; www.aros.dk. Open Tu, Th 10am-5pm, W 10am-10pm. 70kr, students 55kr. AmEx/DC/MC/V.) Fifteen minutes south of town, the **Moesgård Museum of Prehistory,** Moesgård Allé 20, is unremarkable except for the eerie, mummified **Grauballe Man.** Take bus #6 from the train station to the end. (☎8942 1100; www.moesmus.dk. Open Apr.-Sept. daily 10am-5pm; Oct.-Mar. Tu-Su 10am-4pm. 45kr, students 35kr. AmEx/DC/MC/V.) The **Prehistoric Trail** behind the museum reconstructs Danish forests from different ages. The quiet 3km walk leads to a popular **beach.** In summer, bus #19 returns from the beach to the Århus station.

Each July, Århus hosts its acclaimed **jazz festival** (www.jazzfest.dk), followed by the **Århus Festuge** (☎8940 9191; www.aarhusfestuge.dk), a rollicking celebration of theater, dance, and music held from the last weekend in August through early September. For nightlife any time of year, **The Social Club** Klosterg. 34, pumps loud music that polls well with students. (☎8619 4250; www.socialclub.dk. Open Th-Sa 11pm-6am.) **Train,** Tolbodg. 6, has reinvented an enormous dockside warehouse as a nightclub and concert hall. (☎8613 4722; www.train.dk. Concerts all ages, disco 23+. Disco open F-Sa 11pm-late.) The pubs down Skoleg. offer a laidback alternative to the club scene. Gay nightlife in Århus centers around the **Pan Club,** Jægergårdsg. 42, a late-night cafe and disco. Turn left out of the station onto Banegårdspl., left onto MP Bruuns G., and right onto Jægergårdsg. (☎8613 1343. Cover 15kr before 11pm 15kr, 60kr after. Cafe F-Sa 10pm-6am, disco 11pm-5am.)

DAYTRIP FROM ÅRHUS: BILLUND. Billund is the home of **Legoland,** an amusement park filled with intricate, sprawling Lego-sculptures made from over 50 million of the candy-colored blocks. The ferocious **Power Builder** ride will make a convert of any adult skeptic. (☎7533 1333; www.legoland.com. Open daily July to mid-Aug. 10am-9pm; June and late Aug. 10am-8pm; Apr.-May and Sept.-Oct. reduced hours. Day pass 185kr. Free entrance 30min. before rides close.) To get there, take the **train** from Århus to Vejle (45min., every hr., 85kr), then **bus** #244 (dir.: Grinsted; 46kr).

RIBE ☎75, 76

Denmark's oldest settlement, Ribe (pop. 18,000) is a lovely, self-consciously medieval, town situated on the salt plains near Jutland's west coast. Climb the 12th-century **Domkirke tower** for a sweeping view of Ribe's red-shingle roofs. (☎7542 0619. Open July to mid-Aug. M-Sa 10am-5:30pm, Su noon-5:30pm; May-June and mid-Aug. to Sept. M-Sa 10am-5pm, Su noon-5pm; Apr. and Oct. M-Sa 11am-4pm, Su noon-4pm; Nov.-Mar. daily 11am-3pm. 12kr.) Near the Torvet, the **Old Town Hall,** on Von Støckens Pl., houses a former debtors' prison where artifacts of Ribe's medieval "justice" are displayed. (☎7688 1122. Open daily June-Aug. 1-3pm; May and Sept. M-F 1-3pm. 15kr.) Follow the singing **night watchman** for a tour of town, beginning in the Torvet. (40min. June-Aug. 8, 10pm; May and Sept. 10pm. Free.) The open-air **Ribe VikingCenter,** Lustrupv. 4, painstakingly recreates a Viking town unearthed near Ribe. Take bus #711 from Ribe Station (every hr.); ask the driver to stop at the center. Walk towards the train tracks, then continue past them toward the Danish flags. By foot, head 25min. south down Hundeg. Pass through two roundabouts and look for signs. (☎7541 1611; www.ribevikingecenter.dk. Open July-Aug. daily 11am-5pm; May-June and Sept. M-F 10am-3:30pm. 65kr. MC/V.)

The basic **Ribe Vandrerhjem (HI) ❷,** Sct. Pedersg. 16, rents bikes for 60kr per day. From the station, cross the Viking Museum parking lot, bear right, walk down Sct. Nicolajg. to the end, then turn right on Saltg. and immediately left. (☎7542 0620; www.danhostel-ribe.dk. Breakfast 47kr. Linen 42kr. Reception 8am-noon and 4-8pm. Check-in 4-6pm. Open Feb.-Nov. Dorms 125-155kr; singles 305-515kr; doubles 370-550kr. 35kr HI discount. AmEx/MC/V; 4% surcharge.) **Overdammen,** which begins at the Torvet, has plenty of inexpensive cafes; **Seminarievej,** at the end of Saltg., is home to a number of supermarkets. **Trains** arrive from Århus (3½hr., every 1-2hr., 210kr) via Fredricia. The **tourist office,** Torvet 3, books rooms for a 25kr fee. From the train station, walk down Dagmarsg.; the office is in the main square. (☎7542 1500; www.visitribe.dk. Open July-Aug. M-F 9am-6pm, Sa 10am-5pm, Su 10am-2pm; June and Sept. M-F 9am-5pm, Sa 10am-1pm; Jan.-May and Oct.-Dec. M-F 9:30am-4:30pm, Sa 10am-1pm.) The library, next to the Rådhus, offers 30min. free **Internet.** (☎7542 1700. Open M-Tu 10am-5:30pm, W-F 10am-5pm, Sa 10am-1pm.)

AALBORG ☎96, 98, 99

A laidback haven for university students by day, Aalborg (OLE-borg; pop. 162,000) heats up after nightfall, when its renowned bar and club scene takes center stage. To pass the hours until the parties begin, head to the corner of Alg. and Molleg., where an elevator descends from outside the Salling Department Store to the half-excavated ruins of a **Franciscan friary.** (☎9631 0410. Open Tu-Su 10am-5pm. Elevator 20kr per 2-3 people, up to 250kg.) North of town, the starkly solemn grounds of

Lindholm Høje, Vendilav. 11, include 700 ancient Viking graves and an informative—but less-than-essential—museum detailing life in Viking times with artifacts from the excavated graves. Take bus #2C, which departs in front of the Burger King near the tourist office. (☎9931 7400; www.nordjyllandshistoriskemuseum.dk. Grounds open daily 24hr. Museum open mid-Apr. to Oct. daily 10am-5pm; Nov. to mid-Apr. Tu 10am-4pm, Su 11am-4pm. English-language museum tours in July W 2pm. Grounds free. Museum 30kr, students 15kr. MC/V.) After a full day of dusty antiquarianism, turn your attention to the bacchanalia down on **Jomfru Ane Gade,** a teeming pedestrian strip of bars and clubs that's packed with students and party-goers nearly every night. For an even wilder time, hit up Aalborg the last weekend in May for **Karneval i Aalborg** (May 26-27, 2006; www.karnevaliaalborg.dk), when the city welcomes spring with the largest carnival in Northern Europe.

Cozy private cabins double as dorms at **Aalborg Vandrerhjem and Camping (HI) ❷,** Skydebanev. 50, alongside the windswept Lim Fjord. Take bus #13 (dir.: Fjordparken, 2 per hr.) to the end of the line. (☎9811 6044. Reception mid-June to mid-Aug. 8am-11pm; low season 8am-noon and 4-9pm. Breakfast 47kr. Linen 35kr. Laundry 35kr. Free Internet. Dorms 155kr; singles 315-515kr; doubles 410-570kr. 35kr HI discount. Camping electricity 26kr. Tent sites 65-80kr. MC/V; 4% surcharge.) **Ved Stranden,** which runs parallel to the water, is lined with cheap eateries between Vesterbro and Jomfru Ane G.; the restaurants get more expensive near Østerågˌ. The **Føtex** supermarket, Slotsg. 8-14, just past Boomtown on Nytorv., has an ATM. (☎9932 9000. Open M-F 9am-8pm, Sa 8am-5pm. Cash only.)

Trains run to Århus (1½hr., every hr., 147kr) and Copenhagen (5hr., 2 per hr., 326kr). Within the city, **buses** (15kr) include an hour of transfers. To find the **tourist office,** Østerågˌ. 8, head out of the train station, cross JFK Pl. and turn left on Boulevarden, which becomes Østerågˌ. The office distributes copies of *Musik i Aalborg*, which contains info on **free concerts** in Mølleparken. (☎9930 6090; www.visitaalborg.com. Open July M-F 9am-5:30pm, Sa 10am-4pm; late June and Aug. M-F 9am-5:30pm, Sa 10am-1pm; Sept. to mid-June M-F 9am-4:30pm, Sa 10am-1pm.) The public library, near the end of Alg. or Nytorv., has free **Internet.** (☎9931 4300. Open mid-June to Aug. M-F 10am-8pm, Sa 10am-2pm; Sept. to mid-June M-F 9am-8pm, Sa 10am-3pm.) At **Boomtown,** Nytorv. 18, you must reserve a slot in advance on weekends after midnight. (Open M-Th 10am-2am, F-Sa 10am-8am, Su 11am-midnight. 20kr per 30min., 30kr per hr.)

FREDERIKSHAVN ☎96, 98, 99

From its days as a fishing village and naval base, Frederikshavn (fred-riks-HOW-n; pop. 35,000) has evolved into a transportation hub for Scandinavian ferry lines. Little else recommends the town. **Stena Line** ferries (☎9620 0200; www.stenaline.com) leave for Gothenburg, Sweden (2-3½hr.; 100-150kr, 30% Scanrail discount) and Oslo, Norway (8½hr.; 140-280kr, 50% Scanrail discount). **Color Line** (☎9956 1977; www.colorline.com) sails to Larvik, Norway (6¼hr., 180-440kr). To get from the station to the **Frederikshavn Vandrerhjem (HI) ❶,** Buhlsv. 6, walk right on Skipperg. for 10min.; turn left onto Nøorreg., and right on Buhlsv. (☎9842 1475; www.danhostel.dk/frederikshavn. Reception 8am-noon and 4-8pm. Breakfast 46kr. Linen 45kr. Laundry 40kr. Dorms 97-155kr; singles 235-285kr; doubles 310-370kr. 35kr HI discount. Cash only.) Restaurants and shops cluster along the pedestrian **Søndergade** and **Havnegade;** Rådhus Allé has several grocery stores.

SKAGEN ☎98

Perched on Denmark's northernmost tip, the spectacular Skagen (SKAY-en; pop. 10,000) descends into long stretches of white sand dunes lining its ice-blue water, and brightly painted "Skagen yellow" houses topped by red-tiled roofs welcome local fishermen home from the sea. Skagen's colorful, idyllic charms make it worth the long trek north; though Danish tourists discovered it long ago, international tourists are just beginning to venture to this out-of-the-way spot. The elegant **Skagens Museum,** Brøndumsv. 4, features 19th- and 20th-century work by Skagen-based artists. From the train station, walk left down St. Laurentii V. and turn right on Brondumsv. (☎44 64 44; www.skagensmuseum.dk. Open May-Sept. daily 10am-5pm; Oct.-Apr. W-Su 10am-3pm. 60kr. AmEx/MC/V.) At nearby **Grenen,** the powerful currents of the North and Baltic Seas collide in striking rhythm. Unlike the 60km of beach in other areas of Skagen, Grenen is strictly off-limits to bathers due to its life-threatening currents. To get to Grenen, take the bus from the Skagen station (15kr) or walk 2km down Fyrv.; turn left out of the train station and bear left at the fork. About 13km south of Skagen is the spectacular and enormous **Råberg Mile** (ROH-bayrg MEE-leh), a sand dune formed by a 16th-century storm. The vast moonscape migrates 15m east each year. Take bus #99 or the train from Skagen to Hulsig, then walk 4km down Kandestedv.

DENMARK

Book in advance at the popular **Skagen Ny Vandrerhjem ❷,** Rolighedsv. 2. From the station, turn right on Chr. X's V., which becomes Frederikshavnv., then left on Rolighedsv. (☎44 22 00; www.danhostelnord.dk/skagen. Breakfast 45kr. Linen 50kr. Reception 9am-noon and 4-6pm. Open Feb.-Dec. Dorms 155kr; singles 310-515kr; doubles 395-670kr. 35kr HI discount. Cash only.) Bus #99 passes several campgrounds. Turn right out of the station onto Sct. Laurentii V., where restaurants cluster near **Havnevej.** Pick up picnic supplies at **Super Brugsen,** Sct. Laurentii V. 28. (☎44 17 00. Open daily 9am-10pm.) **Trains** run to Frederikshavn (40min., every hr., 45kr). Despite the wind, biking is the best way to experience Skagen. Rent **bikes** at **Cykelhandler,** Kappelborgv. 23; from the station turn right onto Sct. Laurentii V., right onto Havnev. and right again. (☎44 25 28. 20kr per hr., 60kr per day. Open M-F 8am-5:30pm, Sa 9:30am-noon. Cash only.) The **tourist office** is in the station. (☎44 13 77; www.skagen-tourist.dk. Open July M-Sa 9am-6pm, Su 10am-4pm; June and Aug. M-Sa 9am-5pm, Su 10am-2pm; low season reduced hours.) The **library,** Sct. Laurentii V. 23, has free **Internet.** (☎44 28 22; www.skagen.dk/skagbib. Open M, Th 10am-6pm; Tu-W and F 1-6pm, Sa 10am-1pm.)

ESTONIA (EESTI)

Only too happy to sever its Soviet bonds, Estonia has just as eagerly revived ties with its Nordic neighbors. As a result, Finnish tourism and investment have proven a revitalizing force. The material wealth that has accumulated in Tallinn, however, masks the declining living standards that lurk outside of big cities, as well as the chagrin of the ethnically Russian minority over Estonia's Finnish leanings. Still, having overcome successive centuries of domination by the Danes, Swedes, and Russians, Estonians are now proud to take their place as members of modern Europe.

DISCOVER ESTONIA: SUGGESTED ITINERARIES

THREE DAYS If you're arriving in **Tallinn** (p. 287) spend a day exploring the streets and sights of Old Town—don't miss the enthralling **Museum of Occupations.** On your second day, venture outside the city walls to the **Maarjamäe** branch of the Estonian History Museum, before catching some rays at **Pirita Beach.** Spend your third day in the seaside town of **Pärnu** (p. 291), which provides quiet relief from the capital.

ONE WEEK If arriving from the south, enjoy the unique sights and sounds of **Tartu** (2 days; p. 291). Then move west to **Pärnu** (1 day), and its **Lithographic Center** or bizarre **Museum of Contemporary Art.** Next, head out to the beautiful island of **Saaremaa** (2 days; p. 292). Rent a bicycle and take in the unspoiled beauty of the region, including meteorite craters and far-flung peninsulas. Spend your last 2 days in **Tallinn.**

ESSENTIALS

FACTS AND FIGURES

Official Name: Republic of Estonia.
Capital: Tallinn.
Major Cities: Pärnu, Tartu.
Population: 1,330,000.
Time Zone: GMT +2.
Languages: Estonian (official); Russian.
Religions: Evangelical Lutheran, Russian Orthodox, Estonian Orthodox.

WHEN TO GO

The best time to visit Estonia is in the late spring (Apr.-May) and summer (June to early Sept.), with highs reaching 30°C (86°F) in July and August. Winters can be cold, with limited daylight hours, but ideal conditions for skiing, skating, and ice fishing. The fall is frequently damp.

DOCUMENTS AND FORMALITIES

EMBASSIES AND CONSULATES. Embassies of other countries in Estonia are all in **Tallinn** (p. 287). Estonia's embassies and consulates abroad include: **Australia,** 86 Louisa Rd., Birchgrove, NSW 2041 (☎2 9810 7468; eestikon@ozemail.com.au); **Canada,** 260 Dalhousie St., Ste. 210, Ottawa, ON K1N 7E4 (☎613 789 4222; www.estemb.ca); **UK,** 16 Hyde Park Gate, London SW7 5DG (☎20 7589 3428; www.estonia.gov.uk); **US,** 2131 Massachusetts Ave., NW, Washington, D.C. 20008 (☎202-588-0101; www.estemb.org).

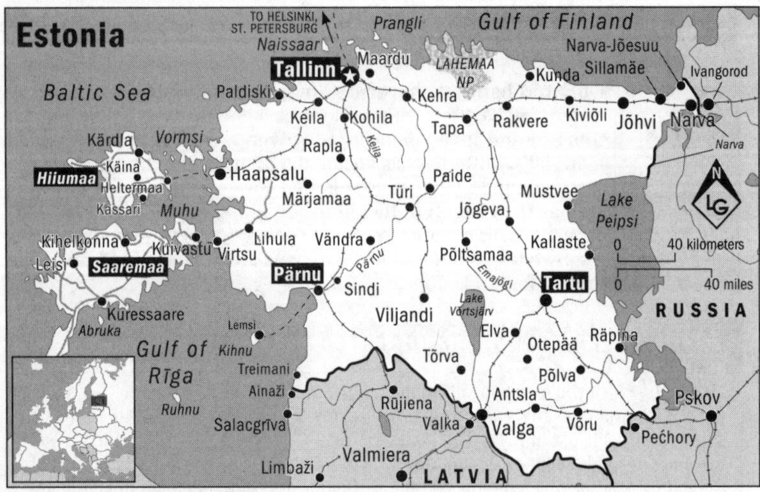

VISA AND ENTRY INFORMATION. Citizens of EU countries, Australia, Canada, New Zealand, and the US can visit Estonia for up to 90 days in a six-month period without a visa. Visa **extensions** are not granted. For more info, consult www.vm.ee/eng. The easiest means of crossing the **border** is from Tallinn to Moscow, St. Petersburg, or Rīga. Visas are not granted at the border.

ENTRANCE REQUIREMENTS

Passport: Required for all travelers.

Visa: Not required for citizens of EU countries, Australia, Canada, New Zealand, the US, and assorted other countries for stays under 90 days.

Letter of Invitation: Not required.

Inoculations: Not required. Recommended up-to-date on DTaP (diphtheria, tetanus, and pertussis), Hepatitis A, Hepatitis B, MMR (measles, mumps, and rubella), Polio booster, and Typhoid.

Work Permit: Required for all foreigners planning to work.

International Driving Permit: Required for all those planning to drive.

TOURIST SERVICES AND MONEY

TOURIST OFFICES. Tourist offices, marked with a small white "i" on a green background, are present in most towns selling maps and offering helpful advice. Offices generally keep extended hours during the summer months.

MONEY. The unit of currency is the **kroon (EEK),** divided into 100 senti. The kroon is pegged to the euro at €1=15.64EEK. **Inflation** is around 3%, so prices should be relatively stable. Many restaurants and shops accept **MasterCard** and **Visa,** and **ATMs** are available everywhere. When purchasing an item, cash is not usually passed between hands, but is placed instead in a small tray. Tipping is becoming more common; 10% is generally expected in restaurants.

Expect to spend between €25-45 a day. Tallinn is very expensive compared to the rest of the country, including the islands. Accommodation, food, and transport in the capital will cost €35-40 per day, whereas outside the city, €25 will allow a fairly comfortable day of sightseeing, eating, and drinking to your heart's content.

KROONI (EEK)		
	AUS$1 = 9.68EEK	10EEK = AUS$1.03
	CDN$1 = 10.54EEK	10EEK = CDN$0.95
	EUR€1 = 15.65EEK	10EEK = EUR€0.64
	NZ$1 = 8.94EEK	10EEK = NZ$1.12
	UK£1 = 23.04EEK	10EEK = UK£0.43
	US$1 = 12.85EEK	10EEK = US$0.78

HEALTH AND SAFETY

Medical services for foreigners are few and far between, and usually require cash payments. There are two kinds of **pharmacies** (both called *"apteek"*). Some only stock prescription medication, but most are well-equipped Scandinavian chains that stock just about everything else. Public **toilets** *(tasuline)*, marked by "N" or a triangle pointing up for women and "M" or a triangle pointing down for men, usually cost 3EEK and include a very limited supply of toilet paper. While Tallinn's tap water is generally safe to drink, **bottled water** is necessary in the rest of the country. Petty **crime** is rare, though pickpocketing is common in Tallinn's Old Town, especially along crowded Viru st. **Women** should not have a problem traveling alone, though you might want to dress conservatively. **Minorities** in Estonia are rare; they receive stares but generally experience little discrimination. For English-speaking help in an emergency, contact your embassy. **Homosexuality** is generally treated with curiosity rather than suspicion, but it is best to refrain from public displays.

EMERGENCY	**Police:** ☎ 110. **Fire** and **Ambulance:** ☎ 112.

TRANSPORTATION

BY PLANE, TRAIN, AND FERRY. Several international airlines offer flights to Tallinn; try **SAS, AirBaltic,** or **Fly Nordic.** If you're coming from another Baltic state or Russia, trains may be even cheaper than ferries, which also connect to Finland, Sweden, and Germany, but expect more red tape when crossing the border. A helicopter service flies from Helsinki, Finland to Tallinn.

BY BUS. **Euroline** buses are the cheapest way of reaching the Baltics. Domestic buses are much cheaper and more efficient than trains, though service can be infrequent between smaller cities. Though buses on the islands can be especially frustrating, it is possible to ride buses from the mainland to island towns (via ferry) for less than the price of a solo ferry ride. During the school year (Sept. to late June), students receive half-price bus tickets.

BY CAR, BIKE, AND THUMB. If entering Estonia by car, avoide routes through Kaliningrad and Belarus, as these both require visas. Although **road conditions** are fair and steadily improving, the availability of **roadside assistance** remains poor. Check out the **Estonian National Road Administration** (www.mnt.ee). **Taxis** (about 7EEK per km) are a safe means of transportation. Bicycling is common in Estonia, though be careful of aggressive motorists. Those who want to **hitchhike** should stretch out an open hand; *Let's Go* does not recommend hitchhiking.

KEEPING IN TOUCH

PHONE CODES	**Country code:** 372. **International dialing prefix:** 800. For more information on how to place international calls, see inside back cover.

EMAIL AND THE INTERNET. Though Internet cafes are not as common as you might expect, wireless Internet is curiously ubiquitous. If you have your own laptop, you can find free wireless connections throughout the country at www.wifi.ee, or look for places with the wifi.ee sign.

TELEPHONE. Pay phones, which are very common at bus stations and shopping malls, require magnetic cards, available at any kiosk. Calls to the Baltic states cost 5EEK per minute, to Russia 10EEK. **Prepaid phonecards** can get you rates of US$0.30-0.50 per minute to phone the US. Otherwise, expect to pay US$1-4 per minute International access codes include: **AT&T** (☎0 800 12 001); **Canada Direct** (☎0 800 12 011); and **MCI** (☎0 800 12 122). Internet access, which is common, usually costs 30-60EEK per hour. If you bring a GSM mobile phone, SIM cards offer a convenient and sometimes cheap way to keep in touch.

PHONE MAYHEM. Tallinn numbers all begin with the number 6 and have 7 digits. Numbers in smaller towns, however, often have only 5 digits. Tallinn, unlike other Estonian cities, has no city code; to call Tallinn from outside Estonia on the digital system, dial Estonia's country code (372) and then the number. To call any city besides Tallinn from outside the country, dial the country code, the city code, and then the number. The 0 listed in parentheses before each city code need only be dialed when placing calls within Estonia.

ESTONIA

MAIL. An airmail letter costs 6.50EEK to Europe and the former Soviet Union, and 8EEK to the rest of the world. Postcards cost 6/7.50EEK. Mail can be received through **Poste Restante.** Address envelopes as follows: First name LAST NAME, POSTE RESTANTE, Post Office address, Postal Code, City, ESTONIA.

LANGUAGE. **Estonian** is a **Finno-Ugric** language, closely related to **Finnish.** Estonians speak the best **English** in the Baltic states; most young people know at least a few phrases. Many also know **Finnish** or **Swedish,** but **German** is more common among the older set and in the resort towns. **Russian** used to be mandatory, but Estonians in remote areas have often forgotten much of it since few Russians live there.

ACCOMMODATIONS AND CAMPING

ESTONIA	❶	❷	❸	❹	❺
ACCOMMODATIONS	under 200 EEK	200-400EEK	400-550EEK	550-600EEK	over 600EEK

Each tourist office has accommodations listings for its town. There is little distinction between **hotels, hostels,** and **guesthouses;** some upscale hotels still have hall toilets and showers. The word *võõrastemaja* (guesthouse) in a place's name usually implies that it's less expensive. Some hostels are wings or floors of larger hotels, so be sure to ask for the cheaper rooms. For info on HI hostels around Estonia, contact the **Estonian Youth Hostel Association,** Narva Mantee 16-25, 10121, Tallinn (☎372 6461 455; www.baltichostels.net). **Camping** is the best way to experience Estonia's islands, but doing so outside of designated areas is illegal and dangerous for wildlife. **Farm stays** are growing popular, and provide a great peek into local life. For more info visit **Rural Tourism,** www.maaturism.ee, or search for a variety of accommodations at www.visitestonia.com.

FOOD AND DRINK

ESTONIA	❶	❷	❸	❹	❺
FOOD	under 50EEK	50-80EEK	80-100EEK	100-140EEK	over 140EEK

Much to the dismay of vegetarians and those trying to keep kosher, *schnitzel* (breaded and fried pork fillet) appears on nearly every menu, and most cheap Estonian cuisine is fried and doused with sour cream. Estonian specialties include *seljanka* (meat stew) and *pelmenid* (dumplings), as well as smoked salmon and trout. Bread is usually dark and dense. Pancakes with cheese curd and berries are a delicious, common dessert. The national brew *Saku* and the darker *Saku Tume* are excellent, but local beers, such as Kuressaare's *Saaremaa*, are less consistent.

HOLIDAYS AND FESTIVALS

Holidays: New Year's Day (Jan. 1); Independence Day (Feb. 24); Good Friday (Apr. 14); Easter Holiday (Apr. 16); Labor Day (May 1); Pentecost (June 4); Victory Day (June 23); Jaanipäev (June 24); Restoration of Independence (Aug. 20); Boxing Day (Dec. 26).

Festivals: In June, Memme-taadi Days, a celebration of Estonian folk culture, climax on the 24th with Jaanipäev, or Midsummer's Day. Haapsalu's White Lady Festival, held around the August full moon, celebrates Estonia's most famous ghost.

BEYOND TOURISM

Bridges for Education, 94 Lamarck Dr., Buffalo, NY 14226 USA (☎716-839-0180; www.bridges4edu.org). Runs 4-week summer "peace camps" in Bulgaria, Estonia, and Romania. US$930 plus travel and other expenses. Scholarships available.

Earthwatch, 3 Clocktower Pl., Ste. 100, P.O. Box 75, Maynard, MA 01754, USA (☎800-776-0188; www.earthwatch.org). Arranges 1- to 3-week environmental conservation-programs in Eastern Europe, including Estonia. Programs average US$2000.

TALLINN ☎0

Crisp sea air gusts over the medieval buildings and spires of Tallinn (pop. 371, 000), the self-proclaimed "Heart of Northern Europe." Unfortunately, wall-to-wall tourists often give the cobblestone streets of Old Town a theme-park feel. Visitors willing to venture beyond the compact center will be delighted by quirky cafes, lush parks, and the seaside promenade.

TRANSPORTATION

Trains: Toompuiestee 35 (☎615 68 51; www.evr.ee). Trams #1 and 5 run between the station and the town center. To: **Moscow, Russia** (14½hr.; 1 per day; 515EEK, sleeper car 723EEK); **St. Petersburg, Russia** (10hr., every 2 days, 390EEK); **Pärnu** (2½hr., 2 per day, 50EEK); **Tartu** (3-4hr., 4 per day, 80EEK).

Buses: Lastekodu 46 (☎680 09 00), 1.5km southeast of Vanalinn. Trams #2 and 4 run between Hotel Viru and the station. Buy tickets at the station or from the driver. **Eurolines** (www.eurolines.ee) runs to: **Rīga, Latvia** (5-6hr., 5 per day, 180-200EEK); **St. Petersburg, Russia** (8-10½hr., 5 per day, 190-270EEK); **Vilnius, Lithuania** (10½hr., 2 per day, 340-400EEK). 10% ISIC discount.

Ferries: (☎631 85 50). At the end of Sadama. Ferries cross to **Helsinki, Finland** (1½-3½hr., 47 per day, 235-705EEK). **Mainedd** travel agency (☎644 47 44; mainedd@datanet.nee), Raekoja pl. 18, books ferry tickets with no commission. Ask for student rates. Open M-F 9:30am-5:30pm. MC/V.

Public Transportation: Buses, trams, minibuses, and **trolleys** run 6am-midnight. Buy tickets *(talong)* from kiosks (10EEK) or from drivers (15EEK). 10-ticket booklet 80EEK. Validate tickets in the metal boxes onboard or face a 600EEK fine.

Taxi: Rate per km should be posted on your taxi's window. Try to call ahead and order a car to avoid a "waiting fee." **Klubi Takso** (☎142 00). 5.50-7EEK per km, min. 35EEK. **Kiisu Takso** (☎655 07 77). 5.50EEK per km. **Linnatakso** (☎644 24 42), 7EEK per km, can provide taxis for disabled passengers.

ORIENTATION AND PRACTICAL INFORMATION

Even locals lose their way along the winding medieval streets of Tallinn's **Vanalinn** (Old Town), an egg-shaped maze ringed by five main streets: **Rannamäe tee, Mere puistee, Pärnu mantee, Kaarli puistee,** and **Toompuies tee.** The best entrance to Vanalinn is through the 15th-century **Viru ärarad,** across from Hotel Viru, Tallinn's central landmark. **Viru,** the main thoroughfare, leads directly to **Raekoja plats** (Town Hall Square), the center of town. It has two sections: **All-linn,** or Lower Town, and **Toompea,** a rocky, fortified hill. In Old Town, **Pikk** and **Vene,** run northeast of Raekoja pl. **Uus,** the first street on your right after entering the Old Town gates, runs north towards the ferry ports. South of Raekoja pl., a number of smaller streets run into each other and eventually cross **Muurivahe,** which borders the southern and eastern edges of Vanalinn.

Tourist Office: Kullassepa 4/Niguliste 2 (☎645 77 77; www.tourism.tallinn.ee). Sells city maps and *Tallinn In Your Pocket* (35EEK). Open July-Aug. M-F 9am-8pm, Sa-Su 10am-6pm; May-June M-F 9am-7pm, Sa-Su 10am-5pm; Sept. M-F 9am-6pm, Sa-Su 10am-5pm; Oct.-Apr. M-F 9am-5pm, Sa 10am-3pm. Another branch at Sadama 25, in Ferry Terminal A (☎631 83 21). Open daily 8am-4:30pm.

Embassies: For more info, contact the Estonian Foreign Ministry (www.vm.ee). **Canada,** Toomkooli 13 (☎627 33 11; tallinn@canada.ee). Open M, W, F 9am-noon. **UK,** Wismari 6 (☎667 47 00; www.britishembassy.ee). Open M-F 10am-noon and 2-4:30pm. **US,** Kentmanni 20 (☎668 81 00, emergency 509 21 29; www.usemb.ee). Open M-F 9am-noon and 2-5pm.

Currency Exchange: Banks have better rates than hotels and private exchange bureaus. Try **Eesti Uhispank,** Pärnu mnt. 12. Open M-F 9am-6pm, Sa 10am-3pm. There are **ATMs** throughout the city.

American Express: Suur-Karja 15 (☎626 62 11; www.estravel.ee). Books hotels and tours, sells airline, ferry, and rail tickets, and provides visa services. Open June-Aug. M-F 9am-6pm, Sa 10am-5pm; Sept.-May M-F 9am-6pm, Sa 10am-3pm.

Emergency: ☎112.

Pharmacy: Raeapteek, Raekoja pl. 11 (☎631 48 30). In business since 1422. Open M-F 9am-7pm, Sa 9am-5pm.

Internet Access: Metro, Viru valjak 4 (☎610 15 19), in the bus station below Viru keskus. 15EEK per 30min., 25EEK per hr., 35EEK per 2hr. Open daily 8am-11pm. **Central Library,** Estonia pst. 8, 2nd fl. (☎683 09 00). 15min. free with advance reservation. Open M-F 11am-7pm, Sa 10am-5pm.

Post Office: Narva mnt. 1 (☎661 66 16), opposite Hotel Viru. **Poste Restante** in basement. Open M-F 7:30am-8pm, Sa 8am-6pm, Su 9am-3pm. **Postal Code:** 10101.

ACCOMMODATIONS AND FOOD

Hostels fill fast, so book ahead. **Rasastra,** Mere pst. 4, second floor, finds private rooms in central Tallinn and anywhere else in the Baltics. (☎661 62 91; www.bedbreakfast.ee. Tallinn singles 275EEK; doubles 500EEK; triples 650EEK. Open daily 9:30am-6pm.) **Tallinn Old Town Backpackers (HI)** ❷, Uus 14, features clean dorms and good company. (☎517 13 37; www.balticbackpackers.com. Linen 25EEK. Dorms 225EEK. 25EEK HI discount.) The helpful and welcoming staff at **Oldhouse Guesthouse and Hostel** ❷, Uus 22, provides clean and cozy dorms. (☎641 14 64;

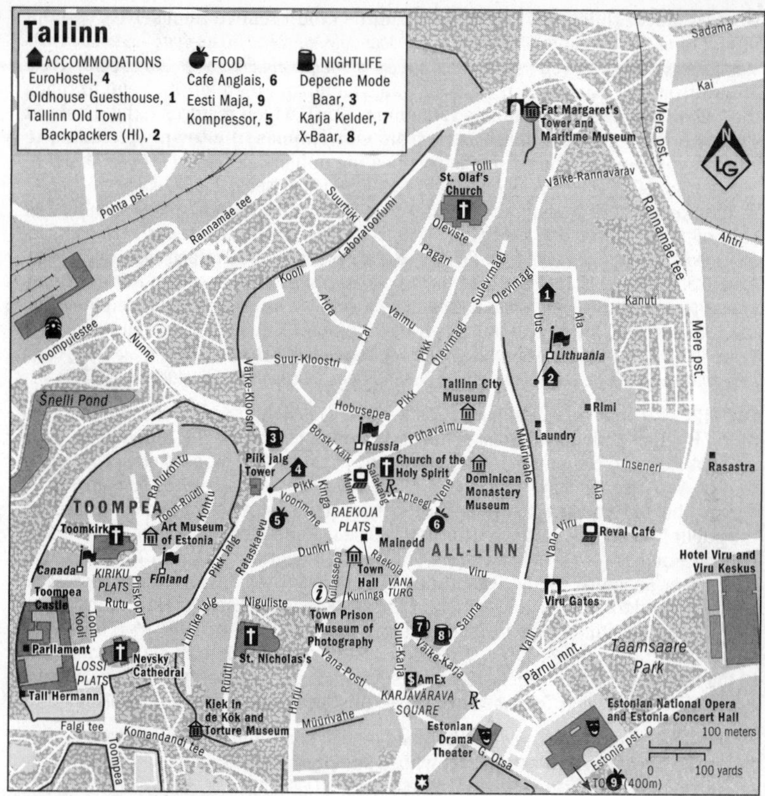

www.oldhouse.ee. Breakfast included. Reception 24hr. Dorms 250-290EEK; singles 450-550EEK; doubles 650EEK; quads 1300EEK. 10% ISIC discount. Cash only.) Modern, clean **Eurohostel ❷,** Nunne 2, offers comfortable bunks right in the midst of Vanalinn's nightlife. (☎644 77 88; www.eurohostel.ee. Dorms 290EEK. Cash only.) **Kompressor ❶,** Rataskaevu 3, is the best place in town for savory Estonian pancakes, offering giant portions with meat, fish, and veggie fillings. (Pancakes 35-45EEK. Kitchen open F-Sa noon-10pm, Su 11am-10pm; bar open to last customer.) **Eesti Maja ❷,** Lauteri 1, just 600m southeast of Vanalinn, offers folksy favorites, including the daring *sült* (jellied pig legs; 80EEK), and its own history magazine. (www.eestimaja.ee. M-F 11am-3pm all-you-can-eat buffet 75EEK. Entrees 45-165EEK. Open daily 11am-11pm.) **Cafe Anglais ❷,** Raekoja pl. 14, offers a menu of fresh sandwiches (75-80EEK) and salads (115EEK), as well as views of the town square. (Open daily 11am-11pm; kitchen closes at 10pm. MC/V.)

SIGHTS

ALL-LINN (LOWER TOWN). Enter Vanalinn through the Viru gate and head up Viru to reach **Raekoja plats,** where beer flows in cafes and local troupes perform throughout the summer. Tallinn's **town hall,** Europe's oldest, is right on the square. It contains several rooms decorated in medieval style and a tower with one of the world's tallest toilets (77m), built so guards could relieve themselves without descending the winding, narrow steps. *(Open July-Aug. M-Sa 10am-4pm. Tower open mid-May to Aug. daily 11am-6pm. Town hall 35EEK, students 20EEK. Tower 25/15EEK.)* Take Mündi from the square, turn right on Pühavaimu, and then left on Vene to reach the **Tallinn City Museum** (Tallinna Linnamuuseum), which features exhibits about Tallinn's most colorful characters, from Old Thomas, the town watchman, to Johann von Uexkyll, the infamous serf-beating nobleman. *(Vene 17. Open M and W-Su Mar.-Oct. 10:30am-5:30pm; Nov.-Feb. 11am-4:30pm. Museum 25EEK, students 10EEK.)* At the north end of All-linn, the 124m tower of **St. Olaf's Church,** offers such a great view of the Old Town that the KGB used it as an observation post to spy on locals. *(Lai 50. Open daily Apr.-Oct. 10am-6pm. Services M and F 6:30pm, Su 10am and noon. Church free. Tower 25EEK, students 10EEK.)* Head to the other end of Pikk and turn left on Rataskaevu to see **St. Nicholas Church** (Niguliste Kirkko). The Soviets destroyed the original 13th-century Gothic building when they bombed Tallinn in 1944, but restored it years later so it could house part of the **Art Museum of Estonia.** *(Open W-Su 10am-5pm. Last entrance 4:30pm. Organ concerts Sa-Su 4-4:30pm. Museum 35EEK, students 20EEK.)*

TOOMPEA. Toompea's **Lossi plats** (Castle Square) is dominated by the onion domes of the Russian Orthodox **Alexander Nevsky Cathedral** named for the 13th-century Russian warrior who conquered much of Estonia. *(From Raekoja pl., head down Kullassepa, right on Niguliste, and uphill on Lühike jalg. Open daily 8am-8pm. Services 9am and 6pm.)* Directly behind **Toompea Castle,** the current seat of the Estonian Parliament (closed to the public), an Estonian flag tops the impressive medieval fortification of **Tall Hermann** (Pikk Hermann). To reach the spires of the 13th-century Lutheran **Toomkirik** that tower over Toompea, follow Toom-Kooli to Kiriku pl. *(Open Tu-Su 9am-5pm. Services Su 10am.)* Next door is the main branch of the **Art Museum of Estonia** (Eesti Kunstimuuseum), which features 18th- through 20th-century Estonian art. *(Kiriku pl. 1. Open W-Su 11am-6pm. 20EEK, students 5EEK.)* To reach the eye-opening **Museum of Occupation and of the Fight for Freedom** which documents Estonia's repression by the Germans and Soviets, walk south on Toompea from Lossi pl. *(Open Tu-Sa 11am-6pm. 10/5EEK.)*

ESTONIA

KADRIORG. Among the quiet paths, shady trees, and fountains of Kadriorg Park is Peter the Great's **Kadriorg Palace,** whose sumptuous grand hall is a fine example of Baroque architecture. *(Open May-Sept. Tu-Su 10am-5pm; Oct.-Apr. W-Su 10am-5pm. 45EEK, students 35EEK.)* The grounds also have two art museums with superb collections of Dutch and Flemish art, as well as the **Peter the Great House Museum** in his former temporary residence. The museum holds many of the tsar's original furnishings, as well as an imprint of his extremely large hand. *(Mäekalda 2. From Vanalinn, follow Narva mnt. and veer right on Weizenbergi or take tram #1 or 3 to Kadriorg. Palace open May-Sept. Tu-Su 10am-5pm; Oct.-Apr. W-Su 10am-5pm. Art museum open W-Su 11am-6pm. House museum open mid-May to Sept. W-Su 10:30am-5:30pm. Palace 45EEK, students 35EEK. Art museum 15/5EEK. House museum 10/5EEK.)*

ROCCA-AL-MARE. On the peninsula of Rocca-al-Mare, 10km west of the city center, is the **Estonian Open-Air Museum** (Eesti Vabaõhumuuseum). The park is filled with 17th- to 20th-century wooden mills and homesteads transplanted from all over the country. Estonian folk troupes perform here regularly. *(Vabaõhumuuseumi tee 12. Take trolley bus #6 from Kaarli Pst., at the edge of Old Town to the Zoo stop. From there, walk across the parking lot and left on Vabaõhumuuseumi tee. Open daily May-Oct. 10am-6pm; Nov.-Apr. 10am-5pm; Oct. 10am-4pm. 28EEK, students 12EEK. Last Tu of each month free.)*

ENTERTAINMENT AND NIGHTLIFE

Pick up a free copy of *Tallinn This Week* at the tourist office. The **Estonia Concert Hall** and the **Estonian National Opera** (Rahvusooper Estonia) are both at Estonia pst. 4. (Concert hall ☎614 77 60; www.concert.ee. Opera ☎626 02 60; www.opera.ee.

Concert box office open M-F noon-7pm, Sa noon-5pm, Su 1hr. before curtain. Opera box office open daily noon-7pm. Tickets 30-270EEK.) Celebrate the power of barley in early July at **Beersummer,** Tallinn's answer to the Oktoberfest. (www.ollesummer.ee). **Depeche Mode Baar,** Nomme 4, plays all Depeche Mode, all day long. For those who just can't get enough, there are mixed drinks (35-60EEK) named after the band's songs, autographed photographs lining the walls, and a TV playing music videos and live concert footage. (Beer 35EEK per 0.5L. Open daily noon-4am. Cash only.) **Karja Kelder,** Vaike-Karja 1, is a cozy cellar with over 40 varieties of beer. (Beer 30EEK per 0.5L. Open July-Aug. M-Th and Su 11am-2am, F-Sa 11am-4am; Sept.-June M and Su 11am-midnight, Tu-Th 11am-1am, F-Sa 11am-3am. MC/V.) **X-Baar,** Sauna 1, offers a relaxed atmosphere for its largely gay clientele. (Beer 30EEK. Live DJ F-Sa 10pm. Open daily 2pm-1am.)

PÄRNU

☎(0)44

Famous for its mud baths, beaches, and festivals, Pärnu (pop. 45,000) is the summer capital of Estonia. The **Mudaravila** health resort, Ranna pst. 1, features the *crème-de-la-crème* of mud. (☎442 55 25; www.mudaravila.ee. Fully body 150EEK.) When you're not soaking in mud, soak up some culture at Pärnu's **Museum of New Art,** Esplanaadi 10, which features a statue of Lenin with a strobe light in his head and an amputated right hand. (Open daily 9am-9pm. 15EEK, students 10EEK.) Stop by the **Estonian Lithograph Center** (Eesti Litograafiakeskus), Kuninga 17, to see print makers at work. (☎55 604 631; www.hot.ee/litokeskus. Hours vary.) The water of the white-sand **beach** warms up in July and August.

Tanni-Vakoma Majutusbüroo, Hommiku 5, behind the bus station, arranges **private rooms.** (☎518 53 19; tanni@online.ee. Open May-Aug. M-F 10am-8pm, Sa 10am-3pm. From 200EEK.) **Georg ❶,** Rüütli 43, is a cafeteria-style eatery packed with locals enjoying fried fish and open-faced sandwiches. (☎443 11 10. Sandwiches 6-8EEK. Open summer M-F 7:30am-10pm, Sa-Su 9am-10pm; winter M-F 7:30am-7:30pm, Sa-Su 9am-5pm.) **Kadri Kohvik ❷,** Nikolai 12, around the corner from the TIC, serves filling dishes in a cafe atmosphere. Head to the Swedish-owned **Veerev Olu** (The Rolling Beer), Uus 3a, in a courtyard behind the TIC, for live rock and folk Saturday 9:30pm-1am. (☎534 03 149. 0.5L beer 20EEK. Entrees 17-35EEK. Open M-Sa 11am-1am, Su noon-1am.) Eurolines **buses** (☎442 78 41) go from Ringi 3 to: Rīga, Latvia (3½hr., 6-8 per day, 110-150EEK); Tallinn (2hr., 42 per day, 55-80EEK); Tartu (2½hr., 21 per day, 70-100EEK). **City Bike,** will deliver a bicycle to you anywhere in Pärnu. (☎566 080 90; www.citybike.ee. 120EEK for 12hr., 150EEK per day.) The **tourist office,** Rüütli 16, sells *Pärnu In Your Pocket* for 25EEK. (☎447 30 00; www.parnu.ee. Open mid-May to mid-Sept. M-F 9am-6pm, Sa 9am-4pm, Su 10am-3pm; mid-Sept. to mid-May M-F 9am-5pm.) **Postal Code:** 80010.

TARTU

☎(0)72

Tartu (pop. 110,000), Estonia's second largest city, is home to prestigious **Tartu University** (Tartu Ülikool). In **Raekoja plats** (Town Hall Square), the building that houses the **Tartu Art Museum** (Tartu Kunstimuuseum) leans a little to the left (just like the city's student population). Stop in to check out new work from Tartu's art schools, or the retrospective exhibit that covers a century of local paintings. From there, follow Ülikooli behind the town hall to the university's main building at Ülikooli 18. In the attic is the **student lock-up** *(kartser)*, which until 1892 was used to detain rule-breaking students; their drawings and inscriptions are still visible. (Open M-F 11am-5pm. 5EEK, students 4EEK.) According to a warning sign, the ruins of the **Cathedral of St. Peter and St. Paul** are "liable to fall down." Next door is the **Tartu University History Museum,** which showcases ancient scientific instruments. Buy tickets here to climb the towers in the ruins of the cathedral. (Open W-Su 11am-5pm. 20EEK, students 5EEK.) The **Tartu Toy**

Museum (Tartu Manguasjamuuseum) includes a massive **playroom** where visitors can entertain themselves with childhood memorabilia. (Open W-Su 11am-6pm. Playroom closes at 4pm. 15EEK, students 10EEK. Playroom 5EEK.)

The university dorms at **Hostel Pepleri ❷**, Pepleri 14, are more luxurious than many hotels, with private kitchenettes and bathrooms. From the bus station, take Vadabuse toward town, turn left on Vanemuise, and then take a left on Pepleri. (☎42 76 08; www.kyla.ee. Singles 250EEK; doubles 400EEK. Cash only.) The tavern **Püssirohukelder ❷** ("Gunpowder Cellar"), Lossi 28, features large, filling meals on its "student menu" and brews its own "Gunpowder Red" beer. (Tu-Sa live music usually 10pm. Open M-Th noon-2am, F-Sa noon-3am, Su noon-midnight. MC/V.) At **Maailm,** Rüütli 12, you can enjoy drinks or delectable ice-cream shakes (25EEK) in velvet armchairs or on wooden swings. (☎742 90 99; www.klubimaailm.ee. Open M-Sa noon-1am, Su noon-10pm. MC/V.) **Wilde Irish Pub,** Vallikraavi 4, records every order of Saku, the national brew, on a digital billboard; the tally reset when it reached 100,000 in 2003. (Entrees 49-170EEK. Open M-Tu and Su noon-midnight, W-Th noon-1am, F-Sa noon-3am. MC/V.)

Buses (☎477 227) leave from Turu 2, 300m southeast of Raekoja pl., for: Pärnu (4hr., 20 per day, 50-95EEK); Tallinn (2-3hr., 46 per day, 50-80EEK); Rīga, Latvia (5hr., 1 per day, 190EEK); St. Petersburg, Russia (9hr., 1 per day, 160EEK). Some routes offer 30-50% ISIC discounts. **Trains** (☎615 68 51), generally less reliable than buses, go from the intersection of Kuperjanovi and Vaksali, 1.5km from the center, to Tallinn (2½-3½hr., 3 per day, 70EEK). Buses #5 and 6 run from the train stop to the city center and then to the bus station. From the bus station, follow Riia mnt. and turn right on Ülikooli to reach Raekoja pl. Pick up the helpful *Tartu Today* (15EEK) at the **tourist office,** Raekoja pl. 14. (☎442 111; www.visitestonia.com. Open June-Aug. M-F 9am-5pm, Sa 10am-3pm; Sept.-May M-F 9am-6pm, Sa-Su 10am-3pm.) **Postal Code:** 51001.

ESTONIAN ISLANDS

Afraid that Estonia's 1500 islands would serve as an escape route to the West, the Soviets cordoned them off from foreign and mainland influence; the islands now remain a preserve for all that is distinctly Estonian, with rugged coasts, thick forest, and quiet, rural living.

SAAREMAA ☎(0)45

Kuressaare (pop. 16,000), the largest town on the island of Saaremaa, is making a comeback with tourists but remains tranquil. Head south from Raekoja pl. (Town Hall Square) along Lossi, through the park, and across the moat to reach the 1260 **Bishopric Castle** (Piiskopilinnus). Inside, the **Saaremaa Museum** chronicles the island's history, with an eclectic collection that includes a stuffed bear and an antique Penny Farthing bicycle. (Open May-Aug. daily 10am-7pm; Sept.-Apr. W-Su 11am-6pm. 30EEK, students 15EEK.) Rent a **bike** (135EEK per day) at **Bivarix,** Tallinna 26, near the bus station, to pedal to the beaches of southwestern Saaremaa (8-12km) or to Karujärve Lake in western Saaremaa (23km).

Sug Hostel ❶, Kingu 6, is your best bet for budget accommodations. (☎45 543 88. Open June-Aug. Singles 210-250EEK; doubles 300-350EEK; quads 480-580EEK.) Grab a delicious bite to eat at **Pannkoogikohvik ❶**, Kohtu 1. (☎45 335 75. Open M-Th 8:15am-midnight, F-Sa 8:15am-2am, Su 9:15am-midnight. MC/V.) Direct **buses** (☎45 316 61) leave from Pihtla tee 2, at the corner with Tallinna, for Pärnu (2½hr., 5 per day, 140EEK) and Tallinn (4-6hr., 9-11 per day, 160EEK). The extremely useful **tourist office,** Tallinna 2, in the town hall, offers free **maps,** arranges private rooms, and provides schedules. (☎45 331 20; www.saaremaa.ee. Open May to mid-Sept. M-F 9am-7pm, Sa 9am-5pm, Su 10am-3pm; mid-Sept. to Apr. M-F 9am-5pm.)

HIIUMAA

☎(0)46

By restricting access to Hiiumaa (pop. 11,500) for 50 years, the Soviets unwittingly preserved the island's rare plant and animal species. The island remains Estonia's most forested region. Creek-laced **Kärdla** (pop. 4100) is the island's biggest town. To explore the sights along the coast, rent a **bike** (100EEK per day) from **Kerttu Sport,** Sadama 15, across the bridge from the bus station. (☎46 321 30. Open M-F 10am-6pm, Sa 10am-3pm.) Bike west from Kärdla toward Kõrgessaare to the chilling **Hill of Crosses** (Ristimägi; 6km). About 2km past the Hill of Crosses, a right turn leads to the cast-iron **Tahkuna Lighthouse** (11km), brought from Paris in 1874. Return to the main road and turn right again toward Kõrgessaare; continue 20km past the town to reach the impressive 16th-century **Kõpu Lighthouse,** which offers a panoramic view of the Baltic Sea. (20EEK, students 10EEK.) The tiny island of **Kassari** is attached to Hiiumaa by a land bridge from Käina, which can be reached from Kärdla by local buses or a 22km bike ride. The island's most beautiful sight is the 1.3m wide **Sääretirp** peninsula, which is covered in wild strawberry and juniper bushes and juts 3km into the sea.

Eesti Posti Hostel ❷, Posti 13, has modern rooms with comfortable beds and clean shared baths. From the bus station, follow Sadama over the little stream, and turn right onto Posti. (☎533 118 60. May-Sept. 200EEK per person; Oct.-Apr. 150EEK.) In the town square, **Arteesia Kohvik ❶,** Keskväljak 5, serves generous portions of home-cooked meat and seafood. (Entrees 30-65EEK. Open daily 9am-9pm. MC/V.) Direct **buses** run from Sadama 13 (☎46 320 77), north of Kärdla's main square, Keskväljak, to Tallinn (4½hr., 2-3 per day, 110-140EEK). Once you're on **Hiiumaa,** you can get to **Saaremaa** via public transportation, but it's difficult to find transportation in the opposite direction. The **tourist office,** Hiiu 1, in Keskväljak, sells maps (5-40EEK) and **The Lighthouse Tour** (20EEK), a handy guide to sights all over the island. (☎462 22 32; www.hiiumaa.ee. Open May-Sept. M-F 9am-6pm, Sa-Su 10am-3pm; Oct.-Apr. M-F 10am-4pm.)

FINLAND (SUOMI)

After seven centuries in the crossfire of warring Sweden and Russia, Finland gained autonomy in 1917 and never looked back. Provincial seaside towns stand against bustling Helsinki, where Aalto's Modernist constructions rise in dramatic contrast to the historic city center. With thousands of lakes and 68% of its land area carpeted in rich boreal forest, the country's geography reels in serious hikers even as its southern cities draw architecture students and art gurus. Budget travelers will find Finland—outside of its stylish capital—more affordable than many of its Scandinavian neighbors.

DISCOVER FINLAND: SUGGESTED ITINERARIES

Start things off in the lakeside capital of **Helsinki** (p. 298), ambling along the tree-lined Esplanadi and veering into some of the city's grade-A museums, leaving time to bike down the Pellinge archipelago south of **Porvoo** (p. 306). Out west, the venerable city of **Turku** (p. 307) is worth a look, but today **Tampere** (p. 309) is the rising star of Finnish urbanity, with a lively music scene and museums taking over renovated factories. Picnic on the islands of **Savonlinna** (p. 310), and daytrip out to the transcendent **Retretti Art Center.** From here, decide between heading back to Helsinki or embarking on the trek north to **Rovaniemi** (p. 313), where you can launch a foray into the wilds of the Arctic Circle.

ESSENTIALS

FACTS AND FIGURES

Official Name: Republic of Finland.

Capital: Helsinki.

Major Cities: Oulu, Tampere, Turku.

Population: 5,210,000.

Land Area: 305,000 sq. km.

Time Zone: GMT +2.

Languages: Finnish, Swedish.

Religions: Evangelical Lutheran (89%).

WHEN TO GO

The long days of Finnish summers make for a tourist's dream, although the two-month polar night *(kaamos)* in the northernmost regions of Finland could give the chirpiest traveler a case of Seasonal Affective Disorder. Watch out for Midsummer festivities (June 23-24, 2006), though, when the entire country shuts down for a weekend-long party. In early February, winter-sport fanatics start hitting the slopes; the skiing continues well into March and April. Temperatures average about 20-25°C (68-77°F) in summer, and dip as low as -20°C (-5°F) in winter.

DOCUMENTS AND FORMALITIES

EMBASSIES AND CONSULATES. All foreign embassies are in Helsinki. Finnish embassies in your home country include: **Australia,** 12 Darwin Ave., Yarralumla, ACT 2600 (☎26 273 38 00; www.finland.org.au); **Canada,** 55 Metcalfe St., Ste. 850, Ottawa, ON K1P 6L5 (☎613-288-2233; www.finland.ca/en); **Ireland,** Russell House, Stokes Pl., St. Stephen's Green, Dublin 2 (☎01 478 1344); **UK,** 38 Chesham Pl., London SW1X 8HW (☎020 7838 6200; www.finemb.org.uk); **US,** 3301 Massachusetts

Ave. NW, Washington, D.C. 20008 (☎202-298-5800; www.finland.org). **New Zealanders** should either contact their consul in Wellington (☎04 499 4599; colin.beyer@simpsongrierson.com) or call the Australian embassy.

VISA AND ENTRY INFORMATION. EU citizens do not need a visa. Citizens of Australia, Canada, New Zealand, and the US do not need a visa for stays of up to 90 days, although this three-month period begins upon entry into any of the countries that belong to the EU's freedom of movement zone. For more info, see p. 16.

TOURIST SERVICES AND MONEY

EMERGENCY	**Police:** ☎10022. **Ambulance** and **Fire:** ☎112.

TOURIST OFFICES. The Finnish Tourist Board (☎09 4176 911; www.visitfinland.com) maintains an official online travel guide, which customizes its travel information and advice by your home country.

MONEY. The **euro (€)** has replaced the **Finnish markka** as the unit of currency in Finland. For exchange rates and more info on the euro, see p. 21. Banks exchange currency for a €2-5 commission, though **Forex** offices and **ATMs** offer the best exchange rates. Food from grocery stores runs €10-17 per day; meals cost somewhere around €8 for lunch and €12 for dinner. Restaurant bills include a service charge, although an extra 5-10% tip is appreciated for particularly good service. Elsewhere in Finland, tips are not expected. All countries who are members of the European Union impose a **Value Added Tax (VAT)** on goods and services purchased within the EU. Prices in Finland already include the country's stiff 22% VAT rate, although partial refunds up to 16% are available for visitors who are not EU citizens. For additional information on the VAT, see p. 23.

TRANSPORTATION

BY PLANE. Several major airlines fly into Helsinki from Europe, North America, and Australia. **Finnair** (Finland ☎0600 140 140, €1.64 per call; US 800-950-5000; UK 087 0241 4411; www.finnair.com) flies from 50 international cities and also covers the domestic market. Finnair gives a domestic discount of up to 50% for ages 17-24 on a limited number of youth tickets, and has summer and snow rates that reduce fares by up to 60%. **Ryanair** (☎353 1249 7700; www.ryanair.com) flies to Tampere.

BY TRAIN. The national rail company is **VR Ltd., Finnish Railways** (☎0600 41 902, €1 per call; www.vr.fi). Travelers pay high prices for efficient trains; seat reservations (€2.40-10) are not required except on InterCity and Pendolino trains. **Eurail** is valid in Finland. A **Finnrail pass,** available only outside

Finland, gives three (€122), five (€163), or 10 travel days (€220) in a one-month period. The **Scanrail pass,** purchased outside Scandinavia, is good for rail travel through Denmark, Finland, Norway, and Sweden, as well as many discounted ferry and bus rides. Passes can also be purchased within Scandinavia, but passholders can only use three travel days in the country of purchase, so a Scanrail pass purchased at home is more economical for those traveling mostly within Finland. See p. 53 for more info. Since student discounts on Finnish trains are available only to students with Finnish student IDs, a Finnrail or Scanrail pass is often your best bet for longer trips.

RAIL SAVINGS. Scanrail passes purchased outside Scandinavia are much more flexible than Scanrail passes purchased once you arrive, and may be less expensive depending on the exchange rate. Check www.scanrail.com for more information on where to purchase passes at home.

BY BUS. Buses are the only way to reach some smaller towns and to travel past the Arctic Circle. **Oy Matkahuolto Ab** (☎02 00 40 00, €1.64 per call; www.matkahuolto.fi) coordinates bus service across Finland. ISIC holders can buy a **student card** (€5.40) at bus stations, which grants a 50% discount on one-way tickets for routes over 80km. **Railpasses** are valid on buses when trains are not in service.

BY FERRY. Viking Line (Helsinki ☎09 123 51, Stockholm 08 452 4000; www.vikingline.fi) runs from Stockholm to Helsinki, Mariehamn, and Turku. **Silja Line** (Helsinki ☎09 180 41, Stockholm 08 666 33 30; www.silja.fi) sails from Stockholm to Helsinki, Mariehamn, and Turku. On Viking ferries, **Scanrail** holders get 50% off and a **Eurail** pass plus train ticket entitles holders to a free passenger fare. (Mention this discount when booking.) Additionally, Viking offers "early bird" discounts of 15-50% for those who book at least 30 days in advance within either Finland or Sweden. On Silja, both Scan- and Eurailers ride either for free or at reduced rates, depending on the route and type of ticket.

BY CAR. Finland honors foreign drivers' licenses for up to one year for drivers aged 18 years or older. **Speed limits** are 120kph on expressways, 50kph in densely populated areas, and 80-100kph elsewhere. Headlights must be used at all times. Driving conditions are good, but take extra care in winter weather and be wary of reindeer crossings. For more info on car rental and driving in Europe, see p. 60.

BY BIKE AND BY THUMB. Finland has a well-developed network of **cycling** paths. **Fillari GT** route maps are available at bookstores (€10-16). Check www.visitfinland.com/cycling/eng/ for pre-trip route planning. **Hitchhiking** is uncommon in Finland and illegal on highways, although www.cs.helsinki.fi/u/kjokisal/liftaus does recommend a number of major routes. *Let's Go* does not recommend hitchhiking.

KEEPING IN TOUCH

PHONE CODES	**Country code:** 358. **International dialing prefix:** 00. For more information on how to place international calls, see inside back cover.

EMAIL AND THE INTERNET. Cybercafes in Helsinki are relatively scarce compared to other European capitals, and in smaller towns they are virtually nonexistent. However, many tourist offices and public libraries offer short (15-30min.) slots of free Internet, and some places in Helsinki do provide free wireless access.

TELEPHONE. To make a long-distance call within Finland, dial 0 and then the number. Prepaid phone cards (€1-10) are available from bus stations, post offices, and R-kiosk convenience stores. **Mobile phones** are extremely popular in the nation that gave the world Nokia, and prepaid mobile phone cards can be used to make international calls (never cheap, but cheapest 5pm-8am). For more info on mobile phones, see p. 33. For operator assistance, dial ☎118; for help with international calls, dial ☎020 208. International direct dial numbers include: **AT&T** (☎0800 1100 15); **Canada Direct** (☎0800 1100 11); **MCI** (☎0800 1102 80); **Sprint** (☎0800 1102 84); **Telecom New Zealand** (☎0800 1106 40); **Telstra Australia** (☎0800 110 610).

MAIL. Mail service is fast and efficient. Postcards and letters under 50g cost €0.65 within Finland, €0.90 within the EU, and €1.20 outside Europe. International letters weighing under 20g cost just €0.65.

LANGUAGES. Finnish is spoken by most of the population, although children learn both Swedish and Finnish from the seventh grade. Three dialects of Sami are also spoken by an ethnic minority in northern Finland, adding up to roughly 2000 speakers. English is also widely spoken, with 66% of Finns reporting that they can speak at least some English. City-dwellers and those under 35 are generally the most proficient. Travelers should note that some town names take a modified form on train and bus schedules. "To Helsinki" is written *Helsinkiin*, while "from Helsinki" is *Helsingistä*. For basic Finnish words and phrases, see p. 1058.

ACCOMMODATIONS AND CAMPING

FINLAND	❶	❷	❸	❹	❺
ACCOMMODATIONS	under €12	€12-23	€23-45	€45-70	over €70

Finland has over 100 **youth hostels** (*retkeilymaja;* RET-kay-loo-MAH-yah), although only half of them are open year-round. The **Finnish Youth Hostel Association** (Suomen Retkeilymajajärjestö; ☎09 565 71 50; www.srmnet.org) is Finland's HI affiliate. Prices are generally around €23 per person for a dorm room, with an HI discount of €2.50. Most have laundry facilities and a kitchen; some have saunas and rent bicycles or skis. **Hotels** are generally expensive (over €50); *kesähotelli* (summer hotels) are usually student lodgings that are vacant from June to August, and cost about €25 per night. Camping is common for both international travelers and Finns. More than 350 **campgrounds** pepper the countryside, 70 of which are open year-round (tent sites €10-25 per night; small cottages from €30). The **Camping Card Scandinavia** (€6) qualifies cardholders for discounts, and includes limited accident insurance. For a campground guide or to purchase the Camping Card, contact the **Finnish Camping Site Association.** (☎09 477 407 40; www.camping.fi. Allow 3 weeks for delivery of the card.) Finland's *jokamiehenoikeudet* (right to public access) means that travelers can temporarily camp for free in the countryside, as long as they stay a reasonable distance from private homes.

FOOD AND DRINK

FINLAND	❶	❷	❸	❹	❺
FOOD	under €8	€8-15	€15-20	€20-30	over €30

Kebab and pizza joints (from €4) are popular, but the local **Kauppatori** market and **Kauppahalli** food court are more likely to serve fresh, recognizably Finnish fare. Finland's traditional diet slants toward hearty grain breads and sausages that last through a long winter—too long to keep perishable meats around. In season, however, menus feature freshly caught trout, perch, pike, and herring, and a new wave of five-star chefs in Helsinki are starting to pair French and Mediterranean ingredients with the fruits of Finland's fisheries. Bowls of reindeer stew are a staple of Lapland, while Kuopio is known for its pillowy rye pastries. A surprising number of adults drink milk with their meals, followed by interminable pots of coffee; the tiny Finnish market accounts for almost 2% of global coffee consumption. You must be 18 to purchase beer and wine, 20 for liquor; the minimum age in bars is usually 18, but can be as high as 25. All alcohol stronger than light beer must be purchased at state-run **Alko** liquor stores, open weekdays until at least 6pm and Saturdays until at least 4pm.

HOLIDAYS AND FESTIVALS

Holidays: New Year's Day (Jan. 1); Epiphany (Jan. 6); Good Friday (Apr. 14); Easter Sunday and Monday (Apr. 16-17); May Day (May 1); Ascension Day (May 25); Whit Sunday (June 4); Midsummer (June 23-24); All Saints' Day (Nov. 4); Independence Day (Dec. 6); Christmas Day (Dec. 25); Boxing Day (Dec. 26).

Festivals: Flags fly high and *kokko* (bonfires) blaze on Midsummer's Eve (June 23), when the Finnish desert their cities for seaside cabins. Those marooned in town still get a touch of the countryside with the birch branches that festoon buses and trams. July is the festival high season in Finland, with gays and lesbians celebrating Helsinki Pride, Turku's youth taking to the mosh pits of Ruisrock, and Pori's residents launching their eclectic Jazz Festival. Savonlinna's Opera Festival continues into early August, while the Helsinki's signature Helsinki Festival, Oulu's Music Video Festival and Lahti's Sibelius Festival, celebrating the renowned composer, close out the summer. Check out www.festivals.fi for more info and 2006 dates.

BEYOND TOURISM

It is relatively difficult for foreigners to secure full-time employment in Finland, but travelers may be able to secure summer work. Check the **CIMO** website (see below) for information on work placement or www.jobs-in-europe.net. The two organizations below coordinate limited work and volunteer opportunities. See p. 66 for Beyond Tourism opportunities throughout Europe.

The American-Scandinavian Foundation (AMSCAN), 725 Park Ave., New York, NY, 10016, USA (☎212-879-9779; www.amscan.org/jobs/index.html). Volunteer and job opportunities throughout Scandinavia. Limited number of fellowships for study in Finland available to Americans.

Centre for International Mobility (CIMO), Hakaniemenk. 2, Helsinki (☎358 1080 6767; finland.cimo.fi). Provides information on youth exchange programs, technical and agricultural internships, and study abroad in Finland. CIMO also organizes **European Voluntary Service** programs (europa.eu.int/comm/youth/program/guide/action2_en.html) for citizens of the EU, which provides a fully funded year of service in another EU country. In Finland, EVS opportunities are largely in social work, including volunteering with children and the disabled.

Council of International Fellowship (CIF) (www.ciffinland.org). Finances exchange programs for human service professionals, including homestays in various Finnish cities. Must have two years work of experience.

HELSINKI (HELSINGFORS) ☎09

With all the appeal of a big city but none of the grime, Helsinki's broad avenues, grand architecture, and green parks make it a model of successful urban planning. A hub of the design world, the city also distinguishes itself with a decidedly multicultural flair: Lutheran and Russian Orthodox cathedrals stand almost face-to-face, and youthful energy mingles with Old World charm. Seaside in both location and character, Baltic Sea produce fills Helsinki marketplaces and restaurants, while St. Petersburg and Tallinn are only a short cruise away.

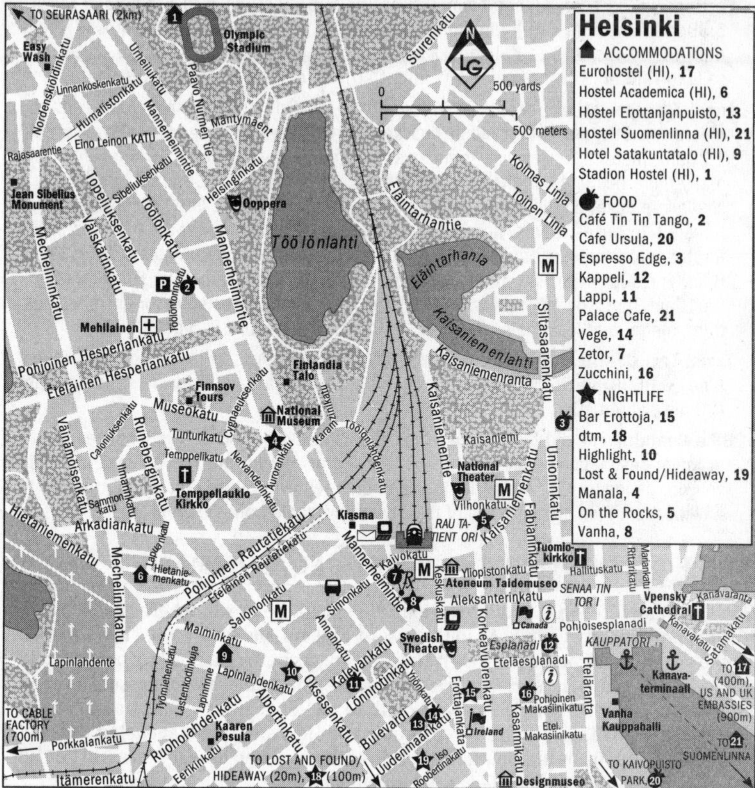

TRANSPORTATION

Flights: Helsinki-Vantaa Airport (HEL; ☎020 01 46 36; www.ilmailulaitos.fi). **Bus** #615 runs between Platform 1b in the airport and the train station (40min.; from the airport: M-F 6am-9pm 3 per hr., 9pm-1am 1-2 per hr., Sa-Su 6am-1am 1-2 per hr.; to the airport: departures 5am-midnight; €3.40). A **Finnair bus** runs between the Platform 1a in the airport and the Finnair building next to the train station (☎0600 14 01 40; www.finnair.com; 25min., 4 per hr. 5am-midnight, €5.20).

Trains: (☎030 072 09 00, English-language info 231 999 02; ww.vr.fi.) Reserve ahead for all long-distance routes. To: **Moscow, Russia** (14hr., daily 5:40pm, €85); **Rovaniemi** (10-13hr., 5-8 per day, €66-71); **St. Petersburg, Russia** (5½hr., 2 per day, €50); **Tampere** (2hr., 8-12 per day, €19-30); **Turku** (2hr., 12 per day, €19-30). See p. 857 for info on documents you'll need before entering Russia.

Buses: The station, Simonk. 3 (☎020 040 00) is between Salomonk. and Simonk.; from the train station, take Postik. past the statue of Mannerheim. Cross Mannerheimintie onto Salomonk. and the station is on your left. To: **Lahti** (1½hr.; 2 per hr.; €18, students €9); **Tampere** (2½hr., 1 per hr., €20/10); **Turku** (2½hr., 2 per hr., €22/11).

Ferries: Viking Line, Mannerheimintie 14 (☎12 35 77), sails to **Stockholm** (17hr., 5:30pm daily, from €46) and **Tallin** (3hr., daily 12:30pm and 9pm, from €17). Take tram #2 or bus #13 to Katajanokka terminal. **Tallink,** Erottajank. 19 (☎22 83 11), sails to **Tallinn** (3¼hr., 2-3 per day, from €20). Take bus #15 to West terminal.

Local Transportation: (☎472 2454; www.hkl.fi/english.html.) **Buses, trams,** and the **metro** run 5:30am-11pm; major bus and tram lines, including tram #3T, run until 1:30am. There is 1 metro line (running approximately east to west), 10 tram lines, and many more bus lines. **Night buses,** marked with an "N," run F-Sa after 2am for €3. A single-fare ticket on the tram without transfers is €1.80. Single-fare tickets with 1hr. of transfers to buses, trams, and the metro are €2. The **City Transport Office** is in the Rautatientori metro station, below the train station. Open in summer M-Th 7:30am-6pm, F 7:30am-4pm, Sa 10am-3pm; low season M-Th 7:30am-7pm, F 7:30am-5pm, Sa 10am-3pm. The office sells the **tourist ticket,** a good investment for unlimited bus, tram, metro, and local trains. 1-day ticket €5.40, 3-day €10.80, 5-day €16.20.

Taxis: Taxi Centre Helsinki (☎0100 06 00). Special prices to the airport with **Yellow Line** (☎0600 55 55 55; www.yellowline.fi). Reserve a day in advance, before 6pm (20min., about €25).

Bike Rental: From mid-June to Aug., the city provides over 300 free, lime-green bikes at major destinations throughout the city; it can be tricky to track one down, but when you do, deposit a €2 coin in the lock and then retrieve it upon "returning" the bike to any location. Free cycling maps of the city are available from the tourist office.

ORIENTATION AND PRACTICAL INFORMATION

Sea surrounds Helsinki in all directions except to the north, where two lakes lie just beyond the city center. As in the rest of Finland, the feel of the city is shaped by the surrounding bodies of water. Helsinki boasts both relaxing city beaches and gorgeous lakeside parks. Helsinki's main street, **Mannerheimintie,** passes between the bus and train stations on its way south to the city center, coming to an end at the **Esplanadi.** This lively tree-lined promenade leads east to **Kauppatori** (Market Square) and the beautiful South Harbor. Both Finnish and Swedish are used on all street signs and maps; *Let's Go* uses the Finnish names.

Tourist Offices: Pohjoisesplanadi 19 (☎169 37 57; www.hel.fi/tourism). From the train station, walk 2 blocks down Keskusk. and turn left on Pohjoisesplanadi; from the ferry terminals, head left on Pohjoisesplanadi. Open May-Sept. M-F 9am-8pm, Sa-Su 9am-6pm; Oct.-Apr. M-F 9am-6pm, Sa-Su 10am-4pm. The **Helsinki Card** (www.helsinkicard.fi), sold at the tourist office, provides unlimited local transportation and free or discounted admission to most museums, although cardholders have to keep up a blistering pace to make their purchase worthwhile. 1-day €25, 2-day €35, 3-day €45. The **Finnish Tourist Board,** across the street at Eteläesplanadi 4 (☎41 76 93 00; www.mek.fi), has info for all of Finland. Open May-Sept. M-F 9am-5pm, Sa-Su 11am-3pm; Oct.-Apr. M-F 9am-5pm. **Finnsov Tours,** Museok. 15 (☎436 69 60) arranges trips to Russia and expedites the visa process. Open M-F 8:30am-5pm.

Embassies: Canada, Pohjoisesplanadi 25B (☎22 85 30; www.canada.fi). Open M-Th 8:30am-noon and 1-4:30pm, F 8:30am-1:30pm. **Ireland,** Erottajank. 7A (☎64 60 06). Open M-F 9am-5pm. **UK,** Itäinen Puistotie 17 (☎22 86 51 00; www.ukembassy.fi). Also handles diplomatic matters for **Australians** and **New Zealanders.** Open M-F 8:30am-3:30pm. **US,** Itäinen Puistotie 14A (☎61 62 50; www.usembassy.fi). Open M-F 8:30am-5pm.

Currency Exchange: Forex (☎020 7512 510) has 4 locations and the best rates in the city. Hours vary; the branch in the train station is open daily 8am-9pm.

Luggage Storage: Lockers in the train station €2-3 per day.

Laundromat: **Café Tin Tin Tango,** Töölöntorink. 7 (☎27 09 09 72), a combination bar, cafe, laundromat, and sauna. Wash €3.50, dry €1.80, detergent €1. Sandwiches €6. Salad €8.50. Sauna €20 per hr. for 2 people. Open M-F 7am-2am, Sa-Su 10am-2am. MC/V. For a more traditional laundromat, try **Kaaren Pesula,** Kalevank. 45 (☎ 67 97 89). Wash €4 per 5kg, dry €3 per 5kg, detergent €1. Higher prices for bigger loads. Open M-Th 10am-8pm, F 10am-6pm, Sa 10am-4pm.

Emergency: ☎112. **Police:** ☎100 22. **24hr. Medical Hotline:** ☎100 23

24hr. Pharmacy: Yliopiston Apteekki, Mannerheimintie 96 (☎41 78 03 00).

Hospital: 24hr. medical clinic **Mehilainen,** Runebergink. 47A (☎010 414 44 44).

Internet Access: Library 10, Elielinaukio 2G, upstairs in the main post office building. Free 30min. slots. Open M-Th 10am-10pm, F 10am-6pm, Sa-Su noon-6pm. **Academic Bookstore,** Keskusk. 1. Free 15min. slots. Open M-F 9am-9pm, Sa 9am-6pm.

Post Office: Elielinaukio 2F (☎20 07 10 00). Open M-F 7am-9pm, Sa-Su 10am-6pm. Address mail to be held in the following format: First name SURNAME, *Poste Restante,* Mannerheiminaukio 1A, 00100 Helsinki, FINLAND.

ACCOMMODATIONS AND CAMPING

Helsinki's hotels tend to be expensive, but its budget hostels are often quite nice. In June and July, make reservations a few weeks in advance for both.

Hostel Erottanjanpuisto (HI), Uudenmaank. 9 (☎64 21 69; www.erottajanpuisto.com). Friendly staff tends well-kept rooms in a centrally-located 19th-century building. Breakfast €5. Lockers €1. Laundry €7. Internet €1 per 10min. Reception 24hr. Summer dorms €22.50; singles €46; doubles €62.50. Low season singles €44; doubles €60.50. €2.50 HI discount. AmEx/MC/V. ❷

Eurohostel (HI), Linnank. 9 (☎622 04 70; www.eurohostel.fi), 200m from the Katajanokka ferry terminal. From the train station, head right to Mannerheimintie, take tram #2 and get off at Linnank. or take tram #4 to Vyök. stop. Bright rooms, cafe, and free morning sauna. Evening sauna €5. Breakfast €6.10. Internet €1 per 10min. Reception 24hr. Singles €38; doubles €46; triples €69. €2.50 HI discount. MC/V. ❸

Hostel Satakuntatalo (HI), Lapinrinne 1A (☎69 58 52 32). M: Kamppi. Spacious, well-equipped rooms close to the city center. Breakfast and sauna included. Linen and laundry each €5.50. Reception 24hr. Open June-Aug. Dorms €19; singles €39; doubles €58; triples €72; quads €84. €2.50 HI discount. AmEx/DC/MC/V. ❷

Stadion Hostel (HI), Pohj. Stadiontie 3B (☎477 84 80; www.stadionhostel.com). Take tram #7A or 3 to Auroran Sairaala. Walk down Pohj. Stadiontie toward the white tower. This hostel might look like a high-school locker room, but it boasts a much healthier social life. Breakfast €5.30. Linen €5. Laundry €2.50. Internet €1 per 15min. Reception June to early Sept. 7am-3am; mid-Sept. to May 7am-2am. Lockout noon-4pm. Dorms €15.50; singles €27.50; doubles €38.50. €2.50 HI discount. MC/V. ❷

Hostel Academica (HI), Hietaniemenk. 14 (☎1311 4334; www.hostelacademica.fi). M: Kamppi. Turn right onto Runebergink. and left shortly after crossing the bridge over the railroad tracks. University housing transforms into a hostel in summer. Morning sauna and swim included. Breakfast and linen included for singles and doubles. Breakfast €6. Linen and towel €5. Internet €2 per 15min. Reception 24hr. Open June-Aug. Dorms €18; singles €38-64; doubles €66-88. €2.50 HI discount. AmEx/DC/MC/V. ❷

Hostel Suomenlinna (HI), building C9 by the main quay on the Iso Mustasaari island in Suomenlinna, next to the supermarket (☎684 74 71; www.leirikoulut.com). High-ceilinged rooms in a squat brick building on Suomenlinna's western island. Breakfast €4.50. Laundry €2. Reception 8am-9pm; call ahead for check-in. Dorms €22.50; doubles €55; triples €82.50. €2.50 HI discount. MC/V. ❷

Rastila Camping, Karavaanik. 4 (☎321 65 51; www.hel.fi/liv/rastila/rastila.html), M: Rastila. The campsite is 100m to the right. A large campsite 12km from the city next to a public beach and public sauna (€4; limited hours). Kitchen, showers and electricity each €4. Mid-May to mid-Sept. reception 24hr; mid-Sept. to mid-May daily 8am-10pm. Tent sites €11, up to 5 extra people €6. Cabins €43-62. MC/V. ❶

FOOD

Restaurants and cafes are easy to find on **Esplanadi** and the streets branching off from **Mannerheimintie** and **Uudenmaankatu.** Cheaper options surround the **Hietalahti** flea market at the southern end of Bulevardi. A large **supermarket** is under the train station. (Open M-F 7:30am-10pm, Sa 9am-10pm, Su 10am-10pm.) Get lunch at the open-air market of **Kauppatori,** by the harbor, where stalls sell a variety of fried fish and farm-fresh produce; it's not hard to assemble a satisfying meal for €6-8. (Open June-Aug. M-Sa 6:30am-5pm; Sept.-May M-F 7am-2pm.) The nearby **Vanha Kauppahalli** is an old-fashioned indoor market. (Open M-F 8am-7pm, Sa 8am-4pm.)

Zetor, Mannerheimintie 3-5 (☎66 69 66; www.zetor.net), in Kaivopiha, the mall opposite the train station. Cheeky dish names, cheekier farm-inspired decor, and ridiculously good Finnish food. Homemade beer €5. Entrees €10-19. Attached bar 22+. Open M, Su 3pm-1:30am, Tu 3pm-2:30am, W-F 3pm-3:30am, Sa 11am-3:30am. ❷

Kappeli, Eteläesplanadi 1 (☎681 24 40), near the Kauppatori. Frequented by well-heeled bohemians since 1839, this lovely cafe serves salads and sandwiches (€6-9) both inside the temple-like pavilion and on its terrace; head inside to the left. Open M-Sa 9am-2am, Su 9am-1am. Kitchen closes at 1am. AmEx/MC/V. ❶

Cafe Ursula (☎65 28 17), near Kaivopuisto park on Ehrenströmintie. Relax in an idyllic setting on the edge of the Baltic Sea. Sandwiches €5-7. Salads €8-9. Open daily 9am-midnight. AmEx/MC/V. ❶

Lappi, Annank. 22 (☎64 55 50; www.lappires.com). Wood-and-fur decor puts diners in the mood to splurge on Lappish specialties like reindeer, elk, lingonberries, and arctic char. M-F noon-3pm lunch entrees €11, dinner entrees from €17. Reservations strongly recommended. Open M-F noon-10:30pm, Sa-Su 1-10:30pm. AmEx/DC/MC/V. ❸

Zucchini, Fabianink. 4 (☎622 29 07), just south of the tourist office. This popular vegetarian eatery features organic produce as well as vegan options. Pizza and salad €4.50. Daily lunch specials €8, with soup €9. Open daily 11am-4pm. AmEx/DC/MC/V. ❷

Espresso Edge, Liisank. 29 (☎278 41 44). Take tram #7B to the Liisank. stop. This artsy neighborhood cafe serves tasty sandwiches (€5) and wraps (€7.90). Soup and sandwich lunch special €7.90. Open M-Th 8am-7pm, F 8am-6pm, Sa-Su 11am-5pm. In July, M-F 8am-6pm only. MC/V. ❶

Vege, Uudenmaank. 9 (☎6227 7550). Vege offers both lunch specials (€11) and restaurant dining during the evenings, including vegan options. Open M-F 11am-11pm, Sa noon-11pm. MC/V. ❷

Palace Cafe, Eteläranta 10 (☎1345 6793). Take Eteläranta from the Kauppatori market place; around the corner from the Palace Hotel. Serves hearty Finnish home cooking at affordable prices. Lunch special €8. Open M-F 11am-3pm. MC/V. ❷

SIGHTS

Helsinki's polished Neoclassical buildings and bold new forms reflect Finnish architect Alvar Aalto's joke: "Architecture is our form of expression because our language is so impossible." Much of the layout and architecture of the old center, however, is the brainchild of a German. After Helsinki became the capital of Finland in 1812,

Carl Engel designed a grand city modeled after St. Petersburg. Today, Helsinki's Art Nouveau *(Jugendstil)* and Modernist structures are home to a bustling design community. Most of the major sights are crammed into the city's compact center, making it ideal for walking tours; pick up *See Helsinki on Foot* from the tourist office for suggested routes. Trams #3T and 3B loop around the major sights in roughly 1hr., providing a cheap alternative to sightseeing buses. Helsinki is dotted with parks, including **Kaivopuisto** in the south, **Töölönlahti** in the north, and **Esplanadi** and **Tähtitorninvuori** in the center of town.

SUOMENLINNA. Five interconnected islands are home to this 18th-century Swedish military fortification, erected to stave off an expected Russian invasion of Helsinki. The old fortress's dark passageways are an adventure to explore. The **Suomenlinna Museum** and the **Coastal Artillery Museum,** located within one of the ramparts, offer a more informative approach to history. *(☎684 1850; www.suomenlinna.fi. Museums open daily May-Aug. 10am-6pm; Sept.-Apr. 11am-4pm; €5, students €4. MC/V.)* The islands also feature the world's only combination church and lighthouse, which contains Finland's largest bell, as well as Finland's only remaining WWII submarine, Vesikko. *(Church ☎684 7471. Open W-F noon-4pm. Submarine ☎1814 5295. Open mid-May to Aug. 11am-6pm. €4, students €2.)* The smooth rocks on the southern island are popular with sunbathers and swimmers. *(City Transport ferries depart from Market Sq. every 20min. 8am-11pm, round-trip €3.60. Combination ticket for the museums plus the submarine €5.50, students €3.)*

SENAATIN TORI (SENATE SQUARE). The square and its gleaming white **Tuomiokirkko** (Dome Church) showcase Engel's work and exemplify the splendor of Finland's 19th-century Russian period. The church's interior is so elegantly simple that every decorative detail becomes magnified tenfold. *(At Aleksanterink. and Unionink. in the city center. Church open June-Aug. M-Sa 9am-6pm, Su noon-8pm; Sept.-May M-Sa 9am-6pm, Su noon-6pm.)* Just around the corner from Tuomiokirkko, at the Hallitusk. stop of trams #7A/7B, is the **Bank of Finland Museum.** It displays money from Finland and abroad, as well as wisely rejected euro designs. *(Snellmanink. 2. ☎010 831 2981. Open Tu-F noon-6pm, Sa-Su 11am-4pm. Free.).* Off of Senate Sq., on a small street running between Unionink. and Snellmanink., the **Helsinki City Museum** focuses on the city's 450-year history through displays and a film. *(Sofiank. 4. ☎169 3933. Open M-F 9am-5pm, Sa-Su 11am-5pm. The City Museum also has other exhibits throughout the city; pick up a list at the museum or at the tourist office. Each exhibit €3, students €1.50. Free Th. DC/MC/V.)* The street itself is an open-air

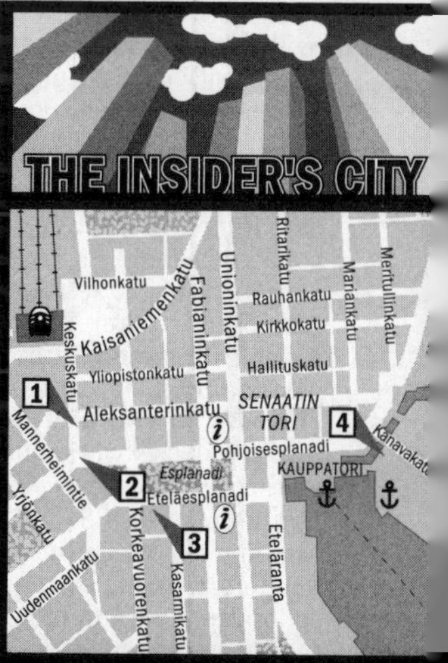

AALTO'S HELSINKI

The curvilinear marble surfaces of Finlandia Hall may be architect Alvar Aalto's most recognizable gift to Helsinki, but a number of his other Modernist creations give a sense of his aesthetic breadth.

1. **Rautatalo** (Iron House), Keskusk. 3. The stark facade conceals an airy atrium meant to recall an Italian *piazza,* one of Aalto's favorite motifs.

2. **Academic Bookstore,** Pohjoisesplanadi 39. The capital's largest bookstore named its upstairs cafe after the architect who designed the building in 1969.

3. **Savoy Restaurant,** Eteläesplanadi 14. The €35 entrees are too pricey for the budget traveler, but the decor is all Aalto's work–right down to the sinuous amber vases.

4. **Stora Enso Headquarters,** Kanavak. 1. This ultramodern "sugar cube" overlooks the South Harbor and provocatively comments on the two churches that flank it.

museum of street pavements and street furniture. On a dramatic hill to the east, the red-brick **Uspenski Orthodox Cathedral** (Uspenskinkatedraadi), the largest Orthodox church in Western Europe, evokes images of Russia with its ornate interior and golden onion domes. *(Open M and W-Sa 9:30am-4pm, Tu 9:30am-6pm, Su noon-3pm.)*

ESPLANADI AND MANNERHEIMINTIE. A lush boulevard dotted with statues and fountains, Esplanadi is an ideal place to people-watch on a sunny day. Turn south onto Korkeavuorenk. to reach the **Designmuseo,** which presents the work of established designers like Aalto and Eliel Saarinen alongside creations by exciting young artists. *(Korkeavuorenk. 3. ☎622 0540; www.designmuseum.fi. Open June-Aug. daily 11am-6pm; Sept.-May Tu 11am-8pm, W-Su 11am-6pm. €7, students €3. AmEx/DC/MC/V.)* At the end of Esplanadi, turn right onto Mannerheimintie and right again onto Kaivok. past the train station to reach the **Ateneum Art Museum** (Ateneum Taidemuseo), Finland's largest, with comprehensive exhibits on Finnish art. Don't miss Aksel Gallen-Kallela's work illustrating episodes from the Kalevala, the Finnish national epic. *(Kaivok. 2, opposite the train station. ☎17 33 64 01; www.ateneum.fi. Open Tu and F 9am-6pm, W-Th 9am-8pm, Sa-Su 11am-5pm. €5.50, €7.50 during temporary exhibits. Free W 5-8pm.)* Continue on Mannerheimintie past the post office to **Kiasma** (Museum of Contemporary Art), a stark, silver warehouse that houses top-flight modern art and calibrates the width of its doors to Fibonacci's golden ratio. Check out the sculpture garden behind the museum for free. *(Mannerheiminaukio 2. ☎17 33 65 01; www.kiasma.fi. Open Tu 9am-5pm, W-Su 10am-8:30pm. €5.50, students €4. Free F 5-8:30pm. AmEx/DC/MC/V.)* After passing the grandiose Parliament building, you'll find yourself between two of Helsinki's most beautiful buildings. On the left is Saarinen's **National Museum of Finland** (Suomen Kansallismuseo), featuring a romp through Finnish cultural history and a magnificent floor-to-ceiling fresco by Gallen-Kallela. *(Mannerheimintie 34. ☎40 501; www.kansallismuseo.fi. Open Tu-W 11am-8pm, Th-Su 11am-6pm. €5.50, students €4. Free Tu 5:30-8pm. AmEx/DC/MC/V.)* On the right is Aalto's majestic **Finlandia Talo,** the white marble home of Helsinki's Philharmonic and Radio Symphony Orchestra. *(Mannerheimintie 13E. ☎402 41; www.finlandia.hel.fi. Tours in summer daily 1:30pm. €4.)* Head back down Mannerheimintie toward the post office, turn right onto Arkadiank. and right again onto Fredrikink. to reach the stunning **Temppeliaukio Kirkko.** Hewn out of a hill of rock with only the roof visible from the outside, the huge domed ceiling inside the church appears to be supported only by rays of sunlight. *(Lutherink. 3. ☎494 698. Usually open M-Tu and Th-F 10am-8pm, W 10am-6:45pm, Sa 10am-6pm, Su noon-1:45pm and 3:30-5:45pm.)*

OTHER SIGHTS. North of Senate Sq. along Unionink. lies the University of Helsinki **Botanic Garden,** where beautiful glass houses shelter lily leaves more than a meter in diameter. *(Unionink. 44. ☎191 24453; www.helsinki.fi/english/botanicgarden. Take trams #3B/3T or 6 to Kaisaniemi. Gardens open M-F 7am-8pm, Sa-Su 9am-8pm. Gardens free. Glass houses open Tu-Su 10am-5pm in Apr.-Sept. and 10am-3pm the remainder of the year. Glass houses €4.20. MC/V.)* In an industrial area west of the city center, the mammoth, vaguely anarchic **Cable Factory** (Kaapeli) houses three museums, dozens of studios and galleries, and various performance areas. Especially worthwhile are the **Finnish Museum of Photography,** with dramatic photographs from the past century, and the **Theater Museum,** with dazzling set models and costume designs from the national theater. The complex also hosts major cultural events. *(Tallbergink. 1. ☎68 50 9121; www.kaapelitehdas.fi. M: Ruoholahti. After exiting, walk 5 blocks down Itämerenk. You can also take tram #8 to the end of the line. Museums open Tu-Su noon-7pm. Photography Museum €6, students €4. Theater Museum €5.50/2.50. MC/V.)* Near the Western Harbor, the well-touristed **Jean Sibelius Monument** pays homage to one of the 20th century's greatest composers with what looks like a stormcloud of organ pipes ascending to heaven. *(On Mechelinink. in Sibelius park. Take bus #24, dir.: Seurasaari, from Mannerheimintie and get off at Rasjasaarentie; the monument will be behind you.)*

ENTERTAINMENT

Helsinki's parks are always animated. A **concert series** enlivens the **Esplanadi** park all summer Monday through Thursday at 4:30pm as well as on Saturdays at 10:30am. Highlights of the program are **Jazz Espa** in July, and **Ethno Espa** showcasing ethno-music (www.kulttuuri.hel.fi/espanlava). The **Helsinki Festival** (www.helsinkifestival.fi) towards the end of August wraps up the summer with cultural events ranging from music and theater to film and visual arts. At the end of September, **Helsinki Design Week** (www.helsinkidesignweek.fi) reinforces Helsinki's image as a city of design, while the **Love and Anarchy Film Festival** (www.hiff.fi) features works from across the globe. All through the summer, concerts rock **Kaivopuisto** (on the corner of Puistok. and Ehrenstromintie, in the southern part of town) and **Hietaniemi Beach** (down Hesperiank. on the western shore). The free English-language papers *Helsinki This Week*, *Helsinki Happens*, and *City* list popular cafes, nightspots, and events; pick up copies at the tourist office. Also check the schedules of the Helsinki Philharmonic and Radio Symphony Orchestra, the National Opera, and the National Theater. **Lippupiste,** Aleksanterink. 52 (☎0600 90 09 00), in the Stockmann department store, sells tickets for most big venues.

NIGHTLIFE

Bars and beer terraces start filling up in the late afternoon; most clubs don't get going until midnight and stay hopping until 4am. With the exception of licensed restaurants and bars, only the state-run liquor store **Alko** can sell alcohol more potent than light beer. Branch at Mannerheimintie 1, in Kaivopiha across from the train station. (Open M-F 9am-8pm, Sa 9am-6pm.) Bars and clubs, ranging from laidback neighborhood pubs to sleek discos, line **Mannerheimintie, Uudenmaankatu,** and **Iso Roobertinkatu.** East of the train station, nightlife flourishes around **Yliopistonkatu** and **Kaisaniemenkatu.**

On the Rocks, Mikonk. 15 (☎612 20 30; www.ontherocks.fi). The legendary rock bar and club draws large crowds to its dungeon-like dance floor. Beer €4.50. Tu-Th live music. 23+. Cover Tu-Th €6-12; F-Sa €7. Open daily 8pm-4am. AmEx/D/MC/V.

Bar Erottoja, Erottajank. 13-17 (☎61 11 96). This art student hangout is packed with people engaged in conversation over blaring hip-hop music. Beer €4. 22+. Open M and Su 2pm-1am, Tu 2pm-2am, W-Sa 2pm-3am. AmEx/D/MC/V.

Manala, Dagmarink. 2 (☎5807 7707; www.botta.fi). This student-owned house draws a varied crowd to its 3 dance floors. Beer €4.40. Live bands F, except in July. 22+. Club open F-Sa 11pm-3:30am. AmEx/D/MC/V.

Vanha, Mannerheimintie 3 (☎13 11 43 46). A student crowd gathers in this historic building for club nights every other weekend and occasional cultural events. Beer €4-5. Cover F-Sa €2-4. Open M-Th 11am-1am, F 11am-2am, Sa 11am-4am. MC/V.

Highlight, Fredrinkink. 42 (☎050 409 00 79). A dance club for the young and fit. Beer €3.80. 19+. Cover F-Sa 11pm-3am €5. Open W and F-Sa 10pm-4am. AmEx/D/MC/V.

dtm, Iso Roobertink. 28 (☎67 63 14; www.dtm.fi). This huge, popular gay club draws a mixed crowd to foam parties, drag bingo, and more. Beer €4. 24+ after 10pm. Cover Sa €5.20, special events €5-10. Open M-Sa 9am-4am, Su noon-4am. MC/V.

Lost and Found/Hideaway, Annank. 6 (☎680 10 10; www.lostandfound.fi). The relaxed atmosphere and a busy dance floor draws regulars to this late-night hetero-friendly gay bar. Beer €4.60. 24+. Open daily 5pm-4am in the winter; 8pm-4am in the summer.

OUTDOOR ACTIVITIES

Just north of the train station lie the two city lakes; the winding paths around them lend to a nice afternoon walk. Northwest of the Sibelius Monument across a lovely white bridge, the island of **Seurasaari** offers respite from the bustle of the city. It is also home to farmsteads and churches transplanted from around Finland, as well as an **open-air museum** that allows entrance into many of the historical buildings. On Midsummer's Eve, drunken revelers light tall bonfires *(kokko)* to celebrate the mild season. *(Take bus #24 from Erottaja, outside the Swedish Theater, to the last stop. The island is always open for hiking. Museum open daily 11am-5pm. €5.)* Much farther out from the city, beyond Espoo, lies the Nuuksio National Park. Known for its flying squirrels that are more common here than anywhere else in Finland. *(☎0205 64 4790; www.outdoors.fi. Take the train to Espoo railway station and bus #85 from there to Nuuksionpää.)*

DAYTRIPS FROM HELSINKI

PORVOO. Picturesque Porvoo (pop. 46,000) lies along **Old King Road,** a network of paths that stretches from St. Petersburg west through Turku all the way to the Norwegian port of Bergen. In 1809, Tsar Alexander I granted Finland autonomy at the simple, whitewashed **cathedral** in Porvoo's old town. (☎66 112 50. Open May-Sept. M-F 10am-6pm, Sa 10am-2pm, Su 2-5pm; Oct.-Apr. Tu-Sa 10am-2pm, Su 2-4pm. Free.) The house of Finland's national poet **Johan Ludvig Runeberg,** Aleksanterink. 3, looks just as it did when he called it home in the mid-1800s; the works of his son, sculptor Walter Runeberg, are on display across the street. (Both houses open May-Aug. M-Sa 10am-4pm, Su 11am-5pm; Sept.-Apr. W-Sa 10am-4pm, Su 11am-5pm. €5, students €2.) Impressionist painter Albert Edelfelt also called Porvoo home, and some of his graceful canvases are on display at the **Edelfelt-Vallgren Museum,** Välikatu 11, next to the **Historical Museum.** (Both museums open May-Aug. M-Sa 10am-4pm, Su 11am-4pm; Sept.-Apr. W-Su noon-4pm. €5.) **Porvoo Pyörätalo,** Mannerheimink. 12 (☎019 58 51 04), rents **bikes** to visitors heading as far south as **Pellinki** (30km) on the Pellinge archipelago. **Buses** run from Helsinki (1hr., every 15min., €8.50). The **tourist office,** Rihkamak. 4, offers free Internet. Follow signs from the bus station. (☎019 520 23 16; www.porvoo.fi. Open mid-June to Aug. M-F 9am-6pm, Sa-Su 10am-4pm; low season reduced hours.)

LAHTI. World-class winter sports facilities make Lahti (pop. 96,000) a popular destination for the snow-bunny set. All year round, the **Ski Museum** has ski-jump and biathalon simulators, as well as exhibits on the history of skiing in Finland. (☎38 14 45 23; www.lahti.fi/museot/ski.html. Open M-F 10am-5pm, Sa-Su 11am-5pm. €5, students €3.) Towering more than 200m above the museum, the tallest of three **ski jumps** is accessible by a chairlift/elevator combination. (Open in summer M-Su 10am-5pm. €4, with ski museum €7.) The extensive network of cross-country **ski trails** (100km) emanating from the sports complex is hikable in summer; the tourist office provides free hiking **maps,** including information about the thickly forested **Ilvesvaellus Trail,** a 30min. bus ride to the northwest. At the northern part of the city, in Kariniemi Park next to the harbor, the Musical Fountains combine water and music daily at 7pm, while at the harbor the Sibelius Hall houses the annual **Sibelius Festival** in September. **Trains** arrive from Helsinki (1½-2hr., every hr., €12-22); Savonlinna (3-3½hr., 5 per day, €36-38); Tampere (2hr., every 1-2hr., €21-23.50). The **tourist office,** Aleksanterink. 16, provides free Internet; walk up Raututienk. 7 blocks and turn left on Aleksanterink. (☎03 814 45 66; www.lahti-travel.fi. Open M-Th 9am-5pm, F 9am-4pm.)

TURKU (ÅBO) ☎02

Finland's oldest city, Turku (pop. 163,000) has grown weatherbeaten with the passing of 775 years. It was the focal point of Swedish and Russian power struggles, the seat of Finnish governance until 1812, and then the victim of the worst fire in Scandinavian history, which almost wiped the city off the map in 1827. Turku has rebuilt itself into a vibrant cultural and academic center that continues to pride itself on what is has endured.

TRANSPORTATION AND PRACTICAL INFORMATION. **Trains** run to Helsinki (2hr., 1 per hr., €19-28) and Tampere (1¾hr., every 1-2hr., €17-26). Viking Line **ferries** sail to Stockholm (10hr., 2 per day, from €24), as do Silja Line ferries (12hr., daily 6:30pm, from €20). To get to the ferry terminal, catch bus #1 from Kauppatori (€2) or walk to the end of Linnank. The **tourist office,** Aurak. 4, offers 15min. of free **Internet** access. (☎262 74 44; www.turkutouring.fi. Open Apr.-Sept. M-F 8:30am-6pm, Sa-Su 9am-4pm; Oct.-Mar. M-F 8:30am-6pm, Sa-Su 10am-3pm.)

ACCOMMODATIONS AND FOOD. The spacious, riverside **Hostel Turku (HI) ❷,** Linnank. 39. From the station, walk west four blocks on Ratapihank., turn left on Puistok., and right at the river. (☎262 76 80. Bike rental €10 per day, €5 per 4hr., with €10 deposit. Breakfast €4.50. Linen €4.70. Laundry €2. Reception 6am-midnight. Check-in 3pm-midnight. Curfew 2am for dorm residents. Dorms €14; singles €33.50; doubles €38; quads €57. €2.50 HI discount. MC/V.) For well-kept rooms in a peaceful setting, try the nun-run **Bridgettine Convent Guesthouse ❸,** Ursinink. 15A, near the corner of Puutarhak. (☎250 19 10. Breakfast included. No kitchen available. Reception 8am-9pm. Singles €42; doubles €62; triples €80. Cash only.) Take bus #8 from Eerikink. to **Ruissalo Camping ❷,** on the tip of leafy Ruissalo Island. (☎262 51 00. Electricity €3.50. Showers included. Reception 7am-11pm. Open May-Aug. Tent sites €14, extra person €4. MC/V.)

Produce fills the outdoor **Kauppatori** (open M-Sa 7am-2pm) and indoor **Kauppahalli** (open M-Th 8am-5pm, F 8am-2pm, Sa 8am-2pm) on Eerikink. Cheap eateries line **Humalistonkatu.** Locals pack **Kertu ❷,** Läntinen Pitkäk. 35, where they feast on traditional Jallupulla meatballs (€9; choice of veggie or meat) and other tasty fare while surfing the free wireless Internet or doing laundry (€2.50 per 2hr.). By night, Kertu becomes a hopping bar. (☎250 69 90; www.kertu.fi. Open M-Tu 10:30am-midnight, W-Th 10:30am-1am, F 10:30am-2am, Sa 2pm-2am. MC/V.)

SIGHTS AND ENTERTAINMENT. Just over a decade ago, when a tobacco magnate's riverside mansion was being renovated into a museum, workers discovered a medieval city block 7m directly beneath the house, and dug it out. Today, the **Aboa Vetus and Ars Nova Museums,** Itäinen Rantak. 4-6, house a modern art collection suspended over the archaeological dig in dramatic juxtaposition. (☎250 05 52; www.aboavetusarsnova.fi. Open Apr. to mid-Sept. daily 11am-7pm; late Sept. to Mar. Tu-Su 11am-7pm. €8, students €7. MC/V.) The blocky **Turku Cathedral,** Tuomiokirkkotori 20, serves as the spiritual center of Finland's Lutheran Church. Finnish public radio has broadcast the cathedral's noontime chiming of the bells since 1944. Skip the boring interior museum. (☎261 7100; www.turunseurakunnat.fi. Open daily mid-April to mid-Sept. 9am-8pm; low season 9am-7pm. Evening concerts June-Aug. Tu 8pm. Cathedral free. Museum €2, students €1.) Around the corner, the **Sibelius Museum,** Piispank. 17, houses memorabilia like the composer's cigar box, as well as a collection of European folk instruments. (☎215 44 94; www.sibeliusmuseum.abo.fi. Open Tu-Su 11am-4pm, W also 6-8pm. Concerts in fall and spring W 8pm. Museum €3, students €1. Concerts €7/3. Cash only.) The 700-

year-old **Turun Linna** (Turku Castle), Linnank. 80, 3km from the town center, contains a labyrinthine historical museum with dark passageways and medieval artifacts. Catch bus #1 (€2) from Market Sq. or walk to the end of Linnank. (☎262 03 00. Open mid-Apr. to mid-Sept. daily 10am-6pm; mid-Sept. to mid-Apr. Tu-Su 10am-3pm. €6.50, students €5.20. MC/V.)

The end of June brings the **Medieval Market** to town, while power chords rock Ruissalo Island at July's **Ruisrock** festival (www.ruisrock.fi). In August, the annual **Turku Music Festival** (www.turkumusicfestival.fi) brings a diverse range of artists to non-traditional venues throughout the city, including Turun Linna. Turku is known throughout Finland for its laidback pubs and breweries, many of which are housed in unusual spaces. In summer, Turku's nightlife centers around the river, where Finns and tourists alike crowd the boats docked by the banks to dance and drink. Pull up a stool to the medicine counter at an old apothecary, **Pub Uusi Apteekki,** Kaskenk. 1, across the Auran bridge from the center. (☎250 25 95; www.kolumbus.fi/uusi.apteekki. 20+. Open daily 10am-3am. DC/MC/V.) A 19th-century girls' school, **Brewery Restaurant Koulu,** Eerikink. 18, offers a broad range of its own brews. (☎274 57 57; www.panimoravintolakoulu.fi. Open M-Th and Su 11am-2am, F-Sa 11am-3am. AmEx/DC/MC/V.) For your fill of toilet humor, head to a former public restroom, **Restaurant Puutorin Vessa,** Puutori. (☎233 81 23; www.puutorinvessa.fi. Open daily noon to midnight. MC/V.)

DAYTRIPS FROM TURKU: RAUMA AND PORI. Farther north on the Baltic Coast, **Rauma** (pop. 37,000) is known for the well-preserved wooden buildings that make up the **old town.** Pick up walking tour maps at the tourist office. Nearby, the frescoed, subtly asymmetrical **Church of the Holy Cross,** which shed its past as a Franciscan monastery to become a Lutheran chapel, is a poster child for the Reformation. Many islands in Rauma's **archipelago** are excellent for hiking; try the trails on **Kuuskajaskari,** a former fortress. (30min. Ferries depart twice daily in summer from the harbor. €7.) The **Finnish Rock Festival** (www.rmj.fi) throws the biggest midsummer party in Finland, while festivals dedicated to the blues (mid-July) and lace (late July; www.rauma.fi/kiku) pack Rauma's calendar later in the summer. Late August brings the **Blue Sea Film Festival** (www.blueseafilmfestival.com), which screens the best new domestic films of the year. **Buses** arrive from Turku every hr., 1½-2hr., €16. To reach the **tourist office,** Valtak. 2, walk down Nortamonk. and turn right. (☎716 68 00; www.visitrauma.fi. Open June-Aug. M-F 8am-6pm, Sa 10am-3pm, Su 11am-2pm; Sept.-May M-F 8am-4pm.)

FINLAND

Each July, the elegant coastal town of **Pori** (pop. 76,000) is mobbed by crowds attending the **Pori Jazz Festival,** an event that has confounded jazz traditionalists by showcasing Macy Gray and Ladysmith Black Mambazo alongside the usual suspects. (☎626 22 00; www.porijazz.fi. July 15-23, 2006. Tickets from €7; some concerts free.) For modern art installations, head to the **Pori Art Museum,** on the corner of Eteläranták. and Raatihuonek. (☎621 10 80. Open Tu-Su 11am-6pm, W until 8pm. €5, students €2.50. Cash only.) In a graveyard 1.5km west of the town center, on Maantiek., the gorgeous **Juselius Mausoleum** is adorned with frescoes painted by Jorma Gallen-Kallela using sketches drawn by his father Akseli. (☎623 87 46. Open May-Aug. daily noon-3pm. Free.) Bus #2 (20min., €2) leads northwest to **Yyteri Beach,** home to windsurfers in summer and cross-country skiers in winter. Loll in the sand while you pound a Karhu beer, brewed in Pori. **Trains** arrive from Helsinki, 3½-4hr., 5-8 per day, €25-32. Buses pull in from Tampere (2hr., 4 per day, €16) and Turku (2hr., 6-7 per day, €21). The **tourist office,** Yrjönk. 17, finds rooms. (☎621 12 73; www.pori.fi. Open M-F June-Aug. 8am-6pm; Sept.-May 8am-4pm.)

TAMPERE ☎03

A striking example of successful urban renewal, Tampere (pop. 200,000) has converted its old brick factories to museums and planted trees along waterways where paddle wheels and turbines once whirred. As telecommunications and information technology edged out textile and metal plants, a contemporary city has emerged to give Turku a run for its money as Finland's second capital.

TRANSPORTATION AND PRACTICAL INFORMATION. Trains head to: Helsinki (2hr., 2 per hr., €19-29); Oulu (4-5hr., 8 per day, €45-56); Turku (2hr., every 1-2hr., €17-26). **City buses** cost €2, and most buses pass through the main square on Hämeenk. The **tourist office,** Verkatehtaank. 2, has free **Internet.** Its officials zip around town on green scooters and offer assistance. From the train station, walk up Hämeenk. four blocks and turn left before the bridge. (☎314 66 800; www.tampere.fi. Open June-Aug. M-F 9am-8pm, Sa-Su 10am-5pm; Sept. M-F 9am-4pm, Sa-Su 10am-5pm; Oct.-May M-F 9am-4pm.) **Postal Code:** 33100.

ACCOMMODATIONS AND FOOD. Tampeeren NNKY (HI) ❷, Tuomiokirkonk. 12A, offers bunks in cramped quarters near the cathedral. From the train station, walk down Hämeenk. and make a right on Tuomiokirkonk. (☎254 40 20; www.tnnky.fi/.hostel.html. Breakfast M-F €5. Linen €4.50. Reception 8-10am and 4-11pm. Open June-Aug. Dorms €13.50-15.50; singles €31; doubles €44 €2.50 HI discount. Cash only.) For slightly less cramped rooms with no bunk beds, make the trek out to **Hostel Tampere (HI) ❷,** Pirkank. 10, on the other side of the city center. Walk 1.5km down Hämeenk. and bear right after the library. (☎222 94 60; www.hosteltampere.com. Breakfast €4.50. No kitchen or lockers. Reception 8am-11pm. Dorms €20; singles €38.50-41.50; doubles €54; triples €69.50; quads €88; quints €105. €2.50 HI discount. Cash only.) Bus #1 (€2) goes to **Camping Härmälä ❷,** Leirintäk. 8, where tightly-packed cabins compete for space on the shore of Lake Pyhäjärvi. (☎265 13 55; www.lomaliitto.fi. Open mid-May to late Aug. Electricity €4. Tent sites €10. Cabins €29-66. MC/V.)

Restaurants line **Hämeenkatu** and **Aleksanterinkatu.** The first building to have electricity in Northern Europe now houses **Plevna Panimoravintola ❷,** Itäinenk. 8, a traditional restaurant serving microbrews and heavy local specialties in a converted weaving mill. (☎260 12 00. Entrees €8-16. Beer €4-6. Open M-Th 11am-1am, F-Sa 11am-2am, Su noon-11pm. MC/V.) The city's oldest pizzeria, **Napoli ❶,** Aleksanterink. 31, serves 100 different varieties. (☎223 88 87. Pizza €7-12. Open M-Th 11am-11pm, F 11am-midnight, Sa noon-midnight, Su 1-11pm. DC/MC/V.) The gastronomically bold can also try *mustamakkara*, a black blood sausage, available starting from €1 at Tampere's vast **Kauppahalli,** Hämeenk. 19, the largest market hall in Scandinavia. (Open M-F 8am-6pm, Sa 8am-4pm.)

SIGHTS. Most of Tampere's museums are housed in renovated factories, including the **Vapriikki Museum Center,** Veturiaukio 4. Seven collections run the gamut from local history to ice hockey, while temporary exhibits add cultural heft to the center's offerings. (☎716 69 66. Open Tu and Th-Su 10am-6pm, W 11am-8pm. €5, students €1.) Scottish cotton magnate James Finlayson gave his name to the **Finlayson Complex,** which includes the **Media Museum Rupriikki** (open Tu-Su 11am-6pm; €4, students €1), the **Central Museum of Labor** (open Tu-Su 11am-6pm; €4), and the interactive **Spy Museum,** Satakunnank. 18A. (☎212 30 07; www.vakoilumuseo.fi. Open May-Aug. M-F noon-6pm, Sa-Su 10am-4pm; Sept.-Apr. M-F noon-6pm, Sa-Su 10am-4pm. €7, students €5. Cash only.) In December 1905, a conference in the Tampere Workers' Hall was the occasion of Lenin and Stalin's first meeting; a century later, the **Lenin Museum,** Hämeenpuisto 28, occupies the same building. (☎276 81 00. Open M-F 9am-6pm, Sa-Su 11am-4pm. €4, students €2.) The daring frescoes of the **Tuomiokirkko,** Tuomiokirkonk. 3 (open daily 9am-6pm) are matched in architectural beauty only by the vaulted wooden ceiling of the **Aleksanterinkirkko,** on Pyynikin kirkkopuisto (open daily May-Aug. 10am-5pm).

At the western edge of the city, the **Pyynikki Observation Tower** offers spectacular views of the surrounding nature conservation area. Enjoy a traditional *munkki*, a doughnut-like pastry dipped in sugar, at the downstairs cafe. (☎212 32 47. Open daily 9am-8pm. €1. Cash only.) The city's northern lakefront is home to **Särkänniemi,** a recreation center that includes the 168m **Näsinneula** observation tower. An amusement park, planetarium, and a dolphinarium round out the attractions. (☎248 82 12; www.sarkanniemi.fi. The Adventure Key grants admission to all attractions, including rides €29. Otherwise, admission to each attraction €5, plus €5 per ride. Hours vary; check website for details.)

ENTERTAINMENT AND NIGHTLIFE. In March, Tampere's internationally recognized **Short Film Festival** draws entries from around the globe (www.tamperefilmfestival.fi; Mar. 8-12, 2006). Mid-July's **Tammerfest** (www.tammerfest.net) fills the city with music, while August's **International Theater Festival** takes over city parks for performances of Finnish works (www.teatterikesa.fi; Aug. 7-13, 2006). **Hämeenkatu, Aleksanterinkatu,** and the surrounding streets are energetic at night, and many hotels host discos. **Cafe Europa,** Aleksanterink. 29, serves drinks in a bohemian lounge with low, rakishly mismatched chandeliers. (☎223 55 26. Beer €4; cider €4.30. Ask about ISIC discounts. Dancing F-Sa 9pm-3am. Live piano Su. F-Sa 18+. Other nights 20+. Open M-Th and Su noon-2am, F-Sa noon-3am. AmEx/DC/MC/V.) **Telakka,** Tullikamarinaukio 3, houses a bar, restaurant, club, and theater in an old warehouse near the train station. (☎225 07 00. Live music F-Sa. Open M-Th 11am-2am, F 11am-3am, Sa noon-3am, Su noon-midnight.) **Doris,** Aleksanterink. 20, is a popular rock club featuring live acts most nights. (☎272 02 12. Cover from €2. Open Tu-Th and Su 9pm-3am, F-Sa 10pm-3am.)

SAVONLINNA ☎015

Each summer, vacationers descend upon Savonlinna, an island region in the heart of Finland's lake country. Built on three of these islands is the town of Savonlinna (pop. 28,700), the region's epicenter. A vacation destination and fashionable spa town since the Russian aristocracy first came to the area in the 19th century, the town is packed with visitors each summer, especially in July, when the world-famous **Savonlinna Opera Festival** (www.operafestival.fi) takes place at the **Olavinlinna Castle.** The castle, perched on an island in the middle of the fast-flowing Kyrönsalmi Straits, was built in 1475 to reinforce the eastern border against the tsars. Learn about soldiers' beer rations and the castle's early forays into plumbing on the free English-language tour, or visit the **Orthodox Museum** and **Castle Museum**, each of which features artifacts discovered during the castle's restoration. (☎531 164. Open daily June to mid-Aug. 10am-5pm; mid-Aug. to May 10am-3pm. Tour departs on the hour. €5, students €3.50. MC/V.) Near the castle, on Riihisaari, the **Provincial Museum** details the history of the region, focusing on the shipping industry that once dominated the area's economy. While you're there, creep around the eerily preserved museum ships moored at the island. (☎571 47 12. Museum open Tu-Su 11am-5pm; July also open M. Ships open mid-May to mid-Sept. €5, students €3. Cash only.) The secluded northern island **Sulosaari** is a peaceful retreat with several walking trails. From the **Kauppatori,** go under the train tracks, cross the footbridge, go through the parking lot, and cross the next footbridge; look for the "no cars" sign to the right of the building.

Try to make time for a daytrip out to the surreal **Retretti Art Center,** where massive caves display beautiful glasswork and dream-like installations. (☎775 22 00; www.retretti.fi. Open daily July 10am-6pm; June and Aug. 10am-5pm. €15, students €9.) Buses (7 per day, €4.50) make the 30min. trip from Savonlinna. From Retretti, walk 20min. along the breathtaking **Punkaharju Ridge** to reach **Lusto** (Finnish Forest Museum), which documents the environmental history of the area. (☎345 10 30; www.lusto.fi. Open daily June-Aug. 10am-7pm; low season reduced hours. 1hr. tour departs July-Aug. daily 3pm. €7, students €6.)

Summer Hotel Vuorilinna ❸, on Kylpylaitoksentie near the casino, has well-equipped student apartments. From the Kauppatori, walk under the tracks and cross the bridge. (☎739 54 30. Reception 7am-11pm. Open June-Aug., but call ahead for specific dates. Dorms €25; singles €55-65; doubles €65-75. AmEx/MC/V.) Bus #3 (€2.50) runs to **Vuohimäki Camping ❶,** a secluded site on the shore of Lake Pihlajavesi. (☎537 353. Open June-Aug. Bike rental €9 per day. Showers €1-2. Electricity €4. Laundry €1-2. Reception and cafe open M-Th 8am-11pm, F-Sa 8am-midnight, Su 8am-10pm. Tent sites €10. Cabins with bath €74-82; June and Aug. 14-28 €56-69. MC/V.) Bars and cafes line **Olavinkatu** and the marketplace area, while terraces on **Linnankatu** look out over the castle.

Trains run from Savonlinna to Helsinki (5-6hr., 3-5 per day, €41-46). The **Savonlinna-Kauppatori** stop is in the center of town, while **Savonlinna Station** is closer to the bus station and the campsite. The **tourist office,** Puistok. 1, is across the bridge from the market. (☎517 510; www.savonlinnatravel.com. Open June-Aug. daily 8am-8pm; Sept.-May M-F 9am-5pm.) **Postal Code:** 57100.

KUOPIO ☎017

Eastern Finland's largest city, Kuopio (pop. 88,000) lies in the midst of the beautiful Saimaa lake district. The archbishop of the Finnish Orthodox Church resides here, and the **Orthodox Church Museum,** Karjalank. 1, shows a collection of textiles and icons. (☎287 22 44. Open May-Aug. Tu-Su 10am-4pm; Sept.-Apr. M-F noon-3pm, Sa-Su noon-5pm. €5, students €3.) The **Kuopio Museum,** Kauppak. 23, which houses both the Natural and Cultural History Museums, frightens children with its life-size reconstruction of a mammoth and entertains sensible older visitors with its exhibit on prehistoric Finland. (☎182 603; www.kulttuuri.kuopio.fi/museo. Open M-F 9am-4pm, W until 7pm, Su 10am-5pm. €4, students €2. Cash only.) The **VB Photographic Center,** Kuninkaank. 14-16, brings temporary exhibits of world-class photography to Kuopio. Check the website for latest exhibit information. (☎261 55 99; www.vb.kuopio.fi. June-Aug. open M-F 10am-7pm, Sa-Su 11am-4pm; reduced hours and rates in winter. €5, students €4. Cash only.) The 2km hike uphill to the **Puijo Tower** is rewarded with a far-ranging view of Lake Kallavesi and the coniferous forests beyond it. From the Kauppatori, walk toward the train station on Puijonk., cross the tracks and the highway, and continue up the hill. (Open daily May-Sept. 9am-9pm. €3.) In mid-June, the **Kuopio Dance Festival** (www.kuopiodancefestival.fi) draws crowds to its performances, and lures wannabe Baryshnikovs with dance lessons for every ability level and age group (adult classes from €60). Happy drunkards toast to a different country every year at the **Wine Festival** (www.kuopiowinefestival.fi), in early July.

All rooms at the **Rautatie Guest House ❸,** Asemak. 1, have their own TVs; more expensive rooms have private baths. Reception is in the Asemagrilli restaurant in the station. (☎580 05 69. Breakfast included. Reception M-F, Su 7am-8pm, Sa until 6pm. Singles €36-46; doubles €56-75; triples €93; quads €119. MC/V.) Embrace your inner schoolmarm at the **Virkkula Youth Hostel ❷,** Asemak. 3, which offers bare-bones accommodations in an old-fashioned schoolhouse. It's the red building to the right out of the station. (☎263 18 39. Linen and towels

€6. Internet €1 per 1st 30min., €0.50 per 30min. after. Reception 24hr. Open June-July. Dorms €15. Cash only.) While the service may be slow at **Muikkuravintola Sampo ❷**, Kauppak. 13, the restaurant draws praise for its imaginative renderings of *muikku*, a local whitefish. (☎261 46 77. Entrees €9-12. Open June-Aug. M-Sa 11am-midnight, Su noon-midnight; Sept.-May M-Sa 11am-10pm, Su noon-10pm. AmEx/DC/MC/V.) Get fresh produce at the **Kauppatori** market in the center of town or inside the lovely **Kauppahalli** market hall, where you can also try the local specialty, kalakukko fish pie, for €2. (www.kuopionkauppahalli.net. Kauppatori open M-Sa 7am-3pm. Kauppahalli open M-F 8am-5pm, Sa 9am-3pm.) **Trains** run to Helsinki (5½hr., 10 per day, €42-55) and Oulu (4½hr., 6 per day, €35-47). To get to **tourist office,** Haapaniemenk. 17, from the station, go right on Asemak. and turn left on Haapaniemenk. (☎18 25 84; www.kuopioinfo.fi. Open June-Aug. M-F 9:30am-5pm, July also Sa 9:30am-3pm; Sept.-May M-F 9:30am-4:30pm.) **Postal Code:** 70100.

OULU ☎08

Most travelers pass through Oulu (pop. 127,000), a relaxed university town at the crossroads of northern and southern Finland, on their way to other destinations. Unless traveling to late August's **Oulu Music Video Festival** (www.omvf.net) or the associated **Air Guitar World Championships,** there is little reason to stop for a long stay. For a brief diversion between trains, stroll through beautiful **Ainola Park,** a short walk from the train station. From the station, walk down Asemak. turn right on Kirkkok. and walk to its end. Down Nahkurinpl. the **Science Center Tietomaa,** Nahkatehtaank. 6, attracts crowds with its interactive exhibits, an IMAX theater, and a 35m observation tower, as well as the free **Oulu Expo**—hands-on presentations of technological innovations used in Oulu, including a surprisingly cool display on the city's recycling program. (☎55 84 13 40; www.tietomaa.fi. Open July daily 10am-8pm; Mar.-June and Aug. daily 10am-6pm; Sept.-Feb. M-F 10am-4pm, Sa-Su 10am-6pm. €10, students €8.50. MC/V. Oulu Expo ☎44 703 1384; www.ouluexpo.fi. Open M-F 10am-4pm, Sa-Su 10am-6pm. Free.) The island of **Pikisaari** draws picnickers with brightly colored wooden cottages and boutiques; take the footbridge at the end of Kaarlenväylä.

Cheap rooms are hard to come by in Oulu. The **Oppimestari Summer Hotel (HI) ❸,** Nahkatehtaank. 3, provides generously furnished rooms with kitchenettes. From the train station, cross Rautatienk. and walk along its pedestrian walkway until turning left onto Nahkatehtaank. Walk towards the brick tower; the hotel is across the street. (☎884 85 27; www.merikoski.fi/oppimestari. Breakfast included. Laundry €3. Open mid-June to July. Reception 24hr. Singles €37; doubles €55. €2.50 HI discount. AmEx/MC/V.) Bus #5 (€2.50) goes to the colorful cottages at **Nallikari Camping ❶,** Hietasaari, located right on the water. (☎55 86 13 50; www.nallikari-camping.fi. Electricity €3.50-5. Showers included. Tent sites €9, extra person €4. 4-person cabins €29-32. MC/V.) Cheap food, on the other hand, is easy to find; it's hard to walk 10m without passing a pizzeria or kebab joint. The **Kauppatori,** at the end of Kauppurienk. by the harbor, sells produce and is flanked by old wooden warehouses that have been pressed into reluctant service as yuppie cafes. (Open M-F 9am-6pm, Sa 8am-3pm.) Nightlife spills out of the pavilion on **Kirkkokatu** and the terraces lining **Otto Karhin Park** and **Kappurienkatu.**

Trains between northern and southern Finland pass through Oulu, heading south to Helsinki (6-7hr., 5-6 per day, €55-66) and north to Rovaniemi (2½hr., 4 per day, €22-26). To reach the **tourist office,** Torik. 10, take Hallitusk. and then the second left after the park. (☎55 84 13 30; www.oulutourism.fi. Open mid-June to Aug. M-F 9am-6pm, Sa-Su 11am-3pm; Sept. to mid-June M-F9am-4pm.) **Postal Code:** 90100.

ROVANIEMI ☎016

Just south of the Arctic Circle, Rovaniemi (pop. 35,000) is the capital of Finnish Lapland and a gateway to the northern wilderness. After retreating German troops burned the city to the ground in October 1944, architect Alvar Aalto stepped in with the Reindeer Antler Plan, a reconstruction scheme that would use rivers and existing highways to rebuild the settlement in the shape of a reindeer's head. Not all of Aalto's plan was executed, but you can look at a modern map of Rovaniemi with east facing up and see the resemblance. The **Arktikum,** housed in a beautiful glass corridor at Pohjoisranta 4, has a treasure trove of info on Arctic peoples and landscapes. (☎31 78 40; www.arktikum.fi. Open daily mid-June to mid-Aug. 9am-7pm; low season reduced hours. €11, students €8.50.) To dash your childhood dreams of Christmas once and for all, head to the **Santa Claus Village,** 8km north of Rovaniemi, where Father Christmas holds office hours. Children may find it difficult to understand why Santa lives in a gift shop. For a somewhat amusing diversion from the gift store trinkets, make a dramatic crossing over the Arctic Circle line, which runs right through the center of the village. Take bus #8 (30min.; €3, €5.20 round-trip) from the train station or the center of the city to Arctic Circle. (☎356 20 96; www.santaclausvillage.info. Open daily June-Aug. and Dec. to mid-Jan. 9am-7pm; Sept. 9am-5pm; Oct.-Nov. and mid-Jan. to May 10am-5pm.)

Hostel Rudolf (HI) ❸, Koskik. 41, has well-furnished rooms with private baths. (☎321 321. Reception 24hr. at the Quality Hotel Santa Claus, Korkalonk. 29. Breakfast €6 at the hotel. Apr. to mid-Nov. dorms €23; singles €34. Mid-Nov. to March dorms €35; singles €46. €2.50 HI discount. AmEx/DC/MC/V.) **Koskikatu** is lined with cafes and bars. **Trains** travel south to Helsinki (10hr., 4-5 per day, €71) via Oulu (2½hr., €23) and Kuopio (8hr., 3-4 per day, €52-56). **Buses** run to destinations throughout northern Finland, and to Nordkapp, Norway (11hr., 1 per day, €101). The **tourist office,** Rovak. 21, books northern wilderness safaris for €20-150. (☎34 62 70; www.rovaniemi.fi. Internet €2 per 15min. Open June-Aug. M-F 8am-6pm, Sa-Su 10am-6pm; Dec. M-F 8am-6pm, Sa-Su 10am-2pm; Sept.-Nov. and Jan.-May M-F 8am-5pm.) The **library,** Jorma Eton tie 6, one of Aalto's signature designs, offers free **Internet.** (Open in summer M-Th 11am-7pm, F 11am-5pm, Sa 11am-3pm; winter M-Th 11am-8pm, F 11am-5pm, Sa 11am-4pm.) **Postal Code:** 96200.

FRANCE

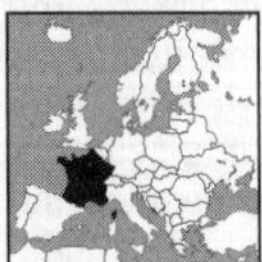

With its lavish chateaux, fields of lavender, medieval streets, and sidewalk cafes, France can rightfully conjure up any number of postcard-ready scenes. To the proud French, it is only natural that outsiders should flock to their history-steeped and art-rich homeland. Even though France may no longer control the course of world events, the vineyards of Bordeaux, the museums of Paris, and the beaches of the Riviera draw more tourists than any other nation worldwide. Centuries-old farms and churches share the landscape with modern architecture, street posters advertise jazz festivals as well as Baroque concerts, and the country's rich culinary tradition rounds out a culture that simply cannot be sent home on a four by six.

DISCOVER FRANCE: SUGGESTED ITINERARIES

THREE DAYS Don't even think of leaving **Paris,** the City of Light (p. 320). Explore the shops and cafes of the **Latin Quarter,** then cross the Seine to reach **Île de la Cité** to admire **Sainte Chapelle.** Visit the wacky **Centre National d'Art et de Culture Georges Pompidou** before seeing a hot spot of 1789, the **Bastille.** Swing through **Marais** for food and fun. The next day, stroll down the **Champs-Elysées,** starting at the **Arc de Triomphe,** meander through the **Jardin des Tuileries,** and over to the **Musée d'Orsay.** See part of the **Louvre** the next morning, then spend the afternoon at **Versailles.**

ONE WEEK After three days in **Paris,** go to **Tours** (1 day; p. 354) a great base for exploring the chateaux of the **Loire Valley** (1 day; p. 352). Head to **Rennes** for medieval sights and modern nightlife (1 day; p. 348), then to the dazzling island of **Mont-St-Michel** (1 day; p. 348).

BEST OF FRANCE, THREE WEEKS Begin with three days in **Paris,** with a daytrip to the royal residences at **Versailles.** Whirl through the **Loire Valley** (2 days) before traveling to the wine country of **Bordeaux** (1 day; p. 358). Check out the rose-colored architecture of **Toulouse** (1 day; p. 361) and the medieval walls of **Carcassonne** (1 day; p. 362) before sailing through **Avignon** (p. 365), **Aix-en-Provence** (p. 366), and **Nîmes** (p. 364) in sunny Provence (3 days). Let loose in **Marseille** (2 days; p. 367), and bask in the glitter of the Riviera in **Nice** (2 days; p. 376). Then show off your tan in the Alps as you travel to **Lyon** (2 days; p. 390) and **Chamonix** (1 day; p. 388). Eat your fill in **Dijon** (1 day; p. 396), and finish your trip with a little German flavor in cosmopolitan **Strasbourg** (1 day; p. 397), where trains will whisk you away to your next European adventure.

ESSENTIALS

FACTS AND FIGURES

Official Name: French Republic.

Capital: Paris.

Major Cities: Lyon, Marseille, Nice.

Population: 60,400,000.

Time Zone: GMT +1.

Language: French.

Religion: Roman Catholic (90%).

Most Expensive Wine: Château d'Yquem Sauternes (1787), a dessert wine from Bordeaux: €46,980-53,685.

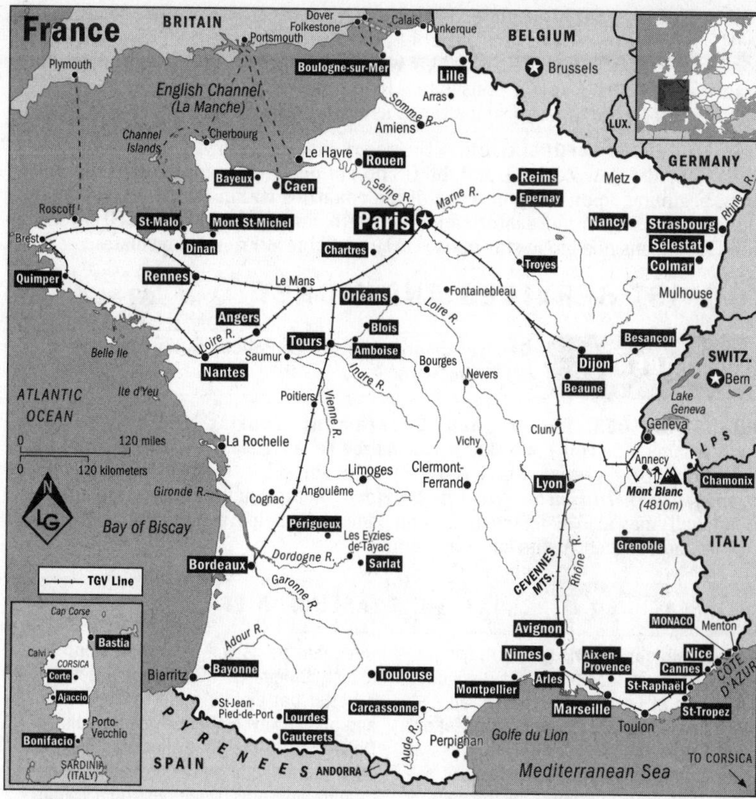

WHEN TO GO

In July, Paris starts to shrink; by August it is devoid of Parisians, animated only by tourists and the pickpockets who love them. The French Riviera fills with Anglophones from June to September. French natives flee to other parts of the country during these months, especially the Atlantic coast. Early summer and fall are the best times to visit Paris—the city has warmed up but not completely emptied out. The north and west have cool winters and mild summers, while the less-crowded center and east have a more continental climate. From December to February, the Alps provide some of the best skiing in the world, while the Pyrenees offer a calmer, if less climatically dependable, alternative.

DOCUMENTS AND FORMALITIES

EMBASSIES AND CONSULATES. Foreign embassies in France are in Paris (p. 322). French embassies at home include: **Australia,** Embassy of France, 6 Perth Ave., Yarralumla, Canberra, ACT 2600 (☎02 62 16 01 00; www.ambafrance-au.org); **Canada,** French Embassy, 42 Sussex Dr., Ottawa, ON K1M 2C9 (☎613-789-1795; www.ambafrance-ca.org); **Ireland,** French Embassy, Consulate Section, 36 Ailesbury Rd., Ballsbridge, Dublin 4 (☎01 227 5000; www.ambafrance.ie); **New Zealand,**

French Embassy and Consulate, 34-42 Manners St., P.O. Box 11-343, Wellington (☎04 384 25 55; www.ambafrance-nz.org); **UK,** French Embassy, 58 Knightsbridge, London SW1X 7JT (☎020 7073 1000; www.ambafrance-uk.org); **US,** Embassy of France and French General Consulate, 4101 Reservoir Rd. NW, Washington, D.C. 20007 (☎202-944-6195; www.ambafrance-us.org).

VISA AND ENTRY INFORMATION. EU citizens do not need a visa. Citizens of Australia, Canada, New Zealand, and the US do not need a visa for stays of up to 90 days, beginning upon entry into any of the countries within the EU's freedom of movement zone. For more information, see p. 16. For stays longer than 90 days, all non-EU citizens need long-stay visas (€99), available at French consulates.

TOURIST SERVICES AND MONEY

EMERGENCY	**General Emergency:** ☎112 **Police:** ☎17. **Ambulance:** ☎15. **Fire:** ☎18.

TOURIST OFFICES. The **French Government Tourist Office** (FGTO; www.franceguide.com), also known as **Maison de la France,** runs tourist offices in France and offers tourist services to travelers abroad. Tourist offices are called *syndicats d'initiative* or *offices de tourisme;* in the smallest towns, the *mairie* (town hall) may also distribute maps and pamphlets, help travelers find accommodations, and suggest sights and excursions.

FEATURED ITINERARY: WINE-TASTING IN FRANCE

Start your tour in **Paris** (p. 320), and preview some of France's most distinctive vintages at **La Belle Hortense,** an egghead wine bar in the Marais. Then set out for **Reims** (p. 401), where the folks at **Champagne Pommery** offer tours of cellars that hold magnums of the bubbly stuff. Spend a night in **Epernay** (p. 401), and saunter down the avenue de Champagne for wine-tastings at blue-blood **Moët & Chandon** and the more populist **Mercier.** Then head for **Strasbourg** (p. 397), the northernmost point on Alsace's legendary **Route du Vin** (p. 398).

Frequent trains will whisk you south to touristy **Colmar** (p. 399), while buses are a better bet as you head to **Riquewihr** and quaint **Kaysersberg.** Catch a train to Dijon—just to the south lies **Beaune** (p. 396), surrounded by the storied Côte de Beaune vineyards. Don't pass up a visit to **Patriarche Père et Fils,** where a tour of the Byzantine cellars includes a mouthful of 13 regional wines. Then dart back to Paris, or extend your itinerary to explore the Médoc region around **Bordeaux** (p. 358) and the ancient vineyards at **St-Emilion** (p. 359).

MONEY. The **euro (€)** has replaced the franc as the unit of currency in France. For more information, see p. 19. As a general rule, it's cheaper to exchange money in France than at home. Be prepared to spend at least €20-40 per day, and considerably more in Paris. **Tips** are generally included in meal prices at restaurants and cafes, as well as in drink prices at bars and clubs; look for the phrase *service compris* on the menu or ask. If service is not included, tip 15-20%. Even when service is included, it is polite to leave a *pourboire* of up to 5% at a cafe, bistro, restaurant, or bar. Workers such as concierges may expect at least a €1.50 tip for services beyond the call of duty; taxi drivers won't expect more than €1. A **Value Added Tax (VAT; TVA** in French) of up to 19.6% is included in the price of a wide range of goods and services (p. 23). Non-EU citizens bringing purchased goods home with them can usually be refunded this tax for purchases over €175 per store. Ask for VAT forms at the time of purchase and present them at the *détaxe* booth at the airport. You must carry these goods with you at all times (at the airport and on the airplane) and you must claim your refund within six months.

TRANSPORTATION

BY PLANE. Most transatlantic flights to Paris land at **Roissy-Charles de Gaulle** (CDG; ☎01 48 62 22 80). Many continental and charter flights use **Orly** (ORY; ☎01 49 75 15 15). **Aéroports de Paris** (www.aeroportsdeparis.fr) has information about both airports. For more info on flying to France, see p. 48. Once in France, you shouldn't need to take a plane unless you're headed to Corsica (p. 384).

BY TRAIN. The French national railway company, **SNCF** (☎08 92 35 35 35; www.sncf.fr), manages one of Europe's most efficient rail networks. **TGV** (high-speed, or *train à grande vitesse*) trains, among the fastest in the world, now link many major cities in France, as well as some other European destinations, including Brussels, Geneva, Lausanne, and Zurich. **Rapide** trains are slower; local **Express** trains are, strangely enough, the slowest option. French trains offer discounts of 25-50% on tickets for travelers under 26 with the **Carte 12-25** (€49; good for 1 year). Locate the ticket counters *(guichets)*, the platforms *(quais)*, and the tracks *(voies)*, and you will be ready to roll. Terminals can be divided into suburb *(banlieue)* and the bigger intercity trains *(grandes lignes)*. Yellow ticket machines *(billetteries)* sell tickets for credit cards with PINs.

VALIDATE = GREAT. Be sure to validate *(composter)* your ticket! Orange validation boxes lie around every station, and you must have it stamped with date and time by the machine before boarding the train.

While seat reservations are required only for select trains, you are not guaranteed a seat without one (usually US$5-18). Consider reserving in advance during peak holiday and tourist seasons. Some railpasses require a **supplement** (US$10-50) or special fare for high-speed or high-quality trains such as TGVs.

If you are planning to spend extensive time on trains, a railpass will be worth it, but in many cases, especially if you are under 26, point-to-point tickets may be cheaper. **Eurail** is valid in France. Standard **Eurail passes,** valid for a given number of consecutive days, are best for those spending extensive time on trains every few days. **Flexipasses,** valid for any 10 or 15 (not necessarily consecutive) days within a two-month period, are more cost-effective for those traveling longer distances less frequently. **Youth passes** and **Youth Flexipasses** provide the same second-class perks for those under 26. It is best to purchase a pass before leaving. For prices and more info, contact student travel agencies, **Rail Europe** (Canada ☎800-361-7245, UK 08 705 848 848, US 877-257-2887; www.raileurope.com), or **DER Travel Services** (☎800-782-2424; www.der.com).

BY BUS. Within France, long-distance buses are a secondary transportation choice, as service is relatively infrequent. However, in some regions buses are indispensable for reaching out-of-the-way towns. Bus services operated by SNCF accept railpasses. *Gare routière* is French for "bus station."

BY FERRY. Ferries across the English Channel *(La Manche)* link France to England and Ireland. The shortest and most popular route is between **Dover** and **Calais** (1-1½hr.), and is run by P&O Stena Line, SeaFrance, and Hoverspeed. Hoverspeed also travels from Newhaven, England to **Dieppe** (2¼-4¼hr.). Brittany Ferries travels from Portsmouth to **Caen** (6hr.) and **St-Malo** (9hr.). For more info on English Channel ferries, see p. 63. For info on ferries to **Corsica,** see p. 384.

BY CAR. Drivers in France should have either an **International Driving Permit (IDP)** or a valid EU-issued driving license. Remember that seatbelts for both drivers and passengers are mandatory by law. Unless you're traveling in a group of three or more, you won't save money going by car instead of by train, thanks to highway tolls, high gasoline costs, and rental charges. To rent a car from most establishments in France, you need to be at least 21 years old. Some agencies require renters to be 25, and most charge those aged 21-24 an additional insurance fee (around €25 per day). Driving in a foreign country can also be stressful, and if you don't know how to drive stick, you'll need to pay a hefty premium for a car with automatic transmission. French roads are usually in great condition, but in Corsica and the Alps rugged landscapes can make for difficult driving.

BY BIKE AND BY THUMB. Of all Europeans, the French may be alone in loving cycling more than soccer. Drivers usually accommodate bikers on wide country roads, and many cities banish cars from select streets each Sunday to make way for cyclists. Renting a bike (€8-19 per day) beats bringing your own if you're only touring one or two regions. Hitchhiking is illegal on French highways, and many people consider France to be the hardest country in Europe for hitchhikers. *Let's Go* does not recommend hitchhiking.

KEEPING IN TOUCH

PHONE CODES	**Country code:** 33. **International dialing prefix:** 00. For more information on how to place international calls, see inside back cover. When calling within a city, dial 0 + city code + local number.

EMAIL AND THE INTERNET. Most major **post offices** offer Internet access at special *cyberposte* terminals, where rechargeable cards provide 1hr. of access for €7 (€4 each additional hr.). A large town in France will usually have at least one **cybercafe**; check www.cybercafes.com for locations.

TELEPHONE. Publicly owned **France Télécom** pay phones charge less than their privately owned counterparts. They accept stylish *Télécartes* (phonecards), available in 50-unit (€7.50) and 120-unit (€15) denominations at *tabacs*, post offices, and train stations. Most pay phones now also accept credit cards such as MasterCard (or EuroCard) and Visa. An expensive alternative is to call collect *(faire un appel en PCV)*; an English-speaking operator can be reached by dialing the appropriate service provider listed below. *Décrochez* means pick up; you'll then be asked to *patientez* (wait) to insert your card; at *numérotez* or *composez*, you can dial. The number for general information is ☎12; for an international operator, call ☎00 33 11. For information on purchasing **mobile phones,** see p. 33. International direct dial numbers include: **AT&T** ☎0 800 99 00 11; **Canada Direct** ☎0 800 99 00 16 or 99 02 16; **MCI** ☎0 800 99 00 19; **Sprint** ☎0 800 99 00 87; **Telecom New Zealand Direct** ☎0 800 99 00 64; **Telstra Australia** ☎0 800 99 00 61.

MAIL. Airmail between France and North America takes five to 10 days; writing "*prioritaire*" on the envelope should ensure delivery in four to five days at no extra charge. To send a 20g airmail letter or postcard from France to another EU destination costs €0.50, to a non-EU European country €0.75, and to Australia, Canada, New Zealand, or the US €0.90. Mail can be held for pickup through *Poste Restante* at almost any city or town with a post office. Address letters to be held according to the following example: [SURNAME First name], *Poste Restante*, Paris France. It's best to use the largest post office, since mail may be sent there regardless. Bring your passport (or other photo ID) for pickup; there may be a small fee.

LANGUAGE AND POLITESSE. Even if your French is near-perfect, waiters and salespeople who detect the slightest accent will often immediately respond in English. If your language skills are good, continue to speak in French; more often than not, the waiter or salesperson will revert to French. The French put a premium on polite pleasantries. Always say *"bonjour Madame/Monsieur"* when you come into a business, restaurant, or hotel, and *"au revoir"* when you leave. If you knock into someone on the street, always say *"pardon."* When meeting someone for the first time, a handshake is appropriate. However, friends and acquaintances greet each other with a kiss on each cheek (the exception is two men). For a traveler's survival kit of basic French, see p. 1059.

ACCOMMODATIONS AND CAMPING

FRANCE	❶	❷	❸	❹	❺
ACCOMMODATIONS	under €15	€15-26	€26-37	€37-55	over €55

The **French Hostelling International (HI)** affiliate, **Fédération Unie des Auberges de Jeunesse** (**FUAJ;** ☎01 44 89 87 27; www.fuaj.org), operates 160 hostels within France. A bed in a hostel averages €11-15. Some hostels accept reservations through the International Booking Network. Two or more people traveling together will often save money by staying in cheap hotels rather than hostels. The French government employs a four-star hotel rating system. *Gîtes d'étapes* are rural accommodations for cyclists, hikers, and other ramblers in less-populated areas; they provide beds, a kitchen facility, and a resident caretaker. After 3000 years of settled history, true wilderness in France is hard to find. It's illegal to camp in most public spaces, including national parks. Instead, look forward to organized *campings* (campsites), full of vacationing families and all manner of programmed fun. Most campsites have toilets, showers, and electrical outlets, though you may have to pay €1.50-6 extra for such luxuries; you'll often need to pay a fee for your car, too (€3-8). In total, expect to pay €8-15 per site.

FOOD AND DRINK

FRANCE	❶	❷	❸	❹	❺
FOOD	under €7	€7-12	€12-18	€18-33	over €33

French chefs cook for one of the most finicky clientele in the world. The largest meal of the day is lunch *(le déjeuner)*. A complete French meal includes an *apéritif* (drink), an appetizer *(entrée)*, a main course *(plat)*, salad, cheese, dessert, fruit, coffee, and an after-dinner drink *(digestif)*. The French drink wine with virtually every meal; *boisson comprise* entitles you to a free drink (usually wine) with your food. Most restaurants offer a *menu à prix fixe* (fixed-price meal) that costs less than ordering *à la carte*. The *formule* is a cheaper, two-course version for the hurried luncher. Odd-hour cravings between lunch and dinner can be satisfied at *brasseries*, the middle ground between casual cafes and structured restaurants. *Service compris* means the tip is included in the check *(l'addition)*. It's easy to get a satisfying dinner for under €10 with staples such as cheese, pâté, wine, bread, and chocolate. For a picnic, get fresh produce at an outdoor market *(marché)* and then hop between specialty shops. Start with a bakery *(boulangerie)* for bread, proceed to a butcher *(charcuterie)* for meats, and then pastry shops *(pâtisseries)* and candy shops *(confiseries)* to satisfy a sweet tooth. When choosing a cafe, remember that those on a major boulevard are more expensive than smaller places a few steps down a side street. Prices are also cheaper at the counter *(comptoir)* than in the seating area *(salle)*. For supermarket shopping, look for the chains Carrefour, Casino, Monoprix, and Prisunic.

HOLIDAYS AND FESTIVALS

Holidays: New Year's Day (Jan. 1); Easter Monday (Apr. 17); Labor Day (May 1); Victory Day (May 8); Ascension Day (May 25); Whit Monday (June 4); Bastille Day (July 14); Feast of the Assumption (Aug. 15); All Saints' Day (Nov. 1); Armistice Day (Nov. 11).

Festivals: Many cities celebrate a pre-Lenten Carnaval—the most over-the-top festivities are in Nice (Feb. 11-28). The Cannes Film Festival (May 17-26; www.festival-cannes.com) caters to directors and stars. Although you may not be biking the Tour de France (starting July 2; www.letour.fr), you'll enjoy all the hype. The Festival d'Avignon (July-Aug.; www.festival-avignon.com) is famous for its theater. The biggest national holiday, Bastille Day (July 14), is marked nationwide with parades and fireworks.

BEYOND TOURISM

As a volunteer in France, you can participate in projects anywhere from Paris to Nice, either on a short- or long-term basis. Though France is a wealthy country, opportunities with aid organizations are readily available.

Care France, CAP 19, 13 r. de Georges Auric, 75019 Paris, France (☎01 53 19 89 89; www.carefrance.org). An international organization providing volunteer opportunities in 6000 locations throughout France, from combatting AIDS to promoting education.

Jeunesse et Reconstruction, 8 et 10 r. de Trevise, 75009 Paris, France (☎01 47 70 15 88; www.volontariat.org). Database of volunteer opportunities for young people in preservation and historical reconstruction. Open June-Sept. M-Sa 9:30am-1pm and 2-6pm.

Trade Art Abroad, Boite No. 45, Maison des Associations du 20eme, 1-3 r. Frederick Lematire, 75020 Paris, France. Brings local art to the communities of Paris and beyond.

PARIS ☎01

FRANCE

From the grand Baroque architecture of the Louvre to the latticework of colorful tubes at Centre Pompidou, Paris (pop. 2,150,000) at once embraces tradition and welcomes innovation. The city blends its spirit of revolution with a reverence for history, devoting as much energy to preserving certain conventions as it does to shattering others. Paris is everything you expect—and a constant surprise.

INTERCITY TRANSPORTATION

Flights: Aéroport Roissy-Charles de Gaulle (CDG; ☎48 62 22 80; www.adp.fr), 23km northeast of Paris, serves most transatlantic flights. For flight info, call the 24hr. English-speaking information center. **Aéroport d'Orly** (ORY; English-language recording ☎49 75 15 15), 18km south of Paris, is used by charters and many continental flights. The cheapest and fastest ways to get into the city are by **RER** or **bus.**

Trains: Paris has 6 major train stations: **Gare d'Austerlitz** (to the Loire Valley, southwestern France, Spain, and Portugal); **Gare de l'Est** (to Austria, eastern France, southern Germany, Hungary, Luxembourg, Prague, and Switzerland); **Gare de Lyon** (to southern France, Greece, Italy, and Switzerland); **Gare du Nord** (to Belgium, Britain, the Netherlands, northern France, northern Germany, and Scandinavia); **Gare Montparnasse** (to Brittany and southwestern France by TGV); **Gare St-Lazare** (to Normandy).

Buses: Gare Routière Internationale du Paris-Gallieni, 28 av. du Général de Gaulle, just outside Paris in Bagnolet. Ⓜ Gallieni. **Eurolines** (☎49 72 57 80; www.eurolines.fr) sells tickets to most destinations in France and neighboring countries.

ORIENTATION

The **Île de la Cité** and **Île St-Louis** sit at the center of the city, while the **Seine,** flowing east to west, splits Paris into two sections: the **Left Bank (Rive Gauche)** to the south and the **Right Bank (Rive Droite)** to the north. The Left Bank, with its older architecture and narrow streets, has traditionally been considered bohemian and intellectual, while the Right Bank, with grand avenues and designer shops, is more ritzy. Paris is divided into 20 **arrondissements** (districts; e.g., 1*er*, 6*ème*) that spiral clockwise around the Louvre. Well-known sights are packed into the central *arrondissements*, though periphery ones should not be overlooked.

On the Left Bank, the **Latin Quarter,** encompassing the 5*ème* and parts of the 6*ème*, has been home to students for centuries. The northwestern corner of the 6*ème* is known as **St-Germain-des-Prés.** Farther west, the gold-domed **Invalides** and the **Ecole Militaire** recall the military past of the 7*ème*, now an upscale neighborhood. The 15*ème* is predominantly residential. **Montparnasse,** mostly contained within the boundaries of the 14*ème*, is a relatively quiet neighborhood with a bohemian history. Much of the eastern Left Bank, in the 13*ème*, is working-class or industrial, but the area around **place d'Italie** is an up-and-coming hot spot.

On the Right Bank, the **Louvre** is located in the sight- and tourist-packed 1*er*. The 2*ème* is more business-oriented and contains the old-fashioned **Montorgeuil** neighborhood. The crooked streets of the **Marais,** in the 3*ème* and 4*ème*, escaped Baron Haussmann's redesign of Paris and now support many diverse communities. From **place de la Concorde,** at the western end of the 1*er*, **avenue des Champs-Elysées** bisects the 8*ème* as it sweeps up toward the **Arc de Triomphe** at **Place Charles de Gaulle-Etoile.** South of the Etoile, old and new money fill the exclusive 16*ème*, bordered to the west by the **Bois de Boulogne** park and to the east by the Seine and the **Trocadéro,** facing the Eiffel Tower across the river. Back toward central Paris, the 9*ème* is defined by broad boulevards to the south and a red-light district, **Pigalle,** to the north. The 10*ème*, not generally frequented by tourists, is known primarily as home to the **Gare du Nord** and **Gare de l'Est.** The **Bastille** area in the 11*ème* and 12*ème* claims the newest hip nightlife scene in Paris. East of Bastille, the party atmosphere gives way to the quieter, more residential 20*ème* and 19*ème*, while the 18*ème* is home to the quaint and heavily touristed **Montmartre.** To the east, the 17*ème* is a mix of wealthy and working-class neighborhoods.

LOCAL TRANSPORTATION

Public Transportation: The efficient **Metro** (Ⓜ) runs 5:30am-12:15am. Lines are numbered and are generally referred to by their number and final destinations; connections are called *correspondances.* **Single-fare tickets** within the city €1.40; **carnet** of 10 €10.50. Buy extras for when ticket booths are closed (after 10pm) and hold onto your ticket until you exit. The **RER (Réseau Express Régional),** the commuter train to the suburbs, serves as an express subway within central Paris; changing to and getting off the RER requires sticking your validated ticket into a turnstile. Watch the signboards next to the RER tracks and check that your stop is lit up before riding. **Buses** use the same €1.40 tickets (bought on the bus; validate in the machine by the driver), but transfers require a new ticket. Buses run 6:30am-8:30pm, *Autobus de Nuit* until 1am, and *Noctambus* (3-4 tickets) 1 per hr. 1:30-5:30am at stops marked with the bug-eyed moon between the Châtelet stop and the *portes* (city exits). The **Mobilis** pass covers the metro, RER, and buses (€5.40 for a 1-day pass in Zones 1 and 2). A weekly pass *(carte orange hebdomadaire)* costs €15.70 and expires on Su; photo ID required. Refer to the front of the book for **color maps** of Paris's transit network.

Taxis: Alpha Taxis (☎45 85 85 85). **Taxis Bleus** (☎49 36 10 10). Taxis are expensive and take 3 passengers (extra passenger; €2-3 surcharge). Meter starts running when you phone. Taxi stands are indicated by a blue light.

Bike Rental: La Maison Roue Libre, 37 bd. Bourdon, *4ème* (☎44 54 19 29; www.ratp.fr). €3 per hr., €21 per half day, €29 per day.

PRACTICAL INFORMATION

Tourist Office: Main Welcome Center, *1er* (☎08 92 68 30 00). Ⓜ Pyramides, Tuileries, and Opera. Open daily June-Aug. 9am-7pm; Sept.-May reduced hours. **Montmartre Tourist Office,** *18ème* (☎42 62 21 21). Ⓜ Anvers. Open daily 10am-7pm. **Bureau Tour Eiffel,** Champs de Mars, *7ème* (☎08 92 68 31 12). Ⓜ Bir-Hakeim. Open daily Mar.-Sept. 11am-6:40pm.

Embassies: Australia, 4 r. Jean-Rey, *15ème* (☎40 59 33 00; www.austgov.fr). Ⓜ Bir-Hakeim. Open M-F 9am-5pm. **Canada,** 35 av. Montaigne, *8ème* (☎44 43 29 02; www.amb-canada.fr). Ⓜ Franklin-Roosevelt. Open daily 9am-noon and 2-5pm. **Ireland,** 12 av. Foch, *16ème* (☎44 17 67 00; www.embassyofirelandparis.com). Ⓜ Trocadéro. Open M-F 9:30am-noon. **New Zealand,** 7ter r. Léonard de Vinci, *16ème* (☎45 01 43 43; www.nzembassy.com/france). Ⓜ Victor-Hugo. Open July-Aug. M-Th 9am-1pm and 2-4:30pm, F 9am-2pm; Sept.-June M-Th 9am-1pm and 2-5:30pm, F 9am-1pm and 2-4pm. **UK,** 18bis r. d'Anjou, *8ème* (☎44 51 31 00; www.amb-grandebretagne.fr). Ⓜ St-Augustin. Open M-F 9:30am-12:30pm and 2:30-5pm. **US,** 2 r. St-Forentin, *1er* (☎43 12 22 22; www.amb-usa.fr). Ⓜ Concorde. Open M-F 9am-1pm. To skip the long line, tell the guard you want American citizen services.

Currency Exchange: Most **ATMs** accept Visa ("CB/VISA") and MasterCard ("EC"). Crédit Lyonnais ATMs take AmEx; Crédit Mutuel and Crédit Agricole ATMs are on the **Cirrus** network; and most Visa ATMs accept **PLUS**-network cards. Hotels, train stations, and airports offer poor rates but have extended hours; Gare de Lyon, Gare du Nord, and both airports have booths open 6:30am-10:30pm.

American Express: 11 r. Scribe, *9ème* (☎47 77 79 28). Ⓜ Opéra or Auber. Open M-Sa 9am-6:30pm; exchange counters also open Su 10am-5pm.

GLBT Resources: Centre Gai et Lesbien, 3 r. Keller, *11ème* (☎43 57 21 47). Ⓜ Ledru Rollin or Bastille. Information on gay services in Paris. Open M-F 4-8pm.

Laundromats: Laundromats are everywhere, especially in the *5ème* and *6ème*. Ask the reception at the hostel or hotel in which you are staying for the closest laundry facilities. **LV84,** 24 pl. Marché St-Honoré, *1er* (☎42 51 04 49).

Emergency: Police: ☎17. **Ambulance:** ☎15. **Fire:** ☎18.

Pharmacies: Every *arrondissement* has a **pharmacie de garde** which opens in emergencies. The locations change, but their names are posted on every pharmacy's door. **Pharmacie Les Champs,** in the Galerie des Champs 84, av. des Champs-Elysées, *8ème* (☎45 62 02 41). Ⓜ George V. Open 24hr. **British and American Pharmacy,** 1 r. Auber, *9ème* (☎42 65 88 29). Ⓜ Auber or Opéra. Open daily 8am-8:30pm.

Hospitals: American Hospital of Paris, 63 bd. Hugo, Neuilly (☎46 41 25 25). Ⓜ Port Maillot, then bus #82 to the end of the line. **Hôpital Franco-Britannique de Paris,** 3 r. Barbès, in the suburb of Levallois-Perret (☎46 39 22 22). Ⓜ Anatole France. Some English spoken. **Centre Médicale Europe,** 44 r. d'Amsterdam, *9ème* (☎42 81 93 33). Ⓜ St-Lazare. Open M-F 8am-7pm, Sa 8am-6pm.

Internet Access: XS arena, 110 bd. St-Germain, *6ème* (☎40 13 02 60). 5 other branches: 17 r. Sufflot, *5ème;* 53 r. de la Harpe, *5ème;* 31 bd. Sébastopol, *1er;* 43 bd. Sébastopol, *1er;* 5 r. d'Odessa, at Montparnasse station. €2 per 30min., €3 per hr., €6 per 2hr., €8 per 3hr., €10 per 4hr., €11 per 5hr., €20 per 12hr. Open 24hr.

Post Office: Poste du Louvre, 52 r. du Louvre, *1er* (☎40 28 20 40). Ⓜ Louvre. Open 24hr. Address mail to be held: SURNAME First name, *Poste Restante,* 52 r. du Louvre, 75001 Paris, FRANCE. **Postal Codes:** 750xx, where "xx" is the *arrondissement* (e.g., 75003 for any address in the *3ème*).

ACCOMMODATIONS

Due to the massive influx of travelers during summer, already high prices climb even further. In a hotel, expect to pay at least €30 for a single and €40 for a double. Hostels are a better option for single travelers; staying in a hotel is a more economical option for groups. Paris's **hostels** skip many standard restrictions (e.g., curfews) and tend to have flexible maximum stays. In cheaper hotels, few rooms have private baths; hall showers cost about €2.50 per use. Rooms fill quickly after check-out; arrive early or reserve ahead. Most hostels and *foyers* include the **taxe de séjour** (€0.10-2 per person, per day) in listed prices, but some do not.

ÎLE DE LA CITÉ, 1ER, AND 2ÈME ARRONDISSEMENTS

Central to the Louvre, the Tuileries, the Seine, and the ritzy pl. Vendôme, this area still has a few budget hotels.

Hôtel Henri IV, 25 pl. Dauphine, Île de la Cité. (☎43 54 44 53). Ⓜ Pont Neuf. One of the most centrally located and least expensive hotels in Paris. The corridors are rundown, but rooms are clean. Showers €2.50. Reserve 2 months ahead. Singles €26; doubles €29, with shower and toilet €56; triples €44; quads €55. MC/V. ❷

Hôtel Vivienne, 40 r. Vivienne (☎42 33 13 26; paris@hotel-vivienne.com). Ⓜ Grands Boulevards. With hardwood floors and spacious rooms with armoires, this newly renovated hotel adds a touch of refinement to budget digs. Breakfast €6. Singles with shower €50, with shower and toilet €80; doubles €67/82. MC/V. ❹

Centre International de Paris (BVJ): Paris Louvre, 20 r. Jean-Jacques Rousseau, 1*er* (☎53 00 90 90). Ⓜ Louvre or Palais-Royal. Bright, dorm-style rooms. Internet €1 per 10min. Book weekends 1 week in advance by phone only. Be on time to your expected check-in. Doubles €60; other rooms €26 per person. Cash only. ❸

Hôtel Tiquetonne, 6 r. Tiquetonne, 2*ème* (☎42 36 94 58). Ⓜ Etienne-Marcel. Small, simple rooms only a stone's throw from the sex shops on r. St-Denis and the market on r. Montorgueil. Breakfast €5. Shower €5. Book 2 weeks in advance. Singles €30, with toilet €38; doubles with bath €46. AmEx/MC/V. ❸

3ÈME AND 4ÈME ARRONDISSEMENTS

Some of the Marais's 17th-century mansions now house budget hotels close to the **Centre Pompidou** and the **Île St-Louis;** the area is also convenient for sampling nightlife, as Paris's night buses converge in the 4*ème* at Ⓜ Châtelet.

Hôtel du Séjour, 36 r. du Grenier St-Lazare, 3*ème* (☎ 48 87 40 36). Ⓜ Rambuteau. Walk toward the Centre Pompidou, turn right on r. St-Martin, and right on r. du Grenier St-Lazare, it's on the left. Renovated hotel in the heart of the Marais. Reception 7am-10:30pm. Book ahead. Singles €35; doubles €47, with bath €57. Cash only. ❸

Hôtel des Jeunes (MIJE), 4*ème* (☎42 74 23 45; www.mije.com). Le Fourcy, Le Fauconnier, and Maubuisson are 3 small hostels on cobblestoned streets in Marais medieval mansions. **Ages 18-30 only.** Breakfast and linen included. Internet €1 per 10min. 7-day max. stay. Reception 7am-1am. Lockout noon-3pm. Strict 1am curfew and quiet time after 10pm. Check-in before noon. Reserve 1 month ahead buy MIJE membership (€2.50). 5-bed dorms €27-28; singles €42; doubles €64; triples €84; quads €108. ❸

Le Fourcy, 6 r. de Fourcy. From Ⓜ St-Paul, walk opposite the traffic on r. François-Miron and turn left on r. de Fourcy. Large courtyard ideal for meeting travelers or open-air picnicking.

Le Fauconnier, 11 r. du Fauconnier. From Ⓜ St-Paul, take r. du Prevôt, turn left on r. Charlemagne, and right on r. du Fauconnier. Ivy-covered building steps away from the Seine and Île St-Louis.

Maubuisson, 12 r. des Barres. From Ⓜ Pont Marie, walk opposite traffic on r. de l'Hôtel-de-Ville and turn right on r. des Barres. A former convent on a silent street by the St-Gervais monastery.

5ÈME AND 6ÈME ARRONDISSEMENTS

The lively Latin Quarter and St-Germain-des-Prés offer proximity to **Notre-Dame,** the **Panthéon,** the **Jardin du Luxembourg,** and a bustling student cafe culture.

Paris Food and Accommodations

FOOD

Name	No.	Grid	Name	No.	Grid
L'Affriolé,	1	A4	L'Epi Dupin,	14	B6
L'As du Falafel,	2	E4	"Jules",	15	D3
Au Rocher de Cancale,	3	D3	Lao Siam,	16	D1
Aux Artistes,	4	A6	Musée du Vin Restaurant,	17	A3
La Boheme du Tertre,	5	C1	Nos Ancêtres Les Gaulois,	18	E5
Café des Lettres,	6	B4	Papou Lounge,	19	D3
Café de la Mosquée,	7	E6	Le Petit Vatel,	20	C5
Camille,	8	E4	Les Sans Culottes,	21	F5
Cantine d'Antoine et Lili,	9	E2	Savannah Café,	22	D6
Le Caveau du Palais,	10	C5	Le Soleil d'Or,	23	D5
Chez Janou,	11	E4	Le Temps des Cerises,	24	C6
Chez Paul,	12	F5	Tricotin,	25	D6
Crêperie Saint Germain,	13	D5	Un Zebre A Montmartre,	26	C1

RER Réseau Express Régional train

A B C

ROME
TO 35 AND 5 (800m), 26 AND 37 (2km)
PIGALLE
ANVERS
LIÈGE
r. Blanche
r. Fontaine
r. Notre-Dame de Lorette
r. des Martyrs
r. Pigalle
r. de Clichy
r. d'Amsterdam
ST-GEORGES
r. Rodier
TRINITÉ
Gare St-Lazare
ST-LAZARE
r. St-Lazare
PL. D'ORVES
r. de Châteaudun
NOTRE DAME DE LORETTE
9ème
LE PELETIER
r. de la Victoire
HAVRE-CAUMARTIN
Opéra Garnier
CHAUSSÉE D'ANTIN LA FAYETTE
Passage Jouffroy
MIROMESNIL
ST-PHILIPPE DE ROULE
AUBER
bd. des Italiens
bd. Montmartre
RICHELIEU-DROUOT
bd. de la Madeleine
OPÉRA
4 SEPTEMBRE
MADELEINE
r. Daunou
av. de l'Opéra
r. du 4 Sept.
BOURSE
FRANKLIN D. ROOSEVELT
CHAMPS ÉLYSÉES/ CLEMENCEAU
av. des Champs-Elysées
r. Boissy d'Anglas
PL. DE LA CONCORDE
r. Chabanais
r. Vivienne
r. de la Sourdière
r. des Petits Champs
av. F. D. Roosevelt
Grand Palais
CONCORDE
r. Royale
PYRAMIDES
8ème
r. de Rivoli
TUILERIES
1er
r. de Richelieu
cours de la Reine
Jardin des Tuilleries
PALAIS ROYAL/ MUSÉE DU LOUVRE
Palais Royal
TO 17 (2.5km)
quai d'Orsay
INVALIDES
Assemblée Nationale
quai des Tuilleries
r. du Louvre
r. St-Honoré
LOUVRE RIVOLI
r. de l'Université
Seine
Louvre
TO 1 (150m)
r. Ste-Dominique
ASSEMBLÉE NATIONALE
MUSÉE D'ORSAY
quai Anatole France
r. de l'Amiral Coligny
quai du Louvre
PONT NEUF
TO 41 (300m)
r. de Grenelle
PL. DES INVALIDES
r. de Bourgogne
SOLFÉRINO
Musée D'Orsay
Pont Neuf
VARENNE
7ème
bd. St-Germain
r. de l'Université
LATOUR MAUBOURG
Hôtel des Invalides
quai St-Michel
RUE DU BAC
r. de Seine
r. Mazarine
r. Dauphine
r. Jacob
r. des Grands Augustins
PL. VAUBAN
r. de Varenne
ST-GERMAIN-DES-PRÉS
bd. St-Germain
ST-MICHEL
av. de Lowenthal
bd. des Invalides
0 300 yards
0 300 meters
MABILLON
ODÉON
CLUNY LA SORBONNE
av. de Ségur
r. de Babylone
ST-SULPICE
r. Bonaparte
r. des Canettes
r. de Tournon
r. de l'Odéon
r. de l'Ec. de Médecine
ST-FRANÇOIS XAVIER
SÈVRES BABYLONE
Sulpice
r. de Sèvres
r. de Rennes
Université de Paris (Sorbonne)
VANEAU
RENNES
av. de Saxe
DUROC
ST-PLACIDE
6ème
Jardin du Luxembourg
r. Soufflot
SÈVRES LECOURBE
r. de Vaugirard
bd. Raspail
r. d'Assas
LUXEMBOURG
MONTPARNASSE BIENVENUE
N.-D. DES CHAMPS
bd. St-Michel
r. Royer-Collard
TO 4 (1km)
FALGUIÈRE
TO 39 (1km)
TO 24 (1km), 32 (1.6km)

FRANCE

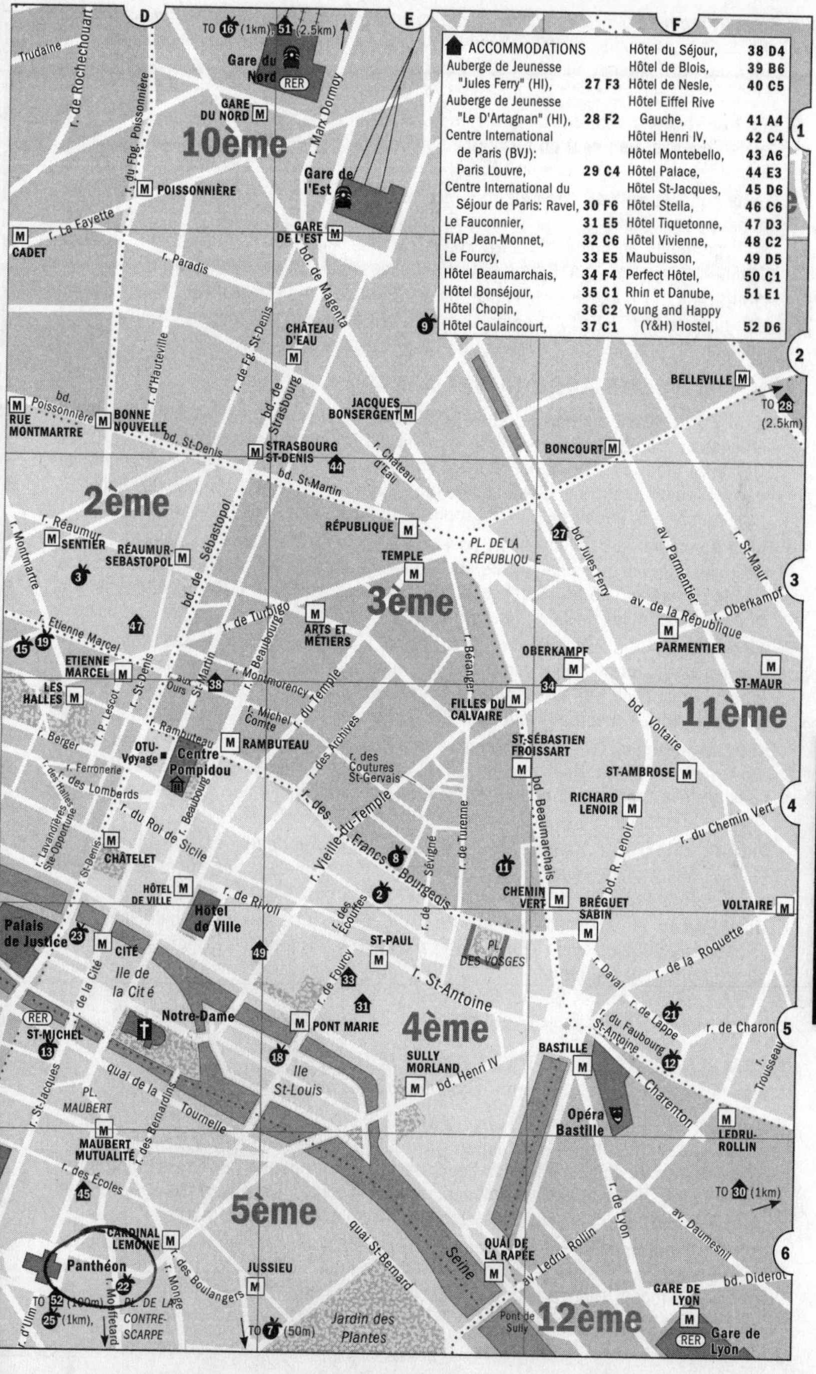

ACCOMMODATIONS
Auberge de Jeunesse "Jules Ferry" (HI), 27 F3
Auberge de Jeunesse "Le D'Artagnan" (HI), 28 F2
Centre International de Paris (BVJ): Paris Louvre, 29 C4
Centre International du Séjour de Paris: Ravel, 30 F6
Le Fauconnier, 31 E5
FIAP Jean-Monnet, 32 C6
Le Fourcy, 33 E5
Hôtel Beaumarchais, 34 F4
Hôtel Bonséjour, 35 C1
Hôtel Chopin, 36 C2
Hôtel Caulaincourt, 37 C1
Hôtel du Séjour, 38 D4
Hôtel de Blois, 39 B6
Hôtel de Nesle, 40 C5
Hôtel Eiffel Rive Gauche, 41 A4
Hôtel Henri IV, 42 C4
Hôtel Montebello, 43 A6
Hôtel Palace, 44 E3
Hôtel St-Jacques, 45 D6
Hôtel Stella, 46 C6
Hôtel Tiquetonne, 47 D3
Hôtel Vivienne, 48 C2
Maubuisson, 49 D5
Perfect Hôtel, 50 C1
Rhin et Danube, 51 E1
Young and Happy (Y&H) Hostel, 52 D6
10ème
2ème
3ème
4ème
5ème
11ème
12ème
Gare du Nord
Gare de l'Est
Centre Pompidou
Hôtel de Ville
Notre-Dame
Ile de la Cité
Ile St-Louis
Palais de Justice
Panthéon
Opéra Bastille
Gare de Lyon
Jardin des Plantes
PL. DE LA RÉPUBLIQUE
PL. DES VOSGES
Seine
TO 16 (1km), 51 (2.5km)
TO 28 (2.5km)
TO 30 (1km)
TO 52 (100m) 25 (1km)
TO 7 (50m)

Hôtel St-Jacques, 35 r. des Ecoles, 5ème (☎44 07 45 45; hotelstjacques@wanadoo.fr). Ⓜ Maubert-Mutualité or RER: Cluny-La Sorbonne. Regal ambience. English spoken. Breakfast €8. Internet. Singles €52, with toilet and shower €80; doubles with toilet and shower €90, with bath €118. AmEx/MC/V. ❹

Hôtel de Nesle, 7 r. du Nesle, 6ème (☎43 54 62 41). Ⓜ Odéon. Walk up r. de l'Ancienne Comédie, turn right on r. Dauphine, then left on r. du Nesle. Rooms with themes like African safari. Singles from €55; doubles €75. Extra bed €12. AmEx/MC/V. ❹

Young and Happy (Y&H) Hostel, 80 r. Mouffetard, 5ème (☎47 07 47 07; www.youngandhappy.fr). Ⓜ Monge. Though slightly cramped, the lively atmosphere and relaxed staff promises an enjoyable stay. English spoken. Internet €2 per 30min. Lockout 11am-4pm. Curfew 2am. Dorms €20-23; doubles €24-26. Cash only. ❷

Hôtel Stella, 41 r. Monsieur-le-Prince, 6ème (☎40 51 00 25). Ⓜ Odéon. Family owned and operated for years. All rooms have bath. Book ahead with deposit. Singles €45; doubles €55; triples €75; quads €85. Cash and traveler's checks only. ❹

7ÈME TO 10ÈME ARRONDISSEMENTS

Hôtel Eiffel Rive Gauche, 6 r. du Gros-Caillou, 7ème (☎45 51 24 56; www.hotel-eiffel.com). Ⓜ Ecole Militaire. Walk up av. de la Bourdonnais, turn right onto r. de la Grenelle, then left. Well-furnished accommodations off a quiet street. Rooms have cable TV, Internet jack, and bath; some have Eiffel Tower views. Breakfast €9. Safe €3. Singles €55-95; doubles €65-105; triples €85-125, quads €95-155. MC/V. ❺

Hôtel Bonséjour, 11 r. Burq, 8ème (☎42 54 22 53). Ⓜ Abesses. On a quiet street just seconds from the bohemian bustle, this family-run hotel is as friendly and clean as it is cheap. Breakfast €5.50. Singles €25-30; doubles with sink €30-36, with sink and shower €42; triples €49/57. Cash only. ❷

Hôtel Chopin, 46 passage Jouffroy, 9ème (☎47 70 58 10). Ⓜ Grands Boulevards. Walk against traffic on bd. Montmartre and turn right into passage Jouffroy. Lavishly decorated rooms, each with a TV, exude a classic Parisian feel. Breakfast €7. Singles €57, with bath €65-73; doubles with bath €75-86; triples with bath €100. AmEx/MC/V. ❺

Hôtel Montebello, 18 r. Pierre Leroux, 7ème (☎47 34 41 18; hmontebello@aol.com). Ⓜ Vaneau. A 15min. walk from the Eiffel Tower. Unbeatable rates for this upscale area. Basic, clean rooms have bath. Reserve at least 2 weeks in advance. Breakfast served 7:30-9:30am; €4. Singles €30; doubles €37-47. Cash only. ❸

Perfect Hôtel, 39 r. Rodier, 9ème (☎42 81 18 86; perfecthotel@hotmail.com). Ⓜ Anvers. Hotel-quality rooms at hostel prices. Breakfast free for *Let's Go* readers. Singles €30, with bath €50; doubles €37/50; triples €53/65. MC/V. ❸

Hôtel Palace, 9 r. Bouchardon, 9ème (☎42 06 59 32; hotel.palace@club-internet.fr). Ⓜ Strasbourg-St-Denis. Walk against traffic on bd. St-Denis until the Roman arch; follow r. René Boulanger on the left, then turn left on r. Bouchardon. Friendly staff welcomes travelers to tidy rooms. Shower €3.50. Book ahead. Singles €19-25, with shower €31; doubles €25-26/36; triples €48; more than 3 people €58-69. AmEx/MC/V. ❷

11ÈME AND 12ÈME ARRONDISSEMENTS

These hotels are close to hopping bars and clubs, but be careful at night.

Auberge de Jeunesse "Jules Ferry" (HI), 8 bd. Jules Ferry, 11ème (☎43 57 55 60; auberge@easynet.fr). Ⓜ République. Walk east on r. du Faubourg du Temple and turn right on the far side of bd. Jules Ferry. Basic rooms, wooden bunk beds, tiled floors. Social atmosphere. Breakfast included. Internet. 1 week max. stay. Lockout 10am-2pm. Check-in by 8am; no reservations. Dorms €20; doubles €20. MC/V. ❷

Hôtel Beaumarchais, 3 r. Oberkampf, 11ème (☎53 36 86 86; www.hotelbeaumarchais.com). Ⓜ Oberkampf. Exit on r. de Malte and turn right on r. Oberkampf. Spacious, renovated rooms with modern furniture, clean bathrooms, A/C, and cable TV. Breakfast €10. Book 2 weeks ahead. Singles €70; doubles €110; suites €170. AmEx/MC/V. ❺

Centre International du Séjour de Paris: CISP "Ravel," 6 av. Maurice Ravel, 12*ème* (☎44 75 60 00; www.cisp.asso.fr). Ⓜ Porte de Vincennes. Bright yellow building houses dorm-style accommodations removed from the major sights. Breakfast included. Reception 6:30am-1:30am. Book 1 month ahead. Dorms €16-20; singles with bath €30; doubles with bath €48. AmEx/MC/V. ❷

13ÈME TO 20ÈME ARRONDISSEMENTS

Just south of the Latin Quarter, the Montparnasse area mixes intellectual charm with thriving commercial centers and cafes.

Hôtel de Blois, 5 r. des Plantes, 14*ème* (☎45 40 99 48; fax 45 40 45 62). Ⓜ Alésia. Recently refurbished rooms are elegant and spacious. Comfortable rooms come with TV and hair dryer. Breakfast €6. Reserve 10 days in advance. Singles €43, with shower €49, with bath €56; doubles €46/53/61; triples €53-65. AmEx/MC/V. ❹

FIAP Jean-Monnet, 30 r. Cabanis, 14*ème* (☎43 13 17 00, reservations 43 13 17 17; www.fiap.asso.fr). Ⓜ Glacière. Spotless rooms all have toilets, shower and phone. Breakfast included. Check-in after 2:30pm. Check-out 9am. Curfew 2am. Book 2-4 weeks ahead; specify if you want a dorm bed or you'll get a single. €15 deposit per person per night by check or credit card. Dorms €23.90-34.20; singles €53. MC/V. ❷

Hôtel Caulaincourt, 2 sq. Caulaincourt, 18*ème* (☎46 06 46 06; bienvenue@caulaincourt.com). Ⓜ Lamarck-Caulaincourt. Friendly establishment with views of the city from the top floors. Breakfast €5.50. Book 1 month in advance. Dorms €24; singles €38, with shower €48, with shower and toilet €58; doubles €52, with shower and toilet €69; triples with shower €76. MC/V. ❷

Rhin et Danube, 3 pl. Rhin et Danube, 19*ème* (☎42 45 10 13; fax 42 06 88 82). Ⓜ Danube. 16 suites are packed with amenities but far from the sights. Each room has kitchen, fridge, dishes, coffee maker, hair dryer, shower, toilet, phone, and satellite TV. Singles €46; doubles €61; triples €73; quads €83; quints €92. MC/V. ❹

Auberge de Jeunesse "Le D'Artagnan" (HI), 80 r. Vitruve, 20*ème* (☎40 32 34 56; www.hostels-in.com). Ⓜ Porte de Bagnolet or Porte de Montreuil. Backpacker's colony includes restaurant, bar, and a small cinema. Breakfast included. TV in 2-person rooms. Laundry €3. 6-night max. stay. Reception 8am-1am. Lockout noon-3pm. Book by email. 9-bed dorms €19.50; 3-to 4-bed €21.50; 2-bed €26. Cash only. ❷

FOOD

Splurging on a delicious French meal should not be considered an additional expense, it should be like paying an entrance fee to see a world renowned sight. Paris offers some of the most exquisite culinary experiences in the world, so indulge, and be aware that chic doesn't equal expensive.

RESTAURANTS

ÎLE DE LA CITÉ AND ÎLE ST-LOUIS

Nos Ancêtres Les Gaulois, 39 r. Saint-Louis en l'Île, Île St-Louis (☎46 33 66 07; www.nosancetreslesgaulois.com). Ⓜ Pont Marie. Take a gastronomic voyage back to France's barbarous past and dine like the king of Gaul. Unlimited feast €35. Open daily 7pm-1:30am. AmEx/MC/V. ❺

Le Caveau du Palais, 19 pl. Dauphine, Île de la Cité (☎43 26 04 28). Ⓜ Cité. This Basque bistro serves steak and fish (€16-19) to satisfied locals. Reservations recommended. Open daily noon-3pm and 7-10:30pm. MC/V. ❹

Le Soleil d'Or, 15 bd. du Palais, Île de la Cité (☎43 54 22 22). Ⓜ Cité. This bustling bodega is right between the Louvre and Notre Dame. Perfect for tourists on the move. Hot dogs €4. Quiches €5. Sandwiches €6. Open daily 9am-10pm. MC/V. ❶

1ER AND 2ÈME ARRONDISSEMENTS

The *1er* and *2ème* are small but packed with flavors from all over the world. Expensive touristy places can be found near the Louvre, Asian cuisine is near the Opera Garnier, and street-side bistros dot r. Montorgueil.

Au Rocher de Cancale, 78 r. Montorgueil, *2ème* (☎42 33 50 29). Ⓜ Les Halles. One of the oldest restaurants in Paris, this trendy mainstay is perfect for a romantic date. Open M-Sa 7-10pm. MC/V. ❸

"Jules", 62 r. Jean-Jacques Rousseau, *1er* (☎40 28 99 04; www.julesrestaurant.com). Ⓜ Etienne Marcel. Enjoy modern incarnations of traditional French cuisine over 4 delectable courses (€29). Open Tu-Sa noon-1:45pm and 7:30-10pm. AmEx/MC/V. ❹

Papou Lounge, 74 r. Jean-Jacques Rousseau, *1er* (☎44 76 00 03). Ⓜ Etienne Marcel. Dine amid tribal paraphernalia with gregarious 20-somethings. Open daily 10am-2am. Kitchen open noon-4:30pm and 7pm-midnight. MC/V. ❸

3ÈME AND 4ÈME ARRONDISSEMENTS

The Marais offers chic bistros, kosher delis, and couple-friendly cafes.

Chez Janou, 2 r. Roger Verlomme, *3ème* (☎42 72 28 41). Ⓜ Chemin-Vert. Take r. St-Gilles and turn left almost immediately on r. des Tournelles. The restaurant is on the corner of r. Roger Verlomme. This French-Mediterranean bistro teems with contented customers sampling perfected Provençal recipes. Vegetarian options available. Open daily noon-3pm and 7:45pm-midnight. Reservations recommended. MC/V. ❸

Camille, 24 r. des Francs-Bourgeois, *3ème* (☎42 72 20 50). From Ⓜ St-Paul, follow r. Mahler away from St-Paul's church, and turn left. Nestled in the narrow medieval streets of the Marais, this classic *brasserie* promises the most for your money. The *crème brûlée* is blow-torched heaven (€6). Open daily until late. AmEx/DC/MC/V. ❸

L'As du Falafel, 34 r. des Rosiers, *4ème* (☎48 87 63 60). Ⓜ St-Paul. This bright green halal and kosher stand/restaurant in the heart of the Jewish Quarter is famous for its long lines and delicious falafel. Open M-F and Su 11:30am-midnight. MC/V. ❶

5ÈME AND 6ÈME ARRONDISSEMENTS

Enjoy the buzzing cafe culture that earned the Latin Quarter its contemporary fame. Tiny, low-priced restaurants and cafes pack the quadrangle bounded by bd. St-Germain, bd. St-Michel, r. de Seine, and the Seine River. **Rue de Buci** hosts Greek restaurants and a street market; **rue Gregoire de Tours** has cheap greasy spoons.

L'Epi Dupin, 11 r. Dupin, *6ème* (☎42 22 64 56; lepidupin@wanadoo.fr). Ⓜ Sevrès Babylone. Exceptional cuisine and presentation is deserving of its many accolades, and well worth the €32 fixed *menu*. Reservation recommended. Open M-F evenings. ❹

Café de la Mosquée, 39 r. Geoffrey St-Hilaire, *5ème* (☎43 31 38 20). Ⓜ Censier-Daubenton. With fountains, marble floors, and an exquisite multilevel terrace, this refined orientalized cafe echoes the lavishness of the mosque. Tea room open daily 9am-11:30pm. Kitchen open daily noon-3pm and 7:30-10:30pm. MC/V. ❸

Le Petit Vatel, 5 r. Lobineau, *6ème* (☎43 54 28 49). Ⓜ Mabillon. Follow traffic on bd. St-Germain, turn right on r. de Seine, and take the 2nd right. A greasy spoon without the grease, serving cheap French-Mediterranean specialties in a non-smoking venue. Vegetarian options. *Plats* €10. Open Tu-Sa noon-2:30pm and 7-10:30pm. Cash only. ❷

Savannah Café, 27 r. Descartes, *5ème* (☎43 29 45 77). Ⓜ Cardinal Lemoine. Follow r. du Cardinal Lemoine uphill, turn right on r. Clovis, and walk 1 block. Cheerfully decorated with swatches of yellow, this English-friendly eatery serves Lebanese favorites for €12.50-14.50. Open M-Sa 7-11pm. MC/V. ❸

Crêperie Saint Germain, 33 r. St-André-des-Arts, *6ème* (☎43 54 24 41). Ⓜ St-Michel. Cross pl. St-Michel and walk down r. St-André-des-Arts. Dine in diamond-shaped adobe booths covered with bright blue-tiled mosaics. Chow down on inventive and delicious crepes (€3-7.60) or a fresh salad (€4.50-8.50). AmEx/MC/V. ❷

7ÈME AND 8ÈME ARRONDISSEMENTS

L'Affriolé, 17 r. Malar, *7ème* (☎44 18 31 33). Ⓜ Invalides. Walk with traffic on r. de l'Université and turn left on r. Malar. This small venue has a delectable, yet changing fixed *menu* (€32). Reservations recommended. Open Tu-Sa for dinner. MC/V. ❹

Café des Lettres, 53 r. de Verneuil, *7ème* (☎4222 5217). Ⓜ Solférino. Exit the metro onto pl. J. Blainville and take r. de Villersexel; turn right on r. de l'Université, left on r. de Poitiers, and right on r. de Verneuil. Scandinavian cafe in a courtyard. Seafood €12-20. Reservations recommended. Open M noon-3pm, Tu-F noon-11pm, Sa noon-7pm. MC/V. ❹

9ÈME TO 11ÈME ARRONDISSEMENTS

Meals close to the Opéra cater to the after-theater and movie crowd and can be quite expensive. **Rue Faubourg-Montmartre** is packed with cheap eateries.

Les Sans Culottes, 27 r. de Lappe, *11ème* (☎48 05 42 92). Ⓜ Bastille. Go northeast on r. de la Roquette and turn right on r. de Lappe. Huge portions of traditional French cuisine. The set *menu* (€23) is a sampling of beautifully presented *entrées* (€8), *plats* (€15), and decadent desserts (€7). Open Tu-F 7:30pm-midnight, Sa-Su noon-3pm and 7:30pm-12:30am. Dinner reservations recommended after 9pm. AmEx/MC/V. ❸

Cantine d'Antoine et Lili, 95 quai de Valmy, *10ème* (☎40 37 34 86). Ⓜ Gare de l'Est. Go down r. Faubourg St-Martin and make a left on r. Récollets; it's on the corner of quai de Valmy. With bursts of bright primary colors, this cafe/bistro attracts relaxed locals. Salads €6.50. Open M-Tu and Su 11am-8pm, W-Sa 11am-1am. AmEx/MC/V. ❶

Chez Paul, 13 r. de Charonne, *11ème* (☎47 00 34 57). Ⓜ Bastille. Go east on r. du Faubourg St-Antoine and turn left on r. de Charonne. Classic bustling bistro downstairs; quaint, quieter dining upstairs. Reservations recommended. Open daily noon-2:30pm and 7pm-2am. Kitchen open until 12:30am. AmEx/MC/V. ❸

12ÈME TO 14ÈME ARRONDISSEMENTS

The *13ème* is a budget gourmand's dream, with scores of Asian restaurants packing Paris's **Chinatown,** south of pl. d'Italie on av. de Choisy, and numerous affordable French restaurants in the **Butte-aux-Cailles** area. The *14ème* is bordered at the top by the busy **boulevard du Montparnasse,** lined with a diverse array of restaurants. **Rue du Montparnasse** has Breton *crêperies;* **rue Daguerre** is lined with vegetarian-friendly restaurants; and inexpensive eateries cluster on **rue Didot, rue du Commerce, rue de Vaugirard,** and **boulevard de Grenelle.**

Tricotin, 15 av. de Choisy, *13ème* (☎45 84 74 44). Ⓜ Porte de Choisy. With 2 large restaurants under 1 roof, each offering unique pan-Asian specialties, customers will surely have a difficult time choosing between delicious dishes. Try the Vietnamese beef *pho* (€5.20). Open daily 9am-11:30pm. MC/V. ❶

Le Temps des Cerises, 18 r. de la Butte-aux-Cailles, *13ème* (☎45 89 69 48). Ⓜ Place d'Italie. Take r. Bobillot and turn right on r. de la Butte-aux-Cailles. Le Temps has been owned cooperatively by its workers since 1976. Lunch €10. *Menus* €14 and €22. Open M-F 11:45am-2:15pm and 7:30-11:45pm, Sa 7:30-11:45pm. AmEx/MC/V. ❸

15ÈME AND 16ÈME ARRONDISSEMENTS

Musée du Vin Restaurant, r. des Eaux or 5-7 pl. Charles Dickens, *16ème.* Ⓜ Passy. Go down the stairs, turn right on Sq. Alboni, and then turn right on r. des Eaux. Stroll past the wine-making wax figurines and enjoy a tasting at the end of your tour (€8, students €5.70) in this cave-like cellar. Stay for lunch (noon-3pm) and enjoy an *entrée* and *plat,* or 3 wines and 3 cheeses for €19. Open Tu-Su 10am-6pm. MC/V. ❹

Aux Artistes, 63 r. Falguière, *15ème* (☎43 22 05 39). Ⓜ Pasteur. Walk away from the exposed train tracks and turn right on r. Falguière. Eclectic assortment of vintage posters, pictures, and rusty license plates matches the exciting *mélange* of items on the extensive menu. Lunch *menu* €10, dinner €13. Open M-F noon-2:30pm and 7pm-12:30am, Sa 7pm-12:30am. ❷

17ÈME TO 20ÈME ARRONDISSEMENTS

The 17ème's **Village des Batignolles** is a great place to dine on a budget, far from the tourist traffic of the city. In the *18ème*, bistros and cafes line **rue des Abbesses** and **rue Lepic.** Ethnic enclaves in the *19ème* and *20ème* offer cheap, funky eats.

SAVE YOUR WALLET, HAVE A PICNIC. As a major tourist attraction, Montmartre has inevitably attracted high prices. Save a couple euro and picnic over Paris. Buy your *croque monsieur* or ham sandwich from a restaurant that offers both takeaway *(à emporter)* and sit-down service; the takeaway is always cheaper—even than stands which only have takeaway.

La Boheme du Tertre, 2 pl. du Tertre, *18ème* (☎46 06 51 69). Ⓜ Abbesses. The swankiest joint in Place du Tertre with suprisingly cheap sandwiches. A great place to rest your feet and enjoy the bustling bohemian square at the base of Sacre Coeur. Ham sandwich €3.20. *Croque monsieur* €6. Open daily 9am-2am. AmEx/MC/V. ❶

Lao Siam, 49 r. de Belleville, *19ème* (☎40 40 09 68). Ⓜ Belleville. In the heart of one of Paris's most diverse quarters, this authentic eatery is worth the trek from the city-center. Open daily noon-4pm and 7:30-11:30pm. MC/V. ❷

Un Zebre A Montmartre, 38 r. Lepic, *18ème* (☎42 23 97 80). Ⓜ Abbesses. Turn right onto r. Abbesses and keep right as it turns into r. Lepic. Fill up on tasty *plats* (€11) like steak tartare or paleron (avoid the fish) and imbibe cheap drinks (starting at €4) while listening to trippy beats spun by the hip bartender/DJ. Open daily 9am-2am. MC/V. ❷

SALONS DE THÉ (TEA ROOMS)

Ladurée, 16 r. Royale, *8ème* (☎42 60 21 79). Ⓜ Concorde. Ever wondered what it would be like to dine inside a Fabergé egg? The Rococo decor of this classic tea salon attracts well-groomed shoppers. 1 large macaroon €4.40. 4 mini macaroons €6.20. Open daily 8:30am-7pm. Lunch served until 3pm. AmEx/MC/V.

Mariage Frères, 30 r. du Bourg-Tibourg, *4ème* (☎42 72 28 11). Ⓜ Hôtel-de-Ville. Also at 260 r. du Faubourg St-Honoré, *8ème* (☎46 22 18 54). Started by 2 brothers who hated British tea, this depot offers 500 varieties (€7-15). Afternoon tea *menu* includes sandwich, pastry, and tea (€25). Brunch *menu* €25. Reservations recommended. Open daily 10:30am-7:30pm. AmEx/MC/V.

SPECIALTY SHOPS

Food shops, particularly *boulangeries* (bakeries) and *pâtisseries* (pastry shops), are on virtually every street in Paris. Your gustatory experiences, particularly when buying breads or pastries, will vary depending on how recently your food has left the oven. The following listings are some of Paris's most famous.

Ice Cream: Berthillon, 31 r. St-Louis-en-l'Île (☎43 54 31 61). Ⓜ Cité or Pont Marie. Swank scoopery boasts the best ice cream in Paris (€2-4). Try the *nougat miel* (honey nougat) here; other shops offer pale imitations. Takeaway W-Su 10am-8pm. Eat-in W-F 1-8pm, Sa-Su 2pm-midnight. Closed 2 weeks in Feb. and Apr. and July 14-Sept.

Bread: Julien, 75 r. du Faubourg St-Honoré, *1er* (☎42 36 24 83). The best of everything: breads, sandwiches, pastries, cakes. For an indulgent breakfast, try the *pain au chocolat* (chocolate croissant) or the very different but equally delicious *pain chocolat* (small loaf of bread with chocolate chips). Long lines at lunch.

Wine: Nicolas, 64 r. St-Louis-en-l'Île, Île St-Louis (☎42 33 58 45). Open since 1822, this is the original location of the popular chain of wine vendors throughout Paris. Wines range from €4 to €400 and come in all shapes and sizes, including a bottle shaped like the Eiffel Tower. Most branches open M-F 10am-8pm. AmEx/MC/V.

Cheese: Barthélémy, 51 r. de Grenelle, *7ème* (☎45 48 56 75). Ⓜ Rue du Bac. One of the finest *fromageries* in Paris, you can smell the cheese from outside. President Chirac has been known to stop in. Open Tu-F 7:30am-7:30pm. Cash only.

MARKETS

Marché Mouffetard, *5ème.* Ⓜ Monge. Walk through pl. Monge and follow r. Ortolan to r. Mouffetard. An exciting market known for its baked goods. A wide variety of cheeses, meat, produce, and fish are also available. Open Tu-Su 8am-1:30pm.

Marché Montorgueil, *2ème.* Ⓜ Etienne Marcel. Walk along r. Etienne Marcel away from the river; take the 2nd right. A center of gastronomy since the 13th century, this market offers home-grown wine, cheese, meat, and produce. Open Tu-Su 8am-7:30pm.

SIGHTS

While it would take weeks to see all of Paris's monuments, museums, and gardens, the city's small size makes sightseeing easy and enjoyable. In a few hours, you can walk from the heart of the Marais in the east to the Eiffel Tower in the west, passing most major monuments along the way. A solid day of wandering will show you how close the medieval Notre Dame is to the modern Centre Pompidou and the funky Latin Quarter to the royal Louvre—Paris's diversity is all the more amazing for the proximity in which it unfolds.

ÎLE DE LA CITÉ AND ÎLE ST-LOUIS

ÎLE DE LA CITÉ

If any one place is the heart of Paris, it is this small island in the Seine. In the 3rd century BC, when it was inhabited by the *Parisii*, a Gallic tribe of merchants and fishermen, the Île was all there was to Paris. Today, all distance-points in France are measured from *kilomètre zéro*, a sundial in front of Notre Dame.

CATHÉDRALE DE NOTRE DAME DE PARIS. This 12th- to 14th-century cathedral, founded under Bishop Maurice de Sully, is one of the world's most famous. After the Revolution, the building fell into disrepair—it was even used to shelter livestock—until Victor Hugo's 1831 novel *Notre Dame de Paris* (a.k.a. *The Hunchback of Notre Dame*) inspired citizens to lobby for restoration. The apocalyptic facade and soaring, apparently weightless walls, effects produced by brilliant Gothic engineering and optical illusions, are inspiring even for the most church-weary. The cathedral's biggest draws are the enormous stained-glass **rose windows** that dominate the northern and southern ends of the transept. A staircase inside the towers leads to a perch from which gargoyles survey the city. *(Ⓜ Cité. ☎53 10 07 02, crypt 55 42 50 10. Cathedral open M-F 8am-6:45pm, Sa-Su 8am-7:45pm. Towers open July-Aug. 9am-7:30pm; Apr.-June and Sept. 9:30am-7:30pm; Jan.-Mar. and Oct.-Dec. 10am-5:30pm. Treasury open M-Sa 9:30am-12:30pm and 1:30-5:30pm, Su 1:30-5:30pm. Crypt open daily 10am-5:30pm. Free tours begin at the booth to the right as you enter. In English W-Th noon, Sa 2:30pm; in French M-F noon, Sa 2:30pm. Cathedral and towers €6, ages 18-25 €4.10. Treasury €2.50, students €2. Crypt €3.90, under 27 €2.20.)*

PALAIS DE JUSTICE, STE-CHAPELLE, AND CONCIERGERIE. The **Palais de la Cité** contains three vastly different buildings. The opulent, Gothic **Ste-Chapelle** was built by St-Louis (Louis IX) to house his most precious possession, Christ's crown of thorns, now in Notre Dame. On sunny days, light pours through the **Upper Chapel's** medieval stained glass, illuminating frescoes of saints and martyrs. *(4 bd. du Palais. Ⓜ Cité. ☎53 73 78 50. Open daily Apr.-Sept. 9:30am-6pm. €6.10, ages 18-25 €4.10, under 18 free.)* Around the corner is the Conciergerie, one of Paris's most famous

FRANCE

prisons; Marie-Antoinette and Robespierre were incarcerated here during the Revolution. *(Ⓜ Cité. Entrance on bd. du Palais, to the right of Palais de Justice. ☎53 73 78 50. Open daily Apr.-Sept. 9:30am-6pm; Oct.-Mar. 10am-5pm. €6.10, students €4.10.)* Built after the great fire of 1776, the Palais de Justice houses France's district courts. *(☎44 32 51 51. Courtrooms open M-F 9am-noon and 1:30-6pm. Free.)*

ÎLE ST-LOUIS

The Île St-Louis has been home to Paris's elite, from Voltaire to Marie Curie. The city's best ice cream is at **Berthillon,** 31 r. St-Louis-en-l'Île (p. 330).

RUE SAINT-LOUIS-EN-L'ÎLE. Rolling down the center of the island, this charming street is a welcome distraction from busy Parisian life. With a small village feel, ambling shoppers with an ice cream cone in hand can enjoy a wealth of specialty shops, quaint bistros, and upscale hotels. Visit the **Église St-Louis-en-Île,** 19bis r. St-Louis-en-l'Île, to see Louis Le Vau's 17th-century Rococo interior.

LOUVRE AND OPÉRA: 1ER, 2ÈME, AND 9ÈME ARRONDISSEMENTS

LOUVRE AND TUILERIES. World-famous art museum and former residence of kings, the **Louvre** (p. 337) occupies about one-seventh of the 1*er arrondissement.* The **Jardin des Tuileries,** at the western foot of the Louvre, celebrates the victory of geometry over nature. It was commissioned by Catherine de Médici in 1564 and improved by André Le Nôtre (designer of Versailles's gardens) in 1649. *(Ⓜ Tuileries. ☎40 20 90 43. Garden open daily Apr.-Sept. 7am-9pm; Oct.-Mar. 7:30am-7:30pm. English-language tours from the Arc de Triomphe du Carrousel.)* North of the Tuileries along r. de Castiglione, **place Vendôme** was built to house embassies, but bankers instead created lavish private homes behind the elegant facades. Today, the smell of money is still in the air: designer shops, perfumers, and jewelers line the square.

PALAIS-ROYAL. One block north of the Louvre along r. du Faubourg St-Honoré lies the once regal and racy Palais-Royal, constructed in the 17th century as Richelieu's Palais Cardinal. Anne d'Autriche moved in with her son, young Louis XIV. In 1781, the Duc d'Orléans, strapped for cash, rented out the buildings around the palace's garden to boutiques, restaurants, theaters, and gambling joints. *(Palace closed to the public. Fountain open daily June-Aug. 7am-11pm; Apr.-May 7am-10:15pm; Sept. 7am-9:30pm; Oct.-Mar. 7am-8:30pm. Free.)*

LES HALLES. A sprawling market since 1135, Les Halles received a much-needed face-lift in the 1850s with the construction of large iron-and-glass pavilions to shelter the vendors' stalls. In 1970, the medieval market was torn down and replaced with an extensive underground shopping mall and cinema called **Forum des Halles,** with its own metro station. The area has seen a recent influx of younger locals.

OPÉRA. The exterior of the **Opéra Garnier,** with its newly restored marble facade, sculpted golden goddesses, and ornate columns and friezes is equally as impressive as it is kitschy. The lavish interior decor transports visitors back to a time when the Opéra was haunted by the famous phantom. *(Ⓜ Opéra. General info ☎08 36 69 78 68, tours 40 01 22 63; www.opera-de-paris.fr. Concert hall and museum open daily Sept. to mid-July 10am-5pm; mid-July to Aug. 10am-6pm. Concert hall closed during rehearsals; call ahead. English-language tours daily noon, 2pm. €7, students €3. Tours €10/8.)*

PIGALLE. Farther north, on the border of the 18*ème*, is the salacious Pigalle district. Stretching along bd. de Clichy from pl. Pigalle to pl. Blanche, this is home to famous old cabarets (Folies Bergère, Moulin Rouge, Folies Pigalle) and overtly raunchy newcomers like Le Coq Hardy and Dirty Dick. Visitors traveling alone should exercise caution. *(Ⓜ Pigalle.)*

MARAIS: 3ÈME AND 4ÈME ARRONDISSEMENTS

PLACE DES VOSGES. At the end of r. des Francs-Bourgeois sits the magnificent pl. des Vosges, Paris's oldest public square. The manicured central park is surrounded by 17th-century Renaissance townhouses. The *place* is one of Paris's most charming spots for a picnic or an afternoon siesta. Victor Hugo lived at no. 6, which is now a museum of his life and work. *(Ⓜ Chemin Vert or St-Paul.)*

RUE DES ROSIERS. In the heart of the Jewish community of the Marais, r. des Rosiers is packed with kosher shops and falafel stands. When Philippe-Auguste expelled Jews from the city in the 13th century, many families moved to this area, just outside the city walls. Since then, the quarter was repopulated by an influx of Russian Jews in the 19th century and North African Sephardim fleeing Algeria in the 1960s. During WWII, many who had fled to France to escape the pogroms of Eastern Europe were murdered by the Nazis. *(Ⓜ St-Paul.)*

HÔTEL DE VILLE. Paris's grandiose city hall dominates a large square scattered with fountains and *Belle Epoque* lampposts. The present edifice is a 19th-century replica of the original medieval structure, a meeting hall for the cartel that controlled traffic on the Seine. *(29 r. de Rivoli. Ⓜ Hôtel-de-Ville. ☎42 76 43 43. Open M-F 9am-6:30pm when there is an exhibit, until 6pm otherwise.)*

LATIN QUARTER AND ST-GERMAIN-DES-PRÉS: 5ÈME AND 6ÈME ARRONDISSEMENTS

The student population is the soul of the Latin Quarter, so named for the prestigious universities that taught here in Latin until 1798. Since the student riots in May 1968, many artists and intellectuals have migrated to the cheaper outer *arrondissements*, and the *haute bourgeoisie* have moved in. The *5ème* still presents the most diverse array of bookstores, cinemas, and jazz clubs in the city. Designer shops and edgy art galleries are found around St-Germain-des-Prés.

RUE MOUFFETARD. South of pl. de la Contrescarpe, r. Mouffetard plays host to one of the liveliest street markets in Paris. The stretch of r. Mouffetard, past pl. de la Contrescarpe, and onto r. Descartes and r. de la Montagne Ste-Geneviève is the quintessential Latin Quarter stroll. *(Ⓜ Cardinal Lemoine or Pl. Monge.)*

JARDIN DU LUXEMBOURG. Parisians flock to these formal gardens to sunbathe or read. A residential area of Roman Paris, the site of a medieval monastery, and later the home of 17th-century French royalty, the gardens were liberated during the Revolution and are now free to all. *(Ⓜ Odéon or RER: Luxembourg. Main entrance on bd. St-Michel. Open daily dawn-dusk.)*

MOSQUÉE DE PARIS. The *Institut Musulman* houses the beautiful Persian gardens, elaborate minaret, and shady porticoes of the Mosquée de Paris, a mosque constructed in 1920 by French architects to honor the role of North African countries in WWI. Exhausted travelers can relax in the baths at the exquisite *hammam* (Turkish bath) or sip mint tea in the equally soothing cafe. *(Ⓜ Censier Daubenton. Walk down r. Daubenton; the mosque is at the end of the street. ☎48 35 78 17. Open daily June-Aug. 10am-noon and 2-6:30pm; Sept.-May until 5:30pm. Guided tour €3, students €2. Hammam open for men Tu 2-9pm, Su 10am-9pm; women M, W-Th, Sa 10am-9pm, F 2-9pm. €15.)*

LA SORBONNE. The Sorbonne is one of Europe's oldest universities, founded in 1253 by Robert de Sorbon as a dormitory for 16 theology students. Visitors can stroll through the **Chapelle de la Sorbonne** (entrance off of the pl. de la Sorbonne), which houses temporary exhibits on arts and letters. Nearby **place de la Sorbonne,** off bd. St-Michel, boasts cafes, bookstores, and, during term-time, students. *(45-47 r. des Ecoles. Ⓜ Cluny-La Sorbonne or RER: Luxembourg.)*

PANTHÉON. The **crypt** of the Panthéon, which occupies the highest point on the Left Bank, houses the tombs of Louis Braille, Victor Hugo, Jean Jaurès, Jean-Jacques Rousseau, Voltaire, and Emile Zola. The building's other attraction is **Foucault's Pendulum,** which proves the rotation of the earth. *(Pl. du Panthéon. Ⓜ Cardinal Lemoine. Walk down r. Cardinal Lemoine, turn right on r. Clovis, and walk around to the front of the building. ☎44 32 18 00. Open daily 10am-6:30pm. Last admission 5:45pm. €7, students €4.50, under 18 free. Oct.-Mar. 1st Su of the month free.)*

JARDIN DES PLANTES. Opened in 1640 to grow medicinal plants for King Louis XIII, the garden now features science museums, rosaries, and a zoo, which Parisians raided for food during the Prussian siege of 1871. *(Ⓜ Gare d'Austerlitz or Jussieu. ☎40 79 37 94. Open daily in summer 7:30am-8pm; in winter 7:30am-5:30pm.)*

7ÈME ARRONDISSEMENT

EIFFEL TOWER. Gustave Eiffel wrote of his creation: "France is the only country in the world with a 300m flagpole." Designed in 1889 as the tallest structure in the world, the Eiffel Tower was conceived as a modern monument to engineering that would surpass the Egyptian pyramids in size and notoriety. Critics dubbed it a "metal asparagus" and a "Parisian tower of Babel." Writer Guy de Maupassant ate lunch every day at its ground-floor restaurant—the only place in Paris, he claimed, from which he couldn't see the offensive thing. Nevertheless, when it was inaugurated in March 1889 as the centerpiece of the World's Fair, the tower earned the love of Paris; nearly two million people ascended during the event. Some still criticize its glut of tourists and trinkets, but don't believe the anti-hype; the tower is a wonder of design and engineering. *(Ⓜ Bir-Hakeim or Trocadéro. ☎44 11 23 23; www.tour-eiffel.fr. Open daily mid-June to Aug. 9am-midnight; Sept. to mid-June 9:30am-11pm. Stairs open 9:30am-6pm). Last access to top 30min. before closing. Elevator to 1st fl. €4, to 2nd fl. €7.30, to 3rd fl. €10.40. Stairs to 1st and 2nd fl. €3.50.)*

INVALIDES. The gold-leaf dome of the Hôtel des Invalides shines at the center of the *7ème.* The grassy **Esplanade des Invalides** runs from the *hôtel* to the **Pont Alexandre III,** a bridge with gilded lampposts from which you can catch a great view of the Invalides and the Seine. The **Musée de l'Armée, Musée des Plans-Reliefs,** and **Musée de l'Ordre de la Libération** are housed in the Invalides complex, as is **Napoleon's tomb,** in the **Église St-Louis.** Enter from either pl. des Invalides or pl. Vauban and av. de Tourville. *(127 r. de Grenelle. Ⓜ Invalides.)*

CHAMPS-ELYSÉES AND NEARBY: 8ÈME AND 16ÈME ARRONDISSEMENTS

ARC DE TRIOMPHE. Napoleon commissioned the Arc, at the western end of the Champs-Elysées, in 1806 to honor his Grande Armée. In 1940, Parisians were brought to tears by the sight of Nazis goose-stepping through the Arc. At the end of the German occupation, a sympathetic Allied army made sure that a French general would be the first to drive under the arch. The terrace at the top has a fabulous view. The **Tomb of the Unknown Soldier** has been under the Arc since November 11, 1920. An eternal flame has been burning strong since 1921. *(On pl. Charles de Gaulle. Ⓜ Charles-de-Gaulle-Etoile. Open daily Apr.-Sept. 10am-11pm; Oct.-Mar. 10am-10:30pm. Last entry 30min. before closing. €7, ages 18-25 €4.50.)*

PLACE DE LA CONCORDE. Paris's most famous public square lies at the eastern end of the Champs-Elysées and the Jardin des Tuileries. Built between 1757 and 1777 as a monument to Louis X, the area soon became the **place de la Révolution,**

site of the guillotine that severed 1343 aristocratic heads. After the Reign of Terror, the square was renamed *concorde* (peace). The huge 13th-century BC **Obélisque de Luxor** depicts the deeds of Egyptian pharaoh Ramses II. Given to Charles X by the Viceroy of Egypt, it is Paris's oldest monument. *(Ⓜ Concorde.)*

AVENUE DES CHAMPS-ELYSÉES. Extending from the Louvre, this wide thoroughfare was a piecemeal project begun under the reign of Louis XIV. By the first half of the 20th century, opulence reigned—ornate mansions towered above exclusive cafes. Today, the Champs-Elysées is one of the most conflicted spots in Paris; shop offerings range from designer fashion to low-budget options. The erstwhile swankiness of the cafe scene is now ruled by hokey tourist traps and McDonald's.

BASTILLE: 10ÈME, 11ÈME, AND 12ÈME ARRONDISSEMENTS

CANAL ST-MARTIN. The most pleasant area of the *10ème* is the tree-lined Canal St-Martin. In recent years, the city has made efforts to improve water quality in the canal and clean up its banks, resulting in a local renaissance. Children line up along the quays to watch the working locks lift barges and boats. *(Ⓜ République or Goncourt will take you to the more beautiful end of the canal.)*

PLACE DE LA BASTILLE. This busy intersection was once the home of the famous Bastille Prison, stormed on July 14, 1789, sparking the French Revolution. Two days later, the National Assembly ordered the prison demolished, but the ground plan of the prison's grand turrets remain embedded in the road near r. du Faubourg St-Antoine. *(Ⓜ Bastille.)*

OPÉRA DE LA BASTILLE. One of Mitterrand's *Grands Projets*, the Opéra opened in 1989 to loud protests over its unattractive design. It has been described as a huge toilet because of its resemblance to the city's coin-operated *pissoirs*. The opera has not struck a completely sour note, though, as it has helped renew local interest in the arts. The guided tour offers a behind-the-scenes view of the largest theater in the world. *(130 r. de Lyon. Ⓜ Bastille. Look for the words "Billeterie" on the building. ☎40 01 19 70; www.opera-de-paris.fr. 1hr. tour almost every day, usually at 1 or 5pm; call ahead. Tours in French, but groups of 10 or more can arrange for English. €10, students and under 26 €5.)*

EASTERN LEFT BANK: 13ÈME ARRONDISSEMENT

QUARTIER DE LA BUTTE-AUX-CAILLES. Historically a working-class neighborhood, the old-fashioned Butte-aux-Cailles Quarter has a long-standing tradition of defiance. The area was one of the first to fight during the Revolution of 1848. Later, it was the unofficial headquarters of the *soixante-huitards*, the student and intellectual activists behind the 1968 Paris riots. Funky new restaurants and galleries have cropped up in recent years. *(Ⓜ Pl. d'Italie. From the large roundabout, walk southeast down r. Bobillot and turn right onto r. de la Butte-aux-Cailles.)*

MONTPARNASSE: 14ÈME AND 15ÈME ARRONDISSEMENTS

THE CATACOMBS. Almost 2km of tunnels 20m below ground were originally excavated to provide stone for building the city. By the 1770s, much of the Left Bank was in danger of caving in and digging was promptly halted. The former quarry was then used as a mass grave, relieving Paris's foul and overcrowded cemeteries. During WWII, the Resistance set up headquarters among the departed. *(1 pl. Denfert-Rochereau. Ⓜ Denfert-Rochereau. ☎43 22 47 63. Exit to pl. Denfert-Rochereau and cross av. du Général Leclerc. Tour lasts 45min. Open Tu-Su 10am-4pm. €5, ages 14-26 €2.50.)*

PARC ANDRÉ CITROËN. The futuristic Parc André Citroën was created by landscapers Alain Provost and Gilles Clément in the 1970s. The hot-air balloon ride that launches from the central garden offers spectacular aerial views of Paris. *(2 r. de la Montagne de la Fage. Ⓜ Javel-André Citroën or Balard. ☎44 26 20 00. Open M-F 7:30am-9:30pm, Sa-Su 9am-9:30pm. Balloon rides €12, ages 12-17 €10.)*

BOULEVARD DU MONTPARNASSE. In the early 20th century, Montparnasse became a center for avant-garde artists like Chagall and Modigliani. Political exiles Lenin and Trotsky talked strategy over cognac in cafes along the boulevard, including **Le Dôme, Le Sélect,** and **La Coupole.** After WWI, Montparnasse attracted American expats and artistic rebels like Calder, Hemingway, and Henry Miller.

MONTMARTRE AND PÈRE-LACHAISE: 18ÈME, 19ÈME, AND 20ÈME ARRONDISSEMENTS

BASILIQUE DU SACRÉ-COEUR. The Basilique du Sacré-Coeur crowns the butte Montmartre like an enormous white meringue. Its onion dome is visible from almost anywhere in the city, and its 112m bell tower is the highest point in Paris. Nearby, pl. du Tertre is full of touristy cafes and amateur artists. *(35 r. du Chevalier-de-la-Barre. Ⓜ Anvers or Abbesses. ☎53 41 89 00. Open daily 6am-11pm. Wheelchair accessible. Dome and crypt open daily 9am-6pm. Church free. Dome and crypt €5.)*

PARC DE LA VILLETTE. La Villette is the product of a successful urban renewal project. Inaugurated by President Mitterrand in 1985 as "the place of intelligent leisure," it contains museums, libraries, and concert halls in the Cité des Sciences and the Cité de la Musique. The **Promenade des Jardins** links several thematic gardens. Every July and August, La Villette hosts a free open-air **film festival.** The **Zénith** concert hall hosts major rock bands, and the **Trabendo** jazz and modern music club holds an extraordinarily popular annual jazz festival. *(Ⓜ Porte de Pantin. General info, including Grande Halle ☎40 03 75 03. Promenade des Jardins open 24hr. Free.)*

CIMETIÈRE PÈRE LACHAISE. The cemetery holds the remains of Balzac, Sarah Bernhardt, Colette, Danton, David, Delacroix, La Fontaine, Haussmann, Molière, Proust, and Seurat within its peaceful paths and elaborate tombs. Foreigners buried here include Modigliani, Gertrude Stein, and Oscar Wilde; the most visited grave is that of Jim Morrison. French Leftists make ceremonious pilgrimage to the **Mur des Fédérés** (Wall of the Federals), where 147 *communards* were executed. *(16 r. du Repos. Ⓜ Père-Lachaise. Open Mar.-Oct. M-F 8am-6pm, Sa 8:30am-6pm, Su 9am-6pm; Nov.-Feb. M-F 8am-5:30pm, Sa 8:30am-5:30pm, Su 9am-5:30pm. Free.)*

MOUNTING MONTMARTRE. One does not merely visit Montmartre; one climbs it. The standard approach is from the south, via Ⓜ Anvers or Ⓜ Abbesses, although other directions provide interesting, less crowded climbs. From Ⓜ Anvers, walk up r. Steinkerque to the ornate switchback stairway. The longer climb from Ⓜ Abbesses passes more worthwhile cafes and shops. The *funiculaire* provides a less tiring way of ascending the more than 200 stairs to the base of Sacré-Coeur. From Ⓜ Anvers, walk up r. Steinkerque and take a left on r. Tardieu. *(Funicular runs every 2min. Accepts normal metro tickets. Open daily 6am-12:30am.)*

BAL DU MOULIN ROUGE. Along the bd. de Clichy and bd. de Rochechouart, you'll find many of the nightclubs that were the definitive hangouts of the Belle Epoque, including the infamous cabaret Bal du Moulin Rouge. The revues are still risqué, but the price of admission is the real shock. *(82 bd. de Clichy. Ⓜ Blanche. ☎53 09 82 82; www.moulin-rouge.com. Shows 7, 9, 11pm. Dinner and show €140-170, 11pm show €87.)*

PERIMETER SIGHTS

LA DÉFENSE. Outside the city limits, west of the 16*ème*, the modern architecture of La Défense make up Paris's newest (unofficial) *arrondissement*, home to the headquarters of 14 of France's top 20 corporations. The **Grande Arche,** inaugurated in 1989, completes the *axe historique* running through the Louvre, pl. de la Concorde, and the Arc de Triomphe. There's yet another stunning view from the top. Trees, shops, and sculptures by Calder and Miró line the esplanade. *(Ⓜ/RER: La Défense, or bus #73. Arche open daily 10am-8pm. €7.50, students and under 18 €5.50.)*

BOIS DE BOULOGNE. By day, this over 2000-acre park, with numerous gardens, several stadiums, and two lakes, is a popular spot for picnics, jogging, and bike-riding. The *bois* is notorious for drugs and prostitution by night. *(On the western edge of the 16ème. Ⓜ Porte Maillot, Sablons, Pont de Neuilly, or Porte Dauphine.)*

MUSEUMS

The **Carte Musées et Monuments** grants immediate entry to 70 Paris museums (no waiting in line) and will save you money if you plan to visit three or more museums and major sights per day. It's available at major museums and metro stations. (1-day €15; 3-day €30; 5-day €45.)

MUSÉE D'ORSAY. If only the *Académiciens* who turned the Impressionists away from the Louvre could see the Musée d'Orsay. Now considered masterpieces, these "rejects" are well worth the pilgrimage to this mecca of modernity. The collection, installed in a former railway station, includes painting, sculpture, decorative arts, and photography from 1848 until WWI. On the ground floor, Classical and Proto-Impressionist works are on display, including Manet's *Olympia*, a painting that caused a scandal when it was unveiled in 1865. Other highlights include: Monet's *La Gare St-Lazare* and *Cathédrale de Rouen* series, Renoir's *Le bal du Moulin de la Galette*, Edgar Dégas's *La classe de danse*, Rodin's *Gates of Hell*, and paintings by Cézanne, Sisley, Seurat, Pissaro, and Morisot. Over a dozen diverse works by van Gogh are also featured. *(62 r. de Lille. 7ème. Ⓜ Solférino; RER: Musée d'Orsay. ☎40 49 48 14; www.musee-orsay.fr. Open Tu-W and F-Sa 10am-6pm, Th 10am-9:45pm; June 20-Sept. 20 also Su 9am-6pm. Last entry 45min. before closing. €7, ages 18-25 and Su €5, under 18 and 1st Su of month free.)*

CROWDLESS CULTURE. Orsay's undeniably amazing collection draws large crowds, marring an otherwise enjoyable museum. A Sunday morning or Thursday evening visit will avoid the tourist throngs and calm the inner artist.

MUSÉE DU LOUVRE. No visitor has ever alotted enough time to thoughtfully ponder every display at the Louvre, namely because it would take weeks to read every caption of the over 30,000 items in the museum. A short list of its masterpieces includes *Hammurabi's Code*, Jacques-Louis David's *The Oath of the Horatii*, Delacroix's *Liberty Leading the People*, Vermeer's *Lacemaker*, da Vinci's *Mona Lisa*, the *Winged Victory of Samothrace*, and the *Venus de Milo*. Enter through I.M. Pei's stunning glass **Pyramid** in the Cour Napoléon, or skip lines by entering directly from the metro. The Louvre is organized into three different wings: Sully, Richelieu, and Denon. Each is divided according to the artwork's date, national origin, and medium; pick up a map for extra guidance. *(1er. Ⓜ Palais-Royal/Musée du Louvre. ☎40 20 51 51; www.louvre.fr. Open M, W 9am-9:45pm, Th-Su 9am-6pm. Last entry 45min. before closing; visitors are asked to leave 15-30min. before closing. Admission M, W-Sa 9am-6pm €8.50, M, W-Sa 6pm-close and Su €6. 1st Su of month free.)*

CENTRE POMPIDOU. This inside-out building has inspired debate since its opening in 1977. Whatever its aesthetic merits, the exterior's chaotic colored piping provides an appropriate shell for the Fauvist, Cubist, Pop, and Conceptual works inside. *(Pl. Georges-Pompidou, 4ème. Ⓜ Rambuteau or Hôtel-de-Ville. ☎44 78 12 33; www.centrepompidou.fr. Centre open M and W-Su 11am-10pm. Museum open M and W-Su 11am-9pm. Last entry 8pm. €7, students €5, under 18 and 1st Su of month free.)*

MUSÉE RODIN. The 18th-century Hôtel Biron holds hundreds of sculptures by Auguste Rodin (and by his student and lover, Camille Claudel), including the *The Thinker*, *The Hand of God*, and *The Kiss*. Bring a book and repose in the fertile gardens amid bending flowers and flexing sculptures. *(77 r. de Varenne, 7ème. Ⓜ Varenne. ☎44 18 61 10; www.musee-rodin.fr. Open Tu-Su Apr.-Sept. 9:30am-5:45pm; Oct.-Mar. 9:30am-4:45pm. Last entry 30min. before closing. €5, ages 18-25 and Su €3.)*

MUSÉE PICASSO. When Picasso died in 1973, his family paid the French inheritance tax in artwork. The French government put this collection, which includes work from his Cubist, Surrealist, and Neoclassical years, on display in 1985 in the 17th-century Hôtel Salé. *(5 r. de Thorigny, 3ème. Ⓜ Chemin Vert. ☎42 71 63 15. Open M and W-Su Apr.-Sept. 9:30am-6pm; Oct.-Mar. 9:30am-5:30pm. Last entry 45min. before closing. €5.50, ages 18-25 and Su €4.)*

MUSÉE JACQUEMART-ANDRÉ. The 19th-century mansion of Nélie Jacquemart and her husband contains a world-class collection of Renaissance art, including *Madonna and Child* by Botticelli and *St-George and the Dragon* by Ucello. *(158 bd. Haussmann, 8ème. Ⓜ Miromesnil. ☎45 62 11 59. Open daily 10am-6pm. Last entrance 5:30pm. €9.50, students and ages 7-17 €6.50. English-language audio tours included.)*

MUSÉE MARMOTTAN MONET. Thanks to donations by Monet's family, this Empire-style house has been transformed into a shrine to Impressionism, with some of Monet's famed water lily canvases in the basement. *(2 r. Louis Boilly, 16ème. Ⓜ La Muette. Follow Chaussée de la Muette, which becomes av. Ranelagh, through the Jardin du Ranelagh park. ☎44 96 50 33. Open Tu-Su 10am-6pm. €6.50, students €4.)*

MUSÉE DE CLUNY. One of the world's finest collections of medieval art, the Musée de Cluny is housed in a medieval monastery built on top of Roman baths. Works include **La Dame et La Licorne** (The Lady and the Unicorn), a striking medieval tapestry series. *(6 pl. Paul Painlevé, 5ème. Ⓜ Cluny-La Sorbonne. ☎53 73 78 00. Open M and W-Sa 9:15am-5:45pm. Last entry 5:15pm. €7; students, under 25, and Su €5.50; under 18 free. 1st Su of every month free.)*

FRANCE

INSTITUT DU MONDE ARABE. Featuring Arabesque art from the 3rd to 18th centuries, the IMA was designed to look like the ships that carried North African immigrants to France. The southern face is comprised of 240 portals which open and close depending on how much light is needed to illuminate the interior without damaging the art. *(1 r. des Fossés St-Bernard, 5ème. Ⓜ Jussieu. ☎40 51 38 38; www.imarabe.org. Open Tu-Su 10am-6pm. Library open Tu-Sa 1-8pm. €4, students €3.)*

FONDATION CARTIER POUR L'ART CONTEMPORAINE. The Fondation Cartier, a gallery of contemporary art, looks like a synthetic indoor forest, with a stunning glass facade surrounding the grounds' natural greenery. *(261 bd. Raspail, 14ème. Ⓜ Raspail. ☎42 18 56 51; www.fondation.cartier.fr. Open Tu-Su noon-8pm. €6, students €4.50.)*

MUSÉE CARNAVALET. Housed in Mme. de Sévigné's 16th-century mansion, this museum traces Paris's history with exhibits from prehistory to Mitterrand's *Grands Projets*. *(23 r. de Sévigné, 3ème. Ⓜ Chemin Vert. Take r. St-Gilles, which turns into r. de Parc Royal, and turn left on r. de Sévigné. ☎44 59 58 58; www.paris.fr/musees/musee_carnavalet. Open Tu-Su 10am-6pm. Last entry 5:15pm. Free.)*

MAISON DE BALZAC. In this three-story hillside *maison*, home of Honoré de Balzac from 1840-47, visitors can view some of the author's original manuscripts. The picturesque garden is filled with flowers in the summertime. *(47 r.*

Raynouard, 16ème. Ⓜ Passy. Walk up the hill and turn left onto r. Raynouard. ☎55 74 41 80. Open Tu-Su 10am-6pm. Last entry 5:40pm. Free.)

PALAIS DE TOKYO. Recently refurbished, this large warehouse space is known as the **site création contemporaine** and is outfitted to host prominent avant-garde sculptures, video displays, and multimedia installations. Exhibits change every two or three months; be on the lookout for each exhibit's *vernissage* (private viewing) for free entrance and refreshments. *(13 av. du Président-Wilson, 16ème. Ⓜ Iéna. Follow av. du Président-Wilson with the Seine on your right. ☎47 23 54 01; www.palaisdetokyo.com. Open Tu-Su noon-midnight. Wheelchair accessible. €6, students under 26 €4.)*

ENTERTAINMENT

Pick up one of the weekly bibles of Parisian entertainment: *Pariscope* and the *Officiel des Spectacles* (both €0.40), on sale at any newsstand or *tabac*. *Pariscope* includes an English-language section. For concert listings, check the free magazine *Paris Selection*, available at tourist offices throughout the city. Free concerts are often held in churches and parks, especially during summer festivals. They are extremely popular, so plan to arrive early.

CONCERT VENUES

Le Bataclan, 50 bd. Voltaire, 11*ème* (☎43 14 35 35). Ⓜ Oberkampf. An 800-person concert space and cafe-bar that hosts the likes of Blur, Metallica, Oasis, and Prince, as well as indie rock bands. Tickets start at €15 and vary with show. Closed Aug. MC/V.

La Cigale, 120 bd. Rochechouart, 18*ème* (☎49 25 89 99; www.lacigale.fr). Ⓜ Pigalle. Seats 2000 for indie, punk, and hardcore bands. Also stages modern dance shows. Box office open M-Sa noon-showtime. Music starts 8:30pm. Tickets €20-35. MC/V.

L'Olympia, 28 bd. des Capucines, 9*ème* (☎55 27 10 00; www.olympiahall.com). Ⓜ Opéra. This 50-year-old music hall is one of Paris's oldest. The Beatles and Sinatra played here. Box office open M-Sa 9am-7pm. Tickets €25-60. MC/V.

OPERA AND THEATER

Opéra Garnier, pl. de l'Opéra, 9*ème* (☎08 92 89 90 90; www.opera-de-paris.fr). Ⓜ Opéra. Hosts symphonies, chamber music, and the Ballet de l'Opéra de Paris. Free performance on Bastille Day. Box office open M-Sa 11am-6pm. Tickets €19-64. Available 2 weeks before show; discount tickets available 1hr. before show. AmEx/MC/V.

BEACH BUMMING

In 2001, the super-fast TGV line to the Mediterranean brought Paris closer to the beach. In 2002, Mayor Bertrand Delanoë did even better: he came up with **Paris Plage,** an annual event that turns the banks of the Seine into a sun-splashed summer paradise.

From mid-July to mid-August kilometers of quai-side are covered with sand and planted with palm trees. The beaches are free and open to all, and Parisians come in droves to sunbathe by the Seine. The city provides hammocks and beach umbrellas. Ice cream carts dot the area.

The festival was such a success in its first two years that in 2004 a 20m swimming pool was thrown into the mix, perhaps to make up for the polluted and unswimmable Seine. The pool held morning aquagym classes for adults and afternoon free swims for kids. Add to that a paddling pool, changing rooms, and a humidified solarium, and Paris felt about as posh as St-Tropez.

In summer 2005, Paris Plage added a restaurant on a floating barge. With other facilities like volleyball courts and trampolines Paris Plage leaves little to complain about but—unlike its Côte d'Azur counterparts—no nude sunbathing. Ultimately, Parisians are thankful that they can still get a tan in the heart of the city—just not a seamless one.

Opéra de la Bastille, pl. de la Bastille, 12*ème* (☎08 92 69 78 68; www.opera-de-paris.fr). Ⓜ Bastille. Opera and ballet with a modern spin. Tickets (€60-105) can be purchased by Internet, mail, fax, phone (M-Sa 9am-7pm), or in person (M-Sa 11am-6:30pm). Student rush tickets for under 25 available 15min. before show. MC/V.

La Cartoucherie, rte. du Champ de Manoeuvre, 12*ème* (www.la-tempete.fr/theatre/cartoucherie.html). Ⓜ Château de Vincennes. From the station, a free shuttle departs every 15min. beginning 1hr. before performances. This 19th-century weapons factory has housed cutting-edge, socially conscious, and refreshingly democratic theater since 1970. Home to 5 collectives, 2 studios, and 7 performance spaces. Tickets €18-25.

JAZZ AND CABARET

Au Duc des Lombards, 42 r. des Lombards, 1*er* (☎42 33 22 88; www.jazzvalley.com/duc). Ⓜ Châtelet. Still the best in French jazz, with occasional American soloists and hot items in world music. 3 sets each night. Beer €5-8. Mixed drinks €9. Cover €12-23. Open M-Sa 8pm-2am. Music 9:30pm-1:30am.

Aux Trois Mailletz, 56 r. Galande, 5*ème* (☎43 54 00 79, before 5pm 43 25 96 86). Ⓜ St-Michel. Basement houses a crowded cafe featuring world music and jazz vocals. Upper floor is packed with a mix of well-dressed students and 40-somethings. Mixed drinks €12.50. F-Sa cover for club €13-19. Bar open daily 5pm-dawn.

SHOPPING

Shopping in Paris is as diverse as the city itself, from the wild clubwear near r. Etienne-Marcel to the boutiques of the Marais to the upscale designer shops of St-Germain-des-Prés. The great *soldes* (sales) of the year begin after New Year's and at the very end of June. Paris's oldest department store and the first to offer *prêt à porter* fashion, **Au Bon Marché,** 22 r. de Sèvres, 7*ème*, is now known for its high prices. Look for the high security shoe displays on the top floor. (Ⓜ Sèvres-Babylone. Open M-W and F 9:30am-7pm, Th 10am-9pm, Sa 9:30am-8pm. AmEx/MC/V.) With 18 floors of stores in three buildings, **Galeries Lafayette,** 40 bd. Haussmann, 9*ème*, is a cosmos of commerce. (Ⓜ Chaussée d'Antin. Open M-W and F-Sa 9:30am-7:30pm, Th 9:30am-9pm. AmEx/MC/V.) Not quite as chic, **Samaritaine,** 67 r. de Rivoli, on the quai du Louvre, 1*er*, fills four historic Art Deco buildings with merchandise at reasonable prices. (Ⓜ Pont Neuf, Châtelet-Les Halles. Open M-W and F-Sa 9:30am-7pm, Th 9:30am-10pm. AmEx/MC/V.)

The fabrics are trendier and cheaper in **Etienne-Marcel** and **Les Halles,** in the 1*er* and 2*ème*, than in many other parts of the city, especially around **rue Tiquetonne. Le Shop,** 3 r. d'Argout, 2*ème*, has 1200 sq. m of sleek clubwear plus a live DJ. (Ⓜ Etienne-Marcel. Open M 1-7pm, Tu-Sa 11am-7pm. AmEx/MC/V.) From Ⓜ Etienne-Marcel, walk against traffic on r. de Turbigo and go left on r. Tiquetonne to reach **Espace Kiliwatch,** 64 r. Tiquetonne, 2*ème*. This is one of Paris's most popular shops, with funky clothes, books, and furnishings. (Open M-Sa 9am-7pm. MC/V.) Shopping in the **Marais,** in the 3*ème* and 4*ème*, is a complete aesthetic experience: boutiques of all colors and flavors brighten up medieval streets. What the Marais does best is independent designer shops. Vintage stores line **rue Vieille-du-Temple, rue de Sévigné, rue Roi de Sicile,** and **rue des Rosiers.** Find your fragrance amongst the myriad all-natural scents at **L'Artisan Parfumeur,** 32 r. du Bourg Tibourg, 4*ème*.(Ⓜ Rambuteau. www.artisanparfumeur.com. Open Tu-Su 11am-7pm.) **Alternatives,** 18 r. de Roi de Sicile, 4*ème*, sells an eclectic collection of second-hand clothes. (Ⓜ St-Paul. ☎42 78 31 50. Open Tu-Sa 11am-1pm and 2:30-7pm. MC/V.)

The **Champs-Elysées** area, in the 8*ème*, is perfect for a day of window shopping. On the **Champs-Elysées,** you can purchase everything from CDs (check out the **Virgin Megastore,** open until midnight) to perfumes to chocolates, usually until a much later hour than in the rest of Paris. Take a break and walk along **avenue Montaigne** to admire the great *couture* houses; their collections change every season but are invariably innovative, gorgeous, and jaw-droppingly expensive. The **Bastille** area , in the 11*ème* and 12*ème*, boasts some of the newest names in Paris fashion. Trendsetters hit the boutiques on **rue de Charonne** and **rue Keller.** Meanwhile, the 18*ème*, around **Montmartre,** has some of the city's most eclectic shops. Explore near **rue de Lavieuville** for funky designer wear, expecially **Spree,** 16 r. de Lavieuville, 18*ème*, is a must. (Ⓜ Abbesses. Open M 2-7pm, Tu-Sa 11am-7:30pm.)

Across the river in the **Latin Quarter,** you'll find plenty of chain stores around **boulevard St-Michel,** numerous little boutiques selling chic scarves and jewelry, as well as bookstores of all kinds. Post-intellectual, materialistic St-Germain-des-Prés, particularly the triangle bordered by **boulevard St-Germain, rue St-Sulpice,** and **rue des Sts-Pères,** is saturated with high-budget names. Dive into endless rows of trendy threads at **La Piscine,** 17 r. de Sèvres, 6*ème*, a former indoor pool. (Ⓜ Sèvres-Babylone. ☎42 22 65 52. Open M-Sa 11am-7:30pm. MC/V.)

NIGHTLIFE

CAFES AND BARS

LES HALLES AND MARAIS (1ER, 2ÈME, 3ÈME, 4ÈME)

Le Champmeslé, 4 r. Chabanais, 1*er*. Ⓜ Pyramides or Quatre Septembre. This friendly lesbian bar is Paris's oldest and most famous, though everyone is welcome. Beer €4. Mixed drinks €8. Popular cabaret show Th 10pm. Open M-Sa 2pm-2am.

Chez Richard, 37 r. Vieille-du-Temple, 4*ème*. Ⓜ Hôtel-de-Ville. A hot spot to people-watch on weekends, but low-key during the week. Happy hour 6-8pm for mixed drinks. Beer €4-6. Mixed drinks €9. Open daily 6pm-2am.

Amnésia Café, 42 r. Vieille-du-Temple, 4*ème*. Ⓜ Hôtel-de-Ville. A diverse crowd lounges on plush sofas under vintage movie posters. 1st fl. cafe, 2nd fl. bar/club. One of the top see-and-be-seen spots in the Marais. Espresso €2. Open daily 10:30am-2am.

L'Apparemment Café, 18 r. des Coutures St-Gervais, 3*ème*. Ⓜ Chemin Vert. Relaxed smoking lounge with games and vintage magazines. Beer €4. MC/V.

Banana Café, 13-15 r. de la Ferronnerie, 1*er*. Ⓜ Châtelet. With bodacious bananas covering the entrance, this popular gay bar is hard miss. Come early for 2-for-1 drinks and stay late for the go-go boys. Happy hour 6-9pm. Beer €6-7. Open daily 4pm-dawn.

LATIN QUARTER AND ST-GERMAIN (5ÈME, 6ÈME, 7ÈME)

Chez Georges, 11 r. des Canettes, 6*ème* (☎43 26 79 15). Ⓜ Mabillon. Walk down r. du Four and turn left. Time-warped upstairs wine bar and groove dungeon in the cellar are constantly crammed with 20-somethings. Beer €3.50. Wine bar open Tu-Sa noon-2am, cellar 1pm-2am. Closed Aug.

Thoumieux, 4 r. de la Comète, 7ème (☎45 51 50 40; www.thoumieux.com). Ⓜ La Tour Maubourg. A swank and smoky tapas bar specializing in a unique assortment of vodka flavors. Open M-F noon-2am, Sa 5pm-2am. Closed 2 weeks in Aug. AmEx/MC/V.

Le Caveau des Oubliettes, 52 r. Galande, 5*ème*. Ⓜ St-Michel. Head away from pl. St-Michel on quai de Montebello and turn right on r. Petit Pont, then left onto r. Galande. Take shots by a real guillotine, mellow out in the basement jazz lounge, or romp through the *caveau des oubliettes* where criminals were locked up and forgotten. Jam session M-Th and Su 10:30pm-1:30am. F-Sa concerts €7.50. Beer €4. Open daily 5pm-2am.

Le 10 Bar, 10 r. de l'Odéon, 6*ème*. Ⓜ Odéon. Walk against traffic on bd. St-Germain and make a left on r. de l'Odéon. A classic student haunt, regulars sip the famous sangria (€3) and chill out amid vintage movie posters. Jukebox plays everything from Edith Piaf to Aretha Franklin. Beer €3.50 before 10pm. Open daily 5:30pm-2am.

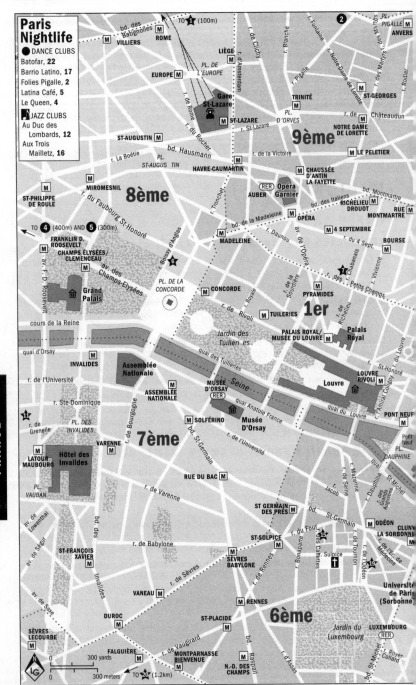

Paris Nightlife

DANCE CLUBS

Batofar, **22**
Barrio Latino, **17**
Folies Pigalle, **2**
Latina Café, **5**
Le Queen, **4**

JAZZ CLUBS

Au Duc des Lombards, **12**
Aux Trois Mailletz, **16**

bd. des Batignolles
ROME
VILLIERS
TO 1 (100m)
LIÈGE
r. d'Amsterdam
r. de Clichy
r. Blanche
r. Fontaine
PL. PIGALLE
ANVERS
r. des Martyrs
PL. DE L'EUROPE
EUROPE
r. Pigalle
r. Notre-Dame de Lorette
r. Rodier
r. de Rome
Gare St-Lazare
TRINITÉ
ST-GEORGES
ST-LAZARE
PL. D'ORVES
r. de Châteaudun
r. du Rocher
r. St-Lazare
NOTRE DAME DE LORETTE
ST-AUGUSTIN
9ème
bd. Hausmann
r. La Boétie
PL. ST-AUGUS TIN
r. de la Victoire
LE PELETIER
HAVRE-CAUMARTIN
CHAUSSÉE D'ANTIN LA FAYETTE
MIROMESNIL
ST-PHILIPPE DE ROULE
8ème
RER
Opéra Garnier
AUBER
bd. Montmartre
r. du Faubourg St-Honoré
r. Tronchet
bd. des Italiens
RICHELIEU DROUOT
RUE MONTMARTRE
bd. de la Madeleine
OPÉRA
TO 4 (400m) AND 5 (300m)
r. Daunou
4 SEPTEMBRE
MADELEINE
av. de l'Opéra
r. du 4 Sept.
BOURSE
FRANKLIN D. ROOSEVELT
CHAMPS ELYSÉES/ CLEMENCEAU
r. Boissy d'Anglas
r. Chabanais
av. des Champs-Elysées
r. Vivienne
r. des Petits Champs
av. F. D. Roosevelt
Grand Palais
PL. DE LA CONCORDE
CONCORDE
r. de la Sourdière
PYRAMIDES
r. Royale
r. de Rivoli
TUILERIES
1er
r. de Richelieu
cours de la Reine
Jardin des Tuilleri es
PALAIS ROYAL/ MUSÉE DU LOUVRE
Palais Royal
quai d'Orsay
quai des Tuilleries
r. du Louvre
INVALIDES
Assemblée Nationale
r. St-Honoré
r. de l'Université
MUSÉE D'ORSAY
Seine
LOUVRE RIVOLI
Louvre
r. de l'Amiral Coligny
ASSEMBLÉE NATIONALE
r. Ste-Dominique
quai Anatole France
quai du Louvre
PONT NEUF
r. de Grenelle
PL. DES INVALIDES
r. de Bourgogne
SOLFÉRINO
Musée D'Orsay
bd. St-Germain
r. de l'Université
Pont Neuf
PL. DAUPHINE
VARENNE
7ème
LATOUR MAUBOURG
Hôtel des Invalides
r. Mazarine
r. de Seine
quai St-Michel
RUE DU BAC
r. Jacob
r. Dauphine
r. des Grands Augustins
PL. VAUBAN
r. de Varenne
ST GERMAIN DES PRÉS
bd. St-Germain
av. de Lowenthal
bd. des Invalides
ODÉON
CLUNY LA SORBONNE
ST-SULPICE
r. du Four
r. des Canettes
r. de Tournon
av. de Ségur
r. de Babylone
r. Bonaparte
r. de l'Ec. de Médecine
ST-FRANÇOIS XAVIER
SÈVRES BABYLONE
St-Sulpice
r. de l'Odéon
r. de Rennes
r. de Sèvres
Université de Paris (Sorbonne)
VANEAU
av. de Saxe
RENNES
DUROC
ST-PLACIDE
6ème
SÈVRES LECOURBE
Jardin du Luxembourg
LUXEMBOURG
RER
bd. Raspail
r. de Vaugirard
r. Royer-Collard
FALGUIÈRE
MONTPARNASSE BIENVENUE
N.-D. DES CHAMPS
r. d'Assas
bd. St-Michel
0 300 yards
0 300 meters
TO 20 (1.2km)

FRANCE

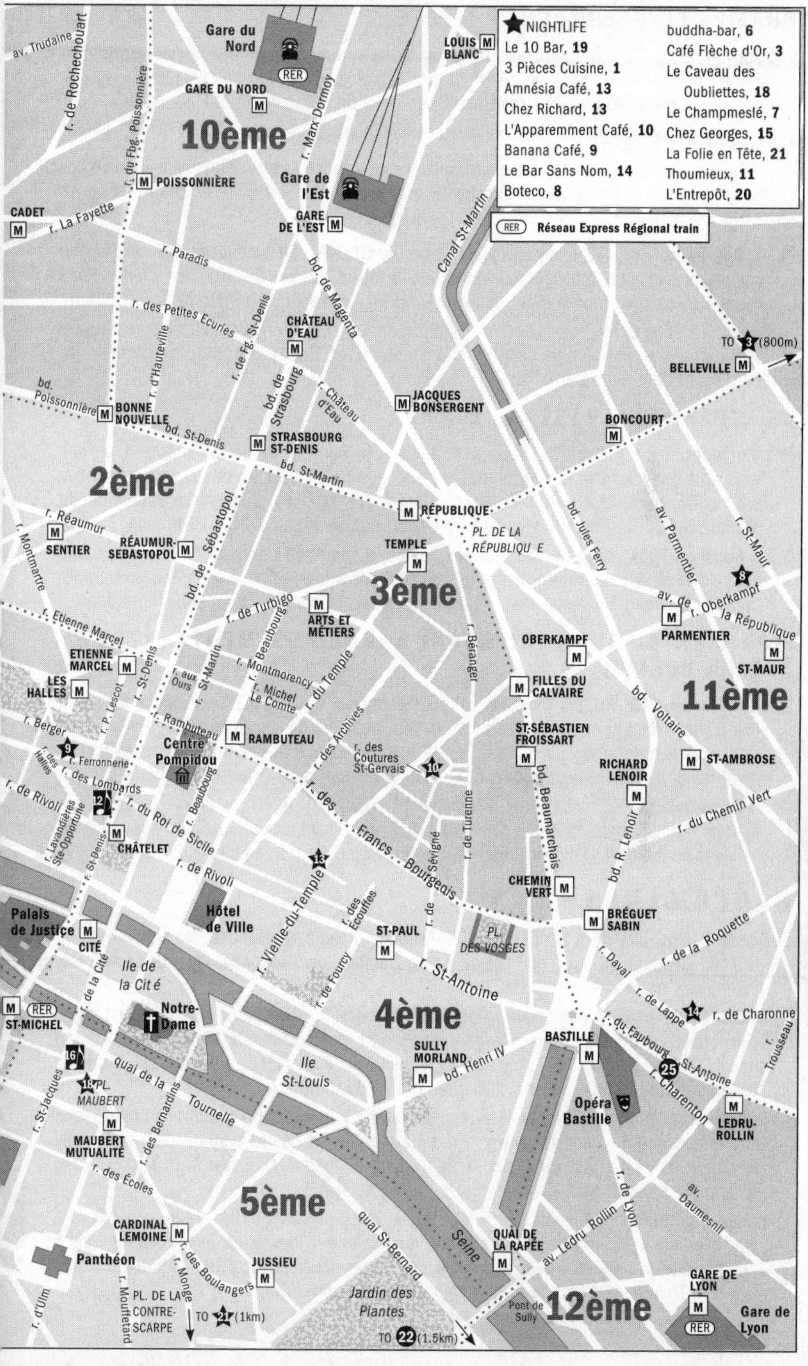

★ NIGHTLIFE

- Le 10 Bar, **19**
- 3 Pièces Cuisine, **1**
- Amnésia Café, **13**
- Chez Richard, **13**
- L'Apparemment Café, **10**
- Banana Café, **9**
- Le Bar Sans Nom, **14**
- Boteco, **8**
- buddha-bar, **6**
- Café Flèche d'Or, **3**
- Le Caveau des Oubliettes, **18**
- Le Champmeslé, **7**
- Chez Georges, **15**
- La Folie en Tête, **21**
- Thoumieux, **11**
- L'Entrepôt, **20**

RER **Réseau Express Régional train**

CHAMPS-ELYSÉES (8ÈME)

buddha-bar, 8 r. Boissy d'Anglas, 8*ème.* Ⓜ Madeleine or Concorde. The giant Buddha is almost as big as this bar's ego. Perfect for people-watching, join the wealthy, beautiful, and pretentious sipping €12 martinis. Open daily 6pm-2am, also M-F noon-3pm.

BASTILLE (11ÈME)

Bar-hoppers spill out onto the narrow lane of **rue de Lappe.** Happy hour ranges from 6-9pm, and promises cheap mixed drinks (around €4.50) and cheaper beers (around €3.50).

Le Bar Sans Nom, 49 r. de Lappe, 11*ème.* Ⓜ Bastille. Seductive lounge swathed in shimmering fabrics. Most famous for creative mixed drinks (€8.50). Don't leave Paris without trying their mojito (€8.50). Beer €5-6.20. Shots €6.20. Open M-Sa 7pm-2am.

Boteco, 131 r. Oberkampf, 11*ème.* Ⓜ Parmentier. A popular Brazilian bar-restaurant with trendy waitstaff, jungle decor, and Amazonian art. Happy hour 6-9pm (mixed drinks €4). Open daily 9am-2am.

MONTPARNASSE (13ÈME, 14ÈME)

L'Entrepôt, 7-9 r. Francis de Pressensé, 14*ème.* Ⓜ Pernety. Cinema, restaurant, art gallery, and bar prove that intellectualism and good times go together. Concerts F-Sa; around €5. Beer €2.50. Su brunch 11:30am-4:30pm (€15). Open M-Sa 9am-midnight or later, Su 11:30am-midnight. Kitchen open noon-3pm and 7:30-11:30pm.

La Folie en Tête, 33 r. de la Butte-aux-Cailles, 13*ème.* Ⓜ Corvisart. World music and exotic instruments line the walls of this beaten-up, wood-fronted hole-in-the-wall. Sept.-June Sa crowded concerts (€8). Happy hour 6-8pm. Beer €3. Open M-Sa 6pm-2am.

MONTMARTRE AND PERIPHERAL ARRONDISSEMENTS (17ÈME, 18ÈME, 20ÈME)

Café Flèche d'Or, 102bis r. de Bagnolet, 20*ème* (☎43 72 04 23; www.flechedor.com). The perfect chill spot, with friendly staff and local bands. Look for a large "Ceinture" sign over the entrance. Live music every night. Restaurant serving traditional French favorites in the back. Cover up to €10. Beer €4. Open daily 10am-2am. MC/V.

3 Pièces Cuisine, 25 r. de Chéroy, 17*ème* (☎44 90 85 10). Ⓜ Villiers. From r. de Lévis, turn right on r. des Dames, its at the corner of r. de Chéroy. Laidback atmosphere with intriguing collages on the wall. Non-smoking section. Margarita €7.50. Open daily noon-2am. MC/V.

DANCE CLUBS

Barrio Latino, 46/48 r. du Faubourg St-Antoine, 12*ème.* Ⓜ Bastille. No wallflowers on this hot Latin dance floor, and not an empty barstool on weekends. Weekend cover €8. Open daily noon-2am. AmEx/MC/V.

Latina Café, 114 av. des Champs-Elysées. Ⓜ George V. Draws one of the largest nightclub crowds on the Champs with energetic world music. Drinks €10-12. Cover women free M-Th and Su; men €7, includes 1 drink. F-Sa cover €16, includes 1st 2 drinks. Cafe open daily 7:30pm-2am; club open daily 10am-5am.

Le Queen, 102 av. des Champs-Elysées. Ⓜ George V. Undeniably the queen of gay clubs in Paris, where hipsters get down to the state-of-the-art sound system. Women warmly welcome. M disco (and unofficial straight night). Drinks €10. Cover M-Th and Su €14, includes 1 drink; F-Sa €20. Open daily midnight-dawn.

Folies Pigalle, 11 pl. Pigalle, 9*ème.* Ⓜ Pigalle. Flashing lights in the shape of a scantily-clad woman welcomes customers to the largest and wildest club in the sleazy Pigalle neighborhood. Very crowded, even at 4am. Drinks €10. Cover €20, includes 1 drink. Open Tu-Th midnight-6am, F-Sa midnight-noon, Su 5pm-6am.

Batofar, facing 11 quai François-Mauriac, 13*ème*. Ⓜ Quai-de-la-Gare. Facing the river, walk right along the quai; Batofar has the red lights. This barge/bar/club has made it big with the electronic music crowd. Cover €7-10, usually includes 1 drink. Open Tu-Th 9pm-3am, F-Sa until 4am; hours vary for special events.

DAYTRIPS FROM PARIS

VERSAILLES. Louis XIV, the Sun King, built and held court at Versailles's extraordinary palace, 12km west of Paris. The chateau embodies the extravagance of the Old Regime, especially in the **Hall of Mirrors** (under renovation until 2007; only portions are open to visitors), the antique-furnished **Queen's Bedchamber,** and fountain-filled **gardens.** Most visitors enter at **Entrance A,** on the right-hand side in the north wing, or **Entrance C,** in the archway to the left, where you can pick up audio tours. **Entrance B** is for groups; **Entrance D** is where tours with a live guide begin; and **Entrance H** is for those in wheelchairs. (Info ☎01 30 83 76 79. Chateau open Tu-Su Apr.-Oct. 9am-6:30pm; Nov.-Mar. 9am-5:30pm. Gardens open dawn-dusk. 1-2hr. tours. Chateau €7.50, after 3:30pm €5.30. Gardens €3, under 18 and after 6pm free. Audio tours €4. Tours €4.) A **shuttle** (round-trip €5) runs behind the palace to Louis's hideaways, the **Grand** and **Petit Trianons,** and to Marie Antoinette's peasant fantasy, the **Hameau.** (Both Trianons open Tu-Sa Apr.-Oct. noon-6:30pm; Nov.-Mar. noon-5:30pm. €5, after 3:30pm €3.) Take any RER C5 **train** beginning with a "V" from Ⓜ Invalides to the Versailles Rive Gauche station (30-40min., every 15min., round-trip €5.20). Buy your RER ticket before getting to the platform; a metro ticket is useless at Versailles.

CHARTRES. Chartres's phenomenal cathedral is one of the most beautiful surviving creations of the Middle Ages. Arguably the finest example of early Gothic architecture in Europe, the cathedral retains several of its original 12th-century stained-glass windows, many featuring the stunning color, "Chartres blue." The rest of the windows and the magnificent sculptures on the main portals date from the 13th century, as does the carved floor in the rear of the nave. You can enter the 9th-century **crypt** only from La Crypte, opposite the cathedral's south entrance. (☎02 37 21 75 02; www.cathedrale-chartres.com. Open daily Easter-Oct. 8am-8pm; Nov.-Easter 8:30am-7pm. Closed to tourists during mass. North Tower open May-Aug. M-Sa 9:30am-noon and 2-5:30pm, Su 2-5:30pm; Sept.-Apr. closes at 4:30pm. Cathedral free. Tower €4.10, Sept.-Apr. 1st Su of the month free.) **Trains** run from Paris's Gare Montparnasse (1hr.; 10 per day; round-trip €25, under 26 €19). From the station, walk straight, turn left into the pl. de Châtelet, right on r. Ste-Même, and left on r. Jean Moulin.

NORMANDY (NORMANDIE)

Fertile Normandy is a land of fields, fishing villages, and cathedrals. Invasions have twice secured the region's place in military history: in 1066, William of Normandy conquered England; on D-Day, June 6, 1944, Allied armies began the liberation of France on Normandy's beaches.

ROUEN ☎02 35

However sharply literature's most famous desperate housewife, Madame Bovary, may have criticized Rouen, Flaubert's hometown (pop. 106,000) is no provincial hamlet. The site of Joan of Arc's 1431 execution, Rouen continues to entrance artists, writers, and a younger crowd with its splendid Gothic cathedrals and *vieille ville*. The most famous of Rouen's "hundred spires" belong to the **Cathédrale de Notre-Dame,** in pl. de la Cathédrale; one of them, standing at 151m, is the tallest in France. Art lovers may also recognize the cathedral's facade from Monet's celebrated studies of light. (Open M 2-7pm, Tu-Sa 7:45am-7pm, Su 8am-6pm.) Combining the disparate themes of Flaubert, who was raised on the premises, and the history of medicine, the **Musée Flaubert et d'Histoire de la Médicine,** 51 r. de Lecat, down r. de Crosne from pl. de Vieux-Marché, houses a large collection of bizarre paraphernalia on both subjects. (☎15 59 95. Open Tu 10am-6pm, W-Sa 10am-noon and 2-6pm. €2.20, ages 18-25 €1.50, under 18 free.) The **Musée des Beaux-Arts,** 26bis r. Jean Lecanuet, down r. Jeanne d'Arc from the train station, houses a worthwhile collection of 16th- to 20th-century art, including works by Monet and Renoir. (☎71 28 40. Open M and W-Su 10am-6pm. €3, ages 18-25 €2, under 18 free.)

Hôtel Solférino ❷, 51 r. Jean Lecanuet, is between the train station and the center of town. (☎71 10 07. Breakfast €5. Singles €25, with shower €28; doubles €28/32. MC/V.) Cheap eateries crowd **place du Vieux-Marché** and the **Gros Horloge** area. A popular on-the-go lunch option for locals, **Estival Eric ❶,** 23 allée Eugène Delacroix, between the Musée des Beaux-Arts and the Palais de Justice, serves 32 different types of fresh bread. (☎98 28 58. Open M-Sa 7am-7pm. MC/V.) A **Monoprix** supermarket is at 73 r. du Gros Horloge. (Open M-Sa 8:30am-9pm.) **Trains** leave r. Jeanne d'Arc, on pl. Bernard Tissot, for Lille (3hr., 3 per day, €27) and Paris (1½hr., every hr., €18). From the station, walk down r. Jeanne d'Arc and turn left on r. du Gros Horloge to reach the **tourist office,** 25 pl. de la Cathédrale. (☎02 32 08 32 40; www.rouentourisme.com. Open May-Sept. M-Sa 9am-7pm, Su 9:30am-12:30pm and 2-6pm; Oct.-Apr. M-Sa 9am-6pm, Su 10am-1pm.) **Postal Code:** 76000.

CAEN ☎02 31

Although Allied bombing leveled three-quarters of its buildings during WWII, Caen (pop. 113,000) has skillfully rebuilt itself into an active university town.

TRANSPORTATION AND PRACTICAL INFORMATION. Trains run to: Paris (2¼hr., 12 per day, €26.20); Rennes (3hr., 2 per day, €27.30); Rouen (2hr., 8 per day, €19.40); Tours (3½hr., 3 per day, €28.40). Bus Verts (☎08 10 21 42 14) **buses** cover the beaches and the rest of Normandy. The **tourist office,** pl. St-Pierre, offers free maps. (☎27 14 14; www.caen.fr/tourisme. Open July-Aug. M-Sa 9am-7pm, Su 10am-1pm and 2-5pm; Apr.-June and Sept. M-Sa 9:30am-6:30pm, Su 10am-1pm; Oct.-Mar. M-Sa 9:30am-1pm and 2-6pm, Su 10am-1pm.) **Postal Code:** 14000.

ACCOMMODATIONS AND FOOD. In a great spot, **Hôtel de la Paix ❷,** 14 r. Neuve-St-Jean, off av. du 6 Juin, is a stone's throw from the chateau. Rooms decorated in bright colors, some with balconies. (☎86 18 99; fax 38 20 74. Breakfast €5. Reception 24hr. Singles €26, with shower €29, with toilet €32; doubles €29/35/37; triples €37/43/45; quads with shower €53. Extra bed €8. MC/V.) Ethnic restaurants, *crêperies*, and *brasseries* are near the chateau and between **Place Courtonne, Eglise St-Pierre,** and **Eglise St-Jean.** Get your groceries at **Monoprix,** 45 bd. du Maréchal Leclerc. (Open M-Th and Sa 9am-8:30pm, F 9am-9pm.)

SIGHTS AND NIGHTLIFE. Caen's biggest draw is the **Mémorial de Caen,** a powerful, tasteful, and creative exploration of the "failure of peace" and the modern prospects for global harmony. Take bus #2 to Mémorial. (☎06 06 44; www.memorial-caen.fr. Open daily mid-July to late Aug. 9am-8pm; early Feb. to mid-July and late Aug. to Oct. 9am-7pm; mid-Jan. to early Feb. and Nov.-Dec. 9am-6pm. Closed first 2 weeks in Jan. Last entry 1¼hr. before closing. €16.50-17.50; students and ages 10-18 €14-16.) The ruins of William the Conqueror's enormous **chateau** sprawl above the center of town. (☎27 14 14; www.chateau.caen.fr. Open daily May-Sept. 6am-1am; Oct.-Apr. 6am-7:30pm. July-Aug. tours M-Sa in French 11am, English-language 3pm. Chateau free. Tours €4, students €3.50.) The **Musée de Normandie,** within the chateau grounds on the left, traces the cultural evolution of people living on Norman soil from the beginning of civilization to the present. (☎30 47 60. www.musee-de-normandie.caen.fr. Open M, W-Su 9:30am-6pm. Free.) The **Musée des Beaux-Arts de Caen,** inside the chateau to the right, is an immense complex housing a collection of 600 works from the 17th-century Classical and Baroque periods. (☎30 47 70; www.ville-caen.fr/mba. Open daily 9:30am-6pm. Free.) Begun in 1066, the **Abbaye-aux-Hommes,** at Esplanade J.M. Louvel off r. Guillaume le Conquérant, functioned as a boys' school and a shelter for 10,000 of the town's inhabitants during WWII; it is now the town hall. (☎30 42 81. Required 1½hr. tours daily at 9:30, 11am, 2:30, 4pm; meet in lobby. €2, students €1, under 18 free. Su free.) The adjacent **Église St-Etienne,** whose 11th-century facade and nave are the oldest parts of the complex, contains William's tomb—home only to the monarch's right femur since pillaging during the Wars of Religion. (Open daily 8:15am-12:30pm and 1:30-7:30pm.) At night Caen's already busy streets turn boisterous; well-attended bars and clubs populate **rue de Bras, rue des Croisiers, quai Vendeuvre,** and **rue St-Pierre.**

BAYEUX ☎02 31

Relatively unharmed by WWII, beautiful Bayeux (pop. 15,000) is an ideal base for exploring the nearby D-Day beaches. Visitors should not miss the 900-year-old **Tapisserie de Bayeux,** 70m of embroidery depicting William the Conqueror's invasion of England. The tapestry is displayed in the **Centre Guillaume le Conquérant,** on r. de Nesmond. (Open daily May-Aug. 9am-7pm; mid-Mar. to Apr. and Sept.-Oct. 9am-6:30pm; Nov. to mid-Mar. 9:30am-12:30pm and 2-6pm. Last entrance 45min. before closing. €7.50, students €3.) Nearby is the original home of the tapestry, the extraordinary **Cathédrale Notre-Dame.** (Open daily July-Sept. 8:30am-7pm; Oct.-Dec. 8:30am-6pm; Jan.-Mar. 9am-5pm; Apr.-June 8am-6pm. French-language tours of the old city, including access to the labyrinth and treasury, daily June-Aug. €4.) The **Musée de la Bataille de Normandie,** bd. Fabian Ware, completely remodeled for the 60th anniversary of the battle, recounts the D-Day landing and subsequent 76-day battle. (☎51 46 90. Open daily May to mid-Sept. 9:30am-6:30pm, last entrance 5:30pm; mid-Sept. to Apr. 10am-12:30pm and 2-6pm, last entrances noon and 5pm. Closed last 2 weeks in Jan. English-language film about every 2hr. €6, students €4.)

From the tourist office, turn right onto r. St-Martin, follow through several name changes, and turn left onto r. Général de Dais for the **Family Home/Auberge de Jeunesse (HI) ❷,** 39 r. Général de Dais. (☎92 15 22; www.fuaj.org. Dorms €20. €2 HI discount. Cash only.) Turn right onto r. Genas Duhomme from r. St-Martin coming from the tourist office, and continue on av. de la Vallée des Prés. Turn right onto bd. d'Eindhoven to get to **Camping Municipal ❶,** on the right. (☎92 08 43. Open May-Sept. Tent sites €6.75, extra person €3.) **Marché Plus** is up the pedestrian walkway from the tourist office. (Open M-Sa 7am-9pm, Su 8:30am-12:30pm.) **Trains** (☎92 80 50) leave pl. de la Gare for Caen (20min., 15 per day, €7.90) and Paris (2½hr., 12 per day, €30). To reach the **tourist office,** pont St-Jean, turn left onto bd. Sadi-Carnot, go right at the roundabout, continue up r. Larcher toward the cathedral, then turn right on r. St-Martin. The office is at the edge of the pedestrian walkway. (☎51 28 28; www.bayeux-bessin-tourism.com. Open June-Aug. M-Sa 9am-7pm, Su 9am-1pm and 2-6pm; low season reduced hours.) **Postal Code:** 14400.

D-DAY BEACHES

On June 6, 1944, over one million Allied soldiers invaded the beaches of Normandy leading to the liberation of France and the downfall of Nazi Europe. Today, reminders of that first devastating battle can be seen in the somber gravestones, remnants of German bunkers, and the pockmarked landscape.

The First US Infantry Division scaled 30m cliffs at the **Pointe du Hoc,** from **Utah** and **Omaha Beaches,** to capture the heavily fortified strategic stronghold of the Germans. Of the 225 men in the division, only 90 survived. The Pointe is considered a military cemetery because so many casualties remain there, crushed beneath collapsed sections of the 5m thick concrete bunkers. Often referred to as "bloody Omaha," **Omaha Beach,** next to Colleville-sur-Mer and east of the Pointe du Hoc, is the most famous of the beaches. Nothing went right at this beach on D-Day: scouts failed to detect a German presence and bombardment of the fortifications was entirely ineffective due to fog. The 9387 graves of the **American Cemetery** overlook the beach. (Open daily 9am-5pm.) Ten kilometers north of Bayeux and just east of Omaha is **Arromanches,** a small town at the center of **Gold Beach,** where the British built Port Winston in a single day to provide shelter while the Allies unloaded their supplies. The **Arromanches 360° Cinéma** combines images of modern Normandy with those of D-Day. To get there, turn left on r. de la Batterie from the museum and climb the steps to get there. (Open daily June-Aug. 9:40am-6:40pm; Sept.-May reduced hours. €4, students €3.50.)

Reaching the beaches can be difficult without a car. Some sites are accessible by **bus** from Caen and Bayeux with Bus Verts on lines #1, 3, 4 (Caen), 70, and 74 (Bayeux), as well as the special summer D-Day line which goes from Bayeux and Caen to sights on Omaha Beach. (☎08 10 21 42 14; www.busverts14.fr. Mid-June to Aug. only. All buses leave 9:20-9:40am. Tickets €1.50-17.20, depending on how far you go and how many times you get off.)

MONT-ST-MICHEL ☎02 33

Regarded as a paradise in the Middle Ages, the fortified island of Mont-St-Michel is a dazzling labyrinth of stone arches, spires, and stairways that climb up to the **abbey.** Adjacent to the abbey church, **La Merveille** (the Marvel), a 13th-century Gothic monastery, encloses a seemingly endless web of corridors and chambers. (Open daily May-Aug. 9am-7pm; Sept.-Apr. 9:30am-6pm. €8, ages 18-25 €5.) Hotels on Mont-St-Michel are expensive, starting at €50 per night. The cheapest beds are at the **Centre Duguesclin (HI) ❶,** r. du Général Patton, Pontorson. (☎/fax 60 18 65. Dorms €9.50. €1 HI discount. Cash only.) The Mont is most stunning at night, but plan ahead; since there's no late-night public transport off the island, consider viewing Mont-St-Michel as a daytrip via **bus.** Courriers Bretons, 104 r. Couesnon in Pontorson (☎02 99 19 70 70), runs buses from Rennes (1½hr., 1-6 per day, €3) and St-Malo (70min., 2-4 per day, €2.50). Biking from Pontorson takes about 1hr. on terrain that is relatively flat but not always bike-friendly. The path next to the Couesnon River may be the best route. The **Pontorson tourist office,** pl. de l'Eglise, helps visitors find affordable lodging. (☎60 20 65; www.mont-saint-michel-baie.com. Open July-Aug. M-F 9am-noon and 2-6pm, Sa 10am-noon and 3-6pm, Su 10am-noon; Sept.-June reduced hours.) **Postal Code:** 50170.

BRITTANY (BRETAGNE)

Lined with spectacular beaches and cliffs gnawed by the sea, Brittany fiercely maintains its Celtic heritage despite Paris's age-old efforts at assimilation. Britons fled Anglo-Saxon invaders to this beautiful peninsula between the 5th and 7th centuries, and have since defended their independence from the Franks, Normans, French, and English. Today, traditional headdresses appear at folk festivals, and lilting *Brezhoneg* (Breton) is spoken at ports in the western part of the province.

RENNES ☎02 99

The cultural capital of Brittany, Rennes (pop 206,000) has a well-deserved reputation as the party mecca of northwestern France. Ethnic eateries, colorful nightspots, and crowds of university students lend interest to the picturesque cobblestones and half-timbered houses of the *vieille ville.*

TRANSPORTATION AND PRACTICAL INFORMATION. Trains leave pl. de la Gare (☎29 11 92) for: Caen (3hr., 8 per day, €29); Paris (3hr., every hr., €49); St-Malo (1hr., 15 per day, €12); Tours (2½-3hr., every 2-3hr., €32) via Le Mans. **Buses** go from 16 pl. de la Gare to Angers (2½-3hr., 2 per day, €13) and Mont-St-Michel (1½hr., 3-4 per day, €12). The **metro** line uses the same ticket (€1.10, day pass €3, *carnet* of 10 €8.40). To get from the train station to the **tourist office,** 11 r. St-Yves, take av. Jean Janvier to quai Chateaubriand. Turn left and walk through pl. de la République, turn right on r. George Dottin, then turn right again on r. St-Yves. (☎67 11 11; www.tourisme-rennes.com. Open Apr.-Sept. M-Sa 9am-7pm, Su 11am-6pm; Oct.-Mar. M-Sa 9am-6pm, Su 11am-6pm.) Access the **Internet** at **Neurogame,** 2 r. de Dinan. (☎65 53 85; www.neurogame.com. €3 per hr. Open July-Aug. M-Sa noon-2am, Su 2-10pm; Sept.-June daily 10am-1am.) **Postal Code:** 35000.

ACCOMMODATIONS AND FOOD. The **Auberge de Jeunesse (HI) ❶,** 10-12 Canal St-Martin, has simple rooms. Take the metro (dir.: Kennedy) to Ste-Anne. Follow r. de St-Malo downhill; the hostel will be on your right. (☎33 22 33; rennes@fuaj.org. Breakfast included. Reception 7am-11pm. Dorms €14. AmEx/MC/V.) **Hôtel Maréchal Joffre ❷,** 6 r. Maréchal Joffre, has small, cheerful, and quiet rooms over an Asian lunch counter on a busy street. (☎79 37 74. Breakfast €5. Reception 24hr. Singles €23.50-32.50; doubles €37; triples €42.50. MC/V.) **Rue St-Malo** has many ethnic restaurants, while the *vieille ville* boasts more traditional brasseries and cheap kebab stands. In general, the best food is found on the outskirts, north and east of the city center, around **rue St-Georges** and the **place de Lices.** Organic vegetarian sandwiches (€6) and *menus* (€12-18) attract patrons to **Le St-Germain des Champs (Restaurant Végétarien-Biologique) ❸,** 12 r. du Vau St-Germain. (Open Tu-Sa noon-2:30pm, F-Sa also 7-10pm. MC/V.) **Crêperie des Portes Mordelaises ❶,** 6 r. des Portes Mordelaises, is one of the best *crêperies* in the city, as long lines of students attest. (☎30 57 40. *Galettes* and crepes €3-11. Salads €2-7.50. Open daily 11:45am-2pm and 6:45-11pm. MC/V.) A **Champion** supermarket is in the basement of a mall on r. d'Isly, near the train station. (Open M-Sa 9am-8pm.)

SIGHTS AND ENTERTAINMENT. Rennes's *vieille ville* is peppered with medieval architecture, particularly on **rue de la Psalette** and **rue St-Guillaume.** At the end of r. St-Guillaume, turn left onto r. de la Monnaie to visit the **Cathédrale St-Pierre,** founded in 1787 on a site previously occupied by a pagan temple, a Roman church, and a Gothic cathedral. The center of attention is the intricately carved altarpiece depicting the life of the Virgin. (Open daily 9:30am-noon and 3-6pm.) Across the street, the **Portes Mordelaises** are the former entrances to the city and the last vestiges of its medieval walls. The **Musée des Beaux-Arts,** 20 quai Emile Zola, houses a small, varied collection, including a few works by Picasso and Gauguin. (☎28 55 85 40. Open Tu-Su 10am-noon and 2-6pm. €4.10, students €2.10, under 18 free.) Across the river and up r. Gambetta is the lush **Jardin du Thabor,** ranked among the most beautiful gardens in France. Concerts are often held here and a gallery on the northern side exhibits local artwork on a rotating basis. (☎38 05 99. Open daily June-Aug. 7:15am-9:30pm; Sept.-June 7:30am-6pm.)

With enough bars for a city twice its size and clubs that draw students from Paris and beyond, Rennes is a partygoer's weekend mecca, more so during the school year. Look for action in **place Ste-Anne, place St-Michel, place de Lices,** and the radiating streets. **Le Zing,** 5 pl. des Lices, packs two floors and four bars with the young and beautiful. (☎79 64 60. Open daily from 3pm, busy midnight-2am. AmEx/MC/V.) **Delicatessen,** 7 allée Rallier du Baty, around the corner from pl. St-Michel in a former prison, has swapped jailhouse bars for dance cages to become one of Rennes's hottest clubs. (Cover €5-14. Open Tu-Sa midnight-5am.)

ST-MALO ☎02 99

St-Malo (pop. 52,000) merges all the best of northern France, with miles of sandy beaches, imposing ramparts and towers guarding a walled *vieille ville*, countless *crêperies*, boutiques, and cafes, and a cosmopolitan worldliness that livens days of sun worship with international festivals, rock concerts, and an active art scene. East of the walled city is **Grande Plage,** the town's largest and longest beach. The slightly more secluded **Plage de Bon Secours** lies to the west and features the curious **Piscine de Bon-Secours,** three cement walls that hold in a pool's worth of warm salt water even when the tide recedes. The best view of St-Malo is from its **ramparts,** which once kept out invaders but now attract tourists in droves. All entrances to the city have stairs leading up to the old walls; the view from the north side reveals a sea speckled with islands, including the **Fort National,** the **Grand Bé,** and the **Petit Bé,** all of which can be reached on foot at low tide.

Auberge de Jeunesse (HI) ❶, 37 av. du Révérend Père Umbricht, has 248 beds near the beach. From the train station, take bus #5 (dir.: Paramé, Davier or Rothéneuf) to Auberge de Jeunesse (last bus 7:30pm) or bus #11 (July to late Aug., 1 per hr. 8am-11:30pm) from St-Vincent or the tourist office. By foot from the station (30min.), take the first right and go straight from the roundabout onto av. de Moka. Turn right on av. Pasteur, which becomes av. du Révérend Père Umbricht; keep right at the "Auberge de Jeunesse" sign. (☎40 29 80. Reception M-F 8:30am-10pm, Sa-Su 8:45am-10pm. Dorms €13.40-16.20.) The best eateries lie close to the center of the *vieille ville*. Try **La Brigantine ❶,** 13 r. de Dinan. (☎56 82 82. *Galettes* €2-8. Crepes €1.50-6. Open M and Th-F 11am-3pm and 6:30-8pm, Sa-Su noon-11pm. MC/V.) **Marché Plus,** 9 r. St-Vincent, is near the Porte St-Vincent entrance within the city walls. (Open M-Sa 7am-9pm, Su 9am-1pm.) **Trains** run from sq. Sean Coquelin to: Dinan (1hr., 4 per day, €7.90); Paris (5hr., 10 per day, €55.50); Rennes (1hr., 7-15 per day, €11.60). From the station, cross bd. de la République and follow av. Louis Martin to esplanade St-Vincent for the **tourist office,** near the *vieille ville*'s entrance. (☎56 64 48; www.saint-malo-tourisme.com. Open July-Aug. M-Sa 9am-7:30pm, Su 10am-6pm; low season reduced hours.) **Postal Code:** 35400.

DINAN ☎02 96

Perhaps the best-preserved medieval town in Brittany, the cobblestone streets of Dinan (pop. 10,000) are lined with 15th-century houses inhabited by traditional artisans. On the ramparts, the 13th-century **Porte du Guichet** is the entrance to the **Château de Dinan,** which has served as a military stronghold, residence, and prison. Included in the ticket is admission to the 15th-century **Tour de Coëtquen,** which houses a collection of medieval sculptures. (Open June-Sept. daily 10am-6:30pm; low season reduced hours. €4, ages 12-18 €1.60.) On the ramparts behind the chateau are the **Jardins "des Petits Diables" du Val Cocherel,** which hold a chessboard scaled for life-sized pieces. (Open daily 8am-7:30pm; Nov.-Mar. closed Su mornings.) A long, picturesque walk down the steep r. du Petit Fort will lead you to the **Maison d'Artiste de la Grande Vigne,** 103 r. du Quai. This former home of painter Yvonne Jean-Haffen (1895-1993) is a work of art, with exhibitions of her work, murals adorning the walls, and a beautiful hillside garden. (☎87 90 80. Open daily July-Aug. 10:30am-6pm; Sept.-June reduced hours. €2.70, students €1.70.)

To reach the **Auberge de Jeunesse (HI) ❷,** in Vallée de la Fontaine-des-Eaux, turn left from the station and cross the tracks, then turn right, and follow the tracks downhill for 1km before turning right again; it will be on your right. (☎39 10 83. Reception July-Aug. 8am-noon and 5-9pm; low season reduced hours. Dorms €15.25, under 26 €10.70. MC/V.) **Rue de la Cordonnerie** and **place des Merciers** have inexpensive *brasseries*. A **Monoprix** supermarket is at 7 pl. du Marchix. (Open M-Sa 9am-7:30pm.) **Trains** run from pl. du 11 Novembre 1918 to

FRANCE

Paris (3hr., 8 per day, €46.20) and Rennes (1hr., 8 per day, €8.80). To get to the **tourist office,** 9 r. du Château, bear left across pl. du 11 Novembre 1918 onto r. Carnot, turn right on r. Thiers, then left into the *vieille ville*, and bear right onto r. du Marchix, which becomes r. de la Ferronnerie; it will be on your right. (☎87 69 76; www.dinan-tourisme.com. Open July-Aug. M-Sa 9am-7pm, Su 10am-12:30pm and 2:30-6pm; Sept.-June M-Sa 9am-12:30pm and 2-6pm.) **Postal Code:** 22100.

QUIMPER ☎02 98

With a central waterway crisscrossed by flower-adorned pedestrian footbridges, Quimper (kam-PAIR; pop. 63,000) has irrepressible charm to fuel its fierce Breton pride. At **Faïenceries de Quimper HB-Henriot,** r. Haute, guides lead visitors through the studios where potters and painters design each piece of the town's renowned earthenware. (☎90 09 36; www.hb-henriot.com. Open July-Aug. M-Sa 9-11:15am and 1:30-4:45pm; Sept.-June closed Sa. Tours available. €3.50.) The dual spires of the **Cathédrale St-Corentin,** built between the 13th and 15th centuries, mark the entrance to the old quarter from quai St-Corentin. (Open May-Oct. M-Sa 8:30am-noon and 1:30-6:30pm, Su 8:30am-noon and 2-6:30pm; Nov.-Apr. M-Sa 9am-noon and 1:30-6pm, Su 1:30-6pm.) The **Musée Départemental Breton,** 1 r. du Roi Gradlon, through the cathedral garden, offers exhibits on Breton history and culture. (Open daily June-Oct. 9am-6pm; Oct.-May reduced hours. €3.80, students €2.50.)

To reach the comfortable **Centre Hébergement de Quimper (HI) ❶,** 6 av. des Oiseaux, take bus #1 (dir.: Kermoysan; last bus 7:30pm) from pl. de la Résistance to Chaptal; the hostel will be up the street on your left. (☎64 97 97; quimper@fuaj.org. HI members only. Breakfast €3.30. Linen €3.10. Dorms €12.40. Cash only.) Next to the hostel, **Camping Municipal ❶,** av. des Oiseaux, offers a forested camping area only 15min. from the town center. (☎55 61 09; expo@mairie-quimper.fr. Reception June-Sept. M 1-7pm, Tu, Th 8-11am and 3-8pm, W 9am-noon, F 9-11am and 3-8pm, Sa 8am-noon and 3-8pm, Su 9-11am; Oct.-May reduced hours. Tent sites €3.85, extra person €3.15.) The **Les Halles market,** off r. Kéréon on r. St-François, has seafood, meat, and cheese. (Open Apr.-Oct. M 7am-8pm, Tu-Th 5:30am-8pm, F-Sa 5am-8pm, Su 7:30am-1pm; Nov.-Mar. reduced hours.) At night, head to the cafes near the cathedral. **Trains** go from av. de la Gare to Brest (1½hr., 4 per day, €14) and Rennes (2¼hr., 10 per day, €30). From the train station, go right onto av. de la Gare and follow it, with the river on your right, until it becomes bd. Dupleix

FRANCE FOR THE FRENCHLESS

It's common for Americans t believe that traveling throug France without speaking French i the kiss of death. When I set ou to spend 45 days in Brittany an Normandy armed with nothin more than a decent Spanis accent and a penchant for overus ing the term *dénoument* i English class, I was nervous— anticipating impatient sighs an outright disdain.

But, fellow Anglophones, tak heart: I discovered that th rumors are baseless. You can no only survive France, but trave through it inspiring goodwill, i you follow one simple rule: just *tr* to speak French. French peopl smiled when I butchered their lan guage. Then they would tur around and ignore my fellow tour ists, the ones who approache the desk in English. Once o twice, they even compliment me on my non-existent French I'm sure my gigantic smile an outpouring of *"mercis"* helped but the biggest hit was my effor with the language—even thoug my knowledge was limited t basics like *bonjour, combien, j voudrais,* and *oui.* That famou French scorn is directed at peopl who assume that everyon speaks English. Even if you're no quite speaking like Gérard Depar dieu by the end of your trip, a li tle practice with your phraseboo (p. 1059) will get you a long way.

—*Julia Reischel*

and leads to pl. de la Résistance. The **tourist office,** 7 r. de la Déesse, is on your left. (☎53 04 05; www.quimper-tourisme.com. Open July-Aug. M-Sa 9am-7pm, Su 10am-1pm and 3-5:45pm; Sept.-June reduced hours.) **Postal Code:** 29000.

NANTES ☎02 40

Successfully shrugging off its violent past, modern Nantes (pop. 270,000), successfully blends a high-tech industry and a professional population with a large university crowd. Make sure to see the **Passage Pommeraye,** off pl. du Commerce, an unusual 19th-century shopping arcade built on three levels around a monumental staircase. (Guided visits available at the tourist office.) Gothic vaults soar 38m in the remarkably bright **Cathédrale St-Pierre.** A complete restoration of the interior has undone the ravages of time—though it could not salvage the stained glass that shattered during WWII. (Open daily 10am-7pm.) The real draw at the **Musée des Beaux-Arts,** 10 r. Georges Clemenceau, is the daring temporary exhibit of contemporary French art on the ground floor. (Open M, W, F-Su 10am-6pm, Th until 8pm. €3.10, students €1.60; half-price daily after 4:30pm, Th 6-8pm free.)

Some of the clean rooms at **Hôtel St-Daniel ❸,** 4 r. du Bouffay, off pl. du Bouffay, overlook a garden. (☎47 41 25; www.hotel-saintdaniel.com. Breakfast €3. Reception 7:30am-10pm, closed Su 2-7pm. Singles and doubles €30, with bath €35; triples and quads with shower and toilet €50. AmEx/MC/V.) From pl. du Commerce, take tram #2 (dir.: Orvault Grand Val) to Morrhonnière and, with your back to the stop, walk right (15min.) to **Camping du Petit Port ❶,** 21 bd. du Petit Port. (☎74 47 94; www.nge-nantes.fr. Reception July-Aug. 8am-9pm; June and Sept. 8:30am-7:30pm; Oct.-May 9am-7pm. In summer, reserve in writing or arrive early in the day. Tent sites €6, extra person €2.90. MC/V.) **La Cigale ❸,** 4 pl. Graslin, is one of the most beautiful bistros in France, filled with painted tiles, huge mirrors, and wall sculptures. The food deserves equal acclaim. (☎02 51 84 94 94; www.lacigale.com. *Menus* €16.50-26.50. Brunch daily 10am-4pm €20. Open daily 7:30am-12:30am. MC/V.) **Monoprix supermarket,** 2 r. de Calvaire, is off cours des 50 Otages. (Open M-Sa 9am-9pm.) **Quartier St-Croix,** near pl. du Bouffay, has about three bars per block and as many cafes. **Trains** leave from 27 bd. de Stalingrad for: Bordeaux (4hr., 5 per day, €40); Paris (2-4hr., every hr., €52); Rennes (2hr., 1-8 per day, €20). The **tourist office,** 3 cours Olivier de Clisson, has excellent maps and a free self-guided walking tour. (☎08 92 46 40 44; www.nantes-tourisme.com. Open M-Sa 10am-6pm.) **Postal Code:** 44038.

LOIRE VALLEY (VAL DE LOIRE)

The Loire, France's longest and most celebrated river, meanders toward the Atlantic through a valley overflowing with the fertile soil of vineyards that produce some of France's best wines. It's hardly surprising that a string of French (and English) kings chose to station themselves in opulent chateaux by these waters rather than in the commotion of their capital cities.

TRANSPORTATION

Faced with such widespread grandeur, many travelers plan overly ambitious itineraries—two chateaux a day is a reasonable goal. The city of Tours is the region's best **rail** hub. However, train schedules are often inconvenient and many chateaux aren't accessible by train. **Biking** is the best way to explore the region. Many stations distribute the invaluable *Châteaux pour Train et Vélo* booklet with train schedules and bike and **car** rental information.

ORLÉANS ☎02 38

A gateway from Paris into the Loire, Orléans (pop. 117,000) cherishes its historical connection to Joan of Arc, who marched triumphantly down **rue de Bourgogne** in 1429 after liberating the city from a seven-month British siege. Most of Orléans's highlights are near **place Sainte-Croix.** With towering buttresses and stained-glass windows that depict Joan's story, the **Cathédrale Sainte-Croix,** pl. Ste-Croix, is Orléans's crown jewel. (Open daily July-Aug. 9:15am-7pm; Sept.-June reduced hours.) The **Musée des Beaux-Arts,** 1 r. Ferdinand Rabier, has a collection of French, Italian, and Flemish works. (☎79 21 83; musee-ba@ville-orleans.fr. Open Tu-Sa 9:30am-12:15pm and 1:30-5:45pm, Su 2-6:30pm. €3, students €1.50, under 16 free.)

To reach the **Auberge de Jeunesse (HI) ❶,** 1 bd. de la Motte Sanguin, walk down r. de la République and continue as it turns into r. Royal. Turn left onto r. de Bourgogne to its end at bd. de la Motte Sanguin. Turn right and walk down two blocks. Alternatively, take bus RS (dir.: Rosette) or SY (dir.: Concyr/La Bolière) from pl. Jeanne d'Arc to Pont Bourgogne, then follow bd. de la Motte Sanguin; the hostel is on the right. (☎53 60 06. Breakfast €3.50. Reception M-F 8am-7pm, Sa-Su 9-11am and 5-7pm. Dorms €8.80. Cash only.) **Rue de Bourgogne** and **rue Sainte-Catherine** have a variety of cheap eateries and a lively bar scene at night. You'll find groceries at **Carrefour,** in the back of the mall at pl. Jeanne d'Arc. (Open M-Sa 8:30am-9pm.)

Trains arrive at the Gare d'Orléans on pl. Albert I from: Blois (30min., 15 per day, €8.80); Paris (1¼hr., 2-4 per hr., €15.90); Tours (1½hr., 2 per hr., €15.40). To reach the **tourist office,** 2 pl. de l'Etape, exit the train station onto r. de la République and continue straight until pl. du Martroi. Hook left onto r. d'Escures to pl. de l'Etape. (☎24 05 05; www.ville-orleans.fr. Open May-Sept. Tu-Sa 9:30am-1pm and 2-6pm; Oct.-Apr. reduced hours.) **Postal Code:** 45000.

BLOIS ☎02 54

Awash in a rich regal history, Blois (pop. 50,000) is one of the Loire's most charming and popular cities. Once home to monarchs Louis XII and François I, Blois's gold-trimmed chateau was the Versailles of the late 15th and early 16th centuries. Housed within are impressive collections and excellent museums: royal apartments showcase extravagant and elegant pieces; the Musée des Beaux-Arts features a gallery of 16th- to 19th-century portraits; the Musée d'Archéologie showcases locally excavated glass and ceramics; and the Musée Lapidaire exhibits sculpted pieces from nearby chateaux. (☎90 33 33. Open daily Apr.-Sept. 9am-6pm; Jan.-Mar. and Oct.-Dec. 9am-12:30pm and 2-5:30pm. €6.50, students under 25 €4.50.) The **Musée de la Résistance, de la Déportation et de la Libération,** 1 pl. de la Grève, is a powerful memorial to the French Holocaust. (☎56 07 02. Open M-F 9am-noon and 2-6pm, Sa 2-6pm. €3, students €1.)

Hôtel du Bellay ❷, 12 r. des Minimes, is at the top of porte Chartraine, two minutes above the city center. It offers comfortable rooms with colorful decor. (☎78 23 62; http://hoteldubellay.free.fr. Breakfast €4.50. Closed Jan. 5-25. Singles and doubles with sink €24, toilet €27, shower €31; triples €49-58; quads €61. MC/V.) Fragrant pâtisseries entice from **rue Denis Papin,** while **rue St-Lubin, place Poids du Roi,** and **place de la Résistance** have more dining options. An **Intermarché** supermarket is at 16 av. Gambetta. (Open M-Sa 9am-7pm.) At night, Blois lights up. Move from the cafes of pl. de la Résistance to the hip combination *discothèque,* lounge bar, and karaoke joint **Z 64,** 6 r. Mal. de Tassigny. (☎74 27 76. Mixed drinks €5-8. Open Th-Sa 10pm-5am. Tu-W, Su 10pm-4am.) **Trains** leave pl. de la Gare for: Orléans (30-50min., 14 per day, €8.80); Paris (1¾hr., 8 per day, €21.50) via Orléans; Tours (1hr., 8-13 per day, €8.50). Transports Loir-et-Cher (TLC; ☎58 55 44) sends **buses** from the station to nearby chateaux (45min.; 2 per day; €10, students €8). Or, rent a **bike** from **Amster Cycles,** 3 av. du Laigret, down the street from the train station. (☎56 07 73; www.amstercycles.com. €13 per day. Open Apr.-Oct. M-Sa 9:15am-1pm and 2-6pm, Su 10am-1:30pm and 3-6pm. MC/V.) The **tourist office** is in pl. du Château. (☎90 41 41; www.loiredeschateaux.com. Open Apr.-Sept. M-Sa 9am-7pm, Su 10am-7pm; Oct.-Mar. reduced hours.) **Postal Code:** 41000.

CHAMBORD AND CHEVERNY ☎02 54

Built between 1519 and 1545 to satisfy François I's egomania, Chambord is the largest and most extravagant of the Loire chateaux. With 440 rooms, 365 chimneys, and 83 staircases, the castle could accommodate the entire royal court—up to 10,000 people. To cement his claim, François stamped 200 of his trademark stone salamanders throughout this "hunting lodge," which also boasts a spectacular double-helix staircase designed by Leonardo da Vinci. (☎50 40 00. Open daily Apr.-Sept. 9am-6:15pm; Oct.-Mar. reduced hours. €8.50, ages 18-25 €6, under 18 free.) Take the TLC **bus** from Blois (45min.; 2 per day; €10, students €8) or **bike** south from Blois on D956 for 2-3km, and then turn left on D33 (1hr.).

Cheverny has been privately owned since 1634 by the Hurault family, whose members have served as financiers and officers to the kings of France. The chateau's magnificent furnishings include elegant tapestries and delicate Delft vases. Fans of Hergé's *Tintin* books may recognize Cheverny's Renaissance facade as the inspiration for Marlinspike, Captain Haddock's mansion. The **kennels** hold nearly 90 mixed English-Poitevin hounds who stalk stags on hunting expeditions. (☎79 96 29. Open daily July-Aug. 9:15am-6:45pm; Apr.-June and early Sept. 9:15am-6:15pm; mid-Sept. to mid-Mar. reduced hours. €6.30, students €4.20.) Cheverny is 45min. south of Blois by bike and is on the TLC bus route (see above). Travelers to Chambord or Cheverny should plan to stay in **Blois** (p. 353).

AMBOISE ☎02 47

Amboise (pop. 12,000) is guarded by the parapets of the 15th-century **chateau** that six cautious French kings called home. In the **Logis du Roi,** intricate 16th-century Gothic chairs stand over 2m tall to prevent attacks from behind. The jewel of the grounds is the **Chapelle St-Hubert,** the final resting place of **Leonardo da Vinci.** (☎57 00 98. Open daily July-Aug. 9am-7pm; Sept.-June reduced hours. €7.70, students €6.50.) Four hundred meters farther is **Clos Lucé,** where da Vinci spent his last three years. The manor's main attraction is a collection of 40 machines realized from da Vinci's visionary designs and built with the materials of his time. (☎57 62 88. Open daily July-Aug. 9am-8pm; Apr.-June and Sept.-Oct. 9am-7pm; Nov.- Dec. 9am-6pm; Jan. 10am- 5pm. €12.50, students €9. Low season €8.50/6.50.)

The **Centre International de Séjour Charles Péguy (HI)** ❶, on Île d'Or, sits on an island in the Loire. (☎30 60 90; www.ucrif.asso.fr. Breakfast €2.80. Linen €3.30. Reception M-F 10-noon and 2-8pm. Dorms €9.) Buy groceries at **Marché Plus,** 5 quai du Général de Gaulle. (Open M-Sa 7am-9pm, Su 9am-1pm.) **Trains** leave 1 r. de Jules-Ferry for: Blois (20min., 14 per day, €5.70); Orléans (1hr., 8 per day, €12.40); Paris (2¼hr., 5 per day, €24.70); Tours (20min., 27 per day, €4.70). To reach the **tourist office** on quai du Général de Gaulle, turn left outside the train station, following r. de Jules-Ferry, and cross both bridges past the residential Île d'Or. (☎57 09 28; www.amboise-valdeloire.com. Open July-Aug. M-Sa 9am-8pm, Su 10am-6pm; Sept.-June reduced hours.) **Postal Code:** 35400.

TOURS ☎02 47

On the surface, Tours (pop. 253,000) sparkles with shops and bars of a modern metropolis. Yet behind streets seeded with stores loom magnificent towers, aged homes, and fine cathedrals. Home to 30,000 students, abundant restaurants, and a booming nightlife, Balzac's birthplace is a comfortable base for chateaux hopping.

The **Cathédrale St-Gatien,** r. Jules Simon, first erected in the 4th century, combines solid Romanesque columns, delicate Gothic carvings, two Renaissance spires, and an intricate facade. (Cathedral open daily 9am-7pm. Cloister open Easter-Sept. daily 9:30am-12:30pm and 2-6pm; Oct.-Easter W-Su 9:30am-12:30pm and 2-5pm. Cathedral free. Cloister €2.50.) Jutting up from modern commercial streets, the imposing **Tours du Basilique St-Martin,** on r. Descartes, include the **Tour de l'Horloge** and **Tour de Charlemagne.** The Nouvelle Basilique St-Martin is an ornate church designed by Victor Laloux, architect of the Tours railway station and of the Musée d'Orsay in Paris. (Open Feb.-Nov. daily 8am-6:45pm. Mass daily 11am.) The **Musée du Gemmail,** 7 r. du Murier and off the northern tip of r. de Bretonneau, showcases the brilliantly colored glass mosaics unique to Tours. (Open Mar.-Oct. Tu-Su 2-6:30pm. €4.70, students €3.10.)

The **Foyer des Jeunes Travailleurs ❷,** 16 r. Bernard Palissy, houses workers, students, and backpackers in simple rooms with private baths. When exiting the tourist office, hook right into r. Bernard Pallisy for 5min. (☎60 51 51. Free Internet. Singles €17; doubles €26.) Try **place Plumereau** and **rue Colbert** for great restaurants, cafes, and bars. Hidden in a peaceful alley off the commercial r. National, **Boccacio ❷,** 9 r. Gambetta, is a gem, with sumptuous wood-oven pizzas (€6.70-12.80) and charming decor. (☎05 45 22. Lunch *menu* €12. Open M-Th noon-2pm, M and W-Th 7:30-9:30pm, F-Sa noon-2pm and 7:30-10pm. MC/V.) At night, the elegantly aged **place Plumereau** is the place to be. The most popular nightclub in town, **Le Pym's,** 170 av. de Grammont, has leopard print plush couches and two hopping dance floors. (☎66 22 22. Mixed drinks €9. Cover with drink W-Th €12, students €7 with drink, €4 without drink; F-Sa €9; after midnight €15. Su free. 18+. Open Tu-Su 11pm-4am. MC/V.) **Trains** leave pl. du Général Leclerc for Bordeaux (2½hr., 9 per day, €39.10) and Paris (2¼hr., 14 per day, €26.50; TGV 1hr., 28 per day, €49.40). To reach the **tourist office,** 78-82 r. Bernard Palissy, from the station, walk through the pleasantly green pl. du Général Leclerc, cross bd. Heurteloup, and veer to the right. The office's neon sign is in plain sight. (☎70 37 37; www.ligeris.com. Open mid-Apr. to mid-Oct. M-Sa 8:30am-7pm, Su 10am-12:30pm and 2:30-5pm; mid-Oct. to mid-Apr. reduced hours.) **Postal Code:** 37000.

CHENONCEAU AND LOCHES

Chenonceau, sometimes called the *château des dames* (castle of the ladies), owes its beauty to the series of women who designed it: first a 16th-century tax collector's wife; then Henri II's lover, Diane de Poitiers; and finally Henri's widowed wife, Catherine de Médici. The part of the chateau bridging the Cher River marked the border between occupied and Vichy France during WWII. (☎02 47 23 90 07. Open daily mid-Mar. to mid-Sept. 9am-7pm; low season reduced hours. €8, students €6.50.) **Trains** from Tours roll into the station in front of the castle. (30min., 8 per day, €5.30). Fil Vert **buses** also run from Amboise (20min., 2 per day, €1.10) and Tours (1¼hr., 2 per day, €2.10).

The chateau of Loches is surrounded by a walled medieval town that merits a visit in itself. The chateau's oldest structures are the 11th-century keep and watchtowers to the north, which were converted into a state prison under Louis XI. The three-story **tower,** the floors of which have fallen out, offers fantastic panoramic views of the village below. The extravagant **Logis Royal** (Royal Lodge) honors the famous ladies who held court here, including Charles VII's lover Agnès Sorel, the first officially-declared Mistress of the King of France. (☎02 47 91 82 82. Open daily Apr.-Sept. 9:30am-7pm; Oct.-Mar. 9:30am-12:30pm and 1:30-6:30pm. Dungeon or *Logis Royal* €5, students €3.50.) **Trains** run from Tours to Loches (1hr., 13 per day, €7.30). Plan to find accommodations in **Tours** (p. 354).

FRANCE

ANGERS ☎02 41

Angers (pop. 151,000) has grown into a sophisticated city, building on its illustrious aristocratic origins. From behind the stone walls of the **Château d'Angers,** pl. Kennedy, the medieval Dukes of Anjou ruled the surrounding area, including the Anglo-Saxon island across the Channel. Inside the chateau is the 14th-century **Tapisserie de l'Apocalypse,** the world's largest tapestry. (Open daily May to mid-Sept. 9:30am-7pm; mid-Sept. to Apr. 10am-5:30pm. €7, students €4.50.) Angers's other woven masterpiece is the 1930 **Chant du Monde** (Song of the World), in the **Musée Jean Lurçat,** 4 bd. Arago. Next door, the **Musée de la Tapisserie Contemporaire** dazzles with its art. (☎24 18 45. Open mid-June to mid-Sept. daily 10am-7pm; mid-Sept. to mid-June Tu-Su 10am-noon and 2-6pm. Both museums €4, students €3.) Creator of the famous liqueur since 1849, the **Musée Cointreau** offers tours of the factory and free tastings. Take bus #7 from the train station to Cointreau. (Open daily July-Aug. 10:30am-6:30pm; low season reduced hours. €5.50.)

Hôtel de l'Univers ❸, 2 pl. de la Gare, across the street from the train station, has simple but pristine rooms. (☎88 43 58; fax 86 97 28. Breakfast €5.60. Singles and doubles €27-54. AmEx/MC/V.) Cheap food is abundant along **rue St-Laud** and **rue St-Aubin.** Grab groceries in **Galeries Lafayette,** at r. d'Alsace and pl. du Ralliement. (Open M-Sa 9:30am-7:30pm.) From r. de la Gare, **trains** leave for Paris (1-2hr., 15 per day, €43.20-55.40) and Tours (1hr., 10 per day, €14.90). **Buses** run from pl. de la République to Rennes (3hr., 2 per day, €16). To get from the station to the **tourist office,** pl. Kennedy, exit straight onto r. de la Gare, turn right at pl. de la Visitation on r. Targot, and turn left on bd. du Roi-René; the office sits on the right, across from the chateau. (☎23 50 00; www.angers-tourisme.com. Open May-Sept. M-Sa 9am-7pm, Su 10am-6pm; low season reduced hours.) **Postal Code:** 49052.

PÉRIGORD AND AQUITAINE

Périgord's green countryside is splashed with yellow sunflowers, white chalk cliffs, and plates of black truffles. First settled 150,000 years ago, the area around Les Eyzies-de-Tayac has seen the excavation of more Stone-Age artifacts than anywhere else on earth, and the prehistoric painted caves of Lascaux are the most extensive in the world. Farther south, Aquitaine grows its grapes in the world-famous vineyards of the Médoc that surround Bordeaux.

PÉRIGUEUX ☎05 53

Rich with tradition and gourmet cuisine, the lovely old quarters of Périgueux (pop. 65,000) preserve architecture from medieval and Gallo-Roman times. The towering steeple and five massive Byzantine cupolas of the **Cathédrale St-Front** dominate the city from above the Isle River. (Open daily 8am-noon and 2:30-7pm.) Just down r. St-Front, the **Musée du Périgord,** 22 cours Tourny, houses one of France's most important collections of prehistoric artifacts, including a set of 2m mammoth tusks. (☎06 40 70. Open Apr.-Sept. M and W-F 10:30am-5:30pm, Sa-Su 1-6pm; Oct.-Mar. reduced hours. €4, students €2.) The **Musée Gallo-Romain,** r. Claude Bertrand, has an intricate walkway over the excavated ruins of the *Domus de Vésone*, once the home of a wealthy Roman merchant. (☎53 00 92. Open daily July-Aug. 10am-7pm; Sept.-June reduced hours; closed Jan. €5.50. English-language audio tours €2.) Across from the train station, **Hôtel des Voyageurs ❶,** 26 r. Denis Papin, has clean, basic rooms. (☎53 17 44. Breakfast €3.50. Singles €14; doubles €16, with shower €19. MC/V.) **Au Bien Bon ❷,** 15 r. de l'Aubergerie, serves regional specialties at affordable prices. (☎09 69 91. *Plats* €9-14. Lunch *menus* €10-14. Open Tu-F noon-2pm and 7:30-10pm, Sa noon-2pm.) **Monoprix** supermarket is on pl. Bugeaud. (Open

M-Sa 8:30am-8pm.) **Trains** leave r. Denis Papin for: Bordeaux (1½hr., 12 per day, €16.30); Lyon (6-8hr., 2 per day, €46.80); Paris (4-6hr., 12 per day, €45.90). The **tourist office,** 26 pl. Francheville, has free maps. From the station, turn right on r. Denis Papin, bear left on r. des Mobiles-de-Coulmierts, which becomes r. du Président Wilson, and take the next right after the Monoprix; it will be on your left. (☎53 10 63; www.ville-perigueux.fr. Open June-Sept. M-Sa 9am-6pm, Su 10am-1pm and 2-6pm; Oct.-May M-Sa 9am-1pm and 2-6pm.) **Postal Code:** 24000.

SARLAT ☎05 53

The medieval *vieille ville* of Sarlat (pop. 11,000) is the best base for exploring the **Caves of Lascaux** (see below), but it has also been the focus of tourist and movie cameras in its own right; Gérard Depardieu's *Cyrano de Bergerac* and *Manon des Sources* were both filmed here. Sarlat's accommodations are expensive since the town's only hostel closed; the best option is to book a room at one of the *chambres d'hôtes* (€25-50; visit the tourist office for a complete list). For the true deal, the campground **Maisonneuve ❶,** 11km from Sarlat and down the river from Castelnaud on the D57, offers a cafe, a river-side swimming hole, and a base for exploring the countryside. (☎29 51 29; www.campingmaisonneuve.com. Reception 9am-10pm. Cafe 8am-11pm. Book ahead July-Aug. Open Mar.-Oct. Tent sites €11.70, extra person €4.90. *Gîte* €10.) A **Champion** supermarket is a 15min. walk from the old city on rte. de Montignac; follow av. de Selves away from the town center. (Open M-Sa 9am-7:45pm. MC/V.) **Trains** rumble from av. de la Gare to Bordeaux (2½hr., 3-4 per day, €20.60) and Périgueux (3hr., 1-2 per day, €12.30). Trans-Périgord **buses** run from pl. Pasteur to Périgueux (1½hr., 1 per day, €10.35). To reach the **tourist office,** off r. Tourny in the *centre ville*, turn left out of the train station onto av. de la Gare and take a right at the bottom of the hill onto av. Thiers, which becomes av. Général Leclerc, then r. de la République. Bear right on r. Lakanal and left on r. de la Liberté; the office is next to the cathedral. (☎31 45 45; www.ot-sarlat-perigord.fr. Open Apr.-Oct. M-Sa 9am-7pm, Su 10am-noon and 2-6pm; Nov.-Mar. M-Sa 9am-noon and 2-7pm.) **Postal Code:** 24200.

CAVES OF THE VÉZÈRES VALLEY ☎05 53

The most spectacular cave paintings ever found line the **Caves of Lascaux,** "the Sistine Chapel of prehistory," near the town of **Montignac,** 25km north of Sarlat. Discovered in 1940 by a couple of teenagers, the caves were closed to the public in 1963—the breath of millions of visitors had fostered algae and micro-stalactites that ravaged the paintings. **Lascaux II** replicates the original cave in the same pigments used 17,000 years ago. Although they may lack ancient mystery, the new caves—filled with paintings of 5m tall bulls, horses, and bison—manage to inspire a wonder all their own. The ticket office (☎51 96 23) shares a building with Montignac's **tourist office** (☎51 82 60), on pl. Bertran-de-Born. (Ticket office open 9am until sold out. Reserve tickets 1 week ahead. €8.) The **train** station nearest Montignac is at Le Lardin, 10km away. From there, you can call a **taxi** (☎50 86 61). During the academic year, CFTA (☎05 55 86 07 07) runs **buses** from Périgueux and Sarlat; call or check at the stations for times and prices. Numerous **campgrounds** dot the Vézères Valley near Montignac; the tourist office has a complete list.

At the **Grotte de Font-de-Gaume,** 1km east of **Les Eyzies-de-Tayac** on D47, 15,000-year-old friezes are still open for viewing. (☎06 86 00; www.leseyzies.com/grottes-ornees. Open mid-May to mid-Sept. M-F and Su 9am-5:30pm; mid-Sept. to mid-May reduced hours. Reserve 2-4 weeks in advance. €6.10, ages 18-25 €4.10.) The **tourist office** is on pl. de la Mairie in Les Eyzies-de-Tayac. (☎06 97 05; www.leseyzies.com. Open July-Aug. M-Sa 9am-7pm, Su 10am-noon and 2-6pm; Sept.-June reduced hours.) From Les Eyzies-de-Tayac, **trains** go to: Paris (6-8hr., 3 per day, €48.70); Périgueux (30min., 5 per day,

€6.30); Sarlat (1hr., 3 per day, €7.50). Rooms tend to be expensive—consider staying in **Périgueux.** The Demaison family runs pleasant and well-located **Chambre d'Hôte ❷,** rte. de Sarlat, 3min. outside of Les Eyzies-de-Tayac. From the train station, follow signs to Sarlat; the house is past the laundromat on the right. (☎06 91 43. Breakfast €5. Reservations required. Singles and doubles €25-36; triples and quads €48.)

BORDEAUX ☎05 56

Enveloped by emerald vineyards, Bordeaux (pop. 215,000) toasts the ruby wine that made it famous. A mecca for wine connoisseurs, this university town also has vibrant nightlife, a world-class opera house, and some of the best food in France.

TRANSPORTATION AND PRACTICAL INFORMATION. Trains leave Gare St-Jean, r. Charles Domercq, for: Lyon (8-10hr., 4 per day, €56.70); Nice (9-10hr., 2 per day, €74.10); Paris (3hr., 15-25 per day, €60.40); Toulouse (2-3hr., 11 per day, €28.40). From the train station, take tramway line B to pl. Gambetta (€1.30) and walk toward the Monument aux Girondins to reach the **tourist office,** 12 cours du 30 juillet, which arranges winery tours and books rooms. (☎00 66 00; www.bordeaux-tourisme.com. Open July-Aug. M-Sa 9am-7:30pm, Su 9:30am-6:30pm; Sept.-June reduced hours.) **Postal Code:** 33000.

ACCOMMODATIONS AND FOOD. A favorite among backpackers, **Hôtel Studio ❷,** 26 r. Huguerie, has clean, newly remodeled rooms with phone, bathroom, and cable TV. (☎48 00 14; www.hotel-bordeaux.com. Breakfast €4. Internet €2.25 per hr. Singles €16-24; doubles €20-29. MC/V.) Run by the same family, **Hôtel de la Boétie ❷,** 4 r. de la Boétie, offers bathroom, shower, and TV in every room. Check in around the corner at Hôtel Bristol, 4 r. Bouffard. (☎81 76 68; fax 81 24 72. Breakfast €4. Singles and doubles €24; triples €31. AmEx/MC/V.) The Bordelais possess a flair for food that rivals their vineyard expertise. Hunt around **rue St-Remi** and **place St-Pierre** for regional specialties: oysters, *foie gras*, and beef braised in wine sauce. Delicious dessert crepes (€3-8) at **La Crêperie ❶,** 20 r. Georges Bonnac, take the French staple to a new level. (☎51 02 33. *Galettes* €3-10. Salads €2-6.80. Open daily noon-midnight. MC/V.) Head to **Le Saint Georges ❸,** on pl. Camille Jullian, for traditional cuisine and a well-stocked cellar of local vintages. (☎44 86 33. *Menus* €17-26. Open M-Sa 8am-2am, Su 2pm-2am. MC/V.) **Auchan** supermarket is at the Centre Meriadeck on r. Claude Bonnier. (Open M-Sa 8:30am-10pm.)

FRANCE

SIGHTS AND ENTERTAINMENT. Nearly nine centuries after its consecration, the **Cathédrale St-André,** in pl. Pey-Berland, sits at the heart of Gothic Bordeaux. Its bell tower, the **Tour Pey-Berland,** rises 50m into the sky. (Cathedral open July-Aug. M 10-11:30am and 2-6:30pm, Tu-F 7:30-11:30am and 2-6:30pm, Sa 9-11:30am and 2-7pm, Su 9am-12:30pm and 2:30-8:30pm; Sept.-June closed Su afternoon. Tower open June-Sept. daily 10am-1:15pm and 2-6pm; Oct.-May Tu-Su 10am-12:30pm and 2-5:30pm. €4.60, under 25 €3.10.) Nearby, the **Musée des Beaux Arts,** 20 cours d'Albret, contains works by masters such as Carvaggio, Matisse, and Picasso. The permanent collection is held in the two buildings that frame the Hôtel de Ville; the temporary exhibits are across the street. (Open M, W-Su 11am-6pm. Permanent collection €4, permanent and temporary collections €5.50. Students and 1st Su of every month free.) For the best cityscape of Bordeaux, look down from the 114m tower of the **Eglise St-Michel.** (Tower open June-Sept. M and Sa-Su 2-7pm, Tu-F 10:30am-7pm. €2.50.) On pl. de Quinconces, the elaborate **Monument aux Girondins** commemorates Revolutionary leaders from towns bordering the Gironde who were guillotined in 1797. Bordeaux's opera house, the **Grand Théâtre,** conceals a breathtakingly intricate interior behind an austere Neoclassical facade. (☎00 85 95; www.opera-bordeaux.com. Open for tours Tu-Sa 11am-6pm. Tickets €8-70, 50% discount for students and those under 25. Tours €5, students €4.)

For an overview of Bordeaux's nightlife, check out the free *Clubs and Concerts* brochure at the tourist office. Students pack the bars in hot spots **Place de la Victoire** and **Place Gambetta.** The atmosphere is more mellow in **St-Michel,** where locals gather at cafe tables from 6pm until midnight. Popular **Le Bodegon,** on pl. de la Victoire, draws wild students with theme nights and giveaways on weekends. (Beer €2.50. Open M-Sa 7am-2am, Su 2pm-2am.) Covered in flashing lights and mirrors, the fashionable gay bar **BHV,** 4 r. de l'Hôtel de Ville, is almost always full. (Beer €3.50. W theme night. Open daily 6pm-2am.)

ST-EMILION ☎05 57

Just 35km northeast of Bordeaux, St-Emilion (pop. 2850) is home to viticulturists who have been refining their technique since Roman times. Today, they gently crush hectares of grapes to produce 23 million liters of wine annually. The medieval village itself is a pleasure to visit, and its Eglise Monolithe is the largest subterranean church in Europe. The tourist office, pl. des Créneaux, near the church tower, rents bikes (€14 per day) and offers guided tours (€9) of the local chateaux. (☎55 28 28; www.saint-emilion-tourisme.com. Open daily July-Aug. 9:30am-8pm; Sept.-June reduced hours.) Trains run from Bordeaux (35min., 4 per day, €7.20). The latest train back to Bordeaux leaves at 6:26pm—plan accordingly.

THE PAYS BASQUE AND GASCONY

South of Aquitaine, the forests recede and the mountains of Gascony rise, shielded from the Atlantic by the Basque Country. While the Gascons have long considered themselves French, the Basques still struggle to maintain their identity; some separatists see themselves as an independent people rather than a part of France or Spain. Today, people come to Gascony to be healed: millions of believers descend on Lourdes in search of miracles, while thousands of others undergo natural treatments in the hot springs of the Pyrenees.

BAYONNE ☎05 59

The pace of life in Bayonne (pop. 42,000) has not changed for centuries. Locals rise early to set up lively markets on the banks of the Nive and shop in the *vieille ville.* In the afternoon, they retreat indoors behind exposed wooden beams and colorful shutters. The **Musée Bonnat,** 5 r. Jacques Laffitte, showcases works by Bayonnais painter Léon Bonnat alongside others by Degas, van Dyck, Goya, Rembrandt, and Reubens. (Open May-Oct. M and W-Su 10am-6:30pm; Nov.-Apr. reduced hours. €5.50, students €3.) Starting the first Wednesday in August, locals let loose for five days during the **Fêtes Traditionnelles** (www.fetes-de-bayonne.com).The **Hôtel Paris-Madrid ❷,** pl. de la Gare, has large rooms and knowledgeable, English-speaking proprietors. (☎55 13 98. Breakfast €4. Reception 6am-12:30am. Singles and doubles €17-22, with shower €26, with bath €29-45; triples and quads with bath €41-45. MC/V.) A **Monoprix** supermarket is at 8 r. Orbe. (Open M-Sa 8:30am-7:30pm.) **Trains** depart from pl. de la Gare for: Biarritz (10min., 11 per day, €2.10); Bordeaux (2hr., 9 per day, €23.30); San Sebastián, Spain (1½hr., 5-6 per day, €8); Toulouse (4hr., 5 per day, €34.30). Local STAB **buses** (☎59 04 61) depart from the Hôtel de Ville for Biarritz (#1, 2, and 6; last bus M-Sa 8pm, Su 7pm; €1.20). From the train station, take the middle fork onto pl. de la République, veer right over pont St-Esprit, pass through pl. Réduit, cross pont Mayou, and turn right on r. Bernède which becomes av. Bonnat. The **tourist office,** pl. des Basques, is on the left. (☎46 01 46; www.bayonne-tourisme.com. Open July-Aug. M-Sa 9am-7pm, Su 10am-1pm; Sept.-June M-F 9am-6:30pm, Sa 10am-6pm.) **Postal Code:** 64100.

BIARRITZ ☎05 59

Once a playground for 19th-century aristocrats, Biarritz (pop. 29,000) can still make a dent in your wallet. Luckily, its sparkling **beaches** are free for both budget travelers and the rich and famous. In summer, thousands of perfect bodies soak up the sun at **Grande Plage,** while thrill-seeking surfers ride its waves. **Plage Miramar,** just to the north, is less crowded. Walk left along av. de l'Impératrice to reach the **Pointe St-Martin** for a fantastic view. Take bus #2 (dir.: Gare SNCF) to Francis Jammes to reach the **Auberge de Jeunesse (HI) ❷,** 8 r. de Chiquito de Cambo, which has an energetic, welcoming staff and a lakefront location. (☎41 76 00; aubergejeune.biarritz@wanadoo.fr. Internet €3 per hr. Dorms €17-18, €14-15 each additional night. AmEx/MC/V.) **Rue Mazagran** and **Place Clemençeau** have cheap but filling crepes and sandwiches. **Shopi** supermarket, 2 r. du Centre, is off r. Gambetta. (Open M-Sa 9am-8pm, Su 9am-12:30pm.) **Trains** (☎50 83 07) leave from Biarritz-la-Négresse, 3km from town, for: Bayonne (10min., 17 per day, €2.10); Bordeaux (2hr., 7 per day, €24.20); Paris (5hr., 5 TGV per day, €73.70). The **tourist office,** 1 sq. d'Ixelles, finds accommodations. (☎22 37 10; www.biarritz.fr. Open daily July-Aug. 8am-8pm; Sept.-June reduced hours.) **Postal Code:** 64200.

LOURDES ☎05 62

In 1858, 14-year-old Bernadette Soubirous saw the first of 18 visions of the Virgin Mary in the Massabielle Grotto in Lourdes (pop. 16,300). Today, five million people from across the globe make the pilgrimage each year. Follow av. de la Gare, turn left on bd. de la Grotte, and follow it to the right and across the River Gave to reach the **Grotte de Massabielle.** There, visitors whisper prayers, receive blessings, and carry home water from the spring where Bernadette washed her face. (No shorts or tank tops. Open daily 5am-midnight.) The **Basilique du Rosaire** and the **Upper Basilica** were built double-decker style above the grotto. The **Basilique St-Pius X,** a huge concrete echo chamber designed to resemble an overturned ship, is hidden underground. (Basilicas open daily Easter-Oct. 6am-7pm; Nov.-Easter 8am-6pm.) **Processions** depart daily from the grotto at 5pm. To get to the centrally located **Hôtel Arbizon ❶,** 37 r. des Petits Fossés, follow av. Helios away from the station, bear right under the bridge on bd. du Lapacca, take the next left uphill onto r. Basse, and turn right onto r. des Petits Fossés. (☎/fax 94 29 36. Breakfast €4. Singles €14, with shower €15; doubles €19/20; triples €24. Cash only.) The cheapest eateries are near the tourist office. Stock up at the **market** at Les Halles, pl. du Champ Commun. (Open daily 8am-1pm, every other Th until 5pm.) **Trains** leave 33 av. de la Gare for: Bayonne (2hr., 5 per day, €18.40); Bordeaux (3hr., 7 per day, €29.50); Paris (7-9hr., 5 TGV per day, €88.40); Toulouse (2½hr., 8 per day, €21.50). To reach the **tourist office,** on pl. Peyramale, turn right onto av. de la Gare, bear left onto av. Maransin, cross the bridge above bd. du Lapacca, and climb uphill. (☎42 77 40; www.lourdes-infotourisme.com. Open May-Oct. M-Sa 9am-7pm; Nov.-Apr. reduced hours.) **Postal Code:** 65100.

THE PYRENEES ☎05 62

The **Parc National des Pyrénées Occidentales** shelters hundreds of endangered species in its snow-capped mountains and lush valleys. Touch base with the friendly **Parc National Office,** Maison du Parc, pl. de la Gare, in Cauterets, before braving the wilderness. The staff has maps (€7-9) and info on the park, the 14 **hiking** trails that begin and end in Cauterets. (☎92 52 56; www.parc-pyrenees.com. Open June to mid-Sept. daily 9:30am-noon and 3-7pm; mid-Sept. to May reduced hours.) The park's trails are appropriate for a wide range of skill levels. From Cauterets, the

GR10, which intersects most other hikes in the area, winds through Luz-St-Saveur, over the mountain, and then on to Gavarnie, another day's trek up the valley (a.k.a. **circuit de Gavarnie.**) One of the most spectacular trails follows the GR10 to the turquoise **Lac de Gaube** and then to the end of the glacial valley (2hr. past the *lac*), where you can spend the night at the **Refuge des Oulettes ❶.** (☎92 62 97. Open June-Sept. Reserve two days ahead. Dorms €13.50.) Other *gîtes* (shelters) in the park, usually located in towns along the GR10, cost about €11 per night.

CAUTERETS ☎05 62

Nestled in a narrow valley on the edge of the **Parc National des Pyrénées Occidentales** is tiny, sleepy Cauterets (pop. 1300). Cauterets's sulfuric hot springs (*thermes*) have long been instruments of healing; for more info, contact **Thermes de César,** av. du Docteur Domer. (☎92 51 60. Open M-Sa 7-11:30am and 2:30-8pm.) Today, most visitors come to ski and hike. Multiple half-day **hikes** depart from a trailhead behind the Thermes de César; for more hiking info and advice, head to Parc National des Pyrénées (p.360). From the Parc National office, cross the street and turn left uphill on the footpath under the funicular depot to reach the idyllically located. **Gîte d'Etape UCJG ❶,** av. du Docteur Domer. (☎92 52 95. Open mid-June to mid-Sept. Dorms €8; tent sites and rental €6.50.) SNCF **buses** run from pl. de la Gare to Lourdes (1hr., 8 per day, €6.20). Rent **bikes** at Le Grenier, 4 av. du Mamelon Vert. (☎92 55 71. Full day €22-53, half-day €16-39. Open daily 8am-1pm and 3-8pm.) The **tourist office,** on pl. Foch, has free trail maps. (☎92 50 50; www.cauterets.com. Open July-Aug. M-Sa 9am-12:30pm and 2-7pm, Su 9am-12:30pm and 3-6pm; Sept.-June reduced hours.) **Postal Code:** 65110.

LANGUEDOC-ROUSSILLON

Occitania was once a region independent of both France and Spain, stretching from the Rhône valley to the foothills of the Pyrenees. When it was eventually integrated into France, Occitania's Cathar religion was persecuted and its language, *langue d'oc,* faded. Regional pride, however, was never lost, and Languedoc's citizens today display it with impromptu street performances, festivals, and frequent protests calling for national attention.

Roussillon, in the far southwest corner of France, was historically part of Catalunya and today its locals still identify more with Barcelona than with Paris. Many speak Catalan, a relative of the *langue d'oc,* which sounds like a hybrid of French and Spanish. Architecture, food, and nightlife all bear the marks of Spanish neighbors. Perfectly situated between the sandy coasts of the Mediterranean and the gorgeous peaks of the Pyrenees, the region has inspired the likes of Matisse and Picasso and now attracts an interesting mix of sunbathers and backpackers.

TOULOUSE ☎05 61

Vibrant Toulouse—*la ville en rose* (city in pink)—provides a change of pace from surrounding villages with its stately rose-colored architecture and a lively twenty-something scene. A rebellious city since the 12th century, Toulouse (pop. 390,000) remains a center of independent thought, pushing the frontiers of knowledge as a university town and the capital of France's aerospace industry.

TRANSPORTATION AND PRACTICAL INFORMATION. Trains leave Gare Matabiau, 64 bd. Pierre Sémard, for: Bordeaux (2-3hr., 14 per day, €27.70); Lyon (6½hr., 3-4 per day, €51); Marseille (4½hr., 8 per day, €40.60); Paris (8-9hr., 4 per day, €59.90). Eurolines, in the bus station, 68-70 bd. Pierre Sémard, sends **buses** to major European cities. (☎26 40 04; www.eurolines.fr. Open M-F 9:30am-6:30pm, Sa 9:30am-5pm.) To get from the station to the **tourist office,** r. Lafayette, in pl. Charles de Gaulle, head straight down r. de Bayard. Veer left around pl. Jeanne d'Arc and continue on r. d'Alsace-Lorraine; the office is on the right. (☎11 02 22; www.ot-toulouse.fr. Open June-Sept. M-Sa 9am-7pm, Su 10am-1pm and 2-6:15pm; Oct.-May reduced hours.) Surf the **Internet** at **Nethouse,** 1 r. des 3 Renards. (☎21 98 42. €3 per hr. Open M-Sa 9am-11pm, Su noon-6pm.) **Postal Code:** 31000.

ACCOMMODATIONS AND FOOD. To reach the spacious and charming **Hôtel des Arts ❷**, 1 bis r. Cantegril, off r. des Arts, take the metro (dir.: Basso Cambo) to pl. Esquirol. Walk down r. de Metz away from the river; r. des Arts is on the left. (☎23 36 21. Breakfast €5. Singles €23-26, with shower €29-31; doubles €28-34/32-38. MC/V.) Take bus #59 (dir.: Camping) from pl. Jeanne d'Arc to camp at **Pont de Rupé ❶,** 21 ch. du Pont de Rupé, at av. des Etats-Unis along N20 north. (☎70 07 35. €9.50 per person, extra person €3.50.) Cheap eateries on **rue du Taur,** in the student quarter, serve meals for €5.50-10. Markets (open Tu-Su 6am-1pm) line **place des Carmes, place Victor Hugo,** and **boulevard de Strasbourg.** There's a **Monoprix** supermarket at 39 r. d'Alsace-Lorraine. (Open M-Sa 9am-10pm.) Neighborhood favorite **Jour de Fête ❶,** 43 r. du Taur, is a relaxed *brasserie* with tastes as creative as the local art on its walls. (☎23 36 48. *Plat du jour* €6.70. Open daily 11am-midnight. Cash only.) Combination restaurant, art gallery, and small theater, **Le Grand Rideau ❸,** 75 r. du Taur, serves a three-course lunch (€9.10) and an evening *menu* (€16) with excellent regional dishes. (☎23 90 19. Open M noon-2pm, Tu-F noon-2pm and 7:30-10pm, Sa 7:30-10pm. Cash only.)

SIGHTS AND NIGHTLIFE. The **Capitole,** the brick palace next door to the tourist office, is Toulouse's most prominent monument. The building was once home to the bourgeois *capitouls,* who unofficially ruled the city for many years in the 12th century. (Open daily 9am-7pm. Free.) R. du Taur leads to the **Basilique St-Sernin,** the longest Romanesque structure in the world. Its **crypt** houses holy relics from the time of Charlemagne. (Church open July-Sept. M-Sa 8:30am-6:30pm, Su 8:30am-7:30pm; Oct.-June reduced hours. Crypt open July-Sept. M-Sa 10am-6pm, Su 11:30am-6pm; Oct.-June reduced hours. Church free. Crypt €2.) From pl. du Capitole, take a right on r. Romiguières, and turn left on r. Lakanal to get to the 13th-century southern Gothic **church,** where the remains of St. Thomas Aquinas are housed in an elevated tomb. (Open daily 9am-7pm. Cloister €2.20.) Just across the St-Pierre bridge, **Les Abbatoirs,** 76 allées Charles-de-Fitte, houses intermittent exhibits by up-and-coming contemporary artists in old slaughterhouses converted into a vast art space. (☎05 62 48 58 00. Open Tu-Su noon-8pm. €6.10, students €3.05.) The restored **Hôtel d'Assézat,** at pl. d'Assézat on r. de Metz, houses the **Fondation Bemberg,** a modest collection of Bonnards, Gauguins, and Pissarros. (Open Tu and F-Su 10am-12:30pm and 1:30-6pm, Th 10am-12:30pm and 1:30-9pm. €4.60, students €2.75.) Numerous cafes flank **place St-Georges** and **place du Capitole,** and late-night bars line **rue de la Colombette** and **rue des Filatiers.** For cheap drinks and a lively atmosphere, try **Café Populaire,** 9 r. de la Colombette, where you can polish off 13 glasses of beer for only €19, €13 on Mondays. (☎63 07 00. Open M-F 9pm-2am, Sa 2pm-4am.)

CARCASSONNE ☎04 68

Walking over the drawbridge and through the stone portals into Carcassonne's *La Cité* (pop. 46,000) is like stepping into a fairy tale; the first-century ramparts still seem to resound with the clang of armor. It's almost enough to make you forget that the only battles raging are between camera-wielding visitors vying for space on the narrow streets. Built as a palace in the 12th century, the **Château Comtal,** 1 r. Viollet-le-Duc, became a citadel after the royal takeover in 1226. (Open daily Apr.-Sept. 9:30am-6:30pm; Oct.-Mar. 9:30am-5pm. €6.10, under 25 €4.10.) Agglo'Bus runs **shuttles** from the train station to the citadel gates (mid-June to mid-Sept. 9:30am-noon and 1:30-

7:30pm every 15min., round-trip €1.50). Converted into a fortress after the city was razed during the Hundred Years' War, the Gothic **Cathédrale St-Michel,** r. Voltaire, in the bastide St-Louis, still has fortifications on its southern side. (Open M-Sa 7:30am-noon and 2-7pm, Su 9:30am-noon.) The evening is the best time to experience *La Cité.*

Nestled in an alley, in the heart of *La Cité,* the **Auberge de Jeunesse (HI) ❷,** r. de Vicomte Trencavel, offers affordable comfort. (☎25 23 16; carcassonne@fuaj.org. Internet €3 per hr. Lockout 10am-3pm. Reception 24hr. Dorms €18.40. €2.90 HI discount. MC/V.) Restaurants in *La Cité* are on the expensive side. For somewhat better deals, head to the lower city. The traditional French cuisine at **Les Fontaines du Soleil ❸,** 32 r. du Plô, is best savored as part of a €13 lunch *menu.* (☎47 87 06. Salads €9-21. Dinner *menu* €18-49. Open daily noon-3:30pm and 7-10:30pm. MC/V.) Save room for crepes and other desserts around **place Marcou.** While Carcassonne has a sizable nightlife during the year, the city quickly falls asleep in summer with most of the regulars gone to the beach. Nonetheless, several bars and cafes along **boulevard Omer Sarraut** and **place Verdun,** both in the lower city, stay open past midnight. **Le Bar à Vins,** 6 r. du Plô, remains popular and full throughout the year. (☎47 38 38. Beer €2.80-5. Wine €2 per glass. Open daily Feb.-Nov. 9am-2am. MC/V.) Pay homage to the 80s and dance the night away at the **Cafe de Nuit,** 31 bd. Omer Sarraut. Monday is gay night with a drag show. (☎92 43 38. 25+. Open M-Sa 7pm-4am.)

Trains (☎71 79 14) depart behind Jardin St-Chenier for: Marseille (3-4hr., 3 per day, €39); Nice (6hr., 5 per day, €57); Nîmes (2-3hr., 9 per day, €28); Toulouse (1hr., 5 per day, €15). Shops, hotels, the cathedral, and the train station are in the **Bastide St-Louis,** once known as the *basse ville* (lower city). From the station, walk down av. de Maréchal Joffre, which becomes r. Clemençeau; after pl. Carnot, turn left on r. de Verdun to reach the **tourist office,** 28 r. de Verdun. (☎10 24 30; www.carcassonne-tourisme.com. Open daily July-Aug. 9am-7pm; Sept.-June M-Sa 9am-6pm, Su 9am-noon.) **Postal Code:** 11000.

MONTPELLIER ☎04 67

Live music brings every street corner to life in Montpellier (pop. 230,000), the most lighthearted city in southern France. The gigantic **Musée Fabre,** 39 bd. Bonne Nouvelle, is undergoing renovations until 2006; it normally displays one of the largest collections of 14th- to 17th-century paintings outside of Paris, with works by Delacroix, Ingres, and Poussin. Temporary exhibits are on display at the **pavilion** on the opposite side of Esplanade Charles de Gaulle. (☎66 13 46. Hours and prices vary; call in advance.) Bd. Henri IV leads to the **Jardin des Plantes,** France's first botanical garden. (Open daily June-Sept. M-Sa noon-8pm; Oct.-May noon-6pm. Free.)

Nova Hôtel ❷, 8 r. Richelieu, hides large, comfortable rooms with clean showers and baths. (☎60 79 85; hotelnova@free.fr. Breakfast €4.60. Reception M-Sa 7am-1am, Su 7-11am and 7pm-1am. Singles €20.90; doubles €23.90, with shower €27.70-34.10, with shower, toilet, and TV €35.85-40.85. 5% *Let's Go* discount. AmEx/MC/V.) Standard French cuisine dominates Montpellier's *vieille ville,* while a number of Indian and Lebanese restaurants have taken hold on **rue des Ecoles Laïques. Crêperie le Kreisker ❶,** 3 passage Bruyas, behind the Credit Lyonnaise on pl. de la Comédie, serves 80 kinds of delicious crepes (€2-6.60) topped with everything from buttered bananas to snails. (☎60 82 50. Open M-Sa 11:45am-2pm and 6:45-11pm. MC/V.) Get groceries at **INNO,** in the basement of the Polygone commercial center, just past the tourist office. (Open M-Sa 9am-8:30pm. MC/V.) At dusk, **rue de la Loge** fills with vendors, musicians, and stilt-walkers. The liveliest bars are in **place Jean-Jaurès.** Popular with 20-somethings, **Cubanito Cafe,** 13 r. de Verdun, just off pl. de la Comédie, starts early and parties late. (☎92 65 82. Mixed drinks €5. Open daily 6pm-2am; low season 6pm-1am. MC/V.) Prominent gay nightlife is centered around **place du Marché aux Fleurs. New THT,** 10 r. St-Firmin, off r. Foch, draws men during the later hours. (☎66 12 52. Beer €4. Open daily mid-June to mid-Sept. 9am-2am; mid-Sept. to mid-June 8pm-1am. MC/V.)

Trains leave pl. Auguste Gibert (☎08 92 35 35 35) for: Avignon (1hr., 12 per day, €14); Marseille (1¾hr., 12 per day, €23); Nice (4hr., 3 per day, €42); Paris (3½hr., 12 per day, €89); Toulouse (2½hr., 13 per day, €29). From the train station, r. Maguelone leads to **place de la Comédie,** Montpellier's modern center. The **tourist office,** 30 allée Jean de Lattre de Tassigny, is a block to the right. (☎60 60 60; www.ot-montpellier.fr. Open July-Aug. M-F 9am-7:30pm, Sa 10am-6pm, Su 9:30am-1pm and 2:30-6pm; Sept.-June reduced hours.) Access the **Internet** at **Cybercafé www,** 12bis r. Jules Ferry, across from the train station. (€1.50 per hr. Open daily 9:30am-1am.) **Postal Code:** 34000.

PROVENCE

Olive groves and vineyards carpet hills dusted with sunflowers and mimosas, while the fierce winds of the *mistral* carry the scents of lavender, rosemary, and sage. From the Roman arena and cobblestone elegance of Arles to Cézanne's lingering footsteps in Aix-en-Provence, life along Provence's shaded paths tastes as good as a bottomless glass of *pastis*.

NÎMES ☎04 66

Southern France flocks to Nîmes (pop. 132,000) for the *férias*, celebrations featuring bullfights, flamenco dancing, and other hot-blooded fanfare (mid-Sept., mid-Feb., and May 27). The city lights up every Thursday night during the summer, when the old town's squares are filled with art and musical performances. Outside of the festival season, Nîmes attracts few visitors, and most don't stay longer than two days. **Les Arènes** is a well-preserved, first-century Roman amphitheater that still holds bullfights and concerts. (Open summer M-F 9am-7pm; winter 10am-6pm. €4.80, students €3.50.) North of the arena stands the **Maison Carrée,** a rectangular temple built in the first century BC. (Open daily mid-Mar. to mid-Oct. 9am-7pm; mid-Oct. to mid-Mar. 10am-5pm. Free.) Across the square, the **Carrée d'Art** displays traveling exhibits of contemporary art. (Open Tu-Su 10am-6pm. €4.65, students €3.40.) Near the mouth of the canals are the spacious grounds, boule courts, and luscious woods of the **Jardins de la Fontaine.** A hike through the park reveals the Roman ruins of the **Tour Magne.** (Garden open daily Apr. to mid-Sept. 7:30am-10pm; mid-Sept. to Mar. reduced hours. Tower open daily July-Aug. 9am-7pm; Sept.-June 9am-5pm. Garden free. Tower €2.60, students €2.10.)

To get to the newly renovated **Auberge de Jeunesse (HI) ❶**, 257 ch. de l'Auberge de la Jeunesse, take bus I (dir.: Alès) from the train station to Stade, rte. d'Alès and follow the signs uphill; call for pickup after 8pm. With brand new rooms and jovial staff, this comfortable hostel is worth the 45min. trek from train station. (☎68 03 20. HI members only. Breakfast €3.35. Internet €3.80 per hr. Reception 24hr. Open Mar.-Sept. Dorms €11.30. Camping €5.65. MC/V.) **Domaine de La Bastide ❶,** rte. de Générac, 5km south of the train station, is a campground complete with a restaurant and laundry. Take bus D (dir.: La Bastide, last bus 8pm) to its terminus. (☎62 05 82. €8.65 per person, €12.80 for 2. MC/V.) For good deals on groceries, head to the **Monoprix,** 3 bd. de la Libération near Esplanade Charles de Gaulle. (Open M-Sa 8:30am-8pm, Su 9am-noon.) **Trains** go from bd. Talabot to: Arles (20min., 8 per day, €7); Marseille (1¼hr., 9 per day, €18); Montpellier (30min., 31-46 per day; €8); Toulouse (3hr., 3-4 per day, €33). **Buses** (☎29 52 00) depart from behind the train station for Avignon (1½hr., M-Sa 3-4 per day, €8). The **tourist office,** 6 r. Auguste, is across from the Maison Carrée. (☎58 38 00; www.ot-nimes.fr. Open July-Aug. M-W and F 8:30am-8pm, Th 8:30am-9pm, Sa 9am-7pm, Su 10am-6pm; Sept.-June reduced hours.) **Postal Codes:** 30000; 30900.

PONT DU GARD

☎04 66

In 19 BC, Augustus's close friend and advisor Agrippa built an aqueduct to channel water 50km to Nîmes from the Eure springs near Uzès. The architectural fruit of this 15-year project is the Pont du Gard, spanning the gorge of the Gardon River and towering over sunbathers and swimmers. An amazing way to experience Pont du Gard is to kayak from Collais, 5.5km from the aqueduct. **Kayak Vert,** situated in Collias, rents canoes, kayaks, and bikes. (☎22 80 76. Canoes and kayaks €18 per day, bikes €15 per day. 10% discount for students and guests at the Nîmes youth hostel. Call a day ahead to make reservations and arrange for pickup at Pont du Gard.) **Camping le Barralet ❶,** in Collias, offers a pool and hot showers. (☎22 84 52; www.barralet.fr. Open Mar-Sept. Tent sites €13, extra person €3. MC/V.) More accommodations are in **Nîmes.** STDG **buses** (☎29 27 29) run to the Pont du Gard from Avignon (45min., 6 per day, €6) and Nîmes (40min.; 7 per day; €5.60, round-trip €9.90).

AVIGNON

☎04 90

Immortalized by the French children's song about its bridge, Avignon (pop. 100,000) also hosts Europe's most prestigious theater festival. The golden **Palais des Papes,** the largest Gothic palace in Europe, is a reminder of the city's brief stint as the center of the Catholic Church. Although revolutionary looting stripped the interior of its lavish furnishings and fires erased its medieval murals, the vast chambers and few remaining frescoes are still remarkable. (☎27 50 74. Open daily July 9am-9pm; Aug.-Sept. 9am-8pm; Oct.-June 9am-7pm. €9.50.) For three weeks in July, the **Festival d'Avignon** holds theatrical performances in at least 30 venues, from factories to cloisters to palaces. (☎14 14 14; www.festival-avignon.com. Tickets €16-33. Reservations accepted from mid-June. Standby tickets available 45min. before shows. Under 25 €12, purchase at IN office or 45min. before show. €8 Carte IN, sold at the tourist office, grants holders a 30% discount on all tickets.) The **Festival OFF,** also in July, is more experimental and almost as well established. (Office on pl. du Palais. ☎01 48 05 01 19; www.avignon-off.org. Tickets under €16. €14 Carte OFF grants holders a 20-50% discount on all tickets.)

Avignon's accommodations fill three to four months before festival season; book ahead or stay in Arles or Nîmes. From the post office, take bus #10 or 11 to La Barthelasse for **Foyer Bagatelle ❶,** Île de la Barthelasse, which has cheap dorms; only groups can reserve in advance for €11. (☎86 30 39; auberge.bagatelle@wanadoo.fr. Reception 8am-8:30pm. Lockout 2-5pm. Dorms €11.) The **hotel ❷** next door houses worn but clean and well-kept rooms. (Singles €26, with shower €27-29; doubles €26-32; triples €35-40; quads €47. Prices increase by 10% during the festival. MC/V.) Pitch your tent at **Camping du Pont d'Avignon ❶,** 300 Île de la Barthelasse. The four-star site has hot showers, laundry facilities, a restaurant, supermarket, pool, jacuzzi, and tennis and volleyball courts. (☎80 63 50; www.camping-avignon.com. Open Mar.-Oct. High season 1-person tent site €15; 2 people €21, extra person €4.10. Low-season prices 60% lower. MC/V.) Chatty owners and a cheerful regular crowd enjoy delicious *tartines* (€4.50) and occasional guitar serenades at **La Cuisine des Méchantes ❶,** 68 r. de la Bonneterie. (☎86 14 81. Open daily noon-2pm and 7:30pm-1:30am.) Restaurants cluster on **rue des Teinturiers.** A **Marche Plus** supermarket hides at 7 r. Portail Matheron. (Open M-Sa 7am-9pm, Su 9am-12:30pm. MC/V.) During the festivals, free theatrical performances spill into the streets at night, and many eateries stay open until 2 or 3am. **Place des Corps Saints** has a few bars that remain lively year-round.

Trains (☎27 81 89) run from bd. St-Roch, porte de la République to: Arles (20min., 19 per day, €6); Lyon (1hr., 5-7 per day, €26.80-36.90); Marseille (1¼hr., 18-22 per day, €16.60); Nîmes (30min., 16-18 per day, €7.70); Paris (TGV 3½hr., 14 per day, €88.80). **Buses** leave to the right of the train station for Arles (1½hr., 5 per day, €9.60) and Marseille (2hr., 1 per day, €17.20). From the train station, walk straight through porte de la République to reach the **tourist office** at 41 cours Jean Jaurès. (☎04 32 74 32 74; www.avignon-tourisme.com. Open July M-Sa 9am-7pm, Su 10am-5pm; Apr.-June and Aug.-Oct. M-Sa 9am-6pm, Su 10am-5pm; low season reduced hours.) **Postal Code:** 84000.

ARLES ☎04 90

All roads in Arles (pop. 35,000), once the capital of Roman Gaul, seem to meet at the great Roman arena. Built in the first century AD to seat 20,000 spectators, **Les Arènes** is still used for bullfights. (Open daily May-Sept. 9am-6pm; Oct.-Apr. reduced hours. €4, students €3.) Provençal daily life and folklore are showcased at the **Muséon Arlatan,** 29 r. de la République. (Open June-Aug. daily 9:30am-1pm and 2-6:30pm; Apr.-May and Sept. Tu-Su 9:30am-12:30pm and 2-6pm; Oct.-Mar. Tu-Su 9:30am-12:30pm and 2-5pm. €4, students €3.) The excellent **Musée de l'Arles Antique,** on av. de la 1er D. F. L., revives the city's Roman past. (Open daily Mar.-Oct. 9am-7pm; Nov.-Feb. 10am-5pm. €5.50, students €4.) The contemporary **Musée Réattu,** r. du Grand Prieuré, houses 57 Picasso drawings inspired by the city. (Open daily May-Sept. 10am-12:30pm and 2-7pm; Mar.-Apr. and Oct. 10am-12:30pm and 2-5:30pm; Nov.-Feb. 1-5:30pm. €4, students €3.) The annual week-long **Fête d'Arles** brings traditional costumes, Provençal dancing, and bullfights to town beginning on the summer Solstice. Every three years, the city elects the Queen of Arles and her six ladies, who represent the city's language, customs, and history at local events and international exchanges. The next election will occur in 2008.

To get from the station to the **Auberge de Jeunesse (HI) ❶,** 20 av. Maréchal Foch, follow directions to the tourist office, but cross bd. des Lices instead of turning onto it, and follow the signs down av. des Alyscamps. Simple but comfortably arranged single-sex dorms with sturdy beds and individual locking cabinets await. (☎96 18 25. English-speaking staff. Breakfast included. Internet €4 per hr. Reception 7-10am and 5-11pm. Lockout 10am-5pm. Curfew midnight, in winter 11pm. Dorms €12.60. MC/V.) The brasseries on **place du Forum** are pricey but popular, while those on **place Voltaire** have cheaper, though not as tasteful, cafes. A **Monoprix** supermarket is on pl. Lamartine on the way to the station. (Open M-Th 8:30am-7:30pm, F-Sa 8:30am-8pm.) **Trains** leave av. P. Talabot for: Avignon (20min., 12-20 per day, €6); Marseille (50min., 18-27 per day, €13); Montpellier (1hr., 5-8 per day, €13); Nîmes (20min., 8-11 per day, €7). **Buses** (☎49 38 01) depart from next to the station for Avignon (55min., 9-11 per day, €7.10) and Nîmes (55min., 4 per day, €6). To get to the **tourist office,** esplanade Charles de Gaulle on bd. des Lices, turn left outside the station and walk to the roundabout. Veer clockwise, hooking left after the Monoprix onto bd. Emile Courbes. At the end of the city walls take a right on bd. des Lices. (☎18 41 20; www.tourisme.ville-arles.fr. Open daily Apr.-Sept. 9am-6:45pm; Oct.-Mar. reduced hours.) **Postal Code:** 13200.

AIX-EN-PROVENCE ☎04 42

Famous for festivals, fountains, and former residents Paul Cézanne and Emile Zola, Aix-en-Provence (pop. 134,000) caters to tourists without being ruined by them. The **Chemin de Cézanne,** 9 av. Paul Cézanne, features a 2hr. self-guided walking tour that leads visitors to the artist's birthplace, his favorite cafes, and his studio. (☎21 06 53. Open daily July-Aug. 10am-6pm; Sept.-June reduced hours. €5.50, students €2.) The **Fondation Vasarely,** av. Marcel-Pagnol, in Jas-de-Bouffan, is a must-see for modern art fans. (☎20 01 09. Open M-Sa May-Sept. 10am-6pm; Oct.-Apr. 10am-5pm. €7, students €4.) An eclectic mix of Romanesque, Gothic, and Baroque, the **Cathédrale St-Saveur,** r. Gaston de Saporta, fell victim to misplaced violence during the Revolution; angry *Aixois* (citizens of Aix) mistook the statues of the apostles for statues of royalty and defiantly chopped off their heads. The statues were recapitated in the 19th century, but remain *sans* neck. (☎23 45 65. Open daily 8am-noon and 2-6pm.) In June and July, famous performers and rising stars descend on Aix for the **Festival d'Aix-en-Provence,** a series of opera and orchestral performances. (☎16 11 70; www.festival-aix.com. Tickets from €8.) Aix also hosts **Danse à Aix,** a two-week dance festival starting in late July. (☎23 41 24; www.danse-a-aix.com. Tickets €7-33.)

Aix has few cheap hotels; travelers should reserve in March for festival season (July). The rooms at the excellent **Hôtel du Globe ❸,** 74 cours Sextius, are spacious and well lit. (☎26 03 58; www.hotelduglobe.com. Singles €36, with shower €39; doubles €54/59; triples €79; quads €85. AmEx/MC/V.) To **camp** at **Arc-en-Ciel ❶,** on rte. de Nice, take bus #3 from La Rotonde to Trois Sautets. (☎26 14 28. €5.90 per person, €5.40 per tent.) The roads north of **cours Mirabeau** are packed with reasonably priced restaurants, as is **rue Verrerie.** You'll find tasty Provençal *tartines* (grilled bread with cheese and toppings; €9.90-12.50) at **Le P'tit Bistrot ❷,** 38 r. Lieutaud. (☎27 52 20. Open Tu-Sa 9am-3pm and 6pm-1am. MC/V.) **Petit Casino** supermarket at 3 cours d'Orbitelle. (Open M-Sa 8am-1pm and 4-7:30pm.) **Rue Verrerie,** off r. des Cordiliers, is lined with bars and clubs. **Bistro Aixois,** 37 cours Sextius, packs in international students with a taste for beer. (Open daily 7pm-2am.)

Trains, at the end of av. Victor Hugo, run to: Cannes (3½hr., 25 per day, €30); Marseille (40min., 27 per day, €6); Nice (3-4hr., 25 per day, €30). **TGV** trains leave for Paris CDG (3½hr., 5 per day, €89) from the TGV station, accessible via a shuttle (20min., every 15min., €4) from the bus station. **Buses** (☎08 91 02 40 25) from av. de l'Europe, run to Marseille (30min., every 10min., €4.30). From the train station, follow av. Victor Hugo, bearing left at the fork, until it feeds into La Rotonde. On the left is the **tourist office,** 2 pl. du Général de Gaulle, which books rooms for free. (☎16 11 61; www.aixenprovencetourism.com. Open July-Aug. M-Sa 8:30am-9pm, Su 10am-1pm and 2-7pm; Sept.-June reduced hours.) **Postal Code:** 13100.

MARSEILLE ☎04 91

Dubbed "the meeting place of the entire world" by Alexandre Dumas, Marseille (pop. 800,000) is a jumble of color and commotion. A walk through its side streets is punctuated by the vibrant hues of West African fabrics, the sounds of Arabic music, and the smells of North African cuisine. A true immigrant city, Marseille offers a taste of both the ancient and modern cultures of the entire Mediterranean.

FRANCE

TRANSPORTATION

Flights: Aéroport Marseille-Provence (MRS; ☎04 42 14 14 14; www.marseille.aeroport.fr). Flights to **Corsica, Lyon,** and **Paris.** Buses connect airport to Gare St-Charles (3 per hr. 5:30am-9:50pm, €8.50).

Trains: Gare St-Charles, pl. Victor Hugo (☎08 92 35 35 35). To: **Lyon** (1½hr., 21 per day, €41.90); **Nice** (2¾hr., 21 per day, €25.60); **Paris** (3hr., 18 per day, €72-80).

Buses: Gare Routière, pl. Victor Hugo (☎08 16 40), near the train station. To: **Avignon** (2hr., 5 per day, €15); **Cannes** (2¼-3hr., 4 per day, €21); **Nice** (2¾hr., 1 per day, €23.50). Open M-F 6:15am-7:30pm, Sa 6:30am-6:30pm, Su 7:30am-12:30pm and 1:30-6:30pm.

Ferries: SNCM, 61 bd. des Dames (☎08 25 88 80 88; www.sncm.fr). To: **Corsica** (12hr.; €35-53, students €20-40) and **Sardinia** (14½hr., €59-69/50-65). Open M-F 8am-6pm, Sa 8am-noon and 2-5:30pm.

Local Transportation: RTM, 6 r. des Fabres (☎91 92 10; www.rtm.fr). Tickets sold at bus and metro stations (€1.60; day pass €4.30; 5- to 11-ride **Carte Liberté** €6.50-13). **Metro** runs M-Th 5am-9pm, F-Su 5am-12:30am.

Taxis: (☎02 20 20) 24hr. €20-30 to hostels from Gare St-Charles.

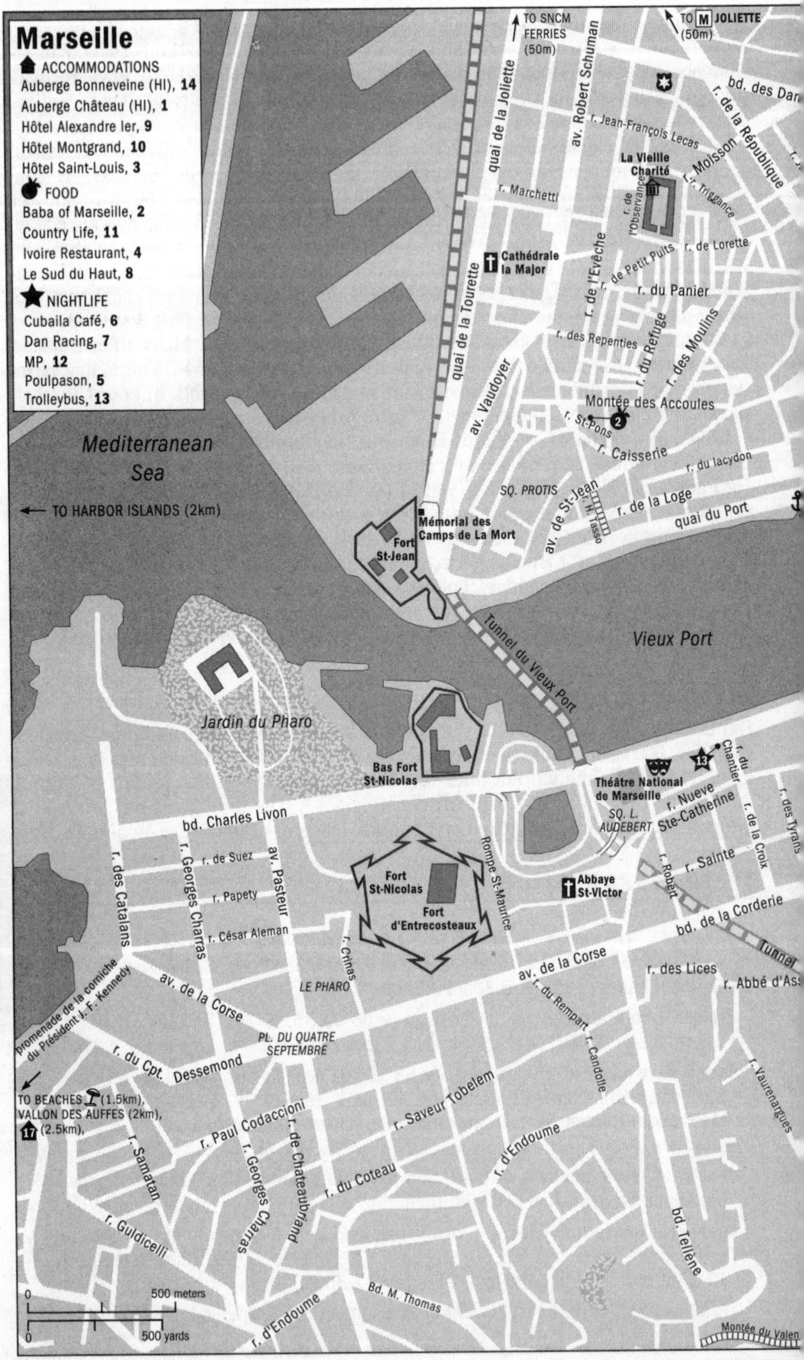

Marseille

ACCOMMODATIONS
Auberge Bonneveine (HI), **14**
Auberge Château (HI), **1**
Hôtel Alexandre Ier, **9**
Hôtel Montgrand, **10**
Hôtel Saint-Louis, **3**

FOOD
Baba of Marseille, **2**
Country Life, **11**
Ivoire Restaurant, **4**
Le Sud du Haut, **8**

NIGHTLIFE
Cubaila Café, **6**
Dan Racing, **7**
MP, **12**
Poulpason, **5**
Trolleybus, **13**

TO SNCM FERRIES (50m)
TO M JOLIETTE (50m)
Mediterranean Sea
TO HARBOR ISLANDS (2km)
quai de la Joliette
av. Robert Schuman
bd. des Dames
r. de la République
r. Jean-François Lecas
La Vieille Charité
r. Moisson
r. de l'Observance
r. Triggance
r. Marchetti
Cathédrale la Major
quai de la Tourette
r. de l'Evêche
r. de Petit Puits
r. de Lorette
r. du Panier
r. des Repenties
r. du Refuge
r. des Moulins
av. Vaudoyer
Montée des Accoules
r. St-Pons
r. Caisserie
r. du lacydon
SQ. PROTIS
av. de St-Jean
r. H. Tasso
r. de la Loge
quai du Port
Mémorial des Camps de La Mort
Fort St-Jean
Tunnel du Vieux Port
Vieux Port
Jardin du Pharo
Bas Fort St-Nicolas
Théâtre National de Marseille
r. du Chantier
r. Nueve Ste-Catherine
SQ. L. AUDEBERT
r. de la Croix
r. des Tyrans
bd. Charles Livon
r. des Catalans
r. Georges Charras
av. Pasteur
r. de Suez
r. Papety
r. César Aleman
Fort St-Nicolas
Fort d'Entrecosteaux
Rompe St-Maurice
Abbaye St-Victor
r. Robert
r. Sainte
bd. de la Corderie
Tunnel
r. Crinas
LE PHARO
av. de la Corse
r. des Lices
r. Abbé d'Ass
r. du Rempart
r. Candolle
promenade de la corniche du Président J. F. Kennedy
PL. DU QUATRE SEPTEMBRE
r. du Cpt. Dessemond
r. Vaurenargues
TO BEACHES (1.5km), VALLON DES AUFFES (2km), 17 (2.5km),
r. Saveur Tobelem
r. Paul Codaccioni
r. Georges Charras
r. de Chateaubriand
r. du Coteau
r. d'Endoume
r. Samatan
r. Guldicelli
bd. Tellène
Bd. M. Thomas
r. d'Endoume
Montée du Valen
0 500 meters
0 500 yards

FRANCE

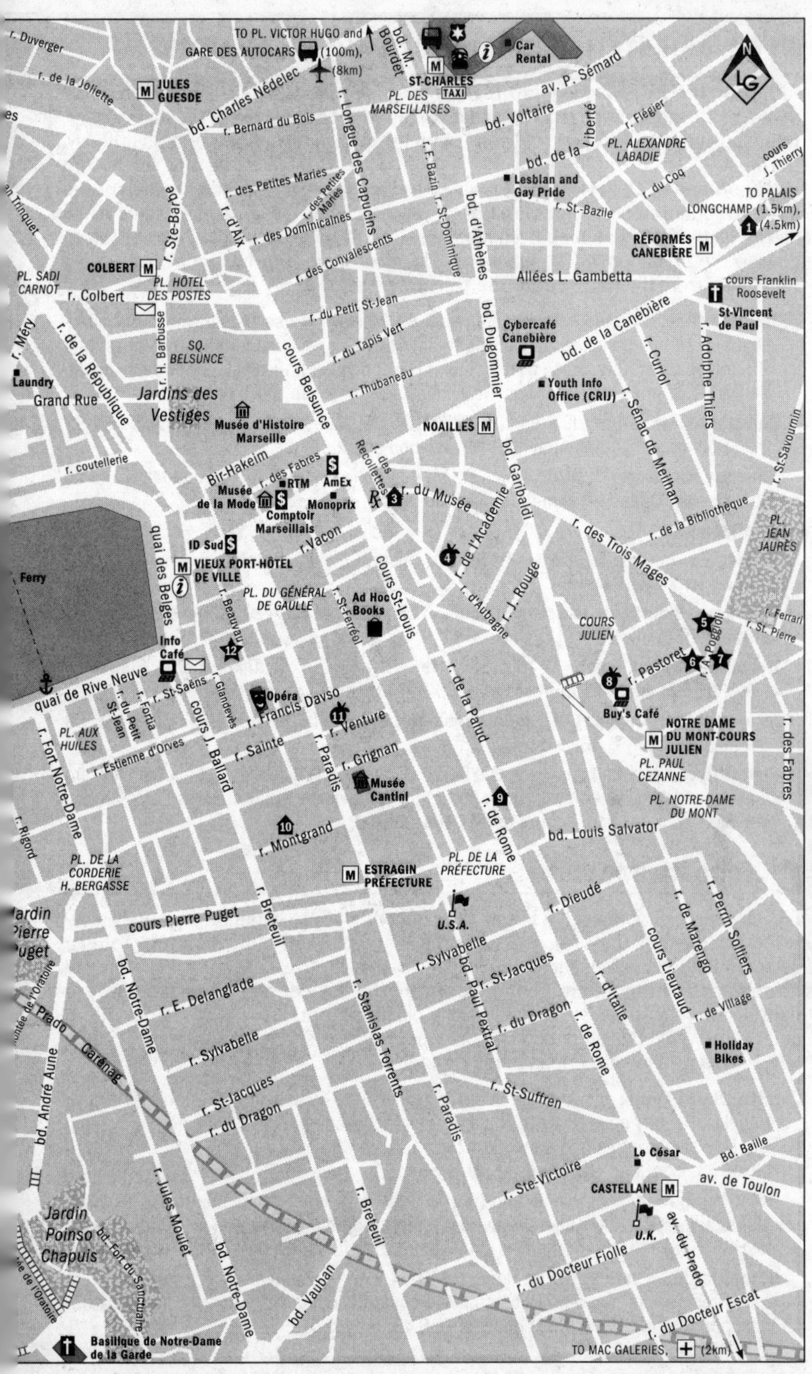
TO PL. VICTOR HUGO and GARE DES AUTOCARS (100m), (8km)
ST-CHARLES
PL. DES MARSEILLAISES
Car Rental
JULES GUESDE
bd. Charles Nédelec
av. P. Sémard
bd. Voltaire
r. Bernard du Bois
r. Longue des Capucins
bd. M. Bourdet
r. des Petites Maries
r. des Dominicaines
r. des Convalescents
r. d'Aix
r. Ste-Barbe
r. F. Bazin
r. St-Dominique
bd. d'Athènes
bd. de la Liberté
PL. ALEXANDRE LABADIE
r. Flégier
cours J. Thierry
r. du Coq
r. St.-Bazile
Lesbian and Gay Pride
TO PALAIS LONGCHAMP (1.5km), (4.5km)
RÉFORMÉS CANEBIÈRE
Allées L. Gambetta
cours Franklin Roosevelt
St-Vincent de Paul
COLBERT
PL. SADI CARNOT
r. Colbert
PL. HÔTEL DES POSTES
r. du Petit St-Jean
r. du Tapis Vert
r. Thubaneau
Cybercafé Canebière
bd. de la Canebière
Youth Info Office (CRIJ)
r. Curiol
r. Adolphe Thiers
r. Méry
r. de la République
r. H. Barbusse
SQ. BELSUNCE
Laundry
Grand Rue
Jardins des Vestiges
Musée d'Histoire Marseille
cours Belsunce
NOAILLES
bd. Dugommier
r. Sénac de Meilhan
r. St-Savournin
r. coutellerie
Bir-Hakeim
r. des Fabres
RTM
AmEx
Monoprix
r. des Recolettes
r. du Musée
bd. Garibaldi
r. de la Bibliothèque
PL. JEAN JAURÈS
Musée de la Mode
Comptoir Marseillais
r. Vacon
r. de l'Académie
r. des Trois Mages
Ferry
ID Sud
VIEUX PORT-HÔTEL DE VILLE
quai des Belges
cours St-Louis
r. d'Aubagne
r. J. Rouge
PL. DU GÉNÉRAL DE GAULLE
r. Beauvau
r. St-Ferréol
Ad Hoc Books
COURS JULIEN
r. Ferrari
r. St. Pierre
Info Café
r. Pastoret
r. A. Poggioli
quai de Rive Neuve
r. St-Saëns
r. Glandevès
Opéra
r. Francis Davso
r. de la Palud
Buy's Café
NOTRE DAME DU MONT-COURS JULIEN
r. du Petit St-Jean
r. Fortia
cours J. Ballard
r. Venture
PL. AUX HUILES
r. Estienne d'Orves
r. Sainte
r. Paradis
r. Grignan
PL. PAUL CEZANNE
r. des Fabres
r. Fort Notre-Dame
Musée Cantini
r. de Rome
PL. NOTRE-DAME DU MONT
r. Rigord
r. Montgrand
bd. Louis Salvator
PL. DE LA CORDERIE H. BERGASSE
ESTRAGIN PRÉFECTURE
PL. DE LA PRÉFECTURE
r. Breteuil
U.S.A.
r. Dieudé
r. de Marengo
r. Perrin Solliers
Jardin Pierre Puget
cours Pierre Puget
r. Sylvabelle
bd. Notre-Dame
r. E. Delanglade
r. St-Jacques
bd. Paul Pextral
r. du Dragon
r. d'Italie
cours Lieutaud
r. de Village
Holiday Bikes
Carénage
r. Sylvabelle
r. Stanislas Torrents
r. de Rome
bd. André Aune
r. St-Jacques
r. du Dragon
r. St-Suffren
r. Paradis
Le César
Bd. Baille
r. Ste-Victoire
CASTELLANE
av. de Toulon
Jardin Poinso Chapuis
r. Jules Moulet
r. Breteuil
U.K.
av. du Prado
bd. Fon du Sanctuaire
bd. Notre-Dame
bd. Vauban
r. du Docteur Fiolle
r. du Docteur Escat
Basilique de Notre-Dame de la Garde
TO MAC GALERIES, (2km)

FRANCE

ORIENTATION AND PRACTICAL INFORMATION

Although the city is divided into 16 *arrondissements*, Marseille is understood by *quartier* (neighborhood) names and major streets. **La Canebière** is the main artery, funneling into the **vieux port** (old port), with its upscale restaurants and nightlife, to the west. North of the *vieux port*, working-class residents pile into the hilltop neighborhood of **Le Panier,** east of which lies the **Quartier Belsunce,** the hub of the city's Arab and African communities. A few blocks to the southeast, **cours Julien** has a young, bohemian feel. Both **metro** lines go to the train station; line #1 (blue) goes to the *vieux port*. The **bus** system is much more thorough but complex—a route map from the tourist office helps enormously.

Tourist Office: 4 bd. de la Canebière (☎13 89 00; www.marseille-tourisme.com). Multilingual staff has brochures of walking tours, free maps, accommodation bookings, and RTM day passes. City tours (€16 by bus, €5 by open-car train) daily. Open July-Aug. M-Sa 9am-7:30pm, Su 10am-6pm; Oct.-June M-Sa 9am-7pm, Su 10am-5pm.

Consulates: UK, 24 av. du Prado (☎15 72 10). **US,** 12 bd. Paul Peytral (☎04 91 54 92 00). Both open by appointment M-F 9am-noon and 2-5pm.

Currency exchange: ID SUD, 3 pl. Général de Gaulle (☎13 09 00). Good rates and no commission. Open M-F 9am-6pm, Sa 9am-5pm.

Emergency: ☎17.

Police: 2 r. Antoine Becker (☎39 80 00). Also in the train station on esplanade St-Charles (☎14 29 97).

Pharmacy: Pharmacie le Cours St-Louis, 5 cours Saint-Louis (☎54 04 58). Open daily 8:30am-7:30pm.

Hospital: Hôpital Timone, 246 r. St-Pierre (☎38 60 00). M: Timone. **SOS Médecins** (☎52 91 52) and **SOS Dentist** (☎85 39 39) connect to on-call doctors.

Internet Access: Cyber Café de la Canebière, 87 r. de la Canebière (☎05 94 24). €2 per hr. Open daily 8:30am-3am.

Post Office: 1 pl. Hôtel des Postes (☎04 91 15 47 00). Follow r. de la Canebière toward the sea and turn right onto r. Reine Elisabeth as it becomes pl. Hôtel des Postes. Open M-F 8am-7pm, Sa 8am-noon. **Postal Code:** 13001.

FRANCE

ACCOMMODATIONS

Like any large city, Marseille has a range of hotel options, from pricey hotels scattered throughout the *vieux port* to the less reputable but temptingly cheap accommodations in Belsunce. Hotels listed here prioritize safety and location. The hostels are far from the city center; this makes them inconvenient—particularly in light of infrequent bus service and early curfews—but quiet. Most places fill up quickly on weekends and in the summer, so call at least a week in advance. Large white signs provide directions to major hotels.

Hôtel Saint-Louis, 2 r. des Recollettes (☎54 02 74; www.hotel-st-louis.com). M: Noailles. Brightly painted, spacious rooms just off bustling r. de la Canebière. Breakfast €5. Free wireless Internet. Reception 24hr. Singles €36; doubles with bath €45-52; triples €63. Extra bed €10. AmEx/V. ❸

Hôtel Montgrand, 50 r. Montgrand (☎00 35 20; www.hotel-montgrand-marseille.com). M: Estragin-Préfecture. Quiet, newly renovated, clean rooms near the *vieux port*. Breakfast €5. Singles €36-44; doubles €44-48; triples and quads €49-61. MC/V. ❸

Hôtel Alexandre Ier, 111 r. de Rome (☎48 67 13). M: Estragin-Préfecture. Large, red-toned rooms with showers. Rooms on the cours St-Louis can be noisy. Breakfast €5. Reception 24hr. Singles €37; doubles €38-42; triples €49; quads €65. MC/V. ❸

Auberge de Jeunesse Bonneveine (HI), impasse Bonfils (☎17 63 30). M: Rond-Point du Prado. Off av. J Vidal. Take bus #44 to pl. Bonnefon, backtrack toward the roundabout and turn left at av. J. Vidal, then left onto impasse Bonfils. A well-organized hostel with an international crowd. HI members only. 6-night max. stay. Reception 9am-12:45pm and 1:30-6pm. Curfew 1am. Closed mid-Dec. to mid-Jan. Dorms Apr.-Aug. €15.60; doubles €17.85. Feb.-Mar. and Sept.-Dec. reduced prices. MC/V. ❷

Auberge de Jeunesse Château de Bois-Luzy (HI), allée des Primevères (☎49 06 18). M: Chartreux. Take bus #6 to Marius Richard, go right onto bd. de l'Amandière. Follow the road around the fields to reach the hostel. A 19th-century chateau east of Marseille. HI members only. Breakfast €3.30. Reception 7:30am-noon and 5-10:30pm. Lockout noon-5pm. Curfew 10:30pm; in summer 11:30pm. Dorms 1st night €11.50, thereafter €9; singles €16/13.50; doubles €13/10.50. Cash only. ❶

FOOD

Marseille's restaurants reflect the cultural diversity of its inhabitants. African eateries and kebab stands line **cours St-Louis,** the streets surrounding the **vieux port** are packed with outdoor cafes and restaurants serving the city's famed seafood and trademark *bouillabaisse* (a fish soup that is a meal in itself), and **cours Julien** offers artsy, eclectic food options. Buy groceries at the **Monoprix** supermarket across from the AmEx office on bd. de la Canebière. (Open M-Sa 8:30am-8:30pm.)

Baba of Marseille, 14 r. St-Pons (☎90 66 36). M: Vieux Port. Delicious southern French dishes earn a loyal clientele. Photos of past diners and a varied collection of lanterns, chandeliers, and trinkets give this welcoming restaurant a familiar feel. Try the *mille feuille d'agneau* (lamb and pastry; €18). Open W-Sa 8pm-midnight. ❹

Ivoire Restaurant, 57 r. d'Aubagne (☎33 75 33). M: Noailles. Head to this no-frills restaurant for authentic West African cuisine and helpful advice from owner "Mama Africa." Côte d'Ivoire specialties include *yassa,* braised fish with plantains and couscous, and *maffé,* meat in peanut sauce, both €7. Open daily noon-midnight. Cash only. ❷

Le Sud du Haut, 80 cours Julien (☎92 66 64). M: Cours Julien. Beautifully presented, traditional Provençal cuisine. The *Saint Marcellin rôti* (roasted cheese dish; €9.20) is particularly excellent. Open M-Sa noon-1:30pm and 8pm-12:30am. AmEx/MC/V. ❷

Country Life, 14 r. Venture (☎04 96 11 28 00). M: Estragin-Préfecture, off r. Paradis. Appetizing vegan buffet with creative hot and cold selections. Patrons choose either a big (€7.50) or a small (€4.50) buffet plate. Open M-F 11:30am-2:30pm; health food store open M-Th 9am-6:30pm, F 9am-3pm. MC/V. ❷

SIGHTS

A walk through the city's streets tops any other sights-oriented itinerary, providing glimpses of lively African and Arabic communities amid ancient Roman ruins and 17th-century forts. Check www.museum-paca.org for the latest info on the region's museums. Unless otherwise noted, all the museums listed below have the same hours (Tu-Sa June-Sept. 11am-6pm; Oct.-May 10am-5pm).

BASILIQUE DE NOTRE DAME DE LA GARDE. A hilltop location has made this church strategically important for centuries, and today it offers visitors a stunning view of the city, surrounding mountains, and stone-studded bay. During the WWII liberation of Marseille, the French Resistance fought to regain the basilica, which remains pocked with bullet holes and shrapnel scars. Towering nearly 230m above the city, the golden statue of the Madonna cradling the infant Christ, known as *la bonne mère,* is often regarded as the symbol of Marseille. *(☎13 40 80. Open daily summer 7am-8pm; low season 7am-7pm.)*

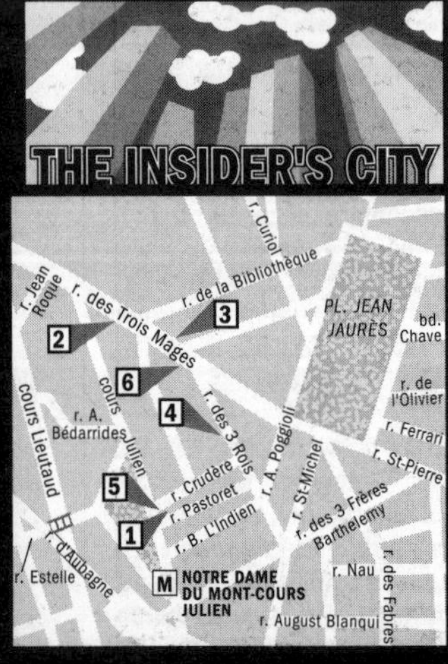

COURS JULIEN

An eclectic collection of murals, vintage music and clothing shops, bookstores, theaters, and cafes and restaurants make cours Julien the perfect place to stroll for a bargain. Many shops are closed on Sunday and Monday.

1. Street artists have turned **rue Pastoret** and **rue Crudère** into impromptu outdoor galleries with cartoonish, spray-paint murals.
2. **Black Music,** 2 r. de la Bibliothèque, has a large assortment of soul and hip-hop.
3. **Kaleidoscope,** 3 r. des Trois Mages, offers eclectic used records and CDs.
4. Tiny **Baluchon Boutique,** 11 r. des Trois Rois, has the best vintage threads.
5. Peruse dusty paperbacks at **Librairie du Cours Julien,** 51 cours Julien.
6. **La Passerelle,** 26 r. des Trois Mages, features comic books and a snappy cafe.

HARBOR ISLANDS. Resembling an elaborate version of a child's sand castle, the **Château d'If** guards the city from its rocky perch outside the harbor. Its dungeon, immortalized in Dumas's *Count of Monte Cristo*, once held a number of hapless Huguenots. Nearby, the **Île Frioul** was only marginally successful in isolating plague victims when an outbreak in 1720 killed half of the city's citizens. A handful of small shops and restaurants, combined with inlets popular for swimming, make the islands a convenient escape from the city. *(Boats depart from quai des Belges for both islands. Societe des Armateurs Côtiers ☎55 50 09. Chateau ☎59 02 30. Round-trip 1hr.; €10 for each island, both €15.)*

LA VIEILLE CHARITÉ. A formidable example of the 17th-century work of local architect Pierre Puget, La Charité was originally constructed to house the hundreds of beggars congesting the entrances to Marseille's churches. Now a national historical monument and home to many of the city's cultural organizations, it also houses several of the city's museums, including the anthropological collections of the **Musée des Arts Africains, Océaniens et Amérindiens.** *(2 r. de la Charité. ☎14 59 30. Temporary exhibits €5, permanent collections €2; students half-price.)*

MUSÉE CANTINI. This memorable museum chronicles the region's 20th-century artistic successes, with major Fauvist and Surrealist collections, including works by Henri Matisse and Paul Signac. *(19 r. Grignan. ☎54 77 75. €2, students €1.)*

MÉMORIAL DES CAMPS DE LA MORT. This small museum is located in a blockhouse built by the Germans during their occupation of Marseille. A collection of photos and news articles recalls the death camps of WWII and the deportation of 20,000 Jews from the *vieux port* in 1943. Sobering quotes by Primo Levi, Louis Serre, and Elie Wiesel, and an unsettling collection of ashes are on display. *(Quai de la Tourette. ☎90 73 15. Open Tu-Su June-Aug. 11am-6pm; Sept.-May 10am-5pm. Free.)*

ABBAYE ST-VICTOR. St-Victor, an abbey fortified against pirates and Saracen invaders, is one of the oldest Christian sites in Europe. The eerie 5th-century crypt and basilica contain pagan and Christian relics. *(On r. Sainte at the end of quai de Rive Neuve. ☎04 96 11 22 60. Open daily 9am-7pm. Crypt €2.)*

OTHER SIGHTS. The fluctuating exhibits at **Musée de la Mode** pay homage to the fashion world, featuring designers from around the globe. *(Espace Mode Méditerranée, 11 bd. de la Canebière. ☎04 16 17 06 00. €1.50, students €1.)* The remains of Marseille's original port rest peacefully in the quiet **Jardin des Vestiges.** Millennia-old artifacts, including pottery pieces and the skeleton of a 6th-century fishing boat, are displayed in the adjacent **Musée d'Histoire de Marseille.** *(Enter through the lowest level of the Centre Bourse mall. ☎90 42 22. Open M-Sa noon-7pm. €2, students €1.)* Bus #83 (dir.: Rond-Point du Prado) takes you from the *vieux port* to Marseille's **public beaches.** Get off just after it rounds the statue of David (20-30min.). Both the north and south **plages du Prado** offer sandy stretches, clear water, and good views of Marseille's surrounding cliffs.

ENTERTAINMENT AND NIGHTLIFE

Late-night restaurants and a few nightclubs center around **place Thiers,** near the *vieux port.* On weekends, tables from the bars along the **quai de Rive Neuve** spill out into the sidewalk, and huge crowds rush to grab a seat and a drink. A more creative, counter-cultural crowd unwinds along the **cours Julien.** Tourists should exercise caution at night, particularly in Panier and Belsunce, and near the Opera on the *vieux port.* Night buses are scarce, taxis are expensive, and the metro closes early (M-Th and Su 9pm, F-Sa 12:30am).

Trolleybus, 24 quai de Rive Neuve. M: Vieux Port. A mega-club in an 18th-century warehouse with 3 separate cave-like rooms for pop-rock, techno, and soul-funk-salsa. Prize-winning French and international DJs have been spinning here for 14 years. Beer from €5. Mixed drinks €3-7. Sa cover €10, includes 1 drink. Open July-Aug. Tu-Sa 11pm-6am; low season Th-Sa only. MC/V.

Dan Racing, 17 r. André Poggioli. M: Cours Julien. Let your inner rock star run wild at this fun, casual bar, where drunken revelers can hop onstage to jam on 15 guitars, 2 drum sets, and countless other instruments. Auto- and bike-racing decor adds to the atmosphere. Drinks €2.50-3.50. Open M-Sa 9pm-2am.

Cubaila Café, 40 r. des Trois Rois (☎48 97 48). M: Cours Julien. Take your mojito from the striped couches of the 1st fl. down to the basement, where you'll find a perfect replica of the Malecon boardwalk in Havana, complete with miniature house facades and a view of the "ocean." Drinks €3-8. Open Tu-Sa 8:30pm-4am.

Poulpason, 2 r. André Poggioli. M: Cours Julien. DJs spin hip hop, funk, jazz, reggae, and electro-house. A giant octopus reaching out from the wall, wave and vortex mosaics, and a black-lit aquarium make for a surreal atmosphere. Drinks €3-5. Cover on concert nights €3-8. Open M-Sa 10pm-2am. MC/V.

MP, 10 r. Beauvau (☎33 64 79) M: Vieux Port. Both men and women relax on plush velour couches at this quiet gay bar. Tall wire stools and pink runner lights add a touch of class. Patrons can snack on paella or couscous and use the free Internet kiosk. Drinks €2.50-6.50. Open daily from 5:30pm.

FRENCH RIVIERA (CÔTE D'AZUR)

Between Marseille and the Italian border, the sun-drenched beaches and warm waters of the Mediterranean form the backdrop for this fabled playground of the rich and famous. Chagall, F. Scott Fitzgerald, Matisse, Picasso, and Renoir are among those who flocked to the coast in its heyday. Now, the Riviera is a curious combination of high-handed millionaires and low-budget tourists. High society steps out every May for the Cannes Film Festival and the Monte-Carlo Grand Prix. Less exclusive are Nice's summer jazz festivals and uproarious *Carnaval.*

ST-TROPEZ ☎04 94

Hollywood stars, corporate giants, and curious backpackers congregate on the spotless streets of St-Tropez (pop. 5400), where the glitz and glamor of the Riviera shines brightest. The young, beautiful, and restless flock to this "Jewel of the Riviera" to flaunt their tans on its infamous **beaches,** and their designer clothing in its lively and expensive nightclubs. The best beaches can be difficult to reach without a car, but a **shuttle** (*navette municipale*) leaves pl. des Lices for **Les Salins,** a secluded sunspot, and **plage Tahiti** (Capon-Pinet stop), the first of the famous **plages des Pampelonne.** (M-Sa, 5 per day, €1. Ask for schedule at the tourist office.) Take a break from the sun at the **Musée de l'Annonciade,** pl. Grammont, which showcases Fauvist and neo-Impressionist paintings. (Open M and W-Su June-Sept. 10am-noon and 2-6pm; Oct.-May 10am-1pm and 4-7pm. €4.60, students €2.30.)

Budget hotels do not exist in St-Tropez, and the closest youth hostel is in Fréjus (see below). **Camping** is the cheapest option; **Kon Tiki ❷** has a choice location near the northern stretch of the Pampelonne beaches. In July and August, Sodetrav sends daily buses (4 per day, €1.60) from the station to the campsite or, take the municipal shuttle from pl. des Lices to Capon-Pinet, and follow the signs downhill to the Plage Tahiti; walk 30-40min. down the beach to reach the site. Campers can soak up sun by day and wild parties by night at Kon Tiki's in-house bar. (☎55 96 96; www.campazur.com. Open Apr. to mid-October. July-Aug. 2 people, tent, and car €50; low season €20-27.) The *vieux port* and the streets behind the waterfront are lined with incredibly pricey restaurants, so create your own meal at **Monoprix** supermarket, 9 av. du Général Leclerc (open daily July-Aug. 8am-10pm, Sept.-June 8am-8:20pm; AmEx/MC/V) or stop by the snack stands and cafes near **place des Lices.**

Sodetrav **buses** (☎97 88 51) leave av. du Général Leclerc for St-Raphaël (2hr., 10-14 per day, €8.90). Les Bateaux de St-Raphaël **ferries** (☎95 17 46; www.tmr-saintraphael.com), at the *vieux port*, serve St-Tropez from St-Raphaël (1hr.; 2-5 per day; €11, round-trip €20). The **tourist office,** on quai Jean Jaurès, has shuttle schedules and copies of the *Manifestations* events guide. (☎97 45 21; www.saint-tropez.st. Open daily late June-Aug. 9:30am-12:30pm and 2-7pm; Sept. to late June reduced hours.) **Postal Code:** 83990.

ST-RAPHAËL AND FRÉJUS ☎04

With affordable accommodations, convenient transport, and proximity to the sea, the twin cities of St-Raphaël (pop. 32,000) and Fréjus (pop. 48,000) provide a good base for exploring the Riviera. In St-Raphaël, golden beaches stretch along the coast and the boardwalk turns into a carnival on summer evenings, while Fréjus trades sandy shores for Roman ruins. The first weekend in July brings the **Compétition Internationale de Jazz New Orleans** (☎98 11 89 00) to St-Raphaël. In Fréjus, the **Roman Amphitheater,** on r. Henri Vadon, holds frequent concerts and occasional bullfights. (Open May-Oct. M-Tu and Th-Sa 10am-1pm and 2:30-6:30pm; Nov.-Apr. M-F 10am-noon and 1:30-5:30pm, Sa 9:30am-12:30pm and 1:30-5:30pm. Bullfights July 14-16 and Aug. 15; €22-61. Contact the tourist office for a concert schedule.)

Take av. du 15ème Corps d'Armée from the Fréjus tourist office and turn left on chemin de Counillier after the second roundabout to reach the **Auberge de Jeunesse de St-Raphaël-Fréjus (HI) ❶,** a friendly hostel located in a secluded 170 acres of forest. (☎94 53 18 75; frejus-st-raphael@fuaj.org. Linen €2.80. Reception 8-11am and 5:30-10pm. Lockout 11am-5:30pm. Curfew June-Aug. 11pm; Sept.-Nov. and Feb.-Mar. 10pm. Closed Dec.-Jan. Camping €10 per person with tent. Dorms €13-15. Cash only.) In St-Raphaël, the **Hôtel les Pyramides ❸,** 77 av. Paul Doumer., offers well-kept rooms near the waterfront. To get to the hotel, turn left out of the station, make a right onto r. Henri Vadon, and take the first left onto av. Paul Doumer. (☎98 11 10 10; www.saint-raphael.com/pyramides. Breakfast €7. Reception 7am-9pm. Open mid-Mar. to mid-Nov. Singles €26; doubles €37-55; triples €57; quads €67. Extra bed €13. MC/V.) St-Raphaël's **Monoprix** supermarket is on 14 bd. de Félix Martin, near the station. (Open M-Sa 8:30am-7:30pm.) St-Raphaël sends **trains** every 30min. from pl. de la Gare to Cannes (25min., €5.60) and Nice (1hr., €9.40). **Buses** leave from behind the train station in St-Raphaël for Fréjus (25min., 1 per hr., €1.10) and St-Tropez (1½hr., 11 per day, €8.90). The **St-Raphaël tourist office,** on r. Waldeck Rousseau, is opposite the train station. (☎94 19 52 52; www.saint-raphael.com. Open July-Aug. daily 9am-7pm; Sept.-June M-Sa 9am-12:30pm and 2-6:30pm.) Take bus #6 from St-Raphaël to pl. Paul Vernet to reach the **Fréjus tourist office,** 325 r. Jean Jaurès. (☎94 51 83 83; www.ville-frejus.fr. Open July-Aug. M-Sa 10am-noon and 2:30-6:30pm, Su 10am-noon and 3-6pm; Sept.-June M-Sa 10am-noon and 2-6pm.) **Postal Codes:** 83700 (St-Raphaël); 83600 (Fréjus).

CANNES ☎04 93

Cannes conjures images of its annual film festival, where countless stars compete for camera time. But for the rest of the year, Cannes (pop. 70,000) rolls up the red carpet and becomes the most accessible of all the Riviera's glam towns. A palm-lined boardwalk, gorgeous sandy beaches, and innumerable boutiques draw the wealthy as well as the young and friendly. Stars and star-seekers descend on Cannes for the world-famous **Festival International du Film** (May 17-28, 2006). The festival is invite-only, though celebrity-spotting is always free. Of the town's three **casinos,** the most accessible is **Le Casino Croisette,** 1 espace Lucien Barrière, next to the Palais des Festivals. (No shorts, jeans, or t-shirts. Jackets required for men. 18+. Cover €10. Gambling daily 8pm-4am. Slots open at 10am.)

Hostels are 10-20min. farther from the beach than other lodgings, but are the cheapest options in town. **Hotel Mimont ❸,** 39 r. de Mimont, is the best budget hotel in Cannes. English-speaking owners maintain basic but clean rooms two streets behind the train station, off bd. de la République. (☎39 51 64; canneshotelmimont65@wanadoo.fr. Singles €29; doubles €38; triples €51. AmEx/MC/V.) Run by a young English-speaking couple, **Hostel Les Iris ❷,** 77 bd. Carnot, was converted from an old hotel into a clean, bright hostel with sturdy bunks, a Mexican-themed terrace restaurant, and small cafe. (☎68 30 20; www.iris-solola.com. Dorms €20. AmEx/MC/V.) The pedestrian zone around **rue Meynadier** has inexpensive restaurants. Stock up at **Champion** supermarket, 6 r. Meynadier. (Open M-Sa 8:30am-7:30pm. MC/V.) Cafes and bars near the waterfront stay open all night and are a great alternative to the expense of gambling and the glitz of posh clubs. Nightlife thrives around **rue Dr. G. Monod.** Try **Morrison's,** 10 r. Teisseire (☎04 92 98 16 17), for casual company in a literary-themed pub. (Beer from €5. Happy hour 5-8pm. Open daily 5pm-2am. MC/V.) Coastal **trains** depart from 1 r. Jean Jaurès for: Antibes (15min., €2.30); Marseille (2hr., €23); Monaco (1hr., €7.40); Nice (40min., €5.20); St-Raphaël (25min., €5.50). The **tourist office,** 1 bd. de la Croisette, helps find accommodations. (☎39 24 53; www.cannes.fr. Open July-Aug. daily 9am-8pm; Sept.-June M-F 9am-7pm.) There is a branch office at the train station. (☎99 19 77. Open M-Sa 9am-7pm.) Access the **Internet** at **Cap Cyber,** 12 r. 24 Août. (☎38 85 63. €3 per hr. Open daily 10am-10:30pm. MC/V.) **Postal Code:** 06400.

ANTIBES ☎04 93

Blessed with beautiful beaches and a charming *vieille ville*, Antibes (pop. 72,000) is less touristy than Nice and more relaxed than St-Tropez; with access to top-notch nightlife in neighboring **Juan-les-Pins,** it provides a much needed middle ground on the swanky coast. The excellent **Musée Picasso,** in the Chateau Grimaldi on pl. Mariejol, which displays works by the former Antibes resident and his contemporaries, is closed for renovations until 2007. The two main public beaches in Antibes, **plage du Ponteil** and neighboring **plage de la Salis,** are crowded all summer. Cleaner and more secluded, the rocky beach on **Cap d'Antibes** has a breathtaking landscape of white cliffs and blue water perfect for snorkeling.

For the cheapest option in Antibes, grab a bunk with a rowdy crowd of yacht-hands in the basic rooms at **The Crew House ❷,** 1 av. St-Roch. From the train station, walk down av. de la Libération; just after the roundabout, make a right onto av. St-Roch. (☎04 92 90 49 39; workstation_fr@yahoo.com. Internet €0.12 per min. Reception M-F 9am-7pm, Sa-Su 10am-6pm. Dorms Apr.-Oct. €20; Nov.-Mar. €15. MC/V.) A variety of restaurants set up outdoor tables along **boulevard d'Aguillon,** behind the *vieux port.*

WATER INTO WINE

France is the place for the frugal traveler who loves wine, and nowhere will budget-conscious oenophiles be more at home than at **Cave Raymond.** Behind a classy storefront of expensive bottles of local *pastis,* the owners keep three enormous vats of red, white, and rosé wines. Customers use a garden hose to transfer the wine from these giant metal vats into their own empty bottles for a mere €1.80 per liter. If you're worried about the quality of the wine you're getting, you're welcome to taste it first.

In order to conserve glass, the *cave* requires its patrons to use a specific wine bottle decorated with glass stars. First-time customers can look for a similar bottle at the supermarket, or pay an extra €0.30 to buy an empty one from the *cave.* But super-thrifty wine lovers can bring in any sort of container—empty water bottles included. Beware: the plastic taste can leech into the wine. After a visit here, that €4 *bouteille de vin* from the supermarket might not seem like such a good deal.

Cave Raymond has been emptying its vats to customers for the past 60 years. Unfortunately, this once-common practice is increasingly rare, so fill your bottles while you can.

***Cave Raymond,** 6 av. Guilllabert. ☎04 93 34 08 68. Open M-Sa 9am-1pm and 4-8pm.*

For cheaper eats, you're better off heading to lively **place Nationale,** a few blocks away. The **Marché Provençal,** on cours Masséna, is considered one of the best fresh produce markets on the Côte d'Azur. (Open Tu-Su 6am-1pm.) Come summer, the young and hip Juan-les-Pins is synonymous with wild nightlife. Frequent **buses** and **trains** run from Antibes, although walking between the two along bd. Wilson is also an option. Boutiques generally remain open until midnight, cafes until 2am, discothèques until 5am, and bars past dawn. **Pam Pam Rhumerie,** 137 bd. Wilson, is a hot Brazilian bar that turns wild when bikinied showgirls take the stage at 9:30pm to dance around and down flaming drinks. (☎61 11 05. Open daily mid-Mar. to early Nov. 2pm-5am.) In psychedelic **Whisky à Gogo,** 5 r. Jacques Leonetti, water-filled columns lit with blacklights frame a young crowd on the intimate dance floor. (Cover €16, €8 for students; includes 1 drink. Open July-Aug. daily midnight-5am; Apr.-June and Sept.-Oct. Th-Sa.)

Trains leave pl. Pierre Semard, off av. Robert Soleau for: Cannes (15min., 23 per day, €2.30); Marseille (2¼hr., 12 per day, €23.80); Nice (15min., 25 per day, €3.50). RCA **buses** leave pl. de Gaulle for Cannes (20min., every 20min., €2.60) and Nice (45min., every 20min., €4.10). From the train station, turn right on av. Robert Soleau, and follow the signs to the **tourist office** at 11 pl. de Gaulle. (☎04 92 90 53 00; www.antibes-juanlespins.com. Open July-Aug. daily 9am-7pm; Sept.-June M-F 9am-12:30pm and 1:30-5pm.) **Postal Code:** 06600.

NICE ☎04 93

Sophisticated and spicy, Nice (pop. 340,000) is the unofficial capital of the Riviera. Its non-stop nightlife, top-notch museums, and bustling beaches are unerring tourist magnets. During the three-week *Carnaval* in February, visitors and *Niçois* alike ring in the spring with grotesque costumes and wild revelry. No matter when you visit Nice, prepare to have more fun than you'll remember.

TRANSPORTATION

Flights: Aéroport Nice-Côte d'Azur (NCE; ☎08 20 42 33 33). **Air France,** 10 av. de Verdun (☎08 02 80 28 02), serves **Bastia, Corsica** (€116; under 25, over 60, and couples €59) and **Paris** (€93; under 25, over 60, and couples €50).

Trains: Gare SNCF Nice-Ville (☎14 82 12), av. Thiers. Open daily 5am-12:30am. To: **Cannes** (40min., every 20min., €5.50); **Marseille** (2½hr., 16 per day, €26.40); **Monaco** (15min., every 10-30min., €3.10); **Paris** (5½hr., 9 per day, €83.50-103.20).

Buses: 5 bd. Jean Jaurès (☎85 61 81). Information booth open M-F 8:30am-5:30pm, Sa 9am-4pm. To **Cannes** (1½hr., every 20-30min., €5.90) and **Monaco** (45min., every 10-15min., €4).

Ferries: Corsica Ferries, Port du Commerce (☎04 92 00 42 93; www.corsicaferries.com). Take bus #1 or 2 (dir.: Port) from pl. Masséna. To **Corsica** (€40).

Public Transportation: Sunbus, 10 av. Félix Faure (☎13 53 13; www.sunbus.com), near pl. Leclerc and pl. Masséna. Buses operate daily 7am-8pm. Individual ticket €1.30, day pass €4, 5-day pass €13, weekly pass €16.77, 8-ticket *carnet* €8.29. Purchase tickets and day passes onboard the bus; *carnet,* 5-day, and weekly pass from the office. The tourist office provides **Sunplan** bus maps, schedules, and route info.

Bike and Scooter Rental: Holiday Bikes, 34 av. Auber (☎16 01 62), a few doors down from the train station. Bikes €14 per day, €65 per week, deposit €230; scooters €32/160/500. Open M-Sa 9am-6:30pm. AmEx/MC/V.

ORIENTATION AND PRACTICAL INFORMATION

Avenue Jean-Médecin, on the left as you exit the train station, and **boulevard Gambetta,** on the right, run directly to the beach. **Place Masséna** is 10min. down av. Jean-Médecin. Along the coast, **promenade des Anglais** is a people-watcher's paradise. To the southeast, past av. Jean-Médecin and toward the bus station, is **Vieux Nice.** Women should not walk alone after sundown, and everyone should exercise caution at night around the train station, *Vieux Nice*, and promenade des Anglais.

Tourist Office: av. Thiers (☎08 92 70 74 07; www.nicetourisme.com), next to the train station. Books rooms. Ask for a map and *Nice: A Practical Guide.* The free *Le Pitchoun* has tips from students on restaurants, entertainment, and nightlife. Open June-Sept. daily 8am-9pm; closed Oct.-May.

Consulates: Canada, 10 r. Lamartine (☎92 93 22). Open M-F 9am-noon. **US,** 7 av. Gustave V (☎88 89 55). Open M-F 9-11:30am and 1:30-4:30pm.

Currency Exchange: Office Provençal, 17 av. Thiers (☎88 56 80), opposite the train station. 4% commission on euro-denominated traveler's checks. Open M-F 7:30am-8pm, Sa-Su 7:30am-7:30pm.

Laundromat: Lavomatique, 7 r. d'Italie (☎85 88 14). Wash €3.50, dry €1 per 18min. Open daily 7am-9pm.

Police: 1 av. Maréchal Foch (☎04 92 17 22 22), at the far end from av. Jean-Médecin.

24hr. Pharmacy: 7 r. Masséna (☎87 78 94).

Hospital: St-Roch, 5 r. Pierre Dévoluy (☎04 92 03 33 75).

Internet Access: Teknosoft, 16 r. Paganini (☎16 89 81). €2.50 per hr. Open daily 10am-11pm. **Alexso Info,** 2 r. de Belgique (☎88 65 00). €2.35 per 30min., €3.90 per hr. Open daily 10am-10pm.

Post Office: 23 av. Thiers (☎82 65 22), near the train station. Open M-F 8am-7pm, Sa 8am-noon. **Postal Code:** 06033.

ACCOMMODATIONS

Come to Nice with reservations; it can be hard to find beds, particularly in the summer. The city has two clusters of budget accommodations: near the train station and near *Vieux Nice.* Those by the station are newer but more remote; the surrounding neighborhood has a deservedly rough reputation, so exercise caution at night. Hotels closer to *Vieux Nice* are more convenient but less modern.

FRANCE

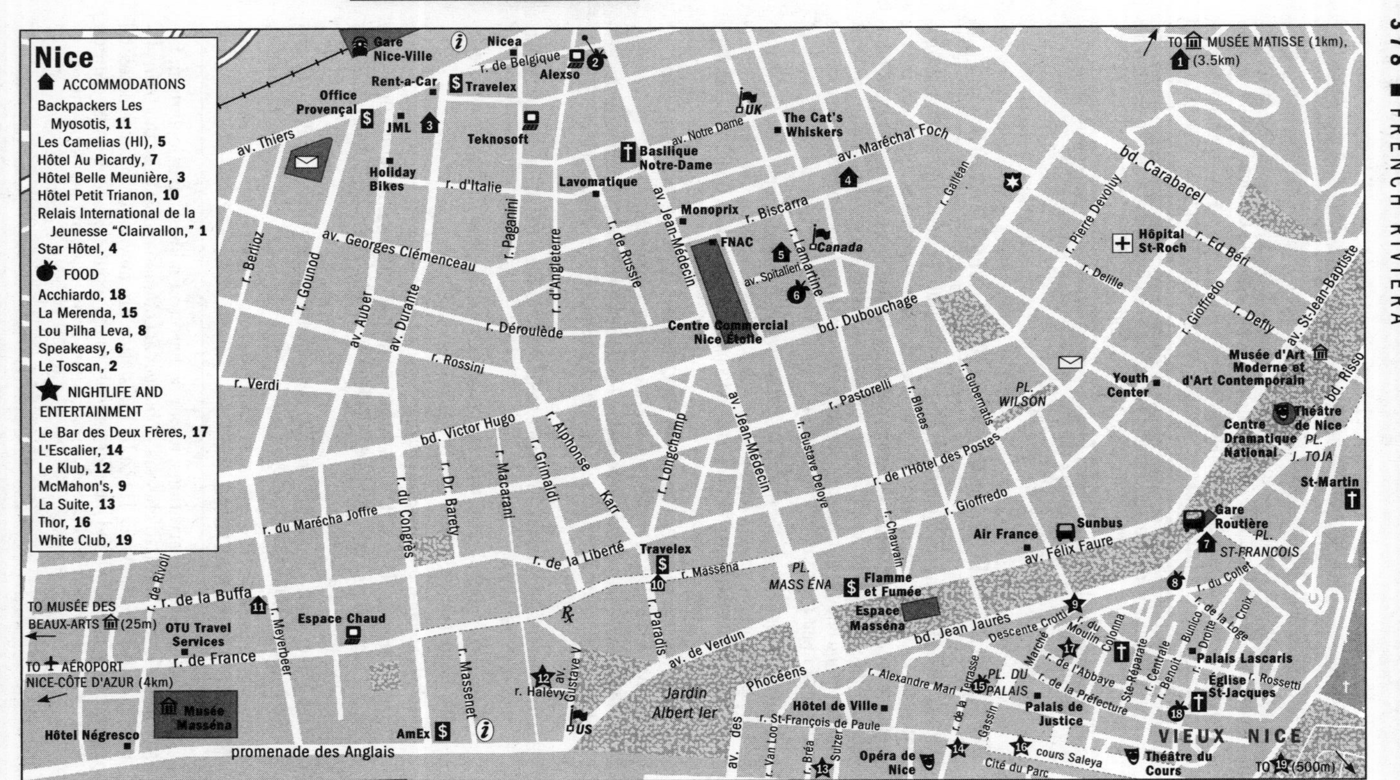
Nice
ACCOMMODATIONS
Backpackers Les Myosotis, 11
Les Camelias (HI), 5
Hôtel Au Picardy, 7
Hôtel Belle Meunière, 3
Hôtel Petit Trianon, 10
Relais International de la Jeunesse "Clairvallon," 1
Star Hôtel, 4
FOOD
Acchiardo, 18
La Merenda, 15
Lou Pilha Leva, 8
Speakeasy, 6
Le Toscan, 2
NIGHTLIFE AND ENTERTAINMENT
Le Bar des Deux Frères, 17
L'Escalier, 14
Le Klub, 12
McMahon's, 9
La Suite, 13
Thor, 16
White Club, 19
TO MUSÉE MATISSE (1km), (3.5km)
TO MUSÉE DES BEAUX-ARTS (25m)
TO AÉROPORT NICE-CÔTE D'AZUR (4km)
TO 19 (500m)
VIEUX NICE
Gare Nice-Ville
Nicea
Alexso
Rent-a-Car
Travelex
Office Provençal
JML
Teknosoft
Holiday Bikes
UK
The Cat's Whiskers
Basilique Notre-Dame
Lavomatique
Monoprix
FNAC
Canada
Centre Commercial Nice Étoile
Hôpital St-Roch
Youth Center
Musée d'Art Moderne et d'Art Contemporain
Théâtre de Nice
Centre Dramatique National
PL. J. TOJA
St-Martin
Gare Routière
PL. ST-FRANCOIS
Sunbus
Air France
PL. WILSON
PL. MASSÉNA
Flamme et Fumée
Espace Masséna
Espace Chaud
OTU Travel Services
Musée Masséna
Hôtel Négresco
AmEx
US
Jardin Albert Ier
Hôtel de Ville
Palais de Justice
PL. DU PALAIS
Palais Lascaris
Église St-Jacques
Opéra de Nice
Théâtre du Cours
av. Thiers
r. de Belgique
r. d'Italie
av. Notre Dame
av. Maréchal Foch
bd. Carabacel
r. Galléan
r. Pierre Devoluy
r. Ed Béri
r. Delille
r. Gioffredo
r. Defly
av. St-Jean-Baptiste
bd. Risso
av. Georges Clémenceau
r. Paganini
r. d'Angleterre
r. de Russie
av. Jean-Médecin
r. Biscarra
r. Lamartine
av. Spitalieri
bd. Dubouchage
r. Berlioz
r. Gounod
av. Auber
av. Durante
r. Déroulède
r. Rossini
r. Verdi
bd. Victor Hugo
r. Alphonse Karr
r. Longchamp
r. Pastorelli
r. Gustave Deloye
r. Blacas
r. Gubernatis
r. de l'Hôtel des Postes
r. du Congrès
r. Dr. Barety
r. Macarani
r. Grimaldi
r. du Marécha Joffre
r. de la Liberté
r. Masséna
r. Chauvain
av. Félix Faure
r. du Collet
r. de Rivoli
r. de la Buffa
r. Meyerbeer
r. de France
r. Massenet
r. Paradis
av. de Verdun
bd. Jean Jaurès
Descente Crotti
r. du Moulin
Colonna
r. Bunico
r. de la Loge
r. Droite
Croix
Marché
r. de l'Abbaye
r. de la Préfecture
Ste-Réparate
r. Centrale
r. Benoît
r. Rossetti
r. Halévy
av. Gustave V
Phocéens
r. Alexandre Mari
r. de la Terrasse
Gassin
av. des
r. Van Loo
r. Bréa
Sulzer
r. St-François de Paule
cours Saleya
Cité du Parc
promenade des Anglais

Hôtel Belle Meunière, 21 av. Durante (☎88 66 15; fax 82 51 76), opposite the train station. A relaxed crowd of backpackers fills high-ceilinged, 4- to 5-bed coed dorms in a former mansion. Showers €2. Laundry €6-10. Reception 7:30am-midnight. Dorms €15, with shower €20; doubles with shower €50; triples €60; quads €80. MC/V. ❷

Auberge de Jeunesse (HI) Les Camelias, 3 r. Spitalieri (☎62 15 54; nice-camelias@fuaj.org), behind the Centre Commerical Nice Etoile. A brand new hostel with clean rooms, located between the train station and the beach. Breakfast included. Laundry €6. Internet €5 per hr. Reception 24hr. Lockout 11am-3pm. Dorms €20. MC/V. ❷

Hôtel Petit Trianon, 11 r. Paradis (☎87 50 46; hotel.nice.lepetittrianon@wanadoo.fr). A motherly owner looks after guests in 8 comfortable, clean rooms just off lively pl. Masséna. Reserve ahead. Singles €30, with bath €35; doubles €40-42/50-53; triples €60-75; quads €76-96. 10% discount on stays longer than a week. MC/V. ❸

Hôtel Au Picardy, 10 bd. Jean Jaurès (☎85 75 51), across from the bus station. Spacious, renovated rooms near *Vieux Nice.* Breakfast €3. Reception 8am-8pm. Singles €25, with bath €34-36; doubles €40; triples and quads €50. Cash only. ❷

Relais International de la Jeunesse "Clairvallon," 26 av. Scudéri (☎81 27 63; clajpaca@cote-dazur.com), in Cimiez, 4km out of town. Take bus #15 to Scudéri (dir.: Rimiez; 20min., every 20min., €1.30) from pl. Masséna; after 9pm, take the N2 bus from pl. Masséna. Clean, 160-bed hostel in a luxurious villa, with sports field, TV room, and pool. Laundry €6. Lockout 9:30am-5pm. Dorms €15. Cash only. ❷

Star Hôtel, 14 r. Biscarra (☎85 19 03; www.hotel-star.com), in a quiet area between the train station and *Vieux Nice.* Spacious pastel rooms with TV, A/C, and soundproof windows. Closed Nov.-Dec. Singles €50-55; doubles with shower €60-65, with bath €63-68; triples with bath €73-78. Prices €10-15 lower Sept.-May. MC/V. ❹

Backpackers Les Myosotis, 19 r. Meyerbeer (☎06 24 72 49 36), on the corner of r. Meyerbeer and r. de la Buffa. A young crowd enjoys the carefree feel of this converted hotel just minutes from the beach. Clean 2- and 4-bed dorms have TVs, showers, and mini-fridges. Linen €1.20. Reception 24hr. 4-day max. stay. Dorms €18. Cash only. ❷

FOOD

Niçois cuisine is flavored with Mediterranean spices. Try crusty *pan bagnat,* a round loaf of bread topped with tuna, sardines, vegetables, and olive oil or *socca,* thin, olive-oil-flavored chickpea bread. The famous *salade niçoise* combines tuna, olives, eggs, potatoes, tomatoes, and a spicy mustard dressing. The eateries along the promenade des Anglais and av. Masséna are expensive and unremarkable. Save your euro for olives, cheese, and produce from the **markets** at cours Saleya and av. Maché de la Libération (both open Tu-Su 7am-1pm). **Avenue Jean-Médecin** features reasonable *brasseries, panini* vendors, and kebab stands. Load up on groceries at **Monoprix,** av. Jean-Médecin, next to the Nice Etoile shopping center. (☎04 92 47 72 62. Open M-Sa 8:30am-8:50pm. AmEx/MC/V.)

La Merenda, 4 r. de la Terrasse. Behind stained-glass exterior and a beaded curtain, this intimate restaurant offers some of the best regional dishes in the city. Reserve in the morning, in person, for dinner. *Plats* €11-16. 2 seatings at 7 and 9pm. Open M-F noon-1:30pm and 7-9pm. Cash only. ❷

Lou Pilha Leva, 10-13 r. du Collet (☎13 99 08), in *Vieux Nice.* At lunch and dinnertime, a line of locals and tourists hungry for inexpensive, tasty *Niçois* fare extends around the corner. Open daily 8am-midnight. Cash only. ❶

Acchiardo, 38 r. Droite (☎85 51 16), in *Vieux Nice.* Long, crowded family-style tables fill with simple but appetizing Italian and French dishes served up by a quick, dedicated team. Open M-F July 7-10pm; Sept.-June noon-1:30pm and 7-10pm. ❶

Le Toscan, 1 r. de Belgique (☎88 40 54), near the train station. Delicious, generous 4-course *menus* (€12.50, €14.50, or €20) use fresh produce purchased daily on the cours Saleya. Open Tu-Sa 11:45am-2pm and 6:45-10pm. MC/V. ❸

THAT LOOKS FAMILIAR!

Nice's big-city status has also earned it a reputation for big-city crime. Anywhere else, victims of theft resign themselves to never seeing their possessions again. However, in Nice, there's a running joke that if one of the city's many thieves robs you, head to the black markets.

Amid designer knock-offs and piles of dirt-cheap junk, you might well spot the leather wallet your grandfather gave you or the mobile phone you thought was safe charging in your hotel room—and the merchant will happily give you a bargain on your stuff. The Niçois readily tell stories of apartments being swept clean by burglars and then almost returned to normal after their owners visited the black markets.

The police do their best to stop the markets, carrying out sweeping arrests every now and then. But the markets are remarkably resilient and, in the end, set up each Sunday off rte. de Grenoble.

Even if the markets sound enticing, steer clear of these rough areas. Despite the deals, remember where all those items come from—tourists like you.

The continuing success of the black markets should serve as a reminder to bolt your hotel room door and watch your purse. Nice may be a party town, but it's a party to enjoy with caution.

Speakeasy, 7 r. Lamartine (☎85 59 50). The stiffest drink you'll find at this tiny hole-in-the-wall is freshly made carrot juice, the perfect complement to a delectable vegan menu. All customers share 3 wooden tables. 2 courses and dessert €11.50-13.50. Open M-F noon-2:15pm and 7-9:15pm, Sa noon-2:15pm. Cash only. ❸

SIGHTS

Many visitors to Nice head straight for the beaches and don't retreat from the sun and water until the day is done. However, whatever dreams you've had about Nice's beach, the hard reality is an endless stretch of pebbles; bring a beach mat if you plan to soak up the sun in comfort. Perfecting your tan has its merits, but don't forget that blue waves and topless sunbathers aren't Nice's only attractions.

MUSÉE NATIONAL MESSAGE BIBLIQUE MARC CHAGALL. Chagall founded this extraordinary concrete and glass museum in 1966 to showcase his 17 *Message Biblique* paintings. Twelve of these strikingly colorful canvases illustrate the first two books of the Old Testament, and the remaining five, done entirely in shades of red, illustrate the Song of Songs. *(Av. du Dr. Ménard. Walk 15min. north of the station, or take bus #15, dir.: Rimiez, to Musée Chagall. ☎53 87 20; www.chagall.fr. Open M and W-Su July-Sept. 10am-6pm; Oct.-June 10am-5pm. Last entrance 30min. before closing. €6.70, students ages 18-25 €5.20, under 18 and 3rd Su of the month free.)*

MUSÉE MATISSE. Henri Matisse visited Nice in 1916 and never left its shores. Originally a 17th-century Genoese villa, this museum contains a small collection of paintings and a dazzling exhibit of Matisse's three-dimensional work. *(164 av. des Arènes de Cimiez. Take bus #15, 17, 20, 22, or 25 to Arènes. Free bus between Musée Chagall and Musée Matisse; ask at either ticket counter. ☎81 08 08. Open M and W-Su 10am-6pm. €4, students €2.50. 1st and 3rd Su of the month free.)*

VIEUX NICE. Though the tourist industry has brought a slew of souvenir shops, ice cream stands, and *brasseries*, *Vieux Nice*, southeast of bd. Jean Jaurès, remains the spiritual heart of the city. Its tall buildings, painted in bright Mediterranean hues overlook a labyrinth of streets crowded with pansy-filled balconies, hand-painted awnings, pristine churches, and lively public squares. Artists of all kinds have shops throughout the neighborhood, particularly on **rue Droigt.** In the morning, the area hosts bustling **markets,** including a fish frenzy at **place St-François** and a flower market on **cours Saleya.** In the evening, cafe tables replace the market stalls, and the quarter becomes the center of Nice's lively nightlife.

MUSÉE D'ART MODERNE ET D'ART CONTEMPORAIN. An impressive glass facade welcomes visitors to this museum, which houses the work of French New Realists and American Pop artists, including Lichtenstein and Warhol. Minimalist galleries enshrine avant-garde pieces. The fantastic statues of Niki de St. Phalle and "color-field" pieces by Yves Klein are standouts. *(Promenade des Arts, at the intersection of av. St-Jean Baptiste and Traverse Garibaldi. Take bus #5, dir.: St-Charles, to Musée Promenade des Arts. ☎62 61 62; www.mamac-nice.org. Open Tu-Su 10am-6pm. €4, students €2.50, under 18 and 1st and 3rd Su of every month free.)*

LE CHÂTEAU. At the eastern end of the promenade, Le Château—the formal name for the ruins of an 11th-century fort—marks the site of the city's birthplace. The chateau itself was destroyed by Louis XIV, but the hilltop does, however, provide a spectacular view of Nice and the sparkling Baie des Anges. In the summer, an outdoor theater hosts orchestral and vocal concerts. The vista can be reached by climbing 400 steps or catching the elevator at the Tour Bellanda. *(Park open daily June-Aug. 9am-8pm; Sept. 10am-7pm; Oct.-Mar. 8am-6pm; Apr.-May 8am-7pm. Elevator runs daily June-Aug. 9am-8pm; Sept.-Mar. 10am-6pm; Apr.-May 10am-7pm. €0.70, round-trip €1.)*

MUSÉE DES BEAUX-ARTS. The former villa of Ukraine's Princess Kotschoubey has been converted into a celebration of French and Italian academic painting. Raoul Dufy, a Niçois Fauvist painter, celebrated the spontaneity of his city with sensational pictures of the town at rest and play. *(33 av. Baumettes. Take bus #38 to Chéret or #12 to Grosso. ☎04 92 15 28 28. Open Tu-Su 10am–6pm. €4, students €2.50, under 18 free. 1st and 3rd Su of every month free.)*

JARDIN ALBERT I. The city's oldest park, Jardin Albert I has plenty of palm trees, benches, and fountains. Its outdoor Théâtre de Verdun presents jazz and drama in summer. Contact the tourist office for a schedule. Unfortunately, the park is one of the most dangerous spots in Nice after dark; women especially should avoid walking here at night. *(Between av. Verdun and bd. Jean Jaurès, off promenade des Anglais. Box office open daily 10:30am-noon and 3:30-6:30pm.)*

OTHER SIGHTS. Named by the rich English community that commissioned it, the **promenade des Anglais,** a posh, palm-lined seaside boulevard, is Nice's answer to the great pedestrian thoroughfares of Paris, London, and New York. Today the promenade is lined by luxury hotels like the stately **Négresco** (toward the western end), where the staff still don top hats and 19th-century uniforms. Just east of the Négresco, the **Espace Masséna** provides a lovely, shady area where romantic picnickers can flirt beside the fountains. The seashore between bd. Gambetta and the Opéra alternates private **beaches** with crowded public strands, but a large section west of bd. Gambetta is reserved entirely for public use.

ENTERTAINMENT AND NIGHTLIFE

Nice's **Jazz Festival,** in mid-July at the Parc et Arènes de Cimiez near the Musée Matisse, attracts world-famous performers. (☎08 20 80 04 00; www.nicejazzfest.com. Tickets €33.) The **Carnaval,** in late February, gives Rio a run for its money with three weeks of parades, floral processions, confetti, fireworks, and parties.

Bars and nightclubs around r. Masséna and *Vieux Nice* pulsate with dance and jazz. Most will turn you away if you are wearing shorts, sandals, or a baseball cap. To experience Nice's nightlife without spending a euro, head down to the **promenade des Anglais,** where street performers, musicians, and pedestrians fill the beach and boardwalk. The free brochure *La Côte d'Azur en Fêtes*, available at the tourist office, provides info on nightlife and festivals. Exercise caution after dark; men have a reputation for harassing lone women on the promenade, near the train station, and in the Jardin Albert I, while the beach becomes a gathering place for prostitutes and thugs. Travelers should walk in groups if possible, and only take main, well-lit avenues to get back to their accommodations.

BARS

McMahon's, 50 bd. Jean Jaurès (☎13 84 07; www.mcmahonspub.com). Locals and expats stay entertained with nonstop contests, theme parties, and drink discounts. Happy hour daily 5-9pm (pints €3; wine €2); Cheap Tu (whisky, vodka, or gin mixed drinks; €2), Sangrian W (€10 pitchers). Open daily 5pm-2am. MC/V.

Thor, 32 cours Saleya (☎62 49 90). Svelte bartenders pour pints for a youthful crowd amid war shields, long wooden oars, and glasses shaped like Viking horns in this raucous faux-Scandinavian pub. Daily live bands blare rock, starting at 10pm. Happy hour 6-9pm (pints €4.50). Open daily 6pm-2:30am. MC/V.

Le Bar Des Deux Frères, 1 r. du Moulin (☎80 77 61). Vinyl records cover the walls of this hip favorite of local students, where nightly DJs keep the young crowd hopping with reggae, electronica, and techno. Open M-Sa 9pm-2:30am. AmEx/MC/V.

L'Escalier, 10 r. de la Terrasse (☎92 64 39). DJs spin R&B, funk, and hip-hop for a mix of locals late into the night. The real party starts around 1am when other bars close, but there's a €10 cover (includes 1 drink) after that point. Open daily 10pm-5am. MC/V.

CLUBS

White Club, 26 quai Lunel (☎26 54 79). A crowd of young fashionistas show off their trendy threads against a backdrop of white vinyl stools and blank tile walls. Cover €15. Open Th-Sa midnight-5am.

La Suite, 2 r. Brea (☎92 92 91). With velvet theater curtains and tall white candles, this swanky *boîte* attracts a well-dressed crowd. Go-go girls help make parties sizzle on weekends. Cover €13. Open Tu-Sa 11pm-2:30am. MC/V.

Le Klub, 6 r. Halévy (☎16 87 26). Nice's most popular gay club attracts a large crowd of men and women to the sleek lounge and active dance floor. Cover €11-14 includes 1 drink. Mixed drinks €6-10. Open W-Su midnight-5am. AmEx/MC/V.

FRANCE

DAYTRIPS FROM NICE: THE CORNICHES

Rocky shores, pebble beaches, and luxurious villas line the coast between hectic Nice and high-rolling Monaco. More relaxing than their glamorous neighbors, these tiny towns have interesting museums, ancient ruins, and breathtaking countryside. The train offers a glimpse of the coast up close, while bus rides on the high roads allow bird's-eye views of the steep cliffs and crashing sea below.

EZE. Three-tiered hilltop Eze owes its fame to the Roman village turned medieval citadel overlooking the Corniches. The **Porte des Maures** was the Moors' golden ticket into Eze during a 10th-century surprise attack; they ended up controlling the village for the next 70 years. The 18th-century **Eglise Paroissial** is adorned with *trompe l'oeil* frescoes and sleek Phoenecian crosses. (Open daily July-Aug. 9:30am-7:30pm; Sept.-June 9:30am-6pm.) To get to these historic landmarks, take the 40min. hike up the **Sentier Friedrich Nietzsche,** where the philosopher found inspiration; the path begins in Eze Bord-du-Mer, 100m east of the train station and tourist office, and ends at the base of the medieval city. Or, take the bus from the train station to the village. Frequent **trains** run from Nice (12min., €2.10).

VILLEFRANCHE-SUR-MER. This town's narrow streets and red-roofed houses have enchanted artists and writers from Aldous Huxley to Katherine Mansfield. As you stroll from the train station along quai Courbet, a sign for the *vieille ville* points to the spooky 13th-century **rue Obscure,** the oldest street in Villefranche. At the end is the **Chapelle St-Pierre,** decorated in bright pastels by Jean Cocteau, former resident, filmmaker, and jack-of-all-arts. (☎04 93 76 90 70. Open summer Tu-sSa 10am-noon and 4-8:30pm, low season reduced hours. €2.) **Trains** run from Nice (8min., 2 per hr., €1.60.) To reach the **tourist office** from the station, exit on quai 1, head inland on av. G. Clémenceau, and follow the right branch of av. Sadi Carnot to its end. (☎04 93 01 73 68; www.villefranche-sur-mer.com. Open July-Aug. daily 9am-7pm; low season reduced hours.)

MONACO AND MONTE-CARLO

Monaco (pop. 7200) has money—lots of it—invested in ubiquitous surveillance cameras, high-speed luxury cars, and sleek yachts. At Monaco's spiritual heart is the famous casino in its capital, Monte-Carlo, a magnet for the wealthy and dissolute since 1885. The sheer spectacle of it all is worth a daytrip from Nice.

CALLING TO AND FROM MONACO

Monaco's country code is 377. To call Monaco from France, dial 00377, then the eight-digit Monaco number. To call France from Monaco, dial 0033 and drop the first zero of the French number.

TRANSPORTATION AND PRACTICAL INFORMATION. Trains run to: Antibes (1hr., every 30min., €6); Cannes (65min., every 30min., €7.70); Nice (25min., every 30min., €3). **Buses** (☎04 93 85 64 44) leave bd. des Moulins and av. Princesse Alice, near the tourist office, for Nice (45min., every 15min., €4). The enormous **Rocher de Monaco** looms over the harbor, with **Monaco-Ville** at the top. The historical heart of the city can be found here, home to the Palais Princier, the Cathédrale de Monaco, and cafe-lined pedestrian streets. **La Condamine** quarter, Monaco's port, sits just below Monaco-Ville, with a colorful morning market, lively bars, and lots of traffic. Ritz and glitz is mostly concentrated in **Monte-Carlo,** home to the casino. Bus #4 links the Ste-Dévote train station entrance to the casino; buy tickets onboard (€1.45, *carnet* of 4 €3.50). At the **tourist office,** 2a bd. des Moulins, a friendly staff provides city maps and books hotels for no fee. (☎92 16 61 16; www.monaco-tourisme.com. Open M-Sa 9am-7pm, Su 10am-noon.) **Fnac,** Le Métropole Shopping Center, 17 av. des Spélugues, offers 20min. free Internet. (☎93 10 81 81. Open M-Sa 10am-5:30pm.) **Postal Code:** MC 98000 Monaco.

ACCOMMODATIONS AND FOOD. There's no need to stay in Monaco itself; the nearby town of **Beausoleil,** in France, has several options and is only a 10min. walk from the casino. **Hôtel Cosmopolite ❹,** 19 bd. du Général Leclerc, has comfortable rooms managed by English-speaking owners. (☎04 93 78 36 00; www.hotelcosmopolite.com. Singles €44; doubles €70; triples €91. Prices €5-10 lower Sept.-June. AmEx/MC/V.) The rooms at **Hôtel Diana ❸,** 17 bd. du Général Leclerc, are a little more modest, but come with A/C and TV. (☎04 93 78 47 58; www.monte-carlo.mc/hotel-diana-beausoleil. Singles €35; doubles €52; triples €63. AmEx/MC/V.) Not surprisingly, Monaco has little in the way of budget fare. Try the narrow streets behind the **place du Palais** for affordable sit-down meals, or fill a picnic basket at the **market** on pl. d'Armes at the end of av. Prince Pierre. (Open daily 6am-1pm.) The bright, bustling **Café Costa Rica ❷,** 40 bd. des Moulins, serves up *bruschetta,* salads, and other flavorful Italian staples at lunchtime, and tea and crepes after 3pm. (☎93 25 44 45. Pasta €8-11. *Plats du jour* €10-11. Open July-Aug. M-F 8am-7:30pm, Sa-Su 8am-3pm; Sept.-June daily 8am-7pm. Closed Aug. 1-15. V.) Just uphill from the casino tourist office is a **Marché U** supermarket, 30 bd. Princesse Charlotte. (☎93 50 68 60. Open M-Sa 8:30am-7:15pm. MC/V.)

SIGHTS AND ENTERTAINMENT. At the notorious **Monte-Carlo Casino,** pl. du Casino, Richard Burton wooed Elizabeth Taylor and Mata Hari shot a Russian spy. The slot machines open at 2pm (July-Aug. noon), while blackjack, craps, and roulette open at noon (cover €10). The exclusive *salons privés*, where French games such as *chemin de fer* and *trente et quarante* begin at noon, have a €10 cover. Next door, the more relaxed **Café de Paris** opens at 10am and has no cover. All casinos have **dress codes** (no shorts, sneakers, sandals, or jeans), and the *salons privés* require coat and tie. Guards are strict about the **18 age minimum;** bring a passport as proof. Perched above the casino is the **Palais Princier,** the occasional home of the tabloid-darling royal family. Visitors curious for a glimpse of royal life can tour the small but lavishly decorated palace. (☎93 25 18 31. Open daily June-Sept. 9:30am-6pm; Oct. 10am-5pm. €6, students €3.) Next door, the **Cathédrale de Monaco,** at pl. St-Martin, is the burial site of 35 generations of the Grimaldi family and was the venue for Prince Rainier and Grace Kelly's 1956 wedding. Princess Grace lies behind the altar in a tomb marked with her Latinized name, "Patritia Gracia." Prince Rainier is buried to the right of her tomb. (Open daily Mar.-Oct. 8am-7pm; Nov.-Feb. 8am-6pm. Free.) The **Private Collection of Antique Cars of His Serene Highness Prince Rainier III,** on les Terraces de Fontvieille, showcases 105 of the sexiest cars ever made. (Open daily 10am-6pm. €6, students €3.) Though Monaco hardly seems like a desert locale, innumerable species of cacti imported from America in the 16th century thrive in the **Jardin Exotique,** 62 bd. du Jardin Exotique. (Open daily mid-May to mid-Sept. 9am-7pm; mid-Sept. to mid-May 9am-6pm or until sundown. €6.80, students €3.50.) The **Musée Océanographique,** on av. St-Martin, holds a 90-tank aquarium full of exotic sea life. (☎93 15 36 00; www.oceano.mc. Open daily July-Aug. 9:30am-7:30pm; Apr.-June and Sept. 9:30am-7pm; Oct.-Mar. 10am-6pm. €11, students €6. MC/V.) Monaco's nightlife offers fashionistas a chance to see and be seen. **La Condamine,** near the port, is cheaper and caters to a younger clientele. Pricier spots near the casino are frequented by a glitzy crowd. **Stars N' Bars,** 6 quai Antoine 1er, draws a young, international crowd with its vintage decor, video games, and the latest pop and techno beats. (Open daily 11am-3am.) **Ras-Casbah,** 1 quai Antoine 1er, hosts live music nightly at 11pm. (Open daily 10am-5am. AmEx/MC/V.)

CORSICA (LA CORSE)

Napoleon claimed that the smell of herbs on Corsica's hillsides was so distinctive that he could identify his home island with his eyes shut. Even if your senses aren't that acute, there's no confusing Corsica with the French mainland. Despite centuries of invasions by Phoenicia, Carthage, Rome, Pisa, and Genoa, it has managed to preserve a unique, fiercely guarded culture. Most of Corsica's visitors come for the endless possibilities offered by its unspoiled and easily accessible landscape. Nearly one-third of the island is a protected nature reserve, with over 100 summits, far-reaching networks of hiking and ski trails, and unbroken coastlines that beckon to kayakers, windsurfers, sailors, and sunbathers alike.

GETTING THERE AND TRANSPORTATION

Air France and its subsidiary **Compagnie Corse Méditerranée (CCM)** fly to Ajaccio and Bastia from: Marseille (€117, students €104); Nice (€121, students €98); Paris (round-trip from €173, students €140). In Ajaccio, the Air France/CCM office is at 3 bd. du Roi Jérôme (☎08 20 82 08 20). **Ferries** between the mainland and Corsica can make for a rough trip, and aren't always much cheaper than a plane. High-speed ferries (3½hr.) run from Nice. Overnight ferries from Marseille take at least 10hr. The Société National Maritime Corse Méditerranée (☎08 91 70 18 01; www.sncm.fr) sends ferries from Marseille (€35-53, under 25 €20-40) and Nice (€30-41, under 25 €15-26) to Ajaccio and Bastia. Get SNCM schedules and prices at travel agencies and ports. Corsica Ferries (☎08 25 09 50 95; www.corsicaferries.com) has similar destinations and prices; it crosses from Livorno and Genoa, Italy to Bastia (€16-26). SAREMAR (☎04 95 73 00 96) and Moby Lines (☎04 95 73 00 29) go from Santa Teresa, Sardinia to Bonifacio. (€6.80-15.)

Train service in Corsica is slow and limited to destinations north of Ajaccio. Rail passes are not valid in Corsica. **Buses** provide more comprehensive service; call Eurocorse Voyages (☎04 95 21 06 30) for more info. **Hiking** is the best way to explore the island's mountainous interior. The **GR20** is an extremely difficult 14- to 15-day, 180km trail that takes hikers across the island from Calenzana to Conca. The popular **Mare e Monti** (7-10 days), **Mare a Mare Sud** (4-6 days), **Mare a Mare Nord** (12 days), and **Mare a Mare Centre** (7 days) trails are shorter and easier. The **Parc Naturel Régional de la Corse,** 2 Sargent Casalonga, in Ajaccio (☎04 95 51 79 00; www.parc-naturel-corse.com), has maps and a guide to *gîtes d'étape* (hostels).

AJACCIO (AIACCIU) ☎04 95

Napoleon must have insisted on the best from the very beginning: the little dictator couldn't have picked a better place to call home. Brimming with more energy than most Corsican towns, Ajaccio (pop. 60,000) has excellent museums and nightlife to complement its palm-lined boulevards, yellow sunlit buildings, and white sand beaches. Inside the **Musée Fesch,** 50-52 r. Cardinal Fesch, an impressive collection of 14th- to 19th-century Italian paintings gathered by Napoleon's art-collecting uncle fill cavernous rooms. Also within the complex is the **Chapelle Impériale,** the final resting place of most of the Bonaparte family—Napoleon himself is buried in Paris. (Open July-Aug. M 2-6pm, Tu-Th 10:30am-6pm, F 2-9:30pm, Sa-Su 10:30am-6pm; Sept.-June reduced hours. Museum €5.35, students €3.80. Chapel €1.50/0.75.) Napoleon's childhood home, the **Musée National de la Maison Bonaparte,** r. St-Charles, between r. Bonaparte and r. Roi-de-Rome, is now a warehouse of memorabilia. (Open May.-Sept. M 2-6pm, Tu-Su 9am-noon and 2-6pm; Oct.-Apr. M 2-4:45pm, Tu-Su 10am-noon and 2-4:45pm. €4, under 26 €2.60)

Ajaccio has many hotels, but from June through August, rates soar and vacancies plummet. The unbelievably welcoming **Pension de Famille Tina Morelli ❹,** 1 r. Major Lambroschini fills quickly; book as far in advance as possible. (☎/fax 21 16 97. Singles with breakfast and 4-course meal €50, with breakfast and 2 full meals €63; doubles €90/115. Cash only.) To camp at **Barbicaja ❶,** take bus #5 from av. Dr. Ramaroni to Barbicaja and walk straight ahead. (☎/fax 52 01 17. Open May to mid-Oct. Electricity €2.40. Tent sites €10.45. Cash only.) Though Ajaccio has no shortage of restaurants, your best option is the fabulous **morning market** on pl. du Marché. (Open Tu-Su 8am-1pm.) Pizzerias, bakeries, and one-stop *panini* shops can be found on **rue Cardinal Fesch;** at night, patios on the festive dock offer affordable seafood and pizza. Get groceries at **Monoprix,** 31 cours Napoléon. (Open July-Sept. M-Sa 8:30am-8pm; Oct.-June 8:30am-7:20pm.) **Boulevard Pascal Rossini,** near the casino, is home to Ajaccio's liveliest strip of bars. TCA bus #8 (€4.50) shuttles from the bus station at quai l'Herminier to **Aéroport Campo dell'Oro** (AJA; ☎23 56 56), where flights serve Lyon, Marseille, Nice, and Paris. **Trains** (☎23 11 03) leave pl. de la Gare for Bastia (3-4hr., 4 per day, €24) and Corte (2½hr., 4 per day, €13). Eurocorse Voyages **buses** (☎21 06 30) go to: Bastia (3hr., 2 per day, €18); Bonifacio (3hr., 2 per day, €21); Corte (1¾hr., 2 per day, €11). The **tourist office** is at 3 bd. du Roi Jérôme. (☎51 53 03; www.ajaccio-tourisme.com. Open July-Aug. M-Sa 8am-8:30pm, Su 9am-1pm and 4-7pm; Sept.-June reduced hours.) **Postal Code:** 20000.

BONIFACIO (BONIFAZIU) ☎04 95

At the southern tip of Corsica, the stone ramparts of Bonifacio (pop. 3000), perched on 70m-tall limestone cliffs, present an imposing visage to miles of empty turquoise sea. Bonifacio's fantastic **boat tours** reveal multicolored cliffs, coves, and stalactite-filled grottoes. Ferries also run to the pristine sands of **Iles Lavezzi,** a

FRANCE

nature reserve with beautiful reefs perfect for **scuba diving.** Companies that offer tours include **Les Vedettes Thalassa.** (☎73 01 17. Grottes-Falaises-Calanques tour every 30min. 9am-6:30pm. €14. Îles Lavezzi-Cavallo 5 departures per day, last boat returns at 5:30pm. €25. Cash only.) To explore the *haute ville*, head up the steep, broad steps of the **montée Rastello,** located halfway down the port, where excellent views of the hazy cliffs to the east await. Continue up montée St-Roch to the lookout at **Porte des Gênes,** a drawbridge built by invaders, then walk to the **place du Marché** to see Bonifacio's famous cliffs and the **Grain de Sable,** an enormous limestone formation that serves as a perch for daring cliff-divers.

Finding affordable rooms is virtually impossible in summer; avoid visiting in August when prices soar. Try **Hôtel des Etrangers ❹,** av. Sylvère Bohn. (☎73 01 09. Reception 24hr. Closed late Oct. to early Apr. July-Aug. singles and doubles €47-74; triples €70-74; quads €82-84. Low-season prices reduced. MC/V.) **Camping** is by far the cheapest option. **L'Araguina ❶,** av. Sylvère Bohn, is at the entrance to town between Hôtel des Etrangers and the port. (☎73 02 96. Open Apr. to mid-Oct. Laundry €6. Tent sites €7.70, extra person €5.60. Cash only.) A few supermarkets dot the port, including **SPAR,** at the start of rte. de Santa Manza. (Open daily July-Aug. 8am-8:30pm; Sept.-June reduced hours.) Eurocorse Voyages (☎21 06 30) sends **buses** to Ajaccio (3½hr., 1-3 per day, €21). To reach the **tourist office,** at the corner of av. de Gaulle and r. F. Scamaroni, walk along the port; before the *gare maritime*, climb the stairs. (☎73 11 88; www.bonifacio.fr. Open July-Aug. daily 9am-8pm; May-June and Sept. daily 10am-7pm; Oct.-Apr. M-F 9am-noon and 2-6pm.) **Postal Code:** 20169.

BASTIA ☎04 95

Bastia (pop. 40,000), Corsica's second-largest city, is one of the island's most trampled gateways, with connections to the French mainland and to more removed villages and vacation spots. Despite heavy tourist traffic, Bastia deserves more than just a passing glance. Its enormous 14th-century **citadel,** also called Terra Nova, has remained almost perfectly intact, with ramparts that reach down the hill toward the *vieux port*, dwarfing adjacent shops and bakeries. The tiny **Eco-Musée,** in the citadel's old powder magazine, contains a detailed replica of a traditional Corsican village, complete with miniature houses, working lights, and authentic vegetation. (Open Apr.-Oct. M-Sa 9am-noon and 2-6pm. €3.50, students €3.) On the other side of the *vieux port*, the 17th-century **Eglise St-Jean Baptiste,** pl. de l'Hôtel de Ville, towers over the city. The immense interior of the largest church in Corsica boasts gilded walls and ornate altars constructed with funds raised by local fishermen. The **Oratoire de l'Imaculée Conception,** on r. Napoléon, contains elaborately painted Baroque ceilings and red-and-gold walls. (Open daily 8am-7pm.) While there are no true budget hotels in Bastia, the welcoming **Hôtel Central ❺,** 3 r. Miot, is a good value, complete with antique furniture in large, well-kept rooms. (☎31 71 12; www.centralhotel.fr. Breakfast €6. May-Oct. singles €55-60; doubles €60-78. Nov.-June €10 less. AmEx/MC/V.) To reach **Camping Les Orangiers ❶,** take bus #4 (€1.15) from the tourist office to Licciola-Miomo. (☎33 24 09. Open May to mid-Oct. Electricity €3.50. Tent sites €7.30, extra person €4.60.) Inexpensive cafes crowd **place St-Nicolas. SPAR** supermarket is at 14 r. César Campinchi. (Open M-Sa 8am-12:30pm and 4-8:30pm, Su 8am-noon. MC/V.) Shuttle buses (30min., €8) leave from the *préfecture*, across from the train station, for the Bastia-Poretta Airport (BIA; ☎54 54 54), where **flights** go to Marseille, Nice, and Paris. **Trains** (☎32 80 61) run from pl. de la Gare to Ajaccio (4hr., 4 per day, €24) and Calvi (3hr., 4 per day, €19). Eurocorse **buses** (☎21 06 31) leave from rte. du Nouveau Port for Ajaccio (3hr., 1-2 per day, €20). The **tourist office,** pl. St-Nicolas, has copies of the bus schedule. (☎54 20 40; www.bastia-tourisme.com. Open daily July-Aug. 8am-8pm; Sept.-June 8:30am-noon and 2-6pm.) **Postal Code:** 20200.

CORTE (CORTI)

☎04 95

Corte (pop. 6000) is an unforgettable eyeful of plunging cliffs, jagged snow-capped summits, and quaint cobblestone streets. The geographical, intellectual, and political heart of Corsica, it harbors an unparalleled pride in its heritage. It is also home to the island's only university, whose students keep prices surprisingly low. The town's *vieille ville*, with its steep streets and 15th-century stone **citadel**, has long been a bastion of Corsican patriotism. It now houses the **Musée de la Corse,** at the top of r. Scolisca, which displays historical island artifacts and provides entrance to the higher forts of the citadel. (Open daily June-Sept. 10am-8pm; Nov.-May reduced hours. €5.30, students €3.) Corte's mountains offer great **hiking, biking,** and **horseback riding.** Rent horses at **Ferme Equestre Albadu,** 1.5km from town on N193. (☎46 24 55. €14 per hr., €75 per day with picnic.)

At the no-frills **Hôtel-Residence Porette ❷,** 6 allée du 9 Septembre, functional, clean rooms and a pleasant garden hide behind an austere cement facade. Head left from the train station and take a right at the roundabout; the hotel is across from the stadium. (☎45 11 11. Breakfast €5. Singles €21-27, with bath €39; doubles €25-29/39; triples and quads €59. AmEx.) **Place Paoli** has sandwiches and pizza joints, while **rue Scolisca** and the side streets off **cours Paoli** abound with cheap local fare. A huge **Casino** supermarket is to the left of station on N193. (Open July-Aug. M-Sa 8:30am-8pm; Sept.-June M-F 8:30am-12:30pm and 3-7:30pm, Sa 8:30am-7:30pm.) **Trains** (☎00 80 17) leave from the roundabout at av. Jean Nicoli and N193 for Ajaccio (2½hr., 4 per day, €13) and Bastia (2hr., 5 per day, €12). Eurocorse Voyages (☎31 73 76) runs **buses** to Ajaccio (1¾hr., M-Sa 2 per day, €11) and Bastia (1¼hr., M-Sa 2 per day, €10). To reach the town center from the train station, turn right on N193, then left at the bridge onto av. Jean Nicoli. Follow the road to cours Paoli, then turn left onto pl. Paoli; at the far right corner, climb the stairs of r. Scolisca and enter the citadel's walls to reach the **tourist office.** (☎46 26 70; www.corte-tourisme.com. Open July-Aug. M and Sa 10am-5pm, Tu-F 9am-7pm, Su 10am-6pm; Sept.-June reduced hours.) Hikers should get advice from the tourist office's knowledgeable staff on the region's best trails. **Postal Code:** 20250.

THE ALPS (LES ALPES)

FRANCE

Nature's architecture is the real attraction of the Alps. The curves of the Chartreuse Valley rise to rugged crags in the Vercors range and ultimately crescendo at Europe's highest peak, Mont Blanc. From bases like Chamonix, winter skiers enjoy some of the world's most challenging slopes. In the summer, hikers take over the mountains for endless vistas and clear air. As a rule, the farther into the mountains you want to go, the harder it is to get there, although service is more frequent from December to April during ski season.

GRENOBLE

☎04 76

Young scholars from all corners of the globe and sizable North and West African populations collide in Grenoble (pop. 168,000), a dynamic city whose surrounding snow-capped peaks are cherished by both athletes and aesthetes.

TRANSPORTATION AND PRACTICAL INFORMATION. **Trains** leave pl. de la Gare for: Annecy (2hr., 18 per day, €16); Lyon (1½hr., 30 per day, €17.50); Marseille (2½-4½hr., 15 per day, €44); Nice (5-6½hr., 5 per day, €58); Paris (3hr., 9 per day, €80). **Buses** leave from the left of the station for Geneva, Switzerland (3hr., 1 per day, €27). Turn right into pl. de la Gare, take the third left on av. Alsace-Lorraine, and follow the tracks on r. Félix Poulat and r. Blanchard to reach the **tourist office,** 14 r. de la République. (☎42 41 41; www.grenoble-isere.info. Open M-Sa 9am-6:30pm, Su 10am-1pm and 2-5pm.) **Celciuscafe.com,** 11 r. Gutéal, has **Internet.** (☎46 43 36. €2.50 per hr. Open daily 9am-11pm.) **Postal Code:** 38000.

ACCOMMODATIONS AND FOOD. From the tourist office, follow pl. Ste-Claire to pl. Notre-Dame and take r. du Vieux Temple on the far right to reach **Le Foyer de l'Etudiante ❶,** 4 r. Ste-Ursule. This stately building serves as a dorm during most of the year, but opens its large, modern rooms to travelers from June to August. (☎42 00 84; www.multimania.com/foyeretudiante. Linen €10. Laundry €2.20. Free Internet. June-Aug. 3-night min. stay for private rooms; 5-night max. stay for dorm. Dorms €8; singles €15; doubles €24.) To reach **Camping Les 3 Pucelles ❶,** 58 r. des Allobroges 4km from town in Seyssins, take tram A (dir.: Fontaine-La Poya) to Louis Maisonnat, then take bus #51 (dir.: Les Nalettes) to Mas des Îles; it's on the left. (☎96 45 73; www.camping-trois-pucelles.com. Tent sites €8, extra person €3.) Regional restaurants cater to locals around **place de Gordes,** while Italian eateries and cheap pizzerias line **quai Perrière** across the river. *Pâtisseries* and North African joints congregate around **rue Chenoise** and **rue Lionne,** between the pedestrian area and the river. **La Belle Etoile ❷,** 2 r. Lionne, has excellent Tunisian dishes. (☎51 00 40. Open Tu-Su 9am-2pm and 6-11pm. *Entrées* €7.40-13. AmEx/MC/V.) Cafes and smaller bistros cluster around **place Notre-Dame** and **place St-André,** in the heart of the *vieille ville.* A **Monoprix** supermarket is opposite the tourist office. (Open M-Sa 8:30am-8pm. AmEx/MC/V.)

SIGHTS AND ENTERTAINMENT. **Téléphériques** (cable cars) depart from quai Stéphane-Jay every 10min. for the 16th-century **Bastille,** a fort perched 475m above the city. (Open July-Aug. M 11am-12:15am, Tu-Su 9:15am-12:15am; Sept.-June reduced hours. €3.90, round-trip €5.70; students €3.20/4.60.) After enjoying the views from the top, you can walk down via the **Parc Guy Pape,** through the other end of the fortress, to the **Jardin des Dauphins** (1hr.). Cross the Pont St-Laurent and go up Montée Chalemont for the **Musée Dauphinois,** 30 r. Maurice Gignoux, which offers futuristic exhibits on the people of the Alps and the history of skiing. (Open M and W-Su June-Sept. 10am-7pm; Oct.-May 10am-6pm. Free.) The **Musée de Grenoble,** 5 pl. de Lavelette, houses one of France's most prestigious art collections. (☎63 44 44; www.museedegrenoble.fr. Open M and W-Su 10am-6:15pm. €5, students €2.) Another attractive aspect of Grenoble is its proximity to the slopes. The biggest and most developed **ski areas** are to the east in **Oisans;** the **Alpe d'Huez** boasts 220km of trails. (Tourist office ☎11 44 44, ski area 80 30 30. Lift tickets €33.50 per day, €202 per week.) The **Belledonne** region, northeast of Grenoble, has both a lower elevation and lower prices; its most popular ski area is **Chamrousse.** (Tourist office ☎89 92 65. Lift tickets €24 per day, €108-139 per week.) Only 30min. from Grenoble by **bus,** the resort also makes a great destination for **hiking** in summer. Whether you've spent your day in the museums or on the slopes, Grenoble's funky cafes, bars, and clubs are a great way to spend the night. Most are in the area between **place St-André** and **place Notre-Dame.** Drunken scholars mix it up at **Le Couche-Tard,** 1 r. du Palais, a small, graffiti-covered bar. (Mixed drinks €2. Happy hour 7-9pm. Open M-Sa 7pm-2am. AmEx/MC/V.)

FRANCE

CHAMONIX ☎04 50

The site of the first winter Olympics in 1924, Chamonix (pop. 10,000) combines the dignity of Mont Blanc, Europe's highest peak (4807m), with the spirit of its energetic visitors. Whether you've come to climb up the mountains or ski down them, be cautious—steep grades and potential avalanches make the slopes as challenging as they are beautiful. The **Aiguille du Midi téléphérique** (cable car) offers a pricey, knuckle-whitening ascent over snowy cliffs to a needlepoint peak, revealing a fantastic panorama from 3842m. (☎08 92 68 00 67. Round-trip €35.) Bring your passport to continue by gondola to **Helbronner, Italy** for views of three countries and of the **Matterhorn** and **Mont Blanc** peaks. (May-Sept., round-trip with Aiguille du Midi €52.) Chamonix has 350km of **hiking;** the tourist office distributes detailed hiking maps (€4). Some are accessible by cable car, which can save time and energy. The mountains that surround Chamonix are ideal for **skiing.** To the south, **Le Tour-Col de Balme** (☎54 00 58; day pass €27), above the village of **Le Tour,** draws beginner and intermediate skiers, while **Les Grands Montets** (☎54 00 71; day pass €36), to the north, is the *grande dame* of Chamonix skiing, with advanced terrain and **snowboarding** facilities. **Compagnie des Guides,** in Maison de la Montagne, facing the tourist office, leads ski trips and hikes. (☎53 00 88; www.cieguides-chamonix.com. Open daily Jan.-Mar. and July-Aug. 8:30am-noon and 3:30-7:30pm; Sept.-Dec. and Apr.-June reduced hours.)

Chamonix's *gîtes* and dorms are cheap, but they fill up fast; call ahead. From the train station, walk down av. Michel Croz and take a right onto r. Joseph Vallot for the **Red Mountain Lodge ❷,** 435 r. Joseph Vallot. The hard-working, English-speaking staff keeps its backpacker clientele happy with plush furnishings, views of Mont Blanc, and frequent barbecues for €10. (☎53 94 97. Breakfast included. Reception 8am-noon and 5-7pm. Dorms €16; private rooms €22.50-35. Cash only.) Restaurants in Chamonix cluster around the town center on **Rue du Docteur Paccard** and **Rue des Moulins,** which also boast Chamonix's most popular nightclubs and bars. Get groceries at **Super U,** 117 r. Joseph Vallot. (Open M-Sa 8:15am-7:30pm, Su 8:30am-noon.) **Trains** leave av. de la Gare (☎53 12 98) for: Annecy (2½hr., 6 per day, €19); Geneva, Switzerland (2½hr., 7 per day, €45); Lyon (3½hr., 7 per day, €34); Paris (6-7hr., 6 per day, €70-90). Société Alpes Transports **buses** (☎53 01 15) leave the train station for Geneva, Switzerland (1½hr., 1-5 per day, €33). Local buses (€1.50) connect to ski slopes and hiking trails. From the station, follow av. Michel Croz, turn left on r. du Dr. Paccard, and take the first right to reach pl. de l'Eglise and the **tourist office,** 85 pl. du Triangle de l'Amitié. (☎53 00 24; www.chamonix.com. Open daily July-Sept. and mid-Dec. to Apr. 8:30am-12:30pm and 2-7pm; May-June and Oct. to mid-Dec. reduced hours.) Access the **Internet** at **Cybar,** 80 r. des Moulins. (☎53 41 78. €0.80 per 10min. Open daily 10am-2am.) **Postal Code:** 74400.

ANNECY

☎04 50

With narrow cobblestone streets, winding canals, and a turreted castle, Annecy (pop. 53,000) appears more like a fabrication of fairy-tale life than a modern city. The **Palais de l'Isle,** in the beautiful *vieille ville,* is a 13th-century chateau that served as a prison for Resistance fighters during WWII. (☎33 87 30. Open June-Sept. daily 10:30am-6pm; Oct.-May M and W-Su 10am-noon and 2-5pm. €3.20, students €1.) The shaded **Jardin de l'Europe** is Annecy's pride and joy. In summer, the crystalline **lake** is a popular spot for windsurfing and kayaking, particularly along the **plage d'Albigny.** Annecy's Alpine forests boast excellent hiking and biking trails. One of the best hikes begins at the **Basilique de la Visitation,** near the hostel, and a scenic 25km *piste cyclable* (bike route) hugs the eastern shore of the lake.

In summer, you can reach the clean, beautifully located **Auberge de Jeunesse "La Grande Jeanne" (HI) ❷,** on rte. de Semnoz, via the *ligne d'été* bus (dir.: Semnoz) from the train station (€1). Alternatively, take bus #6 (dir.: Marquisats) from the station to Hôtel de Police, turn right on av. du Tresum, and follow signs to Semnoz. (☎45 33 19; annecy@fuaj.org. Breakfast included. Reception 8am-10pm. 4- and 5-bed dorms with showers €16.30. MC/V.) **Place Ste-Claire** has morning **markets** (Tu, F, Su 8am-noon) and some of the most charming restaurants in the city. A **Monoprix** supermarket is at pl. de Notre-Dame. (Open M-Sa 8:30am-7:30pm.) **Trains** arrive at pl. de la Gare from: Chamonix (2½hr., 6 per day, €19); Grenoble (2hr., 9 per day, €17); Lyon (2hr., 9 per day, €21); Nice (7-9hr., 7 per day, €72); Paris (4hr., 6 per day, €64). Autocars Frossard **buses** (☎45 73 90) leave from next to the station for Geneva, Switzerland (1¼hr., 8 per day, €10). From the train station, take the underground passage to r. Somellier, go left onto r. Vaugelas for four blocks, and enter the Bonlieu shopping mall to reach the **tourist office,** 1 r. Jean Jaurès, in pl. de la Libération. (☎45 00 33; www.annecytourisme.com. Open daily July-Aug. 9am-6:30pm; Sept.-June reduced hours.) **Postal Code:** 74000.

LYON ☎04 78

Laidback Lyon (pop. 1,260,000), a stopping point between the north and south, elicits cries of "forget Paris" from weary backpackers. Friendlier than that other French city, Lyon also boasts a few more centuries of history—it has been a provincial capital of Gaul, a hub of the silk trade, a center of the French Resistance, and is now an ultra-modern city, though *Vieux Lyon* recalls the city's wealthy past with 16th-century townhouses. France's culinary capital is also a stomping ground for world-renowned chefs and an incubator for new gastronomic genius. If the way to your heart is through your stomach, Lyon will have you at *bon appétit.*

TRANSPORTATION

Flights: Aéroport Lyon-Saint-Exupéry (LYS; ☎08 26 80 08 26), 25km east of Lyon. The TGV, which stops at the airport, is cheaper and more convenient than the 50 daily flights to Paris. **Satobus/Navette Aéroport** (☎04 72 68 72 17) shuttles passengers to Gare de Perrache, Gare de la Part-Dieu, and Metro stops Jean Mace, Grange-Blanche, and Mermoz Pinel (every 20min., €8.50). **Air France,** 5 r. Jessieu, 2*ème* (☎08 20 82 08 20), has flights to Paris's Orly and Charles de Gaulle airports (6 per day, €101-215).

Trains: Trains passing through Lyon stop only at **Gare de la Part-Dieu,** bd. Marius Vivier-Merle (M: Part-Dieu), in the business district on the east bank of the Rhône. Trains terminating at Lyon also stop at **Gare de Perrache,** pl. Carnot (M: Perrache). TGV trains to Paris stop at both. **SNCF** info and reservation desk at Part-Dieu open M-F 9am-7pm, Sa 9am-6:30pm; at Perrache open M-Sa 9am-7pm. SNCF trains go from both stations to: **Dijon** (2hr., 22 per day, €24); **Geneva, Switzerland** (2hr., 11 per day, €22); **Grenoble** (1¼hr., 19 per day, €18); **Marseille** (3hr., 17 per day, €38); **Nice** (6hr., 12 per day, €58); **Paris** (2hr., 26 TGVs per day, €57-70); **Strasbourg** (5½hr., 6 per day, €46).

Buses: On the lowest level of the Gare de Perrache and at Gorge de Loup in the 9*ème* (both ☎04 72 61 72 61). Domestic companies include **Philibert** (☎98 56 00) and **Transport Verney** (☎70 21 01), but it's almost always cheaper, faster, and simpler to take the train. **Eurolines,** on the main floor of Gare de Perrache (☎04 72 56 95 30), travels out of France. Open M-Sa 9am-9pm.

Local Transportation: TCL (☎08 20 42 70 00; www.tcl.fr), has info offices at both train stations and major metro stops. Pocket maps are available from any TCL branch. The efficient **metro** runs 5am-12:20am, as do **buses** and **trams.** Tickets are valid for all mass transport. 1hr. single-fare ticket €1.40; 10-ride *carnet* €11.90, students €10.20. The *Ticket Liberté* day pass (€4.20) allows unlimited use of mass transit.

ORIENTATION AND PRACTICAL INFORMATION

Lyon is divided into nine **arrondissements** (districts). The 1*er*, 2*ème*, and 4*ème* lie on the **presqu'île** (peninsula), which juts south toward the **Saône** River to the west and the **Rhône** to the east. Starting in the south, the 2*ème* (the *centre ville*) includes the **Gare de Perrache** and **place Bellecour.** The 1*er* houses the nocturnal **Terreaux** neighborhood, with its popular cafes and student-packed bars. Farther north are the 4*ème* and the **Croix-Rousse.** The main pedestrian roads on the *presqu'île* are **rue de la République** and **rue Victor Hugo.** West of the Saône, **Fourvière Hill** and its basilica overlook **Vieux Lyon** (5*ème*). East of the Rhône (3*ème* and 6-8*ème*) lie the **Gare de la Part-Dieu** (3*ème*) and most of the city's population.

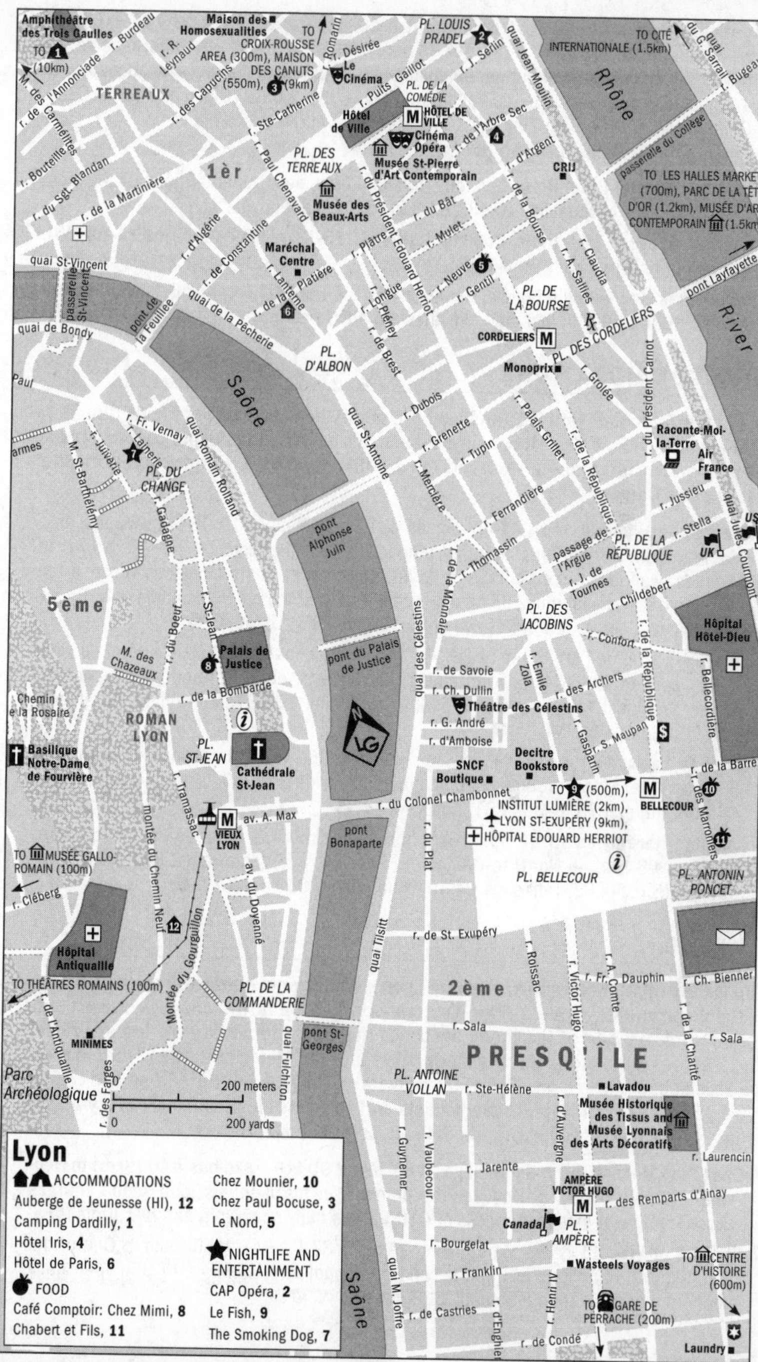
Lyon
ACCOMMODATIONS
Auberge de Jeunesse (HI), 12
Camping Dardilly, 1
Hôtel Iris, 4
Hôtel de Paris, 6
FOOD
Café Comptoir: Chez Mimi, 8
Chabert et Fils, 11
Chez Mounier, 10
Chez Paul Bocuse, 3
Le Nord, 5
NIGHTLIFE AND ENTERTAINMENT
CAP Opéra, 2
Le Fish, 9
The Smoking Dog, 7
Amphithéâtre des Trois Gaulles
TO 1 (10km)
Maison des Homosexualities
TO CROIX-ROUSSE AREA (300m), MAISON DES CANUTS (550m), 3 (9km)
Le Cinéma
PL. LOUIS PRADEL
TO CITÉ INTERNATIONALE (1.5km)
TERREAUX
Hôtel de Ville
HÔTEL DE VILLE
PL. DE LA COMÉDIE
Cinéma Opéra
Musée St-Pierre d'Art Contemporain
PL. DES TERREAUX
Musée des Beaux-Arts
1èr
CRIJ
Rhône
TO LES HALLES MARKET (700m), PARC DE LA TÊTE D'OR (1.2km), MUSÉE D'ART CONTEMPORAIN (1.5km)
Maréchal Centre
quai St-Vincent
passerelle St-Vincent
pont de la Feuillée
quai de Bondy
quai de la Pêcherie
Saône
PL. D'ALBON
PL. DE LA BOURSE
CORDELIERS
PL. DES CORDELIERS
Monoprix
pont Lafayette
River
Raconte-Moi-la-Terre
Air France
PL. DU CHANGE
quai Romain Rolland
quai St-Antoine
pont Alphonse Juin
PL. DE LA RÉPUBLIQUE
US
UK
5ème
PL. DES JACOBINS
Hôpital Hôtel-Dieu
Palais de Justice
pont du Palais de Justice
Théâtre des Célestins
ROMAN LYON
PL. ST-JEAN
Cathédrale St-Jean
Basilique Notre-Dame de Fourvière
SNCF Boutique
Decitre Bookstore
TO 9 (500m), INSTITUT LUMIÈRE (2km), LYON ST-EXUPÉRY (9km), HÔPITAL EDOUARD HERRIOT
BELLECOUR
VIEUX LYON
TO MUSÉE GALLO-ROMAIN (100m)
pont Bonaparte
PL. BELLECOUR
PL. ANTONIN PONCET
Hôpital Antiquaille
TO THÉATRES ROMAINS (100m)
PL. DE LA COMMANDERIE
2ème
MINIMES
pont St-Georges
PRESQU'ÎLE
Parc Archéologique
200 meters
200 yards
PL. ANTOINE VOLLAN
Lavadou
Musée Historique des Tissus and Musée Lyonnais des Arts Décoratifs
AMPÈRE VICTOR HUGO
Canada
PL. AMPÈRE
Wasteels Voyages
TO CENTRE D'HISTOIRE (600m)
TO GARE DE PERRACHE (200m)
Laundry

FRANCE

Tourist Office: In the **Tourist Pavilion** at pl. Bellecour, 2*ème* (☎04 72 77 69 69; www.lyon-france.com). M: Bellecour. Indispensable map and free hotel reservation office. The **Lyon City Card** authorizes unlimited public transport along with admission to 14 museums and various tours. Valid for: 1 day (€18), 2 days (€28), or 3 days (€38). Open May-Oct. M-Sa 9am-7pm, Su 10am-6pm; Nov.-Apr. reduced hours.

Police: 47 r. de la Charité (☎42 26 56).

Hospital: Hôpital Hôtel-Dieu, 1 pl. de l'Hôpital, 2*ème*, near quai du Rhône, is the most central. The city hospital line (☎08 20 08 20 69) will direct you.

Internet Access: Taxiphone Communications, 15-17 r. Montebello (☎14 54 25). €1.50 per hr. Open daily 9am-10pm.

Post Office: 2 pl. Antonin Poncet, 2*ème* (☎04 72 40 65 22), near pl. Bellecour. **Postal Codes:** 69001-69009; last digit indicates *arrondissement*.

ACCOMMODATIONS

As a major financial center, Lyon has more empty beds on the weekends than during the work week. Fall is the busiest season; it's easier and cheaper to find a place in the summer, but making reservations is still a good idea. Budget hotels cluster east of **place Carnot.**

Auberge de Jeunesse (HI), 41-45 montée du Chemin Neuf (☎15 05 50; www.fuaj.org). M: Vieux Lyon. Hike up from near the cathedral, or take the funicular from *Vieux Lyon* to Minimes, walk down the stairs, and go left downhill for 5min. Gorgeous views, a *terrasse*, and a lively bar make up for crowded 4- to 8-bed rooms. HI members only. Breakfast included. Linen €2.90. Reserve online. Dorms €13.75. MC/V. ❶

Hôtel Iris, 36 r. de l'Arbre Sec (☎39 93 80; www.hoteliris.freesurf.fr). M: Hôtel de Ville. A cozy convent-turned-hotel with sunny rooms creatively decorated by the cheerful owner. Breakfast €5. Singles and doubles with sink €35-37, with toilet and shower €45-50; triples €61. MC/V. ❸

Hôtel de Paris, 16 r. de la Platière, 1*er* (☎28 00 95; www.hoteldeparis-lyon.com). M: Hôtel de Ville. Elegant rooms full of character. Breakfast €6.50. Singles €42; doubles €49-68; triples €78; quads €81. AmEx/MC/V. ❹

Camping Dardilly (☎35 64 55). 10km from Lyon. From the Hôtel de Ville metro stop, take bus #3 (dir.: le Nord) to Gargantua. Pool, TV, and game room. Reception 8am-10pm. Electricity €3. Tent sites €4.50, extra person €3.20. MC/V. ❶

FRANCE

FOOD

The galaxy of Michelin stars adorning Lyon's restaurants confirms the city's status as the gastronomic capital of the Western world. But if *haute cuisine* doesn't suit your wallet, try one of the many **bouchons** that serve local fare for lower prices; they can be found along **rue des Marronniers** and **rue Mercière** in the *2ème*, and on **rue St-Jean** in *Vieux Lyon*. There are **markets** on the quais of the Rhône and Saône (Tu-Su 8am-1pm) and small **supermarkets** and **épiceries** close to nearly every major square, including pl. Bellecour, pl. St-Jean, and pl. des Terreaux.

Chez Paul Bocuse, 50 r. de la Plage (☎04 72 42 90 90). Take bus #40 (9km) to Neuville and ask to stop at Bocuse. The pinnacle of the *lyonnais* food scene charges accordingly, with *menus* in excess of €100. Open daily noon-2pm and 8-9:30pm. ❺

Chabert et Fils, 11 r. des Marronniers, 2*ème* (☎37 01 94). M: Bellecour. One of the better-known *bouchons* in Lyon, serving traditional fare. *Menus* €17-33. Open daily noon-2pm and 7-11pm, F-Sa until 11:30pm. MC/V. ❸

Chez Mounier, 3 r. des Marronniers, *2ème* (☎37 79 26). M: Bellecour. Tiny gem offers generously portioned traditional specialties in a cozy setting. 4-course *menus* €10-16. Open Tu-Sa noon-2pm and 7-11pm, Su noon-1:30pm. MC/V. ❷

Le Nord, 1 r. Neuve, *2ème* (☎04 72 10 69 69). M: Cordeliers. This spin-off restaurant of master Paul Bocuse offers a taste of his famous cuisine and for a more reasonable *menu* price (€18). Open M-Sa noon-2:30pm and 7-11pm. AmEx/MC/V. ❹

Café Comptoir: Chez Mimi, 68 r. St-Jean (☎38 09 34). M: Vieux Lyon. This small cafe serves salads (€6.40) and omelettes (€6.50) that are easy on the wallet. Open W-Th 6pm-1am, F-Sa noon-1am, Su noon-9:30pm. ❷

SIGHTS

VIEUX LYON

Stacked against the Saône at the bottom of Fourvière Hill, the narrow streets of *Vieux Lyon* wind between lively cafes and magnificent medieval and Renaissance houses. The striking *hôtels particuliers*, with their delicate carvings, shaded courtyards, and ornate turrets, emerged between the 15th and 18th centuries when Lyon controlled Europe's silk and publishing industries.

TRABOULES. The distinguishing features of *Vieux Lyon* townhouses are the *traboules*, indoor passageways connecting parallel streets through a maze of courtyards, often with vaulted ceilings and exquisite spiral staircases. Although their original purpose is still debated, many of the later *traboules* were constructed to transport silk safely from looms to storage rooms. During WWII, the passageways proved invaluable as info-gathering and escape routes for the Resistance. Many are open to the public, especially in the morning. An English-language tour beginning near the cathedral is the ideal way to see them; the tourist office also has a list of addresses. *(Consult tourist office regarding tours. €9, students €5.)*

CATHÉDRALE ST-JEAN. The cathedral's soaring columns dominate the southern end of *Vieux Lyon;* it was here that Henri IV met and married Maria de Médici in 1600. Some of the stained-glass windows are relatively new replacements; the originals were destroyed when Lyon's bridges exploded during the hasty Nazi retreat in 1944. Inside, every hour between noon and 4pm, automatons pop out of the 14th-century **astronomical clock** in a charming reenactment of the Annunciation. The clock can calculate church feast days until 2019. *(Open M-F 8am-noon and 2-7:30pm, Sa-Su 8am-noon and 2-5pm. Free.)*

DEVOURING LYON

Deciphering a menu in Lyon isn't always easy. Here are a few standards to get you started.

Salade Lyonnaise. A green salad tossed with diced ham sprinkled with croutons, and garnished with a poached egg.

Quenelle. A doughy dish of wheat, flour, eggs, and poultry or fish in a creamy sauce.

Tête de Veau. The translation says it all: "head of veal." Served bouillon-style with a vinaigrette.

Tablier de Sapeur. Only for the lion-hearted. A Lyon specialty since the time of Napoleon III, *tablier* is prepared from the stomach of cattle and marinated in wine, mustard, flour, and oil.

Melettes. An unappealing dish with an interesting history. Made from the testicles of lamb and cooked in lemon, *melettes* lent their name to the Lyonnais phrase *"être comme un chat entre deux melettes"* (being like a cat between two *melettes*)—or, in other words, being torn between two options.

Cervelle de Canut. A holdover from when Lyon was home to France's *canuts* (silk-weavers) this is a white cheese made with herbs, especially chives.

Bugne. This 14th-century Lyonnaise dessert was created at the convent of the St-Pierre church. The dessert was so airy and light that, upon the death of a good Christian, one would say *"il ira au ciel droit comme une bugne"* (he will go straight to heaven like a *bugne*).

FOURVIÈRE AND ROMAN LYON

From the corner of r. du Bœuf and r. de la Bombarde in *Vieux Lyon*, climb the stairs straight up to reach **Fourvière Hill,** the nucleus of Roman Lyon. From the top of the stairs, continue up via the rose-lined **Chemin de la Rosaire,** a series of switchbacks that leads through a garden to the **esplanade Fourvière,** where a model of the city indicates local landmarks. Most prefer to take the less strenuous **funicular** *(la ficelle)* to the top of the hill. It leaves from the *Vieux Lyon* metro station, at the head of av. A. Max. The **Tour de l'Observatoire,** on the eastern edge of the hilltop basilica, offers a different view of the city. On a clear day, scan for Mont Blanc, about 200km to the east. *(Chemin de la Rosaire open daily 6am-9:30pm. Tour de l'Observatoire open M and W-Su 10am-noon and 2-6:30pm. €2.)*

BASILIQUE NOTRE-DAME DE FOURVIÈRE. During the Franco-Prussian War, Lyon's archbishop vowed to build a church if the city was spared from attack. Now, the basilica's white, meringue-like exterior looms over the entire city. While some locals feel the building resembles an *éléphant renversé* (upside-down elephant) from the outside, its ornate, colorful interior is truly stunning. Inside are gigantic, shimmering mosaics depicting religious scenes, Joan of Arc at Orléans, and the naval battle of Lepanto. The low, heavy crypt was conceived by architect Pierre Bossan. *(Behind the esplanade at the top of the hill. Open 8am-7pm.)*

MUSÉE GALLO-ROMAIN. With rooms and corridors that cut deep into the historic hillside of Fourvière, this brilliant museum houses a collection of arms, pottery, statues, and jewelry. Highlights include six large, luminous mosaics, a bronze tablet inscribed with a speech by Lyon's favorite son, Emperor Claudius, and a huge, half-cracked eggshell pot. *(Open Tu-Su 10am-6pm. €3.80, students €2.30. Th free.)*

LA PRESQU'ÎLE AND LES TERREAUX

Monumental squares, statues, and fountains are the trademarks of the *presqu'île*, the lively area between the Rhône and the Saône. At its heart is **place Bellecour,** which is home to the tourist office and links Lyon's two main pedestrian arteries. **Rue Victor Hugo** heads quietly south, lined with boutiques. To the north, crowded **rue de la République,** or "la Ré," is the urban aorta of Lyon. It runs through **place de la République** and ends at **place Louis Pradel** in the *1er*, at the tip of the Terreaux district. Once a marshy wasteland, this area was filled with soil, creating dry terraces *(terreaux)* and establishing the neighborhood as the place to be for chic locals.

MUSÉE DES BEAUX-ARTS. This excellent museum takes visitors on a whirlwind tour through a tantalizing array of exhibits. An archaeological wing displays Egyptian and Roman artifacts. Distinguished French, Dutch, and Spanish paintings, along with works by Picasso, line the third-floor walls, and a lovely sculpture garden graces the inner courtyard. Surrounded by all-star Impressionist collections, even the museum's esoteric local works are delightful. A few surprises await museum-goers, including a fascinating Islamic art display and an unbelievably large coin collection. The museum's courtyard, accessible and free to the public, provides a much-needed sanctuary from the commotion of the square outside. *(20 pl. des Terreaux. Open Tu-Th and Sa-Su 10am-6pm, F 10:30am-8pm. Sculpture wing closed noon-2:15pm, painting wing closed 1-2:15pm. €6, under 26 €4, students free.)*

LA CROIX-ROUSSE AND THE SILK INDUSTRY

Though mass silk manufacturing is based elsewhere today, Lyon is proud of its historical dominance of the industry in Europe. The city's Croix-Rousse district, a steep, uphill walk from pl. des Terreaux, houses the vestiges of its silk-weaving days; Lyon's few remaining silk workers still perform delicate handiwork, reconstructing and replicating rare patterns for museum and chateau displays.

MUSÉE HISTORIQUE DES TISSUS. Exhibits about the history of the silk trade may be interesting, but everyone comes here for the clothes. In dark rooms, rows of costumes recall skirt-flouting, bosom-baring characters of the past. The collection includes examples of 18th-century elite garb (such as Marie-Antoinette's Versailles winter wardrobe), scraps of luxurious Byzantine textiles, and silk wall-hangings that resemble stained-glass windows. Included with admission is the neighboring **Musée des Arts Décoratifs,** in a fully furnished 18th-century *hôtel*, which displays an astounding array of clocks, painted plates, silverware, and furniture dating from the Renaissance to the present. *(34 r. de la Charité, 2ème. Tissus open Tu-Su 10am-5:30pm. Arts Décoratifs open Tu-Su 10am-noon and 2-5:30pm. €5, students €3.)*

EAST OF THE RHÔNE AND MODERN LYON

Lyon's newest train station and monstrous space-age mall form the core of the ultra-modern Part-Dieu district. Locals call the commercial **Tour du Crédit Lyonnais** *"le Crayon"* for its unintentional resemblance to a giant pencil standing on end. Next to it, the shell-shaped **Auditorium Maurice Ravel** hosts major cultural events.

CENTRE D'HISTOIRE DE LA RÉSISTANCE ET DE LA DÉPORTATION. Housed in a building where Nazis tortured detainees during the occupation, this museum presents an impressive but sobering collection of documents, photos, and films of the Resistance, which was based in Lyon. Audio tours in three languages lead visitors past heartbreaking letters and inspiring autobiographies. An excellent video at the end retraces life in concentration camps. *(14 av. Bertholet, 7ème. M: Jean Macé. Open W-Su 9am-5:30pm. €4, students €2, under 18 free. Audio tour included with admission.)*

MUSÉE D'ART CONTEMPORAIN. This mecca for modern art resides in the futuristic **Cité Internationale de Lyon,** a super-modern complex with shops, theaters, and Interpol's world headquarters. All the museum's exhibits are temporary; the walls themselves are built anew for each installation. *(Quai Charles de Gaulle, next to Parc de la Tête d'Or, 6ème. Take bus #4 from M: Foch. Open W-Su noon-7pm. €5, students €2.)*

NIGHTLIFE

Nightlife in Lyon is fast and furious; the city is crawling with bars and nightclubs. The best and most accessible late-night spots are a strip of **riverboat dance clubs** by the east bank of the Rhône. The tourist office lists venues that cater to gay and lesbian communities; the most popular are in the *1er*. For superb tips about gay nightlife, pick up *Le Petit Paumé* at l'EM Lyon, 23 av. de Collonge (€2.65).

Le Fish, across from 21 quai Victor Augagneur, *3ème*. M: Guillotière. Plays hip-hop, jungle, and house in a swanky boat with a dance floor. F-Sa cover €11 includes 1 drink, free before 11pm. Students only. Open W-Th 10pm-5am, F-Sa 10pm-6am. AmEx/MC/V.

The Smoking Dog, 16 r. Lainerie, *5ème*. M: Vieux Lyon. An English pub with sand-packed floors and book-lined walls, this popular spot is a constant lively beach party. Mixed drinks €5. Pints €4.50. Th student night. Open daily 2pm-1am. MC/V.

CAP Opéra, 2 pl. Louis Pradel, *1er*. A popular gay pub, with red lights to match the Opéra next door. A mellow crowd early in the evening spills outside as nighttime descends. Occasional *soirées à thème*. Open daily 2pm-3am.

BERRY-LIMOUSIN AND BURGUNDY

Too often passed over for beaches and big cities, Berry-Limousin offers undisturbed countryside and fascinating towns. While Bourges served as a temporary capital of France in the 15th century, Jacques Coeur, King Charles VII's financier, built a string of chateaux through the area. To the east, Burgundy declined such secular ornaments in favor of abbeys and cathedrals that bear witness to the religious fervor of the Middle Ages. Today, Burgundy draws Epicureans worldwide for its fine wines and delectable dishes like *coq au vin* and *bœuf bourguignon.*

DIJON ☎03 80

Dijon (pop. 150,000) isn't just about the mustard. The capital of Burgundy counters the preserved signs of its historic grandeur with an irreverent, fun-loving lifestyle. The diverse **Musée des Beaux-Arts** occupies the east wing of the colossal **Palais des Ducs de Bourgogne,** on pl. de la Libération at the center of the *vieille ville.* (☎74 52 70. Open M and W-Su May-Oct. 9:30am-6pm; Nov.-Apr. 10am-5pm. €3.40, students and Su free.) Built in only 20 years, the **Eglise Notre-Dame,** pl. Notre Dame, is one of France's most famous churches. Its 11th-century cult statue of the Black Virgin is credited with having liberated the city on two desperate occasions: in 1513 from a Swiss siege and in 1944 from the German occupation. The brightly tiled roof of **Cathédrale St-Bénigne,** in pl. St-Bénigne, is noticeable from anywhere in town; inside, the church features a spooky circular crypt. (☎30 39 33. Open daily 9am-6pm. Crypt €1.) Next door, the **Musée Archéologique,** 5 r. Dr. Maret, displays Neolithic housewares and 17th-century mustard crocks. (☎30 86 23. Open M and W-Su mid-May to Sept. 9am-6pm; Oct. to mid-May 9am-12:30pm and 1:30-6pm. €2.20, students and Su free.) Dijon's **Estivade** (☎30 31 00; tickets under €8) brings dance, music, and theater to the streets and indoor venues from late June to mid-July. In late summer, the week-long **Fêtes de la Vigne** and **Folkloriades Internationales** (☎30 37 95; www.fetesdelavigne.com; tickets €10-46) celebrate the grape harvest with dance and music from around the world.

Hotel Victor Hugo ❸, 23 r. des Fleurs, features antique clocks, armchairs, and tiled bathrooms. (☎43 63 45. Breakfast €5. Reception 24hr. Singles €30.50-38; doubles €38-47. MC/V.) **Rue Amiral Boussin** has charming cafes, while reasonably priced restaurants line **rue Berbisey, rue Monge, rue Musette,** and **place Emile Zola.** Fend for yourself at the **supermarket** in the basement of the Galeries Lafayette department store, 41 r. de la Liberté. (Open M-Sa 8:15am-7:45pm.) **Trains** run from cours de la Gare to: Lyon (2hr., 7 per day, €24); Nice (6-8hr., 6 per day, €68); Paris (1¾-3hr., 20 per day, €35-50). The **tourist office,** in pl. Darcy, is straight down av. Maréchal Foch from the station. (☎08 92 70 05 58; www.dijon-tourism.com. Open daily May to mid-Oct. 9am-7pm; mid-Oct. to Apr. 10am-6pm.) **Postal Code:** 21000.

BEAUNE ☎03 80

Wine has poured out of the well-touristed town of **Beaune** (pop. 24,000), just south of Dijon, for centuries. Surrounded by the famous Côte de Beaune vineyards, the town itself is packed with wineries offering free *dégustations* (tastings). To escape the wine tourists, rent a bike at Bourgogne Randonées and follow their suggested route by the *caves* (cellars). The largest of the *caves* which belongs to **Patriarche Père et Fils,** 5-7 r. du Collège, is a 5km labyrinth of corridors with over four million bottles. (☎24 53 78. Open daily 9:30-11:30am and 2-5:30pm. €10; all proceeds to charity.) Those thirsting for knowledge can learn more about winemaking on the Côte at the **Musée du Vin,** r. d'Enfer, off pl. Général Leclerc. (☎22 08 19. Open Apr.-Nov. daily 9:30am-6pm; Dec.-Mar. W-Su 9:30am-5pm. €4.50, students €2.20.) Beaune is also home to the **Hôtel-Dieu,** 2 r. de l'Hôtel-Dieu, one of France's architectural icons. A hospital built in 1443 to help the city's poor recover from the famine following the Hundred Years' War, it is now a museum. (☎24 45 00. Ticket office open daily Apr.-Nov. 9am-6:30pm; Dec.-Mar. 9-11:30am and 2-5:30pm. Museum closes 1hr. after ticket office. €5.50, students €4.70.)

Hôtel le Foch ❷, 24 bd. Foch, has colorful but cramped rooms close to downtown. (☎24 05 65. Singles and doubles €25, with shower €33-54; triples €38. MC/V.) However, cheap accommodations are hard to come by in Beaune; staying in

FRANCE

Dijon may be a better option. **Trains** run from Dijon (25min., 37 per day, €7). The **tourist office,** 1 r. de l'Hôtel-Dieu, lists *caves* that offer tours. (☎26 21 30; www.ot-beaune.fr. Open mid-June to mid-Nov. M-Sa 9:30am-8pm, Su 10am-12:30pm and 2-6pm; mid-Nov. to mid-June reduced hours.) The staff at Bourgogne Randonnées, 7 av. du 8 Septembre, near the station, rents **bikes** and gives free maps and great advice on suggested routes. (☎22 06 03. Bikes €3 per hr., €15 per day, €28 per 2 days, €75 per week. Credit card deposit required. Open M-Sa 9am-noon and 1:30-7pm, Su 10am-noon and 2-7pm. MC/V.) **Postal Code:** 21200.

ALSACE-LORRAINE AND FRANCHE-COMTÉ

As first prize in the endless Franco-German border wars, France's northeastern frontier has a long and bloody history. Heavily influenced by its tumultuous past, the entire region now maintains a fascinating blend of French and German in the local dialects, cuisine, and architecture. Alsatian towns display half-timbered Bavarian houses, tiny crooked streets, and canals, while Lorraine's wheat fields are interspersed with elegant, well-planned cities. The Jura mountains in Franche-Comté offer some of France's finest cross-country skiing.

STRASBOURG ☎03 88

On the Franco-German border, Strasbourg (pop. 450,000) has been annexed so many times by both sides that even its residents seem unsure of their current nationality. The tower of the ornate Gothic **Cathédrale de Strasbourg** stretches 142m skyward; young Goethe scaled its 332 steps regularly to cure his fear of heights. Inside the cathedral, the **Horloge Astronomique** demonstrates the wizardry of 16th-century Swiss clockmakers daily at 12:30pm, and the **Pilier des Anges** (Angels' Pillar) depicts the Last Judgment. (Cathedral open M-Sa 7-11:40am and 12:40-7pm, Su 12:45-6pm. Tower open Apr.-Oct. M-F 9am-5:30pm, Sa-Su 10am-5:30pm; Nov.-Mar. reduced hours. Clock tickets for sale inside cathedral or at southern entrance; €1. Tower €3, students €1.50.) **Palais Rohan,** 2 pl. du Château, houses three small but excellent museums: the **Musée des Beaux-Arts,** the **Musée des Arts Décoratifs,** and the **Musée Archéologique.** (All 3 open M and W-Su 10am-6pm. €4 each, students €2.50. Free 1st Su of every month.)

There are high-quality, inexpensive hotels all over the city, especially around the train station. Wherever you stay, make reservations early, particularly in the summer. The **Centre International d'Accueil de Strasbourg (CIARUS)** ❷, 7 r. Finkmatt, has brightly painted hallways and clean rooms complete with shower and toilet. From the train station, take r. du Maire-Kuss to the canal, turn left, and follow quai St-Jean through various name-changes; turn left on r. Finkmatt and it will be on your left. (☎15 27 88; www.ciarus.com. Breakfast included. Curfew 1am. Dorms €16.50-20.50; singles €39.50. MC/V.) The **La Petite France** neighborhood, especially along r. des Dentelles, is full of informal *winstubs* with Alsatian specialties such as *choucroute garnie* (spiced sauerkraut with meats). Explore **place de la Cathédrale, rue Mercière,** or **rue du Vieil Hôpital** for restaurants, and **place Marché Gayot,** off r. des Frères, for lively cafes. **El Pimiento ❷,** 52 r. du Jeu des Enfants, a lively, chili-themed tapas joint, serves both traditional favorites and creative variations. (☎21 94 52. Most tapas €3-5. Sangria €2.10. Open M-Sa noon-2pm and 6:30pm-midnight. AmEx/MC/V.) For groceries, swing by **ATAC,** 47 r. des Grandes Arcades, off pl. Kléber. (Open M and Sa 8:30am-8:30pm, Tu-F 8:30am-8pm.) Strasbourg, home to an international university, has bars everywhere. Students often play jazz piano at **Le Gayot,** 18 r. des Frères, whose terraces spill onto lively pl. Marché Gayot. (Beer €3.10. Mixed drinks from €7.50. Live music Th Sept.-June. Open daily June-Aug. 11am-1am; Sept.-May 11am-midnight. MC/

V.) **Bar Exils,** 28 r. de l'Ail, offers an upbeat atmosphere, over 40 beers, and food served until closing. (Beer from €2. Open M-F noon-4am, Sa-Su 2pm-4am. MC/V.) **Trains** (☎08 92 35 35 35) go to: Frankfurt (3hr., 18 per day, €47.50); Luxembourg (2½hr., 14 per day, €32.20); Paris (4hr., 16 per day, €45); Zurich (3hr., 3-4 per day, €39.50). The **tourist office,** 17 pl. de la Cathédrale, makes hotel reservations for a €2 fee plus deposit. (☎52 28 28; www.ot-strasbourg.fr. Open daily 9am-7pm.) There is also a branch at pl. de la Gare, near the train station (☎32 51 49). **Postal Code:** 67000.

LA ROUTE DU VIN

The vineyards of Alsace flourish along the foothills of the Vosges from Strasbourgto Mulhouse—a region known as the Route du Vin. The Romans were the first to ferment Alsatian grapes, and today Alsatians sell over 150 million bottles annually. Hordes of wine-loving and largely middle-aged tourists are drawn to the medieval villages along the route by picture-book houses and wineries offering free dégustations. Consider staying in **Colmar** (p. 399) or **Sélestat** (see below), larger towns that anchor the southern Route, and daytripping to the smaller (and pricier) towns. The best source of info on regional caves is the **Centre d'Information du Vin d'Alsace,** 12 av. de la Foire aux Vins, at the Maison du Vin d'Alsace in Colmar. (☎03 89 20 16 20. Open M-F 9am-noon and 2-5pm.) Tourist offices in Strasbourg (p. 397) or along the Route dispense helpful advice, including the Alsace Wine Route brochure.

TRANSPORTATION

Buses run frequently from Colmar to surrounding towns, but smaller towns are more difficult to reach. **Car** rental from Strasbourg or Colmar smooths out transportation problems, but also drain any wallet. **Biking,** especially from Colmar, is only for those with the stamina to gut out lengthy journeys, but trails and turn-offs are well marked. **Trains** connect Sélestat, Molsheim, Barr, Colmar, and Mulhouse. Country roads are difficult to walk along as they have minimal sidewalks.

SÉLESTAT ☎03 88

Sélestat (pop. 17,200), between Colmar and Strasbourg, is a friendly haven of good vines and good vibes often overlooked by tourists on their way to more "authentic" Route cities. Founded in 1452, the **Bibliothèque Humaniste,** 1 r. de la Bibliothèque, contains a fascinating collection of illuminated manuscripts and handwritten books produced during Sélestat's 15th-century Humanistic boom. (Open July-Aug. M and W-F 9am-noon and 2-6pm, Sa 9am-noon and 2-5pm, Su 2-5pm; Sept.-June closed Su. €3.60, students €2.10.) Nearby, on r. du Sel, the **Maison de Pain** reveals the history of breadmaking from 12,500 BC to the present. Head baker François Baltanas will happily tell you more about his art. (Open Jan.-Nov. Tu 2-6pm, W-F 10am-noon and 2-6pm, Sa 9am-noon and 2-6pm, Su 9am-12:30pm and 2:30-6pm; Dec. daily 10am-7pm. €4.60, students €2.30.)

Hôtel de l'Ill ❸, 13 r. des Bateliers, has 15 cozy rooms with shower and TV. (☎92 91 09. Breakfast €5. Reception 7am-3pm and 6:30-11pm. Singles €28-30; doubles €40; triples €50. MC/V.) A local favorite, **J P Kamm ❶,** 15 r. des Clefs, has outdoor dining and a dazzling selection of desserts. (☎92 85 25. Ice cream from €1.20. Open Tu and Th-F 8am-7pm, W 8:30am-7pm, Sa 8am-6pm, Su 8am-1pm. MC/V; €8 min. charge.) From pl. de la Gare, **trains** run to Colmar (15min., 20 per day, €3.90) and Strasbourg (30min., 20 per day, €7). The **tourist office,** 10 bd. Général Leclerc, in the Commanderie St-Jean, has bus schedules and rents **bikes** (€12.50 per day). From the train station, go straight on av. de la Gare, through pl. du Général de Gaulle, to av. de la Liberté. Turn left onto bd. du Maréchal Foch, which becomes bd. Général Leclerc. (☎58 87 20; www.selestat-tourisme.com. Open July-Aug. M-F 9:30am-12:30pm and 1:30-6:45pm, Sa 9am-12:30pm and 2-5pm, Su 11am-3pm; Sept.-June reduced hours.) **Postal Code:** 67600.

COLMAR ☎03 89

Best used as a base for exploring smaller Route towns, Colmar (pop. 68,000) has bubbling fountains, crooked lanes, pastel houses, and crowds of tourists. The collection of **Musée Unterlinden,** 1 r. d'Unterlinden, ranges from Romanesque to Renaissance, including Grünewald's *Issenheim Altarpiece.* (Open May.-Oct. daily 9am-6pm; Nov.-Apr. M and W-Su 9am-noon and 2-5pm. €7, students €5.) The **Eglise des Dominicains,** on pl. des Dominicains, is a bare-bones container for Colmar's other masterpiece, Schongauer's *Virgin in the Rose Bower.* (Open daily Apr.-Dec. 10am-1pm and 3-6pm. €1.30, students €1.) The 10-day **Foire aux Vins d'Alsace** in mid-August is the region's largest wine fair, with concerts, free tastings, and exhibitions. (☎03 90 50 50 50; www.foire-colmar.com. Festival entrance until 5pm €2.50, afterwards €5.50. Concerts €12-25.)

To reach the **Auberge de Jeunesse (HI) ❶,** 2 r. Pasteur, take bus #4 (dir.: Europe) to Pont Rouge. (☎80 57 39. HI members only. Linen €3.85. Reception Apr.-Sept. 7-10am and 5pm-midnight; Nov. to mid-Dec. and mid-Jan. to Feb. 7-10am and 5-11pm. Closed mid-Dec. to mid-Jan. Lockout 10am-5pm. Curfew midnight, 11pm in winter. Dorms €11.50-12.50; singles €17.50; doubles €28.50. MC/V.) Take bus #1 (dir.: Horbourg-Wihr) to Plage D'Ill and **Camping de l'Ill ❶,** rte. de Neuf-Brisach. (☎41 15 94; www.camping-alsace.com. Open Mar.-Nov. Tent sites €3.50, extra person €3.40.) The quiet **La Pergola et sa Taverne ❷,** 28 r. des Marchands, offers great regional cuisine. (*Tartes flambées* €9-12. Open daily noon-1:30pm and 7-10pm. MC/V.) A **Monoprix** supermarket is on pl. Unterlinden. (Open M-Sa 8am-8pm.) **Trains** depart pl. de la Gare for: Lyon (4½-5½hr., 7 per day, €41.90); Paris (5hr., 21 per day, €49); Strasbourg (40min., 36 per day, €9.70). To get to the **tourist office,** 4 r. d'Unterlinden, from the train station, turn left on av. de la République, which becomes r. Kléber, and follow it to the right to pl. Unterlinden. (☎20 68 92; www.ot-colmar.fr. Open July-Aug. M-Sa 9am-7pm, Su 10am-1pm; Sept.-June reduced hours.) **Postal Code:** 68000.

BESANÇON ☎03 81

Bounded by the river Doubs on three sides and a steep bluff on the fourth, Besançon (pop. 120,000) baffled Julius Caesar and was later made completely impenetrable with an enormous **citadel,** at the end of r. des Fusilles de la Résistance. Though its mountaintop fortifications are more daunting than pretty, Besançon hosts a slew of world-class museums and an active student population. Within the citadel, the **Musée de la Résistance et de la Déportation** chronicles the Nazi rise to power and the events of WWII from a French perspective. (Citadel ☎87 83 33; www.citabelle.com. Open daily July-Oct. 9am-7pm; Nov.-June. reduced hours. Admission to all museums in summer €7.80, students €6.50; in winter €7.20/6.) The **Cathédrale St-Jean,** beneath the citadel, holds two treasures: the 30,000-part 19th-century **Horloge Astronomique** (Astronomical Clock) and the white marble **Rose de St-Jean.** (Open M and W-Su 9am-6pm. Cathedral free. Tour of clock €2.50, students and under 18 free.) The **Musée des Beaux-Arts et d'Archéologie,** on pl. de la Révolution, houses an exceptional collection ranging from ancient Egyptian mummies to works by Matisse, Picasso, and Renoir. (☎87 80 49. Open M and W-Su 9:30am-noon and 2-6pm. €5, Su, students and under 18 free.)

To reach the **Foyer Mixte de Jeunes Travailleurs (HI) ❷,** 48 r. des Cras, take a left from the train station onto r. de la Viotte, the first right onto r. de l'Industrie, then a right on r. de Belfort to pl. de la Liberté. The Liberté bus stop is on r. de la Liberté, right off pl. de la Liberté. Take bus #5 or night line A (both dir.: Orchamps; 3-5 per hr.; €1) to the hostel, at stop Les Oiseaux, which has concerts, movies, and free Internet access in the lobby. (☎40 32 00. Singles €20, second night €18. AmEx/MC/V.) **Hôtel du Nord ❸,** 8-10 r. Moncey, is a fully-outfitted, high-end hotel in a quiet, central location. (☎81 35 56. Breakfast €4.60. Singles and doubles €35-48, with shower or bath €48-55; triples and quads with shower €58-64. AmEx/MC/V.) Restaurants line **rue Claude-Pouillet. La Boite au Sandwich ❶,** 21 r. du Lycée, offers enormous €3-7 salads and sandwiches. (☎81 63 23. Open M-F 11:30am-2:30pm and 7-10:30pm,

Sa 11:30am-2:30pm. MC/V.) Buy groceries at **Monoprix,** 12 Grande Rue. (Open M-Sa 8:30am-8pm.) The area between **rue Claude Pouillet** and **rue Pont Battant** buzzes with nightlife. Shoot pool and sip beer (€2) at the eccentric, but hip **Pop Hall,** 26 r. Proudhon. (☎83 01 90. Open M-Th and Su 2pm-1am, F-Sa 2pm-2am.)

Trains (☎08 36 35 35 35) leave av. de la Paix for: Dijon (1hr., 22 per day, €12.40); Paris (2hr., 8 per day, €47); Strasbourg (3hr., 8 per day, €28). Monts Jura **buses,** 4 r. Berthelot (☎08 25 00 22 44), go to Pontarlier (1hr., 3 per day, €8). Walk downhill from the station; turn onto av. Maréchal Foch and continue to the left as it becomes av. de l'Helvétie. Once you reach pl. de la Première Armée Française, the *vieille ville* is across pont de la République; the **tourist office,** 2 pl. de la 1ère Armée Française, is in the park to the right. (☎80 92 55; www.besancon-tourisme.com. Open June-Sept. M and W-Sa 9:30am-7pm, Tu 10am-7pm, Su 10am-5pm. Oct.-May reduced hours.) **Postal Code:** 25000

PONTARLIER AND THE JURA ☎03 81

The sedate town of Pontarlier (pop. 18,400) is a good base from which to explore the oft-overlooked Haut-Jura Mountains. The Jura are best known for **cross-country skiing;** nine trails cover every skill level. (Day pass, available at the Le Larmont and Le Malmaison trails; €6, under 17 €3.50.) Le Larmont is the closest **Alpine ski** area (☎46 55 20). In summer, **fishing, hiking,** and **mountain biking** are popular. There's a mountain bike departure point to the north just off r. Pompée, and another to the south, about 2km west of Forges. Hikers can choose between the **GR5,** an international 262km trail accessible from Le Larmont, and the **GR6,** which leads to a narrow valley and a dramatic chateau. To get from the tourist office to the quiet, centrally located **Auberge de Pontarlier (HI) ❶**, 2 r. Jouffroy, go left on r. Marpaud; the hostel is the white stucco building on the left. (☎39 06 57. HI members only. Breakfast €2.35. Linen €2.80. Reception 8am-noon and 5:30-10pm. Dorms €9.40. Cash only.) More accommodations are in **Besançon.** Monts Jura **buses** (☎08 25 00 22 44) run to Besançon (1hr., 3 per day, €8). The **tourist office,** 14bis r. de la Gare, has guides and maps. (☎46 48 33; www.pontarlier.org. Open July-Aug. M-Sa 9am-7pm, Su 10am-noon; Sept.-June closed Su.) **Postal Code:** 25300.

NANCY ☎03 83

Nancy (pop. 100,000) combines classical beauty and fresh innovation. The city that spawned the Art Nouveau "Nancy School" is today the artistic and intellectual heart of modern Lorraine. The stunning works on display at the **Musée de L'Ecole de Nancy,** 36-38 r. du Sergent Blandan, reject the straight lines of previous art and architecture, instead using organic forms to recreate aspects of the natural landscape. Take bus #122 or 123 (dir.: Vandoeuvre Cheminots) to Sédillot or Paul-Painlevé. (☎40 14 86; www.ecole-de-nancy.com. Open W-Su 10:30am-6pm. €8 pass buys entry to Nancy's museums.) The elaborately dazzling, newly renovated **place Stanislas** houses three Neoclassical pavilions, with nightly *son et lumière* (sound and light) shows at 10pm in July and August. The collection in the **Musée des Beaux-Arts,** 3 pl. Stanislas, houses works that date from the 14th century to the present, including gems by Monet, Rodin, and Picasso. (☎85 30 72. Open M and W-Su 10am-6pm. €6, students €4. W students free.) Portals of roses lead into the aromatic **Roseraie,** in the relaxing **Parc de la Pépinière,** just north of pl. de la Carrière. (Open daily May-Sept. 6:30am-11:30pm; Oct.-Apr. reduced hours. Free.)

Hôtel L'Academie ❷, 7 r. des Michottes, offers slightly unfinished rooms, but has a convenient location and a great price. (☎35 52 31. Breakfast €3.50. Reception 7am-11pm. Singles €18.60-26.50; doubles €26.50-32.50. AmEx/MC/V.) Restaurants line **rue des Maréchaux, place Lafayette,** and **place St-Epvre.** A **Shopi** supermarket sits at 26 r. St-Georges. (Open M-F 9am-8pm, Sa 9am-7pm. MC/V.) Nancy has a dynamic arts and nightlife scene. **Rue Stanislas** and **Grand Rue** are great places to grab a drink. **Blitz,** 76

r. St-Julien, is smoky suave at its best. (Shots €2.20. Beer €2.20. Mixed drinks €2.80. Absinthe €4. Open Tu-Sa June-Aug. 2pm-2am; Sept.-May 11am-2am. MC/V.) **Trains** (☎22 12 46) depart from the station at 3 pl. Thiers for Paris (3hr., 14 per day, €40) and Strasbourg (1hr., 17 per day, €22.30). Head left, then follow r. Raymond Poincaré away from the station, through a stone archway, and then straight on to pl. Stanislas and the **tourist office.** (☎35 22 41; www.ot-nancy.fr. Open Apr.-Oct. M-Sa 9am-7pm, Su 10am-5pm; Nov.-Mar. M-Sa 9am-6pm, Su 10am-1pm.) **Postal Code:** 54000.

CHAMPAGNE AND THE NORTH

Legend has it that when he first tasted champagne, Dom Perignon exclaimed, "Come quickly! I am drinking the stars!" Few modern-day visitors need further convincing as they flock to the wine cellars in Reims and Epernay, where champagne is produced from regional grapes according to a rigorous, time-honored method. As you head north to the ferry ports, don't overlook the intriguing Flemish culture in Arras or the world-class art collections in Lille.

REIMS ☎03 26

From the 26 monarchs crowned in its cathedral to the bubbling champagne of its famed caves, everything Reims (pop. 187,000) touches turns to gold. The **Cathédrale de Notre-Dame,** built with golden limestone taken from the medieval city walls, features sea-blue stained-glass windows by Marc Chagall. (☎77 45 25. Open daily 7:30am-7:30pm. €6, ages 12-25 €3.50.) The adjacent **Palais du Tau,** pl. du Cardinal Luçon, houses the original statues from the cathedral's facade alongside dazzling 16th-century tapestries. (☎47 81 79. Open May-Aug. Tu-Su 9:30am-6:30pm; Sept.-Apr. reduced hours. €6.10, ages 18-25 €4.10.) **Champagne Pommery,** 5 pl. du Général Gouraud, gives the best tours of Reims's champagne caves. Its 75,000L vat *(tonneau)* is the largest in the world. (☎61 62 56; www.pommery.com. Tours by reservation. Admission includes tour and various tasting options €8-15, students €3.50.) For champagne bargains, look for sales on local brands and check prices at supermarkets. Good bottles start at around €9.50. The small schoolroom where Germany surrendered to the Allies during WWII is now the **Museé de la Reddition,** 12 r. Franklin Roosevelt, a potent time capsule for the momentous event it witnessed. (☎47 84 19. Open M and W-Su 10am-noon and 2-6pm, Tu 2-6pm only. €3 pass includes Musée-Abbaye St-Rémi, Foujita Chapel, Musée de Beaux-Arts, and the planetarium. Students free.) In July, Reims hosts the fantastic **Flâneries Musicales d'Eté** (☎77 45 00), with more than 100 free concerts in 60 days.

The **Centre International de Séjour/Auberge de Jeunesse (HI) ❶,** on chaussée Bocquaine, has comfortable, sunlit rooms. (☎40 52 60; fax 47 35 70. Breakfast €3.30. Reception 24hr. Dorms €14.30-16.30; singles €21.90, with shower €33; doubles €27/35. €3 HI discount. AmEx/MC/V.) A **Monoprix** supermarket is at 21 r. Chativesle. (Open M-Sa 9am-8pm.) Cafes, restaurants and bars crowd **place Drouet d'Erlon,** the choice nightspot. **Trains** (☎88 11 65) leave bd. Joffre for Epernay (20min., 11 per day, €4.80) and Paris (1½hr., 11 per day, €20.90). To get from the train station to the **tourist office,** 2 r. Guillaume de Machault, follow the right-hand curve of the roundabout to pl. Drouet d'Erlon, turn left onto r. de Vesle and right on r. du Trésor; it's on the left before the cathedral. (☎77 45 00; www.reims-tourisme.com. Open mid-Apr. to mid-Oct. M-Sa 9am-7pm, Su 11am-6pm; mid-Oct. to mid-Apr. reduced hours.) **Postal Code:** 51100.

EPERNAY ☎03 26

Epernay (pop. 30,000), at the juncture of three wealthy grape-growing regions, is appropriately ritzy and sparklingly seductive. The aptly named **avenue de Champagne** is distinguished by its palatial mansions, lush gardens, and swanky champagne companies. **Moët & Chandon,** 20 av. de Champagne, produces the king of all champagnes: **Dom Perignon.** (☎51 20 20. Open Mar.-Oct. daily 9:30-11:30am and 2-4:30pm; Nov.-Apr. M-F only. Tours with several tasting options €8-21.) Ten minutes away is **Mercier,** 70 av. de Champagne, the self-proclaimed "most popular champagne in France," which gives tours in laser-guided cars. (☎51 22 22. Open late Mar. to mid-Nov. daily 9:30-11:30am and 2-4:30pm; mid-Nov. to mid-Dec. and mid-Jan. to Mar. M and Th-Su only. 30min. tour €6.50.)

Epernay caters to the champagne set—budget hotels are rare. **Hôtel St-Pierre ❷,** 1 r. Jeanne d'Arc, is your best bet with spacious, antique-furnished rooms. (☎54 40 80; fax 57 88 68. Breakfast €5.50. Reception 7am-10pm. Singles and doubles €23, with shower €26-38. MC/V.) Ethnic options line **rue Gambetta.** The area around **place des Arcades** and **place Hugues Plomb** is dotted with delis and bakeries. A **Marché Plus** supermarket is at 13 pl. Hugues Plomb. (Open M-Sa 7am-9pm, Su 9am-1pm.)**Trains** leave Cours de la Gare for Paris (1¼hr., 18 per day, €18.10) and Reims (25min., 16 per day, €5.30). From the station, walk straight ahead through pl. Mendès France, go one block up r. Gambetta to pl. de la République, and turn left on av. de Champagne to reach the **tourist office,** 7 av. de Champagne. (☎53 33 00; www.ot-epernay.fr. Open Easter to mid-Oct. M-Sa 9:30am-12:30pm and 1:30-7pm, Su 11am-4pm; mid-Oct. to Easter reduced hours.) **Postal Code:** 51200.

TROYES ☎03 25

Although the city plan resembles a champagne cork, little else links Troyes (pop. 60,000) with its grape-crazy northern neighbors. Troyes features Gothic churches, 16th-century mansions, and an abundance of museums complementing an energy and social scene equal to cities many times its size. The enormous **Cathédrale St-Pierre et St-Paul,** pl. St-Pierre, down r. Clemenceau past the town hall, is a flamboyant Gothic church, with ornate detail and flying buttresses. Its stunning stained glass, in the unique Troyes style, has survived several fires, bombings, and other disasters. (Open daily 10am-7pm. Closed M morning. Free.) The **Musée d'Art Moderne,** just next door on pl. St-Pierre, houses over 2000 works by French artists, including Degas, Rodin, and Seurat, in the former Episcopal palace. (☎76 95 02. Open Tu-Su 11am-6pm. €5, students and under 25 free. 1st Su of every month free.) The fresh-water **Grands Lacs** dot the Forêt d'Orient region around Troyes. The **Comité Départemental du Tourisme de l'Aube,** 34 quai Dampierre, provides info on outdoor activities that include fishing, swimming, waterskiing, and windsurfing. (☎42 60 00. Open M-F 8:45am-noon and 1:30-6pm.)

Les Comtes de Champagne ❸, 56 r. de la Monnaie, is in a 16th-century mansion with lace-curtained windows and large, airy rooms. (☎73 11 70; www.comtesdechampagne.com. Reception 7am-10pm. Singles from €29; doubles from €34; triples from €54; quads from €58. MC/V.) To reach **Camping Municipal ❶,** 2km from Troyes on N60, take bus #1 (dir.: Pont St-Marie) and ask to be let off at the campground. (☎81 02 64. Open Apr. to mid-Oct. Tent sites €5.60, €4.10 per person. Cash only.) *Crêperies* and inexpensive eateries lie near **rue Champeaux,** in *quartier* St-Jean, and on **rue Général Saussier,** in *quartier* Vauluisant. Stock up at **Monoprix** supermarket, 78 r. Emile Zola, which also has cheap, tasty cafeteria food. (Open M-Sa 8:30am-8pm.) Cinemas and pool halls rub elbows with chic boutiques on **rue Emile Zola.** On warm nights, locals fill the cafes and taverns of **rue Champeaux** and **rue Molé** near **place Alexandre Israël. Trains** run from av. Maréchal Joffre to Paris (1½hr., 21 per day, €22). The **tourist office,** 16 bd. Carnot, to the right of the station, has bus schedules for the lakes and helps book rooms. (☎82 62 70; www.tourisme-troyes.com. Open M-Sa 9am-12:30pm and 2-6:30pm.) **Postal Code:** 10000.

LILLE

☎03 20

A long-time international hub with rich Flemish ancestry and the best nightlife in the north, Lille (pop. 214,000) has abandoned its industrial days to become a delightfully untouristy metropolis. The impressive **Palais des Beaux-Arts,** on pl. de la République (M: République), is the second-largest art collection in France, with a comprehensive display of 15th- to 20th-century French and Flemish masterpieces. (Open M 2-6pm; Tu, Th, Sa-Su 10am-6pm; F 10am-7pm. €4.60, students €3.) Housed in a renovated indoor pool building, the aptly named **La Piscine,** 23 r. de L'Espérance (M: Gare Jean Lebas), has creative exhibits and a collection that includes paintings and sculptures from the 19th and early 20th centuries. (Open Tu-Th 11am-6pm, F 11am-8pm, Sa-Su 1-6pm. €3, students €2.)

To reach the friendly **Auberge de Jeunesse (HI)** ❷, 12 r. Malpart (M: Mairie de Lille), from Gare Lille Flandres, circle left around the station, then turn right onto r. du Molinel, left onto r. de Paris, and right onto r. Malpart. (☎57 08 94; lille@fuaj.org. Linen €2.80. Reception 24hr. Lockout 11am-3pm. Open Feb. to mid-Dec. Dorms €18.15, under 26 €13.60. HI discount. MC/V.) Restaurants line **rue de Béthune, rue Léon Gambetta,** and **place du Théâtre.** A **Carrefour** supermarket is in the shopping center next to Gare Lille Europe. (Open M-Sa 9am-10pm.) At night, students flock to the pubs along **rue Solférino** and **rue Masséna,** while *vieux* Lille has a more sophisticated scene. A student clientele sips drinks and shoots billiards at **Gino Pub,** 21 r. Masséna. (Beer €1.50. Open M-Sa noon-2am, Su 5pm-2am.)

Trains leave from Gare Lille Flandres, on pl. de la Gare (M: Gare Lille Flandres), for Brussels, Belgium (1½hr., 20 per day, €21) and Paris (1hr., 21 per day, €34.50). Gare Lille Europe, on r. Le Corbusier (☎08 36 35 35 35; M: Gare Lille Europe), sends **Eurostar** trains to Brussels, Belgium (€22.40) and London, England (10 per day, €35-187.50), and **TGVs** to the south of France and Paris (1hr., 4 per day, €46.50). Eurolines **buses** (☎78 18 88) run from Gare Lille Europe to: Amsterdam, Netherlands (round-trip €49); Brussels, Belgium (round-trip €19); London, England (round-trip €47). From Gare Lille Flandres, walk straight down r. Faidherbe and turn left through pl. du Théâtre and pl. Général de Gaulle. The **tourist office,** pl. Rihour (M: Rihour), is behind the huge war monument. (☎21 94 21; www.lilletourism.com. Open M-Sa 9:30am-6:30pm, Su 10am-noon and 2-5pm.) **Postal Code:** 59000.

BOULOGNE-SUR-MER

☎03 21

Boulogne-sur-Mer (pop. 46,000) is by far the most attractive of the Channel ports. Its huge aquarium, **Le Grand Nausicaä,** bd. Ste-Beuve, next to the **beach,** capitalizes on the town's main source of commerce and nutrition. (Open daily July-Aug. 9:30am-7:30pm; Sept.-June 9:30am-6:30pm. €11.50-13, students €8.30.) The **Château-Musée,** r. de Bernet, houses an eclectic collection ranging from an Egyptian mummy to Napoleon's second-oldest hat. (☎10 02 22; fax 10 02 23. Open M and W-Su 10am-12:30pm and 2-6pm. €1.) **Hôtel Au Sleeping** ❹, 18 bd. Daunou, near the train station, has spotless, well-decorated rooms. (☎80 62 79; fax 10 63 97. Breakfast €6.50. Reserve ahead June-Aug. Singles €38; doubles €45. Sept.-May prices about €6 lower. MC/V.) **Champion** supermarket is on bd. Daunou, in the Centre Commercial de la Liane shopping center. (Open M-Sa 8:30am-8pm.) **Trains** leave Gare Boulogne-Ville, bd. Voltaire, for Lille (2½hr., 11 per day, €18.40), and Paris (2-3hr., 11 per day, €20.10). From the station, turn right on bd. Voltaire, turn left on bd. Daunou, and continue to pl. de France past the roundabout for the **tourist office,** 24 quai Gambetta. (☎10 88 10; www.tourisme-boulognesurmer.com. Open July-Aug. M-Sa 9am-7pm, Su 10am-1pm and 3-6pm; Sept.-June reduced hours.) **Postal Code:** 62200.

GERMANY (DEUTSCHLAND)

Whether glittering skyscrapers or the burnished roofs of medieval towns greet you as you enter Germany, this land will be sure to enchant. World-class music rings out of every concert hall in the glitzy big cities, where museums and parks vie for travelers' attention during the day and clubs light up the streets at night. Near these circles of urban sophistication, charming towns crop up from rolling hills while castles beckon from cliffsides. Although the rise of the Nazi regime marked a bitter break in Germany's humanistic tradition and the Cold War divided the nation, Germans today are fashioning a new, united identity for themselves.

DISCOVER GERMANY: SUGGESTED ITINERARIES

THREE DAYS Enjoy two days in **Berlin** (p. 409): stroll along **Unter den Linden** and the **Ku'damm,** gape at the **Brandenburger Tor** and the **Reichstag,** and explore the **Tiergarten.** Walk along the **East Side Gallery** and visit **Checkpoint Charlie** for a history of the Berlin Wall, then pass an afternoon at **Schloß Sanssouci** (p. 430). Overnight it to **Munich** (p. 466) for a stein-themed last day.

ONE WEEK After scrambling through **Berlin** (3 days), head north to racy **Hamburg** (1 day; p. 440). Take in the cathedral of **Cologne** (1 day; p. 449) before slowing down in the bucolic **Lorelei Cliffs** (1 day; p. 460). End your trip Bavarian-style with the castles, cathedrals, and beer gardens of **Munich** (1 day).

THREE WEEKS Start in **Berlin** (3 days). Party in **Hamburg** (2 days), then zip to **Cologne** (1 day) and the former West German capital, **Bonn** (1 day; p. 453). Contrast the Roman ruins at **Trier** (1 day, p. 458) with glitzy **Frankfurt** (1 day; p. 455), then visit Germany's oldest university in **Heidelberg** (2 days; p. 462). Lose your way in the fairy-tale **Black Forest** (2 days; p. 465), before finding it again in **Munich** (2 days). Marvel at **Neuschwanstein** (1 day; p. 478) and tour the wineries of the **Romantic Road** (2 days; p. 477). Get cultured in Goethe's **Weimar** (1 day; p. 437)—then dramatize your learnings in Faust's cellar in **Leipzig** (1 day; p. 436). End your trip in the reconstructed splendor of **Dresden** (1 day; p. 431).

ESSENTIALS

FACTS AND FIGURES

Official Name: Federal Republic of Germany.

Capital: Berlin.

Major Cities: Cologne, Frankfurt, Hamburg, Munich.

Population: 82,431,390.

Land Area: 357,021 sq. km.

Time Zone: GMT +1.

Language: German.

Religions: Protestant (38%), Roman Catholic (34%), Muslim (2%), unaffiliated or other (27%).

WHEN TO GO

Germany's climate is temperate, with rain year-round (especially in summer). The cloudy, mild months of May, June, and September are the best time to go, as there are fewer tourists and the weather is pleasant. In July, Germans head to summer spots en masse with the advent of school vacations. Winter sports gear up from November to April; the ski season takes place from mid-December to March.

DOCUMENTS AND FORMALITIES

EMBASSIES. All foreign embassies are in Berlin (p. 409). German embassies abroad include: **Australia,** 119 Empire Circuit, Yarralumla, Canberra, ACT 2600 (☎02 6270 1911; www.germanembassy.org.au); **Canada,** 1 Waverly St., Ottawa, ON

K2P OT8 (☎613-232-1101; www.ottawa.diplo.de); **Ireland,** 31 Trimleston Ave., Booterstown, Blackrock/Co Dublin (☎01 269 3011; www.germanembassy.ie); **New Zealand,** 90-92 Hobson St., Thorndon, Wellington 6001 (☎04 473 6063; www.wellington.diplo.de); **UK,** 23 Belgrave Sq., London SW1X 8PZ (☎020 7824 1300; www.german-embassy.org.uk); **US,** 4645 Reservoir Rd. NW, Washington, D.C. 20007 (☎202-298-4000; www.germany-info.org).

VISA AND ENTRY INFORMATION. Citizens of Australia, Canada, the EU, New Zealand, and the US do not need visas for stays of up to 90 days, although this three-month period begins upon entry into any of the countries that belong to the EU's freedom of movement zone. Residence and work permits can be obtained after entering the country (see www.germany-info.org for more information).

TOURIST SERVICES AND MONEY

EMERGENCY	**Police:** ☎110. **Ambulance** and **Fire:** ☎112.

TOURIST OFFICES. Every city in Germany has a tourist office, usually near the Hauptbahnhof (main train station) or *Marktplatz* (central square). All are marked by a sign with a thick lowercase "i," and many book rooms for a small fee. Also consult the website of the **National Tourist Board** (www.germany-tourism.de).

MONEY. The **euro (€)** has replaced the **Deutschmark (DM)** as the unit of currency in Germany. For more info, see p. 21. As a general rule, it's cheaper to exchange money in Germany than at home. Costs for those who stay in hostels and prepare their own food may range anywhere from €20-40 per person per day. **Tipping** is not practiced as liberally in Germany as elsewhere—most natives just round up €1. Tips are handed directly to the server with payment of the bill—if you don't want any change, say "*Das stimmt so*" (das SHTIMMT zo). As in other EU nations, most goods and services bought in Germany automatically include a **Value Added Tax (VAT);** see p. 23. You can get VAT refunds for one-time purchases if you carry the goods out of Germany within three months of their purchase. To apply for a refund, notify the retailer at the time of purchase, who will give you either an export invoice or a Tax Free Shopping Check. Submit these to customs along with your passport on your way out of the country. The invoice will be sent to the retailer, who will then send a check to whatever address you specify.

TRANSPORTATION

BY PLANE. Most flights land in Frankfurt; Berlin, Munich, and Hamburg also have international airports. **Lufthansa,** the national airline, is not always the best-priced option. Often it is cheaper to travel domestically by plane than by train; check out **Air Berlin** (www.airberlin.com), among other options.

BY TRAIN. The **Deutsche Bahn (DB)** network (www.bahn.de) is Europe's best—and one of its most expensive. Luckily, all trains have clean and comfy second-class compartments, and there are a wide variety of train lines to choose from. **RegionalExpress (RE)** and the slightly slower **RegionalBahn (RB)** trains include rail networks between neighboring cities. **InterRegio (IR)** trains, covering larger networks between cities, are speedy and comfortable. **D** trains are foreign trains that serve international routes. **EuroCity (EC)** and **InterCity (IC)** trains zoom between major cities every hour from 6am-10pm. You must purchase a supplement *(Zuschlag)* for IC or EC trains. **InterCityExpress (ICE)** trains approach the luxury and kinetics of airplanes, running at speeds up to 280kph.

Eurail is valid in Germany. The **German Railpass** allows unlimited travel for four to 10 days within a one-month period. Non-Europeans can purchase German Railpasses in their home countries and, with a passport, in major German train stations (2nd class 4-day pass €180, 10-day €324; under 26 €142/220). A **Schönes-Wochenende-Ticket** (€33) gives up to five people unlimited travel on any of the slower trains (RE or RB) from 12:01am Saturday or Sunday until 3am the next day; single travelers often find larger groups who will share their ticket.

BY BUS. Bus service runs from the local **ZOB** *(Zentralomnibusbahnhof)*, usually close to the main train station. Buses are usually slightly more expensive than trains. Railpasses are not valid on buses except for a few run by Deutsche Bahn.

BY CAR AND BY BIKE. German road conditions are generally excellent. Rumors are true: there is no speed limit on the *Autobahn*, only a recommendation of 130kph (80 mph). Germans drive fast. Watch for signs indicating the right-of-way (usually designated by a yellow triangle). The *Autobahn* is marked by an "A" on signs; secondary highways, where the speed limit is usually 100kph (60 mph), are accompanied by signs bearing a "B." In cities and towns, speed limits hover around 30-60kph (20-35 mph). **Mitfahrzentralen** are agencies that pair up drivers and riders for a small fee; riders then negotiate payment for the trip with the driver. Seat belts are mandatory. Police strictly enforce driving laws. Germany has designated lanes for **bicycles.** *Germany by Bike*, by Nadine Slavinski (Mountaineers Books, 1994; US$15), details 20 tours throughout Germany.

KEEPING IN TOUCH

EMAIL AND THE INTERNET. Almost all German cities have at least one Internet cafe with web access for about €2-10 per hour. Wireless Internet is often available in bigger cities.

TELEPHONE. Most public phones will accept only a phone card *(Telefonkarte)*, available at post offices, kiosks, and some Deutsche Bahn counters. **Mobile phones** are a popular and economical alternative (p. 33). Phone numbers have no standard length. International access numbers include **AT&T USADirect** (☎0800 225 5288), **British Telecom** (☎0800 180 0144), **Canada Direct** (☎0800 888 0014), **MCI WorldPhone** (☎0800 888 8000), **Sprint** (☎0800 888 0013), **Telecom New Zealand** (☎0800 080 0064), and **Telstra Australia** (☎0800 080 0061).

SHARE A LITTLE...

As railways have begun to demand heftier sums with each passing year, budget travelers have sought out cheaper options, often in vain. Fortunately, Germany's popular *Mitfahrzentrale* (ride-share services) pose a cost-saving solution, matching drivers who have extra space in their vehicles with passengers seeking a cheaper way to the next destination. While a train ticket from Berlin to Dresden comes with a whopping €30 price tag, catching a ride for the same distance costs only €7-14 and takes the same amount of time.

Most major cities have *Mitfahrzentrale* offices near their main train station, but these charge a fee for arranging the match. It's cheapest to arrange rides on websites like www.mitfahrgelegenheit.de and www.mf24.de, which present lists of departure times, destinations, prices, and drivers; once you've chosen a driver, you can make the arrangements yourself. Both websites are in German, but hostel receptionists will sometimes help you book if they're not busy.

Although ride-sharing does pose risks, most matchmakers solicit and provide feedback, allowing customers to rate drivers and view driver profiles before paying. It can be a great way to meet interesting locals, make lifelong friends, and—of course—catch a cheap ride to your next destination.

PHONE CODES	**Country code:** 49. **International dialing prefix:** 00. For more information on how to place international calls, see inside back cover.

MAIL. Airmail (*Luftpost* or *par avion*) usually takes three to six days to Ireland and the UK, four to 10 days to Australia and North America. *Let's Go* lists addresses for mail to be held *(Postlagernde Briefe)* in the **Practical Information** sections of big cities. Mail will go to the main post office unless you specify a subsidiary by street address. Address mail to be held according to the following example: First name Surname, Ludwigstr. 60, 10963 Berlin, GERMANY.

LANGUAGE. Younger Germans often speak at least some English, and residents of Western Germany are usually proficient as well. Recent spelling reforms did not eliminate the letter **ß** (the *ess-tset*); it is equivalent to a double "s" in English. German basics are listed on p. 1060.

ACCOMMODATIONS AND CAMPING

GERMANY	❶	❷	❸	❹	❺
ACCOMMODATIONS	under €15	€15-25	€25-33	€33-50	over €50

Germany currently has about 600 **hostels**—more than any other nation on the planet. Official hostels in Germany are overseen by **DJH** *(Deutsches Jugendherbergswerk)*, Bismarckstr. 8, 32756 Detmold, Germany (☎05231 740 10; www.jugendherberge.de). A growing number of **Jugendgästehäuser** (youth guesthouses) have more facilities than hostels and attract slightly older guests. DJH publishes *Jugendherbergen in Deutschland*, a guide to all federated German hostels. Most hostels charge €15-25 for dorms. The cheapest **hotel-style** accommodations are places with *Pension*, *Gasthof*, *Gästehaus*, or *Hotel-Garni* in the name. Hotel rooms start at €20 for singles and €45 for doubles; in large cities, expect to pay nearly twice as much. Breakfast *(frühstück)* is almost always available, if not included. The best bet for a cheap bed is often a **Privatzimmer** (a room in a family home), where a rudimentary knowledge of German is very helpful. Prices can be as low as €15 per person. Reservations are made through the local tourist office or through a private-room booking office *(Zimmervermittlung)*, sometimes for a small fee. Germans love **camping;** over 2600 campsites dot the landscape. Facilities are well maintained and usually provide showers, bathrooms, and a restaurant or store. Camping costs €7-12 per tent site and €4-6 per extra person, with additional charges for tent and vehicle rental. Blue signs with a black tent on a white background indicate official sites.

FOOD AND DRINK

GERMANY	❶	❷	❸	❹	❺
FOOD	under €4	€4-8	€8-12	€12-20	over €20

A typical breakfast *(frühstück)* consists of coffee or tea with rolls *(brötchen)*, cold sausage *(wurst)*, and cheese *(käse)*. Germans' main meal, lunch *(mittagessen)*, includes soup, broiled sausage or roasted meat, potatoes or dumplings, and a salad. Dinner (*abendessen* or *abendbrot*) is a reprise of breakfast, with beer in place of coffee and a wider selection of meats and cheeses. Many older Germans indulge in a daily ritual of coffee and cake *(kaffee und kuchen)*. To eat on the cheap, stick to the daily menu *(Tagesmenü)*, buy food in supermarkets, or, if you have a student ID, head to a university *Mensa* (cafeteria). Fast-food stands *(imbiß)* also offer cheap eats; the Turkish *döner* resembles a gyro. German beer is maltier and more "bread-like" than Czech, Dutch, or American beers.

HOLIDAYS AND FESTIVALS

Holidays: New Year's Day (Jan. 1); Epiphany (Jan. 6); Good Friday (Apr. 14); Easter (Apr. 16-17); Labor Day (May 1); Ascension (May 25); Pentecost (June 4-5); Corpus Christi (June 15); Assumption (Aug. 15); Day of German Unity (Oct. 3); Reformation Day (Oct. 31); All Saints' Day (Nov. 1); Repentance Day (Nov. 22); Christmas (Dec. 25-26).

Festivals: Fasching, Munich (Feb. 24-28); Karneval, Cologne (Feb. 23-27; p. 452); Berlinale Film Festival (Feb. 9-19); Christopher Street Day parades in major cities (late June; p. 430); Oktoberfest, Munich (Sept. 16-Oct. 1); and the Christmas Market, Nuremberg (Dec. 1-23).

BEYOND TOURISM

Germany's volunteering opportunities often involve environmental preservation, but opportunities for civil service and community building still exist, especially in eastern Germany.

Willing Workers on Organic Farms (WWOOF), Postfach 210259, 01263 Dresden, Germany (www.wwoof.de). €18 membership in WWOOF gives you room and board at a variety of organic farms in Germany in exchange for chores.

Open Houses Network, Goethepl. 9B, D-99423 Weimar (☎03643 502390; www.openhouses.de). A group dedicated to restoring and sharing public space (mostly in the former DDR), providing lodging for anyone who arrives, in return for work.

BERLIN ☎030

Dizzying, electric, and dynamic, this city of 3.5 million is always changing in some way, both in terms of its increasingly diverse population and which neighborhood *(bezirk)* is currently the trendiest. Yet while Berlin surges ahead as one of the continent's most vibrant cities, memories of the past century—in particular, the Nazi regime and the DDR—remain etched into residents' daily life. Psychological division between East and West Germany—the problem dubbed "wall in the head"—is still felt more acutely here than anywhere else in the country.

INTERCITY TRANSPORTATION

Flights: Berlin has 3 airports; for info on any of them, call ☎0180 500 01 86. **Flughafen Tegel** is Western Berlin's main international airport. To get to Tegel, take express bus X9 from Bahnhof Zoo or bus TXL from U2: Potsdamer Pl. To get to the city from Tegel, signs with a bus on them lead you to the BVD *(Berliner Verkehrsbetriebe)* counter, where the staff can help you choose between the TXL, the X9, and the 128. **Flughafen Schönefeld** services intercontinental flights and travel to developing countries. Take S9 or the 45 to Flughafen Berlin Schönefeld. Or, take the Schönefeld Express, which runs every 30min. through most major Bahn stations, including Bahnhof Zoo, Ostbahnhof, Alexanderpl., and Friedrichstr. **Flughafen Tempelhof,** Berlin's smallest airport, has flights to European destinations. Take U6 to Pl. der Luftbrücke.

Train Stations: Scheduled to open in time for the World Cup in May of 2006, **Lehrter Stadtbahnhof** will be Europe's biggest train station. For now, trains to and from Berlin stop at **Zoologischer Garten** (a.k.a. **Bahnhof Zoo**) in the West and at **Ostbahnhof** in the East. Call ☎0180 599 66 33 or visit www.bahn.de for more info on schedules and destination changes. Trains run every hr. to: **Cologne** (4¼hr., €89); **Frankfurt** (4hr., €95); **Hamburg** (1½-2½hr., €45-55). Direct trains run at least every 2hr. to: **Dresden** (2¼hr., €30); **Leipzig** (2hr., €31); **Munich** (6½-7hr., €92). Times and prices for international connections change frequently; check at computers located in stations. Reserving as much as 3 weeks in advance can save up to 50% on listed prices. Destinations include: **Amsterdam** (6½hr.); **Brussels** (7½hr.);

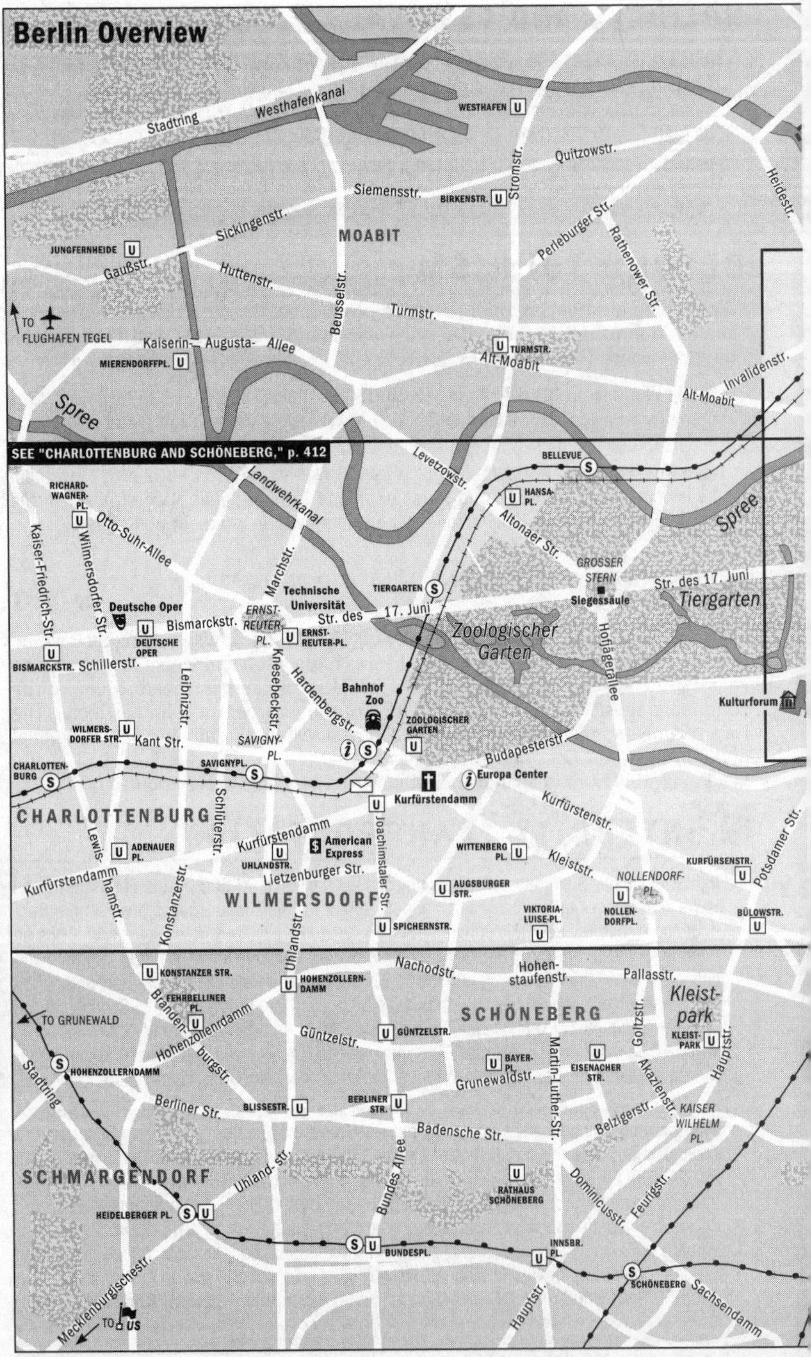

Berlin Overview

Stadtring
Westhafenkanal
WESTHAFEN U
Quitzowstr.
Heidestr.
Siemensstr.
BIRKENSTR. U
Stromstr.
Sickingenstr.
MOABIT
Perleburger Str.
Rathenower Str.
JUNGFERNHEIDE U
Gaußstr.
Huttenstr.
Beusselstr.
Turmstr.
TO FLUGHAFEN TEGEL
Kaiserin- Augusta- Allee
U TURMSTR.
Alt-Moabit
MIERENDORFFPL. U
Invalidenstr.
Alt-Moabit
Spree

SEE "CHARLOTTENBURG AND SCHÖNEBERG," p. 412

Levetzowstr.
BELLEVUE S
U HANSA-PL.
Landwehrkanal
Spree
RICHARD-WAGNER-PL. U
Otto-Suhr-Allee
Altonaer Str.
Kaiser-Friedrich-Str.
Wilmersdorfer Str.
Marchstr.
GROSSER STERN
Str. des 17. Juni
TIERGARTEN S
Technische Universität
Siegessäule
Tiergarten
Deutsche Oper
ERNST-REUTER-PL.
Str. des 17. Juni
Bismarckstr.
U DEUTSCHE OPER
U ERNST-REUTER-PL.
Zoologischer Garten
Hofjägerallee
U BISMARCKSTR.
Schillerstr.
Leibnizstr.
Knesebeckstr.
Hardenbergstr.
Bahnhof Zoo
Kulturforum
WILMERS-DORFER STR. U
Kant Str.
SAVIGNY-PL.
ZOOLOGISCHER GARTEN U
CHARLOTTEN-BURG S
SAVIGNYPL. S
Budapesterstr.
Europa Center
Kurfürstendamm
U
CHARLOTTENBURG
Kurfürstenstr.
Lewis-hamstr.
Schlüterstr.
Joachimstaler Str.
U ADENAUER PL.
Kurfürstendamm
U UHLANDSTR.
American Express
WITTENBERG PL. U
Kleiststr.
Potsdamer Str.
KURFÜRSENSTR. U
Kurfürstendamm
Lietzenburger Str.
NOLLENDORF-PL.
U AUGSBURGER STR.
U NOLLEN-DORFPL.
Konstanzerstr.
WILMERSDORF
VIKTORIA-LUISE-PL. U
BÜLOWSTR. U
U SPICHERNSTR.
Uhlandstr.
Nachodstr.
Hohen-staufenstr.
Pallasstr.
U KONSTANZER STR.
U HOHENZOLLERN-DAMM
FEHRBELLINER PL. U
Kleist-park
TO GRUNEWALD
Branden-burgstr.
Hohenzollerndamm
SCHÖNEBERG
Goltzstr.
Güntzelstr.
U GÜNTZELSTR.
KLEIST-PARK U
Martin-Luther-Str.
Hauptstr.
S HOHENZOLLERNDAMM
U BAYER-PL.
U EISENACHER STR.
Stadtring
Grunewaldstr.
Akazienstr.
Berliner Str.
BLISSESTR. U
BERLINER STR. U
Belzigerstr.
KAISER WILHELM PL.
Badensche Str.
Bundes Allee
SCHMARGENDORF
Uhland-str.
U RATHAUS SCHÖNEBERG
Dominicusstr.
Feurigstr.
HEIDELBERGER PL. S U
S U BUNDESPL.
INNSBR. PL. U
Mecklenburgischestr.
S SCHÖNEBERG
Sachsendamm
Hauptstr.
TO US

GERMANY

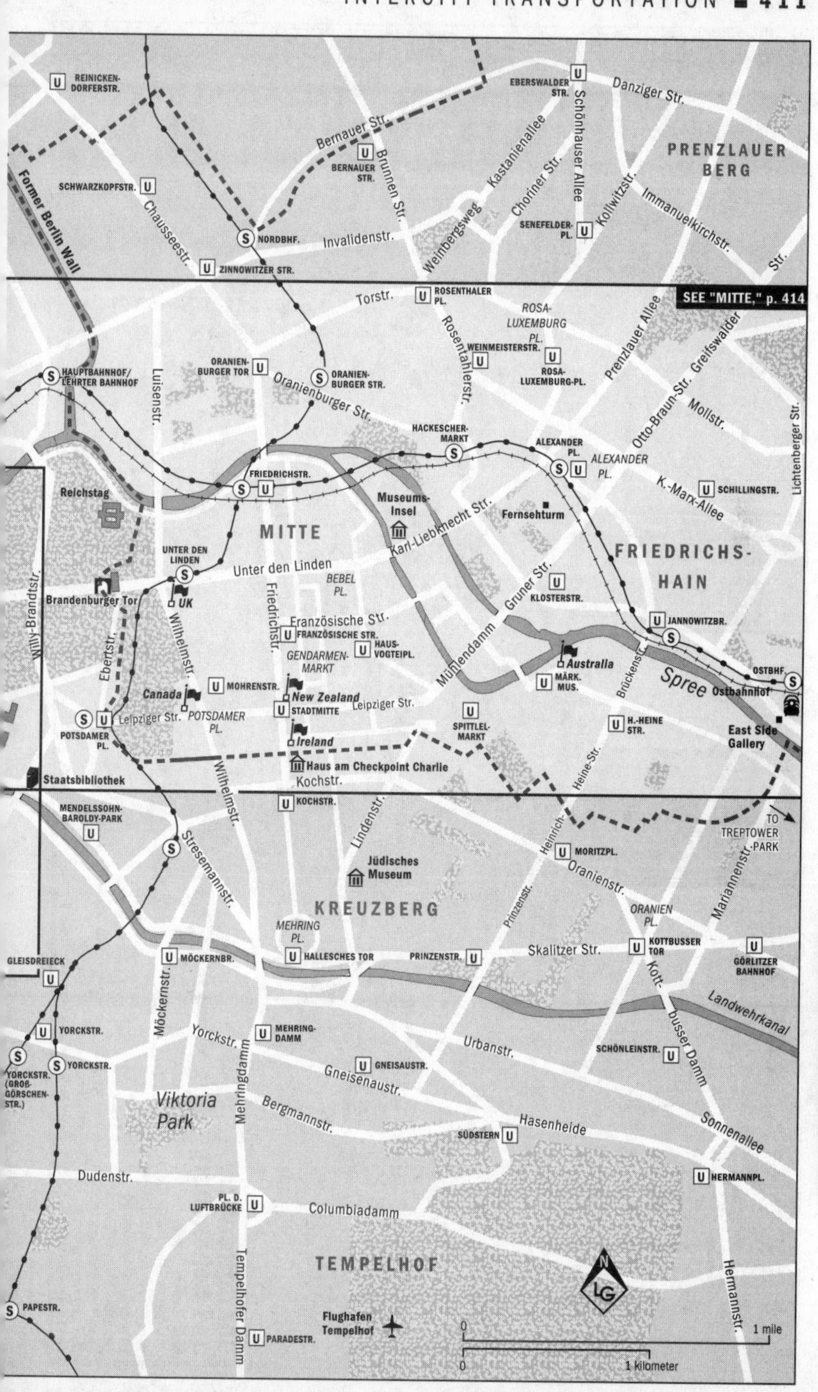

PRENZLAUER BERG
MITTE
FRIEDRICHS-HAIN
KREUZBERG
TEMPELHOF
SEE "MITTE," p. 414
Former Berlin Wall
Reichstag
Brandenburger Tor
Museums-Insel
Fernsehturm
Haus am Checkpoint Charlie
Jüdisches Museum
Staatsbibliothek
East Side Gallery
Viktoria Park
Flughafen Tempelhof
UK
Canada
New Zealand
Ireland
Australia
Spree
Landwehrkanal
TO TREPTOWER PARK
1 mile
1 kilometer

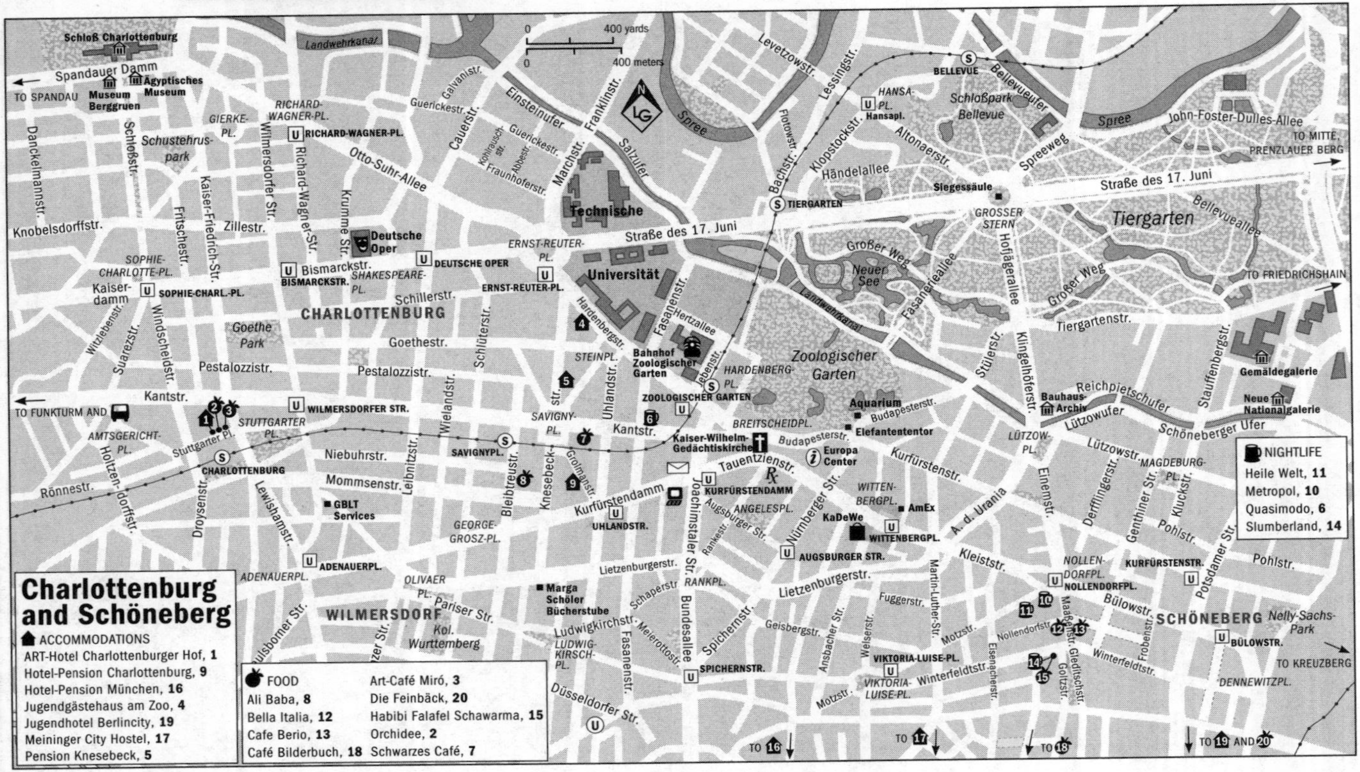

Charlottenburg and Schöneberg
ACCOMMODATIONS
ART-Hotel Charlottenburger Hof, 1
Hotel-Pension Charlottenburg, 9
Hotel-Pension München, 16
Jugendgästehaus am Zoo, 4
Jugendhotel Berlincity, 19
Meininger City Hostel, 17
Pension Knesebeck, 5
FOOD
Ali Baba, 8
Bella Italia, 12
Cafe Berio, 13
Café Bilderbuch, 18
Art-Café Miró, 3
Die Feinbäck, 20
Habibi Falafel Schawarma, 15
Orchidee, 2
Schwarzes Café, 7
NIGHTLIFE
Heile Welt, 11
Metropol, 10
Quasimodo, 6
Slumberland, 14
0 400 yards
0 400 meters
Schloß Charlottenburg
Spandauer Damm
TO SPANDAU
Museum Berggruen
Ägyptisches Museum
TO FUNKTURM AND
TO MITTE, PRENZLAUER BERG
TO FRIEDRICHSHAIN
TO KREUZBERG
CHARLOTTENBURG
WILMERSDORF
SCHÖNEBERG
Tiergarten
Zoologischer Garten
Technische
Universität
Deutsche Oper
Bahnhof Zoologischer Garten
Kaiser-Wilhelm-Gedächtniskirche
Europa Center
KaDeWe
AmEx
Siegessäule
Aquarium
Elefantentor
Bauhaus-Archiv
Gemäldegalerie
Neue Nationalgalerie
GBLT Services
Marga Schöler Bücherstube
Straße des 17. Juni
Kurfürstendamm
Kantstr.
Otto-Suhr-Allee
Bismarckstr.
Tauentzienstr.
Kurfürstenstr.
Spree
Landwehrkanal

Budapest (12hr.); **Copenhagen** (7½hr.); **Kraków** (8½-11hr.); **Moscow** (27-33hr.); **Paris** (9hr.); **Prague** (5hr.); **Rome** (17½-21hr.); **Stockholm** (13-16hr.); **Vienna** (9½hr.); **Warsaw** (6hr.); **Zurich** (8½hr.). **Euraide** counters sell tickets and have English-language information.

Buses: ZOB (☎301 03 80), by the *Funkturm* near Kaiserdamm, in the central bus station. U2 to Kaiserdamm or S4, 45, or 46 to Witzleben. Open M-F 6am-7:30pm, Sa-Su 6am-noon. Check *Zitty* (€2.30) or *Tip* (€2.50) for deals on long-distance buses, which are slower than trains but usually cheaper. **Gullivers,** Hardenbergpl. 14 (☎0800 48 55 48 37; www.gullivers.de), is at the far end of the bus parking lot in Bahnhof Zoo. To **Paris** (14hr., €59); **Vienna** (10½hr., €49). Open daily 9am-2:30pm and 3-7pm. AmEx/MC/V.

Ride-share: Berlin has many ride-share centers *(Mitfahrzentralen)*. Magazines *Zitty, Tip,* and *030* list addresses and phone numbers. Larger centers include: **Citynetz,** Charlottenburg, Joachimstaler Str. 14 (☎194 44). U9 or 15 to Kurfürstendamm. To: **Frankfurt** (€29); **Hamburg** (€19); **Hanover** (€19). Open M-F 9am-8pm, Sa-Su 9am-7pm.

ORIENTATION

Berlin's main landmarks include the **Spree River,** which flows through the city from west to east, and the narrower **Landwehrkanal** that flows into it from the south. The vast central park, the **Tiergarten,** stretches between the waterways. The radio tower looming above it is either the pointed **Funkturm,** in the west, or the globed **Fernsehturm,** rising above **Alexanderplatz** in the east. Major thoroughfares include **Kurfürstendamm** (a.k.a. Ku'damm), which is lined with department stores and runs into the **Bahnhof Zoologischer Garten,** the transportation hub of West Berlin. Nearby are the elegant wreck of the **Kaiser-Wilhelm Gedächtniskirche,** and one of Berlin's few real skyscrapers, the **EuropaCenter.**

Grand, tree-lined **Strasse des 17. Juni** runs east-west through the Tiergarten, ending triumphantly at the **Brandenburger Tor** in the east. The street next becomes **Unter den Linden,** which beelines through most of Berlin's imperial architecture. Neighboring the gate is the **Reichstag.** Several blocks south, **Potsdamer Platz** bustles beneath the glittering Sony Center and the headquarters of the Deutsche Bahn. Berlin's streets change names often; addresses often climb higher and higher and then wrap around to the other side of the street, placing the highest- and lowest-numbered buildings across from one another. Well-indexed maps are invaluable.

Charlottenburg and **Schöneberg,** in former West Berlin, have become the city's commercial heart. Also in the former West, despite its geographical location in the east, **Kreuzberg** is a bastion of counter-culture. **Mitte, Prenzlauer Berg,** and **Friedrichshain,** in the former East, are home to much of the city's chaotic nightlife.

LOCAL TRANSPORTATION

Public Transportation: Berlin is 8 times as large as Paris—fortunately, the extensive **bus, Straßenbahn** (streetcar), **U-Bahn** (subway), and **S-Bahn** (surface rail) systems can take you anywhere. Berlin is divided into 3 transit zones. **Zone A** encompasses central Berlin, including Flughafen Tempelhof. **Zone B** comprises the rest of the downtown. **Zone C** ties in outlying areas, including Potsdam and Oranienburg. **AB tickets** are the best deal, and allow for the purchase of extension tickets for Zone C. A one-way ticket *(Einzelfahrausweis)* is good for 2hr. after validation. (Zones AB €2, BC €2.25, ABC €2.60.) Since single tickets can become pricey, it often makes sense to buy a pass. A **Tageskarte** (AB €5.60, ABC €6) is good until 3am the next day; the **WelcomeCard** (€22; sold at tourist offices) remains valid for 72hr. and discounts sights in addition; the **7-Tage-Karte** (AB €24.30, ABC €30) remains valid for 7 days; and the **Umweltkarte Standard** (AB €64, ABC €79.50) is valid for 1 calendar month. Tickets work on any S-Bahn, U-Bahn, bus, or streetcar. **Bikes** require a supplemental ticket and are permitted on the U- and S-Bahn, but not on buses or streetcars. Buy tickets from *Automaten* (machines), bus drivers, or ticket windows in the U- and S-Bahn stations. When using an *Automat,* make your selection before inserting money. Machines will not give more than €10 change. Validate your ticket in the box marked *"hier entwerfen."*

GERMANY

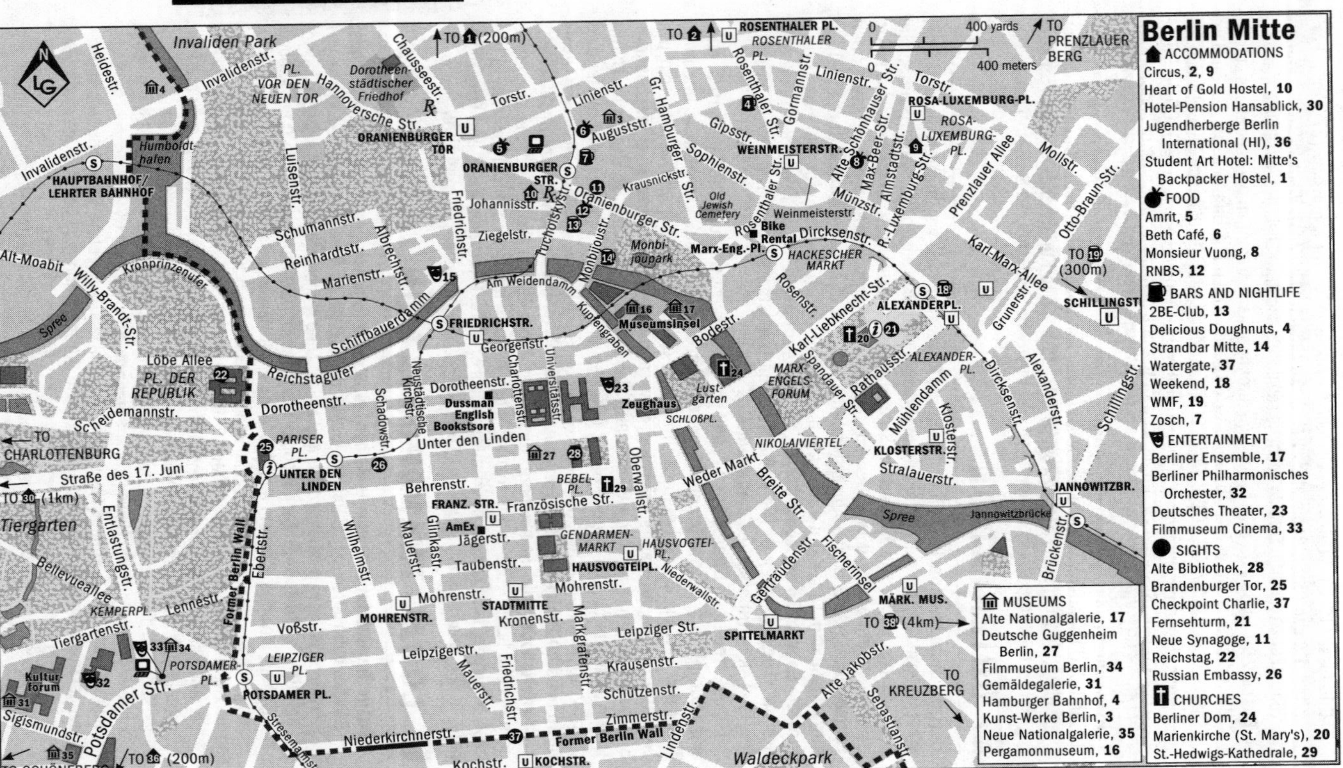
Berlin Mitte
ACCOMMODATIONS
Circus, 2, 9
Heart of Gold Hostel, 10
Hotel-Pension Hansablick, 30
Jugendherberge Berlin International (HI), 36
Student Art Hotel: Mitte's Backpacker Hostel, 1
FOOD
Amrit, 5
Beth Café, 6
Monsieur Vuong, 8
RNBS, 12
BARS AND NIGHTLIFE
2BE-Club, 13
Delicious Doughnuts, 4
Strandbar Mitte, 14
Watergate, 37
Weekend, 18
WMF, 19
Zosch, 7
ENTERTAINMENT
Berliner Ensemble, 17
Berliner Philharmonisches Orchester, 32
Deutsches Theater, 23
Filmmuseum Cinema, 33
SIGHTS
Alte Bibliothek, 28
Brandenburger Tor, 25
Checkpoint Charlie, 37
Fernsehturm, 21
Neue Synagoge, 11
Reichstag, 22
Russian Embassy, 26
CHURCHES
Berliner Dom, 24
Marienkirche (St. Mary's), 20
St.-Hedwigs-Kathedrale, 29
MUSEUMS
Alte Nationalgalerie, 17
Deutsche Guggenheim Berlin, 27
Filmmuseum Berlin, 34
Gemäldegalerie, 31
Hamburger Bahnhof, 4
Kunst-Werke Berlin, 3
Neue Nationalgalerie, 35
Pergamonmuseum, 16
400 yards
400 meters
TO PRENZLAUER BERG
TO KREUZBERG
TO CHARLOTTENBURG
TO SCHÖNEBERG
Former Berlin Wall
Invaliden Park
Tiergarten
Waldeckpark
Spree
Unter den Linden
Friedrichstr.
Karl-Marx-Allee
Alexanderstr.
Museumsinsel
ALEXANDERPL.
FRIEDRICHSTR.
POTSDAMER PL.
Dussman English Bookstsore
Bike Rental

Night Transport: U- and S-Bahn lines shut down 1-4am on weeknights (with final runs around 12:15am), but **night buses** (with numbers preceded by the letter N) run every 20-30min.; pick up the *Nachtliniennetz* map at a *Fahrscheine und Mehr* office.

Taxis: ☎26 10 26, 21 02 02, or 690 22. Call at least 15min. in advance.

Car Rental: Most companies have counters at all 3 airports and at Bahnhof Zoo, Ostbahnhof, and Friedrichstr. **Hertz** (☎261 1053; open M-F 7am-8pm, Sa 8am-4pm, Su 9am-1pm) and **Avis** (☎230 9370; open M-F 7am-7pm, Sa 9am-2pm) also have counters in the EuropaCenter, Budapester Str. 39.

Bike Rental: Fahrradstation, Mitte, 4041 Rosenthaler Str. (☎20 45 45 00), in Hackescher Höfe near the Hackescher Markt S-Bahn station. €15 per day; €10 per day for rentals longer than 3 days. Open daily 10am-7pm. **Pedal Power,** Kreuzberg, Großbeerenstr. 53 (☎78 99 19 39). €10 per day. Open M-F 10am-6pm, Sa 11am-2pm. Bikes are also available for rental at some hostels.

PRACTICAL INFORMATION

Tourist Offices: EurAide, in Bahnhof Zoo's Reisezentrum. Sells rail tickets, maps, phone cards, and walking tour tickets; also recommends hostels. Open May-Sept. daily 9am-1:30pm and 2:30-6pm; Oct.-Dec. and Feb.-Apr. M-F 9am-1:30pm and 2:30-5pm.

City Tours: A city tour lets you take in all of the major sights in just a few hours. **Terry Brewer's Best of Berlin** (www.brewersberlin.com) features guides who are legendary for their vast knowledge of the city and engaging personalities. 8hr. tours (€12) leave daily at 10:30am from Friedrichstr. Station in front of the Australian Ice Cream and at 11am from the Neue Synagoge on Oranienburger Str., near the intersection with Tucholskystr. (S1, 2, or 25 to Oranienburger Str.). **New Berlin Tours** (☎0179 973 0397; www.newberlintours.com) offers free walking and bike tours of the city; be sure to bring some cash to tip the guides. 3½hr. walking tours leave daily at 10:30am and 12:30pm from Zoologischer Garten in front of Dunkin' Donuts; they also pick up visitors at 11am and 1pm at Brandenburger Tor in front of the Starbucks (S1, 2, or 25 to Unter den Linden).

Embassies and Consulates: Australia, Mitte, Wallstr. 76-79 (☎880 08 80; www.australian-embassy.de). U2 to Märkisches Museum. Open M-F 8:30am-5pm, F closes 4:15pm. **Canada,** Mitte, Leipziger Pl. 17 (☎20 31 20; www.canada.de). U2 or S1 to Potsdamer Pl. Open M-F 8:30am-12:30pm and 1:30-5pm. **Ireland,** Mitte, Friedrichstr. 200 (☎22 07 20; www.botschaft-irland.de). U2 or 6 to Stadtmitte. Open M-F 9:30am-12:30pm and 2:30-4:45pm. **New Zealand,** Mitte, Friedrichstr. 60 (☎20 62 10; www.nzembassy.com). U2 or 6 to Stadtmitte. Open M-F 9am-1pm and 2-5:30pm, F closes 4:30pm. **UK,** Mitte, Wilhelmstr. 70-71 (☎20 45 70; www.britischebotschaft.de). S1-3, 5, 7, 9, 25, or 75, or U6 to Friedrichstr. Open M-F 9am-4:30pm. **US,** Clayallee 170 (☎832 9233; www.usembassy.de). U1 to Oskar-Helene-Heim. Open M-F 8:30am-noon. Phone advice M-F 2-4pm; after-hours emergency advice ☎830 50.

Currency Exchange: The best rates are usually found at exchange offices with *"Wechselstube"* signs at most major train stations and large squares. **ReiseBank,** at Bahnhof Zoo (☎881 71 17; open daily 7:30am-10pm) and Ostbahnhof (☎296 43 93; open M-F 7am-10pm, Sa 8am-8pm, Su 8am-noon and 12:30-4pm) has higher rates.

American Express: Main Office, Charlottenburg, Bayreuther Str. 37-38 (☎21 47 62 92). U1, 2, or 15 to Wittenbergpl. Cashes AmEx Travelers Cheques for no commission. Long lines F-Sa. Open M-F 9am-7pm, Sa 10am-1pm. Another branch in Mitte at Friedrichstr. 172 (☎20 17 400). U6 to Französische Str. Same services and hours.

Luggage Storage: In Bahnhof Zoo. Rates start at €0.50 per day. 72hr. max. If lockers are full, try luggage deposit (€2 per piece per day). Open daily 6:15am-10:30pm. Lockers are also available 24hr. at Ostbahnhof and Alexanderpl. stations.

Bookstores: Marga Schöler Bücherstube, Charlottenburg, Knesebeckstr. 33, between Savignypl. and the Ku'damm. S3 to Savignypl. Contemporary reading material in English. Open M-W 9:30am-7pm, Th-F 9:30am-8pm, Sa 9:30am-4pm. **Dussman,** Mitte, Friedrichstr. 90. U6 to Friedrichstr. English books on 2nd fl. Open M-Sa 10am-10pm.

GLBT Resources: Lesbenberatung, Kulmer Str. 20 (☎217 2253), offers counseling for lesbians. Open M-Tu and Th 4-7pm, F 2-5pm. **Schwulenberatung,** Charlottenburg, Mommsenstr. 45 (☎194 46), has similar services for gay men. Open M-F 9am-8pm.

Emergency: Police: ☎110. **Ambulance and Fire:** ☎112.

Crisis Lines: Helpline International (☎44 01 06 07) is Berlin's emergency phone service for English-speaking foreigners. Open daily 2-6pm. **American Hotline** (☎0177 814 15 10) is a crisis and referral service. **Berliner Behindertenverband,** Jägerstr. 63d (☎204 3847), has advice for the disabled. Open M-F 8am-4pm. **Frauenkrisentelefon** (☎614 2242) is a women's crisis line. Open M-T, Th 10am-noon, Th also 7-9pm, F 7-9pm only.

Pharmacies: Pharmacies *(apotheken)* are everywhere. **Europa-Apotheke,** Tauentzienstr. 9-12 (☎261 4142), is conveniently located near Bahnhof Zoo. Open M-F 6am-8pm, Sa 9am-4pm. **Schlecker** drug stores can be found throughout the city.

Medical Services: The American and British embassies list English-speaking doctors. **Emergency doctor:** ☎31 00 31. **Emergency dentist:** ☎89 00 43 33. Both 24hr.

Internet Access: Netlounge, Mitte, Auguststr. 89 (☎24 34 25 97). U-Bahn to Oranienburger Str. €1.50 per hr. Open noon-midnight. **Easy Everything** has locations at: Karl-Marx-Str. 78, Kurfürstendamm 224, Schloßstr. 102, Sony Center, and Rathausstr. 5. Wireless Internet free anywhere in the **Sony Center** (p. 422).

Post Offices: City-wide general service hotline ☎018 02 33 33 (www.deutschepost.de). **Postamt Charlottenburg,** Joachimstaler Str. 7, near Bahnhof Zoo; look for Postbank sign. Open M-Sa 9am-8pm. **Postal Code:** 10623. **Postamt Mitte,** Georgenstr. 17. Open M-F 6am-10pm, Sa-Su 8am-10pm. **Postal Code:** 10117.

ACCOMMODATIONS

Longer stays are most conveniently arranged through one of Berlin's many **Mitwohnzentrale,** which can arrange house-sitting gigs or sublets (from €250 per month). **Home Company Mitwohnzentrale,** Joachimstaler Str. 17, is one of these and has a useful placement website. (☎194 45; www.homecompany.de. U9 or 15 to Kurfürstendamm. Open M-Th 9am-6pm, F 9am-5pm, Sa 11am-2pm. MC/V.)

GERMANY

MITTE

Circus, Weinbergsweg 1a (☎28 39 14 33). U8 to Rosenthaler Pl. Clean, modern, and well run. Wheelchair accessible. Linen €2. Internet €0.60 per 10min. Reception and bar 24hr. Dorms €15-20; singles €32, with shower €45; doubles €48/60; triples €60; apartments with kitchen and balcony €75. Winter reduced rates. Cash only. Another location at Rosa-Luxemburg-Str. 39-41. U2 to Rosa-Luxemburg-Pl. Same prices and hours. ❷

Heart of Gold Hostel, Johannisstr. 11 (☎29 00 33 00; www.heartofgold-hostel.de). S1, 2, or 25 to Oranienburger Str. or U6 to Oranienburger Tor. Designed as a tribute to *The Hitchhiker's Guide to the Galaxy.* Breakfast €3. Laundry €3. Internet €3 per hr. Reception and bar 24hr. Dorms €17-21; singles €24-28; doubles with shower €48-56. ❷

Student Art Hotel: Mitte's Backpacker Hostel, Chausseestr. 102 (☎28 39 09 65). U6 to Zinnowitzer Str. Up Chausseestr. on the left. Look for the giant orange sign—the hotel is across the street. Decorations range from pastels and poetry to a giant metal spider on the ceiling. Large lounge area with big-screen TV and bar. Bike rental €10 per day. Breakfast €1.50. Linen €2.50. Laundry €5. Internet €3 per hr. Reception 24hr. Dorms €15-18; singles €30; doubles €48-56. Winter reduced rates. ❷

TIERGARTEN

Jugendherberge Berlin International (HI), Kluckstr. 3 (☎257 99 808; www.hostel.de). U1 to Kurfürstenstr. Walk up Potsdamer Str., go left on Pohlstr., and right on Kluckstr. Feels like sleeping in your grade school—cafeteria breakfast and kids included—but features a big-screen TV, table tennis, and large common room. Bike rental €10 per day. Internet €3 per hr. Grill for rent €3. Reception and cafe 24hr. Dorms €16, under 27 €12-19; doubles €24/28. Backyard camping €16. MC/V. ❷

Hotel-Pension Hansablick, Flotowstr. 6 (☎390 48 00; www.hotel-hansablick.de). S3, 5, 7, 9, or 75 to Tiergarten. Some rooms have balconies over the Spree; all have bath, phone, and cable TV. Riverboat tours stop 200m away. Breakfast included. Reception 24hr. Singles €82; doubles €101-121. 5% *Let's Go* discount. AmEx/DC/MC/V. ❹

CHARLOTTENBURG

Pension Knesebeck, Knesebeckstr. 86 (☎312 7255; www.pensionknesebeck.de). S3, 5, 7, or 9 to Savignypl. Follow Kantstr. to Savignypl. and go clockwise around the green until Knesebeckstr. Friendly owners and 9 rooms. Breakfast included. Laundry €4. Reception 24hr. Dorms €25-30; singles €35-39, with shower €40-45; doubles €55-61/65-72. AmEx/MC/V. ❸

Jugendgästehaus am Zoo, Hardenbergstr. 9a, 4th fl. (☎312 9410; www.jgh-zoo.de), opposite the Technical University Mensa. Bus #145 to Steinpl., or a short walk from Bahnhof Zoo down Hardenbergstr. Unremarkable decor but decent mattresses. Reception 9am-midnight. Check-in 10am. Check-out 9am. Lockout 10am-2pm. Dorms €20, under 27 €17; singles €28/25; doubles €47/44. Cash only. ❷

Hotel-Pension Charlottenburg, Grolmanstr. 32/33 (☎88 03 29 60; www.pension-charlottenburg.de). S3 to Savignypl. or U1 to Uhlandstr. In this older hotel, clean and simple rooms come with phone and TV; more expensive ones have private shower. Breakfast included. Check-out 11am. Singles €38-58; doubles €72-87. Cash only. ❸

ART-Hotel Charlottenburger Hof, Stuttgarter Pl. 14 (☎32 90 70; www.charlottenburger-hof.de). S3, 5, 7, or 9 to Charlottenburg or U7 to Wilmersdorfer Str. Miró-styled rooms all have phone, TV, and flat-screen computers with free unlimited Internet; some have whirlpool and balcony. Breakfast €8. Laundry €3. Reception 24hr. Singles €60-90; doubles €70-100; quads €125-160. Discounts for online bookings. AmEx/MC/V. ❺

SCHÖNEBERG AND WILMERSDORF

Meininger City Hostel, Meininger Str. 10 (from abroad ☎666 36 100, in Germany 0800 634 6464; www.meininger-hostels.de). U4 or bus #146 to Rathaus Schöneberg. Walk toward the Rathaus tower on Freiherr-vom-Stein-Str., turn left onto Martin-Luther-Str. and right on Meininger Str. This well-run hostel, complete with bar and beer garden, is the best value in town. Friendly, English-speaking staff. Linen deposit €5. Internet €3 per hr. Reception 24hr. Dorms €12.50; 4- to 5-bed dorms €21; singles €33; doubles €46. 10% *Let's Go* discount on 1st night stay. See website for additional specials. Cash only. ❶

Jugendhotel Berlincity, Crellestr. 22 (☎78 70 21 30; www.jugendhotel-berlin.de). U7 to Kleistpark. Fancy lounge and helpful staff make this small hotel fill fast; book ahead. Breakfast included. Cheaper prices for extended stays. Singles €38, with bath €55; doubles €60/79; triples €84/99; quads €108/118. AmEx/MC/V. ❸

Hotel-Pension München, Güntzelstr. 62 (☎857 9120; www.hotel-pension-muenchen-in-berlin.de). U9 to Güntzelstr. Contemporary Berlin art fills the foyer. 8 rooms with cable TV and phones. Breakfast included. Singles €40, with bath €55; doubles with bath €70-80; triples €95; quads €105. AmEx/MC/V. ❹

KREUZBERG

Meininger City Hostel, Hallesches Ufer 30 (from abroad ☎666 36 100, in Germany 0800 634 64 64; www.meininger-hostels.de). Located between Hallesches Tor (U6 or U1), and Möckernbruke (U1 or U7). This location of the popular hostel chain features a bar, big-screen TV, and a comfortable roof terrace. All rooms with bath and TV. Breakfast included. Linen €5 deposit. Reception 24hr. Dorms €13.50; 4- to 5-bed dorms €25; singles €49; doubles €66. 10% *Let's Go* discount on 1st night stay. Cash only. **Branch** across the river at Tempelhofer Ufer 10. ❶

Hotel Transit, Hagelberger Str. 53-54 (☎789 0470; www.hotel-transit.de). U6 or 7; bus #119, 219, or 140; or night bus N4, 6, 19, and 76 to Mehringdamm. Hip hostel with attention to detail: helpful brochures and maps fill the lounge. Breakfast included. Internet €6 per hr. Reception 24hr. Check-in 2pm. Check-out noon. All rooms with bath. Dorms €19; singles €59; doubles €69; triples €90; quads €120. AmEx/MC/V. ❷

Bax Pax, Skalitzer Str. 104 (☎69 51 83 22; www.baxpax.de). U1 or 15 to Görlitzer Bahnhof. At the start of Oranienstr., with a pool table and a bed inside a VW Bug (ask for room #3). Linen €2.50. Internet €3 per hr. Reception 24hr. Dorms €15-17; singles €30; doubles €46; triples €60. Winter reduced rates. MC/V. ❷

FRIEDRICHSHAIN AND PRENZLAUER BERG

Globetrotter Hostel Odyssee, Grünberger Str. 23 (☎29 00 00 81; www.globetrotterhostel.de). U1 or 15 to Warschauer Str. or U5 to Frankfurter Tor. Gothic statues and candlelit tables greet you as you enter, but rooms are modern and spotless. Bar open until dawn. Breakfast €3. Linen deposit €3. Internet €3 per hr. Reception 24hr. Check-in 4pm. Check-out noon. Reserve ahead. Dorms €13; doubles €45-52; triples €57; quads €68. Winter reduced rates. MC/V. ❶

Sunflower Hostel, Helsingforser Str. 17 (☎44 04 42 50; www.sunflower-hostel.de). U1 or 15 to Warschauer Str., turn right and then left onto Helsingforser Str., closest to the river. Lounge adorned with bright sunflowers and stuffed farm animals. Rooms with balconies. Locker deposit €3. Laundry €4.50. Internet €3 per hr. Reception 24hr. Dorms €13-15; singles €35; doubles €45; triples €57; quads €68. MC/V. ❶

East Seven, Schwedter Str. 7 (☎93 62 22 40; www.eastseven.de). U2 to Senefelderpl. A large kitchen, free coffee, and a courtyard with picnic tables, make this new hostel a friendly backpacker destination. Linen €3. Laundry €4. Internet €2 per hr. Dorms €15-17; doubles €44; triples €57; quads €64. Cash only. ❶

Lette'm Sleep Hostel, Lettestr. 7 (☎44 73 36 23; www.backpackers.de). U2 to Eberswalder Str. Cozy red common room and friendly staff make up for occasionally cluttered hallways. Wheelchair accessible. Linen €3. Free Internet. Dorms €15-16; doubles €48; triples €57. 10% discount for stays over 4 nights. AmEx/MC/V. ❷

FOOD

Berlin's Indian, Italian, Thai, and Turkish communities provide a diverse and tasty options. An especially dear culinary tradition is breakfast, which street-side cafes extend well into the afternoon; Germans love to wake up late over a *milchkaffee* (a bowl of coffee with foamed milk). Quick bites are handily supplied by vendors of *currywurst* or *bratwurst*, and 24hr. Turkish *imbiß* stands.

Aldi, Plus, Edeka, and **Penny Markt** are the cheapest supermarket chains, while **Bolle, Kaiser's,** and **Reichelt** are pricier (typically open M-F 9am-6pm and Sa 9am-4pm). Almost every neighborhood has an **open-air market;** Bahnhof Zoo market, on Winterfeldtpl., is particularly lively on Saturday mornings.

MITTE

Monsieur Vuong, Alte Schönhauser Allee 46 (☎30 87 26 43). U2 to Rosa-Luxemburg-Pl. Serves from a limited but delicious menu of Vietnamese food. Outdoor seating available. All entrees €6.40. Open M-Sa noon-midnight, Su 2pm-midnight. ❷

RNBS, Oranienburger Str. 27 (www.rnbs.de). This tiny cafe serves healthful Asian-themed fast food. Meatball with scallions and fresh herbs €1.90. Noodles with sesame tofu, scallions, sprouts, and fresh herbs €3. Open daily noon-midnight. Cash only. ❶

Beth Café, Tucholskystr. 40 (☎281 31 35), off Auguststr. S1, 2, or 25 to Oranienburger Str. Each bench in the garden comes with a red blanket to keep you warm. The kosher menu features falafel (€3.20) and bagels with lox and cream cheese (€2.50). Vegetarian options available. Entrees €3-8. Open M-Th, Su noon-8pm. AmEx/MC. ❷

Amrit, Oranienburger Str. 50 (☎2844 4482; www.amrit.de). S1 or 2 to Oranienburger Str. At this sleek Indian restaurant, entrees (€7-10) can be split and specials are only €5.50. Vegetarian options available. Kreuzberg location at Oranienstr. 202-203 (☎617 5550). Both locations open M-Th, Su 11am-1am, F-Sa 10am-2am. AmEx/MC/V. ❸

CHARLOTTENBURG

Schwarzes Café, Kantstr. 148 (☎313 8038). S3, 5, 7, 9, or 75 to Savignypl. This popular Bohemian cafe boasts candlelit tables and a 24hr. breakfast menu. The ground-floor bathrooms must be seen to be believed. Open 24hr. except Tu 3-10am. Cash only. ❸

Orchidee, Stuttgarter Pl. 13 (☎31 99 74 67; www.restaurantorchidee.de). *Won ton, pho,* and *maki* all under one roof; the Vietnamese food especially stands out. During the 11am-5pm lunch special, get half-price sushi or a free appetizer with any €5-11 entree. Open M-Sa 11am-midnight, Su 3pm-midnight. Cash only. ❸

Ali Baba, Bleibtreustr. 45 (☎881 1350). S3, 5, 7, 9, or 75 to Savignypl. A pizzeria with outdoor seating, mountainous spaghetti (€4), and crispy, fresh-baked pizzas (€3-5). Open daily 11am-3am. MC/V. ❶

Art-Café Miró, Stuttgarter Pl. 14 (☎3290 7404). S3, 5, 7, 9, or 75 to Charlottenburg, or U7 to Wilmersdorfer Str. Breakfast buffet €8. Daily special (€5), including drink, offers a choice of 2 meals. Entrees €5-15. Open 24hr. AmEx/MC/V; €7 minimum charge. ❸

SCHÖNEBERG

Cafe Berio, Maaßenstr. 7 (☎216 1946; www.cafe-berio.de). U1, 2, 4, or 15 to Nollendorfpl. Enjoy a terrific breakfast menu (€3.50-8.50) at the outdoor seating of this relaxing Viennese-style cafe. Open daily 8am-1am. Cash only. ❷

Bella Italia, Maaßenstr. 12. (☎215 3312). U1, 2, 4, or 15 to Nollendorfpl. Best known for its delicious, oven-baked pizza (€1 per slice; €3-4.50 for small pie). Also serves pasta dishes, salads, and omelettes. Entrees €3.50-4. Open daily 11am-1am. ❶

Café Bilderbuch, Akazienstr. 28 (☎78 70 60 57; www.cafe-bilderbuch.de). U7 to Eisenacher Str. Relax in a dramatic Venetian library or sit in the airy courtyard. Customers can choose what CDs to play. Known for their daily breakfasts named after fairy tales (€7-8). Open M-Th 9am-1am, F-Sa 9am-2am, Su 10am-1am. ❸

Habibi Falafel Schawarma, Goltzstr. 24, Am Winterfeldtpl (☎215 3332). With great, cheap food, this place is always packed. Falafel plate €3. M-Th, Su 11am-3am, F-Sa 11am-5am. Cash only. ❶

Die Feinbäck, Vorbergstr. 2 (☎81 49 42 40; www.feinbaeck.de). U7 to Kleistpark or Eisenacher Str. Swabian cuisine as unassuming as the restaurant's tasteful interior. Unbeatable *spätzle* (noodles; €6.50) and weekday lunch special (€4.90; M-F 10am-5pm). Open daily noon-midnight. Cash only. ❷

KREUZBERG

Yellow Sunshine, Wiener Str. 19 (☎21 46 00 66; www.yellow-sunshine.de). Over 25 different kinds of vegetarian burgers (€3-4) and vegetarian gyros, pastas, and stir fries. Fruit shakes €2.50. Open M-Th noon-midnight, F-Su noon-1am. Cash only. ❶

Hannibal, on the corner of Wiener Str. and Skalitzerstr. (☎61 15 16). U1, 12, or 15, or night bus N29 to Görlitzer Bahnhof. Excels in massive burgers (€6) and blueberry pancakes (€4.50). Open M-Th 8am-3am, F-Sa 8am-4am, Su 9am-3am. AmEx/MC/V. ❷

Sarod's Thai Restaurant, Friesenstr. 22 (☎69 50 73 33). U7 to Gneisenaustr. Enjoy the €5 all-you-can-eat lunch on weekdays from noon-4pm. Open M-F noon-11:30pm, Sa-Su 2-11:30pm. Cash only. ❷

Curry 36, Mehringdamm 36. U6 or 7 to Mehringdamm. Berlin's best curry sausages and burgers (€1-4). Open M-F 9am-4am, Sa 10am-4am, Su 10am-4am. Cash only. ❶

Zur Henne, Leuschnerdamm 25 (☎614 7730). U1 or 15 to Kottbusser Tor. Nearly everyone orders the fried chicken (*brathänchen*; €6), arguably Berlin's best. Reserve ahead, as the place is always packed. Open Tu-Su 7pm-late. Cash only. ❷

Abendmahl, Muskauer Str. 9 (☎612 5170; www.abendmahl-berlin.de). U1 or 15 to Görlitzer Bahnhof. Fabulously macabre desserts like coffin-shaped ice cream petit-fours (€8.50). Open W-Su 6pm-1am. Kitchen closes 11:30pm. Cash only. ❹

Melek Bäckerei, Oranienstr. 28. U1, 8, or 15 to Kottbusser Tor. Popular sweets shop sells Turkish pastries like baklava (100g; €0.80). Open 24hr. Cash only. ❶

FRIEDRICHSHAIN AND PRENZLAUER BERG

Massai Afrikanische Bar and Restaurant, Bart Lychener Str. 12 (☎48 62 55 95; www.massai-berlin.de). U2 to Eberswalder Str. African art and carved wooden chairs complement savory entrees (€8-10) and 15 delicious vegetarian options (€7-9). Banana beer €3.30. Open daily noon-2am. Cash only. ❸

Prater Biergarten, Kastanienallee 7-9 (☎448 5688; www.pratergarten.de). U2 to Eberswalder Str. Sit under giant chestnut trees at picnic tables with locals at Berlin's oldest beer garden. Outdoor theater and big-screen TV for watching sports. Bratwurst €2. Beer €2.20-3.10. Open in good weather Apr.-Sept. daily noon-late. Cash only. ❶

Maja's Deli, Pappelallee 11 (☎48 49 48 51). U2 to Eberswalder Str. Escape from smoke-filled eateries to this cozy vegan cafe. The homemade organic lasagna (€4) is a particular stand-out. Fruit shakes €2.80. Open M-F noon-6pm. Cash only. ❶

Nosh, Pappelallee 77 (☎44 04 03 97). U2 to Eberswalder Str. "Borderless cooking" brings together bagels with pesto-olive spread (€4.50), pad thai (€7.50), and the "Brighton Breakfast" (eggs, baked beans, grilled tomatoes, bacon, and toast; €6.50). Open daily 9am-late. Kitchen closes midnight. Cash only. ❸

Café-Restaurant Miró, Raumerstr. 29 (☎44 73 30 17). U2 to Eberswalder Str. Enjoy generous portions of Mediterranean cuisine (€8-11) while sitting on colorful floor cushions. Breakfast €4-7. Soups €3. Large appetizers and salads €4-9. Open 10am-late. Kitchen closes midnight. AmEx/MC/V; €7 minimum charge. ❸

SIGHTS

Most of central Berlin's major sights lie along the route of **bus #100,** which runs every 5min. from Bahnhof Zoo to Prenzlauer Berg. It passes by the **Siegessäule, Brandenburger Tor,** other sights along **Unter den Linden,** the **Berliner Dom,** and **Alexanderplatz.** Remnants of the **Berlin Wall** still survive in a few places: in **Potsdamer Platz;** near the **Haus Am Checkpoint Charlie;** in Prenzlauer Berg, next to the sobering **Documentation Center;** and memorably at the **East Side Gallery** in Friedrichshain.

MITTE

Once the heart of Berlin, Mitte was split down the middle by the wall. Much of it languished in disrepair under the DDR, but the wave of revitalization that swept post-wall Berlin hit Mitte first. Mitte may have received a final coat of polish, but you can still find war wrecks squeezed in among grandiose Prussian palaces, glittering modern constructions, swank galleries, and hyper-hip stores.

UNTER DEN LINDEN

Unter den Linden, one of Europe's best-known boulevards, was the spine of imperial Berlin. During the Cold War it was known as the "Idiot's Mile" because it was often all that visitors to the East saw, and gave them little idea of what the city was like. Beginning in Pariser Pl. in front of Brandenburger Tor, the street extends east through Bebelpl. and the Lustgarten, punctuated by dramatic squares. *(S1, 2, or 25 to Unter den Linden. Bus #100 runs the length of the boulevard every 4-6min.)*

BRANDENBURGER TOR. This gate served as the memorable backdrop for the fall of the Berlin Wall. Built as a tribute to peace in the 18th century, it later came to symbolize the city's division: facing the Berlin Wall, it became a barricaded gateway to nowhere. Today, it is the most powerful emblem of reunited Germany. Visitors can reflect in the **Room of Silence** at the northern end of the gate.

RUSSIAN EMBASSY. Rebuilding the edifices of the rich wasn't a priority in the workers' state of the DDR. One exception was Berlin's largest embassy, which covers almost an entire city block. Although the *Palais* lost its special status after the end of the Cold War, visitors still marvel at its imposing architecture from behind a cast-iron fence. *(Unter den Linden 55.)*

BEBELPLATZ. On May 10, 1933, Nazi students burned nearly 20,000 books here by "subversive" authors such as Heinrich Heine and Sigmund Freud, both of Jewish descent. In the center of the square, a small glass window in the ground reveals empty bookcases beneath and a plaque that translates to: "Wherever they burn books, eventually they will burn people too." On the western side of Bebelpl., the building with a curved facade is the **Alte Bibliothek;** once the royal library, it's now home to the law faculty of Humboldt-Universität. On the eastern side is the **Deutsche Staatsoper,** one of Berlin's three opera houses, fully rebuilt (twice!) after the war from the original sketches. The blue dome at the end of the square belongs to **St.-Hedwigs-Kathedrale,** the first Catholic church built in Berlin after the Reformation. Modeled on the Roman Pantheon and completed in 1773, it was destroyed by Allied bombers. The church was rebuilt in the 1950s in a more modern style. *(Cathedral open M-Sa 10am-5pm, Su 1-5pm. Organ concerts W 3pm. Cathedral free.)*

TIERGARTEN

Once a hunting ground for Prussian monarchs, the lush Tiergarten (Animal Park) is the eye of Berlin's metropolitan storm. Stretching from Bahnhof Zoo to the Brandenburger Tor, the vast landscaped

IN RECENT NEWS

THE POLITICS OF MEMORY

Tilting over uneven walkways, 2700 stone slabs jut out of the ground in rows near Brandenburger Tor in the heart of Berlin. Opened in May 2005 after 17 years of red tape and dispute, the **Monument to the Murdered Jews of Europe** draws an emotional response from all who pass over its stark terrain.

The memorial has stirred controversy ever since architect Peter Eisenman's design was approved in 1999. Early critics felt that the featureless gray stones were too abstract to provide an opportunity for learning and reflection; a visitor's center was added beneath the memorial as a compromise. Others still believe that the focus on the Jews of Europe is too narrow, excluding other victims of the Nazi regime from remembrance.

Even the prospect of graffiti has occasioned debate. Although Eisenman himself felt that scrawlings on the slabs would make the memorial a part of the city, planners decided to treat the slabs with an anti-graffiti agent—only to discover afterwards that the company that manufactured the chemical had once supplied Zyklon B to the Nazi death camps.

The memorial is free and open to the public at all times.

(Cora-Berliner-Str. 1. ☎7407 2929; www.stiftung-denkmal.de. Information Center open daily 10am-8pm. Free.)

park is frequented today by bikers, joggers, and families out for a stroll. **Straße des 17. Juni** bisects the park from west to east, connecting Ernst-Reuter-Pl. to the Brandenburger Tor.

THE REICHSTAG. Today home to the *Bundestag*, Germany's governing body, the Reichstag was central to one of the most critical moments in history. When it mysteriously burned down in 1933, Adolf Hitler declared a state of emergency and seized power. Today, a glass dome offers visitors 360° views of the city as they climb the spiral staircase inside. Go before 8am or after 8pm to avoid long lines. *(☎22 73 21 52. Open daily 8am-midnight. Last entrance 10pm. Free.)*

SIEGESSÄULE. Fondly known as "chick-on-a-stick," this column, topped by the goddess of victory, commemorates Prussia's victory over France in 1870. The goddess is made of melted French cannons. Climb the 285 steps for a panorama of the city. *(Großer Stern. Take bus #100 or 187 to Großer Stern or S5, 7, or 9 to Tiergarten and walk 5min. on Straße des 17. Juni. ☎391 29 61. Open mid-May to mid-Oct. M-Th 8:30am-6:30pm, F-Sa 9:30am-7pm; mid-Oct. to mid-May M-Su 8:30am-5pm.)*

POTSDAMER PLATZ. Originally designed to allow the rapid mobilization of troops under Friedrich Wilhelm I, Potsdamer Pl. is Berlin's commercial center. During the 1990s, it formed the city's largest construction site; now, its ambitious architecture never fails to impress visitors. Most of the new office space is empty, but the central complex includes the towering headquarters of the Deutsche Bahn, Berlin's Film Museum, and the glitzy **Sony Center,** where travelers can watch a movie, enjoy free wireless Internet, or window-shop. *(U2, or S1, 2, or 25 to Potsdamer Pl.)*

MUSEUMSINSEL AND ALEXANDERPLATZ

After crossing the Spree, Unter den Linden becomes Karl-Liebknecht-Str. and cuts through the Museumsinsel (Museum Island), home to five major museums and the **Berliner Dom.** Karl-Liebknecht-Str. then continues onward to Alexanderpl. Take S3, 5, 7, 9, or 75 to Hackescher Markt, or bus #100 to Lustgarten.

BERLINER DOM. Berlin's most recognizable landmark, this multi-domed cathedral proves that Protestants can be as dramatic as Catholics. Built during the reign of Kaiser Wilhelm II, the Dom suffered damage in a 1944 air raid and only recently emerged from two decades of restoration. Inside, keep an eye out for the likenesses of Protestant luminaries Calvin, Zwingli, and Luther, or search out the glorious view of Berlin from the tower. *(Open M-Sa 9am-8pm, Su noon-8pm. Closed for services daily 6:30-7:30pm. Organ recitals W-F at 3pm. Ticket office open M-Sa 10am-8pm, Su noon-8pm. Admission to Dom, crypt, tower, and galleries €5, students €3. Buy tickets to frequent summer concerts in the church or call ☎20 26 91 36.)*

MARIENKIRCHE. A quilt of architectural styles, the church itself is Gothic, its altar and pulpit Rococo, and its tower neo-Romantic. Relatively unscathed by WWII, this inconspicuous church still shelters relics from nearby churches that weren't as lucky. Knowledgeable guides explain the relics and the collection of paintings, which is mainly comprised of Northern Renaissance works. *(☎242 44 67. Open daily in summer 10am-6pm; in winter 10am-4pm.)*

FERNSEHTURM. Berlin's tallest structure at 368m, this bizarre TV tower was built to prove East Germany's technological capabilities—even though Swedish engineers helped build it. The Swedes left a controversial surprise for the DDR, as a crucifix appears when the sun hits the dome, defying the DDR's attempt to rid the city of religious symbols. It is known as the *"Papsts Rache"* (Pope's Revenge). An elevator whisks tourists up to a magnificent view from the spherical node 203m above the city. A cafe one floor up serves international meals for €9-13. *(☎242 33 33. Open daily Mar.-Oct. 9am-midnight; Nov.-Feb. 10am-midnight. €7.50, under 16 €3.50.)*

SCHEUNENVIERTEL AND ORANIENBURGER STRAßE

Northwest of Alexanderpl., near Oranienburger Str. and Große Hamburger Str., is the Scheunenviertel, once the center of Berlin's Orthodox Jewish community. Prior to WWII, Berlin did not have ghettos; the city's assimilated Jews lived in Western Berlin, while Orthodox Jews from Eastern Europe settled here. The district shows traces of Jewish life back to the 13th century; the area now is known mainly for its outdoor cafes. *(S1, 2, or 25 to Oranienburger Str., or U6 to Oranienburger Tor.)*

NEUE SYNAGOGE. This synagogue was used for worship until 1940, when the Nazis occupied it and used it for storage. Amazingly, the building survived *Kristallnacht*—even though the SS torched it, a local police chief managed to bluff his way past SS officers and order the fire to be extinguished. The striking building no longer holds services. Instead, it houses small exhibits on the history of Berlin's Jews. *(Oranienburger Str. 30. ☎88 02 83 00. Open May-Aug. M, Su 10am-8pm, Tu-Th 10am-6pm, F 10am-5pm; Sept.-Apr. M-Th, Sa-Su 10am-6pm, F 10am-2pm. Museum €5, students €3. Permanent exhibit €3/2. Dome €1.50/1.)*

CHARLOTTENBURG

Charlottenburg was originally a separate town huddled around Friedrich I's imperial palace. Now the neighborhood is home to Berlin's main shopping drag, the Ku'damm, full of uppity boutiques. Charlottenburg sights can be expensive; budget travelers come mostly to see the sights near Bahnhof Zoo.

AROUND BAHNHOF ZOO. West Berlin once centered around Bahnhof Zoo, the station that inspired U2's "Zoo TV" tour. In the surrounding area, a welter of peep-shows and department stores mingle with souvenir shops and other G-rated attractions. Many of the animals at the renowned **Zoologischer Garten** live in open-air habitats; the flamingos have no confines. The zoo gates post feeding times. At the second entrance across from EuropaCenter is the famous **Elefantentor,** a pagoda of pachyderms. *(Budapester Str. 34. Open daily May-Sept. 9am-6:30pm; Oct.-Feb. 9am-5pm; Mar.-Apr. 9am-5:30pm. €10, students €7.50.)* Within the walls of the zoo but independently accessible, an **aquarium** contains insects, reptiles, and miles of fish tanks. A wall of translucent sea nettles has a psychedelic effect. *(Budapester Str. 32. Open daily 9am-6pm. €7.50, students €7. Combination ticket to zoo and aquarium €15/12.)*

KAISER-WILHELM-GEDÄCHTNISKIRCHE. Nicknamed "the hollow tooth," this shattered church has been left in its jagged state as a reminder of WWII. Its colorful mosaics are mostly intact, however, and the church also houses an exhibit on its history. *(☎218 5023. Church open daily 9am-7pm. Exhibit open M-Sa 10am-4pm.)*

SCHLOß CHARLOTTENBURG. This monumental Baroque palace occupies a park in northern Charlottenburg and contains more 18th-century paintings than any other location outside of France. The pristine grounds include the beautifully furnished **Altes Schloß,** the marbled receiving rooms of the **Neuer Flugel,** the **Neuer Pavillon,** and the palace **Mausoleum.** The **Belvedere,** which houses the royal family's porcelain collection, also lies within the grounds. Leave time to stroll the **Schloßgarten** behind the main buildings, a paradise of small lakes, fountains, and footbridges. *(Take bus #145 from Bahnhof Zoo to Luisenpl./Schloß Charlottenburg or U2 to Sophie-Charlotte Pl. and walk about 10-15min. up Schloßstr. ☎32 09 14 40. Altes Schloß open Tu-F 9am-5pm, Sa-Su 10am-5pm. Neuer Flugel open Tu-F 10am-6pm, Sa-Su 11am-6pm. Neuer Pavillon open Tu-Su 10am-5pm. Mausoleum open Apr.-Oct. Tu-Su 10am-noon and 1-5pm. Belvedere open Apr.-Oct. Tu-Su 10am-5pm; Nov.-Mar. Tu-F noon-4pm and Sa-Su noon-5pm. Required tour of Altes Schloß €8, students €5. Neuer Flugel €5. Audio tour included in admission. Neuer Pavillon €2/1.50. Mausoleum €1. Belvedere €2/1.50. Entire complex €12/9.)*

OLYMPIA-STADION. At the western edge of Charlottenburg, the Olympic Stadium is one of the most prominent legacies of the Nazi architectural aesthetic. It was erected for the 1936 Olympic Games, in which African-American Jesse Owens won four gold medals. Hitler refused to congratulate him, but there's now a Jesse-Owens-Allee nearby. A neighboring bell tower *(Glockenturm)* has a great view. *(S5 or 7 to Pichelsburg. Turn left onto Schirwindter Allee and left again onto Passenheimerstr. Stadium ☎306 3430, Glockenturm 305 8123. Glockenturm open daily Apr.-Oct. 9am-6pm. €2.50.)*

SCHÖNEBERG

South of the Ku'damm, Schöneberg is a pleasant, residential district notable for its shopping streets and tasty restaurants. Locals lounge here for hours in laidback cafes. In busy **Nollendorfplatz,** the nexus of Berlin's gay and lesbian community, even the military store is draped with rainbow flags.

GRUNEWALD. This 745-acre birch forest is home to the **Jagdschloß,** once a royal hunting lodge. Now a one-room museum, it houses paintings by German masters Graff and Cranach, as well as knives, guns, spears, goblets, antlers, and mounted wild boars. *(Am Grunewaldsee 29. U1 or 7 to Fehrbelliner Pl., or S45 or 46 to Hohenzollerndamm, then bus #115, dir.: Neuruppiner Str., to Pücklerstr. Walk west 15min. on Pücklerstr. to the lodge. ☎813 3597. Open Tu-Su 10am-5pm. €2, students €1.50. Guided tour €1 extra.)*

KREUZBERG

In what was once West Germany, Kreuzberg today is counter-culture central. Much of the area was occupied by squatters *(hausbesetzer)* in the 60s and 70s, but the city government evicted most of them in the early 80s. Protests are still frequent and intense; the most prominent is an annual demonstration on Labor Day. Home to a large portion of the city's immigrant population, the district has recently seen an influx of hipsters amid a wider wave of gentrification.

HAUS AM CHECKPOINT CHARLIE. A strange mix of eastern sincerity and glossy western salesmanship, Checkpoint Charlie documents the history of the Berlin Wall and the dramatic escapes that once centered around its wire-and-concrete barrier. Cluttered with artwork, newspaper clippings, and photographs of the Berlin Wall, the museum also showcases a collection of contraptions used to get over, under, or through it. If you are pressed for time, skip the audio tour—there's plenty of English-language information to keep you busy for an hour. *(Friedrichstr. 43-45. U6 to Kochstr. ☎253 7250; www.mauer-museum.com. Museum open daily 9am-10pm. German films every 2hr. from 9:30am. €9.50, students €5.50.)*

FRIEDRICHSHAIN AND LICHTENBERG

As the alternative scene follows the low rents eastward, **Friedrichshain** is becoming the new hallowed ground of the unpretentiously hip. Not extensively renovated since reunification, the district retains old pre-fab apartments and large stretches of the wall. **Simon-Dach-Straße** is filled with outdoor cafes and a crowd of 20-somethings. The grungier area surrounding **Rigärstraße** is one of the strongholds of Berlin's legendary alternative scene.

GERMANY

EAST SIDE GALLERY. The longest remaining portion of the wall, this 1.3km stretch of cement slabs and asbestos also serves as the world's largest open-air art gallery, unsupervised and open at all hours. The murals are not remnants of Cold War graffiti, but efforts of an international group of artists who gathered here in 1989 to celebrate the end of the city's division. It was expected that the wall would be destroyed soon after and the paintings lost, but in 2000, with this portion still standing, many of the artists reconvened to repaint their work, covering others' scrawlings. Unfortunately, the new paintings are being rapidly eclipsed by graffiti. *(Along Mühlenstr. Take U1 or 15, or S3, 5, 6, 7, 9, or 75 to Warschauer Str.)*

FORSCHUNGS- UND GEDENKSTÄTTE NORMANNENSTRAßE. The Lichtenberg suburb harbors the most feared building of the DDR regime: the headquarters of the **secret police** (*Staatssicherheit*, or *Stasi*). During the Cold War, the *Stasi* kept dossiers on six million East Germans. An exhibit displays a collection of tiny microphones and cameras used by the *Stasi* and a bizarre shrine filled with busts of Lenin. *(Ruschestr. 103, Haus #1. U5 to Magdalenenstr. Walk up Ruschestr. from the exit and turn right on Normannenstr.; it's in the office complex. ☎553 6854; www.stasimuseum.de. All exhibits German-language. Open Tu-F 11am-6pm, Sa-Su 2-6pm. €3.50, students €2.50.)*

PRENZLAUER BERG

Everything in Prenzlauer Berg used to be something else. Brunches unfold every Sunday morning in what once were butcher shops, furniture exhibits bring domestic grace to a former power plant, and kids cavort in breweries-turned-nightclubs.

DOKUMENTATIONSZENTRUM DER BERLINER MAUER. A museum, chapel, and entire city block of the Berlin Wall—two concrete barriers separated by the open *Todesstreife* (death strip)—make up a controversial memorial to "victims of the communist tyranny." The Center assembles historic photos, film clips, and sound bites from wall history. Ascend the spiral staircases for the full, desolate effect. *(Bernauer Str. 111. ☎464 10 30; www.berliner-mauer-dokumentationszentrum.de. U8 to Bernauer Str. Open Tu-Su Apr.-Oct. 10am-6pm; Nov.-Mar. 10am-5pm. Free.)*

MUSEUMS

Berlin is one of the world's great museum cities, with over 170 museums that include collections from every world-historical epoch. *Berlin Programm* (€1.60) lists museums and galleries.

SMB MUSEUMS

Staatliche Museen zu Berlin (SMB) runs over 20 museums in four major areas of Berlin—the **Museumsinsel, Tiergarten-Kulturforum, Charlottenburg,** and **Dahlem**—and elsewhere in Mitte and the Tiergarten. All museums sell single admission tickets (€6, students €3) and the three-day card (*Drei-Tage-Karte;* €12, students €6). Admission is free the first Sunday of every month and Thursdays after 6pm. Unless otherwise noted, all SMB museums are open Tuesday through Sunday 10am-6pm, Thursday until 10pm. All offer free English-language audio tours.

MUSEUMSINSEL (MUSEUM ISLAND)

Germany's greatest cultural treasures reside in five separate museums, separated from the rest of Mitte by two arms of the Spree. Two museums are now undergoing renovations: the **Bodemuseum** should reopen in 2006, the **Neues Museum** in 2008. *(S3, 5, 7, 9 or 75 to Hackescher Markt or bus #100 to Lustgarten. ☎20 90 55 55.)*

PERGAMONMUSEUM. One of the world's great ancient history museums, the museum is named for Pergamon, the Turkish city from which the enormous **Altar of Zeus** (180 BC) was taken. Collections include enormous artifacts from the ancient Near East, including the colossal blue **Ishtar Gate of Babylon** (575 BC) and the Roman **Market Gate of Miletus.** Be sure to get the headsets for your choice of free audio tours. *(Bodestr. 1-3. ☎20 90 55 77. Last entry 30min. before closing.)*

ALTE NATIONALGALERIE. After renovations, this renowned museum is again open to eager 19th-century art lovers. Collections showcase everything from German Realism to French Impressionism, and include works by Caspar David Friedrich and Karl Friedrich Schinkel. Afterward, enjoy a drink at the outdoor Sage Bar under the columns overlooking the water. *(Am Lustgarten. ☎20 90 58 01.)*

TIERGARTEN-KULTURFORUM

A complex of museums at the eastern end of the Tiergarten, near the Staatsbibliothek and Potsdamer Pl., the Tiergarten-Kulturforum is a good place to find fine arts students and local aficionados. *(Take S1, 2, or 25, or U2 to Potsdamer Pl. and walk down Potsdamer Str.; look for Matthäikirchpl. on the right. ☎ 20 90 55 55.)*

GEMÄLDEGALERIE. One of Germany's best-known museums, the Gemäldegalerie beautifully displays nearly 3000 masterpieces by Italian, German, Dutch, and Flemish masters from the 13th to 18th centuries, including works by Botticelli, Dürer, Raphael, Rembrandt, Titian, and Vermeer. *(Stauffenbergstr. 40. ☎ 266 29 51.)*

HAMBURGER BAHNHOF/MUSEUM FÜR GEGENWART. North of the Tiergarten, Berlin's foremost modern art collection occupies a full 10,000 sq. m of this former train station. Its artist roster includes Beuys, Kiefer, and Warhol. With few space constraints, the museum also hosts outrageous sculptures and temporary exhibits. *(Invalidenstr. 50-51. U6 to Zinnowitzer Str. or S3, 5, 7, 9, or 75 to Lehrter Stadtbahnhof. ☎ 39 78 34 11; www.hamburgerbahnhof.de. Open Tu-F 10am-6pm, Sa 11am-8pm, Su 11am-6pm. Tours Su 4pm. €8, students €4. Th 2-6pm free.)*

NEUE NATIONALGALERIE. Designed by Mies van der Rohe, this sleek building hosts temporary exhibits of modern and contemporary art and displays its permanent collection—which includes works by Beckmann, Kirchner, Munch, and Warhol—from time to time as well. Check www.smb.museum to see its current offerings. *(Potsdamer Str. 50. Just past the Kulturforum. ☎ 266 26 62.)*

CHARLOTTENBURG

Many excellent museums surround **Schloß Charlottenburg.** Take bus #145 from Bahnhof Zoo to Luisenpl./Schloß Charlottenburg. Or, take U2 to Sophie-Charlotte-Pl. and walk 10-15min. up the tree-lined Schloßstr.

ÄGYPTISCHES MUSEUM. This stern Neoclassical building displays a wide variety of ancient Egyptian art complemented by dramatic lighting. The most famous work in the collection is the limestone bust of **Queen Nefertiti** (1340 BC), but the sarcophagi and mummified cats will also draw the adventurer out in every traveler. *(Schloßstr. 70. ☎ 34 35 73 11. Open daily 10am-6pm. Th 2-6pm free.)*

MUSEUM BERGGRUEN. Subtitled "Picasso and His Time," this three-story museum explores the work of the groundbreaking 20th-century artist and the art movements that sprung up around him. *(Schloßstr. 1. Across from the Ägyptisches Museum. ☎ 32 69 58 11. Open Tu-Su 10am-6pm.)*

INDEPENDENT (NON-SMB) MUSEUMS

DEUTSCHE GUGGENHEIM BERLIN. Located in a newly renovated building opposite the Deutsche Staatsbibliothek, this joint venture of the Deutsche Bank and the Guggenheim Foundation features new exhibits of contemporary art every few months. *(Unter den Linden 13-15. U2 to Stadtmitte or U6 to Französische Str., or take S1, S2 to Unter den Linden or S3, S5, S7, S9 to Friedrichstr. ☎ 202 0930; www.deutsche-guggenheim-berlin.de. Open daily 11am-8pm, Th until 10pm. €4, students €3. M free.)*

KUNST-WERKE BERLIN. Under the direction of Mitte art luminary Klaus Biesenbach, this former margarine factory now houses artists' studios, rotating modern exhibits, and a garden cafe. *(Auguststr. 69. U6 to Oranienburger Tor. ☎ 243 4590; www.kw-berlin.de. Open Tu-Su noon-6pm. €4, students €2.50.)*

FILMMUSEUM BERLIN. This new museum chronicles the development of German film, with a focus on older films like *Metropolis* and rooms devoted to such superstars as Leni Riefenstahl and Marlene Dietrich. *(Potsdamer Str. 2. On the 3rd and 4th fl. of the Sony Center. S1, 2, 25 or U2 to Potsdamer Pl. ☎ 300 9030; www.filmmuseum-berlin.de. Tickets sold on the ground fl. Open Tu-Su 10am-6pm, Th until 8pm. €6, students €4.)*

JÜDISCHES MUSEUM BERLIN. Daniel Libeskind designed this museum in such a way that no facing walls run parallel. Jagged hallways end in windows overlooking "the void." Wander through the labyrinthine Garden of Exile or shut yourself in the Holocaust Tower, a room virtually devoid of light and sound. *(Lindenstr. 9-14. U6 to Kochstr. or U1, 6, or 15 to Hallesches Tor. ☎25 99 33 00; www.juedisches-museum-berlin.de. Open daily 10am-8pm, M until 10pm. Last entry 1hr. before closing. €5, students €2.50.)*

ENTERTAINMENT

Berlin hosts myriad exhibitions, concerts, plays, and dance performances. Box offices at theaters and concert halls offer student discounts of up to 50% on tickets bought at the *Abendkasse* (evening counter; generally open 1hr. before shows). Other ticket outlets charge 15-18% commissions and offer no discounts. **KaDeWe** has a city-wide ticket counter. (☎217 7754. Open M-F 10am-8pm, Sa 10am-4pm.) Many venues close from mid-July to late August in the season known as *Theaterferien* or *Sommerpause*. The monthly magazine *Berlin Programm* (€1.50) lists opera, theater, and classical music schedules. Spring for *Zitty* (€2.30) or *Tip* (€2.50), which have the most comprehensive listings for film, theater, concerts, and clubs. Check www.berlin.de for more info.

CONCERTS, OPERA, AND DANCE

Berlin's musical calendar peaks in September during the **Berliner Festwochen,** a festival that draws the world's best orchestras and soloists. Contact **Berliner Festspiele** (☎25 48 90; www.berlinerfestspiele.de) for information. In mid-July, the **Bachtage** features classical music, while every Saturday night in August the **Sommer Festspiele** turns the Ku'damm into a multi-faceted concert hall with punk, steel-drum, and folk groups competing for attention.

The monthly *Konzerte und Theater in Berlin und Brandenburg* (free) and *Berlin Programm* (€1.50) both have concert listings, as do the bi-weekly *Tip* and *Zitty*. Tickets for the *Philharmonie* and the *Oper* are nearly impossible to get without writing months in advance, except by standing outside before performances with a small sign marked *"Suche Karte"* (seeking ticket).

Berliner Philharmonisches Orchester, Mitte, Herbert Von Karajanstr. 1 (☎25 48 81 32; www.berlin-philharmonic.com). Take S1, 2, or 25, or U2 to Potsdamer Pl., and walk up Potsdamer Str. This yellow building is acoustically perfect: you hear the music exactly as it is meant to be heard. The Berlin Philharmonic is one of the world's finest orchestras—and one of its greatest steals, with tickets available for as little as €7. Tickets are hard to come by, however; either check 1hr. before concert time or write at least 8 weeks in advance. No performances late June to early Sept. Box office open M-F 3-6pm, Sa-Su 11am-2pm. Standing room tickets from €7, seats from €15.

THEATER

Pamphlets *Kultur!news, 030* (free), *Berlin Programm, Tip,* and *Zitty* all list shows city-wide. In addition to the world's best German-language theater, Berlin has a lively English-language scene. A number of private companies called "off-theaters" also occasionally feature English-language plays.

Deutsches Theater, Mitte, Schumannstr. 13a (☎28 44 12 25; www.deutsches-theater.berlin.net). Take U6 to Friedrichstr., then follow Friedrichstr. north; turn left on Reinhardtstr., then right on Albrechtstr., which curves into Schumannstr. Widely recognized as the best theater in Germany, it interprets playwrights from Büchner to Ibsen. Box office open M-Sa 11am-6:30pm, Su 3-6:30pm. Tickets €4-42, students €8.

Berliner Ensemble, Mitte, Bertolt-Brecht-Pl. 1 (☎28 40 81 55; www.berliner-ensemble.de). U6 or S1-3, 5, 7, 9, 25, or 75 to Friedrichstr. Founded by Bertolt Brecht, this theater has recently enjoyed a renaissance. Its latest repertoire has included works by Brecht, Heiner Müller, and younger Americans. Box office open M-F 8am-6pm, Sa-Su 11am-6pm, and 1hr. before shows. Tickets €2-24, students €7.

FILM

Foreign-language movies listed as *"O.F."* play undubbed; those listed as *"O.m.U."* have German subtitles. Check *Tip* or *Zitty* for schedules. Most theaters reduce rates Monday through Wednesday. Students receive discounts with ID.

Odeon, Hauptstr. 116 (☎78 70 40 19; www.yorck.de). U4 to Rathaus Schöneberg. One of the 1st English-language theaters in Berlin, Odeon shows mainstream American and British flicks, generally with German subtitles. M €4.50, Tu-W €5.50, Th-Su €7.50.

NIGHTLIFE

Bars in Berlin open around 6pm and get going around midnight, just as clubs begin to open. The bar scene winds down between 1 and 6am, as clubs fill up and don't empty until dawn, when they pass the baton to after-parties and 24hr. cafes. Between 1 and 4am, take advantage of the **night buses** and **U-Bahn** 9 and 12, which run all night on Friday and Saturday. For nightlife info, check out *Tip* (€2.50) and *Zitty* (€2.30), available at newsstands, or in *030*, free in hostels, cafes, and bars.

Berlin's largest bar scene sprawls down pricey, packed **Oranienburger Straße** in Mitte. Prices fall only slightly around **Kollwitzplatz** and **Kastanienallee** in Prenzlauer Berg, but areas around **Schönhauser Allee** and **Danziger Straße**, such as the **"LSD" zone** (named for Lychener Str., Schliemannstr., and Dunckerstr.) still harbor an edgy alternative scene. Lively bars decorate **Simon-Dach-Straße** and **Gabriel-Max-Straße** in Friedrichshain, and dance venues for younger crowds are scattered between the car dealerships and empty lots of **Mühlenstraße.** Businessmen and middle-aged tourists drink at bars along the **Ku'damm.** Gay and lesbian nightlife centers on **Nollendorfplatz,** in the West.

BARS AND CLUBS

MITTE

WMF, Karl-Marx-Allee 34. U5 to Schillingstr. Moves often; check www.wmfclub.de for location. In a former cabaret, its 2 dance floors fill with electro-loungers Th and Sa. Gay night Su. Beer €3. Cover €8-12. Open Th and Sa from 11pm, Su from 10pm.

2BE-Club, Ziegelstr. 23 (☎89 06 84 10; www.2be-club.de). U6 to Oranienburger Tor. Reggae and hip-hop in a huge space that includes 2 dance floors and a tented courtyard with palm trees. Cover varies; women free until midnight. Open F-Sa from 11pm.

Zosch, Tucholskystr. 30 (☎280 7664). U6 to Oranienburger Tor. A bright, laidback bar on the ground floor resembles a living room, while the basement has live music, fiction and poetry readings, and a darker bar. W dixieland jazz. Open daily from 4pm.

Strandbar Mitte, Monbijioustr. 3 (☎28 38 55 88). S3, 5, 7, 9, or 75 to Hackescher Markt. Walk down Stadtbogen, which borders Monbijoupark, past bars that line the park's rim. After the last bar, go under the bridge to your right and then left down the path. Area can feel unsafe; consider going in a group. With deep beach chairs and a huge sand pit, this bar radiates sunshine. Beer €2.50-3.50. Mixed drinks €4-7. Open in summer daily from 10pm.

Delicious Doughnuts, Rosenthaler Str. 9 (☎28 09 92 74; www.delicious-doughnuts.de). U8 to Rosenthaler Pl. Curved design draws patrons through the door into one of the bar's low lounge booths—this is the place for the after-party. Nightly DJ, foosball, and a pocket-sized dance floor. Cover €5 F-Sa. Open daily 10pm-7am.

Weekend, Alexanderpl. 5 (www.week-end-berlin.de), on the 12th fl. overlooking the city. A mix of beautiful tourists and locals dance to house music and exchange smiles across the dance floor. Wheelchair accessible. Cover €6-8. Open Th-Sa 11pm-4am.

CHARLOTTENBURG (SAVIGNYPLATZ)

Quasimodo, Kantstr. 12a (www.quasimodo.de). U2 or 12, or S3, 5, 7, 9, or 75 to Zoologischer Garten. Beneath a huge cafe, this cozy venue showcases soul, R&B, and jazz. Cover €5-24. Concert tickets available from 5pm at the cafe upstairs or through the Kant-Kasse ticket service (☎313 45 54). Open M-F from 5pm, Sa-Su from 2pm. Concerts start at 11pm. Call or check the website for schedules.

SCHÖNEBERG

Slumberland, Goltzstr. 24 (☎216 5349). U1, 2, 4, 12, or 15 to Nollendorfpl. Palm trees, African art, a sand floor, and tantalizing mixed drinks encourage kicking back and occasionally napping. Open M-Th 6pm-2am, F 6pm-4am, Sa 11am-4am, Su 4pm-2am.

Metropol, Nollendorfpl. 5 (☎21 73 68 11). U1, 2, 4, or 15, or night buses N5, 19, 26, 48, 52, or 75 to Nollendorfpl. Don't meet a friend here without specifying on which floor. **Tanz Tempel,** the main venue of Metropol, pumps out 650,000 watts of light and 35,800 watts of sound onto its giant dance floor. Also check out the **West-Side Club** and **Love Lounge.** Cover €5-10. Drinks €2.50-4. Music and hours vary.

KREUZBERG

Freischwimmer, vor dem Schlesischen Tor 2 (☎61 07 43 09; www.freischwimmer-berlin.de). U1 or 15 to Schlesisches Tor or night bus N65 to Heckmannufer. Relax by the water amid roses, chill inside on a comfy sofa, or lounge in a beach chair on their floating dock. M summer poetry readings on the dock. €8.20 Su brunch 11am-4pm; reserve ahead. Open M-F noon-midnight, Sa-Su 11am-midnight.

SO36, Oranienstr. 190 (☎61 40 13 06; www.SO36.de). U1, 12, or 15 to Görlitzer Bahnhof or night bus N29 to Heinrichpl. Berlin's best mixed club. A massive dance floor packs in a friendly crowd for techno, hip-hop, and ska; music is often played live. Gay night last Sa of each month. Cover €4-8, concerts €7-18. Open daily from 11pm.

Watergate, Falckensteinstr. 49 (☎61 28 03 95; www.water-gate.de). U1 to Schlesisches Tor. Overlooking the river, this club is currently the hottest night attraction in town. Beer €3. Cover €10. Free entry until the club goes bust. Terrace opens daily at 8pm.

FRIEDRICHSHAIN AND PRENZLAUER BERG

Astro-Bar, Simon-Dach-Str. 40 (☎29 66 16 15). At this retro locale with plastic 70s robots, DJs spin anything from reggae to electronica. Mixed drinks €4.50-5.50. Open daily 6pm-late.

Dachkammer Bar (DK), Simon-Dach-Str. 39 (☎296 1673). U5 to Frankfurter Tor. Brick and wood create a rustic theme. Weekend brunch 10am-3pm; €6.50. With any luck, someone will bring an acoustic guitar and serenade you while you eat snacks (from €3) and sip mixed drinks (€5-7.50). Open M-F noon-late, Sa-Su 10am-late.

KulturBrauerei, Knaackstr. 97 (www.kulturbrauerei.de). U2 to Eberswalder Str. An enormous party space in an old East German brewery, housing the popular clubs **Soda** (www.soda-berlin.de) and **Kesselhaus** (www.kesselhaus-berlin.de), a Russian theater, upscale cafes, and an art school. Dance floors and stages abound. Music includes disco, hardcore, reggae, techno, and *Ostrock.* Cover and hours vary between venues.

TREPTOW

Insel der Jugend (Island of Youth), Alt-Treptow 6 (☎20 91 49 90; www.insel-berlin.net). S4, 6, 8, or 9 to Treptower Park, then bus #265 or N65 to Rathaus Treptow. Located on an island in the Spree River, this club is a 3-story tower crammed with gyrating bodies, multiple bars, and an open-air movie theater. The top 2 floors spin reggae, hip-hop, ska, and house, while a techno scene dominates the basement. Cover Th-Sa €4-6. Open W from 7:30pm, F-Sa from 10pm. In summer, movies M-Tu, Th-Su begin 8:30-9:30pm €6. Cafe open daily from 2pm. Cash only.

GLBT NIGHTLIFE

Berlin is one of the most gay-friendly cities in Europe. **Goltzstraße, Akazienstraße,** and **Winterfeldtstraße** have mixed bars and cafes, while the **"Bermuda Triangle"** of Motzstr., Fuggerstr., and Eisenacherstr. is more exclusively gay.

Siegessäule, *Sergej*, and *Gay-yellowpages* have entertainment listings for gays and lesbians. June culminates in the ecstatic, champagne-soaked floats of the **Christopher Street Day (CSD)** parade, a 6hr.-long street party that draws over 250,000 participants annually (July 22, 2006). Nollendorfpl. hosts the **Lesbisch-schwules Stadtfest** (Lesbian-Gay City Fair) the weekend before the parade.

Heile Welt, Schöneberg, Motzstr. 5 (☎21 91 75 07). U1, 2, 4, or 15 to Nollendorfpl. Clientele pack this bar and spill out into the street. 2 sitting rooms in the back offer quieter ambience for conversation. Mostly male crowd during "prime time," mixed in the early evening and latest hours of the night. Open daily 6pm-4am.

Rose's, Kreuzberg, Oranienstr. 187 (☎615 6570). U1 or U8 to Kottbusser Tor or U1 to Görlitzer Bahnhof. Marked only by a sign over the door that reads "Bar." A friendly, mixed clientele packs this claustrophobic party spot at all hours. The voluptuous dark-red interior is adorned by hearts, glowing lips, furry ceilings, feathers, and glitter. Daiquiris €3.50. Open daily 10pm-6am. Cash only.

SchwuZ, Kreuzberg, Mehringdamm 61 (☎629 0880; www.schwuz.de). U6 or 7 to Mehringdamm. Hidden behind **Sundström,** a popular gay and lesbian cafe, SchwuZ features 2 small dance floors and a lounge area with its own DJ and a young, chill crowd. Music varies. Cover €4-8. Open F-Sa from 11pm. Cash only.

Die Busche, Friedrichshain, Mühlenstr. 12 (www.diebusche.de). U1, 12, or 15, or S3, 5-7, 9, or 75 to Warschauer Str. East Berlin's most famous disco in the DDR days, Die Busche is still a color-saturated haven for dancers, spinning an incongruous rotation of techno, Top 40, and German *Schlager* to a mixed crowd. Cover €3.50-6. Open W, F-Su from 10pm-5am, F-Sa until 6am.

DAYTRIPS FROM BERLIN

KZ SACHSENHAUSEN. Just north of Berlin, the small town of Oranienburg was the setting for the Nazi concentration camp Sachsenhausen, where more than 100,000 Jews, communists, intellectuals, Roma (gypsies), and homosexuals were killed between 1936 and 1945. **Gedenkstätte Sachsenhausen,** a memorial preserving the remains of the camp, was opened in 1961 under the DDR. It includes some of the original cramped barracks, the cell block where "dangerous" prisoners were kept in solitary confinement and tortured daily, and a pathology wing where Nazis experimented on inmates. A stone monolith commemorating the camp's victims stands guard over the windswept grounds and several small museums. (Str. der Nationen 22. S1 to Oranienburg, 40min. Follow the signs from Stralsunderstr., turn right on Bernauer Str., left on Str. der Einheit, and right on Str. der Nationen, 20min. ☎03301 20 00; www.gedenkstaette-sachsenhausen.de. Open mid-Mar. to mid-Oct. 8:30am-6pm; mid-Oct. to mid-Mar. 8:30am-4:30pm. Free. Audio tours €2.50, students €1.50.)

POTSDAM. Anyone disappointed by Berlin's distinctly unroyal demeanor can satisfy cravings for imperial splendor in nearby Potsdam, the glittering city of Friedrich II (the Great). Potsdam is best seen by bike or by tour as the attractions are quite spread out. From the Potsdam S-Bahn station, exit to the North and look beyond the buses for **Fahrradverleihstation.** (☎0331 27 06 210. Open M-F 9am-7pm, Sa-Su until 8pm. €11 per day.) Spread over 600 acres, **Park Sanssouci** is testimony to the size of Friedrich's treasury and the diversity of his aesthetic. For info on the park, stop by the **tourist office** below the windmill and across the road in a yellow house. (Open daily May-Oct. 8:30am-5pm; Nov.-Feb. 9am-4pm.) **Schloß Sanssouci,**

the park's main attraction, was Friedrich's answer to Versailles. (Take bus #695 to Schloß Sanssouci. ☎969 41 90. Open Tu-Su Apr.-Oct. 9am-5pm; Nov.-Mar. 9am-4pm. Required tours €8, students €5.) The gold-plated **Chinesisches Teehaus,** complete with a rooftop Buddha carrying a parasol, contains 18th-century porcelain. Next door, the **Bildergalerie** gathers Caravaggio, van Dyck, and Rubens into one long hall. (☎0331 96 94 181. Open mid-May to mid-Oct. Tu-Su 10am-5pm. €2, students €1.50. Tours €1.) Perhaps the park's most intricate garden, the stunning **Sizilianischer Garten** is at the opposite end of the park from the largest of the four castles, the 200-chambered **Neues Palais.** (Open Apr.-Oct. M-Th, Sa-Su 9am-5pm; Nov.-Mar. 9am-4pm. €6, students €5. Summer tours €1.)

EASTERN GERMANY

Saxony *(Sachsen)* and Thuringia *(Thüringen)*, the most interesting regions in eastern Germany outside of Berlin, encompass Dresden, Leipzig, and Weimar. The architecture of the area is defined by contrasts: castles attest to Saxony's one-time decadence, while boxy GDR-era buildings recall the socialist aesthetic.

DRESDEN ☎0351

The buildings that form the skyline of Dresden's magnificent *Altstadt* (old town) look ancient, but most of them are newly reconstructed—the Allied firebombings in February 1945 that claimed over 40,000 lives also destroyed 75% of the city center. Long-delayed healing has accompanied the city's reconstruction, and today, its Baroque architecture, dazzling views of the Elbe River, world-class museums, and *Neustadt* nightlife make Dresden (pop. 479,000) one of the most celebrated cities of its size in Germany and a frequent stopover on journeys from Berlin to Prague.

TRANSPORTATION

Flights: Dresden's **airport** (☎881 3360; www.dresden-airport.de) is 9km from the city. S2 runs there from both train stations (15min. from *Neustadt,* 20min. from the Hauptbahnhof; 2 per hr. 4am-11:30pm; €1.50).

Trains: Nearly all trains stop at both the **Hauptbahnhof** in the *Altstadt* and **Bahnhof Dresden Neustadt** across the Elbe. Trains run to: **Berlin** (3hr., 2 per hr., €30); **Budapest** (11hr., every 2hr., €81); **Frankfurt** (5hr., 2 per hr., €74); **Leipzig** (1½hr., 1-2 per hr., €18); **Munich** (7hr., 1 per hr., €86); **Prague** (2½hr., 12 per day, €26); **Warsaw** (8hr., 8 per day, €54). Tickets are available from the machines in the main hall of each station, but are cheaper at the *Reisezentrum* desk.

Public Transportation: Streetcars cover the whole city. 1hr. ticket €1.70. Day pass €4.50. The €5.50 Family Card, good for 2 passengers until 4am, is probably the best deal. Weekly pass €15. Tickets are available from *Fahrkarte* dispensers at major stops and on streetcars. For info and maps, go to one of the **Verkehrs-Info** stands in front of the Hauptbahnhof or at Postpl. Open M-F 8am-7pm, Sa 8am-6pm, Su 9am-6pm. Most major lines run hourly after midnight–look for the moon sign marked **Gute-Nacht-Linie.**

Taxis: ☎211 211 and 888 88 88.

Bike Rental: In the Hauptbahnhof (☎461 32 62). €6 per day. Open daily 6am-10pm. Bike rentals also available at many hostels (see **Accommodations,** p. 433).

Ride-Share: Mitfahrzentrale, Dr.-Friedrich-Wolf-Str. 2 (☎194 40; www.mf24.de). On Slesischen Pl., across from Bahnhof Neustadt. Open M-F 9am-8pm, Sa-Su 10am-2pm. Non-German speakers may require assistance from their hostels in order to book.

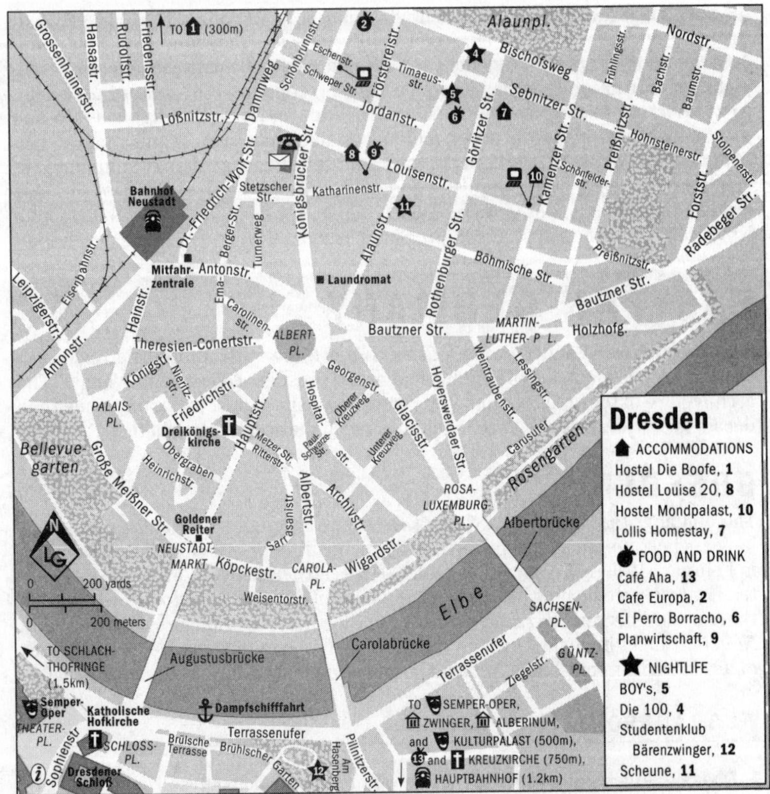

ORIENTATION AND PRACTICAL INFORMATION

The **Elbe** River bisects Dresden 60km northwest of the Czech border, dividing the city into the **Altstadt** in the south (where the Hauptbahnhof is located) and the **Neustadt** in the north. Many of Dresden's attractions lie between the **Altmarkt** and the Elbe in the historic *Altstadt.* Nightlife centers in the *Neustadt* to the north of the river, around **Albertplatz.**

Tourist Office: 2 main branches: Prager Str. 2a, near the Hauptbahnhof (open M-F 10am-6pm, Sa 10am-4pm), and Theaterpl. in the Schinkelwache, a small building in front of the Semper-Oper (☎49 19 20; open M-F 10am-6pm, Sa-Su and holidays 10am-4pm). Staff books rooms (€3 fee, rooms from €18) and sells city maps (€0.30). 2 cards provide transportation and free or reduced admission to Dresden museums: the **Dresden City-Card,** valid for 48hr. of transport in the city-zone (€19), and the **Dresden Regio-Card,** good for 72hr. in the Oberelbe region, including Meißen and Saxon Switzerland (€29). Call the city hotlines for general information (☎49 19 21 00), room reservations (☎4919 2222), tours (☎4919 2140), and advance tickets (☎4919 2233).

Currency Exchange: ReiseBank (☎471 2177), in the main hall of the Hauptbahnhof. 1-1.5% commission to cash **traveler's checks.** Western Union money transfers. Open M-F 8am-7pm, Sa 9am-noon and 12:30-4pm, Su 9am-1pm.

Luggage Storage: At all train stations. Lockers €1-2 per 24hr.

Laundromat: Eco-Express, Königsbrücker Str. 2. Wash €1.90, dry €0.50. Open M-Sa 6am-11pm.

Emergency: Police: ☎110. **Ambulance** and **Fire:** ☎112.

Pharmacy: Apotheke Prager Straße, Prager Str. 3 (☎490 3014). Open M-F 8:30am-7pm, Sa 8:30am-4pm. The Notdienst sign outside lists 24hr. pharmacies.

Hospitals: The Universitätsklinikum hospital is located at Fetscherstr. 74 (☎45 80). Dr. Marion Nadolny speaks English at Königsbrücker Str. 72 (☎804 1375).

Internet Access: Groove Station, Katharinenstr. 11-13. €3 per hr. Open M-Sa 7pm-late, Su 4pm-late. There are also several Internet cafes along Königsbrücker Str.

Post Office: The **Hauptpostamt,** Königsbrücker Str. 21/29 (☎819 1373). In the *Neustadt.* Open M-F 9am-7pm, Sa 10am-1pm. Branch in the *Altstadt* on Weberg. at the *Altmarkt* Galerie. Open daily 9:30am-8pm. **Postal Code:** 01099.

ACCOMMODATIONS

In the *Neustadt,* high-quality hostels with late check-out times neighbor clubs and bars. In the *Altstadt,* quieter hostels and pricier hotels are closer to the sights. Anywhere in the city, reservations are a must from April through November.

Hostel Mondpalast, Louisenstr. 77 (☎563 4050; www.mondpalast.de). Settle down in a comfy bed after a night hanging out in the lively bar downstairs. Bike rental €4 per 3hr. Breakfast €5. Linen €1.50. Internet €3.50 per hr. Reception 24hr. Dorms €13.50-16; singles €29, with bath €39; doubles €37/50; quads €74. AmEx/MC/V. ❶

Hostel Louise 20, Louisenstr. 20 (☎889 4894; www.louise20.de). Above the restaurant Planwirtschaft. Walk through a courtyard to enter this luxurious hostel, where granite floors lead you up a winding staircase to modern rooms. Breakfast €4.50. Linen €2.50. Reception 7am-11pm. Check-out noon. 20-bed ladder-accessible attic dorm €10; other dorms €15; singles €26; doubles €37; triples €48; quads €64. Cash only. ❶

Lollis Homestay, Görlitzer Str. 34 (☎8108 4558; www.lollishome.de). This hostel reproduces the relaxed atmosphere of a student flat with free coffee, tea, and a book exchange. Old bikes are available to borrow for free. Breakfast €3. Linen €2. Laundry €3. Dorms €13; singles €27; doubles €36; triples €48; quads €60. Cash only. ❶

Hostel Die Boofe, Hechtstr. 10 (☎801 33 61; www.boofe.den). From Bahnhof Neustadt, take a left and walk parallel to the tracks on Dammweg. Go left on Bischofsweg and right on Hechtstr. This funky hostel has a sauna in the basement. Wheelchair accessible. Breakfast €5. Internet €2 per hr. Reception 7am-midnight. Dorms €15, with shower €16; singles €26/29; doubles €34/38, quads €60/64. Cash only. ❷

FOOD

It's difficult to find anything in the *Altstadt* not targeting tourists; the cheapest eats are at the *Imbiß* stands along **Prager Straße** and around **Postplatz.** The *Neustadt* area between **Albertplatz** and **Alaunplatz** spawns a new bar every few weeks and is home to most of Dresden's quirky, student-friendly restaurants.

Café Aha, Kreuzstr. 7 (☎496 0673; www.ladencafe.de), across the street from Kreuzkirche. Often exotic, always delicious, Café Aha introduces food from a different developing country each month. Vegetarian options. Entrees €3.50-8.40. Fair trade shop located in the basement. Open daily 10am-midnight. Kitchen closes 10:30pm. ❶

Planwirtschaft, Louisenstr. 20 (☎801 3187). German dishes with ingredients fresh from local farms. Inventive soups, fresh salads (€3.50-6.90), and main dishes (€7-13) from stuffed eggplant to fresh lake fish. Breakfast buffet (€8.60) until 3pm. Outdoor courtyard seating. Open M-Th, Su 9am-midnight, F-Sa 9am-1am. ❸

El Perro Borracho, Alaunstr. 70 (☎803 6723; www.elperro.de). Walk down a hallway to discover the mosaic-filled courtyard of this near-hidden restaurant, where flowing Spanish wines, sangria, and tasty tapas (all €2.90) make happy Dresdeners. Main dishes €5-8. Buffet breakfast (€8) 10am-3pm on weekends. Open M 4pm-2am, Tu-F 11:30am-2am, Sa-Su 10am-2am. Cash only. ❷

Cafe Europa, Königsbrücker Str. 68 (☎804 4810). Open 24hr., this hip cafe draws a crowd of students and 20-somethings with 120 different warm and cold drinks, soups (€2.90-3.20), traditional main dishes (€6-10), and free Internet for customers. ❷

SIGHTS

Saxony's electors once ruled nearly all of central Europe from the banks of the majestic Elbe. Despite the *Altstadt*'s demolition in WWII and only partial reconstruction during communist times, the area remains a formidable cultural center.

ZWINGER. The extravagant collection of Saxon elector August the Strong occupies the magnificent Zwinger palace. A glorious example of Baroque design, the palace narrowly escaped destruction in the 1945 bombings. Gottfried Semper, revolutionary activist and master architect, designed the north wing. The palace now hosts Dresden's finest museums (see **Museums,** p. 434).

SEMPER-OPER. Dresden's opera house echoes the splendor of the Zwinger's north wing. Painstaking restoration has returned the building to its pre-war state. *(Theaterpl. 2. ☎491 14 96. Tours usually M-Sa every 30min. 11am-3pm, but times vary each week; check at the entrance. €6, students €3.)*

DRESDENER SCHLOß. Once the proud home of August the Strong, the Polish king who built most of the castles in and around Dresden, this palace regained its notoriety in 2004 with the return of the **Grünes Gewölbe** (Green Vault). From a collection of rare medieval chalices to the most lavish Baroque jewels, the vault dazzles with some of the finest metal and gem work in Europe. *(☎491 47 14. Open M, W-Su 10am-6pm. €6, students €3.50.)* The 100m tall **Hausmannsturm** hosts a collection of sobering photographs of the city after the firebombings that, combined with the 360-degree view from the tower, convey the enormity of the reconstruction project. *(Open Apr.-Sept. M, W-Su 10am-6pm. €2.50, students €1.50.)*

KREUZKIRCHE. After being leveled three times—by fire in 1669, by the Thirty Years' War in 1760, and by fire again in 1897—the Kreuzkirche survived WWII, although flames ruined its interior. The tower offers a bird's-eye view of town. *(An der Kreuzkirche 6. ☎439 3920; www.dresdner-kreuzkirche.de. Church open in summer M-Sa 10am-6pm; winter M-Sa 10am-4pm; Su after 9:30am services. Church free. Tower €1.50.)* The world-class **Kreuzchor** boys' choir has sung here since the 13th century. *(☎315 3560; www.kreuzchor.de. Concerts 6pm on some Sa during winter. Tickets €4-31.)*

MUSEUMS

If you plan on visiting more than one in a day, consider a **Tageskarte** (€10, students €6), which grants admission to the Albertinum museums, the Schloß, most of the Zwinger, and more. The **Dresden City-Card** and **Dresden Regio-Card** (see **Practical Information,** p. 432) also include admission to museums. For museum information, check www.skd-dresden.de. Most museums are closed on Monday.

ZWINGER. Through the archway from the Semper-Oper, **Gemäldegalerie Alte Meister** has a first-rate collection of Italian and Dutch paintings from 1400 to 1800, including Cranach the Elder's luminous *Adam and Eve*, Rubens's *Leda and the Swan*, and Raphael's *Sistine Madonna*. *(☎491 46 19. Tu-Su 10am-6pm. €6, students €3.50. Tickets include admission to the Rüstkammer.)* The **Rüstkammer** shows shiny but deadly toys from

GERMANY

the court of the Wettin princes: ivory-inlaid guns, chain mail, and the armor of the Wettin toddlers. *(Open Tu-Su 10am-6pm. €3, students €2.)* With over 20,000 pieces, the **Porzellansammlung** boasts the largest collection of European porcelain in the world. *(Open Tu-Su 10am-6pm. €5, students and seniors €3.)* Europe's oldest "science museum," the **Mathematisch-Physikalischer Salon** contains 16th- to 19th-century scientific instruments far more stylish than those in use today. *(Open Tu-Su 10am-6pm. €3, students €2.)*

ALBERTINUM. The **Gemäldegalerie Neue Meister** picks up in the 19th century where the Alte Meister gallery leaves off, with exhibits by hometown Romantic painter Caspar David Friedrich and by the Impressionists Degas, Monet, and Renoir. Check out Otto Dix's renowned *War* triptych and the Expressionist works. *(Open M, W-Su 10am-6pm. €5, students €2.50. The Albertinum may be closed for renovations in 2006. Call ☎49 643 for updates on where exhibits are temporarily located.)*

ENTERTAINMENT

Although most theaters break from mid-July to early September, open-air festivals bridge the gap. Outdoor movies screen along the Elbe during **Filmnächte am Elbufer** in July and August. (Office at Alaunstr. 62. ☎89 93 20. Movies show at around 9pm. Tickets €6.) Like other area palaces, the **Zwinger** has classical concerts on summer evenings; shows start at 6:30pm.

Sächsische Staatsoper (Semper-Oper), Theaterpl. 2 (☎491 1705). Some of the finest opera in the world. It takes work to get a ticket; call ahead. Tickets €3-90. Box office at Schinkelwache open M-F 10am-6pm, Sa 10am-4pm, and 1hr. before performances.

Kulturpalast, Schloßstr. 2, am *Altmarkt* (☎486 6666; www.kulturpalast-dresden.de). Home to the **Dresdner Philharmonie** (☎486 63 06; www.dresdnerphilharmonie.de) and a variety of performances. Open M-F 10am-4pm.

NIGHTLIFE

Little over 10 years ago, the area north of Albertpl. was a maze of gray streets and crumbling buildings. Since then, an alternative community has sprung up in dozens of bars on Louisenstr., Königsbrücker Str., Bischofsweg, Kamenzerstr., and Albertpl. *Kneipen Surfer*, free at *Neustadt* hostels, describes every bar.

Studentenklub Bärenzwinger, Brühlscher Garten 1 (☎495 1409; www.baeren-zwinger.de). Under the garden between the Elbe and the Albertinum. Dresden's former fortress attracts crowds with cheap drinks and unique atmosphere. Beer €1.80. German-language movies M 9pm. Open M-Th from 7pm, F-Sa from 9pm. Cash only.

Scheune, Alaunstr. 36 (☎804 3822). From Albertpl., walk up Königsbrücker Str. and turn right onto Katharinenstr., then take a left on Alaunstr. The granddaddy of the *Neustadt* scene, this huge bar is a starting point for hipsters on a night out. Meals €7-8. Attached club opens 8pm. Bar open M-F 5pm-2am, Sa-Su 10am-2am. Cash only.

Die 100, Alaunstr. 100 (☎801 3957). The candlelit interior and intimate stone courtyard of this well-stocked wine cellar provide an escape from the social flurry elsewhere. Open daily 5pm-3am. Cash only.

BOY's, Alaunstr. 80, just beyond the Kunsthof Passage. A half-clad devil mannequin guards one of Dresden's popular gay bars. Drinks €1.90-6. Tu-Th, Su 8pm-3am, F-Sa until 5am. MC/V.

DAYTRIP FROM DRESDEN: MEIßEN

In 1710, the Saxon elector contracted a severe case of the "porcelain bug," and turned the city's defunct castle into Europe's first porcelain factory. To prevent competitors from learning its techniques, the building was once more tightly guarded than KGB headquarters; today, anyone can tour the brand new **Staatliche Porzellan-Manufaktur Meißen,** Talstr. 9, and watch artists paint petal-perfect flowers before your disbelieving eyes. (☎46 82 08. Open daily May-Oct. 9am-6pm; Nov.-Apr. 9am-5pm. English-language audio tour available. €8, students €4.) Narrow, romantic alleyways lead up to the **Albrechtsburg** Castle and Cathedral (www.albrechtsburg-meissen.de). To get there from the train station, walk straight onto Bahnhofstr. and follow it over the Elbbrücke. Cross the bridge, continue straight to the Markt, and turn right onto Burgstr. Follow the signs to Albrechtsburg up the hill, then look for a long staircase to your right that hugs the alleyway; this will lead you to the castle. (Open daily Mar.-Oct. 10am-6pm; Nov.-Feb. 10am-5pm. Last entry 30min. before closing. €3.50, students €2.50.) **Trains** run to Meißen from Dresden (30min., €4.50). The **tourist office,** Markt 3, across from Frauenkirche, finds private rooms for free. (☎0352 14 19 40. Open daily Apr.-Oct. 9am-6pm; Nov.-Mar. M-F 10am-4pm.)

LEIPZIG ☎0341

Leipzig (pop. 493,000) is known as the city of music, and indeed, it's hard to walk more than a few blocks without being serenaded by a classical quartet or wooed by a Spanish guitar. Large enough to have a life outside the academy, but small enough to feel the influence of its students, Leipzig boasts both world-class museums and corners packed with cafes, cabarets, and second-hand stores.

TRANSPORTATION AND PRACTICAL INFORMATION. Leipzig lies on the Berlin-Munich line. **Trains** run to: Berlin (2-3hr., 1 per hr., €33); Dresden (1½hr., 3 per hr., €25); Frankfurt (5hr., 1 per hr., €60); Munich (7hr., 3 per hr., €90). To find the **tourist office,** Richard-Wagner-Str. 1, cross Willy-Brandt-Pl. in front of the station and hang a left on Richard-Wagner-Str. (☎710 4265. Open M-F 10am-6pm, Sa-Su 9am-4pm.) **Postal Code:** 04109.

ACCOMMODATIONS AND FOOD. To reach **Hostel Sleepy Lion ❶,** Käthe-Kollwitz-Str. 3, take streetcar #1 (dir.: Lausen) to Gottschedstr. Run by young locals, it draws an international crowd with its spacious lounge area, foosball table, and separate non-smoking area. (☎993 9480; www.hostel-leipzig.de. Bike rental €5 per day. Breakfast €3. Linen €2. Internet €2 per hr. Reception 24hr. All rooms with bath. Dorms €14-15; singles €28; doubles €40; quads €64. Winter reduced rates. AmEx/MC/V.) Less than 5min. from the train station, **Central Globetrotter ❶,** Kurt-Schumacher-Str. 41, fills with young backpackers and church choir groups alike. Take the west exit and turn right onto Kurt-Schumacher-Str. (☎149 8960; www.globetrotter-leipzig.de. Group showers. Breakfast €4. Linen €2. Internet €2 per hr. Dorms €13-14; singles €24; doubles €36; quads €60.)

Imbiß stands, bistros, and bakeries line **Grimmaischestraße** in the Innenstadt. Outside the city center, **Karl-Liebknecht-Straße** (streetcar #10 or 11 to Südpl.) is packed with cafes, bars, and cheap *döner* stands. A favorite with many locals, **Aladin Döner,** Burgstr. 12 (☎976 6707), tops off pitas, Turkish pizzas, and falafel with a free cup of tea at the end of every meal. The hip cafe **Bellini's ❷,** Barfußgäßchen 3-5 (☎961 7681), serves baguettes, salads, and pasta in the heart of the Markt. (Open daily noon-late. MC/V.) **Zur Pleißenburg ❷,** Schulstr. 2, down Burgstr. from the Thomaskirche, serves hearty fare. (Open daily 9am-5am. Cash only.) There is a **market** on Richard-Wagner-Pl. at the end of the Brühl. (Open Tu and F 9am-5pm.)

SIGHTS AND NIGHTLIFE. The heart of Leipzig is the **Marktplatz,** a cobblestone square guarded by the slanted 16th-century **Altes Rathaus.** Head down Grimmaischestr. to the **Nikolaikirche,** where massive weekly demonstrations accelerated the fall of the GDR. (Open M-Sa 10am-6pm, Su 9am-6pm. Free.) Backtrack to the Rathaus and follow Thomasg. to the **Thomaskirche.** Bach spent his last 27 years here as cantor; his grave is by the altar. (Open daily 9am-6pm. Free.) Just behind the church is the **Johann-Sebastian-Bach-Museum,** Thomaskirchof 16. (Open daily 10am-5pm. €3, students €2. Free English-language audio tours.) Head back to Thomasg., turn left, then turn right on Dittrichring to reach Leipzig's fascinating **Museum in der "Runden Ecke,"** Dittrichring 24, with blunt exhibits on the GDR-era *Stasi* (secret police). Ask in the office for an English-language brochure. (☎961 2443; www.runde-ecke-leipzig.de. Open daily 10am-6pm. Free.) Outside the city ring, the **Völkerschlachtdenkmal** memorializes the 1813 Battle of Nations against Napoleon. (Tram #15 from the station to Völkerschlachtdenkmal. Open daily Apr.-Oct. 10am-6pm; Nov.-Mar. 10am-4pm. €3, students €2.)

Leipzig's **Gewandhaus-Orchester,** Augustuspl. 8, has been a major orchestra since 1843. (☎127 02 80. Open M-F 10am-6pm, Sa 10am-2pm, and 1hr. before performances; July 11-Aug. 13 M-F 1-6pm. Tickets €12-40. Th 20% student discount.) Free magazines *Fritz* and *Blitz* have nightlife info, as does *Kreuzer* (€1.50 at newsstands). **Barfußgäßchen,** a street just off the Markt, is the gathering place for a student and young professional crowd. A slightly younger crowd and louder music lie just across Dittrichring on **Gottschedstraße** and **Bosestraße.** Leipzig students get their groove on in the **Moritzbastei,** Universitätsstr. 9, with bars and multi-level dance floors under vaulted brick ceilings. (Cover varies. Cafe open daily 2pm-midnight, Su open at 9am for brunch €7.50. Disco open W and F until 6am.)

WITTENBERG ☎03491

Martin Luther inaugurated the Protestant Reformation here in 1517 when he nailed his *95 Theses* to the door of the Schloßkirche; Wittenberg (pop. 48,000) has been fanatical about its native heretic ever since. All major sights surround **Collegienstraße.** The **Lutherhalle,** Collegienstr. 54, chronicles the Reformation through letters, texts, art, and artifacts. (☎420 30. Open daily Apr.-Oct. 9am-6pm; Nov.-Mar. Tu-Su 10am-5pm. €5, students €3.) Down Schloßstr., the **Schloßkirche** allegedly holds Luther's body and a copy of the *Theses;* its tower has a sumptuous view of the *Altstadt*, the countryside, and the Elbe. (Tower ☎40 25 85. Church open M-Sa 10am-5pm, Su 11:30am-5pm. Tower open Easter-Oct. M-F noon-3:30pm, Sa-Su 10am-4:30pm. Church free. Tower €1, students €0.50.)

The musty **Jugendherberge (HI)** ❷ is hidden in the castle opposite the tourist office. Follow signs for the Schloßkeller Restaurant just before the tourist office on your left. Enter the courtyard and look to your right for the entrance. (☎40 32 55. Breakfast included. Linen €3.50. Reception 6:30am-10pm. Check-out 9:30am. Lockout Sa-Su noon-5pm. Dorms €15.20, under 27 €12.50. HI members only. MC/V.) Look for cheap meals along the Collegienstr.-Schloßstr. strip. **Trains** leave for Berlin (1½hr., every 2hr., €17) and Leipzig (1hr., every hr., €9). From the station, follow the street curving right and continue until Collegienstr., the start of the pedestrian zone. The **tourist office,** Schloßpl. 2, provides maps (€.50), books rooms, and gives audio tours (€6) in eight languages. (☎49 86 10. Open Mar.-Oct. M-F 9am-6pm, Sa 10am-3pm, Su 11am-4pm; Nov.-Feb. M-F 10am-4pm, Sa 10am-2pm, Su 11am-3pm.) **Postal Code:** 06886.

WEIMAR ☎03643

The writer Goethe once said of Weimar (pop. 62,000), "Where else can you find so much that is good in a place that is so small...?" Indeed, Weimar's diverse cultural attractions, lustrous parks, and rich history make it a required stop on any tour of eastern Germany. The **Goethehaus** and **Goethe-Nationalmuseum,** Frauenplan 1, preserve the chambers where the poet wrote, entertained guests, and died. Expect a wait on summer weekends. (Open Tu-Su Apr.-Oct. 9am-6pm; Nov.-Mar. 9am-4pm. €6, students €4.50. Museum €2.50/2.) The multi-talented Goethe landscaped the **Park an der Ilm,** Corona-Schöfer-Str., which contains his first Weimar residence, the **Gartenhaus.** (Open M, W-Su Apr. to mid-Oct. 9am-6pm; mid-Oct. to Mar. 9am-4pm. €3, students €2.) South of the town center is the **Historischer Friedhof** cemetery, where Goethe and Schiller rest together in the basement of the **Fürstengruft.** (Cemetery open daily Mar.-Sept. 8am-9pm; Oct.-Feb. 8am-6pm. Tomb open M, W-Su Apr. to mid-Oct. 9am-1pm and 2-6pm; mid-Oct. to Mar. 10am-1pm and 2-4pm. Cemetery free. Tomb €2, students €1.50.) Weimar's **Bauhaus Museum** on Theaterpl. showcases weavings, sculpture, and furniture. (Open Tu-Su Apr.-Oct. 10am-6pm; Nov.-Mar. 10am-4pm. €4.50, students €3.50.) Directly opposite the museum, the **Deutsches Nationaltheater,** which debuted plays by Goethe and Schiller, still presents *Faust* regularly; the Weimar Constitution was also signed there in 1919. (☎75 53 34. Entry to the theater allowed only with ticket. Tickets €8-55. Box office open M 2-6pm, Tu-Sa 10am-6pm, Su 10am-1pm, and 1hr. before performances.)

Jugendherberge Germania (HI) ❷, Carl-August-Allee 13, is near the train station but a 15min. walk from the city center. The beds might be a bit cramped if you're over 6 ft. tall, but they're comfortable and cheap. (☎85 04 90; www.djh-thueringen.de. Breakfast included. Internet €3 per hr. Dorms €20, under 27 €17. Cash only.) Relax in front of the piano at the student-run **Hababusch Hostel ❶,** Geleitstr. 4, in the heart of Weimar, but beware of flies in the summer. To get there, follow Geleitstr. from Goethepl. After a sharp right, you'll come to a statue on your left; the entrance is behind it. (☎85 07 37; www.hababusch.de. Linen €2.50. Reception 24hr. Dorms €10; singles €15; doubles €24. Cash only.) A combination cafe and gallery, **ACC ❷,** Burgpl. 1-2, screens art films in the hallway and offers free Internet. (Open M-F 11am-1am, Sa-Su 10am-1am. AmEx/MC/V.) The **produce market** on Marktpl. has groceries. (Open M-Sa 7am-5pm.)

Trains run to: Dresden (2hr., every hr., €38); Frankfurt (3hr., every hr., €47); Leipzig (1½hr., every hr., €21). To reach **Goetheplatz** from the station, follow Carl-August-Allee downhill to Karl-Liebknecht-Str., which leads into Goethepl. (15min.). The **tourist office,** Marktstr. 10, across from the Rathaus, provides maps (€0.50) and information on outdoor activities. (☎240 00. Open Apr.-Oct. M-F 9:30am-6pm, Sa-Su 9:30am-3pm; Nov.-Mar. M-F 10am-6pm, Sa-Su 10am-2pm.)

BUCHENWALD ☎03643

During WWII, Buchenwald Camp interned 250,000 prisoners, including Jews, gypsies, homosexuals, communists, and other political dissidents. Although it was not built as an extermination camp, over 50,000 died here from malnutrition, medical experimentation, or abominably harsh treatment by the SS. The **Buchenwald National Monument and Memorial** *(Nationale Mahnmal und Gedenkstätte Buchenwald)* has two principal sites. The **KZ-Lager** is what remains of the camp; a large storehouse documents the history of Buchenwald (1937-1945) and of Nazism. The monument built by the former East German government is on the other side of the hill; go up the main road that bisects the two large parking lots or take the footpath uphill from the old Buchenwald train station and continue on the main road. Camp **archives** are open to those searching for records of family and friends between 1937 and 1945; schedule an appointment with the curator. (Archives ☎43 01 54, library 43 01 60. Camp closes daily at sundown.) Sadly, the suffering at Buchenwald did not end with liberation. Soviet authorities later used the site as an internment camp, **Special Camp No. 2,** where more than 28,000 Germans—mostly Nazi war criminals and opponents of communism—were held until 1950. An exhibit on this period opened in 1997; walk from the camp into the woods and look for the path.

The best way to reach the camp is by **bus** #6 from Weimar's train station or from Goethepl. Check the schedule carefully; some #6 buses go to Ettersburg rather than Gedenkstätte Buchenwald. (20min.; M-Sa 1 per hr., Su every 2hr.). Ask at Buchenwald's **information center** for the bus times back to Weimar. The infrequent bus picks up at the KZ-Lager parking lot and at the road by the *Glockenturm* (bell tower). Be sure to watch the info center's half-hour video, which plays every hour, and consider investing in an audio tour (€3 at the info center), which augments the limited written information in English. (☎43 00; www.buchenwald.de. Open Tu-Su May-Sept. 9am-6pm; Oct.-Apr. 8:30am-4:30pm.)

EISENACH ☎03691

Eisenach (pop. 44,000) is best-known as home to **Wartburg Fortress,** which protected Martin Luther in 1521 after his excommunication. It was here, disguised as a bearded noble named Junker Jörg, that Luther famously fought an apparition of the devil with an inkwell. After renovations, much of the castle's interior is not authentically medieval, but Wartburg is still enchanting and the view from its south tower is spectacular. (Open daily Mar.-Oct. 8:30am-5pm; Nov.-Feb. 9am-3:30pm. Accessible only through tours. German-language tour every 20min. English-language tour 1:30pm. €6.50, students €3.50.) Eisenach is also the birthplace of composer **Johann Sebastian Bach.** Although his exact place of birth is unknown, local legend holds that Bach was born in 1685 in the **Bachhaus,** Frauenplan 21. Roughly every hour, a guide plays one of the museum's period keyboard instruments and provides historical context in German. (Open daily 10am-6pm. €4, students €3. English translations available.) Bach was baptized at the 800-year-old **Georgenkirche,** just off the Markt, where members of his family were organists for 132 years. (Open M-Sa 10am-12:30pm and 2-5pm, Su 11am-12:30pm and 2-5pm.) Up the street is the latticed **Lutherhaus,** Lutherpl. 8, where Luther lived during his school days. (Open daily 10am-5pm. €2.50, students €2.)

To reach the renovated **Jugendherberge Arthur Becker (HI) ❷,** Mariental 24, take bus #3 or 10 (dir.: Mariental) to Liliengrund Parkpl. or call a taxi (€5.20). To make the 35min. walk, take Bahnhofstr. from the station to Wartburger Allee, which runs into Mariental. (☎74 32 59. Breakfast included. Reception 8am-11pm. Dorms €18, under 27 €15.) **La Fontana ❶,** Georgenstr. 22, serves pizza and pasta in the center of town—look for the large fountain in front. (☎74 35 39. Open M-Th, Su 11:30am-2:30pm and 5-11pm, F-Sa 11:30am-2:30pm and 5-11:30pm.) For groceries, head to **Edeka** on Johannispl. (Open M-F 7am-7pm, Sa 7am-2pm.) **Trains** run to Weimar (1hr., 1 per hr., €11). The **tourist office,** Markt 9, hands out free maps and books rooms for no charge. From the train station, follow Bahnhofstr. through the tunnel and veer left until taking a right onto the pedestrian Karlstr. (☎194 33. Open M-F 10am-6pm, Sa 10am-4pm.) **Postal Code:** 99817.

NORTHERN GERMANY

Schleswig-Holstein, Germany's gateway to Scandinavia, bases its past and present livelihood on the trade generated at its port towns. Between the western coast of the North Sea and the eastern coast of the Baltic, the velvety plains are populated primarily by sheep and bales of hay. Farther south, the huge, less idyllic Hamburg is notoriously rich and radical, and the small city of Hanover charms visitors with its orderly English gardens and flourishing culture.

HANOVER (HANNOVER) ☎0511

Despite its relatively small size, Hanover (pop. 516,000) has the art, culture, and landscape to rival any European city. Hanover's highlights are the three bountiful **Herrenhausen gardens.** The largest, **Großer Garten,** has geometrically pruned shrubbery and contains the **Große Fontäne,** one of Europe's highest-shooting fountains. From the train station, walk to the far end of the lower shop level and take the U4 or 5 to Herrenhauser Garten. (www.herrenhaeuser-gaerten.de. Garden open May-Aug. 9am-8pm; Apr. and Sept. until 7pm; the first week in Oct. until 6pm. Fountain spurts mid-Mar. to mid-Oct. M-F 11am-noon and 3-5pm, Sa-Su 11am-noon and 2-5pm. €3.) On the outskirts of the *Altstadt* (old town) stands the **Neues Rathaus;** take the elevator up the tower for a lovely view year-round or ascend to the dome on a summer evening. (Open Mar.-Nov. M-F 9:30am-6:30pm, Sa-Su 10am-6:30pm. Evening ascent July to mid-Aug. 9-11:30pm. Elevator €2.50. Evening ascent €4.) Nearby, the **Sprengel Museum,** Kurt-Schwitters-Pl., hosts some of the 20th century's greatest art, including works by Dalí and Picasso. (Open Tu 10am-8pm, W-Su 10am-6pm. €7, students €4.) **Kestner-Museum,** Trammpl. 3, showcases decorative arts, with a focus on chairs from every era. (☎16 84 21 20; www.kestner-museum.de. Open Tu and Th-Su 11am-6pm, W 11am-8pm. €3. F free.)

Jugendherberge Hannover (HI) ❷, Ferdinand-Wilhelm-Fricke-Weg 1, is outside the city center, but worth the trek: balconies in the sun-filled rooms overlook a park. Ask for a room in the new wing. Take U3 or 7 to Fischerhof. From the stop, backtrack 10m, turn right, and cross the tracks; follow the path as it curves and cross Stammestr. Turn right after going over the red footbridge. (☎131 7674. Wheelchair accessible. Breakfast included. Reception 7:30am-1am. Check-out 9am. Dorms €19-30, under 27 €17.50-28. MC/V.) For German fare and great house brews, head to **Uwe's Hannenfaß Hannover ❷,** Knochenhauerstr. 36, in the center of the *Altstadt.* (Entrees €5-7. Open M-Th, Su 4pm-2am, F 4pm-4am, Sa noon-4am. AmEx/MC/V; €25 minimum charge.) A **Euro-Spar** supermarket is by the Kröpke U-Bahn stop. (Open M-Sa 7am-8pm.) **The Loft,** Georgstr. 50a, fills a chic garden with students on weekends. (☎363 1376. M-Th, Su 8-9pm, F-Sa 1-2am half-price mixed drinks. Open W-Sa from 8pm. Cash only.)

Trains leave at least every hour for: Amsterdam (4½-5hr., €58); Berlin (2½hr., €51); Frankfurt (3hr., €70); Hamburg (1½hr., €35); Munich (4½hr., €98). To reach the **tourist office,** Ernst-August-Pl. 2, head out the main entrance of the train station; facing the rear of the king's splendid steed, turn right. (☎12 34 51 11. Open M-F 9am-6pm, Sa 9am-2pm; Su during the summer.) The office also sells the **Hannover Card** (1-day €8, 3-day €12), which covers transportation costs in Hanover and reduces museum and sightseeing tour prices. **Postal Code:** 30159.

HAMBURG ☎040

The largest port city in Germany, Hamburg (pop. 1,700,000) radiates an inimitable recklessness. Riots and restorations defined the post-WWII landscape; today, Hamburg is a haven for contemporary artists, intellectuals, and party-goers who live it up in Germany's self-declared "capital of lust."

TRANSPORTATION

Trains: The Hauptbahnhof has hourly connections to: **Berlin** (2½hr., €45); **Copenhagen** (5hr., €73); **Frankfurt** (4½hr., €90); **Hanover** (1½hr., €34); **Munich** (6hr., €111); and runs frequently to **Amsterdam** (5hr., 3 per day, €75). **DB Reisezentrum** ticket office open M-F 5:30am-10pm, Sa-Su 7am-10pm. **Dammtor** station is near the university; **Harburg** station is south of the Elbe; **Altona** station is to the west of the city; and **Bergedorf** is to the southeast. 24hr. **lockers** (€1-4 per day) are available at stations.

Buses: The **ZOB** is on Steintorpl. across from the Hauptbahnhof, just past the Museum für Kunst und Gewerbe. Terminal open M-Th 5am-10pm, F-Sa 5am-midnight, Su 5am-10pm. **Autokraft** (☎280 86 60) runs to **Berlin** (3¼hr., 8 per day, €23). **Gulliver's** (☎24 71 06) runs to **Amsterdam** (5½hr., 1 per day, €36) and **Paris** (12hr., 1 per day, €55). Student discounts available.

Public Transportation: HVV operates an efficient U-Bahn, S-Bahn, and bus network. One-way tickets within the downtown cost €1.50; prices vary with distance and network. 1-day pass €5.50, €4.65 after 9am or on weekends; 3-day pass €13.30. Tickets can be bought at *Automaten*, but consider buying a **Hamburg Card** instead (p. 442).

Bike Rental: The community-run **Fahrradstation Dammtor/Rothebaum,** Schlüterstr. 11 (☎41 46 82 77), rents bikes at the best rate in Hamburg for €3-6 per day; weekend rentals count as one day. Also offers a free English-language guide to biking in Hamburg and stores luggage for free. Open M-F 9am-6pm.

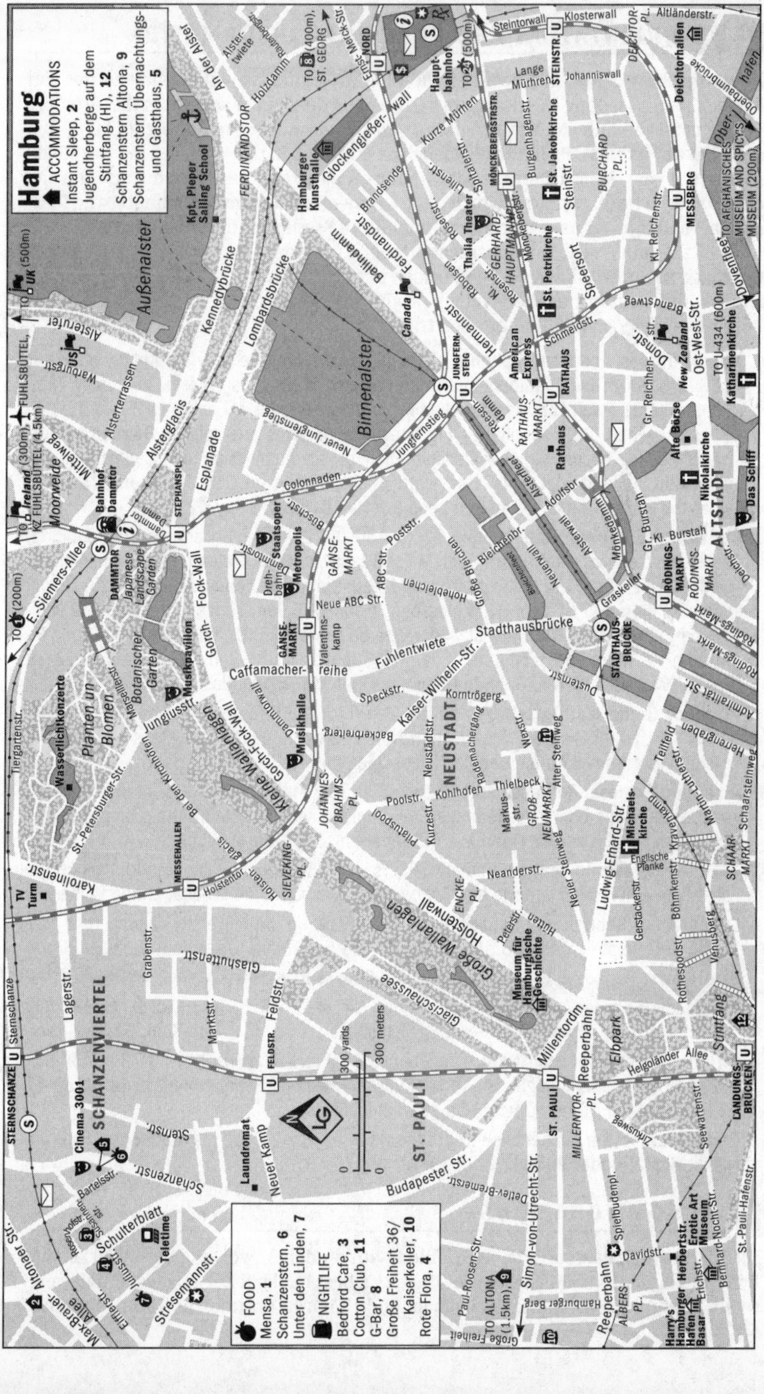

Hamburg

ACCOMMODATIONS
Instant Sleep, **2**
Jugendherberge auf dem Stintfang (HI), **12**
Schanzenstern Altona, **9**
Schanzenstern Übernachtungs- und Gasthaus, **5**

FOOD
Mensa, **1**
Schanzenstern, **6**
Unter den Linden, **7**

NIGHTLIFE
Bedford Cafe, **3**
Cotton Club, **11**
G-Bar, **8**
Große Freiheit 36/ Kaiserkeller, **10**
Rote Flora, **4**

ORIENTATION AND PRACTICAL INFORMATION

Hamburg's city center sits between the Elbe River and two lakes, **Außenalster** and **Binnenalster.** Bisecting the downtown, the Alsterfleet canal separates the *Altstadt* on the eastern bank from the *Neustadt* on the west. Most major sights lie in this area, between the **St. Pauli Landungsbrücken** port area in the west and the **Hauptbahnhof** in the east. **Mönckebergstraße,** Hamburg's most famous shopping street, runs all the way to Rathausmarkt. North of downtown, the **university** dominates the **Dammtor** area and sustains a vibrant community of students and intellectuals. To the west of the university, the **Schanzenviertel** is a politically active community home to artists, squatters, and a sizable Turkish population. At the south end of town, an entirely different atmosphere reigns on the wild **Reeperbahn,** home to both Hamburg's best discos and infamous sex trade.

Tourist Offices: The **Hauptbahnhof** office, in the Wandelhalle near the Kirchenallee exit (☎300 51 300; www.hamburg-tourism.de), books rooms for a €4 fee. Open daily 7am-10pm. The **St. Pauli Landungsbrücken** office, between piers #4 and 5 (☎33 44 22 15), is less crowded. Both supply free English-language maps and sell the **Hamburg Card,** which provides access to public transportation, reduced admission to museums, and discounts on bus and boat tours. 1-day card €7.30, 3-day card €15. The **Group Card** provides the same benefits for up to 5 people. 1-day €13.50, 3-day €23.90.

Consulates: Canada, Ballindamm 35 (☎460 0270). S- or U-Bahn to Jungfernstieg; between Alestertor and Bergstr. Open M-F 9:30am-12:30pm. **Ireland,** Feldbrunnenstr. 43 (☎44 18 61 13). U1 to Hallerstr. Open M-F 9am-1pm. **New Zealand,** Domstr. 19, Zürichhaus 3rd fl. (☎442 55 50). U1 to Messberg. Open M-Th 9am-1pm and 2-5:30pm, F 9am-1pm and 2-4:30pm. **UK,** Harvestehuder Weg 8a (☎448 0320). U1 to Hallerstr. Open M-Th 9am-12:30pm and 1:30-4pm, F 9am-12:30pm and 1:30-3pm. **US,** Alsterufer 26-28 (☎41 17 11 00). S- or U-Bahn to Dammtor. Open M-F 9am-noon.

Currency Exchange: ReiseBank, on the 2nd fl. of the Hauptbahnhof near the Kirchenallee exit (☎32 34 83), has Western Union services, cashes traveler's checks, and exchanges currency for a steep 4-5% fee. Open daily 7:30am-10pm.

American Express: Rathausmarkt 10 (☎30 39 38 11). U3 to Rathaus. Across from the bus stop, on the corner of Hermanstr. All banking services. Mail (letters only) held for members up to 5 weeks. Open M-F 9:30am-6pm, Sa 10am-2pm.

GLBT Resources: The gay community centers in the St. Georg neighborhood. Pick up the useful, free *hinnerk* magazine and *Friends* gay map from **Café Gnosa,** Lange Reihe 93.

Laundromat: Schnell und Sauber, Grindelallee 158, in the university district. Take S21 or 31 to Dammtor. Wash €3.50 per 6kg. Dry €1 per 15min. Open daily 7am-10:30pm.

Emergency: Police: ☎110. **Ambulance** and **Fire:** ☎112.

Pharmacy: Senator-Apotheke, Hachmannpl. 14 (☎32 75 27 or 33 92 92). Turn right from the station's Kirchenallee exit. English spoken. Open M-F 7am-8pm, Sa 8am-8pm.

Internet Access: Internet Cafe, Adenauerallee 10 (☎28 00 38 98). €0.70 per 30min. Open M-Sa 10am-midnight, Su 1pm-midnight. **Teletime,** Schulterblatt 39 (☎41 30 47 30). €0.50 per 10min. Open M-Sa 10am-midnight.

Post Office: At the Kirchenallee exit of the Hauptbahnhof. Open M-F 8am-8pm, Sa 9am-6pm. **Postal Code:** 20099.

ACCOMMODATIONS

The dynamic **Schanzenviertel** area, filled with students, working-class Turks, and left-wing dissenters, houses two of the city's best backpacker hostels. Small, relatively cheap pensions line **Steindamm** and the area around the Hauptbahnhof, although the area's prostitutes and wannabe Mafiosi detract from its charm. **Lange Reihe** has equivalent options in a cleaner neighborhood. More expensive hotels line the **Binnenalster** and eastern **Außenalster.**

Instant Sleep, Max-Brauer-Allee 277 (☎43 18 23 10; www.instantsleep.de). S21 or U3 to Sternschanze. Backpackers become a family in this friendly hostel, where rooms are often left open while guests lounge, read, or gather together to cook dinner. Linen €2. Internet €2 per hr. Reception 9am-2pm. Dorms €15-18; singles €28; doubles €44; triples €60. €1 ISIC discount. Cash only. ❷

Schanzenstern Übernachtungs- und Gasthaus, Bartelsstr. 12 (☎439 8441; www.schanzenstern.de). S21, S31, or U3 to Sternschanze. Left onto Schanzenstr., right on Susannenstr., and left to Bartelsstr. Bright, clean rooms on the upper floors of a renovated pen factory. Wheelchair accessible. Breakfast €4-6. Dorms €18; singles €36; doubles €51; triples €61; quads €74; quints €92. ❷

Schanzenstern Altona, Kleine Rainstr. 24-26 (☎39 91 91 91; www.schanzenstern-altona.de). S1, 11, 21, or 31. Take the Offenser Hauptstr. exit from the Altona station. After 2 blocks, turn right on Große Rainstr., then left on Kleine Rainstr. This hostel makes up for its distance from the city center with a large common area and lively neighborhood scene. Wheelchair accessible. Breakfast €6. Reception 24hr. Dorms €18; singles €40; doubles €55-65; triples €70; quads €80. Cash only. ❷

Jugendherberge auf dem Stintfang (HI), Alfred-Wegener-Weg 5 (☎31 34 88). S1, S3, or U3 to Landungsbrücke. The hostel is above the Landungsbrücke station—look for stairs that lead up the hill to reveal a view of the harbor. Entrance around the left side. Clean and well-furnished rooms look out on the woods or the harbor. Breakfast included (7-8:30am). Lunch and dinner €5. Reception 12:30pm-12:30am. Check-out 9:30am. Curfew 2am. Dorms €22-25, under 27 €19-22; doubles €47. MC/V. ❸

FOOD

Seafood abounds in the port city of Hamburg. In **Schanzenviertel,** avant-garde cafes and Turkish falafel stands entice hungry passersby. **Schulterblatt, Susannenstraße,** and **Schanzenstraße** are home to funky cafes and restaurants, while slightly cheaper establishments abound in the **university** area, especially along **Rentzelstraße, Grindelhof,** and **Grindelallee.** In **Altona,** the pedestrian zone near the train station is packed with food stands and produce shops.

Schanzenstern, Bartelsstr. 12 (☎43 29 04 09; www.schanzenstern.de). Delicious organic masterpieces served in the Schanzenviertel hostel. Lunch €6.50. Dinner €8-12.50. Open M 4pm-1am, Tu-Sa 10:30am-1am, Su 11am-1am. Cash only. ❷

Unter den Linden, Juliusstr. 16 (☎43 81 40). Read complimentary papers over *milchkaffee* (coffee with foamed milk; €3.30), breakfast (€4-7), or salad (€6.50) in a relaxed atmosphere beneath the linden trees. Open daily 10am-1am. Cash only. ❷

Mensa, Von-Melle-Park 5. S21 or 31 to Dammtor, then bus #4 or 5 to Staatsbibliothek (1 stop). Lots of cafeteria food and a bulletin board of university events. Meals €2.20-3.70. Student discount €0.70. Open M-Th 11am-3pm, F until 4:30pm. Cash only. ❶

SIGHTS

ALTSTADT

GROßE MICHAELSKIRCHE. The 18th-century Michaelskirche is the symbol of Hamburg, and with good reason. Destroyed successively by lightning, accidents, and Allied bombs and finally rebuilt after the Cold War, its fate has kept in tandem with the city's. Restored in 1996, the scalloped walls of the interior recall the space of a concert hall. A panoramic view of Hamburg awaits those who climb the 462 stairs of the spire—or those who opt for the elevator. In the crypt, a multimedia presentation on the history of the church screens on weekends. *(U-Bahn to Baumwall, S-Bahn to Stadthausbrücke. ☎37 67 81 00. Church open daily May-Sept. 9am-6pm; Oct.-Apr. 10am-4:30pm. Crypt open June-Oct. daily 11am-4:30pm; Nov.-May M, W, F-Su 11am-4:30pm. Screenings Th, Sa-Su every hr. 12:30-3:30pm. Tower open 9am-5:30pm; winter 10am-4:30pm. Church and crypt €1.25, students €0.75. Screenings €2.50. Tower €2.50.)*

RATHAUS. The city and state governments convene amid the mahogany carvings and two-ton chandeliers of the most richly ornamented building in Hamburg. In front, the **Rathausmarkt** hosts political demonstrations and medieval fairs. *(☎428 31 24 70. English-language tours every hr. M-Th 10:15am-3:15pm, F-Su 10:15am-1:15pm. €2.)*

NIKOLAIKIRCHE. The spire of this neo-Gothic ruin, bombed in 1943, has been preserved as a memorial for victims of war and persecution. *(U3 to Rödingsmarkt. Exhibit in the basement open M-F 11am-5pm, Sa-Su 11am-6pm. €2.)* The buildings along nearby **Trostbrücke** sport huge copper models of clipper ships on their spires in testimony to Hamburg's sea-trade wealth. *(Just south of the Rathaus, off Ost-West-Str.)*

MÖNKEBERGSTRAßE. Two spires punctuate Hamburg's shopping zone, which stretches from the Rathaus to the Hauptbahnhof. The one closest to the Rathaus is **St. Petrikirche,** the oldest church in Hamburg. *(Open M-Sa 10am-5pm, Su 1-5pm. Frequent free concerts.)* The other, **St. Jakobikirche,** is known for its 14th-century Arp-Schnittger organ. *(Open M-Sa 10am-5pm.)*

BEYOND THE ALTSTADT

PLANTEN UN BLOMEN. West of the Außenalster, this huge expanse of manicured flower beds and trees includes the largest Japanese garden in Europe. *(S21 or 31 to Dammtor. Open daily 7am-11pm. Free.)* In summer, performers in the outdoor **Musikpavillon** range from Irish step-dancers to Hamburg's police choir. *(May-Sept. daily 3pm.)* At night, opt for the **Wasserlichtkonzerte,** with a choreographed play of fountains and underwater lights. *(May-Aug. daily 10pm; Sept. 9pm.)* To the north, the tree-lined paths bordering the two **Alster lakes** provide refuge from the city crowds.

ST. PAULI LANDUNGSBRÜCKEN. The harbor lights up at night with ships from all over the world. Look for the 1200m **Elbtunnel,** completed in 1911 and still active today, behind Pier 6 in the building with the copper cupola. At the **Fischmarkt,** vendors hawk fish, produce, and other goods. *(U- or S-Bahn to Landungsbrücken or S-Bahn to Königstr. or Reeperbahn. Open Su Apr.-Oct. 5-9:30am; Nov.-Mar. 7-9:30am.)*

BEYOND THE CENTER

Two different testaments to the atrocities of the Nazi regime are a short trip away from Hamburg's city center.

KZ NEUENGAMME. An idyllic agricultural village east of Hamburg provided the backdrop for the Neuengamme concentration camp, where Nazis killed 55,000 prisoners through slave labor. In 1989, the Hamburg Senate built a memorial on the site. A mile-long path begins at the **Haus des Gedenkens,** a memorial building containing banners inscribed with the names and death dates of the victims; the path eventually leads to the former **Walther-Werke** factory, where visitors can listen to the recorded testimony of survivors. Exhibits are in English. *(Jean-Doldier-Weg 75. S21 to Bergedorf, then bus #227, about 1½hr. from city. Bus runs from Bergedorf M-Sa every hr., Su every 2hr. ☎428 96 03. Museum and memorial open May-Oct. Tu-F 9:30am-4pm, Sa-Su noon-7pm; Oct.-Mar. Tu-Su noon-5pm. Path always open. Tours Su noon, 2:30pm. Museum free.)*

GEDENKSTÄTTE BULLENHUSER DAMM UND ROSENGARTEN. Surrounded by warehouses, this schoolhouse is a memorial to 20 Jewish children brought here for "testing" and murdered by the S.S. only hours before Allied troops arrived. Visitors are invited to plant a rose for the children in the flower garden behind the school. *(Bullenhuser Damm 92. S21 to Rothenburgsort. Follow the signs to Bullenhuser Damm along Ausschläger Bildeich to the intersection with Grossmannstr.; the garden is on the far left side, the school 200m farther. ☎428 13 10. Open Th 2-8pm, Su 10am-5pm. Free.)*

MUSEUMS

The **Hamburg Card** provides free access to all museums except the Deichtorhallen, the Hafen Basar, and the Erotic Art Museum. *Museumswelt Hamburg*, a free newspaper, lists exhibits and events and can be picked up at tourist offices. Most museums are closed on Mondays.

HAMBURGER KUNSTHALLE. This sprawling, first-rate fine arts museum would require many days to appreciate in full. The lower level presents the Old Masters and extensive special exhibits. In the connected four-level **Galerie der Gegenwart,** contemporary art takes a stand, and a loud one at that. *(Glockengießerwall 1. Turn right from the Spitalerstr./City exit of the Hauptbahnhof and cross the street. ☎428 13 12 00; www.hamburger.kunsthalle.de. Open Tu-Su 10am-6pm, Th until 9pm. €8.50, students €5.)*

MUSEUM FÜR KUNST UND GEWERBE. Handicrafts, china, and furnishings from all corners of the earth fill this applied arts museum. A huge exhibit chronicles the evolution of the modern piano with dozens of the world's oldest harpsichords, clavichords, and hammerklaviers. *(Steintorpl. 1. 1 block south of the Hauptbahnhof. ☎428 54 27 32; www.mkg-hamburg.de. Open Tu-Su 10am-6pm, Th until 9pm. €8.20, students €4.10.)*

EROTIC ART MUSEUM. This four-story museum host everything from Victorian pornography to gigantic Russian dolls in varying degrees of undress. Drawings by Picasso add fame—and a dose of propriety—to an otherwise shocking display. *(Bernhard-Nocht-Str. 69. S1 or 3 to Reeperbahn. ☎317 47 57; www.erotic-art-museum.de. Open M-Th, Su 10am-midnight, F-Sa 10am-2am. €8, students €5. Under 16 not admitted.)*

ENTERTAINMENT AND NIGHTLIFE

The **Staatsoper,** Große Theaterstr. 36, houses one of the best **opera** companies in Germany; the associated **ballet** is the nation's acknowledged star. (U2 to Gänsemarkt. ☎35 68 68. Open M-F 10am-6:30pm, Sa 10am-2pm.) **Orchestras** abound: the Philharmonie, the Norddeutscher Rundfunk Symphony, and Hamburg Symphonia all perform at the **Musikhalle** on Johannes-Brahms-Pl. (U2 to Gänsemarkt. ☎34 69 20; www.musikhalle-hamburg.de.) Live music also prospers in Hamburg. Superb traditional jazz swings at the **Cotton Club.** Early on Sundays, musicians talented and otherwise play at the **Fischmarkt.** The **West Port Jazz Festival,** Germany's largest, runs in mid-July; for info, call the Konzertkasse (☎32 87 38 54). The huge **G-Move** (Mar. 3, 2006; www.gmove.de) has been dubbed the "Love Parade of the North."

Hamburg's unrepressed nightlife heats up in the **Schanzenviertel** and **St. Pauli** areas. The infamous **Reeperbahn** runs through the heart of St. Pauli; lined with sex shops, strip joints, and peep shows, it's also home to the best bars and clubs. Though the Reeperbahn is generally safe, women especially may want to avoid adjacent streets. Parallel to the Reeperbahn lies **Herbertstraße,** Hamburg's official prostitution strip, where licensed prostitutes flaunt their flesh. Herbertstr. is open only to men over the age of 18; potential patrons should be warned that engaging with streetwalkers is highly dangerous.

Students head north to the streets of the Schanzenviertel, where cafes create an atmosphere more leftist than lustful. The **St. Georg** district, near Berliner Tor and along Lange Reihe, is the center of Hamburg's **gay scene.** In general, clubs open and close late, with some techno and trance clubs remaining open all night. *Szene* (€2.50), available at newsstands, lists events and parties.

Große Freiheit 36/Kaiserkeller, Große Freiheit 36 (☎317 7780). Everyone from Ziggy Marley to Matchbox 20 has performed on the big stage and dance floor upstairs. Live music or DJs usually 10pm-4am. Cover €5-6. Concerts €10-30, with even higher prices for bigger names. Entry often free until 11pm; if you get your hand stamped, you can return later (not applicable for concerts).

Rote Flora, Schulterblatt 71 (www.roteflora.de). Spraypaint and posters seem to hold together this looming mansion of graffiti in the heart of the Schanzenviertel scene. Entrance hidden on the side; crowds come at midnight. Beer €1.50 on weekends. Cover F-Sa €3-5. Cafe open M-F 6-10pm. Music starts around 10pm. Cash only.

Bedford Cafe, on the corner of Schulterblatt and Suzannesstr. One of the most crowded bars in the Schanzenviertel, it's known to locals as the "no name bar" and is a prime place to see and be seen. Look for the "Pascucci" sign outside. Beer €2-3.40. Mixed drinks €5-6. Open daily 10am-late. Cash only.

G-Bar, Lange Reihe 81 (☎28 00 46 90). Young male waiters could be models at this clean-cut gay bar. Beer €2-3. Mixed drinks €6-7. Open daily 7pm-2am. Cash only.

Cotton Club, Alter Steinweg 10 (☎34 38 78; www.cotton-club.de). U3 to Rödingsmarkt. New Orleans, dixie, swing, and Big Band jazz in a warmly lit setting. Cover €5 for Hamburg bands, around €10 for guest bands. Shows start at 8:30pm. Open M-Th 8pm-midnight, F-Sa 8pm-1am; Sept.-Apr. also open Su 11pm-3am.

LÜBECK ☎0451

Lübeck (pop. 213,000) is easily Schleswig-Holstein's most beautiful city. In its heyday it controlled trade across all Northern Europe. No longer a center of commercial or political influence, today Lübeck is a merchant of delicious marzipan and red-blond Dückstein beer, as well as a gateway to the Baltics. Stop by the famous confectionery **I.G. Niederegger Marzipan Café,** Breitestr. 89, for marzipan, Lübeck's specialty, in the shape of pigs, jellyfish, and even the town gate. (Marzipan box €2.70. Open M-F 9am-7pm, Sa 9am-6pm, Su 10am-6pm. AmEx/MC/V.) Between the station and the *Altstadt* (old town) stands the massive **Holstentor,** one of Lübeck's four 15th-century defensive gates. The museum inside deals equally in trade and torture. (Open Tu-Su Apr.-Sept. 10am-5pm; Oct.-Mar. 10am-4pm. €4, students €2.) The skyline is dominated by the twin brick towers of the **Marienkirche,** a gigantic church housing the largest mechanical organ in the world. (☎39 77 01 80. Open daily in summer 10am-4pm. Donations suggested.) For a sweeping view of the spire-studded *Altstadt,* take the elevator to the top of **Petrikirche.** (☎39 77 30. Church open daily 11am-5pm. Tower open Apr.-Oct. daily 9am-7pm. €2.50, students €1.50.) The **Museum für Puppentheater,** Kolk 14, holds the world's largest private puppet collection. (☎786 26. Open daily 10am-6pm. €3, students €2.50.)

To reach **Rucksack Hotel ❷,** Kanalstr. 70, take bus #1, 11, 21, or 31 to Pfaffenstr. and turn right at the church onto Glockengießerstr. In the middle of an earthy indoor mall with a concert stage in center, this hostel has a social common space. (☎70 68 92. Linen €3. Reception 10am-1pm and 4-9pm. Winter reception until 8pm. Dorms €13; doubles with bath €40; quads €60, with bath €68.) **Tipasa ❷,** Schlumacherstr. 12, has a beer garden where it serves pizza, pasta, and vegetarian dishes. (☎706 0451. Open M-Th, Su noon-midnight, F-Sa noon-1am. Cash only.) Dance aboard the **"Body and Soul"** boat in the water at the corner of Kanalstr. and Hohe Glockenstr. (Cover €4. Open Tu, Sa 10pm-late, F 10:30pm-late.) **Trains** run to Berlin (3½hr., every hr.,

€52) and Hamburg (45min., every hr., €19). Lübeck's **tourist office,** by the Holstentor in the *Altstadt,* books rooms for no commission. Lübeck's **Happy Day Card** (1-day card €5; 3-day card €10) includes free local transport and museum discounts. (☎122 5420. Open M-F 9:30am-6pm, Sa-Su 10am-3pm.) **Postal Code:** 23552.

CENTRAL AND WESTERN GERMANY

Lower Saxony *(Niedersachsen),* which stretches from the North Sea to the hills of central Germany, comprises agricultural plains and foggy marshland. Just south, North Rhine-Westphalia is the most economically powerful area in Germany, and so densely populated that it's nearly impossible to travel through the countryside without glimpsing the next hamlet, village, or metropolis ahead.

DÜSSELDORF ☎0211

As Germany's fashion hub and multinational corporation base, the rich city of Düsseldorf (pop. 571,000) crawls with patricians and would-be aristocrats. The nation's "Hautstadt"—a pun on the German *"Hauptstadt"* (capital) and the French *"haute,"* as in *"haute couture"*—is a stately metropolis with an *Altstadt* (old town) that features stellar nightlife and shopping.

TRANSPORTATION AND PRACTICAL INFORMATION. **Trains** run to: Amsterdam (3hr., 2-3 per hr., €32-42); Berlin (4½hr., 2 per hr., €72-88); Frankfurt (2hr., 3 per hr., €41-64); Hamburg (4hr., 2 per hr., €60-72); Munich (5-6hr., 2-3 per hr., €92-112). Düsseldorf's S-Bahn is integrated into the regional **VRR** *(Verkehrsverbund Rhein-Ruhr)* system, which links most nearby cities and is the cheapest way to get to Aachen and Cologne. Call ☎582 28 for schedule. On the **public transportation** system, single tickets cost €1.10-8. *Tagestickets* (€5-20) let up to five people travel for 24hr. on any line. To reach the **tourist office,** Immermannstr. 65, head straight out of the train station and to the right; look for the Immermannhof building. It books rooms for free on your day of arrival, except during fairs, and has numerous city maps. (☎172 02 22. Open M-F 9:30am-6:30pm, Sa 9am-12:30pm.) The **post office,** on Konrad-Adenauer-Pl., is to the right of the tourist office. (Open M-F 8am-6pm, Sa 9am-2pm.) **Postal Code:** 40210.

ACCOMMODATIONS AND FOOD. Düsseldorf hotels and hostels often double their prices during trade fairs, which take place from August to April. Fairly close to the center of town, **Backpackers Düsseldorf ❷,** Fürstenwall 180, has lime-green beds and a great common room equipped with a TV and DVD player. Take bus #725 (dir.: Lausward/Franziusstr.) from the station and get off at Kirchpl. (☎302 0848; www.backpackers-duesseldorf.de. Breakfast included. Free Internet. Reception 8am-9pm. Book 1-2 weeks ahead on summer weekends. Dorms €20. MC/V.) **Jugendgästehaus Düsseldorf (HI) ❷,** Düsseldorfer Str. 1, is just over the Rheinkniebrücke from the *Altstadt.* Take U70, 74, 75, 76, or 77 to Luegpl., then walk 500m down Kaiser-Wilhelm-Ring, or get off at Belsenpl. and take bus #835 or 836 to the Jugendherberge bus stop. (☎55 73 10; jh-duesseldorf@djh-rheinland.de. Breakfast included. Reception 7am-1am. Curfew 1am. Dorms €24; singles €35.60; doubles €58.20. €3.10 HI discount. Cash only.) **Hotel Weidenhof ❹,** Oststr. 87, is a conveniently located three-star hotel with huge bathtubs and moderate prices. Prices are often lower if you book the same day at the tourist office. From the station, walk down Immermannstr. and turn left onto Oststr. (☎130 6460; www.hotelweidenhof.de. Breakfast included. Singles €40; doubles €60; apartments available from €25 per person. AmEx/MC/V.) To camp at **Kleiner Torfbruch ❶,** take any S-Bahn to Düsseldorf Geresheim, then bus #735 (dir.: Stamesberg) to

Seeweg. (☎899 2038. Open Apr.-Oct. Tent sites €10, extra person €5. Cash only.) For a cheap meal, the eateries in the *Altstadt* can't be beat. **A Tavola ❸**, Wallstr. 11, has meticulously prepared pastas (€7.50-14) and bottomless bread baskets. (☎13 29 23. Open daily noon-3pm and 6-11pm. MC/V.) **Pilsner Urquell ❷**, Grabenstr. 6, specializes in meaty Eastern European fare. (☎868 1411. Entrees €4-11. Open M-Sa 10am-1am, Su 4pm-midnight. MC/V.) The most convenient **supermarket** is at the eastern corner of Carlspl. in the *Altstadt*. (Open M-Sa 8am-8pm.)

SIGHTS AND NIGHTLIFE. Glitzy **Königsallee** (the "Kö"), just outside the *Altstadt*, embodies the vitality and glamor of wealthy Düsseldorf. To reach the Kö, walk 10min. down Graf-Adolf-Str. from the train station. Midway up the street is the marble-and-copper **Kö-Galerie**, a mall showcasing one haughty store after another. Better deals in non-designer stores can be found along Flingerstr. in the *Altstadt*. To get to the Baroque **Schloß Benrath**, Benrather Schloßallee 104, in the suburbs of Düsseldorf, take S6 (dir.: Köln) to Schloß Benrath. Strategically placed mirrors and false exterior windows make the castle appear larger than it is, but the enormous French gardens still dwarf it. (☎892 19 03; www.schloss-benrath.de. Open mid-Apr. to Oct. Tu-Su 10am-6pm; low season Tu-Su 11am-5pm. Tours every hr. €5, students €2.50.) The **Heinrich-Heine-Institut**, Bilker Str. 12-14, is the official shrine of Düsseldorf's melancholic son. (☎899 55 71. Open Tu-F and Su 11am-5pm, Sa 1-5pm. €3, students €1.50.) At the upper end of the Kö is the **Hofgarten**, the oldest public park in Germany. At its eastern end, the 18th-century **Schloß Jägerhof**, Jakobistr. 2, houses a **Goethe Museum.** Take streetcar #707 or bus #752 to Schloß Jägerhof. (☎899 62 62. Open Tu-F and Su 11am-5pm, Sa 1-5pm. €3, students €1.50.) The **Kunstsammlung am Grabbeplatz**, Grabbepl. 5, within the black glass edifice west of the Hofgarten, houses works by Expressionists, Surrealists, Picasso, and former Düsseldorf resident Paul Klee. (U70, 75, 76, 78, or 79 to Heinrich-Heine-Allee, and walk two blocks north. ☎838 10. Tours W 3:30pm, Su 11:30am. Open Tu-F 10am-6pm, Sa-Su 11am-6pm. €6.50, students €4.50.)

By nightfall it's nearly impossible to see where one pub ends and the next begins in Düsseldorf's packed *Altstadt*. **Bolkerstraße** is jam-packed with street performers. *Prinz* (€3) gives tips on the scene; you can often find this newsletter for free at youth hostels. **Unique**, Bolkerstr. 30, lives up to its name, drawing a young, trendy crowd to its red-walled interior. (www.uniqueclub.de. Cover €5-10. Open W-Sa 10pm-late.) **Nachtresidenz**, Bahnstr. 13-15, is half-lounge, half-disco, and caters to an older crowd. (☎136 57 55; www.nachtresidenz.de. 21+. Open F-Sa 10pm-5am. Cash only.) **GLBT nightlife** clusters along Bismarckstr., at the intersection of Charlottenstr. *Facolte* (€2), a gay and lesbian nightlife magazine, is available at newsstands. **Parkhouse**, Charlottenstr. 62, is a popular gay and lesbian club. (☎160 94 94; www.club-parkhouse.de. Open F-Sa 10pm-5am.)

GERMANY

AACHEN ☎0241

The capital of Charlemagne's Frankish empire in the 8th century, Aachen (pop. 246,000) is a trove of historical treasures and a polyglot forum for up-and-coming European artists. Aacheners call it the "city of water"; the natural springs that run through the area scared off early settlers who believed the water came from hell. The Romans realized the advantage of hell-water, however, and constructed the city's first **mineral baths.** These baths are now the luxurious **Carolus Thermen**, Passstr. 79, with eight pools and numerous themed saunas. Take bus #51 to Carolus Thermen. (☎18 27 40; www.carolus-thermen.de. Day-long soak €14, with sauna €28; 2½hr. €9.50/19. Open daily 9am-11pm.) The three-tiered dome and blue-gold mosaics of the **Dom**, in the center of the city, look down on the reliquary behind the altar that houses Charlemagne's remains. (Open M-Sa 7am-7pm, Su 12:30-7pm. Closed during services.) Around the corner is the **Schatzkammer**, Klosterpl. 2, a treasury that contains a silver bust of Charlemagne which holds the emperor's skull, among other sacred art treasures. (Open M 10am-1pm, Tu-W and F-Su 10am-6pm, Th 10am-9pm. €4, students €3.)

Hotel Cortis ❸, Krefelderstr. 52, near the Stadtgarten, is a comfortable B&B with cable TV in each room. Take bus #51 to Rolandstr., walk to the intersection, and turn left on Krefelderstr. (☎977 4110; webmaster@hotel-cortis.de. Breakfast included. Singles €28; doubles €50-55, with bath €60. MC/V.) **Euroregionales Jugendgästehaus (HI) ❷**, Maria-Theresia-Allee 260, has clean, bright rooms about a 20min. bus ride from the city center. From the station, walk left on Lagerhausstr. to Finanzamt bus stop and take bus #2 (dir.: Preusswald) to Ronheide. (☎71 10 10; www.jugendherberge.de/jh/aachen. Breakfast included. Curfew 1am. Dorms €21.50; singles €35; doubles €53.20. Cash only.) **Sausalitos ❸**, Markt 47, is a popular Mexican restaurant with a huge cocktail bar. (☎23 49 200. Entrees €7-13. Open daily noon-11pm. Cash only.) Both the **pedestrian zone** and **Pontstraße,** off Marktpl., also host a number of wallet-friendly restaurants.

Trains run to Brussels (2hr., every hr., €22-28) and Cologne (1hr., 2-3 per hr., €12). The **tourist office,** on Friedrich-Wilhelm-Pl. in the Atrium Elisenbrunnen, provides free maps and books rooms for free. From the station, head up Bahnhofstr.; turn left onto Theaterstr., which becomes Theaterpl., then turn right onto Kapuzinergraben, which becomes Friedrich-Wilhelm-Pl. (☎180 2960. Open M-F 9am-6pm, Sa 9am-2pm; Easter-Christmas also Su 10am-2pm.) **Postal Code:** 52062.

COLOGNE (KÖLN) ☎0221

Although 90% of inner Cologne (pop. 968,000) crumbled in WWII, the magnificent Gothic *Dom* amazingly survived 14 bombings and remains Cologne's main attraction. Today, the city is the largest in North Rhine-Westphalia and is its most important cultural center, with a full range of first-rate museums and theaters.

TRANSPORTATION

Flights: Flights depart from **Köln-Bonn Flughafen** (☎01803 80 38 03; www.koeln-bonn-airport.de). Shuttles fly to Berlin 24 times per day 6:30am-8:30pm. The airport is connected to the train station by the S13 (14min., 2-3 per hr.) and the train (11min., 2-3 per hr.); both €2.10.

Trains: To: **Amsterdam** (3½hr., €37-47); **Berlin** (4½hr., every hr., €75-90); **Düsseldorf** (30-50min., 5-7 per hr., €9-17); **Frankfurt** (2hr., 2 per hr., €35-55); **Hamburg** (4hr., 2-3 per hr., €63-78); **Munich** (4½-5hr., 1-2 per hr., €85-110); **Paris** (4hr., every 2hr., €87-120).

Ride-Share: Citynetz Mitfahrzentrale, Maximinenstr. 2 (☎194 40; www.mitfahr.org). Turn left from the back of the train station. Show up 1-2 days before you want to travel. Open daily 8am-8pm. Cash only.

Ferries: Köln-Düsseldorfer (☎208 83 18; www.k-d.com) begins popular Rhine cruises to **Koblenz** (€35) or **Mainz** (€47.40). Ships to **Bonn** (€11). Eurail valid on most trips.

Public Transportation: VRS (Verkehrsverbund Rhein-Sieg), downstairs in the train station, has free maps of the S- and U-Bahn, bus, and streetcar lines. Day passes €4.40. *Minigruppen-Ticket* (from €6.70) allows up to 5 people unlimited rides M-F 9am-midnight as well as all day Sa-Su. Week-long passes €12.

Bike Rental: Kölner Fahrradverleih, Markmannsg. (☎0171 629 87 96), in the *Altstadt* on the Rhine. €2 per hr., €10 per day, €40 per week. Open daily 10am-6pm.

ORIENTATION AND PRACTICAL INFORMATION

Cologne extends across the Rhine, but the city center and nearly all sights are located on the western side. The *Altstadt* (old town) splits into **Altstadt-Nord,** near the **Hauptbahnhof,** and **Altstadt-Süd,** just south of the **Severinsbrücke** bridge.

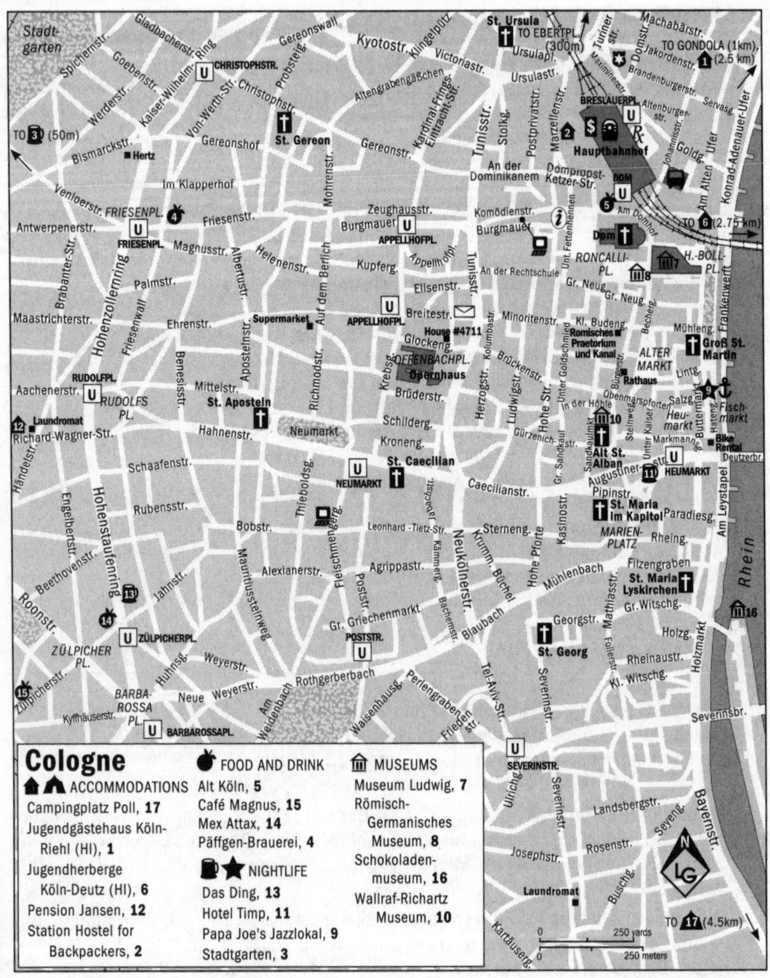

Tourist Office: **KölnTourismus,** Unter Fettenhennen 19 (☎30 400; www.koelntourismus.de), opposite the main entrance to the *Dom,* has city maps (€0.20) and books rooms for €3. Open July-Sept. M-Sa 9am-10pm, Su 10am-6pm; Oct.-June M-Sa 9am-9pm, Su 10am-6pm. **Köln WelcomeCard** includes public transportation and discounts museum admission, Rhine cruises, and bike rentals (1-, 2-, 3-day cards €9/14/19).

Currency Exchange: Reisebank, in the train station. Open daily 7am-10pm.

Emergency: Police: ☎110. **Ambulance** and **Fire:** ☎112.

Pharmacy: Apotheke im Hauptbahnhof (☎139 1112), near Platform 11 in the train station. Open M-F 6am-8pm, Sa 9am-8pm.

Internet Access: Telepoint Callshop & Internet C@fe, Komödenstr. 19 (☎250 99 30), by the *Dom.* €1.50 per hr. Open M-F 8:30am-midnight, Sa-Su 9am-midnight.

Post Office: At the corner of Breite Str. and Tunisstr. in the WDR-Arkaden shopping gallery. Open M-F 9am-7pm, Sa 9am-2pm. **Postal Code:** 50667.

ACCOMMODATIONS

Conventions fill hotels in spring and fall, and Cologne's hostels often sell out in summer. If you're staying over a weekend in the summer, book at least two weeks in advance. **Mitwohnzentrale,** Maximinenstr. 2, behind the train station, arranges apartments for longer stays. (☎194 40. Open daily 8am-8pm.)

Station Hostel for Backpackers, Marzellenstr. 44-56 (☎912 53 01; www.hostel-cologne.de). From the station, walk down Dompropst-Ketzer-Str. and take the 1st right on Marzellenstr. Abuzz with backpackers in a college dorm atmosphere. Breakfast €3. Free Internet. Reception 24hr. Check-in 2pm. Check-out noon. Dorms €16-19.50; singles €28-35; doubles €42-50; triples €66. Cash only. ❷

Pension Jansen, Richard-Wagner-Str. 18 (☎25 18 75; www.pensionjansen.de). U1, 6, 7, 15, 17, or 19 to Rudolfpl. Family-run with beautiful high-ceilinged rooms and colorful walls. Breakfast included. Singles €30-42; doubles €62. Cash only. ❸

Jugendherberge Köln-Deutz (HI), Siegesstr. 5a (☎814 711; www.koeln-deutz.jugendherberge.de), just over the Hohenzollernbrücke. Take U1 or 7-9 to Deutzer Freiheit, then walk under the pedestrian walkway and turn right on Siegesstr. Newly renovated rooms. Breakfast included. Internet €4 per hr. Reception 24hr. Call ahead. Dorms €26.10; singles €42.60; doubles €65.70. €3.10 HI discount. MC/V. ❸

Jugendgästehaus Köln-Riehl (HI), An der Schanz 14 (☎76 70 81; www.djh.de/jugendherbergen/koeln-rieh). U17-19 (dir.: Ebertpl.) to Boltensternstr.; exit station and follow the signs. Carpeted rooms with bath and a tree-lined location on the Rhine. Breakfast included. Laundry €3. Reception 24hr. Call ahead. Dorms €25.30; singles €38.10; doubles €61.20. €3.10 HI discount. MC/V. ❷

Campingplatz Poll, Weidenweg (☎83 19 66), southeast of the *Altstadt* on the Rhine. U16 to Heinrich-Lübke-Ufer, across the Rodenkirchener Brücke. Reception 8am-noon and 5-8pm. Open mid-Apr. to Oct. Tent sites €8, extra person €5. MC/V. ❶

FOOD

The *Kölner* diet includes *rievekoochen,* or fried potato dunked in applesauce, and the city's trademark smooth *Kölsch* beer. Cheap restaurants gather on **Zülpicherstraße** and **Weidengasse** in the Turkish district. Mid-range ethnic restaurants line the perimeter of the *Altstadt,* particularly from **Hohenzollernring** to **Hohenstaufenring.** German eateries surround **Domplatz.**

Alt Köln, Trankg. 7-9 (☎13 74 71). A required stop on visits to Cologne. Regional specialties (€4-18) and cheap *Kölsch* (€1.45). Open daily 8am-midnight. AmEx/MC/V. ❷

Päffgen-Brauerei, Friesenstr. 64. Take U3-6, 12, or 15 to Friesenpl. A local favorite since 1883. *Kölsch* (€1.30) is brewed on the premises, consumed in cavernous halls and in the 600-seat beer garden, and refilled until you put your coaster on top of your glass. Meals €2-19. Open daily 10am-midnight. Kitchen open 11:30am-11pm. Cash only. ❸

Mex Attax, Hohenstaufenring 23. Take U8 or 9 to Zülpicher Pl. Mouth-watering wraps (€3-5), quesadillas (€2-4), and sweet potato soup (€3). At night, grab a mixed drink to go (€3.50). Open M-Th 11am-11pm, F-Sa 11am-1am. Cash only. ❶

Café Magnus, Zülpicherstr. 48 (☎24 14 69). Take U8 or 9 to Zülpicher Pl. Locals flock to this crowded cafe for funky tunes and artfully prepared meals from €4. Vegetarian options €6. Open M-Th 8am-3am, F-Sa 8am-5am, Su 8am-1am. Cash only. ❷

SIGHTS

DOM. Germany's greatest cathedral, the *Dom*, is the perfect realization of the High Gothic style. Built over the course of six centuries, it was finished in 1880 and miraculously escaped destruction during WWII. A chapel on the inside right houses a 15th-century **triptych** depicting the city's five patron saints. Behind the altar in the center of the choir is the **Shrine of the Magi,** the cathedral's most sacred compartment, which allegedly holds the remains of the Three Kings. Before exiting the choir, stop in the **Chapel of the Cross** to admire the 10th-century **Gero crucifix,** which is the oldest intact sculpture of a crucified Christ with his eyes shut. It takes 15min. to scale the 509 steps of the **Südturm** tower. *(Cathedral open daily 6am-7:30pm. 45min. English-language tours M-Sa 10:30am, 2:30pm, Su 2:30pm. Tower open daily May-Sept. 9am-6pm; Nov.-Feb. 9am-4pm; Mar.-Apr. and Oct. 9am-5pm. Cathedral free. Tours €4, children €2. Tower €2, students €1.)*

MUSEUMS. Four words about the **Schokoladenmuseum:** Willy Wonka made real. It presents every step of chocolate production, from the rain forests to the gold fountain that spurts streams of silky free samples. *(Rheinauhafen 1a, near the Severinsbrücke. ☎931 88 80; www.schokoladenmuseum.de. From the train station, head for the Rhine and walk to the right along the river, go under the Deutzer Brücke, and take the 1st footbridge. Open Tu-F 10am-6pm, Sa-Su 11am-7pm. Last entry 1hr. before closing. €5.50, students €3.)* Heinrich-Böll-Pl. houses the **Museum Ludwig,** where the collection includes everything from Impressionism to Cubism to Pop Art. *(Bischofsgartenstr. 1. Open Tu-Su 10am-6pm; 1st F of every month until 11pm. €7.50, students €5.50.)* Masterpieces from the Middle Ages to the Post-Impressionist period are gathered in the **Wallraf-Richartz Museum.** *(Martinstr. 39. ☎276 94; www.museenkoeln.de/wrm. From the Heumarkt, take Gürzenichtstr. 1 block to Martinstr. Open Tu 10am-8pm, W-F 10am-6pm, Sa-Su 11am-6pm. €5.80, students €3.30.)* The **Römisch-Germanisches Museum** displays a large array of artifacts documenting the daily lives of Romans, rich and poor alike. *(Roncallipl. 4. Open Tu-Su 10am-5pm, W until 8pm. €6, students €3.50.)*

HOUSE #4711. The fabled **Eau de Cologne,** once prescribed as a drinkable curative, earned the town worldwide recognition. Today, the house of its origin, labeled #4711 by a Napoleonic system that abolished street names, is a boutique where a fountain flows with the scented water. Visit the gallery upstairs for a history of the fragrance. *(On Glockeng. near the intersection with Tunisstr. From Hohe Str., turn right on Brückenstr., which becomes Glockeng. Open M-F 9am-7pm, Sa 9am-6pm. Free.)*

ENTERTAINMENT AND NIGHTLIFE

Cologne explodes in celebration during **Karneval** (Feb. 23, 2006), a week-long pre-Lenten festival made up of 50 neighborhood processions. **Weiberfastnacht** (Feb. 23, 2006) is the first major to-do: the mayor mounts the platform at Alter Markt and abdicates leadership to the city's women, who then hunt down their husbands at work and chop off their ties. The weekend builds to the out-of-control parade on **Rosenmontag** (Rose Monday; Feb. 27, 2006), when thousands of merry participants dance their way through the city while exchanging *bützchen* (kisses on the cheek). For more info, pick up the Karneval booklet at the tourist office.

Roman mosaics dating back to the third century record the wild excesses of the city's early residents; they've toned it down only a bit since. The best way to know what you'll get is to pick up the monthly magazine *Kölner* (€1). The closer to the Rhine or *Dom* you venture, the faster your wallet will empty. After dark in **Hohenzollernring,** crowds of people move from theaters to clubs and finally to cafes in the early morning. Students congregate around Zülpicherstr. and Zülpicher Pl., as well as along the Hohenstaufenring. Radiating westward from Friesenpl., the **Belgisches Viertel** has slightly more expensive bars and cafes. Gay nightlife thrives in Cologne, centering on the **Bermuda-Dreieck** (Bermuda Triangle), around Rudolfpl., and also on the area running up Matthiasstr. to Mühlenbach, Hohe Pforte, Marienpl., and the Heumarkt neighborhood by **Deutzer Brücke.**

Papa Joe's Jazzlokal, Buttermarkt 37 (☎257 7931). Papa Joe has a legendary reputation for providing good jazz and good times. Grab some peanuts when the sack comes around. *Kölsch* (€3.60) in 0.4L glasses, not the usual 0.2L. Live jazz from 9pm. Open daily 7pm-1am, F-Sa until 3am. Cash only.

Stadtgarten, Venloerstr. 40 (☎95 29 94 33). Take U3, 5, 6, or 12 to Friesenpl. A huge outdoor beer garden complements 2 indoor clubs for the price of one. Downstairs spins techno and house; upstairs, the concert hall is renowned for its live jazz recordings. Cover €5-8. Open M-Th 9pm-1am, F-Sa 9pm-3am. Cash only.

Das Ding, Hohenstaufenring 30 (www.dingzone.de). Smoky and very noir. A popular student bar and disco with varied music and dirt-cheap drink specials (€1). Student ID required. Cover €4. Open Tu, Th, Su 9pm-3am, W 9pm-2am, F-Sa 9pm-4am. Cash only.

Hotel Timp, Heumarkt 25 (☎258 1409; www.timp.de). Across from the U-Bahn stop. This GLBT club and hotel has become a virtual institution in Cologne for gaudy, glittery travesty theater. Drag shows daily 1-4am. No cover, but 1st drink €8 on weeknights and €13 on weekends. Open daily 11am-late. AmEx/MC/V.

BONN ☎0228

Bonn's Rhine-side setting, popular concert scene, and diverse museums attract just enough visitors nowadays to keep Bonn (pop. 306,000) well touristed—but not overly so. Once housed in Bonn, the *Bundestag* moved to Berlin in 1999 and returned Bonn to its low profile.

TRANSPORTATION AND PRACTICAL INFORMATION. Trains run to: Cologne (20min., 5 per hr., €8.60-10.30); Frankfurt (2hr., 3 per hr., €26-62); Koblenz (45min., 3 per hr., €9-14.50). The **tourist office** is at Windeckstr. 1, just off Münsterpl. Walk straight down Poststr. from the station. They provide free maps and book rooms for a €2 fee. (☎194 33; www.bonn.de. Open M-F 9am-6:30pm, Sa 9am-4pm, Su 10am-2pm.) The **Bonn Regio WelcomeCard** (1-day €9, 2-day €14, 3-day €19) covers public transportation after 9am and admission to over 20 museums in the Bonn area. The **post office** is at Münsterpl. 17. (Open M-F 9am-8pm, Sa 9am-4pm.) **Postal Code:** 53111.

ACCOMMODATIONS AND FOOD. Take bus #621 (dir.: Ippendorf Altenheim) to Jugendgästehaus for the super-modern **Jugendgästehaus Bonn-Venusberg (HI) ❷,** Haager Weg 42. (☎28 99 70; www.bonn.jugendherberge.de. Breakfast included. Laundry €3.90. Curfew 1am. Dorms €21.50; singles €33.50; doubles €52. AmEx/MC/V.) Snuggle under feather blankets at the more centrally located **Hotel Bergmann ❹,** Kasernenstr. 13, which is small and well kept; from the station, follow Poststr., turn left at Münsterpl. on Vivatsg., then bear right on Kasernenstr. (☎63 38 91; ajbergmann@web.de. Breakfast included. Singles €35; doubles €50. Cash only.) Descend to the basement of the Kaufhof on Münsterpl. to find a **supermarket.** (Open M-F 9:30am-8pm, Sa 9am-8pm.) Find cheap eats at the second-floor university cafeteria **Mensa ❶,** Nassestr. 11, a 10min. walk down Kaiserstr. from the station. (Open M-F noon-2pm and 5:30-7:30pm, Sa noon-2pm. Cash only.)

SIGHTS AND NIGHTLIFE. Bonn's lively pedestrian zone has many historic nooks. **Beethovenhaus,** Bonng. 20, Beethoven's birthplace, houses a collection of the composer's personal effects, from his first violin to his hearing aids. (☎981 7525; www.beethoven-haus-bonn.de. Open Apr.-Oct. M-Sa 10am-6pm, Su 11am-4pm; Nov.-Mar. M-Sa 10am-5pm, Su 11am-4pm. Last entry 30min.

before closing. €4, students €3.) In its heyday as parliament, the **Bundestag's** see-through walls were meant to symbolize transparency in government. (Take U16, 63, or 66 to Heussallee or bus #610 to Bundeshaus.) Students study within the **Kurfürstliches Schloß,** the huge 18th-century palace that now serves as the linchpin for Bonn's **Friedrich-Wilhelms-Universität.** To reach Bonn's other palace, follow Poppelsdorfer Allee to the 18th-century **Poppelsdorfer Schloß,** around which lie manicured **botanical gardens.** (Gardens open Apr.-Sept. M-F, Su 9am-6pm; Oct.-Mar. M-F 9am-4pm. Free.) The WelcomeCard (p. 453) covers admission to most of Bonn's **Museum Mile.** Take U16, 63, or 66 to Heussallee or Museum König. Interactive exhibits at the **Haus der Geschichte** (House of History), Willy-Brandt-Allee 14, examine post-WWII Germany. (☎91 650; www.hdg.de. Open Tu-Su 9am-7pm. Free.) One block away, the immense **Kunstmuseum Bonn,** Friedrich-Ebert-Allee 2, houses a superb selection of Expressionist and Modern German art. (☎77 62 60; www.bonn.de/kunstmuseum. Open Tu, Th-Su 10am-6pm, W 10am-9pm. €5, students €2.50.)

Schnüss (€1), sold at newspaper stands, has club and concert listings. **Jazz Galerie,** Oxfordstr. 24, is a jumping bar and disco on the weekends. Check the schedule on the door for theme nights. (☎63 93 24. Cover €5-7.50. Open Tu, Th 9pm-3am, F-Sa 10pm-5am.) **Boba's Bar,** Josephstr. 17, is one of Bonn's few gay and lesbian nightspots. Beers only cost €1 during the happy hour 8-9pm, and on Tuesday mixed drinks are only €3. (Open Tu-Su 8pm-3am.)

KASSEL ☎0561

The curious monuments and sweeping green vistas that surround Kassel (pop. 195,000) make it well worth visiting, and both can be found at the antiquated hillside park, **Wilhelmshöhe.** Inside, **Schloß Wilhelmshöhe** is a dressed-down but more authentically furnished version of the Residenz in Würzburg (p. 477). Just uphill, **Schloß Löwenburg** was built by Wilhelm in the 18th century with stones deliberately missing so it would resemble a crumbling medieval castle—he was obsessed with the year 1495 and quixotically imagined himself a knight. Take streetcar #1 from Bahnhof Wilhelmshöhe. (Both castles open Mar.-Oct. Tu-Su 10am-5pm; Nov.-Feb. 10am-4pm. Last entry 1hr. before closing. Required tours every hr. Each castle €3.50, students €2.50.) Park paths lead up to the statue **Herkules,** Kassel's emblem, where visitors can climb onto the pedestal and, if they're brave enough, into a club. (Pedestal and club open daily mid-Mar. to mid-Nov. 10am-5pm. €2, students €1.50. Access to the base of the statue free.)

To reach **Jugendherberge und Bildungsstätte Kassel (HI) ❷,** Schenkendorfstr. 18, take streetcar #4 from the Wilhelmshöhe station to Annastr., backtrack on Friedrich-Ebert-Str., and turn right on Querallee, which becomes Schenkendorfstr. (☎77 64 55; www.djh-hessen.de/jh/kassel. Breakfast included. Reception 11am-11:30pm. Curfew 12:30am. Dorms €24.30, under 26 €21.60; singles €34.30/31.60; doubles €39.30/36.60. €3.10 HI discount. Cash only.) **Friedrich-Ebert-Straße,** the upper part of **Wilhelmshöher Allee,** and the area around **Königsplatz** all have supermarkets and cafes sprinkled amongst clothing stores. **Boys and Girls ❶,** Treppenstr. 9, serves endless varieties of ridiculously cheap pizza (€1.90-5.30), pasta (€6.10-7.30), and other Italian delights. From the Hauptbahnhof, walk straight down Kurfürstenstr., and cross the intersection to the pedestrian street, Treppenstr. (☎701 34 50. Open daily 11am-midnight. Cash only.)

Kassel has two train stations, Bahnhof Wilhelmshöhe and the Hauptbahnhof, but most trains stop only at Wilhelmshöhe. **Trains** run to: Düsseldorf (3½hr., 1-4 per hr., €40-87); Frankfurt (2hr., 3 per hr., €27-42); Hamburg (2½hr., 2-3 per hr., €53-60); Munich (4hr., 1-2 per hr., €82). The **tourist office,** in Bahnhof Wilhelmshöhe, has free maps and books rooms for a €2.50 fee. (☎70 77 07; www.kassel-tourist.de. Open M-F 9am-6pm, Sa 9am-2pm.) **Postal Code:** 34117.

FRANKFURT AM MAIN ☎069

International offices, shiny skyscrapers, and expensive cars define every intersection in Frankfurt (pop. 641,000), lovingly nicknamed "Mainhattan" for its location on the Main river and its glitzy vitality. Both people and money are constantly in motion in this major transportation hub, also home to the central bank of the EU.

TRANSPORTATION

Flights: The ultra-modern airport, **Flughafen Rhein-Main** (☎01805 372 46 36), is connected to the Hauptbahnhof by S8 and 9 (every 15min.; buy tickets for €3.30 from the green machines marked *"Fahrkarten"* before boarding).

Trains: Trains run from the Hauptbahnhof to: **Amsterdam** (4hr., 2 per hr., €70-112); **Berlin** (5-6hr., 2 per hr., €78-95); **Cologne** (1½hr., 3 per hr., €35-55); **Hamburg** (3½-5hr., 2 per hr., €67-86); **Munich** (3½-4½hr., 3 per hr., €56-69); **Paris** (6-8hr., 2 per hr., €71). Call ☎01805 99 66 33 for schedules, reservations, and info.

Public Transportation: Frankfurt's public transportation system runs daily until about 1am. Short-hop tickets (€1.70, rush hour M-F 6-9am and 4-6:30pm, €2) are valid for 1hr. in 1 direction, transfers permitted. **Eurail** is valid only on the S-Bahn. The **day pass** (*Tageskarte;* valid until midnight of the purchase date) provides unlimited transportation on the S-Bahn, U-Bahn, streetcars, and buses and can be purchased from machines in any station (€4.80). Ticketless passengers face €40 fines.

Ride-share: Mitfahrzentrale, Baseler Str. 7 (☎23 64 44). Turn right onto Baseler Str. from the side exit of the Hauptbahnhof (track #1). Arranges rides to: **Berlin** (€29); **Hamburg** (€28); **Munich** (€22); **Paris** (€30); and elsewhere. It's best to book by phone 1-2 days in advance. Open M-F 8am-6:30pm, Sa 8am-4pm, Su 10am-4pm.

ORIENTATION AND PRACTICAL INFORMATION

Frankfurt's Hauptbahnhof opens into its red-light district; from the station, the *Altstadt* is a 20min. walk down Kaiserstr. or Münchener Str. To the north, the commercial heart of Frankfurt lies along **Zeil.** Students, cafes, and services cluster in **Bockenheim** (U6 or 7 to Bockenheimer Warte). Across the Main River, **Sachsenhausen** draws pub-crawlers and museum-goers (U1, 2, or 3 to Schweizer Pl.).

Tourist Office: In the Hauptbahnhof (☎21 23 88 49; www.frankfurt-tourismus.de). Sells maps (€0.50) and the **Frankfurt Card** (1-day €8, 2-day €12), which allows unlimited use of public transportation and provides discounts on sights. Also book rooms for €3, or for free if you call ahead. Open M-F 8am-9pm, Sa-Su and holidays 9am-6pm.

Currency Exchange: At banks. Locations in the airport and station have lousy rates.

Laundromat: Waschsalon, Wallstr. 8, near the hostel in Sachsenhausen. Wash €3, dry €0.50 per 15min. Soap included. Open daily 6am-11pm.

Emergency: Police: ☎110. **Ambulance** and **Fire:** ☎112.

Pharmacy: In the train station's Einkaufspassage (☎23 30 47). Open M-F 6:30am-9pm, Sa 8am-9pm, Su 9am-8pm. For medical emergencies, call ☎192 92.

Internet Access: Alpha, in the Hauptbahnhof's gambling salon, past track #24. (☎23 62 22). €3.50 per hr. Open daily 24hr.

Post Office: In the train station near track #24. Open M-F 7am-7:30pm, Sa 8am-4pm. **Postal Code:** 60313.

ACCOMMODATIONS

Frankfurt's **Westend/University** area has a few cheap options, but deals are rare and frequent trade fairs make rooms even scarcer. Reserve at least 2-3 weeks ahead.

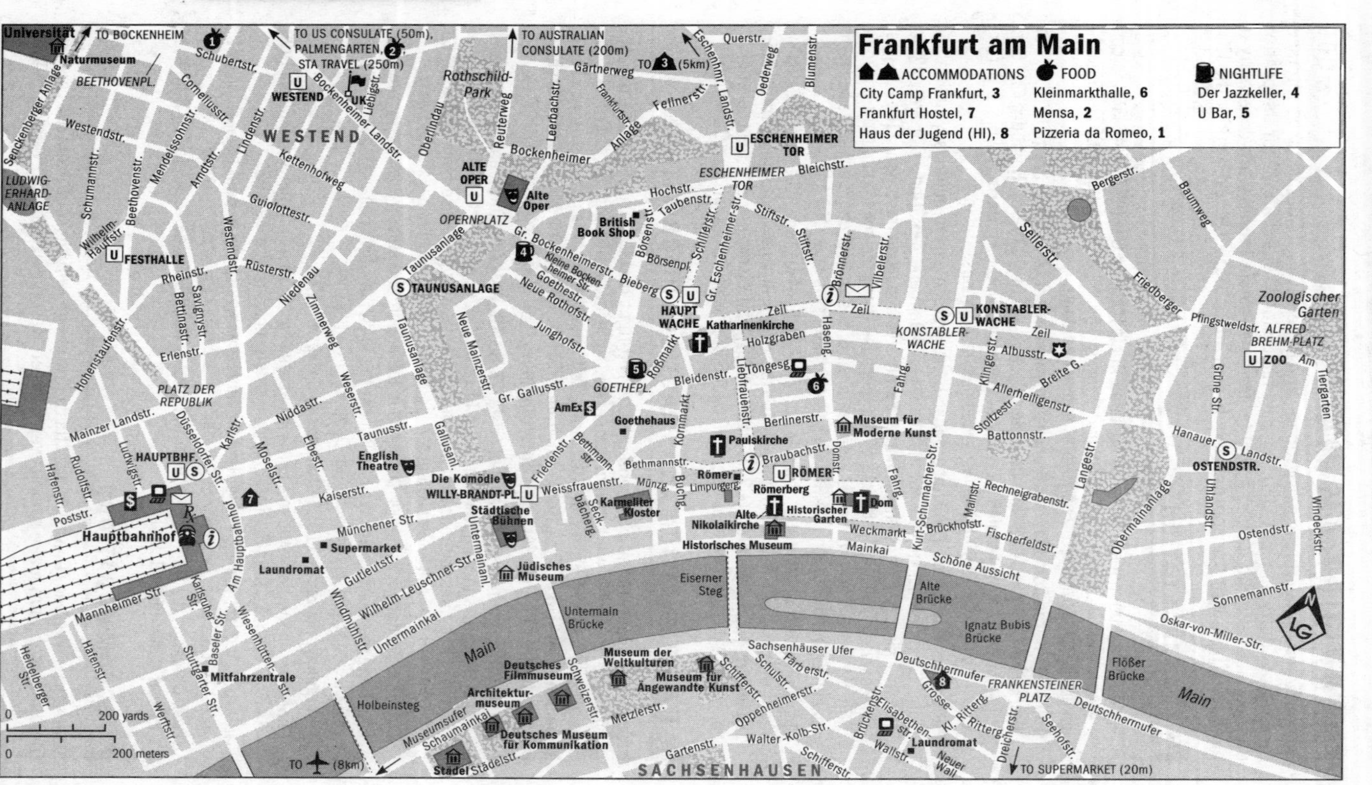

Frankfurt am Main
ACCOMMODATIONS
City Camp Frankfurt, 3
Frankfurt Hostel, 7
Haus der Jugend (HI), 8
FOOD
Kleinmarkthalle, 6
Mensa, 2
Pizzeria da Romeo, 1
NIGHTLIFE
Der Jazzkeller, 4
U Bar, 5
TO BOCKENHEIM
TO US CONSULATE (50m), PALMENGARTEN, 2
STA TRAVEL (250m)
TO AUSTRALIAN CONSULATE (200m)
TO 3 (5km)
TO SUPERMARKET (20m)
TO (8km)
WESTEND
SACHSENHAUSEN
Main
Zoologischer Garten
ALFRED-BREHM-PLATZ
ZOO
KONSTABLER-WACHE
HAUPTWACHE
ESCHENHEIMER TOR
ALTE OPER
OPERNPLATZ
TAUNUSANLAGE
GOETHEPL.
WILLY-BRANDT-PL.
HAUPTBHF.
FESTHALLE
PLATZ DER REPUBLIK
RÖMER
OSTENDSTR.
FRANKENSTEINER PLATZ
LUDWIG-ERHARD-ANLAGE
Rothschild-Park
Universität
Naturmuseum
BEETHOVENPL.
Hauptbahnhof
Alte Oper
British Book Shop
Goethehaus
Paulskirche
Dom
Römer
Römerberg
Historischer Garten
Alte Nikolaikirche
Katharinenkirche
Museum für Moderne Kunst
Historisches Museum
Jüdisches Museum
Städtische Bühnen
English Theatre
Die Komödie
Karmeliter Kloster
Museum der Weltkulturen
Museum für Angewandte Kunst
Deutsches Filmmuseum
Architekturmuseum
Deutsches Museum für Kommunikation
Städel
AmEx
Supermarket
Laundromat
Mitfahrzentrale
Eiserner Steg
Alte Brücke
Ignatz Bubis Brücke
Untermain Brücke
Flößer Brücke
Holbeinsteg
Zeil
Zimmerweg
Mainzer Landstr.
Kaiserstr.
Münchener Str.
Sachsenhäuser Ufer
Schaumainkai
Schöne Aussicht
Deutschherrnufer
200 yards
200 meters

Frankfurt Hostel, Kaiserstr. 74 (☎247 5130; www.frankfurt-hostel.com). Walk straight from the station; it's 2min. ahead on the left. Great location between the Hauptbahnhof and the *Altstadt,* with friendly staff and newly renovated rooms. Undergoing renovation at time of research; call ahead to confirm prices. Breakfast included. Reception 24hr. Dorms €20; singles €45; doubles €50-60. MC/V. ❷

Haus der Jugend (HI), Deutschherrnufer 12 (☎610 0150; www.jugendherberge-frankfurt.de). From the station, take bus #46 to Frankensteiner Pl. Turn left along the river; the hostel is at the end of the block. Its location bordering the pubs and museums of the Sachsenhausen district makes it popular with students. Breakfast included. Check-in after 1pm. Check-out 9:30am. Curfew 2am. Dorms €23-32, under-26 €19-28; singles €37-42/33-38; doubles €64-74/56-66. €3.10 HI discount. AmEx/MC/V. ❷

City Camp Frankfurt, An der Sandelmühle 35 (☎57 03 32; www.city-camp-frankfurt.de). U1, 2, or 3 to Heddernheim. Use the unmarked exit, turn left at Kleingartnerverein sign and continue down road until you reach Sandelmühle sign. Cross stream, turn left, and follow signs. Showers €1 per 4min. Reception 9am-1pm and 4-8pm. Tent sites €8.70, extra person €5.20. Cash only. ❶

FOOD

Cheap meals surround the university in **Bockenheim,** and many **Sachsenhausen** pubs serve food at decent prices. Just blocks from the HI hostel is a well-stocked **HL Markt,** Dreieichstr. 56 (open M-Sa 8am-8pm). An **Alim Markt,** Münchener Str. 37, is near the Hauptbahnhof (open M-F 8:30am-7:30pm, Su 8am-2pm). **Kleinmarkthalle,** on Haseng. between Berliner Str. and Töngesg., is a three-story warehouse with food stands and the best *wurst* in the city (open M-F 8am-6pm, Sa 8am-4pm).

Pizzeria da Romeo, Mendelssohnstr. 83 (☎74 95 01). Italian dishes (from €4.50) and fresh pizzas (€3.50-7.50) accompanied by humor and charm. Vegetarian options abound. Open M-F 10:30am-3pm and 4-9:30pm. Cash only. ❷

Mensa, U6 (dir.: Heerstr.) or 7 (dir.: Hausen) to Bockenheimer Warte. Take the exit to Mensa and then the 1st left before STA travel; it's in the courtyard to the right, beside the fountain. A cafeteria is on the 1st fl. and Mensa is on the 2nd. Guest meals €2.80-4.30. Mensa open M-F 11:30am-3pm. Cafeteria open M-F 8am-5pm. Cash only. ❶

SIGHTS

Since Allied bombing destroyed everything but the cathedral, Frankfurt's historic splendor survives mostly in memories and in reconstructed monuments. If you plan on touring Frankfurt's museums, consider buying a **Frankfurt Card** (p. 455).

RÖMERBERG. Any voyage through Frankfurt should begin here in the center of the *Altstadt* (old town), among the half-timbered homes and seemingly medieval fountains that misleadingly cover most postcards of the city. In celebration of the 13 imperial coronations held in Frankfurt, the Statue of Justice in the center of the square once spouted wine. Unfortunately, she has since sobered up. Across from the Römerberg, the **Paulskirche,** once the birthplace of Germany's 19th-century attempt at liberal government, now memorializes the trials of German democracy. *(Open daily 10am-5pm. Free.)* At the west end of Römerberg, the gables of **Römer** have marked the city hall since 1405. Upstairs, the **Kaisersaal** is an imperial banquet hall adorned with portraits of the 52 German emperors from Charlemagne to Franz II. *(Entrance from Limpurgerg. Open daily 10am-1pm and 2-5pm. €2.)* These emperors were once crowned in the red sandstone **Dom,** lone survivor of the WWII bombings. *(Open Tu-F 10am-5pm, Sa-Su 11am-5pm. Church free. Museum €2, students €1.)*

BEST OF THE *WURST*

So you're finally in Germany and itching to sink your teeth into your first authentic German *wurst.* To eat it, don't try to put it in your *brötchen* (bread roll). Eat it like a true German: take a napkin and wrap it around one end of the sausage, dip the other in mustard, and dive in. You might want to alternate bites with your *brötchen. Guten Appetit!*

Bockwurst: This tasty sausage is commonly roasted or grilled at street stands, and is usually served dripping with ketchup, mustard, and a soft *brötchen.* Although *"bock"* means billy-goat, this *wurst* is made of finely ground veal with parsley and chives. Complement your *bockwurst* with some Bock beer.

Thüringer Bratwurst: Similar to the *bockwurst* both in content and presentation, the *bratwurst* also contains a little pork, ginger, and nutmeg.

Frankfurter: Unlike the American variety, the German Frankfurter can only bear this name if made in Frankfurt. It's made of lean pork ground into a paste and then cold-smoked, which gives it an orange-yellow coloring.

Knockwurst: Shorter and plumper, this sausage is served with sauerkraut. It's made of lean pork and beef, with a healthy dose of garlic.

Weißwurst: Cream and eggs give this "white sausage" its paleness. *Weißwurst* goes best with rye bread and mustard.

STÄDEL. With equally important paintings from nearly every period, the Städel exhibits works by Old Masters, Impressionists, and Modernists. If paintings by Beckmann and Kandinsky aren't your thing, head for the works by Monet and Renoir. *(Schaumainkai 63, between Dürerstr. and Holbeinstr. Open Tu and F-Su 10am-5pm, W-Th 10am-9pm. €6, students €5. English-language audio tours €2.50.)*

ENTERTAINMENT AND NIGHTLIFE

A number of prominent techno DJs and discos are situated in the commercial district between **Zeil** and **Bleichstraße.** Wait until midnight for things to really heat up, and wear something dressier than jeans if you plan to slip by the selective bouncers. If you prefer drinks to dancing, head to the **Alt-Sachsenhausen** district between Brückenstr. and Dreieichstr., home to numerous rowdy pubs and taverns, or make your way over to the complex of cobblestoned streets centering on **Große** and **Kleine Rittergaße,** which teems with cafes, restaurants, bars, and Irish pubs. More info on Frankfurt's club scene can be found at www.nachtleben.de.

U Bar, Roßmarkt (www.u60311.net), on the corner of Goethepl. Frankfurt's best DJs and international stars spin in this old subway station. Cover €6-15. Open from 10pm. Techno/house club opens F-Su 11pm. Lines start at 9pm F nights.

Der Jazzkeller, Kleine Bockenheimer Str. 18a (☎28 85 37; www.jazzkeller.com). Germany's oldest jazz club, established in 1952, has hosted masters like Dizzy Gillespie. Cover €4-15. Open W-Sa from 9pm, Su from 8pm. Cash only.

SOUTHWESTERN GERMANY

There is much to be seen in the Rhine and Mosel River Valleys, and much to be drunk. Vineyards upon vineyards grow the best German wines near the Mosel as it curls downstream along the Rhine Gorge to a shore of castle-studded hills. Farther south, modern cities fade slowly into the beautiful hinterlands of the Black Forest.

TRIER ☎0651

Located at the western end of the Mosel Valley, Trier (pop. 100,000) is the oldest town in Germany. Founded by Romans, it became both the capital of the Western Empire and a stronghold for Christianity by the early 4th century. The Roman ruins decorating the heart of the city will keep history buffs occupied for hours, and the greenery of the riverside promenade offers an escape for walkers, bikers, or those just looking to relax. A one-day **combination ticket** (€6.20, students €3.10) provides access to the city's Roman monuments. The most impressive is the massive and well-preserved 2nd-century **Porta Nigra** (Black Gate), which travelers can climb for a view of Trier. (Open daily Apr.-Sept. 9am-6pm; Oct.-Mar. 9am-5pm. Last admission 30min. before closing. €2.10, students €1.60.) The nearby **Dom** shelters the *Tunica Christi* (Holy Robe of Christ) and the tombs of many archbishops. (Open daily Apr.-Oct. 6:30am-6pm; Nov.-Mar. 6:30am-5:30pm. Free.) The enormous **Basilika** was originally the location of Emperor Constantine's throne room. (Open Apr.-Oct. M-Sa 10am-6pm, Su noon-6pm; Nov.-Mar. Tu-Sa 11am-noon and 3-4pm, Su noon-1pm. Free.) Near the southeast corner of the city walls are the 4th-century **Kaiserthermen** (Emperor's baths), with underground passages that once served as Roman sewers. (Open daily Apr.-Sept. 9am-6pm; Oct.-Mar. 9am-5pm. Last admission 30min. before closing. €2.10, students €1.60.) **Boat cruises** take passengers on 1hr. and 2hr. trips (€7/10), departing from the dock to the right of the Kaiser-Wilhelm-Brücke every 1¼hr. from 10am to 5:45pm (☎266 66).

A talking bird in the lobby of **Jugendgästehaus Trier (HI) ❷,** An der Jugendherberge 4, gives visitors a warm welcome to the riverside setting. To get there, take buses #2 (which leaves from the train station), 8, 12, or 87 to the Zurlaubenerufer stop. The hostel is a 10min. walk downstream from the bus stop. (☎292 92; www.diejugendherbergen.de. Breakfast included. Laundry €5. Dorms €20.60; singles €26.10; doubles €52.20. €3.10 HI discount. MC/V.) **Jugendgästehaus im Kolpinghaus Warsberger Hof ❶,** Dietrichstr. 42, is in the city center. (☎97 52 50; www.warsberger-hof.de. Dorms €15; singles €25; doubles €42. Reception 7:30am-10pm. MC/V.) Moderately priced restaurants line the pedestrian path along the river between the youth hostel and the Kaiser-Wilhelm-Brücke. Two blocks from Viehmarkt-Pl., **Astarix ❷,** Karl-Marx-Str. 11, dishes out large portions of pasta and pizza from €4. (☎722 39. Open M-Th 11:30am-1am, F-Sa 11:30am-2am, Su 2pm-1am. Cash only.) **Plus** supermarket, Brotstr. 54, is near the Hauptmarkt. (Open M-F 8:30am-8pm, Sa 8:30am-6pm.)

Trains run to Koblenz (1½hr., 2 per hr., €16) and Luxembourg City (45min., 1 per hr., €10-14). From the station, walk straight down Theodor-Haus-Allee and turn left under the Porta Nigra to reach the **tourist office,** by the Porta Nigra. (☎97 80 80; www.trier.de. Open May-Sept. M-Sa 9am-7pm, Su 10am-5pm; Oct.-Dec. and Mar.-Apr. M-Sa 9am-6pm, Su 10am-3pm; Jan.-Feb. M-Sa 10am-5pm, Sa 10am-1pm. 2hr. English-language city tours Sa 1:30pm; 1hr. English-language coach tour daily 1pm. Each €6, students €5.) **Postal Code:** 54292.

RHINE VALLEY (RHEINTAL)

Castles tower above tiny villages and green hillsides as the Rhine River carves its way through the 80km stretch of the Rhine Valley. Sailors' nightmares and poets' dreams layer its hills as it flows north from Mainz (an easy journey from Frankfurt) through Bacharach and Koblenz to charming Bonn.

TRANSPORTATION

Two different **train** lines traverse the Rhine Valley, one on each bank; the line on the western side stays closer to the water and has superior views. It's often tricky to switch banks, as train and ferry schedules don't always match up, so plan your trip ahead and remember which side of the river your destination is located on. Although full of tourists, **boats** are probably the best way to see the sights; **Köln-Düsseldorfer (KD)** covers the Mainz-Koblenz stretch four times a day in summer.

MAINZ ☎06131

Pastel-colored buildings decorate the *Altstadt* (old town) of Mainz, attempting to recapture the old-town atmosphere of its pre-war days. Once the greatest Catholic diocese north of the Alps, Mainz's colossal sandstone **Martinsdom** stands as a memorial to its former ecclesiastical power. (Open Mar.-Oct. Tu-F 9am-6pm, Sa 9am-2pm, Su 1-2:45pm and 4-6:30pm; Nov.-Feb. M-F 9am-5pm, Sa 9am-4pm, Su 12:45-3pm and 4-5pm. Free.) South of the *Dom*, the Gothic **Stephanskirche** on Stephansberg. is inlaid with stunning stained-glass windows set by Russian exile Marc Chagall. (Open daily 10am-noon and 2-5pm. Free.) Johannes Gutenberg, the father of movable type, is immortalized at the **Gutenberg-Museum,** Liebfrauenpl. 5, across from the *Dom*, where there is a replica of his original press. (Open Tu-Sa 9am-5pm, Su 11am-3pm. €3, students €2.)

To reach the clean rooms of **Jugendgästehaus (HI) ❷,** Otto-Brunfels-Schneise 4, take bus #62 (dir.: Weisenau) or 63 (dir.: Laubenheim) to Viktorstift/Jugendherberge and follow the signs. (☎853 32; www.diejugendherbergen.de. Breakfast included. Reception 6:30am-10pm. Dorms €20.60; doubles €52.20. €3.10 HI discount. MC/V.) **Der Eisgrub-Bräu ❷,** Weißlilieng. 1a, on the edge of the *Altstadt*, serves breakfast and lunch buffets (€2.90/5.10) and its own house beer. (Open M-Th, Su 9am-1pm, F-Sa 9am-2pm.) **Trains** run to: Frankfurt (30min., €6-9.40); Heidelberg (1hr., €14.60-25); Bacharach (50min., €7); and Koblenz (1hr., €14.60-18). KD **ferries** (☎23 28 00) depart from the wharfs on the other side of the Rathaus. The **tourist office,** in Brückenturm by the river in the *Altstadt*, arranges English-language tours, has free maps, and reserves rooms for a €2.50 fee. From the station, walk straight down Schottstr., turn right onto Kaiserstr. and continue straight until you reach Ludwigstr.; turn left and follow the green signs. (☎28 62 10; www.info-mainz.de/tourist. Open M-F 9am-6pm, Sa 10am-3pm. 2hr. English-language tours May-Oct. W and F-Sa 2pm; low season Sa 2pm. €5.) **Postal Code:** 55001.

BACHARACH ☎06473

Bacharach (Altar of Bacchus) lives up to its name, with wine cellars *(weinkeller)* tucked between every other half-timbered house along the village's cobblestone main street. Try some of the Rhine's best wines and cheeses (€2-5) at **Die Weinstube,** Oberstr. 63. (Open M-F from 1pm, Sa-Su from noon. Cash only.) Nearby, up the path to the hostel, is the 14th-century **Wernerkapelle,** the remains of a red sandstone chapel that took 140 years to build but only hours to destroy during the Palatinate War of Succession in 1689. At the height of hostel greatness—literally—**Jugendherberge Stahleck (HI) ❷** is a gorgeous 12th-century castle with a panoramic view of the Rhine Valley. The steep 15min. hike to the hostel is worth every step. Make a right out of the station and turn left at the stairs between the tourist office and the Peterskirche. (☎12 66; www.diejugendherbergen.de. Breakfast included. Call ahead. Reception 7am-7:30pm. Curfew 10pm. Dorms €19.60; doubles €50.20. HI discount €3.10. MC/V.) At **Café Restaurant Rusticana ❷,** Oberstr. 40, a lovely German couple serves three-course meals (€6-11) and lively conversation. (☎17 41. Open May-Oct. daily 10am-10pm. Cash only.) **Trains** go from Bacharach to Koblenz (40min., 1-2 per hr., €7.20) and Mainz (50min., 1 per hr., €7). The **tourist office,** Oberstr. 45, located at the opposite end of the village from the bus station, books rooms for free. (☎91 93 03. Open Apr.-Oct. M-F 9am-5pm, Sa-Su 10am-2pm; Nov.-Mar. M-F 9am-noon.) **Postal Code:** 55422.

LORELEI CLIFFS AND CASTLES

Sailors were once lured to these cliffs by the infamous Lorelei maiden, but her hypnotic song is now superfluous: today, hordes of travelers are seduced by the scenery alone. **St. Goarshausen** and **St. Goar,** two charming towns on either side of the Rhine, host the spectacular **Rhein in Flammen** (Rhine Ablaze) fireworks celebration on the third Saturday in September (Sept. 16, 2006). St. Goarshausen, on the east bank, provides access by foot to the Lorelei statue and the cliffs. Directly above the town, the fierce **Burg Katz** (Cat Castle) eternally stalks its prey, the smaller **Burg Maus** (Mouse Castle). To get there, face the river, head right, and follow the signs. Burg Maus offers daily falconry demonstrations at 11am and 2:30pm; for info, call ☎76 69 or visit St. Goarshausen's tourist office.

To reach **Jugendheim Loreley ❶**, on the St. Goarshausen side of the Rhine, take bus NVG from the KD ferry dock to the Lorelei statue, then walk from the cliffs past the parking gate down the road a few hundred meters and turn left. (☎06771 26 19. Breakfast included. Linen €3.50. Curfew 10pm. Dorms €8.50. Cash only.) **Trains** run to St. Goarshausen from Cologne (1hr., €18) and Mainz (1hr., €10). The *Lorelei VI* **ferry** (M-F 6am-11pm, Sa-Su 7am-11pm; round-trip €2) crosses the river to St. Goar, which has a spectacular view of the Rhine and surrounding area. St. Goar's **tourist office,** Heerstr. 86, is in the pedestrian zone, about a 5min. walk from the ferry dock. (☎06741 383; www.st-goar.de. Open M-F 9am-12:30pm and 1:30-5pm, Sa 10am-noon.) To reach St. Goarhausen's **tourist office,** Bahnhofstr. 8, turn left from the station and follow the signs. (☎06771 91 00; www.loreley-touristik.de. Open M, Th 9:30am-12:30pm and 2-4:30pm, Tu-W and Sa 9:30am-12:30pm, F 9:30am-12:30pm and 2-5:30pm.) **Postal Code:** 56329.

KOBLENZ ☎0261

A menacing fortress perched high above the city of Koblenz (pop. 108,000) overlooks the crossroads between two of Germany's major rivers, the Rhine and Mosel, which corner the *Altstadt* (old town) far below. Koblenz has long been a strategic hot spot. In the two millennia since its birth, the city has hosted every empire seeking to conquer Europe. It centers around the **Deutsches Eck** (German Corner) at the confluence of the Rhine and Mosel, which purportedly witnessed the birth of the German nation in 1216. To the right, the **Mahnmal der Deutschen Einheit** (Monument to German Unity) is a tribute to Kaiser Wilhelm I. The **Museum Ludwig im Deutschherrenhaus,** Danziger Freiheit 1, behind the *Mahnmal*, features contemporary French art. (☎304 04 16; www.ludwigmuseum.org. Open Tu-Sa 10:30am-5pm, Su 11am-6pm. €2.50, students €1.50.) Head across the river to the **Festung Ehrenbreitstein,** a fortress at the highest point in the city. Today, it contains a youth hostel, numerous museums, and rotating historical exhibits. (Non-hostel guests €1.10, students €0.60. See below for hostel information.)

Jugendherberge Koblenz (HI) ❷, in the fortress, has breathtaking views of the Rhine and Mosel. Take the train to Koblenz-Ehrenbreitstein (10min., every hr.). From there, walk left along the main road for 100m and take the paved path to your right. (☎97 28 70; www.diejugendherbergen.de. Breakfast included. Reception 7:15am-10pm. Curfew midnight. Dorms €19.60; doubles €50.20. €3.10 HI discount. MC/V.) **Ferries** (€0.80) cross the Mosel to **Campingplatz Rhein-Mosel ❶,** Am Neuendorfer Eck. (☎827 19. Reception 8am-1pm and 3-10pm. Open Apr.-Oct. 15. Tent sites €7, extra person €4.50.) **Kaffeewirtschaft ❷,** Münzpl. 14, serves light meals (€5-11) and mouth-watering desserts (€1.50-5) amid fresh roses. (Open M-Th 9am-midnight, F-Sa 9am-2am, Su 10am-midnight.)

Trains run to: Bonn (30min., 3 per hr., €8.70-14.50); Cologne (1½hr., 4 per hr., €14.60-19.70); Frankfurt (2hr., 2-3 per hr., €20-25); Mainz (1hr., 2-3 per hr., €14.60-20.40); Trier (2hr., 2-3 per hr., €16). Directly across from the station is the **tourist office,** Bahnhofpl. 7, where they give out free maps and book rooms for no charge. (☎30 38 80. Open May-Oct. M-F 9am-7pm, Sa-Su 10am-7pm; Nov.-Apr. M-F 9am-6pm, Sa-Su 10am-6pm.) **Postal Code:** 65068.

HEIDELBERG ☎06221

Sun-drenched Heidelberg (pop. 141,000) and its crumbling castle have lured scores of writers and artists over the years, from Goethe to Twain. Today, legions of fannypackers fill the length of Hauptstraße, where postcards and t-shirts sell like hotcakes and every sign is posted in four languages. But even mass tourism can't spoil the experience of Heidelberg's beautiful hillside setting above the Neckar River, Germany's oldest university, or the city's enviable nightlife.

TRANSPORTATION AND PRACTICAL INFORMATION

Trains run to: Frankfurt (50min., 2 per hr., €13-24) and Stuttgart (40min., 2 per hr., €20-26). Within Heidelberg, single-ride **bus** tickets cost €2; day passes (€5) are available on the bus. Rhein-Neckar-Fahrgastschifffahrt (☎201 81; www.rnf-schifffhrt.de), in front of the *Kongresshaus,* runs **ferries** all over Germany and cruises on the Neckar to Neckarsteinach (3hr., Easter to late Oct. every 1½hr. 9:30am-4:50pm, €9.50). Heidelberg's attractions are mostly in the eastern part of the city, along the south bank of the Neckar. From the train station, take any bus or streetcar to Bismarckpl., then walk east down **Hauptstraße,** the city's spine, to the *Altstadt.* The **tourist office,** in front of the station, sells maps with a city guide (€1) and books rooms for a €3 fee and a small deposit. (☎138 8121; www.cvb.heidelberg.de. Open Apr.-Oct. M-Sa 9am-7pm, Su 10am-6pm; Nov.-Mar. M-Sa 9am-6pm.) It also sells the **Heidelberg Card,** which includes unlimited public transit and admission to most sights. (2-day card €14; 4-day card €21.) The **post office** is at Sofienstr. 8-10. (Open M-F 9am-6:30pm, Sa 9:30am-1pm.) **Postal Code:** 69115.

ACCOMMODATIONS AND FOOD

In summer, reserve at least two weeks in advance, or earlier for weekend visits. If you can't do this, arrive early in the day to spare yourself a headache. **Pension Jeske ❷,** Mittelbadg. 2, has a perfect *Altstadt* (old town) location. Take bus #33 (dir.: Ziegelhausen) to Rathaus/Kornmarkt. (☎237 33; www.pension-jeske-heidelberg.de. Reception 11am-1pm and 5-7pm. Singles €20; doubles €50, with bath €60; triples €60/75; quints with bath €100. Cash only.) To reach the large rooms of the **Jugendherberge (HI) ❸,** Tiergartenstr. 5, take bus #33 (dir.: Zoo-Sportzentrum) to Jugendherberge. Located by the zoo, this hostel also teems with wild species, such as *schoolchildus germanius.* (☎65 11 90. Breakfast included. Reception 1-11pm. Lockout 9am-1pm. Reserve at least a week ahead. Dorms €26.10, under 27 €23.10; singles and doubles add €10/5. €3.10 HI discount. AmEx/MC/V.)

Restaurants on and around Hauptstr. are expensive, but historic pubs just outside the central area offer better value. To reach the **Mensa "Zeughaus" ❶,** in the stone fortress on Marstallstr., take bus #12, 41, or 42 to Marstallstr. (Cafeteria meals €0.80 per 100g. CampusCard required; available for €5 inside the cafeteria. Open M-Sa 11:30am-10pm. Cash only.) **Hemingway's Bar-Café-Meeting Point ❷,** Fahrtg. 1, has a crowded, shaded patio along the Neckar. (☎16 50 33. Lunch menu €4.10. Open M-Th, Su 9am-1am, F-Sa 9am-3am. Cash only.)

SIGHTS

HEIDELBERGER SCHLOß. Tourists lay siege to Heidelberg Castle every summer, and for good reason. Thrice destroyed, twice by war (1622 and 1693) and once by lightning (1764), the castle has only gained in beauty over its centuries-long collapse. A cool, musty wine cellar in the castle houses the **Großes Faß,** which,

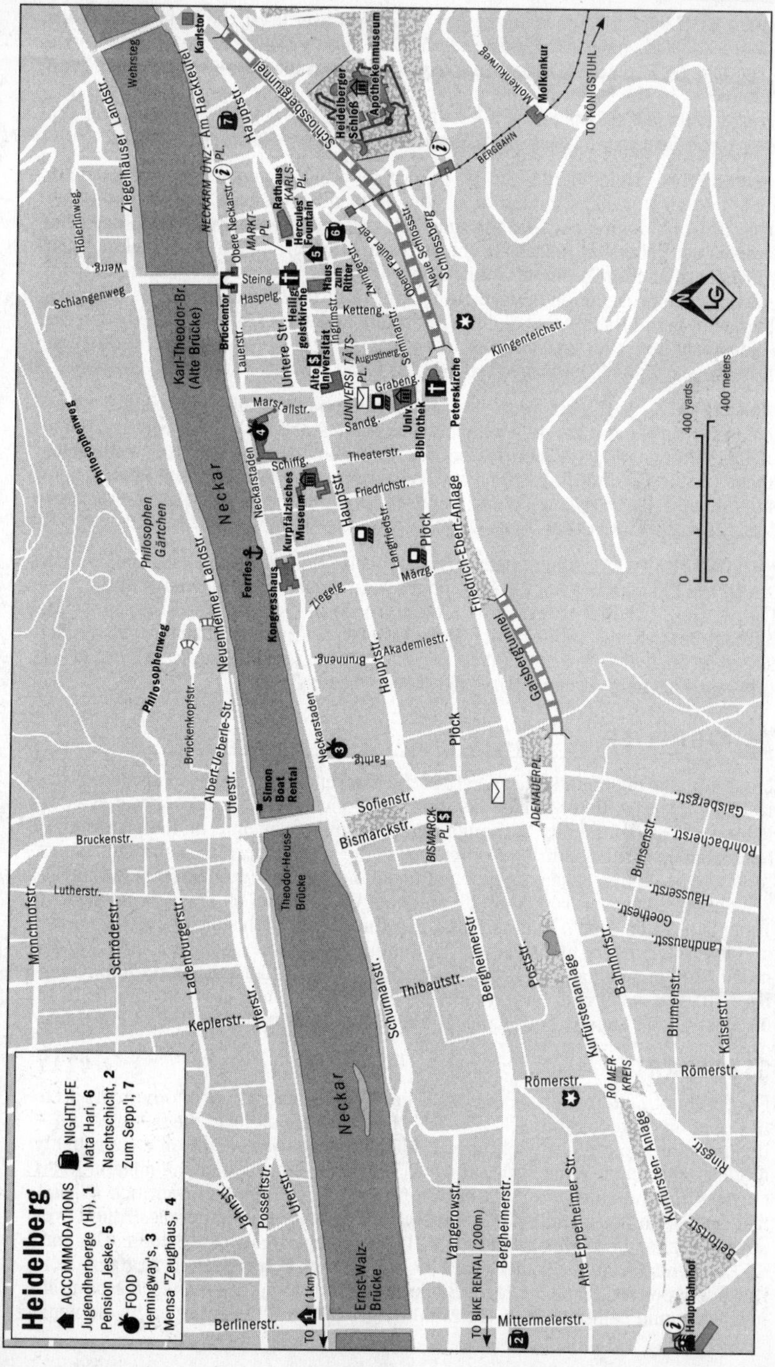

Heidelberg

ACCOMMODATIONS
- Jugendherberge (HI), 1
- Pension Jeske, 5

FOOD
- Hemingway's, 3
- Mensa "Zeughaus," 4

NIGHTLIFE
- Mata Hari, 6
- Nachtschicht, 2
- Zum Sepp'l, 7

Karlstor
Wehrsteg
Ziegelhäuser Landstr.
NECKARMÜNZ- PL.
Am Hackteufel
Hauptstr.
Schlossbergtunnel
Heidelberger Schloß
Apothekenmuseum
Molkenkurweg
Molkenkur
TO KÖNIGSTUHL
BERGBAHN
Rathaus
KARLS- PL.
Hercules' Fountain
Obere Neckarstr.
MARKT- PL.
Hölderlinweg
Werrg.
Steing.
Haspelg.
Brückentor
Heiliggeistkirche
Haus zum Ritter
Zwingerstr.
Oberer Faulerpelz
Neue Schlossstr.
Neue Schlossberg
Schlangenweg
Karl-Theodor-Br. (Alte Brücke)
Lauerstr.
Untere Str.
Ingrimstr.
Ketteng.
Alte Universität
UNIVERSITÄTS- PL.
Augustinerg.
Seminarstr.
Grabeng.
Klingenteichstr.
Peterskirche
Marstallstr.
Sandg.
Univ. Bibliothek
Philosophenweg
Neckar
Neckarstaden
Schiffg.
Theaterstr.
Kurpfälzisches Museum
Friedrichstr.
Hauptstr.
Philosophen Gärtchen
Ferries
Kongresshaus
Langfriedstr.
Plöck
Märzg.
Friedrich-Ebert-Anlage
400 yards
400 meters
0
Neuenheimer Landstr.
Ziegelg.
Brunneng.
Akademiestr.
Gaisbergtunnel
Brückenkopfstr.
Albert-Ueberle-Str.
Uferstr.
Simon Boat Rental
Fahrtg.
Plöck
Sofienstr.
ADENAUERPL.
Gaisbergstr.
Bruckenstr.
Bismarckstr.
BISMARCK- PL.
Rohrbacherstr.
Bunsenstr.
Lutherstr.
Theodor-Heuss-Brücke
Häusserstr.
Goethestr.
Monchhofstr.
Schröderstr.
Ladenburgerstr.
Schurmanstr.
Bergheimerstr.
Poststr.
Landhausstr.
Thibautstr.
Kurfürstenanlage
Bahnhofstr.
Blumenstr.
Keplerstr.
Kaiserstr.
Römerstr.
RÖMER- KREIS
Römerstr.
Ringstr.
Jahnstr.
Posseltstr.
Uferstr.
Vangerowstr.
Bergheimerstr.
Alte Eppelheimer Str.
Kurfürsten-Anlage
Belfortstr.
Ernst-Walz-Brücke
TO (1km)
TO BIKE RENTAL (200m)
Berlinerstr.
Mittermeierstr.
Hauptbahnhof

GERMANY

with a 221,726L capacity, is the largest wine cask ever used; the **Kleines Faß** holds a mere 125,000L. *(Grounds open daily 8am-5:30pm. English-language tours daily every 15min. 10am-4pm. Grounds €3, students €1.50. Tours €4.)* Reach the castle by the uphill path (10min.) or by the **Bergbahn,** one of Germany's oldest cable cars. *(Take bus #11, dir.: Karlstor, to Bergbahn/Rathaus. Trams leave the parking lot next to the bus stop daily Mar.-Oct. every 10min. 9am-8pm; Nov.-Feb. every 20min. 9am-6pm. Round-trip €5, students €4.)*

UNIVERSITÄT. Heidelberg is home to Germany's oldest university, established in 1386. It is also perhaps the nation's most prestigious; its past faculty rosters list over 20 Nobel Laureates, and the university all but gave birth to sociology. The **Museum der Universität Heidelberg** traces the institution's history in a building that contains the school's oldest auditorium, **Alte Aula.** Intriguingly, students were exempt from prosecution by civil authorities until 1914. Instead, crimes from plagiarism to grand theft were tried by the faculty and students were punished in the **Studentenkarzer** jail. *(Augustinerg. 2. Open Apr.-Sept. Tu-Su 10am-6pm; Oct. Tu-Su 10am-4pm; Nov.-Mar. Tu-Sa 10am-4pm. Museum and jail €2.50, students €2.)*

MARKTPLATZ. At the center of the *Altstadt* is the cobblestoned Marktpl., where accused witches and heretics were burned at the stake in the 15th century. Some of Heidelberg's oldest structures border the square: the 14th-century **Heiliggeistkirche** (Church of the Holy Spirit) and the 16th-century inn **Haus Zum Ritter,** opposite the church. *(Church open M-Sa 11am-5pm, Su 1-5pm. Tower open M-Sa 11am-4:45pm, Su 12:15-4:45pm. Church free. Tower €0.50.)*

PHILOSOPHENWEG. A high path on the opposite side of the Neckar from the *Altstadt*, the Philosophenweg (Philosopher's Way) has unbeatable views of the city. On the top of Heiligenberg (Holy Mountain) lie the ruins of the 9th-century **St. Michael Basilika,** the 13th-century **Stefanskloster,** and an **amphitheater** built on the site of an ancient Celtic gathering place. *(To get to the path, take streetcar #1 or 3 to Tiefburg, or use the steep spur trail 10m west of the Karl-Theodor-Brücke.)*

NIGHTLIFE

Most popular nightspots fan out from the **Marktplatz.** On the Neckar side of the Heiliggeistkirche, **Unter Straße** has the most concentrated—and congested—collection of bars in the city, although nightlife spills over onto on **Hauptstraße.** At **Nachtschicht,** in the Landfried-Komplex near the station, university students dance to mixed beats in a basement resembling an old factory. (☎43 85 50; www.nachtschicht.com. Cover €3.50, M and F students €1.50. Open M, Th-Sa 10pm-4am, W 10pm-3am.) **Zum Sepp'l,** Hauptstr. 213, is a student lair with stained-glass windows and live piano every night except for Sunday and Wednesday. (☎230 85. Homemade German specialties €7.50-16. Open daily noon-10:30pm.) **Mata Hari,** Oberbadg. 10, is a small club for gays and lesbians, although all are welcome. (☎18 18 08. Beer €2.80. Tu men only. Open M-Th, SuM-Th, Su 10pm-3am, F-Sa 10pm-4am.)

STUTTGART ☎0711

Forget about *Lederhosen*—Porsche, Daimler-Benz, and a host of other corporate thoroughbreds keep Stuttgart (pop. 587,000) speeding along in the fast lane. After its almost complete destruction in WWII, Stuttgart was rebuilt in a thoroughly modern and uninspiring style. More to its credit are its amazing **mineral baths** *(mineralbäder)*, fueled by Western Europe's most active mineral springs. **Mineralbad Leuze,** Am Leuzebad 2-6, has indoor and outdoor thermal pools. Take U1 or streetcar #2 or 14 to Mineralbäder. (☎216 42 10. Open daily 6am-8:40pm. Day card €13, students €8.30. 2hr. soak €6.40/4.80.) The superb **Staatsgalerie Stuttgart,** Konrad-Adenauer-Str. 30-32, collects Beckmann, Dalí, Kandinsky, and Picasso in its new wing, and paintings from the Middle Ages to the 19th century in its old wing.

(☎47 04 00; www.staatsgalerie.de. Open Tu-W and F-Su 10am-7pm, Th 10am-9pm. First Sa of every month open 10am-midnight. €4.50, students €3. W free.) The **Mercedes-Benz Museum,** Mercedesstr. 137, is a must for car-lovers. Take S1 (dir.: Ploschingen) to Daimlerstadion. (☎172 25 78. Open Tu-Su 9am-5pm. Free.)

Reserve a bed in hostel heaven at least a week or two in advance at **Alex 30 Hostel ❷,** Alexanderstr. 30, where each room comes with a TV; painted murals on the walls see you off to sleep. The bar and outdoor beer garden are open around the clock. Take U5, 6, 7, or 15 to Olgaeck. (☎838 8950; www.alex30-hostel.de. Breakfast €5. Linen €3. Reception 24hr. Dorms €18; singles €29; doubles €48. MC/V.) Overlooking the city are the newly renovated rooms of the **Jugendherberge (HI) ❷,** Haussmannstr. 27. Take U15 to Eugenspl. then walk down Kernerstr. to the intersection with Werastr. and up the stairs to the hostel. (☎24 15 83; www.jugendherberge.stuttgart.de. Breakfast included. Dorms €24.10, under 27 €21.10; doubles €53.20/47.20. €3.10 HI discount. MC/V.) Look for mid-range restaurants in the pedestrian zone between Pfarrstr. and Charlottenstr., and fast food on Rotebühlpl. **Gaststätte Brett ❷,** Katharinepl. 1, serves German food (€3-8) and fills daily with locals. (☎236 5605. Open M-Th 11:30am-1am, F-Sa 11:30am-2am, Su 3pm-1am. Cash only.) Nightlife clusters around **Eberhardstraße, Rotebühlplatz,** and **Calwer Straße,** and runs the length of **Theodor-Heuss-Straße. Suite 212,** Theodor-Heuss-Str. 15, has DJs and video-mixing on weekends. (Beer €2.50. Mixed drinks €3.50-8. No cover, except for VIP parties on the 2nd Sa of every month. Open M-W 11am-2am, Th 11am-3am, F-Sa 11am-5am, Su 2pm-2am.) Gay parties are held at various clubs on rotating weekends; check at the tourist office for information.

Trains run to: Basel (3½hr., 2-4 per hr., €50); Berlin (6hr., 2 per hr., €110); Frankfurt (1-2hr., 2 per hr., €33-47); Munich (2½-3½hr., 2 per hr., €31-45); Paris (6½hr., 4 per day, €88-96). The **tourist office,** Königstr. 1A, to the left across from the train station, provides free maps and books rooms for €3. (☎22 280. Open M-F 9am-8pm, Sa 9am-6pm, Su 11am-6pm.) The **post office,** Arnulf-Klett-Pl. 2, is in the station. (Open M-F 8:30am-6pm, Sa 8:30am-12:30pm.) **Postal Code:** 70173.

BLACK FOREST (SCHWARZWALD)

Once the inspiration for *Hansel and Gretel,* the Black Forest today lures hikers and skiers with more than just gingerbread: natural beauty and castle ruins make it an idyllic vacation spot. The gateway to the forest is **Freiburg,** accessible by train from Basel and Stuttgart. Visitors tend to favor exploring the area by bike or by car, as public transportation is sparse. Many rail lines encircle the forest, but only two cut through it. **Bus** service is more thorough, although slow and infrequent.

FREIBURG IM BREISGAU. Green hills can be seen from downtown Freiburg (pop. 208,000), a city without a city's pace. Freiburg's centerpiece is its **Münster,** a 13th- to 16th-century stone cathedral with a 116m spire that shelters Germany's oldest bell. (Open M-Sa 9:30am-5pm, Su 1-5pm. Tower €1.50, students €1.) For another view of the city, board the **Schloßberg Seilbahn,** a two-person gondola that rises up into the forest; a panoramic view of the area and refreshments in a restaurant await at the top. Take the bridge over Leopoldstr. to the base. (Open Apr.-Oct. 11am-7pm, closed first Tu of every month; Nov.-Mar. W-Su 11am-5pm. €2.10, return €3.60.) Surrounding hills have well-marked **hiking** and **mountain biking** trails; the tourist office (see below) sells trail maps (€3-8). **Bikes** can be rented from **Fahrrad Station Mobile,** Wentzingerstr. 15, the round building to the left out of the back of the station. (☎292 7998. €5 per 3hr., €11 per 7hr., €12.50 per day.)

To reach the **Jugendherberge (HI) ❷,** Kartäuserstr. 151, take bus #1 to Lassbergstr. Turn left, then right onto Fritz-Geiges-Str., and follow the signs. (☎676 56. Breakfast included. Dorms €23, under 27 €20; doubles €50. MC/V.) Stalls at the **Freiburger Markthalle ❶,** next to the Martinstor, serve specialties from all over the world for €3-7. (Open M-F 7am-7pm, Sa 7am-4pm.) **Brennessel ❷,** Eschholzstr. 17, behind the train station, stuffs patrons with everything from ostrich steak to pancakes. (☎28 11 87. Entrees €2-10. Open M-Sa 6pm-1am, Su 5pm-1am.) **Trains** run to Basel (1hr., 3 per hr., €10) and Stuttgart (2hr., every hr., €30). The **tourist office,** Rotteckring 14, down Eisenbahnstr. from the station, gives out free city maps and books private rooms for €3, the city's best budget option. (☎388 1880. Open June-Sept. M-F 9:30am-8pm, Sa 9:30am-5pm, Su 10am-noon; Oct.-May M-F 9:30am-6pm, Sa 9:30am-2pm, Su 10am-noon.) **Phone Code:** 0761. **Postal Code:** 79098.

CONSTANCE (KONSTANZ) ☎07531

Located on the **Bodensee** (Lake Constance) and ranking among Germany's most popular vacation spots, Constance (pop. 79,000) has river promenades and narrow streets that wind around beautiful Baroque and Renaissance facades. Constance emerged unscathed from WWII, since part of the city extends into Switzerland and the Allies were leery of striking neutral territory. Under renovation through 2006, the **Münster** (cathedral) in the center of town displays ancient religious objects beneath its 76m Gothic spire. (Open M-F 10am-6pm, Sa-Su noon-5pm.) Wander down **Seestraße,** near the yacht harbor on the lake, or **Rheinsteig,** along the Rhine, for picturesque promenades. Constance boasts a number of **public beaches;** all are free and open from May to September.

In the center, **Pension Gretel ❹,** Zollernstr. 6-8, has bright rooms. Go right out of the train station (5min.), then make a left onto Zollernstr. (☎45 58 25; www.hotel-gretel.de. Breakfast included. Singles €45; doubles €60-70, with bath €80-90; triples with bath €114; quads with bath €148. Low season reduced rates. Cash only.) **DKV-Campingplatz Bruderhofer ❶,** Fohrenbühlweg 50, is by the lake. Take bus #1 to Staad and walk 10min. with the lake to your left. (☎313 88; www.campingkonstanz.de. Showers €1. Reception 8am-1pm and 3-8pm. Tent sites €8, extra person €3.50. Cash only.) **Groceries** are in the basement of the Karstadt department store on Augustinerpl. Walk straight up Bahnhofstr. from the station and continue until you reach Augustinerpl. (Open M-F 9:30am-8pm, Sa 9:30am-7pm.)

Trains run from Constance to most cities in southern Germany. BSB **ferries** leave hourly from Constance for all ports around the lake. Buy tickets onboard or in the pale yellow building, Hafenstr. 6, behind the train station. (☎364 03 89. Open M-Th 8am-noon and 1-4pm, F 8am-noon and 1-5pm.) The friendly **tourist office,** Bahnhofspl. 13, to the right of the train station, provides free maps of the city and makes hotel reservations for no charge. (☎13 30 30; www.konstanz.de. Open Apr.-Oct. M-F 9am-6:30pm, Sa 9am-4pm, Su 10am-1pm; Nov.-Mar. M-F 9:30am-12:30pm and 2-6pm.) Reserve accommodations a few weeks ahead in summer. **Postal Code:** 78462.

BAVARIA (BAYERN)

Bavaria is the Germany of Teutonic myth and Wagnerian opera. From the Baroque cities along the Danube to mad King Ludwig's castles high in the Alps, the region attracts more tourists than any other part of the country.

MUNICH (MÜNCHEN) ☎089

The capital and cultural center of Bavaria, Munich (pop. 1.3 million) is a sprawling, liberal metropolis where world-class museums, handsome parks and architecture, and a cosmopolitan population create a city of astonishing vitality. *Müncheners* party zealously during *Fasching*, or Mardi Gras (Feb. 24-28, 2006), shop with abandon during the Christ Child Market (Dec. 1-23, 2006), and chug unfathomable quantities of beer during the legendary Oktoberfest (Sept. 16-Oct. 1, 2006).

TRANSPORTATION

Flights: Flughafen München (☎97 52 13 13). S1 and S8 run between the airport and the Hauptbahnhof and Marienpl. (40min., every 20min. 3:57am-12:57am, €8 or 8 strips on the Streifenkarte); buy a *Gesamtz Tageskarte* (€9) that covers all zones. The Lufthansa Airport Bus makes the same trip (40min., every 20min., €9.50).

Trains: Munich's **Hauptbahnhof** (☎118 61) is the transportation hub of southern Germany, with connections to: **Amsterdam** (7-9hr., 15 per day); **Berlin** (6½hr., 2 per hr.); **Cologne** (6hr., 2-4 per hr.); **Frankfurt** (4½hr., 2 per hr.); **Füssen** (2hr., every hr. 6am-9pm); **Hamburg** (6hr., 1-2 per hr.); **Paris** (8-10hr., 9 per day); **Prague** (6-7hr., 7 per day); **Rome** (11hr., 7-8 per day); **Salzburg** (2hr., 2 per hr.); **Vienna** (5hr., every hr.); **Zürich** (4½-5½hr., 14 per day). Purchase **Bayern-Ticket** (single €19, 2-5 people €26) for unlimited train transit in Bavaria and parts of Austria on weekdays 9am-3am, and on weekends midnight-3am. **EurAide,** in the station, provides free train info in English and sells train tickets. **Reisezentrum** info counters at train station open daily 7am-9:30pm.

Ride-Share: Mitfahr-Zentrale, Lämmerstr. 6 (☎194 40). Arranges intercity transportation with drivers going the same way. Around €30. Open M-Sa 8am-8pm. AmEx/MC/V.

Public Transportation: MVV (☎41 42 43 44), Munich's public transport system, has something to satisfy everyone, no matter what hours they keep. The U-Bahn (subway) runs M-Th, Su 5am-12:30am and F-Sa 5am-2am. S-Bahn trains run from 4am until 2 or 3am. Night buses and trams serve Munich's dedicated clubbers (route number prefixed by "N"). Eurail, InterRail, and German railpasses are valid on the S-Bahn (S) but *not* on the U-Bahn (U), streetcars, or buses.

Tickets: Buy tickets at the blue vending machines and validate them in the blue boxes marked with an "E" before entering the platform. If you jump the fare *(Schwarzfahren)*, you risk a €40 fine.

Prices: Single-ride tickets €2.20 (valid 3hr.). **Short-trip** *(Kurzstrecke)* tickets €1.10 (1hr. or 2 stops on the U- or S-Bahn, 4 stops on a streetcar or bus). A **10-strip ticket** *(Streifenkarte)* costs €10 and can be used by more than 1 person. Cancel 2 strips per person for a normal ride, or 1 strip for a short trip; for rides beyond the city center, cancel 2 strips per zone. A **single day ticket** *(Single-Tageskarte)* is valid until 6am the next day (€4.50). At €11, the **3-day pass** is a great deal. The **Munich Welcome Card,** available at the tourist office (p. 468), also has transportation discounts. The **XXL Ticket** gives day-long transit on all transport in Munich and surroundings (€6 single; €10.50 for up to 5 people).

Taxis: Taxi-München-Zentrale (☎216 10 or 194 10) has stands in front of the train station and every 5-10 blocks in the city center. Women may request a female driver.

Bike Rental: Mike's Bike Tours, in Discover Bavaria, 10 Bräuhausstr. (☎25 54 39 87); with your back to the Hofbräuhaus, take a left on Bräuhausstr. and a right onto Hochbrückenstr. All-day bike rental €12, overnight €18. Half off with a tour (p. 468). Open M, F-Sa 8:35am-9:15pm, Su, Tu-Th 10am-1pm and 3-9pm. To return your bike after hours, call ☎0172 722 0435.

ORIENTATION

Downtown Munich is split into quadrants by thoroughfares running east-west and north-south. These intersect at Munich's central square, **Marienplatz,** and link the traffic rings at Karlsplatz (called Stachus by locals) in the west, Isartorplatz in the east, Odeonsplatz in the north, and Sendlinger Tor in the south. In the east beyond the Isartor, the Isar River flows north-south. The **Hauptbahnhof** is just beyond Karlspl. to the west of the ring. To get to Marienpl. from the station, use the main exit and make a right on Bahnhofpl., then a left on Bayerstr. heading east through Karlspl., and continue straight. Or, take any S-Bahn to Marienpl. The **university** is to the north amid the budget restaurants of the **Schwabing** district; to the east of Schwabing is the **English Garden,** to the west, the **Olympiapark.** South of downtown is the

Glockenbachviertel, filled with night hot spots and many gay bars. A seedy area with hotels and sex shops surrounds the Hauptbahnhof. Oktoberfest takes place on the large and open **Theresienwiese,** southeast of the train station on the U4 and 5 lines.

PRACTICAL INFORMATION

The most comprehensive list of services, events, and museums can be found in the English-language monthly *Munich Found* (€3), available at newsstands.

Tourist Offices: Main office (☎23 39 65 55), on the front side of the train station, next to the SB-Markt on Bahnhofpl. Books rooms for free with a 10-15% deposit, sells English-language city maps (€0.30), and sells the **Munich Welcome Card** for discounts and passes to transportation and sights (1-day €6.50, 3-day €16). Open M-Sa 9am-8pm, Su 10am-6pm. **EurAide** (☎59 38 89), room #3 along track 11 of the Hauptbahnhof, near the Bayerstr. exit. Books train tickets for free, explains public transportation, sells maps (€1), and books English-language city tours. Pick up the free brochure *Inside Track.* Open daily except Su pm: June 7:45am-noon and 1-6pm; Aug.-Sept. 8am-12:30pm and 2-5pm; Oct. 7:45am-12:45pm and 2-4pm; Nov.-Apr. 8am-noon and 1-4pm; May 7:45am-12:30pm and 2-4:30pm.

Tours: Mike's Bike Tours, 10 Bräuhausstr. (☎25 54 39 88; www.mikesbike-tours.com). If you only have 1 day in Munich, take this tour. Starting from the Altes Rathaus on Marienpl., the 4hr., 6.5km city tour includes a *Biergarten* break. Tours leave daily June-July 11:30am and 4pm. Look for coupons at youth hostels. €24.

Consulates: Canada, Tal 29 (☎219 95 70). Open M-Th 9am-noon and 2-5pm, F 9am-noon. **Ireland,** Dennigerstr. 15 (☎20 80 59 90). Open M-F 9am-noon. **UK,** Bürkleinstr. 10, 4th fl. (☎21 10 90). Open M-F 8:45-11:30am and 1-3:15pm. **US,** Königinstr. 5 (☎288 80). Open M-F 8-11am.

Currency Exchange: ReiseBank (☎551 08 13; www.reisebank.de), at the front of the train station on Bahnhofpl. Slightly cheaper than other banks. Open daily 7am-10pm.

GLBT Resources: Gay services information (☎260 3056), hotline open 7-10pm. **Lesbian information** (☎725 4272). Phones staffed M, W 2:30-5pm, Tu 10:30am-1pm. The reception desk of **Hotel Deutsche Eiche,** Reichenbachstr. 13, can provide information 24hr. (☎231 1660; www.deutsche-eiche.com.) Also see **GLBT Nightlife,** p. 473.

Laundromat: City SB Waschcenter, Paul-Heyse-Str. 21. Wash €4 (includes detergent), dry €0.60 per 10min. Open daily 7am-11pm; last load 10pm.

Emergency: Police: ☎110. **Ambulance** and **Fire:** ☎112. **Medical service:** ☎192 22.

Pharmacy: Bahnhofpl. 2 (☎59 81 19), on the corner outside the train station. Open M-F 8am-6:30pm, Sa 8am-2pm.

Internet Access: Just around the corner from Mike's Bike Tours (see **Bike Rental,** p. 467), **Glopolis** charges €2.50 for unlimited Internet time. Open M, F-Sa 8:35am-9:15pm; Su, Tu-Th 10am-1pm and 3-9pm.

Post Office: Bahnhofpl. In the yellow building opposite the main train station exit. Open M-F 7:30am-8pm, Sa 9am-4pm. **Postal Code:** 80335.

ACCOMMODATIONS AND CAMPING

Munich's accommodations tend to fall into one of three categories: seedy, expensive, or booked solid. During mid-summer and Oktoberfest, rooms are hard to find and prices jump 10-15%. In summer, it's usually necessary to book a few weeks in advance or to start calling before noon.

HOSTELS AND CAMPING

Euro Youth Hotel, Senefelderstr. 5 (☎59 90 88 11). From the Hauptbahnhof, make a left on Bayerstr. and a right on Senefelderstr. Informed staff, cheerful rooms, and a busy bar make this the best hostel in Munich. Breakfast €3.90, included in private rooms.

Free lockers. Wash €2.80, dry €1.30. Internet €3 per hr. Key deposit €20. Reception 24hr. 22-bed dorms €19.50; 3- to 5-bed dorms €22; 3-bed dorms with shower €25; singles €42; doubles €54, with private shower €70; triples with bath €84. MC/V. ❷

Jugendlager Kapuzinerhölzl (The Tent), In den Kirschen 30 (☎141 43 00). Streetcar #17 from the Hauptbahnhof (dir.: Amalienburgstr.) to Botanischer Garten (15min.). Make a right at Franz-Schrank-Str., follow the signs, and turn left at In den Kirschen. Sleep with 250 others under a big tent on a wooden floor. Evening campfires. Free English-language city tours. Free lockers. Wash €2, dry €1.50. Bike rental open 9-11am, €8 per day. Reception 24hr. Check-in 4:30pm. Open June-Aug. Foam pad, blankets, shower, and breakfast €8.50. Actual beds €11. Camping €11. Cash only. ❶

Wombat's City Hostel, Senefelderstr. 1 (☎599 89 18 0). The first in a row of 3 hostels on Senefelderstr. Check your email in the inner greenhouse courtyard or meet up with other backpackers for free board games and weekly English-language movie nights. Bright, colorful rooms, all with bath. Breakfast €4. Free lockers. Laundry €4.50. Internet €3 per hr. Reception 24hr. Dorms €19-22; singles €49; doubles €62. Cash only. ❷

4 You München, Hirtenstr. 18 (☎552 1660; www.the4you.de), 200m from the Hauptbahnhof. Ecological hostel with wooden beds and basic rooms. Wheelchair accessible. Breakfast included. Wash €2.30, dry €1.40. Reception 24hr. Dorms €18-23, over 26 €21-26; singles €44/47; doubles €70/73; triples €92/95. DC/MC/V. ❷

Jugendherberge München Neuhausen (HI), Wendl-Dietrich-Str. 20 (☎13 11 56; jhmuenchen@djh-bayern.de). U1 or 7 (dir.: Westfriedhof) to Rotkreuzpl. Go down Wendl-Dietrich-Str. past the Galeria Kaufhof. 3km from the center. Lime-green hallways and high ceilings make this hostel feel spacious and cool. Clean, simple rooms. Breakfast included. Dinner €5.40. Free lockers. Wash €2.60, dry €1.10. Key deposit €15. Reception 24hr. Check-in from 11:30am. Closed Dec. Dorms €20-23; doubles €49. ❷

Campingplatz Thalkirchen, Zentralländstr. 49 (☎723 17 07; www.camping.muenchen.de). U1 or 2 to Sendlinger Tor, then U3 to Thalkirchen, and change to bus #135 (every 30min.); Campingpl. is the 3rd stop (8min.). 550 sites on the lush banks of the Isar. TV lounge, convenience store, and cafe. Showers €1. Wash €4, dry €0.50. Reception 7am-11pm. 14-day max. stay. Open mid-Mar. to Oct. Tent sites €12.50, extra person €4.50. Tent rental €3-4. Cash only. ❶

REMINDER. HI-affiliated hostels in Bavaria generally do not admit guests over age 26, except families or groups of adults with young children.

HOTELS AND PENSIONS

Creatif Hotel Elephant, Lämmerstr. 6 (☎55 57 85; www.munich-hotel.net). Take the Arnulfstr. exit out of the station, hang a quick right, turn left on Hirtenstr., then right on Lämmerstr. Uniquely modern rooms, airy and colorful, all with bath, telephone, TV, and tiny stained-glass windows. Free Internet. Reception 24hr. Singles from €35; doubles from €50; triples from €70. Extra bed €10. AmEx/MC/V. ❹

Pension am Kaiserplatz, Kaiserpl. 12 (☎34 91 90). U3 to Münchener Freiheit. With the Karstadt on your right, take a left onto Herzogstr., walk 3 blocks, and turn left on Viktoriastr.; it's on the right at the end of the street. Elegantly furnished rooms a few blocks from nightlife central. Breakfast included and served in room. Reception 7am-8pm. Singles €31, with shower €47; doubles €48/57; triples €66; quads €84. Cash only. ❸

GERMANY

FOOD

For an authentic Bavarian lunch, spread a *brez'n* (pretzel) with *leberwurst* (liverwurst) or cheese. *Weißwürste* (white veal sausages) are a regional specialty; don't eat the skin, just slice them open for their tender meat. The tasty *leberkäse* is a pinkish loaf of ground beef and bacon; *leberknödel* are liver dumplings.

SHEER *BIER*

lthough droves of tourists visit Germany to sample its renowned beer, few understand the intricacies of German *bierkultur*. German beer is typically served by he liter *(Maß)*, sometimes by he half-liter *(halb-Maß)*. Ask for *"Ein Maß, bitte,"* and if you feel short-changed (most glasses have measurement lines on hem), say *"Bitte nachschenken"* or a top-up.

Germany beer comes in endess varieties. A **Helles** is a typical ight, usually Bavarian, beer. The am-crowned **Pils** is a more biter and more alcoholic, but less nalty brew.

Similar to an English shandy, a **Radlermaß** (bikers brew) is a 50-50 blend of *Helles* and sparkling emonade, so named because Germans seem to think that it's safe to cycle as long as you are only half drunk. **Weißbier** is a strong, cloudy beer made with wheat *(weizen)*; many like to add a squeeze of lemon.

A more malty lager, the **Dunkeles** is not the strongest beer. If you're aiming for severe inebriaion, try a strong **Bock** or an even stronger **Doppelbock.** Both of hese beers are often brewed by nonks, presumably because they lone have the self-restraint not o drink it all themselves.

Germany's excellence in beer s a double-edged sword, however. Visitors should be warned hat for a palate weaned on German brews, watery domestics will never taste as good again.

Off **Ludwigstraße,** the university district supplies students with inexpensive, filling meals. Many reasonably priced restaurants and cafes cluster on **Schellingstraße, Amalienstraße,** and **Türkenstraße** (U3 or 6 to Universität). Munich is also the place where someone first connected the "beer" concept to the "garden" concept to create the **beer garden.** Now they're all over the city (see **Nightlife,** p. 472).

Dukatz Kaffee im Literaturhaus, Salvatorpl. 1 (☎291 9600). This sunny, open-air cafe is Munich's unofficial literary hub. Gourmet food from €4 complements creative drinks (€5-8.50). Book discussions and readings are frequent and often free; for more information call ☎29 19 34 27. Open M-Sa 10am-1am. Cash only. ❷

Café Ignaz, Georgenstr. 67 (☎271 6093). U2 to Josephspl. Crepes, pasta, stir-fry, and more at this friendly vegetarian bakery and cafe. Entrees (€5-9) include dessert. Get main dishes to go for €4. Breakfast (€5-7), lunch (€6), and weekend brunch (€8) buffets. M-F 3-6pm entrees €6. Open M, W-Su 8am-11pm, Tu 11am-1pm. Cash only. ❷

Schelling Salon, Schellingstr. 54 (☎272 07 88). Bavarian *knödel* and billiard balls since 1872. Rack up at the tables where Lenin, Rilke, and Hitler once played, €7 per hr. Traditional German entrees include *weißwurst* with mustard (€3.20) and *beuscherl,* or pig's lung, with *knödel* (€4) for the adventurous. Breakfast €3-5. English-language menu available. Restaurant open M, Th-Su 10am-1am. Cash only. ❶

buxs, Frauenstr. 9 (☎291 9550), on the southern edge of the Viktualienmarkt. A delicious variety of fresh, unique salads, as well as hot foods, soups, and desserts. Sit on the terrace or in the modern, upscale cafe. Everything (excluding drinks) €2 per 100g. Open M-F 11am-6:45pm, Sa 11am-3pm. Cash only. ❸

Poseidon, Westenriederstr. 13 (☎29 92 96), off the Viktualienmarkt. Locals squeeze into this bustling fish market for fresh, sushi-quality seafood. Bowls of *bouillabaisse* with bread €10. Other entrees €4-10. Th special sushi menu €20. Open M-W 8am-6:30pm, Th-F 8am-7pm, Sa 8am-4pm. ❷

Zappeforster, Corneilusstr. 16 (☎20 24 52 50). Walk down Reichenbachstr. with the city center at your back from Marienpl., or take the U-Bahn to Sendlinger Tor or Fraunhoferstr. This lively cafe serves toast (€2.50-3.50) grilled with goat cheese, pears, sundried tomatoes, and more. Daily menu €6-8. Open daily 8am-1am. Cash only. ❶

SIGHTS

RESIDENZ. Down the pedestrian zone from Odeonspl., the ornate rooms of the Residenz (palace) celebrate the wealth left behind by the Wittelsbach dynasty. The **Schatzkammer** (treasury) contains crowns, swords, china, precious stones, and ivory. The **Residenzmuseum** comprises the Wittelsbach apartments and State Rooms, a vast collection of European porcelain, and a 17th-century court chapel. *(Max-Joseph-pl. 3. U3-6 to Odeonspl. ☎29 06 71. Open daily Apr. to mid-Oct. 9am-6pm, Th 9am-8pm; mid-Oct. to Mar. 10am-4pm. Last admission 30min. before closing. Schatzkammer and Residenzmusuem each €6, students €5. Combination ticket €9/8.)*

MARIENPLATZ. The **Mariensäule,** an ornate 1683 monument to the Virgin Mary, commemorates the city's survival of the Thirty Years' War. At the **Neues Rathaus,** the **Glockenspiel** pleases tourists with a display of jousting knights and dancing coopers. At 9pm, a mechanical watchman marches out and the Guardian Angel escorts the *Münchner Kindl* (Munich Child) to bed. *(Daily at 11am, noon, 3pm; in summer also 5pm.)* A sweeping view of the plaza makes the tower of the Neues Rathaus worth a visit. *(Tower open M-F 9am-7pm, Sa-Su 10am-7pm. €2, children 6-18 €1.)* Be wary when passing through Marienpl.: with all the tourists looking upward, pickpockets have a field day.

PETERSKIRCHE AND FRAUENKIRCHE. Across from the Neues Rathaus, the 12th-century Peterskirche is the city's oldest parish church. Scale over 300 steps for a spectacular view of Munich. *(Open M-Sa 9am-7pm, Su 10am-7pm; last admission 6:30pm. Tower €1.50, students €1.)* From the Marienpl., take Kaufingerstr. one block toward the Hauptbahnhof to the onion-domed towers of the 15th-century Frauenkirche—one of Munich's most notable landmarks and an emblem of the city. *(1 Frauenpl. Tower open daily Apr.-Oct. 10am-5pm. €3, students €1.50, under 6 free.)*

ENGLISCHER GARTEN. The vast Englischer Garten (English Garden), Europe's largest public metropolitan park, extends from the city center to its outskirts. On sunny days, all of Munich turns out to bike, play badminton, ride horseback, or swim in the Eisbach. The garden includes a Japanese tea house, a Chinese pagoda, a Greek temple, and German beer gardens. Nude sunbathing areas are designated FKK *(Frei-Körper-Kultur)* on signs and park maps.

SCHLOß NYMPHENBURG. Ludwig I celebrated the birth of his son in 1662 by erecting an elaborate summer playground northwest of the city. Today, the swans of Schloß Nymphenburg have become camera fodder for the hundreds of tourists flocking for the perfect shot. Four manors and several lakes also dot the grounds. In the *Marstallmuseum* (Carriage Museum), learn about the means of 17th-century royal travel. *(Streetcar #17, dir.: Amalienburgstr., to Schloß Nymphenburg. ☎17 90 86 68. All attractions open daily Apr. to mid-Oct. 9am-6pm, Th until 8pm; late Oct. to Mar. 10am-4pm. Museum and Schloß open Tu-Su 9am-noon and 1-5pm. Park open daily May-Aug. 6am-9:30pm; Apr. 6am-8:30pm; Sept. 6am-8pm; Oct. 6am-7pm; Nov.-Mar. 6:30am-6pm. Schloß €5, students €4. Marstallmuseum €4/3. Entire complex €10/8. Park grounds are free.)*

MUSEUMS

Many of Munich's museums require days for exhaustive perusal. The *Münchner Volkshochschule* (☎48 00 62 29) gives tours of many exhibits for €6. A **day pass** to all of Munich's state-owned museums is sold at the tourist office and at many larger museums (€15). All state-owned museums are **discounted on Sunday.**

DEUTSCHES MUSEUM. Even if you don't know (or care) how engines power a Boeing 747, the Deutsches Museum's more than 50 departments on science and technology will still keep you entertained and educated. *(Museuminsel 1. S1-8 to Isartor or streetcar #18 to Deutsches Museum. ☎217 91; www.deutsches-museum.de. Open daily 9am-5pm. English-language tour daily 1:15pm. €7.50, students €3. English-language guidebook €4.)*

PINAKOTHEKE. Designed by *Münchener* Stephan Braunfels, the beautiful Pinakothek der Moderne is four museums in one. Subgalleries display architecture, design, drawings, and paintings by a wide range of artists from Picasso to the latest contemporary works. *(Barerstr. 40. U2 to Königspl. ☎2380 5360. Open Tu-W and Sa-Su 10am-5pm, Th-F 10am-8pm. €9, students €5. Su €1.)* Commissioned in 1826 by King Ludwig I, the **Alte Pinakothek** houses Munich's most precious art, including works by da Vinci, Rembrandt, and Rubens. *(Barerstr. 27. ☎2380 5216. Open Tu 10am-8pm, W-Su 10am-5pm. €5, students €3.50. Su €1.)* Next door, the **Neue Pinakothek** exhibits artists of the 19th and 20th centuries, including Cézanne, Manet, and van Gogh. *(Barerstr. 29. ☎2380 5195. Open M, Th-Su 10am-5pm, W 10am-8pm. €9, students €5; Su €1. Combination ticket for the Alte and Neue Pinakotheke €8/5. Day pass to all 3 €12/7.)*

BMW MUSEUM. This sleek driving museum, housed in a silver globe, displays past, present, and future BMW products. An English-language brochure guides you through the exhibit. *(Am Spindon-Louis-Ring. U3 to Olympiazentrum. Next to the Olympic Tower. ☎382 23 307. Open daily 10am-8pm; last admission 7:30pm. €2, students €1.50.)*

ZAM: ZENTRUM FÜR AUSSERGEWÖHNLICHE MUSEEN. Munich's Center for Unusual Museums corrals such treasures as the Peddle-Car Museum, the Museum of Easter Rabbits, and the Chamberpot Museum. *(Westenriederstr. 41. S1-8 or streetcar #17 or 18 to Isartor. ☎290 41 21. Open daily 10am-6pm. €4, students €3.)*

ENTERTAINMENT

Monatsprogramm (€1.50) and *Munich Found* (€3) list schedules for Munich's stages, museums, and festivals. In July, an **opera festival** arrives at the **Bayerische Staatsoper** (Bavarian National Opera), Max-Joseph-pl. 2. (Tickets ☎21 85 01, info 2185 1919; www.bayerische.staatsoper.de. U3-6 to Odeonspl. or streetcar #19 to Nationaltheater. Standing-room, student tickets €4-10, 1hr. before performances; some shows have these available 2 weeks in advance. Box office for standing-room and student tickets at the theater. Box office at 5 Marstallpl.; call ☎2185 1920; open M-F 10am-6pm, Sa 10am-1pm. No performances Aug. to mid-Sept.)

NIGHTLIFE

Munich's nightlife is a curious conglomerate of Bavarian *gemütlichkeit* (comfort) and trendy cliquishness. A typical night begins at a beer garden or beer hall, which usually closes around midnight, weather depending. Cafes and bars keep the alcohol flowing, shutting off taps at 1am (later on weekends). Discos and dance clubs, sedate before midnight, throb until 4am. Trendy spots line **Leopoldstraße** in **Schwabing**, and clubs cluster in the east, near the Ostbahnhof and Haidhausen. Many venues require partiers to don something other than shorts and a t-shirt.

BEER GARDENS (BIERGÄRTEN)

Munich has six great labels: *Augustiner*, *Hacker-Pschorr*, *Hofbräu*, *Löwenbräu*, *Paulaner*, and *Spaten-Franziskaner*. Most establishments have chosen sides and only serve one brewery's beer. Saying "*Ein Bier, bitte*" will order a *Maß* (liter; €4-6). Specify for only a *halb-Maß* (half-liter; €3-4) or a *Pils* (0.3L; €2-3).

Hirschgarten, Hirschgarten 1 (☎17 25 91). Streetcar #17 (dir.: Amalienburgstr.) to Romanpl., near Schloß Nymphenburg. Seating 9000, Europe's largest beer garden should rather be called a beer park. Vast expanses of grass, trees, and giant chess pieces promise something for everyone. Entrees €2-8 in food stands, €5-17 in the restaurant. *Maß* €5.50. Open daily 10am-midnight; last drink 11:30pm; kitchen closes 10pm. Su brunch starts at 11am. MC/V.

Augustinerkeller, Arnulfstr. 52 (☎59 43 93), at Zirkus-Krone-Str. S1-8 to Hackerbrücke. Many view Augustinerkeller, est. 1824, as the finest beer garden in town for its lush grounds, century-old chestnut trees, and sharp Augustiner beer (*Maß;* €6.40). Open daily 10am-1am. Kitchen open daily 10:30am-10pm.

Hofbräuhaus, Platzl 9 (☎29 01 360), 2 blocks from Marienpl. Come here for the full *Biergarten* experience: this is as jolly, as festive, and as loud as it gets. Go in the early afternoon to avoid tourists. *Maß* €6.20. *Weißwürste* €4.20. Open daily 9am-midnight.

BARS

Günther Murphy's, Nikolaistr. 9a (☎39 89 11). U3 or 6 to Giselastr. Irish cheer accompanies every plateful of Irish and American food (€3-15) in this packed pub, which caters to a mostly English-speaking crowd. Guinness €4.20. Live music and DJs some Th-F nights, Su karaoke, M quiz night. Sa-Su mornings rugby. Open M-Th 6pm-1am, F 6pm-3am, Sa noon-3am, Su noon-1am. AmEx/MC/V.

Café Reitschule, Königinstr. 34 (☎38 88 760). U3 or 6 to Giselastr. In summer a backyard *Biergarten* teems with students around rose-filled fountains. At night, chic clientele socialize over mixed drinks (€6-10). Beer €3.20. Open daily 9am-1am. AmEx/MC/V.

CLUBS

Muffathalle, Zellstr. 4 (☎45 87 50 10; www.muffatwerk.de), in Haidhausen. S1-8 to Rosenheimerpl. and walk toward the river on Rosenheimer Str. for 2 blocks, or take streetcar #18 to Deutsches Museum. A former power plant, Muffathalle now generates techno, rock, hip-hop, jazz, dance, and spoken word performances from local and international artists every night. The entire complex features a concert hall (Muffathalle), cafe, beer garden, and club. Cover usually €5-20, depending on venue. Advance tickets available online. Beer garden open May-Sept. Muffathalle open daily 7 or 8pm depending on performance, until 2-3am Su-Th and as late as 5-6am F-Sa.

Backstage, Friedenheimer Brücke 7 (☎12 66 100; www.backstage089.de). Streetcar #16 or 17 to Steubenpl. or #18 or 19 to Lautensackstr. An outdoors underground scene playing hardcore, indie rock, and electronica. 2 concert stages and a beer garden with weekly themes like "indiegarten." *Maß* €3.80 from 7-11pm. F movie nights. Check online or call for concert listings. Open M-Th, Su 7pm-3am, F-Sa 7pm-5am.

GLBT NIGHTLIFE

Despite Bavaria's reputation for being unwelcoming to homosexuality, gay nightlife thrives in Munich. The gay scene centers in the **Glockenbachviertel,** stretching from south of Sendlinger Tor through the Viktualienmarkt/Gärtnerpl. area to the Isartor. *Our Munich,* a gay and lesbian leaflet, is available at the tourist office.

Bei Carla, Buttermelcherstr. 9 (☎22 79 01). S1-8 to Isartor. Walk south on Zweibrückenstr., then turn right on Rumfordstr., left on Klenzestr., and left again onto Buttermelcherstr. A friendly lesbian cafe and bar. Open M-Sa 4pm-1am, Su 6pm-1am.

Cafe Nil, Hans-Sachs-Str. 2 (☎26 55 45). U1 or 2 to Fraunhofer Str. Turn right out of the U-Bahn down Klenzestr., right on Ickstattstr., and right on Hans-Sachs-Str. Casual cafe for gay men in their 20s and 30s. Entrees €5-12. Open daily 3pm-3am. AmEx/MC/V.

DAYTRIP FROM MUNICH: DACHAU

"*Arbeit Macht Frei*" (Work Will Set You Free) was the first thing prisoners saw as they passed through the gate of the **Jourhaus** on the way to Dachau, where over 206,000 "undesirables" were interned between 1933 and 1945. Dachau was a work camp, rather than a death camp like Auschwitz; knowing the Allies would not bomb prisoners, the SS used it for the construction of armaments. The walls, gates, and the crematorium were restored in 1962 and form a memorial to the victims. Located in the former administrative buildings, the **museum** examines pre-1930s anti-Semitism, the rise of Nazism, the concentration camp system, and the lives of prisoners through a gathering of photographs, newspapers, documents, and other artifacts. Most exhibits have English captions; a lengthy guide (€15) translates the propaganda posters, SS files, documents, and letters. A **short film** (22min.) screens in English at 11:30am, 2, and 3:30pm. Displays in the **Bunker,** the former prison and torture chamber, chronicle prisoners' lives and the barbarism of SS guards. Two English-language **tours** depart from the museum: 30min. museum tours (June-Aug. M-F 12:30pm, Sa-Su also 11am; Sept.-May Sa-Su 12:30pm; €1.50) and 2½hr. tours of the memorial. (June-Aug. M-F 1:30pm, Sa-Su also noon; Sept.-May Sa-Su 1:30pm. €3.) Take the S2 (dir.: Petershausen) to Dachau (20min.; €4 or 4 strips on the Streifenkarte). Then take bus #724 (dir.: Kräutergarten) or 726 (dir.: Saubachsiedlung) to KZ-Gedenkstätte (10min.; €1 or 1 strip on the Streifenkarte). The memorial site is open Tuesday through Sunday 9am-5pm.

GARMISCH-PARTENKIRCHEN ☎08821

Garmisch-Partenkirchen (pop. 28,000) is situated at the foot of the **Zugspitze** (2964m), Germany's highest peak. The peak should only be attempted in fair weather. To get there, take the **cog railway** from the **Zugspitzbahnhof,** behind the main train station, to Eibsee (1¼hr., every hr. 8:15am-2:15pm; return every hr. 9:30am-4:30pm), then continue on the **Gletscherbahn** or even steeper **Eibsee Seilbahn** cable car to the top (4-10min., every 30min. 8am-4:45pm, round-trip with train and either cable car €44). Climbers can skip the railways and make the ascent in 10-12hr., but only very experienced hikers should attempt the two-day trek.

To reach **Naturfreundehaus ❶,** Schalmeiweg 21, from the station, walk straight on Bahnhofstr. as it becomes Ludwigstr., follow the bend to the right and turn left on Sonnenbergstr.; continue as it becomes Prof.-Michael-Sachs-Str. and then Schalmeiweg (30min.). (☎43 22; naturfreunde-forelle@t-online.de. Kitchen use €0.50. Breakfast €4. Sleepsack €2. Reception 6-8pm. 10- to 17-bed dorms €8; 3- to 5-bed rooms €10; 1-night stays add €0.60. Cash only.) **Trains** run to Innsbruck (1½hr., every 2hr., €11.90) and Munich (1½hr., every hr., €14.70). **Buses** #9651 and 9606 run to Füssen (2hr., 3 per day, €8). To reach the **tourist office,** Richard-Strauss-Pl. 2, turn left on Bahnhofstr. from the train station and left again onto Von-Brug-Str.; it's the pink building. The staff distributes maps and finds rooms at no charge. (☎18 07 00. Open M-Sa 8am-6pm, Su 10am-noon.) **Postal Code:** 82467..

THE REAL DEAL. As a 50th birthday gift, the Nazi party built Adolf Hitler a mountain retreat near Berchtesgaden. Hitler, who is reputed to have been afraid of heights, rarely visited the **Eagle's Nest,** the name under which the resort has entered into popular tourist mythology. The resort no longer exists, having been built over by an expensive restaurant. Despite all this, the site remains a tourist draw. While the region around Berchtesgaden boasts excellent hiking opportunities and the views are hard to beat, the Eagle's Nest is probably best left off the itinerary of those looking for any meaningful insight into the man it was built for.

PASSAU ☎0851

Baroque arches cast long shadows across the cobblestone alleys of Passau (pop. 51,000), a two-millennium-old city situated at the confluence of the Danube, the Inn, and the Ilz rivers. Passau's crowning attraction is the Baroque **Stephansdom,** Dompl., where the world's largest church organ looms above the choir. (Open daily in summer 6:30am-7pm; low season 6:30am-6pm. Tours Apr.-Oct. M-F 10:30am, 2:30pm, Sa-Su 2:30pm; Nov.-Mar. daily noon; Christmas week daily 12:30pm. Church free. Tours €3, students €1.50.) Behind the cathedral is the **Residenz,** home to the **Domschatz,** an extravagant collection of tapestries and gold. Enter through the back of the Stephansdom, to the right of the altar. (☎39 33 74. Open Easter-Oct. M-Sa 10am-4pm. €2.50, students €1.50.) Over the Luitpoldbrücke is the former palace of the bishopric, **Veste Oberhaus,** now home to the **Cultural History Museum.** A shuttle bus runs every 30min. between the Rathaus and the museum during opening hours. (Open early Mar. to early Nov. M-F 9am-5pm, Sa-Su 10am-6pm; Dec.-Mar. Tu-Su 9am-5pm. €5, students €4.)

In a castle above the Danube, the **Jugendherberge (HI) ❷,** Veste Oberhaus 125, has playroom-like dorms and tons of school groups to match. Catch the Veste Oberhaus bus during museum hours, or prepare for a 30min. walk from the station. Cross the bridge downstream from the Rathaus and follow the signs up the mountain. (☎49 37 80. Breakfast included. Internet €0.50 per 20min. Reception 7-11am and 4-8pm. Dorms €21.55. €3 HI discount. MC/V.) Good, cheap places to eat fill the student district around **Innstraße,** parallel to the Inn River. Get meat, baked goods, sandwiches, and salads at **Schmankerl Passage,** Ludwigstr. 6. (Open M-F 7:30am-6pm, Sa 7:30am-4pm.) **Norma** supermarket, Bahnhofstr. 16b, has groceries. (Open M-F 8:30am-7pm, Sa 8am-2pm.) Students descend upon the lively **Cafe-Bar Uferlos,** 12 Gottfriedstr., for special theme nights and deals with the movie theater next door. (M 8pm mixed drinks €3.90, students and movie-goers €3.30. Open M, W-Th 8pm-3am, F-Sa 10pm-3am.)

Trains depart for: Frankfurt (4½hr., every 2hr., €35); Munich (2hr., 1-2 per hr., €26); Nuremberg (2hr., 1 per hr., €25); Regensburg (1-2hr., 1 per hr., €17); Vienna (3½hr., 1 per hr., €35). To get to the **tourist office,** Rathauspl. 3, follow Bahnhofstr. from the train station to Ludwigspl., then bear left downhill to Ludwigstr., which becomes Rindermarkt, Steinweg, and finally Große Messerg.; continue straight on Schusterg. and turn left on Schrottg. (☎95 59 80. Open Easter-Oct. M-F 8:30am-6pm, Sa-Su 9am-4pm, Oct. weekdays until 4pm; low season M-Th 8:30am-5pm, F 8:30am-4pm.) **Postal Code:** 94032.

NUREMBERG (NÜRNBERG) ☎0911

Before it witnessed the fanaticism of Hitler's massive Nazi rallies, Nuremberg (pop. 491,000) hosted Imperial Diets in the first *Reich*. Today, the remnants of both regimes draw visitors to the city, which new generations have rechristened *Stadt der Menschenrechte* (City of Human Rights). Locally, the city is known more for its Christmas market, toy fairs, sausages, and gingerbread than for its politics.

TRANSPORTATION AND PRACTICAL INFORMATION. **Trains** go to: Berlin (5hr., every 2hr., €64); Frankfurt (2½hr., 1-4 per hr., €37); Munich (1½hr., 2 per hr., €38); Stuttgart (2hr., every 2hr., €32). DB Reisezentrum, located in the central hall of the station, sells tickets. (Open M-F 6am-9pm, Sa-Su 8am-9pm. AmEx/MC/V.) The **tourist office,** Königstr. 93, books rooms for free. Walk through the tunnel from the station to the *Altstadt* (old town) and take a right. (☎233 61 31. Open M-Sa 9am-7pm. MC/V.) **Internet** is available at **Tele Point** on the underground level of the train station, heading toward the old town. (€1 per hr. Open daily 8am-11pm.) On the second floor of the train station, **Flat-S** charges exorbitant rates. (☎815 7521. €1 per 15min., €5 per 3 hr. Open 24hr.) **Postal Code:** 90402.

ACCOMMODATIONS AND FOOD. **Jugendgästehaus (HI) ❷,** Burg 2, sits in a castle above the city. From the tourist office, follow Königstr. through Lorenzerpl. and over the bridge to the Hauptmarkt, head toward the fountain

GERMANY

on the left, and right on Burgstr. (☎230 9360. Breakfast €3.80. Reception 7am-1am. Dorms €19-28; singles €38; doubles €45. MC/V.) The quirkily named rooms of **Lette'm Sleep ❷**, 42 Frauentormauer, are only a short walk away from the train station. Take the first left immediately after entering the old town through Königpl. (☎992 8128. Linen €3. Free Internet. Reception 24hr. 8-bed women-only dorms €16; 6-bed co-ed dorms €17; 4- to 5-bed €18; doubles €44; triples €20.) In the southwestern corner of the *Altstadt*, **Zum Gulden Stern ❷**, Zirkelschmiedg. 26, is the world's oldest bratwurst kitchen. (☎205 9298. 6 for €6. Other entrees €5-10. Open daily 11am-10pm. AmEx/MC/V.) Cheaper Frankish fare can be found at **Bratwursthäusle ❶**, Rathausp. 1. Goods to go include three *rostbratwurst* in a *weckla* (roll) for €1.80 and *spargel* (white asparagus) for €4. (☎22 76 95. Eat-in entrees €3-8. Open daily 10am-11pm. Cash only.) **Super Markt Straub**, Hauptmarkt 12, is near the Frauenkirche. (Open M-F 8:30am-7pm, Sa 8am-4pm.)

SIGHTS AND ENTERTAINMENT. Allied bombing left little of old Nuremberg untouched, but its churches, castle, and other buildings have been reconstructed. The walled-in **Handwerkerhof** near the station is more mall than medieval; head up Königstr. for the real sights. Take a detour to the left for the pillared **Straße der Menschenrechte** (Avenue of Human Rights) as well as the gleaming glass **Germanisches Nationalmuseum**, Kartäuserg. 1, which chronicles German art since prehistoric times. (☎133 10. Open Tu-Su 10am-6pm, W 10am-9pm. €5, students €4. W 6-9pm free.) Across the river is the **Hauptmarktplatz**, site of the annual **Christmas market.** Hidden in the fence of the **Schöner Brunnen** (Beautiful Fountain) in the Hauptmarkt is a seamless golden ring; spinning it brings good luck. Walk uphill to the **Rathaus**, Rathauspl. 2; the **Lochgefängnisse** (dungeons) beneath contain medieval torture instruments. (☎231 2690. Open 10am-4:30pm M-F Feb.-Mar. 18 and Nov.-Dec.; Tu-Su Mar. 19-Oct.; daily Nov. 25-Dec. 23. Tours every hr. €3, students €1.50.) Atop the hill, the **Kaiserburg** (Fortress of the Holy Roman Emperor) looms over Nuremberg as a symbol of the city. (Open daily Apr.-Sept. 9am-6pm; Oct.-Mar. 10am-4pm. Required tours in German every hr. €6, students €5.)

The ruins of **Reichsparteitagsgelände**, site of the Nazi Party Congress rallies, remind visitors of Nuremberg's darker history. On the far side of the lake is the **Tribüne**, the marble platform where throngs gathered to hear Hitler. The Fascination and Terror exhibit, in the **Kongresshalle** at the north end of the park, covers the Nazi era. (☎231 56 66. Open M-F 9am-6pm, Sa-Su 10am-6pm. €5, students €2.50.) Tram #9 from the train station stops directly at the Kongresshalle (Dokumentationszentrum stop). To reach the Tribüne (or Zeppelinwiese), walk around the lake from the Kongresshalle or take S2 (dir.: Feucht/Altdorf) to Dutzendteich, then take the middle of three exits, go down the stairs, and turn left. Nazi leaders faced Allied judges during the Nuremberg war crimes trials on the other side of town, in Room 600 of the **Justizgebäude**, Fürtherstr. 110. (Take U1 to Bärenschanze. English-language tours Sa-Su 1, 2, 3, 4pm. €2, students €1.)

Nuremberg's nightspots cluster in the *Altstadt*, especially by the river in the west. **Cine Città**, Gewerbemuseumspl. 3 (U-Bahn to Wöhrder Wiese), packs in 16 bars and cafes, 17 cinemas, an IMAX, and a disco. (Infoline ☎206 667, reservations 206 666. Open M-Th, Su until 1am, F-Sa until 3am.) **Wies'n Biergarten**, on Johann Sörgel Weg in the Wöhrder Wiese, is next to a gigantic grass field where students pretend to study. (☎240 6668. *Maß* €4.10. Open daily May-Sept. 10am-10pm.) **Cartoon**, An der Sparkasse 6, is a popular gay bar near Lorenzpl. (☎227 170. 0.4L beer €3. Open Su-Th 11am-1am, 3am if they're busy; F-Sa 11am to 3 or 5am.)

ROMANTIC ROAD

Groomed fields of sunflowers, vineyards, and hills checker the landscape between Würzburg and Füssen. Its beauty was not lost on the German tourist industry, which christened the area the Romantic Road *(Romantische Straße)* in 1950, helping to make it the most traveled route in Germany.

TRANSPORTATION

Train travel is the most flexible and economical way to see the Romantic Road. **Europabus** also has a variety of routes; up-to-date reservations and schedule info can be found at www.touring.de or www.romantischestrasse.de. There is a 10% student and under-26 discount, and a 60% Eurail and German Railpass discount.

ROTHENBURG OB DER TAUBER ☎09861

Possibly the only walled medieval city without a single modern building, Rothenburg (pop. 12,000) is *the* Romantic Road stop. After the Thirty Years' War, the town had no money to modernize and remained unchanged for 250 years. Tourism, when it came, brought economic stability and only more reasons to keep the medieval *Altstadt* (old town). The English-language tour led by the **night watchman** gives an entertaining introduction to tidbits about Rothenburg's history. (Starts at the Rathaus on Marktpl. Easter-Christmas daily 8pm. €20.) A long climb up the narrow stairs of the 60m **Rathaus Tower** leads to a panoramic view of the town and valley. (Open Apr.-Oct. daily 9:30am-12:30pm and 1-5pm; Dec. daily noon-3pm; Nov. and Jan.-Mar. Sa-Su noon-3pm; €1.) Anyone who can stomach the thought of iron-maiden justice should inspect the torture instruments at the **Medieval Crime Museum,** Burgg. 3-5. (Open daily Apr.-Oct. 9:30am-6pm; Nov. and Jan.-Feb. 2-4:15pm; Dec. and Mar. 10am-4:15pm. Last entry 45min. before closing. €3.50, university students €2.30.) Occupying the polar opposite slot on the horror spectrum is the cheerful **Weihnachtsdorf** (Christmas Village), Herrng. 1, a museum documenting the history of gift giving. (☎409 365. Open Apr.-Dec. daily 10am-5:30pm; Jan.-Mar. Sa-Su 10am-5:30pm. €4, students €2.50.)

Many private rooms (€15-45) do not register at the tourist office; to find these, look for the *"Zimmer frei"* (free room) signs that many restaurants and stores sport. Antique furniture at **Gästehaus Raidel ❷,** Wengg. 3, makes you feel as if you're sleeping in the past, but spotless modern bathrooms break the illusion. (☎31 15. Breakfast included. Singles €19, with bath €39; doubles €39/49. Cash only.) The sparkling rooms at **Hotel Garni Uhl ❷,** Plönlein 8, have a fantastic view of the valley. (☎48 95. Breakfast €10. Reception 7am-10pm. Singles €22; doubles €44. MC/V.) **Trains** run to Steinach (15min., 1 per hr., €1.80), which has transfers to Munich and Würzburg. The **Europabus** leaves from the Busbahnhof by the train station. The **tourist office,** Marktpl. 2, books rooms and offers free **Internet.** (☎404 800. Open May-Oct. M-F 9am-noon and 1-6pm, Sa-Su 10am-3pm; Nov.-Apr. M-F 9am-noon and 1-5pm, Sa 10am-1pm.) **Postal Code:** 91541.

WÜRZBURG ☎0931

Surrounded by vineyards, the university town of Würzburg retains much of its medieval feel, but its student population and the bars that serve them keep the *Altstadt* (old town) humming with energy late into the night. The Main River flows through the town; visit the ancient stone bridge at sunset for a luminous view of both the Gothic steeples and the striking fortress high above. Inside the **Fortress Marienburg** are the 11th-century **Marienkirche,** the 40m **Bergfried watchtower,** above the Hole of Fear dungeon, and the **Fürstengarten,** built to resemble a ship. (Bus #9 from the station to Festung, or a 20min. walk up the hill. Tours Apr.-Oct. Tu-F 11am, 2, 3pm, Sa-Su every hr. 10am-4pm except noon. Tours €3, students €2.50. Fortress free.) The **Residenz** houses the largest ceiling fresco in the world, by Tiepolo, but will be undergoing restoration until late 2006. Other rooms offer a riot of Rococo stuccoed ceilings and plump cherubs.

The airy dorms and comfortable beds of **Babelfish Hostel ❷**, Prymstr. 3, are very convenient; with your back to the train station, turn left on Haugering and walk about 7min. until the grinning fish sign. (☎304 0430. Free lockers. Linen €2.50. Free Internet. Reception 7am-11pm. Curfew 11pm, but key available with €15 deposit. Dorms €16-22.) **Cafe Uni ❶**, Neubaustr. 2, at Augustinerstr., caters to a lively student crowd with sandwiches, burgers, and toasted baguettes (€2-3). Stuff yourself on the €6 Greek menu Monday through Friday 8am-6pm. (☎156 72. Wireless Internet €3. Open M-Sa 8am-1am, Su 9am-1am. Cash only.)

Trains run to: Frankfurt (1hr., 2-3 per hr., €19); Munich (3hr., 2-5 per hr., €35); Nuremberg (1hr., 2-3 per hr., €11); Rothenburg ob der Tauber (1hr., 1 per hr., €11). The **tourist office,** in a yellow building on Marktpl., has maps and room info. (☎37 23 98. Open Apr.-Dec. M-F 10am-6pm, Sa 10am-2pm; May-Oct. M-F, Su 10am-2pm; Jan.-Mar. M-F 10am-4pm, Sa 10am-1pm.) **Postal Code:** 97070.

FÜSSEN ☎08362

Füssen, which means "feet" in German, seems an apt name for this little town at the foot of the Romantic Road and in the foothills of the Bavarian Alps. Füssen's main attraction is its proximity to Ludwig's famed **Königsschlößer** (below), best seen as a daytrip. Above the pedestrian district, the town's own **Hohes Schloß** (High Castle) features arresting *trompe-l'oeil* windows and towers in its inner courtyard. (Open Tu-Su Apr.-Oct. 11am-4pm; Nov.-Mar. 2-4pm. Castle free.) Inside the **Kloster St. Mang,** the **Annakapelle** holds macabre paintings depicting everyone from the pope to the smallest child caught up in the dance of death *(Totentanz)*, a frenzy of despair that overtook Europe during the plague. Entrance to the Annakapelle is included in the ticket to the **Stadtmuseum,** which explores Füssen's history. (Open Tu-Su Apr.-Oct. 10am-5pm; Nov.-Mar. 1-4pm. €2.50, students €2.)

Turn right from the station and follow the railroad tracks for 15min. to reach the **Jugendherberge (HI) ❷,** Mariahilfer Str. 5. (☎77 54. Laundry €3.20. Reception 7am-noon and 5-11pm; Oct.-Apr. 5-10pm. €2 locker deposit. Dorms €16.15, additional nights €15.55. MC/V.) The salad (€1 per 100g) and entree (€1.45 per 100g) buffet at **Frisch Misch ❷,** Ritterstr. 6, guarantees a "fresh mix" on your plate. (☎91 60 20. Open M-F 11am-6pm, Sa 11am-2pm. AmEx/DC/MC/V.) **Trains** run to Munich (2hr., 7am-5pm every 2hr., €18.80). Füssen can also be reached by bus #9651 or 9606 from Garmisch-Partenkirchen (2¼hr.; 9:35am, 12:35, 4:25pm; €8). To reach the **tourist office** from the train station, Kaiser-Maximilian-Pl. 1, walk the length of Bahnhofstr. and head across the roundabout to the big yellow building on your left; the staff sells hiking maps (€4-7) and finds rooms for no commission. (☎938 50. Open in summer M-F 9am-6pm, Sa 10am-2pm, Su 10am-noon; winter M-F 10am-4pm, Sa 10am-noon.) **Postal Code:** 87629.

KÖNIGSSCHLÖßER (ROYAL CASTLES)

King Ludwig II, a lunatic visionary and fervent Wagner fan, used his cash to turn his passions into fantastic castles. In 1886, a band of nobles and bureaucrats deposed Ludwig, declared him insane, and imprisoned him; three days later, the king and a loyal advisor were mysteriously discovered dead in a nearby lake. The fairy-tale castles that framed Ludwig's life and the enigma of his death still captivate tourists today. The gorgeous **Schloß Neuschwanstein** inspired Disney's Cinderella Castle. Its completed chambers—63 remain unfinished—include a Byzantine throne room, an artificial grotto, and an immense *Sängersaal* (Singer's Hall) built expressly for Wagnerian operas. Hike 10min. up to **Marienbrücke,** a bridge that spans the gorge and waterfall behind the castle, for the fairy godmother of all views. Climb the mountain on the other side of the bridge if you prefer enchantment without the crowds. Ludwig spent his summers in the bright yellow, neo-Gothic **Schloß Hohenschwangau** across the valley. Tickets can be purchased at the **Ticket-Service Center,** Alpseestr. 12, about 100m uphill from the Hohenschwangau bus stop. Arrive early to avoid lines. (☎93 08 30. Both castles open daily Apr.-Sept. 9am-6pm, ticket sales 8am-5pm; Oct.-Mar. castles 10am-4pm, tickets 9am-3pm; Hohenschwangau ticket sales close 30min. later. Mandatory tours each €9, students €8; English available. Combination ticket €17/15.)

Depart from the Füssen train station on **bus** #73, 78, 9696, or 9651, all marked "Castles" (10min., 2 per hr., round-trip €3.10). Hop off in front of the **info booth** (open daily 9am-6pm). Separate paths lead to Hohenschwangau and Neuschwanstein. A *Tagesticket* (€5.60, bought on bus) provides a day of regional bus use.

GREECE (Έλλας)

A land where sacred monasteries are mountainside fixtures, 3hr. seaside siestas are standard issue, and circle dancing and drinking until daybreak is a summer rite: Greece's treasures are impossibly varied. Renaissance men long before the Renaissance, the ancient Greeks sprung to prominence with their philosophical, literary, artistic, and athletic mastery. The all-encompassing Greek lifestyle is a frustratingly delicious mix of high speed and sun-inspired lounging, as old men hold lively debates in town *plateias*, young kids zoom on mopeds around the clock, and unpredictable schedules force a go-with-the-flow take on life.

DISCOVER GREECE: SUGGESTED ITINERARIES

THREE DAYS Spend it all in **Athens** (p. 485). Roam the **Acropolis,** gaze at the treasures of the **National Archaeological Museum,** and pay homage at the **Parthenon.** Visit the ancient **Agora,** then take a trip down to **Poseidon's Temple** at Cape Sounion.

ONE WEEK Begin your week with a sojourn in **Athens** (3 days). Move on to **Corinth** to wander through the **Temple of Apollo** (1 day; p. 498). Sprint to **Olympia** to see where the games began (1 day; p. 495). Take the ferry to **Corfu** (1 day; p. 505) then soak up Byzantine history in **Thessaloniki** (1 day; p. 498).

BEST OF GREECE, THREE WEEKS Explore **Athens** (4 days) before visiting the mansions of **Nafplion** (1 day; p. 496). Race west to **Olympia** (1 day), then take a ferry from **Patras** to the beaches of **Corfu** (2 days). Back on the mainland, wander through **Thessaloniki** (2 days), then climb to the cliffside monasteries of **Meteora** (1 day; p. 503). Consult the gods at **Mount Olympus** (1 day; p. 502) and the Oracle of **Delphi** (1 day). On **Crete** (3 days; p. 511), hike Europe's largest gorge. Seek rest on **Santorini** (1 day; p. 511), debauchery on **Ios** (1 day; p. 510), and sun on **Mykonos** (1 day; p. 508).

ESSENTIALS

FACTS AND FIGURES

Official Name: Hellenic Republic.
Capital: Athens.
Major Cities: Thessaloniki, Patras.
Population: 10,600,000.
Land Area: 131,940 sq. km.
Time: GMT +2.
Language: Greek.
Religion: Eastern Orthodox (98%).

WHEN TO GO

June through August is high season in Greece; consider visiting during May, early June, or September, when gorgeous weather smiles on thinner crowds. The low season brings cheaper lodgings and food prices, but many sights and accommodations have shorter hours or close altogether. Ferries, buses, and trains run considerably less frequently, and life is quieter in general.

DOCUMENTS AND FORMALITIES

EMBASSIES. Foreign embassies in Greece are in Athens (p. 485). Greek embassies abroad include: **Australia,** 9 Turrana St., Yarralumla, Canberra, ACT 2600 (☎2 6273 3011); **Canada,** 80 MacLaren St., Ottawa, ON K2P 0K6 (☎613-238-6271; www.greekembassy.ca); **Ireland,** 1 Upper Pembroke St., Dublin 2 (☎1 676 7254); **New Zealand,** 5-7 Willeston St., 10th fl., Box 24066, Wellington (☎4 473 7775); **the UK,** 1a Holland Park, London W11 3TP (☎020 7229 3850; www.greekembassy.org.uk); and **US,** 2221 Massachusetts Ave. NW, Washington, D.C. 20008 (☎202-939-1306; www.greekembassy.org).

VISA AND ENTRY INFORMATION. EU citizens do not need a visa. Citizens of **Australia, Canada, New Zealand,** and the **US** do not need a visa for stays of up to 90 days, beginning on entry into any of the countries in the EU's freedom of movement zone. Contact your Greek embassy to apply for a visa to work or study in Greece.

TRANSPORTATION

BY PLANE. Most international flights land in Athens (ATH; ☎210 353 0000; www.aia.gr), though some lines also serve Corfu (CFU), Heraklion (HER), Kos (KSG), and Thessaloniki (SKG). **Olympic Airways,** Syngrou 96-100, Athens 11741 (☎21092 69 111; www.olympicairlines.com), offers extensive domestic service. Their website lists info for every office around the globe. A 1hr. flight from Athens (€60-90) can get you to almost any island in Greece. Even in the low season, remote destinations are serviced several times a week, while developed areas may have several flights per day.

BY TRAIN. Greece is served by a number of international train routes that connect Athens, Larisa, and Thessaloniki to most European cities. Train service within Greece, however, is limited and sometimes uncomfortable, and no lines go to the western coast. The new express, air-conditioned, intercity trains, while slightly more expensive and less frequent, are worth the price. **Eurail** passes are valid on all Greek trains. **Hellenic Railways Organization** (OSE; www.osenet.gr) connects Athens to major Greek cities; in Greece, call ☎210 529 7002 for schedules and prices.

BY BUS. There are almost no buses running directly from any European city to Greece. **Busabout,** 258 Vauxhall Bridge Rd., London SW1V 1BS (☎020 7950 1661; www.busabout.com), is one of the few European bus companies that runs to Greece. Domestic bus service is extensive and fares are cheap. **KTEL** (www.ktel.org) operates most domestic buses; always check with an official source about scheduled departures, as posted schedules are often outdated.

BY FERRY. The most popular way of getting to Greece is by ferry from Italy. Boats travel from Brindisi in Italy, to Corfu (p. 505), Kephalonia (p. 505), and Patras (p. 494) and from Ancona, Italy, to Corfu and Patras. Ferries also run from Greece to various points on the Turkish coast. There is frequent ferry service to the Greek islands, but schedules are irregular and faulty information is common. Check schedules posted at the tourist office or the port police, or at www.ferries.gr. Make reservations and arrive at least 1hr. before your departure time. **Hellas Flying Dolphins** (www.dolphins.gr) provides hydrofoil service between the islands at twice the cost and speed of ferries.

BY CAR AND MOPED. You must be 18 to drive in Greece, and 21 to rent a car; some agencies require renters to be at least 23 or 25. Ferries charge a transport fee for cars. Rental agencies may quote low daily rates that exclude the 18% tax and

Collision Damage Waiver (CDW) insurance; expect to pay €30-60 per day for a rental. Foreign drivers are required to have an **International Driving Permit** and an **International Insurance Certificate** to drive in Greece. The **Automobile and Touring Club of Greece (ELPA),** Messogion 395, Athens 15343, provides assistance and offers reciprocal membership to foreign auto club members. (☎21060 68 800, 24hr. emergency roadside assistance ☎104, Infoline for Athens ☎174, elsewhere ☎21060 68 838; www.elpa.gr. Open M-F 7am-3pm.) Mopeds can be great for exploring, but they are also extremely dangerous; wear a helmet.

TOURIST SERVICES AND MONEY

EMERGENCY **Police:** ☎100. **Hospital:** ☎106. **Ambulance:** ☎166.

TOURIST OFFICES. Two national organizations oversee tourism in Greece: **Greek National Tourist Organization (GNTO)** and the **tourist police** *(touristiki astinomia)*. The GNTO, Tsoha 7, Athens (☎2108 70 7000; www.gnto.gr), known as the **EOT** in Greece, can supply general information about sights and accommodations throughout the country. The tourist police deal with local and immediate problems such as bus schedules, accommodations, and lost passports. Offices are open long hours and are willing to help, but English may be limited.

MONEY. The official currency of Greece is the **euro (€).** For exchange rates and more information on the euro, see p. 19. If you're carrying more than €1000 in cash when you enter Greece, you must declare it upon entry. As a general rule, it's cheaper to convert money in Greece than at home. When changing money in Greece, try to go to a bank (τράπεζα; TRAH-peh-za) that has at most a 5% margin between its buy and sell prices. A bare-bones day in Greece costs €40-50. A day with more comforts runs €50-65. There is a 13% **gratuity** included in all restaurant prices; tipping is unnecessary. **Taxi** drivers do not expect tips. Generally, **bargaining** is expected for street wares and in other informal venues, but when in doubt, wait and watch to avoid offending merchants. Bargaining is also common in *domatia* (rooms to let) and small hotels, as well as for unmetered taxi rides. There is a **Value Added Tax (VAT)** of 16% on goods and services sold in mainland Greece, and 11.5% in the Aegean islands. VAT is included in the listed price. Travelers from non-EU countries who spend more than €120 in one shop in one day may be entitled to a VAT refund upon leaving Greece. Claiming your refund can involve complicated paperwork; ask about VAT when making substantial purchases and be sure to save your receipts. For more info, see p. 23.

KEEPING IN TOUCH

PHONE CODES	**Country code:** 30. **International dialing prefix:** 00. For more information on how to place international calls, see inside back cover.

EMAIL AND THE INTERNET. The availability of the Internet in Greece is rapidly expanding. In all big cities, most small cities and large towns, and on most islands, you'll be able to find Internet cafes. Expect to pay €3-6 per hour.

TELEPHONE. Pay phones in Greece use prepaid phone cards. You can buy the cards at streetside kiosks *(peripteros)* in denominations of €3, €12, and €25. Time is measured in minutes or talk units (100 units=30min. of domestic calling). A calling card is the cheapest way to make international phone calls. Mobile phones are an increasingly popular option; for more info, see p. 33.

MAIL. To send a letter anywhere from Greece weighing up to 20g costs €0.65. Mail sent to Greece from the continent generally takes at least three days to arrive; from Australia, New Zealand, and the US airmail will take up to two weeks. Address mail to be held for you at a Greek post office according to the following example: First name SURNAME, Corfu Town Post Office, Corfu, Greece 8900, POSTE RESTANTE.

LANGUAGE. To the non-Greek speaker, the intricate levels of nuance, idiom, irony, and poetry in the language can present a seemingly impenetrable wall to understanding. The Greek language (Ελληνικά, eh-lee-nee-KAH) is one of the most difficult languages for English speakers to learn fluently, but learning enough to order a meal, send a postcard, and get to the airport is surprisingly easy. Greek is obsessively phonetic—though a cursory knowledge of the Greek alphabet (p. 1056) does not always help with the many double consonants and double vowels—and all multisyllabic words come with a handy accent called a *tonos*, which marks the emphasized syllable. Greeks are famously welcoming of foreigners who try their hand at the language, but many Greeks—and certainly most working in the tourist industry—will understand English. For useful phrases, see **Phrasebook: Greek,** p. 1061.

ACCOMMODATIONS AND CAMPING

GREECE	❶	❷	❸	❹	❺
ACCOMMODATIONS	under €17	€17-28	€28-40	€40-60	above €60

Local tourist offices usually maintain lists of inexpensive accommodations. A bed in a **hostel** averages around €15-25. Those not currently endorsed by HI are in most cases still safe and reputable. In many areas, **domatia** (rooms to let) are an attractive and dependable option. Often you'll be approached by locals as you enter town or disembark from your boat, a practice that is common but illegal. Prices vary; expect to pay €20-30 for a single and €25-45 for a double. Always negotiate with *domatia* owners before settling on a price, and never pay more than you would for a hotel in town. If in doubt, ask the tourist police; they may set you up with a room and conduct the negotiations themselves. **Hotel** prices are regulated, but proprietors may try to push you to take the most expensive room. Budget hotels start at €20 for singles and €30 for doubles. Check your bill carefully, and threaten to contact the tourist police if you think you are being cheated. Greece has plenty of official **campgrounds,** which run €4-8 per person, plus €2-3 per tent. Camping on public beaches—sometimes illegal—is common in July and August but may not be the safest option.

FOOD AND DRINK

GREECE	❶	❷	❸	❹	❺
FOOD	under €4	€4-9	€9-16	€16-25	above €25

Penny-pinching carnivores will thank Zeus for lamb, chicken, or pork *souvlaki,* stuffed into a pita to make *gyros* (YEE-ro). Vegetarians can also eat their fill on the cheap; options include *horiatiki* (Greek salad) and savory pastries like *tiropita* (cheese pie) and *spanakopita* (spinach and feta pie). Frothy, iced coffee frappes take the edge off the summer heat. *Ouzo* (a powerful, licorice-flavored spirit) is served with *mezedes* (snacks of octopus, cheese, and sausage). Breakfast, served only in the early morning, is generally very simple: a piece of toast with *marmelada* or a pastry. Lunch, a hearty and leisurely meal, can begin as early as noon but is more likely eaten sometime between 2 and 5pm. Dinner is a drawn-out, relaxed affair served late. Greek restaurants are known as *taverna* or *estiatorio;* a grill is a *psistaria.* Many restaurants don't offer printed menus.

HOLIDAYS AND FESTIVALS

Holidays: Feast of St. Basil/New Year's Day (Jan. 1); Epiphany (Jan. 6); Clean Monday, First day of Lent (Mar. 6); Greek Independence Day (Mar. 25); St. George's Day (Apr. 23); Easter (Apr. 23); Labor Day (May 1); Ascension (June 1); Pentecost (June 11); Feast of the Assumption of the Virgin Mary (Aug. 15); The Virgin Mary's Birthday (Sept. 8); Feast of St. Demetrius (Oct. 26); Ohi Day (Oct. 28).

Festivals: 3 weeks of Carnival feasting and dancing (starting Feb. 12) precede Lenten fasting. April 23 is St. George's Day, when Greece honors the dragon-slaying knight with horse races, wrestling matches, and dances. The Feast of St. Demetrius (Oct. 26) is celebrated with particular enthusiasm in Thessaloniki.

BEYOND TOURISM

There are a wide range of opportunities available if you want to give back to the community on your travels within Greece. There are homestays and study-abroad options for those who want to immerse themselves in the culture and language, and volunteer and work opportunities to help you give something back. For more information and resources see p. 66 or check out www.beyondtourism.com.

Conservation Volunteers Greece (☎21038 25 506; www.cvgpeep.gr), offers summer programs in environmental and cultural conservation, as well as social outreach.

Anglo-Hellenic Teacher Recruitment (☎27410 53 511; www.anglo-hellenic.com), provides employment, training, and support for English teachers in Greece.

ATHENS Αθήνα ☎210

Even more than other ancient Greek cities, Athens is haunted by its illustrious past. The ghosts of antiquity peer down from every hilltop and lurk around each dark alleyway. But Athens is also a daring and modern place. In the shadow of the Acropolis, scores of outdoor theaters play domestic and foreign films. Creatively international menus, hipster bars, and large warehouses converted into performance spaces crowd among Byzantine churches, traditional *tavernas*, and toppled columns. Whether settling in or just passing through, don't miss the chance to explore a city that is more energetic and exciting than ever.

TRANSPORTATION

Flights: Eleftherios Venizelou (ATH; ☎353 0000; www.aia.gr), Greece's new international airport operates as a massive yet easily navigable terminal. Arrivals are on the ground floor, departures are on the 2nd. The new **suburban rail** services the airport from the city center in 30min. 4 bus lines run to Athens, Piraeus, and Rafina.

Trains: Hellenic Railways (OSE), Sina 6 (☎362 4402; www.ose.gr). **Larisis Train Station** (☎210 529 8837) serves northern Greece. Ticket office open daily 5am-midnight. Take trolley #1 from El. Venizelou in Pl. Syndagma (every 10min. 5am-midnight, €0.45) or the Metro to Sepolia. Trains depart for **Thessaloniki** (7hr., 5 per day, €14; express 5½hr., 6 per day, €28). **Peloponnese Train Station** (☎529 8735) serves: **Kalamata** (6½hr., 3 per day, €7); **Nafplion** (3½hr., 2 per day, €4.80); **Patras** (4¼hr., 3 per day, €5.30). From Larisis, exit to your right, and cross the footbridge.

Buses: Terminal A: Kifissou 100 (☎512 4910). Take blue bus #051 from the corner of Zinonos and Menandrou near Pl. Omonia (every 15min. 5am-11:30pm, €0.45). Buses to: **Corfu** (10hr., 4 per day, €30); **Corinth** (1½hr., every 30min., €5); **Patras** (3hr., every 30min., €13); **Thessaloniki** (6hr., 11 per day, €30) and other destinations. **Terminal B:** Liossion 260 (☎831 7153; Open M-F). Take blue bus #024 from Amalias outside the National Gardens (45min., every 20min., €0.45). Buses to **Delphi** (3hr., 6 per day, €11) and other destinations.

Public Transportation: Yellow KTEL (ΚΤΕΛ) **buses** travel all around Attica. Other buses around Athens and its suburbs are blue and designated by 3-digit numbers. Buy bus and trolley tickets at any street kiosk and hold on to your ticket–you can be fined €18-30 if caught without one. **Trolleys** are crowded, sporting 1- or 2-digit numbers; they are distinguished from buses by their electrical antennae. A standard bus/trolley ticket is €0.45. The rebuilt Athens **metro** consists of 3 lines running 5am-midnight. **M1** runs from northern Kifisia to Piraeus, **M2** from Sepolia to Ag. Dimitrios, **M3** from Ethniki Amyna to Monastiraki in central Athens. Buy tickets (€0.30-0.60) in any station. There are 2 **tram** lines. **Line 1** runs from Pl. Syndagma to the coast and Helliniko. **Line 2** runs from Neo Faliro along the Apollo Coast until Glyfada.

Car Rental: Try the places on **Syngrou.** €35-50 for a small car with 100km mileage (including tax and insurance); prices higher in summer. Up to 50% student discount.

Taxis: Meters start at €0.85, with an additional €0.30 per km; midnight-5am €0.53 per km. There is a €3 surcharge from the airport; €0.80 from bus and train stations, plus €0.29 for each piece of luggage over 10kg. Call for pick-up (€1.50-2.50 extra). Companies include **Ermis** (☎411 5200); **Ikaros** (☎515 2800); **Kosmos** (☎1300).

A
B
C
TO (200m)
Filadelfias
TO
Alkamenous
Livaniou
M. Voda
Smirnis
Akharnon
Filis
Aristotelous
Ioulianou
Ferron
Enianos
TO MAROUSI (9km)
Are os Par k
TO KIFISIA (13km)
Leoforos Alexandras
Khomatianou
Mamouri
Neof. Metaxa
Liossion
Alkiviadou
Ipirou
Patission-28 Oktovriou
Mavromateon
Rethimnou
Metsovou
Fotifa
Skilitsi
Psalida
Psellou
Plapduta
Ioustianou
Poulkerias
Psaron
Kritis
Agrou Pavlou
Paleologou
Iliou
Deligianni
Makednoias
Averof
Sourmeli
3 Septemvriou
Vas. Irakliou
30
Kountouriotou
Strefi Hill
Tossitsa
EXARHIA
Marni
Politekniou
Polytechnic University/School of Fine Arts
Bouboulinas
Zaimi
Notara
Trikoupi
Tsamadou
Ikonomou
Zossimadon
Metsovou
M. Themistokleous
5
Mezonos
Akominatou
Sonierou
Magher
PL. VATHIS
Solomou
Stournara
20
Kalidromiou
Elefsinion
Favierou
Laundromat
Kapodistriou
Galaxias
Kaningos
Botassi
Soultani
9
13
Rivera Garden Art Cinema
Methonis
Kodratou
Laundromat
Victor Hugo
1
Marni
Halkokondili
Aristotelous
Tzortz
Koleti
A. Metaxa
Eressou
Dervenion
METAXOURGIO M
Psaron
Karolou
Veranzerou
PL. KANINGOS
Em. Benaki
Arakhovis
Valtetsiou
PL. EXARHIA
Odisseos
PL. KARAISKAKI
OSE
Satovriandou
Koumoundourou
National Theater
Messologiou
Zoõdokou Pigis
Mavromihali
METAXOURGIO
Nikiforou
Dorou
Glad-stonos
Gamveta
Zalongou
TO
Deligiorgi
Kalergi
Agiou Konstantinou
PL. OMONIA
Vilara
M OMONIA
Ippokratous
M. Alexandrou
Kolonou
Iassonos
Zinonos
Voulgari
OMONIA
Fidiou
Har. Trikoupi
Skoufa
Asklipiou
Didotou
Solonos
Gateron
Keramikou
P. Tsaldari
Likourgou
Aiolou
Panepistimiou
Opera House
Leonidou
Kolokinthous
Agisilaou
Menandrou
Geraniou
Sokratous
Klisthenous
Efpolidos
Santaroza
Massalias
34
Milerou
Ghiatrakou
Laundromat
Kratinou
KOTZIA
National Library
University
Akademias-Rouzvelt
Sina
Pireos
Sofokleous
Pesmazoglou
Armodiou
PL THEATROU
Aristogitonos
PANEPISTIMIOU M
Pl. Eleftherias (Koumoundour ou)
Epikorou
Evripidou
Dragatsaniou
Korai
Vissarionos
Omirou
Likavitou
Soutsou
Psaromilingou
Dipilou
Aristofanous
Eshilou
Ag. Dimitriou
Polikitou
Praxitelous
Papargopoulou
El. Venizelou
Amerikis
Valaoritou
Voukourestiou
27
Leokoriou
Sari
Ag. Anargiron
Paladon
3
Hrissospiliotissas
Ag. Markou
Romvis
Khr. Lada
Stadiou
Ag. Arsomaton
PSIRI
Protogenous
Keramik os
Lepeniotou
11
Miaouli
Athinas
Voreou
Aiolou
Kolokotroni
32
Kriezotou
TO ELEUSIS (15km)
Synagogue
Ag. Assomati
Ivis
Kariskaki
Ag. Theklas
Ag. Pitaki
16
Skouze
Evangelistrias
Leka
Smats
Zalokosta
6
Ermou
Athinaidos
Perikleous
Karageorgi Servias
Georgiou A
Thissiou
Ag. Filipou
MONASTIRAKI
MONASTIRAKI M
Mitropoleos
Ermou
4
SYNDAGMA
SYNDAGMA M
M THISSIOU
15
Deka
Pl. Syndagma
38
Amfiktionos
Apostolou Pavlou
Pandrossou
Mitropoleos
Othonos
41
Ago ra
Vrissakiou
Areos
Dexipou
Apollonos
Xenofontos
Iraclidhon
22
Pikilis
33
Adrianou
Diogenous
Voulis
Skoufou
Nikis
Filellinon
Polignotou
14
Kiristou
Nikodimou
Thoukididou
Nat ional Gardens
PLAKA
Lissiou
Flessa
28
Dioskouron
Pritaniou
Iperidou
Asteriou
Kydatheneon
Acr opolis
Tripodon
Adrianou
7
25
Amalias
21
Thespidous
Geronda
Dedalou
Zappeion
32
17
Pny x Hill
Herod Atticus Odeum
Epimenidi
Lysikratous
Vas. Olgas
Thrassilou
Vironos
Frinhou
Dion. Areopagitou
42
Rovertou
29
Kalisperi
Gkalli
ACROPOLIS M
Makri
Diakou
Rogon
Phi lapapp os Hill
Mitseon
Kariatidon
Parthenonos
Erekhtiou
Propileon
Garivaldi
TO VOULIAGMENI (11km)
Makrighiani
Zitrou
Syngrou
TO PIRAEUS (10km)
TO GLYFADA (10km)
Arditou
Meletiou Riga

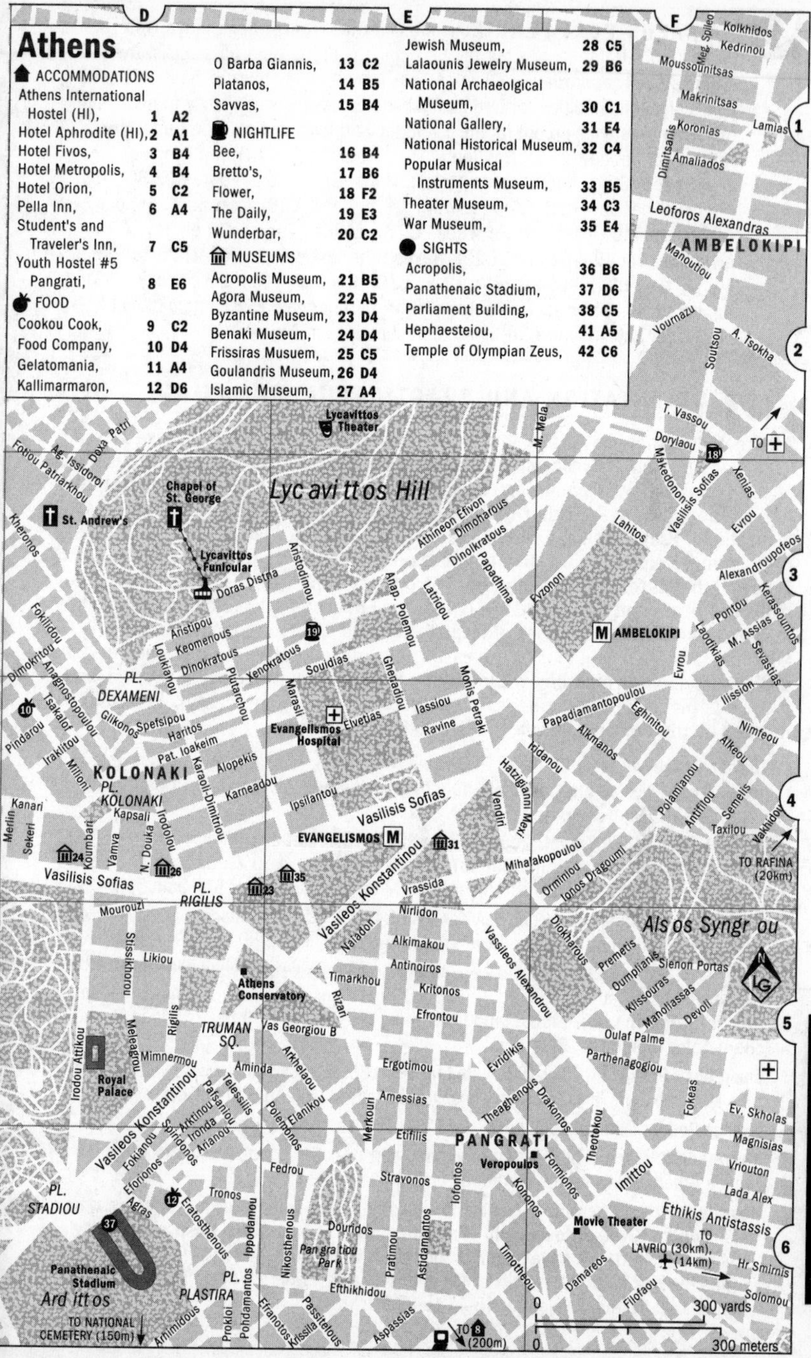

Athens

ACCOMMODATIONS

Athens International Hostel (HI),	1	A2
Hotel Aphrodite (HI),	2	A1
Hotel Fivos,	3	B4
Hotel Metropolis,	4	B4
Hotel Orion,	5	C2
Pella Inn,	6	A4
Student's and Traveler's Inn,	7	C5
Youth Hostel #5 Pangrati,	8	E6

FOOD

Cookou Cook,	9	C2
Food Company,	10	D4
Gelatomania,	11	A4
Kallimarmaron,	12	D6
O Barba Giannis,	13	C2
Platanos,	14	B5
Savvas,	15	B4

NIGHTLIFE

Bee,	16	B4
Bretto's,	17	B6
Flower,	18	F2
The Daily,	19	E3
Wunderbar,	20	C2

MUSEUMS

Acropolis Museum,	21	B5
Agora Museum,	22	A5
Byzantine Museum,	23	D4
Benaki Museum,	24	D4
Frissiras Musuem,	25	C5
Goulandris Museum,	26	D4
Islamic Museum,	27	A4
Jewish Museum,	28	C5
Lalaounis Jewelry Museum,	29	B6
National Archaeolgical Museum,	30	C1
National Gallery,	31	E4
National Historical Museum,	32	C4
Popular Musical Instruments Museum,	33	B5
Theater Museum,	34	C3
War Museum,	35	E4

SIGHTS

Acropolis,	36	B6
Panathenaic Stadium,	37	D6
Parliament Building,	38	C5
Hephaesteiou,	41	A5
Temple of Olympian Zeus,	42	C6

D E F 1 2 3 4 5 6

Lycavittos Hill
Lycavittos Theater
Chapel of St. George
Lycavittos Funicular
St. Andrew's
KOLONAKI
PL. KOLONAKI
PL. DEXAMENI
Evangelismos Hospital
EVANGELISMOS
AMBELOKIPI
PL. RIGILIS
Athens Conservatory
TRUMAN SQ.
Royal Palace
PANGRATI
Veropoulos
Movie Theater
Pangratiou Park
PL. STADIOU
Panathenaic Stadium
Ardittos
PL. PLASTIRA
Alsos Syngrou
TO NATIONAL CEMETERY (150m)
TO RAFINA (20km)
TO LAVRIO (30km), (14km)
TO 8 (200m)
0 300 yards
0 300 meters
Leoforos Alexandras
Vasilisis Sofias
Vasileos Konstantinou
Vassileos Alexandrou
Ethikis Antistassis

PIRAEUS PORT FERRIES. Most ferries from Athens leave from the Piraeus port. Unfortunately the ferry schedule changes on a daily basis; the following are only approximate. Check *Athens News* and the back of the *Kathimerini* English-language edition for updated schedules. Ferries sail directly to nearly all major Greek islands except for the Sporades and Ionians. Ferries to Crete: **Hania** (11hr., 1-2 per day, €20); **Iraklion** (11hr., 1-3 per day, €24); **Rethymno** (11hr., 3 per week, €24). Additional ferries to: **Chios** (9hr., 1-2 per day, €22.30); **Ios** (7½hr., 3 per day, €22); **Kos** (13½hr., 1-2 per day, €36); **Lesvos** (12hr., daily, €26); **Limnos** (18hr., 3 per week, €26); **Milos** (7hr., 1-2 per day, €20); **Mykonos** (6hr., 2-4 per day, €20); **Naxos** (6hr., 5-7 per day, €24); **Paros** (5hr., 4-7 per day, €24); **Patmos** (8hr., daily, €30); **Rhodes** (14hr., 2-5 per day, €43); **Samos** (10hr., daily, €27); **Santorini** (9hr., 3-5 per day, €28); International ferries (2 per day, around €30) head to destinations in **Turkey.**

ORIENTATION AND PRACTICAL INFORMATION

Athenian geography mystifies newcomers. If you lose your bearings, ask for directions back to well-lit **Syndagma.** The **Acropolis** serves as a reference point, as does **Mount Lycavittos.** Syndagma, the central *plateia* containing the Parliament building, is encircled by the other major neighborhoods. Clockwise, they are **Plaka, Monastiraki, Psiri, Omonia, Exarhia, Kolonaki,** and **Pangrati.** Plaka, the center of the old city and home to many accommodations, is bound by the **Temple of Olympian Zeus** and the *plateia* of the Cathedral Mitropolis. Monastiraki is between the outer walls of the ancient Agora and the boulevard **Ermou;** it is the site of a large metro station. Two parallel avenues, **Panepistimiou** and **Stadiou,** connect Syndagma to Omonia. Omonia's neighbor to the east, progressive Exarhia, sports some of Athens's most exciting nightlife, while nearby Kolonaki, on the foothills of Mt. Lycavittos, has plenty of glitz and swanky shops. Pangrati, southeast of Kolonaki, is marked by the **Olympic Stadium** and the **National Cemetery.**

Tourist Office, Amalias 26 (☎331 0392; www.gnto.gr). Provides an indispensable Athens map, as well as the most up-to-date bus, train, and ferry schedules. Open M-F 9am-7pm, Sa-Su 10am-3pm.

Budget Travel: STA Travel, Voulis 43 (☎321 1188; statravel@robissa.gr). Open M-F 9am-5pm, Sa 10am-2pm. **Consolas Travel,** Aiolou 100 (☎321 9228; consolas@hol.gr), 9th fl., above post office. Open M and Sa 9am-2pm, Tu-F 9am-5pm.

Bank: National Bank, Karageorgi Servias 2 (☎334 0500), in Pl. Syndagma. Open M-Th 8am-2:30pm, F 8am-2pm; open for **currency exchange** only M-F 3:30-5pm, Sa 9am-2pm, Su 9am-1pm. 24hr. currency exchange at the airport, but commissions there may be exorbitant.

Laundromats: Most laundromats *(plintirias)* post signs in English. **National,** Apollonos 17, in Syndagma, offers both laundry and dry cleaning. €4.50 per kg. Open M and W 8am-4pm, Tu and Th-F 8am-8pm.

Emergency: Police: ☎100 or 103. **Ambulance:** ☎166. **Medical:** Athens ☎105, or 646 7811; line available 2pm-7am. Emergency hospitals on duty ☎106. **AIDS Help Line:** ☎722 2222.

Tourist Police: Dimitrakopoulou 77 (☎171). English spoken. Open 24hr.

Pharmacies: Marked by a green cross hanging over the street. Many are open 24hr.; check *Athens News* for the current all-night pharmacies.

Hospitals: *Athens News* lists emergency hospitals. Free emergency health care for tourists. **Geniko Kratiko Nosokomio (Y. Gennimatas; Public State Hospital),** Mesogion 154 (☎777 8901). A state hospital, **Aeginitio,** Vas. Sofias 72 (☎722 0811) and Vas. Sofias 80 (☎777 0501), is closer to Athens's center. Near Kolonaki is the public hospital **Evangelismos,** Ypsilantou 45-47 (☎720 1000).

Internet Access: Athens teems with Internet cafes. Expect to pay €3-6 per hr.

Arcade Internet Cafe, Stadiou 5 (☎324 8105), just up Stadiou from Pl. Syndagma, set in a shopping center about 15m from the main thoroughfare. Complimentary coffee. €3 per hr., €0.50 each additional 10min., €2 minimum. Open M-Sa 9am-10pm, Su noon-8pm.

Bits'n Bytes Internet, Kapnikareas 19 (☎382 2545 or 330 6590), in Plaka, or Akadamias 78 (☎522 7717) in Exarhia. This mother of new-age Internet cafes has fast connections in a spacious, black-lit joint with A/C. Midnight-9am €3 per hr., 9am-midnight €5 per hr. Open 24hr.

Cafe 4U, 3 Septemvriou 24 (☎520 1564), in Omonia. A refuge off busy Septemvriou, this cafe offers fast access for €2.50 per hr. €1.50 minimum.

Post Office: Syndagma (☎622 6253), on the corner of Mitropoleos. Open M-F 7:30am-8pm, Sa 7:30am-2pm. Branch offices at Aiolou 100 in Omonia, at the corner of Zaimi and K. Deligiani in Exarhia, and at the Acropolis/Plaka. Currency exchange at all branches except Omonia. **Postal Code:** 10300.

ACCOMMODATIONS

The **Greek Youth Hostel Association,** Damareos 75 in Pangrati, lists hostels in Greece. (☎751 9530; y-hostels@ote.net.gr. Open M-F 9am-3pm.) The **Hellenic Chamber of Hotels,** Stadiou 24, in Syndagma, provides info and makes reservations for all types of hotels throughout Greece. Reservations require a cash deposit; contact at least one month in advance and tell them the length of your stay and number of people. (☎323 7193; www.grhotels.gr. Open May-Nov. M-F 8:30am-1:30pm.)

Student's and Traveler's Inn, Kydatheneon 16 (☎324 4808; www.studenttravelersinn.com), in Plaka. Unrivaled location and lively atmosphere with around-the-clock Internet. Reserve ahead. Co-ed dorms €15; doubles €50, with private bath €60; triples €72/84; quads €88/100. ❷

Pella Inn, Karaiskaki 1 (☎325 0598), 2 blocks west of the Monastiraki metro. Features a large rooftop terrace with views of the Acropolis. Breakfast included in room prices, €3 extra with dorms. Dorms €15; doubles €40-50; triples €60; quads €80. ❷

Hotel Orion, Em. Benaki 105 (☎382 7362; fax 380 5193), in Exarhia. From Pl. Omonia, walk up Em. Benaki or take bus #230 from Pl. Syndagma. Orion rents small rooms with shared baths and A/C. Sunbathers relax on the rooftop. Laundry €3. Internet €2 per hr. Singles €30; doubles €40; triples €48. Bargain for better prices. MC/V. ❸

Hotel Fivos, 23 Athenias (☎322 6657; www.consolas.gr). A few blocks up Athenias from the Monastiraki metro. Unadorned, simply furnished rooms with large windows. A/C and private baths available. Common room with Internet and vending machine. Breakfast included. Singles €45; doubles €55. ❷

Youth Hostel #5 Pangrati, Damareos 75 (☎751 9530; y-hostels@ote.net). From Omonia or Pl. Syndagma, take trolley #2 or 11 to Filolaou. There's no sign for this cheery hostel, just a green door. Bring a sleeping bag to stay on the roof (€6). Hot showers €0.50 per 7min. Linen €2. Laundry (wash only) €4. Quiet hours 2-5pm and 11pm-7am. Dorms €10-12. ❶

Hotel Metropolis, Mitropoleos 46 (☎321 7469; www.hotelmetropolis.gr), in Syndagma. Enjoy full amenities and wonderful views of Cathedral Mitropolis and the Acropolis on a spacious balcony. Elevator and A/C. Laundry €6. Singles €40, with bath €50; doubles €45/60. Traveler's checks and MC/V. ❹

Hostel Aphrodite (HI), Einardou 12 (☎881 0589; www.hostelaphrodite.com), in Omonia. Small, clean rooms with A/C. Internet €5 per hr. Reception 24hr. Dorms €17; doubles €45; triples €60; quads €72. Low season reduced rates. ❷

Athens International Hostel (HI), Victor Hugo 16 (☎523 2540; www.hostelbooking.com), in Omonia. Walk down 30 Septemvriou from Pl. Omonia and take a left on Veranzerou, which becomes Victor Hugo after crossing Marni. Members only. Hot water 6am-midnight. Laundry €6. Reservations required. Dorms €8; doubles €16. ❶

FOOD

Athens offers a mix of fast-food stands, open-air cafes, side-street *tavernas*, and intriguing restaurants. Cheap food abounds in **Syndagma** and **Omonia.** Pick up groceries at the markets and sweet-smelling bakeries that abound in **Plaka.**

Savvas, Mitropoleos 86, right off of Pl. Monastiraki, across from the flea market. Cab drivers and kiosk vendors alike recommend this lively joint for the best *souvlaki* in town. Save money by eating on the fly; restaurant prices for gyros (€6-9) shrink to €1.70 for take out orders. Open daily 10am-3am. ❶

O Barba Giannis, Em. Benaki (☎382 4138). From Syndagma, walk up Stadiou and make a right on Em. Benaki; it's the yellow building on the corner. Tall green doors and high ceilings make this informal *taverna* breezy and elegant. Order one of the satisfying daily specials, on display at the front, and feel like one of the many local regulars. Entrees €5-10. Open M-Sa noon-1:30am. ❷

Food Company, Anagnostopoulou 47, in Kolonaki. A kind of gourmet deli, Food Company offers diners a handful of delicious pre-prepared dishes, all on display under a glass counter. Cute and bright, this popular eatery has outdoor benches and cafe tables. Lentil salad with feta and red peppers €4. Open daily noon-11:30pm. ❷

Kallimarmaron, Eforionos 13, in Pangrati. With your back to the old Olympic Stadium, take the closest street on the left and walk 1½ blocks. Some of the best traditional Greek food in the city. Spiced chicken with raisins (€12) is prepared from an ancient recipe. Open Tu-Sa noon-3pm and 8pm-1am, Su noon-3pm. DC/MC/V. ❸

Platanos, Diogenous 4 (☎322 0666). Just meters away from the hustle of touristy restaurants on Adrianou and Kydatheon, Platanos offers authentic traditional fare under a plant-draped trellis or in the cozy *taverna*. Diners choose from a wide-ranging menu, unchanged since 1932. Tomato salad €3. Lamb with string beans €7. Open M-Sa noon-4:30pm and 7:30pm-midnight, Su noon-4:30pm. ❷

Gelatomania, Agatharou 21 on Taki, in Monastiraki. Ice cream has always been cool, but Gelatomania makes it trendy. Heaping displays of homemade ice cream tempt with creative flavors Rum Raisin, Wafer, and Gum (one scoop €1.70). A great place day or night. Iced chocolate €3.50. Waffle with ice cream €5.50. Open daily 10am-3am. ❶

Cookou Cook, Themistokles 66 (☎330 1369), in Exarhia. Yellow walls, mosaic tables, and eccentric wall decorations, including hanging kitchen utensils, decorate this funky little restaurant, which fuses creative gourmet with speed and informality. Open M-Sa 1pm-1am. Closed 2 weeks in Aug. V. ❸

SIGHTS

ACROPOLIS

Looming majestically over the city, the Acropolis complex has been the heart of Athens since the 5th century BC. Visit as early in the day as possible to avoid crowds and the broiling mid-day sun. *(☎321 0219. Open daily 8am-7pm; low season 8am-2:30pm. Admission includes access to all of the sights below the Acropolis, including Hadrian's Arch, the Temple of Olympian Zeus, and the Agora, within a 48hr. period; tickets can be purchased at any of the sights. €12, students €6, under 19 free.)*

PARTHENON. The **Temple of Athena Parthenos** (Athena the Virgin), commonly known as the Parthenon, keeps vigil over Athens. Ancient Athenians saw their city as the capital of civilization; the **metopes** (scenes in the open spaces above the columns) on the sides of the Parthenon celebrate Athens's rise. The architect Iktinos integrated a variation of the Golden Mean into the design of the temple.

ACROPOLIS MUSEUM. The museum, which neighbors the Parthenon, houses a superb collection of sculptures, including five of the original **Caryatids** that supported the southern side of the Erechtheion. The statues initially seem to be identical, but a close look at the folds of their drapery reveals delicately individualized detail. Compare the stylized face and frozen pose of the Archaic period **Moschophoros** (calf-bearer) sculpture to the idealized, more human Classical period **Kritios Boy** to follow the development of Greek sculpture. *(Open M 11am-7pm, Tu-Su 8am-7pm; low season M 11am-2pm, Tu-Su 8am-2pm. No flash photography.)*

TEMPLE OF ATHENA NIKE. This tiny temple was raised during a lull in the Peloponnesian War. Known as the "jewel of Greek architecture," it houses a statue of Nike, the winged goddess of victory. The Athenians, afraid Nike might abandon them, amputated her wings. The remains of the 5m thick **Cyclopean wall** which once circled the Acropolis are visible below the temple.

ERECHTHEION. To the left of the Parthenon, the Erechtheion was completed in 406 BC, just before Sparta defeated Athens in the Peloponnesian War. The building is named after the snake-bodied hero Erechtheus who was speared during a battle over the city's patronage between Athena and Poseidon; hence, the eastern half is devoted to the goddess of wisdom, and the western half to the god of the sea.

ELSEWHERE ON THE ACROPOLIS. The southwestern corner of the Acropolis looks down over the reconstructed **Odeon of Herodes Atticus,** a functional theater dating from AD 160. See the *Athens News* for a schedule of concerts and plays. *(Entrance on Dionissiou Areopagitou. ☎323 2771. Purchase tickets at the door or by phone.)*

OTHER SIGHTS

AGORA. The Agora served as the city's marketplace, administrative center, and hub of daily life from the 6th century BC to the 6th century AD. Here, the debates of Athenian democracy raged; Socrates, Aristotle, Demosthenes, and St. Paul all instructed here. The 415 BC **Hephaesteion,** on a hill in the northwest corner of the Agora, is the best-preserved Classical temple in Greece, boasting **friezes** depicting Hercules's labors and Theseus's adventures. The **Stoa of Attalos** was a multi-purpose building filled with shops and home to informal gatherings of philosophers. Reconstructed in the 1950s, it now houses the **Agora Museum,** which contains relics from the site. *(Enter the Agora off Pl. Thission, from Adrianou, or as you descend from the Acropolis. ☎321 0185. Open daily 8am-7:30pm. €4, students €2, EU students free.)*

TOP TEN LIST

TOP TEN PLACES TO MEET A GREEK GOD

There once was a time when unicorns, centaurs, and gods roamed the earth. Now, finding the divine is hard, but if Hermes, the traveler god, doesn't befriend you, some other deity just might.

1. Visit the volcanoes of **Nisyros** (p. 516) and **Santorini** (p. 511) to see the forge of Hephaestus, god of fire.

2. Run through the forests of **Samos** (p. 516) or **Kephalonia** (p. 505) in search of Artemis, protectress of the woods.

3. Mykonos (p. 508) will put you in the alcoholic stupor needed to bond with wine god Dionysus, though **Ios** (p. 510) will do just as well.

4. Seek Athena's wisdom at none other than her patron city, **Athens** (p. 485), or try **Ithaka** (p. 506), home of one of her favorites, Odysseus.

5. Corfu's **Canal d'Amour** (p. 505) might help you find Aphrodite, or a mortal replacement.

6. A hike through Crete's **Valley of Death** (p. 511) might lead you to Hades.

7. You may run into Apollo at his oracle at **Delphi** (p. 504) or sanctuary at **Delos** (p. 509).

8. Lesvos (p. 517), home of the tenth Muse, Sappho, is a good place to seek the other nine.

9. Find Poseidon at his temple on **Cape Sounion** (p. 493), if you don't meet him first on a ferry.

10. Mt. Olympus (p. 502). Duh.

ROMAN AGORA. The Roman Agora, built between 19 and 11 BC, was once a lively meeting place. By far the most intriguing structure in the site is the well-preserved **Tower of the Winds.** This octagonal tower, built in the first century BC by the astronomer Andronikos, was initially crowned by a weathervane. *(☎324 5220. Open daily 8am-7:30pm. €2, students €1, EU students free.)*

KERAMIKOS. This geometrically designed site includes a large-scale cemetery built around the **Sacred Way,** the road to Eleusis, and a 40m wide boulevard that ran to the sanctuary of **Akademes,** where Plato founded his academy. The **Oberlaender Museum** displays finds from the burial sites. *(Northwest of the Agora. ☎346 3552. From Syndagma, walk toward Monastiraki on Ermou for 1km. Open Tu-Su 8:30am-7pm. €2, students and EU seniors €1, under 19 and EU students free.)*

TEMPLE OF OLYMPIAN ZEUS AND HADRIAN'S ARCH. On the edge of the National Gardens in Plaka, you can spot traces of the largest temple ever built in Greece. The 15 Corinthian columns of the Temple of Olympian Zeus hint at its mammoth proportions. Started in the 6th century BC, it was completed 600 years later by Roman emperor Hadrian, who added an arch to mark the boundary between the ancient city of Theseus and his new city. *(Vas. Olgas at Amalias. ☎922 6330. Open daily 8am-5pm. Temple €2, students and EU seniors €1, under 19 free. Arch free.)*

PANATHENAIC STADIUM. The Panathenaic Olympic Stadium, also known as the Kallimarmaro, is carved into a hillside between the National Gardens and Pangrati. The site of the first modern Olympic Games in 1896, the stadium seats 70,000 and served as the finish line of the marathon events during the 2004 Summer Olympic Games. *(On Vas. Konstantinou. From Syndagma, walk up Amalias 15min. to Vas. Olgas, then follow it left. Or take trolley #2, 4, or 11 from Syndagma. Open daily 8am-8:30pm. Free.)*

AROUND SYNDAGMA. Be sure to catch the changing of the guard in front of the **Parliament** building. Every hour on the hour, two *evzones* wind up like toy soldiers, kick their tasseled heels in unison, and disappear into guardhouses on either side of the **Tomb of the Unknown Soldier.** Athens's endangered species—greenery and shade—are preserved in the **National Gardens,** but the zoo is uninspiring.

MOUNT LYCAVITTOS. Of Athens's seven hills, Lycavittos is the largest. Ascend at sunset to catch a glimpse of the city lighting up for the night. At the top is the **Chapel of St. George,** a popular spot for weddings. A leisurely stroll around the church provides a view of Athens's panoramic expanse.

OUTDOOR MARKETS. The **Flea Market,** adjacent to Pl. Monastiraki, has a festive atmosphere: picture a massive garage sale where old forks and teapots are sold alongside odd family heirlooms. Try to go on a Sunday. *(Open M, W, Sa-Su 8am-8pm.)* The biggest outdoor food market in Athens, **Varnakios,** is on Athinias between Armodiou and Aristogeitonos. *(Open M-Th 6am-7pm, F-Sa 5am-8pm.)*

MUSEUMS

NATIONAL ARCHAEOLOGICAL MUSEUM. Almost every artifact in this collection is a masterpiece. The museum's highlights include the so-called **Mask of Agamemnon,** excavated from the tomb of a king who lived at least three centuries earlier than Agamemnon himself, and a comprehensive timeline of the development of Greek sculpture. *(Patission 44. ☎821 7717. Take trolley #2, 4, 5, 9, 11, 15, or 18 from the uphill side of Syndagma, or trolley #3 or 13 from the northern side of Vas. Sofias. Open Apr.-Oct. Tu-Su 8:30am-3pm; Nov.-Mar. M 10:30am-5pm, Tu-Su 8:30am-3pm. €6, students €3, EU students free. No flash photography.)*

MUSEUM OF ISLAMIC ART. Large glass windows, spotless marble staircases, and sparkling white walls showcase the collection of brilliant tiles, metalwork, and tapestries documenting the history of the Islamic world from the 12th to 18th century. The exhibit includes a marble reception room transported from a 17th-century Cairo mansion. *(Ag. Asomaton 22, in Psiri. ☎367 1000; www.benaki.gr. M: Thissou. Open Tu and Th-Su 9am-3pm, W 9am-9pm. €5, students and seniors €3. W free.)*

BYZANTINE AND CHRISTIAN MUSEUM. This well-organized museum comprehensively documents the political, religious, and mundane aspects of life during the Byzantine Empire. Its collection of metalware, mosaics, sculpture, and painted icons presents Christianity in its earliest stages. *(Vas. Sofias 22, in Kolonaki. ☎721 1027. Open Tu-Su 8:30am-3pm. €4; students €2; EU students and classicists free.)*

GOULANDRIS MUSEUM OF CYCLADIC AND ANCIENT GREEK ART. Established by the Goulandris shipping family, this museum displays a stunning collection of Cycladic figurines: sleek, abstract marble works, some almost 5000 years old. Visit the extension of the museum in a gorgeously renovated 1895 mansion on the corner of Vas. Sofias and Herodotou. *(Neophytou Douka 4. ☎722 8321. Walk 20min. toward Kolonaki from Syndagma on Vas. Sofias; turn left on Neophytou Douka. Accessible by trolleys #3 and 13. Open M and W-F 10am-4pm, Su 10am-3pm. €5, seniors and students €2.50, archaeologists and archaeology students free with university pass.)*

ENTERTAINMENT AND NIGHTLIFE

The weekly *Athens News* (€1) lists events, as well as news and ferry information. Summertime performances are staged in **Lycavittos Theater** as part of the **Athens Festival.** The Festival Office, Stadiou 4, sells tickets. (☎210 322 1459. Open M-Sa 8am-4pm, Su 9am-2pm and 6-9pm. Tickets €10-110. Student discounts available.) Chic Athenians head to the seaside clubs of **Glyfada.** (Dress well; no shorts. Drinks €4-10. Cover €10-15.) Take the A2, A3, or B3 bus from Vas. Amalias to Glyfada (€0.75), and then catch a cab from there to your club. Taxis to Glyfada run about €8; the return trip typically costs €10-15.

Bretto's, Kydatheneon 41, between Farmaki and Afroditis in Plaka. Serves almost exclusively local alcohol. Colorful bottles and gigantic barrels line the walls, while a handful of wooden stools invite mellow crowds to sample *ouzo* on the spot. €5 per bottle of sweet red wine; €2 per sizable glass. Open daily 10am-midnight.

Wunderbar, Themistokleous 80, on Pl. Exarhia, plays pop and some techno. Star-shaped paper lanterns decorate the interior, while revelers lounge under large umbrellas at the outdoor tables. Beer €5-6. Mixed drinks €8-9. Open M-Th 9am-3am, F-Su 9am-sunrise.

The Daily, Xenokratous 47. Kolonaki's chic student population converges here to drink, listen to Latin and reggae, and watch sports on TV. Fabulous outdoor seating. Mixed drinks €3-6. Open daily 9am-2am.

Bee, Miaouli 6, off Ermou at the corner of Themidos, in Psiri. A melange of neon plastic and illumination, Bee offers margaritas (€9), other mixed drinks (€7), and excellent people-watching on a busy corner. Beer €4. Open Tu-Th, Su noon-3am, F-Sa noon-6am.

Flower, Dorylaou 2, in Pl. Mavili, in Kolonaki. A popular dive bar with European partiers. Shots €3. Mixed drinks €5. Open daily 6pm-late.

DAYTRIP FROM ATHENS

CAPE OF SOUNION. Ancient Greeks built the enormous **Temple of Poseidon** in 600 BC. Today, 16 Doric columns remain from the Periclean reconstruction of 440 BC, drawing flocks of visitors, especially at sunset. Hundreds of names are carved into the monumental structure, including Lord Byron's. Next to the bus station, **Cafe Naos** ❶ has one of the best views in Attica. Buses leave Athens for Sounion from the station at Mavromateon 14 (2hr., every hr. 6:30am-6:30pm, €4.50).

PELOPONNESE Πελοπόννεσος

Stretching its fingers into the Mediterranean, the Peloponnese transports its visitors to another time and place through its rich history and folklore. The achievements of ancient civilizations dot the stunning landscape of the peninsula. Here rest the majority of Greece's most significant archaeological sites, including Corinth, Epidavros, Messini, Mycenae, Mystras, and Olympia. Away from large, urban transportation hubs, serene villages welcome visitors to traditional Greece.

FERRIES TO ITALY

Boats sail from Patras to destinations in Italy, including Ancona, Bari, Brindisi, and Venice. Several ferry lines make the trip, each offering different prices, so make sure to check prices for more than one line. Railpasses won't work for domestic ferries, but for international ferries, **Superfast Ferries,** Oth. Amalias 12 (☎2610 622 500; open 10am-9pm), accepts Eurail passes. Questions about departures from Patras should be directed to the Port Authority (☎2610 341 002).

PATRAS Πάτρας ☎2610

Greece's third-largest city spreads from its harbor in a mixture of urban and classical, Greek and international styles. Location, location, location—on the northwestern tip of the Peloponnese—makes Patras a busy transportation hub. During **Carnival** (mid-Jan. to Ash Wed.), this port city becomes one gigantic dance floor, consumed by pre-Lenten madness. Follow the water to the western end of town to reach **Agios Andreas,** the largest Orthodox cathedral in Greece, which houses magnificent frescoes, an enormous wooden chandelier, and St. Andrew's holy head. (Dress modestly. Open daily 7am-dusk.) Sweet black grapes are made into Mavrodaphne wine at the **Achaïa Clauss Winery,** the country's most famous vineyard. Take bus #7 (30min., €1.20) towards Seravali from the intersection of Kanakari and Gerokostopoulou. (Free English-language tours every hr. Open daily May-Sept. 11am-7pm, tours noon-3pm; Sept.-Apr. 10am-5pm, tours 11am-3pm. Free.) Built atop an ancient acropolis and continuously in use from the 6th century through WWII, Patras's **castle** remains surprisingly intact. It's perfect for a bird's-eye view of the entire city. (Open Tu-Su 8:30am-3pm. Free.) The hippest bar on the Ag. Nikolaou strip, **Cibo Cibo,** serves delicious Italian food during the day (entrees €5-12), and mixed drinks (€6) in the evening. (☎620 761. Open daily 7am-3am.)

Rooms to Let Spyros Vazouras ❸, Tofalou 2, across from the new port entrance, has large rooms with A/C and clean baths. (☎452 152. Singles €30; doubles €40.) Affordable **Pension Nicos** ❷, Patreos 3, two blocks off the waterfront, is close to all the main *plateias*. (☎623 757. Singles €20; doubles €30; triples €40-45.) **Kirineia** ❷, Kolokotroni 63, near the intersection with Karaiskaki, serves Cypriot dishes such as grilled *haloumi* cheese (€5) amid tasteful and romantic rustic decor. (☎274 340, delivery 622 435. Entrees €4-8.)

Trains (☎639 108) leave from Oth. Amalias 47 for Athens (4¼hr., 8 per day 2:30am-7:20pm, €5.30-10) and Kalamata (5½hr., 3 per day 6:30am-5:15pm, €5.60) via Pirgos (2hr., €4), where you can catch a bus to Olympia. KTEL **buses** (☎623 886) leave from Oth. Amalias for: Athens (3hr., every 30min., €13.90); Ioannina (4hr., 3 per day, €17); Kalamata (4hr., 2 per day, €15); Thessaloniki (8hr., 3 per day, €30); Tripoli (4hr., 2 per day, €11). **Ferries** go to Corfu (7hr., 1 per day, €29), Vathy in Ithaka (3½hr., €13.50), as well as to Italy. Free maps are available at the **tourist office** on Oth. Amalias, between 28 Octovriou and Astingos. (☎461 740. Open daily 8am-10pm.) **Postal Code:** 26001.

OLYMPIA Ολυμπία ☎26240

In ancient times, every four years city-states would call a sacred truce and travel to Olympia for a pan-Hellenic assembly which showcased athletic ability as well as fostering peace and diplomacy. Modern Olympia, set among meadows and shaded by cypress and olive trees, is recognized for its pristine natural beauty as much as for its illustrious past. The ancient **Olympic arena** draws hordes of tourists. In **Ancient Olympia,** to the north of the **Bouleuterion** (toward the entrance), are the ruins of the **Temple of Zeus.** Once home to master-sculptor Phidias's awe-inspiring **Statue of Zeus,** one of the Seven Wonders of the Ancient World, the 27m sanctuary was the largest temple on the Greek mainland before the Parthenon. The ruins of the **Temple of Hera,** dating from the 7th century BC, are better preserved than those of Zeus's Temple, and sit to its west, past the temples of Metroön and the Nymphaeum. The **Archaeological Museum** has an impressive sculpture collection that includes the cup engraved with the words "I Belong To Phidias" which indicated the location of his workshop to the excavators. Essential maps (€2-4) are available at the site. (Site open daily in summer 8:30am-7:30pm. Museum open M noon-7:30pm, Tu-Su 8am-7:30pm. Site and museum each €6, both €9.)

The cheap **Youth Hostel ❶,** Kondili 18, is a great place to meet international backpackers. (☎22 580. Linen €1. Dorms €9; doubles €22.) **New Olympia ❸,** on the road leading diagonally to the train station, offers large, retro rooms. (☎22 547. Breakfast included. Singles €30; doubles €50; triples €70.) Mini-markets, bakeries, and fast food establishments line **Kondili.** A walk toward the railroad station or up the hill leads to inexpensive *tavernas.* A filling meal is as Greek as it gets at **Vasilakis Grill ❷,** on the corner of Karamanli and Spiliopoulou. Take a right off Kohili before the Youth Hostel. (☎22 104. Entrees €5-10. Open daily noon-midnight.) **Buses** run to Tripoli (3½hr., 2-3 per day, €9). The **tourist office,** on Kondili, is on the eastern side of town toward the ruins. (☎23 173. Open daily 9am-8pm. Closed low season.) **Postal Code:** 27065.

SPARTA Σπάρτη AND MYSTRAS Μυστράς ☎27310

Citizens of today's Sparta make olive oil, not war. Sparta is by far the best base for visiting **Mystras,** 4km away, which was once the religious center of all of Byzantium and the locus of Constantinople's rule over the Peloponnese. Its extraordinary hillside **ruins** comprise a city of Byzantine churches, chapels, and monasteries. Although churches are the highlight, a visit to the **palace** is a must, where pointed arches and frescoed stone walls tell a history of the region. Modest dress is required at the functioning convent. The ruins can get hot, so go early, bring water, and wear good hiking shoes. (☎83 377. Open daily in summer 8am-7pm; low season 8:30am-3pm. €5, children and students €3, EU students free.) Buses leave from the station and from the corner of Lykourgou and Leonidou in Sparta for the ruins (20min., 10 per day 7:20am-8:20pm, €1). The meager ruins at **Ancient Sparta** are only a 1km walk north down Paleologou from the center of town. **Hotel Cecil ❸,** Paleologou 125, five blocks north of Lykourgou toward Ancient Sparta, has pleasant rooms with TV, A/C, phone, and private bath under its scruffy exterior. (☎24 980. Singles €30-35; doubles €40-45; triples €55-60.) **Parthenon ❶,** on Vrasida, two blocks north of the intersection with Paleologou and one block east toward the bus station, serves glorified fast food in a faux-rustic kitchen, but the low prices will help you forgive it. (☎23767 20 444. *Souvlaki* €1.20-1.80. *Gyros* €1.40-1.60.) **Buses** from Sparta go to: Areopolis (1½hr., 4 per day, €5); Athens (3½hr., 11 per day, €14.30) via Corinth (2½hr., €8.60); Monemvasia (2hr., 4 per

OLLING WITHOUT THE HOMIES

Exploring Greece, land of the shameless stare, as a solo female traveler can be daunting; it's not unusual to be stared at, catcalled, invited to dinner, or propositioned, all before breakfast.

The overt staring will likely be most apparent as you walk down the street in the late afternoon and early evening. If it feels like all the eyes of the men seated at the sidewalk cafes are on you, you're not imagining it. They are. As the night progresses and cocktails replace coffee on cafe tables, the stares are often accompanied by catcalls. Although slightly creepy, the leers and comments are usually harmless. If you continue walking and avoid meeting the onlooker's gaze, you will be left undisturbed. If the man is particularly persistent, continue playing the I-can't-hear-you game or politely refuse and move on. As it is uncommon for women, either alone or in groups, to eat out before sunset, if you buy yourself lunch or coffee, you will likely be the only woman in the taverna save for the occasional waitress; the stares will intensify.

The bar scene is actually less openly intimidating than the sidewalk situation, but potentially more dangerous given the addition of alcohol. On the touristy islands that draw European partiers, a single female out at night is not unusual—just join in the

day, €10.30). To reach the town center from the bus station, walk about 10 blocks west on Lykourgou; the **tourist office** is on the third floor of the glass building in the *plateia*. (☎24 852. Open M-F 8am-2pm.) **Postal Code:** 23100.

MONEMVASIA Μονεμβασία ☎27320

An otherworldly quality shrouds the island of Monemvasia. No cars or bikes are allowed within the walls of the Old Town, so it feels as if time stopped in the Middle Ages. At the edge of the cliffs perches the **Agia Sofia,** a 12th-century church; to get there, turn left at the sign for Kate's Apartments and continue on the path uphill, which will eventually reach the edge of the cliff. The climb is about 20min. on slippery rocks; wear good shoes. It is less expensive to stay in **New Town Monemvasia,** a 15min. walk down the main road and across the causeway from old Monemvasia. The waterfront *domatia* along the harbor are the best option for budget travelers. The tasteful interior of **Hotel Belissis ❸,** with beautiful wood-paneled rooms, A/C, TV, fridge, and private bath, feels like it belongs in the Old Town. From the bus station, walk along Spartis away from the bridge for 5min. It will be on the left, right on the beach. (☎61 217. Singles €30; doubles €45; 4-person apartment with kitchenette €50-60.) With fantastic views and unique ambience, dining in old Monemvasia is a unforgettable. One of the first tavernas on the main road on the right is **Restaurant Matoula ❸,** which offers an unobstructed view of the clear waters below and superb service that justify a €7 *moussaka*. (Entrees €6-15. Open daily noon-midnight. V.) **Buses** leave from Spartis for: Athens (5½hr., €21.60); Ithsmos (4½hr., €16.70); Sparta (2hr., €7.30); Tripoli (3hr., €11.20). The helpful **Malvasia Travel Agency,** in the bus station, provides **currency exchange** (3% commission), and **tickets** for Flying Dolphins and ferries. (☎61 752; fax 61 432. Open daily 7am-3:30pm; high season also 5-8pm.) **Postal Code:** 23070.

NAFPLION Ναύφπλιο ☎27520

After passing from the Venetians to the Ottomans and back again, Nafplion became Greece's first capital in 1821. The town's dynamic history is quite evident today—in the Old Town, Plateia Syndagma alone boasts a Venetian mansion, a Turkish mosque, and a Byzantine church. The town's crown jewel is the 18th-century **Palamidi fortress,** with spectacular views of the town and gulf. Take a taxi up the 3km road, or climb the grueling 999 steps, marked by two cannonballs, starting from Polizoidhou, across the park from the bus station. (Open 8:30am-6:30pm. €4, non-EU students €2, EU students and under 18 free.) To reach **Bouboulinas,** the waterfront promenade, go left out of the bus station and follow Syngrou to the harbor; the **Old Town** is on your left.

Tucked into the mountainside, **Pension Marianna** ❹ provides jaw-dropping views and handsome rooms with TV, A/C, minibar, and bath. Turn right out of the bus station onto Syngrou, then right at Fotomara, and follow the signs. (☎24 256; www.pension-marianna.gr. Singles €50-55; doubles €60-70; triples €75. MC/V.) For rooftop views at **Dimitris Bekas' Domatia** ❷, follow Fotomara past Marianna, turn left up the stairs at the Catholic church, right on Zygomala, then left up the first stairs. (☎24 594. Singles €19; doubles from €25; triples €33. Cash only.) **Ellas** ❷, pl. Syndagma, is cheap and cheerful. (☎27 278. Entrees €4-7. MC/V.)

Buses leave from Syngrou for: Athens (3hr., 15 per day, €9.70) via Corinth (2hr., €4); Epidavros (40min., 4 per day, €2.20); Mycenae (45min., 3 per day, €2.20). The **tourist office** is on 25 Martiou across from the **OTE** telephone office. (☎24 444. Open daily 9am-1pm and 4-8pm.) **Postal Code:** 21100.

EPIDAVROS Επίδαυρος ☎27530

Like Olympia and Delphi, Epidavros was once both a town and a sanctuary—first to an ancient deity Maleatas, then to Apollo, who assumed the former patron's name and aspects of his identity. Eventually the energies of the sanctuary were directed toward the demigod **Asclepius,** the son of Apollo who caught Zeus's wrath (and even worse, his fatal thunderbolt) when the good doctor got a little overzealous and began to raise people from the dead. Under the patronage of Asclepius, Epidavros became famous across the ancient world as a center of medicine. Today, visitors can explore the **sanctuary** and visit a **museum** of ancient medical equipment and other artifacts. (☎22 009. Both open daily 8am-7pm; low season 8am-5pm; during festival F-Sa 8am-9pm. Museum closed M 8am-noon. €6, non-EU students €3, EU students and under 18 free.) With its world-renowned acoustics, the theater, built in the early 2nd century BC, is undoubtedly the most splendid structure at the site. Fortunately for today's visitors, Ancient Greece's top theater has come alive again after centuries of silence: during July and August it hosts the **Epidavros Theater Festival.** The National Theater of Greece and visiting companies perform classical Greek plays. Performances begin at 9pm, and tickets can be purchased at the site. (€17-40, students and children €8.50.) Epidavros is best visited as a daytrip from Nafplion; catch a **bus** from the station at 8 Syngrou. (40min.; 10:15am, 12:14, 2:30, 5:30pm; €2.20.)

drunken crowds and keep your wits about you. In general, however, it's very strange for a woman to go out drinking alone, and this is particularly noticeable in bars frequented by locals. In such establishments, talk with the bartender or with other women (if there are any) to avoid unwanted overtures.

Greeks are not booty-shakers by nature, but enough alcohol will get them dancing. Avoid suggestive bumping and grinding unless you want the added attention, and refuse a potential dance partner unless you want to be dancing with him all night. Although some advise that a wedding band might prevent pick-ups, even the biggest bling won't put off a determined Greek suitor.

If a lusty guy won't stop bothering you, say "AH-se-meh!" meaning "leave me alone." If that fails, get the attention of a local woman, who, used to this game of sexual politics, will likely tell the guy off in not-so-nice terms and send him away, tail between his legs. This is especially effective on smaller islands, where the bar's clientele probably already know each another well.

If you there is someone who sparks your interest, returning the stare will signal to him that it's okay to proceed. If he is still interested, he'll send over a drink. If you're female, he'll be interested. Choose carefully, though—once you start talking, he'll expect to be with you the rest of the night.

—Laurie Schnidman

MYCENAE Μυκήνες ☎27330

The head of the Greek world from 1600 to 1100 BC, Mycenae was ruled by the legendary Agamemnon, leader of the Greek forces in the Trojan War. Excavations of ancient Mycenae have persisted since 1876, turning the area into one of the most visited sites in Greece. The imposing **Lion's Gate,** the portal into the ancient city, has two lions carved in relief above the lintel and is estimated to weigh 20 tons. The **Tomb of Agamemnon** (a.k.a. the Treasury of Atreus) is the large and impressive *tholos* 400m downhill on the way to the town. At the far end of the city, between the palace and the **postern gate,** is the **underground cistern,** a vital component of the ancient city which guaranteed water during sieges. (Sites open daily June-Oct. 8am-7:30pm; Nov.-May 8am-3pm. €8, students €4, EU students free. Keep your ticket or pay twice.) **Buses** from Mycenae go to Nafplion (45min.; 11am, 1, 2:30, 7pm; €2.10) via Argos (30min., €1.10).

CORINTH Κόρινθος ☎27410

Between the Corinthian and Saronic Gulfs, Ancient Corinth was a powerful commercial center in ancient Greece. The city's ruins lie at the base of **Acrocorinth,** a large hill, at the top of which stands a magnificent fortress built in the 10th century; its walls encircle the ruins of towers, mosques, gates, and buildings from the 14th to 18th centuries. Seven of the original 38 columns from the **Temple of Apollo** in the ancient city have defiantly endured since the 6th century BC. Up the stairs from the temple is the excellent **Archaeological Museum,** which houses statues, mosaics, and figurines from the Julian Basilica (27 BC-AD 4). To the left, near the exit at the edge of the site farthest from the museum, a broad stone stairway descends into the monumental **Peirene Fountain.** (☎31 207. Open daily 8:30am-7:30pm. Museum and site €6, non-EU students €3, EU students and under 18 free.)

Hotel Akti ❷, Eth. Antistasis 1, is the best downtown budget lodging, offering clean rooms and private baths. (☎23 337. Singles €20; doubles €30.) In grimy **New Corinth,** a transportation hub and the logical base for viewing the ruins, **buses** leave from terminal A, past the train station, for Athens (1½hr., every 30min., €6.60), and from terminal B, on Koliatsou, halfway through the park, to Ancient Corinth (20min., 15 per day, €1). From terminal C in **Argolis Station** (☎24 403), at the intersection of Eth. Antistasis and Aratou, buses leave for: Argos (1hr., €3.20); Mycenae (45min., €2.70); Nafplion (1½hr., €4). **Trains** go from the station on Dimokratias to Athens (2hr., 7 per day, €2.60; express: 1½hr., 6 per day, €5.20). The **tourist police,** Ermou 51, in the city park, provide tourists with maps, brochures, and other assistance. (☎23 282. Open daily 8am-2pm.) **Postal Code:** 20100.

NORTHERN AND CENTRAL GREECE

For travelers seeking to distance themselves from hectic Athens and the tourist-packed islands, northern and central Greece offer an idyllic escape, ripe with fantastic hiking and Byzantine and Hellenistic heritage. The Greek heartland also boasts several major cities, including Thessaloniki and Ioannina. A region connected both ethnically and historically to its Balkan neighbors, the north is where the multicultural Greek state surfaces.

THESSALONIKI Θεσσαλονίκη ☎2310

Thessaloniki (a.k.a. Salonica; pop. 1,083,000) is one of the most cosmopolitan cities in Greece, second in size only to Athens. From its fashionable cafes by the harbor to its churches and mosques, Thessaloniki dazzles travelers with eastern fragrances and atmosphere while providing a material timeline of Greek history. Most travelers spend a few days in Thessaloniki checking out the world-class museums, clubbing, and touring the nearby archaeological site at Vergina.

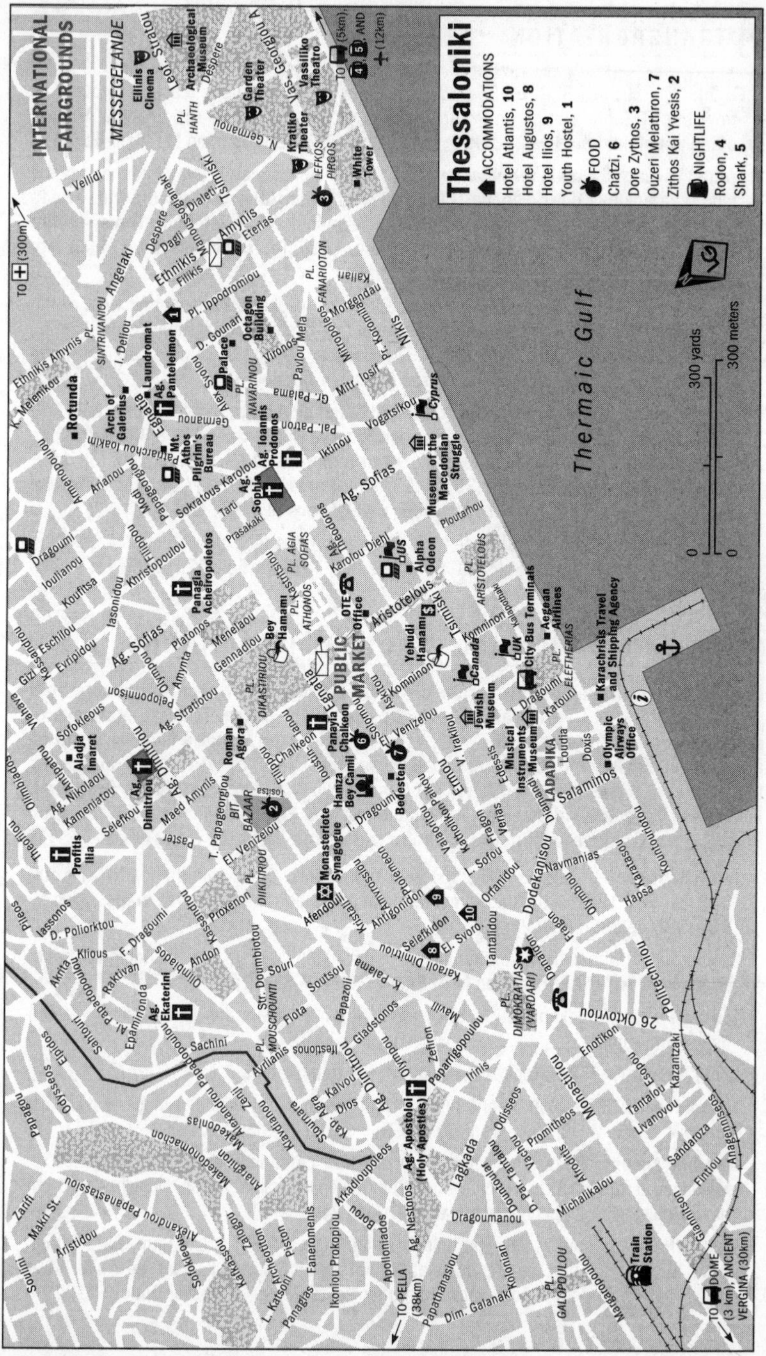
Thessaloniki
ACCOMMODATIONS
Hotel Atlantis, 10
Hotel Augustos, 8
Hotel Ilios, 9
Youth Hostel, 1
FOOD
Chatzi, 6
Dore Zythos, 3
Ouzeri Melathron, 7
Zithos Kai Yvesis, 2
NIGHTLIFE
Rodon, 4
Shark, 5
Thermaic Gulf
INTERNATIONAL FAIRGROUNDS
MESSEGELANDE
Archaeological Museum
White Tower
Rotunda
Arch of Galerius
Ag. Sophia
Ag. Dimitriou
Roman Agora
Museum of the Macedonian Struggle
Jewish Museum
Musical Instruments Museum
City Bus Terminals
Train Station
Ag. Apostoloi (Holy Apostles)
PUBLIC MARKET
LADADIKA
Egnatia
Ag. Sofias
Tsimiski
Mitropoleos
Nikis
26 Oktovriou
300 yards
300 meters

TRANSPORTATION

Flights: The **airport** (SKG; ☎985 000), 16km east of town, can be reached by bus #78 from the KTEL bus station on Pl. Aristotelous, or by **taxi** (€15). The **Olympic Airways** office Kountouriotou 3 (☎368 311, reservations 368 666), is open M-F 8am-4pm.

Trains: To reach the **main terminal** (☎517 517), on Monastiriou in the western part of the city, take any bus down Egnatia (€0.50). Trains go to: **Athens** (7hr., 6 per day 8am-11:45pm, €14; high speed: 5hr., 6 per day 7am-2am, €33); **İstanbul, Turkey** (14hr., 7:17am, €14); **Sofia, Bulgaria** (7hr., midnight, €50). The **travel office** (☎1110) provides schedules and English-language assistance.

Buses: Most **KTEL** buses leave from the central, dome-shaped bus station west of the city center. Bus #1 is a shuttle service between the train and bus stations (every 15min., €0.50). To: **Athens** (6hr., 9 per day, €30); **Corinth** (7½hr., 11:30pm, €36.60); **Ioannina** (6½hr., 6 per day, €23.30); **Patras** (7½hr., 4 per day, €33).

Ferries: Buy tickets at **Karacharisis Travel and Shipping Agency,** Kountouriotou 8 (☎513 005; fax 532 289), across from the Olympic Airways Office. Open M-F 8:30am-8:30pm, Sa 8:30am-2:30pm. Mid-June to early Sept., ferries travel to: **Chios** (20hr., Su 1am, €34.20); **Iraklion** (24hr., Tu 2:30pm, €34) via **Paros** (11hr., €37.50) and **Santorini** (18hr., €41); **Naxos** (14hr., Th 7pm, €36) via **Mykonos** (13½hr., €37.50).

Local Transportation: Local buses run throughout the city. Buy tickets for €0.40 at *periptera* or depot ticket booths, €0.50 on the bus. **Taxis** (☎551 525) gather at stands on Ag. Sophia and Mitropoleos.

ORIENTATION AND PRACTICAL INFORMATION

Egnatia, an old Roman highway, runs down the middle of town and is home to budget hotels. Parallel to the water, the main streets are **Ermou, Tsimiski, Mitropoleos,** and **Nikis,** which runs along the waterfront. Inland from Egnatia is **Agios Dimitriou** and the **old city** beyond. Intersecting all these streets are, in order from the harbor in the west to the White Tower *(Levkos Pyrgos)* in the east, **Ionos Dragoumi, Eleftherias Venizelou, Aristotelous, Agias Sophias,** and **Ethnikis Aminis.** Aristotelous, a wide, breezy boulevard from the ocean to the acropolis, is the city's center.

Tourist Offices: An **EOT** (☎985 215) is at the **airport.** Open 9am-9pm. **GNTO** (☎500 310; fax 566 120), in the passenger terminal of the port, provides **free maps.** Open M-F 9am-9pm, Sa-Su 8am-2pm.

Banks: Banks with currency exchange and 24hr. **ATMs** line Tsimiski, including **Citibank,** Tsimiski 21 (☎373 300). Open M-Th 8am-2:30pm, F 8am-2pm.

Tourist Police: Dodekanissou 4, 5th fl. (☎554 871). Free maps and brochures. Open daily 8am-10pm.

Local Police: (☎553 800 or 100.) Booth at the train station.

Telephones: OTE, Karolou Diehl 33 (☎134), at the corner of Ermou, 1 block east of Aristotelous. Open M-F 8:30am-2pm, Tu and Th-F also 5:30-8:30pm.

Internet Access: There is no shortage of Internet cafes in Thessaloniki. **Meganet,** Pl. Navarinou 5 (☎250 331; www.meganet.gr) by Galerius's palace. Noon-midnight €1.80 per hr., midnight-noon €1 per hr. Laptop access. Open 24hr.

Post Office: Aristotelous 26, just below Egnatia. Open M-F 7:30am-8pm, Sa 7:30am-2pm, Su 9am-1:30pm. Send parcels at the branch on Eth. Aminis near the White Tower (☎227 604). Open M-F 7am-8pm. Both offer *Poste Restante.* **Postal Code:** 54101.

ACCOMMODATIONS

Don't expect to find comfort and cleanliness all at one low price—budget options are available, but you'll get what you pay for. Thessaloniki's less expensive hotels are along the western end of **Egnatia,** between **Plateia Dimokratias** (500m east of the train station) and **Aristotelous.**

Hotel Atlantis, Egnatia 14 (☎540 131). Friendly Standard budget rooms with sinks and balconies. Clean hallway bathrooms. Some rooms with A/C. English spoken. Breakfast €4. Singles €20, with bath €35; doubles €25/40; triples €30/45. ❷

Hotel Ilios, Egnatia 27 (☎512 620), on the western Egnatia budget strip, has modern rooms with big windows, A/C, and TV. If you want to escape the hustle and bustle of Egnatia, ask for a room facing the back. Singles €35; doubles €49; triples €63.70. ❸

Hotel Augustos, El. Svoronou 4 (☎522 955; augustos@hellasnet.gr). Follow Egnatia down to Pl. Dimokratias and take a sharp right onto Karaoli. El. Svoronou is your first right. Cozy rooms with high ceilings, rugs, and wooden floors. Some rooms with balcony. Singles €20, with bath €25; doubles €27/38; triples with bath €50. ❷

Thessaloniki Youth Hostel, Alex. Svolou 44 (☎225 946). Take bus #8, 10, 11, or 31 west down Egnatia; get off at the Arch of Galerius (Kamara stop) and walk down Gounari towards the water. Svolou is your second left. Backpackers talk all night on this cheap hostel's balconies. Mid-July to mid-Sept. dorms €15; mid-Sept. to mid-July €13. 10% ISIC discount. Max. 5-day stay. ❶

FOOD

Near the fortress, the **old city** overflows with *tavernas* and restaurants with sweeping views of the gulf. Thessaloniki restaurants have a delightful custom of giving patrons free watermelon or sweets after a meal.

Dore Zythos, Tsiroyianni 7 (☎279 010; www.zithos.gr), across from the White Tower. Sea breezes and an avant-garde menu make this a local favorite. Try the Samothrakian fava bean salad (€3.70). Entrees €4.50-12. Open 10am-2am. V. ❷

Chatzi, El. Venizelou 50 (☎279 058; www.chatzis.gr), offers sweets ranging from from the banal to the bizzare. Interesting versions of traditional desserts like nuts *kataifi* (€3), or *galaktoboureko,* a cream filled pastry (€2.20). Open daily 6:30am-3am. Cash only. ❶

Ouzeri Melathron, Karypi 21-34 (☎275 016). From Egnatia, walk past the Ottoman Bedesten on El. Venizelou, make a right into the cobblestone passageway, then take the first left. Extensive and wittily subtitled menu. Entrees €4.30-13. Free round of drinks with ISIC. Open daily 1pm-1am. MC/V. ❷

Zithos Kai Yvesis (☎268 746), hidden away near the intersection of El. Venizelou and Filipou. With your back to Egnatia, walk a half-block past the intersection and look for a sign reading "Venizelou 72". The restaurant is through the passageway, on your left. Laughter and conversation continue into the night. The taverna serves a variety of appetizers and traditional Greek food. Dishes €1.50-5.50. Open daily 6pm-2am. Cash only. ❷

SIGHTS AND NIGHTLIFE

The streets of modern Thessaloniki are graced with the reminders of its significance during the Byzantine and Ottoman Empires. **Agios Dimitrios,** on Ag. Dimitriou north of Aristotelous, is the city's oldest and most famous church. Although most of the interior was gutted in a 1917 fire, some lovely mosaics remain. (Open daily 6am-10pm.) Originally part of a grand palatial complex designed for Roman Caesar Galerius when he made Thessaloniki his capital, the **Rotunda** became

Church Agios Georgiou in late Roman times. Under the Ottoman Empire, the huge cylindrical building was converted into a mosque. Its walls were once plastered with some of the city's most brilliant mosaics of saints and New Testament stories; unfortunately, very few remain. (☎968 860. Open Tu-Su 8am-5pm. Free.) At the intersection of D. Gounari and Egnatia stands the striking **Arch of Galerius,** known to locals simply as *Kamara* (arch). It was erected to commemorate Galerius's victory over the Persians. Farther west down Egnatia, don't miss **Bey Hamami,** a perfectly preserved 15th-century bath house, the first the Turks built in Thessaloniki. Formerly host to the Ottoman governor and his retinue, it now houses art exhibits. (Open M-F 8:30am-3pm. Free.) In keeping with its position as second city of the Byzantine Empire, Thessaloniki uses its **Museum of Byzantine Culture,** Stratou 2, to tell a cosmopolitan and secular tale through displays on everyday Byzantine life, economics, engineering, and imperial dynasties. This museum houses the largest collection of early Christian wall paintings outside the Vatican and vividly evokes daily life in early Christendom. (☎868 570; www.mbp.gr. Open M 10:30am-5pm, Tu-Su 8:30am-3pm. €4, non-EU students €2, EU students free.) Once the site of gruesome executions, the **White Tower** is now all that remains of a 15th-century Venetian seawall. Today it is Thessaloniki's most recognizable landmark, presiding over the waterfront like an overgrown chess piece. The Museum of Byzantine Culture presents rotating exhibits in the tower. (☎267 832. Open Tu-Su 8:30am-3pm. €2, students free.) Thessaloniki's **Archaeological Museum,** at the eastern end of Tsimiski, across from the International Helexpo Fairgrounds, is full of Neolithic artifacts, Roman mosaics, and an impressive display of Macedonian gold. (☎861 306; fax 861 306; info@amth.culture.gr. Open M 1-7:30pm, Tu-Su 8:30am-7:30pm; low season reduced hours. €4, non-EU students €2, EU students free.)

There are four main hubs for late-night fun in Thessaloniki: the bars and cafes of the **Ladadika** district, a sea of dance clubs; the bustling **waterfront** cafes where students congregate; the dance-until-you-drop open-air discos around the **airport,** popular with tourists; and the **'Bit Bazar'** area which includes 13 wine bars—every one of which is packed all night long. Rub elbows with the city's hipsters at **Rodon,** one of the most expensive and high-class clubs in Thessaloniki, located 11km east of the city along the main highway. (☎476 720. Cover €10, includes 1 drink. Open 11pm-4:30am.) **Shark,** Themistokli Sofouli and Argonavton 2, has waterfront views of the skyline. (☎416 855. Open 9pm-4am.)

DAYTRIP FROM THESSALONIKI

ANCIENT VERGINA. The tombs of Vergina (Βέργινα), final home to ancient Macedonian royalty, lie only 30km from Thessaloniki. The principal sight is the **Great Tumulus,** a manmade mound 12m tall and 110m wide. Visitors can stroll in to see its magnificent burial treasures, intricate gold work, and brilliant frescoes. The extravagance of these tombs has convinced archaeologists that they hold the bones of **Philip II** and **Alexander IV,** father and son of Alexander the Great. (Open summer M noon-7pm, Tu-Su 8am-7pm; winter Tu-Su 8am-7pm. €8, non-EU students €4, EU students free.) **Buses** run from Thessaloniki to Veria (1hr., 1 per hr., 8:12am-7:15pm, €5). From Veria, take the bus to Vergina's *plateia* (20min., 11 per day 6:50am-8pm, €1); follow the signs to the sights.

MOUNT OLYMPUS Ολύμπος Όρος ☎23520

Erupting out of the Thermaic Gulf, Mt. Olympus, Greece's highest peak, so mesmerized the ancients that they believed it to be the dwelling place of their pantheon. Today, a network of well-maintained **hiking** trails makes the summit accessible to anyone with sturdy legs. Mt. Olympus has eight peaks: Ag. Andonios

(2817m), Kalogeros (2701m), Mytikas (2918m), Profitis Ilias (2803m), Skala (2866m), Skolio (2911m), Stefani (the Throne of Zeus; 2907m), and Toumba (2801m). There are several ways to take on Olympus; all originate in the town of **Litochoro** (elev. 500m). The most popular trail begins at **Prionia** (elev. 1100m), 18km from the village, ascending 4km through a forested ravine to **Zolotas** refuge, also known as Refuge A. There, you'll find reliable resources for all aspects of hiking—updates on weather and trail conditions, advice on itineraries and routes, and reservations for any of the **Greek Alpine Club (EOS)** refuges. The staff has years of experience and dispenses info over the phone in English. (☎81 800. Curfew 10pm. Open mid-May to Oct. 6am-10pm. Camping €5; dorms €10.) After spending the night at the Zolotas refuge, you'll ascend to the summit in the morning. Hikers can spend another night in a mountaintop refuge and walk down the next day to Diastavrosi (3-4hr.), or make the whole trip in one day. All of the trails to the refuges are easy to follow, and most are marked with red and yellow blazes. Unless you're handy with a crampon and an ice axe, make your ascent between May and October. Mytikas, the tallest peak, is inaccessible without special equipment before June.

The night before your hike, head to **Hotel Park ❷,** Ag. Nikolaou 23, where tacky mosaic hallways lead into large rooms with A/C, bath, TV, fridge, phone, and large balcony. (☎81 252. Singles €24; doubles €30; triples €35.) KTEL **buses** (☎81 271) go from Litochoro to Athens (5hr., 3 per day, €25) and Thessaloniki (1½hr., 16 per day, €6.50). The **tourist office,** which offers free maps of the town and a map of the mountain (€4.50), is on Ag. Nikolaou by the park. (☎83 100. Open July-Nov. daily 8am-2pm and 3-9pm.) **Postal Code:** 60200.

METEORA Μετέωρα ☎24320

Atop a series of awe-inspiring pinnacles perches the monastic community of Meteora. These summits were picked as the location of a series of 21 gravity-defying, frescoed Byzantine monasteries in the 14th century. Six of these monasteries are still in use and open to the public. However, don't expect a hidden treasure—tour buses and sweaty faces are as common in Meteora as Byzantine icons. The **Grand Meteora Monastery** is the oldest, largest, and most popular of the monasteries. It houses a **folk museum** and the 16th-century **Church of the Transfiguration,** as well as a collection of early printed secular books by Aristotle, Plato, and others which attest to a once-vibrant intellectual center. **Roussanou,** to the right after the fork in the road, is one of the most spectacularly situated monasteries in the area. (Modest dress required. Open Apr.-Sept. Sa-Su and W 10am-12:30pm and 3:30-5pm; hours vary during the rest of the week. €2 per monastery.)

In the Old Town, at the base of Meteora, **Alsos House ❷,** Kanari 5, has reasonably priced rooms with gorgeous views, private bath, A/C, and balcony. It's an 8min. walk from the central *plateia;* follow Vlachava until it ends, then follow the signs. (☎24 097; www.kalampaka.com/alsoshouse. Laundry €5. Singles €25; doubles €35-40; triples €50; 2-room apartment with kitchen €60. Discounts for students and *Let's Go* travelers.) Meteora is accessible by **bus** from Kalambaka, the nearest town (15min.; 2 per day 9am, 1:20pm; €1). **Trains** leave Kalambaka for Athens (4½hr., 4 per day, €19.10). **Buses** depart Kalambaka for: Athens (5hr., 7 per day, €21); Ioannina (3hr., 2 per day, €9); Patras (5hr.; Tu and Th 10am, F-Su 3pm; €22.30); Thessaloniki (3½hr.; 7:30am, 4:15pm; €14.60). **Postal Code:** 42200.

IOANNINA Ιωάννινα ☎26510

Ioannina (pop. 100,000) is the capital and transportation hub of the Epirus region of northern Greece. The city was captured in 1788 by **Ali Pasha,** an Albanian-born leader and visionary, who planned to make Ioannina the capital of his Empire. The peninsula that extends into Lake Pamvotis is the site of the **Frourio,** a monumental

13th-century fortress which is still home to many of Ioannina's residents. To reach the **Itş Kale** (inner citadel) from the main entrance of the Frourio, turn right, then take the first left and walk up the long ramp. To the left of the main entrance are the remnants of Ali Pasha's **hamam** (baths). Catch a ferry from the waterfront for **Nisi** (10min., 2 per hr., €1.30) to explore the **Ali Pasha Museum,** where he hid from the Turkish soldiers and was ultimately shot to death. (Open daily 9am-9pm; €2.) A hike through the **Vikos Gorge,** the world's steepest canyon, in the Zagorohoria region just north of Ioannina, will rejuvenate anyone tired of city life.

Budget lodging is hard to come by in Ioannina. **Hotel Dioni ❸**, Tsirigoti 10, is near the main bus station, and is probably the best value in town. With your back to the station, follow Zosimadon for one block and turn left onto Tsirigoti. Bright rooms have A/C, TV, phone, spacious baths, and a balcony. (☎27 032; www.epirus.com/dioni. Singles €50; doubles €70. AmEx/MC/V.) Camping is available at **Limnopoula ❶**, Kanari 10 near the town exit on route to Perama, with laundry (€5), a kitchen, swimming, and a mini-market. (☎25 265; fax 38 060. Reception 7am-midnight. Tent sites €10, extra person €6.) **Limni ❷**, Papagou 26, has a charming lakeside patio with views of the mountains and mosque. Portions are huge and prices reasonable. (☎78 988. Entrees €4.50-7. Open daily 10am-3am.) The cafe-bar **Kura Frosuni** is right outside the fort. Always crowded with young people, the cafe has the closest tables to the water and a great view of Nisi. (☎73 984. Beer €3.50. Mixed drinks €7. Open daily 9:30am-3am.) **Buses** run from the terminal at Zosimadon 4 to Athens (5½hr., 10 per day, €28.60); Igoumenitsa (2hr., 8 per day, €7); Thessaloniki (4½hr., 3 per day, €22.30). To reach the **tourist office,** walk 500m down Dodonis; the office is on the left, immediately after the playground. Ask for a free map. (☎46 662; eotioan@otenet.gr. Open M-F 7:30am-2:30pm.) **Postal Code:** 45110.

DELPHI Δελφοι ☎22650

Troubled denizens of the ancient world journeyed to this stunning mountaintop sanctuary of the Oracle of Delphi, where the priestess of Apollo related cryptic prophecies of the gods. The site's fantastic **museum** houses artifacts from the **Temple of Apollo** and the surrounding digs. There is also a **stadium** that once hosted the Delphic Games. Head east out of the town of Delphi to reach the site. (Open daily 7:30am-7:30pm. €6, site and museum €9.) **Hotel Sibylla ❷,** Pavlou 9, has wonderful views and private baths at the best prices in town. (☎82 335. Singles €20; doubles €26; triples €34. €2 discount for *Let's Go* readers.) Buses leave Athens for Delphi from Terminal B, Liossion 260 (3hr., 6 per day, €11.80). Delphi's **tourist office,** Pavlou 12, is in the town hall. (☎82 900. Open M-F 8am-2:30pm.) **Postal Code:** 33054.

OSIOS LOUKAS Όσιος Λουκάς ☎22670

Stunning Byzantine architecture, gold-laden mosaics, vivid frescoes, and intricate brick- and stone-work adorn this striking **monastery.** Founded by Saint Osios Loukas, the **Church of the Panagia** (Church of the Virgin Mary), was finished soon after his death in AD 953, and today holds the shriveled body of the saint himself, lying in a glass coffin. The larger and more ornate **Katholikon of Osios Loukas,** built in 1011, became the site of his reliquary. In addition to the two churches, the monastery contains a crypt, a bell tower, monks' cells, and a museum. (☎22 797. Open daily May 3-Sept. 15 8am-2pm and 4-6pm; Sept. 16-May 2 8am-5pm. Dress modestly. €3, students €2, children and EU students free.) From Delphi, take a **bus** to Arahova (10min., 6 per day, €1), then take a **car** or **taxi** (☎31 566) to the monastery. When you are negotiating the price, ask the driver to also bring you back to town. Most taxis are willing to wait for an hour for a higher fare. (Round-trip €30.)

IONIAN ISLANDS Νησιά Του Ιόνιου

West of mainland Greece, the Ionian Islands entice travelers with their lush vegetation and shimmering turquoise waters. Never conquered by the Ottomans, the islands show traces of Venetian, British, French, and Russian occupants. Today, they are a favorite among Western Europeans and ferry-hopping backpackers.

FERRIES TO ITALY

To catch a ferry from Corfu to Italy, buy your ticket at least a day ahead and ask if the port tax is included. **International Tours** (☎26610 39 007) and **Ionian Cruises** (☎26610 31 649), both across the street from the port on El. Venizelou, can help with scheduling. Destinations include: Bari (10hr., M-F 1 per day, €49); Brindisi (8hr., 1-2 per day, €32); Venice (24hr., 1 per day, €64). Schedules vary; call ahead.

CORFU Κέρκυρα ☎26610

Ever since Homer's Odysseus washed ashore and raved about Corfu's lush beauty, the surrounding seas have brought a constant stream of conquerors, colonists, and tourists to the verdant island. **Corfu Town** enchants an Ionian combination of Greek and Venetian traditions. Discover the pleasures of colonialism at the English-built **Mon Repos Estate,** which features lovely gardens and an exhibit of archaeological treasures from the island. (Estate open daily 8am-7pm. Museum open Tu-Su 8:30am-3pm. Estate free. Museum €3, EU students €2.) The **Palace of St. Michael and St. George** is another impressive, stately home, with a collection of Neoclassical sculpture and Asian artifacts. (Open Tu-Su 8:30am-3pm. €3, students and seniors €2, EU students free.) The lovely beach of **Paleokastritsa,** where Odysseus supposedly washed ashore, lies west of Corfu Town; take a KTEL bus to Paleokastritsa (45min., 3-6 per day, €1.70). The **Disco Strip,** on Eth. Antistaseos, 2km west of the new port is the undisputed epicenter of Corfu Town's nightlife.

The Association of Owners of Private Rooms and Apartments, Iak. Polila 24, has a complete list of rooms in Corfu Town. (☎26 133. Open M-F 9am-3pm and 5-8pm.) KTEL buses also run from Corfu Town to **Agios Gordios** (45min., 2-4 per day, €1.70), home to the **Pink Palace Hotel ❷.** Here, hordes of American and Canadian backpackers trade travel stories and bodily fluids while enjoying the nightclub, clothing-optional cliff-diving (€15), and other water sports. (☎53 103; www.thepinkpalace.com. Breakfast, dinner, and ferry pickup included. Internet €1.50 per 35min. Dorms from €18; singles €20, with A/C and bath €25-40. Flexible prices for *Let's Go* readers.) Lodging in Corfu Town is exorbitant, so if you're looking for more mellow digs, take bus #11 to nearby Pelekas (20min., 7 per day 7am-8:30pm, €0.95), where the friendly owners of the **Pension Tellis and Brigitte ❷** offer homey rooms with balconies and superb views. (☎94 326; matini@pelekas.com. Singles €18; doubles €25-30.) At **Restaurant Antranik/Pizza Pete ❷,** Arseniou 21, order a large entree (€5-8) or choose between 20 flavors of homemade ice cream. (☎22 301. Prawns with feta €15, serves 3. Open daily 9am-midnight. AmEx/MC/V.)

Ferries run from Corfu Town to Igoumenitsa (1½hr., every hr. 5:45am-10:45pm, €5.10); Patras (8hr., 1-2 per day, €27) and various locations in Italy (see above). Green KTEL intercity **buses** depart from between I. Theotaki and the New Fortress; blue municipal buses leave from Pl. San Rocco. The **tourist office** is on Pl. San Rocco in a green kiosk. (☎12 177. Open daily 8am-10pm.) **Postal Code:** 49100.

KEPHALONIA Κεφαλόνια ☎26710

With soaring mountains, subterranean lakes and rivers, caves, and forests, Kephalonia is a nature lover's paradise. The bus schedules are erratic and the taxis expensive, but armed with your own transportation, you can uncover picturesque

GO WITH THE FLOW

)f all the strangely worded and :reatively translated phrases I ıave encountered in the Greek slands, the worst is "ferry sched-ıle," a term which leads one to ɔelieve that a regular pattern of departures and arrivals exists, ınd that ferry companies run ıccordingly. Neither assumption, ıowever, is entirely valid. The 'schedules" change constantly, ınd even if a boat is listed to depart or arrive, it's possible that ıothing will materialize.

As an American trained to swear by my day planner, the Greek people's lack of frustration with the ferries' unpredictably was even more mysterious than the 'schedule" itself. While being stranded drove me crazy, Greeks eacted to my frustration with con-usion: "Go tomorrow, go the next lay, why rush?"

Maybe this nonchalance about scheduling (or lack thereof) stems rom acclimatization; the locals expect ferries not to run on time ınd are surprised when they do. Or perhaps it simply reflects more elaxed cultural values.

Though the ferry system's orced deviances took some get-ing used to, the frustration at ɔeing "stuck" on an island soon ɔecome opportunistic relief. When a planned two-day whirl-wind suddenly became a luxuri-ous five-day stay, it was easy to go beyond the standard beach-ınd-acropolis routine, and delve nto the local culture.

—Laurie Schnidman

villages and never-ending beaches that blend into brilliant sunsets. **Argostoli,** the capital of Kephalonia, is a lively city packed with pastel buildings that offers easy access to other points on the island. The town of **Sami,** 24km from Argostoli on the eastern coast, is close to the underground **Melissani Lake** and **Drogarati Cave,** a large cavern filled with stalactites and stalagmites. (Lake open daily 9am-late afternoon. Cave open daily until nightfall. Lake €5. Cave €3.) **Fiskardo,** at the northern tip of the island, is the most beautiful of Kephalonia's towns. Buses to and from Fiskardo stop at the turn-off for **Myrtos Beach,** with brilliant white pebbles and clear, blue water lapping against sheer cliffs. (Beach 4km from turn-off.)

In Argostoli, **Hotel Agamemnon ❷,** 36 I. Metaxa, on the waterfront five blocks north of the tourist office, has immaculate rooms at half the price of its competitors. (☎90 844. Singles €15-30; doubles €25-50.) **Captain's Grille ❷** has two locations: on the waterfront at 21 Maiou and next to the *plateia* at Rizospaston 3. Its tasty portions and live music blend quality food with Greek tradition. (Vegetarian options. Entrees €5-9.) **Ferries** depart from Argostoli for Kyllini on the Peloponnese (2 per day, €7.30), and from Sami to: Brindisi, Italy (July-Sept., 1 per day, €35); Patras (2½hr.; 8:30am, 5pm; €13.60); Vathy in Ithaka (1hr., 11:30pm, €6). **Buses** leave the southern end of the Argostoli waterfront for Fiskardo (2hr., 10am and 2pm, €4) and Sami (40min., 4 per day, €3). There is also a bus from Sami to Fiskardo (1hr., 10:15am, 2pm; €2). The **tourist office,** beside the Port Authority, near the ferry docks, has free maps. (☎22 248. Open daily 7am-2:30pm.) **Internet** is available in Argostoli at B.B.'s Club in the central *plateia*. (☎25 469. €2.50 per hr. Open 9am-2am.) **Postal Code:** 28100.

ITHAKA Ιθάκη ☎26740

Discovering Ithaka means uncovering 6000 years of history, traversing the homeland of legendary Odysseus, and delighting in the island's pebbled beaches, rocky hillsides, and terraced olive groves. **Vathy,** Ithaka's lovely capital, wraps around a circular bay filled with fishing boats and yachts. *Sholi Omirou* (Homer's School), widely acknowledged as the place where **Odysseus's Palace** once stood, has a plethora of Mycenaean ruins. From the village of **Stavros,** go past the Archaeological Museum on the main road, and follow it to the end. The ruins are about 150m farther down the footpath. (Taxi from Vathy €20 one-way. Ruins free.) The enchanting **Monastery of Panagia Katharon** perches on Ithaka's highest mountain, Mt. Neritos; take a moped or taxi (€25 round-trip) toward the town of Anoghi and follow the signs. The monks have two rules for visitors: close the front door to keep goats from wandering in, and women must cover their legs in the sanctuary. (Open sunrise-sunset. Free.) On the white pebble beaches of **Filiatro** and **Sarakiniko,** the water glows in the sun and trees droop into the sea. From Vathy, walk out of town with the water on your left. The beaches are 3.5 and 2.5km out, respectively.

Sophia's ❸, is a gem of a *domatia*, with spacious bathrooms, satellite TV, and A/C. From Vathy's central *plateia*, bear left at the National Bank, walk straight past Niko's Taverna and to the left of the sports store, then walk uphill for two blocks. (☎32 104. Reservations recommended. Rooms €25.) Local favorite **Taverna To Trexantiri ❷**, one block behind the post office, serves big portions of traditional Greek dishes. (☎33 066. Salads €3-4. Entrees €5-7. Open daily 6pm-late.) **Ferries** depart from Frikes, on the northern tip of Ithaka, to Lefkada (2½hr., 1 per day at 10am, €6). Departures from Piso Aetos go to Sami, Kephalonia (45min., 4 per day, €2) and Patras in the Peloponnese (4hr., 7am, €13.30). Schedules vary seasonally; check with the staff at **Delas Tours** in the main *plateia*. (☎32 104; fax 33 031. Open daily 6-7am, 9am-1pm and 5-9:30pm; low-season closed 6-7am.) **Postal Code:** 28300.

ZAKYNTHOS Ζάκυνθος ☎26950

Known as the greenest of the Ionian Islands, Zakynthos is home to thousands of plant and flower species and a large population of loggerhead sea turtles. Bustling **Zakynthos Town** maintains a romantic, nostalgic air. Boats from Zakynthos Town and the nearby towns of Ag. Nikolaos and Laganas go to the glowing, stalactite-filled **Blue Caves** on the northeastern shore past Skinari. Southwest of the Blue Caves is **Smuggler's Wreck,** a large boat skeleton that has made the beach one of the most photographed in the world. For a more intimate travel experience, skip the huge cruise ships from Zakynthos Town and hire a small fishing boat from the docks in nearby towns. Be aware that you share Zakynthos's beaches with a resident population of **endangered sea turtles,** and respect their nesting grounds.

Athina Marouda Rooms for Rent ❶, on Tzoulati and Koutouzi, has simple rooms with communal baths and backpacker-friendly prices. (☎45 194. Singles €10-15; doubles €25-35.) Dining in the *plateias* and by the waterfront in Zakynthos Town is a treat. The quaint **Village Inn ❸**, Lomvardou 20, has tables facing the water and a lovely garden with live Greek music every evening in August. (☎26 991. Entrees €5-9. Open daily noon-midnight.) **Ferries** for Kyllini in the Peloponnese depart from the southern dock (1½hr., 5-7 per day 5:30am-8pm, €5.80). Buy tickets at Praktoreio Ploion, on Lomvardou past the police station with the water on your right. (☎26278 22 083. Open daily 8:30am-8:30pm.) **Postal Code:** 29100.

CYCLADES Κυκλάδες

White-washed houses, winding stone streets, and trellis-covered tavernas characterize all of the Cycladic islands, but subtle quirks make each distinct. Orange-and-black sands coat the shores of Santorini, rocky cliffs shape arid Sifnos, and celebrated archaeological sites distinguish sacred Delos. Naxos and Paros offer peaceful mountain villages, while notorious party spots Ios and Mykonos uncork some of wildest nightlife on earth. Tourists on any island find plenty of local flavor.

TRANSPORTATION

Ferries run from: Athens to Ios (7½hr., 3 per day, €22); Milos (7hr., 1-2 per day, €20); Mykonos (6hr., 2-4 per day, €20); Naxos (6hr., 5-7 per day, €24); Paros (5hr., 4-7 per day, €24); Santorini (9hr., 3-5 per day, €28). From Iraklion, Crete to: Mykonos (8½hr., 2 per week, €22); Naxos (8hr., 1 per week, €22); Paros (7hr., 2 per week, €24); Santorini (4hr., 3 per week, €16) They also run from Thessaloniki

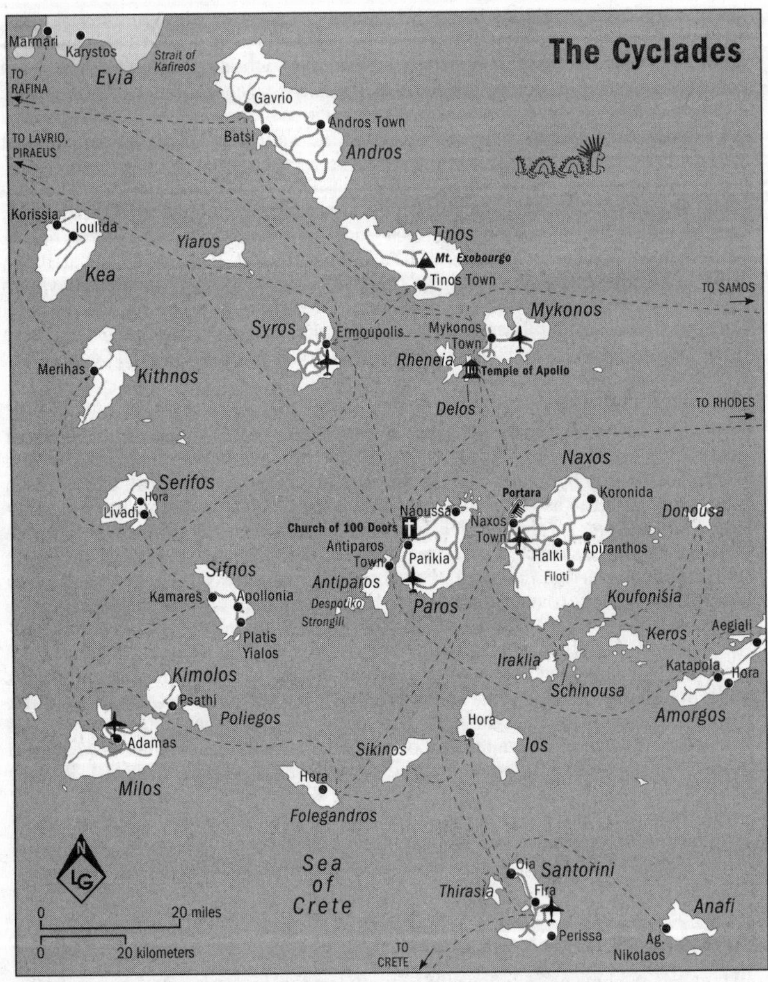

to Mykonos (13½hr., 1 per week, €37.50); Naxos (14hr., 1 per week, €36); Paros (10-12hr., 1 per week, €37.50); Santorini (17-18hr., 1 per week, €36). Frequent ferries run between the islands in the Cyclades. See below for all ferry information. High-speed **hydrofoils** cover some of these routes at twice the cost and speed.

MYKONOS Μύκονος ☎22890

Coveted by pirates in the 18th century, Mykonos is still lusted after by those seeking revelry and excess. Nightlife, both gay and straight, abounds on this island, the expensive playground of chic sophisticates. Ambling down colorful alleyways at dawn or dusk, among the **disturbingly large pink pelicans,** is the way to experience the island, especially **Mykonos Town.** All of Mykonos's beaches are nude, but the degree of bareness varies. **Platis Yialos, Paradise** beach, and **Super Paradise** beach are the most daring; **Elia** is a bit tamer. Buses run south from South Station to Platis Yialos and Paradise (2 per hr. 10am-8pm, €1; 1 per hr. 8pm-10am, €1.30) and from North Station to Elia (30min., 8 per day 11am-7:30pm, €1). **Caprice Bar,** on the water in Little Venice, is a popular post-beach hangout with breathtaking sunsets, funky music, and lively company. (Beer €7. Mixed drinks €10. Open daily 6:30pm-4am.) The **Skandinavian Bar** on the waterfront has something for everyone in its two-building party complex. (Beer and shots €4-6. Mixed drinks from €7. Open daily 9pm-5am.) **Cavo Paradiso,** on Paradise beach, is considered one of the world's top dance clubs, hosting internationally renowned DJs. (Cover €15. Free bus to and from Mykonos Town. Open daily 3am-11am.)

Hotel Philippi ❹, Kalogera 25, across from Zorzis, provides cheerful rooms around a garden with bath, fridge, and A/C. (☎22 294; chriko@otenet.gr. Open Apr.-Oct. Singles €45-70; doubles €60-90; triples €72-108. AmEx/MC/V.). The aptly named **Paradise Beach Camping ❶,** 6km from the village, is lively and right on the beach. (☎25 852. Free pickup at port or airport. Tent sites €2.50-7; extra person €5-8. 2-person beach cabin €15-40.) Cheap *creperies* and *souvlaki* joints line nearly all of Mykonos's streets. **Appaloosa ❸,** D. Mavrogeneous 11, one block from Taxi Square, serves salads, pastas, and Mexican food. (Entrees €7-15. €2 cover includes bread and olive pâté. Open daily 8pm-1am.) **Ferries** run to: Naxos (3hr., F 9:20pm, €9.50); Paros (3hr., M-Sa 1 per day, €8.40); Piraeus (6hr., daily 2:15pm, €25.50). The helpful, English-speaking **tourist police** are located at the ferry landing. (☎22 482. Open daily 8am-9pm.) **Windmills Travel,** on Xenias, around the corner from South Station, books lodgings, scuba and snorkeling trips, and provides maps, as well as GLBT resources. **Postal Code:** 84600.

DELOS Δήλος ☎22890

Delos is the sacred center of the Cyclades. The island-wide **archaeological site** takes several days to explore completely, but its highlights can be seen in about 3hr. From the dock, head straight to the **Agora of the Competaliasts,** then turn left onto the **Sacred Road** to reach the **Sanctuary of Apollo,** a collection of temples that date from Mycenaean times to the 4th century BC. On the right is the biggest and most famous, the **Temple of Apollo.** Continue 50m past the end of the Sacred Road to the beautiful **Terrace of the Lions.** The **museum,** next to the cafeteria, contains an assortment of archaeological finds. (Open Tu-Su 8:30am-3pm. €5, students and seniors €3, EU students free.) From the museum, a path leads to the summit of **Mt. Kythnos** (112m), from which Zeus supposedly watched Apollo's birth. On the descent, you will pass temples to Egyptian gods, including the **Temple of Isis.** The island is best visited as a daytrip from Mykonos. Excursion **boats** leave the dock near Mykonos Town for Delos (35min., Tu-Su 4 per day, round-trip €6.50-7).

PAROS Πάρος ☎22840

Paros is famed for its pure white marble, tall mountains, and long, golden beaches. Behind the commercial surface of **Parikia,** Paros's port and largest city, flower-lined streets wind through archways in the shadow of one of the most treasured basilicas of the Orthodox faith, the **Panagia Ekatontapiliani** (Church of Our Lady of 100 Doors. Dress modestly. Open daily 7am-10pm. Mass daily 7-7:30 pm, Su 7:30-10am. Free.) Just 10km south of town is the shady and undeniably romantic **Petaloudes** (Valley of the Butterflies), where rare *Panaxiaquadripunctaria* moths gather to mate from June to late September. Take the bus from Parikia to Aliki (12min., 7 per day, €0.90) and ask to be let off at Petaloudes. Follow the signs 2km up the road. (Open daily June-Sept. 9am-8pm. €1.50.) Along the waterfront, **The Parian Experience** pulses late into the night with a central courtyard connecting four themed bar areas: The Dubliner, Salsa Club, Scandi (Scandinavian) Bar, and the Paros Rock Cafe. Follow the spotlight and crowds to the far end of the harbor. (☎21 113. Beer €3-5. Mixed drinks €5-6. Cover €3 includes 1 drink.)

Turn left at the dock and turn right after the cemetery to reach the cottage-like **Rena Rooms ❷.** (☎22 220. Doubles €20-40; triples €30-55. 20% discount for *Let's Go* readers.) **Happy Green Cow ❸,** a block off the *plateia* behind the National Bank, serves tasty vegetarian dinners. (☎24 691. Entrees €8-12. Open Apr.-Nov. daily 7pm-midnight.) **Ferry** schedules and prices change regularly. Consult **Kontostavlos A.S Travel Agents** (☎21 353; asc@otenet.gr) for updated information. Approximately, ferries sail to: Crete (3½hr., 2 per week, €43); Ios (2hr., 2-3 per day, €10); Kos (1 per week, €17); Mykonos (5 per week, €8); Naxos (1hr. 4-5 per day, €6); Santorini (3hr., 3-4 per day, €12); Thessaloniki (1 per week, €35). The **tourist police** are on the *plateia*. (☎21 673. Open daily 7am-2:30pm.) **Postal Code:** 84400.

NASOS Νάξος ☎22850

The ancients believed Naxos, the largest of the Cyclades, was once home to Dionysus, the god of wine and revelry. Olive groves, wineries, and chalky white ruins fill its interior, while sandy beaches line its shores. **Naxos Town,** the capital, is crowned by the **Kastro,** a Venetian castle. In the Kastro, the **Venetian Museum** hosts evening concerts with traditional Greek music, dancing, and shadow theater. (☎22 387; venetian@acn.gr. Open daily 10am-3pm and 7-10pm. €3, students €2.) The **Mitropolis Museum,** next to the Orthodox church, is built around the excavated site of a 13th-century BC settlement. (☎24 151. Open Tu-Su 8:30am-3pm. Free.) The 6th-century BC **Portara** archway, visible from the waterfront, is one of the few archaeological sites in Greece that allows you to climb on the ruins.

Pension Irene ❷, about 100m from Ag. Giorgios, is near the center of the town. (☎23 169. All rooms with A/C. Singles €15; doubles €20-30; triples €25-35; 5-person apartments €40-50.) Naxos has three **campsites** along the beach; look for agents on the dock. (Tent sites €2, plus €4-8 per person.) On the old market street at the foot of the Old Town, **O Apolstolis ❷** is a traditional Greek restaurant serving whole, grilled fish (€11) and other fine dishes in an outdoor setting. (Open daily noon-2am. AmEx/MC/V.) **Irini's ❷** is the second taverna along the waterfront after Zas Travel. Try the stuffed green peppers (€5) or the grilled chicken with mushrooms (€6.50) under Irini's leafy terrace. (Open daily noon-late. MC/V.) **Ferries** go from Naxos Town to: Crete (7hr., 1 per week, €20); Ios (1hr., 1 per day, €8.20); Kos (7hr., 1 per week, €16); Mykonos (3hr., 1 per day, €9); Paros (1hr., 4 per day, €5.50); Piraeus (6hr., 4 per day, €20); Rhodes (13hr., 1 per week, €20); Santorini (3hr., 3 per day, €13); Thessaloniki (14hr., €30). A bus goes from the port to the beaches of **Agios Giorgios, Agios Prokopios, Agia Anna,** and **Plaka** (about 1 per hr., €1.20). Buses also run from Naxos Town to **Apiranthos,** a beautiful village with narrow, marble paths (1hr., €2.10). The **tourist office** is 300m up from the dock, next to the bus station. (☎24 358. Open daily 8am-11pm.) **Postal Code:** 84300.

IOS Ίος ☎22860

In recent years, Ios has made a concerted and successful effort to tone down its party-animal reputation and attract families and older travelers. Still, you won't have to look very far to see everything your mother warned you about—wine swilled from the bottle at 3pm, partiers dancing madly in the streets, and even people swimming less than 30min. after they've eaten. Most spend their days at **Mylopotas beach,** a 20min. walk downhill from Hora or a bus ride from the port or town (3-6 per hr. 7:20am-midnight, €1). Various establishments on the beach offer windsurfing, water-skiing, and snorkeling during daylight hours (€14-40). Sunning is typically followed by drinking; head up from the *plateia* to reach the **Slammer Bar** for tequila slammers (€3), then stop by **Disco 69** for some dirty dancing. (Drinks €5. Cover €6 after midnight.) Join in the table dancing at **Sweet Irish Dream** (cover after 2:30am) or grind to techno at **Scorpion Disco,** the island's largest club (cover after 2am). A few hours later, crowds begin to re-gather at the beach.

In the village, take the uphill steps to the left in the *plateia* and take the first left to reach **Francesco's ❶**, where you'll find spectacular harbor views and a terrace bar. (☎91 223; www.francescos.net. Dorms €8-13; private rooms with A/C and bath €10-22 per person.) At the end of Mylopotas beach, **Far Out Beach Club and Camping ❶** offers accommodations for any budget, from tent sites to hotel rooms, as well as pools, parties, and bungee jumping. (☎92 302. Open Apr.-Oct. Tent sites €4-9, tent rental €1; small cabins €5-12; bungalows €8-18. Hotel rooms €10-35 per person.) **Ali Baba's ❷**, next to Ios Gym, offers delicious international fare—from Asian dishes to burgers to duck—to satisfy any taste. (☎91 558. Chicken satay €9. BLT €5.50. Open daily 6:30pm-midnight.) **Ferries** go to: Naxos (1¾hr., 3 per day, €9); Paros (3hr., 3 per day, €9); Piraeus (8hr., 3 per day, €22); Santorini (1¼hr., 3 per day, €7). **Acteon Travel,** next to the bus stop at the port, takes the place of a tourist office. (☎91 343. Open daily 8am-11pm.) **Postal Code:** 84001.

SANTORINI Σαντορίνη ☎22860

Whitewashed towns balanced delicately on cliffs, black-sand beaches, and deeply scarred hills make Santorini's landscape nearly as dramatic as the volcanic cataclysm that created it. Despite the abundant kitsch in touristy **Fira,** the island's capital, nothing can ruin the pleasure of wandering the town's streets or browsing its craft shops. The town of **Oia** is the best place in Greece to watch the sunset. Catch a bus from Fira (25min., 23 per day, €1). On the southwestern side of the island, the archaelogical site of the Minoan city **Akrotiri** has been preserved by lava. (Open Tu-Su 8:30am-3pm. €3, students €2.) Buses run to Akrotiri from Fira (30min., 14 per day, €1.60). Buses also leave Fira for the black-sand **beaches** of Kamari (20min., 32 per day, €1) and Perissa (30min., 21 per day, €1.50). The bus stops before Perissa in Pyrgos; from there, you can hike (40min.) to the **Profitis Ilias Monastery,** whose lofty location provides an island panorama, and continue for 1½hr. to the ruins of **Ancient Thira.** (Open Tu-Su 8:30am-2:30pm. Free.)

Find impeccable rooms, laundry service, and a roof-top bar at **Youth Hostel Oia ❷.** (☎71 465. Breakfast included. Open May-Oct. Dorms €13-15.) The cheery **Mama's Cyclades Cafe ❷,** north of Fira on the road to Oia, serves a big breakfast special. (☎23 032. Entrees €5-8. Open daily 8am-midnight.) At night, head to **Murphy's,** supposedly the first Irish pub in Greece. (Beer €5. Mixed drinks €6.50. Cover €5. Open daily Mar.-Oct. noon-late.) **Ferries** from Fira run to: Ios (1hr., 1-3 per day, €7.50); Iraklion, Crete (4hr., 3 per week, €15.50); Mykonos (6hr., 2 per week, €14.50); Naxos (3hr., 3-4 per day, €12.50); Paros (4hr., 2-5 per day, €13.50); Piraeus (10hr., 2-5 per day, €25); Thessaloniki (15hr., 5 per week, €42). Ferries depart from Athinios Harbor; frequent buses (25min., €1.50) connect to Fira. **Postal Codes:** 84700 (Fira); 84702 (Oia).

CRETE Κρήτη

According to a Greek saying, a Cretan's first loyalty is to his island, his second to his country. Since 3000 BC, Crete has maintained an identity distinct from the rest of Greece. The pride of Cretans is justified, and travelers, too, will find themselves drawn to the island's villages, mosques, grottoes, beaches, and warm hospitality.

GETTING TO CRETE

Olympic Airways (☎21096 66 666) and **Aegean/Cronus Airlines** (☎21099 88 300) fly from Athens to: Hania (45min., 4-5 per day, €55-90) in the west; Iraklion (50min., 4-5 per day, €65-95) in the center; and Sitia (1hr., 2-3 per week, €70) in the east.

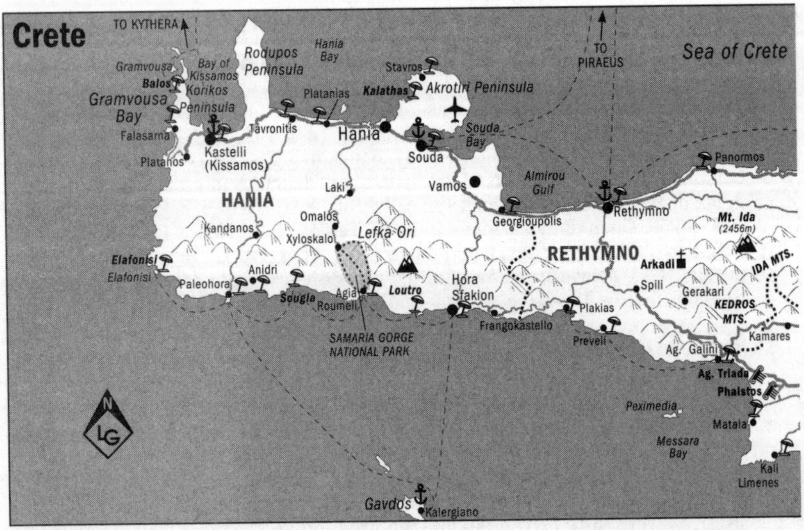

IRAKLION Ηράκλειο ☎2810

Iraklion is Crete's capital and primary port. Iraklion's main attraction after **Knossos** is the superb **Archaeological Museum,** off Pl. Eleftherias. By appropriating major finds from all over the island, the museum has amassed a comprehensive record of the Neolithic and Minoan stages of Cretan history. (Open M 1-7:30pm, Tu-Su 8:30am-7:30pm. €6; non-EU students €3; "classicists," fine arts students, and EU students free.) The **Tomb of Nikos Kazantzakis,** on top of the city walls, offers the best view of the city and is a necessary stop for fans of the author or his creation, Zorba. Iraklion's night spots lie in the maze of streets between **Plateia Venizelou** and **Plateia Eleftherias.** At **Cafe Korais,** Korai 8, patrons watch the parade of bar-hoppers from an expansive deck. (☎346 336. Mixed drinks €6.50. Open daily 9pm-4am.)

Rent a Room Hellas ❶, Handakos 24, two blocks from El Greco Park, has large dorm rooms and a spectacular view. (☎288 851. Dorms €10; doubles €27.) **Hotel Rea ❷,** Kalimeraki 1, offers clean, airy rooms. (☎223 638; www.hotelrea.gr. Doubles €26, with bath €34.) **Ouzeri Tou Terzaki ❷,** Loch. Marineli 17, serves small portions cooked delectably fresh. (☎221 444. Fried squid €6.80. Open M-F 12:30pm-midnight.) From Terminal A, between the old city walls and the harbor, **buses** leave for Agios Nikolaos (1½hr., 20 per day, €5.30) and Hania (3hr., 17 per day, €11.50) via Rethymno (1½hr., €6.50). Buses leave across from Terminal B for Phaistos (1½hr., 9 per day, €4.80). The **tourist office** is on Xandthoudidou 1. (☎246 299. Open M-F 8am-2:30pm.) Use the Internet at **Netc@fé,** 1878 4. (€1.50 per hr. Open M-Sa 10am-2am, Su noon-2am.) **Postal Code:** 71001.

KNOSSOS Κνωσός

At **Knossos,** the most famous archaeological site on Crete and a must-see daytrip from Iraklion, excavations have revealed the remains of the largest and most complicated of Crete's **Minoan palaces.** It is difficult to tell fact and legend apart at the palace of Knossos, famous throughout history as the site of King Minos's machinations, the Minotaur's labyrinth, and the imprisonment of Daedalus and Icarus. The original palace was built around 1700 BC, but was partially destroyed by fire around 1450 BC

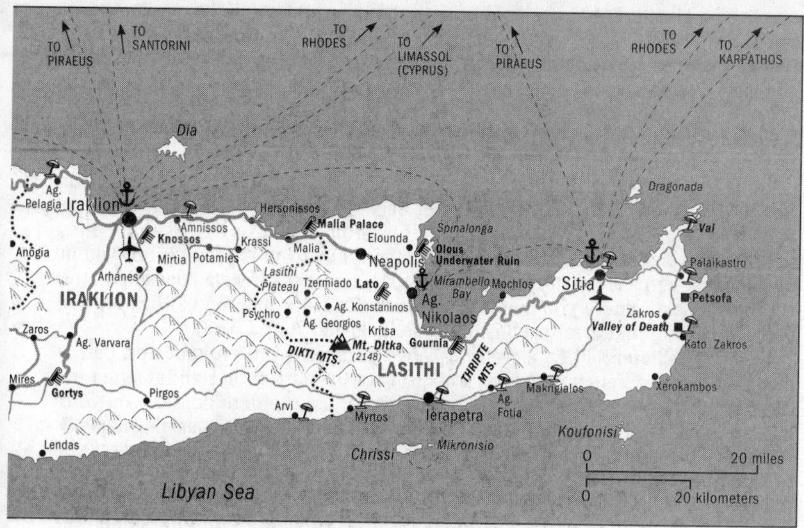

and subsequently forgotten. Sir Arthur Evans, who financed and supervised the excavations, eventually restored large parts of the palace in Knossos. Don't miss the **Queen's Bathroom,** where, over 3000 years ago, she took milk baths while gazing up at dolphin frescoes. Walking north from the royal quarters, you'll stumble across the grand **pithoi**—jars so big that, according to legend, Minos's son met a Pooh Bear-esque fate by drowning in one filled with honey. (Open daily 8am-7:30pm. €6, students €3.) To reach Knossos from Iraklion, take **bus** #2 from Terminal A (€1).

RETHYMNO Ρέθυμνο ☎28310

Crete's many conquerors—Venetians, Ottomans, and even Nazis—have had a profound effect in Rethymno. Arabic inscriptions adorn the walls of the narrow streets, minarets highlight the skyline, and the 16th-century **Venetian Fortezza** stands watch over the harbor. (Open Tu-Su 9am-8pm. €3.) To get from the station to the colorful and inviting **Youth Hostel ❶,** Tombazi 41-45, walk down I. Gavriil, take the first left at Pl. Martiron; Tombazi is the second right. (☎22 848. Reception 8am-noon and 5-9pm. Dorms €7.50.) With complimentary *raki* and honey-drizzled cheese pie after your meal, **Taverna Kyria Maria ❷,** Moskovitou 20, is one of the best deals in town. (☎29 078. Open daily mid-Mar. to Oct. 11am-11pm. MC/V.) The Rethymno-Hania **bus** station (☎29 644) is south of the fortress on the water, with service to Hania (1hr., 20 per day, €6) and Iraklion (1½hr., 21 per day, €6.50). Up the stairs behind the bus station, left on I. Gavriil, which becomes Kountouriotou, and left on Varda Kallergi, is the waterfront and the **tourist office,** on El. Venizelou. (☎29 148. Open M-F 8:30am-2:30pm.) **Postal Code:** 74100.

HANIA Χάνια ☎28210

Crete's second largest city, Hania (pop. 60,000) takes on its avalanche of summer tourists with refined ease. The **Venetian lighthouse** marks the entrance to the city's stunning architectural relic, the Venetian Inner Harbor. Nestled away on the north-western tip of Crete, the heavenly **blue lagoon** of Balos offers bright white sand and warm, shallow waters to those who make the trek out. Daily **boat cruises** leave from Kissamos port, 3km outside of Kissamos Town along the main road heading away from Hania (May-Oct. departs daily 10:15am, returns 5:30pm; round-trip €20). Buy tickets at Kissamos port from companies like **Gramvousa-Balos Daily Cruises** (☎28220 24 344; gramvous@in.gr). Before arriving at Balos, the boat stops at nearby **Gramvousa,** an island with a Venetian fortress perched on its summit.

The most popular excursion from Hania and Iraklion is the 5-6hr. hike down **Samaria Gorge** (Φράγγι της Σαμαριάς), a spectacular 16km ravine extending through the White Mountains, where endangered griffin vultures circle overhead. (Open daily May to mid-Oct. 6am-3pm. €5, under 15 free. Hang on to your ticket.) For more info, call **Hania Forest Service** (☎92 287). The trail starts at **Xyloskalo;** take the 6:15, 7:30, or 8:30am bus from Hania to Xyloskalo (1½hr., €5.40) for a day's worth of hiking. The 1:45pm bus from Hania will put you in **Omalos,** ready to set out the next morning. The trail ends in **Agia Roumeli,** on the southern coast, where you can hop on a boat to Hora Sfakion (1¼hr., 3-4 per day, €5.40) and take a return bus to Hania (6:30 and 7pm, €5.80).

To get to **Hotel Neli ❸,** a well-furnished pension with wrought-iron balconies and loads of Venetian charm, walk toward the harbor on Halidon and turn right onto Athenagora, which becomes Sarpaki. It's the pink building on your left. (☎55 533; www.nelistudios.gr. Singles €28; doubles €35.) **Camping Hania ❶** is close to the beach but walled in by apartment buildings. Take Skalidi west out of town and follow it as it becomes Kisamou; 4km down the road, take a right at the sign. (☎31 138. Tent rental €8. Tent sites €8.50-9.50, €5 per extra person.) **Anaplous ❷,** near the harbor on Sifaka, serves *pilino*, a pork and lamb creation (€25; serves 3) and other traditional Hanian dishes. (Entrees €6-8. Open daily 7:30pm-12:30am. AmEx/MC/V.) **Ferries** arrive in the port of Souda, near Hania; buses connect from the port to Hania's Municipal Market on Zymvrakakidon (25min., €1). **Buses** (☎93 052) leave from the station on the corner of Kidonias and Kelaidi for Iraklion (2½hr., 20 per day, €11) and Rethymno (1hr., 20 per day, €6). The **tourist office** is next to the city hall. (☎36 155; www.chania.gr. Open M-F 9am-8pm, Sa 9am-2pm.) **Postal Code:** 73100.

AGIOS NIKOLAOS Άγιος Νικόλαος ☎28410

Catering to beach-obsessed patrons, one-stop holiday-makers, and hikers on their way to more obscure destinations, Agios Nikolaos's meandering harbor promenades, pedestrian streets, and open-air cafes provide a relaxing rest stop. For an exciting daytrip, catch a bus to Elounda (€1.10) and take a ferry (Apr.-Oct. every 30min. 9:30am-4:30pm, €8) to the ominous and intriguing island of **Spinalonga,** a former Venetian fortress and leper colony. (€2, EU students free.) A great hike runs through the cheerfully named **Valley of Death.** To get there, take the bus to Sitia (1½hr., 8 per day, €5.50) and then to the small village of Zakros (1hr., 3 per day, €2.90). In the city, museums and beaches will keep you busy.

From the tourist office, turn away from the water and right onto the street behind the taxi stand. Walk up the hill and turn left onto Stratigou Koraka to reach the bright, breezy rooms of **Christodoulakis Pension ❷,** Stratigou Koraka 7. The pension, the second building after the corner, is unmarked; look for the profusion of plants. (☎22 525. Singles €20; doubles €20-25; triples €30-40.) **Loukakis Taverna ❷,** S. Koundourou 24, a 10min. walk past the tourist office, dishes up satisfying meals at low prices in a fresh environment. (☎28 022. *Stifado* €6.20. Stuffed green peppers €3.20. Open daily 9am-midnight.) At night, **Sorrento Bar,** S. Koundourou on the harbor waterfront, is a lively scene. (Mixed drinks €2.50-5. Open daily noon-late.) **Ferries** sail to Piraeus (12hr., 3 per week, €30.90) via Milos (7hr., 3 per week, €20.40) and Rhodes (12hr., 2 per week, €25.60). To reach the **tourist office,** S. Koundourou 21A, cross the bridge at the harbor onto S. Koundourou. (☎22 357. Open Apr.-Nov. daily 8am-9:30pm.) **Postal Code:** 72100.

EASTERN AEGEAN ISLANDS

Scattered along Turkey's coast, the islands of the **Dodecanese** are marked by a history of persistence in the face of myriad invasions. The more isolated islands of the **Northeast Aegean** remain sheltered from creeping globalization. Cultural authenticity here is palpable—a traveler's welcome and reward.

FERRIES TO TURKEY

Ferries for Turkey depart from Chios, Kos, Lesvos, and Samos. Ferries run to Bodrum from Kos Town every morning (20min., round-trip €15-40). Daily excursion boats leave Samos Town for Kuşadası (1¼hr., 8:30am, round-trip €50); a guided tour of nearby **Ephesus** costs an additional €20. Turkish entrance **visas** (US$65) must be purchased at the border. From Chios Town, ferries go to Çesme (45min., 1-2 per day, round-trip €50). Mytilini on Lesvos has service to Ayvalik (1½hr., 4 per week, €49).

RHODES Ρόδος ☎22410

The undisputed tourism capital of the Dodecanese, the island of Rhodes has retained a sense of serenity in the sandy beaches along its eastern coast, the jagged cliffs skirting its western coast, and the green mountains in its interior. Rhodes is also known for a sight that no longer exists—the 33m **Colossus,** which was once one of the Seven Wonders of the Ancient World. The pebbled inclines of the Old Town, constructed by the Knights of St. John, lend **Rhodes town** medieval flair. At the top of the hill, a square tower marks the entrance to the **Palace of the Grand Master,** which contains intricate mosaics and medieval artwork. (☎25 500. €6, non-EU students €3, EU students free.) The beautiful halls and courtyards of the **Archaeological Museum,** dominating the **Plateia Argiokastrou,** shelter small treasures, including the exquisite statue of *Aphrodite Bathing* from the first century BC. (☎27 657. Open Tu-Su 8:30am-2:30pm. €3, students €2.) With whitewashed houses clustered at the foot of a castle-capped acropolis, **Lindos,** south of Rhodes town, is less touristy and arguably the most picturesque town on the island.

The vine-enclosed garden-bar of **Hotel Anastasia ❷**, 28 Oktovriou 46, complements bright pastel rooms with private baths. (☎28 007. Singles €25-28; doubles €30-37. V.) **Mama's Pension ❶**, Menekleous 28, has comfortable rooms, and clean shared baths. (☎25 359. Laundry €5. Dorms €10; doubles €25.) **Taverna Romios ❷**, in Pl. Sophokleous, serves divine local recipes. (☎25 549. Entrees €5-12.) Nightlife in Rhodes's Old Town focuses on **Militadou,** off Apelou. **Orfanidou,** in the New Town, is popularly known as Bar Street. **Ferries** leave Rhodes town for: Kos (1-2 per day, €17); Patmos (1-2 per day, €26.60); Piraeus (1 per day, €44.40); Samos (1 per week, €26.80); Agios Nikolaos in Crete (3 per week, €25). Local **buses** run to Lindos from Rhodes town (16 per day, €3.70). There is a **tourist office** in Rhodes town at the intersection of Makariou and Papagou. (☎44 335; www.ando.gr/eot. Open M-F 8am-3pm.) **Postal Code:** 85100.

KOS Κως ☎22420

Antiquity best knew Kos as the sacred land of Asclepius, god of healing, and the birthplace of Hippocrates, the father of modern medicine. Today, **Kos Town** attracts a young, loud, and inebriated crowd more interested in sexual healing. The more sedate can escape to serene mountain villages or **Asclepeion,** 4km southwest of Kos Town, the location of Hippocrates's medical school, which opened in the 5th century BC. In the summer, mini-trains run there from Kos Town. (Open Tu-Su 8am-2:30pm. €4, students €2.) For a steaming daytrip, hop a ferry to the neighboring island of **Nisyros** (1½hr., 4 per week) to take a peek into the craters of active **Mandraki Volcano,** which emit sulfur crystals and hissing steam. The island's best beaches stretch along southern Kos to Kardamena and are all accessible by bus; stops are by request.

Take the first right off Megalou Alexandrou to get to **Pension Alexis ❷**, Irodotou 9, a beloved travel institution with spacious doubles and a kind owner. (☎28 798. Doubles €20-22; triples €28-38.) **Studios Nitsa ❷**, Averof 47, is only 10m from the beach and close to the nightlife. (☎25 810. Doubles with A/C €20-25.) Heaping portions of Greek dishes characterize **Taverna Hellas ❷**, 7 Psaron St, down the street from Pension Alexis at Amerikis and Psaron. (☎22 609. Entrees €4-8. Vegetarian options available. Open daily noon-late.) Most bars are located around **Nafklirou,** in the old city, and along **Porfirou,** between Averof and Zouroudi in the new city. The cavernous **Fashion Club,** Kanari 2, by the Dolphin roundabout, hosts Kos's wildest nights. (F-Sa cover €10, includes 1 drink. Open daily 11pm-4am.) The stone walls of **Haman Club,** Nafklirou 1, a former Turkish bath in the old city, echo with American and Greek hits all night long. (July-Aug. cover €5, includes 1 drink.) **Ferries** run to: Patmos (4hr., 1-2 per day, €10); Piraeus (11-15hr., 1-3 per day, €23); Rhodes (4hr., 2-3 per day, €15). The exceptionally helpful **tourist office** is at Vas. Georgiou B 1 and has free maps. (☎24 460; www.hippocrates.gr. Open M-F 8am-2pm and 5-8pm, Sa 8am-2pm.) **Postal Code:** 85300.

SAMOS Σάμος ☎22730

Visitors frequently stop in Samos en route to Kuşadası and the ruins of Ephesus on the Turkish coast. Yet the island is an excellent destination itself; hiking paths through mountain forests lead to hidden caves and waterfalls, and luminous beaches lie just minutes from the metropolis of **Samos Town.** The **Archaeological Museum,** behind the municipal gardens, houses artifacts from the Temple of Hera. (☎27 469. Open Tu-Su June-Oct. 8am-7:30pm; Nov.-May 8:30am-3pm. €3, students €2, EU students free.) The ancient city of **Pythagorio,** once the island's capital, is 14km south of Vathy. Near the town is the magnificent **Tunnel of Eupalinos,** which supplied water to the city. (Open Tu-Su June-Oct. 8am-7:30pm; Nov.-May 8:30am-3pm. €4, seniors and students €2, EU students free.) Polykrates's greatest feat was the **Temple of Hera,** in Heraion. Though only one of the original 134 columns is still standing, the temple merits a visit. (Bus from Vathy 30min., €1.50. Temple open Tu-Su June-Oct. 8am-7:30pm, Nov.-May 8:30am-3pm. €3, students €2.)

IN RECENT NEWS

COLOSSUS, REDUX

lthough no trace of the ancient olossus, which toppled in 226 C, remains, some creative Rhodesians plan to resurrect the ormer Seventh Wonder of the ncient World in the near future. hough the 100 ft. statue of the un god Helios originally towered ver the entrance to Mandraki arbor in Rhodes Town, neighborng Faliraki has agreed to provide site for a replica of the famed tatue. Attempting to shed their sland's notorious reputation as a necca of debauchery and to estore a flagging tourist economy, aliraki's local authorities hope to reate a substantive site of cultural heritage.

Greek-Cypriot sculptor Nikos otziamanis, who has spearheaded the project in collaboraion with other European artists nd politicians, plans to recreate he Colossus with as much historcal accuracy as possible. Falirakins working on the project have ikened their vision to the Statue f Liberty in New York City, and ope that the reconstructed Colossus and a planned adjacent ultural center will generate the ame kind of tourist appeal as its merican counterpart. And like ady Liberty, the new Colossus vill be hollow, giving visitors dramatic views of the Aegean Sea rom inside the statue's head. lthough a far cry from the tatue's ancient religious purose, the reconstructed version night draw much-needed tourists o Faliraki.

The rooms at **Pythagoras Hotel ❷**, across from the hospital, are clean and the cheapest in town. Private baths, beachfront location, and free port pickup make this a backpacker's haven. (☎28 601; smicha@atenet.gr. Internet €3 per hr. Singles €18-25; doubles €20-35.) **Pension Trova ❷**, Kalomiris 26, has clean, airy rooms with shared baths. (☎27 759. Singles €15-20; doubles €20-35; triples €30-40.) **Ferries** from Samos Town go to: Chios (3½hr., 2 per week, €13); Kos (5hr., 2-3 per day, €25.50); Mykonos (6hr., 4 per week, €21); Piraeus (12-16hr., 1-2 per day, €27.50); Rhodes (10hr., 1 per week, €28). Four buses daily run from Samos Town to Pythagorio. The **tourist office** is on a side street one block before Pl. Pythagoras. (☎28 530. Open July-Aug. M-Sa 10am-1pm.) **Postal Code:** 83100.

LESVOS Λέσβος ☎22510

Olive groves, remote monasteries, art colonies, and a petrified forest harmonize on Lesvos in an irresistible siren song. Modern **Mytilini** is the capital and central port city. At the new **Archaeological Museum**, on 8 Noemvriou, visitors can walk on mosaic floors from Lesvos's Neolithic past. (Open Tu-Su 8am-7:30pm. €3, students €2, EU students and under 18 free.) Only 4km south of Mytilini along El. Venizelou, the village of **Varia** is home to two excellent museums. **Theophilos Museum** features the work of the neo-Primitivist Greek painter Theophilos Hadzimichali. (Open Tu-Su 9am-2:30pm and 6-8pm. €2, students free.) **Musée Tériade** displays lithographs by Chagall, Matisse, Miró, and Picasso. (Open daily 9am-2pm and 5-8pm. €2, students and children free.) Local buses to Varia leave Mytilini every hour (20min., €1). Tell the driver you're going to the museums. **Molyvos** has the sensibility of an artists' colony; though frequented by tourists, its atmosphere remains serene and its prices reasonable. Take a bus from Mytilini (2hr., 4 per day, €4.70). **Eftalou** has beautiful black pebble beaches, accessible by frequent buses from Molyvos. A 20-million-year old **petrified forest,** 4km from Sigri, one of only two such forests in the world, has fossilized trunks preserved in amazing detail. For more info, call the main parks office in Mytilini. (☎40 132. Open daily July-Aug. 8am-7pm; Sept.-June 8am-3pm. €2.)

Mytilini *domatia* are plentiful and well advertised. Doubles should run €20-25 before July 15, and start at €35 during high season. **Alkaios Rooms to Let ❸**, Alkaiou 16, has soothing peach rooms with high ceilings and blue-tiled private baths. (☎47 737. Doubles €30-35; triples €40-50.) At **Arion Rooms to Let ❸**, at the intersection of Alkaiou and Arionos 4, hardwood floors grace rooms with A/C and private bath. (☎42 650. Singles €30; doubles €40.) Fresh octopi hang to dry in front of tables right by the water at **O Stratos ❷**. (☎21 739. Entrees €4.50-6.50. Open daily 11am-late.) **Ferries** go from Mytilini to: Chios (3hr., 11 per week, €14); Limnos (5hr., M-Tu and F-Su 2-3 per day, €20); Thessaloniki (13hr., 2 per week, €35). Book tickets at **NEL Lines,** Pavlou Koudourioti 67 (☎46 595), on the far right side of the waterfront, facing inland. **Postal Code:** 81100.

HUNGARY

HUNGARY (MAGYARORSZÁG)

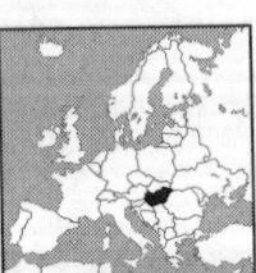

Communism was merely a blip in Hungary's 1100-year history of repression and renewal. Now one year after its accession to the European Union, Hungary appears at ease with its newfound capitalist identity. Teeming Budapest may still be the country's socioeconomic keystone, but those who pass over the countryside for the capital risk mistaking Hungary's heart for its soul. Travelers will be rewarded by visits to the rough-and-tumble cowboy plains to the south, the beach resorts to the east, and the rolling hills with wine valleys to the north.

DISCOVER HUNGARY: SUGGESTED ITINERARIES

THREE DAYS. Three days is hardly enough time for **Budapest** (p. 523). Spend a day at the churches and museums of **Castle Hill,** and an afternoon in the waters of the **Széchenyi Baths** before exploring the rest of the **City Park.** Get a lesson in Hungarian history at the **Parliament** before taking in the **Opera House.**

ONE WEEK. After four days in the capital, head up the Danube Bend to see the rustic side of Hungary: in **Szentendre** (1 day; p. 534), cafes and cobblestone welcome visitors, while farther down the river, **Visegrad's** citadel looms over the town (1 day; p. 535). Next, explore **Eger** (1 day; p. 536) and sample the wines of the **Valley of Beautiful Women.**

ESSENTIALS

WHEN TO GO

Spring is the best time to visit Hungary, as flowers are in bloom throughout the countryside and the tourists have yet to arrive. July through August is Hungary's high season; expect crowds, booked hostels, and sweltering weather; consider going anytime May through June. The fall is gorgeous, with mild weather through October. January and February can average freezing temperatures; many museums and tourist spots shut down or reduce their hours during the winter months.

FACTS AND FIGURES

Official Name: Hungary.

Capital: Budapest.

Major Cities: Eger, Pécs, Siófok.

Population: 10,000,000 (92% Hungarian, 2% Roma, 6% other or unknown).

Land Area: 93,030 sq. km.

Time Zone: GMT +1.

Language: Hungarian.

Religions: Roman Catholic (60%).

DOCUMENTS AND FORMALITIES

EMBASSIES AND CONSULATES. Foreign embassies to Hungary are in Budapest (p. 523). Hungary's embassies and consulates abroad include: **Australia,** 17 Beale Cres., Deakin, ACT 2600 (☎6282 3226; www.hunconsydney.com); **Canada,** 299 Waverley St., Ottawa, ON K2P 0V9 (☎613-230-2717; www.docuweb.ca/Hungary); **Ireland,** 2 Fitzwilliam Pl., Dublin 2 (☎661 2902; www.kum.hu/dublin); **New Zealand,** Consulate-General,

37 Abbott St., Wellington 6004 (☎973 7507; www.hungarianconsulate.co.nz); **UK,** 35 Eaton Pl., London SW1X 8BY (☎020 7235 2664; www.huemblon.org.uk); **US,** 3910 Shoemaker St. NW, Washington, D.C. 20008 (☎202-362-6730; www.hungaryemb.org).

VISA AND ENTRY INFORMATION. Citizens of Australia, Canada, Ireland, New Zealand, the UK, and the US can visit Hungary without visas for up to 90 days, if they do not intend to work. Passports must be valid for six months after your planned departure from the country. If you do need a visa, consult your embassy. There is no fee for crossing a Hungarian border. In general, border officials are efficient; plan on 30min. crossing time.

ENTRANCE REQUIREMENTS

Passport: Required for all travelers.

Visa: Not required for stays under 90 days for citizens of Australia, Canada, Ireland, New Zealand, the UK, and the US.

Letter of Invitation: Not required for citizens of Australia, Canada, Ireland, New Zealand, the UK, and the US.

Inoculations: Not required. Recommended up-to-date on DTaP (diphtheria, tetanus, and pertussis), Hepatitis A, Hepatitis B, MMR (measles, mumps, and rubella), Polio booster, and Typhoid.

Work Permit: Required for all foreigners planning to work in Hungary.

Driving Permit: Required for all those planning to drive in Hungary.

TOURIST SERVICES AND MONEY

TOURIST OFFICES. Tourinform, with branches in most cities, is a useful first stop. They don't make reservations but will find vacancies in university dorms and private *panzió*. Employees generally speak English and German. Most **IBUSZ** offices book private rooms, exchange money, and sell train tickets; they are generally better at assisting in travel plans than at providing info. *Tourist Information: Hungary*, *Budapest in Your Pocket*, and the monthly entertainment guide *Programme in Hungary* are all free and in English. Local agencies may be staffed only by Hungarian and German speakers, but they are often very helpful.

HUNGARY

MONEY. The national currency is the **forint (Ft),** which is divided into 100 **fillérs,** which have almost entirely disappeared from circulation. Hungary has a **Value Added Tax** (VAT) rate of 25%. **Inflation** hovers around 5.3%, so expect price increases. Currency exchange machines are slow but offer good rates, and banks like **OTP Bank** and **Postabank** offer the best exchange rates for traveler's checks. Never change money on the street, and avoid extended-hour exchange offices, which have poor rates. Watch for scams: the maximum legal commission for cash-to-cash exchange is 1%. **ATMs** are common; major **credit cards** are accepted in some establishments. Standard business hours in Budapest are Monday through Thursday 9am-4pm, Friday 9am-1pm. Businesses generally close on holidays.

A bare-bones day in Hungary, including dorm accommodation, transport, and food, costs 4500-5500Ft. For less ascetic living, expect to spend 5500-7000Ft. Tipping is not usually included and while it is not mandatory, it's appropriate to tip around 10%. Don't bother bargaining with cabbies; set a price before getting in.

FORINTS (FT)		
	AUS$1 = 150.13FT	1000FT = AUS$6.66
	CDN$1 = 163.86FT	1000FT = CDN$6.10
	EUR€1 = 243.21FT	1000FT = EUR€4.11
	NZ$1 = 138.83FT	1000FT = NZ$7.20
	UK£1 = 358.33FT	1000FT = UK£2.79
	US$1 = 199.74FT	1000FT = US$5.01

HEALTH AND SAFETY

In Budapest, **medical services** are easily obtained. Embassies have lists of Anglophone doctors, and most hospitals have English-speaking doctors on staff. Outside Budapest, try to bring a Hungarian speaker to the hospital with you. **Tourist insurance** is valid—and necessary—for many medical services. **Tap water** is usually clean, except in Tokaj. **Bottled water** is available at most food stores. Public bathrooms vary in cleanliness: pack soap, towel, and 30Ft for the attendant. Carry **toilet paper,** as many hostels do not provide it, and you get a single square in public restrooms. Women should look for *Nők* signs and men for *Férfi*. Many **pharmacies** *(gyógyszertár)* stock Western brands, tampons, and condoms.

Violent **crime** is low, but in Budapest and other large cities, foreign tourists are targets for petty thieves and pickpockets. Check prices before getting in taxis or ordering food or drinks. In an emergency, your embassy will likely be more helpful than the **police.** Lone **women,** the elderly, and families with children are all safe to travel in Hungary. **Minorities** are generally accepted, though dark-skinned travelers may be mistaken for Roma (gypsies) and encounter prejudice. Though Hungary is known for being open-minded, **GLBT** travelers may face serious discrimination, especially outside Budapest.

EMERGENCY	**Police:** ☎107. **Ambulance:** ☎104 (in English: 1 311 1666). **Fire:** ☎105.

TRANSPORTATION

BY PLANE. Many international airlines arrive in Budapest. The cheapest options to Hungary are **Sky Europe** (www.skyeurope.com) and **WizzAir** (www.wizzair.com), two Eastern European budget airlines, as well as old dependables **Air Berlin** (www.airberlin.com) and **easyJet** (www.easyjet.com), all of which offer service from London or Paris to Budapest. The national airline, **Malév,** flies to Hungary from London, New York, and other major cities.

BY TRAIN. Most trains *(vonat)* pass through Budapest, and are generally reliable and inexpensive. Several types of **Eurail passes** are valid in Hungary. Check schedules and fares at **www.elvira.hu.** *Személyvonat* trains have many local stops and are excruciatingly slow; *gyorsvonat* trains, listed in red on schedules, move much faster for the same price. Large towns are connected by blue *expressz* lines; these InterCity trains are fast and air-conditioned. A *pótjegy* (seat reservation) is required on trains labeled "R," and violators face a hefty fine. A basic vocabulary will help you navigate: *érkezés* (arrival), *indulás* (departure), *vágány* (track), and *állomás* or *pályaudvar* (station, abbreviated *pu*). The *peron* (platform) is rarely indicated until the train approaches the station so look closely out the window as you approach a station; it will sometimes be announced in Hungarian. Many stations are not marked; ask the conductor what time the train will arrive (if your Hungarian is a bit rusty, point at your watch and say the town's name).

BY BUS. Buses, which are cheap (though often slightly more expensive than trains) and clean but crowded, are best for travel between outer provincial centers. Purchase tickets on board, and arrive early for a seat. In larger cities, buy tickets at the kiosk, and they will be punched when you get on. There's a fine if you're caught without a ticket. A ferry runs down the Danube from Vienna and Bratislava to Budapest. For more info, contact **Utinform** (☎322 3600).

BY CAR AND BIKE. Taxi prices should not exceed the following: 6am-10pm base fare 200Ft, 240Ft per km, 60Ft per min. waiting; 10pm-6am are 300/280/70Ft. Beware of taxi scams. Before getting in, check that the meter is working and ask how much the ride will cost. Taxis ordered by phone cost less than those hailed on the street. For info on road conditions, contact ☎322 7052 or 443 5651. Emergency phones are every 2km on motorways. For 24hr. English-language assistance, contact **Magyar Autóklub** (**MAK;** in Budapest ☎345 1800). Biking terrain varies; the northeast is hilly while the south is generally flat. Roads are usually well paved. Though it is common in Hungary, *Let's Go* does not recommend **hitchhiking.**

KEEPING IN TOUCH

PHONE CODES	**Country code:** 36. **International dialing prefix:** 00. For more information on how to place international calls, see inside back cover.

EMAIL AND THE INTERNET. The Internet is readily available in major cities. The Hungarian keyboard differs significantly from English-language keyboards; click the "Hu" icon at the bottom right of the screen and switch the setting to "Angol" to shift to an English keyboard. Most Internet cafes charge 150-300Ft per hour.

TELEPHONE. For **intercity calls,** wait for the tone and dial slowly; "06" goes before the phone code. Use red phones for **international calls.** Phones often require *telefonkártya* (phonecards). Of these, the best for international calls are **Neophone,** available at the post office, and **Micronet,** available at Fotex stores. Calls to Australia, Canada, and Ireland cost 45-50Ft per minute, to the UK 39Ft per minute, to the US 35Ft per minute. Make direct calls from Budapest's phone office. A 20Ft coin is required to start most calls. International access numbers include: **AT&T Direct** (☎06 800 01111); **Australia Direct** (☎06 800 06111); **BT Direct** (☎0800 89 0036); **Canada Direct** (☎06 800 01211); **MCI WorldPhone** (☎06 800 01411); **NZ Direct** (☎06 800 06411); and **Sprint** (☎06 800 01877). **Mobile phones** are common in Hungary; service can be purchased from Pannon GSM, T-Mobile, or Vodafone. Dialing a mobile from anywhere in Hungary is long-distance, requiring the entire 11-digit number.

MAIL. Hungarian mail is usually reliable; airmail *(légiposta)* takes seven to 10 days to the US and Europe. Mailing a letter costs about 36Ft domestically and 140-150Ft internationally. Those without a permanent address can receive mail **Poste Restante.** Use Global Priority mail, as it is reliable. Address envelopes: First name LAST NAME, POSTE RESTANTE, Post office address, Postal code, City, Hungary.

LANGUAGE. Hungarian, a Finno-Ugric language, is distantly related to Estonian and Finnish. After German, English is Hungary's most common second language. Most young people know some English. *"Hello"* is used as an informal greeting. Coincidentally, *"Szia!"* (sounds like "see ya!") is another greeting—friends often cry, "Hello, see ya!" For a few useful sayings, see **Phrasebook: Hungarian,** p. 1061.

ACCOMMODATIONS AND CAMPING

HUNGARY	❶	❷	❸	❹	❺
ACCOMMODATIONS	under 2000Ft	2000-3000Ft	3000-6000Ft	6000-10,000Ft	over 10,000Ft

Tourism is developing rapidly, and rising prices make **hostels** attractive. Hostels are usually large enough to accommodate summer crowds, and **Hostelling International** cards are often useful. Many hostels can be booked through a student travel agency or through local tourist offices. From June to August, many university dorms become hostels. These may be the cheapest options in smaller towns, as hostels are less common outside Budapest. Locations change annually; inquire at Tourinform and call ahead. **Guesthouses** and **pensions** *(panzió)* are more common than hotels in small towns. Private rooms booked through tourist agencies are sometimes a cheaper option. Singles are scarce, though some guesthouses have a singles rate for double rooms—it can be worth finding a roommate, as solo travelers must often pay for doubles. Check prices: agencies may try to rent you the most expensive rooms. Outside Budapest, the best offices are region-specific. After staying a few nights, make arrangements directly with the owner to save the 20-30% commission. There are over 300 **campgrounds** in Hungary. Most are open from May to September and charge for unfilled spaces in their bungalows. For more information, consult *Camping Hungary,* available in most tourist offices, or contact Tourinform in Budapest (p. 526).

FOOD AND DRINK

HUNGARY	❶	❷	❸	❹	❺
FOOD	under 400Ft	400-800Ft	800-1300Ft	1300-2800Ft	over 2800Ft

Hungarian food is more flavorful than many of its Eastern European culinary cohorts, with many spicy meat dishes. **Paprika,** Hungary's chief agricultural export, colors most dishes red. In Hungarian restaurants (*vendéglő* or *étterem*), *halászlé,* a spicy fish stew, is a traditional starter. Or, try *gyümölesleves,* a cold fruit soup with whipped cream. The Hungarian national dish is *bográcsgulyás,* a soup of beef, onions, green peppers, tomatoes, potatoes, dumplings, and plenty of paprika. *Borjúpaprikás* is veal with paprika and potato-dumpling pasta. For **Vegetarians** there is tasty *rántott sajt* (fried cheese) and *gombapörkölt* (mushroom stew). Delicious Hungarian fruits and vegetables abound in summer. Vegetarians should also look for *salata* (salad) and *sajt* (cheese), as these will be the only options in many small-town restaurants. *Túrós rétes* is a chewy pastry filled with sweet cottage cheese, while *Somlói galuska* is a rich, rum-soaked sponge cake of chocolate, nuts, and cream. The Austrians stole the recipe for *rétes* and called it "strudel," but this concoction is as Hungarian as can be.

Hungary produces an array of fine wines. The northeastern towns of Eger and Tokaj produce famous red and white wines, respectively. Hungarian **beer** *(sör)* ranges from first-rate to acceptable. Lighter beers include *Dreher Pils, Szalon Sör, Steffl, Gold Fassl, Gösser*, and *Amstel*. Hungary also produces *pálinka*, similar to brandy; among the tastiest are *barackpálinka* (like apricot schnapps) and *körtepálinka* (pear brandy). *Unicum*, advertised as the national drink, is an **herbal liqueur** that was used by the Hapsburgs to cure digestive ailments.

HOLIDAYS AND FESTIVALS

Holidays: New Year's Day (Jan. 1); National Day (Mar. 15); Easter Sunday and Monday (Apr. 16-17); Labor Day (May 1); Pentecost (June 4); Constitution Day (St. Stephen's Day, Aug. 20); Republic Day (Oct. 23); All Saints' Day (Nov. 1).

Festivals: Central Europe's largest rock festival, **Sziget Festival,** hits Budapest for a week at the end of July or the beginning of August, featuring rollicking crowds and international superstars. Eger's fabulous **World Festival of Wine Songs** celebration kicks off in late September, bringing together boisterous choruses and world-famous vintages.

BEYOND TOURISM

Central European University, Nador u. 9, Budapest 1051, Hungary (☎361 327 30 00; www.bard.edu/ceu). University affiliated with the Open Society Institute-Budapest offers English-language program for international students. Tuition US$14,500 per semester. Financial aid available.

Hungarian Dance Academy, Columbus u. 87-89, Budapest H-1145, Hungary (☎361 273 34 34; www.mtf.hu). Summer dance programs for international students.

Central European Teaching Program, 3800 NE 72nd Ave., Portland, OR 97213, USA (☎503-287-4977; http://www.ticon.net/~cetp/). Places English teachers in state schools in Hungary and Romania for 1 semester (US$1500) or 10 months (US$2000).

BUDAPEST

☎01

A spicy goulash of East and West, medieval and modern, Budapest (pop. 1.9 million) has steamrolled into a nucleus of urban chic. Unlike the toyland center of Prague, Budapest's sites are spread out within the energetic city, giving a sense of independence from the increasing number of tourists. Once two separate cities, Buda and Pest were joined in 1872 and became the Hapsburg Empire's number-two city. Proud Hungarians rebuilt their city from rubble after WWII and weathered 40 years of communist rule. These triumphs resonate through the streets today as Budapest finally resumes its place as a major European capital.

TRANSPORTATION

Flights: Ferihegy Airport (BUD; ☎296 9696). **Malév** (Hungarian Airlines; reservations ☎235 3888) flies to major cities. From the airport, the cheapest way to the city center is by bus #93 (20min., 4 per hr. 4:55am-11:20pm, 150Ft), and then by the M3 to Kőbánya-Kispest (15min. to Deák tér in downtown Pest).

Trains: Major stations are **Keleti Pályaudvar, Nyugati Pályaudvar,** and **Déli Pályaudvar.** (International info ☎461 5500, domestic 461 5400; www.mav.hu.) Most international trains arrive at Keleti pu., but some from Prague go to Nyugati pu. For schedules, check www.elvira.hu. To: **Berlin, Germany** (12-15hr.; 2 per day; 35,852Ft, 1500Ft reservation fee); **Bucharest, Romania** (14hr., 5 per day, 20,986Ft); **Prague, Czech Republic**

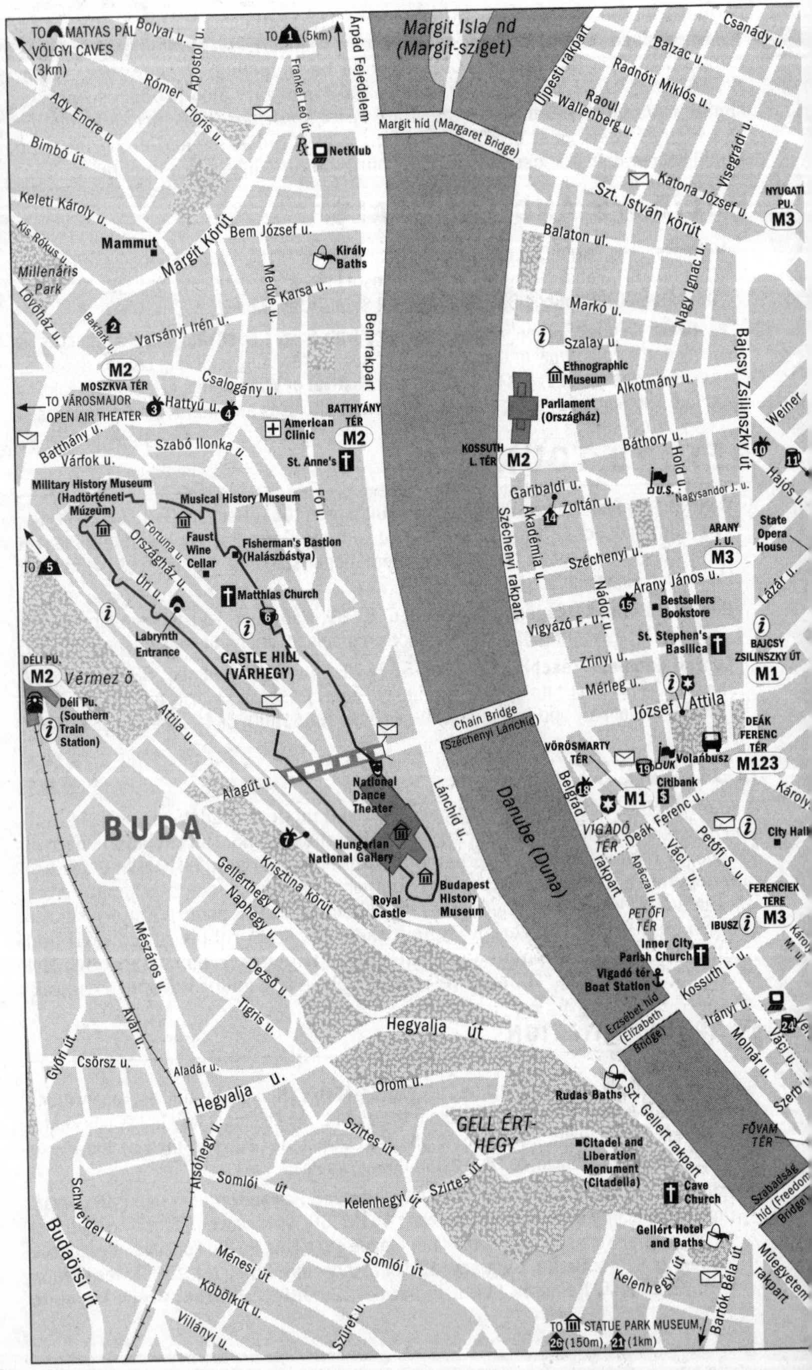
Margit Island (Margit-sziget)
Margit híd (Margaret Bridge)
TO MATYAS PÁL VÖLGYI CAVES (3km)
TO 1 (5km)
NetKlub
Király Baths
Mammut
Millenáris Park
MOSZKVA TÉR
M2
TO VÁROSMAJOR OPEN AIR THEATER
American Clinic
BATTHYÁNY TÉR
St. Anne's
Military History Museum (Hadtörténeti Múzeum)
Musical History Museum
Faust Wine Cellar
Fisherman's Bastion (Halászbástya)
Matthias Church
Labrynth Entrance
CASTLE HILL (VÁRHEGY)
DÉLI PU.
Vérmező
Déli Pu. (Southern Train Station)
National Dance Theater
Hungarian National Gallery
Royal Castle
Budapest History Museum
BUDA
Chain Bridge (Széchenyi Lánchíd)
Danube (Duna)
Ethnographic Museum
Parliament (Országház)
KOSSUTH L. TÉR
U.S.
ARANY J. U.
M3
State Opera House
Bestsellers Bookstore
St. Stephen's Basilica
BAJCSY ZSILINSZKY ÚT
M1
József Attila
VÖRÖSMARTY TÉR
UK
Volánbusz
DEÁK FERENC TÉR
M123
Citibank
VIGADÓ TÉR
City Hall
PETŐFI TÉR
FERENCIEK TERE
IBUSZ
Inner City Parish Church
Vigadó tér Boat Station
Erzsébet híd (Elizabeth Bridge)
Rudas Baths
GELLÉRT-HEGY
Citadel and Liberation Monument (Citadella)
Cave Church
Gellért Hotel and Baths
FŐVAM TÉR
Szabadság híd (Freedom Bridge)
NYUGATI PU.
TO STATUE PARK MUSEUM, 26 (150m), 21 (1km)
TO 5
Bolyai u.
Apostol u.
Rómer Flóris u.
Ady Endre u.
Bimbó út
Keleti Károly u.
Kis Rókus u.
Lövőház u.
Bakfark u.
Margit körút
Bem József u.
Medve u.
Karsa u.
Varsányi Irén u.
Csalogány u.
Hattyú u.
Batthány u.
Várfok u.
Szabó Ilonka u.
Fő u.
Fortuna u.
Országház u.
Úri u.
Attila u.
Alagút u.
Krisztina körút
Gellérthegy u.
Naphegy u.
Dezső u.
Tigris u.
Mészáros u.
Avar u.
Győri út
Csörsz u.
Aladár u.
Hegyalja út
Orom u.
Szirtes út
Alsóhegy u.
Somlói út
Kelenhegyi út
Schweidel u.
Budaörsi út
Ménesi út
Kőbölkút u.
Villányi u.
Szüret u.
Árpád Fejedelem
Frankel Leó út
Bem rakpart
Lánchíd u.
Újpesti rakpart
Balzac u.
Csanády u.
Radnóti Miklós u.
Raoul Wallenberg u.
Katona József u.
Visegrádi u.
Szt. István körút
Balaton ul.
Nagy Ignác u.
Markó u.
Szalay u.
Bajcsy Zsilinszky út
Alkotmány u.
Weiner
Báthory u.
Hold u.
Hajós u.
Garibaldi u.
Nagysandor J. u.
Zoltán u.
Akadémia u.
Széchenyi rakpart
Széchenyi u.
Arany János u.
Lázár u.
Nádor u.
Vigyázó F. u.
Zrinyi u.
Mérleg u.
Belgrád rakpart
Deák Ferenc u.
Apáczai u.
Váci u.
Petőfi S. u.
Károly
Kossuth L. u.
Irányi u.
Molnár u.
Szerb u.
Szt. Gellert rakpart
Bartók Béla út
Műegyetem rakpart

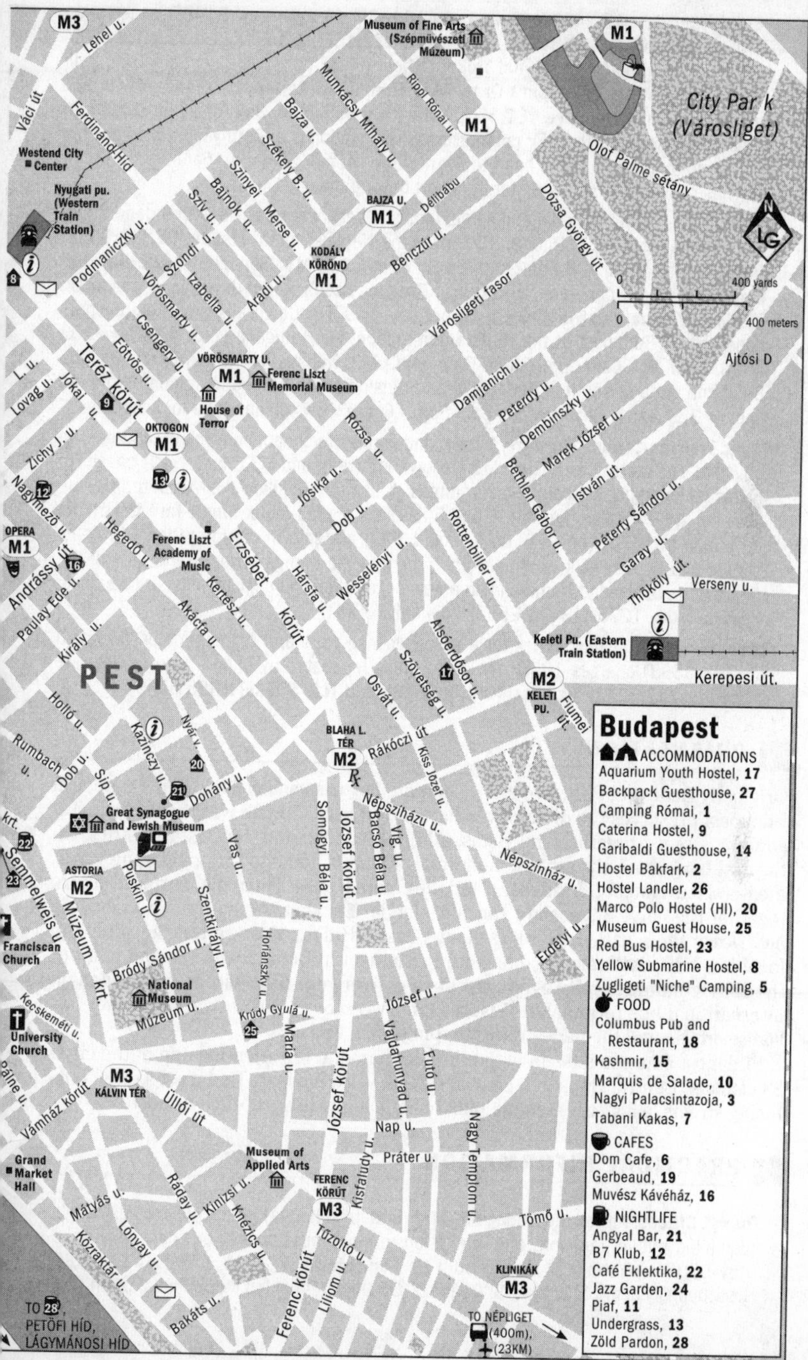
Budapest
ACCOMMODATIONS
Aquarium Youth Hostel, 17
Backpack Guesthouse, 27
Camping Római, 1
Caterina Hostel, 9
Garibaldi Guesthouse, 14
Hostel Bakfark, 2
Hostel Landler, 26
Marco Polo Hostel (HI), 20
Museum Guest House, 25
Red Bus Hostel, 23
Yellow Submarine Hostel, 8
Zugligeti "Niche" Camping, 5
FOOD
Columbus Pub and Restaurant, 18
Kashmir, 15
Marquis de Salade, 10
Nagyi Palacsintazoja, 3
Tabani Kakas, 7
CAFES
Dom Cafe, 6
Gerbeaud, 19
Muvész Kávéház, 16
NIGHTLIFE
Angyal Bar, 21
B7 Klub, 12
Café Eklektika, 22
Jazz Garden, 24
Piaf, 11
Undergrass, 13
Zöld Pardon, 28
PEST
City Par k (Városliget)
Museum of Fine Arts (Szépmüvészeti Múzeum)
Westend City Center
Nyugati pu. (Western Train Station)
Ferenc Liszt Memorial Museum
House of Terror
Ferenc Liszt Academy of Music
Keleti Pu. (Eastern Train Station)
Great Synagogue and Jewish Museum
Franciscan Church
National Museum
University Church
Grand Market Hall
Museum of Applied Arts
TO 28, PETŐFI HÍD, LÁGYMÁNOSI HÍD
TO NÉPLIGET (400m), (23KM)
M1 BAJZA U.
M1 KODÁLY KÖRÖND
M1 VÖRÖSMARTY U.
M1 OKTOGON
M1 OPERA
M2 ASTORIA
M2 BLAHA L. TÉR
M2 KELETI PU.
M3 KÁLVIN TÉR
M3 FERENC KÖRÚT
M3 KLINIKÁK
0 400 yards
0 400 meters
Andrássy út
Teréz körút
Erzsébet körút
József körút
Ferenc körút
Múzeum krt.
Vámház körút
Rákóczi út
Dózsa György út
Városligeti fasor
Olof Palme sétány
Kerepesi út.
Üllői út
Váci út
Podmaniczky u.
Munkácsy Mihály u.
Dohány u.
Wesselényi u.
Király u.
Népszínház u.

(8hr., 4 per day, 13,243Ft); **Vienna, Austria** (3hr.; 17 per day; 8148Ft, reservation 700Ft); **Warsaw, Poland** (11hr.; 2 per day; 17,515Ft, 2000Ft reservation fee). Purchase tickets at an **International Ticket Office.** (Keleti pu. open daily 8am-7pm; Nyugati pu. open M-Sa 5am-9pm.) Or try **MÁV Hungarian Railways,** VI, Andrássy út 35, branches at all stations. (☎461 5500. Open M-F 9am-5pm. Say *"diák"* for student or under 26 discounts.) The HÉV **commuter railway** station is at Batthyány tér, across the river from Parliament. Trains head to **Szentendre** (45min., 4 per hr. 5am-9pm, 268Ft). Purchase tickets at the station for transport beyond the city limits.

Buses: Buses to international and some domestic destinations arrive at and depart from the **Népliget** station, X, Ulloi u. 131, near the Népliget metro station. (☎382 0888. Ticket window open M-F 6am-9pm, Sa-Su 6am-4pm.) M3: Népliget. To: **Berlin, Germany** (14½hr., 6 per week, 16,900Ft); **Prague, Czech Republic** (8hr., 6 per week, 9900Ft); **Vienna, Austria** (3-3½hr., 4 per day, 5490Ft). Catch buses to/from destinations east of Budapest at the **Népstadion** station, XIV, Hungária körút 46-48. (☎252 4498. Open M-F 6am-6pm, Sa-Su 6am-4pm.) M2: Népstadion. Buses to the Danube Bend and parts of northern Hungary depart outside **Árpád híd** metro station on the M3 line. (☎329 1450. Cashier open 6am-8pm.) Check www.volanbusz.hu for schedules.

Public Transportation: Subways, buses, and **trams** are cheap, convenient, and easy to navigate. The **metro** has 3 lines: M1 (yellow), M2 (red), and M3 (blue). Night transit (É) buses run midnight-5am along major routes: #7É and 78É follow the M2 route, #6É follows the 4/6 tram line, and #14É and 50É follow the M3 route. **Single-fare tickets** for all public transport (one-way on 1 line; 160Ft) are sold in metro stations, in *Trafik* shops, and by sidewalk vendors. Punch them in the orange boxes at the gate of the metro or on buses and trams; punch a new ticket when you change lines, or face fines. Passes: 1-day 1275Ft, 3-day 2550Ft, 1-week 3000Ft.

Taxis: Beware of scams; check for a yellow license plate and running meter. **Budataxi** (☎233 3333) charges 135Ft per km for rides requested by phone. Also reliable are **Főtaxi** (☎222 2222), **6x6 Taxi** (☎266 6666), and **Tele 5 Taxi** (☎355 5555).

ORIENTATION

Originally Buda and Pest, two cities separated by the **Danube River** (Duna), modern Budapest preserves the distinctive character of each. On the west bank, **Buda** has winding streets, breathtaking vistas, a hilltop citadel, and the Castle District. On the east bank, **Pest,** the city's commercial center, is home to shopping boulevards, theaters, Parliament (Országház), and the Opera House. Three main bridges suture together the halves: **Széchenyi Lánchíd,** slender **Erzsébet híd,** and green **Szabadság híd.** Down the north slope of Várhegy (Castle Hill) is **Moszkva tér,** the tram and local bus hub. **Batthyány tér,** opposite Parliament in Buda, is the starting point of the HÉV commuter railway. Metro lines converge at **Deák tér,** next to the main international bus terminal at **Erzsébet tér.** Two blocks west toward the river lies **Vörösmarty tér** and the pedestrian shopping zone, **Váci utca.**

Budapest addresses begin with a Roman numeral representing one of the city's 23 **districts.** Central Buda is I; central Pest is V. To navigate Budapest's often confusing streets, a **map** is essential; pick one up at any tourist office or hostel.

PRACTICAL INFORMATION

Tourist Offices: All sell the **Budapest Card** (Budapest Kártya), which provides discounts, unlimited public transport, and admission to most museums. (2-day card 4900Ft, 3-day 5700Ft.) Your first stop should be **Tourinform,** V, Sütő u. 2 (☎438 8080; www.hungary.com). M1, 2, or 3: Deák tér. Off Deák tér behind McDonald's. Open daily

8am-8pm. **Vista Travel Center,** Andrássy u. 1 (☎429 9751; www.vista.hu), arranges tours and accommodations. Open M-F 9am-6:30pm, Sa 9am-2:30pm. **Budapest in Your Pocket** (www.inyourpocket.com; 750Ft) is an up-to-date city guide.

Embassies: Australia, XII, Királyhágo tér 8/9 (☎457 9777; www.australia.hu). M2: Déli pu., then bus #21 or tram #59 to Királyhágo tér. Open M-F 9am-noon. **Canada,** XII, Ganz út 12-14 (☎392 3360). Open M-Th 8:30-10:30am and 2-3:30pm. **Ireland,** V, Szabadság tér 7 (☎302 9600), in Bank Center. M3: Arany J. u. Walk down Bank u. toward the river. Open M-F 9:30am-12:30pm and 2:30-4:30pm. **New Zealand,** VI, Nagymezo u. 50 (☎302 2484). M3: Nyugati pu. Open M-F 11am-4pm by appointment only. **UK,** V, Harmincad u. 6 (☎266 2888; www.britishembassy.hu), near the intersection with Vörösmarty tér. M1: Vörösmarty tér. Open M-F 9:30am-12:30pm and 2:30-4:30pm. **US,** V, Szabadság tér 12 (☎475 4464, after hours 475 4703; www.usembassy.hu). M2: Kossuth tér. Walk 2 blocks down Akadémia and turn on Zoltán. Open M-Th 1-4pm, F 9am-noon and 1-4pm.

Currency Exchange: Banks have the best rates. **Citibank,** V, Vörösmarty tér 4 (☎374 5000). M1: Vörösmarty tér. Cashes traveler's checks for no commission and provides MC/V cash advances. Bring your passport. Open M-Th 9am-5pm, F 9am-4pm.

Luggage Storage: Lockers at all 3 train stations. 150-600Ft.

English-Language Bookstore: Libri Könyvpalota, VII, Rákóczi u. 12 (☎/fax 267 4843). M2: Astoria. A floor of English titles. Open M-F 10am-7:30pm, Sa 10am-3pm. MC/V.

GLBT Resources: GayGuide.net Budapest (☎0630 932 3334; www.budapest.gayguide.net). Volunteers post an online guide and run a hotline (daily 4-8pm) with info about gay- and lesbian-friendly lodgings.

Emergency: ☎112 connects to all. **Police:** ☎107. **Ambulance:** ☎104. **Fire:** ☎105.

Tourist Police: V, Sütő u. 2 (☎438 8080). M1, 2, or 3: Deák tér. Inside the Tourinform office. Often less than helpful. Beware of people pretending to be Tourist Police who may demand your passport. Open 24hr.

Pharmacies: Look for a green-and-white sign labeled Apotheke, Gyógyszertár, or Pharmacie. After-hours service 100-200Ft. **II,** Frankel Leó út 22 (☎212 4406). AmEx/MC/V. **VI,** Teréz krt. 41 (☎311 4439). Open M-F 8am-8pm, Sa 8am-2pm. **VII,** Rákóczi út 39 (☎314 3695). Open M-F 7:30am-9pm, Sa 7:30am-2pm; no after-hours service.

Medical Services: Falck (SOS) KFT, II, Kapy út 49/b (☎200 0100). Ambulance service US$120. **American Clinic,** I, Hattyú u. 14 (☎224 9090; www.americanclinics.com). Open M 8:30am-7pm, Tu-W 10am-6pm, Th 11:30am-6pm, F 10am-6pm. 24hr. emergency ☎224 9090. The US embassy (see above) has a list of English-speaking doctors.

Telephones: Phone cards are sold at kiosks and Metro stations. 50-unit card 800Ft, 120-unit card 1800Ft. Domestic operator and info ☎198; int'l operator ☎190, info ☎199.

Internet Access: Cybercafes are everywhere, but can be expensive and long waits are common. **Ami Internet Coffee,** V, Váci u. 40 (☎267 1644; www.amicoffee.hu). M3: Ferenciek tér. 200Ft per 15min., 700Ft per hr. Open daily 9am-2am. **Libri Könyvpalota,** VII, Rákóczi út 12 (☎267 4843; www.libri.hu). M2: Astoria. Sells coffee and drinks. 250Ft per 30min., 400Ft per hr. Open M-F 10am-7:30pm, Sa 10am-3pm.

Post Office: V, Városház u. 18 (☎318 4811). Poste Restante *(Postán Mar)* in office around the right side of the building. Open M-F 8am-8pm, Sa 8am-2pm. Branches include: Keleti pu.; Nyugati pu.; VI, Teréz krt. 105/107; VIII, Baross tér 11/c. Open M-F 7am-9pm, Sa 8am-2pm. **Postal Code:** Varies by district, taking the form 1XX2, where XX is the 2-digit district number (e.g., district V translates to 1052).

ACCOMMODATIONS AND CAMPING

Call ahead in summer. Travelers arriving at Keleti pu. will be swarmed with hawkers; be cautious and don't believe all promises of special discounts, but keep an open mind if you need a place to stay.

ACCOMMODATION AGENCIES

Private rooms may be slightly more expensive than hostels (3000-5000Ft per person; less with longer stays), but usually offer what hostels can't: peace, quiet, and private showers. Arrive early, bring cash, and haggle.

Best Hotel Service, V, Sütő u. 2 (☎318 4848; www.besthotelservice.axelero.net). M1, 2, or 3: Deák tér. Bus #7 from Keleti pu. Next to McDonald's in the courtyard. Arranges hotel, apartment, and hostel reservations, as well as car rentals and city tours. Rooms in Pest 6000Ft and up. Open daily 8am-8pm. ❹

IBUSZ, V, Ferenciek tér 10 (☎485 2700; accommodation@ibusz.hu). M3: Ferenciek tér. Agency branches across the city. Doubles 5000-10,000Ft; triples 6500-12,000Ft. 1800Ft surcharge if staying fewer than 4 nights. Open M-F 8:15am-5pm. ❸

YEAR-ROUND HOSTELS

Budapest's hostels are centers for the backpacker social scene. Common rooms can be as exciting as expat bars and clubs. Especially for solo travelers, they're a great place to pull together a posse of instant friends. Many hostels are run by the **Hungarian Youth Hostels Association (HI),** which operates from an office in Keleti pu. Representatives wearing Hostelling International t-shirts—and legions of competitors—will accost you and offer free transportation as you get off the train.

Backpack Guesthouse, XI, Takács Menyhért u. 33 (☎209 8406; www.backpackbudapest.hu), in Buda, 12min. from central Pest. From Keleti pu., take bus #7 or 7A toward Buda; get off at Tétenyi u., backtrack, take a left under the railway bridge, another left on Hamzsabégi út, and take the 3rd right. With a common room full of movies, music, and cheap beer, hostel life doesn't get much better. Internet 15Ft per min. Reception 24hr. Reserve ahead. Dorms 3000Ft; doubles 6600Ft. Cash only. ❷

Museum Guest House, VIII, Mikszáth Kálmán tér 4, 1st fl. (☎318 9508; museumgh@freemail.c3.hu). M3: Kálvin tér. Take the left exit onto Baross u.; at the fork, go left on Reviczky u. At the square, go to the right corner and ring buzzer at gate #4. Convenient location, colorful rooms, and loft beds. English spoken. Free Internet. Laundry 1200Ft. Reception 24hr. Check-out 11am. Book ahead. Dorms 3200Ft. Cash only. ❷

Caterina Hostel, III, Teréz krt. 30, apt. #28, ring code: 48 (☎269 5990; www.caterinahostel.hu), in Pest. M1: Oktogon, or trams #4 and 6. Newly renovated, spotless rooms with fresh linen. Internet 400Ft per hr. Reception 24hr. Check-out 10am. Lockout 10am-1pm. Book online. Dorms 2500-3200Ft; doubles 6800Ft; triples 10,200Ft. Low season 2000-3000/6000/9000Ft. Cash only. ❷

Garibaldi Guesthouse, V, Garibaldi u. 5 (☎302 3456; garibaldiguest@hotmail.com). M2: Kossuth tér. A variety of spacious, furnished rooms from singles to quads. Some have kitchenette, TV, and shower. English spoken. Dorms 3200-4000Ft. Private rooms from 6500Ft; apartments 6000-10,000Ft. Discounts for long stays and large groups. ❹

Red Bus Hostel, V, Semmelweis u. 14 (☎266 0136; www.redbusbudapest.hu), in Pest. Spacious dorms in downtown Pest. Internet 12Ft per min. Breakfast included. Laundry 1200Ft. Reception 24hr. Check-out 10am. 10-bed dorms 2900Ft; singles 6500-7500Ft; doubles 7500Ft; triples 10,500Ft. AmEx/MC/V. ❷

Yellow Submarine Hostel, VI, Teréz krt. 56, 3rd fl. (☎331 9896; www.yellowsubmarinehostel.com). Across from Nyugati pu. Known as a party hostel. Doubles and triples in nearby apartments. Internet 10Ft per min. Breakfast included. Laundry 1700Ft. Check-out 9am. Dorms 2900Ft; singles 7500Ft; doubles 9000Ft; triples 10,500Ft; quads 14,000Ft. 10% HI discount. MC/V. ❷

Aquarium Youth Hostel, VII, Alsoérdósor u. 12 (☎322 0502; aquarium@budapesthostels.com), in Pest. A hidden gem—there are no signs outside. Ring buzzer. Close to Keleti pu. and the metro. Laundry 1200Ft. Free Internet. Reception 24hr. Reserve ahead. 4- to 5-bed dorms 3000Ft; doubles 8500Ft. ❷

Hotel Marco Polo (HI), VII, Nyár u. 6 (☎413 2555; www.marcopolohostel.com), in Pest. M2: Astoria or M2: Blaha Lujza tér. Luxurious and spotless, dorm bunk beds are in separate compartments blocked off by curtains. Internet 7Ft per min. Reception 24hr. Book 1-2 days ahead in summer. Dorms 5000Ft; singles 13,750Ft; doubles 18,900Ft. 10% HI and ISIC discount. MC/V. ❸

SUMMER HOSTELS

Many university dorms moonlight as hostels during July and August. The majority are clustered around Móricz Zsigmond Körtér in district XI.

Hostel Bakfark, II, Bakfark u. 1/3 (☎413 2062), in Buda. M2: Moszkva tér. Comfortable dorms with lofts instead of bunks. Check-out 10am. Book ahead. Open mid-June to late Aug. Dorms 3300Ft, students 2000Ft. 10% HI discount. ❸

Hostel Landler, XI, Bartók Béla út 17 (☎463 3621), in Buda. Take bus #7 or 7A across the river and get off at Géllert; take Bartók Béla út away from the river. Comfy dorms. Check-out 9am. Open July to early Sept. Singles 5850Ft; triples 11,700Ft; quads 15,600Ft. 10% HI discount. ❸

CAMPING

Camping Római, III, Szentendrei út 189 (☎388 7167). M2: Batthyány tér. Take HÉV to Római fürdő; walk 100m toward river. Huge complex with swimming pool, shady park, nearby grocery store and restaurants. Breakfast 880Ft. Laundry 800Ft. Electricity 600Ft. Tent sites 2100Ft per person; bungalows 1800-15,000Ft, 990Ft per extra person, children 590Ft. Tourist tax 3%. 10% HI discount. ❶

Zugligeti "Niche" Camping, XII, Zugligeti út 101 (☎200 8346; www.campingniche.hu). Take bus #158 from above Moszkva tér to Laszállóhely, the last stop. Restaurant. Communal showers. Electricity 900Ft. Tent sites 800Ft; large tents 1200Ft. 1200Ft per person. Cars 900Ft, caravans 2200Ft. ❶

FOOD

Cafeterias with *"Önkiszolgáló Étterem"* signs serve cheap food (entrees 300-500Ft), and a neighborhood *kifőzés* (kiosk) or *vendéglő* (vendor) gives you a real taste of Hungary. Corner markets, many with 24hr. windows, stock basics. The **Grand Market Hall,** IX, Fövam tér 1/3, next to Szabadság híd (M3: Kálvin tér), was built in 1897; it now boasts 2½ acres of stalls, making it a tourist attraction itself. Ethnic restaurants inhabit the upper floors of **Mammut Plaza,** just outside the Moszkva tér metro in Buda, and the **West End Plaza,** near the Nyugati metro in Pest.

RESTAURANTS

Nagyi Palacsintazoja, II, Hattyu u. 16 (☎201 5321). Dishes out sweet and savory crepes (118-298Ft) piled with cheese, fruit, chocolate sauce, or whatever you desire. Seating options are squeezed in this tiny, mirror-covered restaurant. Open 24hr. ❶

Columbus Pub and Restaurant (☎266 9013), V, below the chain bridge on the Danube promenade. If you feel you've neglected the beautiful Danube, enjoy a tasty Hungarian meal on this moored ship. Open daily noon-midnight. AmEx/MC/V. ❸

Kashmir, V, Arany János u. 13 (☎354 1806). This Indian restaurant offers a lighter alternative to Hungarian knuckle dishes, with Kashmiri specialties and several vegetarian options. Entrees 850-1750Ft. M-F 11am-11pm, Sa-Su 5-11pm. Cash only. ❷

Tabani Kakas, I, Atilla u. 27 (☎375 7165), behind Castle Hill. A simple restaurant for the serious meat-eater. Pictures of Budapest line the walls, but food is the real draw. The fist-sized goose venison dumplings (1900Ft) will leave you floored. Entrees 1500-2500Ft. English-language menu available. Open daily noon-midnight. Cash only. ❷

Marquis de Salade, VI, Hajós u. 43 (☎302 4086). M3: Arany János. At the corner of Bajcsy-Zsilinszky út, 2 blocks from the metro. Huge menu with dishes from Azerbaijan and Russia. Entrees 1800-3500Ft. Open daily 11am-1am. Cash only. ❹

CAFES

Once the haunts of the literary, intellectual, and cultural elite—as well as political dissidents—Budapest's cafes boast histories as rich as the pastries they serve.

Dom Cafe, I, Szentháromság tér. Astonishing views of the Danube and Pest from atop Castle Hill. Beer and coffee start at 360Ft. Pastries and sandwiches also served. Open daily 10am-10pm.

Gerbeaud, V, Vörösmarty tér 7 (☎429 9020; www.gerbeaud.hu). M1: Vörösmarty tér. This illustrious cafe has been serving its layer cakes (620Ft) and homemade ice cream (250Ft) since 1858. Open daily 9am-9pm. AmEx/MC/V.

Muvész Kávéház, VI, Andrássy út 29 (☎352 1337). M1: Opera. Diagonally across from the Opera. Before or after a show, stop in for a slice of rich cake (350-380Ft) and a cappuccino (330Ft) at the polished stone tables. Open daily 9am-11:45pm.

SIGHTS

In 1896, Hungary's 1000th birthday bash prompted the construction of what are today Budapest's most prominent sights. Among the works commissioned by the Hapsburgs were **Heroes' Square** (Hősök tér), **Liberty Bridge** (Szabadság híd), **Vajdahunyad Castle** (Vajdahunyad vár), and continental Europe's first **metro** system. Slightly grayer for wear, war, and occupation, these monuments attest to the optimism of a capital on the verge of its Golden Age. See the sights, find your way around the city, and meet other travelers with **Absolute Walking and Biking Tours.** Their basic tour (3½hr.; 4000Ft, students 3500Ft) meets daily June through August at 9:30am and 1:30pm on the steps of the yellow church in Deák tér. During low season (Sept.-May) tours leave daily at 10:30am. Specialized tours focus on everything from communism to pubbing. (☎211 8861; www.absolutetours.com. Specialized tours 3½-5½hr. 4000-5000Ft.) **Boat tours** leave from Vigadó tér piers 6-7. The *Danube Legend*, which runs in the evening, costs 4200Ft; its daytime counterpart, the *Duna Bella*, costs 2600Ft for 1hr. and 3600Ft for 2hr.

BUDA

On the east bank of the Danube, Buda sprawls between the base of **Castle Hill** and southern **Gellért Hill,** rambling into the city's main residential areas. Older than Pest, Buda is filled with parks, lush hills, and islands.

CASTLE DISTRICT. Towering above the Danube on Castle Hill, the Castle District (Várhegy) has been razed three times in its 800-year history, most recently in 1945. With its winding, statue-filled streets, breathtaking views, and hodgepodge of architectural styles, the UNESCO-protected district now appears much as it did in Hapsburg times. The reconstructed **Buda Castle** *(Vár)* now houses a number of fine museums (p. 532), but bullet holes in the palace facade recall the 1956 Uprising. *(M1, 2, or 3: Deák tér. From the metro, take bus #16 across the Danube. Alternatively, take the metro to M2: Moszkva tér and walk up to the hill on Várfok u. "Becsi kapu" marks the castle entrance.)* Beneath Buda castle, the **Castle Labyrinths** (Budvári Labirinths) provide a spooky glimpse of the subterranean world of the city. *(Úri u. 9. ☎212 0207. Open daily 9:30am-7:30pm. 1400Ft, students 1100Ft.)*

MATTHIAS CHURCH. The multi-colored roof of Matthias Church (Mátyás templom) is one of Budapest's most photographed sights. The church was converted into a mosque in 1541, then reconverted 145 years later when the Hapsburgs defeated the Turks. Ascend the spiral steps to the exhibits of the **Museum of Ecclesiastical Art.** *(On Castle Hill. Open M-Sa 9am-5pm, Su 1-5pm. High Mass daily 7, 8:30am, 6pm; Su and holidays also 10am, noon. Church and museum 600Ft, students 300Ft.)*

GELLÉRT HILL. After the coronation of King Stephen, the first Christian Hungarian monarch, the Pope sent Bishop Gellért to convert the Magyars. Budapest's principal hill was named Gellérthegy after those unconvinced by the bishop's message hurled him to his death from the summit. The **Liberation Monument** (Szabadság Szobor), which honors Soviet soldiers who died ridding Hungary of Nazis, overlooks Budapest from the hilltop. The view from the adjoining **Citadel,** built as a symbol of Hapsburg power after the foiled 1848 revolution, is especially breathtaking at night. At the base of the hill is Budapest's most famous Turkish bath, the **Gellért Hotel and Baths.** *(XI. Tram #18 or 19, or bus #7, to Hotel Gellért; follow Szabó Verjték u. to Jubileumi Park, continuing on marked paths to the summit. Or take bus #27 to Búsuló Juhász and walk 5min. to the peak. Citadel 1200Ft.)*

PEST

Constructed in the 19th century, the winding streets of Pest now bring together cafes, corporations, and monuments. The crowded **Belváros** (Inner City) is based around the swarming pedestrian boulevards **Váci utca** and **Vörösmarty tér.**

PARLIAMENT. Standing 96m tall, a number that symbolizes the date of Hungary's millennial anniversary, the palatial Gothic Parliament (Országház) was modeled after the UK's, right down to the riverside location and hieratic facade. The **Hungarian crown jewels** were moved from the National Museum to the Cupola Room here in 1999. *(M2: Kossuth tér. ☎441 4000. English-language tours M-F 10am, noon, 2, 2:30, 5, and 6pm; Sa-Su 10am; arrive early. 5-person min. Ticket office at Gate X opens at 8am. Entrance with mandatory tour 2300Ft, students 1150Ft. Free with EU passport.)*

GREAT SYNAGOGUE. The largest synagogue in Europe and the second largest in the world, Pest's Great Synagogue (Zsinagóga) was designed to hold 3000 worshippers. In the garden the enormous metal **Tree of Life,** a Holocaust memorial, sits above a mass grave for thousands of Jews killed near the end of the war. The Hebrew inscription reads: "Whose pain can be greater than mine?", and the Hungarian beneath: "Let us remember." Each leaf bears the name of a family that perished. Next door, the **Jewish Museum** (Zsidó Múzeum) documents Hungary's rich Jewish past. *(VII. M2: Astoria. At the corner of Dohány u. and Wesselényi u. Open May-Oct. M-Th 10am-5pm, F 10am-2pm, Su 10am-2pm; Nov.-Apr. M-Th 10am-3pm, F 10am-1pm, Su 10am-1pm. Services F 6pm. Admissions often start at 10:30am. Covered shoulders required. Tours M-Th 10:30am-3:30pm on the half-hour, F and Su 10:30, 11:30am, 12:30pm. Admission to Synagogue and Museum 1000Ft, students 400Ft. Tours 1900Ft, students 1600Ft.)*

ST. STEPHEN'S BASILICA (SZ. ISTVÁN BAZILIKA). Though seriously damaged in WWII, the neo-Renaissance facade of the city's largest church has been largely restored. The **Panorama Tower** offers an amazing 360° view of the city. A curious attraction is St. Stephen's mummified right hand, one of Hungary's most revered religious relics; a 100Ft donation dropped in the box will illuminate it for 2min. *(V. M1, 2, or 3: Deák tér. Open May-Oct. M-Sa 9am-5pm; Nov.-Apr. M-Sa 10am-4pm. Mass M-Sa 7, 8am, 6pm, Su 8:30, 10am, noon, 6pm. Tower open daily June-Aug. 9:30am-6pm; Sept.-Oct. 10am-5:30pm; Apr.-May 10am-4:30pm. Church free. Tower 500Ft, students 400Ft.)*

ANDRÁSSY ÚT AND HEROES' SQUARE. Hungary's grandest boulevard, Andrássy út, extends from Erzsébet tér in downtown Pest to Heroes' Sq. (Hősök tér) to the northeast. The Hungarian State Opera House (Magyar Állami Operaház), the gilded interior of which glows on performance nights, is a vivid reminder of Budapest's Golden Age. Take a tour if you can't see an opera. *(Andrássy út 22. M1: Opera. ☎332 8197. 1hr. English-language tours daily 3, 4pm. 2000Ft, students 1000Ft. 20%*

discount with Budapest Card.) At the Heroes' Sq. end of Andrássy út, the Millennium Monument (Millenniumi emlékmű) commemorates the nation's most prominent leaders. Also off Heroes' Sq. is the Museum of Fine Arts (see below).

CITY PARK (VÁROSLIGET). Budapest's park is home to a zoo, a circus, an aging amusement park, and the lakeside **Vajdahunyad Castle.** The castle's collage of Baroque, Gothic, and Romanesque styles chronicles the history of Hungarian design. Outside broods the hooded statue of King Béla IV's **anonymous scribe,** to whom we owe much of our knowledge of medieval Hungary. Rent a **rowboat** or **ice skates** on the lake next to the castle. The park's main road is closed to automobiles on weekends. *(XIV. M1: Széchenyi Fürdő. Zoo ☎343 3710. Open May-Aug. M-Th 9am-6:30pm, F-Su 9am-7pm; Mar. and Oct. M-Th 9am-5pm, F-Su 9am–5:30pm; Apr. and Sept. M-Th 9am-5:30pm, F-Su 9am-6pm; Nov.-Jan. daily 9am-4pm. Park ☎363 8310. Open July-Aug. daily 10am-8pm; May-June M-F 11am-7pm, Sa-Su 10am-8pm. Park 300Ft. Zoo 1300Ft, students 1000Ft.)*

MUSEUMS

MUSEUM OF FINE ARTS (SZÉPMŰVÉSZETI MÚZEUM). A spectacular collection of European art is housed here, with paintings perhaps not found in the books but memorable nonetheless. The El Greco room should not be missed. *(XIV. Hősök tér. M1: Hősök tér. English ☎069 036 9300. Open Tu-Su 10am-5:30pm. Free English-language tours Tu-F 11am. Permanent collection free, temporary exhibits 800-100Ft.)*

LUDWIG MUSEUM (LUDVIG MÚZEUM). Newly relocated to the outskirts of the city, the Ludwig Museum ("LuMu") attests to Budapest's rise in the art world, displaying the most recent Hungarian painting and sculpture. *(IX. Komor Marcell u. 1. Take tram #4 or 6 to Boráros tér, then take the HÉV commuter rail one stop to Lagymanyosi híd. ☎555 3444; www.ludwigmuseum.hu. Open Tu, F, Su 10am-6pm; W noon-6pm; Th noon-8pm; Sa 10am-8pm. Permanent collection free. Temporary exhibits 800Ft, students 400Ft.)*

NATIONAL MUSEUM (NEMZETI MÚZEUM). An extensive exhibit on the second floor here chronicles the history of Hungary from the founding of the state through the 20th century; the first floor is reserved for temporary exhibits. *(VIII. Múzeum krt. 14/16. M3: Kálvin tér. ☎338 2122; www.mng.hu. Open Tu-Su 10am-6pm. 600Ft.)*

STATUE PARK. After the collapse of Soviet rule, the open-air Statue Park museum (Szoborpark Múzeum) was created to house Soviet statues removed from Budapest's parks and squares. The indispensable English-language guidebook (1000Ft) explains the statues' histories. *(XXII. On the corner of Balatoni út and Szabadkai út. Take express bus #7 from Keleti pu. to Étele tér, then take the Volán bus from terminal #2 bound for Diósd—15min., every 15min.—and get off at the Szoborpark stop. ☎424 7500; www.szoborpark.hu. Open daily 10am-dusk. 600Ft, students 400Ft.)*

MUSEUM OF APPLIED ARTS (IPARMŰVÉSZETI MÚZEUM). Hungary's 1896 millennium celebration prompted the construction of this Art Nouveau building. Inside is an eclectic collection of impressive handcrafted objects, including furniture and Tiffany glass, as well as excellent temporary exhibits. *(IX. Üllői út 33-37. M3: Ferenc krt. ☎456 5100. Open daily 10am-6pm. 1-2hr. guided tours. Fewer than 6 people 2500Ft total; 6-25 people 200Ft each. English-language pamphlet 100Ft. Museum 1000Ft, students 500Ft.)*

BUDA CASTLE. The reconstructed Buda Castle (p. 530) now houses several museums. **Wings B-D** hold the huge **Hungarian National Gallery** (Magyar Nemzeti Galéria), a definitive collection of Hungarian painting and sculpture. Its treasures include works by Realist Mihály Munkácsy and Impressionist Paál Lászlo, gold medieval altarpieces, and many depictions of national tragedies. *(☎375 7533. Open Tu-Su 10am-6pm. English-language tour by appointment. Permanent collection free; temporary exhibits*

1500Ft, students 800Ft.) **Wing E** houses the **Budapest History Museum** (Budapesti Törtenéti Múzeum), a collection of recently unearthed medieval artifacts, including weapons, tombstones, and glassware. *(I. Szent György tér 2. M1, 2, or 3: Deák tér, then take bus #16 across the Danube to the top of Castle Hill. ☎375 7533. English info. Open Mar.-Nov. M and W-Su 10am-6pm; Nov.-Mar. 10am-4pm. 900Ft, students 450Ft.)*

ENTERTAINMENT

Hungary's largest cultural festival, the **Budapest Spring Festival** (☎486 3311), in late March, showcases Hungary's premier musicians and actors. In August, Óbudai Island hosts the week-long **Sziget Festival,** an open-air rock festival that draws major European and American acts. (☎372 0650; www.sziget.hu. Call for ticket prices.) *Budapest Program*, *Budapest Panorama*, *Pesti Est*, and the essential *Budapest in Your Pocket* are the best English-language entertainment guides, listing everything from festivals to cinemas to art showings. All are available at most tourist offices and hotels. The "Style" section of the *Budapest Sun* (www.budapestsun.com; 300Ft) has a comprehensive 10-day calendar and film reviews. (Tickets 600-1200Ft; cinema schedules change on Th.) Prices to most performances are reasonable; check **Ticket Express Hungary,** Andrássy u. 18. (☎312 0000; www.tex.hu. Open M-F 9:30am-6:30pm.)

The **State Opera House** (Magyar Állami Operaház), VI, Andrássy út 22, is one of Europe's leading performance centers with a glorious hall. (M1: Opera. ☎331 2550, box office 353 0170. Tickets 800-8700Ft. Box office open M-Sa 11am-7pm, Su 4-7pm. Closes at 5pm on non-performance days.) The **National Dance Theater** (Nemzetí Táncszínház), Szinház u. 1-3, on Castle Hill, hosts a variety of shows—modern, alternative, Latin, ballet—but Hungarian folklore is the most popular. (☎201 4407, box office 375 8649; www.nemzetitancszinhaz.hu. Most shows 7pm. Tickets 1200-4000Ft.) Performances in the lovely **Városmajor Open-Air Theater,** XII, Városmajor, include musicals, operas, and ballets. Walk up the big stairs, turn right on Várfok u. and left on Csaba u., then right on Maros u. and left on Szamos u. (M1: Moszkva tér. ☎375 5922. Open June 27-Aug. 18. Box office open W-Su 3-6pm.)

To soak away the city grime, sink into a hot, relaxing thermal bath. First built in 1565, their services—from mud baths to massages—are quite cheap. **Széchenyi,** XIV, Állatkerti u. 11/14, is one of Europe's largest bath complexes. (M1: Hősök tér. ☎321 0310. Open May-Sept. daily 6am-7pm; Oct.-Apr. M-F 6am-7pm, Sa-Su 6am-5pm. 2000Ft, 800Ft returned if you leave within 2hr., 500Ft within 3hr., 200Ft within 4hr.; keep your receipt. 15min. massage 2400Ft. Cash only.) **Gellért,** XI, Kelenhegyi út 4/6, one of the most elegant baths, has a rooftop sundeck and an outdoor wave pool. Take bus #7 or tram #47 or 49 to Hotel Gellért, at the base of Gellérthegy. (Open May-Sept. daily 6am-7pm; Oct.-Apr. M-F 6am-7pm, Sa-Su 6am-5pm. 3000Ft, with scaled refund. 15min. massage 2400Ft. Pedicure 1300Ft. MC/V.)

NIGHTLIFE

All-night outdoor parties, elegant after-hours clubs, nightly thump-and-grind—Budapest has it all. Pubs and bars bustle until 4am, though given the city's energy the streets remain surprisingly empty and poorly lit. Upscale cafes and restaurants in **VI, Ferencz Liszt tér** (M2: Oktogon) attract Budapest's hip youth.

Undergrass, VI, Ferencz Liszt tér 10. M1: Oktogon. The hottest spot in Pest's trendiest area. A soundproof glass door divides a hip bar from a packed disco. Cover up to 1000Ft. Open F-Sa 10pm-4am.

Zöld Pardon, XI, on the Buda side of Petőfi Bridge. If you're wondering where everyone is on weeknights, wonder no more. 3 large screens project the crowd on the giant dance floor. Beer 250-400Ft. Cover 100Ft. Open daily 9am-6am.

Jazz Garden, V, Veres Pálné u. 44a. Low-hanging vines and branches create a laidback atmosphere. Live jazz 9pm daily. Beer 650Ft. Open M-F 3pm-5am, Sa-Su 5pm-5am.

Café Eklektika, V, Semmelweis u. 21 (☎266 2116). This centrally located, gay-friendly bar and cafe serves light meals and precious wines. Smooth jazz, sleek leather chairs and a marble floor. Dance classes daily 6pm. Open M-F noon-1am, Sa-Su 5pm-1am.

B7 Klub, VI, Dessewffy u. 3 (☎633 6000; www.b7.hu), on the corner of Nagymező u. Hip-hop with a smattering of electronica plays to a disco-lit international crowd at this up-and-coming club. Cover varies, usually free before midnight. Open M-Sa 5pm-5am.

Piaf, VI, Nagymező u. 25. A much-loved lounge, frequented by travelers. Knock on the inconspicuous door and kiss cheeks with the club's matron. Cover 800Ft, includes 1 beer. Open M-Th and Su 10pm-6am, F-Sa 10pm-7am, but slow before 1am.

Angyal (Angel) Bar, VII, Kazinczy u. 4 M2: Blaha Lujza tér. Oldest gay bar in Budapest. Huge 3-level disco, cafe, and bar packed for its weekend programs. F-Sa drag shows. Sa men only. Cover 1300Ft. Open F-Sa 10pm-5am.

NIGHTLIFE SCAM. There have been reports of a scam involving English-speaking Hungarian women who ask foreign men to buy them drinks. When the bill comes, accompanied by imposing men, it can be US$1000 per round. If victims claim to have no money, there is an ATM inside the bar. The US Embassy has advised against patronizing serveral places near Váci u. When in doubt, verify the price of a drink before ordering. For a current list of questionable establishments, check the US Embassy website at http://budapest.usembassy.gov/tourist_advisory.html. If you are taken in, call the police. You'll probably still have to pay, but get a receipt to issue a complaint at the Consumer Bureau.

DAYTRIPS FROM BUDAPEST: THE DANUBE BEND

North of Budapest, the Danube sweeps in a dramatic arc called the Danube Bend *(Dunakanyar)*, deservedly one of the favorite tourist attractions in Hungary.

SZENTENDRE. The narrow cobblestone streets of Szentendre (pop. 23,000) brim with upscale art galleries and restaurants. Head up **Church Hill** (Templomdomb) in Fő tér, for an amazing view from the 13th-century church. The **Czóbel Museum,** Templom tér 1, exhibits the work of post-Impressionist Béla Czóbel, including his bikini-clad *Venus of Szentendre.* (Open Tu-Su 10am-6pm. 400Ft, students 200Ft.) The popular **Kovács Margit Museum,** Vastagh György u. 1, off Görög u., displays whimsical ceramics by the 20th-century Hungarian artist. (Open Mar.-Sept. M-Th 10am-5:30pm, F-Su 10am-7:30pm; Sept.-Mar. daily 9am-5pm. 600Ft, students 300Ft.) The real thriller at the **Szabó Marzipan Museum and Confectionery,** Dumtsa Jenő u. 12, is a 80kg white chocolate statue of Michael Jackson. (Open daily May-Sept. 9am-7pm; Oct.-Apr. 10am-6pm. 350Ft.) The **National Wine Museum** (Nemzeti Bormúzeum), Bogdányi u. 10, exhibits wines from across Hungary. (Open daily 10am-10pm. Exhibit 100Ft, tasting and English tour 1600Ft.)

At **Nostalgia Cafe ❶**, Bogdányi u. 2, enjoy a pastry (from 350Ft) and cappuccino (from 300Ft) while serenaded by opera singers. (Open Th-Su 10am-10pm. AmEx/MC/V.) HÉV **trains** travel to Szentendre from Budapest's Batthyány tér (45min., every 20min., 430Ft). **Buses** run from Szentendre to: Budapest's Árpád híd metro station (30min., every 20-40min., 303Ft); Esztergom (1½hr., 1 per hr., 476Ft); Visegrád (45min., 1 per hr., 316Ft). The train and bus stations are 10min. from Fő tér; descend the stairs past the end of the HÉV tracks and head through the underpass up Kossuth u. At the fork, bear right onto Dumtsa Jenő u., which leads to the center. **Tourinform,** Dumtsa Jenő u. 22, between the center and the stations, has maps. (☎026 31 79 65. Open mid-Mar. to Oct. M-F 9am-1pm and 1:30-4:30pm, Sa-Su 10am-1pm and 1:30-2pm; Nov. to mid-Mar. M-F 9:30am-1pm and 1:30-4:30pm.)

VISEGRÁD. Host to the royal court in medieval times, Visegrád was devastated when the Hapsburgs destroyed its 13th-century **citadel** in a struggle against freedom fighters. A former Roman outpost, the edifice provides a dramatic view of the Danube and surrounding hills. To reach it, head north on Fő út., make a right on Salamontorony u., and follow the path. Sprawling across the foothills above Fő út. are the ruins of King Matthias's **Royal Palace** *(Királyi Palota)*, which was considered a myth until unearthed by archaeologists. Exhibits include a computerized reconstruction of the original castle. (Open Tu-Su 9am-5pm; last admission 30min. before close. Free.) The palace grounds relive their glory days with parades, jousting, and music during the mid-July **Viségrad Palace Games.** (☎026 39 81 28; muvelodesihaz@visegrad.hu.) At the end of Salamontorony u., the **King Matthias Museum,** inside Solomon's Tower *(Alsóvár Salamon Torony)*, exhibits artifacts from the palace ruins. (Open May-Oct. Tu-Su 9am-5pm; last admission 4:30pm. Free.)

Gulás Csárda ❸, Nagy Lajos u. 4, serves a variety of excellent Hungarian dishes; let the garlic aromas tempt you from the garden outside. (Entrees 1200-1700Ft. Open daily noon-10pm.) **Buses** run to Budapest's Árpád híd metro station (1½hr., 30 per day, 484Ft). The tourist office, **Visegrád Tours,** Rév út. 15, sells maps for 300Ft. (☎026 39 81 60. Open Apr.-Oct. daily 8am-6pm; Nov.-Mar. M-F 10am-4pm.)

ESZTERGOM. A millennium of religious history revolves around the solemn hilltop cathedral, the **Basilica of Esztergom,** which is now the seat of the Catholic Church in Hungary. Ascend the endless staircases to the **cupola,** with a stunning view of the Danube Bend. (Open Mar.-Oct. Tu-Su 9am-4:30pm; Nov.-Dec. Tu-F 9am-4:30pm, Sa-Su 10am-3:30pm. Cupola 200Ft. Treasury 450Ft, students 220Ft.) The red marble **Bakócz Chapel,** to the left of the nave, is a Renaissance masterwork. (Open daily Mar.-Oct. 6:30am-6pm; Nov.-Dec. 7am-4pm. Free.)

Csülök Csárda ❷, Batthány út 9, below the basilica, offers fine Hungarian cuisine with vegetarian options. (Entrees 480-1800Ft. Open daily noon-10pm. Cash only.) **Trains** go to Budapest (1½hr., 22 per day, 512Ft). To reach the main square from the station, turn left on the main street, Baross Gábor út., and make a right onto Kiss János Altábornagy út., which becomes Kossuth Lajos u. **Buses** run to Szentendre (1½hr., 1 per hr., 476Ft) and Visegrád (45min., 1 per hr., 302Ft). MAHART **boats** depart from the pier at Gőzhajó u. on Primas Sziget Island for: Budapest (4hr., 3 per day, 1200Ft.); Szentendre (2¾hr.; 2 per day; 980Ft.); Visegrád (1½hr.; 2 per day; 700Ft.). **Grantours,** Széchenyi tér 25, at the edge of Rákóczi tér, sells maps (300-500Ft) and books rooms. (☎033 41 70 52; grantour@mail.holop.hu. Open July-Aug. M-F 8am-5pm, Sa 9am-noon; Sept.-June M-F 8am-4pm.)

PÉCS ☎072

Pécs (PAYCH; pop. 180,000), at the foot of the Mecsek mountains, is blessed with a pleasant climate, gorgeous vistas, and lovely architecture. Outdoor activities in the surrounding region and an intense nightlife fueled by university students make Pécs an attractive weekend spot.

TRANSPORTATION AND PRACTICAL INFORMATION. **Trains** run to Budapest (2½hr., 16 per day, 2706Ft), as do **buses** (4½hr., 5 per day, 2540Ft). To reach the train station, just south of the historic district, take bus #30, 32, or 33 from the town center. Local **bus** tickets cost 145Ft in kiosks or 155Ft on the bus. **Tourinform,** Széchenyi tér 9, sells maps and phone cards. (☎511 232. Open May-Oct. Sa-Su 9am-2pm; Nov.-Apr. M-F 8am-4pm. **Postal Code:** 7621.

ACCOMMODATIONS AND FOOD. Private rooms close to the town center are a good budget option. In the center of town, **Pollack Mihály Students' Hostel ❷**, Jokai u. 8, has comfortable rooms and a lounge. (☎315 846. Book ahead. Singles 2700Ft.) Take bus #21 from the main bus terminal to 48-as tér, or walk up the hill to Rákóczi út. and turn right to reach **Szent Mór Kollégium ❶**, 48-as tér 4, in a gorgeous old university wing. (☎503 610. Reception 24hr. Checkout 10am. Curfew midnight; ring the bell after 10pm. Open July-Aug. Triples 1700Ft.)

Pécs's restaurants, cafes, and bars are among the city's biggest attractions. **Aflúm ❷**, Irgalmasok u. 2, has a delicious Italian and Hungarian menu with vegetarian options. (Entrees 700-2800Ft. Open M-F 11am-1am, Su 11am-midnight.) **Cellarium Étterem ❸**, Hunyadi út. 2, is a Hungarian restaurant housed in a wine cellar. (Entrees 950-3200Ft. AmEx/MC/V.) Sink your sweet tooth into pastries (from 100Ft) and sundaes (300-650Ft) amid the antique chandeliers, marble cafe tables, and velvet chairs at **Caflisch Cukrászda ❶**, Király u. 32. (☎310 391. Open daily 10am-10pm.) **Interspar**, Bajcsy-Zsilinszky u. 11, downstairs inside Árkád Shopping Mall, is a fully-stocked grocery store with a salad bar, deli, and bakery. (Open M-Th and Sa 7am-9pm, F 7am-10pm, Su 8am-7pm.)

SIGHTS AND NIGHTLIFE. The family workshop at the **Zsolnay Museum**, Káptalan u. 2, has handcrafted world-famous porcelain since the 19th century. Walk up Szepessy I. u. and turn left on Káptalan u. (Open Tu-Sa 10am-6pm, Su 10am-4pm. 700Ft, students 350Ft. Photography 400Ft, video 800Ft.) Next door, the **Vasarely Museum**, Káptalan u. 3, displays the works of Viktor Vasarely, a pioneer of Op-Art and geometric abstraction, along with those of other 20th-century artists of the same ilk. (☎324 822, ext. 21. Open Apr.-Oct. Tu-Sa 10am-6pm, Su 10am-4pm. 500Ft, students 250Ft. Photography 400Ft, video 800Ft.) At nearby Széchenyi tér stands the **Mosque of Ghazi Kassim** *(Gázi Khasim Pasa dzsámija)*. The church was once a Turkish mosque built on the site of an earlier church. Its fusion of Christian and Muslim traditions has become an emblem of the city. (Open mid-Apr. to mid-Oct. M-Sa 10am-4pm, Su 12:30-4pm; mid-Oct. to mid-Apr. M-Sa 10am-noon, Su open for Mass only 9:30, 10:30, 11:30am. Free; donations requested.) Walk downhill from Széchenyi tér on Irgalmasok u. to Kossuth tér and the 1869 **synagogue**, with intricate ceiling frescoes and a stunning Ark of the Covenant. (Open Mar.-Oct. M-F and Su 10-11:30am and noon-1pm. 300Ft, students 200Ft.) Atop Pécs hill on Dóm tér, the 4th-century Romanesque **cathedral** offers a respite from the bustling city. Organ music reverberates under the painted ceiling supported by patterned columns. (☎513 030. Open M-F 9am-5pm, Sa 9am-2pm, Su 1-5pm. Mass M-Sa 6pm; Su 8, 9:30, 11am, 6pm. 700Ft, students 350Ft.) Chill with the artists and students at **Dante Cafe**, Janus Pannonis u. 11, in the Csontváry Museum building. (Beer 350-420Ft. Sa-Su live jazz. Open M-F 10am-1am, later Sa-Su.) On a quiet side street, slick and spacious **Trafik**, Perczel M. u. 22, invites you to relax with its comfy couches and big-screen TV. (☎212 672. Drinks from 600Ft. Open M-Sa 4pm-1am.)

EGER ☎036

Once the site of Captain István Dobó's legendary struggles against Ottoman conquest, Eger (EGG-air; pop. 57,000) is a much more soothing locale today. The town still prides itself on its rich history, but its real claim to fame is homemade wine. The spirited cellars of the Valley of Beautiful Women lure travelers from Budapest with the alleged strengthening powers of *Egri Bikavér* (Bull's Blood) wine.

TRANSPORTATION AND PRACTICAL INFORMATION. Trains depart from the station on Vasút u. (☎314 264) to Budapest (2hr.; 21 per day, 4 direct; 1036-1242Ft). Indirect trains run to Keleti station in Budapest via Füzesabony.

Trains also go to Szeged (4½hr., 12 per day, 3050Ft). From the **bus** station on Barkóczy u. (☎517 777; www.agriavolan.hu) catch a ride to: **Aggtelek** (3hr., 1 per day at 8:45am, 1330Ft); **Budapest** (2hr., 25-30 per day, 1360Ft); **Debrecen** (3hr., 10 per day, 1296Ft); **Szilvásvárad** (45min., 40 per day, 363Ft). If public transport doesn't do it for you, try **City Taxi** (☎555 555). To walk to the **Dobó tér,** the main square, from the train station (15min.), head straight and take a right on Deák Ferenc út, a right on Kossuth Lajos u., and a left on Tokaj u. To get to the center from the bus station, turn right on Barkóczy u. from terminal #10 and right again at Bródy u. Follow the stairs to the end of the street and turn right on Széchenyi u.; a left down Érsek u. leads to Dobó tér. Most sights are within a 10min. walk of the square. Find free maps at **TourInform,** Bajcsy-Zsilinszky u. 9. (☎517 715; www.ekft.hu/eger. **Internet** access 200Ft for 30min. Open June-Sept. M-F 9am-7pm, Sa-Su 10am-6pm; Oct.-May M-F 9am-5pm, Sa 9am-1pm.) **Postal Code:** 3300.

ACCOMMODATIONS AND FOOD. Private rooms are the best budget option; look for "*Zimmer frei*" or "*szòba eladò*" on signs outside the main square, particularly on Almagyar u. and Mekcsey István u. near the castle. **Eger Tourist ❷,** Bajcsy-Zsilinszky u. 9, next to TourInform, arranges private rooms that cost about 3000Ft. (☎517 000. Open M-F 9am-5pm.) Family-run **Lukács Vendéghaz ❷,** Bárány u. 10, located just next to Eger Castle, has its own garden, an outdoor patio, and large, comfortable rooms. The streets nearby can be dark and empty at night. (☎/fax 411 567. Rooms 3500-5000Ft.) Centrally located **Hotel Minaret ❹,** Knézich K. u. 4, offers a beauty and massage center, swimming pool, restaurant, and gym. (☎410 233; www.hotelminaret.hu. All rooms with satellite TV. Singles 8400Ft; doubles 14,600Ft; triples 19,200Ft; quads 22,900Ft. Nov.-Mar. 1000Ft less. AmEx/MC/V.) Take bus #5 or 11 north to near the Shell station to reach **Autós Caravan Camping ❶,** Rákóczi u. 79. (Open daily mid-Apr. to mid-Oct. 9am-10pm. Lockout midnight-6am. 900Ft, students 700Ft. MC.) **Széchenyi utca** is lined with restaurants. In the Valley of the Beautiful Women, crowds fill the courtyard of **Kulacs Csárda Panzió ❸.** (English-language menu. Entrees 950-2000Ft. Open daily noon-10pm. AmEx/MC/V.) **Dobos Cukrászola ❶,** Széchenyi u. 6, offers mouth-watering desserts. (Confections 200-400Ft. Ice cream 100Ft. Open daily 9:30am-9pm.) **Gyros ❷,** Széchenyi u. 10, serves gyros (450-950Ft) on a patio. There is an **ABC** supermarket between Sandor u. and Szt. Janos u. (Open M-F 6am-7pm, Sa 6am-1pm, Su 6-11am.)

THE HIDDEN DEA

STAYIN' A-LAVA

A bustling town by day, Eger turns suspiciously quiet at night, with cafes closed and few people wandering the streets. Or at least so i seems. Underneath—quite literally—Eger continues to offer festive diversions in the form of clubs built into a series of lava tunnels.

Unknown to most visitors, an elaborate labyrinth lies below Eger, the carved remnants of a 120km bed of lava upon which the city was founded. Locals have converted three sections into nightclubs, invisible to the world above except for small, barel marked entrances.

One of the most popular (and cave-like) of these dens, **Broadway Palace,** on Pyrter 3, along side Kossuth L. u, lies under the Eger Cathedral: Blaspheming youths dance the night away wandering out just hours before the church above begins morning service. (Cover 500Ft. Open W Sa, 10pm-6am.)

Another popular underground spot is **Liget Dance Cafe,** Erksel kert (☎427 754), under Excalibu Restaurant in the Archbishop' Gardens. (Cover 600Ft. Open F-Sa 10pm-6am. AmEx/MC/V.) Clearl marked by spotlights, the club draws a younger crowd to the neon lights of its central dance floor **Hippolit Club and Restaurant** Katona ter 2, is classier and more subdued. (☎411 031. Dancing starts around 11pm. Open M-Th noon-midnight, F-Sa noon-4am).

SIGHTS AND FESTIVALS. Spend an evening in the cellars of the **Valley of the Beautiful Women** (Szépasszonyvölgy). Walk down Széchenyi u. with Eger Cathedral to your right, turn right on Kossuth Lajos u., and left when it dead-ends into Vörösmarty u. Take a right on Kiraly u. and keep walking (25min.). Most of the 25 cellars consist of little more than a few tables with benches, but each has its own personality. Some are hushed while others burst with Hungarian and Gypsy singalongs. (Open from 9am, closing times vary; July-Aug. some open until midnight. 0.1L taste free or 50Ft, 1L 350Ft.) In summer, **open-air baths** offer a break from the sweltering heat. (Open May-Sept. M-F 6am-7pm, Sa-Su 8am-7pm; Oct.-Apr. daily 9am-7pm. Ticket window closes 6pm. 900Ft, students 450Ft.) Eger resonates with opera and early court music during the **Baroque Festival** (late July to mid-Aug.).

BARADLA BAVES

Straddling the Slovak-Hungarian border, Aggtelek National Park is home to the fantastic Baradla Caves. Formed 200 million years ago and spanning over 25km, the limestone caves may be seen as a daytrip from Eger, but if you take a longer hike, you'll miss the return bus. The trip from Eger is long, but passes through lush hills to the caves filled with imposing stone formations. Tours vary in length from 1hr. basic and Bat Branch tours (daily 10am, noon, 1, 3, and 5pm; low season no 5pm tour; 1900Ft, students 1100Ft), to 5hr. guided hikes (6000Ft, students 3600Ft). Arrange longer tours with **TourInform** (☎503 000). The temperature is 10°C year-round, so bring a jacket. **Baradla Hostel ❶**, next to the park, is an excellent base from which to explore the caves and to take hikes into the nearby region. (☎503 005. Dorms 1800Ft, students 1500Ft; cottage triples 4000Ft; quads 5300Ft. Tent sites 1000Ft per person, students 700Ft.) Beside the ticket booth, **Barlang Vendéglo ❸** offers reasonably priced Hungarian favorites (entrees 750-2300Ft) on a pleasant outdoor terrace. The **bus** leaves Eger daily at 8:45am and arrives in Aggtelek at 11:25am, returning from the stop just up and across the street at 3pm. From the bus, cross the street and go down the path to the caves; the park entrance is on the right. (☎503 002. Open daily April-Sept. 8am-6pm; Oct.-Mar. 8am-4pm.)

GYŐR ☎096

In the unspoiled, far western region of Őrség, lively Győr (DYUR; pop. 130,000) overflows with monuments, museums, and 17th- and 18th-century architecture. Turn right out of the train station, left before the underpass, and cross the street to reach the pedestrian-only **Baross Gábor útca.** Walk uphill on Czuczor Gergely u., one street to the right of Baross Gábor u., and turn left at Gutenberg tér to reach the **Ark of the Covenant** statue (Frigylada szobov) and **Chapter Hill** (Káptalandomb). At the top of the hill is the **Episcopal Cathedral** (Székesegyház) with its **Weeping Madonna of Győr;** legend has it that the icon wept blood for persecuted Irish Catholics on St. Patrick's Day in 1697. The **Diocesan Library and Treasury** (Egyházmegyei Kincstár), Káptalandomb 26, in an alley off the cathedral square, displays 14th-century gold and silver. (Open Tu-Su 10am-4pm. 500Ft, students 350Ft.) The **Imre Patkó collection,** Széchenyi tér 4, has contemporary art; enter at Stelczera u. Buy tickets in the Xántus Janos Museum next door. (Open Tu-Su 10am-6pm. 400Ft, students 200Ft.) Across the river is the huge **water park,** Cziráky tér 1, supplied by thermal springs. From Bécsi Kapu tér, take the bridge over the small island and make the first right on the other side, then right again onto Cziráky tér. (Open daily 8am-8pm. 3hr. ticket 1300Ft, students 800Ft; full-day ticket 1600/1000Ft.)

Katalin Kert ❸, Sarkantyú köz 3, off Bécsi Kapu tér, has huge modern rooms with private baths. (☎54 20 88; katalinkert@matavnet.hu. Singles 7100Ft; doubles 9100Ft; triples 12,500Ft. Tax 300Ft per person. Cash only.) **Matróz Restaurant ❷,** Dunakapu tér 3, off Jedlik Ányos u., serves succulent fish, turkey, and pork dishes.

(Entrees 440-1390Ft. Open M-Th and Su 9am-10pm, F-Sa 9am-11pm.) **John Bull Pub ❷**, Aradi u. 3, offers a break from the Hungarian diet with Italian dishes, grilled meat, and salads. (Salads 330-580Ft. Entrees 1200-2850Ft. Open daily 10am-midnight. MC/V.) **Kaiser's** supermarket is at the corner of Arany János u. and Aradi vértanúk. (Open M 7:30am-7pm, Tu-F 6:30am-7pm, Sa 6:30am-3pm. MC/V.) At night, Győr's sophisticates head to **The 20th Century,** Schweidel u. 25. (Beer 195-400Ft. Mixed drinks 500-1250Ft. Open M-F 9am-midnight, Sa-Su 5pm-midnight.) The patio at **Komédiás Biergarten,** Czuczor Gergely u. 30, draws laughing crowds. (Beer 290-460Ft. Open M-Sa 11am-midnight.) **Trains** run from Budapest (2½hr., 34 per day, 1338Ft) and Vienna (2hr., 13 per day, 4488Ft). **Buses** also run to Budapest (2½hr., 1 per hr., 1450Ft). The train station is 3min. from the city center; the underpass that links the platforms leads to the bus station. The **Tourinform kiosk,** Árpád u. 32, at the corner with Baross Gábor u., provides free maps and arranges lodgings. (☎31 17 71. Open June-Aug. M-F 8am-8pm, Sa-Su 9am-6pm.) **Postal Code:** 9021.

ARCHABBEY OF PANNONHALMA. Visible on a clear day from Győr, the hilltop **Archabbey of Pannonhalma** (Pannonhalmi Főapátság) has seen a millennium of destruction and rebuilding since its establishment by the Benedictine order in AD 996. It now houses a 360,000-volume library, 13th-century basilica, and hosts classical concerts. **TriCollis Tourist Office,** to the left of the entrance, leads tours and has concert info. (☎57 01 91; www.bences.hu. Hungarian-language tour with English text every hr. English-language tours June-Sept. daily 11:20am, 1:20 and 3:20pm; Oct.-May Tu-Su 11:20am and 3:30pm. Hungarian tours 1400Ft, students 600Ft. English tours 2000/1200Ft.) From Győr, take the **bus** from platform #11 (45min., 7 per day, 302Ft). Ask for Pannonhalma vár and get off at the huge gates.

LAKE BALATON

A retreat since Roman times, warm Lake Balaton drew the European elite in the 19th century and is now a budget paradise for German and Austrian students. Be aware that storms roll in quickly—when the yellow lights on harbor buildings speed up to one revolution per second, swimmers must get out of the water. Don't worry that storms will ruin your vacation, though: most last less than 30min.

SIÓFOK. The density of tourist offices reflects Siófok's popularity with summer vacationers. The **Strand** is a series of lawns running to the shore; entry is free to some sections, 200-400Ft to others. The largest private beach lies to the right of town as you face the water. (700Ft, children 350Ft. Open M-F 8am-3am.) Bars and clubs line the lakefront, and **disco boats** (☎310 050) push off nightly. **Renegade Pub,** Petőfi sétány 3, is a crowded bar and dance club. (Open daily June-Aug. 8pm-4am.) **Palace Disco,** Deák Ferenc sétány 2, is a party complex with discos, bars, and restaurants. Buses depart every hour from behind the water tower. (Beer from 600Ft. Cover 1500-2500Ft. Disco open daily May to mid-Sept. 10pm-5am.)

Take a 25min. bus or train ride to Balatonszéplak felsö for **Villa Benjamin Youth Hostel ❷**, Siófoki u. 9, which has garden rooms and a beach-bungalow feel. (☎084 350 704. Singles 2500-3000Ft; doubles 5000Ft; triples 7500Ft; 4- to 6-person apartments 14,000-21,000Ft; 8- to 10-person house 28,000-35,000Ft. Tax 300Ft.) **Park Hotel ❹**, Batthány u. 7, offers rooms with A/C right by the Strand. (☎084 310 539. Reception 24hr. Doubles July-Aug. 10,000-15,000Ft, Sept.-June 8000-10,000Ft. MC/V.) **Trains** run to Budapest (2½hr., 20 per day, 1142Ft). Buses head to Budapest (1½hr., 9 per day, 1320Ft) and Pécs (3hr., 4 per day, 2456Ft). **Tourinform,** Fő út. at Szabadság tér, in the base of the water tower opposite the train station, helps find rooms and has free maps. (☎084 315 355; www.siofok.com. Open mid-June to mid-Sept. M-Sa 8am-8pm, Sa-Su 9am-6pm; mid-Sept. to mid-June M-F 9am-4pm.)

TIHANY. Scenic hikes, charming cottages, and panoramic views grace the Tihany peninsula. The **Benedictine Abbey** (Bencés Apátság) draws over a million visitors annually with its luminous frescoes, gilded Baroque altars, and crypt holding one of Hungary's earliest kings. (Open daily Mar.-Oct. 9am-6pm. 500Ft, students 250Ft. Su free.) The well marked **green line trail** runs past the Hermit's Place (Barátlakások), where the cells and chapel hollowed by 11th-century hermits are still visible. MAHART **ferries** go to Tihany from Siófok (1-1¼hr.; 6-9 per day; 1020Ft, students 765Ft). To reach the town from the ferry pier and neighboring **Strand,** walk underneath the elevated road and follow the Apátság signs up the steep hill to the abbey.

KESZTHELY. At the lake's western tip, Keszthely (KEST-hay), once the playground of the powerful Austro-Hungarian Festetics family, is home to year-round thermal springs. The **Helikon Palace Museum** (Helikon Kastélymúzeum) in the Festetics Palace (Kastély) is a storybook Baroque palace with a 90,000-volume library, extravagantly furnished chambers, an exotic arms collection, and a porcelain exhibit. From Fő tér, follow Kossuth Lajos u. toward Tourinform until it becomes Kastély u. (Open Sept.-May Tu-Su 10am-5pm; June Tu-Su 9am-5pm; July-Aug. daily 9am-6pm. 1300Ft, students 700Ft.) The **Strand,** on the coast to the right as you exit the train station, draws crowds with its giant slide, paddle boats, and volleyball nets. From the center, walk down Erzsébet Királyné u. as it curves right into Vörösmarty u., then cut through the park, crossing the train tracks on the other side to get to the beach. (Open daily mid-May to mid-Sept. 9:30am-4pm 440Ft, children 300Ft; 4-6:30pm 380/260Ft; 6:30-7pm free.)

Central **Kiss&Máté Panzió ❸,** Katona J u. 27, has spacious rooms. (☎083 319 072. Free laundry. Singles 5000Ft; doubles 6000Ft; triples 8000Ft.) **Castrum Camping ❶,** Móra Ferenc u. 48, has large sites and tennis courts. (☎083 31 21 20. 900Ft per person. July-Aug. tent sites 600Ft; Sept.-June 480Ft.) **Corso Restaurant ❸,** Erzsébet Királyné u. 23, in the Abbázia Club Hotel, serves fish from Balaton. (Entrees 800-2800Ft. Open M-Sa 7am-10pm. AmEx/MC/V.) **Donatello ❷,** Balaton u. 1/A, serves pizza and pasta in an open courtyard. Though named after the Teenage Mutant Ninja Turtle rather than the artist, the chefs are genuine Italian masters. (☎083 31 59 89. Pasta 410-880Ft. Pizza 440-1080Ft. Open daily noon-11pm.) InterCity **trains** run to Budapest (3hr.; 13 per day; 1926Ft, reservations 400Ft). **Buses** run from near the train station to Pécs (4hr., 5 per day, 1926Ft). From the station, take Mártirok u., which ends in Kossuth Lajos u., and turn left to reach the main square, Fő tér. **Tourinform,** Kossuth Lajos u. 28, on the palace side of Fő tér, has free maps and checks room availability. (☎083 31 41 44. Open July-Aug. M-F 9am-8pm, Sa-Su 9am-6pm; Oct.-June M-F 9am-5pm, Sa 9am-1pm.)

ICELAND (ÍSLAND)

Born from the collision of the European and North American continents, Iceland's landscape is uniquely warped and contorted, forged by the tempers of still-active volcanoes and raked by the slow advance and retreat of impassive glaciers. Nature is the country's greatest attraction—few other places offer visitors the chance to pick their way through sunken ice kettles, dodge scalding water spewing forth from geysers, and bike 200km between fishing villages with no one but seabirds for company.

ESSENTIALS

FACTS AND FIGURES

Official Name: Republic of Iceland.

Capital: Reykjavík.

Major Cities: Akureyri, Ísafjörður, Kópavogur, Hafnarfjörður.

Population: 294,000.

Time Zone: GMT -1.

Language: Icelandic.

Religions: Evangelical Lutheran (87%).

WHEN TO GO

Visitors to Iceland should brave high-season crowds in order to enjoy all that the country has to offer; June, July, and August are still the months to go for the broadest range of accommodations and transportation options. The sun dips below the horizon for a few hours each night, but the sky never really gets dark and it remains warm enough to camp with a jacket. During December and January, the sun is restricted to brief four-hour cameo appearances that temporarily interrupt

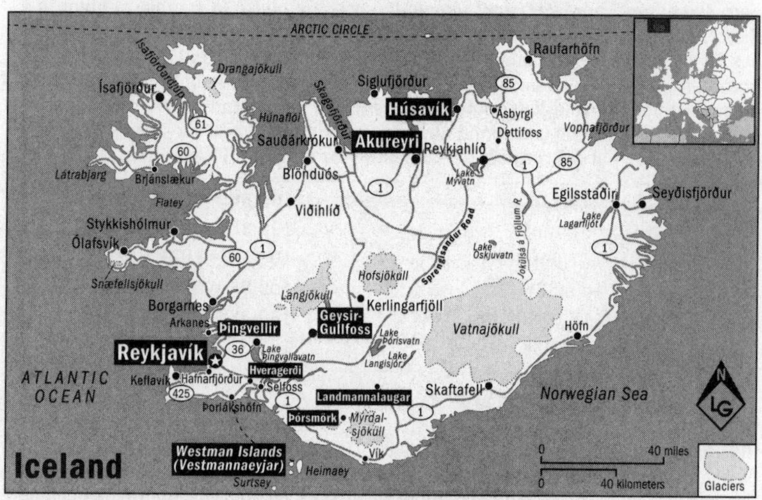

the dazzling Northern Lights. Winter temperatures in Reykjavík average a far-from-Arctic 0°C (32°F), making travel there feasible. Still, you won't be going far, since public transportation in the low season slows to an irregular crawl.

BURNING THE MIDNIGHT OIL. The midnight sun pops its head out June through August. While the near 24hr. sunlight makes for easy all-night partying, it can take its toll on visitors. Bring a sleeping mask and over-the-counter, non-habit forming sleep aids, such as melatonin, to avoid sleepless nights.

DOCUMENTS AND FORMALITIES

EMBASSIES. Foreign embassies in Iceland are in Reykjavík. Icelandic embassies in your home country include: **Canada,** 360 Albert St., Ste. 710, Ottawa, ON KIR 7X7 (☎613-482-1944; www.iceland.org/ca); **UK,** 2A Hans St., London SW1X 0JE (☎020 7259 3999; www.iceland.org/uk); **US,** 1156 15th St. NW, Ste. 1200, Washington, D.C. 20005 (☎202-265-6653; www.iceland.org/us).

VISA AND ENTRY INFORMATION. EU citizens do not need a visa. Citizens of Australia, Canada, New Zealand, and the US do not need a visa for stays of up to 90 days, beginning upon entry into any of the countries within the EU's freedom of movement zone. For more information, see p. 16.

TOURIST SERVICES AND MONEY

EMERGENCY	**Police, Ambulance,** and **Fire:** ☎112.

TOURIST OFFICES. Tourist offices in large towns have maps, brochures, and the must-have BSÍ bus schedule; check at hotel reception desks in smaller towns for local info. The Icelandic Tourist Board website is at www.icetourist.is.

MONEY. Iceland's monetary unit is the **króna** (plural: krónur), which is divided into 100 aurar. There's no way around it: costs are high. On average, a night in a hostel will cost 1700Isk, a guesthouse 3000-4000Isk, and a meal's worth of groceries 700-1200Isk. Restaurants include a service charge on the bill; **tipping** further is unnecessary and even discouraged. All countries who are members of the European Union impose a **Value Added Tax (VAT)** on goods and services purchased within the EU. Prices in Iceland already include the country's steep 24.5% VAT rate, although partial refunds are available for non-EU citizens (p. 23).

ICELANDIC KRÓNUR (ISK)		
	AUS$1 = 48.14ISK	100ISK = AUS$2.08
	CDN$1 = 52.80ISK	100ISK = CDN$1.89
	EUR€1 = 77.84ISK	100ISK = EUR€1.28
	NZ$1 = 44.50ISK	100ISK = NZ$2.25
	UK£1 = 115.02ISK	100ISK = UK£0.87
	US$1 = 64.08ISK	100ISK = US$1.56

TRANSPORTATION

BY PLANE. Icelandair (US ☎800-223-5500, UK 0207 874 1000, Iceland 505 01 00; www.icelandair.net) flies to Reykjavík year-round from the US and Europe. Icelandair provides free stopovers of up to seven days on all transatlantic flights, and runs a Lucky Fares email list that lists discounted flights. No-frills **Iceland Express**

(UK ☎0870 240 5600, Iceland 550 06 00; www.icelandexpress.com) flies from London, Copenhagen and Frankfurt from April through late October. Fares start at €98 one-way. Icelandair's domestic counterpart **Air Iceland** (☎570 30 30; www.airiceland.is) flies from Reykjavík to most major towns in Iceland.

BY BUS. Although flying between destinations is faster and more comfortable, **Bifreiðastöð Íslands (BSÍ)** buses are usually cheaper and provide a closer look at the terrain; Iceland has no intercity train service. **Destination Iceland** (☎585 42 70; www.dice.is), which has offices in the Reykjavík bus terminal, can help you navigate the schedule, available online at www.bsi.is and at tourist offices. From mid-June to August, buses run daily on the **Ring Road,** the highway that circles Iceland, but may only run three times per week in the low season. The going is slow, since some stretches in the east are unpaved. The **Full Circle Passport** lets travelers circle the island at their own pace on the Ring Road (May 20-Sept. 5; 23,900Isk). However, it only allows travel in one direction, so travelers must move either clockwise or counter-clockwise around the country to get back to where they started. For an extra 12,000Isk, the pass provides access to the Westfjords in the extreme northwest (Jun.-Aug.). The **Omnibus Passport** gives a period of unlimited travel on all scheduled bus routes, including non-Ring roads (1-week 26,900Isk, 2-week 39,000Isk, 3-week 47,900Isk, 4-week 52,900Isk; mid-September to May 1-week pass 16,500Isk). Travelers, especially those arriving in groups of two or more, should note that the inflexibility of the **Full Circle** pass and the high cost of the **Omnibus Passport** often makes it wise for those heading to rural Iceland to rent cars.

BY FERRY. The best way to see Iceland's gorgeous and intimidating shores is on the **Norröna** ferry (☎570 86 00; www.smyril-line.fo) that crosses the North Atlantic via: Hanstholm, Denmark; Tórshavn in the Faroe Islands; and Seyðisfjörður, Iceland. (7 days. May 28-Sept. 2. One-way sleeper cabin €336; low season €240; students under 26 receive a 25% discount with ID.) From Tórshavn, you can either continue on to Bergen, Norway, or return to Seyðisfjörður. An **Eimskip** cargo ship leaves Reykjavík at 4pm every Wednesday from March through October, carrying up to three passengers to ports including: Rotterdam, the Netherlands; Hamburg, Germany; Göthenburg, Sweden; and Århus, Denmark. (Reservations ☎585 43 00; travel@dice.is. Fares from 33,030Isk. Bicycles 3150Isk. No student discount.)

BY CAR. Rental cars provide the most freedom to travelers and may even be the cheapest option for those who want to visit rural areas. Car rental *(bílaleiga)* companies charge 4000-8000Isk per day for a small car, and 20,000-25,000Isk for the **four-wheel-drive vehicles** that are imperative outside of settled areas. On these routes, drivers should bring a container of extra fuel, since some roads go 300km without a single refueling station and strong headwinds can significantly affect the rate of fuel consumption. It is not uncommon for local drivers to **ford streams** in their vehicles; do not attempt this in a compact car, and cross in a convoy if possible. (24hr. reports on road conditions ☎800 63 16, June-Aug. in English.) Drivers are required to wear seat belts and to keep their headlights on at all times. Iceland recognizes foreign driver's licenses, but you may need to purchase insurance for the rental vehicle (1500-3500Isk).

BY BIKE AND BY THUMB. Ferocious winds, driving rain, and gravel roads make long-distance cycling difficult. Hug the Ring Road if you prefer company, branch out to the coastal roads that snake their way through the Eastfjords, or check **Cycling in Iceland** (home.wanadoo.nl/erens/icecycle.htm) for a wealth of other itineraries. Travel in the country's rugged interior often require mountain bikes; get in touch with the **Icelandic Mountainbike Club** (☎562 00 99; www.mmedia.is/~ifhk) or drop by their clubhouse in Reykjavík, at Brekkustíg. 2, Thursday nights after 8pm for some friendly advice. Buses will carry bikes for a 500-900Isk fee, depending on the route. Hitchhikers sometimes try the roads in summer, but sparse traffic and harsh weather exacerbate the inherent risks. Nevertheless, hitchhikers can find rides with relative ease between Reykjavík and Akureyri; flagging down a ride is harder in the east and the south. *Let's Go* does not recommend hitchhiking.

KEEPING IN TOUCH

PHONE CODES	**Country code:** 354. **International dialing prefix:** 00. There are no city codes in Iceland. For more information on how to place international calls, see inside back cover.

EMAIL AND THE INTERNET. Internet access is widespread in Iceland, although in small towns it may only be available in public libraries. Internet is generally 200-300Isk per hour, but can sometimes be found for free in libraries.

TELEPHONE. Síminn, the state-owned telephone company, usually has an office in the same building as the post office; these offices sell phone cards, and give the best rates on international calls. Pay phones accept prepaid phone cards, credit cards (cheapest for calls to mobile phones), as well as 10Isk, 50Isk, or 100Isk coins. Iceland uses two different mobile phone networks; digital GSM phones service 98% of the country's population, but only a small fraction of its land area, so hikers, fishermen, and others who travel outside of settled areas rely on analog NMT phones, which reach into rural regions. Prepaid GSM phone cards are available at gas stations and at convenience stores. OG Vodafone generally offers the best prepaid rates. For operator assistance within Iceland, dial ☎118; for international assistance, dial ☎1811. International direct dial numbers include: **AT&T** (☎800 222 55 288); **British Telecom** (☎800 89 0354); **Canada Direct** (☎800 90 10); MCI (☎800 90 02); **Telecom New Zealand** (☎800 90 64); **Telstra Australia** (☎800 90 61)

MAIL. Mailing a letter or postcard from Iceland costs 60Isk to Europe; 65kr outside of Europe. Post offices *(póstur)* are generally open Monday to Friday 9am-4:30pm. Check www.postur.is/haht/English for additional info.

LANGUAGE. Most Icelanders speak Icelandic, which draws its roots from Old Norse. Icelanders, especially those under 35, usually speak at least some English.

ACCOMMODATIONS AND CAMPING

ICELAND	❶	❷	❸	❹	❺
ACCOMMODATIONS	under 2000Isk	2000Isk-3000Isk	3000-5000Isk	5000-10,000Isk	over 10,000Isk

Iceland's 26 **HI youth hostels** are invariably clean and reasonably priced around 1800-2200Isk for nonmembers. HI members should expect to receive a 150-400Isk discount. Visit **Hostelling International Iceland,** Sundlaugarveg. 34, 105 Reykjavík, for locations and information on Iceland's seven eco-friendly **Green Hostels** (☎553 81 10; www.hostel.is). Expect to pay around 2000Isk for **sleeping-bag accommodations** (*svefnpokapláss;* beds with no linen or blankets included), which make guesthouses more affordable and are often the only option when staying in summer hostels or **farmhouses** (☎570 27 00; www.farmholidays.is). Ask about the open voucher program (www.dice.is/Desktopdefault.aspx/tabid-33/m), which enables the holder to receive unlimited accommodation for a fixed rate. Many remote lodgings will pick up tourists in the nearest town for a small fee. **Campers** can choose between one of Iceland's 125 designated campsites or rough it on uncultivated land; squatters need to get permission if they set up camp in a nature reserve or near houses. You should also ask permission if more than three people are sleeping in a tent, or if you plan to stay for longer than three nights. Bring a camp stove; open fires are frowned upon. Designated campsites run the gamut from grassy areas with cold-water taps to sumptuous facilities around Reykjavík; to find the right one, navigate the Icelandic-language website at www.camping.is or check out www.infoiceland.is/infoiceland/accommodation/camping/.

FOOD AND DRINK

ICELAND	❶	❷	❸	❹	❺
FOOD	under 500Isk	500-1000Isk	1000-1400Isk	1400-2000Isk	over 2000Isk

Fresh fish and gamey free-range lamb continue to be staples of the Icelandic diet, while vitamin-rich vegetables grown in greenhouse towns like Hveragerði (p. 553) are weaning the country off its dependence on starchy roots. A trickle of Asian immigrants in the past decade have also introduced methods of cooking that retain more flavor than the traditional regimen of boiling and salting everything in sight. On the other hand, *skyr*, a low-fat dessert made from milk curds, is more popular than ever. Food in Iceland is very expensive, and a cheap restaurant meal will cost at least 800Isk. Grocery stores, which can be found in virtually every town, are the way to go. Alcohol presents the same quandary; beer costs 500-600Isk for a large glass (0.5L, approx. 17 ounces) at pubs and cafes, while the price of hard liquor is even steeper. Perhaps it's no wonder that bootleggers in the countryside cook up batches of *landi*, potent homemade moonshine. *Let's Go* does not recommend moonshine.

HOLIDAYS AND FESTIVALS

Holidays: New Year's Day (Jan. 1); Good Friday (Apr. 14); Easter Sunday and Monday (Apr. 16-17); Labor Day (May 1); Feast of the Ascension (May 25); Whit Sunday and Monday (June 4-5); Proclamation of the Republic (June 17); Commerce Day (Aug. 7); Christmas Eve and Day (Dec. 24-25); Boxing Day (Dec. 26); New Year's Eve (Dec. 31).

Festivals: In past centuries, meager food supplies during mid-winter forced residents to adopt a leaner diet, known as *Thorramatur.* Today, *svið* (singed and boiled sheep's head), *hrútspungur* (ram's testicles), and *hákarl* (shark meat that has been allowed to rot underground) remain part of the month-long Thorrablót celebration (Feb.-Mar. 2006). The Reykjanes Peninsula celebrates *Sjomannadagur* (Seamen's Day) on June 4 with boat races and tug-of-war, while young people head to the countryside on *Verslunnarmannahelgi* (Labor Day Weekend) for wild parties on the 1st weekend of August.

BEYOND TOURISM

Travelers hoping to move Beyond Tourism in Iceland may be able to secure summer work. Check www.jobs-in-europe.net for information on work placement. See p. 66 for Beyond Tourism opportunities throughout Europe.

International Cultural Youth Exchange, Große Hamburger Str. 30, Berlin, Germany. (☎49 30 2839 0550; www.icye.org.) ICYE brings together volunteers and host organizations on a variety of projects worldwide, including several in Iceland. ICYE also organizes European Voluntary Service programs (europa.eu.int/comm/youth/program/guide/action2_en.html) for EU citizens, which provide a fully-funded year of service in another EU country.

Earthwatch Institute, 3 Clock Tower Pl., Ste. 100, Box 75. Maynard, MA USA, 01754 (US/Canada ☎1-800-776-0188; Europe ☎44 1865 318838; Australia ☎03-9682-6828; www.earthwatch.org). For a hefty fee (above $2500/€2000), Earthwatch organizes volunteers, guided by scientists, to conduct geological fieldwork in the Icelandic glaciers. Will also help coordinate fundraising efforts for those unable to afford the fee.

Volunteers for Peace (☎802-259-2759; www.vfp.org). Runs 2800 "workcamps" throughout the world, including several in Iceland. $250 per 2- to 3-week workcamp, including room and board, plus $20 VFP membership fee.

REYKJAVÍK

Despite its modest size, Reykjavík (pop. 180,000), home to three out of five Icelanders, exudes the assured, forward-thinking cosmopolitanism of European capitals several times its size. Bold, modern architecture juts out above the searingly blue waters of the Faxaflói Bay, and the city's refreshingly clear air complements the clean streets and well-kept gardens. Quiet during the week, Reykjavík comes alive on weekends with its legendary nightlife.

TRANSPORTATION

Flights: All international flights arrive at **Keflavík Airport** (KEF), 55km from Reykjavík. From the main exit, catch a **Flybus** (☎562 10 11; 40-50min., 1150lsk) to Reykjavík's BSÍ Bus Terminal. From there ask to take a free Flybus minivan to your hostel or hotel. Flybus also runs from the terminal to City Hall, and city buses #7, 115, 140, and 150 head downtown to Lækjartorg, but it's an easy 2-block walk from the terminal to the city

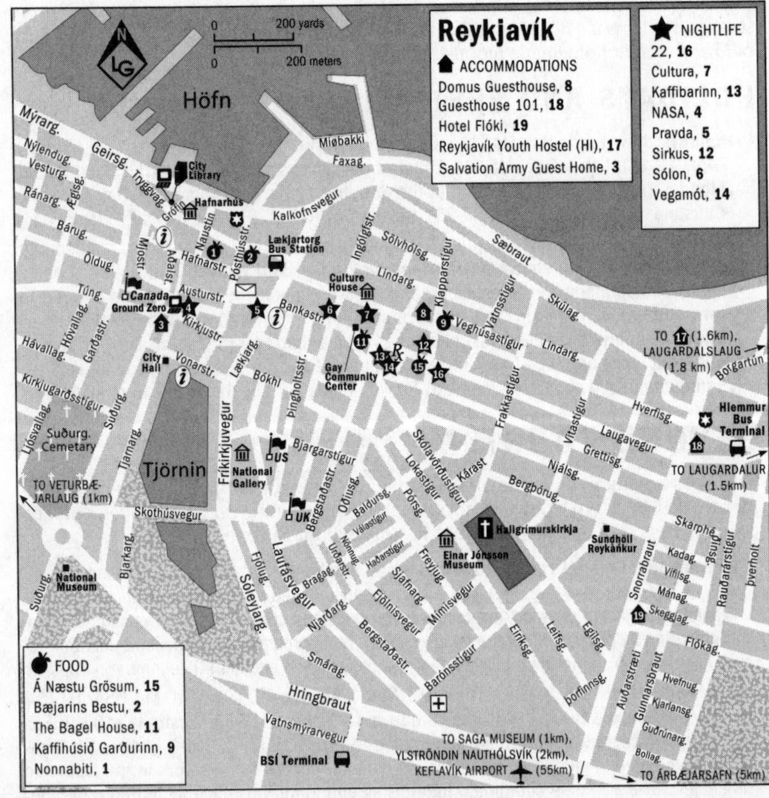

center. Downtown buses depart from the stop next to the horse sculpture. (M-F 7am-midnight, Sa-Su 10am-midnight; 220lkr). Flybus service to the airport departs from the BSÍ Bus Terminal, but most hostels will arrange pick-ups for no additional fee.

Buses: Umferðarmiðstöð BSÍ (BSÍ Bus Terminal), Vatnsmýrarveg. 10 (☎562 10 11; www.bsi.is), off Hringbraut near Reykjavík Airport. Walk 15-20min. south along Tjörnin from the city center, or take bus #7 (every 20min., 220lsk).

Public Transportation: Bus service can be spotty; walking is often a speedier and cheaper option. **Strætisvagnar Reykjavíkur** (Strætó; ☎540 27 00; www.bus.is) operates yellow city buses (220lsk). Pick up Strætó's helpful bus schedule at its terminals. Buy packages of 9 adult fares (1500lsk), or pay bus fare with coins; drivers do not give change. Ticket packages sold at the bus terminals as well as at swimming pools; the 2 major terminals are **Lækjartorg,** on Harfnarst. in the city center (☎510 98 00; open M-F 7am-11:30pm, Sa 8am-11:30pm, Su 10am-11:30pm) and **Hlemmur,** farther east on Hverfisg. (Open M-Sa 7am-11:30pm, Su 10am-11:30pm.) If you need to change buses, ask the driver for a free transfer ticket *(skiptimiði)* when you get on the first bus, valid for 45min. after fare has been paid. Most buses run every 20-30min. M-Sa 7am-midnight, Su and holidays 10am-midnight.

Taxis: BSR (☎561 00 00). 24hr. service. **Hreyfill** (☎588 55 22).

Car Rental: Berg, Bíldshöfða 10 (☎577 60 50; www.carrental-berg.com). Under 100km from 4800lsk per day. Unlimited mileage from 8850lsk per day; low season reduced rates. Pick-up available at Keflavík and Reykjavík Airports for an extra 2000lsk one-way. **Hertz** (☎505 06 00; www.hertz.is), at the Reykjavík Airport. Economy models from 3700lsk per day. Pick-up available at Keflavík Airport for an extra 2300lsk. **Avis** (☎591 4000; www.avis.is), **Budget** (☎462 3400), and **Hasso** (☎464 1030; hasso.co.is) also rent cars from locations in Reykjavík.

Bike Rental: At the **Reykjavík Youth Hostel** campsite (p. 548). 1700lsk per 24hr., 1500lsk 8am-6pm; helmet 200 lsk.

Hitchhiking: Hitchhiking is relatively common in Iceland but never completely safe. Those looking for a ride generally head to the east edge of town. *Let's Go* does not recommend hitchhiking as a safe means of transport.

ORIENTATION AND PRACTICAL INFORMATION

Lækjartorg is Reykjavík's main square and a good base for navigation. **Lækjargata** leads southwest from Lækjartorg to **Tjörnin** (the Pond), which lies halfway between the square and BSÍ Bus Terminal. Reykjavík's main thoroughfare extends out from Lækjartorg, changing names from **Austurstræti** to **Bankastræti** and then **Laugavegur,** as it is most commonly known. Free publications *What's On in Reykjavík*, *Reykjavík City Guide*, and *The Reykjavík Grapevine*, also at the tourist office, provide info about exploring the city.

Tourist Office: Upplýsingamiðstöð Ferðamanna í Reykjavík, Aðalstr. 2 (☎590 15 50; www.visitreykjavik.is). Open June-Aug. daily 8:30am-7pm; Sept.-May M-F 9am-6pm, Sa 10am-4pm, Su 10am-2pm. Sells the **Reykjavík Card** (1-day 1200lsk, 2-day 1700lsk, 3-day 2200lsk), which allows unlimited public transportation, free entry to some sights and the thermal pools (p. 550), as well as limited **Internet** at the tourist center. The **Discount Guide** (www.coupons.is) offers discounts on a variety of services.

Embassies: Canada, Túng. 14 (☎575 65 00). Open M-F 9am-noon. **UK,** Laufásveg. 31 (☎550 51 00). Open M-F 9am-noon. **US,** Laufásveg. 21 (☎562 91 00). Open M-F 8am-12:30pm and 1:30-5pm.

Currency Exchange: Most banks are open M-F 9:15am-4pm. On weekends from mid-May to mid-Sept., try the **BSÍ Bus Terminal.** There are **ATMs** throughout the city. Avoid the **Exchange Group,** in the tourist office, due to steep commissions.

Luggage Storage: At BSÍ Bus Terminal, next to the ticket window. 500Isk per day. Open M-F 7:30am-7pm, Sa-Su 7:30am-4pm.

GLBT Resources: Gay Community Center, Laugaveg. 3, 4th fl. (☎552 78 78; www.samtokin78.is). Includes library and cafe. Office and library open daily 2-4pm. Cafe M 8-11pm, Th 8-11:30pm, Sa 10pm-2am. More info available at www.gayice.is.

Emergency: ☎112.

Police: Hverfisg. 113-115 (☎569 90 00). Station at Tryggvag. 19 (☎569 90 25).

Pharmacies: Lyfja Laugavegi, Laugaveg. 16 (☎552 40 45). Open M-F 10am-7pm, Sa 10am-4pm. **Lyfja Lágmúla,** Lágmúla 5 (☎533 23 00). Open 24hr.

Hospital: National Hospital at Fossvogur (☎525 17 00), on Hringbraut, has a 24hr. emergency ward. From the center of town, take bus #3 southeast.

Internet Access: **Reykjavík Public Library,** Tryggvag. 15. Two Internet terminals on the 1st fl., more on the 5th; coffee included. 200Isk per hr. Open M-Th 10am-7pm, F 11am-7pm, Sa-Su 10am-5pm. **Ground Zero,** Vallarstr. 4. (☎562 77 76). 300Isk per 30min., 450Isk per hr. Open M-F 11am-1am, Sa-Su noon-1am. MC/V.

Post Office: Íslandspóstur, Pósthússtr. 5 (☎580 11 21), at Austurstr. Address mail to be held in the following format: First name SURNAME, *Poste Restante,* ÍSLANDSPÓSTUR, Pósthússtr. 5, 101 Reykjavík, ICELAND. Open M-F 8:30am-4:30pm.

ACCOMMODATIONS AND CAMPING

Gistiheimili (guesthouses) offer "sleeping-bag accommodations" (bed and pillow in a small room; add 300-500Isk for a blanket). Hotels cost at least 5500Isk. Call ahead for reservations, especially from mid-June to August.

Reykjavík Youth Hostel (HI), Sundlaugarveg. 34 (☎553 81 10; www.hostel.is/heimilin/Reykjavik/Eindex.htm). Take bus #5 from Lækjarg. and ask to be let off at the hostel. Easy camaraderie and exceptional facilities make this hostel extremely popular. Breakfast 750Isk. Linen 550Isk. Laundry 300Isk. Internet 200Isk per 20min. Reception 8am-11pm; ring bell after hours. Dorms 2000Isk; doubles 4100Isk. 350Isk HI discount. ❷

Domus Guesthouse, Hverfisgötu 45 (☎561 12 00). Take bus #5 and get off across from the Regnboginn movie theatre on Hverfisgötu. Spacious, comfortable rooms close to the city center. Limited kitchen with fridge and microwave available. Breakfast included, except for sleeping-bag accommodation. Sleeping-bag accommodation 2900Isk; singles 8100Isk; doubles 10,800Isk. Reduced prices Oct.-Apr. MC/V. ❷

Hotel Flóki/Guesthouse Flókagata, Flókag. 1 (☎552 11 55; www.eyjar.is/guesthouse). Indulge in facilities that include a kettle, fridge, and TV in every room. Breakfast included. Reception 24hr. Check-out noon. June-Aug. sleeping-bag accommodation 5500Isk; singles 7300Isk; doubles 10,400Isk, with bath 12,600Isk. Extra bed 3400Isk. Sept.-May. reduced prices and no sleeping-bag accommodation. MC/V. ❹

Salvation Army Guest and Seamen's Home, Kirkjustr. 2 (☎561 32 03; www.guesthouse.is). This pale yellow house boasts a great location and friendly staff, although the inexpensive rooms can be less than luxurious. Breakfast included, except for sleeping bag accommodation. Sleeping-bag accommodation 2000Isk, blanket 400Isk; singles 5000Isk; doubles 7500Isk; triples 9800Isk; quads 12,200Isk. ❷

Guesthouse 101, Laugaveg. 101 (☎562 61 01; www.iceland101.com). Entrance from Snorrabraut on the 3rd floor. This converted office building In a slightly more run-down part of the city is low on atmosphere but offers small, neat rooms. Breakfast included. Wheelchair-accessible. Singles 6300Isk; doubles 8900Isk; triples 11,250Isk. MC/V. ❹

Reykjavík Youth Hostel Campsite (☎568 69 44), next to the youth hostel. Friendly staff and lively campers make this a good alternative to indoor facilities. Open June to mid-Sept. Electricity and storage each 300Isk. Showers included. Reception 24hr. Tent sites 800Isk. 4-person cabins 4000Isk. AmEx/MC/V. ❶

FOOD

An authentic Icelandic meal featuring seafood, lamb, or puffin costs upwards of 1500Isk but is worth the splurge at least once. For days on a leaner budget, hit up any one of the stands hawking *pylsur* (hot dogs) west of Lækjartorg, and be sure to ask for "the works"—remoulade (a spicy mayonnaise-based sauce) and all. Alternately, grab groceries on **Austurstræti, Hverfisgata,** or **Laugavegur.**

Á Næstu Grösum, Laugaveg. 20B (☎552 84 10). Entrance off Klapparstígur. This "one-woman restaurant" dishes out delicious, heaping portions of vegetarian and vegan fare in a homey environment. Bean burgers (1000Isk) and lasagna (1100Isk) are almost always on the menu, although other dishes rotate. Friendly staff knows many customers by name. Soup comes with refill, 650Isk. Lunch special 1200Isk. Dinner 1490Isk. Open M-F 11:30am-10pm, Sa noon-10pm, Su 5-10pm. AmEx/MC/V. ❸

Bæjarins Bestu, corner of Tryggvag. and Pósthússtr. The only restaurant in Iceland allowed to use the word "best" in its name is certainly its best bargain. The weekend crowd heads here to satisfy late-night food cravings with 210Isk hot dogs. Open until 12:30am on weekdays, or as late as there is a crowd–sometimes past 6am. MC/V. ❶

Kaffihúsið Garðurinn, Klapparstíg. 37 (☎561 23 45). Locals on lunch breaks come together to feast on meals made from all-natural ingredients and accompanied by unlimited fresh bread. A different vegetarian meal (950Isk) and soup (550Isk) offered each day. Open M-F 11am-6:30pm, Sa noon-5pm. MC/V. ❷

The Bagel House, Laugaveg. 2. This newcomer offers fast, filling, and cheap bagel sandwiches in an otherwise expensive neighborhood. Read the script of Pulp Fiction under the counter while waiting for your order. Philadelphia breakfast bagel 229Isk. Lunch bagels 500Isk. Open daily 11am-7pm. MC/V. ❶

Nonnabiti, Hafnarstr. 11 (☎551 23 12). Just west of Lækjartorg, toward the main tourist office. A sandwich shop good for filling meals on the cheap. Serves large hot sandwiches, 750Isk. Burgers 380Isk. Open M-F 9am-2am, Sa-Su 11am-5:30am. MC/V. ❶

SIGHTS

Reykjavík's **City Hall,** located on the shore of **Lake Tjörnin** in the heart of the city center, houses an impressive three-dimensional model of Iceland that gives visitors a sense of the country's varied and striking topography. (Open M-F 8am-7pm, Sa-Su noon-6pm. Free.) Just beyond the main entrance of the City Hall lies the oldest street in the city, **Aðalstræti.** Off Aðalstr. stands the **Hafnarhús,** Tryggvag. 17, the most eclectic of the three wings of the Reykjavík Art Museum, with performance art and installation pieces staged within the byzantine corridors of a renovated warehouse. From Aðalstr., walk past the tourist office and turn onto Grófin. (☎590 12 00. Open daily 10am-5pm. 500Isk, includes entrance to all 3 wings.) Follow Tryggvag. to Lækjarg. and Hverfisg. to **Árnarhóll,** where the statue of Ingólfur Arnason, Iceland's first settler, stands, and revel in the view of the mountains to the north. Past Árnarhóll is the **Culture House,** Hverfisg. 15, which carefully preserves vellum manuscripts of the Icelandic Eddas and Sagas. (☎545 14 00. Open daily 11am-5pm. 300Isk, students 200Isk.) To see these mytho-historical texts brought to life, take bus #7 south to Perlan and investigate the **Saga Museum.** (☎511 1517; www.sagamuseum.is. Open Mar.-Nov. 10am-6pm, low season noon-5pm. 800Isk, students 600Isk.) For a more comprehensive overview of Icelandic history, hop bus #4 to the recently renovated **National Museum,** Suðurgt. 41. (☎530 22 00; www.natmus.is. Open daily 10am-6pm; low season Tu-Su 11am-5pm. 600Isk, students 300Isk.) Continue on bus #4 out to **Árbæjarsafn,** the open-air city museum chronicling the lifestyles and architecture of past generations of Icelanders. Check www.reykjavikmuseum.is for special events such as folk dances and Viking games. (☎411 63 00. Open June-Aug. daily 10am-5pm. 600Isk.)

ICELAND

The summer exhibits of the **National Gallery of Iceland,** Fríkirkjuveg. 7, present highlights of Icelandic art in a modern, four-room building. (☎515 96 20. Open Tu-Su 11am-5pm. 400Isk, W free.) The church tower of the monolithic landmark **Hallgrímskirkja,** on Skólavörðustígur, provides a fabulous view from the city's highest point. (☎510 10 00. Church open daily 9am-5pm. Tower open M-W and F-Su 9am-8pm, Th 9am-10pm. Elevator to the top 350Isk.) Across the street, the **Einar Jónsson Museum,** Njarðarg., exhibits 300 of the sculptor's allegorical and emotionally charged works. Don't miss the free sculpture garden behind the museum. (☎551 37 97; www.skulptur.is. Open June to mid-Sept. Tu-Su 2-5pm; mid-Sept. to Nov. and Feb.-May Sa-Su 2-5pm. 400Isk.)

Additional sights cluster around **Laugardalur,** well east of the center city. Orient yourself around **Áskirkja** church, which looks like a ship's prow and stands on a hill at the east side of Laugardalur. The white dome of the **Ásmundarsafn,** the Ásmundur Sveinsson Sculpture Museum, on Sigtún, houses works spanning Sveinsson's career in a building the artist designed. The free sculpture garden surrounding the museum features his larger works, some of which have been designed as interactive pieces ideal for climbing. Take bus #5 to the stop outside the museum. (☎553 21 55. Open daily May-Sept. 10am-4pm, Oct.-Apr. 1-4pm. 500Isk, M free.) From the same bus stop, follow Engjaveg. to the entrance of the **Reykjavík Botanic Garden,** Skúlatún 2, and stroll through one of the few forested areas in all of Iceland. (☎553 88 70. Garden open 24hr. Greenhouse and pavilion open daily Apr.-Sept. 10am-10pm; Oct.-Mar. 10am-5pm. Free.) Just outside the end of the garden, opposite the pavilion and greenhouse, is a free outdoor exhibit on the history of the **Washing Springs,** Reykjavík's geothermal square, where the women of the city once came to do their cooking and laundry. The city's largest thermal swimming pool, **Laugardalslaug** (see **Thermal Pools**, below), is also located in this area.

THERMAL POOLS

Reykjavík's thermal pools are all equipped with hot pot (naturally occurring hot tub) and a steam room or sauna, although each maintains a special character. Freeloaders should seek out the city beach and its free hot pots at Nauthólsvik. All pools listed below charge 250Isk admission, with 10 visits for 1900Isk.

Laugardalslaug, Laugardalslaug-Sundlaugarveg. (☎510 45 00). Take bus #5. Entrance to the right, around the white part of the building. The city's largest thermal pool features a large slide, a children's slide, and 4 hot pots. Swimsuit or towel 300Isk. Swimsuit, towel, and swim 600Isk. Open Apr.-Sept. M-F 6:30am-10:30pm, Sa-Su 8am-10pm; Oct.-Mar. M-F 6:30am-10:30pm, Sa-Su 8am-8pm. MC/V.

Sundhöll Reykjavíkur, Barónsstigur 45 (☎551 40 59). This centrally located pool has a much smaller outdoor area than the other pools, but is the only one equipped with diving boards. Open M-F 6:30am-9:30pm, Sa-Su 8am-7pm. MC/V.

Vesturbæjarlaug, Hofsvallag. (☎551 50 04). Take bus #4 from the city center, get off on Hofsvallag. by the Lyfßheilsa and follow the signs. Popular with Reykjavík University students, this location boasts a 25m outdoor pool as well as a glass-domed steam room and a sauna. Open M-F 6:30am-10pm, Sa-Su 8am-8pm. MC/V.

Ylströndin Nauthólsvík (☎511 66 30). Take bus #7 either to Hotel Loftleiðir and walk down Hlíðarfótur or to Perlan and hike down Öskuhlíð. This city beach is hard to reach using public transportation, but the hot pot in the midst of sea water makes it well worth the trek. Locker 200Isk. Swimming free. Open May-Sept. daily 10am-8pm.

HIKING

Reykjavík features a range of hikes for travelers of different experience levels. Those looking for easier hikes should take bus #7 to a range of trails, one of which features a working model of the *Strókur* geyser at its head; get of at the Perlan stop. At the southwest corner of the park is **Nauthólsvík** beach (see above) and a beautiful trail around the airport that leads back towards the city; if you get tired, catch bus #5 on Skeljanes back to the center. Pick up maps at the tourist office. To bird watch or bask in the midnight sun, visit the bird reserve **Grótta** on the western tip of the peninsula. Take bus #3 out to the Lindarbraut and walk for about 15min. along the sea on Byggarðstangi. Although the Grótta itself is closed off during the nesting season (May-June), the bird-filled sky is still worth it. South of the city lies the **Heiðmörk Reserve,** a large park and sports complex with picnic spots and easy to intermediate hiking trails. There is, however, no direct public transportation. (Take bus #10 or 11, and ask the driver to let you off at Lake Elliðavatn; from there, you can walk or bike 3-4km south to the reserve.)

Quaint and slow-paced **Viðey Island,** home to Reykjavík's oldest house and Iceland's second-oldest church, has been inhabited since the 10th century. (Take the ferry from the Reykjavík harbor *Miðbakki* at 10am or take bus #4 east from Laekjartorg to Sundahöftn. The ferry departs daily at 1, 2, 3, 7, and 9pm, as well as at 8:30am June 10-Aug. 12. Round-trip 750Isk.) Across the bay from Reykjavík looms **Mt. Esja,** which you can ascend via a well-maintained trail (2-3hr.). While the trail is not difficult, hikers should be prepared for rain, hail, or even a summertime **snow squall.** Take bus #10 or 110 to Artún and transfer to bus #20, exiting at Mógilsá. Bus #20 runs once every 1-2hr.; consult SVR city bus schedule before departing.

DOOR-TO-DOOR. Legs ache after a long hike? The friendly drivers on BSÍ buses will generally let you off anywhere along the route upon request.

NIGHTLIFE

Although unnervingly quiet on weeknights, Reykjavík reasserts its reputation as a wild party town each weekend; in few other places can you totter out of a club at 3am to a sky that has barely dimmed to twilight. To avoid vicious drink prices and cover charges, most Icelanders pregame at home and then hit the clubs just before covers kick in; don't bother showing up before 12:30am, and plan to be out until 4 or 5am. Boisterous crowds tend to bar-hop around **Austurstræti, Tryggvagata,** and **Laugavegur.** The establishments listed below are 20+, unless otherwise noted.

The shipyards along the harbor can be unsafe, especially at night. If you are walking along the water, make sure to bring a reliable walking map, and travel with a friend if possible.

22, Laugaveg. 22 (☎517 55 22). Its luminous bar, spacious dance floor, and skull-adorned "conversation room" draw a thoroughly mixed crowd. Beer 500-600Isk. 500Isk cover after 2am. Open M-Th, Su 10am-1am, F-Sa 10am-6am.

Sirkus, Klapparstíg. 30 (☎551 19 99). A tropical outdoor patio and an intimate upstairs bungalow room contribute to a deliciously out-of-place atmosphere frequented by local underground artists. Beer 500Isk. Open M-Th, Su 2pm-1am, F-Sa 2pm-5am.

Kaffibarinn, Bergstaðastr. 1 (☎551 15 88), off Laugaveg. This atmospheric lounge is a brainy, chill alternative to the whirling dervish of dancing elsewhere. Beer 550Isk, 600Isk after 1am. Mixed drinks 750Isk. Th-Sa Live DJ. W night white wine 500Isk. 22+. Open M-Th 10:30am-1am, F 10:30am-5am, Sa 11:30am-5am, Su 2pm-1am.

Sólon, Bankastr. 7a (☎562 32 32). A trendy cafe during the week, Sólon draws shades over its bay windows on the weekend and morphs into a posh nightclub that bounces with grade-A hip-hop. Famous for *Svali,* a fruity, energy-drink based concoction, 700Isk. Beer 600Isk. Th live music. Open M-Th and Su 11am-1am, F-Sa 11am-5:30am.

Pravda, Austurstr. 22 (☎522 92 22) near the Lækjargt. bus terminal. With its dim violet lighting, Pravda is a playground for the trendy fashionista. The crowded dance floor upstairs reverberates with techno tunes, while private alcoves downstairs lend themselves to more intimate forms of interaction. 300Isk cover. F-Sa 8pm-5:30am.

I BRAKE FOR ELVES

celand recently made headlines or its population's staunch belief n elves. With 80% of Iceland ınwilling to rule out the existence ›f "hidden people," it's disre- ;pectful to dismiss this folk reli- ;ion out of hand. After all, the ;taunchly Lutheran nation has vorked elves into the book of ;enesis; some believe that when ;od paid Adam and Eve a visit on vashing day, Eve had only bathed ;ome of her children. She told the ›thers to stay hidden until God eft, but God was irked at the poor urnout and declared that "whom- ;oever hides from me shall be ıidden from me and my people orever."

Excluded from divine favor, ;ome hidden people hope to fall n love with a human and then get ›aptized. Others just care for their ›wn, as in the tale of a human ;randmother who stepped away rom milking her cow only to find ıer bucket half-empty. Puzzled, ;he left a little milk behind every ıight for a week, finding it gone he next morning. On the last ıight, a beautiful elf-woman came o the grandmother in her sleep to ;ay thanks; she had needed the nilk for a potion to cure a sick ;hild. In exchange for the grand- nother's kindness, the elf gave ıer a veil with golden embroidery hat no human had the skill to nake. The old woman's greedy ›rogeny hoped to inherit the veil ıfter she died, but after the uneral they searched her closet ınd found that the veil was gone.

NASA, Thorraldssenstr. 2 (☎511 13 13; www.nasa.is), at the Austurvollur Square. One of the hottest dance clubs in Reykjavík also features live bands every weekend. The large dance floor in the center of this spacious club draws a varied crowd, depending on the evening's band. Beer 700Isk. Cover 500-1500Isk. Open F-Sa 11pm-late. MC/V.

Cultura, Hverfisgt. 18 (☎530 93 14), across from the National Theater. Cafe by day and bar by night, Cultura radiates a multicultural and laidback feel. Converse over round mosaic tables before getting down in the room next door. Beer 600Isk. W Tango night. F-Sa house DJ. Open M-Th and Su 11:30am-1am, F-Sa 11:30am-4am. MC/V.

Vegamót, Vegamótarstíg. 4 (☎511 30 40), off of Laugaveg. The well dressed head to this posh bar to flaunt it and see others do the same. Beer 600Isk. Th-Sa DJ nights. Open M-Th 11pm-1am, F-Sa 11pm-5am. MC/V.

DAYTRIPS FROM REYKJAVÍK

Iceland's true attractions are its mesmerizing natural wonders. **Iceland Excursions** runs the popular Golden Circle tour, which stops at Hveragerði, Kerið, Skálholt, Geysir, Gullfoss, and Þingvellir National Park. (☎562 10 11; www.icelandexcursions.is. 9-10hr. 6200Isk.) **Highlanders** offers exciting, if pricey off-road tours in "super jeeps" that can traverse rivers, crags, and even glaciers. (☎568 30 30; www.hl.is. 10,600-17,500Isk.)

GULLFOSS AND GEYSIR. The glacial river Hvita plunges down 32m to create Gullfoss (Golden Falls). The thunderous cascades can be viewed from only an arm's length away, although the spray may give you a good drenching. Climb the hill adjacent to the falls for a stunning view of the surrounding mountains, plains, cliffs, and glaciers. Nine kilometers down the road is the Geysir area, a rugged tundra with steaming pools of hot water scattered across the landscape. The **Strokkur Geyser** (the Churn) erupts every 5-10min., spewing sulfurous water at heights up to 35m. Watch your footing; more than one tourist has fallen into the nearby **Blesi pool** and has been badly scalded. The excellent **museum** at the visitor's center offers a multimedia show on the science behind these natural phenomena. (450Isk, students 350Isk.) BSÍ (☎562 10 11) runs a round-trip **bus** to both sites, departing Reykjavík from the BSÍ Terminal. (June-Aug. daily 8:30am and 12:30pm, Sa also 5pm; Sept.-May M-Sa 9:30am, Su 12:30pm; 3800Isk.)

BLUE LAGOON. The southwest corner of the Reykjanes peninsula harbors a primordial paradise: a vast pool of geothermally heated water hidden in the middle of a lava field. Though the lagoon has become a tourist magnet, its cloudy blue waters rich in silica, minerals, and algae are famous for their healing powers and well-worth braving the crowds. Bathers who have had their fill of wading through the 36-39°C (97-102°F) waters can indulge in a steam bath, skin-soothing silica facial, or an in-water massage for 1300Isk per 10min. (☎420 88 00; www.bluelagoon.com. Open daily mid-May to Aug. 9am-9pm; low season 10am-8pm. 1300Isk admission plus locker. Towel rental 300Isk. Bathing suit rental 350Isk. AmEx/MC/V.) **Buses** arrive from BSÍ Bus Terminal in Reykjavík (6 per day; last return 8pm; 3000Isk round-trip, including Blue Lagoon admission).

HVERAGERÐI. Hveragerði (pop. 2000) sits on a geothermal hotbed so volatile that geysers have been known to burst through the floors of existing houses. Geothermal energy also powers the town's numerous greenhouses, which allow locals to grow peppers, bananas, and other produce that would not otherwise survive in Iceland's capricious climate. While most of the greenhouses do not run organized tours, many owners will be happy to show you around upon request. **The Garden of Eden,** Austurmörk 25, which boasts a nursery and an ice cream parlor, is one of the few that caters to tourists. (Located across the street from the gas station where the bus stops. ☎483 49 00; www.eden.smart.is. Open daily in summer 8:30am-11pm; low season 9am-7pm.) The **tourist office,** Sunnumörk 2, can steer visitors toward guesthouses and campsites or dispatch them on hiking routes in the surrounding area. (☎483 46 01. Open in summer M-F 9am-5pm, Sa-Su noon-4pm, low season M-F 9am-4:30pm.)

ÞINGVELLIR NATIONAL PARK. Þingvellir National Park straddles the divide between the European and North American tectonic plates. Stand in the chasm between the continents, but don't linger too long—the plates are moving apart at a rate of 2cm per year. The Öxará River, slicing through lava fields and jagged fissures, leads to the **Drekkingarhylur** (Drowning Pool), where adulterous women were once drowned, and to **Lake Þingvallavatn,** Iceland's largest lake. Not far from the Drekkingarhylur lies the site of the **Alþing** (ancient parliament), where for almost nine centuries Icelanders gathered in the shadow of the **Lögberg** (Law Rock) to discuss matters of blood, money, and justice. BSÍ runs a round-trip **bus** from Reykjavík (May 20-Sept. 10 daily 1:30pm, return 4:50pm; 900Isk). Grab maps at the **Þingvellir Information Center.** (☎482 26 60. Open June-Aug. daily 9am-7pm; Apr.-May and Sept.-Oct. daily 9am-5pm; Nov.-Mar. Sa-Su 9am-5pm.)

WESTMAN ISLANDS (VESTMANNAEYJAR)

Jutting from the depths of the North Atlantic, the black cliffs off the Westman Islands are only the most recent offerings of the volcanic fury that created the main island of Iceland. As recently as 1973, the fiery **Eldfell** volcano tore through the northern section of Heimaey, the only inhabited island, spewing lava and ash in a surprise eruption that forced the population to flee overnight. When the eruption tapered off five months later, a third of the town's houses had been destroyed, and the island itself had grown by the same amount. Years later, visitors can still feel the heat of the cooling lava. The **Volcanic Film Show** on Heiðarveg. runs a documentary about the eruption. (☎481 1045. 55min. shows daily mid-June to mid-Aug. 11am, 2, 3:30, 9pm; mid-Aug. to mid-Sept. 11am, 3:30pm. 600Isk.) Head to the **aquarium** across the street, at Heiðarveg. 12, to see some of the island's sea creatures. Only basic information is available in English (☎481 1997 or 899 2540). A combination ticket (750Isk) also grants admission to the **Folkmuseum,** in the town hall on Ráðhúströð, which re-creates 19th-century Heimaey, and to one of the island's oldest houses at **Skansinn,** on the harbor, where visitors can see for themselves why Icelandic buildings cringe at the mention of lava. (Folkmuseum ☎481 1194. Aquarium and museums open May-Sept. daily 11am-5pm; Sept.-Apr. Sa-Su 3-5pm. 400Isk each. AmEx/DC/MC/V.) Though less than 15 sq. km in area, the island offers several spectacular **hikes.** Scenic spots include the cliff's edge at **Há** on the western side of the island and the puffin colony at **Stórhöfði** on the southern tip. Both volcanic peaks can be scaled by hikers, although strong gusts often make for rough going. The three-day **People's Feast** *(Þjóðhátíð)* draws thousands of young people to the island during the first weekend in August for bonfires, binge drinking, and related revelry. Book transportation well in advance.

Friendly, centrally located **Guesthouse Hreiðrið ❷**, Faxastíg. 33, is just past the cinema on Heiðarveg. (☎481 1045; tourist.eyjar.is. Reception 24hr. in summer. Sleeping-bag accommodation 1800Isk; singles 3600Isk; doubles 5800Isk. Low season reduced rates.) **Guesthouse Sunnuhóll ❷**, Vestmannabraut 28b, offers functional rooms in a house behind Hótel Þorshamar. (☎481 2900; http://hotel.eyjar.is. Breakfast 600Isk. Sleeping-bag accommodation in single room 2700Isk; sleeping-bag accommodation in a double room 1800Isk; singles 4200Isk.) **Herjólfsdal Camping ❶**, 10min. west of town on Dalveg., is surrounded by mountains. (☎692 69 52. Showers free. Tent sites 700Isk.) Pick up groceries at **Krónan** on Strandaveg. (Open daily 11am-7pm.) In summer, Air Iceland runs **flights** from Reykjavík Airport. (☎481 3255; www.eyhaflug.is. 30min., from 4500Isk one-way.) The Herjólfur **ferry** departing from Þorlákshöfn is slower but cheaper. (☎481 2800. 2¾hr.; M-F, Su noon, 7:30pm, Sa noon; return M-F and Su 8:15am, 4pm, Sa 8:15am. 1700Isk; Internet tickets 10% discount.) **Buses** go from BSÍ Station to the ferry 1hr. before departure (1000Isk). The **tourist office,** Strandveg. 51, is in the central harbor. (☎481 3555; www.eyjar.is/eyjar. Open M-F 9am-5pm; May-Sept. also Sa-Su 11am-4pm.)

LANDMANNALAUGAR AND ÞÓRSMÖRK

Wedged between the glaciers, lava fields, and colorful rhyolite mountains of southern Iceland, Landmannalaugar and Þórsmörk are popular jumping-off points for **hikers,** especially the intrepid souls who undertake the demanding 4-day trek between the two areas. The 54km trail poses a number of challenges, including volatile weather conditions, even in the middle of the summer. Other trails take day hikers through gentler terrain, including a 2hr. loop through Landmannalaugar's volcanoes and bubbling hot springs, and a walk from Þórsmörk to the peak of **Valahnjukur,** which overlooks a web of rivers and ash fields. **Ferðafélag Islands** (Iceland Touring Association) runs guided hikes. (☎568 25 33; www.fi.is). The footsore can also soak away their aches and pains in Landmannalaugar's soothing **thermal brook.** Austurleið SBS (☎545 17 17; www.austurleid.is) runs **buses** daily from Reykjavík to Landmannalaugar (4½hr.; daily mid-June to mid-Sept. 8:30am, return 2:45pm; round-trip 9000Isk) and Þórsmörk (3½hr.; June to mid-Sept. daily 8:30am, return 3:30pm or 7:20pm; round-trip 7400Isk). Landmannalaugar has a **campsite ❶** and **lodge ❷** run by Ferðafélag Islands; book online at www.fi.is. (☎854 11 92. Open July-Sept. Camping 600Ikr; mountain huts 2000Ikr.) In Þórsmörk, **Húsadalur Þórsmörk ❶** offers hiking tips and simple accommodations. (☎852 55 06; www.thorsmork.is. Open Apr. to mid-Oct. Breakfast 850Ikr. Camping 500Ikr; sleeping-bag dorms 1600Ikr; 5-person cabin with kitchen 6000Ikr.)

AKUREYRI

A town of 15,000 people rarely occupies the position that Akureyri (Ah-KOO-rare-ee) does in Icelandic culture. The island's second biggest population center is not only a bustling college town with trendy hangouts but also an outpost of Icelandic frontier culture. A green city bordered by white mountains and blue water, Akureyri also serves as the gateway to Iceland's outlying lands of fire and ice.

TRANSPORTATION AND PRACTICAL INFORMATION. Flights arrive from Reykjavík daily; booking ahead may snag you lower-than-bus rates. For flight information, contact Air Iceland (☎460 7000; www.airiceland.is). **Buses** run from the SBA bus station to Reykjavík (6hr.; at least once daily, more in high season; 6200Isk). **Car rental** agencies are located at **Akureyri Airport,** 3km south of the city center along the seaside road, Drottningarbraut. Most of the agencies have 24hr. service, but not necessarily on site: **Avis** (☎461 2428; www.avis.is); **Budget** (☎462 3400); **Hasso** (☎464 1030; hasso.co.is); and **Hertz** (☎461 6000; www.hertz.is).

Akureyri is bordered to the west by mountains and the harbor area, and to the east by the imposing Eyjafjörður fjord. Within the city limits, follow **Hafnarstræti** to its end to reach Akureyri's main square, **Rådhustorg.** The SBA bus station shares its space with the **tourist office,** Hafnarstr. 82, which books tours, hostels, and car rentals. (☎ 462 7733; www.eyafjordur.is. Open late June-Aug. M-F 7:30am-7pm, Sa-Su 8am-5pm; low season M-F 7:30am-5pm. MC/V.) Most of the main services such as **banks** can be found around Rådhustorg. **KB Banki** and **Landsbanki** banks (M-F 9:15am-4pm) are just off the square. For **Internet,** walk from Rådhustorg up Brekkugt. to the corner of Oddeyarargt. to the **library.** (☎462 4141. Open mid-June to mid-Sept. M-F 10am-7pm, Sa noon-5pm; low season M-W, F 10am-7pm, Th 10am-10pm. 200Isk per hr.) Wireless-equipped laptops (1st hr. 300Isk, 2nd hr. 200Isk, 3rd hr. and after 100Isk) are also available for rental.

ACCOMMODATIONS AND FOOD. Akureyri's only hostel, **Stórholt ❶,** Stórholt 1, draws an adventurous crowd of Arctic travelers who relax between treks in comfy common spaces. Ask about discount whale-watching tickets. (☎462 3657; storholt@simnet.is. Laundry 600Isk. Dorms 1800Isk; singles 3600Isk; doubles 5400Isk. HI discount 400-600Isk. D/MC/V.) If the hostel is full, try the cottages at **Gula Villan ❷,** Brekkugt. 8 and Þingvallastr. 14, for bright and tidy rooms. (☎461 2860; gulavillan@nett.is. Free laundry. Sleeping-bag accommodation from 2200Isk; singles 3300Isk; doubles 4800Isk; triples 6600Isk. AmEx/DC/MC/V.) The **Hamrar campsite ❶,** is 3km southwest of the city by the Kjarnaskógur Forest. (☎461 2264; www.hamrar.is. Open year-round. Electricity 200Isk. Showers included. Laundry 400Isk. Tent sites 700Isk. 10% student discount. AmEx/DC/MC/V.)

The incredible **Götu grillið ❶,** Strandgt. 11, flavors Icelandic fish with Indian spices. Burgers start from 490Isk, seafood from 795Isk, and the lunch buffet fills you up for 1190Isk, or ask for the day's special. (☎462 1800. Open mid-June to Sept. daily 11am-11pm; winter M-F noon-2pm and 5:30-9pm, Sa-Su 5:30-10pm. MC/V.) Travelers staying at the Stórholt hostel enjoy a 15% discount off meals at **Greyfinn ❸,** Glerárgötu 20, which serves a lunch buffet for a reasonable 1350Isk (before discount) on weekdays. (☎460 1600. Fish dishes from 1350Isk. Sandwiches and burgers from 1290Isk. Open daily 11:30am-11pm, pizza takeaway and delivery F-Sa until 1am. AmEx/D/MC/V.) (Open M-Th 9am-11pm, F 9am-1am, Sa 10am-1am, Su 11am-9pm. MC/V.) Stock up on 18Isk noodles at the **Bonus** supermarket, on Hörgárbraut. (☎466 3500. Open M-Th noon-6:30pm, F 10am-7:30pm, Sa 10am-6pm, Su noon-6pm. MC/V.)

SIGHTS AND NIGHTLIFE. While most travelers use Akureyri as a base for further Arctic exploration, it has a few sights worth visiting in their own right. **Nonnahús,** Aðalstr. 54, offers a glimpse into late 19th-century life in Akureyri by taking visitors into the life of the Icelandic author Jón Sveinsson, whose most famous work, the children's book *Nonni and Manni*, has been translated into over 30 languages. (☎462 3555. Open June-Sept. daily 10am-5pm; call ahead in low season. 350Isk. MC/V.) At the **Botanical Gardens,** tropical and subtropical plants fight off the sub-arctic climate. (On the corner of Hrafnagilsstr. and Eyrarlandsveg.. Open M-F 8am-10pm, Sa-Su 9am-10pm. Free.) Travelers seeking a more traditionally Icelandic natural experience can hike to **Mount Súlur** (1144m) along a trail that starts 4km out of town. More challenging hikes that require specialized gear for glaciers include **Strýta** (1456m) and **Kerling** (1536m). The tourist office provides hiking maps. Culture lovers arrive for the annual **Summer Arts Festival** (www.listagil.is), which runs from late June until late August. It includes art exhibits, theater performances, poetry readings, and history walks. Check for details.

After a day of sightseeing, step into the **Café Amour,** Rådhustorget, a hot spot that rivals that of a major European capital. The well-dressed crowd can make the budget traveler seem like a bit of an oddity, but it also serves as a reminder of life beyond the waterfalls and lava fields. Beers start at 600Isk (try the locally brewed Thule), but keep an eye out for five-bottles-for-1500Isk offers during occasional happy hours. (☎461 3030; www.cafeamour.is. Open Su-Th noon-1am, F-Sa noon-4am. MC/V.) **Kaffi Akureyri,** Strandgt. 7, is the standard for nighttime entertainment, with a crowd ranging from 20- to 60-year-olds. Knock down Opal liquorice shots with the locals for 400Isk. (☎461 3999; siggi@heimsnet.is. 20+. Music cover 500-800Isk. Open M-Th and Su 5pm-1am, F-Sa 3pm-4am. AmEx/DC/MC/V.)

DAYTRIPS FROM AKUREYRI: MÝVATN NATURE BATHS AND GOÐAFOSS.

Icelanders fleeing the tourist hordes at the Blue Lagoon (p. 552) head to the **Mývatn Nature Baths,** 90km east of Akureyri. Mývatn's freshwater baths further distinguish it from its more famous saltwater counterpart. Those traveling by car or bicycle can hike the Dimmuborgir region and the Krafta crater nearby before indulging in a trip to the baths. **Buses** run round-trip from Akureyri to Reynihlíð (daily June-Aug. at 8am, returning at 3:30pm; 4200Isk). From Reynihlíð, it is about a 4km walk to the baths along Rte. 1. Mývatn Baths ☎464 4411; www.naturebaths.com. Open June-Aug. daily 9am-midnight, Sept.-May M-F 4-10pm, Sa-Su noon-10pm. 1100Isk. Towel or swimsuit rental 350Isk; in winter prices may be lower. MC/V.)

Legend holds that in AD 1000, the mastermind of Iceland's conversion to Christianity, Þorgeir, returned to his home in northeastern Iceland after overseeing the *Alþing*'s (ancient parliament) acceptance of Christianity. He celebrated this achievement by throwing statues of pagan gods into the waterfall he passed, thus christening it with the name **Goðafoss** (Waterfall of the Gods). While Goðafoss stands only 12m high, it is set against a beautiful backdrop that makes it a glorious place for travelers on the road to Akureyri to stretch their legs. The inconvenient bus schedule means that bus-bound travelers may want to skip Goðafoss. A **bus** departs Akureyri daily June-Aug. at 8:30am but does not return until 4pm (1100Isk). By **car,** Goðafoss is about 50km from both Akureyri and Húsavik off Rte. 1.

HÚSAVÍK

As Iceland's whale-watching capital, Húsavík (WHO-saah-veek; pop. 2500) boasts a diverse set of attractions that range from the natural to the bizarre. Start your visit at the **tourist office,** Húsavíkurstofa at Garðarsbraut 5, for discount coupons and local maps. (☎464 4300; info@husavik.is. Open June-Aug. M-F 9am-7pm, Sa 9am-6pm, Su 10am-6pm.) For a unique mix of science, art, and humor, head to **The Icelandic Phallological Museum,** at Héðinsbraut 3a. The erect phallus that greets passersby makes the museum hard to miss. Inside, view the reproductive organs of over 86 species—thankfully, none *Homo sapiens*—from the hamster specimen that measures less than 2mm to the 70kg organ of the sperm whale. (☎561 6663; www.phallus.is. Open daily mid-May to mid-Sept. noon-6pm. 500Isk. Cash only.) Moving down Héðinsbraut, the **Húsavík Whale Museum,** just next to the harbor, covers the rest of whale biology with its ever-expanding exhibit on whales and their natural habitat. The video presentations are informative, although slanted towards the anti-whaling case. (☎464 2520; www.icewhale.is. Open daily June-Aug. 9am-9pm, May and Sept. 10am-5pm. 500Isk, students 400Isk. MC/V.) Húsavík has come to be known as Europe's premier whale-watching destination; book a 3hr. tour with **Gentle Giants** or **North Sailing** to hang out with the enormous creatures. (Gentle Giants ☎464 1500; www.gentlegiants.is. Tours May-Sept., call for times. 3600Isk. MC/V. North Sailing ☎464 2350; www.northsailing.is. May-Sept., call for times. 3800Isk. MC/V.)

Two **guesthouse** options are available along Baldursbrekka (the first street on your right when entering the town from the north). **Aðalbjörg Birgisdóttir Guesthouse ❶**, Baldursbrekka 20, has sleek but small rooms. (☎464 1005; mariam@simnet.is. Breakfast 400-500Isk. Sleeping-bag accommodation 1800Isk.; single bed with linens 3200Isk; double bed with linens 4600Isk. Cash only.) Across the street, **Emhild K. Olsen ❶**, Baldursbrekka 17, caters more directly to the sleeping bag crowd and has larger, but more basic, rooms for the same prices. (☎464 1618. Cash only.) For seaside dining and drinks saunter towards the **Salka Restaurant ❷** on the harbor. Try the smoked puffin breast on green salad for 850Isk. (☎464 2551. Entrees from 800Isk and pizzas from 1200Isk. Kitchen open daily 11:30am-10pm. Bar open June-Aug. M-F until 11pm, year-round F-Sa until 3am. MC/V.) During the day, **Heimabakarí konditori,** Garðarsbraut 15, bakes delicious local breads and pastries. (☎464 2900. Marzipan punchcake 166Isk. Open M-F 9am-6pm, Sa 10am-4pm. MC/V.) **SBA buses** (☎550 0771; www.sba.is) run from Húsavík, leaving from the Shell Gas Station at Héðinsbraut 6 (the main street north of the harbor) to Akureyri (1¼hr., late May-Aug. 4-5 per day, 2000-2100Isk) and Reynihilldð on Lake Mývatn (45min., late May-Aug. 2-3 per day, 1600Isk). **Internet** can be found at the Húsavík Public Library, Stórigarður 17. (☎464 1173. Open June-Aug. M-Th 10am-7pm, F 10am-5pm; Sept.-May also open Sa 11am-3pm. 150Isk per hr.)

JÖKULSÁRGLJÚFUR NATIONAL PARK

The Jökulsa á Fjöllum River flows into the Jökulsárgljúfur National Park from the the Vatnajökull glacier in the south, creating astounding waterfalls throughout the region. While Jökulsárgljúfur is a trek from any transport hub, the magnificent **Dettifoss** waterfall rewards those that sit through a long bus ride, book a pricey tour, or rent a car for the occasion. The most powerful waterfall in Europe, Dettifoss's horseshoe-shaped torrent invigorates its surrounding areas in stark contrast with the barren lands to its south. The nearby cliffs allow you to get a too-close-to-be-safe look at the fall. A 1.4km walk upstream, past Icelandic river beaches covered by dark lava sand, lies **Sellfoss,** a smaller but still imposing sight. Jökulsárgljúfur's third major waterfall, Hafragilsfoss, is located 2km downstream from Dettifoss. The Hafragilsfoss parking area offers a majestic view of both the waterfall and the canyon below. Round-trip **buses** run mid-June to August from Akureyri (5hr., 1 per day leaving at 8:30am, 10,800Isk) and Húsavik (3½hr., 1 per day leaving at 10am, 5100Isk). **Nonni Travels,** Brekkugötu 5 in Akureyri, runs bus and Jeep tours to Dettifoss from Húsavik and Akureyri. (☎461 1841; www.nonnitravel.is. Open M-F 9am-5pm. Bus tours leave Húsavik June-Aug. M-F at 8:30am. 7600Isk. Groups of 4 can book the Super Jeep tour departing Mývatn with an optional bus from Akureyri for 10,700Isk, additional fee for bus. AmEx/MC/V.) Private car rental (p. 554), preferably 4WD, is often the cheapest and easiest way to reach Jökulsárgljúfur.

ICELAND

REPUBLIC OF IRELAND AND NORTHERN IRELAND

Jagged coastal cliffs, misty days, and rolling hills are the poetic images of Western Ireland that dominate the idea of Ireland abroad. Stone-Age forts, pre-Christian tombs, millennial monasteries, and high crosses dot this land. Its cosmopolitan centers have modernized significantly, but windswept scenery still lines the coasts and untouched mountain chains stretch across the interior bogland. Despite murmurs of declining native culture, the Irish language lives on in secluded areas known as *gaeltachts* and dark village pubs continue to nurture traditional music.

IRELAND

DISCOVER IRELAND: SUGGESTED ITINERARIES

THREE DAYS Spend it all in **Dublin** (p. 564). Wander through **Trinity College,** admire the **Book of Kells,** then have a drink at the **Old Jameson Distillery.** Take a day to visit the **National Museums,** stopping to relax on **St. Stephen's Green.** Get smart at the **James Joyce Centre** and then work your pubbing potential in **Temple Bar** and on **Grafton Street,** stopping by Leopold Bloom's haunt, **Davy Byrne's.**

ONE WEEK From **Dublin** (2 days) head to historic **Belfast** (1 day; p. 587). Don't miss the **Giant's Causeway** (1 day; p. 594) before heading to artsy **Galway** (1 day; p. 583). Admire the countryside in the **Ring of Kerry** (1 day; p. 579) and return to civilization in **Cork** (1 day; p. 575).

BEST OF IRELAND, THREE WEEKS Land in **Dublin** (4 days) before taking the train up to **Belfast** (3 days). Catch the bus to **Giant's Causeway** (1 day), and stop at Derry/Londonderry (1 day; p. 592). Use **Sligo** (3 days; p. 586) as a base for visiting the surrounding lakes and mountains. From there, head to **Galway** (3 days), the **Ring of Kerry** (2 days), **Killarney National Park** (1 day; p. 578), and **Cork** (2 days). On the way back to Dublin, stop by medieval **Kilkenny** (1 day; p. 574).

ESSENTIALS

WHEN TO GO

Weather on the Irish continent is subject to frequent changes but relatively constant temperatures. The southeastern coast is the driest and sunniest, while western Ireland is considerably wetter and cloudier. May and June are the sunniest months, July and August the warmest. December and January have the worst weather. Take heart when you wake to clouded, foggy mornings—the weather usually clears by noon. Make sure you bring rain gear, regardless of the season.

DOCUMENTS AND FORMALITIES

EMBASSIES AND CONSULATES. All embassies for the Republic of Ireland are in Dublin (p. 564). For Irish embassies in your home country, contact: **Australia,** 20 Arkana St., Yarralumla, Canberra ACT 2600 (☎06 273 3022); **Canada,** Ste. 1105, 130 Albert St., Ottawa, ON K1P 5G4 (☎613-233-6281); **New Zealand,** Consulate-General,

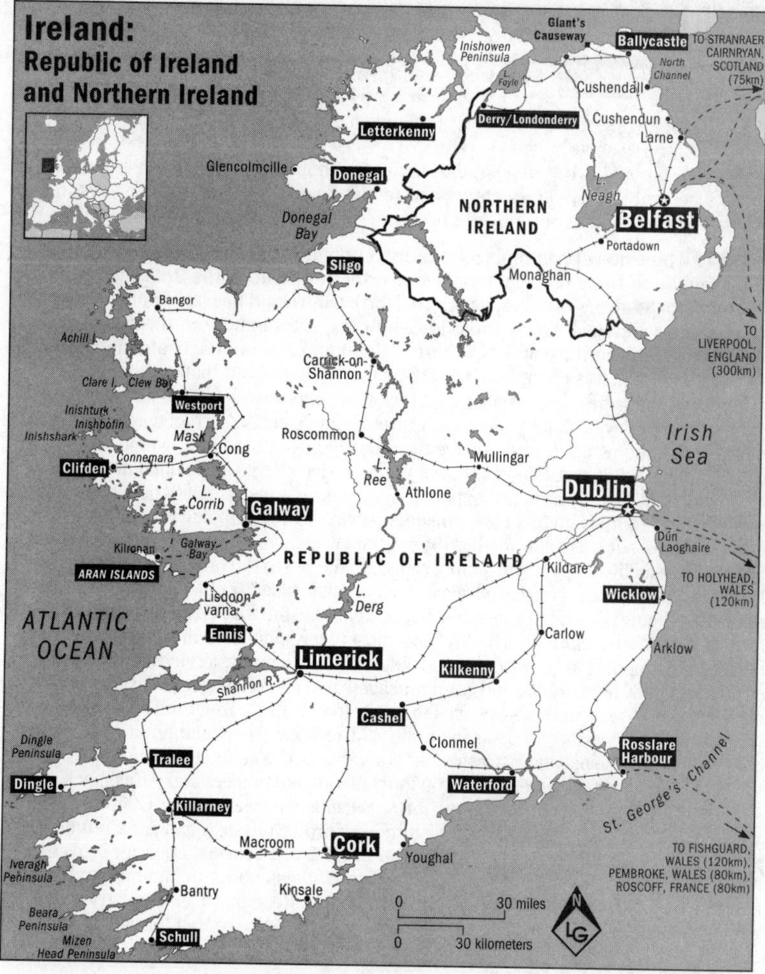

6th fl., 18 Shortland St., Auckland (☎09 977 2252; www.ireland.co.nz); **UK,** 17 Grosvenor Pl., London SW1X 7HR (☎020 7235 2171); **US,** 2234 Massachusetts Ave. NW, Washington, D.C. 20008-2849 (☎202-462-3939).

VISA AND ENTRY INFORMATION. Citizens of Australia, Canada, the EU, New Zealand, the UK, and the US do not need a visa for stays of up to 90 days. For longer stays, nonmembers of the EU should register for free with the **Garda National Immigration Bureau,** 13-14 Burgh Quay, Dublin 2 (☎01 666 9100). If in doubt, or if your home country is not one of these, check with your embassy. Double-check entrance requirements at the nearest Irish embassy or consulate for up-to-date information before departure.

TOURIST SERVICES AND MONEY

EMERGENCY	**Emergency:** ☎112. **Police, Ambulance, Fire:** ☎999.

TOURIST OFFICES. Bord Fáilte (Irish Tourist Board; ☎01 602 4000; www.ireland.ie) operates a nationwide network of offices. Most tourist offices book rooms for a small fee and a 10% deposit, but many fine hostels and B&Bs are not on the board's central list. The **Northern Ireland Tourist Board** (☎028 9023 1221; www.discovernorthernireland.com) offers similar services.

MONEY. The **euro (€)** has replaced the Irish pound (£) as the unit of currency in the Republic of Ireland. Legal tender in Northern Ireland is the **British pound;** for more info on conversion rates, see p. 19. Northern Ireland has its own bank notes, identical in value to English and Scottish notes. Although all of these notes are accepted in Northern Ireland, Northern Ireland notes are not accepted in Britain. As a general rule, it is cheaper to exchange money in Ireland than at home.

If you stay in hostels and prepare your own food, expect to spend about €30/UK£20 per person per day; a slightly more comfortable day (sleeping in B&Bs and the occasional budget hotel, eating out one meal per day, going out at night) would cost €50/UK£35. Menus often indicate whether or not a service charge is included in the price. Most waitstaff, however, do not expect a tip, unless the restaurant is targeted exclusively toward tourists. In that case, consider leaving 10-15%. Tipping is uncommon for other services, such as taxis and hairdressers, especially in rural areas. In most cases, people are usually happy if you simply round up the bill to the nearest euro or pound. Both the Republic and Northern Ireland have a **Value Added Tax (VAT),** a national sales tax on most goods and some services. In the Republic, the 21% VAT does not apply to food and children's clothing. The VAT is almost always included in listed prices. The British rate, applicable to Northern Ireland, is 17.5% on many services (such as hairdressers, hotels, restaurants, and car rental agencies) and on all goods (except books, medicine, and food). Refunds are available only to non-EU citizens and only for goods taken out of the country. In the Republic, **VAT refunds** are available on goods purchased in stores displaying a "Cashback" sticker (ask if you don't see one). Ask for a voucher with your purchase, which you must fill out and present at the Cashback service desk in Dublin or Shannon airports. Purchases greater than €250 must be approved at the customs desk first. Visitors to Northern Ireland can get a refund on goods taken out of the country through the **Retail Export Scheme.** Look for signs like "Tax Free Shopping" or "Tax Free for Tourists" and ask about minimum purchases (usually €65-130) as well as for the appropriate form. Keep purchases in carry-on luggage so a customs officer can inspect the goods and validate refund forms.

TRANSPORTATION

BY PLANE. Flying to London and connecting to Ireland is often easier and cheaper than flying directly. A popular carrier to Ireland is national airline **Aer Lingus** (☎081 836 5000, US 800-474-7424; www.aerlingus.com), which has direct flights to London, Paris, and the US. **Ryanair** (☎081 830 3030; www.ryanair.ie) is a smaller airline that offers a "lowest-fare guarantee." Web-based phenomenon **easyJet** (UK ☎0871 244 2366; www.easyjet.com) offers cheap flights into Belfast from all over Europe. **British Airways** (Republic ☎890 626 747, UK 0870 850 9850, US 800-247-9297; www.ba.com) flies into most Irish airports daily.

BY TRAIN. Iarnród Éireann (Irish Rail; ☎01 850 366 2222; www.irishrail.ie) is useful only for travel to urban areas. The **Eurail** pass is accepted in the Republic but not in Northern Ireland. The **BritRail** pass does not cover travel in Northern Ireland or the Republic, but the month-long **BritRail+Ireland** pass (€350-560) does, with rail options and round-trip ferry service between Britain and Ireland. **Northern Ireland Railways** (☎028 9066 6630; www.nirailways.co.uk) is not extensive but covers the northeastern coastal region well; the major line connects Dublin to Belfast. A valid **Translink Student Discount Card** (UK£7) will get you up to 33% off all trains and 15% discounts on bus fares over UK£1.45 within Northern Ireland. The **Freedom of Northern Ireland** ticket allows unlimited travel by train and Ulsterbus for seven consecutive days (UK£47), three out of eight days (UK£32), or a single day (UK£13).

BY BUS. Bus Éireann (☎01 836 6111; www.buseireann.ie), the national bus company, works in conjunction with ferry services and the bus company **Eurolines** (www.eurolines.com) to reach Britain and the continent. Most buses leave from Victoria Station in London for Belfast (15hr.; €62/UK£42, round-trip €102/UK£69) and Dublin (16hr.; €77/UK£52, round-trip €112/UK£76); other major city stops include Birmingham, Bristol, Cardiff, Glasgow, and Liverpool with services to Cork, Derry/Londonderry, Galway, Limerick, Tralee, and Waterford, among others. Discounted fares are available in the low season and for people under 26 or over 60. Bus Éireann operates both long-distance Expressway buses, which link larger cities, and local buses, which serve the countryside and smaller towns.

Ulsterbus (☎028 9066 6630, Belfast office 028 9033 7011; www.ulsterbus.co.uk) operates routes throughout Northern Ireland. The **Irish Rover** pass covers both Bus Éireann and Ulsterbus services (3 of 8 consecutive days €68/UK£46, children €38/UK£26; 8 of 15 days €152/UK£102, children €84/UK£56; 15 of 30 days €226/UK£152, children €124/UK£83). The **Emerald Card** offers unlimited travel on Ulsterbus, Northern Ireland Railways, Bus Éireann Expressway, and many local services; for more info, see www.buseireann.ie. (8 of 15 consecutive days €198/UK£133, children €99/UK£67; 15 of 30 days €341/UK£229, children €170/UK£114).

BY FERRY. Ferries, more economical than air travel, journey between Britain and Ireland several times per day (€28-55/UK£18-35). Weeknight travel promises the cheapest fares. Students, seniors, families, and youth traveling alone typically receive discounts; **ISIC** holders receive a 20-50% discount from Irish Ferries and a 20-30% discount on Stena Line ferries. Ferries run from Cork to South Wales and Roscoff, France (p. 573), and from Rosslare Harbour to Pembroke, Wales, and Roscoff and Cherbourg, France (p. 573).

WHISKEY BUSINESS

While Guinness is synonymous with Ireland the world over, Irish whiskey comes a close second as the unofficial national drink of the Emerald Isle. Indeed, seasoned Irish drinkers often chase a pint of "a big one" (Guinness) with "a small one" (whiskey).

Whiskey in Ireland was created by medieval monks, who used the fiery tipple as an antidote to cold winters. In later years it was distilled at dangerous strengths in Irish homes, where the phrase "blind drunk" was sometime quite literal. At the end of the 16th century, the English government cited spirits as the source o Irish unrest, and waged wa against all moonshiners. This led to the emergence of illegal estab lishments called *shabeens* sellin extra-potent *poitín*.

Poitín is a 140-proof kick in the face. Culled from potatoes steeped in a mixture of apples berries, and barley, then thrice distilled in a gigantic coppe worm, it is a clear liquid with a bouquet reminiscent of paint thin ner. Because of its high alcoho content and risky mode of prepa ration, *poitín* is illegal. It is no served in pubs or brought out in polite company.

Most whiskey drinkers take their spirits neat, over ice, or with a bit of water. Other popular whis key-based drinks are "hot Irish (whiskey, lemon, cloves, brown sugar, and boiling water) and Irish coffee (black coffee, sugar, and whiskey, topped with cream).

BY CAR. Drivers in Ireland use the left side of the road. Gasoline (petrol) prices are high. Be particularly cautious at roundabouts—give way to traffic from the right. **Dan Dooley** (☎062 53103, UK 0800 282 189, US 800-331-9301; www.dan-dooley.com) and **Enterprise** (☎01 844 5848, UK 0129 360 9090, US 800-261-7331; www.enterprise.com) are the only companies in Ireland that will rent to drivers between 21 and 24, though such drivers incur an additional daily surcharge. Prices are €85-200/UK£58-136 (plus VAT) per week, including insurance and unlimited mileage. If you plan to drive a car in Ireland for longer than 90 days, you must have an **International Driving Permit (IDP).** If you rent, lease, or borrow a car, you will need a **green card** or **International Insurance Certificate** to certify that you have liability insurance that applies abroad. It is always significantly less expensive to reserve a car from the US than from Europe.

BY BIKE, FOOT, AND THUMB. Much of Ireland's countryside is well suited for **biking,** as many roads are not heavily traveled. Single-digit "N" roads in the Republic and "M" roads in the North are more trafficked; try to avoid these. Ireland's mountains, fields, and hills make **walking** and **hiking** arduous joys. The **Wicklow Way** has hostels within a day's walk of each other. Locals do not recommend **hitchhiking** in Northern Ireland, where it is illegal along motorways; some caution against it in Co. Dublin and the Midlands. *Let's Go* does not recommend hitchhiking.

KEEPING IN TOUCH

Country code: 353 (Republic); 44 (Northern Ireland; dial 048 from the Republic). **International dialing prefix:** 00. For more information on how to place international calls, see inside back cover. The city code for all of Northern Ireland is 028. From outside Northern Ireland, dial int'l dialing prefix (see inside back cover) + 44 (from the Republic, 048) + 28 + local number. From inside the Republic, dial the city code only when calling from outside the city.

EMAIL AND THE INTERNET. Internet access is available in cafes, hostels, and most libraries. Using free web-based email accounts (e.g., www.gmail.com and www.yahoo.com) is the fastest way to check email. One hour of web time costs about €3-6/UK£2-4; an ISIC often earns you a discount. Look into a county library membership in the Republic (€2.50-3), which gives unlimited access to participating libraries and their Internet terminals. Online listings of cybercafes in Ireland and Britain are available at Cybercafes.com (www.cybercafes.com).

TELEPHONE. Both the Irish Republic and Northern Ireland have public phones that accept coins (€0.40/UK£0.27 for about 4min.) and prepaid phone cards. In the Republic, dial ☎114 for an international operator, 10 for a national operator, or 11850 for directory assistance. Mobile phones (p. 33) are a popular and economical alternative. International direct dial numbers in the Republic include: **AT&T** (☎800 550 000); **British Telecom** (☎800 550 144); **Canada Direct** (☎800 555 001); **MCI** (☎800 55 1001); and **Telstra Australia** (☎800 55 00 61). In Northern Ireland, call ☎155 for an international operator, 100 for a national operator, or 192 for directory assistance. International direct dial numbers in Northern Ireland include: **AT&T** (☎0800 89 00 16); **Canada Direct** (☎0800 890 016); **MCI** (☎0800 55 1001); and **Telstra Australia** (☎0800 856 6161).

MAIL. In the Republic, postcards and letters up to 25g cost €0.60 domestically and to the UK, and €0.65 to the continent and other international destination. Airmail letters take around six to nine days between Ireland and North America and cost €0.67.

Dublin is the only place in the Republic with postal codes (p. 567). Northern Ireland uses the same postal system as Britain (p. 127). Address *Poste Restante* according to the following example: Firstname SURNAME, *Poste Restante*, [CITY], Ireland. The mail will go to a desk in the central post office, unless you specify otherwise.

ACCOMMODATIONS AND CAMPING

THE REPUBLIC/ NORTHERN IRELAND	❶	❷	❸	❹	❺
ACCOMMODATIONS	under €17/ £14	€17-26/ £14-21	€26-40/ £21-30	€40-56/ £30-46	over €56/ £46

A **hostel** bed will average €16-22 in the Republic and UK£11-15 in the North. **An Óige** (an OYJ), the **HI** affiliate, operates 32 hostels countrywide. (☎01 830 4555; www.irelandyha.org. One-year membership €20, under 18 €10.) Many An Óige hostels are in remote areas or small villages and were designed primarily to serve nature-seekers. They therefore do not offer the social environment typical of other European hostels. The North's HI affiliate is **HINI** (Hostelling International Northern Ireland; formerly known as **YHANI**). It operates only eight hostels, all comfortable. (☎028 9032 4733; www.hini.org.uk. One-year membership UK£13, under 18 UK£6.) A number of hostels in Ireland belong to **Independent Holiday Hostels** (**IHH;** ☎01 836 4700; www.hostels-ireland.com). Most of the 140 IHH hostels have no lockout or curfew, accept all ages, require no membership card, and have a less institutional feel than their An Óige counterparts; all are Bord Fáilte-approved. In virtually every Irish town, **B&Bs** can provide a luxurious break from hostelling; expect to pay €30-35/UK£20-24 for singles and €45-60/UK£31-41 for doubles. "Full Irish breakfasts" are often filling enough to get you through to dinner. **Camping** in Irish State Forests and National Parks is not allowed; camping on public land is permissible only if there is no official campsite nearby. Sites cost €5-13, depending on the level of luxury. Northern Ireland treats its campers royally; there are well-equipped campsites throughout the country (UK£3-9).

FOOD AND DRINK

THE REPUBLIC/ NORTHERN IRELAND	❶	❷	❸	❹	❺
FOOD	under €6/ £4	€6-10/ £4-6	€10-15 /£6-10	€15-20/ £10-15	over €20/ £15

Food in Ireland can be expensive, but the basics are simple and filling. Find quick and greasy staples at chippers (fish 'n' chip shops) and takeaways (takeout joints). Most pubs serve food like Irish stew, burgers, soup, and sandwiches. Soda bread is delicious and keeps well, and Irish cheeses are addictive. Guinness, a rich, dark stout, is revered in Ireland with a zeal usually reserved for the Holy Trinity. Known as "the dark stuff" or "the blonde in the black skirt," its head is so thick it's rumored that you can stand a match in it. Irish whiskey, which Queen Elizabeth once claimed was her only true Irish friend, is sweeter than its Scotch counterpart. Irish monks invented whiskey, calling it *uisce beatha*, or "water of life." Ordering at an Irish **pub** is not to be done willy-nilly. When in a small group, one individual will usually approach the bar and buy a round of drinks for everyone. Once those drinks are downed, another individual will buy the next round. It's considered poor form to refuse someone's offer to buy you a drink.

HOLIDAYS AND FESTIVALS

Holidays: Holidays for the Republic of Ireland include: New Year's Day (Jan. 1); St. Patrick's Day (Mar. 17); and Good Friday and Easter Monday (Apr. 14, 17). There are bank holidays in the Republic and Northern Ireland during the summer months; check tourist offices for dates. Northern Ireland has the same national holidays as the Republic; it also observes Orangemen's Day (July 12).

Festivals: All of Ireland goes green for St. Patrick's Day (Mar. 17). On Bloomsday (June 16), Dublin celebrates James Joyce's *Ulysses*. In mid-July, the Galway Arts Festival hosts theater, trad, rock, and film. Many return home happy from the Lisdoonvarna Matchmaking Festival in early September.

BEYOND TOURISM

As a volunteer in Ireland you can participate in projects ranging from organic farming to peace and reconciliation efforts to advocacy for the homeless, either on a short- or long-term basis. The best way to find opportunities that match up with your interests and schedule may be to check with national volunteer agencies, such as **Volunteering Ireland** (www.volunteeringireland.com) or the **Northern Ireland Volunteer Development Agency** (www.volunteering-ni.org).

L'Arche Ireland, "Seolta," Warrenhouse Rd., Baldoyle, Dublin 13, Ireland (☎01 839 4356; www.larche.ie). Assistants become part of a residential community in Dublin, Belfast, Cork, or Kilkenny to live with, work with, and teach people with learning or mental health disabilities. Room, board, and a small stipend provided. Commitment of 1-2 years expected.

The Donegal Organic Farm, Doorian, Glenties, Co. Donegal, Ireland (☎074 94 95 51286; www.esatclear.ie/~tbecht). Offers opportunities in areas of farming, forestry, habitat maintenance, and wildlife.

Focus Ireland, 9-12 High St., Dublin 8, Ireland (☎01 881 5900; www.focusireland.ie). Volunteers get involved in advocacy and fund raising for the homeless in Dublin, Limerick, and Waterford.

Kilcranny House, 21 Cranagh Rd., Coleraine BT51 3NN, Northern Ireland (☎028 7032 1816; www.kilcrannyhouse.org). A residential and educational center provides a safe space for Catholics and Protestants to interact and explore issues of non-violence, prejudice, and conflict resolution. Volunteer opportunities range from 6 months to 2 years. UK£26 per week for expenses. Room and board provided.

REPUBLIC OF IRELAND

FACTS AND FIGURES

Official Name: Éire.
Capital: Dublin.
Major Cities: Cork, Galway, Limerick.
Population: 3,900,000.
Time Zone: GMT.
Languages: English, Gaelic.
Religion: Roman Catholic (92%).
Longest Serving Barracks: Collins Barracks, Dublin; 290 years (1704-1994).

DUBLIN ☎01

In a country known for its rural charms, the international flavor and frenetic pace of the city of Dublin stand out. Those who live outside the city worry that it has acquired the crime, rapid social change, and unfriendly demeanor characteristic of metropolises elsewhere. Yet traditional Dublin hasn't gone anywhere; its musical, cultural, and drinkable attractions continue to draw droves of tourists. While it may not resemble the rustic "Emerald Isle" promoted on tourist brochures, Dublin retains the country's famous charm while exuding urban sophistication.

TRANSPORTATION

Flights: Dublin Airport (DUB; ☎814 1111; www.aer-rianta.ie). **Dublin buses** #41, 41B, and 41C run from the airport to Eden Quay in the city center (40-45min., every 20min., €1.75). **Airlink shuttle** (☎703 3092) runs nonstop to Busáras Central Bus Station and O'Connell St. (20-25min., every 10-20min. 5:45am-11:30pm, €5), and to Heuston Station (50min., €5). A **taxi** to the city center costs roughly €20-25.

Trains: The **Iarnród Éireann** travel centre, 35 Lower Abbey St., sells tickets. (Centre open M-F 9am-5pm, Sa 9am-1pm. For info, M-Sa 9am-6pm; Su 10am-6pm, call ☎836 6222; www.irishrail.ie.) Dublin's other train station is **Pearse Station,** Pearse St. (☎888 0226).

Connolly Station, Amiens St. (☎703 2358), is north of the Liffey and close to Busáras. Bus #20B heads south of the river, and the DART runs to Tara Station on the south quay. Trains to: **Belfast** (2hr.; M-Sa 8 per day, Su 5 per day; €48); **Sligo** (3hr., 3-4 per day, €33.50); **Wexford** (3hr., 2 per day, €23.50).

Heuston Station (☎703 3299) is south of Victoria Quay, west of the city center. Buses #26, 78, and 79 run to the city center. Trains to: **Cork** (3hr., 6 per day, €56.50); **Galway** (2¾hr., 7 per day, €42); **Limerick** (2½hr., 9 per day, €46.50); **Waterford** (2½hr., 4-5 per day, €28).

Buses: Intercity buses to Dublin arrive at **Busáras Central Bus Station,** Store St. (☎836 6111), behind the Customs House and next to Connolly Station. Info available at the **Dublin Bus Office,** 59 Upper O'Connell St. (☎873 4222; www.dublinbus.ie). The Bus Éireann (www.buseireann.ie) window is open M-F 10am-5pm, Sa 10:30am-2pm. To: **Belfast** (3hr., 6-7 per day, €7); **Derry/Londonderry** (4¼hr., 4-5 per day, €12); **Donegal** (4¼hr., 4-5 per day, €12.50); **Galway** (3½hr., 15 per day, €8.50); **Limerick** (3½hr., 13 per day, €12.50); **Rosslare Harbour** (3hr., 13 per day, €12); **Sligo** (4hr., 4-6 per day, €12.25); **Wexford** (2¾hr., 10-13 per day, €11.50).

Ferries: Irish Ferries, 2-4 Merrion Row (☎661 0511; www.irishferries.com). Open M-F 9am-5pm, Sa 9:15am-12:45pm. Ferries arrive from Holyhead, UK at the **Dublin Port** (☎607 5665), from where bus #20B runs every hr. to Busáras station (€1.05). **Stena Line** ferries arrive from Holyhead at the **Dún Laoghaire** ferry terminal (☎204 7777; www.stenaline.com); from there DART trains run to the Dublin city center. Dublin Bus runs buses timed to fit the ferry schedules (€2.50).

Public Transportation: Dublin Bus, 59 Upper O'Connell St. (☎873 4222; www.dublinbus.ie). Open M 8:30am-5:30pm, Tu-F 9am-5:30pm, Sa 9am-1pm. Dublin Bus runs the **NiteLink** service to the suburbs (M-W 12:30 and 2am, Th-Sa every 20min. 12:30-4:30am; €4-6; passes not valid). **Travel Wide** passes offer unlimited rides for a day (€5) or a week (€19). **DART** trains serve the suburbs and the coast (every 10-15min. 6am-11:30pm, €1.30-1.90).

Taxis: Blue Cabs (☎802 2222) and **ABC** (☎285 5444) have wheelchair-accessible cabs (call in advance). Available 24hr.

Car Rental: Budget, 151 Lower Drumcondra Rd. (☎837 9611; www.budget.ie), and at the airport. From €27 per day. 23+.

Bike Rental: Cycleways, 185-6 Parnell St. (☎873 4748; www.cycleways.com). Open M-W and F-Sa 10am-6pm, Th 10am-8pm. €20 per day.

ORIENTATION AND PRACTICAL INFORMATION

Dublin is refreshingly compact. Street names are usually posted on the sides of buildings at most intersections and never on street-level signs. Buying a map with a street index is a smart idea. The tiniest map of all is the *EZ Map Guide* (€1.50), perfect for the traveler who wants to blend in.

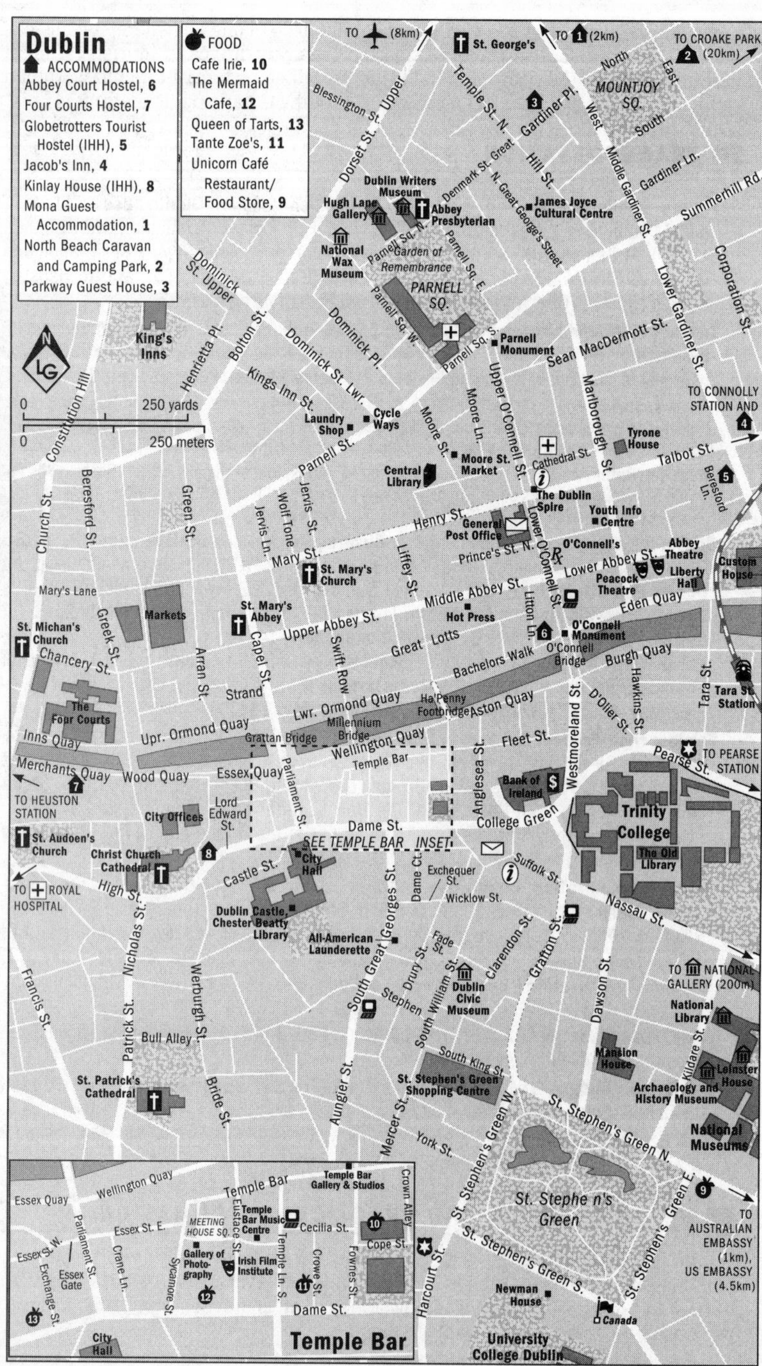
Dublin
ACCOMMODATIONS
Abbey Court Hostel, 6
Four Courts Hostel, 7
Globetrotters Tourist Hostel (IHH), 5
Jacob's Inn, 4
Kinlay House (IHH), 8
Mona Guest Accommodation, 1
North Beach Caravan and Camping Park, 2
Parkway Guest House, 3
FOOD
Cafe Irie, 10
The Mermaid Cafe, 12
Queen of Tarts, 13
Tante Zoe's, 11
Unicorn Café Restaurant/Food Store, 9
0
250 yards
0
250 meters
TO (8km)
St. George's
TO 1 (2km)
TO CROAKE PARK, 2 (20km)
Blessington St.
Dorset St. Upper
Temple St. N.
Gardiner Pl.
North
East
MOUNTJOY SQ.
West
South
Hill St.
Denmark St. Great
N. Great George's Street
Middle Gardiner St.
Gardiner Ln.
Summerhill Rd.
Dublin Writers Museum
Hugh Lane Gallery
Abbey Presbyterian
James Joyce Cultural Centre
National Wax Museum
Parnell Sq. N.
Garden of Remembrance
Parnell Sq. E.
Parnell Sq. W.
PARNELL SQ.
Parnell Sq. S.
Parnell Monument
Lower Gardiner St.
Corporation St.
Dominick St. Upper
Dominick Pl.
Dominick St. Lwr.
Bolton St.
King's Inns
Henrietta Pl.
Kings Inn St.
Sean MacDermott St.
Constitution Hill
Laundry Shop
Cycle Ways
Moore St.
Moore Ln.
Upper O'Connell St.
Marlborough St.
TO CONNOLLY STATION AND 4
Parnell St.
Moore St. Market
Cathedral St.
Tyrone House
Talbot St.
Central Library
The Dublin Spire
Beresford Ln.
5
Church St.
Beresford St.
Green St.
Jervis Ln.
Wolf Tone
Jervis St.
Henry St.
General Post Office
Youth Info Centre
Lower O'Connell St.
Mary St.
Prince's St. N.
O'Connell's
Abbey Theatre
Custom House
St. Mary's Church
Liffey St.
Lower Abbey St.
Peacock Theatre
Liberty Hall
Mary's Lane
Middle Abbey St.
Eden Quay
Markets
St. Mary's Abbey
Hot Press
St. Michan's Church
Greek St.
Capel St.
Upper Abbey St.
Litton Ln.
6
O'Connell Monument
Chancery St.
Great Lotts
O'Connell Bridge
Burgh Quay
Bachelors Walk
Arran St.
Swift Row
Hawkins St.
Tara St.
Tara St. Station
The Four Courts
Strand
Lwr. Ormond Quay
Ha'Penny Footbridge
Aston Quay
Westmoreland St.
D'Olier St.
Inns Quay
Upr. Ormond Quay
Millennium Bridge
Grattan Bridge
Wellington Quay
Fleet St.
Merchants Quay
Wood Quay
Essex Quay
Temple Bar
Anglesea St.
Pearse St.
TO PEARSE STATION
7
TO HEUSTON STATION
Parliament St.
Bank of Ireland
Lord Edward St.
City Offices
Dame St.
College Green
Trinity College
St. Audoen's Church
8
SEE TEMPLE BAR INSET
Christ Church Cathedral
City Hall
Exchequer St.
The Old Library
Castle St.
Dame Ct.
Suffolk St.
TO ROYAL HOSPITAL
High St.
Wicklow St.
Nassau St.
Dublin Castle, Chester Beatty Library
South Great Georges St.
Fade St.
All-American Launderette
Drury St.
Clarendon St.
Grafton St.
Dawson St.
Nicholas St.
Francis St.
Werburgh St.
Dublin Civic Museum
South William St.
TO NATIONAL GALLERY (200m)
Stephen
National Library
Patrick St.
Bull Alley
Aungier St.
South King St.
Kildare St.
Mansion House
Leinster House
St. Patrick's Cathedral
Bride St.
St. Stephen's Green Shopping Centre
Archaeology and History Museum
Mercer St.
St. Stephen's Green W.
St. Stephen's Green N.
National Museums
York St.
Wellington Quay
Temple Bar
Temple Bar Gallery & Studios
Crown Alley
Essex Quay
9
St. Stephe n's Green
TO AUSTRALIAN EMBASSY (1km), US EMBASSY (4.5km)
MEETING HOUSE SQ.
Eustace St.
Temple Bar Music Centre
Cecilia St.
10
Essex St. E.
Parliament St.
Crane Ln.
Essex St. W.
Gallery of Photography
Irish Film Institute
Temple Ln. S.
Crowe St.
Fownes St.
Cope St.
St. Stephen's Green E.
Harcourt St.
St. Stephen's Green S.
Exchange St.
Essex Gate
Sycamore St.
12
11
Newman House
13
Dame St.
Canada
City Hall
Temple Bar
University College Dublin

The **Liffey River** forms a natural boundary between Dublin's North and South Sides. Heuston Station and the more famous sights, posh stores, and upscale restaurants are on the **South Side.** Connolly Station, the majority of hostels, and the bus station are on the **North Side,** which is less expensive than the more touristed South, but also has the reputation of being rougher, especially at night. The streets running alongside the Liffey are called **quays** (KEYS); the name of which changes with every block. **O'Connell Street,** three blocks west of the Busáras Central Bus Station, is the primary link between northern and southern Dublin. **Henry** and **Mary Streets** comprise a pedestrian shopping zone that intersects with O'Connell St. after the **General Post Office,** two blocks from the Liffey. **Fleet Street** becomes **Temple Bar** one block south of the Liffey. **Dame Street** runs parallel to Temple Bar until **Trinity College,** at the southern edge of the district, a main street full of cheap eateries. Trinity College is the nerve center of Dublin's cultural activity.

Tourist Office: Main Office, Suffolk St. (☎669 792 083, international 0800 039 7000; www.visitdublin.com). Near Trinity College, in a converted church. Open M-Sa 9am-5:30pm, Su 10:30am-3pm. Reservation desks close 30min. earlier. **Northern Ireland Tourist Board,** 16 Nassau St. (☎679 1977 or 1850 230 230). Open M-F 9:15am-5:30pm, Sa 10am-5pm.

Embassies: Australia, Fitzwilton House, Wilton Terr., 7th fl. (☎664 5300; www.australianembassy.ie); **Canada,** 65 St. Stephen's Green (☎417 4100); **UK,** 29 Merrion Rd. (☎205 3700; www.britishembassy.ie); **US,** 42 Elgin Rd. (☎668 8777). **New Zealanders** should contact their embassy in London (p. 132).

Banks: Bank branches with **currency exchange** and 24hr. **ATMs** cluster on Lower O'Connell St., Grafton St., and near Suffolk and Dame St. Most open M-W and F 10am-4pm, Th 10am-5pm.

Luggage Storage: Connolly Station. First-come, first-served lockers €4-7. Open daily 7am-10pm. **Busáras.** Lockers €5-10. Open 24hr.

Laundromat: Laundry Shop, 191 Parnell St. (☎872 3541). Wash and dry €9. Open M-F 9am-7pm, Sa 9am-6pm.

Emergency: ☎112.

Police *(Garda)*: Dublin Metro Headquarters, Harcourt Terr. (☎666 9500); Store St. Station (☎666 8000); Fitzgibbon St. Station (☎666 8400); Pearse Station (☎666 9000).

Pharmacy: O'Connell's, 56 Lower O'Connell St. (☎873 0427). Open M-F 7am-10pm, Sa 8am-10pm, Su 10am-10pm. Other branches on Grafton St. and Westmoreland St.

Hospitals: St. James's Hospital, James St. (☎410 3000). Take bus #123. **Mater Misericordiae Hospital,** Eccles St. (☎803 2000), off Lower Dorset St. Buses #3, 10, 11, 16, 22, and 121.

Internet Access: The Internet Exchange, with branches at Cecilia St. (☎670 3000) and Fownes St. (☎635 1680) in Temple Bar. €3 per hr. Cecilia St. location open M-F 8am-2am, Sa-Su 10am-2am; Fownes St. location open M-F 8am-2am, Sa-Su 9am-2am.

Post Office: General Post Office, O'Connell St. (☎705 7000). Open M-Sa 8am-8pm. Smaller post offices open M-Tu and Th-F 9am-6pm, W 9:30am-6pm. **Postal Codes:** The city is organized into regions numbered 1-18, 20, 22, and 24, with even-numbered codes for areas south of Liffey, and odd-numbered ones to the north. The numbers radiate out from the center of the city: North City Centre is 1, South City Centre 2. Dublin is the only city in the Republic with postal codes.

ACCOMMODATIONS AND CAMPING

Reserve accommodations at least a week in advance, especially during summer and holidays. **Hostels** range from €15-26 per night. Quality **B&Bs** are plentiful and most charge €25-50 per person.

HOSTELS

Despite their location in such a cosmopolitan city, some of Dublin's mega-hostels tend towards the institutional. There are gems to be found, though, even in the very heart of Dublin. The beds south of the river fill up the fastest; they also tend to be more expensive than those to the north.

Globetrotters Tourist Hostel (IHH), 46-7 Lower Gardiner St. (☎878 8808; www.townhouseofdublin.com). Gorgeous, hotel-like accommodations at a budget price. Free Internet and luggage storage. Towels €1 with €6 deposit. Dorms €21.50-23; singles €66; triples €114; quads €127. ❷

Abbey Court Hostel, 29 Bachelor's Walk (☎878 0700; www.abbey-court.com), near O'Connell Bridge. Clean, narrow, smoke-free rooms overlook the Liffey. Continental breakfast included. Free luggage storage; security box €1. Laundry €8. Internet €1 per 15min., €2 per 40min. Dorms €18-29; doubles €76-88. ❷

Kinlay House (IHH), 2-12 Lord Edward St. (☎679 6644), a few blocks from Temple Bar, looking out onto Christ Church Cathedral. Bright, spacious rooms and oak banisters in the entrance hall. Continental breakfast included. Laundry €7. Internet €1 per 15min. Dorms €16-27; singles €40-50; doubles €54-64. ❶

Four Courts Hostel, 15-17 Merchants Quay (☎672 5863), on the South Side, along the river. Bus #748 from the airport stops next door. Long-term stays available. Continental breakfast included. Laundry €5. Free Internet. Dorms €16.50-27; singles €45-50; doubles €60-66; triples €60. ❶

Jacob's Inn, 21-28 Talbot Pl. (☎855 5660; www.isaacs.ie), 2 blocks north of the Customs House. Clean, spacious rooms. Breakfast included. Lockout 11am-3pm. Dorms €18-20; doubles €66. ❷

BED AND BREAKFASTS

B&Bs with a green shamrock sign out front are registered and approved by Bord Fáilte. On the North Side, B&Bs cluster along Upper and Lower Gardiner St., on Sheriff St., and near Parnell Sq.

Mona Guest Accommodation, 148 Clonliffe Rd. (☎837 6723). Charming house run for 38 years by an endearing proprietress. Homemade brown bread accompanies the full Irish breakfast. Open May-Oct. Singles €35; twins €66. ❸

Parkway Guest House, 5 Gardiner Pl. (☎874 0469). High-ceilinged, tidy rooms. Ask the owner, a cheery and chatty hurling veteran, for advice on the city's restaurants and pubs. Irish breakfast included. Singles €35; doubles €55-65, with bath €65-80. ❸

CAMPING

Most official campsites are far away from the city center, and while it may seem convenient, camping in **Phoenix Park** is both illegal and unsafe.

North Beach Caravan and Camping Park (☎843 7131; www.northbeach.ie), in Rush. Accessible by bus #33 from Lower Abbey St. (45min., 25 per day) and suburban rail. Open Apr.-Sept. Electricity €2. €8.50 per person, €4.50 per child. Showers €1. ❶

FOOD

Dublin's **open-air markets,** like the fun, cozy one on Sundays in Market Sq., in the heart of Temple Bar, sell fresh and cheap fixings. The cheapest **supermarket** is the **Dunnes Stores** chain; there is one at St. Stephen's Green (☎478 0188; open M and F 8:30am-8pm, Tu-W and Sa 8:30am-7pm, Th 8:30am-9pm, Su 10am-7pm), the ILAC Centre, and North Earl St. **Temple Bar** has creative eateries for every budget.

Queen of Tarts, Dame St. (☎670 7499), across from City Hall. This little red gem offers homemade pastries, scones, cakes, and coffee. Breakfast €4-6. Scrumptious flaky scones €2.95. Open M-F 7:30am-6pm, Sa 9am-6pm, Su 9:30am-6pm. ❷

Unicorn Café Restaurant, 12B Merrion Ct. (☎676 2182). Left off Merrion Row, behind Unicorn Market and Cafe. Legendary Italian restaurant. Entrees from €13. Open M-Th 12:30-3:30pm and 6-11pm, F-Sa 12:30-3:30pm and 6-11:30pm. ❹

Unicorn Food Store and Café, Merrion Row (☎678 8588), offers food from the Unicorn Café Restaurant kitchen for a fraction of the price. Open daily 8am-6pm. ❷

Tante Zoe's, 1 Crowe St. (☎679 4407), across from the back entrance of the Foggy Dew pub. New Orleans Creole cuisine in an elegantly casual setting. Entrees €14-27. Open daily noon-4pm and 5:30pm-midnight. ❹

Cafe Irie, 11 Fownes St. (☎672 5090). On the left above the clothing store Sé Sí Progressive. Small, hidden eatery with impressive selection of sandwiches (€4.50-6.25). Vegan-friendly. Open M-W and F-Sa 9am-7pm, Th 9am-8pm. ❶

The Mermaid Cafe, 69-70 Dame St. (☎670 8236), near Great Georges St. Outstanding Su brunch. Sophisticated entrees €18-28. Open M-Sa 12:30-2:30pm and 6-11pm, Su 12:30-3:30pm and 6-9pm. ❺

SIGHTS

Most of Dublin's sights lie less than 2km from O'Connell Bridge, and the 2hr. **Historical Walking Tour** stops at many of them. Meet at Trinity College's main gate. (☎878 0227. Daily May-Sept. 11am, 3pm; Apr. and Oct. 11am; Nov.-Mar. F-Su 11am. Call for info on group tours. €10, students €8.)

TRINITY COLLEGE AND GRAFTON STREET. The British built Trinity in 1592 as a Protestant seminary that would "civilize the Irish and cure them of Popery"; the Catholic Church still deemed it a cardinal sin to attend Trinity until the 1960s. A not-to-be-missed stop on the tourist trail, the college today is one of Ireland's best universities. *(Between Westmoreland and Grafton St. The main entrance fronts the block-long roundabout now called College Green. ☎608 1724; www.tcd.ie. Grounds always open. Free.)* Trinity's **Old Library** holds an invaluable collection of ancient manuscripts, including the renowned and beautiful *Book of Kells*. Upstairs, the awe-inspiring **Long Room** contains Ireland's oldest harp—the **Brian Ború Harp,** seen on Irish coins—and one of the few remaining copies of the original **1916 proclamations** of the Republic of Ireland. *(On the south side of Library Sq. ☎608 2320; www.tcd.ie/library. June-Sept. M-Sa 9:30am-5pm, Su 9:30am-4:30pm; Oct.-May M-Sa 9:30am-5pm, Su noon-4:30pm. €8, students €7.)* The few blocks south of College Green are off-limits to cars, making the area a playground for pedestrians. Street performers on Grafton Street keep the crowds entertained.

KILDARE STREET AND TEMPLE BAR. The **Natural History Museum** displays fascinating examples of taxidermy, including enormous Irish deer skeletons. *(Upper Merrion St. Open Tu-Sa 10am-5pm, Su 2-5pm. Free.)* The **National Gallery** has a collection of over 2500 paintings, including canvases by Brueghel, Caravaggio, Goya, Rembrandt, and Vermeer. *(Merrion Sq. W. Open M-W and F-Sa 9:30am-5:30pm, Th 9:30am-8:30pm, Su noon-5:30pm. Free.)* The **National Museum of Archaeology and History,** Dublin's largest museum, has artifacts spanning the last two millennia, including the **Tara Brooch** and the bloody vest of nationalist **James Connolly.** *(Kildare St., next to Leinster House. Open Tu-Sa 10am-5pm, Su 2-5pm. Free.)* West of Trinity, between Dame St. and the Liffey, the Temple Bar neighborhood has rapidly become one of Europe's hottest nightspots. The government-sponsored Temple Bar Properties spent over €40 million to build a fleet of arts-related attractions. Among the most inviting are:

The Irish Film Institute, which screens specialty and art-house films; Ireland's only **Gallery of Photography;** and the **Temple Bar Music Centre.** *(The Irish Film Institute, 6 Eustace St. Gallery of Photography, Meeting House Sq. Temple Bar Music Centre, Curved St.)*

DAME STREET AND THE CATHEDRALS. At the **Chester Beatty Library,** behind Dublin Castle, visitors can see the treasures bequeathed to Ireland by American mining magnate Alfred Chester Beatty, including Asian art, sacred scriptures, illustrated texts, and much more. *(Open May-Sept. M-F 10am-5pm, Sa 11am-5pm, Su 1-5pm; Oct.-Apr. closed M. Free.)* King John built **Dublin Castle** in 1204, and for the next 700 years it would be the seat of British rule in Ireland. Since 1938, each president of Ireland has been inaugurated here. *(Dame St., at the intersection of Parliament and Castle St. Open M-F 10am-5pm, Sa-Su 2-5pm. €4.50, students €3.50. Grounds free.)* Sitric Silkenbeard, King of the Dublin Norsemen, built a wooden church on the site of the **Christ Church Cathedral** around 1038; Strongbow rebuilt it in stone in 1169. Fragments of the ancient pillars are now scattered about like bleached bones. *(At the end of Dame St., across from the castle. Take bus #50 from Eden Quay or 78A from Aston Quay. Open daily 9:45am-5pm except during services. €5, students €2.50.)* **St. Patrick's Cathedral,** Ireland's largest, dates to the 12th century, although Sir Benjamin Guinness remodeled much of it in 1864. Jonathan Swift spent his last years as Dean of St. Patrick's; his grave is marked on the floor of the south nave. *(Patrick St. Open Mar.-Oct. daily 9am-6pm; Nov.-Feb. Sa 9am-5pm, Su 10am-3pm. €4.50, students €3.50.)*

GUINNESS BREWERY AND KILMAINHAM. Guinness brews its black magic at the St. James's Gate Brewery, next door to the **Guinness Storehouse.** Take a look at the quirky seven-story atrium containing Arthur Guinness's 9000-year lease on the original brewery. And then drink, pilgrim, drink. *(St. James's Gate. From Christ Church Cathedral, follow High St. west through its name changes: Cornmarket, Thomas, and James. Or, take bus #51B or 78A from Aston Quay or #123 from O'Connell St. Open daily July-Aug. 9:30am-8pm; Sept.-June 9:30am-5pm. €14, students over 18 €9.50.)* Almost all of the rebels who fought in Ireland's struggle for independence from 1792-1921 spent time at **Kilmainham Gaol.** Tours, every 30min., wind through the frigid, eerie limestone corridors of the prison. *(Inchicore Rd. Take bus #51b, 51c, 78a, or 79 from Aston Quay. Open Apr.-Sept. daily 9:30am-5pm; Oct.-Mar. M-F 9:30am-4pm, Su 10am-5pm. €5, students €2.)*

> **THE REAL DEAL.** Though the Guiness Storehouse may be a Dublin tourist hotspot, it's all style and no substance; the only highlight seems to be a complimentary drink in the admittedly snazzy penthouse Gravity Bar. For more interesting and less expensive cultural experience, try one of the city's free national museums. If it's a pint you're after, just head to a pub.

O'CONNELL STREET AND PARNELL SQUARE. O'Connell St., once Europe's widest street, now holds the less honorable distinction of being Dublin's biggest shopping thoroughfare. Statues of Irish leaders such as **Daniel O'Connell, Charles Parnell,** and **James Larkin** adorn the traffic islands. Don't look too hard for **Nelson's Pillar,** though—this free-standing pillar, which had honored Trafalgar for 150 years, was blown up by the IRA in 1966, on the 50th anniversary of the Easter Rising. Today, it may just be a place to send a postcard, but the **General Post Office,** O'Connell St., was the nerve center of the 1916 Easter Rising; Padraig Pearse read the Proclamation of Irish Independence from its steps. Outside, a number of bullet nicks are still visible. *(☎705 7000. Open M-Sa 8am-8pm.)* The city's rich literary heritage comes to life at **The Dublin Writers' Museum,** which displays rare editions, manuscripts, and memorabilia of Beckett, Wilde, Yeats, and other famous Irish writers. *(18 Parnell Sq. N. Open June-Aug. M-F 10am-6pm, Sa 10am-5pm, Su 11am-5pm; Sept.-May M-Sa 10am-5pm, Su 11am-5pm. €6.50, students €5.50.)* The **James Joyce Cultural Centre** features a wide range of

Joyceana, including portraits of the individuals who inspired his characters. Call for info on lectures and Bloomsday events. *(35 N. Great Georges St. ☎878 8547. Open July-Aug. M-Sa 9:30am-5pm, Su 11am-5pm; Sept.-June M-Sa 9:30am-5pm, Su 12:30-5pm. €10, students €9.)*

OTHER SIGHTS. Once a private estate, **St. Stephen's Green** was later bequeathed to the city by the Guinness clan. Today, its 27 acres teem with all sorts of life. During the summer, musical and theatrical productions are given near the old bandstand. *(Open M-Sa 8am-dusk, Su 10am-dusk.)* The dry air in the nave of **St. Michan's Church** has preserved the corpses in the vaults; it was these seemingly living bodies that inspired Bram Stoker to write about the living deadman in *Dracula*. *(Church St. Open Mar. 17-Oct. M-F 10am-12:45pm and 2-4:30pm, Sa 10am-12:45pm; Nov.-Mar. 17 reduced hours. Church of Ireland services Su 10am. Crypt tours €3.50, students €3.)* **Four Courts,** Inn's Quay, has an impressive facade and was once seized by members of the IRA, sparking the Irish Civil War, when members of the Free State Government attacked the garrison there. The building now houses Ireland's highest national court. *(Open M-F 9am-4:30pm. Free.)* At the **Old Jameson Distillery,** learn how science, grain, and tradition come together to create whiskey. Be quick to volunteer in the beginning and you'll get the chance to taste-test a tray of six different whiskeys from around the world. Even those not chosen are blessed, however, with a glass of firewater at the end. *(Bow St. From O'Connell St., turn onto Henry St. and continue straight as the street dwindles to Mary St., then Mary Ln., then May Ln.; the warehouse is down a cobblestone street on the left. Tours daily every 45min. 9:30am-5:30pm. €8.75, students €7.)*

ENTERTAINMENT AND NIGHTLIFE

Whether you fancy poetry or punk, Dublin is equipped to entertain you. The free *Event Guide*, available at the tourist office and Temple Bar restaurants, is a comprehensive listing of the latest on the scene.

THEATER

Dublin has no true theater district, but smaller theater companies thrive off Dame St. and Temple Bar. Call ahead for tickets. Showtime is generally around 8pm.

Abbey Theatre, 26 Lower Abbey St. (☎878 7222). Ireland's national theater was founded in 1904 by Yeats and Lady Gregory to promote Irish culture and modernist theater. Synge's *Playboy of the Western World* premiered here in 1907. Tickets €15-30; Sa 2:30pm matinee €15, students €9.50. Box office open M-Sa 10:30am-7pm.

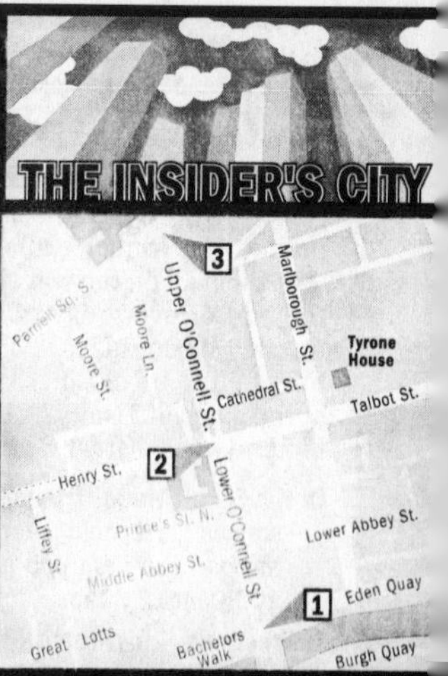

INFIDELITY ON O'CONNELL STREET

This main drag was once called the Street of the Three Adulterers.

1. **O'Connell Monument:** Daniel O'Connell led the 19th-century Catholic Emancipation movement, but he also sparked controversy with his purported infidelity.
2. **Dublin Spire:** Dublin's Millennium Spire, unceremoniously nicknamed "Stiffy by the Liffey," was once the site of a pillar erected in honor of Horatio Nelson, a British Admiral whose extramarital affair produced his only child. The pillar was blown up by former IRA members in 1966.
3. **Parnell Monument:** Charles Stewart Parnell was the leader of the Home Rule Party whose infamous, long-term affair with Kitty O'Shea led to his political downfall. Parnell's statue points in the direction of the Rotunda Hospital, which was formerly Dublin's primary maternity ward.

Peacock Theatre, 26 Lower Abbey St. (☎878 7222). The Abbey's experimental studio theater downstairs offers evening shows in addition to occasional lunchtime plays, concerts, and poetry. Tickets €10-17.

PUBLIN

James Joyce once proposed that a "good puzzle would be to cross Dublin without passing a pub." A radio station later offered €125 to the first person to solve the puzzle. The winner explained that you could take any route—you'd just have to visit them all on the way. Pubs dominate the urban landscape and quickly fill up at the end of every day of the week. Normal pub hours end at 11:30pm Sunday through Wednesday; 12:30am Thursday through Saturday, but an increasing number of pubs are closing "late," meaning at least after midnight. Begin your journey at the gates of Trinity College, moving onto Grafton St., stumble onto Camden St., teeter down S. Great Georges St., and finally, crawl into the Temple Bar area.

The Stag's Head, 1 Dame St. (☎679 3701). Gorgeously atmospheric Victorian pub with stained glass, marble-topped round tables, and a gigantic deer head suspended above the bar. Excellent pub grub. Entrees €7.50-11. Open M-Th 10:30am-11:30pm, F-Sa 10:30am-12:30am. Kitchen open M-F noon-3:30pm and 5-7pm, Sa noon-2:30pm.

Whelan's, 25 Wexford St. (☎478 0766). Dark, busy pub with wood-filled interior is a venue for big-name acts. Live music nightly from 8:30pm (doors open at 8pm). Cover €7-15. Lunch (€8-12) served 12:30-2pm. Open late daily.

The Porter House, 16-18 Parliament St. (☎671 5715). A huge selection of beer including 10 home brews. Live music every night. Open M-Tu and Th 11:30am-11:30pm, W 11:30am-midnight, F-Sa 11:30am-2:30am, Su 11:30am-1:30am.

McDaid's, 3 Harry St. (☎679 4395), off Grafton St. across from Anne St. Old books on high shelves recall McDaid's status as the center of the Irish literary scene in the 50s. The din of the packed crowd fills this high-ceilinged pub. Open M-W 10:30am-11:30pm, Th-Sa 10:30am-12:30am, Su 12:30-11pm.

Davy Byrne's, 21 Duke St. (☎677 5217), off Grafton St. Lively, middle-aged crowd fills the pub where Joyce set *Ulysses*'s Cyclops chapter. Gourmet pub food served all day. Open M-W 9am-11:30pm, Th-Sa 9am-12:30am, Su 12:30-11pm.

Brogan's Bar, 75 Dame St. (☎679 9570). Unassuming little spot ignored by tourists. Marvel at the impressive collection of Guinness paraphernalia as you sip the "black magic." Open M-Th 4-11:30pm, F-Sa 1pm-12:30am, Su 1-11:30pm.

The Celt, 81-82 Talbot St. (☎878 8665). Step out of the city and into Olde Ireland. Small, comfortably worn, and truly welcoming. Nightly trad. Open M-Th 10:30am-11:30pm, F-Sa 10:30am-12:30am, Su 12:30pm-11pm.

CLUBS

As a general rule, clubs open at 10:30 or 11pm, but things don't really heat up in most locations until at least midnight, after some pubs start closing. Clubbing is an expensive way to end the night, since covers run €7-20, and pints can cost more than €5. The gay nightclub scene is alive and well, with venues (usually rented-out clubs) open almost every night. Keep up-to-date by checking out the queer pages of *In Dublin* for gay-friendly pubs, restaurants, and clubs, or try **Gay Switchboard Dublin** for event info and updates. (☎872 1055. M-F and Su 8-10pm, Sa 3:30-6pm.)

The PoD, 35 Harcourt St. (☎478 0225). A futuristic club that's serious about music. **The Red Box,** upstairs, is an intense warehouse-like club. Cover €10-20, Th €5 with ISIC.

The Dragon, 64-65 S. Great Georges St. (☎478 1590), a few doors down from The George. Young, hot–the place to be. Dublin's newest gay club flows seamlessly from lounge to bar to dancefloor and packs a happening crowd on weekends. 18+. No cover. Open M-W 5-11:30pm, Th-Sa 5pm-2:30am, Su 5pm-1am.

The Front Lounge, Parliament St. (☎670 4112). The red velvet seats of this gay bar are filled nightly by a young, trendy crowd. Open M and W noon-11:30pm, Th noon-1:30am, F-Sa noon-2am, Su 4-11:30pm.

Gaiety, S. King St. (☎677 1717), at the end of Grafton St. Elegant theater shows its late-night wild side every F-Sa. 3 bar areas. Best of all worlds with salsa, jazz, swing, Latin, and soul. Cover about €10. Open F-Sa 11:45pm-4am.

DAYTRIP FROM DUBLIN

HOWTH PENINSULA. Only 14.5km from Dublin, Howth (rhymes with "both") Peninsula is an popular destination for Dubliners looking to escape the city. A 4hr. **cliff walk** circles the peninsula, passing heather and thousands of seabird nests. To get to the trailhead from town, turn left at the DART station and follow Harbour Rd. past East Pier for about 20min. Just offshore is **Ireland's Eye,** a former monk sanctuary turned avian refuge. The seals flock to **Nicky's Plaice** on West Pier (☎832 3557; www.nickysplaice.ie) when a bell rings to announce feeding time each day at noon and 3:30pm. To reach the private **Howth Castle,** a charming patchwork of architectural styles, go right as you exit the DART station, walk 400m and then left, at the entrance to the Deer Park Hotel. To get to Howth, take a northbound DART **train** to the end of the line (30min., 6 per hr., €1.80).

SOUTHEASTERN IRELAND

The region is famous for its strawberries and oysters, whose aphrodisiacal powers may account for the gaggles of children playing on its beaches. Roundtowers, those haunting bastions of faith under siege, litter the countryside, from St. Canice's in the medieval city of Kilkenny to the tower perched on the Rock of Cashel, the oldest structure to conquer its heights. Inland, mesmerizingly green fields and stunning mountain views provide an exciting contrast to the trad and rock pumping through the pubs of Waterford, Kilkenny, and Wexford.

FERRIES TO FRANCE AND BRITAIN

Stena Line (☎053 61560) and **Irish Ferries** (☎053 33158) bridge passengers from Rosslare Harbour to Pembroke, Wales (2-6 per day) and to Roscoff and Cherbourg, France (1 every other day). **Eurail** passes are valid on ferries to France.

THE WICKLOW MOUNTAINS ☎0404

Over 600m tall, carpeted in fragrant heather and pleated by sparkling rivers, the Wicklow summits are home to grazing sheep, scattered villages, beautiful lakes, and monastic ruins. Tour the region by the **Wicklow Way,** a 125km hiking trail. The blessed valley of **Glendalough** is home to St. Kevin's 6th-century monastery. **St. Kevin's Bus Service** (☎01 281 8119) arrives in Glendalough from St. Stephen's Green in Dublin (2 per day, round-trip €14). The **National Park Information Office,** between the two lakes, is the best source for hiking advice. (☎45425. Open May-Aug. daily 10am-6pm, closed for lunch; Sept.-Apr. Sa-Su 10am-dusk.) When the park office is closed, call the **ranger office** (☎45800), located in nearby Trooperstown Wood. Shack up at **The Glendalough Hostel (HI) ❷,** 5min. up the road from the Glendalough Visitor Centre. (☎45342. Breakfast €4-6.50. Laundry €5. Dorms June-Oct. €22.50. Nov.-May €18; private rooms €24-25 per person. €2 HI discount.) Just 1.5km up the road, **Laragh** has food options and plenty of B&Bs. Public transportation in the mountains is limited.

ROSSLARE HARBOUR ☎053

Rosslare Harbour is a useful departure point for Wales or France. If staying overnight, try the seaside **Mrs. O'Leary's Farmhouse ❸**, off N25 in Kilrane. It's a 15min. drive from town, so call for pickup from town. (☎33134. Singles €30, low season €27.) **Trains** run from the ferry port to Dublin (3hr., 3 per day, €17.50) and Limerick (2hr., 1-2 per day, €17.50) via Waterford (1hr., €9). **Buses** run from the same area to: Dublin (3hr., 10-12 per day, €15); Galway via Waterford (4 per day, €24); Limerick (M-Sa 5 per day, Su 3 per day; €19); Tralee (M-Sa 4 per day, Su 2 per day; €23). Contact Wexford Tourism (☎52900) for **tourist information.**

KILKENNY ☎056

Nine churches share the streets with 80 pubs in Kilkenny (pop. 30,000), Ireland's best-preserved medieval town. One-hour **Tynan Walking Tours** explore Kilkenny's folkloric tradition. (☎087 265 1745. Tours depart from tourist office. €6, students €5.50.) The 13th-century **Kilkenny Castle,** complete with well-maintained public grounds, housed the Earls of Ormonde until 1932. (☎21450. Open daily June-Aug. 9:30am-7pm; Sept. 10am-6:30pm; Oct.-Mar. 10:30am-12:45pm and 2-5pm; Apr.-May 10:30am-5pm. Required tour €5, students €2.) Climb the 30m tower of **St. Canice's Cathedral,** up the hill off Dean St., for a panoramic view. (☎64971. Open June-Aug. M-Sa 9am-6pm, Su 2-6pm; Apr.-May and Sept. M-Sa 10am-5pm, Su 2-5pm; Oct.-Mar. M-Sa 10am-1pm and 2-4pm, Su 2-4pm.) **Kilkenny Tourist Hostel ❶**, 35 Parliament St., is close to all the pubs. (☎63541. Dorms €16.) **Pordylo's ❹**, on Butterslip Ln. between Kieran and High St., has excellent international cuisine at high prices. (Entrees €17-23. Open daily 5:30-11pm.) A **Dunnes** supermarket is on Kieran St. (☎61655. Open M-Sa 8:30am-10pm, Su 9:30am-7pm.) Start your crawl at the traditional pubs at the end of **Parliament Street,** then work your way to the more modern late bars on **John Street. Trains** (☎22024) arrive at Dublin Rd. from Dublin (2hr.) and Waterford (45min.). **Buses** (☎64933) arrive at Dublin Rd. and the city center from: Cork (3hr., 2-3 per day, €16); Dublin (2hr., 5-6 per day, €10); Galway (5hr., 3-6 per day, €19); Limerick (2½hr., 2-4 per day, €13.30); Rosslare Harbour (2hr., 2-3 per day, €7); Waterford (1½hr., 2 per day, €6.35). The **tourist office** is on Rose Inn St. (☎51500. Open Mar.-Sept. M-F 9am-6pm, Sa 10am-6pm; Oct.-Feb. M-Sa 9am-5pm.)

WATERFORD ☎051

Waterford is Ireland's oldest city, founded in AD 914 by the grandson of Viking Ivor the Boneless. The highlight is the **Waterford Crystal Factory,** 3km away on N25. One-hour tours allow you to witness the transformation of grains of sand into molten glass and finally into sparkling crystal. Catch the City Imp minibus outside Dunnes on Michael St. (10-15min., every 15-20min., €1.20) and request a stop at the factory. (☎332 500. Open daily Mar.-Oct. 8:30am-6pm; Nov.-Feb. 9am-5pm. Tours every 15min. during high season. Tours €7.50, students €3.50. Gallery free.) Head to **Waterford Treasures** at the granary and see Viking artifacts and the only remaining item of Henry VIII's clothing, a velvet hat. (☎304 500. Open Apr.-Sept. M-Sa 9:30am-6pm, Su 11am-6pm; Oct.-Mar. M-Sa 10am-5pm, Su 11am-5pm. €6, students €4.50.) Stellar tour guide Jack Burtchaell keeps audiences entertained and enthralled on his **Walking Tour of Historic Waterford.** (☎873 711. 1hr. tours depart from the Granary Museum Mar.-Oct. daily 11:45am, 1:45pm. €5.)

Let Mrs. Ryan of **Beechwood ❷,** 7 Cathedral Sq., invite you into her charming house. (☎876 677. Doubles €50.) **Haricot's Wholefood Restaurant ❸,** 11 O'Connell St., serves healthy traditional food with bohemian flair. (☎841 299. Entrees €9.50. Open M-F 10am-8pm, Sa 10am-6pm.) The Quay is crowded with pubs. **T&H Doolan's,** on George's St., has been serving crowds for 300 years. (Pub food €13-19.

Trad nightly at 9:30pm.) A younger crowd flocks to the modern late bars at the cross of **John** and **Parnell Streets. Trains** (☎317 889) leave from The Quay across the bridge for: Dublin (2½hr., M-F 5-6 per day, €17-21); Kilkenny (40min., 3-5 per day, €8); Limerick (2¼hr., M-Sa 2 per day, €15.50); Rosslare Harbour (1hr., M-Sa 2 per day, €10). **Buses** depart from The Quay for: Cork (2½hr., 10-13 per day, €14.50); Dublin (2¾hr., 6-12 per day, €10); Galway (4¾hr., 5-6 per day, €18.50); Kilkenny (1hr., 1 per day, €8); Limerick (2½hr.; M-Th, Su 6 per day, F 7 per day; €14.50); Rosslare Harbour (1¼hr., 3-5 per day, €12.50). The **tourist office** is on The Quay, across from the bus station. (☎875 823. Open M-F 9am-6pm, Sa 10am-6pm.)

CASHEL ☎062

Cashel sits at the foot of the 90m **Rock of Cashel** (a.k.a **St. Patrick's Rock** or **Cashel of the Kings**), a huge limestone outcropping topped by medieval buildings. (Open daily mid-June to mid-Sept. 9am-7pm; mid-Mar. to mid-June 9am-5:30pm; mid-Sept. to mid-Mar. 9am-4:30pm. €5, students €2.) Down the cow path from the Rock lie the ruins of **Hore Abbey,** built by Cistercian monks and presently inhabited by sheep. The **GPA-Bolton Library,** on John St., houses ecclesiastical texts and rare manuscripts. (☎61944. Open M-F 10am-4:30pm; inquire at the tourist office about tours.) The internationally acclaimed **Brú Ború Heritage Centre,** at the base of the Rock, stages traditional music and dance performances. (☎61122. Performances mid-June to mid-Sept. Tu-Sa 9pm. €16, with dinner €42.) Ten minutes out of town on Dundrum Rd. is **O'Brien's Farmhouse Hostel ❶.** (☎61003. Laundry €8-10. Camping €7.50 per person. Dorms €15; doubles €50.) **Buses** (☎061 33333) leave from Main St. near the tourist office for Dublin (3hr., 6 per day, €15) and Cork (1½hr., 6 per day, €12). The **tourist office** is in City Hall on Main St. (☎62511. Open mid-Mar. to mid-Sept. daily 9:30am-5:30pm; mid-Sept. to mid-Mar. M-F only.)

IRELAND

SOUTHWESTERN IRELAND

With a dramatic landscape that ranges from lakes and mountains to stark ocean-battered cliffs, Southwestern Ireland is a land rich in storytellers and artists. Outlaws and rebels once lurked in the hidden coves and glens now overrun by visitors. The Ring of Kerry and Cork's southern coast offer stunning scenery.

FERRIES TO FRANCE AND BRITAIN

Swansea-Cork Ferries (☎021 427 1166) goes between Cork and Swansea, South Wales (10hr., 1 per day, from €39). **Brittany Ferries** (☎021 427 7801) sails from Cork to Roscoff, France (12hr., Sa only, from €99).

CORK ☎021

Cork (pop. 150,000) hosts most of the cultural activities in the southwest. River quays and pub-lined streets reveal architecture both grand and grimy, evidence of "Rebel Cork's" history of resistance, ruin, and reconstruction.

TRANSPORTATION

Trains: Kent Station, Lower Glanmire Rd. (☎450 6766; www.irishrail.ie), across the river from the city center. Open M-Sa 6:30am-8pm, Su 7:50am-8pm. To: **Dublin** (3hr.; M-Sa 9 per day, Su 8 per day; €55); **Killarney** (2hr.; M-Sa 7 per day, Su 4 per day; €25.50); **Limerick** (1½hr., 5 per day, €25.50); **Tralee** (2½hr., 3 per day, €30.50).

Buses: Parnell Pl. (☎450 8188), 2 blocks east of St. Patrick's Bridge on Merchant's Quay. Info desk open daily 9am-5:30pm. **Bus Éireann** goes to all major cities: **Dublin** (4½hr.; M-Sa 6 per day, Su 5 per day; €23); **Galway** (4hr., 12 per day, €17); **Killarney** (2hr.; M-Sa 13 per day, Su 11 per day; €13); **Limerick** (2hr., 14 per day, €13.20); **Rosslare Harbour** (4hr., 3 per day, €18.50); **Sligo** (7hr., 5 per day, €23); **Tralee** (2½hr., 12 per day, €14); **Waterford** (2¼hr., M-Sa 13 per day, €14.50).

Public Transportation: Downtown **buses** run M-Sa every 10-30min. 7:30am-11:15pm, with reduced service Su 10am-11:15pm. Fares from €1. From downtown, catch buses (and their schedules) along St. Patrick St., across from the Father Matthew statue.

ORIENTATION AND PRACTICAL INFORMATION

Cork is compact and pedestrian-friendly. **St. Patrick Street** becomes **Grand Parade** to the west; to the north it crosses **Merchant's Quay,** home of the bus station. North across **St. Patrick's Bridge, MacCurtain Street** runs east to **Lower Glanmire Road** and the train station before becoming the N8 to Dublin. Downtown action concentrates on the generally parallel **Paul, Oliver Plunkett,** and **St. Patrick Streets.**

Tourist Office: Tourist House, Grand Parade (☎425 5100), near the corner of South Mall, offers accommodations booking (€4), souvenirs, and a free Cork city guide and map. Open June-Aug. M-F 9am-7pm, Sa 9am-5pm; July-Aug. M-F 9am-7pm, Sa 9am-5pm, Su 10am-5pm; Sept.-May M-Sa 9:15am-5:15pm.

Banks: Ulster Bank Limited, 88 St. Patrick St. (☎427 0618). Open M 10am-5pm, Tu-F 10am-4pm. **Bank of Ireland,** 70 St. Patrick St. (☎427 7177). Open M 10am-5pm, Tu-F 10am-4pm. Most banks in Cork have 24hr. **ATMs.**

Police (*Garda*): Anglesea St. (☎452 2000).

Pharmacies: Regional Late-Night Pharmacy (☎434 4575), on Wilton Rd. opposite the Regional Hospital on bus #8. Open M-F 9am-10pm, Sa-Su 10am-10pm. **Phelan's Late Night,** 9 Patrick St. (☎427 2511). Open M-F 8:30am-10pm, Su 10am-10pm.

Hospitals: Mercy Hospital (☎427 1971), on Grenville Pl. €45 fee for emergency room visits. **Cork University Hospital,** Wilton Rd. (☎454 6400), on the #8 bus route.

Internet Access: Web Workhouse (☎427 3090), near the post office between St. Patrick and Oliver Plunkett St. 8am-5pm €3 per hr., 5pm-3am €2.50 per hr., 3-8am €1.50 per hr.; Su €2.50 per hr. all day. Open 24hr.

Post Office: (☎485 1049), on Oliver Plunkett St. Open M-Sa 9am-5:30pm.

ACCOMMODATIONS

B&Bs cluster along **Patrick's Hill,** on **Glanmire Road,** rising upward from St. Patrick's Bridge, and on **Western Road** near University College. Call ahead in summer.

Sheila's Budget Accommodation Centre (IHH), 4 Belgrave Pl. (☎450 5562; www.sheilashostel.ie), at Wellington Rd. and York St. Hill. Sauna €2 for 40min. Breakfast €2.50. Internet €1 per 20min. Reception 24hr. Check-out 10:30am. Dorms €14-16.50; singles €28-30; doubles €44-50. ❶

Kinlay House (IHH), Bob and Joan's Walk (☎450 8966; www.kinlayhouse.ie), to the right of St. Anne's Church. Bright rooms and sunny yellow walls, with a plush lounge area and Internet room. Continental breakfast included. Internet €1 per 15min. Laundry €8. Free parking. Dorms €14-16; doubles €44. ❶

Roman House, 3 St. John's Terr. (☎450 3606), on Upper John St. across from Kinlay House. Colorful Roman House is Cork's only B&B catering specifically to GLBT travelers. Walls display proprietor's artwork. Singles from €45; doubles €65. ❹

Cork International Hostel (An Óige/HI), 1-2 Redclyffe, Western Rd. (☎454 3289), a 15min. walk from the Grand Parade. Continental breakfast €4. Internet €1 per 15min. Reception 10:30am-midnight. Dorms €15-17. ❶

FOOD

Restaurants and cafes abound on the lanes connecting **Patrick Street, Paul Street,** and **Oliver Plunkett Street.** On Paul St., **Tesco** is the biggest grocery store in town. (☎427 0791. Open M-W 9am-8pm, Th-F 9am-10pm, Sa 8:30am-8pm, Su noon-6pm.)

Tribes (☎427 6070), on Tuckey St. Full menu and a global spectrum of coffee keeps a young crowd buzzing into the early hours. Open M-Th 10:30am-midnight, F-Sa 10:30am-4am, Su 3pm-midnight. ❶

Quay Co-op, 24 Sullivan's Quay (☎431 7660). Delicious vegetarian and vegan meals. Soups €4. Specials €8.90. Open M-Sa 9am-9pm. ❷

Amicus, 14A French Church St. (☎427 6455). Sophisticated decor. Artistic, delicious dishes served in a spacious dining room. Lunch €7-10. Dinner €10-23. Open M-Sa 8am-10:30pm, Su noon-9:30pm. ❸

SIGHTS

All Cork's sights can be reached by foot; pick up the *Cork Area City Guide* (€1.90) at the tourist office. In the western part of town lie the brooding Gothic buildings, manicured lawns, and sculpture-studded grounds of the 1845 **University College Cork.** *(☎490 3000; www.ucc.ie.)* Across the walkway from UCC's front gate, **Fitzgerald Park** has beautiful rose gardens and art exhibits courtesy of the **Cork Public Museum.** *(☎427 0679. Open M-F 11am-1pm and 2:15-5pm, Su 3-5pm. Free.)* At the western end of Fitzgerald Park is a white footbridge; cross it and make a right on Sunday's Well Rd. to reach **Cork City Gaol.** Cork's social history comes alive in multimedia tours of the former prison. *(☎430 5022. Open daily Mar.-Oct. 9:30am-6pm; Nov.-Feb. 10am-5pm. €6, students €5. Audio tour included.)* In the old city, **St. Finbarr's Cathedral,** Bishop St., is a testament to the Victorian obsession with the neo-Gothic and houses contemporary art exhibits during the summer. *(☎496 3387. Open M-Sa 10am-5:30pm. €3, students €1.50.)* North across the river in the Shandon neighborhood, the steeple of **St. Anne's Church** houses the famous "Bells of Shandon." Its four clock faces are notoriously out of sync and has earned the church its nickname, "the four-faced liar." *(Open June-Sept. M-Sa 10am-5:30pm. €6, students €5.)*

NIGHTLIFE

The lively streets of Cork make finding entertainment easy. *WhazOn! Cork*, free at local shops, helps stay on top of the scene and **Oliver Plunkett Street, Union Quay,** and **South Main Street** for pubs and live music. **The Old Oak,** Oliver Plunkett St. across from the General Post Office, is huge, packed, and great for the young crowd. (☎427 6165. Open M-Sa noon-2am, Su noon-1am. Kitchen open M-Sa noon-3pm.) For those craving good alternative rock, **An Brog** (☎427 1392), at the corner of Oliver Plunkett St. and Grand Parade, is ideal. Techno and dance is spun nightly for the trendy at **One,** 1 Phoenix St., off of Smith St. (☎480 6707. Cover €5-10.)

DAYTRIP FROM CORK

BLARNEY. Tourists eager for quintessential Irish scenery and a cold kiss head northwest from Cork to see Blarney Castle and its legendary Blarney Stone. Some insist that those who kiss it will acquire the gift of eloquence. Visitors can explore the castle's many rooms, retracing the steps of medieval royalty. (Buses run from Cork to Blarney 10-16 per day, round-trip €4.50. Open June-Aug. M-Sa 9am-7pm, Su 9:30am-5:30pm; Sept. M-Sa 9am-6:30pm, Su 9:30am-sundown; Oct.-Apr. M-Sa 9am-sundown, Su 9:30am-sundown; May M-Sa 9am-6:30pm, Su 9:30am-5:30pm. Last admission 30min. before closing. Castle and grounds €7, students €5.)

SCHULL AND THE MIZEN HEAD PENINSULA ☎028

The seaside hamlet of Schull is an ideal base for exploring the craggy southwest tip of Ireland. A calm harbor and numerous shipwrecks make it a diving paradise; the **Watersports Centre Ltd.** rents gear. (☎28554. Open June-Oct. M-F 9:30am-1pm and 2-5:30pm, Sa 10am-1pm and 2-5:30pm.) The coastal road winds past **Barley Coast Beach** and continues on to **Mizen Head.** The Mizen becomes more scenic and less populated farther west from Schull, but it's mobbed during July and August when sun-loving vacationers pack the sandy beaches. **Betty Johnson's Bus Hire** offers tours of the area. (☎28410. Call ahead. €10.) Confident **bicyclists** can daytrip to Mizen Head (29km from Schull). The homey **Schull Backpackers' Lodge (IHH) ❶,** on Colla Rd., has simple but cozy rooms, and a terraced backyard for campers. Its friendly, welcoming staff readily shares info on local walks and rides. (☎28681. Bike rental €11 per day for the general public, €10 per day for hostelers. Dorms €15; singles €20; doubles €40-44, with bath €44-48. Tent sites €7.50 per person.) **Adele's Bakery ❶,** on Main St., sells mouthwatering pastries and breads (€2-5) and has a tempting lunch menu. (☎28459. Open July-Aug. Tu-Th 9:30am-6pm, F-Sa 9:30am-8pm, Su 11am-8pm; Sept.-June W-Sa 9:30am-6pm, Su 11am-6pm.) In summer, **ferries** (☎28138) depart from Schull for Cape Clear Island (June-Aug. 2-3 per day, round-trip €12). **Buses** arrive in Schull from Cork (2-3 per day, €12.10). There is no other public transportation on the peninsula.

CAPE CLEAR ISLAND ☎028

Although the scenery visible from the ferry landing at Cape Clear Island *(Oileán Chléire)* is desolate and foreboding, the island's beautiful interior scenery keeps visitors coming back. A history as the seat of the O'Driscoll clan makes Cape Clear a place of ancestral affection. The island provides asylum for gulls, petrels, cormorants, and their attendant flocks of ornithologists at the **Cape Clear Bird Observatory** (☎39181), on North Harbor. The **Cape Clear Heritage Centre** has everything from a family tree of the ubiquitous O'Driscolls to a well-preserved deck chair from the *Lusitania.* (Open June-Aug. M-Sa noon-5pm, Su 2-5pm. €3, students €2.) On the road to the center, **Cléire Goats** claims that its **goat's milk ice cream** (€1.50) is creamier and more scrumptious than the generic bovine variety (☎39126). **Cape Clear Island Youth Hostel (HI) ❶,** has simple but clean rooms and a fantastic location on the secluded and swimming-friendly South Harbor. It's a 10min. walk from the pier; turn right onto the main road past the pottery shop and stay to the left. (☎41968. Dorms €15.) To reach **Cuas an Uisce Campsite ❶,** follow the directions to the hostel but bear right before Ciarán Danny Mike's; it's 400m up on the left. (☎39119. Open June-Sept. Tent sites €6 per person.) Groceries are available at pier-side **An Siopa Beag.** (☎39099. Open June-Aug. daily 10am-8:30pm; Sept.-May M-Th 11am-6pm.) **Ferries** (☎28138) go to Schull (45min.; 3-4 per day; €7, round-trip €12). There is an **information office** in the pottery shop at the end of the pier. (☎39100. Open daily June-Aug. 11am-1pm and 3-6pm; Sept. 3-5pm.)

KILLARNEY AND KILLARNEY NATIONAL PARK ☎066

The town of Killarney is just minutes from some of Ireland's most glorious natural scenery. Outside of town, forested mountains rise from the famous **Lakes of Killarney** in the 95 sq. km national park. Five kilometers south of Killarney on Kenmare Rd. is **Muckross House,** a massive 19th-century manor with a garden that blooms brilliantly each year. A path leads to the 20m high **Torc Waterfall,** the starting point for several short trails along beautiful **Torc Mountain.** It's a 3.5km stroll in the opposite direction to the **Meeting of the Waters.** The paved path is nice, but the dirt trail through the **Yew Woods** is more secluded and inaccessible to bikes. To get to the 14th-century **Ross Castle,** the last stronghold in Munster to fall to Cromwell's army, take a right on Ross Rd. off Muckross Rd., 3km from Killarney. The footpaths from Knockreer (out of town on New St.) offer a more scenic route. (☎35851. Open daily June-Aug. 9am-6:30pm; May and Sept. 10am-6pm; mid-Mar. to Apr. and Oct. 10am-5pm. €5, students €2.)

The immense and immaculate **Neptune's (IHH) ❶,** on Bishop's Ln., has an ideal location, excellent common spaces, and a friendly staff. (☎35255. Breakfast €2.50. Dorms €12.50-16; doubles €34-42.) For delicious chicken, meat, and vegetarian dishes, try **The Stonechat ❷,** on Fleming's Ln. A sophisticated but unpretentious atmosphere makes this the best restaurant in Killarney. (☎34295. Lunch €7-9. Dinner €13-18. Open M-Sa noon-4pm and 6:30-10pm.) A trendy 20-something crowd gets down to a huge variety of live music in the loungelike **McSorley's,** College St. (☎39770. Trad/live band/disco progression nightly. Sa cover €13.) **Trains** (☎31067 or 1890 200 493) arrive at Killarney station, off E. Avenue Rd., from: Cork (2hr., 7-8 per day, €20); Dublin (3½hr., 2-3 per day, €53); Limerick (3hr., 2-3 per day, €22). **Buses** (☎30011) leave from Park Rd. for: Belfast (3-4 per day, €31); Cork (2hr., 11-14 per day, €14); Dublin (6hr., 5-6 per day, €21). **O'Sullivan's,** on Bishop's Ln., rents **bikes.** (☎31282. Free locks and maps. Open daily 8:30am-6:30pm. €12 per day, €70 per week.) The **tourist office** is on Beech St. (☎31633. Open July-Aug. M-Sa 9am-8pm, Su 10am-1pm and 2:15-6pm; June, Sept. and Oct.-May reduced hours.)

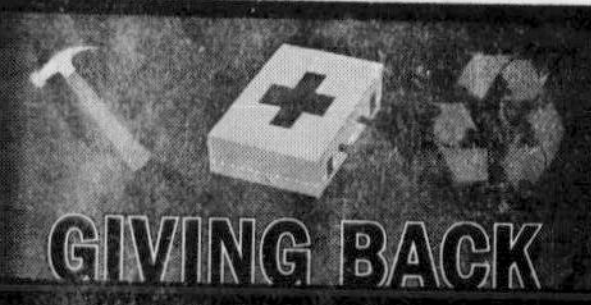

DOWN WITH THE RHODODENDRONS

Killarney National Park is home to some of Ireland's most spectacular scenery and its most diverse flora and fauna, but its future is in danger. *Rhododendron ponticum,* a common rhododendron native to parts of Eastern Europe and the Iberian peninsula, grows like wildfire on the forest floor, blocking much-needed light from the oak acorns that fall to the ground in order to take root. As a result, the Irish oak population has been severely depleted.

This poses a problem, as oaks are vital to Ireland's ecosystem. The Groundwork Conservation Workcamps were established in 1981 to get rid of the rebel rhododendrons and preserve Ireland's native forest. Anyone with a green thumb or merely an interest in the environment can help: from June to September, the organization runs one- and two-week work sessions where volunteers clear away the rhododendrons throughout the park. A fee of €35 for one week or €45 for two weeks guarantees food and accommodation in a hostel, as well as the chance to preserve the glory that is Killarney National Park.

For more information, visit www.groundwork.ie or call Muckross House's information center at ☎0643 1440.

RING OF KERRY ☎066

The Southwest's most celebrated peninsula offers picturesque villages, ancient forts, and rugged mountains. Although tour buses often hog the roads, rewards await those who take the time to explore the landscape on foot or by bike.

TRANSPORTATION

The term "Ring of Kerry" usually describes the entire **Iveragh Peninsula,** though it technically refers to the ring of roads circumnavigating it. Hop on the circuit run by **Bus Éireann,** based in Killarney and stopping at the major towns on the Ring (mid-June to Aug., 2 per day; entire ring in 1 day €18.50), including Cahersiveen (from Killarney 2½hr., €11.50) and Caherdaniel (from Cahersiveen 1hr., €4.25).

CAHERSIVEEN ☎066

Although best known as the birthplace of patriot Daniel O'Connell, Cahersiveen (CAR-sah-veen) also serves as a useful base for jaunts to the Skelligs and local archaeological sites. The ruins of **Ballycarbery Castle** are past the barracks on Bridge St., left over the bridge, and left off the main road. About 200m past the castle turn-off stands a pair of Ireland's best-preserved stone forts, **Cahergall** and **Leacanabuaile Fort.** Enjoy scenic views of the countryside from the second-floor balcony at **Sive Hostel (IHH) ❶**, 15 East End, Main St. (☎947 2717. Laundry €5.10. Dorms €14; doubles €31-35. Camping €7 per person.) The pubs on **Main Street** still retain the authentic feel of their former proprietors' main business, be it general store, blacksmithy, or leather shop. The Ring of Kerry **bus** stops in front of Banks Store on Main St. (mid-June to Aug., 2-4 per day) and continues on to Killarney (2½hr., €11.50) and Caherdaniel (1hr., €4.25). The **tourist office** is across from the bus stop. (☎947 2589. Open June to mid-Sept. M, W, F 9:15am-1pm and 2-5:15pm, Tu and Th 9:15am-1pm.)

CAHERDANIEL

There's little in the village of **Caherdaniel** to attract the Ring of Kerry's droves of buses. However, nearby **Derrynane National Park,** 2.5km from the village, holds 3km of gorgeous beach circled by picture-perfect dunes. Follow signs for **Derrynane House,** once the residence of Irish patriot Daniel O'Connell. (☎947 5113. Open May-Sept. M-Sa 9am-6pm, Su 11am-7pm; Apr. and Oct. Tu-Su 1-5pm; Nov.-Mar. Sa-Su 1-5pm. Last admission 45min. before closing. €2.75, students €1.25.) Rest at **The Travellers Rest Hostel ❶.** (☎947 5175. Dorms €14.50; singles €17.50.)

DINGLE PENINSULA

For decades, the Ring of Kerry's undertouristed counterpart has maintained a healthy ancient site to tour bus ratio. Only recently has the Ring's tourist blitz begun to encroach upon the spectacular cliffs and sweeping beaches of this Irish-speaking peninsula.

TRANSPORTATION

Dingle Town is most easily reached by **Bus** Éireann from Tralee (1¼hr.; M-Sa 4-6 per day, Su 2-5 per day; €9). Many visitors explore the area by **bike.**

DINGLE TOWN ☎915

Lively Dingle Town, adoptive home of **Fungi the Dolphin** (now a focus of the tourist industry), is a good base for exploring the peninsula. **Sciúird Archaeology Tours** leave from the pier for 2½hr. whirlwind bus tours of the area's ancient spots. (☎1606. 2 per day, €15.) **Moran's Tours** runs great trips to Slea Head, passing through majestic scenery and stopping at historic sites. (☎1155. 2 per day, €15.) **Ballintaggart Hostel (IHH) ❶**, 25min. east of town on Tralee Rd., is supposedly haunted by the murdered wife of the Earl of Cork. (☎1454. Open May-Oct. Dorms €13.50-19; doubles €52-70. Tent sites €8.) Busy **Homely House Cafe ❷**, Green St., has an extensive and exotic menu. (☎2431; www.homelyhouse.com. Entrees €4-9.50. Open M-Sa 11am-5pm; July-Aug. also open W-Sa 7-10pm.) The **tourist office** is on Strand St. (☎1188. Open mid-June to mid-Sept. M-Sa 9am-7pm, Su 10am-5pm; mid-Sept. to mid-June reduced hours.)

SLEA HEAD, VENTRY, AND DUNQUIN ☎915

By far the most rewarding way to see the cliffs and crashing waves of Dunquin and Slea Head is to **bike** along the predominantly flat **Slea Head Drive.** Past Dingle Town toward Slea Head sits the village of Ventry *(Ceann Trá)*, home to a sandy **beach** and the **Celtic and Prehistoric Museum,** a massive collection that includes a 50,000-year-old woolly mammoth. (☎9191. Open daily Mar.-Nov. 10am-5:30pm; Dec.-Feb. call ahead. €5, students €4.) While in Ventry, stay at the secluded yet convenient **Ballybeag Hostel ❶.** (☎9876; www.iol.ie/~balybeag. Bike rental €8 per day. Laundry €3. Dorms €15; doubles €44.)

North of Slea Head and Ventry, the scattered settlement of Dunquin *(Dún Chaoin)* consists of stone houses, a pub, and little else. Past Dunquin on the road to Ballyferriter, the **Great Blasket Centre** has outstanding exhibits about the isolated Blasket Islands. (☎6444. Open daily July-Aug. 10am-7pm; Easter-June and Sept.-Oct. 10am-6pm. €3.50, students €1.25.) At **An Óige Hostel (HI) ❶,** on the Dingle Way across from the turn-off to the Blasket Centre, each bunk has an ocean view. (☎6121. Breakfast €4.50. Reception 9-10am and 5-10pm. Lockout 10am-5pm. Dorms €14-16; doubles €32.) **Kruger's,** the westernmost pub in Europe, features pub grub, music sessions, and great views (☎6127).

TRALEE

The economic and residential capital of Co. Kerry, Tralee (pop. 20,000) is a good departure point for the Ring of Kerry or the Dingle Peninsula. **Kerry the Kingdom,** in Ashe Memorial Hall on Denny St., features a high-tech history of Ireland from 8000 BC to the present. (☎712 7777; www.kerrymuseum.ie. Open June-Aug. daily 9:30am-5:30pm; Sept.-Dec. Tu-Sa 9:30am-5pm; Jan.-Mar. Tu-F 10am-4:30pm; Apr.-May Tu-Sa 9:30am-5:30pm. €8, students €6.50.) During the last week of August, the nationally known **Rose of Tralee Festival** brings lovely Irish lasses to town to compete for the title "Rose of Tralee." A few extra euro stretch to the extreme at the **Whitehouse Budget Accommodation and B&B ❷,** in Boherboy. (☎712 9174; www.whitehousetralee.com. Wheelchair accessible. Breakfast included. Dorms €19; singles €30; doubles €50.) **Trains** depart from the station on Oakpark Rd. for: Cork (2½hr., 3-5 per day, €26); Dublin (4hr., 3-6 per day, €52.50); Galway (5-6hr., 3 per day, €52.50); Killarney (40min., 4 per day, €7.50). **Buses** leave from the train station for: Cork (2½hr., 4 per day, €15); Galway (7-8 per day, €19.50); Killarney (40min., 10-14 per day, €7); Limerick (2¼hr., 8-9 per day, €14). To get from the station to the **tourist office** in Ashe Memorial Hall, head down Edward St., turn right on Castle St., and then left on Denny St. (☎712 1288. Open July-Aug. M-Sa 9am-7pm, Su 10am-6pm; Sept.-May M-Sa 9am-6pm.)

WESTERN IRELAND

Even Dubliners will say the west is the "most Irish" part of Ireland; in many remote areas you'll hear Gaelic as often as English. The potato famine that plagued the island was most devastating in the west—entire villages emigrated or died. In fact, the current population is still less than half of what it was in 1841. The mountainous landscapes from Connemara north to Ballina are great for hiking and cycling.

LIMERICK ☎061

Although its 18th-century Georgian streets and parks are both regal and elegant, 20th-century industrial and commercial developments cursed Limerick (pop. 80,000) with a featureless urban feel. Frank McCourt's celebrated memoir *Angela's Ashes* revealed the squalor of the city. However, with help from the EU and a strong art and student scene, Limerick is a city on the rise and a fine place to stay en route to points west. The **Hunt Museum,** in the Custom House on Rutland St., holds a gold crucifix given by Mary Queen of Scots to her executioner and a coin reputed to be one of the infamous 30 pieces of silver paid to Judas by the Romans. (☎312 833. Open M-Sa 10am-5pm, Su 2-5pm. €6.80, students €5.50.)

A number of B&Bs can be found on O'Connell St. or the Ennis road. Limerick suffered from a series of hostel closures in 2002, and another smaller wave in 2005. Close to the city center, **Gerard B&B ❸**, O'Connell St. has rooms in a Victorian house. (☎314 981. Breakfast included. €35 per person.) **O'Grady's Cellar Restaurant ❷**, 118 O'Connell St., serves traditional favorites. (☎418 286. Beef and Guinness stew with soda bread €8. Open M-Th and Su 9am-10pm, F-Sa 9am-10:30pm.) The area where **Denmark Street** and **Cornmarket Row** intersect is a good place for nighttime fun. **Dolan's**, 4 Dock Rd., hosts rambunctious local patrons and nightly trad. (☎314 483. Entrees €6-10. Lunch menu €3.50-8. Food served M-Sa 8am-10pm, Su 10am-10pm. Lunch served noon-7pm.) **Trains** (☎315 555) leave for Cork (2½hr., 5-6 per day, €21) and Dublin (2½hr., 8-9 per day, €40). **Buses** (☎313 333) leave **Colbert Station**, off Parnell St., for: Cork (2hr., 14 per day, €14); Dublin (3½hr., 13 per day, €14.50); Galway (2½hr., every hr., €14). The **tourist office** is on Arthurs Quay. From the station, walk down Davis St., turn right on O'Connell St. and then go left at Arthurs Quay Mall. (☎317 522. Open July-Aug. M-Su 9:30am-5:30pm; Sept.-June reduced hours.)

IRELAND

ENNIS AND DOOLIN ☎065

Ennis's proximity to Shannon Airport and the Burren makes it a common stopover for tourists. **Abbey Tourist Hostel ❶**, Harmony Row, welcomes guests with flowers. (☎682 2620. Dorms €14-16; singles €25; doubles €40.) Scrumptious, overfilled sandwiches bring locals to **Henry's ❶**, by the Abbey St. parking lot. (☎682 2848. Open M 10:30am-6pm, Tu-Sa 10:30am-6pm and 7-11pm.) At **Cruises Pub**, on Abbey St., local musicians appear nightly for cozy trad sessions in one of the oldest buildings in Co. Clare (est. 1658). **Trains** leave from Station Rd. for Dublin (1-2 per day, €30). **Buses** also leave from Station Rd. every hour for: Cork (3hr., €16); Dublin (4hr., €16); Galway (1hr., €12); Limerick (40min., €8.20); Shannon Airport (40min., €5.50). The **tourist office** is on Arthur's Row, off O'Connell Sq. (☎28366. Open July-Sept. daily 9am-1pm and 2-6pm; Apr.-June and Oct. M-Sa 9:30am-1pm and 2-6pm; Nov.-Mar. closed Sa.)

Something of a shrine to Irish music, the little village of **Doolin** draws thousands every year to its three pubs. **McDermott's** (in the Upper Village), **O'Connor's** (in the Lower), and **McGann's** (Upper) all have trad sessions nightly at 9:30pm. **Aille River Hostel (IHH) ❶**, halfway between the Upper and Lower Villages, has a friendly atmosphere and a gorgeous location. (☎707 4260. Free Internet. Dorms €14. Camping €7.) **Buses** leave from Doolin Hostel for Dublin via Ennis and Limerick (#15; 2 per day) and Galway (#50; 1½hr., 2-4 per day).

THE CLIFFS OF MOHER AND THE BURREN ☎065

Plunging 213m straight down to the open sea, the **Cliffs of Moher** afford views of the Kerry Mountains, the Twelve Bens, and the Aran Islands. Be careful of extremely strong winds; they blow a few tourists off every year. *Let's Go* strongly discourages straying from the established paths. The shop and cafe have basic tourist information and a schedule of bus service to the cliffs. (☎708 1171. Open daily mid-July to mid-Aug. 9am-7:30pm; mid-Aug. to mid-July 9:30am-5:30pm.) To reach the cliffs, head 5km south of Doolin on R478, or hop on the Galway-Cork bus (in summer 2-3 per day). From Liscannor, Cliffs of Moher Cruises (☎708 6060; www.mohercruises.com) sails directly under the cliffs (1¾hr., 2-3 per day, €20).

Entering the magical 260 sq. km landscape of nearby **Burren** is like happening upon an enchanted fairyland. Lunar limestone stretches end in secluded coves, wildflowers peek brightly from cracks in 1.5km long rock planes, and 28 of Ireland's 33 species of butterfly flutter by. The Burren town of **Lisdoonvarna** is synonymous with its **Matchmaking Festival**, a six-week long *craic*-and-snogging celebration that attracts over 10,000 singles each September. The **Hydro Hotel ❹** has nightly music and festival information. (☎707 4005; www.whites-hotelsireland.com. Open Mar.-Oct. €45 per person.) A **bus** (☎682 4177) connects Galway to towns in and near the Burren a few times a day in summer but infrequently in winter. In Ballyvaughan, stay at **O'Brien B&B ❶**, on Main St., and enjoy its fireplaces and hearty Irish breakfasts. (☎707 7003. Doubles from €30.)

GALWAY

☎091

In the past few years, Co. Galway's reputation as Ireland's cultural capital has brought flocks of young Celtophiles to Galway (pop. 70,000), the fastest-growing city in Europe. Street performers dazzle with homegrown tricks while locals and tourists lounge in outdoor cafes. In addition to its quiet quay-side walks and hot club scene, Galway is not that far from the Clare Coast and beautiful Connemara.

TRANSPORTATION AND PRACTICAL INFORMATION. **Trains** leave the station on Eyre Sq. (☎561 444; open M-Sa 9am-6pm) for Dublin (3hr., 4-5 per day, €28-39) via Portarlington (€22-30); transfer at Portarlington for all other lines. **Buses,** which also leave from Eyre Sq. (☎562 000), head to: Belfast (7½hr., 14 per day, €28); Donegal (4hr., 4 per day, €12.50); Dublin (4hr., 14 per day, €13.50). The **tourist office,** on Forster St., stocks Aran Islands info, exchanges currency, and books accommodations. (☎537 700. Open daily 9am-5:45pm.) To access the **Internet,** head to **Fun World,** Eyre Sq., above Supermac's. (☎561 415. €5 per hr.; 8-11pm €3 per hr. Open M-Sa 10am-11pm, Su 11am-11pm.) The **post office** is on 3 Eglinton St. (☎534 727. Open M and W-Sa 9am-5:30pm, Tu 9:30am-5:30pm.)

ACCOMMODATIONS AND FOOD. **Barnacle's Quay Street House (IHH) ❶,** 10 Quay St., has bright, spacious rooms in a location perfect for post-pub-crawl crashing. (☎568 644; www.barnacles.ie. Light breakfast included. All rooms with bath. Laundry €6.50. Internet €1 per 15min. 4- to 10-bed dorms €15-22; doubles €53. Low season reduced rates.) At **St. Martin's ❸,** 2 Nun's Island Rd., on the west bank of the river at the end of O'Brien's Bridge, the gorgeous back garden spills into the river. This friendly B&B is located near Galway's best pubs and just across the river from the main commercial district. (☎568 286. All rooms with bath. Singles €35; doubles €70; large family room €30 per person.) At **The Home Plate ❷,** Mary St., diners enjoy massive helpings on tiny wooden tables. (Sandwiches and entrees €6-10. Open M-Sa noon-8pm.) **Anton's ❶,** just over the bridge near the Spanish Arch and a 3min. walk up Father Griffin Rd., lets the food do all the talking. (Scrambled eggs with smoked salmon; €4.50. Open M-F 8am-6pm.)

SIGHTS AND ENTERTAINMENT. The **Nora Barnacle House,** 8 Bowling Green, has hardly changed since James Joyce's life-long companion left. Check out the author's original love letters to Ms. Barnacle. (☎564 743. Open mid-May to mid-Sept. W-F 10am-1pm and 2-5:30pm, otherwise by appointment; last admission 5pm. €2.50.) Head to **Claddagh,** an area that until the 1930s was an Irish-speaking, thatch-roofed fishing village. Across the river, south of Dominick St., the famous **Claddagh rings,** traditionally used as wedding bands, are today's mass-produced reminders of yesteryear. Say a prayer at the **Church of St. Nicholas,** the patron saint of travelers. A stone, on Market St., behind the castle, marks the spot where Columbus supposedly stopped to pray before sailing the ocean blue. (Open daily May-Sept. 9am-5:45pm. Free.)

Pubs on Quay St. and Eyre Sq. cater primarily to tourists, while locals stick to the more trad-oriented **Dominick Street** pubs. At **Roisín Dubh** (The Black Rose), Dominick St., a bookshelved front hides one of Galway's hottest live music scenes. (☎586 540. Sa stand-up comedy 9pm. Cover €5-23 most nights for music in the back room, front room always free.) **The King's Head,** High St., has three floors and a huge stage devoted to nightly rock. (☎566 630. Su brunch 1-3pm.) Between midnight and 12:30am, the pubs drain out and the tireless go dancing. Follow the crowd after last call to find the hot spot for the night. **Cuba,** on Prospect Hill, right past Eyre Sq., is far and away the best club in the city, and features wonderfully varied but danceable live music. (Cover €5-10.)

ARAN ISLANDS (OILEÁIN ÁRANN) ☎099

On the westernmost edge of Co. Galway, isolated by 32km of swelling Atlantic, lie the spectacular Aran Islands *(Oileáin Árann)*. Ruins, forts, churches, and holy wells rise from the stony terrain of **Inishmore** (*Inis Mór;* pop. 900). Don't miss the **Dún Aengus** ring fort, where stones circle a sheer 100m drop. The **Inis Mór Way** is a mostly paved route that passes the majority of the island's sights; pick up a map at the tourist office (€2). **Inisheer** (*Inis Oírr;* pop. 260), the smallest island, and windswept **Inishmaan** (*Inis Meáin;* pop. 200) feature similar paths.

The **Kilronan Hostel ❷**, adjacent to Tí Joe Mac's pub, has great rooms and a helpful staff. (☎61255. Bike rental €10. Dorms €17, all with bath.) The **Spar** supermarket in Kilronan functions as an unofficial community center. (Open July-Aug. M-Sa 9am-8pm, Su 9am-7pm; Mar.-June and Sept.-Oct. M-Sa 9am-8pm, Su 10am-5pm; Nov.-Feb. M-Sa 9am-7pm, Su 10am-5pm.) Island **Ferries** (☎091 561 767) go from Rossaveal, west of Galway, to Inishmore (2-4 per day, round-trip €25) and Inisheer (2 per day). Clan Eagle II (☎566 535) also leaves from Rossaveal for Inishmore (4 per day, round-trip €25). Both companies run **buses** to Rossaveal (€6, students €5); they depart from Kinlay House, on Merchant St. in Galway, 1½hr. before ferry departure. Ferries to Inishmore arrive at Kilronan. The **tourist office** stores luggage (€1) and helps find accommodations. (☎61263. Open daily June-Aug. 10am-7pm; Apr.-May and Sept.-Oct. 10am-5pm; Nov.-Mar. 11am-5pm.)

IRELAND

CONNEMARA

Connemara, a largely Irish-speaking region in northwest Co. Galway, is comprised of a lacy net of inlets and islands in the Atlantic Ocean. Offshore islands look out over two major mountain ranges, the Twelve Bens and the Maamturks.

CLIFDEN (AN CLOCHÁN) ☎095

Busy, English-speaking Clifden attracts crowds of tourists who use it as a base for exploring the region. Visit the **Connemara Walking Centre,** Market St., and take a tour led by Michael Gibbons, the critically acclaimed archaeologist and raconteur. The tours explore the history, folklore, geology, and archaeology of the region. (☎21492; www.walkingireland.com. Open Mar.-Oct. M-Sa 9am-9pm. Boat tours daily Easter-Oct.) **White Heather House ❸,** The Square, boasts panoramic views and an Irish breakfast. (☎21655. Singles €30; doubles €60.) **Clifden Town Hostel (IHH) ❶,** Market St., endears itself to guests with spotless rooms, a helpful owner, quiet atmosphere, and proximity to the pubs. (☎21076; www.clifdentownhostel.com. Open year-round, but call ahead Nov.-Feb. Dorms €13-15; doubles €32-34; triples €48; quads €60-64.) **Cullen's Bistro and Coffee Shop ❹,** Market St., is a family-run establishment that cooks up hearty meals. (☎21983. Thick Irish stew €15.50. Open Apr.-Nov. daily 11:30am-10pm.) **O'Connor's SuperValu** is on Market St. (Open June-Aug. M-Sa 9am-9pm; Su 10am-6pm. Sept.-May M-Th and Sa 9am-7pm, F 9am-8pm, Su 10am-6pm.) Bus Éireann runs **buses** from the library on Market St. to Galway via Oughterard (1½hr., 1-6 per day, €9) and to Westport via Leenane (1½hr., late June to Aug. M-Sa 1 per day). Michael Nee buses go from the courthouse to Galway (2hr.; 2 per day; €10, €13 round-trip). Rent a **bike** at **Mannion's,** on Bridge St. (☎21160. July-Aug. €15 per day, €70 per week; Sept.-June €10 per day. €2 deposit. Open daily 9:30am-6pm.) The **tourist office** is on Galway Rd. (☎21163. Open July-Aug. M-Sa 10am-6pm; Mar.-June and Sept.-Oct. M-Sa 10am-5pm.)

CONNEMARA NATIONAL PARK

☎095

Connemara National Park occupies 12.5 sq. km of mountainous countryside. Bogs, often deceptively covered by a thin screen of grass and flowers, constitute much of the park's terrain. The **Srufanboy Nature** and **Ellis Wood** trails are easy 20min. hikes. The newly constructed pathway up **Diamond Hill** offers a more difficult climb that rewards climbers with views of bog, harbor, and forest (or impenetrable mist). Experienced hikers head for the **Twelve Bens** (*Na Benna Beola;* the Twelve Pins), a rugged range that reaches heights of 2200m. A tour of six takes a day. **Biking** the 65km circle through Clifden, Letterfrack, and the Inagh Valley is truly captivating, but only appropriate for fit bikers. Hikers often stay at the **Ben Lettery Hostel (HI) ❶**, in Ballinafad, 13km east of Clifden. (☎51136. Dorms €15, €13 with student ID.) A guidebook mapping out walks (€6.40) and additional help in planning hikes is available at the **Visitors Centre.** (☎41054. Open daily June-Aug. 9:30am-6:30pm; Mar.-May and Sept. 10am-5:30pm. €2.75, students €1.25.) Turn off from N59, 13km east of Clifden, to reach the park.

WESTPORT

☎098

Palm trees and steep hills lead down to Westport's busy Georgian streets. Nearby, the conical **Croagh Patrick** rises 650m over Clew Bay. The summit has been revered as a holy site for thousands of years. St. Patrick worked here in AD 441, praying for 40 days and nights to banish the snakes from Ireland. Climbers start their excursion from the 15th-century **Murrisk Abbey,** several kilometers west of Westport on R335 toward Louisburgh. **Buses** go to Murrisk (2-3 per day). For groups, cabs (☎087 2588384; €8-10) are cheaper and more convenient.

B&Bs cluster on **Altamont Road** and **The Quay.** Great breakfasts and incredible hospitality at **Altamont House ❸,** Altamont Rd., have kept travelers coming back for 42 years. (☎25226. Rooms €30, with bath €33.) Restaurants are concentrated on **Bridge Street.** The **SuperValu** supermarket is on Shop St. (Open M-Sa 8:30am-9pm, Su 10am-6pm.) **Trains** arrive at the Altamont Rd. Station (☎25253), a 5min. walk up the North Mall, from Dublin (2-4 per day, €22-25) via Athlone. **Buses** leave from Mill St. for Galway (2hr., 4-8 per day, €12). The **tourist office** is on James St. (☎25711. Open daily 9am-5:45pm.)

NORTHWESTERN IRELAND

A mere sliver of land connects the mountains, lakes, and ancient monuments of Co. Sligo to Co. Donegal. Among Ireland's counties, Donegal (DUN-ee-gahl) is second only to Cork in size and second to none in glorious wilderness. Its *gaeltacht* is the largest sanctuary of the living Irish language in Ireland, and its geographic isolation and natural beauty embrace travelers sick of the tourist hordes.

DONEGAL TOWN (DÚN NA NGALL)

☎074 97

A gateway for travelers heading to more isolated destinations in the north and northwest, this sometimes sleepy town erupts with live music in pubs on weekends; things reach fever pitch when festivals arrive in late June and early July. Six craftsmen open their studios to the public around the pleasant courtyard of the **Donegal Craft Village,** 1.6km south of town on the Ballyshannon Rd. (☎22225. Open July-Aug. M-Sa 10am-6pm, Su noon-6pm; Sept.-June call ahead.) For a different perspective on the area, the **Waterbus** shuttle provides aquatic tours of Donegal Bay. (Ferry leaves from the quay next to the tourist office. ☎23666. Departure times depend on tides; call ahead. €10.) During the last weekend in June, the varied **Donegal Summer Festival** doubles the town's size. Contact the tourist office for details. For two weeks in July, the **Earagail Arts Festival** celebrates the arts throughout County Donegal. (Info ☎074 91 20777, tickets ☎074 91 29186; www.donegalculture.com. Prices range from free to €25.)

A 10min. walk from town, family-run **Donegal Town Independent Hostel (IHH/IHO) ❶**, Killybegs Rd., warmly welcomes road-weary backpackers. (☎20749. Open June-Aug. Dorms €13; doubles €28. Tent sites €7.50 per person.) **The Blueberry Tea Room ❷**, Castle St., buzzes with patrons packing in for the all-day breakfasts (€6) and delicious daily specials (€8). Check email at their cybercafe on the second floor. (☎22933. €2 for 30min. Open M-Sa 9am-7pm.) For groceries, head to **SuperValu**, minutes from the Diamond down Ballyshannon Rd. (Open M-W and Sa 9am-7pm, Th-F 9am-9pm, Su 10am-6pm.) Lantern-lit **The Schooner Bar and B&B** (☎21671), Upper Main St., draws a mix of hostelers and locals for the best trad sessions in town on weekends between June and August. **Buses** (☎21101) stop outside the Abbey Hotel on the Diamond from: Derry/Londonderry (3-7 per day, €11.30) via Letterkenny (€6.35); Dublin (4-7 per day, €14.40); Galway (3-4 per day, €15.80); Sligo (4-6 per day; €10). The center of town is called **the Diamond**, a triangle bordered by Donegal's main shopping streets. Facing away from the Abbey Hotel, turn right; the **tourist office** is outside the Diamond on the Ballyshannon/Sligo Rd., next to the quay. (☎21148; www.donegaltown.ie. Open July-Aug. M-Sa 9am-6:30pm, Su 10am-3pm; Sept.-Oct. and Easter-June M-Sa 10am-6pm.)

IRELAND

SLIGO ☎071 91

Since the beginning of the 20th century, Sligo has seen a literary pilgrimage of William Butler Yeats devotees; the poet spent summers in town as a child and set many of his poems around Sligo Bay. **Sligo Town**, the commercial center, is an excellent base for exploration. The well-preserved former Dominican friary, **Sligo Abbey**, is on Abbey St. (Open daily Apr.-Dec. 10am-6pm; Jan.-Mar. reduced hours. €2, students €1.) **Model Arts and Niland Gallery**, on the Mall, houses one of the finest collections of modern Irish art. (Open June-Oct. Tu-Sa 10am-5:30pm, Su 11am-5:30pm; Nov.-May closed Su. Free.) Yeats is buried in **Drumcliffe Churchyard**, on the N15, 6.5km northwest of Sligo. Catch a bus from Sligo to the Derry stop at Drumcliffe (10min., 9 per day, round-trip €5).

B&Bs cluster on **Pearse Road. Eden Hill Holiday Hostel (IHH) ❶**, off Pearse Rd., has Victorian decor and a friendly staff. From the town center, follow Pearse Rd., turn right at the Marymount sign, and take another right after one block. (☎43204. Laundry €6. Dorms €14.) A **Tesco** supermarket is on O'Connell St. (☎62788. Open M-Sa 24hr., Su 10am-8pm.) **McLaughlin's Bar**, 9 Market St., is a true musician's pub; with pick-up jam sessions in the back room on Friday and Saturday nights. (Open M-Th 5-11:30pm, F-Sa 5pm-12:30am, Su 5-11pm.) **Trains** (☎69888; www.irishrail.ie) leave from Lord Edward St. to Dublin (3hr., 3-4 per day, €24 round-trip) via Carrick-on-Shannon and Mullingar. From the same station, **buses** (☎60066; www.buseireann.ie) head to: Belfast (4hr.; 2-3 per day; €24, student €19); Derry/Londonderry (3hr., 3-7 per day, €15.50/12.50); Donegal (1hr., 3-7 per day, €11.50/9.20); Dublin (3-4hr., 4-6 per day, €16/12.5); Galway (2½hr., 4-6 per day, €13/10.60); Westport (2½hr., 2-3 per day, €15/12). Turn left on Lord Edward St., then follow the signs right onto Adelaide St. and around the corner to Temple St. to find the **tourist office.** (☎61201. Open July-Aug. M-F 9am-6pm, Sa 10am-4pm, Su 10am-2pm; Sept.-May M-F 9am-6pm; June M-F 9am-6pm, Sa 10am-3pm.)

LETTERKENNY ☎074 91

Letterkenny, though difficult to navigate, is a lively place to make bus connections to the rest of Donegal, the Republic, and Northern Ireland. **Buses** leave from the junction of Port (Derry) and Pearse Rd., in front of the shopping center. Bus Éireann (☎21309) runs to: Derry/Londonderry (30min.; 3-7 per day; €7, students €5.20); Dublin (4½hr., 4-6 per day, €16/13.50); Galway (4¾hr., 3 per day, €27.50/22) via Donegal Town (50min., €8/6.20); Sligo (2hr., 4-5 per day, €12/11). Lough Swilly (☎22863) buses run to Derry (M-Sa 12 per day, €6) and the Inishowen Peninsula (M-F 2-3 per day, €6). The **tourist office** is off the second roundabout at the intersection of Port (Derry) and Blaney Rd. (☎21160. Open July-Aug. M-F 9am-6pm, Sa 11am-5pm, Su noon-3pm; Sept.-June M-F 9am-5pm.) **The Port Hostel (IHO) ❶,** Orchard Crest, the town's only hostel, is run by a registered nurse. (☎25315. Laundry €5. Dorms €15.) There is a **Tesco** supermarket in the shopping center behind the bus station. (Open M-Sa 8am-10pm, Su 10am-8pm.)

NORTHERN IRELAND

In Northern Ireland, hillside castles coexist with fishing villages and the city of Belfast. The calm tenor of everyday life has long been overshadowed by headlines screaming about riots and bombs. Negotiations continue to help make the region as peaceful as it is beautiful. Beyond its urban cities, Ireland and Northern Ireland still hold fast to their old-world welcome.

FACTS AND FIGURES

Official Name: Northern Ireland.
Capital: Belfast.
Population: 1,700,000.
Time Zone: GMT.
Language: English.
Religions: Protestant (40%), Roman Catholic (40%), other (20%).
Largest Permanent Hedge Maze: Peace Maze, Castlewellan Forest Park, Co. Down; 11,215 sq. m.

BELFAST ☎028

Despite the violent associations conjured by the name Belfast (pop. 330,000), the capital feels more peaceful than most visitors expect. Today, its reputation as an artistic center is maintained by such renowned writers as Nobel Prize-winner Seamus Heaney and by the annual Queen's University Festival. The Belfast bar scene, a mix of Irish-British pub culture and international trends, entertains locals, foreigners, and a student population as lively as any in the world.

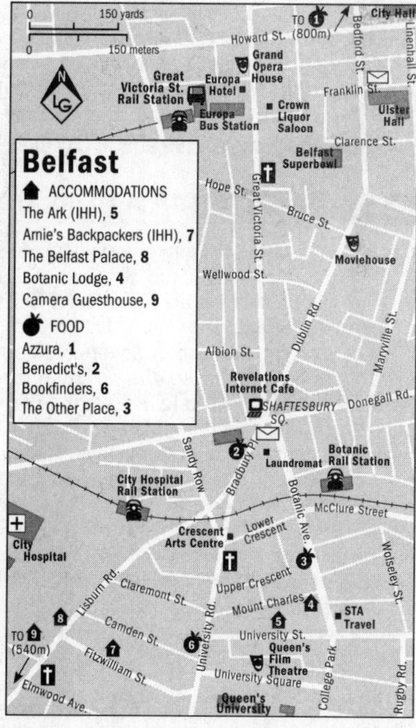

TRANSPORTATION

Flights: Belfast International Airport (BFS; ☎9442 2448; www.belfastairport.com) in Aldergrove, serves: **Aer Lingus** (☎0845 084 4444); **British Airways** (☎0845 850 9850); **British European** (a.k.a **Flybe;** ☎087 0567 6676); **BMI** (☎0870 607 0555); **Easyjet** (☎0870 600 0000; www.easyjet.com). **Airbus** (☎9066

6630) runs to Laganside and Europa Bus Stations in the city center (40min.; M-Sa 2 per hr. 5:45am-10:30pm, Su about every hr. 6:15am-9:30pm; £6, round-trip £9). **Belfast City Airport** (☎9093 9093; www.belfastcityairport.com), at the harbor, serves **British European.** Trains run from City Airport to Central Station (M-Sa 25-33 per day, Su 12 per day; £1).

Trains: Translink (☎9066 6630; www.translink.co.uk). **Trains** arrive at **Central Station,** E. Bridge St. Some also stop at **Botanic Station,** Botanic Ave. in the University area, or **Great Victoria Station,** next to Europa Hotel. To **Derry/Londonderry** (2hr.; M-F 10 per day, Sa 9 per day, Su 4 per day; £8.20, students £4) and **Dublin** (2hr.; M-F 8 per day, Sa 9 per day, Su 5 per day; £20).

Buses: Buses to the south and west operate out of **Europa Bus Station** (☎9066 6630), off Great Victoria St., behind the Europa Hotel. To **Derry/Londonderry** (1¾hr.; M-Sa 19 per day, Su 7 per day; £7.50, students £5) and **Dublin** (3hr.; M-Sa 7 per day, Su 6 per day; £12/10). Buses to the west and north operate out of **Laganside Station** (☎9066 6630), off Donegall Quay.

Ferries: The docks can be unsafe late at night and early in the morning; take a cab. **SeaCat** (☎087 0552 3523), from the ferry terminal off Donegall Quay, sails to the **Isle of Man** (2¾hr.; Apr.-Nov. M, W, F 1 per day) and **Troon, Scotland** (2½hr., 2-3 per day). **Norse Merchant Ferries** (☎087 0600 4321; www.norsemerchant.com) run to **Liverpool, England** (8hr.).

Local Transportation: The new **Metro** bus service (☎9066 6630; www.translink.co.uk) is supplemented by **Ulsterbus's** suburban "blue buses." Travel within the city center £1.20, concessions £0.50. 5-journey ticket £5.25-7.25/3.38-4.48. The bus system centers at **Donegall Square** and runs 12 high-frequency routes covering all of the major areas of Belfast, including Europa Bus Station, Castlecourt Shopping Centre, Central Train Station, and Laganside Bus Station. To reach Donegall Sq. from Central Station, walk down E. Bridge St., turn right on Oxford St., and take a left on May St. **Nightlink** buses shuttle the tipsy from Donegall Sq. W. to various small towns outside Belfast (Sa 1, 2am; £3.50). Pay onboard or at the Donegall Sq. W. kiosk.

Taxis: Value Cabs (☎9080 9080); **City Cab** (☎9024 2000); **Fon a Cab** (☎9033 3333).

ORIENTATION AND PRACTICAL INFORMATION

City Hall is in **Donegall Square.** A busy shopping district spans north for four blocks to the enormous Castlecourt Shopping Centre. In the eastern part of the shopping district, the **Cornmarket** area shows off Belfastian architecture and pubs in its narrow entries (small alleyways). The stretch of Great Victoria St. between Europa Bus Station and **Shaftesbury Square** is known as the **Golden Mile** for its high-brow establishments and Victorian architecture. **Botanic Avenue** and **Bradbury Place** (which becomes University Rd.) extend south to **Queen's University,** where student pubs and budget accommodations await. In this southern area, the busiest neighborhoods center around **Stranmillis, Malone,** and **Lisburn Roads.** Divided from the rest of Belfast by the **Westlink Motorway,** working-class **West Belfast** is more politically volatile than the city center. There remains a sharp division between sectarian neighborhoods: the Protestant neighborhood stretches along **Shankill Road,** just north of the Catholic neighborhood, centered around **Falls Road.** The **peace line** separates them. **River Lagan** splits industrial **East Belfast** from Belfast proper. The city's shipyards and docks extend north on both sides of the river as it grows into **Belfast Lough.** During the week, the area north of City Hall is deserted after 6pm. Although muggings are rare in Belfast, use taxis after dark.

Tourist Office: Belfast Welcome Centre, 47 Donegall Pl. (☎9024 6609; www.gotobelfast.com). Free booklets on Belfast and surrounding areas. Books accommodations in Northern Ireland (£2) and the Republic (£3). Open June-Sept. M-Sa 9am-7pm, Su noon-5pm; Oct.-May M-Sa 9am-5pm.

Banks: Banks and **ATMs** are plentiful. Most banks are open M-F 9am-4:30pm. **Thomas Cook,** 10 Donegall Sq. W. (☎9088 3800). No commission on cashing **traveler's checks.** Open M-W and Sa 8am-7pm, Th 8am-9pm, F 8am-8pm, Su 1-5pm.

Luggage Storage: For security reasons, there is no luggage storage at airports, bus stations, or train stations. The tourist office stores luggage for 4hr. (£3) or longer (£4.50), but not overnight. All hostels listed hold bags during the day for guests.

Laundromat: Globe Drycleaners and Launderers, 37-39 Botanic Ave. (☎9024 3956). £4.65 for use of machines. Open M-F 8am-9pm, Sa 8am-6pm, Su noon-6pm.

Police: 65 Knock Rd. (☎9065 0222).

Hospital: Belfast City Hospital, 91 Lisburn Rd. (☎9032 9241).

Internet Access: Belfast Central Library. £2 per hr. **Revelations Internet Cafe,** 27 Shaftesbury Sq. (☎9032 0337). £4 per hr., students and hostelers £3 per hr. Open M-F 10am-10pm, Sa 10am-6pm, Su 11am-7pm.

Post Office: Central Post Office, 25 Castle Pl. (☎0845 722 3344). Open M-Sa 9am-5:30pm. **Postal Code:** BT1 1BB.

IRELAND

ACCOMMODATIONS

Most budget accommodations are near Queen's University. Walk 10-20min. south from Europa Bus Station or the train stations. Alternatively, catch Metro bus #8 toward Shaftesbury Sq.

Arnie's Backpackers (IHH), 63 Fitzwilliam St. (☎9024 2867), a short walk from Europa Bus Station. Friendly Arnie welcomes hostelers into his Victorian townhouse with a cup of tea and a library of travel info. Dorms £7-9.50. ❶

Camera Guesthouse, 44 Wellington Park (☎9066 0026). Pristine Victorian house in quiet, leafy neighborhood. Breakfast offers organic options. Singles £35, with bath £45; doubles £54/60. ❹

The Belfast Palace, 68 Lisburn Rd. (☎9033 3367), at the corner of Fitzwilliam St. The new kid on the block, this sociable hostel offers some of the most modern amenities, including free Internet (daily 8am-10:30pm), satellite TV, and complimentary videos. Breakfast included. Laundry facilities. Car park. Dorms from £8.50. ❶

The Ark (IHH), 18 University St. (☎9032 9626), 10min. from Europa Station on Great Victoria St. Recently upgraded to a new location with the same great sense of community and helpful, friendly staff. Also books tours of Belfast (£8) and Giant's Causeway (£16). Laundry £5. Internet £3 per hr. Curfew 2am. Dorms £10; doubles £36. ❶

Botanic Lodge, 87 Botanic Ave. (☎9032 7682), at the corner of Mt. Charles Ave. Larger B&B is right in the heart of the Queen's University area, surrounded by eateries and close to the city center. Singles £25, with bath £35; doubles £40/45. ❸

FOOD

Dublin Road, Botanic Avenue, and the **Golden Mile** have the most options. For produce, visit **St. George's Market,** E. Bridge St., between Victoria and Oxford St. (Open F 8am-2pm, Sa 6am-noon.) For gourmet pizzas and pastas fresh from the oven (under £5), try **Azzura** ❷, 8 Church Ln. (☎9024 2444. Open M-Sa 9am-5pm.) **Benedict's** ❷, 7-21 Bradbury Pl., is a swanky hotel restaurant with a "Beat the Clock" meal deal: order fine meals from 5:30-7:30pm with the time ordered as the price. (☎9059 1999.Open M-Sa noon-2:30pm and 5:30-10:30pm, Su noon-3:30pm and 5:30-9pm.) The bustling eatery, **The Other Place** ❶, 79 Botanic Ave., serves fried breakfasts from £2.85, until 5pm. (☎9020 7200. Open daily 8am-10pm.) Or, eat at cozy **Bookfinders** ❶, 47 University Rd., a dusty bookstore/cafe

THE CATHOLIC MURALS

The murals of West Belfast are a powerful testament to the volatile past and fierce loyalties of the divided neighborhoods. Many of the most famous Catholic murals are on Falls Rd., an area that saw some of the worst of the Troubles.

1. This mural illustrates protestors during the **Hunger Strikes of 1981,** which ultimately won political prisoner status for paramilitary captives.
2. A portrayal of **Bobby Sands,** the first hunger-striker to die, is located on the side of the Sinn Féin Office, Sevastopol St. Sands was elected as a member of the British Parliament under a "political prisoner" ticket during this time and is remembered as the North's most famous martyr.
3. Formerly operating as Northern Ireland's National RUC Headquarters, the most bombed of any police station in England, the Republic, or the North. Its fortified, barbed-wire facade is on Springfield St.

with mismatched dishes, counter-culture paraphernalia, and occasional poetry readings. (☎9032 6677. Open M-Sa 10am-5:30pm.)

SIGHTS

DONEGALL SQUARE. The most impressive piece of architecture in Belfast is also its administrative and geographic center. Dominating the grassy square that serves as the locus of downtown Belfast, **City Hall's** green copper dome (52m) is visible from nearly any point in the city. At the entrance, a marble **Queen Victoria** grimaces formidably. *(☎9027 0456. 1hr. tours June-Sept. M-F 11am, 2, 3pm, Sa 2:30pm; Oct.-May M-F 11am, 2:30pm, Sa 2:30pm. Tour times prone to change. Free.)* The **Linen Hall Library** contains a famous collection of Northern Irish political documents. *(Enter via 52 Fountain St. ☎9032 1707. Open M-F 9:30am-5:30pm, Sa 9:30am-1pm. Free tours.)*

CORNMARKET AND ST. ANNE'S CATHEDRAL. North of the city center, this shopping district envelops eight blocks around **Castle Street** and **Royal Avenue.** Relics of the old city remain in the **entries,** or tiny alleys. St. Anne's Cathedral, also known as the **Belfast Cathedral,** was begun in 1899. Each of its interior pillars names one of Belfast's professions: Agriculture, Art, Freemasonry, Healing, Industry, Music, Science, Shipbuilding, Theology, and "Womanhood." *(Donegall St., near the city center. Open M-Sa 10am-4pm, Su before and after services.)*

THE DOCKS AND EAST BELFAST. Belfast's newest mega-attraction, **Odyssey,** 2 Queen's Quay, a gigantic center housing five different science attractions. Its best feature is the **W5 Discovery Centre,** a playground for curious minds and hyperactive schoolchildren. *(☎9046 7700; www.w5online.co.uk. Open M-Th 10am-5pm, F-Sa 10am-6pm, Su noon-6pm. £6, students £4.50, families £17.)* The **Sheridan IMAX Cinema** shows both 2D and 3D films on its 19 by 25m screen. *(☎9046 7014; www.belfastimax.com. £5, students M-Th £4.50.)* For nautical enthusiasts, the **Sinclair Seamen's Church** is sure to please. Here, the minister delivers his sermons from a pulpit carved in the shape of a ship's prow, collections are taken in miniature lifeboats, and an organ with port and starboard lights carries the tune. *(Corporation St. Open W 2-5pm and Su services.)*

THE GOLDEN MILE. This strip along Great Victoria St. contains many of Belfast's historical jewels. Of these, the **Grand Opera House,** is the city's pride and joy, sadly making it a repeated bombing target for the IRA. *(☎9024 1919. Office open 8:30am-9pm. Tours* *begin across the street at the office Sa 11am. £3, students £2.)* If opera is not your thing, visit the popular **Crown Liquor Saloon,** 46 Great Victoria St., a showcase of carved wood and stained glass recently restored by the National Trust. Finally, check out the **Europa Hotel,** which has the dubious distinction of being "Europe's most bombed hotel," having survived 31 blasts.

WEST BELFAST. West Belfast is not a "sight" in the traditional sense. The streets display political **murals.** Visitors should definitely take a **black cab tour** of the murals, easily booked at most hostels. **Black Taxi Tours** (☎0800 052 3914; www.belfasttours.com) offer witty, objective presentations. The Catholic neighborhood is centered around **Falls Road** where the **Sinn Féin** office is easily spotted: one side of it is covered with an enormous portrait of Bobby Sands and an advertisement for the *Sinn Féin* newspaper, *An Phoblacht.* On **Divis Street,** a high-rise apartment building marks the site of the **Divis Tower,** formerly an IRA stronghold and now occupied by the British army. Farther north is **Shankill Road** and the Protestant neighborhood. Between the Falls and Shankill is the **peace line.** The side streets on the right guide you to the **Shankill Estate** and more murals. **Crumlin Road,** through the estate, is the site of the oldest Loyalist murals.

! Be advised that it is illegal to photograph military installations, and the Protestant Orangemen's **Marching Season** (July 4-12) is a risky time to visit the area, since the parades are underscored by mutual antagonism.

ENTERTAINMENT AND NIGHTLIFE

Belfast's cultural events and performances are covered in the monthly *Arts Council Artslink* (free at the tourist office). The **Grand Opera House,** on Great Victoria St., stages a mix of opera, ballet, musicals, and drama. Buy tickets at the box office, 2-4 Great Victoria St. (☎9024 1919; www.goh.co.uk. Tickets from £12.50.) The **Queen's University Festival** (☎9066 7687; www.belfastfestival.com) in November hosts ballet, comedy, films, and opera.

Pubs close early, so start crawling while the sun's still up; *Let's Go* suggests starting downtown, moving through Cornmarket, and finishing near the university. Begin with a pint at **The Duke of York,** 7-11 Commercial Ctr., which in former days was a boxing venue and communist printing

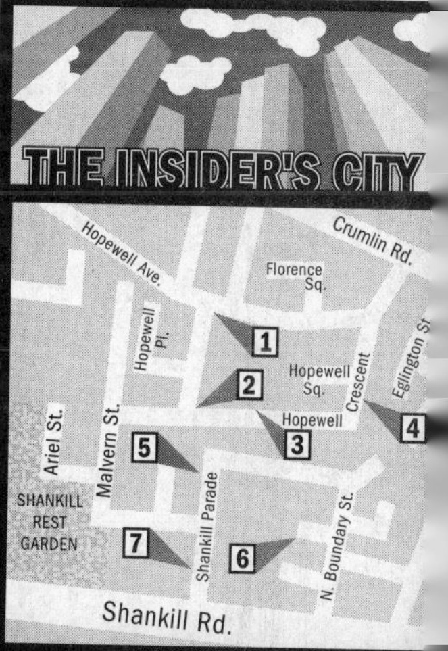

THE PROTESTANT MURALS

The Protestant murals, in the Shankill area of West Belfast, tend to be overtly militant. Most are found near Hopewell St. and Hopewell Crescent, to the north of Shankill Rd., or down Shankill Parade, and are accessed by traveling south from Crumlin Rd.

1. This mural commemorates the **Red Hand Commando,** a militant Loyalist group.
2. Painting of a **Loyalist martyr,** killed in prison in 1997.
3. Depiction of the **Grim Reaper,** with gun and British flag.
4. A collage featuring Loyalist militant groups including the **UVF, UDU,** and **UDA.**
5. Mural of the **Battle of the Boyne,** commemorating William of Orange's 1690 victory over James II.
6. The **Marksman's** gun seems to follow you as you pass by.
7. Portrait of the infamous **Top Gun,** a man responsible for the deaths of many high-ranking Republicans.

OCK YOUR SOCKS OFF

ust over 60 million years ago, fter the last dinosaurs had died, he supercontinent Laurasia began o split up. The movement of the earth's plates caused zones of weakness in crustal rock, one of hem in the Irish Sea. The lava that erupted through fissures in the weakened northern Irish coastline eventually pooled into a lake 90m deep, and cracks in the cooling ava formed the 40,000 basalt coulmns of the Giant's Causeway. Many are hexagonal, but others have seven or eight sides.

Some deposits of fresh lava were broken down by Irish wind and rain, forming the mineral-rich red soil that would delight farmers millions of years later. Others stood up to the elements as well as the Causeway steps did, and can still be seen today as formations like the Giant's Harp (a hardened lava waterfall) and Giant's Eye (the cross-section of a column that weathered in many colorful, concentric rings).

At the end of the second Ice Age, about 15,000 years ago, glaciers carved out Ireland's dramatic coastline. Eventually the ice melted and sea levels rose around the Causeway columns and the surrounding cliffs.

Though the Causeway Coast is he only place in Ireland with such dramatic geology, similar volcanic structures can also be found in Scotland, Israel, Thailand, and New Zealand. Those countries just don't have giants to blame for hem.

press. It's now home to the city's largest selection of Irish whiskeys. (☎9024 1062. Open M-W 11:30am-11pm, Th-F 11:30am-1am, Sa 11:30am-2am.) Move on to **White's Tavern,** 2-4 Winecellar Entry, Belfast's oldest tavern. (☎9024 3080. Open M-W 11:30am-11pm, Th-Sa 11:30am-1:30am.) Farther south, **Apartment,** 2 Donegall Sq. W., the preferred cafe/bar/bistro of Belfast's hip and beautiful is perfect for pre-clubbing mixed drinks from £3.75. (Open M-F 8am-1am, Sa 9am-1am, Su noon-midnight.) Explore the club scene at **The Fly,** 5-6 Lower Crescent. Don't let the insect decor scare you off. The first floor is for pints, the second for mingling, and the third for a 40-flavor vodka test-tube-shot bar. (☎9050 9750. Open M-W 7pm-1am, Th-Sa 5pm-1:15am.) **The Kremlin,** 96 Donegall St., is Belfast's best gay nightspot. Doors close at 1am, but the party only heats up inside. (☎9080 9700. Bar open Tu-Th 4pm-3am, F-Su 1pm-3am.)

DERRY/LONDONDERRY ☎028

Originally christened *Diore,* meaning "oak grove," the city's name was anglicized to Derry and finally to Londonderry. The city's label remains a source of contention, as the minority Protestant population uses the official title while many Republican Northerners and informal Protestants refer to the city as Derry. In an effort to remain impartial, the BBC reported on "Derry-stroke-Londonderry" at the height of the troubles.

Modern Derry/Londonderry is trying to cast off the legacy of its political Troubles, with much success. Although the landscape was razed by years of bombings, and violence still erupts occasionally during the marching season (July 4-12), recent years have been relatively peaceful. Today's rebuilt city is beautiful and intimate with a manageable but cosmopolitan vibe. The **city walls,** 5.5m high and 6m thick, erected between 1614 and 1619, have never been breached—hence Derry/Londonderry's nickname "the Maiden City." The tower topping the southeast wall past New Gate was built to protect **St. Columb's Cathedral,** off Bishop St., the symbolic focus of the city's Protestant defenders. (Open M-Sa Easter-Oct. 9am-5pm; Nov.-Mar. 9am-4pm. Tours £2.) At Union Hall Pl., just inside Magazine Gate, the **Tower Museum's** engaging exhibits recount Derry/Londonderry's history. (☎7137 2411. Open July-Aug. M-Sa 10am-5pm, Su 2-5pm; Sept.-June Tu-Sa 10am-5pm. Last admission 4:30pm. Call for prices.) West of the city walls, Derry/Londonderry's residential neighborhoods—both the Protestant **Waterside** and **Fountain Estate,** as well as the Catholic **Bogside**—display brilliant murals.

Go down Strand Rd. and turn left up Great James to reach the friendly and social **Derry City Independent Hostel ❶**, 44 Great James St. (☎7137 7989. Breakfast included. Free Internet. Dorms £10; doubles £28.) **The Saddler's House (No. 36) ❸**, 36 Great James St., offers elegant rooms in a lovely Victorian home. (☎7126 9691. Breakfast included. Singles £30; doubles £45-50.) Modern Italian eatery **Danano ❸**, 2-4 Lower Clarendon St., has the only wood-burning pizza oven in Northern Ireland. (☎7126 9034. M-Tu 2-for-1 pizzas. Open daily 5pm-midnight.) The **Tesco** supermarket is in the Quayside Shopping Centre, a short walk from the walled city along Strand Rd. (Open M-Th 9am-9pm, F 8:30am-9pm, Sa 8:30am-8pm, Su 1-6pm.) After dark, check out **Peadar O'Donnell's,** 53 Waterloo St., where Celtic and Orangeman paraphernalia hang beside chalkboards of specials. (☎7137 2318. Open M-Sa 11am-1am, Su 7pm-midnight.) The stained-glass ceilings at **Mullan's,** 13 Little James St., are a surreal backdrop for thumping dance beats. (☎7126 5300. W-Th live music. Open M-Sa 10am-2am, Su noon-12:30am.)

Trains (☎7134 2228) arrive on Duke St., Waterside, from Belfast (2hr., 4-9 per day, £9). A free Rail-Link bus connects the **train station** and the **bus station,** on Foyle St., between the walled city and the river. Ulsterbus **buses** (☎7126 2261) go to Belfast (1½-3hr., 10-36 per day, £8) and Dublin (4¼hr., 4-6 per day, £13). The **tourist office** is at 44 Foyle St. (☎7126 7284; www.derryvisitor.com. Open July-Sept. M-F 9am-7pm, Sa 10am-6pm, Su 10am-5pm; Nov.-June reduced hours.) **Postal Code:** BT48.

CAUSEWAY COAST ☎028

Sea-battered cliffs and castle ruins tower over white beaches before giving way to the spectacular geology of **Giant's Causeway,** for which the region is named. Thousands of visitors swarm to the site today, but few take time to explore the rest of the stunning and easily accessible coastline that stretches beyond.

TRANSPORTATION. Bus (☎7032 5400) #172 runs between Ballycastle and Portrush along the coast (1hr., 3-5 per day, £7.80). The Antrim Coaster #252 runs from Belfast to Portstewart via most small towns along the coast (2 per day). The open-topped Bushmills Bus traces the coast between Coleraine, 8km south of Portrush, and the Causeway (July-Aug. 5 per day).

LOCAL LEGEN

WHAT A BABY

If the geological explanation of the Giant's Causeway seems too prosaic, a little story time is in order One of the best known yarns in the Irish oral tradition claims that the Giant's Causeway was forme when the famed giant Finn Mac Cool *(Finn mac Cumaill)*, leader o the warrior clan *Fianna*, foun himself, as warrior giants are won to be, in a row with his hulkin Scottish counterpart, Benandonner. Excited at the prospect of a showdown, the cavalier Finn constructed an ornate walkway for his opponent to cross from his home on Staffa Island off Scotland.

Upon hearing rumors o Benandonner's colossal stature and strength, the deflated Finn did what any good leader of a warrior clan of giants would do he asked his wife, Oonagh, to hide him. Oonagh did what any fine lady giant would do: she dressed her husband up as a baby and placed him in a huge cradle in plain sight.

When the hunkering Sco crossed the bridge and saw the oversized baby, he imagined the size of the father and quickly turned and fled back to Scotland in terror, ripping up the Causeway to ensure that Papa Finn would not pursue. The rock known as the Giant's Boot was Benandonner's cast-off, left in the haste of his cowardly retreat.

BALLYCASTLE AND ENVIRONS. The Causeway Coast leaves the sleepy glens behind when it hits **Ballycastle,** a seaside town sheltering tourists bound for Giant's Causeway. **Bus** #162A goes to Cushendall via Cushendun (50min., M-F 1 per day, £3), and #131 goes to Belfast (3hr., M-Sa 5-6 per day, £6.50). The **tourist office** is in Sheskburn House, 7 Mary St. (☎2076 2024. Open July-Aug. M-F 9:30am-7pm, Sa 10am-6pm, Su 2-6pm; Sept.-June M-F 9:30am-5pm.) A bright orange-and-yellow facade beckons budget travelers to the comfortable and homey **Castle Hostel (IHH)** ❶, 62 Quay Rd. (☎2076 2337. Dorms £8.)

Just off the coast of Ballycastle, bumpy, boomerang-shaped **Rathlin Island** ("Fort of the Sea") is home to more puffins (pop. 20,000) than people (pop. 100). **Raghery Tours** (☎2076 3949) drives to the **Kebble Bird Sanctuary,** 7km from the harbor (20min., every 45min., £3). Caledonian MacBrayne (☎2076 9299) **ferries** run to the island from the pier at Ballycastle, up the hill from Quay Rd. (45min., 2-4 per day, round-trip £8.60). Eight kilometers west of Ballycastle, the modest village of **Ballintoy** attracts the crowds on their way to the tiny **Carrick-a-rede Island.** From the mainland, cross the fishermen's rope bridge (about 2m wide) over the dizzying 30m drop to the rocks and sea below; be extremely careful in windy weather. A sign marks the turn-off for the bridge from the coastal road east of Ballintoy. The **Sheep Island View Hostel (IHH)** ❶ is at 42A Main St. (☎2076 9391; www.sheepisland-view.com. Laundry £2. Dorms with breakfast £12. Camping £5 per person.)

GIANT'S CAUSEWAY. Advertised as the eighth natural wonder of the world, the Giant's Causeway is Northern Ireland's most popular attraction, so don't be surprised to find that 2000 other travelers picked the same day to visit; arrive early in the morning or after the visitors' center closes to avoid crowds. Geologists believe that the unique rock formations were formed 60 million years ago. Comprised of over 40,000 perfectly symmetrical hexagonal basalt columns, the site resembles a large descending staircase that leads out from the cliffs to the ocean floor below. Ulsterbus #172 to Portrush, the #252 Antrim Coaster, and the Bushmills Bus all drop visitors off at the Giant's Causeway Visitors' Centre. A minibus (£1.20) runs the 1km from the center to the columns. *(Causeway open 24hr. Free. Centre ☎2073 1855; www.northantrim.com. Open May daily 10am-5:30pm; June daily 10am-6pm; July-Aug. daily 10am-7pm; Sept.-Oct. M-F 10am-5pm, Sa-Su 10am-5:30pm.)*

ITALY (ITALIA)

Italy's breathtaking vistas range from steep Alpine peaks in the north to the rolling olive hills of the interior to the aquamarine waters of the southern shoreline. Civilizations evolved piecemeal throughout the country, creating an people with distinct regional characteristics. Visitors find romance infused in the sculpture of old masters, the vibrancy of the people, and the finesse of gourmet food. Italians embrace the pleasures of life: indulging in daily siestas, dressing in the latest fashions, and hosting family feasts on a regular basis. The openness of the Italian people lets any traveler ease into this country's relaxed and admired way of life.

DISCOVER ITALY: SUGGESTED ITINERARIES

THREE DAYS Spend it all in the Eternal City of **Rome** (p. 601). Go back in time at the **Ancient City:** be a gladiator in the **Colosseum,** explore the **Roman Forum** and stand in the well-preserved **Pantheon.** Spend the next day admiring the fine art in the **Capitoline Museums** and the **Galleria Borghese,** then satiate your other senses in a disco. The next morning, redeem your debauched soul in **Vatican City,** gazing at the ceiling of the **Sistine Chapel,** gaping at **St. Peter's Cathedral,** and enjoying the **Vatican Museums.**

ONE WEEK Spend 3 days taking in the sights in **Rome** before heading north to **Florence** (2 days; p. 658) to immerse yourself in Italy's amazing Renaissance art at the Uffizi Gallery. Move to **Venice** (2 days; p. 642) to float through the canals.

BEST OF ITALY IN 3 WEEKS Begin among the waterways of **Venice** (2 days). Find your Romeo or Juliet in **Verona** (1 day; p. 655). Take a hike in **Lake Como** (1 day; p. 631) before heading to cosmopolitan **Milan** (2 days; p. 624). Move coastward to **Finale Ligure** (1 day; p. 634), and the beautiful **Cinque Terre** (2 days; p. 636). Next, take in the culture of **Florence** (3 days), then cheer on horses in **Siena** (1 day; p. 669). Immerse yourself in the sights and history of **Rome** (3 days), before heading south to **Naples** (2 days; p. 676); be sure to visit preserved, ancient **Pompeii** (1 day; p. 680). Then hike and swim along the **Amalfi Coast** (1 day; p. 681), and see the Grotto Azzura on the island of **Capri** (1 day; p. 682).

ESSENTIALS

FACTS AND FIGURES

Official Name: Italian Republic.

Capital: Rome.

Major Cities: Florence, Milan, Naples, Venice.

Population: 58,060,000.

Time Zone: GMT +1.

Language: Italian; some German, French, and Slovenian.

Religion: Roman Catholic (98%).

Longest Salami: Made by Rino Parenti in Zibello, displayed on Nov. 23, 2003; 486.8m in length.

WHEN TO GO

Traveling to Italy in late May or early September, when the temperature drops to a comfortable 77°F (25°C), will ensure a calmer, cooler vacation. Also keep weather patterns, festival schedules, and tourist congestion in mind. Tourism goes into

overdrive in June, July, and August: hotels are booked solid, with prices limited only by the stratosphere. In August, Italians flock to the coast for their summer vacation; northern cities become tourist-infested infernos.

DOCUMENTS AND FORMALITIES

EMBASSIES AND CONSULATES. Foreign embassies are in Rome (p. 601). Italian embassies abroad include: **Australia,** 12 Grey St., Deakin, Canberra ACT 2600 (☎02 627 333 33; www.ambitalia.org.au); **Canada,** 275 Slater St., 21st fl., Ottawa, ON K1P 5H9 (☎613-232-2401; www.italyincanada.com); **Ireland,** 63/65 Northumberland Rd., Dublin (☎660 1744; www.italianembassy.ie); **New Zealand,** 34-38 Grant Rd., Wellington (☎4473 5339; www.italy-embassy.org.nz); **UK,** 14 Three Kings Yard, London W1K 4EH (☎020 731 222 00; www.embitaly.org.uk); and **US,** 3000 Whitehaven St., Washington, D.C. 20008 (☎202 612 4400; www.italyemb.org).

VISA AND ENTRY INFORMATION. EU citizens do not need a visa. Citizens of Australia, Canada, New Zealand, and the US do not need a visa for stays of up to 90 days, beginning upon entry into any of the countries within the EU's freedom of movement zone. For more information, see **One Europe,** p. 16.

TOURIST SERVICES AND MONEY

EMERGENCY	**Emergency:** ☎113. **Carabinieri Military Police:** ☎112. **Ambulance:** ☎118. **Fire:** ☎115.

TOURIST OFFICES. In provincial capitals, look for the **Ente Provinciale per il Turismo (EPT)** or **Azienda di Promozione Turistica (APT)** for info on the town and the entire province. Local tourist offices, **Informazione e Assistenza ai Turisti (IAT)** and **Azienda Autonoma di Soggiorno e Turismo (AAST),** are generally the most useful. **Italian Government Tourist Board (ENIT)** has offices in: **Australia,** Level 26, 44 Market St., NSW 2000 Sydney (☎02 9262 1666); **Canada,** 175 E. Bloor St., #907 South Tower, Toronto, ON M4W 3R8 (☎416-925-4882); **UK,** 1 Princes St., London WIR 2AY (☎020 7399 3562); **US,** 630 5th Ave., #1565, New York, NY 10111 (☎212-245-5618). Visit www.enit.it for a list of all ENIT locations.

MONEY. The **euro (€)** has replaced the **lira** as the unit of currency in Italy. For more information, see p. 19. The **Value-Added Tax (VAT,** or **IVA** in Italy) is a sales tax levied in the EU. Foreigners making any purchase over €335 are entitled to an additional 20% VAT refund. Some stores take off 20% on site; the alternative is to fill out forms at the customs office upon leaving the EU and send receipts from home, upon which the refund will be mailed to you. Not all storefront "Tax-Free" stickers imply an immediate, on-site refund; ask before making a purchase.

BUSINESS HOURS. Nearly everything closes 1-3 or 4pm for *siesta.* Most museums open 9am-1pm and 3-6pm; some open through lunch, however. Monday is often their *giorno di chiusura* (day of closure).

TRANSPORTATION

BY PLANE. Rome's international airport (FCO), known as both Fiumicino and Leonardo da Vinci, is served by most major airlines. Other hubs are Milan's Malpensa or Linate airports and Florence's Amerigo Vespucci airport. **Alitalia** (☎800-223-5730; www.alitalia.com) is Italy's national airline and offers low-season fares.

SEEING GREEN. If you're under 26 or over 60 and plan to travel extensively in Italy, your first purchase should be a Carta Verde (€26), which offers a year-long 20% discount on all train tickets.

BY TRAIN. The Italian State Railway **Ferrovie dello Stato,** or **FS** (national information line ☎848 88 80 88; www.fs-on-line.com), offers inexpensive, efficient service. There are several types of trains: the *locale* stops at every station on a particular line; the *diretto* makes fewer stops than the *locale;* and the *espresso* stops only at major stations. The air-conditioned *rapido,* an **InterCity** (IC) train, zips along but costs more. Tickets for the fast, pricey **Eurostar** trains require reservations. **Eurail** is valid without a supplement on all trains except Eurostar.

BY BUS. Intercity buses serve points inaccessible by train and occasionally arrive in convenient places in large towns. Buy city bus tickets in *tabacchi* (kiosks).

VALIDATE=GREAT. Always **validate** your train ticket **before boarding.** Validation machines, usually yellow or orange, are located all over train stations. Insert and remove your ticket from the slot and check to see if the machine stamped it. Failure to validate may result in steep fines, and train operators do not accept ignorance as an excuse. The same goes for bus tickets, which should be validated immediately after boarding the bus using the machines onboard.

BY FERRY. Portside ferries in Ancona (p. 675), Bari, and Brindisi connect Italy to Greece. Boats from Trieste (p. 657) serve the Istrian Peninsula down to Croatia's Dalmatian Coast. Ferries also connect Italy's islands to the mainland. For Sardinia, boats leave from Genoa (p. 633), La Spezia (p. 637), and Naples (p. 676). Travelers to Sicily (p. 684) take the ferry from Naples (p. 676) or Reggio di Calabria.

BY CAR. There are four kinds of roads: *autostrada* (superhighways; mostly toll-roads); *strade statali* (state roads); *strade provinciali* (provincial); and *strade communali* (local). Driving in Italy is frightening; congested traffic is common in large cities and in the north. On three-lane roads, the center lane is for passing. **Mopeds** (€30-40 per day) can be a great way to see the islands and more scenic areas but can be disastrous in the rain and on rough roads. Always exercise caution; practice in empty streets and learn to keep with the flow of traffic. Drivers in Italy—especially in the south—are notorious for ignoring traffic laws. Call the **Automobile Club Italiano (ACI)** at ☎116 if you break down. If you plan to drive a car while in Italy, you must be 18 or older and have an **International Driving Permit** if you don't have an EU license.

BY BIKE AND BY THUMB. Bicycling is popular, but bike trails are rare and most terrain is challenging. Drivers can be reckless. *Let's Go* does not encourage hitchhiking, which can be unsafe in Italy, especially in areas south of Rome or Naples.

KEEPING IN TOUCH

PHONE CODES

Country code: 39. **International dialing prefix:** 00. For more information on how to place international calls, see inside back cover. When calling within a city, dial 0 + city code + local number. All 10-digit numbers listed in this chapter are mobile phones and do not require a city code.

EMAIL AND THE INTERNET. Though Italy initially lagged behind in jumping on the information superhighway, it's now playing catch-up like a pro. It's easy to find access in large cities, and in many small towns and southern cities. Rates are €5-8 per hour. For free Internet access, try local universities and libraries. For a list of Italian cyberspots, check www.cybercaptive.com.

TELEPHONE. Prepaid phone cards, available from *tabacchi*, vending machines, and phone card vendors, carry a certain amount of time depending on the card's denomination (€5, €10, or €20). International calls start at €1.05 and vary depending on where you are calling. A collect call is a *contassa a carico del destinatario* or *chiamata collect.* For info on purchasing and using a **mobile phone** in Italy, see p. 33. International direct dial numbers include: **AT&T** ☎172 10 11; **Canada Direct** ☎172 10 01; **MCI** ☎172 10 22; **Sprint** ☎172 18 77.

MAIL. Airmail letters sent from Australia, North America, or the UK to Italy take anywhere from three to seven days. Since Italian mail is notoriously unreliable, it is usually safer and quicker to send mail priority *(prioritaria)* or registered *(raccomandata)*. *Fermo Posta* is Italian for *Poste Restante* and should be addressed like so: First name SURNAME, Fermo Posta [postal code, city] Italy.

LANGUAGE. The Italian language has evolved into something completely different from its structural and lexical basis: Latin. As a result of the country's fragmented history, variations in dialects are strong. The throaty **Neapolitan** can be difficult for a northerner to understand; **Ligurians** use a mix of Italian, Catalan, and French; **Sardo,** spoken in Sardinia, bears little resemblance to standard Italian; and many **Tuscan** dialects differ from Italian in pronunciation. Some inhabitants of the northern border regions don't speak Italian at all: the population of Valle d'Aosta speaks mainly French, and Trentino-Alto Adige harbors a German-speaking minority. In the southern regions of Puglia, Calabria, and Sicily, entire villages speak a form of Albanian called **Arbresh.** In order to facilitate conversation, locals do their best to employ standard Italian when speaking with foreigners, although some may be shy or hesitant to do so. Many Italians, especially older people or those living in rural areas, do not speak English, although most young people and those in the tourist industry do. Any knowledge of French, Portuguese, Spanish, or Latin will help you understand Italian. For a traveler's survival kit of basic Italian, see p. 1062.

ACCOMMODATIONS AND CAMPING

ITALY	❶	❷	❸	❹	❺
ACCOMMODATIONS	under €16	€16-25	€25-40	€40-60	over €60

Associazione Italiana Alberghi per la Gioventù (AIG), the Italian hostel federation, is a Hostelling International (HI) affiliate. A full list of AIG affiliates is available online at www.ostellionline.org. Prices start at about €8 per night for dorms. Hostels are the best option for solo travelers (single rooms are relatively scarce in hotels), but curfews, lockouts, distant locations, and less-than-perfect security detract from their appeal. Italian **hotel** rates are set by the state. Hotel owners will need your passport to register you; don't be afraid to hand it over for a while (usually overnight), but ask for it as soon as you think you will need it. Hotel singles *(camera singola)* usually start at around €25-50 per night, and doubles *(camera doppia)* start at €40-82. A room with a private bath *(con bagno)* usually costs 30-50% more. Smaller **pensioni** are often cheaper than hotels. Be sure to confirm charges before checking in; Italian hotels are notorious for tacking on additional costs at check-out time. The **Azienda di Promozione Turismo (APT),** provides lists of hotels that have paid to be listed; some of the hotels *Let's Go* recommends may not be on the list. **Affittacamere** (rooms for rent in private houses) are another inexpensive option. For more info, inquire at local tourist offices. There are over 1700 **campsites** in Italy; tent sites average €4.20. The **Touring Club Italiano** (www.touringclub.it) publishes books and pamphlets on the outdoors.

FOOD AND DRINK

ITALY	❶	❷	❸	❹	❺
FOOD	under €7	€7-15	€15-20	€20-25	over €25

Breakfast time in Italy often goes unnoticed; lunch is the main feast of the day. A *pranzo* (full meal) is a true event, consisting of an *antipasto* (appetizer), a *primo* (first course of pasta or soup), a *secondo* (meat or fish), a *contorno* (vegetable side dish), and then finally a *dolce* (dessert or fruit), a *caffè*, and often an after-dinner liqueur. If you don't have a big appetite, you can buy authentic snacks for a picnic at *salumeria* or *alimentari* (meat and grocery shops). Grab a lighter lunch at an inexpensive *tavola calda* (hot table), *rosticceria* (grill), or *gastronomia* (serving hot, prepared dishes). *Osterie*, *trattorie*, and *ristoranti* are, in ascending order, fancier and more expensive. Many restaurants offer a fixed-price tourist menu *(menù turistico)* that includes *primo*, *secondo*, bread, water, and wine. Italian dinner is typically a lighter meal. In the north, butter and cream sauces dominate, while Rome and central Italy are notoriously spicy regions. Farther south, tomatoes play a significant role. Coffee is another rich and varied focus of Italian life; for a standard cup of espresso, request a *caffè; cappuccino* is a breakfast beverage. *Caffè macchiato* (spotted coffee) has a touch of milk, while *latte macchiato* is heavier on the milk and lighter on the coffee. Wines from the north of Italy, such as the Piemonte's *Asti Spumante* or Verona's *Soave*, tend to be heavy and full-bodied; stronger, fruitier wines come from southern Italy. Almost every shop sells Italy's greatest contribution to civilization: gelato (ice cream).

THE UGLY DUCKLING. Before shelling out the euro for a *piccolo cono* (small cone), assess the quality of an establishment by looking at the banana gelato: if it's bright yellow, it's been made from a mix. If it's slightly gray, real bananas were used. *Gelati* in metal bins also tend to be homemade, whereas plastic tubs indicate mass-production.

ITALY

HOLIDAYS AND FESTIVALS

Holidays: New Year's Day (Jan. 1); Epiphany (Jan. 15); Easter Sunday and Monday (Apr. 16 and 17); Liberation Day (Apr. 25); Labor Day (May 1); Assumption of the Virgin (Aug. 15); All Saints' Day (Nov. 1); Immaculate Conception (Dec. 8); and Santo Stefano (Dec. 26).

Festivals: The most common excuse for a local festival is the celebration of a religious event—a patron saint's day or the commemoration of a miracle. Most include parades, music, wine, and obscene amounts of food. Carnevale, a country-wide celebration, is held during the 10 days leading up to Lent. In Venice, costumed Carnevale revelers fill the streets and canals. During Scoppio del Carro, held in Florence's P. del Duomo on Easter Sunday, Florentines set off a cart of explosives, remembering Pazziano dei Pazzi who returned from the crusades with a few splinters from the holy sepulcher, which he used to light a simple fireworks display. The Spoleto Festival (known as the Festival dei Due Mondi; Festival of Two Worlds) is one of the world's most prestigious international arts events. Each June and July it features concerts, operas, ballets, film screenings, and modern art shows (www.spoletofestival.it).

BEYOND TOURISM

One of the most satisfying ways to develop a deeper understanding of Italian culture is through personal interaction, made possible by Italy's many volunteer organizations and international programs. From harvesting grapes on vineyards in Siena to restoring and protecting marine life in the Mediterranean, there is something for everyone interested in working for a cause. Those in search of a more lucrative experience might consider working as an intern for the Italian press or teaching English in Italian schools. For more info on Beyond Tourism opportunities throughout Europe, see **Beyond Tourism,** p. 66.

Abruzzo National Park, V. Roma s.n.c., 67030 Villetta Barrea, AQ Italy (☎0864 89 102; www.parcoabruzzo.it.), hosts 1000 summer volunteers. Opportunities range from park maintenance to nature education programs. Program fee €110-170. Write to apply.

Gruppi Archeologici d'Italia, V. Tacito 41, I-00193 Rome, Italy (☎06 687 40 28; www.gruppiarcheologici.org). Organizes 1- 3-week long volunteer programs at archaeological digs throughout Italy. Offers links to various programs hoping to promote cultural awareness about archaeological preservation. Program fee €205-380.

ROME (ROMA) ☎06

From the winding medieval streets to the majestic triumphal vistas on the Via del Corso and the Via dei Fori Imperiali, from the chill late-night atmosphere on a *piazza* to the awe of standing in the middle of the Roman Forum, Rome (pop. 2,545,000) is an animated city set in a backdrop of a lengthy and glorious history. Romans celebrate their city, with a warmth and eagerness to share its masterpieces, colossal testaments to the centuries of power and wealth that have thrived here. Even though the Roman Empire has long since crumbled, Rome's glory has not been diminished, but instead transformed.

INTERCITY TRANSPORTATION

Flights: Da Vinci International Airport (FCO; ☎659 51), known as **Fiumicino,** handles most flights. The **Termini** line runs nonstop to Rome's main station, **Stazione Termini** (30min., 8 and 38min. past the hr., €9.50). After hours, take the blue COTRAL **bus** to Tiburtina from outside the main doors after customs (€5). From Tiburtina, take bus #492, 175, or metro B to Termini. Most charter flights arrive at **Ciampino** (CIA; ☎79 49 41). To get to Rome, take the COTRAL bus (every 30min., €1) to Anagnina station.

Trains: From Stazione Termini to: **Bologna** (2½-3½hr., €27-38); **Florence** (1½-3¾hr., €15-30); **Milan** (4½-8hr., €31-47); **Naples** (1¾-2½hr., €11-23); **Venice** (4½-5½hr., €36-58). Trains arriving in Rome between midnight and 5am arrive at **Stazione Tiburtina** or **Stazione Ostiense,** which are connected to Termini by the #175 bus.

ITALY

ORIENTATION

Navigating Rome's narrow winding streets is difficult, so many speak of locations in relation to nearby landmarks or main arteries. The **Tiber River,** which snakes north-south through the city, is a useful reference point. Most trains arrive in Termini Station, east of Rome's **centro storico** (historic center). **Termini,** and the neighborhood of **San Lorenzo** to the east are home to the city's largest university and the most budget accommodations. **Via Nazionale** originates two blocks northwest of Termini Station in **Piazza della Repubblica** and leads to **Piazza Venezia,** the focal point of the city marked by the immense wedding-cake-like **Vittorio Emanuele II monument.** From P. Venezia **Via dei Fori Imperiali** runs southeast to the Ancient city, where the **Colosseum** and the **Roman Forum** speak of former glory. **Via del Corso** stretches from P. Venezia to **Piazza del Popolo** in the north, marked by a black obelisk at its center. The **Trevi fountain, Piazza Barberini,** and the streets around **Piazza di Spagna** lie to the east of V. del Corso. **Villa Borghese** with its impressive gardens and museums is northeast of P. di Spagna. To the west of V. del Corso is the *centro storico*, a tangle of sights around the **Pantheon, Piazza Navona, Campo dei Fiori,** and the old **Jewish Ghetto. Largo Argentina,** west of P. Venezia, marks the start of **Corso Vittorio Emanuele II,** which runs through the *centro storico* to the Tiber. West across the river is **Vatican City** and the **Borgo-Prati** neighborhood. South of the Vatican is **Trastevere** and residential **Testaccio.** Arm yourself with a map; pick up a free copy at Enjoy Rome (p. 607).

LOCAL TRANSPORTATION

Public Transportation: The 2 **Metropolitana** subway lines (A and B) meet at Termini and run 5:30am-11:30pm. **Buses** run 5am-midnight (with limited late-night routes); validate your ticket in the machine when you board. Buy tickets (€1) at *tabacchi*, newsstands, and station machines; they're valid for 1 metro ride or unlimited bus travel

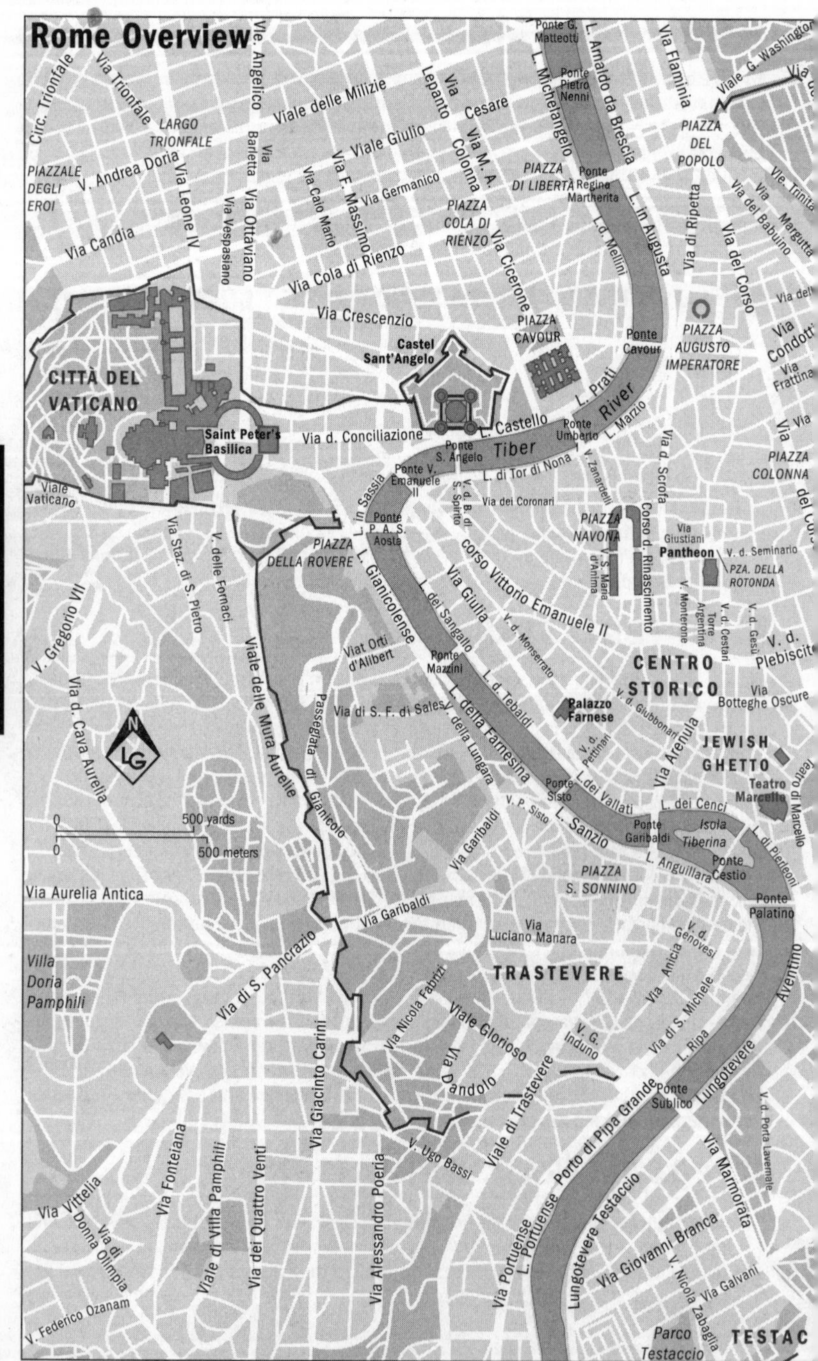
Rome Overview
CITTÀ DEL VATICANO
Saint Peter's Basilica
Castel Sant'Angelo
Tiber River
PIAZZA NAVONA
Pantheon
CENTRO STORICO
Palazzo Farnese
JEWISH GHETTO
Teatro Marcello
Isola Tiberina
TRASTEVERE
PIAZZA DEL POPOLO
PIAZZA AUGUSTO IMPERATORE
PIAZZA COLONNA
PIAZZA CAVOUR
PIAZZA DI LIBERTÀ
PIAZZA COLA DI RIENZO
PIAZZALE DEGLI EROI
LARGO TRIONFALE
PIAZZA DELLA ROVERE
PIAZZA S. SONNINO
PZA. DELLA ROTONDA
Villa Doria Pamphili
Parco Testaccio
TESTAC
0 500 yards
0 500 meters
Via Aurelia Antica
Via di S. Pancrazio
Via Garibaldi
Viale delle Mura Aurelie
Via Cola di Rienzo
Via Crescenzio
Via d. Conciliazione
Corso Vittorio Emanuele II
Via Giulia
Viale di Trastevere
Lungotevere
Via Marmorata
Via Giovanni Branca
Via Flaminia
Via del Corso
Via di Ripetta
Via Ottaviano
Viale Giulio Cesare
Viale delle Milizie
Via Candia
Via Leone IV
V. Andrea Doria
Via Trionfale
Circ. Trionfale
Via Cicerone
Via Arenula
Ponte Garibaldi
Ponte Sisto
Ponte Mazzini
Ponte Cavour
Ponte Umberto
Ponte S. Angelo
Ponte Palatino
Ponte Cestio
Ponte Sublicio
Ponte Regina Martherita
Ponte Pietro Nenni
Ponte G. Matteotti
L. Arnaldo da Brescia
L. in Augusta
L. Michelangelo
L. Gianicolense
L. della Farnesina
L. Sanzio
L. dei Cenci
L. Anguillara
Via Giacinto Carini
Viale Glorioso
Via Dandolo
V. Ugo Bassi
Via Luciano Manara
Via dei Quattro Venti
Viale di Villa Pamphili
Via Fonteiana
Via Vitellia
V. Federico Ozanam
Via Portuense
Porto di Pipa Grande
Lungotevere Testaccio
Viale G. Washington
Via Condotti
Via Frattina
V. d. Plebiscito
Via Botteghe Oscure
V. Gregorio VII
Via d. Cava Aurelia
Via Staz. di S. Pietro
V. delle Fornaci
Viale Vaticano
Passeggiata di Gianicolo
Via di S. F. di Sales
Via dei Coronari
Via Lepanto
Via M. A. Colonna
Via F. Massimo
Via Caio Mario
Via Germanico
Via Vespasiano
Via Barletta
Vle. Angelico
Corso d. Rinascimento
Via d. Scrofa
L. Prati
L. Castello
L. di Tor di Nona
L. d. Mellini
L. Marzio
Via dei Vallati
V. d. Monserrato
L. d. Tebaldi
L. dei Sangallo
Via d. Lungara
Via Nicola Fabrizi
Via Alessandro Poeria
Via Anicia
Via di S. Michele
V. G. Induno
L. Ripa
Via Galvani
V. Nicola Zabaglia
V. d. Porta Lavernale

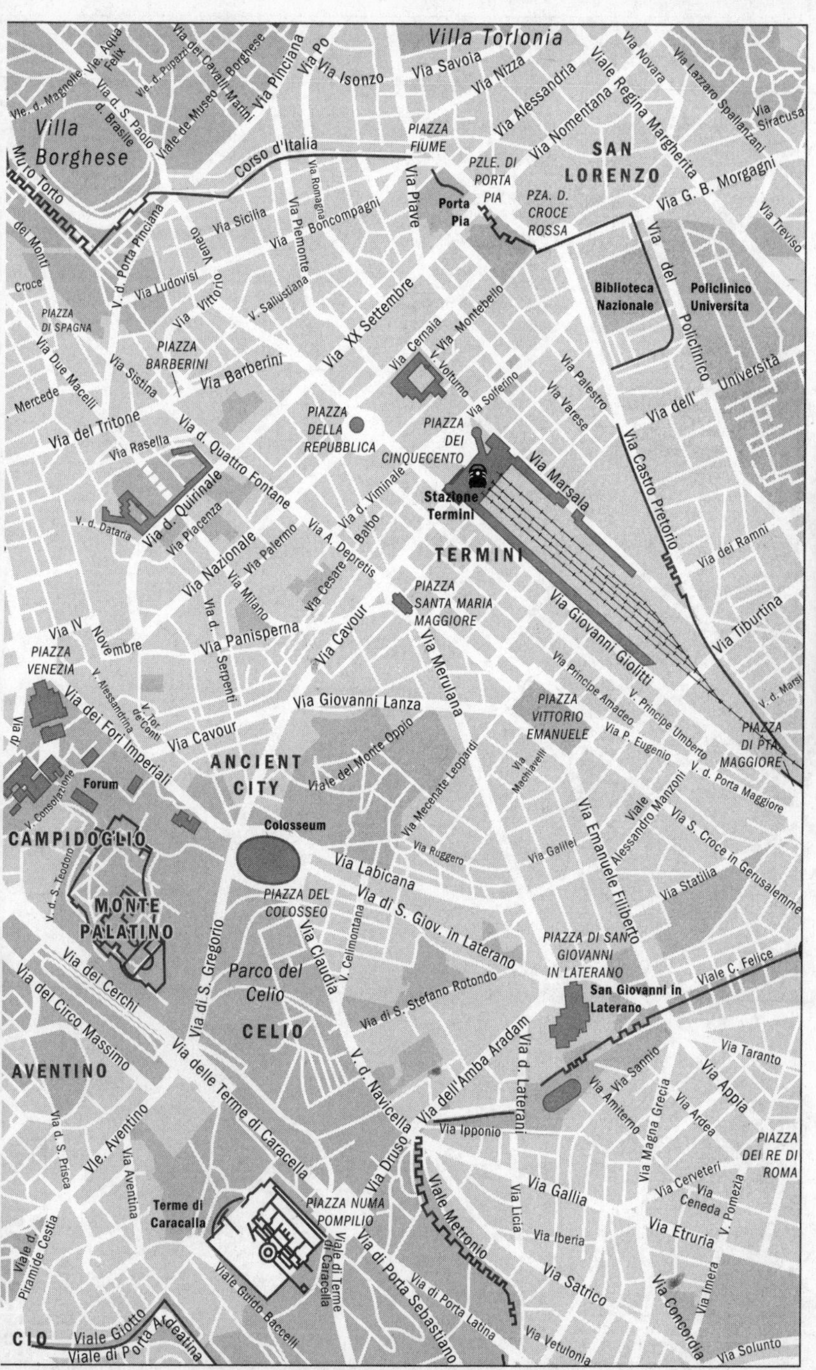
Villa Torlonia
Villa Borghese
SAN LORENZO
Porta Pia
Biblioteca Nazionale
Policlinico Universita
PIAZZA FIUME
PZLE. DI PORTA PIA
PZA. D. CROCE ROSSA
PIAZZA DI SPAGNA
PIAZZA BARBERINI
PIAZZA DELLA REPUBBLICA
PIAZZA DEI CINQUECENTO
Stazione Termini
TERMINI
PIAZZA SANTA MARIA MAGGIORE
PIAZZA VENEZIA
PIAZZA VITTORIO EMANUELE
PIAZZA DI PTA. MAGGIORE
ANCIENT CITY
Forum
Colosseum
CAMPIDOGLIO
MONTE PALATINO
PIAZZA DEL COLOSSEO
Parco del Celio
CELIO
PIAZZA DI SAN GIOVANNI IN LATERANO
San Giovanni in Laterano
AVENTINO
Terme di Caracalla
PIAZZA NUMA POMPILIO
PIAZZA DEI RE DI ROMA
Via Po
Via Isonzo
Via Savoia
Via Nizza
Via Alessandria
Via Nomentana
Viale Regina Margherita
Via Novara
Via Lazzaro Spallanzani
Via Siracusa
Via G. B. Morgagni
Via Treviso
Via Pinciana
Corso d'Italia
Via Piave
Via Sicilia
Via Boncompagni
Via Piemonte
Via Romagna
Via Veneto
Via Ludovisi
Via Vittorio
V. Sallustiana
V. d. Porta Pinciana
Muro Torto
Via XX Settembre
Via Cernaia
V. Volturno
Via Montebello
Via Solferino
Via Palestro
Via Varese
Via Marsala
Via dell' Università
Via del Policlinico
Via Castro Pretorio
Via dei Ramni
Via Tiburtina
V. d. Marsi
Via Barberini
Via Sistina
Via Due Macelli
Via del Tritone
Via Rasella
Via d. Quattro Fontane
Via d. Quirinale
V. d. Dataria
Via Piacenza
Via Nazionale
Via Palermo
Via Milano
Via d. Viminale
Via A. Depretis
Via Cesare Balbo
Via Panisperna
Via IV Novembre
Via d. Serpenti
Via Cavour
Via Merulana
Via Giovanni Giolitti
Via Principe Amadeo
V. Principe Umberto
Via P. Eugenio
V. d. Porta Maggiore
Via Machiavelli
Via Giovanni Lanza
V. Alessandrina
V. Tor de' Conti
Via dei Fori Imperiali
Viale del Monte Oppio
Via Mecenate Leopardi
Via Ruggero
Via Galilei
Via Emanuele Filiberto
Viale Alessandro Manzoni
Via S. Croce in Gerusalemme
Via Statilia
V. Consolazione
V. d. S. Teodoro
Via Labicana
Via di S. Giov. in Laterano
Via Claudia
V. Celimontana
Via di S. Gregorio
Via dei Cerchi
Via del Circo Massimo
Via di S. Stefano Rotondo
Viale C. Felice
Via Taranto
Via Appia
Via Sannio
Via Amiterno
Via Magna Grecia
Via Ardea
Via delle Terme di Caracalla
V. d. Navicella
Via dell'Amba Aradam
Via d. Laterani
Via Ipponio
Via Druso
Viale Metronio
Via Gallia
Via Licia
Via Iberia
Via Cerveteri
Via Ceneda
V. Pomezia
Via Etruria
Via Satrico
Via Imera
Via Concordia
Via Vetulonia
Via Solunto
Vle. Aventino
Via Aventina
Via d. S. Prisca
Viale d. Piramide Cestia
Viale di Terme di Caracalla
Via di Porta Sebastiano
Via di Porta Latina
Viale Guido Baccelli
Viale Giotto
Viale di Porta Ardeatina
Via Mercede
Croce
dei Monti
Vle. Aqua Felix
Via dei Cavalli Marini
Viale de Museo Borghese
Via d. S. Paolo d. Brasile
Vle. d. Magnolie
Vle. d. Pupazzi

ITALY

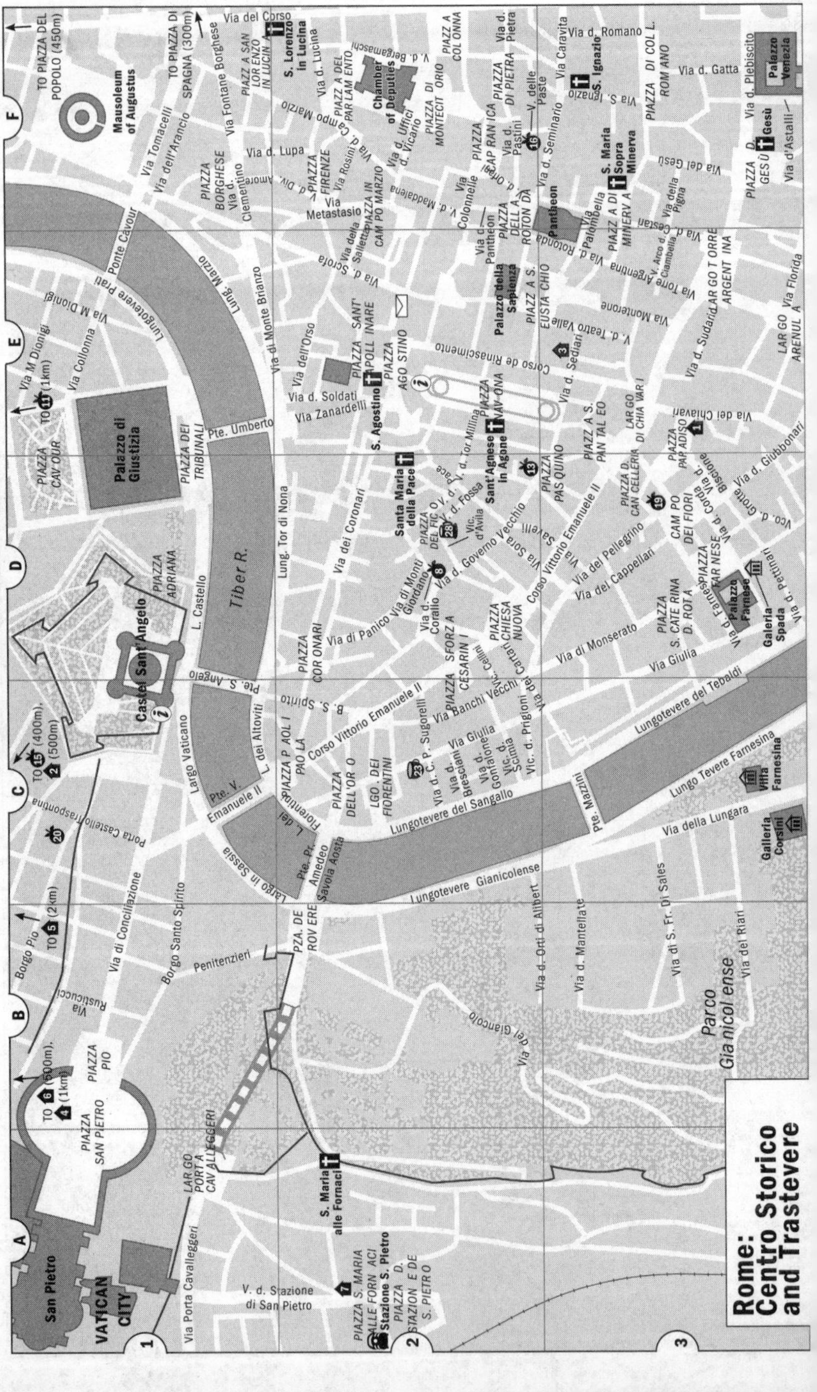

ITALY

Rome: Centro Storico and Trastevere

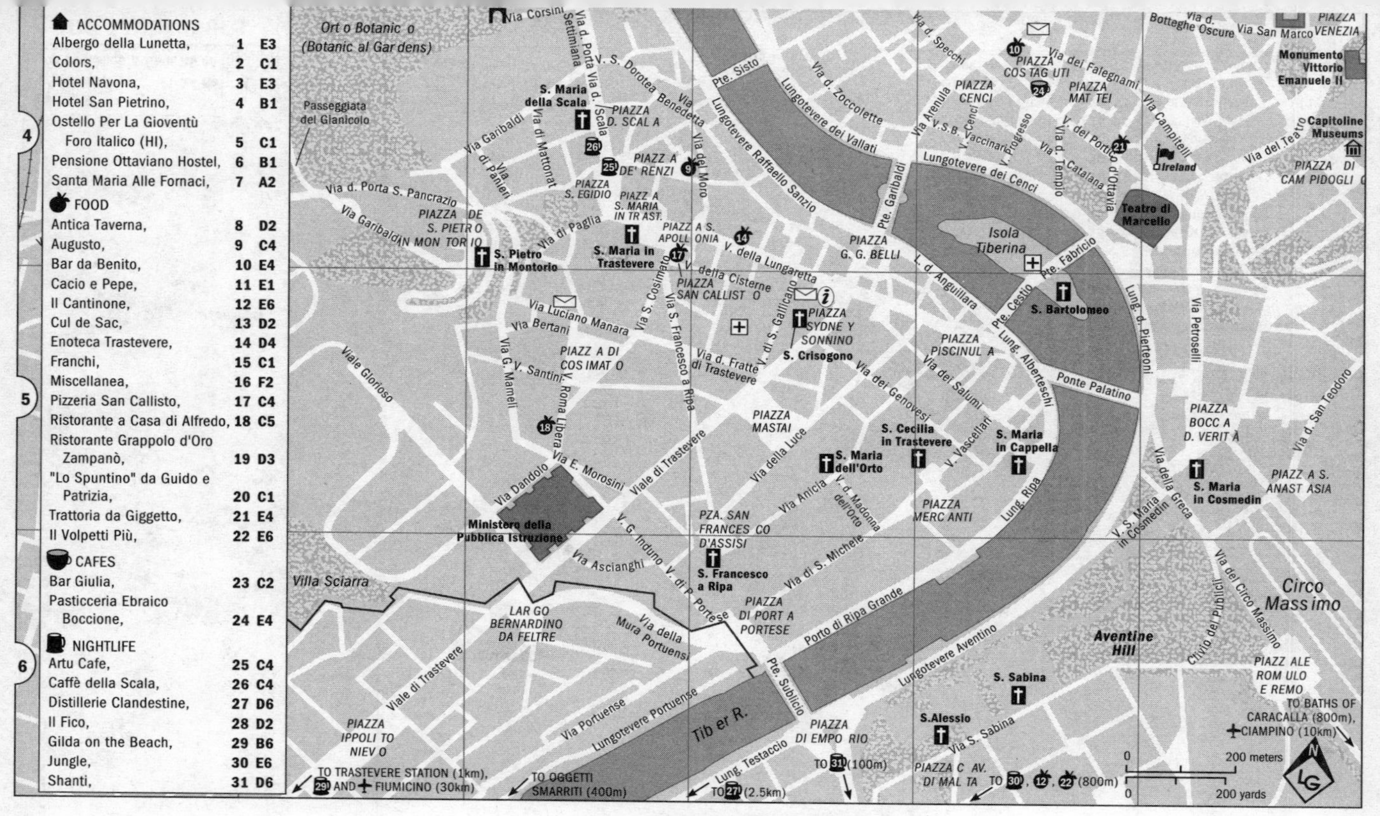
ACCOMMODATIONS
Albergo della Lunetta, 1 E3
Colors, 2 C1
Hotel Navona, 3 E3
Hotel San Pietrino, 4 B1
Ostello Per La Gioventù Foro Italico (HI), 5 C1
Pensione Ottaviano Hostel, 6 B1
Santa Maria Alle Fornaci, 7 A2
FOOD
Antica Taverna, 8 D2
Augusto, 9 C4
Bar da Benito, 10 E4
Cacio e Pepe, 11 E1
Il Cantinone, 12 E6
Cul de Sac, 13 D2
Enoteca Trastevere, 14 D4
Franchi, 15 C1
Miscellanea, 16 F2
Pizzeria San Callisto, 17 C4
Ristorante a Casa di Alfredo, 18 C5
Ristorante Grappolo d'Oro Zampanò, 19 D3
"Lo Spuntino" da Guido e Patrizia, 20 C1
Trattoria da Giggetto, 21 E4
Il Volpetti Più, 22 E6
CAFES
Bar Giulia, 23 C2
Pasticceria Ebraico Boccione, 24 E4
NIGHTLIFE
Artu Cafe, 25 C4
Caffè della Scala, 26 C4
Distillerie Clandestine, 27 D6
Il Fico, 28 D2
Gilda on the Beach, 29 B6
Jungle, 30 E6
Shanti, 31 D6
4
5
6
Orto Botanico (Botanical Gardens)
Passeggiata del Gianicolo
Villa Sciarra
Monumento Vittorio Emanuele II
Capitoline Museums
PIAZZA VENEZIA
Teatro di Marcello
Isola Tiberina
S. Bartolomeo
Circo Massimo
Aventine Hill
S. Sabina
S.Alessio
S. Maria in Cosmedin
S. Maria in Cappella
S. Cecilia in Trastevere
S. Maria dell'Orto
S. Crisogono
S. Francesco a Ripa
S. Maria in Trastevere
S. Maria della Scala
S. Pietro in Montorio
Ministero della Pubblica Istruzione
Ireland
Tiber R.
Pte. Sisto
Pte. Garibaldi
Pte. Fabricio
Pte. Cestio
Ponte Palatino
Pte. Sublicio
Lungotevere Raffaello Sanzio
Lungotevere dei Vallati
Lungotevere dei Cenci
Lung. d. Pierleoni
Lung. Alberteschi
Lung. Ripa
Lungotevere Aventino
Lungotevere Portuense
Lung. Testaccio
Viale di Trastevere
V. della Lungaretta
Via dei Genovesi
Via della Luce
Via Anicia
Via S. Francesco a Ripa
Via S. Cosimato
Via Luciano Manara
Via Garibaldi
Via G. Mameli
Via Dandolo
Via E. Morosini
V. Roma Libera
Via Portuense
Via della Mura Portuensi
Porto di Ripa Grande
Via della Greca
Via del Circo Massimo
Clivo dei Publicii
Via Petroselli
Via d. San Teodoro
Via del Teatro
Via Arenula
Via d. Specchi
Via d. Zoccolette
Via del Moro
Via d. Porta Settimiana
Via Corsini
Viale Glorioso
Via d. Porta S. Pancrazio
PIAZZA S. MARIA IN TRAST.
PIAZZA MASTAI
PIAZZA DI COSIMATO
PIAZZA SAN CALLISTO
PIAZZA G. G. BELLI
PIAZZA SYDNEY SONNINO
PIAZZA PISCINULA
PIAZZA DI PORTA PORTESE
PZA. SAN FRANCESCO D'ASSISI
PIAZZA MERCANTI
PIAZZA BOCCA D. VERITÀ
PIAZZA S. ANASTASIA
PIAZZALE ROMULO E REMO
PIAZZA C. AV. DI MALTA
PIAZZA DI EMPORIO
PIAZZA IPPOLITO NIEVO
LARGO BERNARDINO DA FELTRE
TO BATHS OF CARACALLA (800m), CIAMPINO (10km)
TO TRASTEVERE STATION (1km), AND FIUMICINO (30km)
TO OGGETTI SMARRITI (400m)
200 meters
200 yards

ITALY

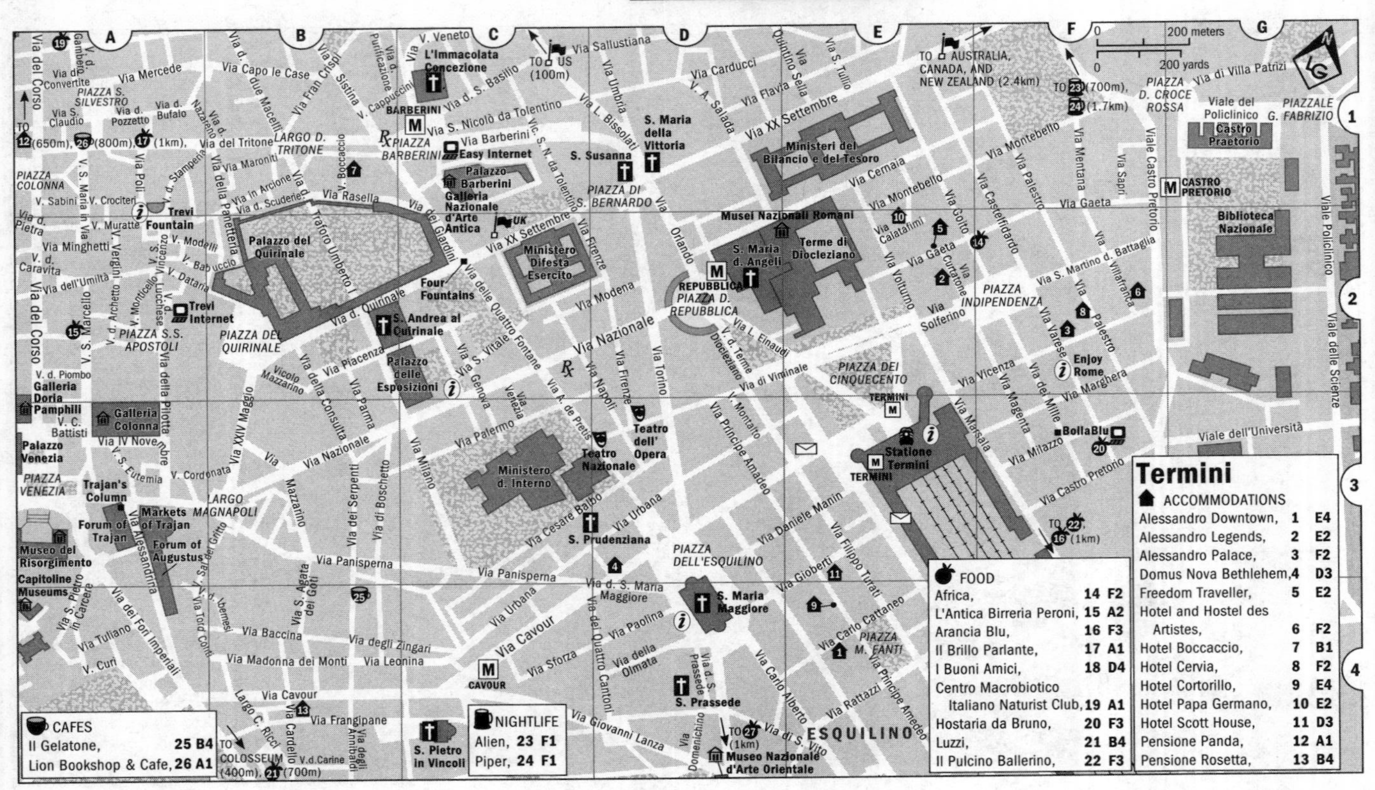
ITALY
Termini
ACCOMMODATIONS
Alessandro Downtown, 1 E4
Alessandro Legends, 2 E2
Alessandro Palace, 3 F2
Domus Nova Bethlehem, 4 D3
Freedom Traveller, 5 E2
Hotel and Hostel des Artistes, 6 F2
Hotel Boccaccio, 7 B1
Hotel Cervia, 8 F2
Hotel Cortorillo, 9 E4
Hotel Papa Germano, 10 E2
Hotel Scott House, 11 D3
Pensione Panda, 12 A1
Pensione Rosetta, 13 B4
FOOD
Africa, 14 F2
L'Antica Birreria Peroni, 15 A2
Arancia Blu, 16 F3
Il Brillo Parlante, 17 A1
I Buoni Amici, 18 D4
Centro Macrobiotico Italiano Naturist Club, 19 A1
Hostaria da Bruno, 20 F3
Luzzi, 21 B4
Il Pulcino Ballerino, 22 F3
NIGHTLIFE
Alien, 23 F1
Piper, 24 F1
CAFES
Il Gelatone, 25 B4
Lion Bookshop & Cafe, 26 A1
200 meters
200 yards
TO AUSTRALIA, CANADA, AND NEW ZEALAND (2.4km)
TO US (100m)
TO 23 (700m), 24 (1.7km)
TO 12 (650m), 26 (800m), 17 (1km),
TO COLOSSEUM (400m), 21 (700m)
TO 22, 16 (1km)
TO 27 (1km)
L'Immacolata Concezione
BARBERINI
PIAZZA BARBERINI
Easy Internet
Palazzo Barberini
Galleria Nazionale d'Arte Antica
UK
S. Susanna
S. Maria della Vittoria
PIAZZA DI S. BERNARDO
Ministeri del Bilancio e del Tesoro
Musei Nazionali Romani
S. Maria d. Angeli
Terme di Diocleziano
REPUBBLICA
PIAZZA D. REPUBBLICA
PIAZZA INDIPENDENZA
PIAZZA DEI CINQUECENTO
Enjoy Rome
BollaBlu
Stazione Termini
TERMINI
CASTRO PRETORIO
Castro Pretorio
Biblioteca Nazionale
PIAZZA D. CROCE ROSSA
PIAZZALE G. FABRIZIO
Ministero Difesta Esercito
Four Fountains
Palazzo del Quirinale
PIAZZA DEL QUIRINALE
S. Andrea al Quirinale
Palazzo delle Esposizioni
Trevi Fountain
Trevi Internet
PIAZZA S.S. APOSTOLI
PIAZZA COLONNA
PIAZZA S. SILVESTRO
LARGO D. TRITONE
Galleria Doria Pamphili
Galleria Colonna
Palazzo Venezia
PIAZZA VENEZIA
Trajan's Column
Forum of Trajan
Markets of Trajan
Forum of Augustus
LARGO MAGNAPOLI
Museo del Risorgimento
Capitoline Museums
Ministero d. Interno
Teatro Nazionale
Teatro dell' Opera
S. Prudenziana
PIAZZA DELL'ESQUILINO
S. Maria Maggiore
S. Prassede
PIAZZA M. FANTI
ESQUILINO
Museo Nazionale d'Arte Orientale
CAVOUR
S. Pietro in Vincoli
Via del Corso
Via Nazionale
Via XX Settembre
Via Cavour
Via Torino
Via Marsala
Via Giovanni Lanza
Via Principe Amedeo
Via Carlo Alberto
Via dei Fori Imperiali
Viale Castro Pretorio
Viale del Policlinico
Viale delle Scienze
Viale dell'Università
Via di Villa Patrizi

within 1¼hr. of validation. **B.I.G. daily tickets** (€4) and **CIS weekly tickets** (€16) allow for unlimited public transport, including Ostia but not Fiumicino. For a short stay, buy the 3-day tourist pass for €11. Pickpocketing is rampant on buses and trains.

Taxis: Taxis are expensive. Find them at stands, or flag them down in the street. Ride only in yellow or white taxis, and make sure your taxi has a meter (if not, negotiate the price before you get in the car). **Surcharges** apply at night (€2.60), on Su (€1), and when heading to or from Fiumicino (€7.25) or Ciampino (€5.50). Fares run about €7.75 from Termini to Vatican City; around €35 between the city center and Fiumicino.

Bike and Moped Rental: Bikes cost €3 per hr. or €10 per day while mopeds cost €40-50 per day; the length of a "day" varies according to the shop closing time. In summer, try the stands on V. del Corso at P. di San Lorenzo and V. di Pontifici. Open daily 10am-7pm.

PRACTICAL INFORMATION

Tourist Office: Enjoy Rome, V. Marghera 8/A (☎445 18 43; www.enjoyrome.com). From the middle concourse of Termini, exit right, with the trains behind you; cross V. Marsala and follow V. Marghera for 3 blocks. The helpful staff makes reservations at museums and shows, books accommodations, and orients visitors. Open Apr.-Oct. M-F 8:30am-7pm, Sa 8:30am-2pm; Nov.-Mar. M-F 9am-6pm, Sa 9am-2pm.

Embassies: Australia, V. Antonio Bosio 5 (☎85 2721). Open M-F 8:30am-5pm. **Canada,** V.G.B. de Rossi (☎44 59 81; www.canada.it). Open M-F 9am-5pm. **Ireland,** P. di Campitelli 3 (☎697 91 21). Open M-F 10am-12:30pm and 3-4:30pm. **New Zealand,** V. Zara 28 (☎441 71 71). Open M-F 8:30am-12:45pm and 1:45-5pm. **UK,** V. XX Settembre 80/A (☎482 54 41; www.grbr.it). Open M-F 9:15am-1:30pm. **US,** V. Vittorio Veneto 119/A (☎467 41; www.usembassy.it/mission). Open M-F 8:30am-5:30pm.

American Express: P. di Spagna 38 (☎676 41, lost cards 722 82). Open Sept.-July M-F 9am-7:30pm, Sa 9am-3pm; Aug. M-F 9am-6pm, Sa 9am-12:30pm.

Luggage Storage: In Termini, underneath track #24. €3.60.

GLBT Resources: Arci-Gay, V. Goito 35/B (☎340 347 57 10; www.arcigay.it). Membership card (€10) gains admission to gay clubs. **Coordinamento Lesbico Italiano,** V.S. Francesco di Sales 1/A (☎686 42 01), off V. d. Lungara in Trastevere.

Laundromat: OndaBlu, V. La Mora 7 (☎800 86 13 46). Locations throughout Rome. Wash €3.50 per 6.5kg, dry €3.50 per 6.5kg. Open daily 8am-10pm.

Emergency: ☎113. **Police:** ☎112. **Ambulance:** ☎118. **Fire:** ☎115.

24hr. Pharmacies: Farmacia Internazionale, P. Barberini 49 (☎487 11 95). MC/V. **Farmacia Piram,** V. Nazionale 228 (☎488 07 54). MC/V.

Hospitals: International Medical Center, V. Firenze 47 (☎488 23 71; www.imc84.com). Call ahead. Referral service to English-speaking doctors. General visit €100. Open M-Sa 9am-8pm; on-call 24hr. **Rome-American Hospital,** V.E. Longoni 69 (24hr. service ☎225 51, appointments 225 52 90; www.rah.it). No emergency room.

Internet Access: Internet cafes are located throughout the city. **Splashnet,** V. Varese 33 (☎493 82 073), 3 blocks north of Termini. €1.50 per hr. Open daily in summer 8:30am-1am; in winter 8:30am-11pm. **Trevi Internet,** V. d. Lucchesi 31-32 (☎/fax 692 007 99). €4 per hr. Open daily 10am-8:30pm.

Post Office: Main Post Office (Posta Centrale), P. San Silvestro 19 (☎697 66 320). Open M-F 8am-7pm, Sa 8am-1:15pm. Another branch at V. d. Terme di Diocleziano 30 (☎488 869 20), near Termini.

ACCOMMODATIONS

Rome swells with tourists around Easter, May through July, and in September. Prices vary widely with the time of year, and a proprietor's willingness to negotiate increases with length of stay and group size. Termini swarms with hotel scouts. Many are legitimate and have IDs issued by tourist offices; however, some imposters have fake badges and direct travelers to run-down locations with exorbitant rates. The three **Hostels Alessandro** (www.hotstelsalessandro.com) around the Termini station offer great prices and a fun, social atmosphere.

HOTELS AND HOSTELS

CENTRO STORICO AND ANCIENT CITY

If being a bit closer to the sights is important to you, then choosing Rome's medieval center over the area near Termini may be worth the higher prices.

Pensione Rosetta, V. Cavour 295 (☎47 82 30 69), a few blocks past the Fori Imperiali. Buzz to get through. 18 comfortable rooms, with simple decor. Rooms have bath, TV, phone, and fan. Singles €60; doubles €80; triples €90; quads €100. AmEx/MC/V. ❹

Hotel Navona, V. dei Sediari 8, 1st fl. (☎686 42 03; www.hotelnavona.com). Take V. d. Canestrari from P. Navona, cross C. del Rinascimento, and go straight; the hotel sign is tiny. Opulent rooms have housed historical greats including Keats. A/C €15. Breakfast, TV, and bath included. Check-out 10:30am. Singles €90-110; doubles €125-140; triples €160-185. Reservations with credit card and deposit; otherwise cash only. ❺

Albergo della Lunetta, P. del Paradiso 68 (☎68 61 080; www.albergodellalunetta.it), on the 1st right off V. dei Chiavari from C. Vittorio Emanuele II. Great location between Campo dei Fiori and P. Navona. Reserve ahead with credit card or check. Singles €60, with bath €70; doubles €90/120; triples €120/150; quads €180. MC/V. ❹

ITALY

NEAR PIAZZA DI SPAGNA AND ENVIRONS

Though prices near P. di Spagna can be very steep, accommodations are often newer than in the *centro storico* and closer to the metro.

Pensione Panda, V. della Croce 35 (☎678 01 79; www.hotelpanda.it). M: A-Spagna. Between P. di Spagna and V. del Corso. 28 rooms on a quiet side street with faux marble statues and arched, frescoed ceilings. A/C €6 per day. Free Internet. Book ahead. Singles €48, with bath €68; doubles €68/98; triples €130; quads €170. Jan.-Feb. €5 less. 5% *Let's Go* discount when paying in cash. AmEx/MC/V. ❹

Hotel Boccaccio, V. del Boccaccio 25 (☎488 59 62; www.hotelboccaccio.com). M: A-Barberini. Off V. del Tritone near P. Barberini. Step out of simply furnished rooms onto the hotel's cozy terrace. Singles €43; doubles €73, with bath €93. AmEx/MC/V. ❹

BORGO AND PRATI (NEAR VATICAN CITY)

Pensioni near the Vatican offer some of the best deals in Rome and the sobriety one would expect from a neighborhood with this kind of nun-to-tourist ratio.

Colors, V. Boezio 31 (☎687 40 30; www.colorshotel.com). M: A-Ottaviano. Turn right onto V. Terenzio off V. Cola di Rienzo, then right onto V. Boezio. Fl. 3 is a hotel. Floors 1 and 4 boast the best hostel amenities in Rome. Free A/C. Internet €2 per hr. Dorms €23; doubles with bath €80; triples €100. Reserve private rooms with credit card; for dorms, call by 9pm the night before. Call or check website for low-season and hotel information. Cash only. ❷

Pensione Ottaviano Hostel, V. Ottaviano 6, 2nd fl. (☎397 38 138; www.ottavianohostel.com). M: A-Ottaviano. Follow V. Ottaviano toward S. Pietro. Hostel is on left, just before P. di Risorgimento. Simple but roomy co-ed dorms with minifridges, some with shower. Free Internet. Lockout 11:30am-2:30pm in high season. High-season check-in by 2:30pm, low season 6:30pm. Dorms €12-20; doubles €50-80; triples €60-90. Credit card required for reservations, but payment in cash only. ❶

Ostello Per La Gioventù Foro Italico (HI), V. delle Olimpiadi 61 (☎323 62 67; bookingrome@tiscali.it). M: A-Ottaviano, then bus #32 from P. di Risorgimento to "LGT Cadorna Ostello Gioventù" (15min.). Barracks-style marble building holds massive dorm rooms on single-sex floors and a huge cafeteria and common area. HI members only. Breakfast included. Dinner €9. Laundry and Internet access with phone card. Reception 7am-midnight. Curfew midnight. Dorms €18. Cash only. ❷

Hotel San Pietrino, V.G. Bettolo 43, 3rd fl. (☎37 00 132; www.sanpietrino.it) M: A-Ottaviano. Exit on V. Barletta, walk 3 blocks and turn left on V.G. Bettolo. Friendly staff and an army of frogs characterize this small hotel. Spacious rooms have A/C, TV, DVD, and Internet. Singles €30-45; doubles with bath €70-98; triples €90-125. AmEx/MC/V. ❸

SAN LORENZO AND EAST OF TERMINI

Welcome to budget traveler and backpacker central. While Termini is chock-full of traveler's services, use caution when walking in the area, especially at night, and keep close watch on your pockets and/or purse.

Hotel and Hostel Des Artistes, V. Villafranca 20, 5th fl. (☎44 70 28 68; www.hoteldesartistes.com). From the middle concourse of Termini, exit right, turn left on V. Marsala, right on V. Vicenza, then take the 5th left. An elegant hotel and a newly-renovated hostel floor with bright rooms. Rooftop terrace. Free Internet 2pm-12:30am. Buffet breakfast included with hotel rooms, otherwise €12. Reception 24hr. Dorms €12-23; singles €34-70; doubles €39-84; triples €54-104. Discount when paying cash. AmEx/MC/V. ❶

Hotel Cervia, V. Palestro 55, 2nd fl. (☎49 10 57; www.hotelcerviaroma.com). From Termini, exit on V. Marsala, head down V. Marghera and take the 4th left. Common TV room and clean rooms, with very friendly staff. Some rooms with A/C. Breakfast €3. Reception 24hr. Check-out 11am. In summer, 4- and 5-bed dorms €20; singles €35, with bath €50; doubles €55/75; triples €60/75. 5% *Let's Go* discount. AmEx/MC/V. ❷

ITALY

VIA XX SETTEMBRE AND NORTH OF TERMINI

Dominated by government ministries and private apartments, this area is less noisy and touristy than the nearby Termini.

Freedom Traveller, V. Gaeta 23 (☎478 23 862; www.freedom-traveller.it). Walk down V. Marsala which becomes V. Volturno, and make a right onto V. Gaeta. Known for pub crawls and Tu Pizza and Beer Party. Breakfast included. Free Internet. Lockout 10am-2pm. Dorms €23, with bath €25; doubles €80; triples €105; quads €120. ❷

Alessandro Legends, V. Curtatone 12 (☎447 03 217). Farther away from the main streets, the quiet rooms here are suitable for the less rowdy. All rooms have bath and fan. Dorms €18-23; doubles €45-75; quads €80-108. AmEx/MC/V. Reserve online. ❷

Hotel Papa Germano, V. Calatafimi 14/A (☎48 69 19; www.hotelpapagermano.com). From Termini, exit right; turn left on V. Marsala, which becomes V. Volturno, and take the 4th right onto V. Calatafimi. Clean, simple rooms with TV. English spoken. Breakfast included. Internet €2 per hr. Check-out 11am. Dorms €23-28; singles €30-40; doubles €55-70, with bath €70-95; triples €85-110; quads €95-130. AmEx/MC/V. ❷

ESQUILINO AND WEST OF TERMINI

Esquilino, south of Termini, has tons of cheap hotels close to the major sights. The area west of Termini is more inviting than Esquilino, with busy shop-lined streets.

Alessandro Palace, V. Vicenza 42 (☎446 19 58). Exit Termini from track #1. Turn left on V. Marsala, then right on V. Vicenza. The Palace houses recently renovated 4-person dorms, all with bath and A/C, and a guests-only bar. Mixed or all-female dorms €18-22; doubles €50-80; triples €60-99; quads €80-120. Reserve online. ❷

Alessandro Downtown, V.C. Cattaneo 23 (☎443 40 147). Exit Termini by track #22, make a left on V. Giolitti, then a right onto V.C. Cattaneo. A cheap and worthwhile alternative when the Palace is booked. Large dorms, mixed or female-only €18-23; doubles €40-60; quads with bath €100. Reserve online. ❷

Hotel Scott House, V. Gioberti 30 (☎446 53 79; www.scotthouse.com). Wonderfully colorful, modern rooms have bath, A/C, phone, and satellite TV. English spoken by helpful staff. Breakfast included. Free Internet 7-9pm. Check-out 11am. Dorms €22-25; singles €35-68; doubles €60-90. AmEx/MC/V. ❷

Hotel Cortorillo, V. Principe Amedeo 79/A, 5th fl. (☎446 69 34; www.hotelcortorillo.it). This newly renovated hotel has bath, TV, and A/C in all 14 spacious rooms. Breakfast with espresso bar included. Check-out 10am. Singles €35-90; doubles €50-120; larger rooms €120-210. AmEx/MC/V. ❸

RELIGIOUS HOUSING

Don't automatically think cheap; these can run up to €155 for a single. And don't think Catholic. A few require letters of introduction from local dioceses, but most are open to all. Do think sober: early curfews or chores are standard.

Domus Nova Bethlehem, V. Cavour 85/A (☎478 24 41; www.suorebambinogesu.it). Take V. Cavour from Termini, past P. d. Esquilino on the left. Modern, central hotel, with religious icons throughout. Rooms have A/C, bath, and TV. Breakfast included. Curfew 1am. Singles €70; doubles €99; triples €129; quads €148. AmEx/MC/V. ❺

Santa Maria Alle Fornaci, P.S. Maria alle Fornaci 27 (☎393 676 32; ciffornaci@tin.it). Facing St. Peter's, turn left through a gate in the basilica walls onto V. d. Fornace. Take 3rd right onto V. d. Gasperi, which leads to P.S. Maria alle Fornaci. This *casa per ferie* has 54 rooms with bath and phone. Simple, small, and clean. Breakfast included. Singles €55; doubles €85; triples €120. AmEx/MC/V. ❹

FOOD

Traditional Roman cuisine includes *spaghetti alla carbonara* (with a light egg and cream sauce sprinkled with bacon), *spaghetti all'amatriciana* (spicy, with thin tomato sauce, chiles, and bacon), *carciofi alla giudeia* (deep fried artichokes found most commonly in the Jewish Ghetto) and *fiori di zucca* (stuffed, fried zucchini flowers—unexpectedly delicious). Try *pizza romana* instead of the bread, which is more like what we think of as *focaccia:* a flat bread rubbed with olive oil, sea salt, and rosemary, sometimes with toppings. Lunch is typically the main meal, although some Romans now eat lunches of *panini* on the go during the week. Restaurants tend to close between 3 and 7:30pm.

BY NEIGHBORHOOD

ANCIENT CITY

The area around the Fora and the Colosseum is home to some of Italy's finest tourist traps. The best way to get a great meal at an even better price is to avoid the streets directly surrounding the Colosseum and Fora and head for the side streets.

I Buoni Amici, V. Aleard Aleardi 4 (☎704 91 993). M: B-Colosseo. From the Colosseum, take V. Labicana, then take a right onto V. Merulana, and turn left on V.A. Aleardi. The cheap, excellent food is worth the hike. Most popular is the *linguine alle vongole* (with clams in the shell, €7). The self-serve *antipasto* bar is phenomenal. *Secondi* €7-10. Cover €1. Open M-Sa noon-3pm and 7:30-11:30pm. AmEx/MC/V. ❷

Luzzi, V.S. Giovanni in Laterano 88 (☎70 96 332), 3 blocks past the Colosseum coming from V. dei Fori Imperiali. Huge portions bring locals to this casual *hostaria.* The crowning glory is the *pasta alla vongole* (with clams; €5.50). *Primi* €3.50-6. Open M-Tu and Th-Su noon-3pm and 7pm-midnight. AmEx/MC/V. ❷

L'Antica Birreria Peroni, V. San Marcello 19 (☎679 53 10; www.anticabirreriaperoni.it), facing away from the Vittoriano, take a right onto V.C. Battisti and a left into the P. dei S.S. Apostoli. 1 block down on the left. Italian with a German twist, this restaurant provides a fun alternative to omnipresent *enoteche.* Beer lovers can ask for a *rosso* (Italian red ale). *Primi* €3-5. Cover €1. Open M-Sa noon-midnight. AmEx/MC/V. ❷

CENTRO STORICO

The restaurants in the *centro storico* can be frightfully expensive and generic, especially those near famous landmarks. Head to **Via del Governo Vecchio** and its tiny cross streets for more authentic fare. The **Campo dei Fiori,** a daily food and clothing market, is surrounded by a labyrinth of crooked streets that can be frustrating, but almost invariably worthwhile, to navigate.

Antica Taverna, Vicolo dell'Avila 13, off V. del Governo Vecchio. Just steps away from the P. Navona; you'll be able to smell the garlic. This *taverna* serves Roman specialties and flavorful meat dishes for pocket change. Great house wine. *Primi* €6-7. *Secondi* €7-8. Open daily noon-midnight. Cash only. ❷

Miscellanea, V. delle Paste 10a, just around the corner from the Pantheon. At this "International Student's Pub," complete with a jukebox, old Chicago pizzeria-style lampshades, and vintage Coca-Cola ads, locals crowd around for cheap lunch and classic American surroundings. *Antipasti* €3-5. *Panini* €3. Cash only. ❶

Ristorante Grappolo d'Oro Zampanò, P. della Cancelleria 80/83 (☎689 70 80), between C. Vittorio Emanuele II and Campo dei Fiori. This multi-award winning, slightly upscale *hostaria* offers over 200 wines served on a pristine patio or beneath wine bottle-lined ceilings. *Primi* €9.50. *Secondi* €13-19. Open M and W-Su noon-2:30pm and 7:30-11pm, Tu 7:30-11pm, Sa 7:30-11:30pm. AmEx/MC/V. ❸

JEWISH GHETTO

The Jewish Ghetto, about a 10min. walk south of the Campo, serves many Roman specialties as well as traditional Jewish and kosher dishes. Keep in mind that much of the ghetto is closed on Saturdays.

Bar Da Benito, V. dei Falegnami 14 (☎686 15 08), easiest to approach from V. del Portico D'Ottavia or V. Arenula. This 40-year-old establishment is fast moving and always full. 2 hot pastas prepared daily (€4.50), along with fresh *secondi* like prosciutto with vegetables (€5). Open M-Sa 6:30am-7pm. Lunch noon-4pm. Closed Aug. ❶

Trattoria da Giggetto, V. del Portico d'Ottavia 21-22 (☎686 11 05). It doesn't get any better than this patio, right next to the ruins of the Portico d'Ottavia. The Roman tradition of using all of an animal's meat is alive and well here, serving *fritto di cervello d'abbacchino* (brains with vegetables; €12) among other traditional delicacies. *Primi* €7.50-12. *Secondi* €8-18. Cover €1.50. Dinner reservation required. Open Tu-Su 12:15-3pm and 7:30-11pm. Closed last 2 weeks of July. AmEx/MC/V. ❸

PIAZZA DI SPAGNA

The area around P. di Spagna and the Trevi Fountain, though busy late into the night and closer to most tourist destinations, tends to be on the disappointing side of the quality-for-money spectrum. As always, we recommend heading off the main drags (V. del Corso and V. dei Condotti) to find the best eateries.

Trattoria da Settimio all'Arancio, V. dell'Arancio 50-52 (☎687 61 19). Take V. dei Condotti from P. di Spagna; take 1st right after V. del Corso, then 1st left. Portions are generous and dishes are decadent. The *tagliatelle* with truffles (€20) are a divine splurge. *Primi* from €7.50. *Secondi* from €8.50. Reservations recommended. Open M-Sa 12:30-3pm and 7:30-11:30pm. AmEx/MC/V. ❸

Centro Macrobiotico Italiano Naturist Club, V. della Vite 14, 4th fl. (☎679 25 09). Heading toward P. del Popolo on V. del Corso, make a right onto V. della Vite. A mother-daughter duo take traditional Roman cuisine to vegetarian heaven. Vegan dishes available. Lunch *menù* €14. Dinner *menù* €20-25. Reservation required for dinner. Open M-Sa 12:30-3pm and 7:30-11pm. Cash only. ❸

Il Brillo Parlante, V. Fontanella 12 (☎324 33 34; www.ilbrilloparlante.com). Take V. del Corso away from P. del Popolo and turn left on V. Fontanella. The wood-oven pizza (€7-10), handmade pasta, and innovative small plates such as *pecorino* cheese with honey and walnuts (€8.50) set this place apart. In the summer, patrons flood the shady outdoor tables. Open M 5pm-1am, Tu-Su 12:30pm-1am. Tu-Su lunch served 12:30-3:30pm, 3:30-5pm pizza only, 5-7:30pm bar only. MC/V. ❷

BORGO AND PRATI (NEAR VATICAN CITY)

As at all other major tourist destinations, the streets near the Vatican are paved with bars and pizzerias that serve mediocre sandwiches at inflated prices. For better, much cheaper food, venture down **Via Cola di Rienzo** for several blocks toward P. Cavour and explore the residential side streets.

Franchi, V. Cola di Rienzo 204 (☎687 46 51; www.franchi.it). Benedetto Franchi has been serving phenomenal lunches and luxurious picnic supplies to the citizens of Prati for nearly 50 years. 2 people can stuff themselves for under €15, but be careful to look at the prices before you buy. Open M-Sa 8:15am-9pm. AmEx/MC/V. ❷

Cacio e Pepe, V. Giuseppe Avezzana 11 (☎321 72 68). From P. Mazzini, make a right onto V. Settembrini, and at P. dei Martiri di Belfiore take a left on V. Avezzana. Great pasta and low prices, though a 20min. walk from the Vatican. The specialty of the house is *cacio e pepe:* perfect *al dente* pasta piled high with olive oil, grated cheese, and fresh ground pepper. Full lunch €5-10; M-Sa 12:30-3pm, M-F 7pm-12:30am. Cash only. ❷

"Lo Spuntino" da Guido e Patrizia, Borgo Pio 13 (☎687 54 91), near Castel Sant'Angelo. With plastic utensils and a casual atmosphere, this homey spot is popular with lunching locals. Guido holds court behind a well-stocked *tavola calda.* Full meal (*primo, secondo,* and wine) runs less than €8. Open M-Sa 8am-8pm. Cash only. ❷

ITALY

TRASTEVERE

This beautiful old neighborhood is famous for its medieval streets and distance from the tourist crowds, though recently it has become a stronghold of Rome's thriving expatriate community and English can be heard on every street corner. The waits are long and the street-side tables are always cramped, but you can't get more Roman than Trastevere.

Pizzeria San Callisto, P.S. Callisto 9/A (☎581 82 56), off P.S. Maria. Simply the best pizza (€4.20-7.80) in Rome, though there are as many foreigners as Romans. Avoid long waits for a table by ordering to go. Open Tu-Su 7pm-midnight. AmEx/MC/V. ❷

Ristorante a Casa di Alfredo, V. Roma Libera 5-7 (☎588 29 68). Off P.S. Cosimato. This rustic restaurant presents a family-style approach with a bent toward affordable cuisine, as the chef's tasting menu—€18 for 3 courses—suggests. *Antipasti* €5-8. *Primi* €5-8. *Secondi* €7-9. Open daily noon-3pm and 7:30-11:30pm. AmEx/MC/V. ❸

Augusto, P. de' Renzi 15 (☎ 580 37 98), before P.S. Maria in Trastevere from the river. Augusto nourishes a back-to-basics, neighborhood atmosphere. Daily lunch pasta specials (€5) are fresh and tasty, and service is quick. Open M-F 12:30-3pm and 8-11pm, Sa 12:30-3pm. Closed Aug. ❶

TERMINI AND SAN LORENZO

Tourist traps abound in the Termini area. A well-stocked **CONAD** supermarket is on the lower floor of the Termini Station, down the escalator just inside the V. Marsala entrance. (Open daily 8am-midnight.) An **alimentari-salumeria,** 68 V. Marsala, serves excellent *panini* for under €2. An abundance of students with discriminating palates in San Lorenzo makes for inexpensive food with local character. Plan your route beforehand and avoid walking alone at night in this area.

Arancia Blu, V. d. Latini 65 (☎445 41 05), off V. Tiburtina. This elegant and popular vegetarian restaurant greets you with 3 wine glasses (white, red, and champagne) and an inspired menu that is extremely affordable in spite of its adventurous style and fine ingredients. Especially phenomenal are the warm pesto salad and the fried eggplant ravioli (€8.50). English-language menus available. Extensive wine list €12-130 per bottle. Chocolate-tasting *menù* (€13). Open daily 8:30pm-midnight. MC/V. ❷

Africa, V. Gaeta 26-28 (☎494 10 77), near P. Indipendenza. Decked out in yellow and black, Africa continues its 20-year tradition of Eritrean/Ethiopian food. The meat-filled *sambusas* (€3) are a flavorful starter. Cover €1. Open Tu-Su 8am-1:30am. MC/V. ❷

Hostaria da Bruno, V. Varese 29 (☎49 04 03). From V. Marsala, take V. Milazzo and turn right on V. Varese. Italians who work in the Termini area relax with lunches at this bastion of authentic food amid tourist traps. Open M-Sa noon-3:15pm and 7-10:15pm. AmEx/MC/V. ❷

Il Pulcino Ballerino, V. d. Equi 66-68 (☎494 12 55). The cook stirs up traditional pastas alongside hard-to-find steak dishes. *Primi* €6-7.50. *Secondi* €9.50-13.50. Open M-Sa 1-3:30pm and 8pm-midnight. AmEx/MC/V. ❸

TESTACCIO

This residential neighborhood is the seat of many excellent restaurants serving meat-heavy fare.

Il Cantinone, P. Testaccio 31/32 (☎574 62 53). M: B-Piramide. Go up V. Marmorata and take a left on V.G.B. Bodoni; P. Testaccio is just past V. Luca della Robbia. In spite of slightly kitschy decor, Il Cantinone is a down-to-earth Italian restaurant. Massive portions of pasta and hearty meat-and-gravy dishes (most around €9). Long tables make it great for groups. Open M and W-Su noon-3pm and 7pm-midnight. AmEx/MC/V. ❷

Il Volpetti Più, V. Alessandro Volta 8 (☎574 43 06). Turn left off of V. Marmorata. This *tavola calda* serves lunch in large portions at self-service tables–pick out your food cafeteria-style and battle locals for a seat. Fresh salads, pasta, pizza, and daily specials from €4. Call ahead for 3:30-6pm meals. Open M-Sa 10am-10pm. Cash only. ❶

DESSERT AND COFFEE

While gelato is everywhere in Rome, good gelato is not. Look for the signs of quality (See **The Ugly Duckling,** p. 600), or head to these *Let's Go* favorites. Coffee is taken either standing up at the bar or sitting down at a table, with higher prices for table service. In Rome, cafes are crammed with men in neat business suits starting at about 12:30pm.

Pasticceria Ebraico Boccione, Jewish Ghetto, V. del Portico d'Ottavia 1 (☎687 86 37), on the corner of P. Costaguti. This tiny, family-run bakery only makes about 8 items, but they are all fantastic and served with a smile by one of the quick-moving elderly ladies. The sugar-dusted, custard-filled *ciambelle* (doughnuts) are divine (€0.80). Open all day M-F and Sa. Closed for lunch Su 2-4pm in summer. F closes early.

Il Gelatone, V. dei Serpenti 28 (☎48 20 187), from V. dei Fori Imperiali take a left on V. Cavour, and the 1st major left onto V. dei Serpenti. Creamy, smooth, and vividly flavored. Their specialty is *Gelatone,* a blend of chocolate and vanilla with chocolate chips. Cones €1.50-3. 3-flavor cone-bowls €4. Open daily 11am-1am.

The Lion Bookshop and Café, P. di Spagna, V. dei Greci 33/36 (☎326 54 007; www.thelionbookshop.com). Turn right on V. dei Greci from V. del Corso. This huge English-language bookstore has a delightful cafe inside. All of the espresso drinks (€1.50-2.50) come with biscuits, so that you can dip, sip, and crunch while you read. Bookshop hours M 3:30-7:30pm, Tu-Su 10am-7:30pm. AmEx/MC/V.

Bar Giulia (a.k.a. Cafe Peru), V. Giulia, 84 (☎06 686 13 10), near P. Vittorio Emanuele II. Raphael once called this building home; today the owner, Alfredo, adds your favorite liqueur at no charge to your coffee (€0.60, at table €0.70). You may have to crowd surf to get your cup of fresh-squeezed orange juice. Open M-Sa 4am-9:30pm.

ENOTECHE (WINE BARS)

Wine bars range from laidback and local to chic and international, acting sometimes as simple afternoon cafes and other times as urban nightclub-lounge spots. No matter what the scene, *enoteche* usually serve a variety of small dishes and plates, such as cheese selections, smoked meats, *antipasti*, and salads. Romans like to eat dinner around 9pm, so they either go to *enoteche* beforehand for a small bite to eat, or sip and nibble their way through the entire night.

Enoteca Trastevere, Trastevere, V. della Lungaretta 86 (☎588 56 59). A block off of P.S. Maria in Trastevere. This casual *enoteca* has a terrace populated with romantic couples and jovial groups alike. A helpful staff will help you choose from the small, high-caliber list. Busiest around midnight. Open M-Sa 6pm-2:30am, Su 6pm-1am.

Cul de Sac, P. Pasquino 73 (☎688 010 94), near P. Navona. One of Rome's first wine bars, Cul de Sac has kept customers coming with an extensive wine list (from €2 per glass), outdoor tables, and divine dishes. Specialty homemade pâtés (such as boar and chocolate; €5.70) are exquisite. Open daily noon-4pm and 6pm-12:30am. MC/V.

SIGHTS

ITALY

From ancient temples, medieval churches, and Renaissance basilicas to Baroque fountains and contemporary museums, *La Città Eterna* is a city bursting with masterpieces from every era of Western Civilization. Remember to dress modestly when visiting churches or the Vatican.

ANCIENT CITY

THE COLOSSEUM. This enduring symbol of the Eternal City—a hollowed-out marble ghost that dwarfs every other ruin in Rome—once held as many as 50,000 spectators. Within 100 days of its AD 80 opening, some 5000 wild beasts perished in the arena. The floor covers a labyrinth of brick cells, ramps, and elevators used to transport wild animals from cages up to arena level. Beware the men dressed as gladiators: they want to take a picture with you for €5. *(M: B-Colosseo. Open daily Mar.-Aug. 9am-7:30pm; Sept. 9am-7pm; Oct. 9am-6:30pm; Nov. to mid-Feb. 9am-4pm; mid-Feb. to Mar. 9am-5pm. Combined ticket to the Colosseum and the Palatine Hill €10.)*

THE PALATINE HILL. The best way to attack the Palatine is from the stairs near the Forum's **Arch of Titus.** Throughout the garden complex, terraces provide breathtaking views. Farther down, excavations continue on the 9th-century BC village, the **Casa di Romulo.** To the right of the village is the podium of the 191 BC **Temple of Cybele.** The stairs to the left lead to the **Casa di Livia,** which is connected to the **Casa Augusto** next door. Around the corner, the spooky **Cryptoporticus** connected Tiberius's palace with nearby buildings. The path around the Casa Augusto leads to the vast ruins of a giant palace divided into two wings. The solemn **Domus Augustana** was the private space for the emperors; the adjacent wing, the sprawling **Domus Flavia,** once held a gigantic octagonal fountain. Between the Domus Augustana and the Domus Flavia stands the **Stadium Palatinum,** the museum that houses the artifacts found during the excavations of the Palatine Hill. Outside, on the right, the palace's east wing contains the curious **Stadium of Domitian,** or *Hippodrome*, a sunken oval space once surrounded by a colonnade but now decorated with fragments of porticoes, statues, and fountains. The **Arch of Constantine** lies between the Colosseum and the Palatine Hill, marking the tail end of the V. Sacra. One of the best-preserved monuments in the area, it commemorates Constantine's victory over Maxentius at the Milvian Bridge in AD 315. *(South of the Forum. Same hours and prices as Colosseum.)*

DOMUS AUREA. This park houses just a portion of Nero's "Golden House," which once covered a huge chunk of Rome. After deciding that he was a god, Nero had architects build a house worthy of his divinity. The Forum was reduced to a vestibule of the palace; Nero crowned it with the 35m *Colossus*, a huge statue of himself as the sun. *(On the Oppian Hill. From the Colosseum, walk up V. della Domus Aurea and make the 1st left. Reservations ☎399 677 00. Open M and W-Su 9am-6:40pm. Groups of 30 admitted every 40min. €5.)*

ROMAN FORUM. The pre-Romans founded a thatched-hut shanty town here in 753 BC. The entrance ramp leads to **Via Sacra,** Rome's oldest street, near the area once known as the Civic Forum. Off V. Sacra to the right is the **Curia** (Senate House); it was converted to a church in AD 630 and restored by Mussolini. The broad space in front of the **Curia** was the **Comitium,** where male citizens came to vote. The **market square** holds a number of shrines and sacred precincts, including the *Lapis Niger* (Black Stone), where Romulus was supposedly murdered by Republican senators. Below the *Lapis Niger* are the underground ruins of a 6th-century BC altar and the oldest known Latin inscription in Rome. In the square, the **Three Sacred Trees of Rome**—olive, fig, and grape—have been replanted by the Italian state. The most recent addition to the Forum is the **Column of Phocas,** erected in AD 608. The temples of the **Lower Forum** have been closed off for excavations; however, the eight columns of the 5th-century BC **Temple of Saturn** have been restored. At the far end, three marble columns mark the podium of the recently restored **Temple of Castor and Pollux,** built to celebrate the Roman defeat of the Etruscans. The circular building is the **Temple of Vesta,** where Vestal Virgins tended the city's sacred fire, keeping it lit for more than 1000 years.

In the Upper Forum lies the **House of the Vestal Virgins.** For 30 years, the six virgins who officiated over Vesta's rites lived in seclusion here from the ripe old age of seven on. Nearby, V. Sacra runs over the **Cloaca Maxima,** the ancient sewer that still drains water from the otherwise marsh-like valley. V. Sacra leads to an exit on the other side of the hill to the Colosseum; the path that crosses before the Arch of Titus heads to the Palatine Hill. *(M: B-Colosseo, or bus to P. Venezia. Main entrance is on V. dei Fori Imperiali, at Largo C. Ricci, between P. Venezia and the Colosseum. Open daily in summer 9am-6:30pm; in winter 9am-3:30pm. Guided tour 11am. Tour €3.50. Audio tour €4.)*

FORI IMPERIALI. Across the street from the Ancient Forum are the **Fori Imperiali,** a complex of temples, basilicas, and public squares constructed in the first and 2nd centuries. Much of the surrounding area is being excavated and is closed to the public, but passersby can still peer over the railing from V. dei Fori Imperiali. Built between AD 107 and 113, the **Forum of Trajan** included a colossal equestrian statue of Trajan and an immense triumphal arch. At one end of the now-decimated Forum, 2500 carved legionnaires march their way up the almost perfectly preserved **Trajan's Column,** one of the greatest specimens of Roman relief-sculpture. The crowning statue is St. Peter, who replaced Trajan in 1588. The gray rock wall of the **Forum of Augustus** commemorates Augustus's victory over Caesar's murderers in 42 BC. The aptly named **Forum Transitorium** (a.k.a. **Forum of Nerva**) was a narrow space connecting the Forum of Augustus with the Republican Roman Forum. The only remnant of **Vespatian's Forum** is the mosaic-filled **Church of Santi Cosma e Damiano** across V. Cavour, near the Roman Forum. *(Open daily 9am-6:30pm.)*

CAPITOLINE HILL. Home to the original capitol, the **Monte Capitolino** still serves as the seat of the city government. Michelangelo designed its **Piazza di Campidoglio,** now home to the **Capitoline Museums** (p. 621). Stairs lead up to the rear of the 7th-century **Chiesa di Santa Maria in Aracoeli.** The gloomy **Mamertine Prison,** consecrated as the **Church of San Pietro in Carcere,** lies down the hill from the back stairs of the Aracoeli. Imprisoned here, St. Peter baptized his captors with the waters that flooded his cell. *(Open daily 9am-12:30pm and 2:30-6:30pm. Donation requested.)* At the far end of the *piazza*, opposite the stairs, lies the turreted **Palazzo dei Senatori**, the home of Rome's mayor. *(Take any bus that goes to P. Venezia. From P. Venezia, walk around to the right to P. d'Aracoeli, and take the stairs up the hill.)*

VELABRUM. The Velabrum area lies in a flood plain south of the Jewish Ghetto. At the bend of V. del Portico d'Ottavia, a shattered pediment and a few ivy-covered columns are all that remain of the once magnificent **Portico d'Ottavia.** The **Teatro di Marcello** next door is named for Augustus's nephew, whose sudden death remains a mystery. Farther down V. di Teatro di Marcello, **Chiesa di San Nicola in Carcere** incorporates Roman temples dedicated to Juno, Janus, and Spes. *(☎686 99 72. Open Sept.-July M-Sa 7:30am-noon and 2-5pm, Su 9:30am-1pm and 4-8pm.)* Across the street, the **Chiesa di Santa Maria in Cosmedin** harbors lovely medieval decorations. The film *Roman Holiday* made the portico's relief, the **Bocca della Verità,** famous. According to legend, the aging face will chomp on the hand of a liar. *(Portico open daily Apr.-Sept. 9am-6:30pm; Oct.-Mar. 9am-5pm.)*

CENTRO STORICO

VIA DEL CORSO AND PIAZZA VENEZIA. The **Via del Corso** takes its name from its days as Rome's premier race course, running between P. del Popolo and the rumbling P. Venezia. **Palazzo Venezia** was one of the first Renaissance *palazzi* built in Rome; Mussolini used it as an office and delivered his famous orations from its balcony, but now it's only a regal roundabout dominated by the **Vittorio Emanuele II monument.** Off the northwestern corner of the *piazza* is the **Piazza di Montecitorio,** dominated by Bernini's **Palazzo Montecitorio,** the seat of the Chamber of Deputies.

ITALY

THE PANTHEON. Architects still wonder how this 2000-year-old temple was erected; its dome—a perfect half-sphere made of poured concrete without the support of vaults, arches, or ribs—is the largest of its kind. The light that enters the roof was used as a sundial to indicate the passing of the hours and the dates of equinoxes and solstices. In AD 606, it was consecrated as the **Church of Santa Maria ad Martyres.** *(In P. della Rotonda. Open M-Sa 8:30am-7:30pm, Su 9am-6pm. Free.)*

PIAZZA NAVONA. Originally a first-century stadium, the *piazza* hosted wrestling matches, track and field events, and mock naval battles in which the stadium was flooded and filled with fleets skippered by convicts. Each of the river god statues in Bernini's **Fountain of the Four Rivers** represents one of the four continents of the globe (as known then): the Ganges for Asia, the Danube for Europe, the Nile for Africa, and the Río de la Plata for the Americas. *(Open daily 9am-noon and 4-7pm.)*

CAMPO DEI FIORI. Across C. Vittorio Emanuele II from P. Navona, Campo dei Fiori is one of the last authentically Roman areas of the *centro storico*. Home to a bustling market in the morning Monday through Saturday, at night it transforms into a hip hot spot. The Renaissance **Palazzo Farnese,** built by Alessandro Farnese, the first Counter-Reformation pope, dominates P. Farnese, south of the Campo.

THE JEWISH GHETTO

The Jewish community in Rome is the oldest in Europe—Israelites came in 161 BC as ambassadors from Judas Maccabei, asking for help against invaders. The Ghetto, the tiny area to which Pope Paul IV confined the Jews in 1555, was closed in 1870 but is still the center of Rome's thriving Jewish population of 16,000. In the center of the Ghetto are **Piazza Mattei** and the 16th-century **Fontana delle Tartarughe.** Nearby is the **Church of Sant'Angelo in Pescheria;** Jews were forced to attend mass here every Sunday and quietly resisted by stuffing their ears with wax. *(Toward the eastern end of V. del Portico d'Ottavia. Both fountain and church under restoration as of Aug. 2005.)*

PIAZZA DI SPAGNA AND ENVIRONS

FONTANA DI TREVI. The extravagant **Fontana di Trevi** emerges from the back wall of **Palazzo Poli.** Legend says that a traveler who throws a coin into the fountain is ensured a speedy return to Rome; a traveler who tosses two will fall in love there. Forget about funding your trip with an early morning swim: several homeless men were arrested in 2002 and fined €500. Opposite is the Baroque **Chiesa dei Santi Vincenzo e Anastasio,** rebuilt in 1630. The crypt preserves the hearts and lungs of popes who served from 1590 to 1903. *(Open daily 7:30am-12:30pm and 4-7pm.)*

THE SPANISH STEPS. Designed by an Italian, funded by the French, named for the Spaniards, occupied by the British, and currently under the sway of American ambassador-at-large Ronald McDonald, the **Scalinata di Spagna** exude an international air. The pink house to the right of the Steps was the site of John Keats's death in 1821; it's now the **Keats-Shelley Memorial Museum.** *(Open M-F 9am-1pm and 3-6pm, Su 11am-2pm and 3-6pm. €3.)*

PIAZZA DEL POPOLO. In the center of the "people's square," once the venue for the public execution of heretics, is the 3200-year-old **Obelisk of Pharaoh Ramses II** that Augustus brought back as a souvenir from Egypt in the first century BC. Behind an early-Renaissance shell, the **Church of Santa Maria del Popolo** contains Renaissance and Baroque masterpieces. Two exquisite Caravaggios, *The Conversion of St. Paul* and *Crucifixion of St. Peter*, are found in the **Cappella Cerasi.** Raphael designed the **Cappella Chigi** for the great Renaissance financier Augustino Chigi. *(Open M-Sa 7am-noon and 4-7pm, Su 7:30am-1:30pm and 4:30-7:30pm.)*

VILLA BORGHESE. To celebrate his purchase of a cardinalship, Scipione Borghese built the **Villa Borghese** north of P. di Spagna and V.V. Veneto. Its huge park houses three art museums: world-renowned **Galleria Borghese,** stark **Galleria Nazionale d'Arte Moderna,** and intriguing **Museo Nazionale Etrusco di Villa Giulia.** North of the Borghese are the **Santa Priscilla catacombs.** *(M: A-Spagna and follow the signs. Open M-F 9:30am-6pm, Sa-Su 9:30am-7pm. €8.50.)*

ITALY

VATICAN CITY

Occupying 108½ independent acres within Roman boundaries stands the foothold of the Roman Catholic Church, which was once the mightiest power in Europe. The Vatican has symbolically preserved its independence by minting coins (Italian *lire* and euro with the Pope's face), running a separate press and postal system, maintaining an army of Swiss Guards, and hoarding fine art in the **Musei Vaticani.** *(M: A-Ottaviano. Alternatively, catch bus #64, 271, or 492 from Termini or Largo Argentina, #62 from P. Barberini, or #23 from Testaccio. ☎698 1662.)*

BASILICA DI SAN PIETRO (ST. PETER'S). A colonnade by Bernini leads from **Piazza San Pietro** to the church. The **obelisk** in the *piazza*'s center is framed by two fountains; stand on the round discs set in the pavement and the quadruple rows of the colonnade will visually resolve into one perfectly aligned row, courtesy of the Counter-Reformation popes' battery of architects. Above the colonnade are 140 statues; those on the basilica represent Christ, John the Baptist, and the Apostles (except for Peter, naturally). The pope opens the **Porta Sancta** (Holy Door) every 25 years by knocking in the bricks with a silver hammer; the last opening was in 2000, so don't hold your breath. The basilica itself rests on the reputed site of St. Peter's tomb. To the right, Michelangelo's *Pietà* has been protected by bullet-proof glass since 1972, when an axe-wielding fiend smashed Christ's nose and broke Mary's hand. Arnolfo di Cambio's *Peter* has been crippled by centuries' worth of pilgrims rubbing his foot. The climb to the top of the **dome** might very well be worth the heart attack it will undoubtedly cause. An elevator will take you up about 300 of the 350 stairs. *(No shorts, skirts above the knee,* *sleeveless shirts, or sundresses. Multilingual confession available. Church: Open daily Apr.-Sept. 7am-7pm; Oct.-Mar. 7am-6pm. Mass M-Sa 8:30, 10, 11am, noon, 5pm; Su 9, 10:30, 11:30am, 12:10, 1, 4, 5:30pm. Free. Dome: From inside the basilica, exit the building, and re-enter the door to the far left. Open daily Apr.-Sept. 8am-5:45pm; Oct.-Mar. 7am-4:45pm. Dome €4, elevator €7.)*

SISTINE SIGHTSEEING. The Sistine Chapel is at the end of the standard route through the Vatican Museums (p. 620), and it's extremely crowded. You may want to go straight to the Sistine Chapel to enjoy Michelangelo's masterpiece or, when it's relatively empty, early in the morning.

SISTINE CHAPEL. Since its completion in the 16th century, the **Sistine Chapel** (named for its founder, Pope Sixtus IV) has served as the chamber in which the College of Cardinals elects new popes. Michelangelo's ceiling, at the pinnacle of artistic creation, gleams from its restoration. The meticulous compositions hover above, each section depicting a story from Genesis. The scenes are framed by the famous *ignudi* (young nude males). Contrary to legend, Michelangelo did not paint flat on his back, but standing up and craning backward, causing irreparable strain to his neck and eyes. In *The Last Judgment* filling the altar wall, the figure of Christ as judge hovers in the upper center, surrounded by his saintly entourage and the supplicant Mary. Michelangelo painted himself as a flayed human skin hanging symbolically between heaven and hell. The cycle was completed by 1483 by a team of artists under Perugino, including Botticelli, Ghirlandaio, Roselli, Pinturicchio, Signorelli, and della Gatta. The frescoes on the side walls pre-date Michelangelo's ceiling; on the right, scenes from the life of Moses complement parallel scenes of Christ's life on the left. *(Admission included with Vatican Museums,* p. 620.*)*

ITALY

CASTEL SANT'ANGELO. Built by Hadrian (AD 117-138) as a mausoleum for himself and his family, this mass of brick and stone has served as a fortress, prison, and palace. When Rome was wracked with the plague in AD 590, Pope Gregory the Great saw an angel sheathing his sword at the top of the complex; the plague abated soon after, and the edifice was rededicated to the angel. *(Walk along the river with St. Peter's behind you and the towering castle to your left; follow the signs to the entrance. Open Tu-Su 9am-7pm. €5, EU students ages 18-25 €2.50.)*

TRASTEVERE

Right off the **Ponte Garibaldi** stands the statue of the famous dialect poet G. G. Bellie. On V. di Santa Cecilia, through the gate, and beyond the courtyard is the **Basilica di Santa Cecilia in Trastevere;** Carlo Maderno's famous statue of Santa Cecilia lies under the altar. *(Open daily 7am-1pm and 3:30-7pm. Cloister open Tu and Th 10-11:30am, Su 11:30am-noon. Donation requested. Crypt €2.)* From P. Sonnino, V. della Lungaretta leads west to P.S. Maria in Trastevere, home to stray dogs, expatriates, and the **Chiesa di Santa Maria in Trastevere,** built in the 4th century. *(Open M-Sa 9am-5:30pm, Su 8:30-10:30am and noon-5:30pm.)* North of the *piazza* are the Rococo **Galleria Corsini,** V. della Lungara 10, and, across the street, the **Villa Farnesina,** the jewel of Trastevere. Atop the Gianicolo Hill is the **Chiesa di San Pietro in Montorio,** built on the spot once believed to be the site of St. Peter's upside-down crucifixion. The church contains del Piombo's *Flagellation,* which uses Michelangelo's designs. Next door in a small courtyard is Bramante's tiny **Tempietto.** Rome's **botanical gardens** contain a garden for the blind as well as a rose garden that holds the bush from which all the world's roses are supposedly descended. *(Church and Tempietto open Tu-Su May-Oct. 9:30am-12:30pm and 4-6pm; Nov.-Apr. 9:30am-12:30pm and 2-4pm.)*

NEAR TERMINI

These sights are concentrated northwest of the station and near P. Vittorio Emanuele II, to the south.

PIAZZA DEL QUIRINALE. At the southeastern end of V. del Quirinale, this *piazza* occupies the summit of the tallest of Rome's seven hills. In its center, the enormous statues of Castor and Pollux stand on either side of an obelisk from the Mausoleum of Augustus. The President of the Republic resides in the imposing **Palazzo del Quirinale** *(closed to the public)*, a Baroque architectural collaboration by Bernini, Maderno, and Fontana. Down V. del Quirinale, V. Ferrara on the right leads down the steps to V. Milano. Farther along the street lies the marvelous facade of Borromini's pristine **Chiesa di San Carlo alle Quattro Fontane.** *(Open M-F 10am-1pm and 3-7pm, Sa-Su 10am-1pm.)*

BASILICA OF SANTA MARIA MAGGIORE. This basilica, crowning the Esquiline Hill, is officially part of Vatican City. To the right of the altar, a marble slab marks the **Bernini's tomb.** The 14th-century mosaics in the **loggia** recount the story of the August snowfall that showed the pope where to build the church. *(Dress code strictly enforced. Open daily 7am-7pm. Loggia open daily 9:30am-12:30pm. Tickets in souvenir shop €3.)*

SOUTHERN ROME

The area south of the center is a mix of wealthy and working-class neighborhoods and is home to the city's best nightlife as well as some of its grandest churches.

APPIAN WAY. Since burial inside the city walls was forbidden during ancient times, fashionable Romans made their final resting places along the Appian Way. At the same time, early Christians secretly constructed maze-like catacombs under the ashes of their persecutors. *(M: A-San Giovanni. Take bus #218 from P. di S. Giovanni to the intersection of V. Ardeatina and V. delle Sette Chiese.)* **San Callisto,** V. Appia Antica 110, is the largest catacomb in Rome, with nearly 22km of subterranean paths. Its four levels once held 16 popes, St. Cecilia, and 500,000 other Christians. *(Take the private road that runs northeast to the entrance to the catacombs. Open Mar.-Jan. M-Tu and Th-Sa 8:30am-noon and 2:30-5pm.)* **Santa Domitilla** houses an intact 3rd-century portrait of Christ and the Apostles. *(Facing V. Ardeatina from the exit of S. Callisto, cross the street and walk up V. d. Sette Chiese. Open Feb.-Dec. M and W-Su 8:30am-noon and 2:30-5pm.)*

CAELIAN HILL. Southeast of the Colosseum, the Caelian is home to some of the city's greatest chaos. Split into three levels, each from a different era, the **Chiesa di San Clemente** is one of Rome's most intriguing churches. A fresco cycle by Masolino dating from the 1420s graces the **Chapel of Santa Caterina.** *(M: B-Colosseo. Turn left out of the station and walk down V. dei Fori Imperiali away from the Forum. Open M-Sa 9am-12:30pm and 3-6pm, Su 10am-12:30pm and 3-6pm. €3.)* The immense **Chiesa di San Giovanni in Laterano** was the seat of the papacy

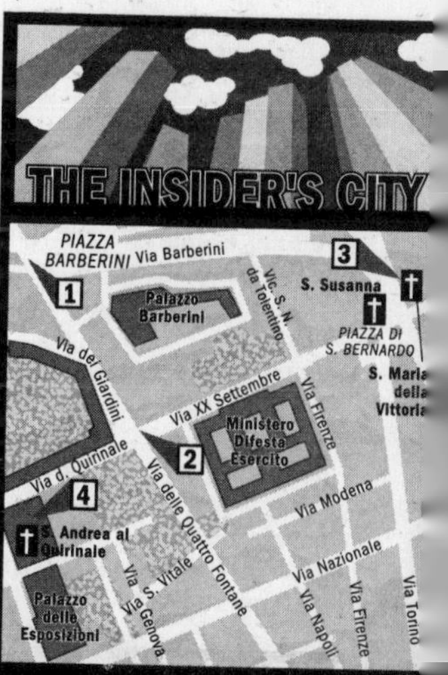

OBSCURE BERNINI

Multi-talented Gianlorenzo Bernini (1598-1680) worked under every pope in his lifetime, in the process defining 17th-century Roman sculpture. Although his most famous works are hard to miss, take an afternoon to explore the lesser-known masterpieces.

1. P. Barberini has the Triton-crowned **Fontana del Tritone** for its centerpiece, while the **Fontana dei Api** (Fountain of the Bees) on the corner of V. V. Veneto spectacularly displays the Bernini family coat of arms.
2. Bernini's **Four Fountains,** representing the four seasons, are built into each corner of this busy intersection.
3. The sculpture **Ecstasy of St. Theresa** in S. Maria della Vittoria is controversial for its depiction of the saint pierced by an angel's dart in a pose resembling sexual climax.
4. Bernini only asked for bread from the Jesuit novitiate for the construction of his beloved oval **San Andrea de Quirinal.**

until the 14th century; founded by Constantine in AD 314, it is Rome's oldest Christian basilica. The two golden reliquaries over the altar contain the skulls of St. Peter and St. Paul. Across the street is the **Scala Santa,** which houses what are believed to be the 28 steps used by Jesus outside Pontius Pilate's house. *(Dress code enforced. M: A-San Giovanni or bus #16 from Termini. Open daily 9am-6pm. €2, students €1.)*

AVENTINE HILL. The **Roseto Comunale,** Rome's official rose garden, is host to the annual Premio Roma, the worldwide competition for the best blossom. *(V. delle Valle Murcia, across the Circus Maximus from the Palatine Hill. Open daily 8am-7:30pm.)* The 5th-century **Church of Santa Sabina** and its monastery were home to St. Dominic, Pius V, and St. Thomas Aquinas. *(At the southern end of Parco Savello.)* V.S. Sabina continues along the crest of the hill to **Piazza dei Cavalieri di Malta.** Hedges perfectly frame the dome of St. Peter's through the **keyhole** in the cream-colored gate.

MUSEUMS

Etruscans, emperors, popes, and *condottiere* have been busily stuffing Rome full of artwork for several millennia, leaving behind a city teeming with galleries. Museums are generally closed on Mondays, Sunday afternoons, and holidays.

GALLERIA BORGHESE. The exquisite Galleria's **Room I,** on the right, houses Canova's statue of **Paolina Borghese** portrayed as Venus triumphant. The next rooms display Bernini's most famous sculptures: a striking **David,** crouching with his slingshot; **Apollo and Daphne;** the weightless body in **Rape of Proserpina;** and weary-looking Aeneas in **Eneo e Anchise.** Don't miss six **Caravaggio** paintings, including his *Self Portrait as Bacchus* and *St. Jerome.* The collection continues in the *pinacoteca* upstairs, accessible from the gardens around the back by a winding staircase. **Room IX** holds Raphael's **Deposition** while Sodoma's *Pietà* graces **Room XII.** Look for Bernini's self portraits, del Conte's *Cleopatra and Lucrezia,* Rubens's *Pianto sul Cristo Morto,* and Titian's *Amor Sacro e Amor Profano.* *(M: A-Spagna; take the Villa Borghese exit, walk to the right past the metro stop to V. Muro Torto and then to P. Porta Pinciana; Viale del Museo Borghese ahead leads to the museum. Open Tu-Su 9am-7:30pm. Entrance every 2hr. Limited capacity; reserve ahead. Tickets €8.50.)*

VATICAN MUSEUMS. The Vatican Museums constitute one of the world's greatest art collections, with ancient, Renaissance, and modern statues, paintings, and papal odds and ends. A good place to start a tour is the stellar **Museo Pio-Clementino,** the world's greatest collection of antique sculpture. The last room contains the enormous red sarcophagus of Sant'Elena, Constantine's mother. From here, the Simonetti Stairway climbs to the **Museo Etrusco,** with artifacts from Tuscany and northern Lazio. Back on the landing of the Simonetti Staircase is the **Stanza della Biga** (room of an ancient marble chariot) and the **Galleria della Candelabra** (chandelier). The long trudge to the Sistine Chapel begins here, passing through the **Galleria degli Arazzi** (tapestries), the **Galleria delle Mappe** (maps), the **Appartamento di Pio V** (where there is a shortcut to *la Sistina*), the **Stanza Sobieski,** and the **Stanza della Immaculata Concezione.** A door leads into the first of the four **Stanze di Rafaele,** apartments built for Pope Julius II in the 1510s. From here, there are two paths: a staircase leading to the brilliantly frescoed Borgia Apartments, the **Museum of Modern Religious Art,** and another route leading to the Sistine Chapel (p. 618). On the way out of the chapel, peak at the **Room of the Aldobrandini Marriage,** a series of rare, ancient frescoes. Finally, the Vatican's painting collection, the **Pinacoteca,** spans eight centuries and is one of Rome's best. *(Walk north from P.S. Pietro along the wall of Vatican City for about 10 blocks. ☎698 849 47. Open Mar.-Oct. M-F 8:45am-3:20pm, Sa 8:45am-12:20pm; Nov.-Feb. M-Sa 8:45am-12:20pm. Last entrance 1hr. before closing. €10, with ISIC €8. Free last Su of the month 8:45am-1:45pm. Plan to spend at least 4-5hr.)*

CAPITOLINE MUSEUM. This collection of ancient sculpture is one of the largest in the world. The Palazzo Nuovo contains the original statue of **Marcus Aurelius** that once stood in the center of the *piazza*. The collections continue across the *piazza* in the Palazzo dei Conservatori. See fragments of the **Colossus of Constantine** and the famous **Capitoline Wolf,** an Etruscan statue that has symbolized the city of Rome since antiquity. At the top of the stairs, the **pinacoteca's** masterpieces include Caravaggio's *St. John the Baptist*, Rubens's *Romulus and Remus Fed by the Wolf*, and Titian's *Baptism of Christ*. *(On Capitoline Hill behind the Vittorio Emanuele II monument. ☎67 10 24 75. Open Tu-Su 9am-8pm. €7.80, with ISIC €5.80.)*

OTHER COLLECTIONS. The **Villa Farnesina** was the sumptuous home of the one-time wealthiest man in Europe, Agostino "il Magnifico" Chigi, and now displays decadent artwork. The **Stanza delle Nozze** (Marriage Room), is particularly noteworthy. *(V. della Lungara 230. Across from Palazzo Corsini on Lungotevere Farnesina. Open M-Sa 9am-1pm. €4.50.)* The **Museo Nazionale D'Arte Antica's** collection of 12th- through 18th-century art is split between Palazzo Barberini and Palazzo Corsini, in different parts of the city. **Palazzo Barberini** contains paintings from the medieval through Baroque periods, while the **Galleria Corsini** holds a collection of works by 17th- and 18th-century painters. *(Palazzo: V. Barberini 18. M: A-Barberini. Bus #492 or 62. Open Tu-Su 9am-7pm. €5. Galleria Corsini: V. della Lungara 10. Opposite Villa Farnesina in Trastevere. Open Tu-Su 8:30am-7:30pm; July-Aug. 8:30am-2pm. €4.)* Cardinal Bernardino Spada bought a grandiose assortment of paintings and sculpture and commissioned an even more opulent set of great rooms to house them; a visit to the **Galleria Spada** offers a glimpse of the luxury surrounding Baroque courtly life. *(P. Capo di Ferro 13, in the Palazzo Spada. Open Tu-Su 8:30am-7:30pm. €5.)*

ENTERTAINMENT

The weekly *Roma C'è* (with a section in English) and *Time Out*, both available at newsstands, have comprehensive and up-to-date club, movie, and event listings.

THEATER AND CINEMA

The **Festival Roma-Europa** (www.romace.it) in late summer brings a number of world-class acts to Rome; for year-round performances of classic Italian theater, **Teatro Argentina,** Largo di Torre Argentina 52, is the matriarch of all Italian venues. (☎684 000 345. Box office open M-F 10am-2pm and 3-7pm, Sa 10am-2pm. Tickets €14-26, students €10-13. AmEx/D/MC/V.) **Teatro Colosseo,** V. Capo d'Africa 5/A, usually features work by foreign playwrights translated into Italian, but it also hosts an English-language theater night. (☎700 49 32. M: B-Colosseo. Box office open Sept.-Apr. Tu-Sa 6-9:30pm. Tickets €10-20, students €8.)

Most English-language films are dubbed into Italian; for films in their original languages, check newspapers or *Roma C'è* for listings with a **v.o.** or **l.o. Il Pasquino,** P. San Egidio 10, off P.S. Maria in Trastevere, screens English-language films daily. (☎580 36 22. €6.20, students €4.20.) **Nuovo Sacher,** Largo Ascianghi 1 (☎581 81 16), the theater of famed Italian director Nanni Moretti, shows a host of independent films. (Films in the original language M-Tu. €7, matinee and W €4.50.)

MUSIC

Founded by Palestrina in the 16th century, the **Accademia Nazionale di Santa Cecilia** remains the best in classical music performance. Concerts are held at the Parco della Musica, V. Pietro di Coubertin 30, near P. del Popolo. (www.musicaperroma.it. Tickets at Parco della Musica. Regular season runs Sept.-June. €15, students €8.) Known as one of Europe's best jazz clubs, the smoky atmosphere at **Alexanderplatz Jazz Club,** V. Ostia 9, conveys the feeling of a 40s jazz joint. Read messages on the wall from old greats. (☎397 421 71. M: A-Ottaviano, near Vatican

City. Cover €7. Open daily Sept.-May 9pm-2am. Shows start at 10pm.) The **Cornetto Free Music Festival Roma Live** (www.cornettoalgida.it.) has attracted the likes of Pink Floyd and the Backstreet Boys to the city during the summer.

SPECTATOR SPORTS

Though May brings tennis and equestrian events, sports revolve around *calcio*, or soccer. Rome has two teams in Serie A, Italy's prestigious league: **S.S. Lazio** and the 2000 European champion **A.S. Roma.** Matches are held at the **Stadio Olimpico,** in Foro Italico, most Sundays from September to June, with international matches often played mid-week. The can't-miss matches of the season are the two Roma-Lazio games, which often prove decisive in the race for the championship. Single-game tickets, typically starting at €15.50, can be bought at team stores like **A.S. Roma,** P. Colonna, 360 (☎678 65 14; www.asroma.it; tickets sold daily 10am-6:30pm; AmEx/MC/V); and **Lazio Point,** V. Farini 34/36, near Termini. (☎482 66 88. Open M-F 9am-7pm, Sa 9am-1pm. AmEx/MC/V.) Tickets can also be obtained at the stadium before a game, but beware long lines and the possibility of tickets running out; if you're buying last minute, watch out for overpriced or fake tickets.

SHOPPING

ITALY

No visit to Italy is complete without a "sight-seeing" pilgrimage to Gucci and Prada. These designer shrines with their cardiac arrest-inducing prices center around the Spanish Steps and V. dei Condotti. Tiny boutiques with off-brand fare, such as Ethic and Havana, showcase fashion without sky-high prices at locations throughout the city. Skip the chain outfits and techno-blasting teen stores that dominate V. del Corso and V. Cola di Rienzo. Remember that all purchases of over €155 at a single store are eligible for a VAT refund.

BOUTIQUES

Dolce & Gabbana, V. dei Condotti 52 (☎699 249 99). Open M-Sa 10am-7:30pm.

Emporio Armani, V. del Babuino 140 (☎360 02 197). Houses the less expensive Armani line. Open M 3-7:30pm, Tu-Su 10am-7:30pm.

Gianni Versace, Men: V. Borgognona 24-25 (☎679 50 37); women: V. Bocca di Leone 25-27 (☎678 05 21). Open M-Sa 10am-7pm.

Giorgio Armani, V. dei Condotti 75 (☎699 14 60). Open M-Sa 10am-7pm.

Gucci, V. dei Condotti 8 (☎678 93 40). Open Sept.-July M-F 10am-7pm, Sa 10am-2pm; Aug. M 3-7pm.

Prada, V. dei Condotti 92/95 (☎679 08 97). Open daily 10am-7pm.

CHEAP AND CHIC

Diesel, V. del Corso 186 (☎678 10 45). Italian-made Diesel is *the* label in urban European fashion. Stock up on jeans and t-shirts at prices far lower than anywhere else. Open M-Sa 10:30am-8pm, Su 3:30-8pm.

Mariotti Boutique, V. della Frezza 20 (☎322 71 26). This elegant boutique sells modern, sophisticated clothes in gorgeous fabrics. Prices are steep, so watch for sales. Open M-F 10am-7pm. Closed Aug.

NIGHTLIFE

PUBS

Though *enoteche* tend to be the primary destination for many locals, pubs are still a fun way to knock a few back without covers or sweaty polyester. Many are of the Irish variety; the best being in Campo dei Fiori. Crowds of people flood the P. Navona after bars close at 2am to continue the revelry.

Shanti, V. dei Conciatori 11 (☎330 46 56 62), in Testaccio. M: B-Piramide. Head down V. Ostiense; take 2nd right. The drinks may seem pricey at first (€7 per shot plus mixer), but all worries dissipate after a few puffs of one of Shanti's hookahs (€2.50 per person). Settle into the opulent Middle Eastern decor and enjoy the evening. Belly dancing in winter W-F 11pm-1am. Open daily 9pm-1am. Closed Aug., Su in July.

Caffé della Scala, P. della Scala 60 (☎580 37 63) on V. della Scala before it intersects with P. San Egidio in Trastevere. In nice weather the tables at this casual cafe/bar line V. della Scala. The drink menu has creative options, such as the very Italian *Spritz* (campari, white wine, and soda; €5.50). Open daily 5pm-2am. AmEx/MC/V.

Il Fico, P. del Fico 26 (☎686 52 05), take V. del Tor Millina off P. Navona, and continue past V. del Pace. This bar has an outdoor patio shaded by fig trees and live jazz within. Fantastic mixed drinks (aperitifs €4; full mixed drinks €7). Open daily 9am-2:30am.

Artu Café, Largo Fumasoni Biondi 5 (☎588 03 98), in P. San Egidio, directly behind Santa Maria in Trastevere. Patrons swear this small bar is the best in Trastevere. Beer €4.50. Wine €3-5.50 per glass. Free snacks 6:45-9pm. Open Tu-Su 6pm-2am. MC/V.

CLUBS

Italian discos are flashy and fun, yet often have spoken or unspoken dress codes. Although clubs in many areas of the city close in the summer in favor of more distant desinations such as Fregene or Frascati, Testaccio is dependable through early August. Check *Roma C'è* for the latest news on club openings and closings. *Time Out* covers Rome's sparse but solid collection of gay nightlife listings, many of which require an ARCI-GAY pass (€10, see **GLBT Resources,** p. 607).

Distillerie Clandestine, V. Libetta 13 (☎573 051 02). Speakeasy-like nightspot hosts a restaurant with live music and DJ. Cover F-Sa €20, W-Th free. Open W-Sa 8:30pm-3am.

Jungle, V. di monte Testaccio 95. (☎33 37 20 86 94; www.jungleclubroma.com). Smoky bar full of Italian Goths on Sa, with more of a rock feel on F. Extravagant yet disorienting light effects. Cover €10. Open F-Sa 10:30pm-5am.

Gilda-Alien-Piper, (www.gildabar.it). With steep covers and exclusive guest lists, this nightclub empire caters to the hipsters of Roman nightlife. In the summer, Piper and Alien move to Gilda on the Beach, located in Fregene near Fiumicino, 30km from Rome.

Alien, V. Velletri 13-19 (☎841 22 12). One of the biggest discos in Rome attracts a well-dressed crowd. Cover about €15, includes 1 drink; Sa €20. Open Tu-Su 11pm-5:30am.

Piper, V. Tagliamento 9 (☎855 53 98). North of Termini. From V. XX Settembre, take V. Piave (V. Salaria). Turn right on V. Po (V. Tagliamento). Or take bus #319 from Termini to Tagliamento. Caters to a more exclusive crowd, with international DJs spinning 70s, rock, disco, house, and underground. Cover €15-20, includes 1 drink. Open F-Sa 11pm-4:30am.

Gilda on the Beach, Lungomare di Ponente 11 (☎665 606 49). From May-Sept., ultra-cool clientele make the pilgrimage to Gilda for 4 dance floors, a private beach, a pool, and a restaurant. Cover €20. Disco open 11pm-4am. Dinner served from 8:30pm. AmEx/MC/V.

DAYTRIP FROM ROME: TIVOLI

Take M: B-Rebibbia. Follow signs for Tivoli through an underpass to reach the other side of V. Tiburtina. Take the blue COTRAL bus to Tivoli. Tickets (€1.60) are sold in the metro station. Once the bus reaches Tivoli (25min.), get off past P. Garibaldi at P. delle Nazioni Unite. The bus back to Rome leaves from P. Garibaldi. The tourist office is on the street leading from P. Garibaldi, with info on villas, maps, and bus schedules. (☎0774 31 12 49. Open M and W 9am-1pm, Tu and Th-Sa 9am-3pm and 4-7pm.) Villa d'Este is through the souvenir stands in P. Trento and to the left. For Villa Adriana, 5km from Tivoli proper, take the orange bus #4 or 4x from P. Garibaldi's newsstand, which also sells tickets (€1). The COTRAL bus also runs to and from Villa Adriana: from the parking lot, take a right away from the villa and head uphill until you reach a small bus stop sign.

ITALY

Tivoli is a beautifully preserved hilltop town, with winding streets, steep stone stairs, and views of the surrounding valleys. Though Tivoli's main attractions are three extravagant villas, the tourist office provides a fantastic map with three walking tours of different lengths. **Villa d'Este,** a castle-garden, was laid out by Cardinal Ercole d'Este with the idea of recreating an ancient Roman *nymphaea* and pleasure palace. (☎0774 31 20 70; www.villadestetivoli.com. Open May-Aug. Tu-Su 9am-6:45pm; Sept.-Apr. 9am-4pm. €9.) **Villa Gregoriana,** at the other end of town, is a park with hiking trails and spectacular lookout points that wind over waterfalls and "the caves of Neptune and the Sirens." (€4. Audio tour €4). On the way back from Tivoli, visit the vast remains of **Villa Adriana,** the largest and most expensive villa ever built in the Roman Empire. Look for the *pecile*, built to recall the famous *Stoa Poikile* (Painted Porch) of Athens. (☎0774 38 27 33. Open daily 9am-1½hr. before sunset. €8.50. Archaeologist tour €3.50, audio tour €4.)

LOMBARDY (LOMBARDIA)

ITALY

Ever since the Celts snatched this fertile region from the Etruscans, Lombardy has been under attack. It has been coveted in turn by the Romans, Goths, French, Spaniards, and the Austrians. However, the disputing powers failed to rob Lombardy of its prosperity, as the region remains the wealthiest in Italy. While Milan may bask in the cosmopolitan spotlight, equally important are the rich culture and beauty of Bergamo, Mantua, and the foothills of the Alps.

MILAN (MILANO) ☎02

Unlike Rome, Venice, or Florence, which wrap themselves in a veil of historic allure, Milan (pop. 1,400,000) presents itself as it is: rushed, refined, and cosmopolitan. The city has its share of urban sores—thirsty mosquitoes, traffic congestion, and notoriety as one of the most expensive cities in Europe. But true *Milanesi* claim their city proudly. Once the capital of the western half of the Roman Empire, Milan is now the center of Italian style, financial markets, and industry.

TRANSPORTATION

Flights: Malpensa Airport (MXP), 48km from the city. Handles intercontinental flights. **Malpensa Express** leaves Cadorna metro station and Stazione Nord for the airport (40min., €9). **Linate Airport** (LIN), 7km away, covers domestic and European flights. Take bus #73 from MM1: P.S. Babila (€1). Information for both ☎748 52 200.

Trains: Stazione Centrale (☎848 888 088), in P. Duca d'Aosta on MM2. Trains leave for: **Bergamo** (1hr., every hr., €4); **Florence** (3½hr., 5 per day, €22); **Rome** (7hr., every hr., €39); **Turin** (2hr., every hr., €8); **Venice** (3hr., every hr., €20).

Buses: Stazione Centrale. Intercity buses tend to be less convenient and more expensive than trains. **SAL, SIA, Autostradale,** and other carriers leave from P. Castello (MM1: Cairoli) and Porta Garibaldi for **Bergamo,** the **Lake Country, Trieste,** and **Turin.**

Public Transportation: The **Metro** (Metropolitana Milanese, or **MM**) runs 6am-midnight. Use the **bus** system for trips outside the city proper. Metro tickets can be purchased at *tabacchi,* ticket booths, and station machines. Always keep a few extra tickets, as *tabacchi* close at 8pm and ticket machines can be unreliable, especially in Stazione Centrale. Single-fare tickets €1, 1-day pass €3, 2-day €5.50, 10-ticket pass €9.20.

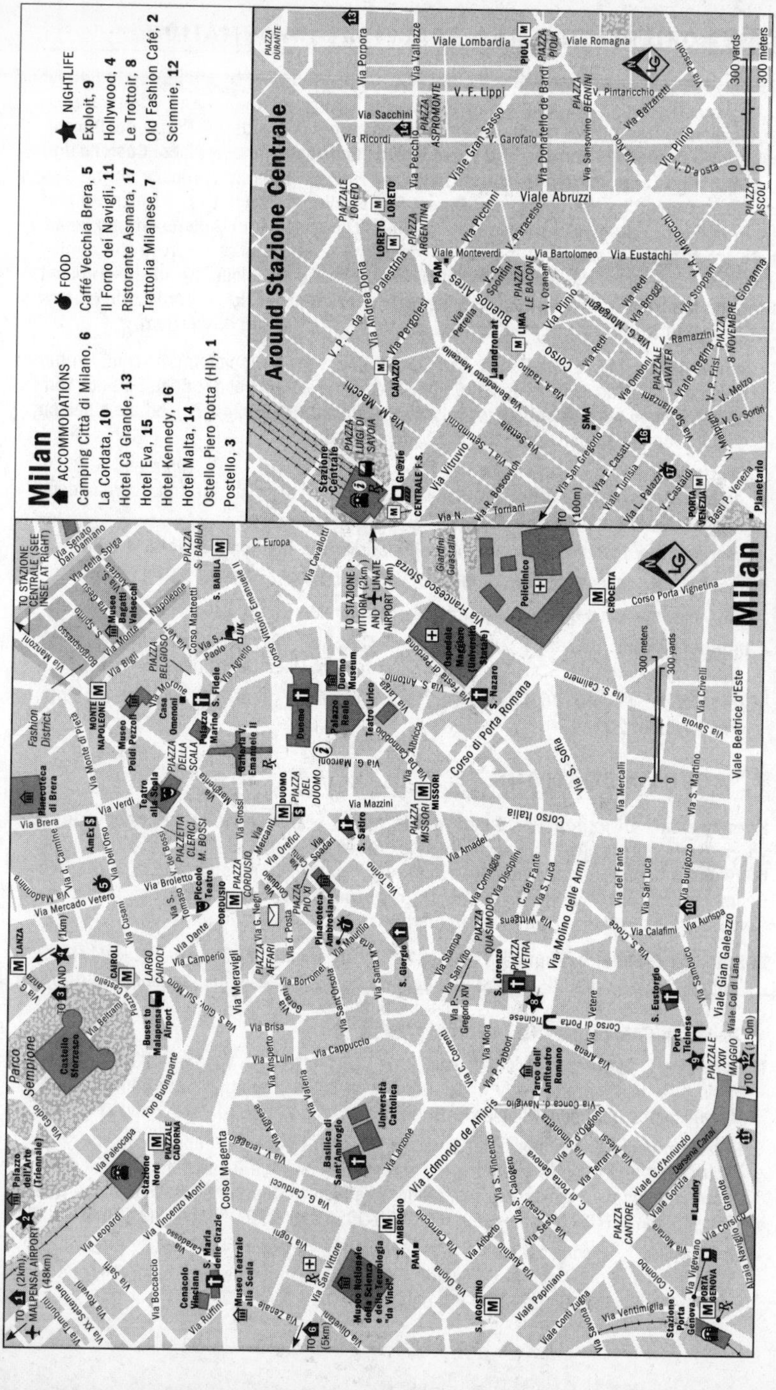

Milan

ACCOMMODATIONS

- Camping Città di Milano, **6**
- La Cordata, **10**
- Hotel Cà Grande, **13**
- Hotel Eva, **15**
- Hotel Kennedy, **16**
- Hotel Malta, **14**
- Ostello Piero Rotta (HI), **1**
- Postello, **3**

FOOD

- Caffé Vecchia Brera, **5**
- Il Forno dei Navigli, **11**
- Ristorante Asmara, **17**
- Trattoria Milanese, **7**

NIGHTLIFE

- Exploit, **9**
- Hollywood, **4**
- Le Trottoir, **8**
- Old Fashion Café, **2**
- Scimmie, **12**

Around Stazione Centrale

Milan

ORIENTATION AND PRACTICAL INFORMATION

The layout of the city resembles a giant bull's-eye, encircled by ancient, concentric city walls. In the outer rings lie suburbs built during the 50s and 60s to house southern immigrants. In the inner circle are four central squares: **Piazza del Duomo,** where **Via Orefici, Via Mazzini,** and **Corso Vittorio Emanuele II** meet; **Piazza Castello** and the attached **Largo Cairoli,** near the Castello Sforzesco; **Piazza Cordusio,** connected to Largo Cairoli by **Via Dante;** and **Piazza San Babila,** entrance to the business and fashion district along C. Vittorio Emanuele II. The **duomo** and **Galleria Vittorio Emanuele** are roughly at the center of the downtown circle. Radiating from the center are two large parks, the **Giardini Pubblici** and the **Parco Sempione.** From the colossal **Stazione Centrale** train station, farther northeast, you can take a scenic ride on bus #60 or the more efficient commute on subway line #3 to the downtown.

Tourist Office: IAT, V. Marconi 1 (☎725 24 301; www.milanoinfotourist.com), in the Palazzo di Turismo in P. del Duomo. Open M-Sa 8:45am-1pm and 2-6pm, Su 9am-1pm and 2-5pm. Another **branch** is in Stazione Centrale (☎725 24 370), off main hall on 2nd fl. Open M-Sa 9am-6pm, Su 9am-1pm and 2-5pm.

American Express: V. Larga 4 (☎721 04 010), on the corner of V. Larga and S. Clemente. Handles wire transfers and holds mail for up to 1 month for AmEx cardholders. Also **exchanges currency.** Open M-F 9am-5:30pm.

Emergency: ☎118. **Police:** ☎113. **Carabinieri:** ☎112. **Medical Services:** ☎38 83.

Hospital: Ospedale Maggiore di Milano, V. Francesco Sforza 35 (☎550 31).

24hr. Pharmacy: (☎669 07 35). In Stazione Centrale's 2nd fl. galleria.

Internet Access: Gr@zia, P. Duca d'Aosta 14 (☎303 127 149; www.grazianet.com). MM2/MM3: Central F.S. €1 for 15min., €15 for 5hr. Open daily 8am-1am.

Post Office: V. Cordusio 4 (☎724 82 126). Open M-F 8am-7pm, Sa 9:30am-2pm. **Postal Code:** 20100.

ITALY

ACCOMMODATIONS

Every season in expensive, fashionable Milan is high season—except August when many hotels close. September, November, March, and April are particularly busy when business conventions bring hotel capacity to a maximum. For the best deals, try one of the hostels on the city's periphery or the areas east of Stazione Centrale. Make reservations well in advance.

Hotel Cà Grande, V. Porpora 87 (☎261 45 295; www.hotelcagrande.it). MM1/MM2: Loreto. 7 blocks from P. Loreto in a yellow house. Spotless, homey rooms with A/C, phone, and TV. Friendly owners serve included breakfast in the garden. Singles €40, with bath €45; doubles €60/70. AmEx/MC/V. ❹

Hotel Eva, V. Lazzaretto 17, 4th fl. (☎67 06 093). MM1: Porta Venezia. Take V.F. Casati, then turn right. Large, lovely white rooms with lace curtains, all with phone and TV. Clean shared bathroom. Singles €30; doubles €45; triples €70. Cash only. ❸

Hotel Kennedy, Viale Tunisia 6, 6th fl. (☎294 00 934; www.kennedyhotel.it). MM1: Porta Venezia. Exit on C. Buenos Aires, and turn left on Viale Tunisia. Homey pink rooms have fans, phones, sinks, and TVs. Modern bathrooms. Singles €35-40; doubles €50-55, with bath €70-75; triples with bath €85-90; quads €90-95. AmEx/MC/V. ❸

Hotel Malta, V. Ricordi 20 (☎20 49 615; www.hotelmalta.it). MM1/MM2: Loreto. Take V. Porpora and turn right on V. Ricordi. Floral-decorated rooms have bath, fan, and TV; many with balcony. Singles €36-60; doubles €50-90. MC/V. ❸

Ostello per la Gioventù AIG Piero Rotta (HI), V.M. Bassi 2 (☎392 67 095; www.ostellionline.org). MM1: QT8. Exit and turn right facing the white church; the hostel is on the right. Institutional building with 6-bed dorms and a larger rooms. Breakfast included. Laundry €5.50. 3-night max. stay. Lockout 9am-3:30pm. Reserve online. Closed Dec. 24-Jan. 12. Dorms €21.50; family rooms €25 per person. €3 HI discount. MC/V. ❷

Postello, V. Pergola 5 (☎33 317 52 272). MM2: P. Garibaldi. Take the V. Pepe exit, then turn left and immediately right on V. Carmagnola. V. Pergola is 3 blocks ahead after P. le C. Archinto. Milan's newest, cheapest hostel is right behind painted, postered gates. Clean, no frills 4- and 8-bed dorms without locks. Frequent movies, book talks, and DJ performances in the garden courtyard and bar create community but can make sleeping difficult. Free wireless Internet and luggage storage. Dorms €18. Cash only. ❶

La Cordata, V. Burigozzo 11 (☎583 14 675). MM3: Missori. From P. Missori, take tram #15 to Italia S. Lucia, keep walking 1 block, and go right on V. Burigozzo. Enter around the corner from La Cordata camping store. Sky-blue walls, whimsical murals, and backpackers looking to party in Navigli. Curfew 12:30pm. Dorms €18. Cash only. ❷

Camping Città di Milano, V.G. Airaghi 61 (☎48 20 01 34; www.parcoaquatica.com). MM1: De Angeli, then bus #72 to S. Romanello Togni. Backtrack 10m and turn right onto V. Togni. Enter at Aquatica waterpark. Large campground with modern facilities. Grills available. Laundry €5. Closed Dec.-Jan. Tent sites €14-16, €6.50 per car. 2- to 6-person cabins €37-88; deluxe cabins with bath and A/C €80-120. MC/V. ❶

ITALY

FOOD

Old-style *trattorias* still follow *Milanesi* culinary traditions with *risotto alla Milanese* (rice with saffron), *cotoletta alla Milanese* (breaded veal cutlet with lemon), and *osso buco* (shank of lamb, beef, or veal). The cheapest dinners in town are at bars that offer discount buffets, starting around 6:30pm, with the purchase of a mixed drink. **PAM** supermarket, V. Piccinni 2, is off C. Buenos Aires or at Viale Olona 1/3, just outside the MM2: S. Ambrogio. (Open M-Sa 8am-9pm.)

Trattoria Milanese, V.S. Marta 11 (☎864 51 991). MM1/3: Duomo. Take V. Torino from P. del Duomo, turn right on V. Maurilio and right again. Authentic *cucina milanese,* under brick arches and sketches of old Milan. The *cotolette alla milanese* (breaded rib; €15) is a work of culinary art. *Primi* €6-8. *Secondi* €7-19. Cover €2. Service 11%. Closed last 2 weeks of July. Open M, W-Su 10am-3pm and 7pm-1am. AmEx/MC/V. ❷

Ristorante Asmara, V. Lazzaro Palazzi 5 (☎295 22 453). MM1: Porta Venezia. Take C. Buenos Aires to V. Lazzaro Palazzi. Large African restaurant specializing in spicy Eritrean food, including vegetarian options. Cover €1.60. Large *piatti* €8-11.50. Open M-Tu and Th-Su 10am-4pm and 6pm-midnight. AmEx/MC/V. ❷

Caffè Vecchia Brera, V. Dell'Orso 20 (☎864 61 695). MM1: Cairoli. Head across V. Cusani; restaurant is through intersection with V. Mercado Vetero on the left corner. This classic spot serves Parisian chic with an Italian kick in its crepes filled with cheese and proscuitto. Dessert crepes are a favorite of the cast of *La Scala.* Cover €1. Crepes €3.50-7. *Primi* and *secondi* €6-14. Open daily 7am-3am. ❷

Il Forno dei Navigli, V.A. Naviglio Pavese 2 (☎83 23 372). At the corner with Ripa di Porta Ticinese. Out of "the oven of Navigli" come the most decadent pastries in the city. Pastries and breads €0.50-6. Open M-Sa 7am-7:30pm, Su 9am-7:30pm. Cash only. ❶

SIGHTS

DUOMO. The geographical and spiritual center of Milan and a good starting point for any walking tour of the city, the *duomo* is one of the largest churches in the world. **Gian Galeazzo Visconti** began construction of the *duomo* in 1386 and was finally completed at Napoleon's command in 1809. Meanwhile, the cathedral accumulated more than 3400 statues, 135 spires, and 96 gargoyles. Climb (or ride) to the **roof walkway,** where you'll find yourself among turrets and spires with views of the Alps. *(MM1: Duomo. Cathedral open daily 7am-7pm. Modest dress required. Free. Roof open daily 9am-5:45pm. €4, elevator €6.)*

PINACOTECA AMBROSIANA. The 23 palatial rooms of the Ambrosiana display exquisite works from the 14th through 19th centuries, including Botticelli's circular *Madonna of the Canopy*, Brueghel's *Allegories*, Caravaggio's *Basket of Fruit* (the first Italian still-life), Raphael's wall-sized *School of Athens*, Titian's *Adoration of the Magi*, and da Vinci's captivating *Portrait of a Musician*. The statue-filled courtyard is also enchanting. *(P. Pio XI 2. Follow V. Spadari off V. Torino and make a left onto V. Cantù. Open Tu-Su 10am-5:30pm. €7.50.)*

MUSEO POLDI PEZZOLI. Poldi Pezzoli, an 18th-century nobleman and art collector, bequeathed his house and its eclectic collection to the city "for the enjoyment of the people" in 1879. Today, the masterpieces hang in the Golden Room overlooking the garden. Smaller collections fill Pezzoli's former private chambers, where the decor reflects his fine taste. Particularly impressive is a tiny but sublime display of Italian military armaments. *(V. Manzoni 12. Open Tu-Su 10am-6pm. €6.)*

TEATRO ALLA SCALA. Founded in 1778, La Scala has established Milan as the opera capital of the world. Its understated Neoclassical facade and lavish interior set the stage for premieres of works by Mascagni, Rossini, Puccini, and Verdi, performed by virtuosos like Maria Callas and Enrico Caruso. Visitors can soak up La Scala's historical glow at the Museo Teatrale alla Scala. From poster art to a plaster cast of Toscanini's hand, the museum offers a glimpse into the past of opera's premier house. *(Access through the Galleria Vittorio Emanuele from P. del Duomo. ☎88 79 24 73; www.teatroallascala.org. Museum: C. Magenta 71. MM1: Conciliazione. Open daily 9am-12:30pm and 1:30-5:30pm. Last entry 30min. before closing. €5, students €4.)*

GALLERIA VITTORIO EMANUELE II. Light pours through an immense glass and steel cupola (48m) and into a five-story arcade of cafes, shops, and offices. Elegant mosaics representing different continents besieged by the Romans adorn the floors and walls. Once considered the drawing room of Milan, the statue-bedecked Galleria is now a graceful mall. *(North of the duomo. Free.)*

CASTELLO SFORZESCO. Restored after extensive bomb damage in 1943, the Castello Sforzesco is one of Milan's best-known monuments. Constructed in 1368 as a defense against Venice, it was used as an army barrack, a horse stall, and a storage house before da Vinci made it his studio. Inside are the 10 **Musei Civici** (Civic Museums), which include the **Museum of Musical Instruments** and the **Museum of Decorative Art.** The ground floor contains a sculpture collection most renowned for Michelangelo's unfinished, angular *Pietà Rondanini* (1564), his last work. The Museum of Decorative Art showcases ornate household furnishings, Murano glass, and a giant porcelain crab. The underground level has a small Egyptian collection. *(MM1: Cairoli. Open Tu-Su 9am-5:30pm. Combined admission €3, student €1.50.)*

CHIESA DI SANTA MARIA DELLA GRAZIE. The church's Gothic nave is dark and elaborately patterned with frescoes, contrasting the airy Renaissance tribune Bramante added in 1497. To the left of the church entrance, in what was once the dining hall, is the **Cenacolo Vinciano** (Vinciano Refectory), home to one of the most important pieces of art in the world: Leonardo da Vinci's **Last Supper.** Following a 20-year restoration effort, the painting was put back on public display, though rumors persist that it may again be closed. Make reservations well in advance or risk missing it. *(P. di S. Maria delle Grazie 2. MM1: Conciliazione. From P. Conciliazione, take V. Boccaccio and then right onto V. Ruffini for about 2 blocks. Reservations ☎89 42 11 46. Wheelchair accessible. Open Tu-Su 8:15am-6:45pm. €6.50. Reservation fee €1.50.)*

PINACOTECA DI BRERA. The Brera Art Gallery presents a collection of 14th- to 20th-century paintings, with an emphasis on the Lombard School. Works include Bellini's *Pietà*, Caravaggio's *Supper at Emmaus*, Mantegna's brilliant *Dead Christ*, and Raphael's *Marriage of the Virgin*. *(V. Brera 28. MM2: Lanza. Wheelchair accessible. Open Tu-Su 8:30am-7:15pm. €5.)*

SHOPPING AND ENTERTAINMENT

In a city where clothes really do make the man (or woman), fashion pilgrims arrive in spring and summer to watch the newest styles take their first sashaying steps down the runway. Once the music fades and designers take their bows, window displays and world-famous **saldi (sales)** in July and January usher new collections into stores. For window shopping, take the Metro to MM1: S. Babila and stroll around the **Golden Triangle**, especially **Via Monte Napoleone** and **Via Sant'Andrea**, with their two **Prada** and four **Armani** stores. Designer creations are available to mere mortals at the trendy boutiques along **Corso di Porta Ticinese.** *Fashionistas* who can tolerate being a season behind can purchase famous designer wear from *blochisti* (stocks or wholesale outlets), such as the well-known **Il Salvagente,** V. Bronzetti 16, off C. XXII Marzo (MM2/3: Stazione Centrale), or **Gruppo Italia Grandi Firme,** V. Montegani, #7/A (MM2: Famagosta), which offers famous designer duds at 70% off. If all else fails, pick up the free *Shopping Map* at the tourist office.

Milan sponsors many free cultural and artistic events that can be found in the monthly *Milano Mese* (free), distributed at the tourist office, or in *Milano è Milano*, a booklet published in English and Italian with entertainment and cultural venues (€3) available at the tourist office and bookstores. Milan's famed tradition and unrivalled audience enthusiasm make **La Scala** one of the best places in the world to see an opera. (Infotel Scala ☎720 037 44; www.teatroallascala.org. Season runs Jan.-July and Sept.-Nov. Central box office located at Galleria V. Emanuele, open daily noon-6pm. Tickets €10-105.) The La Verdi season of the **Milan Symphony Orchestra** runs during summer at the **Auditorium di Milano** (☎833 89 201; www.orchestrasinfonica.milano.it. Tickets €13-50, with student discount €10-25.)

Inter and **Milan A.C.** soccer clubs face off in their shared stadium, Stadio Guiseppe Meazza (capacity 87,000; MM2: Lotto), once a year. Ticket One sells tickets for both teams (☎02 39 22 61). **Stadium tours,** including a visit to the superb soccer museum, are available on non-game days M-Sa 10am-6pm. (☎40 42 432. €12.50.)

From June to September the tourist office sponsors both the **Festa della Cultura** featuring myriad events of dance, music, and food from Milan's many immigrant cultures (call the tourist office ☎884 645 33), and the **Serate al Museo** celebration with both classical and contemporary concerts throughout Milan's museum courtyards and great halls. (☎88 45 65 55; www.comune.milano.it/museiemostre.)

NIGHTLIFE

The **Navigli district** is a nightlife area popular with students. The **Brera district** invites tourists and Milanese to test their vocal skills while sipping mixed drinks at one of its piano bars. **Corso di Porta Ticinese** is the sleek land of the all-night happy hour buffet, where the price of an enormous mixed drink (€6-8) also buys dinner. A single block of **Corso Como** near **Stazione Garibaldi** is home to the most exclusive clubs in Milan. Bars and clubs dot the city, especially around **Largo Cairoli,** where the summer brings Milan's hottest outdoor dance venues, and southeast of **Stazione Centrale,** where there is a mix of bars and much of Milan's gay and lesbian scene. Pick up the free *Nightlife Map* at the tourist office for more suggestions.

Scimmie, V. Sforza 49 (☎894 02 874). A legendary nightclub in 3-part harmony: the pizza pub on the river barge; the chill, polished *ristorante;* and the cool, blue bar with nightly performances. Talented underground musicians play fusion, jazz, blues, Italian swing, and reggae. Concerts 10:30pm. Barge: pizza €4-8. Restaurant: *primi* and *secondi* €6-17. Bar: drinks €5-9. Barge and restaurant open M-F noon-3pm and 7pm-2am, Sa-Su 6pm-2am. Bar open daily 8pm-3am. MC/V.

Old Fashion Café, Viale Alemagna 6 (☎02 805 62 31; www.oldfashion.it). MM1/2: Cadorna F. N. Walk up V. Paleocapa next to the station and then veer right onto Viale Alemagna before the bridge on the left. To the left of Palazzo dell'Arte along a dirt path. Hot lounge and dance club spills outside in the summer to become a writhing dance party. The stylishly under-dressed reign; Tu is the most popular night, with mixed music, while F is R&B night. Dancing midnight-4am. M-Sa cover €20 includes 1 drink, W cover often €5-10 cheaper and students free. Su cover €15 for dancing. MC/V.

Exploit, V. Pioppette 3 (☎89 40 86 75; www.exploitmilano.com) on C. Porta Ticinese near Chiesa di S. Lorenzo Maggiore down V.E. de Amicis. Locals flock to this trendy bar/restaurant to enjoy romantic candlelit dining inside on spotless white tablecloths or to sip cocktails outside in the shadow of Roman ruins at mosaic-topped tables. Mixed drinks €6-8. Wine €5 or €18-20 for a bottle. *Primi* €10. *Secondi* €18-22. Happy hour buffet daily 6-9pm. Open Tu-Su noon-4pm and 6pm-2am. MC/V.

Le Trottoir, P. XXIV Maggio 1 (☎83 78 166). This alternative club with DJ and live underground music from 10:30pm-2am may be the loudest, most crowded bar in the Navigli. Mixed drinks €7. Pizza and sandwiches €8, until 2am. Happy hour daily 6-8pm with €3.50 beer and €5 mixed drinks. Open daily 3pm-3am. Cash only.

Hollywood, C. Como 15 (☎659 89 96; www.discotecahollywood.com). Get primped to pout for the bouncer; this disco selects its revelers with the utmost discrimination. Su tends to be an invite-only party for sports stars and celebs. Mixed drinks €10. Cover €20 including 1 drink. Students with ID €13-18. Open Tu-Su 11pm-5am. MC/V.

MANTUA (MANTOVA) ☎0376

Mantua (pop. 47,000) owes its literary fame to its famous son, the poet Virgil. Its grand *palazzi*, including the opulent **Palazzo Ducale,** P. Sordello 40, were built by the powerful Gonzaga family who, after ascending to power in 1328, ruled for 400 years, importing well-known artists to leave their mark on the town's mansions and churches. Inside, check out an unending array of facades, gardens, and frescoes, including Mantegna's painted **Bridal Chamber,** featuring the entire Gonzaga clan, in the Castello di San Giorgio wing. (Open Tu-Su 8:45am-7:15pm. €6.50, students €3.25.) Music lovers first filled the **Teatro Bibiena,** V. Accademia 4, when 14-year-old Mozart inaugurated the building in 1769. Its rose and gray stone balconies create the illusion of a fairy-tale castle. (Open Tu-Su 9:30am-12:30pm and 3-6pm. €2.10.) Down V.P. Amedeo and V. Acrebi, through P. Veneto, and down Largo Parri, lies the **Palazzo del Te,** built as a suburban retreat for Federico II Gonzaga. It is considered the finest building in the Mannerist style; visit its frescoed **Room of Giants,** depicting the demise of the titans at the hands of Jupiter. (Open M 1-6pm, Tu-Su 9am-6pm. €8, students €2.50.) South of P. Sordello is the 11th-century Romanesque **Piazza delle Erbe.** Opposite the piazza is Leon Alberti's **Chiesa di Sant'Andrea,** one of the first monumental classical buildings since imperial Rome. (Open daily 8am-noon and 3-7pm. Free.)

The modern **Hotel ABC ❹,** P. Don E. Leoni 25, opposite the station, features comfortable rooms with lodge-like wooden ceilings, A/C, TV, and modern bathrooms. (☎0372 32 23 29; www.hotelabcmantova.it. Breakfast included. Singles Apr.-Aug. €40-45; doubles €60-66; triples €80-88. Sept.-Mar. €50-55/70-77/90-99. MC/V; discounts for cash.) Young Mantuan professionals dine at **Trattoria con Pizza da Chiara ❷,** V. Corridonia 44/A, a tastefully chic, upscale pizzeria. From C. Libertà turn left on V. Roma, then right on the narrow V. Corridonia. (☎22 35 68. Pizza and *primi* €4-8. *Secondi* €8.50-13. Cover €2. Open M and W-Su noon-3pm and 7pm-midnight. AmEx/MC/V.) Head to **CompraBene Supermercati,** V. Porto 31/A, for groceries. (Open M-Sa 8am-7:30pm.) **Trains** go from P. Don E. Leoni to Milan

(2¼hr., 8 per day, €8.45) and Verona (40min., every hr., €2.40). From the train station, head left on V. Solferino, which becomes V. Fratelli Bandiera, and right on V. Verdi to reach the **tourist office,** P. Mantegna 6, next to Chiesa Sant'Andrea. (☎32 82 53; www.aptmantova.it. Open daily 9am-7pm.) **Postal Code:** 46100.

BERGAMO

☎035

Bergamo's (pop. 117,000) two distinct neighborhoods reflect its colorful history: the *città bassa* (lower city) is a modern commercial metropolis packed with Neoclassical buildings, while the *città alta* (upper city), is a compact medieval town, accessible by funicular, born as a Venetian outpost. The cobbled pedestrian path **Via Noca** ascends to the medieval *città alta* through the 16th-century **Porta San Agostino.** Stroll down V. Porta Dipinta to the main thoroughfare **Via Gambito,** which ends at **Piazza Vecchia,** an ensemble of medieval and Renaissance buildings. Behind it lies 12th-century **Basilica di Santa Maria Maggiore,** with its ornate Baroque interior. (Open Apr.-Oct. M-Sa 9am-12:30pm and 2:30-6pm, Su 9am-1pm and 3-6pm; Nov.-Mar. reduced hours. Free.) Climb the **Torre Civica** (Civic Tower) in the piazza for a marvelous panoramic view. (Open Apr.-Oct. Tu-F 9:30am-7pm, Sa 9:30am-9:30pm; Nov.-Mar. Tu-F 9:30am-7pm to groups of 5+, Sa 9:30am-4:30pm. €3.)

The train station, bus station, and many budget hotels are in the *città bassa,* though the best food is in the *città alta.* To get from the train station to **Ostello Città di Bergamo (HI) ❷,** V.G. Ferraris 1, head to Porta Nuova and take bus #4 to Leonardo da Vinci, then walk up the stairs on the hill. (☎36 17 24; www.ostellodibergamo.it. All rooms with bath and balcony. Dorms €18; singles €26; doubles €43. HI discount. MC/V.) **Trattoria Casa Mia ❷,** V.S. Bernardino 20, in the *città bassa,* serves lunch (€8.50) and dinner (€11). From the train station walk straight along V.P. Giovanni to Largo Pta. Nuova. Turn left on V.G. Tiraboschi, which becomes V. Zambonate, then turn left. (☎22 06 76. Open daily noon-2pm and 7-10pm. Bar open 11am-3:30pm and 6pm-midnight. Cash only.) Pick up staples at **Pellicano** supermarket, V.V. Emanuele 17, straight up from the train station. (Open M 8:30am-1:30pm, Tu-F 8:30am-1:30pm and 3:30-8pm, Sa 8:30am-8pm.)

Trains (☎21 02 04; 1hr., 1 per hr., €3.90) and **buses** (every 30min., €4.35) pull into P. Marconi from Milan. The **airport bus** runs to and from Bergamo's airport (30min., 5:30am-10:05pm, €1.55). To get to the *città alta* from the train station, take bus #1 to the *funicolare di città alta,* which ascends from **Via Vittorio Emanuele** to the Mercato delle Scarpe. The **tourist office** in the *città alta* is located at V. Gombito 13, on the ground floor of the tower. (☎24 22 26; www.provincia.bergamo.it.) In the *città bassa,* it is the building in the center of P. Marconi in front of train station. **Postal Code:** 24122.

ITALY

THE LAKE COUNTRY

When Italy's monuments and museums start blurring together, escape to the natural beauty of the northern Lake Country, where clear waters lap the encircling mountains. Artistic visionaries like Liszt, Longfellow, and Wordsworth sought rest among the serene shores of the northern lakes. Today, a young crowd descends upon Lake Garda for its watersports by day and thriving club scene at night.

LAKE COMO (LAGO DI COMO)

A heavenly magnificence lingers over the reaches of Europe's deepest lake (410m). *Bougainvillea* and lavish villas adorn the peaceful lake's craggy backdrop, warmed by sun and cooled by lakeside breezes. Industrial Como, the largest city on the lake, is an ideal transportation hub. Three lakes form the forked Lake Como, joined at the more relaxing towns of Centro Lago: Bellagio, Menaggio, and Varenna. **Ostello Villa Olmo (HI) ❷,** V. Bellinzona 2, offers cramped but clean rooms in a familial atmosphere. From the train station, walk 20min. down V. Borgo Vico, which becomes V. Bellinzona. (☎031 57 38 00; ostellocomo@tin.it. Bike rentals. Breakfast included. Reception 7-10am and 4-11:30pm. Lockout 10am-4pm. Strict curfew 11:30pm. Open Mar.-Nov. Reserve ahead. Dorms €17.50. €3 HI discount.) To get from the train station to the **tourist office,** P. Cavour 17, walk down the steps, turn left on V. Fratelli Ricchi, and right on V. Fratelli Rosselli, which leads to P. Cavour via Lungo Lario Trento. (☎031 26 97 12; www.lakecomo.org. Open M-Sa 9am-1pm and 2:30-6pm, Su 9:30am-1pm; Oct.-Apr. closed Su.) **Trains** roll into Stazione San Giovanni (☎0147 88 80 88) from Milan (1hr., every 30min., €4.85) and Zurich, Switzerland (4hr., 6 per day, €40). **Bus** C46 leaves P. Matteotti for Bergamo (2hr., every hr., €5). From Como, take the C10 bus near Ferrovia Nord to Menaggio (1hr., every hr., €3). The C30 buses also serve Bellagio (1hr., every hr., €3). Spend the day zipping between the stores, gardens, villas, and wineries of the remaining towns by **ferry** (day pass €5-18). **Postal Code:** 22100.

LAKE MAGGIORE (LAGO MAGGIORE)

Lacking the frenzy of its eastern neighbors, Lake Maggiore combines temperate mountain waters with idyllic shores. The romantic resort town of **Stresa** is only 1hr. from Milan by **train** (every hr., €4.20). **Orsola Meublé ❷,** V. Duchessa di Genova 45, has large, affordable rooms. Turn right from the station, walk downhill to the intersection, and turn left. (☎0323 310 87. Breakfast included. Singles €20, with bath €25; doubles €40/50. AmEx/MC/V.) To reach the **tourist office** in P. Martini, from the station, turn right on V.P. Piemonte, and left on V. Duchessa di Genova. At the waterfront turn right. (☎0323 301 50. Open Mar.-Oct. daily 10am-12:30pm and 3-6:30pm; Nov.-Feb. M-F 10am-12:30pm and 3-6:30pm, Sa 10am-12:30pm.)

ITALY

BORROMEAN ISLANDS. Stresa is a perfect stepping-stone to the gorgeous Borromean Islands. Daily excursion tickets (€9) allow you to hop back and forth between Stresa and the three islands—**Isola Bella, Isola Superiore dei Pescatori,** and **Isola Madre**—which boast lush, manicured botanical gardens and elegant villas. The opulent, Baroque **Palazzo e Giardini Borromeo,** on Isola Bella, features meticulously designed rooms with priceless masterpieces, tapestries, and sculptures, as well as 10 terraced gardens. (Open Mar. 19-Oct. 23 daily 9am-6pm. €9.)

LAKE GARDA (LAGO DI GARDA)

Garda has staggering mountains and breezy summers. **Desenzano,** the lake's southern transport hub, is only 30min. from Verona, 1hr. from Milan, and 2hr. from Venice. Sirmione and Gardone Riviera, easily accessible by bus and boat, are best explored as daytrips; accommodations are scant and pricey.

SIRMIONE. Exploring Sirmione's 13th-century castle and Roman ruins can fill a leisurely day or a busy afternoon. The **Albergo Grifone ❸,** V. Bocchio 4, has country-style rooms with lake views and bath just past the castle. (☎030 91 60 14. Reserve ahead. Singles €36; doubles €57. Cash only.) **Buses** run every hour from Verona (1hr., €3.50). **Ferries** run until 8pm to: Gardone (1¼-2hr., €6-11.50) and Riva (2-4hr., €9-14). The **tourist office,** V. Guglielmo Marconi 6, is in the circular building. (☎030 91 61 14; www.comune.sirmione.bs.it. Open Apr.-Oct. daily 9am-8pm; Nov.-Mar. M-F 9am-12:30pm and 3-6pm, Sa 9am-12:30pm.) **Postal Code:** 25019.

RIVA DEL GARDA. Riva's pebble beaches are Lake Garda's compromise for the budget traveler put off by steep local prices. Visitors **swim, windsurf, hike,** and **climb** near the most stunning portion of the lake, where cliffs crash into the sea. Sleep at **Ostello Benacus (HI) ❶,** P. Cavour 10. (☎0464 55 49 11. Breakfast included. Laundry €4. Internet €2 per hr. Reception 7-9am and 3pm-midnight. Silence at 11pm; ask for key to return after midnight. Book ahead. Dorms €14. AmEx/MC/V.) Riva is accessible by **bus** (☎0464 55 23 23) from Trent (1½hr., 20 per day, €3.50) and Verona (2hr., 14 per day, €5.50). **Ferries** (☎030 914 95 11) leave from P. Catena for Gardone (1½-3hr., €7-10) and Sirmione (2-4hr., €8-12). The **tourist office** is at Giardini di Porta Orientale 8. (☎0464 55 44 44; www.gardatrentino.it. Open M-Sa 9am-noon and 3-6pm, Su 10am-noon and 4-6:30pm.) **Postal Code:** 38066.

ITALIAN RIVIERA (LIGURIA)

The Italian Riviera, stretching along the Mediterranean between France and Tuscany, is the most famous and most touristed area of the Italian coastline. Genoa divides the crescent-shaped strip into the **Riviera di Levante** (Rising Sun) to the east and the **Riviera di Ponente** (Setting Sun) to the west. The elegant coast, where Riviera glamour mixes with a seaside relaxation, beckons with lemon trees, almond blossoms, and turquoise seas. Especially lovely is the **Cinque Terre** area (p. 636), just west of **La Spezia** (p. 637). The coastal towns are all linked by a major **rail** line, that runs between Ventimiglia (near the French border) in the west and La Spezia (near Tuscany) in the east, but slow local trains lengthen short trips. Frequent intercity **buses** pass through all big towns, and local buses run to inland hillside towns. **Boats** connect most resort towns.

ITALY

GENOA (GENOVA) ☎010

Genoa (pop. 640,000), city of grit and grandeur, has little in common with its resort neighbors. What it may lack in intimacy, Genoa makes up for with its rich cultural history. Since falling into decline in the 18th century, modern Genoa has turned its attention to the restoration of its bygone splendor, once more claiming its position as one of Italy's most important cultural centers.

TRANSPORTATION. Colombo Internazionale **Airport** (GOA), in Sesti Ponente, services European destinations. Take Volabus #100 from Stazione Brignole to the airport (every 30min. 5:30am-9:30pm, €2) and get off at Aeroporto. Most visitors arrive at one of Genoa's two train stations: Stazione Principe, in P. Acquaverde, or Stazione Brignole, in P. Verdi. **Trains** go to Rome (5-6hr., 12 per day, €32.50) and Turin (2hr., 19 per day, €8-12). AMT **buses** (☎558 24 14) run throughout the city (€1; all-day passes €3). **Ferries** to Olbia, Sardinia and to Palermo, Sicily depart from the Ponte Assereto section of the port; buy tickets at the Stazione Marittima.

ORIENTATION AND PRACTICAL INFORMATION. From Stazione Principe, take **Via Balbi** to **Via Cairoli,** which becomes **Via Garibaldi.** Turn right on **Via XXV Aprile** at P. delle Fontane Maroseo to get to **Piazza de Ferrari** in the center of town. From Stazione Brignole, turn right out of the station then left on **Via Fiume,** and right onto **Via XX Settembre.** Or, take bus #18, 19, or 20 from Stazione Principe, or bus #19 or 40 from Stazione Brignole. The **centro storico** (historic center) contains many of Genoa's monuments. The **tourist office** is on V. Roma, near the aquarium on Porto Antico. (☎57 67 91; www.genovatouristboard.net. Open daily 9am-1pm and 2-6pm.) Log on to the Internet at **Number One Bar/Cafe,** P. Verdi 21r. (☎54 18 85. €4 per hr. Open daily 7:30am-11:30pm.) **Postal Code:** 16121.

ACCOMMODATIONS AND FOOD. Delight in views of the city or relax in comfortable, spacious rooms at **Ostello per la Gioventù (HI)** ❶, V. Costanzi 120. From Stazione Principe, take bus #35 to V. Napoli and transfer to #40, which runs to the hostel. From Stazione Brignole, take bus #40 (30min., every 15min.) to the hilltop. (☎242 24 57; www.geocities.com/hostelge. HI members only. Breakfast included. Reception open until 12:30am. Dorms €15.) **Albergo Carola ❸**, V. Gropallo 4/12, offers meticulously decorated rooms, some overlooking a garden. (☎839 13 40; albergocarola@libero.it. Singles €28; doubles €46, with bath €56; triples €65/75; quads €85. Cash only.) **Camping** is popular; check the tourist office for availability or try **Genova Est ❶**, on V. Marcon Loc Cassa. Take the train from Stazione Brignole to the suburb of Bogliasco (10min., 6 per day, €1); a free van (5min., every 2hr. 8:10am-6pm) runs from there to the cliffside campsite. (☎347 20 53; www.camping-genova-est.it. Laundry €3.50 per load. Electricity €1.80 per day. Tent sites €15.05.) **Trattoria da Maria ❷**, V. Testa d'Oro 14r, off V. XXV Aprile, has authentic Genovese atmosphere. (☎58 10 80. *Menù* €9. Open M-Sa 8am-2pm.)

SIGHTS AND NIGHTLIFE. Genoa boasts a multitude of *palazzi* built by its famous merchant families. These are best seen along **Via Garibaldi,** on the edge of *centro storico*, and on **Via Balbi,** in the heart of the university quarter. The 17th-century **Palazzo Reale,** V. Balbi 10, is filled with Rococo rooms bathed in gold and upholstered in red velvet. (Open Tu-W 9am-1:30pm, Th-Su 9am-7pm. €4, ages 18-25 €2.) Follow V. Balbi through P. della Nunziata and continue to L. Zecca, where V. Cairoli leads to V. Garibaldi, Genoa's most impressive street. The **Galleria di Palazzo Bianco,** V. Garibaldi 11, exhibits Dutch, Flemish, and Ligurian paintings. Across the street, the 17th-century **Galleria Palazzo Rosso,** V. Garibaldi 18, has magnificent furnishings in a lavishly frescoed interior. (Both open Tu-F 9am-7pm, Sa-Su 10am-7pm. One gallery €5, both galleries €7.) From P. de Ferrari, take V. Boetto to P. Matteotti for a glimpse of the ornate interior of **Chiesa di Gesù.** (Open daily 7:15am-12:30pm and 4-7:30pm. Closed to tourists during Su mass. Free.) **Centro storico,** the eerily beautiful historical center bordered by the port, V. Garibaldi, and P. Ferrari, is a mass of winding streets that contain some of Genoa's most memorable sights, including the **duomo** and the medieval **Torre Embraici.** Steer clear of this area after sunset. From P. Matteotti, go down V.S. Lorenzo toward the water, turn left on V. Chiabrera and left on V. di Mascherona to reach the **Chiesa Santa Maria di Castello,** a labyrinth of chapels, courtyards, cloisters, and crucifixes. (Open daily 9am-noon and 3:30-6:30pm. Closed to tourists during Su mass. Free.)

Corso Italia is an upscale promenade home to much of Genoa's nightlife. Most get to clubs by car, however, as they are difficult to reach on foot and the city streets can be dangerous at night. Students flock to bars in **Piazza Erbe** and along **Via San Bernardo,** where lively conversations are held in many languages. Try the swanky bar, **Al Parador,** P. della Vittoria 49r, which is easy and fairly safe to reach from Stazione Brignole. (☎58 17 71. Mixed drinks €4.50. Open M-Sa 24hr.)

RIVIERA DI PONENTE

FINALE LIGURE ☎019

A beachside plaque proclaims the town of Finale Ligure (pop. 12,000) the place for "*il riposo del popolo*" (the people's rest). From bodysurfing in choppy waves to browsing through chic boutiques to scaling the 15th-century ruins of **Castello di San Giovanni,** *riposo* takes many forms. Climb the tough trail starting from Finalborgo's post office to the ruins of **Castel Govone** for an amazing view. The nearby medieval hamlets are also worth exploring. Skip the packed beaches in town and walk east along V. Aurelia through the first tunnel, turning right for a less populated and free **beach.** Within its ancient walls, **Finalborgo,** Finale Ligure's historic quarter, is a 1km walk or 2min. ACTS bus ride up V. Bruneghi from the station.

With immaculate rooms and a unique atmosphere, **Castello Wuillerman (HI) ❶**, V. Generale Caviglia, is worth the hike. From the train station, turn left onto V. Raimondo Pertica. After passing a church on the left, turn left onto V. Alonzo and trudge up the steps to the red-brick *castello*. (☎69 05 15; www.hostelfinaleligure.com. HI members only. Breakfast included. Internet €4 per hr. Reception 7-10am and 5-10pm. Midnight curfew. Dorms €14. MC/V.) **Pensione Enzo ❷,** Gradinata d. Rose 3, has jovial owners and a fantastic view. (☎69 13 83. Breakfast included. Open mid-Mar. to Sept. Doubles €40-60.) **Camping Del Mulino ❶,** on V. Castelli, has a restaurant and mini-market. Take the Calvisio bus from the station to the Boncardo Hotel, turn left on V.G.F. Orione and follow the signs up the hill. (☎60 16 69; www.campingmulino.it. Reception 8am-8pm. Open Apr.-Sept. Tent sites €9.50-13.50. MC/V.) Cheap restaurants hug **Via Rossi, Via Roma,** and **Via Garibaldi.** Fill up on huge two-person portions of pasta at **Spaghetteria Il Posto ❷,** V. Porro 21. (☎60 00 95. Entrees around €7. Cover €1. Open Tu-Su 7-10:30pm. Closed 1st 2 weeks of Mar.) **Di per Di Express** supermarket is at V. Alonzo 10. (Open M-Sa 8:30am-1pm and 3:45-7:45pm, Su 9am-1pm. MC/V.)

Trains leave from P. V. Veneto for Genoa (1hr., 1 per hr., €4). SAR **buses** run from the train station to Borgo Verezzi (10min., 8 per day, €1). The city has three sections: **Finalpia** to the east, **Finalmarina** in the center, and **Finalborgo** farther inland. The train station and most sights are in Finalmarina. The IAT **tourist office,** V.S. Pietro 14, has free maps. (☎68 10 19; www.inforiviera.it. Open M-Sa 9am-12:30pm and 3-6:30pm, Su 9am-noon; low season closed Su.) **Postal Code:** 17024.

RIVIERA DI LEVANTE ☎0185

CAMOGLI

Postcard-perfect Camogli shimmers with color. Sun-faded peach houses crowd the hilltop, red and turquoise boats bob in the water, piles of fishing nets cover the docks, and umbrellas dot the dark stone beaches. Exit the train station, walk down the stairway to the right, and look for the blue sign of **Albergo La Camogliese ❹,** V. Garibaldi 55, near the beach. (☎77 14 02; www.lacamogliese.it. Internet €2 per hr. Singles €55; doubles €80; triples €90-120. 10% *Let's Go* discount with cash payment. AmEx/MC/V.) **Trains** run on the Genoa-La Spezia line to Genoa (40min., 38 per day, €1.60) and La Spezia (1½hr., 24 per day, €3.95). Golfo Paradiso **ferries,** V. Scalo 3 (☎77 20 91; www.golfoparadiso.it), near P. Colombo, go to Cinque Terre (round-trip €20) and Portofino (round-trip €12). Buy tickets on the dock; call ahead for the schedule. Turn right from the station to find the **tourist office,** V. XX Settembre 33, which helps find rooms. (☎77 10 66. Open M-Sa 9am-12:30pm and 3:30-7pm, Su 8:30am-12:30pm; low season reduced hours.) **Postal Code:** 16032.

SANTA MARGHERITA LIGURE

Santa Margherita Ligure was a calm fishing village until the early 20th century, when it fell into favor with Hollywood stars. Today, glitz and glamor paint the shore, but the serenity of the town's early days still lingers. If ocean waves prove spiritually insufficient, try the holy water in seashell basins at the **Basilica di Santa Margherita,** at P. Caprera. **Hotel Nuova Riviera ❸,** V. Belvedere 10/2, is a quiet yellow villa just behind P. Mazzin. (☎28 74 03; www.nuovariviera.com. Breakfast included. English spoken. Doubles €65, with bath €98; triples €90/120; quads €150. MC/V.) **Trattoria Da Pezzi ❷,** V. Cavour 21, is popular with the locals for its homestyle *Genovese* cuisine. (☎28 53 03. *Primi* €3.50-6.50. *Secondi* €3.10-9. Open M-F and Su 10am-2:15pm and 5-9:15pm. MC/V.) **Trains** along the Pisa-Genoa line go from P. Federico Raoul Nobili, at the top of V. Roma, to Genoa (50min., 2-4 per hr., €2.10) and La Spezia (1½hr., 1-2 per hr., €3.95). Tigullio **ferries,** V. Palestro 8/B (☎28 46 70), run tours to Cinque Terre (July-Sept. W-Th and Sa, 8:45am, €22 round-trip) and Portofino (1 per hr., 9:15am-4:15pm, €4.50). Turn right out of the train station, right on C. Rainusso and take the first left on V. Gimelli to find the **tourist office,** V. XXV Aprile 2/B, which arranges lodging. (☎28 74 85; www.apttigullio.liguria.it. Open M-Sa 9am-12:30pm and 3-7:30pm, Su 9:30am-12:30pm and 4:30-7:30pm.) **Postal Code:** 16032.

CINQUE TERRE ☎0187

The five fishing villages of Cinque Terre seem to exist apart from the rest of Italy. Hiking through the savage cliffs and lush tropical vegetation surrounding the towns, gazing at the vast turquoise sea, it is hard to believe that so much natural beauty could possibly fit in one place. The villages themselves, five tiny clusters of rainbow-colored houses surrounded by terraced hillsides of olive groves and vineyards, offer winding streets full of good company and great restaurants. Once a hidden treasure, the Cinque Terre have become fodder for a booming tourism industry; English and German are now just as commonly heard as Italian.

TRANSPORTATION AND PRACTICAL INFORMATION. **Trains** run along the Genoa-La Spezia line. A **Cinque Terre Card** (€4.20) allows unlimited trips among the five towns and to La Spezia and Levanto; it can be purchased at **Cinque Terre National Park Office** in each town. Monterosso is the most accessible town by train; the Monterosso park office is at P. Garibaldi 20. (☎81 78 38. Open daily 8am-8pm.) From the station on V. Fegina, in the northern end of town, trains run to: Florence (3½hr., 1 per hr., €8-17) via Pisa (2½hr., 1 per hr., €4.65); Genoa (1½hr., 1 per hr., €4.45); La Spezia (20min., 2 per hr., €1.35); Rome (7hr., every 2hr., €31). Local trains connect the five towns (5-20min., 1 per hr., €1-1.50). **Ferries** run from La Spezia to Monterosso (1hr., 2 per day, €18). The five villages stretch along the shore between Levanto and La Spezia, connected by trains, roads (although cars are not allowed inside the towns), and footpaths. **Monterosso** is the easternmost town and the largest, containing most of the services for the area, followed by picturesque **Vernazza,** cliffside **Corniglia,** and the quiet towns of **Manarola** and **Riomaggiore.** The Pro Loco **tourist office,** V. Fegina 38, Monterosso, below the train station, provides information and accommodations service. (☎81 75 06; fax 81 78 25. Open daily 9:30am-6:30pm.) **Postal Codes:** 19016 (Monterosso); 19017 (Manarola and Riomaggiore); 19018 (Corniglia and Vernazza).

ITALY

ACCOMMODATIONS AND FOOD. Most hotels are in Monterosso, and they fill quickly during the summer. Try the tourist office for help finding the more plentiful *affittacamere* (private rooms). The modern **Albergo Della Gioventù-Ostello Cinque Terre ❷,** V.B. Riccobaldi 21, and its sweeping roof terrace, is in Manarola. Turn right from the train station and continue up the hill. (☎92 02 15; www.hostel5terre.com. Breakfast €3.50. Laundry wash €4, dry €3. Ask about kayak, bike, and snorkeling equipment rental. Curfew 1am, in winter midnight. Dorms €17-22.50. MC/V.) Popular with students, lively **Hotel Souvenir ❷,** V. Gioberti 30, Monterosso, has 30 beds, a friendly staff, and an outdoor garden. (☎/fax 81 75 95. Breakfast €5. Dorms €25; private rooms €40. Cash only.) All rooms at **Hotel Gianni Franzi ❹,** P. Marconi 1, Vernazza, have lovely antique decor; some have a balcony views. (☎82 10 03; www.giannifranzi.it. Singles €42; doubles €60-65, with bath €77; triples €100. AmEx/MC/V.) While Vernazza is reputed to have the best food in the Cinque Terre, delicious options exist in all of the towns. Call ahead for free taxi service to **Il Ciliegio ❷,** Località Beo, Monterosso, near P. Garibaldi. Savor fresh food made daily with ingredients from the owner's garden. (☎81 78 29. *Primi* €6-8. *Secondi* €7-11. Open Tu-Su 12:30-2:30pm and 7:30-10:30pm.) Stock up on groceries at **SuperCONAD Margherita,** P. Matteotti 9, Monterosso. (Open June-Sept. M-Sa 8am-1pm and 5-8pm, Su 8am-1pm. MC/V.)

OUTDOOR ACTIVITIES AND NIGHTLIFE. The best sights in Cinque Terre are the five villages themselves and the gorgeous paths that connect them. Monterosso has the largest free **beach,** in front of the historic center, sheltered by a cliff cove. The hike between Monterosso and Vernazza is the most difficult of the four, with steep climbs over dry, rugged cliffs. The trail winds its way through terraced vineyards and past hillside cottages before steeply descending into town. From there, the trip to Corniglia offers breathtaking views of the sea and olive groves. Near Corniglia, the secluded **Guvano Beach,** accessed through a tunnel, is popular with young backpackers. The subsequent hike to youthful Manarola lacks the flora of the previous two, but retains the sweeping sea views. The most famous hike, the **Via dell'Amore,** from Manarola to Riomaggiore is a 20min. slate-paved walk featuring a stone tunnel painted with love scenes. Together, the hikes take about five hours, not including time spent exploring the towns themselves.

At night, the most happening towns are Monterosso, Manarola, and Riomaggiore. In Monterosso, **Il Casello,** V. Lungo Fessario 70, lures backpackers with occasional live music and a location near the beach. (Beer and mixed drinks from €2.50. Internet €4 per hr. Open daily noon-2am.)

LA SPEZIA ☎0187

An unavoidable stopover to and from Cinque Terre, La Spezia (pop. 96,000), a naval town in the Gulf of Poets, serves as a great starting point for daytrips into the surrounding area. **Museo Navale,** in P. Chiodo, shows diving suits from WWII, massive iron anchors, and vessel replicas. (Open M-Sa 8am-6:45pm, Su 8am-1pm. €1.55.) **Albergo Il Sole ❷,** V. Cavalloti 3, off V. Prione, offers spacious rooms. (☎73 51 64. Singles €25-36; doubles €39-45, with bath €47-55; triples €53-61; quads €66-92. AmEx/MC/V.) Reasonably priced *trattorie* line V. del Prione. Groceries are available at **Supermercato Spesafacile,** V. Colombo 101-107. (Open daily 8:30am-1pm and 4:15-8pm. MC/V.) La Spezia lies on the Genoa-Pisa **train** line. **Navigazione Golfo dei Poeti,** V. d. Minzoni 13 (☎73 29 87; www.navigazionegolfodeipoeti.it), runs ferries that stop in each village of Cinque Terre (€11; round-trip M-Sa €19, Su €22). The **tourist office,** V. Mazzini 45, is at the port. (☎77 09 00. Open M-Sa 9:30am-1pm and 3:30-7pm, Su 9:30am-1pm.) **Postal Code:** 19100.

EMILIA-ROMAGNA

Go to Florence, Venice, and Rome to sightsee; come to Emilia-Romagna to eat. Italy's wealthy wheat- and dairy-producing region covers the fertile plains of the Po River Valley, and celebrates the finest culinary traditions on the peninsula. The Romans originally settled here, but the towns later fell under the rule of great Renaissance families whose names adorn every *palazzo* and *piazza* in the region.

BOLOGNA ☎051

Home to Europe's oldest university as well as rich, flavorful cuisine, Bologna (pop. 500,000) has been known since ancient times as the *dotta* (learned) and *grassa* (fat) city. Today, academic liberalism drives political activism—minority groups, student alliances, and the national gay organization all find a voice, and attentive ears, in Bologna, encouraged by a well-run city government that offers free Internet access, clean streets, and urban planning that's second to none.

TRANSPORTATION AND PRACTICAL INFORMATION. Bologna is a rail hub for all of Italy and the Adriatic coast. **Trains** leave the northern tip of the walled city for: Florence (1½hr., 53 per day, €4.65); Milan (3hr., 63 per day, €10.12); Rome (4hr., 39 per day, €19.37); Venice (2hr., 25 per day, €7.90). **Buses** #25 and 30 run between the train station and the historic center at **Piazza Maggiore** (€1). The **tourist office,** P. Maggiore 1, in Palazzo del Podestà. (☎24 65 41; www.iperbole.bologna.it/bolognaturismo. Open daily 9am-8pm.) **Postal Code:** 40100.

ACCOMMODATIONS AND FOOD. Take V. Ugo Bassi from P. del Nettuno, then take the third left to reach **Albergo Panorama ❹**, V. Livraghi 1, fourth floor, where sunny rooms with high ceilings look out over V. Ugo Bassi or a cheery rooftop terrace. (☎22 18 02; www.hotelpanoramabologna.it. Curfew 3am. Singles €50-60; doubles €60-70; triples €75-85; quads €85-95; quints €100. AmEx/DC/MC/V.) Six kilometers northeast of the *centro*, **Ostello due Torre San Sisto (HI) ❷**, V. Viadagola 5, has a basketball court and a reading room with satellite TV. Take bus #93 from V. Marconi 69 (M-Sa every 30min.); ask the driver for the San Sisto stop. The hostel is the yellow building on the right. (☎/fax 50 18 10. Lockout 10am-3:30pm. Curfew 11:30pm. Dorms €18; doubles €36. €3 HI discount. AmEx/DC/MC/V.) Scout **Via Augusto Righi, Via Piella,** and **Via Saragozza** for traditional *trattorie* offering Bologna's signature *spaghetti alla Bolognese.* **Nuova Pizzeria Gianna ❶**, V.S. Stefano 76a, has some of the freshest pizza in Italy, made in front of your eyes in 10min. (☎22 25 16. Pizzas from €2.90. Open M-Sa 8:30am-11pm. Closed 2 weeks in Aug. Cash only.) Some of the best gelato in Italy is created at **Il Gelatauro,** V.S. Vitale 98b, where flavors like ginger and cinnamon squash are surprisingly smooth and wildly popular. (☎23 00 49. 2 scoops €1.90. Open daily 11am-11pm. Closed Aug. Cash only.) A **PAM** supermarket, V. Marconi 26, is by the intersection with V. Riva di Reno. (Open M 8am-7pm, Tu-Su 11am-midnight. AmEx/MC/V.)

SIGHTS AND NIGHTLIFE. Forty kilometers of porticoed buildings line the streets of Bologna in a mix of Gothic, Renaissance, and Baroque styles. The ancient *palazzi* and expensive boutiques in **Piazza Maggiore** speak of Bologna's historical and contemporary wealth, all lorded over by the nearby basilica. The cavernous Gothic interior of the city's *duomo*, **Basilica di San Petronio,** P. Maggiore 3, was to be larger than St. Peter's in Rome, but the jealous church leadership ordered that the funds instead be used to build the nearby Palazzo Archiginnasio. The pomp and pageantry of the exercises at the church allegedly inspired a disgusted Martin Luther to reform religion in Germany. (Open daily 7:30am-1pm and 2:30-6pm. Free.) The **Palazzo Archiginnasio,** V. Archiginnasio 1, behind S. Petronio, was the first home of Bologna's modern university; the upstairs theater was built in 1637 to teach anatomy. (Open daily 9am-6:45pm. Closed 1st 2 weeks of Aug. Free.) On the northern side of P. Maggiore is the 15th-century **Palazzo del Podestà. Piazza del Nettuno** contains Giambologna's bronze 16th-century fountain, *Neptune and Attendants.* From P. Nettuno, go down V. Rizzoli to **Piazza Porta Ravegana,** where seven streets converge to form Bologna's medieval quarter. Two towers that constitute the city's emblem rise magnificently from the *piazza;* the **Torre degli Garisenda** cants violently to one side, but the fit can still climb the 498 steps of the **Torre degli Asinelli** for a breathtaking view of the city and nearby hillsides. (Open daily 9am-6pm. €3.) From V. Rizzoli, follow V.S. Stefano to P.S. Stefano, where four of the seven churches of the **Chiesa Santo Stefano** remain. (☎22 32 56. Modest dress required. Open M-Sa 9am-noon and 3:30-6pm, Su 9am-12:45pm and 3:30-6:30pm. Free.)

Bologna's hip students ensure raucous nighttime fun. **Cluricaune,** V. Zamboni 18/b, a dimly-lit Irish pub, is filled with students listening to Celt rock amid classic pub decor. (☎26 34 19. Pints €3.10-4.20. Happy hour W 7-10:30pm with €2.50 pints. Open M-F and Su noon-2am, Sa 4pm-3am.) **Cassero,** in the Porta Saragozza, is a lively gay club in a 17th-century salt warehouse. Both men and women are welcome. (☎649 44 16. Drinks €3-6. €14 ARCI-GAY card, available at www.arcigay.it/eng, required. Open M-F 10pm-2am, Sa-Su 10pm-3am.)

PARMA ☎0521

Though famous for its *parmigiano* cheese and *prosciutto*, Parma's (pop. 172,000) artistic excellence is not confined to the kitchen. Mannerist painting came into full bloom here under native artists Parmigianino and Correggio, and

Giuseppe Verdi composed some of his greatest works here. The town centers around the 11th-century **duomo** where Correggio's *Virgin* ascends to a golden heaven in a spiral of white robes and gray clouds in its spectacular dome. From P. Garibaldi, follow Str. Cavour and take the third right on Str. al Duomo. The pink-and-white marble **baptistry** displays fine early medieval frescoes of enthroned saints and apostles that rise to the pinnacle of the dome on each of its 16 sides. (Duomo open daily 9am-12:30pm and 3-7pm. Baptistry open daily 9am-12:30pm and 3-6:45pm. Duomo free. Baptistry €4, students €2.) Built in 1521 to house a picture of the Virgin Mary, supposedly miraculous, the **Chiesa Magistrale di Santa Maria della Staccata,** up V. Garibaldi from P. Garibaldi, features impressive frescoes by Parmigianino on the arch above the presbitery. (Open daily 7:30am-noon and 3-6:30pm. Free.) From P. del Duomo, follow Str. al Duomo across Str. Cavour, walk one block down Str. Piscane, and cross P. della Pace to reach the 17th-century **Palazzo della Pilotta,** an artistic treasure chest housing the **Galleria Nazionale** and the elegant, entirely wooden **Teatro Farnese.** (Both open Tu-Su 8:30am-1:45pm. Ticket office closes 1pm. Theater €2, students €1. Gallery €6, students €4.)

From the train station, take bus #9 (€0.85) and get off when the bus turns left on V. Martiri della Libertà for the **Ostello/Camping Cittadella (HI) ❶,** on V. Passo Buole. The hostel is in a corner of a 15th-century fortress with a campground beside it. (☎96 14 34; ostellocittadella@libero.it. HI members only. Lockout 9:30am-5pm. Curfew 11pm. Open Apr.-Oct. 3-night max. stay. Dorms €10.50. Camping tent sites €11. Cash only.) **Albergo Leon d'Oro ❸,** V. Fratti 4, off Str. Garibaldi, has basic rooms close to the train station. (☎77 31 82. Closed in Aug.; call ahead for exact dates. Singles €35; doubles €55. AmEx/MC/V.) To reach **Trattoria Sorelle Picchi ❸,** Str. Farini 27, walk down Str. Farini from P. Garibaldi; the restaurant is on your left behind a *salumeria* of the same name. (☎23 35 28. *Primi* €7.50-8. *Secondi* €8.50-13. Cover €2. Open M-Sa noon-3pm. MC/V.) **Dimeglio** supermarket is at Str. Ventidue Luglio 27/c. (Open daily 8:30am-1:30pm and 4:30-8pm.) **Trains** go from P. Carlo Alberto della Chiesa to: Bologna (1hr., every hr., €4.70); Florence (2hr., 2 per day, €14.46); Milan (1½hr., every hr., €11.47). Walk left from the station, turn right on V. Garibaldi, then turn left on V. Melloni to reach the **tourist office,** V. Melloni 1/a. (☎21 88 89; http://turismo.comune.parma.it. Open M-Tu and Th-Sa 9am-7pm, W 9am-1pm and 3-7pm, Su 9am-1pm.) **Postal Code:** 43100.

RAVENNA ☎0544

Ravenna (pop. 130,000) enjoyed its 15 minutes of fame 14 centuries ago, when Justinian and Theodora, rulers of the Byzantine Empire, made it the headquarters of their campaign to restore order in the anarchic west. That 15 minutes has filled the city with the art and has turned it into the mosaic capital of the world. Take V. Argentario from V. Cavour to reach the 6th-century **Basilica di San Vitale,** V.S. Vitale 17. A courtyard overgrown with greenery leads to the glowing mosaics that coat the interior; those of the emperor and empress adorn the lower left and right panels of the apse. Behind V.S. Vitale, the city's oldest and most intriguing mosaics cover the shimmering interior of the **Mausoleo di Galla Placidia.** (☎21 62 92. Open daily Apr.-Sept. 9am-7pm; Mar. and Oct. 9am-5:30pm; Nov.-Feb. 9am-4:30pm.) To see the astounding pastoral mosaics in the **Basilica di Sant'Apollinare,** take bus #4 or 44 across from the train station (€0.75) to Classe. (Open M-Sa 8:30am-7:30pm, Su 9am-1pm. Ticket booth closes 30min. before basilica. €2. Su free.) Much to Florence's dismay, Ravenna is also home to the **Tomb of Dante Alighieri,** the unpretentious final resting place of Florence's exiled native son. In the adjoining **Dante Museum,** Dantephiles pore over Wostry Carlo's illustrations of the poet's works, the fir chest that held Dante's bones, and 18,000 scholarly volumes on his works. From P. del Popolo, cut through P. Garibaldi to V. Alighieri. (☎30252. Tomb open daily 9am-7pm. Museum open Tu-Su Apr.-Sept. 9am-noon and 3:30-6pm; Oct.-Mar. 9am-noon. Tomb free. Museum €2.)

ITALY

Walk down V. Farini, and go right at P. Mameli for rooms with carpet, TV, fan, and sink just outside the *centro* at **Albergo Al Giaciglio ❷**, V. Rocca Brancaleone 42. (☎394 03; mmambo@racine.ra.it. Breakfast €5. Singles €25-38, with bath €30-43; doubles €42-55/60-65. MC/V.) **Piazza del Popolo** has a number of authentic restaurants and cafes nearby. **Trains** (☎89 20 21) leave P. Farini for Ferrara (1hr., 22 per day, €4.20) and Bologna (1hr., 19 per day, €4.60). Follow V. Farini from the station to V. Diaz, which runs to the central P. del Popolo and the **tourist office,** V. Salara 8. (☎354 04; www.turismo.ravenna.it. Open Apr.-Sept. daily 8:30am-7:30pm; Oct.-Mar. M-Sa 8:30am-6pm.) **Postal Code:** 48100.

RIMINI ☎0541

The Ibiza of the Adriatic, Rimini is the party town of choice for young European fashionistas. Beaches, nightclubs, and boardwalks crammed with boutiques, fortune tellers, and artists all contribute to a society where it is perfectly acceptable—and admirable—to collapse into bed and bid the rising sun good night. Rimini's most treasured attraction is its remarkable **beach** of fine sand and mild Adriatic waves. Hotels reserve strips of beach with chairs and umbrellas for their guests, though non-guests can slip in for €3.50; everyone else must use the public beach, located at the end of the shore. After dark, Rimini's nightlife heats up around the *lungomare* in southern Rimini and surrounding areas. **Bus #11** is an institution in and of itself: early in the evening, families and older locals steel themselves in the seats as the bus fills with scantily clad teenagers. **Embassy,** V. Vespucci 22, a 5min. walk from P. Kennedy, stays dependably active as the only club within walking distance of Rimini *centro*. (☎23934. Drinks €6. Cover €13-25. Open daily midnight-4am.) **Life,** V.R. Margherita, 11, hosts two floors of party-goers, from the teenage glitterati to a mixed crowd later in the night. The top level has a laidback bar, while the bottom kicks it up a notch with a fog machine and an elevated stage. Take bus #11 to stop 22. (☎37 34 73. Free drink at 2:30am. Cover €9 with discount pass, available near the door. Open daily 10pm-4am. Cash only.)

Hotel Cirene ❸, V. Cirene 50, has richly upholstered rooms with bath, phone, and TV; some rooms have a balcony. (☎39 09 04; www.hotelcirene.com. Breakfast included. Open May-Sept. Singles €30-35; doubles €46-50; triples €55-60; quads €65-70. AmEx/MC/V.) After spending your budget on drinks and club cover, pick up groceries at the **STANDA** supermarket, V. Vespucci 13. (Open daily 8am-9pm. AmEx/DC/MC/V.) **Trains** (☎89 20 21) run from P. C. Battisti and V. Dante to: Bologna (1½hr., 58 per day, €6.45); Milan (3hr., 25 per day, €15.44); Ravenna (1hr., 34 per day, €2.90). **Postal Code:** 47900.

FERRARA ☎0532

Rome has mopeds, Venice has gondolas, and Ferrara (pop. 135,000) has bicycles. Wrinkled old men, gum-popping girls in stilettos, and harried businesspeople zip through the city, dodging the cars that race bravely through the winding medieval streets. The 14th-century **Castello Estense** towers over the center of town surrounded by a fairy-tale moat. Inside, duck through dungeon tunnels or admire frescoed apartments for a medieval experience. (☎29 92 33. Open Tu-Su 9:30am-5pm. €6, students €5.) From the *castello*, take C. Martiri della Libertà to P. Cattedrale and the ornate **Duomo San Romano,** across V.S. Romano from the **Museo della Cattedrale.** (*Duomo* open M-Sa 7:30am-noon and 3-6:30pm, Su 7:30am-12:30pm and 3:30-7:30pm. Museum open Tu-Su 9am-1pm and 3-6pm. €5, students €3.) From the *castello*, cross Largo Castello to C. Ercole I d'Este and walk to the intersection with C. Rossetti to reach the **Palazzo Diamanti.** Eighty-five hundred white pyramids cover its facade. Inside, the **Pinacoteca Nazionale** holds many of the finest works of the Ferrarese school of painting, as well as some panels by El Greco. (Open Tu-W and F-Sa 9am-2pm, Th 9am-7pm, Su 9am-1pm. €4, EU students €2.)

Ferrara has plenty of inexpensive and comfortable accommodations. Walk down C. Ercole I d'Este from the *castello* to reach the central, fresco-ceilinged **Ostello della Gioventù Estense (HI) ❷**, C. B. Rossetti 24. (☎20 42 27. Breakfast included. Internet €5.16 per hr. Lockout 10am-3:30pm. Curfew 11:30pm. Dorms €19; 2- to 5-person private rooms €19 per person. €3 HI discount. AmEx/DC/MC/V.) **Casa degli Artisti ❷**, V. Vittoria 66, near P. Lampronti, is in the historic center of Ferrara. (☎76 10 38. Singles €25; doubles €43, with bath €60. Cash only.) Gorge on local specialties such as triangular meat ravioli served in broth, or the traditional Ferrarese dessert of luscious *pampepato* (chocolate-covered almond and fruit cake). **Osteria Al Brindisi ❸**, V.G. degli Adelardi 11, has been wining and dining the likes of Titian and Pope John Paul II amid dusty wine bottles since 1435. (☎20 91 42. Cover €2. Open Tu-Su 9am-1am. MC/V.) For picnic supplies, stop by the **Supermercato Conad,** V. Garibaldi 53. (Open daily 8:30am-8pm. MC/V.)

Trains go to: Bologna (30min., 52 per day, €2.90); Padua (1hr., 39 per day, €4.30); Ravenna (1hr., 22 per day, €4.20); Rome (3-4hr., 11 per day, €30.73); Venice (1½hr., 26 per day, €6.10). ACFT (☎59 94 92) and GGFP **buses** leave the train station for Bologna (1½hr., 15 per day, €3.31) and Ferrara's beaches (1½hr., 12 per day, €4.23). Rent **bikes** at **Pirani e Bagni,** P. Stazione 2. (☎77 21 90. €2 per hr., €7 per day. Open M-F 5:30am-8pm, Sa 6:30am-noon. Cash only.) To get to the *centro*, turn left out of the train station onto **Viale Costituzione.** This road becomes **Viale Cavour** and runs to the **Castello Estense** (1km). Or, take bus #2 to Castello (every 20min., €0.83). The **tourist office** is in Castello Estense. (☎20 93 70. Open M-Sa 9am-1pm and 2-6pm, Su 9:30am-1pm and 2-5:30pm.) **Postal Code:** 44100.

THE DOLOMITES (DOLOMITI)

The Dolomites offer a naturally beautiful setting for nearly any outdoor enthusiast, from steep mountain trails to trendy lodges. The near-impenetrable dolomitic rock has slowed major industrialization, preserving the jagged pink-purple cliffs and thick evergreen forests that Le Corbusier once called "the most beautiful natural architecture in the world."

TRENT (TRENTO) ☎0461

Between the Dolomites and the Veneto, Trent (pop. 105,000) offers an affordable sampling of northern Italian life with cultural festivals, delicious food, and spectacular scenery. The **Piazza del Duomo,** Trent's bustling epicenter, is stoically guarded by the massive, trident-wielding **Fontana del Nettuno** in the center of the *piazza*. Nearby is the **Cattedrale di San Vigilio,** where the Council of Trent planned the Counter-Reformation. (Open daily 6:40am-12:15pm and 2:30-8pm. Free.) Walk down V. Belenzani and head right on V. Roma to reach the well-preserved **Castello del Buonconsiglio,** home to the famed **Ciclo dei Mesi,** a series of frescoes depicting the prince-bishop's vision of an ideal feudal system. (Open Apr.-Sept. Tu-Su 9am-noon and 2-5:30pm; Oct.-Mar. Tu-Su 9am-noon and 2-5pm. €5, students €2.50.) **Monte Bondone** looms across the river for a daytrip or an overnight excursion. Catch the **cable car** (☎23 21 54; every 15-30min., €0.90) to **Sardagna** on Mt. Bondone from V. Lung'Adige Monte Grappa, between the river and the station. From the station, turn right on V. Pozzo then right on V. Torre Vanga to get to the tidy rooms of **Ostello Giovane Europa (HI) ❶**, V. Torre Vanga 11. (☎26 34 84. Breakfast included. Reception 7:30am-11pm. Ask for door code if returning after 11:30pm. Dorms €13; singles €25; doubles €40. AmEx/MC/V.) **Piazza del Duomo** and surrounding areas are lined with cafes and host a Thursday morning market. **Trains** (☎89 20 21) leave V. Dogana for: Bologna (3hr., 9 per day, €11); Bolzano (45min., 35 per day, €3); Venice (3hr., 12 per day, €8); Verona (1hr., 2 per hr., €4.70). Atesina **buses** (☎82 10 00) go from V. Pozzo, next to the train station, to Riva del Garda (1¾hr., every hr., €3.20) and Rovereto (1hr., every hr., €3.60). Turn right from the train station and turn left on V. Roma, which becomes V. Manci, to reach the **tourist office,** V. Manci 2, which offers advice on local trails, festivals, and guided tours. (☎98 38 80; www.apt.trento.it. Open daily 9am-7pm.) **Postal Code:** 38100.

BOLZANO (BOZEN) ☎0471

As German street names begin to appear alongside their Italian equivalents, Bolzano's (pop. 100,000) Italian-Austrian cultural fusion becomes increasingly obvious. A spiny Gothic bell tower tops the Romanesque **duomo,** off P. Walther. (Open M-F 9:45am-noon and 2-5pm, Sa 9:45am-noon. Free.) The fascinating **South Tyrol Museum of Archaeology,** V. Museo 43, near Ponte Talvera, houses the freezer home of **Ötzi,** a 5000-year-old **Ice Man,** and his well-preserved personal effects. (Open Tu-Su 10am-5pm, Th until 7pm. €8, students €5.50.) Take a right from the train station and walk 5min. to reach the **Youth Hostel Bolzano ❷,** V. Renon 22, where guests enjoy ultra-clean rooms and ultra-slick decor at this brand-new hostel. (☎39 04 71. Breakfast included. Internet €2 per hr. Reception 8am-9pm. €21 per person. €2 discount for multi-night stays. AmEx/MC/V.) Sample some of Bolzano's Austrian-influenced fare around **Via Argentieri** and the markets of the **Piazza della Erbe. Trains** leave P. Stazione for Trent (45min., 32 per day, €3) and Verona (2hr., 25 per day, €7). The **tourist office,** P. Walther 8, is near the *duomo.* (☎30 70 00; www.bolzano-bozen.it. Open M-F 9am-7pm, Sa 9am-6pm.) **Postal Code:** 39100.

THE VENETO

From the rocky foothills of the Dolomites to the fertile valleys of the Po River, the Veneto region has a geography as diverse as its historical influences. Once loosely linked to the Venetian Empire, these towns have retained their cultural independence; in fact, visitors are more likely to hear regional dialects than standard Italian. The tenacity of local culture and custom will come as a pleasant surprise for those who come expecting only mandolins and gondolas.

VENICE (VENEZIA) ☎041

There is a mystical, defeated quality to Venice's (pop. 274,000) decadence. Lavish palaces stand proudly on a steadily sinking network of wood, treading in the clouded waters of age-old canals lapping at the wet, mossy steps of abandoned front doors. The maze of knotted streets leads to a treasury of Renaissance art, housed in scores of palaces, churches, and museums that are themselves architectural delights. The same narrow streets that once earned the name *La Serenissima* (most serene) are now saturated with visitors, as Venice struggles to retain its authenticity in a climate where 70% of economic growth comes from tourism.

TRANSPORTATION

The **train station** is on the northwest edge of the city; be sure to get off at **Santa Lucia,** not at Mestre on the mainland. Buses and boats arrive at **Piazzale Roma,** just across the Canal Grande from the train station. To get from either station to **Piazza San Marco** or the **Ponte di Rialto** (Rialto Bridge), take *vaporetto* #82 or follow the signs for a 40min. walk—from the train station, exit left on Lista di Spagna.

Flights: Aeroporto Marco Polo (VCE; ☎260 92 60; www.veniceairport.it), 10km north of the city. Take the **ATVO shuttlebus** (☎042 138 36 72) from the airport to P. Roma (30min., every hr., €3).

Trains: Stazione Santa Lucia, northwest corner of the city. Open daily 3:45am-12:30am. **Information office** (☎89 20 21) to the left as you exit the platforms. Open daily 7am-9pm. To: **Bologna** (2hr., 27 per day, €8); **Florence** (3hr., 9 per day, €19); **Milan** (3hr., 24 per day, €23); **Rome** (4½hr., 7 per day, €35).

Buses: ACTV (☎24 24; www.hellovenezia.it), in P. Roma. Local buses and boats. **ACTV long-distance carrier** runs buses to **Padua** (1½hr., 2 per hr., €4).

Public Transportation: The **Canal Grande** can be crossed on foot only at the Scalzi, Rialto, and Accademia *ponti* (bridges). **Vaporetti** (water buses) provide 24hr. service around the city, with reduced service midnight-5am. Single-ride €3.50, €5 for the Canal Grande. 24hr. *biglietto turistico* pass €10.50, 3-day €22 (€13 with Rolling Venice Card, see **Practical Information,** p. 643). Buy tickets from booths at *vaporetti* stops, self-serve kiosks at the ACTV office in P. Roma and the Rialto stop, or from conductors. Pick up extra *non timbrati* (non-validated) tickets to use when the booths aren't open; validate before boarding to avoid fines. **Lines #1** (slow) and **82** (fast) run from the station down Canal Grande and Canale della Giudecca; **line #52** goes from the station through Canale della Giudecca to Lido and along the city's northern edge, then back to the station; **line LN** runs from Fondamente Nuove to Burano, Murano, and Torcello.

ORIENTATION

Venice is composed of 118 bodies of land in a lagoon and is connected to the mainland by a thin causeway. The city is a veritable labyrinth and can confuse even its natives, most of whom simply set off in a general direction and then patiently weave their way. If you allow yourself to do likewise, you'll discover some of the unexpected surprises that make Venice spectacular. A few tips will help you to orient yourself. Locate the following landmarks on a map: **Ponte di Rialto** (the bridge in the center), **Piazza San Marco** (central south), **Ponte Accademia** (the bridge in the southwest), **Ferrovia** (the train station, in the northwest), and **Piazzale Roma** (directly south of the station). The **Canal Grande** winds through the city, creating six *sestieri* (sections): Cannaregio, Castello, Dorsoduro, Santa Croce, San Marco, and San Polo. Within each *sestiere*, there are no street numbers—door numbers in a section form one long, haphazard set consisting of around 6000 numbers. While these boundaries are nebulous, they can give you a general sense of location; **Cannaregio** is in the north and includes the train station, Jewish ghetto, and Cà d'Oro; **Castello** extends east toward the Arsenale; **Dorsoduro,** across the bridge from S. Marco, stretches the length of Canale della Giudecca and up to Campo S. Pantalon; **Santa Croce** lies west of S. Polo, across the Canal Grande from the train station; **San Marco** fills in the area between the Ponte di Rialto and Ponte Accademia; and **San Polo** runs north from Chiesa S. Maria dei Frari to the Ponte di Rialto.

PRACTICAL INFORMATION

Tourist Office: APT, Cal. della Ascensione, S. Marco 71/F (☎ 529 87 40; www.doge.it), directly opposite the basilica. Open daily 9am-3:30pm. Avoid the eternally mobbed branch at the train station. The **Rolling Venice Card** offers discounts on transportation and at over 200 restaurants, cafes, hotels, museums, and shops for ages 14-29. APT provides a list of participating vendors. Cards cost €3 and are valid for 1 year from date of purchase. The card can be purchased at APT or **ACTV VeLa** office (☎274 76 50) in P. Roma. Open daily 7am-8pm. Other ACTV VeLa kiosks are next to the Ferrovia, Rialto, S. Marco, and Vallaresso *vaporetto* stops. **VeneziaSi** (☎800 843 006), next to the tourist office in the train station. Books rooms for a €2 fee. Open daily 8am-10pm. Other branches in P. Roma (☎522 86 40) and the airport (☎541 51 33).

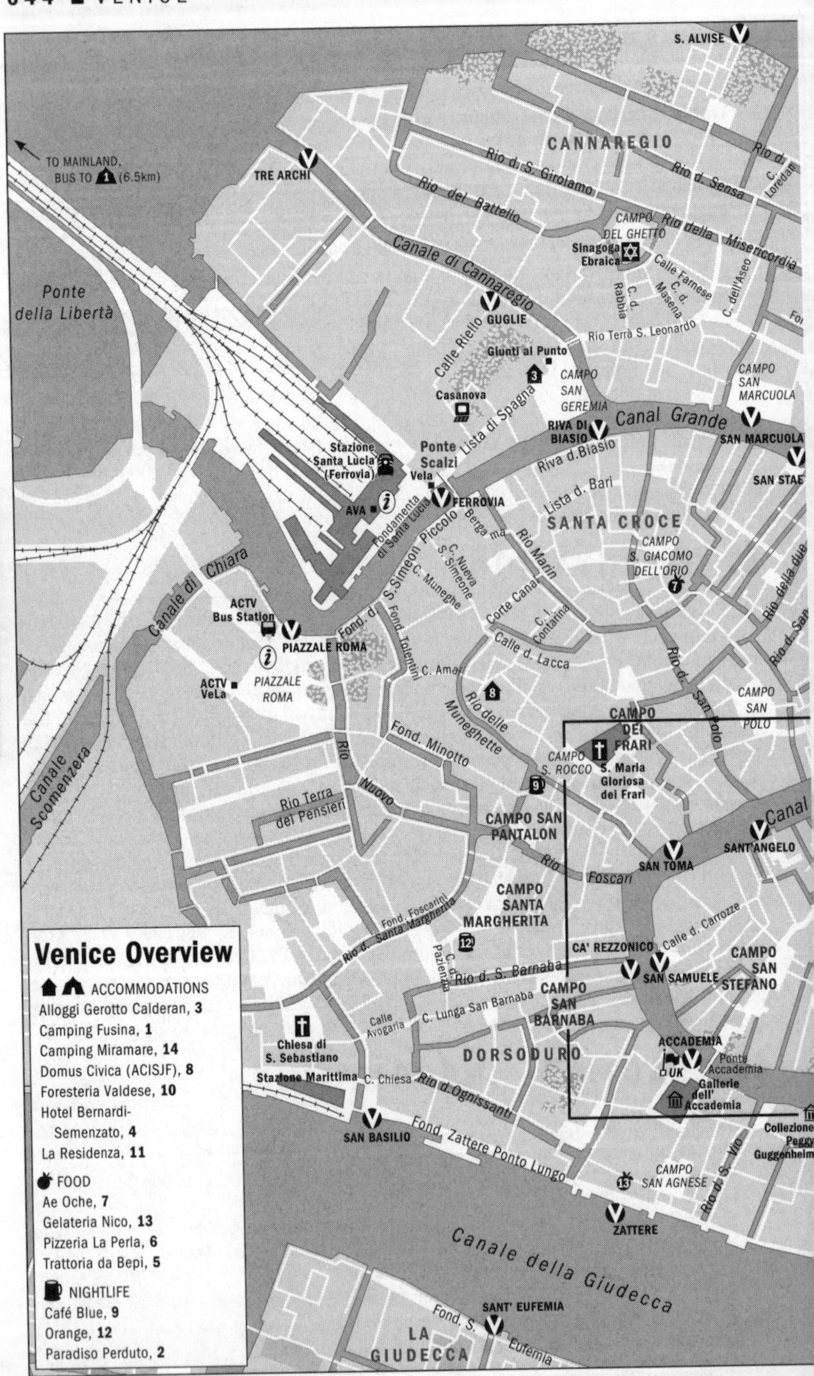
ITALY
TO MAINLAND, BUS TO 1 (6.5km)
S. ALVISE
TRE ARCHI
CANNAREGIO
Rio d. S. Girolamo
Rio d. Sensa
Rio del Battello
CAMPO DEL GHETTO
Rio della Misericordia
Sinagoga Ebraica
Canale di Cannaregio
Ponte della Libertà
GUGLIE
Calle Riello
Giunti al Punto
Rio Terrà S. Leonardo
CAMPO SAN GEREMIA
Casanova
Lista di Spagna
CAMPO SAN MARCUOLA
RIVA DI BIASIO
Canal Grande
SAN MARCUOLA
SAN STAE
Stazione Santa Lucia (Ferrovia)
Ponte Scalzi
Vela
Riva d.Biasio
AVA
FERROVIA
Lista d. Bari
SANTA CROCE
CAMPO S. GIACOMO DELL'ORIO
Canale di Chiara
ACTV Bus Station
PIAZZALE ROMA
ACTV VeLa
Corte Canal
Calle d. Lacca
Rio delle Muneghette
CAMPO SAN POLO
CAMPO DEI FRARI
S. Maria Gloriosa dei Frari
CAMPO S. ROCCO
Fond. Minotto
Rio Nuovo
Rio Terra dei Pensieri
Canale Scomenzera
CAMPO SAN PANTALON
SAN TOMA
SANT'ANGELO
Rio Foscari
CAMPO SANTA MARGHERITA
Rio d. Santa Margherita
CA' REZZONICO
Calle d. Carrozze
SAN SAMUELE
CAMPO SAN STEFANO
Rio d. S. Barnaba
CAMPO SAN BARNABA
C. Lunga San Barnaba
Chiesa di S. Sebastiano
DORSODURO
ACCADEMIA
Ponte Accademia
Gallerie dell' Accademia
UK
Stazione Marittima
Rio d.Ognissanti
SAN BASILIO
Fond. Zattere Ponto Lungo
Collezione Peggy Guggenheim
CAMPO SAN AGNESE
ZATTERE
Canale della Giudecca
SANT' EUFEMIA
LA GIUDECCA
Venice Overview
ACCOMMODATIONS
Alloggi Gerotto Calderan, 3
Camping Fusina, 1
Camping Miramare, 14
Domus Civica (ACISJF), 8
Foresteria Valdese, 10
Hotel Bernardi-Semenzato, 4
La Residenza, 11
FOOD
Ae Oche, 7
Gelateria Nico, 13
Pizzeria La Perla, 6
Trattoria da Bepi, 5
NIGHTLIFE
Café Blue, 9
Orange, 12
Paradiso Perduto, 2

TO MURANO, BURANO, TORCELLO, AND AEROPORTO MARCO POLO
CIMITERO
Canale delle Fondamente Nuove
Isola di San Michele
ORTO
Sacca della Misericordia
FONDAMENTA NUOVE
Chiesa dei Gesuiti
S. Fosca
Fondamenta Zen
OSPEDALE
CA' D'ORO
Strada Nuova
CAMPO DEI S.S. APOSTOLI
Vaporetti Stops
S.S. Giovanni e Paolo
S. Giucomo di Rialto
Ponte di Rialto
SAN POLO
CAMPO S. BARTOLOMEO
CAMPO S. MARIA FORMOSA
CELESTIA
CAMPO SAN LORENZO
Scuola Dalmata San Giorgio Degli Schiavoni
TO ARSENALE
CASTELLO
RIALTO
SAN SILVESTRO
CAMPO MANIN
PIAZZA SAN MARCO
Palazzo Ducale
S. Zaccaria
CAMPO S. ZACCARIA
CAMPO BANDIERA E MORO
TO GIARDINI PUBLICI
SAN MARCO
Riva degli Schiavoni
S. ZACCARIA
ARSENALE
SAN MARCO
GIGLIO
SALUTE
SEE "CENTRAL VENICE," p. 646
FERROVIA
Canale di San Marco
S. Maria della Salute
SAN GIORGIO
San Giorgio Maggiore
Isola di S. Giorgio Maggiore
ZITELLE
Fond. delle Zitelle
TO LIDO, 14
200 yards
200 meters
ITALY

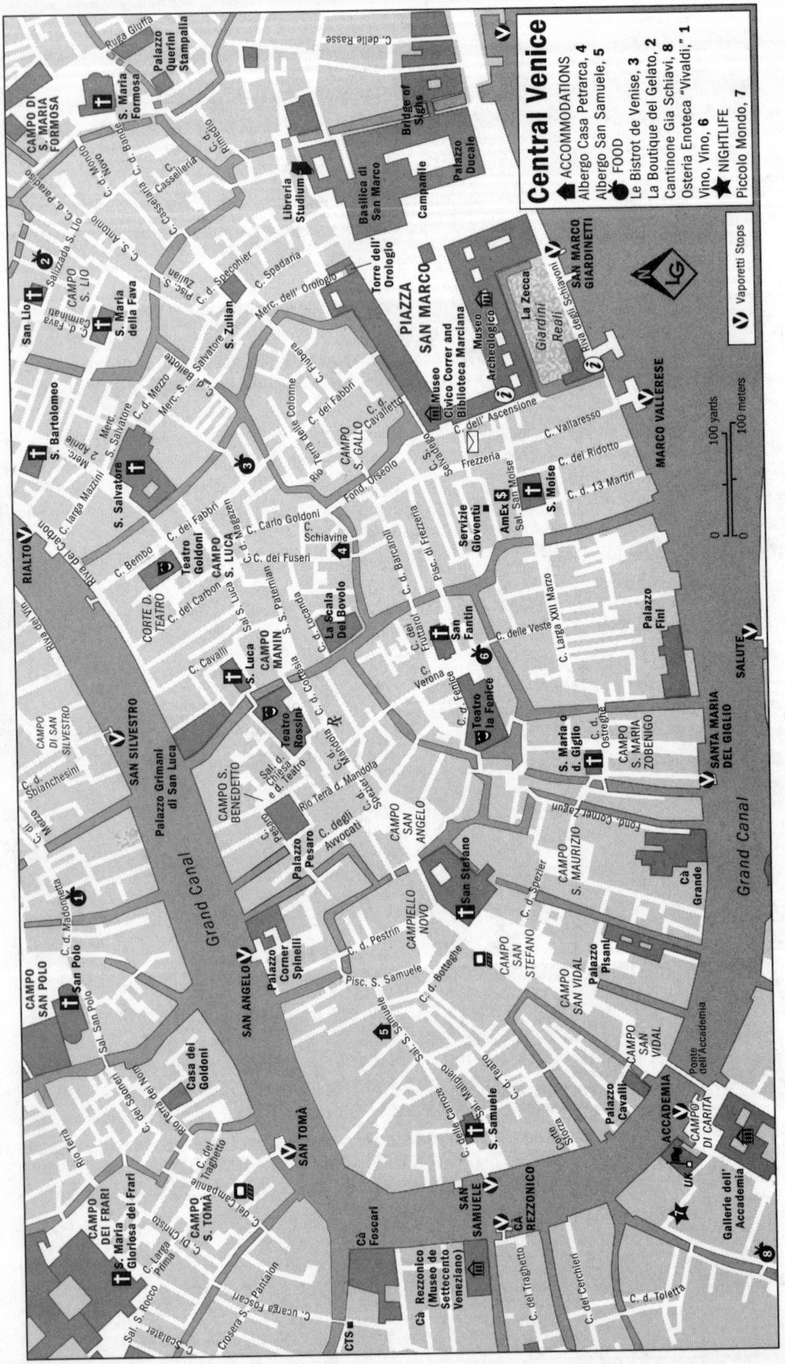

Central Venice

ACCOMMODATIONS
Albergo Casa Petrarca, 4
Albergo San Samuele, 5

FOOD
Le Bistrot de Venise, 3
La Boutique del Gelato, 2
Cantinone Gia Schiavi, 8
Osteria Enoteca "Vivaldi," 1
Vino, Vino, 6

NIGHTLIFE
Piccolo Mondo, 7

Vaporetti Stops

0 — 100 yards
0 — 100 meters

Budget Travel: CTS, Fond. Tagliapietra, Dorsoduro 3252 (☎520 56 60; www.cts.it). From Campo S. Barnaba, cross the bridge and follow the road through the *piazza.* Turn left at the foot of the bridge. Sells discounted student plane tickets and issues ISICs. English spoken. Open M-F 9:30am-1:30pm and 2:30-6pm. MC.

Currency Exchange: Exchange offices charge high prices for service. Use banks whenever possible and inquire about fees beforehand. The streets around S. Marco and S. Polo are full of **banks** and **ATMs.**

Emergency: ☎113 or 112. **Ambulance:** ☎118. **Fire:** ☎115.

Carabinieri (tourist police): Campo S. Zaccaria, Castello 4693/A (☎27 41 11). **Questura,** Fta. S. Lorenzo, Castello 5056 (☎270 55 11). Contact the Questura if you have a serious complaint about your hotel.

Pharmacy: Farmacia Italo-Inglese, Cal. della Mandola, S. Marco 3717 (☎522 48 37). Follow C. Cortesia out of Campo Manin. Open Apr.-Nov. M-F 9am-1:30pm and 2:30-7:30pm, Sa 9am-12:45pm; Dec.-Mar. M-F 9am-12:30pm and 3:45-7:30pm, Sa 9am-12:45pm. MC/V. There are no 24hr. pharmacies in Venice; late-night and weekend pharmacies rotate—check the list posted in the window of any pharmacy.

Hospital: Ospedale Civile, Campo S. S. Giovanni e Paolo, Castello (☎529 41 11).

Internet Access: **Casanova,** Lista di Spagna, Cannaregio 158/A (☎275 01 99). Hip bar with Internet access on high-speed computers. €7 per hr., students €4. Open daily 9am-11:30pm. AmEx/MC/V; €10 min. purchase.

Post Office: Poste Venezia Centrale, Salizzada Fontego dei Tedeschi, S. Marco 5554 (☎271 71 11), off Campo S. Bartolomeo. Open M-Sa 8:30am-6:30pm. **Postal Codes:** 30121 (Cannaregio); 30122 (Castello); 30123 (Dorsoduro); 30135 (S. Croce); 30124 (S. Marco); 30125 (S. Polo).

ITALY

ACCOMMODATIONS

Venetian hotels are more expensive than elsewhere in Italy, but savvy travelers can sniff out cheaper options by starting early in summer. Agree on a price before booking and make reservations one month ahead. Dorm rooms may be available without reservations even in summer. The **VeneziaSi** (see **Tourist Offices,** p. 643) finds rooms with same-day availability, but prices are high. If you're looking for a miracle, try religious institutions, which often offer rooms in summer for €25-70. Options include: **Casa Murialdo,** Fond. Madonna dell'Orto, Cannaregio, 3512 (☎71 99 33); **Patronato Salesiano Leone XIII,** Cal. S. Domenico, Castello, 1281 (☎240 36 11); **Domus Cavanis,** Dorsoduro 896 (☎528 73 74), near the Ponte Accademia.

HOSTELS AND HOTELS

CANNAREGIO AND SANTA CROCE

The station area, around the Lista di Spagna, has some of Venice's best budget accommodations. Although a 20min. *vaporetto* ride and a 15-25min. walk from most major sights, the neighborhood bustles at night with students and young travelers and offers easy *vaporetti* access from Fond. Nuove.

Alloggi Gerotto Calderan, Campo S. Geremia 283 (☎71 55 62; www.casagerottocalderan.com). Half hostel, half hotel, all good. Location makes it the best deal in Venice. Check-in 2pm. Check-out 10am. Curfew 12:30am. Reserve at least 15 days ahead. Dorms €21; singles €36, with bath €41; doubles €60/93; triples €84/93. 10% Rolling Venice discount; lower prices for extended stays. Cash only. ❷

Hotel Bernardi-Semenzato, Cal. dell'Oca, Cannaregio 4366 (☎522 72 57; www.hotelbernardi.com). From V: Cà d'Oro, turn right on Str. Nuova, left on Cal. del Duca, then right. Helpful staff, great views, and decor that manages to be both elegant and homey. Singles with shared bath €30; doubles €45-60, with bath €60-90; triples €78-90; quads €85-118. 10% Rolling Venice discount on larger rooms. AmEx/MC/V. ❸

SAN MARCO AND SAN POLO

Surrounded by designer boutiques, souvenir stands, scores of restaurants, near-domesticated pigeons, and many of Venice's most popular sights, these accommodations are pricey options for those in search of Venice's showy side.

Albergo Casa Petrarca, Cal. Schiavine, S. Marco 4386 (☎520 04 30). From Campo S. Luca, follow Cal. Fuseri, take the 2nd left and then a right. Cheerful proprietors run a tiny hotel with 7 bright rooms, most with bath and A/C. Singles €55-65; doubles €90-110. Cash only. ❹

Albergo San Samuele, Salizzada S. Samuele, S. Marco 3358 (☎522 80 45; www.albergosansamuele.it). Follow Cal. delle Botteghe from Campo S. Stefano and turn left on Salizzada S. Samuele. This centrally located, quirky treasure boasts a mix of antique and retro furniture. Reception until midnight. Reserve 1-2 months ahead. Singles €26-45; doubles €50-100, with bath €60-105; triples €135. Cash only. ❸

Domus Civica (ACISJF), Campiello Chiovere Frari, S. Polo 3082 (☎72 11 03). From the station, cross Ponte Scalzi and turn right. Turn left on Fond. dei Tolentini and left through the courtyard onto Corte Amai. The hostel's rounded facade is after the bridge. Spartan white rooms with shared TV, piano, and bath. Free Internet. Reception 7am-12:30am. Strict curfew 11:30pm. Open June-Sept. 25. Singles €28.50; doubles and triples €52. 15% Rolling Venice discount; 20% ISIC discount. AmEx/MC/V. ❸

CASTELLO

Castello, the *sestiere* where most Venetians live, is arguably the prettiest part of Venice. A second- or third-floor room with a view of the sculpted skyline is worth the inevitability of getting lost in the dead ends and barricaded alleys of some of the narrowest and most tightly clustered streets in the city.

Foresteria Valdese, Castello 5170 (☎528 67 97; www.diaconiavaldese.org/venezia). From Campo S. Maria Formosa, take Cal. Lunga S. Maria Formosa; it's over the 1st bridge. A crumbling but grand 18th-century guest house run by Venice's largest Protestant church. 2min. from major sights. Breakfast included. Internet €5 per hr. Lockout 10am-1pm. Reservations for groups only. Dorms €21-22; doubles with TV €58, with bath and TV €75; quads with bath and TV €106. Rooms larger than singles require 2-night min. stay. €1 Rolling Venice discount. MC/V. ❷

La Residenza, Campo Bandiera e Moro, Castello 3608 (☎528 53 15; www.venicelaresidenza.com). From V: Arsenal, turn left on Riva degli Schiavoni and right on Cal. del Dose into the *campo*. Sumptuously decorated 15th-century palace looks out onto a courtyard. All rooms with bath, safe, A/C, TV, and minibar. Breakfast included. Reception 24hr. Singles €50-100; doubles €80-160. MC/V. ❹

CAMPING

Plan on at least a 20min. boat ride from Venice. In addition to these listings, the Litorale del Cavallino, on the Lido's Adriatic side, has multiple beach campsites.

Camping Miramare, Lungomare Dante Alighieri 29 (☎96 61 50; www.camping-miramare.it). A 40min. ride on V #LN from P.S. Marco to Punta Sabbioni. Campground is 700m along the beach on the right. 2-night min. in high season. Open Apr.-Oct. Tent sites €13.20-15.60; cabins €27-60 plus per person charge. MC/V. ❶

Camping Fusina, V. Moranzani 93 (☎547 00 55; www.camping-fusina.com), in Malcontenta. From Mestre, take bus #11. Restaurant, garden, laundromat, ATM, Internet, and TV on-site. Call ahead to reserve cabins. Free hot showers. Tent sites €12. Cabin singles €22; doubles €26. AmEx/MC/V. ❶

FOOD

Beware the overpriced restaurants that line the canals around San Marco. With few exceptions, the best restaurants hide along less traveled alleyways. *Sarde in saor* (sardines in vinegar and onions) is available only in Venice and can be sampled cheaply at most bars with *cicchetti* (tidbits of seafood, rice, meat, and the ever-famous Venetian sardines; €1-3). For informal alternatives to traditional dining, visit an *osteria* or *bacaro* for stuffed pastries, seafood, rice, or *tramezzini* (soft white bread with any imaginable filling). The BILLA **supermarket,** Str. Nuova, Cannaregio 3660, has groceries, a small bakery, and a deli near Campo S. Fosca. (Open M-Sa 8:30am-8:30pm, Su 9am-8:30pm. AmEx/MC/V.)

Le Bistrot de Venise, Cal. dei Fabbri, S. Marco 4685 (☎523 66 51; www.bistrotdevenise.com). From P.S. Marco, head through 2nd Sottoportego dei Dai under the awning. Follow road around and over a bridge; turn right. Scrumptious Venetian pastas listed with century of origin served in an art-adorned dining room. *Primi* from €15. *Secondi* from €24. Service 12%. Open daily noon-1am. 10% Rolling Venice discount. MC/V. ❺

Cantinone Gia Schiavi, Fond. Meraviglie, Dorsoduro 992 (☎523 00 34). From the Frari, follow signs for Ponte Accademia. Just before Ponte Meraviglie, turn right toward the church of S. Trovaso. Cross the 1st bridge. Friendly owner serves chilled wine, including a delicate strawberry variety (€8.50 per bottle), at a broad marble bar. Enjoy a glass (€0.80-3) with flavorful *cicchetti* (from €1). Open M-Sa 8am-8pm. Cash only. ❶

Gelateria Nico, Fond. Zattere, Dorsoduro 922 (☎522 52 93). Near V: Zattere, with a great view of the Giudecca Canal. For a guilty pleasure, try the Venetian **gianduiotto de passeggio,** a brick of dense chocolate-hazelnut ice cream dropped into a cup of dense whipped cream (€2.50). Gelato €1, 2 scoops €1.50, 3 scoops €2, more if eaten at tables. Open M-W and F-Su 6:45am-11pm. Cash only. ❶

Trattoria da Bepi, Cannaregio 4550 (☎/fax 528 50 31; dabepi@tin.it). From Campo S.S. Apostoli, turn left on Salizzada del Pistor. Traditional Venetian trattoria attracts tourists and locals who come for the warm atmosphere and the expertly prepared cuisine. *Primi* €7-11. *Secondi* from €10. Cover €1.50. Reservations suggested for outdoor seating. Open M-W and F-Su noon-2:30pm and 7-10pm. MC/V. ❸

La Boutique del Gelato, Salizzada S. Lio, Castello 5727 (☎522 32 83). From Campo Bartolomeo, walk under Sottoportego de la Bissa, then cross the bridge into Campo S. Lio and follow Salizzada S. Lio. Popular stand doles out generous portions of rich, heavy gelato. 1 scoop €0.80, 2 scoops €1.50. Open daily July-Aug. 10am-11pm; Sept.-June 10am-8:30pm. Cash only. ❶

Ae Oche, Santa Croce 1552A/B (☎524 11 61). From Campo S. Giacomo, take Cal. del Trentor. 60s American advertisements painted onto the unfinished wooden walls make strange bedfellows with the cartoonish duck logo everywhere, but the overall effect is charming, if a bit strange. *Primi* €5.50-7. *Secondi* €7.50-12.50. Cover €1.40. Open daily noon-3pm and 7pm-midnight. Service 12%. MC/V. ❷

Osteria Enoteca "Vivaldi", S. Polo 1457 (☎523 81 85). From the Campo. S. Polo, opposite the church, cross the bridge to Cal. della Madonnetta. Tiny neighborhood restaurant has classical instruments hanging from its rafters, but the real appeal is the hearty Venetian cuisine. *Primi* €5.50-11. *Secondi* from €8.50. Cover €1.50. Service 10%. Reservations recommended F night. Open daily 10:30am-2:30pm and 5:30-10:30pm. Kitchen opens at noon. AmEx/MC/V. ❷

Pizzeria La Perla, Rio Terra dei Franceschi, Cannaregio 4615 (☎528 51 75). From Str. Nuova, turn left on Salizzada del Pistor in Campo SS. Apostoli. Follow to the end, then follow signs for the Fondamente Nuove. Satisfied diners savor sizable pizzas served by friendly staff. Pizza and pasta €4.65-8.20. Cover €1.10. Service 10%. Open daily M-Tu and Th-Su noon-3pm and 7-9:45pm. AmEx/MC/V. ❶

Vino, Vino, Ponte delle Veste, S. Marco 2007/A (☎241 76 88). From Cal. Larga XXII Marzo, turn on Cal. delle Veste. No-frills wine bar serves over 350 kinds, but you can also fill up on their traditional *Sarde in Saor. Primi* €5.50. *Secondi* €9-10.50. Cover €1. Open M and W-Su 10:30am-midnight. 10% Rolling Venice discount. Cash only. ❸

SIGHTS

Venice's maze-like layout of narrow streets and winding canals make sightseeing a time-consuming and slightly disorienting affair. While most sights center around the sinking city's **Piazza San Marco,** getting lost in Venice can be an better experience than braving the tourist crowds of the busy *piazza.*

AROUND PIAZZA SAN MARCO

BASILICA DI SAN MARCO. Venice's crown jewel graces **Piazza San Marco** with symmetrical arches and incomparable mosaic portals. The city's largest tourist attraction, the **Basilica di San Marco** also has the longest lines. Visit in the early morning for the shortest wait or in late afternoon for the best natural light. Begun in the 9th century to house the remains of St. Mark, the interior now sparkles with mosaics from the 13th-century Byzantine and 16th-century Renaissance periods. Behind the altar, the **Pala D'Oro** relief frames a parade of saints in thick, gem-encrusted gold. Farther back, the tomb of St. Mark rests within the altar, adorned with a single gold-stemmed rose. To the right rests the **Tesoro** (treasury), containing gold and relics from the Fourth Crusade. Steep stairs in the atrium lead to the **Galleria della Basilica,** which provides an eye-level view of the tiny golden tiles that compose the basilica's vast ceiling mosaics, an intimate view of the original bronze **Cavalli di San Marco** (Horses of St. Mark), and a balcony overlooking the *piazza. (Basilica open M-Sa 9:30am-5pm, Su 2-4pm. Modest dress required. Pala D'Oro open M-Sa 9:45am-5pm. Treasury open M-Sa 9:45am-5pm. Galleria open M-F 9:45am-4:15pm, Sa-Su 9:45am-4:45pm. Basilica free. Pala D'Oro €1.50. Treasury €2. Galleria €3.)*

ITALY

PALAZZO DUCALE (DOGE'S PALACE). Once the home of Venice's *doge* (mayor), the Palazzo Ducale museum now contains spectacular artwork. In the courtyard, Sansovino's enormous sculptures, *Mars* and *Neptune*, flank the **Scala dei Giganti** (Stairs of the Giants), upon which new *doges* were crowned. The Council of Ten, the *doge*'s assistants who acted as judges and administrators, would drop the names of those they suspected to be guilty of crimes into the **Bocca di Leone** (Lion's Mouth), on the balcony. The *doge*'s private apartments and the massive state rooms of the Republic contain huge quantities of ornate wooden carving, thick gold leaf, and enormous oil canvases. Climb the elaborate **Scala d'Oro** (Golden Staircase) to the **Sala delle Quatro Porte** (Room of the Four Doors), where the ceiling is covered in pictorial biblical judgements, and the **Sala dell'Anticollegio** (Antechamber of the Senate) is decorated with mythological tales related to events in Venetian history. More doors lead through the courtrooms of the much-feared Council of Ten, the even-more-feared Council of Three, and the **Sala del Maggior Consiglio** (Great Council Room), dominated by Tintoretto's *Paradise*, the largest oil painting in the world. Near the end, thick stone lattices and uneven stones line the **Ponte dei Sospiri** (Bridge of Sighs) and continue into the prisons. Casanova was condemned by the Ten to walk across this bridge, which gets its name from the mournful groans of prisoners descending into the damp cells. *(☎520 90 70. Wheelchair accessible. Open daily Apr.-Oct. 9am-7pm; Nov.-Apr. 9am-5pm. €11, students €5.50.)*

PIAZZA SAN MARCO. Unlike the labyrinthine streets that fill most of Venice, P.S. Marco, Venice's only official *piazza*, is a magnificent expanse of light, space, and architectural harmony. Enclosing the *piazza* are rows of cafes and expensive shops along the Renaissance **Procuratie Vecchie** (old treasury offices), the Baroque **Procuratie Nuove** (new treasury offices), and the Neoclassical **Ala Napoleonica** (also treasury offices). The 96m brick **campanile** (bell tower), which stands on Roman foundations, provides one of the best views of the city. Though it originally served as a watch tower and lighthouse, cruel and unusual Venice took advantage of its location to create a medieval tourist attraction by dangling state prisoners in cages from its top. During a 1902 restoration project, it collapsed into a pile of bricks only to be reconstructed in 1912 with the enlightened addition of an elevator. On a clear day, Croatia and Slovenia are visible from the top; a panorama of the entire island of Venice is guaranteed. *(Campanile open daily 9am-9pm. €6.)*

AROUND THE PONTE RIALTO

THE GRAND CANAL. The Grand Canal is Venice's "main street." Over 3km long and nearly 50m wide, it loops through the city and passes under three bridges: the **Ponte Scalzi, Rialto,** and **Accademia.** The candy-cane posts used for mooring boats on the canal are called "bricole"; they are painted with the family colors of the adjoining *palazzo*. *(For great facade views, ride vaporetto #82, 4, or the slower #1 from the train station to P.S. Marco. The facades are flood-lit at night, producing dazzling reflections.)*

RIVOALTUS LEGATORIA. Step into the book-lined **Rivoaltus** on any given day and hear Wanda Scarpa shouting greetings from the attic, where she has been sewing leather bound, antique-style **journals** for an international cadre of customers and faithful locals for more than three decades. The floor-to-ceiling shelves of the shop, overflow with the products of Wanda's efforts. *(Ponte di Rialto 11. Basic notebooks €18-31. Photo albums €31-78. Open daily 10am-7:30pm.)*

ITALY

SAN POLO

SCUOLA GRANDE DI SAN ROCCO. The most illustrious of Venice's *scuola*, or guild halls, stands as a monument to Jacopo Tintoretto, who left Venice only once in 76 years and who sought to combine "the color of Titian with the drawing of Michelangelo." The school commissioned Tintoretto to complete all the paintings in the building, which took 23 years. The *Crucifixion* in the last room upstairs is the collection's crowning glory. Step outside to admire this masterpiece to classical music performed by street musicians. *(Behind Basilica dei Frari in Campo S. Rocco. Open daily Apr.-Oct. 9am-5:30pm; Nov.-Mar. 10am-4pm. €5.50, students and Rolling Venice €4.)*

DORSODURO

COLLEZIONE PEGGY GUGGENHEIM. Guggenheim's Palazzo Venier dei Leoni displays works by Dalí, Duchamp, Ernst, Kandinsky, Klee, Magritte, Picasso, and Pollock. The Marini sculpture *Angel in the City*, in front of the *palazzo*, was designed with a detachable penis so that Ms. Guggenheim could make emergency alterations to avoid offending her more prudish guests. *(Fond. Venier dei Leoni, Dorsoduro 710. V: Accademia. Turn left and follow the yellow signs. Open M and Th-Su 10am-6pm. €8, ISIC or Rolling Venice €5.)*

GALLERIE DELL'ACCADEMIA. The Accademia houses the world's most extensive collection of Venetian art. At the top of the staircase, **Room I,** topped by a ceiling full of cherubim, houses Gothic works. Among the enormous altarpieces in **Room II,** Giovanni Bellini's *Madonna Enthroned with Child, Saints, and Angels* stands out for its lush serenity. **Rooms IV** and **V** display more Bellinis and **Giorgione's** enigmatic *La Tempesta*. In **Room VI,** three paintings by Tintoretto, *The Creation of the Animals, The Temptation of Adam and Eve*, and *Cain and Abel* grow progressively darker. In **Room XX,** works by Gentile Bellini and Carpaccio display Venetian processions and cityscapes so accurately that scholars use them as "photos" of Venice's past. *(V: Accademia. Open M 8:15am-2pm, Tu-Su 9:15am-7pm. €6.50. Cash only.)*

CASTELLO

SCUOLA DALMATA SAN GIORGIO DEGLI SCHIAVONI. Some of Carpaccio's finest paintings, including episodes from the lives of St. George and St. Tryfon, decorate this early 16th-century building. *(Castello, 3259/A. V: S. Zaccaria. Modest dress required. Open Apr.-Oct. Tu-Sa 9:30am-12:30pm and 3:30-6:30pm, Su 9:30am-12:30pm; Nov.-Mar. reduced hours. €3, Rolling Venice €2.)*

CANNAREGIO

JEWISH GHETTO. In 1516 the *doge* forced Venice's Jewish population into the old cannon-foundry area, creating the first Jewish ghetto in Europe. The word "ghetto" is the Venetian word for "foundry." The **Schola Grande Tedesca** (German Synagogue), the oldest synagogue in the area, now shares a building with the **Museo Ebraica di Venezia** (Hebrew Museum of Venice) in the Campo del Ghetto Nuovo. *(Cannaregio 2899/B. V: S. Marcuola. Museum open M-F and Su June-Sept. 10am-7pm; Oct.-May 10am-4:30pm. Entrance to synagogue by 40min. guided tour only. English-language tours leave from the museum every hr. June-Sept. 10:30am-5:30pm; Oct.-May 10:30am-4:30pm. Hebrew Museum €3, students €2. Museum and tour €8.50/7. MC/V.)*

CÀ D'ORO AND GALLERIA GIORGIO FRANCHETTI. The most spectacular facade on the Canal Grande and the premier example of the Venetian Gothic style, the Cà d'Oro, built from 1425 and 1440, now houses a Franchetti collection. For the best view of the palace, take the *traghetto* (ferry) across the canal to the Rialto Markets. *(V: Cà d'Oro. Open M 8:15am-2pm, Tu-Su 8:15am-7pm. €5, under 35 €2.50. Cash only.)*

CHURCHES

The Foundation for the Churches of Venice sells the **Chorus Pass** (☎275 0462), which provides admission to all of Venice's churches. A yearly pass (€8, students €5) is available at all participating churches except S. Maria Gloriosa dei Frari.

CHIESA DI SAN ZACCARIA. Designed in the late 1400s by Coducci, among others, and dedicated to the father of John the Baptist, this Gothic-Renaissance church holds S. Zaccaria's incorruptible corpse in an elevated, windowed sarcophagus along the right wall of the nave. Nearby, watch for Bellini's *Virgin and Child Enthroned with Four Saints*, one of the masterpieces of Venetian Renaissance painting. *(S. Marco. V: S. Zaccaria. Open daily 10am-noon and 4-6pm. Free.)*

CHIESA DI SAN GIACOMO DI RIALTO. Between the Ponte di Rialto and surrounding markets stands Venice's first church. An ornate clock face adorns its *campanile*. Across the *piazza*, a statue called *il Gobbo* (the hunchback) supports the steps. It was at the foot of this sculpture that thieves, forced to run naked from P.S. Marco and lashed all the way by bystanders, could finally collapse. *(S. Polo. V: Rialto. Turn right past bridge. Open daily 10am-5pm. Free.)*

BASILICA DI SANTA MARIA GLORIOSA DEI FRARI. Franciscans began construction on this enormous Gothic church, also known simply as *I Frari*, in 1340. Today it is a mausoleum of art, boasting two paintings by Titian as well as the Renaissance master himself, who is entombed within the cathedral's cavernous terra-cotta walls. His **Assumption** (1516-1518) on the high altar marks the height of the Venetian Renaissance. Titian's elaborate tomb, a lion-topped triumphal arch with bas relief scenes of Paradise, stands across from the enormous pyramid in which the sculptor Canova (1757-1822) rests. *(S. Polo. V: S. Tomà. Follow signs back to Campo dei Frari. Open M-Sa 9am-6pm, Su 1-6pm. €2.50.)*

CHIESA DI SANTA MARIA DELLA SALUTE. The theatrical *Salute* (Italian for "health") is a hallmark of the scattered Venetian skyline: its domes are visible from everywhere in the city. The fat gray domes, accented with gesturing marble statuary and spiral cement flourishes, are prime examples of the Venetian Baroque style, which sought to draw spectators fully into the architectural space. In 1631, the city commissioned Longhena to build the church for the Virgin, whom they believed would return the favor by ending the plague. When nearby construction ends, walk along the *fondamenta* to the tip of Dorsoduro, where a superb **panorama** of the city awaits. *(Dorsoduro. V: Salute. ☎522 55 58. Open daily 9am-noon and 3-5:30pm. Free. Entrance to sacristy with donation.)*

CHIESA DI SAN SEBASTIANO. The Renaissance painter Veronese took refuge in this small 16th-century church when he fled Verona in 1555 after allegedly killing a man. By 1565 he had filled the church with an amazing cycle of paintings and frescoes. His breathtaking *Stories of Queen Esther* covers the ceiling, while the artist himself rests under the gravestone by the organ. Also displayed are works by Titian and Bordone. *(Dorsoduro. V: S. Basilio. Continue straight. Open M-Sa 10am-5pm, Su 1-5pm. Tickets close at 4:45pm. €2.50. Cash only.)*

ISLANDS OF THE LAGOON

LIDO. The sunny, breezy resort island of Lido provided the tragic setting for Thomas Mann's haunting novella of love and lust, *Death in Venice.* Visonti's film version was also shot here at the famous Hotel des Bains, Lungomare Marconi 17. Today, people flock to Lido to enjoy the surf at the popular **public beach.** An impressive shipwreck looms at one end. The island also offers a casino, horseback riding, and one of Italy's finest golf courses, the Alberoni Golf Club. *(V #1 and 82: Lido. Beach open daily 9am-8pm. Free.)*

MURANO. Famous for its glass since 1292 (when Venice's artisans were forced off Venice proper because their kilns started fires), the island of Murano affords visitors the opportunity to witness resident artisans blowing and spinning crystalline creations. Don't be fooled by the vendors near the train station or in P.S. Marco who sell tickets to see glass demonstrations—the studios in Murano are free. Look for signs directing to the *fornace*, concentrated around the Colona, Faro, and Navagero *vaporetti* stops. The speed and grace of these artisans are stunning, and some studios let visitors blow their own glass creations. The **Museo Vetrario** (Glass Museum) houses a collection featuring pieces from the last two millennia. *(V #12 or 52: Faro from S. Zaccaria. Museo Vetrario: Fond. Giustian 8. ☎73 95 86. Open M-Tu and Th-Su Apr.-Oct. 10am-5pm; Nov.-Mar. 10am-4pm. Museo Vetrario €4, students and Rolling Venice €2.50. Basilica open daily 8am-7pm. Modest dress required. Free.)*

ENTERTAINMENT

Admire Venetian houses and *palazzi* via their original canal pathways. Rides are most romantic about 50min. before sunset and most affordable if shared by six people. The rate that a gondolier quotes is negotiable, and the most price-flexible gondoliers are those standing by themselves rather than those in groups at the "taxi-stands" throughout the city. The "official" price starts at €73 per 50min., with a maximum of six people; prices rise at night.

Teatro Goldoni, Cal. del Teatro, S. Marco 4650/B (☎240 20 11; teatrogoldini@libero.it), near the Ponte di Rialto, showcases varying types of live productions, often with a seasonal theme. Check with the theater for upcoming listings. The **Mostra Internazionale di Cinema** (Venice International Film Festival), held annually from late August to early September, draws established names and rising phenoms from around the world. Movies are shown in their original language. (☎521 88 78. Tickets sold throughout the city €20. Some late-night outdoor showings are free.) The weekly *A Guest in Venice*, free at hotels and tourist offices or online at www.unospitedivenezia.it, lists current festivals, concerts, and gallery exhibits.

ITALY

During the 10 days preceding Ash Wednesday, masked figures jam the streets while outdoor concerts and street performances spring up throughout the city. Venice's second-most colorful festival is the **Festa del Redentore** (3rd Su in July), originally held to celebrate the end of a 16th-century plague.

NIGHTLIFE

Though pubs and bars are not uncommon, most residents agree that truly world-class nightlife in Venice is virtually nonexistent. Most locals would rather spend an evening sipping wine and listening to string quartets in P.S. Marco than bumping and/or grinding in a disco, and the island's fluctuating population means that new establishments spring up (and wither and die) with some regularity. Venetian student nightlife is concentrated around **Campo Santa Margherita,** in Dorsoduro, while the areas around the **Lista di Spagna,** in Cannaregio, are more touristy.

Paradiso Perduto, Fond. della Misericordia, Cannaregio 2540 (☎099 45 40). From Str. Nuova, cross Campo S. Fosca, cross the bridge, and continue in the same direction, crossing 2 more bridges. Dreadlocked students flood this unassuming bar, where waitstaff dole out large portions of *cicchetti* (mixed plate; €19). F nights live jazz. Open M-Sa 9:30am-3pm and 7pm-2am.

Piccolo Mondo, Accademia, Dorsoduro 1056/A (☎520 03 71). Facing away from the canal toward the Accademia, turn right. Disco, hip-hop, and vodka with Red Bull (€10) keep a full house at this small, popular *discoteca.* Framed collages of the wide-ranging clientele include notables like Michael Jordan and Prince Albert of Monaco. Ring bell to enter. Drinks from €7. Cover free with *Let's Go.* Open nightly 10pm-4am. AmEx/MC/V.

Café Blue, Campo S. Pantalon, Dorsoduro 3778 (☎71 02 27). From S. Maria Frari, take Cal. Scalater and turn right at the end. Grab some absinthe (€6) and a stool in the brick-walled back room and watch the daytime coffee crowd turn into a chill and laid-back set as night falls. Free Internet. Live music F evenings in winter, DJ Wed nights. Open in summer noon-2am; in winter 8pm-2am. MC/V.

Orange, Dorsoduro 3054/A (☎523 47 40; www.orangebar.it). Across from Duchamp in Campo S. Margherita. The good-looking gather at this minimalist bar on the garden terrace, in the orange interior, or outside right on the *campo.* Match the theme with a €6 tequila sunrise. Beer from €2. Wine from €1.50. Open M-Sa 7am-2pm, Su 6pm-2am. AmEx/MC/V.

PADUA (PADOVA) ☎049

Ancient Padua (pop. 205,000) was once a wealthy center of commerce, but centuries of barbarian attacks and natural disasters left few of its architectural treasures intact. Padua's university, founded in 1222 and second in seniority only to Bologna's, hosted such luminaries as Galileo, Copernicus, Giotto, and Donatello, and now keeps a young and energetic population buzzing in the streets well past dusk. The starry blue ceiling of the **Cappella degli Scrovegni,** P. Eremitani 8, overlooks Giotto's epic 38-panel fresco cycle, illustrating the lives of Biblical figures. Buy tickets at the attached **Musei Civici Eremitani,** which displays an overwhelming art collection, including Giotto's beautiful crucifix, which once adorned the Scrovegni Chapel. (☎820 45 51; www.padovanet.it/museicivici. Open daily Feb.-Oct. 9am-7pm; Nov.-Jan. 9am-6pm. Museum €10; combined with chapel €12, students €5. AmEx/DC/MC/V.) Throngs of pilgrims visit St. Anthony's displayed jawbone, tongue, and tomb at the **Basilica di Sant'Antonio,** in P. del Santo. (☎824 28 11; www.basilicadelsanto.org. Modest dress required. Open daily Apr.-Sept. 6:30am-7:45pm; Nov.-Mar. 6:30am-6:45pm. Free.) From here, follow signs to **Orto Botanico,** V. Orto Botanico 15, a circular oasis of colorful water lilies, medicinal herbs, and a 420-year-old palm tree. (Open Apr.-Sept. daily 9am-1pm and 3-6pm; Oct.-Mar. M-F 9am-1pm. €4, students €1.) Next to the **duomo,** in P. Duomo, sits the tiny 12th-century **Battistero,** with a domed interior coated with colorful New Testament frescoes. (*Duomo* open M-Sa 7:30am-noon and 3:45-7:45pm, Su 7:45am-1pm and 3:45-8:30pm. Battistero open daily 10am-6pm. €2.50, students €1.50. *Duomo* free.) Ancient buildings from the university are scattered throughout the city, especially near the student-heavy **Palazzo Bó,** which is also the nexus for nightlife.

Go to V. Aleardi and turn left; walk to the end of the block and **Ostello Città di Padova (HI) ❷,** V. Aleardi 30, will be on the left. (☎875 22 19; pdyhtl@tin.it. Internet €6 per hr. Wheelchair accessible. Lockout 9:30am-3:30pm. Curfew midnight. Book ahead. Dorms €18. €3 HI discount. MC/V.) Enjoy Paduan favorites with dim mood lighting at **Antica Trattoria Paccagnella ❷,** V. del Santo 113. (☎875 05 49. *Primi* €6-9.50. *Secondi* €4.50-17. Cover €2. Open daily noon-2:30pm and 7-10pm. AmEx/MC/V.) The cavernous **Highlander Pub,** V.S. Martino e Solferino 69, is a little piece of Scotland in the heart of Italy. (Pints from €4.50. Open daily 11am-3pm and 6pm-2am. AmEx/MC/V.) **Trains** depart from P. Stazione for: Bologna (1½hr., 34 per day, €5.73); Milan (2½hr., 25 per day, €11.21); Venice (30min., 82 per day, €2.50); Verona (1hr., 44 per day, €4.30). **Buses** (☎820 68 34) leave from P. Boschetti for Venice (45min., 2 per hr., €3.05). To reach the *centro* from the train station, follow the main street through town and turn right on V. Rogati. The **tourist office** is in the train station. (☎875 20 77. Open M-Sa 9am-7pm, Su 8:30am-12:30pm.) **Postal Code:** 35100.

VERONA ☎045

Bright gardens and breathtakingly realistic sculptures fill Verona (pop. 245,000) with enough artistic majesty to overwhelm any hopeless romantics who wander into its walls. From dank tombs to dizzying towers, Verona offers all the perks of a large city as well as rich wines, authentic local cuisine, and an world-renowned opera with low student prices. The city's medley of monuments and natural splendor inspired Shakespeare to use it as the setting of his *Romeo and Juliet.*

TRANSPORTATION AND PRACTICAL INFORMATION. **Trains** (☎89 20 21) go from P. XXV Aprile to: Bologna (2hr., 27 per day, €6); Milan (2hr., 37 per day, €7); Trent (1hr., 25 per day, €5); Venice (1½hr., 41 per day, €7). From the train station, walk 20min. up **Corso Porta Nuova** or take bus #11, 12, 13, 51, 72, or 73 (Sa-Su take #91, 92, or 93) to Verona's epicenter, the **Arena** in **Piazza Brà.** The **tourist office** is right of the *piazza* at V. D. Alpini 9. (☎806 86 80; iatverona@provincia.vr.it. Open M-Sa 9am-7pm, Su 9am-3pm.) **Postal Code:** 37100.

ACCOMMODATIONS AND FOOD. Reserve hotel rooms ahead, especially in opera season (June-Sept.). The **Ostello della Gioventù (HI) ❶,** Villa Francescatti, Salita Fontana del Ferro 15, is in a renovated 16th-century villa with gorgeous gardens and aging frescoes. From the station, take bus #73 or night bus #90 to P. Isolo, turn right, and follow the yellow signs uphill. (☎59 03 60. HI members only. Includes breakfast and communal showers. Lockout 9am-5pm. Curfew 11:30pm; flexible for opera-goers. Dorms €13.50; family rooms €15. Cash only.) To get to the classically decorated **Locanda Catullo ❹,** Vicolo Catullo 1, walk from V. Mazzini, turn onto V. Catullo, and turn left on Vicolo Catullo. (☎800 27 86. Reservations only for stays of 3 or more nights. Singles €40; doubles €55-65; triples €81. Cash only.) Verona is famous for its wines, including the dry white *soave* and red *valpolicella.* Prices in **Piazza Isolo** are cheaper than those in P. delle Erbe. **Enoteca dal Zovo ❶,** Vicolo S. Marco in Foro 7/5, near P. Brà, was once the private chapel of Verona's archbishop. Now it plays the role of wine bar and resembles an apothecary's shop with cluttered bottles on every horizontal surface. (☎803 43 69. Open M-Th 8am-1pm and 2-8:30pm, F-Su 8am-1pm and 2-9pm. Cash only.) **Pam** supermarket is at V. dei Mutilati 3. (Open M-Sa 8am-8pm, Su 9am-7pm. AmEx/MC/V.)

OUT, OUT, BRIEF CANDLE

On August 10, 1913, Giuseppe Verdi's *Aida* opened the Verona Opera Festival. Performed before thousands of spectators in the Arena di Verona, it echoed through the theater on a particularly balmy and auspicious evening, Verdi's 100th birthday. Still several years before the installation of electric lights, the theater was dark, the stage dim, and the programs impossible to read. Despite the less-than-ideal conditions, the audience remained eager, as on that night each audience member had brought a candle, the light of which kept the arena glowing throughout the night.

Soon after, the advent of electricity meant that the Arena di Verona traded candlelight for the spotlight and the tradition quickly fell out of favor. But in the mid-1980s, a wealthy patron of the arts decided to revive the ritual by making candles available to modern opera-goers. Now boxes of candles greet spectators as they enter the theater for every summer performance. Just before the first act, as if on silent cue, everyone in the theater lights a candle, setting the entire arena ablaze with twinkling lights. Over the course of the performance, the candles are left to burn out on their own. As the acts unfold individual candles wink out, leaving only the actors to shine.

SIGHTS AND ENTERTAINMENT. The heart of Verona is the tiered first-century **Arena** in P. Brà. (☎800 32 04. Open M 1:45-6:30pm, Tu-Su 8:30am-6:30pm. Closes 4:30pm on opera nights. Ticket office closes 45min. before Arena. €4, students €3. Cash only.) From late June to early September, tourists and singers from around the world descend on the Arena for the city's annual **Opera Festival.** *Aida*, *Carmen*, and *Madama Butterfly* are among the 2006 highlights. (☎800 51 51; www.arena.it. Box office open M-F 9am-noon and 3:15-5:45pm, Su 9am-noon. June 24-Aug. 27 2006, box office open on performance days 10am-9pm, non-performance days 10am-5:45pm. General admission M-Th and Su €16.50-24.50, F-Sa €18.50-26.50. AmEx/DC/MC/V.) From P. Brà, V. Mazzini leads to the markets and medieval architecture of **Piazza delle Erbe.** The 83m **Torre dei Lambertini,** in P. dei Signori, offers a great view of Verona. (Open M 1:30-7:30pm, Tu-Su 8:30am-7:30pm. €4, students €3. Cash only.) The **Giardino Giusti,** V. Giardino Giusti 2, is a magnificent 16th-century garden filled with limbless Roman sculptures, meticulously trimmed hedges, and a thigh-high floral labyrinth. (☎803 40 29. Open daily 9am-8pm. €4.50. Cash only.) The della Scala fortress, **Castelvecchio,** down V. Roma from P. Brà, is filled with walkways, parapets, and an art collection that includes Pisanello's *Madonna della Quaglia*. (☎806 26 11. Open M 1:30-7:30pm, Tu-Su 8:30am-7:30pm. €4, students €3. Cash only.) Thousands of tourists have immortalized **Casa di Giulietta** (Juliet's House), V. Cappello 23, although the Capulet family never actually lived there. The famed balcony overlooks a courtyard full of tourists adding their love notes to walls covered in scraps of paper and graffiti. (☎803 43 03. Open M 1:30-7:30pm, Tu-Su 8:30am-7:30pm. Ticket office closes at 6:45pm. €4, students €3. Courtyard free. Cash only.)

FRIULI-VENEZIA GIULIA

Friuli-Venezia Giulia usually receives less than its fair share of recognition, but this region has served as inspiration to prominent literary figures. James Joyce wrote the bulk of *Ulysses* in coffeehouses that still dot the cityscape of Trieste; Ernest Hemingway found part of his plot for *A Farewell to Arms* in the region's white Carso cliffs; and Franz Liszt, Sigmund Freud, and Rainer Maria Rilke all worked around Friuli, taken by its beauty. Smaller towns of idyllic charm and growing cities with a quicker heartbeat make Friuli-Venezia Giulia an adventure.

TRIESTE (TRIEST)

☎040

After being volleyed between Italian, Austrian, and Slavic powers for hundreds of years, Trieste (pop. 241,000) celebrated its 50th anniversary as an Italian city in 2004. Subtle reminders of Trieste's Eastern European past are manifest in its arches, the subtle spices of its cuisine, and the Hapsburg rulers smirking from portraits on its museums' walls. While Trieste's fast-paced center is undeniably urban, the surrounding Carsoian hillside and tranquil Adriatic Sea temper the metropolis with stunning natural beauty. The Città Nuova, centers around the Canale Grande. Facing the canal is the bright blue-domed Serbian Orthodox **Chiesa di San Spiridione.** (Open Tu-Sa 9am-noon and 5-8pm, Su 9am-noon. Modest dress required.) The ornate Municipio is in the P. dell'Unità d'Italia, the largest waterfront *piazza* in Italy. P. della Cattedrale overlooks the town center and the sea from the remains of a Roman basilica. Archduke Maximilian of Austria commissioned the now lavishly decorated **Castello Miramare** in the mid-19th century. Legend holds that visitors can still hear the wailing ghost of Carlotta, Maximilian's wife, whose player piano plucks notes in an eerie upper room. Take bus #36 (15min., €0.90) to the *ostello* stop and walk along the water for 15min. (Open M-Sa 9am-7pm, Su 8:30am-7pm. Ticket office open daily 9am-6:30pm. €4.)

Hotel Alabarda ❸, V. Valdirivo 22, is near the city center. All rooms have modern furnishings, phone, and satellite TV. From the train station, head south on Corso Cavour and turn left onto V. Valdirivo. (☎63 02 69; www.hotelalabarda.it. Internet €5 per hr. Singles €35, with bath €52; doubles €45/68; triples €63/92. AmEx/MC/V.) The setting sun highlights happy diners munching at **Pizzeria Barattolo ❶,** P.S.P.S. Antonio 2. A multilingual menu describes favorites like *schiacciata* (€7), a pizza with grilled vegetables, cheese, basil, and garlic. (☎63 14 80; www.albarattolo.it. Pizza €4.90-8. *Primi* €5.20-9.50. *Secondi* €5.20-11. Service 15%. Open daily 8:30am-midnight. AmEx/MC/V.) Find groceries at **Euro Spesa** supermarket, V. Valdirivo 13/F, off C. Cavour. (Open M-Sa 8am-8pm.) **Trains** leave P. della Libertà 8, down C. Cavour from the quays, for Budapest, Hungary (12hr., 2 per day, €80-90) and Venice (2hr., 20 per day, €8). The APT **tourist office** is at P. dell'Unità d'Italia 4/E, near the harbor. (☎347 83 12. Open daily 9:30am-7pm.) **Postal Code:** 34100.

PIEDMONT (PIEMONTE)

Piedmont has been a politically influential region for centuries. Turin served as the capital from 1861 to 1865 when Vittorio Emanuele II and Camillo Cavour united Italy. In addition to its political activity, Piedmont has proven itself a producer of fine food and wine, which *Piemontese* insist is the best in Italy.

TURIN (TORINO)

☎011

Renowned for its chocolate and *caffè* culture, commercial Turin (pop. 1,000,000) remains an elegant and manageable city, filled with green spaces and cradled by the Alps. Turin vibrates with modern economic energy as headquarters of the **Fiat Auto Company** and host of the **2006 Winter Olympic Games.** To experience the Turin of the future and relive past Olympic glories in a multimedia extravaganza, hit the ultra-modern **Olympic Atrium,** in P. Solfieri. (Open daily 9:30am-7pm. Free.) The city also has one of the more famous relics of Christianity: the **Holy Shroud of Turin,** which is housed in the **Cattedrale di San Giovanni,** behind the **Palazzo Reale.** With rare exceptions, a life-sized photo is as close as anyone gets to the real thing. (Open daily 7am-noon and 3-7pm. Free.) The **Museo Egizio,** in the **Palazzo dell'Accademia delle Scienze,** V. dell'Accademia delle Scienze 6, boasts a world-class collection of Egyptian artifacts. (Open Tu-Su 8:30am-7:30pm. €6.50, ages 18-25 €3.) The same building houses the **Galleria Sabauda,** and its large collection of Renaissance paintings, including works by van Dyck and Rembrandt. (Open Tu and F-Su 8:30am-2pm, W 2-7:30pm, Th 10am-7:30pm. €4, ages 18-25 €2.) Begun as a synagogue in 1863, the **Mole Antonelliana,** V. Montebello 20, dominates Turin's skyline. It is home to the eccentric **Museo Nazionale del Cinema,** which plays hundreds of movie clips in oddly designed settings. (Open Tu-F and Su 9am-8pm, Sa 10am-11pm. Museum €5.40, students €4.20. Elevator to the observation deck €3.62/2.58. Combined ticket €6.80/5.20.) The sleek **Castello di Rivoli Museo D'Arte Contemporanea,** P. Mafalda di Savoia in Rivoli, houses one of the most impressive collections of modern art in Europe. (☎95 65 222. Open Tu-Th 10am-5pm, F-Su 1am-9pm. €6.50, students €3.50.)

To get to the clean, comfortable **Ostello Torino (HI) ❶**, V. Alby 1, take bus #52 (#64 on Su) from Stazione Porta Nuova to the "Lanza" stop on V. Crimea. Continue along the road 300m, following the signs. (☎660 29 39; ostello.torino@libero.it. Lockout 10am-3:30pm. Curfew 11:30pm; ask for a key if coming in late. Closed late Dec. to mid-Jan. Dorms €13; doubles €36.) Sample some of the city's specialty *bicerin* chocolate and coffee drink at **Caffè Cioccolateria al Bicerin,** V. della Consolata 5 (☎43 69 325; www.bicerin.it). The **open-air market** under Porta Palazzo in P. della Repubblica has cheap food, clothing, and odds and ends. (Open M-F 8:30am-1:30pm, Sa 8:30am-6:30pm.) On summer nights, the bars and clubs of **I Murazzi** along the River Po stay open until 4am or later. The former railroad depot area at **Docks Dora** along the Milan train tracks is the place to be in winter. **Trains** (☎66 53 098) leave Porta Nuova on C. Vittorio Emanuele II for: Genoa (2hr., every hr., €8); Milan (2hr., every hr., €8); Rome (6-7hr., 6 per day, €41); Venice (5hr., 5 per day, €31). The Olympics are sure to bring changes; be sure to contact the **tourist office,** in the Olympic Atrium, for updated info and free maps. (☎53 51 81; www.turismotorino.org. Open M-Sa 9:30am-7pm, Su 9:30am-3pm.) **Postal Code:** 10100.

TUSCANY (TOSCANA)

The vision of Tuscany has inspired countless artists, poets, and hordes of tourists. Its rolling hills, prodigious olive groves, and cobblestone streets beg visitors to slow their frenetic pace, sip some wine, and relax in fields of brilliant sunflowers. Tuscany fostered some of Italy's, and the world's, greatest cultural achievements under the tender care—and devious machinations—of the powerful Medici family.

FLORENCE (FIRENZE) ☎055

The setting sun shimmers over a sea of burnt-orange roofs and towering domes to reveal the breathtaking concentration of beauty in Florence (pop. 376,000). A busy trading town in the 13th century, Florence took a decidedly different path under Medici rule. By the mid-15th century, the city was the European capital of art, architecture, commerce, and political thought. Present-day Florence is an electric mix of young and old: street graffiti quotes Marx and Malcolm X, businessmen whiz by on Vespas, and children play soccer in front of the *duomo.*

TRANSPORTATION

Flights: Amerigo Vespucci Airport (FLR; ☎30 615), in Peretola. The **ATAF** bus #62 connects the train station to the airport (€1).

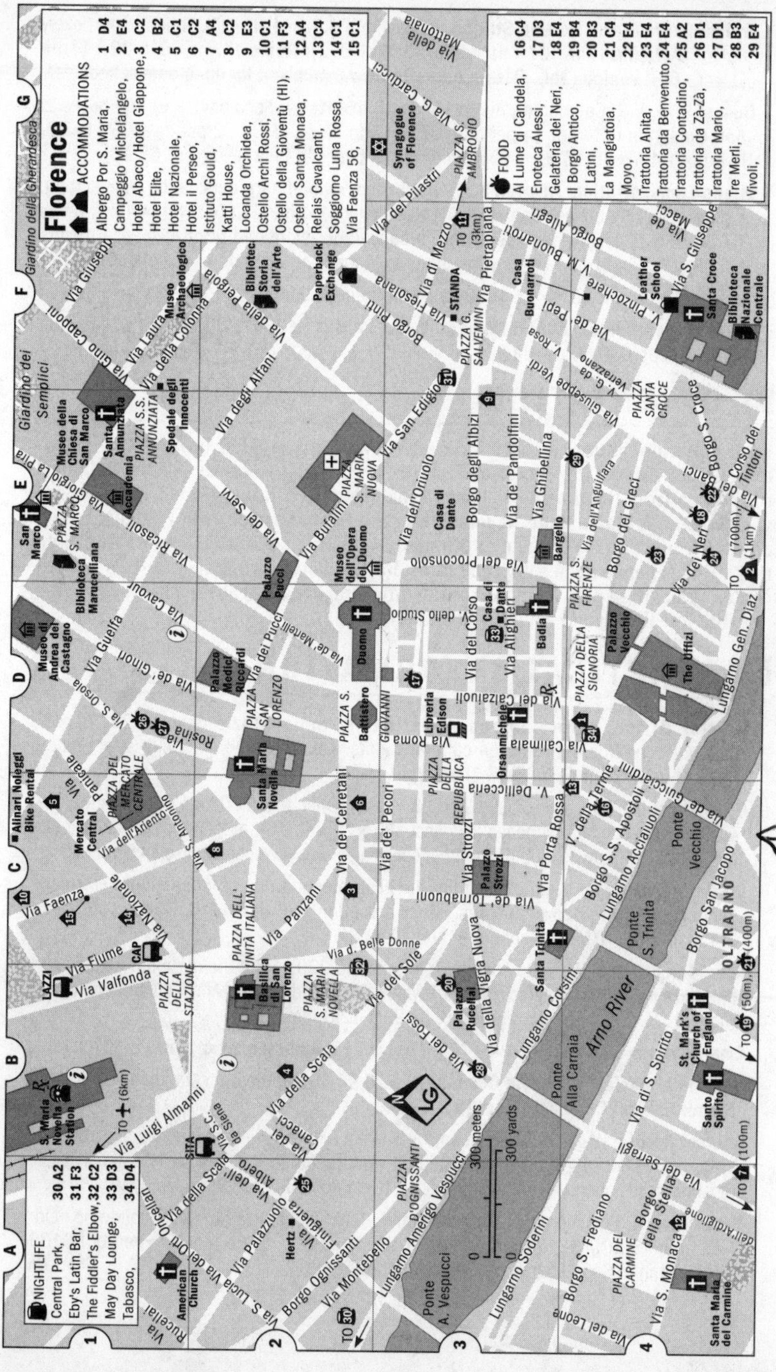

Florence

ACCOMMODATIONS

Albergo Por S. Maria,	1	D4
Campeggio Michelangelo,	2	E4
Hotel Abaco/Hotel Giappone,	3	C2
Hotel Elite,	4	B2
Hotel Nazionale,	5	C1
Hotel il Perseo,	6	C2
Istituto Gould,	7	A4
Katti House,	8	C2
Locanda Orchidea,	9	E3
Ostello Archi Rossi,	10	C1
Ostello della Gioventù (HI),	11	F3
Ostello Santa Monaca,	12	A4
Relais Cavalcanti,	13	C4
Soggiorno Luna Rossa,	14	C1
Via Faenza 56,	15	C1

FOOD

Al Lume di Candela,	16	C4
Enoteca Alessi,	17	D3
Gelateria dei Neri,	18	E4
Il Borgo Antico,	19	B4
Il Latini,	20	B3
La Mangiatoia,	21	C4
Moyo,	22	E4
Trattoria Anita,	23	E4
Trattoria da Benvenuto,	24	E4
Trattoria Contadino,	25	A2
Trattoria da Zà-Zà,	26	D1
Trattoria Mario,	27	D1
Tre Merli,	28	B3
Vivoli,	29	E4

NIGHTLIFE

Central Park,	30	A2
Eby's Latin Bar,	31	F3
The Fiddler's Elbow,	32	C2
May Day Lounge,	33	D3
Tabasco,	34	D4

ITALY

Trains: Santa Maria Novella Station, across from S. Maria Novella. Trains depart every hr. for: **Bologna** (1hr., €7.75); **Milan** (3½hr., €22); **Rome** (3½hr., €15-22); **Siena** (1½hr., €6); **Venice** (3hr., €16). Check out www.trenitalia.it for up-to-date schedules.

Buses: SITA, V.S. Caterina da Siena 15r (☎28 46 61; www.sita-on-line.it), run buses to **San Gimignano** (1½hr., 14 per day, €7.60) and **Siena** (1½hr., 2 per day, €6). **LAZZI,** P. Adua 1-4r (☎35 10 61; www.lazzi.it) sends buses to **Pisa** (every hr., €6.10).

Public Transportation: ATAF (☎800 42 45 00; www.ataf.net), outside the train station, runs orange city buses (6am-1am). 1hr. tickets €1, 3hr. €1.80, 24hr. €4.50, 3-day €7.20. Buy tickets at any newsstand, *tabacchi,* or automated ticket dispenser before boarding. Validate your ticket using the orange machine onboard or risk a €50 fine.

Taxis: ☎43 90, 47 98, or 42 42. Outside the train station.

Bike/Moped Rental: Alinari Noleggi, V. Guelfa 85r (☎28 05 00). Bikes €15-20 per day. Mopeds €30-60 per day.

ORIENTATION

From the train station, a short walk on V. Panzani and a left on V. dei Cerretani leads to the **duomo,** the center of Florence. A bustling walkway, **Via dei Calzaiuoli** runs south from the *duomo* to **Piazza della Signoria.** V. Roma leads from P.S. Giovanni through **Piazza della Repubblica** to the **Ponte Vecchio** (old bridge), which crosses from central Florence to **Oltrarno,** the district south of the **Arno River.** Note that streets change names unpredictably. For guidance through Florence's tangled center, grab a free map from the tourist office. Sights are scattered throughout the city, but few lie beyond walking distance.

ITALY

PRACTICAL INFORMATION

Tourist Office: Informazione Turistica, P. della Stazione 4 (☎21 22 45; turismo3@comune.fi.it). Info on cultural events. Ask for a free map with street index. Open M-Sa 8:30am-7pm, Su 8:30am-2pm.

Consulates: UK, Lungarno Corsini 2 (☎28 41 33). Open M-F 9:30am-12:30pm and 2:30-4:30pm. **US,** Lungarno Amerigo Vespucci 38 (☎239 82 76), at V. Palestro, near the station. Open M-F 9am-12:30pm. For other consulates, see www.corpoconsolarefirenze.it.

Currency Exchange: Local banks offer the best rates; beware of independent exchange services with high commissions. Most are open M-F 8:20am-1:20pm and 2:45-3:45pm. 24hr. **ATMs** are common throughout the city.

American Express: V. Dante Alighieri 22r (☎50 98 220). From the *duomo,* walk down V. dei Calzaiuoli and turn left on V. dei Tavolini. Mail held free for AmEx customers, otherwise €1.55. Open M-F 9am-5:30pm, Sa 9am-12:30pm.

Emergency: ☎113. **Police:** ☎49 771. **Fire:** ☎115. **Ambulance:** ☎118.

24hr. Pharmacies: Farmacia Comunale (☎28 94 35), at the train station by track #16. **Molteni,** V. dei Calzaiuoli 7r (☎28 94 90).

Internet Access: Walk down almost any busy street and you'll find an Internet cafe. **Internet Train** has 15 locations in the city listed on www.internettrain.it. €4 per hr., students €3. Most branches open M-F 9am-midnight, Sa 10am-8pm, Su noon-9pm. AmEx/MC/V.

Post Office: V. Pellicceria (☎273 648), off P. della Repubblica. Address mail to be held: First name SURNAME, In Fermo Posta, L'Ufficio Postale, V. Pellicceria, Firenze, 50100 ITALY. Open M-Sa 8:15am-7pm. **Postal Code:** 50100.

ACCOMMODATIONS AND CAMPING

Lodging in Florence generally doesn't come cheap. **Consorzio ITA,** in the train station by track #16, can find rooms for a €3-8.50 fee. (☎28 28 93. Open daily 8:45am-8pm.) It is best to make reservations *(prenotazioni)* in advance.

HOSTELS

Ostello Archi Rossi, V. Faenza 94r (☎29 08 04; www.hostelarchirossi.com). Exit left from the station on V. Nazionale and take the 2nd left on V. Faenza. Outdoor patio is packed with young travelers after dark. Hearty breakfast included. Laundry €5.20. Free Internet. Lockout 11am-2:30pm. Curfew 2am. Book online. Dorms €18-26. ❷

Istituto Gould, V. dei Serragli 49 (☎21 25 76; www.istitutogould.it), in the Oltrarno. Take bus #36 or 37 from the train station to the 2nd stop across the river. Spotless rooms. Reception M-F 8:45am-1pm and 3-7:30pm, Sa 9am-1:30pm. Dorms €21; singles €36, with bath €41; doubles €50/58. MC/V. ❷

Ostello Santa Monaca, V.S. Monaca 6 (☎26 83 38; www.ostello.it). Follow the directions to the Istituto Gould, but turn left off V. dei Serragli onto V.S. Monaca. Breakfast €2.50-3.50. Laundry €6.50 per 5kg. Internet €5 per hr. 7-night max. stay. June-Sept. check-in before 9am. Curfew 1am. Book ahead. 10-bed dorms €17. AmEx/MC/V. ❷

Ostello della Gioventù Europa Villa Camerata (HI), V. Augusto Righi 2-4 (☎60 14 51), northeast of town. Take bus #17 from outside the train station (near track #5); ask for Salviatino stop. From the street entrance, walk 10min. up driveway past a vineyard. Tidy and crowded, in a beautiful villa. Breakfast included. Laundry €5.20. 3-night max. stay. Lockout 10am-2pm. Strict midnight curfew. Dorms €19.10. €3 HI discount. ❷

HOTELS

OLD CITY (NEAR THE DUOMO)

Hotel Il Perseo, V. de Cerretani 1 (☎21 25 04; www.hotelperseo.com), en route to the *duomo* from the station, opposite the Feltrinelli bookstore. Immaculate rooms with fans. Breakfast included. Internet €1.50 per 15min. Singles €55; doubles €75, with bath €95; triples €97-120; quads €118-140. MC/V with 3-night min. stays. ❹

Locanda Orchidea, Borgo degli Albizi 11 (☎248 03 46; hotelorchidea@yahoo.it). Turn left off V. Proconsolo from the *duomo.* Dante's wife was born in this 12th-century *palazzo,* built around a still-intact tower. Helpful, English-speaking staff. Carefully decorated rooms with marble floors, some of which open onto a garden. Singles €55; doubles €75; triples with shower €100; quads with shower €120. Cash only. ❹

Relais Cavalcanti, V. Pellicceria 2 (☎21 09 62). Supreme location just steps from P. della Repubblica, near the central post office. Ring bell to enter. Beautiful gold-trimmed rooms with antique wardrobes. Singles €70-85; doubles €90-125; triples €130-160. 10% *Let's Go* discount. MC/V. ❺

Albergo Por S. Maria, V. Calimaruzza 3 (☎21 63 70). Between the Uffizi and P. della Repubblica. Pleasant, airy rooms. Matronly proprietor strikes up conversations in Italian. Singles €50, with shower €55; doubles €85, with bath €95. Cash only. ❹

PIAZZA SANTA MARIA NOVELLA AND ENVIRONS

Hotel Abaco, V. dei Banchi 1 (☎238 19 19; www.abaco-hotel.it). From the train station, cross to the back of S. Maria Novella church. Walk past church into P.S. Maria Novella and go left onto V. dei Banchi. 7 beautifully extravagant rooms, each named after a Renaissance master, with 17th-century headboards. Breakfast and A/C included when paying in cash, otherwise €5 each. Laundry €7. Free Internet. Doubles €75, with bath €90; triples €110; quads €135. 10% *Let's Go* discount. MC/V. ❺

Soggiorno Luna Rossa, V. Nazionale 7 (☎230 21 85; www.touristhouse.com). Exit train station left on V. Nazionale. Large, airy rooms. Small shared baths. Breakfast included. Dorms €20-22; singles €25, with bath €30; doubles €60; triples €75, with shower €90; quads with shower €100. Book ahead. Cash only. ❷

Hotel Elite, V. della Scala 12 (☎21 53 95). Exit right from the train station onto V. degli Orti Oricellari; turn left on V. della Scala. Brass bedposts glow in the lovely rooms. Breakfast €6. Singles €70; doubles with shower €75, with full bath €90; triples €110; quads €120. AmEx/MC/V. ❺

Hotel Giappone, V. dei Banchi 1 (☎21 00 90; www.hotelgiappone.com). Follow directions to Hotel Abaco. 10 clean, centrally located rooms have phone, TV, A/C, and Internet jack. Singles €50, with bath €55; doubles €72/85. MC/V. ❹

AROUND VIA NAZIONALE

Katti House, V. Faenza 21 (☎21 34 10). Exit train station onto V. Nazionale; walk 1 block and turn right onto V. Faenza. Lovingly kept lodgings, recently renovated. 400-year-old antiques and an attentive staff. Large rooms with A/C, TV, and bath. Singles €55; doubles €75; triples and quads €105. Nov.-Mar. prices drop. MC/V. ❹

Hotel Nazionale, V. Nazionale 22 (☎238 22 03; www.nazionalehotel.it). Turn left from train station. 9 sunny rooms with comfy beds and A/C. Breakfast brought to your room 8-9:30am (€6). Singles €63-95; doubles €70-95; triples €100-125. MC/V. ❺

Via Faenza 56 houses 5 *pensioni* that are among the best deals in the area. From the train station, exit left onto V. Nazionale, walk 1 block, and turn left on V. Faenza.

Pensione Azzi (☎21 38 06; www.hotelazzi.com) has large rooms and a terrace. Styled as an artists' inn. Breakfast included. Singles €70; doubles €110. AmEx/MC/V. ❺

Hotel Anna's (☎230 27 14; www.hotelannas.com), on the 2nd fl. Large, bright rooms with TV, phone, A/C, and bath. Breakfast €5. Singles €40-60; doubles €80-130. AmEx/MC/V. ❹

Locanda Paola (☎21 36 82) has doubles with views of the surrounding hills. Flexible 2am curfew. Dorms €25; doubles €65. Extra bed €25. Breakfast included. Cash only. ❸

Hotel Merlini (☎21 28 48; www.hotelmerlini.it) has some rooms with views of the *duomo*. Breakfast €5. Curfew 1am. Doubles €75, with bath €90; triples €105; quads €115. MC/V. ❺

Albergo Armonia (☎21 11 46). All rooms have high ceilings and wood-framed beds. Singles €30-42; doubles €35-60; triples €90; quads €100. Prices drop in winter. ❸

CAMPING

Campeggio Michelangelo, V. Michelangelo 80 (☎681 19 77; www.ecvacanze.it), beneath P. Michelangelo. Take bus #13 from the bus station (15min.; last bus 11:25pm). Crowded, but with a great view of Florence. Reception 7am-11:30pm. Tent sites €11, €9.50 per person. ❶

FOOD

Specialties include *bruschetta* (grilled bread soaked with olive oil and garlic and topped with tomatoes, basil, and anchovy, or liver paste) and *bistecca alla Fiorentina* (thick sirloin steak). No Tuscan meal is complete without wine, and genuine *chianti classico* commands a premium price. A liter costs €4-5.20 in Florence's *trattorie;* stores sell bottles for as little as €3. Florence's own Buontalenti family supposedly invented gelato; this is as good an excuse for indulgence as any. Pick up fresh produce and meat at the **Mercato Centrale,** between V. Nazionale and S. Lorenzo. (Open June-Sept. M-Sa 7:30am-2pm; Oct.-May M-F 7am-2pm, Sa also 4-8pm.) To get to **STANDA** supermarket, V. Pietrapiana 1r, turn right on V. del Proconsolo, take the first left on Borgo degli Albizi, and continue straight through P. G. Salvemini. (Open M-Sa 8am-9pm, Su 9:30am-1:30pm and 3:30-6:30pm.)

RESTAURANTS

OLD CITY (THE CENTER)

Trattoria Anita, V. del Parlascio 2r (☎21 86 98), behind the Bargello. Dine by candlelight, surrounded by shelves of expensive wine. Traditional Tuscan fare—including pasta, roast chicken, and steak. *Primi* €4.70-5.20. *Secondi* from €5.20. Great lunch *menù* €5.50. Cover €1. Open M-Sa noon-2:30pm and 7-10pm. AmEx/MC/V. ❷

Al Lume di Candela, V. delle Terme 23r (☎265 65 61), between P.S. Trinità and P. della Signoria. Candlelight illuminates the bright yellow walls of this restaurant that serves Tuscan, Venetian, and southern Italian favorites. *Primi* €6.80-9.50. *Secondi* €8.90-15.90. Open M-Sa noon-2:30pm and 7:30pm-1am. AmEx/MC/V. ❸

Moyo, V. dei Banchi 23r (☎247 97 38), near P. Santa Croce. New lunch spot crowded with young Italians. Fresh salads and surprisingly tasty burgers. Lunch options from €5. Open daily noon-4pm. AmEx/MC/V. ❷

Trattoria da Benvenuto, V. della Mosca 16r (☎21 48 33). Comfortable dining amid pastel decor and linen tablecloths. *Spaghetti alle vongole* (with clams) €5.50. *Primi* €5-10. *Secondi* €6-15. Set dinner *menù* €12.50. Cover €1.50. Service 10%. Open M-Sa noon-2:30pm and 7-10:30pm. AmEx/MC/V. ❷

PIAZZE SANTA MARIA NOVELLA AND ENVIRONS

Il Latini, V. dei Palchetti 6r (☎21 09 16). From Ponte alla Carraia, walk up V. del Moro; V. dei Palchetti is on the right. Crowds line up nightly for the *bistecca alla fiorentina* (€16). Waiters keep the house wine flowing. Reserve ahead. *Primi* €6-8. *Secondi* €10-18. Open Tu-Su 12:30-2:30pm and 7:30-10:30pm. AmEx/MC/V. ❸

Trattoria Contadino, V. Palazzuolo 71r (☎238 2673). Filling, homestyle, fixed-price *menù* includes *primo, secondo,* bread, water, and 0.25L of wine (€9.50). Open daily 11am-2:30pm and 7-9:30pm. June-July closed Sa-Su. AmEx/MC/V. ❷

Tre Merli, entrance on V. del Moro 11r (☎28 70 62). Beautiful red mushroom lights create romantic vibe. *Primi* €7.50-14. *Secondi* €12-19. Lunch *menù* €12. Cover €2. Open daily 11am-11pm. Discount and free glass of wine with *Let's Go.* AmEx/MC/V. ❹

THE STATION AND UNIVERSITY QUARTER

Trattoria da Zà-Zà, P. del Mercato Centrale 26r (☎21 54 11). Wooden-beam ceilings and brick archways inside, lively patio outside. Try the *tris* (mixed bean and vegetable soup; €7) or the *tagliata di manzo* (cut of beef; €13-18). Cover €1.55. Reservations recommended. Open M-Sa noon-3pm and 7-11pm. AmEx/MC/V. ❸

NICE TO MEAT YOU

Meat, and plenty of it, has been a hearty staple at Tuscan tables fo centuries. Use this quick guide t distinguish between the numer ous options for carnivores.

Carpaccio, paper-thin slices o raw beef, is usually seen on *anti pasti* menus, served with slices o parmesan cheese and drizzle with olive oil.

Porchetta, found in market and local *macellerie* (butche shops) are thick pieces of por are carved straight from the roas for the perfect sandwich.

For more adventurous eaters **cinghiale,** the flavorful wild boa that is popular throughout th region is always a hit. Die-har fans eat it plain, but it's bes when accompanied by a thic pasta like *tagliatelle.*

On the rare occasion of ba weather, **osso bucco,** a heart beef stew, is sure to warm yo bones to belly. It is best comple mented by a glass of red win and a side of *patate frittate* (frie potatoes, similar to French fries).

Coniglio, or rabbit, is a sophis ticated choice often found on five star menus and in local *osterie* This tender meat is usually serve in an olive sauce.

Those looking to go for the ca nivore gold medal should orde **bistecca alla fiorentina,** trad tionally served extremely rar Don't necessarily expect silve ware—it's perfectly acceptable t pick up your steak and attack i with gusto.

Trattoria Mario, V. Rosina 2r (☎21 85 50), around the corner from P. del Mercato Centrale. Incredible pasta. *Primi* menu offers traditional Tuscan soups (€3.10-3.40). *Secondi* €3.10-10.50. Cover €0.50. Open M-Sa noon-3:30pm. Closed Aug. Cash only. ❷

OLTRARNO

Il Borgo Antico, P.S. Spirito 6r (☎21 04 37). Trendy spot with young staff and student-heavy clientele. Memorable pastas and fantastic salads (€7). *Primi* €7. *Secondi* €10-20. Pizza €7. Cover €2. Reservation recommended. Open June-Sept. daily 1pm-12:30am; Oct.-May 12:45-2:30pm and 7:45pm-1am. AmEx/MC/V. ❸

La Mangiatoia, P.S. Felice 8r (☎22 40 60). Continue straight on V. Guicciardini from Ponte Vecchio. Quality Tuscan fare. Extensive takeaway menu. *Primi* €3.50-5.50. *Secondi* €4-9. Cover €1.50. Open Tu-Su 11am-3pm and 6:30-10pm. AmEx/MC/V. ❷

GELATERIE

Vivoli, V. Isole della Stinche 7 (☎29 23 34), behind the Bargello. A renowned Florentine *gelateria* and long-time contender for the distinction of the best ice cream in Florence. Cups from €1.50. Open Tu-Sa 7:30am-1am, Su 9:30am-1am.

Gelateria dei Neri, V. dei Neri 20-22r (☎210 034). Stand outside and watch through the window as dozens of delicious flavors are mixed right before your eyes. Try *crema giotto* (coconut, almond, and hazelnut). Cones and cups from €1.40.

ENOTECHE (WINE BARS)

Check out an *enoteca* to sample Italy's finest wines. A meal can often be made out of complimentary side dishes (cheeses, olives, toast and spreads, and salami).

Enoteca Alessi, V. della Oche 27/29r (☎21 49 66), 1 block from the *duomo*. Among Florence's finest, stocking over 1000 wines. Sizable and cool. Doubles as a candy store, offering bites between sips. Open M-F 9am-1pm and 4-8pm. AmEx/MC/V.

SIGHTS

With the views from Brunelleschi's dome, the perfection of San Spirito's nave and the overwhelming array of art in the Uffizi Galleries, it's hard to take a wrong turn in Florence. For a full list of museum openings, check out www.firenzeturismo.it. For museum reservations, call **Firenze Musei** (☎294 883; www.firenzemusei.it).

PIAZZA DEL DUOMO

THE DUOMO (CATTEDRALE DI SANTA MARIA DEL FIORE). In 1296 the city fathers commissioned Arnolfo di Cambio to erect a cathedral so magnificent that it would be "impossible to make it either better or more beautiful with the industry and power of man." Arnolfo succeeded, completing the massive but domeless nave by 1418. Filippo Brunelleschi came up with his revolutionary double-shelled construction that utilized interlocking bricks to construct the enormous dome. The *duomo* claims the world's third longest nave, after St. Peter's in Rome and St. Paul's in London. *(Open M-Sa 10am-4:45pm, Su 1:30-4:45pm. Mass daily 7am, 12:30, 5-7pm. Free.)* Climb the 463 steps inside the dome to **Michelangelo's lantern,** which offers an expansive view of the city from the 100m high external gallery. *(Open M-F 8:30am-7pm, Sa 8:30am-5:40pm. €6.)* The 82m high **campanile,** next to the *duomo*, also has spectacular views. *(Open daily 8:30am-6:30pm. €6.)* Most of the *duomo*'s art resides behind the cathedral in the **Museo dell'Opera del Duomo.** Up the first flight of stairs is a late *Pietà* by Michelangelo, who, according to legend, destroyed Christ's left arm with a hammer in a fit of frustration; soon after, an over-eager pupil touched up the work, leaving visible scars on parts of Mary Magdalene's head. The museum also houses four frames from the baptistry's *Gates of Paradise.* *(P. del Duomo 9, behind the duomo. ☎23 02 885. Open M-Sa 9am-6:50pm, Su 9am-1pm. €6.)*

ORSANMICHELE. Built in 1337 as a granary, the Orsanmichele was converted into a church after a fire convinced officials to move grain operations outside the city walls. Secular and spiritual concerns mingle in the statues on the facade. Within the numerous niches, the patient searcher will find Ghiberti's *St. John the Baptist* and *St. Stephen*, Donatello's *St. Peter* and *St. Mark*, and Giambologna's *St. Luke*. Across the street, the **Museo di Orsanmichele** exhibits paintings and sculptures from the original church. *(V. Arte della Lana, between the duomo and P. della Signoria. ☎28 49 44. Museum open daily 9am-noon. Both closed 1st and last M of the month. Free.)*

BATTISTERO. Built between the 5th and 9th centuries, the *battistero* (baptistry) was the site of Dante's christening; its Byzantine-style mosaics inspired the details of his *Inferno*. The **bronze doors** were products of an intense competition among Florentine artists; Ghiberti was eventually commissioned to forge reliefs depicting Biblical scenes. In the resulting product, which Michelangelo dubbed the **Gates of Paradise,** Ghiberti exchanged his earlier 28-panel design for 10 large, gilded squares, each of which employs mathematical perspective to create the illusion of depth. The gates are best admired in the morning or late evening after the tourist crowds have thinned. *(Opposite the duomo. Open M-Sa noon-7pm, Su 8:30am-2pm. €3.)*

PIAZZA DELLA SIGNORIA AND ENVIRONS

From P. del Duomo, the bustling **Via dei Calzaiuoli,** one of the city's oldest streets, runs south through crowds and chic shops to P. della Signoria.

THE UFFIZI. Designed this in 1554 for the offices (*uffizi*) of Duke Cosimo's administration, this gallery now holds one of the world's top art collections. Botticelli, da Vinci, Michelangelo, Raphael, Titian, Giotto, Fra Angelico, Caravaggio, Bronzino, Cimabue, della Francesca, Bellini; even Dürer, Rubens, and Rembrandt—you name it, it's here. A few rooms are usually closed each day, and famous pieces often go on loan, so not all works will always be on display. *(Extends from P. della Signoria to the Arno River. ☎238 86 51. Open Tu-Su 8:15am-6:35pm. €8.50; reserve tickets in advance for €3 extra. Pick up reserved tickets at door #1 before entering.)*

PALAZZO VECCHIO. Arnolfo del Cambio designed this fortress-like *palazzo* in the late 13th century as the seat of government. Michelangelo decorated the **courtyard** after it became the Medici family home in 1470. The **Monumental Apartments,** housing the *palazzo*'s extensive art collections, are now a museum. The **Activities Tour,** well worth the extra €2 (students €1), includes the **Secret Routes,** which reveal hidden stairwells and chambers tucked behind exquisite oil paintings, and **Invitation to Court,** a reenactment of court life. *(☎276 82 24. Call ahead for tours. Open M-W and F-Sa 9am-7pm, Su 9am-1pm. Palazzo and Monumental Apartments each €6, ages 18-25 €4.50. Courtyard free.)*

PIAZZA DELLA SIGNORIA. The Palazzo Vecchio and the Uffizi border this 13th-century *piazza*, now a crowded center of tourism. With the construction of the Palazzo Vecchio in 1299, the square became Florence's civic and political center. In 1497, religious zealot Girolamo Savonarola convinced Florentines to light the **Bonfire of the Vanities,** a grand roast in the square that consumed some of Florence's best art. A year later, the citizens sent Savonarola up in smoke on the same spot, marked today by a granite disc. The graceful 14th-century **Loggia dei Lanzi,** built as a stage for civic orators, now displays world-class sculpture free of charge. From the Uffizi, follow V. Georgofili left and turn right along the river to reach the nearby **Ponte Vecchio** (old bridge), the oldest bridge in Florence. From the neighboring **Ponte alle Grazie,** the **view** of the Ponte Vecchio is breathtaking, and the bridge itself buzzes with pedestrians and street performers, especially at night.

THE BARGELLO AND ENVIRONS

BARGELLO. This 13th-century fortress, which was once the residence of the chief magistrate and later a brutal prison with public executions in its courtyard, was restored in the 19th century. It now houses the sculpture-filled, largely untouristed **Museo Nazionale.** Donatello's bronze *David*, the first free-standing nude since antiquity, stands opposite the two bronze panels of the *Sacrifice of Isaac*, submitted by Ghiberti and Brunelleschi in the baptistry door competition (p. 665). Michelangelo's early works are on the ground floor. *(V. del Proconsolo 4, between the duomo and P. della Signoria. ☎238 86 06. Open daily 8:15am-1:50pm. Closed 2nd and 4th M of each month, though hours and additional closing days vary by month. €4.)*

BADIA. The site of medieval Florence's richest monastery, the Badia is now buried in the interior of a residential block, making it a quiet respite from the busy city streets. The church's simple facade belies the treasures that lie within. Filippino Lippi's *Apparition of the Virgin to St. Bernard*, one of the most famous paintings of the 15th century, hangs in eerie gloom to the left of the entrance to the church. Visitors are asked to walk silently among the prostrate, white-robed worshippers. *(Entrance on V. Dante Alighieri, off V. Proconsolo. Open to tourists M 3-6pm, but respectful visitors can walk through at any time.)*

MUSEO DI STORIA DELLA SCIENZA. This impressive collection boasts scientific instruments from the Renaissance, including telescopes, astrological models, clock workings, and wax models of anatomy and childbirth. The highlight of the museum is **Room 4,** where a number of Galileo's tools are on display, including the objective lens through which he first observed the satellites of Jupiter in 1610. *(P. dei Giudici 1, behind Palazzo Vecchio and the Uffizi. ☎26 53 11. Open M and W-F 9:30am-5pm, Tu and Sa 9:30am-1pm; Oct.-May also open 2nd Su of each month 10am-1pm. €6.50.)*

ITALY

PIAZZA DELLA REPUBBLICA AND FARTHER WEST

CHIESA DI SANTA MARIA NOVELLA. This church, near the train station, houses the chapels of the wealthiest merchants. Santa Maria Novella was home to the order of Dominicans, or *Domini canes* (Hounds of the Lord), who took a bite out of sin and corruption. The 14th-century *chiesa* boasts a Romanesque-Gothic facade made of Florentine marble, considered one of the greatest masterpieces of early Renaissance architecture. Thirteenth-century frescoes covered the interior until the Medici commissioned Vasari to paint new ones. Fortunately, Vasari spared Masaccio's powerful **Trinity,** the first painting to use geometric perspective. *(Open M-Th and Sa 9am-5pm, F and Su 1-5pm. €2.50, ages 13-18 €1.50.)*

PIAZZA DELLA REPUBBLICA. The largest open space in Florence, this *piazza* teems with crowds and street performers in the evenings. An enormous arch filling in the gap over V. Strozzi marks the western edge of the square. The rest of the *piazza* is lined with overpriced *caffès*, restaurants, and *gelaterie*. The inscription "*Antico centro della città, da secolare squalore, a vita nuova restituito*" ("Ancient center of the city, squalid for centuries, restored to new life") makes a derogatory reference: the *piazza* is the site of the old Jewish ghetto, which slowly disappeared as a result of the "liberation of the Jews" in Italy in the 1860s that allowed members of the Jewish community to live elsewhere.

CHIESA DI SANTA TRINITÀ. Hoping to spend eternity as they had lived—in elite company—the most fashionable *palazzo* owners commissioned family chapels in this church. The facade, designed by Bernardo Buontalenti in the 16th century, is an exquisite example of late-Renaissance architecture; its ornamentation verges on Baroque. Scenes from Ghirlandaio's *Life of St. Francis* decorate the **Sassetti Chapel** in the right arm of the transept. The famous altarpiece, Ghirlandaio's *Adoration of the Shepherds*, resides in the Uffizi—this one is a convincing copy. *(In P.S. Trinità. Open M-Sa 8am-noon and 4-6pm, Su 4-6pm.)*

MERCATO NUOVO. The *loggie* of the New Market have housed gold and silk traders since 1547 under their Corinthian-columned splendor. Today, the occasional piece of gold or silk makes a quiet appearance amongst the more prominent vendors selling imitation designer wares. Pietro Tacca's pleasantly plump statue, *Il Porcellino* (The Little Pig; actually a wild boar)—appeared some 50 years after the market first opened. Rubbing its snout is reputed to bring good luck, but don't expect it to turn that purse you've got your eye on into real leather. *(Off V. Calimala, between P. della Repubblica and the Ponte Vecchio. Open from dawn until dusk.)*

SAN LORENZO AND FARTHER NORTH

ACCADEMIA. It doesn't matter how many pictures of him you've seen—when you come around the corner and see Michelangelo's triumphant **David** in person, towering in self-assured perfection under the rotunda designed just for him, you will momentarily stop in your tracks. In a series of unfortunate incidents, the statue's base was struck by lightning in 1512, damaged by anti-Medici riots in 1527, and was finally moved here from P. della Signoria in 1873 after a stone hurled during a riot broke David's left wrist in two places. In the hallway leading up to the *David* are Michelangelo's four **Slaves** and a **Pietà.** The master left these intriguing statues intentionally unfinished—chipping away only enough to show the figures emerging from the marble, he remained true to his theories about "releasing" his figures from the living stone. *(V. Ricasoli 60, between the churches of S. Marco and S. S. Annunziata. ☎29 48 83. Most areas wheelchair accessible. Open Tu-Su 8:15am-6:50pm. €8.)*

ITALY

BASILICA DI SAN LORENZO. Designed in 1419 by Brunelleschi, the Basilica di San Lorenzo was funded by the Medici family. They cunningly used this authority to place Cosimo Medici's grave in front of the high altar, making the entire church his personal mausoleum. Michelangelo designed the exterior, but, disgusted by Florentine politics, he abandoned the project to study architecture in Rome, which accounts for the basilica's still unadorned facade. *(Open daily M-Sa 10am-5pm. €2.50.)* To reach the **Cappelle dei Medici** (Medici Chapels), walk around to the back entrance on P. Madonna degli Aldobrandini. Michelangelo sculpted the **Sacrestia Nuova** (New Sacristy) to hold two Medici tombs. *(Open daily 8:15am-5pm. Closed the 1st, 3rd, and 5th M and the 2nd and 4th Su of every month. €6.)* Don't miss Michelangelo's entrance portico; the *pietra serena* sandstone staircase is one of his most innovative architectural designs. *(Open daily 8:30am-1:30pm. Free with entrance to San Lorenzo.)*

MUSEO DELLA CHIESA DI SAN MARCO. Works by Fra Angelico adorn the Museo della Chiesa di San Marco, one of the most peaceful and spiritual places in Florence. A large room to the right of the lovely courtyard contains some of the painter's major works, including the church's altarpiece. The second floor houses Angelico's famous *Annunciation*, as well as the monks' quarters. Every cell in the convent contains its own Fra Angelico fresco, each painted in flat colors and with sparse detail to facilitate the monks' somber meditation. In cells #17 and 22, you can see underground excavated artwork from the medieval period through the glass floor. Toward the exit are two rooms housing the **Museo di Firenze Antica,** which has numerous archaeological fragments on display; most of them from Etruscan and Roman buildings in the area. Be sure to peek in to the church itself, next door to the museum, to admire the elaborate altar and beautifully vaulted ceiling. *(Enter at P.S. Marco 3. ☎238 86 08. Open daily 8:15am-6:50pm. Closed 2nd and 4th M and 1st, 3rd, and 5th Su of every month. €4.)*

PALAZZO MEDICI RICCARDI. The palace's facade is the work of Michelozzo and the archetype for all Renaissance *palazzi*. The chapel inside features Benozzo Gozzoli's beautiful fresco of the **Three Magi** and several Medici portraits. The *palazzo* hosts rotating from Renaissance architectural sketches to Fellini memorabilia. *(V. Cavour 3. ☎276 03 40. Open M-Tu and Th-Su 9am-7pm. €4, children €2.50.)*

PIAZZA SANTA CROCE AND ENVIRONS

CHIESA DI SANTA CROCE. The Franciscans built this church as far as possible from their Dominican rivals at S. Maria Novella. Started in 1210 as a small oratory, the ascetic Franciscans ironically produced what is arguably the most splendid church in the city. Among the luminaries buried here are Galileo, Machiavelli, Michelangelo (in the right aisle in a tomb designed by Vasari), and humanist Leonardo Bruni. *(Open M-Sa 9:30am-5:30pm, Su 3-5:30pm. €4.)* Intricate *pietra serena* pilasters and statues of the evangelists by Donatello grace Brunelleschi's small **Cappella Pazzi,** at the end of the cloister next to the church. A humble marvel of perfect proportions, among them are Luca della Robbia's *tondi* of the apostles and Brunelleschi's moldings of the evangelists. The **Museo dell'Opera di Santa Croce** forms three sides of the church's peaceful courtyard. *(Enter through the* loggia *in front of Cappella Pazzi. Hours same as church. Free with entrance to church.)*

ITALY

THE OLTRARNO

Historically disdained by downtown Florentines, the far side of the Arno remains a lively and unpretentious quarter, filled with students and young people and, thankfully, not too many tourists.

PALAZZO PITTI. Luca Pitti, a 15th-century banker, built his *palazzo* east of P.S. Spirito against the Boboli hill. The Medici acquired the *palazzo* and the hill in 1550 and expanded it in every way possible. Today, it houses six museums, including the **Galleria Palatina,** one of only a few public galleries when it opened in 1833, which now houses Florence's most important art collection after the Uffizi. Works by Raphael, Titian, Caravaggio, and Rubens line the walls. Other museums display Medici family treasures, costumes, porcelain, carriages, and Royal Apartments—lavish reminders of the time when the *palazzo* was the living quarters of the royal House of Savoy. *(Open Tu-Su 8:15am-6pm. €8.50, EU students €4.25.)*

BOBOLI GARDENS. With geometrically sculpted hedges, contrasting groves of holly and cypress trees, and bubbling fountains, the gardens are an exquisite example of stylized Renaissance landscaping. A large oval lawn is just up the hill from the back of the palace, with an Egyptian obelisk in the middle and marble statues dotting the perimeter. *(Open daily June-Aug. 8:15am-7:30pm; Apr.-May and Sept.-Oct. 8:15am-6:30pm; Nov.-Feb. 8:15am-4:30pm; Mar. 8:15am-5:30pm. €6, EU students €3.)*

SAN MINIATO AL MONTE AND ENVIRONS

PIAZZALE MICHELANGELO. Laid out in 1860, Piazzale Michelangelo offers a fine panorama of the entire city, which is breathtaking at sunset. Views from here are even better (and certainly cheaper) than those from the top of the *duomo*. Make the challenging uphill trek at around 8:30pm during the summer to arrive at the *piazza* in time for sunset. Unfortunately, the *piazza* doubles as a large parking lot, and is home to hordes of tour buses during summer days; it occasionally hosts concerts as well. *(Cross the Ponte Vecchio and turn left, walk through the piazza, and turn right up V. de Bardi. Follow it uphill as it becomes V. del Monte alle Croci, where a staircase to the left heads to the piazza.)*

SAN MINIATO AL MONTE. One of Florence's oldest churches gloriously surveys the skyline. The inlaid marble facade and 13th-century mosaics provide a prelude to the incredible floor inside, patterned with lions, doves, and astrological signs. The **Chapel of the Cardinal of Portugal** holds a collection of della Robbia terracottas. The cemetery is an overwhelming profusion of tombs and mausoleums in many architectural styles. For a special treat, visit at 5:40pm, when monks perform beautifully haunting chants. *(Take bus #13 from the station or climb the stairs from Piazzale Michelangelo. ☎234 27 31. Open daily 8am-7:30pm. Free.)*

ENTERTAINMENT

May starts the summer music festivals with the classical **Maggio Musicale.** In June, the *quartieri* of Florence turn out in costume to play their own medieval version of soccer, **calcio storico,** in which two teams of 27 players face off over a wooden ball in one of the city's *piazze*. These games often blur the line between athletic contest and riot. Tickets (€10-40) are sold at the box office across from P.S. Croce. Check with the tourist office for match times and locations. The **Estate Fiesolana** (June-Aug.) fills the Roman theater in Fiesole with concerts, opera, theater, ballet, and film events. September brings the **Festa dell'Unità,** a concert series at Campi Bisenzia (take bus #30). Info on all festivals available at the tourist office.

NIGHTLIFE

For info on hot nightlife, consult the monthly *Firenze Spettacolo* (€2), available at newsstands. Begin your nighttime *passeggiata* along V. dei Calzaiuoli and end it with coffee or gelato in a ritzy cafe on **Piazza della Repubblica,** where singers prance about the stage in front of **Bar Concerto.** In the Oltrarno, **Piazza San Spirito** has plenty of bars and restaurants, and live music in summer.

May Day Lounge, V. Dante Alighieri 16r (www.maydayclub.it). Aspiring artists display their work on the walls of this eclectic lounge that fills with offbeat Italians. Play Pong on the early 80s gaming system or sip mixed drinks (€4.50-6.50) to the beat of the background funk. Happy hour 8-10pm. Beer €4.50. Open daily 8pm-2am. AmEx/MC/V.

Central Park, in Parco della Cascinè. Open-air dance floor pulses with hip-hop, reggae, and rock. Favored by Florentine and foreign teens and college students. Mixed drinks €8. No cover for foreign students before 12:30am; after 12:30am, cover €11. Open M-Tu and Th-Sa 11pm-late, W 9pm-late. AmEx/MC/V.

The Fiddler's Elbow, P.S. Maria Novella 7r (☎21 50 56). Irish pub where expat bartenders serve cider, Guinness, and other beers (pints €4.50) to crowds of convivial foreigners. Popular outdoor patio looks onto P.S. Maria Novella. Happy hour until 8pm. Open M-Th and Su 3pm-1am, F-Sa 2pm-2am. AmEx/MC/V.

Eby's Latin Bar, V. dell'Oriuolo 5r (☎338 650 89 59). Eby blends fresh mixed drinks from seasonal fruit. Great nachos, a raucous young crowd, and salsa music. Happy hour 6-9pm. Beer €3.50. Mixed drinks €5.50-7. Open M-Sa noon-3pm and 6pm-3am.

Tabasco Gay Club, P.S. Cecilia 3r, from Palazzo Vecchio. Smoke machines and strobe lights on dance floor. Florence's most popular and classy gay disco caters primarily to men. 18+. Cover €13, includes 1 drink. Open Tu-Su 10pm-4am. AmEx/MC/V.

SIENA ☎0577

Many travelers rush from Rome to Florence, ignoring medieval Siena (pop. 60,000) despite its history rich in arts, politics, and trade. One of Siena's proudest celebrations is **Il Palio,** an intoxicating display of pageantry in which jockeys from the city's 17 *contrade* (districts) race horses around **Il Campo,** the central square.

TRANSPORTATION AND PRACTICAL INFORMATION. Trains leave P. Rosselli for Florence (1¾hr., 19 per day, €6) and Rome (3hr., 12 per day, €17) via Chiusi. TRA-IN/SITA **buses** (☎20 42 46) depart from P. Gramsci and the train station

HORSE POWER

The Palio is only about 90 seconds long. The rope suddenly drops, the horses lunge onto the track, and then, in a minute-and-a-half blur of trampling hooves and bright jerseys, it's over, and a new *contrada* can claim victory. At least until August.

Though the semi-annual bareback horse race around Siena's Il Campo is very brief, ceremonies leading up to the event begin several days in advance, as 10 *contrade,* or districts, of Siena prepare their horses and jockeys with trial runs around the converted *piazza.* The night before the race, Siena's streets are full of music and revelry as locals toast victories past, sing rewritten (and often obscene) lyrics to popular children's songs, and rekindle old *contrada* rivalries.

Spectators begin to pack Il Campo early on the morning of the race, with prime free spots near the rails going to die-hard Palio fans. Those lucky (or wealthy) enough to secure bleacher seats file in at around 3pm, after the horses have been led into their *contrada* churches and blessed. A 2hr. parade of heralds, flag-throwers, and city dignitaries follows, prefacing the anarchy to come with regal pomp. The final piece is the victory prize, the Palio itself, a banner depicting the Madonna and Child alongside a rearing horse, which is drawn in a cart by four white oxen.

for Florence (every hr., €6.50) and San Gimignano (31 per day, €5.20). Across from the train station, take TRA-IN/SITA buses #3, 4, 7-10, 14, 17, or 77 (€0.90) into the center of town at **Piazza del Sale** or **Piazza Gramsci.** The central APT **tourist office** is at P. del Campo 56. (☎28 05 51; infoaptsiena@terresiena.it. Open mid-Mar. to mid-Nov. daily 9:30am-1pm and 2:30-6pm; mid-Nov. to mid-Mar. M-Sa 8:30am-1pm and 3-7pm, Su 9am-1pm.) **Prenotazioni Alberghi e Ristoranti,** in P.S. Domenico, finds rooms for a €2 fee. (☎94 08 09. Open M-Sa Apr.-Oct. 9am-8pm; Nov.-Mar. 9am-7pm.) Check email at **Cafe Internet,** Galleria Cecco Angiolieri 16. (€0.99 per 20min., €0.03 per min. thereafter. Open daily 9am-11pm.) **Postal Code:** 53100.

ACCOMMODATIONS AND FOOD. Finding a room in Siena can be difficult between Easter and October. Book at least a month ahead for *Il Palio.* **Piccolo Hotel Etruria ❹,** V. Donzelle 3, is only a stone's throw from Il Campo and has carefully decorated, spacious rooms. (☎28 80 88; www.hoteletruria.com. Breakfast €5. Curfew 1am. Singles €45-50; doubles €80; triples €105. AmEx/MC/V.) Bus #10 and 15 from P. Gramsci stop at the spotless **Ostello della Gioventù "Guidoriccio" (HI) ❶,** V. Fiorentina 89, in Località Lo Stellino. (☎522 12. Curfew midnight. Dorms €13.75. MC/V.) To camp at **Colleverde ❶,** Str. di Scacciapensieri 47, take bus #3 or 8 from P. del Sale; confirm destination with driver. (☎28 00 44; www.terresiena.it. Open late Mar. to mid-Nov. Tent sites €3.50, €7.75 per person. MC/V.)

Siena specializes in rich pastries, of which the most famous is *panforte*, a confection of honey, almonds, and citron. Indulge (€2.10 per 100g) at **Bar/Pasticceria Nannini ❶,** V. Banchi di Sopra 22-24, the oldest *pasticceria* in Siena. Next to Santuario di S. Caterina is the lively **Osteria La Chiacchera ❷,** Costa di S. Antonio 4, which serves hearty pasta dishes. (☎28 06 31. *Primi* €4.50-5. *Secondi* €5-5.50. Open M and W-Su noon-3:30pm and 7pm-midnight. AmEx/MC/V.) A **CONAD** supermarket is in P. Matteoti. (Open M-Sa 8:30am-8:30pm, Su 9am-1pm and 4-8pm.)

SIGHTS AND ENTERTAINMENT. Siena offers two **biglietto cumulativi** (cumulative tickets). The first is good for two days (€10) and allows entry into the Museo Civico, Spedale di S. Maria della Scala, and the Palazzo Papesse; the second is valid for seven days (€16) and covers three additional sights, including the Museo dell'Opera della Metropolitana. Both may be purchased at any of the sights. Siena radiates from **Piazza del Campo (Il Campo),** a shell-shaped brick square. At the top of Il Campo is the **Fonte Gaia,** fed by the same aqueduct used in the 1300s. At the bottom, the **Torre del Mangia** bell tower looms over the Gothic **Palazzo Pubblico.** Inside the *palazzo*, the **Museo Civico** contains Gothic and early Renaissance paintings; check out the **Sala del Mappamondo** and the **Sala della Pace.** (*Palazzo*, museum, and tower open daily Mar.-Oct. 10am-7pm; Nov.-Feb. 10am-5:30pm. Museum €7. Tower €6, both €10.) From the *palazzo* facing Il Campo, take the left side stairs and cross V. di Città to Siena's Gothic **duomo.** To prevent the apse from hanging in mid-air, the lavish **baptistry** was constructed below. (Open mid-Mar. to Oct. M-Sa 7:30am-7:30pm, Su 2-5pm; Nov. to mid-Mar. M-Sa 7:30am-5:30pm, Su 2-5pm. €3, when floor is uncovered in Sept. €4-5.50.) The **Libreria Piccolomini,** off the left aisle, holds frescoes and 15th-century music scores. (Open mid-Mar. to Oct. M-Sa 9am-7:30pm, Su 2-4:45pm; Nov. to mid-Mar. M-Sa 10am-1pm and 2-5pm, Su 2-4:45pm. €1.50.) The **Museo dell'Opera della Metropolitana,** to the right of the *duomo*, houses overflow art from the church. (Open daily mid-Mar. to Sept. 9am-7:30pm; Oct. to mid-Mar. reduced hours. €6.) Siena's **Il Palio** (July 2 and Aug. 16) is a traditional bareback horse race around Il Campo. Arrive three days early to watch the trial runs and to pick a *contrada* to root for. During *Il Palio*, the jockeys take about 90 seconds to tear around Il Campo three times.

DAYTRIP FROM SIENA: SAN GIMIGNANO. The hilltop village of San Gimignano looks like an illustration from a medieval manuscript. The city's 14 famous towers, all that survive of its original 72, earned San Gimignano the nickname of *Città delle Belle Torri* (City of Beautiful Towers). The **Museo Civico,** on the second floor of **Palazzo Comunale,** has an amazing collection of Sienese and Florentine artwork. Within the museum is the entrance to the **Torre Grossa,** the tallest remaining tower. (Open daily Mar.-Oct. 9:30am-7pm; Nov.-Feb. 10am-5:30pm. €5.) Not for the faint of heart, **Museo Della Tortura,** V. del Castello 1, off P. della Cisterna, offers morbidly fascinating displays of torture tools from medieval Europe to the present. (Open daily Apr.-Oct. 10am-8pm; Nov.-Mar. 10am-6pm. €8, students €5.) TRA-IN **buses** leave P. Montemaggio for Florence (1½hr., every hr., €6) via Poggibonsi and Siena (1½hr., every 1-2hr., €5.20). From the bus station, pass through Porta S. Giovanni, climb the hill, and follow V.S. Giovanni to the city center, **Piazza della Cisterna,** which runs into P. del Duomo. The **tourist office** is at P. del Duomo 1. (☎94 00 08; prolocsg@tin.it. Open daily Mar.-Oct. 9am-1pm and 3-7pm; Nov.-Feb. 9am-1pm and 2-6pm.) The tourist office and the **Associazione Strutture Extralberghiere,** P. della Cisterna 6, both find private rooms. (☎94 31 90. Open daily Mar.-Nov. 9:30am-7:30pm.) **Postal Code:** 53037.

By 7:30pm, the starting time of the race, the energy and volume of the crowd has reached a fever pitch. But suddenly, absolute silence engulfs the *piazza* as the crowd waits with bated breath to hear the line-up order of the horses, randomly decided in secret just before the race. Riders battle for spots behind the starting line until the announcer decides that all is in order and signals for the rope to drop without warning. During the three laps around the *piazza,* traditional medieval rules apply, and jockeys have free rein to whip, jostle, or push their opponents as they like. This becomes especially precarious around the first curve, notoriously the most difficult, where it is not uncommon for riders to be thrown, trampled, or even killed. The frenzied crowd, however, is focused only on the horse at the head of the pack, and as the cannon shot announces the winner of the race, the *piazza* erupts into outbursts of joy, despair, mania, and disbelief. Only 90 seconds, true. But what a 90 seconds it is.

Celebration by the winning *contrada* continues until the fall, when the official victory dinner is held in the *piazza.* And occupying the seat of honor? Why, the winning horse, of course.

The Palio is run every year on July 2 and Aug. 16. Contact Siena's APT tourist office for more info and a copy of the program.

PISA ☎050

Tourism hasn't always been Pisa's (pop. 96,000) prime industry. During the Middle Ages, the city was a major port with its own Mediterranean empire, but when the Arno River filled with silt and the tower started leaning, the city's power and wealth declined with it. Today, Pisa seems resigned to welcoming tourists and myriad t-shirt and ice cream vendors to the **Piazza del Duomo,** also known as the **Campo dei Miracoli** (Field of Miracles), a grassy expanse enclosing the tower, *duomo*, baptistry, Camposanto, Museo delle Sinopie, and Museo dell'Opera del Duomo. An **all-inclusive ticket** to the Campo's sights—excluding the tower—costs €10.50 and is available at the two *biglietteria* on the *Campo dei Miracoli* (at the Museo del Duomo and next to the tourist office behind the tower). Begun in 1173, the famous **Leaning Tower** began to tilt when the soil beneath it suddenly shifted. In June 2001, a multi-year stabilization effort was completed; the tower is presently considered stable, meaning there's little chance the tower's going to collapse with a satisfying thwump on the tourists pretending to hold it up for a picture. Tours of 30 visitors are permitted to ascend the 294 steps once every 30min. (Tours depart daily June-Aug. 8:30am-11pm; Sept.-May 8:30am-7:30pm. Make reservations at adjacent tourist office. €15.) Also on the Campo, the dazzling **duomo,** a collection of splendid art, is considered one of the finest Romanesque cathedrals in the world. (Open Apr.-Sept. M-Sa 10am-7:45pm, Su 1-7:45pm; Mar. and Oct. M-F 10am-5:30pm, Su 1-5:45pm; Nov.-Feb. M-F 10am-12:30pm and 3-4:30pm, Su 3-4:30pm. €2.) Next door is the **baptistry,** whose precise acoustics allow an unamplified choir to be heard 2km away. (Open daily Apr.-Sept. 8am-7:30pm; Mar. and Oct. 9am-5:30pm; Nov.-Feb. 9am-4:30pm. €6, includes admission to one other monument.) The adjoining **Camposanto,** a cloistered cemetery, was once considered to be one of the architectural wonders of the world, and is filled with Roman sarcophagi. (Open daily Apr.-Sept. 8am-7:30pm; Mar. and Oct. 9am-5:30pm; Nov.-Feb. 9am-4:30pm. €6, includes admission to one other monument.) The **Museo delle Sinopie,** near the baptistry, displays preliminary fresco sketches discovered in the Camposanto during post-WWII restoration. (Both open daily Apr.-Sept. 8am-7:20pm; Mar. and Oct. 9am-5:20pm; Nov.-Feb. 9am-4:20pm. €6 for both museums.)

Two minutes from the duomo, the **Albergo Helvetia ❸,** V. Don G. Boschi 31, off P. Archivescovado, has large, clean rooms and a multilingual staff. (☎55 30 84. Singles €35, with bath €45; doubles €50/62.) Cheap dining options line **Corso Italia,** south of the river, and **Via Santa Maria,** as long as you're not too close to the duomo, where prices skyrocket. Try the heavenly *risotto* at the lively **Il Paiolo ❶,** V. Curtatone e Montanara 9. (*Menù* with *primi* and *secondi* €4-6. Open M-F 12:30-3pm and 7:30pm-1am, Sa-Su 7:30pm-2am only. Cash only.) Get groceries at **Pam,** V. Pascoli 8, just off C. Italia. (Open M-Sa 8am-8pm.) **Trains** (☎147 808 88) leave P. della Stazione, in the southern end of town, for: Florence (1hr., every hr., €5.05); Genoa (2½hr., €7.90); Rome (3hr., 12 per day, €16-24). To reach the **tourist office,** walk straight out of the train station and take a left onto P. V. Emanuele. (☎422 91; www.turismo.toscana.it. Open M-F 9am-7pm, Sa 9am-1:30pm.) To reach the Campo from the train station, take bus #3 (€0.85). **Postal Code:** 56100.

UMBRIA

Umbria, a land rich in natural beauty, is known as the "Green Heart of Italy." Christianity transformed Umbria's architecture along with its regional identity, turning it into a breeding ground for saints and religious movements. It was here that St. Francis of Assisi shamed the extravagant church with his humility.

ITALY

PERUGIA ☎075

With its gorgeous countryside, big-city vitality, and world-renowned chocolate, Perugia (pop. 160,000) gives its residents much to smile about. The city's most popular sights frame **Piazza IV Novembre.** In its center, the **Fontana Maggiore** is adorned with sculptures and bas-reliefs by Nicolà and Giovanni Pisano. At the end of the *piazza*, the imposing Gothic **Cattedrale di San Lorenzo,** also known the *duomo*, houses the purported wedding ring of the Virgin Mary. (Open M-Sa 9am-12:45pm and 4-5:15pm, Su 4-5:45pm.) The 13th-century **Palazzo dei Priori,** presiding over the *piazza*, contains the impressive **Galleria Nazionale dell'Umbria,** C. Vannucci 19, which displays magnificent 13th- and 14th-century religious works. (Open daily 8:30am-7:30pm. Ticket office closes at 6:30pm. Closed 1st M each month. €8.50, EU students €4.25.) Past Porta S. Pietro at the end of town, the **Basilica di San Pietro,** on Borao XX Guigo, has a beautiful medieval garden. The basilica's interior is covered with brilliant paintings and frescoes; an impeccably preserved Etruscan tomb lies underground. (Open daily 8am-noon and 3-6:30pm.) **Ostello della Gioventù/Centro Internazionale di Accoglienza per la Gioventù ❶,** V. Bontempi 13, offers clean rooms, a social setting, and panoramic views. From P. IV Novembre, keep to the right past the *duomo* and P. Danti into P. Piccinino, and onto V. Bontempi. (☎572 28 80; www.ostello.perugia.it. Linen €1.50. Lockout 9:30am-4pm. Curfew 1am, midnight in winter. Closed mid-Dec. to mid-Jan. Dorms €13. AmEx/MC/V.) Local favorite **Trattoria Dal Mi Cocco ❷,** C. Garibaldi 12, provides prompt service and an extensive fixed menu at a reasonable price. (*Menù* €13. Reservations recommended. Open Tu-Su 1-3pm and 8:30pm-midnight. MC/V.) Perugia is full of bakeries peddling local confections and chocolates. The famous **Perugina** store is at C. Vannucci 101. (Open M 2:30-7:45pm, Tu-Sa 9:30am-1:30pm and 2:30-7:45pm, Su 10:30am-1:30pm and 3:30-7:45pm.) The **COOP,** P. Matteotti 15, has groceries. (Open M-Sa 9am-8pm.) **Trains** leave Perugia FS in P. V. Veneto, Fontiveggio, for: Assisi (25min., every hr., €1.65); Florence (2½hr., 18 per day, €8); Rome (2½hr., 6 per day, €10) via Terontola or Foligno. From the station, take bus #6, 7, 9, 13d, or 15 to the central P. Italia (€0.90), then walk down C. Vannucci or V. Baglioni to P. IV Novembre and the **tourist office,** P. IV Novembre 3. (☎572 332. Open M-Sa 8:30am-1:30pm and 3:30-6:30pm, Su 9am-1pm.) **Postal Code:** 06100.

ITALY

ASSISI ☎075 81

Assisi (pop. 25,000) owes its serene atmosphere and renowned spirituality to the legacy of St. Francis, Italy's patron saint and the town's favorite son. The town's jewel is the 13th-century **Basilica di San Francesco.** The subdued art of the lower church celebrates St. Francis's modest lifestyle, while Giotto's renowned fresco cycle, the *Life of St. Francis*, on the walls of the upper church, pays tribute to the saint's consecration. (Lower basilica open daily 9am-6:45pm. Upper basilica open daily 8:30am-6:45pm. Modest dress code is strictly enforced.) The fortress **Rocca Maggiore** offers a breathtaking panoramic view of the town and countryside. (Open daily 10am-dusk. €2, students €1.50.) The pink-and-white **Basilica of Santa Chiara** houses the crucifix that is said to have spoken to St. Francis. (Open daily 6:30am-noon and 2-7pm.) **Camere Martini ❷,** V.S. Gregorio 6, has sunny rooms and a family atmosphere. (☎35 36; cameremartini@libero.it. Singles €24-26; doubles €38; triples €55; quads €62. Cash only.) **Ostello Fontemaggio ❷,** V. per L'Eremo delle Carceri 8, has a hostel, hotel, bungalows, campground, and restaurant. Take V. per L'Eremo from P. Matteotti about 1.5km. (☎36 36. Curfew 11pm. Camping €5.50; dorms €20; singles €35; doubles €52; triples €72.50; quads €96. Cash only.) Grab a personal pizza (€5-7) at **Pizzeria Otello ❶,** V. San Antonio 1. (Open daily noon-4pm and 7-10:30pm. AmEx/MC/V.) From the station near the Basilica Santa Maria degli Angeli, **trains** go to: Ancona (2hr., 8 per day, €9); Florence (2½hr., 13 per day, €9); Rome (2½hr., 14 per day, €9). **Buses** run from P. Unita D'Italia to Florence (2½hr.,

ON A WING AND A PRAYER

Father Pasquale Magro is a monk of the Franciscan order who has lived in the Convent of the Basilica di San Francesco for 13 years. He is also in charge of the historical research library Biblioteca del Sacroconvento in Assisi.

On his youth: My mother was a housewife and my father was a government worker. I was an altar boy from very young age. I wanted to become a pilot, an air pilot, but this was only a child's dream.

On becoming a monk: My brother had to become a priest but I had no intention. I don't know how or when I entered the convent. It was quite smooth, no shock, nothing. It was not possible to become a pilot in Malta.

On the monastic lifestyle: One has to control and guide his instincts, otherwise life becomes instinctive. Life is hard for everybody. You have to live courageously as a friar or nun. Life is not advantages. Life is advantages and disadvantages.

On the basilica: This is one of the greatest places of Christendom. It's the explosion of human spirit. There is one exhibition happening here of religious Christian images made of bombs from WWI. There is a dove made out of a hand bomb, which splinters into wings.

7am, €6.40) and Perugia (1½hr., 12 per day, €2.70). From P. Matteotti, follow V. del Torrione, bear left in P.S. Rufino, and take V.S. Rufino to **Piazza del Comune,** the town center and location of the **tourist office.** (☎25 34; www.assisi.umbria2000.it. Open M-Sa 8am-2pm and 3-6pm, Su 9am-1pm.) **Postal Code:** 06081.

ORVIETO ☎0763

Orvieto (pop. 25,000) perches on a volcanic plateau above the rolling farmlands of Umbria. Below the surface, caves and tunnels attest to the town's long history; Etruscans began burrowing into the hillside in the 7th century BC. **Underground City Excursions** offers a tour of the ancient Etruscan city beneath modern Orvieto. (☎34 48 91. Tours leave the tourist office daily 11am, 12:15, 4, 5:15pm. €5.50, students €3.50.) Six-hundred years of labor went into the construction of the **duomo,** whose spires, sculptures, and mosaics are the town's pride and joy. The **Capella della Madonna di San Brizio,** off the right transept, houses the dramatic apocalypse frescoes of Luca Signorelli, whose compositions inspired Michelangelo. (Modest dress required. *Duomo* open M-Sa 7:30am-12:45pm and 2:30-7pm, Su 2:30-6:45pm. *Capella* open Apr.-Sept. M-Sa 10am-12:45pm and 2:30-7:15pm, Su 2:30-6pm; Oct.-Mar. reduced hours. €3.) Walk up V. del Duomo to **Hotel Posta ❸**, V. Luca Signorelli 18, an old *palazzo* with antique decorations. (☎34 19 09. Singles €26-31, with bath €37; doubles €43/56. Cash only.) **Hostaria Nonnamelia ❷**, V. del Duomo 25, serves elegant dishes with unique, fresh flavors. (☎34 24 02. Pizza €6-7.50. *Primi* €5-7. *Secondi* €7-13. Open daily noon-3pm and 7-11pm. Cash only.) For a free tasting of *Orvieto Classico* and other wines, try **Cantina Freddano,** C. Cavour 5. (☎30 82 48. Bottles from €4. Open daily 9:30am-7:30pm.) **Trains** run hourly to Florence (2½hr., €9.90) and Rome (1½hr., €6.82). From the train station, take a shuttle to the **tourist office**, P. del Duomo 24. (☎34 17 72. Open M-F 8:15am-1:50pm and 4-7pm, Sa 10am-1pm and 4-7pm, Su 10am-1pm and 3-6pm.) **Postal Code:** 05018.

THE MARCHES (LE MARCHE)

In the Marches, green foothills separate the gray shores of the Adriatic from Apennine peaks and traditional hill towns from umbrella-laden beaches. Inland villages, easily accessible by train, rely on agriculture and preserve the region's historical legacy in the architectural remains of the Gauls and Romans.

URBINO

☎0722

With stone dwellings scattered along its steep city streets and a turreted palace ornamenting its skyline, Urbino (pop. 15,000) encompasses all that is classic Italy. The city's most remarkable monument is the Renaissance **Palazzo Ducale,** in P. Rinascimento. Stairs in the central courtyard lead to the former apartments of the duke, now home to the **Galleria Nazionale delle Marche.** Look for Raphael's *Portrait of a Lady* in **Room 25,** and don't miss the servants' tunnels. (☎32 26 25. Open M 8:30am-2pm, Tu-Su 8:30am-7:15pm. €4, EU students ages 18-25 €2.) Walk back across P. della Repubblica onto V. Raffaello to Raphael's birthplace, the **Casa Natale di Raffaello,** V. Raffaello 57, now a museum of period furniture, works by local masters, and the *Madonna col Bambino*, attributed to Raphael. (☎32 01 05. Open Mar.-Oct. M-Sa 9am-1pm and 3-7pm, Su 10am-1pm; Nov.-Feb. M-Sa 9am-2pm, Su 10am-1pm. €3.) Five doors down from Raphael's birthplace, **Pensione Fosca ❷**, V. Raffaello 67, has modest rooms and good prices. Call ahead for check-in time. (☎32 96 22. Singles €21; doubles €35; triples €45. Cash only.) **Hotel San Giovanni ❷,** V. Barocci 13, has basic but comfy rooms. (☎32 90 55. Closed July. Singles €25, with bath €35; doubles €38/55.) **Margherita** supermarket, V. Raffaello 37, stocks everything but produce. (☎32 97 71. Open M-Sa 7:30am-2pm and 4:30-8pm. Cash only.) Bucci **buses** (☎0721 32 401) from Borgo Mercatale to Rome (5hr., 4pm, €22). Blue SOGET buses (☎223 33) run from P. Matteotti and the train station to Pesaro (55min.; M-Sa 11 per day, Su 6 per day; €2.05). **Trains** go from Pesaro to Ancona (1hr., 55 per day, €3.10). From Borgo Mercatale, a short walk uphill on V.G. Mazzini leads to P. della Repubblica, the city center. The **tourist office,** V. Puccinotti 35, is opposite the palace. (☎26 13; iat.urbino@regione.marche.it. Maps available. Open M and Sa 9am-1pm, Tu-F 9am-1pm and 3-6pm.) **Postal Code:** 61029.

ANCONA

☎071

Ancona (pop. 100,000) is Italy's major transportation hub for those heading east. While a gorgeous vista of the harbor below is worth a look, Ancona has little else to recommend it. The P. del Duomo, atop Monte Guasco, a vigorous hike up a set of stairs, offers a view of the rooftops and waters below. Across the *piazza* is the **Cattedrale di San Ciriaco,** a marble church with its namesake under velvet in the basement. (☎52 688. Open summer M-Sa 8am-noon and 3-7pm; winter M-Sa 8am-noon and 3-6pm. Su hours vary.) From the train station, cross the *piazza*, turn left, take the first right, and make a sharp right behind the newsstand to reach **Ostello della Gioventù (HI) ❶**, V. Lamaticci 7. (☎/fax 42 257. HI members only. Lockout 11am-4:30pm. Dorms €15. Cash only.) Sparse rooms offer little more than an cheap place to sleep at **Pensione Euro ❷**, C. Mazzini 142, 2nd fl., off P. Cavour. (☎20 34 22. Singles €25; doubles €40; triples €50. Cash only.) **Di per Di** supermarket is at V. Matteotti 115. (Open M-W and F 8:15am-1:30pm and 5-7:35pm, Sa 8:15am-1pm and 5-7:40pm. Cash only.) **Ferries** leave Stazione Marittima for Croatia, Greece, and northern Italy. Adriatica (☎502 11 621; www.adriatica.it.), Jadrolinija (☎20 43 05; www.jadrolinija.tel.hr/jadrolinija), and SEM Maritime Co. (☎20 40 41; www.marittimamauro.it) run to Croatia (from €40). ANEK (☎207 23 46; www.anekitalia.com) ferries go to Patras, Greece (from €70). All lines accept AmEx/MC/V. Schedules vary; be sure to check at the station. **Trains** leave P. Rosselli for: Bologna (2½hr., 43 per day, €10); Milan (5hr., 24 per day, €19.37); Rome (3-4hr., 10 per day, €13.22); Venice (5hr., 4 per day, €22.20). Take bus #1/4 (€0.90) up C. Stamira to reach P. Cavour, the city center. The **tourist office** across from Stazione Marittima provides ferry info. (☎207 90 29. Open summer M 9am-7pm, Tu 11am-7pm, W-Su 10am-7pm.) **Postal Code:** 60100.

SOUTHERN ITALY

An introduction to *mezzogiorno* (Southern Italy) should begin in Campania, the cradle of the Bay of Naples and the Gulf of Salerno. The shadow of Mt. Vesuvius hides the ruins of Pompeii, lost to time and a river of lava, while the Amalfi Coast cuts a dramatic course down the Tyrrhenian shore. The region remains proud of its open-hearted populace, traditions, ruins, and relatively untouristed beaches.

NAPLES (NAPOLI) ☎081

Italy's third-largest city, Naples (pop. 1,000,000) is also its most chaotic—Neapolitans run red lights, drive the wrong way on one-way streets, order things not on the menu, and stand in the middle of busy streets finishing up conversations. The birthplace of pizza and modern-day home of tantalizing seafood, Naples will please even the pickiest gourmand. Once you submit to the quick heartbeat of Naples, every other place seems a bit slow in comparison.

TRANSPORTATION

Flights: Aeroporto Capodichino, V. Umberto Maddalena (NAP; ☎789 6259), northeast of the city. Connects to all major Italian and European cities. An **Alibus** (☎531 1706) departs P. Municipio and P. Garibaldi (20min., 6am-11:30pm, €3).

Trains: Ferrovie dello Stato (☎892 021) goes from Stazione Centrale to: **Brindisi** (5hr., 5 per day, €9.25); **Milan** (8hr., 13 per day, €50); **Rome** (2hr., 34 per day, €10). **Circumvesuviana** (☎772 2444) runs to **Herculaneum** (2 per hr., €1.70) and **Pompeii** (2 per hr., €2.30).

Ferries: Depart from **Molo Angioino** and **Molo Beverello,** at the base of P. Municipio. From P. Garibaldi, take tram #1; from P. Municipio, take the R2 bus. **Caremar,** Molo Beverello (☎551 3882), runs frequently to **Capri** and **Ischia** (both 1½hr., €5). **Tirrenia Lines,** Molo Angioino (☎199 12 31 199), goes to **Palermo, Cagliari,** and **Sardinia.** Schedules and prices vary; check *Qui Napoli* (free at the tourist office).

Public Transportation: UnicoNapoli tickets (€1 per 1½hr., full-day €3) are valid on **buses, metro, trains,** and **funiculars.**

Taxis: Free (☎551 5151) or **Napoli** (☎556 4444). Only take metered taxis, and ask about prices up front; even well-known companies try to get away with overcharging.

ORIENTATION AND PRACTICAL INFORMATION

The main train and bus terminals are in the immense **Piazza Garibaldi** on the east side of Naples. From P. Garibaldi, broad **Corso Umberto I** leads southwest to P. Bovi, from which V. de Pretis leads left to **Piazza Municipio,** the city center, as well as to **Piazza Trieste e Trento** and **Piazza Plebiscito.** Below P. Municipio lie the **Stazione Marittima** ferry ports. From P. Trieste e Trento, **Via Toledo** (a.k.a **Via Roma**) leads through the Spanish quarter to **Piazza Dante.** Make a right into the historic **Spaccanapoli** neighborhood, which follows **Via dei Tribunali** through the middle of town. While violent crime is rare in Naples, theft is fairly common, so exercise caution.

Tourist Offices: EPT (☎26 87 79), at Stazione Centrale. Helps with hotels and ferries. Grab **Qui Napoli,** a free monthly publication full of schedules and listings. Open M-Sa 8:30am-8pm, Su 8am-2pm. Another **branch** at Stazione Mergellina (☎761 21 02).

Consulates: Canada, V. Carducci 29 (☎40 13 38). **UK,** V. dei Mille 40 (☎423 89 11). **US,** P. della Repubblica (☎583 81 11, emergency 033 794 50 83), at the west end of Villa Comunale.

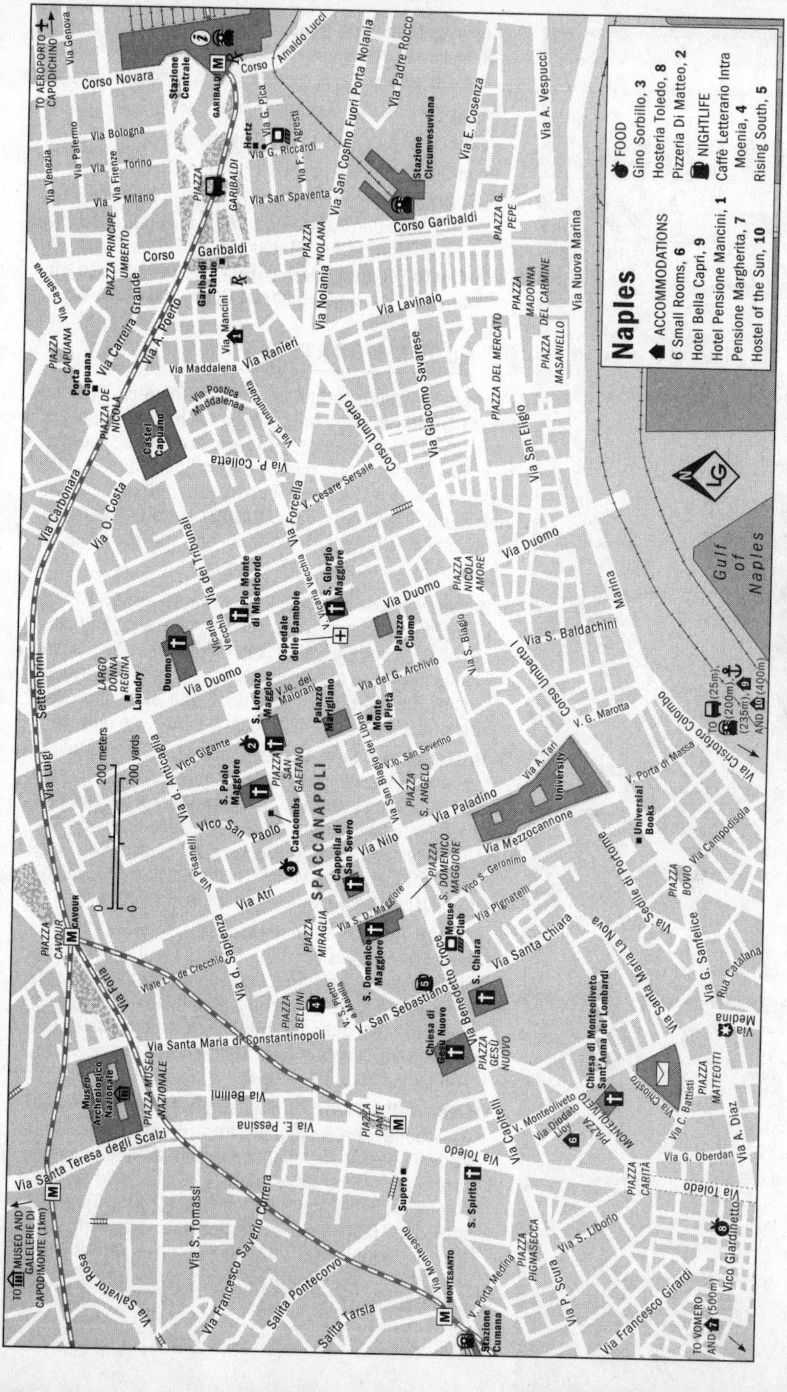

Naples
ACCOMMODATIONS
6 Small Rooms, 6
Hotel Bella Capri, 9
Hotel Pensione Mancini, 1
Pensione Margherita, 7
Hostel of the Sun, 10
FOOD
Gino Sorbillo, 3
Hosteria Toledo, 8
Pizzeria Di Matteo, 2
NIGHTLIFE
Caffè Letterario Intra Moenia, 4
Rising South, 5

ITALY

DIRT CHEAP

I should have left well before I discovered ants crawling up my arm in the morning. Stepping into the peeling, foul-smelling bathrooms, and realizing that they hadn't been cleaned for weeks, I should have left at once. In fact, it would have been better had I turned around as soon as I passed through swarms of mosquitoes in the lemon grove, ran into roosters squabbling by the front door, and noticed stray cats roaming in the yard. I probably should have never come at all after the gruff voice at the other end of the line demanded how I got the number.

But for some reason I wanted to give the place a chance. I couldn't just write it off because it was an illegal hostel. It was recommended by a worker at a great hostel in Naples, it was relatively inexpensive, and everyone spoke English. I realize in hindsight that just knowing its unregistered status should have been reason enough not to waste my time and money. Since I did go, however, and I did stay the night, I have a better understanding of what an illegal hostel really is. It's a place that doesn't pay taxes or contribute to the local economy, a place that doesn't adhere to health or sanitation standards, a place that exploits disoriented travelers for personal gain.

One night was enough for me to get out of there; I just hope others don't wait that long.

—Lauren Holmes

Currency Exchange: Thomas Cook, at the airport and in P. Municipio 70 (☎551 83 99). Open M-F 9:30am-1pm and 3-6:30pm.

Emergency: ☎113. **Ambulance:** ☎752 82 82.

Police: ☎113 or 794 11 11. English spoken.

Hospital: Cardarelli (☎747 28 59), on the R4 line.

Post Office: P. Matteotti (☎552 42 33), at V. Diaz on the R2 line. Unreliable *Fermo Posta.* Address mail to be held: First name, SURNAME, *In Fermo Posta,* P. Matteotti, Naples 80100, ITALY. Open M-F 8:15am-6pm, Sa 8:15am-noon. **Postal Code:** 80100.

ACCOMMODATIONS

Fantastic bargain lodgings do exist, especially near **Piazza Garibaldi,** but be cautious when choosing a room. Avoid hotels that solicit customers at the station, never give your passport until you've seen the room, agree on the price before unpacking, and be alert for hidden costs. The **ACISJF/Centro D'Ascolto,** at Stazione Centrale, helps women find rooms. (☎28 19 93. Open M-Tu and Th 3:30-6:30pm.)

Hostel Pensione Mancini, V. Mancini 33 (☎553 67 31; www.hostelpensionemancini.com), off the far end of P. Garibaldi from the train station. Friendly owners share their knowledge of Naples. Spacious, newly renovated rooms. Dorms €20; singles €35, with bath €45; doubles €50/60; triples €80; quads €90. Cash only. ❷

Hostel of the Sun, V. Melisurgo 15 (☎420 63 93; www.hostelnapoli.com). Take R2 bus, exit at V. de Pretis, cross the street to V. Melisurgo. Buzz #51. First-rate hostel with large rooms. Breakfast included. Laundry €3. Fast Internet €3 per hr. Dorms €20; singles €45, with bath €50; doubles €55/70; triples €80/90; quads €90/100. 10% *Let's Go* discount. AmEx/MC/V. ❷

6 Small Rooms, V. Diodato Lioy 18 (☎790 13 78; www.6smallrooms.com). up from P. Monteolovieto. No sign; look for the name on the call button. Friendly atmosphere and larger rooms than the name suggests. Call for dorms after 10pm the night before arrival; call anytime for private rooms. Dorms €20; doubles €55, with bath €65. Cash only. ❷

Hotel Bella Capri, V. Melisurgo 4 (☎55 29 494; www.bellacapri.it). Across from Hostel of the Sun. Perfect spot for spending the night before ferry departures. All rooms have bath, A/C, TV, and phone. Dorms available starting in summer 2006. Breakfast included. Dorms €22; singles €45-50, with bath €57-69; doubles €50-60/66-80; triples €66-84/80-100; quad €80-96/90-110. 10% *Let's Go* discount. AmEx/MC/V. ❷

Pensione Margherita, V. Cimarosa 29, 5th fl. (☎578 2852; pensione.margherita@tiscali.it), in the same building as the funicular station (go outside and around the corner to the right; buzz to enter). Large rooms share spotless baths; some have terraces. Curfew 1am. Closed Aug. 1-15. Singles €40; doubles €70; triples €95. Cash only. ❹

FOOD

If you ever doubted that Neapolitans invented pizza, Naples's *pizzerie* will take that doubt, beat it into a ball, throw it in the air, spin it on their collective finger, punch it down, and bury it with sauce and mozzarella. Nothing can compare to Neapolitan **seafood;** the **waterfront** offers a traditional Neapolitan fare and a culinary change of pace from the plethora of pizza. Some of the cheapest, most authentic options lie along **Via dei Tribunali** in the heart of Spaccanapoli.

Gino Sorbillo, V. dei Tribunali 32 (☎44 66 43; www.accademiadellapizza.it). The only *pizzeria* that boasts a grandfather who invented the *ripieno al forno* (calzone) and 21 pizza-making children in this generation alone. Peer inside the kitchen to see the original brick oven. *Margherita* €3. Open daily noon-3:30pm and 7-11:30pm. MC/V. ❶

Pizzeria Di Matteo, V. dei Tribunali 94 (☎45 52 62), near V. Duomo. The *marinara* is the best cheap bite (€2). Flavorful pies attracts pizza enthusiasts–put your name on the list and expect a short wait. Open M-Sa 9am-midnight. Cash only. ❶

Hosteria Toledo, Vicolo Giardinetto 78A (☎42 12 57), in the Spanish Quarter. Get ready for Neapolitan comfort food aplenty. The *gnocchi* (€6) is hearty enough to be a meal on its own. *Primi* €6-12. *Secondi* €5-10. Open daily 8pm-midnight. AmEx/MC/V. ❷

SIGHTS

MUSEO ARCHEOLOGICO NAZIONALE. Situated in a 16th-century *palazzo* and former barracks, one of the world's most important archaeological museums houses exquisite treasures from Pompeii and Herculaneum, from the personal collection of Charles Bourbon. The mezzanine contains a room filled with mosaics, most noticeably the Alexander Mosaic, which shows a young and fearless Alexander the Great routing the Persian army. A sporadically open **Egyptian Collection** quietly inhabits the museum's basement. Peeking out from a beautifully painted sarcophagus is the foot of a mummy. *(M: P. Cavour. Turn right from the station and walk 2 blocks. ☎44 01 66. Open M and W-Su 9am-7:30pm. €6.50, EU students €3.25.)*

MUSEO AND GALLERIE DI CAPODIMONTE. Housed in a royal *palazzo*, the museum resides inside a park filled with playful youngsters. In addition to its plush royal apartments, the palace houses the Italian National Picture Gallery. Among these incomparable works are Bellini's *Transfiguration*, Masaccio's *Crucifixion*, and Titian's *Danae*. *(Take bus #24, 110, M4, or M5 from the Archaeological Museum and exit at the gate to the park, on the right. The park has 2 entrances, Pta. Piccola and Pta. Grande. ☎749 91 11. Open Tu-Su 8:30am-7:30pm. €7.50, after 2pm €3.75.)*

PALAZZO REALE AND MASCHIO ANGIONO. The 17th-century Palazzo Reale contains opulent royal apartments, the **Museo di Palazzo Reale,** and a fantastic view from the terrace of the **Royal Chapel.** *(Take the R2 bus from P. Garibaldi to P. Trieste e Trento and walk around the palazzo to the entrance on P. Plebiscito. Open M-Tu and Th-Su 9am-7:30pm. €7.50, students €3.75.)* The **Biblioteca Nazionale** stores 1.5 million volumes, including the scrolls from the **Villa dei Papiri** in Herculaneum. The **Teatro San Carlo** is reputed to top the acoustics in Milan's La Scala. *(Theater entrance on P. Trieste e Trento. Open daily 9am-6:30pm. Tours €5, students €3.)* It's impossible to miss Mascio Angiono, a five-turreted landmark towering over the Bay of Naples. Its

A PROBLEM OF MOUNTAINS

olcanoes have fascinated Domi-ique di Salvo since she was a irl. Twenty-nine years ago, she raded her native Paris for the immering setting of Sicily's Mt. tna. When the volcano erupted n summer 2002, destroying her estaurant, di Salvo wasn't ready o give in.

G: How many people live on Mt. tna?

: Three. There are three of us vho live here at 2000m: my hus-band, my son, and me. Other peo-ple come only to work.

G: And you're not afraid?

: Not at all. This is not like Pompeii that has explosions. No, tna is not like Pompeii or Vesu-ius. Here, lava takes a long time o come down the mountain.

G: Your restaurant was lestroyed by an eruption ecently, is that correct?

: Yes, I said it was safe for peo-ple, but not for buildings. I am vorking in this restaurant while I ebuild mine, and when other res-aurants in the area have been lestroyed, the owners come to vork in mine. We help each other out when an eruption occurs.

G: What if Etna erupts again?

: There is always time to leave. Most people who die [here] do so rom heart problems or asthma. his happens to people who don't now that at 2000m, or 3000m, people don't feel that well. This is a problem of mountains, not tna.

most stunning feature is the triumphal entrance, with reliefs commemorating the arrival of Alphonse I of Aragon in 1443. *(P. Municipio. Take the R2 bus from P. Garibaldi or walk from anywhere in the historic center. ☎795 58 77. Open M-Sa 9am-7pm. €5.)*

VIRGIL'S TOMB. Anyone who studied Latin in high school may have at least a passing interest in seeing the poet's resting place at V. Salita della Grotta. Below the tomb is the entrance to the closed *Crypta Neapolitana*, a tunnel built during the reign of Augustus; the metro line of antiquity, it connected ancient Neapolis to Pozzuoli and Baia. Call ahead and arrange a translator to describe and explain the inscriptions, or just come for the amazing view. *(M: Mergellina. From the station, take 2 quick rights. Entrance between overpass and tunnel. ☎66 93 90. Guided tours upon request. Open daily 9am-1hr. before sunset. Free.)*

DUOMO. The main attraction of the 14th-century *duomo* is the **Capella del Tesoro di San Gennaro,** decorated with Baroque paintings. A 17th-century bronze grille protects the high altar, which possesses a reliquary containing the saint's head and two vials of his coagulated blood. According to legend, disaster will strike the city if the blood does not liquify on the celebration of his **festa** (3 times a year); miraculously, it always does. Behind the main altar of the church lies the saint's crypt, decorated with Renaissance carvings in marble. Visitors can also view the newly opened **excavation site.** *(Walk 3 blocks up V. Duomo from C. Umberto I or take bus #42 from P. Garibaldi. Open M-F 9am-noon and 4:30-7pm, Su 9am-noon. Free. Excavation site €3.)*

NIGHTLIFE

Piazza Vanvitelli in Vomero draws young people to relax and socialize. Take the funicular from V. Toledo or bus C28 from P. Vittoria. **Via Santa Maria La Nova** is another hot spot. Outdoor bars and cafes are a popular choice in **Piazza Bellini,** near P. Dante. **Caffè Letterario Intra Moenia,** P. Bellini 70, appeals to intellectuals by keeping books amid the wicker furniture. (Open daily 10am-2am. Cash only.) **Rising South,** V.S. Sebastiano 19, nearby P. Gesu Nuovo, does it all: *enoteca*, bar, cultural association, cinema. (Drinks around €4. Bar open daily Oct.-May, with special events in the summer. Cash only.) **ARCI-GAY/Lesbica** (☎552 88 15) has info on gay and lesbian club nights.

DAYTRIPS FROM NAPLES

HERCULANEUM. Herculaneum city is less excavated than Pompeii because it was buried much deeper and a modern city sits on top. One highlight is the **House of Deer.** (Open daily 8:30am-7:30pm. €10.) The **House of the Mosaic of Neptune and Anfitrite** is famous for its breathtaking **mosaic.** The city is 500m downhill from the *Ercolano* stop on the Circumvesuviana **train** from Naples (dir.: Sorrento; 20min.). Stop at the **tourist office,** V. IV Novembre 84 (☎081 788 12 43), for a free map.

POMPEII. On the morning of August 24, AD 79, a deadly cloud of volcanic ash from Mt. Vesuvius overtook the Roman city of Pompeii, catching the prosperous residents by surprise and engulfing the city in black clouds. Mere hours after the eruption, stately buildings, works of art, and human bodies were sealed in hardened casts of ash. These natural tombs would remain undisturbed until 1748 when excavations began to unearth a well-preserved picture of daily Roman life. The site hasn't changed much since then, and neither have the victims. Walk down V. della Marina to reach the colonnaded **Forum,** which was once the civic and religious center of the city. Exit the Forum through the upper end by the cafeteria, and head right on V. della Fortuna to reach the **House of the Faun,** where a bronze dancing faun and the spectacular Alexander Mosaic (today in the Museo Archeologico Nazionale) were found. Continue on V. della Fortuna and turn left on V. dei Vettii to reach the **House of the Vettii** and the most vivid frescoes in Pompeii. Backtrack on V. dei Vettii, cross V. della Fortuna to V. Storto, turn left on V. degli Augustali and take a quick right to reach a small brothel (the Lupenare). Prepare for a wait: the brothel remains the most popular spot in town even 2000 years later, although modern visitors come for the frescoes. V. dei Teatri, across the street, leads to the oldest standing **amphitheater** in the world (80 BC), which once held up to 12,000 spectators. To get to the **Villa of the Mysteries,** the complex's best-preserved villa, head west on V. della Fortuna, right on V. Consolare, and go up Porta Ercolano. (Site open daily Apr.-Oct. 8:30am-7:30pm; Nov.-Mar. 8:30am-5pm. €10.) Take the Circumvesuviana **train** (☎081 772 24 44) from Naples to the Pompei Scavi stop (dir.: Sorrento; 40min., 2 per hr., €2.30). To reach the **tourist office,** V. Sacra 1, walk right from the station and continue down the hill. (Open M-F 8am-3:30pm, Sa 8am-2pm.)

Pompeii's sites afford visitors few water fountains and little shade. Bring water, sunblock, and a parasol. Around 15 people per year die of heat-related illness at Pompeii. If you need medical attention, flag down a guide or call ☎113.

MOUNT VESUVIUS. You can peer into the only active volcano on mainland Europe at Mt. Vesuvius. Although it hasn't erupted since March 31, 1944 (scientists estimate that the volcano becomes active on average every 30 years), experts deem the trip relatively safe. Trasporti Vesuviani **buses** (buy ticket onboard; €7.60 round-trip) run from the Ercolano Circumvesuviana station to the crater.

AMALFI COAST ☎089

Tucked between the jagged rocks of the Sorrentine Peninsula and the azure waters of the Adriatic, the Amalfi Coast has much to recommend it. Its local population is spirited and lively, and its monuments reflect the area's history as a maritime powerhouse. Still, the region's natural beauty remains its main attraction.

TRANSPORTATION. The coast is accessible from Naples, Salerno, Sorrento, and the islands by ferry and by blue SITA buses. **Trains** run directly to Salerno from Naples (45min., 40 per day, €5-11) and Rome (2½-3hr., 22 per day, €22-33). Trains also run to Sorrento from Naples (1hr., 39 per day, €3.20). **Buses** link Paestum and Salerno (1½hr., 12 per day, €2.50). From Salerno, Travelmar (☎87 29 50) runs **fer-**

ries to Amalfi (35min., 6 per day, €4) and Positano (1¼hr., 6 per day, €6). From Sorrento, Linee Marittime Partenopee (☎081 807 18 12) ferries (40min., 5 per day, €7.50) and **hydrofoils** (20min., 19 per day, €10.50) run to Capri.

AMALFI AND ATRANI. Breathtaking natural beauty surrounds the narrow streets and historic monuments of Amalfi. Visitors crowd P. del Duomo to admire the elegant 9th-century **Duomo di Sant'Andrea** and the nearby **Fontana di Sant'Andrea,** a marble nude with water trickling from her nipples. **A'Scalinatella ❶**, P. Umberto 12, runs dorms, private rooms, and camping all over Amalfi and Atrani. (☎87 19 30; www.hostelscalinatella.com. Tent sites €5 per person. Dorms €10-21; doubles €30-60, with bath €50-83. Cash only.) Amalfi's many *paninoteche* (sandwich shops) are perfect for a tight budget. The tiny beachside village of Atrani is a 15min. walk from Amalfi. The **Path of the Gods,** a spectacular 4hr. **hike,** follows the coast from Bomerano to Positano and offers spectacular views. The 2hr. hike to Ravello via Scalla also makes for a pleasant trip. **Postal Code:** 84011.

RAVELLO. Atop 330m cliffs, Ravello has long been a haven for celebrity artists. The Moorish cloister and gardens of **Villa Rufolo,** off P. del Duomo, inspired Boccaccio's *Decameron* and Wagner's *Parsifal.* (Open daily 9am-8pm. €4.) The villa puts on a summer concert series in the gardens; tickets are sold at the Ravello Festival box office, V. Roma 10-12 (☎85 84 22; www.ravellofestival.com). The small road to the right leads to the impressive **Villa Cimbrone,** whose gardens hide temples and statue-filled grottoes, as well as magnificent views. (Open daily 9am-7:30pm. €4.50.) **Hotel Villa Amore ❹**, V. dei Fusco 4, has 12 tidy rooms and a garden overlooking the cliffs and the sea. Follow V. San Francesco out of P. del Duomo toward Villa Cimbrone, and take a left onto V. dei Fusco. (☎/fax 85 71 35. Breakfast included. Singles €48-56; doubles €80-90. MC/V.) **Postal Code:** 84010.

ITALY

SORRENTO. The most touristed town on the peninsula, lively Sorrento makes a convenient base for daytrips around the Bay of Naples. The **tourist office,** L. de Maio 35, is off P. Tasso, in the C. dei Forestieri compound. (☎081 807 40 33. Open M-Sa Apr.-Sept. 8:45am-7:45pm; Oct.-Mar. 8:30am-2pm and 4-6:15pm.) Halfway to the **beach** at **Punta del Capo** (bus A), **Hotel Elios ❸**, V. Capo 33, has clean rooms. (☎081 878 18 12. Open Apr.-Oct. Singles €30-40; doubles €60-65.) Savory menus abound. After dark, a crowd gathers for drinks in the rooftop lemon grove above **The English Inn,** C. Italia 56. (Open daily 9am-1am.) **Postal Code:** 80067.

SALERNO. While industrial Salerno is best used as a base for daytrips to **Paestum,** the town is home to most of the peninsula's nightlife. Paestum is the site of preserved **Doric temples,** including the **Temples of Ceres** and **Poseidon,** as well as a **museum** of artifacts taken from the sites. (Temples open daily 9am-7:30pm. Museum open daily 9am-6:30pm. Both closed the 1st and 3rd M of each month. Low season reduced hours. Both sights €6.50, EU students €3.25.) To reach the clean **Ostello Ave Gratia Plena ❶**, V. Canali, take C.V. Emanuele to the old district where it becomes V. dei Mercanti; head right onto V. Canali. (☎23 47 76. Curfew 12:30am. Dorms €14; doubles €34. MC/V.) **Postal Code:** 84100.

BAY OF NAPLES ISLANDS

CAPRI ☎081

Glittery Capri has been a hot spot for the rich and famous for thousands of years. There are two towns on the island—**Capri,** near the ports, and **Anacapri,** higher up the mountain. Visitors flock to the renowned **Blue Grotto,** a sea cave where waters shimmer with neon-blue light. (Short boat ride from Marina Grande €8. Open M-

Sa 9am-1pm and 3:30-7pm, Su 9am-12:30pm.) In the summer, crowds and prices increase; the best times to visit are in late spring and early fall. Buses departing from V. Roma make the trip up the mountain to Anacapri every 15min. until 1:40am. Away from the throngs flitting among Capri's pricey boutiques, Anacapri is home to budget hotels, spectacular vistas, and quiet mountain paths. Upstairs from P. Vittoria in Anacapri, **Villa San Michele** sports lush gardens, ancient sculptures, and a remarkable view. (Open daily 9am-6pm. €5.) Take the chairlift up **Monte Solaro** from P. Vittoria to see the Apennines looming ahead and the Alabrian mountains sitting to your right. (Open Mar.-Oct. daily 9:30am-4:45pm. Round-trip €6.50.) For those who prefer cliff to coastline, Capri's **hiking** trails are worth sampling; try the short, steep hike to the ruins of Emperor Tiberius's **Villa Jovis,** the largest of his 12 Capri villas. The view from the **Cappella di Santa Maria del Soccorso,** part of the villa, is unrivaled. (1½hr. Open daily 9am-6pm.)

Bussola di Hermes ❸, V. Traversa La Vigna 14, in Anacapri, has a friendly proprietor and is one of the best deals on the island. Call from P. Vittoria in Anacapri for pickup. (☎838 20 10; www.bussolahermes.com. Dorms €27-30; doubles €70-110. AmEx/MC/V.) For more convenient access to the beach and the center of Capri, stay at **Vuotto Antonio ❸**, V. Campo di Teste 2. Take V.V. Emanuele out of P. Umberto, a left onto V. Camerelle, a right onto V. Cerio, and left onto V. Campo di Teste. Housed in "Villa Margherita," simple, airy rooms are decorated in antiques and majolica tiles. (☎837 02 30. Doubles €60-90. Cash only.) The **supermarket,** V.G. Orlandi 299, in Anacapri, is well stocked. (Open M-Sa 8:30am-1:30pm and 5-8:30pm, Su 8:30am-noon.) In the evenings, Italians, dressed-to-kill, come out for Capri's nightlife; bars around **Piazza Umberto** in Capri proper keep the music pumping late, while cheaper Anacapri draws a younger crowd.

Caremar (☎837 07 00) **ferries** run from Marina Grande to Naples (1¼hr., 3 per day, €6) and Sorrento (25min., 4 per day, €6). LineaJet (☎837 08 19) runs **hydrofoils** to Naples (40-50min., 11 per day, €12) and Sorrento (25min., 15 per day, €10). Ferries and hydrofoils to Ischia and Amalfi run much less frequently; check with the lines at Marina Grande for information. The Capri **tourist office** (☎837 06 34) sits at the end of Marina Grande; in Anacapri, it's at V. Orlandi 59 (☎837 15 24), to the right of the P. Vittoria bus stop. (Both open June-Sept. M-Sa 9am-1pm and 2:30-7:40pm; Oct.-May reduced hours.) **Postal Codes:** 80073 (Capri); 80021 (Anacapri).

ISCHIA

☎081

Augustus fell in love with Capri's fantastic beauty in 29 BC, but later swapped the island for its more fertile neighbor. Ischia (pop. 55,000), just across the bay, offers sandy beaches, hot springs, ruins, forests, vineyards, and lemon groves. SEPSA **buses** #1, CD, and CS (every 15-30min.; €1.20, 1-day pass €4) depart from the ferry landing and follow the coast in a circular route, stopping at: **Ischia Porto,** a port formed by the crater of an extinct volcano; **Casamicciola Terme,** with a crowded beach and legendary thermal waters; **Lacco Ameno,** the oldest Greek settlement in the western Mediterranean; and popular **Forio,** home to lively bars. The **Mortella Gardens,** V. Calese 39, feature over 800 rare and exotic plants, manmade streams, and views of Ischia. (Open Tu, Th, Sa-Su 9am-7pm. €10.) The **Ostello "Il Gabbiano" (HI) ❷**, Str. Statale Forio-Panza 162, is accessible by buses #1, CS, and CD. The hostel has a pool and beach access. (☎90 94 22. Curfew 2am. Open Apr.-Sept. Dorms €16.) **Emiddio ❸**, V. Porto 30, a family-run restaurant, features locally caught fish. (*Primi* €5-7. *Secondi* €10-16. Cover €1. Open daily noon-3pm and 7pm-midnight. AmEx/MC/V.) Caremar **ferries** (☎98 48 18) arrive from Naples (1½hr., 8 per day, €6). Alilauro (☎99 18 88) runs **hydrofoils** to Sorrento (1 per day, €13). The **tourist office** is on V. Iasolino. (☎507 42 31. Open M-Sa 9am-2pm and 3-8pm.) **Postal Code:** 80077.

SICILY (SICILIA)

Ancient Greeks lauded the golden island of Sicily as the second home of the gods; now, eager tourists seek it as the home of *The Godfather*. While the *Cosa Nostra* remains a presence in Sicily, it makes up only a small part of the varied culture.

TRANSPORTATION

From southern Italy, take a **train** to Reggio di Calabria, then a Meridiano **ferry** (40min., M-Sa 12 per day, €1.50) or Ferrovie Statale **hydrofoil** (25min., 14 per day, €3) to Messina, Sicily's transport hub. Tirrenia ferries (☎091 60 21 111) also go to Palermo from Sardinia (14hr., every Sa, €30-60) and Naples (10hr., 1 per day, €35-80). **SAIS buses** (☎090 77 19 14) serve destinations throughout the island. **Trains** head to Messina directly from Naples (7hr., 11 per day, €22) and Rome (9hr., 17 per day, €42), and continue west to Palermo (3½hr., 14 per day, €11).

PALERMO ☎091

From twisting streets lined with ancient ruins to the shrinking shadow of organized crime, gritty Palermo (pop. 680,000) is a city whose recent history provides texture to a rich cultural heritage. To get to the magnificent **Teatro Massimo,** where the climactic opera scene of *The Godfather: Part III* was filmed, walk up V. Maqueda past Quattro Canti at the intersection with V. Vittorio Emanuele. (Open for tours Tu-Su 10am-3:30pm. Closed during rehearsals. €3.) From Quattro Canti, a left on V. Vittorio Emanuele will take you to the **Palazzo dei Normanni** and the **Cappella Palatina,** full of golden mosaics. (Open M-Sa 8:30am-noon and 2-5pm, Su 8:30am-12:30pm. M and F-Su entire palace €6, chapel only €4; Tu-Th €4/2.) At the haunting **Cappuccini Catacombs,** 8000 corpses line the tunnels in various states of decay: some are nothing but skeletons, others appear to be heavy sleepers. Take bus #109 or 318 from Stazione Centrale to P. Indipendenza and transfer to bus #327. (Open daily 9am-noon and 3-5pm. €1.50.) Homey **Hotel Regina ❷,** C. Vittorio Emanuele 316, is off V. Maqueda. Triple-check your reservation before arriving. (☎611 42 16; fax 612 21 69. Singles €23, with bath €37; doubles €42/50; triples with bath €72. AmEx/MC/V.) The area around **Teatro Massimo** has a variety of cheap restaurants and bars. **Trains** leave Stazione Centrale, in P. Giulio Cesare, at V. Roma and V. Maqueda, for Florence (15hr., 11 per day, €58) and Rome (11hr.; 9 per day; €45, €70 with bunk). All four **bus** lines run from V. Balsamo, next to the train station. After purchasing tickets, ask the ticket agent exactly from where your bus will depart. Pick up a metro and bus map from an **AMAT** or **metro** information booth. Buses #101 and 102 (€1 for 2hr.) circle the downtown area. To reach the **tourist office,** P. Castelnuovo 34, in the Banco di Sicilia building, take a bus to P. Politeama, at the end of V. Maqueda. (☎605 81 11; www.palermotourism.com. Open M-F 8:30am-2pm and 2:30-6pm.) **Postal Code:** 90100.

SYRACUSE (SIRACUSA) ☎0931

Never having regained the glory of its Grecian golden days, the modern city of Syracuse (pop. 130,000) takes pride in its extraordinary ruins and in the architectural beauty of its island Ortigia. Syracuse's one-time role as a Mediterranean superpower is still evident in the **Archaeological Park,** on the north side of town. To reach the 2nd-century **Roman theater,** as well as the park, follow C. Gelone until it meets V. Teocrito, then walk left down V. Augusto. (Open daily 9am-2hr. before sunset; low season 9am-3pm. €6.) Across from the tourist office on V.S. Giovanni are the **Catacomba di San Giovanni,** 20,000 now-empty tombs carved into the remains of a Greek aqueduct. (☎64 694. Open Tu-Su 9am-12:30pm and 2:30-5:30pm. €3.50.)

ITALY

More ruins lie over the Ponte Umbertino on **Ortigia,** the serene island on which the Greeks first landed. The ruined **Temple of Apollo** has a few columns standing, but those at the **Temple of Diana** are more impressive. For those who prefer tans to temples, take bus #21 or 22 to **Fontane Bianche. Hotel Centrale ❷,** C. Umberto I 141, has rooms with gorgeous views. (☎605 28. Singles €17; doubles €28-30, with bath €35-50; triples with bath €65.) For cheap food, try **Via Savoia** and **Via Cavour,** or the **open-air market** in Ortigia, on V. Trento, off P. Pancali. (Open M-Sa 8am-1pm.) **Trains** leave V. Francesco Crispi for Messina (3hr., 9 per day, €9) and Rome (10-13hr., 11 per day, €38). Interbus **buses,** V. Trieste 40 (☎667 10), leave for Palermo (3hr., 3 per day, €13.40). To get from the train station to the **tourist office,** V.S. Sebastiano 45, take V.F. Crispi to C. Gelone, turn right on V. Teocrito, left on V.S. Sebastiano; it's on the left. (☎67 710. Open M-F 8:30am-1:30pm and 3-6:30pm, Sa 9am-1pm and 3:30-6:30pm, Su 9am-1pm. Low season reduced hours.) **Postal Code:** 96100.

TAORMINA ☎0942

Legend has it that Neptune wrecked a boat off the eastern coast of Sicily in the 8th century BC, and the sole survivor founded Taormina. As historians tell it, the Carthaginians founded Tauromenium at the turn of the 4th century BC only to have it wrested away by the Greek tyrant Dionysius. Taormina's Greek roots are apparent in its best-preserved treasure, the **Greek theater.** (Open daily May-Aug. 9am-1hr. before sunset; Apr. and Sept. 9am-6:30pm; Oct. and Mar. 9am-5pm; Nov.-Feb. 9am-4pm. €4.15.) The 5000-seat theater offers views of Mt. Etna and hosts the annual **Taormina Arte** summer festival. (Box office at C. Umberto 19. www.taormina-arte.com.) The 13th-century **duomo,** rebuilt during the Renaissance, takes center stage. (Hours vary; inquire at Museo Sacra next door.) For a place to stay the night, go from the intersection of C. Umberto and V.L. Pirandello and take V.C. Patrizio to V. Cappuccini. When it forks, veer right onto V. Fontana Vecchia and follow the signs to **Taormina's Odyssey Youth Hostel ❷,** which offers clean rooms and a social atmosphere that makes it worth the hike. (☎24 533. Breakfast included. Dorms €15-18; doubles €45-50. Cash only.) **SMA** supermarket is at V. Apollo Arcageta 21, at the end of C. Umberto, near the post office. (Open M-Sa 8:30am-1pm and 4:30-8:30pm.) **Trains** run from: Messina (40min., 22 per day, €3); Palermo (4hr., 5 per day, €13); Syracuse (2hr., 11 per day, €10). The **tourist office** is in the courtyard of Palazzo Corvaja, off C. Umberto across from P. V. Emanuele. (☎23 243. Open M-Sa 9am-2pm and 4-7pm.) **Postal Code:** 98039.

AEOLIAN ISLANDS (ISOLE EOLIE) ☎090

Sparkling seas, smooth beaches, and fiery volcanoes testify to the area's beauty.

TRANSPORTATION. The *archipelago* lies off the Sicilian coast, north of **Milazzo,** the principal and least expensive departure point. Hop off a **train** from Palermo (3hr., 12 per day, €9.20) and onto an orange AST **bus** to get to the port (10min., 2 per hr., €1). Siremar (☎928 32 42) and Navigazione Generale Italiana (NGI; ☎928 40 91) **ferries** depart for Lipari (2hr., €6.20); Stromboli (6hr., €10); Vulcano (1½hr., €6.30). Ticket offices on V. dei Mille in Milazzo. Ferries run less frequently from the Molo Beverello port in Naples.

LIPARI. Lipari, the largest and most developed of the islands, is renowned for its beaches and stunning hillside views. To reach the beaches of **Spiaggia Bianca** and **Porticello,** take the Lipari-Cavedi **bus** a few kilometers north to Canneto. Lipari also offers a rebuilt medieval **castello** on the site of an ancient Greek acropolis. The fortress shares its hill with an **archaeological park,** the **San Bartolo church,** and the **Museo Archeologico Eoliano.** (Museum open daily June-Aug. 9am-1:30pm and 4-7pm; Sept.-May reduced hours. €4.50.) **Casa Vittorio ❷,** Vico Sparviero 15, is on a

ITALY

quiet street in the center of town. Rooms range from singles to a five-person penthouse. (☎981 15 23. Rooms €15-40. AmEx/MC/V.) **Da Gilberto e Vera ❶**, V. Marina Garibaldi 22-24, is known for its sandwiches. (☎981 27 56. *Panini* €4. Open daily Mar.-Oct. 7am-4am; Nov.-Feb. 7am-2am. AmEx/MC/V.) Shop at **UPIM** supermarket, C.V. Emanuele 212. (Open M-Sa 8am-10pm.) The **tourist office,** C.V. Emanuele 202, is near the ferry dock. (☎988 00 95. Open July-Aug. M-F 8am-2pm and 4:30-9:30pm, Sa 8am-2pm; Sept.-June M-F 8am-2pm and 4:30-7:30pm.) **Postal Code:** 98050.

VULCANO. Black beaches, bubbling seas, and natural mud spas attract visitors from around the world to Vulcano. A steep 1hr. **hike** to the inactive **Gran Cratere** (Grand Crater) snakes between the volcano's noxious yellow fumaroles. On a clear day, you can see the other islands from the top. The allegedly therapeutic **Laghetto di Fanghi** (mud pool) is just up V. Provinciale to the right from the port; this natural spa's odor is impossible to miss. If you would prefer not to bathe in sulfuric radioactive mud, step gingerly into the scalding waters of the **acquacalda,** where underwater volcanic outlets make the sea bubble like a jacuzzi, or visit the black sands and clear waters of **Sabbie Nere** (follow the signs off V. Ponente). To get to Vulcano, take the **hydrofoil** from the port at nearby Lipari (10min., 11 per day, €2.50). For more info, check the **tourist office,** V. Provinciale 41. (☎985 20 28. Open daily Aug. 8am-1:30pm and 3-5pm.) For **private rooms** *(affittacamere)*, call ☎985 21 42. The Lipari tourist office also has information on Vulcano. **Postal Code:** 98050.

STROMBOLI. If you find luscious beaches and hot springs tame, visit Stromboli's active **volcano,** which spews cascades of lava and molten rock about every 10min. **Hiking** the volcano on your own is **illegal** and **dangerous,** but **Magmatrek** offers tours, which also should be taken at your own risk. The group once ran excursions to the craters, but new laws prohibit tours from going any higher than 450m. This still provides a close-up view of the eruptions—the most exciting way to see the volcano. Bring sturdy shoes, a flashlight, snacks, water, and warm clothes; don't wear contact lenses, as the wind sweeps ash everywhere. (☎/fax 986 57 68. Tours depart from V.V. Emanuele. Helmets provided. €22.) From the main road, follow the side street across from St. Bartholomew's church to reach **Casa del Sole ❶**, on V. Cincotta, the best value in town. Large rooms face a shared terrace. (☎/fax 98 60 17. Open Mar.-Oct. Dorms €13-24; doubles €30-50. Prices vary by season.) Siremar (☎98 60 16) runs **ferries** and **hydrofoils** from Milazzo to Stromboli, and rents boats. From July to September, you won't find a room without a reservation; your best bet may be one of the *affittacamere*. **Postal Code:** 98050.

ITALY

SARDINIA (SARDEGNA)

Sardinian legend says that when God finished making the world, He had a handful of dirt left. He took the dirt, threw it into the Mediterranean, and stepped on it, creating the island of Sardinia and some of the world's most spectacular landscapes.

TRANSPORTATION

Tirrenia **ferries** (☎081 317 29 99; www.tirrenia.it) run to Olbia from Civitavecchia, just north of Rome (4-8hr., 1-2 per day, €20-45), and Genoa (10¼-13¼hr., 1 per day, from €21). They also chug to Cagliari from: Civitavecchia (14½-16¾hr., 1 per day, from €25); Naples (16hr., 1-2 per week, from €27); Palermo (13½hr., 1 per week, from €21). **Trains** run from Cagliari to Olbia (4hr., 1 per day, €13) via Oristano (1½hr., 16 per day, €4.55) and to Sassari (4hr., 2 per day, €12.10). From Sassari, trains run to Alghero (50min., 13 per day, €1.50). PANI **buses** connect Cagliari to Oristano (1½hr., 4 per day, €6) and Sassari (3hr., 7 per day, €13-14).

CAGLIARI

☎070

Cagliari combines the energy of a modern Italian city with the rural atmosphere of the rest of the island. Its Roman ruins, medieval towers, and cobblestone streets contrast with the tree-lined streets and sweeping beaches downtown. Climb Largo Carlo Felice to reach the city's **duomo,** P. Palazzo 4. Gold mosaics top each of its entryways. (Open M-F 8am-12:30pm and 4:30-8pm, Su 8am-1pm and 4-8pm.) The 2nd-century **Roman amphitheater** comes alive during the **arts festival** in July and August. If you prefer to sun-worship, take city bus P, PQ, or PF to **Il Poetto** beach (20min., €0.77), famous for its white sand until the government dumped a coarse brown variety on top to prevent erosion; the clear waters are beautiful regardless. **Albergo Palmas ❸,** V. Sardegna 14, is the town's best budget option, with clean rooms and shared bath. Cross V. Roma, turn right; take the first left on Largo Carlo Felice, and right onto V. Sardegna. (☎65 16 79. Singles €25; doubles €35-40. AmEx/MC/V.) The **tourist office** is in P. Matteotti. (☎66 92 55. Open M-Sa 8:30am-1:30pm; low season reduced hours.) **Postal Code:** 09100.

ALGHERO

☎079

Vineyards, ruins, and horseback rides are a short trip away from Alghero's parks and medieval streets. Reach the **Grotte di Nettuno,** a 70-million-year-old, stalactite-filled cavern in Capo Caccia, by bus (1hr., 3 per day, round-trip €1.80) or boat (2½hr.; 3-8 per day; round-trip €12, includes tour). Visitors descend the 632 steps between massive cliffs. (Open daily Apr.-Sept. 9am-7pm; Oct. 10am-4pm; Nov.-Mar. 9am-1pm. €10.) Take bus AF from the port to Fertilia to reach **Hostal del'Alguer (HI) ❷,** V. Parenzo 79. Staff offer bike rental, bar, pool table, and Internet. (☎93 20 39. HI members only. Breakfast included. Dinner €10. 4- to 6-bed dorms €16; 2-bed family rooms €18-25.) Two kilometers away from Alghero toward Fertilia, **La Mariposa ❶** campgrounds, V. Lido 22, offer a restaurant, bar, bike rentals, diving excursions, and beach access. (☎95 03 60; www.lamariposa.it. Mar.-Oct. tent sites €5-12, €7-10.50 per extra person; Apr.-June tents and cars free. 4-person bungalows €44-75. AmEx/MC/V.) The **tourist office,** P. Porta Terra 9, is to the right of the bus stop. (☎97 90 54; www.infoalghero.it. Open M-Sa 8am-8pm.) **Postal Code:** 07041.

ORISTANO AND THE SINIS PENINSULA

☎0783

The town of Oristano is an excellent base for excursions to the Sinis Peninsula. From the train station, follow V. Vittorio Veneto to P. Mariano, then take V. Mazzini to P. Roma to the town center. Rent a moped or car to explore the tranquil beaches, stark white cliffs, and ancient ruins on the Sinis Peninsula. At the tip, 17km west of Oristano, lie the ruins of the ancient Phoenician port of **Tharros.** To get there, take the ARST bus to San Giovanni di Sinis (dir.: Is Arutas; 40min., 5 per day, €1.45). Slightly to the north off the road to Cuglieri is **S'Archittu,** where people leap from a 15m limestone arch into the waters of a rocky inlet. ARST **buses** go to S'Archittu (30min., 8 per day, €1.45). The secluded white sands of **Is Arutas** are well worth the trip. The ARST bus to Is Arutas runs only during July and August (50min., 5 per day, €1.45). The **Piccolo Hotel ❸,** V. Martignano 19, is on a quiet side street in the historic center. All rooms have bath; some have TV and balcony. (☎71 500. Singles €32; doubles €53. Cash only.) **SISA** supermarket is on V. Amiscora 26. (Open M-Sa 8am-8pm. MC/V.) The **tourist office,** V. Ciutadella de Minorca 8, has maps and information on local festivals. (☎/fax 70 621. Open daily 9am-noon and 4:30-7:30pm.) **Postal Code:** 09170.

LATVIA (LATVIJA)

At the Baltic crossroads, Latvia has been caught for hundreds of years in international political struggles. The country has been conquered and reconquered so many times that the year 2006 will only be Latvia's 37th year of independence—ever. National pride, however, abounds, from patriotically renamed streets to a rediscovery of native holidays predating the Christian invasions. Rīga, Latvia's only city, lures international investors, while the rest of the country is a provincial expanse of green hills, tall birches and pines, dairy pastures, and quiet towns.

DISCOVER LATVIA: SUGGESTED ITINERARIES

THREE DAYS Settle into **Rīga** (p. 692) to enjoy stunning **Art Nouveau** architecture, **cafe culture**, and the best **music and performing arts** scene in the Baltics. Take a daytrip to lavish **Rundāle Palace.**

ONE WEEK After four days in **Rīga,** head to **Cēsis** (3 days; p. 696) to enjoy **Cēsis Castle** and the wilds of **Gaujas Valley National Park.**

ESSENTIALS

FACTS AND FIGURES

Official Name: Republic of Latvia.

Capital: Rīga.

Major Cities: Daugavpils, Rēzekne.

Population: 2,300,000 (58% Latvian, 30% Russian, 4% Belarussian, 3% Polish, 3% Ukrainian, 2% Other).

Land Area: 63,589 sq. km.

Time Zone: GMT +2.

Language: Latvian.

Religions: Lutheran (55%), Roman Catholic (25%), Russian Orthodox (9%), Jewish (0.5%).

LATVIA

WHEN TO GO

Latvia is wet year-round, with cold, snowy winters, and short, rainy summers. Tourism peaks in July and August; if you'd prefer not to experience central Rīga in the company of throngs of British stag parties, late spring or early fall is the best time to visit. Much of the coast is delightfully untouristed even in summer.

DOCUMENTS AND FORMALITIES

EMBASSIES AND CONSULATES. Embassies of other countries in Latvia are in **Rīga** (p. 692). Latvia's embassies abroad include: **Australia,** 2 Mackennel St., East Ivanhoe, Victoria 3079; P.O. Box 23 Kew, VIC 3101 (☎61 9499 6920); **Canada,** 350 Sparks St., Ste. 1200, Ottawa, ON K1R 7S8 (☎613-238-6014); **Ireland,** "On a Clearday," Ballyedmonduff Rd., Kilternan, County Dublin (☎353 1 295 41 82); **UK,** 45 Nottingham Pl., London W1M 3FE (☎020 7312 0040); **US,** 4325 17th St. NW, Washington, D.C. 20011 (☎202-726-8213; www.latvia-usa.org).

VISA AND ENTRY INFORMATION. Citizens of Australia, Canada, New Zealand, the UK, and the US do not need a visa for stays of up to 90 days. If you are staying longer, you will need a temporary residency permit. For special visas and residency permits, consult The Foreigners' Service Centre of the Citizenship and Migration Board, Alunàna 1, Rīga, Latvia (☎721 9656; aad@pmlp.gov.lv).

ENTRANCE REQUIREMENTS

Passport: Required for all travelers.

Visa: Not required for stays under 90 days for citizens of Australia, Canada, Ireland, New Zealand, the UK, and the US.

Letter of Invitation: Not required for citizens of Australia, Canada, Ireland, New Zealand, the UK, and the US.

Inoculations: None required. Recommended up-to-date on DTaP (diphtheria, tetanus, and pertussis), Hepatitis A, Hepatitis B, MMR (measles, mumps, and rubella), Polio booster, and Typhoid.

Work Permit: Required for all foreigners planning to work in Latvia.

Driving Permit: Required for all those planning to drive in Latvia.

TOURIST SERVICES AND MONEY

TOURIST OFFICES. Look for the green "i" marking official **tourist offices,** which are rather scarce. In Rīga, employees of such establishments will speak fluent English, but elsewhere, they may not. Private tourist offices such as **Patricia** (p. 693) are much more helpful.

MONEY. The Latvian currency unit is the **Lat** (1Ls=100 santîmi). **Inflation** averages around 2% per year. There are many MC/V **ATMs** in Rīga, and at least one or two in larger towns. Larger businesses, restaurants, and hotels catering to Westerners accept **MasterCard** and **Visa. Traveler's checks** are more difficult to use, but both AmEx and Thomas Cook checks can be converted in Rīga. It's often difficult to exchange non-Baltic currencies other than US dollars or euro.

LATI (LS)		
	AUS$1 = 0.43LS	1LS = AUS$2.31
	CDN$1 = 0.47LS	1LS = CDN$2.13
	EUR€1 = 0.70LS	1LS = EUR€1.43
	NZ$1 = 0.40LS	1LS = NZ$2.51
	UK£1 = 1.03LS	1LS = UK£0.97
	US$1 = 0.57LS	1LS = US$1.76

HEALTH AND SAFETY

Latvia was hotlisted after outbreaks of incurable varieties of tuberculosis, though none have been reported since 2000. As a precaution, drink bottled water or boil tap water before drinking. **Medical facilities** do not meet Western standards. **Pharmacies** carry tampons, condoms, and bandages. **Restrooms** are marked with an upward-pointing triangle for women, downward for men.

Foreigners in Rīga may be targets for petty crime. **Pickpocketing** is a problem, especially in crowded areas. At night, beware of drunken crowds around bars. Both men and women should avoid walking alone at night. If you feel threatened, *"Ej prom"* (EY prawm) means "go away"; *"Lasies prom"* (LAH-see-oos PRAWM) says it more offensively; and *"Lasies lapās"* (LAH-see-oos LAH-pahs; "go to the leaves") is even ruder. You are more likely to find help in English from your **consulate** than from the police. **Women** may be verbally hassled, especially if traveling alone, but there is generally no physical threat. **Minorities** in Latvia are rare; they receive stares but generally experience little discrimination. **Homosexuality** is legal, but public displays may result in violence. Women walk down the street holding hands, but this is strictly a sign of friendship. Expect less tolerance outside Rīga. Call the Latvian Gay and Lesbian Hotline at ☎959 2229.

EMERGENCY	**Police:** ☎02. **Ambulance:** ☎03. **Fire:** ☎01.

TRANSPORTATION

BY PLANE. Airlines flying to Latvia use the Rīga airport (RIX). **Air Baltic, SAS, Finnair, Lufthansa,** and others make the hop to Rīga from their hubs.

BY TRAIN, BUS, AND FERRY. Trains and long-distance buses link Latvia to the major Eastern European capitals. Trains are cheap and efficient, but stations aren't well marked, so make sure to have a map. The commuter rail system renders the entire country a suburb of Rīga. Domestic buses are quicker than trains, but beware of the standing-room-only long-distance jaunt. Ferries go to Kiel and Lübeck, Germany and Stockholm, Sweden, but are slow and expensive.

BY CAR. Road conditions in Latvia are improving after years of deterioration. For more info, consult the **Latvian Road Administration** (www.lad.lv). Taxi stands in front of hotels charge higher rates. Hitchhiking is common, but drivers may ask for a fee comparable to bus fare. *Let's Go* does not recommend hitchhiking.

KEEPING IN TOUCH

PHONE CODES	**Country code:** 371. **International dialing prefix:** 00. For more information on how to place international calls, see inside back cover.

TELEPHONE AND INTERNET. Pay phones take **cards** (2, 3, or 5Ls denominations), sold at post offices, telephone offices, kiosks, and state stores. To call abroad from an analog phone, dial 1, then 00, then the country code. If it's digital, dial 00, then the country code. Phone offices and *Rīga in Your Pocket* have the latest updates on the phone system. International access codes include **AT&T Direct** (☎800 2 288) and **MCI WorldPhone** (☎800 8888). Internet is readily available in Rīga but rarer elsewhere; it generally costs 0.5Ls per hour.

Rīga's phone code is ☎2 for all 6-digit numbers; there is no phone code for 7-digit numbers. **Info:** ☎800 80 08. **Latvian operator:** ☎116. **International operator:** ☎115. **Directory services:** ☎118, 722 22 22, or 777 07 77.

MAIL. Ask for *gaisa pastu* to send by **airmail.** The rate for a letter to Europe is 0.30Ls, to anywhere else 0.40Ls; for a postcard 0.20/0.30Ls. Mail can be received general delivery through **Poste Restante.** Address envelopes: First name LAST NAME, POSTE RESTANTE, post office address, postal code, City, LATVIA.

LANGUAGE. Influenced by German, Russian, Estonian, and Swedish, **Latvian** is one of two languages in the Baltic language group. Life, however, is bilingual. **Russian** is widespread in Rīga; it is still spoken in the countryside but its popularity is waning. Many young Latvians study **English;** the older set knows some **German.**

ACCOMMODATIONS AND CAMPING

LATVIA	❶	❷	❸	❹	❺
ACCOMMODATIONS	under 8Ls	8-15Ls	15-20Ls	20-25Ls	over 25Ls

There is one HI **hostel** in Rīga and a scattering of hostels along the coast. Beware the raucous European parties who invade such hostels, especially on summer weekends. Contact the **Latvian Youth Hostel Association,** Aldaru 8, Rīga LV-1050 (☎921 8560; www.hostellinglatvia.com), for more info. In summer, **college dormitories** are often the cheapest option. Rīga's array of **hotels** satisfy any budget. Most small towns outside the capital have only one hotel (if any) in the budget range; expect to pay 3-15Ls per night. **Camping** isn't very popular. Campgrounds exist in the countryside, but camping beyond marked areas is prohibited.

FOOD AND DRINK

LATVIA	❶	❷	❸	❹	❺
FOOD	under 2Ls	2-4Ls	4-6Ls	6-7Ls	over 7Ls

Latvian food is heavy, starchy, and—not coincidentally—delicious. Tasty specialties include *maizes zupa* (soup made from cornbread, currants, and cream), and the warming *Rīgas* (or *Melnais*) *balzams,* a black liquor. Dark rye bread is a staple. Try *speķa rauši,* a warm pastry, or *biezpienmaize,* bread with sweet curds. Regional Latvian beers are great, particularly *Porteris* from the Aldaris brewery.

HOLIDAYS AND FESTIVALS

Holidays: New Year's Day (Jan. 1); Good Friday (Apr. 14); Easter Holiday (Apr. 16); Labor Day (May 1); Ligo Day (June 23); St. John's Day (June 24); Independence Day (Nov. 18); Boxing Day (Dec. 26); New Year's Eve (Dec. 31).

Festivals: Gadatirgus is an annual festival of arts and crafts, held the first weekend in June. Midsummer celebrations (June 23-24) involve strewing grass around the house and feasting in the countryside. In July, the Rīga Summer Festival presents chamber and classical music around the city. The ARSENALS film festival hits Rīga in September.

BEYOND TOURISM

American Field Service (AFS), 71 W. 23rd St., 17th fl., New York, NY 10010 USA (☎212-807-8686; www.afs.org). Homestay exchange programs for high school students in Eastern Europe, including Latvia. Community service programs for young adults 18+. Teaching programs for current and retired teachers. Financial aid available.

The Baltic Times (www.balticitimes.com). English-language newspaper with classified employment ads.

RĪGA ☎8(2)

Rīga is the cosmopolitan center of Latvia's cultural and economic life, and boasts an interesting mix of Russian and Latvian influences. The city's calendar is filled with music, theater, and opera festivals, and visitors can enjoy the city's spectacular Art Nouveau architecture any time of year. Soviet Realist sculptures still dot the streets between museums and medieval churches.

TRANSPORTATION

Flights: Lidosta Rīga (RIX; ☎720 70 09; www.riga-airport.com), 8km southwest of Vecrīga. Take bus #22 from 13 Janvara Iela (30min., 0.20-0.25Ls). **Air Baltic** (☎720 77 77; www.airbaltic.com) flies cheaply to many European cities.

Trains: Centrālā Stacija (Central Station), Stacijas laukums (☎723 31 13), next to the bus station south of the Old Town. International tickets are sold at counters 1-6 and 24; destinations include: **Moscow, Russia** (18hr., 2 per day, 10.60Ls); **St. Petersburg, Russia** (14hr., 1 per day, 9Ls); **Vilnius, Lithuania** (8hr., 2 per day on odd-numbered days, 10-14Ls).

Buses: Autoosta, Prāgas 1 (☎900 00 09; www.autoosta.lv), 100m from the train station, across the canal from the Central Market. To: **Kaunas, Lithuania** (5-6hr., 2 per day, 8Ls); **Minsk, Belarus** (12hr., 1 per day, 12Ls); **Tallinn, Estonia** (4-6hr., 8 per day, 5.50Ls); **Vilnius, Lithuania** (5hr., 4-6 per day, 7Ls). **Ecolines** (☎721 45 12; http://ecolines.lv), in the bus station, goes to **Prague, Czech Republic** (25½hr., 1 per week).

ORIENTATION AND PRACTICAL INFORMATION

The city is divided in half by **Brīvības bulvāris,** which leads from the outskirts to the **Freedom Monument** in the center, becomes **Kaļķu iela,** and passes through **Vecrīga** (Old Rīga). To reach Vecrīga from the train station, turn left on **Marijas iela** and then right on any of the small streets beyond the canal.

Tourist Office: Rātslaukums 6 (☎703 43 77; www.rigatourism.com), in the town square, next to the House of the Blackheads. Sells maps and provides advice and brochures, including the free *Rīga This Week*. Open daily 9am-7pm; low season 10am-6pm.

Embassies and Consulates: Australia, Alberta iela 13 (☎733 63 83; acr@latnet.lv). Open Tu 10am-noon and Th 3-5pm. **Canada,** Baznīcas 20/22. (☎781 39 45; riga@dfait-maeci.qc.ca). Open Tu and Th 10am-1pm. **Ireland,** Brīvības bul. 54. (☎702 52 59; fax 702 52 60). Entrance on Blaumana. Open M-Tu and Th-F 10am-noon. **UK,** Alunāna iela 5 (☎777 47 00; www.britain.lv). Open M-F 9:30am-noon. **US,** Raiņa bul. 7 (☎703 62 00; www.usembassy.lv). Open M-Tu and Th 9-11:30am.

Currency Exchange: At any of the **Valutos Maiņa** kiosks. **Unibanka,** Pils iela 23, gives MC/V cash advances and cashes both **AmEx** and **Thomas Cook traveler's checks** without commission. Open M-F 9am-5pm.

24hr. Pharmacy: Vecpilsetas Aptieka, Audeju 20 (☎721 33 40).

Internet Access: Elik, Kaļķu iela 11 (☎722 70 79; www.elikkafe.lv), in the center of Vecrīga; branch at Čaka iela 26 (☎728 4506). 0.50Ls per hr., 4Ls per day. Open 24hr.

Post Office: Stacijas laukumā 1 (☎701 88 04; www.pasts.lv/en), near the train station. *Poste Restante* at window #9. Open M-F 7am-8pm, Sa 8am-6pm, Su 8am-4pm. Another Branch at Brīvības bul. 19. Address mail to be held: First name SURNAME, *POSTE RESTANTE,* Stacijas laukumā 1, Rīga, LV-1050 LATVIA. **Postal Code:** LV-1050.

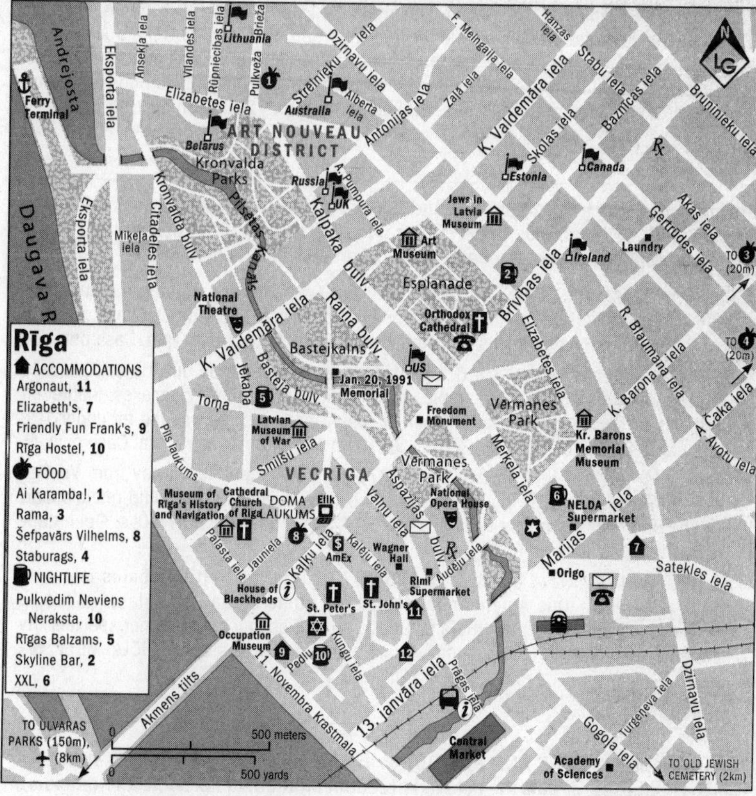

ACCOMMODATIONS

Make reservations well in advance during the high season. **Patricia,** Elizabetes iela 22 (☎728 48 68; patricia@parks.lv), arranges homestays from 22Ls; apartments 40-60Ls. (Open M-F 9am-6pm, Sa-Su 11am-4pm.)

Rīga Hostel, Mārstalu 12 (☎988 9915; www.riga-hostel.com). Upstairs of the 'Foxy' strip club, Rīga Hostel has the cheapest beds in Old Town in clean, well-decorated rooms with fresh linen. Friendly English-speaking staff will answer any question and ensure that your stay is enjoyable. Free Internet, and a bright common area. Airport pickup or drop off 4Ls. Dorms 6-17Ls; doubles 20Ls. Cash only. ❶

Argonaut, Kalēju 50 (☎614 7214; www.argonauthostel.com). Mysteriously, this hostel is also located above a strip club. Key-card door access to each room ensures security. The dorms are slightly crowded, with mosquitoes in the summer, but staff are friendly and informative. Free Internet. Prices fluctuate. 4- to 12-bed dorms from 8Ls. MC/V. ❷

Elizabeth's, Elizabetes iela 101 (☎670 5476; info@youthhostel.lv). Walk north along Marijas and turn left onto Elizabetes. New, wooden bunk beds and freshly painted rooms make for a quiet, comfortable stay close to the train station and Old Town. Common room and free Internet. 14-bed dorm 8Ls, 8-bed 10Ls, 6-bed 12Ls. Cash only. ❷

Friendly Fun Frank's, 11 Novembra krastmala 29 (☎599 0612; www.franks.lv). From the bus/train stations, walk toward the river and turn right onto Novembra krastmala. Continue walking and look for the large peach building with a small koala beside the buzzer. Spacious dorms, a large common room, and nightly outings to pubs and clubs in Rīga. 1 free beer when you arrive. 12-bed dorms from 12Ls. Cash only. ❷

FOOD

For midnight snackers, 24hr. food and liquor stores are at Marijas 5 *(Nelda)* and Brīvības bul. 68. **Centrālais Tirgus** (Central Market), behind the bus station, is the largest market in Europe. (Open m and Su 8am-4pm, Tu-Sa 8am-5pm.)

Rama, K. Barona iela 56 (☎727 24 90). Between Gertrudes and Stabu iela. Eat well for about 1Ls at this Hare-Krishna-run cafeteria, which dishes out hearty Indian-style vegetarian fare and donates profits to feed the poor. Open M-Sa 11am-7pm. Cash only. ❶

Šefpavārs Vilhelms, Škuņu iela 6. Look for the large chef statue outside this pancake house that offers meat, potato, apple, banana, cheese, and plain pancakes. Slather on jam or sour cream, grab a glass of milk or yogurt, and you'll be well fed for under 1Ls. Open M-Th 9am-10pm, F 10am-11pm, Sa 10am-11pm, Su 10am-10pm. Cash only. ❶

Staburags, A. Čaka iela 55 (☎729 97 87). Follow A. Čaka iela away from Vecrīga until it intersects with Stabu iela. Authentic Latvian cuisine served amid rustic decor. Try the unprocessed house beer (0.70Ls per 0.5L). Entrees 1.80-7.30Ls. Open daily noon-midnight. Cash only. ❷

Ai Karamba!, Pulkveza Brieza 2 (☎733 4672). Turn right off Elizabetes iela onto Pulkveza Brieza. This American-themed diner offers all-day breakfast, including omelettes (0.99-2.85Ls) and BLTs (0.99Ls), as well as lunch and dinner specials. Try the fresh mint leaf tea (0.65Ls) after a hard night out. Entrees 1.90-2.85Ls. MC/V. ❷

SIGHTS

FREEDOM MONUMENT AND ENVIRONS. In the center of the winding streets of Vecrīga (Old Rīga) stands the beloved Freedom Monument (Brīvības Piemineklis), affectionately known as "Milda." *(At the corner of Raiņa bul. and Brīvības bul.)* Continuing along Kaļķu iela toward the river, you'll see one of the few Soviet monuments not torn down: the **Latvian Riflemen Monument** (Latviešu Strēlnieku Laukums), honoring Lenin's famous bodyguards. Rising behind the statues are the black walls of the **Occupation Museum** (Okupācijas muzejs), Strēlnieku laukums 1, where the initial Soviet occupation is vividly depicted. *(Open May-Sept. daily 11am-6pm; Oct.-Apr. Tu-Su 11am-5pm. Donations accepted.)* Just beyond the museum stands the **House of the Blackheads** (Melngalvju nams) Rātslaukums 7. Built in 1344 and destroyed by the Nazis and Soviets, the unusual but magnificent building was reconstructed in honor of Rīga's 800th birthday. The structure houses a museum and an assembly hall and occasionally hosts concerts. *(Open Tu-Su 10am-5pm. 1Ls, students 0.50Ls.)*

ELSEWHERE IN VECRĪGA. Follow Kaļķu iela from the Freedom Monument and turn right on Škūņu iela to reach the cobblestone **Dome Square** (Doma laukums), and the **Cathedral Church of Rīga** (Doma baznīca). The organ boasts over 6700 pipes. *(Open May-Oct. Tu-F 11am-4pm, Sa 10am-2pm. 0.50Ls, students 0.30Ls.)* Next to the cathedral is the **Museum of Rīga's History and Navigation** (Rīgas Vēstures un Kugnie-cības Muzejs), Palasta iela 4. Established in 1773, this collection helped rekindle Latvia's cultural heritage after Soviet efforts to suppress it. *(Open W-Su May-Sept. 10am-5pm; Oct.-Apr. 11am-5pm. 1.20Ls, students 0.40Ls. Tours 3/2Ls.)* From the top of the 123m spire of **St. Peter's Church** (Sv. Pētera baznīca), you can see the city and the Baltic Sea. *(On Skāmu iela, off Kaļķu iela. Open in summer Tu-Su 10am-6pm; low season 10am-5pm. Ticket office closes for lunch. Church free. Tower 2Ls, students 1Ls.)* The magnificent Neoclassical **State Museum of Art** (Valsts mākslas muzejs), Kr. Valdemāra iela 10a, has 18th- to 20th-century Latvian art and occasional concerts. *(Near the corner of Elizabetes iela and Kr. Valdemāra iela. Open Apr.-Oct. M, W, F-Su 11am-5pm, Th 11am-7pm; Oct.-Apr. M and W-Su 11am-5pm. 0.50Ls, students 0.40Ls.)* The newer areas of Rīga host elaborate **Art Nouveau** Jugendstil architecture; most is on Alberta iela, Elizabetes iela, and Strēlnieku laukums.

BASTEJKALNS. Rīga's central park, surrounded by the old city moat (Pīlsētas kanāls), houses ruins of the old city walls. Across and around the canal, five red slabs of stone stand as **memorials** to the events of January 20, 1991, when Soviet special forces stormed the Interior Ministry on Raiņa bul. At the northern end of Bastejkalns, on K. Valdemāra iela, sits the **National Theater,** where Latvia first declared its independence on November 18, 1918. *(Open daily 10am-7pm.)*

ENTERTAINMENT AND NIGHTLIFE

The night scene is centered in **Vecrīga.** **Skyline Bar,** Elizabetes iela 55, on the 26th floor of the Reval Hotel Latvija, has the best view in the city. (Open M-Th and Su 3pm-2am, F-Sa 3pm-3am. MC/V.) If you prefer a more relaxed, alternative scene, spend the evening with great DJs at **Pulkvedim Neviens Neraksta,** Peldu 26/28. The dark upstairs bar and dance floor contrasts the colorful basement lounge. (Open M-Th noon-3am, F-Sa noon-5am, Su 4pm-1am. MC/V.) Try *balzams*, Latvia's national liquor—a mysterious herb and berry brew—at **Rigas Balzams,** Torņa iela 4, in Vecrīga, 100m east of the Powder Tower. (Open M-Th and Su 11am-midnight, F-Sa 11am-1am). The gay bar and club **XXL,** A. Kalniņa iela 4, is off K. Barona iela; buzz to be let in. (www.xxl.lv. Cover Tu-Sa 1-5Ls. Open daily 6pm-6am.

DAYTRIPS FROM RĪGA

JŪRMALA. Boardwalks and sun-bleached sand cover the narrow spit of Jūrmala. Visitors, including the Soviet elite, have been drawn to its warm waters since the 19th century. The coastal towns between **Bulduri** and **Dubulti** are popular for sunning and swimming, but Jūrmala's social center is **Majori,** where masses flock to the crowded beach or wander along **Jomas iela,** a pedestrian street lined with cafes and

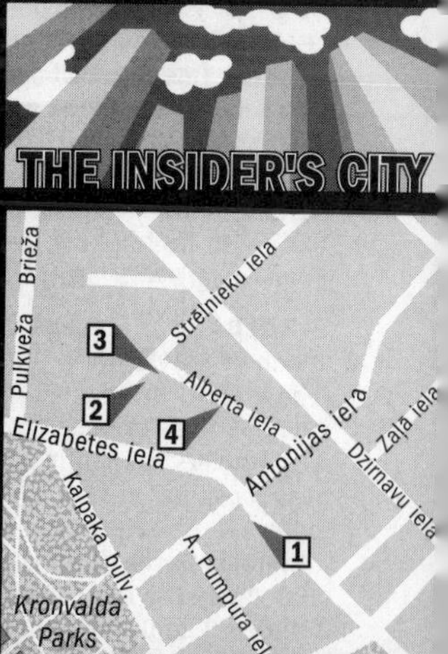

ART NOUVEAU RĪGA

Look up while you wander the streets of Rīga to appreciate the city's remarkable architecture. About 40% of the downtown is built in the unique Art Nouveau style, with an international mix of influences. For a short tour of some of the most impressive buildings, take this walk:

1. From K. Valdemāra iela, turn left on Elizabetes iela to reach 10b, on your left. Admire the work from across the street.
2. Turn right on Strēlnieku to take in the blue-and-white masterpiece at 4b. The 1905 building is now the home of the Stockholm School of Economics.
3. Next door is the massive, cream-colored corner edifice at Alberta iela 13. Recently repaired, it has pronounced details and pointed turrets.
4. Turn on Alberta iela. Numbers 8, 6, 4, 2, and 2a, in various states of repair, showcase a colorful and impressive catalogue of Art Nouveau balconies and brickwork.

shops. **Bicycles** are a popular mode of transportation; rent one along the beach (1.50Ls per hr.). **Sue's Asia ❹**, Jomas 74, offers Chinese, Indian, and Thai cuisine, serving the same fine fare that scored Rīga's branch a spot on *Conde Naste*'s list of the 100 best restaurants in the world. (☎775 59 00. Entrees 3-10Ls. Open M-Th noon-11pm, F-Su noon-midnight.) The **commuter rail** runs from Rīga to Jūrmala (30min., every 30min., 0.50Ls). **Public buses** (0.18Ls) and **microbuses** (0.20-0.30Ls) string together Jūrmala's towns. The **tourist office,** Jomas iela 42, arranges accommodations (from 6Ls) with no booking fee. (☎877 642 76; www.jurmala.lv. Open daily in summer 10am-7pm; low season 10am-5pm.) **Postal Code:** LV-2105.

SIGULDA. The Knights of the Sword, the Germanic crusaders who Christianized much of Latvia in the 13th century, staked their base at Segewald—now Sigulda. The knights are gone, but the Gauja National Park Administration has planted its headquarters in this picturesque town 50km from Rīga. The area offers great biking, bobsledding, bungee-jumping, horseback riding, and hot-air ballooning, as well as skiing in winter. **Makars Tourism Agency,** Peldu 1, arranges all kinds of outdoor excursions. (☎924 49 48; www.makars.lv.) The restored brick fortifications of **Turaida Castle** (Turaidas Pils), Turaidas iela 10, across the river from Sigulda and 2km down the road, are visible throughout the Gauja Valley and from surrounding hilltops. Climb the staircase in the main tower for a view of the region. (Tower open daily 8am-9pm.) Take Turaidas iela 10-15min. back down the hill to reach the famous **caves** of Sigulda. Inscriptions and coats of arms from as early as the 16th century cover the chiseled mouth of **Gutman's Cave** (Gūtmaņa ala). On a ridge to the right of Gaujas iela, on the near side of the gorge, is the **Sigulda Dome** palace, behind which lie the ruins of the 13th-century **Sigulda Castle** (Siguldas pilsdrupas).

Pilsmuižas Restorāns ❸, Pils iela 16, in Pilseta Dome, serves generous portions of Latvian fare. (Entrees 3-12Ls. Open daily noon-2am. MC/V.) For a cheap bite, try **Trīs Draugi ❶**, Pils iela 9, a Soviet-style cafeteria. (Open daily 8am-10pm. MC/V.) **Trains** run from Rīga on the Rīga-Lugaži commuter rail line (1hr., 9 per day, 0.71Ls). From the station, walk up Raiņa iela, passing the bus station, to the town center. **Buses** run from Rīga hourly (1Ls). Continue on as Raiņa iela turns into Gaujas iela, which, after the Gaujas Bridge, becomes the steep Turaidas iela and passes Turaida Castle. Bus #12 runs directly to Turaida Castle (1 per hr., 0.20Ls). From the station, Raiņa iela runs 1km north to the **Gauja National Park Visitor Centre,** Baznicas 3, which offers the essential map of the park for 1.40Ls. (☎797 13 45; www.gnp.gov.lv. Open M 9am-5:30pm, Tu-Su 9am-7pm.) **Postal Code:** LV-2150.

CĒSIS. Sprawling medieval ruins and Cēsu, the local brew, make Cēsis the quintessential Latvian town. Crusading Germans came to town in 1209 and built the famous **Cēsis Castle.** The new castle's **tower** offers stunning views of the Gauja Valley. Explore the old castle's **ruins** with a hard-hat and lantern, or check out the fallen Lenin at the garden entrance. (☎412 26 15. Open mid-May to Sept. Tu-Su 10am-6pm; Nov. to mid-May W-Su 10am-5pm. 1Ls.) Cēsis is served by infrequent suburban **trains** from Rīga via Sigulda (1½-2hr., 2 per day, about 1Ls). **Buses** are more convenient (2hr., 1-2 per hr., 1.30Ls). The **tourist office,** Pils laukums 1, across from the castle, offers free maps and arranges **private rooms** in the Cēsis region for a 0.50Ls fee, or elsewhere in Latvia for 1Ls. (☎412 18 15; www.cesis.lv. Open mid-May to mid-Sept. M-F 9am-6pm, Sa-Su 10am-5pm.) **Postal Code:** LV-4101.

LIECHTENSTEIN

A tourist brochure once amusingly mislabeled the already tiny 160-square-kilometer country an even tinier 160 square meters. That's just about how much most tourists see of the world's only German-speaking monarchy, even though its cliff-hugging roads are gateways to unspoiled mountains with great biking and hiking.

ESSENTIALS

FACTS AND FIGURES

Capital: Vaduz.

Major Villages: Malbun, Schaan.

Population: 33,000.

Form of Government: Hereditary constitutional monarchy.

Land Area: 160 sq. km.

Major Exports: Dental products.

Language: German (see p. 1060).

Religions: Roman Catholic (80%), Protestant (7.4%), other (12.6%).

DOCUMENTS AND FORMALITIES. Citizens of Australia, Canada, New Zealand, the UK, and the US do not need visas for stays of up to 90 days.

TRANSPORTATION. To enter Liechtenstein, catch a **bus** from Buchs or Sargans in Switzerland, or from Feldkirch, just across the Austrian border (20-30min., 3.60SFr). Liechtenstein has no rail system. Instead, its cheap, efficient **PostBus** system links all 11 villages (short trips 2.40SFr, long trips 3.60SFr; students half-price; SwissPass valid). A **one-week bus ticket** (10SFr, students 5SFr) covers all of Liechtenstein and buses to Swiss and Austrian border towns.

EMERGENCY. **Police:** ☎117. **Ambulance:** ☎144. **Fire:** ☎118.

MONEY. Liechtenstein uses the **Swiss Franc (SFr).** Go to Switzerland to exchange currency at reasonable rates. Conversion rates for the franc are listed on p. 1016.

BEYOND TOURISM. Travelers wishing to volunteer in Liechtenstein should visit the local tourist office to see if there are any opportunities available in one of the country's many forests. Travelers should also consider contacting the **Special Olympics,** Im Bühl 101 9498 Planken Fürstentum (423 768 60 77; brigitte.marxer@adon.li) to see if there are volunteer positions available.

VADUZ AND LOWER LIECHTENSTEIN ☎00423

As the national capital, Vaduz (pop. 5000) attracts the most visitors of any village in Liechtenstein. Above town, the 12th-century **Schloß Vaduz** (Vaduz Castle) is home to Hans Adam II, Prince of Liechtenstein. After transferring day-to-day running of the country to his son Alois in 2004, he invited the entire country to a garden party to celebrate. Its interior is off-limits, but visitors can hike up to the castle for a closer look and for a view of Vaduz. The 20min. trail begins down the street from the tourist office, heading away from the post office, and is lined with information about the country. Facing the tourist office is the **Kunstmuseum Liechtenstein,** Städtle 32, home to yearly rotating art exhibits; 2006 will feature a "Princely Exhibition," with paintings from the Biedermeier period. (☎235 0300; www.kunstmuseum.li. Open Tu-W, F-Su 10am-5pm, Th 10am-8pm. 8SFr, students 5SFr.)

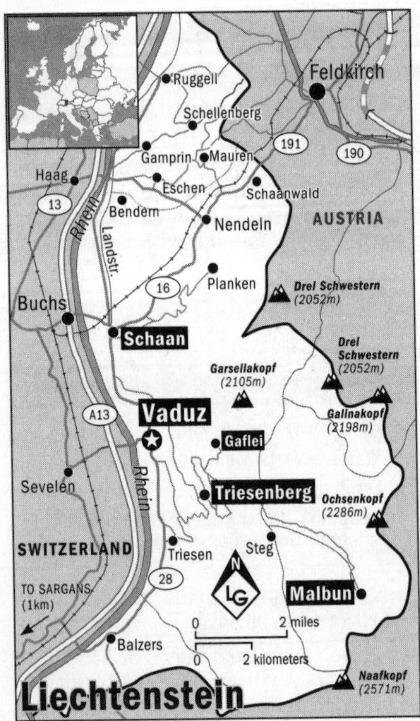

Nearby **Schaan** houses Liechtenstein's sole **Jugendherberge (HI) ❷**, Untere Rüttig. 6. From Vaduz, take bus #1 to Mühleholz, walk toward the intersection with traffic lights, and turn left on Marianumstr. Walk 5min. and follow the signs to this spotless pink hostel on the edge of a farm. (☎232 5022. Breakfast included. Laundry 6SFr. Internet 1SFr per 5min. Reception 7:30-10am and 5-10pm. Open Mar.-Oct. Dorms 36.50SFr; singles 61.50SFr; doubles 93SFr. 6SFr HI discount. AmEx/DC/MC/V.) Just around the corner from the Jugendherberge lies **Restaurant Forum ❷**, Gapetschstr. 87, which serves generous portions of pasta (11-15SFr) and a daily menu (*Tagesmenü;* 15.50SFr), which includes a soup, salad, and main entree. (☎232 5710. Open M-Th 9:30am-11pm, F 9:30am-midnight. Cash only.) In Vaduz, the country's 20- and 30-somethings pack the candlelit outdoor patio of **B'eat ❷**, Städtle 3, where they enjoy good food by day and even better drinks by night. The lunch *Tagesmenü* (18SFr, vegetarian 15SFr) includes a main dish, soup or salad, and dessert. (☎232 8484. Open M-Th 10:30am-1am, F-Sa until 3am, Su noon-1am. Cash only.) There is a **Migros** supermarket at Aulestr. 20 in Vaduz. (Open M-F 8am-1pm and 1:30-6:30pm, Sa-Su 8am-6pm.) Stamp your passport (2SFr) or pick up a **hiking map** (16SFr) at the **tourist office,** Städtle 37, just up the hill from the Vaduz PostBus stop. (☎239 6300; www.tourismus.li. Open July-Sept. daily 9am-5pm at the welcome desk at the bus stop; Oct.-June M-F 9am-noon and 1:30-5pm.)

LIECHTENSTEIN

UPPER LIECHTENSTEIN ☎00423

Rising up into the tree-studded mountains on the eastern bank of the Rhine are the villages of Upper Liechtenstein. Full of winding roads, ski lifts, and hiking trails, these villages are where the country's real beauty lies. Spanned by a series of switchbacks and foothills 800m above the river, **Triesenberg** (bus #10; 20min., every 20min.), the principal town, offers spectacular views of the Rhine Valley. The local **tourist office** shares a building with the **Walser Heimatmuseum,** which chronicles the history of the region. (Both ☎262 19 26. Open Sept.-May Tu-F 1:30-5:30pm, Sa 1:30-5pm; June-Aug. also Su 2-5pm. Museum 2SFr.) Aside from the museum, there's not much else to see in Triesenberg, so head to **Gaflei,** take bus #10 to Triesenberg, then change to bus #30 (20min., every hr.) for a lovely 2hr. hike through green forests and fields, passing through Silum, then Sücka and into Steg. Although neither of these towns offer much more than beautiful scenery, they're worth a short stop.

Malbun sits in an Alpine valley in the southeastern corner of Liechtenstein, accessible by bus #10 (40min., every hr.). Undoubtedly the hippest place in the principality, it boasts approachable people, the best hiking in the country, and affordable ski slopes (day pass 37SFr). The most popular and most scenic hiking trail follows the Fürstin-Gina-Weg, and takes about 4-5hr. The route starts at the base of the chairlift *(Bergbahnen)* at the Malbun Zentrum bus stop, leads to the top of the lift, then passes along the crest of Augstenberg Mountain to Bettlerjoch Mountain and back to Malbun. (Chairlift open daily 8am-12:15pm and 1:15-4:50pm. 7.50SFr, students 5.90SFr; round-trip 11.70/9SFr.) The Hotel Galina, several buildings past the tourist office heading away from the chairlift, offers **falconry** demonstrations from mid-May to mid-October, as long as the weather cooperates and spectators show up. (☎263 34 24. Tu-Su 3pm. 6SFr.)

Hotel Steg ❶, in the nearby village of Steg, offers the cheapest accommodations in the country. With 10 beds barely separated in the cozy dorm, you will get to know your neighbors extremely well. Take bus #10 to Hotel Steg; it's right across from the bus stop. (☎263 21 46. Breakfast included. In the dorm, a blanket and pillow are provided but no linen available. Linen included for private rooms. Dorms 25SFr; singles 45SFr; doubles 80SFr. MC/V.) **Alpen Hotel ❸** is the red building across from the Malbun PostBus stop; it has an indoor pool. (☎263 11 81; www.alpenhotel.li. Reception 8am-10pm. Open mid-May to Oct. and mid-Dec. to Apr. Singles 40-65SFr, with bath 60-95SFr; doubles 80-130/120-170SFr. AmEx/MC/V.) The **Schädler-Shop,** between the chairlift and the tourist office, has groceries. (Open M-F 8am-12:30pm, 1:30-5pm, Sa-Su 8am-6pm.) The **tourist office,** just down the street from the Malbun Zentrum bus stop, provides more information on skiing and hiking in the area. (☎263 65 77. Open June-Oct. and mid-Dec. to mid-Apr. M-F 8am-6pm, Sa-Su 9am-5pm.)

LITHUANIA (LIETUVA)

Once part of the largest country in Europe, Lithuania shrank significantly in the face of oppression from Tsarist Russia, Nazi Germany, and the Soviet Union. Since the fall of the USSR, Lithuania has become more Western with every passing year, culminating in its recent admission to the European Union. The spectacular capital of Vilnius welcomes visitors into the largest Old Town in Europe, recently covered in a bright new coat of paint. In the other corner of the country, the mighty Baltic Sea washes up against Palanga and the towering dunes of the Curonian Spit.

DISCOVER LITHUANIA: SUGGESTED ITINERARIES

THREE DAYS. Head straight to the **Baltic Coast** to enjoy the stunning–and surprisingly untouristed–sands of the **Drifting Dunes of Parnidis** (p. 709), then leave the **Curonian Spit** and head up the coast to the electric nightlife and seaside park of **Palanga** (p. 709).

ONE WEEK After three days on the **Baltic Coast,** go inland to cosmopolitan **Vilnius** (3 days; p. 704), where you can explore the cobblestoned **Old Town,** wander offbeat **Užupis,** and take a daytrip to **Trakai Castle,** the ancient capital.

ESSENTIALS

FACTS AND FIGURES

Official Name: Republic of Lithuania.

Capital: Vilnius.

Major Cities: Kaunas, Klaipėda.

Population: 3,596,617 (83% Lithuanian, 7% Polish, 6% Russian).

Land Area: 65,200 sq. km.

Time Zone: GMT +2.

Language: Lithuanian.

Religions: Roman Catholic (79%).

WHEN TO GO

Lithuanian summers are brief but glorious, while winters are long and cold. Tourist season peaks in July and August, especially along the coast. June and September are pleasant times to visit. A winter visit also has its charms, especially in the major cities. Be aware that many coastal establishments close in the off-season.

DOCUMENTS AND FORMALITIES

EMBASSIES AND CONSULATES. Foreign embassies for Lithuania are in Vilnius (p. 704). For Lithuanian embassies and consulates abroad, contact: **Australia,** 40B Fiddens Wharf Rd., Killara, NSW, 2071 (☎02 9498 2571); **Canada,** 130 Albert St., Ste. 204, Ottawa, Ontario, K1P 5G4 (☎613-567-5458; litemb@storm.ca); **Ireland,** 90 Merrion Rd. Ballsbridge, Dublin 4 (☎1 668 8292); **New Zealand,** 28 Heather St. Parnell, Auckland (☎64 9 379 66 39; saul@f1rst.co.nz); **UK,** 84 Gloucester Pl., London W1U 6AU (☎020 7486 6401; http://lithuania.embassyhomepage.com); **US,** 2622 16th St., NW, Washington, D.C. 20009 (☎202-234-5860; info@ltembassyus.org).

VISA AND ENTRY INFORMATION. Citizens of Australia, Canada, New Zealand, the UK, and the US do not need a visa for stays of up to 90 days. Special visas (€60), for temporary residence are valid for up to one year, and can be purchased from the Migration Department of the Ministry of the Interior. Avoid crossing through Belarus to enter or exit Lithuania: not only will you need to obtain a visa (US$100) for Belarus in advance, but guards may hassle you at the border.

ENTRANCE REQUIREMENTS

Passport: Required for all travelers.
Visa: Not required for stays under 90 days for citizens of Australia, Canada, Ireland, New Zealand, the UK, and the US.
Letter of Invitation: Not required for citizens of Australia, Canada, Ireland, New Zealand, the UK, and the US.
Inoculations: Not required. Recommended up-to-date on DTaP (diphtheria, tetanus, and pertussis), Hepatitis A, Hepatitis B, MMR (measles, mumps, and rubella), Polio booster, and Typhoid.
Work Permit: Required for all foreigners planning to work in Lithuania.
Driving Permit: Required for all those planning to drive in Lithuania.

TOURIST SERVICES AND MONEY

TOURIST OFFICES. Major cities have official **tourist offices. Litinterp** reserves accommodations and rental cars, usually without a surcharge. Kaunas, Klaipėda, Nida, Palanga, and Vilnius each have an edition of the *In Your Pocket* series, available at kiosks and some hotels. Employees at tourist offices will often speak English, though they cannot be counted upon to do so.

MONEY. The unit of **currency** is the **Lita** (1Lt=100 centas), plural Litai, fixed to the euro at €1 = 3.4528Lt. Prices are stable, with inflation hovering at just under 1%. **ATMs** are readily available in most cities, though few accept AmEx. Exchange bureaus near the train station usually have poorer rates than banks. Most banks cash **traveler's checks** for 2-3% commission. Visa **cash advances** can usually be obtained with minimum hassle. **Vilniaus Bankas,** with outlets in major cities, accepts major credit cards and traveler's checks for a small commission. Outside Vilnius, most places catering to locals don't take credit cards. Additionally, some establishments that claim to take MasterCard and/or Visa may not actually do so.

LITAI (LT)		
	AUS$1 = 2.14LT	1LT = AUS$0.47
	CDN$1 = 2.32LT	1LT = CDN$0.43
	EUR€1 = 3.45LT	1LT = EUR€0.30
	NZ$1 = 1.97LT	1LT = NZ$0.51
	UK£1 = 5.08LT	1LT = UK£0.20
	US$1 = 2.81LT	1LT = US$0.36

HEALTH AND SAFETY

Well-stocked **pharmacies** are common and carry most medical supplies, tampons, condoms, and toiletries. Drink bottled mineral water, and **boil tap water** for 10min. before drinking. An upward-pointing triangle indicates women's **restrooms;** a triangle pointing downward indicates men's bathrooms. Many restrooms are nothing but a hole in the ground, so carry your own **toilet paper.** Lithuania's **crime rate** is generally low, though cab drivers will think nothing of ripping off a tourist. Lithuanian **police** are generally helpful but understaffed, so your best bet for assistance in English is still your **consulate.**

Women traveling alone will be noticed but shouldn't encounter too much difficulty. Skirts, blouses, and heels are more common than jeans, shorts, tank tops, or sneakers, though showing skin is more acceptable in clubs. **Minorities** traveling to

Lithuania may encounter unwanted attention or discrimination, though most is directed toward Roma (gypsies). Lithuania has made little effort to provide for **disabled** travelers. **Homosexuality** is legal but not always tolerated. Vilnius has the most nightclubs, hotlines, and services for gays and lesbians in the Baltics.

EMERGENCY	**Police, Ambulance,** and **Fire:** ☎ 112.

TRANSPORTATION

BY PLANE AND TRAIN. Finnair, LOT, Lufthansa, SAS, and other airlines fly into Vilnius International Airport (VNO). Trains are more popular for international and long-distance travel. Two major lines cross Lithuania: one north-south from Latvia through Šiauliai and Kaunas to Poland; the other east-west from Belarus through Vilnius and Kaunas to Kaliningrad, branching out around Vilnius and Klaipėda.

BY BUS. Domestic buses are faster, more common, and only a bit more expensive than trains, which are often crowded. When possible, try to catch an express bus, typically marked with an asterisk or an "E" on the timetable. They are normally direct and can be up to twice as fast. Vilnius, Kaunas, and Klaipėda are easily reached by train or bus from Estonia, Latvia, Poland, and Russia.

BY FERRY. Ferries connect Klaipėda with Århus and Aabenra, Denmark; Kiel and Mukran, Germany; and Åhus and Karlshamn, Sweden.

BY CAR. All travelers planning to drive in Lithuania must purchase a **Liability Insurance Policy** at the Lithuanian border (79Lt for the 15-day min.). These policies may only be purchased with Litai, so make sure to convert some cash before reaching the border. **US** citizens may drive with an American driver's license for up to three months; all others must have an **International Driving Permit.** Inexpensive taxis are available in most cities. Agree on a price before getting in. Hitchhiking is common; many drivers charge a fee comparable to local bus or train fares. Locals line up along major roads leaving large cities. *Let's Go* does not recommend hitchhiking.

KEEPING IN TOUCH

PHONE CODES	**Country code:** 370. **International dialing prefix:** 810. For more information on how to place international calls, see inside back cover

EMAIL AND THE INTERNET. Internet is widely available, though rarely for free. Most well-located Internet cafes charge 3-6Lt per hour.

TELEPHONE. There are two kinds of pay phones: rectangular ones take magnetic strip cards and rounded ones take chip cards. Phone cards (8-30Lt) are sold at phone offices and kiosks. Calls to **Estonia** and **Latvia** cost 1.65Lt per minute; **Europe** 5.80Lt; and the **US** 7.32Lt. International access numbers include: **AT&T Direct** (☎800 90028); **Canada Direct** (☎800 90004); **Sprint** (☎800 95877).

MAIL. Airmail *(oro pastu)* letters abroad cost 1.70Lt (postcards 1.20Lt) and take about one week to reach the US. **Poste Restante** is available in Vilnius but hard to find elsewhere. Address envelope as follows: First name LAST NAME, POSTE RESTANTE, Post office address, postal code City, LITHUANIA.

LANGUAGE. Lithuanian is one of only two Baltic languages (Latvian is the other). All "r"s are trilled. **Polish** is helpful in the south and **German** on the coast. **Russian** is understood in most places, although it is not as prominent as in Latvia. Most Lithuanians understand basic English phrases. If someone seems to sneeze at you, he might be saying *ačiu* (ah-choo; thank you). For a few helpful phrases see **Phrasebook: Lithuanian** p. 1063.

ACCOMMODATIONS AND CAMPING

LITHUANIA	❶	❷	❸	❹	❺
ACCOMMODATIONS	under 30Lt	30-80Lt	80-130Lt	130-180Lt	over 180Lt

Lithuania has several youth **hostels,** particularly in Vilnius and Klaipėda. HI membership is nominally required, but an LJNN guest card (10.50Lt at any hostel) will suffice. The head office is in Vilnius (see **Vilnius: Practical Information,** p. 704). Their *Hostel Guide* is a handy booklet with info on bike and car rentals, hotel reservations, and maps. **Hotels** across the price spectrum abound in Vilnius and most major towns. **Litinterp,** with offices in Vilnius, Kaunas, and Klaipėda, assists in finding homestays or apartments for rent. **Camping** is gaining popularity, but it is restricted by law to marked campgrounds; the law is well enforced.

FOOD AND DRINK

LITHUANIA	❶	❷	❸	❹	❺
FOOD	under 11Lt	11-20Lt	20-30Lt	30-40Lt	over 40Lt

Lithuanian cuisine is heavy and sometimes greasy. Keeping a **vegetarian** or **kosher** diet is difficult, but possible. Restaurants serve various types of *blynai* (pancakes) with *mėsa* (meat) or *varske* (cheese). *Cepelinai* are heavy, potato-dough missiles of meat, cheese, and mushrooms; *saltibarščiai* is a beet and cucumber soup prevalent in the east; *karbonadas* is breaded pork fillet; and *koldunai* are meat dumplings. Good Lithuanian **beer** flows freely. *Kalnapis* is popular in Vilnius and most of Lithuania, *Baltijos* reigns supreme around Klaipėda, and the award-winning *Utenos* is everywhere. Lithuanian **vodka** *(degtinė)* is also very popular.

HOLIDAYS AND FESTIVALS

Holidays: New Year's Day and Flag Day (Jan. 1); Independence Day (Feb. 16); Restoration of Independence (Mar. 11); Easter Holiday (Apr. 16); Labor Day (May 1); Statehood Day (July 6); Feast of the Assumption (Aug. 15); All Saints' Day (Nov. 1).

Festivals: Since the 19th century, craftsmen from around Eastern Europe have gathered to display their wares each March in Vilnius at the **Kaziukas Fair.**

BEYOND TOURISM

The Baltic Times (www.baltictimes.com). English-language newspaper with classified ads for short-term and long-term employment.

Lithuanian Academy of Music, Gedimino pr. 42, 2600 Vilnius, Lithuania (☎370 5 261 26 91; www.lma.lt). Classes in music, art, and theater in Lithuania. Offers music classes in English.

VILNIUS ☎(8)5

Although still rough around the edges, Vilnius (pop. 579,000), is quickly developing new commerce and tourism. Founded in 1321 after a prophetic dream by Grand Duke Gediminas, Vilnius has flourished throughout the centuries, surviving WWII, the Holocaust, and the iron grip of the Soviet Union. Vilnius today remains a rich cultural and commercial center, welcoming and affordable for travelers.

TRANSPORTATION

Flights: Vilnius Airport (Vilniaus oro uostas), Rodūnės Kelias 2 (info ☎230 6666), is 5km south of town. Take bus #1 to the Old Town.

Trains: Geležinkelio Stotis, Geležinkelio 16 (☎233 0086; www.litrail.lt). Domestic tickets are sold to the left of the entrance, international to the right (reservations for Western Europe ☎269 3722). Open daily 6-11am and noon-6pm. Most international trains pass through Belarus, requiring a Belarussian transit visa (US$30). To: **Moscow, Russia** (17hr., 3 per day, 103Lt); **Rīga, Latvia** (7½hr., 1 per day, 80Lt); **St. Petersburg, Russia** (18hr., 3 per day, 91Lt); **Warsaw, Poland** (8hr., 2 per day, 85Lt).

Buses: Autobusų Stotis, Sodų 22 (☎290 1661, reservations 216 2977), opposite the train station. **Eurolines** (☎215 1377; www.eurolines.lt) serves **Rīga, Latvia** (5hr., 4 per day, 40Lt); **St. Petersburg, Russia** (18hr., 4 per day, 45Lt); **Tallinn, Estonia** (9hr., 2 per day, 90Lt); **Warsaw, Poland** (9-10hr., 3 per day, 97Lt). ISIC discount.

Public Transportation: Buses and **trolleys** run daily 6am-midnight. Buy tickets at any kiosk (0.80Lt) or from the driver (1Lt). Tickets are checked frequently; punch them onboard to avoid the 20Lt fine. Monthly passes available for students (5Lt).

Taxis: Martino (☎240 0004, from a mobile 1422). Cabbies notoriously overcharge foreigners; get a local to hail one for you, if at all possible.

ORIENTATION AND PRACTICAL INFORMATION

Geležinkelio runs right from the train and bus stations to **Aušros Vartų,** which leads downhill through the **Aušros Vartai** (Gates of Dawn) and into the **Senamiestis** (Old Town). Aušros Vartų becomes **Didžioji** and then **Pilies** before reaching the base of

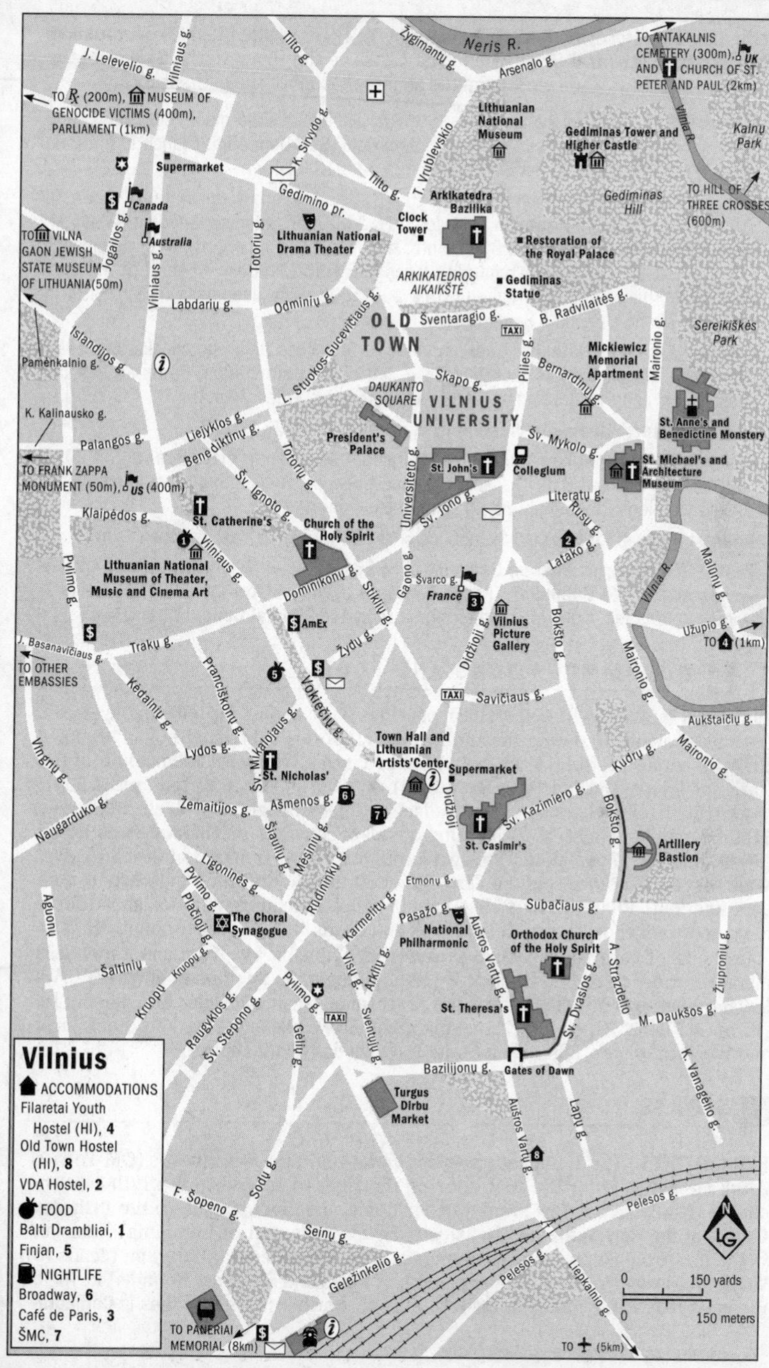
Vilnius
ACCOMMODATIONS
Filaretai Youth Hostel (HI), 4
Old Town Hostel (HI), 8
VDA Hostel, 2
FOOD
Balti Drambliai, 1
Finjan, 5
NIGHTLIFE
Broadway, 6
Café de Paris, 3
ŠMC, 7
OLD TOWN
VILNIUS UNIVERSITY
Neris R.
Lithuanian National Museum
Gediminas Tower and Higher Castle
Arkikatedra Bazilika
Clock Tower
Restoration of the Royal Palace
Gediminas Statue
ARKIKATEDROS AIKAIKŠTĖ
Lithuanian National Drama Theater
Supermarket
Canada
Australia
TO VILNA GAON JEWISH STATE MUSEUM OF LITHUANIA(50m)
TO (200m), MUSEUM OF GENOCIDE VICTIMS (400m), PARLIAMENT (1km)
TO ANTAKALNIS CEMETERY (300m), UK AND CHURCH OF ST. PETER AND PAUL (2km)
Kalnų Park
Gediminas Hill
TO HILL OF THREE CROSSES (600m)
Sereikiškes Park
Mickiewicz Memorial Apartment
St. Anne's and Benedictine Monstery
St. Michael's and Architecture Museum
DAUKANTO SQUARE
President's Palace
St. John's
Collegium
TO FRANK ZAPPA MONUMENT (50m), US (400m)
St. Catherine's
Church of the Holy Spirit
Lithuanian National Museum of Theater, Music and Cinema Art
France
Vilnius Picture Gallery
AmEx
TO OTHER EMBASSIES
TO (1km)
Town Hall and Lithuanian Artists'Center
Supermarket
St. Nicholas'
St. Casimir's
Artillery Bastion
The Choral Synagogue
National Philharmonic
Orthodox Church of the Holy Spirit
St. Theresa's
Gates of Dawn
Turgus Dirbu Market
TO PANERIAI MEMORIAL (8km)
TO (5km)
0 150 yards
0 150 meters
TAXI
J. Lelevelio g.
Vilniaus g.
Tilto g.
Žygimantų g.
Arsenalo g.
K. Sirvydo g.
Gedimino pr.
T. Vrublevskio
Jogailos g.
Totorių g.
Labdarių g.
Odminių g.
L. Stuokos-Gucevičiaus g.
Šventaragio g.
B. Radvilaitės g.
Pilies g.
Bernardinų g.
Maironio g.
Islandijos g.
Pamėnkalnio g.
K. Kalinausko g.
Skapo g.
Liejyklos g.
Benediktinų g.
Palangos g.
Šv. Mykolo g.
Šv. Ignoto g.
Universiteto g.
Šv. Jono g.
Literatų g.
Rusų g.
Klaipėdos g.
Latako g.
Vilnia R.
Malūnų g.
Pylimo g.
Dominikonų g.
Stiklių g.
Gaono g.
Švarco g.
Didžioji g.
Bokšto g.
Užupio g.
J. Basanavičiaus g.
Trakų g.
Žydų g.
Pranciškonų g.
Kėdainių g.
Vokiečių g.
Savičiaus g.
Aukštaičių g.
Vingrių g.
Lydos g.
Šv. Mikalojaus g.
Kudrų g.
Šv. Kazimiero g.
Ašmenos g.
Žemaitijos g.
Naugarduko g.
Šiaulių g.
Mėsinių g.
Rūdininkų g.
Ligoninės g.
Etmonų g.
Subačiaus g.
Aguonų
Plačioji g.
Karmelitų g.
Pasažo g.
Aušros Vartų g.
A. Strazdelio
Žiupronių g.
Šaltinių
Kruopų g.
Kruopų
Raugyklos g.
Šv. Stepono g.
Visų g.
Arklių g.
Šventųjų g.
Šv. Dvasios g.
M. Daukšos g.
Gėlių g.
Bazilijonų g.
K. Vanagėlio g.
Lapų g.
Sodų g.
F. Šopeno g.
Pelesos g.
Seinų g.
Geležinkelio g.
Liepkalnio g.

LITHUANIA

Gediminas Hill. Here, the **Gediminas Tower** of the Higer Castle presides over **Arkikatedros Aikštė** (Cathedral Square) and the banks of the River Neris. **Gedimino,** the commercial artery, leads west from the square in front of the cathedral.

Tourist Office: Vilniaus 22 (☎262 9660; www.vilnius.lt). Free maps, schedules, and bicycle rentals (1Lt per day). Open M-F 9am-6pm, Sa 10am-4pm. Branch in the train station (☎269 2091). Open M-F 9am-6pm, Sa-Su 10am-4pm.

Embassies: Australia, Vilniaus 23 (☎212 3369; australia@consulate.lt). Open Tu 10am-1pm, Th 2-5pm. **Canada,** Jogailos 4 (☎249 0950; vilnius@canada.lt). Visas M, W, F 9am-noon. Open daily 8:30am-5pm. **UK,** Antakalnio 2 (☎246 2900, emergency mobile 869 83 7097; www.britain.lt). Visas M-F 8:30-11:30am. Open M-Th 8:30am-5pm, F 8:30am-4pm. **US,** Akmenų 6 (☎266 5500; www.usembassy.lt). Visas M-Th 8:30-11:30am. Open M-F 8am-5:30pm.

Currency Exchange: Vilniaus Bankas, Vokiečių 9, cashes traveler's checks. Open M-F 8am-6pm. **Parex Bankas,** Geležinkelio 6, left of the train station. Rates are not the best, but it's convenient and accepts many currencies. Open 24hr.

24hr. Pharmacy: Gedimino Vaistinė, Gedimino pr. 27 (☎261 0135).

Hospital: Baltic-American Medical and Surgical Clinic, Nemenčinės 54a (☎234 2020 or 698 526 55; www.bak.lt). Accepts major American, British, and other international insurance plans. Open daily 7am-11pm; doctors on call 24hr.

Internet Access: Klubas Lux, Svitrigailos 5 (☎233 3788). 2Lt per hr. Open 24hr.

Post Office: Lietuvos Paštas, Gedimino 7 (☎261 6759; www.post.lt), west of Arkikatedros Aikštė (the Cathedral). **Poste Restante** at the window labeled "iki pareikalavimo"; 0.50Lt fee. Open M-F 7am-8pm, Sa 9am-4pm. **Postal Code:** LT-01001.

ACCOMMODATIONS AND FOOD

VDA Hostel ❶, Latako 2 (☎212 0102), provides basic rooms for unbeatable prices. Dorms are available during the summer only. (Dorms 18Lt; singles 43Lt; doubles 52-60 Lt; triples 66-78 Lt. Cash only.) Tucked into a courtyard 100m south of the Gates of Dawn, the **Old Town Hostel (HI) ❷,** Aušros Vartų 20-15a (☎262 5357; www.balticbackpackers.com) is a budget traveler's delight. (Book ahead. Dorms 34Lt, HI members 32Lt. MC/V.) Young travelers converge on **Filaretai Youth Hostel (HI) ❶,** Filaretv 17 (☎215 4627; www.filaretaihostel.lt.), 1km east of the Old Town. Walk east on Užupio across the Vilnia River. At the fork, bear left onto Krivių, then bear right onto Filaretų. (Linen 5Lt. Laundry 10Lt. Free Internet. Book ahead June-Sept. and weekends. Dorms 28Lt; triples and quads 42Lt. 4Lt HI discount. MC/V.)

In a city of carnivores, **Balti Dramblìai ❷,** Vilniaus 41, maintains a meatless menu. (Entrees from 8Lt. Open M-F 11am-midnight, Sa-Su noon-midnight. MC/V.) Locals linger over Middle Eastern and Argentinian cuisine at **Finjan ❸,** Vokiečių 18. (Entrees 10-45Lt. Open daily 11am-midnight. MC/V.) **Iki** supermarkets stock local and Western brands. (Branch at Sodu 22. Open daily 8am-10pm.)

SIGHTS

SENAMIESTIS. The 16th-century **Aušros Vartai** guard the Senamiestis (Old Town). After the gates, enter the first door on the right to ascend to the 17th-century **chapel** (Koplyčia). A few steps farther down, a gateway leads to the **Orthodox Church of the Holy Spirit** (Šv. Dvasios bažnyčia), the seat of Lithuania's Russian Orthodox Archbishop. The street merges with the pedestrian Pilies and leads to **Vilnius University** (Vilniaus Universitetas), at Pilies and Šv. Jono. Founded in 1579, the university is the oldest in Eastern Europe. Farther north on Pilies is **Cathedral**

Square (Arkikatedros aikštė); its **cathedral** contains the ornate **Chapel of St. Casimir** (Šv. Kazimiero koplyčia) and the royal mausoleum. *(Didžioji 34. ☎222 1715. Open M-Sa 4-6:30pm, Su 9am-1pm. Free.)* From behind the cathedral, walk up Castle Hill to **Gediminas Tower** for a great view. Off Pylimo, between Kalinausko 1 and 3, is the continent's most unexpected monument: a 4m steel shaft topped with a bust of the late freak-rock legend **Frank Zappa,** depicted in the Socialist realist style.

THE OLD JEWISH QUARTER AND PANERIAI MEMORIAL. Vilnius was once a center of Jewish life comparable to Warsaw and New York, with 105 synagogues and a Jewish population of 100,000 (in a city of 230,000) at the start of WWII. Nazi persecution left only 6000 survivors, and the **synagogue** at Pylimo 39 is the only one still standing. The **Paneriai Memorial,** Agrastų 15, in **Paneriai,** is 10min. away by train (0.90Lt). Go right from the train station and follow Agrastų to the memorial. During WWII, Nazis butchered 100,000 Lithuanians, 70,000 of them Jews, in this eerie forest. The memorials are at pits that served as mass graves. Return by bus #8, on the other side of the tracks. *(Open M, W-F 11am-5pm. Free.)* The **Vilna Gaon Jewish State Museum of Lithuania** preserves and commemorates Vilnius's Jewish heritage at three sites, including "The Green House," Pamenkalnio 12. The exhibits provide an honest account of Lithuanians' persecution of their Jewish neighbors on the eve of the German invasion. *(Open M-Th 9am-5pm, F 9am-4pm. Donations requested.)* For info on the Jewish Quarter or on locating ancestors, visit the **Chabad Lubavitch Center.** *(Šaltiniv 12. ☎215 03 87; www.jewish.lt. Open daily 9am-6pm.)*

MUSEUM OF GENOCIDE VICTIMS. The horrors of the Soviet regime are on full display at this former KGB headquarters, which served as a Gestapo outpost during WWII. The basement remains as it was in 1991, with isolation rooms, torture chambers, and the execution cell open to the public. The exhibit upstairs honors Lithuanian resistance fighters. *(Aukų 2a, at the intersection with Gedimino. Open Tu-Sa 10am-5pm, Su 10am-3pm. Museum 2Lt, Sept.-May 1Lt ISIC discount. Sept.-May W free.)*

ENTERTAINMENT AND NIGHTLIFE

The National Philharmonic's **Vilniaus Festivalis,** starts in late May (www.filharmonija.lt/vilniausfestivalis). Check *Vilnius in Your Pocket* and *Exploring Vilnius*, distributed at hotels, for more on festivals and performances. Stay on the lookout for postcards announcing events and club nights in cafes. For info on gay nightlife, check the Lithuanian Gay and Lesbian Homepage (www.gayline.lt).

The outdoor patio at **ŠMC** (Contemporary Art Center), Vokiečių 2, fills with the young and hip. (Beer 5Lt. Open M-Th, Su 11am-midnight, F 11am-3am, Sa noon-1am. Cash only.) **Broadway** (Brodvėjus), Mėsiniu 4, is enormously popular with teenie-boppers. (Cover 10Lt, includes 2 drinks. Open M noon-3am, Tu noon-4am, W-Sa noon-5am, Su noon-2am. MC/V.) Musicians, artists, and expats feel at home at **Cafe de Paris,** Didžioji 1, next to the French Embassy. (Open M-Tu 11am-10pm, W-Th 11am-2am, F 11am-3am, Sa noon-3am, Su noon-10pm. MC/V.)

KAUNAS ☎37

Kaunas (pop. 420,000), served as capital of Lithuania between the world wars and remains a cultural center. At the eastern end of **Laisvės,** the city's main pedestrian boulevard, the sparkling blue domes of **Church of St. Michael the Archangel** loom over the city. (Open M-F 9am-3pm, Sa-Su 8:30am-2pm. Free.) Nearby, the **Devil Museum,** V. Putvinskio 64, exhibits more than 2000 depictions of the devil, who was revered as a guardian in Lithuanian folklore until Christianity came to rain on the Satanic parade. (Open Tu-Su 10am-5pm. 5Lt, students 2.50Lt.) On the western end of Laisvės is the well-preserved **Old Town** and a 15th-century **cathedral.** (Open daily 7am-7pm. Free.) Walk west from the Old Town Square to reach the meeting of the Neris and Nemunas rivers and the beautiful **Santakos Parkas.** Take the bus from the station to reach the **Ninth Fort** (20min., 2 per hr., 1Lt), where 50,000 prisoners, including 30,000 Jews, were killed during WWII. The fort now holds an exhibit on Lithuanians sent to Siberia by Stalin's purges. (Open M, W-Su 10am-6pm. 4Lt, students 2Lt.) The **Sugihara House,** Valzganto 30, details the courage of Diplomat Sugihara, the "Japanese Schindler," who helped 6000 Jews escape the Nazis by issuing them travel visas to Japan. (Open M-F 10am-5pm, Sa-Su 11am-6pm. Free.)

Litinterp ❸, Gedimino 28, arranges private rooms. (☎22 87 18; www.litinterp.lt. Open M-F 8:30am-5:30pm, Sa 9:30am-3pm. Singles 80-120Lt; doubles 140-160Lt. MC/V.) In the evenings, traditional music fills **Žalias Ratas ❷,** Laisvės 36b. (Entrees 5-28Lt. Open daily 11am-midnight. MC/V.) The brewery **Avilys,** Vilniaus 34, has a wide selection of its own brews and Tibetan teas. (Tea 4Lt. Beer 6Lt per 0.5L. Open M-Th 11am-midnight, F-Sa noon-2am, Su noon-midnight.) There is a **grocery** store in the basement on the corner of Daukanto and Laisvės. (Open daily 8am-10pm.) To reach Kaunas from Vilnius, take a **train** (2hr., 12 per day, 10.40Lt) or **bus** (1½hr., 2 per hr., 14.50Lt). The **tourist office** is at Laisvės 36. (☎32 34 36; http://visit.kaunas.lt. Open M-F 9am-6pm, Sa-Su 9am-1pm and 2-6pm.) **Postal Code:** LT-3000.

KLAIPĖDA ☎846

Strategically located on the tip of the Neringa peninsula, Klaipėda (pop. 194,000) was briefly the Prussian capital in the 19th century. On mainland Klaipėda, the **Clock Museum** (Laikrodžių Muziejus), Liepų 12, displays everything from Egyptian sundials to Chinese candle clocks. From S. Daukanto, turn left on H. Manto and left on Liepų. (Open Tu-Su noon-6pm. 4Lt, students 2Lt.) **Klaipėda Drama Theater** (Klaipėdos Dramos Teatras), Teatro aikštė, on the other side of H. Manto, was one of Wagner's favorite haunts. (☎31 44 53. Open Tu-Su 11am-2pm and 4-7pm.) The main attraction in **Smiltynė,** across the lagoon, is the **Sea Museum** (Lietuvos Jūrų Muziejus), Smiltynė 3, and its spectacular **sea lion show.** (www.juru.muziejus.lt. Open June-Aug. Tu-Su 10:30am-6:30pm; May and Sept. W-Su 10:30am-6:30pm; Oct.-Apr. Sa-Su 10:30am-5pm. Sea lion show June-Aug. 11am, 1, 3pm; May and Sept. 11am, 1pm. Museum 8Lt, students 4Lt.) Paths lead 500m west to gorgeous **beaches.**

Klaipėda Traveller's Guesthouse (HI) ❷, Butkų Juzės 7-4, near the bus station, has spacious dorms, hot showers, and friendly staff. (☎21 18 79; oldtown@takas.lt. Bike rental 30Lt per day. Dorms 34Lt.) Heading away from the Danė River on Tiltų, turn left on Kulių Vartų, left again onto Bangų to reach the modern **Aribė Hotel ❹,** Bangų 17a, with private bath. (☎49 09 40; vitetur@klaipeda.omnitel.net. Singles 140Lt; doubles 180Lt. Low season 20Lt less. MC/V.) **Trys Mylimos ❷,** Taikos 23, 500m southeast of the Old Town, dishes out deep-fried regional cuisine. (☎41 14 79. Entrees 6-16Lt. Live music F-Sa 8-11pm. Open daily 11am-midnight. MC/V.) The **central market** is on Turgaus aikštė. (Open daily 8am-6pm.) The best bars line H. Manto on the mainland. **Kurpiai,** Kurpių 1a, is an excellent jazz club. (Live jazz nightly 9:30pm. Cover F-Sa 5-10Lt. Open M, Su noon-midnight, Tu-Sa noon-2am. MC/V.) **Buses** (☎41 15 47, reservations 41 15 40) go from Butkų Juzės 9 to: Kaunas (3hr., 14 per day, 34Lt); Palanga (30-40min., 23 per day, 2.50-3Lt); Vilnius (4-5hr., 10-14 per day, 44Lt). **Ferries** (☎31 42 17, info 31 11 17) run from Old Port Ferry Terminal, Žvejų 8, to Smiltynė (7min., every 30min., 1.50Lt) and connect with buses to Nida (1hr., 7Lt). If arriving at the International Ferry Terminal, take microbus 8a (2Lt) to the city center. The **tourist office,** Turgaus 7, arranges tours and offers free maps and guidebooks. (☎41 21 86; www.klaipeda.lt. Open June-Aug. M-F 9am-6pm, Sa-Su 10am-4pm; May and Sept. M-F 10am-6pm, Sa 10am-4pm; Oct.-Apr. M-F 9am-6pm.) **Postal Code:** LT-5800.

NIDA

☎8469

Windswept white sand dunes have long drawn summer vacationers to **Nida.** From the remains of the town's immense sundial on the highest of the **Drifting Dunes of Parnidis,** you can look down on the Curonian Lagoon and the Baltic. Please stay on the paths to preserve the delicate landscape. From the center of town, follow the promenade by the water and bear right on Skruzdynės to reach the **Thomas Mann House** (Thomo Manno Namelis), up a large staircase at #17. Mann built the cottage in 1930 and wrote a novel here, but had to leave when Hitler invaded. (Open June-Aug. daily 10am-6pm; Sept.-May Tu-Sa 10am-5pm. 2Lt, students 0.50Lt.)

Luxurious **camping,** with toilets, showers, and a Chinese restaurant, is just beyond the top of the hill at Taikos 45a. (☎37 96 82. Gear rental available. Tent sites 25Lt, extra person 15Lt.) From Naglių 18e, **buses** (☎524 72) run to Klaipėda/Smiltynė (1hr., 1 per hr., 7Lt). The **tourist office,** Taikos 4, opposite the bus station, arranges private rooms for a 5Lt fee and offers free **Internet.** (☎523 45; www.neringainfo.lt. Rooms 40-50Lt. Open June-Aug. M-F 10am-7pm, Sa 10am-6pm, Su 10am-3pm; low season M-F 9am-1pm and 2-6pm, Sa-Su 10am-3pm.) **Postal Code:** LT-5872.

PALANGA

The largest park in the country, over 20km of shoreline, and an exuberant nightlife make Palanga (pop. 20,000) the hottest summer spot in Lithuania. While the beach is the main attraction, Palanga's pride and joy is the **Amber Museum** (Gintaro Muziejus) in a mansion at the expansive Botanical Gardens. The collection consists of 15,000 pieces of the fossilized resin—known as "Baltic Gold"—with primeval flora and fauna trapped inside. (Open June-Aug. Tu-Sa 10am-8pm, Su 10am-7pm; Sept.-May daily 11am-4:30pm. 5Lt, students 2.50Lt.) **Vytauto,** which runs parallel to the beach and passes the bus station, and **J. Basanavičiaus,** perpendicular to Vytauto, are lined with cafes and restaurants that have outdoor seating. **Buses** (☎533 33) or **microbuses** from Klaipėda (30min., 2 per hr., 2.50Lt) arrive at Kretinjos 1. The **tourist office** to the right of the station books private rooms by email. (☎488 11; palangaturinfo@is.lt. Open daily 9am-2pm and 3-6pm.) During the summer, bicycle rental kiosks line J. Basanavičiaus, Vytauto, and Jurates. Rates average 6Lt per hour or 25-30Lt per day.

LUXEMBOURG

The forgotten "lux" of the Benelux countries, tiny Luxembourg is often overlooked by travelers smitten by Dutch windmills or impatient to press east into Germany. Yet Luxembourg's castles can go toe to toe with those of the Rhineland, and the charming villages of the Ardennes are less touristed than their Belgian cousins to the northwest. White-collar financiers keep prices in Luxembourg City high, but the eminently walkable capital remains a promising destination for those who have drunk their fill of Bruges or Ghent.

DISCOVER LUXEMBOURG

Budget two days for **Luxembourg City** (p. 713), exploring the capital's maze of well-fortified tunnels by day and its lively nightlife after hours. The towns of **Echternach** (p. 718) and **Vianden** (p. 717) should be your next stops, the former for its historic basilica and the latter for its hilltop chateau. From here, the route coils south to the fly-speck village of **Esch-sur-Sûre** (p. 718) for hiking through wooded river valleys.

ESSENTIALS

FACTS AND FIGURES

Official Name: Grand Duchy of Luxembourg.

Capital: Luxembourg City.

Population: 468,000.

Land Area: 2,600 sq. km.

Time Zone: GMT +1.

Languages: Lëtzebuergesch; French, German, and English are widely spoken.

Religions: Roman Catholic (87%).

WHEN TO GO

The sea winds that routinely douse Belgium with rain have usually shed their moisture by the time they reach Luxembourg; good weather prevails from May through October, although travelers leery of crowds may want to avoid July and August. Temperatures average 17°C (64°F) in summer, and 1°C (34°F) in winter.

DOCUMENTS AND FORMALITIES

EMBASSIES AND CONSULATES. All foreign embassies and consulates are in Luxembourg City. For Luxembourg's embassies and consulates at home: **Australia,** Level 4, Quay West, 111 Harrington St., Sydney NSW 2000 (☎02 9253 4708); **UK,** 27 Wilton Crescent, London SW1X 8SD (☎20 7235 6961); **US,** 2200 Massachusetts Ave. NW, Washington, D.C. 20008 (☎202-265-4171; www.luxembourg-usa.org). **Canadians** can reach their ambassador from Luxembourg at the American embassy in Washington, **Irish** citizens can reach their ambassador from Luxembourg at the British embassy in London, and **New Zealanders** should contact the Belgian embassy for economic questions and the Dutch embassy for all other concerns.

VISA AND ENTRY INFORMATION. EU citizens do not need a visa. Citizens of Australia, Canada, New Zealand, and the US do not need a visa for stays of up to 90 days, although this three-month period begins upon entry into any of the countries belonging to the EU's freedom of movement zone.

TOURIST SERVICES AND MONEY

EMERGENCY	Police: ☎113. Ambulance: ☎112. Fire: ☎112.

TOURIST OFFICES. For general info, contact the **Luxembourg National Tourist Office,** P.O. Box 1001, L-1010 Luxembourg (☎42 82 82 1; www.ont.lu).

MONEY. On January 1, 2002, the **euro (€)** replaced the **Luxembourg Franc** as the unit of currency in Luxembourg. For exchange rates and more info on the euro, see p. 19. The cost of living in Luxembourg City is quite high, although the surrounding countryside is more reasonable. All countries who are members of the European Union impose a **Value Added Tax (VAT)** on goods and services purchased within the EU. Prices in Luxembourg already include the country's 15% VAT rate, one of the lowest in Europe. Partial refunds are also available for visitors who are not EU citizens (p. 23). Restaurant bills usually include a service charge, although an extra 5-10% tip can be a classy gesture. Tip taxi drivers 10%.

TRANSPORTATION

BY PLANE. The Luxembourg City airport (LUX) is serviced by **Luxair** (☎2456 4242; www.luxair.lu) and a slew of other European airlines. Cheap last-minute flights on Luxair (from €129) are available online.

BY TRAIN AND BUS. A **Benelux Tourrail Pass** (€126, under 26 €95; see p. 105) allows five days of unlimited train travel in a one-month period in Belgium, the Netherlands, and Luxembourg. Within Luxembourg itself, the **Billet Réseau** (€4.60, book of 5 €18.50) is good for one day of unlimited bus and train travel. The **Luxembourg Card** (€9-22) includes 1-3 days of unlimited transportation along with free or discounted admission to 50+ sights around the country.

BY BIKE AND THUMB. An 460km network of **cycling paths** already snakes its way through Luxembourg, and plans are in place to add another 440km to the network in the near future. Bikes aren't permitted on buses but domestic trains will transport them for a small fee. While *Let's Go* does not recommend hitchhiking as a safe means of transport, service areas in Luxembourg are popular places to hitch rides into Belgium, France, and the Netherlands, since many motorists stop to take advantage of relatively low fuel prices.

KEEPING IN TOUCH

TELEPHONES. There are no city codes in Luxembourg; from outside the country, dial 352 plus the local number. Public phones can only be operated with a phone card, available at post offices, train stations, and newspaper stands. **Mobile phones** are an increasingly popular and economical alternative (p. 33). International direct dial numbers include: **AT&T** (☎8002 0111); **British Telecom** (☎0800 89 0352); **Canada Direct** (☎8002 0119); **MCI** (☎8002 0112); **Sprint** (☎8002 0115); **Telecom New Zealand** (☎800 20064); **Telstra Australia** (☎0800 0061).

PHONE CODES	**Country code:** 352. **International dialing prefix:** 00. Luxembourg has no city codes. For more information on how to place an international call, see inside back cover.

LANGUAGE. French and German are the administrative languages, but most citizens use a West Germanic language called *Lëtzebuergesch* in everyday conversation. *Lëtzebuergesch* is almost never written, however, so signs and official documents appear in French. German is most common in smaller towns, and English is commonly spoken as a second, third, or fourth language.

ACCOMMODATIONS AND CAMPING

LUXEMBOURG	❶	❷	❸	❹	❺
ACCOMMODATIONS	under €18	€18-24	€24-34	€34-55	over €55

Luxembourg's 12 **HI youth hostels** (*Auberges de Jeunesse*) are often booked solid with school groups during the summer, so it's wise to reserve ahead. Half of the hostels close from mid-November to mid-December, and the other half close from mid-January to mid-February. Prices range from €17-20; members receive a €3 discount. Contact **Centrale des Auberges de Jeunesse Luxembourgeoises** (☎26 27 66 40; www.youthhostels.lu) for more info. **Hotels** are typically expensive, costing upwards of €40 per night. Happily, Luxembourg is a **camper's** paradise, and most towns have campsites close by. One person with a tent will typically pay €8-12 per night. Contact **Camprilux** (www.camping.lu/gb/gbstart.htm) for more info.

FOOD AND DRINK

LUXEMBOURG	❶	❷	❸	❹	❺
FOOD	under €5	€5-9	€9-14	€14-22	over €22

Traditional Luxembourgish cuisine combines elements of French and German cooking. Some specialties include *Judd mat Gaardenbou'nen* (smoked neck of pork with beans), *Friture de la Moselle* (fried fish), *Gromperekichelcher* (potato fritters), and *Quetscheflued* (plum tart). Fruity Riesling wines are produced in the Moselle Valley, and show up most Chardonnays in terms of subtlety.

HOLIDAYS AND FESTIVALS

Holidays: New Year's Day (Jan. 1); Easter Sunday and Monday (Apr. 16-17); Labor Day (May 1); Ascension (May 25); Whit Sunday and Monday (June 4-5); National Day (June 23); Assumption (Aug. 15); All Saints' Day (Nov. 1); Christmas (Dec. 25).

Festivals: The weeks leading up to Lent bring parades and masked balls under the guise of Carnival. Echternach hosts the International Music Festival in May and June, while Riesling Open wine festivals kick off in Wormeldange on the third weekend of Sept.

LUXEMBOURG CITY

With a medieval fortress perched on a cliff that overlooks high bridges and a lush green river valley, Luxembourg City (pop. 84,000) is one of the most beautiful and dramatic capitals in Europe. As an international banking capital, it is home to thousands of frenzied foreign business executives; even so, most visitors find it surprisingly relaxed and pleasant.

TRANSPORTATION

Flights: Findel International Airport (LUX), 6km from the city. Bus #16 (€1.20) is the cheapest option to get from the airport to the train station, and runs every 15-30min. Taxis are around €20 from the airport to the city center.

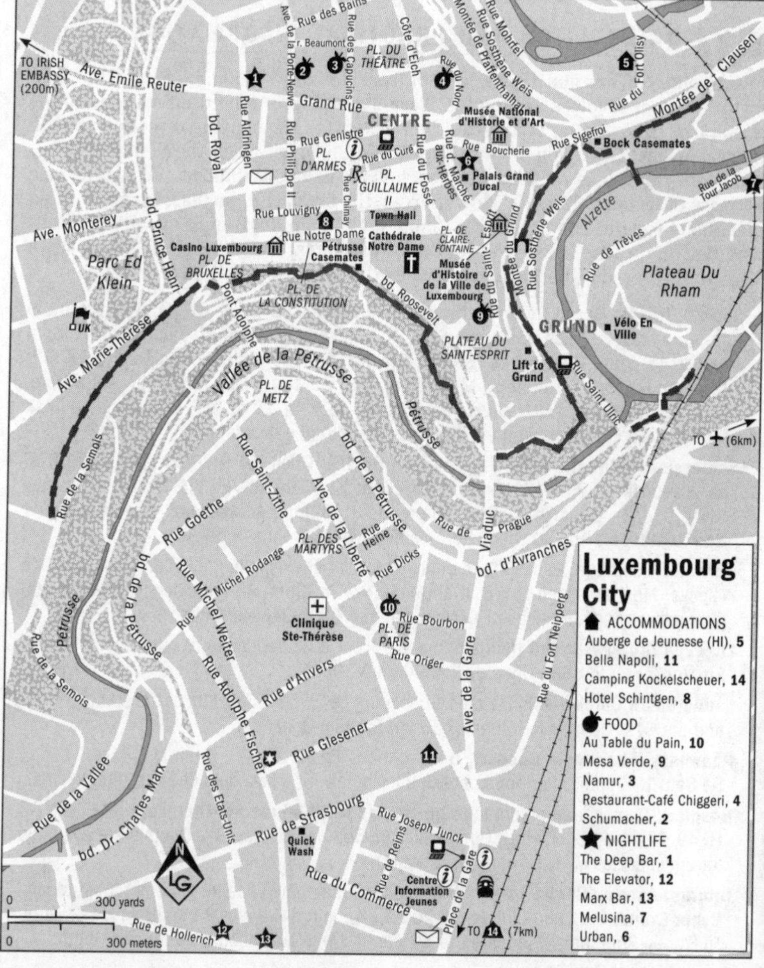

Trains: Gare CFL, av. de la Gare (☎49 90 49 90; www.cfl.lu), a 15min. walk south of the city center. To: **Amsterdam** (6hr.; every hr.; €48.20, under 26 €33.50); **Brussels** (2¾hr., every hr., €27.40/15); **Ettelbrück** (25min., 2 per hr., €3.60); **Frankfurt** (4½hr., every hr., €49.20); **Paris** (4hr., every 2hr., €44.80/33.70).

Buses: For travel exclusively within the city, buy a short-distance ticket (*billet courte distance;* €1.20, book of 10 €9.20), valid for 1hr. A network pass (*billet réseau;* €4.60, book of 5 €18.50), also accepted on trains, allows for unlimited travel throughout the entire country for one day and is the most economical option for intercity travel. Most buses run until midnight; night buses run on weekends in the city center midnight-4am.

Taxis: €2 per km. 10% more 10pm-6am. **Colux Taxis:** ☎48 22 33.

Bikes: Rent from **Vélo en Ville,** 8 r. Bisserwé (☎47 96 23 83), in the Grund. Open daily Apr.-Nov. 10am-noon and 1-8pm. €5 per hr., €12.50 per half-day, €20 per day, €37.50 per weekend, €75 per week. Under 26 20% discount for full day and longer.

ORIENTATION AND PRACTICAL INFORMATION

Five minutes by bus and 15min. by foot from the train station, Luxembourg City's historic center revolves around the **Place d'Armes.** From the train station, follow av. de la Gare or av. de la Liberté, then watch for signs giving directions to the city's main sights. Facing the tourist office in the pl. d'Armes, the Pétrusse Valley is to your right; take r. Chimay to reach **Place de la Constitution** and the historic **Pétrusse Casemates.** The city's lower areas, the **Grund** and the **Clausen,** are located diagonally to your right and left, 10min. and 15min. on foot, respectively. Halfway between these areas are the **Bock Casemates;** from the pl. d'Armes, walk straight down r. du Curé, which becomes r. Boucherie and then r. Sigefroi.

Tourist Offices: Grand Duchy National Tourist Office (☎42 82 82 20; www.ont.lu), in the train station. Open daily June-Sept. 8:30am-6:30pm; Oct.-May 9:15am-12:30pm and 1:45-6pm. **Luxembourg City Tourist Office,** pl. d'Armes (☎22 28 09; www.lcto.lu). Open Apr.-Sept. M-Sa 9am-7pm, Su 10am-6pm; Oct.-Mar. M-Sa 9am-6pm, Su 10am-6pm. Also, during the summer, look for the helpful, yellow-shirted **"Ask Me"** representatives around the city–they give out free tourist info.

Embassies: Ireland, 28 rte. d'Arlon (☎45 06 10). Open M-F 9:30am-12:30pm. **UK,** 5 bd. Joseph II (☎22 98 64). Open M-F 9:30am-12:30pm. **US,** 22 bd. Emmanuel Servais (☎46 01 23). Open Th 8:30-11:30am and 1:30-3pm. **Australians, Canadians,** and **New Zealanders** should contact their embassies in France or Belgium.

Currency Exchange: Banks are the only option for changing money or cashing traveler's checks. Most are open M-F 8:30am until 4 or 4:30pm. All are closed on weekends. Expect to pay commissions of €5 for cash and €8 for traveler's checks.

Luggage Storage: In the train station. €2-4 per day, depending on the size of locker. Storage for up to 48hr. Open daily 6:30am-9:30pm.

Laundromat: Quick Wash, 31 r. de Strasbourg (☎26 19 65 42), near the station. Wash and dry €12. Open M-F 8:30am-6:30pm, Sa 8am-6pm.

Pharmacy: Pharmacie Goedert, 5 pl. d'Armes (☎22 23 99). Open M-F 8am-6:15pm, Sa 8am-12:30pm. After hours, check the window for a schedule of 24hr. pharmacies.

Hospital: Doctors and pharmacies on call ☎112. **Clinique Ste-Thérèse,** r. Ste-Zithe 36 (☎49 77 61 or 49 77 65). Open M-F 7am-5pm for office visits. Doctors are available for emergencies M-W, F 7am-7pm, Th 24hr.

Internet Access: Centre Information Jeunes (see above) has free Internet for students. **Cyber-Grund,** 2 r. Saint-Ulric (☎26 20 39 98), in the Grund. €2 per 30min., €3 per hr. Tu-F noon-3pm rates discounted to €2 per hr. Open Tu-F noon-6:30pm, Sa 1-5pm.

Post Office: 38 pl. de la Gare, across the street and to the left of the train station. Open M-F 6am-7pm, Sa 6am-noon. Address mail to be held in the following format: First name SURNAME, *Poste Restante,* L-1009 Luxembourg G-I Gare, LUXEMBOURG. Another branch, 25 r. Aldringen, near pl. d'Armes. Open M-F 7am-7pm, Sa 7am-5pm.

ACCOMMODATIONS AND CAMPING

The city hostel is the only budget option in Luxembourg City. Hotels are cheaper near the train station than in the city center.

Auberge de Jeunesse (HI), 2 r. du Fort Olisy (☎22 19 20). Take bus #9 and ask to get off at the hostel. Head under the bridge and turn right down the steep path. Call ahead to book shuttles from the airport (€3) and train station (€2). This brand-new hostel has a beautiful riverside setting, lively restaurant, and bar. Book in advance. Breakfast included. Reception 24hr. Dorms €19.60. €3 HI discount. AmEx/MC/V. ❷

Bella Napoli, 4 r. de Strasbourg (☎48 46 29). From the train station, go straight down r. de la Liberté and turn left onto r. de Strasbourg. Simple rooms with hardwood floors and full bath. Breakfast included. Reception 8am-midnight. Singles €38; doubles €45; triples €60. AmEx/MC/V. ❹

Hotel Schintgen, 6 r. Notre Dame (☎22 28 44). Down r. Chimay from the pl. d'Armes, turn right onto r. Notre Dame. One of the best deals in the Old Center, as long as you don't mind the noise of the street below. Breakfast included. Reception 7am-11pm. Singles €55-67; doubles €80-87; triples €90; quads €95. AmEx/MC/V. ❺

Camping Kockelscheuer (☎47 18 15), 7km outside Luxembourg City. Take bus #5 from the station or city center to Kockelscheuer-Camping. Free showers. Snack bar open 5-8:30pm. Open Easter-Oct. Reception 7am-noon and 2-10:30pm. Tent sites €8.25, extra person €3.75. Cash only. ❶

FOOD

Although the area around the pl. d'Armes teems with a strange mix of fast-food joints and upscale restaurants, there are a few affordable and appealing alternatives. Stock up on groceries at **Supermarché Boon,** in Galerie Kons across from the train station. (Open M-F 8am-8pm, Sa 8am-6pm, Su 8am-noon.)

Restaurant-Café Chiggeri, 15 r. du Nord (☎22 82 36). From pl. du Théatre, walk down r. du Nord; Chiggeri is on the right after the bend. Serves traditional French food amid shimmery, night-sky decor. Wine list offers an amazing 2300 vintages. Entrees €10-14. Open M-Th 8:30am-1am, F-Sa 8am-3am, Su 10am-1am. Kitchen closes at midnight. Bar closes at 1am. AmEx/MC/V. ❸

Mesa Verde, 11 r. du St-Esprit (☎46 41 26), down the street from the pl. de Clairefontaine. A local favorite, this bright vegetarian restaurant features an ever-changing array of hand-painted murals and billowing fabrics. Entrees €18-25. Open Tu-Sa 6:30pm-midnight. Open for lunch W-F noon-2pm. MC/V. ❹

Au Table du Pain, 37 av. de la Liberté (☎29 56 63), on the way to the train station. Serves soups, salads (€8-10), sandwiches (€4-8), and baked goods on wooden tables in a country home atmosphere. Open M-F 7am-6pm. Cash only. ❷

Namur, 27 r. des Capucins (☎22 34 08), down the street from pl. d'Armes. Marble floors and an elegant ambience make the selection of pastries, chocolates, and sundaes (€4-6) even sweeter. Open M 2-6pm, Tu-Sa 8:30am-6pm. MC/V. ❷

MAKE A WISH, YOUR HIGHNESS

uxembourg's diminutive size oesn't stop it from throwing one normous royal birthday party. he circumstances around the une 23 bash are a little puzzling, ince Grand Duke Henri was born n April 16, 1955. But Henri nherited the tradition from his randmother, Grand Duchess harlotte, born on January 23, 896. When her court realized hat mid-winter doesn't lend itself o open-air wingdings, they udged official celebrations up by ive months. Reluctant to further onfuse their subjects, both rand Duke Henri and his father ean took June 23 as their own.

A long procession through the ld city starts things off early in he evening on June 22. At 11pm, ireworks rip through the air, and vaterfalls of fire make silhouettes ut of the city's tall bridges. Then, n a flash, the narrow streets are ransformed into impromptu bars nd dance floors; alcohol flows ike water, spirits are high, and it akes the rising sun to finally reak up the party. The dishev-eled revelers pour into the Place l'Armes for breakfast before stag-gering home to sleep. June 23 is public holiday, so once the city vakes around noon, everyone eads downtown to see Henri trolling through the streets. With is aged parents in tow and royal ecurity out of sight, the duke estores calm and a sense of rou-ine to a city unaccustomed to uch glorious commotion.

Schumacher, 18 av. de la Porte-Neuve (☎22 90 09). This popular sandwich spot lends itself well to last-minute picnics in the Pétrusse Valley. Sandwiches €2-4. Open M-F 7am-6pm, Sa 7am-6pm. AmEx/DC/MC/V. ❶

SIGHTS

Luxembourg City is compact enough to be explored on foot. The most spectacular views of the city can be seen from **Place de la Constitution** and from the bridge closest to the **Bock Casemates.** For guidance on your stroll, follow the signs pointing out the **Wenzel Walk.** It leads visitors through 1000 years of history as it winds around the old city, from the **Chemin de la Corniche** down into the casemates.

FORTRESSES AND THE OLD CITY. The city's first fortress, built in AD 963, has has seen its network of fortifications expand so much over the years that the city has earned the nickname "Gibraltar of the North." The fortress also contains the **casemates,** an intricate 23km network of tunnels through the fortress walls. During WWII, these tunnels sheltered 35,000 people during bomb raids. Start your tour with the **Bock Casemates** fortress, part of Luxembourg's original castle, which looms over the Alzette River Valley and offers a fantastic view of the **Grund** and the **Clausen.** An invaluable brochure allows visitors to tour this system of casements on their own without getting lost. *(Entrance on r. Sigefroi, just past the bridge leading to the hostel. Open Mar.-Oct. daily 10am-5pm. €1.75, students €1.50.)* A visit to the **Pétrusse Casemates,** built by the Spanish in the 1600s, takes explorers down 250 steps into historic chambers while providing views of the Pétrusse Valley. A tour is required, but it's interesting and cheap. *(On pl. de la Constitution. English-language tours every hr., on the hr. July-Sept. 11am-4pm. €1.75, students €1.50.)* Visitors can also catch one of the **Pétrusse Express tourist trains** that depart from pl. de la Constitution and meander through the city and into the valley. *(Mid-Mar. to Oct. every 30min. 10am-6pm except 1pm. Trip lasts 1hr. €8.)* Double decker, roofless **tourist buses** allow you to get on and off as you please; they depart every 20min. from several marked stops throughout the city. *(Info for train and buses ☎26 65 11; www.sightseeing.lu. €12, students €10.)*

MUSEUMS. The **Luxembourg Card** covers transportation and entrance to 51 museums and tourist attractions throughout the country. *(Available at tourist offices and most train stations. www.luxembourgcard.lu. 1-day card €9, 2-day €16, 3-day €22.)* The eclectic collection at the

Musée National d'Histoire et d'Art features an exhibit that chronicles the influences of conquering powers on Luxembourg's art. *(Marché-aux-Poissons, at r. Boucherie and Sigefroi. ☎479 33 01; www.mnha.lu. Open Tu-Su 10am-5pm. €5, students €3.)* The only gamble at **Casino Luxembourg** is on the changing exhibits of contemporary art. *(41 r. Notre Dame, near pl. de la Constitution. ☎22 50 45; www.casino-luxembourg.lu. Open M, W-Su 11am-6pm, Th until 8pm. €4, under 26 €3.)*

NIGHTLIFE

There is no central location for nightlife in Luxembourg City, so an evening of bar-hopping also involves hopping on and off of the city's night bus. In the summer, the **Place d'Armes** comes to life with free concerts and stand-up comedy. Pick up a copy of *Nico* at the tourist office for a list of nightlife action and events.

Marx Bar, 42-44 r. de Hollerich (☎48 84 26; www.marx-bar.lu). Take bus #1 or 22, or walk down av. de la Gare away from the city center. Live music at a classy outdoor bar and DJs inside. Dress to impress. Beer €2.20. Open daily 5pm-1am. MC/V.

Melusina, 145 r. de la Tour Jacob (☎43 59 22). Cross the bridge from the Grund lift, then follow the left side of r. de Trèves and veer left as it becomes r. de la Tour Jacob. Dance the night away at this cafe and weekend nightspot. Cafe open M-Th 11:30am-2pm and 7-11pm, F-Sa 11:30am-2pm and 7-11pm. Club open F-Sa 11pm-late. Cover €7.50-12. Free drink 11pm-midnight. Cash only.

Urban, at the corner of r. de la Boucherie and r. du Marché-aux-Herbes (☎26 47 85 78; www.urban.lu). A friendly, crowded bar in the heart of the downtown. Food served until 7pm. Open daily noon-1am. Cash only.

The Elevator, 48 r. de Hollerich (☎29 41 64), down the road from The Complex. A local favorite, with lively crowds and outside-the-mainstream electronic music. W happy hour 5-8pm with half-price drinks. Open M-F 5pm-1am, Sa-Su 7pm-1am.

The Deep Bar, 11 r. Aldringen (☎26 20 04 23; www.deepbar.lu). Friendly gay bar. All are welcome. Beer €2. Open M 7am-9pm, Tu-Th 7am-1am, F 7am-3am, Sa 8pm-3am.

THE ARDENNES

In 1944, the Battle of the Bulge raged through the rolling hills of this region. Today, quiet towns, looming castles, and pleasant hiking trails are powerful draws.

ETTELBRÜCK. The main railway line linking Luxembourg City to Liège, Belgium, runs through Ettelbrück (pop. 7500), making the town the transportation hub for the Ardennes. Little else recommends the place, although history buffs waiting out a layover might investigate the **General Patton Memorial Museum,** 5 r. Dr. Klein, which commemorates Luxembourg's liberation during WWII. (☎81 03 22. Open June to mid-Sept. daily 10am-noon and 1-5pm; mid-Sept. to June M-Sa 10am-noon and 1-5pm, Su 2-5pm. €2.50.) Buy groceries at **Match,** near the train station. (Open M-Th 7:30am-7:30pm, F 7:30am-8pm, Sa 7:30am-6pm, Su 9am-12:30pm.) **Trains** go to: Clervaux (30min., every hr.); Liège (2hr., every 2hr.); Luxembourg City (25min., 3 per hr.). The **tourist office** is in the station. (☎81 20 68; www.sit-e.lu. Open M-F 9am-noon and 1:30-5pm, Sa 10am-noon and 2-4pm; Sept.-June closed Sa.)

VIANDEN. The village of Vianden (pop. 2000) is home to one of the most impressive castles in Western Europe. A weathered patchwork of Carolingian, Gothic, and Renaissance architecture, the stoic **Chateau de Vianden** holds several displays of armor, furniture, and tapestries. The real attraction, however, is the view from the top of the hill, where you can look down at the towers and battlements of the castle. (☎83 41 08; www.castle-vianden.lu. Open daily Apr.-Sept. 10am-6pm;

Nov.-Feb. 10am-4pm; Oct. and Mar. 10am-5pm. €5.50, students €4.50.) Delicious home-cooked dinners await at the social **Auberge de Jeunesse (HI) ❷,** 3 Montée du Château, near the foot of the castle. To get there, climb Grande Rue up the hill and toward the castle; the road will change to Montée du Château. (☎83 41 77; www.youthhostels.lu/site/Viandenauberge.html. Breakfast included. Dinner €7.50; order ahead. Reception 8-10am and 5-9pm. Closed mid-Nov. to Dec. Dorms €17.70. €3 HI discount.) **Buses** head to Ettelbrück (#570; 30min., 2 per hr., €2.40) via Diekirch, and to Clervaux (40min., 4 per day). From the bus station, take r. de la Gare to the center of town; the **tourist office,** 1 r. du Vieux Marché, is next to the bridge. (☎83 42 57; www.tourist-info-vianden.lu. Internet €2 per hr. Open in summer M-F 8am-6pm, Sa-Su 10am-2pm; winter 8am-noon and 1-5pm.)

ESCH-SUR-SÛRE. Cradled by the green Ardennes mountains and almost encircled by the Sûre River, this tiny village (pop. 320) is an ideal base of operations for those looking to explore the beautiful **Haute-Sûre nature reserve** (☎899 3311; www.naturpark-sure.lu) or to strike out along the area's 700km of nature trails. The dramatic ruins of Luxembourg's oldest **castle** overlook the village. English-language audio tours (1½hr.) of the castle are available at the nature reserve for €4. (Open Apr.-Nov. M-Tu, Th-F 10am-noon and 2-6pm, Sa-Su 2-6pm; Nov.-Apr. closes 5pm.) **Hotel de la Sûre ❸,** 1 r. du Pont, the village's unofficial tourist office and best bet for lodgings, offers small luxuries like a sauna in a relaxed and social setting. (☎83 91 10; www.hotel-de-la-sure.lu. F 10pm guided mountain hike. Bike rental €5 per hr.; €12 per half-day, hotel guests €11; €22 per day, hotel guests €19. Free canoe loan for guests. Breakfast included. Free Internet. Reception 7am-midnight. M-F singles from €25.50, weekends €28. AmEx/MC/V.) The **bus** to Ettelbrück runs on weekdays (25min., every 2-4hr., €2). Hotel de la Sûre offers daily **shuttles** to Ettelbrück for its guests (€15; call ahead to arrange pickup).

ECHTERNACH. In the heart of the Little Switzerland region, Echternach (pop. 4500) is a paradise for **hikers** and **bikers** who venture out into the surrounding woodlands. In town, the turrets of the 15th-century **town hall** share the skyline of the pl. du Marché with the towering **Basilica of St. Willibrord.** (Basilica open daily 8:30am-7:30pm. Free.) St. Willibrord draws more than 10,000 pilgrims every Whit Tuesday (7th Tu after Easter) for a **Dancing Procession** of penance and healing. The basilica and the intimate Église Saints Pierre-et-Paul host Echternach's renowned **International Music Festival** in May and June. (☎72 83 47; www.echternachfestival.lu. Tickets €8-55, students from €7.) The remains of a **Roman villa** can be found near the river; a museum and open-air exhibit cast light on its history. (☎26 72 09 74. Open daily Easter-May and Oct.-Nov. 11am-1pm and 2-5pm; June and Sept. 11am-6pm; July-Aug. 10am-6pm. €2.)

A new **Auberge de Jeunesse (HI) ❷,** set on the lake on r. Grégoire, is scheduled to open in January of 2006. Call ahead for shuttle service or walk 15min. to the lake from the bus station. (☎72 01 58. Breakfast included. Reception 24hr. Dorms €19.60. €3 HI discount. MC/V.) Pick up groceries at **Match,** near pl. du Marché. (Open M-F 8am-7pm, Sa 8am-6pm, Su 8am-noon.) **Buses** run to Ettelbrück (50min., every hr.) and Luxembourg City (1hr., 2 per hr.). To get from the bus station to the town center, walk past the cafes lining r. de la Gare. Rent **bikes** at Trisport, 31 rte. de Luxembourg. (☎72 00 86. €2.50 per hr., €15 per day.) The **tourist office,** 9 parvis de la Basilique, provides information on hikes and bike routes in the area. (☎72 02 30; www.echternach-tourist.lu. Open July-Aug. daily 9:30am-12:30pm and 1:30-5:30pm; low season M-F 9:30am-12:30pm and 1:30-5:30pm.)

THE NETHERLANDS (NEDERLAND)

With most of the Netherlands's land area below sea level, the task of keeping its iconic tulips and windmills on dry ground has become something of a national pastime. Early planners built dikes to hold back the sea, but a new "flexible coast" policy depends on spillways and reservoirs to contain potentially disastrous floods. For a people treading water, the Dutch have deep cultural roots and a down-to-earth friendliness that keep them better grounded than most land-locked nations. Time-tested art, ambitious architecture, and dynamic nightlife make the Netherlands one of the most popular destinations in Europe.

DISCOVER THE NETHERLANDS: SUGGESTED ITINERARIES

Start with at least two days dallying amid the canals and coffeeshops of **Amsterdam** (p. 723). **Museumplein** is home to some of the finest art collections in Europe, while the houses of ill repute in the **Red Light District** are delightfully lurid. Zip out to the beach parties in **Zandvoort** (p. 743), and take a day to recover in historic **Haarlem** (p. 742). Head south to amble among the monuments of **The Hague** (p. 744), before bracing yourself for hypermodern Rotterdam (p. 746). Explore the museums in the college town of **Utrecht** (p. 746). Spend the night in **Arnhem,** and the next day roaming the trails and galleries of **De Hoge Veluwe National Park** (p. 747). The trendy, underappreciated city of **Groningen** (p. 748) marks the end of the trail up north.

ESSENTIALS

FACTS AND FIGURES

Official Name: Kingdom of the Netherlands.

Capital: Amsterdam; The Hague is the seat of government.

Major Cities: The Hague, Rotterdam, Utrecht.

Population: 16,407,491.

Time Zone: GMT +1.

Language: Dutch; English is spoken almost universally.

Religions: Catholic (31%), Protestant (20%), Muslim (5.5%).

WHEN TO GO

July and August are lovely months to travel to the Netherlands, as the crowded hostels and lengthy lines during those months will confirm. If you fancy a bit more elbow room, you may prefer April, May, and early June, as tulips and fruit trees roar into bloom and temperatures hover around 12-20°C (53-68°F). The Netherlands is famously drizzly year-round, so travelers should bring raingear.

DOCUMENTS AND FORMALITIES

EMBASSIES AND CONSULATES. All foreign embassies and most consulates are in The Hague (p. 744). Both the US and the UK have consulates in Amsterdam (p. 723). Dutch embassies abroad include: **Australia,** 120 Empire Circuit, Yarralumla

Canberra, ACT 2600 (☎02 62 20 94 00; www.netherlands.org.au); **Canada,** 350 Albert St., Ste. 2020, Ottawa ON K1R 1A4 (☎613-237-5030; www.netherlandsembassy.ca); **Ireland,** 160 Merrion Rd., Dublin 4 (☎012 69 34 44; www.netherlandsembassy.ie); **New Zealand,** P.O. Box 840, at Ballance and Featherston St., Wellington (☎04 471 63 90; http://netherlandsembassy.co.nz); **US,** 4200 Linnean Ave. NW, Washington, D.C. 20008 (☎202-244-5300; www.netherlands-embassy.org); **UK,** 38 Hyde Park Gate, London SW7 5DP (☎020 75 90 32 00; www.netherlands-embassy.org.uk).

VISAS AND ENTRY INFORMATION. EU citizens do not need a visa. Citizens of Australia, Canada, New Zealand, and the US do not need a visa for stays of up to 90 days, beginning upon entry into any of the countries in the EU's freedom of movement zone. For more information, see p. 16.

TOURIST SERVICES AND MONEY

EMERGENCY	**Police, Ambulance,** and **Fire:** ☎112.

TOURIST OFFICES. VVV (vay-vay-vay) tourist offices are marked by triangular blue signs. The website www.visitholland.com is also a useful resource.

MONEY. The **euro (€)** has replaced the guilder as the unit of currency in the Netherlands. For more info on the euro, see p. 21. As a general rule, it's cheaper to exchange money in the Netherlands than at home. A bare-bones day traveling in the Netherlands will cost €35-40; a slightly more comfortable day will run €50-60. Hotels, shops, and restaurants always include a service charge in the bill; additional tips are appreciated but not necessary. Taxi drivers are generally tipped 10% of the fare. Retail goods in the Netherlands bear a 19% **Value Added Tax (VAT),** included in the listed price. In the airport, upon departure, non-EU citizens who have stayed in the EU fewer than 180 days can claim a refund on the tax paid for purchases at participating stores, as long as they meet minimum spending requirements. Ask shops to supply you with a tax return form.

TRANSPORTATION

BY PLANE. Many major airlines, including the Dutch **KLM,** fly into Amsterdam's **Schiphol Airport** (AMS). **Ryanair** flies from London Stansted into secondary airports in Aachen (AAH), Eindhoven (EIN), and Groningen (GRQ), all accessible by rail. For more info on flying to Europe, see p. 48.

BY TRAIN. The national rail company is the efficient **Nederlandse Spoorwegen** (NS; Netherlands Railways; www.ns.nl). Train service tends to be faster than bus service. *Sneltreinen* are the fastest, while *stoptreinen* make many local stops. One-way tickets are called *enkele reis;* same-day, round-trip tickets *(dagretour)* are valid only on the day of purchase, but are roughly 15% cheaper than normal round-trip tickets. *Weekendretour* tickets are not quite as cheap, but are valid from Friday at 7pm through Monday at 4am. A day pass *(dagkaart)* allows unlimited travel throughout the country for one day, for the price equivalent of the most expensive one-way fare across the country. **Eurail** and **InterRail** are valid in the Netherlands. The **Holland Railpass** is good for three or five travel days in any one-month period. Although available in the US, the Holland Railpass is cheaper in the Netherlands at DER Travel Service or RailEurope offices. For more information on train travel in Europe, see p. 53.

WHERE'S THE RAIL? Nederlandse Spoorwegen is the Dutch national rail company, operating the country's intercity train service. Their website, www.ns.nl, has an English-language section where you can check train times and costs, and get door-to-door directions for all stops in the Netherlands.

BY BUS. A nationalized fare system covers city buses, trams, and long-distance buses. The country is divided into zones; a trip between destinations in the same zone costs two strips on a *strippenkaart* (strip card), while a trip that traverses two zones will set you back three strips. On buses, tell the driver your destination and he or she will cancel the correct number of strips; on trams and subways, stamp your own *strippenkaart* in either a yellow box at the back of the tram or in the subway station. Tram and bus drivers sell cards with two, three, and eight strips, but it's cheaper to buy 15-strip or 45-strip cards at tourist offices, post offices, and some newsstands near a rail station. Day passes *(dagkaarten)* are valid for travel throughout the country and are discounted as special summer tickets *(zomerzwerfkaarten)* during the months of June, July, and August. Riding without a ticket can result in a fine.

BY CAR. As a general rule, tourists with a driver's license valid in their home country can drive in the Netherlands for fewer than 185 days. The country has well-maintained roadways, although drivers may cringe at high fuel prices and at the congestion around Amsterdam, The Hague, and Rotterdam. The yellow cars of the **Royal Dutch Touring Association** (ANWB) patrol many major roads, and will offer prompt roadside assistance. In the case of a breakdown, call the ANWB (☎080 08 88) toll-free from any yellow phone booth.

BY BIKE AND BY THUMB. Cycling is the way to go in the Netherlands—distances between cities are short, the countryside is absolutely flat, and most streets have separate bike lanes. Bike rentals run €6-7 per day and €25-40 per week. For a database of bike rental shops across the country, visit www.holland.com/global/discover/active/cycling. **Hitchhiking** is illegal on motorways but common elsewhere; droves of hitchhikers can be found along roads leading out of Amsterdam. Those choosing this mode of transport often take public transportation to a nearby town before trying their luck. *Let's Go* does not recommend hitchhiking.

KEEPING IN TOUCH

PHONE CODES	**Country code:** 31. **International dialing prefix:** 00. For more information on how to place international calls, see inside back cover.

EMAIL AND THE INTERNET. Email is easily accessible within the Netherlands. In small towns, try the public library. Travelers with wireless-enabled computers may be able to take advantage of an increasing number of hot spots, which offer wireless Internet for free or for a small fee. Websites like www.jiwire.com, www.wi-fihotspotlist.com, and www.locfinder.net can help locate hot spots.

TELEPHONE. Some pay phones still accept coins, but phone cards are the rule. KPT and Telfort are the most widely accepted varieties, the former available at post offices and the latter at train stations (from €5). **Mobile phones** are an increasingly popular and economical alternative (p. 33). For directory assistance, dial ☎09 00 80 08; for collect calls, dial ☎08 00 01 01. International direct dial numbers include: **AT&T** (☎0800 022 91 11); **British Telecom** (☎0800 089 00 31); **Canada Direct** (☎0800 022 91 16); **MCI** (☎0800 023 5103); **Sprint** (☎0800 022 91 19); **Telecom New Zealand** (☎0800 022 44 64); **Telstra Australia** (☎0800 022 00 61).

MAIL. Post offices are generally open Monday through Friday 9am-5 or 6pm, while in larger towns some remain open Thursday or Friday night, or Saturday 10am-1pm. Mailing a postcard or letter (up to 20g) in the EU or a postcard outside of Europe costs €0.54; letters outside of Europe cost €0.75.

LANGUAGE. Dutch is the official language of the Netherlands. Most natives speak excellent English, thanks to mandatory English education in schools and English-language media exports.

ACCOMMODATIONS AND CAMPING

THE NETHERLANDS	❶	❷	❸	❹	❺
ACCOMMODATIONS	under €25	€25-32	€32-45	€45-55	over €55

VVV offices supply accommodation listings and can almost always reserve rooms for a €2-5 fee. **Private rooms** cost about two-thirds as much as hotels, but they are harder to find; check with the VVV. During July and August, many cities add a tourist tax (€1-2) to the price of all rooms. The country's 30 **Hostelling International (HI) youth hostels,** run by **Stayokay** (www.stayokay.com), are dependably clean and modern. **Camping** is available across the country, although campsites tend to be crowded during the summer months; **CityCamps Holland** has a network of 17 well-maintained sites. Visit www.strandheem.nl for more information.

FOOD AND DRINK

THE NETHERLANDS	❶	❷	❸	❹	❺
FOOD	under €7	€7-11	€11-16	€16-21	over €21

Traditional Dutch cuisine is hearty, heavy, meaty, and wholesome. Expect bread and cheese for breakfast and lunch, and generous portions of meat and fish for dinner, traditionally the only hot meal of the day. Seafood is popular, including all sorts of grilled fish and shellfish, fish stews, and raw herring. For a truly authentic Dutch meal (most commonly available in May and June), ask for white asparagus, served with potatoes, ham, and eggs. Light snacks include *tostis* (hot grilled cheese sandwiches, sometimes with ham) and *broodjes* (light, cold sandwiches), while colonial history has added Surinamese and Indonesian cuisine into the mix. Wash it all down with a foamy glass of Heineken or Amstel.

HOLIDAYS AND FESTIVALS

Holidays: New Year's Day (Jan. 1); Good Friday (Apr. 14); Easter Sunday and Monday (Apr. 16-17); WWII Remembrance Day (May 4); Liberation Day (May 5); National Windmill Day (May 13); Ascension Day (May 25); Whit Sunday and Monday (June 4-5); Boxing Day (Dec. 26).

Festivals: Koninginnedag (Queen's Day; Apr. 30) turns the country into a huge carnival. The Holland Performing Arts Festival (June 24) is a massive celebration of the arts. Bloemen Corso (Flower Parade; Sept. 2) runs from Aalsmeer to Amsterdam. Many historical canal houses and windmills are open to the public for National Monument Day (2nd Sa in Sept.). The High Times Cannabis Cup (Late Nov.) celebrates the weed that is rumored to have had a positive effect on Amsterdam's tourism industry.

BEYOND TOURISM

Volunteer, study, and work opportunities in the Netherlands revolve around the hallmarks of Dutch culture, with environmental-, political-, and community-based programs featuring most prominently.

Het Vrouwenhuis (The Women's House), Nieuwe Herengracht 95, Amsterdam (☎625 20 66). A center for several organizations and magazines dedicated to supporting women. Also offers classes and workshops; mostly in Dutch, some in English.

University of Amsterdam, Spui 21, Amsterdam (☎525 80 80 or 525 33 33; www.uva.nl/english). Amsterdam's largest university offers a full range of degree programs in Dutch. Open to college and graduate students. The Summer Institute on Sexuality, Culture, and Society (www.ishss.uva.nl/summerinstitute), set in the heart of one of the world's most tolerant cities, offers participants a foray into the ins and outs of all things sexual. Tuition €1445-10,000 per year, depending on the program. Discounts offered for EU citizens.

AMSTERDAM ☎020

Amsterdam's reputation precedes it—and what a reputation it is. Born out of a murky bog and cobbled together over eight centuries, the "Dam on the River Amstel" (pop. 735,000) coaxes visitors with an alluring blend of grandeur and decadence. Geometry-defying canals support palatial museums and narrow, gabled houses. Thick clouds of marijuana smoke waft from subdued coffeeshops, and countless bicycles whoosh past blooming tulip markets. Yet there is more to Amsterdam than postcard icons. Against the backdrop of Van Gogh's thick swirls and Vermeer's luminous figures, gritty street artists spray a graffiti of protest. Squatters sharpen the city's defiant edge, while politicians push the boundaries of progressive reform. Gay and lesbian citizens blend seamlessly into a social landscape that defines tolerance, but one that today faces difficult questions, including Muslim integration into Dutch secularism; the limits of liberalism in an interdependent world; and of course, the endless fight to fend off the encroaching seas.

TRANSPORTATION

Flights: Schiphol Airport (AMS; ☎0800 72 44 74 65). Light rail **sneltrains** connect the airport to Centraal Station (20min., every 10min., €2.90).

Trains: Centraal Station, Stationspl. 1 (☎09 00 92 92, €0.30 per min.; www.ns.nl), at the northern end of the Damrak. To: **Brussels, Belgium** (2½-3hr., 1-2 per hr., €40); **Groningen** (2½hr., 2 per hr., €23.80); **Haarlem** (20min., 6-7 per hr., €3.10); **The Hague** (50min., 2-3 per hr., €9.40); **Leiden** (35min., 2-4 per hr., €7.40); **Paris, France** (4hr., 10 per day, €94); **Rotterdam** (1hr., every hr., €12.40); **Utrecht** (40min., 3-8 per hr., €7.60).

Buses: Trains are quicker, but the **GVB** (see below) will direct you to a bus stop for domestic destinations not on a rail line. **Muiderpoort** (2 blocks east of Oosterpark) sends buses east; **Marnixstation** (at the corner of Marnixstr. and Kinkerstr.) west; and the **Stationsplein depot** north and south.

Public Transportation: GVB (☎09 00 92 92, €0.30 per min.), on Stationspl. in front of Centraal Station. Open M-F 7am-9pm, Sa-Su 8am-9pm. **Tram, metro,** and **bus** lines radiate from Centraal Station. Trams are most convenient for inner-city travel; the metro leads to farther-out neighborhoods. Normal public transportation runs daily 6am-12:30am; **night buses** traverse the city 12:30am-7am—pick up a schedule and map at the GVB. *Strippenkaarten* (strip cards) are used on all public transportation in Amsterdam; 2 strips (€1.60) get you to almost all sights within the city center and include unlimited transfers for 1hr. *Strippenkaarten* are cheapest bought in bulk (up to bundles of 45) and are available everywhere, especially at newsstands and tourist offices.

Bike Rental: Frederic Rent a Bike, Brouwersgr. 78 (☎624 55 09; www.frederic.nl), in the Shipping Quarter. Bikes €10 per day, €40 per week. Lock, theft insurance, and personalized map of the city included. Open daily 9am-6pm. AmEx/MC/V. **MacBike Rentals,** Stationspl. 12 (☎620 09 85; www.macbike.nl), has 2 locations in the south of the city at Weteringschans 2, near Museumpl., and at Mr. Visserpl. 2. Bikes €6.50-9.75 per day, plus €3-5 for theft insurance. €50 deposit. Open daily 9am-5:45pm. AmEx/MC/V.

ORIENTATION

Let the canals guide you through Amsterdam's cozy but confusing neighborhoods. In the city center, water runs in concentric circles, beginning at Centraal Station. The **Singel** runs around the **Centrum,** which includes the **Oude Zijd** (Old Side), the infamous **Red Light District,** and the **Nieuwe Zijd** (New Side). Barely a kilometer in diameter, the Centrum overflows with brothels, bars, clubs, and tourists wading through wafts of marijuana smoke. The next three canals—the

Amsterdam

ACCOMMODATIONS
Aivergo Youth Hostel, **6**
Bicycle Hotel, **35**
Bob's Youth Hostel, **8**
Euphemia Budget Hotel, **31**
Flying Pig Downtown, **7**
Flying Pig Palace, **30**
Frederic Rent a Bike, **2**
The Golden Bear, **4**
Hemp Hotel, **32**
Hotel Asterisk, **33**
Hotel Bema, **36**
Hotel Brouwer, **5**
Hotel Clemens, **11**
Hotel Fantasia, **26**
Hotel Pension Kitty, **27**
Hotel Royal Taste, **12**
Quentin Hotel, **24**
The Shelter Jordan, **10**
StayOkay Amsterdam Stadsdoelen, **17**
StayOkay Amsterdam Vondelpark, **29**
Weichmann Hotel, **16**
The Winston Hotel, **9**

BEST OF FOOD
Eat at Jo's, **22**
Harlem: Drinks and Soulfood, **3**
In de Waag, **13**

BEST OF COFFEESHOPS
Abraxas, **14**
Barney's Coffeeshop, **1**

BEST OF NIGHTLIFE
Bourbon Street Jazz & Blues Club, **25**
Cafe de Jaren, **18**
Club NL, **15**
Escape, **21**
Melkweg, **23**
Paradiso, **28**
De Trut, **19**

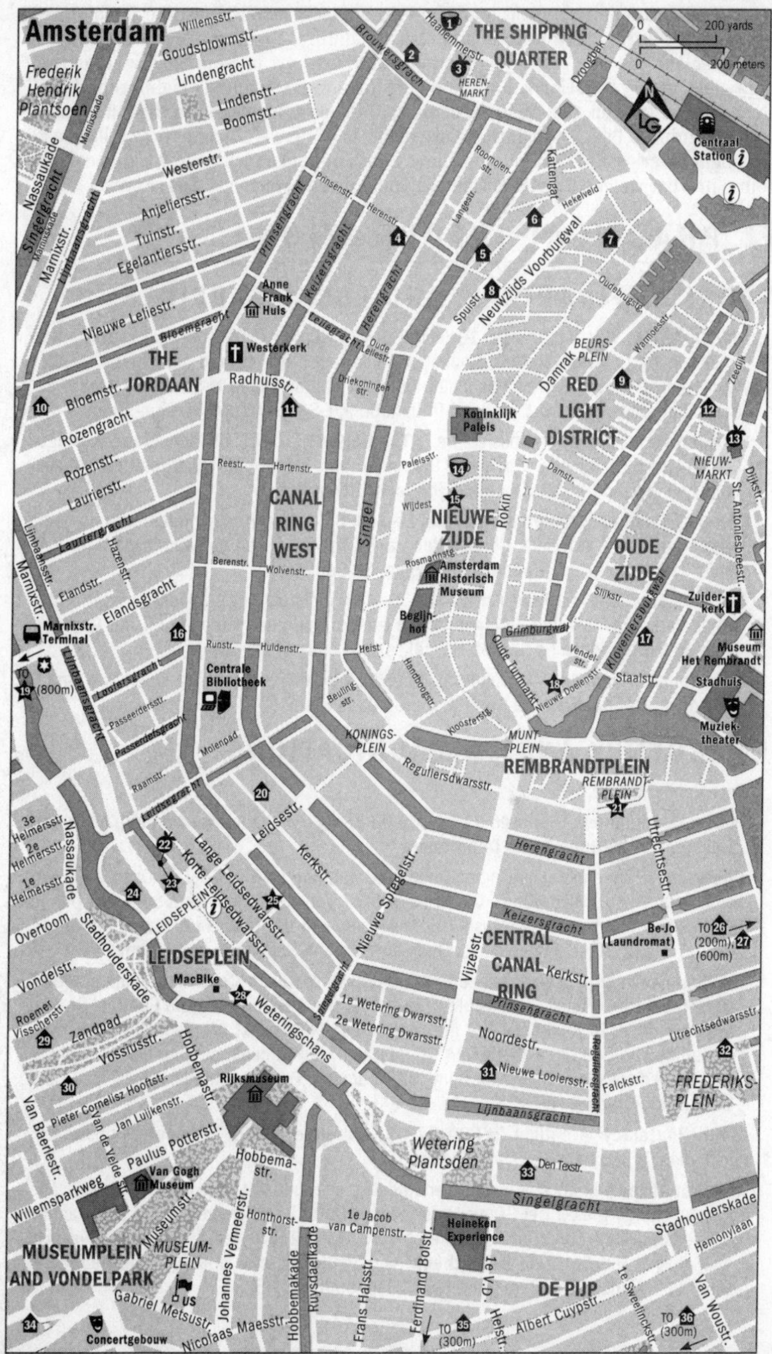

Amsterdam
THE SHIPPING QUARTER
THE JORDAAN
CANAL RING WEST
NIEUWE ZIJDE
RED LIGHT DISTRICT
OUDE ZIJDE
REMBRANDTPLEIN
CENTRAL CANAL RING
LEIDSEPLEIN
MUSEUMPLEIN AND VONDELPARK
DE PIJP
Centraal Station
Anne Frank Huis
Westerkerk
Koninklijk Paleis
Amsterdam Historisch Museum
Begijnhof
Zuiderkerk
Museum Het Rembrandt
Stadhuis
Muziektheater
Centrale Bibliotheek
Marnixstr. Terminal
Rijksmuseum
Van Gogh Museum
Heineken Experience
Concertgebouw
MacBike
Be-Jo (Laundromat)
Wetering Plantsden
FREDERIKSPLEIN
200 yards
200 meters

Herengracht, the **Keizersgracht,** and the **Prinsengracht**—constitute the **Canal Ring,** home to beautiful canal houses and classy nightlife. Just over the Singelgracht, **Museumplein** is home to the city's most renowned art museums as well as the sprawling, grassy **Vondelpark.** Farther out lie the more residential neighborhoods: to the west, the **Jordaan, Oud-West, Westerpark;** to the east, **Plantage** and the **Jodenbuurt;** to the south, **De Pijp.** Though these are districts of dense housing, they still boast excellent eateries and brilliant museums. South of Leidseplein, a few sights can be found in what we call **Greater Amsterdam,** including **Amsterdamse Bos** (Forest).

PRACTICAL INFORMATION

TOURIST, FINANCIAL, AND LOCAL SERVICES

Tourist Office: VVV, Stationspl. 10 (☎0900 400 40 40, €0.55 per min.), to the left when exiting Centraal Station. Books rooms for a €3.50 fee and sells maps for €2. Open daily 9am-5pm. Branches inside Centraal Station (open M-Sa 8am-7:45pm, Su 9am-5pm) and Leidsepl. 1 (open M-Th 9am-6pm, F-Sa 9am-7pm, Su 9am-5pm).

Consulates: All foreign embassies are in **The Hague** (p. 744). **UK Consulate,** Koningslaan 44 (☎676 43 43). Open M-F 9am-noon and 2-5:30pm. **US Consulate,** Museumpl. 19 (☎575 53 09). Open M-F 8:30am-11:30am.

Currency Exchange: American Express, Damrak 66, offers the best rates, with no commission on AmEx Traveler's Cheques and a €4 flat fee for all non-euro cash and non-AmEx traveler's checks. Open M-F 9am-5pm, Sa 9am-noon.

GLBT Resources: Pink Point (☎428 10 70; www.pinkpoint.org), a kiosk in front of the Westerkerk, provides info on nightlife and events. Open daily noon-6pm. The **Gay and Lesbian Switchboard** (☎623 65 65) takes calls daily 10am-10pm.

Laundromat: Happy Inn, Warmoesstr. 30 (☎624 84 64). €4 per 5kg. Open M-W and F 8am-7pm, Th 8am-9pm, Sa 8am-10pm, Su 9am-10pm.

EMERGENCY AND COMMUNICATIONS

Emergency: ☎112.

Police: Headquarters, Elandsgr. 117 (☎09 00 88 44), at the intersection with Marnixstr. Call here for the **Rape Crisis Department.**

Crisis Lines: General counseling at **Telephone Helpline** (☎675 75 75). Open 24hr. For drug counseling, call **Jellinek Clinic** (☎408 77 77). Open M-F 9am-5pm. For phone counseling about sexually transmitted diseases, call the **STD Line,** Groenburgwal 44 (☎555 58 22). Free testing clinic. Open for calls M-F 8am-noon and 1-4pm.

Medical Services: For hospital care, **Academisch Medisch Centrum,** Meibergdreef 9 (☎566 91 11), is easily accessible by bus #59, 60, 120, or 158 from Centraal Station (ask the driver to announce the medical center). **Kruispost Medisch Helpcentrum,** Oudezijds Voorburgwal 129 (☎624 90 31), is a walk-in clinic offering first aid only to non-insured travelers daily 7am-9pm. €25 per visit. For 24hr. medical help, call **Centrale Doktorsdienst** (☎592 34 34).

24hr. Pharmacy: A hotline (☎694 87 09) will direct you to the nearest pharmacy, including 24hr. pharmacies after hours.

Internet Access: Many coffeeshops and hostels offer Internet access for customers and guests, charging €1-2 per 30min. **easyInternetCafe,** Reguliersbreestr. 22 and Damrak 34, generally €1 per 26min., but rates vary. Open 24hr. Free 30min. slots are also available at the **Centrale Bibliotheek** (☎523 09 00; www.oba.nl), Prinsengr. 587. Open M 1-9pm, Tu-Th 10am-9pm, F-Sa 10am-5pm, Su 1-5pm.

Post Office: Singel 250, at Radhuisstr. Address mail to be held in the following format: First name, SURNAME, *Poste Restante,* Singel 250, 1016 AB, Amsterdam, THE NETHERLANDS. Open M-W and F 9am-6pm, Th 9am-8pm, Sa 10am-1:30pm.

ACCOMMODATIONS

The chaos of the Red Light District prompts accommodations near **Centraal Station** to enforce strong security measures, while hostels and hotels near **Museumplein** and out in the **Jordaan** can afford to be more laissez-faire. These locations are close to bars and coffeeshops and are a mere 2min. by tram from the heart of the city. Accommodations in the center of the **Red Light District** are often bars with beds over them. Before signing up for a bunk, consider just how much noise and drug use you can tolerate from your neighbors.

NIEUWE ZIJDE, OUDE ZIJDE, AND THE RED LIGHT DISTRICT

Aivergo Youth Hostel, Spuistr. 6 (☎421 36 70). Brightly tiled walls sprinkled with jewels endow this hostel with a uniformly cool vibe. Small safe-deposit box. Free Internet. 2-night min. stay on weekends. Lockout 1-5pm. No reservations; arrive before 11am for a room. Closed during part of Dec. Dorms €20-25; doubles €60. Cash only. ❶

Flying Pig Downtown, Nieuwendijk 100 (☎420 68 22; www.flyingpig.nl). Helpful staff, a great location, and a happening lounge keep backpackers coming. Breakfast and linen included. Free Internet. Key deposit €10. Online reservations strongly recommended. Dorms €21-27; singles and twins €76. AmEx/MC/V. ❶

The Winston Hotel, Warmoesstr. 129 (☎623 13 80; www.winston.nl). Rooms painted by local artists make every room feel like an installation art piece. Breakfast included. Singles €60-65; doubles €75-83; triples €110-118; quads 124-137. AmEx/MC/V. ❺

StayOkay Amsterdam Stadsdoelen (HI), Kloveniersburgwal 97 (☎624 68 32; www.hostel-booking.com). Clean, drug-free canalside lodgings in a quiet corner of Oude Zijde. Breakfast included. Laundry €4.50. Internet €5 per hr. Reception 7am-midnight. Dorms €22.50. €2.50 HI discount. AmEx/MC/V. ❶

Hotel Royal Taste, Oudezijds Achterburgwal 47 (☎623 24 78; www.hotelroyaltaste.com). Clean, almost-fancy accommodations at reasonable prices. All rooms with private bath, fridge, and TV; some with kitchen. Breakfast included. Singles €50; doubles €90; triples €135, quads €180. Cash only. ❹

Hotel Brouwer, Singelgr. 83 (☎624 63 58; www.hotelbrouwer.nl). 8 gorgeously restored rooms, each named for a Dutch painter. Breakfast included. Reception 8am-6pm. Reserve in advance. Singles €50; doubles €85. Cash and traveler's checks only. ❹

Bob's Youth Hostel, Nieuwezijds Voorburgwal 92 (☎623 00 63; www.bobsyouthhostel.nl). Big, no-frills dorms are popular with backpackers. Bar downstairs. Breakfast included. Key deposit €20. 2-night min. weekend stay. Reception 8am-3am. No reservations; arrive before 10am. Dorms €19; doubles €70; triples €90. Cash only. ❶

SHIPPING QUARTER, CANAL RING WEST, AND THE JORDAAN

Frederic Rent a Bike, Brouwersgr 78 (☎624 55 09; www.frederic.nl). In addition to bikes, Frederic also rents unique, beautiful rooms, apartments, and houseboats. The best options are 3 homey, cheerful rooms in the back of the rental shop— 1 has private bath with sauna jets, while the other 2 share a bath. Reception 9am-6pm. Singles €50-80; doubles €60-90; houseboats for 2-3 people €100-140. Apartments available for short-term stays. Cash only; AmEx/MC/V required for reservation. ❹

Wiechmann Hotel, Prinsengr. 328-332 (☎626 33 21; www.hotelwiechmann.nl). 3 restored canal houses with spacious rooms and grandma's-attic details. Breakfast included. Singles €75-95; doubles €120-140; triples and quads €180-230. MC/V. ❺

Hotel Clemens, Raadhuisstr. 39 (☎624 60 89; www.clemenshotel.nl). Each elegant suite has a safe. Breakfast €5. Key deposit €20. Book well in advance. 3-night min. stay on weekends. Singles €60; doubles €75, with bath €120; triples with bath €130. AmEx/MC/V. ❺

The Shelter Jordan, Bloemstr. 179 (☎624 47 17; www.shelter.nl). Religious but not proselytizing, this Christian hostel provides a quiet retreat. No smoking or alcohol. Under 35 only. Breakfast included. Lockers €5 deposit. Internet €1.50 per hr. Curfew 2am. July-Aug. dorms €19; Sept.-June €18. MC/V; 5% surcharge. ❶

LEIDSEPLEIN AND MUSEUMPLEIN

StayOkay Amsterdam Vondelpark (HI), Zandpad 5 (☎589 89 96; www.stayokay.com/vondelpark). One of the most palatial hostels in the StayOkay empire, in a lovely park-side location. Breakfast included. Lockers €2. Laundry €4.50. Internet €5 per hr. Reception 7:30am-midnight. Book well in advance. Dorms €24-29; doubles €80. Low season reduced rates. €2.50 HI discount. AmEx/MC/V. ❶

Quentin Hotel, Leidsekade 89 (☎626 21 87). A chic lobby leads to white, almost minimalist rooms with canal views. Reception 24hr. Singles €40, with bath €65; doubles €80-100; triples €125. AmEx/MC/V; 5% surcharge. ❸

Hotel Bema, Concertgebouwpl. 19b (☎679 13 96; www.bemahotel.com). Charming 7-room hotel with skylights and neo-hippie style. Breakfast included. Reception 8am-midnight. Singles €35-45; doubles €55, with bath €85; triples €75/90; quads €90-105. AmEx/MC/V; 5% surcharge. ❸

Flying Pig Palace, Vossiusstr. 46-47 (☎400 41 87; www.flyingpig.nl). Friendly attitude with views of Vondelpark. Online bookings don't guarantee you the room you reserved, so be prepared to switch rooms or pay extra to upgrade. Popular bar downstairs. Under 35 only. Breakfast included. Free Internet. Reception 8am-9pm. 7-night max. stay. Dorms €23-28; doubles €64; triples €90. Low season reduced rates. AmEx/MC/V. ❶

CENTRAL CANAL RING AND REMBRANDTPLEIN

Hemp Hotel, Frederikspl. 15 (☎625 44 25; www.hemp-hotel.com). 5 rooms are homages to all things hemp, using the material in everything from towels to soap. Unwind as you sip—what else?—hemp beer in the adjacent hotel bar. Breakfast included. Reception 11am-3am. Singles €50; doubles €65-80. MC/V; 5% surcharge. ❹

The Golden Bear, Kerkstr. 37 (☎624 47 85; www.goldenbear.nl). Opened in 1948, The Golden Bear may be the world's oldest openly gay hotel. Mainly male couples frequent the summery rooms, though lesbians are welcome. Breakfast included. Singles €60, with bath 105; doubles €74/118. Cash only. AmEx/MC/V required for reservations. ❺

Euphemia Budget Hotel, Fokke Simonszstr. 1-9 (☎622 90 45; www.euphemiahotel.com). Quiet, budget digs draw an older crowd to this former monastery. Internet €1 per 15min. Reception 8am-11pm. Doubles €80; triples €90; quads €120. 10% discount on 1st night with online reservation. AmEx/MC/V; 5% surcharge. ❸

Hotel Asterisk, Den Texstr. 16 (☎626 23 96 or 624 17 68; www.asteriskhotel.nl). Quiet hotel with 40 sunny rooms that include cable TV, phone, and safe. Free breakfast if you pay in cash (€8 otherwise). Singles €44, with bath €48-85; doubles €65, with bath €115-125; triples €130-136; quads €150. MC/V; 4% surcharge. ❸

DE PIJP, JODENBUURT, AND THE PLANTAGE

Bicycle Hotel, Van Ostadestr. 123 (☎679 34 52; www.bicyclehotel.com). Park in the bike garage and get trip recommendations. Breakfast included. Free Internet. Doubles €70, with bath €105; triples €95/130; quads €150. AmEx/MC/V; 4% surcharge. ❸

Hotel Pension Kitty, Plantage Middenlaan 40 (☎622 68 19). Look out for the small sign. Gentle, aged proprietress provides for those seeking a peaceful stay in this historic house. No children. Singles €50; doubles €60; triples €75. Cash only. ❹

Hotel Fantasia, Nieuwe Keizersgr. 16 (☎623 82 59; www.fantasia-hotel.com). Family-owned hotel in an 18th-century house on a quiet canal. Ask for a top floor room. Breakfast included. Reception 8am-10pm. Closed Dec. 14-27 and Jan. 6-Mar. 1. Singles €55-63; doubles €86-97; triples €124; quads €145. AmEx/MC/V; 3% surcharge. ❺

MUNCHIES

In most areas the sheer number of options—from Shawarma snack-bars to Argentinian barbecue to pan-Asian noodle joints—can be dizzying. Cheap restaurants cluster around **Leidseplein, Rembrandtplein,** and **De Pijp.** Cafes, especially in the **Jordaan,** serve inexpensive sandwiches (€2-5) and good meat-and-potatoes fare (€5.50-9). Bakeries line **Utrechtsestraat,** south of Prinsengr., and De Pijp is home to several cheap ethnic restaurants. Fruit, cheese, flowers, and even live chickens fill the markets on **Albert Cuypstraat,** behind the Heineken brewery. (Open M-Sa 9am-6pm.) **Albert Heijn** supermarkets line the streets in Amsterdam. Two of the most popular reside in Dam Sq. and underneath Museumplein. Check for more locations at www.ah.nl. Hours vary depending on location.

NIEUWE ZIJDE AND OUDE ZIJDE

In de Waag, Nieuwmarkt 4 (☎452 77 72; www.indewaag.nl). In the late 1400s, this castle served as the eastern entrance to the city. Today, it serves sandwiches and salads (€5-10) on the patio for lunch. Italian, French, and Norwegian specialties served at night amid hundreds of candles. Entrees €17-22. Open M-Th and Su 10am-midnight, F-Sa 10am-1am; often open until 3am. ❹

Pannenkoekenhuis Upstairs, Grimburgwal 2 (☎626 56 03). Scale the steep staircase to this tiny nook for sweet, filling pancakes (up to €9). Open M-F noon-7pm, Sa noon-6pm, Su noon-5pm. ❷

Cafe Latei, Zeedijk 143 (☎625 74 85). Nearly everything is for sale at this unique cafe, —even your plate. Hanging lamps, old-fashioned crockery, and wall hangings may come and go, but the affable atmosphere remains. Large sandwiches about €3. All-day continental breakfast €6.40. Open M-F 8am-6pm, Sa 9am-6pm, Su 11am-6pm. ❶

Ristorante Caprese, Spuistr. 259-261 (☎620 00 59). From Dam Sq., follow Spuistr. south a few blocks. Authentic Italian food, relaxed jazz, peach-colored walls, and comforting candlelight. All meat is organically raised. Main pasta dishes €10-11. Open daily M-F 5:15-11:15pm, Sa-Su 11am-4pm and 5:15-11:15pm. ❷

Green Planet, Spuistr. 122 (☎625 82 80; www.greenplanet.nl). Stylish vegetarian restaurant with salads from €4.50; add ingredients for €1.50 each. Asian wok stir-fry €12.50. Organic wines and beers from €2.50. You can rest easy: takeout meals come with biodegradable packaging. Open M-Sa 11am-11pm. ❷

Aneka Rasa, Warmoesstr. 25-29 (☎626 15 60). If grim Warmoesstr. is beginning to take its toll, you'll appreciate this clean, relaxed Indonesian joint. Main dishes, like the popular beef in spicy coconut sauce, satisfy the palate (€11-13.40). Vegetarian plates €8. Open daily 5-10:30pm. AmEx/MC/V. ❸

SHIPPING QUARTER, CANAL RING WEST, AND THE JORDAAN

Harlem: Drinks and Soulfood, Haarlemmerstr. 77 (☎330 14 98). When American-style soul food collides with Cajun and Caribbean flavors, the crowds arrive. Sandwiches €6.80-7.50. Creative dinner entrees €12-17. Open M-Th 10am-1am, F-Sa 10am-3am, Su 11am-1am. Food served until 10pm. MC/V. ❸

Hein, Berenstr. 20 (☎623 10 48). Watch your own meals prepared fresh in the open kitchen. Menu changes daily, according to the owner's tastes. Entrees average €10. Reservations accepted. Open M-Sa 8:30am-4pm, Su 9am-4pm. Cash only. ❷

De Vliegende Schotel, Nieuwe Leliestr. 162-168 (☎625 20 41; www.vliegendeschotel.com). Simple, organic, and delicious vegetarian fare. Entrees €7.50-9.50. Open daily 4-11:30pm. Food served until 10:45pm. AmEx/MC/V. ❷

Foodism, Oude Leliestr. 8 (☎427 51 03). Bright colors and a cozy atmosphere complement a variety of vegetarian choices and inspired pasta dishes (€8-9). All-day breakfast €8.50. No alcohol, but you're welcome to bring your food to Café Zool, the bar across the street. Open M-Sa 11:30am-10pm, Su 1-10pm. Cash only. ❷

Cinema Paradiso, Westerstr. 186 (☎623 73 44). Word of mouth has filled this cavernous, windowless former cinema with fans of its purist Italian food and candlelit charm. *Antipasti* €4-10. *Bruschette* €5-7. Pasta €9-15. No reservations, so be prepared for a wait unless you arrive early. Open Tu-Su 6-11pm. Kitchen closes 11pm. AmEx/MC/V. ❷

LEIDSEPLEIN AND MUSEUMPLEIN

Eat at Jo's, Marnixstr. 409 (☎624 17 77; www.melkweg.nl), inside Melkweg (see **Live Music,** p. 742). Jo may hail from the American Midwest, but her restaurant's multi-ethnic menu and arty, modular decor suggest that she's seen the world outside Milwaukee. Large bowls of soup €4.40. Entrees €12. Open W-Su noon-9pm. Cash only. ❷

Cafe Vertigo, Vondelpark 3 (☎612 30 21; www.vertigo.nl). Pop over to Vertigo's tree-lined terrace for some sunshine before you get too pasty watching movies at the Filmmuseum next door. The dinner menu's pricey, but light sandwiches (€4) and pastries (€2) hit the spot at lunch. Open daily 10am-1am. MC/V. ❶

Papa Pasta, Leidsekruisstr. 12 (☎623 13 47). Over 24 types of pasta (€5-8), and 2-for-1 drinks before 7pm. Open daily 5pm-midnight. AmEx/MC/V. ❶

Het Blauwe Theehuis, Vondelpark 5 (☎662 02 54; www.blauwetheehuis.nl). Peering through the trees in Vondelpark, you may glimpse a blue structure shaped like a flying saucer, brimming with a convivial crowd. Reach for your ray gun, or else pull up a chair on this teahouse's outdoor terrace. Sandwiches €4. Tapas €3-4. DJs spin F-Sa nights. Open M-Th and Su 9am-midnight, F-Sa 9am-2am. Kitchen closes 10pm. Cash only. ❶

CENTRAL CANAL RING AND REMBRANDTPLEIN

Lanskroon, Singel 385 (☎623 77 43). Traditional Dutch pastries baked on site. *Koningsstroopwafels* (honey-filled cookies) €1.50. Fresh fruit pies €2.50. Open Tu-F 8am-5:30pm, Sa 9am-6pm, Su 10am-6pm. Cash only. ❶

Maoz Falafel, Regulierbreestr. 45 (☎624 92 90; www.maozfalafel.nl). Crisp, flavorful falafel and all-you-can-stack salad bar make this string of kiosks a reliable bet for budget meals on the go. Falafel €2.50. Other locations: outside Centraal Station; Ferdinand Bolstr. 67; Leidsestr. 85; Muntpl. 1. Open daily at least 11am-11pm. ❶

Coffee and Jazz, Utrechtsestr. 113 (☎624 58 51). Dutch-Indonesian fusion turns colonialism on its ear, as fresh mackerel shares the menu with beef satay (€10.50). Nurse a cup of dark coffee by the window, and talk a waiter into taking out the glass on sunny days. Open Tu-F 9:30am-8pm, Sa 10am-4pm. ❷

Ristorante Pizzeria Firenze, Halvemaansteeg 9-11 (☎627 33 60; www.pizzeria-firenze.nl). A delightful Italian restaurant and pizzeria—one of the least expensive stops for a sit-down meal in the Rembrandtplein. 25 types of pizza (€3.30-6.90) and pasta (€3.30-6.60). Open daily noon-midnight. MC/V. ❶

DE PIJP, JODENBUURT, AND PLANTAGE

Abe Veneto, Plantage Kerklaan 2 (☎639 23 64). A dizzying selection of freshly made pizza (€4.50-9.50), pasta (€6.50-9.50), and salad (most under €5). Takeout and delivery available to nearby hotels. Open daily noon-midnight. Cash only. ❷

Cafe De Pijp, Ferdinand Bolstr. 17-19 (☎670 41 61). Fusion fare in stylish surroundings. Tapas €3.90-7.50. Entrees €13-15. Open M-Th and F-Sa noon-3am. Cash only. ❷

Eeetkunst Asmara, J.D. Meyer Pl. 8 (☎627 10 02). Operated by a group of Eritrean immigrants, this small restaurant caters to neighborhood visitors and a friendly crowd of regulars. East African specialties €8.50. Vegetarian options available. Cash only. ❷

The Bazar, Albert Cuypstr. 182 (☎664 71 73). A 2-story, Oriental-carpeted wonder in a former church. Cuisine from North Africa, Lebanon, and Turkey. Lunch menu €9.90 per person (2-person min.). Dinner entrees around €10. Open M-Th 8am-1am, F-Sa 8 or 9am-2am, Su 9am-midnight. ❷

King Solomon Restaurant, Waterloopl. 239 (☎625 58 60). Run by a hospitable Orthodox family, this is the only kosher restaurant in sight of the old Jewish quarter. Falafel €7.25. Veggie platters €13.50. *Malaouakh* €6.25. Open M-Th and Su noon-10pm, F noon-5pm; in winter Sa 45min. after sundown-10pm. AmEx/MC/V. ❷

SIGHTS

Amsterdam is fairly compact, so tourists can easily explore the area from the Rijksmuseum to the Red Light District on foot. For those not inclined toward pedestrian navigation, the tram system will get you to any of the city's major sights within minutes. For a peaceful, if pricey, view of the city from the water, **Museumboot Canal Cruise** allows you to hop on and off along its loop from the tourist office to the Anne Frank Huis, the Bloemenmarkt, the Rijksmuseum, Waterlooplein, and the old shipyard. (☎530 10 90. Boats pass every 15-40min. Day pass €16.)

NIEUWE ZIJDE, OUDE ZIJDE, AND THE RED LIGHT DISTRICT

THE RED LIGHT DISTRICT. No trip to Amsterdam would be complete without witnessing the notorious spectacle that is the Red Light District. After dark, the area actually glows red—sex theaters throw open their doors, and the main streets are thick with people gawking at lingerie-clad prostitutes pressing themselves against windows; **Warmoesstraat** and **Oudezijds Achterburgwal** boast wall-to-wall brothels. There are also **sex shows,** in which actors perform strictly choreographed fantasies on stage; the most famous live sex show takes place at **Casa Rosso,** Oudezijds Achterburgwal 106-108, where €40 will buy you admission to eight consecutive acts and €45 includes complimentary drinks. The show is quite tame, and probably not worth the money. *(☎627 89 54; www.janot.com. Afternoon shows daily 1:30-7:30pm. Evening shows M-Th and Su 7:30pm-2am, F-Sa 7:30pm-3am. Afternoon shows €20.)*

FLESH PHOTOGRAPHY. As tempting as it may be, **do not** take pictures in the Red Light District, especially of prostitutes. Taking pictures is incredibly rude and can land the picture-taker in trouble.

OUDE KERK. Amsterdam's Old Church comes as a welcome, wholesome shock, smack in the middle of the otherwise lurid Red Light District. The stunning structure in place today began as a narrow, crude basilica around 1300 and took on new architectural features into the 16th century. Today, Oude Kerk's enormous interior and magnificent stained-glass windows host photography and modern art exhibitions. At the head of the church is the massive Vater-Müller organ, built in 1724 and still played in public concerts every Saturday or Sunday. Check the schedule posted in the church. *(Oudekerkspl. 23. ☎625 82 84; www.oudekerk.nl. Open M-Sa 11am-5pm, Su 1-5pm. €4.50, students €3.50. Exhibits usually €5. Concerts €6, students €5.)*

NIEUWMARKT. On the border between the Oude Zijde and the Jodenbuurt, Nieuwmarkt is worth a visit simply for a look at the **Waag,** Amsterdam's largest surviving medieval building. Dating from the 15th century, the Waag was one of

Amsterdam's fortified city gates and later housed the Surgeons Guild's amphitheater. Public dissections and private anatomy lessons were once held there, as Rembrandt's *The Anatomy Lesson of Dr. Tulp* famously depicts.

DAM SQUARE AND KONINKLIJK PALEIS. The **Koninklijk Paleis** (Royal Palace) was completed in 1655 and functioned as the town hall until Louis Napoleon had it renovated in 1808 to better look the part of a royal residence. Today, Queen Beatrix still uses the building for official receptions, although she makes her home in The Hague. The palace's indisputable highlight is the **Citizen's Hall,** designed to replicate the universe in a single room. Across the large Dam Sq. is the Dutch **Nationaal Monument,** unveiled on May 4, 1956, to honor Dutch victims of WWII. Inside the 21m white stone obelisk is soil from all 12 of Holland's provinces as well as the Dutch East Indies. *(Koninklijk Paleis ☎620 40 60; www.koninklijkhuis.nl. Palace open daily July-Aug. 11am-5pm; Sept and June hours vary. €4.50.)*

BEGIJNHOF AND SPUI. You don't have to take vows to enter this secluded courtyard—the 14th-century home of the Beguines, a sect of religiously devoted laywomen—but you will have to get up early. Begijnhof's rose-lined gardens and beautifully manicured lawns afford a welcome respite from the excesses of the Nieuwe Zijde. *(Open daily July-Aug. 9-11am; Sept.-June 9am-5pm. Free.)* Just to the south, **Spui** (pronounced "spow") is a tree-lined square perfect for lounging. Walled in by bookstores, Spui is home to a Friday book market and a Sunday art market.

CANAL RING WEST AND THE JORDAAN

WESTERKERK. This stunning Protestant church was designed by Roman Catholic architect Hendrick de Keyser and completed in 1631. It is one of the last structures to be built in the Dutch Renaissance style, although the bare, white interior raises the question of whether Classicism was such a bad idea after all. Rembrandt is believed to be buried here, though his exact resting place has not yet been located. Climb the **Westerkerkstoren** tower in a 30min. tour for a great view of the city. *(Prinsengr. 281. ☎624 77 66. Church open Apr.-Sept. M-F 11am-3pm; July-Aug. M-Sa 11am-3pm. Tower closed Oct.-Mar. Tower tours Apr.-Sept. every 30min. 10am-5:30pm. €5.)*

HOMOMONUMENT. Homomonument, in front of Westerkerk, serves as a memorial to people of all genders persecuted for being anything other than happily heterosexual. Since 1987, the monument has stood in the center of Amsterdam as a testament to the strength and resilience of the city's queer community. Karin Daan's design, three pink granite triangles, allude to the emblem that homosexuals were forced to wear in Nazi concentration camps. During Amsterdam Pride, held in the first week of August, the monument takes on a happier cast, drawing DJs and performers for a four-night "Summer Camp" party.

LEIDSEPLEIN AND MUSEUMPLEIN

LEIDSEPLEIN. Leidseplein proper is a crush of cacophonous street musicians, blaring neon lights, and clanging trams. Daytime finds the square packed with shoppers, smokers, and drinkers lining the busy sidewalks. When night falls, tourists flock to the square, while locals fade to the less populated surrounding streets. **Max Euweplein,** a square along Weteringschans named for the famous Dutch chess master, sports an enormous chess board with people-sized pieces.

VONDELPARK. With meandering walkways, green meadows, several ponds, and a paved path for bikers and skaters, this English-style park—the largest in the city center—is a lovely meeting place for seniors, stoners, soccer players, and sidewalk acrobats. Named after 17th-century poet and playwright Joost van den Vondel, Vondelpark is home to the open-air **Openluchttheater** (☎673 14 99;

www.openluchttheater.nl), where visitors can enjoy free summer concerts from Wednesday through Sunday. Check the schedule posted beside the theater. *(In the southwest of the city, outside the Singelgr. A short walk across the canal from the Leidsepl.)*

CENTRAL CANAL RING AND REMBRANDTPLEIN

CENTRAL CANAL RING. YThe Central Canal Ring is the city's highest rent district and arguably its most beautiful. **Prinsengracht** (Prince's canal), **Keizersgracht** (Emperor's canal), and **Herengracht** (Gentlemen's canal) are collectively known as the *grachtengordel* (literally "canal girdle"). The Ring is home to some of Amsterdam's most important and breathtaking architecture, particularly on a stretch of the Herengr. between Leidsegr. and Vijzelstr. known as the **Golden Bend** for its wide, lavish homes. *(Over the Singel and just south of Centrum.)*

REMBRANDTPLEIN. Rembrandtplein proper consists of a grass rectangle surrounded by scattered flowerbeds. A bronze likeness of the famed master, Rembrandt van Rijn, peers at the hordes of out-of-towners who elbow their way into the bars and cafes in the surrounding area. South and west of the square you'll find **Reguliersdwarsstraat,** ground zero for Amsterdam's gay nightlife. *(In the northeastern corner of the Central Canal Ring, just south of the Amstel.)*

DE PIJP, JODENBUURT, AND THE PLANTAGE

HEINEKEN EXPERIENCE. Heineken stopped producing beer at their original Amsterdam brewery in 1988, opting to turn the place into a sort of multimedia amusement park devoted to their green-bottled lager. A visit includes three beers and a free gift. *(Heinekenpl. ☎523 96 66; www.heinekenexperience.com. Open Tu-Su 10am-6pm; last entry at 5pm. Guests under 18 must be accompanied by a parent. €10.)*

PORTUGEES-ISRAELIETISCHE SYNAGOGUE. This beautifully maintained Portuguese synagogue dates to 1675, when it was founded by Jews fleeing the Spanish Inquisition. It has remained largely unchanged since then and still holds services every Saturday at 9am. *(Mr. Visserpl. 1-3. ☎624 53 51; www.esnoga.com. Open Apr.-Oct. M-F and Su 10am-4pm; Nov.-Mar. M-Th and Su 10am-4pm, F 10am-3pm. €5.)*

HOLLANDSCHE SCHOUWBURG. This historic building was founded as a Dutch theater on the edge of the old Jewish quarter. In 1941, Nazi occupiers converted it into the Joodsche Schouwburg, the sole establishment to which the city's Jewish performers and patrons were granted access. Not long after, the building became an assembly point for Dutch Jews who were to be deported to transit camps. Today, the building houses a memorial to Holocaust victims. *(Plantage Middenlaan 24. ☎626 99 45; www.jhm.nl. Open daily 11am-4pm. Closed on Yom Kippur. Free.)*

HORTUS BOTANICUS. Founded in 1638, these gardens were originally established as "Hortus Medicus," medicinal gardens for the city's physicians. Among 6000 flourishing species, one highlight is the *Victoria amazonica*, the world's largest water lily, strong enough to hold a baby on its blossoms. When it blooms on summer evenings, it emits a baby-enticing pineapple scent. *(Plantage Middenlaan 2A. ☎638 16 70; www.dehortus.nl. Open July-Aug. M-F 9am-9pm, Sa-Su 10am-9pm; Feb.-June and Sept.-Nov. daily 9am-5pm; Dec.-Jan. daily 9am-4pm. Guided tours Su 2pm. €6. Tours €1.)*

DE PIJP. South of the tourist-filled canal rings, De Pijp (pronounced "pipe") is a mash of ethnicities and cultures. Constructed in the 19th century to ease cramped working-class housing in the Jordaan, De Pijp is now home to more upper-crust overflow, though far from erasing its labor-class roots. The best place to start is amid the crowded din of the **Albert Cuypmarkt,** a lively market and home to some of the best no-name eateries in the city. The market is along Albert Cuypstr., between **Ferdinand Bolstraat** (the district's largest thoroughfare) and Van Woustr.

To see Amsterdam as locals do, spend a day on bike. The nicest biking routes are those that run through the canal districts; places toward the center of town (especially congested pedestrian walkways near the Red Light District) should always be avoided. Our tour starts and ends at **Frederic Rent a Bike,** Brouwersgr. 78. (☎624 55 09. Open daily 9am-noon, 1-6pm.) Though his are the best quality, Frederic's is not the only place to rent bikes; see p. 724 for more rental options.

Begin your tour by biking down **Prinsengracht.** Turn left onto **Reestraat,** which becomes **Hartenstraat** and **Gasthuismolensteeg.** Continue over the **Singel** to **Dam Square.**

1 DAM SQUARE. Amsterdam's central square is surrounded by the Nieuwe Kerk, Nationaal Monument, and Koninklijk Paleis, home to the Dutch royal family. Stop and check out the street performers in good weather.

2 SPUI. Go back toward Singel, turn left on Nieuwezijds Voorburgwal and go south for a few minutes. Pronounced "spow," the square (p. 731) is home to a Sunday art market, a Friday book market, and is surrounded by bookstores. If you're up early, head into the **Begijnhof**, the peaceful courtyard for observant laywomen. Ride back to the Western Canal Ring via Heistr. Turn left onto Herengr. and right onto Leidsegr.; pause at the beautiful intersection of Leidsegracht and Keizersgr.

3 DE APPEL. Continue down Leidsegr., turn left at Keizersgr., and left on Nieuwe Spiegelstr. Stop at Nieuwe Spiegelstr. 10 to tour Amsterdam's premier space for contemporary art. (p. 738).

4 GOLDEN BEND. After some art-gazing, head to this stretch of Herengr.t, between Leidsestr. and Vijzelstr., known as the "Golden Bend" because of its opulent houses. Officials bent the strict house-width rules for wealthy citizens who were willing to invest in the construction of the Herengr., or Gentleman's Canal.

5 MAGERE BRUG. Turn right at Utrechtsestr. and then left at Prinsengr. Continue until you hit the Amstel. Turn left; the Magere Brug (Skinny Bridge) is on your right. This is the oldest of the city's pedestrian bridges, and the only one operated by hand.

6 NIEUWMARKT. Cross the bridge, turn left, and head north along the Amstel; cross at Herengr. Veer left, go right around the far side of the Stadhuis, and cross the bridge at Staalstr. When you hit Groenburgwal, turn right, right again at Raamgr., and then left at the first bridge. Cross over, turn left and double back along the far side of Raamgr. Turn right at Kloveniersburgwal and follow it to Nieuwmarkt, an open-air market. Head back to Frederic's via Zeedijk, which becomes Prins Hendrikkade and passes Centraal Station.

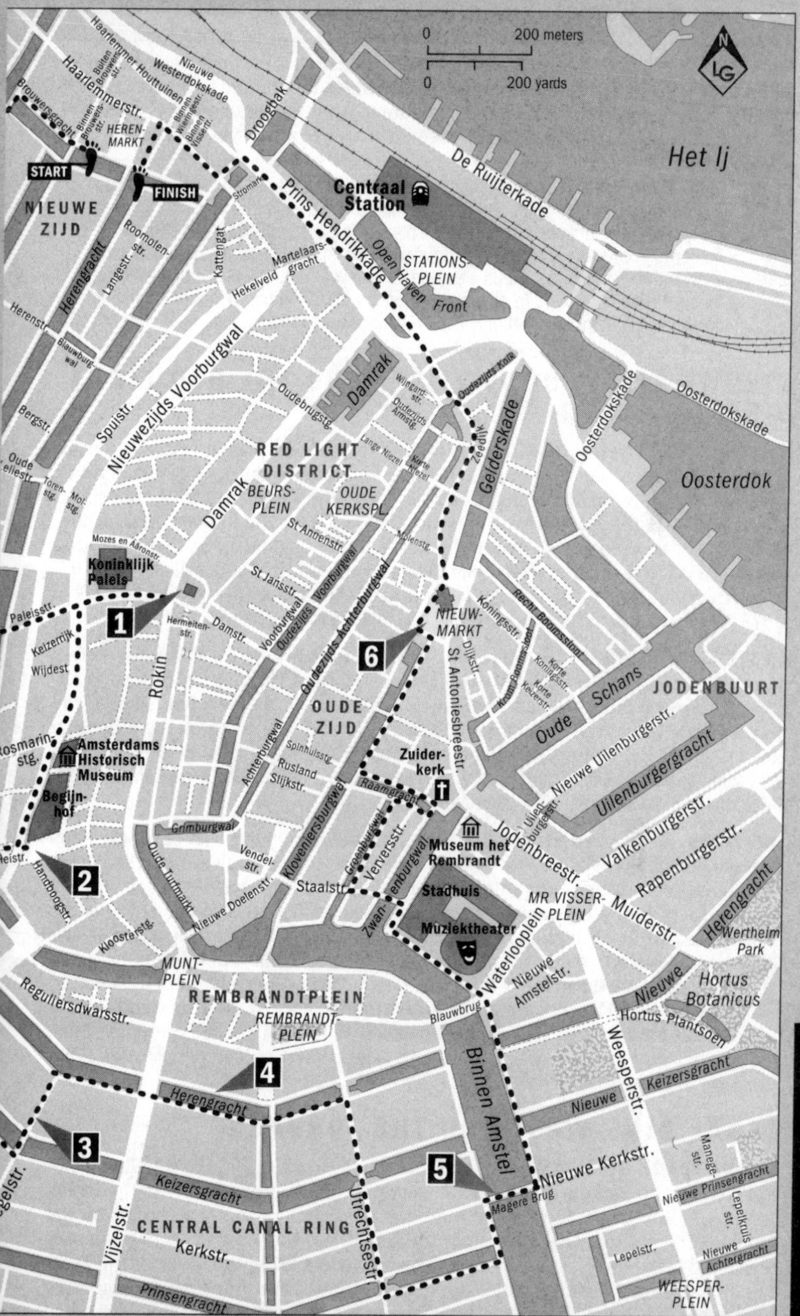

MUSEUMS

Amsterdam's museums contain enough art and history to arouse even the most indifferent curiosities. Whether you want to admire Rembrandts and Van Goghs, observe cutting-edge photography, pay tribute to Anne Frank's memory, or marvel at sexual oddities, Amsterdam has a museum geared toward every purpose.

THE REAL DEAL. Amsterdam has more museums per square meter than any other city in the world. Visitors planning to see even a handful may want to invest in a Museumjaarkaart (MJK). The pass (€30, under 25 €17.55) entitles the holder to admission at most major museums in Amsterdam and many museums all over the Netherlands. Cards are good for one year, but can be worth it even for those staying one week. To buy the MJK, bring a passport photo to a participating museum. For more information, check www.museumjaarkaart.nl.

NIEUWE ZIJDE, OUDE ZIJDE, AND THE RED LIGHT DISTRICT

STEDELIJK MUSEUM OF MODERN ART. The Stedelijk has amassed a world-class collection on par with MoMA or the Tate Modern. But new art sometimes needs a new home, and a distinguished jury spent the summer of 2004 choosing a Dutch architect to design a new museum building, to open in 2008. Meanwhile, selected pieces are being shown in the Post-CS Building, to the left when exiting Centraal Station. Dinner at **Restaurant Club 11,** on the 11th floor, will set you back at least €30, although the spectacular view of the city is free. *(Oosterdokskade 5. ☎573 27 45; www.stedelijk.nl. Open M-W and F-Su 10am-6pm, Th 10am-9pm. €8.)*

AMSTERDAM HISTORISCH MUSEUM. The Amsterdam Historical Museum offers an introduction to the city's historical development through medieval manuscripts, Baroque paintings, and multimedia displays. In the covered passageway between this converted orphanage and Begijnhof, be sure to catch the extensive collection of 17th-century paintings depicting Amsterdam's civic guards. *(Nieuwezijds Voorburgwal 357, Sint Luciensteeg 27, and Kalverstr. 92. ☎523 18 22; www.ahm.nl. Open M-F 10am-5pm, Sa-Su 11am-5pm. Closed Apr. 30. €6.)*

THE VICES. If it's weed that interests you, far and away your best bet is the staggeringly informative **Cannabis College,** Oudezijds Achterburgwal 124. The center for "higher" education offers info on everything from the uses of medicinal marijuana to facts about the war on drugs to creative applications of industrial hemp. Downstairs, artificial lighting in the Cannabis Garden simulates the summer and fall growing seasons so that visitors can always see a plant in full bloom. For a curated taste of the seaminess that runs down Amsterdam's underbelly, head to the **Amsterdam Sex Museum,** Damrak 18, less than a 5min. walk from Centraal Station. If walls plastered with pictures of bestiality and S&M are not your cup of tea, you may wish to look elsewhere for a cup of tea. *(Cannabis College open daily 11am-7pm. Free. Sex Museum open daily 10am-11:30pm. 16+. €2.50.)*

CANAL RING WEST AND THE JORDAAN

ANNE FRANK HUIS. A visit to the Anne Frank House is a must, whether or not you've read the famous diary. The museum chronicles the two years the Frank family and four other Jews spent hiding in the annex of this warehouse on the Prinsengr. The rooms are no longer furnished, but personal objects in display cases and text panels with excerpts from the diary bring the story of the eight inhabitants to life. The magazine clippings and photos that Anne used to decorate her room still hang on the wall. Footage of interviews with Otto Frank, Miep Gies (who ran food and supplies to the refugees), and childhood friends of Anne round out the story. Arrive around 5 or 6pm for the shortest lines. *(Prinsengr. 267. ☎556 71 00; www.annefrank.nl. Open daily Apr.-Aug. 9am-9pm; Sept.-Mar. 9am-7pm. Closed on Yom Kippur. Last admission 30min. before closing. €6.50.)*

ELECTRIC LADYLAND: THE FIRST MUSEUM OF FLUORESCENT ART. Endearingly eccentric owner Nick Padalino has collected a singularly impressive assortment of fluorescent objects, including gorgeous rocks that glow green in black light and an array of everyday objects that reveal hidden shades. During personal guided tours, visitors are encouraged to dive into the interactive space and play with the many switches and buttons that turn various lights on and off. *(2e Leliedwarsstr. 5. ☎420 37 76; www.electric-lady-land.com. Open Tu-Sa 1-6pm. €5.)*

STEDELIJK MUSEUM BUREAU AMSTERDAM. This adjunct of the Stedelijk (p. 736) devotes itself to exhibiting the newest in Amsterdam art. A pure white space made light and breezy by a vaulted glass ceiling, the museum bureau is something of a testing ground for avant-garde artists and material designers. The temporary shows last for eight weeks, and range from traditional forms of painting and sculpture to outrageous attempts at installation, as well as furniture and fashion design. The museum closes for one to two weeks between exhibits; check the website for a schedule. *(Rozenstr. 59. ☎422 04 71; www.smba.nl. Open Tu-Su 11am-5pm. Free.)*

MUSEUMPLEIN

VAN GOGH MUSEUM. This architecturally breathtaking museum houses the largest collection of Van Goghs in the world and a diverse group of 19th-century paintings by contemporaries like Gaugin and Emile Bernard. While the Rijksmuseum and the Stedelijk are juggling their collections during renovations, this museum's substantial collection of Impressionist, post-Impressionist, Realist, and Symbolist art acquires a new luster. *(Paulus Potterstr. 7. ☎570 52 00; www.vangoghmuseum.nl. Open daily 10am-6pm; ticket office closes 5:30pm. €9. Audio tours €4. Tickets more expensive during major temporary exhibitions.)*

RIJKSMUSEUM AMSTERDAM. Amsterdam's "state museum" has long been known as the continent's preeminent destination for art from the Dutch Golden Age. Even though the main building is closed for renovations, the Rijksmuseum is still a mandatory outing. During the restoration, the smaller Philips Wing will remain open to show 400 masterpieces of 17th-century painting, including works by Rembrandt, Vermeer, Frans Hals, and Jan Steen. Other pieces from the collection are on display around the city; check the website for details. *(Jan Luijkenstr. 1. ☎674 70 00; www.rijksmuseum.nl. Open daily 10am-5pm. €8.50. Audio tour €4.)*

FILMMUSEUM. Most visitors come here to see movies, not exhibits. As the national center for Dutch cinema, the museum's collection includes 35,000 titles stretching back to 1898. In addition to screening several films a day, they maintain an information center at 69 Vondelstr. (across the path from the entrance), with the country's largest collection of books and periodicals on film, many of them in English. Friday nights in July and August bring outdoor screenings to the museum; a €3 ticket includes a drink, although squatters can sit across the pond and watch for free. *(Vondelpark 3, between the Roemer Visscherstr. and Vondelstr. entrances. ☎589 14 00; www.filmmuseum.nl. Open M-F 9am-10:15pm. Free. Film screenings €7.20-7.80.)*

CENTRAL CANAL RING

FOAM PHOTOGRAPHY MUSEUM. Inside a traditional canal house, Foam stages a fearless exploration of modern photography. Every genre of the photographed image is fair game, from the purely aesthetic to the explicitly political, from fashion photography to historical exhibits. *(Keizersgr. 609. ☎551 65 00; www.foam.nl. Open M-W and Sa-Su 10am-5pm, Th-F 10am-9pm. €5, students €4. Cafe open W-Su 10am-5pm.)*

DE APPEL. This contemporary art museum houses a small permanent collection and draws compelling, cutting-edge temporary exhibits. *(Nieuwe Spiegelstr. 10. ☎625 56 51; www.deappel.nl. Open Tu-Th and Sa-Su 11am-6pm, F 11am-10pm. €2.50.)*

MUSEUM WILLET-HOLTHUYSEN. In 1895, Sandrina Holthuysen donated the 17th-century canal house she shared with her collector husband Abraham Willet to the Amsterdam Historisch Museum. The mansion has been redone with gilt-edged walls, glittering chandeliers, family portraits, Rococo furnishings, and other signs of conspicuous consumption. The French Neoclassical garden out back remains as finely manicured as it was in the Golden Age. *(Herengr. 605. ☎523 18 70; www.ahm.nl. Open M-F 10am-5pm, Sa-Su 11am-5pm. €4.)*

JODENBUURT AND PLANTAGE

NEMO (NEW METROPOLIS). The half-submerged green structure shaped like a ship's hull by the Oosterdok is NEMO, the coolest science museum you have ever seen. Renzo Piano's whimsical architecture pays tribute to the Netherlands's seafaring past. Inside, four stories littered with science exhibits beg to be poked at, jumped on, and experimented with. NEMO targets children ages 4-16, but adult visitors soon find themselves shooting each other conspiratorial grins as they blow meter-wide bubbles or don lab coats to view creepy-crawlies through a light microscope. Afterward, don't miss the spectacular view of the shipyard and the historic city from the structure's slanted roof. *(Oosterdok 2, east of Centraal Station. ☎0900 919 11 00, €0.35 per min.; www.e-nemo.nl. Open Tu-Su 10am-5pm. €11, students €6.)*

MUSEUM HET REMBRANDT. Dutch master Rembrandt van Rijn's house at Waterlooplein is home to 250 of his etchings, as well as a number of paintings by his pupils. See the claustrophobic box-bed in which Rembrandt slept and tour the studio in which he mentored promising painters. *(Jodenbreestr. 4. ☎520 04 00; www.rembrandthuis.nl. Open M-Sa 10am-5pm, Su 1-5pm. €7, students €5.)*

REMBRANDT AT 400. In 2006, Amsterdam will be celebrating Rembrandt's 400th birthday with exhibits, shows, and festivals at the city's countless art galleries in honor of one of Amsterdam's most famous residents. Check www.rembrandt400.com for more information.

JOODS HISTORISCH MUSEUM. In the heart of Amsterdam's oldest Jewish neighborhood, the Jewish Historical Museum aims to document the religious heritage and cultural legacy of Dutch Jews. The museum presents a comprehensive picture of Jewish life through a permanent collection of photographs, religious artifacts, artwork, and traditional clothing. *(Jonas Daniel Meijerpl. 2-4. ☎626 99 45; www.jhm.nl. Open daily 11am-5pm; closed Yom Kippur. €6.50, students €4. Audio tour €1.)*

VERZETSMUSEUM (DUTCH RESISTANCE MUSEUM). Though the Nazis quickly overran Dutch armed forces in May 1940, the Netherlands maintained an active resistance throughout WWII. The Resistance Museum focuses on the members of this secret army, providing visitors with the details of their lives and struggles. Model streets, buildings, and tape-recorded radio reports recreate the rebels' experiences—from smuggling food to issuing counterpropaganda on an illicit printing press. *(Plantage Kerklaan 61. ☎620 25 35; www.verzetsmuseum.org. Open M and Sa-Su noon-5pm, Tu-F 10am-5pm, public holidays noon-5pm. €5.)*

COFFEESHOPS AND SMART SHOPS

COFFEESHOPS

The coffee at Amsterdam's coffeeshops is generally beside the point. Establishments calling themselves coffeeshops often sell pot or hash or will let customers buy a drink and smoke their own stuff. Look for the **green-and-white sticker** signifying the shop's affiliation with the Bond voor Cannabisdetaillisten (BCD), an organized union of coffeeshops. Reputable independent shops do exist, and between fairly steep union dues and a decade-long freeze on new licenses, it's easy to understand why not all shops get union-certified. Still, establishments with the BCD sticker remain the safest bet for visitors new to the city. While Amsterdam was once known as the **hashish** capital of the world, **marijuana** is today the soft drug of choice. Technically, pot is illegal in the Netherlands, but the country's tolerance policy means that you are unlikely to face legal action if you carry no more than 30g (1.05 oz.) on your person, and buy no more than 5g (0.17 oz.) at a time. Possession of harder drugs like cocaine and heroin can and will be severely punished. For more info on the legal ins and outs, call the **Jellinek clinic** (☎408 77 77).

TALKING BEFORE TOKING. Amsterdam may be a liberal city, but smoking marijuana outside of a coffeeshop is not acceptable. Although smoking cigarettes is permitted in most restaurants, smoking weed is not. If you are unsure and really want to toke up, ask first.

Let's Go does not recommend drug use in any form. Those who decide to partake should use common sense and remember that any experimentation with drugs can be dangerous. **Never buy drugs from street dealers,** because there is no way of knowing whether they are laced with more harmful drugs or are simply expensive oregano. Coffeeshops are licensed to sell cannabis and hashish, and the good ones carefully regulate the quality of their smokeables. When customers walk into a coffeeshop, they should ask for a menu, because the shops are not allowed to leave menus out or otherwise advertise their wares. The legal age to enter a coffeeshop is 18, and it's not unusual for staff to ask for ID when you enter.

Marijuana is the dried, cured flower of the cannabis plant, and costs anywhere from €3 to €15 per gram. Different strains fall in and out of favor, but are divided into two main subspecies: Sativa strains (like "Kali Mist" or anything marked "Thai") gets users high, giggly, and energized, while Indica strains (like "Northern Lights") gets users really stoned and relaxed. Increasingly popular hybrid strains (like "White Widow" or "AK-47") combine both effects. Keep in mind that pot in the Netherlands is very potent; visitors report that they smoke noticeably less than they would at home and still achieve the same high. Prerolled joints are sometimes available, but smoking one clearly identifies its user as a tourist, as does smoking out of a pipe. Staff at coffeeshops are not going to be enthusiastic about explaining how to roll a joint, but they will be happy to explain the different menu options.

Hashish is made from the resin crystals extracted from the flowers of the cannabis plant, and it comes in three varieties: black (Indian), blonde (Moroccan), and Dutch (also called ice-o-lator). The first two grades run €4-35 per gram, averaging somewhere around €7, while increasingly popular **ice-o-lator hash** tops out at €20-35 per gram. Typically, the cost of the hash is proportional to its quality and strength; black hash hits harder than blonde, and ice-o-lator can send even a seasoned smoker off his head. Hash can be smoked directly out of a glass hash pipe, or sprinkled into a joint containing either tobacco or marijuana. Both hash and weed can be used to make **space cakes** and other fortified food items. Because these treats need to be digested, they take longer to affect the body (up to 2hr.) and longer to rinse out. Experts warn against eating another brownie just because you don't feel the effects immediately.

DRUG DICTION. A Dutch slang term for marijuana is "blow," not to be confused with the American-English slang use of the same word to signify cocaine, a hard drug neither tolerated nor legal in the Netherlands.

SMART SHOPS

Smart shops peddle a variety of **"herbal enhancers"** and **hallucinogens** that walk the line between soft and hard drugs. Always remember that experimentation with drugs is dangerous and can cause both short- and long-term damage. If you're interested in experimenting with magic mushrooms ('shrooms), it is crucial, as with all soft drugs, that you do your research beforehand. Here's a brief rundown of the types of mushrooms and a few guidelines. **Magic mushrooms** start to work 30min. to 1hr. after consumption and act on your system for 4-8hr., depending on how much you weigh and whether you've eaten beforehand. Different types give different highs: **Mexican** and **Thai** mushrooms are generally used by beginners; they are the least potent and give a laughing, colorful, and speedy high with some visual hallucination. **Philosophers' stones** (colors and lights swirl together as you think deep thoughts) and **Hawaiians** (a visual trip similar to LSD) are significantly more intense, and should be taken only by experienced users. Wandering the city tripping on mushrooms can be a majestic, mind-expanding experience, but it can also leave you lost and unable to think straight enough to find your way home. It's often more pleasant to stay in familiar surroundings, like a favorite coffeeshop or a corner of the Vondelpark. Never look for mushrooms in the wild and never buy from a street dealer; it's extremely difficult to tell the difference between hallucinogenic mushrooms and flat-out poisonous ones. **Don't mix hallucinogens with alcohol,** and if you have a bad trip, call ☎ 122 to go to the hospital or ask someone for help—you won't be arrested, and they've seen it all before.

LAWS ONLINE. Although for the uninitiated and unfamiliar, it may seem like anything goes in Amsterdam, there are, in fact, very strict regulations regarding both cannabis consumption and prostitution. A good resource to check up on the latest laws is the English-language website of the Dutch Ministry of Justice, www.justitie.nl/english.

WHERE TO GO

Barney's Coffeeshop, Haarlemmerstr. 102. Wine and cheese, coffee and cigarettes—some pairings are just meant to be. Pot and all-day breakfast (€4.50-12.50) falls into the same category, especially when the coffeeshop in question is a three-time "best marijuana strain" winner at the Cannabis Cup. Open daily 7am-8pm.

Abraxas, J. Roelensteeg 12-14. Hot spots come and go, but Abraxas has remained one of Amsterdam's largest, most beautiful coffeeshops. Plush couches fill 3 floors decorated with abstract designs and a stylized tree-branch motif. Open daily 9am-1am.

Dampkring, Handboogstr. 29. Several scenes from the 2004 film *Ocean's Twelve* were filmed in this chill, subterranean space. But don't take Brad Pitt's word for it; locals are unanimously enthusiastic. Open M-Th 10am-1am, F-Sa 10am-2am, Su 11am-1am.

Hill Street Blues, Warmoesstr. 52. If you don't want to smoke (weed and hash €4.50-11.50 per g; pre-rolled joints €3), you won't be able to resist the incredibly cheap beer (pint €2.80). Space shakes €4.60. Space tea €4. Space cakes €3.20. Happy hour 6-9pm; beer €2.10. Open M-Th and Su 9am-1am, F-Sa 9am-3am.

Amnesia, Herengr. 133. Fuschia walls, pink tabletops, and cushioned benches make for a comfortable, newbie-friendly atmosphere that has found a niche in a city with many standoffish, veterans-only shops. Vaporizer available for guests looking for alternatives to smoking. Open daily 9:30am-1am.

Paradox, 1e Bloemdwarsst. 2. This bright, nonchalant coffeeshop jives with the neighborhood's relaxed vibe, counting many of the area's artists among its clientele. Beginning smokers or those looking to unwind can try a "bluff," a light joint (€2). Open daily 10am-8pm. Kitchen closes 3pm.

tWEEDy, Vondelstr. 104, at 2e Constantijn Huygenstr. Low-key coffeeshop with a pool table. Great place to grab a joint for a munchies picnic in Vondelpark. Weed is cheap at €4-7 per g for several varieties. Open daily 11am-11pm.

NIGHTLIFE

Leidseplein and **Rembrandtplein** are the liveliest areas for nightlife, with coffeeshops, loud bars, and tacky clubs galore. Near Leidsepl., pricey discos abound on **Prinsengracht,** near **Leidsestraat,** and on **Lange Leidsedwarsstraat.** Some clubs charge a membership fee in addition to normal cover. Amsterdam's finest cafes are the old, dark, wood-paneled *bruin café* (brown cafes) mainly on the **Jordaan;** those lining **Prinsengracht** often have outdoor seating. In Amsterdam, the concept of a "straight" versus a "gay" nightlife does not really apply; most establishments are gay-friendly and have a mixed-orientation crowd. Around Rembrandtpl., gay bars almost exclusively for men line **Amstelstraat** and **Reguliersdwarsstraat. Kerkstraat,** five blocks north of Leidsepl., is another gay hot spot. Pick up a *Clu* guide, free at cafes and coffeeshops, for a club map of the city, or the free monthly *Gay and Night,* for more comprehensive GLBT listings.

LEARNED DRINKING. Student travelers: don't forget to ask bartenders if there is a student discount; it's almost always worth a shot.

BARS AND CAFES

Club NL, Nieuwezijds Voorburgwal 169 (www.clubnl.nl). This is the unmarked destination for Amsterdam's slickest, best-dressed, and most savvy insiders. Mixed drinks €8. F-Su cover €5. Mandatory €1 coat check. Open M-Th and Su 10pm-3am, F-Sa 10pm-4am.

Café de Jaren, Nieuwe Doelenstr. 20-22. Spacious, glamorous cafe on par with the best of Paris or Vienna. 2 sprawling floors offer various indoor and outdoor seating options an arm's length away from the Klovenierburgswal canal. Beer and mixed drinks €1.80-3.10. Open M-Th and Su 10am-1am, F-Sa 10am-2am.

Wijnand Fockink, 31 Pijlsteeg (www.wynand-fockink.nl), on an alleyway just off Dam Sq. Over 300 years old, with unequivocally the best *fockink* liquor (Dutch gin) in the city. Made especially for this tiny bar and available in over 60 flavors, including appletart, peppermint, and the famous half-and-half. Glass €2. Open daily 3-9pm. Cash only.

Club Magazijn, Warmoesstr. 170 (www.clubmagazijn.nl). Just off Dam Sq., a new club popular with local students. Huge bar and dance floor, and smaller upstairs lounge. Cover varies (usually around €5). Open M-Th 8pm-3am, F-Sa 8pm-4am. Cash only.

Café Brandon, Kiezersgracht 157. Café Brandon is like a voyage through time. An older, local crowd relaxes to Pink Floyd and late 70s English rock. Amstel on tap from €1.60. Open M-Th and Su noon-1am, F-Sa noon-3am. Cash only.

Cafe April, Reguliersdwarsstr. 37 (www.april-exit.com). Popular gay bar that's laidback by day, increasingly active and cruisey as the night wears on. Beer €2. Mixed drinks €6.20. 2-for-1 happy hour M-Sa 6-7pm, Su 6-8pm makes it a popular after-work stop. Open M-Th and Su 2pm-1am, F-Sa 2pm-3am. Cash only.

CLUBS AND DISCOS

De Trut, Bilderdijkstr. 165. A low-ceilinged basement in an apartment building west of the city center hosts Su night parties for gay and lesbian locals skipping the cruisy downtown scene. Don't be chased off by 2m pictures of genitalia on the doors; the emphasis inside is on dancing and mingling. Beer €1. Cover €1.50. Doors open 11pm and close once the club fills, so join the queue on the sidewalk by 10:30pm.

Escape, Rembrandtpl. 11 (www.escape.nl). Party animals pour into this massive venue, a nightlife institution with 6 bars on 2 floors. Well-dressed club kids groove to house, trance, and disco tunes. 1st F of month gay Salvation dance party. Beer €2.30. Mixed drinks €7.50. Cover €10-15. Open Th and Su 11pm-4am, F-Sa 11pm-7am. Cash only.

Meander, Voetboogstr. 3b. Smoky atmosphere, constant clamor, and dense crowds make for a raucous, high-energy good time. Beer €1.80. M student night, F-Sa disco with live music. Cover €2.50-5. Open M-Th and Su 9pm-3am, F-Sa 9pm-4am.

Dansen Bij Jansen, Handboogstr. 11-13. *The* student dance club in town, popular with locals from the University of Amsterdam and backpackers too. You must show a student ID or be accompanied by a student. Beer €1.70-3.30. Mixed drinks from €3.30. Cover M-W and Su €2, Th-Sa €4. Open M-Th and Su 11pm-4am, F-Sa 11pm-5am.

Exit, Reguliersdwarsst. 42 (☎625 87 88). Enter Exit to find one of the most popular gay discos in the Netherlands. Downstairs bar plays dance classics for the laidback boys; upstairs is a DJ-driven, high-energy techno party where a young, handsome crowd sheds its inhibitions. Darkroom reserved just for men. Th cover €4, F-Sa €9. Open M-Th and Su 11pm-4am, F-Sa 11pm-5am. Cash only.

LIVE MUSIC

Melkweg, Lijnbaansgr. 234a (☎531 81 81; www.melkweg.nl). A legendary nightspot in an old milk factory, it's one-stop shopping for live music, food (see **Eat At Jo's,** p. 730), films, and dance parties. Concert tickets €9.50-22 plus €2.50 monthly membership fee. Box office open M-F 1-5pm, Sa-Su 4-6pm; show days from 7:30pm to end of show.

Paradiso, Weteringschans 6-8 (☎626 45 21; www.paradiso.nl). Hosts a summertime line-up of big-name acts. Upstairs a smaller stage showcases up-and-coming talent. Tickets €5-25; required membership fee €2.50. M and Th-Su after the shows, usually around 11:30pm, the space morphs into a dance club. M-Th nightclub cover €6, F-Su €12.50. Open until 2am. Hours vary; check website for details.

Bourbon Street Jazz and Blues Club, Leidsekruisstr. 6-8 (☎623 34 40; www.bourbon-street.nl). A slightly older crowd comes for blues, soul, funk, and rock bands. Check postings in the window for events. Beer €2.50. Th and Su cover €3, F-Sa €5; free daily 10-10:30pm. Open M-Th and Su 10pm-4am, F-Sa 10pm-5am.

HAARLEM ☎023

Haarlem's (pop. 150,000) narrow cobblestone streets, rippling canals, and fields of tulips make for a great escape from the urban frenzy of Amsterdam, but the city also bustles with a relaxed energy that befits its urban size, as coffeeshops and a slew of restaurants ensure that there's fun to be had even after the sun goes down.

TRANSPORTATION AND PRACTICAL INFORMATION. Reach Haarlem by **train** from Amsterdam's Centraal Station (20min.; €3.10). The **tourist office,** Stationspl. 1, to your right as you walk out of the station, sells maps of the city (€2) and finds private rooms for a €5 fee. (☎090 06 16 16 00; www.vvvzk.nl. Open Apr.-Sept. M-F 9am-5:30pm, Sa 10am-4pm; Oct.-Mar. M-F 9am-5:30pm, Sa 10am-2pm.)

ACCOMMODATIONS AND FOOD. Three kilometers from the train station is **Stayokay Haarlem (HI) ❶,** Jan Gijzenpad 3. Take bus #2 (dir.: Haarlem-Noord; every 10min. until 6pm, every 15min. 6pm-12:30am) to this hostel on the banks of a placid canal. (☎537 3793; www.stayokay.com/haarlem. Bikes €8 per day. Breakfast included. Dorms €25. AmEx/MC/V.) **Hotel Carillon ❸,** Grote Markt 27, is in the town square, to the left of the Grote Kerk. Despite their small size, most rooms include a shower, phone, and TV. (☎531 05 91; www.hotelcarillon.com. Breakfast included.

Reception in summer 7:30am-1am; in winter until midnight. Singles €33, with bath €58; doubles €58/76; triples €92; quads €99. MC/V.) For cheap meals, try cafes in the **Grote Markt** or **Botermarkt;** many offer outdoor patios. **Grand Café Doria ❷,** Grote Houtstr. 1a, right in the Grote Markt, to the west of the Grote Kerk, looks deceptively like a standard Dutch cafe, though it actually specializes in Italian fare. Doria turns into a lively nightspot after dark. (☎531 33 35; www.doria.nl. Main courses €6-19.50. *Broodjes* €2.50-7. Open M-Th and Su 9am-midnight, F-Sa 9am-2am. AmEx/MC/V.)

SIGHTS AND ENTERTAINMENT. The action centers on the **Grote Markt,** Haarlem's bustling main square, which gets taken over by a flea market on Monday afternoons. To get there from the train station, head south along Kruisweg, which becomes Kruisstr. and then Barteljorisstr. Nearby is the poignant **Corrie Ten Boomhuis,** Barteljorisstr. 19, a museum in the former headquarters of Corrie Ten Boom's movement to protect Jews during WWII. The savior of an estimated 800 lives, Corrie was caught and sent to a concentration camp but survived to write *The Hiding Place.* (Open Tu-Sa 10am-4pm. Donations accepted.) The **Grote Kerk,** on the Grote Markt, houses portraitist Frans Hals's tomb, a mammoth Müller organ once played by Handel and Mozart, and even a small cafe. (☎553 20 40; www.bavo.nl. Open Mar.-Oct. Tu-Su 10am-4pm; Nov.-Feb. M-Sa 10am-4pm. €1.50.) From the front of the church, take a right onto Warmoesstr. and walk three blocks to the **Frans Hals Museum,** Groot Heiligland 62, which houses 11 of Hals's canvases and work by other Golden Age Dutchmen in a 17th-century almshouse and orphanage. (☎511 57 75; www.franshalsmuseum.nl. Open Tu-Sa 11am-5pm, Su noon-5pm. €5.40, under 19 free.) The museum also organizes modern art exhibits at **De Hallen,** Grote Markt 16. (Open Tu-Sa 11am-5pm, Su noon-5pm. €4, under 19 free.) **Teyler's Museum,** Spaarne 16, is the oldest museum in the country and contains a merry hodgepodge of scientific instruments, fossils, paintings, and drawings. Walk behind the church, turn left onto Damstr. and take a left at the river. (Open Tu-Sa 10am-5pm, Su noon-5pm. €5.50.) Nightlife clusters around the Grote Markt. **Cafe Stiel's,** Smedestr. 21, features live music from soul and jazz to disco. (☎531 69 40; www.stiels.nl. Open M-Th and Su 6pm-2am, F-Sa 6pm-4am.)

CARPE HAARLEM. Not sure what those three V-words sprayed across this tulip country town mean? Haarlem's motto is *Vicit Vim Virtus:* "Virtue triumphs over violence."

DAYTRIPS FROM HAARLEM: ZANDVOORT. A mere 11km from Haarlem, the seaside town of **Zandvoort** (pop. 16,000) draws sun-starved Germans and Dutchmen to its miles of sandy beaches. From the train station, follow the signs to the Raadhuis, and from there head west along Kerkstr. until you fall into the warm sand. **Beach clubs** boast patios along the shore where revelers carouse on lounge chairs. These clubs open early each morning, close at midnight, and are only in service during the summer. Each offers distinct personality and food, with themes ranging from Australian to tapas, and admission is free as long as you're buying drinks or food. The irresistible hippie-style club **Woodstock 69,** Zeedijk 8 (☎573 21 52; www.woodstock69.nl), hosts **Beach Bop,** the party that takes over the beach the last Sunday of every month (check www.beachbop.info for details). **Bloomingdale** reclines in chic elegance with tan sofas and plush pillows thrown into a background of pulsing music. The club's laidback grace makes it the local favorite (☎0900 606 06 66). **Trains** arrive in Zandvoort from Haarlem (10min., round-trip €2.50). The **tourist office,** Schoolpl. 1, is east of the town square, off Louis Davidstr. (☎571 79 47; www.vvvzk.nl. Open M-Sa 9am-5:15pm.) Most visitors stay the night in Haarlem; the tourist office books inexpensive B&Bs in Zandvoort for a €4 fee.

LEIDEN ☎071

Home to one of the oldest and most prestigious universities in Europe, Leiden (pop. 118,000) brims with bookstores, windmills, gated gardens, and hidden walkways. The city that gave the world Rembrandt has more than its fair share of outstanding museums, while the botanical gardens where Carolus Clusius first cultivated **tulips** still draw admirers of the Netherlands's beloved bulbs. Make your own pilgrimage to the **Hortus Botanicus,** Rapenburg 73, and picnic on the grassy knolls alongside the **Witte Singel** canal. (☎527 72 49; www.hortusleiden.nl. Open Apr.-Oct. daily 10am-6pm; Nov.-Apr. M-F and Su 10am-4pm. €4.) Head indoors to the spacious **Museum Naturalis,** a natural history museum that traces the formation of the earth and its inhabitants through splashy, interactive displays. (☎568 76 00; www.naturalis.nl. Open July-Aug. daily 10am-6pm; Sept.-June Tu-Su 10am-6pm. €9.) See the inside of an 18th-century windmill and look out over Leiden's tiled roofs at **Molenmuseum "De Valk,"** 2e Binnenvestgr. 1. (☎516 53 53. Open Tu-Sa 10am-5pm, Su 1-5pm. €2.50.)

The **Hotel Pension Witte Singel ❷,** Witte Singel 80, overlooks serene canals and gardens. (☎512 45 92; www.pension-ws.demon.nl. Singles €38.50-45; doubles €58.50-72.) A budget traveler's dream, **Olive Garden ❶,** Lange Mare 71, is a small Italian shop known for its killer food and delicious prices. (☎514 44 66; www.olive-garden.nl. Homemade pasta €6.75. Open Tu-F 10:30am-6:30pm, Sa 10am-6:30pm, Su noon-6:30pm.) For up-to-date information on Leiden's entertainment scene, grab a copy of the free magazine *L.O.S.*, with features on bars, restaurants, and theme nights. **Trains** run to Amsterdam (35min., every 30min., €7.40) and The Hague (20min., every 30min., €2.90). To get to the **tourist office,** Stationsweg 2d, take the city center exit from the train station and walk straight ahead. The office sells maps and walking tour brochures (€2-3), and reserves rooms for €2.25 for one person, plus €1.75 per extra person. (☎090 02 22 23 33; www.leiden.nl. Open M 11am-5:20pm, Tu-F 10am-5:20pm, Sa 10am-4:30pm, Su 11am-4:30pm.)

THE HAGUE (DEN HAAG) ☎070

With its international lawyers, elected officials, embassies, and imposing government buildings, The Hague (pop. 470,000) might seem a bit stiff in the collar. But world-class art museums, a lively (if a bit confusing) city center, and an incredible jazz festival combine to make the Netherlands's political capital anything but boring.

TRANSPORTATION AND PRACTICAL INFORMATION. **Trains** run from Amsterdam (50min., €9.40) and Rotterdam (30min., €4) to both of The Hague's major stations, **Centraal Station** and **Holland Spoor.** Trams #1, 9, and 12 connect the two stations, but get off at Den Haag Centraal if you can; it is much closer to the city center and main attractions. From Amsterdam, the stop for Holland Spoor comes first, so just stay on until the train reaches Den Haag Centraal or Centraal Station. The **tourist office,** Kon. Julianapl. 30, just outside the north entrance to Centraal Station, sells detailed city maps (€2). You can book hotels on the computer outside the tourist office 24hr. (☎090 03 40 35 05; www.denhaag.com. Open Aug.-May M and Sa 10am-5pm, Tu-F 9am-5:30pm; June-Sept. also Su 11am-3pm.)

ACCOMMODATIONS AND FOOD. The **StayOkay City Hostel Den Haag (HI) ❷,** Scheepmakerstr. 27, is near Holland Spoor; turn right from the station, follow the tram tracks, and turn right at the big intersection; Scheepmakerstr. is 3min. ahead. From Centraal Station, take tram #1 (dir.: Delft), 9 (dir.: Vrederust), or 12 (dir.: Duindorp) to Rijswijkseplein, cross left in front of the tram, and cross the intersection; Scheepmakerstr is straight ahead. (☎315 78 88; www.stayokay.com/denhaag. Breakfast included. Reception daily 7:30am-10:30pm. Dorms €25.25; singles €55.25; doubles €61-66. €2.50 HI discount. MC/V.) Budget fare is plentiful on

Lange Poten and **Korte Poten** near the Binnenhof. Tasty tapas await at the antiqued **Cafe de Oude Mol ❶**, Oude Molstr. 61, near Grote Halstr. (☎345 16 23. Entrees €3.50-6.50. Open M-W 5pm-1am, Th 5pm-1:30am, F-Sa 5pm-2am. Cash only.)

SIGHTS AND ENTERTAINMENT. The Hague's **Peace Palace** (Het Vredespaleis), at Carnegiepl. 2, was donated to the city in 1913 by American industrialist Andrew Carnegie and is today the opulent home of the International Court of Justice. (Take tram #8, dir.: Scheveningen, to Vredespaleis. ☎302 42 42; www.vredespaleis.nl. Tours M-F 10, 11am, 2, 3pm. Reserve in advance. €3.50.) Spend an afternoon in the courtyard of the **Binnenhof,** The Hague's Parliament complex. Tours of the complex leave from Binnenhof 8a and visit the 13th-century Ridderzaal (Hall of Knights) as well as the Second Chamber of the States General. (☎364 61 44; www.eerstekamer.nl. Open M-Sa 10am-4pm. Tour €5.) Near the Binnenhof's entrance, the 17th-century **Mauritshuis,** Korte Vijverberg 8, features an impressive collection that includes works by Rembrandt and Jan Steen, as well as Vermeer's famous *Girl With a Pearl Earring.* (☎302 34 35; www.mauritshuis.nl. Open Tu-Sa 10am-5pm, Su 11am-5pm. €7.50, under 18 free. Audio tour €2.50.) Piet Mondrian's 1944 canvas *Victory Boogie Woogie* stands out from a collection of his earlier sketches at the **Gemeentemuseum,** Stadhouderslaan 41, which also features early musical instruments and historical costumes. Take tram #10 from Holland Spoor; from Centraal, take bus #4. (☎338 11 11; www.gemeentemuseum.nl. Open Tu-Su 11am-5pm. €7.50.) Windsurfers and kite-flying tots pack the beach in nearby **Scheveningen,** which doubles as a popular nightlife destination.

In late June of every year, The Hague hosts the largest free public pop concert in Europe—**Parkpop.** Held on 3 big stages in the Zuiderpark, the concert has seen acts including the Dandy Warhols, Suzanne Vega, and the Bloodhound Gang (☎523 90 64; www.parkpop.nl). Experimental theater, opera, jazz and blues, world-class classical ensembles, indie music, and modern dance all find a home at **Theater aan het Spui,** Spui 187, with its funky stage design and hip approach to entertainment. Though some plays are in Dutch, regular concerts feature the latest cutting-edge sound. Pick up a free schedule of events at the box office or the tourist office. Take tram #16 or 17 to Spui. (Ticket office ☎880 03 33, main office 880 03 00; www.theateraanhetspui.nl. Closed late June-Aug. Ticket office open noon-6pm.)

DAYTRIP FROM THE HAGUE: DELFT. The lilied canals and stone footbridges that line the streets of Delft (pop. 97,000) offer the same views that native Johannes Vermeer immortalized in paint over 300 years ago. It's best to visit on Thursdays and Saturdays, when townspeople flood the marketplace. The town is renowned for **Delftware,** blue-on-white earthenware developed in the 16th century. Watch Delftware being made from scratch at homey **De Candelaer,** Kerkstr. 13a-14, located in the center of town. (☎213 18 48; www.candelaer.nl. Open daily 9am-6pm. Free.) To see a larger factory, take tram #1 to Vrijenbanselaan and take in the free demonstration at **De Delftse Pauw,** Delftweg 133. (☎212 47 43; www.delftsepauw.com. Open Apr.-Oct. daily 9am-4:30pm; Nov.-Mar. M-F 9am-4:30pm, Sa-Su 11am-1pm.) Built in 1381, the **Nieuwe Kerk** holds the restored mausoleum of Dutch liberator William of Orange. Climb the 109m tower, which shelters a 36-bell carillon and offers a magnificent view of old Delft. (Church open Apr.-Oct. M-Sa 9am-6pm; Nov.-Mar. M-F 11am-4pm, Sa 11am-5pm. Tower closes 1hr. earlier. Church €2.50. Tower €2.) Founded in 1200, the brighter **Oude Kerk** lays claim to Vermeer's gravestone and a leaning 75m tower erected in 1325. (Open Apr.-Oct. M-Sa 9am-6pm; Nov.-Mar. M-F 11am-4pm, Sa 11am-5pm. €2.50.) The easiest way into Delft is the 15min. ride on **tram** #1 from The Hague to Delft station (2 strips). **Trains** also arrive from Amsterdam (1hr., €9). The **tourist office,** Hippolytusbuurt 4, near the Stadhuis, distributes a free map of the city. (☎215 40 51; www.delft.nl. Open M and Su 10am-4pm, Tu-F 9am-6pm, Sa 9am-5pm.) There aren't any budget accommodations in Delft; stay in The Hague. Restaurants line **Volderstraat** and **Oude Delft.**

ROTTERDAM ☎010

Festivals, art galleries, and a dynamic nightlife make Rotterdam (pop. 660,000) a hub of cultural activity, as well as the most up-and-coming city in the Netherlands. It's also the country at its multicultural best, with the largest traditional immigrant population in the Netherlands. Find works by Dalí, Magritte, and Rothko at the **Museum Boijmans van Beuningen,** Museumpark 18-20. (Take the subway to Eendractspl. or tram #5 to Witte de Withstr. ☎441 91 75; www.boijmans.nl. Open Tu-Sa 10am-5pm, Su 11am-5pm. €7.) Walk through the Museumpark to reach the linear **Kunsthal,** Westzeedijk 341, which Rem Koolhaas designed to feature constantly changing temporary exhibits on architecture, photography, and painting. (☎440 03 00; www.kunsthal.nl. Open Tu-Sa 10am-5pm, Su 11am-5pm. €8.50.) Although the **Euromast,** built in 1958, feels a bit dated, the tallest structure in the Netherlands is the best way to take in the breathtaking view of Rotterdam's skyline. (Parkhaven 20. Take tram #8 to Euromast. ☎436 48 11; www.euromast.nl. Open July-Aug. Tu-Sa 10am-10:30pm; Apr.-June and Sept. 10am-7pm; Jan.-Mar. and Oct.-Dec. daily 10am-5pm.) Down by the wharf, floodlights illuminate the cables of the **Erasmus Bridge** each night in a ghostly white haze.

StayOkay Rotterdam (HI) ❶, Rochussenstr. 107-109, is a great place to meet other young travelers. Take the Metro to Dijkzigt. Friendly staff and comfortable rooms compensate for slightly crowded conditions. Downstairs bar with pool table, bike rental (€6.45 per day), and laundry (€3.40) available. (☎436 57 63; www.stayokay.com/rotterdam. Internet €5 per hr. Reception 7am-midnight. Dorms €22.50; singles €39.75-44.25; doubles €55.50-64.50. MC/V.) **Bazar ❷,** on a hotel of the same name, shines with glittering colored lights, bright blue tables, and amazing Middle Eastern fusion cuisine. (☎206 51 51. Sandwiches €4. Entrees €8-15. Open M-Th 8am-1am, F 8am-2am, Sa 10am-2am, Su 10am-midnight. AmEx/MC/V.) Shop for groceries at **Spar,** Witte de Withstr. 36. (Open M-F 8:30am-7pm, Sa 8:30am-5pm.) Coffeeshops line **Oude Binnenweg** and **Nieuwe Binnenweg.** For the inside scoop on Rotterdam nightlife, shows, and special events, pick up a free copy of *Zone 010* or *The Gaymap*. **Trains** run to: Amsterdam (1¼hr., 1-5 per hr., €12.40) and The Hague (30min., 1-4 per hr., €4). The **tourist office,** Coolsingel 67, opposite the Stadhuis, books rooms for a €1.60 fee and provides free maps. (☎414 00 00; www.vvvrotterdam.nl. Open M-Th 9:30am-6pm, F 9:30am-9pm, Sa 9:30am-5pm.) **Use-It Rotterdam,** Conradstr. 2, is also a great service for backpackers, publishing the *Simply the Best* guide to the city (☎240 91 58; www.use-it.nl).

UTRECHT ☎030

Utrecht (pop. 250,000), with its robust student population, is free of tourist hordes and chock-full of cultural events, museums, and a swinging nightlife. Even the canals are visitor-friendly: they lie below street level and are ideal for picnicking and strolling. Get info on churches and museums at **RonDom,** Dompl. 9. (☎233 30 36; www.domtoren.nl. Open M-Sa 10am-5pm, Su noon-5pm.) Then make your first stop the awe-inspiring **Domkerk,** started in 1254 and finished a good 250 years later. (Open May-Sept. M-F 10am-5pm, Sa 10am-3:30pm, Su 2-4pm; Oct.-Apr. M-F 11am-4pm, Sa 11am-3:30pm, Su 2-4pm. Free.) The 112m **Domtoren,** the tallest tower in the Netherlands, was attached to the cathedral until a medieval tornado blew away the nave in 1674. (Tickets for tours sold at RonDom. Tours daily July-Aug. 10am-4:30pm every 30min.; Sept.-June 10am-4pm on the hr. €6.) The **Museumkwartier** is the nucleus of Utrecht's extended family of museums, and includes the labyrinthine **Centraal Museum,** Nicolaaskerkhof 10, founded in 1838. The collection ranges from oil paintings in the style of Caravaggio to Gerrit Thomas Rietveld's 1918 *Red and Blue Chair*. (☎236 23 62; www.centraalmuseum.nl. Open Tu-Su 11am-5pm. €8.) The **Nationaal Museum Van Speelklok tot Pierement,** Steenwag 6, traces the history of mechanical musical instruments. Amid the kitsch, check out the collection of automats from the 17th to 20th centuries. (☎231 27 89; www.museumspeelklok.nl. Open Tu-Sa 10am-5pm, Su noon-5pm. Guided tours every hr. €7.)

At **B&B Utrecht City Centre ❶,** Lucasbolwerk 4, European backpackers use their knees to balance plates from the 24hr. buffet in between turns in the inflatable pool. From the station, walk toward the city center down Vredenburg, which eventually turns into Nobelstr. (☎0650 43 48 84; www.hostelutrecht.nl. Free Internet. Dorms €16; singles €55; doubles €65. MC/V.) **Strowis Hostel ❶,** Boothstr. 8, has colorful rooms and an outdoor terrace overlooking a garden. Walk toward the city center down Vredenburg, turn left on Janskerkhof, and left on Boothstr. (☎238 02 80; www.strowis.nl. Breakfast €5. Linen €1.25. Free Internet. Dorms €13-16; doubles €50.) Cheap fare can be found along **Nobelstraat.** Sit out by the canal or inside the cozy lounge at **Het Nachtrestaurant ❷,** Oudegrt. 158, which boasts great tapas (€3-6) and sangria (€3.20) by the glass. (☎230 30 36. Open M-Sa 6-11pm. Sa nightclub after 11pm. MC.) Utrecht is the Netherlands's largest college town, and has the social scene to prove it. Pick up a copy of *Uit-Loper* at bars to scout out cultural events. Big stepping-out nights are Wednesday through Friday; on Saturday many students leave town. **'t Oude Pothuys,** Oudegr. 279, is a converted cellar that hosts live music nightly. (Beer €1.90. Open daily 10pm-3am.) Once the rest of Utrecht has shut down, students party at fraternity-run **Woolloo Moollo** (the "Wo"), Janskerkhof 14. (Student ID required. Cover €3. Open daily 11pm-late.) **De Winkel van Sinkel,** Oudegr. 158, is the city's most popular grand-cafe, with martini glasses lining the walls of a huge, mandarin-colored complex. (Beer from €2.30. Sa DJs spin house. Cover €12.50. Open M-F and Su 11pm-2am, Sa 11pm-5am.)

Trains depart from Hoog Catharijne station for Amsterdam (30min., 3-6 per hr., €7.60). To reach the **tourist office,** Vinkenbrugstr. 19, follow Vredenberg over the canal; after a block, turn right into the square. Pick up a city map and a complete listing of museums for €2. (☎0900 128 87 32; www.utrechtstad.nl. Open June-Sept. M-W and F 9:30am-6:30pm, Th 9:30am-9pm, Sa 10:30am-5pm, Su 10am-2pm.)

DE HOGE VELUWE NATIONAL PARK ☎0318

The impressive **De Hoge Veluwe National Park** (HO-geh VEY-loo-wuh) is a 13,565-acre preserve of woods, heath, dunes, red deer, and wild boars. (☎59 16 27; www.hogeveluwe.nl. Park open daily Apr. 8am-8pm; May and Aug. 8am-9pm, June-July 8am-10pm; Sept. 9am-8pm, Oct. 9am-7pm; Nov.-Mar. 9am-5:30pm. €6. May-Sept. 50% discount after 5pm.) Deep in the park, the **Kröller-Müller Museum** has troves of Van Goghs from an outstanding private collection, as well as key works by Giacometti, Gris, Mondrian, Picasso, and Seurat. The museum's striking **sculpture garden,** one of the largest in Europe, is home to works by Rodin and Serra, and Jean Dubuffet's delightfully wacky *Jardin d'email.* (☎59 12 41; www.kmm.nl. Open Tu-Su 10am-5pm. Sculpture garden closes 4:30pm. €12.) Explore over 40km of paths with one of the 1000 free **bikes** in the park and a map (€2.50) from the **visitors center.** Find the center by following signs reading "*Bezoekerscentrum.*"

Arnhem (pop. 140,000) is a good base for exploring the park; **bus** #107 (6 strips) traverses the 15km from Arnhem to the park's northwestern entrance. From the Otterlo stop, you can walk to the park entrance and grab a bike, or transfer to bus #110 (free), which heads through the middle of the park and stops at both the museum and the visitors center. Contact Arnhem's **tourist office,** Willemspl. 8, for more information. (☎0900 202 40 75; www.vvvarnhem.nl. Open M 11am-5:30pm, Tu-F 9am-5:30pm, Sa 10am-4pm.) To get to the **Stayokay Hostel (HI) ❶,** Diepenbrocklaan 27, take bus #3 (€2.10 round-trip) from the Arnhem train station to Rijnstate Hospital; as you face the hospital, turn right and then left on Cattepoelseweg.

About 150m ahead, turn right up the brick steps, and at the top go right. (☎442 01 14; www.stayokay.com/arnhem. Breakfast included. Reception 8am-11pm. Dorms €22-23; singles €30-31; doubles €53-55. MC/V.)

MAASTRICHT ☎043

Situated on a narrow strip of land between Belgium and Germany, Maastricht's (pop. 125,000) strategic location has made it a frequent target for military conquest throughout history. Today, it is known for its abundance of galleries and antique stores, and as the home of the prestigious **Jan van Eyck Academie,** an institute for modern art and high-flown theory. The futuristic **Bonnefantenmuseum,** ave. Ceramique 250, houses collections of medieval sculpture, Northern Renaissance painting, and pieces by up-and-coming Dutch artists. (☎329 01 90; www.bonnefanten.nl. Open Tu-Su 11am-5pm. €7.) Centuries of territorial conflicts around Maastricht prompted the city to invest in an innovative subterranean defense system; the 20,000 underground passages of the **Mount Saint Pieter Caves** were used as a siege shelter as late as WWII, and contain inscriptions and artwork by generations of inhabitants. Access is possible at two locations, and only with a tour guide. The **Northern System,** Luikerweg 71, suffices during low season (English-language tours mid-Apr. to June and Sept. to Oct. at 1:30pm; €3.25), but opt for the **Zonneberg Caves,** Slavante 1, during high season. (English-language tours June-Aug. 1:45pm; €3.25.) Back above ground, the **Basilica of St. Servatius,** Keizer Karelpl., off central Vrijthof Sq., contains 11th-century crypts and one of the country's largest bells, affectionately known as *Grameer*, meaning "Grandmother." (Open daily Jan.-June and Sept.-Dec. 10am-5pm; July-Aug. 10am-6pm. €3.50.)

Maastricht's popularity with gourmands and art dealers means that good budget lodgings can be difficult to find. **Hotel Pierre Zenden ❸,** St. Bernardusstr. 5, is a terrific value if you can book a room. (☎321 22 11; www.sportsschool-zenden.nl. All rooms with bath. Breakfast included. M-Th €37.50 per person, F-Su €47.80 per person. Cash only.) The tiny cabins of the floating **Botel ❷,** Maasboulevard 95, are the cheapest options in town, but can be reminiscent of unusually roomy telephone booths. Try to get a cheerier room above-deck. (☎321 90 23. Breakfast €4. Reception 24hr. Singles €27-30; doubles €41-43. Cash only.) **'T Liewe ❸,** Grote Gracht 62, is a small restaurant serving French and Mediterranean cuisine in an old-world atmosphere. (☎321 04 59. Daily special €6. Entrees €11-19. Open Tu-Su 4:30pm-midnight. Kitchen closes 11pm. Cash only.) **Slagery Franssen ❶,** St. Pietersstraat 42, offers a seemingly endless array of hot and cold sandwiches (€1.25-4) and traditional meat-filled rolls (€3). It has been family-owned for four generations; all food is cooked fresh daily, including the bread. (☎321 29 00. No tables. Open Tu-F 8am-6pm, Sa 8am-4pm. Cash only.) There is always something to do at night. For the best value, try the bars like **De Uni,** Brusselsestr. 31, run by groups of fraternity brothers and filled with hordes of local students. At many of the student-run bars, a €10 card buys you 12 beers. After 2am, partiers head over to the **Allebonner,** a dance club open until the sun comes up. **Trains** go from the east side of town, away from most of the action, to Amsterdam (2½hr., every 30min., €26.50). To reach the **tourist office,** Kleine Str. 1, walk straight on Stationstr., cross the bridge, and take a right. (☎325 21 21; www.vvvmaastricht.nl. Open May-Oct. M-Sa 9am-6pm, Su 11am-3pm; Nov.-Apr. M-F 9am-6pm, Sa 9am-5pm.)

GRONINGEN ☎050

Groningen pulses with youthful energy. More than half of the city's 175,000 inhabitants are under 35, adding to Groningen's reputation as a great party city. Heavily bombed in WWII, the city rebuilt itself completely yet managed to keep the old-world appeal that Rotterdam consciously kicked to the curb.

TRANSPORTATION AND PRACTICAL INFORMATION. Trains arrive from Amsterdam (2½hr., 2 per hr., €23.80), though passengers sometimes need to switch trains at Amersfoot; ask the conductor to be sure. The **tourist office,** Grote Markt 25, is in the far corner of the Markt next to the Martinitoren. The office books accommodations for around a €5 fee. (☎313 97 41; www.vvvgroningen.nl. Open M-W 9am-6pm, Sa 10am-5pm; July-Aug. also Su 11am-3pm.)

ACCOMMODATIONS AND FOOD. A staff of heavy-metal enthusiasts tends clean, imaginatively decorated rooms at **Simplon Jongerenhotel ❶,** Boterdiep 73-2. Take bus #1 from the station (dir.: Korrewegwijk) to Boterdiep; the hostel is through the yellow- and black-striped entrance. (☎313 52 21; www.simplon-jongerenhotel.nl. Breakfast €4, included with private rooms. Free lockers. Linen €2.80. Reception 24hr. Lockout noon-3pm. All-female dorm available. Dorms €13-17; singles €32.50-39; doubles €46.50-55. Cash only.) To get to **Hotel Friesland ❶,** Kleine Pelsterstr. 4, cross the canal at the Groninger Museum and walk up Ubbo Emmiusstr., turn right on Gedempte Zuiderdiep, left on Pelsterstr., and right onto Kleine Pelsterstr. The beds are slightly saggy, but clean. (☎312 13 07. Breakfast included. Singles €23.50; doubles €43.50. AmEx/MC/V.) Attune your palate to the spices of the East at **De Kleine Moghul ❷,** Nieuwe Boteringstr. 62, an Indian restaurant serving inventive, seasonal fare. (☎318 89 05. Entrees around €9. Open daily 5-10pm. MC/V.) At **Ben'z ❷,** Peperstr. 17, dinner is served by lantern-light in a Bedouin tent. Recline on Turkish cushions after your meal and take a puff on the *nargileh*, a traditional water pipe. (☎313 79 17; www.restaurantbenz.nl. Student menu €7.60-9.10. Open daily 4:30pm-midnight. Cash only.)

SIGHTS AND NIGHTLIFE. The town's spectacular **Groninger Museum,** housed in three whimsical, angular pavilions, exhibits modern art, traditional paintings, and ancient artifacts. The multi-colored galleries create a futuristic laboratory atmosphere for daring exhibitions. (☎366 65 55; www.groningermuseum.nl. Open July-Aug. M 1-5pm, Tu-Su 10am-5pm; Sept.-June Tu-Su 10am-5pm. €7.) Admire the city from atop the Grote Markt's **Martinitoren,** a 97m tower that weathered the German attacks during WWII. Midway up the tower, you can pull cords to simulate ringing the tower's bells. Book tickets at the tourist office. (Open daily Apr.-Oct. 11am-5pm; Nov.-Mar. noon-4pm. €2.50.) Soak up the sunshine in the serene **Prinsenhoftuin** (Princes' Court Gardens); the entrance is on the canal by the Maagden bridge. (Open daily Apr. to mid-Oct. 10am-dusk.) Inside the gardens, the tiny **Theeschenkerij Tea Hut** offers 130 kinds of tea (€0.80) under charming canopied underpasses. (Open M-F 10am-6pm, Sa-Su noon-6pm.) At day's end, cool off at **Noorderplantsoen,** a rolling, fountain-filled park that hosts late August's **Noorderzon Festival,** 10 days of outdoor theater and concerts.

Groningen parties beyond its size; there are 160 pubs and discotheques crammed in this medium-sized city. For cheap pitchers of beer and bars packed shoulder-to-shoulder, head to the corner of the Grote Markt on Poelestr. and Peperstr. For outdoor nightlife, try the megabar overlooking the Grote Markt, known familiarly as the **Zuid Zijd** (South Side). The staff at **Vera,** Oosterstr. 44, proclaim it to be the "club for the international pop underground." Pick up a copy of the newsletter in the box outside for a schedule of events. (☎313 46 81; www.vera-groningen.nl. Open daily 1pm-3 or 4am.) Candlelit **Jazzcafe de Spieghel,** Peperstr. 11, offers two floors of live jazz, funk, or blues nightly at 11pm or later. Pick up a free copy of *UILoper* from the tourist office to find out what's on. (☎321 63 00. Wine €2.20 per glass. Open daily 8pm-4am.) Groningen's **coffeeshops** offer cheap alternatives to their Amsterdam brethren. **Dee's Cafe,** Papengang 3, tucked unassumingly into a small alley, is a perfect spot for night owls. (www.cafedees.nl. Marijuana sold in €5 and €12 denominations. Internet €2 per hr. Space cakes €2.50. Open M-W 11am-midnight, Th noon-1am, F 11am-3am, Sa noon-3am.)

WADDEN ISLANDS (WADDENEILANDEN)

Wadden means "mudflat" in Dutch, but sand is the defining characteristic of these islands; gorgeous beaches hide behind dunes covered in golden grass. Deserted, tulip-lined bike trails carve through vast, flat stretches of grazing land to the sea. Sleepy and isolated, these islands are truly the Netherlands's best-kept secret.

TRANSPORTATION. The islands arch clockwise around the northwestern coast of the Netherlands: Texel (closest to Amsterdam), Vlieland, Terschelling, Ameland, and Schiermonnikoog. To reach Texel, take the train from Amsterdam to Den Helder (1½hr., €11), then grab bus #33 (2 strips) and a ferry to 't Hoorntje, the island's southernmost town (20min., every hr. 6:30am-9:30pm, round-trip €4). **Buses** depart from Texel's ferry dock to various locales around the island, though the best way to travel is to rent a **bike** from **Verhuurbedrijf Heijne,** opposite the dock. (Bikes from €4.50 per day. Open daily Apr.-Oct. 9am-8pm; Nov.-Mar. 9am-6pm.) To reach the other islands from Amsterdam, catch a **train** from Centraal Station to Harlingen Haven (3hr., €27.90). From Harlingen, **ferries** (☎05 17 49 15 00; www.doeksen.nl) depart for Terschelling (1-2hr., 3-5 per day, €17.63). **Ferries** also run between Texel, Vlieland, and Terschelling. From Texel, ferries depart for Vlieland (25min., Tu-Th and Su 1 per day, €9).

TEXEL. The largest and most populous of the Wadden Islands, Texel (pop. 14,000) is home to more sheep than people. Stunning **beaches** lie near De Koog, on the western side of the island, and *naakstranden* (nude beaches) beckon the uninhibited; you can bare it all near Paal 9 (2km southwest of Den Hoorn) or Paal 27 (5km west of De Cocksdorp). Watch seal feedings at the **EcoMare Museum and Aquarium,** Ruijslaan 92, south of De Koog. (Take bus #28. ☎02 22 31 77 41; www.ecomare.nl. Open daily 9am-5pm. Feeding 11am, 3pm. €7.50.) On the other side of the island, in the quaint burg of **Oudeschild,** the **Maritime and Beachcomber's Museum** (Maritiem en Jutters Museum), Barentzstr. 21, invites visitors to tour a windmill or stroll across a canal to peer into life-sized replicas of a smithy and fishermen's houses from the turn-of-the-century. (☎02 22 31 49 56; www.texelsmaritiem.nl. Open July-Aug. M-Sa 10am-5pm; Sept.-June Tu-Sa 10am-5pm. €4.50.)

The island's hostel, **StayOkay Texel ❶,** Schansweg 7, is 3km outside of Den Burg and accessible via bus #29 from the ferry (4 strips); tell the bus driver your destination. Although the hostel will move to a new building in mid-2006, its phone number won't change; call ahead. (☎02 22 31 54 41; www.stayokay.com. Reception 8:30am-10:30pm. Dorms €21.50; single €38.75; doubles €59.50. €2.50 HI discount.) Ask the tourist office about **campgrounds.** A **Texel Ticket** (€4.50), which you can buy on any bus, allows one day of unlimited travel on the island's bus system. The **tourist office,** Emmaln 66, is located just outside Den Burg, about 300m south of the main bus stop; look for the blue signs. (☎02 22 31 47 41; www.texel.net. Open M-Th 9am-6pm, F 9am-9pm, Sa 9am-5:30pm; July-Aug. also Su 10am-1:30pm.)

TERSCHELLING. With 80% of the island covered by protected nature reserves, Terschelling offers secluded beaches that stretch around its western tip and across the northern coast. To explore the island's striking scenery, rent a bike from **Haantjes Fietsverhuur,** W. Barentzskade 23. (☎05 62 44 29 29. Bikes €4.50 per day, €20 per week. Open M-Sa 9:30am-5:30pm.) To reach waterfront **Terschelling StayOkay Hostel (HI) ❶,** van Heusdenweg 39, from the boat dock, turn right and walk for 15min. (☎05 62 44 23 38; www.stayokay.com/terschelling. Breakfast included. Laundry €3.50. Reception 9am-10pm. Dorms €25.75; low season €20.25. €2.50 HI discount.) It's well worth the 13km trek out to **The Heartbreak Hotel ❶,** in Oosterend, which doubles as a shrine to Elvis. The restaurant serves great diner-style food (Burning Love Burger; €4.50) in red pleather booths, and hosts live rock 'n' roll each night during the summer. (☎05 62 44 86 34. Open daily 10am-1am. Cash only.) The most convenient place to grab a bite is in the island's main village, West Terschelling. **Zeezicht ❸,** W. Barentszkade 20, has enormous dinner portions and a sweeping view of the sea. (☎05 62 44 22 68. Entrees €12-16.50. Open daily 10am-midnight. AmEx/MC/V.) From mid-July to mid-August, every wild child in the Netherlands flocks to Terschelling. Head to **Braskoer,** Torenstr. 32, to join a young crowd on the sweaty, packed dance floor. (☎05 62 46 21 97. Beer €2. Cover €5 after 9pm. Open daily 10am-2am.) If the high-energy pop leaves you feeling a bit long in the tooth, take your brooding thoughts over to dimly lit **Cafe De Zeevaart,** Torenstr. 22, where a seaside groghouse feel prevails. (☎05 62 44 26 77. Beer €1.50. Open daily 10am-2am. Cash only.) The **tourist office,** W. Barentszkade 19a, is opposite the ferry landing. (☎05 62 44 30 00. Open M-Sa 9:30am-5:30pm.)

NORWAY (NORGE)

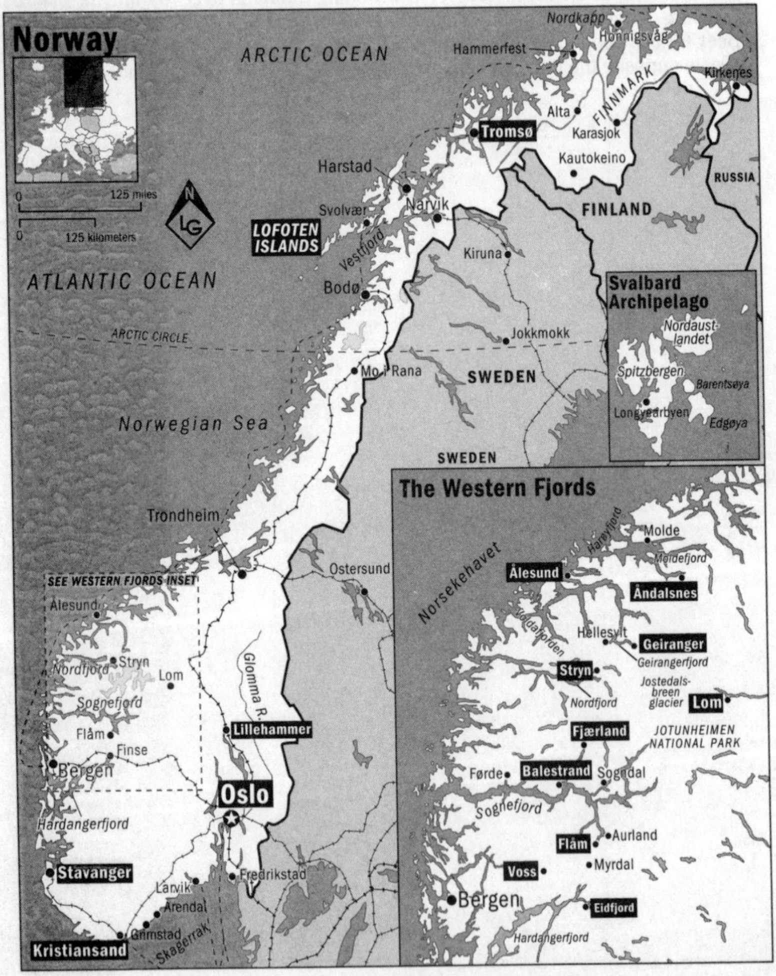

The rugged fjords and remote mountain farms of Norway gave birth to one of the most fabled and feared seafaring civilizations of pre-medieval Europe, the Vikings. Modern-day Norwegians have inherited their Norse ancestors' independent streak, voting against joining the EU in 1994 and drawing the ire of environmental groups for their refusal to ban commercial whaling. Although much of the country's oil revenues get socked away to pay for social programs, Norwegians place a priority on self-reliance. The spectacular scenery of the fjords and the icy beauty of the glacial regions make Norway one of the world's most unique destinations—but be warned, sky-high prices and spotty public transportation in rural areas make it a practical destination for only the most well-prepared budget traveler.

DISCOVER NORWAY: SUGGESTED ITINERARIES

Oslo (p. 758) is the classic jumping-off point for travels in Norway, although the capital city's many museums and ethnic restaurants may leave you spoiling to stay. Tear yourself away long enough to visit seaside **Stavanger** (p. 766), and then catch a westbound train for the long, scenic ride to **Bergen** (p. 768). Let yourself get sidetracked by a trip up the **Flåm Railway** (p. 775), or try hiking on the unspoiled Hardangervidda plateau near **Eidfjord** (p. 774). Plan a few days to explore Bergen's museums and relaxed cafes, but then head north to picture-postcard **Geirangerfjord** (p. 778) and less-trafficked **Sognefjord** (p. 775). Soak up some civilization in **Ålesund** (p. 779) or **Trondheim** (p. 780) before shooting north to the tumbledown fishing villages of the **Lofoten Islands** (p. 783). Vibrant **Tromsø** (p. 781) ties it all together with echoes of the cosmopolitan south.

ESSENTIALS

FACTS AND FIGURES

Official Name: Kingdom of Norway.

Capital: Oslo.

Major Cities: Bergen, Stavanger, Tromsø, Trondheim.

Population: 4,570,000.

Land Area: 310,000 sq. km.

Time Zone: GMT +1.

Language: Norwegian; Swedish and English widely spoken.

Religions: Evangelical Lutheran (86%).

WHEN TO GO

Oslo averages 18°C (63°F) in July and -4°C (24°F) in January. The north is colder and wetter than the south or east; Bergen and its surrounding mountains are especially rainy. For a few weeks around the summer solstice (June 21), the area north of Bodø basks in the midnight sun. The **Northern Lights,** spectacular night-time displays formed when solar flares produce plasma clouds that run head-on into atmospheric gases, peak out November to February from above the Arctic Circle. Skiing is best just before Easter.

DOCUMENTS AND FORMALITIES

EMBASSIES. Foreign embassies for Norway are in Oslo. For Norwegian embassies in your home country: **Australia** and **New Zealand,** Royal Norwegian Embassy, 17 Hunter St., Yarralumla, Canberra, ACT 2600 (☎02 6273 3444; www.norway.org.au/info/embassy.htm); **Canada,** 90 Sparks St., Ste. 532, Ottawa, ON K1P 5B4 (☎613-238-6571; www.emb-norway.ca); **Ireland,** 34 Molesworth St., Dublin 2 (☎01 662 18 00; www.norway.ie/info/embassy.htm); **UK,** 25 Belgrave Sq., London SW1X 8QD (☎020 7591 5500; www.norway.org.uk/embassy); **US,** 2720 34th St. NW, Washington, D.C. 20008 (☎202-333-6000; www.norway.org/embassy).

VISA AND ENTRY INFORMATION. EU citizens do not need a visa. Citizens of Australia, Canada, New Zealand, and the US do not need a visa for stays of up to 90 days, although this three-month period begins upon entry into any of the countries within the EU's freedom of movement zone. For more information, see p. 16.

TOURIST SERVICES AND MONEY

EMERGENCY	**Police:** ☎112. **Ambulance:** ☎113. **Fire:** ☎110.

TOURIST OFFICES. Virtually every town and village has a **Turistinformasjon** office; look for a white "i" on a square green sign. From the latter half of June through the first half of August, most tourist offices are open daily; expect reduced hours at other times. Check www.visitnorway.com for a directory of local offices.

MONEY. The Norwegian **krone** (plural: kroner) is divided into 100 *øre.* Banks and large post offices change money, usually for a small commission. As a general rule, it's cheaper to exchange money in Norway than at home. **Tipping** is not essential, but an extra 5-10% is always welcome for good restaurant service. It is customary to leave coins on the counter or table rather than putting the tip on a credit card. Hotel bills often include a 15% service charge. Refunds for the 24% **Value Added Tax (VAT)** are available for single-item purchases of more than 315kr in a single store for customers who are not Norwegian citizens, although the amount needed for a refund is subject to change. See p. 23 for additional information on the VAT.

NORWEGIAN KRONER (KR)		
	AUS$1 = 4.90KR	10KR = AUS$2.04
	CDN$1 = 5.27KR	10KR = CDN$1.90
	EUR€1 =7.90KR	10KR = EUR€1.27
	NZ$1 = 4.97KR	10KR = NZ$2.24
	UK£1 = 11.47KR	10KR = UK£0.87
	US$1 = 6.33KR	10KR = US$1.58

TRANSPORTATION

BY PLANE. The main international airport is in Oslo, though a few international flights land at Trondheim and Bergen. **SAS** (Scandinavian Airlines; Norway ☎915 05 400, UK 0870 6072 7727, US 800-221-2350) flies to Norway, as do Finnair and Icelandair. Students and travelers under 25 qualify for special youth fares when flying domestically on SAS. The new budget airline, **Norwegian** (www.norwegian.no), has introduced price competition into the internal market, as well as cheap fares to destinations throughout Europe. Book early for the best fares on both SAS and Norwegian, or try your luck with SAS domestic standby tickets *(sjanse billetter)* that can be purchased at the airport on the day of travel for around 400kr. Travel on standby tickets is not guaranteed and is subject to availability of seats, which may be determined only minutes before departure.

BY TRAIN. Norway's train system includes an extensive commuter train network around Oslo and long-distance lines running from Oslo to Bergen and to Stavanger via Kristiansand. Contact **Norwegian State Railways** for timetables and to purchase tickets. (☎815 00 888, press 4 for an English-speaking operator; www.nsb.no.) The unguided **Norway in a Nutshell** tour combines a ride along the **Flåm Railway,** a **cruise** through narrow Aurlandsfjord and Nærøyfjord to the port of Gudvangen, and a twisting **bus** ride over the mountains to Voss. Tickets can be purchased in advance as a package from tourist offices or train stations in Oslo and Bergen. (☎81 56 82 22; www.norwaynutshell.com. Round-trip fare from Voss 490kr; Bergen 760kr; Oslo from 1515kr.). Overnight trains may be best option for travel as far north as Bodø and Trondheim; from there, you'll need buses or ferries to get farther north. Seat reservations (30kr) are compulsory on many trains, including high-speed **Signatur** trains, which cover some long-distance lines. **Eurail** is valid in Norway. The **Norway Railpass,** which cannot be purchased in Norway, allows three days of unlimited travel in a one-month period (US$209, under 26 US$151). A **Scanrail pass** purchased in Norway allows five travel days in a 15-day period (1956kr, under 26 1360kr) or 21 consecutive travel days (3044kr, under 26 2117kr) of unlimited rail travel, as well as heavily discounted fares on many ferries and buses. However, only three of those travel days can be used in the country of purchase, so a Scanrail pass purchased at home (p. 59) is more economical for those traveling mostly within Norway. Neither pass includes trips on the Flåm Railway.

RAIL SAVINGS. For rail travel within Norway, the **Minipris** offered by NSB is an almost unbeatable deal. A limited number of seats are made available on regional trains for 199kr and 299kr, even on the most expensive routes. Go to www.nsb.no to purchase Minipris tickets; when you are asked to choose the type of ticket, select Minipris. (If it is not on the menu, tickets are sold out.) Minipris tickets purchased outside Norway are 50kr cheaper than those purchased in the country. Additionally, **Scanrail** passes purchased outside Scandinavia are much more flexible than Scanrail passes purchased once you arrive, and may be less expensive depending on the exchange rate. Check www.scanrail.com for more information on where to purchase passes at home.

BY BUS. Buses can be quite expensive but are the only land option north of Bodø and in the fjords. **Norway Bussekspress** (☎81 54 44 44; www.nor-way.no) operates most of the domestic bus routes and publishes a timetable *(Rutehefte)* with schedules and prices, available at bus stations and on buses. Scanrail holders are entitled to a 50% discount on most routes, and students with ISIC are eligible for a 25-50% discount—be insistent, and follow the rules listed in the *Norway Bussekspress* booklet. Bus passes, valid for 10 or 21 consecutive travel days (1300/2400kr), are good deals for those exploring the fjords or the north.

BY FERRY. **Car ferries** *(ferjer)* are usually much cheaper (and slower) than the many passenger **express boats** (*hurtigbat* or *ekspressbat*) cruising the coasts and fjords; both often have student, Scanrail, and InterRail discounts. The **Hurtigruten** (☎81 03 00 00; www.hurtigruten.com) takes six days for the incredible voyage from Bergen to Kirkenes on the Russian border; there is one northbound and one southbound departure daily from each of its 34 stops (from 6000kr in high season, 3500kr in low season). Discounts for railpasses are limited to a 50% discount on the Bergen-Stavanger route, but some ferry lines offer a 50% discount for students. The most common ports for international ferries are Oslo, Bergen, Kristiansand, and Stavanger. **DFDS Seaways** (☎38 10 55 00; www.dfdsseaways.co.uk) sails from Oslo and Kristiansand to Copenhagen, Denmark and Gothenburg, Sweden. **Color Line** (☎81 00 08 11; www.colorline.com) operates ferries between Norway and Denmark, as well as several domestic routes.

BY CAR. Citizens of Canada, the EU, and the US need only a valid driver's license in their home country to drive in Norway for up to one year. Insurance is required and is usually included in the price of rental. Roads in Norway are in good condition, although blind curves are common and roads are frighteningly narrow in some places. Drivers should remember to be cautious, especially on mountain roads and in tunnels. Driving around the fjords can be frustrating, as only Nordfjord has a road completely circumnavigating them; there are numerous car ferries, so check timetables in advance. Rental cars are expensive, but can be more affordable than trains and buses when traveling in a group. Vehicles are required to keep headlights on at all times. For more info on driving in Europe, see p. 60.

BY BIKE AND BY THUMB. The beautiful scenery around Norway is rewarding for cyclists, but the hilly terrain can be rough on bikes. Contact **Syklistenes Landsforening** (☎22 47 30 30; www.slf.no) for maps, suggested routes, and other info. **Hitchhik-**

ing is notoriously difficult in mainland Norway, but easier on the Lofoten and Svalbard Islands. Some successfully hitchhike beyond the rail lines in northern Norway and the fjord areas of the west; many others try for hours and end up exactly where they started. Hitchhikers should bring several layers of clothing, rain gear, and a warm sleeping bag. *Let's Go* does not recommend hitchhiking.

KEEPING IN TOUCH

PHONE CODES	**Country code:** 47. **International dialing prefix:** 095. There are no city codes in Norway. For more information on how to place international calls, see inside back cover.

EMAIL AND THE INTERNET. Oslo and Bergen have a good number of Internet cafes. Expect to pay about 1kr per min. Smaller cities might have one or two Internet cafes, and most have a public library open on weekdays that offers 15-30min. of free Internet. Free wireless connections for travelers with laptops are also readily available. **Peppes Pizza** restaurants across Norway have free wireless

TELEPHONE. There are three types of **public phones;** black and gray phones accept 1kr, 5kr, 10kr, and 20kr coins; green phones accept only phone cards; and red phones accept coins, phone cards, and major credit cards. **Phone cards** (*telekort;* 40kr, 90kr, or 140kr at post offices and Narvesen kiosks) are the most economical option, especially when prices drop from 5pm-8am. **Mobile phones** are increasingly popular and cheap; for more info, see p. 33. In Norway, **Netcom** offers the best prepaid deals for those traveling with a GSM mobile phone. A starter pack sells for 200kr that includes 150kr worth of calling time. **Telenor,** which has the widest coverage, sells starter packs for 200kr that include 100kr of calling time. "Top-up" refills for both operators are widely available. For help with domestic calls, dial ☎117; for help with international calls, dial ☎115. International direct access numbers include: **AT&T** (☎800 190 11); **British Telecom** (☎800 199 44); **Canada Direct** (☎800 191 11); **MCI** (☎800 199 12); **Sprint** (☎800 198 77); **Telecom New Zealand** (☎800 199 64); **Telstra Australia** (☎800 199 61).

MAIL. Mailing a first-class postcard or letter (under 20g) within Norway costs 6kr; outside Norway costs 7.50-10.50kr. Address mail to be held in the following format: First name SURNAME, *Poste Restante*, 5811 Bergen, NORWAY.

LANGUAGE. Norwegian is universally spoken, although most Norwegians also speak excellent English. The Sami languages are spoken by the indigenous people of northern Norway. For basic Norwegian words and phrases, see p. 1063.

ACCOMMODATIONS AND CAMPING

NORWAY	❶	❷	❸	❹	❺
ACCOMMODATIONS	under 160kr	160-260kr	260-400kr	400-550kr	over 550kr

HI youth hostels *(vandrerhjem)* are run by **Norske Vandrerhjem** (☎23 13 93 00; www.vandrerhjem.no). Beds run 175-250kr for nonmembers, though hostels out on the Lofoten Islands are closer to 125kr. HI members receive a 25kr discount. Linen typically costs 45-60kr per stay. Few hostels have curfews. Most hostels open in mid- to late June and close after the third week in August. Many tourist offices book **private rooms** and hotels for a fee (usually 30kr). Norwegian law allows free **camping** anywhere on public land for fewer than three nights, provided that you keep 150m from buildings and leave no trace behind. **Den Norske Turist-**

forening (DNT; Norwegian Mountain Touring Association) sells excellent maps (60-70kr), offers guided hiking trips for novice and experienced hikers alike, and maintains more than 350 **mountain huts** *(hytter)* throughout the country. A one-year membership (445kr, under 26 260kr) entitles the holder to discounts on DNT lodgings (☎ 22 82 28 00; www.dntoslo.no). The 43 staffed huts are open in summer; most have showers and serve dinner. Unstaffed huts are open from mid-February to mid-October; a sizable minority have basic provisions for sale on the honor system. Leave a 200-500kr deposit at any tourist office to borrow a key. Official campgrounds ask 60-130kr for tent sites, 300-700kr for cabins.

FOOD AND DRINK

NORWAY	❶	❷	❸	❹	❺
FOOD	under 60kr	60-100kr	100-150kr	150-250kr	over 250kr

Eating in Norway is pricey; markets and bakeries are the way to go. **Rema 1000** and **Rimi** supermarkets have the best prices, while outdoor markets are your best bet for cheap seafood and fruit. Many restaurants have inexpensive *dagens ret* (dish of the day; 70-80kr); otherwise, you'll rarely spend less than 150kr on a full Norwegian meal. Fish in Norway—cod, salmon, and herring—is fresh and relatively inexpensive. Non-fish national specialties include cheese *(ost)*; pork and veal meatballs *(kjøttkaker)* with boiled potatoes; and, for more adventurous carnivores, reindeer, ptarmigan, and whale meat *(hval)*. Around Christmas, steel yourself for a special meal of dried fish soaked in water and lye *(lutefisk)*. Beer is very expensive in bars (45-60kr for 0.5L), though 0.33L bottles hover around 10-13kr in supermarkets. Try the local favorite, *Frydenlund*, or go rock-bottom with Danish *Tuborg*. You must be 18 to buy beer, and 20 to buy wine and alcohol at the aptly named **Vinmonopolet** (wine monopoly) stores.

HOLIDAYS AND FESTIVALS

Holidays: New Year's Day (Jan. 1); Maundy Thursday (Apr. 13); Good Friday (Apr. 14); Easter Sunday and Monday (Apr. 16-17); Labor Day (May 1); Ascension Day (May 25); Whit Sunday and Monday (June 4-5); Constitution Day (May 17); Christmas Eve and Day (Dec. 24-25); Boxing Day (Dec. 26).

Festivals: Norway throws festivals virtually year-round, from the Tromsø International Film Festival (Jan. 17-22; www.tiff.no) to Bergen's operatic Festpillene (May 31-June 1; www.fib.no). The Norwegian Wood festival (mid-June; www.norwegianwood.no) brings together pop, folk, and classic rock acts for one of Norway's largest open-air festivals. Heavy metal enthusiasts might prefer Inferno, held in the capital on Easter weekend. A searchable database of other festivals can be found at www.norwayfestivals.com.

BEYOND TOURISM

From May 15 to September 30, foreigners may seek employment in Norway without a work permit. It makes sense to seek employment either before or after mid-June through mid-July, when competition from Norwegians will be fiercest. Check www.jobs-in-europe.net for listings. At all other times during the year, foreigners must procure work permits. Information on obtaining work permits is available at www.aetat.no. Citizens of the 39 signatory countries of the Svalbard Treaty, which include Australia, Canada, India, New Zealand, South Africa, the United Kingdom and the United States, may work without a permit on the Svalbard archipelago (p. 785). For those interested in volunteering, several opportunities are listed below. See p. 66 for Beyond Tourism opportunities throughout Europe.

The American-Scandinavian Foundation (AMSCAN), 725 Park Ave., New York, NY 10016, USA (☎212-879-9779; www.amscan.org/jobs/index.html). Volunteer and job opportunities throughout Scandinavia. Limited number of study fellowships in Norway available to Americans.

Norsk Økologisk Landbrukslag (APØG), Langeveien 18, Bergen, Norway (☎47 55 32 04 80). The Norse Organic Farmers Union is sometimes willing to organize volunteer service on organic farms throughout Norway.

OSLO ☎21, 22, 23

Scandinavian capitals consent to being urban without renouncing the landscape around them, and Oslo (pop. 550,000) is no exception. The pine-covered hills to the north and Oslofjord to the south bracket the cultural institutions, busy cafes, and elegant boutiques that give the city its metropolitan edge. While most of Norway remains distinctly homogeneous, Oslo boasts a small, multiethnic immigrant community. The residents of the Norwegian capital both embrace their past and move toward the future, creating an enthralling urban experience.

TRANSPORTATION

Flights: The high-speed **FlyToget** train runs between **Gardermoen Airport** (GEN; ☎815 50 250) and downtown Oslo (19-22min.; M-F every 10min., Sa-Su every 20min. 4:45am-midnight from train station to airport, 5:36am-12:36am from airport to downtown; 120-190kr, 50% student discount with ID). White SAS **Flybussen** drive a similar route (40min.; every 20-30min. 4:05am-9:50pm from bus terminal to airport, 5:20am-1am from airport to downtown; 110kr, 50% student discount, round-trip 170kr).

Trains: Oslo Sentralstasjon (Oslo S; ☎81 50 08 88). Trains run to: **Bergen** (6-8hr., 4-5 per day, 693kr); **Copenhagen** (7-8hr., 2 per day, from 736kr); **Stockholm** (4¾hr.; 3 per day; from 498kr); **Trondheim** (6-8hr., 2-5 per day, 772kr). Mandatory seat reservations for all long-distance domestic trains cost 41-71kr.

Buses: Norway Bussekspress, Schweigårdsgt. 8 (☎81 54 44 44). Follow the signs from the train station through the Oslo Galleri Mall to the Bussterminalen Galleriet. Schedules available at the info office. 25-50% student discount with ISIC.

Ferries: Color Line (☎81 00 08 11; www.colorline.com). To: **Hirtshals, Denmark** (12½hr.; 7:30pm; 190-460kr, students 95kr-230kr) and **Kiel, Germany** (19½hr.; 2pm; 740-1490kr, 50% student discount daily except F). **DFDS Seaways** (☎21 62 13 40; www.dfdsseaways.com) goes to **Copenhagen, Denmark** (16hr.) and **Helsingborg, Sweden** (14½hr.) daily at 5pm (both from 488-988kr). Color Line departs from 20min. west of the train station, DFDS from 10min. south.

Public Transportation: Bus, tram, subway, and **ferries** all cost 30kr per ride, or 20kr in advance. Tickets include 1hr. of unlimited transfers. If you are caught traveling without a valid ticket, you can be fined 750kr. **Trafikanten** (☎177), in front of Oslo S, also sells the **Dagskort** (day pass) for 55kr, **Flexicard** (8 trips) for 150kr, and **7-day Card** for 190kr. Open M-F 7am-8pm, Sa-Su 8am-6pm. Tickets also available at Narvesen kiosks and Automat machines.

Bike Rental: The city's bike-share system allows visitors to borrow one of the 1000+ bikes available at racks throughout the city center. Both the main tourist office and the Oslo S branch sell system enrollment cards (60kr) that are valid for 1 year.

Hitchhiking: Hitchers heading south to Kristiansand or Stavanger take bus #31 or 32 to Maritim. Hitchers to Bergen take bus #161 to the last stop. Those bound east into Sweden ride bus #81, 83, or 85 to Bekkelaget. *Let's Go* does not recommend hitchhiking.

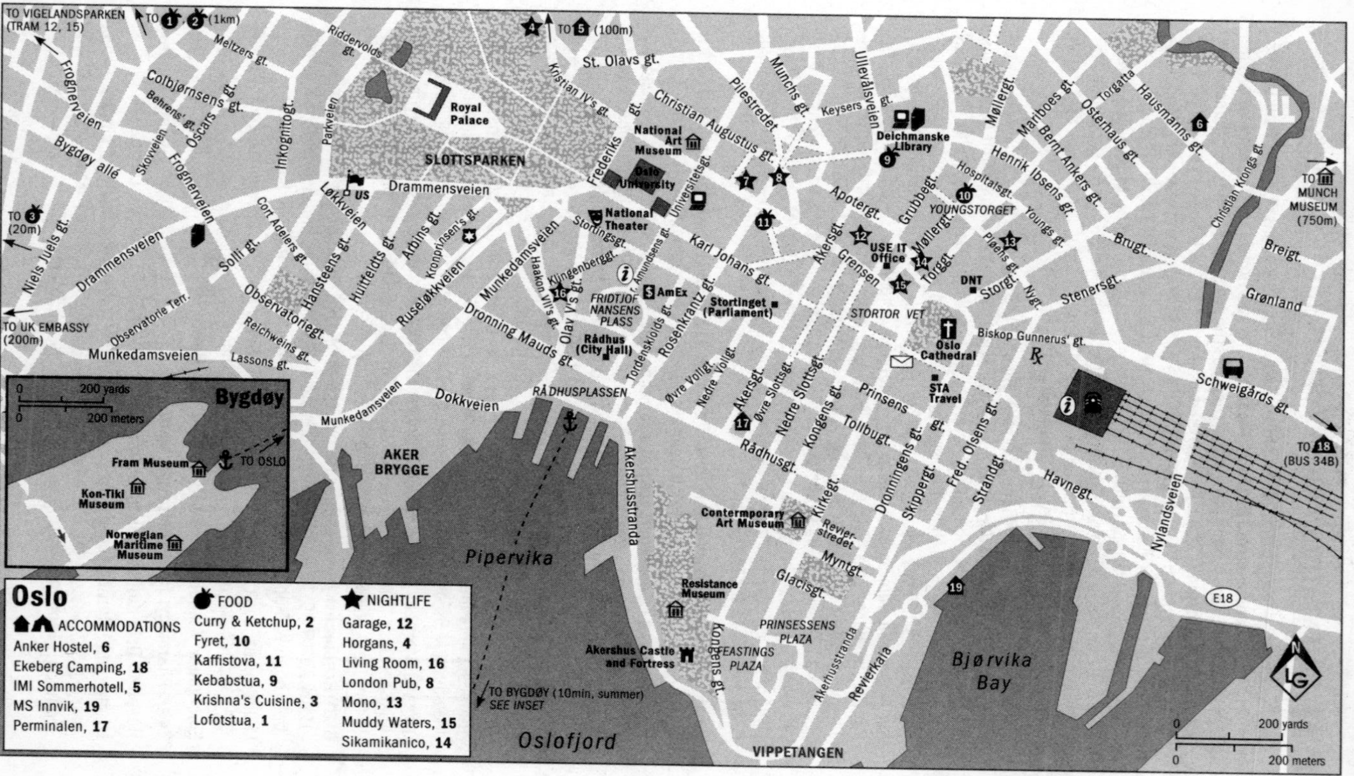
Oslo
ACCOMMODATIONS
Anker Hostel, 6
Ekeberg Camping, 18
IMI Sommerhotell, 5
MS Innvik, 19
Perminalen, 17
FOOD
Curry & Ketchup, 2
Fyret, 10
Kaffistova, 11
Kebabstua, 9
Krishna's Cuisine, 3
Lofotstua, 1
NIGHTLIFE
Garage, 12
Horgans, 4
Living Room, 16
London Pub, 8
Mono, 13
Muddy Waters, 15
Sikamikanico, 14
Bygdøy
Fram Museum
Kon-Tiki Museum
Norwegian Maritime Museum
TO OSLO
200 yards
200 meters
TO VIGELANDSPARKEN (TRAM 12, 15)
TO UK EMBASSY (200m)
TO MUNCH MUSEUM (750m)
TO 18 (BUS 34B)
TO BYGDØY (10min, summer) SEE INSET
Royal Palace
SLOTTSPARKEN
National Art Museum
Oslo University
National Theater
Stortinget (Parliament)
Rådhus (City Hall)
FRIDTJOF NANSENS PLASS
RÅDHUSPLASSEN
AKER BRYGGE
Pipervika
Oslofjord
Akershus Castle and Fortress
Resistance Museum
Contermporary Art Museum
PRINSESSENS PLAZA
FEASTINGS PLAZA
VIPPETANGEN
Bjørvika Bay
Oslo Cathedral
STORTOR VET
YOUNGSTORGET
Deichmanske Library
USE IT Office
STA Travel
DNT
AmEx
US
Karl Johans gt.
Drammensveien
Grønland
Schweigårds gt.
Nylandsveien
Akershusstranda
E18

NORWAY

ORIENTATION AND PRACTICAL INFORMATION

At Oslo's center is the garden plaza **Slottsparken,** which lies just beside **Oslo University** and the **Nationaltheatret (National Theater)** and surrounds the **Royal Palace.** The city's main street, **Karl Johans gate,** runs through the heart of town to **Jernbanetorget** and **Oslo Sentralstasjon** (Oslo S) at the eastern end. The harbor is south of the city, the **Bygdøy** peninsula farther southwest. Parks are scattered throughout Oslo, especially north of the Nationaltheatret. An excellent network of public trams, buses, and subways makes transportation through the outskirts quick and simple. Don't get mired down on Karl Johans gt. and miss exploring neighborhoods outside the downtown area; the latest urban trends are evident in parks, boutiques, and cafés in **Grünerløkka** to the north and in **Grønland** to the east.

Tourist Offices: Tourist Office, Fridtjof Nansenspl. 5 (☎23 14 77 00; www.visitoslo.com). From Oslo S, walk 15min. down Karl Johans gt., turn left on Roald Amundsens gt.; the office is on the right just before City Hall. Sells the **Oslo Pass,** which includes unlimited public transportation as well as admission to most of the city's museums. 1-day pass 195kr, 2-day 285kr, 3-day 375kr. Open daily June-Aug. 9am-7pm; Sept. and Apr.-May M-Sa 9am-5pm; Oct.-Mar. M-F 9am-4pm. Branch at Oslo S also books last-minute pensions for a 45kr fee. Open May-Aug. daily 8am-11pm; Sept. M-Sa 8am-11pm; Oct.-Apr. M-Sa 8am-5pm. **Use It,** Møllergt. 3 (☎24 14 98 20; http://ung-info.oslo.no/useit) targets students and backpackers. Books accommodations for free, offers free Internet, and puts out the invaluable *Streetwise Budget Guide to Oslo.* Go up Karl Johans gt. from Oslo S and turn right onto Møllergt. Open July-Aug. M-F 9am-6pm; Sept.-June M-W, F 11am-5pm, Th 11am-6pm.

Budget Travel: STA Travel, Karl Johans gt. 8 (☎81 55 99 05; www.statravel.no), a few blocks up from Oslo S. Books student airfares. Open M-F 10am-5pm, Sa 11am-3pm.

Embassies and Consulates: Australia, Strandvn 20, Lysaker (☎6758 4848). Open M-F 10am-3pm. **Canada,** Wergelandsv. 7, 4th fl. (☎22 99 53 00). Open June-Aug. M-F 8am-3:30pm; Sept.-May M-F 8:30am-4:45pm. **Ireland,** Haakon VII's gt. 1 (☎22 01 72 00; hibernia@online.no). Open M-F 8:30am-4:30pm. **UK,** Thomas Heftyes gt. 8 (☎23 13 27 00). Open in summer M-F 8:30am-4pm; in winter M-F 9am-4pm. **US,** Drammensv. 18 (☎22 44 85 50). Open M-F 8:30am-5pm.

Currency Exchange: Forex, Fridtjof Nansens pl. 6 (☎22 41 30 60), across from the Rådhus, offers the best rates. **Nordea Bank** in Oslo S, also exchanges currency. Open May-Sept. M-F 7am-6pm, Sa-Su 9am-4pm; Oct.-Apr. M-F 10am-6pm, Sa 8am-5pm.

Luggage Storage: Lockers at Oslo S and at the Nationaltheatret station. 7-day max. 20-45kr per 24hr. Available 4:30am-1:10am. Office open M-F 9am-3pm. Bags can be left in the Use It office (see above) for an afternoon or night.

GLBT Resources: Landsforeningen for Lesbisk og Homofil fri gjøring (LLH), Kongensgt. 12 (☎23 10 39 39; www.llh.no). Open June-Aug. M-F 8am-3pm; Sept.-May 8am-4pm. Cafe open W 6-9pm. Sells *Blikk* (60kr), a newspaper with nightlife listings.

Laundromat: Look for the word *"myntvaskeri."* **Selva AS,** Ullevålsveien 15 (☎41 64 08 33). Wash 40kr, dry 30kr. Open daily 8am-9pm.

Emergency: Ambulance: ☎113. **Fire:** ☎110. **Police:** ☎112.

24hr. Pharmacy: Jernbanetorvets Apotek (☎23 35 81 00), opposite the train station.

Hospital: Oslo Kommunale Legevakt, Storgt. 40 (☎22 11 80 80). Open 24hr.

Library and Internet Access: Free terminals at the stately **Deichmanske Library,** Henrik Ibsensgt. 1. Sign up for 1hr. or use a terminal for 15min. Open June-Aug. M-F 10am-6pm, Sa 11am-2pm; Sept.-May M-F 10am-7pm, Sa 10am-3pm.

Post Office: Main post office at Kirkegt. 20 (☎23 35 86 90). From Oslo S, head down Karl Johans gt. and turn left on Kirkegt. Address mail to be held in the following format: First name SURNAME, *Poste Restante,* Oslo Central Post Office, N-0101 Oslo, NORWAY. Open M-F 9am-5pm, Sa 10am-3pm. The post office at Oslo S is open M-F until 8pm.

ACCOMMODATIONS AND CAMPING

Hostels in Oslo fill up quickly in the summer—make reservations, especially if traveling in a group. The **private rooms** available through **Use It** (see **Practical Information,** p. 760) are a good deal at upwards of 125kr. **Pensions** *(pensjonater)* are centrally located, but can be more expensive since they don't offer dorm options. Check with the tourist office for last-minute accommodation deals. You can **camp** for free in the forest north of town (no open fires); try the end of the Sognsvann line #3. Although young Norwegians often drink at home before heading out on the town, most hostels, including HI, prohibit alcohol consumption on their premises.

Anker Hostel, Storgt. 55 (☎22 99 72 00, bookings 22 99 72 10; www.ankerhostel.no). Walk 12min. from the city center or take tram #11, 12, 13, or 17 to Hausmanns gt.; it's 100m up Storgt. Friendly atmosphere around the TV area, foosball table, and cafe accompanies comfortable rooms with kitchenettes. Breakfast 60kr. Linen 45kr. Internet. Reception 24hr. in summer. Dorms 150-175kr; doubles 440kr. AmEx/D/MC/V. ❶

Oslo Vandrerhjem Haraldsheim (HI), Haraldsheimvn. 4 (☎22 22 29 65; www.haraldsheim.oslo.no). Take tram #17 from Stortorvet for 15min. to Sinsenkrysset and walk up the hill. Rooms in good condition, if relatively small. Breakfast included. Linen 50kr. Reception 24hr. Dorms 200kr, with bath 220kr; singles 320/390kr; doubles 435/515kr. 25kr HI discount. MC/V. ❷

MS Innvik, Langkaia 49 (☎22 41 95 00; www.msinnvik.no). Cross the large white overpass and head right along the harbor. Let the waters of Bjørvika Bay rock you to sleep in this artsy, boat-borne B&B. Compact cabins come with bathrooms; ask for the captain's room for more space and comfort. Breakfast included. Reception 24hr. Singles 400kr; doubles 700kr. MC/V. ❹

Perminalen, Øvre Slottsgt. 2 (☎23 09 30 81; www.perminalen.com). Take tram #12 to Christiania Torv. Spotless rooms with cable TV, phones, and big bathrooms only 5min. from the heart of Oslo. Breakfast included. Internet 15kr per 15min. Reception 24hr. Dorms 295kr; singles 495kr; doubles 670kr. AmEx/D/MC/V. ❸

IMI Sommerhotell, Staffeldgt. 4 (☎95 42 28 59). Walk 20min. down Karl Johans gt., staying to the right of Slottsparken, and turn right on Linstows gt. Or take tram #10, 11, 17, or 18 to Holbergs pl. Open May 15 to July. Dorms consist of floor space; bring your own sleeping bag and mat. Rooms are well equipped and comfortable. Reception 24hr. Dorms 100kr; singles 350kr; doubles 500kr. Cash only. ❶

Ekeberg Camping, Ekebergveien 65 (☎22 19 85 68; www.ekebergcamping.no). Take bus #34A or 40 (10min.). Vast camping ground 3km from town with 24hr. security. Grocery store open daily 8am-10pm. Showers 10kr per 6min. Laundry 40kr. Reception 7:30am-11pm. Open late May to Aug. 2-person tent sites 150kr, 4-person 220kr; extra person 50kr. AmEx/D/MC/V. ❶

FOOD

Visitors to Oslo can choose between authentic Norwegian fare and a wide array of ethnic dishes, but either way they will usually feel robbed blind once the check arrives. The smart backpacker will raid the city's **grocery stores;** look for the chains **Rema 1000** or **Kiwi,** often open until 11pm, or invest in fresh produce at the **open-air market** on Youngstorget (M-Sa 7am-2pm). Vendors in the **Grønland** district east of

VENTURING EAST

Norway's sky-high prices can bring even trust-fund travelers to tears. Luckily, those looking to conserve *kroner* can venture beyond Karl Johan's gt. for a taste of Norway's spicier—and happily less expensive—cultural flavors.

Immigrants from Pakistan and India have settled just east of Oslo S in the neighborhood of Grønland over the past two decades, bringing with them incredible home cooking. **Tasty Grill and Tandoori** ❶, Norbygt. 56, serves lamb or chicken curry for 49kr in a relaxed setting. Take bus #60 to Norbygt. or walk up Grønland and turn onto Tøyengt. until you reach Norbygt. (☎22 67 75 15. Open daily noon-10pm. MC/V.) Cram in next to locals at **Tandoori Curry Corner** ❶, Grønland 22 (corner of Motzfield gt.), where a curry dish with rice and salad costs a mere 45kr. Take Brenersgt. from Jernbanetorget and cross Vaterlands bridge. ☎92 43 80 75. M-Th, Su 11am-4am, F-Sa 11am-6am. MC/V.)

After dinner, sashay your full belly down Grønlandsleiret 61 to **Restaurant Grønlandshagen** ❷, which stages live music every night of the week, including blues, jazz, rock, reggae, afrobeat, and Arabic dance. Take bus #37 from Oslo S to Politihuset. (☎90 74 99 11. Open daily noon-12:30am. Beer 43kr. D/MC/V.) By the time the band is done playing, you may be ready for another round of curry.

the train station hawk **kebabs** (around 40kr) and **falafel** (35kr), and the district's halal butchers can provide Muslim travelers with cooking meat.

Kaffistova (☎22 20 51 82), at the intersection of Rosenkrantz gt. and Kristian IV gt. Quiet, convenient cafeteria-style eatery with big portions of traditional Norwegian meat, fish, porridges, and desserts. Vegetarian options. Daily dish 156kr. Open M-F 9:30am-9pm, Sa-Su 10:30am-7pm. AmEx/D/MC/V. ❹

Lofotstua, Kirkeveien 40 (☎22 46 93 96). One of Oslo's best fish restaurants, drawing on the cuisine and the spare aesthetic of the Lofoten Islands (p. 781). Try the spiced Captain's Seal (235kr). Entrees 150-260kr. Open M-F 3-10pm. AmEx/D/MC/V. ❹

Fyret, Youngstorg. 6 (☎22 20 51 82). Down the stairs at the intersection of Møllergt. and Pløens gt. Cozy restaurant and bar serves fresh meat, shellfish, and Oslo's largest selection of potent aquavit, as well as stellar views of the square. Entrees 65-110kr. Live jazz M 8pm. Open M-W 11am-1am, Th-Sa 11am-2am. AmEx/D/MC/V. ❷

Curry and Ketchup, Kirkeveien 51 (☎22 69 05 22). Generous helpings of Indian mainstays served to a young crowd. Entrees 74-99kr. Open daily 1-11pm. Cash only. ❷

Krishna's Cuisine, Kirkeveien 59b (☎22 60 62 50). Huge portions of spicy, mercifully inexpensive Indian fare. Exclusively vegetarian, although their reliance on *ghee* (clarified butter) rules out vegans. Entrees 60-90kr. Open M-F noon-8pm. Cash only. ❷

Kebabstua, Ullevålsveien 13 (☎22 11 17 28). Fill up on 25kr kebabs while watching football with the friendly owner. Open Su-Th 10am-4am, F-Sa 10am-5am. Cash only. ❶

SIGHTS

Although visitors can wander Oslo's tree-lined streets and extensive network of parks for free, museums and other sights are often pricey. If you plan to visit more than a couple, it may make sense to purchase an Oslo Pass (p. 758).

VIGELANDSPARKEN. This 80-acre expanse is home to over 200 of Gustav Vigeland's sculptures, each of which depicts a stage of the human life cycle. Vigeland's mammoth art is controversial and purposefully puzzling, but worth deciphering. Each year the park draws more than a million visitors, who read and in-line skate amid works like the *Monolith*, a towering granite column of intertwining bodies. *(Entrance on Kirkeveien. Take bus #20 or tram #12 or 15 to Vigelandsparken. Open 24hr. Free.)*

ART MUSEUMS. The **Munchmuseet** has finally reopened after security improvements following the daring (and embarrassing) 2004 theft of two extremely valuable paintings, including a version of **The Scream** *(Shrik)*, Munch's most famous work. *(Tøyengt. 53. Take the subway to Tøyen or bus #20 to Munchmuseet. ☎23 49 35 00. Open June-Aug. daily 10am-6pm; Sept.-May Tu-F 10am-4pm, Sa-Su 11am-5pm. 65kr, students 35kr. Free with Oslo Pass. AmEx/D/MC/V.)* The definitive version of *The Scream* can still be found at the **Nasjonalgalleriet,** which boasts an impressive collection of Norwegian and foreign works from artists such as Cézanne, Gauguin, van Gogh, Matisse, Picasso, and Sohlberg. *(Universitetsgt. 13. ☎21 98 20 00. Open Tu-W, F 10am-6pm, Th 10am-8pm, Sa-Su 10am-5pm. Free.)* Next door at Oslo University's **Aulaen** (Assembly Hall), several of Munch's late, dreamy murals show his interest in bringing art to the masses. *(Enter through the door by the columns off Karl Johans gt. Open late June to July M-F 10am-2:45pm. Free.)* At the **Museet for Samtidskunst** (Contemporary Art Museum), in Kvadraturen, Oslo's old town, spacious halls display works from the museum's heavily Norwegian permanent collection, as well as avant-garde temporary exhibits. *(Bankplassen 4. Take bus #60 or tram #10, 12, 13, or 19 to Koongens gt. ☎22 86 22 10. Open Tu-W, F 10am-6pm, Th 10am-8pm, Sa-Su 10am-5pm. Free.)*

NORWAY

AKERSHUS CASTLE AND FORTRESS. Originally built in 1299, this waterfront complex was reconstructed as a Renaissance palace after most of Oslo burned to the ground in 1624. Norway's most famous traitor, Vidkun Quisling, was imprisoned here prior to his execution for collaborating with the Nazi invasion of 1940. *(☎23 09 39 17. Take tram #10 or 12 to Rådhusplassen. Fortress complex open daily 6am-9pm. Castle open May to mid-Sept. M-Sa 10am-4pm, Su 12:30-4pm; mid-Sept. to Oct. Su 12:30-4pm. Guided tours in English and Norwegian mid-June to early Aug. M-Sa 11am, 1, 3pm; Su 1, 3pm. Fortress free. Castle 40kr, students 20kr. Free with Oslo Pass. Cash only.)* The castle grounds include the powerful **Resistance Museum,** which documents the country's efforts to subvert Nazi occupation. *(Open mid-June to Aug. M, W, F 10am-5pm, Tu and Th 10am-6pm, Sa 10am-5pm, Su 11am-5pm; Sept. to mid-June closed 1-2hr. earlier. 30kr, students 15kr.)*

BYGDØY. The Bygdøy peninsula is directly across the inlet from downtown Oslo; although mainly residential, its beaches and museums more than justify a visit. In the summer, a public ferry leaves from Pier 3 in front of City Hall for the peninsula. *(10min.; runs Apr.-Sept. and late May to mid-Aug. every 15-30min. daily 8:45am-8:45pm; 20kr. ☎177; www.boatsightseeing.com. Or take bus #30 from Oslo S to Folkemuseet or Bygdøynes.)* Uphill from the ferry port is the **Norsk Folkemuseum** which traces Norwegian everyday life since 1200 through its architecture. Visit the 800-year-old stave church for a glimpse into the country's simple past. Nearby, the **Vikingskiphuset** (Viking Ship Museum) showcases three wooden burial vessels promoted as the best preserved of their kind. *(Walk away from the dock up the hill and follow signs to the right for 10min., or take bus #30 15min. from Nationaltheatret to Folkemuseet. Folkemuseum ☎22 12 37 00; www.norskfolkemuseum.no. Open mid-May to mid-Sept. daily 10am-6pm; mid-Sept. to mid-May M-F 11am-3pm, Sa-Su 11am-4pm. Summer 90kr, students 60kr. Winter 70/45kr. AmEx/D/MC/V. Viking Ship Museum ☎22 13 52 80; www.khm.uio.no. Open daily May-Sept. 9am-6pm; Oct.-Apr. 11am-4pm. 40kr, students 20kr. Free with Oslo Pass. MC/V.)* The **Kon-Tiki Museet** details Oscar-winning documentarian Thor Heyerdahl's daring 1947 ocean crossing from South America to Polynesia on a papyrus raft, a voyage that strengthened anthropologists' hypotheses about migration between the continents. *(Walk 15min. toward Bygdøynes, or take bus #30b. Kon-Tiki Museum ☎23 08 67 67; www.kon-tiki.no. Open daily June-Aug. 9am-5:30pm; Apr.-May and Sept. 10am-5pm; Oct.-Mar. 10:30am-4pm. 45kr, students 25kr. Both museums free with Oslo Pass. MC/V.)* The southwestern side of Bygdøy is home to two popular beaches: **Huk** appeals to a younger crowd, while **Paradisbukta** is more family-oriented. A stretch of shore between them is a nude beach. *(Take bus #30 or walk south for 25min. from the Bygdøynes ferry stop.)*

OTHER SIGHTS. The **Royal Palace,** on a hill at the western end of Karl Johans gt., is open to the public via guided tours, although tickets sell out well in advance. You can watch the daily changing of the guard for free at 1:30pm in front of the palace. *(Tram #12, 15, 19, or bus #30-32, 45 to Slottsparken. Open late June to mid-Aug. Tours in English daily 2, 2:20pm. Purchase tickets at any post office. 80kr, students 70kr.)* You can watch the changing of the guard daily at 1:30pm in front of the palace. For a panoramic view of Oslofjord and the city, bound up the stairs of the Holmenkollen ski jump (after an elevator-ride halfway up) and explore 4000 years of skiing history at the world's oldest **Ski Museum,** founded in 1923. A simulator recreates the rush of a leap off a ski jump and a blisteringly swift downhill run. *(Kongeveien 5. ☎22 92 32 64; www.skiforeningen.no. Take subway #1 on the Frognerseteren line to Holmenkollen, and walk 10min. uphill. Open daily June-Aug. 9am-8pm; Sept. and May 10am-5pm; Oct.-Apr. 10am-4pm. Museum 60kr, students 50kr. Free with Oslo Pass. Simulator 50kr, 40kr with Oslo Pass. AmEx/D/MC/V.)* The **Domkirke,** just next to Stortorvet, is hard to miss. The otherwise classically simple Lutheran cathedral gains additional character from its colorful ceiling, which is covered with biblical motifs. *(Karl Johans gt. 11. ☎23 3146 00; www.oslodomkirke.no. Open M-F 10am-3pm, Sa 10am-1pm. Free.)*

ENTERTAINMENT AND NIGHTLIFE

The monthly *What's On in Oslo*, free at tourist offices, follows the latest in opera, symphony, and theater. **Filmens Hus,** Dronningens gt. 16, is the center of Oslo's indie film scene. (☎22 47 45 00. Open Tu-W, F noon-5pm, Th noon-7pm, Sa noon-4pm. 70kr per movie, members 45kr, 100kr to join.) Jazz enthusiasts head to town for the **Oslo Jazz Festival** in mid-August (☎22 42 91 20; www.oslojazz.no). Countless bars along **Karl Johans gate** and in the **Aker Brygge** harbor complex host a hard-partying crowd, while mellowness prevails at the cafe-by-day, bar-by-night lounges along **Thorvald Meyers gate** in Grüner Løkka. Alcohol tends to be egregiously expensive out on the town, so young Norwegians have taken to the custom of the *Vorspiel*—gathering at private homes to sip comparatively cheap, store-bought liquor before wobbling out to paint the town red.

Mono, Pløens gt. 4 (☎22 41 41 66), livens up a relaxed, funky bar atmosphere with frequent concerts and DJs. If you're not lucky enough to be in Oslo for the weekend, Mono is a good bet for a sweaty night out. Beer 52kr. M-Th and Su 20+, F-Sa 22+. Cover for concerts 50-70kr. Open M-Sa 3pm-3:30am, Su 6pm-3:30am. MC/V.

Garage, Grensen 9 (☎22 42 77 66), caters to the Norwegian metal scene but also draws international acts. Bands play several nights a week during the summer. At Fight Club on W nights, bands compete against one another. Beer 48-58kr. M-Th, Su 20+, F-Sa 22+. Cover for concerts 50-180kr. M-Sa 2pm-3:30am, Su 6pm-3:30am. MC/V.

Muddy Waters, Grensen 13 (☎22 41 06 40), lives up to its claim as being one of the top blues clubs in Europe. It attracts an older crowd with live music almost every night. Beer from 54kr. 20+. Cover F-Sa around 90kr. Open daily 2pm-3am. AmEx/D/MC/V.

Horgans, Hegdehaugsv. 24 (☎22 60 81 87), is one of the most boisterous sports bars in Oslo. Come see how seriously Norwegians take their football. 21+. Cover Sa 50kr. Open M-Tu 5pm-midnight, W-Th and Su 5pm-1:30am, F-Sa 5pm-3am. AmEx/D/MC/V.

Living Room, Olav V's gt. 1 (☎40 00 33 60; www.living-room.no), is a fixture on the city's lounge scene. On weekends, Room morphs into heated dance floor. Beer 55kr. 24+. Cover F-Sa 100kr. Open W-Su 10pm-3am. AmEx/D/MC/V.

Sikamikanico, Møllergt. 2 (☎22 41 44 09; www.sikamkanico.no), is the club for thumping drum'n'bass and experimental house. Beer 47kr. 20+. Cover F-Sa 50-100kr. Open Tu-W 9pm-3am, Th-Sa 9pm-3:30am, Su 10pm-3am. MC/V.

London Pub, C.J. Hambros pl. (☎22 70 87 00; www.londonpub.no). This relaxed bar has been the "gay headquarters" of the city since 1979. Beer 48kr after 9pm and 32kr during the day. 21+. Cover F-Sa 40kr. Open daily 3pm-3:30am. AmEx/D/MC/V.

DAYTRIPS FROM OSLO

AROUND OSLO. Short, scenic harbor cruises show off the nearby islands of inner **Oslofjord.** The ruins of a **Cistercian Abbey,** as well as a picnic-friendly southern shore, lie on the landscaped island of **Hovedøya,** while **Langøyene** has Oslo's best **beach.** Take bus #60 (22kr) from City Hall to Vippetangen to catch a ferry to either island. The **Villmarkshuset,** Christian Krohgs gt. 16, rents canoes and kayaks for trips on the Akerselva river. (☎22 05 05 25; www.schlytter.no. Open M-F 10am-6pm, Sa 10am-3pm. 220kr per 2hr., 600kr per weekend.) The fortress town of **Fredrikstad** is less than 2hr. south of Oslo. Explore the 28km **Glommastien** bike path that winds through abandoned brickyards and timber mills along the Glomma River, or hop a ferry bound for seaside resorts on the lovely **Hvaler Islands.** The **train** (1hr.; 156kr, students 117kr) runs every 2hr. The **tourist office,** Toyhusgt. 98, has ferry schedules. (☎69 30 46 00. Open M-F 9am-5pm, Sa-Su noon-5pm.)

LILLEHAMMER. A small city set in the Lagen River valley at the edge of Lake Mjøsa, Lillehammer (pop. 25,000) still cherishes the laurels it earned as host of the 1994 Winter Olympics. The **Norwegian Olympic Museum** in Olympic Park traces the history of the Games from their genesis in ancient Greece and their rebirth in 1896 through their return to Athens in the summer of 2004. From the train station, it's a 15-20min. walk; head 2 blocks uphill, turn left on Storgt., right on Tomtegt., go up the stairs and follow the road uphill to the left. Or take bus #5 to Sigrid Undsetsveg (5min., 17kr). The museum is in the far dome. (☎61 25 21 00; www.ol.museum.no. Open June-Aug. daily 10am-6pm; Sept.-May Tu-Su 11am-4pm. 60kr, students 50kr. AmEx/D/MC/V.) Climb up the endless steps of the Olympic **ski jump,** or give your spine a jolt on the **bobsled simulator** at the bottom of the hill. (☎61 26 46 93; www.olympiaparken.no. Open daily June 11-Aug. 21 9am-8pm; May 28-June 10 and Aug. 22-Sept. 11 9am-6pm. Ski jump 15kr. Simulator 45kr. Combination ticket including chairlift ride 65kr.) For those who are interested in activities beyond skiing, the open-air museum **Maihaugen** provides a glimpse into rural Norwegian life of the past 300 years. From the train station head up Jernbanegt., turn right onto Gågt. and take the next left onto Bankgt., which you follow until turning right S. Undsets veg. (☎61 28 89 00; www.maihaugen.no. Open mid-May to Sept. daily 10am-5pm; Oct. to mid-May Tu-Su 11am-4pm. 75kr, students 60kr. AmEx/D/MC/V.) Accommodations at **Gjeste Bu ❶,** Gamleveien 110, come with a dose of mountainside charm. (☎61 25 43 21; gjestebu@lillehammer.online.no. Reception M-Sa 9am-11pm, Su 11am-11pm. Dorms 120kr; singles 275kr; doubles 375kr. Cash only.) **Trains** run to Oslo (2¼hr., 10-19 per day, 294kr) and Trondheim (4½hr., 4 per day, 577kr). The **tourist office,** in the station, has info on hiking and attractions. (☎61 28 98 00; www.lillehammerturist.no. Open mid-June to mid-Aug. M-Sa 9am-6pm, Su 11am-6pm; mid-Aug. to mid-June M-F 9am-4pm, Sa 10am-2pm.)

SOUTHERN NORWAY

Norway's southern coastline has become a summer holiday destination, and town after tidy town whispers "moneyed leisure" with red-tiled bungalows and jetties full of small powerboats. Luckily for the budget traveler, the region's rocky archipelagos *(skjærgarden)* can be explored on the cheap by hopping a local ferry with a packed picnic lunch or fishing gear.

KRISTIANSAND ☎38

Each year, vacationers on their way from the Danish ferry (p. 766) to Oslo tarry in Kristiansand (pop. 75,000), one of the jewels of the Norwegian Riviera. Meander through the old town of **Posebyen,** where the single-story wooden houses quartered soldiers over the centuries and hid Jewish refugees during WWII. Walking tour pamphlets and free English-language **guided tours** are both available at the tourist office. The **skerries,** a string of tiny islands and coves just off the coast, break the waves of the Skagerrak before they wash up on the harbor. Take in the view on a **ferry cruise** (2½hr.), or befriend a local and sail out on your own for a secluded swim or to camp (Departs daily at 11am from Nupen Park in East Harbor; round-trip 100kr). Back on land, **Dyreparken,** 11km east of the city, includes an amusement park and a zoo with prowling lynxes and Nordic wolves. Catch bus #1 (dir.: Sørlandsparken; 33kr) around the corner from the tourist office. (☎04 97 00; www.dyreparken.com. Open late June to late Aug. daily 10am-7pm; late Aug. to May M-F 10am-3pm, Sa-Su 10am-5pm; 250kr; low season from 90kr.)

The **Kristiansand Youth Hostel (HI) ❶,** Skansen 8, is a 25min. walk from the center of town. Walk away from the water until you reach Elvegt., turn right, then turn left onto Skansen. The hostel's beachfront location draws travelers of all ages. (☎02 83 10. Breakfast included. Linen 50kr. Internet 2kr per 15min. Mid-June to Aug. reception 24hr.; Sept. to mid-June 5-9pm. Dorms 220kr; singles 420kr; doubles 480kr. 25kr HI discount. D/MC/V.) Restaurants are expensive in Kristiansand, even by Norwegian standards. For cheaper fare, head to the **harbor** between 11am and 4pm, when families of fishermen cook up part of the morning's catch and sell it out of stalls. Groceries are available at **Rimi,** on the corner of Festningsgt. and Gyldenløves gt. (☎02 95 16. Open M-F 9am-9pm, Sa 9am-6pm. Cash only.)

Trains run to Oslo (4½-5½hr.; 4 per day; 551kr, students from 413kr) and Stavanger (3hr.; 6 per day; 370kr, students from 278kr). Color Line **ferries** (☎81 00 08 11; www.colorline.no) sail to Hirsthals, Denmark (2½-4hr.; 1-5 per day; in summer M-F 420kr, Sa-Su 460kr, low season 190-300krx ; students 50% discount). The **tourist office,** opposite the train station at Henrik Wegerlandsgt. and Vestre Strandgt., books rooms and can arrange **elk safaris** for groups of six or more for 250kr per person; call ahead by 3 pm. (☎12 13 14. Open June 20-Aug. 14 M-F 8:30am-6pm, Sa 10am-6pm, Su noon-6pm; low season M-F 8:30am-3:30pm.) The public library on Rådhusgt. offers free **Internet** in 15min. slots. (Sept. to mid-June. M-Th 10am-7pm, F 10am-5pm, Sa 10am-3pm; mid-June to Aug. M-F 10am-5pm.) **Postal Code:** 4601.

STAVANGER ☎51

A port town with cobblestone streets and a lively fish market, Stavanger (pop. 110,000) draws a delightfully contradictory mix of tree huggers and budding oil magnates to its great hikes and eclectic Petroleum Museum. On the western side of the harbor is the old town, Gamle Stavanger, where narrow lanes nose their way between well-preserved cottages by lamp light. The 12th-century **Stavanger Domkirke** is Norway's oldest cathedral, although time and overzealous renovations have not been kind to its Anglo-Norman towers. (Open June-Aug. daily 11am-7pm; Sept.-May Tu-Th and Sa 11am-4pm. Free.) A short walk down Kirkegt. from the church, the architecturally innovative **Norwegian Petroleum Museum** (Norsk Oljemuseum) explains drilling, refining and life on drilling platforms with interactive, if somewhat romanticized, displays. (☎93 93 00; www.norskolje.museum.no. Open June-Aug. daily 10am-7pm; Sept.-May M-Sa 10am-4pm, Su 10am-6pm. 80kr, students 40kr. AmEx/D/MC/V.) In nearby Lysefjord, perennial postcard-pick **Pulpit Rock** (Preikestolen) affords travelers a magnificent view from an altitude of 600m. If the crowds and your sense of vertigo permit, lie flat on this mountain plateau and look down into the abyss below. Take the ferry to Tau from the Fiskepiren dock (runs June-Aug. M-Sa 8am, 1pm, Su 8:25, 9:45am, 1, 2:25pm; Sept. Su only, 8:25, 9:45am, 1, 2:25pm; 33kr), catch the waiting bus (50kr) and then make the easy hike up the well-marked trail (1½-2hr.). Ferries return at 2:50 and 4:25pm.

To reach the **Jæren Vandrerhjem (HI)** ❷, Nordsjøvegen, from the train station, take bus #4 to Vigrestad, then walk across the road and through the small tunnel to your right. Head through the campground, then turn left. (☎54 36 36. Breakfast 65kr. Linen 60kr. Dorms 185kr; doubles 370kr. 25kr HI discount. MC/V.) Back in town, eat amid the maritime decorations of **N.B. Sørensens Dampskibssexpedition** ❹, Skagen 26. Dinner at this Stavanger institution can be a major investment, with some entree prices soaring above 200kr, but a salmon burger makes for a decently priced lunch at 74kr. (☎84 38 20. Open M-Th 11am-12:30am, F-Sa 11am-1:30am, Su 1pm-12:30am. AmEx/D/MC/V.) For less expensive fare, sample native strawberries at the **market** opposite the cathedral (open M-F 8am-5pm), or take a **Stavanger Cruise** around the harbor for fresh mussels accompanied by glittering shoreline views. (☎71 48 00. Departs Th-Sa 7pm. 100kr, including mussels.) Cheap beer often comes with questionable company in Norway, but **Cementen Pub,** Nedre Strandgt. 25, manages to have both rock-bottom prices and a great vibe. On Sundays the laidback crowd drinks its beers for only 31kr a piece. (☎56 78 00. Drinks M-Sa before 10pm 39kr. Open M-Th 7pm-3am, F-Sa 3pm-3am, Su 1pm-3am. V.)

Trains run to Kristiansand (4hr., every 3hr., 370kr) and Oslo (8hr., 4 per day, 806kr). **Buses** to Bergen (5-6hr., 400kr, students 300kr) leave from Stavanger Byterminal every 30min. The Flaggruten **express boat** (4hr., 620kr) sails past many a fjord and still makes the trip from Bergen in record time. (☎81 52 21 20; www.hsd.no. M-F 4 per day, Sa-Su 1-2 per day. Eurail and Scanrail holders 50% discount. Students 40% discount.) Fjordline **ferries** (☎81 53 35 00; www.fjordline.co.uk) also go to Newcastle, England (19½hr.; 2-3 per week; one-way from 760kr, students 50% discount). Fjordline ferries depart and arrive from Strandkaien, on the western side of the harbor. The **tourist office,** Domkirkeplassen 3, books rooms for a 30kr fee and provides info about bike rental. (☎85 92 00; www.regionstavanger.com. Open June-Aug. daily 9am-8pm; Sept.-May M-F 9am-4pm, Sa 9am-2pm.) **Postal Code:** 4001.

THE FJORDS AND WEST COUNTRY

Spectacular views and idyllic towns await at the end of the scenic train ride from Oslo to Bergen. From the rugged peaks of Jotunheim National Park to the humbling depths of Sognefjord, western Norway possesses a dramatic natural grandeur that thoroughly upstages the region's settlements.

TRANSPORTATION

Although transportation around the fjords can be complicated, the scenery out the window is half the fun. Plan your route ahead of time, as times vary from day to day. Call ☎177 for transportation info. Tourist offices, boat terminals, and bus stations can also help plan itineraries. **Bergen** is the major port serving the region; HSD **express boats** (☎55 23 87 80; www.hsd.no; ticket office at Strandkaiterminalen) run to Stavanger and points south of the city, while **Fylkesbaatane** (☎55 90 70 710; www.fylkesbaatane.no; ticket office at Strandkaiterminalen) sails north into Sognefjord, Nordfjord and Sunnfjord. Almost all destinations around the fjords connect via **bus** to Bergen. Visit www.nor-way.no for timetables and fares.

BERGEN ☎55

Situated in a narrow valley between steep mountains and the waters of the Puddefjorden, Bergen (pop. 235,000) bills itself as the "Gateway to the Fjords." Norway's second-largest city has a pedestrian-friendly downtown, which plays host to a slew of international students. Although it lacks the urban thrills of Oslo, Bergen's natural beauty and attentiveness to its history make it a world-class city.

TRANSPORTATION

Trains: The **station** (☎96 69 00), is 10min. south of the harbor. Trains run to: **Myrdal** (2¼hr., 6-8 per day, 219kr); **Oslo** (6½-7½hr., 4-5 per day, 693kr); **Voss** (1¼hr., every 1-2hr., 144kr).

Buses: Busstasjon, Strømgt. 8, inside the Bergen Storsenter mall. (☎177, outside Bergen 55 90 70). Buses run to: **Ålesund** (9-10hr., 2 per day, 54kr); **Oslo** (9-11hr., 4 per day, 660kr); **Trondheim** (14½hr., 2 per day, 695kr). 25% student discount.

Ferries: The **Hurtigruten** steamer (☎81 03 00 00; www.hurtigruten.com) begins its journey up the coast from **Bergen** and stops in **Ålesund,** the **Lofoten Islands, Tromsø,** and **Trondheim.** (Departs mid-Apr. to mid-Sept. daily 8pm, 613-5688kr; mid-Sept. to mid-Apr. 10:30pm, 30% discount except on Tu. 50% student discount.) **Flaggruten** express boats (☎81 52 21 20; www.flaggruten.no) head south to **Stavanger** (4hr.; M-F 4 per day, Sa-Su 1-2 per day; 620kr; 40% student and 50% Scanrail discount). **Fjord Line** (☎81 53 35 00; www.fjordline.co.uk) sends ships to **Hanstholm, Denmark** (16hr.; 3-4 per week; mid-June to mid-Aug. from 300kr, low season from 200kr) and **Newcastle, England** (25hr.; 2-3 per week; mid-May to early Sept. from 400kr; low season from 300kr). **Smyril Line** (☎59 65 20; www.smyril-line.no) departs June-Aug. on Tu 3pm for: the **Faroe Islands** (24hr.; 880-1160kr; low season from 690kr, students from 520kr) and **Iceland** (41hr.; 1560-2100kr, low season 900/750kr). Check website for low-season hours. All international ferries depart from **Skoltegrunnskaien,** a 10-15min. walk past Bryggen along the right side of the harbor.

Public Transportation: Buses are 23kr within the city center, 31-38kr outside. The **Bergen Card** (1-day 170kr, 2-day 250kr), available at the train station, includes unlimited rides on city buses as well as free admission to most of the city's museums.

ORIENTATION AND PRACTICAL INFORMATION

Central Bergen is small enough for visitors to explore on foot. Using the **Torget** (fish market) by the harbor as a basis for navigation, the city center can be broken down into a few basic areas. North of the Torget where the main street **Bryggen** curves around the harbor, the well-tended old city features artisans from an earlier era; southwest of the Torget is **Torgalmenningen,** the city's main shopping street. Locals tend to stay farther down Torgalmenningen, past **Håkons gaten** and **Nygårdsgaten.** The train and bus stations are about 10min. south of the Torget.

Tourist Office: Vågsalmenningen 1 (☎55 20 00; www.visitbergen.com), just past the Torget in the Fresco Hall. Crowded in summer; friendly, dedicated staff make it worth the wait. Books private rooms for a 30kr fee and helps visitors plan travel through the fjords. Open June-Aug. daily 8:30am-10pm; May and Sept. daily 9am-8pm; Oct.-Apr. M-Sa 9am-4pm. **DNT,** Tverrgt. 4-6 (☎33 58 10), off Marken, sells maps (94-119kr) and provides hiking info. Open M-W and F 10am-4pm, Th 10am-6pm, Sa 10am-2pm.

Budget Travel: STA Travel, Vaskerelven 32 (☎55 99 05; bergen@statravel.no). Take Torgalmenningen southwest from the Torget; turn left on Vaskerelven. Sells student tickets for international flights and books accommodations. Open M-F 10am-5pm. D/MC/V.

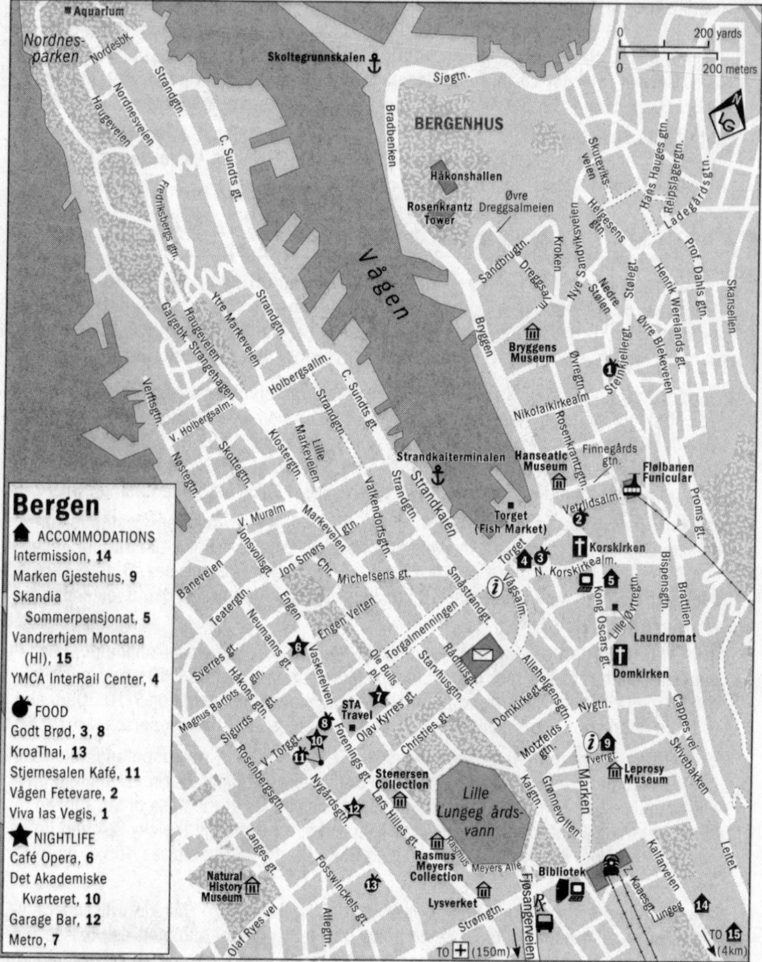

Currency Exchange: At banks near the harbor and the post office. Usually open M-W and F 9am-3pm, Th 9am-4:30pm; low season reduced hours. Tourist office changes currency at a less favorable rate.

Luggage Storage: At train and bus stations. 20-40kr per day depending on locker size.

Laundromat: Jarlens Vaskoteque, Lille Øvregt. 17 (☎32 55 04; www.jarlens.no). Wash and dry 70kr. Open M-Tu and F 10am-6pm, W-Th 10am-8pm, Sa 10am-3pm.

Emergency: Ambulance: ☎113. **Fire:** ☎110. **Police:** ☎112.

Pharmacy: Apoteket Nordstjernen (☎21 83 84) 2nd fl. of bus station. Open M-Sa 8am-11pm, Su 10am-11pm. AmEx/D/MC/V.

Hospital: 24-Hour Clinic, Vestre Strømkai 19 (☎56 87 00).

Internet Access: The public library, Strømgt. 6, at the intersection of Strømgt. and Vestre Strømkai (☎55 56 85), offers free 15-30min. slots. Open May-Aug. M-Th 10am-6pm, F 10am-4:30pm, Sa 10am-4pm; Sept.-Apr. M-Th 10am-8pm, F 10am-4:30pm, Sa 10am-4pm. **Bergen Internet C@fe,** Kong Oscars gt. 2B (☎96 08 36). Open M-F 9am-11pm, Sa-Su 10am-10pm. 1kr per min. Minimum 15min. Students 25kr for 30min. Cash only.

Post Office: Småstrandgt. (☎81 00 07 10). Open M-F 9am-8pm, Sa 9am-6pm. Address mail to be held in the following format: First name SURNAME, *Poste Restante,* 5014 Bergen, NORWAY. *Poste Restante* office closes M-Sa at 3pm.

ACCOMMODATIONS

In the summer, it's wise to reserve ahead. The tourist office books **private rooms** in local homes for a 30kr fee, a good deal for duos who can sometimes nab doubles for as little as 300kr. You can also **camp** for free on the far side of the hills above town; walk 30min. up the slopes of Mount Fløyen or take the funicular.

Intermission, Kalfarveien 8 (☎30 04 00; www.intermissionhostel.com). American college students staff this hostel, cultivating a chatty, open vibe. Waffle night M and Th. Breakfast 35kr. Linen deposit 30kr. Laundry free. Reception M-Th, Su 7-11am and 5pm-midnight, F-Sa until 1am. Lockout 11am-5pm. Curfew M-Th, Su midnight, F-Sa 1am. Open mid-June to mid-Aug. Dorms 120kr. Camping in backyard 70kr. Cash only. ❶

Marken Gjestehus, Kong Oscars gt. 45 (☎31 44 04; www.marken-gjestehus.com). Immaculate, sunny rooms draw travelers of all ages. Breakfast 55kr. Linen 55kr. Reception May-Sept. 9am-11pm; Oct.-Apr. 11am-6pm. All dorms single-sex. 6- to 8-person dorms 155-165kr; 4-person dorms 195kr; singles 355kr; doubles 470kr. Book ahead for dorms. AmEx/D/MC/V. ❶

YMCA InterRail Center, Nedre Korskirkealm. 4 (☎60 60 55; ymca@online.no). Backpackers clamber to the rooftop balcony of this central hostel, but 40+ bed dormitory can be overwhelming. Offers short-term work in summertime. Reception 7-10:30am and 3:30pm-midnight. Dorms 125kr; 4- to 6-person room 160-175kr per person. MC/V. ❶

Vandrerhjem Montana (HI), Johan Blyttsvei 30 (☎20 80 70; www.montana.no). Take bus #31 from the tourist office to Montana and follow the signs. Backpackers and traveling families trek 5km out of the city for clean, basic digs at the base of Mt. Ulriken. A perfect starting-point for hiking, but less convenient for exploring the city. 24-bed dorm can feel crowded. Breakfast included. Linen 65kr. Dorms 185kr; singles 465kr; doubles 710kr. 25kr HI discount. MC/V. ❷

Skandia Sommerpensjonat, Kong Oscars gt. 22 (☎21 00 35). Mingle with local students at bright student flats converted into private rooms for summer; ask to see the available rooms, as some are bigger than others. Laundry 30kr. Reception 8am-midnight. Most rooms with kitchenettes. Open mid-June to mid-Aug. Singles 375kr; doubles 500kr, with kitchen 600kr. Discount available for longer stays. MC/V. ❸

FOOD

Bergen's irresistible outdoor **fish market** panders to tourists on the Torget with colorful tents, raucous fishmongers, and free samples of salmon, caviar, whale, reindeer, and wild shrimp. (Open June-Aug. M-F 7am-5pm, Sa 7am-4pm, Su 7am-5pm; low season M-Sa 7am-4pm. Most vendors cash only.)

Viva las Vegis, Steinkjellergt. 2 (☎92 66 99 11). This neon-colored and irony-rich vegetarian eatery celebrates the carnivorous Elvis with veggie burgers for 39-89kr. Ask about student discount. Open M-Th and Su 11am-11pm, F-Sa 11am-1am. AmEx/D/MC/V. ❶

Godt Brød, V. Torggt. 62 and N. Korskirkealm. 12 (V. Torggt. ☎56 33 10, Korskirkealm. ☎32 80 00; www.bakeverksted.no). Prepares thick sandwiches (30-62kr) on fresh organic bread. V. Torggt. open M-F 7am-6pm, Sa 8am-5pm, Su 10am-5pm. N. Korskirkealm open M-F 7am-6pm, Sa 7am-4:30pm, Su 10am-5pm. Cash only. ❶

Vågen Fetevare, Kong Oscars gt. 10 (☎31 65 13). A favorite for leisurely morning coffee (16-33kr) or browsing through secondhand books. Open M-Th 8am-11pm, F 8am-9pm, Sa 9am-7pm, Su 11am-11pm. Cash only. ❶

KroaThai, Nygårdsgt. 29 (☎32 58 50). Saunter up to the counter for generous portions of cheap Asian fare from 70kr. Open M-Sa noon-10pm. MC/V. ❷

Stjernesalen Kafé, Olav Kyrres gt. 49-53 (☎58 99 10). Inside **Det Akademiske Kvarteret** (see **Nightlife,** p. 772). Serves soups, snack fare, and dinner dishes (30-60kr) until late in the night. Open M-F noon-1am, Sa-Su noon-2am. MC/V. ❶

SIGHTS

BRYGGEN AND BERGENHUS. Gazing down the right side of the harbor from the Torget brings Bryggen's signature pointed gables into view. This row of medieval buildings is rightfully the most visited tourist attraction in Bergen. Its charming, narrow alleys and crooked balconies have survived numerous fires and the explosion of a Nazi munitions ship to provide insight into the city's medieval past—and its busy present. While Bryggen is home to numerous galleries and craftshops whose spirit stems from the Middle Ages, their high prices are definitely in tune with 21st-century Norway. The **Bryggens Museum** displays archaeological artifacts, including fragments from the oldest buildings in Bergen, and a multimedia display on the Hanseatic trading league that dominated the history of the city for 400 years from the late Middle Ages. *(Dreggsalm. 3, behind a small park at the end of the Bryggen houses. ☎58 80 10. Open May-Aug. daily 10am-5pm; Sept.-Apr. M-F 11am-3pm, Sa noon-3pm, Su noon-4pm. 40kr, students 20kr. AmEx/D/MC/V.)* Tickets for walking tours of Bryggen are available at the museum. *(1½hr.; June-Aug. daily 11am, 1pm; 80kr.)* History buffs can continue their education at the **Hanseatic Museum,** located in an old trading house on the right side of the harbor, close to the Fløibanen funicular station. *(Finnegaardsgt. 1a. ☎31 41 89; www.hanseatisk.museum.no. Open June-Aug. daily 9am-5pm. Low season generally Tu-Su 11am-2pm; call for exact hours. May-Sept. 45kr, Oct.-Apr. 25kr. MC/V.)* **Bergenhus,** the city's fortress, is home to the 16th-century **Rosenkrantz Tower,** which features splendid views of the city, while the cavernous **Håkonshallen** displays the history of the Norwegian medieval monarchy in a grand architectural setting. *(☎55 31 43 80. Walk along the harbor away from the Torget. Hall and tower open daily mid-May to Aug. 10am-4pm; Sept. to mid-May hall open M-W and F-Su noon-3pm, Th 3-6pm; tower open Su noon-3pm only. In summer, guided tours every hr. on Su included in admission. 25kr, students 12kr. Cash only.)*

MUSEUMS. Three branches of the **Bergen Art Museum** line the western side of the Lille Lungegårdsvann. The 13th-century Russian icons and 15th-century Dutch Masters in **Lysverket** anticipate the canvases of Munch, Dahl, and Norway's neo-Impressionists in the **Rasmus Meyers Collection,** while the **Stenersen Collection** specializes in temporary exhibits as well as Northern Europe's most extensive collection of Paul Klee's work. *(Rasmus Meyers allé 3, 7, and 9. ☎56 80 00; www.bergenartmuseum.no. Open Tu-Su 11am-5pm. 50kr for all 3 museums, students 35kr, temporary exhibits 15kr. AmEx/D/MC/V.)* Bergen's **Leprosy Museum,** Kong Oscars gt. 59, is on the site of one of the first hospitals dedicated to the study of the disease. Poke your nose into the tiny cells where patients were kept and observed until the 1940s. *(☎96 11 55; www.lepra.no. Open June-Aug. 11am-3pm; Sept. to mid-June by appointment. 30kr, students 15kr. Cash only.)*

HIKING

Bergen is the only city in the world surrounded by **seven fjords** and **seven mountains.** While visits to all the waterways require careful planning—and usually a private vessel—the peaks are all easily accessible from the city center and have well-kept **hiking trails.** As locals are keen to inform visitors: you have not seen Bergen until you have seen it from above. Free hiking maps are available at the tourist and DNT offices, but if you plan to spend the night in the mountains, or if the weather seems less than perfect, invest in a detailed, full-size map of the area.

The four mountains east of the city center are most popular, largely due to their proximity to town. **Mount Fløyen** is the most-visited. It can be reached by the **Fløibanen funicular** or by hiking up a steep—but paved—road for 45min. Board funicular 150m from the fish market, on the right side of the harbor; the road up the mountain begins next to it. (☎33 68 09. Funicular open May-Aug. M-F 7:30am-midnight, Sa 8am-midnight, Su 9am-midnight; Sept.-May closes at 11pm. 30kr. MC/V.) At the summit, you'll find terrific views and several relatively easy, well-marked **trailheads.** The trails lead away from the crowds into a forest whose mammoth kerns and secluded ponds open occasionally to reveal stunning vistas. A bus and cable car combination also runs from the city center to the top of **Mt. Ulriken,** the highest of the peaks above Bergen. The mountain affords a panoramic view over the city, fjords, mountains, and nearby islands. Take bus #31 to Haukeland Sykehus and walk up the winding Haukelandsbakken until you reach the cable car. (☎20 20 20. Cable car daily May-Sept. 9am-10pm; Oct.-Apr. 10am-5pm. 40kr. Cash only.) Once on top, check the weather forecast at the **restaurant** before heading out on the trails or hiking down. Thick fogs can roll in quickly, creating danger for unprepared hikers. Ask at the tourist office about other hiking options.

Many of the mountains near Bergen are close to the city, which often provides hikers with a false sense of comfort. The peaks can be downright dangerous, especially if inclement weather hits. Always check in with the tourist office or the DNT for up-to-date weather and safety information before departing for a hike.

ENTERTAINMENT AND NIGHTLIFE

As spring sets up shop in western Norway, Bergen gears up for two simultaneous festivals in late May and early June. **Festspillene,** a 12-day program of music and dance, will bring Latvia's National Opera to perform Wagner's *Ring of the Nibelungs* in June 2006. (☎21 06 30; www.festspillene.no. 100-450kr.) **Nattjazz,** a series of more than 60 jazz concerts held in a converted sardine factory, as well as other sites around the city, tests the boundaries between jazz, rock, ethno, and electronica. (☎30 72 50; www.nattjazz.no. Day pass 330kr.) October rings in the up-and-coming **Bergen International Film Festival.** (www.biff.no. 1 film 65kr, 10 films 500kr.) Bergen nightlife rarely picks up until around 11:30pm on weekend nights; many locals throw back a round or two at home to avoid high beer prices at bars and clubs. Steer clear of pricey harborside tourist traps and take Torgallm. to **Nygårdsgaten,** home to an array of pubs and cafes.

Det Akademiske Kvarteret, Olav Kyrres gt. 49-53 (☎58 99 10). This half-salon, half-cultural center is run by student volunteers from the University of Bergen. Inside, the happening **Grøhndals** bar sells some of the cheapest beer in Bergen (M-W and Su 43kr, Th-Sa 39kr), while the **Teglverket** stage hosts jazz and rock concerts several nights a week during the summer. Concerts usually at 10pm; tickets 30-100kr. 18+; low season 20+. Open M-W and Su 7pm-1am, Th 7pm-2am, F-Sa 7pm-3am.

Café Opera, Engen 18 (☎23 03 15). Draws a mixed clientele with light meals, drinks, and DJs spinning after 11pm. F and Sa club nights pound a lively mix of house, disco, and funk. Open M 11am-12:30am, Tu-Th noon-3am, F-Sa noon-3:30am, Su noon-12:30am. AmEx/D/MC/V.

Garage Bar, at the corner of Nygårdsgt. and Christies gt. (☎32 02 10). A friendly crowd queues up for Bergen's most popular alt-rock pub. 20+. Cover 30kr after 1am. Open M-Sa 1pm-3:30am, Su 3pm-3:30am. MC/V.

Metro, Ole Bulls pl. 4 (☎55 57 30 37). The young and trendy come for hip-hop beats and spicy "mixology" fruit drinks in summer. M-Th and Su 20+, F-Sa 24+. Cover 90kr. Open daily 10pm-3am. AmEx/D/MC/V.

ALONG THE OSLO-BERGEN RAIL LINE

The 7hr. journey from Oslo to Bergen is one of the most scenic rides in the world. From Oslo, trains climb 1222m to remote Finse, stop in Myrdal for transfers to the Flåm railway, and then pass through Voss en route to Bergen. The 100km stretch along the desolate Hardangervidda plateau exemplifies stark beauty.

FINSE. Outdoor enthusiasts hop off at Finse and hike several days north through the Aurlandsdalen valley into **Aurland,** 53km from Flåm. Before you set out, be sure to ask about trail conditions at Finse's train station or at the DNT offices in Oslo and Bergen (p. 756); the trails are usually snow-free and accessible between early July and late September. You can sleep in DNT *hytte* (mountain huts), spaced one day's walk apart along the Aurland trails. **Bikers** can pick up the rutted **Rallarvegen** trail, which parallels the Oslo-Bergen train and extends 81km west to Voss. Most of the ride is downhill; bikers should exercise extreme caution on the steep curves in the **Flåmdalen valley.** Break up the ride by staying in a DNT *hytte* in Hallingskeid (21km from Finse) or forge on to Flåm (57km). Rent bikes at **Finsehytta.** (☎56 52 67 32. Open July-Aug. 495kr for 2 days).

VOSS. Stretched along a glassy lake that reflects the towering, snow-capped peaks above, Voss (pop. 14,000) is an adventurer's dream. Deep powder and 40km of marked trails attract skiers during the winter, while adventure sports including kayaking, paragliding, and parabungy (a jump from a flying parasail) draw devotees in summer. The safety-conscious staff at **Nordic Ventures,** behind the Park Hotel in a mini-mall, runs a variety of adventure expeditions. Their **kayaking** trips to nearby Nærøyfjord

NO VEGANS HERE

Dine at the farm of Ivar Løne, and nights spent counting sheep will never be the same. You'll eat in a converted meat storeroom where the forks and candlesticks are stamped with sheep heads. "In Voss," Løne's daughter-in-law explains, "there have always been sheep." Then Løne himself turns up, carrying half a cooked sheep's head on a long platter. "And as long as there have been sheep, there has been *smalahove!*"

Smalahove is a specialty of western Norway, eaten by farmers who used every scrap of meat on their sheep in the lean winter months. Løne's farm, 8km north of Voss, uses both old and new techniques to prepare the gory masterpiece. Instead of scraping the heads clean by hand, a large spinning rack allows them to be shaved en masse. Each head gets sawed in half, cleaned, soaked in salt for three days, and cured in a traditional smokehouse.

Løne gives his guests a tour of the facilities before sitting them down for the feast, flashing a sweet smile as they devour the sheep's eye in a single bite. Falafel may have taken Oslo by storm, but in Voss, carnivores still rule the roost. Løne's farm sells 55,000 heads a year, satisfying local demand but also shipping *smalahove* overseas to soldiers and oil executives hungering for a taste of home.

Call ☎56 51 69 65 to arrange a farm visit. Dinner starts at 300kr.

allow beginners to visit otherwise inaccessible areas of the fjord. (☎56 51 00 17; www.nordicventures.com. Open daily May to mid-Oct. 9am-9pm; mid-Oct. to Apr. 10am-5pm. Kayaking daytrips 890kr; 2 days 1495kr; 3 days including hiking 2250kr. All trips fully catered. MC/V.) For more ways to get yourself wet, contact **Voss Rafting Center,** Nedkvitnesvegen 25, based 3.5km from Voss in Skulestadmo. Pickup from Voss can be arranged. (☎56 51 05 25; www.vossrafting.no. Open in summer daily 9am-5pm, phone bookings until 10pm; winter M-F 9am-4pm. Rafting trips from 450kr per person. MC/V.) If you'd rather stick to *terra firma,* take the easy 30min. walk to **Bordal Gorge,** where water rushes through a narrow path lined by overhanging cliffs. Hikers should only make the trek in the months of July and August, when the path is safest. To reach Bordal, turn left from the train station, walk along the shore, and turn right onto the gravel path; after crossing the bridge, turn right and follow signs to Bordalgjelet.

Turn right as you exit the station and walk along the lake to take in the views from **Voss Vandrerhjem (HI) ❷.** If money is short, economize by sleeping on a foam mattress in the attic for 150kr. (☎56 51 20 17. Bike, canoe, and kayak rental. Breakfast included. Linen 60kr. Internet 1kr per min. Reception 24hr. Dorms 225kr; singles 450kr; doubles 600kr. 25kr HI discount. MC/V.) To reach **Voss Camping ❶,** head left from the station, stick to the lake shore, and turn right onto the gravel path at the church. Book ahead and be rewarded with a lakeside location. (☎56 51 15 97; www.vosscamping.no. Reception May-Sept. 8am-10pm. Showers 10kr per 6min. Tent sites 90kr. 5-person cabin 400kr. MC/V.) Pick up groceries at **Kiwi,** on the main street past the post office. (☎56 51 27 35. Open M-F 9am-9pm, Sa 9am-8pm.)

Trains leave for Bergen (1¼hr., every 1-2hr., 144kr) and Oslo (5½-6hr., 4-5 per day, 603kr). Get hiking maps and check weather conditions at the **tourist office,** Hestavangen 10. Turn left as you exit the train station and bear right at the fork by the church. (☎56 52 08 00; www.visitvoss.no. Open June-Aug. M-F 8am-7pm, Sa 9am-7pm, Su 2-7pm; Sept.-May M-F 8am-3:30pm. MC/V.) The Voss Public Library, Vångsgt. 22B, provides 30min. free **Internet.** (☎56 51 94 70. June-Aug. M-F 10am-3pm, Sa 10am-1pm; low season additional hours.) **Postal Code:** 5702.

EIDFJORD. Tucked into an eastern arm of the orchard-lined Hardangerfjord, tiny Eidfjord (pop. 950) draws hikers to the nearby **Hardangervidda** mountain plateau, the largest of its kind in Europe. Greenhorns stick to the plateau's eastern half, while more seasoned adventurers head for the **Hardangerjøkulen Glacier** up north or to the virtually untouched southern tip. In Eidfjord itself, the austere 14th-century **old church** hugs the harbor. (Open daily July to mid-Aug. 9am-3pm. Free.) A 2hr. walk along a trail from the harbor leads to a **Viking burial place** on top of a plateau in **Hereid.** Pick up a map of the trail from the tourist office and then head out along Simadalvegen. After passing the bridge, turn right and walk along the river; follow the path as it goes by the lake and winds uphill. A **mini-tour** whisks a mixed-age crowd to **Hardangervidda Nature Center** (☎53 66 59 00; www.hardangervidda.org. Open daily June-Aug. 10am-8pm; Apr.-May and Sept.-Oct. 10am-6pm. 80kr; admission included in tour price. MC/V.) From there, the tour continues on to the roaring **Vøringfossen Waterfall,** which plummets 182m into a serrated glacial valley. Be careful; stones are slippery and safety rails are few and far between. (Mini-tour daily mid-June to mid-Aug. Departs after ferry arrival from the harbor. 195kr.)

For a spectacular lakeside location, try **Sæbø Camping ❶,** 7km from town, close to the Nature Center. Buses leave from the HSD station across the street from the tourist office; ask the driver to let you off at the campground. (☎53 66 59 27. Open mid-May to mid-Sept. Showers 5kr per 2min. Tent sites 60kr, extra person 15kr. Basic, clean cabins from 310kr, one available for 260kr. MC/V.) Eidfjord is best reached from Voss via Ulvik. **Buses** leave Voss at 8:45am (1 per day; 69kr, students 57kr) and arrive in Ulvik at 11:10am. From there, the **ferry** travels the rest of the way to Eidfjord, returning at 2:40pm (runs June-Aug.). **HSD** offers a bus tour of Eidfjord and Vøringfossen starting from Bergen and ending with a cruise through the Hardangerfjord. (☎55 23 87 00; www.hsd.no. Mid-May to mid-Sept. depart Bergen 8:40am, return 7pm; 620kr.) Ask at the **tourist office,** in the town center, for info about hiking on the plateau. The office also has information on bike rental and finds accommodations for a 50kr fee. (☎53 67 34 00. Open mid-June to mid-Aug. M-F 9am-6pm, Sa-Su noon-6pm; May to mid-June and mid-Aug. to Sept. M-F 8:30am-4pm; low season M, W, and every other F 10am-4pm.)

FLÅM AND THE FLÅM RAILWAY. The historic railway connecting Myrdal, a stop on the Oslo-Bergen line, with the tiny fjord town of Flåm (pop. 450) is one of Norway's most celebrated attractions. The railway is an incredible feat of engineering, boasting the steepest descent of any railway in the world and ducking through hand-excavated tunnels. The highlight of the 55min. ride is a view of the thunderous **Kjosfossen** waterfall. To avoid the dancing nymphs and other clichéd routines set up to amuse tourists, ride the railway later in the evening. (☎57 63 14 00; www.flaamsbana.no. 55min.; 8-10 per day; 160kr, round-trip 250kr, 30% discount with ScanRail or Eurail.) A 20km **hike** (4-5hr.) on the well-tended paths between Myrdal to Flåm more or less mirrors the train route and allows hikers to tarry by smaller cascades before camping along the valley's goat-dotted knolls. Take the train uphill to Myrdal to cycle back down; check your brakes beforehand, and be ready to dismount on the steepest sections. The **Flåm Vandrerhjem (HI) ❶,** half-hostel, half-campground, is your best bet for cheap overnighting. (☎57 63 21 21. Shower 10kr per 5min. Dorms 155kr; singles 225kr; doubles 380-430kr. Tent sites 100kr. Cabins 450-750kr. 25kr HI discount. MC/V.) Flåm's **tourist office** is beside the train station. (☎57 63 21 06; www.visitflam.com. Open daily June-Aug. 8:30am-8pm; May 8:30am-4pm; Sept. 8:45am-4pm. Closed Oct.-Apr.) During the rest of the year, direct questions about Flåm to the tourist office in nearby Aurland, 9km to the north. (☎57 63 33 13; www.alr.no. Bike rental 30kr per hr., 175kr per day. Open M-F 8:30am-3:30pm.) Fylkesbaatane **express boats** run daily to Aurland (15min.), Balestrand (1½hr.), and Bergen (5hr.); check www.fylkesbaatane.no for a full schedule. **Postal Code:** 5742.

SOGNEFJORD

The slender fingers of Sognefjord, the longest fjord in Europe, reach all the way to the foot of the Jotunheimen Mountains in central Norway. The **Fylkesbaatane** company (☎55 90 70 70; www.fylkesbaatane.no) sends boats on daytrips to towns on Sognefjord and back to Bergen, and offers day tours of Sognefjord and the Flåm valley. The boats depart from Bergen's Strandkaiterminalen; buy tickets there or at the city's tourist office. Due to uncertain road conditions and the limited number of bus routes, overland transportation is often more confusing than it's worth.

BALESTRAND. Balestrand (pop. 1400) is an ideal base for exploration of Sognefjord. Adventure companies such as **Jostedalen Breførarlag** (☎57 68 31 11; www.bfl.no) run easy glacier walks (from 150kr), as well as offer courses in rock climbing and advanced glacier walking (from 2050kr, not including equipment). **Icetroll** (☎57 68 32 50; www.icetroll.com) also runs kayaking trips on glacial lakes within Jostedalsbreen National Park (from 690kr); during the summer, kayakers watch agape as huge boulders of ice splinter off the glacier into the water. In front of the ferry docks, **Sognefjord Akvarium** showcases the rarely seen marine life of the fjords. Admission includes a short slideshow and 1hr. of canoeing on the fjord. (☎57 69 13 03. Open daily late June to mid-Aug. 9am-10pm; May to late June and mid-Aug. to early Sept. 10am-6pm. 60kr. 50% discount for Kringsjå Hostel guests. AmEx/D/MC/V.) **Hiking** in the area is excellent, with clear, color-coded trails that promise exquisite views. From the harbor, head uphill to the right, take your second left, and walk along the main road for 10min.; turn right on Sygna and follow the signs. The trails range from gentle strolls to arduous treks for experienced hikers; their difficulty is clearly marked at the trailhead. The 5hr. hike to **Raudmelen** culminates in a far-ranging 360° view on a clear day.

Walk up the hill past the tourist office and take your second left to reach the **Kringsjå Hotel and Youth Hostel (HI)** ❶ overlooking the mountains. (☎57 69 13 03; www.kringsja.no. Breakfast included. Linen 40kr. Laundry 15kr. Open July to mid-Aug. Dorms 210kr; doubles 600kr; triples 750kr. 20kr HI discount. MC/V.) **Sjøtun Camping** ❶ is past the brown church on the coastal road. (☎57 69 12 23; www.sjotun.com. Open June to early Sept. Reception 9-9:30am, 6-6:30pm, and 9-9:30pm; call for other arrival times. Showers free. Tent sites 50kr. 4- to 6-person cabins 225-310kr. Cash only.) Fylkesbaatane **express boats** connect Bergen and Balestrand (4hr.; 2 per day M-Sa; 400kr, students 200kr). For hiking info and free maps, head to the **tourist office** near the quay. (☎57 69 12 55. Internet 15kr per 15min. Open mid-June to mid-Aug. M-F 7:30am-7pm, Sa-Su 8am-5:30pm; May to mid-June and mid-Aug. to Sept. M-F 10am-5pm, Sa-Su 10am-3pm; Oct.-Apr. M-F 8:30am-3:30pm.)

FJÆRLAND AND FJÆRLANDSFJORD. Fjærlandsfjord branches off Sognefjord in a thin northward line past Balestrand to the tiny town of **Fjærland** (pop. 300), perched at the base of the looming **Jostedalsbreen.** (*"Breen"* means glacier in Norwegian.) To reach the 1000m level, **hike** 2-3hr. up the Flatbreen, one of the arms of the bigger Jostedalsbreen, to the Flatbrehytta self-service cabin. (Cabin ☎57 69 32 29. Limited availability June-Aug. Bring sleeping bag.) While this hike is only moderately difficult, it can pass through areas covered with snow well into July; bring cold weather gear. The hike begins 5km northeast from the Norsk Bremuseum (see below) at the Øygard parking lot. The **Norsk Bremuseum** (Glacier Museum), 3km outside town along the only road, screens a beautiful panoramic film about the glacier and national park. (☎57 69 32 88. Open daily June-Aug. 9am-7pm; Apr.-May and Sept.-Oct. 10am-4pm. 80kr, students 40kr. AmEx/D/MC/V.) Back in town, **The Norwegian Booktown** attracts bookworms with a network of 12 secondhand bookstores that hold over 200,000 volumes. (☎57 69 22 10; www.booktown.net. Open May-Sept. daily 10am-6pm. MC/V.)

Accommodations are cheaper back in Balestrand, but sleeping on a budget is possible at **Bøyum Camping** ❶, right next to the Norsk Bremuseum. Ask to see your cabin; some are nicer than others. (☎57 69 32 52. Reception 9am-10pm during the summer. Dorms 125kr. Showers 10kr per 6min. Laundry 60kr. Tent sites 95kr. Cabins from 530kr. MC/V.) **Ferries** connect Fjærland and Balestrand (1¼hr.; 2 per day; 152kr, students 76kr). Local buses shuttle passengers to the Norsk Bremuseum, whisk them to view two Jostedalsbreen outcroppings, then return them to the harbor. (9:40am bus 120kr, 1:25pm bus 90kr.) From the Norsk Bremuseum, **buses** run to Ålesund (6hr.; 4 per day; 320kr, students 233kr) and Sogndal (30min.; M-Sa 2-5 per day; 56kr, students 41kr). The **tourist office,** near the harbor, solves transportation woes, rents bikes (25kr per hr.), and provides hiking maps. (☎57 69 32 33; info@fjaerland.org. Open daily 10am-6pm.)

LOM AND JOTUNHEIMEN NATIONAL PARK

Between the last tributaries of the western fjords and the remote towns of the interior lies the pristine landscape of Jotunheimen National Park. Hunters chased wild reindeer across its heights for thousands of years. Norwegian writers and painters discovered it anew in the 19th century, channeling its rugged beauty into a National Romantic artistic movement. In 1862, the poet Aasmund Olavsson Vinje christened the region "Jotunheimen," the home of the giants in Norse mythology.

LOM. Lom (pop. 2500) has become a major hub for excursions farther into the park. The park itself is the main attraction here, including the popular trek to the summit of 2469m **Galhøpiggen,** northern Europe's tallest mountain, and the **Memurubu-Gjendsheim** trail mentioned in Henrik Ibsen's *Peer Gynt.* Ask at the tourist office for the best location from which to base your excursion, since the best departure point varies according to skill level and weather conditions; options include **Juvashytta, Krossbu,** and **Spiterstulen.** The 6hr. journey from Juvashytta is the most popular route; a bus leaves for the base from Lom mid-June to mid-August daily at 8:30am (60kr). From Krossbu, the hike is a 4-6hr. glacier walk; from Spiterstulen, plan to hike 8-9hr., although not on the glacier. No extensive hiking should be done before early July; locals tend to tackle the mountains between mid-July and mid-August. Back in town, the 12th-century **stave church,** whose tumbledown, wood-carved interior includes graffiti carved in runes by some medieval wag, still holds weekly services. (☎97 07 53 97. Open daily mid-June to mid-Aug. 8am-8pm; mid-May to mid-June 10am-4pm. Adults 40kr, students 35kr. Cash only.)

With the nearest HI hostel more than 20km away, opt instead for a simple room with kitchenette at **Furulund Camping ❶.** Walk left as you exit the tourist office and follow the right branch of the main road for 600m. (☎61 21 10 57. Reception 8am-11pm. Trampoline. Showers 5kr per 5min. Laundry 80kr. Doubles 200kr; quads 300kr, with running water 450kr. Cash only.) Pick up groceries at **Kiwi,** just off the central roundabout. (Open M-F 9am-9pm, Sa 9am-6pm. Cash only.) **Buses** run to: Bergen (8½hr., 2 per day, 514kr); Oslo (6-6½hr., 5 per day, 440kr); Sogndal (3½hr., mid-June to mid-Sept. 2 per day, 200kr); Trondheim (5½hr., 2 per day, 305kr). The **tourist office,** in the Fjellmuseum, provides crucial transportation info, suggests outdoor activities for all levels of experience, and directs travelers to accommodations within the park. To reach it from the bus station, turn left and cross the bridge. (☎61 21 29 90; www.visitlom.com. Open mid-June to mid-Aug. M-F 9am-7pm, Sa-Su 10am-7pm; low season reduced hours.) Across the street, sign up for 30min. free **Internet** at the public library. (☎61 21 16 30. Open in summer M-Tu and Th-F 10am-3pm.)

NORDFJORD AND JOSTEDALSBREEN

Nordfjord is less popular than Geirangerfjord and Sognefjord, but the towering, ice-blue expanse of the nearby Jostedalsbreen has drawn more tourists to the region in recent years. Although solo trips onto the glacier are tempting, guided tours are essential, due to the glacier's dangerous soft spots and crevasses.

STRYN. Jostedalsbreen is comprised of several smaller glaciers (see **Fjærland,** p. 776), including the easily accessible Briksdalsbreen. Stryn (pop. 6600) provides an excellent base for glacier walks and other excursions on Briksdalsbreen. The **Glacier Bus** (69kr) runs to the base of the glacier from Stryn's bus terminal daily June to August at 9:30am, returning at 1:40pm. The young, energetic staff of **Olden Aktiv** (☎57 87 38 88; www.briksdalsbreen.com) run a variety of glacier tours and ice climbs for different fitness and skill levels (300-550kr; reserve ahead) from Melkevoll Bretun (see below) at the base of the glacier. The bus timetable makes it difficult to squeeze in any of Olden Aktiv's longer tours and still make it back to Stryn for the night; if you plan to spend most of the day on the glacier, consider staying at Melkevoll Bretun. Thumbing a ride back to Stryn is also possible, although *Let's Go* does not recommend hitchhiking.

Melkevoll Bretun ❶ sits in the shadow of Briksdalbreen, 45min. from Stryn. In addition to camping huts and relatively palatial holiday cabins, the campsite also features an open-air **cave dorm,** where guests sleep on wooden slabs swaddled in reindeer skins with 800 tons of rock overhead. Bring an insulated sleeping bag. (☎57 87 38 64. Showers 10kr per 5min. Firewood 50kr. Huts from 290kr. Cabins 570-690kr. Cave dorm 90kr per person; call ahead to check availability. MC/V.) To reach friendly **Stryn Vandrerhjem (HI)** ❶ from the bus station, turn left onto Setrevegen, head up the hill, and look for signs. If you arrive in the evening, call to ask about pickup. (☎57 87 11 06. Breakfast included. Laundry 20kr. Internet 15kr per 15min. Reception 7-11am and 4-11pm. Lockout 11am-4pm. Open June-Aug. Dorms 210kr; singles 325kr; doubles with bath 550kr. 25kr HI discount. MC/V.)

Bus #440 leaves Stryn daily at 3pm for Trondheim (7½hr., 500kr) via Lom (2hr., 185kr). Buses also run to Ålesund (3½hr., 4-5 per day, 230kr) and Bergen (6hr., 4 per day, 419kr). All fares are discounted 25% for students. Check www.nor-way.no for a schedule. The knowledgeable staff at Stryn's **tourist office,** Perhusveien 19, past the Esso station, sells mountain maps (30kr) and recommends hikes. (☎57 87 40 40; www.nordfjord.no. Internet 15kr per 15min. Open July daily 8:30am-8pm; June and Aug. daily 8:30am-6pm; Sept.-May M-F 8:30am-3:30pm.) For free **Internet,** book a 30min. slot at the public library, right next to the bus station. (☎57 87 48 86. Open mid-June to mid-Aug. M-F 10am-4pm; mid-Aug. to mid-June M, W, F 9am-5pm, Tu, Th 9am-6pm, Sa 10am-2pm.)

GEIRANGERFJORD

Only 16km long, Geirangerfjord is lined with narrow cliffs and waterfalls that make it one of the most spectacular—and most heavily touristed—places in Norway. While cruising through the iridescent water, watch for the Seven Sisters waterfalls and the Suitor geyser opposite them. Geirangerfjord can be reached from the north via the famous Trollstigen road from Åndalsnes or by the bus from Ålesund or Stryn that stops in sleepy Hellesylt.

GEIRANGER. A tiny jewel of a town, Geiranger (pop. 210) is situated at Geirangerfjord's glorious eastern end. An endpoint of the famous Trollstigen road, Geiranger is one of this nation's most visited destinations. In July and early August, masses of tourists overrun the minuscule town, fighting to take in its spectacular views of its spectacular glacier. The well-marked nature trails allow a brief escape from the crowds, although even here, you are unlikely to be alone. **Hikers** can peer down from **Flydalsjuvet Cliff** (2hr. round-trip), sidle behind the **Storseter Waterfall** (2½hr.), or catch a glimpse of the Seven Sisters waterfalls from **Skageflå Farm** (5hr.), abandoned in 1916. **Buses** (2 per day 9:30am, 2pm; 140kr) leave from opposite the ferry docks for the 1hr. ride to Lanfvaten, where hikers disembark and climb up into the cloud cover that shrouds the top of the **Dalsnibba Mountain Plateau.** If you prefer to explore the fjord on your own, call ahead to rent a motor boat from **Holenaustet.** (☎95 10 75 21. From 110kr per hr. AmEx/D/MC/V.) The only true budget accommodation in town is **Geiranger Camping** ❶, 100m from the town center down by the water. (☎70 26 31 20. Open mid-May to early Sept. Reception 8am-10pm. Shower 10kr per 5min. Laundry 80kr. Tent sites 79kr. MC/V.) **Buses** run to Ålesund (3hr., 2-4 per day, 176kr). There is no bus station; buy tickets onboard with cash. For hiking maps, head to the **tourist office,** up the path from the ferry landing. (☎70 26 30 99; www.geiranger.no. Open daily mid-June to Aug. 9am-7pm; mid-May to mid-June 9am-5pm.)

ROMSDAL AND TRØNDELAG

Between the western fjords and the long, sparsely inhabited stretch of Norway that extends north past the Arctic Circle, a string of small coastal cities forms the third point of a triangle with Oslo and Bergen. Hemmed in by the spiny Trollstigen range and the fertile valleys along the Trondheimsfjord, travelers are only just now beginning to discover this Norwegian heartland.

ÅLESUND

☎70

Often described as a scaled-down version of Bergen, seaside Ålesund (OH-less-oont; pop. 40,000) welcomes travelers emerging from fjord country with splashy Art Nouveau architecture. The best view of the city and the distant mountains calls for scampering up 418 steps to the **Aksla** viewpoint. Head through the park across from the youth hostel and start climbing; the 25min. walk to the top is well worth the slight exertion, especially late at night when the city lights sear the inky sky. The Time Machine exhibit at the centrally located **Art Nouveau Center,** Apotekergt. 16, transports visitors back to the city's devastating fire of 1904. This informative and engaging introduction to the city then traces its century-long renaissance. (☎10 49 70. Open June-Aug. M-F 10am-7pm, Sa-Su noon-5pm; Aug.-May Tu-F 11am-4pm, Sa 11am-4pm, Su noon-4pm. 50kr, students 40kr. AmEx/MC/V.) To head back even further, the **Sunnmøre Museum** features reconstructed farm-houses and the excavated remains of an 11th-century trading post. On Wednesdays between noon and 3pm, locals demonstrate traditional handicrafts and at 1:30pm, a replica Viking ship takes visitors out on the water for a short cruise. Take bus #13 or 18 (10min.) to Sunnmøre. (☎17 40 00; www.sunnmore.no. Open late May to early Sept. M-Sa 11am-5pm, Su noon-5pm; low season M-Tu, F 11am-3pm, Su noon-3pm. Cruise 30kr. Museum 60kr, students 45kr. MC/V.)

It's a 5min. walk from the bus station to the **Ålesund Vandrerhjem (HI) ❶,** Parkgt. 14, where tight bunks stacked three high bring travelers closer together. Head down Keiser Wilhelmsgt., keeping the water on your right, turn left onto Rådstugt. and head uphill to Parkgt.; the hostel is around the corner. (☎70 11 58 30. Breakfast included. Linen 50kr. Laundry free. Reception 8:30-11am and 3:30pm-midnight. Open May-Sept. Dorms 200kr; singles 415kr; doubles 550kr. 25kr HI discount. MC/V.) Arrive at trendy **Tango ❷,** Keiser Wilhelmsgt. 23, around midnight for a chatty bar scene. (☎12 10 12. F in summer mixed drinks 49kr. Beer 48kr. Open W-Sa 9:30pm-3am. AmEx/D/MC/V.) **Rema 1000** stocks groceries at the corner of Storgt. and Keiser Wilhelmsgt. (☎12 42 57. Open M-F 9am-10pm. Cash only.)

Buses go to Stryn (3½hr., 2-3 per day, 230kr) and Trondheim (8hr., 2 per day, 500kr). A slightly shorter route involves a bus to Åndalsnes (2½hr., 3 per day, 176kr) and a seat on the waiting train to Trondheim (4-5hr., 508kr). Hurtigruten **express boats** are costly, but trips include one night of accommodation; beware that "dormitory accommodations" can mean a space on the floor. (Departs daily 6:45pm, arrives in Trondheim 8:15am. 988kr, students 494kr.) The **tourist office,** at the Skateflukaia dock arranges walking tours of the city (60kr) that depart daily at 2pm. (☎70 15 76 00; www.visitalesund.com. Internet 10kr per 10min. Open June-Aug. M-F 8:30am-7pm, Sa 9am-5pm, Su 11am-5pm; Sept.-May M-F 8:30am-4pm.)

ÅNDALSNES

☎71

Åndalsnes (pop. 2700), on Romsdalsfjord, is a brawny, lightly industrialized port on the perimeter of fjord country. **Hikes** along the **Trollstigen** (Troll's Road) climb to 850m above sea level along the zigzag turns. The trail becomes enwreathed in mist as it passes the 180m **Stigfossen** waterfall and approaches the sheer **Trollveggen** (Troll's Wall). The alluring lip of the wall drew base jumpers for years until the burden of making helicopter rescues drove the town into debt and the activity was outlawed. Thrill-seeking scofflaws continue to make jumps on the sly. Trace your way back down to Åndalsnes (5hr.) on the **Kløvstien path,** recently smoothed over for walkers but still steep enough to require a hand-rail on certain segments. In mid-July, these paths fill with outdoor enthusiasts who have come to Åndalsnes for the concerts of the **Norwegian Mountain Festival** (www.norsk-fjellfestival.no). During the first week of August, Åndalsnes holds the **Rauma Rock Festival** (www.raumarock.com; 2-day pass 500kr), while the outdoor theater in nearby Klungnes hosts the **Sinclairfestival,** an

NORWAY

open-air re-enactment of a 1612 battle between Scottish mercenaries and Norwegian farmers. An annual rowboat regatta provides Romsdal-style sporting thrills. (www.sinclairfestivalen.com. Adults 250kr, students 150kr.) The wooden cabins and friendly proprietor of **Åndalsnes Vandrerhjem (HI)** ❶, Setnes, are just 2km outside of town. The Ålesund bus will stop at the hostel upon request. (☎22 13 82. Breakfast included. Linen 50kr. Internet 15kr per 15min. Reception 4pm-10am. Dorms 200kr; singles 350kr; doubles 500kr. MC/V.) **Trains** run to Oslo (5½hr., 2-4 per day, 670kr). **Buses** depart outside the train station for Ålesund (2½hr., 1-2 per day, 176kr), where the Hurtigruten stops en route to Bergen. For hiking maps and help booking rooms, duck into the **tourist office,** in the same building as the train station. (☎22 16 22; www.visitandalsnes.com. Open mid-May to mid-Sept. M-Sa 9am-6pm, Su noon-6pm.)

TRONDHEIM ☎73

A thousand years have come and gone since Viking kings turned Trondheim (pop. 150,000) into Norway's seat of power. Today, almost 30,000 university students lend Trondheim's well-kept canals and restored townhouses youthful energy during term time, while summer turns this gateway to the north country into a bustling meeting point for travelers.

TRANSPORTATION AND PRACTICAL INFORMATION. **Trains** go to Bodø (11hr., 2 per day, 894kr) and Oslo (6½hr., 3-5 per day, 772kr). **Buses** leave the train station for Ålesund (8hr.; 4 per day; 500kr, students 375kr) and Bergen (14½hr.; 2 per day; 714kr, students 536kr). The **Hurtigruten** departs daily at noon for Stamsund, in the Lofoten Islands (31hr.; 1964kr, students 982kr). To get to the **tourist office,** Munkegt. 19 from the station, cross the bridge, walk six blocks down Søndregt., turn right on Kongensgt., and look to your left as you approach the roundabout. (☎80 76 60; www.visit-trondheim.com. Open July to early Aug. M-F 8:30am-8pm, Sa-Su 10am-6pm; low season reduced hours) **DNT,** Sandgt. 30, has maps and hiking info. (☎92 42 00. Open May-Sept. M-F 8am-4pm, Th until 6pm.)

ACCOMMODATIONS AND FOOD. The fun-loving atmosphere at **Trondheim InterRail Center** ❶, Elgesetergt. 1, in the Studentersamfundet (p. 781), more than makes up for its thin mattresses and large dorms. Cross the roundabout to Kongensgt., turn left onto Prinsens gt., and the hostel will be on the left after the bridge. (☎89 95 38; www.tirc.no. Breakfast included. Linen 60kr deposit; does not rent pillow or quilts. Free Internet. Open late June to mid-Aug. Dorms 135kr. Cash only.) For equally basic, but quieter, lodging, take Lillegårdsbakken, off Øvre Bakklandet, uphill to **Singsaker Sommerhotell** ❶, Rogertsgt. 1. (☎89 31 00; http://sommerhotell.singsaker.no. Breakfast included. Linen 35kr. Open mid-June to mid-Aug. Dorms 155kr; singles 380-485kr; doubles 580-690kr; triples 795kr. MC/V.)

Gluttony may be one of the seven deadly sins, but the all-you-can-eat **cake buffet** (54kr) at **Mormors Stue** ❷, Nedre Enkeltskillingsveita 2, is more fun than wrath and sloth combined. Throw in all-you-can-eat pasta for an extra 55kr, and then nestle down into the restaurant's plush couches as your starch headache sets in. (☎52 20 22. Su buffet 1-7pm. Open M-Sa 10am-11:30pm, Su 1-11:30pm. MC/V.) For a paltry 99kr, the early-bird dinner crowd can snap up fresh fish platters prepared by some of Trondheim's finest chefs at the riverside **Den Gode Nabo** ❷, Øvre Bakklandet 66, just over the old bridge. After dinner, students arrive to sample the largest beer selection in town. (☎87 42 40. Dinner special daily 4-6pm. Beer M 40kr, Tu-Su 50kr. Open daily 1pm-1:30am. MC/V.) Alternakids nibble on eco-friendly lamb burgers (70kr) at eclectic **Ramp** ❷, Strandv. 25a in the small Svartlamon district, occupied by over 300 squatters just north of Solsiden. (☎51 80 20. Daily menu 80-100kr for main course. Beer 43kr. Open M-W 10am-midnight, Th-F 10am-1am, Sa noon-1am, Su noon-midnight. MC/V).

A ROOM OF ONE'S OWN. If you fall in love with this funky neighborhood, inquire for a cheap apartment (from 100kr per night) at **Ramp.**

SIGHTS. Most sights huddle in the southern end of town around **Nidaros Cathedral.** If you choose to see only one church in Norway, visit Nidaros, built on King Olof's tomb in the 11th century and completed around 1300. Norway's crown jewels are housed here, as is one of five large organs built by Joachim Wagner, one of Bach's contemporaries; free organ concerts are held throughout the year. (☎53 91 60; www.nidarosdomen.no. Open mid-June to mid-Aug. M-F 9am-6pm, Sa 9am-2pm, Su 1-4pm; low season reduced hours. Organ concerts mid-June to mid-Aug. M-Sa 1pm; low season Sa 1pm. Mid-June to mid-Aug. 40kr admission includes the nearby Archbishop's Palace. Low season cathedral free, palace 40kr. AmEx/D/MC/V.) To the north, the **Nordenfjeldske Kunstindustrimuseum** (National Museum of Decorative Arts), Munkeg. 3-7, features a collection of 20th-century tapestries. (☎80 89 50; www.nkim.museum.no. Open June to late Aug. M-Sa 10am-5pm, Su noon-5pm; late Aug. to May Tu-Sa 10am-3pm, Th 10am-5pm, Su noon-4pm. 50kr, students 25kr. Cash only.) The Medieval exhibit at **NTNU Vitenskapsmuseet** (Museum of Natural History and Archaeology) tells the 700-year story of Trondheim through a boy named Little Ivar. (☎59 83 94; www.ntnu.no/vmuseet. Open May to mid-Sept. M-F 9am-4pm, Sa-Su 11am-4pm. 25kr, students 15kr. Cash only.) Across the scenic **Gamle Bybro** (Old Town Bridge) to the east is the **old district's** former fishing houses, which have subtly morphed into chic galleries and cafes even as they outwardly maintain their weather-worn maritime charm.

ENTERTAINMENT AND NIGHTLIFE. Every year from the end of July through early August, the **Olavsfestdagena Medieval Festival** fills the city with everyone from pop bands to pilgrims (☎84 14 50; www.olavsfestdagena.no). The **Studentersamfundet,** the university's student society, houses a cafe with cheap food and beer next to the InterRail Center. (☎89 95 00; www.samfundet.no. Beer 48kr; 38kr for guests of the InterRail Center. Tu and F 8pm-10pm beer 25kr. Open daily until 2am.) Befriend some of the local students and you may discover one of the 18 private bars behind locked doors in this maze-like building. The Solsiden ("sunny side") district is home to popular **Club Blæst,** TMV kaia 17, which hosts concerts and DJs most weekends. (☎60 01 06; www.blaest.no. 20+. Beer 56kr during the summer; low season 49kr. Concerts from 50kr. Open daily noon-3:30am. AmEx/D/MC/V.) **Cafe Bare Blåbær,** 50m away at Innherredsveien 16, serves pizza (99-129kr) until midnight, after which it turns into a busy bar. (☎53 30 32. 20+ after 6pm. Beer 53kr. Open M-Th 11am-1:30am, F-Sa 11am-3:30am, Su 3-11:30pm. D/MC/V.) When school is in session, the clubs and bars along **Brattorgata** offer everything from tapas to fine malt whiskey. During the summer a stroll along **Carl Johans gata** or **Nordre gata** is your best bet for nightlife beyond Solsiden.

FARTHER NORTH

TROMSØ

☎77

The undisputed capital of northern Norway, Tromsø (pop. 60,000) exudes a worldly cosmopolitanism that belies its location, 720km north of the Arctic Circle. In between hikes in the Norwegian wilderness, a few days wandering the pedestrian-friendly center by day or club hopping by night can do wonders for any case of city-sickness.

TRANSPORTATION AND PRACTICAL INFORMATION. The **Hurtigruten express boat** arrives in Tromsø from Stamsund, in the Lofoten Islands (departs 7:30pm, arrives 2:30pm the next day; 1056kr, students 528kr). **Buses** go to Narvik (4½hr.; 2-4 per day; 330kr, students and Scanrail holders 165kr), a transportation hub for Finnish and Swedish destinations. The **tourist office,** Storgt. 63, books private rooms, as well as dogsled, snowmobile, or raft excursions. (☎61 00 00; www.destinasjontromso.no. Open June-Aug. M-F 8:30am-6pm, Sa 10am-5pm, Su 10:30am-5pm; low season reduced hours.) **Postal Code:** 9253.

NORWAY

ACCOMMODATIONS AND FOOD. To reach **Tromsø Vandrerhjem (HI)** ❷, Åsgårdv. 9, from the tourist office, turn right and walk two blocks down Storgt., take another right on Fr. Langes gt., and then catch bus #26. The dorms are basic but clean. (☎65 76 28. Linen 50kr. Reception 8-10:30am and 4-10pm. Open mid-June to mid-Aug. Dorms 175kr; doubles 430kr. 25kr HI discount. MC/V.) Housed in a Bible school, the **Fjellheim Sommerhotell** ❶, Mellomvn. 96, has the cheapest accommodations in town, with thick mattresses laid on the floor of the dorm. Take bus #28 to Bjerkely from the center or walk along Mellomvn. for 15min. (☎75 55 60; fjellheim@nlm.no. Open mid-June to mid-Aug. Breakfast included. Linen included. Free laundry and Internet. Reception 24hr. Dorms 150kr; singles 400kr; doubles 600kr. AmEx/D/MC/V.) For year-round accommodations with a central location, the **Ami Hotel** ❷, Skoleg. 24, just off Kongsbakken, has clean and pleasant rooms. Book early during the summer, as beds fill up fast. (☎62 10 00; www.amihotel.no. Reception M-F 7:30am-3pm, Sa-Su 9am-3pm. Dorms 200kr, with bath 250kr; singles 450/550kr; doubles 550/650kr. MC/V.) Mountainside **Tromsø Camping** ❶ has comfortable cabins and convenient access to outdoor activities. Take bus #20 or 24 to Kraftforsyninga, walk back across the red bridge, turn left and follow the road 400m. (☎63 80 37; www.tromsocamping.no. Reception 7am-11pm. Tent sites 150kr. 2- to 5-person cabins 400-950kr; Oct. to Apr. 400-700kr. MC/V.) Stock up on **groceries** along and just off Gågt. and Storgt.

SIGHTS. At the Tromsdalen end of the Tromsøbua bridge, the **Arctic Cathedral** resembles a glacier; metallic plates covering its surface reflect natural light in long, diaphanous streaks. Eleven tons of glass were used to fashion the huge, triangular stained-glass window behind the altar. (Open June to mid-Aug. M-Sa 10am-8pm, Su 1-8pm; mid-Aug. to May daily 4-6pm. 22kr. Services Su 11am.) Just off Strandv. at the other end of the city center, **Polaria,** Hjarlmar Johansens gt. 12, is a sleek, interactive museum and aquarium focused on Arctic ecosystems; watch the bearded seals strut their stuff at the daily feeding. (☎75 01 00; www.polaria.no. Open daily mid-May to mid-Aug. 10am-7pm; mid-Aug. to Apr. noon-5pm. Seal meals 12:30, 3:30pm. 80kr, students 55kr. AmEx/D/MC/V.) The **Tromsø University Museum** delves into geology, zoology, and the indigenous Sami culture, then dazzles visitors with a short video about the Northern Lights. Take bus #28 from the city center or walk along Mellomvegen for 25min. (☎64 50 00; www.tmu.uit.no. Open mid-June to mid-Aug. daily 9am-8pm; low season reduced hours. 30kr, students 15kr. MC/V.) To see the midnight sun hovering above Tromsø in June and early July, take the **Fjellheisen** cable car, Solliveien 12, up 420m to the top of Mt. Storsteinen. (☎63 87 37; www.fjellheisen.no. Cable car daily every 30min. 10am-1am. 80kr.) Students are fond of taking the lift late at night for a serene, introspective evening at the **Fjellstua** cafe. (☎63 86 55. Open daily mid-May to mid-Aug. 10am-1am; Apr. to mid-May and mid-Aug. to Sept. 10am-5pm. AmEx/D/MC/V.) The tour at the **Mack Mircrobrewery,** Storgt. 5-13, introduces visitors to both the art of brewing and the intricacies of Norwegian alcohol legislation. (☎65 86 77; www.olhallen.no. Open M-Th 9am-5pm, F 9am-6pm, Sa 9am-3pm; June-Aug. also M-Th 5-6pm. English-language tours M-Th 1pm; June-Aug. also M-Sa 3:30pm. 110kr, including 1 beer. AmEx/D/MC/V.)

ENTERTAINMENT AND NIGHTLIFE. The **Tromsø International Film Festival** (Jan. 17-22, 2006) is Norway's largest film festival, bringing over 40,000 visitors to town annually. In 2006, it will showcase "Films from the North," all shot in arctic Scandinavia and Russia. (☎75 30 90; www.tiff.no.) Tromsø is famous for its nightlife, which crackles on **Stortorget** and along **Sjøgata** until late. Board games and cappuccino await at **Amtmandens Datter,** Grønne gt. 81, a student hangout with leather chairs straight out of a professor's study. (☎68 49 06. Internet 20kr per 20min. Beer 53kr, 2-for-1 on summer weekends. DJ spins Sept.-May F-Sa. 20+. Cover F-Sa 50kr. Open June-Aug. M-Th and Su 3pm-2am, F 3pm-3:30am, Sa noon-3:30am; Sept.-May M-Sa noon-3:30am, Su 3pm-3:30am. AmEx/D/MC/V.) Nosh on hamburgers (from 89kr) at **Blå Rock,** Strandgt. 14/16, and return for the bar's famous Monday night parties. (☎77 63 59 99. Beer 56kr, M 33kr, 2-for-1 F-Sa 8pm-12:30am. Cover F-Sa 30kr. 18+ and 20+ areas. Open M-Th 11:30am-2am, F-Sa 11:30am-3:30am, Su 1pm-2am. MC/V.) Tuesday nights at **Kaos,** Strandgt. 22, are famous for their underground edge. During the weekend, a young crowd parties the night away to avant-garde tunes spun by some of Norway's best DJs. (☎63 59 99. Beer 54kr, M all night and Sa 6-11pm 35kr. 18+. Cover 30kr. Concerts W-Th 30-80kr. Open M-Th and Su 6pm-2am, F-Sa 6pm-3:30am. Cash only.) On other nights, try **Strøket** (W), **Meieriet** (Th), **Hawk** (Su), and **Abboteke Bar** (Su).

LOFOTEN ISLANDS

A jumble of emerald mountains, glassy waters, and colorful villages, the Lofotens prove that there is more to Norwegian beauty than the western fjords. As late as the 1950s, isolated fishermen lived in *rorbuer*, raised red wooden shacks along the coast; today, the same shacks are rented out to tourists venturing above the Arctic Circle to visit fishing villages aglow with the wan rays of the midnight sun.

TRANSPORTATION. To get to the Lofotens from Trondheim, take the **Hurtigruten express boat** to Stamsund (31hr.; departs daily at noon, arrives at 7pm the next day; 1964kr, students 982kr) or take a **train** to Bodø (11hr., 2 per day, 894kr) and then a **ferry** to Moskenes (3-4hr.; 4-7 per day; 138kr, students 69kr) or the Hurtigruten to Svolvær (6hr., daily 3pm, 391kr) via Stamsund (4hr., 417kr). Bodø's **tourist office** is down Sjogt. from the train station. (☎75 54 80 00; www.visitbodo.com. Open June-Aug. M-F 9am-8pm, Sa 10am-6pm, Su noon-8pm; Sept.-May M-F 9am-4pm, Sa 10am-2pm.)

HUNTING FOR CONTROVERSY

Since 1993, Norway has rejected the International Whaling Commission's ban on whale hunting, making it the only country in the world to sanction the activity. While Japan and Iceland allow whaling for scientific purposes, Norway is the only country to support hunting for its own sake, creating widespread controversy within both the country and the international community.

During the 2005 whaling season, 31 boats captured 797 minke whales, the highest number since Norwegians resumed hunting in 1993. Although the debate between activists and whalers quieted down in the late 1990s, the rising number of whale deaths has turned the Lofoten Islands, which serve as the base of Norway's whaling industry, into a battleground for the fight between whalers and environmental activists. Supporters of Norwegian whaling argue that they are protecting an ancient and indigenous way of life, while opponents point to the danger that modern hunting methods pose to many already endangered species.

For now, adventurous visitors can still seek out a truly unique Norwegian dish—red-meat whale steak. Just don't be surprised if your four-star dinner is disrupted by the protests outside.

Within the islands, **local buses** are the main form of transport; pick up the *Nordtrafikk* timetable at the tourist office. Hitchhiking is common by boat and by car; *Let's Go* does not recommend hitchhiking.

MOSKENES AND FLAKSTAD. The southernmost inhabited islands, Moskenes (pop. 1300) and Flakstad (pop. 1600) are linked by the E10 highway. Challenging mountainous hikes are one of the principal reasons to visit, although trails are often sparsely marked; pick up a hiking map (95kr) at the tourist office. Make the 3hr. trek up to the DNT's **Munkebu cabin** and stay the night if you prefer running water and beds to sleeping bags in the rough. DNT membership (p. 756) and a 500kr deposit are required for key rental, but nonmembers may accompany members. (200kr, under 25 100kr. Members 100/50kr.) Key available at the Sørvågen Handel (☎76 09 12 15) and KIN Trykk, Ramberg (☎76 09 34 20). South of Moskenes, the lovely, well-preserved fishing village of **Å** (OH) is the poster child for the Lofotens' tourist industry. **Buses** depart from behind the tourist office. The **Norsk Fiskeværsmuseum** uses reenactments to explain the island's maritime economy and offers visitors with strong stomachs a spoonful of homemade cod-liver oil. For a more conventional snack, sample cinnamon rolls from the birch-fired oven at the museum's historic bakery. (☎76 09 14 88. Open mid-June to mid-Aug. daily 10am-5:30pm; mid-Aug. to mid-June M-F 11am-3pm. 50kr, students 25kr. AmEx/D/MC/V.) Experienced hikers can tackle the 8hr. **Stokkvikka hike** by heading down the southern bank of Lake Ågvatnet and up 400m to cross the Stokkvikskaret Pass; bring a map. A less difficult, but still challenging, 3hr. hike from **Sørvågen** (between Å and Moskenes; 2.5km from each) leads up **Tinstinden** to its 490m peak, where you can take in the region's best view of Å and its surroundings. Information on this and other hikes can be found at the Å Lofoten Vandrerhjem (see below).

Private residences around town rent doubles. For cheaper digs, the dorms at **Å Lofoten Vandrerhjem (HI)** ❷ provide simple accommodations in a converted attic above the Fiskværsmuseum bakery. (☎76 09 11 21; www.lofoten-rorbu.com. Linen 30kr. Dorms 165kr; doubles 310kr. 30kr HI discount. MC/V.) Groups of four or more should consider renting out one of the comfortable *rorbuer* cabins at **Å Hamna Rorbuer As.** Very basic dorms are also available. (☎76 09 12 11. Reception June-Sept. 10am-10pm; call ahead at other times. Dorms 100kr. Cabins 400-1000kr. AmEx/D/MC/V.) Groceries can be found at **Service-mat.** (☎76 09 12 06. Open M-F 9am-7pm, Sa 9am-5pm, Su 4-7pm. Cash only.) The **tourist office,** 100m from the Moskenes ferry landing, offers rafting tours (3-6hr., 500-900kr) that go through the **Maelstrom,** one of the most dangerous ocean currents in the world, past the abandoned fishing hamlet of **Hell,** and into the ancient **Refsvikhula caves** to view their 3000-year-old drawings. The office also arranges 3hr. fishing trips (300kr) with locals. (☎76 09 15 99; www.lofoten-info.no. Internet 15kr per 15min. Open late June to early Aug. daily 10am-6pm; early June and late Aug. M-F 10am-5pm.)

VESTVÅGØY. Farther north is Vestvågøy (pop. 11,000). **Hikers** are serenaded by *ptarmigans,* a local species of bird, on the way up to the peaks of **Stein Tinden** (500m) or **Justad Tinden** (732m); both treks take roughly 6hr. round-trip and provide panoramic views of the Lofotens. A visit during June and early July provides opportunities for tanning into the wee hours under the midnight sun. Clear nights in late autumn or early spring could mean seeing the **Northern Lights.** The endearingly gruff, knowledgeable proprietor and homey common rooms at **Stamsund Vandrerhjem (HI)** ❶ have kindled enough friendships between travelers to earn the hostel a reputation across Norway. Guests catch fish during their stay and share it freely, keeping food costs low. (☎76 08 93 34. Wheelchair accessible. Fishing gear 100kr deposit. Free use of rowboats. Bike rental 100kr per day. Showers 5kr per 5min. Laundry 30kr. Open mid-Dec. to mid-Oct. Dorms 115kr; doubles 350kr. 25kr

HI discount. Cabins 400-650kr. Cash only.) Given the island's sporadic bus schedules, a car may be the best way to go, as long as you drive carefully on the one-lane roads. The gas station (☎76 08 97 40; open M-Sa 8am-11pm, Su 10am-11pm; MC/V) uphill from the hostel rents **cars.** (☎99 63 92 10; 300kr per day.)

SVALBARD ARCHIPELAGO ☎79

Frozen between the North Pole and the Arctic Circle, the Svalbard archipelago is home to some of the earth's most hostile territory; if the bone-chilling temperatures don't frighten you, the 3000+ polar bears should. Outside the mining and research community Longyearbyen (pop. 1800) on the main island of Spitsbergen, the bears are so prevalent that visitors are strongly encouraged to carry rifles. Still, tens of thousands of tourists arrive every year to experience Svalbard's wild beauty. Its vast, windswept spaces are not all fraught with peril, and constitute some of the world's most awesome scenery.

TRANSPORTATION AND PRACTICAL INFORMATION. Getting to Svalbard doesn't have to break the bank. Planes to Svalbard arrive at Longyearbyen Airport from Tromsø (1½hr., 1-3 per day in summer, from 500kr) and Oslo (3hr., 1-3 per day in summer, from 800kr). The airport bus (40kr) will take you directly to your hotel or hostel. **SAS Braathens** (www.sasbraathens.no) offers the lowest fares, but the best deals require plenty of flexibility and advance planning. The best time to visit Svalbard is the last week of July and first week of August, when temperatures can climb as high as 6°C (43°F). Tourists arrive both in "winter" (April to May) and summer (July to August); the remaining months comprise the dark season, when minimal sunlight and ice-cold temperatures send visitors packing. Whenever you visit, bring plenty of cold weather gear.

The exceptional **tourist office,** in Longyearbyen center, should be your first stop for navigating around address-less Longyearbyen and the rest of Svalbard. (☎02 55 50; www.svalbard.net. Open M-F 8am-6pm, Sa 9am-4pm, Su noon-4pm.) The library at the Lompensenteret provides 30min. free **Internet.** (☎02 23 70. Open July to mid-Aug. M-Th 10am-5pm, F 10am-4pm.) Svalbard's weather makes **taxis** an attractive option (call ☎02 13 75 or 02 13 05), but **hitchhiking** around Longyearbyen is both common and relatively easy. *Let's Go* does not recommend hitchhiking.

TIP **BEYOND TOURISM.** Svalbard is technically a part of Norway, but is governed by a special treaty that, among other provisions, allows many foreigners to **work** without a permit. Students with an interest in the hard sciences might prefer the **University Center in Svalbard (UNIS)**, where hundreds of students at all levels spend a semester or two every year. (☎02 33 00; www.unis.no.)

ACCOMMODATIONS AND FOOD. Accommodations on Svalbard are understandably limited. Book well in advance. For a warm community at budget prices, opt for the basic **Gjestehuset 102 ❸,** 25min. from the town center. (☎02 57 16; 102@wildlife.no. Breakfast included. Mar.-Sept. dorms 290kr; singles 475kr; doubles 790kr. Oct.-Feb. 280/350/550kr. AmEx/D/MC/V.) The neighboring **Spitsbergen Guesthouse ❸** is less social, but similarly basic. (☎02 63 00; spitsbergen.guesthouse@spitsbergentravel.no. Breakfast included. Open Mar.-Sept. Mar. to mid-Apr. dorms 295kr; singles 495kr; doubles 840kr. Mid-Apr. to Sept. 295/500/850kr. D/MC/V.) The greenhouse bar at centrally-located **Mary-Ann's Polarrigg ❹,** is excellent for midnight sunbathing in summer. (☎02 37 42; info@polarriggen.com. Mar.-Sept. singles 595kr, doubles 850kr. Oct.-Feb. 495/750kr. Breakfast 95kr. Beer 45kr. AmEx/D/MC/V.) Since camping on public land is strictly prohibited, try **Longyearbyen Camp-**

ground ❶, 4.5km outside of town next to the airport. Late arrivals can pay the next morning. Rest assured: no polar bears have been found at the site since 1985. (☎02 14 44; info@longyearbyen-camping.no. Open late June to early Sept. Tent sites 80kr. Tent rental 100kr per night. Sleeping bag rental 100kr 1st night, 50kr thereafter. Cash only. Reception 8-10am and 8-10pm.)

Food is very expensive on Svalbard, but other goods (including alcohol) are often cheaper due to the archipelago's tax-free status. To sample Arctic cuisine, order the Chef's Lunch (94kr) at **Kroa ❷**, in the Basecamp Spitsbergen in the town center. This frontier restaurant serves hearty fare to its big wooden tables. (☎02 34 50; kroa@longyearbyen.net. Beer 38kr. Open daily 11:30pm-2am. AmEx/D/MC/V.) **Svalbard Butiken** stocks groceries and duty-free goods. (☎02 25 20; www.svalbard-butiken.no. M-F 10am-8pm, Sa 10am-6pm, Su 3-6pm. AmEx/D/MC/V.)

SIGHTS AND NIGHTLIFE. Before venturing off into the wilderness, stop by the new Svalbard Museum at UNIS to learn more about these unique islands. Exhibits fill travelers in on the flora and fauna of the islands, as well as the history of the settlements. (☎02 13 84; www.svalbardmuseum.no. Opening June-Sept. daily 10am-6pm; Oct.-May M-W and F-Su noon-5pm. 50kr. AmEx/D/MC/V.) In July and August, join **Historical Wanderings with Anne,** a long-time Svalbard resident. (Tours depart the museum Tu and F 6pm. 100kr. Cash only.)

Since 20-somethings arrive in Svalbard from around the world to work by day and party by night, Longyearbyen's nightlife is surprisingly hot for a town of its size. The **Karls-Bergers Pub** stocks 1020 liquors in a dark, friendly room. (☎02 25 11; www.karlsbergerpub.com. Beer 36kr. Open M-F 5pm-2am, Sa-Su 3pm-2am. MC/V.) Barents Pub at the Radisson draws locals with its cheap beer. (☎02 34 66. Beer 39kr. Open daily 4pm-2am. AmEx/D/MC/V.) For a longer night out, throw back 25kr beers at the bar of the **Gjestehuset 102** (p. 785), then make your way to the **Huset** nightclub. (☎02 25 00; huset@longyearbyen.net. Beer 39kr. Open F-Sa; check local publications for more exact hours. AmEx/D/MC/V.)

OUTDOOR ACTIVITIES

No activity in Svalbard is perfectly safe; the widespread glacial cover and wandering polar bears make any trip outside Longyearbyen center dangerous. Travel on the archipelago requires careful planning and preparation. Basic safety information can be found at the Governor's Office website, www.sysselmannen.svalbard.no. Be aware, however that even the most experienced hikers often choose to travel with guided tours. Those who do decide to venture beyond Longyearbyen without a guide must first register with the Governor. Registration requires proof of insurance to cover potential rescue operations. Do not, under any circumstances, leave Longyearbyen alone; always travel with at least one person.

GUIDED TOURS. For most travelers, tours are by far the safest and most practical option. Unfortunately, they are expensive; expect to pay 500-1000kr for a day-trip. In winter, activities include dogsledding trips, ice caving, skiing, and snowmobiling. In summer, boat trips offer a great way for less intrepid travelers to explore. Other summer activities include glacier crossing, fossil hunting, and hiking. Mining tours and visits to the Wilderness Center are possible year-round.

For a complete listing of tours and tour companies, visit www.svalbard.net. Tours can be booked online in advance, or at guesthouses and hotels; plan to book at least the first few days of your tour ahead of time. A boat trip to either the abandoned mining town of **Pyramiden** or the inhabited Russian settlement of **Barentsburg** should be included in every itinerary. The energetic guides at **Svalbard Wildlife Service,** in the town center, run trips to both destinations. (☎02

56 60; info@wildlife.no. Office open in summer M-F 8am-6pm, Sa 10am-1pm; in winter M-F 10am-4pm. All trips include a hot lunch. Barentsburg 990kr. Pyramiden 930kr.) Join the wildlife-oriented **Svalbard Villmarksenter** for a 6-7hr. tour of Foxfonna, a region just outside Longyearbyen that has been declared a "no-go" zone for snowmobiles. Hikers and skiers arrive year-round to spot Svalbard reindeer. (☎02 19 85; www.svalbard-adventure.com. All trips include lunch. Foxfonna hike 550kr.) Climb up the **Trollsteinen** mountain for a stunning view of Spitsbergen; on a clear summer evening, the horizon extends for miles over a barren landscape. The biggest tour provider in Svalbard, **Spitsbergen Travel** organizes a trip up the mountain, crossing a glacier along the way. Tours leave several times per week in summer. (☎02 61 00; www.spitsbergentravel.no. Trip includes sandwiches and hot drinks. 540kr.) For **polar bear** spotting in a safe setting, book a multi-day boat tour with Spitsbergen Travel or Svalbard Wildlife Service.

INDEPENDENT TRAVEL. Only very experienced hikers should venture into the Svalbardean wilderness without a guide, even in summer. Quick-flaring foul weather makes even brief hikes from Longyearbyen surprisingly challenging; the polar bears that roam the islands ensure that overnight trips require the use of emergency beacons, trip-wire with flares, and a rifle. If you do not know how to use a rifle, do not travel on your own. Those experienced with rifles can rent equipment at the **Sportscenteret** in the Lompensenteret Mall. (☎02 15 35; sports.centeret@longyearbyen.net. Rifle rental 100kr per day, 500kr per week. 1000kr cash-only deposit for rifle plus 200kr for ammunition. AmEx/D/MC/V.) Permits are not required by law in Svalbard, but some stores may ask for one. Solo travelers should spend several days in Longyearbyen to plan routes and meet up with other travelers to form hiking groups. Bear in mind, however, that relatively few travelers arrive alone; most groups have planned their trips well in advance. One of the most popular routes is the three-day hike from Longyearbyen to Barentsburgh. Several companies (p. 786) run boat trips between the two destinations; arrange to travel at least part of the way with them.

Svalbard is dangerous. We mean it. If you don't know what you are doing, do not venture outside of Longyearbyen without a well-trained guide. In recent years, several tourists have been killed by polar bears and glacier accidents.

POLAND (POLSKA)

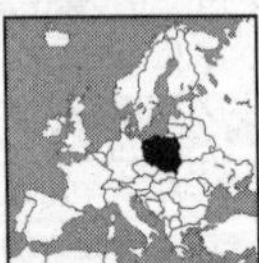

Caught at the threshold of East and West, Poland's moments of independence have always been brief. Between 1795 and 1918, the country did not exist on any map of Europe. Ravaged in WWII, then subsumed into the USSR, Poland is now taking advantage of its breathing room, raising its economic output and entering both NATO and the EU. Although capitalism has brought with it rising crime and unemployment—the shocks of transition—Poles have also spent their new wealth to reinvent their cultural roots and restore their architecture to its former glory.

DISCOVER POLAND: SUGGESTED ITINERARIES

THREE DAYS In **Kraków** (p. 801), enjoy stunning **Wawel Castle,** medieval **Stare Miasto,** and the bohemian nightlife of **Kazimierz.** Take a daytrip to the sobering **Auschwitz-Birkenau** concentration camp

ONE WEEK After three days in **Kraków,** go to **Warsaw** (2 days; p. 793), where the **Uprising Museum** and **Russian Market** can't be missed; head north to **Gdańsk** (2 days; p. 813) and soak up the sun on the beach of **Sopot.**

BEST OF POLAND, THREE WEEKS Begin with five days in **Kraków,** including a daytrip to **Auschwitz-Birkenau** or the **Wieliczka** salt mines. Spend two days in lovely **Wrocław** (p. 810), then enjoy the mountain air of **Zakopane** (1 day; p. 809). After a night at the edgy bars and clubs of **Poznań** (p. 811), head east to dynamic **Warsaw** (4 days), then take a break in scenic **Toruń** (2 days; p. 812). In **Gdańsk** (4 days), don't miss **Sopot** or **Malbork Castle.**

ESSENTIALS

FACTS AND FIGURES

Official Name: Republic of Poland.
Capital: Warsaw.
Major Cities: Katowice, Kraków, Lódź.
Population: 39,000,000.
Land Area: 312,000 sq. km.
Time Zone: GMT +1.
Language: Polish.
Religions: Roman Catholic (95%).

WHEN TO GO

Poland has warm summers and cold, snowy winters; summer weather can be capricious, and rain is frequent in July. Tourist season runs from late May to early September, except in mountain areas, which also have a winter high season (Dec.-Mar.). Late spring and early fall are pleasantly mild—though they too can be rainy. Late April, May, September, and early October are the best times to travel in Poland. Many attractions are closed for the winter.

DOCUMENTS AND FORMALITIES

EMBASSIES AND CONSULATES. Foreign embassies for Poland are in Warsaw and Kraków. Polish embassies and consulates abroad include **Australia,** 7 Turrana St., Yarralumla, Canberra, ACT 2600 (☎02 6273 1208; www.poland.org.au); **Canada,** 443 Daly Ave., Ottawa, ON, K1N 6H3 (☎613-789-0468; www.polishembassy.ca); **Ireland,** 5 Ailesbury Rd., Ballbridge, Dublin 4 (☎01 283 0855; www.polishembassy.ie); **New Zealand,** 17 Upland Rd., Kelbum, Wellington (☎04 475 9453; polishem-

bassy@xtra.co.nz); **UK,** 47 Portland Pl., London W1B 1JH (☎087 0774 2700; www.polishembassy.org.uk); **US,** 2640 Sixteenth St. NW, Washington, D.C. 20009 (☎202-234-3800; www.polandembassy.org).

VISA AND ENTRY INFORMATION. Citizens of Australia, Canada, New Zealand, the UK, and the US do not need a visa for stays of up to 90 days. Single-entry visas cost US$60, students US$45; multiple-entry visas cost US$100/75; 2-day transit visas cost US$20/15. Applications require a passport, two photos, and payment by money order, certified check, or cash. Regular service takes four days with a US$10 surcharge; 24hr. rush service costs an extra US$35. To extend your stay, apply in the city where you are staying to the regional government *(voi vodine)* or to the **Ministry of Internal Affairs,** ul. Stefana Batorego 5, Warsaw 02-591 (☎022 621 02 51; fax 849 74 94). **Passports** must be valid for at least three months after the scheduled departure from Poland and have at least one blank page.

TOURIST SERVICES AND MONEY

TOURIST OFFICES. City-specific tourist offices are the most helpful. Almost all provide free English-language info and help arrange accommodations. Most have good free maps and sell more detailed ones. **Orbis,** the state-sponsored travel

ENTRANCE REQUIREMENTS

Passport: Required for all travelers.

Visa: Not required for stays under 90 days for citizens of Australia, Canada, Ireland, New Zealand, the US, and the UK.

Letter of Invitation: Not required of most travelers.

Inoculations: Not required. Recommended up-to-date on DTaP (diphtheria, tetanus, and pertussis), Hepatitis A, Hepatitis B, MMR (measles, mumps, and rubella), Polio booster, and Typhoid.

Work Permit: Required for all foreigners planning to work in Poland.

Driving Permit: Required for all those planning to drive.

POLAND

bureau, operates hotels in most cities and sells transportation tickets. **Almatur,** the student travel organization, offers ISICs, arranges dorm stays, and sells discounted transportation tickets. The state-sponsored **PTTK** and **IT** *(Informacji Turystycznej)* bureaus, in nearly every city, are helpful for basic traveling needs. Try the *Polish Pages,* a free guide available at hotels and tourist agencies.

MONEY. The Polish currency is based on the **złoty** (1 złoty=100 groszy), plural: złotych. **Inflation** is around 3%, so prices should be reasonably stable. **Kantory** (except those at the airport and train stations, which often attempt to scam tourists) offer better exchange rates than banks. **Bank PKO SA** and **Bank Pekao** have decent exchange rates; they cash traveler's checks and give **cash advances. ATMs** *(bankomat)* are common, and are all in English; MasterCard and Visa are widely accepted at ATMs. Budget accommodations rarely accept **credit cards,** but some restaurants and upscale hotels do. **Normal business** hours in Poland are 8am-4pm.

ZŁOTYCH (ZŁ)		
	AUS$1 = 2.49ZŁ	1ZŁ = AUS$0.40
	CDN$1 = 2.70ZŁ	1ZŁ = CDN$0.37
	EUR€1 = 4.02ZŁ	1ZŁ = EUR€0.25
	NZ$1 = 2.30ZŁ	1ZŁ = NZ$0.44
	UK£1 = 5.92ZŁ	1ZŁ = UK£0.17
	US$1 = 3.28ZŁ	1ZŁ = US$0.31

HEALTH AND SAFETY

Medical clinics in major cities have private, English-speaking doctors, but they may not be up to Western standards. Expect to pay 50zł per visit. Avoid state hospitals. In an emergency, go to your embassy. **Pharmacies** are well stocked, and some stay open 24hr. **Public restrooms** are marked with a triangle for men and a circle for women. They range from pristine to squalid and cost up to 0.70zł; soap, towels, and toilet paper may cost extra. **Tap water** is drinkable in theory, but **bottled water** will spare you from some unpleasant metals and chemicals.

Crime rates are low, but tourists are sometimes targeted. Watch for muggers and **pickpockets,** especially on trains and in lower-priced hostels. Cab drivers will invariably attempt to cheat those who do not speak Polish, and "friendly locals" looking to assist tourists are sometimes merely setting them up for scams. **Minorities** may receive unwanted attention. Darker-skinned people may be mistaken for Roma (gypsies) and discriminated against. There may be lingering prejudice against Jews despite great efforts on the part of the government. **Homosexuality** is legal and a frequent topic of media debate, although it remains fairly underground; discretion is advised.

EMERGENCY	**Police, Ambulance,** and **Fire:** ☎999.

TRANSPORTATION

BY PLANE. Warsaw's modern **Okęcie Airport** (WAW) is the hub for international flights. **LOT,** the national airline, flies to major cities.

BY TRAIN. Trains are faster and more comfortable than buses. For a **timetable,** see **www.pkp.pl.** *Odjazdy* (departures) are in yellow, *przyjazdy* (arrivals) in white. *InterCity* and *ekspresowy* (express) trains are listed in red with an "IC" or "Ex" before the train number. *Pośpieszny* (direct; in red) are almost as fast and a bit cheaper. Low-priced *osobowy* (in black) are the slowest and have no restrooms. If you see a boxed "R" on the schedule, ask the clerk for a *miejscówka* (reservation). Students and seniors buy *ulgowy* (half-price) tickets instead of *normalny* tickets, but **foreign travelers are not eligible for discounts** on domestic buses and trains. **Eurail** is not valid in Poland. **Wasteels** tickets and **Eurotrain** passes, sold at Almatur and Orbis, get 40% off international train fares for those under 26. Buy tickets in advance or wait in long lines. Stations are not announced and can be poorly marked. **Do not take night trains,** as they are plagued with theft and crime.

BY BUS. PKS buses are cheapest and fastest for short trips. There are *pośpieszny* (direct; in red) and *osobowy* (slow; in black). In the countryside, PKS markers (yellow steering wheels that look like upside-down Mercedes-Benz symbols) indicate stops. Buses have no luggage compartments. **Polski Express,** a private company, offers more luxuries, but does not run to all cities.

BY CAR. For **taxis,** either arrange the price before getting in (in Polish, if possible) or be sure the driver turns on the meter. The going rate is 1.50-3zł per kilometer. Try to arrange cabs by phone. **Rental cars** are available in Warsaw and Kraków. Though legal, **hitchhiking** is rare and can be dangerous for foreigners. Hand-waving is the accepted sign. *Let's Go* does not recommend hitchhiking.

POLAND

KEEPING IN TOUCH

PHONE CODES	**Country code:** 48. **International dialing prefix:** 00. For more information on how to place international calls, see inside back cover.

EMAIL AND THE INTERNET. Poland is wired. Some **Telekomunikacja Polska** offices offer Internet. Most mid-sized towns have at least one Internet cafe and larger cities have several. Cost ranges from 2-5zł per hour.

TELEPHONE. Pay phones take phone cards, sold at post offices, Telekomunikacja Polska offices, and kiosks. Before using a card, break off its perforated corner. To make a **collect call,** hand the clerk the name of the city or country and the number plus "*Rozmowa 'R'.*" International access codes include: **AT&T Direct** (☎800 111 11 11); **Australia Direct** (☎800 611 11 61); **BT Direct** (☎800 89 0036); **Canada Direct** (☎800 111 41 18); **MCI WorldPhone** (☎800 111 21 22); **Sprint** (☎800 111 31 15).

MAIL. Mail is efficient. Airmail *(lotnicza)* takes two to five days to Western Europe and seven to 10 days to Australia, New Zealand, and the US. Mail can be received via **Poste Restante.** Address the envelope thus: First Name LAST NAME, POSTE RESTANTE, post office address, postal code City, POLAND. Letters cost about 2.20zł. Bring your passport to pick up *Poste Restante* or pay a 1.10zł fee.

LANGUAGE. Polish is a West Slavic language written in the Latin alphabet, and closely related to **Czech** and **Slovak.** The language varies little across the country (see **Phrasebook: Polish,** p. 1064). The two exceptions are in the **Kaszuby** region, whose Germanized dialect is sometimes classified as another language, and in **Karpaty,** where the highlander accent is thick. In western Poland, **German** is the most common foreign language, though many Poles in big cities speak **English.** Most can understand other Slavic languages if they're spoken slowly. The older generation may speak **Russian.** One more thing: the English word "no" means "yes" in Polish.

ACCOMMODATIONS AND CAMPING

POLAND	❶	❷	❸	❹	❺
ACCOMMODATIONS	under 45zł	45-65zł	65-80zł	80-120zł	over 120zł

Hostels *(schroniska młodzieżowe)* abound and cost 15-40zł. They are often booked solid by tour groups; call ahead. **PTSM** is the national hostel organization. **Dom Wycieczkowy** and **Dom Turystyczny** hostels, both geared toward adults, cost around 50zł. **University dorms** open to travelers in July and August, and are an especially good option in Kraków. The **Almatur** office in Warsaw arranges stays throughout Poland. PTTK runs several **hotels** called *Dom Turysty,* which have multi-bed rooms and budget singles and doubles. Hotels generally cost 80-180zł. **Pensions** are often the best deal; the owner's service more than makes up for the small sacrifice in privacy. **Private rooms** *(wolne pokoje)* are common, but be sure to establish the terms beforehand. Find rooms at the tourist office. Private rooms should cost 20-60zł. **Campsites** average 10-15zł per person, 20zł with a car. They may rent **bungalows;** a bed costs 20-30zł. *Polska Mapa Campingów,* available at tourist offices, lists campsites. Almatur runs a number of sites in summer; ask them for a list. Only camp in designated campsites or risk a night in jail.

FOOD AND DRINK

POLAND	❶	❷	❸	❹	❺
FOOD	under 8zł	8-18zł	18-30zł	30-45zł	over 45zł

Polish cuisine blends French, Italian, and Slavic traditions. Meals begin with **soup,** usually *barszcz* (beet or rye), *chłodnik* (cold beets with buttermilk and eggs), *ogórkowa* (sour cucumbers), *kapuśniak* (cabbage), or *rosól* (chicken). **Main courses** include *gołąbki* (cabbage rolls with meat and rice), *kotlet schabowy* (pork cutlet), *naleśniki* (crepes filled with cheese or jam), and *pierogi* (dumplings). Finding **vegetarian** food is feasible if one sticks to dumplings and crepes, but **kosher** eating is very difficult; you will eat lots of pizza. Poland bathes in **beer, vodka,** and **spiced liquor.** *Żywiec* is the most popular beer. Even those who dislike beer will enjoy sweet **piwo z sokiem,** beer with raspberry syrup. *Wyborowa, Żytnia,* and *Polonez* are popular vodka *(wódka)* brands while *Belweder* (Belvedere) is Poland's main alcoholic export. *Żubrówka* vodka comes with a blade of grass from Woliński, where bison roam. It's often mixed with apple juice *(z sokem jabłkowym). Miód* and *krupnik* (mead) are beloved by the gentry; grandmas make *nalewka na porzeczce* (black currant vodka).

HOLIDAYS AND FESTIVALS

Holidays: New Year's Day (Jan. 1); Easter Holiday (Apr. 16); May Day (May 1); Constitution Day (May 3); Corpus Christi (June 15); Assumption Day (Aug. 15); All Saints' Day (Nov. 1); Independence Day (Nov. 11); Christmas (Dec. 25-26).

Festivals: Festivals are tied to Catholic holidays, though folk tradition adds variety. Businesses close on holidays like **Corpus Christi** (June 15) and **Assumption Day** (Aug. 15), which are not as widely observed elsewhere.

BEYOND TOURISM

Auschwitz Jewish Center, 36 West 44th St., Ste. 310, New York, NY 10036 USA (☎212-575-1050; www.acjf.org). Offers fully paid 2-week or 8-week programs for college students and recent graduates, focusing on cultural exchange and pre-war Jewish life in Poland, with visits to the Auschwitz-Birkenau State Museum and other sites.

Jagiellonian University, Center for European Studies, ul. Garbarska 7a, 31-131 Kraków, Poland (☎48 12 431 1575; www.ces.uj.edu.pl). University founded in 1364 offers undergraduates summer and semester programs in Central European studies and Polish language. Semester tuition €3500. Scholarships available.

WorldTeach, 79 JFK St., Cambridge, MA 02138 USA (☎800 483 2240; www.worldteach.org). Arranges work teaching English in high schools and homestays with families in Poland. US$3990.

WARSAW (WARSZAWA) ☎022

After rebuilding itself from the rubble after WWII, and weathering the further blow of a half-century of communist rule, Warsaw has now sprung to life as a dynamic center of business, politics, and culture. With Poland's recent entrance into the European Union, things are moving even faster in the busy, youthful capital. A proud survivor and an unabashed striver, underrated Warsaw is a city on the rise.

TRANSPORTATION

Flights: Port Lotniczy Warszawa-Okęcie (Terminal 1), ul. Żwirki i Wigury (☎650 41 00). Take bus #175 (bus #611 after 10:40pm) for a 20min. ride to the city center. Buy tickets at the *Ruch* kiosk in the departure hall. Open M-F 5:30am-10:30pm.

Trains: Warszawa Centralna, al. Jerozolimskie 54 (☎94 36), is the most convenient of Warsaw's 3 major train stations. The **IT office** provides schedules and translations. Yellow signs list departures *(odjazdy)*, white signs arrivals *(przyjazdy)*. English is rare; write down when and where you want to go, then ask "*Który peron?*" (Which platform?). To: **Berlin, Germany** (6hr., 4 per day, 160zł); **Budapest, Hungary** (10-13hr., 2 per day, 280zł); **Gdańsk** (4hr., 12 per day, 50-117zł); **Kraków** (2½-5hr., 15 per day, 80-105zł); **Łódź** (1½-2hr., 17 per day, 25-45zł); **Lublin** (2½hr., 17 per day, 25-92zł); **Poznań** (2½-3hr., 20 per day, 80-115zł); **Prague, Czech Republic** (9-12hr., 3 per day, 270-310zł); **St. Petersburg, Russia** (25-30hr., 1 per day, 300zł); **Toruń** (2½-5hr., 5 per day, 40-105zł); **Wrocław** (4½-6hr., 11 per day, 55-125zł).

Buses: Both PKS and Polski Express buses serve Warsaw.

Polski Express, al. Jana Pawła II (☎844 55 55), in a kiosk next to Warszawa Centralna. To: **Gdańsk** (6hr., 2 per day, 65zł); **Kraków** (8hr., 2 per day, 62zł); **Łódź** (2½hr., 7 per day, 30zł); **Lublin** (3hr., 8 per day, 31zł); **Toruń** (4hr., 15 per day, 45zł). Kiosk open daily 6:30am-10pm.

PKS Warszawa Zachodnia, al. Jerozolimskie 144 (☎822 48 11, info 94 33, int'l info 823 55 70; www.pks.warszawa.pl), Zachodnia station. Take bus #127, 130, 508, 517, or E5 to the center. To: **Gdańsk** (7hr., 14 per day, 50zł); **Kraków** (6hr., 4 per day, 38zł); **Kyiv, Ukraine** (14½hr., 1 per day, 155zł); **Lublin** (3hr., 20 per day, 25zł); **Toruń** (4½hr., 11 per day, 35zł); **Vilnius, Lithuania** (9½hr., 3 per day, 115zł); **Wrocław** (9½hr., 3 per day, 43zł). Open daily 6am-9:30pm.

Centrum Podróży AURA, al. Jerozolimskie 144 (☎ 823 68 58; www.aura.pl), Zachodnia station. More international routes than PKS. To: **Amsterdam, Netherlands** (23hr., 2 per day, 300-320zł); **Minsk, Belarus,** this service can be irregular (12hr., 2 per week, 55zł); **Geneva, Switzerland** (27hr., 2 per day, 370-400zł); **London, England** (27hr., 3 per day, 280-450zł); **Paris, France** (25hr., 1-3 per day, 300-470zł); **Prague, Czech Republic** (11½hr.; 3 per week, M, W, F; 115zł); **Rome, Italy** (28hr., 1 per day, 350-400zł). Open M-F 9am-6pm, Sa 9am-2pm.

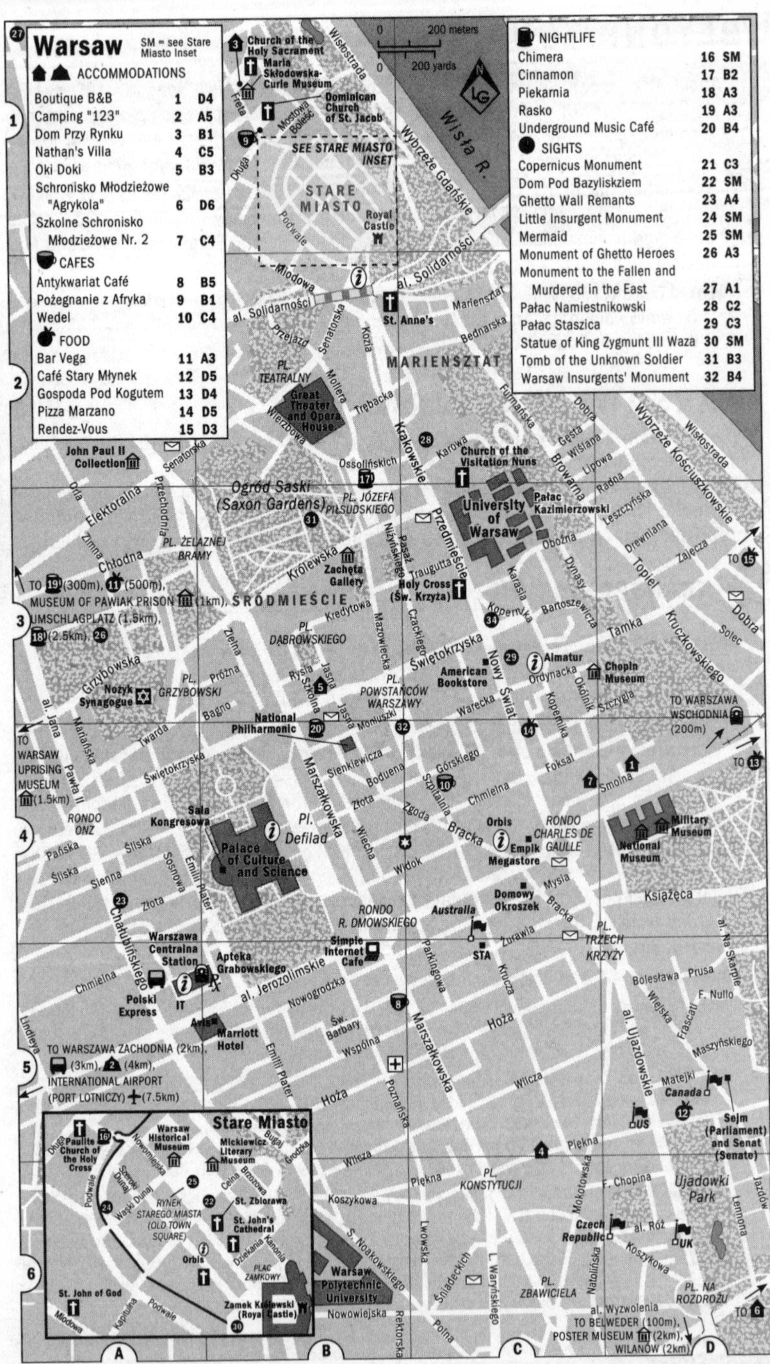
Warsaw
SM = see Stare Miasto Inset
ACCOMMODATIONS
Boutique B&B 1 D4
Camping "123" 2 A5
Dom Przy Rynku 3 B1
Nathan's Villa 4 C5
Oki Doki 5 B3
Schronisko Młodzieżowe "Agrykola" 6 D6
Szkolne Schronisko Młodzieżowe Nr. 2 7 C4
CAFES
Antykwariat Café 8 B5
Pożegnanie z Afryka 9 B1
Wedel 10 C4
FOOD
Bar Vega 11 A3
Café Stary Młynek 12 D5
Gospoda Pod Kogutem 13 D4
Pizza Marzano 14 D5
Rendez-Vous 15 D3
NIGHTLIFE
Chimera 16 SM
Cinnamon 17 B2
Piekarnia 18 A3
Rasko 19 A3
Underground Music Café 20 B4
SIGHTS
Copernicus Monument 21 C3
Dom Pod Bazyliskziem 22 SM
Ghetto Wall Remants 23 A4
Little Insurgent Monument 24 SM
Mermaid 25 SM
Monument of Ghetto Heroes 26 A3
Monument to the Fallen and Murdered in the East 27 A1
Pałac Namiestnikowski 28 C2
Pałac Staszica 29 C3
Statue of King Zygmunt III Waza 30 SM
Tomb of the Unknown Soldier 31 B3
Warsaw Insurgents' Monument 32 B4
200 meters
200 yards
Wisła R.
Church of the Holy Sacrament
Maria Skłodowska-Curie Museum
Dominican Church of St. Jacob
SEE STARE MIASTO INSET
STARE MIASTO
Royal Castle
St. Anne's
MARIENSZTAT
PL. TEATRALNY
Great Theater and Opera House
John Paul II Collection
Church of the Visitation Nuns
Ogród Saski (Saxon Gardens)
PL. JÓZEFA PIŁSUDSKIEGO
University of Warsaw
Pałac Kazimierzowski
PL. ŻELAZNEJ BRAMY
Zachęta Gallery
Holy Cross (Św. Krzyża)
ŚRÓDMIEŚCIE
TO (300m), (500m), MUSEUM OF PAWIAK PRISON (1km), UMSCHLAGPLATZ (1.5km), (2.5km),
PL. DĄBROWSKIEGO
Almatur
Chopin Museum
American Bookstore
PL. GRZYBOWSKI
Nożyk Synagogue
PL. POWSTAŃCÓW WARSZAWY
National Philharmonic
TO WARSZAWA WSCHODNIA (200m)
TO WARSAW UPRISING MUSEUM (1.5km)
RONDO ONZ
Sala Kongresowa
Pl. Defilad
Palace of Culture and Science
Orbis
Empik Megastore
RONDO CHARLES DE GAULLE
Military Museum
National Museum
Domowy Okroszek
RONDO R. DMOWSKIEGO
Australia
STA
PL. TRZECH KRZYŻY
Warszawa Centralna Station
Apteka Grabowskiego
Simple Internet Cafe
Polski Express
IT
Avis
Marriott Hotel
TO WARSZAWA ZACHODNIA (2km), (3km), (4km), INTERNATIONAL AIRPORT (PORT LOTNICZY) (7.5km)
Canada
Sejm (Parliament) and Senat (Senate)
US
PL. KONSTYTUCJI
Ujadowski Park
Czech Republic
UK
Warsaw Polytechnic University
PL. ZBAWICIELA
PL. NA ROZDROŻU
TO BELWEDER (100m), POSTER MUSEUM (2km), WILANÓW (2km)
Stare Miasto
Paulite Church of the Holy Cross
Warsaw Historical Museum
Mickiewicz Literary Museum
RYNEK STAREGO MIASTA (OLD TOWN SQUARE)
St. Zbiorawa
St. John's Cathedral
Orbis
PLAC ZAMKOWY
St. John of God
Zamek Królewski (Royal Castle)
A
B
C
D
1
2
3
4
5
6

Public Transportation: (☎0300 300 130 from a land line, 720 8383 from a mobile phone; www.ztm.waw.pl.) **Trams, buses,** and the **metro** run 4:30am-midnight. 2.40zł, with ISIC 1.25zł; **day pass** 7.20/3.70zł; **weekly pass** 26/12zł. Punch the ticket in the machines on-board or face a 120zł fine. Bus #175 runs from the airport to Stare Miasto via Warszawa Centralna and ul. Nowy Świat. Warsaw's 1 metro line runs north-south through the center. There are 2 **sightseeing bus routes:** #180 (M-F) and 100 (Sa-Su).

Taxis: Try **MPT Radio Taxi** (☎91 91), **Euro Taxi** (☎96 62), or **Halo Taxi** (☎96 23). Beware of overcharging. State-run cabs with a mermaid logo tend to be safer. 5-6zł base fare, 1.80-3zł per km.

ORIENTATION

Warsaw lies mainly west of the **Wisła River.** Although the city is large, its grid layout and efficient public transportation system make it easy to navigate. The main east-west thoroughfare is **aleja Jerozolimskie,** which intersects **ulica Marszałkowska,** a major tram route. **Warszawa Centralna** train station sits at the intersection of al. Jerozolimskie and **aleja Jana Pawła II.** To the east lies **Rondo Charles de Gaulle.** Intersecting al. Jerozolimskie at a roundabout east of the city center, the **Trakt Królewski** (Royal Way) takes different names as it runs north-south. Running north it becomes **Nowy Świat** (New World Street) and then **ulica Krakówskie Przedmieście** as it leads into **Stare Miasto** (Old Town). Running south, it becomes **aleja Ujazdowskie** as it runs past Embassy Row, more palaces, and **Łazienki Park. Praga,** the part of the city on the east bank of the Wisła, is accessible by tram via **aleja Jerozolimskie** and **aleja Solidarności,** and the two most trafficked north-south thoroughfares are **ulica Targowa,** near the zoo, and **ulica Francuska,** south of al. Jerozolimskie.

POLAND

PRACTICAL INFORMATION

Tourist Offices: Informacji Turystyczna (IT), al. Jerozolimskie 54 (☎94 31; www.warsawtour.pl), inside the central train station. Informative, English-speaking staff. Provides maps (free-4zł) and arranges accommodations (no charge). The free *Warsaw In Short* lists restaurants and events. Open daily May-Sept. 8am-8pm; Oct.-Apr. 8am-6pm. **Branches:** al. Jerozolimskie 144, open daily 9am-5pm. At the PKS bus station. Open daily 9am-5pm. In the airport, open daily May-Sept. 8am-8pm; Oct.-Apr. 8am-6pm.

Budget Travel: Almatur, ul. Kopernika 23 (☎826 35 12). Discounted plane and bus tickets. ISIC 44zł. Open M-F 9am-7pm, Sa 10am-5pm. AmEx/MC/V. **Orbis,** ul. Bracka 16 (☎827 38 57), entrance on al. Jerozolimskie. Plane, train, ferry, and international bus tickets. Open M-F 8am-6pm, Sa 9am-3pm. Branch at ul. Świętokrzyska 23/25 (☎831 82 99; orbis.bis@pbp.com.pl). Open M-F 9am-6pm, Sa 10am-3pm. MC/V.

Embassies: Australia, ul. Nowogrodzka 11 (☎521 34 44; ambasada@australia.pl). M-F 9am-1pm and 2-5pm. **Canada,** al. Matejki 1/5 (☎584 31 00; wsaw@international.gc.ca). Open M-F 8:30am-4:30pm. **Ireland,** ul. Mysia 5 (☎849 66 33; ambasada@irlandial.pl). Open M-F 9am-1pm and 2-5pm. **UK,** al. Róż (☎311 00 00). Open M-F 8:30am-12:30pm and 1:30-4:30pm. **US,** al. Ujazdowskie 29/31 (☎504 20 00; www.poland.usembassy.gov). Open M-F 8:30am-5pm.

Currency Exchange: Except at tourist sights, *kantory* have the best rates, though rates may rise at night. 24hr. currency exchange at Warszawa Centralna and al. Jerozolimskie 61. **Bank PKO SA,** pl. Bankowy 2 (☎521 84 40), in the blue-glass skyscraper, or ul. Grójecka 1/3 (☎59 88 28), in Hotel Sobieski, cashes AmEx/V traveler's checks for 1-2% commission and gives MC/V cash advances. Open M-F 8am-6pm, Sa 10am-2pm. **Bank Zachodni,** al. Jerozolimskie 91 (☎635 47 00). Open M-F 8am-6pm.

American Express: al. Jerozolimskie 65/79 (☎630 69 52). Offers **Western Union** services. Open M-F 9am-7pm, Sa 10am-6pm.

Luggage Storage (Kasa Bagażowa): At Warszawa Centralna train station. 5zł per item per day, plus 2.25zł per 50zł of declared value for optional insurance. Lockers also available. Open 24hr.

English-Language Bookstores: American Bookstore (Księgarnia Amerykańska), ul. Nowy Świat 61 (☎827 48 52; american@americanbookstore.pl). Good but pricey selection of fiction, history, and maps. Open M-Sa 10am-7pm, Su 10am-6pm. AmEx/MC/V. **Empik Megastore,** ul. Nowy Świat 15-17 (☎627 06 50). Great selection of maps. Open M-Sa 9am-10pm, Su 11am-5pm.

GLBT Resources: Lambda (☎628 52 22; www.lambda.org.pl), in English and Polish. Open Tu-W 6-9pm, F 4-10pm. Also try http://warsaw.gayguide.net. The GLBT scene in Warsaw is generally discrete, and lacks widespread political support.

24hr. Pharmacy: Apteka Grabowskiego "21" (☎825 69 86), upstairs at Warszawa Centralna train station. AmEx/MC/V.

Hospitals: Centrum Medyczyne LIM, al. Jerozolimskie 65/79, 9th fl. (24hr. **emergency line** ☎458 70 00, 24hr. **ambulance** 430 30 30; www.cm-lim.com.pl), in the Marriott. English-speaking doctors. 85zł. Open M-F 7am-9pm, Sa 8am-8pm, Su 9am-1pm. **Branch** at ul. Domaniewski 41 (☎458 70 00). Open M-F 7am-9pm, Sa 8am-8pm. **Central Emergency Station,** ul. Hoża 56 (☎999) has a 24hr. ambulance.

Telephones: Phones are at the post office, train station, and scattered throughout the city. All but a few only accept cards, available at the post office and many kiosks. Ask for a *karta telefoniczna*. Directory assistance ☎118 913.

Internet Access: **Simple Internet Cafe,** ul. Marszałkowska 99/101 (☎628 31 90), at the corner of al. Jerozolimskie and ul. Marszałkowska, has the best hourly rates and English-speaking staff. The largest and orangest Internet cafe in Warsaw. Open daily 24hr., rates vary from 1zł per hr. late at night to 4zł per hr. midday. Several 24hr. Internet cafes line the bowels of the Centralna train station.

Post Office: Main branch, ul. Świętokrzyska 31/33 (☎827 00 52). Take a number at the entrance. For stamps and letters push "D"; packages "F." For Poste Restante, inquire at window #42. Open 24hr. *Kantor* open daily 7am-10pm. Most other branches open 8am-8pm. **Postal Code:** 00 001.

ACCOMMODATIONS AND CAMPING

Although accommodations options are rapidly improving, demand still outpaces supply so, reserve ahead, especially in the summer. The **Informacji Turystyczna (IT)** (p. 795) maintains a list of accommodations in the city, including private rooms, and from July to September also arranges stays for 25-30zł in **university dorms.**

Oki Doki, pl. Dąbrowskiego 3 (☎826 51 12; www.okidoki.pl). From the city center, take any tram north on Marszałkowska to Świętokrzyska. Walk 1 block north and turn right on Rysia. In the heart of town but facing a quiet park, this hostel is also an awesome art gallery. Enthusiastic English-speaking staff. Bike rental 26zł per day, 6zł per hr. Laundry 10zł. Internet free. Reception 24hr. Check-in 3pm. Check-out 11am. Dorms 45-60zł; singles 110zł; doubles 135zł, with bath 185zł. Prices lower Sept.-Apr. MC/V. ❷

Boutique Bed and Breakfast, ul. Smolna 14/7 (☎0605 199 289). Take any tram east on al. Jerozolimskie to Rondo Charles de Gaulle; half a block north on ul. Nowe Świat, turn right on ul. Smolna and walk three blocks. Enter through the unmarked wooden double-doors; it is the first door on your right. Large, sophisticated rooms have independent entry from the stairwell. Classy atmosphere, low price, and central location make this B&B impossible to turn down. Singles 45zł; doubles 60zł; suites 75zł. Cash only. ❷

Nathan's, ul. Piękna 24/26 (☎0509 358 487; www.nathansvilla.com). From Płac Konstytucji, south of city center, go left on ul. Piękna. Near downtown, Nathan's has clean, brightly colored dorms, restrooms that could pass for Ikea showcases, and a tireless party atmosphere. English-speaking staff eagerly dispense advice. Breakfast included. Internet 30min. per day. Reception 24hr. Flexible check-out. Dorms 45-60zł; private rooms 120-140zł. Book ahead. Cots rented to the truly desperate when beds fill up. MC/V. ❷

Dom Przy Rynku, Rynek Nowego Miasta 4 (☎/fax 831 50 33; www.cityhostel.net). Take bus #175 from the center to Franciszkańska; turn right, then right again into the Rynek; the hostel is downhill on your left. In summer, this school for disadvantaged children is one of Warsaw's most spotless budget accommodations. Reception 24hr. Open July-Aug. daily; Sept.-June F-Su. Dorms 40zł. Cash only. ❶

Schronisko Młodzieżowe "Agrykola," ul. Myśliwiecka 9 (☎622 91 10; www.hotelagrykola.pl). Near Łazienki Park. Take bus #151 from the train station, or bus #107, 420, or 520 from Marszałkowska to Rozbrat. From the bus stop, walk downstairs to the corner of ul. Myśliwiecka and al. Armii Ludowej; enter from al. Armii Ludowej. Serene, parkside Agrykola includes a hostel and mid-range hotel. English-speaking staff and an escape from the ubiquitous bunk bed. Bath, TV, and included breakfast in the hotel, but not hostel. Hostel beds 47zł; hotel singles 270zł; hotel doubles 320zł. Cash only. ❷

Szkolne Schronisko Mlodziezowe Nr 2, ul. Smolna 30 (☎827 89 52). 2 blocks up ul. Smolna from Nowy Świat. From the center, take any tram east on al. Jerozolimskie and get off at Rondo Charles de Gaulle. At the base of one of the most popular streets in Warsaw, this quiet, air-conditioned hostel has clean dorms and small, well-kept rooms. The lockout is not party-friendly, but the atmosphere is safe and friendly. Reception 24hr. Lockout 10am-4pm and midnight-6am. Dorms 36zł; singles 65zł. Cash only. ❶

Camping 123, ul. Bitwy Warszawskiej 15/17 (☎/fax 822 91 21). By Warszawa Zachodnia bus station. Take bus #508, 127, 130, or 517 to Zachodnia, cross al. Jerozolimskie, walk right to the roundabout and turn left on Bitwy Warszawskiej. Few amenities. Also offers spartan rooms. Singles 40zł; doubles 70zł; triples 100zł; quads 120zł. Tent sites 10zł, plus 10zł per person and per vehicle. Open May-Sept. Cash only. ❶

POLAND

FOOD

At countless roadside stands across the city the food of choice is the **kebab turecki,** a pita stuffed with spicy meat, cabbage, and pickles (5-10zł). **Kebab Bar,** ul. Nowy Świat 31, serves up an excellent version. **Domowy Okruszek,** ul. Bracka 3, just south of al. Jerozolimskie, sells baked goods and ready-to-cook dishes like *naleśniki* (pancakes) and *pierogi* (dumplings) for 15-20zł per kg. (☎628 70 77. Open M-Sa 10am-6pm, Su 10am-3pm.) Grocery stores open 24hr. include **MarcPol** by the central train station and **Albert** on ul. Marszałkowska in the Galleria Centrum.

RESTAURANTS

Gospoda Pod Kogutem, ul. Freta 48 (☎822 05 00). A rare treat in touristy Stare Miasto: delectable and authentic local food without the kitsch. Beer 6zł. Entrees 15-40zł. Open daily 11am-midnight. MC/V. ❷

Rendez-Vous, ul. Francuska 24 (☎616 13 23), 3 blocks south of Praga's Russian Market, is evidence of Praga's increasing vogue. Sophisticated atmosphere complements excellent contemporary cuisine. Try the sautéed vegetables with roasted feta cheese entree (14.50zł). Desserts 8-16zł. English-language menu. Open daily 9am-9pm. ❸

Bar Vega, ul. Jana Pawła II 36c (☎652 27 54). Tasty, vegetarian Indian dishes such as *pakora* (deep-fried vegetables) and *kofta* (cabbage patty). Proceeds go to feed the hungry children of Warsaw. Open daily noon-8pm. Small/large plate 8/11zł. Cash only. ❶

Cafe Stary Młynek, al. Ujazdowskie 6 (☎622 92 64). Smaller dishes offer a sampling of modern Polish food in the bare but comfy cellar of a renovated mill. Dishes 10-25zł. Open M-F 10am-10pm, Sa noon-11pm, Su noon-9pm. AmEx/MC/V. ❸

Bar Universitat, ul. Krakówskie Przedmiescie 20/22 (☎826 07 93) resembles milk bars as they truly were. The simple, camp-like interior and long lines set the tone for extremely traditional dishes for as little as 5zł. Near the university, it's a favorite among the students. Cash only. ❶

Pizza Marzano, ul. Nowy Świat 42 (☎826 21 33). This trustworthy chain cooks up richly flavored pizzas (15-25zł), with Polish spiced meats adding a local touch. Serves beer and wine. Open M-Th and Su 11am-11pm, F-Sa 11am-midnight. AmEx/MC/V. ❷

CAFES

Pożegnanie z Afryka, ul. Freta 4/6 (☎602 356 287), ul. Ostrobranmska 75c, and ul. Dobra 56/66. Incredible coffee and iced coffee (8-15zł). Adventurous decor and wide selection of exotic blends. Open M-Th 10am-9pm, F-Su 10am-10pm.

Antykwariat Cafe, ul. Źurawia 45 (☎629 99 29), 2 blocks south of Rondo Charles de Gaulle. Staff invites the weary to lounge in plush chairs amid the book-lined walls of this old-fashioned cafe. Coffees 5-17zł. Open M-F 11am-11pm, Sa-Su 1-11pm. Cash only.

Wedel, ul. Szpitalnia 17 (☎827 29 16). A rare glimpse of pre-war Warsaw and unbelievable hot chocolate (8zł). Enjoy stained glass, rich mahogany, doilies, and the suspicion that you've traveled back in time. Open M-Sa 10am-10pm, Su noon-5pm. AmEx/MC/V.

SIGHTS

At first glance, Warsaw offers two strains of architecture: impeccably restored historical facades and Soviet-era concrete blocks. However, from cutting-edge art installations in a rebuilt castle to the sobering stillness of the Jewish Cemetery, the city holds out its most compelling sights to those who get to know it better. The tourist bus routes #100 and 180 are convenient; they begin at pl. Zamkowy and run along pl. Teatralny, ul. Marszałkowska, al. Ujazdowskie, Łazienki Park, and back up the Royal Way, then loop through Praga before returning to pl. Zamkowy.

STARE MIASTO. Warsaw's postwar reconstruction shows its finest face in the narrow cobblestone streets and colorful facades of Stare Miasto. *(Take bus #175 or E3 from the city center to Miodowa.)* The landmark **Statue of King Zygmunt III Waza,** constructed in 1644 to honor the king who moved the capital from Kraków to Warsaw, towers over the entrance to Stare Miasto. To the right stands the impressive **Royal Castle** (Zamek Królewski), the royal residence since the late 16th century. When it was plundered and burned by the Nazis in September 1939, many Varsovians risked their lives hiding priceless works in the hope they might one day be returned. Today, the palace houses the **Royal Castle Museum,** which has paintings, artifacts, and the stunning Royal Apartments. *(Pl. Zamkowy 4. ☎657 21 70; www.zamek-krolewski.art.pl. Tickets and guides at the kasa inside the courtyard. Open M and Su 11am-6pm, Tu-Sa 10am-6pm. 18zł, students 12zł. Highlights tour Su 11am-6pm. English-language tour M-Sa. Highlights tour free. English-language tour 70zł per group. MC/V.)* Across ul. Świętojańska sits Warsaw's oldest church, **St. John's Cathedral** (Katedra św. Jana), decimated in the 1944 uprising but rebuilt after the war. *(Open daily 10am-1pm and 3-5:30pm. Entrance to crypts 1zł.)* Ul. Świętojańska leads to the restored Renaissance and Baroque **Rynek Starego Miasta** (Old Town Square); the statue of the **Warsaw Mermaid** (Warszawa Syrenka) still marks the center. According to legend, a greedy merchant kidnapped the mermaid from the Wisła River, but local fishermen rescued her. In return, she swore to defend the city, and now protects it with a shield and raised sword. Ul. Krzywe Koło runs from the northeast corner of the *Rynek* to the restored **Barbican** *(barbakan)*, a rare example of 16th-century Polish fortification and popular spot to relax. The *barbakan* opens onto ul. Freta, the edge of **Nowe Miasto** (new town). Nobel Prize-winning physicist and chemist **Marie Curie** was born at ul. Freta 16.

TRAKT KRÓLEWSKI. The Trakt Królewski (Royal Way) begins at the entrance to the Stare Miasto on pl. Zamkowy and stretches 4km south toward Kraków, the former capital. On the left as you leave pl. Zamkowy, the 15th-century **St. Anne's Church** (Kościół św. Anny), features a striking gilded altar. *(Open daily dawn-dusk.)* Frederick Chopin grew up near ul. Krakówskie Przedmieście, and gave his first public concert in **Pałac Radziwiłłów,** ul. Krakówskie Przedmieście 46/48. Guarded by four stone lions; the building is now known as **Pałac Namiestnikowski,** the Polish presidential mansion. A block down the road and set back from the street behind a grove of trees, the **Church of the Visitation Nuns** (Kościół Wizytówek) once resounded with the mop-topped composer's romantic ivory pounding. *(Open daily dawn-1pm and 3pm-dusk.)* Chopin died abroad at the age of 39 and was buried in Paris, but his heart belongs to Poland; it now rests in an urn in **Holy Cross Church.** *(Kościół św. Krzyża. Ul. Krakówskie Przedmiescie 3. Open daily dawn-dusk.)* For more Chopin relics, visit the **Frederick Chopin Museum** (Muzeum Fryderyka Chopina), which has a collection of original letters, scores, paintings, and keepsakes, including the composer's last piano and a section of his first *polonaise*, penned when he was seven years old. *(Ul. Okólnik 1, in Ostrogski Castle. Enter from ul. Tamka. ☎826 59 35; www.chopin.pl. Open May-Sept. M, W, F 10am-5pm, Th noon-6pm, Sa-Su 10am-2pm; Oct.-Apr. M-W and F-Sa 10am-2pm, Th noon-6pm. 8zł, students 4zł. Audio tours 4zł. Concerts 30zł, students 15zł. Cash only.)*

The Royal Way continues down fashionable **ul. Nowy Świat.** Turn left just after Rondo Charles de Gaulle to reach Poland's largest museum, the **National Museum** (Muzeum Narodowe), which holds 16th- to 20th-century Polish paintings and ancient statuary. *(Al. Jerozolimskie 3. ☎629 30 93, English-language tours 629 50 60; www.mnw.art.pl. Open Tu-W and F 10am-5pm; Th and Sa-Su 10am-6pm. Permanent exhibits 12zł, students 7zł. Special exhibits 17zł, students 10zł. AmEx/MC/V.)* Farther down, the Royal Way turns into al. Ujazdowskie and runs alongside **Łazienki Park.** In the park is the striking Neoclassical **Palace on Water** (Pałac na Wodzie or Pałac na Wyspie), while outbuildings house rotating art exhibits. *(Take bus #116, 180, or 195 from ul. Nowy Świat or #119 from the city center to Bagatela. Park open daily dawn-dusk. Palace open Tu-Su 8:30am-3:30pm. 12zł, students 9zł.)* Just north of the park, off ul. Agrykola, the **Center of Contemporary Art** (Centrum Sztuki Współczesnej), al. Ujazdowskie 6, hosts installations of contemporary Polish art in the reconstructed 17th-century Ujazdowskie Castle. *(Open Tu-Th and Sa-Su 11am-5pm, F 11am-9pm. 12zł, students 6zł. Cash only.)*

THE FORMER WARSAW GHETTO AND SYNAGOGUE. Muranów, the former ghetto, is the walled neighborhood north of the city center. It holds few traces of the nearly 400,000 Jews who made up one-third of the city's population prior to WWII. The **Umschlagplatz,** at the corner of ul. Dzika and ul. Stawki, was the railway platform where the Nazis gathered 300,000 Jews for transport to death camps. *(Take tram #35 from ul. Marszałkowska to Dzika.)* With the Umschlag pl. monument to your left, continue down Stawki and turn right on ul. DuBois, which becomes ul. Zamenhofa; along the road, a stone monument marks the location of the command bunker of the 1943 Ghetto Uprising. Farther on, in the large park to the right, the **Monument of the Ghetto Heroes** (Pomnik Bohaterów) honors the uprising's leaders. Continue along ul. Zamenhofa for two blocks and take a right on ul. Dzielna. On the corner of ul. Dzielna and al. Jana Pawła II, the **Museum of Pawiak Prison** (Muzeum Więzienia Pawiaka) exhibits the artwork and poetry of many former prisoners. Over 100,000 Polish Jews were imprisoned here from 1939 to 1944; 37,000 were executed and 60,000 were moved to concentration camps. *(Ul. Dzielna 24/26. ☎/fax 831 13 17. Open Su 10am-4pm, W 9am-5pm, Th and Sa 9am-4pm, F 10am-5pm. Donation requested.)* Follow al. Jana Pawła II, take a left on ul. Anielewicza, and continue for five blocks to reach the **Jewish Cemetery** (Cmentarz Żydowski), in the western corner of Muranów. The thickly wooded cemetery is the final resting place of 250,000 Polish Jews. *(Tram #22 from the center to Cm. Żydowski. ☎838 26 22; www.jewishcem.waw.pl. Open Apr.-Oct. M-Th 10am-5pm, F 9am-1pm, Su 11am-4pm; Nov.-Mar. cemetery closes at dusk. Closed Jewish holidays. 4zł.)* The beautifully reconstructed **Nożyk Synagogue** (Synagoga Nożyka) is a living remnant of Warsaw's Jewish heritage. Warsaw's only synagogue to survive the war, Nożyk now serves as the spiritual home for the few hundred observant Jews remaining in Warsaw. *(Ul. Twarda 6. From* *the center, take any tram along al. Jana Pawła II to Rondo Onz. Turn right on ul. Twarda and left at the Teatr Żydowski, the Jewish Theater. ☎620 10 37. Open Su-F Apr.-Oct. 10am-5pm, Nov.-Feb. 10am-3pm. Closed on Jewish holidays. Morning and evening prayer daily. 5zł.)*

ELSEWHERE IN WARSAW. Warsaw's commercial district, southwest of Stare Miasto, is dominated by the 70-story Stalinist **Palace of Culture and Science** (Pałac Kultury i Nauki) on ul. Marszałkowska. Locals claim the view from the top is the best in Warsaw—partly because you can't see the building itself. *(☎656 60 00. Open daily 9am-8pm. Observation deck on 33rd fl. 18zł, students 12zł. After 9pm 20zł.)* Adjacent to the **Saxon Garden** (Ogród Saski) is the **John Paul II Collection,** with works by Dalí, van Gogh, Goya, Rembrandt, Renoir, and others. *(Pl. Bankowy 1. ☎620 27 25. Open May-Oct. Tu-Su 10am-5pm; Nov.-Apr. 10am-4pm. 11zł, students 5.50zł. Polish tour 1zł.)*

Though a bit far from the center, the recently opened **Warsaw Uprising Museum** is one of Poland's finest. Educational without being pedantic and somber without being heavy-handed, the museum recounts the tragic 1944 Uprising with full-scale replica bunkers and ruins haunted by the sound of approaching bombs. Excellent English-language subtitles. *(Ul. Grzybowska 79, enter on ul. Przyokopowa. ☎539 79 01; www.1944.pl. Open W and F-Su 10am-6pm, Th 10am-8pm. 4zł, students 2zł. Su free. From the center, take tram #20, 22, or 12 to ul. Grzybowska; the museum will be on your left. Cash only.)*

PRAGA. Across the **Wisła River** from central Warsaw, the formerly run-down district of Praga is undergoing a renaissance, though you should still exercise caution, especially after dark. Located in the Stadion Dziesięciolecia, the **Russian Market** offers great deals on anything from sunglasses and baked goods to t-shirts with subversive Polish phrases. Keep a low profile and beware of pickpockets. *(Take any train from al. Jerozolimskie going east, and get off at the 1st stop over the river. The market is across the street on your left. Open daily dawn-dusk.)* The onion domes of the **St. Mary Magdalene Cathedral** hint at the pre-Soviet Russian presence in Warsaw. *(Al. Solidarnosci 52. From the Russian Market, take tram #2, 8, 12, or 25 to the intersection of Targowa and al. Solidarnosci: the church will be across the street on your left. ☎619 84 67. Su-M 1-4pm, Tu-Sa 11am-3pm. Donation requested.)* **Skaryszewski Park,** the most serene of Praga attractions, contains sculptures by early 20th-century Polish artists and a lovely network of willow-lined ponds and streams. *(East of al. Zieleniecka. Free.)*

WILANÓW. In 1677, King Jan III Sobieski bought the sleepy village of Milanowo, rebuilt the existing mansion into a Baroque palace, and named the new residence Villa Nova (Wilanów). Since 1805, **Pałac Wilanowski** has served as a public museum and a residence for the highest-ranking guests of the Polish state. Surrounded by elegant gardens, the palace is filled with frescoed rooms, portraits, and extravagant royal apartments. English-language captions allow you to leave the slow-moving Polish-language tour to explore on your own. *(Take bus #180 from ul. Krakówskie Przedmiesce, #516 or 519 from ul. Marszałkowska south to Wilanów, or #116 or 180 south along the Royal Way. From the bus stop, cross the highway and follow signs for the Pałac. ☎842 07 95. Open May 15-Sept. 15 M and W-Su 9:30am-4:30pm; Sept. 16-May 14 M and Th-Sa 9:30am-4pm, W 9:30am-6pm, Su 9:30am-7pm. Last entrance 1½hr. before closing. Call ahead for English-language tour. Gardens open M and W-F 9:30am-dusk. Orangery open M and W-F Su 9:30am-3:30pm. Wilanów 20zł, students 10zł. Th free. Gardens 4.5/2.5zł. Cash only.)*

ENTERTAINMENT AND NIGHTLIFE

Warsaw boasts an array of live music, and free outdoor concerts abound in summer. Classical music performances are rarely sold out; standby tickets cost as little as 10zł. Inquire at the **Warsaw Music Society** (Warszawskie Towarzystwo Muzyczne), ul. Morskie Oko 2 (☎849 56 51). Take tram #4, 18, 19, 35, or 36 to Morskie Oko from ul. Marszałkowska. Nearby Łazienki Park has free Sunday performances at the **Chopin Monument.** (Pomnik Chopina; concerts mid-May to Sept. Su noon, 4pm.) The first week of June brings the **International Festival of Sacred Music,** with performances at Warsaw's historic churches. **Jazz Klub Tygmont** (☎828 34 09), ul. Mazowiecka 6/8, hosts free concerts M-F at 9pm. From July through September, the Old Market Square of Stare Miasto swings with free jazz nightly at 7pm.

Teatr Dramatyczny, in the Pałac Kultury, has a stage for big productions and a studio theater playing more avant-garde works. (☎620 21 02; www.teatrdramatyczny.pl. Tickets 18-40zł; standby tickets 11-17zł.) **Teatr Żydowski,** pl. Grzybowski 12/16 (☎620 70 25), is a Jewish theater with primarily Yiddish-language shows. **Kinoteka** (☎826 1961), in the Pałac Kultury, shows Hollywood blockbusters in a Stalinist setting. **Kino Lab,** ul. Ujazdowskie 6 (☎628 12 71), features independent films. See **Center for Contemporary Art,** p. 798.

In the evenings, Warsaw is full of energy. *Kawiarnie* (cafes) around Stare Miasto and ul. Nowy Świat are open late into the night, and a variety of pubs attract crowds with live music. In summer, outdoor beer gardens complement the pub scene. Several publications, including *Gazeta Wyborcza,* list gay nightlife.

Chimera, ul. Podwale 29. An unusual bar with slightly sinister decor. Crowded with lively and relaxed university students. Beer 6zł. Open M-F 3pm-late, Sa-Su 2pm-late. MC/V.

Piekarnia, ul. Mlocinska 11 (☎636 49 79), has a packed dance floor and expert DJs. Cover F 20zł, Sa 25zł. Open F-Sa 10pm-late.

Underground Music Cafe, ul. Marszalkowska 126/134 (☎826 70 48). A 2-level dance club with a guaranteed party on weeknights. Beer 8.50zł. Cover W, F 10zł, students 5zł; Sa 20/10zł; Th 10zł; Su-Tu free. Open daily 10pm-late.

Rasko, ul. Krochmalna 32A (☎890 02 99; www.rasko.pl). A staple in Warsaw's underground GLBT scene, this secluded, bohemian club attracts a varied clientele. Friendly staff can direct you to other GLBT nightlife. Beer 7zł. Open daily 5pm-3am. Cash only.

Cinnamon, pl. Pilsudskiego 1 (☎323 76 00), is a bar with attitude, favored by the hottest locals and expats. Open daily 9am-late. MC/V.

KRAKÓW ☎012

Although Kraków (KRAHK-oof; pop 758,000) only recently emerged as an international hot spot, it has long been Poland's darling. The regal architecture, rich cafe culture, and palpable sense of history that now bewitch foreign visitors have drawn kings, artists, and scholars for centuries. Kraków, unlike most Polish cities, emerged from WWII and years of socialism miraculously unscathed. The maze-like Old Town and the old Jewish quarter of Kazimierz hide scores of museums, galleries, cellar pubs, and clubs, with 130,000 students adding to the spirited nightlife. Still, the city's gloss and glamor can't completely hide the scars of the 20th century: the Auschwitz-Birkenau Nazi death camps that lie just 70km outside the city are a sobering reminder of the atrocities committed in the not-so-distant past.

TRANSPORTATION

Flights: Balice Airport (☎411 19 55; www.lotnisko-balice.pl), 18km west of the center. Take northbound bus #192 (40min.) or 208 (1hr.) to the main train station. Taxis to downtown Kraków cost 50-60zł.

Trains: Kraków Główny, pl. Kolejowy 1 (☎624 54 39, info 624 15 35). Trains to: **Bratislava, Slovakia** (8hr., 1 per day, 188zł); **Budapest, Hungary** (11hr., 1 per day, 227zł); **Gdańsk** (7-10hr., 4 per day, 60-100zł); **Kyiv, Ukraine** (22hr., 21 per day, 230zł); **Poznań** (6-8hr., 4 per day, 49-81zł); **Prague, Czech Republic** (9hr., 2 per day, 196zł); **Vienna, Austria** (8½hr., 2 per day, 223zł); **Warsaw** (4½-5hr., 10 per day, 45-85zł); **Zakopane** (3-5hr., 4 per day, 19-56zł). *Let's Go* does not recommend night trains.

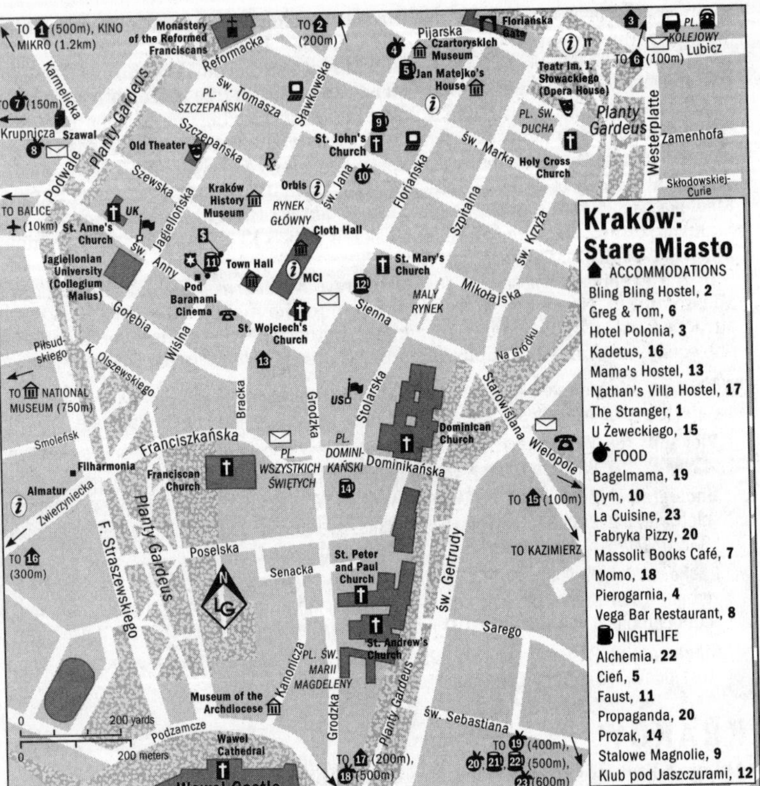

Buses: ul. Cysterów 15 (☎93 16), about a 12min. tram ride from the old town. The bus station is subject to move because of construction. Open 5am-11pm. Buses to: **Łódź** (6½hr., 5 per day, 40zł); **Warsaw** (6hr., 3 per day, 50zł); **Wrocław** (6½hr., 2 per day, 43zł); **Zakopane** (2hr., 33 per day, 11zł). **Sindbad** (☎421 02 40) in the main hall, sells international tickets. Open M-F 8am-5:30pm, Sa 9am-2pm. To: **Vienna, Austria** (9hr.; 7 per week; 100-125zł, under 26 10% discount).

Public Transportation: Buy **bus** and **tram** tickets at *Ruch* kiosks (2.50zł) or from drivers (3zł) and punch them onboard. Large backpacks need their own tickets. Night buses from 11pm 5zł. Day pass 10.40zł.

Taxis: Reliable taxi companies include: **Barbakan Taxi** (☎96 61 or 0800 400 400); **Euro Taxi** (☎96 64); **Radio Taxi** (☎919 or 0800 500 919); **Wawel Taxi** (☎96 66). It is up to 30% cheaper to call a taxi than to hail one.

ORIENTATION

The heart of the city is the huge **Rynek Główny** (Main Marketplace), in the center of **Stare Miasto** (Old Town). Stare Miasto is encircled by the **Planty** gardens and, a bit farther out, a broad ring road, which is confusingly divided into sections with different names: **Basztowa, Dunajewskiego, Podwale,** and **Westerplatte.** South of Rynek Główny looms the celebrated **Wawel Castle.** The **Wisła River** (VEE-swah) snakes past the castle and borders the old Jewish district of **Kazimierz.** The bus and train stations sit northeast of Stare Miasto. A large, well-marked (and well-kiosked) underpass cuts beneath the ring road and into the Planty gardens; from there a number of paths lead into the Rynek (10min.). Turn left from the train station or right from the bus station to reach the underpass.

PRACTICAL INFORMATION

Tourist Office: City Tourist Information, Szpitalna 25 (☎432 01 10; www.krakow.pl/en). Arranges accommodations and tours, and sells maps (7-12zł). English spoken. **MCI,** Rynek Główny 1/3 (☎421 77 06; www.mcit.pl), in the main square, sells maps, *Kraków in Your Pocket* (5zł, English 10zł), and the cultural guide *Karnet* (4zł). Open May-Sept. M-F 9am-7pm, Sa 9am-1pm; Oct.-Apr. M-F 9am-5pm, Sa 9am-1pm.

Budget Travel: Orbis, Rynek Główny 41 (☎422 40 35; www.orbis.krakow.pl). Sells train tickets and arranges trips to Wieliczka and Auschwitz (each 120zł, both 238zł), cashes traveler's checks, and exchanges currency. Open M-F 9am-7pm, Sa 9am-3pm.

Consulates: UK, św. Anny 9, 4th fl. (☎421 56 56). Open M-F 9am-4pm. **US,** Stolarska 9 (☎424 51 00; http://krakow.usconsulate.gov). Open M-F 8:30am-5pm.

Currency Exchange: ATMs, found all over the city, offer the best rates. *Kantory* (exchange kiosks) have widely varying rates. Avoid those around the train station and near Floriańska Gate. Check rates carefully around Rynek Główny. **Bank PKO SA,** Rynek Główny 31 (☎422 60 22). Cashes **traveler's checks** for 1-2% commission (min. 10zł) and gives MC/V **cash advances.** Open M-F 8am-6pm, Sa 9am-2pm.

Luggage Storage: At the train station. 1% of value per day plus 3.90zł for the 1st day and 2zł for each additional day. Lockers near the exit. Small 4zł. Large 8zł. Open 24hr.

English-Language Bookstore: Massolit, Felicjanek 4 (☎432 41 50). Impressive selection of over 25,000 popular, classic, and academic English-language books. Open M-Th, Su 10am-8pm, F-Sa 10am-10pm.

Laundromat: Piastowska 47 (☎622 31 81), in the basement of Hotel Piast. Take tram #4, 13, or 14 to WKS Wawel and turn left on Piastowska. Wash 15zł, dry 15zł, detergent 3zł. Open Tu and Th 11am-4pm, Sa 11am-2pm.

Pharmacy: Apteka Pod Zółtym Tygrysem, Szczepańska 1 (☎422 92 93), just off Rynek Główny. Posts a list of 24hr. pharmacies. Open M-F 8am-8pm, Sa 8am-3pm. MC/V.

Medical Services: Medicover, Krótka 1 (☎616 10 00). Ambulance services available. English spoken. Open M-F 8am-8pm, Sa 9am-2pm.

Telephones: At the post office and throughout the city. **Telekomunikacja Polska,** Wielpole 2 (☎421 64 57), sells phonecards. Open M-F 10am-6pm, Sa 10am-2pm.

Internet Access: Internet Cafe, Rynek Główny 23. 2zł per 30min., 3zł per hr. 24hr.

Post Office: Westerplatte 20 (☎422 24 97). Poste Restante at counter #1. Open M-F 7:30am-8:30pm, Sa 8am-2pm, Su 9am-2pm. **Postal Code:** 31075.

ACCOMMODATIONS

Kraków's budget accommodations fill up in summer; call ahead. **Travel Agency Jordan,** Długa 9, books private rooms, apartments, hotels, and hostels. (☎421 21 25; www.jordan.krakow.pl. Open M-F 8am-6pm, Sa 9am-2pm. Singles 65-100zł; doubles 130-160zł; triples 180-240zł. AmEx/MC/V.) University dorms open up in July and August; the booklet *Kraków in Your Pocket* has a list.

Nathan's Villa Hostel, ul. św. Agnieszki 1 (☎422 35 45; www.nathansvilla.com). Excellent, social hostel. Fantastic cellar bar and gallery. Breakfast, wireless Internet, and laundry included. Reception 24hr. Dorms 50-60zł. MC/V; 3% surcharge. ❷

POLAND

THE ORIGINAL

According to legend, a Jewish baker in Vienna concocted the first bagel in 1683 as a gift to Polish king Jan Sobieski to thank Sobieski for routing Turkish invaders. The bread (the story goes) was shaped like a stirrup "beugal" in honor of Sobieski's heroic horsemanship. The historical record, however, first spots the bagel in Kraków in 1610: community regulations decreed that bagels be given to pregnant women for easy childbirth, and to teething babies. Whatever the bagel's origins, it thrived in Poland, especially in the Kraków region. A 1915 chronicle of the Jewish neighborhood of Kazimierz recalls that the smell of freshly baked bagels often wafted through the streets, especially near the Tempel Synagogue, where a tiny shop called Pan Bejgul (Mr. Bagel) stood at the end of Podbrzezie Street.

In Kraków today, street vendors hawk the Polish descendent of the original bagel, a crisp ring of bread known as *obwarzanki*, for about a złoty. The smell of baking bagels, meanwhile, has returned to Podbrzezie St. **Bagelmama,** facing the Tempel Synagogue at Podbrzezie 2, opened in 2001. Run by an American expat chef, Navara, it is currently the only shop in Poland that sells fresh bagels as they have evolved among Polish Jewish immigrants to North America: soft and chewy, with cream cheese spreads.

☒ **Mama's Hostel,** ul. Bracka 4 (☎429 59 40; www.mamashostel.com.pl). Centrally located with excellent facilities. Breakfast and laundry included. Reception 24hr. Flexible check-in and check-out. Dorms 50-55zł. MC/V; 3% surcharge. ❷

The Stranger, ul. Kochanowskiego 1 (☎634 25 16; www.thestrangerhostel.com). Social atmosphere and simple, clean dorms. Common room with fantastic entertainment system and free Internet. The friendly staff even does guests' laundry daily. Reception 24hr. Dorms 55-60zł. Cash only. ❷

Hotel Polonia, Basztowa 25 (☎422 12 33; www.hotel-polonia.com.pl), across from the train station. Neoclassical exterior, modern rooms, and see-through bathtubs in suites. Breakfast 17zł, included for rooms with bath. Reception 24hr. Check-out noon. Singles 89zł, with bath 295zł; doubles 109/345zł; triples 139/409zł; suites 509zł. MC/V. ❹

Bling Bling Hostel, ul. Pędzichow 7 (☎634 05 32; www.blingbling.pl). Small, familial hostel with warm staff. Breakfast and laundry included. Free Internet. Reception 24hr. Flexible check-in and check-out. Dorms 55zł. MC/V. ❷

Greg and Tom, ul. Pawia 12/15 (☎422 41 00; www.gregtomhostel.com). Look past the climb to the 4th fl. of a weary Soviet-era building: this small hostel is clean, attractive, and right next to the train and bus stations. Reception 5:30am-10pm. Free laundry and Internet. Dorms 45zł; one double 60zł. Cash only. ❷

Kadetus, ul. Zwierzyniecka 25 (☎422 36 17; www.kadetus.com). Simple dorms with modern pastel furnishings. Free laundry and Internet. Reception 24hr. Dorms 55zł; doubles 60zł. Cash only. ❷

U Żeweckiego, Librowszczyzna 1 (☎429 55 96; www.zewecki.com). Dorms and private rooms with bright, multi-colored bedspreads and modern bathrooms. Laundry 20zł. Reception 24hr. Dorms 40zł; private rooms 110-220zł. Cash only. ❶

FOOD

Many restaurants, cafes, and grocery stores are located on and around the *Rynek*. More grocery stores surround the bus and train stations.

☒ **Bagelmama,** Podbrzezie 2 (☎431 19 42), facing the Tempel Synagogue. Poland is the mother of the bagel; here the blessed foodstuff returns home in triumph. (2.50zł, 5-8zł with cream cheese or hummus). As if that wasn't enough: the best burritos in Kraków (12-14zł). Open Tu-Su 10am-9pm. Cash only. ❶

☒ **Pierogarnia,** Szpitalna 30/32 (☎422 74 95). By the counter in this miniscule dumpling outpost, a window reveals a cook rolling dough and shaping delicious *pierogi* (7-10zł). Also serves excellent *gołąbki* (cabbage rolls; 8zł). Open daily 10am-9pm. Cash only. ❶

Dym (Smoke), św. Tomasza 13 (☎429 66 61). A hub for sophisticated locals, Dym earns high praise for unbeatable coffee (4.50zł), though many prefer to enjoy the relaxed atmosphere over beer (5.50zł). The cheesecake (4zł) is divine. Open daily 10am-midnight. Cash only. ❶

Vega Bar Restaurant, Krupnicza 22 (☎430 08 46). Fresh flowers set the mood for delightful, largely vegetarian cuisine (3-10zł). Faux-meat dishes like cheese-and-soy cutlet (5zł). 32 varieties of tea (2.50zł). Another branch at św. Gertrudy 7 (☎422 34 94). Both open daily 9am-9pm. MC/V. ❶

Massolit Books Café, Felicjanek 4 (☎432 41 50). Fantastic wood-lined bookstore cafe with a *fin-de-siècle* atmosphere and decadent desserts. Open mic 1st and 3rd Su of each month, 7pm. Open M-Th, Su 10am-8pm, F-Sa 10am-10pm. MC/V. ❷

Momo, Dietla 49 (☎609 68 5775). This simple Kazimierz outfit serves fresh, mostly vegan dishes amid spare yet funky decor. Open daily 11am-8pm. Cash only. ❶

Fabryka Pizzy, Józefa 34 (☎433 80 80). This wildly popular Kazimierz pizza place lives up to its hype. Open M-Th and Su 11am-11pm, F-Sa noon-midnight. MC/V. ❷

La Cuisine, Warszauera 3 (☎429 60 18; www.lacuisine.pl). Small, chic, and full of brushed metal, this pastry shop resembles an iPod. *Naleśniki* 4-12zł. Cakes 4-8zł. Open M-Th and Su noon-11pm, F-Sa 10am-2am. Cash only. ❷

SIGHTS

STARE MIASTO. In center of Stare Miasto is Rynek Główny, a sea of cafes and bars surrounded by multi-colored row houses. Nearby, **Collegium Maius** of Kraków's **Jagiellonian University** (Uniwersytet Jagielloński) dates from 1364, making it the third-oldest university in Europe. Alumni include astronomer Mikołaj Kopernik, or Copernicus, and painter Jan Matejko. Once a lecture hall and professors' quarters, the Collegium became a museum in 1964, and boasts an extensive collection of historical scientific instruments. *(ul. Jagiellońska 15. Walk down św. Anny in the corner of the* Rynek *near the Town Hall and turn left onto Jagiellońska. ☎422 05 49. Open M-W and F 10am-3pm, Th 10am-6pm, Sa 10am-2pm. Guided visits only; tours begin every 20min. English-language tour daily 1pm. 12zł, students 6zł. Sa free.)* A trumpet call blares every hour from Wieża Mariacka, the taller tower of **St. Mary's Church** (Kościół Mariacki), and cuts off abruptly to recall the near-destruction of Kraków in 1241, when invading Tatars shot down the trumpeter as he attempted to warn the city. A stunning blue and gold interior encases the world's oldest Gothic altarpiece, a 500-year-old treasure dismantled, but not destroyed, by the Nazis. *(At the corner of the* Rynek *closest to the train station. Cover shoulders and knees. Church open daily 11:30am-6pm. Wieża Mariacka open Tu, Th, Sa 9-11am and 2-6pm. Smaller tower open daily 10am-1:15pm and 2-5pm. Each tower 5zł, students 2.50zł. Altar 4/2zł.)* In the middle of the *Rynek*, the yellow **Cloth Hall** (Sukiennice) houses hawkers of souvenirs and a gallery of Polish painting and sculpture. *(Open Tu and F-Sa 10am-7pm, W-Th 10am-4pm, Su 10am-3pm. 8zł, students 5zł. Th free.)* Letters by Copernicus and paintings by Matejko, da Vinci, and Rembrandt can be found in the **Czartoryskich Museum.** *(Św. Jana 19, parallel to ul. Florianska. Open Tu, Th 10am-4pm; W, F 11am-7pm; Sa-Su 10am-3pm. Closed 3rd Su of each month. 9zł, students 6zł. Th free.)* **Ulica Floriańska** runs to the *Rynek* from the **Barbakan** and **Floriańska Gate,** which formed the entrance to the old city and are now the only remnants of the city's medieval fortifications. From the *Rynek*, walk down Grodzka and turn right to reach the brightly colored **Franciscan Church,** which displays Stanisław Wyspiański's stained-glass window *God the Father*. *(Open daily until 7:30pm. Free English-language tours.)*

WAWEL CASTLE AND SURROUNDINGS. **Wawel Castle** (Zamek Wawelski) is an architectural masterpiece and arguably *the* sight to see in Poland. Begun in the 10th century and remodeled in the 16th, the castle contains 71 chambers, including a magnificent sequence of 16th-century tapestries commissioned by the royal family. Royal treasures can be seen in the **Komnaty** (state rooms), the royal lifestyle in the **Apartamenty** (royal chambers). Also see the treasury's cache of armor, swords, spears, and ancient guns. *(☎422 64 64; www.wawel.krakow.pl. Open Apr.-Oct. M 9:30am-noon; Tu, W, and Sa 9:30am-3pm; Th-F 9:30am-4pm, Su 10am-3pm. Nov.-Mar. Tu-Sa 9:30am-3pm, Su 10am-3pm. Royal Chambers and Oriental Collection closed M. Castle 18zł, students 13zł. M free. Lost Wawel and Oriental Collection 6/4zł each. Royal Apartments, Treasury and Armory 14/8zł each.)* Next door is **Wawel Cathedral** (Katedra Wawelska), which once hosted the coronations and funerals of Polish monarchs. Kraków native Karol Wojtyła was archbishop here before becoming Pope John Paul II. Steep wooden stairs from the church lead to **Sigismund's Bell** (Dwon Zygmunta); the view of the city rewards the climb. *(Open M-Sa 9am-2:45pm, Su 12:15-2:45pm. 10zł, students 5zł.)* In the complex's southwest corner is the entrance to the **Dragon's Den** (Smocza Jama). Legend has it that a shepherd left a poisoned sheep outside the cave as bait; the dragon ate it and became so thirsty that it drank itself to death at the Wisła River. *(Open daily Apr.-Oct. 10am-5pm. 3zł.)*

KAZIMIERZ. South of Stare Miasto lies Kazimierz, Kraków's 600-year-old **Jewish quarter.** On the eve of WWII, 68,000 Jews lived in the Kraków area, many of them in Kazimierz. The Nazis deported all by March 1943, many to the nearby Płaszów and Auschwitz-Birkenau concentration camps. Only about 100 practicing Jews now live here, but modern Kazimierz, with its cafes and bars, is both a favorite haunt of Kraków's artists and intellectuals and the center of a resurgence of Central European Jewish culture. *(From the Rynek, go down ul. Sienna past St. Mary's Church; ul. Sienna turns into Starowiślna. After 1km, turn right onto Miodowa, then left onto Szeroka.)* The unconventional **Galicia Jewish Museum** documents the past and present of Galicia, a region that in southern Poland that was once the heart of Ashkenazi Jewish culture, and poses difficult questions about the future of Judaism in Poland. *(Dajwór 18. ☎421 68 42; www.galiciajewishmuseum.org. Open daily 10am-8pm. 7zł, students 5zł.)* The tiny **Remuh Synagogue** is surrounded by **Remuh's Cemetery,** which has graves dating to the plague of 1551-1552 and a wall constructed from tombstones recovered after WWII. For centuries, the cemetery was covered with sand, protecting it from 19th-century Austrian invaders as well as from the Nazis who used the area as a garbage dump. *(ul. Szeroka 40. Open M-F, Su 9am-6pm. Services F at sundown and Sa morning. 6zł, students 3zł.)* Back on Szeroka is Poland's earliest example of Jewish religious architecture, the **Old Synagogue,** which houses a museum of traditions and art. *(ul. Szeroka 24. Open Apr.-Oct. M 10am-2pm, Tu-Su 10am-5pm; Nov.-Mar. M 10am-2pm, W-Th, Sa-Su 9am-4pm, F 11am-6pm. 7zł, students 5zł. M free.)* The **Center for Jewish Culture** organizes cultural events and arranges heritage tours. *(Rabina Meiselsa 17, off pl. Nowy. ☎430 64 49; www.judaica.pl. Open M-F 10am-6pm, Sa-Su 10am-2pm. Closed Jewish holidays.)*

ENTERTAINMENT

The **Cultural Information Center,** ul. św. Jana 2, sells the comprehensive monthly guide *Karnet.* (3zł; www.karnet.krakow2000.pl. Center ☎421 77 87. Open M-F 10am-6pm, Sa 10am-4pm.) Notable summer festivals include the **International Short Film Festival** (late May), the **Floating of Wreaths on the Wisła** (Wianki; June), **Festival of Jewish Culture** (early July), the **Street Theater Festival** (early July), and the **Jazz Festival** (late July). The city jumps with jazz. Check out **U Muniaka,** Floriańska 3 (☎423 12 05; open daily 6:30pm-2am) and **Harris Piano Jazz Bar,** Rynek Główny 28 (☎421 57 41; shows 9pm-midnight; open daily 9am-3am). The opera performs at **J. Słowacki Theater,** pl. św. Ducha 1. (☎422 40 22; www.slowacki.krakow.pl. Box office open M-Sa 11am-2pm and 3-7pm, Su 2hr. before performance. Tickets 30-50zł, students 25-30zł.) **Stary Teatr** hosts movies, plays, and other exhibits. (☎422 40 40. Open Tu-Sa 10am-1pm and 5-7pm, Su 5-7pm. Tickets 30-60zł, students 20-35zł.) European films roll at **Kino Mikro,** ul. Lea 5. (☎634 28 97. Open daily 30min. before 1st showing. M-F 10zł, Sa-Su 12zł.)

NIGHTLIFE

Kraków in Your Pocket has up-to-date info on the hottest club and pub scenes, while the free monthly English-language *KrakOut* magazine has day-by-day listings of events. Most dance clubs are in **Stare Miasto,** while bohemian pubs and cafes cluster in **Kazimierz.** For more info, see www.puby.krakow.pl. Be advised that Kraków's nightlife establishments have a high turnover rate. For tips on Kraków's **gay nightlife,** see http://gayeuro.com/krakow.

Alchemia, Estery 5 (☎292 09 70). Frequented by students, artists, and young Brits, this quintessential Kazimierz bar masquerades by day as a smoky cafe. Occasional live music and film screenings. Open M-Sa 11am-4am, Su 10am-4am.

Prozak, Dominikańska 6 (☎429 11 28; www.prozak.pl). Hipster students, porn star lookalikes, foreigners, and more dance floors, bars, and intimate nooks than you'll be able to count, make Prozak one of the top clubs in town. Beer 7zł. Mixed drinks 12-22zł. No sneakers or sandals. Cover F-Sa 10zł. Open daily 4pm-2am.

Cień, św. Jana 15 (☎422 21 77). The underground vaults filled with Kraków's beautiful people and house techno. Open W-Th 7pm-3am, F-Sa 7pm-6am. Cash only.

Faust, Rynek Główny 6 (☎423 83 00). Sell your soul in this underground labyrinth, with long wooden tables and techno-pop hits. Occasional *klezmer* or metal nights. Beer 4-6zł. Cover F-Sa 5zł. Open M-Th and Su noon-1am, F-Sa noon-4am. Cash only.

Propaganda, Miodowa 20. Despite the candles and wobbly tables, Propaganda's take on Kazimierz bohemia has a punk rock feel. Decor mixes posters of Stalin with guitars of Polish rockers. Open daily 2pm-late. Cash only.

Stalowe Magnolie, ul. św. Jana 15 (☎422 60 84). Scarlet lights illuminate this decadent jazz club and student hangout complete with comfy, king-size beds. Beer 6-10zł. Mixed drinks 14-25zł. Tu-Th live jazz. Sa-Su rock. Open daily 6pm-3am.

Klub pod Jaszczurami (Club under the Lizards), Rynek Główny 8 (☎292 22 02). A students-only cafe by day and thumping club party by night. Beer 5.50zł. Open M-Th and Su 10am-1am, F-Sa 10am-late.

DAYTRIPS FROM KRAKÓW

AUSCHWITZ-BIRKENAU. An estimated 1.5 million people, mostly Jews, were murdered—and thousands more suffered unthinkable horrors—in the Nazi concentration camps at **Auschwitz** (in Oświęcim) and **Birkenau** (in Brzezinka). The gates over the smaller **Konzentrationslager Auschwitz I** are inscribed with the ironic dictum "*Arbeit Macht Frei*" (Work Will Set You Free). Tours begin at the **museum** at Auschwitz. As you walk past the leavings of thousands of lives—suitcases, shoes, glasses, kilos upon kilos of women's hair—the sheer enormity of the atrocity begins to come into focus. A 15min. English-language film (3.50zł), with footage shot by the Soviet Army that liberated the camp on January 27, 1945, is shown at 11am and 1pm. Children under 14 are strongly advised not to visit the museum. (☎843 20 22. Open daily June-Aug. 8am-7pm; Sept. and May 8am-6pm; Oct. and Apr. 8am-5pm; Nov. and Mar. 8am-4pm; Dec.-Feb. 8am-3pm. English-language tour daily 11:30am. Museum free. Tours 3½hr., 25zl; film and bus included.)

The larger, starker **Konzentrationslager Auschwitz II-Birkenau** is in the countryside 3km from the original camp, a 30min. walk along a well-marked route or a quick **shuttle** ride from the parking lot of the Auschwitz museum (every hr. 11:30am-5:30pm, 2zł). Birkenau was built later in the war, when the Nazis developed a more brutally efficient means of killing massive numbers of people. Little is left of the camp today; most was destroyed by retreating Nazis to conceal the genocide. The reconstructed train tracks lead to the ruins of the crematoria and gas chambers.

Near the monument lies a pond still gray from the ashes deposited there 60 years ago. (Open mid-Apr. to Oct. 8am-dusk. Free.) **Auschwitz Jewish Center and Synagogue** features exhibits on pre-war Jewish life in the town of Oświęcim, films based on survivors' testimonies, genealogy resources, and a reading room. Guides offer tours of the compound. Take a taxi for about 17zł, or take bus #1, 3-6, or 8 from the train station in the town center, get off at the first stop after the bridge, and backtrack. (Pl. Ks. Jana Skarbka 5. ☎844 70 02; www.ajcf.pl. Open M-F, Su 8:30am-8pm.)

Buses from Kraków's central bus station go to **Oświęcim** (1½-2hr., 5 per day, 10-15zł). Return buses leave from the stop on the other side of the parking lot; turn right out of the museum. Less convenient **trains** leave from Kraków Płaszów, south of the town center. Buses #2-5, 8-9, and 24-29 connect the Oświęcim train station to the Muzeum Oświęcim stop; alternatively, walk a block to the right out of the station, turn left onto ul. Więźniów Oświęcimia, and continue 1.6km to Auschwitz.

WIELICZKA. A 700-year-old **salt mine** sits at ul. Daniłowicza 10 in the tiny town of Wieliczka, 13km southeast of Kraków. Pious Poles carved the immense underground complex of chambers out of salt; in 1978, UNESCO declared the mine one of the 12 most priceless monuments in the world. The most spectacular cavern is **St. Kinga's Chapel,** complete with salt chandeliers, an altar, and relief works. (☎278 73 02; www.kopalnia.pl. Open daily Apr.-Oct. 7:30am-7:30pm; Nov.-Mar. 8am-4pm. English-language tours available July-Aug. 2 per hr.; June and Sept. 8 per day; Oct.-May 2 per day. 2hr. 50zł, students under 25 40zł. MC/V.) Most travel companies, including **Orbis** (p. 803), organize trips to the mines, but it's cheapest to take a private **minibus,** like "Lux-Bus," that departs from between the train and bus stations (30min., every 15min., 2zł). Look for "Wieliczka" marked on the door. In Wieliczka, follow the path of the former tracks, then signs marked *"do kopalni."*

LUBLIN ☎081

Unlike most cities in Poland, Lublin (LOO-bleen; pop. 400,000) survived WWII with cobblestones and medieval buildings intact. The 14th-century **Lublin Castle** (Zamek Lubelski), in the **Rynek** (main square) of the **Stare Miasto** (Old Town), was used as a Gestapo jail during Nazi occupation. The adjacent **Holy Trinity Chapel** contains stunning Russo-Byzantine frescoes from 1418. (☎532 50 01, ext. 35. Museum open W-F 9am-4pm, Sa 10am-5pm, Su 9am-5pm. Chapel open M-Sa 9am-3:30pm, Su 9am-4:30pm. Entrance to each 6.50zł, students 4.50zł. Tours 45zł each, 55zł for both.) Take eastbound bus #28 from the train station, trolley #153 or 156 from al. Racławickie, or walk along Droga Męczenników Majdanka (Road of the Martyrs of Majdanek; 30min.) to Zamość in order to reach **Majdanek,** the second-largest WWII concentration camp. Nazis did not have time to destroy it, so the original structures still stand. (☎744 26 48; www.majdanek.pl. Open May-Sept. Tu-Su 8am-6pm; Mar.-Apr. and Oct.-Nov. Tu-Su 8am-3pm. Children under 14 not permitted. Free. English-language tours 100zł per group; call ahead. English guidebooks 7zł.)

From the bus station, walk through Zamkowy Sq., past the castle, and through the gate to reach **Domu Rekolekcyjnym ❶,** ul. Podwale 15, a rectory with simple but pleasant rooms, friendly nuns, and an unbeatable location. (☎532 41 38; j.halasa@kuria.lublin.pl. Dorms 20-40zł.) Lublin's eateries cluster near **ulica Krakówskie Przedmieście;** a dozen beer gardens can be found in **Stare Miasto. Café Szeroka 28 ❹,** ul. Grodzka 21, looks out onto the castle. The traditional Polish food is tasty, and upstairs you'll find an avant-garde theater and a free exhibit of pre-WWII Lublin. (Entrees 30zł. Sa live klezmer. Open M-Th and Su 11am-11pm, F-Sa 11am-late. AmEx/MC/V.) **Cafe Vanilla,** ul. Krakowskie Przedmieście 12, serves *naleśniki* (Polish crepes; 8-20zł) and unusually elaborate ice cream desserts. (15-20zł. Coffee 9-14zł. Open daily 10am-11pm. AmEx/MC/V.) **Trains** (☎94 36) run from pl. Dworcowy 1 to: Kraków (4hr., 3 per day,

43zł); Warsaw (3hr., 4 per day, 27zł); Wrocław (9½hr., 3 per day, 43zł). The **tourist office,** ul. Jezuica 1/3, is near the Kraków Gate. (☎532 44 12; itlublin@onet.pl. Open May-Aug. M-Sa 9am-6pm, Su 10am-3pm; Sept.-Apr. M-F 9am-5pm, Sa-Su 10am-3pm.) **Postal Code:** 20-950.

ZAKOPANE

☎018

The year-round resort of Zakopane (zah-ko-PAH-neh; pop. 28,000) lies in a valley surrounded by jagged Tatran peaks and alpine meadows. During peak seasons (Jan.-Feb. and June-Sept.), the town fills with skiers and hikers headed for the magnificent **Tatra National Park.** (Tatrzański Park Narodowy; 5zł, students 2.50zł.)

Signs marked "*pokój*" and "*noclegi*" indicate private rooms; owners may greet you at the station. **Schronisko Morskie Oko ❶,** by the Morskie Oko lake, is a gorgeous hostel in an ideal hiking location. Take a bus (45min., 11 per day, 4zł) from the station to Palenice Białczańska or a direct minibus (20min., 5zł) from opposite the bus station, and then hike (1-2hrs., 9km) up the paved road. (☎207 76 09. Book ahead. Linen 7zł. June-Oct. space on floor 34zł; 3- to 6-bed dorms 44zł. Nov.-June 24/34zł. Cash only.) **Schronisko PISM "Szarotka" ❷,** ul. Notowarska 45G, is a traditional hostel with small, clean rooms, and fresh bathrooms. (☎201 36 18. Linens 5zł. Reservations recommended. English spoken. Dorms 40zł. Cash only.) Waiters at **Zbojecka ❸,** ul. Krupówki 28, serve regional fare in traditional costume. (☎201 38 54. Open 10am-midnight. Cash only.) At ul. Kościuszki 3 there is a Super Sam **grocery store.** (Open 24hr.; low season M-Sa 24hr., Su 6am-7pm. AmEx/MC/V.)

The bus station (☎201 46 03) sits on the corner of ul. Kościuszki and ul. Jagiellońska, facing the train station (☎201 45 04). **Buses** run to Kraków (2-2½hr., 22 per day, 8zł) and Warsaw (8½hr., 2 per day, 53zł). A private express line runs between Zakopane and Kraków (2hr., 15 per day, 10zł), leaving from a stop on ul. Kościuszki 50m toward the center from the station. **Trains** go to Kraków (3-4hr., 19 per day, 20zł) and Warsaw (8hr., 8 per day, 46-80zł). To reach the town center, walk down ul. Kościuszki, which intersects the central ul. Krupówki (15min.). The **tourist office,** ul. Kościuszki 17, provides info on topics from dining to hiking, sells maps (5-9zł), offers help in locating a room, and books English-language rafting trips on the Dunajec. (☎201 22 11. Open daily July-Sept. 8am-8pm; Oct.-June 9am-6pm. Rafting 70-80zł.) **Postal Code:** 34-500.

HIKING NEAR ZAKOPANE. **Kuźnice,** south of central Zakopane, is the best and most popular place to begin hikes. Head uphill on ul. Krupówki to ul. Zamoyskiego; follow this road as it becomes ul. Chałubińskiego, which turns into ul. Przewodników Tatrzańskich and continues to the trailheads (1hr. from Zakopane center). You can also take a "mikro-bus" (2zł) from in front of the bus station. From Kuźnice, start one of the hikes listed below, or try the 1987m Kasprowy Wierch **cable car,** where you can enjoy the amazing views from atop **Kasprowy Mountain** with one foot in Poland and one in Slovakia. (Round-trip 29zł, students 19zł; ascent 19/14zł, descent 15/10zł. Open July-Aug. 7am-7pm; June and Sept. 7:30am-6pm; Oct. 7:30am-3pm.) Trails are well marked, but pick up the *Tatrzański Park Narodowy* map (7zł) at a kiosk or bookstore before hiking.

The **Valley of the Five Polish Tarns** (Dolina Pięciu Stawów Polskich; 1 day) is an intense, beautiful hike. It starts at Kuźnice and follows the yellow trail through **Dolina Jaworzynka** (Jaworzynka Valley) to the steep blue trail, which leads to **Hala Gasienicowa** (2½hr.). The blue trail ends at Morskie Oko (2hr.). Mind the crowds and be careful on the steep final ascent to the peak of **Mount Giewont** (1894m; 6½hr.). The mountain's silhouette resembles a man lying down; you'll envy him after the climb. From Kuźnice, take the moderately difficult blue trail (7km) to the peak for a view of Zakopane, the Tatras, and Slovakia.

POLAND

Morskie Oko ("Sea Eye"; 1406m) is a dazzling glacial lake. Take a bus from the Zakopane station (45min., 11 per day, 4zł) or a private minibus from opposite the station (30min., 5zł) to **Palenice Białczańska.** Hike the popular paved 18km loop (5-6hr.) or take the green trail to the blue trail (4hr.) for a majestic view of the lake.

WROCŁAW ☎071

Wrocław (pop. 657,000), the capital of Lower Silesia, is a city of spires, islands, gardens, and stone bridges. Passed among competing powers for centuries, in WWII the city became Festung Breslau (Fortress Wrocław), one of the last Nazi holdouts en route to Berlin. Although it has been a favorite of middle-aged German tourists for years, new investments from abroad are expanding cultural attractions; today, Wrocław offers beautiful sights and energetic nightlife.

TRANSPORTATION AND PRACTICAL INFORMATION. Trains, ul. Piłsudskiego 105 (☎367 58 82), run from Wrocław Główny to: Berlin, Germany (6¼hr., 2 per day, 185zł); Bratislava, Slovak Republic (7½hr., 10:30pm, 240zł); Kraków (4½hr., 14 per day, 25-44zł); Poznań (3¼hr., 29 per day, 19-31zł); Prague, Czech Republic (5¼hr., 2 per day, 125zł); Warsaw (4¼hr., 12 per day, 27-42zł). Buses leave from behind the train station. From the train station, turn left on ul. Piłsudskiego, take a right on ul. Świdnicka, and go past Kościuszki pl. over the Fosa River to reach the Rynek (main square). The tourist office, Rynek 14, can help book student dorms. (☎344 11 09; fax 344 29 62. Dorms 20-50zł. Free Internet. Bike rental 50zł per day, 10zł for the 1st hr., and 5zł every hr. after, 400zł deposit required. Open daily 9am-9pm.) Surf the web at Internet Klub Navig@tor Podziemia, ul. Kuźnicza 11/13. (3zł per hr. Open daily 9am-10pm.) Postal Code: 50-900.

ACCOMMODATIONS AND FOOD. **The Stranger Hostel ❷**, ul. Kołłątaja 16/3, opposite the train station, is on the third floor behind an unmarked wooden doorway (ring buzzer #3). New and filled with quirky touches like decorated glass toilet seats, it features large dorms with eclectic, comfortable stylings, and an entertainment center. (☎634 25 16. Free laundry and Internet. Reception 24hr. Dorms 50zł. AmEx/MC/V.) The colorful but worn **Youth Hostel Mlodziezowy Dom Kultury im. Kopernika (HI) ❶**, ul. Kołłątaja 20, is opposite the train station on the road perpendicular to ul. Piłsudskiego, with standard dorms and new bathrooms. (☎343 88 56. Lockout 10am-5pm. Curfew 10pm. Book ahead. Dorms 22zł; doubles 58zł. Discount after 2 nights.) Art Nouveau **Hotel Monopol ❹**, ul. Modrzejewskiej 2, has satellite TV, telephones, and a princely breakfast buffet. (☎343 70 41. Check-in and check-out 2pm. Singles 120zł, with bath 180zł; doubles 160/260zł; triples with bath 310zł. AmEx/MC/V.) **Bazylia ❶**, ul. Kuźnicza 42, is a traditional Polish milk bar serving cheap, filling meals. (Open M-F 7am-7pm, Sa 8am-5pm. Cash only.) **Kuchinia Marche ❶**, ul. Świdnicka 53, is a tasty alternative to milk bars. This popular and hip *marche* offers fresh pastries (1-3zł), pasta cooked before your eyes (8-10.50zł), Polish dishes (3.50-6zł), milkshakes (2.50zł), and salads (1.50-4zł) from different stations. (☎343 95 65. Open M-F 9am-8pm, Sa-Su noon-8pm. MC/V.) Skip the grocery stores and stock up at **Hala Targona,** at the corner of Plaskowa and Ducha Św. where you'll find a massive selection of fresh produce and meats within this towering 1908 building. (Open M-F 8am-6:30pm, Sa 9am-3pm.)

SIGHTS AND NIGHTLIFE. The Gothic **Ratusz** (town hall) towers over the **Rynek** in the heart of the city. Past the *Rynek* runs the beautiful central street, **Ulica Świdnicka.** The rotunda containing the 120-by-five meter **Racławice Panorama,** ul. Purkyniego 11, transports visitors into the 18th-century peasant insurrection against the Russian occupation. To reach it, face away from the *Ratusz*, bear left onto ul. Kuźnicza, then turn right onto ul. Kotlarska, which becomes ul.

Purkyniego. (☎344 23 44. Open Tu-Su 9am-5pm. Shows every 30min. 9:30am-5pm. 20zł, students 15zł.) Across the street is the **Muzeum Narodowe** (National Museum), pl. Powstańców Warszawy 5, with exhibits ranging from medieval sculpture to modern art. (Open W, F, and Su 10am-4pm, Th 9am-4pm, Sa 10am-6pm. 15zł, students 10zł. Sa free.) In Wrocław's cultural center, the beautiful **Uniwersytet Wrocławski** (Wrocław University), the **Mathematical Tower,** pl. Uniwersytecka 1, provides a sweeping view of the city. (Open M-Tu and Th-Su 10am-3pm. 4zł, students 2zł.) Across the Oder River lies the serene **Plac Katedralny** (Cathedral Square) and the spires of the 13th-century **Katedra Św. Jana Chrzciciela** (Cathedral of St. John the Baptist. Open M-Sa 10am-5:30pm, Su 2-4pm. 4zł, students 3zł.)

Students and self-described "alternative" bar-goers crowd into dimly lit **REJS Pub,** ul. Kotlarska 32a. (Beer 4.50zł. Open M-Sa 9:30am-late, Su 11am-late.) The bar and cafe **Kawiarnia "Pod Kalamburem,"** ul. Kuźnicza 29a, was founded by an experimental theater group and now hosts readings and film screenings. (Beer 3-10zł. Open M-Th 1pm-midnight, F-Sa 1pm-late, Su 4pm-midnight.) On ul. Ruska, near the corner with Nowy Św., is a complex containing several clubs and bars filled every night of the week. The hip-hop dance floor of **MPJ** and its surrounding beer garden are popular. (Beer 5zł. Open daily 11am-late. Disco after 8pm.) Next door, **Niebo Cafe** offers alt rock and New Age concerts in a lovingly worn interior filled with plush velvet chairs. (Beer 4.50zł. Open M-F 1pm-late, Sa-Su 5pm-late.)

POLAND

POZNAŃ ☎061

International trade fairs throughout the year fill Poznań (pop. 600,000), the capital of Wielkopolska (Greater Poland), with businessmen and tourists. Opulent 15th-century merchant homes surround the ornate, Renaissance **Town Hall** *(Ratusz)*, now home to a history museum. (Open M-Sa 10am-4pm, Su 10am-3pm. Museum 5.50zł, students 3.50zł. Sa free.) The **Museum of Musical Instruments** (Muzeum Instrumentów Muzycznych), Stary Rynek 45, exhibits one of Chopin's pianos. (Open Tu-Sa 11am-5pm, Su 11am-4pm. 5.50zł, students 3.50zł. Sa free.) Sculpted ceilings and columns spiral heavenward in the **Parish Church of the City of Poznań of St. Mary Magdalene,** at the end of ul. Świętosławska off Stary Rynek. (Free concerts Sa 12:15pm.) On the outskirts of town is the first Polish cathedral, the **Cathedral of St. Peter and St. Paul** (Katedra Piotra i Pawła). In the **Golden Chapel** (Kaplica Złota) are the tombs of Prince Mieszko I and his son Bolesław Chrobry, the first king of Poland. (Cathedral open M-Sa 9am-6pm, Su 1:15-6:30pm. Crypt 2zł.)

Reasonably priced accommodations near the center are extremely elusive; make arrangements in advance. **Przemysław ❶,** ul. Głogowska 16, arranges private rooms near the center. (☎866 35 60; przemyslaw@przemyslaw.com.pl. Singles 42zł; doubles 64zł. Open M-F 8am-6pm, Sa 10am-2pm.) From train station, turn left on Roosevelta, which becomes Glogowska; at the third stoplight, go right on Berwinskiego to reach **Schronisko Młodziezowe #3 (HI) ❶,** Berwinskiego 2/3. Though outside the center and short on frills, this hostel has clean dorms and reliably low prices. (☎866 40 40. Reception 5-9pm. Lockout 10am-5pm. Curfew 10pm. Dorms 24-30zł. Cash only.) The traditional Polish food at **Bar Mleczny Pod Kuchcikiem ❶,** św. Marcin 75, is a student favorite. (☎853 60 94. Entrees 3-5zł. Open M-F 8am-8pm, Sa 8am-5pm, Su 10am-5pm. Cash only.) **W Starem Kinie,** ul. Nowowieskiego 8, draws students and artists with its film screenings and live rock and jazz shows. (Beer 6.50zł. 18+. Open M-Sa 10am-1am, Su 6pm-midnight.) **Trains** run from Poznań Główny, ul. Dworcowa 1 (☎866 12 12), to: Berlin, Germany (3½hr., 7 per day, 138zł); Kraków (5hr., 10 per day, 45-79zł); Warsaw (3hr., 23 per day, 57-87zł). To reach Stary Rynek (Old Market), take any tram to the right down św. Marcin from the end of ul. Dworcowa, and get off at ul. Marcinkowskiego. The **tourist office,** Stary Rynek 59/60, has free maps and books rooms. (☎852 61 56. Open June-Aug. M-F 9am-6pm, Sa 10am-4pm; Sept.-May reduced hours.) **Postal Code:** 61-890.

TORUŃ ☎056

Toruń (pop. 210,000) bills itself as the hometown of Mikolaj Kopernik, or Copernicus. Before the astronomer eclipsed its other attractions, his hometown was known far and wide as "beautiful red Toruń" for its brick and stone structures.

TRANSPORTATION AND PRACTICAL INFORMATION. Across the Wisła River from the city center, the train station, ul. Kujawska 1, serves: Gdańsk (3¼hr., 7 per day, 36zł); Łódz (2¾hr., 4 per day, 32zł); Poznań (2¼hr., 5 per day, 31zł); Warsaw (2¾hr., 6 per day, 37zł). Dworzec PKS **buses,** ul. Dąbrowskiego 26, leave for Berlin, Germany (9½hr., 1 per day, 120zł) and Kołobrzeg (7hr., 2 per day, 40zł). Polski Express buses leave from Ruch Kiosk just north of pl. Teatralny for many of the same destinations, with student discounts. The IT **tourist office,** Rynek Staromiejski 25, offers free maps and helps find lodgings. From the train station, take bus #22 or 27 across the river to pl. Rapackiego and head through the park. (☎621 09 31; www.it.torun.pl. Open May-Dec. M and Sa 9am-4pm, Tu-F 9am-6pm, Su 9am-1pm; Sept.-Apr. closed Su.) **Postal Code:** 87-100.

ACCOMMODATIONS AND FOOD. Inexpensive hotels are frequently the best value and are centrally located. **Hotel Kopernik ❸,** ul. Wola Zamkowa 16, decks out its rooms with satellite TV and fluffy towels. (☎652 25 73. Breakfast 11zł. Reception 24hr. Check-in and check-out 2pm. Dorms 25zł; singles 76zł, with bath 115zł; doubles 136/180zł. 25% discount Sa-Su. MC/V.) Fresh wood furnishings and floral bedspreads are among the appealing comforts that help make up for the inexplicable bright-green paint job at **Hotelik w Centrum ❸,** ul. Szumana 2 (☎652 22 46). From Rynek Staromiejski, follow ul. Szeroka, veer left on ul. Królowej Jadwigi through the Rynek Nowomiejski and cross ul. Szumana, the hotel will be on your left. (☎652 22 46. Internet 2zł per hr. Breakfast 10zł. Check-in 2pm. Check-out noon. Singles 70zł, with bath 90zł; doubles 110-120zł.) To reach the student-filled **PTTK Dom Turystyczny ❶,** ul. Legionów 24, from the Rynek, follow ul. Chełmińska past pl. Teatralny; take the second right after the park and turn left on ul. Legionów. The simple rooms and large but aging bathrooms are popular with Polish school groups. (☎/fax 622 38 55. Dorms 27-37zł; singles 60zł; doubles 77zł.) **Manekin ❶,** ul. Wysoka 5, serves massive and delicious *nalesniki* (filled pancakes; 2-9.50zł), made to order. (☎652 28 85. Open M-Th 10am-10pm, F-Sa 10am-11pm, Su 10am-10pm.) **Kopernik Factory Store ❷,** Rynek Staromiejski 6, sells the best and most collectible dessert in town: gingerbread effigies of Polish kings, saints, and astronomers. (0.70-26zł. Open M-F 9am-7pm, Sa-Su 10am-2pm. MC/V.) Look for a 24hr. grocery store, **Supersam,** at ul. Chełmińska 22.

SIGHTS AND NIGHTLIFE. **Stare Miasto** (Old Town), on the right bank of the Wisła River, was constructed by the Teutonic Knights in the 13th century. The 14th-century **Town Hall** (Ratusz) that dominates **Rynek Stromiejski** (Old Town Square) is a fine examples of monumental burgher architecture. (Museum open May-Aug. Tu-W and Sa noon-6pm, Th and Su 10am-4pm; Sept.-Apr. Tu-Su 10am-4pm. Medieval tower open May-Sept. Tu-Su. Museum 10zł, students 6zł. Su free. Tower 10/6zł.) Copernicus was born at ul. Kopernika 15/17; the restored **Dom Kopernika** features historical artifacts and a sound and light show. (Open Tu, Th, Sa noon-6pm; W, F, Su 10am-4pm. 10zł, students 6zł. Sound and light show 10/6zł. Both 18/11zł.) A revolt in 1454 led to the destruction of the **Teutonic Knights' Castle,** but its ruins, on ul. Przedzamcze, still impress. (Open daily 9am-8pm. 1zł.) The 15m **Leaning Tower** (Krzywą Wieżą), ul. Krzywą Wieżą 17, was built in 1271 by a Teutonic Knight as punishment for infringing his order's rule of celibacy. The **Cathedral of St. John the Baptist and St. John the Evangelist** (Bazylika Katedralna pw. sw. Janów), at the corner of ul. Żeglarska and sw. Jana, is the most impressive of the many Gothic churches in the area. (Open Apr.-Oct. M-Sa 8:30am-5:30pm, Su 2-5:30pm. 2zł, students 1zł.) Just across the Rynek Stromiejski are the stained-glass windows of the **Church of the Virgin Mary** (Kosciól sw. Marii) on ul. Panny Marii. (Open M-Sa 8am-5pm. 2zł.) **Niebo,** Rynek Staromiejski 1, a sophisticated Gothic cellar in the Old Town Hall, has excellent *szarlotka* (apple cake), live jazz and cabarets, and outdoor seating in summer. (Beer 4-5zł. Open M-Th and Su noon-midnight, F-Sa noon-2am.)

ŁÓDŹ

☎042

Poland's second-largest city, Łódź (WOODGE; pop. 1,055,000) has few postcard-worthy attractions, but nonetheless possesses a charisma of its own. It has always been a working-class town, and once had the largest Jewish ghetto in Europe. The **Jewish cemetery** (Cmentarz Żydowski), on ul. Zmienna, is eerily beautiful, with over 200,000 time-worn graves. Near the entrance is a memorial to the Jews killed in the ghetto; signs lead to the **Ghetto Fields** (Pole Ghettowe), which are lined with faintly marked graves. Take tram #1 from ul. Kilinskiego or #6 from ul. Kosciuszki or Zachnodnia north to the end of the line (20min.); continue up the street, turn left on ul. Zmienna, and enter through a small gate on the right. (☎656 70 19. Open May-Sept. M-F and Su 9am-5pm; Oct.-Apr. M-F and Su 9am-3pm. Closed Jewish holidays. 4zł, free for those visiting the graves of relatives.) The **Jewish Community Center** (Gmina Wyznaniowa Żydowska), ul. Pomorska 18, in the town center, has information on those buried in the cemetery. (☎633 51 56. Open M-F 10am-2pm. English spoken.)

Convenient **PTSM Youth Hostel (HI) ❶,** ul. Legionów 27, has quiet rooms and spacious baths. Take tram #4 toward Helenówek from Fabryczna station to pl. Wolnosci; walk on Legionów past Zachodnia. (☎630 66 80; www.youthhostellodz.w.pl. Curfew 11pm. Dorms 30zł; one single 45zł; singles with bath and TV 65zł; doubles with TV 80zł; triples with TV 120zł. MC/V.) **Anatewka ❸,** ul. 6 Sierpnia 2-4, elegantly evokes the rich Jewish culture of pre-war Łódź. (Meals 20-50zł. Open daily 11am-11pm.) **Green Way Bar Wegetarianski ❷,** ul. Piotrkowska 8, serves healthy vegetarian meals with an emphasis on the fresh and seasonal. (☎632 08 52. Entrees 7.50zł. Open daily 10am-9pm.) Designed by an arts collective, legendary bar and club **Łódź Kaliska,** ul. Piotrkowska 102, draws famous Polish actors and artists to its quirky dance floor. (Beer 7zł. F-Sa disco. Open M-Sa noon-3am, Su 4pm-3am.)

Trains run from the **Łódź Fabryczna** (☎664 54 67), pl. B. Salacinskiego 1, to Kraków (3¼hr., 3 per day, 41zł) and Warsaw (2hr., 17 per day, 28zł), and from **Łódź Kaliska** (☎41 02), al. Unii 1, to Gdansk (7½hr., 3 per day, 45zł) and Wrocław (3¾hr., 3 per day, 35zł). Polski Express **buses** also depart from Łódź Fabryczna to Kraków (5hr., 10 per day, 34-49zł) and Warsaw (2½hr., 6 per day, 12.50-36zł). Łódź's main thoroughfare, **ulica Piotrkowska,** is a bustling pedestrian shopping drag by day and a lively pub strip by night. **IT,** al. Kosciuszkiul 88, has tourist info and can help book lodgings, including university dorms in summer. (☎/fax 638 59 56; cit@uml.lodz.pl. Open M-F 8:30am-4:30pm, Sa 9am-1pm.) **Postal Code:** 90-001.

GDAŃSK

☎058

Gdańsk's (pop. 481,000) strategic location at the mouth of the Wisła River, on the Baltic Coast, has put it at the forefront of Polish history. As the free city of Danzig, it was the Polish gateway to the sea during years of occupation in the 18th and 19th centuries. In WWII, it was the site of the first casualties and of the German army's last stand. Recently, reconstruction has restored the charm of the old quayside town, and efficient transportation makes it a good starting point to explore Sopot and Gdynia, which, with Gdańsk, form the Trójmiasto (Tri-City Area).

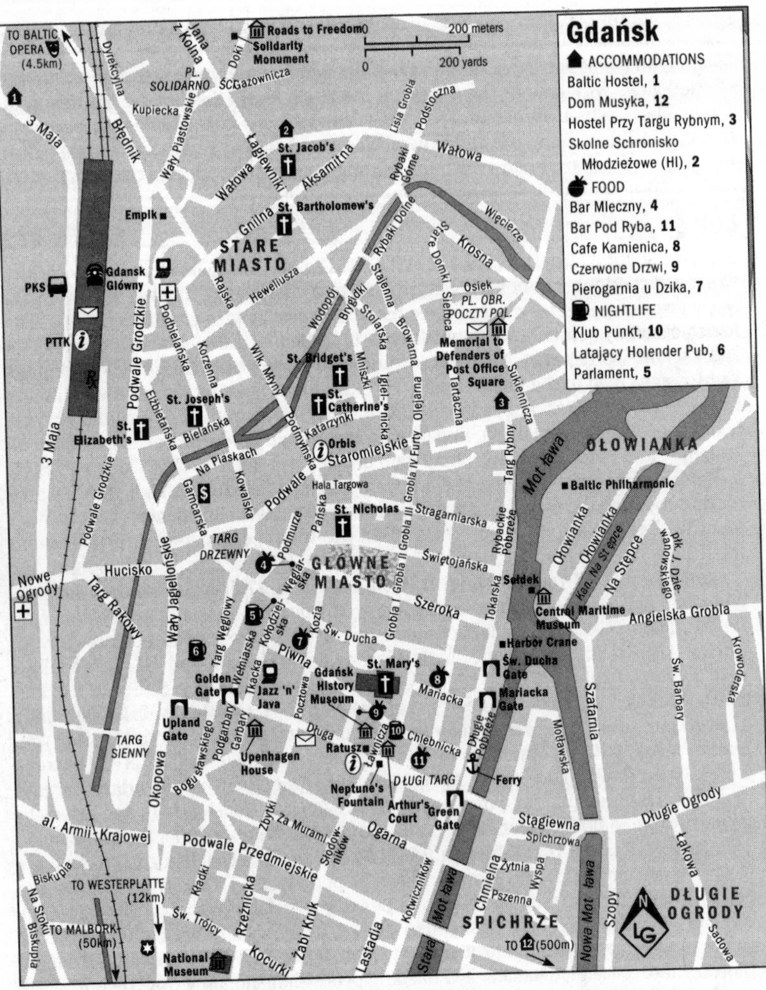

TRANSPORTATION

Trains: Gdańsk Główny, ul. Podwale Grodzkie 1 (☎94 36). To: **Kołobrzeg** (2¾hr., 8 per day, 41zł); **Kraków** (7hr., 13 per day, 58zł); **Łódź** (8hr., 6 per day, 46zł); **Lublin** (8hr., 3 per day, 51zł); **Malbork** (50min., 40 per day, 15-30zł); **Poznań** (4½hr., 7 per day, 42-73zł); **Toruń** (3¼hr., 7 per day, 36zł); **Warsaw** (4hr., 22 per day, 46-79zł); **Wrocław** (6-7hr., 4 per day, 47-80zł). **SKM** (Fast City Trains; ☎628 57 78) run to **Gdynia** (35min.; 4zł, students 2zł) and **Sopot** (20min., 2.80/1.40zł) every 10min. during the day. Punch your ticket in a *kasownik* (ticket machine) before boarding.

Buses: Ul. 3-go Maja 12 (☎302 15 32), behind the train station. To: **Kołobrzeg** (6hr., 1 per day, 47zł); **Kraków** (10¾hr., 1 per day, 68zł); **Łódź** (8hr., 4 per day, 57zł); **Malbork** (1hr., 8 per day, 9.40-13zł); **Toruń** (2½hr., 2 per day, 31zł); **Warsaw** (5¾hr., 9 per day, 66zł). Comfortable **Polski Express** buses run to **Warsaw** (4½hr., 2 per day, 45zł).

Ferries: Żegluga Gdańska (☎301 49 26; www.zegluga.gda.pl) runs summer ferries that leave the Green Gate (Zielona Brama) for **Sopot** (1hr.; 5 per day; 38zł, students 25zł).

Local Transportation: Gdańsk has an extensive **bus** and **tram** system. 10min. 1.10zł; 30min. 2.20zł; 45min. 2.70zł; 1hr. 3.30zł; day pass 6.20zł. Buses run 6am-10pm. **Night buses** 30min. 3.30zł; night pass 5.50zł. Bags over 60cm need their own tickets.

Taxis: MPT (☎96 33; www.artusmpt.gda.pl) is a state-run taxi service.

ORIENTATION AND PRACTICAL INFORMATION

While Gdańsk technically sits on the Baltic Coast, its center is 5km inland. Just blocks southeast of the **Gdańsk Główny** train and bus stations, the center borders **Wały Jagiellońskie** on the west, and the **Motława River** on the east. Take the underpass in front of the stations, go right, and turn left on **ulica Heweliusza.** Turn right on **ulica Rajska** and follow the signs to **Główne Miasto** (main town), turning left on **ulica Długa.** Długa becomes **Długi Targ** as it widens near the Motława. Gdańsk's suburbs all lie north of Główne Miasto.

Tourist Offices: PTTK Gdańsk, ul. Długa 45 (☎301 91 51; www.pttk-gdansk.pl), in Główne Miasto. Tour guides (☎301 60 96) May-Sept. for groups of 3-10, 80zł per person. Open May-Sept. M-F 9am-5pm, Sa-Su 9am-3pm; Oct.-Apr. M-F 9am-6pm.

Budget Travel: Almatur, Długi Targ 11, 2nd fl. (☎301 24 03), in Główne Miasto. Sells ISIC (59zł), and books int'l air and ferry tickets. Open M-F 10am-5pm, Sa 10am-2pm.

Currency Exchange: Bank Pekao SA, ul. Garncarska 31 (☎801 365 365), cashes **traveler's checks** for 1% commission and provides MC/V **cash advances** for no commission. Open M-F 8am-6pm and the 1st and last Sa of each month 10am-2pm.

English-Language Bookstore: Empik, ul. Podwale Grodzkie 8 (☎301 62 88, ext. 115). Sells maps and *Gdańsk in Your Pocket* (5zł). Open M-Sa 9am-9pm, Su 11am-8pm.

24hr. Pharmacy: Apteka Plus (☎763 10 74), at the train station. Ring bell at night.

Medical Services: Private doctors, ul. Podbielańska 16 (☎301 51 68). Sign says "Lekarze Specjaliści." 50zł per visit. Open daily 7am-7pm. For **emergency care,** go to **Szpital Specjalistyczny im. M. Kopernika,** ul. Nowe Ogrody 5 (☎302 30 31).

Internet Access: Jazz'n'Java, ul. Tkacka 17/18 (☎305 36 16), in the Old Town. 3zł per 30min., 5zł per hr. Open daily 10am-10pm.

Post Office: Ul. Długa 23/28 (☎301 88 53). For *Poste Restante,* enter on ul. Pocztowa. Currency exchange, and fax. Open M-F 8am-8pm, Sa 9am-3pm. **Postal Code:** 80-801.

ACCOMMODATIONS

With Gdańsk's limited tourist infrastructure and increasing popularity, it's best to reserve ahead, especially in summer. **University dorms** open to travelers in July and August; for further info consult **PTTK** (see above). Private rooms (20-80zł) can be arranged through either PTTK or **Grand-Tourist** (Biuro Podróży i Zakwaterowania), ul. Podwale Grodzkie 8, connected to the train station. (☎301 26 34; www.grand-tourist.pl. Singles 50-60zł; doubles 80-100zł; 2- to 4-person apartments 180-280zł. Open July-Aug. daily 8am-8pm; Sept.-June M-Sa 10am-6pm.)

Hostel Przy Targu Rybnym, ul. Grodzka 21 (☎301 56 27; www.gdanskhostel.com). Off Targ Rybny, across from the *baszta* (tower). At Poland's wackiest hostel, guests enjoy the chummy common room, free bowls of homemade pickles, free Internet, and included breakfast. Reception 24hr. Dorms 40zł; doubles 120-140zł; quads 250zł. ❶

Baltic Hostel, ul. 3-go Maja 25 (☎721 96 57; www.baltichostel.com). From the train station, take the KFC underpass to the bus station, turn right on ul. 3-go Maja and take the path on your right. In an aging brick apartment building, Baltic offers the nicest hostel rooms in Gdańsk, with hardwood floors and eclectic furnishings. Free Internet, breakfast, and bike and kayak use. Reception 24hr. Dorms 35-40zł; doubles 50zł. ❷

ETURN OF THE BATTLE OF GRUNWALD

From under the smoke, you can make out the flash of swords and he cascade of arrows. Across the battlefield, a horn calls to the soldiers—or is that the soundtrack rom a Hollywood battle epic? Well, it is the 21st century. Every year in mid-July, almost 100,000 Poles gather to reenact the famed 1410 Battle of Grunwald, to honor a crucial Polish victory over the Teutonic Knights. Walking the fine ine between historical chaos and amily barbeque, Grunwald on July 15 is perhaps the best sight in Poland. Camps of soldiers gather or the two weeks before the battle, carousing at night and honing heir crafts by day. Daily Latin Mass and oratory competitions punctuate drinking and training. Local historical organizations often sponsor one or two soldiers and archers who train for several hours a week in preparation.

Upon arrival at the battlefield, be sure to change your złotych for medieval Talar (1 Talar=4 Złotych) at the numerous *kasy* in order to sample the abundant supply of sausages, lard, and—of course—beer. While waiting for the knights o suit up, you can try your hand at archery or peruse the stalls of homemade period goods. A small museum under the stone monument explains the battle sequence in great detail. (Open daily May-Sept. 9am-9pm. Entrance 6zł, students 3zł.) When he loudspeakers start to blare

Skolne Schronisko Młodzieżowe (HI), ul. Wałowa 21 (☎301 23 13). From the train station, follow ul. Karmelicka, turn left on ul. Rajska, and then right on ul. Wałowa. Unusually spacious rooms are clean and well lit. No smoking or drinking. Reception 8am-10pm. Curfew midnight. Dorms 16-21zł; singles 25-30zł; doubles 50-60zł. ❶

Dom Musyka, ul. Łąkowa 1/2 (☎300 92 60; www.amuz.gda.pl). From the train station, take tram #8 or 13 to Akamia Muzycza. On the corner of Podwale Przedmiejskie, behind the gate of the yellow building, a block across the Motława from the Old Town. Extremely rare among the 300zł beds of Gdańsk, this new hotel has plenty of space and brand new furnishings. Singles 155-165zł; doubles 220-230zł; suites 345-350zł. ❹

FOOD

Gdańsk has a wealth of excellent traditional food options. For fresh produce, try **Hala Targowa** on ul. Panska, just off Podwale Staromiejskie. (Open M-F 9am-6pm, first and last Sa of each month 9am-3pm.) For a more indoor shopping experience, head to **Esta,** ul. Podwale Staromiejskie 109/112, in Targ Drzewny. (Open M-Sa 10am-10pm, Su noon-10pm.)

Cafe Kamienica, ul. Mariacka 37/39, in the shadow of St. Mary's Church, masters casual elegance. Superb *szarlotka* (apple pie; 5zł). Tea 4zł. Coffee 5zł. Light entrees 12-19zł. Open daily June-Sept. 9am-midnight; Oct.-May 10am-10pm. AmEx/MC/V. ❷

Pierogarnia u Dzika, ul. Piwna 59/60. Locals swear by these *pierogi* (10 pieces; 12-18zł) stuffed with everything from soy to caviar. Open daily 10am-10pm. MC/V. ❷

Bar Pod Ryba, Długi Targ 35/38/1. Their limited menu specializes in stuffed baked potatoes overflowing with cheeses and meat. Entrees 6-20zł. Open daily July-Aug. 11am-10pm; Sept.-June 11am-7pm. AmEx/MC/V. ❶

Czerwone Drzwi, ul. Piwna 52. Elegant decor and a rotating menu with herring and Baltic salmon staples. Entrees 14-28zł. Open daily noon-11pm. AmEx/MC/V. ❸

Bar Mleczny Turystyczny, ul. Szeroka 8/10. If you look past the plastic furniture and burnt-orange trays at this old-fashioned milk bar, you'll find truly delicious Polish food for pocket change. *Gołąbki* (stuffed cabbage; 4.20zł), is among their meaty specialties. Entrees 3-6zł. Open M-F 8am-6pm, Sa-Su 9am-4pm. Cash only. ❶

SIGHTS

DŁUGI TARG. Długi Targ (long market) is the handsome square at the heart of **Główne Miasto** (main town). Gdańsk's row houses line the cobblestone ul. Mariacka, ul. Chlebnicka, and ul. Św. Ducha. The stone Upland Gate and the elegant blue-gray Golden Gate, emblazoned with gold leaf moldings and the shields of Poland, Prussia, and Germany, mark the entrance to ul. Długa. In the square proper, the **Fontanna Neptuna** (Neptune Fountain) faces the 16th-century facade of **Dwór Artusa** (Arthur's Court), a palace with a Renaissance interior and wood-carved spiral staircase that was restored in 1997. By the fountain, at the intersection of ul. Długa and Długi Targ, is the 14th-century **Ratusz** (town hall). It houses a branch of the **Gdańsk History Museum** (Muzeum Historii Gdańska) which covers city's past from its first historical mention to the rubble that overspread it after WWII. *(Court and museum open June-Sept. M 10am-3pm, Tu-Sa 10am-6pm, Su 11am-6pm; Oct.-May Tu-Sa 10am-4pm, Su 11am-4pm. Each branch 8zł, students 4zł; combined ticket 15/7zł. W free.)* A block toward the train station is the brick **Church of the Blessed Virgin Mary** (Kościół Najświętszej Marii Panny), which has an intricate 15th-century astronomical clock and panoramic view of the city. *(Open June-Aug. M-Sa 9am-5:30pm, Su 1-5:30pm; low-season reduced hours. 3zł, students 1.50zł.)*

ELSEWHERE IN GŁÓWNE MIASTO. In the vaults of a former Franciscan monastery, the **National Museum** (Muzeum Narodowe Gdańsku) has a large collection of 16th- to 20th-century art and furniture, including Hans Memling's *Last Judgement*. *(Ul. Toruńska 1, off Podwale Przedmiejskie. Open June to mid-Sept. Tu-F 9am-4pm, Sa-Su 10am-5pm; mid-Sept. to May Tu-Su 9am-4pm. 10zł, students 6zł. Sa free.)* The **Memorial to the Defenders of the Post Office Square** (Obrońców Poczty) honors the postal workers who bravely defended themselves on September 1, 1939, at the start of WWII. *(From Podwale Staromiejskie, go north on Olejarna and right at the sign for Urzad Poctowy Gdańsk 1. Open M and W-F 10am-4pm, Sa-Su 11am-4pm. 3zł, students 2zł.)* Cobblestone ul. Mariacka, lined with stone porches and gaping dragon-head gutter spouts, leads to riverside ul. Długie Pobrzeże. To the left is the huge **Gothic Harbor Crane** (Żuraw), part of **Central Maritime Museum** (Centralne Muzeum Morskie). Two more branches lie across the river: one on land, the other on the ship *Sołdek*. *(Open June-Aug. daily 10am-6pm; Sept.-May Tu-Su 9:30am-4pm. Crane 6zł, students 4zł. Museum 6/4zł. Sołdek 6/4zł. Shuttle boat round-trip 3/1.50zł. All museums and shuttle boat 14/8zł.)* The flags of Lech Wałęsa's trade union *Solidarność* (Solidarity), the Soviet bloc's first, fly again at the **Solidarity Monument,** pl. Solidarności, north of the center at the end of ul. Wały Piastowskie. At the **Roads to Freedom** *(Drogi do wolnisci)* exhibit in the Gdańsk Shipyard (Stocznia Gdańska), a moving multimedia epic shows the movement's rise. *(Ul. Doki 1. Open Tu-Su 10am-5pm. 6zł, students 4zł. W free.)*

vaguely familiar full-orchestra Hollywood movie themes, join the crowds flocking to the battlefield where a thousand knights kneel in prayer. An elaborately scripted and rehearsed exchange among cavalry, archers, and soldiers kicks off. The battle itself lasts about 50min., with emotional peaks and real casualties—though more frequently from drunken heatstroke than combat. Although the advances and retreats have been planned, soldier-to-soldier combat is very real—mediators police the fields, making sure that soldiers lay down "dead" when they have suffered would-be fatal blows. As the battle draws to an end, everyone recommences drinking, eating, and shopping.

Getting to Grunwald might seem daunting, but is quite easy, as transport systems brace themselves for overflow. From Gdańsk or Warsaw, make connections in nearby Olsztyn. Buses leave the Olsztyn PKS station every 25 min. 1hr. from the 2nd bus stop for Olsztynek (50min., 3.7zł). From Olsztynek, PKS buses as well as private shuttle services ferry the crowds to the battlefield (25min. 3-5.10zł). When the festivities come to an end, it is easy to find a ride directly back to Olsztyn from one of the PKS buses that line up in anticipation of the crowds to come (1½hr., 8.80zl).

WESTERPLATTE. When Germany attacked Poland on September 1, 1939, the little island fort guarding Gdańsk's harbor gained the unfortunate distinction of being the first target of WWII. Outnumbered 20 to one, its defenders held out bravely for a week until lack of food and munitions forced them out. **Guardhouse #1** has been converted into a museum. *(Take bus #106 or 606 south from the train station to the last stop. Open May-Sept. daily 9am-7pm. 3zł, students 2zł.)* Beyond the museum, a path passes bunker ruins and the **Memorial to the Defenders of the Coast** (Pomnik Obrońców Wybrzeża). Giant letters below spell "Nigdy Więcej Wojny" (No More War).

NIGHTLIFE

Długi Targ hums at night as crowds of all ages pack its pubs, clubs, and beer gardens. *City* magazine and *Gdańsk in Your Pocket* have the latest club listings. Toward the end of ul. Długa in the basement of the LOT building, **Latający Holender Pub,** ul. Waly Jagiellońskie 2/4, draws a lively crowd. (Beer 6zł. Coffee 4zł. Open daily noon-midnight.) Debaucherous, bohemian **Klub Punkt,** ul. Chlebnicka 2, stands apart from Gdańsk's tamer bars. (Beer 7zł. Open M-Th and Su 4pm-1am, F-Sa 4pm-3am.) The sleek and young flock to **Parlament,** ul. Św. Ducha 2, for Friday hip-hop and Saturday clubbing hits. (Beer 5zł. 18+. Cover Th after 10pm 5zł; F-Sa 10zł, 5zł with ISIC. Open Tu-Sa 8pm-late. Dance floor opens Th-Sa 10pm.)

POLAND

DAYTRIP FROM GDAŃSK

MALBORK. Malbork (pop. 40,000) is home to the largest brick **castle** in the world, built by the Teutonic Knights in the 14th century. Spectacular collections of amber and weaponry lie inside. Turn right out of the station onto ul. Dworcowa, then left at the fork. Go around the corner to the roundabout and cross to ul. Kościuszki, then veer right on ul. Piasłowska and follow the signs for the castle. (☎055 647 08 00. Open Tu-Su May-Sept. 9am-7pm; Oct.-Apr. 9am-3pm. Courtyards, terraces, and moats open Tu-Su May-Sept. 9am-8pm; Oct.-Apr. 9am-4pm. 6/4zł. Castle 30zł, students 17zł. Polish tour included.) Kiosks sell English-language booklets (7zł). Call ahead for English-language tour (150zł). Both **trains** (40-60min.; 40 per day; 9.30zł, express 32zł) and **buses** (1hr., 8 per day, 9.40-13zł) run from Gdańsk to Malbork.

SOPOT ☎058

Poland's premier resort town, magnetic Sopot (pop. 50,000), draws throngs of visitors to its sandy beaches and legendary nightlife. Restaurants, shops, and street musicians dot Sopot's graceful pedestrian promenade, **ulica Bohaterów Monte Cassino,** and the longest wooden pier in Europe rewards seaside amblers with spectacular Baltic views. (Beach M-F 2.50zł, Sa-Su 3.30zł.) **Soho clubogaleria,** ul. Monte Cassino 61, brandishes art and attitude at every turn, with jazz and alternative music playing during the week and full-throttle house and techno Friday and Saturday. (☎551 69 27. Beer 6.50zł. Open daily noon-5am.) Relive the communist era's wackiest moments at the cluttered **Remanent,** al. Niepodległości 786/2, at the base of ul. Monte Cassino. (☎888 33 44. Beer 5zł. Open daily 4pm-2am.) **Mandarynka,** ul. Bema 6, off ul. Monte Cassino, offers three floors of partying, with each floor bringing faster music and even faster drinking than the one below it. (☎550 45 63. Beer 6zł. Open M 1pm-late, Tu-Su noon-late.)

University dorms, which can be arranged through the tourist office, are affordable and available throughout the summer. **Hotel Wojskowy Dom Wypoczynkowy (WDW) ❶,** ul. Kilińskiego 12, off ul. Grunwaldzka, in the building marked "Meduza," offers the cheapest sea views in Sopot, well-kept bathrooms, TV, and tennis courts. (☎551 06 85. Breakfast included. Check-in 2pm. Check-out noon.

Book at least one month ahead July-Aug. Singles 120-175zł; doubles 220-260zł; triples 310-330zł; apartments 410zł. "Tourist Class" rooms without bath or breakfast 30zł. Oct.-May 10-15zł discount.) *Naleśniki* (filled pancakes) are serious business at **Parasolka ❶**, ul. Monte Cassino 31, where you can enjoy 50 different fillings in their garden seating area complete with avant-garde fountain. (☎550 46 44. Entrees 7-18zł. Open daily 10am-10pm. Cash only.) Local institution **Przystań ❶,** al. Wojska Polskiego 11, along the beach, serves seafood, grilled and fried, under fishing nets and hanging dried blowfish. (☎550 02 41; www.barprzystan.pl. Fresh fish 4.20-7zł per 100g. *Hevelius* 5zł. Open daily 11am-11pm. Cash only.) The **SKM commuter rail** connects Sopot to Gdańsk (20min.; 1-6 per hr.; 2.80zł, students 1.40zł). Ul. Dworcowa begins at the station and leads to ul. Bohaterów Monte Cassino, which runs along the sea to the 512m pier *(molo)*. **Ferries** (☎551 12 93) run from the end of the pier to Gdańsk (1hr.; 2 per day; round-trip 53zł, students 36zł) and Gdynia (35min., 2 per day, 39/22zł). IT **tourist office,** ul. Dworcowa 4, by the train station, sells maps (4-5zł) and arranges rooms. (☎550 37 83. Open daily June to mid-Sept. 10am-5pm; mid-Sept. to May M-F 10am-3pm.)

PORTUGAL

Once one of the world's most powerful empires, Portugal today has the unfortunate reputation of being little more than a beach town on the western coast of Spain. However, a look past the resorts swarming with British beach bunnies reveals an impressive capital, pristine wilderness, and rich artistic traditions. We could all stand to learn something from the Portuguese way of life: relax, and take in the beauty around you.

DISCOVER PORTUGAL: SUGGESTED ITINERARIES

THREE DAYS Make your way through **Lisbon's** (1 day; p. 825) famous Moorish district, the Alfama, up to the Castelo de São Jorge, and then to the Parque das Nações. By night, listen to *fado* and hit the clubs in Barrio Alto. Daytrip to **Sintra's** fairy-tale castles (p. 834) before sipping wine in **Porto** (1 day; p. 839).

ONE WEEK After wandering the streets of **Lisbon** (2 days) and **Sintra** (1 day), lounge on the beaches of **Lagos** (1 day; p. 836) and admire the windswept cliffs of **Sagres** (1 day; p. 838). From there, move to vibrant **Coimbra** (1 day; p. 834) before ending your week in **Porto** (1 day).

BEST OF PORTUGAL, TWO WEEKS After the sights, sounds, and cafes of **Lisbon** (3 days), daytrip to enchanting **Sintra** (1 day). Head down to the infamous beach-and-bar town **Lagos** (2 days), where hordes of visitors dance the night away. Head over to **Sagres** (1 day), once considered the edge of the world, then check out the macabre bone chapel in **Évora** (1 day; p. 836). Head north to the university town of **Coimbra** (2 days) and **Porto** (2 days), then finish your tour in the impressive squares of **Viana do Castelo** (1 day; p. 842).

PORTUGAL

ESSENTIALS

FACTS AND FIGURES

Official Name: Portuguese Republic.

Capital: Lisbon.

Major Cities: Coimbra, Porto.

Population: 10,566,212.

Land Area: 92,000 sq. km.

Time Zone: GMT.

Language: Portuguese.

Religion: Roman Catholic (94%).

Number of Grape Varieties Authorized for Making Port: 48.

WHEN TO GO

Summer is high season, but the southern coast draws tourists between March and November. While Lisbon and some of the larger towns burst with vitality year-round, many smaller towns virtually shut down in winter; sights reduce their hours, hotels slash their prices, and reservations are seldom necessary.

DOCUMENTS AND FORMALITIES

EMBASSIES AND CONSULATES. Most foreign embassies in Portugal are in Lisbon. For Portuguese embassies at home, contact: **Australia** and **New Zealand,** 23 Culgoa Circuit, O'Malley, ACT 2606; P.O. Box 9092, Deakin, ACT 2600 (☎612

6290 1733); **Canada,** 645 Island Park Dr., Ottawa, ON K1Y 0B8 (☎613-729-0883); **Ireland,** Knocksinna Mews, 7 Willow Park, Foxrock, Dublin 18 (☎01 289 4416); **UK,** 11 Belgrave Sq., London SWIX 8PP (☎020 7235 5331); **US,** 2125 Kalorama Rd. NW, Washington, D.C. 20008 (☎202-328-8610).

VISA AND ENTRY INFORMATION. EU citizens do not need a visa. Citizens of Australia, Canada, New Zealand, and the US do not need a visa for stays up to 90 days, beginning upon entry into any of the countries within the EU's freedom of movement zone. For more information, see p. 16.

TOURIST SERVICES AND MONEY

TOURIST OFFICES. The official tourism website is www.portugalinsite.pt. When in Portugal, stop by municipal and provincial tourist offices, listed in the **Practical Information** section of each city and town, for maps and advice.

EMERGENCY	Police, ambulance, fire: ☎112.

MONEY. The **euro (€)** has replaced the escudo as the unit of currency in Portugal. For more information, see p. 21. As a general rule it's cheaper to exchange money in Portugal than at home. **ATMs** offer the best exhange rates. Expect to spend €40-60 per day. **Tips** of 5-10% are customary only in fancy restaurants or hotels. Some cheaper restaurants include a 10% service charge; if they don't and you'd like to leave a tip, round up and leave the change. Taxi drivers do not expect a tip unless the trip was especially long. Retail goods in Portugal bear a 19% **Value Added Tax (VAT),** usually included in the listed price. In the airport, upon departure, non-EU citizens who have stayed in the EU fewer than 180 days can claim a refund on the tax paid for purchases at participating stores. Ask the shop where you have made the purchase to supply you with a tax return form, but note that stores will often provide them only for purchases of more than €50-100. **Bargaining** is not customary in shops, but you can give it a shot at the local market *(mercado)* or when looking for a private room *(quarto)*.

TRANSPORTATION

BY PLANE. Most major international airlines fly to Lisbon (LIS; ☎218 494 323); some also go to Faro (FAO; ☎289 818 582) and Porto (OPO; 229 412 534). **TAP Air Portugal** (US and Canada ☎800-221-7370, UK 845 601 09 32, Lisbon 707 20 57 00; www.tap.pt) is Portugal's national airline, serving all domestic locations and many international cities. **Portugália** (☎218 93 80 49; www.flypga.pt) is a smaller airline that flies between Faro, Lisbon, Porto, major Spanish cities, and other Western European destinations. For more information on European air travel, see p. 48.

BY TRAIN. Caminhos de Ferro Portugueses (☎808 21 57 00; www.cp.pt) is Portugal's national railway, serving Paris, Madrid, and domestic destinations. For long-distance travel outside the Braga-Porto-Coimbra-Lisbon line, however, the bus is better. The exception is around Lisbon, where local trains are fast and efficient. Trains often leave at irregular hours, and posted schedules *(horários)* aren't always accurate; check station ticket booths upon arrival. Fines for riding without a ticket *(sem bilhete)* are exorbitant. **Youth discounts** are only available to Portuguese citizens. The Portugal Flexipass is not worth buying. For more information on getting to Portugal, see p. 53.

BY BUS. Buses are cheap, frequent, and connect to just about every town in Portugal. **Rodoviária** (☎212 94 71 00), the national bus company, has recently been privatized. Each company name corresponds to a particular region of the country, such as Rodoviária Alentejo or Minho e Douro, with a few exceptions such as EVA in the Algarve. Private regional companies also operate, including **AVIC, Cabanelas,** and **Mafrense.** Beware of non-express buses in small regions like Estremadura and Alentejo, which stop every few minutes. Express coach service *(expressos)* between major cities is especially good, and cheap city buses often run to nearby villages. Portugal's main **Euroline** (p. 60) affiliates are Internorte, Intercentro, and Intersul. **Busabout** coaches stop in Portugal at Lisbon, Lagos, and Porto. Every coach has a guide onboard to answer questions and make travel arrangements.

BY CAR. Portugal has the highest rate of automobile accidents per capita in Western Europe. The new highway system *(itinerarios principais)* is quite good, but off the main arteries, the narrow roads are difficult to negotiate. Speed limits are ignored, recklessness is common, and lighting and road surfaces are often inadequate. In short, buses are safer. Moreover, parking space in cities is nonexistent. Portugal's national automobile association, the **Automóvel Clube de Portugal (ACP),** Shopping Center Amoreiras, Loja 1122 Lisbon (☎213 71 47 20), provides **breakdown** and **towing service** and **first-aid.**

BY THUMB. In Portugal, **hitchhiking** is rare. Beachbound locals occasionally hitchhike in summer, but otherwise stick to the inexpensive bus system. Rides are easiest to come by between smaller towns and at gas stations near highways and rest stops. *Let's Go* does not recommend hitchhiking.

KEEPING IN TOUCH

PHONE CODES	**Country code:** 351. **International dialing prefix:** 00. Within Portugal, dial city code + local number. For more information on how to place international calls, see inside back cover.

EMAIL AND THE INTERNET. Cybercafes, listed in cities and most towns, charge around €1.20-4 per hour for Internet access. When in doubt, try the library, where there is often at least one computer equipped for (often free) Internet access.

TELEPHONE. Portugal's national telephone company is **Portugal Telecom.** Pay phones use the **Credifone** and **Portugal Telecom** systems. For both systems, the basic unit for all calls (and the price for local ones) is €0.10. Telecom phone cards, using "patch" chips, are most common in Lisbon and Porto and increasingly elsewhere. Credifone cards with magnetic strips are most useful outside these two big cities. Find them at drugstores, post offices, and locations posted on phone booths. City codes all begin with a 2; local calls do not require dialing the city code. For directory assistance dial ☎118. **Calling cards** are probably the best method of making international calls. For information on using **mobile phones** in Portugal, see p. 33.

MAIL. Mail in Portugal is somewhat inefficient—**airmail** *(via aerea)* takes at least one to two weeks to reach the US or Canada. It is slightly quicker for Europe and longer for Australia and New Zealand. **Surface mail** *(superficie)*, for packages only, takes up to two months. **Registered** or **blue mail** takes five to eight business days for roughly three times the price of airmail. **EMS** or **Express Mail** will probably get there in three to four days for more than double the blue mail price. Mail to be held should be addressed as follows: SURNAME, First Name; Posta Restante; Post Office Street Address; City; Postal Code; PORTUGAL; PAR AVION.

LANGUAGE. Portuguese is the official language of Portugal. Although many residents, especially in heavily touristed areas, speak English or French, the Portuguese appreciate it when travelers try to speak at least a few phrases of their language. As your mother always told you, please *(por favor)* and thank you *(obrigado/a)* are especially important. Be aware that the sounds of Brazilian and continental Portuguese are quite different, due to variations in pronunciation and vocabulary. For some helpful Portuguese phrases, see p. 1065.

ACCOMMODATIONS AND CAMPING

PORTUGAL	❶	❷	❸	❹	❺
ACCOMMODATIONS	under €16	€16-20	€20-30	€30-40	over €40

Movijovem, R. Lúcio de Azevedo 27, 1600-146 Lisbon (☎707 20 30 30; www.pousadasjuventude.pt), the Portuguese Hostelling International affiliate, oversees the country's HI hostels and handles bookings. A bed in a *pousada da juventude* (not to be confused with plush *pousadas*) costs €9-15 per night, slightly less in the low season, including breakfast and linen. Though often the cheapest option, hostels may be far from the town center. To reserve a bed in high season, obtain an **International Booking Voucher** from Movijovem (or your country's HI affiliate) and send it to the desired hostel four to eight weeks ahead. In low season (Oct.-Apr.), double-check that the hostel is open. **Hotels** in Portugal are pricey. Fees typically include breakfast and showers, and most rooms without bath or shower have a sink. When business is slow, try bargaining—the "official price" is just the maximum allowed. **Pensões,** or **residencias,** are a budget traveler's mainstay. Far cheaper than hotels, they are less crowded than youth hostels and still provide sheets and towels. For the few *pensões* that do take reservations, booking a week ahead in high season is advisable. **Quartos** are rooms in private residences, similar to Spain's *casas particulares*. These rooms may be the only option in smaller towns or the cheapest one in bigger cities; tourist offices can help you find one. Prices are flexible and bargaining expected. Portugal has over 150 **official campgrounds** *(parques de campismo)*, often with supermarkets and cafes. Urban and coastal parks may require reservations. Police are cracking down on illegal camping, so don't try it. Tourist offices stock *Portugal: Camping and Caravan Sites*, a free guide to campgrounds. Otherwise, write the **Federação de Campismo e Montanhismo de Portugal,** Av. Coronel Eduardo Galhardo 24D, 1199-007 Lisbon (☎218 12 68 90; www.fcmportugal.com).

FOOD AND DRINK

PORTUGAL	❶	❷	❸	❹	❺
FOOD	under €6	€6-10	€10-15	€15-20	over €20

Portuguese dishes are seasoned with olive oil, garlic, herbs, and sea salt, but few spices. The fish selection includes *choco grelhado* (grilled cuttlefish), *linguado grelhado* (grilled sole), and *peixe espada* (swordfish). Portugal's renowned cheeses *(queijos)* are made from the milk of cows, goats, and ewes. For dessert, try *pudim*, or *flan* (caramel custard). A hearty lunch *(almoço)* is eaten between noon and 2pm; dinner *(jantar)* is served between 8pm and midnight. *Meia dose* (half-portions) cost more than half-price but are often more than adequate; full portions may satisfy two. The special of the day *(prato do dia)* and the set *menú (ementa)* of appetizer, bread, entree, and dessert are also filling choices. Standard pre-meal bread, butter, cheese, and pâté may be served without your asking, but these pre-meal munchies are not free (€1-3 per person). Since chefs start cooking only after you order, you may be grateful for these appetizers. It may not be an international star, but the cheap, high quality Portuguese wine *(vinho)* is astounding. The pinnacle, *vinho do porto* (port), is a dessert in itself. Coffees include *bica* (black espresso), *galão* (with milk, in a glass), and *café com leite* (with milk, in a cup).

NO SUCH THING AS A FREE LUNCH. Waiters in Portugal will put an assortment of snacks, ranging from simple bread and butter to sardine paste, cured ham, or herbed olives, on your table before the appetizer is served. But check the menu for the prices before you dig in: you nibble it, you bought it.

PORTUGAL

HOLIDAYS AND FESTIVALS

Holidays: New Year's Day (Jan. 1); Good Friday (Apr. 14); Easter (Apr. 16); Liberation Day (Apr. 25); Labor Day (May 1); Corpus Christi (June 15); Portugal Day (June 10); Feast of the Assumption (Aug. 15); Republic Day (Oct. 5); All Saints' Day (Nov. 1); Restoration of Independence Day (Dec. 1); Feast of the Immaculate Conception (Dec. 8).

Festivals: All of Portugal celebrates *Carnaval* (Feb. 28) and Holy Week (Apr. 9-16). Coimbra holds the *Queima das Fitas* (Burning of the Ribbons) festival in early May, celebrating the end of the school year. In June, Lisbon hosts the *Festas da Cidade,* honoring the birth of St. Anthony with music, games, and parades. For more information on Portuguese festivals, see www.portugal.org.

BEYOND TOURISM

As a **volunteer** in Portugal, you can contribute to efforts concerning environmental protection, social welfare, or political activism. While not many students think of **studying** abroad in Portugal, most Portuguese universities open their gates to foreign students. Being an au pair and teaching English are popular options for long-term **work,** though many people choose to seek more casual—and often illegal—jobs in resort areas. *Let's Go* does not recommend any type of illegal employment.

Grupo de Acção e Intervenção Ambiental (GAIA), Faculdade de Ciências e Tecnologia, 2829-516 Caparica (☎212 94 96 50; www.gaia.org.pt). Works to educate the Portuguese public about environmental issues and campaigns against the production and sale of genetically modified food.

Teach Abroad (www.teach.studyabroad.com). Brings you to listings around the world for paid or stipend positions to teach English.

Universidade de Lisboa, Rectorate Al. da Universidade, Cidade Universitária, 1649-004 Lisbon (☎217 96 76 24; www.ul.pt). Allows foreign students to enroll directly.

LISBON (LISBOA)

☎21

A rare combination of glorious history and bittersweet memory awaits in Lisbon (pop. 2,500,000), where a sense of *saudade* (nostalgia) permeates everyday life. Travelers hear it in the traditional *fado* music, drink it in the celebrated wines, and, above all, see it in local faces. Such is the glory of Lisbon—it can fill you with wonder and break your heart all at once.

TRANSPORTATION

Flights: Aeroporto de Lisboa (LIS; ☎841 3500). From the terminal, turn right and follow the path to the bus stop. Take the express AeroBus #91 (15min., every 20min., €1) to Pr. dos Restauradores, in front of the tourist office, or take bus #44 or 45 to the same location (20min., every 12-15min., €1.20). A taxi from downtown costs €10 plus a €1.50 baggage fee. Trips are billed by time. Ask at the tourist office (☎845 0660) inside the airport about buying prepaid vouchers for taxi rides from the airport (M-F €14, Sa-Su €17. Open daily 7am-midnight). Major airlines have offices at Pr. Marquês do Pombal and along Av. da Liberdade.

Trains: Caminhos de Ferro Portugueses (☎808 20 82 08; www.cp.pt). Individual stations do not have phone numbers; use the main number above. 5 main stations, each serving different destinations. Trains in Portugal–slow, inconsistent, and confusing–are the bane of every traveler's existence; buses, though more expensive and without toilet, are faster and more comfortable.

Estação do Barreiro, across the Rio Tejo. Serves southern destinations. Ferries to the station leave from the Terreiro do Paço dock off Pr. do Comércio. (Ferry ride 30min., every 30min., €1.35.) To: **Évora** and **Lagos,** take train to **Pinhal Novo** (25min., every 20-60min.,€1.30) and transfer. From: Pinhal Novo to **Évora** (1½hr., 2 per day, €7). From Pinhal Novo to **Lagos** (3½hr., 2 per day, €17).

Estação Cais do Sodré, just beyond R. do Alecrim, near Baixa. M: Cais do Sodré. Take the metro or bus #1, 44, or 45 from Pr. dos Restauradores or bus #28 from Estação Santa Apolónia. To: the monastery in **Belém** (10min., every 15min., €1); **Cascais** and **Estoril** (30min., every 15min., €1.30); the youth hostel in **Oeiras** (20min., every 15min., €1.30).

Estação Rossio, M: Rossio or Restauradores. Serves western destinations. Estação Rossio is closed until June 2006 due to tunnel construction. To reach its destinations, **Sintra** and **Queluz,** take the metro to another train station or travel directly by bus.

Estação Santa Apolónia, Av. Infante Dom Henrique, runs the international, northern, and eastern lines. All trains to Santa Apolónia also stop at **Estação Oriente** (M: Oriente) by the Parque des Nações. The international terminal has currency exchange and an info desk (English spoken). To reach downtown, take bus #9, 39, 46, or 90 to Pr. dos Restauradores. To: **Aveiro** (3-3½hr., 15 per day, €21.50); **Braga** (5hr., 3 per day, €27); **Coimbra** (2½hr., 16 per day, €18.50); **Madrid, Spain** (10hr., 10:05pm, €54); **Porto** (4½hr., 20 per day, €24.50).

Buses: The bus station is at M: Jardim Zoológico. In the metro station, follow exit signs to Av. C. Bordalo Pinheiro, cross the street, and follow the path up the stairs. Look for signs saying "autocarros." **Rede Expressos** buses (☎707 22 33 44; www.rede-expressos.pt) go to: **Braga** (5hr., 13 per day, €14.50); **Coimbra** (2½hr., 25 per day, €9.50); **Évora** (2hr., 20 per day, €9.80); **Faro** (5hr., 16 per day, €15); **Lagos** (5hr., 16 per day, €15); **Porto** (4hr., 19 per day, €13.50) via **Leiria** (2hr., €8).

Public Transportation: CARRIS (☎361 3000; www.carris.pt) runs **buses, trams,** and **funiculars** (each €1.20). If you plan to stay in Lisbon for any length of time, consider a *passe turístico,* good for unlimited travel on all CARRIS transports. 1-, 5-, and 30-day passes are sold in CARRIS booths located in most network train stations and busier metro stations. (Open daily 8am-9pm. €3.50/12.60/26.65.) The 4 lines of the **metro** (☎355 8457; www.metrolisboa.pt) cover downtown and the modern business district. Single ride €0.70; unlimited daily use ticket €3.50; book of 10 tickets €6.15. Trains run daily 6:30am-1am, though some stations close earlier.

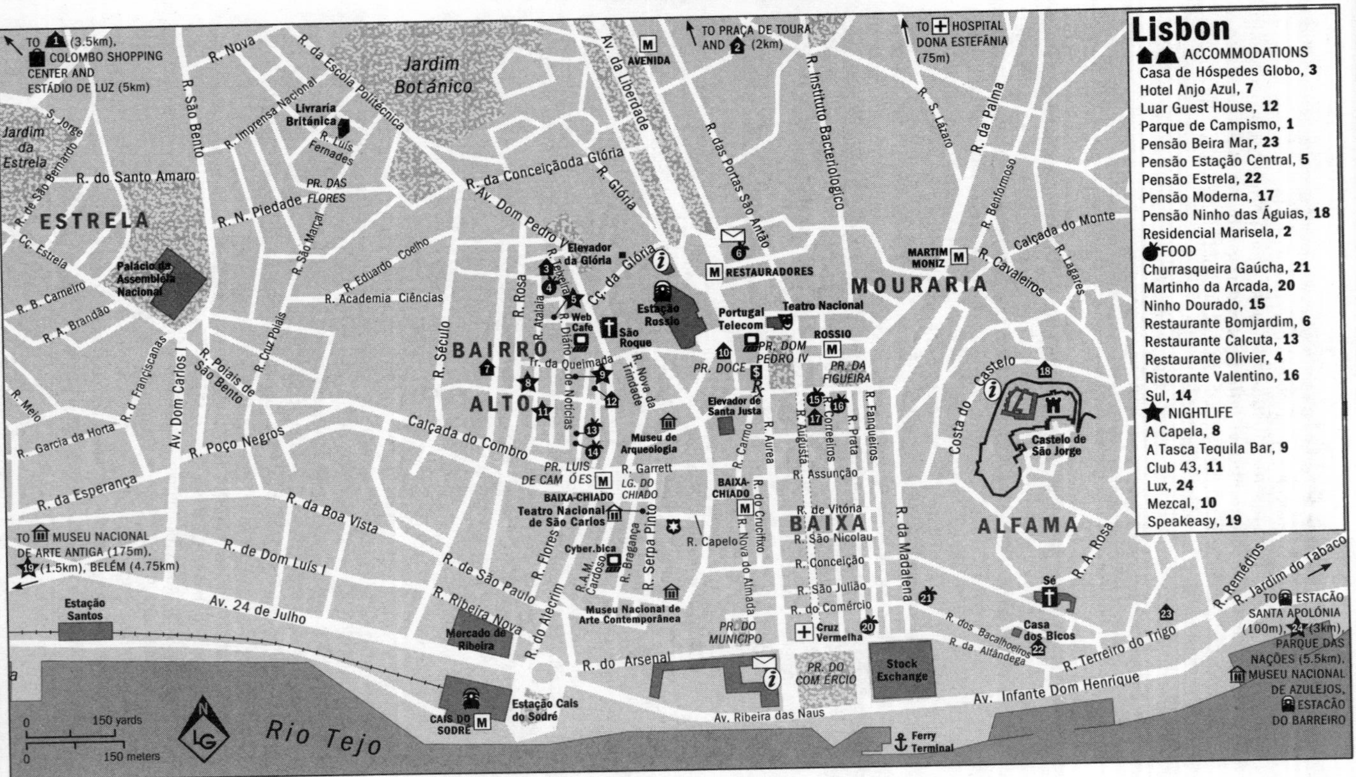
Lisbon
ACCOMMODATIONS
Casa de Hóspedes Globo, 3
Hotel Anjo Azul, 7
Luar Guest House, 12
Parque de Campismo, 1
Pensão Beira Mar, 23
Pensão Estação Central, 5
Pensão Estrela, 22
Pensão Moderna, 17
Pensão Ninho das Águias, 18
Residencial Marisela, 2
FOOD
Churrasqueira Gaúcha, 21
Martinho da Arcada, 20
Ninho Dourado, 15
Restaurante Bomjardim, 6
Restaurante Calcuta, 13
Restaurante Olivier, 4
Ristorante Valentino, 16
Sul, 14
NIGHTLIFE
A Capela, 8
A Tasca Tequila Bar, 9
Club 43, 11
Lux, 24
Mezcal, 10
Speakeasy, 19
TO 1 (3.5km), COLOMBO SHOPPING CENTER AND ESTÁDIO DE LUZ (5km)
TO PRAÇA DE TOURA AND 2 (2km)
TO HOSPITAL DONA ESTEFÂNIA (75m)
TO MUSEU NACIONAL DE ARTE ANTIGA (175m), 19 (1.5km), BELÉM (4.75km)
TO ESTAÇÃO SANTA APOLÓNIA (100m), 24 (3km), PARQUE DAS NAÇÕES (5.5km), MUSEU NACIONAL DE AZULEJOS, ESTAÇÃO DO BARREIRO
Jardim Botánico
Jardim da Estrela
ESTRELA
BAIRRO ALTO
MOURARIA
BAIXA
ALFAMA
Palácio da Assembleia Nacional
Livraria Británica
Elevador da Glória
Web Cafe
São Roque
Estação Rossio
Portugal Telecom
Teatro Nacional
RESTAURADORES
ROSSIO
AVENIDA
MARTIM MONIZ
BAIXA-CHIADO
CAIS DO SODRÉ
Elevador de Santa Justa
Museu de Arqueologia
Teatro Nacional de São Carlos
Cyber.bica
Museu Nacional de Arte Contemporânea
Cruz Vermelha
Stock Exchange
Castelo de São Jorge
Sé
Casa dos Bicos
Estação Santos
Mercado de Ribeira
Estação Cais do Sodré
Ferry Terminal
PR. DAS FLORES
PR. DOM PEDRO IV
PR. DA FIGUEIRA
PR. DOCE
PR. LUIS DE CAM ÕES
LG. DO CHIADO
PR. DO MUNICÍPIO
PR. DO COM ÉRCIO
R. Nova
R. da Escola Politécnica
R. São Bento
R. Imprensa Nacional
R. Luís Fernades
S. Jorge
R. de São Bernardo
R. do Santo Amaro
R. N. Piedade
R. São Marçal
Cç. Estrela
R. B. Carneiro
R. A. Brandão
R. Eduardo Coelho
R. Academia Ciências
R. Cruz Poiais
R. Poiais de São Bento
R. d. Franciscanas
Av. Dom Carlos I
R. Melo
R. Garcia da Horta
R. Poço Negros
R. da Esperança
R. da Boa Vista
R. de Dom Luís I
R. de São Paulo
R. Ribeira Nova
Av. 24 de Julho
R. do Alecrim
R. Flores
R. do Arsenal
Av. Ribeira das Naus
Av. Infante Dom Henrique
R. da Conceiçãoda Glória
Av. Dom Pedro V
R. Glória
Av. da Liberdade
R. das Portas São Antão
R. Instituto Bacteriológico
R. S. Lázaro
R. da Palma
R. Benformoso
Calçada do Monte
R. Lagares
R. Cavaleiros
Cç. da Glória
R. Teixeira
R. Rosa
R. Atalaia
R. Século
R. Diário de Notícias
Tr. da Queimada
R. Nova da Trindade
Calçada do Combro
R. Garrett
R. Carmo
R. Aurea
R. Augusta
R. Correeiros
R. Prata
R. Fanqueiros
R. Assunção
R. de Vitória
R. São Nicolau
R. Conceição
R. São Julião
R. do Comércio
R. do Crucifixo
R. Nova do Almada
R. Capelo
R. Serpa Pinto
R. Bragança
R.A.M. Cardoso
R. da Madalena
Costa do Castelo
R. A. Rosa
R. Remédios
R. Jardim do Tabaco
R. dos Bacalhoeiros
R. da Alfândega
R. Terreiro do Trigo
Rio Tejo
150 yards
150 meters

Taxis: Rádio Táxis de Lisboa (☎811 9000), **Autocoope** (☎793 2756), and **Teletáxis** (☎811 1100). Along Av. da Liberdade and Rossio. Luggage €1.50.

ORIENTATION AND PRACTICAL INFORMATION

The city center is made up of three neighborhoods: **Baixa** (low district), **Bairro Alto** (high district), and hilly **Alfama.** The suburbs extending in both directions along the river are some of the fastest-growing areas and are interesting for their contrast with the historic districts. Other places of interest several kilometers from downtown include **Belém** (p. 831), a walk into Portugal's past, **Alcântara,** whose docks are home to much of Lisbon's party scene, and the **Parque das Nações,** site of the 1998 World Expo. Baixa's grid of pedestrian streets is bordered to the north by **Rossio** (a.k.a. Praça Dom Pedro IV) and to the south by **Praça do Comércio,** on the Rio Tejo. East of Baixa is Alfama, Lisbon's oldest, labyrinthine district, and west of Baixa is Bairro Alto with its upscale shopping district, the **Chiado,** crossed by R. do Carmo and R. Garrett. **Avenida da Liberdade** runs north from Pr. dos Restauradores.

Tourist Office: Palácio da Foz, Pr. dos Restauradores (☎346 3314). M: Restauradores. The largest office, open daily 9am-8pm. The **Welcome Center,** Pr. do Comércio (☎031 2810) is the city's main office. It sells the Lisboa Card, which includes transportation and entrance to most sights (1-, 2-, and 3-day €13.50/23/28). English spoken. Open daily 9am-8pm. Kiosks at Santa Apolónia, Belém, and elsewhere provide tourist info.

Currency Exchange: Banks are open M-F 8:30am-3pm. **Cota Câmbios,** Pr. Dom Pedro IV 41 (☎322 0480), exchanges currency. Open daily 9am-8pm. The main post office, most banks, and travel agencies also change money.

Emergency: ☎112.

Police: R. Capelo 13 (☎346 6141 or 342 1634). English spoken.

Late-Night Pharmacy: Look for the green cross at every intersection, or try **Farmácia Azevedos,** Pr. Dom Pedro IV 31 (☎343 0482), at the base of Rossio in front of the metro.

Hospital: Hospital de Saint Louis, R. Luz Soriano 182 (☎321 6500), Bairro Alto. Open daily 9am-6pm.

Internet Access: Web C@fé, R. Diário de Notícias 126 (☎342 1181). €3 per hr. Open daily 4pm-2am. **Cyber.bica,** R. Duques de Bragança 7 (☎322 5004), in Bairro Alto. €3 per hr. Open M-Sa 11am-midnight.

Post Office: Main office Ctt Correios, Pr. dos Restauradores (☎323 8700). Open M-F 8am-10pm, Sa-Su 9am-7pm. Often crowded. Branch at Pr. do Comércio (☎322 0920). Open M-F 8:30am-6:30pm. Cash only. Central Lisbon **Postal Code:** 1100.

ACCOMMODATIONS

Hotels cluster in the center of town on **Avenida da Liberdade,** while many convenient budget hostels are in **Baixa** along the **Rossio** and on **Rua da Prata, Rua dos Correeiros,** and **Rua do Ouro.** Lodgings near the **Castelo de São Jorge** are quieter and closer to the sights. If central accommodations are full, head east to the hostels along **Avenida Almirante dos Reis.** At night, be careful in Baixa, Bairro Alto, and especially Graça; many streets are isolated and poorly lit.

BAIRRO ALTO

Hotel Anjo Azul, R. Luz Soriano 75 (☎213 47 80 69; www.anjoazul.com). Caters to gay travelers, but accepts all sexual preferences. Laundry €10 for 6kg. Internet €2 per hr. Check-out 11:30am. Singles €20; doubles €25-35; triples €45-50. AmEx/MC/V. ❷

Casa de Hóspedes Globo, R. Teixeira 37 (☎346 2279), across from the Parque São Pedro de Alcântara. Popular with young travelers. All rooms with phone and TV. Laundry €10 for 6kg. Internet €2 per hr. Singles €15, with bath €22.50; doubles €25/30; triples with bath €40; quads with bath €50; quints with bath €55. ❷

PORTUGAL

Luar Guest House, R. das Gáveas 101 (☎346 0949). Simple, clean rooms far enough away from the nightlife to ensure a good night's sleep. Rooms on the R. das Gáveas can smell like the fish shops below. Check-in noon. Check-out 11:30am. Singles €20; doubles €35; triples €45; quads €60. ❷

BAIXA

Pensão Moderna, Rua dos Correeiros 205, 4th fl. (☎346 0818). M: Rossio. Family-owned hostel has big rooms full of furniture. Shared bathrooms. Singles €15; doubles €25; triples €35; quads €45. Low season reduced prices. Cash only. ❶

Pensão Estação Central, Calçada da Carmo 17, 2nd-3rd fl. (☎342 3308). M: Rossio. Small, plain rooms with little more than a bed and bath are inexpensive and centrally located overlooking the downtown streets. Singles have shared bath. Singles €20; doubles €35; triples €45. Low-season prices €5 fewer. Cash only. ❷

ALFAMA

Pensão Ninho das Águias, Costa do Castelo 74 (☎885 4070), behind the Castelo. Spectacular terrace and garden looks out over the old city. Singles €30; doubles €45, with bath €50; triples €60. Low-season prices €5-10 fewer. Cash only. ❷

Pensão Beira Mar, R. Terreiro do Trigo 16 (☎887 1528). Likely the cheapest option in Alfama for solo travelers. Rooms with river views are €5-10 more. Singles €15-20; doubles €30-40; quads €60. Low season €10-15/20-30/40, if you bargain. Cash only. ❶

Pensão Estrela, R. dos Bacalhoeiros 8 (☎886 9506), in the lower part of Alfama. Basic rooms look out on the square below. Check-out 11am. Singles €20-25; doubles €35; 1 triple €53. Low season €15/30-35/45. Cash only. ❷

PORTUGAL

ELSEWHERE AND CAMPING

Residencial Marisela, R. Filipe Folque 19 (☎353 3205, ext. 62 or 316 0423, ext. 4; www.residencialmarisela.pt). M: Picoas. Atypical large rooms and dorm-style beds. Dorms €10; doubles with bath €40. Low season €5/35. MC/V. ❶

Parque de Campismo Municipal de Lisboa (☎760 9620), on the road to Benfica. Take bus #14 to Parque Florestal Monsanto; campsite is at entrance to park. Pool and supermarket. Reception daily 9am-9pm. High-season tent sites €4.80, €4.80 per person, €3.10 per car. Low-season prices are slightly lower. ❶

FOOD

Lisbon has some of the best wine and cheapest restaurants of any European capital. Dinner costs about €12 per person; the *prato do dia* (daily special) is often only €6. Head to the **Calçada de Santa Ana** and **Rua dos Correeiros** to find small restaurants that cater to locals. Snack on surprisingly filling and incredibly cheap Portuguese pastries; *pastelarias* are everywhere. For groceries, look for any **Pingo Doce** supermarket. (Most open M-Sa 8:30am-9pm.)

BAIRRO ALTO

Restaurante Olivier, R. do Teixeira 35 (☎342 1024; www.hed-web.com/olivier). Next to Casa de Hóspedes Globo. The set menu of excellent French food includes 10 (yes 10!) different appetizers followed by a main course (€28). Reservations recommended. M-Sa 8pm-2am. MC/V. ❸

Restaurante Calcuta, R. do Norte 17 (☎342 8295), near Lg. Camões. Indian restaurant in a soothing setting with wide selection of vegetarian entrees (€5.50-6). Meat entrees €6.50-9. Open M-F noon-3pm and 7-11pm, Sa-Su 7-11pm. AmEx/MC/V. ❷

Sul, R. do Norte 13 (☎346 2449). Romantic decor and candlelight. Comes alive when it turns into a bar after 10pm. Entrees €12-16. Open Tu-Su noon-2am. Cash only. ❸

BAIXA AND ALFAMA

Churrasqueira Gaúcha, R. dos Bacalhoeiros 26C-D (☎887 0609), 1 block from the river toward Alfama, near Pr. do Comércio. Incredibly fresh Argentine-style *churrasco* (grilled meat) in large quantity. Entrees €5-12. Open M-Sa 9am-midnight. AmEx/MC/V. ❷

Ristorante Valentino, R. Jardim do Regedor 45 (☎213 46 17 27). Ristorante Valentino offers quality Italian food with a touch of elegance and charm. Watch your pizza cook over the open flames in the brick oven. Entrees €7-17. Pizzas €3-10. AmEx/MC/V. ❷

Martinho da Arcada, Pr. do Comércio 3 (☎887 9259). Lisbon's oldest restaurant and a famed haunt of poet Fernando Pessoa. Entrees €15-32. Open M-Sa noon-3pm and 7-10:30pm. AmEx/MC/V. ❹

Ninho Dourado, R. Augusta 278. Pleasant outdoor seating, a huge menu, and decent prices make Ninho Dourado perfect for a dinner at sunset. Sandwiches €3-4. Pizza €7.50. Entrees €8. Open daily 8am-midnight. Cash only. ❷

Restaurante Bomjardim, Tv. Santo Antão 12 (☎342 4389), off Pr. dos Restauradores. This self-proclaimed *rei da brasa* (king of the grill) satiates customers with savory grilled meats (€8-11). Open daily noon-11:30pm. AmEx/MC/V. ❷

SIGHTS

BAIXA

Though Baixa has few historic sights, the lively atmosphere and dramatic history of the neighborhood make it a monument in its own right.

AROUND THE ROSSIO. Begin in the heart of Lisbon, the Rossio (also known as Pr. Dom Pedro IV). Once a cattle market, the site of public executions, a bullring, and carnival ground, the *praça* is now the domain of tourists and ruthless local motorists who circle a statue of Dom Pedro IV. A statue of Gil Vicente, Portugal's first great dramatist, peers from the top of the **Teatro Nacional de Dona Maria II** (easily recognized by its large columns) at one end of the *praça*. Adjoining the Rossio is the elegant **Praça da Figueira,** on the border of Alfama.

AROUND PRAÇA DOS RESTAURADORES. Just past the Rossio train station, an obelisk and a bronze sculpture of the "Spirit of Independence" commemorate Portugal's independence from Spain in 1640. Numerous shops line the *praça* and C. da Glória—the hill that leads to Bairro Alto. Pr. dos Restauradores also begins **Avenida da Liberdade,** Lisbon's most elegant promenade. Modeled after the wide boulevards of 19th-century Paris, this shady thoroughfare ends at **Praça do Marquês de Pombal** where an 18th-century statue of the Marquês overlooks the city.

BAIRRO ALTO

In the Bairro Alto, the only place in Lisbon that never sleeps, pretentious intellectuals mix with teens and idealistic university students. At the center of the neighborhood is **Praça Luís de Camões,** which adjoins **Largo do Chiado** at the top of R. Garrett, a good place to rest and orient yourself while sightseeing. To reach R. Garrett from the Rossio, take R. do Carmo uphill; it's the first street on the right.

BASÍLICA DA ESTRELA. Directly across from the Jardim da Estrela, the Basílica da Estrela dates back to 1796 Its dome, behind a pair of belfries, towers over surrounding buildings to take its place in the Lisbon skyline. Half-mad Dona Maria I, desiring a male heir, promised God anything and everything if she were granted a son. When a baby boy was finally born, she built this church, and admirers of beautiful architecture and ornate decor have been grateful ever since. Ask to see the 10th-century nativity. *(Pr. da Estrela. Accessible by metro or tram #28 from Pr. do Comércio. ☎396 0915. Open daily 7:30am-1pm and 3-8pm. Free.)*

MUSEU DO CHIADO. The Museu do Chiado's collection mostly features pieces by Portugal's most famous post-1850 artists, juxtaposing fascist-era works with those of democratic Portugal. The museum also showcases 19th- and 20th-century French art and exhibits on famous contemporary artists. *(R. Serpa Pinto 4. ☎343 2148. Open Tu 2-6pm, W-Su 10am-6pm. €3; students and teachers €1.50. Su before 2pm free.)*

ALFAMA

Alfama, Lisbon's medieval quarter, was the only neighborhood to survive the infamous 1755 earthquake. This labyrinth of *escandinhas* (narrow stairways), alleys, and unmarked streets is a challenge to navigate; be especially wary after nightfall. Visitors can hop on tram #28 from Pr. do Comércio (€1.20), which winds past most of the neighborhood's sights.

CASTELO DE SÃO JORGE. At the end of a winding uphill walk lies the Castelo de São Jorge, which offers spectacular views of Lisbon and the ocean. Built by the Visigoths in the 5th century and enlarged by the Moors in the 9th, the castle was again improved and converted into a playground for the royal family between the 14th and 16th centuries. Today, a village bustles within its walls. Wander around the ruins, soak in the views, explore the ponds, or gawk at the exotic birds in the gardens. The castle also includes a string of souvenir shops and restaurants. *(☎880 0620; www.egeac.pt. Open daily Mar.-Oct. 9am-9pm; Nov.-Feb. 9am-6pm. €3, students €1.50.)*

PORTUGAL

THE LOWER ALFAMA. R. da Alfândeo, beginning two blocks away from Pr. do Comércio, connects Baixa and lower Alfama. Veer right when you see **Igreja da Madalena** in Lg. da Madalena on the right. Take R. de Santo António da Sé and follow the tram tracks to the small **Igreja de Santo António,** built in 1812 over the beloved saint's alleged birthplace. Construction was funded with money collected by the city's children, who built miniature altars bearing saintly images to place on doorsteps. This custom is reenacted every June 13, the saint's feast day and Lisbon's largest holiday. *(☎886 9145. Open daily 8am-7pm. Mass daily 11am, 5, 7pm.)* In the square beyond the church is the **Sé de Lisboa,** with its relic-filled treasury. *(☎886 6752. Church open daily 9am-7pm except during mass. Mass Tu-Sa 6:30pm, Su 11:30am and 7pm. Treasury open M-Sa 10am-5pm. Church free. Treasury €2.50, students €1.50.)*

GRAÇA

PANTEÃO NACIONAL. The massive building that is now the Panteão Nacional (National Pantheon) was originally meant to be the Igreja da Santa Engrácia. The citizens of Graça started building the church in 1680 to honor their patron saint, but their ambitions soon outstripped their finances and the building project was abandoned. Salazar's military regime eventually took over construction, completing the project and dedicating it in 1966 as the Panteão Nacional, a burial ground for important statesmen. Ironically, when democracy was restored in 1975, the new government relocated the remains of prominent anti-fascist opponents to this building and prohibited those who had worked with Salazar from entering. Today, the building houses the honorary tombs of explorers like Vasco da Gama, and the remains of important Portuguese artists, including Amália Rodrigues, the queen of *fado*. *(To reach Graça and the Panteão, take the #12 bus or the #28 tram from the bottom of R. dos Correeiros. ☎885 4820. Open Tu-Su 10am-5pm. €2, under 25 €1.)*

IGREJA DE SÃO VICENTE DE FORA. The igreja, built between 1582 and 1692, is dedicated to Lisbon's patron saint. Ask the church attendant to see the *sacristia* with inlaid walls of Sintra marble and the geometrically confused walls at the base of the center dome. *(From the bottom of R. dos Correeiros in Baixa, take bus #12 or tram #28; €1. Open daily 9am-noon and 1-6pm, except for during mass. Mass Tu and Th-F 9:30am, Sa 6:30pm, Su 11:30am. Free. Chapel next door with scenic view €4, students €2.)*

SÃO SEBASTIÃO

Located north of Baixa, this area features busy avenues, department stores, and scores of stripmalls. São Sebastião, however, also houses two of the finest art museums in Portugal (both legacies of oil tycoon Calouste Gulbenkian).

MUSEU CALOUSTE GULBENKIAN. When Calouste Gulbenkian died in 1955, he left his extensive art collection to his beloved Portugal. Though the philanthropist was a British citizen of Armenian descent, it was Portugal he chose to call home. The collection is divided into sections of ancient art and European pieces from the 15th to 20th centuries. *(Av. Berna 45. M: São Sebastião. Exit the metro onto R. Testa and take a right when you reach El Corte Inglés. Follow the road until it ends and then take another right. Bus #18, 46, or 56. ☎782 3000; www.museum.gulbenkian.pt. Open Tu-Su 10am-6pm. Museum €3, museum and Centro de Arte Moderna combination pass €5, students free. Su free.)*

CENTRO DE ARTE MODERNA. Though not as famous as its neighbor, the Museu Calouste Gulbenkian, this museum, also funded by Gulbenkian's foundation, houses a large modern collection dedicated to promoting Portuguese talent. Don't miss the sculpture gardens. *(R. Dr. Nicolau Bettencourt. M: São Sebastião. From the station, head downhill. Bus #16, 31, or 46. ☎795 0241. Open Tu-Su 10am-5:45pm. €3. Sa free.)*

BELÉM

Belém is more of a suburb than a neighborhood of Lisbon, but its concentration of monuments and museums makes it a crucial stop on any tour of the capital. To reach Belém, take tram #15 from Pr. do Comércio (15min.) or bus #28 or 43 from Pr. da Figueira (15min.) to the Mosteiro dos Jerónimos stop. Or, take the train from Estação Cais do Sodré (10min., every 15min., €0.90). From the train station, cross the tracks, cross the street, and go left. The Padrão dos Descobrimentos is to your left, while the Mosteiro dos Jerónimos is on the right.

TORRE DE BELÉM. The best known tower in all of Portugal, the Torre de Belém offers panoramic views of Belém, the Rio Tejo, and the Atlantic. Built as a harbor fortress, it originally sat right on the shoreline; today, due to the receding beach, it is only accessible by a small bridge. *(From the monastery, a 10min. walk along the water away from Lisbon. Use the underpass to cross the highway. Open Tu-Su Oct.-Apr. 10am-5pm; May-Sept. 10am-6:30pm. Last admission 30min. before closing. €3, students €1.50.)*

MOSTEIRO DOS JERÓNIMOS. The Mosteiro dos Jerónimos was established in 1502 to give thanks for the success of Vasco da Gama's expedition to India. The monastery showcases Portugal's native Manueline style, combining Gothic forms with minute Renaissance detail. On the main door of the church, to the right of the monastery entrance, Prince Henry the Navigator mingles with the Twelve Apostles. The symbolic tombs of Luís de Camões and Vasco da Gama lie in two opposing transepts. Inside the monastery, the octagonal cloisters of the courtyard surround rose gardens. *(☎362 0034. Open Tu-Su Oct.-Apr. 10am-5pm; May-Sept. 10am-6:30pm, last admission 30min. before closing. Church free, cloisters €4.50, ages 15-25 €2.25.)*

PARQUE DAS NAÇÕES

The Parque das Nações (Park of Nations) inhabits the former Expo '98 grounds. Until the mid-1990s, the area was a muddy wasteland of run-down factories and warehouses, but the government transformed it in preparation for the World Exposition and afterward spent millions converting the grounds into the Parque das Nações. The entrance leads through the Centro Vasco da Gama **shopping mall** (open daily 10am-midnight) to the center, where information kiosks provide maps. *(From Lisbon, take the metro to Oriente at the end of the red line. City buses #5, 10, 19, 21, 25, 28, 44, 50, 68, 208, and 210 all stop at the Oriente station; €1.20. Parque ☎893 0601; www.parquedasnacoes.pt. Open daily 10am-midnight.)* The park's biggest attraction, the

Oceanário has interactive exhibits that explore the four major oceans, complete with sounds and smells; every section connects to the main tank, which houses fish, sharks, and other sea creatures. *(☎891 7002; www.oceanario.pt. Open daily Apr.-Oct. 10am-7pm; Nov.-Mar. 10am-6pm. €10, under 12 €5.)* Pavilions scattered around the park appeal to a variety of interests. The **Pavilhão do Conhecimento** (Pavilion of Knowledge) hosts an interactive science museum *(☎891 7100; www.paconhecimento.pt; open Tu-F 10am-6pm, Sa-Su 11am-7pm; €6, under 18 €3)* while the **Virtual Reality Pavilion** holds a ride which challenges the senses. The **Atlantic Pavilion** hosts many of Lisbon's concerts and the **International Fairgrounds** accommodate rotating exhibits.

ENTERTAINMENT

Agenda Cultural and *Follow Me Lisboa*, free at the tourist office and at kiosks in the Rossio on R. Portas de Santo Antão, have information on concerts, *fado*, movies, plays, and bullfights. They also have lists of museums, gardens, and libraries.

FADO

Lisbon's trademark is **fado,** an art combining singing and narrative poetry that expresses sorrowful *saudade* (nostalgia). The Bairro Alto has many *fado* joints off R. da Misericórdia and on streets by the Igreja de São Roque, but the prices alone may turn a knife in your heart. All of the popular houses have high minimum consumption requirements (normally €15-20). To avoid these, explore nearby streets where various bars and small venues offer free shows.

Cafe Luso, Tv. da Queimada 10 (☎342 2281; www.cafeluso.pt), around the corner from the Igreja S. Roque in Bairro Alto. Lisbon's premier *fado* club combines the best in Portuguese music, cuisine, and atmosphere. Entrees €22-29. Min. consumption €20. *Fado* 9-10:30pm and 11pm-2am. Open M-Sa 8pm-2am. AmEx/MC/V.

O Faia, R. Barroca 56 (☎342 6742; www.ofaia.com), between R. Atalaia and R. Diário de Notícias. O Faia offers performances by famous *fadistas* like Anita Guerreiro, as well as excellent Portuguese cuisine. Entrees €23-30. Min. consumption €17.50, includes 2 drinks. *Fado* 9:30pm. Open M-Sa 8pm-2am. AmEx/MC/V.

O Forcado, R. da Rosa 219-221 (☎346 8579). A traditional restaurant that features *fado* from Coimbra and Lisbon, as well as folk music and dance. Entrees €16-25. Minimum consumption €15. *Fado* 9pm. Open M-Tu and Th-Su 8pm-1am. AmEx/MC/V.

BULLFIGHTING

The drama that is Portuguese bullfighting differs from the Spanish variety in that the bull is not killed in the ring, a tradition that dates back to the 18th century. These spectacles take place most Thursdays from late June to late September at **Praça de Touros de Lisboa,** Campo Pequeno. (☎793 2143. Open daily 10pm-2am.) The newly renovated *praça* would be the perfect venue in which to observe the distinctly Portuguese *toureio equestre* (horseback bullfighting) but the stadium is shut down for construction until at least summer 2006.

FESTIVALS

In June, the people of Lisbon spill into the city for a summer's worth of revelry. Open-air *feiras* (fairs)—smorgasbords of food, drink, live music, and dance—fill the streets. On the night of June 13, the streets explode in song and dance during the **Festa de Santo António.** Lisbon also has a number of commercial *feiras*. From late May to early June, bookworms burrow for three weeks in the **Feira do Livro** in the Parque Eduardo VII. The **Feira Internacional de Lisboa** occurs every few months in the Parque das Nações. Year-round *feiras* include the **Feira de Oeiras** (antiques;

4th Su of the month) and the **Feira de Carcanelos** (clothes; Th 8am-2pm). Packrats will enjoy the **Feira da Ladra** (flea market), held behind the Igreja de São Vicente de Fora in Graça (Tu and Sa 7am-3pm). To get there, take bus #104 or 105 or tram #28.

NIGHTLIFE

Bairro Alto, where small bars and clubs fill the side streets, is the first place to go at night. **Rua do Norte, Rua do Diário Notícias,** and **Rua da Atalaia** have many small clubs packed into three short blocks, making club-hopping as easy as crossing the road. Several gay and lesbian clubs are between Pr. de Camões and Tv. da Queimada, aand in the **Rato** area near the edge of Bairro Alto. Later at night, the **Docas de Santo Amaro** host a strip of waterfront clubs and bars while **Avenida 24 de Julho** and **Rua das Janelas Verdes** in the **Santos** area have some of the most popular clubs and discos. New hot spots include the area along the river across from the **Santa Apolónia** train station. At clubs, jeans, sandals, and sneakers are generally not allowed. Inside, beer runs €3-5. Crowds tend to flow in around 2am and stay until dawn.

A Tasca Tequila Bar, Tv. da Queimada 13-15 (☎343 3431). This classy Mexican bar is the perfect stopover between dinner and the louder bars and clubs. Mixed drinks €5. Open daily 6pm-2am.

Club 43, 43 R. da Barroca (☎937 71 29). In the absolute heart of nighttime activity, futuristic Club 43 is a great pre-party hangout. Open M-Sa 10pm-2am.

Speakeasy, Cais das Oficinas, Armazém 115 (☎390 9166; www.speakeasy-bar.com), between M: Santos and M: Alcântara. Lisbon's premier jazz and blues center. Live shows every night. Beer €3. Open M-Sa noon-3am. AmEx/MC/V.

Lux, Av. Infante Dom Henrique A (☎882 0890). Across from the Santa Apolónia train station. In a class of its own, Lux is one of the hottest spots in Lisbon. Arrive after 2am. Beer €1.50-2.50. Min. consumption €10. Open Tu-Sa 6pm-6am. AmEx/MC/V.

Mezcal, on the corner of Tr. Agua da Flor and R. Diário de Notícias. This tiny Mexican bar has the cheapest drinks in Bairro Alto. Tacos, burritos, and nachos €2-4. Sangria €1.50. *Caipirinhas* €3.50. Shots €1-2. Margaritas €3.50. Open daily 10pm-4am.

A Capela, R. Atalaia 45. A spacious bar with gold walls and red velvet cushions. Popular in the late hours. Beer €3. Mixed drinks €5. Open daily 9:30pm-4am.

DAYTRIPS FROM LISBON

ESTORIL AND CASCAIS

Trains from Lisbon's Estação Cais do Sodré (M: Cais do Sodré) run to Cascais via Estoril (30min., every 20min. 5:30am-1:30am, €1.40). Cascais is also a pleasant 20min. walk from Estoril; take a right onto the walkway at Praia Estoril Tamariz and walk along the coast. Scott URB has a bus terminal in downtown Cascais; it is underground, next to the blue glass tower of the shopping center by the train station. Bus #417 leaves from the Cascais bus terminal for Sintra via Estoril (40min., every hr., €2.95).

Glorious beaches draw sun-loving tourists to Estoril (pop. 24,000) and neighboring Cascais (pop. 33,000). In balmy weather, Cascais's shores, especially **Praia da Ribeira, Praia da Rainha,** and **Praia da Duquesa,** are filled with sunbathers. To reach Praia da Ribeira from the tourist office, go right and walk down Av. dos Combatantes de Grande Guerra. Praia da Rainha and Praia da Duquesa are a short walk toward Estoril. For the beach-weary, the marvelous (air-conditioned) **Casino Estoril,** one of Europe's largest casinos and quality *fado* venue, is worth a visit even for non-gamblers. It's on Pr. José Teodoro across from the Estoril train station. (☎466 7700; www.casino-estoril.pt. No sneakers, jeans, shorts, swimwear, or hats anywhere in the casino; jackets and ties, required for the game room, can be borrowed at the entrance with ID. 18+ to gamble; passport required for game room. *Fado* W 11:30pm in the Wonder-Bar; reserve at least a day ahead. Open daily 3pm-3am.)

Estoril's **tourist office,** on Arcadas do Parque, is across the street from the train station; the friendly and multilingual staff will gladly provide you with a mountain of information. (☎466 3813; www.estorilcoast.com. Wheelchair accessible. Luggage storage. Open in summer M-Sa 9am-8pm, Su 10am-6pm; in winter M-Sa 9am-7pm, Su 10am-6pm.) To get to Cascais's tourist office, Av. dos Combatantes de Grande Guerra 25, exit the train station through the ticket office, cross Lg. da Estação, and take a right onto Av. Valbom; the office is at the end of the street. (☎486 8204. English, French, and Spanish spoken. Luggage storage. Open in summer M-Sa 9am-8pm, Su 10am-6pm; in winter M-Sa 9am-7pm, Su 10am-6pm.)

SINTRA ☎21

Trains (☎923 26 05) run to Av. Dr. Miguel Bombarda from Lisbon's Estação Sete Rios (45min., every 15min., €1.40). ScottURB buses (☎469 9100; www.scotturb.com) leave Av. Dr. Miguel Bombarda for Cascais (#417) and Estoril (#418; both buses 40min., every hr., €3) Down the street, Mafrense buses go to Ericeira (50min., every hr., €2.70).

PORTUGAL

With fairy-tale castles, enchanting gardens, and spectacular mountain vistas, Sintra (pop. 20,000) is a favorite among backpackers. One of Portugal's only UNESCO World Heritage Sites, **Quinta da Regaleira** is a stunning palace whose architecturally diverse rooms were designed around a common theme: the passage from one world to another. To get to the palace from the tourist office, follow R. Consiglieri Pedroso out of town as it turns into R. M.E.F. Navarro. (☎910 6650. Open daily June-Sept. 10am-8pm; Oct. and Feb.-May 10am-6:30pm; Nov.-Jan. 10am-5:30pm. Tours 11am, 12:30, 2:30, 4pm. €5, students €4. Guided tours €10/8.) The equally embellished **Palácio de Pena** features a great view and an *azulejo* toilet once used by the Queen of Portugal. (☎910 5340; www.parquesdesintra.pt. Open daily June-Sept. 10am-5:30pm; Oct.-May 10am-4pm. €6, students €4. Guided tours €3.50.)

The spacious rooms of **Casa de Hospedes Dona Maria Parreirinha ❸**, R. João de Deus 12/14, near the train station in Estefania, are the cheapest available within 15min. of the town center. (☎923 2490. Rooms €35,with bath €45. Low season prices €5-10 fewer.) Restaurants crowd **Rua João de Deus** and **Avenida Heliodoro Salgado.** For tasty pastries try the historic **Fábrica das Verdadeiras Queijadas da Sapa ❶**, Volta do Duche 12. (☎923 0493. Pastries and other desserts €0.65-2. Open M-F 9am-6pm, Sa-Su 9am-7pm. Cash only.) **Tourist offices** are located in Pr. da República 23 (☎923 1157) and in the train station (☎924 1623). Both have multilingual staff. (Both open daily June-Sept. 9am-8pm; Oct.-May 9am-7pm.)

CENTRAL PORTUGAL

Jagged cliffs and whitewashed fishing villages line the Costa de Prata of Estremadura, with beaches that rival even those in the Algarve. In the fertile region of the Ribatejo (banks of the Rio Tejo), lush greenery surrounds historic sights.

COIMBRA ☎239

Coimbra (pop. 200,000) possesses the cosmopolitan charm of a metropolis many times its size. For centuries, the Universidade de Coimbra was the only university in the country. Today, local university students and backpackers give Coimbra a youthful exuberance unlike any other city in Portugal.

TRANSPORTATION AND PRACTICAL INFORMATION. Regional **trains** (☎808 20 82 08; www.cp.pt) stop at both at both Estação Coimbra-B (Velha) and Estação Coimbra-A (Nova), two blocks from the lower town center, while long-distance trains stop only at Coimbra-B. A train connects the two stations, departing after regional trains arrive (4min.; €0.80, free if transferring from another train). Trains run to Lisbon (2-3hr., 27 per day, €8.50-9.50) and Porto (1-2hr., 28 per day, €5.60-6.40). **Buses** (☎23 87 69) go from the end of Av. Fernão de Magalhães, 15min. past Coimbra-A, to Lisbon (2½hr., 18 per day, €9.40) and Porto (1½hr., 14 per day, €9). From the bus station, turn right, follow the avenue to Coimbra-A, then walk to Largo da Portagem to reach the **tourist office.** The multilingual staff distributes maps and provides short-term luggage storage. (☎85 59 30; www.cm-coimbra.pt. Open June-Sept. M-F 9am-7pm, Sa-Su 10am-1pm and 2:30-5:30pm; Oct.-May M-F 9am-6pm, Sa-Su 10am-1pm and 2:30-5:30pm.) **Espaço Internet,** Pr. 8 de Maio, offers free **Internet,** but you may have to wait 15-30min. (Passport required. Open M-F 10am-8pm, Sa-Su 10am-10pm.) **Postal Code:** 3000.

ACCOMMODATIONS AND FOOD. **Residência Solar Navarro ❶**, Av. Emídio Navarro 60-A, on the second floor, offers simple rooms with bath and TV; some have balconies with views of the park. (☎82 79 99. Reception 24hr. Singles €15; doubles €25; triples €38; quints €60. Cash only.) **Residencial Vitória ❷**, R. da Sota 11-19, has spacious rooms newly renovated with bath, phone, cable TV, and A/C. Older rooms are cheaper, but still roomy and quiet. (☎82 40 49. Breakfast €5. Summer singles €15-30; doubles €25-45; triples €60. Winter €15-25/25-40/50. AmEx/MC/V.) **Pastelaria Arco Iris ❶**, Av. Fernão de Magalhães 22, serves a veritable rainbow of pastries (€0.80-1). The cheapest meals in Coimbra (under €2) are at **UC Cantina ❶**, the university student cafeteria, on the right side of R. Oliveiro Matos, but you'll need an ISIC. (Opens daily at noon.) **Porta Romana ❷**, R. Martins de Carvalho 8/10, is a popular Italian restaurant which also serves Portuguese food. (☎82 84 58. Half-portions €4.50. Entrees €6-8. Open daily 10am-2am.) Supermarket **Pingo Doce,** R. João de Ruão 14, is a 3min. walk up R. da Sofia from Pr. 8 de Maio. (☎85 29 30. Open daily 8:30am-9pm.)

PORTUGAL

SIGHTS AND ENTERTAINMENT. Take in the sights in the **old town** by following the narrow stone steps from the river up to the university. Begin your ascent at the **Arco de Almedina,** a remnant of the Moorish town wall, one block uphill from Largo da Portagem. The looming 12th-century Romanesque **Sé Velha** (old cathedral) is at the top. (Open M-Th and Sa 10am-6pm, F 10am-1pm. Cloister €1, students €0.75.) Follow signs to the Jesuit-built **Sé Nova** (new cathedral), with its blinding gold altar. (Open Tu-Sa 9am-noon and 2-6:30pm. Free.) Just a few blocks uphill is the 16th-century **Universidade de Coimbra.** Enter through the **Porta Férrea** (Iron Gate), off R. São Pedro, to the **Pátio das Escolas,** which has an excellent view of the rural outskirts of Coimbra. (Open daily May-Sept. 9am-7:30pm; Oct.-Apr. 9:30am-12:30pm and 2-5:30pm.) The stairs to the right lead to the **Sala dos Capelos** (Graduates' Hall), which houses portraits of Portugal's kings. (Open daily 9:30am-12:30pm and 2-5:30pm. €2.50, students €2.) The **Capela de São Miguel** (university chapel), adorned with magnificent *talha dourada* (gilded wood) carvings, and the mind-boggling 18th-century **Biblioteca Joanina** (university library) lie past the Baroque clock tower. (Library ☎85 98 00. Open daily mid-Mar. to Oct. 8:30am-7pm; Nov. to mid-Mar. 9:30am-5pm. Only 20 people allowed in every 20min. €2.50, students €1.75. Ticket to all university sights €4, students €2.80. Purchase tickets in the main quad.)

Coimbra's nightlife scene is best from October to July, when the students are in town. **A Capella,** R. Corpo de Deus, a former chapel converted into a small bar, is the best place to hear Coimbra-style *Fado*, which is performed by both students and professionals from the chapel's altar. (☎83 39 85. Mixed drinks €4-5. Cover €5. *Fado* at 9:30, 10:30, 11:30pm. Open M-F 1pm-2am, Sa-Su 1pm-3am.) **Quebra Club,** Parque Verde do Mondego, blasts jazz and funk by the riverside. (☎83 60 36. Beer €1-3. Mixed drinks €4-5. Open M-Th and Su noon-2am, F-Sa noon-4am. AmEx/MC/V.) Students run wild during the **Queima das Fitas** (Burning of the Ribbons), Coimbra's infamous week-long festival in the first or second week of May. The festivities commence when graduates burn the narrow ribbons they got as first-years and receive wide ribbons in return.

ÉVORA ☎266

Évora (pop. 55,000) is the capital and largest city of the Alentejo region. Attached to the pleasant **Igreja Real de São Francisco** in Pr. 1 de Mayo, the bizarre **Capela dos Ossos** (Chapel of Bones) was built by three Franciscan monks out of the bones of 5000 people as a hallowed space to reflect on the profundity of life and death. From Pr. do Giraldo, follow R. República; the church is on the right and the chapel is around back to the right of the main entrance. (☎70 45 21. Open May-Sept. M-Sa 9am-1pm and 2:30-6pm, Su 10am-1pm; Oct.-Apr. M-Sa 9am-1pm and 2:30-5:30pm, Su 10am-1pm. €1, photographs €0.25.) According to legend, the 2nd-century **Templo Romano,** on Largo Conde do Vila Flor, was built for the goddess Diana. Facing the temple is the **Igreja de São João Evangelista,** whose interior is covered with dazzling *azulejos.* (Open Tu-Su 10am-12:30pm and 2-6pm. €2.50.) From Pr. do Giraldo, head up R. 5 de Outubro to the colossal 12th-century **Basílica Catedral;** the 12 apostles on the doorway are masterpieces of medieval Portuguese sculpture. Climb the stairs of the cloister for a great view of the city. The **Museu de Arte Sacra,** above the nave, houses religious artifacts. (Cathedral open daily 9am-noon and 2-5pm. Cloisters open daily 9am-noon and 2-4:30pm. Museum open Tu-Su 9am-12:30pm and 2-4:30pm. Cathedral free. Cloisters and museum €3, students €1.50.)

Pensões cluster around **Praça do Giraldo.** Turn right out of the tourist office and then right onto R. Bernardo Matos to get to cozy **Casa Palma ❷,** R. Bernardo Matos 29A, which has very reasonable prices for the petite rooms on the top floor. (☎70 35 60. Singles €15-25; doubles €30-35. Cash only.) Budget restaurants cluster near Pr. do Giraldo, particularly along **Rua Mercadores.** Intimate **Restaurante Burgo Velho ❷,** R. de Burgos 10, serves large portions of *alentejano* cuisine. (☎22 58 58. Entrees €5-9. Open M-Sa noon-3pm and 7-10pm. AmEx/MC/V.) **Trains** (☎808 20 82 08; www.cp.pt) run from Av. dos Combatentes de Grande Guerra to Faro (5hr., 2 per day, €17.20) and Lisbon (2½hr., 4 per day, €10.30). **Buses** (☎76 94 10; www.rede-expressos.pt) go from Av. São Sebastião to: Braga (7¾-9¾hr., 6 per day, €17.50) via Porto (6-8½hr., 10 per day, €18); Faro (5hr., 3 per day, €17.20); Lisbon (3hr., 20 per day, €5-8.80). The **tourist office** is at Pr. do Giraldo 73. (☎77 70 30. Open daily Apr.-Oct. 9am-7pm; Nov.-Mar. 9am-6pm.) **Postal Code:** 7999.

ALGARVE

Nearly 3000 hours of sunshine per year have transformed the Algarve, a desert on the sea, into a popular vacation spot. In July and August, sun-seeking tourists mob the resorts, packing bars and discos from sunset until long after sunrise. In the low season, the resorts become pleasantly de-populated.

LAGOS ☎282

As the town's countless international expats will attest, Lagos (pop. 17,500) is a black hole: come for two days and you'll stay for two months. Lagos keeps you soaking in the ocean views, the sun on the beach, and the drinks at the bars.

PORTUGAL

TRANSPORTATION AND PRACTICAL INFORMATION. Trains (☎79 23 61) run from across the river to Évora (5-5½hr., 3 per day, €16) and Lisbon (3½-4½hr., 5-6 per day, €16). The bus station (☎76 29 44), off **Avenida dos Descobrimentos,** is across the river from the train station. **Buses** run to Faro (2½hr., 6 per day, €4); Lisbon (5hr., 6 per day, €15); Sagres (1hr., 16 per day, €3). Running along the channel, Av. dos Descobrimentos is the main road carrying traffic to and from Lagos. From the train station, walk through the marina and cross the suspension bridge, then turn left onto Av. dos Descobrimentos. From the bus station, walk straight until Av. dos Descobrimentos, then turn right; after 15m, take another right onto R. Porta de Portugal to reach **Praça Gil Eanes,** the center of the old town. The local **tourist office** is on Lg. Marquês de Pombal, up R. Lima Leitão, which extends from Pr. Gil Eanes. (☎76 41 11. Open M-Sa 10am-6pm.) Check email and the inferior weather back home at **Inter-Net,** Av. dos Descobrimentos 19. (☎08 95 96. €3.50 per hr. Open M-Sa 10am-10pm, Su 10am-6pm.) **Postal Code:** 8600.

ACCOMMODATIONS AND FOOD. In summer, budget lodgings fill quickly; reserve more than a week in advance. If full, the youth hostel will happily refer you to a *quarto* nearby for about the same price. Locals trying to rent rooms in their homes will greet you at the station. Though these rooms are often inconveniently located, they are frequently the best deals (€10-15 per person). A short walk from most of Lagos's bars, the recently renovated **Rising Cock ❷,** Travessa do Forno 14, keeps up Lagos's famous party-town reputation with two patios, a beer garden, "Hard Cock Cafe," and DVD library. (☎966 20 77 02; www.risingcock.com. Free Internet. Dorms €15.) The friendly staff and lodgers at **Pousada da Juventude de Lagos (HI) ❷,** R. Lançarote de Freitas 50, congregate in the courtyard or TV room with billiards and foosball. (☎76 19 70. In summer, book through the central Movijovem office ☎213 59 60 00. Breakfast €1. Mid-June to mid-Sept. dorms €15; doubles with bath €45. Mid-Sept. to mid-June €10/28. Cash only.) **Olinda Teresa Maria Quartos ❷,** R. Lançarote de Freitas 37, is a crowded hostel in a large house. (☎289 08 23 29. Mid-June to mid-Sept. dorms €15; doubles €24. Mid-Sept. to mid-June €10/30.)

Peruse multilingual menus around **Praça Gil Eanes** and **Rua 25 de Abril.** A dedicated following "get stuffed" for €5 at **Casa Rosa ❶,** R. do Ferrador 22. (☎18 02 38. Many vegetarian options. Free Internet for diners. Open daily 5-11pm.) **Mediterraneo ❷,** R.

FABULOUS FIGS

Thanks to the area's Moorish leg acy, the Algarve produces some of the best almonds and figs in the world. Long ago, a North Afr can prince planted the region's white-flowering almond groves to appease his Scandinavian prin cess, who missed the snowy hills of her childhood. While the figs don't boast such a fairy-tale his tory, they are still tasty. Both ingredients find their way into almost every traditional desser along Portugal's southern coast and most *pastelarias* and *confei arias* tout their own homemade almond concoctions. Bot almonds and figs are equally del cious eaten raw—the freshes (and often cheapest) morsels car be found at produce markets.

For the best of both worlds, tr your hand at making this Portu guese dessert that combines both of the Algarve's favorite foods. Soak about 10 figs in port for a least an hour. While you're wai ing, preheat an oven to 350° (175°C). Grind up a few handful of almonds and mix in some finely ground chocolate, lemon pee scrapings, cinnamon, and enough sugar to suit your taste. Then, with a sharp knife, slice off the tops o the figs and make small cavities in the middle with your fingers. Fill the figs with the almond paste, put them on a baking sheet and let them brown in the oven for about 5min. Ta da You've made *figos cheios.*

Senhora da Graça 2, has an extensive menu of Mediterranean and Thai cuisine. (☎76 84 76. Entrees €9-16.50. Open Tu-Sa 6:30-10:30pm.) The indoor **market** is on Av. dos Descobrimentos (open Sa). **Supermercado Marrachinho** is just up the street on Av. dos Descobrimentos 9. (☎54 02 00. Open daily 8am-9pm. MC/V.)

SIGHTS AND BEACHES. Though sunbathing and non-stop debauchery have long erased memories of Lagos's rugged, seafaring past, it's worth taking some time away from the beach or bars to visit the city's sights. The **Fortaleza da Ponta da Bandeira,** a 17th-century fortress with maritime exhibits, overlooks the marina. (☎76 14 10. Open Tu-Sa 10am-1pm and 2-6pm, Su 10am-1pm. €2, students €1.) Also on the waterfront is the old **Mercado dos Escravos** (slave market), site of the first sale of African slaves in Portugal in 1441. Opposite the Mercado dos Escravos is the gilded **Igreja de Santo António,** which houses a museum filled with artifacts from Lagos's past rulers.(Church and museum open Tu-Su 9:30am-12:30pm and 2-5pm. Church free. Museum €2.)

For a lazier day, head to one of Lagos's many beaches. Flat, smooth sands can be found at the 4km **Meia Praia,** across the river from town. Hop on the quick ferry near Pr. Infante Dom Henrique (€0.50). For less crowded beaches, caves, and beautiful cliffs, follow Av. dos Descobrimentos toward Sagres to **Praia de Pinhão** (20min.). A bit farther, **Praia Dona Ana** features the sculpted cliffs and grottoes that grace many Algarve postcards. If you're up for more than lounging on the beach, Lagos offers a wide variety of outdoor sports—from scuba diving to surfing to (booze) cruising. Companies offering tours of the coastal cliffs and grottoes line Av. dos Descobrimentos. Most tours last 45min. and begin at €25 for two people. The very popular **Booze Cruise** offers swimming, snorkeling, tours of the grottoes, a live DJ, and, of course, cheap drinks. (☎963 01 26 92. Cruises on M, W, and Sa. Purchase tickets at the youth hostel. €15.)

NIGHTLIFE. As the sun sets on Lagos, beachgoers head en masse to bars and cafes between **Praça Gil Eanes** and **Praça Luis de Camões.** For late-night bars and clubs, try **Rua Cândido dos Reis** and **Rua do Ferrador,** as well as the intersection of **Rua 25 de Abril, Rua Silva Lopes,** and **Rua Soeiro da Costa.** Brits and Aussies flood **The Red Eye,** R. Cândido dos Reis 63, in search of classic rock, cheap liquor, and casual games of pool. (Beer €1.50-3. Mixed drinks €3-4. Shots €2.50-3. Free shot with first drink. Happy hour 8-10pm. Open daily 8pm-2am.) Backpackers from all over cram into **Whyte's Bar,** R. do Ferrador 7A, to try the the nine Deadly Sins shot contest. (☎968 13 90 62. Beer €2-3. Huge variety of mixed drinks €2.50-5. Nightly happy hour. Open daily 8pm-2am.) At **Metro Bar,** R. Lançarote de Freitas 30, a mixed crowd moves to acid jazz in a stylish, cosmopolitan setting. (Beer €1.50. Mixed drinks €2.25-3. Happy hour 9-11:30pm. Open daily 7pm-2am.)

SAGRES ☎282

Perched atop a desert plateau at the southwesternmost point in Europe, desolate Sagres (pop. 2500) and its cape were once considered the edge of the world. Near the town stands the **Fortaleza de Sagres,** where Prince Henry stroked his beard, decided to map the world, and founded his famous school of navigation. The pentagonal 15th-century fortress and surrounding paths yield striking views of the cliffs and sea. (Open May-Sept. 9:30am-8pm; Oct.-Apr. 9:30am-5:30pm. €3, under 25 €1.50.) Six kilometers west lies the dramatic **Cabo de São Vicente,** where the second most powerful lighthouse in Europe shines over 100km out to sea. To get there on weekdays, take the bus from R. Comandante Matoso near the tourist office (10min.; 11:15am, 12:30, 4:15pm; €1). Alternatively, hike 1hr. past the fortresses perched atop the cliffs. The most notable beach in the area is **Mareta,** at the bottom of the road leading from the town center. The nearby coves of **Salema** and

Luz are picturesque. At night, a young surfer crowd fills **Água Salgada,** on R. Comandante Matoso, 75m past the tourist office, away from the fortress. (☎62 42 97. Beer €1-2. Mixed drinks €3.50-4.50. Open daily June-Aug. 10am-4am; Sept.-May closed Tu.) Next door is **O Dromedário,** where a DJ keeps the party bumping. By day, O Dromedário serves a wide variety of crepes. (☎62 42 97. Crepes €2.20-4. Beer €1-2. Mixed drinks €3.50-5. Open M-Th and Su 10am-2am, F-Sa 10am-4am.)

Finding a bed in Sagres is not hard; windows everywhere display multilingual signs for rooms, many in boarding houses with guest kitchens. Haggle with owners and be sure to check out a room before you agree. Follow R. Comandante Matoso toward the tourist office and take a left on R. Patrão António Faustino to reach **Atalaia Apartamentos ❷,** which features beautiful, fully furnished rooms with bath, TV, and refrigerator. Apartments for rent have a bath, kitchen, living room, and terrace. (☎62 46 81. Doubles July-Sept. €40, Oct.-June €25. 2-person apartments July-Sept. €50, 3- to 4-person apartments €70-80; Apr.-June €30/50-60; Oct.-Mar. €25/40-50.) **Alisuper,** on R. Comandante Matoso, has groceries. (☎62 44 87. Open daily 9am-8pm.) EVA **buses** (☎76 29 44) run to Lagos (1hr., 14 per day, €3). From July to September, buses also run to Lisbon (daily 4pm, €15). The **tourist office,** on R. Comandante Matoso, is up the street from the bus stop. (☎62 48 73. Open Tu-Sa 9:30am-12:30pm and 1:30-5:30pm.) **Postal Code:** 8650.

PORTUGAL

FARO ☎289

The Algarve's capital, largest city, and transportation hub, Faro (pop. 55,000) is largely untouristed despite being perfectly charming. The **Cidade Velha** (old town), is a medley of museums, handicraft shops, and churches. On Lg. do Carmo is the **Igreja de Nossa Senhora do Carmo** and its **Capela dos Ossos** (Chapel of Bones), built from the remains of monks once buried in the church's cemetery. (☎82 44 90. Open May-Sept. daily 10am-1pm and 3-6pm; Oct.-Apr. M-F 10am-1pm and 3-5pm, Sa 10am-1pm. Church free. Chapel €0.75.) To get to sunny beach **Praia de Faro,** take bus #16 in front of the tourist office (5-10min.; 5 per day, return 9 per day; €1).

Pousada da Juventude (HI) ❶, R. Polícia de Segurança Pública, is near the police station. (☎82 65 21. Dorms €7, HI members €5; doubles €24, with bath €30. The **Alisuper** grocery store is on Lg. de Carmo, next to the church. (☎82 49 20. Open daily 8:30am-8pm.) **Trains** (☎82 64 72) run from Lg. da Estação to Évora (4½-6hr., 3-4 per day, €13) and Lagos (1½hr., 9 per day, €16.85). EVA **buses** (☎89 97 00) go from Av. da República to Lagos (2hr., 8 per day, €4.30). Renex (☎81 29 80), across the street, sends buses to Porto (7½hr., 6-13 per day, €22) via Lisbon (4hr., 9 per day, €15). Turn left past the garden on Av. República to reach the **tourist office,** R. da Misericórdia 8. (☎80 36 04. Open June-Sept. daily 9:30am-7pm; Oct.-May M and F-Su 9:30am-1pm and 2-5:30pm, Tu-Th 9:30am-7pm.) **Postal Code:** 8000.

NORTHERN PORTUGAL

The unspoiled Costa da Prata (Silver Coast), plush greenery of the interior, and rugged peaks of the Serra Estrela comprise the Three Beiras region. Beyond trellised vineyards, *azulejo*-lined houses grace charming streets.

PORTO (OPORTO) ☎22

Porto (pop. 264,200) is famous for its namesake product—a strong, sugary wine developed by English merchants in the early 18th century. The port industry is at the root of the city's successful economy, but Porto has more to offer than fine wine. The city retains traditional charm with granite church towers, orange-tiled houses, and graceful bridges alongside a sophisticated modern lifestyle.

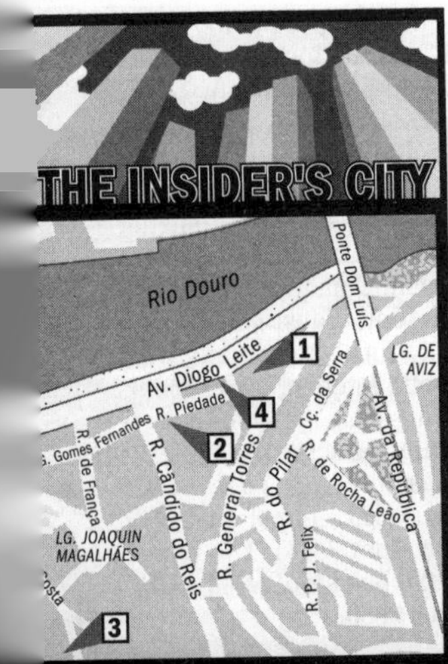

À SUA SAÚDE!

You haven't really been to Porto until you cross the Ponte de Dom Luís I into the Vila Nova da Gaia district and immerse yourself in the city's namesake. Be careful though: excessive tasting along the beautiful Douro may make you want to stay in Porto forever. *À sua saúde!* (Cheers!)

1 **Cálem,** Av. Diogo Leite 26. The house of Cálem has been a major player in the port industry for 200 years, since it began shipping its precious product to Brazil in 1859. Today, its knowledgeable guides offer tours in several languages, explaining the port-making process and history of the powerful Cálem family. (☎374 6660; www.calem.pt. Open M-Sa summer 10am-7pm; winter 10am-6pm. Tours every 15-20min. €2. AmEx/MC/V.)

2 **Sandeman,** Lg. Miguel Bombarda 3, just off Av. Diogo Leite. Founded by a Scottish merchant two centuries ago, Sandeman now offers a very tourist-

TRANSPORTATION AND PRACTICAL INFORMATION. Most **trains** (☎808 20 82 08; www.cp.pt) pass through Porto's main station, **Estação de Campanhã,** on R. da Estação. Trains run to: Aveiro (1¼hr., 47 per day, €4.50-9.50); Braga (1½hr., 26 per day, €9.50); Coimbra (2hr., 24 per day, €7.50-12); Lisbon (3½-4½hr., 18 per day, €14.50-22.50); Madrid, Spain (13-14hr., daily 8:10pm, €64; transfer at Entroncamento); Viana do Castelo (1½-2hr., 11 per day, €5.50). **Estação São Bento,** Pr. Almeida Garrett, serves local and regional trains. Internorte (☎605 2420), Pr. Galiza 96, sends **buses** to Madrid, Spain (10hr., daily at 10am, €40) and other international cities. Rede Expresso buses (☎200 6954; www.redeexpresso.pt), R. Alexandre Herculano 366, travel to: Braga (1¼hr., 10 per day, €4.70); Coimbra (1½hr., 11 per day, €7.50); Lisbon (4hr., 12 per day, €14); Viana do Castelo (1¾hr., 4 per day, €8.20). Transdev (☎200 3152), R. Dr. Alfredo Magalhães 94, two blocks from Pr. República, sends buses to Braga (1hr., 5-17 per day, €3.30). Renex (☎200 3395), Campo Mártires da Pátria, has express service to Lagos (8½hr., 6 per day, €18) via Lisbon (3½hr., 12 per day, €3.50). Buy tickets for the intracity buses and **trams** at kiosks around the city or at the **STCP** office, Pr. de Almeida Garrett 27, across the street from Estação São Bento (€0.70, day-pass €4). The **tourist office,** R. Clube dos Fenianos 25, is off Pr. da Liberdade. (☎339 3470; www.portoturismo.pt. Open July-Sept. daily 9am-7pm; Oct.-June M-F 9am-5:30pm, Sa-Su 9:30am-4:30pm.) **Portweb,** Pr. Gen. Humberto Delgado 291, has **Internet** and plays MTV. (€1.20 per hr., wireless €0.60 per hr. Open M-Sa 10am-2am, Su 3pm-2am.) The **post office** is in Pr. Gen. Humberto Delgado. (☎340 0200. Open M-F 8am-9pm, Sa 9am-6pm, Su 9am-12:30pm and 2-6pm.) **Postal Code:** 4000.

ACCOMMODATIONS AND FOOD. For good accommodation deals, look west of **Avenida dos Aliados** or on **Rua Fernandes Tomás** and **Rua Formosa,** perpendicular to Av. dos Aliados. **Pensão Duas Nações ❶**, Pr. Guilherme Gomes Fernandes 59, has the best combination of low price and high comfort. (☎208 9621. Book ahead or arrive well before noon. Laundry €7. Internet €2.40 per hr. Singles €13.50-16, with bath €22.50; doubles €22.50/30; triples €33/40; quads €44/48. Cash only.) **Pensão Douro ❷**, R. do Loureiro 54, is perfect for those who want to spend little but stay close to the action. (☎205 3214. Singles €15-20, with bath €13-30; doubles €25/30.)

Quality budget meals can be found near Pr. da Batalha on **Rua Cimo de Vila** and **Rua Cativo.** Places selling *bifanas* (small pork sandwiches) line R. Bomjardim. **Ribeira** is the place to go for a high-quality, affordable dinner. Perfect for a night of classy dining without tourists, **Restaurante Tripeiro ❸**, R. de Passos Manuel 195, serves well-prepared regional specialties. (☎200 5886. Entrees €8-15. Open M-Sa noon-3pm and 7-10pm. AmEx/MC/V.) The sprawling **Mercado de Bolhão** has a huge selection of fresh food, including bread, cheese, meat, and olives. The upper level has produce. (Open M-F 8:30am-5pm, Sa 8:30am-1pm.)

SIGHTS AND ENTERTAINMENT. Your first brush with Porto's rich stock of fine artwork may be the celebrated collection of *azulejos* in the **São Bento train station.** From the station, follow signs downhill on R. Mouzinho da Silveira to R. Ferreira Borges and the **Palácio da Bolsa** (Stock Exchange), the epitome of 19th-century elegance. The most striking room of the *Palácio* is the extravagant **Sala Árabe** (Arabian Hall). Its gold and silver walls are covered with the oddly juxtaposed inscriptions "Glory to Allah" and "Glory to Dona Maria II." (☎339 9000. Multilingual tours every 30min. Open daily Apr.-Oct. 9am-7pm; Nov.-Mar. 9am-1pm and 2-6pm. €5, students €3.) Nearby on R. Infante Dom Henrique, the Gothic **Igreja de São Francisco** glitters with an elaborately gilded wood interior. The neighboring museum houses religious art and artifacts; in the basement lies the *Ossário*, a creepy cemetery with countless mass graves. (☎206 2100. Open daily in summer 9am-8pm; winter 9am-5:30pm. €3, students €1.50.) Up R. dos Clérigos from Pr. da Liberdade rises the **Torre dos Clérigos** (Tower of Clerics), adjacent to the 18th-century **Igreja dos Clérigos,** which is adorned with Baroque carvings. (☎200 1729. Tower open daily Apr.-Oct. 9:30am-1pm and 2-7pm; Nov.-Mar. 10am-noon and 2-5pm. Church open M-Sa 9am-noon and 3:30-7:30pm, Su 10am-1pm. Tower €1.50, church free.) Porto is not a party city after hours. Most people congregate around the bar-restaurants of **Ribeira,** where spicy Brazilian music plays until 2am. To get to Porto's rocky and polluted (but popular) **beach** at Matosinhos at any hour, take bus #1 from Pr. da Liberdade.

BRAGA ☎253

The beautiful gardens, plazas, museums, and markets of Braga (pop. 166,000) have earned it the nickname "Portuguese Rome." The treasury of the **Sé,** Portugal's oldest cathedral, showcases the archdiocese's most precious paintings and relics. (☎26 33 17. Open daily June-Aug. 8am-7pm; Sept.-May 8am-6:30pm. Mass daily 5:30pm. Cathedral free. Treasury and chapels €2.) Braga's most famous landmark, **Igreja do Bom Jesús,** is actually 5km outside of town. This church was built in an effort to recreate

friendly dive into the world of port, complete with costumed guides, a souvenir shop, and a museum. (☎374 0500, ext. 594. Open Apr.-Oct. daily 10am-12:30pm and 2-6pm; Nov.-Mar. M-F 9:30am-12:30pm and 2-5pm. Tours every 20min. €3. AmEx/MC/V.)

3 **Taylor's,** R. do Choupelo 250. Perhaps the most prestigious name in the industry, Taylor's expert staff will amaze you with their knowledge; the beautiful outdoor gardens, complete with peacocks, are the perfect environment in which to enjoy the delicious wine. (☎374 2800; www.taylor.pt. Open July-Aug. M-Sa 10am-6pm; Sept.-June closed Sa; last visit starts 5pm. Free tours every 20-30min. and free tasting. AmEx/MC/V.)

4 **Quinta do Noval,** Av. Diogo Leite 256. One of the better-known brands of port worldwide, Quinta do Noval has long focused on the foreign markets, particularly the United States and the United Kingdom. Founded in 1715, the makers makers of one of the finest ports on the market got their start when the mighty Marquês de Pombal gave a vineyard to a noble family. (☎377 0282; www.quinta-donoval.com. Free tours June-Sept. 10am-7pm; Oct.-May M-F 9am-5pm.)

Jerusalem in Braga, providing Iberian Christians with a pilgrimage site closer to home. Take the bus "#02 Bom Jesús" at 10 and 40min. past the hour from in front of Farmacia Cristal, Av. da Liberdade 571 (€1.15). At the site, take the 285m ride on the antique funicular (8am-8pm; €1) or walk 20-25min. up the granite-paved pathway that leads to a 365-step zig-zagging staircase. If you walk, you'll pass several spots that you can't see from the cable car, including fountains representing the five senses and prophets carved from stone.

Take a taxi (€5) from the train station to **Pousada da Juventude de Braga (HI)** ❶, Av. da Liberdade 738, second floor, a conventient hostel with a friendly atmosphere. (☎61 61 63. Reception 8am-noon and 6pm-midnight. Lockout noon-6pm. Dorms €7; doubles €16. €2 HI discount. Cash only.) Cafes on **Praça da Republica** are perfect for light meals and people-watching. The **market** is in Pr. do Comércio. (Open M-Sa 7am-3pm.) **Trains** (☎808 20 82 08) pull into Estação da Braga, 1km from Pr. da Republica, from Lisbon (4hr., 3 per day, €27) via Porto (45-60min., 26 per day, €9.50). Take R. do Souto and pass through the town gate; the station is 400m on the left. **Buses** leave Central de Camionagem (☎61 60 80) for: Coimbra (3hr., 6 per day, €10); Faro (12-15hr., 3-6 per day, €21); Lisbon (5¼hr., 10-11 per day, €14.50); Porto (1¼hr., 11 per day, €4.70). The **tourist office** is on Av. da Liberdade 1. (☎26 25 50. Open June-Sept. M-F 9am-7pm, Sa-Su 9am-12:30pm and 2-5:30pm; Oct.-May M-Sa 9am-12:30pm and 2-5:30pm.) **Postal Code:** 4700.

VIANA DO CASTELO ☎258

Viana do Castelo (pop. 37,000) is one of the loveliest coastal cities in all of Portugal. Though visited mainly as a beach resort, Viana also has a lively historic district centered around the stately **Praça da República.** Here, the **Museu de Traje** provides a glimpse into the region's distinctive attire. (☎80 01 71. Open Tu-Su 10am-1pm and 3-7pm. €2, students €1.) Across the plaza, granite columns support the flowery facade of the **Igreja da Misericórdia,** known for its *azulejo* interior. (Open daily 9:30am-12:30pm and 2-5:30pm. Free.) The **Monte de Santa Luzia,** overlooking the city, is guarded by the **Templo de Santa Luzia.** This early 20th-century church isn't much to look at, but the view from the hill is fantastic. Either brave the hundreds of stairs (20-30min.) or take a taxi (€5) to the top. (*Templo* open daily in summer 8am-7pm; in winter 8am-5pm. Mass daily 4pm. Free.) Viana do Castelo and the surrounding coast have superb beaches.

For accommodations and restaurants, try the side streets off Av. dos Combatentes da Grande Guerra. A 15min. walk from the town center, you'll find **Pousada de Juventude de Viana do Castelo (HI)** ❶, R. de Límia, right on the marina off R. da Argaçosa and Pr. da Galiza. This welcoming hostel has rooms with balconies, a pool, ping-pong tables, and a bar. (☎80 02 60. HI members only. Breakfast included. Laundry €2.50. Internet €3 per hr. Reception 8am-midnight. Check-out noon. Mid-June to mid-Sept. dorms €12.50; doubles with bath €35. Mid-Sept. to mid-June €10/28. MC/V.) It is essential that you try the warm *bolos de berlim* (cream-filled pastries; €0.75) at **Confeitaria Natário** ❶, R. Manuel Espregueira 37. (☎82 23 76. Open M and W-Su 9am-10pm.) Buy groceries at **Estação Supermercado** on the second floor of the mall next to the train station. (☎288 10 08 10. Open daily 9am-11pm.) **Trains** (☎82 13 15) run from the station at the top of Av. dos Combatentes da Grande Guerra, to Porto (2hr., 13 per day, €5.50-6). **Buses** (☎82 50 47) run from the basement of the mall to: Braga (1½hr., 4-9 per day, €3.20); Lisbon (5½hr., 2-3 per day, €14); Porto (2hr., 9-11 per day, €5). The **tourist office** is in a lovely building on Tr. do Hospital Velho 8. (☎82 26 20. Open M-F 9am-12:30pm and 2:30-6pm, Sa 9:30am-1pm and 2:30-6pm, Su 9:30am-1pm.) **Postal Code:** 4900.

ROMANIA (ROMÂNIA)

As it emerges from decades of dictatorship under Nicolae Ceauşescu, modern Romania is in a state of transition. Some citizens are eager to Westernize, while others prefer to follow the rural lifestyles of their ancestors. The resulting state of confusion, combined with a largely undeserved reputation for poverty and crime, discourages foreign visitors. But travelers who dismiss Romania do themselves an injustice—it is a country rich in history, rustic beauty, and hospitality. Romania's fascinating legacy draws visitors to Dracula's dark castle and to the Bucovina monasteries, famous for their colorful frescoes. Meanwhile, new Romania is in evidence in the heavily touristed resort towns of the Black Sea Coast.

DISCOVER ROMANIA: SUGGESTED ITINERARIES

THREE DAYS. Head for **Transylvania,** a budget traveler's paradise, to relax in the Gothic hillside towns of **Sighişoara** (p. 853) and **Sinaia** (p. 852) and hike the **Fagaras Mountains.**

ONE WEEK. After three days in **Transylvania,** head to medieval **Bran** (1 day; p. 855) and stylish **Braşov** (1 day; p. 854), before ending in **Bucharest** (2 days; p. 848), the enigmatic capital.

ESSENTIALS

FACTS AND FIGURES

Official Name: Romania.
Capital: Bucharest.
Major Cities: Constanta, Iasi, Oradea.
Population: 22,400,000.
Land Area: 230,340 sq. km.
Time Zone: GMT +2.
Language: Romanian.
Religions: Eastern Orthodox (87%).

WHEN TO GO

Romania's varied climate makes it a year-round destination. The south has hot summers and mild winters, while winters are harsh and summers are cooler in the north, especially in the mountains. Summer tourist season reaches a fever pitch in July and August only along the Black Sea Coast; elsewhere, travelers will find a refreshing lack of crowds even in mid-summer; they should, however, remember that summer can be brutally hot in much of Romania.

DOCUMENTS AND FORMALITIES

EMBASSIES AND CONSULATES. Foreign embassies for Romania are in Bucharest (p. 848). Romanian embassies and consulates abroad include: Australia, 4 Dalman Cres., O'Malley, ACT 2606 (☎26 286 2343); Canada, 655 Rideau St., Ottawa, ON K1N 6A3 (☎613 789 4037; www.cyberus.ca/~romania); Ireland, 47 Ailesbury Rd., Ballsbridge, Dublin 4 (☎01 269 2852; romemb@iol.ie); UK, 4 Palace Green, London W8 40D (☎0207 937 9666; www.roemb.co.uk); US, 1607 23rd St. NW, Washington, D.C. 20008 (☎202-332-4848; www.roembus.org).

VISA AND ENTRY INFORMATION. Romanian visa rules change frequently; check with your embassy or consulate for the most accurate and specific information. Citizens of Canada, the UK, and the US can visit Romania for up to 90 days without

a visa while citizens of Ireland may visit for up to 30 days without visas. Citizens of Australia and New Zealand need visas for any length of stay. In all cases, passports are required and must be valid six months after the date of departure. Consult the Romanian embassy in your country of origin to apply for a visa. A visa application requires a passport, one application form per visa, a recent photograph, and the application fee. For Americans, a single-entry visa costs US$35; multiple-entry US$70. Visas are not available at the border. Romanian embassies estimate 30-day processing time for some visas. Apply early to allow the bureaucratic process to run its slow, frustrating course. **Visa extensions** and related services are available at police headquarters in large cities or at Bucharest's **passport office,** Str. Luigi Cazzavillan 11. Long lines are common at the border. Bags are rarely searched, but customs officials are strict about visa laws.

ENTRANCE REQUIREMENTS

Passport: Required for all travelers.

Visa: Not required for stays under 90 days for citizens of Canada, the UK, and the US. Citizens of Ireland may stay only for 30 days without a visa, and citizens of Australia and New Zealand require a visa for any length of stay.

Letter of Invitation: Not required for citizens of Australia, Canada, Ireland, New Zealand, the UK, and the US.

Inoculations: Not required. Recommended up-to-date on DTaP (diphtheria, tetanus, and pertussis), Hepatitis A, Hepatitis B, MMR (measles, mumps, and rubella), Polio booster, and Typhoid.

Work Permit: Required for all foreigners planning to work in Romania.

Driving Permit: Required for all those planning to drive in Romania.

TOURIST SERVICES AND MONEY

TOURIST OFFICES. Romania has limited tourist resources, but the National Tourist Office can be useful. Check its website at www.romaniatourism.com. It can help to walk into the most expensive hotel in town and pretend to be important. **Cluj-Napoca,** however, is a welcome relief with its many tourist offices.

MONEY. The Romanian currency is the **leu,** plural lei (abbreviated L), which was revalued in 2005. Bank notes are issued in amounts of L1, L5, L10, and L50; coins come in amounts of 1, 5, 10, and 50 bani (singular ban; L1=100 bani). **Inflation** rates have dropped dramatically and now hover around 10%. Romania has a **Value Added Tax (VAT)** of 19%. **ATMs** generally accept MasterCard and sometimes Visa, and are the best way to get money. ATMs are found everywhere but the smallest towns, usually operate 24hr., and occasionally run out of cash. Many locals carry US dollars; **private exchange bureaus,** which often offer better exchange rates than **banks,** are everywhere and deal in common foreign currencies. However, few take **credit cards** or **traveler's checks.** Compare rates before exchanging money. Most banks will cash traveler's checks in US dollars, then exchange them for lei, with high fees. **American Express Traveler's Cheques** are most useful. Changing money on the street is both illegal and a surefire way to get cheated.

LEI (L)		
	AUS$1 = L2.20	L1 = AUS$0.45
	CDN$1 = L2.40	L1 = CDN$0.42
	EUR€1 = L3.56	L1 = EUR€0.28
	NZ$1 = L2.03	L1 = NZ$0.49
	UK£1 = L5.24	L1 = UK£0.19
	US$1 = L2.92	L1 = US$0.34

HEALTH AND SAFETY

If possible, avoid Romanian **hospitals,** as most are not up to Western standards. Pack a **first-aid kit.** Go to a private doctor for medical emergencies; your embassy can recommend a good one. Some **American medical clinics** in Bucharest have English-speaking doctors; pay in cash. *Farmacies* (pharmacies) stock basic medical supplies. *Antinevralgic* is for headaches; *aspirină* or *piramidon* for colds and the flu; and *saprosan* for diarrhea. *Prezervatives* (condoms), *tampoane* (tampons), and *şerveţele igienice* (sanitary napkins) are available at drugstores and kiosks. Most **public restrooms** lack soap, towels, and toilet paper, and many on trains and in stations smell rank. Attendants may charge L1-1.50 for a single square of toilet paper. Pick up a roll at a drugstore and carry it with you. Beware of **stray dogs,** common everywhere including major cities, as they often carry **rabies.** Water quality in Romania is less contaminated than it once was. Still, avoid untreated **tap water** and do not use **ice cubes;** boil water before drinking it or drink imported **bottled water.** Beware of water-contaminated ice and vendor food.

Violent **crime** is not a major concern, but petty crime against tourists is common. Be especially careful on public transport and night trains. Beware of distracting children and con artists dressed as policemen who ask for your passport or wallet. If someone shows a badge and claims to be a plainclothes policeman, he is probably trying to scam you; ask the "officer" to escort you to the nearest police station. Pickpocketing, money exchange, and taxi scams are prevalent. Many scammers speak good English and German. The **drinking age,** which is 18, is not enforced. **Drug laws,** however, are strictly enforced. Single **female travelers** shouldn't go out alone after dark and should say they are traveling with a male. Tank tops, shorts, and sneakers may attract unwanted attention. **Minorities,** especially those with darker skin, may encounter discrimination, as they may be mistaken for Roma (Gypsies) and therefore considered untrustworthy. Practitioners of **religions** other than Orthodox Christianity may feel uncomfortable in Moldavia. **Homosexuality** is now legal, but public displays are ill-advised. Most Romanians hold conservative attitudes toward sexuality, which may translate into harassment of GLBT travelers and often manifests itself in the form of anti-gay propaganda in major cities. Still, women who walk arm-in-arm will not draw any attention.

EMERGENCY	**Police:** ☎955. **Ambulance:** ☎961. **Fire:** ☎981.

TRANSPORTATION

BY PLANE. Many airlines fly into Bucharest's **Otopeni International Airport** (OTP) which, though recently improved, is not completely modern. **TAROM** (Romanian Airlines; ☎21 201 4000; www.tarom.ro) recently updated its fleet; it flies directly from Bucharest to New York and major European and Middle Eastern cities.

BY TRAIN. Trains are better than buses for international travel. To buy tickets to the national railway, go to the **CFR** (Che-Fe-Re) office in larger towns. You must buy international tickets in advance. Train stations sell tickets 1hr. in advance. The English-language timetable *Mersul Trenurilor* (hardcopy L12; online at www.cfr.ro) is very useful. There are four types of trains: *InterCity* (indicated by an "IC" on timetables and at train stations); *rapid* (in green); *accelerat* (red); and *personal* (black). International trains (blue) are indicated with an "i." *InterCity* trains stop only at major cities. *Rapid* trains are the next fastest; *accelerat* trains start with "1" and are slower and dirtier. The sluggish and decrepit *personal* trains stop at every station. The difference between **first class** (*clasa întâi;* clah-sa un-toy; 6 people per compartment) and **second class** (*clasa doua;* 8 people) is small, except on *personal* trains. In an **overnight train,** shell out for a *vagon de dormit* (sleeping carriage), and buy both compartment tickets if you don't want to share.

BY BUS. Traveling to Romania by bus is often cheaper than entering by plane or train. Tourist agencies may sell timetables and tickets, but buying tickets from the carrier is often cheaper. Use the slow **local bus system** only when trains are unavailable. Local buses are slightly cheaper but are packed, poorly ventilated, and make perfect locations for pickpocketing and other forms of petty theft. Cheap, fast, and clean, **minibuses** are a good option for short distances. Rates are posted inside.

BY FERRY, CAR, AND BIKE. In the Danube Delta, boats are the best mode of transport. A ferry runs down the new European riverway from Rotterdam, the Netherlands to Constanţa, and in the Black Sea between Istanbul, Turkey and Constanţa. Be wary of **taxis;** only use cars that post a company name, phone number, and rate per kilometer. Be sure the driver uses the meter. Your ride should cost no more than L6 per kilometer plus a L7 flat fee. If you wish to drive a car, you must bring an International Driving Permit; make sure you are insured and have your registration papers. MyBike (www.mybike.ro) provides excellent info on biking.

BY THUMB. *Let's Go* does not recommend **hitchhiking.** Hitchhikers stand on the side of the road and put out their palm, as if waving. Drivers generally expect a **payment** similar to the price of a train or bus ticket for the distance traveled. In some places, hitchhiking is the only way to get around.

KEEPING IN TOUCH

PHONE CODES	**Country code:** 40. **International dialing prefix:** 00. For more information on how to place international calls, see inside back cover.

TELEPHONE AND INTERNET. Most pay phones are orange and accept **phone cards,** sold at telephone offices, metro stops, some post offices and kiosks. Only buy cards sealed in plastic wrap. Rates are around L1.20 per minute to neighboring countries, L1.60 per minute to most of Europe, and L2 per minute to the US. Phones operate in English if you press "i." At an analog phone, dial ☎971 for international calls. You may need to make a phone call *prin comandă* (with the help of the operator) at the telephone office; this takes longer and costs more. There are **no toll-free calls** in Romania—you even need a phone card to call the police, an ambulance, or the operator. People with European mobile phones can avoid roaming charges by buying a **SIM card** at **Connex, Dialog,** or **CosmoRom.** General info ☎931, operator ☎930. International access codes include: **AT&T Direct** (☎800 42 88); **Canada Direct** (☎800 50 00); **MCI WorldPhone** (☎800 18 00); and **Sprint** (☎800 08 770). **Internet** cafes are common in cities and cost L1.50-3 per hour. When calling from a mobile phone, you must always use the city code.

MAIL. At the post office, request *par avion* for **airmail,** which takes two weeks for delivery. Postcards or letters cost L2.10 to Europe and L3.10 for the rest of the world. **Mail** can theoretically be received through **Poste Restante.** However, you may run into problems picking up your package. Address envelopes as follows: First name LAST NAME, Oficiul Postal Post Office Address City-POSTE RESTANT, Romania, Postal Code. Major cities have **UPS,** and **Federal Express.**

LANGUAGE. Romanian is a Romance language, but with a Slavic-influenced vocabulary. Those familiar with French, Italian, Portuguese, or Spanish should be able to decipher many words. **German** and **Hungarian** are widely spoken in Transylvania. Throughout the country, **French** is a common second language for the older generation; **English** is common for the younger. Avoid **Russian,** which is often understood but disliked. For useful words and expressions see **Phrasebook: Romanian,** p. 1066.

ACCOMMODATIONS AND CAMPING

ROMANIA	❶	❷	❸	❹	❺
ACCOMMODATIONS	under L40	L40-70	L70-100	L100-200	over L200

Hostels are often fairly pleasant, but few are accredited. Some have perks like free beer and breakfast. While some **hotels** charge foreigners 50-100% more than Romanians, lodging is still inexpensive (US$7-20). Reservations are helpful, but not vital, in July and August. **Guesthouses** and **pensions** are simple and comfortable but rare. In summer, many towns rent low-priced rooms in **university dorms;** consult local tourist offices for help locating these deals. **Private rooms** and **homestays** are a great option, but hosts rarely speak English. Renting a room "together" means sharing a bed. Rooms cost US$7-12 in the countryside and US$15-20 in cities. Look at the room and fix a price before accepting. **Campgrounds** can be crowded and have frightening bathrooms. **Bungalows** are often full in summer; reserve far ahead. Hotels and hostels often provide the best information for tourists.

FOOD AND DRINK

ROMANIA	❶	❷	❸	❹	❺
FOOD	under L7	L7-11	L11-15	L15-20	over L20

A complete **Romanian meal** includes an appetizer, soup, fish, entree, and dessert. Lunch includes **soup,** called *supă* or *ciorbă* (the former has noodles or dumplings, the latter is saltier, with vegetables), an entree (typically grilled meat), and dessert. Soups can be very tasty; try *ciorbă de perişoare* (with vegetables and meatballs) or *supă cu găluște* (with fluffy dumplings). **Pork** comes in several varieties; *mușchi* and *cotlet* are of the highest quality. Common entrees include *mici* (rolls of fried meat), *sarmale* (stuffed cabbage), and *mămăligă* (polenta). **Beef** and **lamb** are other common meats. *Clătite* (crepes), *papanași* (doughnuts with jam and sour cream), and *torts* (creamy cakes), *mere în aluat* (doughnuts with apples) and sugary *gogoși* (fried doughnuts) are delectable. In the west, you'll find lots of **Hungarian food.** Some restaurants charge by weight rather than by portion;

it's difficult to predict how many grams you will receive. *Garnituri*, extras, are usually charged separately. This means you're paying for everything, even a bit of butter or a dollop of mustard. Pork rules in Romania, so keeping **kosher** is difficult, though possible. **Vegetarian** eating is also feasible, if you are willing to eat foods that are not traditionally Romanian. Local **drinks** include *ţuică*, a brandy distilled from plums and apples, and *palincă*, a stronger version of *ţuică* that approaches 70% alcohol. A delicious liqueur called *vişnată* is made from wild cherries.

HOLIDAYS AND FESTIVALS

Holidays: New Year's Holiday (Jan. 1-2); Epiphany (Jan. 6); Mărţişor (Mar. 1); Easter Holiday (Apr. 11-12); Labor Day (May 1); National Unity Day/Romania Day (Dec. 1).

Festivals: For Mărţişor locals wear *porte-boneurs* (good-luck charms) and give snow-drop flowers to friends and lovers. Romania Day commemorates the day in 1918 that Transylvania became a part of Romania.

BEYOND TOURISM

Central European Teaching Program, 3800 NE 72nd Ave., Portland, OR 97213, USA (☎503-287-4977; http://www.ticon.net/~cetp/). Places English teachers in state schools in Hungary and Romania for a semester (US$1500) or 10 months (US$2000).

University of Bucharest, 36-46 M. Kogălniceanu Bd., Sector 5, 70709 Bucharest, Romania (☎40 21 307 7300; www.unibuc.ro). Accepts international students.

BUCHAREST (BUCUREŞTI) ☎021

Bucharest (pop. 2,000,000) was a fabled beauty on the Orient Express until communist dictator Nicolae Ceauşescu rose to power and systematically replaced the grand boulevards and Ottoman ruins with wide highways and concrete blocks.

TRANSPORTATION

Flights: Otopeni Airport (☎204 10 00), 16km from the city. Bus #783 to Otopeni runs from Pţa. Unirii with stops throughout the center. Buy **tickets** at the **TAROM office,** Spl. Independenţei 7. (☎337 04 00; www.tarom.ro.) Open M-F 9am-7pm, Sa 9am-1pm.

Trains: Gara de Nord (☎223 08 80) is the main station. M1: Gara de Nord. To: **Braşov** (4hr., 16 per day, L24.70); **Budapest, Hungary** (14hr., 4 per day, L141.24); **Cluj-Napoca** (10hr., 6 per day, L47.60); **Kraków, Poland** (27hr., 1 per day, L286); **Prague, Czech Republic** (36hr., 1 per day, L330); **Sighişoara** (6hr., 9 per day, L35.20); **Sofia, Bulgaria** (13hr., 2 per day, L77). **CFR,** Str. Domniţa Anastasia 10-14 (☎313 26 43; www.cfr.ro) books train tickets. Open M-F 7:30am-7:30pm, Sa 9am-1:30pm. Inside Gara de Nord, **Wasteels** (☎222 78 44; www.wasteelstravel.ro), books international tickets. Open M-F 8am-7pm, Sa 8am-2pm.

Buses: Filaret, Cuţitul de Argint 2 (☎335 11 40). M2: Tineretului. Near the center. To **Athens, Greece,** buy tickets from **Ager Agency** (☎336 67 83). To **Istanbul, Turkey,** try a **Toros** (☎223 18 98; 2 per day, L125) or **Murat** (☎224 92 93) from outside Gara de Nord. **Double T,** Calea Victoriei 2 (☎313 36 42), a Eurail affiliate, and **Eurolines Touring,** Str. Ankara 6 (☎230 03 70), travel to Western Europe.

Public Transportation: Buses, trolleys, and **trams** run daily 5:30am-11:30pm. Tickets (L1) sold at kiosks only; validate on-board or face fines. **Express buses** take only magnetic cards (L4.4 for 2 trips; sold at kiosks). Pickpocketing is a problem during peak hours. The **metro** offers reliable and less-crowded service to major points. Open daily 5am-11:30pm. Magnetic cards L1.8 for 2 trips, L6 for 10 trips.

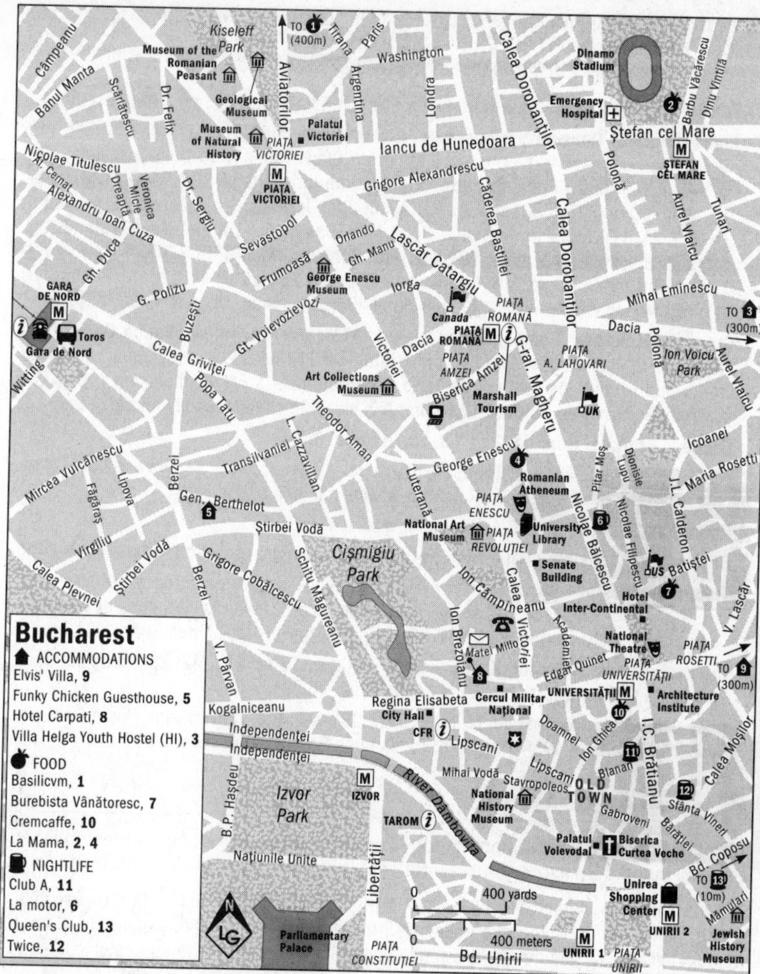

Taxis: Taxi drivers will cheerfully rip off foreigners; only use taxis with a company name, phone number, and per km rate posted in the window. Official rates are L1 base fee plus L1 per km. Drivers rarely speak English. More reliable companies include **Meridien** (☎94 44), **ChrisTaxi** (☎94 61), and **Taxi2000** (☎94 94).

ORIENTATION AND PRACTICAL INFORMATION

The main street changes its name from **Bulevardul Lascăr Catargiu** to **Bulevardul General Magheru** to **Bulevardul Nicolae Bălcescu** to **Bulevardul I.C. Brătianu** as it runs north-south through Bucharest's four main squares: **Piața Victoriei, Piața Romană, Piața Universității,** and **Piața Unirii. Gara de Nord,** the train station, lies along the M1 metro line. From there, to reach the city center take the M1 (dir.: Dristor) one stop to Pţa. Victoriei, then change to the M2 (dir.: Depoul IMGB). One stop reaches Piaţa Romană, two stops Pţa. Universităţii, and three stops Pţa. Unirii. The helpful *Bucharest In Your Pocket* is free at museums, bookstores, and hotels.

Tourist Information: Gara de Nord has a booth but hotels tend to be better resources.

Embassies and Consulates: Australia, Bd. Unirii 74, 5th fl. (☎320 98 02). M2: Pţa. Unirii, then bus #104, 123, or 124 to Lucian Blaga. Open M-Th 9am-1pm and 1:30-5:30pm, F 9am-2:30pm. **Canada,** Str. Nicolae Iorga 36 (☎307 50 00). M2: Pţa. Romană. Open M-Th 8:30am-5pm, F 8:30am-2pm. **Ireland,** Str. V. Lascăr 42-44, 6th fl. (☎212 21 81). M2: Pţa. Romană. Open M-F 10am-noon. **UK** and **New Zealand,** Str. Jules Michelet 24 (☎201 72 79). M2: Pţa. Romană. Open M-Th 8:30am-1pm and 2-5pm, F 8:30am-1:30pm. **US,** Str. Nicolae Filipescu 26 (☎210 40 42; after-hours 210 01 49). M2: Pţa. Universităţii, behind Hotel Intercontinental. Open M-Th 8am-5pm.

Currency Exchange: Exchange agencies and **ATMs** are everywhere. **Banca Comercială Română,** in Pţa. Victoriei and Pţa. Universităţii (☎312 61 85; www.bcr.com), has good rates and exchanges **AmEx Traveler's Cheques** for a 1.5% commission. Open M-F 8:30am-5:30pm, Sa 8:30am-12:30pm. It is illegal to change money on the street.

Luggage Storage: Gara de Nord. L3. Large bags L6. 24hr.

GLBT Resources: Accept Romania, Str. Lirei 10 (☎252 16 37; www.accept-romania.ro). News on gay rights in Romania, social info, and useful links.

Emergency: Police: ☎955. **Ambulance:** ☎961. **Fire:** ☎981.

Pharmacies: Sensiblu pharmacies (☎0800 080 234) are ubiquitous, some open 24hr.

Telephones: Phone cards (L10, or L15) are necessary for emergency numbers and worthwhile for domestic and some international calls. Place collect calls at **Romtelecom,** Calea Victoriei 35 (☎313 36 35). M2: Pţa. Universităţii. Open 24hr.

Internet Access: Jazz Club, Calea Victoriei 120 (☎312 48 41). M2: Pţa. Romană. 9am-11pm L3 per hr., 11pm-9am L1.5 per hr. Open 24hr.

Post Office: Str. Matei Millo 10 (☎315 87 93). M2: Pţă. Universităţii. *Poste Restante* available. Open M, W, F 7am-3pm; Tu, Th noon-8pm. **Postal Code:** 014700.

ACCOMMODATIONS

Renting private rooms is uncommon. Travelers won't go wrong with established hostels, but should avoid "representatives" that greet them at Gara de Nord.

Elvis' Villa, Str. Avram Iancu 5 (☎312 16 53; www.elvisvilla.ro). M2: Pţa. Universităţii. Or, from Gara de Nord, take trolley #85 to Calea Moşilor. Continue along Bd. Carol I, turn right on Str. Sfântul Ştefan, and left onto Str. Avram Iancu. Newer hostel in a quiet, older part of town. A/C. Breakfast and laundry included. Dorms €10. Cash only. ❶

Villa Helga Youth Hostel (HI), Str. Salcâcmilor 2 (☎610 22 14). M2: Pţa. Romană. Take bus #86, 79, or 133 2 stops from Pţa. Romană or 6 stops from Gara de Nord to Pţa. Gemeni. Go 1 block on Bd. Dacia and take a right on Str. Viitorului. Comfortable beds and friendly staff. Breakfast and laundry included. Book ahead in summer. Check-out noon. Dorms €10; singles €14; doubles €24. 5% HI discount. Cash only. ❶

Funky Chicken Guesthouse, Str. General Berthelot 63 (☎312 14 25), from Gara de Nord, go right on Calea Griviţei, right on Str. Berzei, and left onto Str. General Berthelot. Bucharest's newest, cheapest, and best-located hostel. Dorms €8. Cash only. ❶

Hotel Carpati, Str. Matei Millo 16 (☎315 01 40; fax 312 18 57). M2: Pţa. Universităţii. Walk or take the bus down Bd. Regina Elisabeta to Str. I. Brezoianu and turn right. Central location, clean rooms, new furnishings, balconies, and a professional staff. Most rooms with shared bath. Breakfast included. Singles €20-22; doubles €30-39. ❷

FOOD

The **Open-air market** at Pţa. Amzei, near Pţa. Română has meat, cheese, and produce. A large **La Fourmi Supermarket** is in the basement of the Unirea Shopping Center on Pţa. Unirii. (Open M-F 8am-9:30pm, Sa 8:30am-9pm, Su 8am-4pm.)

Burebista Vânătoresc, Str. Batistei 14 (☎211 89 29). M2: Pţa. Universităţii. Off Bd. Nicolae Bălcescu. Traditional atmosphere, complete with a stuffed bear and live folk band. Choose from a menu featuring several tasty wild game dishes, including bear and wild boar. Entrees L10-59. Full bar. Open daily noon-midnight. MC/V. ❸

Basilicvm, Str. Popa Savu 7 (☎222 67 79). M2: Aviatorilor. Praiseworthy food and Italian menu are complemented by a refined setting and attentive service. Weekend lunch special puts everything at half-price. Entrees L14-65. Open daily 11am-1am. MC. ❹

La Mama, Str. Barbu Văcărescu 3 (☎212 40 86; www.lamama.ro). M1: Ştefan cel Mare. Other branches: Str. Delea Veche 51 (☎320 52 13), M1: Pţa. Muncii; Str. Episcopiei 9 (☎312 97 97), M2: Pţa. Română. Lives up to its motto "like at mom's house," with traditional Romanian dishes, low prices, and relaxed atmosphere. Reservations recommended. Entrees L10-14. Open daily 10am-2am. AmEx/MC/V. ❷

Cremcaffe, Str. T. Caragiu 3 (☎313 97 40). M2: Pţa. Universităţii. Just off Bd. Regina Elisabeta and between the statues, in Pţa. Universităţii. Elegant Italian coffeehouse features delicious foccacia sandwiches from L10. Coffee/liqueur blends from L12; ice cream from L8. Open M-F 7:30am-midnight, Sa-Su 9am-midnight. Cash only. ❷

SIGHTS

CIVIC CENTER. To create his ideal Socialist capital, Ceauşescu destroyed five sq. km of Bucharest's historical center, demolishing over 9000 19th-century houses and displacing more than 40,000 people. The Civic Center (Centru Civic) he built lies at the end of the 6km Bd. Unirii, built 1m wider than its inspiration, the Champs-Elysées. Its centerpiece, the **Parliamentary Palace** (Palatul Parlamentului), is the world's second-largest building after the Pentagon. Between 1984 and 1989, in the last years of the Ceauşescu regime, over 20,000 workers assembled it from Romanian wood and marble. *(M1 or 3: Izvor, M2: Unirii. Visitors' entrance is on the north side of the building. Open daily 10am-4pm. English tours L20, students L5.)*

SIGHTS OF THE REVOLUTION. The first shots of the Revolution were fired at **Piaţa Revoluţiei** on December 21, 1989. The square contains the **University Library,** the **National Art Museum,** and the **Senate Building** (formerly Communist Party Headquarters), on whose balcony Ceauşescu delivered his final speech. A white marble triangle with the inscription "*Glorie martirilor nostri*" (Glory to our martyrs) commemorates the rioters who overthrew the dictator. *(M2: Pţa. Universităţii. With Hotel Intercontinental on your left, turn right on Bd. Regina Elisabeta and right again on Calea Victoriei.)* **Piaţa Universităţii** houses memorials to victims of the 1989 revolution and the protests of 1990. Crosses line the center of Bd. Nicolae Bălcescu—the black one marks the spot where the first victim died. In June of 1990, the *piaţa* was again gripped by student riots. Ceauşescu's replacement, Ion Iliescu, bussed in over 10,000 miners to put down the protest, killing 21 students. He has since been democratically elected, but anti-Iliescu graffiti persists on the walls of **Bucharest University** and the **Architecture Institute.** *(M2: Piaţa Universităţii.)*

MUSEUMS. The **Village Museum** (Muzeul Satului), Şos. Kiseleff 28-30, is an open-air replica of a traditional rural village. *(M2: Aviatorilor. ☎222 90 68. Open M 9am-4pm, Tu-Su 9am-6pm. L5, students L2.50.)* The **National Art Museum** (Muzeul Naţional de Artă al României) has works by famous Westerners, but the highlights are paintings by Nicolae Grigorescu and sculpture by Constantin Brâncuşi. *(Calea Victoriei 49-53, in Pţă. Revoluţiei. M2: Pţă. Universităţii. ☎315 51 93. Open W-Su summer 11am-7pm; winter 10am-6pm. L12, students L6.)* The **Museum of the Romanian Peasant** (Muzeul Ţăranului Român) captures Romanian rural life. *(Şos. Kiseleff 3. M2 or 3: Pţa. Victoriei. Open Tu-Su 10am-6pm. L6, students L2.)* Extensive collections of gold and jewels are on display at the **National History Museum** (Muzeul Naţional de Istorie al României) as well as a replica of Trajan's Column. *(Calea Victoriei 12. M2: Pţă. Universităţii. ☎315 70 56. Open Tu-Su 10am-6pm. L3.06, students L1.53.)*

OTHER SIGHTS. Several of modern Bucharest's most fashionable streets, including **Calea Victoriei, Şoseauna Kiseleff, Bulevardul Aviatorilor,** and **Bulevardul Magheru,** are sights in themselves. Side streets just off Pţa. Victoriei and Pţa. Dorobanţilor brim with villas and houses typical of beautiful 19th-century Bucharest. The sole vestiges of Bucharest's **old center** lie west of Bd. Brătianu and south of Bd. Regina Elisabeta, in the vicinity of Str. Lipscani and Str. Gabroveni.

ENTERTAINMENT AND NIGHTLIFE

Theater, symphony, and **opera** performances are cheap (from L3); for the best deals, stop by the box office about a week before a show. No performances are staged from June to September. At night, pack a map and cab fare—streets are poorly lit and public transportation stops at 11:30pm. **La motor,** Bd. Bălcescu 1-3, atop the National Theater, is a student bar with a lively terrace in summer. (☎315 85 08. M2: Pţa. Universităţii. Open daily noon-2am.) Nightclub **Twice,** Str. Sfânta Vineri 4, has two dance floors. (☎313 55 92. M2: Pţa. Universităţii. Cover M-Tu, Th, Su free; W L5; F-Sa men L10, women free. Open Tu-Su 9pm-5am.) **Club A,** Str. Blănari 14, is Bucharest's most famous nightspot, with absurdly cheap drinks and loud rock music. (☎315 68 53; www.cluba.ro. M2: Pţa. Universităţii. Cover F-Sa men L5, women L2. Open daily 11am-5am.) Popular **Queen's Club,** Str. Iuliu Barasch 12-14, near the Jewish Theater, is the only GLBT nightspot in central Bucharest. Head up Calea Coposu, and turn right onto Iuliu Barasch. (☎0722 642 891; www.queen-s-club.ro. M1 and M2: Unirii. Cover L20 includes 1 drink. Open F-Sa 11pm-5am.)

SINAIA ☎0244

Sinaia (sih-NAI-uh; pop. 15,000) first made its mark in the late 1880s as an Alpine getaway for Romania's royal family. Carol I, king of the newly independent country, oversaw construction of the fantastically opulent **Peleş Castle** (Castelul Peleş), completed in 1914. The more modest **Pelişor Castle,** built in 1902, was furnished in the Art Nouveau style by the wife of Carol's cousin Ferdinand, Queen Maria. (Both open Tu 11am-5pm, W-Su 9am-5pm; low season closed Tu. Peleş L10, students L5. Pelişor L8/3.) The nearby **Bucegi Mountains** are good for hiking in the summer and skiing in the winter. A cable car *(telecabină)* to the mountains leaves from behind Hotel New Montana, Bd. Carol I 24, to two stops: one at 1400m and the other at 2000m. (Cars run Tu-F 8:30am-4pm, Sa-Su 8:30am-5pm. In summer, the last car can be as early as 3:45pm. L9 to 1400m; L18 to 2000m.)

The **Cabana Mioriţa ❶,** at the Cota 2000 station, with a bar and restaurant, is the queen of the mountain cabin system. (Dorms L30; private rooms L50.) For traditional fare in a small-town cafe atmosphere, head to **Restaurant Bucegi ❶,** near the top of the stairs by the station. (Entrees L5.50-29. Open daily 9am-10pm. Cash only.) After a long day of hiking, grab a beer (from L4) at the Canadian-style **Old Nick's Pub,** Bd. Carol I 8, by the Hotel Sinaia. (☎31 24 91. Open daily 9am-2am.) **Trains** (☎31 00 40) run to Braşov (1hr., 15 per day, L7.30); Bucharest (2hr., 15 per day, L15.70); Cluj-Napoca (5hr., 5 per day, L29). To get to the center of town, climb the second set of stone steps across from the station. The friendly, English-speaking staff at the **tourist office,** Bd. Carol I 47, has an official list of **private rooms,** as well as information about hiking and skiing. (☎315 656; www.infosinaia.ro. Rooms €7-12. Open M-F 8:30am-4:30pm.) **Postal Code:** 106100.

TRANSYLVANIA (TRANSILVANIA)

In Western imagination, Transylvania evokes a dark land of black magic and vampires, the nest of Nosferatu. Those seeking the Transylvania of legend will not be disappointed by the region's tilted, jagged, and harshly Gothic buildings. Architecture aside, Transylvania is actually a relatively Westernized region with beautiful green hills descending from the Carpathians to the Hungarian Plain.

CLUJ-NAPOCA ☎0264

Cluj-Napoca (KLOOZH nah-POH-kah; pop. 400,000) is Transylvania's student center and unofficial capital. The city is a good base for a journey into Transylvania or north to Maramureş. The 80m Gothic steeple of the Catholic **Church of St. Michael** (Biserica Sf. Mihail) rises from **Piaţa Unirii.** Take Str. Regele Ferdinand across the river, turn left on Str. Dragalina, and climb the stairs on your right to reach the dazzling city view from **Cetătuie Hill.** Over 12,000 plant species grow in the **Botanical Garden** (Grădina Botanica), Str. Republicii 42, off Str. Napoca. (Open daily 9am-7pm. L4.) Hotels distribute the free *Şapte Seri,* which lists the latest nightlife.

Retro Youth Hostel ❷, Str. Potaissa 13, has clean rooms near the university and arranges excursions. (☎450 452; www.retro.ro. Breakfast L10. Laundry L10. Free Internet. Dorms L40. MC/V.) Location doesn't get any better than **Hotel Melody-Central ❹,** Pţa. Unirii 29, with a helpful tourist bureau in the lobby. (☎597 465; www.hcm.ro. Breakfast included. Free Internet. Singles L130; doubles L150-190. MC/V.) **Roata ❷,** Str. Alexandru Ciura 6a, off Str. Emil Isac, is a traditional Romanian restaurant. (☎192 022. Entrees L12.50-22. Open Su-M 1pm-midnight, Tu-Sa noon-midnight. MC/V.) Students shoot pool to rock, jazz, and techno at **Music Pub,** Str. Horea 5. (☎432 517. F-Sa 9 or 10pm live music. Open daily 4pm-3am.)

Trains go to: Bucharest (8-13hr., 5 per day, L34.10) via Braşov (5-7hr., L28); Budapest (6½-7hr., 2 per day, L117); Sibiu (4hr., 1 per day, L30); Timişoara (6hr., 3 per day, L28). Local **buses** and **trams** run 5am-10pm; tickets (L1.10) are sold at **RATUC** kiosks. **ATMs** line Bd. Ferdinand. **Club Internet,** Str. Oberth 3, is just off Bd. Erialor. (L1 per hr.; midnight-8am L0.50 per hr. Open 24hr.) **Postal Code:** 400110.

SIGHIŞOARA ☎0265

Vlad Ţepeş, the model for Bram Stoker's *Dracula* (see **Bran,** p. 855), was born in the enchanting hilltown of Sighişoara (pop. 39,000). Its gilded steeples and old clock tower have survived centuries of attacks, fires, and floods. The **Cetatea** (citadel), built by the Saxons in 1191, is now a tiny medieval city-within-a-city. Enter through the **turnul cu ceas** (clock tower), off Str. O. Goga; pass by the museum and ascend for the view. To the left as you leave the clock tower, the **Colecţia de Arme Medievale** (Museum of Medieval Armory) offers a modest, English-captioned exhibit on Vlad Ţepeş and international weaponry. The **torture room** houses a very small collection of pain-inflicting instruments. (Open M 10am-4:30pm, Tu-F 9am-6:30pm, Sa-Su 9am-4:30pm. Clock tower L4.08, students L2.55; museum L2.55/1.53; torture room L1.53.) Turn right from the station to reach **Nathan's Villa Hostel ❶,** Str. Libertăţii 8. The friendly, multilingual staff organizes daytrips. (☎772 546. Dorms L30.) **Trains** go to Bucharest (5hr., 6 per day, L37.1) via Braşov (2hr., L23.1), and Cluj-Napoca (3½hr., 3 per day, L29.4). To reach the city center, turn right on Str. Libertății and left onto Str. Gării; veer left at the Russian cemetery, turn right onto the footbridge over Târana Mare, and walk down Str. Morii. There is no tourist office, but info is available at the train station. **Postal Code:** 545400.

BRAȘOV ☎0268

Brașov (pop. 353,000) is an ideal departure point for trips into the mountains. A cable car *(telecabină)* goes up **Muntele Tâmpa;** to reach it from **Piața Sfatului,** walk down Apollonia Hirscher, make a left on Str. Castelui, a right on Suișul Castelui, and head up the stairs to the beige building on the right. (Cable car runs M noon-6pm, Tu-W and F 9:30am-6pm, Th 9:30am-5pm, Sa-Su 9:30am-7pm. L6 round-trip.) Alternatively, follow the red triangle markings to hike to the top (1½hr.). Brașov itself is a picturesque town with peaceful side streets. Beyond the square along Str. Gh. Barițiu is Romania's most celebrated Gothic edifice, the Lutheran **Black Church** (Biserica Neagră), which received its name after being charred by fire in 1689. (Open M-Sa 10am-5pm. L3, students L1.50.) Tickets to the **opera** and **orchestra** may be purchased at the Agencia Teatrală de Bilete box office on Str. Republicii 4. (☎471 889. Open Tu-F 10am-5pm, Sa 10am-2pm. Opera tickets L6.30, students L3.15. Orchestra L8/4. Cash only.) The **International Chamber Music Festival** is held here in early September. Each summer, Pță. Sfatului hosts the **Golden Stag Festival** (Cerbul de Aur), which attracts international musicians.

Locals offer **private rooms** at the train station; expect to pay €10-15. **Kismet Dao Villa Hostel ❷,** Str. Democrației 2b, includes breakfast, laundry, a daily drink, and 1hr. of Internet. From Pță. Unirii, walk up Str. Bâlea and turn right. (☎514 296. Dorms €10-11; doubles €25. MC/V.) Romantic, candlelit **Bella Muzica ❷,** Str. G. Barițiu 2, has an eclectic Romanian-Mexican menu, as well as free chips and free shots of *palincă*. (☎476 946. Entrees L7-38.50. Open daily noon-11pm. MC/V.) **Taverna ❸,** Str. Politehnicii 6, serves Romanian, Hungarian, and French cuisine in an elegant setting. (☎474 618; www.taverna.ro. Entrees L10.90-41.90. Open daily noon-midnight. MC/V.) **Trains** run to: Bucharest (3-4hr., 20 per day, L25.80); Cluj-Napoca (5-6hr., 5 per day, L39.70); Iași (9-10hr., 1 per day, L31); Sibiu (4hr., 4 per day, L22.8). Buy tickets at **CFR,** Bd. 15 Noiembrie 43. (☎47 70 18. Open M-F 8am-7:30pm.) From the station, take bus #4 (dir.: Pță. Unirii) to Pță. Sfatului (10min.); get off in front of Black Church. The **tourist office,** Pța. Sfatului 30, gives out free maps. (☎419 078; www.brasovcity.ro. Open daily 9am-6pm.) **Postal Code:** 500000.

SON OF A...

'es, Dracula did exist–sort of. He vas not the ruler of Transylvania, out of Wallachia; he was not a count, but a *voivod* (a local governor or "prince"); and he was not a ampire. Still, the truth about lad Țepeș (1431-1476) is enough to make anyone lock the id to his coffin at night.

Dracula's story begins with his ather, Vlad Basarab, who was icknamed Dragul (dragon) for nis skill with arms–and his ruthessness. Dragul sent his son, Dragula (son of the dragon), to he Ottoman Empire as a hostage n 1442, at the tender age of 10. During his six years as a hostage, lad learned what was to become nis preferred method of torture: mpalement. Victims of impalement–which involved inserting a arge wooden stake through the victim's body without piercing the ital organs–usually begged for a swift death throughout the slow, agonizing process.

Vlad the Impaler earned his itle during his reign as *voivod*. In addition to murderers, thieves, iars, and political rivals, he mpaled the old, the destitute, and the crippled. His crowning achievement was in turning the Turks' gruesome practice against hem. In 1462, the invading Turks urned tail at Wallachia's border, which had been decorated with 20,000 of their impaled countrymen. As his terror tactics became nfamous, the son of the dragon was renamed the son of the devil, Vlad Dracula.

BRAN

☎0268

Vlad Ţepeş, the model for the hero-villain of Bram Stoker's novel *Dracula*, once lived in Bran. Dracula's exploits pale in comparison with Ţepeş's: as a local governor of the Wallachia region, he protected the Bran pass from encroaching Turks, garnering infamy for impaling his enemies. Turks invading Wallachia in 1462 swiftly retreated in horror after they were welcomed to Ţepeş's territory by the sight of some 20,000 of their kinsmen on stakes. Known to many as Vlad the Impaler, he was also a member of the Order of the Dragon, which undertook to defend the faith from infidels—hence the name "Dracula," from Vlad Dracul, or "Dragon." While Ţepeş may have been a guest at **Bran Castle,** built under Hungarian rule in 1377-1382, there is little evidence that he lived there—nor, in fact, did Stoker, an Irishman, ever visit Romania. (Castle open M noon-6pm, Tu-Su 9am-6pm. L10, students L5.) To reach Bran from Braşov, take a taxi or city **bus** #5 or 12 to Autogară 2 (45min., 1-2 per hr. 7am-11:30pm, L2.50). Get off at the souvenir market or at the sign marked "Cabana Bran Castle—500m." Backtrack along the road toward Braşov; the castle is on the right. **Postal Code:** 507025.

TIMIŞOARA

☎0256

Timişoara (pop. 334,000), Romania's westernmost city, is also one of the country's liveliest. In 1989 an anti-Ceauşescu rally in **Piaţă Victoriei** ignited the revolution that overthrew the Communists. At one end of the square stands the imposing **Metropolitan Cathedral,** with a brightly-tiled roof in the Byzantine and Moldavian folk style. (Open daily 6:30am-8pm, Vespers daily 6pm.) In nearby **Huniade Castle,** the **Banat Museum** *(Muzeul Banatului)*, traces Timişoara's history. (Open Tu-Su 10am-4:30pm. Two floors; L2 each, students L1.) Across the square is the **National Theater and Opera** (Box office open daily Sept.-June 10am-1pm and 5-7pm. Theater L10; opera L5.) **Hotel Nord ❷**, Str. Gen. Ion Dragalina 47, by the train station, has comfy rooms with TV and fridge. (☎497 504. Breakfast included. Singles €18; doubles €28. MC/V.) **Trains** run from Timişoara Nord to: Braşov (9hr., 1 per day, L31); Bucharest (8hr., 5 per day, L48.50) and Cluj-Napoca (7hr., 4 per day, L26.50). From the station, take city bus #11 or 14 eastward to the center of town (L1.20; buy tickets at **RATT** kiosks). **Librăria Mihai Eminescu,** Str. Macesilor 2, in Pţa. Victoriei, sells maps. (Open M-F 9am-8pm, Sa 10am-1:30pm.) **Postal Code:** 300005.

MOLDAVIA AND BUCOVINA

Eastern Romania, known as Moldavia (Moldova), extends from the Carpathians to the Prut River. Starker than Transylvania but more developed than Maramureş, Moldavia contains the painted monasteries of Bucovina tucked amid green hills and farming villages. Their exquisite structures mix Moldavian and Byzantine architecture with Romanian Christian images. The best way to see the monasteries is through organized tours from Gura Humorului or Suceava; dress modestly.

GURA HUMORULUI

☎0230

Gura Humorului is an ideal base for monastery tours. Bucovina's oldest frescoes are at **Humor,** known for its life cycle of the Virgin Mary. Walk right on Str. Ştefan cel Mare from the train or bus station to the center of town. At the fork near a park on the right, take Str. Manasteria Humorului to the left and continue 6km to the monastery. (Open daily 7am-8pm. L4, students L2.) The well-preserved frescoes of **Moldoviţa,** painted in 1537, portray the Last Judgment, Jesse's Tree, and a monumental Siege of Constantinople. (Open daily 7am-8pm. L4, students L2.) Take an early **train** from Gura Humorului to Vama (20min., 9 per day, L3.90) and continue to Vatra Moldoviţei (45min., 3 per day, L2.40). Ştefan cel Mare built **Voroneţ** in 1488, and in 1524 his illegitimate son, Petru Rareş, added its famous frescoes. (Open daily 7am-8pm. L4, students L2.) Take a **bus** from Gura Humorului (15min., mid-Sept. to mid-June M-F 3 per day, L1), or walk left from the train station, turn left again onto Cartierul Voroneţ, and follow the signs for a scenic 5km.

Pensiune Casa Ella ❷, Str. Cetaţii 7, off Bd. Bucovina, offers soft beds and home-cooked breakfasts. (☎23 29 61. Breakfast L8. Singles L40; doubles L60. Cash only.) The more luxurious **Vila Fabian ❸**, is across Str. Voroneţ from Dispecerat de Cazare. (☎153 724. Breakfast included. Singles L50; doubles L100. Cash only.) On Bd. Bucovina, past the park from the main square, **Restaurant Lions ❷** has an international menu in a royalty-themed setting. (Pizza L7-10. Entrees L10-26. Open daily 9am-11:30pm. MC/V.) **Trains** go to: Bucharest (6hr., 2 per day, L45.20); Cluj-Napoca (5hr., 4 per day, L25.60); Suceava (1hr., 6 per day, L3.20-5.80). From the station, turn right onto Str. Ştefan cel Mare and continue over the bridge to reach the city center. **Dispecerat de Cazare,** where Str. Câmpului ends at Str. Voroneţ, has tourist info; from the station, head left off Str. Ştefan cel Mare and left onto Str. Câmpului. The office arranges car tours (€30-35) and rooms. (☎23 38 63. Open Mar.-Nov. daily 11am-9pm.) **Postal Code:** 725300.

SUCEAVA ☎0230

Once Moldavia's capital, Suceava is home to the grand 1388 **Citadel of the Throne** (Cetatea de Scaun). Climb the ramparts for a spectacular view. Taxis (5min., L3) from the main square, Pţă. 22 Decembrie, spare travelers the 10min. walk through the seedy park. (Open daily 8am-8pm; low season 10am-5pm. L3, students L1.50). On Str. Ana Ipătescu, walk past the bus shelter and turn left, to find the 1535 **Biserica St. Dumitru,** covered with brilliantly colorful frescoes that feature a particularly vicious Hellmouth on the portico. (Open daily 8am-7pm.)

The spacious **Class Hostel ❶**, Str. Aurel Vlaicu 195, arranges monastery tours and cooks for vegetarians. (☎723 782 328. Breakfast included. Dorms €13. MC/V.) **Pub Chagall ❷**, on the corner of Str. N. Bălcescu and Str. Ştefan cel Mare, serves filling pub food in a cozy cellar. (Entrees L5.40-15.60. Open M-Sa 10am-midnight, Su 11am-midnight. Cash only.) **Trains** run to: Braşov (8hr., 1 per day, L34.10); Bucharest (6hr., 5 per day, L34.10); Cluj-Napoca (6hr., 4 per day, L27.90); Gura Humorului (1hr., 10 per day, L7.30). Buy tickets at **CFR**, Str. N. Bălcescu 4. (☎21 43 35. Open M-F 7:30am-7pm.) **Buses** (☎52 43 40) run from the intersection of Str. N. Bălcescu and Str. V. Alecsandri to: Bucharest (8hr., 4 per day, L32); Cluj-Napoca (7hr., 1 per day, L31); Gura Humorului (1hr., 12 per day, L4.50). **Librăria Lidana,** on Str. Ştefan cel Mare off the main square, sells **maps.** (☎377 324. Open M-F 9am-6pm, Sa 9am-3pm. Maps L11.90.) **Postal Code:** 720290.

RUSSIA (РОССИЯ)

More than a decade after the collapse of the Soviet Union, vast Russia stumbles along with no clear direction; former Communists run the state, while impoverished pensioners long for a rose-tinted Soviet past. Heedless of surrounding provinces, cosmopolitan Moscow gorges on hyper-capitalism, while majestic St. Petersburg struggles to remain one of Europe's major cultural centers. Although traveling here can be a bureaucratic nightmare, Russia is in many ways the ideal destination for a budget traveler—inexpensive and well served by public transportation, with hundreds of monasteries, kremlins, and onion-domed churches.

ESSENTIALS

FACTS AND FIGURES

Official Name: Russian Federation.
Capital: Moscow.
Population: 143,421,000.
Land Area: 16,995,800 sq. km.
Time Zone: GMT +3.
Language: Russian.
Religion: Russian Orthodox (72%).

WHEN TO GO

It may be wise to plan around the high season (June-Aug.). The fall and spring (Sept.-Oct. and Apr.-May) are better times to visit; the weather is reasonable and flights are cheaper. If you intend to visit the large cities and linger indoors at museums and theaters, the bitter winter (Nov.-Mar.) is most economical. Keep in mind, however, that sights and accommodations often close or run reduced hours, especially in rural areas. Another factor to consider is hours of daylight—in St. Petersburg, summer light lasts almost to midnight, but in winter the sun may set as early as 3:45pm. Whenever you go, it will rain; have warm, waterproof clothing on hand.

DOCUMENTS AND FORMALITIES

EMBASSIES AND CONSULATES. Foreign embassies for Russia are in Moscow (p. 864). Russian embassies abroad include: **Australia,** 78 Canberra Ave., Griffith, ACT 2603 (☎6 6295 9033; rusemb@dynamite.com.au); **Canada,** 285 Charlotte St., Ottawa, ON K1N 8L5 (☎613-235-4341; rusemb@magma.ca); **Ireland,** 186 Orwell Rd., Rathgar, Dublin 14 (russiane@indigo.ie); **New Zealand,** 57 Messines Rd., Karori, Wellington (☎64 4 476 6113, visa info 476 6742; eor@netlink.co.nz); **UK,** 13 Kensington Palace Gardens, London W8 4QX (☎44 171 229 3628, visa info 229-8027; dom.harhouse1@harhouse1.demon.co.uk); **US,** 2650 Wisconsin Ave., NW, Washington, D.C. 20007 (☎202-298-5700; www.russianembassy.org).

VISA AND ENTRY INFORMATION. Almost every visitor to Russia needs a visa. Several types exist; the standard tourist visa is valid for 30 days, a business visa up to three months, and both come in single- and double-entry varieties. All applications for Russian visas require an **invitation** stating the traveler's itinerary and dates of travel. Hostels and hotels can often provide invitations for tourist visas to those who make reservations with them (and sometimes those who don't, for a fee). **Visa services** and **travel agencies** (see p. 858) can provide you with invitations (US$30-80), and or get you an actual visa (from US$160, depending on type of visa and processing speed). Students and employees may be able to obtain student visas from

ENTRANCE REQUIREMENTS

Passport: Required for all travelers.

Visa: Required for all travelers.

Letter of Invitation: Required for all travelers.

Inoculations: Recommended up-to-date on DTaP (diphtheria, tetanus, and pertussis), Hepatitis A, Hepatitis B, MMR (measles, mumps, and rubella), Polio booster, and Typhoid.

Work Permit: Required for all foreigners planning to work in Russia.

Driving Permit: Required for all those planning to drive in Russia.

their school or host organization. Upon arrival, travelers are required to fill out an immigration card, part of which must be kept until departure from Russia, and to **register** their visa within three working days (see **Entering Russia,** below).

GETTING A VISA ON YOUR OWN. If you have an invitation from a travel agency or Russian organization and want to get a visa on your own, apply for the visa in person or by mail at a Russian embassy or consulate. (You can download an application form at www.ruscon.org.) Bring your original invitation; your passport; a completed application; three passport-sized photographs; a cover letter stating your name, dates of arrival and departure, cities you plan to visit in Russia, date of birth, and passport number; and a money order or certified check. (Single-entry, 60-day visas: 6 business day processing US$100; 3 business days US$150; 2 business days US$200; same-day US$300. Double-entry visas add US$50, except on 6-day processing. Multiple-entry 6 business days US$100; 3 business days US$300; 2 business days US$350; same-day US$450. Prices change constantly, so check with the embassy.) If you have even tentative plans to visit a city, add it to your visa.

VISA AGENCIES. Travel agencies that advertise discounted tickets to Russia often are also able to provide invitations and visas to Russia. HOFA and Red Bear Tours (see below) require that you book accommodations with them. American Express offices in Moscow (p. 866) and St. Petersburg (p. 876) can arrange train and theater tickets. Non-cardholders will have to pay a fee.

Host Families Association (HOFA), 3 Linia, 6, V.O., St. Petersburg, 199053, Russia (☎812 275 19 92; www.hofa.us). Arranges homestays in 60+ Russian cities. Single rooms with breakfast start at US$20. US$5 discount per day for non-central locations and after the 1st week of a stay with the same family; US$10 after the 2nd week. Visa invitations (US$30, non-guests US$40) available for Russia, Ukraine, and Belarus.

VISAtoRUSSIA.com, 309A Peters St. Atlanta, GA 30313, USA (☎404-837-0099; www.visatorussia.com). Russian visa invitations start at US$30.

OLNA, Inc., Embassy Row, 2005 Massachusetts Ave. NW, Washington, D.C. 20036, USA (☎800-567-4175; www.russia-visa.com). Cheap, reliable visa service starts at US$160. Cheaper if you provide the invitation. UK service available.

Star Travel, Metro station Sokol, 9 Baltiyskaya, 3rd fl., Russia (☎095 797 95 55; www.startravel.ru). Catering to those on a budget, this Russian budget travel agency arranges train and air travel around the region.

ENTERING RUSSIA. The best way to cross the **border** is to fly directly into Moscow or St. Petersburg. Another option is to take a train or bus into one of the major cities. Expect long delays and red tape. Russian law dictates that all visitors must **register** their visas within three days of arrival. Many travelers skip this purgatory, but it is the law and taking care of it will leave one less thing over which bribe-seeking authorities can hassle you—typical fines for visa non-registration run about US$150. While in Russia, carry your passport on your person at all times.

TOURIST SERVICES AND MONEY

TOURIST OFFICES. There are two types of Russian tourist office—those that only arrange tours and those that offer general travel assistance. Offices of the former type are often unhelpful or even rude, but those of the latter are usually eager to assist, particularly with visa registration. While Western-style tourist offices are not very common, big hotels are often home to tourist agencies with English-speaking staffs (see also **Visa Agencies** p. 858). Buy maps at kiosks on the street.

MONEY. The Russian unit of currency is the **ruble,** which comes in 1 and 5R coins and 10, 50, 100, 500, and 1000R bills. One hundred kopecks make a ruble. Government regulations require that you show your passport when exchanging money. Most *Obmen Valyuti* (Обмен Валюты; Currency Exchange) will only exchange

RUSSIA

PAYING IN RUSSIA. Due to the fluctuating value of the Russian ruble, some establishments list their prices in US dollars. For this reason, some prices in this book may also appear in US$, but be prepared to pay in rubles.

US dollars and euro. With **inflation** around 12%, expect prices quoted in rubles and **exchange rates** to undergo frequent changes. **Do not exchange money on the street.** Banks offer the best combination of good rates and security. You'll have no problem changing rubles back at the end of your trip. **ATMs** *(bankomat)*, linked to major networks and credit cards, can be found in most cities. Banks, ATMs, and currency exchanges often accept major **credit cards,** especially Visa. Main branches of banks will usually accept **traveler's checks** and give cash advances on credit cards. It's wise to keep a small amount (around US$20) of dollars on hand. Be aware that most establishments don't accept crumpled, torn, or written-on bills of any denomination. Russians are also wary of old US dollars; bring new bills.

RUBLES		
	AUS$1 = 21.50R	10R = AUS$0.47
	CDN$1 = 23.44R	10R = CDN$0.43
	EUR€1 = 34.79R	10R = EUR€0.29
	NZ$1 = 19.86R	10R = NZ$0.50
	UK£1 = 51.25R	10R = UK£0.20
	US$1 = 28.58R	10R = US$0.35

HEALTH AND SAFETY

In a **medical emergency,** either leave the country or go to the American Medical Centers in St. Petersburg or Moscow; these clinics have American doctors who speak English. Russian **bottled water** is often mineral water; you may prefer to boil or filter your own, or buy imported bottled water at a supermarket. Water is drinkable in much of Russia, but not in Moscow and St. Petersburg. Men's **toilets** are marked with an "M," women's with a "Ж." The 0.5-5R charge for public toilets generally gets you a hole in the ground and a single piece of toilet paper; carry your own. **Pharmacies** abound and offer a range of Western medicine and hygiene products; look for the "Аптека" (apteka) signs.

Crimes against foreigners are on the rise, particularly in Moscow and St. Petersburg. Although it is often tough to blend in (especially with a huge pack on your back), try not to flaunt your nationality. It is extremely unwise to take pictures of anything **military** or to do anything that might attract the attention of a man in uniform—doing something suspicious provides an excuse to detain you or extort money. Generally, avoid interaction with the police unless an emergency necessitates it; officers will attempt to cheat foreigners and locals alike. Do not let officials go through your possessions, and if they try to detain you unreasonably, threaten to call your embassy *("ya pozvonyu svoyu posolstvu.")* The concept of **sexual harassment** has yet to reach Russia. While traveling alone as a **woman** is generally safe, local men will try to pick up women and will get away with offensive language and actions. The routine usually starts with an innocent-sounding *"Devushka..."* (young lady); just say *"Nyet"* (No) or simply walk away. Those who do not speak Russian will also receive unwanted attention, often in the form of ludicrous price hikes. The authorities on the metro will frequently stop and question people with **dark skin,** who may also receive rude treatment in shops and restaurants. Outside of Moscow and St. Petersburg, where a growing gay scene thrives and people are generally accepting, **homosexuality** is still largely taboo; discretion is best.

EMERGENCY **Police:** ☎02. **Ambulance:** ☎01. **Fire:** ☎03.

TRANSPORTATION

BY PLANE. Most major international airlines fly into **Sheremetyevo-2** (SVO) in Moscow, or **Pulkovo-2** (LED) in St. Petersburg. **Aeroflot,** Frunzenskaya Naberezhnaya 4 (☎095 156 80 19; www.aeroflot.org) is the most popular domestic carrier. Most domestic routes are served by Soviet-era planes, many of which are in disrepair and have a poor safety record. While flying to Russia from the US, Europe, and Asia can be expensive, indirect routes offer a cheaper, if less efficient entrance. A number of European budget airlines fly into Tallinn, Estonia, Rīga, Latvia, or Helsinki, Finland, from which a bus or train can carry you into Russia.

BY TRAIN. Avoid entering Russia through Belarus; you need a visa and the border crossing is singularly unpleasant. Trains are generally the best option for **domestic** travel. Weekend or holiday trains between St. Petersburg and Moscow sometimes sell out a week in advance. If you plan ahead, you'll have your choice of four **classes.** The best is *lyuks*, with two beds, while the second-class *kupeyny* has four bunks. The next class down is *platskartny*, an open car with 52 shorter, harder bunks. Aim for places #1-33. Places #34-37 abut the unnaturally foul bathroom, while places #38-52 are on the side of the car; during the summer they can get incredibly hot. **Women traveling alone** can try to buy out a *lyuks* compartment for security, or can travel *platskartny* with the regular folk and depend on the crowds to shame would-be harassers. *Platskartny* is also a good idea on the theft-ridden St. Petersburg-Moscow line, as you are less likely to be targeted there. This logic can only be taken so far; there may be no crooks in fourth class, *obshchy*, but you'll be traveling with livestock. Try to board your train on time, as changing your ticket to suit a later departure could carry a fee of up to 25% of the ticket cost.

BY BUS. Buses, slightly less expensive than trains, are better for shorter distances. However, they are often crowded and overbooked; don't be shy about ejecting people who try to sit in your seat.

BY BOAT. Cruise ships stop in the main Russian ports: St. Petersburg, Murmansk, and Vladivostok. However, they usually only allow travelers less than 48hr. in the city. In December 2002, a regular ferry route opened between Kaliningrad and St. Petersburg, which operates one to two times per week. Kaliningrad ferries also operate to Poland and Germany. Ferries also traverse Khabarovsk-China, Novorossiysk-Georgia, Sochi-Turkey, Sochi-Georgia, Vladivostok-Japan, and Vladivostok-Korea routes. A river cruise runs from Moscow to St. Petersburg.

BY CAR AND BY BIKE. Russia's highly variable road conditions and weather create an interesting driving experience. Police officers may pull you over seemingly without provocation, and gasoline can be difficult to find. Biking is relatively rare, but motorists are generally polite to bikers.

BY TAXI AND BY THUMB. Hailing a car is indistinguishable from **hitchhiking,** and should be treated with equal caution. Most drivers who stop will be private citizens trying to make a little extra cash. Those seeking a ride should stand off the curb and hold out a hand into the street, palm down; when a car stops, riders tell the driver the destination before getting in; he will either refuse altogether or ask "*Skolko?*" (How much?), leading to protracted negotiations. Non-Russian speakers will get ripped off unless they manage a firm agreement on the price—if the driver agrees without asking for a price, you must ask "*Skolko?*" yourself (sign language works too). **Never get into a car that has more than one person in it.** *Let's Go* does not recommend hitchhiking.

KEEPING IN TOUCH

PHONE CODES	**Country code:** 7. **International dialing prefix:** 00. For more information on placing international calls, see inside back cover.

EMAIL AND THE INTERNET. Email is your best bet for keeping in touch in Russia. Internet cafes are readily available in St. Petersburg and Moscow. Rates vary from 35-70R per hour depending on time of day. Many Internet cafes are open 24hr.

TELEPHONE. Most pay phones take phonecards, good for both local and intercity calls and sold at central telephone offices, metro stations, and newspaper kiosks. When you are purchasing phonecards from a telephone office or metro station, the attendant will often ask, "Na ulitsu?" ("На улицу?"; On the street?) to find out whether you want a card for the phones in the station/office or for outdoor public phones. Be careful: phonecards in Russia are very specific, and it is easy to purchase the wrong kind. Often, hostels, Internet cafes and similar locations will try to sell you phonecards that work only in their establishments.

For five-digit numbers, insert a "2" between the dialing code and the phone number. Make direct **international** calls from telephone offices in St. Petersburg and Moscow: prices run US$1-1.50 per minute to Europe, US$1.50-2 to the US and Australia. International access codes include: **AT&T** ☎755 5042, in Moscow ☎325 5042; **Canada Direct** ☎810 800 110 1012; **MCI** in Moscow ☎960 2222, elsewhere ☎747 3322; **Sprint** ☎747 3324, in Moscow ☎8095 747 3324.

Mobile phones have become a popular accessory among Russians and a comforting safety blanket for visitors. Most new phones are compatible with Russian networks and mobile phone shops are common, but service can be costly. On average, a minute costs US$0.20, and unlike in much of Europe, users are charged for incoming calls. Major providers Megafon, BeeLine GSM, and MTS have stores throughout the cities, as do rental chains like Euroset and Svyaznoy.

MAIL. Mail service is more reliable leaving the country than coming in. Letters to the US will arrive as soon as a week after mailing; letters to other destinations take two to three weeks. Domestic mail will usually reach its destination; from abroad, send letters to Russia via friends who are traveling there. Airmail is *avia* (Авия). Send your mail "заказное" (certified; 40R) to reduce the chance of it being lost. Letters to the US cost 16R; postcards 11R. **Poste Restante** is "Pismo Do Vostrebovania." Address envelopes as follows: LAST NAME First name, 103 009 (postal code), Москва (city), Письмо До Востребования, RUSSIA.

LANGUAGE. Russian is an East Slavic language written in the Cyrillic alphabet. Once you get the hang of the Cyrillic alphabet (p. 1056), you can pronounce just about any Russian word. Although **English** is increasingly common, come equipped with at least a few helpful Russian phrases. For a phrasebook and glossary, see **Phrasebook: Russian,** p. 1066.

ACCOMMODATIONS AND CAMPING

RUSSIA	❶	❷	❸	❹	❺
ACCOMMODATIONS	under 400R	400-700R	700-1200R	1200-2000R	over 2000R

The **hostel** scene in St. Petersburg and Moscow often involves less-than-stellar service and facilities and isn't particularly cheap: US$18-25 per night is average. Still, the hostels that do exist are often English-speaking. Reserve in advance. **Hotels** offer several classes of rooms. "Lux," usually two-room doubles with TV, phone, fridge, and bath, are the most expensive. "Polu-lux" rooms are singles or doubles with TV, phone, and bath. The lowest priced rooms are *bez udobstv*, one room with a sink. Expect to pay 300-450R for a single in a budget hotel. As a rule, only cash is accepted as payment. In many hotels, **hot water**—sometimes all water—is only turned on for a few hours each day. **University dorms** offer cheap rooms; some accept foreign students for US$5-10 per night. The rooms are livable, but don't expect sparkling bathrooms or reliable hot water. Make arrangements through an educational institute from home. In the cities, **private rooms** and **apartments** can often be found for very low prices (about US$6 per night). Outside major train stations, there are usually women offering private rooms to rent—be sure to bargain.

FOOD AND DRINK

RUSSIA	❶	❷	❸	❹	❺
FOOD	under 70R	70-150R	150-300R	300-500R	over 500R

Russian cuisine is a medley of dishes both delectable and unpleasant; tasty *borscht* (beet soup) can come in the same meal as *salo* (pig fat). The main meal of the day, *obed* **(lunch)**, is eaten at midday and includes: *salat* (salad), usually cucumbers and tomatoes or beets and potatoes with mayonnaise or sour cream; *sup* (soup); and *kuritsa* (chicken) or *myaso* (meat), often called *kotlyety* (cutlets) or *bifshteks* (beefsteaks). Other common foods include *shchi* (cabbage soup) and *blini* (pancakes). Ordering a number of *zakuski* (small appetizers) instead of a main dish can save money. **Desserts** include *morozhenoye* (ice cream) or *tort* (cake) with *cofe* (coffee) or *chai* (tea), which Russians drink at the slightest provocation. **Vegetarians** and **kosher** travelers in Russia will probably find it easiest to eat in foreign restaurants and pizzerias. On the streets, you'll see a lot of *shashlyki* (barbecued meat on a stick) and *kvas*, a slightly alcoholic dark-brown drink. Beware of meat hawked from sidewalk vendors; it may be several days old. Kiosks often carry **alcohol;** imported cans of beer are safe (though warm), but be wary of Russian labels—you have no way of knowing what's really in the bottle. *Russky Standart* and *Flagman* are the best **vodkas;** the much-touted *Stolichnaya* is primarily made for export. Among local **beers,** *Baltika* (numbered 1 through 7 according to brew and alcohol content) is the most popular and arguably the best. *Baltika* 1 is the weakest (10.5%), *Baltika* 7 the strongest (14%).

HOLIDAYS AND FESTIVALS

Holidays: New Year's Holiday (Jan. 1-2); Orthodox Christmas (Jan. 7); Defenders of the Motherland Day (Feb. 23); Women's Day (Mar. 8); Orthodox Easter Holiday (Apr. 23); Labor Day (May 1); Victory Day (May 9); Independence Day (Accord and Reconciliation Day (Nov. 7); Constitution Day (Dec. 12).

Festivals: Midnight services, gift-giving, and candlelit folk celebrations mark Easter, Christmas, and the secular New Year, while national holidays are occasions for large military parades. In June and early July, Petersburg stays up late to celebrate the sunlight of **White Nights** *(Beliye Nochi)*, with concerts and fireworks. *Maslyanitsa* (Butter Festival/Shrovetide; end of Feb.) is a farewell to winter, during which people eat delectable pancakes covered in honey, caviar, fresh cream, and butter.

BEYOND TOURISM

Kitezh Children's Community (http://atschool.eduweb.co.uk/ecoliza/files/kitezh.html). Teach English to Russian orphans in a rural setting. Young people taking a "gap year" between high school and college are especially welcome as volunteers.

The School of Russian and Asian Studies, 175 E. 74th, Ste. 21B, New York, NY 10021, USA (☎800-557-8774; www.sras.org). Provides study-abroad opportunities at language schools and arranges work and volunteer programs throughout Russia.

The Russia Journal (www.russiajournal.com). English-language newspaper with classified job ads.

MOSCOW (МОСКВА) ☎8095

Moscow (pop. 9,000,000) has long regulated the pulse of Russia. When communism swept through Moscow, it leveled most of the capital's golden domes and left behind massive buildings, crumbling outskirts, and countless statues of Lenin. But things change quickly in this audacious city, and in the midst of its debauchery and corruption, Moscow is recreating itself using the same resourcefulness that helped it engineer, and then survive, the most ambitious social experiment in history.

TRANSPORTATION

Flights: International flights arrive at **Sheremetyevo-2** (Шереметьево-2; ☎956 46 66). Take the van under the "автолайн" sign in front of the station to M2: Rechnoy Vokzal (Речной Вокзал). **Taxis** to the center tend to be overpriced; bargain down at least to US$30. **Yellow Taxi** (☎940 88 88) has fixed prices. Cars outside the departures level charge US$15-20; agree on a price before getting in.

Trains: Moscow has 8 train stations arranged around the M5 (circle) line. Tickets for longer trips within Russia can be bought at the **Moskovskoye Zheleznodorozhnoye Agenstvo** (Московское Железнодорожное Агенство; Moscow Train Agency: ☎266 93 33; www.mza.ru), on the far side of Yaroslavskiy Vokzal from the metro station. Cyrillic schedules of trains, destinations, departure times, and station names are posted on both sides of the hall. (*Kassa* open M-F 8am-7pm, Sa 8am-6pm, Su 8am-5pm.) Buying more expensive tickets through a hotel or hostel spares you the *kassa* hassle.

Belorusskiy Vokzal (Белорусский), pl. Tverskoi Zastavy 7 (☎251 60 93). To: **Berlin, Germany** (27hr., 1 per day, 3500R); **Prague, Czech Republic** (35hr., 1 per day, 2860R); **Vilnius, Lithuania** (16hr., 1 per day, 1950R); **Warsaw, Poland** (21hr., 2 per day, 2520R).

Kievskiy Vokzal (Киевский), pl. Kievskogo Vokzala 2 (Киевского Вокзала; ☎240 04 15). M3, 5: Kievskaya (Киевская). To destinations in Ukraine, including: **Kyiv** (14hr., 5 per day, 950R); **Lviv** (26hr., 1 per day, 1100R); **Odessa** (25-28hr., 2-4 per day, 1100R).

Leningradskiy Vokzal (Ленинградский), Komsomolskaya pl. 3 (Комсомолская; ☎262 91 43). M1 or 5: Komsomolskaya. To: **St. Petersburg** (8hr., 10-15 per day, 700R); **Helsinki, Finland** (13hr., 1 per day, 2720R); **Tallinn, Estonia** (14hr., 1 per day, 1550R).

Rizhskiy Vokzal (Рижский), Prospekt Mira 79/3 (☎631 15 88). M6: Rizhskaya (Рижская). To: **Rīga, Latvia** (16hr., 2 per day, 2050R); and destinations in **Estonia.**

Yaroslavskiy Vokzal (Ярославский), Komsomolskaya pl. 5a (☎921 59 14). M1, 5: Komsomolskaya. The starting point for the legendary **Trans-Siberian Railroad.** To: **Novosibirsk** (48hr., every other day, 1900R); **Siberia** and the **Far East.**

Public Transportation: The **Moscow Metro** (Метро) is fast, clean, and efficient—a masterpiece of Soviet urban planning. Trains run daily 6am-1am. A station serving multiple lines may have multiple names. Buy token-cards (10R, 10 trips for 75R) from the *kassas* in stations. Buy **bus** and **trolley** tickets from kiosks labeled "проездные билеты" or from the driver (10R). Punch your ticket when you get on, or risk a 100R fine. Buses run 24hr., but the metro stops running at 1am.

METRO MADNESS. *Let's Go* has tried to simplify navigation by numbering each metro line; for a key, see this guide's color map of the Moscow Metro. When speaking with Russians, use the color or name, not the number.

RUSSIA

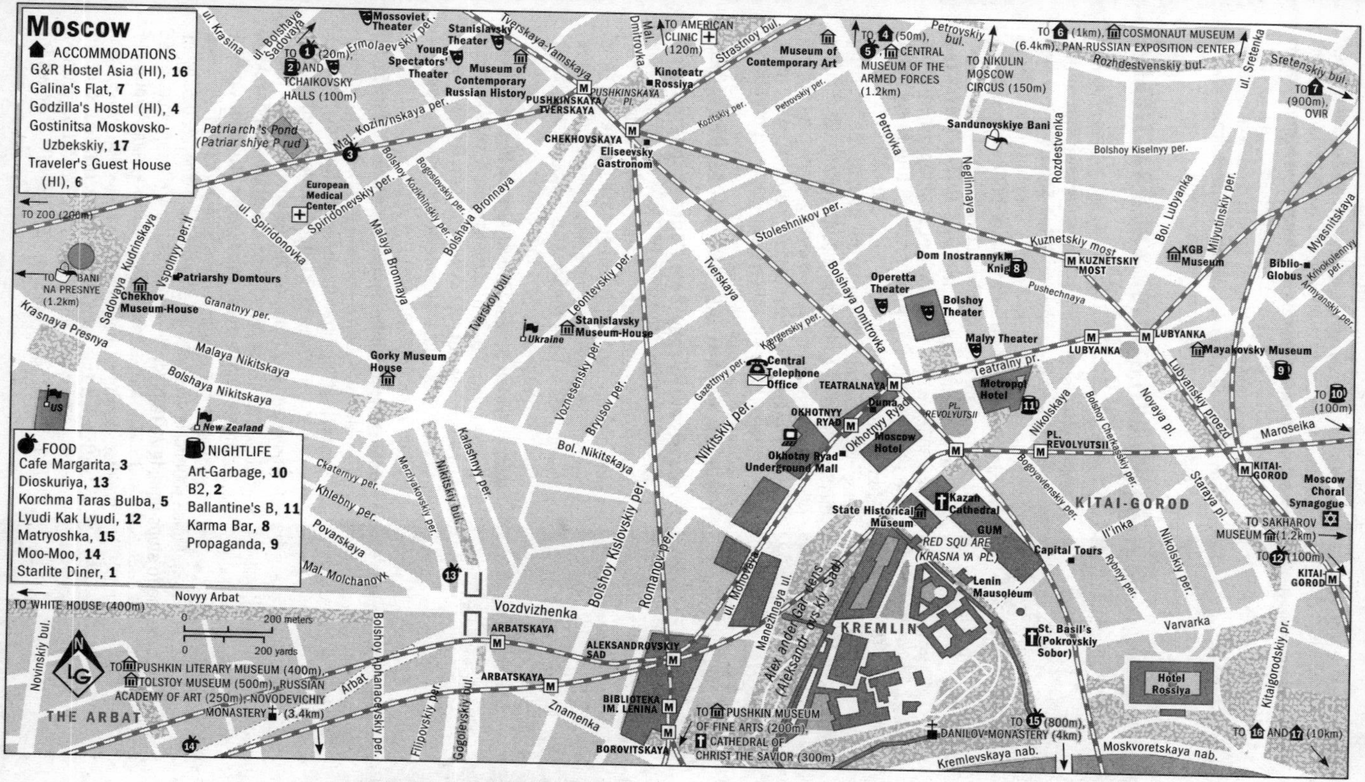

Moscow

ACCOMMODATIONS
- G&R Hostel Asia (HI), **16**
- Galina's Flat, **7**
- Godzilla's Hostel (HI), **4**
- Gostinitsa Moskovsko-Uzbekskiy, **17**
- Traveler's Guest House (HI), **6**

FOOD
- Cafe Margarita, **3**
- Dioskuriya, **13**
- Korchma Taras Bulba, **5**
- Lyudi Kak Lyudi, **12**
- Matryoshka, **15**
- Moo-Moo, **14**
- Starlite Diner, **1**

NIGHTLIFE
- Art-Garbage, **10**
- B2, **2**
- Ballantine's B, **11**
- Karma Bar, **8**
- Propaganda, **9**

THE LOCAL STORY

FORM AND FUNCTION

With over 165 stations and almost 9 million passengers per day, the Moscow metro system is a tourist attraction in itself. Add the fact that many stations were designed by the Soviet Union's leading architects and artists, and you've got a virtual museum of Socialist Realist art available to anyone for the price of a metro ticket. Construction began on the first stations in 1931, executed by men and women drafted from all across the nation, soldiers from the Red Army, and more than 13,000 volunteers from the *Komsomol*, or Communist Youth League.

The yellow-and-gold **Komsomolskaya** station (M:1 and 5), named after the organization, was planned by Aleksey Shchusev, who won a prize at the New York World's Fair for its elaborate chandelier-accented design. Station art quickly developed a functional dimension. Some acted as state propaganda, like the red star formed by the station entrance to **Arbatskaya** (M:3). Similarly, **Ploshchad Revolutsii** (M:3) features two rows of bronze statues commemorating the role ordinary citizens played in establishing the Soviet State. Others were built deep underground to function as bomb shelters during war time. **Mayakaovskaya** (M:2), also a winner at the New York World's Fair, became the headquarters of the Anti-Aircraft Defense Forces in 1941.

Taxis: Most taxis do not use meters and tend to overcharge. **Yellow Taxis** charge 10R per km (15R after midnight) and are easily picked out on the street. It is common and cheaper to hail a private car, done by holding your arm out horizontally. Before getting in, tell the driver your destination and agree on a price (usually 50-100R across town). *Let's Go* does not recommend hitchhiking.

ORIENTATION AND PRACTICAL INFORMATION

A series of concentric rings spread outward from the **Kremlin** (Кремль; Kreml) and **Red Square** (Красная Площадь; Krasnaya ploshchad). The outermost **Moscow Ring Road** marks the city limits, but most sights lie within the **Garden Ring** (Садовоне Кольцо; Sadovoe Koltso). Main streets include **Ulitsa Tverskaya** (Тверская), which extends north along the metro's green line, as well as **Arbat** (Арбат) and **Novyy Arbat** (Новый Арбат), which run west parallel to the blue lines. Orient yourself using the metro. All over the city, kiosks sell English-language and Cyrillic maps (35-60R). Be careful when crossing streets, as drivers are oblivious to pedestrians; for safety's sake, most intersections have an underpass (переход; perekhod).

TOURIST, FINANCIAL, AND LOCAL SERVICES

Tours: Patriarshy Dom Tours, Vspolny per. 6 (Вспольный; from the US ☎650 678 70 76; in Russia 095 795 09 27; http://russiatravel-pdtours.netfirms.com). M5, 7: Barrikadnaya. Wide range of English-language tours including a special behind-the-scenes tour of the former KGB headquarters ($18). Open M-F 9am-6pm, Sa 11am-5pm.

Budget Travel: Student Travel Agency Russia (STAR), Baltiyskaya ul. 9, 3rd fl. (Балтийская; ☎797 95 55; www.startravel.ru). M2: Sokol (Сокол). Discount plane tickets, ISICs, and worldwide hostel booking. Open M-F 10am-7pm, Sa 11am-4pm.

Embassies: Australia, Podkoloniy per. 10/2 (☎956 60 70). M6: Kitai Gorod (Китай Город). M3, 5: Smolenskaya/Park Kultury (Смоленская/Парк Культуры). Open M-F 9:30am-12:30pm. **Canada,** Starokonyushennyy per. 23 (Староконюшенный; ☎105 60 00). M1: Kropotkinskaya or M4: Arbatskaya (Арбатская). Open M-F 8:30am-1pm and 2-5pm. **Ireland,** Grokholskiy per. 5 (Грохольский; ☎937 59 11). M5, 6: Prospekt Mira. Open M-F 9:30am-1pm and 2:30-5:30pm. **New Zealand,** Povarskaya ul. 44 (Поварская; ☎956 35 79). M7: Barikadnaya (Барикадная). Open M-F 9am-5:30pm. **UK,** Smolenskaya nab. 10 (Смоленская; ☎956 72 00; www.britemb.msk.ru). M3: Smolenskaya. Open M-F 9am-1pm and 2-5pm. **US,** Novinskiy 19/23 (Новинский; ☎728 50 00; www.usembassy.ru). M5: Krasnoprenenskaya (Краснопресненская). Open M-F 9am-6pm. **American Citizen Services** (☎728 55 77, after-hours 728 50 00) lists English-speaking establishments. Open M-F 9-10:30am and 2-4pm.

Currency Exchange: Banks are everywhere; check for ads in English-language newspapers. Typically only main branches change **traveler's checks** or issue **cash advances.** Almost all banks and hotels have **ATMs.** Avoid machines protruding from buildings; they work erratically, and withdrawing cash on busy streets makes you a target for muggers.

American Express: ul. Usacheva 33 (☎933 84 00). M1: Sportivnaya. Use the exit at the front of the train, turn right, and then right again after the Global USA shop onto Usacheva. Open M-F 9am-6pm.

English-Language Bookstore: Angliya British Bookshop, Vorotnikovskiy per. 6 (Воротниковский). Open M-F 10am-7pm, Sa 10am-6pm, Su 10am-5pm. AmEx/MC/V.

EMERGENCY AND COMMUNICATIONS

Emergency: Police: ☎02. **Ambulance:** ☎03. **Fire:** ☎01.

24hr. Pharmacies: Tverskaya ul. 25 (☎299 24 59), M2: Tverskaya/Mayakovskaya; ul. Zemlyanoi Val 25 (☎917 12 85), M5: Kurskaya; Kutozovskiy Prospekt 24 (Кутозовский; ☎249 19 37), M4: Kutuzovskaya (Кутузовская).

Medical Services: American Clinic, Grokholskiy per. 31 (☎937 57 57; http://americanclinic.ru). M5, 6: Prospekt Mira. American board-certified doctors; family and internal medicine. Consultations US$100. Open 24hr. MC/V.

Internet Access: Timeonline (☎363 00 60), on the bottom level of the Okhotnyy Ryad underground mall. M1: Okhotnyy Ryad. Over 100 computers in the center of the city. 30-75R per hr. Open 24hr. **Cafemax** (☎787 68 58; www.cafemax.ru) has 3 locations: ul. Pyatnitskaya 25/1m (M2: Novokuznetskaya), Akademika Khokhlova 3 (M1: Universitet), and ul Novoslobodskaya 3 (M9: Novoslobodskaya). 70R per hr. Open 24hr.

Telephones: Local calls require phone cards, sold at kiosks and some metro stops.

Post Offices: Moscow Central Telegraph, Tverskaya ul. 7, uphill from the Kremlin. M1: Okhotnyy Ryad. International calls in the second phone hall; prepay at the counter, 9-20R per min. to the US, 12-35R per min. to Europe. International mail at window #23; faxes at #11-12. *Poste Restante* at window #24. Bring packages unwrapped. Open M-F 8am-2pm and 3-8pm, Sa-Su 7am-2pm and 3-7pm. **Postal Code:** 103 009.

ACCOMMODATIONS

Older women standing outside major rail stations often rent private rooms (сдаю комнату) or apartments (сдаю квартиру)—be sure to haggle.

Godzilla's Hostel (HI), Bolshoy Karetniy 6/5 (Большой Каретний; ☎299 42 23; www.godzillashostel.com). M9: Tsvetnoy Bulvar. 7min. from Pushkin Square and 20min. from the Kremlin. Helpful, English-speaking staff. Co-ed dorms unless you specify in advance. Reception 24hr. Check-out noon. Dorms US$25, doubles US$60. ❷

Galina's Flat, ul. Chaplygina 8, 5th fl. #35 (Чаплыгина; ☎921 60 38; galinas.flat@mtu-net.ru). M1: Chistyye Prudy. Head down Chistoprudnyy bul., take a left on Bol. Kharitonevskiy per., then a right on ul. Chaplygina. Go into the courtyard at #8, and enter at the "KB35-36" sign. Galina and her cats provide real Russian hospitality. Breakfast 60R. Book ahead. Dorms US$10; singles US$18; doubles US$25. ❷

Traveler's Guest House (HI), Bolshaya Pereslavskaya ul. 50, 10th fl. (Большая Переславская; ☎631 40 59; www.tgh.ru). M5, 6: Prospekt Mira. Turn right across from Prospekt Mira 61; at the end, go left on B. Pereyaslavskaya. Friendly, English-speaking staff. Visa invitations US$30. Internet 1R per min. Laundry 130R per 3kg. Check-out 11am. Dorms US$25; singles US$50; doubles US$60, with bath US$65. MC/V. ❷

Gostinitsa Moskovsko-Uzbekskiy, Zelenodolskaya ul. 3/2 (Зеленодольская; ☎378 33 92 or 378 21 77; hotel@caravan.ru). M7: Ryazanskiy Prospekt (Рязанский). A "Гостиница" sign marks the hotel. Wide range of rooms; non-renovated ones are clean and ultra-cheap. 500R key deposit. Singles 750-1200R; doubles 1000-2000R. ❷

G&R Hostel Asia (HI), Zelenodolskaya ul. 3/2 (Зеленодольская; ☎378 00 01; www.hostels.ru). M7: Ryazanskiy Prospekt (Рязанский). On the 5th fl. of the Gostinitsa Moskovsko-Uzbekskiy. Clean rooms. Helpful staff. Visa invitations €25-35. Reception 8am-midnight. Singles €25-40; doubles €40-55; triples €81. €1 HI discount. V. ❸

FOOD

Many restaurants offer business lunch specials (бизнес ланч; typically noon-3pm; US$4-8). **Eliseevskiy Gastronom** (Елисеевский), ul. Tverskaya 14, is Moscow's most famous supermarket. (☎209 07 60. Open M-Sa 8am-9pm, Su 10am-8pm.) For fresh produce, try the **markets** by the Turgenyevskaya and Kuznetsky Most metro stops. (Daily 10am-8pm.) Grocery stores are marked by "продукти" (produkty) signs.

RESTAURANTS

Korchma Taras Bulba (Корчма Тарас Бульба), Sadovaya-Samotechnaya ul. 13 (☎200 00 56). M9: Tsvetnoy Bulvar (Цветной Бульвар). 12 locations around the city. From the metro, turn left and walk up Tsvetnoy Bulvar. Delicious Ukrainian specialities. Menu in 38 languages. Entrees 140-400R. Open 24hr. MC/V. ❸

Lyudi Kak Lyudi (Люди как Люди; People like People), Solyanskiy Tupik 1/4 (☎921 12 01). Enter from Solyanka ul. Order cheap eats at the bar. Business lunch (soup, salad, and sandwich or pirogi) 110R. Sandwiches 70R. Smoothies 80R. No English-language menus. Open M-Th 8am-11pm, F 8am-6am, Sa 11am-6am, Su 11am-10pm. ❶

Cafe Margarita (Кафе Маргарита), Malaya Bronnaya ul. 28 (Малая Вронная; ☎299 65 34), at the intersection with Malyy Kozikhinskiy per. (Малый Козихинский). M2: Mayakovskaya. Turn left on Bolshaya Sadovaya, then again left on Malaya Bronaya. Locals love this Russian cafe and restaurant. Entrees 250-450R. Open daily 1pm-midnight. ❸

Dioskuriya, (Диоскурия) Merzlyakovskiy per. 2 (Мерзляковский; ☎290 69 08). M4: Arbatskaya. Good Georgian eats close to the city center. Live Georgian music daily 7-11pm. Entrees 100-280R. Open daily 11am-midnight. ❷

Matryoshka, (Матрёшка) Klimentovskiy per. 10 (☎953 94 00). Also at Triumfalnaya 1 (☎727 96 51). Exit the metro and restaurant is on nearby Klimentovskiy, off Bol. Ordynka ul. Tasty, inexpensive Russian entrees from 150R. Open noon-midnight. ❷

Moo-Moo (Му-Му), Koroviy Val 1 (☎237 29 00) M5 Dobryninskaya; ul. Arbat 45/42 (☎241 13 64) M4: Smolenskaya. Look for the chain's signature cow statue outside. Moo-moo's many locations offer cheap, tasty European and Russian home cooking, served cafeteria-style. Pork cutlets 54R. Salads 40R. Open daily 9am-11pm. ❶

Starlite Diner, Bolshaya Sadovaya 16 (☎290 96 38; starlite@starlite.ru). M2: Mayakovskaya. Down Bolshaya Sadovaya toward the Mayakovskiy statue. American diner packed with expats on weekends. Cheeseburgers with fries 210R. Milkshakes 280R. Free WiFi. All-day breakfast. Entrees 350-599R. Open 24hr. AmEx/MC/V. ❸

SIGHTS

Moscow's sights reflect the city's interrupted history: because St. Petersburg was the tsar's seat for 200 years, there are 16th-century churches and Soviet-era museums, but little in between. Though Moscow has no grand palaces and 80% of its pre-revolutionary splendor was demolished by the Soviet regime, the city's museums contain the very best of Russian art, and there is history around every corner.

THE KREMLIN

The Kremlin (Кремль; Kreml) is the geographical and historical center of Moscow. In the Kremlin's Armory and in its magnificent churches, the glory and the riches of the Russian Empire are on display. Besides the sights listed below, the only other place in the triangular complex visitors may enter is the **Kremlin Palace of Congresses,** the white square behemoth built by Khrushchev in 1961 for the Communist Party, and since converted into a theater. English-speaking guides offer **tours** of the complex at insane prices; haggle away. *(☎202 37 76; www.kremlin.museum.ru. M1, 3, 4, 9: Aleksandrovskiy Sad. Open M-W and F-Su 10am-5pm. Buy tickets at the kassa in the Alexander Gardens. Large bags not allowed. 300R, students 150R.)*

ARMORY MUSEUM AND DIAMOND FUND. At the southwest corner of the Kremlin, the Armory Museum (Оружейная Палата; Oruzheynaya Palata) shows the opulence of the Russian court. The legendary Fabergé Eggs in Room 2, each reveal an intricate jewelled miniature. In an annex, the Diamond Fund (Выставка Алмазного Фонда; Vystavka Almaznogo Fonda) has even more glitter, as well as Soviet finds, including the world's largest chunks of platinum. *(Both open M-W and F-Su. The Armory lets in groups at 10am, noon, 2:30, and 4:30pm. Diamond Fund open 10am-1pm and 2-6pm. Armory 350R, students 175R; Diamond Fund 350/250R.)*

CATHEDRAL SQUARE. Russia's most famous golden domes can be seen in Cathedral Square. The church closest to the Armory is the **Annunciation Cathedral** (Благовещуиский Собор; Blagoveshchenskiy Sobor), which guards luminous icons by Andrei Rublev and Theophanes the Greek. The square **Archangel Cathedral** (Азчангельский Собор; Arkhangelskiy Sobor), which gleams with vivid icons and metallic coffins, is the final resting place for many tsars who ruled before Peter the Great, including Ivans III (the Great) and IV (the Terrible), and Mikhail Romanov. The 15th-century **Assumption Cathedral** (Успенский Собор; Uspenskiy Sobor), at the center of the square, was used as Napoleon's stable in 1812. To the right of Assumption Cathedral, the **Ivan the Great Bell Tower** (Колокольная Ивана Великого; Kolokolnya Ivana Velikovo) now houses temporary exhibits. Directly behind the tower is the **Tsar Bell** (Царь-колокол; Tsar-kolokol), the world's largest bell. It has never rung and probably never will—a 1737 fire caused an 11½-ton piece to break off. *(All cathedrals included in Kremlin entrance.)*

AROUND RED SQUARE

The 700m-long Red Square (Красная площадь; Krasnaya Ploshchad) has hosted everything from farmer's markets to public hangings, from Communist parades to renegade Cessna landings. Across from the Kremlin is **GUM,** once the world's largest purveyor of Soviet "consumer goods," now an upscale shopping mall. Also flanking the square are **St. Basil's Cathedral,** the **State Historical Museum,** the **Lenin Mausoleum,** and the pink-and-green **Kazan Cathedral.**

ST. BASIL'S CATHEDRAL. Moscow has no more familiar symbol than the colorful onion domes of St. Basil's Cathedral (Собор Василия Блаженного; Sobor Vasiliya Blazhennovo). Ivan the Terrible commissioned it to celebrate his victory over the Tatars in Kazan in 1552, and it was completed in 1561. "Basil" is the English equivalent of Vasily, the name of a holy fool who correctly predicted that Ivan would murder his own son. St. Basil's labyrinthine interior, unusual for Orthodox churches, is filled with both decorative and religious frescoes. *(M3: Ploshchad Revolutsii (Площадь Революции). Open daily 11am-6pm. 100R, students 50R.)*

LENIN'S MAUSOLEUM. Lenin's likeness can be seen in bronze all over the city, but he appears in the eerily luminescent flesh in Lenin's Mausoleum (Мавзолей В. И. Ленина; Mavzoley V.I. Lenina). In the Soviet era, this squat red structure was guarded fiercely, and the wait to get in took three hours. Today's line is still long, and the guards remain stone-faced, but the atmosphere is more curious than reverent. Exit along the **Kremlin wall,** where Stalin, Brezhnev, Andropov, Gagarin, and John Reed, founder of the American Communist Party, are buried. *(No cameras, mobile phones, or large bags. Open Tu-Th and Sa-Su 10am-1pm. Free.)*

NORTH OF RED SQUARE

Just outside the main gate to Red Square is an elaborate gold circle marking **Kilometer 0,** the spot from which all distances from Moscow are measured. Don't be fooled by this tourist attraction—the real Kilometer 0 lies underneath the Lenin Mausoleum. Just a few steps away, the **Alexander Gardens** (Александровский Сад; Aleksandrovskiy Sad) are a green respite from the pollution of central Moscow. At the northern end of the gardens is the **Tomb of the Unknown Soldier** (Могила Неизвестного Солдата; Mogila Neizvestnovo Soldata), where an **eternal flame** burns in memory of the catastrophic losses suffered in the Great Patriotic War (WWII). To the west is **Manezh Square** (Манежная Площадь; Manezhnaya Ploshchad), only recently converted into a pedestrian area. The famous **Moscow Hotel**—demolished in 2004 and scheduled to be rebuilt within two years—separated it from the older, smaller **Revolution Square** (Площадь Революции; Ploshchad Revolyutsii). Both squares are connected in the north by **Okhotnyy Ryad** (Охотный Ряд; Hunters' Row), an underground mall. *(Open daily 11am-10pm. Enter directly from the square or through the underpass.)* Across Okhotnyy Ryad from the Moscow Hotel is the **Duma,** the lower house of Parliament. Across from Revolution Square is **Theater Square** (Театральная Площадь; Teatralnaya Ploshchad), home of the **Bolshoy** and **Malyy Theatres** (see **Entertainment,** p. 872). More posh hotels, chic stores, and government buildings line **Tverskaya Ulitsa,** Moscow's main street and home to some of its richest residents, which starts at Manezh Square and runs northwest.

CHURCHES, MONASTERIES, AND SYNAGOGUES

CATHEDRAL OF CHRIST THE SAVIOR. Moscow's most controversial landmark is the enormous gold-domed Cathedral of Christ the Savior (Храм Христа Спасителя; Khram Khrista Spasitelya). Stalin demolished Nicholas I's original cathedral on this site to make way for a gigantic Palace of the Soviets, but Khrushchev abandoned the project and built a heated outdoor pool instead. In 1995, after the pool's water vapors damaged paintings in the nearby Pushkin Museum, Mayor Yury Luzhkov and the Orthodox Church won a renewed battle for the site and built the US$250 million cathedral in only five years. *(Volkhonka 15, between ul. Volkhonka (Волхонка) and the Moscow River. M1: Kropotkinskaya. Open daily 10am-5pm. No cameras, hats, shorts, or bare arms. Cathedral free.)*

NOVODEVICHY CONVENT AND CEMETERY. Moscow's most famous monastery (Новодевичий Монастырь; Novodevichiy Monastyr) is hard to miss thanks to its high brick walls, golden domes, and tourist buses. In the center, the **Smolensk Cathedral** (Смоленский Собор; Smolenskiy Sobor) shows off icons and frescoes. As you exit the gates, turn right and follow the exterior wall back around to the cemetery (кладбище; kladbishche), a pilgrimage site that holds the graves of such famous figures as Krushchev, Bulgakov, Chekhov, Shostakovich, and Stanislavsky. *(M1: Sportivnaya. Take the metro exit that does not lead to the stadium, then turn right. ☎246 56 07. Open M and W-Su 10am-5:15pm; kassa closes at 4:45pm. Closed 1st M of each month. Cathedral closed on humid days. Cemetery open daily 9am-7pm; low season 9am-6pm. Grounds 40R, students 20R. Cathedral and special exhibits 150R each, students 75R.)*

MOSCOW CHORAL SYNAGOGUE. Constructed in the 1870s, the synagogue is a break from the city's ubiquitous onion domes. Though it remained open during Soviet rule, all but the bravest Jews were deterred by KGB agents who photographed anyone who entered. According to official statistics, more than 200,000 Jews now live in Moscow. Services are increasingly well attended, but the occasional graffiti is a sad reminder that anti-Semitism in Russia is not dead. *(M6, 7: Kitai-Gorod. Go north on Solyanskiy Proyezd (Солянский Проезд) and take the 1st left. Open daily 8am-10pm. Services M-F 8:30am and 8pm, Sa-Su 9am and 9pm.)*

OTHER SIGHTS

MOSCOW METRO. All the beautiful Moscow Metro (Московское Метро) stations are unique. Those inside the circle line have sculptures, stained glass, elaborate mosaics, and unusual chandeliers. See the Baroque elegance of **Komsomolskaya** (Косомолская), the stained glass of **Novoslobodskaya** (Новослободская), and the bronze statues of revolutionary archetypes from farmer to factory worker, of **Ploshchad Revolutsii** (Площадь Революции) all for the price of a metro ticket.

THE ARBAT. Now a commercial pedestrian shopping arcade, the Arbat (Арбат) was once a showpiece of *glasnost* and a haven for political radicals, Hare Krishnas, street poets, and *metallisty* (heavy metal rockers). Some of that eccentric flavor remains in the street performers and guitar-playing teenagers. Intersecting but nearly parallel to the Arbat runs the bigger, newer, and uglier **Novyy Arbat,** lined with gray high-rises and massive modern stores. *(M3: Arbatskaya or Smolenskaya.)*

VICTORY PARK. On the left past the **Triumphal Arch,** which celebrates the 1812 defeat of Napoleon, is Victory Park (Парк Победы; Park Pobedy), a monument to WWII. It includes the **Museum of the Great Patriotic War** (Музей Отечественной Войны; Muzey Otechestvennoy Voyny) and the gold-domed **Church of St. George the Victorious** (Храм Георгия Победаносного; Khram Georgiya Pobedonosnova) which honors the 27 million Russians who died in battle. *(M4: Kutuzovskaya.)*

MUSEUMS

Moscow's museum scene is by far the most patriotic part of the city. Government museums and small galleries alike proudly display Russian art, and dozens of historical and literary museums are devoted to the nation's past.

STATE TRETYAKOV GALLERY. A treasury of 18th- to early 20th-century Russian art, the Tretyakov Gallery (Государственная Третьяковская Галерея; Gosudarstvennaya Tretyakovskaya Galereya) also has a superb collection of icons, including works by Andrei Rublev and Theophanes the Greek. *(Lavrushinskiy per. 10. M8: Tretyakovskaya (Третьяковская). Turn left out of the metro, left again, then take an immediate right on Bolshoy Tolmachevskiy per.; turn right after 2 blocks onto Lavrushinskiy per. Open Tu-Su 10am-7:30pm. Kassa closes at 6:30pm. 225R, students 130R.)*

NEW TRETYAKOV GALLERY. Where the first Tretyakov chronologically leaves off, the new gallery (Новая Третьяковская Галерея; Novaya Tretyakovskaya Galereya) begins. The collection starts on the third floor with early 20th-century art and moves through the neo-Primitivist, Futurist, Suprematist, Cubist, and Social Realist schools. The second floor holds temporary exhibits that draw huge crowds; it's best to go on weekday mornings. Behind the gallery to the right lies a graveyard for Soviet statues. Once the main dumping ground for decapitated Lenins and Stalins, it now contains captioned sculptures of Gandhi, Einstein, Niels Bohr, and Dzerzhinsky, the founder of the Soviet secret police. *(Ul. Krymskiy Val 10 (Крымский Вал). M5: Oktyabraskaya. Walk toward the big intersection at Kaluzhskaya pl. (Калужская пл.) and turn right onto ul. Krymskiy. Open Tu-Su 10am-7:30pm; kassa closes at 6:30pm. 225R, students 130R.)*

PUSHKIN MUSEUM OF FINE ARTS. Moscow's most important collection of non-Russian art, the Pushkin Museum (Музей Изобразительных Искусств им. А.С. Пушкина; Muzey Izobrazitelnykh Iskusstv im. A.S. Pushkina) houses major Renaissance, Egyptian, and classical works, as well as superb pieces by Van Gogh, Chagall, and Picasso. *(Ul. Volkhonka 12 (Волхонка). M1: Kropotkinskaya. Open Tu-Su 10am-7pm; kassa closes at 6pm. 300R, students 150R.)* The smaller building to the right of the main entrance houses the Pushkin **Museum of Private Collections** (Музей Личныч Коллеций; Muzey Lichnych Kolletsiy), with artwork by Kandinsky, Rodchenko and Stepanov. *(Open Tu-Su 10am-7pm; kassa closes 6pm. 100R, students 50R.)*

KGB MUSEUM. Documenting the history and strategies of Russian secret intelligence from Ivan the Terrible to Putin, the KGB Museum (Музей КГБ; Muzey KGB) features guides with intriguing anecdotes and a chance to quiz a current FSB agent. *(Ul. Bul. Lubyanka 12. M1: Lubyanka. Behind the concrete behemoth towering over the northeast side of the square. Pre-arranged tours only. Patriarshy Dom Tours, p. 866, leads periodic 2hr. group tours. US$18 per person.)*

STATE HISTORICAL MUSEUM. A comprehensive exhibit on Russian history, from the Neanderthals through Kyivan Rus to modern Russia, is accessible to English-speaking travelers at the State Historical Museum (Государственный Исторический Музей; Gosudarstvennyy Istoricheskiy Muzey) due to its extensive printed info in English. *(Krasnaya pl. 1/2. M1: Okhotnyy Ryad. Enter by Red Square. Open M and W-Sa 10am-6pm, Su 11am-8pm. Kassa closes 1hr. earlier. Closed 1st M of each month. 150R, students 75R.)*

HOMES OF THE LITERARY AND FAMOUS. If you've never seen Pushkin-worship first-hand, the **Pushkin Literary Museum** (Литературный Музей Пушкина; Literaturnyy Muzey Pushkina) with its large collection of Pushkin memorabilia will either convert or frighten you. *(Ul. Prechistenka 12/2; Пречистенка. Entrance on Khrushchevskiy per. M1: Kropotkinskaya. Open Tu-Su 10am-6pm; kassa closes at 5:30pm. 50R.)* The **Mayakovsky Museum** (Музей им. В. В. Маяковского; Muzey im. V. V. Mayakovskovo) is a walk-through work of Futurist art, created as a biography the Revolution's greatest poet. Mayakovsky lived and died in a communal apartment on the fourth floor of this building. *(Lubyanskiy pr. 3/6; Лубянский. M1: Lubyanka. Behind a bust of Mayakovsky on ul. Myasnitskaya; Мясницкая. Open M-Tu and F-Su 10am-6pm, Th 1-9pm. Closed last F of each month. 60R.)* The **Tolstoy Museum** (Музей Толстого; Muzey Tolstovo) in the neighborhood of Tolstoy's first Moscow residence displays original texts, paintings, and letters related to the author's masterpieces. *(Ul. Prechistenka 11. M1: Kropotkinskaya. Open Tu-Su 11am-6pm; kassa closes at 5pm. Closed last F of each month. 100R, students 30R.)*

RUSSIA

ENTERTAINMENT

From September through June, Moscow boasts some of the world's best theater, ballet, opera, and orchestral performances. Tickets can be purchased from the theater *kassa* or from kiosks; advance tickets are often very cheap (from US$5).

Bolshoi Theater (Большой Театр), Teatralnaya pl. 1 (Театральная; ☎250 73 17; www.bolshoi.ru). M2: Teatralnaya. Home to the opera and world-renowned ballet company. *Kassa* open daily 11am-3pm and 4-8pm. Performances Sept.-June daily 7pm, occasional matinees. Tickets 250-3500R. MC/V. Main stage under renovation until at least 2007. Performances continue on the secondary stage.

Moscow Operetta Theater, Bolshaya Dmitrovka 6 (Большая Дмитровка; ☎692 12 37; www.operetta.org.ru), left of the Bolshoi. Famous operettas staged year-round. *Kassa* open daily 11am-7:30pm. Performances daily 6 or 7pm. Tickets 100-500R.

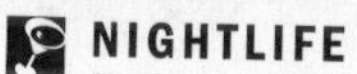

NIGHTLIFE

Moscow's nightlife is the most varied, expensive, and debaucherous in Eastern Europe. Many clubs flaunt their exclusivity. Check the weekend editions of *The Moscow Times* or *The Moscow Tribune* for club reviews and music listings.

Propaganda (Пропаганда), Bolshoy Zlatoustinskiy per. 7 (Большой Златоустинский; ☎924 57 32). M6, 7: Kitai Gorod. Exiting the Metro, walk down Maroseyka and turn left on Bolshoy Zlatoustinsky per. Get down to house music without feeling like you're in a meat market. Dancing after midnight. Th night is the most popular. Beer 70R. Sangria 120R per 0.5L. Sa cover 100R. Open daily noon-6am.

Karma Bar, Pushechnaya 3 (☎924 56 33; www.karma-bar.ru). M1, 7: Kuznetzky Most. Go through the arch on your left and turn right on Pushechnaya. Crowd-pleasing dance music emanates from this hip club. Beer 100-140R per 0.33L. Vodka 80-150R. Mixed drinks 180R. Cover F-Sa 300R for men, 200R for women. Open Th-Su 7pm-6am.

B2, Bolshaya Sadovaya 8 (☎209 99 09; www.b2club.ru). M5: Mayakovskaya. This multi-story complex truly has it all: a quiet beer garden, restaurant, sushi bar, karaoke, jazz club, billiard room, several dance floors, and ballroom dancing on weekends. Concerts 200-500R. Beer 60-160R. Open noon-6am.

Ballantine's Bar, Nikolskaya ul. 17 (Николская; ☎928 46 92). M3: Ploshchad Revolyutsii. Great dance music and a lively student crowd. Beer 55R-165R. Live DJ Th-Sa at 10pm. Cover F-Sa 100R. Open daily 11am-6am. AmEx/MC/V.

Art-Garbage, Starosadskiy per. 5 (☎928 87 45; www.art-garbage.ru). M6, 7: Kitai Gorod. This refreshingly laidback gallery and cafe is better for relaxing than for hardcore clubbing. Vodka tonic 90R. Cover F-Sa 150R-300R. Open daily 12pm-6am.

DAYTRIP FROM MOSCOW

SERGIYEV POSAD. Russia's most famous pilgrimage site, Sergiyev Posad (Сергиев Посад; pop. 200,000) attracts believers to several churches huddled around its main sight: **St. Sergius's Trinity Monastery** (Свято-Троицкая Сергиева Лавра; Svyato-Troitskaya Sergiyeva Lavra). After decades of state-propagated atheism, the stunning monastery, founded in about 1340, is once again a thriving religious center. The splendid **Assumption Cathedral** (Успенский Собор; Uspenskiy Sobor) was modeled after its namesake cathedral in Moscow's Kremlin (p. 869). The magnificent frescoes of the **Refectory** (Трапезная; Trapeznaya) and the gilded icons by Andrei Rublev at **Trinity Cathedral** (Троицкий Собор; Troitskiy Sobor) are equally colorful and captivating. (Monastery open daily 9am-6pm.) **Commuter trains** *(elektrichki)* run to Sergiyev Posad from Moscow's Yaroslavskiy Vokzal (1½-2hr., 2-3 per hr., round-trip 128R). From the station, turn right and look for the domes, cross the street, and walk down the road until you see the city (10-15min.).

ST. PETERSBURG (САНКТ-ПЕТЕРБУРГ) ☎8812

St. Petersburg's wide boulevards and bright facades are exactly what Peter the Great envisioned when he founded his "window on the West." The curtain closed, however, when St. Petersburg (pop. 4,600,000) hosted the 1917 February Revolution that turned Russia into a Communist state. Recently, the city has also rediscovered the artistic genius of its former residents Dostoevsky, Gogol, Tchaikovsky, and Stravinsky, reawakening its latent majesty and sophistication.

0 300 meters
0 300 yards
PETROGRAD SIDE
VASILEVSKIY ISLAND
Malaya Monetnaya ul.
Malaya Posadskaya ul.
Kropotkina ul.
Vonkova ul.
Sytninskaya ul.
Markina ul.
Vvedenskaya ul.
Liry Chaukinoy ul.
Bolshaya Pushkarzkaya ul.
Bolshoy pr.
Sezzhinskaya ul.
Kronverkskiy pr.
Zrerinskaya ul.
ul. Blokhina
ul. Yablochkova
Dobrolyubova ul.
Tuchkov most
SPORTIVNAYA
Kronverkskaya nab.
Alexandrovskiy Park
Military and Artillery Museum
Mosque
GORKOVSKAYA
Museum of Russian Political History
Kamennoostrovskiy pr.
ul. Kuybysheva
Peter's Cabin Museum
Petrovskaya nab.
Peter and Paul Cathedral
Nevskiy Gate
Fortress of Peter and Paul
Timbekshoy Bastion
Trotskiy most
Birzhevoy most
Malaya Neva
Rostral Column
nab. Makarova
Tuchkov pr.
Volkhovkyy pr.
Birchevoy pr.
Birchovaya l.
Central Naval Museum
Mendeleevckaya l.
Zoological Museum
Rostral Column
Kunstkamera Anthropological and Enthnographic Museum
Dvortsovy most
Dvortsovaya nab.
ul. Millionnaya
Sezdovnkaya l.
Repina ul.
Filoigicheskiy pr.
St. Petersburg State University
Menshikov Palace
Universitetskaya nab.
Bolshaya Neva
Hermitage
Winter Palace
DVORTSOVAYA PLOSHCHAD
Alexander Column
Pushkin Museum
Konyushennaya ul.
BA
Swissair
Quo Vadis
Admiralteyskaya nab.
The Admiralty
Bronze Horseman
Malaya Morskaya ul.
Bolshaya Morskaya ul.
Kazan Cathedral
Central Ticket Off
AmEx
most Leytenanta Shmidta
Angliyskaya nab.
Vodka Museum
Manezh
St. Isaac's Cathedral
nab. Reki Moyki
nab. Reki Moyki
Konnogvardeyskiy Bulvar
ul. Galemaya
ul. Yakubovicha
Pochtamtskaya ul.
ul. Truda
Moyka River
Voznesenskiy pr.
American Medical Center
Grivtsova pr.
Kazanskaya ul.
Griboyedov Canal
Bankovskiy per.
Sadovaya ul.
Gorokhovaya ul.
New Holland
SENNAYA PLOSHCHAD
SADOVAYA
SENNAYA PL.
Stolyarnyy pr.
ul. Dekabristov
ul. Pisareva
Mariinskiy Theater/ Kirov Opera and Ballet
Conservatory
Great Choral Synagogue
Cadovaya ul.

RUSSIA

St. Petersburg

ACCOMMODATIONS
Hostel "Zimmer Freie," **7**
International Youth Hostel (HI), **15**
Nord Hostel, **8**
Puppet Hostel (HI), **5**
Sleep Cheap, **3**

FOOD
Cafe Zoom, **12**
Chaynaya Samovar, **13**
City Bar, **4**
Gin no Taki, **2**
Lenin's Mating Call, **14**
Literaturnoye Kafe, **9**
Traktir Shury Mury, **6**

NIGHTLIFE AND CAFES
CCCP, **11**
Che, **17**
Greshniki, **10**
JFC Jazz Club, **1**
Moloko, **16**

VYBORG SIDE
Bolshaya Nevka
Cruiser Aurora
PLOSHCHAD LENINA
Finlyandskiy Vokzal
Akademika Lebedevaul
ul. Komsomola
Pl. Lenina
Mikhailova ul.
nab. Arsenalnaya
Liteinyy most
Neva
ul. Robespyera
Shpalernaya ul.
Zakharevskaya ul.
nab. Kutuzova
Gagarinskaya ul.
pr. Chernyshevskogo
ul. Chaikovskogo
Mokhovaya ul.
Solyanoy pr.
Furshtatskaya ul.
US
CHERNYSHEVSKAYA
Summer Gardens
Kirochnaya ul.
Tavricheskiy Gardens
ul. Ryleeva
Pestelya ul.
Mars Field
Liteyniy pr.
Korolenko ul.
ul. Mayakovskovo
ul. Vosstaniya
Radishcheva
Paradnaya ul.
Vilenskyy pr.
Church of the Bleeding Savior
Maltevskiy Rynok
ul. Nekrasova
Russian Museum
Russian Ethnographic Museum
Tsirk
Ozernyy p.
8-ya Sovetskaya ul.
7-ya Sovetskaya ul.
6-ya Sovetskaya ul.
5-ya Sovetskaya ul.
4-ya Sovetskaya ul.
3-ya Sovetskaya ul.
2-ya Sovetskaya ul.
1-ya Sovetskaya ul.
ul. Belinskovo
Sadovaya ul.
Inzhenernaya ul.
Kcenovaya
Karavannaya ul.
Chekova ul.
Kovenskiy pr.
Mussorgsky Theater
Sheremetyev Palace
Anna Akhmatova Museum
ul. Zhukovskovo
Shostakovich Philharmonic Hall
Italyanskaya ul.
24hr. Supermarket
NEVSKIY PROSPECT
Marionette Theater
Merchant's Yard
Anglia Bookshop
Eliseevskiy Market
Nevskiy pr.
GOSTINYY DVOR
Statue of Catherine the Great
Gostinyy Dvor
Cafemax
PL. OSTROVSKOVO
PLOSHCHAD VOSSTANIYA
Suvorovskiy pr.
Sindbad
Aleksandrinskiy Theater
MAYAKOVSKAYA
UPRISING SQUARE
Maly Dramatichesky Theater
Stremyannaya ul.
Moskovskiy Vokzal
TO 16 (20m)
Theater and Music Museum
Vladimirskiy pr.
PLOSHCHAD VOSSTANIYA
Nevskiy pr.
nab. Reki Fontanka
ul. Marata
Pushkinskaya ul.
Ligovskiy pr.
PRASKIN DVOR.
Kolokolnaya ul.
Poltavskaya ul.
Shcherbakor pr.
DOSTOEVSKAYA
ul. Rubinshteyna
Torgovgy pr.
ul. Lomonosova
Kuznechnyy per.
Arctic and Antarctic Museum
Mirgorodskaya ul.
VLADIMIRSKAYA
Dostoevsky Museum
Fontanka
Covered Market
Leshtukov pr.
Razyezzhaya ul.
Postoevskogo ul.
Berodinskaya ul.
Zagorodny pr.
TO VITEBSKIY VOKZAL (650m)
TO (1.5km)

TRANSPORTATION

Flights: The main airport, **Pulkovo** (Пулково), has 2 terminals: Pulkovo-1 (☎104 38 22) for domestic flights, and Pulkovo-2 (☎104 34 44) for international flights. From M2: Moskovskaya (Московская), take bus #39 to Pulkovo-1 (25min.) or bus #13 to Pulkovo-2 (20min.). Hostels can arrange taxis (usually US$30-35).

Trains: Central Ticket Offices (Центральные Железнодорожные Кассы; Tsentralnye Zheleznodorozhnye Kassy), Canal Griboyedova 24 (Грибоедого). Tickets to Moscow sold at *kassas* on the left. **Intourist** offices in train stations also sell tickets. Check the ticket to see from which station the train leaves. Open M-Sa 8am-8pm, Su 8am-4pm.

Finland Station (Финляндский Вокзал; Finlyandskiy Vokzal; ☎168 76 87). M1: Pl. Lenina (Ленина). To **Helsinki, Finland** (6hr., 2 per day, 1375R).

Moscow Station (Московский Вокзал; Moscovskiy Vokzal; ☎168 45 97). M1: Pl. Vosstaniya (Восстания). To: **Moscow** (5-8hr., 12-15 per day, 300-1300R); **Novgorod** (3-4hr., 2 per day, 66R); **Sevastopol, Ukraine** (35hr., 2 per day, 754-1186R).

Vitebskiy Station (Витебский Вокзал; Vitebskiy Vokzal; ☎168 58 07). M1: Pushkinskaya (Пушкинская). To: **Kaliningrad** (26hr., 1 per day, 550-3300R); **Kyiv, Ukraine** (25hr., about 1 per day, 506-637R); **Odessa, Ukraine** (36hr., 1 per day, 654R); **Rīga, Latvia** (13hr., 1 per day, 887R); **Tallinn, Estonia** (9hr., 1 per day, 350R); **Vilnius, Lithuania** (14hr., every 2 days, 647R).

Buses: Nab. Obvodnovo Kanala 36 (Обводного Канала; ☎166 57 77). M4: Ligovskiy pr. Take tram #19, 25, 44, or 49 or trolley #42 to the stop just across the canal. Facing the canal, turn right and walk 2 long blocks alongside it. The station will be on your right, behind the abandoned building. Surcharge for advance tickets. Open daily 6am-8pm.

Local Transportation: St. Petersburg's **metro** (Метро) runs daily 5:45am-12:15am. Tokens (жетон; zheton) cost 10R. Passes available for 7, 15, or 30 days. **Buses, trams,** and **trolleys** (7R) run fairly frequently 6am-midnight. Licensed private **mini-buses** (маршрутки; *marshrutki;* 7-20R) move much more quickly through traffic and will stop on request (routes are displayed in the windows).

Taxis: Both marked and private cabs operate in St. Petersburg. Marked cabs have a metered rate of 11R per km; add 35R if you call ahead. **Taxi Millionnaya** (Такси Миллионная, ☎100 00 00) has an English-speaking operator. Instead of taking a taxi, many locals hail private cars, which is usually cheaper but unsafe for travelers new to the area. Never get in a car with more than 1 person in it. *Let's Go* does not recommend hitchhiking.

ORIENTATION AND PRACTICAL INFORMATION

St. Petersburg sits at the mouth of the **Neva River** (Нева) on 44 islands among 50 canals. The heart of the city lies on the mainland, between the south bank of the Neva and the **Fontanka River.** Many of St. Petersburg's major sights—including the Hermitage and the three main cathedrals—are on or near **Nevskiy Prospekt** (Невский Проспект), the city's main street, which extends from the **Admiralty** to the **Alexander Nevskiy Monastery**; **Moscow Train Station** (Московский Вокзал; Moskovsky Vokzal) is near the midpoint. Trolleys #1, 5, and 22 run along Nevskiy pr. North of the center and across the Neva lies **Vasilevskiy Island** (Василевский Остров; Vasilevskiy Ostrov), the city's largest island. On the north side of the Neva is the **Petrograd Side** archipelago, where the **Peter and Paul Fortress** stands.

Tourist Office: City Tourist Information Center, ul. Sadovaya 14/52 (☎310 82 62). M: Gostinly Dvor. English-language advice, brochures, postcards, and souvenir books. Open M-F 10am-7pm. *Where* and *St. Petersburg Times* (www.sptimes.ru), available for free in hotels and hostels, provide culture, entertainment and nightlife listings.

Budget Travel: Sindbad Travel (FIYTO), 3-ya Sovyetskaya 28 (☎332 20 20; www.sindbad.ru), in the International Hostel. Books plane, train, and bus tickets. 10-80% student discounts on flights. English spoken. Open M-F 9am-10pm, Sa-Su 10am-6pm.

Consulates: In an emergency, citizens of **Ireland** and **New Zealand** can call the UK consulate, otherwise call embassy in Moscow. **Australia:** Italyanskaya 1 (☎/fax 325 73 33; www.australianembassy.ru). M2: Nevskiy Pr. Open M-F 9am-6pm. **Canada:** Malodetskoselskiy pr. 32/B (Малодетскосельский; ☎325 84 48; www.dfait-maeci.gc.ca/canadaeuropa/russia.) M2: Frunzenskaya. Open M-F 9am-1pm and 2-5pm. **UK:** Pl. Proletarskoy Diktatury 5 (Пролетарской Диктатуры; ☎320 32 00; www.britain.spb.ru). M1: Chernyshevskaya. Open M-F 9am-5pm. **US:** Furshtatskaya 15 (Фурштатская; after hours emergency line ☎331 28 88; ☎331 26 00; www.stpetersburg-usconsulate.ru). M1: Chernyshevskaya. Open M-Tu and Th-F 2-5pm, W 10am-1pm. Phone inquiries M-Tu and Th-F 10am-1pm, W 3-5pm.

Currency Exchange: ATMs are ubiquitous downtown and occasionally dispense dollars and/or euros, but the exchange rates make it favorable to withdraw rubles. "обмен валюты" (obmen valyuty) means currency exchange.

American Express: Mikhailovskaya ul. 1, inside the Grand Hotel Europe (☎19 60 19). Open M-F 9am-5pm.

Emergency: Police: ☎02. **Ambulance:** ☎03. **Fire:** ☎01.

Tourist Police: ☎278 30 14.

24hr. Pharmacy: PetroFarm, Nevskiy pr. 22 (☎314 54 01), stocks Western medicines and toiletries. Pharmacist daily 9am-10pm. MC/V.

Medical Services: American Medical Center, nab. Reki Moyki 78, #78 (Реки Мойки; ☎140 20 90). M2/4: Sennaya Pl./Sadovaya. Follow per. Grivtsova across Griboyedov Canal to the Moyka River. English-speaking doctors provide comprehensive services, including house calls. Consultation US$50. Open 24hr. AmEx/MC/V.

Internet and Telephones: Quo Vadis, Nevskiy pr. 24 (☎311 80 11; www.quovadis.ru). Internet 80R per hr., with ISIC 70R. Long-distance calls to the US and Australia, 19R per min.; UK 14R per min. Also sells mobile phones. Open 24hr. V/MC.

Post Office: Pochtamtskaya ul. 9 (Почтамтская; ☎312 83 02). From Nevskiy pr., go west on ul. Malaya Morskaya, which becomes Pochtamtskaya; the office is about 2 blocks past St. Isaac's Cathedral. Currency exchange and telephone service. International mail at windows #24-30. *Poste Restante* held up to 1 month at windows #1 and 2. Open M-Sa 9am-7:45pm, Su 10am-5:45pm. **Postal Code:** 190 000.

RUSSIA

ACCOMMODATIONS

Hostels geared towards international tourists may be pricier than Soviet-style hotels, but staff generally speaks English and can provide tourist information.

Nord Hostel, Bolshaya Morskaya 10 (☎571 03 42; www.nordhostel.com). M2: Nevskiy Prospekt. Free drinking water, free international calls, and free Internet. Dorms are co-ed, except by request. Breakfast included. Check-out 11am. Dorms €24, Feb.-Mar. €18. ❸

Sleep Cheap, Mokhovaya ul. 18/32 (☎115 13 04; www.sleepcheap.spb.ru). M1: Chernyshevskaya. Enter the courtyard at 18 Mokhovaya; the hostel is 30m in on the right. Light pine floors, modern furnishings. A/C. Breakfast included. Pickup available. Laundry 150R. Internet 86R per hr. Dorms 700R. Cash only. ❸

Hostel "Zimmer Freie," Liteyniy pr. 46 (Литейный; ☎273 08 67; www.zimmer.ru). Through the archway, bear left; enter at the sign "Fast Link." Rooms are clean, and prices are sensational for the location. Laundry free. Check-out noon. May-Sept. dorms US$18, singles US$39; Oct.-Apr. US$11/29. 5% HI and ISIC discount. Cash only. ❶

International Youth Hostel (HI), 3-ya Sovetskaya 28 (Советская; ☎329 80 18; www.ryh.ru). M1: Pl. Vosstaniya. Walk along Suvorovskiy pr. (Суворовский) for 3 blocks, then turn right on 3-ya Sovetskaya. Rooms with large windows in a quiet neighborhood. Breakfast included. Laundry US$4. Reception 8am-1am. Check-out 11am. Dorms US$23; doubles $56. US$2 HI discount, US$1 ISIC discount. Cash only. ❷

Puppet Hostel (HI), Nekrasova 12. (Некрасова; ☎272 54 01; www.hostel-puppet.ru), on the 4th fl. M3: Mayakovskaya. Walk up Mayakovskogo (Маяковского) and take the 2nd left on Nekrasova. Breakfast included. Reception 24hr. Check-out noon. Mar.-Oct. Dorms 672R; doubles 1664R; Nov. to mid-Dec. and mid-Jan. to Feb. 480/1216R; mid-Dec. to mid-Jan. 512/1344R. 32R HI or ISIC discount. Cash only. ❷

FOOD

The **covered market,** Kuznechny per. 3 (Кузнечьный), around the corner from M1: Vladimirskaya, and the **Maltsevskiy Rynok** (Мальцевский Рынок), ul. Nekrasova 52 (M1: pl. Vosstaniya), at the top of Ligovskiy pr. (Лиговский), are largest and most exciting; don't be afraid to bargain. There are **24-hour supermarkets** on side streets off Nevskiy Prospekt; look for "24 Часа" (24hr.) signs.

St. Petersburg lacks an effective water purification system, making exposure to **giardia** (p. 29) very likely, so boil tap water, use iodine, or buy bottled water.

Cafe Zoom, Gorokhovaya 22 (Гороховая; ☎972 18 05). With sleek black and white decor and menus made from wooden card catalogue trays, it's no wonder artists and literati swarm to this hip European and Russian eatery. Entrees 90-200R. English spoken. Open daily 11am-midnight. 20% lunch discount before 4pm. Cash only. ❸

Literaturnoye Kafe (Литературное Кафе), 18 Nevskiy pr. (☎312 60 57). M2: Gostiniy Dvor. Pushkin came here the night before his fatal duel. Sumptuously decorated. An excellent menu, reasonable prices. *Blini* with mushrooms 100R. Black caviar 450R. Cover 20R. English-language menu. Open daily 11am-11pm. Cash only. ❸

Lenin's Mating Call, Kazanskaya 34 (Казанская; ☎371 86 41). Above the fine dining, TVs juxtapose the wisdom of Russia's first socialist dictator with erotic scenes forbidden during Soviet times. Caviar tasting menu (980R; serves 2). Business lunch 160-260R. Usually no erotica until 9pm. Open daily 1pm-2am. AmEx/MC/V. ❹

Traktir Shury Mury (Трактир Шуры Муры), Belinskogo 8 (Белинского; ☎279 85 50). M1: Vladimirskaya. Russian cuisine served in a rustic setting by waiters in traditional garb. Entrees 100-400R. English-language menu. Open daily 11am-6am. MC/V. ❷

Chaynaya Samovar (Чайная Самовар), Gorokovaya 27 (☎314 39 45). M2: Sennaya Pl. Perhaps the best place in St. Petersburg for *blini,* branches of this popular chain can be found all over the city. English-language menu. Блины с мяслом (blini s myaslom; pancakes with butter; 16R). *Blini* 12-67R. Open M-F 10am-9pm, Sa-Su 11am-9pm. ❶

Gin no Taki (Гин но Таки), Chernishevskogo 17 (Чернышевского; ☎272 09 58). M: Chernyshevskaya. Popular Japanese restaurant in a quiet neighborhood combines an upscale atmosphere with fantastic prices and service. 1 pc. sushi 40R. *Maki* 60-235R. Fried dishes 70-270R. English-language menu. Open daily 11am-6pm. MC/V. ❸

City Bar, Millionnaya 10 (Миллионная; ☎314 10 37; www.citybar.ru). American food in a relaxed atmosphere. Cheeseburgers 180-240R. Breakfast 100-180R. Business lunch 150R. Portions come in 'regular' or 'American-sized.' Library of English-language movies and books. Open M-Su noon-last customer; food served noon-11pm. AmEx/MC/V. ❸

SIGHTS

Museums and sights often charge foreigners several times more than Russians. Avoid paying the higher price by handing the cashier the exact amount for a Russian ticket, and saying "adeen" (one). Walk as if you know where you are going, and do not keep your map, camera, or *Let's Go* in plain view.

THE HERMITAGE. Originally a collection of 255 paintings bought by Catherine the Great in 1764, the State Hermitage Museum (Эрмитаж; Ermitazh) houses the world's largest art collection; it rivals the Louvre and the Prado in architectural, historical, and artistic significance. The collection is housed in the **Winter Palace** (Зимний Дворец; Zimny Dvorets), commissioned in 1762. Tsars lived in the complex until 1917, when the museum was nationalized. Only 5% of the three-million-piece collection is on display at a time. English-language plans are available at the info desk near the *kassa. (Nab. Dvortsovaya 34 (Дворцовая).* ☎ *311 34 20; www.hermitagemuseum.org. M2: Nevskiy pr. Turn left onto Nevskiy pr. to the Admiralty. The Hermitage is to the right; enter through the gates on Palace Sq. Open Tu-Sa 10:30am-6pm, Su 10:30am-5pm; cashier and upper floors close 1hr. earlier. Long lines; arrive early. 350R, students free.)*

ST. ISAAC'S CATHEDRAL. Glittering, intricately carved masterpieces of iconography are housed under the awesome 19th-century dome of St. Isaac's Cathedral (Исаакиевский Собор; Isaakievskiy Sobor). On a sunny day, the 100kg of pure gold that coats the dome is visible for miles. The stunning 360-degree view of the city from atop the **colonnade** is worth the 260-step climb. *(M2: Nevskiy pr. Turn left onto Nevskiy pr. and walk almost to the end; turn left onto ul. Malaya Morskaya.* ☎ *315 97 32. Cathedral open M-Tu and Th-Su summer 10am-8pm; winter 11am-7pm. Kassa closes 1hr. earlier. Colonnade open summer M-Tu and Th-Su 10am-7pm; winter Tu-Th 11am-3pm. Cathedral 270R, students 150R. Collonade 120/70R.)*

PALACE SQUARE. (Дворцовая Площадь; Dvortsovaya Ploshchad) This huge, windswept expanse in front of the Winter Palace has witnessed many turning points in Russia's history. Catherine took the crown here after overthrowing Tsar Peter III, her husband; far later, Nicholas II's guards fired into a crowd of protestors on "Bloody Sunday," which precipitated the 1905 revolution. Finally, Lenin's Bolsheviks seized power from the provisional government during the storming of the Winter Palace in October 1917. The 700-ton **Alexander Column,** held in place by its massive weight alone, commemorates Russia's defeat of Napoleon in 1812.

BLAST IN THE BANYA

The *banya* is the real Russiar bathing experience—it has been a part of Slavic culture since long before there was a Russia to claim it as Russian. A moderr *banya* is usually single-sex anc involves several stages. During the first, you enter the *parilka* (парилка), a steam room tha reaches temperatures upward o 70°C. The idea is to stay in the *parilka* as long as you can stanc it, then cool down under a showe before going out into the open air. This is repeated several times in order to acclimate the body intc cardiac workout, before a plunge into the icy cold pool (холодный бассейн) is added to the cycle. A this point, it is also customary tc offer and receive a beating with a wet birch-tree switch—this actually feels like a pleasant massage.

Bring sandals and a sheet i you have them, or rent them upor arrival. Also bring shampoo anc soap for a Western-style showe to wrap things up. Birch switche can be bought for 40-50R.

There is a public banya at 1 Bolshoy Kazachiy per. (☎315 0 34). M1: Pushkinskaya. Enter th banya through the courtyard o Dom 11. Open M and W noor 10pm, Tu and F-Su 9am-10pm Th (women's day) 10am-10pm 50R. There is a private banya a Gagarinskaya (☎272 96 82), i Dom 32. M1: Chernashevskaya Call ahead to book for a group Open 11am-2am. 450R per hr.

PETER AND PAUL FORTRESS. Across the river from the Hermitage stand the walls and golden spire of the Peter and Paul Fortress (Петропавловская Крепость; Petropavlovskaya Krepost). Construction of the fortress, supervised by Peter the Great himself, began on May 27, 1703, which is considered the city's birthday. Originally built as a defense against the Swedes, the fortress came to be used as a prison for political dissidents. Inside, the **Peter and Paul Cathedral** (Петропавловский Собор; Petropavlovskiy Sobor) glows with rosy marble walls and a breathtaking Baroque partition covered with intricate iconography. The cathedral holds the remains of Peter the Great and his successors. Before the main vault sits the **Chapel of St. Catherine the Martyr.** The remains of the last Romanovs—Tsar Nicholas II and his family—were moved here from the Artists' Necropolis on July 17, 1998, the 80th anniversary of their murder at the hands of the Bolsheviks. Condemned prisoners awaited their fate at **Trubetskoy Bastion** (Трубецкой Бастон), where Peter the Great tortured his first son, Aleksei. Dostoevsky, Gorky, and Trotsky all served time here. *(M2: Gorkovskaya. Turn right out of the metro, continue to the river and cross the wooden bridge to the island fortress. Open M and W-Su 11am-6pm, Tu 11am-5pm; closed last Tu of each month. A single ticket covers most sights. Purchase at the central kassa or in the smaller kassa just inside the main entrance. 120R, students 60R.)*

ALEXANDER NEVSKIY MONASTERY. Alexander Nevskiy Monastery (Александро-невская Лавра; Aleksandro-Nevskaya Lavra) is a major pilgrimage site and peaceful strolling ground. The **Artists' Necropolis** (Некрапол Мастеров Искусств; Nekropol Masterov Iskusstv) is the resting place of Fyodor Dostoevsky and composers Tchaikovsky, Rimsky-Korsakov, and Mussorgsky. The **Church of the Annunciation** (Благовещенская Церков; Blagoveshchenskaya Tserkov), along the stone path on the left, holds the remains of war heroes. At the end of the path is the **Holy Trinity Cathedral** (Свято-Тройтский Собор; Svyato-Troitskiy Sobor), teeming with devout *babushki. (M3/4: Pl. Aleksandra Nevskovo. ☎274 04 09. Grounds open daily 6am-10pm. Cathedral open daily 6am-8pm. Artists' Necropolis open daily 9:30am-6pm. Kassa open Tu-W and F-Su 11am-4:30pm. 60R, students 30R.)*

ALONG NEVSKIY PROSPEKT. Many sights cluster around the western end of bustling Nevskiy pr., the city's 4.5km main thoroughfare. Unfortunately, there is no metro station immediately nearby; one was built, but after the station was completed, local residents refused to allow the construction of an entrance or exit connecting it to the surface. The **Admiralty** (Адмиралтейство; Admiralteystvo) towers over the surrounding gardens and most of Nevskiy pr. In the park to the left of the Admiralty is the **Bronze Horseman** statue of Peter the Great, one of the most widely recognized symbols of the city. *(M2: Nevskiy pr. Walk to the end of Nevskiy pr. toward the golden spire.)* Walking back east on Nevskiy pr., the enormous, Roman-style **Kazan Cathedral** (Казанский Собор; Kazanskiy Sobor) looms to the right. It houses the remains of General Kutuzov, commander of the Russian army in the war against Napoleon. *(☎318 45 28. M2: Nevskiy pr. Open daily 8:30am-7:30pm. Free.)* Half a block down, looking up Canal Griboyedova to the left, you can see the brilliantly colored **Church of the Savior on the Blood** (Спас На Крови; Spas Na Krovi), which sits on the site of the 1881 assassination of Tsar Aleksandr II. *(☎315 16 36. Open Tu-Th in summer 10am-8pm; low season 11am-7pm. Kassa closes 1hr. earlier. 270R, students 150R.)* The 220-year-old **Merchants' Yard** (Гостиный Двор; Gostiniy Dvor), one of the world's oldest indoor shopping malls, is to the right. *(M3: Gostiniy Dvor. Open M-Sa 10am-10pm, Su 10am-9pm.)* Nearby **Ostrovskovo Square** (Островского) houses the historic Aleksandrinskiy Theater and the **public library** which contains Voltaire's private library, purchased in its entirety by Catherine the Great. *(Foreigners can obtain a library card for free; bring passport, visa, and two photographs. Library open July-Aug. M and W 1-9pm, Tu and Th-Su 9am-5pm; Sept.-June daily 9am-9pm.)*

SUMMER GARDENS AND PALACE. The long, shady paths of the Summer Gardens and Palace (Летний Сад и Дворец; Letny Sad i Dvorets) are a lovely place to rest and cool off. Peter's modest **Summer Palace,** in the northeast corner, reflects his diverse tastes, with everything from Spanish and Portuguese chairs to Dutch tile and German clocks. **Mars Field** (Марсово Поле; Marsovo Pole), a memorial to the victims of the Revolution and Civil War (1917-1919), extends out from the Summer Gardens. *(M2: Nevskiy pr. Turn right on nab. Kanala Griboyedova (Канала Грибоедова), pass the Church of the Bleeding Savior, cross the Moyka, and turn right on ul. Pestelya (Пестеля); look for the sights on your left. ☎314 03 74. Garden open daily May-Oct. 10am-9:30pm; Nov.-Apr. 10am-8pm. Palace open Tu-Su 10am-5pm; closed last Tu of each month. Kassa closes 4pm. Gardens free. Palace 300R, students 150R. 3rd Th of each month free.)*

OTHER MUSEUMS. The **Russian Museum** (Русский Музей; Russkiy Muzey) boasts the world's second-largest collection of Russian art. *(M3: Gostiniy Dvor. Open M 10am-5pm, W-Su 10am-6pm; kassa closes 1hr. earlier. 270R, students 135R.)* **Dostoevsky's House** (Дом Достоевского; Dom Dostoyevskovo) is where the author penned *The Brothers Karamazov*. *(M1: Vladimirskaya. On the corner of ul. Dostoevskovo, just past the market. ☎311 40 31. Open Tu-Su 11am-6pm; closed last W of each month. Kassa closes 5pm. 90R, students 45R.)* The **Museum of Russian Political History** (Музей Политической Истории России; Muzey Politicheskoi Istorii Rossii) has a vast collection of Soviet propaganda and artifacts from WWII. *(M2: Gorkovskaya. Go down Kamennoostrovskiy (Каменноостровский) toward the mosque and turn left on Kuybysheva. ☎233 70 52. Open M-W and F-Su 10am-6pm. 80R, students 40R.)*

FESTIVALS AND ENTERTAINMENT

Throughout June, when the evening sun barely touches the horizon, the city holds a series of outdoor concerts as part of the **White Nights Festival.** Bridges over the Neva River go up at 1:30am; most don't touch back down until 4:30 or 5:30am.

The home of Tchaikovsky, Prokofiev, and Stravinsky still lives up to its reputation as a mecca for the performing arts. *Yarus* (ярус), the cheapest seats, cost as little as 100R. The **Mariinskiy Teatr** (Марийнский; a.k.a. Kirov), Teatralnaya pl. 1 (Театральная), M4: Sadovaya or bus #3, 22, or 27, is perhaps the world's most famous ballet hall. Tchaikovsky's *Nutcracker* and *The Sleeping Beauty*, Baryshnikov, and Nijinsky all premiered here. Tickets go on sale 20 days in advance. (☎114 43 44. Tickets 160-4800R for foreigners. *Kassa* open Tu-Su 11am-7pm.) **Mussorgsky Opera and Ballet Theater** (Театр Имени Муссоргского; Teatr Imeni Mussorgskovo), pl. Iskusstv 1, is open from July to August, when the Mariinskiy is closed. (☎318 19 78. Bring your passport. Tickets 240-1800R for foreigners. *Kassa* open M and W-Su 11am-3pm, and 4-7pm, Tu 11am-3pm and 4-6pm.) **Shostakovich Philharmonic Hall,** ul. Mikhailovskaya 2, opposite the Russian Museum, has classical and modern concerts. (☎314 10 58. M3: Gostiniy Dvor. Tickets from 480-800R. *Kassa* open daily noon-3pm and 4-7:30pm.) **Aleksandrinskiy Teatr** (Александринский Театр), pl. Ostrovskovo 2, M3: Gostiniy Dvor, attracts famous Russian actors and companies. (☎315 44 64. Tickets 70-680R. *Kassa* open daily noon-6pm.)The Friday issue of the *St. Petersburg Times* has comprehensive listings of entertainment and nightlife and lists what performances are in English.

RUSSIA

NIGHTLIFE

JFC Jazz Club, Shpalernaya 33 (Шпалерная; ☎272 98 50). M1: Chernyshevskaya. Go right on pr. Chernyshevskogo (Чернышевского), take a left on Shpalernaya and go into courtyard 33. Quality jazz in a relaxed atmosphere. Beer 50-400R. Shots 40-150R. Live music 8-10pm. Cover 100-200R. Come early or call ahead. Open daily 7-11pm.

Che, Poltavskaya 3 (Полтавская; ☎277 76 00). M1: Vosstaniya. Walk east on Nevskiy pr., turn right on Poltavskaya. Relax with trendy bourgeoisie largely oblivious to the irony. Drinks 110-400R. Live latin/jazz music 10pm-2am. Open 24hr. AmEx/MC/V.

Moloko (Молоко; Milk), Perekupnoy per. 12 (Перекупной; ☎274 94 67). Off Nevskiy pr., halfway between M1: Pl. Vosstaniya and M3/4: Pl. Aleksandra Nevskogo. Heading toward Pl. A. Nevskovo, turn left off Nevskiy pr. on the unmarked street past the pharmacy. Catch the best Petersburg bands or mingle with the student crowd in this smoky, lively club. Beer 30R. Cover 100-200R. Live music 8-11pm. Open Tu-Su 7pm-midnight.

CCCP, Nevskiy pr. 54 (310-4929). M: Nevskiy Prospect. Though many of its patrons are too young to remember what its name stands for, the cafe milks its Soviet theme for all it's worth. The 2 cafes next door, the Bistro and Cafe Jili-Bili are also popular chill-out spots all nights of the week. Open daily 1pm-6am. Dancing F-Sa nights. AmEx/MC/V.

Greshniki (Грешники; Sinners), nab. Kanala Griboyedova 28 (☎318 42 91), 2 blocks off Nevskiy pr., past Kazan Cathedral. M2: Nevskiy pr. Rocker-dungeon-themed 4fl. gay club, primarily for men. Drinks 40-250R. Drag shows W-Su 1 and 2am. Male strip shows daily. 18+. Cover for men 50-150R, women 300-500R. Open daily 10pm-6am.

DAYTRIP FROM ST. PETERSBURG

PETERHOF (ПЕТЕРГОФ). Now the largest and the best-restored of the Russian palaces, Peterhof was burned to the ground during the Nazi retreat, but Soviet authorities provided the staggering sums needed to rebuild it. The gates open onto the **Lower Gardens,** a perfect place for a picnic along the shores of the Gulf of Finland. (Open daily 10:30am-6pm. 300R, students 150R. Fountains operate May-Oct. 10:30am-5pm.) Bent on creating his own Versailles, Peter started building the first residence, the **Grand Palace** (Большой Дворец; Bolshoy Dvorets), in 1714; his daughter Empress Elizabeth and later Catherine the Great expanded and remodeled it. (☎427 74 25. Open Tu-Su 10:30am-6pm; closed last Tu of each month. 420R, students 210R.) The 64 fountains of the **Grand Cascade** shoot from the palace into the Grand Canal. To enter the stone grotto underneath the fountains, buy tickets just outside the palace. (Grotto open daily 11am-5pm. *Kassa* open 11am-4:30pm. 110R, students 55R.) Take the **train** from Baltiyskiy station (Балтийский; M1: Baltiyskaya; 35min., 1-6 per hr., 12R). Tickets are sold at the courtyard office (Пригородная касса; prigorodnaya kassa). Get off at Novy Peterhof (Новый Петергоф). From the station, take any minivan (5min.; 10R) or bus (10min.; 7R) to Petrodvorets (Петродворец; Peter's Palace); get off when you see the palace. Or, in summer, take the **hydrofoil** from the quay on nab. Dvortsovaya (Дворцовая) in front of the Hermitage (30-35min.; 5 per hr. 9:30am-6pm; 350R, round-trip 600R.)

RUSSIA

SLOVAK REPUBLIC (SLOVENSKA REPUBLIKA)

After centuries of nomadic invasions and Hungarian domination, as well as 40 years of Soviet rule, the Slovak Republic has finally emerged as an independent nation. While still part of Czechoslovakia, Slovaks rejected communism in the 1989 Velvet Revolution, then split from the Czechs in 1993. The two were reunited in 2004 by Slovakia's accession to the European Union. Now in flux between industry and agriculture, many rural Slovaks still cling to peasant traditions, while their children trickle away to the cities. Meanwhile, in Bratislava and the surrounding countryside, budget travelers continue to discover breathtaking castle ruins and spectacular terrain.

ESSENTIALS

FACTS AND FIGURES

Official Name: Slovak Republic.

Capital: Bratislava.

Major City: Košice.

Population: 5,400,000. (86% Slovak, 10% Hungarian, 2% Roma).

Land Area: 48,845 sq. km.

Time Zone: GMT +2.

Language: Slovak.

Religions: Roman Catholic (69%), Protestant (11%), Greek Catholic (4%).

WHEN TO GO

High season occurs in the Tatras during July and August, at which time it is advisable to book rooms in advance. The dorms that open up during high season tend to be the cheapest accommodations in the country. The Slovak Republic is mostly mountainous, with plains to the south. The lower elevations tend to be warmer; summers in the mountains are cool, and winter brings good conditions for skiing.

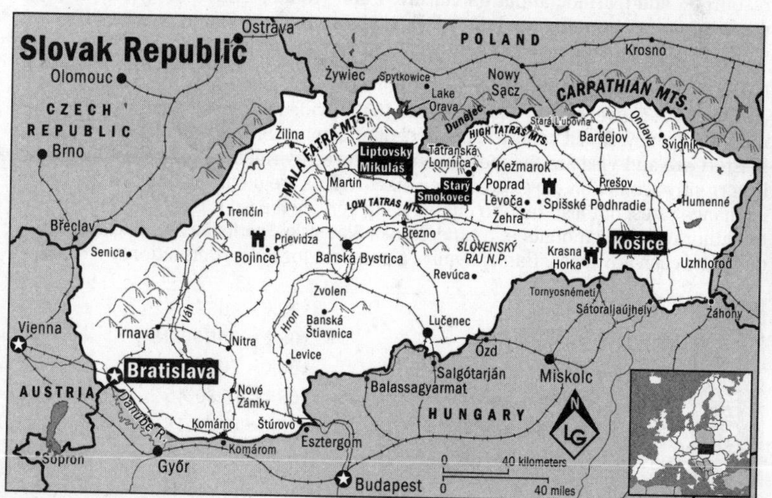

DOCUMENTS AND FORMALITIES

EMBASSIES AND CONSULATES. Foreign embassies in the Slovak Republic are in Bratislava (p. 887). Slovak embassies at home include: **Australia,** 47 Culgoa Circuit, O'Malley, Canberra, ACT 2606 (☎2 6290 1516; www.slovakemb-aust.org); **Canada,** 50 Rideau Terr., Ottawa, ON K1M 2A1 (☎613-749-4442; www.ottawa.mfa.sk); **Ireland,** 20 Clyde Rd., Ballsbridge, Dublin 4 (☎1 660 0012); **UK,** 25 Kensington Palace Gardens, London W8 4QY (☎20 7243 0803; www.slovakembassy.co.uk); **US,** 3523 International Ct. NW, Washington, D.C. 20008 (☎202-237-1054; www.slovakembassy-us.org).

VISA AND ENTRY INFORMATION. Citizens of Australia, Canada, Ireland, New Zealand, the UK, and the US can visit without a visa for up to 90 days. Those traveling to the Slovak Republic for employment, study, or specific program purposes must obtain a temporary residence permit. Contact your embassy for info.

ENTRANCE REQUIREMENTS

Passport: Required for all travelers.

Visa: Not required for stays under 90 days for citizens of Australia, Canada, New Zealand, the UK, and the US.

Letter of Invitation: Not required for citizens of Australia, Canada, Ireland, New Zealand, the UK, and the US.

Inoculations: Not required. Recommended up-to-date on DTaP (diphtheria, tetanus, and pertussis), Hepatitis A, Hepatitis B, MMR (measles, mumps, and rubella), Polio booster, and Typhoid.

Work Permit: Required for all foreigners planning to work.

Driving Permit: Required for all those planning to drive.

TOURIST SERVICES AND MONEY

TOURIST OFFICES. The **Slovak Tourist Board** (☎48 413 61 46; www.sacr.sk) provides useful links for finding accommodations, enjoying the country's natural resources, and learning about its culture. Public tourist offices are marked by a green square containing a white "i." English is often spoken at tourist offices, which usually provide maps and information about transportation.

MONEY. The Slovak Republic is a member of the EU and plans to switch to the euro in 2008. Currently, the **Slovak koruna (Sk),** divided into 100 halier, is the main unit of currency. **Credit cards** are not accepted in many Slovak establishments, but MasterCard and Visa are the most useful, followed by American Express. **Inflation** is currently around 8%, so expect price hikes. ATMs are plentiful and give the best exchange rates, but also tend to charge a flat service fee, so it is most economical to withdraw large amounts at a time. Banks **Slovenská-Sporiteľňa** and **Unibank** handle MC/V cash advances. Banks require a passport for most transactions.

KORUNY (SK)		
	AUS$1 = 23.85SK	10SK = AUS$0.42
	CDN$1 = 26.01SK	10SK = CDN$0.38
	EUR€1 = 38.60SK	10SK = EUR€0.25
	NZ$1 = 22.04SK	10SK = NZ$0.45
	UK£1 = 56.86SK	10SK = UK£0.18
	US$1 = 31.70SK	10SK = US$0.32

HEALTH AND SAFETY

In an emergency, dial ☎ 112 for English and German operators. Tap **water** varies in quality and appearance–water bubbles may make it appear cloudy--but is generally safe. Drug stores *(drogerii)* stock Western brands. Bandages *(obväz)*, aspirin *(aspirena)*, tampons *(tampony)*, and condoms *(kondómy)* are all available. Petty crime is common; be wary in crowded areas and secure passports and valuables at all times. Few accommodations exist for **disabled** travelers. **Women** traveling alone will likely have few problems but may encounter stares. Avoid walking or riding public transportation at night. **Minority** travelers with darker skin may encounter discrimination and should exercise caution at all times. **Homosexuality** is not accepted by all Slovaks; GLBT couples may experience stares or insults.

EMERGENCY	**Police:** ☎ 150. **Ambulance:** ☎ 155. **Fire:** ☎ 158.

TRANSPORTATION

BY PLANE AND TRAIN. Flying to Bratislava may be inconvenient and expensive because many international carriers have no direct flights. Flying to Vienna, Austria and taking a bus or train is often much cheaper and doesn't take much longer. EastPass is valid in the Slovak Republic, but Eurail is not. *InterCity* or *EuroCity* fast trains cost more. A boxed "R" on the timetable means a reservation *(miestenka;* 7Sk) is required. There is a fine for boarding an international train without a reservation. ŽSR is the national rail company. Master schedules *(cestovný poriadok;* 58Sk) are available for sale at info desks and are posted on boards in most stations. Reservations are advisable and often required for express *(expresný)* trains and first-class seats, but are not necessary for *rychlík* (fast), *spešný* (semi-fast), or *osobný* (local) trains. Both first and second class are relatively comfortable and considered safe. Buy tickets before boarding the train, except in very tiny towns. For train info, check www.zsr.sk.

BY BUS. In hilly regions, **ČSAD** or **SAD buses** are the best and sometimes only option. Except for very long trips, buy tickets on board. You can probably ignore most footnotes on schedules, but the following are important: "X" (crossed hammers) means weekdays only; "a" is Saturday and Sunday; "b" is Monday through Saturday; "n" is Sunday; and "r" and "k" mean excluding holidays. *"Premava"* means including; *"nepremava"* is except; following those words are often lists of dates (day is listed before month). Check www.eurolines.sk for bus schedules.

BY BIKE AND BY THUMB. Rambling wilds and castle ruins inspire ever-popular bike tours, especially in the Tatras, the western foothills, and Šariš. **VKÚ** publishes color bike maps (70-80Sk). *Let's Go* does not recommend hitchhiking.

KEEPING IN TOUCH

PHONE CODES	**Country code:** 421. **International dialing prefix:** 00. For more information on placing international calls, see inside back cover.

EMAIL AND THE INTERNET. Internet is common in the Slovak Republic, even in smaller towns. Internet cafes usually have fast access for around 1Sk per hour.

TELEPHONE. Recent modernization of the Slovak phone system has required many businesses and individuals to switch phone numbers. The phone system is still somewhat unreliable, however, so try multiple times if you don't get through. Some pay phones allow international calls, while others do not. Both types of phones exist in each city, but there is no good way to distinguish them. Card phones are common and are usually more reliable than the coin-operated variety. Purchase cards (100-500Sk) at the post office. Be sure to buy the "Global Phone" card if you plan to make an international call.

MAIL. The Slovak Republic has an efficient mail service. Letters abroad take two to three weeks to arrive. Letters to Europe cost 11-14Sk; letters to the US cost 21Sk. Those without permanent addresses can receive mail through **Poste Restante.** Address envelopes as follows: First Name LAST NAME, POSTE RESTANTE, Horná 1 (post office address), 97400 (postal code) Banská Bystrica (city), SLOVAK REPUBLIC. Almost every post office *(pošta)* provides express mail. To send a package abroad, go to a customs office *(colnice)*.

LANGUAGE. Slovak is a West Slavic language written in the Latin alphabet. It is similar enough to **Czech** and **Polish** that speakers of one will understand the others. A traveler's attempts to speak Slovak itself, however, will be appreciated. Older people will speak a little Polish. **English** is common among Bratislava's youth, but **German** is more useful outside the capital. **Russian** is occasionally understood but is sometimes unwelcome. The golden rules of speaking Slovak are to pronounce every letter and stress the first syllable. Accents over vowels lengthen them. For a phrasebook and glossary, see **Phrasebook: Czech,** p. 1057.

ACCOMMODATIONS AND CAMPING

SLOVAK REPUBLIC	❶	❷	❸	❹	❺
ACCOMMODATIONS	under 250Sk	250-500Sk	500-800Sk	800-1000Sk	over 1000Sk

Beware of scams and overpricing. Foreigners are often charged up to twice as much as Slovaks for the same room. Finding cheap accommodations in Bratislava before student dorms open in July is difficult. Those without reservations may also have trouble in Slovenský Raj and the Tatras. In other regions, finding a bed is relatively easy if you call ahead. The tourist office, **SlovakoTourist,** and other tourist agencies can usually help. The Slovak Republic has few hostels; most are in and around Bratislava. These usually provide towels and a bar of soap. **Hotel** prices are dramatically lower outside Bratislava and the Tatras, with budget hotels running 300-600Sk. **Pensions** *(penzióny)* are smaller and less expensive than hotels. Campgrounds are common and are located on the outskirts of most towns; they usually rent bungalows to travelers without tents. Camping in national parks is illegal. In the mountains, mountain huts (*chaty*) range from plush quarters around 600Sk per night to friendly bunks with outhouses (about 200Sk).

FOOD AND DRINK

SLOVAK REPUBLIC	❶	❷	❸	❹	❺
FOOD	under 120Sk	120-190Sk	190-270Sk	270-330Sk	over 330Sk

The national dish, *bryndzové halušky* (small dumplings in sauce), is a godsend for **vegetarians** and those keeping **kosher.** Pork products, however, are central to many meals. *Knedliky* (dumplings) often accompany entrees, but it's often possible to opt for *zemiaky* (potatoes) instead. Enjoy *kolačky* (pastry), baked with cheese, jam or poppy seeds, and honey, for dessert. White **wines** are made northeast of Bratislava, while *Tokaj* wines (distinct from the Hungarian wine) are produced near Košice. Enjoy them at a *vináreň* (wine hall). *Pivo* (beer) is served at a *pivnica* or *piváreň* (tavern). The favorite Slovak beer is the slightly bitter *Spis.*

HOLIDAYS AND FESTIVALS

Holidays: Origin of the Slovak Republic (Jan. 1); Epiphany (Jan. 6); Good Friday (Apr. 9); Easter (Apr. 11-12); May Day (May 1); St. Cyril and Methodius Day (July 5); Anniversary of Slovak National Uprising (Aug. 29); Constitution Day (Sept. 1); Our Lady of the 7 Sorrows (Sept. 15); All Saint's Day (Nov. 1); Day of Freedom and Democracy (Nov. 17).

Festivals: Banská Bystrica's Festival of Ghosts and Spirits, in late spring, is a celebration for the dead. Folk dancers gather in Poprad for the mid-summer Vychodna Folk Festival.

BEYOND TOURISM

Brethren Volunteer Service, 1451 Dundee Ave., Elgin, IL 60120 USA (☎800-323-8039, ext. 410; www.brethrenvolunteerservice.org). Places volunteers with environmental and civic groups in the Slovak Republic.

BTVC, 163 Balby Rd., Balby, Doncaster DN4 ORH, UK (☎01302 572 224). Week-long wildlife and wilderness preservation projects throughout Central and Eastern Europe. Book early for the trip to the Slovak Republic, which monitors bear and wolf predator populations in the Tatras Mountains. Fee including accommodations €450-700.

The Slovak Spectator (www.slovakspectator.sk). A Slovak English-language newspaper with classified job ads.

BRATISLAVA ☎02

One of only two regions in Eastern Europe with living standards above the EU average, Bratislava (pop. 450,000) surprises those who take the time to discover it. While villages, vineyards, and castles lace the city's outskirts, the city's streets are lined with shops, restaurants, and chic cafes. After the Velvet Revolution of 1989, the fall of communism, and the dissolution of Czechoslovakia in 1993, Bratislava has blossomed far more than its neighbors.

TRANSPORTATION

Trains: Bratislava Hlavná Stanica. To get downtown, take tram #2 to the 6th stop. International tickets at counters #5-13. **Wasteels** (☎52 49 93 57) sells discounted tickets to those under 26. Open M-F 8:30am-4:30pm. MC/V. To **Prague, Czech Republic** (4½-5½hr., 3 per day, 750-840Sk) and **Warsaw, Poland** (8hr., every day, 1500-1800Sk).

Buses: Mlynské nivy 31 (☎55 42 16 67). Take trolley #202, or turn right on Mlynské nivy and continue to Dunajská, which leads to Kamenné nám. and the center of town. To: **Berlin, Germany** (12hr., every day, 1200Sk); **Budapest, Hungary** (4hr., every day, 550Sk); **Prague, Czech Republic** (4¾hr., 5 per day, 410Sk); **Vienna, Austria** (1½hr., every 1-2hr., 380Sk); **Warsaw, Poland** (13hr., every day, 670Sk). Check ticket for bus number (*č. aut.*) since several different buses may depart from the same stand.

Public Transportation: Tram and **bus** tickets (10min. 14Sk, 30min. 18Sk, 1hr. 22Sk) are sold at kiosks or at the orange *automats* in bus stations. Use an *automat* only if its light is on. Stamp your ticket when you board; 1200Sk fine for riding ticketless. Trams and buses run 4am-11pm. **Night buses,** marked with black and orange numbers in the 500s, run midnight-4am; 2 tickets required. Some kiosks and ticket machines sell **passes** (1-day 90Sk, 2-day 170Sk, 3-day 210Sk).

Taxis: BP (☎169 99); **FunTaxi** (☎167 77); **Profi Taxi** (☎162 22).

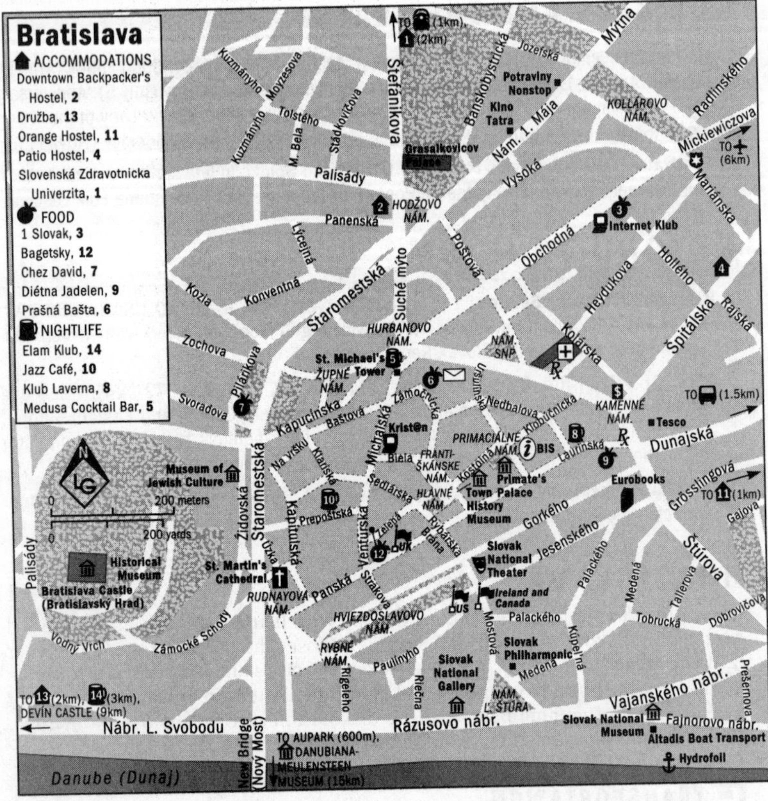

ORIENTATION AND PRACTICAL INFORMATION

The **Dunaj** (Danube) flows east-west. The castle **Bratislavský Hrad** towers on a hill to the west while the center lies between the river and **Námestie Slovenského Národného Povstania** (Nám. SNP; Slovak National Uprising Square). **Nový Most** (New Bridge), the largest of four bridges spanning the Danube, connects central **Staromestská** to the commercial and entertainment district on the southern bank.

Tourist Office: Bratislavská Informačná Služba (BIS), Klobúčnicka 2 (☎161 86). Books private and hotel rooms (rooms 800-3000Sk; 50Sk fee); arranges tours (1000Sk per hr.; max. 19 people), sells maps (free-80Sk), and a **pass** (75Sk) for 4 museums and zoo. Open June to mid-Oct. M-F 8:30am-7pm, Sa 9am-5pm, Su 9:30am-4pm; mid-Oct. to May M-F 8am-6pm, Sa 9am-2pm.

Embassies: Canada, Mostová 2 (☎59 20 40 31). **Ireland,** Mostová 2 (☎59 30 96 11; mail@ireland-embassy.sk). Open M-F 9am-12:30pm. **UK,** Panská 16 (☎59 98 20 00; www.britishembassy.sk). Visa office open M-F 8:30-11am. **US,** Hviezdoslavovo nám. 5 (☎54 43 08 61, emergency 09 03 70 36 66; www.usembassy.sk). Open M-F 8am-4:30pm. Visa office open M-F 8-11:30am. In an emergency, citizens of **Australia** and **New Zealand** should contact the UK embassy.

Currency Exchange: Ľudová Banka, Nám. SNP 15 (☎54 41 89 84; www.luba.sk) cashes AmEx/V **traveler's checks** for 1% commission and offers MC/V **cash advances.** Open M-F 8am-7pm. **ATMs** are at the train station and throughout the city center.

Emergency: Police: ☎158. **Ambulance:** ☎155. **Fire:** ☎150.

Late-Night Pharmacy: Lekáreň Pod Manderlom, Nám. SNP 20 (☎54 43 29 52). Open M-F 7:30am-7pm, Sa 8am-7pm, Su 9am-7pm. Ring bell after hours in an emergency.

Internet Access: There are Internet cafes all over central Bratislava, especially along Michalská and Obchodná. **Megainet,** Šancová 25, has new PCs in a relaxed cafe. 1Sk per min. Open daily 9am-10pm. **Internet Centrum,** Michalská 2, is a cramped 6-computer cafe with friendly staff. M-F 2Sk per min. Sa-Su 1Sk per min. Open daily 9am-midnight.

Post Office: Nám. SNP 35 (☎59 39 33 30). Offers fax service. *Poste Restante* and phone cards at counters #5-6. *Poste Restante* M-F 7am-8pm, Sa 7am-2pm. Open M-F 7am-8pm, Sa 7am-6pm, Su 9am-2pm. **Postal Code:** 81000.

ACCOMMODATIONS

In July and August, several **university dorms** open as hostels; they are sometimes run-down but quite cheap (from 150Sk). Pensions or private rooms are an inexpensive and comfy alternative. **BIS** (see **Practical Information,** p. 888) has more info.

Downtown Backpacker's Hostel, Panenska 31 (☎546 411 91; www.backpackers.sk). In a swank, centrally located 19th-century building with dark-wood floors and brick walls, backpackers relax under a bust of Lenin, enjoying beers from the bar. Laundry 100Sk. Internet 120Sk per hr. Reception 24hr. Check-out noon. Reserve ahead. Dorms 600Sk; doubles 800Sk. 60/80Sk HI discount. Tourist tax 30Sk. MC/V. ❷

Patio Hostel, Spitalska 35 (☎529 257 97; www.patiohostel.com). The entrance is tucked behind a dimly lit, run-down archway, but the hostel itself is clean and comfortable, with sunny rooms and a colorful common area. Free Internet. Check-in 1pm. Check-out 10pm. 2- to 12-person dorms 550-870Sk. MC/V. ❷

Orange Hostel, Dobrovicova 14 (☎902 842 900; www.hostelinbratislava.com). Clean and just 5-10min. from the main square. Free Internet and laundry. Reception 24hr. Check-out 10am. Open mid-July to late Aug. Dorms 550Sk. AmEx/MC/V. ❷

Družba, Botanická 25 (☎654 200 65; www.hotel-druzba.sk). Tram #1 (dir.: Pri Kríži) to Botanická Záhrada. Cross the pedestrian overpass and go to the farther of the 2 red, blue and green concrete blocks. The combination university dorm/hotel is far from the Old Town, with remarkably cheap dorms, but overpriced hotel rooms. Dorms open early July to late Aug. Reception 24hr. Dorms 380Sk, students 190Sk. Hotel open year-round. Reception M-Th 7am-3:30pm, F 7am-1pm. Singles 730Sk; doubles 1280Sk. MC/V. ❶

Slovenská Zdravotnicka Univerzita, Limbová 12 (☎593 701 00; www.szu.sk). From the train station, take bus #32 or tram #204 5 stops to Nemocnica Kramárel. This dirty-green concrete tower is far from the city center, but rooms are clean and comfortable and the doubles are a bargain. Reception 24hr. Check-out 11am. Singles 600Sk; doubles 700Sk; apartments 1000-1200Sk. Tourist tax 30Sk. Cash only. ❷

FOOD

In a square full of fast food, look for groceries at **Tesco Potraviny,** Kamenné nám. 1. (Open M-F 8am-9pm, Sa 8am-7pm, Su 9am-7pm.) Or try the nearby indoor fruit market at Stará Trzníćá, Kamenné nám. (Open M-F 7am-6pm, Sa 7am-1pm.)

Prašná Bašta, Zámočnícka 11 (☎544 349 57; www.prasnabasta.sk). Sit outside on the leafy terrace or downstairs with the sculptures and modern wood decor. A 20-something crowd comes here for generous portions of Slovak cuisine. Entrees 95-325Sk. Open daily 11am-11pm. MC/V. ❹

1 Slovak, Obchodná 62 (☎09 053 532 30). Join the largely student crowd at one of Bratislava's largest and cheapest traditional Slovak restaurants. The labyrinth themed wooden rooms include a reconstructed country cottage. Lunch (until 5pm) 35-89Sk. Dinner entrees 79-179Sk. 10% discount for Patio Hostel guests. Cash only. ❷

Diétna Jadelen, Laurinská 8. A popular lunchtime destination. Choose your treat while standing in the long line; the terrific food is worth the wait. English menu. Entrees 55-85Sk. Open M-F 11am-3pm. Cash only. ❶

Bagetsky, Zelená 8. A relaxed sandwich bar, Bagetsky keeps it simple. Limited seating. Entrees 50-90Sk. Open M-Sa 9:30am-9pm, Su 2-9pm. Cash only. ❶

Chez David, Zámocká 13 (☎544 138 24). The only kosher restaurant in Bratislava. Elegant decor and excellent, if expensive, dishes. Entrees 90-397Sk. Open M-Th and Su 11:30am-10pm, F 11:30am-3pm. MC/V. ❹

SIGHTS

NÁMESTIE SNP AND ENVIRONS. Most of the city's major attractions are in **Old Bratislava** *(Stará Bratislava)*. From Nám. SNP, which commemorates the bloody 1944 Slovak National Uprising, walk down Uršulínska to the Baroque **Primate's Palace** *(Primaciálný Palác)*. In its **Hall of Mirrors** *(Zrkadlová Sieň)*, Napoleon and Austrian Emperor Franz I signed the 1805 Peace of Pressburg. *(Primaciálné nám. 1. Open Tu-Su 10am-5pm. 40Sk, students free.)* Turn left down Kostolná as you exit to reach **Hlavné námestie.** Turn left at the square for the **Town History Museum** (Muzeum História Mesta) and its impressive 1:500 scale model of Bratislava in the era 1945-1955. *(Hlavné nám. 1. ☎592 051 30. Open Tu-F 10am-5pm, Sa-Su 11am-6pm. Museum 50Sk, students 20Sk.)* Continue to the opposite end of the square and go left onto Rybárska Brana to **Hviezdoslavovo námestie,** in which stands the gorgeous 1886 **Slovak National Theater** *(Slovenské Národné Divadlo)*. Go through the square, take Mostová, and turn left at the river to reach the **Slovak National Gallery** *(Slovenská Národná Galéria)*, which displays Gothic and Baroque art and some modern sculptures. *(Rázusovo nábr. 2. ☎544 345 87; www.sng.sk. Open Tu-Su 10am-5:30pm. 80Sk, students 40Sk.)* With the Danube on your left, continue to the gaudy neon-lit **Nový Most** (New Bridge), designed by the Communist government in the 70s. Backtrack from the bridge, turn left on Rigoleho, go straight onto Strakova (which becomes Ventúrska, then Michalská), and pass through **St. Michael's Tower** *(Michalská Brána)*, the city's last remaining medieval gateway. Turn left onto Kapucínska; cross the pedestrian bridge over the highway to the **Museum of Jewish Culture.** *(Múzeum Zidovskej Kultúry; Židovská 17. ☎54 41 85 07; www.slovak-jewish-heritage.org. Open M-F and Su 11am-5pm; last admission 4:30pm. 200Sk, students 50Sk.)*

CASTLES. Visible from much of the city, the four-towered **Bratislava Castle** *(Bratislavský hrad)* is the city's defining landmark. It burned in 1811 and was bombed during WWII; today's castle is a Communist-era restoration. Its towers provide fantastic views of the Danube. From Nový Most, climb the stairs to Židovská; turn left and climb another set of stairs to the castle. *(Museum ☎544 114 44; www.snm-hm.sk. Castle open daily Apr.-Sept. 9am-8pm; Oct.-Mar. 9am-6pm. Museum open Tu-Su 9am-5pm; last admission 4:15pm. Castle free. Museum 80Sk, students 40Sk.)* **Devín Castle's** ruins perch atop an imposing cliff above the Danube and Morava Rivers, a stone's throw from Austria. Take bus #29 from below Nový Most to the last stop, 9km west of Bratislava. Originally a Celtic fortification, the castle was owned by the Romans, Slavs, and Hungarians before Napoleon destroyed it in 1809. A museum highlights its history. *(☎657 301 05. Open July-Aug. Tu-F 10am-5pm, Sa-Su 10am-6pm; May-June and Sept.-Oct. Tu-Su 10am-5pm; last admission 30min. before closing. Museum 70Sk, students 35Sk.)*

ENTERTAINMENT AND NIGHTLIFE

The theater season runs September through June. BIS (p. 888) carries the monthly *Kam v Bratislave*, with film, concert, and theater schedules. Ballets and operas at the **Slovenské Národné Divadlo** (Slovak National Theater), Hviezdoslavovo nám. 1, draw crowds from neighboring Austria. (☎544 330 83; www.snd.sk. Box office open Sept.-June M-F 8am-5:30pm, Sa 9am-1pm. Tickets 100-200Sk.) The **Slovenská Filharmónia** (Slovak Philharmonic), Medená 3, has two to three performances per week in fall and winter. The box office, Palackého 2, is around the corner. (☎544 333 51; www.filharm.sk. Open M-Tu and Th-F 1-7pm, W 8am-2pm. 100-200Sk.)

By day, **Hlavné námestie** has souvenir stands and free outdoor concerts; by night, it fills with couples and teens. The chic and expensive **Medusa Cocktail Bar,** Michalská 89, is the place to see and be seen. (Drinks 130-240Sk. Open M-Th 11am-1am, F-Sa 11am-3am, Su 11am-midnight.) **Klub Laverna,** Laurinská 19, has a packed dance floor and a slide between its levels. (Cover 100Sk. Open daily 8pm-6am.) Take bus #31 or 39 from Nám. Mája to the line's end for the student crowd at **Elam Klub,** Staré Grunty 53. (☎654 263 04; www.elam.sk. Cover 39-100Sk. Open daily 9pm-6am.) The slick **Jazz Café,** Ventúrska 5, has drinks and live jazz. (Jazz Th-Sa 9pm-1am. Cafe open daily 10am-2am. Club open M-F 2pm-2am, Sa-Su 11am-2am.)

THE TATRA MOUNTAINS (TATRY)

The Tatras are a great place to hike, but many of the hikes are extremely demanding and require experience, even in summer. In winter, a guide is almost always necessary. For current conditions, check **www.tanap.sk.**

The mesmerizing High Tatras, which span the border between the Slovak Republic and Poland, offer hiking and skiing trails along the highest Carpathian peaks (2650m). One of the world's most compact ranges, the High Tatras feature sky-scraping hikes, glacial lakes, and deep snows. Many of the lower slopes on the Slovak side of the High Tatras were devastated by freak storms and mudslides in the fall of 2004, and even though vast swaths of the formerly lush pine forest are now brown fields of broken trees, the upper regions escaped largely unscathed.

STARÝ SMOKOVEC ☎052

Spectacular trails run from Starý Smokovec, the High Tatras' central resort. To reach **Hrebienok** (1285m), which leads to hiking country, ride the funicular. (July-Aug. ascent 90Sk, descent 40Sk, round-trip 110Sk. Sept.-June 80/30/90Sk. Open daily 8:30am-4pm.) Or, from the funicular station behind the train station, hike 35min. up the green trail. The green trail continues 20min. north from Hrebienok to the foaming **Cold Stream Waterfalls** *(Volopáday studeného potoka)*. From the falls, take the red trail, which connects with the eastward blue trail to **Tatranská Lomnica** (1¾hr.). The hike to **Little Cold Valley** *(Malá studená dolina)* is also fairly relaxed. Take the red trail (40min.) from Hrebienok to **Zamkovského chata** ❷ (☎442 26 36; dorms 380Sk) and onto the green trail (2hr.) which climbs above the treeline to a high lake and **Téryho chata** ❷. (☎442 52 45. Dorms 280Sk.)

What **Hotel Palace** ❷ lacks in appearance it makes up for in price and spacious, well-furnished rooms--those with bath are especially nice. (☎442 24 54. Breakfast 120Sk. Reception 24hr. Singles 300Sk, with bath 450-550Sk; doubles 600-700Sk. Cash only.) To reach the well-furnished, family-run **Penzión Gerlach** ❸, turn left out of the TEŽ station to the main road; the pension is on the right just past the church. (☎442 32 80; www.penziongerlach.sk. Reception 10am-6pm. Book ahead in high season. 1 single 800Sk; doubles 1000-1200Sk; triples 1500-1600Sk. Low season 600/800-1000/1200-1400Sk. Cash only.) More budget options are two TEŽ stops away in **Horný Smokovec.** Worthwhile restaurants cluster above the bus and train stations. Buy supplies at the **supermarket** in the shopping complex opposite the bus station. (Open M-F 8am-6pm, Sa-Su 8am-12:30pm. MC/V.)

TEŽ trains run to Poprad (30min., 1 per hr., 20Sk). **Buses** run to: Bratislava (6hr., 2 per day, 409Sk); Košice (3hr., 2-3 per day, 132Sk); Levoča (20-50min., 2-4 per day, 67Sk). The **Tatranská Informačná Kancelária (TIK),** in Dom Služieb, has forecasts, sells the essential VKÚ map #113 (89Sk) and other hiking maps, and books private rooms. (☎442 34 40; www.zcrvt.szm.sk. Rooms 200-250Sk; pensions 400Sk; hotels 600Sk. Open July-Aug. daily 8am-6pm; Sept.-Dec. 26 and Jan. 12-June M-F 9am-noon and 12:30-4pm, Sa 9am-1pm; Dec. 27-Jan. 11 daily 8am-5pm.)

HIKING NEAR STARÝ SMOKOVEC. The town of **Štrbské Pleso** is the base for many beautiful hikes. From the **tourist office,** across from the train station (open M-Sa 8am-11:30am and noon-4pm; low season reduced hours), pass the souvenir lot and go left at the junction. Head uphill to a lift that carries visitors to **Chata pod Soliskom** (1840m), overlooking the lake and valleys. (☎449 22 21. Open late May to Sept. and Dec.-Mar. 8:30am-4pm. Last lift up 3:30pm. 130Sk, children 90Sk; round-trip 190/130Sk.) Alternatively, continue on the challenging **yellow trail** and along **Mlynická dolina** past several enchanting mountain lakes and the dramatic **Vodopády Skok** waterfalls. The path (6-7hr.) involves strenuous ascents, mounting **Bystré Sedlo** (2314m) and **Veľké Solisko** (2412m). At the end of the yellow trail, turn left onto the red trail to complete the loop and return to Štrbské Pleso (30min.). A TEŽ **train** serves Štrbské Pleso from Starý Smokovec (30min., 1-2 per hr., 20Sk).

LIPTOVSKÝ MIKULÁŠ. Liptovský Mikuláš (pop. 33,000) is a springboard for the **Low Tatras** (Nízke Tatry). To scale **Mt. Ďumbier** (2043m), the region's tallest peak, catch an early bus from to Liptovský Ján (25-30min., every 1-2hr., 16-20Sk), then follow the blue trail up the Štiavnica River toward the **Svidovské Sedlo** and go right at the red trail (2hr.) to climb Sedlo Javorie (1½hr.). Head left on the yellow trail to summit Mt. Ďumbier (2½hr.). Descend the ridge and follow the red sign to **Chopok** (2024m), the second-highest peak in the range. From Chopok, it's a winding walk down the blue trail to the bus stop behind the Hotel Grand at Otupné (1¾hr.).

Hotel Kriváň ❷, Štúrova 5, opposite the tourist office, has small and worn but central rooms. (☎044 552 24 14. Singles 350Sk, with bath 450Sk; doubles 550/770Sk. Cash only.) The simple **Liptovská Izba Reštaurácia ❶,** nám. Osloboditeľov 22, serves delicious local dishes. (☎044 551 48 53. Entrees 55-115Sk. Open daily 10am-10pm. Cash only.) Buy supplies at **Coop Supermarket,** ul. 1 Maja 54, in the Prior Building. (Open M-F 7am-8pm, Sa 7am-7pm, Su 8am-5pm. MC/V.) **Trains** to Liptovský Mikuláš from Bratislava (4hr., 12 per day, 364Sk) are cheaper than buses. To reach the center, follow Štefánikova toward the gas station at the far end of the lot, go right on Hodžu and left on Štúrova. The **tourist office,** nám. Mieru 1, in the Dom Služieb complex, books private rooms and sells hiking maps. (☎044 552 24 18; www.lmikulas.sk. Rooms 245-400Sk. Maps 110-140Sk. Open mid-June to mid-Sept. M-F 8am-6pm, Sa 8am-noon, Su 11am-4pm; low season reduced hours.)

DEMÄNOVSKÁ JASKYŇA SLOBODY (DEMÄNOV CAVE OF LIBERTY). Take the bus from platform #3 in Liptovský Mikuláš to Demänovská Dolina, get off at Demänovská jaskyňa slobody (20-35min., every hr. 6:25am-5pm, 20Sk), and walk to the cave on the blue trail toward Pusté Sedlo Machnate (1½hr.). Named for its role in WWII, this two-million-year-old cave stored Slovak Uprising supplies. Tours are mandatory. The short tour covers 1.5km and passes through breathtaking underground chambers, lakes, and a magnificent waterfall, all carved of rock by water falling at a rate of one drop per day. The long tour includes 2km of additional corridors. Bring a sweater. (☎559 16 73; www.ssj.sk. Open June-Aug. Tu-Su 9am-4pm, entrance every hr.; Sept. to mid-Nov. and mid-Dec. to May 9:30am-2pm, entrance every 1½hr. 45min. tour 150Sk, 30Sk ISIC discount. 2hr. tour 300/240Sk.)

SLOVENSKÝ RAJ. Southeast of the Nízke Tatry is the less-touristed Slovenský Raj (Slovak Paradise) National Park, filled with forested hills, deep ravines, and fast-flowing streams. The excellent trail guide, **VKÚ map #4,** is available at many hotels. The **Dobšinská Ice Caves** (Dobšinská ľadová jaskyňa) are composed of 110,000 cubic meters of water still frozen from the last Ice Age. Tours cover 475m, passing halls of frozen columns, gigantic ice wells, and waterfalls that don't. Dress warmly. From **Dedinky** (pop. 400), on the park's southern border, take the train two stops toward **Červana Skala** (15min., 3 per day, 11Sk). Head 100m to the main road. Turn left, and head to the parking lot. From there, the steep blue trail (20min.) leads up to the caves. (☎788 14 70; www.ssj.sk. July-Aug. 9am-4pm, entrance every hr.; mid-May to June and early to mid-Sept. 9:30am-2pm, entrance every 1½hr. Guided tour only; min. 40 people for English-language. 150Sk. 30Sk ISIC discount.)

"Privat," "ubytowanie," or *"Zimmer frei"* signs mark private rooms (200-350Sk). **Penzión Pastierňa ❶,** Dedinky 42, has a restaurant serving Slovak cuisine and spacious bedrooms with unvarnished pine floors. (☎058 798 11 75. Breakfast 40-60Sk. Entrees 60-170Sk. Reception 8:30am-9:30pm. Check-out 11am. 2- to 4-bed rooms 350Sk. Tourist tax 15Sk. Cash only.) **Hotel Priehrada ❷,** Dedinky 107, rents older rooms with well-kept bathrooms. It also runs a campground by the lake. (☎798 12 12. Reception 24hr. Check-in 2pm. Check-out 10am. Rooms 450Sk, extra bed 310Sk. Tent sites 80Sk, extra person 40Sk. Cash only.) The **bus** from Poprad (dir.: Rožňava, 1hr., 4 per day, 65Sk) stops at a junction 2km south of Dedinky. Watch for the huge blue road signs at the intersection just before the bus stop. From the intersection, walk down the road the bus did not take, go right at the next intersection, cross the dam after the train station, turn left, and walk to Dedinky. Or, take a bus directly from Spisska Nová Ves (1¼-1½hr., 8-9 per day, 71Sk).

KOŠICE ☎055

Only 20km north of Hungary, Košice (KO-shih-tseh; pop. 236,000) is the Slovak Republic's second-largest city. The city has a modern cosmopolitan flair to match the enchantments of its *Staré Mesto* (Old Town), but away from the center, concrete block architecture scars the city's otherwise beautiful landscape.

TRANSPORTATION AND PRACTICAL INFORMATION. Trains (☎613 21 75) run from the station on Predstaničné nám. to: Bratislava (6hr., 13 per day, 550Sk); Budapest, Hungary (5hr., 3 per day, 850Sk); Kraków, Poland (6-7hr., 3 per day, 850-900Sk); Poprad (1¼hr., 1 per day, 138Sk); Prešov (50min., 10 per day, 60Sk). **Buses** (☎625 16 19), slightly cheaper and slower, run from the terminal to the left of the train station. To reach the center, exit the train station and follow the "*Centrum*" signs across the park. Walk down **Mlynská** to reach the main **Hlavná námestie** and turn right to find the **tourist office,** Hlavná nám. 58. (☎625 88 88; www.kosice.sk/icmk. Internet 40Sk per hr. Open M-F 9am-6pm, Sa 9am-1pm.) Check email at **Internet Centrum,** Hlavná nám. 27. (www.kosez.sk. 30Sk per hr. Open daily 9am-10pm.) Košice's **post office,** Poštová 20, has *Poste Restante* at window #16. (☎617 14 01. Open M-F 7am-7pm, Sa 8am-noon.) **Postal Code:** 04001.

ACCOMMODATIONS AND FOOD. University dorms ❶, far from the center, are the cheapest choice in July and August. (☎643 94 84. 200-400Sk.) Hotels and pensions add a tax of 20Sk per person per night. **K2 Tourist Hotel ❷,** Štúrova 32, is a bargain and is near the Old Town. Go down Hlavná nám. from the main square and turn right on Štúrova. (☎625 59 48. Reception 24hr. Check-in and check-out noon. 3- to 4-bed dorms 350Sk.) Farther away, **Hotel Kohal ❷**, Trieda SNP 61, contains a hostel with plain singles and doubles. Hotel rooms have TV and apartments have private bath. Take tram #6 from the train/bus station to the fifth stop, called "Ferrocentrum" or "Spoločenský Pavilón." (☎/fax 642 55 72. Breakfast 90Sk. Laundry 10-70Sk per item. Reception 24hr. Check-out 11am. Hostel singles 325Sk; doubles 600Sk. Hotel singles 580Sk; doubles 1040Sk. Apartments 1300Sk. AmEx/MC/V.)

Reštaurácia Veverička (Squirrel Restaurant) ❸, Hlavná nám. 97, serves local dishes on its sun-drenched patio. (☎622 33 60. English menu. Entrees 68-250Sk. Open daily 9am-10pm. Cash only.) Vegetarians praise the organic Slovak and Mexican food at **Reštaurácia Ajvega ❶**, Orlia 10. (☎622 04 52; www.ajvega.sk. Meat options. Soups 30-40Sk. Entrees 89-155Sk. Open M-Th and Su 11am-11pm, F-Sa 11am-midnight. Cash only.) **Tesco** supermarket can be found at Hlavná nám. 109. (☎670 48 10. Open M-F 8am-8pm, Sa-Su 8am-4:30pm. MC/V.)

SIGHTS AND NIGHTLIFE. Begun in the high Gothic style in 1378, the **Cathedral of St. Elizabeth** *(Dom sv. Alžbety)* has been renovated repeatedly in many styles. It is the grave of local revolutionary hero Ferenc Rakóczi II. Climb the north tower for a view of the Old Town and the intricate cathedral roof. (☎090 866 70 83. Crypt open M-F 9:30am-4:30pm. Tower open Apr.-Nov. M-F 9:30am-4:30pm. 30Sk, students 20Sk.) The **East Slovak Museum** *(Východnoslovenské Múzeum)*, Hrnčiarska 7, houses **Rakóczi's House,** an exhibit on a local rebellion leader, and **Mikluš's Prison** *(Miklusova väznica)*, an exposé of life behind bars from the 17th to 19th centuries. Walking up Hlavná nám., take a right at the state theater onto Univerzitná. (Open Tu-Sa 9am-5pm, Su 9am-1pm. Mandatory Slovak-language tours every hr. 40Sk, students 15Sk.) The **archaeological branch,** Hviezdoslavova nám. 2, chronicles the Sariš region with tools, bones, and photos. (☎622 05 71. Open Tu-Sa 9am-5pm, Su 9am-1pm. 40Sk, students 15Sk. English guidebook 30Sk.) Stylish and contemporary **Jazz Club,** Kováčska 39, plays jazz and funk Monday and Wednesday; disco Tuesday and Thursday through Saturday; and classical piano Sunday. (☎622 42 37. Beer 25-35Sk. Disco nights cover 30-50Sk. Open daily 4pm-2am, disco nights until 3am.) The Caribbean-themed **Aloha Cocktail Club,** Hlavná nám. 69, attracts a young crowd with its mixed drinks (60-140Sk) and R&B, rap, and pop playlist. (Open M-Th noon-midnight, F-Sa noon-2am, Su 3-11pm.)

SLOVENIA (SLOVENIJA)

Slovenia, the most prosperous of Yugoslavia's breakaway republics, has reveled in its new independence and has quickly separated itself from its neighbors. With a hungry eye westward, Slovenia has used its liberal politics and high economic output to enter prestigious clubs like NATO and the EU. Modernization has not adversely affected the tiny country's natural beauty and diversity, however. It is still possible to eat breakfast on an Alpine peak, lunch under the Mediterranean sun, and dinner in a Pannonian vineyard, all in one day.

DISCOVER SLOVENIA: SUGGESTED ITINERARIES

THREE DAYS. In **Ljubljana** (p. 899), enjoy the charming cafe culture and nightlife, especially in eclectic, Soviet-chic Metelkova, is worth at least a two-day stay, followed by a tranquil digression in fairytale **Bled** (1 day; p. 902).

ONE WEEK. After a day in **Ljubljana,** enjoy **Bled** (1 day) and its cousin **Bohinj** (1 day; p. 903). Train down the coast to the mini-Venice of **Piran**, (2 days; p. 903) and make a stop in the spectacular **Škocjan Caves** on the way back to Ljubljana.

ESSENTIALS

FACTS AND FIGURES

Official Name: Republic of Slovenia.

Capital: Ljubljana.

Major Cities: Celje, Kranj, Maribor.

Population: 2,012,000.

Land Area: 20,151 sq. km.

Time Zone: GMT +1.

Language: Slovenian.

Religions: Roman Catholic (58%).

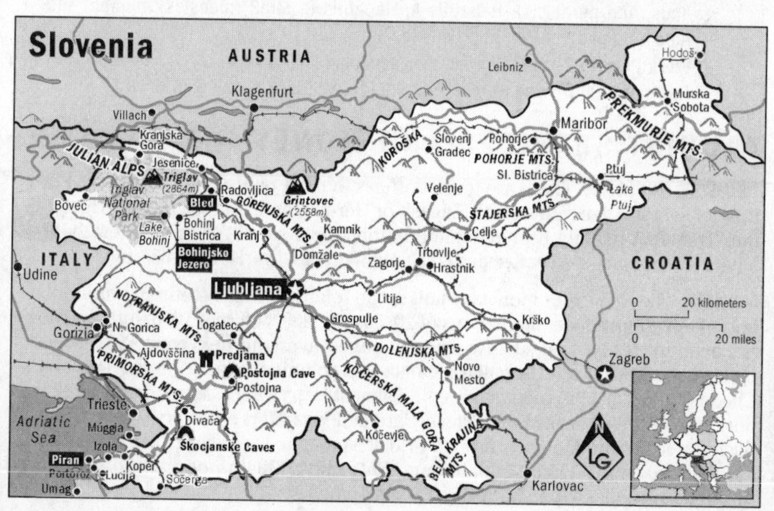

WHEN TO GO

In every way, July and August are the hot months in Slovenia; tourists flood the coast and accommodation prices often rise with the temperature. In early autumn or spring you will be blessed with sparse crowds and great weather for hiking and exploring the countryside. Skiing is popular from December to March.

DOCUMENTS AND FORMALITIES

EMBASSIES AND CONSULATES. Embassies of other countries in Slovenia are all in Ljubljana (p. 899). Slovenia's embassies and consulates abroad include: **Australia,** Level 6, Advance Bank Center, 60 Marcus Clarke St., Canberra, ACT 2601 (☎2 6243 4830; vca@mzz-dkp.gov.si); **Canada,** 150 Metcalfe St. Ste. 2101, Ottawa, ON K2P 1P1 (☎613-565-5781; vot@mzz-dkp.gov.si); **Ireland,** Morrison Chambers, 2nd fl., 32 Nassau St., Dublin 2 (☎1 670 5240; vdb@mzz-dkp.gov.si); **New Zealand,** 201-221 Wastern Hutt Rd., Pmare, Lower Hutt (☎4 567 0027); **UK,** 10 Little College St., London SW1P 3SJ (☎20 7222 5400; vlo@mzz-dkp.gov.si); **US,** 1525 New Hampshire Ave., NW, Washington, D.C. 20036 (☎202-667-5363; www.embassy.org/slovenia).

VISA AND ENTRY INFORMATION. Citizens of Australia, Canada, Ireland, New Zealand, the UK, and the US do not need **visas** for stays of up to 90 days. Visas take four to seven business days to process: send your passport, a money order for the proper fee (5-day transit €10; 1-month single entry €25; 3-month single-entry €30; 3-month multiple-entry €35), two passport-size photos, a voucher from your travel agency or hotel reservations if available, and a self-addressed, stamped envelope. Visas are not available at the **border,** and there is no fee for crossing.

ENTRANCE REQUIREMENTS

Passport: Required for all travelers.
Visa: Not required for stays under 90 days for citizens of Australia, Canada, Ireland, New Zealand, the UK, and the US.
Letter of Invitation: Not required.
Inoculations: Not required. Recommended up-to-date on DTaP (diphtheria, tetanus, and pertussis), Hepatitis A, Hepatitis B, MMR (measles, mumps, and rubella), Polio booster, and Typhoid.
Work Permit: Required for all foreigners planning to work.
International Driving Permit: Required for all those planning to drive.

TOURIST SERVICES AND MONEY

TOURIST OFFICES. There are tourist offices in most major cities and tourist destinations. Staffs generally speak English or German and, on the coast, perfect Italian. They can usually find accommodations for a small fee and generally give advice and maps for free. **Kompas** is the main private tourist organization.

MONEY. The Slovenian monetary unit is the tolar (1Sit=100 stotins), plural tolarjev, which comes in denominations of 20, 50, 100, 200, 500, and 1000. Inflation hovers around 2%, so expect few price changes over the next year. **SKB Banka, Ljubljanska Banka,** and **Gorenjska Banka** are common banks. AmEx Traveler's Cheques and Eurocheques are accepted almost everywhere. Major **credit cards** are not consistently accepted, but MasterCard and Visa **ATMs** are everywhere. Normal business hours are Monday through Friday 8am-4pm; banks and exchange offices Monday through Friday 7:30am-6pm, Saturday 7:30am-noon; shops Monday through Friday 8am-7pm, Saturday 7:30am-1pm.

TOLARJI (SIT)		
	AUS$1 = 147.95SIT	100SIT = AUS$0.68
	CDN$1 = 161.37SIT	100SIT = CDN$0.62
	EUR€1 = 239.49SIT	100SIT = EUR€0.42
	NZ$1 = 136.71SIT	100SIT = NZ$0.73
	UK£1 = 352.70SIT	100SIT = UK£0.28
	US$1 = 196.65SIT	100SIT = US$0.51

HEALTH AND SAFETY

Medical facilities are of high quality, and most have English-speaking doctors. UK citizens receive free medical care with a valid passport; other foreigners must pay cash. **Pharmacies** are stocked to Western standards; ask for band-aids *(obliž)*, tampons *(tamponi)*, and sanitary pads *(vložki)*. **Tap water** is safe to drink. **Crime** is rare in Slovenia. Even in large cities, overly friendly drunks and bad drivers are the greatest public menace. **Female travelers** should, as always, exercise caution and avoid being out alone after dark. There are few **minorities** in Slovenia; but minority travelers don't tend to get any trouble, just curious glances. Navigating Slovenia with a **disability** can be difficult and requires caution on slippery cobblestones. **Homosexuality** is legal, but may elicit unfriendly reactions outside urban areas.

EMERGENCY	**Police, Ambulance,** and **Fire:** ☎112.

TRANSPORTATION

BY PLANE AND BOAT. Commercial flights all arrive at **Ljubljana Airport** (LJU). Most major airlines offer connections to the national carrier **Adria Airways.** To enter the country cheaply, consider flying to Vienna, Austria and taking a train to Ljubljana. A regular **ferry** service connects Portorož to Venice, Italy during the summer.

BY TRAIN AND BUS. First and second class do not differ much; save your money and take the latter. Travelers under 26 can get a 20% discount on most international rail fares. ISIC holders get 30% off domestic tickets; ask for a *popust* (discount). Some useful transportation terms are arrivals *(prihodi vlakov)*, departures *(odhodi vlakov)*, and daily *(dnevno)*. Though usually more expensive than trains, buses are often the only option in mountainous regions. Buy tickets at the station or on board. Large backpacks cost 220Sit extra.

BY CAR AND BIKE. Car rental agencies in Ljubljana offer reasonable rates, and Slovenia's roads are in good condition. Nearly every town has a bike rental office; renting one will generally cost you 2000-3000Sit per day. While those who partake in it insist upon its safety, **hitchhiking** is not recommended by *Let's Go*.

KEEPING IN TOUCH

PHONE CODES	**Country code:** 386. **International dialing prefix:** 00. For more information on placing international calls, see inside back cover.

EMAIL AND THE INTERNET. Internet connections are very fast and common. Though free Internet access is rare, there are Internet cafes in most major tourist destinations. Expect to pay 1000-1500Sit per hour.

TELEPHONE. All phones take **phonecards,** sold at post offices, kiosks, and gas stations (750Sit per 50 units=1½min. to the US). Only **MCI WorldPhone** (☎080 88 08) has an international access number in Slovenia. Dial ☎115 for collect calls. Dial ☎1180 for the international operator. Calling abroad is expensive (over US$6 per min. to the US). Use phones at the post office and pay when you're finished.

MAIL. Airmail *(letalsko)* takes one to two weeks to reach North America, Australia, and New Zealand. Letters to the US cost 105Sit and postcards cost 100Sit; to the UK 100/90Sit; to Australia and New Zealand 110/100Sit. Mail can be received through **Poste Restante.** Address envelopes as follows: First name LAST NAME, Poste Restante, Post office address, postal code City, SLOVENIA.

LANGUAGE. Slovenian is a South Slavic language written in the Latin alphabet. Most young Slovenes speak at least some **English,** but the older generations are more likely to understand **German** or **Italian.** The tourist industry is generally geared toward Germans, but most tourist office employees speak English.

ACCOMMODATIONS AND CAMPING

SLOVENIA	❶	❷	❸	❹	❺
ACCOMMODATIONS	under 3500Sit	3500-5000Sit	5000-6500Sit	6500-8000Sit	over 8000Sit

All establishments charge a nightly **tourist tax. Youth hostels** and **student dormitories** are cheap (2500-3500Sit) and fun, but generally open only in summer (June 25-Aug. 30). **Hotels** fall into five categories—L (deluxe), A, B, C, and D—and are expensive. **Pensions** are the most common form of accommodation; usually they have private singles as well as inexpensive dorms. **Private rooms** are the only cheap option on the coast and at Lake Bohinj. Prices vary, but rarely exceed US$30. Inquire at the tourist office or look for *Zimmer frei* or *Sobe* signs. **Campgrounds** can be crowded, but are in excellent condition. Camp in designated areas to avoid fines.

FOOD AND DRINK

SLOVENIA	❶	❷	❸	❹	❺
FOOD	under 800Sit	800-1200Sit	1200-1800Sit	1800-2400Sit	over 2400Sit

For homestyle cooking, try a *gostilna* or *gostišče* (country-style inn or restaurant). Traditional meals begin with *jota*, a soup with potatoes, beans and sauerkraut. Pork is the basis for many dishes, such as *Svinjska pečenka* (roast pork) or Karst ham. **Kosher** eating thus becomes very difficult, as does finding a **vegetarian** meal. Those with such dietary restrictions might consider such generic options as pizza and bakery items. Slovenia's **wine-making** tradition dates from antiquity. *Renski*, *Rizling*, and *Šipon* are popular whites and *Cviček* and *Teran* are favorite reds. Brewing is centuries old as well; good beers include *Laško* and *Union*. For something stronger, try *žganje*, a fruit brandy, or *Viljamovka*, distilled by monks who know the secret of getting a whole pear inside the bottle.

HOLIDAYS AND FESTIVALS

Holidays: New Year's Day (Jan. 1); Culture Day, Prešeren Day (Feb. 8); Easter Holiday (Mar. 27-28); National Resistance Day (WWII; Apr. 27); Labor Day (May 1).

Festivals: In July and August, Ljubljana's International Summer Festival is the nation's most famous, featuring ballet, music, and theater. The Peasant's Wedding Day *(Kmecka ohcet)*, held in Bohinj at the end of July, and the Cows Ball *(Kravji Bal)* in mid-September, which celebrates the return of the cows to the valleys from higher pastures, are a couple of the country's many summertime folk exhibitions.

BEYOND TOURISM

Central Bureau for Educational Visits and Exchanges, 10 Spring Gardens, London SW1A 2BN, UK (www.britishcouncil.org/education/students). Places qualified British undergraduates and teachers in teaching positions in Hungary, Russia, and Slovenia.

World Wide Opportunities on Organic Farms (WWOOF), Main Office, P.O. Box 2675, Lewes BN7 1RB, UK (www.wwoof.org). Arranges volunteer work on organic and eco-conscious farms in Slovenia and around the world.

LJUBLJANA

☎01

The average traveler only stops in Ljubljana (loob-lee-AH-na; pop. 280,000) for an hour on the way from Vienna or Venice to Zagreb or Budapest, but those who stay discover a town full of folklore. Dragons protect the main bridge, hammocks sway in the city's public parks, and Baroque monuments, Art Nouveau facades, and modern high rises tell of the city's richly layered history.

TRANSPORTATION

Trains: Trg O.F. 6 (☎291 33 32). To: Bled (1hr., 14 per day, 890Sit); **Budapest, Hungary** (9hr.; 3 per day; 14,836Sit); **Munich, Germany** (7hr.; 3 per day; 15,200Sit); **Zagreb, Croatia** (2hr., 9 per day, 2700Sit); **Trieste, Italy** (3¾hr., 3 per day, 4110Sit); **Vienna, Austria** (5-6hr.; 3 per day; 12,800Sit).

Buses: Trg O.F. 4 (☎090 42 30; www.ap-ljubljana.si). To: **Bled** (1½hr., 14 her day, 1400Sit); **Zagreb, Croatia** (3hr., 2 per day, 3310Sit).

Public Transportation: Buses run until 10:30pm. Drop 300Sit in the box by the driver or buy 190Sit tokens *(žetoni)* at post offices or kiosks. Day passes (900Sit) sold at **Ljubljanski Potniški Promet,** Celovška c. 160. Open M-F 6:45am-7pm, Sa 6:45am-1pm.

ORIENTATION AND PRACTICAL INFORMATION

The train and bus stations are on **Trg Osvobodilne Fronte** (Trg O.F. or O.F. Sq.). Turn right as you exit the train station, then left on **Miklošičeva cesta** and follow it to **Prešernov Trg,** the main square. Cross the **Tromostovje** (Triple Bridge) over the **Ljubljanica River** to **Stare Miasto** (Old Town) at the base of the castle hill.

Tourist Office: Tourist Information Center, Stritarjeva 1 (☎306 12 15, 24hr. English-language info 090 939 881; www.ljubljana.si). Pick up **free maps** and the useful, free *Ljubljana From A to Z.* Open daily June-Sept. 8am-9pm; Oct.-May 8am-7pm.

Embassies: Australia, Trg Republike 3 (☎425 42 52). Open M-F 9am-1pm. **Canada,** Miklošičeva cesta 19 (☎430 35 70). Open M-F 9am-1pm. **Ireland,** Poljanski nasip 6 (☎300 89 70). Open M-F 9am-noon. **UK,** Trg Republike 3 (☎200 39 10). Open M-F 9am-noon. **US,** Prešernova 31 (☎200 55 00). Open M-F 9am-noon and 2-4pm.

Currency Exchange: *Menjalnice* booths abound. **Ljubljanska banka** branches throughout town exchange currency for no commission and cash **traveler's checks** for a 1.5% commission. Open M-F 9am-noon and 2-7pm, Sa 9am-noon.

Luggage Storage: Lockers *(garderoba)* at train station. 500Sit per day. Open 24hr.

24hr. Pharmacy: Lekarna Miklošič, Miklošičeva cesta 24 (☎231 45 58).

Internet: Most hostels in Ljubljana offer free Internet. **Cyber Cafe Xplorer,** Petkovško nab. 23 (☎430 19 91; www.sisky.com), has fast connections. 530Sit per 30min., students 477Sit. 20% discount 10am-noon. Open M-F 10am-10pm, Sa-Su 2-10pm.

Post Office: Slovenska 32 (☎426 46 68). **Poste Restante** at *izročitev pošiljk* (outgoing mail) counter. Open M-F 7am-8pm, Sa 7am-1pm. **Postal Code:** 1000.

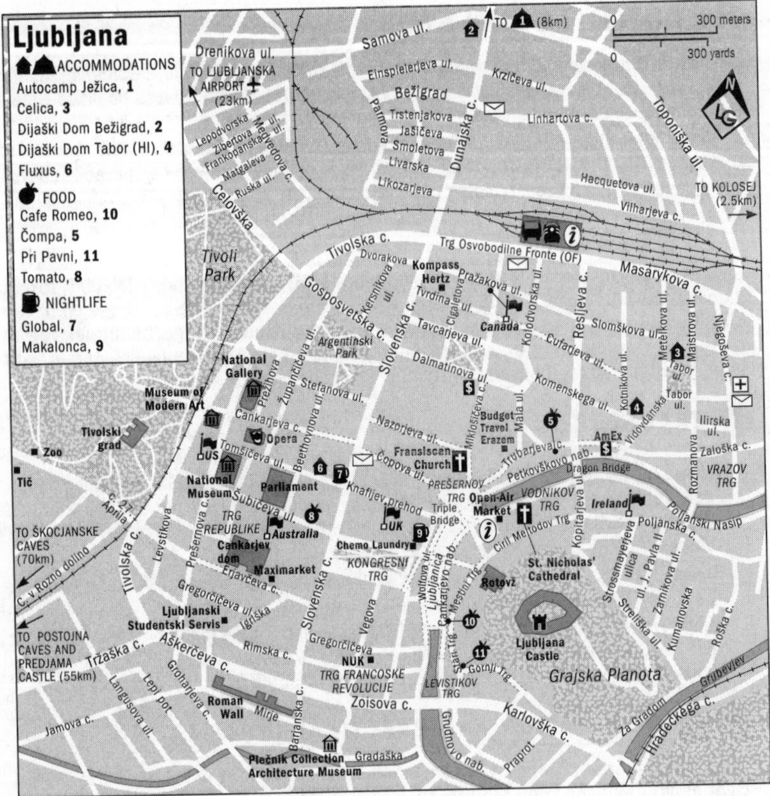

ACCOMMODATIONS

Finding cheap accommodations in Ljubljana is easier in July and August, when university dorms open to travelers. The **Slovene National Hostel Association** (PZS; ☎231 21 56) provides info on youth hostels throughout Slovenia. The **Tourist Info Center** can help find private rooms (singles 4000-10,000Sit; doubles 7000-15,000Sit). There is a daily **tourist tax** (240Sit) at all establishments which is not included in the rates below.

Celica, Metelkova 8 (☎430 18 90; www.hostelcelica.com). With your back to the train station, walk left down Masarykova, then right on Metelkova. Blue signs will lead the way. Local and foreign artists have transformed this former prison into a modern work of art. Bar, cafe, free Internet, and cultural arts programs. Breakfast included. Reception 24hr. Reserve ahead July-Aug. Dorms 3750-5250Sit. ❷

Dijaški Dom Tabor (HI), Vidovdanska 7 (☎234 88 40; ssljddta1s@guest.arnes.si). Turn left out of the train station, right on Resljeva, left on Komenskega, and left on Vidovdanska. Clean and popular with backpackers. Breakfast included. Free Internet. Open June 25-Aug. 25. Dorms 2500-3700Sit per person. 200Sit HI discount. ❶

Fluxus, Tomšičeva 4 (☎251 57 60; www.fluxus-hostel.com). The closest hostel to the river and main square. The high ceilings, long, gauzy curtains, and beautiful winding staircase in the lobby make Fluxus seem fancier than it is. Free Internet. Reception 24hr. Book early. Dorms 4900Sit; 1 double 13,000Sit. Cash only. ❷

Dijaški Dom Bežigrad, Kardeljeva pl. 28 (☎534 00 61). From the train station, cross the street and turn right; at the intersection with Slovenska, take bus #6 (Črnuče) or 8 (Ježica) and get off at Stadion (5min.), then walk 1 block to the crossroads. Negotiable check-out. Singles 3600Sit, with shower 4800Sit; doubles 4800/7200Sit; triples 7200/8400Sit. Open June 20-Aug. 25. ❷

Autocamp Ježica, Dunajska 270 (☎568 39 13; ac.jezica@gpl.si). Take bus #6 or 8 to Ježica's wooded campgrounds. Bungalows have spacious, impeccably clean rooms with TV and private shower. Reception 24hr. Reserve ahead. Camping 1680-2160Sit per person. Bungalow singles 11,000Sit; doubles 15,000Sit. MC/V. ❶

FOOD

Maximarket, on Trg Republike, has a basement grocery store. (Open M-Th 9am-8pm, F 9am-10pm, Sa 8am-3pm.) Buy fruits and vegetables at the **open-air market** by St. Nicholas's Cathedral. (Open M-Sa June-Aug. 6am-6pm; Sept.-May 6am-4pm.)

Cafe Romeo, Stari trg 6. Popular with local hipsters for its retro decor, and of few places serving food on Su. Toast grande sandwich with ham, peppers, cucumbers, tomatoes, and cheese 550Sit. Nachos 800-1000Sit. Dessert crepes 650-890Sit. Open for drinks daily 10am-1am; kitchen open M-Sa 11am-midnight, Su 11am-11pm. Cash only. ❷

Čompa, Trubarjeva ul. 4c. This cozy, leisurely little restaurant serves delicious, light Slovenian cuisine. Baked potato with cheese, meat goulash, mixed veggies, and sour cream 1600Sit. Complimentary after-dinner drink with every meal. Open June-Aug. M-Sa 11am-1am, Su noon-10pm; Sept.-May M-Sa 11am-11pm, Su noon-10pm. Cash only. ❹

Pri Pavni, Stari trg 21. Serving authentic Slovenian cuisine and recognized by the "Society for the Recognition of Sauteed Potato and Onions as an Independent Dish," Pri Pavni offers generous portions of flavorful, filling dishes. Try the "smoked meat with turnips and hard-boiled corn mush" with a side of roasted potatoes (1850Sit). ❸

Tomato, Šubičeva ul. 1 (☎252 75 55). Fast, cheap, and tasty hot and cold sandwiches (380-820Sit; 20% off after 4pm). Salads 1050-1150Sit. Entrees 1150-1500Sit. Vegetarian options. Eat in or take out. Open M-F 7am-10pm, Sa 9am-4pm. ❷

SIGHTS

A good way to see the sights is a 2hr. walking tour, in English and Slovenian, that departs from in front of the city hall (rotovž), Mestni Trg 1. (July-Aug. M-F 1am, Su 11am; May-Sept. daily 10am; Oct.-Apr. F-Su 11am. 1500Sit, students 800Sit. Buy tickets at the tour or at TIC.) A short walk from the rotovž, down Stritarjeva and across the Tromostovje, leads to Prešernov Trg with its pink 17th-century **Franciscan Church** (Frančiškanska cerkev). Cross back to Stare Miasto and take a left to reach the dazzling **St. Nicholas's Cathedral.** (Stolnica Sv. Nikolaia; open daily 6am-noon and 3-7pm. Free.) Continue along the river to Vodnikov Trg, where **Zmajski Most** (Dragon Bridge) stretches across the Ljubljanica. On the far side of Vodnikov Trg, the narrow path Studentovska leads uphill to Ljubljana Castle (Ljubljanski Grad), which has a breathtaking view. (Open daily May-Oct. 10am-9pm; Nov.-Apr. 10am-7pm. English-language tours 1100Sit, students 790Sit.) Cross the Dragon Bridge back to Resljeve cesta, turn left on Tubarjea cesta, continue to Prešernov Trg, take a left on Volfova (which becomes Gosposka), then take a right on Zoisova cesta and a left onto Emonska ul. Across a bridge is the **Plečnik Collection** (Plečnikova Zbrika), Karunova 5, which exhibits the works of Ljubljana's best-known architect. (Open Tu-Th 10am-2pm. 1000Sit, students 500Sit.) Walking back from the museum, take a left on Soistova and a right onto Slovenska; after the Ursuline Church, take a left to find **Trg Republike,** home to the National Parliament and Cankarjev Dom, the city's cultural center. Two blocks bast the square the **National Museum** (Narodni Musei) contains one of the oldest musical instruments in the world and a truly impressive taxidermy collection. (Open Tu-W, F and Su 10am-6pm. 1000Sit, students 700Sit. 1st Su of each month free.)

ENTERTAINMENT AND NIGHTLIFE

Ljubljana International Summer Festival hosts music, opera, and theater from mid-June to mid-September. The neighborhood surrounding the former military compound in **Metelkova Mesto,** behind the Celica hostel from Trg Osvobodilne Fronte to the Ethnographic Museum, is now a graffiti-covered artists' colony with plenty of bars and clubs. You might find Sierra Leone cuisine, an art-house movie screening or an impromptu sing-along. On a terrace below the waterfront, the cavernous bar **Makalonca,** Hribarjevo nab., just past the Triple Bridge, has gorgeous views of the river, fewer crowds, and more attitude than its neighbors. (Sangria 350Sit. Mixed drinks 500-900Sit. Open M-Sa 10am-1am, Su 10am-3pm.) With castle views, eclectic music, and a disco-era ambience, rooftop **Global** is Ljubljana's top dance club. (Mixed drinks 900-1400Sit. Sept.-June 1000Sit cover after 9pm; July-Aug. no cover. Bar open M-Sa 8am-9pm. Disco open Th-Sa 9pm-5am.)

DAYTRIPS FROM LJUBLJANA: ŠKOCJANSKE CAVES

Škocjanske is an amazing system of UNESCO-protected **caverns** with limestone formations and a 120m gorge created by the Reca River. (☎057 63 28 40; www.gov.si/parkskj. Mandatory tours daily June-Sept. 10am-5pm, on the hour; Oct.-May 10am, 1 and 3:30pm. 2500Sit, students 1800Sit.) **Trains** run from Ljubljana to Divača (1½hr., 10 per day, 1340Sit). Follow signs out of town, over the highway, through the village, and onto a narrow path across the woods to the ticket booth (40min.).

BLED ☎04

Alpine hills, snow-covered peaks, a turquoise lake, and a stately castle make Bled (pop. 11,000) one of Slovenia's most striking destinations. The **Church of the Assumption** *(Cerkev Marijinega Vnebovzetja)* rises from the island in the center of the lake. To get there, either rent a boat (2400-2880Sit per hr.), hop on a gondola (round-trip 2400Sit), or just swim (500m from the west side of the lake, next to the campground). Rising 100m above the shores is **Bled Castle** *(Blejski grad)*, built in 1004. It offers a museum detailing the history of the Bled region and an amazing view from the tower. (Open daily May-Sept. 8am-8pm; Oct.-Apr. 9am-5pm. 1200Sit, students 1100Sit.) **Blejski Vintgar,** a 1.6km gorge carved by the waterfalls and rapids of the Radovna River, winds through the rocks of the **Triglav National Park** *(Triglavski Narodni Park)*. To see the 16m **Šum Waterfall,** go over the hill on Grajska c. and turn right at the bottom. After 100m, turn left and follow the signs for Vintgar.

Agency Kompas, Ljubljanska 4, on the top floor of the shopping center, books private rooms. (☎572 75 00; www.kompas-bled.si. Rooms around 5000Sit. Open June-Oct. M-Sa 8am-8pm, Su 8am-noon and 4-7pm; Nov.-May 8am-7pm, Su 8am-noon and 4-7pm. AmEx/MC/V.) With comfortable beds and spotless private baths, **Bledec Youth Hostel (HI) ❸,** Grajska c. 17, feels more like a pension. Turn left from the bus station and follow the street to the top, bearing left at the fork. (☎574 52 50; bledec@mlino.si. Breakfast included. Reception 24hr. Book ahead July-Aug. Dorms 4560Sit. 480Sit HI discount.) To reach **Camping Bled ❶,** Kidričeva 10c, walk downhill on c. Svobode from the bus station, then turn left and walk 25min. along the lake. (☎575 20 00; info@camping.bled.si. Reception 24hr. Open Apr.-Oct. 1600-2400Sit.) Big portions and excellent service distinguish **Gostilna pri Planincu ❸,**

Grajska c. 8, near the bus station. (☎574 16 13. Pizza 1100-2500Sit. Crepes 600-800Sit. Entrees 900-1700Sit. Open daily 9am-11pm.) **Trains** from Ljubljana arrive at the Lesce-Bled station, about 4km from Bled (1hr., 11 per day, 1150Sit). **Buses** from Bled go to: Ljubljana (1½hr., 1 per hr., 5am-9:30pm, 1400Sit); Bohinjsko Jezero (35min., 1 per hr. 7:20am-8:20pm, 790Sit); Lesce (10min., 4 per hr. 5am-10pm, 300Sit); Vintgar (June-Sept. 1 per day 10am, returns 12:30pm; 600Sit, round-trip 1080Sit.) The **tourist office,** c. Svobode 10, sells detailed maps (1400-1750Sit) of Bled and nearby hiking trails. (☎574 11 22; www.bled.si. Open M-Sa June-Sept. 8am-7pm; Nov.-Feb. 9am-5pm; Mar.-May 9am-7pm.) **Postal Code:** 4260.

LAKE BOHINJ (BOHINJSKO JEZERO) ☎04

Although it is only 26km southwest of Bled, Bohinjsko Jezero (BOH-heen-sko YEH-zeh-roh) feels worlds away. The three farming villages that border the glacial lake, Ribčev Laz, Stara Fužina, and Ukranc, retain a traditional Slovene atmosphere. Surrounded by **Triglav National Park,** Lake Bohinj is Slovenia's center for alpine tourism. Hikes from its shores range from casual to nearly impossible. Trails are marked with a white circle inside a red circle; look for blazes on trees and rocks. Maps are available at the tourist office in **Bohinjska Bistrica,** the nearest town, 6km to the east. The most popular hike, **Savica Waterfall** *(Slap Savica)*, is underwhelming and often crowded; strike out on your own.

Take the bus to Hotel Zlatorog and backtrack 300m to reach **AvtoCamp Zlatorog ❶**, Ukanc 2. (☎572 34 82. Sept.-May and July-Aug. 1800-2300Sit; May-June and Sept. 1300-1700Sit. Tourist tax 121Sit.) Cafe **Gostišče Kramar ❶**, Stara Fužina 3, looks out over the lake in Bohinjska Bistrica. From Ribčev Laz, walk over the stone bridge and follow the first path on your left for 7min. through the woods. (Fast food and pizza 200-900Sit. Open M-Th and Su 11am-midnight, F-Sa 11am-9pm.) A **Mercator** supermarket neighbors the tourist office. (Open M-Sa 7am-8pm.) **Trains** arrive there from Ljubljana (2½hr., 8 per day, 1250Sit). More conveniently, **buses** from Ljubljana (2hr., 1 per hr., 1950Sit) pass through Bled (35min., 790Sit) and Bohinjska Bistrica (15min., 1 per hr., 380Sit) en route to the lake; they stop at Hotel Jezero in Ribčev Laz or at Hotel Zlatorog in Ukanc, across the lake. The friendly and helpful **tourist office,** Ribčev Laz 48, sells maps, books private rooms, and plans guided excursions. (☎574 60 10; www.bohinj.si. Open July-Aug. M-Sa 8am-8pm, Su 8am-7pm; Sept.-June M-Sa 8am-6pm, Su 9am-3pm.) **Postal Code:** 4265.

PIRAN ☎05

Unlike more modern towns on the Istrian Peninsula, Piran has retained its Venetian old-world charm, with beautiful churches and dilapidated medieval architecture. A short walk uphill from Tartinijev trg, the commercial center, leads to the Gothic **Church of St. George** *(Crkva sv. Jurja)* and the 17th-century **St. George's Tower,** with a spectacular view of Piran and the Adriatic. (Church and tower open daily 10am-10pm. Church free. Tower 150Sit.) From the tower, head uphill away from the church and continue parallel to the shoreline to the old **city walls.** Piran's real attraction, however, is the sea. **Scuba diving** can be arranged through **Sub-net,** Prešemovo nab. 24, which runs certification classes and guided dives. (☎673 22 18; www.sub-net.si. 1-3hr. dives 6000-8400Sit for certified divers; 1hr. dives 9600Sit for beginners. Equipment 3000Sit. Open M-F 10am-4pm, Sa 9am-7pm. Cash only.) The **Maritime Museum** *(Pomorski Muzej)*, just off Tartinijev trg on Cankarjevo nab., has three stories of exhibits on marine archaeology and seamanship, as well as an impressive collection of ship replicas. (Open Tu-Su 9am-noon and 6-9pm. 600Sit, students 500Sit.) July welcomes the **Primoska Summer Festival,** featuring outdoor plays, ballets, and concerts; inquire at the tourist office for schedules.

Maona Travel Agency, Cankarjevo nab. 7, on the waterfront before Tartinijev trg, books private rooms. (☎673 45 20; www.maona.si. Open daily 8am-7pm. Singles 4300-5500Sit; doubles 6900-8000Sit.) **Youth Hostel Val ❸,** Gregorčičeva 38a, has spotless two- to four-bed suites. From the bus station, follow the coast past Tartinijev trg as it curves away from the harbor; the hostel is three blocks up. (☎673 25 55; www.hostel-val.com. Breakfast included. Reception 8am-10pm. Mid-May to mid-Sept. 5760Sit per person; mid-Sept. to mid-May 4800Sit.) Waterfront cafes line Prešemovo nab., but **Tri Vdove ❷** stands out for its tasty seafood, meat, and pasta dishes. (☎673 02 90. Entrees 1300-3600Sit. Open daily 10am-midnight.) There is a **Mercator** supermarket at Levstikova 5. (Open M-F 7am-8pm, Sa 7am-1pm, Su 8-11am. AmEx/MC/V.) **Buses** arrive from Ljubljana (2¾hr.; M-F 8 per day, Sa 4 per day, Su 6 per day; 2670Sit). The **tourist office,** Tartinijev trg 2, has bus schedules and free maps. (☎673 02 20. Open daily 9am-1pm and 3-9pm.) **Postal Code:** 6330.

SPAIN (ESPAÑA)

The fiery spirit of flamenco; the energy of artistic genius; the explosive merging of cosmopolitan style and archaic tradition—this is Spain. Here, golden plains give way to rugged coastline, and modern architecture rises from ancient plazas. Lose yourself in winding medieval alleyways that blossom into bustling city centers, or watch curiously hairstyled youth pass by from a sidewalk cafe. In Spain, there is always a reason to stay up late, and there is always time for an afternoon *siesta*.

DISCOVER SPAIN: SUGGESTED ITINERARIES

THREE DAYS Soak in **Madrid's** (p. 910) art and cosmopolitan life as you walk through the **Retiro's** gardens and peruse the halls of the **Prado, Thyssen-Bornemisza,** and **Nacional Centro de Arte Reina Sofía.** By night, move from the tapas bars of Huertas to the wild parties of Chueca. Daytrip to **Segovia** (p. 925) or **El Escorial** (p.921). Alternatively, spend your time in **Barcelona** (p. 949) admiring the fabulously strange works of Antoni Gaudí and soaking up the sun.

ONE WEEK Begin in southern Spain, exploring the Alhambra's Moorish palaces in **Granada** (1 day; p. 941) and the mosque in **Córdoba** (1 day; p. 929). After two days in **Madrid,** travel northeast to **Barcelona** (2 days) and the beaches of **Costa Brava** (1 day; p. 963).

BEST OF SPAIN, THREE WEEKS Begin in **Madrid** (3 days), with a daytrip to **El Escorial.** Take the high-speed train to **Córdoba** (2 days), and on to **Seville** (2 days; p. 932). Catch the bus to the white town of **Arcos de la Frontera** (1 day; p. 939) before heading south to charming **Málaga,** on the **Costa del Sol** (1 day, p. 941). Head inland to **Granada** (2 days), then seaward again to **Valencia** (1 day; p. 947) before traveling up the coast to **Barcelona** (3 days). Daytrip to the **Costa Brava,** taking care not to miss the Teatre-Museu Dalí or the Casa-Museu Salvador Dalí. From Barcelona, head to the beaches and tapas bars of **San Sebastián** (1 day; p. 969) and **Bilbao** (2 days; p. 973), home of the world-famous Guggenheim Museum.

ESSENTIALS

FACTS AND FIGURES

Official Name: Kingdom of Spain.

Capital: Madrid.

Government: Parliamentary monarchy.

Major Cities: Barcelona, Granada, Sevilla, Valencia.

Population: 40,341,462.

Time Zone: GMT +1.

Languages: Spanish (Castilian), Catalan, Galician, Basque.

Religions: Roman Catholic (94%).

Largest Paella Ever Made: 20m in diameter; fed 100,000 people (1992).

WHEN TO GO

Summer is high season. In many parts of the country, *Semana Santa* (Holy Week; Apr. 9-16, 2006) and festival days are particularly busy. Tourism peaks in August, when the coastal regions overflow while inland cities empty out. Traveling in the low season has the advantage of lighter crowds and lower prices, but tourist offices and sights reduce their hours.

DOCUMENTS AND FORMALITIES

EMBASSIES. Foreign embassies in Spain are in Madrid. All countries have consulates in Barcelona. Australia, the UK, and the US also have consulates in Seville. Spanish embassies at home include: **Australia** and **New Zealand,** 15 Arkana St., Yarralumla, ACT 2600; P.O. Box 9076, Deakin, ACT 2600 (☎612 6273 3555; www.embaspain.com); **Canada,** 74 Stanley Ave., Ottawa, ON K1M 1P4 (☎613-747-2252; www.embaspain.ca); **Ireland,** 17a Merlyn Park, Ballsbridge, Dublin 4 (☎353 269 1640; www.mae.es/embajadas/dublin); **UK,** 39 Chesham Pl., London SW1X 8SB (☎0207 235 5555); **US,** 2375 Pennsylvania Ave. NW, Washington, D.C. 20037 (☎202-452-0100; www.spainemb.org).

VISAS AND ENTRY INFORMATION. EU citizens do not need a visa. Citizens of Australia, Canada, New Zealand, and the US do not need a visa for stays of up to 90 days, beginning upon entry into any of the countries in the EU's freedom of movement zone. For more information, see p. 16.

TOURIST SERVICES AND MONEY

TOURIST OFFICES. Spain's official tourist board operates an extensive website at www.tourspain.es.

EMERGENCY **General Emergency:** ☎112. **Local Police:** ☎092. **National Police:** ☎091. **Ambulance:** ☎061. **Fire:** ☎080.

MONEY. The **euro (€)** is the unit of currency in Spain. For more information, see p. 21. As a general rule it's cheaper to exchange money in Spain than at home. Expect to spend €40-70 per day. In restaurants, all prices include a service charge. Satisfied customers occasionally toss in some spare change—usually no more than 5%—and while it is purely optional, **tipping** is becoming increasingly widespread in restaurants and other places that cater to tourists. Many people give train, airport, and hotel porters €1 per bag, while taxi drivers sometimes get 5-10%. **Bargaining** is only common at flea markets and with street vendors. Spain has a 7% **Value Added Tax (VAT),** known as IVA, on all restaurant meals and accommodations. The prices listed in *Let's Go* include IVA. Retail goods bear a 16% IVA, usually included in the listed price. In the airport, upon departure, non-EU citizens who have stayed in the EU fewer than 180 days can claim a refund on the tax paid for purchases at participating stores. Ask the shop to supply you with a tax return form, but note that stores will often provide them only for purchases of more than €50-100.

TRANSPORTATION

BY PLANE. Flights into Spain land mainly at Madrid's Barajas (MAD; ☎913 93 60 00) and Barcelona's El Prat (BCN; ☎932 98 38 38) airports. Contact AENA (☎902 40 47 04; www.aena.es) for more information. See p. 48 for more information on flying to Spain.

BY TRAIN. Direct trains are available to Madrid and Barcelona from several European cities, including Geneva, Lisbon, and Paris. Spanish trains are clean, relatively punctual, and reasonably priced. However, many train routes bypass small towns, and buses are often more efficient. Spain's national railway is **RENFE** (☎902 24 02 02; www.renfe.es). Avoid *transvía, semidirecto,* or *correo* trains—they are very slow. *Estrellas* are slow night trains with bunks and showers. *Cercanías* (commuter trains) go from cities to suburbs and nearby towns. See www.raileurope.com for more information on the following passes. The **Spain Flexipass** offers three days of unlimited travel in a two-month period. The **Spain Rail 'n' Drive Pass** is good for three days of unlimited first-class train travel and two days of unlimited mileage in a car rental. The **Spain 'n' Portugal Pass** is good for unlimited first-class travel in Spain and Portugal. For more info, see p. 53.

> TIP **JUST SAY NO.** Transportation is relatively cheap in Spain and Portugal. If these are the only countries you're visiting, a Eurail pass is not the way to go.

BY BUS. In Spain, buses are cheaper and provide far more comprehensive routes than trains. Bus routes provide the only public transportation to many isolated areas. For those traveling primarily within one region, **buses are the best method of transport.** Spain has numerous private companies; the lack of a centralized bus company may make itinerary planning difficult. Companies' routes rarely overlap, so it is unlikely that more than one will serve your intended destination. **Alsa/Enatcar** (☎913 27 05 40; www.alsa.es) serves Asturias, Castilla y León, Galicia, and Madrid, as well as international destinations including France, Germany, Italy, Morocco, and Portugal. **Auto-Res/Cunisa, S.A.** (☎902 02 00 52; www.auto-res.net) serves Castilla y León, Extremadura, Galicia, Madrid, and Valencia.

BY CAR. Spain's four-lane *autopistas* connect major cities. **Speeders beware:** police can "photograph" the license plate of your car and issue a ticket without pulling you over. If you are pulled over, fines must be paid on the spot. **Renting** a car in Spain is considerably cheaper than in many other European countries. The driver must be at least 21-25 and have had a license for at least one year. Spain accepts Canadian, EU, and US driver's licenses; otherwise, an International Driving Permit is required. Try **Atesa** (Spain ☎902 10 01 01, elsewhere 10 05 15; www.atesa.es), Spain's largest rental agency. The Spanish automobile association is **Real Automóvil Club de España** (**RACE;** ☎902 40 45 45; www.race.es.)

BY FERRY. Spain's islands are accessible by ferry. For specifics on island travel, see the **Balearic Islands** (p. 974). Ferries are also the least expensive way of traveling between Spain and **Tangier** or the Spanish enclave of **Ceuta** in Morocco.

BY THUMB. Hitchhikers report that Castilla and Andalucía are long, hot waits, and hitchhiking out of Madrid is virtually impossible. The Mediterranean coast and the islands are much more promising; remote areas in Cataluña, Galicia, or the Balearic Islands may be best accessible by hitchhiking if renting a car is not an option. Approaching people for rides at gas stations near highways and rest stops purportedly gets results. *Let's Go* does not recommend hitchhiking.

KEEPING IN TOUCH

PHONE CODES	**Country code:** 34. **International dialing prefix:** 00. Within Spain, dial city code + local number, even when dialing inside the city. For more information on how to place international calls, see inside back cover.

EMAIL AND THE INTERNET. Email is easily accessible within Spain. An increasing number of bars offer Internet access for a fee of €1-4 per hour. Cybercafes are listed in most towns and all cities. In small towns, if Internet is not listed, check the library or the tourist office, which may have public Internet access. For a list of cybercafes in Spain, consult www.cybercafes.com.

TELEPHONE. The central Spanish phone company is *Telefónica.* The best way to make local calls is with a phone card, issued in denominations of €5-20 and sold at kiosks, tobacconists (*estancos* or *tabacos;* identifiable by brown signs with yellow lettering and tobacco leaf icons), and most post offices. Calling internationally with a Spanish phone card is quite inexpensive and easy. For information on using a mobile phone in Spain, see p. 33.

MAIL. Airmail *(por avión)* takes five to eight business days to reach the US or Canada; service is faster to the UK and Ireland and slower to Australia and New Zealand. Standard postage is €0.80 to North America. While less expensive than airmail, surface mail *(por barco)* can take over a month, and packages take two to three months. Registered mail *(registrado)* is the most reliable way to send a letter or parcel and takes four to seven business days. Spain's overnight mail is not actually overnight, and therefore is probably not worth the expense. Address mail to be held *Poste Restante* as follows: SURNAME, First Name; Lista de Correos; City Name; Postal Code; SPAIN; AIRMAIL.

LANGUAGE. Castilian Spanish is the official language of the Kingdom of Spain, but each region has its own specific language which, in addition to Castilian, is official in that region. Under Francisco Franco's dictatorship, local languages were repressed, but today, protected under the Spanish constitution, local languages are again a source of great regional pride and identity. Most Spaniards are at least bilingual, speaking Castilian in addition to their regional language. The languages with the highest number of speakers are Catalan (spoken in Cataluña), Euskera (spoken in the Basque Country), and Galician (spoken in Galicia). However, there are many other region-specific languages, all of which are protected.

ACCOMMODATIONS AND CAMPING

SPAIN	❶	❷	❸	❹	❺
ACCOMMODATIONS	under €15	€15-25	€25-35	€35-40	over €40

The cheapest and most basic options are *casas de huéspedes* and *hospedajes*, while *pensiones* and *fondas* tend to be a bit nicer. All are essentially boarding houses with basic rooms, shared bath, and no A/C. Higher up the ladder, *hostales* generally have sinks in bedrooms and provide sheets and lockers, while *hostal-residencias* are similar to hotels in overall quality. The government rates *hostales* on a two-star system; even establishments receiving one star are typically quite comfortable. The system also fixes *hostal* prices, posted in the lounge or main entrance. Prices invariably dip below the official rates in the low season (Sept.-May), so bargain away. **Red Española de Albergues Juveniles** (REAJ), the Spanish Hostelling International (HI) affiliate (Seville ☎954 21 62 03; www.reaj.com), runs over 165 hostels year-round. Prices depend on season, location, and services offered, but are generally €9-15 for guests under 26 and higher for those 26 and over. Breakfast is usually included; lunch and dinner are occasionally offered at an additional charge. Hostels usually lock guests out around 11:30am and have curfews between midnight and 3am. To reserve a bed in high season (July-Aug. and during festivals), call at least a few weeks in advance. A national **Youth Hostel Card** is usually required. **Campgrounds** are generally the cheapest choice for two or more people. Most charge separate fees per person, per tent, and per car; others charge for a *parcela* (a small plot of land), plus per-person fees. Tourist offices can provide more info, including the *Guía de Campings.*

FOOD AND DRINK

SPAIN	❶	❷	❸	❹	❺
FOOD	under €6	€6-10	€10-15	€15-20	over €20

Spanish food is becoming increasingly sophisticated and cosmopolitan, but fresh local ingredients are still an integral part of the cuisine. Specific options vary according to each region's climate, geography, and history. Many argue that Spanish food can only be spoken of in local terms.

Spaniards start the day with a light breakfast *(desayuno)* of coffee or thick, liquid chocolate and pastry. The main meal of the day *(la comida)* consists of several courses and is eaten around 2 or 3pm. Supper at home *(la cena)* tends to be light. Dining out begins anywhere between 8pm and midnight. Going out for tapas is an integral part of the Spanish lifestyle; groups will often spend hours barhopping. Some restaurants are "open" from 8am until 1 or 2am, but most serve meals only from 1 or 2-4pm and 8pm-midnight. Many restaurants offer a *plato combinado* (main course, side dish, bread, and sometimes a beverage) or a *menú del día* (two or three set dishes, bread, beverage, and dessert) for roughly €5-9. If you ask for a *menú*, this is what you may receive; *carta* is the word for menu.

Tapas (small, savory dishes cooked according to local recipes) are quite tasty and in some regions complimentary with beer or wine. *Raciones* are large tapas served as entrees. *Bocadillos* are sandwiches on hunks of bread. Spanish specialties include *arroz* (rice), *chorizo* (spicy sausage), *gazpacho* (cold tomato-based soup), *lomo de cerdo* (pork loin), paella (steamed saffron rice with seafood, chicken, and vegetables), and *tortilla de patata* (potato omelette). Vegetarians should learn the phrase *"yo soy vegetariano"* (I am a vegetarian) and specify this means no *jamón* (ham) or *atún* (tuna). A normal-sized draft beer is a *caña de cerveza;* a *tubo* is a little bigger. A *calimocho*, popular with young crowds, is a mix of Coca-Cola and red wine. Sangria is a drink of red wine, sugar, brandy, and fruit. *Café solo* means black coffee; add a touch of milk for a *nube;* a little more and it's a *café cortado;* half milk and half coffee makes a *café con leche.*

HOLIDAYS AND FESTIVALS

Holidays: New Year's Day (Jan. 1); Epiphany (Jan. 6); Holy Week (Apr. 9-16); Maundy Thursday (Apr. 13); Good Friday (Apr. 14); Easter (Apr. 16); Easter Monday (Apr. 17); Labor Day (May 1); Assumption Day (Aug. 15); National Day (Oct. 12); All Saints' Day (Nov. 1); Constitution Day (Dec. 6); Feast of the Immaculate Conception (Dec. 8).

Festivals: Almost every town in Spain has several—in total there are more than 3000—and nearly everything closes during festivals. All of Spain celebrates *Carnaval* the week before Ash Wednesday (Mar. 1); the biggest parties are in Cataluña and Cádiz. During the annual festival of *Las Fallas* (mid-Mar.) Valencia honors St. Joseph with parades, fireworks, and the burning of effigies. Apr. 9-16, the entire country honors the Holy Week, or *Semana Santa.* Seville's *Feria de Abril* (Apr. 12-17) has events showcasing many different Andalusian traditions, including bullfighting and flamenco. *San Fermines* (The Running of the Bulls) charges haphazardly through Pamplona July 6-14.

BEYOND TOURISM

As a **volunteer** in Spain, you can participate in projects from protecting dolphins on the Costa del Sol to fighting for immigrants' rights. Universities in major cities host thousands of foreign students every year. Language schools are a good alternative for those seeking to focus on language or a slightly less rigorous courseload.

Escuela de Cocina Luis Irizar, C. Mari 5, 20003 San Sebastián (☎943 43 15 40; www.escuelairizar.com). Learn how to cook Basque cuisine at this culinary institute. Programs range from week-long summer courses to the comprehensive 2-year apprenticeship. Some of the summer courses may be taught in English.

Don Quijote, Placentinos 2, 37008 Salamanca (☎923 26 88 60; www.donquijote.org). A nationwide language school offering Spanish courses for all levels throughout Spain. Very social atmosphere. 2-week intensive courses (20hr. language plus 5hr. "culture") start at €375. €33 enrollment fee. Discounts for longer sessions.

MADRID ☎91

After Franco's death in 1975, young *Madrileños* celebrated their liberation from totalitarian repression with raging, all-night parties in bars and streets across the city. This revelry became so widespread that it defined an era, and *la Movida* (the Movement) is now recognized as a world-famous nightlife renaissance. While new generations are too young to recall the Franco years, they have kept the spirit of *la Movida* alive. Young people have taken over the streets, shedding their parents' decorous reserve and blurring the distinction between 4pm and 4am.

TRANSPORTATION

Flights: Flights land at **Aeropuerto Internacional de Barajas** (MAD; ☎902 40 47 04), 20min. northeast of Madrid. **Barajas metro line** connects the airport to Madrid (€1). Another option is the blue **Bus-Aeropuerto** #89 (look for EMT signs outside the airport doors), which runs to the city center. (☎914 31 61 92. Every 10-15min., €2.50.) The bus stops beneath the Jardines del Descubrimiento in Pl. de Colón (M: Colón).

Trains: 2 *Largo Recorrido* (long distance) **RENFE** stations connect Madrid to the rest of Europe. Call RENFE (☎902 24 02 02; www.renfe.es) for reservations and info.

Estación Atocha (☎506 6137). M: Atocha Renfe. Domestic service only. AVE (☎902 24 02 02) offers high-speed service to the south of Spain, including **Málaga** (4½hr., 6 per day, €50-56) and **Seville** (2½hr., 22 per day, €61-67) via **Córdoba** (1¾hr., €45-50), and Grandes Lineas leave for **Barcelona** (4½-5hr., 6 per day, €60.50-93.50).

Estación Chamartín (☎300 6969). M: Chamartín. Bus #5 runs to and from Puerta del Sol (45min.). Or, take a red Cercanías train (15min., every 5-10min., €1) from M: Atocha Renfe. Chamartín serves international and domestic destinations in the northeast and south. Major destinations include: **Barcelona** (9hr.; 10, 11pm; €35-42); **Bilbao** (6½-8¾hr., 3 per day, €32-81); **Lisbon, Portugal** (9¼hr., 10:45pm, €54); **Paris, France** (13½hr., 7pm, €112-129). Chamartín has many useful services, including a **tourist office,** Vestíbulo, Puerta 14 (☎315 9976; open M-Sa 8am-8pm, Su 8am-2pm), **currency exchange, accommodations service, post office, car rental, police,** and **luggage storage** (*consignas;* €2.40-4.50; open daily 7am-11pm).

Intercity Buses: Numerous private companies, each with its own station and set of destinations, serve Madrid; most buses pass through the Estación Sur de Autobuses and Estación Auto-Res.

Estación Auto-Res: C. Fernández Shaw 1 (☎902 02 09 99; www.auto-res.net). M: Conde de Casal. Info open daily 6:30am-1am. To: **Cuenca** (2½hr., 5-10 per day, €12); **Salamanca** (3-3¼hr., 9-16 per day, €11-15); **Valencia** (5hr., 10-11 per day, €20.40-25).

Estación La Sepulvedana: Po. de la Florida 11 (☎530 4800; www.sepulvedana.es). M: Príncipe Pío (via extension from M: Ópera). To **Segovia** (1½hr., 2 per hr., €5.84).

Estación Sur de Autobuses: C. Méndez Álvaro (☎468 4200). M: Méndez Álvaro. Info desk open daily 6am-1am. **ATMs** and **luggage storage** (€1.25 per bag per day) available. Destinations include: **Alicante, Santiago de Compostela,** and **Toledo.**

Local Transportation: Madrid's **metro** is safe, speedy, and spotless (☎902 44 44 03; www.metromadrid.es). Individual tickets cost €1; a *metrobus* (ticket of 10 rides valid for both the metro and bus system) is €5.80. Buy both at machines in any metro stop, *estanco* (tobacco shop), or newsstand. Also available are 1-, 2-, 3-, 5-, and 7-day unlimited ride tickets (*abono turístico;* €3.50-37). Spanish-language **bus** info ☎406 8810. Buses run 6am-11:30pm. Bus fares are the same as metro fares and tickets are interchangeable. Búho (owl), the **night bus** service, runs every 20min. midnight-3am, every hr. 3-6am. Look for buses N1-24.

Taxis: Call **Radio Taxi** (☎405 5500), **Radio-Taxi Independiente** (☎405 1213), or **Teletaxi** (☎371 3711). A *libre* sign in the window or a green light indicates availability. Base fare €1.60, plus €0.70-0.90 per km. Teletaxi charges a flat rate of €1 per km.

ORIENTATION

Marking the epicenter of both Madrid and Spain, **"Kilometro 0"** in **Puerta del Sol** ("Sol" for short) is within walking distance of most sights. To the west are the **Plaza Mayor,** the **Palacio Real,** and the **Ópera** district. East of Sol lies **Huertas,** the heart of cafe, theater, and museum life. The area north of Sol is bordered by **Gran Vía,** which runs northwest to **Plaza de España.** North of Gran Vía are three club- and bar-hopping districts, linked by Calle de Fuencarral: **Malasaña, Bilbao,** and **Chueca.** Modern Madrid is beyond Gran Vía and east of Malasaña and Chueca. East of Sol, the tree-lined **Paseo de la Castellana, Paseo de Recoletos,** and **Paseo del Prado** split Madrid in two, running from **Atocha** in the south to **Plaza Castilla** in the north, passing the Prado, the fountains of **Plaza de Cibeles,** and **Plaza de Colón.** Madrid is safer than many European cities, but some plazas are still intimidating late at night.

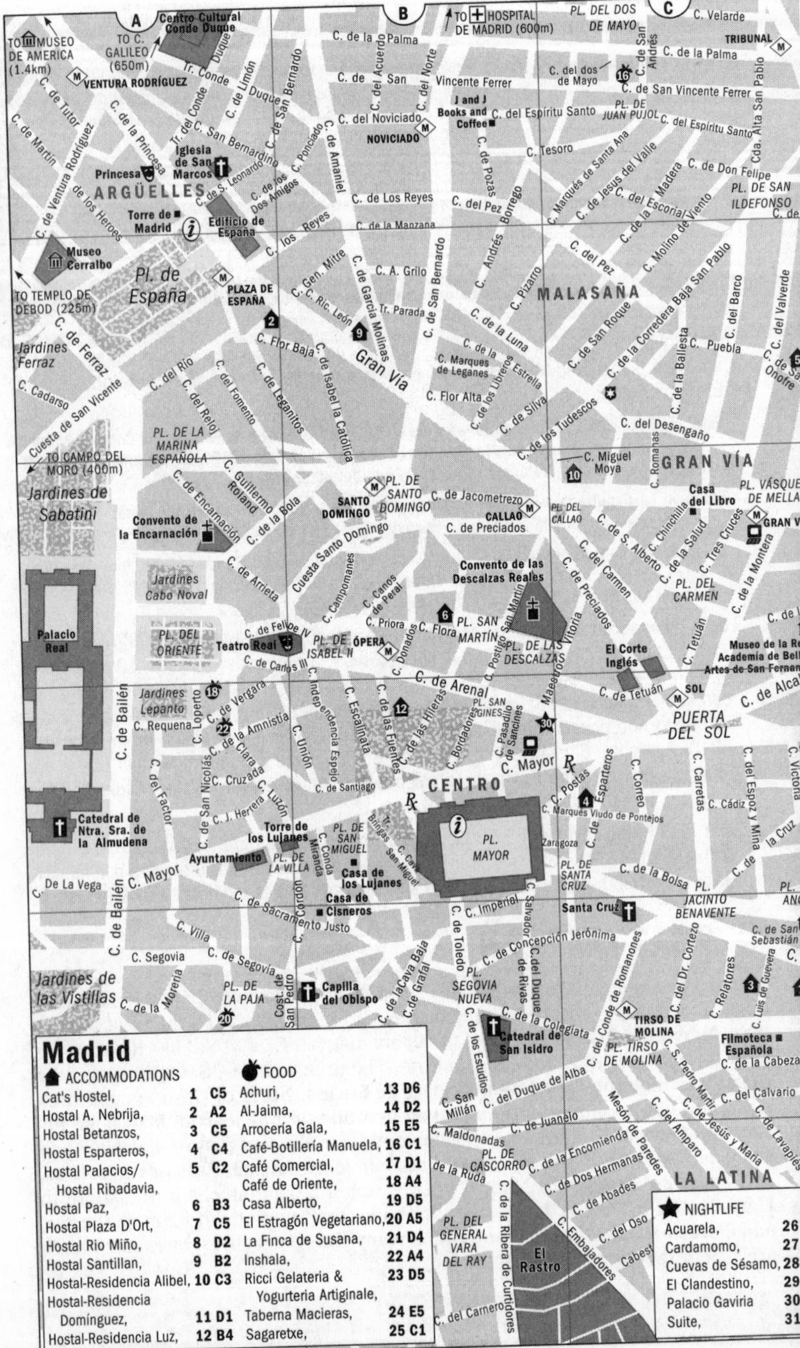
Madrid
ACCOMMODATIONS
Cat's Hostel, 1 C5
Hostal A. Nebrija, 2 A2
Hostal Betanzos, 3 C5
Hostal Esparteros, 4 C4
Hostal Palacios/ Hostal Ribadavia, 5 C2
Hostal Paz, 6 B3
Hostal Plaza D'Ort, 7 C5
Hostal Rio Miño, 8 D2
Hostal Santillan, 9 B2
Hostal-Residencia Alibel, 10 C3
Hostal-Residencia Domínguez, 11 D1
Hostal-Residencia Luz, 12 B4
FOOD
Achuri, 13 D6
Al-Jaima, 14 D2
Arrocería Gala, 15 E5
Café-Botillería Manuela, 16 C1
Café Comercial, 17 D1
Café de Oriente, 18 A4
Casa Alberto, 19 D5
El Estragón Vegetariano, 20 A5
La Finca de Susana, 21 D4
Inshala, 22 A4
Ricci Gelateria & Yogurteria Artiginale, 23 D5
Taberna Macieras, 24 E5
Sagaretxe, 25 C1
NIGHTLIFE
Acuarela, 26
Cardamomo, 27
Cuevas de Sésamo, 28
El Clandestino, 29
Palacio Gaviria 30
Suite, 31
Centro Cultural Conde Duque
TO MUSEO DE AMERICA (1.4km)
TO C. GALILEO (650m)
TO HOSPITAL DE MADRID (600m)
VENTURA RODRÍGUEZ
NOVICIADO
TRIBUNAL
ARGÜELLES
MALASAÑA
GRAN VÍA
CENTRO
LA LATINA
PUERTA DEL SOL
Pl. de España
PLAZA DE ESPAÑA
Museo Cerralbo
Torre de Madrid
Edificio de España
Iglesia de San Marcos
Princesa
J and J Books and Coffee
TO TEMPLO DE DEBOD (225m)
TO CAMPO DEL MORO (400m)
Jardines Ferraz
Jardines de Sabatini
Convento de la Encarnación
Jardines Cabo Noval
Palacio Real
PL. DEL ORIENTE
Teatro Real
ÓPERA
SANTO DOMINGO
CALLAO
SOL
Convento de las Descalzas Reales
El Corte Inglés
Casa del Libro
Museo de la Real Academia de Bellas Artes de San Fernando
Catedral de Ntra. Sra. de la Almudena
Jardines Lepanto
Torre de los Lujanes
Ayuntamiento
Casa de los Lujanes
Casa de Cisneros
PL. MAYOR
Santa Cruz
Jardines de las Vistillas
Capilla del Obispo
Catedral de San Isidro
TIRSO DE MOLINA
Filmoteca Española
El Rastro
Gran Vía
C. Mayor
C. de Arenal
C. de Bailén
C. de Toledo
C. de Segovia
C. de Atocha

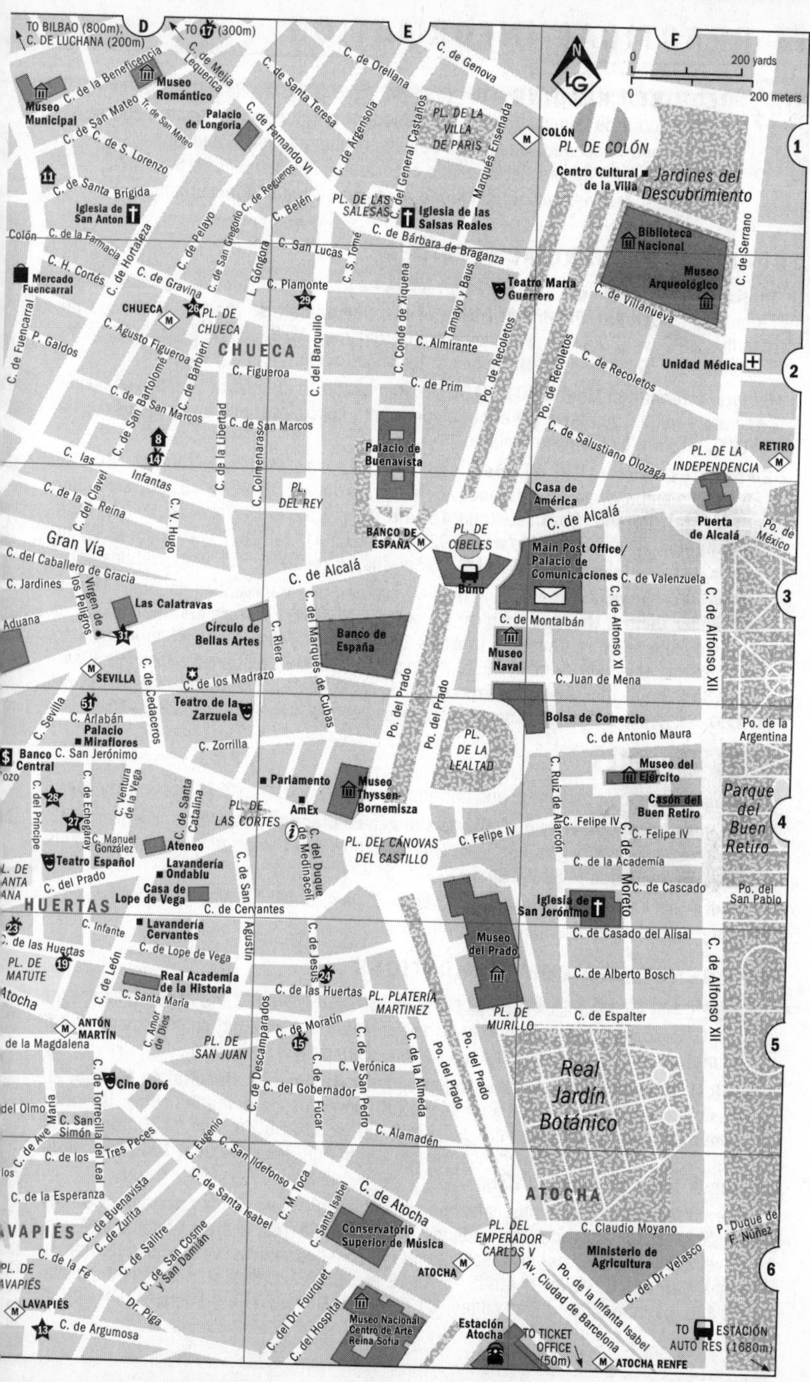
TO BILBAO (800m), C. DE LUCHANA (200m)
TO 17 (300m)
Museo Romántico
Museo Municipal
Palacio de Longoria
PL. DE LA VILLA DE PARIS
COLÓN
PL. DE COLÓN
Centro Cultural de la Villa
Jardines del Descubrimiento
Biblioteca Nacional
Museo Arqueológico
Iglesia de San Anton
PL. DE LAS SALESAS
Iglesia de las Salsas Reales
Mercado Fuencarral
Teatro María Guerrero
CHUECA
PL. DE CHUECA
Unidad Médica
Palacio de Buenavista
PL. DE LA INDEPENDENCIA
RETIRO
Casa de América
Puerta de Alcalá
PL. DEL REY
BANCO DE ESPAÑA
PL. DE CIBELES
Main Post Office/ Palacio de Comunicaciones
Buho
Gran Vía
Las Calatravas
Círculo de Bellas Artes
Banco de España
Museo Naval
SEVILLA
Teatro de la Zarzuela
Bolsa de Comercio
Palacio Miraflores
Banco Central
PL. DE LA LEALTAD
Museo del Ejército
Casón del Buen Retiro
Parlamento
Museo Thyssen-Bornemisza
AmEx
Parque del Buen Retiro
PL. DE LAS CORTES
PL. DEL CÁNOVAS DEL CASTILLO
Ateneo
Teatro Español
Lavandería Ondablu
Casa de Lope de Vega
HUERTAS
Iglesia de San Jerónimo
Lavandería Cervantes
Museo del Prado
PL. DE MATUTE
Real Academia de la Historia
PL. PLATERÍA MARTINEZ
PL. DE MURILLO
ANTÓN MARTÍN
PL. DE SAN JUAN
Real Jardín Botánico
Cine Doré
ATOCHA
LAVAPIÉS
PL. DE LAVAPIÉS
Conservatorio Superior de Música
PL. DEL EMPERADOR CARLOS V
Ministerio de Agricultura
ATOCHA
Museo Nacional Centro de Arte Reina Sofía
Estación Atocha
TO TICKET OFFICE (50m)
ATOCHA RENFE
TO ESTACIÓN AUTO RES (1680m)
C. de Alcalá
Po. del Prado
Po. de Recoletos
C. de Alfonso XII
C. de Atocha
C. de Serrano
C. de Fuencarral
C. de Hortaleza
0 200 yards
0 200 meters

PRACTICAL INFORMATION

TIP **REQUIRED READING.** The *Guía del Ocio* (€1), available at any news kiosk, should be your 1st purchase in Madrid. It has concert, theater, sports, cinema, and TV schedules and lists exhibits, restaurants, bars, and clubs. Spanish-language listingsare decipherable even to non-speakers. For a free English-language magazine, pick up *In Madrid* at tourist offices and restaurants.

TOURIST AND FINANCIAL SERVICES

Tourist Offices: Municipal, Pl. Mayor 27 (☎366 5477). M: Sol. Open M-F 8am-8pm, Su 9am-2pm. **Regional/Provincial Office of the Comunidad de Madrid,** C. Duque de Medinaceli 2 (☎429 4951; www.comadrid.es/turismo). M: Banco de España. Open M-Sa 9am-7pm, Su 9am-3pm. **Branches** at Estación Chamartín and the airport.

General Information Line: ☎901 30 06 00. Run by the Ayuntamiento. English-speaking operators will tell you anything about Madrid, from police locations to zoo hours. Or try ☎010, also run by the Ayuntamiento.

Embassies: Australia, Pl. Descubridor Diego de Ordás 3 (☎441 6025; www.spain.embassy.gov.au). **Canada,** C. Núñez de Balboa 35 (☎423 3250; www.canada-es.org). **Ireland,** Po. Castellana 46, 4th fl. (☎436 4093; fax 435 1677). **New Zealand,** Pl. Lealtad 2, 3rd fl. (☎523 0226; fax 523 0171). **UK,** C. Fernando el Santo 16 (☎700 8200; fax 700 8272). **US,** C. Serrano 75 (☎587 2200; www.embusa.es).

Currency Exchange: Avoid changing money at airport and train station counters. **Banco Santander Central Hispano** charges no commission on AmEx **Travelers Cheques** up to €300. **Main branch,** Pl. Canalejas 1 (☎558 1111). M: Sol. Follow Ctra. de San Jerónimo to Pl. Canalejas. Open Apr.-Sept. M-F 8:30am-2pm; Oct.-Mar. M-Th 8:30am-4:30pm, F 8:30am-2pm, Sa 8:30am-1pm. **American Express,** Pl. de las Cortés 2 (currency exchange ☎393 69 72 00). M: Banco de España. Currency exchange open M-F 9am-7:30pm, Sa 9am-2pm.

LOCAL SERVICES

Luggage Storage: At the airport and bus and train stations (€1.25-2.75 per bag per day).

GLBT Resources: Colectivo de Gais y Lesbianas de Madrid (COGAM), C. Fuencarral 37 (☎522 4517; www.cogam.com), M: Gran Vía, provides a wide range of services and activities. Reception M-Sa 5-10pm.

Laundromat: Lavandería Cervantes, C. León 6. (☎429 4985). Wash €2, dry €1. Free detergent and softener. Open daily 9am-11pm.

EMERGENCY AND COMMUNICATIONS

Police: C. de los Madrazos 9 (☎541 7160). M: Sevilla. From C. de Alcalá take a right onto C. Cedacneros and a left onto C. de los Madrazos. To report crimes committed in the **metro,** go to the office in the Sol station (open daily 8am-11pm).

Medical Services: In a medical emergency, dial ☎061 or 112. **Hospital de Madrid,** Pl. del Conde del Valle Suchil 16 (☎447 6600; www.hospitaldemadrid.com). **Hospital Ramón y Cajal,** Ctra. Colmenar Viejo, km 9100 (☎336 8000). Bus #135 from Pl. de Castilla. For non-emergency concerns, call **Anglo-American Medical Unit,** Conde de Aranda 1, 1st fl. (☎435 1823).

Internet Access: New Internet cafes are surfacing everywhere with an average of €2 per hr. **SATS XXI,** Ctra. de San Jerónimo (☎915 32 09 70), shares a floor with Asatej travel agency. €1.60 per hr. Discounts for multiple-hour blocks. Open daily 10am-midnight. **Euronet,** C. Mayor 1, 4th fl., office 13 (☎915 23 20 89). M: Sol. Take the elevator and buzz the office. . Free coffee. €1 per hr. Open daily 10am-10pm.

Post Office: Palacio de Comunicaciones, C. de Alcalá 51, on Pl. de Cibeles (☎902 19 71 97). M: Banco de España. Windows open M-Sa 8:30am-9:30pm, Su 9am-2pm for stamp purchases, certified mail, and fax service. Poste Restante *(Lista de Correos)* at windows #80-82; passport required. **Postal Code:** 28080.

ACCOMMODATIONS

Book ahead for summer visits. Expect to pay €17-50 per person, depending on location, amenities, and season. Tourist offices provide information about the 22 **campsites** within 50km of Madrid. Prices in **El Centro,** the triangle between Puerta del Sol, Ópera, and Pl. Mayor, are as good as they get, especially if you are planning to brave the legendary nightlife. **Huertas,** framed by Ctra. de San Jerónimo, C. de las Huertas, and C. de Atocha, is almost as central and more fun. Festive **Malasaña** and **Chueca,** bisected by C. Fuencarral, boast cheap rooms in the heart of the action, but the sleep-deprived should beware; the party never stops. *Hostales*, like temptations, are everywhere among **Gran Vía's** sex shops and scam artists.

EL CENTRO: SOL, ÓPERA, AND PLAZA MAYOR

Hostal-Residencia Luz, C. Fuentes 10, 3rd fl. (☎542 0759), off C. Arenal. M: Ópera. Bright, modern, inexpensive, and friendly. Elegant rooms have hardwood floors, tasselled curtains, and satiny sheets. Singles €20; doubles €34-39; triples €39-45. ❷

Hostal Paz, C. Flora 4, 1st and 4th fl. (☎547 3047). M: Ópera. On a quiet street, parallel to C. Arenal, off C. Donados or C. Hileras. Unbeatable hospitality. Peaceful rooms with large windows, satellite TV, and A/C are sheltered from street noise. Reservations recommended. Laundry €9. Singles €30; doubles €38-42; triples €54. MC/V. ❸

Hostal Esparteros, C. Esparteros 12, 4th fl. (☎521 0903). M: Sol. The 4-flight hike is worth it for unbeatable location and large rooms, some with private bath. Jovial, English-speaking owner. Singles €20-25; doubles €35; triples €42. ❷

HUERTAS

Cat's Hostel, C. Cañizares 6 (☎ 902 88 91 92; www.catshostel.com). M: Antón Martín. High-tech hostel in an 18th-century palace. Fantastic Mudéjar patio area, bar, and cafe. Cheap beer (€1.50-2). Breakfast included. Laundry €2.50. Free Internet and lockers. Reception 24hr. English spoken. Key deposit €10; cash only. Dorms €16; singles €21. MC/V. ❷

Hostal Plaza D'Ort, Pl. del Angel 13 (☎429 9041; www.plazadort.com). Beautifully decorated rooms exude comfort. All with TV, phone, A/C, and Internet. Reception 24hr. Singles €30, with bath €35; doubles €50/55; triples €75. MC/V. ❸

Hostal Betanzos, C. Luis de Guevera 8, 3rd fl. (☎369 1440). M: Antón Martín. Old-fashioned pension with high ceilings. Singles €15; doubles €25. Cash only. ❶

GRAN VÍA

Hostal-Residencia Alibel, Gran Vía 44, 8th fl. (☎521 0051). M: Callao. Well-lit rooms with great views and high ceilings. All have private bath, TV, fan, and balcony. Free wireless Internet. Singles with shower €30, with bath €35; doubles €35/40; triples €50. ❸

Hostal A. Nebrija, Gran Vía 67, 8th fl., elevator A (☎547 7319). M: Pl. de España. Pleasant, spacious rooms with TV and fan offer magnificent views of the city. Singles €28; doubles €39. AmEx/MC/V. ❸

Hostal Santillan, Gran Vía 64, 8th fl. (☎548 2328; www.hostalsantillan.com). M: Pl. de España. Friendly staff offers simple rooms with shower, sink, TV, and fan. Doubles €50; triples €66. MC/V. ❸

SPAIN

MALASAÑA AND CHUECA

Hostal-Residencia Domínguez, C. de Santa Brígida 1, 1st fl. (☎532 1547). M: Tribunal. The hospitable young owner is always ready with tips on local nightlife. Immaculate singles €29.45; doubles with bath and A/C €40.90. ❸

Hostal Rio Miño, C. de Babieri 3, 1st fl. (☎522 1417). M. Chueca. Clean, simple rooms at an unbeatable price. Book 2 weeks ahead. Singles €17; doubles €25. ❷

Hostal Palacios and **Hostal Ribadavia,** C. Fuencarral 25, 1st-3rd fl. (☎531 1058). M: Gran Vía. Both run by the same cheerful family. Palacio (1st-2nd fl.) has large, tiled rooms with bath, TV, and A/C. Older Ribadavia (3rd fl.) has comfortable rooms with TV and fans. Singles €25, with bath €30; doubles €35/38; triples €57. MC/V. ❷

FOOD

Small eateries line **Calles Echegaray, Bentura de la Vega,** and **Manuel Fernández González** in Huertas; **Calle Agurrosa** at Lavapiés has outdoor cafes; **Calle Fuencarral** in Gran Vía is lined with cheap eats. **Bilbao** boasts ethnically diverse culinary choices. Bars along **Calle Hartzenbusch** and **Calle Cardenal Cisneros** offer cheap tapas. The *Guía del Ocio* has a complete listing of Madrid's vegetarian options. **%Día** and **Champion** are the cheapest supermarket chains.

La Finca de Susana, C. de Arlabán 4 (☎369 3557). M: Sevilla. Student chefs make this probably the most popular lunch eatery in all of Madrid. Be prepared to wait in line. *Menú* M-F €7.75. Open daily 1-3:45pm and 8:30-11:45pm. AmEx/MC/V. ❷

Ricci Gelateria and Yogurteria Artiginale, C. de las Huertas 9 (☎687 98 96 12). M: Antón Martín. Forget tapas and *jamón;* this ice cream is euphoric. Most patrons request 2 flavors, which counts as one scoop. Vegan-soy ice cream available Sa-Su. Small €2, but you want a €3 large. Open M-Th and Su 9am-12:30am, F-Sa 9am-1:30am. Cash only. ❶

El Estragón Vegetariano, Pl. de la Paja 10 (☎365 8982; www.guiadelocio.com/estragonvegetariano). M: La Latina. Vegetarian offerings so good they'd tempt a puma. Lunch *menú* M-F €9.50. Open daily 1:30-4:30pm and 8pm-1am. AmEx/MC/V. ❸

Arrocería Gala, C. de Moratín 22 (☎429 2562; www.paellas-gala.com). M: Antón Martín. €13 *menú* offers choice of paella with salad, bread, wine, and dessert. Reservations recommended on weekends. Open daily 1-5pm and 9pm-midnight. Cash only. ❸

Inshala, C. Amnistia 10 (☎548 2632). M: Ópera. Diverse menu of Italian, Japanese, Mexican, Moroccan, and Spanish food. M-F lunch *menú* €9. Dinner *menú* €10-26. Reservations recommended. Open M-Sa noon-2am. MC/V. ❸

Al-Jaima, Cocina del Desierto, C. de Barbieri 1 (☎523 1142). M: Gran Vía or Chueca. Serves Lebanese, Moroccan, and Egyptian food to patrons lounging on pillows on the floor. 1st courses €4. Main courses €8. Dinner reservations highly recommended, sometimes required. Open daily 1:30-4pm and 9pm-midnight. ❷

Taberna Macieras, C. de Jesús 7 (☎429 1584). M: Antón Martín. Galician seafood served in a lively Irish setting at reasonable prices. Open M 8pm-12:45am, Tu-F 1-4:15pm and 8:30pm-12:45am, Sa-Su 1-4:45pm and 8:30pm-1:30am. ❸

Achuri, C. Argumosa 2 (☎468 7856). M: Lavapiés. A young crowd gathers on the patio for music and cheap food. *Bocadillos* €2.70. Entrees €4.80. Wine €0.80-2.20 per glass. Open daily July-Aug. 6pm-12:30am; Sept.-June 3:30pm-12:30am. Cash only. ❶

TAPAS

Not so long ago, bartenders in Madrid used to cover *(tapar)* drinks with saucers to keep the flies out. Later, servers began putting little sandwiches on top of the saucers. These became known as "*tapas.*" Many tapas bars *(tascas or tabernas)* cluster around **Plaza Santa Ana** and **Plaza Mayor.**

Casa Alberto, C. de las Huertas 18 (☎429 9356; www.casaalberto.es). M: Antón Martín. Patrons spill out into the night air to wait for a spot at the bar. All tapas are original house recipes. Open Tu-Sa noon-5:30pm and 8pm-1:30am. AmEx/MC/V. ❷

Sagaretxe: La Sidería Vasca, C. Eloy Gonzalo 26 (☎446 2588). M: Iglesia. Sideria delights locals with an ever-rotating menu of *pintxos* (fancy *tostas* from the Basque region; €1.70 each, €12 for 8, €16 for 12). Bar open daily 1-5pm and 6pm-1am. ❷

CAFES

Linger for an hour or two in these historic cafes—an economical way to soak up a little of Madrid's culture. You won't be bothered with the check until you ask.

Café-Botillería Manuela, C. de San Vicente Ferrer 29 (☎531 7037). M: Tribunal. Upbeat music and occasional, impromptu piano playing add to Manuela's atmosphere. Coffee €3.50-4.50. Mixed drinks €3-5. Traditional tapas €2-8. Open June-Aug. M-Th 6pm-2am, F-Su 4pm-3am; Sept.-May daily 4pm-2am.

Café de Oriente, Pl. del Oriente 2 (☎547 1564). M: Ópera. An old-fashioned cafe catering to a ritzy older crowd. Spectacular view of the Palacio Real from the *terraza*. Specialty coffees €2.50-6.50. Open M-Th and Su 8:30am-1:30am, F-Sa 8:30am-12:30am.

Café Comercial, Glorieta de Bilbao 7 (☎521 5655). M: Bilbao. Founded in 1887, Madrid's oldest cafe boasts high ceilings, cushioned chairs, and huge mirrors. Coffee €1.20-1.90. Open M-Th 8am-1am, F 7:30am-2am, Sa 8am-2am, Su 10am-1am.

SIGHTS

Madrid's public transportation should only be used for longer distances or between the day's starting and ending points; the city is made for walking, and you don't want to miss the beauty above ground. While Madrid is perfect for walking, it also offers some of the world's best places to relax. Whether soothing tired feet after perusing the triangulo de arte or seeking shelter from the summer's sweltering heat, there's nothing better than a shaded sidewalk cafe or a romantic park.

EL CENTRO

El Centro, spreading out from Puerta del Sol (Gate of the Sun), is the gateway to Madrid's history. Although several rulers carved the winding streets, the Hapsburgs and Bourbons built El Centro's most celebrated monuments. As a result, the easily-navigable area is divided into two major sections: Hapsburg Madrid and Bourbon Madrid. Unless otherwise specified, Hapsburg directions are given from Puerta del Sol and Bourbon directions from Ópera.

TAPAS FROM A TO Z

Tapas, the tasty little dishes tha are Spain's answer to *hors d'oeu vres*, have more taste and less pretension. To experience the *madrileño* lifestyle, you have to give them a try. The only problem is: what are you going to order?

To the untrained reader, tapas menus are often undecipherable—if the bar has even bothered to print any. To make sure you don' end up eating the stewed parts o the ox you rode in on, keep the following words in mind before *tapeando*. Servings come in three sizes: *pincho* (normally eaten with toothpicks between sips of beer) *tapa* (small plate), or *ración* (meal portion). *Aceitunas* (olives), *albóndigas* (meatballs) *anchoas* (anchovies), *callos* (tripe), *chorizo* (sausage), *croquetas* (croquettes), *gambas* (shrimp), *jamón* (ham), *patatas bravas* (fried potatoes with spic sauce), *pimientos* (peppers) *pulpo* (octopus), and *tortilla española* (onion and potato omelette) comprise any basic menu. Many are served with a thick mayonnaise; ask for them *"sin mayonesa"* if you're not a fan. More adventurous taster should try *morcilla* (blood sausage) or *sesos* (cow's brains).

Often, bartenders will offe tastes of tapas with your drink and strike up a conversation. I you're not given some with you drink, be sure to ask for them. To ensure the full treatment and local respect, the house *cerveza* is always a good choice.

PUERTA DEL SOL

Kilómetro 0, the origin of six national highways, marks the city's center in the most chaotic of Madrid's plazas. A crossroads, or better yet a cattle chute, Puerta del Sol blazes day and night with taxis and street performers. *Madrileños* and tourists alike converge upon **El oso y el madroño,** a bronze statue of the bear and berry tree that grace the city's heraldic coat of arms *(M: Sol)*.

HAPSBURG MADRID

PLAZA MAYOR. Juan de Herrera, architect of El Escorial (p. 921), also designed this plaza. Its elegant arcades, spindly towers, and open verandas, erected for Felipe III in 1620, are defining elements of the "Madrid-style," which inspired architects throughout the country. Toward evening, Pl. Mayor awakens as *Madrileños* resurface, tourists multiply, and cafes fill with lively patrons. Live flamenco performances are a common treat. While the cafes are a nice spot for a drink, food is overpriced; have dinner elsewhere. *(M: Sol. Walk down C. Mayor. The plaza is on the left.)*

CATEDRAL DE SAN ISIDRO. Although San Isidro, Madrid's patron saint, was humble, his final resting place is anything but. The cathedral received the saint's remains in 1769, but during the Civil War, rioting workers burned the exterior and damaged much of the cathedral—all that survived were the main *Capilla*, a 17th-century banner, and the mummified remains of San Isidro and his wife. *(M: La Latina. Take C. Mayor to Pl. Mayor, cross the plaza, and exit onto C. de Toledo. The cathedral is located at the intersection of C. de Toledo and C. de Sacramento. Open daily in summer 7:30am-1:30pm and 5:30-9pm; in winter 7:30am-1pm and 5:30-8:30pm. Free.)*

PLAZA DE LA VILLA. Plaza de la Villa marks the heart of old Madrid. Though only a few medieval buildings remain, the plaza still features a stunning courtyard, beautiful tile-work, and eclectic architecture. Across the plaza is the 17th-century **Ayuntamiento (Casa de la Villa),** designed in 1640 by Juan Gomez de Mora as both the mayor's home and the city jail. *(M: Sol. Go down C. Mayor and past Pl. Mayor.)*

BOURBON MADRID

PALACIO REAL. Palacio Real sits at the western tip of central Madrid, overlooking the Río Manzanares. Felipe V commissioned Giovanni Sachetti to replace the Alcázar, which had burned down in 1734, with a palace that would dwarf all others—he succeeded. Today, the unfinished palace is used by King Juan Carlos and Queen Sofía only on special occasions. The **Salón del Trono** (Throne Room) contains a ceiling fresco outlining the qualities of the ideal ruler, and the **Salón de Gasparini** houses Goya's portrait of Carlos IV. Perhaps the most beautiful is the **Chinese Room,** whose walls swirl with green tendril patterns. The **Biblioteca** shelves first editions of *Don Quixote*. *(M: Ópera. From Pl. de Isabel II, head toward the Teatro Real. ☎454 8800. Open Apr.-Sept. M-Sa 9am-6pm, Su 9am-3pm; Oct.-Mar. M-Sa 9:30am-5pm, Su 9am-2pm. €8, with tour €9; students €3.50/8. Arrive early to avoid lines.)*

PLAZA DE ORIENTE. A minor architectural miscalculation was responsible for this sculpture park. Most of the statues here were designed for the palace roof, but because the queen had a nightmare about the roof collapsing under their weight, they were placed in this shady plaza instead. The **Jardines de Sabatini,** just to the right as you face the palace, is the romantic's park of choice. *(M: Ópera. From Pl. de Isabel II, walk past Teatro Real. Across the street from the Palacio Real.)*

ARGÜELLES

Argüelles and the zone surrounding C. de San Bernardo form a mix of elegant homes, student apartments, and bohemian hangouts. Unlike most of Madrid, it is easily navigable due to its gridlike orientation. By day, families and joggers roam the city's largest park, **Casa del Campo.** Night tends to bring unsafe activity. The **Parque de la Montaña** is home to Spain's only Egyptian temple. Built by Pharaoh Zakheramon in the 4th century BC, the **Temple de Debod** was a gift commemorating the Spanish archaeologists who helped rescue monuments in the Aswan Dam floods. *(M: Pl. de España or Ventura Rodríguez. Buses #1 and 74. From the metro, walk down C. Ventura Rodríguez to Parque de la Montaña; the temple is on the left. ☎765 1008; www.munimadrid.es/templodebod. Open Apr.-Sept. Tu-F 10am-2pm and 6-8pm, Sa-Su 10am-2pm; Oct.-Mar. Tu-F 9:45am-1:45pm and 4:15-5:15pm, Sa-Su 10am-2pm. Park open daily. Both free.)*

OTHER SIGHTS

PARQUE DEL BUEN RETIRO. Join vendors, palm-readers, soccer players, and sunbathers in the area Felipe IV converted from a hunting ground into a *buen retiro* (nice retreat). The finely landscaped 300-acre park is centered around a monument to King Alfonso XII and a rectangular lake, the **Estanque Grande.** Rowboats can be rented for €4.20 per 45min. for four people. Sundays from 5pm to midnight, over 100 percussionists gather for an intense **drum circle** by the colonnaded monument on the Estanque; hypnotic rhythms and hash smoke fill the air.

MUSEUMS

Considered individually to be among the world's best art galleries, the Museo del Prado, Museo de Thyssen-Bornemisza, and the Museo Nacional Centro de Arte Reina Sofía together form the impressive "Avenida del Arte." You won't be able to visit museums of such renown within such easy walking distance anywhere else.

MUSEO DEL PRADO. The Prado is Spain's pride and joy and one of Europe's finest art museums. The museum provides a free and indispensible guide describing each room. English-language audio tours are available for €3. The sheer quantity of paintings means you'll have to be selective—walk past the imitation Rubens and Rococo cherubs to the groves of the masters. On the second floor, keep an eye out for the unforgiving realism of **Diego Velázquez** (1599-1660). His technique of "illusionism" climaxed in the magnificent opus **Las Meninas.** Court portraitist **Francisco de Goya y Lucientes** (1746-1828) created the *Pinturas Negras (Black Paintings)*, named for the darkness of both their color and their subject matter. The Prado also displays many of **El Greco's** religious paintings along with a formidable collection of Italian works, including pieces by **Botticelli, Raphael, Rubens, Tintoretto,** and **Titian.** As a result of the Spanish Hapsburgs' control of the Netherlands, Flemish holdings are top-notch. Works by **van Dyck** and **Albrecht Durer** are here, as well as **Peter Breugel the Elder's** delightful *The Triumph of Death*, in which death drives a carriage of skulls on a decaying horse. **Hieronymus Bosch's** moralistic *The Garden of Earthly Delights* depicts hedonists and the destiny that awaits them. *(Po. del Prado at Pl. Cánovas del Castillo. M: Banco de España or Atocha. ☎330 2800; http://museoprado.mcu.es. Open Tu-Su 9am-7pm. €6, students €3, Su free.)*

MUSEO NACIONAL CENTRO DE ARTE REINA SOFÍA. Since Juan Carlos I decreed this renovated hospital a national museum in 1988, the Reina Sofía's collection of **20th-century art** has grown steadily. The building itself is a work of art, and is much easier to navigate than the Prado. Rooms dedicated to Dalí, Gris, and Miró display Spain's contributions to the Surrealist movement. Picasso's masterwork **Guernica** is the permanent collection's highlight. It depicts the Basque town (p. 974) bombed by the Germans during the Spanish Civil War. *(C. Santa Isabel 52. M: Atocha. ☎467 5062; http://museoreinasofia.mcu.es. Open M and W-Sa 10am-9pm, Su 10am-2:30pm. €3, students €1.50, Sa after 2:30pm, Su, and holidays free.)*

SPAIN

MUSEO THYSSEN-BORNEMISZA. The Thyssen-Bornemisza exhibits works ranging from 14th-century paintings to 20th-century sculptures. Tthe museum's over 775 pieces constitute the world's most extensive private showcase. To view the evolution of styles and themes, begin on the top floor. The top floor is dedicated to the **Old Masters** collection, which includes El Greco's *Annunciation*. The highlight of the museum is the **20th-century** collection on the first floor. *(On the corner of Po. del Prado and C. Manuel González. M: Banco de España or Atocha. Bus #1, 2, 5, 9-10, 14-15, 20, 27, 34, 37, 45, 51-53, 74, 146, or 150. ☎369 0151; www.museothyssen.org. Open Tu-Su 10am-7pm. Last entrance 6:30pm. €6, ISIC holders €4. Audio tours €3.)*

ENTERTAINMENT

EL RASTRO (FLEA MARKET)

The market begins in La Latina at Pl. Cascorro off C. de Toledo and ends at the bottom of C. Ribera de Curtidores. As crazy as the market seems, it is actually thematically organized. The main street is a labyrinth of clothing, cheap jewelry, leather goods, incense, and sunglasses. Antique-sellers contribute their peculiar mustiness to C. del Prado to shops in small plazas off C. Ribera de Cortidores. Collections of old books and LPs are sold in Pl. del Campillo del Mundo, at the bottom of C. de Carlos Arnides. Tapas bars and small restaurants lining the streets provide a cool respite for market-weary bargainers. The flea market is a pickpocket's paradise. Fortunately, police are ubiquitous. *(Open Su and holidays 9am-2pm.)*

MUSIC AND FLAMENCO

Anyone interested in live entertainment should stop by the **Círculo de Bellas Artes.** *(C. de Alcalá 42. From Pl. de Santa Ana, go up C. del Príncipe, cross C. San Jerónimo, and continue toward C. de Alcalá. Turn right onto C. de Alcalá. ☎360 5400. Open Tu-F 5-9pm, Sa 11am-2pm and 5-9pm, Su 11am-2pm.)* Their free magazine, *Minerva*, is indispensable. Check the *Guía del Ocio* (€1) for information on city-sponsored movies, plays, and concerts. Flamenco in Madrid is tourist-oriented and expensive. A few nightlife spots are authentic, but pricey. **Casa Patas,** C. Cañizares 10, is well priced for the quality. *(C. Cañizares 10. M: Antón Martín. ☎369 0496; www.casapatas.com. €25-30. Shows M-Th 10:30pm, F-Sa 9pm and midnight.)* Flamenco enthusiasts should also check out **Corral de la Morería.** *(C. Morería 17. M: Ópera. ☎365 8446. Shows daily 10:30pm and midnight. €28-32. Call for reservations.)*

FÚTBOL

A local team plays at home every Sunday and some Saturdays from September to June. **Real Madrid** (in white) plays at Estadio Santiago Bernabéu. *(Av. Cochina Espina 1. M: Santiago Bernabéu. ☎457 1112.)* **Atlético de Madrid** (in red and white stripes) plays at Estadio Vicente Calderón. *(Po. de la Virgen del Puerto 67. M: Pirámides or Marqués de Vadillos. ☎366 4707.)*

BULLFIGHTS

Bullfights are a Spanish tradition, and locals joke that they are the only events in Spain to start on time. Hemingway-toting Americans and true fans of this struggle between man and beast clog Pl. de las Ventas for the heart-pounding, albeit gruesome, events. From early May to early June, the **Fiestas de San Isidro** provide a daily *corrida* (bullfight) with the top *matadores* and the fiercest bulls. Advance tickets are recommended; those without a seat crowd into bars to watch on TV. There are bullfights every Sunday from March to October and less often during the rest of the year. Look for posters in bars and cafes (especially on C. Victoria, off Ctra. de San Jerónimo). **Plaza de las Ventas,** C. de Alcalá 237, is the biggest ring in Spain. *(M: Ventas. ☎356 2200; www.las-ventas.com. Seats €5-92, more expensive in the shade,* sombra, *than in the sun,* sol. *Tickets available in person only F-Su.)* **Plaza de Toros**

Palacio de Vista Alegre also hosts bullfights and cultural events. *(M: Vista Alegre. ☎422 0780. Call for schedule and prices.)* To watch amateurs, head to the **bullfighting school,** which has its own *corridas. (M: Batán. ☎470 1990. Tickets €7.)*

NIGHTLIFE

Spaniards average an hour less sleep per night than other Europeans, and *Madrileños* claim to need even less. *Madrileños* start in the tapas bars of **Huertas,** move to the youthful scene in **Malasaña,** and end at the wild parties of **Chueca** or late-night clubs of **Gran Vía.** Students fill the streets of **Bilbao** and **Moncloa.** Madrid's superb gay scene centers on **Plaza Chueca.** Establishments in the Chueca area carry *Shanguide*, a free guide to gay nightlife. Most clubs don't heat up until 2am; don't be surprised to see lines at 5am. Disdainful bouncers love to make examples; dress well to avoid being overcharged or denied. Women may not be charged.

Palacio Gaviria, C. Arenal 9 (☎526 6069; www.palaciogaviria.com). M: Sol or Ópera. Party like royalty in this palace-turned-disco. Mixed drinks €9. Cover Tu-Th and Su €9, F-Sa €15; includes 1 drink. Open Tu-W and Su 11pm-3:30am, Th 10:30pm-4:30am, F-Sa 11pm-6am.

Cuevas de Sesamo, C. del Príncipe 7 (☎429 0524). M: Antón Martín. Cheap pitchers of sangria (€5.50-8.50) and live jazz piano draw suave crowds of all ages to this literally underground, smoke-filled gem. Open M-Th and Su 6pm-2am, F-Sa 6pm-2:30am.

Acuarela, C. de Gravina 10 (☎522 2143). M: Chueca. A welcome alternative to the club scene. Buddhas and candles surround cushy antique furniture. Coffee and tea €2-4.50. Mixed drinks €3.20-5. Open daily in summer 3pm-3am; in winter 11pm-3am.

Suite, C. Virgen de los Peligros 4 (☎521 4031; www.suitecafeclub.com). M: Sevilla. Retro-chic restaurant, bar, and club boasts a lunch *menú* (€10) by day and sleek drinks by night (€7). Upstairs dance floor. Mixed crowd. Open daily 2-4pm and 9pm-3:30am.

Cardamomo, C. de Echegaray 15 (☎369 0757; www.cardamomo.net). M: Sevilla. A local crowd dances all night to Flamenco and Latin music or retreats to the quieter lounge area. W live music. Beer €4. M no cover before 10pm. Open daily 9pm-3:30am.

Clamores Jazz Club, C. Albuquerque 14 (☎445 7938), off C. Cardenal Cisneros. M: Bilbao. Swanky, neon setting and interesting jazz. Music starting daily around 10pm. Arrive early for a seat. Cover €4-20. Open summer M-Th and Su 6:30pm-3am, F-Sa 6pm-4am; winter M-Th and Su 7:30pm-1:30am, F-Sa 7:30pm-3am.

El Clandestino, C. del Barquillo 34 (☎521 5563). M: Chueca. A chill crowd of 20-somethings drinks and debates at the bar upstairs and dances in the downstairs caves. Live music most Th-Sa at 11 or 11:30pm. Beer €3. Mixed drinks €6. Open M-Sa 6pm-3am.

La Casa de los Jacintos, C. Arganzuela 11 (www.lacasadelosjacintos.net). M: La Latina or Puerta de Toledo. This intimate venue hosts the cheapest flamenco in town (F 9:30pm-midnight) and improv comedy (Th 10:30pm-midnight). Performances, movies, and mojitos €3. Open Tu and Th-Su during performances. Call ahead for schedule.

El Truco, C. de Gravina 10 (☎532 8921). M: Chueca. This packed gay and lesbian-friendly bar features local artists' works and pop artists' hits. F-Sa cover €8, includes 1 drink. Open M-Th 5:30pm-2:30am, F-Su 5pm-3am.

DAYTRIP FROM MADRID

EL ESCORIAL. Though "El Escorial" loosely translates to "The Slag Heap," the enormous complex was better described by Felipe II as "majesty without ostentation." The **Monasterio de San Lorenzo del Escorial** was a gift from Felipe II to God, the people, and himself, commemorating his 1557 victory over the French at the battle of San Quintín in 1557. Near the town of San Lorenzo, El Escorial is filled with artistic treasures, two palaces, two pantheons, a church, and a magnificent library. To avoid crowds, enter via the gate on C. Floridablanca, on the western side. The adjacent **Museo de Arquitectura y Pintura** has an exhibit comparing El Escorial's construction to that of similar structures. Most of the collection is now housed in Madrid's Museo del Prado (p. 919), though masterpieces by Bosch, Durer, El Greco, and Titian still adorn the walls. The **Palacio Real,** lined with azulejo tiles, includes the majestic **Salón del Trono** (Throne Room), Felipe II's spartan 16th-century apartments, and the luxurious 18th-century rooms of Carlos III and Carlos IV. (Autocares Herranz buses run between El Escorial and Madrid's Moncloa metro station. (50min., every 10-30min., €3.20.) Complex ☎918 90 59 03. Open Apr.-Sept. Tu-Su 10am-7pm; Oct.-Mar. 10am-6pm. Last admission 1hr. before closing. Monastery €7, with guide €9; students €3.50. Joint admission to El Escorial and El Valle de los Caídos €8.50/10/5.)

CENTRAL SPAIN

Medieval cities and olive groves fill Castilla La Mancha, the land south and east of Madrid. Castilla y León's dramatic cathedrals are testaments to its glorious history. Farther west, bordering Portugal, stark Extremadura was the birthplace of world-famous explorers such as Hernán Cortés and Francisco Pisarro.

CASTILLA LA MANCHA

Castilla La Mancha, a battered, wind-swept plateau, is one of Spain's least developed regions. Its austere beauty shines through its tumultuous history, gloomy medieval fortresses, and awe-inspiring crags.

TOLEDO ☎925

Cossío called Toledo (pop. 66,000) "the most brilliant and evocative summary of Spain's history." Today, the city may be marred by armies of tourists, but this former capital of the Holy Roman, Visigoth, and Muslim empires mantains a wealth of Spanish culture. Churches, synagogues, and mosques share twisting alleyways, emblematic of a time when Spain's three religions coexisted peacefully.

TRANSPORTATION AND PRACTICAL INFORMATION. From the station on Po. de la Rosa, just over Puente de Azarquiel, **trains** (RENFE info ☎902 24 02 02) run to Madrid (1¼-1½hr., 6 per day, €5.15). **Buses** run from Av. Castilla La Mancha (☎21 58 50), 5min. from Pta. de Bisagra (the city gate) to Madrid (1½hr., 2 per hr., €4) and Valencia (5½hr., M-F 3pm, €22). Within the city, buses #5 and 6 serve the bus and train stations and the central **Plaza de Zocodóver.** Buses (€0.85; at night €1.10) stop to the right of the train station, underneath and across the street from the bus station. Toledo is an almost unconquerable maze of narrow streets. Though they are well labeled, it's easy to get lost; pick up a map at the **tourist office,** at Pta. de Bisagra. (☎22 08 43. English spoken. Open July-Sept. M-Sa 9am-7pm, Su 9am-3pm; Oct.-June M-F 9am-6pm, Sa 9am-7pm, Su 9am-3pm.) **Postal Code:** 45070.

ACCOMMODATIONS AND FOOD. Toledo is full of accommodations, but finding a bed during the summer can be a hassle, especially on weekends. Last-minute planners should try the tourist office for help. Young children outnumber backpackers at the **Residencia Juvenil San Servando (HI) ❶,** Castillo San Servando, uphill on Subida del Hospital from the train station, a 14th-century castle with a pool, TV room, and Internet. (☎22 45 54. Dorms €10.60, with breakfast €13.80;

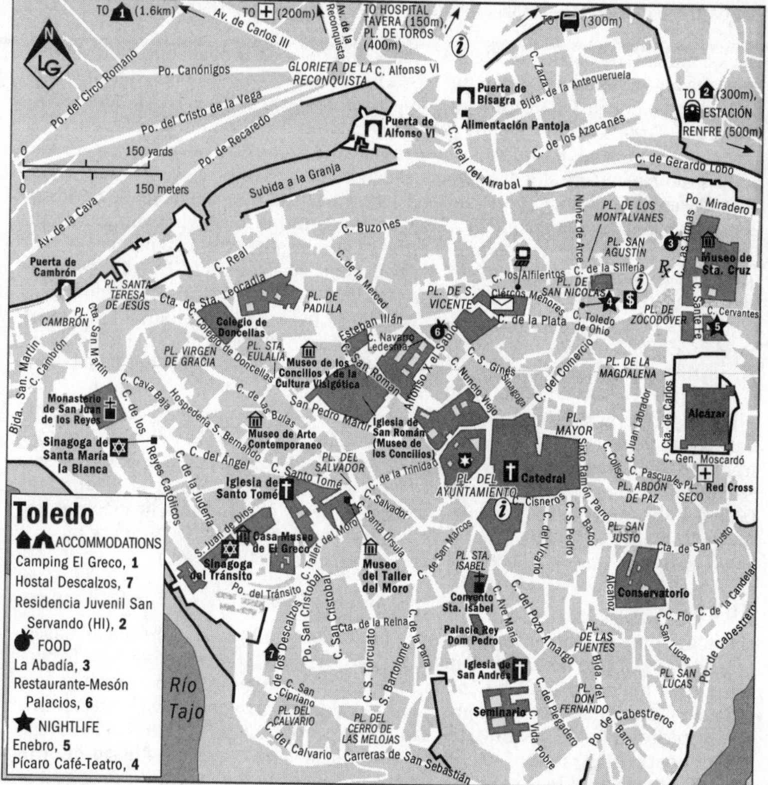

under 30 €8.90/10.60.) **Hostal Descalzos ❸,** C. de los Descalzos 30, down the steps off Po. del Tránsito, has a jacuzzi and modern rooms with stunning views. (☎22 28 88; www.hostaldescalzos.com. June-Oct. singles €30; doubles €56; triples €75.60. Nov.-Apr. €25-27/48-52/56. VAT not included. MC/V.) Take bus #7 from Pl. de Zocodóver to get to **Camping El Greco ❶,** 1.5km from town on Ctra. CM-4000, km 0.7. The shady site features a restaurant, bar, pool, and supermarket. (☎22 00 90. €4.90 per person, per tent, and per car. VAT not included. MC/V.) Toledo is famous for its marzipan; *pastelerías* beckon on every corner. The **market** is in Pl. Mayor, behind the cathedral. (Open M-Sa 9am-8pm.) Homey **Restaurante-Mesón Palacios ❷,** C. Alfonso X El Sabio 3, has two *menús* (€6.95-11.90), one including Toledo's famous partridge dish. (☎21 59 72. Entrees €5-12. Open M-Sa 1-4pm and 7-11pm, Su noon-4pm. Closed Su in Aug. AmEx/MC/V.) To reach **La Abadía ❷,** Pl. de San Nicolás 3, bear left when C. de la Sillería splits and look right. Dine on the regional lunch *menú* (€10) in a maze of cave-like underground rooms. (☎25 11 40. Open M-Th 8am-12:30am, F 8am-1:30am, Sa noon-1:30am. AmEx/MC/V.)

SIGHTS AND NIGHTLIFE. Toledo's collection of museums, churches, synagogues, and mosques make the city impossible to see in one day. Within the fortified walls, Toledo's attractions form a belt around its middle. Most sights are closed Mondays. At Arco de Palacio, up C. del Comercio from Pl. de Zocodóver, Toledo's **cathedral** boasts five naves, delicate stained glass, and unapologetic flashiness.

Beneath the dome is the **Capilla Mozárabe,** the only place where the ancient Visigoth Mass (in Mozarabic) is still held. The **Sacristía** is home to 18 El Grecos, two Van Dycks, and a Caravaggio. (☎22 22 41. Cathedral open daily 10am-noon and 4-6pm. Sacristía and capilla open June-Aug. M-Sa 10:30am-6:30pm, Su 2-6pm; Sept.-May M-Sa 10:30am-6pm, Su 2-6pm. Cathedral free. Sacristía and capilla €5.50. Modest dress required.) Greek painter Doménikos Theotokópoulos, commonly known as El Greco, spent most of his life in Toledo. Though the majority of his masterpieces live at the Prado, many are still displayed throughout town. The best place to start is the **Casa Museo de El Greco,** C. Samuel Leví 2. (☎22 40 46. Open in summer Tu-Sa 10am-2pm and 4-9pm, Su 10am-2pm; in winter Tu-Sa 10am-2pm and 4-6pm, Su 10am-2pm. €2.40; students, Sa afternoon and Su free.) On the same street is the deceptively ornate **Sinagoga del Tránsito,** one of two remaining synagogues in Toledo's *judería* (Jewish quarter). Inside, the **Museo Sefardí** documents early Jewish history in Spain; highlights include a Torah, parts of which are over 400 years old, and a set of Sephardic wedding costumes. (☎22 36 65; www.museosefardi.net. Open Mar.-Nov. Tu-Sa 10am-2pm and 4-9pm, Su 10am-2pm; Dec.-Feb. Tu-Sa 10am-2pm and 4-6pm, Su 10am-2pm. €2.40, students €1.20. Sa after 4pm and Su free.)

For nightlife, head through the arch and to the left from Pl. de Zocodóver to **Calle Santa Fé. Enebro,** on Pl. Santiago de los Caballeros 4 off C. Cervantes, serves free tapas with every drink in the evenings. (Beer €1.30. Open M-F 8:30am-1am, Sa-Su noon-11pm.) For more upscale bars and clubs, try **Calle de la Sillería** and **Calle los Alfileritos,** west of Pl. de Zocodóver. Relax in the candlelit **Pícaro Café-Teatro,** C. Cadenas 6, to escape the rowdiness and noise. (☎22 13 01; www.picaro-cafeteatro.com. Pints €1.50-2.50. *Copas* €4. Open daily 3pm-4am.)

CUENCA ☎969

Cuenca's (pop. 50,000) urban planners were either totally insane or total geniuses; perched atop a hill, the city is flanked by two rivers and the stunning rock formations they have carved. The enchanting **old city** safeguards most of Cuenca's unique charm, including the famed **casas colgadas** (hanging houses) that perch precariously on the cliffs above the Río Huécar. Walk across the San Pablo Bridge for a spectacular view of the *casas* and cliffs. The excellent **Museo de Arte Abstracto Español,** in Pl. Ciudad de Ronda, is housed in the only *casa* open to the public. (☎21 29 83. Open July-Sept. Tu-F 11am-2pm and 5-7pm, Sa 11am-2pm and 4-9pm, Su 11am-2:30pm; Oct.-June reduced hours. €3, students €1.50.)

It's worth spending extra to stay in the quaint old city with its stunning views of the gorge. **Posada de San José ❷,** C. Julián Romero 4, a block up from the left side of the cathedral, has comfortable rooms with gorgeous views. (☎21 13 00. Breakfast €7. Singles €22, with bath €44; doubles €32/62; triples with bath €73; quads with bath €113. *Semana Sant*a increased prices; weeknights and low season reduced prices. AmEx/MC/V.) Enjoy delicious *bocadillos* and omelettes (€2-4) on the terrace of Posada de San José's **restaurant ❷.** (☎21 13 00. Entrees €3.50-9. Open Tu-Su 8-11am and 6-10:30pm. AmEx/MC/V.) Budget eateries line **Calle Cervantes** and **Avenida de la República Argentina;** the cafes off **Calle Fray Luis de León** are even cheaper. Buy groceries at **%Día,** on Av. Castilla La Mancha. (Open M-Th 9:30am-2pm and 5:30-8:30pm, F-Sa 9am-2:30pm and 5:30-9pm.)

Trains (☎902 24 02 02) run from C. Mariano Catalina 10 to Madrid (2½-3hr., 5-6 per day, €9.40) and Valencia (3-4hr., 3-4 per day, €10.35). **Buses** (☎22 70 87) run from C. Fermín Caballero 20 to: Barcelona (9hr.; M-Sa 9:30am, Su 2pm; €32); Madrid (2½hr., 8-9 per day, €9-11); Toledo (2¼hr., 1-2 per day, €10-12). To get to Pl. Mayor from the stations, take a left onto C. Fermín Caballero, which becomes C. Cervantes and C. José Cobo, then bear left through Pl. Hispanidad onto C. Carretería. The **tourist office** is in Pl. Mayor. (☎24 10 51; www.cuenca.org. Open July-Sept. M-F 11am-2pm and 5-7pm, Sa 11am-2pm and 4-8pm, Su 11am-2:30pm; Oct.-June M-Sa 9am-2pm and 4-6:30pm, Su 9am-2pm.) **Postal Code:** 16002.

CASTILLA Y LEÓN

Castilla y León's cities rise like green oases from a desert of burnt sienna. The aqueduct of Segovia, the Gothic cathedrals of León, and the sandstone of Salamanca stand out as regional and national images.

SEGOVIA

☎921

Legend has it that the devil built Segovia's (pop. 56,000) famed aqueduct in an effort to win the soul of a Segovian water-seller named Juanilla. With or without the help of the devil, Segovia's attractions and winding alleyways draw their share of Spanish and international tourists.

TRANSPORTATION AND PRACTICAL INFORMATION. **Trains** (RENFE info ☎902 24 02 02), run from Po. Obispo Quesada, rather far from town, to Madrid (2hr., 7-9 per day, €5.20). La Sepulvedana **buses** (☎42 77 07) run from Estación Municipal de Autobuses, Po. Ezequiel González 12, to Madrid (1½hr., every 30min., €6) and Salamanca (3hr., 3 per day, €9). From the train station, take any bus (€0.73) to **Plaza Mayor,** the city's historic center and site of the regional **tourist office.** Segovia is impossible to navigate without a map, so pick one up here. (☎46 03 34. Open daily July to mid-Sept. 9am-8pm; mid-Sept. to June 9am-2pm and 5-8pm.) The **public library,** C. Juan Bravo 11, offers free, fast **Internet.** (☎46 35 33. Limit 30min. Passport required. Open July-Aug. M-F 9am-3pm, Sa 9am-2pm; Sept.-June M-F 9am-9pm, Sa 9am-2pm.) **Postal Code:** 40001.

ACCOMMODATIONS AND FOOD. Book hotels in advance, arrive early to ensure space, and expect to pay €21 or more for a single. *Pensiones* are cheaper, with basic rooms and shared baths. To reach **Hospedaje El Gato ❷,** Pl. del Salvador 10, which has rooms with comfortable wooden beds, satellite TV, A/C, and private baths. Follow the aqueduct up the hill, turning left on C. Ochoa Ondategui; it meets San Alfonso Rodríguez which leads into Pl. del Salvador. (☎42 32 44. Singles €23; doubles €38; triples €52. MC/V.) For tiled rooms with TV and sink, head to **Hostal Don Jaime ❷,** C. Ochoa Ondategui 8. (☎44 47 87. Breakfast €3. Singles €22, with bath €30; doubles with bath €40; triples with bath €50. MC/V.)

Sample Segovia's famed lamb, *cochinillo asado* (roast suckling pig), or *sopa castellana* (soup with bread, eggs, and garlic), but steer clear of pricey Pl. Mayor and Pl. del Azoguejo. At the casual but classy **Bar-Meson Cueva de San Esteban ❸,** C. Vadelaguila 15, off Pl. Esteban and C. Escuderos, the owner really knows his wines, and the friendly staff is no less attentive to the excellent food. (☎46 09 82. Lunch *menús* M-F €8, Sa-Su €10. Entrees €7-18. Wine €1-3. Open daily 11am-midnight. MC/V.) For tasty vegetarian and meat dishes (€4-10.50), try **Restaurante La Almuzara ❷,** C. Marqués del Arco 3, past the cathedral. (☎46 06 22. Open Tu 8-11:30pm, W-Su 12:45-4pm and 8-11:30pm. MC/V.) Buy groceries at **%Día,** C. Gobernador Fernández Giménez 3, off Av. Fernández Ladreda. (Open M-Th 9:30am-2pm and 5:30-8:30pm, F-Sa 9am-9pm.)

SIGHTS AND ENTERTAINMENT. The serpentine **Roman aqueduct,** built in 50 BC and spanning 813m, commands the entrance to the old city. Some 20,000 granite blocks were used to construct it—without a drop of mortar. This spectacular feat of engineering, restored in the 15th century and used until the late 1940s, can transport 30L of water per second. The 23 chapels of the **cathedral,** towering over Pl. Mayor, earned it the nickname "The Lady of all Cathedrals." The interior may look less impressive than the facade, but its enormity will make you feel truly tiny. (☎46 22 05. Open daily Apr.-Oct. 9am-6:30pm;

MADLY IN LOVE

One of the most enigmatic figures in Spanish history, Queen Juana of Castilla earned the title "La Loca" (the Mad) for her bizarre obsession with her arranged husband, Felipe el Hermoso (the Fair). Born to Fernando and Isabel in 1479, Juana grew into an enviably influential position as heir to Isabel's throne. Although the men in her life deprived her of power after Isabel's death, Juana's worries were hardly political. Supposedly, she was so jealously enamored of her husband that she stabbed a lady-in-waiting, ordered her hair cut off, and thereafter did not allow women to serve in her palace.

Felipe died in 1506, and Juana had the corpse embalmed, organizing a massive funeral procession that would travel for three years on its way to Granada, where Felipe had requested to be buried. Although she is said to have lost her sanity by this point, documentation of her mental state is lacking and rumors abound; some even claim that she put Felipe's corpse on a throne every day as they traveled south. In 1509, upon returning home, rumor has it that the queen was locked inside the Convento de Santa Clara until her death in 1555. However, it seems that Juana really spent her last 50 years in the Palacio Real. She was buried in the convent, though, and was later moved south, where her body was laid alongside her husband's.

Nov.-Mar. 9:30am-6pm. Mass M-Sa 10am, Su 11am and 12:30pm. €2, Su until 2:30pm free.) With its pointed turrets, Segovia's **Alcázar** resembles a fairy-tale castle. In the **Sala de Solio** (throne room), an inscription reads: *Tanto monta, monta tanto* ("she mounts, as does he"). Get your mind out of the gutter—it means Ferdinand and Isabella had equal authority as rulers. The 80m **Torre de Juan II,** 140 steps up a nausea-inducing spiral staircase, affords a marvelous view of Segovia and the surrounding plains. (Pl. de la Reina Victoria Eugenia. ☎46 07 59. Open Apr.-Sept. daily 10am-7pm; Oct. M-Th and Su 10am-6pm, F-Sa 10am-7pm; Nov.-Mar. daily 10am-6pm. Tower closed Tu. Tower €1.50. Palace and tower €3.50, students €2.30. Audio tours in English €3.)

Though the city isn't known for its sleepless nights, *segovianos* know how to party. The **Plaza Mayor** is the center of it all; head for **Calle Infanta Isabel,** appropriately nicknamed *calle de los barres* (street of the bars). A casual, older crowd frequents **Bar Santana,** C. Infanta Isabel 18. (☎46 35 64. Tu and Th live music. Open daily 9am-midnight.) Clubs abound on **Calle Ruíz de Alda,** off Pl. del Azoguejo. You can count on a party every night at **La Luna,** C. Puerta de la Luna 8, where a young crowd downs cheap shots (€1) and Heineken. (☎46 26 51. Beer €1.50. Open daily 4:30pm-4am.) From June 23 to 29, Segovia holds a **fiesta** in honor of San Juan and San Pedro, featuring free open-air concerts, dances, and fireworks.

SALAMANCA ☎923

Salamanca la blanca, city of scholars, saints, royals, and rogues, glows with the finest examples of Spanish Plateresque stonework by day and a vivacious club scene by night. The prestigious Universidad de Salamanca, grouped in medieval times with Bologna, Paris, and Oxford as one of the "four leading lights of the world," continues to add the energy of its thousands of students.

TRANSPORTATION AND PRACTICAL INFORMATION. Trains go from Po. de la Estación (☎12 02 02) to Lisbon, Portugal (6hr., daily 4:51am, €45.70) and Madrid (2½hr., 5-6 per day, €15). **Buses** leave from the station (☎23 67 17) on Av. Filiberto Villalobos 71-85 for: Barcelona (11hr.; daily 7:30am, noon; €42); León (2½hr., 4-6 per day, €11.60); Madrid (2½hr., 16 per day, €10.20-15); Segovia (2¾hr., 2 per day, €9). Gorgeous **Plaza Mayor** is the social and geographic center of Salamanca. From the train station, catch bus #1 (€1) to Gran Vía and ask to be let off at Pl. San Julián, a block from Pl.

Mayor. It's a 20min. walk from the train station and a 15min. walk from the bus station. The **tourist office** is at Pl. Mayor 32. (☎21 83 42. Open June-Sept. M-F 9am-2pm and 4:30-8pm, Sa 10am-8pm, Su 10am-2pm; Oct.-May reduced hours.) *DGratis*, a free weekly newspaper about events in Salamanca, is available from newsstands, tourist offices, and locations in Pl. Mayor. For free **Internet,** try the **public library,** C. Compañia 2 in the Casa de las Conchas. (☎26 93 17. Limit 30min. Open July to mid-Sept. M-F 9am-3pm, Sa 9am-2pm; mid-Sept. to June M-F 9am-9pm, Sa 9am-2pm.) **Postal Code:** 37080.

ACCOMMODATIONS AND FOOD. Reasonably priced *hostales* and *pensiones* cater to the floods of student visitors, especially off Pl. Mayor and C. Meléndez. **Pensión Las Vegas ❷**, C. Meléndez 13, first floor, has a friendly staff and spotless rooms. (☎21 87 49; www.lasvegascentro.com. Singles with shower €24; doubles with bath €36. MC/V.) At nearby **Pensión Barez ❶**, C. Meléndez 19, first floor, a common room with a terrace makes up for tiny spaces. (☎21 74 95. €12 per person. Cash only.) Cafes and restaurants surround **Plaza Mayor,** where three-course meals run about €9. *Salamantinos* crowd **El Patio Chico ❷**, C. Meléndez 13, but hefty portions are worth the wait. (☎26 51 03. *Menú* €11. Entrees €4-8. Open daily 1-4pm and 8pm-midnight.) Good, cheap food keeps the students coming back to **La Fábrica ❶**, C. Libreros 47-49. (☎26 95 74. Coffee and a pastry €1.50. *Bocadillos* €3.60-6. Open M-F 9am-10pm, Sa-Su 9am-midnight.) The closest supermarket is **Champion,** C. Toro 82. (☎21 22 08. Open M-Sa 9am-9:30pm.)

SIGHTS AND NIGHTLIFE. From Pl. Mayor, follow R. Mayor, veer right onto T. Antigua and left onto C. Libreros to reach **La Universidad de Salamanca** (est. 1218), the city's focal point. Entering the stone foyer feels like stepping into another era. The 15th-century classroom **Aula Fray Luis de León** has been left in more or less its original state. Located on the second floor atop a Plateresque staircase is the **Antigua Biblioteca,** one of Europe's oldest libraries. Don't miss the 800-year-old scrawlings on the walls of the **Capilla del Estudiante.** (University ☎29 44 00, museum 29 12 25. Both open M-F 9:30am-1:30pm and 4-7:30pm, Sa 9:30am-1:30pm and 4-7pm, Su 10am-1:30pm. University and museum €4, students €2.) It took 220 years to build the stunning **Catedral Nueva,** in Pl. de Anaya. The church is best viewed from the ground first, but be sure to climb the tower for a spectacular **view.** (Open daily Apr.-Sept. 9am-8pm; Oct.-Mar. 9am-1pm and 4-6pm. Tower open daily 10am-7pm. Cathedral free. Tower €2.50.) The smaller **Catedral Vieja** was built in in AD 1140. The **cupola,** assembled from intricately carved miniature pieces, is one of the most detailed in Spain. Be sure to check out the **Patio Chico** behind the cathedral, where students and tourists congregate for a spectacular view of both cathedrals. (Enter through the Catedral Nueva. Open daily Oct.-Mar. 10am-1:30pm and 4-7:30pm; Apr.-Sept. 10am-7:30pm. €3.50, students €2.75.)

According to *salmantinos*, Salamanca is the best place in Spain to party; it is said that there is one bar for every 100 people living in the city. Nightlife centers on **Plaza Mayor** and spreads out to **Gran Vía, Calle Bordadores** and side streets. **Calle Prior** and **Rúa Mayor** are also full of bars, while intense partying occurs off **Calle Varillas.** After a few candy-colored shots (€0.90-1) at **Bar La Chupitería,** Pl. Monterrey, wander from club to club on C. Prior and C. Compañía, where young Americans mingle with tireless *salmantinos*. Once you get past the picky bouncers, **Niebla,** C. Bordadores 18 (☎26 86 04), **Gatsby,** C. Bordadores 16 (☎21 72 74), **Camelot,** C. Bordadores 3 (☎21 21 82), and **Cum Laude,** C. Prior 5-7 (☎26 75 77) all offer an ambience of tight pants and loose morals. The party doesn't peak until 2:30-3:30am and stays strong for another two hours. (Beer €3-4. Mixed drinks €5.50-6.50. Dress to impress. All clubs have no cover and are cash only.)

DAYTRIP FROM SALAMANCA: ZAMORA

Perched atop a rocky cliff over the Río Duero, Zamora (pop. 70,000) is an intriguing mix of modern and medieval: 15th-century palaces harbor Internet cafes and the magnificent 12th-century cathedral overlooks modern steel bridges. Though Zamora owes its character to the medieval churches dotting its streets, the **Museo de Semana Santa,** Pl. Santa María la Nueva 9, is a fun diversion. Hooded mannequins guard elaborate floats, which are used during the *romería* processions of *Semana Santa* (Holy Week; Apr. 9-16, 2006). The crypt-like setting and impressive collection make this museum an eerie yet worthwhile stop. (☎980 53 22 95. Open M-Sa 10am-2pm and 5-8pm, Su 10am-2pm. €2.70. Photography €3.) Twelve striking **Romanesque churches** remain within the old city's walls. A self-guided tour of all of the churches is available from the tourist office, though they tend to blend together after a while. (All churches open Mar.-Sept. Tu-Sa 10am-1pm and 5-8pm. Free.) Zamora's chief monument is its Romanesque **cathedral.** Inside the cloister, the **Museo de la Catedral** features the 15th-century Black Tapestries, which tell the story of Achilles's defeat during the Trojan War. (☎980 53 06 44. Cathedral and museum open Tu-Su 10am-2pm and 5-8pm. Mass M-F 10am, Sa also 6pm, Su also 1pm. Cathedral free. Museum €3, students €1.50.) The best way to reach Zamora is by bus. **Buses** run from Salamanca to the station on Av. Alfonso Peña (☎980 52 12. 1hr., 6-15 per day, €4). Information on sights can be found at the **tourist office,** C. Santa Clara 20. (☎980 53 18 45; www.ayto-zamora.org. Open July to mid-Sept. M-Th and Su 9am-8pm, F-Sa 9am-9pm; mid-Sept. to June daily 9am-2pm and 5-8pm.)

LEÓN ☎987

Formerly the center of Christian Spain, León (pop. 165,000) is best known today for its 13th-century Gothic **cathedral,** Pl. Regla, arguably the most beautiful in Spain. Its 1800 spectacular meters of stained glass have earned León the nickname *La Ciudad Azul* (The Blue City). The cathedral's **museum** displays gruesome wonders, including a sculpture depicting the skinning of a saint. (☎87 57 70; www.catedraldeleon.org. Cathedral open July-Sept. M-Sa 8:30am-1:30pm and 4-8pm; Oct.-June until 7pm. Museum open June-Sept. M-Sa 9:30am-1:30pm and 4-6:30pm; Oct.-May M-F 9:30am-1pm and 4-6pm. Cathedral free. Museum €3.50, cloisters €1.) The **Basílica San Isidoro,** Pl. San Isidoro, houses the remains of myriad royals in the frescoed *Panteón Real.* From Pl. Santo Domingo, walk up C. Ramón y Cajal; the basilica is up the stairs on the right. (Open July-Aug. M-Sa 9am-8pm, Su 9am-2pm; Sept.-June M-Sa 10am-1:30pm and 4-6:30pm, Su 10am-1:30pm. €3, Th afternoon free.)

The warm, yellow rooms of **Hostal Bayón ❶,** C. Alcazar de Toledo 6, 2nd flr., are just off C. Ancha. (☎23 14 46. Singles €15, with shower €25; doubles €25/35. Cash only.) Cheap eats hug the cathedral and the small streets off C. Ancha. Fresh food is available at the **Mercado Municipal del Conde,** Pl. del Conde, off C. General Mola. (Open M-Sa 9am-3:30pm.) For bars, discos, and techno music, head to the *barrio húmedo* (drinker's neighborhood) around **Plaza de San Martín** and **Plaza Mayor.** RENFE **trains** (☎902 24 02 02) run from Av. de Astorga 2 to: Barcelona (9½hr., 2-3 per day, €39-50); Bilbao (5½hr., 3:16pm, €23); Madrid (4½hr., 7 per day, €22-29). **Buses** (☎21 00 00) leave from Po. del Ingeniero Sáenz de Miera for Madrid (4½hr., 7-12 per day, €20-30) and Salamanca (2½hr., 5-6 per day, €12). The **tourist office,** Pl. Regla 3, has free maps. (☎23 70 82; www.turismocastillayleon.com. Open M-F 9am-2pm and 5-7pm, Sa-Su 10am-2pm and 5-8pm.) **Postal Code:** 24004.

EXTREMADURA

Arid plains bake under the intense summer sun, relieved only by scattered patches of golden sunflowers. This land of harsh beauty and cruel extremes hardened New World conquistadors such as Hernán Cortés and Francisco Pizarro.

TRUJILLO

☎927

The gem of Extremadura, hilltop Trujillo (pop. 10,000) is an enchanting old-world town. Scattered with medieval palaces, Arabic fortresses, and churches of all eras, Trujillo is a hodgepodge of histories and cultures. Crowning the hill are the ruins of a 10th-century **Moorish castle.** Pacing the ramparts is like playing in your best Lego creation. (Open daily June-Sept. 10am-2pm and 5-8:30pm; Oct.-May 9:30am-2pm and 4:30-8pm. €1.30.) Trujillo's **Plaza Mayor** was the inspiration for the Plaza de Armas in Cuzco, Perú, constructed after Francisco Pizarro defeated the Incas. To reach the Gothic **Iglesia de Santa María la Mayor,** take C. de las Cambroneras from the *plaza* in front of the Iglesia de San Martín and turn right on C. de Sta. María. The steps leading to the top of the Romanesque church tower are exhausting, but the **360° view** from the top is worth the effort. (Open May-Oct. 10am-2pm and 4:30-8pm; Nov.-Apr. 10am-2pm and 4-7pm. Su Mass 11am. €1.25.) At the bottom of the hill, far from most other sights, lies the **Museo del Queso y el Vino,** which offers history and advice on how to enjoy artisanal wine and cheese. (☎32 30 31. Open daily May-Sept. 11am-3pm and 6-8pm, Oct.-Apr. 11am-3pm and 5:30-7:30pm. Tickets €2.30 with tasting, €1.30 without.) A *Bono* ticket (€4.70), available at the tourist office, allows entrance to the **Casa-Museo de Pizarro,** the **Moorish castle,** and **Iglesia de Santiago,** and includes a guide book. For €5.30, the *Bono* ticket also gains entrance to **Iglesia de San Martin** and the **Museo del Queso y el Vino.**

Find the pleasant rooms of **Camas Boni ❷** on C. Mingos Ramos 11, off Pl. Mayor on the street directly across from Iglesia de San Martín. (☎32 16 04. Singles €14; doubles €28, with bath €30-35. Cash only.) Exit Pl. Mayor by the church, and walk four blocks down the street to reach **La Tahona ❶,** C. Afueras 2, which serves homemade pizza (€3.05-8.80), pasta (€4-5.20), and other tasty, wallet-friendly meals. (☎32 18 49. Open M 7:30pm-midnight, Tu-Su 1-4pm and 7:30pm-midnight.) **Buses** (☎32 18 22) run from the corner of C. de las Cruces and C. del M. de Albayada to Madrid (2½hr., 5 per day, €14-18). The **tourist office** is in Pl. Mayor, on the left when facing Pizarro's statue. Info is posted in the windows when it's closed. (☎32 26 77. English spoken. Open daily June-Sept. 10am-2pm and 4:30-7:30pm; Oct.-May 9:30am-2pm and 4-7pm.) **Postal Code:** 10200.

SOUTHERN SPAIN

Southern Spain (Andalucía) is all that you expect of Spanish culture—flamenco shows, bullfighting, pitchers of sangria, whitewashed villages, and streets lined with orange trees. The *festivales*, *ferias*, and *carnavales* of Andalucía are world-famous for their extravagance.

CÓRDOBA

☎957

Captivating Córdoba (pop. 310,000), perched on the south bank of the Río Guadalquivir, was once the largest city in Western Europe. The city remembers its heyday with amazingly well-preserved Roman, Jewish, Islamic, and Catholic monuments. Today, lively festivals, balconies dripping with flowers, and nonstop nightlife make Córdoba one of Spain's most beloved cities.

TRANSPORTATION. RENFE **Trains** (☎902 24 02 02; www.renfe.es) run from Pl. de las Tres Culturas, off Av. de América, to: Barcelona (10-11hr., 4 per day, €50-76); Cádiz (2½hr., 5 per day, €17-33); Madrid (2-4hr., 21-31 per day, €27-50); Málaga (2-3hr., 8-11 per day, €12-22); Seville (45min., 20-30 per day, €8-25). **Buses** (☎40 40 40) leave from Estación de Autobuses, on Glorieta de las Tres Culturas across from the train station. Alsina Graells Sur (☎27 81 00) sends buses to: Cádiz

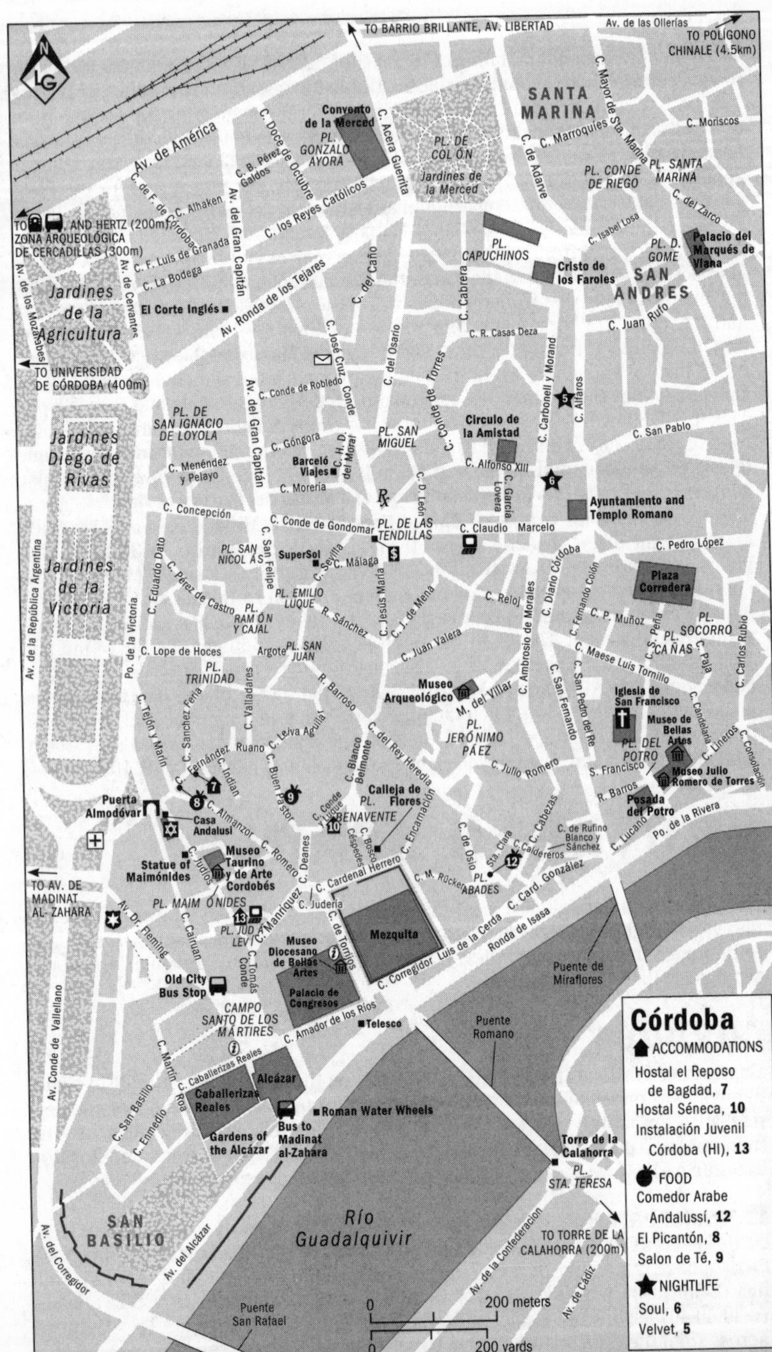

TO BARRIO BRILLANTE, AV. LIBERTAD
Av. de las Ollerías
TO POLÍGONO CHINALE (4.5km)
SANTA MARINA
C. Mayor de Sta. Marina
C. Moriscos
C. Marroquíes
C. de Adarve
PL. CONDE DE RIEGO
PL. SANTA MARINA
C. del Zarco
Convento de la Merced
PL. GONZALO AYORA
C. Acera Guerrita
PL. DE COLÓN
Jardines de la Merced
C. Doce de Octubre
C. B. Pérez Galdós
Av. de América
C. de F. de Córdoba
C. Alhaken
C. los Reyes Católicos
TO AND HERTZ (200m)
ZONA ARQUEOLÓGICA DE CERCADILLAS (300m)
C. F. Luis de Granada
C. La Bodega
Av. de Cervantes
Av. de los Mozárabes
Jardines de la Agricultura
El Corte Inglés
Av. del Gran Capitán
Av. Ronda de los Tejares
C. del Caño
PL. CAPUCHINOS
C. Isabel Losa
Cristo de los Faroles
PL. D. GOME
Palacio del Marqués de Viana
SAN ANDRES
C. Cabrera
C. Juan Rufo
C. R. Casas Deza
C. José Cruz Conde
C. del Osario
C. Conde de Torres
C. Carbonell y Morand
C. Alfaros
TO UNIVERSIDAD DE CÓRDOBA (400m)
C. Conde de Robledo
PL. DE SAN IGNACIO DE LOYOLA
Jardines Diego de Rivas
Circulo de la Amistad
PL. SAN MIGUEL
C. San Pablo
C. Góngora
C. H. D. del Moral
C. Menéndez y Pelayo
Barceló Viajes
C. Alfonso XIII
C. D. León
C. García Lovera
C. Morería
Ayuntamiento and Templo Romano
C. Concepción
C. Conde de Gondomar
PL. DE LAS TENDILLAS
C. Claudio Marcelo
C. Pedro López
PL. SAN NICOLÁS
SuperSol
C. Sevilla
C. Málaga
C. San Felipe
C. Jesús María
C. Diario Córdoba
Plaza Corredera
Jardines de la Victoria
Av. de la República Argentina
C. Eduardo Dato
C. Pérez de Castro
PL. EMILIO LUQUE
PL. RAMÓN Y CAJAL
R. Sánchez
C. J. de Mena
C. Reloj
C. Ambrosio de Morales
C. Fernando Colón
C. P. Muñoz
PL. SOCORRO
C. S. Peña
PL. CAÑAS
C. Carlos Rubio
C. Paja
Po. de la Victoria
C. Lope de Hoces
Argote
PL. SAN JUAN
C. Juan Valera
C. Maese Luis Tornillo
PL. TRINIDAD
C. Valladares
R. Barroso
Museo Arqueológico
M. del Villar
C. San Fernando
C. San Pedro del Re
Iglesia de San Francisco
C. Candelaria
C. Tejón y Marín
C. Sanchez Feria
C. Leiva Aguilar
C. del Rey Heredia
PL. JERÓNIMO PÁEZ
Museo de Bellas Artes
C. Lineros
C. Consolación
C. Fernández Ruano
C. Indian
C. Buen Pastor
C. Blanco Belmonte
C. Julio Romero
PL. DEL POTRO
S. Francisco
Museo Julio Romero de Torres
Puerta Almodóvar
Casa Andalusí
C. Almanzor
Calleja de Flores
PL. BENAVENTE
C. Conde y Luque
C. Encarnación
R. Barros
Posada del Potro
C. Lucano
Po. de la Rivera
C. Romero
C. Deanes
C. Bosco
C. Céspedes
C. de Osio
Sta. Clara
C. Cabezas
C. de Rufino Blanco y Sánchez
C. Calderereros
TO AV. DE MADINAT AL-ZAHARA
Statue of Maimónides
C. Judíos
Museo Taurino y de Arte Cordobés
C. Cardenal Herrero
C. M. Rücker
PL. ABADES
C. Card. González
PL. MAIMÓNIDES
C. Manríquez
C. Judería
C. de Torrijos
Mezquita
C. Luis de la Cerda
Ronda de Isasa
Av. Dr. Fleming
C. Cairuan
PL. JUDÁ LEVÍ
Museo Diocesano de Bellas Artes
Palacio de Congresos
C. Tomás Conde
C. Corregidor
Puente de Miraflores
Av. Conde de Vallellano
Old City Bus Stop
CAMPO SANTO DE LOS MÁRTIRES
C. Amador de los Ríos
Telesco
Puente Romano
C. Martín Roa
C. Caballerizas Reales
Alcázar
Caballerizas Reales
Roman Water Wheels
C. San Basilio
C. Enmedio
Gardens of the Alcázar
Bus to Madinat al-Zahara
Torre de la Calahorra
PL. STA. TERESA
SAN BASILIO
Río Guadalquivir
Av. del Corregidor
Av. del Alcázar
Av. de la Confederación
TO TORRE DE LA CALAHORRA (200m)
Av. de Cádiz
Puente San Rafael
0
200 meters
0
200 yards
Córdoba
ACCOMMODATIONS
Hostal el Reposo de Bagdad, 7
Hostal Séneca, 10
Instalación Juvenil Córdoba (HI), 13
FOOD
Comedor Arabe Andalussí, 12
El Picantón, 8
Salon de Té, 9
NIGHTLIFE
Soul, 6
Velvet, 5

(4-5hr., 1-2 per day, €19) via Seville (2hr., 9-10 per day, €9); Granada (3hr., 8 per day, €11); Málaga (3-3½hr., 5 per day, €11). Bacoma (☎902 42 22 42) runs to Barcelona (10hr., 3 per day, €59-69). Secorbus (☎902 22 92 92) buses go to Madrid (4½hr., 3-6 per day, €13). Autocares Priego (☎40 44 79) and Empresa Rafael Ramírez (☎42 21 77) run buses to nearby towns and campsites.

ORIENTATION AND PRACTICAL INFORMATION. Córdoba is split into two parts: the old city and the new city. The modern and commercial northern half extends from the train station on Av. de América down to **Plaza de las Tendillas,** the city center. The old section in the south is a medieval maze known as the **Judería** (Jewish quarter). The easiest way to reach the old city from the train station is to walk (20min.). Exit left from the station, cross the parking plaza and take a right onto Av. de los Mozárabes. When you reach the Roman columns, turn left and cross Gta. Sargentos Provisionales. Take a right on Po. de la Victoria and continue until you reach Puerto Almodóvar and the old city.

To get to the **tourist office,** C. Torrijos 10, from the train station, take bus #3 along the river until the Puente Romano leading across the river. Walk under the stone arch and the office will be on your left. (☎47 12 35. English spoken. Open May-Sept. M-F 9:30am-7pm, Sa 10am-7pm, Su 10am-2pm; Oct.-Apr. M-F 9:30am-6pm, Su 10am-2pm.) In the old city, **NavegaWeb,** Pl. Judá Leví, has **Internet.** Enter through the youth hostel. (☎29 00 66. €1.50 per hr. Open daily 10am-10pm.) The **post office** is located at C. de José Cruz Conde 15. (☎47 97 96. Open M-F 8:30am-8:30pm, Sa-Su 9:30am-2pm.) **Postal Code:** 14070.

ACCOMMODATIONS AND FOOD. Accommodations cluster around the the Judería and in old Córdoba between the Mezquita and C. de San Fernando. Reserve well in advance during *Semana Santa* and May-June. Popular **Instalación Juvenil Córdoba (HI)** ❷, Pl. Judá Leví, is a former mental asylum converted into a backpacker's paradise. The large rooms all have A/C. (☎29 01 66. Wheelchair accessible. Breakfast included. Linen €1.10. Laundry €4. Reception 24hr. Mar.-Oct. dorms €22, under 26 €17.50; Nov.-Feb. dorms €2.10 less. €3.50 HI member discount. Private rooms available. MC/V.) A lush courtyard, comfy rooms, and an Arab-inspired teahouse make **Hostal el Reposo de Bagdad** ❷, C. Fernández Ruano 11, an amazing deal. (☎20 28 54. Singles €20; doubles €36; triples €45. MC/V.) A beautiful patio and large rooms await at **Hostal Séneca** ❷, C. Conde y Luque 7. All rooms have fans or A/C. (☎47 32 34. Breakfast included. Singles €22, with bath €34; doubles €39/46; triples and one quad €87. Cash only.)

Córdobeses converge on the *terrazas* between **Calle Dr. Severo Ochoa** and **Calle Dr. Jiménez Díaz** for pre-dinner drinks and tapas. Cheap eateries cluster in **Barrio Cruz Conde** and around **Avenida Menéndez Pidal** and **Plaza de las Tendillas.** Tiny **El Picantón** ❶, C. Fernández Ruano 19, has an irresistable Spanish take on subs—tapas in a baguette with fresh toppings for €1-3. (☎629 58 28 64. Takeaway only. Beer €1. Open roughly M-Sa 10am-3:30pm and 8pm-midnight. Cash only.) Family-run **Comedor Arabe Andalussí** ❷, Pl. Abades 4, serves Middle Eastern cuisine at budget-friendly prices. (☎47 51 62. Half-portions €2-3.70. Entrees €6-15. Open W-Su noon-6pm and 8:30pm-midnight. Closed mid-July to mid-Aug. MC/V.) For a taste of the old Moorish Córdoba, head to **Salon de Té** ❶, C. Buen Pastor 13, a recreated 12th-century teahouse with a huge variety of teas, juices, and Arab pastries. (☎48 79 84. Beverages €2-4. Pastries €1.50-3. Open daily 11am-11pm.) **El Corte Inglés,** Av. Ronda de los Tejares 30, has a grocery store. (Open M-Sa 10am-10pm.)

SIGHTS. Built in AD 784, Córdoba's **Mezquita** is considered the most important Islamic monument in the Western Hemisphere. Visitors enter through the **Patio de los Naranjos,** an arcaded courtyard featuring fountains and orange trees. Inside the mosque, 850 granite and marble columns support hundreds of striped arches. In the center, intricate pink-and-blue marble mosaics shimmer across the arches of the **Mihrab** (prayer niche), which is covered in Kufic inscriptions of the 99 names of Allah. Although the town rallied violently against the proposed erection of a **cathedral** in the center of the mosque, after the Crusaders conquered Córdoba in 1236, the towering **crucero** (transept) and **coro** (choir dome) were built. (☎47 05 12. Open July-Oct. daily 10am-7pm; Apr.-June M-Sa 10am-7:30pm; Dec.-Jan. daily 10am-5:30pm; Nov. and Feb. daily 10am-6pm. Open M-Sa 8:30am for 9:30am mass. Su mass 11am, noon, 1pm. €8. Free during mass M-Sa.)

The **Judería** is the area northwest of the Mezquita. Past the statue of Maimónides, the small **Sinagoga,** C. Judíos 20, is one of the few to survive the Inquisition. (☎20 29 28. Open Tu-F 9:30am-3pm, Sa 9:30am-1:30pm. €0.30.) Along the river left of the Mezquita is the **Alcázar,** constructed for Catholic monarchs in 1328 during the *Reconquista.* Ferdinand and Isabella bade Columbus *adios* here; later, it served as Inquisition headquarters. (☎42 01 51. Open Tu-Sa 10am-2pm and 4:30-6:30pm, Su 9:30am-2:30pm. Gardens open June-Sept. 8pm-midnight. Alcázar €4, students €2. F free. Gardens free.) The **Museo Taurino y de Arte Cordobés,** on Pl. Maimónides, details the history of bullfighting. (☎20 10 56. Open Tu-Sa 10:30am-2pm and 5:30-7:30pm, Su 9:30am-2pm. €3, students €1.50. F free.) A **combined ticket** for the Alcázar, Museo Taurino, and the **Museo Julio Romero,** which displays Romero's sensual portraits, is available at all three locations. (€7.10, students €3.60. F free.)

ENTERTAINMENT AND NIGHTLIFE. For the latest cultural events, pick up a free copy of the *Guía del Ocio* at the tourist office. Hordes of tourists flock to see the prize-winning dancers at the **Tablao Cardenal,** C. Torrijos 10. (☎48 33 20. €18, includes 1 drink. Shows M-Sa 10:30pm.) **La Bulería,** C. Pedro López 3, is even more affordable. (☎48 38 39. €11, includes 1 drink. Shows daily 10:30pm.) **Soul,** C. Alfonso XIII 3, is relaxed bar with cozy tables and friendly bartenders. (☎49 15 80; www.bar-soul.com. Beer €1.50-2.10. Mixed drinks €4.50. Open Sept.-June daily 9am-4am.) **Velvet,** C. Alfaros 29, is a popular retro-style pub. (☎48 60 92. Beer €1.50-2.40. Mixed drinks €3.60-4.80. Open in summer 10pm-4am; in winter 5pm-4am.) Starting in June, the **Barrio Brillante,** uphill from Av. de América, is packed with young *córdobeses* hopping between dance clubs and outdoor bars. Bus #10 goes to Brillante from the train station until about 11pm, but the bars don't wake up until around 1am (most are open until 4am); a lift from **Radio Taxi** (☎76 44 44) costs €4-6. If you're walking, head 30min. up Av. Brillante from the Judería. Trendy pubs with crowded *terrazas* on nearby **Avenida Libertad.** An alternative to partying is a nighttime stroll along the **walk-through fountains** and falling sheets of water that line Av. de América between Pl. de Colón and the train station.

Of Córdoba's festivals, floats, and parades, **Semana Santa** (Holy Week; Apr. 9-16, 2006) is the most extravagant. The first few days of May are dedicated to the **Festival de las Cruces,** during which residents make crosses decorated with flowers. During the **Festival de los Patios** in the first two weeks of May, the city erupts with classical music concerts, flamenco dances, and a city-wide patio-decorating contest. Late May brings the **Feria de Nuestra Señora de Salud** *(La Feria de Córdoba)*, a week of colorful garb, dancing, music, and wine-drinking. Every July, Córdoba hosts a guitar festival, attracting talented strummers from all over the world.

SEVILLE (SEVILLA) ☎954

Site of a Roman acropolis, capital of the Moorish empire, focal point of the Spanish Renaissance, and guardian of traditional Andalusian culture, romantic Seville (pop. 700,000) overflows with influences. Flamenco, tapas, and bullfighting are at their best here, and Seville's cathedral is among the most impressive in Spain. But it's the city's infectious spirit that defines it, and, fittingly, its *Semana Santa* and *Feria de Abril* celebrations are among the most elaborate in Europe.

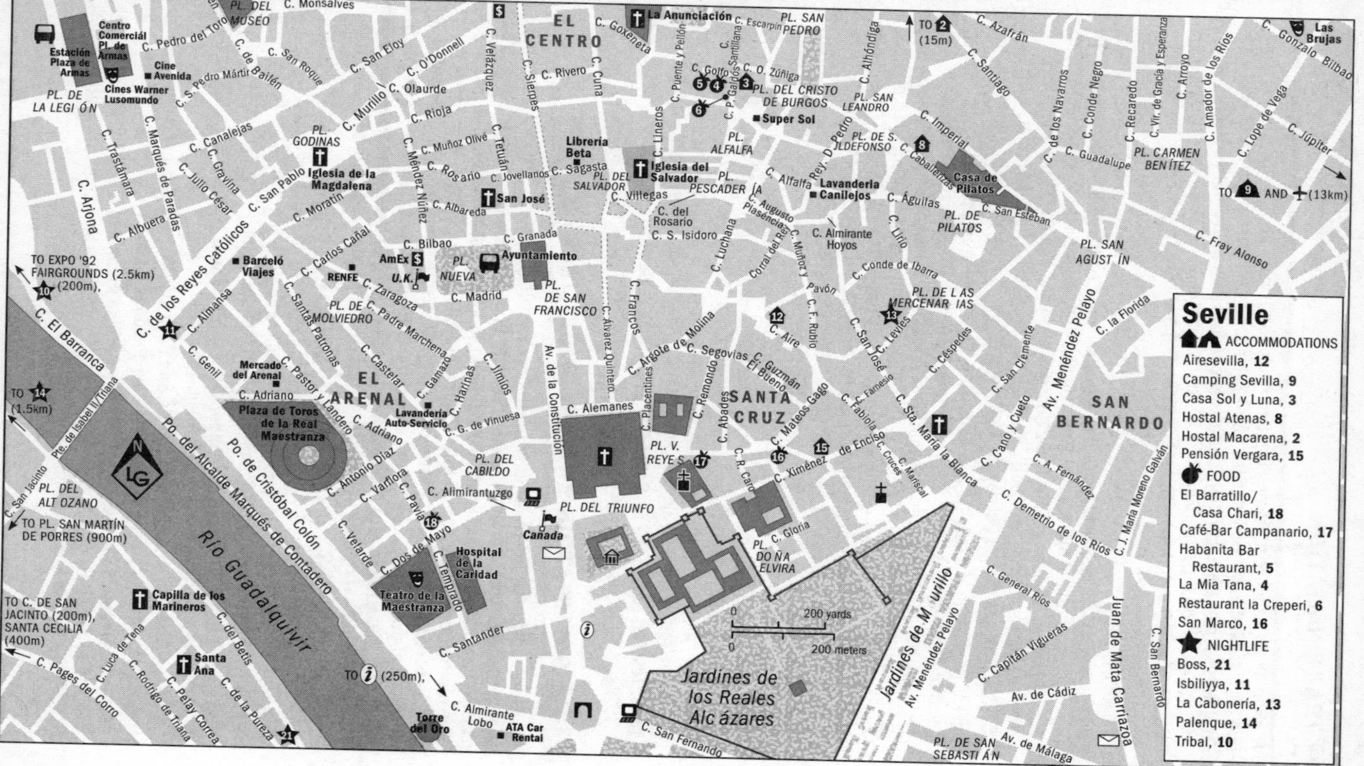
Seville
ACCOMMODATIONS
Airesevilla, 12
Camping Sevilla, 9
Casa Sol y Luna, 3
Hostal Atenas, 8
Hostal Macarena, 2
Pensión Vergara, 15
FOOD
El Barratillo/
Casa Chari, 18
Café-Bar Campanario, 17
Habanita Bar
Restaurant, 5
La Mia Tana, 4
Restaurant la Creperi, 6
San Marco, 16
NIGHTLIFE
Boss, 21
Isbiliyya, 11
La Cabonería, 13
Palenque, 14
Tribal, 10
EL CENTRO
SANTA CRUZ
SAN BERNARDO
EL ARENAL
Río Guadalquivir
Jardines de los Reales Alc ázares
Jardines de M urillo
Plaza de Toros de la Real Maestranza
Av. de la Constitución
Av. Menéndez Pelayo
Po. de Cristóbal Colón
Po. del Alcalde Marqués de Contadero
Estación Plaza de Armas
Centro Comercial Pl. de Armas
Cines Warner Lusomundo
Cine Avenida
Iglesia de la Magdalena
Iglesia del Salvador
La Anunciación
San José
Ayuntamiento
Casa de Pilatos
Hospital de la Caridad
Teatro de la Maestranza
Capilla de los Marineros
Santa Ana
Torre del Oro
Mercado del Arenal
Librería Beta
Super Sol
Lavandería Canilejos
Lavandería Auto-Servicio
Barceló Viajes
AmEx
U.K.
RENFE
Canada
ATA Car Rental
Las Brujas
TO EXPO '92 FAIRGROUNDS (2.5km)
TO PL. SAN MARTÍN DE PORRES (900m)
TO C. DE SAN JACINTO (200m), SANTA CECILIA (400m)
200 yards
200 meters

TRANSPORTATION

Flights: All flights arrive at **Aeropuerto San Pablo** (SVQ; ☎44 90 00), 12km out of town on Ctra. de Madrid. A taxi ride to the town center costs €18-20. **Los Amarillos** (☎98 91 84) buses run to the airport from outside Hotel Alfonso XIII at the Pta. de Jerez (1-2 per hr., €2.40). **Iberia,** C. Guadaira 8 (☎22 89 01, nationwide 902 40 05 00; open M-F 9am-1:30pm) flies to **Barcelona** (1hr., 6 per day) and **Madrid** (45min., 6 per day).

Trains: Estación Santa Justa (☎902 24 02 02), is on Av. de Kansas City. Near Pl. Nueva is the **RENFE** office, C. Zaragoza 29. (☎54 02 02. Open M-F 9am-1:15pm and 4-7pm.) *Altaria* and *Talgo* trains run to: **Barcelona** (10½-13hr., 3 per day, €51.50-79.50); **Córdoba** (1hr., 4-6 per day, €12.80); **Madrid** (3½hr., 2 per day, €52.50); **Valencia** (9hr., 8:20am, €43.50). AVE trains go to **Córdoba** (45min., 15-21 per day, €19) and **Madrid** (2½hr., 15-21 per day, €61). *Regionale* trains run to: **Cádiz** (2hr., 7-12 per day, €8.75); **Córdoba** (1½hr., 6 per day, €7.20); **Granada** (3hr., 4 per day, €19); **Málaga** (2½hr., 4-7 per day, €15.30).

Buses: The station at **Prado de San Sebastián,** C. Manuel Vázquez Sagastizabal, serves most of Andalucía. (☎41 71 11. Open daily 5:30am-1am.) **Estación Plaza de Armas** (☎90 80 40) mainly serves areas outside of Andalucía. To: **Arcos de la Frontera** (2hr., 2 per day, €6.75); **Cádiz** (1½hr., 12-15 per day, €10); **Córdoba** (2hr., 8-10 per day, €9); **Granada** (3hr., 10 per day, €17); **Lagos, Portugal** (7hr., 2 per day, €17); **León** (11hr., 3 per day, €38); **Lisbon, Portugal** (6¼hr., 9:30am, €28.25); **Madrid** (6hr., 14 per day, €17); **Málaga** (2½hr., 10-12 per day, €14); **Ronda** (2½hr., 3-5 per day, €9.60); **Salamanca** (8hr., 5-6 per day, €27); **Valencia** (9-11hr., 3 per day, €44-51).

Public Transportation: TUSSAM (☎900 71 01 71; www.tussam.es) bus lines run 6am-11:15pm and converge on Pl. Nueva, Pl. de la Encarnación, or the cathedral. Especially useful are C3 and C4, which circle the city center, and #34, which serves the university, cathedral, and Pl. Nueva. **Night service** departs from Pl. Nueva (M-Th and Su every hr. midnight-2am, F-Sa every hr. all night). Fare €1, 10-ride *(bonobús)* ticket €4.50.

Taxis: TeleTaxi (☎62 22 22). **Radio Taxi** (☎58 00 00). Base rate €1, €0.40 per km, Su 25% surcharge. Extra charge for luggage and night taxis.

ORIENTATION AND PRACTICAL INFORMATION

The **Río Guadalquivir** flows roughly north-south through the city. Most of the touristed areas of Seville, including **Santa Cruz** and **El Arenal,** are on the east bank. The historic *barrios* of **Triana, Santa Cecilia,** and **Los Remedios,** as well as the Expo '92 fairgrounds occupy the west bank. The cathedral, next to Santa Cruz, is Seville's centerpiece. **Avenida de la Constitución** runs alongside the cathedral. **El Centro,** a commercial pedestrian zone, lies north of the cathedral, starting where Av. Constitución hits **Plaza Nueva** and **Plaza de San Francisco,** site of the Ayuntamiento. **Calle Tetuán,** a popular shopping street, runs north from Pl. Nueva through El Centro.

Tourist Offices: Centro de Información de Sevilla, Pl. de San Francisco 19 (☎23 44 65; www.turismo.sevilla.org). English spoken. Free Internet; 1hr. limit. Open M-F 9am-8pm, Sa-Su 9am-3pm. **Turismo Andaluz,** Av. de la Constitución 21B (☎22 14 04). Info on all of Andalucía. Open M-F 9am-7pm, Sa 10am-2pm and 3-7pm, Su 10am-2pm.

Currency Exchange: Banco Santander Central Hispano, C. Tetuán 10 (☎902 24 24 24). Open M-F 8:30am-2pm, Sa 8:30am-1pm.

Luggage Storage: At Estación Prado de San Sebastián (€1 per bag per day), Estación Plaza de Armas (€3 per day), and the train station (€3 per day).

GLBT Resources: Colectiva de Lesbianas y Gays de Andalucía (COLEGA; ☎50 13 77). Pl. de la Encarnación 23, 2nd fl. Look for the sign in the window; the door is not marked. Open M-F 10am-2pm.

Laundromat: Lavandería Roma, C. Castelar 2 (☎21 05 35). Wash and dry €6 per load. Open M-F 9:30am-1:30pm and 5-8:30pm, Sa 9am-2pm.

24hr. Pharmacy: Check list posted at any pharmacy for those open 24hr.

Medical Services: Red Cross (☎913 35 45 45). **Ambulatorio Esperanza Macarena** (☎42 01 05). **Hospital Universitario Virgen Macarena,** Av. Dr. Fedriani (☎24 81 81).

Internet Access: Distelco, C. Ortiz Zuñiga 3 (☎22 99 66). €2 per hr., €1.10 per hr. with *bono.* Open M-F 10:30am-11pm, Sa 6pm-midnight.

Post Office: Av. de la Constitución 32 (☎21 64 76), opposite the cathedral. *Lista de Correos* and fax. Open M-F 8:30am-8:30pm, Sa 9:30am-2pm. **Postal Code:** 41080.

ACCOMMODATIONS

Rooms vanish and prices soar during *Semana Santa* and the *Feria de Abril;* reserve several months in advance. In Santa Cruz, the streets around **Calle Santa María la Blanca** are full of cheap, central hostels. Those by the **Plaza de Armas** bus station are convenient for visits to **El Centro** and **Calle del Betis** across the river.

Pensión Vergara, C. Ximénez de Enciso 11, 2nd fl. (☎21 56 68). Elegant rooms with lace bedspreads, antique-style furniture, and a sunny courtyard. All rooms with fans. Towels provided on request. Singles €20; doubles €40; triples €60; quads €80. Cash only. ❷

Airesevilla, C. Aire 13 (☎50 09 05; www.airesevilla-gay.com). This gorgeous guesthouse tastefully merges Andalusian styles with modern art for gay guests. Singles €35-45; doubles €55-75. Prices vary with season. MC/V. ❹

Casa Sol y Luna, C. Pérez Galdós 1A (☎21 06 82). Beautiful, homey rooms make you feel like you're staying at a friend's amazing house. Laundry €7. Singles €22; doubles €35, with bath €42; triples €54; quads €72. 2-night min. stay. Cash only. ❷

Hostal Atenas, C. Caballerizas 1 (☎21 80 47), near Pl. Pilatos. Everything about this hostel is appealing, from the old-fashioned indoor patio to modern, spotless rooms. All rooms with A/C and bath. Singles €35; doubles €58; triples €70. MC/V. ❸

Hostal Macarena, C. San Luis 91 (☎37 01 41). Relaxing rooms with A/C in a quite neighborhood. Singles €20; doubles €30, with bath €36; triples €50. MC/V. ❷

Camping Sevilla, Ctra. Madrid-Cádiz km 534 (☎51 43 79), near the airport. From Pr. San Sebastián, take bus #70 (stops 800m away at Parque Alcosa). Hot showers, supermarket, and pool. 1-person tent site €8.50. ❶

FOOD

Tapas bars cluster around **Plaza San Martín** and along **Calle San Jacinto.** Popular venues for "el tapeo" (tapas barhopping) are **Barrio de Santa Cruz** and **El Arenal. Mercado de la Encarnación,** near the bullring in Pl. de la Encarnación, has fresh meat and produce. (Open M-Sa 9am-2pm.) There is an enormous supermarket in the basement of **El Corte Inglés,** in Pl. del Duque de la Victoria. (Open M-Sa 9am-10pm.)

Restaurante-Bar El Baratillo/Casa Chari, C. Pavía 12 (☎22 96 51), off C. Dos de Mayo. Order at least 1hr. in advance for the tour-de-force: homemade paella (vegetarian options available) with a pitcher of wine, beer, or sangria (€18; serves 2). *Menu* €4-9. Open M-F 10am-10pm, Sa 10am-5pm; stays open later when busy. Cash only. ❷

Habanita Bar Restaurant, C. Golfo 3 (☎606 71 64 56; www.andalunet.com/habanita), off C. Pérez Galdós, next to Pl. Alfalfa. Exquisite Cuban fare. Entrees €4.80-10. Open daily 12:30-4:30pm and 8pm-12:30am. Closed Su evenings. MC/V. ❷

La Mia Tana, C. Pérez Galdós 24 (☎22 68 97). The smell of pizza and pasta wafts out to the streets, drawing locals to the intimate setting. Pizza €4.20-12. Pastas €4-4.60. Open daily 1-4:30pm and 8pm-1am. DC/MC/V. ❶

Restaurant La Creperi, C. Pérez Galdós 22 (☎22 28 02). Scrumptious salty (€2.50-6) and dessert (€2-5) crepes. Open daily 1:30-4:30pm and 8pm-midnight. MC/V. ❶

San Marco, C. Mesón del Moro 6 (☎21 43 90), in Santa Cruz's *casco antiguo.* Pizza, pasta, and dessert in an 18th-century house with 17th-century Arab baths. Entrees €5-10. Open Tu-Su 1:15-4:30pm and 8:15pm-12:30am. AmEx/DC/MC/V. ❷

Café-Bar Campanario, C. Mateos Gago 8 (☎56 41 89). Vegetarian-friendly tapas bar. Sit outside and gaze at the cathedral as you sip sangria (0.5L €7.25, 1L €9.65). Tapas €1-2.40. *Raciones* €6.40-9.60. Open daily noon-midnight. AmEx/DC/MC/V. ❷

SIGHTS

CATEDRAL. Legend has it that the *Reconquistadores* wished to show their religious fervor by building a church so great that "those who come after us will take us for madmen." With 44 chapels, the Cathedral of Seville is the world's third largest (after St. Peter's in Rome and St. Paul's in London) and the biggest Gothic edifice ever constructed. Not surprisingly, it took over a century to build. In 1401, a mosque was razed to clear space for the cathedral; all that remains of it is the **Patio de Los Naranjos,** the **Puerta del Perdón** entryway, and the **La Giralda** minaret.

In the center of the cathedral, the **Capilla Real** stands opposite **choir stalls** made of mahogany recycled from a 19th-century Austrian railway. The **retablo mayor** is a golden wall of intricately wrought saints and disciples. Nearby is the **Sepulcro de Cristóbal Colón** (Columbus's tomb), which supposedly holds the explorer's remains. The black-and-gold pallbearers represent the eternally grateful monarchs of Castilla, León, Aragón, and Navarra. Farther on, the **Sacristía Mayor** (treasury) holds gilded panels of Alfonso X el Sabio, works by Ribera and Murillo, and a glittering Corpus Christi icon, **La Custodia Processional.** In the northwest corner of the cathedral lies the stunning **Sala de Las Columnas.** *(☎21 49 71. Entrance by the Pl. de la Virgen de los Reyes. Open M-Sa 11am-5pm, Su 2:30-6pm. Last entrance 1hr. before closing. Mass held in the Capilla Real M-Sa 8:30, 10am, noon; Su 8:30, 10, 11am, noon, 1pm. Cathedral €6, students €1.50, under 12 and Su free.)*

ALCÁZAR. The oldest European palace still used as a private royal residence, Seville's Alcázar oozes extravagance. Though the Granada's Alhambra gets more press, the Alcázar has equally impressive features. Built by the Moors in the 7th century, the palace was embellished greatly during the 15th century and now displays an interesting mix of Moorish and Christian architecture, including Mudéjar arches, tiles, and ceilings. Ferdinand and Isabella are the palace's most well-known former residents. Visitors enter through the **Patio de la Montería,** directly across from the intricate Almohad facade. Through the archway lie the Arabic residences, including the **Patio del Yeso** and the **Patio de las Muñecas** (Patio of the Dolls), so named because of miniature faces carved into the bottom of one of the room's pillars. Of the Christian additions, the most notable is the **Patio de las Doncellas.** Court life in the Alcázar revolved around this columned quadrangle, which is encircled by archways of glistening tilework. The golden-domed **Salón de los Embajadores** (Embassadors' Room) is allegedly the site where Ferdinand and Isabella welcomed Columbus back from the New World. The upstairs **private residences** are the official home of the king and queen of Spain and their accommodations when they visit Seville. The residences are accessible only by 25min. guided tours. *(Pl. del Triunfo 7. ☎50 23 23. Open Tu-Sa 9:30am-7pm, Su 9:30am-5pm. Tours of the upper palace living quarters every 30min. June-July 10am-1:30pm; Aug.-May 10am-1:30pm and 3:30-5:30pm; 15 people max. per tour, so buy tickets in advance. Alcázar €5; students free. Tours €3.)*

CASA DE PILATOS. Inhabited continuously by Spanish aristocrats since the 15th century, this large private residence combines all the virtues of Andalusian architecture and art and has only recently been opened to the public. Some sections are still used as a private home. *(Pl. Pilatos 1. ☎22 52 98. Open daily 9am-7pm. Guided tours every 30min. €5 ground level only, €8 ground level and upper chambers.)*

MUSEO PROVINCIAL DE BELLAS ARTES. This museum contains Spain's finest collection of works by painters of the *Sevillana* School, as well as some by El Greco and Dutch master Jan Breughel. Although the art (displayed more or less chronologically) is biased toward religious themes, later works include some landscape paintings and portraits depicting Seville, its environs, and residents. *(Pl. del Museo 9. ☎22 07 90. Open Tu 3-8pm, W-Sa 9am-8pm, Su 9am-2pm. €1.50, EU citizens free.)*

PLAZA DE TOROS DE LA REAL MAESTRANZA. Home to one of the two great bullfighting schools (the other is in Ronda, p. 939), Plaza de Toros de la Real Maestranza fills to capacity (13,800) for weekly fights and the 13 *corridas* of the *Feria de Abril.* Visitors must follow the multilingual tours through the small but informative **Museo Taurino de la Real Maestranza,** as well as behind the ring to the chapel where *matadores* pray before fights and the site of the medical emergency room, used when their prayers go unanswered. *(☎22 45 77. Open non-bullfight days 9:30am-7pm, bullfight days 9:30am-3pm. Tours every 20min., €4.)*

ENTERTAINMENT

The tourist office distributes *El Giraldillo*, a free monthly magazine with complete listings on all things entertaining. It can also be found at www.elgiraldillo.es.

FLAMENCO

Flamenco is at its best in Seville. Flamenco can be seen either in highly touristed *tablaos*, where skilled professional dancers perform, or in *tabernas*, bars where locals merrily dance *sevillanas*. Both have merit, but the *tabernas* tend to be free. The tourist office provides a complete list of both *tablaos* and *tabernas*. Be sure to ask about student discounts. **Los Gallos,** Pl. de Santa Cruz 11, is probably the best tourist show in Seville. (☎21 69 81; www.tablaolosgallos.com. Shows daily 8, 10:30pm. Cover €27, includes 1 drink.) Less expensive alternatives are the impressive 1hr. shows at the cultural center **Casa de la Memoria Al-Andalus,** C. Ximénez de Enciso 28. Swing by their ticket office or the tourist office for a schedule of themed performances. (☎ 56 06 70. Shows daily 9pm, also 10:30pm in summer. Limited seating; buy tickets in advance. €12, students €10.)

BULLFIGHTING

Seville's beautiful bullring hosts fights from *Semana Santa* through October. The cheapest place to buy tickets is at the ring's ticket office on Po. Alcalde Marqués de Contadero. However, when there's a good *cartel* (line-up), the booths on C. las Sierpes, C. Velázquez, and Pl. de Toros might be the only source of advance tickets. Prices vary depending on the quality of both seat and *matador;* they can run from €20 for a *grada de sol* (nosebleed seat in the sun) to €75 for a *barrera de sombra* (front-row seat in the shade). *Corridas de toros* (professional bullfights) and *novilladas* (bullfights featuring apprentice bullfighters and younger bulls) are held around the *Feria de Abril* and into May, every Sunday April through June and September through October, and during the *Feria de San Miguel* near the end of September. During July and August, *corridas* occur every Thursday at 9pm; check posters around town. (For schedules and ticket sales, call ☎50 13 82.)

FESTIVALS

If you're in Spain during any of the major festivals, head straight to Seville. Book rooms a few months ahead, and expect to pay two or three times the normal rate.

SEMANA SANTA. Seville's world-famous *Semana Santa* lasts from Palm Sunday to Easter Sunday (Apr. 9-16, 2006). In each neighborhood, thousands of robed penitents guide *pasos* (huge, extravagant floats) through the streets, illuminated by hundreds of candles. The climax is Good Friday, when the entire city turns out for the procession along the bridges and through the oldest neighborhoods.

FERIA DE ABRIL. The city rewards itself for its Lenten piety with the *Feria de Abril* (Apr. 12-17, 2006). Circuses, and bullfights, and flamenco roar into the night in a showcase of local customs and camaraderie. A spectacular array of flowers and lanterns decorates over 1000 kiosks, tents, and pavilions (collectively called *casetas*) for eating, drinking, and socializing, There are bullfights daily during the festival; buy tickets in advance. *(The fairgrounds are on the southern end of Los Remedios.)*

NIGHTLIFE

Most clubs don't get going until well after midnight, and the real fun often starts after 3am. Popular bars can be found around **Calle Mateos Gago** near the cathedral, **Calle Adriano** by the bullring, and **Calle del Betis** across the river in Triana.

La Carbonería, C. Levies 18 (☎21 44 60), off C. Santa María La Blanca. Guitar-strumming Romeos abound on the massive outdoor patio. Th free live flamenco. Tapas €1.50-2. Beer €1.50. Mixed drinks €5. Sangria pitchers €8. Open July-Aug. M-Sa 8pm-4am, Su 8pm-2:30am; Sept.-May M-Sa 8pm-4am, Su 7pm-3am.

Boss, C. del Betis. Irresistable beats and a hip atmosphere make this a wildly popular destination. Beer €3.50. Mixed drinks €6. Open daily 9pm-5am. MC/V.

Palenque, Av. Blas Pascal (☎46 74 08). Cross Pte. de la Barqueta, turn left, and follow C. Materático Rey Pastor to the first big intersection. Turn left and look for the entrance on the right. Gigantic dance club, complete with 2 dance floors and a small ice skating rink (€3; includes skate rental). Dress to impress. Mainly *sevillano* university crowd. Beer €3. Mixed drinks €5. F-Sa cover €7, Th free. Open June-Sept. Th-Sa midnight-7am.

Isbiliyya, Po. de Cristóbal Colón 2 (☎21 04 60). Popular riverfront gay and lesbian bar with outdoor seating. Tu, Th, Su drag shows. Beer €2-2.50. Open daily 8pm-5am.

Tribal, Av. de los Descubrimientos, next to Pte. de la Barqueta. Popular discoteca plays American hip-hop, Latin favorites, and lots of reggaeton. W hip-hop nights draw an international crowd. Pitchers €5-10. Open W-Sa midnight-6am.

DAYTRIPS FROM SEVILLE

CÁDIZ

RENFE trains (☎956 25 43 01) go from the station at Pl. de Sevilla to: Barcelona (12hr., 2 per day, €73); Córdoba (3hr., 4 per day, €15.50); Madrid (5hr., 8am, €55-85); Seville (2hr., 12 per day, €8.50-20). Transportes Generales Comes buses (☎956 22 78 11) arrive at Pl. de la Hispanidad 1 from Seville (2hr., 14 per day, €10).

Cádiz (pop. 155,000) is renowned for its extravagant *Carnaval*, the only festival of its size and kind not suppressed during the Franco regime. Dazzling *Carnaval* makes Cádiz an essential stop on February itineraries, but the city offers golden **beaches** year-round. **Playa de la Caleta** is the most convenient to the old city, but better sand awaits in the new city; take bus #1 from Pl. España to Pl. Glorieta Ingeniero (€0.80), or walk along the *paseo* by the water (20-30min. from behind the cathedral) to reach gorgeous **Playa de la Victoria,** whose clean shore is a local favorite. Back in town, in Pl. de la Catedral, visit the museum in the gold-domed **cathedral** for treasures and art. (☎956 28 61 64. Cathedral and museum open Tu-F 10am-1:30pm and 4:30-7:30pm, Sa 10am-1:30pm. Both €4. W and F 7-8pm and Su 11am-1pm free.) To get to the **tourist office,** Pl. San Juan de Dios 11, from the bus station, walk 5min. down Av. Puerto with the port on your left; the plaza is after the park on your right. The staff offers free maps. (☎956 24 10 01. Open summer M-F 9am-2pm and 5-8pm; winter 9am-2pm and 4-6pm. Kiosk in front of office open daily June-Sept. 10am-1pm and 5-7:30pm; Oct.-May 10am-1:30pm and 4-6pm.)

ARCOS DE LA FRONTERA

Los Amarillos buses (☎956 70 49 77) run from C. Corregidores to Seville (2hr.; 7am, 5pm; €6.30). Transportes Generales Comes buses go to Cádiz (1½hr., 6 per day, €4.80) and Ronda (1¾hr., 3 per day, €6).

Peaceful and romantic, Arcos (pop. 33,000) is a prime example of a Spanish *pueblo blanco*. Wander through alleys of ruins and hanging flowers in the **old quarter** and marvel at the stunning view from **Plaza del Cabildo.** In the square is the **Basilica de Santa María de la Asunción,** a hodgepodge of architectural styles. (Open M-F 10am-1pm and 3:30-6:30pm, Sa 10am-2pm. €1.50.) The **Iglesia de San Pedro** stands on the site of an Arab fortress in the old quarter. A collection of religious paintings by Murillo, Ribera, and Zurbarán adorns the interior. (Open daily 10am-1:30pm. €1.) To reach the old quarter from the bus station, exit left, take the first left, and continue uphill on C. Josefa Moreno Seguro. Turn right on C. Muñoz Vásquez, continue until Pl. de España, then veer left onto C. Debajo del Coral, which becomes C. Corredera; the old quarter is 500m ahead. The **tourist office** is on Pl. del Cabildo. (☎956 70 22 64. Open mid-Mar. to mid-Oct. M-Sa 10am-2pm and 4-8pm, Su 10am-2pm; mid-Oct. to mid-Mar. M-Sa 10am-2pm and 3:30-7:30pm, Su 10am-2pm.)

RONDA

Trains (☎902 24 02 02) depart from Av. Alferez Provisional for: Granada (3hr., 3 per day, €10.30); Madrid (4½hr., 2 per day, €40-48.50); Málaga (2hr., 1 per day, €7.60). Buses (☎952 18 70 61) go from Pl. Concepción García Redondo 2, near Av. Andalucía, to Cádiz (4hr., 3 per day, €11.80) and Seville (2½hr., 3-5 per day, €9.30).

Ancient bridges, pretty views, and a famous bullring attract visitors to Ronda (pop. 35,000), which has all the charm of a small, medieval town with the amenities and cultural opportunities of a thriving city. A precipitous 100m gorge, carved by the Río Guadalevín, drops below the **Puente Nuevo,** opposite Pl. España. The views from the Puente Nuevo, and its neighboring **Puente Viejo** and **Puente San Miguel,** are unparalleled. Take the first left after crossing the Puente Nuevo to Cuesta de Santo Domingo 17, and descend the steep stairs of the **Casa Del Rey Moro** into the 14th-century water mine for an otherworldly view of the ravine. (☎952 18 72 00. Open daily 10am-8pm; in winter 10am-7pm. €4.) Bullfighting aficionados charge over to Ronda's **Plaza de Toros,** Spain's oldest bullring (est. 1785) and cradle of the modern *corrida*. In early September, the Pl. de Toros hosts *corridas goyescas* (bullfights in traditional costumes) as part of the **Feria de Ronda.** The small but comprehensive **Museo Taurino** traces the history of bullfighting. (☎952 87 15 39; www.rmcr.org. Bullring and museum open daily mid-Apr. to Oct. 10am-8pm; Nov.-Feb. 10am-6pm; Mar. to mid-Apr. 10am-7pm. €5. Museum audio tour €3.) The **tourist office** is at Po. Blas Infante, across from the bullring. (☎952 18 71 19. English spoken. Open June-Aug. M-F 9:30am-7:30pm, Sa-Su 10am-2pm and 3:30-6:30pm; Sept.-May M-F 9:30am-6:30pm, Sa-Su 10am-2pm and 3:30-6:30pm.)

SPAIN

GIBRALTAR

The craggy face of the Rock of Gibraltar emerges imposingly from the morning mist just off the southern shore of Spain. Ancient seafarers called "Gib" one of the Pillars of Hercules, believing it marked the end of the world. Among history's most contested plots of land, Gibraltar today is officially a self-governing British colony, though Spain continues to campaign for sovereignty. Gibraltar has a culture all its own, a curious enclave of not-quite-British, definitely-not-Spanish culture that makes it a sight worth visiting, despite being something of a tourist trap.

PHONE CODES	☎350 from the UK or the US. ☎9567 from Spain.

TRANSPORTATION AND PRACTICAL INFORMATION. **Buses** arrive in the Spanish border town of La Línea from: Algeciras (40min., every 30min., €1.70); Cádiz (3hr., 4 per day, €10.20); Granada (5hr., 2 per day, €17.60); Madrid (7hr., 2 per day, €23); Seville (6hr., 3 per day, €18.40). Turner & Co., 65/67 Irish Town St. (☎783 05), runs **ferries** to Tangier, Morocco (1¼hr.; 1 per day; £18/€32, under 12 £9/€16.20). Gibraltar's **airport** (GIB; ☎730 26) also sends daily 20min. flights to Morocco. Before heading to Gibraltar, make sure you have a valid passport. From the bus station, walk toward the Rock; the border is 5min. away. Catch bus #9 or 10 (£0.60/€1) or walk across the airport tarmac into town (20min.). Stay left on Av. Winston Churchill when the road forks. The **tourist office** is at Duke of Kent House, Cathedral Sq. (☎450 00; www.gibraltar.gi. Open M-F 9am-5:30pm.)

THE REAL DEAL. Although euros are accepted almost everywhere (except in pay phones and post offices), the **pound sterling (£)** is the preferred method of payment in Gibraltar. ATMs dispense money in pounds, and merchants and sights sometimes charge a higher price in euros than in the pound's exchange equivalent. Unless stated otherwise, assume an establishment will accept euros, although change is often given in British currency. The exchange rate fluctuates around £1 to €1.50. As of press date, **£1 = €1.47.**

ACCOMMODATIONS AND FOOD. Gibraltar is best as a daytrip. The few accommodations in the area are relatively pricey and often full, especially in the summer, and camping is illegal. **Emile Youth Hostel Gibraltar ❷,** Montague Bastian, behind Casemates Sq., has bunk beds and clean communal bathrooms. (☎511 06. Breakfast included. Luggage storage £1. Towels £1. Lockout 10:30am-4:30pm. Dorms £15/€25; doubles £34/€51.) Spending the night at La Línea across the border may be a cheaper option. International restaurants are easy to find, but you may choke on the prices. **Marks & Spencer** on Main St. has a small grocery/bakery with a selection of pre-packaged foods, baked goods, and a good exchange rate. (Open M-F 8:30am-8pm, Sa 10am-6pm, Su 10am-3pm. MC/V.)

SIGHTS. No trip to Gibraltar is complete without a visit to the legendary **Rock of Gibraltar.** About halfway up is the infamous **Apes' Den,** where Barbary Macaques cavort on the sides of rocks, the tops of taxis, and the heads of tourists. At the northern tip of the Rock, facing Spain, are the **Great Siege Tunnels.** Originally used to fend off a Franco-Spanish siege in the 18th century, the underground tunnels were expanded during WWII to span 53km. The eerie chambers of **St. Michael's Cave,** 500m from the siege tunnels, were cut into the rock by thousands of years of erosion. At the Gibraltar's southern tip, guarded by three machine guns and a lighthouse, **Europa Point** commands a view of the straits. (Cable car up the Rock daily every 10min. 9:30am-5:15pm. Combined ticket to all sights, including one-way cable car ride, £14.50/€21.50.)

COSTA DEL SOL

The Costa del Sol mixes rocky beaches with chic promenades and swank hotels. While some spots are over-developed and expensive, elsewhere the coast's stunning landscape remains untouched. Tourists swarm in summer, but nothing takes away from the main attraction: eight months of spring and four of summer.

MÁLAGA

☎952

Málaga (pop. 550,000) is the busiest city on the coast, and while its beaches are known more for bars than for natural beauty, the city has much to offer. While many see Málaga en route to other coastal stops, it is worth a day or two in its own right. Guarding the east end of Po. del Parque, the **Alcazaba** was originally a military fortress and royal palace for Moorish kings. (Open June-Aug. Tu-Su 9:30am-8pm; Sept.-May Tu-Sa 8:30am-7pm. €1.80, students €0.60.) Málaga's breathtaking **cathedral,** C. Molina Lario 4, has been nicknamed *La Manquita* (One-Armed Lady) in reference to the fact that one of its two towers was never completed. (☎22 03 45. Open M-F 10am-6:45pm, Sa 10am-5:45pm. Mass daily 9am. €3.50, includes audio tour.) Picasso's birthplace at Pl. de la Merced 15 is now home to the **Casa Natal y Fundación Picasso,** which organizes exhibitions, concerts, and lectures. Upstairs is a permanent collection on Picasso's life and works. (☎06 02 15. Open M-Sa 10am-8pm, Su 10am-2pm. €1, students free.)

One of the few spots in Málaga just for backpackers, friendly **Picasso's Corner ❷,** Pl. de la Aduana 2, third floor, boasts free Internet and an elegant bathroom. (☎21 22 87. Dorms €18; doubles €40. MC/V.) Sit amid stacks of books and magazines at **Café Con Libros ❶,** Pl. de la Merced 19, as you enjoy wholesome breakfasts for €1.50-3. (Open M 4pm-1am, Tu-Su 11am-1am.) RENFE (☎902 24 02 02) **trains** leave from Explanada de la Estación for: Barcelona (13hr.; 7am, 9pm; €50); Córdoba (2hr., 12 per day, €13); Madrid (5hr., 7 per day, €53); Seville (3hr., 5 per day, €13.60). **Buses** run from Po. de los Tilos (☎31 82 95), one block from the RENFE station along C. Roger de Flor, to: Cádiz (5hr., 5 per day, €18); Córdoba (3hr., 5 per day, €11); Granada (2hr., 17 per day, €8.10); Madrid (7hr., 12 per day, €18); Marbella (1½hr., every hr., €4.20); Ronda (3hr., 4 per day, €8.10); Seville (3hr., 11-12 per day, €13.10). To get to the city center from the bus station, exit right onto Callejones del Perchel, walk straight through the intersection with Av. de la Aurora, turn right on Av. de Andalucía, and cross Puente de Tetuán. From here, Alameda Principal leads into Pl. de la Marina, where the **tourist office** is located. (☎12 20 20. Open M-F 9am-7pm.) **Postal Code:** 29080.

GRANADA

☎958

Legend has it that in 1492, when Moorish ruler Boabdil fled Granada, Spain's last Muslim stronghold, his mother berated him for casting a longing look back at the Alhambra. "You do well to weep as a woman," she told him, "for what you could not defend as a man." The Albaicín, a maze of Moorish houses and twisting alleys, is Spain's best-preserved Arab quarter and the only part of the Muslim city to survive the *Reconquista.* Granada has grown into a university city infused with the energy of international students, backpackers, and Andalusian youth.

TRANSPORTATION

Trains: RENFE Station, Av. Andaluces (☎902 24 02 02; www.renfe.es). To: **Barcelona** (12-13hr., 1-2 per day, €50-51.50); **Madrid** (5-6hr., 2 per day, €30-34); **Seville** (4-5hr., 4 per day, €19).

SPAIN

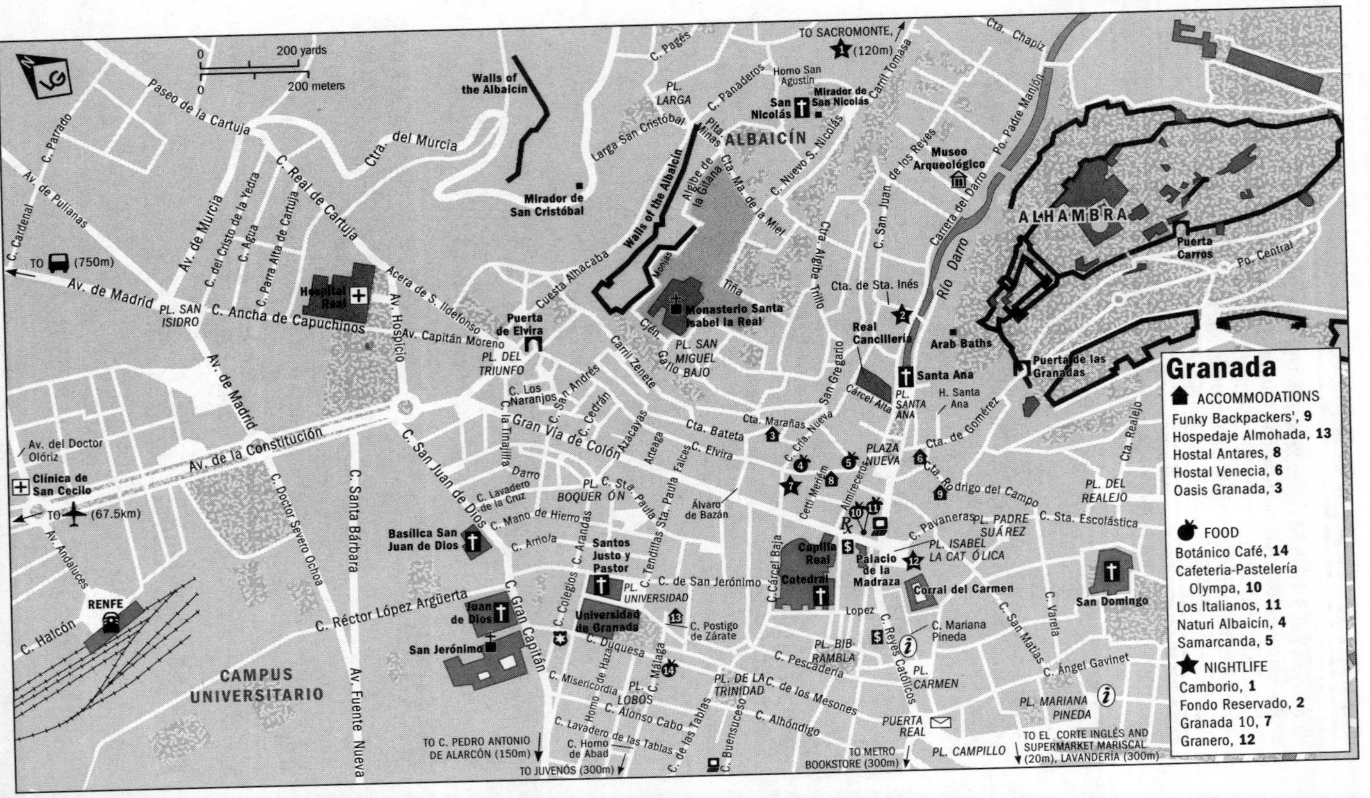
Granada
ACCOMMODATIONS
Funky Backpackers', 9
Hospedaje Almohada, 13
Hostal Antares, 8
Hostal Venecia, 6
Oasis Granada, 3
FOOD
Botánico Café, 14
Cafetería-Pastelería Olympa, 10
Los Italianos, 11
Naturi Albaicín, 4
Samarcanda, 5
NIGHTLIFE
Camborio, 1
Fondo Reservado, 2
Granada 10, 7
Granero, 12
ALHAMBRA
ALBAICÍN
Puerta Carros
Puerta de las Granadas
Arab Baths
Santa Ana
Real Cancillería
Museo Arqueológico
Mirador de San Nicolás
San Nicolás
Monasterio Santa Isabel la Real
Walls of the Albaicín
Mirador de San Cristóbal
Puerta de Elvira
Capilla Real
Catedral
Palacio de la Madraza
Corral del Carmen
San Domingo
Santos Justo y Pastor
Universidad de Granada
Basílica San Juan de Dios
Juan de Dios
San Jerónimo
Hospital Real
Clínica de San Cecilio
RENFE
CAMPUS UNIVERSITARIO
PLAZA NUEVA
PL. ISABEL LA CAT ÓLICA
PL. BIB-RAMBLA
PL. DE LA TRINIDAD
PL. DEL TRIUNFO
PL. SAN ISIDRO
PL. LARGA
PL. SAN MIGUEL BAJO
PL. DEL REALEJO
PL. MARIANA PINEDA
PL. CARMEN
PL. CAMPILLO
PL. UNIVERSIDAD
PL. LOBOS
PL. SANTA ANA
PL. PADRE SUÁREZ
PUERTA REAL
Gran Vía de Colón
C. Reyes Católicos
C. San Juan de Dios
Av. de la Constitución
Av. de Madrid
Av. Hospicio
C. Gran Capitán
C. Réctor López Argüerta
C. Santa Bárbara
Av. Fuente Nueva
C. Doctor Severo Ochoa
C. Real de Cartuja
C. Ancha de Capuchinos
Av. de Murcia
Paseo de la Cartuja
Av. de Pulianas
Av. Andaluces
C. Halcón
Río Darro
Carrera del Darro
Po. Padre Manjón
Po. Central
TO SACROMONTE, (120m)
TO EL CORTE INGLÉS AND SUPERMARKET MARISCAL (20m), LAVANDERÍA (300m)
TO METRO BOOKSTORE (300m)
TO JUVENÓS (300m)
TO C. PEDRO ANTONIO DE ALARCÓN (150m)
TO (750m)
TO (67.5km)
200 yards
200 meters

Buses: The bus station is on the outskirts of Granada on Ctra. de Madrid, near C. Arzobispo Pedro de Castro. **Alsa** (☎902 42 22 42) goes to: **Alicante** (6hr., 6 per day, €25); **Barcelona** (14hr., 6 per day, €60); **Valencia** (10hr., 6 per day, €36.50). **Alsina Graells** (☎18 54 80) runs to: **Cádiz** (4hr., 4 per day, €26); **Córdoba** (3hr., 7 per day, €11-12); **Madrid** (5hr., 12-16 per day, €14.20); **Málaga** (2hr., 16 per day, €8.30); **Marbella** (2hr., 8 per day, €13); **Seville** (3hr., 10 per day, €16.50).

Public Transportation: Pick up a free bus map at the tourist office. Important buses include: Alhambra bus #30 from Gran Vía de Cólon or Pl. Nueva to the Alhambra; #31 from Gran Vía or Pl. Nueva to the Albaicín; #10 from the bus station to C. de Ronda, C. Recogidas, and C. Acera de Darro; #3 from the bus station to Av. de la Constitución, Gran Vía, and Pl. Isabel la Católica. Rides €0.95, *bonobus* (10 rides) €5.20.

ORIENTATION AND PRACTICAL INFORMATION

The geographic center of Granada is the small **Plaza Isabel la Católica,** at the intersection of the city's two main arteries, **Calle de los Reyes Católicos** and **Gran Vía de Colón.** The **cathedral** is on Gran Vía. Two blocks uphill on C. de los Reyes Católicos sits **Plaza Nueva.** Downhill on C. de los Reyes Católicos lies Pl. Carmen, site of the **Ayuntamiento** and **Puerta Real.** The **Alhambra** commands the hill above Pl. Nueva.

Tourist Office: Junta de Andalucía, C. Mariana Pineda (☎22 59 90). Posts bus and train schedules. Open M-Sa 9am-7pm, Su 10am-2pm. **Oficina Provincial,** Pl. Mariana Pineda 10 (☎24 71 28; www.turismodegranada.org). English spoken. From Pta. Real, turn right onto C. Angel Ganivet, then take a right 2 blocks later to reach the plaza. Open M-F 9am-8pm, Sa 10am-7pm, Su 10am-4pm.

American Express: C. de los Reyes Católicos 31 (☎22 45 12), between Pl. Isabel la Católica and Pta. Real. Open M-F 9am-1:30pm and 2-9pm, Sa 10am-2pm.

Luggage Storage: 24hr. storage at the train station (€3).

Police: C. Duquesa 21 (☎80 80 00). English spoken.

Medical Services: Clínica de San Cecilio, C. Dr. Olóriz 16 (☎28 02 00), toward Jaén.

Internet Access: NavegaWeb, C. de los Reyes Católicos 55. English spoken. €1.50 per hr., students €1. 5hr. *Bono* cards (€5/4.50); 10hr. (€9/8). Open daily 10am-11pm.

Post Office: Pta. Real (☎22 48 35). *Lista de Correos* and fax service. Open M-F 8:30am-8:30pm, Sa 9:30am-2pm. **Postal Code:** 18009.

ACCOMMODATIONS

Hostels line **Cuesta de Gomérez, Plaza Trinidad,** and **Gran Vía.** Call ahead during *Semana Santa.*

Oasis Granada, Cuesta de Gomérez 2, 3rd fl. (☎22 39 87). Exactly what a youth hostel should be. Modern facilities include free wireless Internet, satellite TV, bath, and fridges in each suite. Weekly parties and daily activities like tapas tours and pub crawls. Breakfast included. 3-course dinner (often cooked outside on the hostel's Argentine grille) €3.50. Dorms €15; doubles €40. MC/V. ❶

Hospedaje Almohada, C. Postigo de Zarate 4 (☎20 74 46 or 627 47 25 53). A communal atmosphere will make you feel at home. Laundry €3. Dorms €14; singles €16; doubles €30; triples €40. Cash only. ❶

Funky Backpackers', Cuesta de Rodrigo del Campo 13 (☎22 14 62). The young, friendly staff at this hostel hangs out with travelers in the living room or on the roof terrace. Breakfast included. Free lockers and Internet. Dorms €16; doubles €36. MC/V. ❷

Hostal Venecia, Cuesta de Gomérez 2, 3rd fl. (☎22 39 87). Sergio and María del Carmen offer cozy rooms, attentive service, and morning tea or coffee. Singles €15; doubles €28; triples €39; quads €52. Cash only. ❷

Hostal Antares, C. Cetti Meriém 10 (☎22 83 13; www.hostalantares.com). All bright, clean rooms have TV and A/C. Singles €18; doubles €28, with bath €36. Cash only. ❷

SPAIN

FOOD

Cheap North African cuisine can be found around the Albaicín, while more typical *menús* await in Pl. Nueva and Pl. Trinidad. The adventurous eat well in Granada—try *tortilla sacromonte* (omelette with calf brains, bull testicles, ham, shrimp, and veggies). Picnickers can gather fresh fruit, vegetables, and meat at the large indoor **market** on Pl. San Agustín. (Open M-Sa 9am-3pm.)

Naturi Albaicín, C. Calderería Nueva 10 (☎22 73 83; www.vivagranada.com/naturi). Excellent vegetarian cuisine served in a serene Moroccan ambience. No alcohol served. *Menús* €6.90-8.30. Open M-Th and Sa 1-4pm and 7-11pm; F 7-11pm. MC/V. ❷

Cafeteria-Pasteleria Olympia, Gran Vía 4 (☎22 40 34). Jam-packed with locals at almost any time of day for unbeatable, hearty Spanish breakfast. Stand at the bar or sit in the air-conditioned *salón.* Breakfast €1.50-3. Pastries €0.30-2. Cash only. ❶

Botánico Café, C. Málaga 3 (☎27 15 98), 2 blocks from Pl. Trinidad. This trendy restaurant draws in fashionable students for fusion cuisine. Appetizers €5-10. Entrees €6-14. Open M-Th and Su noon-1am, F-Sa noon-2am. MC/V. ❸

Los Italianos, Gran Vía 4 (☎22 40 34). Very tasty ice cream for extremely affordable prices. Cups and cones from €0.50. Open daily 9am-3am. Cash only. ❶

Samarcanda, C. Calderería Vieja 3 (☎21 00 04). Delicious Lebanese food. Entrees €10. Open M-Tu and Th-Su 1-4:30pm and 7:30pm-midnight. MC/V. ❷

SIGHTS

THE ALHAMBRA. From the streets of Granada, the Alhambra appears blocky and practical. Up close, you will discover elaborate and detailed architecture that unites water, light, wood, stucco, and ceramics in a fortress-palace of rich aesthetic and symbolic grandeur. The age-old saying goes: *"Si mueres sin ver la Alhambra, no has vivido."* (If you die without seeing the Alhambra, you have not lived.) Follow signs to the *Palacio Nazaries* to see the **Alcázar,** a 14th-century royal palace full of stalactite archways and sculpted fountains. The walls of the *Patio del Cuarto Dorado* are topped by the shielded windows of the harem. Off the far side of the patio, archways open onto the *Cuarto Dorado,* whose carved wooden ceiling is inlaid with ivory and mother-of-pearl. From the top of the patio, glimpse the 14th-century *Fachada de Serallo,* the palace's intricately carved facade. In the *Sala de los Abencerrajes,* Boabdil had the throats of 37 sons of the Abencerrajes family slit after one of them allegedly had amorous encounters with the sultana. Rust-colored stains in the basin are said to be traces of the massacre.

Over a bridge, across the *Callejón de los Cipreses* and the shady *Callejón de las Adelfas,* are the vibrant blossoms, towering cypresses, and streaming waterways of **El Generalife,** the sultan's vacation retreat. Over the centuries, the estate passed through private hands until it was finally repatriated in 1931. The two buildings of El Generalife, the *Palacio* and the *Sala Regia,* connect across the *Patio de la Acequia,* embellished with a narrow pool fed by fountains.

When the Christians drove the first Nasrid King Alhamar from the Albaicín to this more strategic hill, he built the series of rust-colored brick towers which form the **Alcazaba** (fortress). A dark, spiraling staircase leads to the *Torre de la Vela,* where visitors have a 360° view of Granada and the surrounding mountains. Compared to the rest of the Alhambra, the Alcazaba is the least impressive.

After the Reconquista drove the Moors from Spain, Ferdinand and Isabella restored the Alcázar. Only two generations later, Emperor Charles V demolished part of it to make way for his **Palacio.** Although it is incongruous with the surrounding Moorish splendor, scholars concede that the palace is one of the most beautiful

Renaissance buildings in Spain. *(Walk up Cuesta de Gomérez from Pl. Nueva (20min.), or take the quick Alhambra minibus from Pl. Nueva (every 5min., €1).* ☎ *22 15 03, reservations 902 22 44 60; online reservations www.alhambratickets.com. Open Apr.-Sept. daily 8:30am-8pm; Oct.-Mar. M-Sa 9am-5:45pm. Night visits June-Sept. Tu, Th, Sa 10-11:30pm; Oct.-May Sa 8-10pm. €10. Worthwhile English-language audio tour €3. Tickets and audio tour cash only; credit cards accepted for online reservations. Admission is limited, so arrive early or reserve tickets in advance at local banks (reservation fee €0.88) or online. Enter the Palace of the Nasrids (Alcázar) during the time specified on your ticket, but stay as long as you wish.)*

THE ALBAICÍN. A labyrinth of steep, narrow alleys, the Albaicín was the only Moorish neighborhood to escape the torches of the *Reconquista*. After the fall of the Alhambra, a small Muslim population remained here until their expulsion in the 17th century. Today, with its abundance of North African cuisine, outdoor bazaars blasting Arabic music, tea houses, and the mosque near Pl. San Nicolás, the Albaicín attests to the persistence of Islamic influence in Andalucía. The best way to explore this maze is to proceed along Carrera del Darro off Pl. Santa Ana, climb the Cuesta del Chapiz on the left, then wander through the Muslim ramparts and gates. On Pl. Santa Ana, the 16th-century **Real Cancillería,** with its beautiful arcaded patio and stalactite ceiling, was the Christians' Ayuntamiento. Farther uphill are the 11th-century **Arab baths.** *(Carrera del Darro 31.* ☎ *02 78 00. Open Tu-Sa 10am-2pm. Free.)* The **mirador** adjacent to **Iglesia de San Nicolás** offers the best view of the Alhambra. *(From C. Elvira, go up C. Calderería Nueva to C. San Gregorio and continue uphill past Pl. Algibe de Trillo, where it becomes Cta. Algibe de Trillo. At Pl. Camino, take a left on Cta. Tomasa and a left on Atarazana Cta. Cabras. The mirador will be on your right.)* Although generally safe, the Albaicín is disorienting and should be approached with caution at night. *(Bus #12 runs from beside the cathedral to C. Pagés at the top of the Albaicín.)*

CAPILLA REAL. Downhill from the Alhambra's Arab splendor, Ferdinand and Isabella's private chapel exemplifies Christian Granada. During their prosperous reign, the Catholic Monarchs funneled almost a quarter of the royal income into the chapel's construction (1504-1521) to build a proper burial place. Intricate Gothic masonry and meticulously rendered figurines, as well as **La Reja,** the gilded iron grille of Master Bartolomé, grace the couple's resting place. The adjacent **Sacristía** houses Isabella's private **art collection** and the **royal jewels.** *(The Capilla is on C. Oficios through the Pta. Real off Gran Vía.* ☎ *22 92 39. Capilla and Sacristía open M-Sa 10:30am-1pm and 4-7pm, Su 11am-1pm and 4-5pm. €2.50 for both.)*

CATHEDRAL. Behind the Capilla Real and the Sacristía is Granada's cathedral. After the *Reconquista*, construction of the cathedral began upon the smoldering embers of Granada's largest mosque. Outside, Monday through Saturday, vendors sell spices and tea leaves for every taste and malady. *(☎ 22 29 59. Cathedral open Apr.-Sept. M-Sa 10:45am-1:30pm and 4-7pm, Su 4-7pm; Oct.-Mar. M-Sa 10:30am-1:30pm and 3:30-6:30pm, Su 11am-1:30pm. Market open early morning until about 8pm. Cathedral €2.50.)*

NIGHTLIFE

Granada's "free tapas with a drink" tradition lures students and tourists out to its many pubs and bars. Great tapas bars can be found off the side streets near Pl. Nueva. The most boisterous nightspots belong to **Calle Pedro Antonio de Alarcón,** between Pl. Albert Einstein and Ancha de Gracia, while hip new bars and clubs line **Calle Elvira** from Cárcel to C. Cedrán. Gay bars cluster around Carrera del Darro. The *Guía del Ocio*, sold at newsstands (€1), lists clubs, pubs, and cafes.

Camborio, Camino del Sacromonte 48 (☎ 22 12 15). Walk 20min. uphill from Pl. Nueva, or take nightbus #31 before 2am. Pop music echoes from dance floors to rooftop patio. Great view. Beer €1.80-3. Mixed drinks €5-6. Cover F-Sa €5. Open Tu-Sa 11pm-dawn.

Granero, Pl. Luis Rosales (☎22 89 79). A new-age salsa bar pulsing with energy and local style. Beer €2.50. Mixed drinks €6. Open M-Th and Su 8am-3am, F-Sa 8am-4am.

Granada 10, C. Cárcel Baja 3 (☎22 40 01). Movie theater by evening (shows at 8, 10pm), raging dance club by night. Flashy and opulent. No sneakers or sportswear. Open M-Th and Su 12:30am-4am, F-Sa 12:30am-5am.

Fondo Reservado, Cuesta de Sta. Inés, off Carrera del Darro. Gay-friendly bar with a trendy crowd. Beer €2.60. Mixed drinks €4-5. Open Tu-Th 11pm-3am, F-Sa 11pm-4am.

EASTERN SPAIN

Rich soil and famous orange groves, fed by Moorish irrigation systems, have earned Eastern Spain (Valencia) the nickname *Huerta de España* (Spain's Orchard). Dunes, sandbars, jagged promontories, and lagoons mark the grand coastline, while lovely fountains and pools grace carefully landscaped public gardens in Valencian cities. The famed rice dish *paella* was born in this region.

ALICANTE (ALICANT) ☎965

While undboutedly a Spanish city in every way, there is an extra sparkle and unique energy to Alicante (pop. 306,000). The residents are friendlier, the nightlife is livelier, and even the beaches seem sunnier. Alicante is an unforgettable stop along the Mediterranean that is not to be missed.

TRANSPORTATION AND PRACTICAL INFORMATION. RENFE **trains** (☎902 24 02 02) run from Estación Término on Av. Salamanca to: Barcelona (4½-6hr., 5-6 per day, €45.50-74.50); Madrid (4hr., 4-9 per day, €37-60.50); Valencia (1½hr., 10 per day, €10.80-23.50). **Buses** leave C. Portugal 17 (☎13 07 00) for: Barcelona (7hr., 15 per day, €35.66-42.70); Granada (6hr., 10 per day, €24-30); Madrid (5hr., 15 per day, €24-32); Málaga (8hr., 5 per day, €32.60-40); Seville (10hr., 11:45pm, €42); Valencia (2½hr., 14-21 per day, €15.35-17.55). The **tourist office** is at C. Portugal 17 (☎92 98 02; www.alicanteturismo.com. Open M-Sa 9am-2pm and 4-8pm.) Use the **Internet** at **Fundación BanCaja,** Rbla. Méndez Nuñez 4, 2nd fl. (1hr. free with ISIC. Open M-F 10am-2pm and 5-9pm, Sa 9am-2pm.) **Postal Code:** 03070.

ACCOMMODATIONS AND FOOD. Cheap hostels are everywhere and easy to find. For simple, sunny rooms with A/C, try **Residencia La Milagrosa ❷**, C. Villa Vieja, which boasts a rooftop terrace for socializing and admiring the great view of the castle. (☎21 69 18. Laundry €2. Internet €1 per hr. June-Aug. dorms €20; Sept.-May €15. Cash only.) **Kebap ❶**, Av. Dr. Gadea 5, has the best Middle Eastern food in Alicante. (☎13 28 54. Entrees €5.70-7. Open M-Th and Su 1-4pm and 8pm-midnight; F-Sa 1-4pm and 8pm-1am. MC/V.) For a more local taste, try the family-run bar-restaurants in the *casco antiguo*. Buy groceries at **Supermarket Mercadona,** C. Alvarez Sereix 5, off Av. Federico Soto. (☎21 58 94. Open M-Sa 9am-9pm.)

SIGHTS AND NIGHTLIFE. With drawbridges, dark passageways, and hidden tunnels, the ancient **Castell de Santa Bárbara** keeps silent guard over Alicante's beach. (☎26 31 31. Open daily Apr.-Sept. 10am-7:30pm; Oct.-Mar. 9am-6:30pm. Elevator €2.40.) The **Museu Arqueológico Provincial de Alicante,** Pl. Dr. Gomez Ulls, beautifully showcases artifacts from a variety of periods, including an entire hall dedicated to objects found at sea. (☎14 90 00; www.marqalicante.com. Open Tu-Sa 10am-7pm, Su 10am-2pm. €3, students €1.50.) Alicante's **Playa del Postiguet** attracts beach-lovers, as do nearby **Playa de San Juan** (TAM bus #21, 22, or 31) and **Playa del Mutxavista** (TAM bus #21). Buses (€0.80) depart every 15min.

Nightlife in Alicante is fantastic. Most begin their night bar-hopping in the *casco antiguo*, locally referred to as "el barrio." The complex of bars that overlooks the water in Alicante's **main port** and the discos on **Puerto Nuevo** tend to fill up around 2:30am. Don't miss **Z-Klub,** C. Coloma 3, with its chic decor and gorgeous mixed crowd. Z-Klub is well worth the cover. (☎98 01 36. Cover €10-15, includes 1 drink. Open Th-Sa midnight-6am.) For an even crazier time, the **Trensnochador** night train runs from Estación Marina to disco gardens that stay packed until 6am (July-Aug. M-Th and Su 4 per night 9pm-5am, F-Sa every hr. 9pm-5am; round-trip €4.20). During the hedonistic **Festival de Sant Joan** (June 20-29), *fogueres* (paper mâché effigies) are erected and then burned in the streets during *la Cremà;* afterwards, firefighters soak everyone during *la Banyà* and the party continues until dawn.

VALENCIA

☎963

Valencia's white beaches and palm tree-lined avenues are noticeably less touristed than Spain's other major cities. And yet, it seems to possess all the best aspects of its sisters: the energy of Madrid, the vibrant spirit of Alicante, the offbeat sophistication of Barcelona, and the warmth of Seville. In a city where ultra-modern styles go hand in hand with the oldest traditions, there is truly something for everyone.

TRANSPORTATION AND PRACTICAL INFORMATION. **Trains** arrive at Estació del Nord, C. Xàtiva 24 (☎52 02 02). RENFE (24hr. ☎902 24 02 02) runs to: Alicante (2-3hr., 12 per day, €9.40-23.50); Barcelona (3hr., 8-16 per day, €29-35.50); Madrid (3½hr., 12 per day, €19.75-39); and Seville (8½hr., 11:20am, €43.50). **Buses** (☎49 72 22) go from Av. Menéndez Pidal 13 to: Alicante via the Costa Blanca (4½hr., 10-30 per day, €15.70-17.55); Barcelona (4½hr., 19 per day, €21); Granada (8hr., 9 per day 4:45am-2:30am, €35.45-42.80); Madrid (4hr., 13 per day, €20.40-25.15); Málaga (11hr., 9 per day, €43.60-52.80); Seville (11hr., 3-4 per day, €42.60-49.80). Trasmediterránea **ferries,** Estació Marítima (☎902 45 46 45; www.trasmediterranea.com) sail to the Balearic Islands (p. 974). Take bus #1 or 2 from the bus station. The main **tourist office,** C. de la Paz 48, has branches at the train station and at C. Poeta Querol. (☎98 64 22; www.valencia.es. Open M-F 9am-6:30pm, Sa 10am-6:30pm.) **Ono,** C. San Vicente Mártir 22, has **Internet.** (☎28 19 02. €1-4 per hr. depending on time of day. Open M-F 9am-1am, Sa-Su 10am-1am.) The **post office** is at Pl. del Ajuntament 24. (☎10 27 97. Open M-F 8:30am-8:30pm, Sa 9:30am-2pm.) **Postal Code:** 46080.

ACCOMMODATIONS AND FOOD. The best lodging deals are around **Plaça del Ajuntament** and **Plaça del Mercat.** The **Home Youth Hostel ❶,** C. Lonja 4, is across from the Mercado Central, on a side street off Pl. Dr. Collado. A lounge and beer vending machine make this the most social hostel in town. (☎91 62 29; www.likeathome.net. Linen included. Laundry €5.50. Internet €0.50 per 15min. Dorms €14; singles €21.) From Pl. Ayuntamiento, turn right on C. Barcas, left on C. Poeta Querol, and right on C. Salvá to reach **Pensión Paris ❷,** C. Salvá 12, and its clean, sunny rooms with balconies. (☎52 67 66. Most rooms have sinks. Linen included. Singles €19; doubles €29, with shower €32; triples €41/45.)

Paella is the most famous of Valencia's 200 rice dishes; try as many of them as you can. **Sugar Cafe ❶,** C. de la Paz 1, one block from Pl. de la Reina, is sophisticated restaurant serving sandwiches (€2-2.75), salads (€3.50-3.95) and beer (€1.85-3.45) to the sound of smooth jazz. (☎15 38 47. Open M-F 8:30am-9:30pm, Sa 10am-2pm.) Dine with some of the world's finest art at **Cafeteria N'Scala ❷,** C. Sant Pío V 9, at the Museu Provincial de Belles Artes. Four-course meals (€8.50 inside, €11 on the terrace) include coffee or tea, bread, one tapa, two entrees, and dessert. (☎69 15 99. Open Tu-Su 10am-7:30pm.) The **Mercado Central** sells fresh fish, meat, and fruit

UP IN SMOKE

or one week in March, fires rage n the streets of Valencia. The mell of smoke drifts in and out of alcony doors and gunshots ring ut throughout the city. This isn't he Apocalyse; it's Las Fallas, one f Spain's biggest and most elab- rate festivals. *Papier mâché,* ireworks, and gunpowder fill the treets and the city's population wells to six times its normal size; ittle kids and firecrackers find ach other; women young and old dorn intricately beautiful gowns nd alien-like headwear to com- ete for *fallera,* Queen of Las Fal- as. Special *fallas* commissions re set up to build elaborate effi- ies of wood, cardboard, *papier nâché,* wax, and whatever else hey can find; these amazingly reative (and large) constructions ommemorate the events of the ast year, poke fun at public offi- ials and celebrities, and are ach burned to the ground on St. oseph's day, which marks the nd of the festival. At midnight n March 19, up to 300 fires are it around the city, and the *fallas* o up in smoke; the prize-winning ffigies are the last to go, and at east one is always saved for pos- erity in the Fallas Museum in Pl. le Monteolivete. Then it's all over: he ash is swept away, the *papier nâché* is saved for another day, nd fire-hungry *valencianos* start ounting the days until next year.

(including Valencia's famous oranges) from an Art Nouveau building on Pl. del Mercat. (Open M-Sa 7am-3pm. Cash only.) For groceries, try the basement of **El Corte Inglés,** C. Colón. (Open M-Sa 10am-10pm.)

SIGHTS. Most sights line Río Turia or cluster near Pl. de la Reina. EMT bus #5, dubbed the **Bus Turistic** makes a loop around the old town sights. (☎15 85 15. €1.) Take bus #35 from Pl. Ayuntamiento to reach the ultra-modern and thoroughly fascinating **Ciutat de les Arts i de les Ciències.** The complex is divided into five large spaces including **L'Hemisfèric** with an IMAX theater and planetarium, the **Museu de les Ciències Príncipe Felipe,** an interactive playground for science and technology fiends, and **L'Oceanogràfic,** an enormous aquarium which recreates different aquatic environments. The **Palau de les Arts** houses performance and practice space, while the **L'Umbracle** is an enormous garden terrace and sculpture garden. (☎902 10 00 31; www.cac.es. Shows at L'Hemisfèric IMAX and planetarium every hour M-Th 11am-7pm, F-Sa 11am-9pm. Museum open mid-June to Sept. 14 daily 10am-8pm; Mar. to mid-June and mid-Sept. to Jan. M-F and Su 10am-6pm, Sa 10am-8pm. L'Oceanogràfic open Aug. daily 10am-midnight; mid-June to Aug. and Sept. daily 10am-8pm; Jan. 2 to mid-June and mid-Sept. to Jan. M-F, Su 10am-6pm, Sa 10am-8pm. Combination tickets for the entire complex €28.80.) The 13th-century **Catedral** in Pl. de la Reina is an impressive mix of Romanesque, Gothic, and Baroque architecture. Catch incredible views of Valencia's skyline atop the **Miguelete,** the cathedral tower. (☎91 01 89. Cathedral open daily 7:30am-1pm and 4:30-8:30pm. Closes earlier in winter. Tower open daily 10am-1pm and 4:30-7pm. Cathedral free. Tower €2.) The **Museu de la Catedral** squeezes an impressive number of treasures into three tiny rooms. (☎91 81 27. Open Mar.-Nov. M-Sa 10am-1pm and 4:30-6pm, Su 10am-1pm; Dec.-Feb. daily 10am-1pm. €2.) Across the river, the **Museu Provincial de Belles Artes,** C. Sant Pío V, displays superb 14th- to 16th-century Valencian art and is home to El Greco's *San Juan Bautista,* Velázquez's self-portrait, and a number of works by Goya. (☎60 57 93. Open Tu-Sa 10am-8pm. Free.) Next door, check out the gorgeous **Jardines del Real** (€3, students €1.50). West across the river, the **Institut Valencià d'Art Modern** (IVAM), C. Guillem de Castro 118, lets you get up close to 20th-century masterpieces. (☎86 30 00. Open Tu-Su 10am-10pm. €2, students €1. Su free.)

ENTERTAINMENT AND NIGHTLIFE. The most popular beaches are **Las Arenas** and **Malvarrosa.** Get there on bus #20, 21, 22, or 23. To get to the more attractive **Salér,** 14km from the city, take an Autocares

Herca bus from the intersection of Gran Vía de Germanias and C. Sueca. (☎49 12 50. 25min., every hr. 7am-10pm, €1.) Bars and pubs abound in the El Carme district, while discos dominate the university area. The gay and lesbian scene centers on **Calle Quart** and around **Plaza Vicente Iborra.** Follow C. Bolsería out of Pl. del Mercat to guzzle *agua de Valencia* (orange juice, champagne, and vodka) at outdoor terraces in Pl. Tossal. In El Carme, **Bolsería Café,** C. Bolsería 41, is packed with only with the beautiful and very cool. (☎91 89 03. Mixed drinks €6. W hip hop, Sa-Su house. Open daily 7pm-3:30am.) **Venial,** C. Quart 34, is a popular gay club with a huge dance floor. Try the gin and tonic—it glows in the dark. (☎91 73 56. Beer €4. Mixed drinks €6. €10 cover includes 1 drink. Open daily 1-7:30am.) For more info, consult the weekly *Qué y Dónde* (€1), available at newsstands, the weekly entertainment supplement *La Cartelera* (€0.75), or the free *24/7 Valencia*, available at hostels and cafes everywhere. The most famous festival in Valencia is **Las Fallas** (Mar. 12-19), which culminates with the burning of gigantic papier-mâché effigies.

NORTHEASTERN SPAIN

Northeastern Spain encompasses the country's most avidly regionalistic areas. From rocky Costa Brava to chic Barcelona, the prosperous Cataluña is graced with the nation's richest resources. However, Cataluña isn't the only reason to head northeast. The area is also home to the awesome mountains of the Pyrenees, the running bulls of Navarra, the industrious cities of Aragón, the beautiful coasts of Basque Country, and the crazy parties of the Balearic Islands.

BARCELONA ☎93

From the urban carnival of Las Ramblas to buildings with no straight lines, from wild festivals to even wilder nightlife, Barcelona pushes the limits in everything it does—with amazing results. The center of the whimsical and daring *Modernisme* architectural movement and once home to Pablo Picasso and Joan Miró, the city is grounded in an alternate reality through its art. Yet Barcelona's draw extends beyond its artistic merits. Its residents exhibit the same energy when it comes to fashion, food, and above all, hospitality. Since the end of Franco's oppressive regime, Barcelona has led the autonomous region of Cataluña in a cultural resurgence. The result is a city of striking colors and shapes. Don't worry if you don't speak Spanish—neither does Barcelona.

INTERCITY TRANSPORTATION

Flights: El Prat de Llobregat Airport (BCN; ☎298 3838; www.barcelona-airport.com), 13km southwest of Barcelona. To get to the central Pl. Catalunya, take a **RENFE** train (17min. to Estació Barcelona-Sants, 23min. to Pl. Catalunya; every 30min.; €2.30) or the **Aerobus** (☎415 6020; 30min., every 12-13min., €3.60).

Trains: Barcelona has 2 main train stations. **Estació Barcelona-Sants,** in Pl. Països Catalans (M: Sants-Estació), is the main terminal. **Estació França,** on Av. Marquès de l'Argentera (M: Barceloneta), serves regional destinations and some international arrivals. **RENFE** (Spain ☎902 24 02 02, elsewhere 934 90 11 22; www.renfe.es) has extensive service in Spain and Europe. Trains to: **Bilbao** (8-9hr.; 12:30, 10:30pm; €35-44); **Madrid** (5-9hr., 7 per day, €34-59); **Seville** (10-12hr., 3 per day, €50-78); **Valencia** (3-5hr., 15 per day, €29-35). 20% discount on round-trip tickets.

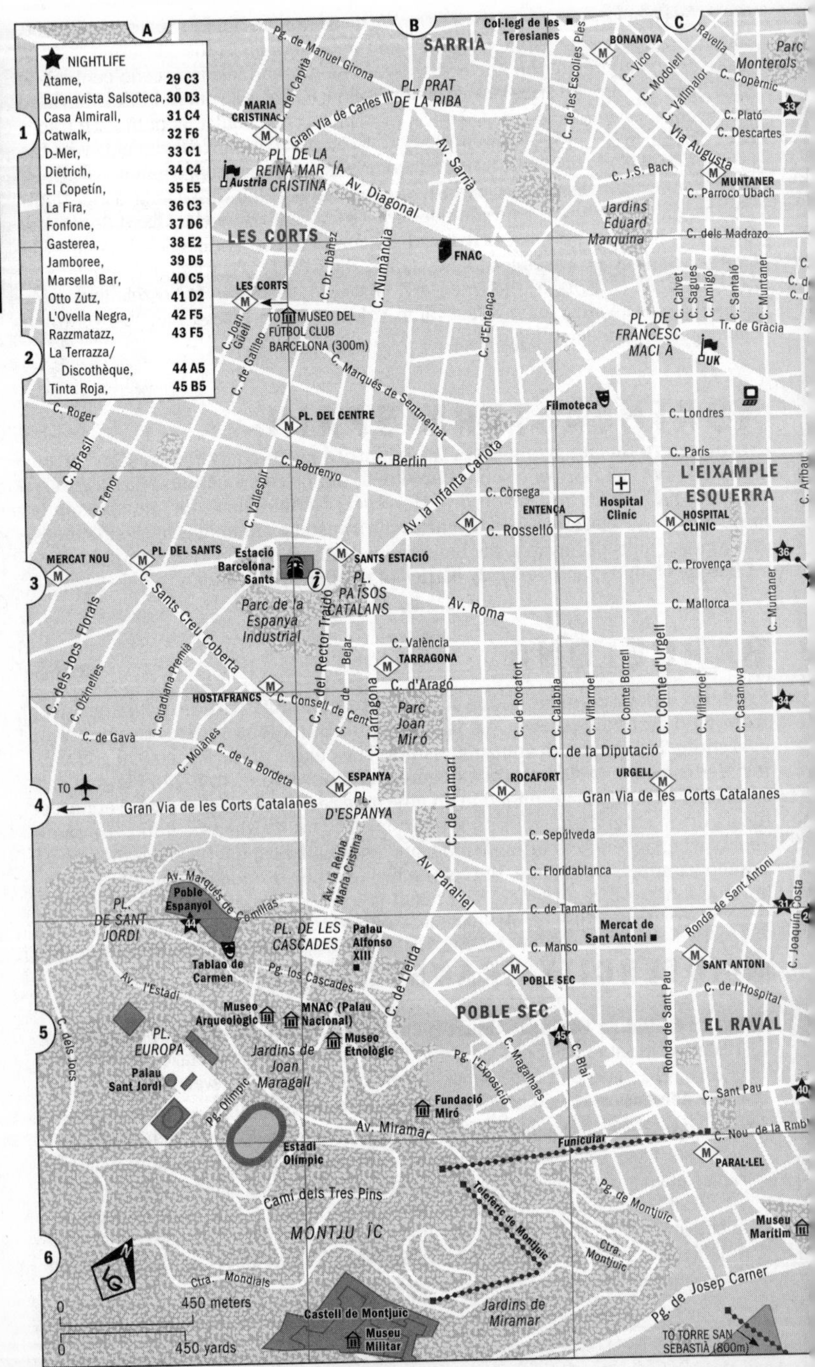
NIGHTLIFE
Àtame, 29 C3
Buenavista Salsoteca, 30 D3
Casa Almirall, 31 C4
Catwalk, 32 F6
D-Mer, 33 C1
Dietrich, 34 C4
El Copetín, 35 E5
La Fira, 36 C3
Fonfone, 37 D6
Gasterea, 38 E2
Jamboree, 39 D5
Marsella Bar, 40 C5
Otto Zutz, 41 D2
L'Ovella Negra, 42 F5
Razzmatazz, 43 F5
La Terrazza/ Discothèque, 44 A5
Tinta Roja, 45 B5
SARRIÀ
Col·legi de les Teresianes
BONANOVA
Parc Monterols
PL. PRAT DE LA RIBA
MARIA CRISTINA
Gran Via de Carles III
PL. DE LA REINA MARÍA CRISTINA
Austria
Av. Diagonal
Av. Sarrià
Via Augusta
MUNTANER
Jardins Eduard Marquina
LES CORTS
FNAC
TO MUSEO DEL FÚTBOL CLUB BARCELONA (300m)
PL. DE FRANCESC MACIÀ
UK
Filmoteca
PL. DEL CENTRE
C. Berlin
L'EIXAMPLE ESQUERRA
ENTENÇA
Hospital Clínic
HOSPITAL CLINIC
C. Rosselló
MERCAT NOU
PL. DEL SANTS
Estació Barcelona-Sants
SANTS ESTACIÓ
PL. PAÏSOS CATALANS
Parc de la Espanya Industrial
Av. Roma
TARRAGONA
HOSTAFRANCS
Parc Joan Miró
C. de la Diputació
ESPANYA
PL. D'ESPANYA
ROCAFORT
URGELL
Gran Via de les Corts Catalanes
TO
PL. DE SANT JORDI
Poble Espanyol
PL. DE LES CASCADES
Palau Alfonso XIII
Tablao de Carmen
Mercat de Sant Antoni
SANT ANTONI
POBLE SEC
Museo Arqueològic
MNAC (Palau Nacional)
Museo Etnològic
PL. EUROPA
Palau Sant Jordi
Jardins de Joan Maragall
EL RAVAL
Fundació Miró
Av. Miramar
Funicular
Estadi Olímpic
PARAL·LEL
Telefèric de Montjuïc
Camí dels Tres Pins
MONTJUÏC
Museu Marítim
Jardins de Miramar
Castell de Montjuïc
Museu Militar
Pg. de Josep Carner
TO TORRE SAN SEBASTIÀ (800m)
0 450 meters
0 450 yards

SPAIN

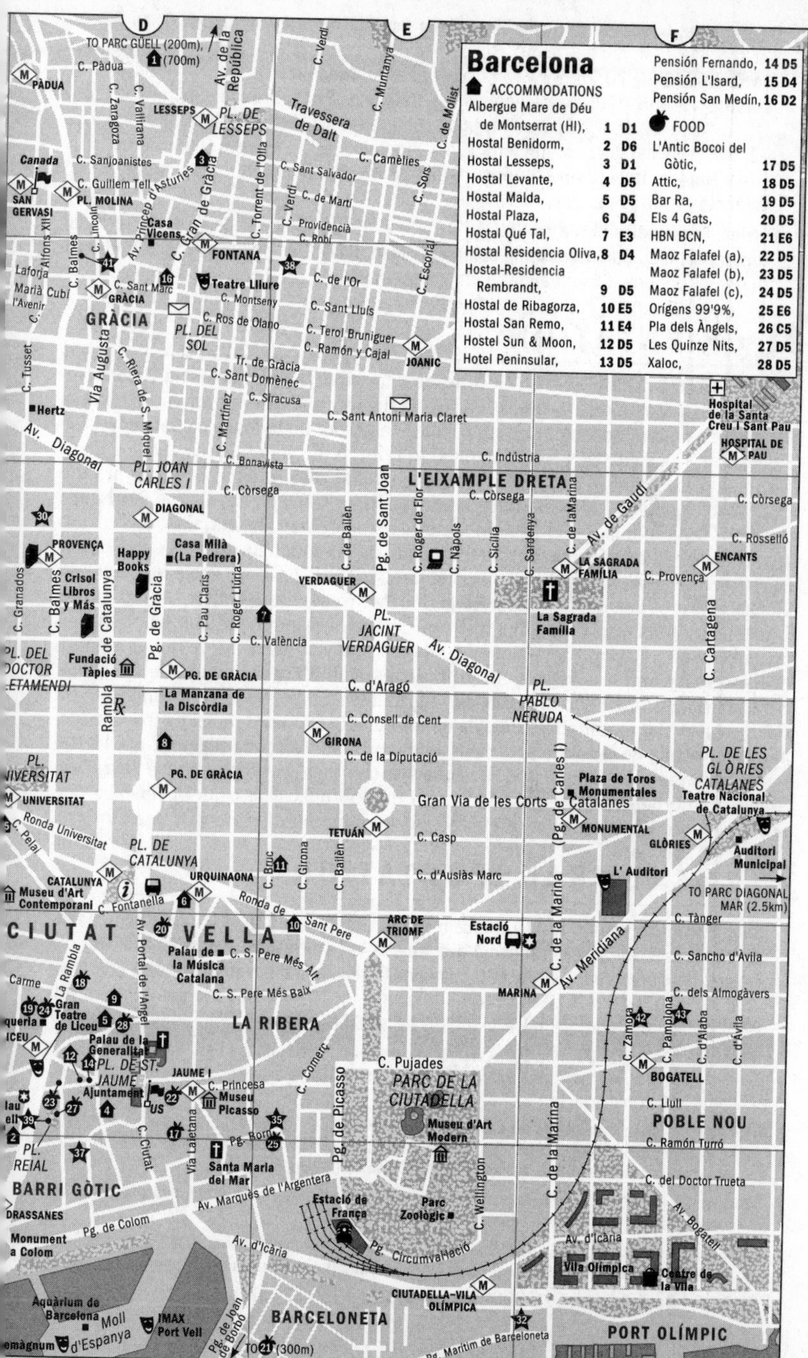

D
E
F
Barcelona
ACCOMMODATIONS
Albergue Mare de Déu de Montserrat (HI), 1 D1
Hostal Benidorm, 2 D6
Hostal Lesseps, 3 D1
Hostal Levante, 4 D5
Hostal Malda, 5 D5
Hostal Plaza, 6 D4
Hostal Qué Tal, 7 E3
Hostal Residencia Oliva, 8 D4
Hostal-Residencia Rembrandt, 9 D5
Hostal de Ribagorza, 10 E5
Hostal San Remo, 11 E4
Hostel Sun & Moon, 12 D5
Hotel Peninsular, 13 D5
Pensión Fernando, 14 D5
Pensión L'Isard, 15 D4
Pensión San Medín, 16 D2
FOOD
L'Antic Bocoi del Gòtic, 17 D5
Attic, 18 D5
Bar Ra, 19 D5
Els 4 Gats, 20 D5
HBN BCN, 21 E6
Maoz Falafel (a), 22 D5
Maoz Falafel (b), 23 D5
Maoz Falafel (c), 24 D5
Orígens 99'9%, 25 E6
Pla dels Àngels, 26 C5
Les Quinze Nits, 27 D5
Xaloc, 28 D5
TO PARC GÜELL (200m), (700m)
C. Pàdua
PÀDUA
Av. de la República
LESSEPS
PL. DE LESSEPS
Travessera de Dalt
C. Verdi
C. Muntanya
C. de Molist
C. Zaragoza
C. Vallirana
Canada
C. Sanjoanistes
C. Camèlies
C. Sant Salvador
C. Guillem Tell
Av. Príncep d'Astúries
C. Torrent de l'Olla
C. de Martí
C. Sors
SAN GERVASI
PL. MOLINA
C. Gran de Gràcia
C. Providència
C. Robí
Casa Vicens
FONTANA
C. Escorial
Alfons XII
C. Lincoln
C. Balmes
Laforja
Marià Cubí
l'Avenir
C. Sant Marc
GRÀCIA
Teatre Lliure
C. Montseny
C. de l'Or
C. Sant Lluís
C. Ros de Olano
PL. DEL SOL
C. Terol Bruniguer
C. Ramón y Cajal
JOANIC
Tr. de Gràcia
C. Sant Domènec
C. Siracusa
C. Tusset
Via Augusta
C. Riera de S. Miquel
Hertz
C. Martínez
C. Sant Antoni Maria Claret
Hospital de la Santa Creu I Sant Pau
HOSPITAL DE PAU
Av. Diagonal
C. Bonavista
PL. JOAN CARLES I
C. Indústria
L'EIXAMPLE DRETA
C. Còrsega
Av. de Gaudí
DIAGONAL
PROVENÇA
Happy Books
Casa Milà (La Pedrera)
Crisol Libros y Más
C. Granados
C. Balmes
Rambla de Catalunya
Pg. de Gràcia
C. Pau Claris
C. Roger Llúria
C. València
C. de Bailèn
Pg. de Sant Joan
C. Roger de Flor
C. Nàpols
C. Sicília
C. Sardenya
C. de laMarina
LA SAGRADA FAMÍLIA
La Sagrada Família
C. Provença
ENCANTS
C. Rosselló
C. Cartagena
VERDAGUER
PL. JACINT VERDAGUER
PL. DEL DOCTOR LETAMENDI
Fundació Tàpies
PG. DE GRÀCIA
C. d'Aragó
PL. PABLO NERUDA
La Manzana de la Discòrdia
C. Consell de Cent
GIRONA
C. de la Diputació
PL. UNIVERSITAT
UNIVERSITAT
PG. DE GRÀCIA
Gran Via de les Corts Catalanes
(Pg. de Carles I)
Plaza de Toros Monumentales
PL. DE LES GLÒRIES CATALANES
Teatre Nacional de Catalunya
MONUMENTAL
GLÒRIES
Auditori Municipal
Ronda Universitat
C. Pelai
PL. DE CATALUNYA
TETUÁN
C. Casp
C. Bruc
C. Girona
C. Bailèn
C. d'Ausiàs Marc
L' Auditori
CATALUNYA
Museu d'Art Contemporani
C. Fontanella
URQUINAONA
Ronda de Sant Pere
TO PARC DIAGONAL MAR (2.5km)
CIUTAT VELLA
Av. Portal de l'Àngel
Palau de la Música Catalana
C. S. Pere Més Alt
ARC DE TRIOMF
Estació Nord
C. Tànger
C. Sancho d'Àvila
C. de la Marina
Av. Meridiana
MARINA
Carme
La Rambla
Gran Teatre de Liceu
C. S. Pere Més Baix
LA RIBERA
C. dels Almogàvers
C. Zamora
C. Pamplona
C. d'Alaba
C. d'Àvila
LICEU
Palau de la Generalitat
PL. DE ST. JAUME
Ajuntament
JAUME I
C. Princesa
Museu Picasso
C. Comerç
C. Pujades
PARC DE LA CIUTADELLA
BOGATELL
C. Llull
Museu d'Art Modern
POBLE NOU
C. Ramón Turró
US
Pg. Born
C. Ciutat
Via Laietana
Pg. de Picasso
PL. REIAL
Santa Maria del Mar
C. Wellington
BARRI GÒTIC
Av. Marquès de l'Argentera
C. del Doctor Trueta
DRASSANES
Estació de França
Parc Zoològic
C. de la Marina
Av. Bogatell
Monument a Colom
Pg. de Colom
Av. d'Icària
Pg. Circumval·lació
Vila Olímpica
Centre de la Vila
Aquàrium de Barcelona
Moll d'Espanya
IMAX Port Vell
CIUTADELLA-VILA OLÍMPICA
BARCELONETA
Pg. de Joan de Borbó
TO 21 (300m)
Pg. Marítim de Barceloneta
PORT OLÍMPIC

Buses: Most buses arrive at the **Barcelona Estació Nord d'Autobuses,** C. Alí Bei 80 (☎265 6132; M: Arc de Triomf). Buses also depart from Estació Sants and the airport. **Sarfa** (☎902 30 20 25; www.sarfa.com) goes to **Cadaqués** (2½hr., 5 per day, €16). **Linebús** (☎265 0700; www.linebus.es) travels to **Paris, France** via Tours or Lyon (15hr.; M-Sa 12:15am, 8pm; €84) and southern France. **Alsa/Enatcar** (☎902 42 22 42; www.alsa.es) goes to: **Alicante** (9hr., 3 per day, €33); **Madrid** (8hr., 20 per day, €24); **Naples, Italy** (24hr., 4:45pm, €115); **Paris, France** (15hr., 1-3 per day, €84); **Valencia** (4hr., 19 per day, €21).

Ferries: Trasmediterránea (☎902 45 46 45; www.trasmediterranea.com), in Terminal Drassanes, Moll Sant Bertran. In summer only to: **Ibiza** (9hr., 1 per day, €50); **Mahón** (8-9hr., 1 per day, €50); **Palma** (3½hr., 1 per day, €70).

ORIENTATION

Imagine yourself perched on Columbus's head at the **Monument a Colom** (on Passeig de Colom, along the shore), viewing the city with the sea at your back. **Las Ramblas,** the main thoroughfare, runs from the harbor up to **Plaça de Catalunya,** the city center. *Let's Go* uses "Las Ramblas" to refer to the general area and "La Rambla" in address listings. The heavily touristed **Ciutat Vella** (old city) centers around Las Ramblas and includes the Barri Gòtic, La Ribera, and El Raval. The **Barri Gòtic** is east of Las Ramblas, enclosed on the other side by **Vía Laietana.** East of V. Laietana lies maze-like **La Ribera,** bordered by Parc de la Ciutadella and Estació França. Beyond La Ribera—farther east, outside the *Ciutat Vella*—are **Poble Nou** and **Port Olímpic.** West of Las Ramblas is **El Raval.** Farther west rises **Montjuïc,** with the 1992 Olympic grounds, gardens, and a fortress. Directly behind the Monument a Colom is the **Port Vell** (old port) development, where a wavy bridge leads to the ultra-modern shopping and entertainment complexes **Moll d'Espanya** and **Maremàgnum.** North of the *Ciutat Vella* is **l'Eixample,** a gridded neighborhood sprawling from Pl. Catalunya to the mountains. **Gran Via de les Corts Catalanes** defines its lower edge, and the **Passeig de Gràcia** bisects the neighborhood. **Avinguda Diagonal** marks the border between l'Eixample and the **Zona Alta** (uptown), which includes **Pedralbes, Gràcia,** and other older neighborhoods in the foothills. The peak of **Tibidabo,** the northwest border of the city, offers the most comprehensive view of Barcelona.

LOCAL TRANSPORTATION

Public Transportation: ☎010. Barcelona's public transportation is quick and cheap. There are several passes *(abonos)* available, all of which work interchangeably for the metro, bus, urban lines of the FGC commuter trains, and the Nitbus. A single ride *(sencillo)* costs €1.15. A **T-10 Pass** (€6.30) is valid for 10 rides; a **T-Día pass** entitles you to unlimited bus and metro travel for 1-5 days (€4.80-19).

Metro: ☎486 0752; www.tmb.net. Vending machines and ticket windows sell passes. Hold on to your ticket until you exit or risk a €40 fine. Trains run M-Th 5am-midnight, F-Sa 5am-2am, Su and holidays 6am-midnight.

Ferrocarrils de la Generalitat de Catalunya (FGC): ☎205 1515; www.fgc.es. Commuter trains to local destinations; main stations at Pl. de Catalunya and Pl. d'Espanya. After Tibidabo, rates increase by zone. Info office at the Pl. de Catalunya station open M-F 7am-9pm.

Buses: Go just about anywhere, usually 5am-10pm. Most stops have maps posted. Buses run every 10-15min. in central locations.

Nitbus: ☎901 511 151. Bus lines run every 20-30min. 10:30pm-4:30am. Buses depart from Pl. de Catalunya, stop in front of most club complexes, and travel through *Ciutat Vella* and *Zona Alta.*

Taxis: Try **RadioTaxi** (☎225 0000) or **ServiTaxi** (☎330 0300).

PRACTICAL INFORMATION

TOURIST AND FINANCIAL SERVICES

Tourist Offices: ☎907 30 12 82; www.barcelonaturisme.com. In addition to several tourist offices, Barcelona has numerous mobile information kiosks.

Aeroport El Prat de Llobregat, terminals A and B (☎478 0565). Info and last-minute accommodation booking. Open daily 9am-9pm.

Estació Barcelona-Sants, Pl. Països Catalans. M: Sants-Estació. Info and last-minute accommodation booking. Open in summer daily 8am-8pm; in winter M-F 8am-8pm, Sa-Su 8am-2pm.

Oficina de Turisme de Catalunya, Pg. de Gràcia 107 (☎238 4000; www.gencat.es/probert). M: Diagonal. Open M-Sa 10am-7pm, Su 10am-2:30pm.

Plaça de Catalunya, Pl. de Catalunya 17S. M: Catalunya. The biggest, best, and busiest tourist office. Free maps, brochures on sights and public transportation, booking service for last-minute accommodations, gift shop, money exchange, and box office. Open daily 9am-9pm.

Plaça de Sant Jaume, Pl. de Sant Jaume 1. M: Jaume I. Open M-F 9am-8pm, Sa 10am-8pm, Su and holidays 10am-2pm.

Budget Travel Offices: usit UNLIMITED, C. Rocafort 116-122 (☎483 8379). Open M-F 10am-2pm and 4-8pm.

Currency Exchange: ATMs give the best rates; the next best rates are available at banks. General banking hours are M-F 8:30am-2pm. Las Ramblas has many exchange stations open late, but the rates are not as good.

LOCAL SERVICES

Luggage Storage: Estació Barcelona-Sants. €4.50 per day. Open daily 5:30am-11pm. **Estació de França.** €3 per day. Open daily 7am-10pm.

Library: Biblioteca Sant Pau, C. de l'Hospital 56 (☎302 0797). M: Liceu. Walk to the far end of the courtyard; the library is on the left. Do not confuse it with the Catalan library you'll see first, which requires permission to enter. Open M and F 3:30-8:30pm, W-Th and Sa 10am-2pm. Closed July to mid-Sept.

Laundromat: Tintorería Ferrán, C. Ferran 11. M: Liceu. Open M-F 9am-8pm.

EMERGENCY AND COMMUNICATIONS

Local Police: ☎092. La Rambla 43 (☎344 1300). M: Liceu. Multilingual officers. Open 24hr.

Tourist Police: C. Nou de La Rambla 80 (☎344 1300), off La Rambla in El Raval. 3 blocks from the port.

Late-Night Pharmacy: Rotates; check any pharmacy window for the nearest on duty.

Medical Services: Medical Emergency: ☎061. **Hospital Clìnic,** C. de Villarroel 170 (☎227 5400). M: Hospital Clìnic. Main entrance at C. Roselló and C. Casanova.

Internet Access:

Easy Internet Café, La Rambla 31 (www.easyinternetcafe.com). M: Liceu. Reasonable prices and over 300 terminals in a bright, modern center make this Internet heaven. Digital camera, CD burning, faxing, copying, and scanning services. €2.20 per hr., 24hr. unlimited pass €4, 7-day €10, 30-day €20. Open daily 8am-2:30am. Branch at Ronda Universitat 35. M: Catalunya. €2 per hr., 24hr. pass €3, 7-day €7, 30-day €15. Open daily 8am-2am. Cash only.

Navegaweb, La Rambla 88-94 (☎317 9193; navegabarcelona@terra.es). M: Liceu. Good rates on international calls. Internet €1.80 per hr. Open daily 10am-10pm.

World Telecom Network, C. Unió 16. (☎933 42 51 42). Many fast, fully equipped new computers. €1 per hr., €1.80 per 2hr. Open daily 10am-10pm.

Post Office: Pl. d'Antoni López (☎902 19 71 97). M: Jaume I or Barceloneta. Fax and *Lista de Correos.* Open M-F 8:30am-9:30pm, Su 8:30am-2:30pm. **Postal Code:** 08003.

SPAIN

ACCOMMODATIONS

Finding an affordable room in Barcelona can be difficult. To crash in touristy **Barri Gòtic** or **Las Ramblas** during the busier months (June–Sept. and Dec.), make reservations weeks or months in advance. Consider staying outside touristy *Ciutat Vella;* many nice hostels in **l'Eixample** and **Gràcia** tend to have more vacancies. A few campsites lie on the outskirts of the city, accessible by intercity buses (€1.50; 20-45min.); contact the **Associació de Càmpings de Barcelona,** Gran Via de les Corts Catalanes 608 (☎412 5955; www.campingsbcn.com).

LOWER BARRI GÒTIC

Backpackers flock to these hostels, all between C. Ferran and the water, to be close to happening Las Ramblas.

Hostal Levante, Baixada de San Miquel 2 (☎317 9565; www.hostallevante.com). M: Liceu. The best deal in Barri Gòtic. Singles €33; doubles €56, with bath €65; 4- to 8-person apartments €120-240. MC/V. ❸

Pensión Fernando, C. Ferran 31 (☎301 7993; reservas@hfernando.com). M: Liceu. So convenient, it fills almost entirely from walk-ins. Dorms with A/C €18-19; singles €30-34; doubles €46-47, with bath €60-64, triples with bath €70. MC/V. ❷

Hostel Sun and Moon, C. Ferran 17 (☎270 2060; www.smhostel.net). Its dorms are a bit cramped, but this hostel offers an unbeatable location. Bike rental and Internet (€2 per hr.). Linen €1.50, towel €1, blanket €2. Dorms €17-26. AmEx/MC/V. ❷

Hostal Benidorm, La Rambla 37 (☎302 2054). M: Drassanes or Liceu. One of the best values on La Rambla, with phone and bath in each room. Some have balconies. Singles €35; doubles €55; triples €75; quads €90; quints €105. €5 extra in Aug. MC/V. ❸

UPPER BARRI GÒTIC

Between C. Fontanella and C. Ferran, accommodations are pricier but more serene than in the lower Barri Gòtic. Early reservations are essential in summer.

Hostal-Residencia Rembrandt, C. de la Portaferrissa 23 (☎318 1011; hostrembrandt@yahoo.es). M: Liceu. Nicest rooms in the area; some with TV, large bath, or patio. Fans €2 per night. Breakfast €5. Reception 9am-11pm. Reserve with credit card. Singles €28, with bath €38; doubles €45/55; triples €65/70. MC/V. ❸

Hostal Malda, C. Pi 5 (☎317 3002), entrance inside a small shopping center. M: Liceu. Great quality rooms at a great price. No reservations; show up between 9-11am to claim a room. Singles €13; doubles €28; triples with shower €40. Cash only. ❶

Hostal Plaza, C. Fontanella 18 (☎301 0139; www.plazahostal.com). M: Catalunya. Kind Texan owners rent bright rooms in a great location. Internet €4 per hr. Singles €35-50, with bath €60; doubles €57/67. Nov. and Feb. 10% discount. AmEx/MC/V. ❹

LA RIBERA AND EL RAVAL

Be careful in the areas near the port and farther from Las Ramblas at night.

Pensión L'Isard, C. Tallers 82 (☎302 5183). M: Universitat. Friendly couple offers the absolute lowest price in the area for 14 impeccable rooms, 4 of which have balconies. Singles €21; doubles €39, with bath €53; triples €55. AmEx/MC/V. ❷

Hotel Peninsular, C. de Sant Pau 34 (☎302 3138). M: Liceu. This building is now one of the sights on the *Ruta del Modernisme.* Rooms with telephone and A/C. Breakfast included. Singles €30, with bath €50; doubles €50/70. MC/V. ❸

Hostal de Ribagorza, C. Trafalgar 39 (☎319 1968; www.hostalribagorza.com). M: Urquinaona. Rooms in a Modernist building have TV, fan, and homey decorations. Singles €40; doubles €50, with bath €50-55. Low season reduced prices. MC/V. ❹

L'EIXAMPLE

Although L'Eixample may be far from the sights of Las Ramblas and the Barri Gòtic, it is the home of Barcelona's most beautiful architecture, and accommodations in this area tend to be much nicer than those in *Ciutat Vella*.

Hostal Residencia Oliva, Pg. de Gràcia 32, 4th fl. (☎488 0162; www.lasguias.com/hostaloliva). M: Pg. de Gràcia. Elegant decorations grace this classy hotel. All rooms with TV and fan. Singles €33; doubles €55, with bath €66; triples with bath €90. ❸

Hostal Qué Tal, C. Mallorca 290 (☎ 459 2366; www.quetalbarcelona.com), near C. Bruc. M: Pg. Gràcia or Verdaguer. A high-quality gay- and lesbian-friendly hostel with colorful, snazzy decor. Singles €39; doubles €58, with bath €74. Cash only. ❹

Hostal San Remo, C. Bruc 20 (☎302 1989; www.hostalsanremo.com). M: Urquinaona. All rooms have TV, A/C, and soundproof windows; 4 have terraces. Book ahead. Singles €28, with bath €32-35; doubles €52/57-58. Low season reduced prices. MC/V. ❸

ZONA ALTA: GRÀCIA AND OUTER BARRIS

Gràcia is Barcelona's "undiscovered" quarter, so last-minute arrivals may find vacancies here, even though options are few.

Pensión San Medín, C. Gran de Gràcia 125 (☎217 3068). M: Fontana. Embroidered curtains and ornate tiling adorn this extremely friendly family-run *pensión.* Reception 8am-midnight. Singles €42, with bath €54; doubles €54/75. MC/V. ❺

Hostal Lesseps, C. Gran de Gràcia 239 (☎218 4434). M: Lesseps. Spacious, classy rooms sport red velvet wallpaper. All rooms have TV and bath. A/C €5 extra. Singles €40; doubles €65; triples €80; quads €95-100. MC/V. ❹

Albergue Mare de Déu de Montserrat (HI), Pg. Mare de Déu del Coll 41-51 (☎210 5151; www.tujuca.com). This pretty 220-bed hostel is a good way to meet other backpackers in spite of its distance from the city center. Members only. Breakfast included. Flexible 3-day max. stay. Dorms €21.60, under 25 €18.10. AmEx/MC/V. ❷

FOOD

The eateries on **Carrer Aragó** by Pg. de Gràcia have lunchtime *menús*, and the **Passeig de Gràcia** has outdoor dining. Gràcia's **Plaça Sol** and La Ribera's **Santa Maria del Mar** are the best tapas spots. For fruit, cheese, and wine, head to **La Boqueria (Mercat de Sant Josep),** off La Rambla outside M: Liceu. (Open M-Sa 8am-8:30pm.) Buy groceries at **Champion,** La Rambla 13. (M: Liceu. Open M-Sa 9am-10pm.)

BARRI GÒTIC

Les Quinze Nits, Pl. Reial 6 (☎317 3075). M: Liceu. Surprisingly quick lines halfway through the plaza. Satisfying Catalan entrees at shockingly low prices (€3.50-9). Don't miss the desserts. Open daily 1-3:45pm and 8:30-11:30pm. AmEx/MC/V. ❷

L'Antic Bocoi del Gòtic, Baixada de Viladecols 3 (☎310 5067). M: Jaume I. A rustic, romantic restaurant. Excellent salads (€6.50-7.50), pâtés (€9-12), and cheese plates (€12). Reservations recommended. Open M-Sa 8:30pm-midnight. AmEx/DC/V. ❸

Els 4 Gats, C. Montsió 3 (☎302 4140). M: Catalunya. An old hangout of Picasso with lots of bohemian character. Lunch *menú* (€11) is the best deal and comes with epic desserts. Live piano 9pm-1am. Open daily 1pm-1am. Closed Aug. AmEx/MC/V. ❹

Maoz, 3 locations: at C. Ferran 13; La Rambla 95; and C. Jaume I 7 (☎412 1261; www.maozfalafel.com). Vegetarian chain selling only falafel (€2.70-3.50), with an array of fresh vegetable toppings. Open M-Th and Su 11am-1:30am, F-Sa 11am-2:30am. ❶

Attic, La Rambla 120 (☎302 4866). M: Liceu. It is hard to believe this chic, modern restaurant with top-rate service is right on touristy La Rambla. Mediterranean fusion entrees €6-14. Open daily 1-4:30pm and 7:30pm-12:30am. AmEx/DC/MC/V. ❷

Xaloc, C. de la Palla 13-17 (☎301 1990). M: Liceu. This big, classy delicatessen popular with locals is centered around a butcher counter. Tasty baguette sandwiches €4-10. Lunch *menú* €10.50. Open daily 9am-midnight. AmEx/MC/V. ❶

ELSEWHERE IN BARCELONA

Orígens 99'9%, C. Enric Granados 9 (☎453 1120), and C. Vidrieria 6-8 (☎310 7531). M: Jaume I. This restaurant-store sticks to natural ingredients. Great atmosphere but small portions. Soups €3-9. Entrees €3-5. Open 12:30pm-1:30am. MC/V. ❷

Bar Ra, Pl. de la Garduña (☎301 4163; www.ratown.com). M: Liceu. This creative fusion restaurant has colorful outdoor seating, massive portions, and many vegetarian options. Entrees €9-15. Open daily 9:30am-1:30am. Kitchen open 1:30-4pm and 9:30pm-midnight. Dinner by reservation only. AmEx/MC/V. ❸

HBN BCN, C. Escar 1 (☎225 0263), on Platja Sant Sebastià in Barceloneta, on the right at the end of Pg. Joan de Borbó. Offers Mediterranean and Cuban fare and mojitos near the beach. Th and Su live band 6pm. Dinner reservations recommended. Cuban tapas platter €8. *Menú* €8.30. Kitchen open 1-4pm and 9pm-midnight. AmEx/MC/V. ❷

Pla dels Àngels, C. Ferlandina 23 (☎349 4047). M: Universitat. Colorful, inexpensive eatery is a great choice for vegetarians. Entrees €5-6. Open M-Th 1:30-4pm and 9-11:30pm, F-Sa 1:30-4pm and 9pm-midnight. MC/V. ❶

SIGHTS

The **Ruta del Modernisme** pass is the cheapest and most flexible option for those with a few days in the city and an interest in seeing the major sights. Passes (€3.60; students €2.60) are good for a month and give holders a 25-30% discount on attractions including Palau de la Música Catalana, the Museu de Zoología, tours of Hospital de la Santa Creu i Sant Pau, and the facades of La Manzana de la Discòrdia. Purchase passes at Casa Amatller, Pg. de Gràcia 41. (☎488 0139. M: Pg. de Gràcia.)

LAS RAMBLAS

Las Ramblas, a pedestrian-only strip roughly 1km long, is a jumble of performers, fortune-tellers, human statues, flower stands, and artists. A stroll along this bustling avenue can be an adventure at almost any hour. The wide, tree-lined thoroughfare, also known as La Rambla or, in Catalan, Les Rambles, is actually composed of six distinct *ramblas* (promenades) that together form one boulevard starting at the Pl. de Catalunya and the **Font de Canaletes.** Pass the **Monument a Colom** on your way out to Rambla del Mar and a beautiful view of the Mediterranean.

LA BOQUERIA (MERCAT DE SANT JOSEP). Besides being one of the cheapest places to get food in the city, La Boqueria is a sight in itself. It is a traditional Catalan market located in a giant, all-steel Modernist structure. Inside, vendors sell delicious produce, fish, and meat from a seemingly infinite number of independent stands. *(La Rambla 89. M: Liceu. Open M-Sa 8am-8:30pm.)*

GRAN TEATRE DEL LICEU. The Liceu has been ravaged by anarchists, bombs, and fires during its 150-year history. Considered one of Europe's top stages, this theater features Catalan opera, and is adorned with palatial ornamentation, gold facades, and sculptures. Be sure to check out the hall of mirrors. *(La Rambla 51-59, by C. de Sant Pau. M: Liceu, L3. ☎485 9913; www.liceubarcelona.com. Box office open M-F 2-8:30pm, Sa 1hr. before show. Also by ServiCaixa ☎902 33 22 11. Open to public daily 10am-1pm. Guided 30min. tours 10am by reservation only; call 9am-2pm. €5.)*

MONUMENT A COLOM. Ruis i Taulet's Monument a Colom towers at the port end of Las Ramblas. Nineteenth-century *Renaixença* enthusiasts convinced themselves that Columbus was Catalan, but historians agree that he was from Italy. Oddly enough, the explorer proudly points toward Libya, not the Americas. Take the elevator to the top to enjoy the view. *(Portal de la Pau. M: Drassanes. Elevator runs daily June-Sept. 9am-8:30pm; Oct.-May 10am-6:30pm. €2.20.)*

BARRI GÒTIC

Brimming with cathedrals, palaces, and unabashed tourism, Barcelona's oldest zone masks its age with 24hr. energy. Catalan commercialism persists in all its glory with store-lined streets and fine restaurants, but the soul of the neighborhood lies deeper than these attractions.

ESGLÉSIA CATEDRAL DE LA SANTA CREU. This cathedral is one of Barcelona's most recognizable and popular monuments. Beyond the choir are an altar designed by Frederic Marès in 1976 and the sunken Crypt of Santa Eulalia, one of Barcelona's patron saints. The cathedral museum holds Bartolomé Bermejo's *Pietà.* Catch a performance of the *sardana* in front of the cathedral on Sundays after mass; services begin at noon and 6:30pm. *(M: Jaume I. In Pl. Seu, up C. Bisbe from Pl. Sant Jaume. Cathedral open daily 8am-12:45pm and 5:15-7:30pm. Cloister open 9am-12:30pm and 5:15-7pm. Elevator to the roof runs M-Sa 10:30am-6pm. Choir area open M-F 9am-12:30pm and 5:15-7pm, Sa-Su 9am-12:30pm. Elevator €2. Choir €2. English-language audio tour €4. Guided tours 1-5pm include all sights for €4.)*

MUSEU D'HISTÒRIA DE LA CIUTAT. There are two components to the Museu d'Història de la Ciutat (Museum of the History of Barcelona). Built on top of the 4th-century city walls, the **Palau Reial Major** served as the residence of the Catalan-Aragonese monarchs. The second part of the museum lies underground; this 4000 sq. m **archaeological exhibit** was excavated between 1930 and 1960 and displays incredibly intact first- to 6th-century remains of the Roman city of Barcino. *(Pl. del Rei. M: Jaume I. ☎315 1111; www.museuhistoria.bcn.es. Open mid-May to Oct. M-Sa 10am-8pm, Su 10am-3pm; Oct. to mid-May Tu-Sa 10am-2pm and 4-8pm, Su 10am-3pm. Palace €4, students €2.50. Archaeological exhibit €3.50/2. Both €6/4.)*

LA RIBERA

This neighborhood has recently evolved into a bohemian nucleus, with art galleries, chic eateries, and exclusive bars. La Ribera's streets are even closer together than those in the Barri Gòtic, but the atmosphere is far less congested.

PALAU DE LA MÚSICA CATALANA. Modernist Luis Domènech i Montaner was commissioned to design this must-see concert venue, which glows with stained-glass, marble reliefs, intricate woodwork, and ceramic mosaics. Concerts at the Palau include pop, rock, and jazz, in addition to symphonic and choral music. *(C. Sant Francesc de Paula 2. M: Jaume I. ☎295 7200; www.palaumusica.org. Required 40min. English-language tours almost every hr. Open daily Aug. 10am-7pm; Sept.-July 10am-3:30pm. €8, students €7. Check the* Guía del Ocio *for concert listings. Concert tickets €6-330. MC/V.)*

MUSEU PICASSO. The most-visited museum in Barcelona traces Picasso's artistic development with the world's most comprehensive collection of work from his formative Barcelona period. Picasso donated over 1700 of his works to the museum; it now boasts 3600, although not all are on display. *(C. Montcada 15-19. M: Jaume I. Open Tu-Sa 10am-8pm, Su 10am-3pm. €6, students €3, under 16 and 1st Su of each month free. Admission and temporary exhibit €8.50/5.)*

PARC DE LA CIUTADELLA. Host of the 1888 World's Fair, the park harbors several museums, well-labeled horticulture, the Cascada fountains, a pond, and a zoo. Buildings of note include Domènech i Montaner's Modernist **Castell dels Tres Dracs**

(now the **Museu de Zoología**), the geological museum, and Josep Amergós's **Hivernacle.** The **Parc Zoològic** is home to several threatened and endangered species, including the Iberian wolf and the Sumatran tiger. *(M: Ciutadella. Park open daily 8am-9pm. Zoo open daily May-Aug. 9:30am-7:30pm; Apr. and Sept. 10am-7pm; Mar. and Oct. 10am-6pm; Nov.-Feb. 10am-5pm. Zoo €13.)*

MUSEU DE LA XOCOLATA (CHOCOLATE MUSEUM). Arguably the most delectable museum in Spain presents gobs of information about the history, production, and ingestion of this sensuous treat. Perhaps more interesting are the exquisite chocolate sculptures, particularly the edible La Sagrada Família. Others include soccer star Ronaldo and Dalí-inspired pieces. The small cafe offers chocolate tasting and workshops on cake baking. *(Pl. Pons i Clerch, by C. Comerç. M: Jaume I. ☎268 7878; www.museudelaxocolata.com. Open M and W-Sa 10am-7pm, Su 10am-3pm. €3.80, students €3.30, with Barcelona Card €2.70. Workshops from €6.30; reservations required.)*

EL RAVAL

Next to Las Ramblas and the Barri Gòtic, the northern part of El Raval tends to be a favorite of Barcelona's natives rather than its tourists. Where over-crowding once led to rampant crime, prostitution, and drug use, revitalization efforts, especially since the '92 Olympic Games, have worked wonders; new museums and cultural centers have paved the way for trendy restaurants and bars.

PALAU GÜELL. Gaudí's 1886 Palau Güell, the Modernist residence built for patron Eusebi Güell (of Park Güell fame), has one of Barcelona's most spectacular interiors. Güell spared no expense on this house, considered to be the first true representation of Gaudí's revolutionary style. The Palau is closed for renovations until December 2006. *(C. Nou de La Rambla 3-5. M: Liceu. Required tour every 15min. Open Mar.-Oct. M-Sa 10am-8pm, Su 10am-2pm; Nov.-Dec. M-Sa 10am-6pm. €3, students €1.50.)*

CENTRE DE CULTURA CONTEMPORÀNIA DE BARCELONA (CCCB). The center stands out for its mixture of architectural styles, consisting of an early 20th-century theater and its 1994 addition, a sleek wing of black glass. The institute shows a variety of temporary exhibits, film screenings, and music performances; check the *Guía del Ocio* for scheduled events. *(Casa de Caritat. C. Montalegre 5. M: Catalunya or Universitat. ☎306 4100; www.cccb.org. Open late June to late Sept. Tu-Sa 11am-8pm, Su 11am-3pm; late Sept. to late June Tu and Th-F 11am-2pm and 4-8pm, W and Sa 11am-8pm, Su 11am-7pm. Tours Tu and F 6pm, Sa-Su and holidays 11:30am. €4, students and W €3.)*

L'EIXAMPLE

The Catalan Renaissance and the growth of Barcelona during the 19th century pushed the city past its medieval walls and into modernity. Ildefons Cerdà drew up a plan for a new neighborhood where people of all social classes could live side by side; however, l'Eixample (luh-SHOMP-luh) did not thrive as a utopian community but rather as a playground for the bourgeoisie. Despite gentrification, L'Eixample remains an innovative, pretty neighborhood full of idealistic Modernist oddities.

LA SAGRADA FAMÍLIA. Antoni Gaudí's unfinished masterpiece is without a doubt the world's most visited construction site. Despite the fact that only eight of the 18 planned towers have been completed and the church still doesn't have an interior, millions of people make the touristic pilgrimage to witness its work-in-progress majesty. Of the three proposed facades, only the Nativity Facade was finished under Gaudí, and there is some controversy over recent additions being inconsistent with the Modernist's original plans. *(C. Mallorca 401. M: Sagrada Família. Open daily Apr.-Sept. 9am-8pm, elevator open 9:30am-7:45pm; Oct.-Mar. both open 9:30am-5:45pm. English-language tours 11am, 1pm; in summer tours also 3, 5:30pm. €8, students with ISIC €5. Combined ticket with Casa-Museu Dali €9/6. Tour €3. Elevator €2. Cash only.)*

CASA MILÀ (LA PEDRERA). Modernism buffs argue that the Casa Milà apartment building, a mass of granite popularly known as *La Pedrera* (the Quarry), is Gaudí's most refined work. Note the intricate ironwork of the balconies and the irregular, egg-shaped window panes of the front gate. Some say the design represents the sea—others say it feels like being in a video game. The entrance fee entitles visitors to tour an apartment, the roof, and the brick attic, now the **Espai Gaudí,** a multimedia look at Gaudí's life and works. *(Pg. de Gràcia 92. ☎902 40 09 73. Open daily 10am-8pm. Free English-language tours M-F 4pm. €7, students €3.50. Audio tours €3.50.)*

LA MANZANA DE LA DISCÒRDIA. The odd-numbered side of Pg. de Gràcia between C. Aragó and Consell de Cent is popularly known as *la manzana de la discòrdia* (block of discord), referring to the stylistic clashing of three buildings. Regrettably, the bottom two floors of **Casa Lleó i Morera,** by Domènech i Montaner, were destroyed to make room for a store, but with the **Ruta del Modernisme** pass (sold on the ground floor), you can take a short tour of the upper floors with their sprouting flowers, stained glass, and legendary doorway sculptures. Puig i Cadafalch opted for a geometric, Moorish-influenced pattern on the facade of **Casa Amatller** at #41. Gaudí's balconies ripple like water and purple-blue tiles sparkle on **Casa Batlló,** #43. The most popular interpretation of Casa Batlló is that the building represents Cataluña's patron Sant Jordi (St. George) slaying a dragon; the chimney plays the lance, the scaly roof is the dragon's back, and the bony balconies are the remains of its victims. *(☎216 0306; www.casbatllo.es. Open daily 9am-8pm. €10, €16 including attic and chimneys. Audio tours free.)*

HOSPITAL DE LA SANTA CREU I SANT PAU. Designated a UNESCO monument in 1997, the Modernist Hospital de la Santa Creu i Sant Pau was Domènech i Montaner's crowning achievement. The entire complex covers nine full l'Eixample blocks; its whimsically decorated pavilions resemble gingerbread houses and little Taj Mahals. The outdoor spaces boast more than 300 types of plants. *(Sant Antoni M. Claret 167. M: Hospital de Sant Pau, L5. ☎488 2078. Hospital grounds open 24hr.)*

MONTJUÏC

Historically, whoever controlled Montjuïc (mon-joo-EEK; Hill of the Jews) controlled the city. Dozens of rulers have modified the **Castell de Montjuïc,** a fortress built atop the ancient Jewish cemetery; Franco made it one of his "interrogation" headquarters. The fort was not given back to the city until 1960. Since then, Barcelona has given Montjuïc a new identity, transforming it from a military stronghold into a peaceful park by day and a debaucherous playground by night.

FUNDACIÓ MIRÓ. Designed by Miró's friend Josep Lluis Sert and tucked into the side of Montjuïc, the Fundació links modern spaces with massive windows and outdoor patios. Skylights illuminate an extensive collection of Miró's sculptures, drawings, and paintings, ranging from small sketches to wall-sized canvases. The gallery downstairs displays experimental works by young artists. Garden paths run down the hill to the Palau Nacional. The Fundació also sponsors music and film festivals; check the *Guía del Ocio* for listings. *(Av. Miramar 71-75. Take the funicular from M: Paral·lel. Open Tu-W and F-Sa 10am-7pm, Th 10am-9:30pm, Su and holidays 10am-2:30pm. €7.20, students €5. Temporary exhibits €4/3. Under 14 free.)*

MUSEU NACIONAL D'ART DE CATALUNYA (PALAU NACIONAL). Designed by Enric Catá and Pedro Cendoya, the Palau Nacional has housed the Museu Nacional d'Art de Catalunya (MNAC) since 1934. Its main hall is an event space, while the wings house the world's finest collection of Catalan Romanesque art and a variety of Gothic pieces. The chronological tour of the galleries stresses the influence of Italy on Cataluña's artistic development. The Palau Nacional recently acquired the entirety of the Museu d'Art Modern's holdings, making MNAC the principal art museum of Cataluña. The **Fonts Luminoses** (Illuminated Fountains) in front of the building are used in summer laser shows. *(From M: Espanya, walk up Av. Reina María Cristina, away from the brick towers, and take the escalators to the top. Open Tu-Sa 10am-7pm, Su 10am-2:30pm. Permanent Romanesque exhibit €5. Temporary exhibits each €3-4.20; both temporary exhibits €5; 1 temporary plus permanent €6; all exhibits €8.50. 30% student discount.)*

CASTELL DE MONTJUÏC. A visit to this historic fortress and its **Museu Militar** is a great way to get an overview of the city's layout and history. The castle's external *mirador* offers spectacular views of the city. Taking the *telefèric* (funicular) to and from the castle is half the fun. *(From M: Paral·lel, walk up the hill on C. Foc, next to the funicular station. Or, take the funicular to Av. Miramar and then the* Teleféric de Montjuïc *cable car to the castle.* Teleféric *open M-Sa 11:15am-9pm; low season 11am-7:15pm. Fortress and* mirador *open daily 9am-10pm. Museum open Tu-Sa Mar.-Nov. 9:30am-8pm; Dec.-Feb. 9:30am-5pm. Funicular €3.60, round-trip €5. Fortress and* mirador *€1. Including museum €2.50.)*

WATERFRONT

TORRE SAN SEBASTIÀ. One of the easiest and best ways to view the city is on the cable cars which span the Port Vell, connecting beachy Barceloneta with mountainous Montjuïc. The full ride, which takes about 10min. each way and makes an intermediate stop at the Jaume I tower near Colom, gives a bird's-eye view of the city. *(Pg. Joan de Borbó. M: Barceloneta. In Port Vell, as you walk down Joan de Borbó with the beaches on your left, stay right and look for the high tower. Open daily 11am-8pm. Elevator to the cable cars €3.50; to Jaume I round-trip €7.50; to Montjuïc €7.50, round-trip €9.)*

MUSEU D'HISTÒRIA DE CATALUNYA. Set in the old general stores of the Port of Barcelona, the Museu provides an exhaustive and patriotic introduction to Catalan history, politics, and culture. Touring the exhibit is a full sensory experience—you will touch, hear, and even smell the region's dynamic and often tragic history. And, of course, extra points if you talk to the guards in Catalan. *(Pl. Pau Vila 3. Near the entrance to the Moll d'Espanya; to the left as you walk out toward Barceloneta. ☎225 4700. Open Tu and Th-Sa 10am-7pm, W 10am-8pm, Su 10am-2:30pm. €3, students €2.40.)*

L'AQUÀRIUM DE BARCELONA. Barcelona's aquarium—the largest in Europe—is an aquatic wonder, featuring countless octopi and penguins. The highlight is a 75m glass tunnel through a tank of sharks, sting rays, and seahorses. *(Moll d'Espanya, next to Maremàgnum. M: Drassanes or Barceloneta. Advance tickets ☎221 7474; www.aquarium-bcn.com. Open daily July-Aug. 9:30am-11pm; Sept.-June 9:30am-9:30pm. €14, students €13.)*

VILA OLÍMPICA. The Vila Olímpica, beyond the eastern side of the zoo, was built to house 15,000 athletes and entertain millions of tourists for the 1992 Summer Olympics. It's the newest part of Barcelona and home to several public parks, a shopping center, and business offices. Nearby **Barceloneta,** with its beaches stretching out from the port, is the city's best spot for sunning. *(M: Ciutadella/Vila Olímpica. Walk along the waterfront on Ronda Litoral toward the 2 towers.)*

ZONA ALTA

Zona Alta (uptown) lies at the top of most maps of Barcelona. The most visited part of *Zona Alta* is Gràcia, which was incorporated into Barcelona in 1897 despite the protests of its residents. The area has always had a political streak, and calls for Gràcian independence crop up sporadically even today. Gràcia packs a surprising number of Modernist buildings and parks, international restaurants, and chic shops into a relatively small and untouristed area.

PARK GÜELL. This fantastic park was designed entirely by Gaudí but—in typical Gaudí fashion—was not completed until after his death. Gaudí intended Park Güell to be a garden city; its dwarfish buildings and sparkling ceramic-mosaic stairways were designed to house the city's elite. Only one house was actually built, which is now the **Casa-Museu Gaudí.** Two mosaic staircases flank the park, leading to a towering Modernist pavilion that Gaudí originally designed as an open-air market. The longest park bench in the world, a multicolored serpentine wonder made of tile shards, decorates the top of the pavilion. *(Bus #24 from Pl. Catalunya stops at the upper entrance. Park open daily 10am-sundown. Museum open daily Apr.-Sept. 10am-8pm; Oct.-Mar. 10am-6pm. Park free. Museum €4, ISIC holders €3.)*

MUSEU DEL FÚTBOL CLUB BARCELONA. A close second to the Picasso as Barcelona's most-visited museum, the FCB merits all the attention it gets from soccer fanatics who appreciate the team's storied history. The high point is the chance to enter the stadium and take in the enormity of 120,000-seat Camp Nou. It costs extra to see the facilities, such as the field and dressing rooms. *(C. Arístides Maillol, next to the stadium. Enter through access gates 7 or 9. M: Collblanc. ☎496 3608. Open M-Sa 10am-6:30pm, Su and holidays 10am-2pm. €6, students €4.50. Facilities and museum €9.50/7.50.)*

ENTERTAINMENT AND FESTIVALS

For tips on entertainment, nightlife, and food, pick up the *Guía del Ocio* (www.guiadelociobcn.es; €1) at any newsstand. The best shopping in the city is in the **Barri Gòtic,** but if you feel like dropping some extra cash, check out the posh **Passeig de Gràcia** in l'Eixample. Grab face paint to join league champion Barça at the Camp Nou stadium for **fútbol.** (Box office C. Arístedes Maillol 12-18. ☎902 18 99 00. Tickets €30-60.) **Barceloneta** and **Poble Nou** feature tons of sand for topless tanning and many places to rent sailboats and water-sports equipment. Head up to Montjuïc to take advantage of the **Olympic Facilities,** which are now open for public use, including **Piscines Bernat Picornell,** a gorgeous pool complex. (☎423 4041. Pool €4.40. Gym €8.80. Open M-F 7am-midnight, Sa 7am-9pm, Su 7am-8pm.)

Remember to double-check sight and museum hours during festival times, as well as during the Christmas season and *Semana Santa.* The **Festa de Sant Jordi** (St. George; Apr. 24) celebrates Cataluña's patron saint with a feast. Men give women roses, and women give men books. In the last two weeks of August, city folk jam at Gràcia's **Festa Mayor;** lights blaze in *plaças* and music plays all night. The three-day **Sónar** music festival comes to town in mid-June, attracting renowned DJs and electronica enthusiasts from all over the world. During July and August, the **Grec Festival** hosts dance performances, concerts, and film screenings. On

BULLISH ON BARCELONA

Flamenco and bullfight-themed souvenirs may line the shelves of tourist shops on Las Ramblas, but those seeking the real-life counterparts of these knick-knacks will have to venture beyond Cataluña. With their own language, cuisine, and dance, Catalonians have historically had a shaky relationship with the rest of the nation. This separatist push has recently taken on a new form: Cataluña may ban bullfighting once and for all. While the rest of the country continues to revere the *matadores* splashed across tabloid covers, more than 250,000 people have signed a petition calling for its abolition, following a campaign by animal rights groups. Though a few *aficionados* have threatened to protest, the ban now hinges on a vote by the regional government, and secret ballots predict an overwhelming victory. Only 100 bulls are killed in Barcelona each year, compared to 20,000 in all of Spain. Catalan distaste for the sport may include a desire to continue to forge an identity separate from that of Spain. While the living statues of *matadores* on Las Ramblas may persist for the amusement of tourists, soon enough, Cataluña will likely take a step toward defining—even if only symbolically—its own personality as separate from that of the rest of Spain.

September 11, the **Festa Nacional de Cataluña** brings traditional costumes, dancing, and Catalan flags hanging from balconies. **Festa de Sant Joan** takes place the night before June 24; ceaseless fireworks will prevent any attempts to sleep.

NIGHTLIFE

Barcelona's wild nightlife treads a precarious line between slick and kitschy. In many ways, the city is a tourist's clubbing heaven: things don't get going until late (don't bother showing up at a club before 1am) and continue until dawn. Yet for every full-blown dance club, there are 100 more relaxed bars. Check the *Guía del Ocio* for up-to-date listings of nighttime fun, as the hot spots change often.

CIUTAT VELLA

Main streets such as C. Ferran have cookie-cutter *cervecerías* and *bar-restaurantes* every five steps. C. Escudellers is the location for post-bar dancing, while Pl. Reial remains packed until the early morning. Las Ramblas, while lively, becomes a bit questionable late at night, with prostitutes replacing families. In recent years, La Ribera has evolved into a hip, artsy district, attracting a young crowd of locals and a few expats and tourists in the know. The streets of El Raval are densely packed with a place for every variety of bar-hopper.

Jamboree, Pl. Reial 17 (☎319 1789). M: Liceu. What was once a convent is now one of the city's most popular live music venues. Dance club later at night. Drinks €8-10. Cover M €3, Tu-Su €8. Open daily 11pm-1am; club open 2-5am. Upstairs, the attached club **Tarantos** (☎318 3067) hosts flamenco shows (€3). Open M-Sa 10pm-2am.

El Copetín, Pg. del Born 19. M: Jaume I. Cuban rhythm infuses everything in this casual nightspot. Awe-inspiring mojitos €5. Open M-Th and Su 7pm-2:30am, F-Sa 7pm-3am.

Marsella Bar, C. de Sant Pau 65. M: Liceu. A rollicking good time with amiable bartenders and a crowd from all over. Religious figurines grace the walls of Barcelona's oldest bar, open since 1820. Absinthe €3.40. Mixed drinks €2-6. Open M-Sa 10pm-3am.

Fonfone, C. Escudellers 24 (☎317 1424; www.fonfone.com). M: Liceu or Drassanes. Atmospheric blue and green lighting and funky music draw crowds from 1-3am. International DJs nightly. Beer €3.50. Mixed drinks €6-8. Open daily 10pm-2:30 or 3am.

Casa Almirall, C. Joaquim Costa 33. M: Universitat. Cavernous space with weathered couches and cool, dim lights. Absinthe €6.50. Beer €3-4. Mixed drinks €6-8. Open M-Th and Su 7pm-2:30am, F-Sa 7pm-3am. Cash only.

L'EIXAMPLE

L'Eixample has upscale bars and some of the best gay nightlife in Europe.

Buenavista Salsoteca, C. Rosselló 217 (☎237 6528; www.salsabuenavista.com). M: Diagonal. This over-the-top club lures in a fun-loving crowd with its Latin beats. W free salsa lessons 10:30pm. Th "Rueda Cubana" party. Cover F-Sa €9, includes 1 drink. Open W-Th 11pm-4am, F-Sa 11pm-5am, Su 8:30pm-2am.

Dietrich, C. Consell de Cent 255. M: Pg. de Gràcia. An unflattering painting of Marlene Dietrich in the semi-nude greets a mostly gay crowd. Nightly dance and trapeze show 1:30am. Beer €3.50. Mixed drinks €5-8. Open M-F and Su 6pm-2:30am, Sa 6pm-3am.

La Fira, C. Provença 171. M: Hospital Clìnic or FGC: Provença. Bartenders serve a crowd dangling from carousel swings and surrounded by funhouse mirrors. DJs spin funk, disco, and oldies. Open Tu-Th 10pm-3am, F-Sa 7pm-4:30am, Su 6pm-1am.

Átame, C. Consell de Cent 257. M: Pg de Gràcia. This bar, frequented mainly by gay men, is not as scandalous as its name ("tie me up") might imply. A great spot for relaxed drinks and conversation. Beer €3. Mixed drinks €3-8. Open daily 5pm-3am.

MONTJUÏC

Lower Montjuïc is home to **Poble Espanyol,** Av. Marqués de Comillas, a re-creation of famous buildings and sights from all regions of Spain. At night the complex becomes a disco theme park. (☎508 6300; www.poble-espanyol.com. M: Espanya.) Poble Espanyol offers the craziest clubbing experience in all of Barcelona at some of the most popular (and surreal) venues.

Tinta Roja, C. Creus dels Molers 17 (☎443 3243), near Poble Espanyol. Live tango show. Open W-Su 8pm-2:30am.

La Terrazza, Poble Espanyol (☎423 1285). Fantastic outdoor dance floor. Cover €15, includes 1 drink. Open May-Oct. F-Sa 1am-7am.

Discothèque, Poble Espanyol (☎423 1285). Winter counterpart of La Terrazza. Dress to impress. Cover €18, includes 1 drink. Open Oct.-May F-Sa midnight-7am.

WATERFRONT

Poble Nou and **Port Olímpic** are home to a long strip of nightclubs. The entire waterfront area, which stretches from **Maremàgnum** to **Port Vell,** may be as hedonistic and touristy as Barcelona gets. At night, Maremàgnum, the city's biggest mall, turns into a tri-level maze of clubs packed with crowds even on weeknights. There is no cover; clubs make their money by charging exorbitant drink prices (beer €5; mixed drinks €8-10). Catching a cab home can be difficult.

L'Ovella Negra (Megataverna del Poble Nou), C. Zamora 78 (☎309 5938). M: Bogatell. The place to come for the first few beers of the night. Large beers €2. Mixed drinks from €2. Open Th 10pm-2:30am, F-Sa 5pm-3am, Su 5pm-midnight.

Razzmatazz, C. Pamplona 88 and Almogàvers 122, across the street (☎272 0910; www.salarazzmatazz.com). M: Marina. A huge warehouse-turned-entertainment complex now houses 5 clubs. Beer €3. Mixed drinks €6. Cover €12, includes all 5 clubs. Call ahead for concert prices. Open F-Sa and holidays 1-5am. MC/V.

Catwalk, C. Ramón Trias Fargas 2-4 (☎221 6161). M: Port Olímpic. One of the hottest and most exclusive places in town. Dress like you've never dressed before, or miss out on the fun. All house music all the time. Cover varies. Open Th-Su midnight-6am.

ZONA ALTA

The area around C. de Marià Cubí has great nightlife undiscovered by tourists, but you'll have to take a taxi. For more accessible fun in Gràcia, head to Pl. del Sol.

Otto Zutz, C. Lincoln 15 (☎238 0722; www.ottozutz.com). FGC: Pl. Molina. Groove to house, hip-hop, and funk. Beer €5. Cover €15, includes 1 drink; email ahead or look for flyers for a discount. Open Tu-W midnight-5am, Th-Sa midnight-6am.

Gasterea, C. Verdi 39. M: Fontana. Yellow walls cast a warm glow in this table-less bar. Tapas €1.05. Mixed drinks €5. Open M-Tu, Th, Su 7pm-1am; F-Sa 7pm-2am.

D-Mer, C. Plató, 13 (☎201 6207). FCG: Muntaner. A blue-hued heaven for lesbians of all ages. A touch of class, a dash of whimsy, and a ton of fun in this small club. Cover €8, includes 1 drink. Beer €3.50. Mixed drinks €6. Open Th-Sa 11pm-3:30am.

DAYTRIPS FROM BARCELONA

THE COSTA BRAVA: FIGUERES AND CADAQUÉS

From Figueres, trains (☎902 24 02 02) leave Pl. de l'Estació for Barcelona (2hr., 27 per day, €8.50) and Girona (30min., 13-23 per day, €2.55). Buses (☎972 67 33 54) run from Pl. de l'Estació to: Barcelona (2¼hr., 2-4 per day, €13.40); Cadaqués (1hr., 6-9 per day, €3.70); Girona (1hr., 2-5 per day, €4). Buses leave Cadaqués for: Barcelona (2½hr., 5 per day, €16.50); Figueres (1hr., 3-7 per day, €4); Girona (2hr., 2 per day, €7.30).

BORN AND BREAD IN CATALUÑA

Once you hit Cataluña, it is inescapable: at each meal, expect to spend some quality time with your new best friend, *pa amb tomàquet*, known to the rest of Spain as *pan con tomate*. A step up from the ubiquitous dry bread basket, this Catalan specialty is an interactive experience. The premise is simple (and frankly, locals like to make it out to be more elaborate than it really is): slice the tomato in half, rub it on the bread to saturate the slice with juice, then do the same with a clove of garlic and add some olive oil. Then eat.

Of course, there are variables at play. Some establishments present the bread pre-rubbed. Usually the bread is toasted, but sometimes it is not. Furthermore, you will find an extensive range of breads being used; the crusty *pan de pagès* (farmer's bread) is most common, but baguettes and smaller rolls have been known to make appearances on the table. Whatever the case, learn it and love it. Waiters delight in instructing travelers on the proper method of dressing the bread, supplementing tradition with their own lively opinions on just how high to pour the oil from and how much garlic to use.

Fundamentally a simple appetizer, *pa amb tomàquet* takes on a new life at the Catalan table. Plus, it's fun to say.

The Costa Brava's jagged cliffs cut into the Mediterranean Sea from Barcelona to the French border. Despite its name, the Brave Coast cowers under the the planeloads of Europeans dumped onto its once-tranquil beaches in July and August. In 1974, Salvador Dalí chose his native, beachless **Figueres** (pop. 35,000) as the site to build a museum to house his works, catapulting the city into international fame. His personal tribute is a Surreal masterpiece, the second most popular museum in Spain, and a prime example of ego run delightfully amok. The **Teatre-Museu Dalí** is in Pl. Gala. From La Rambla, take C. Girona, which becomes C. Jonquera, and climb the steps to your left. The museum contains the artist's nightmarish landscapes and bizarre installations, as well as his tomb. (☎972 67 75 00; www.salvador-dali.org. Open July-Sept. daily 9am-7:45pm; Oct.-June Tu-Su 10:30am-5:45pm. €10, students €7. Summer nights 10pm-12:30am €11.) The **tourist office** is in Pl. Sol. (☎972 50 31 55. Open July-Aug. M-Sa 9am-8pm, Su 10am-3pm; Sept. M-Sa 9am-8pm; Apr.-June and Oct. M-F 9am-3pm and 4:30-7pm, Sa 10am-2pm and 3:30-6:30pm; Nov.-Mar. M-F 9am-3pm.) **Postal Code:** 17600.

The whitewashed houses and small bay of **Cadaqués** (pop. 2000) have attracted artists, writers, and musicians—not to mention tourists—ever since Dalí built his summer home in nearby Port Lligat. Facing uphill with your back to the bus station, take the right fork and follow the signs to Port Lligat and then to the Casa de Dalí (30min.). Alternatively, take a trolley to Port Lligat (1hr., 6 per day, €6) from Pl. Frederic Rahola. **Casa-Museu Salvador Dalí** was the home of Dalí and his wife until her death in 1982. The real artwork is the decorations, including a lip-shaped sofa and a pop-art miniature Alhambra. (☎972 25 10 15. Open mid-June to mid-Sept. daily 10:30am-9pm; mid-Sept. to Nov. and mid-Mar. to mid-June Tu-Su 10:30am-6pm. Tours are the only way to see the house; make reservations 1-2 days in advance. Last tour 45-50min. before closing. €8, students €6.) With your back to the bus station, walk right along Av. Caritat Serinyana to get to Plaça Frederic Rahola; the **tourist office,** C. Cotxe 2, is to the right of the *plaça*, opposite the beach. (☎972 25 83 15. Open July-Aug. M-Sa 9am-2pm and 3-8pm, Su 10:30am-1pm; Sept.-June M-Sa 9am-2pm and 4-7pm.) **Postal Code:** 17488.

THE COSTA DORADA: SITGES

Cercanías (a.k.a. Rodlies; RENFE) trains (☎934 90 02 02) run from Barcelona to Sitges (30-40min., every 15-30min. 5:40am-11pm, €2.30). Mon Bus (☎938 93 70 60) runs late-night buses between Pg. de Villagranca in Sitges and Rbla. de Catalunya in Barcelona midnight-4am (€2.85).

A mecca of gay nightlife, the town of Sitges is perhaps better seen as a night trip from Barcelona than as a daytrip. The town's gorgeous beaches are often less crowded than those of neighboring towns, as Sitges is better known for partying than for tanning. The places to be at sundown are **Calle Primer de Maig** (which runs directly from the beach and Pg. de la Ribera) and **Calle Marquès Montroig,** off C. Parellades. Bars and clubs welcoming a mixed crowd line both sides of the small street, blasting pop and house from 10pm until 3am. Bar- and club-hopping is made easy by the universal lack of cover charge. Beers at most places go for about €3, mixed drinks for €6. A wilder party can be found at the "disco-beach" **Atlàntida,** in Sector Terramar (☎938 94 26 77; Th and Su foam parties), or at legendary **Pachá,** on Pg. de Sant Didac in nearby Vallpineda (☎938 94 22 98). Buses run all night on weekends to the two discos from C. Primer de Maig. Other popular nightspots can be found on **Calle Bonaire** and **Calle Sant Pau;** most open only on weekends. Gay clubs include **Ricky's,** C. Sant Pau 25 (☎938 94 96 81; open daily midnight-6am) and **Trailer,** C. Àngel Vidal 14 (☎938 94 04 01), with infamous foam parties. For more information on nightlife, pick up a *Guía del Ocio* from the **tourist office,** C. Sinia Morera 1. (☎938 94 50 04; www.sitges.com. Open July-Sept. daily 9am-8pm; Oct.-June M-F 9am-2pm and 4-6:30pm.) **Postal Code:** 08870.

GIRONA

RENFE trains (☎902 24 02 02) run from Pl. de Espanya to: Barcelona (1½hr., 28 per day, €6); Figueres (40min., 27 per day, €2.50); Madrid (10½hr., 1 per day, €36). Next door, Barcelona Bus (☎972 20 24 32; www.barcelonabus.com) sends express buses to Barcelona (1¼hr., 3-6 per day, €9.50-11.50) and Figueres (1hr., 3-6 per day, €4-5).

Girona (pop. 81,000) is really two cities in one: a hushed medieval masterpiece on one riverbank and a thriving, modern metropolis on the other. The **Riu Onyar** separates the new city from the old. Nine bridges connect the two banks, including **Pont de Pedra,** which heads into the old quarter by way of C. dels Ciutadans, which becomes C. Bonaventura Carreras i Peralta and then C. Força. This street leads to the cathedral and **El Call,** a thriving Jewish community in the Middle Ages that was virtually wiped out by the Inquisition. Uphill and to the right on C. Força, the imposing Gothic **Cathedral de Girona** rises 90 steps from the plaza below. Within, the **Tresor Capitular** contains some of Girona's most precious art. (☎972 21 44 26; www.lacatedraldegirona.com. Open Tu-Sa July-Sept. 10am-8pm; Mar.-June 10am-2pm and 4-7pm; Oct.-Feb. 10am-2pm and 4-6pm; year-round Su 10am-2pm. Cathedral free. Tresor and cloister €3, students €2.) Join Girona's renowned **Passeig de la Muralla,** a trail along the fortified walls of the old city, at the Jardins de la Francesa (behind the cathedral), at the Jardins d'Alemanys (behind the Museu d'Art), or at the main entrance at the bottom of La Rambla in Pl. de la Marvà. (Open daily 8am-10pm.)

Carrer Cort-Reial is the best place to find good, cheap food, while cafes on **Plaza de la Independencia** offer outside seating on the beautiful square. Pick up groceries at **Caprabo,** C. Sèquia 10, a block off Gran Via de Jaume I. (☎972 21 45 16. Open M-Sa 9am-9pm.) The **tourist office,** Rbla. de la Libertat 1, is by Pont de Pedra on the old bank. (☎972 22 65 75. Open M-F 8am-8pm, Sa 8am-2pm and 4-8pm, Su 9am-2pm.) **Postal Code:** 17070.

THE PYRENEES

The jagged green mountains, Romanesque churches, and tranquil towns of the Pyrenees draw hikers and skiers in search of outdoor adventure.

VICIOUS CYCLING

he Tour de France zooms through he French Pyrenees every year, out on the Spanish side, a slightly lower pace characterizes this popular pastime. Spain offers the same heart-pounding ascents as ts northern neighbor, but with a more Mediterranean philosophy: be sure to take a break to shout an "¡Hola!" to your fellow bikers as you power up those hills. In Cataluña, many of the small, medieval towns are connected by well-marked paths, to be used by bikers and hikers alike. The cycling routes (known as Centres BTT), have distance markers every 500m, to keep even the dizziest biker on track.

Town-to-town biking is a great option for the "thighs of steel" sector, especially between Ripoll, Selva, Baix Empordà, Pla de l'Estany, and Girona, where Lance Armstrong has trained for races since 2001. The fit-but-not-foolhardy will probably prefer some simple, visually rewarding day rides. Two especially popular options run from Ripoll to Olot, a gradual 60km climb, and from Girona to Sant Feliu de Guíxols, a flat, 45km ride ending with an ocean view. Over 100km of smooth, dirt-packed trails follow the old railway lines as well.

For more info on all-terrain cycling, check out www.costabrava.org.

VAL D'ARAN ☎973

Some of the most dazzling peaks of the Catalan Pyrenees cluster around the Val d'Aran, in the northwest corner of Cataluña, best known for its chic ski resorts. The Spanish royal family's favorite slopes are those of **Baquiera-Beret.** For skiing info and reservations, contact the **Oficeria de Baquiera-Beret.** (☎63 90 00.) The palatial **Auberja Era Garona (HI) ❶,** on Ctra. de Vielha, is in the lovely town of Salardú. (☎64 52 71; www.aranweb.com/garona. Breakfast included. Linen €3. Laundry €3.70. Internet €3 per hr. Reception 8am-11pm. Rooms €15-22, with bath €18-25; under 25 €14-19/17-22.) Salardú's 13th-century **Església de Sant Andreu** houses beautifully restored 16th-century murals.

The biggest town in the valley, **Vielha** (pop. 7000) welcomes hikers and skiers with many services for the eager wilderness adventurer. Several inexpensive *pensiones* cluster at the end of C. Reiau, off Pg. Libertat. **Ostau d'Óc ❷,** C. Castéth 13, across the traffic rotary on the main road and up the hill to the left, has clean, spacious rooms with full bath. (☎64 15 97. Singles €17-32; doubles €31-45; quads €53-75.) **Era Plaça ❶,** Pl. de Glèisa, serves up big pizzas (€5.50-7.50) and even bigger sandwiches for €3.50-4. (☎973 64 02 49. Open daily 9am-midnight.) Alsina Graells (Lleida office ☎27 14 70) runs **buses** from Vielha to Barcelona (5hr.; 5:30am, 1:30pm, July to mid-Sept. also 11:45am; €23.70); Lleida (2hr.; 5:30am, 1:30pm); Salardú (20min., 7-13 per day, €0.80). The **tourist office,** C. Sarriulèra 10, is one block upstream from Pl. de Glèisa in the center of town. (☎64 01 10; www.aran.org. Open daily 9am-9pm.)

PARQUE NACIONAL DE ORDESA ☎974

The beauty of Ordesa's Aragonese Pyrenees will enchant even the most seasoned traveler. Its well-maintained trails cut across idyllic forests, jagged rock faces, snow-covered peaks, and rushing rivers. The main **trail** that runs up the Río Arazas to the foot of Monte Perdido and Refugio Góriz, with three spectacular waterfalls within 1hr. of the trailhead, is the most practical and rewarding hike, especially for inexperienced mountaineers. Local companies offer expeditions and adventure sports. For more information, visit www.ordesa.net.

In the park, many *refugios* (mountain huts) allow overnight stays. Right in the center of Torla, across from the tourist office, is **La Casa de Laly ❶,** C. Fatas. (☎48 61 68. Doubles €24-33.) Pick up food at **Supermercado Torla,** on C. Francia. (☎48 63 88. Open May-Oct. daily 9am-2pm and 5-9pm; Nov.-Apr. closed Su. MC/V.) La Oscense (☎48 00 45) sends a **bus** from Jaca to

Sabiñánigo (20min., 4-6 per day, €1.60), and all **trains** on the Zaragoza-Huesca-Jaca line stop at Sabiñánigo. From here, Compañía Hudebus (☎21 32 77) runs to Torla (55min., 1-2 per day, €2.60). From July to October a bus shuttles between Torla and Ordesa (15min.; about every 15min.; €2.20, round-trip €3.20). In low season, you'll have to hike the beautiful 8km to the park entrance or catch a Jorge Soler **taxi** (☎48 62 43; €12), which also offers van tours for up to eight people. The **tourist office** 1.8km past the park entrance, on the left,. (Open July-Aug. daily 9am-2pm and 4-7pm; June Sa-Su only.) The **park info center** in Torla, across the street from the bus stop, takes over in low season. Here you can pick up free maps and the **Senderos Sector Ordesa** trail guide. (☎48 64 72. Open July-Sept. M-F 8am-3pm, Sa-Su 9am-2pm and 4:30-7pm; Oct.-June M-F 8am-3pm.) **Postal Code:** 22376.

NAVARRA

Bordered by Basque Country to the west and Aragón to the east, Navarra's villages—from rustic Pyrenean *pueblos* to bustling Pamplona—are seldom visited except during the festival of *San Fermín*.

PAMPLONA (IRUÑA) ☎948

El encierro, la Fiesta de San Fermín, the Running of the Bulls, utter debauchery: call it what you will, the outrageous festival is the principal reason tourists come to Pamplona (pop. 200,000). Since its immortalization in Hemingway's *The Sun Also Rises*, travelers flock to town the week of July 6-14 for the 8min. event and ensuing chaos. The city's parks, museums, and monuments also merit visits.

Although Pamplona is usually very safe, crime skyrockets during *San Fermín*. Beware of assaults and muggings, do not walk alone at night, and take care in the *casco antiguo*.

TRANSPORTATION AND PRACTICAL INFORMATION. **Trains** (☎902 24 02 02) run from the inconveniently located station, Av. de San Jorge, to: Barcelona (6-8hr., 3-9 per day, €29.50-38); Madrid (3¾hr., 3 per day, €45.50); San Sebastián (2-3 per day, €12.50-16). **Buses** (☎22 38 54) leave from the corner of C. Conde Oliveto and C. Yanguas y Miranda for: Barcelona (5½hr., 4 per day, €20); Bilbao (2hr., 4-7 per day, €11.20); Madrid (5hr., 6-10 per day, €22.20); Valencia (2 per day, €19.50). From Pl. del Castillo, take C. San Nicolás, turn right on C. San Miguel, and walk through Pl. San Francisco to reach the **tourist office,** C. Hilarión Eslava 1. (☎20 65 40; www.cfnavarra.es. Open *San Fermín* daily 8am-8pm; July-Aug. M-Sa 9am-8pm, Su 10am-2pm; Sept.-June M-F 10am-2pm and 4-7pm, Sa 10am-2pm.) During *San Fermín*, there is **luggage storage** at the Escuelas de San Francisco, at the end of Pl. San Francisco. (€2 per day. Open July 3-15 24hr.) **Postal Code:** 31001.

ACCOMMODATIONS AND FOOD. Smart *San Ferministas* book their rooms at least five months ahead to avoid paying rates up to four times higher than those listed below; without a reservation, it's nearly impossible to find a room. Check the newspaper *Diario de Navarra* for *casas particulares* (private homes that rent rooms); be aware, though, that many owners prefer Spanish guests. Roomless backpackers are forced to fluff up their sweatshirts and sleep outside. Be careful—if you can't store your backpack, sleep on top of it and stay in large groups. During the rest of the year, finding a room in Pamplona is no problem. Budget accommodations line **Calle San Gregorio** and **Calle San Nicolás** off Pl. del

Castillo. Deep within the *casco antiguo*, **Pensión Eslava ❶**, C. Hilarión Eslava 13, on the second floor, is quieter and less crowded than other *pensiones*. These older rooms have a balcony and shared bath. (☎22 15 58. Singles €10-15; doubles €20-30. *San Fermín* doubles only €100. Cash only). To get to **Camping Ezcaba ❶**, 7km from the city in Eusa, take city bus line 4-1 (4 per day, 26 per day during *San Fermín;* €0.78) from Pl. de las Merindades. (☎33 03 15. €3.50 per person, per tent, and per car. *San Fermín* €9 per person, per tent, and per car. AmEx/MC/V.) Look for hearty *menús* at the cafe-bars above **Plaza de San Francisco** and around **Paseo de Ronda. Calle Navarrería** and **Paseo de Sarasate** are home to good *bocadillo* bars. **Café-Bar Iruña ❸**, Pl. del Castillo, a former casino made famous by Hemingway, is even more notable for its grand interior than for its stellar *menú* (€11) and amiable staff. (☎22 20 64. Open M-Th 8am-11pm, F 8am-2am, Sa 9am-2am, Su 9am-11pm. MC/V.) Get groceries at **Vendi Supermarket,** C. Hilarión Eslava and C. Mayor. (Open M-F 9am-2pm and 5:30-7:30pm, Sa 9am-2pm; *San Fermín* M-Sa 9am-2pm. MC/V.)

SIGHTS AND NIGHTLIFE. Pamplona's rich architectural legacy is reason enough to visit during the 51 other weeks of the year. The restored 14th-century **Catedral de Santa María,** at the end of C. Navarrería, has a kitchen with five chimneys, one of only four of its kind in Europe. (☎21 08 27. Open M-F 10am-1:30pm and 4-7pm, Sa 10am-2:30pm. Guided tours €4.) The walls of the pentagonal **Ciudadela** once humbled Napoleon; today, the Ciudadela hosts free exhibits, summer concerts, and an amazing *San Fermín* fireworks display. Follow Po. de Sarasate to its end, take a right on C. Navas de Tolosa, a left onto C. Chinchilla and follow it to its end. (☎22 82 37. Open M-Sa 7:30am-9:30pm, Su 9am-9:30pm. Closed for *San Fermín*. Free.) Throughout the year, Pl. del Castillo, with outdoor seating galore, is the heart of the social scene. A young crowd boozes up in the *casco antiguo*, around bar-studded **Calle San Nicolás, Calle Jarauta,** and **Calle San Gregorio,** before hitting the **Travesía de Bayona,** a plaza of bars and *discotecas* off Av. de Bayona (follow Av. del Ejército past the Ciudadela for 600m).

FIESTA DE SAN FERMÍN (JULY 6-14). Visitors overcrowd the city as Pamplona delivers an eight-day frenzy of bullfights, concerts, dancing, fireworks, parades, parties, and wine. Pamplonese, clad in white with red sashes and bandanas, literally throw themselves into the merry-making, displaying obscene levels

RUNNING SCARED. So, you're going to run, and nobody's going to stop you. Because nobody—except the angry, angry bulls—wants to see you get seriously injured, here are a few words of *San Fermín* wisdom:

1. Research the *encierro* before you run; the tourist office has a pamphlet that outlines the route and offers tips for inexperienced runners. Running the entire 850m course is highly inadvisable. (This would mean 4min. of evading 6 bulls running at 24kph.) Instead, pick a 50m stretch.
2. Don't stay up all night drinking and carousing. Experienced runners get lots of sleep the night before and arrive at the course around 6:30am.
3. Take a fashion tip from the locals: wear the white-and-red outfit with close-toed shoes. Ditch the baggy clothes, backpacks, and cameras.
4. Give up on getting near the bulls and concentrate on getting to the bullring in one piece. Though some whack the bulls with rolled newspapers, runners should never distract or touch the animals; this will annoy both the bulls and the locals.
5. Never stop in doorways, alleys, or corners; you can be trapped and killed.
6. Run in a straight line; if you cut someone off, they can easily fall.
7. Be particularly wary of isolated bulls—they seek company in the crowds.
8. If you fall, stay down. Curl up into a fetal position, lock your hands behind your head, and do not get up until the clatter of hooves has passed.

of both physical stamina and alcohol tolerance. The "Running of the Bulls," called the *encierro*, is the highlight of *San Fermines;* the *encierro* first takes place on July 7 at 8am and is repeated at 8am every day for the next week. Hundreds of hungover, hyper-adrenalized runners flee large bulls as bystanders cheer from barricades, windows, balconies, and doorways. Both the bulls and the mob are dangerous; terrified runners react without concern for those around them. To participate in the bullring excitement without the risk of the *enceierro*, don't run. Instead, arrive at the bullring around 6:45am to watch. Tickets for the *Grada* section of the ring are available before 7am (M-F €3.80, Sa-Su €4.40). As one fight ends, the next day's tickets go on sale; wait in the line that forms at the bullring around 6:30pm. (Prices vary from €5 to €888; check www.feriadeltoro.com for details.) Once the running ends, energy spills into the streets and gathers steam until nightfall, when it explodes with singing, dancing, spontaneous parades, and a no-holds-barred party in Pl. del Castillo, Europe's largest open-air dance floor.

BASQUE COUNTRY (PAÍS VASCO)

Basque Country's varied landscape resembles a nation complete in itself, combining cosmopolitan cities, verdant hills, industrial wastelands, and quaint fishing villages. Many believe that the strongly nationalistic Basques are the native people of Iberia, as their culture and language cannot be traced to any known source.

SAN SEBASTIÁN (DONOSTIA) ☎943

Glittering on the shores of the Cantabrian Sea, coolly elegant San Sebastián (pop. 180,000) is known for its world-famous beaches, bars, and scenery. Locals and travelers down *pintxos* (tapas) and drinks in the *parte vieja* (old city), which claims the most bars per square meter in the world. Residents and posters lend a constant reminder: you're not in Spain, you're in Basque Country.

TRANSPORTATION

Trains: San Sebastián has 2 train stations. **Estación de Amara** runs *cercanías* to local destinations and to **Bilbao** (3hr., every hr., €6). **RENFE** (☎902 24 02 02) sends trains from **Estación del Norte,** Po. de Francia, to: **Barcelona** (9hr., 1-2 per day, €35); **Madrid** (8hr., 2-3 per day, €33-44); **Salamanca** (6½hr., 2-3 per day, €29).

Buses: San Sebastián has no actual bus station, only a platform and a series of ticket windows at Av. de Sancho el Sabio 31-33 and Po. de Vizcaya 16. Buses run to: **Barcelona** (7hr., 3 per day, €25); **Bilbao** (1¼hr., 1-2 per hr., €8.30); **Madrid** (6hr., 7-9 per day, €27.40); **Pamplona** (1hr., 6-10 per day, €6); **Paris, France** (12hr., 8pm, €65).

Public Transportation: Local **buses** (☎28 71 00). €1. Map and schedule available at tourist office. Bus #16 runs from Alameda del Boulevard to campground and beaches.

Taxis: Vallina (☎40 40 40) and **Donostia** (☎46 46 46).

ORIENTATION AND PRACTICAL INFORMATION

The **Río Urumea** splits San Sebastián down the middle with the **parte vieja** (old city) and **El Centro** (the new downtown) to the west, separated by the wide walkway **Alameda del Boulevard.** The city center, most monuments, and the two most popular beaches, Playa de la Concha and Playa de Ondaretta, also line the peninsula on the western side of the river. At the tip of the peninsula sits **Monte Urgull.** The **bus station** is south of the city center on Pl. Pío XII. To get to the *parte vieja* from the

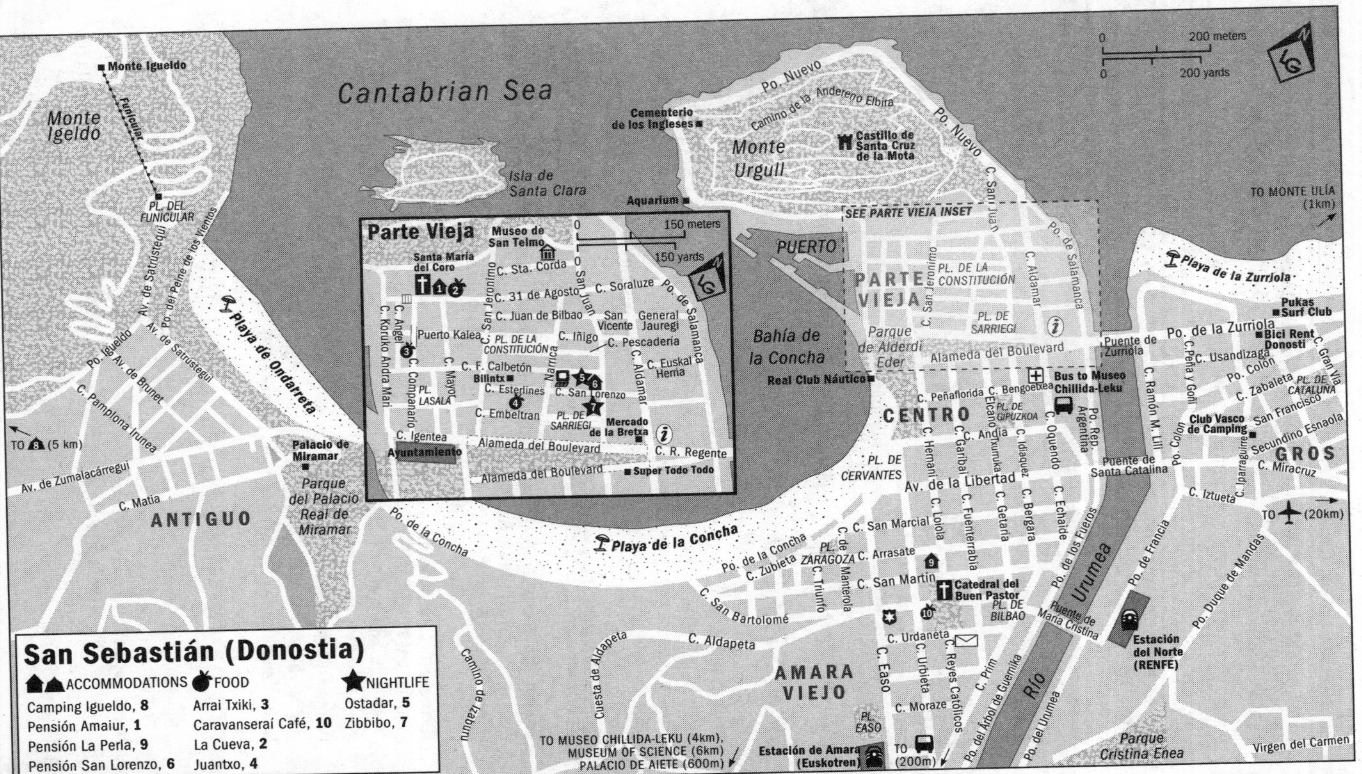
San Sebastián (Donostia)
ACCOMMODATIONS
Camping Igueldo, 8
Pensión Amaiur, 1
Pensión La Perla, 9
Pensión San Lorenzo, 6
FOOD
Arrai Txiki, 3
Caravanseraí Café, 10
La Cueva, 2
Juantxo, 4
NIGHTLIFE
Ostadar, 5
Zibbibo, 7
Cantabrian Sea
Isla de Santa Clara
Monte Urgull
Castillo de Santa Cruz de la Mota
Cementerio de los Ingleses
Aquarium
Monte Igueldo
Monte Igeldo
Funicular
PL. DEL FUNICULAR
Playa de Ondarreta
Palacio de Miramar
Parque del Palacio Real de Miramar
Playa de la Concha
Bahía de la Concha
PUERTO
Real Club Náutico
PARTE VIEJA
SEE PARTE VIEJA INSET
Parque de Alderdi Eder
CENTRO
GROS
AMARA VIEJO
ANTIGUO
Playa de la Zurriola
Pukas Surf Club
Bici Rent Donosti
Club Vasco de Camping
Bus to Museo Chillida-Leku
Catedral del Buen Pastor
Estación del Norte (RENFE)
Estación de Amara (Euskotren)
Parque Cristina Enea
Río Urumea
TO MONTE ULÍA (1km)
TO (20km)
TO (200m)
TO 8 (5 km)
TO MUSEO CHILLIDA-LEKU (4km), MUSEUM OF SCIENCE (6km) PALACIO DE AIETE (600m)
200 meters
200 yards
Parte Vieja
150 meters
150 yards
Santa María del Coro
Museo de San Telmo
Mercado de la Bretxa
Bilintx
Super Todo Todo
Ayuntamiento
PL. DE LA CONSTITUCIÓN
PL. DE SARRIEGI
PL. LASALA
C. Sta. Corda
C. 31 de Agosto
C. Juan de Bilbao
C. Iñigo
C. Pescadería
C. San Lorenzo
C. Esterlines
C. F. Calbetón
C. Embeltran
C. Mayor
Puerto Kalea
C. Companario
C. Angel
C. Koruko Andra Mari
C. Igentea
C. R. Regente
Narrica
San Vicente
General Jauregi
C. Euskal Herria
C. Soraluze
Alameda del Boulevard
Po. de Salamanca
Po. Nuevo
Camino de la Andereno Elbira
C. San Juan
C. Aldamar
C. San Jeronimo
Puente de Zurriola
Puente de Santa Catalina
Puente de María Cristina
Po. de la Zurriola
C. Ramón M. Lili
Po. Colon
Po. de Francia
Po. Duque de Mandas
Po. de los Fueros
Po. del Urumea
Po. del Árbol de Guernika
Po. Rep. Argentina
C. Oquendo
C. Echaide
C. Idiaquez
C. Bergara
C. Getaria
C. Fuenterrabia
C. Loiola
C. Hernani
C. Garibai
C. Andia
Txurruka
Elcano
C. Bengoetxea
C. Peñaflorida
PL. DE GIPUZKOA
Av. de la Libertad
PL. DE CERVANTES
C. San Marcial
C. Arrasate
C. San Martín
C. Urdaneta
C. Urbieta
C. Moraze
C. Easo
PL. EASO
C. Reyes Católicos
C. Prim
PL. DE BILBAO
C. de Manterola
C. Triunfo
PL. ZARAGOZA
C. Zubieta
Po. de la Concha
C. San Bartolomé
C. Aldapeta
Cuesta de Aldapeta
Camino de Izaburu
Virgen del Carmen
C. Miracruz
Secundino Esnaola
San Francisco
C. Iparraguirre
C. Iztueta
C. Gran Via
PL. DE CATALUÑA
C. Zabaleta
Po. Colon
C. Usandizaga
C.Peña y Goñi
Po. del Peine de los Vientos
Av. de Satrústegui
Po. Igueldo
Av. de Brunet
C. Pamplona Irunea
C. Matia
Av. de Zumalacárregui

train station, cross the Puente María Cristina and turn right at the fountain. Continue four blocks north to Av. de la Libertad, then turn left and follow it to the port; the *parte vieja* fans out to the right and Playa de la Concha sits to the left.

Tourist Office: Municipal Centro de Atracción y Turismo, C. Reina Regente 3 (☎48 11 66; www.sansebastianturismo.com), in front of Puente de la Zurriola. English, French, and German spoken. Open June-Sept. M-Sa 9am-8pm, Su 10am-2pm and 3-8pm; Oct.-May M-Sa 9am-1:30pm and 3:30-7pm, Su 10am-2pm.

Bike Rental: Bici Rent Donosti, Po. de la Zurriola 22 (☎29 08 54). Has bike trail maps. Bikes €12 per 4hr., €16 per day. Tandem bikes €6 per hr., €20 per 4hr., €36 per day. Open daily July-Sept. 10am-9pm; Oct.-June 10am-2pm and 4-8:30pm.

Luggage Storage: At the train station. €3 per day. Buy tokens at the ticket counter. Open daily 7am-11pm.

Laundromat: 5 á Sec, inside Mercado de la Bretxa. Open M-Sa 9am-9pm.

Police: C. Easo 41 (☎48 13 20).

Medical Services: Casa de Socorro, C. Bengoetxea 4 (☎44 06 33). Services only available to EU citizens, but others should come here to be redirected to a private clinic.

Internet Access: Zarr@net, C. San Lorenzo 6 (☎43 33 81). €3 per hr. Also ells phone cards. Open M-Sa 10am-10pm, Su 4-10pm. **Biblioteca Central,** Pl. Ajuntamiento,to the right of Casa Consistorial. Free up to 1hr. Open M-F 10am-8:30pm, Sa 10am-1pm, 4:30-8:30pm.

Post Office: C. Urdaneta (☎902 19 71 97), behind the cathedral. Open M-F 8:30am-8:30pm and Sa 9:30am-2pm. **Postal Code:** 20012.

ACCOMMODATIONS

Small *pensiones* are scattered throughout the streets of the noisy *parte vieja*. For a more restful night's sleep, look for hostels and *pensiones* on the outskirts of El Centro. Desperate backpackers scrounge for rooms in July and August, particularly during *San Fermines* (July 6-14) and *Semana Grande* (Aug. 17-25, 2006); September's film festival is just as booked. Many *pensiones* don't take reservations in summer; come early in the day and be prepared to shop around.

Pensión Amaiur, C. 31 de Agosto 44, 2nd fl. (☎42 96 54; www.pensionamaiur.com). From Alameda del Boulevard, follow C. San Jerónimo to its end and turn left. Friendly, English-speaking owner offers lovely rooms in a historic house. Singles €20-35; doubles €33-45, with balcony €38-50; triples €51-72; quads €60-85. MC/V. ❷

Pensión San Lorenzo, C. San Lorenzo 2 (☎42 55 16; www.infonegocio.com/pensionsanlorenzo), off C. San Juan. Sunny doubles with TV and spotless private baths. Internet €1.50 per hr. July-Aug. doubles €48. June and Sept. €36. Oct.-May €25. ❷

Pensión La Perla, C. Loyola 10, 2nd fl. (☎42 81 23; www.pensionlaperla.com), on the street in front of the cathedral. English spoken. Private baths, hardwood floors, and balconies in each room. July-Sept. singles €35; doubles €48. Oct.-June €25/35. MC/V. ❸

Camping Igueldo (☎943 21 45 02; www.campingigueldo.com), 5km west of town atop Monte Igueldo. Beautiful views. Bus #16 (dir.: Barrio de Igueldo-Camping) runs between the site and Alameda del Boulevard (every hr. 7:30am-10pm, €1). Electricity and water included. 2-person tent site mid-June to mid-Sept. and *Semana Santa* €25, extra person €4. Mid-Sept. to mid-June €15-20. MC/V. ❶

FOOD

Pintxos (tapas; €1.50 each), chased down with the fizzy regional white wine *txacoli*, are a religion here. The clean and modern **Mercado de la Bretxa,** in an underground shopping center, sells everything from fresh produce and meat to *pintxos*. The huge supermarket inside offers a choice of groceries. (Open M-Sa 9am-9pm.)

Arrai Txiki, C. del Campanario 3 (☎43 13 02). Delicious, organic vegetarian cuisine in a simple, elegant setting. Entrees €3-6. *Menú* €12. Open in summer M and W-Su 1-3:45pm, Th-Sa also 8:45-11pm. Call ahead for winter hours. Cash only. ❶

Juantxo, C. Esterlines (☎42 74 05). Wide selection of *bocadillos* (€2-3), *pintxos* (€1-2), and *raciones* (€2-5). Open M-Th 9am-11:30pm, F-Su 9am-1:45am. Cash only. ❶

La Cueva, Pl. Trinidad (☎42 54 37), off C. 31 de Agosto. A cavernous restaurant serving traditional seafood dishes. Grilled tuna, cod, and squid entrees €8-15. M-F *menú* €15. Open Tu-Su 1-3:30pm and 8-11pm. MC/V. ❸

Caravanseraí Café, Pl. del Buen Pastor 1 (☎47 54 18). Chic and artsy without pretentious prices. Breakfast deal €1.90. Tasty vegetarian options €3.70-4.30. Entrees €5-8. €0.60 surcharge for patio. Open M-Th 8am-midnight, Sa-Su 10:30-11:30am. MC/V. ❶

SIGHTS AND OUTDOOR ACTIVITIES

MUSEO CHILLIDA-LEKU. The Museo Chillida-Leku features a beautiful permanent exhibit of Eduardo Chillida's work spread throughout the extensive garden of a 16th-century farmhouse restored by the sculptor himself. The farmhouse, a spectacular construction of interlaced wood beams and arching stone, is home to some of the artist's earliest works. *(Autobuses Garayar, line G2, leave from C. Oquendo every 30min., €1.20. Bo. Jauregui 66. 15min. from the town center. ☎33 60 06; www.museochillidaleku.com. Open July-Sept. Sa 10:30am-8pm, Su 10:30am-3pm; Sept.-June M and W-Su 10:30am-3pm. Tours and audio tours included in admission. €7, under 12 €5.)*

MONTE IGUELDO. Though the views from both of San Sebastián's mountains are spectacular, those from Monte Igueldo are far superior. The sidewalk toward the mountain ends just before the base of Monte Igueldo with Eduardo Chillida's sculpture *El Peine de los Vientos*. The road leading to the top is bordered by a low cliffside stone wall, a local favorite for romantic picnics at sunset. A funicular (€1.90) runs every 15min. to the summit. *(☎21 02 11. Open June-Sept. daily 10am-10pm; Oct.-Feb. Sa-Su 11am-8pm; Mar.-June Sa 11am-8pm, Su 11am-9pm.)*

PALACES. When Queen Isabella II started vacationing here in the mid-19th century, fancy buildings sprang up like wildflowers. The **Palacio de Miramar** has passed through the hands of the Spanish court, Napoleon III, and Bismarck; it now serves as the País Vasco University. The adjacent **Parque de Miramar** has beautiful views of the bay. *(Between Playa de la Concha and Playa de Ondarreta. Open daily June-Aug. 8am-9pm; Sept.-May 8am-7pm. Free.)* The other royal residence, **Palacio de Aiete,** is closed to the public, but surrounding trails are not. *(Head up Cta. de Aldapeta or take bus #19 or 31. Grounds open daily June-Aug. 8am-9pm; Sept.-May 8am-7pm. Free.)*

BEACHES AND WATER SPORTS. Lovely **Playa de la Concha** curves from the port to the **Pico del Loro,** home of the Palacio de Miramar. The flat beach disappears during high tide. Sunbathers crowd onto the steeper **Playa de Ondarreta,** beyond the Palacio de Miramar, and surfers flock to **Playa de la Zurrida,** across the river from Monte Urgull. Picnickers head for the **Isla de Santa Clara** in the bay. *(Motorboat ferry 5min., June-Sept. every 30min., round-trip €3.10.)* Check the portside kiosk for more info. **Surfers** should check out the **Pukas Surf Club,** Po. de la Zurriola 23, for lessons and rentals. *(☎42 12 05. Open M-Sa 9:30am-9pm. AmEx/MC/V.)* For general info on sports, pick up the *UDA-Actividades Deportivas* brochure at the tourist office.

ENTERTAINMENT AND NIGHTLIFE

The *parte vieja* pulls out all the stops in July and August, particularly on **Calle Fermín Calbetón,** three blocks in from Alameda del Boulevard. During the year, when students outnumber backpackers, nightlife moves beyond the *parte vieja*. **Osta-**

dar, C. Fermín Calbetón 13, attracts locals and tourists alike with its hip dance mix. (☎42 62 78. Beer €2. Mixed drinks €5. Open M-Th and Su 5pm-3am, F-Sa 5pm-4am.) **Zibbibo,** Pl. de Sarriegi 8, is perhaps the most popular dance club for young tourists in the *parte vieja.* (☎42 53 34. 2-pint Heineken €4. Happy hour M-Th and Su 10-11:30pm. Open M-W 4pm-2:30am, Th-Sa 4pm-3:30am. MC/V.)

BILBAO (BILBO) ☎944

Bilbao (pop. 370,000) is a city transformed; what was once a gritty industrial town is now a beautifully modern city with wide boulevards lined by grand buildings, expansive parks, a host of exciting galleries and museums, and a sleek and efficient subway system. The shining Guggenheim Museum has been the most visible contribution to Bilbao's rise to international prominence, but it doesn't take long to realize that there is much more to Bilbao than its oddly shaped claim to fame.

TRANSPORTATION AND PRACTICAL INFORMATION. **Flights** arrive at the airport (BIO; ☎86 93 00), 8km from Bilbao. To reach the airport, take the Bizkai bus (☎902 22 22 65) marked *Aeropuerto* from P. Moyúa, in front of the Hacienda building (25min., 2 per hr., €1.10). RENFE **trains** (☎902 24 02 02) arrive at the Estación de Abando, Pl. Circular 2, from: Barcelona (9-10hr., 2 per day, €36-49); Madrid (6hr., 3 per day, €31.50-40); Salamanca (5½hr., 2:05pm, €26). **Buses** leave from the Termibús terminal, C. Gurtubay 1 (☎39 50 77; M: San Mamés), for: Barcelona (7¼hr., 4 per day, €37); Madrid (4-5hr., M-F and Su 10-18 per day, €24); Pamplona (2hr., 4-6 per day, €11.60); San Sebastián (1¼hr., 1-2 per hr., €8.30).

The city's main thoroughfare, **Gran Vía de Don Diego López de Haro,** or just **Gran Vía,** connects three of Bilbao's main plazas. Heading east from Pl. de Sagrado Corazón, Gran Vía continues through the central Pl. Moyúa, and ends at Pl. Circular. Past Pl. Circular, you will cross the Río de Bilbao on **Puente del Arenal,** which deposits you on **Plaza de Arriaga,** the entrance to the **casco viejo** and **Plaza Nueva.** The **tourist office** is at Pl. Ensanche 11. (☎79 57 60; www.bilbao.net. Open M-F 9am-2pm and 4-7:30pm.) Surf the **Internet** at **Zona Gris,** Fernandez del Campo 2. (☎44 29 96. €2 per hr. Open daily 9am-11pm.) **Postal Code:** 48008.

ACCOMMODATIONS AND FOOD. **Plaza Arriaga** and **Calle Arenal** have budget accommodations galore. Rates climb during *Semana Grande* (Aug. 17-25, 2006). **Pensión Méndez ❷,** C. Sta. María 13, on the fourth floor, offers sunlit rooms with spacious balconies. (☎16 03 64. Singles €25; doubles €30-35; triples €50.) **Hostal Méndez ❸,** on the first floor of the same building, is even more comfortable; good-sized rooms all have big windows, full bath, and TV. (☎16 03 64. Singles €36; doubles €50-55; triples €65-70.) Restaurants in the *casco viejo* offer a wide selection of local dishes, *pintxos,* and *bocadillos.* The new city has even more variety. As its English-Basque name suggests, **New Inn Urrestarazu ❶,** Alameda de Urquijo 9, is perfect if you just can't decide between authentic local cuisine and comfort food. Try the Idiazábal cheese (€5.40) or €5 onion rings. (☎944 15 40 53. Open M-Th 7:30am-10pm, F-Sa 7am-midnight, Su 10am-10pm. Cash only.) At **Restaurante-Bar Zuretzat ❷,** C. Iparraguirre 7, near the Guggenheim, the walls are lined with helmets signed by the workmen who built the Guggenheim from 1993 to 1997. (☎24 85 05. *Menú* €9-11. Open daily 7:30am-11pm. MC/V.) **Mercado de la Ribera,** on the riverbank, is the biggest indoor **market** in Spain; it's worth a trip even if you're not eating. (Open M-Th and Sa 8am-2:30pm, F 8am-2:30pm and 4:30-7:30pm.)

SIGHTS. Although the **Museo de Bellas Artes,** Pl. del Museo 2, can't boast the name recognition of the Guggenheim, it still wins the favor of locals. Behind an unassuming facade, the museum holds an impressive collection including 15th- to 17th-century Flemish paintings, canvases by Basque artists, and works by Francis Bacon,

Mary Cassatt, El Greco, Gauguin, Goya, and Velázquez. Take C. Elcano to Pl. del Museo or bus #10 from Pte. del Arenal. (☎39 60 60, guided tours 39 61 37. Open Tu-Sa 10am-8pm, Su 10am-2pm. €4.50, students €3, under 12 and W free.) As every tourist pamphlet points out, Frank Gehry's **Museo Guggenheim Bilbao,** Av. Abandoibarra 2, is breathtaking. The US$100 million titanium, limestone, and glass building is said to resemble either an iridescent fish or a blossoming flower, and has catapulted Bilbao into cultural stardom. The interior features a towering atrium and a series of unconventional spaces hosting rotating exhibits from the Guggenheim Foundation's eccentric collection; don't be surprised if you are asked to lie on the floor or sing during your visit. (☎35 90 80; www.guggenheim-bilbao.es. Open July-Aug. daily 10am-8pm; Sept.-June Tu-Su 10am-8pm. Admission includes English-language guided tours Tu-Su 11am, 12:30, 4:30, and 6:30pm. Sign up 30min. before tour at the info desk. €12, students €7, under 12 free.) **Monte Artxanda,** north of the old town, offers the best view of Bilbao's surrounding landscape. (Funicular 3min.; every 15min. M-F 7:15am-10pm, additional service June-Sept. Sa 7:15am-11pm; €0.70)

ENTERTAINMENT AND NIGHTLIFE. In the *casco viejo*, revelers spill out into the streets to sip their *txikitos* (chee-KEE-tos; small glasses of wine), especially on **Calle Barrenkale.** Teenagers and 20-somethings fill **Calle Licenciado Poza** on the west side of town, especially in between C. General Concha and Alameda de Recalde. **The Cotton Club,** C. Gregorio de la Revilla 25 (entrance on C. Simón Bolívar), decorated with over 30,000 beer bottle caps, draws a huge crowd Friday and Saturday nights, while the rest of the week is a little more low-key. (☎944 10 49 51. Beer €3. Over 100 whiskeys €6. Open M-Th 5pm-3:30am, F-Sa 5pm-6am, Su 6:30pm-3:30am.) There is a massive fiesta in honor of *Nuestra Señora de Begoña* during **Semana Grande,** a nine-day party of fireworks, concerts, and theater (Aug. 17-25, 2006). Pick up a *Bilbao Guide* from the tourist office for event listings.

DAYTRIP FROM BILBAO: GUERNICA (GERNIKA). Founded in 1366, Guernica (pop. 15,600) long served as the ceremonial seat of the Basque Country. On April 26, 1937, at the behest of Franco, the Nazi "Condor Legion" released 29,000kg of explosives on Guernica, obliterating 70% of the city in three hours. The thought-provoking **Gernika Peace Museum,** Pl. Foru 1, features a variety of multimedia exhibits. From the train station, walk 2 blocks up C. Adolfo Urioste and turn right on C. Artekale. (☎946 27 02 13. Open July-Aug. Tu-Sa 10am-7pm, Su 10am-2pm; Sept.-June Tu-Sa 10am-2pm and 4-7pm, Su 10am-2pm. Guided English-language tours at noon and 5pm, or call for an appointment. €4, students €2.) The atrocity is immortalized in Picasso's masterpiece, **Guernica** (p. 919), a replica of which stands on C. Pedro de Elejalde, two blocks up San Juan. **Trains** (☎902 54 32 10; www.euskotren.es) roll in from Bilbao (45min., every 30-45min., €2). Bizkai Bus (☎902 22 22 65) sends more frequent and convenient **buses** between Guernica and Bilbao's Estación Abando (lines A-3514 and A-3515; 45min.; buses leave from Hdo. Amezaga in front of the Bilbao RENFE station; 15-30min.; return buses leave from train station; €2). To reach the **tourist office,** C. Artekale 8, from the train station, walk three blocks up C. Adolfo Urioste, turn right on C. Barrenkale, and turn left at the alleyway; look for the signs. (☎946 25 58 92; www.gernika-lumo.net. Open July-Aug. daily 10am-7pm; Sept.-June M-Sa 10am-2pm and 4-7pm, Su 10am-2pm.)

BALEARIC ISLANDS ☎971

While all of the *Islas Baleares* are famous for their gorgeous landscapes, each island has its own special character. Mallorca absorbs the bulk of high-class, package-tour invaders, Ibiza affords some of the best nightlife in Europe, and quieter Menorca offers empty white beaches, hidden coves, and Bronze Age megaliths.

TRANSPORTATION

Flying is the easiest way to reach the islands. Students with an ISIC can often get discounts from **Iberia** (☎902 40 05 00; www.iberia.com), which flies to Palma de Mallorca and Ibiza from Barcelona (40min., €60-120) and Madrid (1hr., €150-180). **Vueling** (☎902 33 39 33; www.vueling.com), **Air Europa** (☎902 40 15 01; www.air-europa.com), and **Spanair** (☎902 92 91 91; www.spanair.com) offer budget flights to and between the islands. Another cheap option is a **charter flight,** which may include a week's stay in a hotel; some companies, called *mayoristas*, sell leftover spots on package-tour flights as "seat-only" (find them through travel agencies).

Ferries to the islands are less popular and take longer. Trasmediterránea (☎902 45 46 45; www.trasmediterranea.com) departs from Barcelona's Estació Marítima Moll and Valencia's Estació Marítima for Mallorca, Menorca, and Ibiza (€68-100). Fares between the islands run €28-63. Buquebus (☎902 41 42 42) has fast catamaran service between Barcelona and Palma de Mallorca (4hr., 2 per day, €55). The three major islands have extensive **bus** systems with fares ranging €1.20-6, though transportation comes to a halt Sundays in most locations; check schedules. **Car** rental costs about €36 per day, **mopeds** €18, and **bikes** €6-10.

MALLORCA

A favorite of Spain's royal family, Mallorca has long attracted the rich and famous. Lemon groves and olive trees adorn the jagged cliffs of the northern coast, while lazy beaches sink into calm bays to the east. The capital of the Balearics, **Palma** (pop. 323,000) is a resort haven for Germans and Brits, but still retains genuine local flavor. In many of its cafes and traditional tapas bars, the native dialect of *mallorquí* is the only language heard. The tourist office distributes a list of over 40 nearby **beaches.** One popular choice (especially with sunburned German tourists) is **El Arenal** (S'Arenal; Platja de Palma; bus #15), 11km southeast of town toward the airport. The *casco viejo* is the place to be for your first drink of the evening. For fantastic cookies during the day and a chill scene at night, try **Costa Galana,** Av. Argentina 45. (Cookies €1.20. Beer €2. Mixed drinks €3-5. Open daily 8am-3am. MC/V.) After sunset, **La Bodeguita del Medio,** C. Vallseca 18, grooves to Cuban rhythms and features a shrine to Ernest Hemingway. (Mixed drinks €4-5. Open M-W and Su 8pm-1am, Th-Sa 8pm-3am.) Palma's clubbers start their night in the *bares-musicales* lining the **Passeig**

¿TIENE FUEGO?

Better watch where you use tha lighter—starting in January 2006 you could get fined €30 600,000. At one time, it seemec that nowhere on the Iberian pen insula was safe from the cancer ous yet atmospheric fumes o *cigarrillos*. Signs prohibitin smoking and laws mandating tha one-third of every cigarette carto be covered with the warnin *"fumar puede matar"* ("smokin can kill)", never prevented th telltale wisps from rising in th metro, in the airport, and even i the Royal Palace. Beginning Janu ary 2006, however, smoking wil be illegal in public buildings, rec reational facilities, private work places, or locations where food i bought and sold. The newl approved anti-smoking measure also raise the legal age for pur chase from 16 to 18 and regulat tobacco companies' advertisin more strictly. The rather sweepin reform is part of the Socialis party's agenda to combat th more than 50,000 deaths pe year from smoking-related dis eases; this number is greater tha fatalities due to car accidents drugs, alcohol, and AIDS com bined. Because nearly a third o Spanish adults currently smoke the new measures are unlikely t be popular. Tourists are responsi ble for 10% of cigarette sales and French smokers often cros the border for cheaper prices Popular or not, *cigarrillos* are i for a nasty shock in the new year

Marítim strip. When the bar scene fades at 3am, partiers move down the strip to the *discotecas.* **Tito's,** in a gorgeous art deco palace on Pg. Marítim, is the city's coolest club. (Beer €3. Mixed drinks €5. Cover €15-18, includes 1 drink. Open daily 11pm-6am. MC/V.)

Hostal Cuba ❷, C. Sant Magí 1, offers spotless rooms private bath and wood furniture. From Pl. Joan Carles I, turn left and walk down Av. Jaume III, cross the river, and turn left on Av. Argentina; the hostel is several blocks down. Bus #1 from the airport drops you at the Sa Faixima stop, half a block away. (☎73 81 59. Singles €22; doubles €40; triples €48. Cash only.) Hungry travelers on a budget head to the side streets off **Passeig del Born,** the cafes along **Avinguda Joan Miró,** or the carbon-copy pizzerias along **Passeig Marítim.** At **Diner ❶,** C. Sant Magí 23, an awesome international staff serves homestyle American favorites. Most dishes cost around €5, but keep an eye out for the daily special. (☎73 62 20. Open 24hr. MC/V.) **Servicio y Precios,** on C. Felip Bauzá, sells groceries. (☎900 70 30 70. Open M-F 8:30am-8:30pm, Sa 9am-2pm.) From the airport, take bus #1 to **Plaza d'Espanya** (15min., every 20min., €1.85). To reach the **tourist office,** Pg. del Born 27, in the bookshop of Casa Solleric, walk up Pg. del Born from Pl. de la Reina. (☎72 40 90; www.a-palma.es. Open M-F 9am-8pm, Sa 9am-1:30pm.) **Postal Code:** 07080.

IBIZA

Nowhere on Earth does style rule over substance (and substances rule over style) more than on Ibiza (pop. 84,000). A hippie enclave in the 1960s, Ibiza has entered new age of decadence. Discogoers, fashion gurus, movie stars, and party-hungry backpackers arrive to debauch in the island's outrageous clubs and gorgeous beaches. None of Ibiza's beaches are within walking distance of **Eivissa** (Ibiza City), but most, including bar-lined **Platja d'en Bossa** and **Platja Figueredes,** are a 20min. bike ride away; bus #14 also leaves from Av. d'Isidor Macabich 20 for Platja d'en Bossa (every 30min., €1.55). The closest beach to the city is **Playa de Las Salinas,** where you can groove to music of top DJs warming up for their club gigs. (Bus #11 runs every 30min. to Salinas from Av. d'Isidor Macabich.)

The crowds return from the beaches by nightfall. The bar scene centers around **Carrer de Barcelona,** while **Carrer de la Verge** is the nexus of gay nightlife. The island's **discos** are world-famous and virtually all gay-friendly. The best sources of information on parties and DJs are posters (often with discounts) plastered around town and the free pamphlet *DJ.* Club promoters are everywhere, and while their insistence on selling you a ticket can be off-putting, don't be afraid to approach them and bargain. The **Discobus** runs to major hot spots (leaves Eivissa from Av. d'Isidor Macabich every hr. 12:30am-6:30am, €1.50). Elegant **Pachá,** on Pg. Perimitral, is a 15min. walk or a 2min. cab ride from the port. (☎31 36 00; www.pacha.com. F "Fuck Me I'm Famous" party. Cover €50. Open daily midnight-7:30am.) At **Amnesia,** on the road to San Antonio, you can forget who you are and who you came with. (☎19 80 41; W drag performances and foam party. Th house or trance. Cover from €40. Open daily midnight-8am. MC/V at bar, cash only for tickets.) Cap off your night in **Space,** on Platja d'en Bossa, which starts hopping around 8am, peaks mid-afternoon, and doesn't wind down until 5pm. (☎39 67 93; www.space-ibiza.es. Cover €30-40. MC/V at bar, cash only for tickets.)

Cheap *hostales* in town are rare, especially in the summer; reserve well in advance. The letters "CH" *(casa de huéspedes)* mark many doorways; call the owners at the phone number on the door. **Hostal Residència Ripoll ❸,** C. Vicent Cuervo 10-14, has spacious rooms with fans and pretty bedspreads, but the apartments are cheaper and more fun. (☎31 42 75. July-Sept. singles €35; doubles €45;

triples €60; 3-person apartments with TV, patio, and kitchen €85. Oct.-June €20/30/33; apartments €450 per month. Cash only.) Grab a slice with a variety of toppings at **Pizza Loca ❶**, C. Lluís Tur i Palau 15. (☎31 45 68. Slices €2-3. Open daily noon-5am.) The **Mercat Vell**, at the end of the bridge leading to *D'alt Villa*, sells meat and produce. (Open M-Sa 7am-1pm.) The **tourist office**, Pl. d'Antoni Riquer 2, is across from the Estació Marítima. (☎30 19 00. June-Nov. M-F 9am-9pm, Sa 9:30am-7:30pm; Dec.-May M-F 8:30am-3pm, Sa 10:30am-1pm.) **Postal Code:** 07815.

MENORCA

Menorca's (pop. 72,000) rustic 200km coastline draws ecologists, sun worshippers, photographers, and wealthy families. Atop a steep bluff, **Mahón** (Maó; pop. 25,000) is the gateway to the island. When cruise ships stop in the harbor, the town becomes considerably more crowded with tourists. The popular **beaches** outside Mahón are accessible by **bus.** Transportes Menorca buses leave from the bus station, up C. Vasallo at the far end of Pl. de s'Esplanada, for **Platges de Son Bou** (30min., 7 per day, €1.85), the island's largest beach, with 4km of gorgeous but crowded sand on the southern shore. Autobuses Fornells buses leave Mahón for the breathtaking **Arenal d'en Castell** (30min., 3-5 per day, €2), while TMSA buses go to touristy **Cala'n Porter** (7 per day, €1.35) and its whitewashed houses, orange stucco roofs, and red sidewalks. While there, don't miss the **Covas d'en Xoroi**, a collection of caves in the cliffs above the sea. The naturally air-conditioned caves house several bars during the day (cover €5-8.50, includes 1 drink; open Apr.-Oct. daily 10:30am-10:30pm) and a crowded disco at night. (☎37 72 36. Th foam parties. Beer €3. Mixed drinks €5-8. Cover €15-25. Open Apr.-Oct. daily 11pm-late.)

To get to the exquisitely decorated rooms of **Posada Orsi ❷**, C. de la Infanta 19, from Pl. de s'Esplanada, take C. Moreres, which becomes C. Hannover; turn right at Pl. Constitució and follow C. Nou through Pl. Reial. (☎36 47 51. Fans available on request. Singles €17-33; doubles €28-38, with shower €35-47. MC/V.) Mahón takes its restaurants very seriously. **Grand General (G.G.) Delicatessan ❷**, Moll. De Llevant 319, the best-kept secret among seaside restaurants, serves mouthwatering Italian food. To get there, head to the port, take a right, and continue for 20min. (☎35 28 05. Sandwiches €3.50-5. Entrees €5-9. Open M-Sa noon-midnight. Cash only.) The Mahón **tourist office**, Moll. de Lavant 2, at the port, is supplemented by mobile tourist booths with yellow umbrellas marked with an "I." (☎35 59 52; www.e-menorca.org. Open M-Sa 8am-9:30pm, Su 9am-1pm and 5-8pm.) **Postal Code:** 07700.

NORTHWESTERN SPAIN

Northwestern Spain is the country's best-kept secret; its seclusion is half its charm. Rainy Galicia hides mysterious Celtic ruins, and on the northern coast tiny Asturias allows access to the dramatic Picos de Europa mountain range.

GALICIA (GALIZA)

If, as the Galician saying goes, "rain is art," then there is no gallery more beautiful than the Northwest's misty skies. Often veiled in silvery drizzle, it is a province of fern-laden eucalyptus woods, slate-roofed fishing villages, and endless white beaches. Locals speak *gallego*, a linguistic hybrid of Castilian and Portuguese.

SPAIN

SANTIAGO DE COMPOSTELA ☎981

Santiago (pop. 94,000) is a city of song. From outdoor operas to roving bands of *guita* players to all-night discos, every street and plaza is filled with musical celebration. Each facade of Santiago's **cathedral** is a masterpiece of a different era, with entrances opening to four different plazas: Inmaculada, Obradoiro, Praterías, and Quintana. (☎58 35 48. Open daily 7am-7pm. Free.) Entrance to the cathedral **museums** includes a visit to the Treasury and Relics, the crypt, the Cloister, the Tapestry room, the Archaeology rooms, the Chapter house, the library, and the archives. (☎58 11 55. Open June-Sept. M-Sa 10am-2pm and 4-8pm, Su and holidays 10am-2pm; Oct.-May M-Sa 10am-1:30pm and 4-6:30pm, Su and holidays 10am-1:30pm. €5, students €3.) Those curious about the *Camino de Santiago* can head to the **Museo das Peregrinacións,** R. de San Miguel 4. (☎58 15 58; www.mdperegrinacions.com. Open Tu-F 10am-8pm, Sa 10:30am-1:30pm and 5-8pm, Su 10:30am-1:30pm. €2.40. Free during special exhibits and most of the summer.)

Nearly every street in the *ciudad vieja* has at least one *pensión.* In the center of the *ciudad vieja,* **Hospedaje Ramos ❷,** R. da Raíña 18, second floor, has well-lit rooms with shining floors, tight windows to keep out the noise, and private baths. Reserve two weeks in advance in summer. (☎58 18 59. Singles €18; doubles €30. Cash only.) Most restaurants are on R. do Vilar, R. do Franco, R. Nova, and R. da Raíña. Literally a hole in the wall, **A Tulla ❷,** R. de Entrerúas 1, is a tiny family restaurant accessible only through an obscure alley between R. do Vilar and R. Nova. The *menús* (€9-11.80) are a superb value. (☎58 08 89. Entrees €6.50-8.50. Open M-Sa noon-midnight. Cash only.) Santiago's **market,** a spectacle in itself, is located between Pl. San Felix and Convento de Santo Agustín. (Open M-Sa 7:30am-2pm.) At night, take R. Montero Ríos to the bars and clubs off **Praza Roxa** to party with local students. **Casa das Crechas,** Vía Sacra 3, is a cavernous, witchcraft-themed drinking hole, renowned for live jazz and Galician folk concerts. (☎56 07 51. Beer €2. Open daily in summer noon-4am; in winter 4pm-3am. MC/V.)

Trains (☎904 24 02 02) run from R. do Hórreo to Bilbao (10¾hr., 9am, €3.50) via León (6½hr., €25.50), and Madrid (8hr., €39). To reach the city, take bus #6 to Pr. de Galicia or walk up the stairs across the parking lot from the main entrance, bear right onto R. do Hórreo, and continue uphill for about 10min. **Buses** (☎54 24 16) run from R. de Rodríguez to Madrid (8-9hr.; 4-6 per day; €36, round-trip €58) and San Sebastián (13½hr.; 3 per day; €50, round-trip €94) via Bilbao (11¼hr., 4 per day, €44/59). To get to the old city from the bus station, walk 20min. or take bus #5 or 10 to Pr. de Galicia. The **tourist office** is at R. do Vilar 63. (☎55 51 29; www.santiagoturismo.com. Multilingual staff. Open daily June-Sept. 9am-9pm; Oct.-May 10am-3pm and 5-8pm.) **Postal Code:** 15701.

ASTURIAS

Spaniards call Asturias a *paraíso natural* (natural paradise). Thanks to its insurmountable peaks and dense alpine forests, Asturias remained untouched for centuries, but a sort of invasion is finally at hand: today, visitors rush to take part in the booming adventure tourism industry. Unlike tourists in the rest of the country, travelers don't come here to see the sights; they come here to brave them.

PICOS DE EUROPA

This mountain range is home to **Picos de Europa National Park,** one of the largest national parks in Europe. The most popular trails and peaks lie near the **Garganta del Cares** (Cares Gorge) in the *Macizo Central* (Central Massif). For a list of mountain *refugios* (cabins with bunks but no blankets), hiking advice, and general park info, contact the **Picos de Europa National Park Visitors' Center** in Cangas de Onís. (☎ 985 84 86 14. Open daily 9am-2pm, W-F also 5-6:30pm, Sa-Su also 4-7pm.)

CANGAS DE ONÍS

☎985

Cangas's (pop. 6370) accessibility makes it an ideal base for exploring the Picos de Europa National Park. In summer, the streets are packed with mountaineers and vacationing families looking for outdoor adventures. Cangas, if not particularly thrilling, is a relaxing, history-rich town. Founded in AD 718, it was the first capital of what would become present-day Spain, and its sights demonstrate the impact of former Paleolithic, Celtic, and Roman inhabitants. Moderately priced pensions abound along Av. Covadonga. On a quiet street off the main road, **Hotel Monteverde ❷,** C. Sargento Provisional 5, offers comfortable rooms facing the mountains and river. (☎84 80 79 or 84 83 70; www.hotelmonteverde.net. Breakfast included. Aug. singles €45; doubles €60; triples €74. July and Sept. €32/42/57. Oct.-June €22/32/43. AmEx/MC/V.) Grab groceries at **Alimerka Supermercado,** Av. de Covadonga, 13. (☎84 94 13. Open M and Su 9am-2pm, Tu-Sa 9am-9:30pm.) **Alsa,** Av. de Covadonga 18 (☎84 81 33), across from the tourist office, sends **buses** to Madrid (7hr., 3:20pm, €27). Find info on lodgings, adventure tourism, and town history at the **tourist office,** Jardines del Ayuntamiento 2, in the Pl. del Ayuntamiento, across from the bus stop. (☎84 80 05. Open *Semana Santa*-Oct. M-Sa 9am-10pm, Su 9am-3pm; Nov.-*Semana Santa* M-Sa 9am-2pm and 4-7pm.)

SPAIN

SWEDEN (SVERIGE)

With the design world cooing over bright, blocky Swedish furniture and college students donning faux-designer wear from H&M, Scandinavia's largest nation has earned a reputation abroad for its cosmopolitan yet highly mass-marketable style. At home, Sweden's struggle to balance a market economy with its generous social welfare system stems from its belief that all citizens should have access to education and affordable health care. Cradle-to-grave programs like these come at a price, and top wage-earners pay out as much as 60% of their annual incomes in taxes. This resolutely neutral nation's zest for spending money on butter instead of guns has also shored up a strong sense of national solidarity, whether you're talking to grain farmers in Skåne or loggers in Norrland's desolate interior.

DISCOVER SWEDEN: SUGGESTED ITINERARIES

Plan for three days in the capital city of **Stockholm** (p. 985), including one sunny afternoon out on the rocky **Skärgård archipelago** (p. 996). Daytrip north to the university town of **Uppsala** (p. 1001), or else take an eastbound ferry out to the island of **Gotland** (p. 997), where serene bike paths and medieval towns overlook the Baltic Sea. Neither **Malmö** (p. 1000) nor **Lund** (p. 1001) are known for their serenity, with clamorous ethnic markets in the former and bombastic student nightlife in the latter. Soak up some high culture in the museums of elegant **Gothenburg** (p. 1003), then get ready to rough it on hikes out of **Åre** (p. 1010) and **Örnsköldsvik** (p. 1011). **Kiruna** (p. 1013) is the end of the line up in mountainous Lappland, where ore miners and the indigenous Sami share vast stretches of Arctic wilderness.

ESSENTIALS

FACTS AND FIGURES

Official Name: Kingdom of Sweden.

Capital: Stockholm.

Major Cities: Gothenburg, Malmö.

Population: 9,002,000.

Land Area: 410,000 sq. km.

Time Zone: GMT +1.

Language: Swedish.

Religions: Lutheran (87%).

WHEN TO GO

July and August are the most popular months to visit Sweden, when temperatures average 20°C (68°F) in the south and 16°C (61°F) in the north. Travelers who arrive in May and early June can take advantage of low-season prices and drink in the late-spring wildflowers, although some attractions don't open until late June. The 24hr. days known as the **midnight sun** are best experienced between early June and mid-July. During the winter, keep an eye out for the **Northern Lights** (p. 753) and bring heavy cold-weather gear; temperatures hover around -5°C (23°F).

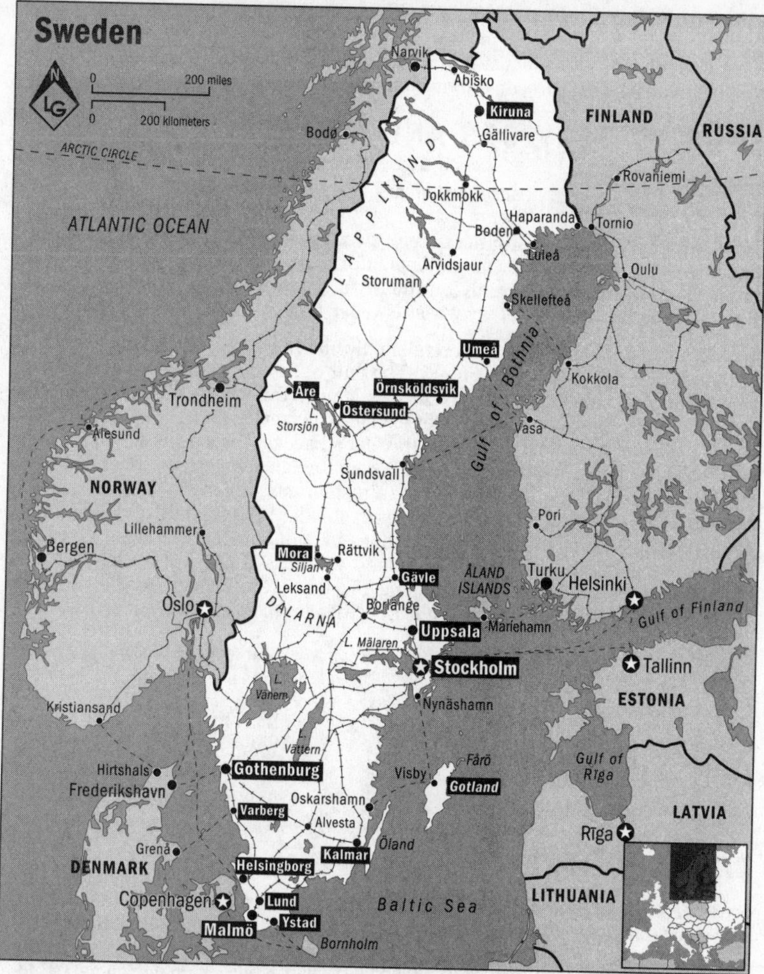

DOCUMENTS AND FORMALITIES

EMBASSIES AND CONSULATES. All foreign embassies are in Stockholm (p. 988). Swedish embassies in your home country include: **Australia,** 5 Turrana St., Yarralumla, Canberra, ACT 2600 (☎02 62 70 27 00; www.swedenabroad.com/canberra); **Canada,** 377 Dalhousie St., Ottawa, ON K1N 9N8 (☎613-244-8200; www.swedenabroad.com/ottawa); **Ireland,** 13-17 Dawson St., Dublin 2 (☎01 474 44 00; www.swedenabroad.com/dublin); **UK,** 11 Montagu Pl., London W1H 2AL (☎020 79 17 64 00; www.swedish-embassy.org.uk); and **US,** 1501 M St. NW, Ste. 900, Washington, D.C. 20005 (☎202-467-2600; www.swedish-embassy.org). Citizens of **New Zealand** should contact the Consulate-General at the Vogel Building, Level 13, Aitken St., Wellington (☎04 499 98 95; sweden@extra.co.nz).

VISA AND ENTRY INFORMATION. EU citizens do not need a visa. Citizens of Australia, Canada, New Zealand, and the US do not need a visa for stays of up to 90 days, although this three-month period begins upon entry into any of the countries that belong to the EU's freedom of movement zone. For more info, see p. 16.

TOURIST SERVICES AND MONEY

EMERGENCY	**Police, Ambulance,** and **Fire:** ☎112.

TOURIST OFFICES. Tourist offices are of two types: those marked with a yellow and blue "I" have both local and national information, while those marked with a green "I" have information only on the town they serve. The Swedish Tourist Board can be found online at www.visit-sweden.com.

MONEY. In a September 2003 referendum, Sweden's voters rejected the adoption of the euro as the country's currency. The unit of Swedish currency remains the **krona** (plural: kronor), divided into 100 *öre.* Many ATMs do not accept non-Swedish debit cards. Banks and post offices exchange currency; expect to pay a 20-35kr commission for cash, and 5-15kr for traveler's checks. **Forex** generally offers the best exchange rates, and has ATMs that accept foreign debit cards. Although a service charge is usually added to the bill at restaurants, tipping is becoming more common and a 7-10% tip is now considered standard. Tip taxi drivers 5-10%. All countries who are members of the European Union impose a Value Added Tax (VAT) on goods and services purchased within the EU. Prices in Sweden already include the country's whopping 25% tax rate, although partial refunds are available for visitors who are not EU citizens (p. 23).

SWEDISH KRONOR (KR)		
	AUS$1 = 5.77KR	10KR = AUS$1.73
	CDN$1 = 6.25KR	10KR = CDN$1.60
	EUR€1 = 9.30KR	10KR = EUR€1.08
	NZ$1 = 5.28KR	10KR = NZ$1.89
	UK£1= 13.56KR	10KR = UK£0.74
	US$1 = 7.47KR	10KR = US$1.34

TRANSPORTATION

BY PLANE. Most international flights arrive in or near Stockholm, with domestic and charter flights connecting to other airports throughout the country. **SAS** (Scandinavian Airlines) offers youth fares (under 26) on some flights within Scandinavia (☎08 797 4000, UK 0870 6072 7727, US 800-221-2350; www.scandinavian.net). Budget airline **Ryanair** (☎353 1249 7700; www.ryanair.com) flies at rock-bottom prices to Västerås Airport, located 1hr. outside of Stockholm.

BY TRAIN. Statens Järnväger (SJ), the state railway company, runs reliable trains throughout southern Sweden, and offers a 30% discount for travelers under 26 (☎0771 75 75 75; www.sj.se/english). Seat reservations (28-55kr) are required on InterCity and high-speed **X2000** trains; they are included in the ticket price but not in railpasses. On other routes, check to see how full the train is; don't bother with reservations on empty trains. In northern Sweden, **Connex** runs trains from Stockholm through Umeå and Kiruna to Narvik, Norway (☎0771 26 00 00; www.connex.info). The 35min. trip over the **Øresund bridge** connecting Malmö to Copenhagen (70kr) is the fastest way to travel from continental Europe; book ahead, especially during the summer. Timetables for all SJ and Connex trains can be found at www.resplus.se. **Eurail** is valid on all of these trains. In the south, purple **pågatågen** trains service local traffic between Helsingborg, Lund, Malmö, and Ystad; **Scanrail** and **Eurail** passes are valid, or purchase tickets from special vending machines. The **Scanrail pass,** purchased outside Scandinavia, is good for rail travel through Sweden, Denmark, Finland, Norway, as well as many discounted ferry and bus rides. Passes can also be purchased within Scandinavia, but passholders can only use three travel days in the country of purchase, so a Scanrail pass purchased at home is more economical for those traveling mostly within Sweden.

RAIL SAVINGS. Scanrail passes purchased outside Scandinavia are much more flexible than Scanrail passes purchased once you arrive, and may be less expensive depending on the exchange rate. Check www.scanrail.com for more information on where to purchase passes at home.

BY BUS. In the north, buses may be a better option than trains. **Swebus** (☎08 546 300 00) is the main carrier nationwide; **Swebus Express** serves the region around Stockholm and Gothenburg exclusively. **Biljettservice** (p. 987), inside Stockholm's Cityterminalen, will reserve tickets for longer routes. Students and travelers aged 17-21 get a 30% discount on express buses. Bicycles are not allowed on board.

BY FERRY. Ferries run from Stockholm (p. 987) to the Åland Islands, Gotland, Finland, and the Baltic states. Ystad (p. 1002) sends several ferries a day to Bornholm, Denmark. Ferries from Gothenburg (p. 1003) serve Frederikshavn, Denmark; Kiel, Germany; and Newcastle, England. Popular lines include the **Silja Line,** Kungsg. 2 (☎22 21 40; www.silja.com/english) and the **Viking Line** (☎452 40 00; www.vikingline.fi). On Silja, both Scan- and Eurailers ride either for free or at reduced rates. On Viking ferries, Scanrail holders get 50% off and a Eurailpass plus a train ticket entitles holders to a free passenger fare. (Mention this discount when booking.) Additionally, Viking offers "early bird" discounts of 15-50% for those who book at least 30 days in advance within Finland or Sweden.

BY CAR. Sweden honors foreign drivers' licenses for a period of up to one year, although drivers under 18 cannot take the wheel, even if they have a valid license in their home country. **Speed limits** are 110kph on expressways, 50kph in densely populated areas, and 70-90kph elsewhere. Headlights must be used at all times. Swedish roads are remarkably uncrowded and in good condition, but take extra care in winter weather and be wary of reindeer or elk in the road. Many gas stations are open until 10pm; after hours, look for cash-operated pumps marked *sedel automat.* For more info on car rental and driving in Europe, see p. 60.

BY BIKE AND THUMB. Bicycling is easy in Sweden; city and regional bike paths are common, and both the **Sverigeleden** (National Route) and the **Cykelspåret** (Bike Path) traverse the entire country. **Cykelfrämjandet,** Tulegaten 43, in Stockholm, publishes a brochure with descriptions of many routes (☎08 545 910 30). **Hitchhiking** is uncommon in Sweden. *Let's Go* does not recommend hitchhiking.

KEEPING IN TOUCH

EMAIL AND THE INTERNET. There are a limited number of cybercafes in Stockholm and other big cities. Expect to pay about 20kr per hr. In smaller towns, Internet is available for free at most tourist offices marked with the yellow and blue "I" (p. 982), as well as for a small fee at most public libraries.

TELEPHONE. Pay phones only accept phone cards *(Telefonkort)*; buy them at newsstands or other shops (30-120kr). **Mobile phones** are an increasingly popular and economical alternative; for more info, see p. 33. International direct dial numbers include: **AT&T** (☎020 79 91 11); **British Telecom** (☎0800 89 0046); **Canada Direct** (☎020 79 90 15); **MCI** (☎0200 89 54 38); **Sprint** (☎020 79 90 11); **Telecom New Zealand** (☎020 79 90 64); **Telstra Australia** (☎020 79 90 61).

PHONE CODES	**Country code:** 46. **International dialing prefix:** 00. For more information on how to place international calls, see inside back cover.

MAIL. Postcards and letters under 50g can be sent for 14-15kr.

LANGUAGE. Sweden has no official language, although Swedish is universally spoken. The region around Kiruna is home to a small minority of Finnish speakers, as well as 7000 speakers of the Sami languages. Almost all Swedes speak English fluently. For basic Swedish words and phrases, see p. 1068.

ACCOMMODATIONS AND CAMPING

SWEDEN	❶	❷	❸	❹	❺
ACCOMMODATIONS	under 160kr	160-230kr	230-350kr	350-500kr	over 500kr

Youth hostels *(vandrarhem)* cost between 120-200kr per night. The 315 hostels run by the **Svenska Turistföreningen (STF)** and affiliated with HI are uniformly top-notch. Nonmembers should expect to pay between 200-240kr per night; HI members receive a 45kr discount. Most hostels have kitchens, laundry facilities, and common areas. To reserve ahead, call the hostel directly or contact STF headquarters in Stockholm (☎08 463 21 00; www.svenskaturistforeningen.se). Tourist offices often book beds in hostels for no fee, and can help find **private rooms** (200-350kr). STF also manages **mountain huts** in the northern wilds (150-350kr). Many **campgrounds** (tent sites 80-110kr; www.camping.se) offer multi-occupant *stugor* (cottages) for 100-300kr per person. International Camping Cards aren't valid in Sweden; **Swedish Camping Cards,** available at all SCR campgrounds, are mandatory (90kr for a one-year sticker of validity). The Swedish tradition of *allemansrätten* (right of public access) means travelers can camp for free in the countryside, as long as they stay a reasonable distance from private homes. For info on how to exercise this right responsibly, check www.allemansratten.se.

FOOD AND DRINK

SWEDEN	❶	❷	❸	❹	❺
FOOD	under 50kr	50-75kr	75-100kr	100-160kr	over 160kr

Restaurant fare is usually expensive in Sweden, but **saluhallen** (food halls), open-air markets, and **varmkorv** (hot dog stands) make budget eating easy enough. Many restaurants offer affordable **dagens rätt,** daily lunch specials, for 60-75kr. The Swedish palate was long attuned to simple, hearty meat-and-potatoes fare, but immigrant communities in Malmö and Stockholm have spiced things up for budget travelers. A coterie of five-star chefs in Gothenburg are tossing off increasingly imaginative riffs on herring and salmon. The Swedish love **drip coffee** (as opposed to espresso) and have institutionalized coffee breaks as a near-sacred rite of the workday. Aside from light beer containing less than 3.5% alcohol, booze can be purchased only at **Systembolaget** liquor stores and in licensed bars and restaurants. You can buy light beer at 18, but it's 20+ otherwise and you will be carded. Some classier bars and clubs have age restrictions as high as 25.

HOLIDAYS AND FESTIVALS

Holidays: New Year's Day (Jan. 1); Epiphany (Jan. 6); Good Friday (Apr. 14); Easter Sunday and Monday (June 4-5); May Day (May 1); Ascension Day (May 25); Whit Sunday and Monday (June 4-5); National Day (June 6); All Saints' Day (Nov. 1); Christmas Eve and Day (Dec. 24-25); Boxing Day (Dec. 26).

Festivals: Valborgsmässoafton (Walpurgis Eve; Apr. 30) celebrates the arrival of spring with roaring bonfires in Dalarna and choral singing in Lund and Uppsala. Dalarna erects flowery maypoles in time for Midsummer (June 23-24), as young people flee to the islands of Gotland, Öland, and the Skärgård archipelago for all-night parties. July welcomes the Stockholm Jazz Festival to the capital city, and crayfish parties in August and eel parties in September leave the timid swimming for sanctuary.

BEYOND TOURISM

Summer employment is often easier to find than long-term work, since Sweden has fairly strict regulations governing the employment of foreigners. See p. 66 for Beyond Tourism opportunities throughout Europe.

The American-Scandinavian Foundation (AMSCAN), 725 Park Ave., New York, NY 10016, USA (☎001 212-879-9779; www.amscan.org/jobs/index.html). Volunteer and job opportunities throughout Scandinavia. Limited number of fellowships for study in Sweden available to Americans.

Council of International Fellowship (CIF) (www.cif-sweden.org). Funds exchange programs for human service professionals, including home stays in various Swedish cities. Must have 2 years work experience.

Internationella Arbetslag, Tegelviksgatan 40, Stockholm, Sweden (☎46 864 308 89; www.ial.nu). The Swedish branch of Service Civil International (SCI; www.sciint.org) organizes a broad range of "workcamps" throughout Sweden. 700kr camp fee plus 150kr SCI membership fee.

STOCKHOLM

☎08

Surrounded by water, elegant Stockholm (pop. 1,250,000) exists by virtue of a delicate latticework of bridges that connects its islands and peninsulas and brings together individual neighborhoods that have developed characters of their own. Regardless of which quarters of the city you happen upon during your visit, sophistication and style are the orders of the day.

TRANSPORTATION

Flights: Arlanda Airport (ARN; ☎797 60 00), 45km north of the city. **Flygbussar** shuttles (☎686 16 00) run between Arlanda and the bus station (40min.; every 15min. 4am-10pm; 90kr, students 59kr), as do **Arlanda Express** trains (☎020 22 22 24; 20min.; every 15min.; 180kr, students 90kr). **Bus** #583 runs to the T-bana stop Märsta (10min., 30kr or 2 coupons); then take the T-bana to T-Centralen in downtown Stockholm (40min., 30kr or 2 coupons). Flygbussar also operates shuttles to **Vasteras Airport** (VST; ☎021 80 56 10) timed to line up with Ryanair departures (1½hr., 100kr).

Trains: Centralstationen (☎762 25 80). T-bana: T-Centralen. Trains to: **Copenhagen** (6hr.; 5 per day; 608-1088kr, under 26 450-935kr); **Gothenburg** (3-5hr.; every 1-2hr.; 434-1180kr, under 26 305-942kr); **Oslo** (5-8hr.; 5 per day; 778kr, under 26 662kr).

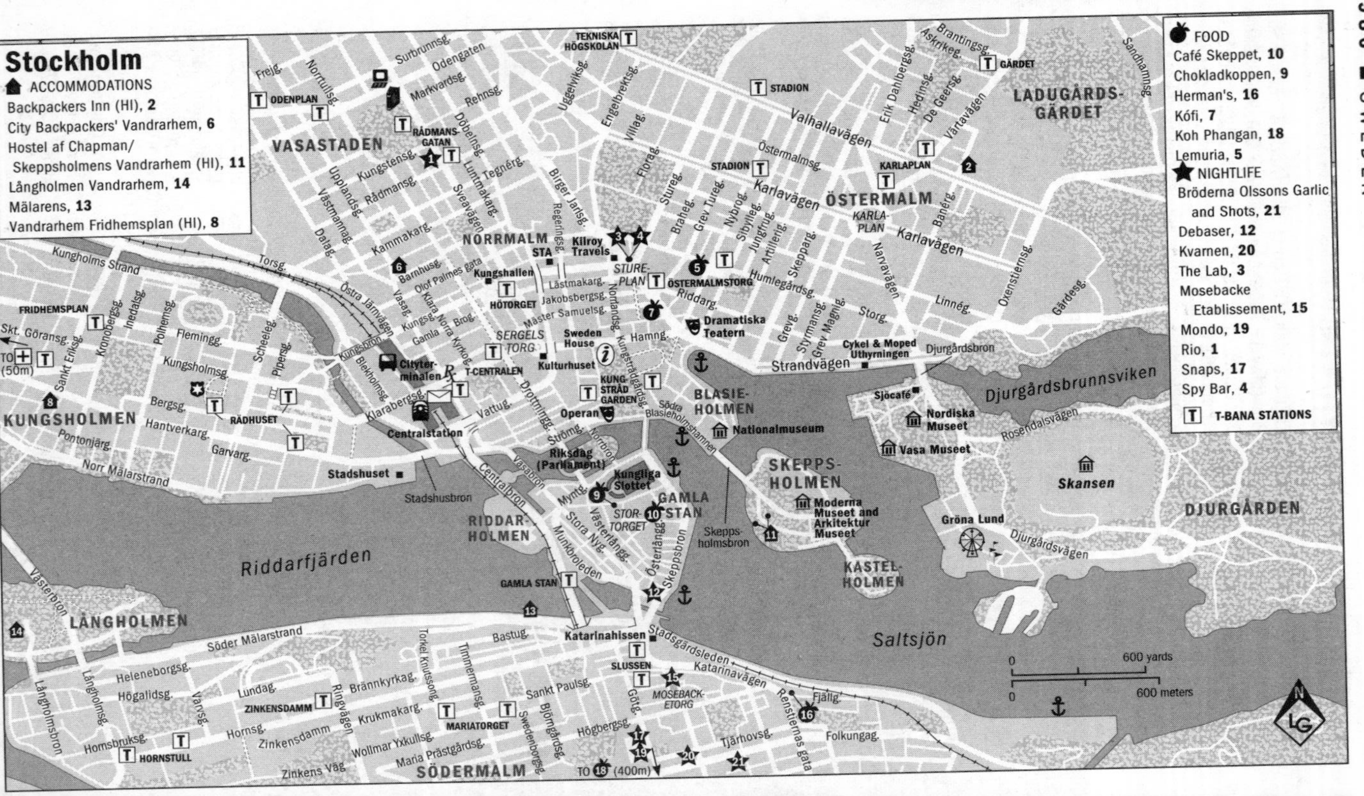
Stockholm
ACCOMMODATIONS
Backpackers Inn (HI), 2
City Backpackers' Vandrarhem, 6
Hostel af Chapman/
Skeppsholmens Vandrarhem (HI), 11
Långholmen Vandrarhem, 14
Mälarens, 13
Vandrarhem Fridhemsplan (HI), 8
FOOD
Café Skeppet, 10
Chokladkoppen, 9
Herman's, 16
Kőfi, 7
Koh Phangan, 18
Lemuria, 5
NIGHTLIFE
Bröderna Olssons Garlic and Shots, 21
Debaser, 12
Kvarnen, 20
The Lab, 3
Mosebacke Etablissement, 15
Mondo, 19
Rio, 1
Snaps, 17
Spy Bar, 4
T-BANA STATIONS
600 yards
600 meters
LADUGÅRDS-GÄRDET
DJURGÅRDEN
Skansen
Djurgårdsbrunnsviken
ÖSTERMALM
NORRMALM
VASASTADEN
KUNGSHOLMEN
GAMLA STAN
SKEPPS-HOLMEN
KASTEL-HOLMEN
BLASIE-HOLMEN
RIDDAR-HOLMEN
LÅNGHOLMEN
SÖDERMALM
Riddarfjärden
Saltsjön
Gröna Lund
Nordiska Museet
Vasa Museet
Moderna Museet and Arkitektur Museet
Nationalmuseum
Dramatiska Teatern
Kungliga Slottet
Riksdag (Parliament)
Operan
Kulturhuset
Sweden House
Kilroy Travels
Centralstation
Cityterminalen
Stadshuset
Cykel & Moped Uthyrningen
Sjöcafé
Katarinahissen
TO 18 (400m)
TO (50m)
Skt. Göransg.
ODENPLAN
RÅDMANSGATAN
TEKNISKA HÖGSKOLAN
STADION
KARLAPLAN
GÄRDET
ÖSTERMALMSTORG
STUREPLAN
KUNGSTRÄDGÅRDEN
T-CENTRALEN
HÖTORGET
GAMLA STAN
SLUSSEN
MARIATORGET
ZINKENSDAMM
HORNSTULL
FRIDHEMSPLAN
RÅDHUSET
Strandvägen
Karlavägen
Valhallavägen
Birger Jarlsg.
Drottningg.
Sveavägen
Kungsholmsg.
Hornsg.
Ringvägen
Götg.

Buses: Cityterminalen, upstairs on the north end of Centralstationen. **Terminal Service** (☎762 59 97) to airport (80kr) and Gotland ferries (70kr). **Biljettservice** (☎762 59 79) makes reservations with Sweden's numerous bus companies for longer routes. **Swebus,** one of the largest, runs to: **Copenhagen** (9hr., 3 per day, 380kr); **Gothenburg** (7hr., 7 per day, 295kr); **Malmö** (8½hr., 3 per day, 370kr).

Ferries: Silja Line, Kungsg. 2 (☎22 21 40; www.silja.com), sails overnight to Finland: **Helsinki** (16hr., daily, from 450kr) and **Turku** (12hr., 2 per day, from 140kr). To get to the terminal, take T-bana to Gärdet and follow signs to Värtahamnen, or take the Silja bus (20kr) from Cityterminalen. 50% Scanrail discount. **Viking Line** (☎452 40 00; www.vikingline.fi) sails to **Helsinki** (15hr.; 1 per day; mid-June to mid-Aug. 430kr, low season from 300kr) and **Turku** (12hr.; 2 per day; mid-June to mid-Aug. 230kr, low season from 130kr). Office in Cityterminalen. **Tallink** (☎666 60 01; www.tallink.ee) sails to **Tallinn, Estonia** (16hr.; 1 per day; from 375kr, low season from 215kr). Shuttle buses (20kr) run from Cityterminalen to the Tallink port.

Public Transportation: T-bana (*Tunnelbana;* subway) runs 5am-12:30am. **Nightbuses** run 12:30am-5:30am. Most destinations cost 2 coupons (30kr, 1hr. unlimited transfer). Coupon books *(rabattkuponger)* are sold at Pressbyrån news agents. 10 coupons 80kr, 20 coupons 145kr. The **SL Tourist Card** *(Turistkort)* is valid on all public transportation. 1-day 95kr; 3-day 180kr. Office in the basement of Centralstationen (☎600 10 00). T-bana: T-Centralen. Open M-Sa 6:30am-11:15pm, Su 7am-11:15pm.

Taxis: Many cabs have fixed prices to certain destinations; ask when you enter the cab. Expect to pay 450kr from Arlanda to Centralstationen. Major companies include **Taxi 020** (☎020 20 20 20), **Taxi Kurir** (☎30 00 00), and **Taxi Stockholm** (☎15 00 00).

Bike Rental: Cykel & Moped Uthyrningen, Strandvägen, Kajplats 24 (☎660 79 59). Bikes from 220kr per day. Open May-Sept. daily 10am-6pm. MC/V. **Djurgårdsbrons Sjöcafé,** Galärvarvsvägen 2 (☎660 57 57). Bikes 250kr per day. In-line skates 200kr per day. Canoes 300-500kr per day. Open June-Aug. daily 9am-9pm. MC/V.

ORIENTATION AND PRACTICAL INFORMATION

Compact Stockholm spans a number of small islands (linked by bridges and the T-bana) at the junction of **Lake Mälaren** to the west and the **Baltic Sea** to the east. The large northern island is divided into two sections: **Norrmalm,** home to Centralstationen and the crowded shopping district around Drottningg., and **Östermalm,** which boasts the elegant **Strandvägen** waterfront and upscale nightlife fanning out from **Stureplan.** The mainly residential western island, **Kungsholmen,** holds grassy beaches, waterside promenades, and the majestic Stadhuset (city hall). The southern island of **Södermalm** retains a traditional feel in the midst of a budding cafe culture and club scene. Nearby **Långholmen** is a nature preserve, as is much of the eastern island **Djurgården,** which houses a number of museums on its western side. At the center of these five islands is the cobblestoned **Gamla Stan** (old town). Gamla Stan's neighbor (via Norrmalm) is **Skeppsholmen,** home to many of the city's art museums. Stockholm's streets are easy to navigate: each begins with number "1" at the end closest to the Kungliga Slottet (p. 990) in Gamla Stan; the lower the numbers, the closer you are to the old town.

Tourist Offices: Sweden House, Hamng. 27 (☎508 28 508; www.stockholmtown.com), entrance off Kungsträdsgården. From Centralstationen, walk up Klarabergsg. to Sergels Torg (the plaza with the 37m glass obelisk), bear right on Hamng. and turn right at the park. Friendly, multilingual agents sell the **SL card** and **Stockholm Card** *(Stockholmskortet)*, which includes public transportation, admission to 75 museums and attractions, and discounts on boat tours. 1-day 260kr; 2-day 390kr; 3-day 540kr. Open M-F 9am-7pm, Sa 10am-5pm, Su 10am-4pm. The **HotellCentralen** branch, located in Centralstationen (☎789 24 56), books rooms for a 60kr fee. Open June-Aug. daily 8am-8pm; Sept.-May M-F 9am-6pm, Sa 9am-4pm, Su 10am-4pm.

PEDESTRIAN TACTICS 101. Stockholm lends itself to exploration on foot, but the network of elevated streets and footbridges can be confusing. To get from Centralstationen to Sergels Torg, turn left out of the station onto Vasag., take the stairs up to Klarag. and head straight. To get to the Stadhuset, turn right out of the station and walk to Vasabron, then walk down the steps to the water just before the bridge and follow the quay under Centralbron. There are different ways to navigate the cloverleaf bridge from Gamla Stan to Södermalm, depending on your destination; to reach Södermalmstorg or the cliffs, stay on the bridge to the left. To reach Södermalärstrand, stay as far to the right as possible and then take the ramp down to the water.

Budget Travel: Kilroy Travels, Kungsg. 4 (☎0771 54 57 69; www.kilroytravels.com). Open M-F 10am-6pm. **STA Travel,** Kungsg. 30 (☎0771 61 10 10; www.statravel.se). Open M-F 10am-6pm; Sept.-June also Sa 11am-2pm.

Embassies: Australia, Sergels Torg 12, 11th fl. (☎613 29 00; www.sweden.embassy.gov.au). Open M-F 8:30am-4:50pm. **Canada,** Tegelbacken 4, 7th fl. (☎453 30 00; www.canadaemb.se). Open 8:30am-noon and 1-5pm. **Ireland,** Ostermalmsg. 97 (☎661 80 05). Open M-F 10am-noon and 2:30-4pm. **UK,** Skarpög. 6-8 (☎671 30 00; www.britishembassy.se). Open M-F 9am-5pm. **US,** Daghammarskjölds Väg 31 (☎783 53 75; www.usemb.se). Open M-Th 9-11am and 1-3pm, F 9-11am.

Currency Exchange: Forex offices in **Centralstationen** (☎411 67 34; open daily 7am-9pm) and **Cityterminalen** (☎21 42 80; open M-F 7am-8pm, Sa 8am-5pm). 15-20kr commission.

Luggage Storage: Lockers are available at Centralstationen (20-60kr per day) and Cityterminalen (25-35kr per day).

GLBT Resources: RFSL, Sveav. 57-59 (☎457 13 20; www.rfsl.se). T-bana: Rådmansgatan. Located above *Rio* (see **Nightlife,** p. 995). Open M-F 9am-5pm. **Rosa Rummet,** Sveav. 57 (☎736 02 15), is a gay and lesbian bookstore on the same block. *Queer Extra (QX)* and the *QueerMap,* available at Rosa Rummet and Sweden House, give info about Stockholm's gay hot spots.

Emergencies: ☎112.

24hr. Pharmacy: Look for green-and-white *Apoteket* signs. **Apoteket C. W. Scheele,** Klarabergsg. 64 (☎454 81 30), at the overpass over Vasag. T-bana: T-Centralen.

Medical Services: ☎32 01 00.

Hospitals: Karolinska (☎517 700 00), north of Norrmalm near Solnavägen. T-Bana: Skt. Eriksplan. **Sankt Göran** (☎587 100 00), on Kungsholmen. T-Bana: Fridhemsplan.

Internet Access: Stadsbiblioteket (library), Odeng. 59, in the annex. T-bana: Odenplan. 10min. free, but slots fill early in the morning. Open M-F 9am-7pm, Sa noon-4pm. **Inferno Online,** Odeng. 60, across from the library, has more than 100 terminals. 19kr per hr. Open daily 10am-midnight. **Sidewalk Express** Internet stations are located throughout the city, including one in Cityterminalen. 19kr per hr. Open 24hr.

Telephones: Almost all public phones require Telia phone cards; buy them at Pressbyrån newsstands in increments of 50 (50kr) or 120 (100kr) units. Local calls are 6 units for 1st min., 2 for each additional min.; international calls use up to 12 units per min.

Post Office: In Centralstationen (☎781 24 25). Open in summer M-F 7am-8pm, Sa-Su 10am-4pm; winter M-F 7am-8pm, Sa-Su 9am-6pm. Address mail to be held in the following format: First name SURNAME, *Poste Restante,* 10110 Stockholm 1, SWEDEN.

ACCOMMODATIONS AND CAMPING

Reservations are indispensable in summer, and many HI hostels limit stays to five nights. If you haven't booked ahead, arrive around 8am. Some non-HI hostels are hotel/hostels; specify that you want to stay in a dorm-style hostel, or risk paying hotel rates. Stockholm's several **botels** (boat-hotels) are a novel solution to space issues, but they can be cramped, noisy, and a recipe for seasickness—request a room on the water side of the boat. There are also various **B&B booking services,** including the **Bed and Breakfast Agency.** (☎643 80 28; www.bba.nu. Open M 10am-5pm, Tu-W 9am-5pm.) An SL or Stockholm Card is the cheapest way for **campers** to reach some of the more remote campsites. Note that the right of public access (p. 984) does not apply within the city limits, although camping is allowed on most of the Skärgård archipelago (p. 996).

Hostel af Chapman/Skeppsholmens Vandrarhem (HI), Flaggmansväg. 8 (☎463 22 66; www.stfchapman.com). T-bana: Kungsträdgården. Exit the station toward Kungsträdgården, walk to the water, and take the bridge to Skeppsholmen. Modern on-shore hostel and a 19th-century schooner pinch-hitting as a roomy botel. Great view of Gamla Stan. Breakfast 70kr. Linen 65kr. Laundry 35kr. Internet 1kr per min. Reception 24hr. Lockout 11am-3pm. Dorms 185-230kr; doubles 510kr. 45kr HI discount. MC/V. ❷

City Backpackers' Vandrarhem, Upplandsg. 2A (☎20 69 20; www.citybackpackers.se). Dorms are a bit crowded, but the free pasta, coffee, and tea make up for it. Free morning sauna, 20kr other times. Linen 50kr. Laundry 50kr. Free Internet. Reception 9am-noon and 2-7pm. Dorms from 190kr; doubles 520kr. MC/V. ❷

Backpackers Inn (HI), Banérg. 56 (☎660 75 15; www.backpackersinn.se). T-bana Karlaplan, Valhallav. exit. From Valhallav., turn right and look for the brick building on the left. Classrooms transform into summer dorms and a gymnasium into communal showers at this school-turned-summer hostel in a quiet Östermalm neighborhood. Open mid-June to mid-Aug. No kitchen available. Breakfast 50kr. Linen 40kr, plus 60kr deposit. Laundry 45kr. Internet 1kr per min. Reception 24hr. 14-bed dorms 175kr. 45kr HI discount. MC/V. ❷

Mälarens, Södermälarstrand, Kajplats 6 (☎644 43 85; www.theredboat.com). T-bana: Gamla Stan. Take Centralbron across the river and walk right 100m along the shore–it's the red boat. This old canal steamer has small rooms with low ceilings, but a lovely view and maritime decor add to the experience. Breakfast 60kr. Reception 8am-11pm. Dorms 195kr; singles 430kr; doubles 490kr; triples 690kr; quads 920kr. MC/V. ❷

Vandrarhem Fridhemsplan (HI), S:t Eriksg. 20 (☎653 88 00; www.fridhemsplan.se) T-bana: Fridhemsplan. Walk 150m along S:t Eriksg. away from the bridge. The trek from the city is rewarded by bright, spacious rooms with great views. Wheelchair accessible. Breakfast 60kr. Lockers 20kr. Linen 50kr. Laundry 50kr. Free Internet. Reception 24hr. Dorms 240kr; singles 435kr; doubles 585kr. 45kr HI discount. AmEx/MC/V. ❸

Långholmen Vandrarhem (HI), Långholmsmuren 20 (☎668 05 10; www.langholmen.com). T-bana: Hornstull. Walk north on Långholmsg., turn left onto Högalidsg., and then right onto Långholmsbron. The cozy rooms of this renovated former prison on the island of Långholmen still bear authentic cell doors. Breakfast 80kr. Linen 40kr. Laundry 100kr. Reception 24hr. Dorms 250kr; doubles 585kr. 45kr HI discount. MC/V. ❸

Ängby Camping, Blackebergsv. 24 (☎37 04 20; www.angbycamping.se), on Lake Mälaren. T-bana: Ängbyplan. Go downstairs, turn left on Färjestadsvägen, and bear left at the fork. Wooded campsite with swimming area. Reception June-Aug. daily 8am-10pm, May and Sept. 9am-9pm; low season M-F 4-8pm, Sa-Su noon-6pm. 2-person tent sites 135kr, extra person 80kr. Cabins 400-550kr. AmEx/MC/V. ❶

Bredäng Camping, Stora Sällskapets Väg (☎97 70 71; www.camping.se/plats/A04), near Lake Mälaren. T-bana: Bredäng. Turn left under the tunnel onto Stora Sällskapets Väg and follow the street 700m, past Ålgrytevägen. Reception 7am-10pm. Open mid-Apr. to late Oct. Tent sites 175kr. Quad rooms 450kr. AmEx/MC/V. ❷

FOOD

Ethnic restaurants line **Götgatan** and **Folkunggatan** in Södermalm, while pizza and kebabs are plentiful on Vasastaden's **Odengatan.** Grocery stores are easy to find around any T-bana station—popular chains include **Coop, Hemköp,** and **ICA.** Head to the outdoor fruit market at **Hötorget** for your Vitamin C fix (open M-Sa 7am-6pm), or to the **Kungshallen** food hall, Kungsg. 44, off the market place, for a meal from one of the international food stands. (www.kungshallen.com. Open M-F 9am-11pm, Sa 11am-11pm, Su noon-11pm.) The **Östermalms Saluhall,** Nybrog. 31 (T-bana: Östermalmstorg), is a more traditional indoor market that contains bustling fish and meat stands, as well as more expensive restaurants serving Swedish dishes. (www.ostermalmshallen.se. Open M-Th 9:30am-6pm, F 9:30am-6:30pm, Sa 9:30am-2pm.) Prices in Stockholm are lowest at lunch time; track down lunch specials *(dagens rätt;* 50-80kr) to save money.

Herman's, Fjällg. 23A (☎643 94 80). T-bana: Slussen. Head uphill on Katarinav. Excellent vegetarian fare, served buffet-style, with phenomenal views off the Söder cliffs. Lunch (78-98kr) and dinner (128-168kr) include dessert and a drink. Open daily in summer 11am-11pm; spring and fall 11am-10pm; winter 11am-9pm. MC/V. ❹

Koh Phangan, Skåneg. 57 (☎642 68 65). T-Bana: Skanstull. Head north on Götg. and turn right onto Skåneg. Splurge on Thai food in the city's trendy SoFo ("south of Folkungagata") neighborhood. A stream runs between tables in what looks like a tree-house transplanted from a South Asian jungle, and a simulated monsoon may interrupt your waiter in mid-sentence. Vegetarian entrees 125-140kr. Meat dishes 150-165kr. Seafood 180-195kr. Open M-Th 11am-11pm, F-Su 2-11pm. MC/V. ❺

Chokladkoppen, Stortorg. 18-20 (☎20 31 70). T-bana: Gamla Stan. Friendly staff serves light meals (34-65kr) and generous desserts (from 34kr). One of the best people-watching spots on the Stortorget sq. Open in summer M-Th and Su 9am-11pm, F-Sa 9am-midnight; low season M-Th and Su closes 10pm. Cash only. ❷

Lemuria, Nybrog. 26 (☎660 02 21). T-bana: Östermalmstorg. Across from the Östermalms Saluhall. Serves carefully balanced, gluten- and lactose-free vegetarian and vegan lunch (55kr). Open M-F 11am-3pm. AmEx/MC/V. ❶

Café Skeppet, Österlångg. 9 (☎23 74 00). On the corner of Österlångg. and Skeppar Karls Gränd. Hidden in Gamla Stan's street maze, this cozy cafe prepares quick wraps (45-55kr) and soup (50kr). Open M-F 10am-6pm, Sa-Su noon-6pm. MC/V. ❶

Kófi, Birger Jarlsg. 11 (☎611 33 35). T-bana: Östermalmstorg. The rent must be sky-high in this tony part of town, but Kófi keeps things affordable with sandwiches (36-49kr) for a light lunch. Open M-W 7am-11pm, Th-Sa 8am-1am, Su 9am-11pm. AmEx/MC/V. ❶

SIGHTS

SOMETHING FOR NOTHING. It may be expensive to get by in Stockholm, but many of the city's excellent museums are free. The **Sweden House** (p. 987) provides a complete listing, for all your wallet-saving cultural needs.

Break up your walking tour (p. 992) of Stockholm's inner neighborhoods with T-bana rides to more remote locations in order to get a sense of the capital's sweeping scope. The T-bana has been called the world's longest art exhibit, since over the past 50 years the city has commissioned more than 140 artists to decorate its stations. The murals and sculptures of T-Centralen remain the best-recognized example of T-bana artistry, although Madonna cast her vote for the space-age Hötorget station when she featured it in her 1998 "Ray of Light" music video.

GAMLA STAN (OLD TOWN). The Baltic trading port of Stockholm was once confined to the small island of Staden. Today, the island is the epicenter of the city and is dominated by the magnificent 1754 **Kungliga Slottet** (Royal Palace), one of the largest palaces in Europe and the winter home of the Swedish royal family. The **Royal Apartments** and the adjacent **Rikssalen** (State Hall) and **Slottskyrkan** (Royal Chapel) are dizzyingly lavish. In the former wine cellar, the **Skattkammaren** (Royal Treasury) houses a small but impressive collection of jewel-encrusted objects, including the 16th-century sword of King Gustav Vasa. The statues in the **Gustav III Antikmuseum** are forgettable, but the **Museum Tre Konor,** on the lower level, includes the foundation of the 13th-century castle that once stood on the same site. Expect lines in summer. *(The main ticket office and information area are at the rear of the complex, near the Storkyrkan. ☎402 61 30; www.royalcourt.se. Open mid-May to June daily 10am-4pm; July to mid-Aug. daily 10am-5pm; Sept. to early May Tu-Su noon-3pm. Each attraction 70kr, students 35kr. Combination ticket 110/65kr.)* The **Livrustkammaren** (Armory) presents an extensive collection of swords, suits of armor, and carriages that seem like they are straight out of Cinderella. *(Slottsbacken 3. ☎519 555 44; www.livrustkammaren.se. Open June-Aug. daily 10am-5pm; Sept.-May Tu-W and F-Su 11am-5pm, Th 11am-8pm. Free.)* A broad plaza separates the palace from the **Storkyrkan** church, where winners of the Nobel Peace Prize speak after accepting their awards. Don't miss the statue of St. George slaying the dragon. *(Open daily 9am-4pm. In summer tower tours 2, 3pm. Church 20kr. Tours 30kr.)* Around the corner on **Stortorget,** the main square, the small **Nobelmuseet** traces the story of the Nobel Prize and its winners through engrossing multimedia exhibits. *(☎534 818 00; www.nobelprize.org/nobelmuseum. Open mid-May to mid-Sept. M and W-Su 10am-5pm, Tu 10am-8pm; mid-Sept. to mid-May Tu 11am-8pm, W-Su 11am-5pm. 50kr, students 40kr.)* Gamla Stan's main pedestrian street, **Västerlånggatan,** is a lively tourist mob scene during the summer. Wander the maze of small side streets to see a less touristy face of the old town. *(T-bana: Gamla Stan. Tours of Gamla Stan June-Aug. M and W-Th 7:30pm. Meet at the obelisk in front of Storkyrkan. 60kr.)*

KUNGSHOLMEN. Perched on the eastern tip of Kungsholmen, the red brick **Stadshuset** (City Hall) hides intricately designed rooms behind its muscular red brick exterior. The required tour of the interior takes you through the council room, whose roof suggests an inverted Viking ship, and then into the enormous Blue Hall, where a 10,000-pipe organ overlooks a miniature Italian *piazza.* In the breathtaking **Gold Room,** millions of shimmering tiles make up an Art Deco mosaic celebrating the history of Stockholm. The 106m **tower** provides the best panoramic view of the city center. *(Hantverkarg. 1. T-bana: T-Centralen. Walk toward the water and turn right on Stadshusbron. ☎508 29 058; www.stockholm.se/stadshuset. Tower open daily May-Sept. 10am-4:30pm. 20kr. Tours daily June-Aug. 10, 11am, noon, 2, 3pm; Sept. 10am, noon, 2pm; Oct.-May 10am, noon. 60kr, students 50kr.)*

SKEPPSHOLMEN AND BLASIEHOLMEN. The huge, well-organized collection at the **Moderna Museet,** on the island of Skeppsholmen (SHEPS-hole-men), spans canvases by Matisse, Picasso, Klee, and Rauschenberg, as well as more recent, lesser-known work. In the same building, the permanent collection of the **Arkitekturmuseet** uses 3-D models to display the history of Swedish design, while temporary exhibits examine cross-cultural aesthetics. *(Moderna Museet ☎519 552 00; www.modernamuseet.se. Arkitekturnuseet ☎587 270 00; www.arkitekturmuseet.se. Both museums open Tu-W 10am-8pm, Th-Su 10am-6pm. Free.)* Across the bridge on the Blasieholmen peninsula, the **Nationalmuseum** features an underwhelming collection; Rembrandt's *Conspiracy of the Batavians* and the folkloric canvases of Anders Zorn are highlights, as is the exhibit on the history of Swedish design. *(T-bana: Kungsträdgården. Museum is on the left before Skeppsholmsbron bridge. ☎51 95 44 10; www.nationalmuseum.se. Open Tu 11am-8pm, W-Su 11am-5pm; Sept.-May also open Th 11am-8pm. Permanent collection free, temporary exhibits 40-80kr. AmEx/MC/V.)*

SWEDEN

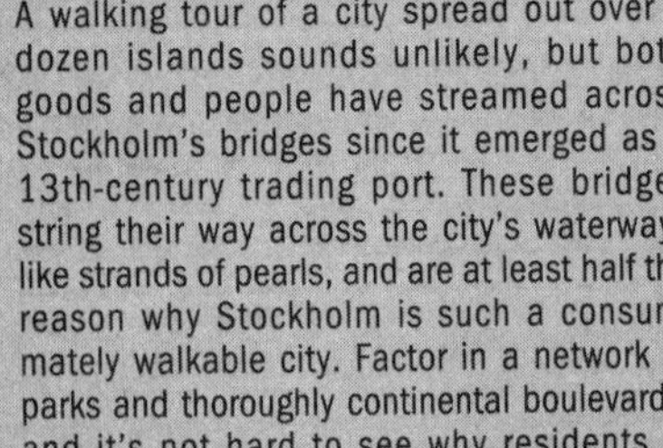

A walking tour of a city spread out over a dozen islands sounds unlikely, but both goods and people have streamed across Stockholm's bridges since it emerged as a 13th-century trading port. These bridges string their way across the city's waterways like strands of pearls, and are at least half the reason why Stockholm is such a consummately walkable city. Factor in a network of parks and thoroughly continental boulevards, and it's not hard to see why residents of Stockholm happily hoof it during the summer months—even though comfortable mass transit options are never very far away.

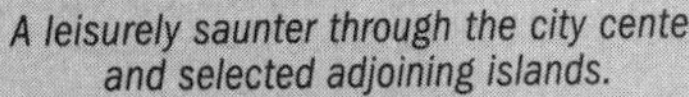

A leisurely saunter through the city center and selected adjoining islands.

TIME: 4hr., 5-6hr. with visits to the Stadhuset, Moderna Museet, or Kungliga Slottet.

DISTANCE: About 6km.

SEASON: Mid-April to late October.

This tour starts at **Sweden House** (p. 987), Stockholm's main tourist office, and ends in the old town of **Gamla Stan.**

1 SERGELS TORG. Begin by walking west on Hamngatan past the exclusive **NK** department store. Make for the 37m glass obelisk at the center of Sergels Torg, the plaza that was carved out of Lower Norrmalm after WWII in what the Swedes called "the great demolition wave." Modernist city planners were convinced that they could arbitrarily designate a new city center and have civic life revolve around it, but they got more than they bargained for with the covey of drug dealers who flocked to the western side of Sergels Torg. Known as the **Plattan,** this sunken plaza should be avoided at night. The glassy **Kulturhuset** (p. 994), on the southern side of the square, is a more wholesome point of interest; check the schedule of events posted inside **Lava,** a popular hangout with Stockholm's university students.

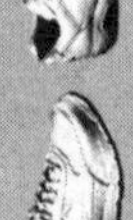

2 STADSHUSET. Turn left onto Drottninggatan, Norrmalm's main pedestrian thoroughfare, and then turn right just before the bridge onto Strömgatan. Take the steps down to the quay just before the Centralbron overpass, go under the bridge, and walk toward the majestic Stadshuset (p. 991). Guided tours leave on the hour, lasting around 1hr. and costing 50kr. If time or money is short, however, make a point of walking around the manicured waterside grounds before continuing on your way.

3 RIDDARHOLMEN. Head back to Centralbron, take the steps up, and then turn right onto the bridge. Make a right into the plaza on Riddarholmen (The Knight's Island). Stockholm's 17th-century elite built private palaces around the **Riddarholmskyrkan** church. Parts of the church date back to the 13th century, when it was used as a Franciscan monastery, although Lutherans threw the Franciscans out on their ears after the Protestant Reformation and then set aside the church as the burial place for Swedish monarchs in 1807. Today, the island's elegant palaces are used as courthouses and offices for government agencies.

WALKING TOUR

4 SKEPPSHOLMEN. Head straight out of the plaza, cross Centralbron, and make a right onto charming Stora Nygatan. Turn left down any of the side streets and then left onto Västerlånggatan, lined with shops and confectionaries. Cross two bridges, cutting through the back of the **Riksdag** (Parliament), then turn right onto Strömgatan and right again back across the water, this time past the Riksdag's long east-facing facade. Turn left onto Slottskajen alongside the royal palace of **Kungliga Slottet** (p. 990), and left again onto the bridge toward the Granc Hotel. Bear right onto Södra Blasieholmshamnen and then cross the scenic Skeppsholmbror bridge onto the island of Skeppsholmen. The main attraction here is the **Moderna Museet** (p 991), home to one of Marcel Duchamp's infamous fountains and plenty of other work from bott ends of the 20th century. Admission is deliciously free.

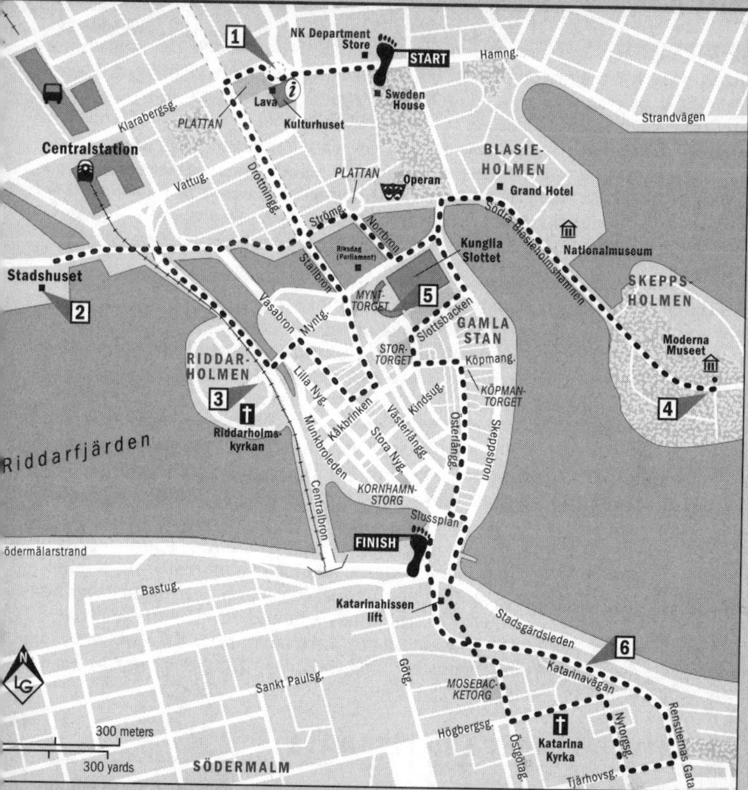

KUNGLIGA SLOTTET. Retrace your steps and turn left back onto Gamla Stan, flanking palace on Skeppsbron this time. You could spend a full day wandering through the pal-e's museums and courtyards, but for the sake of time confine your visit to the **Royal artments.** Turn into the plaza leading up to Storkyrkan; the ticket office is on the right.

SÖDERMALM. Hug the waterfront as you make your way south to the bridge connecting mla Stan to the southern island of Södermalm. Keep to the left as you cross the bridge, the **Katarinahissen lift** (10kr), and cross the bridge to the north-facing cliffs for one of best views of the city. Head straight to intimate Mosebacke Torg and continue south down götagatan. Take your first left onto Högbergsgatan, passing by the octagonal tower of the **tarina kyrka,** devastated by fire in 1990 but rebuilt to its former Baroque splendor. At the of Högbergsgatan, turn right onto Nytorgsgatan, left onto Tjärhovsgatan, and then right Renstiernas gata. As the street begins its languid arch to the west, a beautiful view of ckholm's spires spreads out before you. Finish by heading down to Slussen and crossing k onto Gamla Stan to rest your weary legs.

OSTERMALM. Tucked away among the residential houses of this quiet neighborhood are a number of small and occasionally quirky museums. The **Musikmuseet** (Music Museum) features a room dedicated completely to Swedish pop sensations ABBA, as well as a collection of over 6000 musical instruments. *(Sibylleg. 2. T-bana: Östermalmstorg, Sibylleg. exit. ☎519 554 90; http://stockholm.music.museum. Open Tu-Su July-Aug. 10am-5pm; Sept.-June noon-5pm. Free.)* Less than a block away, the Armémuseum brings to life Swedish military history from Viking times through the present. *(Riddarg. 13. T-bana: Östermalmstorg, exit Sibylleg. ☎788 95 60; www.armemuseum.se. Open Tu 11am-8pm, W-Su 11am-4pm. Free.)* For a more complete account of Sweden's history head to the **Historiska Museet,** which occasionally puts on cool temporary exhibits. *(Narvav. 13-17. T-bana: Karlaplan. ☎519 556 00; www.historiska.se. Open May-Sept. daily 10am-5pm; Oct.-Apr. M-W and F-Su 11am-5am, Th 11am-8pm. Free.)*

SWEDEN

DJURGÅRDEN. Djurgården, a lush national park close to the heart of the city, is a perfect spot for a summer picnic. The main attraction is the haunting **Vasamuseet,** which contains a massive salvaged warship that sank in the middle of Stockholm's harbor on its maiden voyage in 1628. *(☎519 548 00; www.vasamuseet.se. Galärvarvet. Take bus #44, 47, or 69. Open mid-June to mid-Aug. daily 9:30am-7pm; mid-Aug. to mid-June M-Tu and Th-Su 10am-5pm, W 10am-8pm. English-language tours daily every hr. 10:30am-6:30pm. 80kr, students 40kr. AmEx/DC/MC/V.)* The **Gröna Lund** amusement park features a handful of exciting rides, including the 80m Fritt Fall Tilt, which offers a great view of the city before catapulting you downward at high G-forces. *(Open daily mid-May to late Aug., usually 11am-11pm; check www.gronalund.se for detailed schedule. Admission 60kr. Rides 15-60kr each.)* Djurgården is also home to **Skansen,** a huge open-air museum featuring 150 historical buildings, handicrafts, and a small zoo. Costumed actors inhabit the homes, and their attention to period authenticity somehow redeems the project from kitschiness. *(☎442 8000; www.skansen.se. Take bus #44 or 47. Park and zoo open daily June-Aug. 10am-10pm; Sept.-Apr. 10am-5pm; May 10am-8pm. Homes open daily June-Aug. 11am-7pm; Sept.-May 11am-5pm. 70kr, low season 50kr.)*

ENTERTAINMENT AND FESTIVALS

Stockholm's smaller performance venues are showcased in *What's On,* available at the tourist office. There are also a number of larger, more widely known performance spots. The six stages of the national theater, **Dramatiska Teatern,** Nybroplan (☎667 06 80), feature performances of works by August Strindberg and other playwrights (50-260kr). **Backstage** highlights for more experimental material. The **Kulturhuset** at Sergels Torg (☎508 15 08), an arts complex built in the 1960s, houses art galleries, performance spaces, and a variety of cultural venues that are often free to the public. It also plays host to **Lava** (☎508 31 44; closed in July), a popular hangout with a stage, library, and cafe that lend themselves to poetry readings and other student events. Check www.kulturhuset.se for details. The **Operan,** Jakobs Torg 2 (☎24 82 40), stages operas and ballets from late August through mid-June. (Tickets 135-460kr. Student rush tickets available.) The imposing **Konserthuset,** Hötorg. 8 (☎10 21 10), hosts the Stockholm Philharmonic, which performs concerts there in summer (100-270kr). Culture buffs on a budget should sample the sights and sounds of the **Parkteatern** (☎506 20 299; www.stadsteatern.stockholm.se), a summer-long program of free theater, dance, and music staged in parks around the city. Call **BiljettDirect** (☎07 7170 7070; www.ticnet.se) for tickets. The world-class **Stockholm Jazz Festival** arrives in mid- to late July. (☎556 924 40; www.stockholmjazz.com.) Other festivals include the gay blowout **Stockholm Pride** (late July or early Aug.; ☎33 59 55; www.stockholmpride.org) and late August's **Strindberg Festival** for the turtlenecked, furrowed-brow literati.

NIGHTLIFE

For a city where "night" barely exists during the summer, Stockholm knows a thing or two about nightlife. The scene in Stockholm varies by neighborhood, with particular social codes prevailing in different parts of the city. The posh, upscale **Stureplan** area in Östermalm (T-bana: Östermalmtorg), is where beautiful people party until 5am. Expect long lines outside nearly every club; the most pretentious honor exclusive guest lists. High up on the cliffs across the river, **Södermalm's** (T-bana: Mariatorget) nightlife is less glitzy but just as popular, with a diverse mix of bars and clubs along Götg. and around Medborgarpl. In the northern part of town, a grab-bag of nightlife options line **Sveavägen** and the **Vasastaden** area (T-bana: Odenplan or Rådmansg.) while **Kungsgatan** (T-bana: Hötorget) is the main party street in Norrmalm. Stockholm is compact enough to walk between all the islands, although nightbuses cover most of the city. Pick up *Queer Extra (QX)* and the *QueerMap* at Rosa Rummet (p. 988) for invaluable tips on gay nightlife.

Mondo, Medborgarpl. 8 (☎673 10 32). T-bana: Medborgarpl. On the left across from the station. This massive complex with 5 bars, 4 dance floors, and 3 stages packs in well-dressed young Swedes listening to live rock, hip-hop, or reggae. Drinks from 50kr. 20+. Cover 40-150kr M and F-Sa. Open M-Sa 10pm-3am.

Mosebacke Etablissement, Mosebacke Torg 3 (☎55 60 98 90). T-bana: Slussen. Take the Katarina lift (10kr) to Söder Heights. Next to the Söder Teatern. Enjoy the glorious view from the terrace, or head indoors, where the stage features live music in low season. Beer 44kr. Mixed drinks 74kr. 20+. Cover 60-120kr. Terrace open daily in summer 11am-1am. Indoors open M-Th and Su 5pm-1am, F-Sa 5pm-2am. AmEx/DC/MC/V.

Rio, Sveav. 57 (☎32 98 00; www.riostockholm.com). T-bana: Rådmansg. Walk 1 block left of the station. Popular gay club draws a large mixed crowd on the weekends. Beer 34-44kr. 18+. Cover 50-100kr. Bar open M-Sa 6pm-1am. Club open Th-Sa 10pm-3am.

Debaser, Karl Johans Torg 1 (☎462 98 60; www.debaser.nu). T-bana: Slussen. Stockholm's most popular rock club draws crowds year-round with live music. Beer 42kr. 18+. Cover 60-100kr. Open daily 5pm-3am.

Kvarnen, Tjärhovsg. 4 (☎643 03 80). T-bana: Medborgarpl. The slick cocktail lounge **H2O,** the energetic **Eld** dance club, and a 200-year-old beer hall somehow coexist under the same roof. Beer 29kr, 39kr after 7pm. 21+, 23+ after 10pm. Beer hall open daily 5pm-3am. Lounge open M-Sa 7pm-3am, Su 9pm-3am. Club open W-Th 11pm-3am, F-Sa 10pm-3am. AmEx/DC/MC/V.

The Lab, Birjer Jarlsg. 20 (☎545 03 700). T-bana: Östermalmtorg. Stureplan's most down-to-earth–and smallest–venue gets packed with people dancing to 80s and 90s hits. Beer 46kr. Mixed drinks 72kr. 23+. Cover 80kr F-Sa 1-4:30am. Open M-Sa 5pm-5am, Su noon-5am. AmEx/DC/MC/V.

Snaps, Götg. 48 (☎640 28 68). T-bana: Medborgarpl. On the corner of Medborgarpl. Intimate basement dance floor starts to get surreal around midnight, with luminescent walls and skittering jungle beats. Beer 42kr. Mixed drinks from 70kr. W-Th 21+, F-Sa 23+. Cover F-Sa 60kr. Open M-W 5pm-1am, Th-Sa 5pm-3am. AmEx/DC/MC/V.

Bröderna Olssons Garlic and Shots, Folkungag. 84 (☎640 84 46; www.garlicandshots.com). T-bana: Medborgarpl. Follow your nose 3 blocks up Folkungag. Tattooed bartenders serve garlic beer (35-50kr) and a repertoire of 101 shots (35kr) to a crowd sporting both leather and sport coats. Cafe 18+, bar 23+. Open daily 5pm-1am.

Spy Bar, Birjer Jarlsg. 20 (☎545 03 700) T-bana: Östermalmtorg. Once open only to the rich and famous, the Spy Bar maintains its exclusive vibe, especially late-night Sa. Brave the pretense to hear the eclectic mixes spun by a famous DJ inside. Beer 56kr. Mixed drinks 92kr. 23-25+. Cover 100-120kr. Open W-Sa 10pm-5am. AmEx/DC/MC/V.

DAYTRIPS FROM STOCKHOLM

Stockholm is situated in the center of an archipelago, where the mainland gradually crumbles into the Baltic. The islands in either direction—east toward the Baltic or west toward Lake Mälaren—are a lovely escape from the city. **Ferries** to the archipelago leave from in front of the Grand Hotel on the **Stromkajen** docks between Gamla Stan and Skeppsholmen or the **Nybrohamnen** docks (T-bana: Kungsträdgården). Visit the **Excursion Shop** in Sweden House (p. 987) for more info.

THE ARCHIPELAGO (SKÄRGÅRD). The wooded islands of the Stockholm archipelago become less developed as the chain coils its way out into the Baltic Sea. Ritzy **Vaxholm** (tourist office ☎08 541 314 80; www.vaxholm.se) is the archipelago's most popular island to visit. Its pristine beaches and 16th-century fortress have spawned pricey sidewalk cafes and hordes of tourists. Three hours from Stockholm, **Sandhamn** is a bit quieter, although the white sands of Trouville Beach have plenty of devotees. Hikers can escape the crowds by exploring the coastal trails on **Finnhamn** and **Tjockö** to the north. Ask at Sweden House about **hostels;** they tend to be booked up months in advance, but the islands are a promising place to exercise the right of public access. Waxholmsbolaget runs **ferries** to even the tiniest islands year-round. (☎08 679 58 30; www.waxholmsbolaget.se.) Sweden House sells the **Båtluffarkort,** good for unlimited Waxholmsbolaget rides; the pass pays for itself in a few long trips. (5-day 170kr, 30-day 300kr.)

LAKE MÄLAREN. The island of **Björkö** on Lake Mälaren is home to **Birka,** an 8th-century trading port where St. Ansgar established Sweden's first Christian congregation. The settlement was abandoned by the late 10th century, but excavation continues in the surrounding bay. Artifacts uncovered there are displayed in the **Birka Museum.** Closer to town, **Drottningholms Slott** was built for the queens of Sweden in the late 17th century and has served as the royal family's residence since 1981, when they left Kungliga Slottet (p. 990). The Rococo interior and sprawling formal gardens are impressive, but the highlight is the 1766 **Court Theater,** where artistic director Per-Erik Öhrn uses 18th-century sets and stage equipment to mount provocative modern productions. Tickets start at 165kr; guided tours are also available. (Open May-Aug. daily 10am-4:30pm; Sept. daily noon-3:30pm; Oct.-Apr. Sa-Su noon-3:30pm. 60kr, students 30kr. English-language tours mid-June to Aug. daily every hr. 11am-3pm; May to mid-June Sa-Su every hr. 11am-3pm.) Strömma Kanalbolaget **ferries** depart Stockholm May to early Sept. from the Stadshusbron docks next to the Stadshuset. (☎587 140 00; www.strommakanalbolaget.com. July-Aug. 9:30am, 1:15pm, return 3, 6:45pm; Sept. and May 9:30am, return 3pm. Guided tour, museum admission, and round-trip ferry 255kr.)

UPPSALA ☎018

Archbishop Jakob Ulvsson founded Uppsala University in 1477, but the Reformation wrested control away from the Catholic Church and set the stage for secular inquiry in this college town. Today, the footbridges and side streets of Uppsala (pop. 127,000) teem with almost 40,000 undergraduates. Rome may no longer be calling the shots in Uppsala's classrooms, but the city's red-brick **Domkyrka,** Domkyrkoplan 5-7, is still the largest cathedral in Sweden; its 118m towers are as tall as the cathedral is long. Many famous Swedes, ranging from spiritualist Emanuel Swedenborg to scientist Carl Linnaeus, are buried within. (☎18 72 01; www.uppsaladomkyrka.se. Open daily 8am-6pm. Free. Tours mid-June to Aug. M-Sa 10am, 2pm.) Just across Akademig. from the church, the **Gustavianum,** Akademig. 3, houses the university's collection of artifacts and scientific curiosities.

Make your way to the top floor to see the Anatomical Theater, where public dissections were conducted in the late 17th century. (☎471 75 71. Open Tu-Su late June to late Aug. 10am-4pm; Jan. to late June 11am-4pm. Guided tours Sa-Su 1pm. 40kr, students 30kr.) A walk through the center of town along the Fyrisån River is an excellent way to get a taste of the city's flourishing gardens and cafes. Wander down Drottning. to **Carolina Rediviva,** Dag Hammarskjölds v. 1, the university's main library, which houses some five million volumes. (☎471 39 00; www.ub.uu.se. Open mid-Aug. to mid-June M-F 9am-8pm, Sa 10am-5pm, Su 11am-4pm; mid-June to mid-Aug. M-F 9am-5pm, Sa 10am-5pm, Su 11am-4pm. 20kr.) On the other side of the river, the **Linnéträdgården,** Svartbäcksg. 27, reconstructs the botanical gardens tended by Carl Linnaeus using his own 1745 sketch. The grounds also include a small museum in Linnaeus's former home. (☎471 25 76; www.linnaeus.uu.se. Gardens open daily May-Aug. 9am-9pm; Sept. 9am-7pm. 30kr. Museum open June to mid-Sept. Tu-Su noon-4pm. 25kr.) The *M/S Kung Carl Justaf* sails 2hr. south of Uppsala to **Skoklosters Slott,** a lavish 17th-century castle with an impressive armory. (☎38 60 77; www.lsh.se/skokloster. Tours daily June-Aug. every hr. 11am-4pm; May every hr. noon-3pm; Apr. and Sept. reduced hours. Boat departs mid-May to mid-Aug. Tu-Su 10:30am from Islandsbron on Östra Åg. and Munkg.; returns 4:30pm. Castle 40kr. Boat round-trip 200kr. Purchase tickets at the tourist office or upon departure. Cash only.)

Bars cluster around **Stortorget,** especially on **Sysslomansgatan, Västra Ågatan,** and the pedestrian areas of **Svartbäcksgatan** and **Kungsgatan.** During the academic year, nightlife in Uppsala revolves around the university's **"nations"**—student organizations comprised of every student at the university. Each nation owns a house, most with their own restaurants or bars, where prices are lower than at other establishments in town. However, only students are allowed in; non-Uppsalans can pick up a guest pass at **Ubbo,** Övre Slottsg. 7. (☎480 31 50; www.kuratorskonventet.se. Open Tu-F 5-7pm. 1-week pass 50kr; 2-week 70kr; 4-week 90kr. A valid student ID as well as another form of ID required. Cash only.)

The dorms at **Hotel Uppsala ❷,** Kungsg. 27, are luxurious, with in-room shower, kitchen, and TV. (☎480 50 00. Breakfast 60kr. Laundry 10kr. Linen 60kr. Dorms 225kr; singles 410kr; doubles 540kr. AmEx/DC/MC/V.) Pick up groceries at **Hemköp,** Kungsg. 95. (Open daily 8am-10pm.) **Trains** run to Stockholm (40min., 1-4 per hr., 64kr). To get from the station to the **tourist office,** Fyristorg 8, walk right on Kungsg., left on St. Persg., and across the bridge. The office books rooms for free. (☎727 48 00; www.uppland.nu. Open in summer M-F 10am-6pm, Sa 10am-3pm, Su noon-4pm; winter closed Su.) **McDonald's,** Dragarbrunnsg. 29, has 24hr. Internet access for 19kr per hr. **Postal Code:** 75320.

GOTLAND

☎0498

Along the shores of Gotland, Sweden's largest island, families flock to sandy beaches in the east before making their way back to the town of Visby, which recalls the Middle Ages with its winding alleyways and historic city wall. The summer months are busy ones, but even in high season visitors can leave the crowds behind to walk along the northern limestone cliffs or track ospreys on the southern coast. Each May, Gotland's 30 species of orchids come into bloom.

TRANSPORTATION. Destination Gotland **ferries** (☎0771 22 33 00; www.destinationgotland.se) sail to Visby from **Nynäshamn** (3hr.) and **Oskarshamn** (2½hr.). Fares are highest on weekends and in summer, and lowest for early-morning and late-night departures. (June-Aug. 2-6 per day; Oct.-May 1-3 per day. 228-511kr, students 174-238kr; 40% Scanrail discount.) To get to Nynäshamn from **Stockholm,** take the Båtbussen bus from Cityterminalen (1hr.; leaves 1¾hr. before ferry departures; 80kr, 110kr on bus) or the Pendeltåg train from Centralstationen (1hr.; 90kr, SL passes valid). To get to Oskarshamn from **Kalmar,** hop a KLT bus (1½hr., every 1-2hr., 76kr). If you're planning your trip from Stockholm, **Gotland City,** Kungsg. 57A, books ferries. (☎08 406 15 00. Open June-Aug. M-F 9:30am-6pm, Sa 10am-2pm; Sept.-May M-F 9:30am-5pm.) On Gotland, it's worth picking up a bus timetable at the ferry terminal or at the Visby **bus station** (☎21 41 12; www.gotland.se/kollektivtrafiken), Kung Magnusväg 1, outside the wall east of the city. However, buses are fairly expensive (59kr) and only three or four buses cover the routes each day, making it almost impossible to daytrip. **Cycling** is a far better way to explore Gotland's terrain; extensive paths and bike-friendly motorways can be supplemented by strategic bus rides, since buses will carry bikes for an extra 40kr. Bike rental shops are plentiful in Visby and in most towns across the island.

VISBY. Sleepy Visby (pop. 22,500), with its knotted cobblestone streets and medieval **Ringmuren** (Ring Wall), often seems straight out of a fairy tale. The wall encloses the ruins of nine churches; both **S:ta Karin** and **Drotten** can be explored by visitors. (Open in summer M-F and Su 8am-9pm, Sa 8am-7pm.) Stairs behind the towering **Domkyrka** lead to a scenic terrace; follow the path along the cliff for a far-flung view of the town and sea. Visby awakens the first week of August for **Medieval Week,** complete with a jousting tournament, seminar on runes, and wandering minstrels strumming their lutes. (☎29 10 70; www.medeltidsveckan.se.)

Private rooms generally cost 240-290kr for singles and 380-430kr for doubles. The spacious dorms at **Vandrarhem Visby (HI) ❷,** Fältg. 30, are 2.5km from the docks at the Alléskolan but within walking distance of the wall. (☎26 98 42. Linen 55kr. Laundry 30kr. Open late June to mid-Aug. Reception 8-10am and 5-7:30pm. Dorms 165kr; doubles 470kr. 45kr HI discount. Cash only.) **Visby Fängelse Vandrarhem ❷,** Skeppsbron 1, is 300m to the left as you exit the ferry terminal. You'll recognize it by the barbed wire atop its yellow walls, the only remnants of the 19th-century prison that preceded this airy, whimsically decorated hostel. (☎20 60 50. Reception in summer 4-7pm; low season 11am-2pm. Call ahead at other times. Dorms 200kr; doubles 600kr; quads 1200kr.) Outdoor bars and cafes are everywhere in Visby, but especially on **Stora Torget** and down by the harbor, as well as on Adelsg. as it winds toward the south wall. Take advantage of lunch specials (70-90kr), or stock up on groceries at the **ICA** on Stora Torg. (Open daily 8am-10pm.)

From the ferry terminal, walk to the left to reach the **tourist office,** Skeppsbron 4-6, which tends to be jam-packed after summer ferry arrivals. The office arranges-guided tours from June to August. (☎20 17 00; www.gotland.info. Internet 2kr per min. Tours 65kr. Open mid-June to mid-Aug. daily 8am-7pm; low season reduced hours.) **Gotlandsresor,** Färjeleden 3, 75m to the right of the ferry terminal, books ferries, finds private rooms, and rents bikes. (☎20 12 60; www.gotlandsresor.se. Open daily June-Aug. 6am-10pm; Sept.-May 8am-6pm.) Dozens of other **bike rental** shops surround the ferry terminal; prices start at 65kr per day. **Postal Code:** 62101.

ELSEWHERE ON GOTLAND. Use Visby as a launchpad to popular **Tofta** beach at the village of **Klintehamn** (bus #10, 40min.), or the calcified cliffs of **Hoburgen,** at the island's southernmost tip (bus #11, 3hr.). Bus #20 runs from Visby to Fårösund (1½hr.), connecting passengers to a free 15min. ferry ride past the monoliths of austere **Fårö,** a small island off Gotland's northern tip. Take the earliest bus to Hoburgen and Fårösund unless you plan to stay overnight. **Gotlandsresor** (see above) can book accommodations at more than 30 hostels and campgrounds outside of Visby, although hardier souls take advantage of the right of public access (p. 984) and **camp** by the brackish waters of the Baltic Sea.

SOUTHERN SWEDEN

Once a fiercely contested no-man's-land during 17th-century wars between Sweden and Denmark, this region still bears witness to its martial past with well-preserved castles and fortifications. Today, the only invaders are the cranes and cormorants that nest alongside marshes and lakes, and the flocks of vacationers who savor seaside zephyrs at the region's beaches and exult in Malmö and Gothenburg's cosmopolitan flair.

KALMAR

☎0480

An important border city when southern Sweden was part of Denmark, Kalmar (pop. 60,000) is no longer at the center of Scandinavian politics, but retains much of the dignity of its glory days. Perched elegantly across from downtown, the medieval **Kalmar Slott** is the town's greatest attraction. In 1397, the castle witnessed the birth of the Union of Kalmar, a short-lived arrangement that united Denmark, Norway, and Sweden under the rule of Queen Margaret I. King Johann III gave the castle a Renaissance makeover in the 1580s, and today it houses lavish exhibits on its own fascinating history. (☎45 14 90. Open daily July 10am-6pm; June and Aug. 10am-5pm; Apr.-May and Sept. 10am-4pm; low season reduced hours. Free tours mid-June to mid-Aug. 75kr, students 50kr.) Adjoining the castle's seaside grounds are the tree-lined **Kyrkogarden** cemetery and the lush **Stadspark.** In the center of town, Kalmar's luminous **Domkyrkan** is a beautiful example of a 17th-century Baroque church. If you have an extra day, duck across the Kalmar Sound to the long, thin island of **Öland,** whether to laze about on the white-sand beaches of Böda in the northeast or to bike through the orchid-dotted steppe of Stora Alvaret in the south. The Träffpunkt Öland **tourist office** can furnish a list of shops that rent bikes; follow signs from the first bus stop after the bridge to the mainland. (☎04 85 56 06 00; www.olandsturist.se. Open May to mid-July M-F 9am-6pm, Sa 9am-4pm, Su 10am-4pm; low season reduced hours.) Bus #106 goes from Kalmar's train station to Borgholm, the island's main town (50min., 46kr).

To reach **Vandrarhem Svanen (HI) and Hotel ❷,** Rappeg. 1, on the island of Ängö, from the tourist office, turn left onto Larmg., right on Södra Kanalg., continue to the end, and turn left across the bridge onto Ängöleden. (☎129 28. Breakfast 60kr. Linen 50kr. Laundry 30kr. Internet 1kr per min. Reception mid-June to mid-Aug. 7:30am-10pm; low season 7:30am-9pm. Dorms 205kr; doubles 410kr; triples 615kr. 45kr HI discount for dorms.) **Söderportshotellet ❹,** Slottsväg. 1, near Kalmar Slott, rents centrally-located student housing during the summer. (☎125 01. Breakfast included. Open mid-June to mid-Aug. Check-in 2-4pm; reception in the cafe. Singles 495kr; doubles 695kr.) Seaside **Stensö Camping ❶** is 3km south of Kalmar; take bus #121 to Lanssjukhuset, turn right onto Stensbergsv., and right onto Stensöv. (☎888 03. Open Apr.-Sept. Tent sites 155kr. Cabins from 400kr.) Hunt for cheap eats along **Larmtorget, Larmgata,** and **Storgata,** or pick up groceries at **ICP** in Baronen pl. near the station. (Open M-F 10am-8pm, Sa 10am-5pm, Su 11am-4pm.)

Trains and **buses** arrive in Kalmar south of the center, across the bay from the castle. Trains go to: Gothenburg (4-5hr.; every 2hr.; 400kr, under 26 297kr); Malmö (3hr., every 2hr., 337/235kr); and Stockholm (4½hr., every 2hr., 1150/940kr). Buses run directly to Stockholm (3 per day; 325kr, students 260kr). The **tourist office,** Ölandskajen 9, offers **Internet** (10kr per 15min.). From the train station, turn right onto Stationsg., and then right onto Ölandskajen. (☎41 77 00; www.kalmar.se. Open July to mid-Aug. M-F 9am-9pm, Sa-Su 10am-5pm; June and late Aug. M-F 9am-7pm, Sa-Su 10am-4pm; Sept.-May M-F 9am-5pm.) **Postal Code:** 39101.

MALMÖ ☎040

Within a (vigorous) stone's throw of Copenhagen, Sweden's third-largest city boasts a cultural diversity unmatched elsewhere in the country. Malmö (pop. 265,000) melds Arabic and Vietnamese flavors with Swedish traditionalism. Intimate and full of outdoor cafes, Lilla Torg, which adjoins the larger Stortorget, is a mecca for people-watching, especially as outdoor patios light up under the warm glow of heating lamps in the evenings. Möllevångstorget, south of the city center, has a lively open-air market, folksy local bars, and affordable ethnic eateries.

TRANSPORTATION AND PRACTICAL INFORMATION. The train station and harbor lie just north of the old town. **Trains** go to: Copenhagen (35min., every 20min., 87kr); Gothenburg (3½hr., every hr., 250-335kr); Stockholm (4½hr., every hr., 300-1000kr). Malmö has an efficient **bus** system; rides within most of the city are 15kr, and many buses pass by the train station. The **tourist office** is located in the station and offers the **Malmö Card,** which provides free public transportation, parking, sightseeing bus tours, and admission to various museums. (1-day 130kr, 2-day 160kr, 3-day 190kr.) The office also books rooms for a 50-70kr fee. (☎34 12 00; www.malmo.se/tourist. Open June-Aug. M-F 9am-7pm, Sa-Su 10am-5pm; low season reduced hours.) **Internet** can be found at the atmospheric **Cyberspace Cafe,** on Engelbrektsg. between Lilla Torg and Gustav Adolfs Torg. (☎23 81 28. 44kr per hr. until 6pm, 30kr per hr. after 6pm. Open daily 10am-midnight.) **Postal Code:** 20110.

ACCOMMODATIONS AND FOOD. Though decidedly out of the way, **Vandrarhem Malmö (HI) ❶,** Backav. 18, is the cheapest option in town. Roadside rooms are noisy, so ask for a room on the yard. Brace yourself for the communal showers. Take bus #21 from the train station to Vandrarhemmet. (☎822 20; www.malmohostel.com. Breakfast 50kr. Linen 50kr. Reception May-Aug. 8-10am and 4-10pm; Sept.-Apr. 8-10am and 4-8pm. Dorms 175kr; singles 340kr; doubles 460kr; triples 615kr. 45kr HI discount. MC/V.) **Hotel Pallas ❹,** Norra Vallg. 74, across the canal from the train station and to the right, makes you pay for its prime location. (☎611 50 77. Breakfast 50kr. Singles 420kr; doubles 470-545kr. Cash only.) **Gök Boet ❶,** Lilla Torg 3, is an intimate spot that serves creative sandwiches (35-55kr) by day and turns into a popular bar at night. (Open M-Th 11am-midnight, F-Sa 11am-2am, Su 11am-11pm.) Next door, the **Saluhallen** is a massive food court with inexpensive restaurants ranging from Greek to Japanese. (Open M-Sa 10am-6pm, Su 10am-3pm.) **Vegegården ❷,** Stora Nyg. 18, features all-vegetarian Chinese dishes (65-75kr) and a buffet (M-F 55kr, Sa-Su 88kr) for the thrifty herbivore. Turn away from the gardens at Gustav Adolfs Torg. (☎611 38 88. Open M-W 11am-5pm, Th-F 11am-9pm, Sa-Su noon-9pm. Buffet M-F 11am-3pm, Sa-Su 4-8pm.)

SIGHTS AND ENTERTAINMENT. Malmö's west end is dominated by the **Malmöhus Castle** complex, which encompasses five eclectic museums. Within the castle walls, the **Stadsmuseet** documents the city's history and opens onto the fun-house interior of the castle proper. Breeze through the **Konstmuseum's** underwhelming art collection on your way to the **Aquarium** and the charming lizards in the **Tropicarium.** Across the moat, the **Kommendanthuset** hosts rotating exhibits on popular culture. The **Teknikens och Sjöfartens Hus** (Technology and Maritime Museum) down the road is an orgy of shiny ships and airplane mock-ups. Squeeze inside the **U3 Submarine,** part of Sweden's navy from 1943 to 1964; on Sunday and Tuesday afternoons, veterans gather by the vessel to swap old war stories. (All 5 museums ☎040 34 44 37; www.malmo.se/museer. Open daily June-Aug. 10am-4pm; Sept.-May noon-4pm. Combination ticket 40kr, students 20kr.) The **Form Design Center,** Lilla Torg 9, shows off the cutting edge of Swedish design for the Ikea generation. (☎664 51 50; www.formdesigncenter.com. Open Tu-W and F 11am-5pm, Th 11am-6pm, Sa-Su 11am-4pm. Free.) The sprawling **Malmö Konsthall,** St. Johannesg. 7, hosts exhibits covering a wide range of modern art. (☎34 12 93; www.konsthall.malmo.se. Open M-Tu and Th-Su 11am-5pm, W 11am-9pm. Guided tours daily 2pm. Free.) After trawling through all these museums, kick back at the **bars** on Lilla Torg and Möllevångstorget, or case the **club** scene around Stortorg.

LUND

☎046

What Oxford and Cambridge are to England, Lund (pop. 100,400) and Uppsala are to Sweden. **Lund University's** antagonism toward its scholarly northern neighbor in Uppsala has inspired countless pranks, in addition to the drag shows and drinkfests that grace Lund's busy streets. With its vibrant student life and proximity to Malmö and Copenhagen, Lund makes an excellent base for exploring Skåne. The Romanesque **Lunds Domkyrka** is a massive 900-year-old reminder of the time when Lund was the religious center of Scandinavia. Its floor-to-ceiling astronomical clock rings on the hour at noon and 3pm, and its 7074-pipe organ is Sweden's largest. To reach the cathedral from the train station, turn right onto Bang, and left onto Klosterg. (☎35 88 80; www.lundsdomkyrka.org. Free tours mid-June to mid-Aug. daily 2:50pm. Open M-F 8am-6pm, Sa 9:30am-5pm, Su 9:30am-6pm.) The **university campus** is just across the park from the cathedral; get briefed on upcoming events at **Student Info,** Sang. 2, in the Akademiska Föreningen building. (☎38 49 49; http://af.lu.se. Open late Aug. to May M-F 10am-4pm.) **Kulturen,** an open-air museum behind the Student Union at the end of Sankt Anneg. on Tegnerplastén, weaves visitors into the daily lives of Lund residents from the Middle Ages on through a series of reconstructed houses. Wide-ranging temporary exhibits, including contemporary art installations, delve into the modern. (☎35 04 00; www.kulturen.com. Open mid-Apr. to Sept. daily 11am-5pm; Oct. to mid-Apr. Tu-Su noon-4pm. 50kr, free with student ID.) As in Uppsala (p. 997), Lund's nightlife revolves around the "nations," student clubs that throw parties and serve as social centers. Stop by Student Info for tips on snagging a guest pass. Another popular option is **Kulturmejeriet,** Stora Söderg. 64, an arthouse cinema, concert venue, and bar. (☎211 00 23; www.kulturmejeriet.se. Films Th 7pm. Free. Concerts 25-100kr.) **Stortorget/Herkules Bar,** Stortorg. 1, started off as a bank and morphed into a bar and club with theme nights. (☎13 92 90. 22+. Bar open M-W and Su 11:30am-midnight, Th 11:30am-1am, F-Sa 11:30am-2am. Club open Th-Sa 11pm-3am.)

The cramped **Vandrarhem Tåget (HI) ❷,** Vävareg. 22, is housed in the sleeping compartments of a 1940s train. Take the overpass to the park side of the train station. (☎14 28 20; www.trainhostel.com. Breakfast 50kr. Linen 60kr. Hot water 1kr per 2min. Reception Apr.-Oct. 8-10am and 5-8pm; Nov.-Mar. 8-10am and 5-7pm. Dorms 175kr. 45kr HI discount. Cash only.) To get to **Källby Camping ❶,** next to the Källby Bad outdoor swimming pool, take bus #1 (dir.: Klostergården; 18kr) 2km south of the city center. A free swim is included with your stay. (☎35 51 88. Laundry 40kr. Open mid-June to Aug. Tent sites 50kr. MC/V.) The **open-air market** at Mårtenstorg. (open daily 7am-2pm) and the adjoining **Saluhallen** (open M-F 9:30am-6pm, Sa 9am-3pm) are the best bet for budget food; cafes around Stortorg. and the cathedral are pricier. Decorated by caricatures of professors, **Conditori Lundagård ❶,** Kyrkog. 17, serves tasty salads (63kr), sandwiches (22-42kr), and pastries. (☎211 13 58. Open mid-June to mid-Aug. daily 10am-6pm; Sept. to mid-June M-F 7:30am-8pm, Sa 8:30am-6pm, Su 10am-6pm. AmEx/DC/MC/V.)

Lund is accessible from Malmö on SJ **trains** and by local **pågatågen** trains (10min., 1-5 per hr., 36kr). Trains also run to: Gothenburg (3½-4½hr., every hr., 482kr); Kalmar (3hr., every 2hr., 3329kr); and Stockholm (4-5½hr.; every 1-2hr.; 1060kr, under 26 899kr). The **tourist office,** Kyrkog. 11, across from the cathedral,

SWEDEN

sells maps (50-120kr) of the nearby **Skåneleden trail.** (☎35 50 40; www.lund.se. Open June-Aug. M-F 10am-6pm, Sa-Su 10am-2pm; May and Sept. M-F 10am-5pm, Sa 10am-2pm; Oct.-Apr. M-F 10am-5pm.) **Postal Code:** 22101.

AUGUST AND EVERYTHING AFTER. Many establishments in Lund, from restaurants to museums to the otherwise invaluable Student Info office, are **closed** from June through August. Consult www.lund.se before planning a trip.

YSTAD ☎0411

Best known as a ferry port for those heading on to Bornholm, Denmark (p. 275), Ystad (pop. 27,000) also has one of Sweden's best-preserved downtowns, a tight network of cobblestone streets just inland of the terminal. A handful of the town's half-timbered houses date back to the 15th century; you'll find the oldest one in Scandinavia at the corner of Pilgr. and Stora Österg. The **Klostret** (monastery), on Klosterg., showcases rotating exhibits about church and town history and has a lovely rose garden. From the tourist office, turn left onto Lingsg., left onto Stora Österg., and right out of the Stortorg. onto Klosterg. (Open June-Aug. Tu-F 10am-5pm, Sa-Su noon-4pm; low season reduced hours. 40kr.) Next to the tourist office, the **Konstmuseum** features work by Swedish and Danish artists. (☎57 72 85. Open Tu-F noon-5pm, Sa-Su noon-4pm. 20kr.) Near the village of Kåseberga, 18km southeast of town, **Ales Stenar** may have been a Nordic Stonehenge; its 59 stones are set in the shape of a ship, with the bow and stern aligned to the position of the sun at the solstices. Take bus #322 (30min., 3 per day, 24kr), but resist the temptation to scale one of the stones for a photo-op; it's considered disrespectful.

The train station houses the **Vandrarhemmet Stationen ❷,** a sunny hostel conveniently located for travelers passing through. (☎07 08 57 79 95. Linen 60kr. Reception June-Aug. 9-10am and 5-7pm; Oct.-May 5-6pm. Dorms 185kr; doubles 360kr. Cash only.) Stora Österg., or Gågatan (pedestrian street), passes through the main square and teems with cafes and shops. The Saluhallen market is just off Stortorg. (Open daily 8am-9pm.) Bornholms Trafikken (☎55 87 00) **ferries** sail to Bornholm (70min., up to 4 per day, 204kr). **Trains** run to Malmö (45min., every hr., 74kr). The **tourist office** across from the station offers 15min. of free Internet. (☎57 76 81. Open mid-June to mid-Aug. M-F 9am-7pm, Sa-Su 10am-2pm; low season reduced hours.) **Postal Code:** 27101.

HELSINGBORG ☎042

Warring armies carrying the standards of the Swedish and Danish crowns passed Helsingborg (pop. 119,000) back and forth 12 times during the 17th century. When Magnus Stenbock gained the town for the Swedes once and for all in 1710, most of the town lay in shambles. It wasn't until the industrial era that Helsingborg was restored to affluence; more recently, it has transformed into an elegant cultural center. The city's urban renewal showpiece, **Knutpunkten,** houses train, bus, and ferry terminals, restaurants, and shops under one glass roof. Exit Knutpunkten and make a left on Järnvägsg. to reach **Stortorget,** the long, wide main square that branches out into pedestrian shopping streets like swanky **Kullagatan.** Stortorget ends at the majestic **Terrassen,** a fountain-strewn series of steps that climb the rocky ridge leading up to **Kärnan.** A remnant of the 12th-century fortress that once loomed over the city, the Kärnan tower offers a view all the way to Copenhagen for those who mount its 154 twisting steps on a clear day. (☎015 99 91. Open June-Aug. daily 11am-7pm; low season reduced hours. 20kr. Cash only.) Closer to sea level, the harborside **Dunkers Kulturhus,** Kungsg. 11, is the city's newest cultural venue, featuring a concert hall and theater as well as a multimedia installation on the city's history and modern art exhibits. From the tourist office, turn right onto Drottningg. and left into Sundstorg. (☎10 74 00; www.dunkerskulturhus.com.

Open Tu-W, F-Su 10am-5pm, Th 10am-8pm. 70kr, students 35kr. MC/V.) Just north of Helsingborg, the former royal retreat of **Sofiero Slott** sits on a hillside overlooking the sound. The castle is nothing to write home about, but ponds and grottoes on the densely forested grounds as well as the extensive flower gardens beg for exploration on a sunny afternoon. Take bus #219 (18kr) from Knutpunkten to Sofiero Huvudentréen. (☎ 13 74 00; www.sofiero.helsingborg.se. Open daily May-Aug. 10am-6pm; Sept.-Apr. 11am-5pm. Grounds 70kr, with castle 80kr. MC/V.)

To reach the well-kept **Helsingborgs Vandrarhem ❷**, Järnvägsg. 39, from Knutpunkten, cross Järnvägsg., turn right and walk three blocks. (☎ 14 58 50; www.hbg-turist.com. Linen 40kr. Laundry 25kr. Reception 3-6pm. Dorms 185kr; singles 275kr; doubles 395kr. MC/V.) Inexpensive cafes line S. Storg., the last right off of Stortorg. before Terrassen. Behind the Mariakyrkan, waiters at **Cafe Mmmums ❶**, Södra Storg. 3, bring sandwiches (20-43kr) and large salads (48-58kr) out to outdoor tables. (☎ 14 33 40. Open M-F 10am-7pm, Sa 10am-5pm. AmEx/DC/MC/V.) Pick up **groceries** at the ICA, Drottningg. 48, past the Rådhuset. (☎ 13 15 70. Open M-Sa 8am-8pm, Su 10am-8pm. MC/V) The harbor area has a handful of late-night bars and clubs, although the rowdy Helsingør ferries (see below) can be more fun than terrestrial options during the summer.

Trains depart for: Gothenburg (2½hr.; every 2hr.; 285kr, under 26 240kr); Malmö (50min., every hr., 88kr); Stockholm (4-6hr.; 2-4 per day; 1085kr, under 26 930kr). **Ferries** leave almost continuously for Helsingør, Denmark (p. 273), near Copenhagen; popular Scandlines boats depart every 20min. (☎ 18 61 00. 20min.; 22kr, round-trip 40kr.) Most **city buses** (18-20kr) pass Knutpunkten and include 1hr. of free transfers. To reach the **tourist office,** which books rooms for free, exit the station in the direction of the towering Rådhuset; the office is through the doors next to the closest turret. (☎ 10 43 50; www.helsingborg.se. Open mid-June to Aug. M-F 9am-8pm, Sa 9am-5pm, Su 10am-3pm; Sept. to mid-June M-F 10am-6pm, Sa 10am-2pm.) **Postal Code:** 25225.

GOTHENBURG (GÖTEBORG) ☎031

Occasionally dismissed as Sweden's industrial center, Gothenburg (YO-teh-bor-ee; pop. 460,000) is a sprawling, youthful metropolis threaded with parks, bristling with museums and theaters, and intersected by the glitzy Avenyn thoroughfare that slashes through the heart of the city. While Gothenburg is easily overlooked on whirlwind tours of northern Europe, it has the cultural attractions of any of the Scandinavian capitals, but with a relaxed, friendly twist.

TRANSPORTATION

Trains run from Central Station to: Malmö (2¾-3¾hr.; every 1-2hr.; 329kr, under 26 280kr); Oslo, Norway (5¾-8hr., 3 per day, 392/274kr); Stockholm (3-5½hr., every 1-2hr., 489/418kr). Stena Line **ferries** (☎ 704 00 00; www.stenaline.com) sail to Frederikshavn, Denmark (2-3¼hr.; 6-10 per day; 140-200kr, 50% Scanrail or Eurail discount) and Kiel, Germany (13½hr., daily 7:30pm, 340-780kr). DFDS Seaways (☎ 65 06 50; www.dfdsseaways.co.uk) sails to Newcastle, England (24hr., Th and Su 10am, 695-1195kr). Gothenburg has an extensive **tram** and **bus** system; rides are 20kr, and most trams and buses pass by the train station or through Brunnsparken, south of the Nordstan mall. A **day pass,** valid on both trams and buses, is available at kiosks throughout the city for just 50kr.

ORIENTATION AND PRACTICAL INFORMATION

Central Gothenburg is on the southern bank of the Göta River. The city's transportation hub is located in **Nordstaden,** the northernmost part of the center. Across the Stora Hamn canal lies the busy central district of **Inom Vallgraven**. The main street,

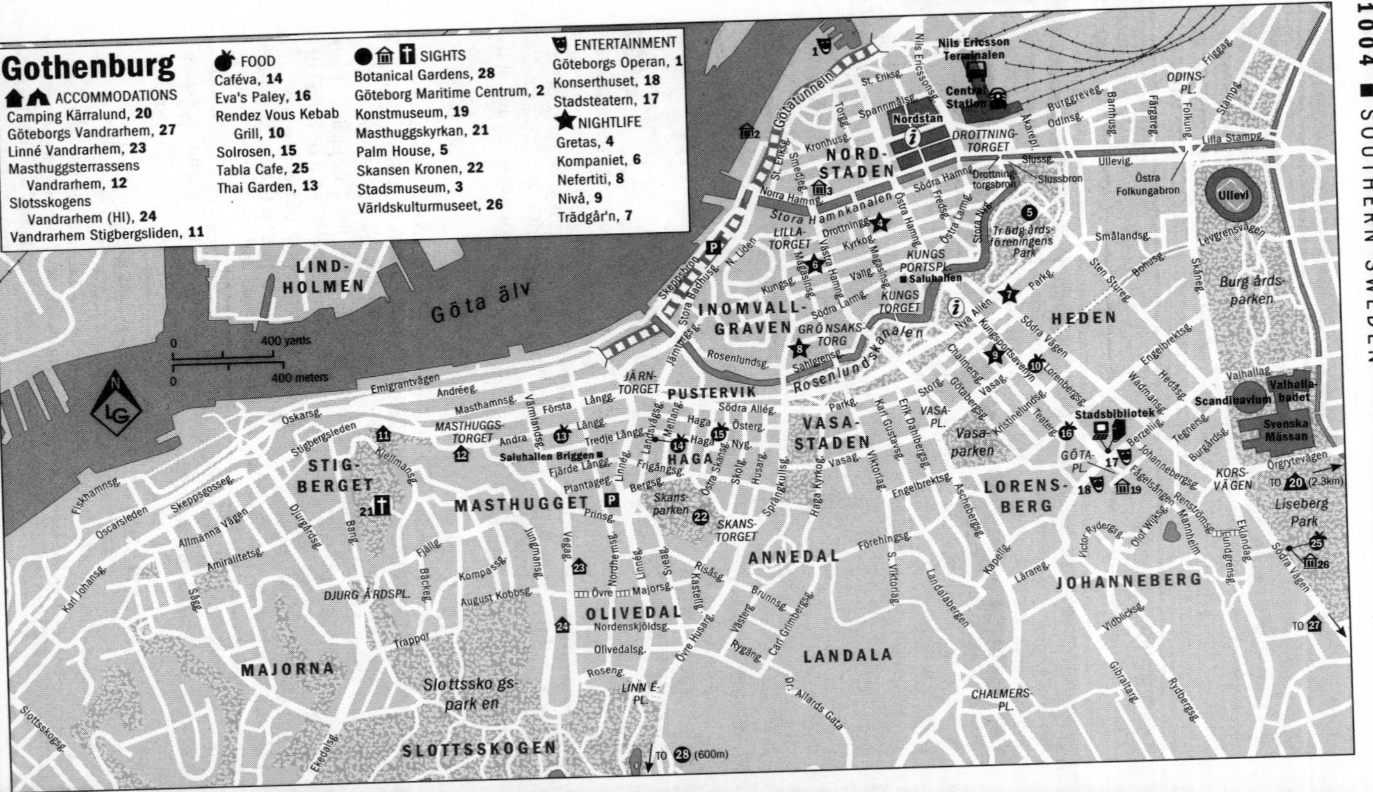
Gothenburg
ACCOMMODATIONS
Camping Kärralund, 20
Göteborgs Vandrarhem, 27
Linné Vandrarhem, 23
Masthuggsterrassens Vandrarhem, 12
Slotsskogens Vandrarhem (HI), 24
Vandrarhem Stigbergsliden, 11
FOOD
Caféva, 14
Eva's Paley, 16
Rendez Vous Kebab Grill, 10
Solrosen, 15
Tabla Cafe, 25
Thai Garden, 13
SIGHTS
Botanical Gardens, 28
Göteborg Maritime Centrum, 2
Konstmuseum, 19
Masthuggskyrkan, 21
Palm House, 5
Skansen Kronen, 22
Stadsmuseum, 3
Världskulturmuseet, 26
ENTERTAINMENT
Göteborgs Operan, 1
Konserthuset, 18
Stadsteatern, 17
NIGHTLIFE
Gretas, 4
Kompaniet, 6
Nefertiti, 8
Nivå, 9
Trädgår'n, 7
400 yards
400 meters
LIND-HOLMEN
Göta älv
NORD-STADEN
INOMVALL-GRAVEN
PUSTERVIK
VASA-STADEN
HEDEN
HAGA
STIG-BERGET
MASTHUGGET
ANNEDAL
OLIVEDAL
LANDALA
LORENS-BERG
JOHANNEBERG
MAJORNA
SLOTTSSKOGEN
Slottsskogsparken
Nils Ericsson Terminalen
Central Station
Nordstan
DROTTNING-TORGET
Ullevi
Burgårdsparken
Trädgårdsföreningens Park
KUNGSPORTSPL.
KUNGSTORGET
Saluhallen
GRÖNSAKSTORG
LILLA-TORGET
JÄRN-TORGET
MASTHUGGS-TORGET
Saluhallen Briggen
SKANS-TORGET
Skansparken
Vasaparken
VASA-PL.
GÖTA-PL.
Stadsbibliotek
Scandinavium
Valhallabadet
Svenska Mässan
KORS-VÄGEN
Liseberg Park
DJURG ÅRDSPL.
LINNÉ-PL.
CHALMERS-PL.
ODINS-PL.
TO 20 (2.3km)
TO 27
TO 28 (600m)
Götatunneln
Stora Hamnkanalen
Rosenlundskanalen
Emigrantvägen
Skeppsbron
Nya Allén
Kungsportsavenyn
Södra Vägen
Östra Folkungabron
Drottningtorgsbron
Slussbron
Lilla Stampg.
Ullevig.
Dr. Allards Gata
Allmänna Vägen
Oscarsleden
Stigbergsleden

Kungsportsavenyn ("Avenyn") begins just north of the Vallgraven canal at Kungsportsplatsen and continues south 1km to **Götaplatsen,** the main square in the Lorensberg district, where theaters and museums cluster. Vasagatan leads west through Vasastaden to the city's oldest suburb, the **Haga** district.

The **tourist office** has a branch in the Nordstan shopping center near the train and bus stations. (Open M-F 10am-6pm, Sa 10am-5pm, Su noon-4pm.) The crowded main branch at Kungsportspl. 2, books rooms for a 60kr fee and sells the **Göteborg pass** (1-day 210kr, 2-day 285kr), which includes unlimited public transit and admission to many attractions, although it's probably only worthwhile for those planning to see at least four sights. (☎61 25 00; www.goteborg.com. Open late June to early Aug. daily 9:30am-8pm; low season M-F 9am-5pm, Sa 10am-2pm.) The **Stadsbibliotek** (public library), off Götapl., provides free **Internet** in 15min. slots. Book at the desk. (Open M-F 10am-8pm, Sa 11am-5pm.) **Postal Code:** 40401.

SWEDEN

ACCOMMODATIONS AND CAMPING

Most of Gothenburg's hostels are found in the west end of the city, in and around Masthugget, but trams and buses make it an easy ride to the city center. It's wise to book ahead, especially in July.

Slottsskogens Vandrarhem (HI), Vegag. 21 (☎42 65 20; www.sov.nu). Bus #60 (dir.: Masthugget) to Vegag. Spacious dorms and common areas greet you after the trek from the city center. Bike rental 90kr per day. Breakfast 50kr. Linen 50kr. Laundry 40kr. Internet 1kr per min. Reception 8am-noon and 2-6pm. 12- to 14-bed dorms 165kr; 3- to 6-bed dorms 185kr; singles 305kr; doubles 420kr. 45kr HI discount. MC/V. ❷

Masthuggsterrassens Vandrarhem, Masthuggsterr. 10H (☎42 48 20; www.mastenvandrarhem.com). Tram #3, 9, or 11 to Masthuggstorget. Cross the square diagonally, walk up the stairs, then follow the signs. Relax in sugar-cube themed rooms above a supermarket. Breakfast 55kr. Linen 55kr, with towel 20kr. Laundry 45kr. Reception 8-10am and 5-7pm. Dorms 160kr; doubles 400kr; triples 480kr; quads 580kr. MC/V. ❷

Vandrarhem Stigbergsliden (HI), Stigbergsl. 10 (☎24 16 20). Tram #3, 9, or 11 to Masthuggstorget. Walk the way the tram is going, then bear right up the hill. Cozy rooms organized around a lovely courtyard, though common areas are somewhat cramped. Bike rental 50kr per day. Breakfast 45kr. Linen 50kr. Reception 8am-noon and 4-10pm. Dorms 165kr; singles 295kr; doubles 390kr. 45kr HI discount. AmEx/MC/V. ❷

Linné Vandrarhem, Vegag. 22 (☎12 10 60; www.vandrarhemmet-linne.com). Take bus #60 (dir.: Masthugget) to Vegagtn. Bright private rooms turn into dorms when space is available. Breakfast 45kr. Linen 45kr. Reception 8am-8pm. Dorms 180kr; doubles 380kr; triples 540kr; quads 720kr. AmEx/DC/MC/V. ❷

Göteborgs Vandrarhem, Mölndalsv. 23 (☎40 10 50; www.goteborgsvandrarhem.se). Tram #4 (dir.: Mölndal) to Geterbergsäng. Walk the way the tram is going. Generic rooms near Liseberg Park. Breakfast 55kr. Linen 50kr. Reception May-Aug. 8am-8pm, Sept.-Apr. 8am-noon and 4-8pm. Dorms 180kr; doubles 450kr. AmEx/MC/V. ❷

Camping Kärralund, Olbersg. 9 (☎84 02 00; www.liseberg.se). Take tram #5 to Welanderg. and turn right onto Olbersg. Conveniently located in Liseberg Park, but pricey. Breakfast 65kr. Laundry 20-30kr. Reception May-Aug. 7am-11pm; low season reduced hours. July-Aug. tent sites 205kr; Sept.-June 100-165kr. AmEx/D/MC/V. ❷

FOOD

The Avenyn is a great place for a stroll, but steer clear of its pricey eats in favor of the affordable restaurants and cafes on **Vasagatan, Linnégatan,** and near the **Haga** neighborhood. Cheap food is also abundant at food halls; the **Saluhallen,** in Kung-storg., has the iron arches and a glass ceiling of a huge train station. (Open M-F 9am-6pm, Sa 9am-3pm.) **Saluhallen Briggen,** Nordhemsg. 28, is housed in a old fire station. (Open M-F 9am-6pm, Sa 9am-2pm.)

Solrosen, Kaponjärg. 4 (☎711 66 97). Even hardcore carnivores come to chow down at this cozy, flower-themed vegetarian haven in the heart of Haga. Entrees 70kr. Soup 50kr. Open M-F 11:30am-1am, Sa 2pm-1am. Kitchen closes at 9pm. AmEx/MC/V. ❷

Thai Garden, Andra Långg. 18 (☎12 76 60). Fill up on the delicious buffet (65kr M-F 11am-3pm; 98kr weekends) at this stand-out on a street lined with Thai eateries. Open M-F 11am-11pm, Sa noon-midnight, Su noon-11pm. AmEx/DC/MC/V. ❷

Tabla Cafe, Södra Vägen 54 (☎63 27 21). Upstairs in the Världskulturmuseet. Even the tea bags are a work of art at this trendy cafe, where the renowned Dahlbom brothers craft magnificent creations for reasonable prices. Try the exquisite salads (75-80kr) or breads (35-40kr). Open Tu and Sa-Su noon-5pm, W-F noon-9pm. AmEx/DC/MC/V. ❸

Caféva, Haga Nyg. 5E (☎711 63 64). Locals flock here for the fresh-baked bread, and stay for the hearty soups (48kr) and sandwiches (18-32kr) at low prices. Open June-Aug. M-F 10am-6pm; Sept.-May M-F 9am-6pm and Sa 11am-4pm. Cash only. ❶

Eva's Paley, Avenyn 39 (☎16 30 70), at the Götaplatsen end. Tasty food and a quality location without an astronomical tab. Sandwiches 59kr. Salads 75-85kr. Open M-Th 8am-11pm, F 8am-midnight, Sa-Su 10am-11pm. AmEx/MC/V. ❷

Rendez Vous Kebab and Grill House, Vasag. 43 (☎330 52 30). Cheap kebab and falafel stand draws barflies to its late-night location near Avenyn. Open M-Th 10am-4am, F 10am-6am, Sa noon-6am, Su noon-4am. AmEx/MC/V. ❶

SIGHTS

CITY CENTER. Nordstan, Scandinavia's largest indoor shopping center and a city unto itself, sits just across from the train station. *(Open M-F 10am-7pm, Sa 10am-6pm, Su 11am-5pm.)* Follow Norra Hamng. along the Stora Hamn canal to reach the **Stadsmuseum,** Norra Hamng. 12, which lavishly recalls the city's history—from its Viking past to its post-industrial rebirth. *(☎61 27 70; www.stadsmuseum.goteborg.se. Open May-Aug. daily 10am-5pm; Sept.-Apr. Tu and Th-Su 10am-5pm, W 10am-8pm. 40kr, under 20 free.)* Turn right at the end of Norra Hamng. to reach the **Göteborg Maritime Centrum,** a floating museum comprised of more than a dozen moored vessels. *(☎10 59 50; www.goteborgs-maritimacentrum.com. Open May-Aug. daily 10am-6pm; Sept.-Oct. and Mar.-Apr. daily 10am-4pm; Nov. F-Su 10am-4pm. 75kr.)* **Trädgårdsföreningens Park,** to the left as you cross the Avenyn bridge, is one of a series of green spaces that line the southern bank of the main canal. Wend your way to the rosarium and **Palm House,** built in 1878 as a reproduction of London's Crystal Palace. *(☎365 58 58; www.tradgardsforeningen.se. Park open daily May-Aug. 7am-9pm; Sept.-Apr. 7am-7:30pm. May-Aug. 15kr, free until 10am and after 6pm; Sept.-Apr. free. Palm House open daily May-Aug. 10am-5pm; Sept.-Apr. 10am-4pm. 20kr.)* Avenyn ends at Götapl., the site of Carl Milles's famous **Poseidon fountain.** Even the bronze sea god is dwarfed by the imposing **Konstmuseum,** which encompasses a spectacular sculpture collection, standout exhibits on Nordic art and French Impressionism, and an incredible photography collection at the Hasselblad Center. Temporary exhibits at the Stenasalen are free. *(☎61 29 80; www.konstmuseum.goteborg.se. Open Tu and Th 11am-6pm, W 11am-9pm, F-Su 11am-5pm. 40kr, under 20 free. AmEx/DC/MC/V.)* Adjacent to the Konstmuseum, the **Konsthall** showcases contemporary art. *(☎61 50 40; www.konsthallen.goteborg.se. Open Tu and Th 11am-6pm, W 11am-9pm, F-Su 11am-5pm. Free.)*

HAGA. Westward, the gentrifying Haga district boasts art galleries, bookstores, and cafes along its pedestrian streets, especially the main thoroughfare, **Haga Nygata.** The steep flight of steps at the southern end of Kaponjärg. leads to **Skansen**

Kronen, the most impressive of the hilltop towers that surround Gothenburg; the climb may be strenuous, but the view of the city from the tower's base is stellar. For a bird's-eye view of Gothenburg's harbor, head out to the **Masthuggskyrkan,** Storebackeg. 1, a brick church with a timber ceiling that suggests the inside of a Viking ship. Take tram #3, 9, or 11 to Masthuggstorg. *(☎731 92 30. Open in summer daily 9am-6pm; low season usually M-F 11am-4pm.)* South of the church, the vast **Slottsskogsparken** invites you to wander among its ponds, meadows, and aviaries. Take tram #1 or 6 to Linnépl. Across the highway lies Sweden's largest **Botanical Gardens,** Carl Skottsbergs G. 22A, home to an herb garden, bamboo grove, and some 12,000 plant species from across the globe, as well as a number of orchid hothouses. Take tram #1, 7, 8, or 13 to Botaniska Trädgården. *(☎741 11 00; www.gotbot.se. Open daily 9am-sunset. 20kr. Hothouses 20kr.)*

NEAR LISEBERG PARK. In the southeastern part of the city, near the Svenska Mässan, the city's newest museum, the **Världskulturmuseet** (Museum of World Culture), Södra Vägen 54, challenges visitors with bold exhibits, including one on AIDS in the era of globalization. *(☎63 27 00; www.varldskulturmuseet.se. Open Tu and Sa-Su noon-5pm, Th-F noon-9pm. Free.)* Scandinavia's largest amusement park, **Liseberg,** is behind the museum. Strap yourself in good and tight for a ride on **Balder,** the park's bone-rattling wooden rollercoaster, or experience the sensation of weightlessness on the park's newest rollercoaster, **Kanonen.** Take tram #4, 5, 6, 8, 13, or 14 to Korsvägen. *(☎40 01 00. Open mid-May to late Aug. daily; Sept. Th-Su. Hours vary; check www.liseberg.se for schedule. Entry 60kr; rides 15-60kr each; 1-day ride pass 265kr.)*

GÖTEBORGS SKÄRGÅRD. Beachgoers should venture out onto the **Göteborgs Skärgård,** a string of islands dribbling out into the waters of the Kattegat Bay. The islands of Brännö and Styrsö have shops and other resort amenities, while the cliffs and beaches of Vargö are wilder and more secluded. *(Take tram #11 to Saltholmen: 30min, and make a free transfer to the ferry: 20-50min.)*

ENTERTAINMENT AND NIGHTLIFE

The enormous **Göteborgs Operan,** at Lilla Bommen, hosts opera, musical theater, and concerts from August through May. (☎13 13 00; www.opera.se. Tickets from 105-215kr, students 25% off except F-Sa.) Gothenburg's **Stadsteatern** (☎61 50 50) and **Konserthuset** (☎726 53 00) round out its highbrow theater and music scene; swing by the tourist office for the latest issue of *What's on in Göteborg* for details. Gothenburg's annual **film festival** (www.filmfestival.org), the largest in Scandinavia, will draw more than 100,000 film lovers to the city for 10 days, starting January 27, 2006. Mid-August brings the **Göteborgskalaset,** an annual party that transforms the city with music, entertainment, and culinary arts.

Gothenburg's club scene is one of the most exclusive and chic in Scandinavia. Many posh restaurants on Avenyn morph into equally posh clubs after nightfall; expect lines, steep covers, and strict dress codes. **Nivå,** Kungsportsavenyn 9, is the scene's standard-bearer. (☎701 80 90. 27+. F cover 70kr, Sa 100kr. Open Tu 11:30am-midnight, W-Th 11:30am-3am, F 11:30am-4am, Sa 6pm-4am.) For a little less attitude, head for **Trädgår'n,** on Nya Allén, an ivy-clad concert venue, club, and patio bar that spills into the adjacent park. (☎10 20 80. 21+. Cover from 100kr. Club open F-Sa 10pm-5am.) A younger crowd packs the two levels of **Kompaniet/Underground,** Kungsg. 19, and jives to an eclectic mix of music. (☎711 99 46. Beer 49kr, students 35kr. Happy hour M-Th 5pm-3am, F-Sa 5pm-midnight; beer 25kr. 18+. Cover 40-100kr. Open M-Sa 5pm-3am.) The biggest gay club in Sweden, **Gretas,** Drottningg. 35, has plenty of room to party in its upstairs bar and on its dance floor. (☎13 69 49; www.gretas.nu. 20+. Club cover 50-60kr. Open W 6pm-

2am, Th 6pm-1am, F 5pm-4am, Sa 6pm-4am.) On a more down-tempo evening, head to **Nefertiti,** Hvitfeldtspl. 6, an intimate jazz bar that reinvents itself as a dance club after 1am. (☎711 15 33; www.nefertiti.se. 20+. Cover for club 80kr. Tickets 120-250kr. Concerts in summer Tu-W and F-Sa 8:30 or 9pm.)

DAYTRIP FROM GOTHENBURG: VARBERG. This summer paradise, a sunny town replete with expansive beaches and charming bath houses, beckons from between Gothenburg and Helsingborg. Varberg's spectacular **fortress** is home to a number of attractions. The **Länsmuseet Varberg** features the **Bockstén Man,** a bog corpse from 1360 found with his clothing intact. To reach the fortress, turn right out of the station and right onto S. Hamnv. (☎18 52 00; www.lansmuseet.varberg.se. Museum open June to mid-Aug. daily 10am-5pm; mid-Aug. to May M-F 10am-4pm, Sa-Su noon-4pm. Mid-June to mid-Aug. 50kr; low season 30kr.) Follow the boardwalk 2km south of town to reach the shallow **Apelviken Bay,** which offers some of the best surfing and windsurfing in Northern Europe. **Surfers Paradise,** Söderg. 22, rents gear and gives both formal lessons and informal tips. Turn right out of the station, pass the tourist office, and turn right onto Söderg. (☎03 40 67 70 55. Open May-June and Aug. M-F 1-7pm, Sa 10am-2pm, Su noon-4pm; July M-F noon-6pm, Sa 10am-2pm, Su noon-4pm; low season reduced hours.) The boardwalk also passes several **nude beaches:** Kärringhålan for women and Goda Hopp for men. **Trains** arrive from Gothenburg (45min., 77kr) and Helsingborg (1½hr., 250kr). To reach the **tourist office,** in Brunnsparken, turn right out of the station and walk four blocks. (☎03 40 887 70. Open May-June M-F 9:30am-6pm, Sa 10am-2pm; July M-Sa 9:30am-7pm, Su 1pm-6pm; Aug. M-F 9:30am-6pm, Su 10am-2pm; Sept.-Apr. M-F 9:30am-5pm.) **Postal Code:** 43201.

DALARNA

The county of Dalarna extends from the swampy foothills along the Norwegian border through sleepy lakeside villages in the center of the country. When farming could no longer support the population, Dalarna turned to handicrafts to bolster its economy; by the 19th century, its stylized religious paintings and garish wooden horses filled the homes of the eastern urban bourgeoisie. Today, Dalarna is home to some of the country's premier cross-country and downhill skiing.

MORA. The quiet town of Mora (pop. 20,000) sits in the crater hollowed out by a meteorite more than 360 million years ago, bordered to the north by Lake Orsa and to the south and east by shimmering **Lake Siljan.** On the first Sunday in March, Mora serves as the finish of the **Vasaloppet,** the world's oldest and longest cross-country ski race; it draws 14,000 contestants to the 90km course annually and hosts a week-long **festival** (www.vasaloppet.se; Feb. 24-Mar. 5, 2006) in conjunction with the race. The **Vasaloppet Museum** screens a 30min. film about the race and chases the hero worship of past winners down with warm blueberry soup. (☎0250 392 25. Open mid-June to mid-Aug. daily 10am-5pm; mid-Aug. to mid-June M-F 10am-5pm; W closes at 3pm year-round. 30kr, including guided tour and soup.) Tucked away behind the city's church, **Zorngården,** Vasag. 37, is the 19th-century home of Anders Zorn, a Swedish painter best remembered for his nude portraits. Tour the estate and then move on to the **Zornmuseet,** which showcases a collection of Zorn's work as well as canvases by his contemporaries. (☎0250 59 23 10; www.zorn.se. Required English-language estate tours daily 2:10pm; call for alternate times. 50kr, students 45kr. Museum open mid-May to mid-Sept. M-Sa 9am-5pm, Su 11am-5pm; mid-Sept. to mid-May M-Sa noon-5pm, Su 1-5pm. 40kr, students 35kr. AmEx/

MC/V.) Hikers can tackle the **Siljansleden** network of trails that circles the two lakes, including a well-marked 310km **bike trail** skirting the shore and a 340km **walking trail** that edges its way farther inland, past shady pastures and creeks. In the winter, a ploughed track across Lake Orsa draws long-distance **skaters.** (☎0250 17 230; www.frilufts.se/mora/is.)

Homey **Vandrarhem Mora (HI) ❷,** Fredsg. 6, offers comfortable dorm rooms 500m from the train station; turn left on the main road and right on Fredsg. (☎0250 381 96; www.maalkullann.se. Breakfast 60kr. Linen 80kr. Reception 8-10am and 5-7pm. Dorms 230kr; singles 320kr; doubles 440kr. 45kr HI discount on dorms. AmEx/MC/V.) **Mora Parken Camping ❶** sits on the last strech of the Vasaloppet track. (☎0250 27600; www.moraparken.se. Breakfast 60kr. Linen 70kr. Laundry 20kr. Free showers. Late June to mid-Aug. tent sites 85kr. 2-person cabins 320kr; 4-person cabins 455kr. Low season reduced rates. AmEx/DC/MC/V.) Get groceries at **Hemköp** on Kyrkog. (☎0250 13600. Open M-Sa 8am-10pm, Su 10am-10pm. V.)

Trains run to Östersund (6hr., 2 per day mid-June to early Aug., 347kr) and Stockholm (4hr., 7 per day, 303kr). **Buses** also head to Östersund year-round (5¼hr., 2 per day, 175kr). The **tourist office,** in Mora's train station, books rooms (200-345kr) for a 25kr fee. (☎0250 592 020. Open mid-June to mid-Aug. and during the ski race M-F 10am-7pm, Sa-Su 10am-5pm; mid-Aug. to mid-June M-F 10am-5pm.) **Internet** is available at the city library, Köpmang. 4, off of the main street Kyrkog., a block away from the bus station. (☎0250 267 70. Open June-Aug. M-F 10am-7pm, Sa 10am-2pm. 10kr per 30min. Cash only.) **Postal Code:** 79200.

ÖSTERSUND. Travelers heading north into Lappland often tarry for a few days in hilly Östersund (pop. 58,000). Deep, reedy Lake Storsjön laps against the town's western shores, and many residents sincerely believe that the lake is home to the **Storsjöodjuret monster.** In 1894, the town called in a Norwegian harpooner to flush out the creature, but appeals by local Quakers and then the tourist office resulted in an 1986 ban on future hunting. The steamer *S/S Thomée* runs cruises and monster-spotting tours. (2-3 per day. 70-100kr. Advance tickets at the tourist office, or at the harbor before departure.) Rent a **bike** at the Badhusparken, next to where the *S/S Thomée* docks, and pedal over the footbridge to **Frösön Island,** a green getaway aptly named for the Norse god of crops and fertility. (☎0730 629972. Open June-Aug. M-F 8am-5pm. 50kr per half day, 100kr per day. In-line skates 25/50kr. Cash only.) Swedish couples have taken the hint by making the island's 12th-century **church** one of the country's most popular wedding chapels. Take bus #3 (18kr) from the center, or make the 4km trek by bike. (☎063 43573. Open daily 8am-8pm.) On the edge of the island closer to town, at the top of Frösö's highest point, stands the **Frösötornet** (Frösö Tower) and the Frösötornets Vandrarhem (see below). From the top, the Norwegian mountains can be seen on a clear day. (☎063 128169. Open daily late June to mid-Aug. 9am-9pm, mid-Aug. to mid-Sept. 10am-4pm, mid-Sept. to late June 11am-6pm. 10kr. Cash only.) Skip the open-air **Jamtli** museum; others in the region (p. 1011) are more authentic and less expensive.

Wild strawberries grow on the roof of the 255-year-old cabin at **Frösötornets Vandrarhem ❶,** Utsiktv. 10, Frösön. Bus #5 runs from the city center 11am-10:20pm, and stops at the bottom of a long, steep hill. The fairy-tale setting is worth the difficult climb. (☎063 51 57 67; vandrarhem@froson.com. No lockers available. Linen 50kr. Call for reception. Dorms 140kr; singles 180kr. Cash only.) Travelers chatter in the roomy kitchen of the more centrally located—if less charming—**Hostel Rallaren ❶,** Bangårdsg. 6, 300m to the left of the station along the tracks. (☎063 13 22 32; sventa_rallaren@hotmail.com. Linen 40kr. No lockers available. Reception 9:30am-3pm. Dorms 150kr; singles 200kr; doubles 340kr. Cash only.) Pick up groceries at **Hemköp,** Kyrkg. 56. (Open M-Sa 8am-10pm, Su 10am-10pm.)

Trains run to Stockholm (6hr.; 6 per day; 572kr, under 26 482kr) and Trondheim, Norway (4hr., 2 per day, 268/187kr). From mid-June to early August, a Inlandsbanan train (☎0771 53 53 53; www.inlandsbanan.se) runs to Mora (6hr., 2 per day, 347kr). The **tourist office,** Rådhusg. 44, books rooms and offers storage facilities, both for free. From the station, walk up the hill on the left and continue down Prästg.; turn right one block up Postgränd. (☎063 144001; www.turist.ostersund.se. Internet 2kr per min. Open July M-Sa 9am-9pm, Su 10am-7pm; June and Aug. M-F 9am-5pm, Sa-Su 10am-3pm; Sept.-May M-F 9am-5pm.) **Postal Code:** 83100.

ÅRE. The **Åre Ski Resort** (☎0647 177 00; www.skistar.com/english/are) is the largest in Sweden, with a rich variety of beginner and intermediate trails as well as an excellent ski school. Even after the snow melts, the town of Åre (pop. 10,000) is a promising base for outdoor activities on and around **Åreskutan,** the highest peak in the region. Serious cyclists can take their chances at **downhill mountain biking,** a sport extreme enough to justify sky-high bike rental prices (300-800kr per day). Rental shops abound around the base of the mountain, and the **World Cup** chairlift brings you halfway up the mountain to a number of trailheads. (Lift runs daily July to Aug. 10am-4pm. Round-trip 60kr.) Ambitious **hikers** make their way up the difficult 7km **Åreskutan trail** from the town square to a 1420m peak, while the **Kabinbanan** cable car shortens the trip to under a kilometer. (Cable car runs July-Aug. 10am-4pm. Round-trip 100kr.) The 26km **Åreskutan Runt** hike cuts a broad circle around the mountain and generally requires a stay in the cabins by the Bjelke mines, while the gentle 2.5km walk to **Totthummeln** can be completed in 2hr. The **Åre Ski Lodge ❶,** Trondheimsleden 44, accents well-equipped rooms with vintage photographs. (☎0647 510 29. Linen 90kr. Laundry available. Dorms 110kr; doubles 290kr. Reserve ahead during ski season. Cash only.) **Trains** run from Åre to Östersund (1¼hr.; 2 per day; 130kr, students 65kr) and Trondheim, Norway (2¾hr., 2 per day, 180kr). The Nabotåget website (www.nabotaget.nu) has the best fares. The **tourist office,** in the station, sells essential hiking maps (9kr), organizes outdoor activities, and provides free **Internet.** (☎0647 177 20; www.areturistbyra.com. Open late June to Aug. and mid-Dec. to Apr. daily 9am-6pm; Sept. to mid-Dec. and May to late June M-F 9-11:30am and 12:30-5pm, Sa-Su 10am-3pm.) **Postal Code:** 83013.

GULF OF BOTHNIA

The Gulf of Bothnia region is deservedly well known for its deep forests, stark ravines, and stretches of pristine coastline. Its quiet, friendly cities show a Sweden outside of the glittery metropolitan centers to the south, but a visit to the region is most worthwhile mostly due to its proximity to short wilderness excursions.

GÄVLE. Two hours north of Stockholm, Gävle (pop. 90,000) is the first stop on the way to northern Sweden. The cobblestone streets and 17th-century houses of **Gamle Gefle** (old town), the only part of Gävle that survived a ravaging 19th-century fire, lie just across the canal from the train station. On the edge of the old town next to the canal, at the **Länsmuseet Gävleborg,** Södra Strandg. 20, contemporary art confronts tradition in themed exhibits drawn from the museum's collection of Swedish art. (☎026 65 56 35; www.lansmuseetgavleborg.se. Open June-Aug. M-F 10am-4pm, Sa-Su noon-4pm; Sept.-May Tu and Th-F 10am-4pm, W 10am-9pm, Sa-Su noon-4pm. 40kr, students free. W free. AmEx/MC/V.) Farther inland along the river, the **Gävle Konstcentrum,** Kungsbäcksv. 32, mounts ever-changing exhibits of international contemporary art. (☎026 17 94 24; www.galve.se/konstcentrum. Open June to mid-Aug. Tu-Su noon-4pm; mid-Aug. to May Tu-F noon-5pm, Th noon-7pm, Sa-Su noon-4pm. Free.) On the opposite bank, stroll through the city park's free **sculpture garden.**

Vandrarhem Gävle (HI) ➊, Södra Rådmansg. 1, has well-lit rooms and a flower-filled courtyard in the middle of the old town. From the train station, turn left, cross the canal, and turn right on Södra Strandg. At the library, make a left, go through the square, then up the stairs and past the parking lot. (☎026 62 17 45. Breakfast 50kr. Linen 70kr. Laundry 30kr. Reception 8-10am and 5-7pm. Dorms 180kr; singles 305kr; doubles 375kr. 45kr HI discount. MC/V.) For a light lunch (55kr) in a traditional Swedish setting, head to **Mamsell**, Kyrkog. 14, in the Berggrenska Gårdens. From the market square, walk one block on N. Stottsg. toward the canal. (☎026 12 34 10. Open M-F 11am-5pm, Sa 11am-3pm. MC/V.) Pick up **groceries** at the ICA across the street from the train station. (Open M-Sa 9am-8pm, Su 11am-8pm. MC/V.) **Trains** run from Gävle to Östersund (4-5hr., 2-4 per day, 252kr) and Stockholm (1½hr., every hr., 177kr). To get to the **tourist office**, Drottningg. 9, head straight out of the train station down Drottningg. to the market square; it is in the center of the Gallerian Nian store complex. (☎026 14 74 30; www.gastrikland.com. Open M-F 10am-7pm, Sa 10am-4pm, Su noon-4pm.) **Postal Code:** 80250.

SWEDEN

ÖRNSKÖLDSVIK. Burly high-rises dominate the center of drab Örnsköldsvik (urn-SHULDS-vik; "Ö-vik" to locals; pop. 30,000), but the town is a popular base for **hiking** excursions. The 127km **High Coast Trail** (Höga Kusten Leden) winds south through Skuleskogen National Park as far as Veda, just north of Sundsvall. Flanked by sea cliffs that drop dizzyingly into the Gulf of Bothnia, the trail is divided into 13 segments with free mountain huts at the end of each leg; bring an insulated sleeping bag or arrive early enough to cut firewood. Day hikes include the 6km **Yellow Trail** loop; although the hike is easy, steep drop-offs along the path may frighten some travelers. You'll find the trailhead on Hantverkareg.; from the tourist office, walk up Centralespl., turn left on Storg. and then left again. **Vandrarhem Örnsköldsvik (HI) ➊**, Högsnäsgården, lies outside town in a gracious country house. Take bus #421 out to the hostel; the last bus leaves town at 9pm on weekdays and 3pm on weekends. (☎06 60 702 44. Reception 9-10am and 5-7pm. Dorms 175kr. 45kr HI discount. MC/V.) Pick up groceries at **Hemköp**, Stora Torg. 3. (Open daily 8am-10pm. MC/V.) **Buses** run to Östersund (4½hr.; M-F 3 per day, Sa-Su 1 per day; 252kr) and Umeå (2hr., 7 per day, 111kr). The **tourist office**, Strandg. 24, next to the station, books rooms for a 40kr fee. (☎06 60 881 00; www.ornskoldsvik.se. Free Internet. Open late June to mid-Aug. M-F 9am-6pm, Sa-Su 10am-2pm; mid-Aug. to late June M-F 9am-6pm, Sa 10am-2pm.) **Postal Code:** 89188.

UMEÅ. In the 1970s, lefty students in Umeå (OOM-eh-oh; pop. 110,000) earned their alma mater the nickname "the red university." Times change, though, and today northern Sweden's largest city is better known for its birch-lined boulevards and genial youth culture than its Marxist leanings, although echoes of its egalitarian past live on in a slew of free attractions. At the **Gammlia** open-air museum, a 20min. walk east of the city center, period actors gives visitors a crack at 19th-century crafts like churning butter and working a pre-industrial loom, as well as the opportunity to sample freshly baked *tunnbröd* (20kr), traditional flatbread from northern Sweden. In the same complex, the **Västerbottens Museum** houses not only the world's oldest ski but also the modern **forUm** exhibit about the town, where visitors can relax on comfortable couches while listening to recordings by local artists. Connected to the museum, the **BildMuseet** displays Swedish and international contemporary art. (Open summer W-Su noon-5pm; low season Tu-Sa noon-4pm, Su noon-5pm. Free.) Nearby, the **Fishing and Nautical Museum** sheds light on the history of seal hunting in the region. Guided tours leave Gammlia daily at 1pm and the Fishing and Nautical Museum

THE BIG SPLURGE

COLD COMFORT

Rising out of the Torne River in tiny Jukkasjärvi, the remarkable **Icehotel** melts away each May and then crystallizes anew in November. Take the name at face value—the entire building is made out of ice. Artists spray tall metal frames with snow cannons to form walls, while ice pillars support the cavernous ceiling from which ice chandeliers dangle. The masterminds behind the Icehotel also allow for innovation; each year it's built with a new set of blueprints, so that artists are never simply replicating the same design.

However, innovation has yet to reveal how to pipe hot water into an ice hotel. Washroom facilities are outside, but the hotel gives its guests thermal suits for the wintry dash to the showers. Reindeer skins line the ledges that serve as beds, and thermal sleeping bags keep guests toasty until the staff shows up mid-morning with cups of hot lingonberry juice. More potent drinkables are on tap at the Absolut Icebar, while the nearby Ice Chapel has become a popular wedding spot for the matching parka set. Meanwhile, the Ice Globe Theater stages the Bard's plays inside a faithful reproduction of the original. Except that Hamlet wears mittens.

Icehotel *(☎980 668 00; www.icehotel.com.) Take bus #501 from Kiruna M-F. Breakfast and sauna included. Open mid-Dec. to Apr. Tours daily noon-6pm. Doubles 2800kr. 120kr, students 100kr.*

at 2:30pm. (☎090 17 18 00; www.vasterbottensmuseum.se. Gammlia, the Västerbottens Museum, and the Fishing and Nautical Museum open daily mid-June to mid-Aug. 10am-5pm; low season Tu-F 10am-4pm, Sa noon-4pm, Su noon-5pm. All free.) West of the city, the 30km **Umeleden** bike and car trail snakes past 5000-year-old rock carvings, an arboretum, one of Europe's largest hydropower stations, and **Baggböle Herrgård,** a cafe nestled into a 19th-century manor house that opens for business in summer. Pick up the trail at the **Gamla Bron** (Old Bridge) and veer across the Norvarpsbron to cut the route in half. Hikers can follow the **Tavelsjöleden** trail (30km) along a boulder ridge, or brave the **Isälvsleden** trail (60km), carved out of the stone by melting pack ice. Mingle with students at the **bars** along Rådhusg. and Kungsg.

The convenient, comfortable **Vandrarhem Umeå (HI) ❷,** V. Esplanaden 10, is one block past the tourist office, to the left off Skolg. (☎090 77 16 50; www.umeavandrarhem.com. No lockers available. Breakfast 50kr. Linen 45kr, with towel 55kr. Reception 8-10am and 5-7pm. Closed 2 weeks around Christmas and New Years. Dorms 175kr, with toilet 195kr, with bath 215kr. 45kr HI discount. DC/MC/V.) **Starz Coffee and Food ❷,** Kungsg. 55, has outdoor seating on the plaza. (☎090 14 14 90. Open M-Th 10am-10pm, F-Sa 10am-midnight, Su 11am-10pm. DC/MC/V.) **Trains** run to Gothenburg (14½hr.; 1 per day; 490kr, with sleeping berth 670kr). Ybuss **buses** (☎090 70 65 00) run to Stockholm (10hr.; 3 per day; 330kr, students 240kr). The **bus terminal** is across from the train station on the right. The **tourist office,** Renmarkstorg. 15, runs free English-language tours of the city in summer. From the stations, walk straight down Rådhusespl. and turn right on Skolg. (☎090 16 16 16; www.umea.se. Free Internet. Tours Sa 2pm. Open mid-June to mid-Aug. M-F 8:30am-7pm, Sa 10am-4pm, Su noon-4pm; low season reduced hours.) **Cykel och Mopedhandlaren,** Kungsg. 101, rents **bikes.** (☎090 14 01 70. Open M-F 9:30am-5:30pm, Sa 10am-1pm. 70kr per day, 195kr per week.) **Postal Code:** 90326.

LAPPLAND (SÁPMI)

Known as Europe's last wilderness, Lappland's mountains and alpine dales sprawl across northern Sweden, touristed only by the most mosquito-proof hikers. Today, the region's indigenous Sami people use technology like helicopters and snowmobiles to tend their herds of reindeer while they continue to wrangle with Stockholm over the hunting and grazing rights their ancestors enjoyed for centuries.

BUG CONTROL. While locals swear by a concoction of diluted vinegar—imbibed every morning—to keep the mosquitoes at bay, most travelers will want to carry a large supply of good old-fashioned bug spray when heading up north.

TRANSPORTATION

There are two **rail** routes to Lappland. **Connex** runs trains along the coastal route from Stockholm through Boden, Umeå, and Kiruna to Narvik, Norway, along the ore railway. If your travel plans are set in stone, call 90 days in advance and Connex will book a non-refundable ticket to anywhere else in Sweden for only 159kr. Head to www.connex.info/booking/booking_en for more info. From late June to early August, the privately run **Inlandsbanan** runs north from Mora (p. 1008) through the northern countryside. (☎063 19 44 12; www.inlandsbanan.se.) **Buses** are the only way to reach smaller towns; call ☎020 47 00 47 for schedules.

KIRUNA ☎098

The only large settlement in Lappland, Kiruna (pop. 23,000) retains the rough edges of a mining town, even as ski teams headed for the 2006 Winter Olympics arrive to practice at **Riksgänsen,** the world's northernmost ski resort. The state-owned mining company LKAB hauls an astonishing 20 million tons of iron ore out of the ground each year and caters to visitors with 3hr. **InfoMine** tours, which descend 540m to an informative museum. (2-3 per day. Tickets available at the tourist office. 220kr, students 140kr. MC/V.) Scientists at **Esrange,** a space center 40km outside Kiruna, launch short-range sounding rockets to conduct research on the ozone layer using high-altitude weather balloons. (☎04 02 70. 4hr. tours late June to mid-Aug. Tu, Th 9:15am. Includes snack. Reserve at the tourist office at least 24hr. in advance. 290kr, students 200kr.) Hikers take bus #92 from Kiruna to Nikkaluokta (1¼hr., 1-2 per day, 67kr) and pick up the well-marked **Kungsleden** trail at Kebnekaise Fjällstation. A week's trek north brings travelers into the mountain passes of Abisko National Park; the STF runs cabins spaced 10-20km apart on the trail. (☎084 63 21 00; www.stfturist.se. Prices vary. Cabins mid-July to mid-Sept. 255-355kr; late Feb. to mid-July 190-235kr. 100kr HI discount.) Closer to Kiruna, the village of **Jukkasjärvi** is home to a 1608 **wooden church** used to convert the Sami to Christianity. (Open 8am-8pm. Free.) Nearby, an open-air **Sami Museum** affords the opportunity to talk with guides about their struggle to preserve a Sami cultural identity in between lessons on how to lasso a reindeer. Take bus #501 (26kr) from the bus station. (☎02 13 29; www.nutti.se. Open daily early June to mid-Aug. 10am-6pm. Tours daily 11am, 12:30, 2pm. 75kr.)

The **Yellow House Hostel ❶,** Hantverkareg. 25, resembles an old farmhouse and has bright, spacious rooms. From the tourist office, walk uphill and turn left onto Vänortsg., which turns into Hantverkareg. (☎01 37 50; www.yellowhouse.nu. Breakfast 50kr. Linen 50kr. Reception 2pm-midnight. Dorms 150-160kr; singles 300kr; doubles 400kr. Cash only.) For a two-course lunch special (9am-2pm; 63-65kr) or a sandwich (30-50kr), head to **Svarta Björn ❷,** Hj. Lundbohmsv. 42, across the street from the Stadshus and the clock tower. (☎01 57 90. Vegetarian options available. Open July-Aug. M-F 8am-11pm, Sa-Su 11am-7pm; Sept.-June M-F 6:30am-9pm, Sa-Su 11am-3pm. Cash only.) Pull up to one of the outdoor tables at **Kaffekoppen ❷,** Föreningsg. 13B, for a reindeer meat wrap (*souvasrulle;* 37kr) and a mug of hot chocolate (25kr) the size of small mixing bowl. (☎01 80 61. Open M-Sa 9am-10pm, Su 10am-10pm. MC/V.) Pick up groceries at **ICA** in the central square. (Open M-F 9am-7pm, Sa 10am-4pm, Su 11am-4pm.)

Connex **trains** run to Stockholm (19hr., 3-4 per day, from 430kr) and Narvik, Norway (2¾hr., 3-4 per day, 221kr). **Flights** to Stockholm depart from Kiruna Flygplats. (KRN; ☎028 48 10. 3-4 per day; 500kr, students 350kr.) The **tourist office,** L. Janssonsgat. 17, is in the Folkets Hus. Walk straight from the train station, follow the footpath through the tunnel, and then go up the stairs through the park to the top of the hill and cross the plaza. The office arranges dogsled excursions and moose safaris, among other adventures. (☎01 88 80; www.lappland.se. Internet 25kr per 20min. Open mid-June to Aug. M-F 8:30am-8pm, Sa-Su 8:30am-6pm; Sept. to mid-June M-F 8:30am-5pm, Sa 8:30am-2pm.) **Postal Code:** 98122.

SWITZERLAND (SCHWEIZ, SUISSE, SVIZZERA)

Switzerland's gorgeous lakes and formidable peaks entice outdoor enthusiasts from around the globe. Three-fifths of the country is dominated by mountains: the Jura cover the northwest region bordering France and the Alps stretch gracefully across the lower half of Switzerland, with the eastern Rhaetian Alps bordering Austria. While stereotypes of Switzerland as a country of bankers and watchmakers are to some extent true, an energetic youth culture belies its staid reputation. Although the country is not known for being cheap, the best things—warm hospitality and Europe's most impressive Alpine playland—remain priceless.

DISCOVER SWITZERLAND: SUGGESTED ITINERARIES

THREE DAYS Experience the great outdoors at **Interlaken** (1 day; p. 1022), and then head to **Luzern** (1 day; p. 1030) for the perfect combination of city culture and natural splendor before jetting to international **Geneva** (1 day; p. 1036).

ONE WEEK Begin in **Luzern** (1 day), where your vision of a typical Swiss city will, strangely, be all too true. Then head to the capital, **Bern** (1 day; p. 1019), before getting your adventure thrills in **Interlaken** (1 day). Get a taste of Italian Switzerland in **Locarno** (1 day; p. 1044), then traverse northern Italy to reach **Zermatt** (1 day; p. 1035). End your trip in the cosmopolitan city of **Geneva** (2 days).

TWO WEEKS Start in **Geneva** (2 days), then check out **Lausanne** (1 day; p. 1041) and **Montreux** (1 day; p. 1042). Tackle the Matterhorn in **Zermatt** (1 day) and keep hiking above **Interlaken** (1 day). Bask in **Locarno's** Mediterranean climate (1 day) then explore the **Swiss National Park** (1 day; p. 1035). Head to **Zurich** (2 days; p. 1025) and **Luzern** (1 day). Unwind in tiny, romantic **Stein am Rhein** (2 day; p. 1031) and then return to civilization via the capital, **Bern** (1 day).

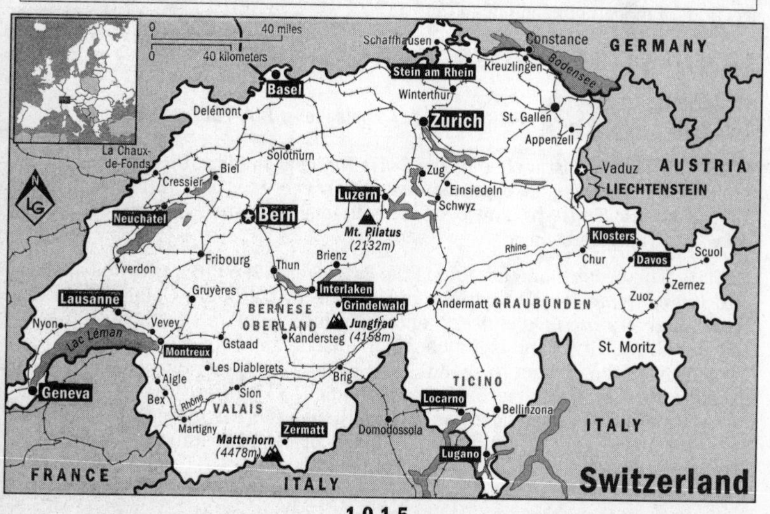

ESSENTIALS

FACTS AND FIGURES

Official Name: Swiss Confederation.

Capital: Bern.

Major Cities: Basel, Geneva, Zurich.

Population: 7,490,000 (65% German, 18% French, 10% Italian).

Time Zone: GMT +1.

Languages: German, French, Italian, Romansch.

Religions: Roman Catholic (46%), Protestant (40%), other or unaffiliated (14%).

WHEN TO GO

During ski season—from November to March—prices double in eastern Switzerland and travelers need reservations months in advance. The situation reverses in the summer, especially July and August, when the flatter, western half of Switzerland fills with vacationers and hikers. A good budget option is to travel during the shoulder season: sights and accommodations are cheaper and less crowded May-June and September-October. Many mountain towns throughout Switzerland shut down completely in May and June, though, so call ahead to make sure that the attractions you want to visit will be open.

DOCUMENTS AND FORMALITIES

EMBASSIES. Most foreign embassies are in **Bern** (p. 1019). Swiss embassies abroad include: **Australia,** 7 Melbourne Ave., Forrest, Canberra, ACT 2603 (☎02 6162 8400); **Canada,** 5 Marlborough Ave., Ottawa, ON K1N 8E6 (☎613-235-1837); **Ireland,** 6 Ailesbury Rd., Ballsbridge, Dublin 4 (☎353 12 18 63 82); **New Zealand,** 22 Panama St., Wellington 6001 (☎04 472 15 93); **UK,** 16-18 Montague Pl., London W1H 2BQ (☎020 76 16 60 00); **US,** 2900 Cathedral Ave. NW, Washington, D.C. 20008-3499 (☎202-745-7900).

VISA AND ENTRY INFORMATION. EU citizens do not need a visa. Citizens of Australia, Canada, New Zealand, and the US do not need a visa for stays of up to 90 days. Although not a member of the EU, Switzerland is expected to join the EU freedom of movement zone in 2007.

TOURIST SERVICES AND MONEY

EMERGENCY **Police:** ☎117. **Ambulance:** ☎144. **Fire:** ☎118.

TOURIST OFFICES. Branches of the **Swiss National Tourist Office,** marked by a standard blue "i" sign, are represented in nearly every town in Switzerland; most agents speak English. The official tourism website for Switzerland is www.myswitzerland.com.

MONEY. The Swiss monetary unit is the **Swiss Franc (SFr/CHF),** which is divided into 100 *centimes* (called *rappen* in German Switzerland). Coins come in 5, 10, 20, and 50 *centimes* and 1, 2, and 5SFr; bills come in 10, 20, 50, 100, 500, and 1000SFr. Switzerland is not cheap; if you stay in hostels and prepare most of your own food, expect to spend 55-80SFr per day. Generally, it's cheaper to exchange money in Switzerland than at home. ATMs offer the best exchange rates. There is no **Value Added Tax (VAT),** although there is often a small tourist tax for a hostel stay. **Gratuity** is included in prices at restaurants and cafes; however, it is polite to round up your bill 1-2SFr.

SWISS FRANC (SFR)		
	AUS$1 = 0.96SFR	1SFR = AUS$1.05
	CDN$1 = 1.06SFR	1SFR = CDN$0.94
	EUR€1 = 1.55SFR	1SFR = EUR€0.65
	NZ$1 = 0.88SFR	1SFR = NZ$1.14
	UK£1 = 2.27SFR	1SFR = UK£0.44
	US$1 = 1.26SFR	1SFR = US$0.80

TRANSPORTATION

BY PLANE. Major international airports are in Bern (BRN), Geneva (GVA), and Zurich (ZRH). From London, **easyJet** (☎0871 244 23 66; www.easyjet.com) has flights to Geneva and Zurich. From Ireland, **Aer Lingus** (☎0818 365 000; www.aerlingus.ie) sells tickets from Dublin to Geneva. For more information on flying to Switzerland from other locations, see p. 48.

BY TRAIN. Federal **(SBB, CFF)** and private railways connect most towns, with frequent trains. For times and prices, check online (www.sbb.ch). **Eurail, Europass,** and **Interrail** are all valid on federal trains. The **SwissPass,** sold worldwide, offers four, eight, 15, 21, or 30 consecutive days of unlimited rail travel. In addition, it entitles you to unlimited public transportation in 36 cities and on some private railways and lake steamers. (2nd class 4-day pass US$180, 8-day US$255, 15-day US$310, 21-day US$360, 1-month US$400.)

BY BUS. PTT Post Buses, a barrage of government-run yellow coaches, connect rural villages and towns that trains don't service. In mountainous areas, they tend to be the fastest means of travel. **SwissPasses** are valid on many buses; **Eurail** passes are not. Even with the SwissPass, you might have to pay 5-10SFr extra if you're riding certain buses.

BY CAR. With armies of mechanized road crews ready to remove snow at a moment's notice, roads at altitudes of up to 1500m generally remain open throughout winter. The speed limit is 50kph in cities, 80kph on open roads, and 120kph on highways. Many small towns forbid cars to enter; some require special permits or restrict driving hours. Call ☎140 for roadside assistance.

BY BIKE. Cycling, though strenuous, is a splendid way to see the country; most train stations rent bikes and let you return them at another station. The Touring Club Suisse, Chemin de Blandonnet 4, Case Postale 820, 1214 Vernier (☎022 417 27 27; www.tcs.ch), is a good source for maps and route descriptions.

KEEPING IN TOUCH

PHONE CODES	**Country code:** 41. **International dialing prefix:** 00. For more information on how to place international calls, see inside back cover.

EMAIL AND THE INTERNET. Most Swiss cities, as well as a number of smaller towns, have at least one Internet cafe with web access available for about 5-12SFr per hour. Hostels and restaurants frequently offer Internet access as well, but it seldom comes for free: rates can climb as high as 15SFr per hour.

TELEPHONE. Use a calling card for international phone calls, as long-distance rates are often exorbitant for national phone services. Most pay phones in Switzerland accept only prepaid phone cards, available at kiosks, post offices, and train stations. Direct access numbers include: **AT&T** (☎0800 89 00 11); **British Telecom** (☎0800 55 25 44); **Canada Direct** (☎0800 55 83 30); **MCI Worldphone** (☎0800 89 02 22); **Sprint** (☎0800 899 777); **Telecom New Zealand** (☎0800 55 64 11); and **Telstra Australia** (☎0800 555 004). For info about using mobile phones abroad, see p. 33.

MAIL. Airmail from Switzerland averages four to seven days to North America, although times are unpredictable from smaller towns. Domestic letters take one to three days. Address mail to be held according to the following example: Firstname SURNAME, *Postlagernde Briefe*, CH-8021 Zurich, SWITZERLAND.

LANGUAGE. German, French, Italian, and Romansch are the national languages. **German** is spoken by 64% of the population, throughout central and eastern Switzerland; in western Switzerland, **French** is the language of choice for 19% of the Swiss; 8% speak **Italian,** primarily in the southern Ticino region. **Romansch** is spoken by less than 1% of the population, but it has historical and ethnic significance, having survived for hundreds of years in the isolated mountain valleys of Graubünden (p. 1033). Most urban Swiss speak English fluently. For basic German words and phrases, see p. 1060; for French, see p. 1059; for Italian, see p. 1062.

ACCOMMODATIONS AND CAMPING

SWITZERLAND	❶	❷	❸	❹	❺
ACCOMMODATIONS	under 26SFr	26-42SFr	42-65SFr	65-125SFr	over 125SFr

There are **hostels** (*Jugendherbergen* in German, *Auberges de Jeunesse* in French, *Ostelli* in Italian) in all big cities and in most small towns. **Schweizer Jugendherbergen** (SJH; www.youthhostel.ch) runs HI hostels in Switzerland. Non-HI members can stay in any HI hostel, where beds are usually 30-44SFr; members typically receive a 6SFr discount. The more informal **Swiss Backpackers (SB)** organization (www.backpacker.ch) has 31 hostels aimed at the young, foreign traveler interested in socializing. Most Swiss **campgrounds** are not idyllic refuges but large plots glutted with RVs. Prices average 12-20SFr per tent site and 6-9SFr per extra person. **Hotels** and **pensions** tend to charge at least 65-80SFr for a single room and 80-120SFr for a double. The cheapest have *Gasthof*, *Gästehaus*, or *Hotel-Garni* in the name. **Privatzimmer** (rooms in a family home) run about 30-60SFr per person. Breakfast is included at most hotels, pensions, and *Privatzimmer*.

HIKING AND SKIING. Nearly every town has **hiking trails;** consult the local tourist office. Luzern (p. 1030), Interlaken (p. 1022), Grindelwald (p. 1024), and Zermatt (p. 1035) offer particularly good hiking opportunities. Trails are usually marked with either red-white-red markers (only sturdy boots and hiking poles needed) or blue-white-blue markers (mountaineering equipment needed). **Skiing** in Switzerland is often less expensive than in North America–if you avoid pricey resorts. **Ski passes** run 40-70SFr per day, 100-300SFr per week; a week of lift tickets, equipment rental, lessons, lodging, and *demi-pension* (breakfast plus one other meal) averages 475SFr. **Summer skiing** is less common than it once was but is still available in a few towns such as Zermatt and Saas Fee.

FOOD AND DRINK

SWITZERLAND	❶	❷	❸	❹	❺
FOOD	under 9SFr	9-23SFr	23-32SFr	32-52SFr	over 52SFr

Switzerland is not for the lactose intolerant. The Swiss are serious about dairy products, from rich and varied **cheeses** to decadent **milk chocolate**—even the major Swiss soft drink, **Rivella,** contains dairy. Swiss dishes vary from region to region.

Bernese *rösti*, a plateful of hash-brown potatoes (sometimes flavored with bacon or cheese), is prevalent in the German regions; cheese or meat **fondue** is popular in the French regions. Try Valaisian *raclette*, made by melting cheese over a fire, scraping it onto a baked potato, and garnishing it with meat or vegetables. Supermarkets **Migros** and **Co-op** double as cafeterias; stop in for a cheap meal and groceries. Each canton has its own local beer, which is often cheaper than Coca-Cola.

HOLIDAYS AND FESTIVALS

Holidays: New Year's Day (Jan. 1); Good Friday (Mar. 25); Easter Monday (Mar. 28); Labor Day (May 1); Swiss National Day (Aug. 1).

Festivals: Two raucous festivals are the Fasnacht (Carnival; late Feb. to early Mar.) in Basel and the Escalade (early Dec.) in Geneva. Music festivals occur throughout the summer, including Open-Air St. Gallen (late June) and the Montreux Jazz Festival (July).

BEYOND TOURISM

Although Switzerland's volunteer opportunities are limited, a number of ecotourism and rural development organizations allow you to give back to the country; your best bet is to go through a placement service. Look for opportunities for short-term work on websites like www.emploi.ch.

Bergwald Projekt/Mountain Forest Project, Hauptstr. 24, 7014 Trin, Switzerland (☎+41 81 630 4145; www.bergwaldprojekt.ch). Organizes week-long conservation projects in Austria, Germany, and Switzerland.

Workcamp Switzerland, Bastionweg 15, 4500 Solothurn, Switzerland (☎+41 32 621 50 37; www.workcamp.ch). Offers 2-week long sessions in which volunteers live in a group environment and work on a common community service project.

GERMAN SWITZERLAND

BERNESE OBERLAND

The peaks of the Bernese Oberland shelter a pristine wilderness that lends itself to discovery through scenic hikes up the mountains and around the twin lakes, the Thunersee and Brienzersee. Not surprisingly, the area's opportunities for paragliding, mountaineering, and whitewater rafting are unparalleled. North of the mountains lies exuberant Bern, Switzerland's capital and the heartbeat of the region.

BERN

☎031

Bern (pop. 127,000) has been Switzerland's capital since 1848, but don't expect fast tracks, power politics, or men in suits—the Bernese prefer to focus on the more leisurely things in life, nibbling the local Toblerone chocolate and lolling along the banks of the serpentine Aare.

TRANSPORTATION AND PRACTICAL INFORMATION. Bern's **airport** (BRN; ☎960 21 11) is 20min. from the city. An **airport bus** runs from the train station 50min. before each flight (10min., 14SFr). **Trains** run from the station at Bahnhofpl. to: Geneva (2hr., 3 per hr., 45SFr); Luzern (1½hr., every 30min., 30SFr); Munich (6hr., every hr., 124SFr); Paris (6hr., approx. 1 per hr., 115SFr); Salzburg (7¼hr., 2 per day, 142SFr); Zurich (1¼hr., every 30min., 45SFr). Local Bernmobil **buses** run 5:45am-midnight. (☎321 86 41. Day pass 12SFr.) **Free bikes** are available from **Bern**

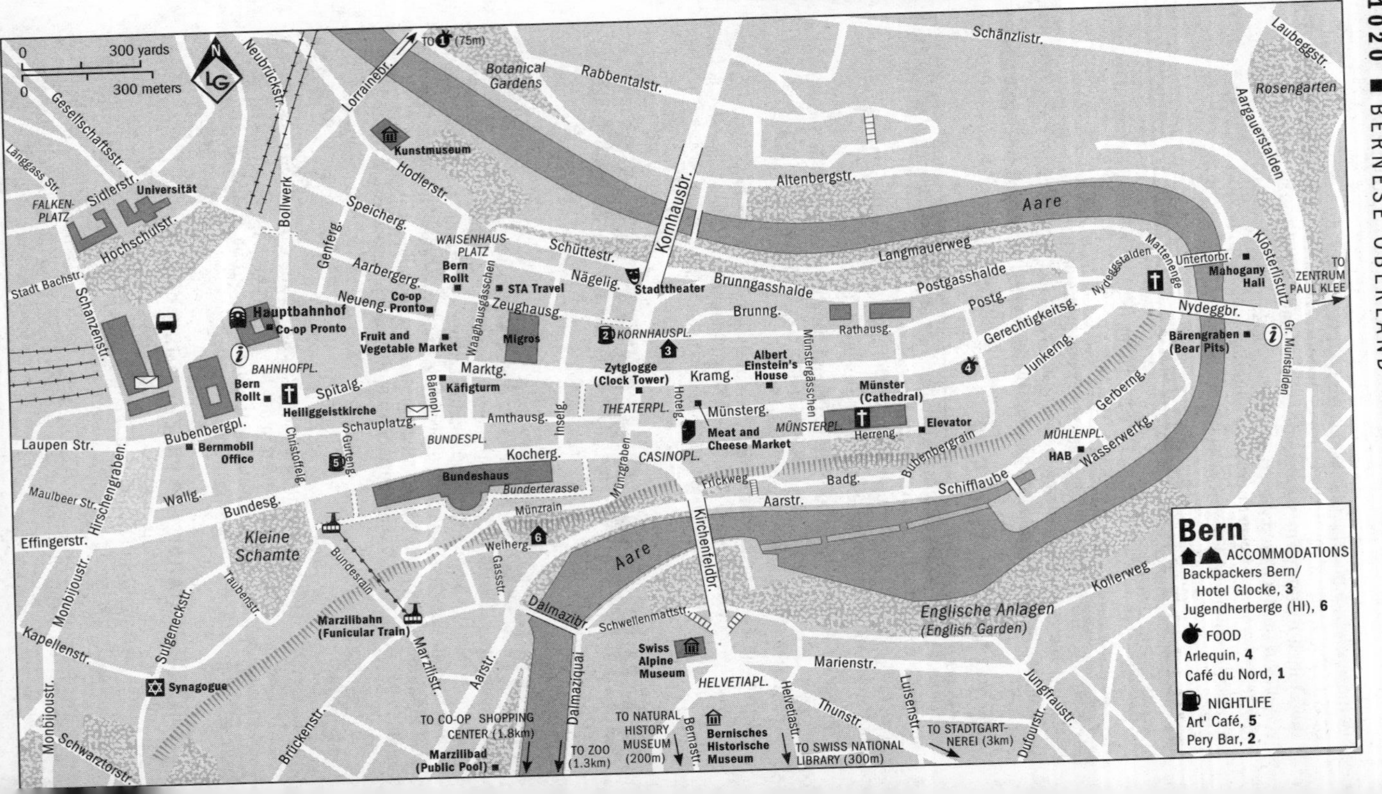
Bern
ACCOMMODATIONS
Backpackers Bern/ Hotel Glocke, 3
Jugendherberge (HI), 6
FOOD
Arlequin, 4
Café du Nord, 1
NIGHTLIFE
Art' Café, 5
Pery Bar, 2
0 300 yards
0 300 meters
Aare
Kornhausbr.
Kirchenfeldbr.
Nydeggbr.
Lorrainebr.
TO (75m)
TO ZENTRUM PAUL KLEE
Gr. Muristalden
Klösterlistutz
Mahogany Hall
Bärengraben (Bear Pits)
Untertorbr.
Mattenenge
Nydeggstalden
Aargauerstalden
Laubeggstr.
Rosengarten
Schänzlistr.
Altenbergstr.
Rabbentalstr.
Botanical Gardens
Kunstmuseum
Hodlerstr.
Langmauerweg
Postgasshalde
Brunngasshalde
Postg.
Gerechtigkeitsg.
Junkerng.
Gerberng.
Wasserwerkg.
MÜHLENPL.
HAB
Schifflaube
Bubenbergrain
Elevator
Münster (Cathedral)
MÜNSTERPL.
Herreng.
Badg.
Aarstr.
Rathausg.
Münstergässchen
Brunng.
Albert Einstein's House
Kramg.
Münsterg.
Meat and Cheese Market
Hotelg.
CASINOPL.
Frickweg
Stadttheater
KORNHAUSPL.
Zytglogge (Clock Tower)
THEATERPL.
Münzgraben
Nägelig.
Schüttestr.
Zeughausg.
STA Travel
Migros
Inselg.
Amthausg.
Marktg.
Käfigturm
Kocherg.
Bundeshaus
Bunderterasse
Münzrain
Weiherg.
Gassstr.
WAISENHAUS-PLATZ
Waaghausgässchen
Bern Rollt
Bärenpl.
BUNDESPL.
Speicherg.
Aarbergerg.
Co-op Pronto
Neueng.
Fruit and Vegetable Market
Schauplatzg.
Gurteng.
Spitalg.
Heiliggeistkirche
Genferg.
Hauptbahnhof
BAHNHOFPL.
Christoffelg.
Bollwerk
Neubrückstr.
Bubenbergpl.
Bernmobil Office
Bundesg.
Kleine Schamte
Bundesrain
Marzilibahn (Funicular Train)
Marzilistr.
Wallg.
Laupen Str.
Effingerstr.
Maulbeer Str.
Hirschengraben
Monbijoustr.
Kapellenstr.
Schwarztorstr.
Sulgeneckstr.
Synagogue
Taubenstr.
Brückenstr.
Aarstr.
Marzilibad (Public Pool)
TO CO-OP SHOPPING CENTER (1.8km)
TO ZOO (1.3km)
Dalmazibr.
Dalmaziquai
Schwellenmattstr.
Swiss Alpine Museum
TO NATURAL HISTORY MUSEUM (200m)
Bernastr.
Bernisches Historische Museum
HELVETIAPL.
Helvetiastr.
TO SWISS NATIONAL LIBRARY (300m)
Thunstr.
Marienstr.
Luisenstr.
TO STADTGART-NEREI (3km)
Englische Anlagen (English Garden)
Jungfraustr.
Dufourstr.
Kollerweg
Universität
Hochschulstr.
Sidlerstr.
Gesellschaftsstr.
FALKEN-PLATZ
Länggass Str.
Schanzenstr.
Stadt Bachstr.

rollt at two locations, one at Bahnhofpl., in front of the station, and another on Zeugausg., near Waisenhauspl. (☎079 277 2857; www.bernrollt.ch. Deposit of passport and 20SFr required. Open May-Oct. daily 7:30am-9:30pm.)

Most of medieval Bern lies in front of the station and along the Aare River. The **tourist office,** on the street level of the station, books hotel rooms and provides maps, both for free. (☎328 1212; www.berninfo.ch. Open June-Sept. daily 9am-8:30pm; Oct.-May M-Sa 9am-6:30pm, Su 10am-5pm.) The **post office,** Schanzenpost 1, is one block from the station. (Open M-F 7:30am-9pm, Sa 8am-4pm, Su 4-9pm.) **Postal Codes:** CH-3000 to CH-3030.

ACCOMMODATIONS AND FOOD. To reach the **Backpackers Bern/Hotel Glocke ❷,** Rathausg. 75, from the train station, cross the tram lines and turn left on Spitalg., continuing onto Marktg.; turn left at Kornhauspl., then right on Rathausg. (☎311 3771; www.bernbackpackers.ch. Internet 2SFr per 15min. Dorms 31-34SFr; singles 75SFr; doubles 80SFr, with bath 160SFr. AmEx/DC/MC/V; 35SFr minimum charge.) At **Jugendherberge (HI) ❷,** Weiherg. 4, a free swimming pool welcomes travelers. From the station, go down Christoffelg.; take the stairs to the left of the park gates, go down the slope, and turn left onto Weiherg. (☎311 6316; www.jugibern.ch. Breakfast included. Closed 2nd and 3rd weeks of Jan. Dorms 36-42SFr; singles 56-61SFr; doubles 92-102SFr. 6SFr HI discount. MC/V.) **Arlequin ❶,** Gerechtigkeitsg. 51, serves meat fondue (30SFr) and tasty sandwiches. (☎311 3946. Sandwiches 4-7.50SFr. Open Tu-W 10am-11:30pm, Th-F 10am-12:30am, Sa 11:30am-12:30am. AmEx/MC/V.) A diverse crowd smokes and socializes under stained-glass at **Café du Nord ❷,** Lorrainestr. 2. (☎332 2328. Entrees 22-32SFr. Pasta 18-25SFr. Open M-F 8am-12:30am, Sa 9am-12:30am. Kitchen open M-Sa 11:30am-2pm and 6:30-10pm, Su 4:30-11:30pm. MC/V.) For groceries, head to **Migros,** Marktg. 46. (Open M 9am-6:30pm, Tu 8am-6:30pm, W-F 8am-9pm, Sa 7am-4pm.)

SIGHTS. The **Bundeshaus,** center of the Swiss government, rises high over the Aare. (www.parlament.ch. 45min. tour every hr. M-Sa 9-11am and 2-4pm. English-language tour usually at 2pm. Arrive 30min. before tour starts. Free.) From the Bundeshaus, Kocherg. and Herreng. lead to the 15th-century **Münster** (cathedral); above the main entrance, a golden sculpture depicts the torments of hell. (Open Easter-Oct. Tu-Sa 10am-5pm; Nov.-Easter Tu-F 10am-noon and 2-4pm, Sa 10am-noon and 2-5pm, Su 11am-2pm. Last entrance 30min. before closing. Tower 4SFr.) **Albert Einstein's house,** Kramg. 49, where he conceived the theory of general relativity, is now filled with his photos and letters. (☎312 0091; www.einstein-bern.ch. Open Feb.-Nov. Tu-F 10am-5pm, Sa 10am-4pm. 6SFr, students 4.50SFr.) Several steep walkways lead down from the Bundeshaus to the **Aare River.**

A recent addition to Bern's plethora of museums is the **Zentrum Paul Klee,** Monument im Fruchtland 3, which houses the world's largest Klee collection. Take bus #12 to Zentrum Paul Klee. (☎359 0101; www.zpk.org. Open Tu-Su 9am-6pm, Th until 9pm. 14SFr, students 12SFr; 2-4SFr more for exhibits.) Near Lorrainebrücke, the **Kunstmuseum,** Hodlerstr. 8-12, has paintings from the Middle Ages to the contemporary era and features a smattering of big 20th-century names: Giacometti, Kirchner, Picasso, and Pollock. (☎328 0944; www.kunstmuseumbern.ch. Open Tu 10am-9pm, W-Su 10am-5pm. 7SFr, students 5SFr.) Across the Nydeggbr. lie the **Bärengraben** (bear pits), which were recently renovated to provide the bears with trees and rocks to clamber over—perhaps an attempt to make up for the indignity of being on display for the gawking crowds. (Open daily June-Sept. 9am-5pm; Oct.-May 10am-4pm.) The path up the hill to the left leads to the **Rosengarten** (Rose Garden), which provides one of the best views of Bern's *Altstadt* (old town).

ENTERTAINMENT AND NIGHTLIFE. Check out *Bewegungsmelder*, available at the tourist office, for events. July's **Gurten Festival** (www.gurtenfestival.ch) has attracted such luminaries as Bob Dylan, Elvis Costello, and Björk, while jazz-lovers arrive in early May for the **International Jazz Festival** (www.jazzfestivalbern.ch). The orange grove at **Stadtgärtnerei Elfenau** (take tram #19, dir.: Elfenau, to Luternauweg) has free Sunday concerts in summer. From mid-July to mid-August, **OrangeCinema** (☎0800 078 078; www.orangecinema.ch) screens recent films in the open air; tickets are available from the tourist office in the train station.

At night, the fashionable folk linger in the *Altstadt*'s bars and cafes while a leftist crowd gathers under the gargoyles of the Lorrainebrücke, behind the station down Bollwerk. When new DJs come to town, they can invariably be found at **Art' Café,** Gurteng. 6, a cafe by day and club by night. (☎318 2070; www.artcafe.ch. Open M-W 7am-8pm, Th-Sa 7am-2:30am, Su 7am-12:30pm. Cash only.) The candlelit interior at **Pery Bar,** Schmiedenpl. 3, provides a romantic setting for early-evening drinks before the DJs begin spinning. (☎311 5908. Wine 7SFr. DJs W-Sa. Open M-W 5pm-1:30am, Th 5pm-2:30am, F-Sa 5pm-3:30am. AmEx/MC/V.)

SWITZERLAND

JUNGFRAU REGION

The most famous (and most visited) region of the Bernese Oberland, Jungfrau draws tourists with glorious hiking trails, turquoise glacier lakes, and permanently snow-capped peaks. From Interlaken, the valley splits at the foot of the Jungfrau Mountain: the eastern valley contains Grindelwald, with easy access to two glaciers, while the western valley hosts many smaller towns, each with unique hiking opportunities. The two valleys are divided by an easily hikable ridge.

INTERLAKEN ☎033

Interlaken (pop. 21,000) lies between the Thunersee and the Brienzersee at the foot of the largest mountains in Switzerland. The countless hiking trails, raging rivers, beautiful lakes, and skyward-reaching peaks have turned Interlaken into one of Switzerland's prime tourist attractions and its top adventure sports destination.

TRANSPORTATION AND PRACTICAL INFORMATION. The Westbahnhof (☎826 4750) and Ostbahnhof (☎828 7319) have **trains** to: Basel (2-3hr., 1-2 per hr., 53SFr); Bern (1hr., 1-2 per hr., 25SFr); Geneva (61SFr); Lugano/Locarno (5:30am-4:35pm, 74SFr); Luzern (2hr., every hr., 30SFr); Zurich (2hr., every 2hr., 61SFr). The Ostbahnhof also sends trains to Grindelwald (June-Sept. every 30min., Sept.-May every hr.; 12.60SFr).

The **tourist office,** Höheweg 37, in Hotel Metropole, gives out maps and books hotel rooms, both for free. (☎826 53 00; www.interlakentourism.ch. Open July-Aug. M-F 8am-7pm, Sa 8am-5pm, Su 10am-noon and 4-6pm; May-June and Sept.-Oct. M-F 8am-6pm, Sa 8am-noon; Nov.-Apr. M-F 8am-noon and 1:30-6pm, Sa 9am-noon.) Both train stations rent **bikes.** (31SFr per day. Open daily 7am-7:30pm.) For **snow** and **weather info,** call ☎828 79 31. In case of **emergency,** call the **police** (☎117) or the **hospital** (☎826 26 26). The **post office** is at Marktg. 1. (Open M-F 8am-noon and 1:45-6pm, Sa 8:30-11am.) **Postal Code:** CH-3800.

ACCOMMODATIONS AND FOOD. Interlaken is a backpacking hot spot, especially in the summer, so hostels tend to fill up quickly; book about a month in advance. Diagonally across the Höhenmatte from the tourist office, the low-key **Backpackers Villa Sonnenhof ❷,** Alpenstr. 16, includes free admission to a nearby spa for the duration of your stay. (☎826 7171. Mountain bike rental 28SFr per day.

Breakfast included. Free lockers. Laundry 10SFr. Internet 1SFr per 5min. Reception 7:30-11am and 4-10pm. May to mid.-Sept. and mid-Dec. to mid-Jan. dorms 33-38SFr; doubles 96-106SFr; triples 129-144SFr. Mid-Sept. to mid.-Dec. and mid-Jan. to Apr. 29-32/88-98/117-132SFr. AmEx/MC/V.) **Balmer's Herberge ❶**, Hauptstr. 23, Switzerland's oldest private hostel (est. 1945), is the best place to party in Interlaken. Services include mountain bike rental (35SFr per day), nightly movies, free sleds, and an extremely popular bar. (☎822 1961. Breakfast included. Internet 12SFr per hr. Reception 24hr. in summer; in winter 6:30-10am and 4:30-10pm. Dorms 25-27SFr; singles 41-43SFr; doubles 70-74SFr; triples 93-99SFr; quads 124-132SFr. AmEx/MC/V.) At the friendly **Walter's Bed and Breakfast Guest House ❶**, Oelestr. 35, enormous rooms with hardwood floors and great views await. From the Ostbahnhof, follow Allmendstr. until it becomes Oelestr. (☎822 7688; walter.rooms@gmx.ch. Breakfast 7SFr. Laundry 6SFr. Internet 3SFr per 15min. Reception 11am-9pm. Doubles 46SFr; quads 80SFr. Cash only.) **Funny Farm ❶**, just off Hauptstr., also attracts party-goers with bonfires and a climbing wall above a swimming pool. (☎079 652 6127; www.funny-farm.ch. Laundry 10SFr. Internet 5SFr per 25min. Reception 24hr. Dorms 20-29SFr, with bath 30-39SFr. MC/V.)

My Little Thai ❷, Hauptstr. 19, fills with hungry backpackers in the evening. (☎821 1017. Pad thai 14.50-20.50SFr. Vegetarian options available. Internet 8SFr per hr. Open daily 11:30am-10pm. Cash only.) **El Azteca ❷**, Jungfraustr. 30, serves cactus salad (15.50SFr), fajitas (24-35SFr), and other Mexican fare. (☎822 7131. Open daily noon-3pm and 6-11pm. AmEx/MC/V.) There are **Migros** supermarkets by both train stations. (Open M-Th 8am-6:30pm, F 8am-9pm, Sa 7:30am-5pm.)

OUTDOOR ACTIVITIES. With the incredible surrounding Alpine scenery, it's no wonder that many of Interlaken's tourists seem compelled to try otherwise unthinkable adventure sports. **Alpin Raft,** Hauptstr. 7, the most established company in Interlaken, has qualified and entertaining guides that offer a wide range of activities, including paragliding (150SFr), river rafting (95-110SFr), skydiving (380SFr), and hanggliding (185SFr). They also offer two different **bungy jumping** locations, the 85m Glacier Bungy Jump (125SFr) and the Alpin Rush Jump (165SFr). There are daily trips to Glacier Bungy, and the bus to Alpin Rush departs Interlaken Monday, Wednesday, Friday, and Saturday at 4:30pm. One of the most popular adventure activities at Alpin Raft is **canyoning** (110-170SFr), which involves rappelling down a series of gorge faces, jumping off cliffs into pools of churning water, and swinging, Tarzan-style, from ropes and zip

5, 4, 3, 2, 1...

"We have one rule here in the gondola," said Mark, our bungee-jumping guide. "No nervous farts." Those were the last instructions I received as I shuffled to the gondola's platform, high above the Stockhorn Lake, wondering what I had gotten myself into. I curled my toes around the edge of the metal platform with the heavy beats of AC/DC in the background. Then, with the countdown shouted out by those waiting behind me, I took a deep breath and dove headfirst into the silence below.

After the initial rush of my exhilarating five-second freefall, I shakily took in the incredible—now inverted—surroundings. Green peaks encircled the lake, and herds of cows grazed lazily below. One by one, the gondola was emptied of about 20 other Interlaken backpackers, and a rowboat at the bottom carted each jumper safely to shore. Even the rain that had started to drizzle couldn't dampen our spirits or stop the adrenaline rush as we huddled around the campfire at the edge of the lake, eating barbequed sausages and toasting a complimentary celebratory beer to our 134m plunge.

-Laura Maludzinksi

cords through the canyon. All prices include transportation to and from any hostel in Interlaken, as well as a beer upon completion. **Swissraft,** Jungfraustr. 72 (☎821 66 50; www.swissraft.ch), offers the cheapest river rafting in Interlaken (half-day 90-110SFr), as well as **hydro-speeding** (aided body-surfing down the river; 95SFr). At **Skydive Xdream,** you can skydive with one of the best in the world; the owner, Stefan Heuser, was on the Swiss skydiving team for 12 years and won three world championship medals. (☎079 759 34 83; www.justjump.ch. Skydiving 380SFr per tandem plane jump; 430SFr per tandem heli jump. Open Apr.-Oct. Pick-up times 9am, 1pm, Sa-Su also 4pm. Call for winter availability.) **Swiss Alpine Guides,** the only company in Interlaken that offers **ice climbing,** runs full-day trips to a nearby glacier and provides all the equipment needed to scale vertical glacier walls. (☎822 60 00; www.swissalpineguides.ch. Trips May-Nov. daily, weather permitting. 160SFr.)

SWITZERLAND

Interlaken's most traversed trail climbs to the **Harder Kulm** (1310m). From the Ostbahnhof, head toward town, take the first road bridge right across the river, and follow the yellow signs that later give way to white-red-white rock markings. From the top, signs lead back down to the Westbahnhof. The hike should be about 2½hr. up and 1½hr. down. For flatter trails, turn left from the train station and left before the bridge, then follow the canal over to the nature reserve on the shore of the Thunersee. The trail winds along the Lombach River, through pastures at the base of the Harder Kulm, and back toward town (3hr.).

Interlaken's adventure sports industry is thrilling, but accidents do happen. On July 27, 1999, 21 tourists were killed by a sudden flash flood while canyoning. Be aware that you participate in all adventure sports at your own risk.

GRINDELWALD ☎033

Grindelwald (pop. 4500), the launching point to the only glaciers accessible by foot in the Bernese Oberland, crouches beneath the north face of the Eiger and peers up at the Jungfraujoch. The **Bergführerbüro** (Mountain Guide's Office), in the sports center near the tourist office, sells hiking maps and coordinates glacier walks, ice climbing, and mountaineering. (☎853 1200. Open June-Oct. M-F 9am-noon and 2-5pm.) The **Untere Grindelwaldgletscher** (Lower Glacier) hike is moderately steep (5hr.). To reach the trailhead, walk up the main street away from the station and follow the signs downhill to Pfinstegg. Hikers can walk the first forested section of the trail (1hr.), following signs up to Pfinstegg. hut or take the funicular. From the hut, signs lead up the glacier-filled valley to Stieregg. hut.

Pet goats greet you at the **Jugendherberge (HI)** ❷, whose rooms have terraces that offer spectacular views of the Jungfraujoch. To reach the lodge, head left out of the train station for 400m, then cut uphill to the right and follow the trail all the way up the hill. (☎853 1009; www.youthhostel.ch/grindelwald. Breakfast included. Reception 7:30-10am and 3-11pm. Dorms 35-37SFr; singles 59SFr, with bath 77SFr; doubles 88/114SFr. 6SFr HI discount. AmEx/MC/V.) **Grindelwald Downtown Lodge** ❷ is located 200m past the tourist office, to the right of the train station. (☎853 0825; www.downtown-lodge.ch. Breakfast included. Dorms 25-35SFr; doubles 70-90SFr. AmEx/MC/V.) Hotel Eiger, on Hauptstr. near the tourist office, houses two restaurants, **Memory** and **Barry's.** (☎854 3131. Memory open daily 8:30am-midnight, Barry's open daily 5:30pm-midnight. AmEx/MC/V.) There's a **Co-op** supermarket on Hauptstr., across from the tourist office. (Open M-F 8am-6:30pm, Sa 8am-6pm.)

The **Jungfraubahn** train runs to Grindelwald from Interlaken's Ostbahnhof (35min., every hr., 9.80SFr). The **tourist office,** located in the Sport-Zentrum 200m to the right of the station, provides chairlift information and a list of free guided excursions. (☎854 1212. Open July-Aug. M-F 8am-noon and 1:30-6pm, Sa 8am-noon and 1:30-5pm, Su 9am-noon and 1:30-5pm; Sept.-June M-F 9am-noon and 2-5pm, Sa-Su 2-5pm.) **Postal Code:** CH-3818.

CENTRAL SWITZERLAND

Considerably more populous than the mountainous cantons to the south, central Switzerland overflows with culture. Innovative museums, enchanting castles, and lovely old towns in Zurich and Luzern add richness to life along the lake shore, while visitors revel in an atmosphere that's alternatingly cosmopolitan and quaint.

ZURICH (ZÜRICH)

☎044

Battalions of briefcase-toting executives charge daily through the world's largest gold exchange and fourth-largest stock exchange, bringing with them enough money to keep Zurich's upper-crust boutiques thriving. 20th-century Zurich (pop. 363,000) enjoyed an avante-garde radicalism that attracted thinkers like Joyce and Lenin. A walk through Zurich's student quarter immerses you in the energetic counter-culture that encouraged these thinkers and countless others, only footsteps away from the showy capitalism of the Bahnhofstr. shopping district.

SWITZERLAND

TRANSPORTATION

Flights: Unique Airport (ZRH; ☎816 22 11; www.unique.ch) is a major stop for Swiss International Airlines (☎084 885 20 00). Daily connections to **Frankfurt, Paris, London,** and **New York.** Trains connect the airport to the Hauptbahnhof in the city center. (Every 10-20min., 5.80SFr. Eurail and SwissPass valid.)

Trains: Run to: **Basel** (1hr., 1-2 per hr., 30SFr); **Geneva** (3hr., every hr., 77SFr) via **Bern** (1¼hr., 1-2 per hr., 45SFr); **Luzern** (1hr., 2 per hr., 22SFr); **Milan** (4hr., every hr., 72-87SFr); **Munich** (5hr., every hr., 90SFr); **Paris** (5hr.; every hr.; 112-140SFr, under 26 86SFr); **Salzburg** (5hr., every hr. 6am-7pm, 10SFr); **Vienna** (9hr., every hr., 12SFr).

Public Transportation: Trams criss-cross the city, originating at the Hauptbahnhof. Tickets for rides of more than 5 stops cost 3.80SFr and are valid for 1hr. (press the blue button on automatic ticket machines); rides of fewer than 5 stops cost 2.40SFr (yellow button). Police will fine you 60SFr if you ride without a ticket. If you plan to ride several times, buy a 24hr. **Tageskarte** (7.60SFr), valid on trams, buses, and ferries. **Night buses** run from the city center to outlying areas (F-Su 1-4am).

LOOSE CHANGE. Travelers should keep change on them for local transportation on buses in Switzerland. You have to buy your tickets from machines before you get on the bus, and the machines don't give change.

Taxis: Dial ☎777 77 77, 444 44 44, or 222 22 22.

Car Rental: The tourist office offers a 20% discount and free upgrade deal with **Europcar** (☎804 4646; www.europcar.ch). Prices start at 152SFr per day for 1-2 days with unlimited mileage. 20+. Branches at Josefstr. 53 (☎271 5656) and Lindenstr. 33 (☎383 1747). Try to rent in the city, as renting at the airport incurs a 40% tax.

Bike Rental: Bike loans are free at **Globus** (☎079 336 36 56), the green hut on the edge of the garden between Bahnhofstr. and Löwenstr. and **Opernhaus** (☎079 352 70 10), at Bellevuepl. **Hauptbahnhof** (☎079 336 36 56), on Museumstr., behind the castle, will merge with Globus by 2006. Passport and 20SFr deposit. Same day return. Open May-Oct. daily 7am-9:30pm.

ORIENTATION AND PRACTICAL INFORMATION

Zurich is in north-central Switzerland, close to the German border and on some of the lowest land in the country. The **Limmat River** splits the city down the middle on its way to the **Zürichsee.** On the western side of the river are the **Hauptbahnhof**

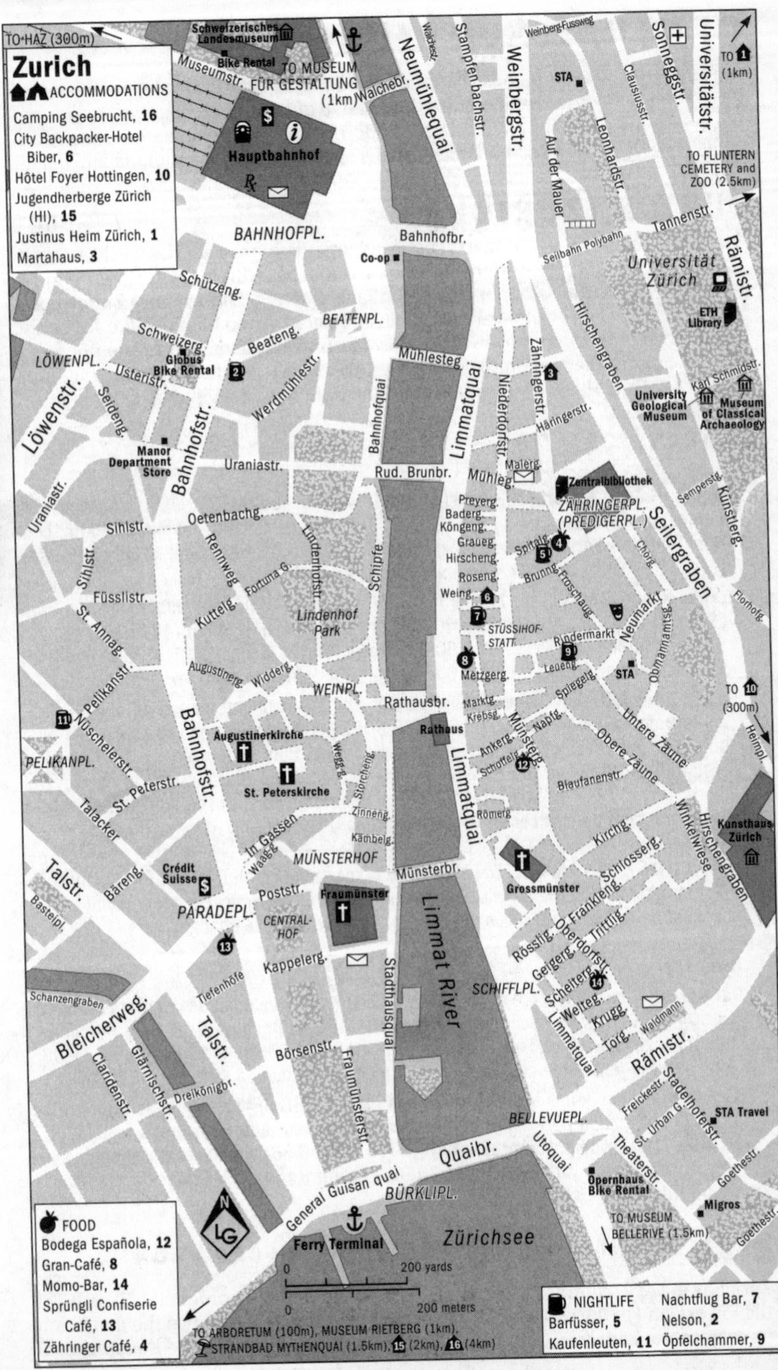

Zurich
ACCOMMODATIONS
Camping Seebrucht, 16
City Backpacker-Hotel Biber, 6
Hôtel Foyer Hottingen, 10
Jugendherberge Zürich (HI), 15
Justinus Heim Zürich, 1
Martahaus, 3
FOOD
Bodega Española, 12
Gran-Café, 8
Momo-Bar, 14
Sprüngli Confiserie Café, 13
Zähringer Café, 4
NIGHTLIFE
Barfüsser, 5
Kaufenleuten, 11
Nachtflug Bar, 7
Nelson, 2
Öpfelchammer, 9
TO HAZ (300m)
Schweizerisches Landesmuseum
Bike Rental
TO MUSEUM FÜR GESTALTUNG (1km)
Hauptbahnhof
BAHNHOFPL.
Bahnhofbr.
Co-op
Neumühlequai
Weinbergstr.
Universitätstr.
Sonneggstr.
TO 1 (1km)
TO FLUNTERN CEMETERY and ZOO (2.5km)
Universität Zürich
ETH Library
University Geological Museum
Museum of Classical Archaeology
Zentralbibliothek
ZÄHRINGERPL. (PREDIGERPL.)
Seilergraben
Limmatquai
Globus Bike Rental
LÖWENPL.
Löwenstr.
Bahnhofstr.
Manor Department Store
Lindenhof Park
STÜSSIHOF-STATT
STA
TO 10 (300m)
Rathaus
Rathausbr.
WEINPL.
Augustinerkirche
St. Peterskirche
PELIKANPL.
MÜNSTERHOF
Münsterbr.
Grossmünster
Kunsthaus Zürich
Crédit Suisse
PARADEPL.
Fraumünster
CENTRAL-HOF
Limmat River
SCHIFFLPL.
Rämistr.
BELLEVUEPL.
Quaibr.
BÜRKLIPL.
General Guisan quai
Ferry Terminal
Zürichsee
STA Travel
Opernhaus Bike Rental
Migros
TO MUSEUM BELLERIVE (1.5km)
Talstr.
Bleicherweg.
Stadthausquai
0 200 yards
0 200 meters
TO ARBORETUM (100m), MUSEUM RIETBERG (1km), STRANDBAD MYTHENQUAI (1.5km), 15 (2km), 16 (4km)

(train station) and **Bahnhofstraße**, the city's main shopping street. Two-thirds of the way down Bahnhofstr. lies **Paradeplatz,** the town center. On the eastern side of the river is the university district, which stretches above the narrow **Niederdorfstraße** and pulses with bars, restaurants, and hostels.

Tourist Office: In the Hauptbahnhof (☎215 40 00; www.zuerich.com). Books hotel rooms by phone and provides maps of the city, both free of charge. An electronic hotel reservation board is at the front of the station. Also sells the **ZürichCARD,** which is good for unlimited public transportation, free museum admission, and discounts on other sights and tours. 1 day 15SFr, 3 days 30SFr. Open May-Oct. M-Sa 8am-8:30pm, Su 8:30am-6:30pm; Nov.-Apr. M-Sa 8:30am-7pm, Su 9am-6:30pm.

Currency Exchange: On the top floor of the main train station. Cash advances for DC/MC/V with photo ID; 200SFr min. and 1000SFr max. Open daily 6:30am-9:30pm. **Crédit Suisse,** Paradepl. 2.50SFr commission. Open M-F 8:15am-4:30pm.

GLBT Resources: Homosexuelle Arbeitsgruppe Zürich (HAZ), Sihlquai 67 (☎271 22 50; www.haz.ch), offers a library, meetings, and the free newsletter *InfoSchwül.* Open W 2-6pm. **Frauenzentrum Zürich,** Matteng. 27 (☎272 85 03), provides information for lesbians and a library of magazines and other resources. Open Tu and Th 6-8pm.

Emergency: Police: ☎117. **Fire:** ☎118. **Ambulance:** ☎144.

24hr. Pharmacy: Bellevue Apotheke, Theaterstr. 14, on Bellevuepl. (☎266 6222).

Internet Access: Quanta Virtual Fun Space, Limmatquai 94 (☎260 7266), at the corner of Mühleg. and the busy Niederdorfstr. 3SFr per 15min. Open daily 9am-midnight.

Post Office: Sihlpost, Kasernestr. 95-97, just behind the station. Open M-F 7:30am-6:30pm, Sa 8am-5pm. Branches throughout the city. Address mail to be held as follows: First name Last name, Sihlpost, Postlagernde Briefe, CH-8021 Zurich. **Postal Code:** CH-8021.

ACCOMMODATIONS

The few budget accommodations in Zurich are easily accessible by foot or via public transportation. Reserve at least a day in advance, especially during the summer.

Justinus Heim Zürich, Freudenbergstr. 146 (☎361 3806; justinuszh@bluewin.ch). Take tram #9 or 10 (dir.: Bahnhof Oerlikon) to Seilbahn Rigiblick, then take the funicular to the top (runs daily 5:20am-12:40am). Quiet, private rooms with a beautiful view of the city. Breakfast included. Laundry available. Reception 8am-noon and 5-9pm. Singles 35-50SFr, with shower 60SFr; doubles 85/100SFr; triples 120-140SFr. V. ❷

Martahaus, Zähringerstr. 36 (☎251 4550; www.martahaus.ch). 3 walls and a thick curtain separate you from your neighbors, who are probably American college students. Breakfast included. Free Internet. Dorms 38SFr; singles 75-85, with shower 115SFr; doubles 98-114/150-160SFr; triples 135SFr; quads 200SFr; studio with kitchen for 1-2 people 150SFr. AmEx/DC/MC/V. ❷

Hôtel Foyer Hottingen, Hottingenstr. 31 (☎256 1919; www.foyer-hottingen.ch). Take tram #3 (dir.: Kluspl.) to Hottingerpl. Families and student backpackers fill this newly renovated house a block from the Kunsthaus. Dorms women only. Breakfast included. Reception 7am-11pm. Partitioned dorms 35SFr; singles 75-90SFr, with bath 110-125SFr; doubles 115/160-175SFr; triples 145/190SFr; quads 180SFr. MC/V. ❷

The City Backpacker-Hotel Biber, Niederdorfstr. 5 (☎251 9015; www.city-backpacker.ch). With Niederdorfstr. nightlife right outside, you may not even need your bunk bed. Linen and towels both 3SFr, blanket provided. Laundry next-day service 10SFr. Internet 12SFr per hr. Reception 8-11am and 3-10pm. Check-out 10am, strictly enforced. Dorms 31SFr; singles 66SFr; doubles 92SFr. MC/V. ❷

Jugendherberge Zürich (HI), Mutschellenstr. 114 (☎399 7800; www.youthhostel.ch/zuerich). From the station, take tram #7 (dir.: Wollishofen) to Morgental, then backtrack 20m and head down Mutschellenstr. Breakfast included. Reception 24hr. Dorms 43.50SFr; singles with shower 105SFr; doubles with shower 128SFr; triples 153SFr, with shower 168SFr; quads 174/196SFr. 6SFr HI discount. MC/V. ❸

Camping Seebrucht, Seestr. 559 (☎482 1612), on the edge of the lake. Take tram #11 to Bürklipl. then bus #161 or 165 to Stadtgrenze. Showers 2SFr. Reception 8am-noon and 3-9pm. Tent sites 20SFr, extra person 8SFr. MC/V. ❶

FOOD

Zurich's more than 1300 restaurants offer a little bit of everything. The cheapest meals are available at *würstli* stands for about 5SFr. The **farmer's markets** at Bürklipl. (Tu and F 6-11am) and Rosenhof (Th 10am-8pm and Sa 10am-5pm) sell produce, baked goods, and flowers.

SWITZERLAND

Zähringer Café, Zähringerpl. 11 (☎252 05 00; www.cafe-zaehringer.ch). Enjoy mainly vegetarian and vegan fare in this colorful cafe. Try their *kefirwasser,* a purple, fizzy drink made from dates and mushrooms fed with sugar (4SFr). Order at the front. Stir-fries 15.50-26.50SFr. Open M 6pm-midnight, Tu-Su 8am-midnight. ❷

Bodega Española, Münsterg. 15. Catalan delights served by charismatic waiters since 1874. Egg-and-potato tortilla dishes 17.50SFr. Tapas 4.80SFr. Open daily 10am-midnight. Kitchen open noon-2pm and 6-10pm. AmEx/DC/MC/V. ❷

Sprüngli Confiserie Café, Paradepl. (☎224 4711), a Zurich landmark, was founded by one of the original Lindt chocolate makers. Pick up a handful of the bite-size *Luxemburgerli,* try the homemade sundaes, or eat a full meal (19-28SFr). Confectionary open M-F 7:30am-6:30pm, Sa 8am-4pm. Cafe open M-F 7:30am-6:30pm, Sa 8am-6pm, Su 9:30am-5:30pm. AmEx/DC/MC/V. ❷

Gran-Café, Limmatquai 66 (☎252 3119). Across from the Limmat River. Alongside soups (7SFr) and salads (8.50-17.50SFr), they also serve *geschnetzeltes* (26.50SFr). Save room for sundaes (8-10SFr). Open M-Th 7am-11:30pm, F 7am-midnight, Sa 7:30am-midnight, Su 7:30am-11:30pm. AmEx/MC/V. ❷

Momo-Bar, Oberdorfstr. 9 (☎043 343 9688), specializes in Tibetan *momos,* vegetable- or meat-filled dumplings (14-20SFr). Noodle dishes from 11SFr. Lunch buffet 12-15SFr. Open M-F 10am-9:30pm, Sa 4-10pm. AmEx/MC/V. ❷

SIGHTS

It's virtually inconceivable to start a tour of Zurich anywhere but the stately **Bahnhofstraße,** which bustles with shoppers during the day but falls dead quiet at 6pm. At the Zürichsee end of Bahnhofstr., **Bürkliplatz** is a good place to explore the lake shore. The *platz* itself hosts a colorful Saturday **flea market** (May-Oct. 6am-3pm). On the other side of the river, the pedestrian zone continues on Niederdorfstr. and Münsterg., where shops run from the ritzy to the erotic. **Fraumünster, Grossmünster,** and **St. Peterskirche** straddle the Limmat river. For a view of Zurich from the water, **boat tours** leave every half hour from the ferry terminal at Bürklipl. A Kleine Rundfahrten, the shortest tour, lasts 1½hr. (May-Sept. daily 11am-6:30pm. 7.60SFr.)

FRAUMÜNSTER. This cathedral's Gothic flourishes are juxtaposed with **Marc Chagall's** modern stained-glass windows, which depict biblical stories. Outside, a mural decorating the courtyard's archway shows Felix and Regula (the decapitated patron saints of Zurich) with their heads in their hands. *(Off Paradepl. Open May-Nov. M-Sa 10am-6pm, Su 11:30am-6pm; Nov.-Apr. M-Sa 11am-4pm, Su 11:30am-4pm. Free.)*

GROSSMÜNSTER. The twin towers of this church can be best viewed on the bridge near the Fraumünster. Considered the mother church of the Swiss-German Reformation, it has come to be a symbol of Zurich. One of Zwingli's Bibles lies in a protected case near his pulpit. Downstairs in the cavernous 12th-century crypt are the forbidding statue of Charlemagne and his 2m-long sword. *(Church open daily mid-Mar. to Oct. 9am-6pm; Nov. to early Mar. 10am-5pm. Steeple access 9:15am-5pm. Tower open daily 9am-5pm. Church and steeple free. Entrance to the tower 2SFr.)*

BEACHES. The city has numerous free swimming spots, which are labeled on the map from the tourist office. The convenient and popular **Arboretum** is about 100m down from the Quaibrücke. Take tram #5 to Rentenanstalt and head to the water.

MUSEUMS

KUNSTHAUS ZÜRICH. The Kunsthaus, the largest privately funded museum in Europe, houses a collection ranging from religious works by the Old Masters to 21st-century American pop art. Works by Chagall, Dalí, Gauguin, Picasso, Rembrandt, Renoir, Rubens, and van Gogh stretch from wall to wall in a patchwork of rich color. The Kunsthaus also houses the largest Munch collection outside of Norway. The collection is continually expanding: a new wing devoted to Alberto Giacometti and his artistic kin opened in May 2002. *(Heimpl. 1. Take tram #3, 5, 8, or 9 to Kunsthaus. ☎253 84 84; www.kunsthaus.ch. English-language audio tours and brochures. Bag storage required. Open Tu-Th 10am-9pm, F-Su 10am-5pm. 12SFr, students 6SFr. W free.)*

MUSEUM RIETBERG. Rietberg presents an exquisite collection of Asian, African, and other non-European art, housed in two spectacular mansions in the Rieter-Park. **Park-Villa Rieter** features internationally acclaimed exhibits of Chinese, Japanese, and Indian paintings. **Villa Wesendonck** houses a sculpture collection. *(Gablerstr. 15. Take tram #7 to Museum Rietberg. ☎206 31 31; www.rietberg.ch. Both buildings open Apr.-Sept. Tu and Th-Su 10am-5pm, W 10am-8pm; Oct.-Mar. Tu-Su 10am-5pm. 6SFr, students 3SFr, under 16 free. MC/V; only at Wesendonck.)*

ENTERTAINMENT AND NIGHTLIFE

For information on after-dark happenings, check ZüriTipp (www.zueritipp.ch), or pick up a free copy of *ZürichGuide* or *ZürichEvents* from the tourist office. On **Niederdorfstraße,** the epicenter of Zurich's *Altstadt* nightlife, bars are packed to the brim almost every night. **"Kreis 5,"** once the industrial area of Zurich, has recently developed into party central, with clubs, bars, and lounges taking over former factories; it lies northwest of the Hauptbahnhof, with Hardstr. as its axis. To get there, take tram #4 (dir.: Bahnhof Tiefenbrumen) or tram #13 (dir.: Albisgütli) to Escher-Wyss-Pl. and follow the crowds. As with any urban center, women should be cautious about walking alone at night. Other hot spots include **Münstergasse** and **Limmatquai,** both of which are lined with overflowing cafes and bars. Beer in Zurich is pricey (from 6SFr), but a number of cheap bars have established themselves on Niederdorfstr. near Mühleg.

Most movies (from 15SFr) are screened in English with French and German subtitles (marked "E/D/F"). Films generally cost 15SFr and up, less on Mondays. From mid-July to mid-August, the **Orange Cinema,** an open-air cinema at Zürichhorn (take tram #4 or 2 to Fröhlichstr.), attracts huge crowds to its lakefront screenings. Every August, the **Street Parade** (Aug. 12, 2006) brings together ravers from all over the world for a giant techno party.

Kaufenleuten, Pelikanstr. 18 (☎225 3322; www.kaufleuten.ch). This trendy club decked out in red velvet attracts the who's-who of Zurich with nightly themed parties; check website to see what's going on any given evening. Cover 10-30SFr. Hours vary, but generally open M-Th, Su 11pm-2am, F-Sa 11pm-4am. MC/V.

Nelson, Beateng. 11 (☎212 6016). Locals, backpackers, and businessmen alike chug beer (8.50SFr per pint) at this large English pub. 20+. Open M-W 11:30am-2am, Th 11:30am-3am, F 11:30am-4:30am, Sa 3pm-4:30am, Su 3pm-2am. AmEx/MC/V.

Lady Hamilton's, Beateng. 11 (☎043 344 8860). At this sedate bar a floor above Nelson, wine and whiskey are preferred to brews. 20+. Open M-W 5pm-midnight, Th 5pm-1am, F-Sa 5pm-4:30am. AmEx/MC/V.

Nachtflug Bar, Café, and Lounge, Stüssihofstatt 4, boasts a popular outdoor bar. Wine from 6SFr. Beer from 4.90SFr. Open M-Th, Su 11am-midnight, F-Sa 11am-1:30am. Outdoor bar Th-Su 10pm-midnight. AmEx/MC/V.

Barfüsser, Spitalg. 14 (☎251 4064), off Zähringerpl. At Switzerland's oldest gay bar, mixed drinks (14-17SFr), wine (6-9SFr), and daily concoctions flow freely. Open M-Th, Su 11am-1am, F-Sa 11am-3am. AmEx/DC/MC/V.

Öpfelchammer, Rindermarkt 12 (☎251 2336). This popular Swiss wine chamber (3-5SFr per glass) has low ceilings and wooden crossbeams covered with initials and messages from 200 years of merry-making. Those who climb the rafters and drink a free glass of wine from the beams get to engrave their names on the furniture. It's harder than it looks. Open mid-Aug. to mid-July Tu-Sa 11am-12:30am. AmEx/DC/MC/V.

LUZERN (LUCERNE) ☎041

Luzern (pop. 60,000) welcomes busloads of tourists each day in the summer, and with good reason. Engaging streets lead down to a placid lake, the covered bridges over the river are among the most photographed sights in Switzerland, and the sunrise over the famous Mt. Pilatus has hypnotized hikers and artists for centuries.

TRANSPORTATION AND PRACTICAL INFORMATION. **Trains** leave Bahnhofpl. for: Basel (1hr., 1-2 per hr., 30SFr); Geneva (3½hr., every 2-3hr., 70SFr); Zurich (1hr., 2 per hr., 22SFr). VBL **buses** depart from in front of the station and provide extensive coverage of Luzern; route maps are available at the **tourist office** in the station, which also offers free city guides, sells the **Museum Pass** (30SFr, valid for one month all over Switzerland), and makes reservations. (☎227 1717; www.luzern.org. Open May-Oct. M-F 8:30am-6:30pm, Sa-Su 9am-6:30pm; Nov.-Apr. M-F 8:30am-5:30pm, Sa-Su 9am-1pm.) The **post office** is by the train station. Address mail to be held: First name SURNAME, *Postlagernde Briefe*, Hauptpost, CH-6000 Luzern 1, SWITZERLAND. (Open M-F 7:30am-6:30pm, Sa 8am-noon.) **Postal Code:** CH-6000.

ACCOMMODATIONS AND FOOD. Inexpensive beds are limited, so call ahead. To reach **Backpackers ❷**, Alpenquai 42, turn right from the station on Inseliquai and follow it for 20min. until it turns into Alpenquai; the hostel is on the right. Balconies in the rooms look out on the lake. (☎360 0420; www.backpackerslucerne.ch. Bike rental 18SFr per day. Internet 10SFr per hr. Laundry 6SFr. Reception 7:30-10am and 4-11pm. Dorms 28SFr; singles 45SFr; doubles 68SFr. Cash only.) The **Tourist Hotel ❷**, St. Karliquai 12, offers plain rooms and a prime location. From the station, walk along Bahnhofstr., cross the river at the second covered bridge, and make a left onto St. Karliquai. (☎410 2474; www.touristhotel.ch. Breakfast included. Dorms 35SFr; singles 75SFr; doubles 98SFr. AmEx/MC/V; dorms cash only.) There's a **Migros** supermarket at the train station. (Open M-Sa 6:30am-9pm, Su 8am-9pm.)

SIGHTS AND ENTERTAINMENT. The *Altstadt*, across the river over the Spreuerbrücke from the station, is famous for its frescoed houses; the best examples are those on Hirschenpl. and Weinmarkt. The 14th-century **Kapellbrücke,** a wooden-roofed bridge, runs from left of the train station to the *Altstadt* and is decorated with Swiss historical scenes; farther down the river, the **Spreuerbrücke** is decorated by Kaspar Meglinger's eerie *Totentanz* (Dance of Death) paintings. To the east is the magnificent **Löwendenkmal,** the dying lion of Luzern, carved into a cliff on Denkmalstr. The **Verkehrshaus der Schweiz** (Swiss Transport Museum), Lidostr. 5, has interactive displays on all kinds of vehicles, but the real highlight is the warehouse of trains. Take bus #6, 8, or 24 to Verkehrshaus. (☎375 75 75; www.verkehrshaus.ch. Open daily Apr.-Oct. 10am-6pm; Nov.-Mar. 10am-5pm. 24SFr, students 22SFr, with Eurail 14SFr.) The **Picasso Museum,** Am Rhyn Haus, Furreng. 21, displays a large collection of Picasso's lesser-known works. From Schwanenpl., take Rathausquai to Furreng. (☎410 35 33. Open daily Apr.-Oct. 10am-6pm; Nov.-Mar. 11am-5pm. 8SFr, students 5SFr.)

The Loft, Haldenstr. 21, hosts special DJs and theme nights. (Beer 8-9SFr. Open W 9pm-2am, Th-Su 10am-4am.) The mellower **Jazzkantine,** Grabenstr. 8, is a product of the Jazz School of Luzern. (Sandwiches 6-8SFr. Open M-Sa 7am-12:30am, Su 4pm-12:30am; mid-July to mid-Aug. M-F, Su 4pm-12:30am, Sa 10am-12:30am. MC/V.) Gay nightlife centers around the industrial area intersected by Tribschenstr., in the south end of the city. Try the Queer Beer (4SFr) at **Uferlos,** Geissensteinring 14, which hosts disco parties on Saturday nights and a low-key bar on Tuesdays. (☎534 64 61. 2nd Sa of every month women only. Open Tu 8-11pm, Sa 10pm-4am. Cash only.) Luzern attracts big names for its two jazz festivals: **Blue Balls Festival** (last week of July) and **Blues Festival** (second week of Nov.).

STEIN AM RHEIN ☎052

The tiny medieval *Altstadt* of Stein am Rhein (pop. 3000) is postcard-perfect. The houses on the square date back to the 15th century and have paintings on their facades depicting the animal or scene after which each house is named. However, it was the 12th-century establishment of the **Kloster St. George** that first made Stein am Rhein prominent. You can reach the Benedictine monastery by heading up Chirchhofpl. from the Rathauspl. Inside the gorgeous **Festsaal,** the tiled floor is off-limits to feet. Try to go when it's bright outside for the best view of the paintings. (☎741 2142. Open Apr.-Oct. Tu-Su 10am-5pm. 3SFr, students 1.50SFr.) On Understadt, the main road running through the village, visitors to the **Museum Lindwurm** are greeted by roosters that wander along with them as they tour this large house depicting 19th-century life. (Open Mar.-Oct. daily 10am-5pm. 5SFr, students 3SFr.)

The family-oriented **Jugendherberge (HI)** ❷ is at Hemishoferstr. 87. From the train station, take bus #7349 (dir.: Singen) to Strandbad and walk 5min. farther in the same direction. (☎741 1255; www.youthhostel.ch/stein. Breakfast included. Internet 1SFr per 5min. Reception 8-10am and 5-10pm. Open Mar.-Nov. Dorms 30.50SFr; singles 46SFr; doubles 80SFr; family rooms 40SFr per person. 6SFr HI discount. AmEx/MC/V.) Though full meals are not available at **Rothen Ochsen Wine Bar** ❷, Rathauspl. 9, built in 1466, their soups (8.50SFr) and wines (4-14SFr) are sustenance enough. (☎741 2328. Open Tu-Sa 11:30am-late, Su 10:30am-6pm.) A **supermarket** is located at Rathauspl. 17. (Open M-F 8:15am-6:30pm, Sa 8am-4pm.)

Trains connect Stein am Rhein to Constance (40min., 1 per hr., 10SFr) via Kreuzlingen, and to Zurich (1hr., 1-2 per hr., 21SFr) via Winterthur. **Boats** (☎634 0888; www.urh.ch) depart for Schaffhausen (1¼hr., 230SFr) and other Bodensee towns. Rent **bikes** from **River Bike,** Rathauspl. 15. (☎741 5541. 15-18SFr per 2hr.; 29-32SFr per day. Open M 1:30-5:30pm, Tu-F 9am-6:30pm, Sa 9am-4pm, Su 11am-5pm.) The **tourist office,** Oberstadt. 3, on the other side of the Rathaus, has free maps and books rooms for free. From the station, walk straight down Bahnhofstr., turn right on Wagenhauserstr., and then head left over the bridge. (☎742 2090; www.steinamrhein.ch. Open July-Aug. M-F 9:30am-noon and 1:30-5pm, Sa 9:30am-noon and 1:30-4pm; Sept.-June M-F 9:30am-noon and 1:30-5pm.) **Postal Code:** CH-8260.

NORTHWESTERN SWITZERLAND

The cantons of Basel-Stadt, Basel-Land, Solothurn, and Aargau inspire peaceful contentment. Despite Basel's reputation as a transportation hub, the city and its surrounding area have more to offer than just a train station, with excellent museums, colorful houses, and relaxing riverside promenades.

BASEL (BÂLE) ☎061

Situated on the Rhine near France and Germany, Basel is home to a large medieval quarter as well as one of the oldest universities in Switzerland—graduates include Erasmus and Nietzsche. Though Basel is predominantly known as a transportation hub, the city and its surrounding area also offer excellent museums, colorful houses, and relaxing riverside promenades.

TRANSPORTATION AND PRACTICAL INFORMATION. Basel has three train stations: the French (SNCF) and Swiss (SBB) stations on Centralbahnpl., near the *Altstadt*, and the German (DB) station across the Rhine. **Trains** leave from the SBB to: Bern (1¼hr., every hr., 36SFr); Geneva (3hr., every hr., 67SFr); Lausanne (2½hr., every hr., 57SFr); Zurich (1hr., every 15-30min., 30SFr). Make international connections at the French (SNCF) or German (DB) stations. The **tourist office** on Steinenbergstr. is in the Stadt Casino building on Barfüsserpl. From the SBB station, take tram #6, 8, 14, 16, or 17 to Barfüsserpl. (☎268 68 68; www.basel-tourismus.ch. Open M-F 8:30am-6:30pm, Sa 10am-5pm, Su 10am-4pm.) For information on **GLBT** establishments, stop by **Arcados,** Rheing. 69, at Clarapl. (☎681 31 32; www.arcados.com. Open Tu-F 1-7pm, Sa noon-4pm.) To reach the **post office,** Rüdeng. 1, take tram #1 or 8 to Marktpl. and backtrack one block, away from the river. (Open M-W and F 7:30am-6:30pm, Th 7:30am-8pm, Sa 8:30am-5pm.) Address mail to be held as follows: *Postlagernde Briefe für* first name SURNAME, Rüdeng., CH-4001 Basel, Switzerland. **Postal Codes:** CH-4000 to CH-4059.

ACCOMMODATIONS AND FOOD. The **Jugendherberge (HI) ❷**, St. Alban-Kirchrain 10, has a convenient location, just down the hill from the *Altstadt.* To get there, take tram #2 to Kunstmuseum; turn right on St. Alban-Vorstadt, then follow the signs. (☎272 0572; www.youthhostel.ch/basel. Breakfast included. Laundry 7SFr. Internet 5SFr per 25min. Reception Mar.-Oct. 7-10am and 2-11:30pm; Nov.-Feb. 2-11pm. Dorms 37-41SFr; singles 86SFr; doubles 96-112SFr. 6SFr HI discount. MC/V.) **Basel Back Pack ❷,** Dornacherstr. 192, is a good distance from the city center, but the hostel provides free tickets for all trams and buses. Take the south exit from the station, turn left until Tellpl., and follow the signs. (☎333 0037; www.baselbackpack.ch. Breakfast 7SFr. Internet 1SFr per 5min. Laundry 6SFr. Reception 8-11:30am, 2-6pm, and 8-11:30pm. Dorms 31SFr; singles 80SFr; doubles 96SFr; triples 123SFr; quads 144SFr. AmEx/MC/V; 60SFr min. charge.)

Barfüsserplatz, Marktplatz, and the streets connecting them are full of satisfying restaurants. **Restaurant Hirscheneck ❷,** Lindenberg 23, is popular with students, vegetarians, and the alternative crowd of Basel. (☎692 7333. Daily menu 12-23SFr, smaller portions 9-14SFr. Open M, Sa 6-10:30pm, Tu-F noon-2pm and 6-10:30pm, Su 10am-4pm and 6:30-10pm. Cash only.) Head to **Migros,** in the SBB station, for groceries. (Open M-F 6am-10pm, Sa-Su 7:30am-10pm.)

SIGHTS AND ENTERTAINMENT. Greater Basel *(Groß-Basel)* and the train station are separated from Lesser Basel *(Klein-Basel)* by the Rhine. The very red **Rathaus** brightens Marktpl. in Greater Basel with its blinding facade and gold-and-green statues. Behind the Marktpl. is the 775-year-old **Middle Rhine Bridge** *(Mittlere Rheinbrücke)* which connects the two halves of Basel. Take tram #6, 10, 16, or 17 to Theater to see the spectacular **Jean Tinguely Fountain,** also known as the **Fasnachtsbrunnen,** whose moving metal parts spray water in all directions. Behind Marktpl. stands the red sandstone **Münster** (cathedral), where you can visit the tomb of Erasmus or climb the tower for a spectacular view of the city. (Open Easter to mid-Oct. M-F 10am-5pm, Sa 10am-4pm, Su 1-5pm; mid-Oct. to Easter M-Sa 11am-4pm, Su 2-4pm. Tower closes 30min. before the church. Church free. Tower 3SFr.) Basel has over 30 museums; pick up the comprehensive museum guide at the tourist office. The **Basel Card,** also available at the tourist office, provides admission to all museums as well as discounts around town. (1-day card 20SFr, 2-day card 27SFr, 3-day card 35SFr.) At **Museum Tinguely,** Paul-Sacher-Anlage 1, everything rattles and shakes in homage to the Swiss sculptor's vision of metal and movement. Take tram #2 or 15 to Wettsteinpl. then bus #31 or 36 to Museum Tinguely. (Open Tu-Su 11am-7pm. 10SFr, students 7SFr.) The **Kunstmuseum** (Museum of Fine Arts), St. Alban-Graben 16, houses outstanding collections of new and old masters; admission also gives access to the **Museum für Gegenwartskunst** (Museum of Modern Art), St. Alban-Rheinweg 60. (Kunstmuseum open Tu, Th-Su 10am-5pm, W 10am-7pm. Gegenwartskunst open Tu-Su 11am-5pm. Both 10SFr, students 5SFr. Free daily 4-5pm and 1st Su of every month.) The **Fondation Beyeler,** Baselstr. 101, has one of Europe's finest private art collections. Take tram #6 to Riehen Dorf then walk 5min. in the direction of the tram. (☎645 9700. Open M-Tu and Th-Su 10am-6pm, W 10am-8pm. 18SFr; students 10SFr.)

In a year-round party town, Basel's carnival, the **Fasnacht,** still manages to distinguish itself. The festivities commence the Monday before Lent with the *Morgestraich*, a three-day parade with a 600-year tradition. During the rest of the year, head to **Barfüsserplatz** for an evening of bar-hopping. **Atlantis,** Klosterberg 10, is a multi-level, sophisticated bar with reggae, jazz, and funk. (☎228 96 96. Summer drink special 12SFr. Open M 11:30am-2pm, Tu-Th 11:30am-2pm and 6pm-midnight, F 11:30am-2pm and 6pm-4am, Sa 6pm-4am. AmEx/MC/V.) **Brauerei Fischerstube,** Rheing. 45, serves such literally intoxicating dishes as beer soup. (☎692 6635. Beer 4.30SFr. Full dinner menu 42SFr, served from 6pm. Open M-Th 10am-12:30am, F-Sa 10am-1:30am, Su 5pm-midnight. AmEx/MC/V.)

GRAUBÜNDEN

Graubünden's rugged gorges, fir forests, and eddying rivers give the region a wildness seldom found in comfortably settled Switzerland. Visitors should plan their trips carefully, especially in ski season when reservations are absolutely required, and in May and June, when nearly everything shuts down.

DAVOS ☎081

Davos (pop. 12,000) sprawls along the valley floor under seven mountains laced with chair-lifts and cable cars. Originally a health resort, the city catered to such *fin de siecle* giants as Robert Louis Stevenson and Thomas Mann. The influx of tourists in recent decades has given the city an impersonal feel, but the thrill of carving down the famed, wickedly steep ski slopes may make up for it. Europe's largest natural **ice rink** (22,000 sq. m), between Platz and Dorf, allows curling, figure skating, hockey, ice dancing, and speed skating. (☎415 36 004. Open July-Aug. and Dec. 15-Feb. 15 M-W, F-Su 10am-4pm, Th 8-10pm.

5SFr. Skate rental 6.50SFr.) At the **Davosersee Surfcenter,** board rentals are 30SFr per hr., 60SFr per day. (Take bus #1 to Flueelastr. and follow the yellow signs to the lake. ☎079 712 0414; www.davossurf.ch. Open mid-June to mid-Sept. daily 11am-6:30pm.) Davos provides direct access to two mountains—**Parsenn** and **Jakobshorn**—and four skiing areas. Parsenn, with long runs and fearsome vertical drops, is the mountain around which Davos built its reputation. (www.fun-mountain.ch. Day pass 60SFr.) Jakobshorn has found a niche with the younger crowd since it opened a snowboarding park with two half-pipes (day pass 55SFr). Cross-country trails cover 75km as they run through the valley, and one is even lit at night. In the summer, ski lifts connect to **hikes,** such as the 2hr. **Panoramaweg.**

Overlooking Davos-Dorf, **Youthpalace Davos (HI) ❸,** Horlaubenstr. 27, has spacious rooms with bath. Go left out of the Dorf train station, take the first right and turn left at the major street, Promenade. Take a right onto Horlaubenstr. and walk up the hill for 15min. (☎410 1920; www.youthhostel.ch/davos. Breakfast, dinner, linen, and towel included. Wireless Internet available. Reception 8-10am and 3-10pm. Mid-Dec. to mid.-Mar. dorms 61-101SFr; singles 145SFr; doubles 230SFr. Early June to mid.-Oct. dorms 51-71/81/162SFr. Low-season rates discounted. 6SFr HI discount. AmEx/MC/V.) At Jakobshorn Ski Mountain's **Snowboardhotel Bolgenschanze ❸,** Skistr. 1, dorm rooms are sold as a package with ski passes, but it's only open during ski season. (☎414 90 20; www.davosklosters.ch. 18+. 1-night, 2-day ski pass 195-405SFr; 6-night, 7-day pass 650-865SFr. AmEx/MC/V.)

Davos is accessible by **train** from Chur (1½hr., 7 per day, 27SFr) via Landquart or from Klosters (25min., 2 per hr., 9.20SFr) on the Rhätische Bahn lines. The town is divided into two areas, Davos-Platz and Davos-Dorf, each with a train station. Platz has the main tourist office, post office, and most places of interest to budget travelers; Dorf is closer to the Davosersee. **Buses** (2.70SFr) run between the two train stations. The main **tourist office,** Promenade 67, is up the hill from the Platz station. (☎415 2121; www.davos.ch. Open Dec. to mid-Apr. and mid-June to mid-Oct. M-F 8:30am-6:30pm, Sa 9am-5pm, Su 10am-noon and 3-5:30pm; mid-Oct. to Dec. and mid-Apr. to mid-June M-F 9am-6pm, Sa 9am-noon.) **Postal Code:** CH-7270.

KLOSTERS ☎081

Davos's sister resort, Klosters (pop. 3000), lies across the Gotschna and Parsenn mountains. Though Klosters is only 25min. from Davos by train, it's a world away in atmosphere. Davos makes every effort to be cosmopolitan, while Klosters capitalizes on its natural serenity and cozy chalets. Most ski packages include mountains from both towns, and Klosters's main lift leads to a mountain pass where one can ski down to either. In summer, Klosters has better access to fantastic biking trails. **Ski passes** for the Klosters-Davos region run 121SFr for two days and 279SFr for six days, including public transportation. The **Madrisabahn** leaves from Klosters-Dorf (1-day pass; 47SFr). The **Grotschnabahn** gives access to Parsenn and Strela in Davos and Madrisa in Klosters. (1-day pass 60SFr; 6-day pass 324SFr.) Summer cable car passes (valid on Grotschnabahn and Madrisabahn) are also available (4-day pass; 80SFr). **Bananas,** operated out of Duty Boardsport, Bahnhofstr. 16, gives snowboard lessons. (☎422 6660. Lessons 70SFr per 4hr. Board rental 38SFr per day. MC/V.) **Ski rental** is also available at **Sport Gotschna,** Alte Bahnhofstr. 5, across from the tourist office. (☎422 1197. Skis and snowboards 28-50SFr per day plus 10% insurance. Open M-F 8am-6:30pm, Sa-Su 8am. AmEx/MC/V.) On the lush green valley floor, **hikers** can make a large loop, from Klosters's Protestant church on Monbielstr. to Monbiel. The route continues to an elevation point of 1488m and turns left, passing through Bödmerwald, Fraschmardintobel, and Monbieler Wald before climbing to its highest elevation of 1634m and returning to Klosters via Pardels. Several adventure companies offer a variety of activities including **river rafting, canoeing, horseback riding, paragliding,** and **glacier trekking.**

To get to **Jugendherberge Soldanella (HI)** ❷, Talstr. 73, from the station, go left uphill past Hotel Alpina to the church, then cross the street and head up the alleyway to the right of the Kirchpl. bus station sign. Walk 10min. along the gravel path. This massive, renovated chalet has a comfortable reading room, couches on a flagstone terrace, and friendly English-speaking owners. (☎422 1316; www.youthhostel.ch/klosters. Breakfast included. Reception 7-10am and 5-10pm. Open mid-Dec. to mid-Apr. and late June to mid-Oct. Dorms 34SFr; singles 45SFr; doubles 88SFr; family rooms 44SFr per person. 6SFr HI discount. AmEx/DC/MC/V.)

Klosters-Platz and Klosters-Dorf connect to Chur by **train** via Landquart (1¼hr., every hr. 5:20am-9:30pm, 20SFr). The same line connects Klosters and Davos (25min., every hr., 8SFr). The main **tourist office,** in Platz by the station, sells hiking (17.50SFr) and biking (7.50SFr) maps of the area. (☎410 20 20; www.klosters.ch. Open May-Nov. M-F 8:30am-6pm, Sa 8:30am-noon and 2-4pm; July to mid-Aug. also Su 9-11am; Dec.-Apr. M-Sa 8:30am-noon and 2-6pm, Su 9-11:30am and 4-6pm.) **Andrist Sport,** Gotschnastr. 8, rents **bikes.** Prices change throughout the year; call to confirm. (☎410 2080. 38SFr per day, 6 days 130SFr. Open M-F 8am-noon and 2-6:30pm, Sa 8am-noon and 2-4pm. AmEx/MC/V.) **Postal Code:** CH-7250.

THE SWISS NATIONAL PARK ☎081

No other area can so beautifully match the Swiss National Park's isolation from man-made structures. A network of 20 hiking trails runs throughout the park, mostly concentrated in the center. Few of the trails are level; most involve a lot of climbing, often into snow-covered areas. All trails are clearly marked, and it is against park rules to wander off the designated trails. Trails that require no mountaineering gear are marked with white-red-white blazes. Keep in mind, though, that even some of the no-gear routes can be tricky.

Zernez is the main gateway to the park and home to its main headquarters, the **National Parkhouse.** The staff provides helpful trail maps as well as up-to-date information on which trails are navigable. (☎856 1378. Headquarters open June-Oct. daily 8:30am-6pm.) From Zernez, **trains** and **post buses** run to other towns in the area, including Scuol, Samedan, and S-chanf. The park is closed November through May. The Swiss National Park is one of the most strictly regulated nature reserves in the world. Camping and campfires are prohibited in the park, as is collecting flowers and plants. A team of wardens patrols the park at all times, so it's better not to test the rules. The nearby towns Zernez, Scuol, and S-chanf have campsites right outside the park boundaries.

VALAIS

The Valais occupies the deep glacial gorge traced by the Rhône River. The clefts of the valley divide the land linguistically: in the west, French predominates, and in the east, Swiss-German is used. Though its mountain resorts can be over-touristed, the region's spectacular peaks make fighting the traffic worthwhile.

ZERMATT AND THE MATTERHORN ☎027

The shape of the valley blocks out most of the great Alpine summits that ring Zermatt (pop. 3500), allowing the monolithic **Matterhorn** (4478m) to rise alone above town. The area has attained mecca status with Europe's longest **ski** run, the 13km trail from Klein Matterhorn to Zermatt, and more **summer ski trails** than any other Alpine ski resort. A one-day ski pass for any of the area's mountains runs 60-72SFr. The **Zermatt Alpin Center,** which houses both the **Bergführerbüro** (Mountain Guide's Office; ☎966 2460) and the **Skischulbüro** (Ski School Office; ☎966 2466), is located on Bahnhofstr., past the post office. The Bergführerbüro provides ski passes, four-day weather forecasts, and information on guided climbing. (Open daily July-Sept. 8:30am-noon and 3-7pm; late Dec. to mid-May 4-7pm.) Bergführerbüro is also the only company to lead formal expeditions above Zermatt. Groups scale Breithorn (150SFr), Pollux (260SFr), and Castor (270SFr) daily in summer. Prices do not include equipment, insurance, hut accommodations, or lifts to departure points. Rental prices for skis and snowboards are standardized throughout Zermatt (28-50SFr per day). For a new perspective on the Matterhorn, **paraglide** with **Air Taxi Zermatt** (☎967 6744) for 150-190SFr.

Hotel Bahnhof ❷, on Bahnhofpl. 54, to the left of the station, provides hotel housing at hostel rates. The central location, mountain views, and clean rooms make up for the slightly cramped space. (☎967 2406; www.hotelbahnhof.com. Reception 8am-8pm. Dorms 33SFr; singles 65SFr, with shower 76SFr; doubles 90/104SFr. MC/V.) Get groceries at the **Co-op Center,** opposite the station. (Open M-Sa 8:15am-7pm, Su 4-7pm.) Although the menu is small at **The North Wall Bar ❷,** Steinmattenstr. 71, the pizza (12SFr, 1SFr per topping) is the cheapest in town. From Bahnhofstr., turn left before the church, cross the big river and take your second right. (☎966 3412. Open daily 6:30pm-12:30am. AmEx/MC/V.) **The Pipe Surfer's Cantina,** on Kirchstr., specializes in Mexican-Thai-Indian fusion cuisine, and by night throws the craziest "beach parties" in the Alps. (☎079 213 3807; www.gozermatt.com/thepipe. Sandwiches 20-24SFr. Salads 11-17SFr. Happy hour daily 6-7pm, in winter 4-5pm. Open daily 3:30pm-1:30am. MC/V.)

To preserve the Alpine air, cars and buses are banned in Zermatt; the only way in is the hourly **BVZ** (Brig-Visp-Zermatt) rail line, which connects to Lausanne (71SFr) and Bern (78SFr). The **tourist office,** in the station, gives out free town maps and sells hiking maps for 26SFr. (☎966 81 00; www.zermatt.ch. Open mid-June to mid-Oct. M-Sa 8:30am-6pm, Su 8:30am-noon and 1:30-6pm; mid-Oct. to mid-Dec. and May to mid-June M-F 8:30am-noon and 2-6pm, Sa 9:30am-noon, Su 9:30am-noon and 4-6pm; mid-Dec. to Apr. 8:30am-noon and 2-6pm, Sa 8:30am-6:30pm, Su 9:30am-noon and 4-6pm.) **Postal Code:** CH-3920.

FRENCH SWITZERLAND

Around Lac Léman and Lac Neuchâtel, hills sprinkled with villas and blanketed by patchwork vineyards seem tame and settled—until the haze clears. Mountain peaks surge from behind the hills, and trees descend from wilderness to each shore. Some travelers suffer financial anxiety when they consider venturing to the expensive cities of refined French Switzerland. However, visitors are often relieved to find that tranquility lies in a simple stroll along a tree-lined avenue, and that the best entertainment is not always the kind money can buy.

GENEVA (GENÈVE) ☎022

The most international city in Switzerland, Geneva is a brew of 178,000 unlikely neighbors: wealthy businessmen speed past dreadlocked skaters in the street while families stroll by artists squatting in abandoned factories. Birthplace of the League of Nations and current home to dozens of multinational organizations (including the Red Cross and the United Nations), Geneva emanates worldliness.

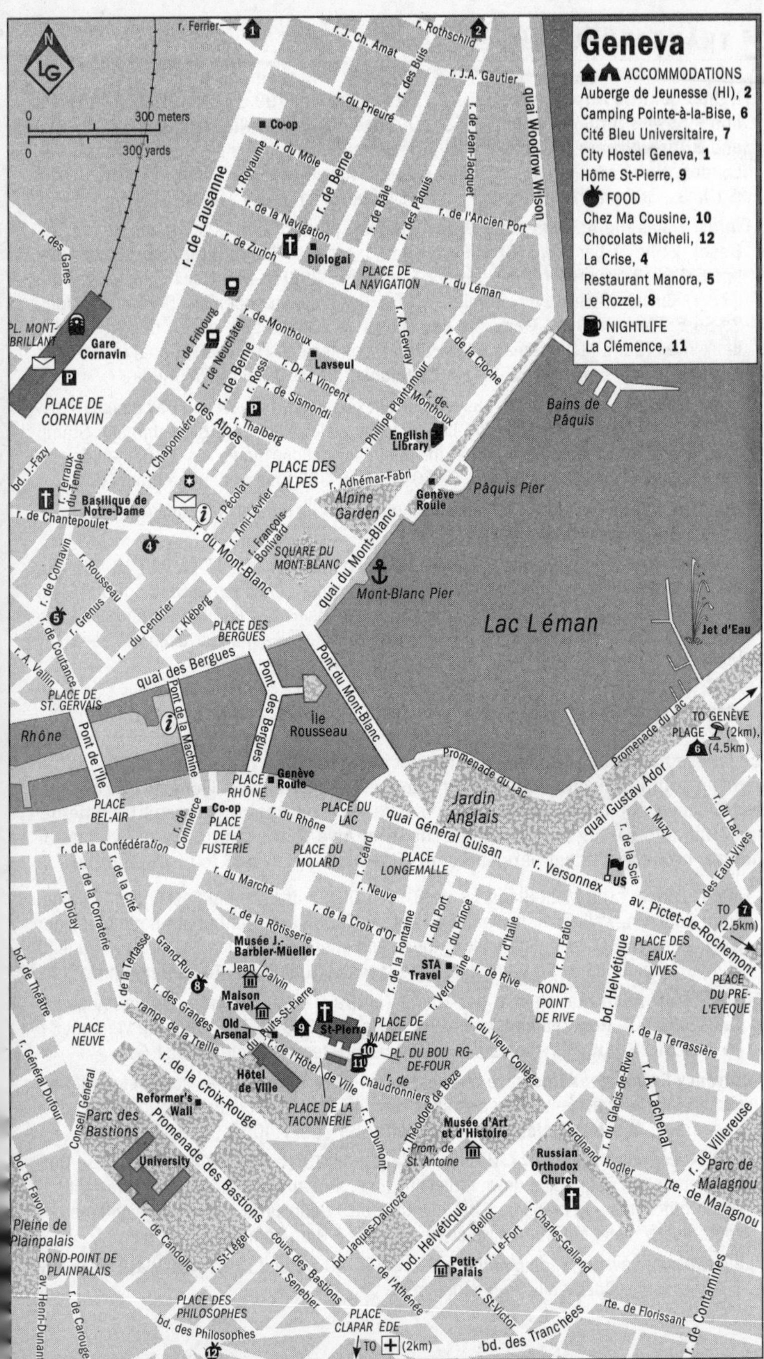
Geneva
ACCOMMODATIONS
Auberge de Jeunesse (HI), 2
Camping Pointe-à-la-Bise, 6
Cité Bleu Universitaire, 7
City Hostel Geneva, 1
Hôme St-Pierre, 9
FOOD
Chez Ma Cousine, 10
Chocolats Micheli, 12
La Crise, 4
Restaurant Manora, 5
Le Rozzel, 8
NIGHTLIFE
La Clémence, 11
Lac Léman
Jet d'Eau
Gare Cornavin
PLACE DE CORNAVIN
Basilique de Notre-Dame
PLACE DES ALPES
Alpine Garden
SQUARE DU MONT-BLANC
Mont-Blanc Pier
Pâquis Pier
Bains de Pâquis
English Library
Diologal
Lavseul
Co-op
PLACE DE LA NAVIGATION
Île Rousseau
Rhône
Jardin Anglais
PLACE DU MOLARD
PLACE LONGEMALLE
Musée J.-Barbier-Müeller
Maison Tavel
Old Arsenal
St-Pierre
Hôtel de Ville
Reformer's Wall
Parc des Bastions
University
Musée d'Art et d'Histoire
Russian Orthodox Church
Petit-Palais
Parc de Malagnou
STA Travel
Genève Roule
TO GENÈVE PLAGE (2km), (4.5km)
TO (2.5km)
TO (2km)
quai du Mont-Blanc
quai des Bergues
quai Général Guisan
quai Gustav Ador
quai Woodrow Wilson
Pont du Mont-Blanc
Pont des Bergues
Pont de l'Île
Pont de la Machine
r. de Lausanne
r. de Berne
r. du Mont-Blanc
r. des Alpes
bd. Helvétique
av. Pictet-de-Rochemont
r. de la Croix-Rouge
Promenade des Bastions
bd. des Tranchées
PLACE NEUVE
PLACE DE PLAINPALAIS
PLACE DES PHILOSOPHES
PLACE CLAPARÈDE
ROND-POINT DE RIVE
300 meters
300 yards

TRANSPORTATION

Flights: Cointrin Airport (GVA; ☎717 71 11, flight info 799 31 11 or 717 71 05) is a hub for **Swiss Airlines** (☎0848 85 20 00) and also serves **Air France** (☎827 87 87) and **British Airways** (☎0848 80 10 10). Several direct flights per day to **Amsterdam, London, New York, Paris,** and **Rome.** Bus #10 runs to the Gare Cornavin (15min., every 5-10min., 3SFr), although the train trip is shorter (6min., every 10min., 3SFr).

Trains: Trains run 4:30am-1am. **Gare Cornavin,** pl. Cornavin, is the main station. To: **Basel** (2¾hr., 1 per hr., 67SFr); **Bern** (2hr., 1 per hr., 45SFr); **Interlaken** (3hr., 1 per hr., 63SFr); **Lausanne** (40min., every 15-30min., 20SFr); **Montreux** (1hr., 2 per hr., 27SFr); **Zurich** (3½hr., every 30min., 77SFr). Ticket counter open M-F 5:15am-9:30pm, Sa-Su 5:30am-9:30pm. **Gare des Eaux-Vives** (☎736 16 20), on av. de la Gare des Eaux-Vives (tram #12 to Amandoliers SNCF), connects to France's regional rail through **Annecy** (1½hr., 6 per day, 15SFr) or **Chamonix** (2½hr., 4 per day, 25SFr).

Public Transportation: Geneva has an efficient bus and tram network. **Day passes** 7SFr-18SFr; price varies depending on how many travel "zones" you pass through. Stamp multi-use tickets before boarding at machines in station. Buses run 5:30am-midnight; **Noctambus** (F and Sa nights only 12:30-4:30am, 3SFr) runs when the others don't.

Taxis: Taxi-Phone (☎331 41 33). 6.80SFr plus 2.90SFr per km. 15-20min. taxi from airport to city 30SFr, 4-person max.

Bike Rental: Behind the station, **Genève Roule,** pl. Montbrillant 17 (☎740 13 43), has **free bikes** available (deposit of 50SFr and passport; fines run upwards of 300SFr if bike is lost or stolen). Two other locations, one at Bains des Pâquis and another at pl. du Rhône. Arrive before 9am, as bikes go quickly. Free bike maps available. Open daily May-Oct. 7:30am-9:30pm; Nov.-Apr. 8am-6pm. Cash only.

ORIENTATION AND PRACTICAL INFORMATION

The labyrinthine cobbled streets and quiet squares of the historic *vieille ville* (old town), around **Cathédrale de St-Pierre,** make up the heart of Geneva. Across the **River Rhône** to the north, five-star hotels give way to lakeside promenades, **International Hill,** and rolling parks. Across the **River Arve** to the south lies the village of **Carouge,** home to student bars and clubs (take tram #12 or 13 to pl. du Marché).

Tourist Office: r. du Mont-Blanc 18 (☎909 70 00), in the Central Post Office Building. From Cornavin, walk 5min. toward the Pont du Mont-Blanc. Staff books hotel rooms for 5SFr, leads English-language walking tours, and offers free city maps. Open mid-June to Aug. M 10am-6pm, Tu-Su 9am-6pm; low season M 10am-6pm, Tu-Sa 9am-6pm.

Consulates: Australia, chemin des Fins 2 (☎799 91 00). **Canada,** av. de l'Ariana 5 (☎919 92 00). **New Zealand,** chemin des Fins 2 (☎929 03 50). **UK,** r. de Vermont 37 (☎918 24 26). **US,** r. Versonnex 7 (☎840 51 60, recorded info 840 51 61).

Currency Exchange: ATMs have the best rates. **Gare Cornavin** has good rates with no commission on traveler's checks, makes cash advances on credit cards (200SFr min.) and arrange **Western Union** transfers. Open M-Sa 7am-7:40pm, Su 9:15am-6pm.

GLBT Resources: Diologai, r. de la Navigation 11-13 (☎906 4040). From Gare Cornavin, turn left, walk 5min. down r. de Lausanne, and turn right onto r. de la Navigation. Offers brochures and maps on GBLT nightlife; also doubles as a cafe and nighttime hot spot. Mostly male, but women welcome. Open M-F 9am-6pm, Su noon-3pm.

Laundromat: Lavseul, r. de-Monthoux 29 (☎735 90 51 or 732 61 46). Wash 5SFr, dry 1SFr per 9min. Open daily 7am-midnight.

Emergency: Police: ☎117. **Ambulance:** ☎144. **Fire:** ☎118.

Police Station, r. de Berne 6. Open M-F 9am-noon and 3-6:30pm, Sa 9am-noon.

Hospital: Hôpital Cantonal, r. Micheli-du-Crest 24 (☎372 33 11). Bus #1 or 5 or tram #12. Door #2 is for emergency care. For consultations use door #3. For info on walk-in clinics, contact the **Association des Médecins** (☎320 84 20).

Internet Access: 12Mix, r. de-Monthoux 58 (☎731 67 47; www.12mix.com). 3SFr per 30min., 5SFr per hr. Copier available. Open daily 10am-midnight.

Post Office: Poste Centrale, r. du Mont-Blanc 18, 1 block from Gare Cornavin. Open M-F 7:30am-6pm, Sa 9am-4pm. *Poste Restaunte.* **Postal Code:** CH-1211.

ACCOMMODATIONS

The indispensable *Info Jeunes* lists about 50 budget options, and the tourist office publishes *Budget Hotels*, which stretches the definition of budget to 120SFr per person. Cheap beds are relatively scarce, so be sure to book in advance.

Auberge de Jeunesse (HI), r. Rothschild 30 (☎732 6260; www.yh-geneva.ch). Huge building kept so clean that some rooms smell like varnish. Breakfast included. Laundry 8SFr. Internet available. 6-night max. stay. Reception 6:30-10am and 2pm-midnight. Dorms 32SFr; doubles 97SFr; triples 137SFr. 6SFr HI discount. AmEx/MC/V. ❷

City Hostel Geneva, r. Ferrier 2 (☎901 1500; www.city-hostel.ch). From the train station, head down r. de Lausanne for 5min., and make your 1st left onto r. du Prieuré, which becomes r. Ferrier. Delicious smells wafting out of the kitchens will make you want to take a break from restaurant fare. Lockers 10SFr deposit. Linen 3.50SFr. Internet 8SFr per hr. Reception 7:30am-noon and 1pm-midnight. Check-out 10am. Single-sex dorms 28SFr; singles 58SFr; doubles 85SFr. MC/V. ❷

Hôme St-Pierre, Cour St-Pierre 4 (☎310 3707; info@homestpierre.ch). Take bus #5 to pl. Neuve or walk from the station. This 150-year-old "home" has comfortable beds and a great location in the middle of the old town, beside the cathedral. Be aware that the church bells ring every 15min. Breakfast M-Sa 7SFr. Reception M-Sa 9am-noon and 4-8pm, Su 9am-noon. Dorms 23SFr; singles 40SFr; doubles 60SFr. MC/V. ❶

Cité Bleu Universitaire, av. Miremont 46 (☎839 2211). Take bus #3 (dir.: Crets-de-Champel) from the station to the last stop. TV rooms, restaurant, disco (Th and Sa, free to guests), and a small grocery. Hall show-

DEALS ON WHEELS

While French Switzerland is ofter considered hostile territory for the budget traveler, access to the region's breathtaking landscapes comes free of charge—with a little sweat and deal-hunting—in many major cities and towns. Geneva Lausanne, and Neuchâtel (as wel as Zurich in German-speaking Switzerland) all offer free bike rentals, allowing tourists tc escape from the beaten pedestrian path and coast along the lakeshore. The program originatec in Geneva a few years ago in ar effort to combat automobile pollution and provide work for asylum seekers, and has since spread around the country.

All you need to borrow a bike is your passport and a deposit o 20-50SFr, and the bike is yours until 9:30pm that evening. A worc of caution: take good care to us your lock, since a lost or stoler bike comes with a hefty 300SF fine. Most locations will provide a free lock upon request; some alsc offer free maps highlighting specific bike paths through the city and all have staff who are willing to make suggestions about scenic trips around the area.

For more information about specific locations, see Genève Roule (p. 1038), Lausanne Roule (p. 1042) Neuchâtel Roule (p. 1043), and Zu ich bike rental (p. 1025).

ers. Reception M-F 8am-noon and 2-10pm, Sa 8am-noon and 6-10pm, Su 9-11am and 6-10pm. Check-out 10am. Dorm lockout 11am-6pm. Dorm curfew 11pm. Dorms (July-Sept. only) 22SFr; singles 55SFr, students 46SFr; doubles 84/65SFr; studios with kitchenette and bath 84SFr. AmEx/MC/V. ❶

Camping Pointe-à-la-Bise, chemin de la Bise (☎752 1296). Take bus #8 to Rive, then bus E north to Bise and walk 10min. to lake. Reception July-Aug. 8am-noon and 2-9pm; Apr.-June and Sept. 8am-noon and 4-8pm. Closed in winter. Tent sites 17SFr, extra person 6.60SFr. No tents provided. 4-person bungalows 95SFr. AmEx/MC/V. ❶

FOOD

Resourceful cheapskates can pick up basics at *boulangeries*, *pâtisseries*, or at supermarkets. Many supermarkets have attached cafeterias; try the **Co-op** on the corner of r. du Commerce and r. du Rhône, in the Centre Rhône Fusterie. Relatively cheap restaurants center in the **Les Pâquis** area, bordered by r. de Lausanne and Gare Cornavin on one side and Quais Mont-Blanc and Wilson on the other. To the south, **Carouge** is known for its cozy pizzerias and funky *brasseries*.

Restaurant Manora, r. de Cornavin 4 (☎909 490), to the right of the station in the Placette department store. This self-serve restaurant has a varied selection and free water (a rarity in Switzerland). Entrees 5-12SFr. Open M-W, F 7:30am-9:30pm, Th 7:30am-10pm, Su 9am-9:30pm. AmEx/DC/MC/V. ❶

Chocolats Micheli, r. Micheli-du-Crest 1 (☎329 9006). Take tram #13 to Plainpalais and walk up bd. des Philosophes until it intersects r. Micheli-du-Crest. Confectionary masterpieces and croissants (1-3SFr) abound in this Victorian cafe. Coffee 3.40SFr. Open Tu-F 8am-7pm, Sa 8am-5pm. MC/V. ❶

La Crise, r. de Chantepoulet 13 (☎738 0264). Arrive in the morning to watch the vegetables being prepared at the next table for the day's soup (3.50SFr) at this tiny but popular snack bar. *Plat du jour* 15SFr; 11SFr for a smaller portion. Open M-F 6am-3pm and 5-8pm, Sa 6am-3pm. Lunch served after noon. Cash only. ❶

Chez Ma Cousine, pl. du Bourg-de-Four 6 (☎310 9696), near the cathedral. With only 3 chicken dishes on the menu, this cheerful restaurant has had plenty of opportunities to perfect them. *Salade de poulet thai* 14SFr. Open M-F 7am-11:30pm, Sa 11am-11:30pm, Su 11am-10:30pm. AmEx/DC/MC/V. ❷

Le Rozzel, Grand-Rue 18. Take bus #5 to pl. Neuve, then walk up the hill past the cathedral on r. Jean-Calvin to Grand-Rue. Outdoor seating in the *Altstadt*. Crepes 4-18SF. Open M, W, F 7:30am-8:30pm, Tu, Th 7:30am-7pm, Sa 7:30am-6pm. MC/V. ❶

SIGHTS

The city's most interesting historical sites are located within a dense, easily walkable area. The tourist office offers 2hr. English-language walking tours. (Mid-June to Sept. M-Sa 10am; Oct. to mid-June Sa only 10am. 15SFr, students 10SFr.)

VIEILLE VILLE. From 1536 to 1564, Calvin preached at the **Cathédrale de St-Pierre.** The **north tower** provides a commanding view of the old town. *(Open June-Sept. M-F 9:30am-6:30pm, Sa 9:30am-5pm, Su noon-6:30pm; Oct.-May daily 10am-5:30pm. Tower 4SFr.)* Ruins, including a Roman sanctuary and a 4th-century basilica, rest in an **archaeological site** below the cathedral. *(Open June-Sept. Tu 11am-5pm, Sa-Su 11am-5:30pm; Oct.-May Tu-F 2-5pm, Sa-Su 1:30-5:30pm. 8SFr, students 4SFr.)* At the western end of the *vieille ville* sits the 14th-century **Maison Tavel,** which now houses a museum showcasing Geneva's history. *(Open Tu-Su 10am-5pm. Free.)* Across the street is the **Hôtel de Ville** (town hall), where world leaders met on August 22, 1864 for the Geneva Convention, the results of which still govern war conduct today. The **Grand-Rue,**

which begins at the Hôtel de Ville, is lined with medieval workshops and 18th-century mansions; plaques commemorate famous residents like Jean-Jacques Rousseau, who was born at #40. Below the cathedral, along r. de la Croix-Rouge, the **Parc des Bastions** stretches from pl. Neuve to pl. des Philosophes and includes **Le Mur des Réformateurs** (Reformers' Wall), a sprawling collection of bas-relief figures depicting Protestant Reformers. The park's center walkway leads to the **Petit-Palais,** Terrasse St-Victor 2, a beautiful mansion containing art by Chagall, Gauguin, Picasso, and Renoir, as well as themed exhibits. *(Bus #36 to Petit-Palais or #1, 3, or 5 to Claparède. Open M-F 10am-6pm, Sa-Su 10am-5pm. 10SFr, students 5SFr.)*

WATERFRONT. Down quai Gustave Ardor, the **Jet d'Eau,** Europe's highest fountain, spews a seven-ton plume of water 134m into the air. The **floral clock** in the **Jardin Anglais** pays homage to Geneva's watch industry. For a day at the beach, head down to **Genève Plage,** on the south side of the lake about halfway to the campground, where a water slide and an enormous pool await. *(☎736 24 82; www.geneve-plage.ch. Open mid-May to mid-Sept. daily 10am-8pm. 7SFr, students 4.50SFr.)*

INTERNATIONAL HILL. The International Red Cross building contains the impressive **International Red Cross and Red Crescent Museum,** av. de la Paix 17. *(Bus #8 or F to Appia or bus V or Z to Ariana. Open M, W-Su 10am-5pm. 10SFr, students 5SFr. English-language audio tour 3SFr.)* The nearby European headquarters of the **United Nations** is in the same building that once sheltered the League of Nations. The constant traffic of international diplomats provides more excitement than the dull guided tour. *(Open July-Aug. daily 10am-5pm; Apr.-June and Sept.-Oct. daily 10am-noon and 2-4pm; Nov.-Mar. M-F 10am-noon and 2-4pm. 9SFr, students 7SFr.)*

ENTERTAINMENT AND NIGHTLIFE

Genève Agenda, available at the tourist office, features event listings ranging from major festivals to movies. Be warned—a movie runs about 17SFr. In July and August, the **Cinelac** turns Genève Plage into an open-air cinema screening mostly American films, and free **jazz concerts** take place in Parc de la Grange. Geneva hosts the biggest celebration of **American Independence Day** outside the US (July 4), and the **Fêtes de Genève** in early August fills the city with music and fireworks.

Diverse nightlife offerings in Geneva cluster in its distinct neighborhoods. **Place Bourg-de-Four,** below the cathedral in the *vieille ville,* attracts students and professionals to its charming terraces. **Place du Molard,** on the right bank by the pont du Mont-Blanc, has terrace cafes and loud bars and clubs. **Les Pâquis,** near Gare Cornavin and pl. de la Navigation, is the city's red-light district, but it also has a wide array of rowdy, low-lit bars. This neighborhood is also home to many of the city's gay bars. **Carouge,** across the river Arve, is a student-friendly locus of nightlife activity. In the *vieille ville,* generations of students have eaten at the famous **La Clémence,** pl. du Bourg-de-Four 20. You can count on it to be open, even when the rest of the city has shut down. (Open M-Th 7am-12:30am, F-Sa 7am-1:30am.)

LAUSANNE

☎021

The unique museums, distinctive neighborhoods, and lazy Lac Léman waterfront of Lausanne (pop. 125,000) make it well worth a stay. In the *vieille ville,* two flights of medieval stairs lead to the Gothic **Cathédrale.** (Open July to mid-Sept. M-F 7am-7pm, Sa-Su 8am-7pm; mid-Sept. to June daily 8am-5:30pm.) Below the cathedral is the **Hôtel de Ville,** on pl. de la Palud, the meeting point for **guided tours** of the town. (☎321 77 66; www.lausanne.ch/visites. Tours May-Sept. M-Sa 10am, 3pm. 10SFr, students free.) The **Musée Olympique,** quai d'Ouchy 1, is a high-tech shrine to modern Olympians. Take bus #2 to Ouchy and follow the signs. (☎621 65

SWITZERLAND

11; www.olympic.org. Open daily 9am-6pm; Oct.-Apr. closed M. 14SFr, students 9SFr.) The **Collection de l'Art Brut,** av. Bergières 11, is filled with unusual sculptures, drawings, and paintings by fringe artists—schizophrenics, peasants, and criminals. Take bus #2 or 3 to Jomini. (Open July-Aug. daily 11am-6pm; Sept.-June closed M. 8SFr, students 5SFr.) In Ouchy, several booths along quai de Belgique offer **water skiing** or **wake boarding** (35SFr per 15min.). **Lausanne Roule,** Haldimand 15, rents **free bikes** beside pl. de l'Europe. (☎076 441 8378. Required deposit of passport and 20SFr. Open mid-Apr. to late-Oct. daily 7:30am-9:30pm.)

Lausanne Guesthouse and Backpacker ❷, chemin des Epinettes 4, is conveniently located and boasts an equipped kitchen, cozy living room with games, and rose garden. Head left and downhill out of the station on W. Fraisse; take the first right on chemin des Epinettes. (☎601 8000; www.lausanne-guesthouse.ch. Linen 5SFr. Laundry 5SFr. Reception 7:30am-noon and 3-10pm. Dorms 30SFr; singles 81SFr, with bath 89SFr; doubles 88/100SFr. 5% ISIC discount. MC/V.) Restaurants, cafes, and bars cluster around **Place St-François** and the *vieille ville,* while *boulangeries* sell cheap sandwiches on every street and grocery stores abound. Stop by **Le Barbare ❶,** Escaliers du Marché 27, near the cathedral and halfway down the covered staircase, for a sandwich (5.50SFr) or omelette (7.50-16SFr), both excellent deals. (☎312 2132. Open M-Sa 8:30am-midnight. AmEx/MC/V.)

Trains leave for: Basel (2½hr., every hr., 57SFr); Geneva (50min., every 20min., 20SFr); Montreux (20min., every 30min., 10SFr); Paris (4hr., 4 per day, 104SFr); Zurich (2½hr., 3 per hr., 65SFr). The **tourist office** in the train station reserves rooms for 4SFr and provides free city maps. (☎613 7373. Open daily 9am-7pm.)

SWITZERLAND

MONTREUX ☎021

Along the Montreux shore, tree-covered mountains frame the clear blue of Lac Léman and rise to snow-capped peaks. A resort town past its Jazz Age heyday, Montreux continues to draw travelers the music that still swings during the annual **Montreux Jazz Festival,** which erupts for 15 days starting the first Friday of July and has hosted icons like Bob Dylan and Miles Davis. (www.montreuxjazz.com. Tickets 59-179SFr.) If you can't get tickets, come for **Montreux Jazz Under the Sky,** 500 hours of free, open-air concerts on three stages. The **Château de Chillon,** a gloomy medieval fortress on a nearby island, features all the comforts of home: prison cells, a torture chamber, and a weapons room. Take the CGN ferry (15SFr) or bus #1 (3SFr) to Chillon. (☎966 8910; www.chillon.ch. Open daily Apr.-Sept. 9am-6pm; Mar. and Oct. 9:30am-5pm; Nov.-Feb. 10am-4pm. 10SFr, students 8SFr.)

Cheap rooms in Montreux are scarce year-round and almost nonexistent during the Jazz Festival, so book ahead. **Riviera Lodge ❷,** pl. du Marché 5, in the neighboring town of Vevey, is worth the commute for its friendly staff, water views, and unbeatable deals. Guests also get a pass that includes free bus transportation and discounts on museums and attractions. Take bus #1 to Vevey (20min., every 10min., 2.80SFr). From the bus stop, head to the left away from the train station on the main road and follow the brown signs to the lodge, located in the main square on the water. (☎923 8040; info@rivieralodge.ch. Linen 5SFr. Laundry 6SFr. Internet 3SFr per 15min. Reception 8am-noon and 4-8pm. Call ahead if arriving late. Dorms 26SFr; singles 60SFr; doubles 80SFr. MC/V.) For an affordable meal, **Babette's ❷,** Grand Rue 60, downstairs from the station and to the left, serves crepes for lunch and dessert. (☎963 7796. Crepes 7-14SFr. Open daily 7am-7pm. MC/V.) Grand Rue and av. de Casino have inexpensive markets. The **Co-op** supermarket is at Grand Rue 80. (Open M-F 8am-12:15pm and 2-6:30pm, Sa 8am-5pm.)

Trains leave for: Bern (1½hr., 2 per hr., 37SFr); Geneva (1hr., 2 per hr., 27SFr); Lausanne (20min., 3-5 per hr., 9.80SFr). Descend the stairs opposite the station, head left on Grand Rue for 5-10min., and look to the right for the **tourist office,** on pl. du Débarcadère, which provides free maps of the town and helps book private rooms during the peak seasons. (☎962 8484; www.montreux-vevey.com. Open mid-June to mid-Sept. M-F 9am-6pm, Sa-Su 10am-5pm; late Sept. to early June M-F 9am-noon and 1-5:30pm, Sa-Su 10am-2pm.) **Postal Code:** CH-1820.

NEUCHÂTEL

☎032

Alexandre Dumas once said that Neuchâtel (pop. 164,000) appeared to be carved out of butter; visitors gazing down street after street filled with yellow stone architecture will immediately see why. The old town centers around **place des Halles,** a block from **place Pury,** the hub of every bus line. From pl. des Halles, turn left onto r. de Château and climb the stairs on the right to reach **Collégiale Church** and the **château** that gives the town its name. (Church open daily Apr.-Sept. 9am-8pm; Oct.-Mar. 9am-6:30pm.) Entrance to the château is available only through a free tour. (1 per hr., every hr. Apr.-Sept. M-F 10am-noon and 2-4pm, Sa 10-11am and 2-4pm, Su 2-4pm.) The nearby **Tour des Prisons** (Prison Tower), on r. Jeanne-Hochberg, has a prime view of the entire city and the lake. (Open daily Apr.-Sept. 8am-6pm. 1SFr.) The **Musée d'Histoire Naturelle,** off r. de l'Hôpital, has a great collection of just about every stuffed creature that you could imagine. Turn right from pl. des Halles onto Croix du Marché, which becomes r. de l'Hôpital. (☎717 7960; www.ne.ch/neuchatel/mhn. Open Tu-Su 10am-6pm. 6SFr, students 3SFr. W free.) The **Musée d'Arts et d'Histoire,** esplanade Léopold-Robert 1, houses an eclectic collection of paintings, weapons, textiles, and teacups. Exit tram station, head to the right along the lake promenade about 100m. (Open Tu-Su 10am-6pm. 7SFr, students 4SFr. W free.) Close to the tourist office, **Neuchâtel Roule** lends free bikes. (☎717 7675; www.newride.ch. Required deposit of 20SFr and passport. Open Apr.-Sept. daily 7:30am-9:30pm.) For the best views of the area, take bus #7 to La Coudre, where you can hop on the **funiculaire** that rises to the village of Chaumont. (1 lift per hr. First run around 9am; last run around 7pm. 4SFr; round-trip 8SFr.)

If lodgings in Neuchâtel leave your wallet sad and frightened, catch the train (3 per hr., 11.40SFr) to nearby Biel, where **Lago Lodge ❶,** Uferweg 5, has a lakeside location and downstairs brewery. Head straight out the back entrance of the Biel train station, walk for 3min. and cross the bridge. Make an immediate right onto Uferweg, then take your first left to the lodge. (☎331 3732; www.lagolodge.ch. Breakfast 8SFr. Dorms 25SFr; doubles 37SFr. MC/V.) At **A.R. Knecht Boulangerie et Pâtisserie ❶,** on the corner of pl. des Halles and r. du Coq d'Inde, locals munch *pain noix* (bread with nuts; 3SFr) while watching passersby. (☎725 1321. Open Tu-Sa 6am-6:30pm. Cash only.) **Migros,** r. de l'Hôpital 12, sells groceries. (Open M-W 8am-6:30pm, Th 8am-10pm, F 7:30am-6:30pm, Sa 7:30am-7pm.)

Trains run to: Basel (1¾hr., every hr., 34SFr); Bern (45min., every hr., 18SFr); Geneva (1½hr., every hr., 37SFr). A free underground **tram** runs from the station to the shore area. Head to the right after disembarking and walk 5min. along the lake to the **tourist office,** in the same building as the post office. They provide free city maps and book rooms at no extra charge. (☎889 6890; www.neuchateltourisme.ch. Open July-Aug. M-F 9am-6:30pm, Sa 9am-4pm, Su 10am-2pm; Sept.-June M-F 9am-noon and 1:30-5:30pm, Sa 9am-noon.) **Postal Code:** CH-2001.

ITALIAN SWITZERLAND

Ever since Switzerland won Ticino, the only Italian-speaking Swiss canton, from Italy in 1512, the region has been renowned for its mix of Swiss efficiency and Italian *dolce vita.* It's no wonder the rest of Switzerland vacations here among jasmine-laced villas painted in the muted pastels of Italian gelato.

LUGANO

☎091

Set in a valley between sloping mountains, Lugano (pop. 52,000) draws plenty of visitors with its seamless blend of artistic flair and historic religious sites. The frescoes of the 16th-century **Cattedrale San Lorenzo,** just south of the train station, are still vivid despite their advanced age. The most spectacular fresco in town, however, is the gargantuan crucifix in the **Chiesa Santa Maria degli Angiuli,** 200m to the right of the tourist office. Armed with topographic maps and trail guides (sold at the tourist office), **hikers** can tackle the rewarding Monte Boglio (5hr.), while tamer souls can reach the peaks of Monte Bré (933m) and Monte San Salvatore (912m) by **funicular.** The **Hotel Continental,** V. Basilea 28 (☎966 11 14), provides information on various adventure sports in the area, from snowshoeing and skiing (full-day 90SFr) to paragliding (165SFr) and canyoning (from 90SFr).

Hotel and Backpackers Montarina ❶, V. Montarina 1, is surrounded by palm trees and elevated even further by its swimming pool and terrace. (☎966 7272; www.montarina.ch. Breakfast 12SFr. Linen 4SFr. Laundry 4SFr. Reception 8am-10:30pm. Open Mar.-Oct. Dorms 25SFr; singles 70SFr, with bath 80SFr; doubles 100/120SFr. AmEx/MC/V.) The **Migros** supermarket, V. Pretoria 15, also has a food court. (Open M-W, F 8am-6:30pm, Th 8am-9pm, Sa 7:30am-5pm.) **Trains** leave P. della Stazione for: Locarno (1hr., every 30min., 16.20SFr); Milan (45min., every hr., 21SFr); Zurich (3hr., 8 per day, 57SFr). The **tourist office,** across from the ferry station at the corner of P. Rezzonico, provides free maps and makes hotel reservations for 4SFr. Free guided walks of the city on Monday at 9am. (☎913 3232; www.lugano-tourism.ch. Open Apr.-Oct. M-F 9am-7pm, Sa 9am-6pm, Su 10am-6pm; Nov.-Mar. M-F 9am-noon and 2-5pm.) **Postal Code:** CH-6900.

LOCARNO

☎091

A Swiss vacation spot on the shores of Lago Maggiore, Locarno (pop. 30,000) gets over 2200 hours of sunlight per year—more than anywhere else in Switzerland. For centuries, visitors have journeyed here solely to see the orange-yellow church of **Madonna del Sasso** (Madonna of the Rock), founded in 1487. A 20min. walk up V. al Sasso leads to the top and passes life-sized wooden niche statues along the way. Hundreds of heart-shaped medallions on the church walls commemorate acts of Mary's intervention in the lives of worshippers who have journeyed here. (Grounds open daily 6:30am-6:45pm.) For 10 days at the beginning of each August, Locarno swells with pilgrims of a different sort and prices shoot through the roof when its world-famous **film festival** draws over 150,000 movie-lovers.

To reach **Pensione Città Vecchia ❷,** V. Toretta 13, turn right onto V. Toretta from P. Grande. (☎751 4554. Breakfast included. Reception hours vary, so be sure to call ahead. Dorms 40SFr; doubles 80SFr; triples 120SFr. Cash only.) Left of the station, **Ristorante Manora ❶,** V. della Stazione 1, offers cheap, self-service dining. (Salad bar 4.50-10SFr. Entrees 10.50-16.50SFr. Open Nov.-Feb. M-Sa 7:30am-9pm, Su 8am-9pm; Mar.-Oct. M-Sa 7:30am-10pm, Su 8am-9pm. V.) Get groceries at the **Aperto** in the station. (Open daily 6am-10pm.) **Trains** run from P. Stazione to: Lugano (1hr., every 30min., 17SFr); Luzern (2½hr., every 30min., 54SFr); Milan (2hr., every hr., 37SFr) via Bellinzona. The **tourist office,** on P. Grande in the casino *(kursaal),* makes hotel reservations and has free maps. From the station, go left down V. della Stazione until you reach P. Grande. (☎791 00 91; www.maggiore.ch. Open Apr.-Oct. M-F 9am-6pm, Sa 10am-6pm, Su 10am-1:30pm and 2:30-5pm; Nov.-Mar. closed Su.) **Postal Code:** CH-6600.

UKRAINE (УКРАЇНА)

"Ukraine" literally means "borderland," and the country has occupied this precarious position for most of its history. Only last year, Ukraine redefined the border between East and West when the popular Orange Revolution took back the state from Russia's overbearing influence. With no beaten path from which to stray, travelers to Ukraine are rewarded by fascinating, uncrowded museums, age-old castles, and the magnificent, spirited Black Sea Coast.

DISCOVER UKRAINE: SUGGESTED ITINERARIES

THREE DAYS. Stick to **Kyiv,** the epicenter of the Orange Revolution. Check out **Independence Square,** stop by **Shevchenko Park** to enjoy real Ukrainian fare at **O'Panas,** and ponder your mortality among the mummified monks of the **Kyiv-Cave Monastery** (p. 1052).

ONE WEEK. After three days in **Kyiv,** take a train to **Lviv** (2 days; p. 1053), the cultural capital of Ukraine. Spend your last two days in **Odessa** (p. 1054); soak up the sun on the beach and experience high culture for cheap at the **Theater of Opera and Ballet.**

UKRAINE

ESSENTIALS

FACTS AND FIGURES

Official Name: Ukraine.

Capital: Kyiv.

Major Cities: Lviv, Odessa.

Population: 47,430,000 (78% Ukrainian, 17% Russian).

Time Zone: GMT +2.

Language: Ukrainian.

Religions: Ukrainian Orthodox (29%), Eastern Orthodox (16%), Ukrainian Greek Catholic (6%), other (38%).

WHEN TO GO

Ukraine has a diverse climate; generally speaking, aim to visit in spring or summer. Reserve in advance from June to August in Odessa and Crimea, which heat up to just barely subtropical temperatures. Kyiv enjoys a moderate climate, while the more mountainous west remains cool even in summer. Winter tourism is popular in the Carpathians. Book accommodations early around the May 1 holiday.

DOCUMENTS AND FORMALITIES

EMBASSIES AND CONSULATES. Foreign embassies for Ukraine are in Kyiv (p. 1050). Ukrainian embassies abroad include: Australia, Level 12, St. George Centre, 60 Marcus Clarke St., Canberra ACT 2601 (☎02 6230 5789; www.ukremb.info); Canada, 310 Somerset St., Ottawa, ON K2P 0J9 (☎613-230-2400; www.infoukes.com/ukremb); UK, 60 Holland Park, London W11 3SJ (☎020 7727 6312, consular/visas 020 7243 8923; www.ukremb.org.uk); US, 3350 M St., NW, Washington, D.C. 20007 (☎202-333-0606; www.ukraineinfo.us).

VISA AND ENTRY INFORMATION. Ukraine's visa requirements changed in 2005 and are likely to continue to do so as the government works to encourage tourism. As of August 2005, a **visa** is no longer required of US citizens returning to Ukraine

after an absence of less than six months. Visas are no longer required of Canadian citizens or citizens of the EU. All visas are valid for 90 days, and all visa-free regimes are applicable for stays of up to 90 days.

Single-entry visas cost US$100, double-entry US$110, multiple-entry US$165. Three business-day rush service costs US$200, double-entry US$220; multiple-entry US$330. There is no next-day service. Transit visas cost an additional US$10, or US$20 for rush service. The visa fee is waived for children under 16 years of age and American students with proper documents. Submit a completed visa application, your passport, one passport-size photo, and payment by money order. US citizens can find applications and information at www.ukraineinfo.us. Citizens of Australia and New Zealand require a letter of invitation, but citizens of Canada, the EU, and the US do not. Perplexingly, an invitation is required even when a "letter of invitation" is not; such invitations are available on request from info@hihostels.com.ua. Make sure to allow time for processing and to fill out the application thoroughly: consulates will return an application to you if it contains any problems. Wherever the application asks for a name, supply an address and telephone number as well. You can extend your visa in Ukraine, at the OVYR office in Kyiv.

When proceeding through **customs** you will be required to declare all cash, traveler's checks, and jewelry regardless of value. Check with your country's Ukrainian embassy for more restrictions. **Do not lose the paper given to you when entering the country to supplement your visas.** The **Office of Visas and Registration** (OVYR;

ОВИР)—in Kyiv at bul. Tarasa Shevchenka 34, or at police stations in smaller cities—extends visas. Make sure to carry your passport and visa at all times.

ENTRANCE REQUIREMENTS

Passport: Required for all travelers.

Visa: Not required for citizens of EU countries, nor US citizens **returning** to Ukraine within six months of a previous visit, but mandatory for all other citizens of the US and for citizens of Canada, Australia, and New Zealand planning on staying for over 90 days.

Letter of Invitation: Required for citizens of Australia and New Zealand.

Inoculations: Not required. Recommended up-to-date on DTaP (diphtheria, tetanus, and pertussis), Hepatitis A, Hepatitis B, MMR (measles, mumps, and rubella), Polio booster, and Typhoid.

Work Permit: Required for all foreigners planning to work in Ukraine.

Driving Permit: Required for all those planning to drive in Ukraine.

TOURIST SERVICES AND MONEY

TOURIST OFFICES. Lviv's tourist office is extremely helpful; it is also the only official tourist office in Ukraine. The remains of the Soviet giant **Intourist** have offices in hotels, rarely speak English. They're used to dealing with groups, to whom they sell "excursion" packages to nearby sights. Local travel agencies can be helpful, but they rarely speak English and are delighted to lighten your wallet.

UKRAINE

HRYVNY (HV)	
AUS$1 = 3.79HV	1HV = AUS$0.26
CDN$1 = 4.10HV	1HV = CDN$0.24
EUR€1 = 6.10HV	1HV = EUR€0.16
NZ$1 = 3.47HV	1HV = NZ$0.29
UK£1 = 8.99HV	1HV = UK£0.11
US$1 = 4.96HV	1HV = US$0.20

MONEY. The Ukrainian unit of currency is the **hryvnya** (hv), and **inflation** is around 12%. If you're looking to **exchange currency,** (Обмшн Валют; Obmin Valyut) kiosks in the center of most cities offer the best rates. **Traveler's checks** can be changed for small commissions in many cities. **Western Union** franchises and **ATMs** are everywhere. Most banks give Mastercard and Visa cash advances for a high commission. The lobbies of fancier hotels usually exchange US dollars at lousy rates. Do not exchange money with **private money changers;** it's illegal and a good way to get ripped off. The Ukrainian work week is eight hours Monday through Friday with a lunch break from 1-2pm; banks are open Monday through Friday 9am-1pm.

HEALTH AND SAFETY

EMERGENCY	**Police:** ☎02. **Ambulance:** ☎03. **Fire:** ☎01.

Hospital facilities in Ukraine are limited and do not meet Western standards. Often basic supplies are missing and patients may be required to supply their own medical supplies (e.g., bandages). Foreigners are required to have medical insurance to receive health care, but be prepared to front the bill yourself. When in doubt, go to your embassy, and they will find you adequate care or fly you out of the country; medical evacuations to Western Europe cost US$25,000 and upwards of US$50,000 to the United States. Boil all **water** or brush your teeth with soda water. Peel or wash **fruits and vegetables** from open markets. Meat purchased at markets should be checked carefully and cooked thoroughly; refrigeration is infrequent and insects run rampant. Embassy officials declare that Chernobyl-related **radiation** poses negligible risk to short-term travelers. **Public restrooms** are horrifying. Pay toilets (платні; platni) are cleaner and may provide toilet paper, but bring your own anyway. **Pharmacies** (Аптеки; Apteky) are common and carry basic Western products. Anything more complicated should be brought from home. **Sanitary napkins** (гігієнчні пакети; hihienchni pakety), **condoms** (презервативи; prezervativy), and **tampons** (прокладки; prokladky) are sometimes sold at kiosks.

While Ukraine is politically stable, it is poor. **Pickpocketing** and wallet scams are the most common crimes, although cases of armed robbery and assault have been reported. Don't exchange money on the street. Do not accept drinks from strangers, as this could result in your being drugged and robbed. Credit card and ATM fraud are endemic; it is best not to use credit or ATM cards while in Ukraine. Be careful when crossing the street—drivers do not stop for pedestrians. It's wise to **register** with your embassy once you get to Ukraine for safety purposes. **Women** traveling alone will be addressed by men anywhere they go, but usually will be safe beyond that. Ukrainian women rarely go to restaurants alone, so expect to feel conspicuous if you do. Women may request to ride in female-only compartments during long train rides, though most travel co-ed. Although minorities may experience **discrimination,** the biggest problems stem from the militia, which often stops people whom it suspects to be non-Slavic. **Disabled** travelers will encounter difficulties, as few locations are wheelchair accessible. **Homosexuality** was decriminalized in 1991, but it is not yet accepted in Ukraine; caution is advised.

TRANSPORTATION

BY PLANE. Ukraine is expensive to reach by plane. Ground transportation is safer and more pleasant, but can take a long time. If you need to get somewhere quickly, **Air Ukraine** flies to Kyiv, Lviv, and Odessa from many European capitals; **Aerosvit, Air France, ČSA, Delta, Lufthansa, LOT, Malév,** and **SAS** fly to Kyiv.

BY TRAIN. The national rail system, *Ukrainski Zaliznitsi*, runs frequently from all of Ukraine's neighbors and is the best way to travel. Trains usually run overnight and are timed to arrive in the morning. While *Let's Go* generally discourages use of night trains, Ukraine's system is relatively, though not completely safe. When coming from a non-ex-Soviet country, expect a 2hr. stop at the border. You must present a passport when purchasing train tickets. Once onboard, present both your ticket and ID to the *konduktor*. On most Ukrainian trains, there are three classes: плацкарт, or *platskart*, crammed with *babushki* and baskets of strawberries; купе, or *kupe*, a clean, more private, four-person compartment; and first class, referred to as "СВ" in Cyrillic, or *SV* in the Latin alphabet—twice as roomy and expensive as *kupe*. *Kupe* is worth the extra money. The *kasa* will sell you a *kupe* seat unless you say otherwise. Except in larger cities, where platform numbers are posted on an electronic board, the only way to figure out which platform your train leaves from is a distorted announcement. Show your ticket to cashiers or fellow passengers and ask "plaht-FORM-ah?"

BY BUS. Buses cost about the same as trains, but are often shabbier. One exception is **AutoLux** (АвтоЛюкс), which runs buses with A/C, snacks, and movies. Bus schedules are generally reliable, but low demand sometimes causes cancellations. Buy tickets at the ticket office *(kasa)*; if they're sold out, try going directly to the driver who might just magically find a seat and pocket the money. Navigating the bus system can be tough for those who do not speak Ukrainian or Russian; memorize departure times and ticket prices in advance.

BY CAR AND BY THUMB. Taxi drivers love to rip off tourists, so negotiate prices beforehand. In urban areas, road conditions are fair; in rural areas they are not. *Let's Go* does not recommend hitchhiking. Few Ukrainians hitchhike; those who do hold a sign with their desired destination or just wave an outstretched hand.

KEEPING IN TOUCH

PHONE CODES	**Country code:** 380. **International dialing prefix:** 00. For more information on placing international calls, see inside back cover.

TELEPHONE AND INTERNET. Telephones in Ukraine are stumbling toward modernity. The easiest way to make an international call is with **Utel.** Buy a phonecard (sold at most Utel phone locations) and dial the number of your international operator (considered a local call). International access codes include: **AT&T Direct** (☎8 100 11); **Canada Direct** (☎8 100 17); **MCI WorldPhone** (☎8 100 13). Or call at the central telephone office—estimate how long your call will take, pay at the counter, and they'll direct you to a booth. Local calls from gray pay phones cost 10-30hv. For an English-speaking operator, dial ☎8192. Internet cafes in major cities typically charge 3-7hv per hour.

MAIL. Mail is cheap and reliable, taking about eight to 10 days to reach North America. Sending a letter internationally costs 3.34hv. Mail can be received through **Poste Restante** (до запитання; do zapytannya). Address envelopes as follows: First name LAST NAME, "до запитання" post office address, postal code City, UKRAINE.

LANGUAGE. Traveling in Ukraine is much easier if you know **Ukrainian** or **Russian.** Ukrainian is an East Slavic language written in the Cyrillic alphabet. In Kyiv, Odessa, and Crimea, Russian is more commonly spoken than Ukrainian (but official signs are in Ukrainian). If you're trying to get by with Russian in Western Ukraine, be forewarned that while everyone understands Russian, some people will answer in Ukrainian out of habit or nationalist sentiment. Try to preface Russian statements with "I'm sorry, I don't speak Ukrainian." This will be appreciated. Practically no English is spoken outside of Kyiv and very little there. *Let's Go* provides all city names in Ukrainian; Ukrainian street names are given for Kyiv and Western Ukraine; Russian street names are used for Crimea and Odessa.

ACCOMMODATIONS AND CAMPING

UKRAINE	❶	❷	❸	❹	❺
ACCOMMODATIONS	under 55hv	55-105hv	105-265hv	265-480hv	over 480hv

Not all **hotels** accept foreigners, and those that do often charge them more than Ukrainians. Room prices in Kyiv are astronomical, but singles run 50-90hv elsewhere. Youth **hostels** are practically nonexistent in Ukraine, though a few can be found in Lviv, Kyiv, and Yalta; budget accommodations are usually in unrenovated Soviet-era buildings. More expensive lodgings aren't necessarily nicer. In some hotels, solo women may be mistaken for prostitutes. You will be given a *vizitka* (hotel card) to show to the *dezhurnaya* (hall monitor) to get a key; return the key upon leaving. **Hot water** is rare—ask before checking in. **Private rooms** are the best bargain at 20-50hv and can be arranged through overseas agencies or bargaining at the train station. Most cities have a **camping** facility—usually a remote spot with trailers. Camping outside designated areas is illegal, and enforcement is merciless.

FOOD AND DRINK

UKRAINE	❶	❷	❸	❹	❺
FOOD	under 11hv	11-27hv	27-54hv	54-105hv	over 105hv

New, fancy restaurants accommodate tourists and the few Ukrainians who can afford them, while *stolovayas* (cafeterias) serve cheap, hot food. *Vavenyky* (pierogi-like dumplings) are usually delicious. **Vegetarians** beware: meat has a tendency to show up even in so-called "vegetarian" dishes. Finding **kosher** foods can be a daunting task, but it helps to eat non-meat items or to dine in primarily Jewish areas. **State food stores** are classified by content: *hastronom* (packaged goods); *moloko* (milk products); *ovochi-frukty* (fruits and vegetables); *myaso* (meat); *khlib* (bread); *kolbasy* (sausage); and *ryba* (fish). *Kvas* is a popular, nonalcoholic fermented-bread drink. Grocery stores are often simply labeled *mahazyn* (store).

HOLIDAYS AND FESTIVALS

Holidays: Orthodox Christmas (Jan. 7); Orthodox New Year (Jan. 14); International Women's Day (Mar. 8); Easter (May 1); Labor Day (May 1-2); Victory Day (May 9); Holy Trinity Day (June 19); Constitution Day (June 28); Independence Day (Aug. 24).

Festivals: One of the most widely celebrated festivals is the **Donetsk Jazz Festival,** usually held in March. The conclusion of the 20th century brought the **Chervona Ruta Festival** which occurs in different Ukrainian cities each year, celebrating modern Ukrainian pop as well as more traditional music. The **Molodist Kyiv International Film Festival,** held in the last week of October, sets the stage for student films and film debuts.

BEYOND TOURISM

The Kyiv Post (www.kyivpost.com). English-language newspaper with classified job ads.

Odessa Language Center (☎380 482 345 058; www.studyrus.com). Spend a year or a summer in Ukraine learning Russian and taking courses on history and culture.

KYIV (КИЇВ) ☎8044

Birthplace of the empire of the Kyivan Rus and no stranger to foreign control, Kyiv (pop. 2,600,000) weathered the Nazis only to be rebuilt with Stalinist pomp by the Soviets. Kyiv has reemerged as a proud capital since Ukraine gained its independence from the USSR, and recently earned international acclaim as the epicenter of the Orange Revolution. Today, streets buzz with optimistic energy, even as the cost of living rises and the government struggles to institute promised reforms.

TRANSPORTATION

Flights: Boryspil International Airport (Бориспіль; ☎490 47 77), 30km southeast of the capital. **Polit** (Політ; ☎296 73 67), just to the right of the main entrance, sends buses to Ploscha Peremohi and the train station; buy tickets onboard (1-2 per hr., 20hv). A taxi to the center costs 70-100hv.

Trains: Kyiv-Pasazhyrskyy (Київ-Пасажирський), Vokzalna pl. (☎005). MR: Vokzalna (Вокзальна). Ticket counters in the main hall require passports. For international tickets, go to window #40 or 41 in the newest section, across the tracks. An **Advance Ticket Office** is next to Hotel Express, blv. Shevchenka 38. To: **Bratislava, Slovakia** (18hr., 1 per day, 440hv); **Budapest, Hungary** (24hr., 1 per day, 550hv); **Lviv** (10hr., 5-6 per day, 50hv); **Moscow, Russia** (15-17hr., 12-15 per day, 150hv); **Prague, Czech Republic** (35hr., 1 per day, 540hv); **Odessa** (11hr., 4-5 per day, 60hv); **Warsaw, Poland** (17hr., 2 per day, 350hv).

Buses: Tsentralny Avtovokzal (Центральний Автовокзал), Moskovska pl. 3 (Московська; ☎525 57 74), 10min. from MB: Libidska. Turn right and then left out of the metro; take trolley #4 or walk 100m down the big highway and follow it 500m right. Window #10 sells international tickets. Buses to: **Lviv** (10hr., 4 per day, 53hv); **Moscow, Russia** (20hr., 2 per day, 96-115hv); **Odessa** (8-10hr., 8 per day, 55-60hv); **Prague, Czech Republic** (28hr.; 1 per day Tu, Th-F, Su; 420hv).

Public Transportation: The 3 **metro** lines—blue (MB), green (MG), and red (MR)—cover the city center. Purchase tokens (житон; zhyton; 0.50hv) at the kasa (каса). "Вхід" *(vkhid)* indicates an entrance, "перехід" *(perekhid)* a walkway to another station, and "вихід у місто" *(vykhid u misto)* an exit onto the street. **Trolleys, buses,** and **marshrutki** (private vans) go where the metro doesn't. Bus tickets are sold at kiosks; punch your ticket onboard or face a 10hv fine. *Marshrutki* tickets (0.60-1hv) are sold onboard; request stops from the driver. Public transport runs 6am-midnight. The *elektrychka* (електричка) commuter rail, leaves from Prymiskyy Vokzal (Приміский Вокзал).

ORIENTATION AND PRACTICAL INFORMATION

Most attractions and services lie on the west bank of the Dniper River. Three metro stops from the train station is the main avenue, **vulitsa Khreshchatyk** (Хрещатик; MR line). The center of Kyiv is vul. Khreshchatyk's fountained **Independence Square** (Майдан Незалежності; Maidan Nezalezhnosti; MB line).

Tourist Offices: Kyiv lacks official tourist services. Representatives of various agencies at the airport offer vouchers, excursion packages, hotel arrangements, and other services. Try **Carlson Wagonlit Travel,** Ivana Franka 33/34, 2nd fl. (☎238 61 56). Open daily 9am-9pm. Students should check out **STI Ukraine,** Priorizna 18/1 (Пріорізна) #6, 2nd fl. (☎490 5960). Open M-F 9am-9pm, Sa-Su 10am-4pm.

Embassies: Australia, Kominternu 18/137 (Комінтерну; ☎235 75 86). Open M-Th 10am-1pm. **Canada,** Yaroslaviv Val 31 (Ярославів Вал; ☎270 71 44). Open M-F 8:30am-1pm and 2-5pm. **UK,** Desyatynna 9 (Десятинна; ☎490 36 60). Consular section at Hlybochytska 4 (Глибочицька; ☎494 34 00). Open M-Th 9am-1pm and 2-5:30pm, F 9am-1pm and 2-4pm. **US,** Yu. Kotsyubynskoho 10 (Ю. Коцюбинського; ☎490 40 00; www.usembassy.kiev.ua). Consular section at Pymonenka 6 (Пимоненка; ☎490 44 22). Open M-F 8:30am-12:30pm.

Medical Services: Emergency: ☎03. **American Medical Center,** Berdycherska 1 (Бердичерска; ☎490 76 00; www.amcenters.com), has English-speaking doctors, and takes patients without documents or insurance. Open 24hr. MC/V.

Internet Access: C-Club, Byesarabskaye pl. 1 (Бесарабскае; ☎247 56 47), in the underground mall between the market and the Lenin statue. 3hv per hr. Open 24hr.

Telephones: Telephone-Telegraph (Телефон-Телеграф; telefon-telehraf) at the post office around the corner (enter on Khreshchatyk). Open daily 8am-10:30pm. Buy cards for **public telephones** (таксофон; taksofon) at any post office. **English-language operator** ☎81 92. **Utel phones** are in the post office, train station, hotels, and nice restaurants. Buy cards at the post office and upscale hotels.

Post Office: vul. Khreshchatyk 22 (☎278 11 67). **Poste Restante** at counters #28 and 30. To pick up packages, enter on Maidan Nezalezhnosti. Internet, copy, fax, and photo services available. Open M-Sa 8am-9pm, Su 9am-7pm. **Postal Code:** 01 001.

ACCOMMODATIONS AND FOOD

Hotels in Kyiv tend to be expensive; the *Kyiv Post* (www.kyivpost.com) lists short-term apartment rentals and private rooms. People at train stations offer even cheaper rooms (from US$5). Another way to find budget lodging is through the commission-free telephone service **Okean-9.** (☎443 6167. Open M-F 9am-5pm, Sa 9am-3pm.) Backpackers flock to **International Youth Hostel Yaroslav ❸** (Ярослав), vul. Yaroslavska 10 (Ярославська), located in the historic Podil district. (☎417 31 89. MB: Kontraktova Plosha. Dorms 114-132hv.) A 15min. walk from MG: Luk'yanivska behind the US consulate, **Youth Hostel Kyiv ❸,** vul. Artema 52-A (Артема), building #2, 9th floor, is well kept and offers a host of amenities. (☎482 2817. 110hv per person.) Down vul. Kominternu from the train station, **Hotel**

UKRAINE

IN RECENT NEWS

SEEING ORANGE

)n November 21, 2004, a seem-ngly routine runoff election was ıeld between two candidates for ɔresident: Prime Minister Viktor 'anukovich, favored by the departing current regime, and eform candidate Viktor Yush-:henko. The next day, Yush-:henko's camp contested the official count, which pronounced 'anukovich the winner. Hundreds gathered in Kyiv's Independence Square to protest the election esults. The square was awash in ɔrange: protestors wore orange ınd stuck orange ribbons on sub-vay cars, monuments, anywhere ribbon would stay. People ɔoured into Kyiv from across Jkraine, and a tent city quickly vent up. It was reported that ɔolice were stopping most traffic rom entering the city, so taxi driv-ers began to shuttle people from he outskirts to metro stations ree of charge. Independence Square became the center of the Orange Revolution, protesting not ɔnly the election results, but also he perceived corruption of the status quo. Babushki delivered ıome-cooked meals to protesters n the square and debated presi-dential politics with neighbors. As he ranks of protestors in Kyiv continued to swell, the departing egime conceded to an unprece-dented third round of voting. 'ushchenko won. A bloodless rev-ɔlution had taken place, and the vorld watched to see how Ukraine vould live up to its new dedica-ion to democracy.

Express ❸ (Експрес), bul. Shevchenka 38/40, has clean rooms. (☎239 8995. Singles 144-160hv, with showers 270-300; doubles 225-250/387-430hv.)

Antresol (Антресоль) ❸, bul. Shevchenka 2, has a hip bookstore-cafe downstairs and a restaurant upstairs. (☎235 8347. English-language menus. Entrees 37-75hv. Tu and Th Live piano 8-10pm. Open daily 9am-last customer.) **O'Panas** ❸ (О'Панас), Tereshchenkivska vul. 10 (Терещенківська), in the Taras Shevchenko Park, serves Ukrainian dishes amid beautiful decor. (☎235 2132. Entrees 28-98hv. Open daily 10am-2am. MC/V.) **King David's** ❹, Esplanadna 24 (Еспланадна) is one of Ukraine's few kosher restaurants. (☎235 74 36. MG: Palats Sportu; Палац спорту. Entrees 40-110hv. Open M-Th, Su 10am-11pm, F 10am-8:30pm. Cash only.)

SIGHTS

KYIV-CAVE MONASTERY. Allot a full day for Kyiv's oldest, holiest site, the mysterious Kyiv-Cave Monastery (Киево-Печерська Лавра; Kyivo-Pecherska Lavra). Inside are the **Refectory Church,** the 12th-century **Holy Trinity Gate Church,** and several **museums** and caves where monks lie mummified. The **Great Lavra Bell Tower** has views of the churches' golden domes. *(MR: Arsenalna; Арсенальна. Turn left out of the metro and go 10min. down vul. Sichnevoho Povstaniya. Open daily May-Aug. 9am-7pm, cashier until 6pm; Sept.-Apr. 9:30am-6pm, cashier until 5pm. Monastery 10hv, students 5hv.)*

ST. SOPHIA MONASTERY. Once the religious center of Kyivan Rus, the St. Sophia Monastery, with its onion domes, ornamented facades, and Byzantine mosaics, is now a focal point of Ukrainian nationalism. *(vul. Volodymyrska. MG: Zoloti Vorota or trolley #16 from Maidan Nezalezhnasti. Grounds open daily 8:30am-8pm. Museums open M-Tu and Th-Su 10am-6pm, W 10am-5pm. Grounds 1hv. Ticket for both museums 11hv, students 4hv.)*

VULITSA KHRESHCHATYK AND ENVIRONS. Kyiv's spinal cord, vul. Khreshchatyk (Хрещатик), begins at the intersection with bul. Shevchenka and extends to **Independence Square** (Майдан Незалежності; Maidan Nezalezhnosti), atop an underground mall. This square hosted a massive tent city that persevered through bitterly cold weather during the Orange Revolution. **Khreshchaty Park,** past the silver **Friendship of the Peoples Arch,** contains a monument to Prince Volodymyr, the man who converted the Kyivan Rus to Christianity. *(MR: Khreshchatyk; Хрещатик.)*

ANDRIYIVSKYY RISE AND THE PODIL DISTRICT. Full of cafes, vendors, and galleries, the cobblestone Andriyivskyy Rise (Андріївский узвіз; Andriyivskyy uzviz) can be reached by walking down Desyatynna from Mikhaylivska Sq. *(MB: Poshtova; Поштова.)* The **Museum of One Street,** Andriyivskyy uzviz 2b, recounts the street's colorful history with a collection of photos and old documents. *(Open Tu-Su noon-6pm. 5hv. 45min. English-language tour 50hv.)* At the corner of Desyatinna and Andriyivskyy uzviz is **St. Andrew's Church.** One block down Andriyivskyy uzviz, steep wooden stairs lead to a great view of **Podil,** Kyiv's oldest district. To the east, the **Chernobyl Museum,** Provulok Khoryva 1, details the nuclear disaster's aftermath. *(Open M-Sa 10am-6pm. Closed last M of each month. 5hv, with ISIC 1hv.)*

ENTERTAINMENT AND NIGHTLIFE

The last Sunday of May brings **Kyiv Days,** with performances all over the city. The **National Philharmonic,** Volodymyrsky uzviz 2, holds regular concerts. (☎278 16 97. *Kasa* open Tu-Su noon-3pm and 4-7pm.) **Shevchenko Opera and Ballet Theater,** Volodymyrska 50, has several shows each week. (MR: Teatralna; Театральна. ☎279 1169. Shows noon, 7pm. Ticket office open M 3-7pm, Tu-Su 11am-2pm and 3-7:30pm.) If you're in town between late spring and fall, don't miss **Dynamo Kyiv,** one of Europe's top soccer teams. (Ticket office in front of stadium. 2-30hv.) On hot days, head to **Hydropark** (Гідропарк), an **amusement park** and **beach** on an island in the Dniper (MR: Hydropark).

Check out *What's On* (www.whatson-kiev.com) and the *Kyiv Post* (www.kyivpost.com) for the latest nightlife listings. Kyiv's popular jazz club, **Artclub 44,** vul. Khreshchatyk 44, is in a courtyard through an unmarked brown door. (☎279 4137. Live music daily 10pm-midnight. Cover Th-Sa 10-50hv. Open daily 10am-2am.) **Eric's Bierstube,** vul. Chervonoarmiyiska 20 (Червоноармійська) draws a crowd of expats and locals. From MB: pl. Lva Tolstoho walk 10m toward Khreshchatyk on vul. Chervonoarmiyiska. At #20, follow the sign that reads "КАФЕ БАР"; cafe bar. (☎235 9472. Beer 5-22hv. M live music. Open daily 8am-2am. Cash only.) **Caribbean Club,** vul. Kominternu 4 (Комінтерну), is packed with salsa experts. (Mixed drinks 26-46hv. W striptease; cover 30hv for men. Cover F-Sa women 30hv, men 50hv. Open daily 6pm-6am.) **Androhyn** (Андрогин), vul. Harmatna 26/2, is a gay-friendly club. (MR: Shulyavska. Cover 20-40hv. Open Tu-Su 7pm-6am.)

LVIV (ЛЬВІВ) ☎80322

Teeming with energy and more affordable than Kyiv, Lviv (pop. 830,000) offers an open invitation to tourists that has gone largely unnoticed in recent years. Those who do visit can meander down cobblestone streets, sip coffee in a cafe, and watch Ukraine's cultural and patriotic center come into its own.

TRANSPORTATION AND PRACTICAL INFORMATION. Trains go from pl. Vokzalna (Вокзальна) to: **Budapest, Hungary** (13hr., 1 per day, 420hv); **Kraków, Poland** (7½hr., every other day, 220hv); **Kyiv** (9hr., 9 per day, 55hv); **Moscow, Russia** (25hr., 3 per day, 210hv); **Odessa** (12hr., 2 per day, 51hv); **Prague, Czech Republic** (24hr., 1 per day, 400hv); **Warsaw, Poland** (13½hr., 1 per day, 230hv). Tickets can be bought at the railway *kasa* at Hnatyuka 20. (Гнатюка; ☎35 25 79. Open M-Sa 8am-2pm and 3-8pm, Su 8am-2pm and 3-6pm.) **Buses** run from the main station, vul. Stryyska 189 (Стрийська; ☎294 98 17) to: **Kraków, Poland** (8-9hr., 1 per day, 98hv) and **Warsaw, Poland** (10hr., 3 per day, 109hv). The English-speaking staff at **Lviv Tourist Info Center,** vul. Pidvalna 3, sells maps. (☎297 57 51; www.tourism.lviv.ua. Open M-F 10am-1pm and 2-6pm.) **Internet Club,** vul. Dudaeva 12, has 24hr. high-speed Internet access (4hv per hr.). For local phone calls from a landline, prefix a "2" to numbers that begin with a "9". **Postal Code:** 79 000.

ACCOMMODATIONS AND FOOD. Most backpackers stay at cheap, clean **Hotel Lviv ❶**, vul. Chornovola 7 (Чорновола), behind the opera house. Take tram #6 from the train station. (☎79 22 72. Singles 55hv, with bath 100hv; doubles 90/140hv; triples 105hv; quads 140/260.) Located where pr. Svobody meets pr. Shevchenko, **Hotel George ❸** (Готель Жорж), pl. Mitskevycha 1, has a helpful reception desk. (☎72 59 52; www.georgehotel.com.ua. Breakfast included. Singles 140hv, with bath 335-430hv; doubles 165/360-455hv. MC/V.) **Veronika ❶** (Вероніка), pr. Shevchenko 21, serves pastries (2-7hv) and coffee. (☎97 81 28. Entrees 10-98hv. Open daily 10am-11pm. V.)

SIGHTS AND ENTERTAINMENT. Climb up the **High Castle Hill** (Високий Замок; Vysokyy Zamok), the former site of the Galician King's Palace, for a panoramic view of Lviv. **Ploschad Rynok,** the historic market square, is surrounded by churches and richly decorated homes. The **History Museum** (Історичний Музей; Istorichnyy Muzey) complex is at pl. Rynok #4, 6, and 24. Exhibits at #4 tell the history of WWII. (Open M-Tu and Th-Su 10am-5:00pm. Each museum 2-3hv.) Walk up vul. Staroyevreiska (Old Jewish Street) to reach the ruins of the **Golden Rose Synagogue,** a center of Jewish culture before its destruction by the Nazis. **Club-Cafe Lyalka** (Клуб-Кафе Лялька), vul. Halytskoho 1, is a popular disco at night. (☎98 08 09. Wine 3-6hv. Cover free-25hv. Open daily 1pm-7am. Cash only). The party at the more pretentious **Millennium,** vul. Chornovola 2, revolves around its dance floor. (☎40 35 91; www.favorite-club.com. Beer 5hv. Cover 30hv. Open T-Su 9pm-4am.)

ODESSA (ОДЕСА) ☎80482

Odessa (pop. 1,100,000) has been blessed by prosperity and cursed with corruption ever since its founding by Catherine the Great in 1794. With a full set of European influences, life in this port town has been kept lively by *mafiosi* and intellectuals, and has inspired writers from Alexander Pushkin to Isaac Babel. Turn right on ul. Preobrazhenskaya, left on ul. Sofiyevskaya (Софиевкая) and walk up two blocks to reach the **Odessa Art Museum** (Художний Музей; Khudozhniy Muzey), ul. Sofiyevskaya 5a, which has a collection of 19th-century art. (☎23 84 62. Open M, W-Su 10:30am-6pm. 2hv.) Odessa's most beautiful street is **ulitsa Pushkinskaya.** The **Pushkin Museum and Memorial** (Литературно-мемориальный Музей Пушкина; Literaturno-memorialnyy Muzey Pushkina) at #13, was the hotel where Pushkin lived during his 1823-1824 exile from St. Petersburg. (Open Tu-Su 10am-5pm. 3.50hv.) Underneath the city is the world's longest series of **catacombs.** During the Nazi occupation, the resistance based itself here; Odessa has established a subterranean **museum** in its honor. FGT (see below) runs 2hr. English-language tours, more affordable with a group. (Guides 150hv, transportation 315hv. Dress warmly.) Odessa's **beaches** are easily accessible. To reach nearby **Lanzheron** (Ланжерон) beach, walk through Shevchenko park or take *marshrutkas* 253, 233, or 2MT. Tram #5 goes to **Arkadiya** (Аркадия), the city's most popular beach.

Buy theater tickets for all shows at the **box office** at ul. Preobrazhenskaya 28. (☎22 02 45. Open daily 10am-5pm.) At the end of ul. Rishelyevskaya, the **Opera and Ballet Theater** (Театр Оперы и Балета; Teatr Opery i Baleta) performs almost daily. Restaurants, cafes, and bars stay open late on **ulitsa Deribasovskaya,** with music from techno to Slavic folk. Street performers gather on **ulitsa Derbasovskaya. Arkadiya** beach attracts dancers nightly to its open-air discos.

Private rooms (from 30hv) are the cheapest option. Hosts solicit customers at the train station. **Hotel Passage ❷** (Пассаж), ul. Preobrazhenskaya 34, is the best budget hotel. (☎22 48 49. Singles 55hv, with bath 95-295hv; doubles 85/125-295hv. Cash only.) The cafeteria **Zharu Paru ❶** (Жару Пару), ul. Grechevskaya 45

(Гречевская), serves excellent Ukrainian fare. (☎22 44 30. Entrees 5-6hv. Open daily 8am-10pm. Cash only.) **Pulcinella ❷**, ul. Lanzheronovskaya 17 (Ланжероновская), is a brick-oven pizzeria. (Open daily 11am-11pm. MC/V.)

Trains run from pl. Privokzalnaya 2 (Привокзальная; tickets ☎005), at the northern end of ul. Pushkinskaya, to: Kyiv (10hr., 4 per day, 57hv); Moscow, Russia (25hr., 2-4 per day, 215hv); Warsaw, Poland (24hr., even-numbered days, 374hv). To reach the bus station, take tram #5 to the last stop. **Buses** run from ul. Kolontayevskaya 58 (Колонтаевская) to Kyiv (8-10hr., 8 per day, 63hv). **FGT Travel,** ul. Deribasovskaya 13 (Дерибасовская), in Hotel Frapolli, provides info. (☎37 52 01; www.odessapassage.com. Open daily 8:30am-8pm.) **Postal Code:** 65 001.

YALTA (ЯЛТА) ☎80654

A former rest spot for the Russian elite, Yalta's tree-lined avenues and open sea welcome visitors to the city that inspired Chekhov and Tolstoy. Many of Yalta's best sights are located outside town. **Massandra Palace** was once housed the tsars before Stalin moved in. Take trolley #2 from Yalta to Massandra (Массандра), cross the street, and go uphill until you see the sign marked "Дворец". (☎32 17 28. Open July-Aug. Tu-Su 9am-6pm; May-June and Sept.-Oct. Tu-Su 9am-5pm; Nov.-Apr. W-Su 9am-4pm. 15hv.) The **Great Livadiya Palace,** which hosted the Yalta Conference in WWII, and **Vorontsov Palace** are also worthwhile daytrips. At ul. Kirova 112, explore the **white dacha** that Anton Chekhov built in 1899. Take *marshrutka* #8 from Kinoteatr Spartak on ul. Pushkinskaya. (☎39 49 47. Open June-Sept. Tu-Su 10am-5:15pm; Oct.-May W-Su 10am-4pm. Closed last day of the month. 15hv.) Follow the shore away from the harbor to reach Yalta's **beaches** (2-5hv).

Reserve at least two months ahead for July and August. If you arrive without a booking in summer, negotiate with locals at the bus station or contact **Eugenia Travel** (☎27 18 29) to rent an apartment (150hv). **Gostinitsa Krym ❶**, ul. Moskovskaya 1/6, between pl. Lenina and pl. Sovetskaya, is cheap and central. (☎27 17 10. Singles 30-210hv; doubles 40-310hv.) **Pension T. M. M. ❸**, ul. Lesi Ukrayinki 16, has views of the sea and rooms with balcony, TV, and bath. (☎23 09 50; www.firmatmm.com.ua. 3 meals included. Singles 160hv; doubles 300-415hv.) Several **cafeterias** (столовая; stolovaya) in the center serve cheap fare (10-20hv); **Stolovaya Krym ❶**, next to Gostinitsa Krym, is one of the better ones. (Open daily 9am-9pm.) **Cafe Voschod ❷**, ul. Ignatenko 2, near pl. Sovetskaya, serves Turkish and Russian cuisine. (☎23 39 43. Open June-Sept. 24hr.; Oct.-May daily 8am-midnight.) Overlooking the waterfront is the nightclub **Tornado,** nab. Lenina 11, upstairs through the arch and to the left. (☎32 20 36. Beer 8hv. Cover 50-100hv. Open July-Sept. daily 10pm-5am; Oct.-Nov. Th-Sa 10am-5pm; Dec.-May F-Sa 10am-5pm.)

Yalta is not accessible by train. **Buses** run from ul. Moskovskaya to Kyiv (17½hr., 2 per day, 110-150hv) and Odessa (14½hr., 2 per day, 70-100hv). **Eugenia Travel,** ul. Rusvelta 10, offers tours and helps book rooms. (☎27 18 29; www.eugeniatours.com.ua. English spoken. Open M-F 9am-6pm.) **Postal Code:** 98 600.

APPENDIX

LANGUAGE PHRASEBOOK

CYRILLIC ALPHABET

Bulgaria and **Ukraine** use variations of the Russian Cyrillic alphabet.

CYRILLIC	ENGLISH	PRONOUNCE	CYRILLIC	ENGLISH	PRONOUNCE
А а	a	*ah* as in Prague	Р р	r	*r* as in **r**evolution
Б б	b	*b* as in **B**osnia	С с	s	*s* as in **S**erbia
В в	v	*v* as in **V**olga	Т т	t	*t* as in **t**ank
Г г	g	*g* as in **G**lasnost	У у	u	*oo* as in **Bu**dapest
Д д	d	*d* as in **d**ictatorship	Ф ф	f	*f* as in **F**ormer USSR
Е е	e	*yeh* as in **yellow**	Х х	kh	*kh* as in Ba**ch**
Ё ё	yo	*yo* as in **yo!**	Ц ц	ts	*ts* as in Let'**s** Go
Ж ж	zh	*zh* as in mira**ge**	Ч ч	ch	*ch* as in Khrush**ch**ev
З з	z	*z* as in communi**s**m	Ш ш	sh	*sh* as in Khru**sh**chev
И и	i	*ee* as in Gr**ee**k	Щ щ	shch	*shch* in Khru**shch**ev
Й й	y	*y* as in bo**y** or ke**y**	Ъ ъ	(hard sign)	(not pronounced)
К к	k	*k* as in **K**remlin	Ы ы	y	*y* as in s**i**lver
Л л	l	*l* as in **L**enin	Ь ь	(soft sign)	(not pronounced)
М м	m	*m* as in **M**acedonia	Э э	e	*eh* as in **E**stonia
Н н	n	*n* as in **n**uclear	Ю ю	yu	*yoo* as in **U**kraine
О о	o	*o* as in Cr**o**atia	Я я	ya	*yah* as in **Ya**lta
П п	p	*p* as in **P**oland			

GREEK ALPHABET

SYMBOL	NAME	PRONOUNCE	SYMBOL	NAME	PRONOUNCE
α Α	alpha	*a* as in f**a**ther	ν Ν	nu	*n* as in **n**et
β Β	beta	*v* as in **v**elvet	ξ Ξ	xi	*x* as in mi**x**
γ Γ	gamma	*y* as in **yo** or *g* as in **go**	ο Ο	omicron	*o* as in r**o**w
δ Δ	delta	*th* as in **th**ere	π Π	pi	*p* as in **p**eace
ε Ε	epsilon	*e* as in j**e**t	ρ Ρ	rho	*r* as in **r**oll
ζ Ζ	zeta	*z* as in **z**ebra	σ Σ	sigma	*s* as in **s**ense
η Η	eta	*ee* as in qu**ee**n	τ Τ	tau	*t* as in **t**ent
θ Θ	theta	*th* as in **th**ree	υ Υ	upsilon	*ee* as in gr**ee**n
ι Ι	iota	*ee* as in tr**ee**	φ Φ	phi	*f* as in **f**og
κ Κ	kappa	*k* as in **k**ite	χ Χ	chi	*h* as in **h**orse
λ Λ	lambda	*l* as in **l**and	ψ Ψ	psi	*ps* as in oo**ps**
μ Μ	mu	*m* as in **m**oose	ω Ω	omega	*o* as in Let's G**o**

CROATIAN

ENGLISH	CROATIAN	PRONOUNCE	ENGLISH	CROATIAN	PRONOUNCE
Yes/No	Da/Ne	da/neh	**Train/Bus**	Vlak/Autobus	vlahk/aw-TOH-bus
Please	Molim	MO-leem	**Station**	Kolodvor	KOH-loh-dvor
Thank you	Hvala lijepa	HVAH-la lye-pa	**Airport**	Zračna Luka	ZRA-chna lu-kah
Good day	Dobardan	Do-bar-DAHN	**Ticket**	Kartu	KAHR-too
Goodbye	Zbogom	ZBO-gohm	**Taxi**	Taksi	TAH-ksi
Sorry/Excuse me	Oprostite	o-PRO-sti-teh	**Hotel**	Hotel	HOH-tel
Help!	U pomoć!	OO po-moch!	**Bathroom**	WC	VAY-tsay
I'm lost (m/f)	Izgubljen(a) sam	iz-GUB-lye-n(a) sahm	**Open/Closed**	Otvoreno/ Zatvoreno	OHT-voh-reh-noh/ZAHT-voh-reh-noh
Police	Policija	po-LEE-tsee-ya	**Left/Right**	Lijevo/Desno	lee-YEH-voh/ DEHS-noh
Embassy	Ambasada	ahm-bah-sah-da	**Bank**	Banka	BAHN-kah
Passport	Putovnica	POO-toh-vnee-tsah	**Exchange**	Mjenjačnica	myehn-YAHCH-nee-tsah
Doctor/Hospital	Liječnik/Bolnica	li-YECH-nik/bol-NI-tsa	**Grocery/Market**	Trgovina	TER-goh-vee-nah
Pharmacy	Ljekarna	lye-KHAR-na	**Post Office**	Pošta	POSH-tah

ENGLISH	CROATIAN	PRONOUNCE
Where is...?	Gdje je...?	GDYE yeh
How much does this cost?	Koliko to košta?	KO-li-koh toh KOH-shta
When is the next...?	Kada polazi sljedeći...?	ka-DA po-LA-zi SLYE-de-tchi
Do you have (a vacant room)?	Imate li (slobodne sobe)?	ee-MAH-teh lee (SLOH-boh-dneh SOH-beh)
I would like...	Želim...	ZHE-lim...
I don't eat...	Ne jedem...	ne YEH-dem
Do you speak English?	Govorite li engleski?	GO-vor-i-teh lee eng-LEH-ski
I don't speak Croatian.	Ne govorim hrvatski.	neh goh-VOH-reem KHR-va-tskee

CZECH

ENGLISH	CZECH	PRONOUNCE	ENGLISH	CZECH	PRONOUNCE
Yes/No	Ano/Ne	AH-no/neh	**Train/Bus**	Vlak/Autobus	vlahk/OUT-oh-boos
Please	Prosím	PROH-seem	**Station**	Nádraží	NA-drah-zhee
Thank you	Děkuji	DYEH-koo-yih	**Airport**	Letiště	LEH-tish-tyeh
Hello	Dobrý den	DO-bree den	**Ticket**	Lístek	LIS-tek
Goodbye	Nashledanou	NAH-sleh-dah-noh-oo	**Taxi**	Taxi	TEHK-see
Sorry/Excuse me	Promiňte	PROH-mihn-teh	**Hotel**	Hotel	HOH-tel
Help!	Pomoc!	POH-mots	**Bathroom**	WC	VEE-TSEE
I'm lost. (m/f)	Zabloudil(a) jsem.	ZAH-bloh-dyil-(ah) sem.	**Open/Closed**	Otevřeno/ Zavřeno	O-te-zheno/ZAV-rzhen-o
Police	Policie	PO-lits-iye	**Left/Right**	Vlevo/Vpravo	VLE-voh/VPRAH-voh
Embassy	Velvyslanectví	VEHL-vi-slah-nehts-vee	**Bank**	Banka	BAN-ka

APPENDIX

ENGLISH	CZECH	PRONOUNCE	ENGLISH	CZECH	PRONOUNCE
Passport	Cestovní pas	TSEH-stohv-nee pahs	**Exchange**	Směnárna	smyeh-NAR-na
Doctor	Lékař	LEK-arzh	**Grocery**	Potraviny	PO-tra-vee-nee
Pharmacy	Lékárna	LEE-khaar-nah	**Post Office**	Pošta	POSH-tah

ENGLISH	CZECH	PRONOUNCE
Where is...?	Kde je...?	k-DEH
How much does this cost?	Kolik to stojí?	KOH-lihk STOH-yee
When is the next...?	Kdy jede příští...?	gdi YEH-deh przh-EESH-tyee
Do you have (a vacant room)?	Máte (volný pokoj)?	MAA-teh (VOHL-nee POH-koy)
I would like...	Prosím...	PROH-seem
I do not eat...	Nejím...	NEH-yeem
Do you speak English?	Mluvíte anglicky?	MLOO-vit-eh ahng-GLIT-ski
I don't speak Czech.	Nemluvim Česky.	NEH-mloo-veem CHESS-kee

FINNISH

ENGLISH	FINNISH	PRONOUNCE	ENGLISH	FINNISH	PRONOUNCE
Yes/No	Kyllä/Ei	KEW-la/ay	**Ticket**	Lipun	LIP-ooh
Please	Olka hyvä	OHL-ka HEW-va	**Train/Bus**	Juna/Bussi	YU-nuh/BUS-si
Thank you	Kiitos	KEE-tohss	**Boat**	Vene	VEH-nay
Hello	Hei	hay	**Departures**	Lähtevät	lah-teh-VAHT
Goodbye	Näkemiin	NA-keh-meen	**Market**	Tori	TOH-ree
Sorry/Excuse me	Anteeksi	ON-take-see	**Hotel/Hostel**	Hotelli/Retkeily-maja	HO-tehl-lee/reht-kayl-oo-MAH-yuh
Help!	Apua!	AH-poo-ah	**Pharmacy**	Apteekki	UHP-teehk-kee
Police	Poliisi	POH-lee-see	**Bathroom**	Vessa	VEHS-sah
Embassy	Suurlähetystö	SOOHR LA-heh-toos-ter	**Telephone**	Puhelin	POO-heh-lin
I'm lost!	Olen kadok-sissa!	Oh-lehn cou-doc-sissa	**Open/Closed**	Auki/Kiinni	Ouh-kee/Keen-ne
Railway sta-tion	Rautatieasema	Row-tah-tiah-ah-seh-ma	**Hospital**	Sairaala	Saih-raah-lah
Bank	Pankki	PAHNK-kih	**Left/Right**	Vasen/oikea	VAH-sen/
Currency exchange	Rahanvaihto-piste	RAA-han-vyeh-tow-pees-teh	**Post Office**	Posti	PAUS-teeh
Airport	lentokenttä	LEH-toh-kehnt-tah			

ENGLISH	FINNISH	PRONOUNCE
Where is...?	Missä on...?	MEE-sah OHN
How do I get to...?	Miten pääsen...?	MEE-ten PA-sen
How much does this cost?	Paljonko se maksaa?	PAHL-yon-ko SEH MOCK-sah
I'd like to buy...	Haluaisin ostaa...	HUH-loo-ay-sin OS-tuh
Do you speak English?	Puhutteko englantia?	POO-hoot-teh-kaw ENG-lan-tee-ah
When is the next...?	Milloin on seuraava...?	MEEHL-loyhn OHN SEUH-Raah-vah
I don't speak Norwegian.	En puhu suomea.	EHN POO-Hoo SUA-meh-ah
I'm allergic to/I cannot eat...	En voi syödä ...	EHN VOY SEW-dah

APPENDIX

FRENCH

ENGLISH	FRENCH	PRONOUNCE	ENGLISH	FRENCH	PRONOUNCE
Hello	Bonjour	bohn-ZHOOR	**Exchange**	L'échange	lay-SHANZH
Please	S'il vous plaît	see voo PLAY	**Grocery**	L'épicerie	lay-PEES–ree
Thank you	Merci	mehr-SEE	**Market**	Le marché	leuh ma-RZH-chay
Excuse me	Excusez-moi	ex-KU-zay MWAH	**Police**	La police	la poh-LEES
Yes/No	Oui/Non	wee/nohn	**Embassy**	L'ambassade	lahm-ba-SAHD
Goodbye	Au revoir	oh ruh-VWAHR	**Passport**	Le passeport	leuh pass-POR
Help!	Au secours!	oh-skoor!	**Post Office**	La poste	la POHST-e
I'm lost	Je suis perdu	zhe SWEE pehr-doo	**One-way**	Le billet simple	leuh bee-AY SAMP
Train/Bus	Le train/Le bus	leuh tran/leuh boos	**Round-trip**	Le billet aller-retour	leuh bee-AY a-LAY-re-TOOR
Station	La gare	la gahr	**Ticket**	Le billet	leuh bee-AY
Airport	L'aéroport	la-ehr-o-POR	**Single room**	Une chambre simple	oon SHAM-br samp
Hotel	L'hôtel	lo-TEL	**Double room**	Une chambre pour deux	oon SHAM-br poor duh
Hostel	L'auberge	lo-BERZH	**With shower**	Avec la douche	a-VEK la DOOSH
Bathroom	La salle de bain	la SAL de BAN	**Taxi**	Le taxi	leuh tax-EE
Open/Closed	Ouvert/Fermé	oo-VEHR/fer-MAY	**Ferry**	Le bac	leuh bak
Doctor	Le médecin	leuh mehd-SEN	**Tourist office**	Le bureau de tourisme	leuh byur-OH de toor-EESM
Hospital	L'hôpital	loh-pee-TAL	**Town hall**	L'hôtel de ville	lo-TEL de VEEL
Pharmacy	La pharmacie	la far-ma-SEE	**Vegetarian**	Végétarien	vay-jay-ta-ree-EHN
Left/Right	À gauche/À droite	a GOSH/a DWAT	**Kosher/Halal**	Kascher/Halal	ka-SHAY/ha-lal
Straight	Tout droit	too DWA	**Newsstand**	Le tabac	leuh ta-BA
Turn	Tournez	toor-NAY	**Cigarette**	La cigarette	la see-ga-RET
Bank	La banque	la bahnk	**Condom**	Le préservatif	leuh pray-sehr-va-TEEF

ENGLISH	FRENCH	PRONOUNCE
Do you speak English?	Parlez-vous anglais?	PAR-lay VOO ahn-GLAY
Where is...?	Où se trouve...?	OO s'TRHOOV
When is the next...?	À quelle heure part le prochain...?	ah KEL ur par leuh PRO-chan
How much does this cost?	Ça fait combien?	SAH fay com-bee-EN
Do you have rooms available?	Avez-vous des chambres dis-ponibles?	AV-ay VOO day SHAM-br DEES-pon-IB-bl
I would like ...	Je voudrais...	zhe voo-DRAY
I don't speak French.	Je ne parle pas Français.	zhe neuh PARL pah FRAWN-say
I'm allergic to...	Je suis allergique à...	zhe SWEE al-ehr-ZHEEK a
I love you.	Je t'aime.	zhe TEM

APPENDIX

GERMAN

Every letter is pronounced. Consonants are pronounced as in English with the following exceptions: ***j*** is pronounced as "y"; ***qu*** is pronounced "kv"; a single ***s*** is pronounced "z"; ***v*** is pronounced "f"; ***w*** is pronounced "v"; and ***z*** is pronounced "ts." ***Sch*** is "sh"; ***st*** is "sht"; and ***sp*** is "shp." The ***ch*** sound, as in "ich" ("I") and "nicht" ("not"), is tricky; you can substitute a "sh." The letter ß (ess-tset) spells a double "s"; pronounce it "ss."

ENGLISH	GERMAN	PRONOUNCE	ENGLISH	GERMAN	PRONOUNCE
Yes/No	Ja/Nein	yah/nein	**Train/Bus**	Zug/Bus	tsoog/boos
Please	Bitte	BIH-tuh	**Station**	Bahnhof	BAHN-hohf
Thank you	Danke	DAHNG-kuh	**Airport**	Flughafen	FLOOG-hah-fen
Hello	Hallo	HAH-lo	**Taxi**	Taxi	TAHK-see
Goodbye	Auf Wiedersehen	owf VEE-der-zayn	**Ticket**	Fahrkarte	FAR-kar-tuh
Excuse me	Entschuldigung	ent-SHOOL-digung	**Departure**	Abfahrt	OBB-fart
Help!	Hilfe!	HIL-fuh!	**One-way**	Einfache	AYHN-fah-kuh
I'm lost.	Ich habe mich verlaufen.	Ish HAH-buh mish fer-LAU-fun	**Round-trip**	Rundreise	RUND-RYE-seh
Police	Polizei	poh-leet-ZAI	**Reservation**	Reservierung	reh-zer-VEER-ung
Embassy	Botschaft	BOAT-shaft	**Ferry**	Fährschiff	FAYHR-shiff
Passport	Reisepass	RYE-zeh-pahss	**Bank**	Bank	bahnk
Doctor/Hospital	Arzt/Krankenhaus	AHRTZT/KRANKen-house	**Exchange**	Wechseln	VEHK-zeln
Pharmacy	Apotheke	AH-po-TAY-kuh	**Grocery**	Lebensmittelgeschäft	LAY-bens-mit-telguh-SHEFT
Hotel/Hostel	Hotel/Jugendherberge	ho-TEL/YOO-gend-air-BAIR-guh	**Tourist office**	Touristbüro	TU-rist-byur-oh
Single room	Einzellzimmer	EIN-tsel-tsim-muh	**Post Office**	Postamt	POST-ahmt
Double room	Doppelzimmer	DOP-pel-tsim-muh	**Old town/City center**	Altstadt	AHLT-shtat
Dorm	Schlafsaal	SHLAF-zahl	**Vegetarian**	Vegetarier	veh-geh-TAYR-ee-er
With shower	Mit dusche	mitt DOO-shuh	**Vegan**	Veganer	VAY-gan-er
Bathroom	Badezimmer	BAH-deh-tsim-muh	**Kosher/Halal**	Koscher/Halaal	KOH-shayr/hah-LAAL
Open/Closed	Geöffnet/Geschlossen	geh-UHF-net/geh-shlos-sen	**Nuts/Milk**	Nüsse/Milch	NYOO-seh/milsh
Left/Right	Links/Rechts	links/rekhts	**Bridge**	Brücke	BRUKE-eh
Straight	Geradeaus	geh-RAH-de-OWS	**Castle**	Schloß	shloss
(To) Turn	Drehen	DRAY-ehn	**Square**	Platz	plahtz

ENGLISH	GERMAN	PRONOUNCE
Where is...?	Wo ist...?	vo ist
How do I get to...?	Wie komme ich nach...?	vee KOM-muh ish NAHKH
How much does that cost?	Wieviel kostet das?	VEE-feel KOS-tet das
Do you have...?	Haben Sie...?	HOB-en zee
I would like...	Ich möchte...	ish MERSH-teh
I'm allergic to...	Ich bin zu ___ allergisch.	ish bihn tsoo ___ ah-LEHR-gish
Do you speak English?	Sprechen sie Englisch?	SHPREK-en zee EHNG-lish
I do not speak German.	Ich spreche kein Deutsch.	ish-SHPREK-eh kine DOYCH

ENGLISH	GERMAN	PRONOUNCE
Leave me alone or I'll call the police!	Lassen sie mich in ruhe oder ich rufe die polizei!	LAH-sen see mish in ROO-eh OH-dur ish ROO-fuh dee poh-leet-ZAI
I'm waiting for my boyfriend/ husband.	Ich warte auf meinen Freund/ Mann.	Ish VAHR-tuh owf MYN-en froynd/mahn

GREEK

ENGLISH	GREEK	PRONOUNCE	ENGLISH	GREEK	PRONOUNCE
Yes/No	Ναι/Οχι	NEH/OH-hee	**Train/Bus**	Τραινο/ Λεωφορειο	TREH-no/leh-o-fo-REE-o
Please	Παρακαλώ	pah-rah-kah-LO	**Ferry**	Πλοιο	PLEE-o
Thank you	Ευχαριστώ	ef-khah-ree-STO	**Station**	Σταθμοζ	stath-MOS
Hello/Good-bye	Γεια σας	YAH-sas	**Airport**	Αεροδρομιο	ah-e-ro-DHRO-mee-o
Sorry/Excuse me	Συγνομη	sig-NO-mee	**Taxi**	Ταξι	tah-XEE
Help!	ΒοητηειαΆ!	vo-EE-tee-ah	**Hotel/Hostel**	Ξενοδοχειο	kse-no-dho-HEE-o
I'm lost	Εχω χαθει	EH-o ha-THI	**Room to let**	Δωματια	do-MA-tee-ah
Police	Αστυνομεια	as-tee-no-MEE-a	**Bathroom**	Τουαλεττα	tou-ah-LET-ta
Embassy	Πρεσβεια	prez-VEE-ah	**Open/closed**	Ανοικτο/ Κλειστο	ah-nee-KTO/ klee-STO
Passport	Διαβατηριο	dhee-ah-vah-TEE-ree-o	**Left/Right**	Αριστερα/ Δεξια	aris-te-RA/ de-XIA
Doctor	Γιατροσ	yah-TROSE	**Bank**	Τραπεζα	TRAH-peh-zah
Pharmacy	Φαρμακειο	fahr-mah-KEE-o	**Exchange**	Ανταλλασσω	an-da-LAS-so
Post Office	Ταχυδρομιο	ta-chi-dhro-MI-o	**Market**	Αγορα	ah-go-RAH

ENGLISH	GREEK	PRONOUNCE
Where is...?	Που ειναι...?	poo-EE-neh
How much does this cost?	Ποσο κανει?	PO-so KAH-nee
Do you have (a vacant room)?	Μηπῶς εχετε (ελευθερα δωμάτια)?	mee-POSE EK-he-teh (e-LEF-the-ra dho-MA-ti-a)
I would like...	Θα ηθελα...	THAH EE-the-lah
Do you speak English?	Μιλάς αγγλικά?	mee-LAHS ahn-glee-KAH
I don't speak Greek.	Δεν μιλαώ ελληνικά.	DTHEN mee-LOW el-lee-nee-KAH

HUNGARIAN

ENGLISH	HUNGARIAN	PRONOUNCE	ENGLISH	HUNGARIAN	PRONOUNCE
Yes/No	Igen/Nem	EE-ghen/Nehm	**Train/Bus**	Vonat/Autóbusz	VAW-noht/OW-toh-boos
Please	Kérem	KAY-rehm	**Station**	Pályaudvar	pah-yoh-OOT-vahr
Thank you	Köszönöm	KUH-suh-nuhm	**Airport**	Repülőtér	rehp-ewlu-TAYR
Hello	Szervusz	SAYHR-voose	**Ticket**	Jegyet	YEHD-eht
Goodbye	Viszontlátásra	Vi-sohnt-lah-tah-shraw	**Tram**	Villamos	vil-LAH-mosh
Excuse me	Elnézést	EHL-nay-zaysht	**Hotel**	Szálloda	SAH-law-dah
Help!	Segitség!	she-GHEET-sheg	**Toilet**	WC	VAY-tsay
I'm lost.	Eltévedtem.	el-TEH-ved-tem	**Open/Closed**	Nyitva/Zárva	NYEET-vah/ ZAHR-vuh
Police	Rendőrség	REN-dur-shayg	**Left/Right**	Bal/Jobb	bol/yowb
Embassy	Követséget	ker-vet-SHE-get	**Bank**	Bank	bohnk

APPENDIX

ENGLISH	HUNGARIAN	PRONOUNCE	ENGLISH	HUNGARIAN	PRONOUNCE
Passport	Az útlevelemet	ahz OOT-leh-veh-leh-meht	**Exchange**	Pénzaváltó	pehn-zah-VAHL-toh
Doctor/Hospital	Orvos/Kórház	OR-vosh/kohr-HAAZ	**Grocery**	Élelmiszerbolt	AY-lel-meser-balt
Pharmacy	Gyógyszertár	DYAW-dyser-tar	**Post Office**	Posta	pawsh-tuh

ENGLISH	HUNGARIAN	PRONOUNCE
Where is...?	Hol van...?	hawl von
How much does this cost?	Mennyibe kerül?	MEHN-ye-behe KEH-rewl
When is the next...?	Mikor indul a következő...?	mi-KOR in-DUL ah ker-VET-ke-zoer
Do you have (a vacant room)?	Van üres (szoba)?	vahn ew-REHSH (SAH-bah)
Can I have...?	Kaphatok...?	KAH-foht-tohk
I do not eat...	Nem eszem...	nem EH-sem
Do you speak English?	Beszél angolul?	BESS-ayl ON-goal-ool
I don't speak Hungarian.	Nem tudok magyarul.	Nehm TOO-dawk MAH-dyah-rool

ITALIAN

ENGLISH	ITALIAN	PRONOUNCE	ENGLISH	ITALIAN	PRONOUNCE
Hello(informal/formal)	Ciao/ Buongiorno	chow/ bwohn-johr-noh	**Bank**	La banca	lah bahn-KAH
Please	Per favore/Per piacere	pehr fah-VOH-reh/pehr pyah-CHAY-reh	**Exchange**	Il cambio	eel CAHM-bee-oh
Thank you	Grazie	GRAHT-see-yeh	**Grocery**	Gli alimentari	li ah-li-mehn-TA-ri
Sorry/Excuse me	Mi dispiace/ Scusi	mee dees-PYAH-cheh/SKOO-zee	**Police**	La Polizia	lah po-LEET-ZEE-ah
Yes/No	Sì/No	see/no	**Embassy**	L'Ambasciata	lahm-bah-shee-AH-tah
Goodbye	Arrivederci	ah-ree-veh-DAIR-chee	**Passport**	Il passaporto	eel pahs-sah-POHR-toh
Help!	Aiuto!	ah-YOO-toh	**Post Office**	L'ufficio postale	loof-FEETCH-io pohs-TAL-e
I'm lost	Sono perso	So-noh PERH-so	**One-way**	Solo andata	SO-lo ahn-DAH-tah
Train/Bus	Il treno/Il autobus	eel TRAY-no/ aow-toh-BOOS	**Round-trip**	Andata e ritorno	ahn-DAH-tah ay ree-TOHR-noh
Station	La stazione	lah staht-see-YOH-neh	**Ticket**	Il biglietto	eel beel-YEHT-toh
Airport	L'aeroporto	LAYR-o-PORT-o	**Single room**	Una camera singola	OO-nah CAH-meh-rah SEEN-goh-lah
Hotel/Hostel	L'albergo	lal-BEHR-go	**Double room**	Una camera doppia	OO-nah CAH-meh-rah DOH-pee-yah
Bathroom	Un gabinetto/ Un bagno	oon gah-bee-NEHT-toh/oon BAHN-yoh	**With shower**	Con doccia	kohn DOH-cha
Open/Closed	Aperto/Chiuso	ah-PAIR-toh/ KYOO-zoh	**Taxi**	Il tassì	eel tahs-SEE
Doctor	Il medico	eel MEH-dee-koh	**Ferry**	Il traghetto	eel tra-GHEHT-toh
Hospital	L'ospedale	lohs-sped-DAL-e	**Tourist office**	L'Azienda Promozione Turistica	lah-tzi-EHN-da pro-mo-tzi-O-nay tur-EES-tee-kah

ENGLISH	ITALIAN	PRONOUNCE	ENGLISH	ITALIAN	PRONOUNCE
Pharmacy	La farmacia	lah far-mah-SEE-ah	**Vegetarian**	Vegetariano	ve-ge-tar-i-AN-o
Left/Right	La sinistra/ destra	lah see-NEE-strah/DEH-strah	**Kosher/Halal**	Kasher/Halal	KA-sher/HA-lal
Straight	Sempre diritto	SEHM-pray DREET-toh	**Cover charge**	Il coperto	eel koh-PEHR-toh
Turn	Gira a	JEE-rah ah	**Bill**	Il conto	eel COHN-toh
Stop	Ferma/ Smetta	FEHR-mah/ SMEHT-tah	**Tip**	La mancia	lah MAHN-chee-yah

ENGLISH	ITALIAN	PRONOUNCE
Do you speak English?	Parla inglese?	PAHR-lah een-GLAY-zeh
Where is...?	Dov'è...?	doh-VEH
When is the next...?	A che ora è la prossima...?	AH keh OH-rah eh lah pross-SIM-a
How much does this cost?	Quanto costa?	KWAN-toh CO-stah
Do you have rooms available?	Hai camere libere?	I CAH-mer-reh LEE-ber-eh
I would like...	Vorrei...	VOH-ray
I don't speak Italian.	Non parlo italiano.	nohn PARL-loh ee-tahl-YAH-noh
I'm allergic to...	Ho delle allergie...	OH DEHL-leh ahl-lair-JEE-eh

LITHUANIAN

ENGLISH	LITHUANIAN	PRONOUNCE	ENGLISH	LITHUANIAN	PRONOUNCE
Yes/no	Taip/ne	TAYE-p/NEH	**Train/Bus**	Traukinys/auto-busas	TROW-kin-ees/ ow-to-BOO-sahs
Please	Prašau	prah-SHAU	**Station**	Stotis	STOH-tees
Thank you	Ačiū	AH-chyoo	**Airport**	Oro uostas	OH-roh oo-OH-stahs
Hello	Labas	LAH-bahss	**Ticket**	Bilietas	BEE-lee-tahs
Goodbye	Viso gero	VEE-soh GEh-roh	**Hotel**	Viešbutis	vee-esh-BOO-tis
Sorry/excuse me	Atsiprašau	aHT-sih-prh-SHAU	**Bathroom**	Tualetas	too-ah-LEH-tas
Help!	Gelbėkite!	GYEL-behk-ite	**Open/Closed**	Atidarytas/ uždarytas	ah-ti-DAH-ri-tas/ oozh-DAH-ri-tas
Police	Policija	po-LEET-siya	**Exchange**	Valiutos keiti-mas	vali-OOT-os kay-TEE-mahs
Market	Turgus	TOORG-us	**Post Office**	Paštas	PAHSH-tahs

ENGLISH	LITHUANIAN	PRONOUNCE
Where is...?	Kur yra...?	Koor ee-RAH
How much does this cost?	Kiek kainuoja?	KEE-yek KYE-new-oh-yah
Do you speak English?	Ar kalbate angliškai?	AHR KULL-buh-teh AHN-gleesh-kye
I do not speak Lithuanian.	Aš nekalbu lietuviškai	ash ne-KAL-boo lut-VEESH-ki

NORWEGIAN

ENGLISH	NORWEGIAN	PRONOUNCE	ENGLISH	NORWEGIAN	PRONOUNCE
Yes/No	Ja/Nei	yah/nay	**Ticket**	Billett	bee-LEHT
Please	Vær så snill	vay sho SNEEL	**Train/Bus**	Toget/Buss	TOR-guh/büs
Thank you	Takk	tuhk	**Airport**	Lufthavn	LUFT-hahn
Hello	Goddag	gud-DAHG	**Departures**	Avgang	AHV-gahng
Goodbye	Ha det bra	HUH deh brah	**Market**	Torget	TOHR-geh

APPENDIX

ENGLISH	NORWEGIAN	PRONOUNCE	ENGLISH	NORWEGIAN	PRONOUNCE
Sorry/Excuse me	Unnskyld	ÜN-shül	**Hotel/Hostel**	Hotell/Vandrerhjem	hoo-TEHL/VAN-drair-yaim
Help!	Hjelp!	yehlp	**Pharmacy**	Apotek	ah-pu-TAYK
Police	Politit	po-lee-TEE-uh	**Toilets**	Toalettene	tuah-LEHT-tuh-nuh
Embassy	Ambassade	uhm-bah-SAH-duh	**City center**	Sentrum	SEHN-trum
I'm lost!	Jeg har gätt meg bort!	Yeh haar got meh boo't	**Open/Closed**	Åpen/Stengt	AW-pen/Stengt
Railway station	Jernbanestasjon	YEH-'N-baa-ner-stah-shuh-nern	**Hospital**	Sykehus	Shuck-hoos
Bank	Bank	Banhk	**Left/Right**	Venstre/Høyre	VEHN-stre/Huhr-uh
Currency exchange	Vekslingskontor	VEHK-shlings-koon-toohr	**Post Office**	Postkontor	POST-koon-toohr

ENGLISH	NORWEGIAN	PRONOUNCE
Where is...?	Hvor er...?	VORR ayr
How do I get to...?	Hvordan kommer jeg til...?	voor-duhn KOM-morr yay teel
How much is...?	Hvor mye koster det...?	vorr moo-yuh KOS-tor deh
Do you speak English?	Snakker du engelsk?	sna-koh du EHNG-olsk
When is the...?	När gär...?	Nor gawr...?
I don't speak Norwegian.	Jeg snakker ikke norsk.	Yeh SNAH-kerr IK-ker noshk
Do you have any vegetarian dishes?	Har dere noen vegetariske retter?	Haar DAY-rer NUH-ern veh-ger-TAA–risk-er REH-terr?
Do you have any vacancies?	Har dere noen ledige rom?	Haar DAY-rer NUH-ern LAY-dee-yer room?

POLISH

ENGLISH	POLISH	PRONOUNCE	ENGLISH	POLISH	PRONOUNCE
Yes/No	Tak/Nie	tahk/nyeh	**Train/Bus**	Pociąg/Autobus	POH-chawnk/ow-TOH-booss
Please	Proszę	PROH-sheh	**Station**	Dworzec	DVOH-zhets
Thank you	Dziękuję	jen-KOO-yeh	**Airport**	Lotnisko	loht-NEE-skoh
Hello	Cześć	cheshch	**Ticket**	Bilet	BEE-leht
Goodbye	Do widzenia	doh veedz-EN-yah	**Hostel**	Schronisko młodzieżowe	srah-NIHS-kah mwa-jee-eh-SHAH-veh
Sorry/Excuse me	Przepraszam	psheh-PRAH-shahm	**Bathroom**	Toaleta	toh-uh-LEH-tuh
Help!	Na pomoc!	nah POH-mots!	**Open/Closed**	Otwarty/Zamknięty	ot-FAHR-tih/zahmk-NYENT-ih
I'm lost (m/f)	Zgubiłem/am się	zgoo-BEE-wem/wam she	**Left/Right**	Lewo/Prawo	LEH-voh/PRAH-voh
Police	Policja	poh-LEETS-yah	**Bank**	Bank	bahnk
Embassy	Ambasada	am-ba-SA-da	**Exchange**	Kantor	KAHN-tor
Doctor/Hospital	Lekarz/Szpital	LE-kash/SHPEE-tal	**Grocery/Market**	Sklep spożywczy	sklehp spoh-ZHIV-chih
Pharmacy	Apteka	ahp-TEH-ka	**Post Office**	Poczta	POHCH-tah

ENGLISH	POLISH	PRONOUNCE
Where is...?	Gdzie jest...?	g-JEH yest
How much does this cost?	Ile to kosztuje?	EE-leh toh kohsh-TOO-yeh
When is the next...?	O której jest następny...?	o KTOO-rey yest nas-TEMP-ni

APPENDIX

ENGLISH	POLISH	PRONOUNCE
Do you have (a vacant room)?	Czy są (jakieś wolne pokoje)?	chih SAWM (yah-kyesh VOHL-neh poh-KOY-eh)
I'd like to order...	Chciałbym zamówić...	kh-CHOW-bihm za-MOOV-eech
I do not eat...	Nie jadam...	nye YA-dam
Do you (male/female) speak English?	Czy pan(i) mówi po angielsku?	chih PAHN(-ee) MOO-vee poh ahn-GYEL-skoo
I don't speak Polish.	Nie mowię po polsku.	nyeh MOO-vyeh poh POHL-skoo

PORTUGUESE

Vowels with a *til* (ã, õ, etc.) or before *m* or *n* are pronounced with a nasal twang. At the end of a word, *o* is pronounced "oo" as in "room," and *e* is sometimes silent. *S* is pronounced "sh" or "zh" when it occurs before another consonant. *Ch* and *x* are pronounced "sh." *J* and *g* (before *e* or *i*) are pronounced "zh." The combinations *nh* and *lh* are pronounced "ny" and "ly," respectively.

ENGLISH	PORTUGUESE	PRONOUNCE	ENGLISH	PORTUGUESE	PRONOUNCE
Hello	Olá	oh-LAH	**Hotel**	Pousada	poh-ZAH-dah
Please	Por favor	pohr fah-VOHR	**Bathroom**	Banheiro	bahn-YAY-roo
Thank you	Obrigado (m)/ Obrigada (f)	oh-bree-GAH-doo/dah	**Open/Closed**	Aberto/ Fechado	ah-BEHR-toh/ feh-CHAH-do
Sorry/Excuse me	Desculpe	dish-KOOLP-eh	**Doctor**	Médico	MEH-dee-koo
Yes/No	Sim/Não	seem/now	**Pharmacy**	Farmácia	far-MAH-see-ah
Goodbye	Adeus	ah-DAY-oosh	**Left/Right**	Esquerda/Dire-ita	esh-KER-dah/di-RAY-tah
Help!	Socorro!	soh-KOO-roh!	**Bank**	Banco	BAHN-koh
I'm lost	Estou perdido (m)/perdida (f)	ish-TOW per-DEE-doo/dah	**Exchange**	Câmbio	CAHM-bee-yoo
Ticket	Bilhete	beel-YEHT	**Market**	Mercado	mer-KAH-doo
Train/Bus	Comboio/Auto-carro	kom-BOY-yoo/ OW-to-KAH-roo	**Police**	Polícia	po-LEE-see-ah
Station	Estação	eh-stah-SAO	**Embassy**	Embaixada	ehm-bai-SHAH-dah
Airport	Aeroporto	aye-ro-POR-too	**Post Office**	Correio	coh-RAY-yoh

ENGLISH	PORTUGUESE	PRONOUNCE
Do you speak English?	Fala inglês?	FAH-lah een-GLAYSH?
Where is...?	Onde é...?	OHN-deh eh...?
How much does this cost?	Quanto custa?	KWAHN-too KOOSH-tah?
Do you have rooms available?	Tem quartos disponíveis?	teng KWAHR-toosh dish-po-NEE-veysh?
I want/would like...	Eu quero/gostaria...	eh-oo KER-oh/gost-ar-EE-uh...
I don't speak Portuguese.	Não falo Português	now FAH-loo por-too-GEZH
I cannot eat...	Não posso comer...	now POH-soh coh-MEHR...
Another round, please.	Mais uma rodada, por favor.	mighsh OO-mah roh-DAH-dah pohr fah-VOHR

APPENDIX

ROMANIAN

ENGLISH	ROMANIAN	PRONOUNCE	ENGLISH	ROMANIAN	PRONOUNCE
Yes/No	Da/Nu	dah/noo	**Train/Bus**	Trenul Autobuz	TRAY-nool aw-toh-BOOS
Please/ Thank you	Vă rog/ Mulţumesc	vuh rohg/ mool-tsoo-MESK	**Station**	Gară	GAH-ruh
Hello	Bună ziua	BOO-nuh zee-wah	**Airport**	Aeroportul	air-oh-POR-tool
Goodbye	La revedere	lah reh-veh-DEH-reh	**Ticket**	Bilet	bee-LEHT
Sorry	Îmi pare rău	im PA-reh rau	**Taxi**	Taxi	tak-SEE
Excuse me	Scuzaţi-mă	skoo-ZAH-ts muh	**Hotel**	Hotel	ho-TEHL
Help!	Ajutor!	AH-zhoot-or!	**Bathroom**	Toaletă	toh-ahl-EH-tah
I'm lost	Sînt pierdut	sunt pyer-dut	**Open/Closed**	Deschis/închis	DESS-kees/un-KEES
Police	Poliţie	poh-LEE-tsee-eh	**Left/Right**	Stânga/ Dreapta	STYN-gah/ drahp-TAH
Embassy	Ambasada	ahm-bah-sah-da	**Bank**	Banca	BAHN-cah
Passport	Paşaport	pah-shah-PORT	**Exchange**	Birou de schimb	bee-RO deh skeemb
Doctor/ Hospital	Doctorul/ spitalul	DOK-to-rul/ SPI-ta-lul	**Grocery**	Alimentară	a-lee-men-TA-ra
Pharmacy	Farmacistul	fahr-ma-CHIS-tul	**Post Office**	Poşta	POH-shta

ENGLISH	ROMANIAN	PRONOUNCE
Where is...?	Unde e...?	OON-deh YEH
How much does this cost?	Cât costă?	kyht KOH-stuh
When is the next...?	Cînd este următorul...?	keend es-te ur-muh-TO-rul
Do you have (a vacant room)?	Aveţi (camere libere)?	a-VETS (KUH-mer-eh LEE-ber-e)
I would like...	Aş vrea...	ahsh VREH-ah
I do not eat...	Eu nu mănînc...	eu nu MUH-nink
Do you speak English?	Vorbiţi englezeşte?	vor-BEETS ehng-leh-ZESH-te
I don't speak Romanian.	Nu vorbesc Româneşte.	noo vohr-BEHSK roh-myn-EHS-HTE

RUSSIAN

For the Cyrillic alphabet, see p. 1056.

ENGLISH	RUSSIAN	PRONOUNCE	ENGLISH	RUSSIAN	PRONOUNCE
Yes/No	Да/нет	Dah/Nyet	**Train/Bus**	Поезд/автобус	POH-yizt/av-TOH-boos
Please	Пожалуйста	pa-ZHAL-sta	**Station**	вокзал	vak-ZAL
Thank you	Спасибо	spa-SEE-bah	**Airport**	аэропорт	ai-roh-PORT
Hello	Добрый день	DOH-bri DYEHN	**Ticket**	билет	bil-YET
Goodbye	До свидания	da svee-DAHN-ya	**Hotel**	гостиница	gahs-TEE-nee-tsah
Sorry/ Excuse me	Извините	iz-vi-NEET-yeh	**Dorm/Hostel**	общежитие	ob-sheh-ZHEE-tee-yeh
Help!	Помогите!	pah-mah-GIT-yeh!	**Bathroom**	туалет	twah-LYET
I'm lost. (m/f)	Я потерен(а)	ya po-TYE-ren-(ah)	**Open/Closed**	открыт/ закрыт	ot-KRIHT/ za-KRIHT
Police	милиция	mee-LEE-tsi-ya	**Left/Right**	налево/нап-раво	nah-LYEH-vah/ nah-PRAH-vah

APPENDIX

ENGLISH	RUSSIAN	PRONOUNCE	ENGLISH	RUSSIAN	PRONOUNCE
Embassy	посольство	pah-SOHL'-stva	**Bank**	банк	bahnk
Passport	паспорт	PAS-pahrt	**Exchange**	обмен валюты	ab-MYEHN val-iy-YU-tee
Doctor/Hospital	Врач/больница	vrach/bol-NI-tsa	**Grocery/Market**	гастроном/рынок	gah-stroh-NOM/REE-nohk
Pharmacy	аптека	ahp-TYE-kah	**Post Office**	Почта	POCH-ta

ENGLISH	RUSSIAN	PRONOUNCE
Where is...?	Где находится...?	gdyeh nah-KHOH-di-tsah
How much does this cost?	Сколько это стоит?	SKOHL-ka EH-ta STOY-it
When is the next...?	Когда будет следуший...?	kog-DAH BOOD-yet SLYED-ooshi
Do you have (a vacant room)?	У вас есть (свободный номер)?	oo vahs yehst (svah-BOHD-neey NOH-mehr)
I'd like (male/female)...	Я хотел(а) бы	ya khah-TYEL(a) bwee
I do not eat...	Я не ем...	ya nye yem
Do you speak English?	Вы говорите по-английски?	vy gah-vah-REE-tyeh pa-an-GLEE-ski
I don't speak Russian.	Я не говорю по-русски.	yah neh gah-vah-RYOO pah ROO-skee

SPANISH

ENGLISH	SPANISH	PRONOUNCE	ENGLISH	SPANISH	PRONOUNCE
Hello	Hola	OH-lah	**Hotel/Hostel**	Hotel/Hostal	oh-TEL/OH-stahl
Please	Por favor	pohr fah-VOHR	**Bathroom**	Baño	BAHN-yoh
Thank you	Gracias	GRAH-see-ahs	**Open/Closed**	Abierto(a)/Cerrado(a)	ah-bee-AYR-toh/sehr-RAH-doh
Sorry/Excuse me	Perdón	pehr-DOHN	**Doctor**	Médico	MEH-dee-koh
Yes/No	Sí/No	see/no	**Pharmacy**	Farmácia	far-MAH-see-ah
Goodbye	Adiós	ah-di-OHS	**Left/Right**	Izquierda/Derecha	ihz-kee-EHR-da/deh-REH-chah
Help!	¡Ayuda!	¡ay-YOOH-duh!	**Bank**	Banco	BAHN-koh
I'm lost	Estoy perdido (a)		**Exchange**	Cambio	CAHM-bee-oh
Ticket	Boleto	boh-LEH-toh	**Grocery**	Supermercado	soo-pehr-mer-KAH-doh
Train/Bus	Tren/Autobús	trehn/ow-toh-BOOS	**Police**	Policía	poh-lee-SEE-ah
Station	Estación	es-tah-see-OHN	**Embassy**	Embajada	em-bah-HA-dah
Airport	Aeropuerto	ay-roh-PWER-toh	**Post Office**	Oficina de correos	oh-fee-SEE-nah day coh-REH-ohs

ENGLISH	SPANISH	PRONOUNCE
Do you speak English?	¿Habla inglés?	AH-blah een-GLEHS?
Where is...?	¿Dónde está...?	DOHN-day eh-STA...?
How much does this cost?	¿Cuánto cuesta...?	KWAN-toh KWEHS-tah...?
Do you have rooms available?	¿Tiene habitaciones libres?	tee-YEH-neh ah-bee-tah-see-YOH-nehs LEE-brehs?
I want/ would like...	Quiero/Me gustaría...	kee-YEH-roh/may goos-tah-REE-ah...
I don't speak Spanish.	No hablo español.	NO AH-bloh ehs-pahn-YOHL
I cannot eat...	No puedo comer...	NO PWAY-doh coh-MEHR...
Please do not arrest me.	Por favor no me detenga.	pohr fah-VOHR no meh deh-TEHN-gah

SWEDISH

ENGLISH	SWEDISH	PRONOUNCE	ENGLISH	SWEDISH	PRONOUNCE
Yes/No	Ja/Nej	yah/nay	**Ticket**	Biljett	bil-YEHT
Please	Tack	tahk	**Train/Bus**	Tåget/Buss	TOH-get/boos
Thank you	Tack	tahk	**Ferry**	Färjan	FAR-yuhn
Hello	Hej	hay	**Departure**	Avgångar	uhv-GOANG-er
Goodbye	Hejdå	HAY-doh	**Market**	Torget	TOHR-yet
Excuse me	Ursäkta mig	oor-SHEHK-tuh MAY	**Hotel/Hostel**	Hotell/Vandrar-hem	hoo-TEHL/vun-DRAR-um
Help!	Hjälp!	yehlp!	**Pharmacy**	Apotek	uh-poo-TEEK
Police	Polisen	poo-LEE-sehn	**Toilets**	Toaletten	too-uh-LEHT-en
Embassy	Ambassad	uhm-bah-SAHD	**Post Office**	Posten	POHS-tehn
I'm lost	Yag är bortkom-men	Yuh air BORT-kummen	**Open/Closed**	Öppen/Stängd	UH-pen/Staingd
Railway sta-tion	Järnvägssta-tionen	Yairnvasgues-stah-SHO-nen	**Hospital**	Sjukhus	Shuhk-huhs
Bank	Bank	Bahnk	**Left/Right**	Vänster/Höger	VAIN-ster/HUH-ger
Currency exchange	Växel	Vaixil	**Condoms**	Smokkar	Smoke-ahrr

ENGLISH	SWEDISH	PRONOUNCE
Where is...?	Var finns...?	vahr FINS
How much does this cost?	Hur mycket kostar det?	hurr MÜK-keh KOS-tuhr deh
I'd like to buy...	Jag skulle vilja köpa...	yuh SKOO-leh vil-yuh CHEU-pah
Do you speak English?	Talar du engelska?	TAH-luhr du EHNG-ehl-skuh
When is the next...?	Hur dags är nästa...?	hurr DAHx air nai-stah
I don't speak Swedish.	Jag talar inte svenska.	yuh tahlahr intuh svenskah
I'm allergic to/I cannot eat...	Jag är allergisk mot/Jag kan inte ata...	yuh air ALLEHR-ghisk moot/yuh kahn intuh aitah
Do you have rooms available?	Har Ni rum tillgängliga?	harh nih ruhm till-YAING-lih-gah

WEATHER CHART

City	January			April			July			October		
	High (F/C)	Low (F/C)	Rain (in.)	High (F/C)	Low (F/C)	Rain (in.)	High (F/C)	Low (F/C)	Rain (in.)	High (F/C)	Low (F/C)	Rain (in.)
Amsterdam	41/5	34/1	3.1	53/11	40/4	1.5	69/20	55/12	2.9	57/13	46/7	4.1
Athens	55/12	44/6	1.9	66/18	52/11	0.9	89/31	73/22	0.2	73/22	60/15	2.1
Berlin	35/1	26/-3	1.7	54/12	37/2	1.7	73/22	56/13	2.1	56/13	42/5	1.4
Copenhagen	37/2	30/-1	1.7	49/9	36/2	1.6	69/20	55/12	2.6	53/11	44/6	2.1
Dublin	46/7	37/2	2.5	52/11	41/5	1.9	66/18	54/12	2.6	55/12	46/7	2.9
London	44/6	34/1	3.1	54/12	38/3	2.1	71/21	53/11	1.8	58/14	44/6	2.9
Madrid	51/10	32/0	1.8	63/17	42/5	1.8	90/32	61/16	0.4	68/20	47/8	1.8
Paris	43/6	34/1	2.2	57/13	42/5	1.7	75/23	58/14	2.3	59/15	46/7	2.0
Rome	55/12	39/3	3.2	63/17	47/8	2.6	83/28	66/18	0.6	71/21	56/13	4.5
Vienna	36/2	27/-2	1.5	57/13	41/5	2.0	77/25	59/15	2.5	57/13	43/6	1.6

INDEX

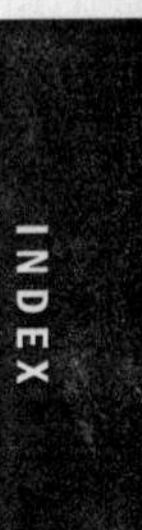

T

U

V

W

Y

Z

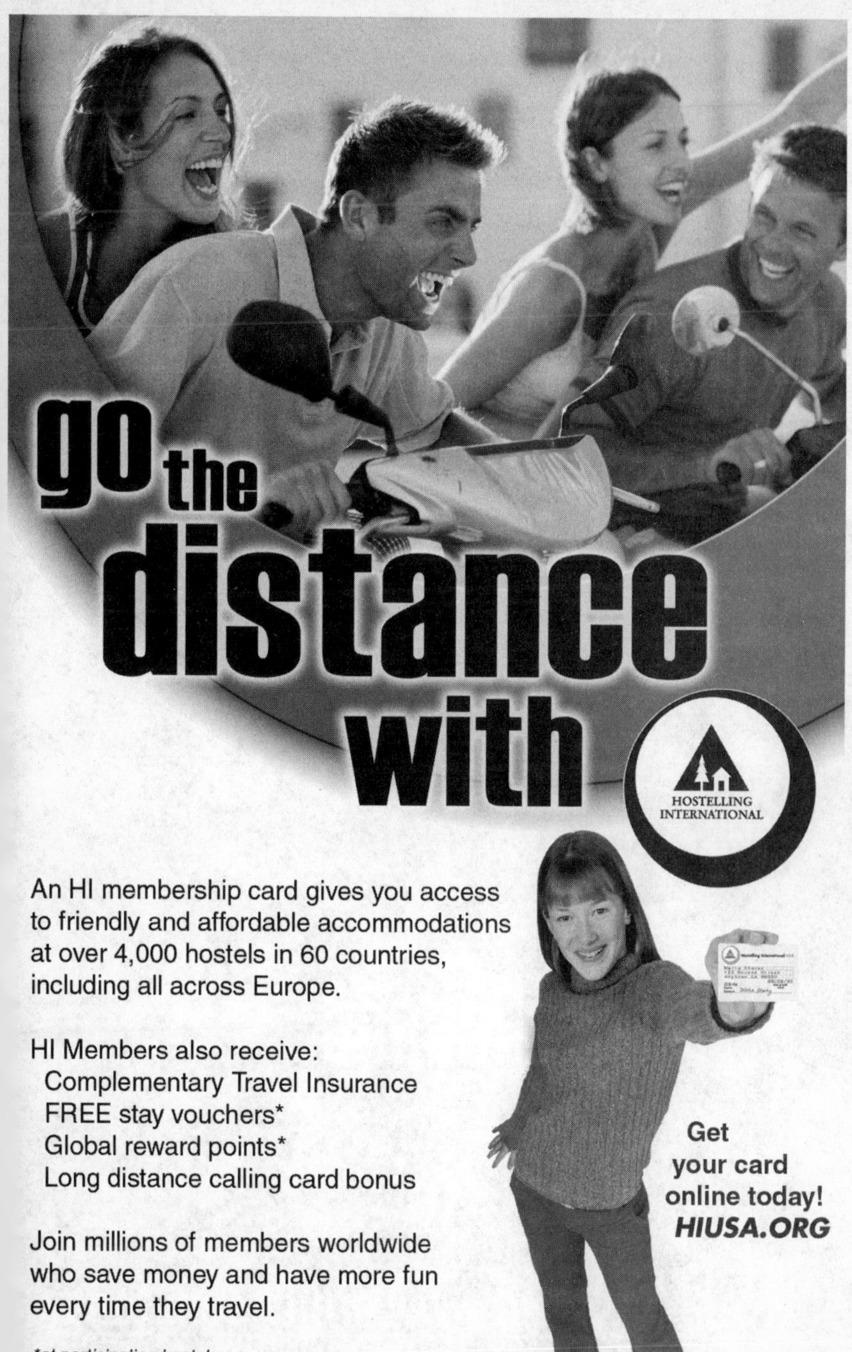
go the distance with
HOSTELLING INTERNATIONAL
An HI membership card gives you access to friendly and affordable accommodations at over 4,000 hostels in 60 countries, including all across Europe.
HI Members also receive:
Complementary Travel Insurance
FREE stay vouchers*
Global reward points*
Long distance calling card bonus
Join millions of members worldwide who save money and have more fun every time they travel.
Get your card online today!
HIUSA.ORG
*at participating hostels

MAP INDEX

MAP LEGEND

Point of Interest
Accommodation
Camping
Food
Café
Museum
Sight
Bar/Pub
Nightlife
Airport
Arch/Gate
Bank
Beach
Bus Station/Stop
Capital City
Castle
Church
Consulate/Embassy
Convent/Monastery
Ferry Landing
347 Highway Sign
Hospital
Internet Cafe
Library/Bookstore
M M Metro Station
Mountain
Mosque
Pharmacy
Police
Post Office
Skiing
Synagogue
Telephone Office
Theater
Tourist Office
Train Station
Park
Water
Beach
Building
Pedestrian Zone
Stairs
The Let's Go compass always points NORTH.

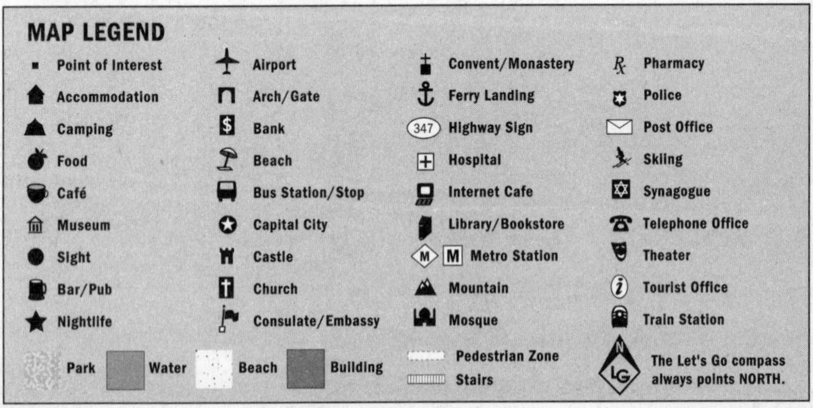